More than ever, THE BEDFORD INTRODUCTION TO ... is
especially suited for courses in which writing in ...
component. In addition to extensive questions a... ...ing assignments that offer
over 2,000 specific occasions for writing – including a new First Response question
for selections in the text chapters – this book provides all the resources listed here.

Nicole Lynn Haynes

FIFTH EDITION

THE BEDFORD INTRODUCTION TO LITERATURE

Reading · Thinking · Writing

Michael Meyer

University of Connecticut

BEDFORD/ST. MARTIN'S   Boston  New York

FOR BEDFORD / ST. MARTIN'S

Developmental Editor: Alanya Harter
Production Editor: Sherri Frank
Marketing Manager: Karen Melton
Associate Developmental Editor: Aron Keesbury
Editorial Assistant: Ellen Thibault
Production Assistants: Deborah Baker, Helaine Denenberg, Arthur Johnson
Copyeditor: Rosemary Winfield
Text Design: Claire Seng-Niemoeller
Cover Design: Hannus Design Associates
Cover Art: Reading Aloud, 1884, by Albert Moore. The Burrell Collection, Glasgow Museum, Scotland, U.K.
Composition: Stratford Publishing Services
Printing and Binding: Quebecor Printing

President: Charles H. Christensen
Editorial Director: Joan E. Feinberg
Director of Editing, Design, and Production: Marcia Cohen
Managing Editor: Elizabeth M. Schaaf

Library of Congress Catalog Card Number: 98-85194

Manufactured in the United States of America.

3   2   1   0   9   8

f   e   d   c   b   a

For information, write: Bedford/St. Martin's
75 Arlington Street, Boston, MA 02116
(617-426-7440)

ISBN: 0-312-17140-4

Acknowledgments

FICTION

"A Letter Home from an Irish Emigrant in Australia" from *Oceans of Consolation: Personal Accounts of Irish Migration to Australia* by David Fitzpatrick (Cornell UP, 1994). Reprinted by permission of David Fitzpatrick and Nancy Lunch.

Isabel Allende. "The Judge's Wife." Reprinted with the permission of Scribner, a Division of Simon & Schuster from *The Stories of Eva Luna* by Isabel Allende, translated from the Spanish by Margaret Sayers Peden. Copyright © 1989 by Isabel Allende. English translation copyright © 1991 by Macmillan Publishing Company. Printed with permission from Key Porter Books.

Margaret Atwood. "There Was Once" from *Good Bones and Simple Murders* by Margaret Atwood. Copyright © 1983, 1992, 1994 by O. W. Toad Ltd. A Nan A. Talese Book. Used by permission of Doubleday, a division of Bantam Doubleday Dell Publishing Group, Inc. Used by permission also of McClelland & Stewart, Inc., *The Canadian Publishers* of *Good Bones* by Margaret Atwood.

For My Wife
Regina Barreca

About Michael Meyer

Michael Meyer has taught introductory writing and literature courses for more than twenty-five years—since 1981 at the University of Connecticut and before that at the University of North Carolina at Charlotte and the College of William and Mary.

In addition to being an experienced teacher, Meyer is a highly regarded literary scholar. His scholarly articles have appeared in distinguished journals such as *American Literature, Studies in the American Renaissance,* and *Virginia Quarterly Review.* An internationally recognized authority on Henry David Thoreau, Meyer is a former president of the Thoreau Society and coauthor (with Walter Harding) of *The New Thoreau Handbook,* a standard reference source. His first book, *Several More Lives to Live: Thoreau's Political Reputation in America,* was awarded the Ralph Henry Gabriel Prize by the American Studies Association. He is also the editor of *Frederick Douglass: The Narrative and Selected Writings* and the author of *The Little, Brown Guide to Writing Research Papers,* Third Edition. His other books for Bedford/ St. Martin's include *The Compact Bedford Introduction to Literature,* Fourth Edition; *Poetry: An Introduction,* Second Edition; and *Thinking and Writing about Literature.*

Preface for Instructors

The fifth edition of *The Bedford Introduction to Literature* incorporates a wide range of distinctive features that have been class-tested in thousands of literature courses and carefully revised over five editions. With its balance of classic and contemporary, traditional, and multicultural works, along with its in-depth treatment of selected writers, provocative secondary materials, and its pervasive concern with critical reading, thinking, and writing, this text-anthology addresses all the requirements of the contemporary introductory literature course. Like its predecessors, the fifth edition of *The Bedford Introduction to Literature* reflects the assumptions that understanding enhances the enjoyment of literature and that reading literature offers a valuable and unique means of apprehending life in its richness and diversity. The book also reflects the hope that the selections included will encourage students to become lifelong readers of imaginative literature. Designed to accommodate a variety of teaching styles, this rich collection of 62 stories (21 of them new to the fifth edition), 417 poems (100 of them new), and 22 plays (4 of them new) represents a wide range of periods, nationalities, and voices. Each selection has been carefully chosen for its appeal to students today and for its usefulness in demonstrating the effects, significance, and pleasures of literature. To enhance these selections, this edition includes more than forty images, including photographs of selected authors and a portfolio of photographs of plays in performance.

Again, like its predecessors, the fifth edition of *The Bedford Introduction to Literature* is designed for the introductory course as it is taught today, which varies — from school to school and from instructor to instructor — more than ever before. Even the traditional course emphasizing the elements of literature and a broad range of works from the Western canon is changing in response to important developments in literary studies and, more generally, in higher education and in American society. The course is now viewed by many teachers as a rich opportunity to supplement classics of Western literature with the work of writers previously excluded from the traditional canon. Increasingly, it now also serves as an introduction to the discipline of literary study, a challenging development that brings to the undergraduate classroom important trends in literary theory and provocative new readings of both familiar and unfamiliar texts. Finally, and perhaps most often, the introduction to literature course is now also taught as a second course in composition in which the critical thinking and writing that students do are as important as the reading that they do. The fifth edition of *The Bedford Introduction to Literature* responds to these developments with distinctive features that address the needs of instructors who teach a traditional course but who are also concerned about canonical issues, literary theory, and writing about literature.

Writing about Literature

The book's concern with helping students write about literature is pervasive. The fifth edition of *The Bedford Introduction to Literature* is especially suited for courses in which writing in response to literature is a central component. Five chapters cover every step of the writing process — from generating topics to documenting sources — and offer advice on different kinds of writing assignments. Two extensive chapters — "Reading and Writing" and "The Literary Research Paper" — discuss and illustrate the writing process while offering models of the different types of papers usually assigned in an introductory course, including explication, analysis, and comparison-contrast. A detailed chapter on the literary research paper, including a student model (with a new discussion of using and documenting on-line sources in the MLA style), provides the necessary information for finding, evaluating, and documenting sources.

In addition, three chapters — "Writing about Fiction," "Writing about Poetry," and "Writing about Drama" — focus on genre-specific writing assignments, each with questions for responsive reading and writing along with sample student papers. The first of these chapters, "Writing about Fiction," includes a new model of every stage of a student's paper in progress, leading from a reader's initial responses to the final draft. Also integrated throughout the book are three "Questions for Writing" units, one on incorporating outside sources, one on writing about an author covered in depth, and one on applying a critical strategy to a work. Each of these units is illustrated by a sample paper. The book includes a total of twelve sample papers that provide concrete, accessible models for a wide range of assignments. Students will also find useful a chapter on developing strategies for taking essay examinations assigned in literature courses. Finally, a quick-reference chart of all the writing-about-literature features is provided on the front endpapers of the book to help students (and instructors) find the writing advice they need. In sum, this expanded coverage offers a comprehensive overview of writing about literature; indeed, this material is strong enough to have been separately published in an earlier version as *Thinking and Writing about Literature* (1995).

Focus on Critical Reading and Thinking

To encourage the critical reading and thinking that are an integral part of the writing process, advice on how to read imaginative literature appears at the beginning of each genre section. It offers practical advice about the kinds of questions active readers ask themselves as they read. To provoke students' interest, sharpen their thinking, and help them improve their discussion and writing skills, the number and variety of questions related to the readings have been increased in the fifth edition. New to this edition are "First Response" questions that can be used as in-class or at-home writing prompts as well as provocative means of generating the kind of critical thinking that promotes class discussion. In addition to the more than two thousand questions that comprise the "Considerations for Critical Thinking and Writing" and "Connections to Other Selections" (questions and suggestions useful for class discussion or writing assignments), the chapter entitled "Reading and Writing" describes how to read a work closely, annotate a text, take notes, keep a reading journal, and develop a topic into a thesis. This chapter also includes a section on arguing about literature that discusses how to generate arguments on literary topics and make those arguments persuasive. A list of questions based on the critical approaches covered in the chapter "Critical Strategies for Reading" helps students to discover the significant issues regarding a short story, poem, or play that may be arguable. In addition, an annotated list of important reference sources for literary research is provided.

Selected Major Authors Treated in Depth

For each genre, the book includes chapters focusing on two or more major figures. There are four stories each by Nathaniel Hawthorne, Flannery O'Connor and Alice Munro (new to this edition); an extensive selection of poems by Emily Dickinson, Robert Frost, and Langston Hughes; and two plays by Sophocles and three by Shakespeare. Substantial introductions provide useful biographical and critical information about each of these important writers, and new photographs of the writers help to engage students more fully with the writers' works. A selection of "Perspectives" — excerpts from letters, journals, and critical commentaries — follows each writer's works to provide a context for discussion and writing. In addition, "Considerations for Critical Thinking and Writing" follow both selections and "Perspectives"; these questions for discussion or writing encourage critical thinking and provide stimulating opportunities for student essays.

Also included are chronologies summarizing important dates for the eight major writers featured and complementary critical readings on a particular work by each of the eight authors. These critical readings offer students examples of the variety of approaches they can take in reading and writing about literature. The two readings on Hawthorne, for instance, focus on feminist and psychological approaches to "The Birthmark." By reading commentaries by two critics who argue competing ideas about one text or who illuminate different aspects of that text, students can see immediately that there is no single way to read a work of literature, an important and necessary step for learning how to formulate their own critical approaches in their essays.

Albums of Contemporary and World Literature

For each genre an album of contemporary selections offers some of the most interesting and lively stories, poems, and plays published in the recent past, including works by Richard Ford, Gish Jen, Tobias Wolff, Martín Espada, Donald Hall, Robert Hass, Linda Hogan, Wendy Wasserstein, and August Wilson. Biographical information about the album authors is included in the text to introduce instructors and students to these important but, perhaps, unfamiliar writers.

In addition, albums of world literature in each genre section offer students a sampling of stories, poems, and plays from other cultures, including the work of Isabel Allende (Chile), Yukio Mishima (Japan), Naguib Mahfouz (Egypt), Claribel Alegría (El Salvador), Octavio Paz (Mexico), Wislawa Szymborska (Poland), Tomas Transtromer (Sweden), Brian Friel (Ireland), and Wole Soyinka (Nigeria), among many others. Half the stories and a third of the poems and plays in this edition are by women and minority writers and writers from other cultures. Related to this multicultural emphasis is a new section on poetry in translation in Chapter 16, "Word Choice, Word Order, and Tone." This section presents different versions of poems that help students understand the significance of a translator's choices concerning diction and tone. The translated poems encourage students to explore the nuances of poetic language as well as larger issues related to translation. This is complemented in the fiction section by two translations — also new — of a portion of a Chekhov story, and in the drama section by a translation of a scene from *Oedipus the King*.

"Connections to Other Selections" consist of questions that link the selections in the albums of contemporary and world literature to more traditional selections in the text. For example, August Wilson's *The Piano Lesson* is linked with Arthur Miller's *Death of a Salesman* and Ralph Ellison's "Battle Royal," while Wole Soyinka's play *The Strong Breed* is connected to Sophocles' *Oedipus the King*. These questions provide engaging writing opportunities and provocative topics for class discussion. "Connections to Other Selections" questions also appear after most of the works in the chapters on the elements of fiction, poetry, and drama.

Perspectives on Literature

This popular feature has been revised in ways that make the fifth edition's 149 "Perspectives" — journal notes, letters, classic and contemporary theoretical essays, interviews, and student responses — even more useful for class discussion and student writing. "Perspectives" are included in five different places in the text: in the chapters treating major authors in depth; in the three "Critical Case Study" chapters focusing on a particular work in each genre; in the new "Cultural Case Study" chapters in each genre; at the end of Chapter 37, on literary theory; and, finally, throughout the text's discussion chapters. Individual "Perspectives" in these chapters follow the works to which they refer and, in many cases, discuss a literary work in terms of the elements of literature for which they serve as illustrations. A variety of "Perspectives" are integrated throughout the book to teach students how to think critically and write effectively about literature.

Sensible and Useful Coverage of Literary Theory

Chapter 37, "Critical Strategies for Reading," deepens the introductory discussions of active reading by focusing on the different reading strategies employed by contemporary literary theorists. This chapter, which can be assigned at any point in the course, introduces students to a wide variety of major contemporary theoretical approaches — formalist, biographical, psychological, historical (including literary history criticism, Marxist criticism, new historicist criticism, and cultural criticism), gender strategies (including feminist criticism and gay and lesbian criticism), mythological, reader-response, and deconstructionist approaches. In brief examples the approaches are applied in analyzing Kate Chopin's "The Story of an Hour," as well as other works, so that students will have a sense of how to use these strategies in their own reading and writing. A selected bibliography for the approaches and a set of "Perspectives" by contemporary literary critics conclude this important chapter.

A "Critical Case Study" chapter in each genre section gathers four or more critical analyses of a single work — such as T. S. Eliot's "The Love Song of J. Alfred Prufrock" — to illustrate the variety of approaches covered in Chapter 37. The questions following these readings encourage students to analyze a particular critical strategy. Included in the critical case study on Ibsen's *A Doll House* is a "Questions for Writing" unit that shows students how to draw on critical approaches in their own writing and features a sample paper.

New to this edition is a "Cultural Case Study" for each genre that invites students to practice cultural criticism by using cultural and historical documents to ask new questions of a text. For fiction, the focus is on James Joyce's "Eveline"; for poetry, Julia Alvarez's "Queens, 1963"; and for drama, David Henry Hwang's *M. Butterfly*. The accompanying documents range from photographs and advertisements to interviews, letters, popular arts, and newspaper stories, all followed by questions designed to shed light on the literary work under consideration.

Although the emphasis in this text is on critical reading and understanding rather than on critical terminology, terms such as *symbol, irony,* and *metaphor* are defined and illustrated to equip students with a basic working vocabulary for discussing and writing about literature. When first defined in the text, these terms appear in boldface italic type. An "Index of Terms" appears inside the back cover of the book for easy reference, and a

"Glossary of Literary Terms" provides thorough explanations of more than two hundred terms central to the study of literature.

Connections between "Popular" and "Literary" Culture

As in previous editions, *The Bedford Introduction to Literature,* Fifth Edition, features introductions to each genre section that draw on carefully chosen examples from popular culture to explain the elements of the genre, inviting students to make connections between what they already know and what they will encounter in subsequent selections. Comparisons between popular culture and more canonical literary selections offer excellent writing opportunities, and suggestions are provided after each popular culture example. The examples include excerpts from a romance novel and from *Tarzan of the Apes,* greeting-card verse, and, new to this edition, Queen Latifah's "The Evil That Men Do" as well as scenes from a television script for *Seinfeld.*

Resources for Teaching THE BEDFORD INTRODUCTION TO LITERATURE, *Fifth Edition*

This thorough and practical instructor's manual — now more than 500 pages long and spiral bound — discusses every selection, suggests answers to many of the questions posed in the text, and provides teaching tips from instructors who have taught from previous editions. The manual also offers questions and writing assignments for the selections in the collection chapter at the end of each genre section. It includes biographical information for authors whose backgrounds are not discussed in the text and offers selected bibliographies for authors treated in depth, as well as a bibliography of articles on teaching literature. The manual also gives several suggestions for teaching thematic units, a list of selections linked by "Connections" questions, and an annotated list of videos, films, and recordings related to the works of literature in the text.

Moreover, additional works of literature from any of Bedford Books' literary reprint series are available at a special price with *The Bedford Introduction to Literature.* Titles from the highly praised Case Studies in Contemporary Criticism include *The Awakening, The Dead, Death in Venice, Frankenstein, Great Expectations, Gulliver's Travels, Hamlet, Heart of Darkness, The House of Mirth, Howards End, Jane Eyre, A Portrait of the Artist as a Young Man, The Scarlet Letter, The Secret Sharer, Tess of the D'Urbervilles, The Turn of the Screw, The Wife of Bath,* and *Wuthering Heights.* Volumes from the Bedford Cultural Editions, the Bedford Shakespeare Series, and Case Studies in Critical Controversy include *Adventures of Huckleberry Finn, The Blithedale Romance, The Commerce of Everyday Life: Selections from* THE SPECTATOR *and* THE TATLER, *Evelina, The First Part of King Henry the Fourth, Life in the Iron-Mills, The Rape of the Lock, Reading the West: An Anthology of Dime Westerns, The Taming of the Shrew,* and *The Yellow Wallpaper.*

Literature Aloud

A CD — also available as an audiotape — of selected poems, stories, and scenes is available to instructors who adopt *The Bedford Introduction to Literature*, Fifth Edition. This rich resource for instructors and students offers the voice of literature as read by celebrated writers and actors.

Robert Frost: Poems, Life, Legacy

This comprehensive CD-ROM on the life and works of Robert Frost includes searchable text of his poetry, audio performances of Frost reading sixty-nine of his finest poems, over 1,500 pages of biography and literary criticism, and a new documentary film narrated by Richard Wilbur. It is available to qualified adopters of *The Bedford Introduction to Literature*.

Bedford Links to Resources in Literature

Because trying to do literary research on the Web can be a daunting task for an undergraduate, Bedford Books has provided research links to get them started. Concise annotations guide students to over 250 professionally maintained sites built around the most often assigned writers, texts, and literary periods. These can be accessed at <http://www.bedfordstmartins.com>.

Acknowledgments

This book has benefited from the ideas, suggestions, and corrections of scores of careful readers who helped transform various stages of an evolving manuscript into a finished book and into subsequent editions. I remain grateful to those I have thanked in previous prefaces, particularly Robert Wallace of Case Western Reserve University. In addition, many instructors who used the fourth edition of *The Bedford Introduction to Literature* responded to a questionnaire on the book. For their valuable comments and advice I am grateful to Colleen Breese, University of Toledo; Kathy DelMonico, Sacred Heart University; Jerry Dyer, York College of Performing Arts; James Guimond, Rider University; Ann R. Hawkins, Austin Pear State University; John Haydock, Hampton University; Dr. Philip Heltrich, Oklahoma State University; Daryl Holmes, Nicholls State University; Mickey Jackson, Golden West College; Claudia Jannone, University of South Florida; Kelly Jennings, Idaho State University; Donald Johns, University of California at Davis; Sally Joranko, John Carroll University; Laureen Beth Kalberer, University of South Carolina; Donald L. Kaplar, University of South Carolina at Columbia; Shannon Kelly, University of South Carolina; Josephine Keese King, Georgia College and State University; Mary Ann Klein, Quincy University; William Lawlor, University of Wisconsin at Steven's Point; Gary F. Leising, University of South Carolina; Pamela

Main, Widener University; Miles S. McCrimmon, J. Sargeant Reynolds Community College; Darlene McElfresh, Northern Kentucky University; Jude R. Meche, Texas A&M University; Joseph Mills, University of California at Davis; Hugh H. Paschal, Hillsborough Community College; Rhonda Pettit, Northern Kentucky University; Teresa P. Reed, Jacksonville State University; Jacob F. Rivers III, University of South Carolina at Columbia; John E. Ryan, Gettysburg College; Don Schweda, Quincy University; Judy Sieg, Spartanburg Technical College; Rick Simmons, University of South Carolina; Enedina G. Snodgrass, University of Massachusetts at Dartmouth; Al Starr, Essex Community College; Trisha Stubblefield, University of South Carolina; Dr. Debra Sutton, Jefferson College; James Tonek, Delta State University; R. B. Weeke, Spartanburg Technical College; Linch Wiley, Howard Community College; Sally Wolf, Arapahoe Community College; and Sonya Wozniak, University of California at Davis. We also received thoughtful reviews from Charles J. Bailey, San Jacinto College Central; Elizabeth H. Curtin, Salisbury State University; Barry Edwards, Santa Fe Community College; Jo N. Farrar, San Jacinto College; Robert Finegan, Drexel University; Alan Hall, North Harris College; Laurie F. Leach, Hawaii Pacific University; Marta Magellen, Miami-Dade Community College; Thomas P. Miller, University of Arizona; Robert C. Peterson, Middle Tennessee State University; James L. Senefeld, Columbia State Community College; Dolly Tarver, Virginia Highlands Community College; Colin Wells, St. Olaf College; and Helen Wilson, Virginia Highlands Community College.

I would also like to give special thanks to the following instructors who contributed teaching tips to the fifth edition of *Resources for Teaching* THE BEDFORD INTRODUCTION TO LITERATURE: Sandra Adickes, Winona State University; Helen J. Aling, Northwestern College; Sr. Anne Denise Brennan, College of Mt. St. Vincent; Robin Calitri, Merced College; James H. Clemmer, Austin Peay State University; Robert Croft, Gainesville College; Thomas Edwards, Westbrook College; Elizabeth Kleinfeld, Red Rocks Community College; Olga Lyles, University of Nevada; Timothy Peters, Boston University; Catherine Rusco, Muskegon Community College; Robert M. St. John, De Paul University; Richard Stoner, Broome Community College; Nancy Veiga, Modesto Junior College; Karla Walters, University of New Mexico; and Joseph Zeppetello, Ulster Community College.

I am also indebted to those who cheerfully answered questions and generously provided miscellaneous bits of information. What might have seemed to them like inconsequential conversations turned out to be important leads. Among these friends and colleagues are Raymond Anselment, Ann Charters, Karen Chow, John Christie, Eleni Coundouriotis, Irving Cummings, William Curtin, Patrick Hogan, Lee Jacobus, Thomas Jambeck, Bonnie Januszewski-Ytuarte, Greta Little, George Monteiro, Brenda Murphy, Joel Myerson, Thomas Recchio, William Sheidley, Stephanie Smith, Milton Stern, Kenneth Wilson, and the dedicated reference librarians at the Homer Babbidge Library, University of Connecticut.

I continue to be grateful for what I have learned from teaching my students and for the many student papers I have received over the years that I have used in various forms to serve as good and accessible models of student writing. I am also indebted to Quentin Miller, Julie Nash, Rob Spirko, and Anne Phillips for their extensive work on the fifth edition of *Resources for Teaching* THE BEDFORD INTRODUCTION TO LITERATURE.

At Bedford Books, my debts once again require more time to acknowledge than the deadline allows. Charles H. Christensen and Joan Feinberg initiated this project and launched it with their intelligence, energy, and sound advice. Karen Henry and Kathy Retan tirelessly steered earlier editions through rough as well as becalmed moments; their work was as first-rate as it was essential. Alanya Harter flawlessly carried on that tradition as developmental editor for this edition; her savvy and quick takes were matched by her patience and prodigious appetite for work, qualities that helped to make this project both a success and a pleasure. Associate Editor Aron Keesbury oversaw *Resources for Teaching* THE BEDFORD INTRODUCTION TO LITERATURE with clear-headed intelligence, meticulous attention, and welcome enthusiasm; he also shared the Herculean labor of clearing permissions with the unflappable Arthur Johnson. Ellen Thibault cheerfully juggled a variety of tasks, including reviewing, researching, preparing the indexes, and developing the new CD/audiotape to accompany the text, *Literature Aloud*. The difficult tasks of production were skillfully managed by Sherri Frank, whose attention to details and deadlines was essential to the completion of this project. She was ably assisted by Deborah Baker, Helaine Denenberg, and Arthur Johnson. Rosemary Winfield provided careful copyediting, and Janet Cocker and Mary Lou Wilshaw proofread. Numerous other people at Bedford Books — including Amanda Bristow, Donna Lee Dennison, Susan Pace, and Stephanie Westnedge — helped to make this enormous project a manageable one.

Finally, I am grateful to my sons Timothy and Matthew for all kinds of help, but mostly I'm just grateful they're my sons. And always for making all the difference, I dedicate this book to my wife, Regina Barreca.

Brief Contents

DRAMA   1167

CRITICAL THINKING AND WRITING   2019

Contents

A Sample Student Paper in Progress 43

3. Plot 60

4. Character 97

5. Setting 143

6. Point of View 174

Third-Person Narrator 175
First-Person Narrator 177

7. Symbolism 215

8. Theme 243

9. Style, Tone, and Irony 268

Style 268
Tone 270
Irony 271

10. A Study of Three Authors: Nathaniel Hawthorne, Flannery O'Connor, and Alice Munro 306

Nathaniel Hawthorne 306

11. Critical Case Study: William Faulkner's "Barn Burning" 480

12. Cultural Case Study: James Joyce's "Eveline" 507

13. A Collection of Stories 523

POETRY   669

14. Reading Poetry 671

20. Sounds 826

Listening to Poetry 826

Rhyme 832

Sound and Meaning 837

Poems for Further Study 838

21. Patterns of Rhythm 856

22. Poetic Forms 876

24. A Study of Three Poets: Emily Dickinson, Robert Frost, and Langston Hughes 925

Emily Dickinson 925

Chronology 932

25. Critical Case Study: T. S. Eliot's "The Love Song of J. Alfred Prufrock"   1044

26. Cultural Case Study: Julia Alvarez's "Queens, 1963"   1060

DRAMA

34. Experimental Trends in Drama 1644

Beyond Realism 1644

35. Cultural Case Study: David Henry Hwang's *M. Butterfly* 1672

Photos: Plays in Performance   Between pages 1684 and 1685

36. A Collection of Plays 1729

CRITICAL THINKING AND WRITING 2019

38. Reading and Writing 2063

39. The Literary Research Paper 2099

INTRODUCTION

Reading
Imaginative Literature

THE NATURE OF LITERATURE

Literature does not lend itself to a single tidy definition because the making of it over the centuries has been as complex, unwieldy, and natural as life itself. Is literature everything that has been written, from ancient prayers to graffiti? Does it include songs and stories that were not written down until many years after they were recited? Does literature include the television scripts from *Seinfeld* as well as Shakespeare's *King Lear*? Is literature only writing that has permanent value and continues to move people? Must literature be true or beautiful or moral? Should it be socially useful?

Although these kinds of questions are not conclusively answered in this book, they are implicitly raised by the stories, poems, and plays included here. No definition of literature, particularly a brief one, is likely to satisfy everyone because definitions tend to weaken and require qualification when confronted by the uniqueness of individual works. In this context it is worth recalling Herman Melville's humorous use of a definition of a whale in *Moby-Dick* (1851). In the course of the novel Melville presents his imaginative and symbolic whale as inscrutable, but he begins with a quotation from Georges Cuvier, a French naturalist who defines a whale in his nineteenth-century study *The Animal Kingdom* this way: "The whale is a mammiferous animal without hind feet." Cuvier's description is technically correct, of course, but there is little wisdom in it. Melville understood that the reality of the whale (which he describes as the "ungraspable phantom of life") cannot be caught by isolated facts. If the full meaning of the whale is to be understood, it must be sought on the open sea of experience, where the whale itself is, rather than in exclusionary definitions. Facts and definitions are helpful; however, they do not always reveal the whole truth.

Despite Melville's reminder that a definition can be too limiting and even comical, it is useful for our purposes to describe literature as a fiction consisting of carefully arranged words designed to stir the imagination. Stories, poems, and plays are fictional. They are made up — imagined — even when based on actual historic events. Such imaginative writing differs from other kinds of writing because its purpose is not primarily to transmit facts or ideas. Imaginative literature is a source more of pleasure than of information, and we read it for basically the same reasons we listen to music or view a dance: enjoyment, delight, and satisfaction. Like other art forms, imaginative literature offers pleasure and usually attempts to convey a perspective, mood, feeling, or experience. Writers transform the facts the world provides — people, places, and objects — into experiences that suggest meanings.

Consider, for example, the difference between the following factual description of a snake and a poem on the same subject. Here is *Webster's Ninth New Collegiate Dictionary* definition:

> any of numerous limbless scaled reptiles (suborder Serpentes or Ophidia) with a long tapering body and with salivary glands often modified to produce venom which is injected through grooved or tubular fangs.

Contrast this matter-of-fact definition with Emily Dickinson's poetic evocation of a snake in "A narrow Fellow in the Grass":

A narrow Fellow in the Grass
Occasionally rides —
You may have met Him — did you not
His notice sudden is —

The Grass divides as with a Comb —   5
A spotted shaft is seen —
And then it closes at your feet
And opens further on —

He likes a Boggy Acre
A floor too cool for Corn —   10
Yet when a Boy, and Barefoot —
I more than once at Noon
Have passed, I thought, a Whip lash
Unbraiding in the Sun
When stooping to secure it   15
It wrinkled, and was gone —

Several of Nature's People
I know, and they know me —
I feel for them a transport
Of cordiality —   20

But never met this Fellow
Attended, or alone
Without a tighter breathing
And Zero at the Bone —

The dictionary provides a succinct, anatomical description of what a snake is, while Dickinson's poem suggests what a snake can mean. The definition offers facts; the poem offers an experience. The dictionary would probably allow someone who had never seen a snake to sketch one with reasonable accuracy. The poem also provides some vivid subjective descriptions — for example, the snake dividing the grass "as with a Comb" — yet it offers more than a picture of serpentine movements. The poem conveys the ambivalence many people have about snakes — the kind of feeling, for example, so evident on the faces of visitors viewing the snakes at a zoo. In the poem there is both a fascination with and a horror of what might be called snakehood; this combination of feelings has been coiled in most of us since Adam and Eve.

That "narrow Fellow" so cordially introduced by way of a riddle (the word *snake* is never used in the poem) is, by the final stanza, revealed as a snake in the grass. In between, Dickinson uses language expressively to convey her meaning. For instance, in the line "His notice sudden is," listen to the *s* sound in each word and note how the verb *is* unexpectedly appears at the end, making the snake's hissing presence all the more "sudden." And anyone who has ever been surprised by a snake knows the "tighter breathing / And Zero at the Bone" that Dickinson evokes so successfully by the rhythm of her word choices and line breaks. Perhaps even more significant, Dickinson's poem allows those who have never encountered a snake to imagine such an experience.

A good deal more could be said about the numbing fear that undercuts the affection for nature at the beginning of this poem, but the point here is that imaginative literature gives us not so much the full, factual proportions of the world as some of its experiences and meanings. Instead of defining the world, literature encourages us to try it out in our imaginations.

THE VALUE OF LITERATURE

Mark Twain once shrewdly observed that a person who chooses not to read has no advantage over a person who is unable to read. In industrialized societies today, however, the question is not who reads, because nearly everyone can and does, but what is read. Why should anyone spend precious time with literature when there is so much reading material available that provides useful information about everything from the daily news to personal computers? Why should a literary artist's imagination compete for attention that could be spent on the firm realities that constitute everyday life? In fact, national best-seller lists much less often include collections of stories, poems, or plays than they do cookbooks and, not surprisingly, diet books. Although such fare may be filling, it doesn't stay with you. Most people have other appetites too.

Certainly one of the most important values of literature is that it nourishes our emotional lives. An effective literary work may seem to speak directly to us, especially if we are ripe for it. The inner life that good writers reveal in their characters often gives us glimpses of some portion of ourselves. We can be moved to laugh, cry, tremble, dream, ponder, shriek, or rage with a character by simply turning a page instead of turning our lives upside down. Although the experience itself is imagined, the emotion is real. That's why the final chapters of a good adventure novel can make a reader's heart race as much as a 100-yard dash or why the repressed love of Hester Prynne in *The Scarlet Letter* by Nathaniel Hawthorne is painful to a sympathetic reader. Human emotions speak a universal language regardless of when or where a work was written.

In addition to appealing to our emotions, literature broadens our perspectives on the world. Most of the people we meet are pretty much like ourselves, and what we can see of the world even in a lifetime is astonishingly limited. Literature allows us to move beyond the inevitable boundaries of our own lives and culture because it introduces us to people different from ourselves, places remote from our neighborhoods, and times other than our own. Reading makes us more aware of life's possibilities as well as its subtleties and ambiguities. Put simply, people who read literature experience more life and have a keener sense of a common human identity than those who do not. It is true, of course, that many people go through life without reading imaginative literature, but that is a loss rather than a gain. They may find themselves troubled by the same kinds of questions that reveal Daisy Buchanan's restless, vague discontentment in F. Scott Fitzgerald's *The Great Gatsby:* "What'll we do with ourselves this afternoon?" cried Daisy, "and the day after that, and the next thirty years?"

Sometimes students mistakenly associate literature more with school than with life. Accustomed to reading it in order to write a paper or pass an examination, students may perceive such reading as a chore instead of a pleasurable opportunity, something considerably less important than studying for the "practical" courses that prepare them for a career. The study of literature, however, is also practical because it engages you in the kinds of problem solving important in a variety of fields, from philosophy to science and technology. The interpretation of literary texts requires you to deal with uncertainties, value judgments, and emotions; these are unavoidable aspects of life.

People who make the most significant contributions to their professions — whether in business, engineering, teaching, or some other area — tend to be challenged rather than threatened by multiple possibilities. Instead of retreating to the way things have always been done, they bring freshness and creativity to their work. F. Scott Fitzgerald once astutely described the "test of a first-rate intelligence" as "the ability to hold two opposed ideas in the mind at the same time, and still retain the ability to function." People with such intelligence know how to read situations, shape questions, interpret details, and evaluate competing points of view.

Equipped with a healthy respect for facts, they also understand the value of pursuing hunches and exercising their imaginations. Reading literature encourages a suppleness of mind that is helpful in any discipline or work.

Once the requirements for your degree are completed, what ultimately matters are not the courses listed on your transcript but the sensibilities and habits of mind that you bring to your work, friends, family, and, indeed, the rest of your life. A healthy economy changes and grows with the times; people do too if they are prepared for more than simply filling a job description. The range and variety of life that literature affords can help you to interpret your own experiences and the world in which you live.

To discover the insights that literature reveals requires careful reading and sensitivity. One of the purposes of a college introduction to literature class is to cultivate the analytic skills necessary for reading well. Class discussions often help establish a dialogue with a work that perhaps otherwise would not speak to you. Analytic skills can also be developed by writing about what you read. Writing is an effective means of clarifying your responses and ideas because it requires you to account for the author's use of language as well as your own. This book is based on two premises: that reading literature is pleasurable and that reading and understanding a work sensitively by thinking, talking, or writing about it increase the pleasure of the experience of it.

Understanding its basic elements — such as point of view, symbol, theme, tone, irony, and so on — is a prerequisite to an informed appreciation of literature. This kind of understanding allows you to perceive more in a literary work in much the same way that a spectator at a tennis match sees more if he or she understands the rules and conventions of the game. But literature is not simply a spectator sport. The analytic skills that open up literature also have their uses when you watch a television program or film and, more important, when you attempt to sort out the significance of the people, places, and events that constitute your own life. Literature enhances and sharpens your perceptions. What could be more lastingly practical as well as satisfying?

THE CHANGING LITERARY CANON

Perhaps the best reading creates some kind of change in us: we see more clearly; we're alert to nuances; we ask questions that previously didn't occur to us. Henry David Thoreau had that sort of reading in mind when he remarked in *Walden* that the books he valued most were those that caused him to date "a new era in his life from the reading." Readers are sometimes changed by literature, but it is also worth noting that the life of a literary work can also be affected by its readers. Melville's *Moby-Dick*, for example, was not valued as a classic until the 1920s, when critics rescued the novel from the obscurity of being cataloged in many libraries (including Yale's) not under fiction but under cetology, the study of whales. Indeed, many writers contemporary to Melville who were important and popular in the nineteenth century — William Cullen Bryant, Henry Wadsworth Longfellow, and James Russell Lowell, to name a few — are now mostly unread; their names appear more often on elementary schools built early in this century than in anthologies. Clearly, literary reputations and what is valued as great literature change over time and in the eyes of readers.

Such changes have accelerated during the past thirty years as the literary *canon* — those works considered by scholars, critics, and teachers to be the most important to read and study — has undergone a significant series of shifts. Writers who previously were overlooked, undervalued, neglected, or studiously ignored have been brought into focus in an effort to create a more diverse literary canon, one that recognizes the contributions of the many cultures that make up American society. Since the 1960s, for example, some critics have reassessed writings by women who had been left out of the standard literary traditions dominated by male writers. Many more female writers are now read alongside the male writers who traditionally populated literary history. Hence, a reader of Mark Twain and Stephen Crane is now just as likely to encounter Kate Chopin in a literary anthology. Until fairly recently Chopin was mostly regarded as a minor local colorist of Louisiana life. In the 1960s, however, the feminist movement helped to establish her present reputation as a significant voice in American literature owing to the feminist concerns so compellingly articulated by her female characters. This kind of enlargement of the canon also resulted from another reform movement of the 1960s. The civil rights movement sensitized literary critics to the political, moral, and aesthetic necessity of rediscovering African American literature, and more recently Asian and Hispanic writers have been making their way into the canon. Moreover, on a broader scale the canon is being revised and enlarged to include the works of writers from parts of the world other than the West, a development that reflects the changing values, concerns, and complexities of the past several years, when literary landscapes have shifted as dramatically as the political boundaries of Eastern Europe and the former Soviet Union.

No semester's reading list — or anthology — can adequately or accurately echo all the new voices competing to be heard as part of the mainstream literary canon, but recent efforts to open up the canon attempt to sensitize readers to the voices of women, minorities, and writers from all over the world. This development has not occurred without its urgent advocates or passionate dissenters. It's no surprise that issues about race, gender, and class often get people off the fence and on their feet (these controversies are discussed further in Chapter 37, "Critical Strategies for Reading"). Although what we regard as literature — whether it's called great, classic, or canonical — continues to generate debate, there is no question that such controversy will continue to reflect readers' values as well as the writers they admire.

FICTION

1

Reading Fiction

READING FICTION RESPONSIVELY

Reading a literary work responsively can be an intensely demanding activity. Henry David Thoreau — about as intense and demanding a reader and writer as they come — insists that "books must be read as deliberately and reservedly as they were written." Thoreau is right about the necessity for a conscious, sustained involvement with a literary work. Imaginative literature does demand more from us than, say, browsing through *People* magazine in a dentist's waiting room, but Thoreau makes the process sound a little more daunting than it really is. For when we respond to the demands of responsive reading, our efforts are usually rewarded with pleasure as well as understanding. Careful, deliberate reading — the kind that engages a reader's imagination as it calls forth the writer's — is a means of exploration that can take a reader outside whatever circumstance or experience previously defined his or her world. Just as we respond moment by moment to people and situations in our lives, we also respond to literary works as we read them, though we may not be fully aware of how we are affected at each point along the way. The more conscious we are of how and why we respond to works in particular ways, the more likely we are to be imaginatively engaged in our reading.

In a very real sense both the reader and the author create the literary work. How a reader responds to a story, poem, or play will help to determine its meaning. The author arranges the various elements that constitute his or her craft — elements such as plot, character, setting, point of view, symbolism, theme, and style, which you will be examining in subsequent chapters and which are defined in the Glossary of Literary Terms (p. 2123) — but the author cannot completely control the reader's response any more than a person can absolutely predict how a remark or action will be received by a stranger, a friend, or even a family member. Few authors *tell* readers how to respond. Our sympathy, anger, confusion, laughter, sadness, or whatever the feeling might be is left up to us to experience. Writers may have the talent to evoke such feelings, but they don't have the power and authority to enforce them. Because of the range of possible responses produced by imaginative literature, there is no single, correct, definitive response or interpretation. There can be readings that are wrongheaded or foolish, and some readings are better than others — that is, more responsive to a work's details and more persuasive — but that doesn't mean there is only one possible reading of a work (see Chapter 2, "Writing about Fiction").

Experience tells us that different people respond differently to the same work. Consider, for example, how often you've heard Melville's *Moby-Dick* described as one of the greatest American novels. This, however, is how a reviewer in *New Monthly Magazine* described the book when it was published in 1851: it is "a huge dose of hyperbolical slang, maudlin sentimentalism and tragic-comic bubble and squeak." Melville surely did not intend or desire this response; but there it is, and it was not a singular, isolated reaction. This reading — like any reading — was influenced by the values, assumptions, and expectations that the readers brought to the novel from both previous readings and life experiences. The reviewer's refusal to take the book seriously may have caused him to miss the boat from the perspective of many other readers of *Moby-Dick,* but it indicates that even "classics" (perhaps especially those kinds of works) can generate disparate readings.

Consider the following brief story by Kate Chopin, a writer whose fiction (like Melville's) sometimes met with indifference or hostility in her own time. As you read, keep track of your responses to the central character, Mrs. Mallard. Write down your feelings about her in a substantial paragraph when you finish the story. Think, for example, about how you respond to the emotions she expresses concerning news of her husband's death. What do you think of her feelings about marriage? Do you think you would react the way she does under similar circumstances?

KATE CHOPIN (1851–1904)

The Story of an Hour   1894

Knowing that Mrs. Mallard was afflicted with a heart trouble, great care was taken to break to her as gently as possible the news of her husband's death.

It was her sister Josephine who told her, in broken sentences; veiled hints that revealed in half concealing. Her husband's friend Richards was there, too, near her. It was he who had been in the newspaper office when intelligence of the railroad disaster was received, with Brently Mallard's name leading the list of "killed." He had only taken the time to assure himself of its truth by a second telegram, and had hastened to forestall any less careful, less tender friend in bearing the sad message.

She did not hear the story as many women have heard the same, with a paralyzed inability to accept its significance. She wept at once, with sudden, wild abandonment, in her sister's arms. When the storm of grief had spent itself she went away to her room alone. She would have no one follow her.

There stood, facing the open window, a comfortable, roomy armchair. Into this she sank, pressed down by a physical exhaustion that haunted her body and seemed to reach into her soul.

She could see in the open square before her house the tops of trees that 5 were all aquiver with the new spring life. The delicious breath of rain was in the air. In the street below a peddler was crying his wares. The notes of a distant song which some one was singing reached her faintly, and countless sparrows were twittering in the eaves.

There were patches of blue sky showing here and there through the clouds that had met and piled one above the other in the west facing her window.

She sat with her head thrown back upon the cushion of the chair, quite motionless, except when a sob came up into her throat and shook her, as a child who has cried itself to sleep continues to sob in its dreams.

She was young, with a fair, calm face, whose lines bespoke repression and even a certain strength. But now there was a dull stare in her eyes, whose gaze was fixed away off yonder on one of those patches of blue sky. It was not a glance of reflection, but rather indicated a suspension of intelligent thought.

There was something coming to her and she was waiting for it, fearfully. What was it? She did not know; it was too subtle and elusive to name. But she felt it, creeping out of the sky, reaching toward her through the sounds, the scents, the color that filled the air.

Now her bosom rose and fell tumultuously. She was beginning to recog- 10 nize this thing that was approaching to possess her, and she was striving to beat it back with her will—as powerless as her two white slender hands would have been.

When she abandoned herself a little whispered word escaped her slightly parted lips. She said it over and over under her breath: "free, free, free!" The vacant stare and the look of terror that had followed it went from her eyes. They stayed keen and bright. Her pulses beat fast, and the coursing blood warmed and relaxed every inch of her body.

She did not stop to ask if it were or were not a monstrous joy that held her. A clear and exalted perception enabled her to dismiss the suggestion as trivial.

She knew that she would weep again when she saw the kind, tender hands folded in death; the face that had never looked save with love upon her, fixed and gray and dead. But she saw beyond that bitter moment a long procession of years to come that would belong to her absolutely. And she opened and spread her arms out to them in welcome.

There would be no one to live for her during those coming years; she would live for herself. There would be no powerful will bending hers in that blind persistence with which men and women believe they have a right to impose a private will upon a fellow-creature. A kind intention or a cruel intention made the act seem no less a crime as she looked upon it in that brief moment of illumination.

And yet she had loved him — sometimes. Often she had not. What did it 15
matter! What could love, the unsolved mystery, count for in face of this possession of self-assertion which she suddenly recognized as the strongest impulse of her being!

"Free! Body and soul free!" she kept whispering.

Josephine was kneeling before the closed door with her lips to the keyhole,
imploring for admission. "Louise, open the door! I beg; open the door — you
will make yourself ill. What are you doing, Louise? For heaven's sake open the
door."

"Go away. I am not making myself ill." No; she was drinking in a very elixir
of life through that open window.

Her fancy was running riot along those days ahead of her. Spring days,
and summer days, and all sorts of days that would be her own. She breathed a
quick prayer that life might be long. It was only yesterday she had thought
with a shudder that life might be long.

She arose at length and opened the door to her sister's importunities. 20
There was a feverish triumph in her eyes, and she carried herself unwittingly
like a goddess of Victory. She clasped her sister's waist, and together they descended the stairs. Richards stood waiting for them at the bottom.

Some one was opening the front door with a latchkey. It was Brently Mallard who entered, a little travel-stained, composedly carrying his gripsack and
umbrella. He had been far from the scene of accident, and did not even know
there had been one. He stood amazed at Josephine's piercing cry; at Richards'
quick motion to screen him from the view of his wife.

But Richards was too late.

When the doctors came they said she had died of heart disease — of joy
that kills.

Did you find Mrs. Mallard a sympathetic character? Some readers think
that she is callous, selfish, and unnatural — even monstrous — because she
ecstatically revels in her newly discovered sense of freedom so soon after
learning of her husband's presumed death. Others read her as a victim of
her inability to control her own life in a repressive, male-dominated society.
Is it possible to hold both views simultaneously, or are they mutually exclusive? Are your views in any way influenced by your being male or female?
Does your age affect your perception? What about your social and economic background? Does your nationality, race, or religion in any way
shape your attitudes? Do you have particular views about the institution of
marriage that inform your assessment of Mrs. Mallard's character? Have
other reading experiences — perhaps a familiarity with some of Chopin's
other stories — predisposed you one way or another to Mrs. Mallard?

Understanding potential influences might be useful in determining
whether a particular response to Mrs. Mallard is based primarily on the
story's details and their arrangement or on an overt or subtle bias that is
brought to the story. If you unconsciously project your beliefs and assumptions onto a literary work, you run the risk of distorting it to accommodate
your prejudice. Your feelings can be a reliable guide to interpretation, but
you should be aware of what those feelings are based on.

Often specific questions about literary works cannot be answered definitively. For example, Chopin does not explain why Mrs. Mallard suffers a heart attack at the end of this story. Is the shock of seeing her "dead" husband simply too much for this woman "afflicted with a heart trouble"? Does she die of what the doctors call a "joy that kills" because she is so glad to see her husband? Is she so profoundly guilty about feeling "free" at her husband's expense that she has a heart attack? Is her death a kind of willed suicide in reaction to her loss of freedom? Your answers to these questions will depend on which details you emphasize in your interpretation of the story and the kinds of perspectives and values you bring to it. If, for example, you read the story from a feminist perspective, you would be likely to pay close attention to Chopin's comments about marriage in paragraph 14. Or if you read the story as an oblique attack on the insensitivity of physicians of the period, you might want to find out whether Chopin wrote elsewhere about doctors (she did) and compare her comments with historic sources. (A number of "Critical Strategies for Reading," including feminist and historical approaches, appear in Chapter 37.)

Reading responsively makes you an active participant in the process of creating meaning in a literary work. The experience that you and the author create will most likely not be identical to another reader's encounter with the same work, but then that's true of nearly any experience you'll have, and it is part of the pleasure of reading. Indeed, talking and writing about literature is a way of sharing responses so that they can be enriched and deepened.

A SAMPLE PAPER

Differences in Responses to Kate Chopin's "The Story of an Hour"

The following paper was written in response to an assignment that called for a three- to four-page discussion of how different readers might interpret Mrs. Mallard's character. The paper is based on the story as well as on the discussion of reader-response criticism (pp. 2039–2041) in Chapter 37, "Critical Strategies for Reading." As that discussion indicates, reader-response criticism is a critical approach that focuses on the reader rather than on the work itself in order to describe how the reader creates meaning from the text.

Wally Villa
Professor Brian
English 210
March 12, 19--

Differences in Responses to

Kate Chopin's "The Story of an Hour"

Kate Chopin's "The Story of an Hour" appears merely
to explore a woman's unpredictable reaction to her husband's assumed death and reappearance, but actually Chopin
offers Mrs. Mallard's bizarre story to reveal problems
that are inherent in the institution of marriage. By offering this depiction of a marriage that stifles the woman
to the point that she celebrates the death of her kind and
loving husband, Chopin challenges her readers to examine
their own views of marriage and relationships between men
and women. Each reader's judgment of Mrs. Mallard and her
behavior inevitably stems from his or her own personal
feelings about marriage and the influences of societal
expectations. Readers of differing genders, ages, and
marital experiences are, therefore, likely to react differently to Chopin's startling portrayal of the Mallards'
marriage, and that certainly is true of my response to
the story compared to my father's and grandmother's
responses.

Marriage often establishes boundaries between people
that make them unable to communicate with each other. The
Mallards' marriage was evidently crippled by both their
inability to talk to one another and Mrs. Mallard's conviction that her marriage was defined by a "powerful will
bending hers in that blind persistence with which men and
women believe they have a right to impose a private will
upon a fellow-creature." Yet she does not recognize that
it is not just men who impose their will upon women and

that the problems inherent in marriage affect men and women equally. To me, Mrs. Mallard is a somewhat sympathetic character, and I appreciate her longing to live out the "years to come that would belong to her absolutely." However, I also believe that she could have tried to improve her own situation somehow, either by reaching out to her husband or by abandoning the marriage altogether. Chopin uses Mrs. Mallard's tragedy to illuminate aspects of marriage that are harmful and, in this case, even deadly. Perhaps the Mallards' relationship should be taken as a warning to others: sacrificing one's own happiness in order to satisfy societal expectations can poison one's life and even destroy entire families.

When my father read "The Story of an Hour," his reaction to Mrs. Mallard was more antagonistic than my own. He sees Chopin's story as a timeless "battle of the sexes," serving as further proof that men will never really be able to understand what it is that women want. Mrs. Mallard endures an obviously unsatisfying marriage without ever explaining to her husband that she feels trapped and unfulfilled. Mrs. Mallard dismisses the question of whether or not she is experiencing a "monstrous joy" as trivial, but my father does not think that this is a trivial question. He believes Mrs. Mallard is guilty of a monstrous joy because she selfishly celebrates the death of her husband without ever allowing him the opportunity to understand her feelings. He believes that, above all, Brently Mallard should be seen as the most victimized character in the story. Mr. Mallard is a good, kind man, with friends who care about him and a marriage that he thinks he can depend on. He "never looked save with love" upon his wife, his only "crime" was coming home from work one day, and yet he is the one who is bereaved at the end of the story, for

reasons he will never understand. Mrs. Mallard's passion
for her newly discovered freedom is perhaps understandable, but according to my father, Mr. Mallard is the character most deserving of sympathy.

Maybe not surprisingly, my grandmother's interpretation of "The Story of an Hour" was radically different
from both mine and my father's. My grandmother was married
in 1936 and widowed in 1959 and therefore can identify
with Chopin's characters, who live at the turn of the century. Her first reaction, aside from her unwavering support for Mrs. Mallard and her predicament, was that this
story demonstrates the differences between the ways men
and women related to each other a century ago and the way
they relate today. Unlike my father, who thinks Mrs. Mallard is too passive, my grandmother believes that Mrs.
Mallard doesn't even know that she is feeling repressed
until after she is told that Brently is dead. In 1894,
divorce was so scandalous and stigmatized that it simply
wouldn't have been an option for Mrs. Mallard, and so her
only way "out" of the marriage would have been one of their
deaths. Being relatively young, Mrs. Mallard probably
considered herself doomed to a long life in an unhappy
marriage. My grandmother also feels that, in spite of all
we know of Mrs. Mallard's feelings about her husband and
her marriage, she still manages to live up to everyone's
expectations of her as a woman both in life and in death.
She is a dutiful wife to Brently, as she is expected to
be, she weeps "with sudden, wild abandonment" when she
hears the news of his death, she locks herself in her room
to cope with her new situation, and she has a fatal heart
attack upon seeing her husband arrive home. Naturally the
male doctors would think that she died of the "joy that
kills"; nobody could have guessed that she was unhappy

Villa 4

with her life, and she would never have wanted them
to know.

    Interpretations of "The Story of an Hour" seem to
vary according to the gender, age, and experience of the
reader. While both male and female readers can certainly
sympathize with Mrs. Mallard's plight, female readers--as
was evident in our class discussions--seem to relate more
easily to her predicament and are quicker to exonerate her
of any responsibility for her unhappy situation. Conversely, male readers are more likely to feel compassion
for Mr. Mallard, who loses his wife for reasons that will
always remain entirely unknown to him. Older readers probably understand more readily the strength of social forces
and the difficulty of trying to deny societal expectations
concerning gender roles in general and marriage in particular. Younger readers seem to feel that Mrs. Mallard is too
passive and that she could have improved her domestic life
immeasurably if she had taken the initiative to either improve or end her relationship with her husband. Ultimately,
how each individual reader responds to Mrs. Mallard's story
reveals his or her own ideas about marriage, society, and
how men and women communicate with each other.

Before beginning your own writing assignment on fiction, you should
review Chapter 2, "Writing about Fiction," as well as Chapter 38, "Reading
and Writing," which provides a step-by-step explanation of how to choose
a topic, develop a thesis, and organize various types of writing assignments. If you use outside sources, you should also be familiar with the conventional documentation procedures described in Chapter 39, "The Literary Research Paper."

EXPLORATIONS AND FORMULAS

Each time we pick up a work of fiction, go to the theater, or turn on the television, we have a trace of the same magical expectation that can be heard in the voice of a child who begs, "Tell me a story." Human beings have enjoyed stories ever since they learned to speak. Whatever the motive for creating stories—even if simply to delight or instruct—the basic human impulse to tell and hear stories existed long before the development of written language. Myths about the origins of the world and legends about the heroic exploits of demigods were among the earliest forms of storytelling to develop into oral traditions, which were eventually written down. These narratives are the ancestors of the stories we read on the printed page today. Unlike the early listeners to ancient myths and legends, we read our stories silently, but the pleasure derived from the mysterious power of someone else's artfully arranged words remains largely the same. Every one of us likes a good story.

The stories that appear in anthologies for college students are generally chosen for their high literary quality. Such stories can affect us at the deepest emotional level, reveal new insights into ourselves or the world, and stretch us by exercising our imaginations. They warrant careful reading and close study to appreciate the art that has gone into creating them. The following chapters on plot, character, setting, and the other elements of literature are designed to provide the terms and concepts that can help you understand how a work of fiction achieves its effects and meanings. It is worth acknowledging, however, that many people buy and read fiction that is quite different from the stories usually anthologized in college texts. What about all those paperbacks with exciting, colorful covers near the cash registers in shopping malls and corner drugstores?

These books, known as *formula fiction,* are the adventure, western, detective, science fiction, and romance novels that entertain millions of readers annually. What makes them so popular? What do their characters, plots, and themes offer readers that accounts for the tremendous sales of stories with titles like *Caves of Doom, Silent Scream, Colt .45,* and *Forbidden Ecstasy?* Many of the writers included in this book have enjoyed wide popularity and written best-sellers, but there are more readers of formula fiction than there are readers of Hemingway, Faulkner, or Oates, to name only a few. Formula novels do, of course, provide entertainment, but that makes them no different from serious stories, if entertainment means pleasure. Any of the stories in this or any other anthology can be read for pleasure.

Formula fiction, though, is usually characterized as escape literature. There are sensible reasons for this description. Adventure stories about soldiers of fortune are eagerly read by men who live pretty average lives doing ordinary jobs. Romance novels about attractive young women falling in love with tall, dark, handsome men are read mostly by women who dream themselves out of their familiar existences. The excitement, violence, and passion that such stories provide are a kind of reprieve from everyday experience.

And yet readers of serious fiction may also use it as a refuge, a liberation from monotony and boredom. Mark Twain's humorous stories have, for example, given countless hours of pleasurable relief to readers who would rather spend time in Twain's light and funny world than in their own. Others might prefer the terror of Edgar Allan Poe's fiction or the painful predicament of two lovers in a Joyce Carol Oates story.

Thus, to get at some of the differences between formula fiction and serious literature, it is necessary to go beyond the motives of the reader to the motives of the writer and the qualities of the work itself.

Unlike serious fiction, the books displayed next to the cash registers (and their short story equivalents on the magazine racks) are written with only one object: to be sold. They are aimed at specific consumer markets that can be counted on to buy them. This does not mean that all serious writers must live in cold garrets writing for audiences who have not yet discovered their work. No one writes to make a career of poverty. It does mean, however, that if a writer's primary purpose is to anticipate readers' generic expectations about when the next torrid love scene, bloody gunfight, or thrilling chase is due, there is little room to be original or to have something significant to say. There is little if any chance to explore seriously a character, idea, or incident if the major focus is not on the integrity of the work itself.

Although the specific elements of formula fiction differ depending on the type of story, some basic ingredients go into all westerns, mysteries, adventures, science fiction, and romances. From the very start, a reader can anticipate a happy ending for the central character, with whom he or she will identify. There may be suspense, but no matter what or how many the obstacles, complications, or near defeats, the hero or heroine succeeds and reaffirms the values and attitudes the reader brings to the story. Virtue triumphs, love conquers all, honesty is the best policy, and hard work guarantees success. Hence, the villains are corralled, the wedding vows are exchanged, the butler confesses, and gold is discovered at the last moment. The visual equivalents of such formula stories are readily available at movie theaters and in television series. Some are better than others, but all are relatively limited by the writer's goal of giving an audience what will sell.

Although formula fiction may not offer many surprises, it provides pleasure to a wide variety of readers. College professors, for example, are just as likely to be charmed by formula stories as anyone else. Readers of serious fiction who revel in exploring more challenging imaginative worlds can also enjoy formulaic stories, which offer little more than an image of the world as a simple place in which our assumptions and desires are confirmed. The familiarity of a given formula is emotionally satisfying because we are secure in our expectations of it. We know at the start of a Sherlock Holmes story that the mystery will be solved by that famous detective's relentless scientific analysis of the clues, but we take pleasure in seeing how Holmes unravels the mystery before us. Similarly, we know that James Bond's wit, grace, charm, courage, and skill will ultimately prevail over the diabolic schemes of eccentric villains, but we volunteer for the mission anyway.

Perhaps that happens for the same reason that we climb aboard a roller coaster: no matter how steep and sharp the curves, we stay on a track that is both exciting and safe. Although excitement, adventure, mystery, and romance are major routes to escape in formula fiction, most of us make that trip only temporarily, for a little relaxation and fun. Momentary relief from our everyday concerns is as healthy and desirable as an occasional daydream or fantasy. Such reading is a form of play because we — like spectators of or participants in a game — experience a formula of excitement, tension, and then release that can fascinate us regardless of how many times the game is played.

Many publishers of formula fiction — such as romance, adventure, or detective stories — issue a set number of new novels each month. Readers can buy them in stores or subscribe to them through the mail. These same publishers send "tip sheets" on request to authors who want to write for a particular series. The details of the formula differ from one series to another, but each tip sheet covers the basic elements that go into a story.

There are many kinds of formulaic romance novels; some include psychological terrors, some use historical settings, and some even incorporate time travel so that the hero or heroine can travel back in time and fall in love, and still others create mystery and suspense. Several publishers have recently released romances that reflect contemporary social concerns and issues; multicultural couples and gay and lesbian relationships as well as more explicit descriptions of sexual activities are now sometimes featured in these books. In general, however, the majority of romance novels are written to appeal to a readership that embraces more traditional societal expectations and values.

The following composite tip sheet summarizes the typical advice offered by publishers of romance novels. These are among the most popular titles published in the United States; it has been estimated that four out of every ten paperbacks sold are romance novels. The categories and the tone of the language in this composite tip sheet are derived from a number of publishers and provide a glimpse of how formula fiction is written and what the readers of romance novels are looking for in their escape literature.

A Composite of a Romance Tip Sheet

Plot

The story focuses on the growing relationship between the heroine and hero. After a number of complications, they discover lasting love and make a permanent commitment to each other in marriage. The plot should move quickly. Background information about the heroine should be kept to a minimum. The hero should appear as early as possible (preferably in the first chapter and no later than the second), so that the hero's and heroine's feelings about each other are in the foreground as they cope with misperceptions that keep them apart until the final pages of the story. The more tension created by their uncertainty about each other's love, the greater the excitement and anticipation for the reader.

Love is the major interest. Do not inject murder, extortion, international intrigue, hijacking, horror, or supernatural elements into the plot. Controversial social issues and politics, if mentioned at all, should never be allowed a significant role. Once the heroine and hero meet, they should clearly be interested in each other, but that interest should be complicated by some kind of misunderstanding. He, for example, might find her too ambitious, an opportunist, cold, or flirtatious; or he might assume that she is attached to someone else. She might think he is haughty, snobbish, power hungry, indifferent, or contemptuous of her. The reader knows what they do not: that eventually these obstacles will be overcome. Interest is sustained by keeping the lovers apart until very near the end so that the reader will stay with the plot to see how they get together.

Heroine

The heroine is a modern American woman between the ages of nineteen and twenty-eight who reflects today's concerns. The story is told in the third person from her point of view. She is attractive and nicely dressed but not glamorous; glitter and sophistication should be reserved for the other woman (the heroine's rival for the hero), whose flashiness will compare unfavorably with the heroine's modesty. When the heroine does dress up, however, her beauty should be stunningly apparent. Her trim figure is appealing but not abundant; a petite healthy appearance is desirable. Both her looks and her clothes should be generously detailed.

Her personality is spirited and independent without being pushy or stubborn because she knows when to give in. Although sensitive, she doesn't cry every time she is confronted with a problem (though she might cry in private moments). A sense of humor is helpful. Because she is on her own, away from parents (usually deceased) or other protective relationships, she is self-reliant as well as vulnerable. The story may begin with her on the verge of an important decision about her life. She is clearly competent but not entirely certain of her own qualities. She does not take her attractiveness for granted or realize how much the hero is drawn to her.

Common careers for the heroine include executive secretary, nurse, 5 teacher, interior designer, assistant manager, department store buyer, travel agent, or struggling photographer (no menial work). She can also be a doctor, lawyer, or other professional. Her job can be described in some detail and made exciting, but it must not dominate her life. Although she is smart, she is not extremely intellectual or defined by her work. Often she meets the hero through work, but her major concerns center on love, marriage, home, and family. White wine is okay, but she never drinks alone — or uses drugs. She may be troubled, frustrated, threatened, and momentarily thwarted in the course of the story, but she never totally gives in to despair or desperation. She has strengths that the hero recognizes and admires.

Hero

The hero should be about ten years older than the heroine and can be foreign or American. He needn't be handsome in a traditional sense, but he must be strongly masculine. Always tall and well built (not brawny or thick) and usually dark, he looks as terrific in a three-piece suit as he does in sports clothes. His clothes reflect good taste and an affluent life-style. Very successful professionally and financially, he is a man in charge of whatever work he's engaged in (financier, doctor, publisher, architect, business executive, airline pilot, artist, etc.). His wealth is manifested in his sophistication and experience.

His past may be slightly mysterious or shrouded by some painful moment (perhaps with a woman) that he doesn't want to discuss. Whatever the circumstance—his wife's death or divorce are common—it was not his fault. Avoid chronic problems such as alcoholism, drug addiction, or sexual dysfunctions. To others he may appear moody, angry, unpredictable, and explosively passionate, but the heroine eventually comes to realize his warm, tender side. He should be attractive not only as a lover but also as a potential husband and father.

Secondary Characters

Because the major interest is in how the heroine will eventually get together with the hero, the other characters are used to advance the action. There are three major types:

(1) *The Other Woman:* Her vices serve to accent the virtues of the heroine; immediately beneath her glamorous sophistication is a deceptive, selfish, mean-spirited, rapacious predator. She may seem to have the hero in her clutches, but she never wins him in the end.

(2) *The Other Man:* He usually falls into two types: (a) the decent sort who is 10 there when the hero isn't around and (b) the selfish sort who schemes rather than loves. Neither is a match for the hero.

(3) *Other Characters:* Like furniture, they fill in the background and are useful for positioning the hero and heroine. These characters are familiar types such as the hero's snobbish aunt, the heroine's troubled younger siblings, the loyal friend, or the office gossip. They should be realistic, but they must not be allowed to obscure the emphasis on the lovers. The hero may have children from a previous marriage, but they should rarely be seen or heard. It's usually simpler and better not to include them.

Setting

The setting is usually contemporary. Romantic, exciting places are best: New York City, London, Paris, Rio, the mountains, the ocean—wherever it is exotic and love's possibilities are the greatest. Marriage may take the heroine and hero to a pretty suburb or small town.

Love Scenes

The hero and heroine may make love before marriage. The choice will depend largely on the heroine's sensibilities and circumstances. She should reflect modern attitudes. If the lovers do engage in premarital sex, it should be made clear that neither is promiscuous, especially the heroine. Even if their relationship is consummated before marriage, their lovemaking should not occur until late in the story. There should be at least several passionate scenes, but complications, misunderstandings, and interruptions should keep the couple from actually making love until they have made a firm commitment to each other. Descriptions should appeal to the senses; however, detailed, graphic close-ups are unacceptable. Passion can be presented sensually but not clinically; the lovemaking should be seen through a soft romantic lens.

Violence and any out-of-the-way sexual acts should not even be hinted at. No coarse language.

Writing

Avoid extremely complex sentences, very long paragraphs, and lengthy descriptions. Use concise, vivid details to create the heroine's world. Be sure to include full descriptions of the hero's and heroine's physical features and clothes. Allow the reader to experience the romantic mood surrounding the lovers. Show how the heroine feels; do not simply report her feelings. Dialogue should sound like ordinary conversation, and the overall writing should be contemporary English without slang, difficult foreign expressions, strange dialects, racial epithets, or obscenities (*hell, damn,* and a few other mild swears are all right).

Length

55,000 to 65,000 words in ten to twelve chapters.

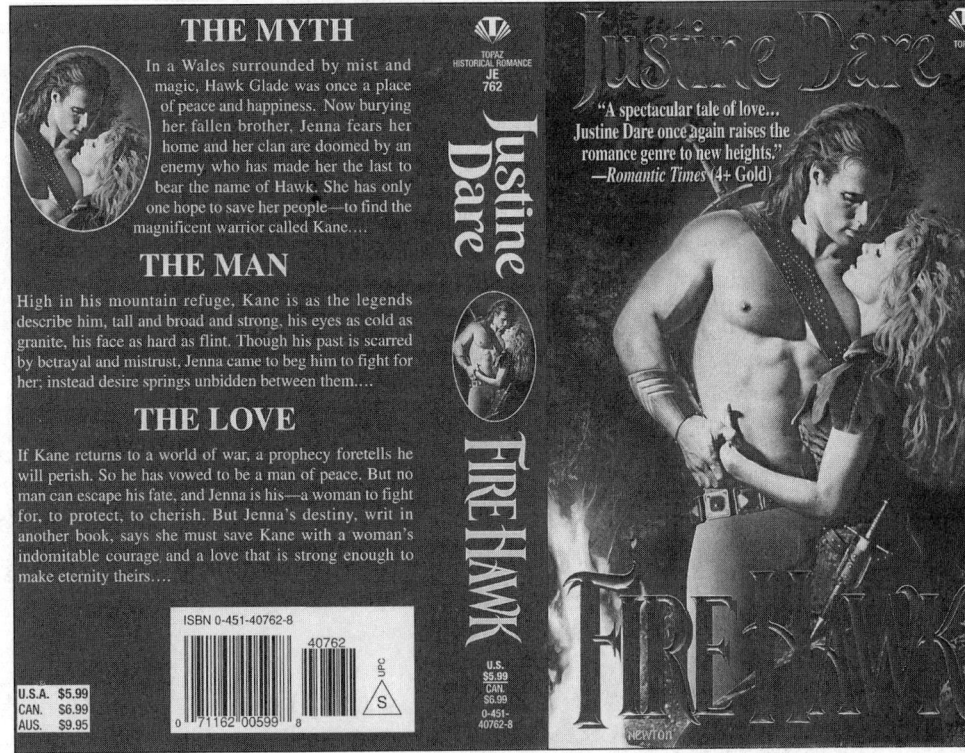

The cover for FireHawk *(Penguin, 1997) illustrates another convention of romance formula fiction: its packaging demands an image of a man clasping a passionate beauty to his manly chest. As the back-cover copy suggests, this Topaz novel is a historical romance—a subcategory of the romance formula—and so a few of the guidelines on the tip sheet are modified (the setting is medieval Wales rather than contemporary America, for example). But most of the guidelines apply: Kane is strong and so is Jenna's powerful love.*

CONSIDERATIONS FOR CRITICAL THINKING AND WRITING

1. FIRST RESPONSE. Given the expectations implied by the tip sheet, what generalizations can you make about those likely to write formula fiction? Does the tip sheet change the way you think about romantic fiction or other kinds of formula fiction?

2. Who is the intended audience for this type of romance? Try to describe the audience in detail: How does a romance novel provide escape for these readers?

3. Why is it best that the heroine be "attractive and nicely dressed but not glamorous"? Why do you think publishers advise writers to include detailed descriptions of her clothes? Do you find the heroine appealing? Why or why not?

4. Why should the hero be "about ten years older than the heroine"? If he is divorced, why is it significant that "it was not his fault"?

5. Why do you think the hero and heroine are kept apart by complications until the end of the story? Does the outline of the plot sound familiar to you or remind you of any other stories?

6. Why do you think restrictions are placed on the love scenes?

7. Why are "extremely complex sentences, very long paragraphs, and lengthy descriptions" discouraged?

8. To what extent does the tip sheet describe the strategies used in popular television soap operas? How do you account for the appeal of these shows?

9. Explain how the tip sheet confirms traditional views of male and female roles in society. Does it accommodate any broken traditions?

10. Carefully examine the Topaz Historical Romance cover. How do the cover's images and copy reinforce what readers can expect from a romance novel?

11. Included in the marketing material that accompanies the Topaz Historical Romance is this notation: "Topaz is an Official Sponsor of the Mrs. America Pageant." Why do you suppose the publishers support this contest?

12. Write a tip sheet for another kind of popular formula story, such as a western or a detective story, that you have observed in a novel, television show, or film. How is the plot patterned? How are the characters made familiar? How is the setting related to the story? What are the obligatory scenes? How is the overall style consistent? To get started, you might consider an Agatha Christie novel, an episode from a police series on television, or a James Bond film.

13. Try writing a scene for a formula romance, or read the excerpt from Edgar Rice Burroughs's *Tarzan of the Apes* (p. 62) and try an adventure scene.

A COMPARISON OF TWO STORIES

Each of the following contemporary pieces of fiction is about a woman who experiences deep sorrow. The first, from *A Secret Sorrow* by Karen Van Der Zee, is an excerpt from a romance by Harlequin Books, a major publisher of formula fiction that has sold well over a billion copies of its romance titles — enough for about 20 percent of the world's population. The second piece, Gail Godwin's "A Sorrowful Woman," is a complete short story that originally appeared in *Esquire;* it is not a formula story. Unlike *A Secret Sorrow,* Godwin's story does not have a standard plot pattern employing familiar character types that appear in a series of separate but similar works.

Read each selection carefully and look for evidence of formulaic writing in the chapters from *A Secret Sorrow.* Pay particular attention to the advice on plotting and characterization offered in the composite tip sheet. As you read Godwin's short story, think about how it is different from Van Der Zee's excerpt; note also any similarities. The questions that follow the stories should help you consider how the experiences of reading the two are different.

KAREN VAN DER ZEE (B. 1947)

This excerpt consists of the final two chapters of *A Secret Sorrow.* This is what has happened so far: the central character, Faye, is recuperating from the psychological effects of a serious car accident in which she received a permanent internal injury. After the accident, she quits her job and breaks her engagement to Greg. She moves into her brother Chuck's house and falls in love with Kai, a visiting Texan and good friend of her brother. At the end of Chapter 10, Kai insists on knowing why she will not marry him and asks, "Who is Doctor Jaworski?"

From A Secret Sorrow   *1981*

Chapter Eleven

Faye could feel the blood drain from her face and for one horrifying moment she thought she was going to faint right in Kai's arms. The room tilted and everything swirled around in a wild madman's dance. She clutched at him for support, fighting for control, trying to focus at some point beyond his shoulder. Slowly, everything steadied.

"I . . . I don't know him," she murmured at last. "I. . . ."

He reached in the breast pocket of his shirt, took out a slip of paper, and held it out for her to see. One glance and Faye recognized it as the note from Doctor Martin with Doctor Jaworski's name scrawled on it, thickly underlined.

"How did you get that?" Her voice was a terrified whisper. She was still holding on, afraid she would fall if she let go.

"I found it on the floor in my bedroom. It must have fallen out of your 5 wallet along with everything else on Saturday morning."

Yes — oh God! Her legs were shaking so badly, she knew it was only his arms that kept her from falling.

"Who is Doctor Jaworski, Faye?" His voice was patiently persistent.

"I . . . he. . . ." Her voice broke. "Let me go, please let me go." She felt as if she were suffocating in his embrace and she struggled against him, feebly, but it was no use.

"He's a psychiatrist, isn't he?" His voice was gentle, very gentle, and she looked up at him in stunned surprise.

He knew, oh God, he knew. She closed her eyes, a helpless sense of inevitability engulfing her.

"You know," she whispered. "How do you know?"

"Simple. Two minutes on the phone to Chicago." He paused. "Doctor Martin — was he one of the doctors who treated you at the hospital?"

"Yes."

"Why did he give you Doctor Jaworski's name? Did he want you to make an appointment with him?"

"Yes." Despondency overtook her. There was no going back now. No escape from the truth. No escape from his arms. Resistance faded and she felt numbed and lifeless. It didn't matter any more. Nothing mattered.

"Did you?" Kai repeated.

"Did I what?"

"See him — Doctor Jaworski."

"No."

"Why did Doctor Martin want you to see a psychiatrist?"

"I. . . ." Faye swallowed miserably. "It's . . . it's therapy for grieving . . . mourning." She made a helpless gesture with her hand. "When people lose a . . . a wife, or husband for instance, they go through a more or less predictable pattern of emotions. . . ." She gave him a quick glance, then looked away. "Like denial, anger. . . ."

". . . depression, mourning, acceptance," Kai finished for her, and she looked back at him in surprise.

"Yes."

His mouth twisted in a little smile. "I'm not totally ignorant about subjects other than agronomy." There was a momentary pause as he scrutinized her face. "Why did you need that kind of therapy, Faye?"

And then it was back again, the resistance, the revolt against his probing questions. She stiffened in defense — her whole body growing rigid with instinctive rebellion.

"It's none of your business!"

"Oh, yes, it is. We're talking about our life together. Your life and mine."

She strained against him, hands pushing against his chest. "Let me go! Please let me go!" Panic changed into tears. She couldn't take his nearness any more, the feel of his hard body touching hers, the strength of him.

"No, Faye, no. You're going to tell me. Now. I'm not letting you go until you've told me everything. Everything, you hear?"

"I can't!" she sobbed. "I can't!"

"Faye," he said slowly, "you'll *have* to. You told me you love me, but you don't want to marry me. You have given me no satisfactory reasons, and I'll be damned if I'm going to accept your lack of explanations."

"You have no right to demand an explanation!"

"Oh, yes, I have. You're part of me, Faye. Part of my life."

"You talk as if you own me!" She was trembling, struggling to get away from him. She couldn't stand there, so close to him with all the pent-up despair inside her, the anger, the fear of what she knew not how to tell him.

His hands were warm and strong on her back, holding her steady. Then, with one hand, he tilted back her head and made her look at him. "You gave me your love—I own that," he said softly. "True loving involves commitment, vulnerability, trust. Don't you trust me, Faye?"

New tears ran silently down her cheeks. "If I told you," she blurted out, "you wouldn't . . . you wouldn't. . . ."

"I wouldn't *what?*"

"You wouldn't want me any more!" The words were wrenched from her in blind, agonizing grief. "You wouldn't *want* me any more!"

He shook his head incredulously. "What makes you think you can make that decision for me? Do you have so little trust in my love for you?"

Faye didn't answer, couldn't answer. Through a mist of tears he was noth-   40
ing but a blur in front of her eyes.

"What is so terrible that you can't tell me?"

She shrank inwardly, as if shriveling away in pain. "Let me go," she whispered. "Please let me go and I'll tell you."

After a moment's hesitation Kai released her. Faye backed away from him, feeling like a terrified animal. She stood with her back against the wall, glad for the support, her whole body shaking. She took a deep breath and wiped her face dry with her hand.

"I'm afraid . . . afraid to marry you."

"Afraid?" He looked perplexed. "Afraid of what? Of me? Of marriage?"   45

Faye closed her eyes, taking another deep breath. "I can't be what you want me to be. We can't have the kind of life you want." She looked at him, standing only a few feet away, anguish tearing through her. "I'm so afraid . . . you'll be disappointed," she whispered.

"Oh God, Faye," he groaned, "I love you." He came toward her and panic surged through her as he held her against the wall, his hands reaching up to catch her face between them.

"Don't," she whispered. "Please, don't touch me." But it was no use. His mouth came down on hers and he kissed her with a hard, desperate passion.

"I love you," he said huskily. "I love you."

Faye wrenched her face free from his hands. "Don't touch me! Please don't   50
touch me!" She was sobbing now, her words barely audible. Her knees gave way and her back slid down along the wall until she crumpled on to the floor, face in her hands.

Kai took a step backward and pulled her up. "Stand up, Faye. For God's sake stand up!" He held her against the wall and she looked at him, seeing every line in his dark face, the intense blue of his eyes, and knew that this was the moment, that there was no more waiting.

And Kai knew it too. His eyes held hers locked in unrelenting demand. "Why should I be disappointed, Faye? *Why?*"

Her heart was thundering in her ears and it seemed as if she couldn't breathe, as if she were going to drown.

"Because . . . because I can't give you children! Because I can't get pregnant! I can't have babies! That's why!" Her voice was an agonized cry, torn from the depths of her misery. She yanked down his arms that held her locked against the wall and moved away from him. And then she saw his face.

It was ashen, gray under his tan. He stared at her as if he had never seen   55
her before.

"Oh my God, Faye. . . ." His voice was low and hoarse. "Why didn't you tell me, why. . . ."

Faye heard no more. She ran out the door, snatching her bag off the chair as she went by. The only thought in her mind was to get away — away from Kai and what was in his eyes.

She reached for Kai's spare set of car keys in her bag, doing it instinctively, knowing she couldn't walk home alone in the dark. How she managed to get the keys in the door lock and in the ignition she never knew. Somehow, she made it home.

The phone rang as Faye opened the front door and she heard Chuck answer it in the kitchen.

"She's just got in," he said into the mouthpiece, smiling at Faye as she   60
came into view. He listened for a moment, nodded. "Okay, fine with me."

Faye turned and walked up the stairs, taking deep breaths to calm her shattered nerves. Kai hadn't wasted any time checking up on her. She didn't care what he was telling Chuck, but she wasn't going to stand there listening to a one-sided conversation. But only a second later Chuck was behind her on the stairs.

"Kai wanted to know whether you'd arrived safely."

"I did, thank you," she said levelly, her voice surprisingly steady.

"I take it you ran out and took off with his car?"

"Did he say that?"   65

"No. He was *worried* about you. He wanted to make sure you went home." He sounded impatient, and she couldn't blame him. She was making life unbearable for everyone around her. Everybody worried about her. Everybody loved her. Everything should be right. Only it wasn't.

"Well, I'm home now, and I'm going to bed. Good night."

"Good night, Faye."

Faye lay in bed without any hope of sleep. Mechanically she started to sort through her thoughts and emotions, preparing mentally for the next confrontation. There would be one, she didn't doubt it for a moment. But she needed time — time to clear her head, time to look at everything in a reasonable, unemotional way.

It was a temptation to run — get in the car and keep driving, but it would   70
be a stupid thing to do. There was no place for her to go, and Kai would find her, no matter what. If there was one thing she knew about Kai it was his stubbornness and his persistence. She had to stick it out, right here, get it over with, deal with it. Only she didn't know how.

She lay listening to the stillness, just a few sounds here and there — the house creaking, a car somewhere in the distance, a dog barking. She had to think, but her mind refused to cooperate. She *had* to think, decide what to say to Kai the next time she saw him, but she couldn't think, she *couldn't think*.

And then, as she heard the door open in the silence, the quiet footsteps coming up the stairs, she knew it was too late, that time had run out.

Without even knocking he came into her room and walked over to the bed. She could feel the mattress sag as his weight came down on it. Her heart was pounding like a sledgehammer, and then his arms came around her and he drew her against him.

"Faye," he said quietly, "please marry me."

"No," she said thickly. "No." She could feel him stiffen against her and she   75
released herself from his arms and slid off the bed. She switched on the light and stood near the window, far from the bed, far from Kai. "I don't expect you

to play the gentleman, I don't expect you to throw out a life of dreams just for the sake of chivalry. You don't have to marry me, Kai." She barely recognized her own voice. It was like the cool calm sound of a stranger, unemotional, cold. "You don't have to marry me," she repeated levelly, giving him a steady look.

Her words were underlined by the silence that followed, a silence loaded with a strange, vibrating energy, a force in itself, filling the room.

Kai rose to his feet, slowly, and the face that looked at her was like that of a stranger, a dangerous, angry stranger. Never before had she seen him so angry, so full of hot, fuming fury.

"Shut up," he said in a low, tight voice. "Shut up and stop playing the martyr!"

The sound of his voice and the words he said shocked Faye into silence. She stared at him open-mouthed, and then a slow, burning anger arose inside her.

"How dare you! How. . . ." 80

He strode toward her and took her upper arms and shook her. "Shut up and listen to me! What the hell are you thinking? What the hell did you expect me to do when you told me? You throw me a bomb and then walk out on me! What did you expect my reaction to be? Was I supposed to stay cool and calm and tell you it didn't matter? Would you have married me then? Well, let me tell you something! It matters! It matters to me! I am not apologizing for my reaction!" He paused, breathing hard. "You know I always wanted children, but what in God's name makes you think you're the only one who has the right to feel bad about it? I have that right too, you hear! I love you, dammit, and I want to marry you, and if we can't have children I have all the right in the world to feel bad about it!"

He stopped talking. He was still breathing hard and he looked at her with stormy blue eyes. Faye felt paralyzed by his tirade and she stared at him, incapable of speech. She couldn't move, she couldn't think.

"Why do you think I want you for my wife?" he continued on a calmer note. "Because you're some kind of baby factory? What kind of man do you think I am? I love *you*, not your procreating ability. So we have a problem. Well, we'll learn to deal with it, one way or another."

There was another silence, and still Faye didn't speak, and she realized she was crying, soundlessly, tears slowly dripping down her cheeks. She was staring at his chest, blindly, not knowing what to think, not thinking at all.

He lifted her chin, gently. "Look at me, Faye." 85

She did, but his face was only a blur.

"Faye, we're in this together—you and I. Don't you see that? It's not just *your* problem, it's *ours*."

"No," she whispered. "No!" She shook her head wildly. "You have a choice, don't you see that? You don't have to marry me. You could marry someone else and have children of your own."

"Oh, God, Faye," he groaned, "you're wrong. Don't you know? Don't you see? I *don't* have a choice. I never did have a choice, or a chance. Not since I met you and fell in love with you. I don't *want* anybody else, don't you understand that? I want you, only you."

She wanted to believe it, give in to him. Never before had she wanted 90 anything more desperately than she wanted to give in to him now. But she couldn't, she couldn't. . . . She closed her eyes, briefly, fighting for reason, common sense.

"Kai, I . . . I can't live all my life with your regret and your disappointment. Every time we see some pregnant woman, every time we're with somebody else's children I'll feel I've failed you! I. . . ." Her voice broke and new sobs came unchecked.

He held her very tightly until she calmed down and then he put her from him a little and gave her a dark, compelling look.

"It's not *my* regret, or *my* disappointment," he said with quiet emphasis. "It's *ours*. We're not talking about *you* or *me*. We're talking about *us*. I love you, and you love me, and that's the starting point, that comes first. From then on we're in it together."

Faye moved out of his arms, away from him, but her legs wouldn't carry her and she sank into a chair. She covered her face with her hands and tried desperately to stop the crying, to stop the tears from coming and coming as if they would never end.

"How . . . how can I ever believe it?"

"Because I'm asking you to," he said quietly. He knelt in front of her, took her hands away from her wet face. "Look at me, Faye. No other woman can give me what you can—yourself, your love, your warmth, your sense of humor. All the facets of your personality that make up the final you. I've known other women, Faye, but none of them have ever stirred in me any feelings that come close to what I feel for you. You're an original, remember? There's no replacement for an original. There are only copies, and I don't want a copy. To me you're special, and you'll have to believe it, take it on faith. That's what love is all about." 95

He was holding her hands in his, strong brown hands, and she was looking down on them, fighting with herself, fighting with everything inside her to believe what he was saying, to accept it, to give in to it.

Leaning forward, Kai kissed her gently on the mouth and smiled. "It's all been too much too soon for you, hasn't it? You never really got a chance to get over the shock, and when I fell in love with you it only made things worse." He smiled ruefully and Faye was surprised at his insight.

"Yes," she said. "It all happened too fast."

"Bad timing. If only we could have met later, after you'd sorted it all out in your mind, then it would never have been such a crisis." 100

She looked at him doubtfully. "It wouldn't have changed the facts."

"No, but it might have changed your perspective."

Would it have? she wondered. Could she ever feel confident and secure in her worth as a woman? Or was she at this moment too emotionally bruised to accept that possibility?

"I don't understand," he said, "why I never guessed what was wrong. Now that I know, it all seems so obvious." He looked at her thoughtfully. "Faye," he said gently, "I want you to tell me exactly what happened to you, what Doctor Martin told you."

She stared at him, surprised a little. A thought stirred in the back of her mind. Greg. He had never even asked. The why and the what had not interested him. But Kai, he wanted to know. She swallowed nervously and began the story, slowly, word for word, everything Doctor Martin had said. And he listened, quietly, not interrupting. "So you see," she said at last, "we don't have to hope for any miracles either." 105

"We'll make our own miracles," he said, and smiled. "Come here," he said then, "kiss me."

She did, shyly almost, until he took over and lifted her up and carried her to the bed. He looked down on her, eyes thoughtful. "I won't pretend I understand your feelings about this, the feelings you have about yourself as a woman, but I'll try." He paused for a moment. "Faye," he said then, speaking with slow emphasis, "don't *ever*, not for a single moment, think that you're not good enough for me. You're the best there is, Faye, the very best."

His mouth sought hers and he kissed her with gentle reassurance at first, then with rising ardor. His hands moved over her body, touching her with sensual, intimate caresses.

"You're my woman, Faye, you're mine. . . ."

Her senses reeled. She could never love anyone like she loved him. No one 110 had ever evoked in her this depth of emotion. This was real, this was forever. Kai wanted her as much as ever. No chivalry, this, no game of pretense, she was very sure of that. And when he lifted his face and looked at her, it was all there in his eyes and the wonder of it filled her with joy.

"Do you believe me now?" he whispered huskily. "Do you believe I love you and want you and need you?"

She nodded wordlessly, incapable of uttering a sound.

"And do you love me?"

Again she nodded, her eyes in his.

"Okay, then." In one smooth flowing movement he got to his feet. He 115 crossed to the closet, opened it, and took out her suitcases. He put one on the end of the bed and began to pile her clothes in it, taking armfuls out of the closet.

Faye watched incredulously. "What are you doing?" she managed at last.

Kai kept on moving around, opening drawers, taking out her things, filling the suitcase until it could hold no more. "Get dressed. We're going home."

"Home . . . ?"

For a moment he stopped and he looked at her with a deep blue glitter in his eyes. "Yes, *home* — where you belong. With me, in my house, in my bed, in my arms."

"Oh, Kai," she said tremulously, smiling suddenly. "It's midnight!"   120

His eyes were very dark. "I've waited long enough, I'm not waiting any more. You're coming with me, now. And I'm not letting you out of my sight until we're safely married. I don't want you getting any crazy ideas about running off to save me from myself, or some such notion."

Her throat was dry. "Please, let's not rush into it! Let's think about it first!"

Calmly he zipped up the full suitcase, swung it off the bed, and put it near the door. "I'm not rushing into anything," he said levelly. "I've wanted to marry you for quite a while, remember?"

He crossed to the bed, sat down next to her, and put his arm around her. "Faye, I wish you wouldn't worry so. I'm not going to change my mind. And I haven't shelved my hopes for a family, either." There was a brief silence. "When we're ready to have kids, we'll have them. We'll adopt them. There are orphanages the world over, full of children in need of love and care. We'll do whatever it takes. We'll get them, one way or another."

Faye searched his face, faint hope flickering deep inside her.   125

"Would you want that?"

"Why not?"

"I don't know, really. I thought you . . . it isn't the same."

"No," he said levelly, "it isn't. Adoption is a different process from pregnancy and birth, but the kids will be ours just the same and we'll love them no less."

"Yes," she said, "yes." And suddenly it seemed as if a light had been turned on inside her, as if suddenly she could see again, a future with Kai, a future with children. 130

A bronzed hand lifted her face. "Look, Faye, I'll always be sorry. I'll always be sorry not to see you pregnant, not to see you with a big stomach knowing you're carrying my child, but I'll live."

Faye lowered her eyes and tears threatened again. With both his hands he cupped her face.

"Look at me, Faye. I want you to stop thinking of yourself as a machine with a defect. You're not a damaged piece of merchandise, you hear? You're a living, breathing human being, a warm-blooded female, and I love you."

Through a haze of tears she looked at him, giving a weak smile. "I love you too." She put her arms around him and he heaved an unsteady breath.

"Faye," he said huskily, "you're my first and only choice." 135

Chapter Twelve

Kai and Faye had their family, two girls and a boy. They came to them one at a time, from faraway places, with small faces and large dark eyes full of fear. In their faces Faye could read the tragedies of war and death and poverty. They were hungry for love, hungry for nourishment and care. At night they woke in terror, screaming, their memories alive in sleep.

Time passed, and in the low white ranch house under the blue skies of Texas they flourished like the crops in the fields. They grew tall and straight and healthy and the fear in the dark eyes faded. Like their father they wore jeans and boots and large-brimmed hats, and they rode horses and played the guitar. They learned to speak English with a Southern twang.

One day Kai and Faye watched them as they played in the garden, and joy and gratitude overflowed in Faye's heart. Life was good and filled with love.

"They're all ours," she said. Even now after all these years she sometimes still couldn't believe it was really so.

Kai smiled at her. His eyes, still very blue, crinkled at the corners. "Yes, and you're all mine." 140

"They don't even look like us," she said. "Not even a tiny little bit." No blondes, no redheads.

Taking her in his arms, Kai kissed her. "They're true originals, like their mother. I wouldn't want it any other way."

There was love in his embrace and love in his words and in her heart there was no room now for doubt, no room for sorrow.

Sometimes in the night he would reach for her and she would wake to his touch, his hands on her breast, her stomach, searching. In the warm darkness of their bed she would come to him and they would hold each other close and she knew he had been dreaming.

She knew the dream. She was walking away from him, calling out that she couldn't marry him, the words echoing all around. *"I can't marry you! I can't marry you!"* And Kai was standing there watching her go, terrified, unable to move, his legs frozen to the ground. He wanted to follow her, keep her from leaving, but his legs wouldn't move. 145

Kai had told her of the dream, of the panic that clutched at him as he watched her walk out of his life. And always he would wake and search for her in the big bed, and she knew of only one way to reassure him. And in the warm afterglow of lovemaking, their bodies close together, she knew that to him she was everything, to him she was the only woman, beautiful, complete, whole.

GAIL GODWIN (B. 1937)

A Sorrowful Woman   1971

Once upon a time there was a wife and mother one too many times

One winter evening she looked at them: the husband durable, receptive, gentle; the child a tender golden three. The sight of them made her so sad and sick she did not want to see them ever again.

She told the husband these thoughts. He was attuned to her; he understood such things. He said he understood. What would she like him to do? "If you could put the boy to bed and read him the story about the monkey who ate too many bananas, I would be grateful." "Of course," he said. "Why, that's a pleasure." And he sent her off to bed.

The next night it happened again. Putting the warm dishes away in the cupboard, she turned and saw the child's gray eyes approving her movements. In the next room was the man, his chin sunk in the open collar of his favorite wool shirt. He was dozing after her good supper. The shirt was the gray of the child's trusting gaze. She began yelping without tears, retching in between. The man woke in alarm and carried her in his arms to bed. The boy followed them up the stairs, saying, "It's all right, Mommy," but this made her scream. "Mommy is sick," the father said, "go wait for me in your room."

The husband undressed her, abandoning her only long enough to root beneath the eiderdown for her flannel gown. She stood naked except for her bra, which hung by one strap down the side of her body; she had not the impetus to shrug it off. She looked down at the right nipple, shriveled with chill, and thought, How absurd, a vertical bra. "If only there were instant sleep," she said, hiccuping, and the husband bundled her into the gown and went out and came back with a sleeping draught guaranteed swift. She was to drink a little glass of cognac followed by a big glass of dark liquid and afterwards there was just time to say Thank you and could you get him a clean pair of pajamas out of the laundry, it came back today.

The next day was Sunday and the husband brought her breakfast in bed 5 and let her sleep until it grew dark again. He took the child for a walk, and when they returned, red-cheeked and boisterous, the father made supper. She heard them laughing in the kitchen. He brought her up a tray of buttered toast, celery sticks, and black bean soup. "I am the luckiest woman," she said, crying real tears. "Nonsense," he said. "You need a rest from us," and went to prepare the sleeping draught, find the child's pajamas, select the story for the night.

She got up on Monday and moved about the house till noon. The boy, delighted to have her back, pretended he was a vicious tiger and followed her from room to room, growling and scratching. Whenever she came close, he would growl and scratch at her. One of his sharp little claws ripped her flesh, just above the wrist, and together they paused to watch a thin red line materialize on the inside of her pale arm and spill over in little beads. "Go away," she said. She got herself upstairs and locked the door. She called the husband's office and said, "I've locked myself away from him. I'm afraid." The husband told her in his richest voice to lie down, take it easy, and he was already on the phone to call one of the baby-sitters they often employed. Shortly after, she heard the girl let herself in, heard the girl coaxing the frightened child to come and play.

After supper several nights later, she hit the child. She had known she was going to do it when the father would see. "I'm sorry," she said, collapsing on the floor. The weeping child had run to hide. "What has happened to me, I'm not myself anymore." The man picked her tenderly from the floor and looked at her with much concern. "Would it help if we got, you know, a girl in? We could fix the room downstairs. I want you to feel freer," he said, understanding these things. "We have the money for a girl. I want you to think about it."

And now the sleeping draught was a nightly thing, she did not have to ask. He went down to the kitchen to mix it, he set it nightly beside her bed. The little glass and the big one, amber and deep rich brown, the flannel gown and the eiderdown.

The man put out the word and found the perfect girl. She was young, dynamic, and not pretty. "Don't bother with the room, I'll fix it up myself." Laughing, she employed her thousand energies. She painted the room white, fed the child lunch, read edifying books, raced the boy to the mailbox, hung her own watercolors on the fresh-painted walls, made spinach soufflé, cleaned a spot from the mother's coat, made them all laugh, danced in stocking feet to music in the white room after reading the child to sleep. She knitted dresses for herself and played chess with the husband. She washed and set the mother's soft ash-blonde hair and gave her neck rubs, offered to.

The woman now spent her winter afternoons in the big bedroom. She made a fire in the hearth and put on slacks and an old sweater she had loved at school, and sat in the big chair and stared out the window at snow-ridden branches, or went away into long novels about other people moving through other winters. 10

The girl brought the child in twice a day, once in the later afternoon when he would tell of his day, all of it tumbling out quickly because there was not much time, and before he went to bed. Often now, the man took his wife to dinner. He made a courtship ceremony of it, inviting her beforehand so she could get used to the idea. They dressed and were beautiful together again and went out into the frosty night. Over candlelight he would say, "I think you are better, you know." "Perhaps I am," she would murmur. "You look . . . like a cloistered queen," he said once, his voice breaking curiously.

One afternoon the girl brought the child into the bedroom. "We've been out playing in the park. He found something he wants to give you, a surprise." The little boy approached her, smiling mysteriously. He placed his cupped hands in hers and left a live dry thing that spat brown juice in her palm and leapt away. She screamed and wrung her hands to be rid of the brown juice. "Oh, it was only a grasshopper," said the girl. Nimbly she crept to the edge of the curtain, did a quick knee bend, and reclaimed the creature, led the boy competently from the room.

"The girl upsets me," said the woman to her husband. He sat frowning on the side of the bed he had not entered for so long. "I'm sorry, but there it is." The husband stroked his creased brow and said he was sorry too. He really did not know what they would do without that treasure of a girl. "Why don't you stay here with me in bed," the woman said.

Next morning she fired the girl who cried and said, "I loved the little boy, what will become of him now?" But the mother turned away her face and the girl took down the watercolors from the walls, sheathed the records she had danced to, and went away.

"I don't know what we'll do. It's all my fault, I know. I'm such a burden, I 15 know that."

"Let me think. I'll think of something." (Still understanding these things.)

"I know you will. You always do," she said.

With great care he rearranged his life. He got up hours early, did the shopping, cooked the breakfast, took the boy to nursery school. "We will manage," he said, "until you're better, however long that is." He did his work, collected the boy from the school, came home and made the supper, washed the dishes, got the child to bed. He managed everything. One evening, just as she was on the verge of swallowing her draught, there was a timid knock on her door. The little boy came in wearing his pajamas. "Daddy has fallen asleep on my bed and I can't get in. There's not room."

Very sedately she left her bed and went to the child's room. Things were much changed. Books were rearranged, toys. He'd done some new drawings. She came as a visitor to her son's room, wakened the father and helped him to bed. "Ah, he shouldn't have bothered you," said the man, leaning on his wife. "I've told him not to." He dropped into his own bed and fell asleep with a moan. Meticulously she undressed him. She folded and hung his clothes. She covered his body with the bedclothes. She flicked off the light that shone in his face.

The next day she moved her things into the girl's white room. She put her 20 hairbrush on the dresser; she put a note pad and pen beside the bed. She stocked the little room with cigarettes, books, bread, and cheese. She didn't need much.

At first the husband was dismayed. But he was receptive to her needs. He understood these things. "Perhaps the best thing is for you to follow it through," he said. "I want to be big enough to contain whatever you must do."

All day long she stayed in the white room. She was a young queen, a virgin in a tower; she was the previous inhabitant, the girl with all the energies. She tried these personalities on like costumes, then discarded them. The room had a new view of streets she'd never seen that way before. The sun hit the room in late afternoon and she took to brushing her hair in the sun. One day she decided to write a poem. "Perhaps a sonnet." She took up her pen and pad and began working from words that had lately lain in her mind. She had choices for the sonnet, ABAB or ABBA for a start. She pondered these possibilities until she tottered into a larger choice: she did not have to write a sonnet. Her poem could be six, eight, ten, thirteen lines, it could be any number of lines, and it did not even have to rhyme.

She put down the pen on top of the pad.

In the evenings, very briefly, she saw the two of them. They knocked on her door, a big knock and a little, and she would call Come in, and the husband

would smile though he looked a bit tired, yet somehow this tiredness suited
him. He would put her sleeping draught on the bedside table and say, "The boy
and I have done all right today," and the child would kiss her. One night she
tasted for the first time the power of his baby spit.

"I don't think I can see him anymore," she whispered sadly to the man. 25
And the husband turned away, but recovered admirably and said, "Of course,
I see."

So the husband came alone. "I have explained to the boy," he said. "And we
are doing fine. We are managing." He squeezed his wife's pale arm and put the
two glasses on her table. After he had gone, she sat looking at the arm.

"I'm afraid it's come to that," she said. "Just push the notes under the
door; I'll read them. And don't forget to leave the draught outside."

The man sat for a long time with his head in his hands. Then he rose and
went away from her. She heard him in the kitchen where he mixed the draught
in batches now to last a week at a time, storing it in a corner of the cupboard.
She heard him come back, leave the big glass and the little one outside on the
floor.

Outside her window the snow was melting from the branches, there were
more people on the streets. She brushed her hair a lot and seldom read anymore. She sat in her window and brushed her hair for hours, and saw a boy fall
off his new bicycle again and again, a dog chasing a squirrel, an old woman
peek slyly over her shoulder and then extract a parcel from a garbage can.

In the evening she read the notes they slipped under her door. The child 30
could not write, so he drew and sometimes painted his. The notes were
painstaking at first; the man and boy offering the final strength of their day to
her. But sometimes, when they seemed to have had a bad day, there were only
hurried scrawls.

One night, when the husband's note had been extremely short, loving but
short, and there had been nothing from the boy, she stole out of her room as
she often did to get more supplies, but crept upstairs instead and stood outside their doors, listening to the regular breathing of the man and boy asleep.
She hurried back to her room and drank the draught.

She woke earlier now. It was spring, there were birds. She listened for
sounds of the man and the boy eating breakfast; she listened for the roar of
the motor when they drove away. One beautiful noon, she went out to look at
her kitchen in the daylight. Things were changed. He had bought some new
dish towels. Had the old ones worn out? The canisters seemed closer to the
sink. She got out flour, baking powder, salt, milk (he bought a different brand
of butter), and baked a loaf of bread and left it cooling on the table.

The force of the two joyful notes slipped under her door that evening
pressed her into the corner of the little room; she had hardly space to breathe.
As soon as possible, she drank the draught.

Now the days were too short. She was always busy. She woke with the first
bird. Worked till the sun set. No time for hair brushing. Her fingers raced the
hours.

Finally, in the nick of time, it was finished one late afternoon. Her veins 35
pumped and her forehead sparkled. She went to the cupboard, took what was
hers, closed herself into the little white room and brushed her hair for a while.

The man and boy came home and found: five loaves of warm bread, a roast
stuffed turkey, a glazed ham, three pies of different fillings, eight molds of the

boy's favorite custard, two weeks' supply of fresh-laundered sheets and shirts and towels, two hand-knitted sweaters (both of the same gray color), a sheath of marvelous watercolor beasts accompanied by mad and fanciful stories nobody could ever make up again, and a tablet full of love sonnets addressed to the man. The house smelled redolently of renewal and spring. The man ran to the little room, could not contain himself to knock, flung back the door.

"Look, Mommy is sleeping," said the boy. "She's tired from doing all our things again." He dawdled in a stream of the last sun for that day and watched his father roll tenderly back her eyelids, lay his ear softly to her breast, test the delicate bones of her wrist. The father put down his face into her fresh-washed hair.

"Can we eat the turkey for supper?" the boy asked.

CONSIDERATIONS FOR CRITICAL THINKING AND WRITING

1. FIRST RESPONSE. How did you respond to the excerpt to *A Secret Sorrow* and "A Sorrowful Woman"? Do you like one more than the other? Is one of the women — Faye or Godwin's unnamed wife — more likable than the other? Why do you think you respond the way you do to the characters and the stories — is your response intellectual, emotional, a result of authorial intent, a mix of these, or something else entirely?

2. Describe what you found appealing in each story. Can you point to passages in both that strike you as especially well written or interesting? Was there anything in either story that did not appeal to you? Why?

3. How do the two women's attitudes toward family life differ? How does that difference constitute the problem in each story?

4. How is the woman's problem in "A Sorrowful Woman" made more complex than Faye's in *A Secret Sorrow*? What is the purpose of the husband and child in Godwin's story?

5. How would you describe the theme — the central point and meaning — in each story?

6. To what extent might "A Sorrowful Woman" be regarded as an unromantic sequel to *A Secret Sorrow*?

7. Can both stories be read a second or third time and still be interesting? Why or why not?

8. Explain how you think a romance formula writer would end "A Sorrowful Woman," or write the ending yourself.

9. Contrast what marriage means in the two stories.

10. Discuss your feelings about the woman in "A Sorrowful Woman." How does she remain a sympathetic character in spite of her refusal to be a traditional wife and mother? (It may take more than one reading of the story to see that Godwin does sympathize with her.)

11. The happy ending of *A Secret Sorrow* may seem like that of a fairy tale, but it is realistically presented because there is nothing strange, mysterious, or fabulous that strains our ability to believe it could happen. In contrast, "A Sorrowful Woman" begins with an epigraph (*"Once upon a time..."*) that causes us to expect a fairy-tale ending, but that story is clearly a fairy tale gone wrong. Consider the two stories as fairy tales. How might "A Sorrowful Woman" be read as a dark version of "Sleeping Beauty"?

12. Read the section on feminist criticism in Chapter 37, "Critical Strategies for Reading." Based on that discussion, what do you think a feminist critic might have to say about these two stories?

PERSPECTIVES

TANIA MODLESKI (B. 1949)
The Popularity of Romance Novels   *1982*

In Harlequin romances, the need of women to find meaning and pleasure in activities which are not wholly male-centered such as work or artistic creation is generally scoffed at. Soap operas also undercut, though in subtler fashion, the idea that a woman might obtain satisfaction from these activities. A soap-opera woman might very well be engaged in important work like law or medicine, but even on the job she is likely to be obsessed with her love-life or perhaps actually carrying on her love-life, simultaneously weeping over and operating on the weak heart of her intended. Thus, while popular feminine texts provide outlets for women's dissatisfaction with male-female relationships, they never question the primacy of these relationships. Nor do they overtly question the myth of male superiority or the institutions of marriage and the family. Indeed, patriarchal myths and institutions are, on the manifest level, wholeheartedly embraced, although the anxieties and tensions they give rise to may be said to provoke the need for the texts in the first place.

It is useless to deplore the texts for their omissions, distortions, and conservative affirmations. It is crucial to understand them: to let their very omissions and distortions speak, informing us of the contradictions they are meant to conceal and, equally importantly, of the fears that lie beneath them. For the texts often do speak profoundly to us, even those of us who like to think we have shed our "false consciousness" and are actively engaged in challenging patriarchal authority. We cannot rest content with theories which would attribute the texts' popularity to the successful conspiracy of a group of patriarchal capitalists plotting to keep women so happy at home that they remain unwilling to make demands which would greatly restructure the work place and the family. Such changes are frightening to *most* of us, for they involve an entire reorganization not just of our social lives, but of our psychic lives as well. Given the radical nature of the feminist task, it is no wonder that college students occasionally cut their women's studies classes to find out what is going on in their favorite soap opera.

From *Loving with a Vengeance: Mass-Produced Fantasies for Women*

CONSIDERATIONS FOR CRITICAL THINKING AND WRITING

1. Does the excerpt from the Harlequin romance *A Secret Sorrow* (p. 25) reflect what Modleski characterizes as a "myth of male superiority"? Explain how evidence from the text supports or refutes Modleski's assertion that romances contain "omissions, distortions, and conservative affirmations."

2. Explain why you agree or disagree that "anxieties and tensions" account for the popularity of Harlequin romances. From your perspective, what does account for their enormous popularity?

3. Write an essay in which you consider a book, film, or television program that appeals to male fantasies, and explore some of the similarities and differences between male and female popular tastes.

THOMAS JEFFERSON (1743–1826)

On the Dangers of Reading Fiction   *1818*

A great obstacle to good education is the inordinate passion prevalent for novels, and the time lost in that reading which should be instructively employed. When this poison infects the mind, it destroys its tone and revolts it against wholesome reading. Reason and fact, plain and unadorned, are rejected. Nothing can engage attention unless dressed in all the figments of fancy, and nothing so bedecked comes amiss. The result is a bloated imagination, sickly judgment, and disgust towards all the real businesses of life. This mass of trash, however, is not without some distinction; some few modeling their narratives, although fictitious, on the incidents of real life, have been able to make them interesting and useful vehicles of a sound morality. . . . For a like reason, too, much poetry should not be indulged. Some is useful for forming style and taste. Pope, Dryden, Thompson, Shakespeare, and of the French, Molière, Racine, the Corneilles, may be read with pleasure and improvement.

Letter to Nathaniel Burwell, March 14, 1818,
in *The Writings of Thomas Jefferson*

CONSIDERATIONS FOR CRITICAL THINKING AND WRITING

1. Jefferson voices several common objections to fiction. What, according to him, are the changes associated with reading fiction? Are these concerns still expressed today? Why or why not? To what extent are Jefferson's arguments similar to twentieth-century objections to watching television?

2. Explain why you agree or disagree that works of fiction should serve as "useful vehicles of a sound morality."

3. How do you think Jefferson would regard Harlequin romances?

2

Writing about Fiction

FROM READING TO WRITING

There's no question about it: writing about fiction is a different experience than reading it. The novelist William Styron amply concedes that writing to him is not so much about pleasure as it is about work: "Let's face it, writing is hell." Although Styron's lament concerns his own feelings about writing prose fiction, he no doubt speaks for many other writers, including essayists. Writing is, of course, work, but it is also a pleasure when it goes well—when ideas feel solid and the writing is fluid. You can experience that pleasure as well, if you approach writing as an intellectual and emotional opportunity rather than merely a sentence.

Just as reading fiction requires an imaginative, conscious response, so does writing about fiction. Composing an essay is not just recording your interpretive response to a work because the act of writing can change your response as you explore, clarify, and discover relationships you hadn't previously considered or recognized. Most writers discover new ideas and connections as they move through the process of rereading and annotating the text, taking notes, generating ideas, developing a thesis, and organizing an argumentative essay (these matters are detailed in Chapter 38, "Reading and Writing"). To become more conscious of the writing process, first study the following questions specifically aimed at sharpening your response to reading and writing about fiction. Then examine the case study of a student's paper in progress that takes you through writing a first response to reading, brainstorming for a paper topic, writing a first draft, revising, and writing the final paper.

QUESTIONS FOR RESPONSIVE READING AND WRITING

The following questions can help you consider important elements of fiction that reveal your responses to a story's effects and meanings. The questions are general, so they will not always be relevant to a particular story. Many of them, however, should prove useful for thinking, talking, and writing about a work of fiction. If you are uncertain about the meaning of a term used in a question, consult the Glossary of Literary Terms beginning on page 2123 of this book. You should also find useful the discussion of various critical approaches to literature in Chapter 37, "Critical Strategies for Reading."

Plot

1. Does the plot conform to a formula? Is it like those of any other stories you have read? Did you find it predictable?
2. What is the source and nature of the conflict for the protagonist? Was your major interest in the story based on what happens next or on some other concern? What does the title reveal now that you've finished the story?
3. Is the story told chronologically? If not, in what order are its events told, and what is the effect of that order on your response to the action?
4. What does the exposition reveal? Are flashbacks used? Did you see any foreshadowings? Where is the climax?
5. Is the conflict resolved at the end? Would you characterize the ending as happy, unhappy, or somewhere in between?
6. Is the plot unified? Is each incident somehow related to some other element in the story?

Character

7. Do you identify with the protagonist? Who (or what) is the antagonist?
8. Did your response to any characters change as you read? What do you think caused the change? Do any characters change and develop in the course of the story? How?
9. Are round, flat, or stock characters used? Is their behavior motivated and plausible?
10. How does the author reveal characters? Are they directly described or indirectly presented? Are the characters' names used to convey something about them?
11. What is the purpose of the minor characters? Are they individualized, or do they primarily represent ideas or attitudes?

Setting

12. Is the setting important in shaping your response? If it were changed, would your response to the story's action and meaning be significantly different?
13. Is the setting used symbolically? Are the time, place, and atmosphere related to the theme?
14. Is the setting used as an antagonist?

Point of View

15. Who tells the story? Is it a first-person or third-person narrator? Is it a major or minor character or one who does not participate in the action at all? How much does the narrator know? Does the point of view change at all in the course of the story?
16. Is the narrator reliable and objective? Does the narrator appear too innocent, emotional, or self-deluded to be trusted?
17. Does the author directly comment on the action?
18. If told from a different point of view, how would your response to the story change? Would anything be lost?

Symbolism

19. Did you notice any symbols in the story? Are they actions, characters, settings, objects, or words?
20. How do the symbols contribute to your understanding of the story?

Theme

21. Did you find a theme? If so, what is it?
22. Is the theme stated directly, or is it developed implicitly through the plot, characters, or some other element?
23. Is the theme a confirmation of your values, or does it challenge them?

Style, Tone, and Irony

24. Do you think the style is consistent and appropriate throughout the story? Do all the characters use the same kind of language, or did you hear different voices?
25. Would you describe the level of diction as formal or informal? Are the sentences short and simple, long and complex, or some combination?
26. How does the author's use of language contribute to the tone of the story? Did it seem, for example, intense, relaxed, sentimental, nostalgic, humorous, angry, sad, or remote?
27. Do you think the story is worth reading more than once? Does the author's use of language bear close scrutiny so that you feel and experience more with each reading?

Critical Strategies

28. Is there a particular critical approach that seems especially appropriate for this story? (See the discussion of "Critical Strategies for Reading" beginning on p. 2021.)
29. How might biographical information about the author help you to determine the central concerns of the story?
30. How might historical information about the story provide a useful context for interpretation?
31. What kinds of evidence from the story are you focusing on to support your interpretation? Does your interpretation leave out any important elements that might undercut or qualify your interpretation?
32. To what extent do your own experiences, values, beliefs, and assumptions inform your interpretation?
33. Given that there are a variety of ways to interpret the story, which one seems the most useful to you?

A SAMPLE STUDENT PAPER IN PROGRESS

The following student paper was written in response to an assignment that asked for a comparison and contrast of the treatment of marriage in the excerpt from Karen Van Der Zee's novel *A Secret Sorrow* (p. 25) and in Gail Godwin's short story "A Sorrowful Woman" (p. 33). The final draft of the paper is preceded by four distinct phases of composition: (1) an initial response, (2) a brainstorming exercise, (3) a preliminary draft of the paper, and (4) an annotated version of the preliminary draft that shows how the student thought about revising the paper. Maya Leigh's First Response is an informal paper based on questions supplied by the instructor: "How did you respond to each story? Do you like one more than the other? Is one of the women more likable than the other? Why do you think you respond the way you do? Is your response to the characters and the stories primarily intellectual, emotional, a result of authorial intention, a mix of these, or something else entirely?" (Spelling and grammatical errors in Maya's preliminary drafts have been silently corrected so as not to distract from her developing argument.)

First Response:

    Reading the excerpt from the Harlequin I was irritated
    by the seeming helplessness of Faye; in the first chapter
    she is constantly on the edge of hysteria and can hardly
    stand up. I could do without all of the fainting, gasping,

and general theatrics. I've read Harlequins before, and I usually skim through that stuff to get to the good romantic parts and the happy ending. What I like about these kinds of romance novels is the happy ending. Even though the ending is kind of clichéd with the white fence and blue skies, there is still something satisfying about having everything work out okay.

The Godwin story, of course, does not have a happy ending. It is a much more powerful story, and it is one that I could read several times, unlike the Harlequin. The Godwin woman bothers me too, because I can't really see what she has to complain about. Her husband is perfectly accommodating and understanding. It seems that if she were unhappy with her life as a wife and mother and wanted to work or do something else, he wouldn't have a problem with it. She seems to throw away her life and hurt her family for nothing.

I enjoyed reading the Godwin story more just because it is well written and more complex, but I liked the ending of the Harlequin more. I think on an emotional level I liked the Harlequin better, and on an intellectual level I liked the Godwin story more. It is more satisfying emotionally to see a romance develop and end happily than it is to see the deterioration of a marriage and the suicide of a depressed woman. I don't really find either character particularly likable; toward the end when the Godwin woman comes out of her room and starts doing things again I begin to feel sympathy for her--I can understand her having a period of depression, but I want her to pull herself out of it, and when she doesn't, I am disappointed. Even though Faye is annoying in the beginning, because everything ends happily I am almost willing to forgive and forget my previous annoyance with her. If the Godwin woman hadn't killed herself and had returned to her family life, I would have liked her better, but because she doesn't I leave the story feeling discouraged.

Brainstorming

By listing these parallel but alternate treatments of marriage in each story, Maya begins to assemble an inventory of relevant topics related to the assignment. What becomes clear to her is that her approach will emphasize the differences in each story's portrayal of marriage.

Marriage

Godwin	Harlequin
marriage as end of life — confining, weighty	marriage as end, goal — dreamlike, idyllic
husband — durable, receptive, understanding	husband — understanding, <u>manly</u>
p. 33 sight of family makes her sad and sick	p. 32 watching kids she feels that life is good + filled with love
house in winter — <u>girl</u> paints room white	white house in Texas under blue skies
the power of his baby spit and looking at arm p. 36	in husband's embrace no room for doubt or sorrow p. 32
family makes her sad	family makes her happy
weight pressing on her	weight lifted off her
impersonal — the husband, the child emphasis on roles	Kai, Faye, our children
dead in the end	beautiful, whole, complete in the end
crisis due to fear of <u>always</u> having husband and kid	crisis due to fear of <u>never</u> having husband and kids
feels incomplete and depressed as only wife and mother	feels incomplete and depressed not being wife and mother

Revising: First and Second Drafts

Maya's first draft of the paper pursues and develops many of the topics she noted while brainstorming. She explores the differences between each story's treatment of marriage in detail by examining each protagonist's role as wife and mother, her husband's response, the role played by her children, and the ending of each story. The second draft's annotations indicate that Maya has been able to distance herself enough from her first draft to critique its weak moments. In the annotations she recognizes, for example, that she needs a clearer thesis, some stronger transitions between paragraphs, some crisper and more detailed sentences to clarify points, and a more convincing conclusion as well as a more pointed title.

Separate Sorrows

In both the excerpt from A Secret Sorrow and "A Sorrowful Woman," by Gail Godwin, the story is centered around ideas of marriage and family. However, marriage and family are presented in very different lights in the two stories. Karen Van Der Zee presents marriage with children as perfect and somewhat dream-like; it is what Faye, the heroine of A Secret Sorrow, wants, and what is necessary for her happiness. For Godwin's heroine, marriage and family are almost the antithesis of happiness; her home life seems to suffocate her and eventually leads her to commit suicide.

Both of the female protagonists in the two stories experience a crisis of sorts. In A Secret Sorrow Faye's crisis comes before marriage. She is distraught and upset because she cannot have children and fears that this will prevent her from marrying the man she loves. Both she and her beloved, Kai, have always wanted a marriage with children, and it is assumed that only under these circumstances will they truly be happy. Faye feels that her inability to have children is a fatal flaw. "Every time we see some pregnant woman, every time we're with somebody else's children I'll feel I've failed you!" (30). In "A Sorrowful Woman," however, the crisis comes after the marriage, when the woman has already procured her husband and child. Faye would be ecstatic in this woman's situation. The protagonist of the Godwin story, however, is not. Her husband and son bring her such sorrow that eventually she is unable to see them at all, and communicates only through notes stuck under her bedroom door. Faye's anxiety and fear is based on the thought of losing her man and never having children. In contrast, Godwin's character has a loving husband and child and is still filled with grief. In a Harlequin such as A Secret Sorrow, this is unimaginable; it goes against every formula of romance writing, where books always end with a wedding, and happiness after that is just assumed.

In A Secret Sorrow, marriage is portrayed as the end, as in the goal. It is what the heroine wants. The author works to let the reader know that only in this way will Faye be fulfilled and happy; it is what the entire story, with all the plot twists and romantic interludes, has been working toward. In "A Sorrowful Woman," marriage is the end, but not as in the goal--it is quite literally the end of the woman's life. Though we don't see what her life was like before her emotional crisis, there are hints of it. When she moves into the new room she mentions seeing the streets from a whole new perspective, suggesting the previous monotony of her daily life. In addition, in the final paragraphs of the story when the character bakes pies and bread and washes and folds the laundry, her son says, "she's tired from doing all our things again," (37) giving us an idea of what "our things" were, and what the woman did with her time before becoming ill.

In A Secret Sorrow Faye's inability to have children does not end Kai's love for her, and the two go on to get married and adopt children. Faye's married life is described in a very idyllic way--she raises her son and two daughters in a "white ranch house under the blue skies of Texas" (32). In other words, once she is married and has children there is no more anxiety, nothing more to fear. The author leads us to the conclusion that marriage solves all problems and is a source of unending happiness for all. This is a great difference from the Godwin tale, which takes place in the winter and maintains a sense of cold throughout the whole thing. Whenever Godwin describes the family it is not in the light, glowing terms of Van Der Zee, but always with a sense of weight or guilt or failure about it. The child's trusting gaze makes the protagonist begin "yelping without tears" (33). Any sign of life or love increases her sorrow and makes her want to be rid of it. For example, when the hired girl brings her son to visit her with a grasshopper he's found--something both alive and from the outside world--she gets very upset and forces her husband to fire her. The girl is too much of an infringement on her space, and too much of a reminder of what she can no longer be.

Never is the difference between the two authors' portrayals of marriage more apparent than when both the women are viewing their families. Faye, sitting with her husband and watching her children play, felt that "life was good and filled with love" (32). Godwin's protagonist, on the other hand, says, "The sight of them made her so sad and sick she did not want to see them ever again" (33). When Kai, now her husband, embraces Faye, she feels that, "There was love in his embrace and love in his words and in her heart there was no room now for doubt, no room for sorrow" (32). When Godwin's heroine feels the loving touch of her husband's arm and the kiss of her child she cannot bear it and cuts off all direct contact with them. The situation of her marriage pushes her into a self-imposed imprisonment and lethargy. She feels unbearably sad because she can no longer be who they want and need her to be. She avoids them not because she does not love them, but rather because she loves them so much that it is too painful to see them and feel her failure.

When Faye's fears of losing Kai are assuaged, and she is happily married, it is as though a great weight has been lifted off of her. Godwin's character, on the other hand, feels her marriage as a great weight pressing in on her. The love of her husband and child weighs on her and immobilizes her. When she leaves her room for a day and

leaves out freshly baked bread for her husband and son,
they express their happiness in the notes they write to
her that night, and "the force of the two joyful notes . . .
pressed her into the corner of the little room; she hardly
had space to breathe" (36). Faye can be a traditional wife
and mother, so her family is a source of joy. Godwin's
character can no longer do this, and so her family is a
representation of her failure, and the guilt presses her
further and further into herself, until she can retreat no
further and ends her life.

The endings of the two stories are powerful illustrations of the differences between them. In the end of
A Secret Sorrow the author shows us Faye feeling "beautiful, complete, whole" (33) in her role as wife and mother.
Godwin, on the other hand, shows us her heroine dead on
her bed. Godwin first gives the reader hope, by showing
all that the woman has done, and saying that "the house
smelled redolently of renewal and spring" (37). This makes
the blow even harder when we then discover, along with the
husband and child, the woman's suicide.

Karen Van Der Zee creates a story full of emotional
highs and lows, but one that leads up to--and ends
with--marriage. After the marriage all plot twists and
traumas come to a halt. Faye is brought to new life by
her marriage and children; in it she finds completion
of herself and total happiness. Godwin's tale, on the
other hand, is full of anguish and emotion, but it all
takes place after the marriage. The character she creates
is stifled and killed by her marriage. There is no portrayal of unending happiness in her tale, but rather
unending woe.

Maya Leigh
Professor Herlin
English 104
October 10, 19--

title works for Godwin—but does it for Van Der Zee?

Separate Sorrows)→

                Karen Van Der Zee's novel   Gail Godwin's short story

In both the excerpt from A Secret Sorrow and "A Sor-
                                    ^
                                   plot   ^
                                                             s
rowful Woman," ~~by Gail Godwin,~~ the ~~story is~~ centered
                                        ^   ^
around ideas of marriage and family. However, marriage and

family are presented in very different lights in the two

stories. Karen Van Der Zee presents marriage with children
                          totally fulfilling
as perfect and ~~somewhat dream-like~~; it is what Faye, the
protagonist
~~heroine~~ of A Secret Sorrow, wants/ and what is necessary
                              unnamed protagonist
for her happiness. For Godwin's ~~heroine~~, marriage and

family are almost the antithesis of happiness; her

does she?   home life seems to suffocate her and eventually leads
or is she
consumed   her to commit suicide.
by her role?
                    Both of the female protagonists in the two stories

experience a crisis ~~of sorts~~. In A Secret Sorrow Faye's

crisis comes before marriage. She is distraught and upset

because she cannot have children and fears that this will

prevent her from marrying the man she loves. Both she and

her beloved, Kai, have always wanted a marriage with chil-
                    unclear
                    referent
dren, and (it) is assumed that only under these

circumstances will they truly be happy. Faye feels that
                              that cuts her off from Kai's love
her inability to have children is a fatal flaw. "Every
                                                   ^
time we see some pregnant woman, every time we're with

somebody else's children I'll feel I've failed you!" (30).

insert from In "A Sorrowful Woman," however, the crisis comes after
*next page*ᴧ
                                                  secured
           the marriage, when the woman has already ~~procured~~ her

need a c
thesis
here—is
that SS
endorse
marriag
while SW
problem
tizes it?

husband and child. Faye would be ecstatic in this woman's
Unlike who

situation., The protagonist of the Godwin story / however,
Inexplicably, 's

is not. Her husband and son bring her such sorrow that

eventually she is unable to see them at all, and communi-

cates only through notes stuck under her bedroom door.
~ing

Faye's anxiety and fear is based on the thought of losing

her man and never having children. In contrast, Godwin's
yet she

character has a loving husband and child and is still

filled with grief. In a Harlequin such as A Secret Sorrow,
sense of defeat would be   in a Harlequin romance because one of the most popular

this is unimaginable, it goes against every formulas of
the plot   's

romance writing; where books always end with a wedding,
with the assumption that the rest is happily ever after.

and happiness after that is just assumed.

In A Secret Sorrow, marriage is portrayed as the end,
Van Der Zee

as in the goal. It is what the heroine wants. The author

works to let the reader know that only in this way will

Faye be fulfilled and happy; it is what the entire story,

with all the plot twists and romantic interludes, has been

working toward. In "A Sorrowful Woman," marriage is the end
's   also

but not as in the goal: it is quite literally the end of
I like this!

the woman's life. Though we don't see what her life was

like before her emotional crisis, there are hints of it.

When she moves into the new room, she mentions seeing the
need p. ref

streets from a whole new perspective, suggesting the pre-

vious monotony of her daily life. In addition, in the

final paragraphs of the story--when the character bakes

pies and bread and washes and folds the laundry--her son

says, "She's tired from doing all our things again," (37)

giving us an idea of what "our things" were and what the

woman did with her time before becoming ill.
is she really ill? or just withdrawing from her life?

insert on first page

need transition | In <u>A Secret Sorrow</u> Faye's inability to have children

does not end Kai's love for her, and the two go on to get

married and adopt children. Faye's married life is

described in a very idyllic way--she raises her son and two

daughters in a "white ranch house under the blue skies of

Texas" (32). ~~In other words,~~ once she is married and has

because the plot
children there is no more anxiety, ~~nothing more to fear.~~

~~The author~~ leads us to the conclusion that marriage solves

all problems and is a source of unending happiness☺ ~~for~~

ly   *~~is~~*
~~all.~~ This ~~is a~~ great, difference from ~~the~~ Godwin's tale,

which takes place in ~~the~~ winter and maintains a sense of

cold☺ ~~throughout the whole thing.~~ Whenever Godwin

describes the family it is ~~not~~ in ~~the light, glowing~~ terms

that suggest
~~of Van Der Zee, but always with a sense of~~ weight, ~~or~~

guilt, or failure☺ ~~about it.~~ The child's trusting gaze

makes the protagonist begin "yelping without tears" (33),

while
Any sign of life or love increases her sorrow and makes

unclear referent
her want to be rid of (it) For example, when the hired

girl brings her son to visit her with a grasshopper he's

found --something both alive and from the outside world --

the girl.
she gets very upset and forces her husband to fire ~~her.~~

Apparently,
The girl is too much of an infringement on her space, ~~and~~

too much of a reminder of what she can no longer be.

Never is the difference between the two authors' por-

trayals of marriage more apparent than when both the women

are viewing their families. Faye, sitting with her husband

and watching her children play, felt that "life was good

and filled with love" (32). Godwin's protagonist, on the

other hand, says, "The sight of them made her so sad and

sick she did not want to see them ever again" (33). When
Kai, now her husband, embraces Faye, she feels, "There was
love in his embrace and love in his words and in her heart
there was no room now for doubt, no room for sorrow" (32).
When Godwin's heroine feels the loving touch of her husband's arm and the kiss of her child, she cannot bear it
and cuts off all direct contact with them. The situation
of her marriage pushes her into a self-imposed imprisonment and lethargy. She feels unbearably sad because she
can no longer be who they want and need her to be. She
avoids them not because she does not love them but rather
because she loves them so much that it is too painful to
see them and feel her failure.

should I use epigram here? or work into the thesis?

need → *transition* When Faye's fears of losing Kai are assuaged, and she
is happily married, it is as though a great weight has
been lifted off her. Godwin's character, on the other
hand, feels her marriage as a great weight pressing ~~in~~ on
her~ *and* ~~The love of her husband and child weighs on her and~~
immobiliz~~ed~~ *cing* her. When she leaves her room for a day and
puts ~~leaves~~ out freshly baked bread for her husband and son,
they express their happiness in the notes they write to
her that night, and "the force of the two joyful notes . . .
pressed her into the corner of the little room; she had
hardly space to breathe" (36). Faye can be ~~a~~ *the* traditional
wife and mother, so her family is a source of joy.
Godwin's character can no longer do this, and so her fam-
ily ~~is a~~ representation~~s~~ *s* ~~of~~ her *own* failure, and the guilt
presses her further and further into herself/ until she
can retreat no further and ends her life.

The endings of the two stories are powerful illustrations of the differences between them. In the end of
A Secret Sorrow the author shows us Faye feeling "beautiful, complete, whole" (33) in her role as wife and mother.
Godwin, on the other hand, shows us her ~~heroine~~ protagonist dead on
her bed. Godwin ~~first~~ give*s* seems to the reader hope / by showing
all that the woman has done / and saying that "the house

*same
idyllic
surroundings
as VDZ's
blue skies?*

smelled redolently of renewal and spring" (37). This makes
the blow even harder when we then discover, along with the
husband and child, the woman's ~~suicide~~ death.

Karen Van Der Zee creates a story full of emotional
highs and lows / but one that leads up to--and ends with--
marriage. After the marriage all plot twists and traumas
come to a halt. Faye is brought to new life by her mar-
riage and children: ~~in it~~ she finds ~~completion of herself~~ fulfillment
and total happiness. Godwin's ~~tale, on the other hand,~~ story, however, is
full of anguish and ~~emotion, but it~~ confusion (?) that all take*s* place after

*need
some
very
brief
quotes
to make
conclusion
stronger?*

the marriage. The character she creates is stifled and
killed by her marriage. There is no portrayal of unending
happiness in her tale, but rather unending (woe.) *is this the right
word, since she
dies?*

Final Draft

The changes noted in Maya's annotations on her second draft are put
to good use in the following final draft. By not insisting that Godwin's protagonist actually commits suicide, Maya shifts her attention away from
this indeterminable death to the causes and effects of it. This shift leads
her to a stronger thesis—that Godwin raises questions about the efficacy
of marriage rather than endorsing it as a certain recipe for happiness the
way Van Der Zee does. Maya also incorporates additional revisions, such as
transitions (see, for example, the revision between paragraphs 3 and 4), sentence clarity, and a fuller and more persuasive concluding paragraph.

Maya Leigh

Professor Herlin

English 104

October 10, 19—

Fulfillment or Failure?

Marriage in A Secret Sorrow and "A Sorrowful Woman"

In both the excerpt from Karen Van Der Zee's novel
A Secret Sorrow and in Gail Godwin's short story "A Sorrowful Woman," the plots center around ideas of marriage
and family. However, marriage and family are presented
in very different lights in the two stories. Karen Van
Der Zee presents marriage with children as perfect and
totally fulfilling; it is what Faye, the protagonist of
A Secret Sorrow, wants and what is necessary for her happiness. For Godwin's unnamed protagonist marriage and family are almost the antithesis of happiness; her home life
seems to suffocate her and eventually leads to her death.
A Secret Sorrow directly endorses and encourages marriage,
whereas "A Sorrowful Woman" indirectly questions and dis-
courages it.

Both of the female protagonists in the two stories
experience a crisis. In A Secret Sorrow Faye's crisis
comes before the marriage. She is distraught and upset
because she cannot have children and fears that this will
prevent her from marrying the man she loves. Both she and
her beloved, Kai, desire marriage with children, and Van
Der Zee suggests that only with these things will they
truly be happy. Faye feels that her inability to have
children is a fatal flaw that cuts her off from Kai's
love. "Every time we see some pregnant woman, every time
we're with somebody else's children I'll feel I've failed
you!" (30). Faye's anxiety and fear are based on the

thought of losing her man and never having children. In "A Sorrowful Woman," however, the crisis comes after the marriage, when the woman has already secured her husband and child. Unlike Faye, who would be ecstatic in this woman's situation, the protagonist of Godwin's story is not. Inexplicably, her husband and son bring her such sorrow that eventually she is unable to see them at all, communicating only through notes stuck under her bedroom door. Godwin's character has a loving husband and child, yet she is still filled with grief. This sense of defeat would be unimaginable in a Harlequin romance because it goes against one of the most popular formulas of romance writing: the plot always ends with a wedding, with the assumption that the rest is happily ever after.

In A Secret Sorrow, marriage is portrayed as the goal. Van Der Zee works to let the reader know that only in this way will Faye be fulfilled and happy; it is what the entire story, with all the plot twists and romantic interludes, works toward. Marriage is also the end in "A Sorrowful Woman" but not as in the goal: it is quite literally the end of the woman's life. Though we don't see what her life was like before her emotional crisis, there are hints of it. When she moves into a new bedroom--away from her husband--she mentions seeing the streets from a whole new perspective (35), suggesting the previous monotony of her daily life. In addition, in the final paragraphs of the story--when the character bakes pies and bread and washes and folds the laundry--her son says, "She's tired from doing all our things again," (37) giving us an idea of what "our things" were and what the woman did with her time before her crisis.

This monotony of marriage is absent in A Secret Sorrow. Faye's inability to have children does not end Kai's

Leigh 3

love for her, and the two go on to marry and adopt children. Faye's married life is described in a very idyllic way: she raises her son and two daughters in a "white ranch house under the blue skies of Texas" (32). Once she is married and has children, there is no more anxiety because the plot leads us to the conclusion that marriage solves all problems and is a source of unending happiness. This greatly differs from Godwin's tale, which takes place in winter and maintains a sense of cold. Whenever Godwin describes the family, it is in terms that suggest weight, guilt, or failure. The child's trusting gaze makes the protagonist begin "yelping without tears" (33), and any sign of life or love increases her sorrow and makes her want to be alone. For example, when the hired girl brings her son to visit her with a grasshopper he's found (34)-- something both alive and from the outside world--she gets very upset and forces her husband to fire the girl. Apparently, the girl is too much of an infringement on her space, too much of a reminder of what she can no longer be.

Never is the difference between the two authors' portrayals of marriage more apparent than when both women are viewing their families. Faye, sitting with her husband and watching her children play, feels that "life was good and filled with love" (32). Godwin's protagonist, on the other hand, says, "The sight of them made her so sad and sick she did not want to see them ever again" (33). When Kai, now her husband, embraces Faye, she feels, "There was love in his embrace and love in his words and in her heart there was no room now for doubt, no room for sorrow" (32). When Godwin's heroine feels the loving touch of her husband's arm and the kiss of her child, she cannot bear it and cuts off all direct contact with them. The situation

of her marriage pushes her into a self-imposed imprisonment and lethargy. She feels unbearably sad because she can
no longer be who they want and need her to be. She avoids
them not because she does not love them but rather because
she loves them so much that it is too painful to see them
and feel her failure. The epigram to Godwin's story tells
us that "Once upon a time there was a wife and a mother
one too many times" (33). The addition of "one too many
times" to this traditional story opening forces the idea
of repetition and monotony: it suggests that it is not
that state of being a wife and mother that is inherently
bad but rather the fact that that is all Godwin's character is. Day in and day out, too many times over, the woman
is just a wife and a mother, and it isn't enough for her.

In Van Der Zee's story there could be no such thing
as too much motherhood or too much of being a wife. When
Faye's fears of losing Kai are assuaged, and she is happily married, it is as though a great weight has been
lifted off her. Godwin's character, on the other hand,
feels her marriage as a great weight pressing on her
and immobilizing her. When she leaves her room for a day
and puts out freshly baked bread for her husband and son,
they express their happiness in the notes they write to
her that night, and "the force of the two joyful notes . . .
pressed her into the corner of the little room; she
hardly had space to breathe" (36). Faye can be a traditional wife and mother, so her family is a source of joy.
Godwin's character can no longer be the traditional wife
and mother, and so her family represents her own failure,
and the guilt presses her further and further into herself
until she can retreat no further and ends her life.

The endings of the two stories are powerful illustrations of the differences between them. In the end of

A Secret Sorrow the author shows us Faye feeling "beautiful, complete, whole" (33) in her role as wife and mother.
Godwin, on the other hand, shows us her protagonist dead
on her bed. Godwin seems to give the reader hope by showing all that the woman has done and saying that "the house
smelled redolently of renewal and spring" (37). This makes
the blow even harder when we then discover, along with the
husband and child, the woman's death. The ambiguous way
the death of Godwin's unnamed protagonist is dealt with
reinforces the author's negative portrayal of marriage. It
isn't explicitly written as a suicide, and Godwin seems to
encourage her readers to see it as the inevitable consequence of her marriage.

Van Der Zee creates a story full of emotional highs
and lows, but one that leads up to and ends with marriage.
After the marriage all of the plot twists and traumas
come to a halt, replaced with peace and happiness. Faye
is brought to new life by her marriage and children; she
finds fulfillment of all of her desires in them. Godwin's
story, however, is full of postmarital anguish and confusion. The character she creates is stifled and most definitely unfulfilled by her marriage. A burst of creative
energy right before her death produces, among other
things, "a sheath of marvelous watercolor beasts accompanied by mad and fanciful stories nobody could ever
make up again, and a tablet full of love sonnets addressed to the man" (37). It is clear that the woman had
talents and desires not met by the routine duties of her
marital life. For Faye, the protagonist of A Secret
Sorrow, marriage is the happily-ever-after ending she has
wanted all of her life; for Godwin's protagonist, on the
other hand, marriage is just a monotonous and interminable
ever after.

3

Plot

Created by a writer's imagination, a work of fiction need not be factual or historically accurate. Although actual people, places, and events may be included in fiction, facts are not as important as is the writer's use of them. We can learn much about Russian life in the early part of the nineteenth century from Leo Tolstoy's *War and Peace*, but that historical information is incidental to Tolstoy's exploration of human nature. Tolstoy, like most successful writers, makes us accept as real the world in his novel no matter how foreign it may be to our own reality. One of the ways a writer achieves this acceptance and engagement — and one of a writer's few obligations — is to interest us in what is happening in the story. We are carried into the writer's fictional world by the plot.

Plot is the author's arrangement of incidents in a story. It is the organizing principle that controls the order of events. This structure is, in a sense, what remains after a writer edits out what is irrelevant to the story being told. We don't need to know, for example, what happens to Rip Van Winkle's faithful dog, Wolf, during his amiable master's twenty-year nap in the Catskill Mountains in order to be enchanted by Washington Irving's story of a henpecked husband. Instead, what is told takes on meaning as it is brought into focus by a skillful writer who selects and orders the events that constitute the story's plot.

Events can be presented in a variety of orders. A chronological arrangement begins with what happens first, then second, and so on, until the last incident is related. That is how "Rip Van Winkle" is told. The events in William Faulkner's "A Rose for Emily," however, are not arranged in chronological order because that would give away the story's surprise ending; instead, Faulkner moves back and forth between the past and present to provide information that leads up to the final startling moment (which won't be given away here either; the story begins on p. 72).

Some stories begin at the end and then lead up to why or how events worked out as they did. If you read the first paragraph of Yukio Mishima's "Patriotism" (p. 593), you'll find an example of this arrangement that will make it difficult for you to stop reading. Stories can also begin in the middle of things (the Latin term for this common plot strategy is *in medias res*). In this kind of plot we enter the story on the verge of some important moment. John Updike's "A & P" (p. 576) begins with the narrator, a teenager working at a checkout counter in a supermarket, telling us: "In walks these three girls in nothing but bathing suits." Right away we are brought into the middle of a situation that will ultimately create the conflict in the story.

Another common strategy is the *flashback*, a device that informs us about events that happened before the opening scene of a work. Nearly all of Ralph Ellison's "Battle Royal" (p. 223) takes the form of a flashback as the narrator recounts how his identity as a black man was shaped by the circumstances that attended a high-school graduation speech he delivered twenty years earlier in a hotel ballroom before a gathering of the town's leading white citizens, most of whom were "quite tipsy." Whatever the plot arrangement, you should be aware of how the writer's conscious ordering of events affects your responses to the action.

EDGAR RICE BURROUGHS (1875–1950)

A great many stories share a standard plot pattern. The following excerpt from Edgar Rice Burroughs's novel *Tarzan of the Apes* provides a conventional plot pattern in which the *character*, an imagined person in the story, is confronted with a problem leading to a climactic struggle that is followed by a resolution of the problem. The elements of a conventional plot are easily recognizable to readers familiar with fast-paced, action-packed mysteries, spy thrillers, westerns, or adventure stories. These page-turners are carefully plotted so that the reader is swept up by the action. More serious writers sometimes use similar strategies, but they do so with greater subtlety and for some purpose that goes beyond providing a thrill a minute. The writer of serious fiction is usually less concerned with what happens next to the central character than with why it happens. In Burroughs's adventure story, however, the emphasis is clearly on action. *Tarzan of the Apes* may add little or nothing to our understanding of life, but it is useful for delineating some important elements of plot. Moreover, it is great fun.

Burroughs's novel, published in 1914 and the first of a series of enormously popular Tarzan books and films, charts the growth to manhood of a child raised in the African jungle by great apes. (See Gore Vidal's discussion of the popularity of Tarzan books in the Perspective on p. 68.) Tarzan struggles to survive his primitive beginnings and to reconcile what he has learned in the jungle with his equally powerful instincts to be a civilized human being. One of the more exciting moments in Tarzan's development is his final confrontation with his old enemy, Terkoz, a huge tyrannical ape that has kidnapped Jane, a pretty nineteen-year-old from Baltimore, Maryland, who has accompanied her father on an expedition to the jungle.

In the chapter preceding this excerpt, Tarzan falls in love with Jane and writes this pointed, if not eloquent, note to her: "I am Tarzan of the Apes. I want you. I am yours. You are mine." Just as he finishes the note, he hears "the agonized screams of a woman" and rushes to their source to find Esmeralda, Jane's maid, hysterical with fear and grief. She reports that Jane, the fair and gentle embodiment of civilization in the story, has been carried off by a gorilla. Here is the first half of the next chapter, which illustrates how Burroughs plots the sequence of events so that the emphasis is on physical action.

From Tarzan of the Apes   *1914*

From the time Tarzan left the tribe of great anthropoids in which he had been raised, it was torn by continual strife and discord. Terkoz proved a cruel and capricious king, so that, one by one, many of the older and weaker apes, upon whom he was particularly prone to vent his brutish nature, took their families and sought the quiet and safety of the far interior.

But at last those who remained were driven to desperation by the continued truculence of Terkoz, and it so happened that one of them recalled the parting admonition of Tarzan:

"If you have a chief who is cruel, do not do as the other apes do, and attempt, any one of you, to pit yourself against him alone. But, instead, let two or three or four of you attack him together. Then, if you will do this, no chief will dare to be other than he should be, for four of you can kill any chief who may ever be over you."

And the ape who recalled this wise counsel repeated it to several of his fellows, so that when Terkoz returned to the tribe that day he found a warm reception awaiting him.

There were no formalities. As Terkoz reached the group, five huge, hairy 5 beasts sprang upon him.

At heart he was an arrant coward, which is the way with bullies among apes as well as among men; so he did not remain to fight and die, but tore himself away from them as quickly as he could and fled into the sheltering boughs of the forest.

Two more attempts he made to rejoin the tribe, but on each occasion he was set upon and driven away. At last he gave it up, and turned, foaming with rage and hatred, into the jungle.

For several days he wandered aimlessly, nursing his spite and looking for some weak thing on which to vent his pent anger.

It was in this state of mind that the horrible, manlike beast, swinging from tree to tree, came suddenly upon two women in the jungle.

He was right above them when he discovered them. The first intimation 10
Jane Porter had of his presence was when the great hairy body dropped to the
earth beside her, and she saw the awful face and the snarling, hideous mouth
thrust within a foot of her.

One piercing scream escaped her lips as the brute hand clutched her arm.
Then she was dragged toward those awful fangs which yawned at her throat.
But ere they touched that fair skin another mood claimed the anthropoid.

The tribe had kept his women. He must find others to replace them. This
hairless white ape would be the first of his new household, and so he threw her
roughly across his broad, hairy shoulders and leaped back into the trees, bearing Jane away.

Esmeralda's scream of terror had mingled once with that of Jane, and
then, as was Esmeralda's manner under stress of emergency which required
presence of mind, she swooned.

But Jane did not once lose consciousness. It is true that that awful face,
pressing close to hers, and the stench of the foul breath beating upon her nostrils, paralyzed her with terror; but her brain was clear, and she comprehended
all that transpired.

With what seemed to her marvelous rapidity the brute bore her through 15
the forest, but still she did not cry out or struggle. The sudden advent of the
ape had confused her to such an extent that she thought now that he was bearing her toward the beach.

For this reason she conserved her energies and her voice until she could
see that they had approached near enough to the camp to attract the succor
she craved.

She could not have known it, but she was being borne farther and farther
into the impenetrable jungle.

The scream that had brought Clayton and the two older men stumbling
through the undergrowth had led Tarzan of the Apes straight to where Esmeralda lay, but it was not Esmeralda in whom his interest centered, though pausing over her he saw that she was unhurt.

For a moment he scrutinized the ground below and the trees above, until
the ape that was in him by virtue of training and environment, combined with
the intelligence that was his by right of birth, told his wondrous woodcraft the
whole story as plainly as though he had seen the thing happen with his own
eyes.

And then he was gone again into the swaying trees, following the high-flung 20
spoor which no other human eye could have detected, much less translated.

At boughs' ends, where the anthropoid swings from one tree to another,
there is most to mark the trail, but least to point the direction of the quarry;
for there the pressure is downward always, toward the small end of the branch,
whether the ape be leaving or entering a tree. Nearer the center of the tree,
where the signs of passage are fainter, the direction is plainly marked.

Here, on this branch, a caterpillar has been crushed by the fugitive's great
foot, and Tarzan knows instinctively where that same foot would touch in the
next stride. Here he looks to find a tiny particle of the demolished larva, oft-
times not more than a speck of moisture.

Again, a minute bit of bark has been upturned by the scraping hand, and
the direction of the break indicates the direction of the passage. Or some great

limb, or the stem of the tree itself has been brushed by the hairy body, and a tiny shred of hair tells him by the direction from which it is wedged beneath the bark that he is on the right trail.

Nor does he need to check his speed to catch these seemingly faint records of the fleeing beast.

To Tarzan they stand out boldly against all the myriad other scars and 25 bruises and signs upon the leafy way. But strongest of all is the scent, for Tarzan is pursuing up the wind, and his trained nostrils are as sensitive as a hound's.

There are those who believe that the lower orders are specially endowed by nature with better olfactory nerves than man, but it is merely a matter of development.

Man's survival does not hinge so greatly upon the perfection of his senses. His power to reason has relieved them of many of their duties, and so they have, to some extent, atrophied, as have the muscles which move the ears and scalp, merely from disuse.

The muscles are there, about the ears and beneath the scalp, and so are the nerves which transmit sensations to the brain, but they are underdeveloped because they are not needed.

Not so with Tarzan of the Apes. From early infancy his survival had depended upon acuteness of eyesight, hearing, smell, touch, and taste far more than upon the more slowly developed organ of reason.

The least developed of all in Tarzan was the sense of taste, for he could eat 30 luscious fruits, or raw flesh, long buried, with almost equal appreciation; but in that he differed but slightly from more civilized epicures.

Almost silently the ape-man sped on in the track of Terkoz and his prey, but the sound of his approach reached the ears of the fleeing beast and spurred it on to greater speed.

Three miles were covered before Tarzan overtook them, and then Terkoz, seeing that further flight was futile, dropped to the ground in a small open glade, that he might turn and fight for his prize or be free to escape unhampered if he saw that the pursuer was more than a match for him.

He still grasped Jane in one great arm as Tarzan bounded like a leopard into the arena which nature had provided for this primeval-like battle.

When Terkoz saw that it was Tarzan who pursued him, he jumped to the conclusion that this was Tarzan's woman, since they were of the same kind — white and hairless — and so he rejoiced at this opportunity for double revenge upon his hated enemy.

To Jane the strange apparition of this godlike man was as wine to sick 35 nerves.

From the description which Clayton and her father and Mr. Philander had given her, she knew that it must be the same wonderful creature who had saved them, and she saw in him only a protector and a friend.

But as Terkoz pushed her roughly aside to meet Tarzan's charge, and she saw the great proportions of the ape and the mighty muscles and the fierce fangs, her heart quailed. How could any vanquish such a mighty antagonist?

Like two charging bulls they came together, and like two wolves sought each other's throat. Against the long canines of the ape was pitted the thin blade of the man's knife.

Jane — her lithe, young form flattened against the trunk of a great tree, her hands tight pressed against her rising and falling bosom, and her eyes wide with mingled horror, fascination, fear, and admiration — watched the primordial ape battle with the primeval man for possession of a woman — for her.

As the great muscles of the man's back and shoulders knotted beneath 40 the tension of his efforts, and the huge biceps and forearm held at bay those mighty tusks, the veil of centuries of civilization and culture were swept from the blurred vision of the Baltimore girl.

When the long knife drank deep a dozen times of Terkoz's heart's blood, and the great carcass rolled lifeless upon the ground, it was a primeval woman who sprang forward with outstretched arms toward the primeval man who had fought for her and won.

And Tarzan?

He did what no red-blooded man needs lessons in doing. He took his woman in his arms and smothered her upturned, panting lips with kisses.

For a moment Jane lay there with half-closed eyes. For a moment — the first in her young life — she knew the meaning of love.

But as suddenly as the veil had been withdrawn it dropped again, and an 45 outraged conscience suffused her face with its scarlet mantle, and a mortified woman thrust Tarzan of the Apes from her and buried her face in her hands.

Tarzan had been surprised when he had found the girl he had learned to love after a vague and abstract manner a willing prisoner in his arms. Now he was surprised that she repulsed him.

He came close to her once more and took hold of her arm. She turned upon him like a tigress, striking his great breast with her tiny hands.

Tarzan could not understand it.

A moment ago, and it had been his intention to hasten Jane back to her people, but that little moment was lost now in the dim and distant past of things which were but can never be again, and with it the good intention had gone to join the impossible.

Since then Tarzan of the Apes had felt a warm, lithe form close pressed to 50 his. Hot, sweet breath against his cheek and mouth had fanned a new flame to life within his breast, and perfect lips had clung to his in burning kisses that had seared a deep brand into his soul — a brand which marked a new Tarzan.

Again he laid his hand upon her arm. Again she repulsed him. And then Tarzan of the Apes did just what his first ancestor would have done.

He took his woman in his arms and carried her into the jungle.

This episode begins with *exposition,* the background information the reader needs to make sense of the situation in which the characters are placed. The first eight paragraphs let us know that Terkoz has been overthrown as leader of the ape tribe and that he is roaming the jungle "looking for some weak thing on which to vent his pent anger." This exposition is in the form of a flashback. (Recall that the previous chapter ended with Esmeralda's report of the kidnapping; now we will see what happened.)

Once this information supplies a context for the characters, the plot gains momentum with the *rising action,* a complication that intensifies the situation: Terkoz, looking for a victim, discovers the vulnerable Esmeralda and Jane. His first impulse is to kill Jane, but his "mood" changes when he remembers that he has no woman of his own after having been forced to leave the tribe (more exposition). Hence, there is a further complication in the rising action when he decides to carry her off. Just when it seems that the situation could not get any worse, it does. The reader is invited to shudder even more than if Terkoz had made a meal of Jane because she may have to endure the "awful face," "foul breath," and lust of this beast.

At this point we are brought up to the action that ended the preceding chapter. Tarzan races to the rescue by unerringly following the trail from the place where Jane was kidnapped. He relentlessly tracks Terkoz. Unfortunately, Burroughs slows down the pursuit here by including several paragraphs that abstractly consider the evolutionary development of human reliance on reason more than on their senses for survival. This discussion offers a rationale for Tarzan's remarkable ability to track Jane, but it is an interruption in the chase.

When Tarzan finally catches up to Terkoz, the **conflict** of this episode fully emerges. Tarzan must save the woman he loves by defeating his long-standing enemy. For Terkoz seeks to achieve a "double revenge" by killing Tarzan and taking his woman. Terkoz's assumption that Jane is Tarzan's woman is a **foreshadowing**, a suggestion of what is yet to come. In this conflict Tarzan is the **protagonist** or **hero,** the central character who engages our interest and empathy. *Protagonist* is often a more useful term than hero or **heroine,** however, because the central character of a story can be despicable as well as heroic. In Edgar Allan Poe's "The Tell-Tale Heart," for example, the central character is a madman and murderer. Terkoz is the **antagonist,** the force that opposes the protagonist.

The battle between Tarzan and Terkoz creates **suspense** because the reader is made anxious about what is going to happen. Burroughs makes certain that the reader will worry about the outcome by having Jane wonder, "How could any vanquish such a mighty antagonist?" If we are caught up in the moment, we watch the battle, as Jane does, with "mingled horror, fascination, fear, and admiration" to see what will happen next. The moment of greatest emotional tension, the **climax,** occurs when Tarzan kills Terkoz. Tarzan's victory is the **resolution** of the conflict, also known as the **dénouement** (a French word meaning the "untying of the knot"). This could have been the conclusion to the episode except that Jane and Tarzan simultaneously discover their "primeval" selves sexually drawn to each other. Burroughs resolves one conflict — the battle with Terkoz — but then immediately creates another — by raising the question of what a respectable professor's daughter from Baltimore is doing in the sweaty arms of a panting, half-naked man.

For a brief moment the cycle of conflict, suspense, and resolution begins again as Jane passionately kisses Tarzan; then her "outraged conscience" causes her to regain her sense of propriety and she pushes him away. Although Tarzan succeeds in the encounter with Terkoz, he is not successful with Jane. However, Burroughs creates suspense for a third time at the very end of the episode, when the "new Tarzan," having been transformed by this sexual awakening, "took his woman in his arms and carried her into the jungle." What will he do next? Despite the novel's implausibility (beginning with the premise that apes could raise a human child) and its heavy use of coincidences (not the least of which is Tarzan's donning a loincloth for the first time only four pages before he meets Jane), the story is difficult to put down. The plot swings us swiftly and smoothly from incident to incident, even if there is an occasional interruption, such as Burroughs's discussion of evolution, in the flow of the action.

Although this pattern of exposition, rising action, conflict, suspense, climax, and resolution provides a useful outline of many plots that emphasize physical action, a greater value of this pattern is that it helps us to see how innovative artists move beyond formula fiction by manipulating and changing the pattern for their own purposes. At the furthest extreme are those modern storytellers who reject traditional plotting techniques in favor of experimental approaches. Instead of including characters who wrestle with conflicts, experimental fiction frequently may concern the writer's own efforts to create a story. Rather than ordering experience, such writers disrupt it by insisting that meanings in fiction are as elusive — or nonexistent — as meanings in life; they are likely to reject both traditional values and traditional forms of writing. Most writers, however, use conflicts in their plots to reveal characters and convey meanings. The nature of those conflicts can help determine how important physical action is to the plot.

The primary conflict that Tarzan experiences in his battle with Terkoz is external. External conflict is popular in adventure stories because the protagonist's physical struggles with a formidable foe or the ever-present dangers of a dense jungle echoing wild screams provide plenty of excitement. External conflicts may place the protagonist in opposition to another individual, nature, or society. Tarzan's battle with societal values begins the moment he instinctively takes Jane in his arms to carry her off into the jungle. He will learn that an individual's conflict with society can be as frustrating as it is complex, which is why so many plots in serious fiction focus on this conflict. It can be seen, to cite only two examples, in a mysterious stranger's alienation from a materialistic culture in Herman Melville's "Bartleby, the Scrivener" (p. 113) and in a young black man's struggle with racism in Ralph Ellison's "Battle Royal" (p. 223).

Conflict may also be internal; in such a case some moral or psychological issue must be resolved within the protagonist. Inner conflicts frequently accompany external ones, as in Godwin's "A Sorrowful Woman" (p. 33). Godwin's story is quiet and almost uneventful compared with *Tarzan of the Apes*. The conflict, though puzzling, is more significant in "A Sorrowful Woman" because that story subtly explores some troubling issues that cannot be resolved simply by "huge biceps" or a "lithe, young form." The protagonist struggles with both internal and external forces. We are not told why she withdraws from her considerate husband and beautiful son. There is no exposition to explain why she is hopelessly "sad and sick" of them. There is no readily identifiable antagonist in her way, but there are several possibilities. Her antagonist is some part of herself that cannot find satisfaction in playing the roles of wife and mother, yet her husband and child also seem to bear some of the responsibility, as does the domestic environment that defines her.

Godwin creates questions for the reader rather than suspense. We are compelled to keep asking why the protagonist in her story is so unhappy instead of what is going to happen next. The story ends with her flurry of domestic activity and her death, but we do not feel as if we have come to a resolution. "A Sorrowful Woman" will not let us go because we keep coming back to what causes the protagonist's rejection of her role. Has she gone mad? Are the husband and child not what they seem to be? Is her domestic life stifling rather than nourishing? Does her family destroy rather than support her? Who or what is to blame? No one is able to rescue the sorrowful woman from her conflict, nor does the design of Godwin's plot relieve the reader of the questions the story raises. The meaning of the action is not self-evident as it is in *Tarzan of the Apes*. It must be drawn from a careful reading of the interrelated details and dialogues that constitute this story's action.

Although Burroughs makes enormous demands on Tarzan to survive the perils of the jungle, the author makes few demands on the reader. In part, that's why *Tarzan of the Apes* is so much fun: we sit back while Tarzan does all the work, struggling heroically through all the conflicts Burroughs has planted along his jungle paths. Godwin's story, in contrast, illustrates that there are other kinds of plots, less dependent on action but equally full of conflict. This kind of reading is more demanding, but ultimately more satisfying, because as we confront conflicts in serious fiction we read not only absorbing stories but also ourselves. We are invited not to escape life but to look long and hard at it. Although serious fiction can be as diverting and pleasurable as most standard action-packed plots, serious fiction offers an additional important element: a perspective on experience that reflects rather than deflects life.

PERSPECTIVE

GORE VIDAL (b. 1925)
The Popularity of the Tarzan Books   *1963*

These books are clearly for men. I have yet to meet a woman who found Tarzan interesting: no identification, as they say in series land.

Though Burroughs is innocent of literature . . . he does have a gift very few writers of any kind possess: he can describe action vividly. I give away no trade secrets when I say that this is as difficult for a Tolstoi as it is for a Burroughs (even William). Because it is so hard, the draftier contemporary novelists usually prefer to tell their stories in the first person, which is simply writing dialogue. In character, as it were, the writer settles for an impression of what happened rather than creating the sense of a happening. Tarzan *in action* is excellent.

There is something basic in the appeal of the 1914 Tarzan which makes me think that he can still hold his own as a daydream figure, despite the sophisticated challenge from his two contemporary competitors, Ian Fleming and Mickey Spillane. For most adults, Tarzan (and John Carter of Mars) can hardly compete with the conspicuous consumer consumption of James Bond or the sickly violence of Mike Hammer, but for children and adolescents, the old appeal continues. All of us need the idea of a world alternative to this one. From Plato's *Republic* to Opar to Bondland, at every level, the human imagination has tried to imagine something better for itself than the existing society. Man left Eden when we got up off all fours, endowing most of his descendants with nostalgia as well as chronic backache. In its naïve way, the Tarzan legend returns us to that Eden where, free of clothes and the inhibitions of an oppressive society, a man can achieve in reverie his continuing need, which is, as William Faulkner put it in his high Confederate style, to prevail as well as endure. . . . The individual's desire to dominate his environment is not a desirable trait in a society which every day grows more and more confining. Since there are few legitimate releases for the average man, he must take to daydreaming. James Bond, Mike Hammer, and Tarzan are all dream-selves, and the aim of each is to establish personal primacy in a world which in reality diminishes the individual. Among adults, increasing popularity of these lively inferior fictions strikes me as a most significant (and unbearably sad) phenomenon.

From "Tarzan Revisited" in *Esquire*

CONSIDERATIONS FOR CRITICAL THINKING AND WRITING

1. What does Vidal see as the lasting appeal of the Tarzan books? Is this true of most popular literature?

2. Explain why you agree or disagree with Vidal's view that "these books are clearly for men" rather than for women.

3. Vidal praises Burroughs's writing when he says, "Tarzan *in action* is excellent." Do you think the excerpt from *Tarzan of the Apes* (p. 62) supports this view? Explain why or why not.

CONNECTIONS TO OTHER SELECTIONS

1. How might the excerpts from *Tarzan of the Apes* (p. 62) and *A Secret Sorrow* (p. 25) be regarded as stories that return us to what Vidal calls a kind of "Eden"? What constitutes Eden in each story? How does each author's gender help to explain the difference in their versions of an ideal existence?

2. Write an essay exploring the differences between how Burroughs writes about action in the Tarzan excerpt and how Tim O'Brien handles action in the plot of "How to Tell a True War Story" (p. 555).

The following three stories—Mark Halliday's "Young Man on Sixth Avenue," William Faulkner's "A Rose for Emily," and Andre Dubus's "Killings"—are remarkable for the different kinds of tension produced in each by a subtle use of plot.

MARK HALLIDAY (B. 1949)

Born in Ann Arbor, Michigan, Mark Halliday earned a B.A. and an M.A. from Brown University and a Ph.D. from Brandeis University. A teacher at the University of Pennsylvania, his short stories and poems have appeared in a variety of periodicals, including *The Massachusetts Review, Michigan Quarterly Review, Chicago Review,* and *The New Republic.* His collection of poems, *Little Star,* was selected by the National Poetry Series for publication in 1987. He has also written a critical study on poet Wallace Stevens titled *Stevens and the Interpersonal* (1991).

Young Man on Sixth Avenue   *1995*

He was a young man in the big city. He was a young man in the biggest, the most overwhelming city—and he was not overwhelmed. For see, he strode across Fifth Avenue just before the light changed, and his head was up in the sharp New York wind and he was thriving upon the rock of Manhattan, in 1938. His legs were long and his legs were strong; there was no question about his legs; they were unmistakable in their length and strength; they were as bold and dependable as any American machine, moving him across Fifth just in time, his brown shoes attaining the sidewalk without any faltering, his gait unaware of the notion that legs might ever want to rest. Forty-ninth Street! He walked swiftly through the haste and blare, through the chilly exclamation points of taxis and trucks and people. He was a man! In America, '38, New York, two o'clock in the afternoon, sunlight chopping down between buildings, Forty-ninth Street. And his hair was so dark, almost black, and it had a natural wave in it recognized as a handsome feature by everyone, recognized universally, along with his dark blue eyes and strong jaw. Women saw him, they all had to see him, all the young women had to perceive him reaching the corner of Forty-ninth and Sixth, and they had to know he was a candidate. He knew they knew. He knew they knew he would *get* some of them, and he moved visibly tall with the tall potential of the not-finite twentieth-century getting that would be his inheritance; and young women who glanced at him on Sixth Avenue knew that he knew. They felt that they or their sisters would have to take him into account, and they touched their scarves a little nervously.

He was twenty-five years old, and this day in 1938 was the present. It was so obviously and totally the present, so unabashed and even garish with its presentness, beamingly right there right now like Rita Hayworth, all Sixth Avenue was in fact at two o'clock a thumping bright Rita Hayworth and the young man strode south irresistibly. If there was only one thing he knew, crossing Forty-eighth, it was that this day was the present, out of which un-counted glories could and must blossom — when? — in 1938, or in 1939, soon, or in the big brazen decade ahead, in 1940, soon; so he walked with fistfuls of fu-tures that could happen in all his pockets.

And his wavy hair was so dark, almost black. And he knew the right restau-rant for red roast beef, not too expensive. And in his head were some sharp ideas about Dreiser, and Thomas Wolfe, and John O'Hara.

On Forty-seventh between two buildings (buildings taller even than him) there was an unexpected zone of deep shade. He paused for half a second, and he shivered for some reason. Briskly then, briskly he moved ahead.

In the restaurant on Seventh Avenue he met his friend John for a witty late *5* lunch. Everything was — the whole lunch was good. It was right. And what they said was both hilarious and notably well-informed. And then soon he was tak-ing the stairs two at a time up to an office on Sixth for his interview. The pow-erful lady seemed to like his sincerity and the clarity of his eyes — a hard com-bination to beat! — and the even more powerful man in charge sized him up and saw the same things, and he got the job.

That job lasted three years, then came the War, then another job, then Judy, and the two kids, and a better job in Baltimore, and those years — those years. And those years. "Those years" — and the kids went to college with new typewriters. In the blue chair, with his work on his lapboard, after a pleasant dinner of macaroni and sausage and salad, he dozed off. Then he was sixty. Sixty? Then he rode back and forth on trains, Judy became ill, doctors offered opinions, comas were deceptive, Judy died. But the traffic on Coleytown Road next morning still moved casually too fast. And in a minute he was seventy-five and the phone rang with news that witty John of the great late lunches was dead. The house pulsed with silence.

Something undone? What? The thing that would have saved — what? Waking in the dark — maybe something unwritten, that would have made peo-ple say "*Yes* that's why you matter so much." Ideas about Wolfe. Dreiser. Or some lost point about John O'Hara.

Women see past him on the street in this pseudo-present and he feels they are so stupid and walks fierce for a minute but then his shoulders settle closer to his skeleton with the truth about these women: not especially stupid; only young. In this pseudo-present he blinks at a glimpse of that young man on Sixth Avenue, young man as if still out there in the exclamation of Sixth Av-enue — that young man ready to stride across — but a taxi makes him step back to the curb, he'll have to wait a few more seconds, he can wait.

Considerations for Critical Thinking and Writing

1. FIRST RESPONSE. Do you identify with the young man as he is described in the first paragraph? Is he appealing to you? Why or why not?

2. Why do you think this story opens in 1938? Why is the Manhattan setting important?

3. The American novelists Theodore Dreiser, Thomas Wolfe, and John O'Hara are mentioned in paragraphs 3 and 7. Of what significance are these novel-ists in this story? You may have to look up these writers in an encyclope-dic entry or a dictionary of American literary biographies to answer this question.

4. What is the conflict in the story?

5. Locate the climax in the story. Is there a resolution to the conflict? Explain.

6. How might paragraph 4 be described as an example of foreshadowing?

7. What does the plotting of this story suggest about the nature of the protagonist's life?

8. What do you think is the cenral point of this story?

CONNECTIONS TO OTHER SELECTIONS

1. Discuss the significance of the Manhattan setting in "Young Man on Sixth
Avenue" and in Herman Melville's "Bartleby, the Scrivener" (p. 113).

2. Write an essay comparing the ending of Halliday's story with that of Raymond Carver's "Popular Mechanics" (p. 272). What is the effect of the ending on your reading of each story?

WILLIAM FAULKNER (1897–1962)

Born into an old Mississippi family that had lost its influence and wealth
during the Civil War, William Faulkner lived nearly all his life in the South
writing about Yoknapatawpha County, an imagined Mississippi county similar to his home in Oxford. Among his novels based on this fictional location
are *The Sound and the Fury* (1929), *As I Lay Dying* (1930), *Light in August* (1932), and
Absalom, Absalom! (1936). Although his writings are regional in their emphasis
on local social history, his concerns are broader. In his 1950 acceptance speech
for the Nobel Prize for literature, he insisted that the "problems of the human
heart in conflict with itself . . . alone can make good writing because only
that is worth writing about, worth the agony and the sweat." This commitment is evident in his novels and in *The Collected Stories of William Faulkner*
(1950). "A Rose for Emily," about the mysterious life of Emily Grierson, presents a personal conflict rooted in her southern identity. It also contains a
grim surprise.

A Rose for Emily   *1931*

I

When Miss Emily Grierson died, our whole town went to her funeral: the men
through a sort of respectful affection for a fallen monument, the women
mostly out of curiosity to see the inside of her house, which no one save an old
manservant — a combined gardener and cook — had seen in at least ten years.

It was a big, squarish frame house that had once been white, decorated with
cupolas and spires and scrolled balconies in the heavily lightsome style of the
seventies, set on what had once been our most select street. But garages and cotton gins had encroached and obliterated even the august names of that neighborhood; only Miss Emily's house was left, lifting its stubborn and coquettish

decay above the cotton wagons and the gasoline pumps — an eyesore among eye-sores. And now Miss Emily had gone to join the representatives of those august names where they lay in the cedar-bemused cemetery among the ranked and anonymous graves of Union and Confederate soldiers who fell at the battle of Jefferson.

Alive, Miss Emily had been a tradition, a duty, and a care; a sort of heredi-tary obligation upon the town, dating from that day in 1894 when Colonel Sar-toris, the mayor — he who fathered the edict that no Negro woman should ap-pear on the streets without an apron — remitted her taxes, the dispensation dating from the death of her father on into perpetuity. Not that Miss Emily would have accepted charity. Colonel Sartoris invented an involved tale to the effect that Miss Emily's father had loaned money to the town, which the town, as a matter of business, preferred this way of repaying. Only a man of Colonel Sartoris' generation and thought could have invented it, and only a woman could have believed it.

When the next generation, with its more modern ideas, became mayors and aldermen, this arrangement created some little dissatisfaction. On the first of the year they mailed her a tax notice. February came, and there was no reply. They wrote her a formal letter, asking her to call at the sheriff's office at her convenience. A week later the mayor wrote her himself, offering to call or to send his car for her, and received in reply a note on paper of an archaic shape, in a thin, flowing calligraphy in faded ink, to the effect that she no longer went out at all. The tax notice was also enclosed, without comment.

They called a special meeting of the Board of Aldermen. A deputation waited upon her, knocked at the door through which no visitor had passed since she ceased giving china-painting lessons eight or ten years earlier. They were admitted by the old Negro into a dim hall from which a stairway mounted into still more shadow. It smelled of dust and disuse — a close, dank smell. The Negro led them into the parlor. It was furnished in heavy, leather-covered furniture. When the Negro opened the blinds of one window, they could see that the leather was cracked; and when they sat down, a faint dust rose sluggishly about their thighs, spinning with slow motes in the single sun-ray. On a tarnished gilt easel before the fireplace stood a crayon portrait of Miss Emily's father.

They rose when she entered — a small, fat woman in black, with a thin gold chain descending to her waist and vanishing into her belt, leaning on an ebony cane with a tarnished gold head. Her skeleton was small and spare; perhaps that was why what would have been merely plumpness in another was obesity in her. She looked bloated, like a body long submerged in motionless water, and of that pallid hue. Her eyes, lost in the fatty ridges of her face, looked like two small pieces of coal pressed into a lump of dough as they moved from one face to another while the visitors stated their errand.

She did not ask them to sit. She just stood in the door and listened quietly until the spokesman came to a stumbling halt. Then they could hear the invis-ible watch ticking at the end of the gold chain.

Her voice was dry and cold. "I have no taxes in Jefferson. Colonel Sartoris explained it to me. Perhaps one of you can gain access to the city records and satisfy yourselves."

"But we have. We are the city authorities, Miss Emily. Didn't you get a no-tice from the sheriff, signed by him?"

"I received a paper, yes," Miss Emily said. "Perhaps he considers himself   10
the sheriff . . . I have no taxes in Jefferson."

"But there is nothing on the books to show that, you see. We must go by
the —"

"See Colonel Sartoris. I have no taxes in Jefferson."

"But, Miss Emily —"

"See Colonel Sartoris." (Colonel Sartoris had been dead almost ten years.)
"I have no taxes in Jefferson. Tobe!" The Negro appeared. "Show these gentlemen out."

II

So she vanquished them, horse and foot, just as she had vanquished their   15
fathers thirty years before about the smell. That was two years after her father's death and a short time after her sweetheart — the one we believed would
marry her — had deserted her. After her father's death she went out very little;
after her sweetheart went away, people hardly saw her at all. A few of the ladies
had the temerity to call, but were not received, and the only sign of life about
the place was the Negro man — a young man then — going in and out with a
market basket.

"Just as if a man — any man — could keep a kitchen properly," the ladies
said; so they were not surprised when the smell developed. It was another link
between the gross, teeming world and the high and mighty Griersons.

A neighbor, a woman, complained to the mayor, Judge Stevens, eighty
years old.

"But what will you have me do about it, madam?" he said.

"Why, send her word to stop it," the woman said. "Isn't there a law?"

"I'm sure that won't be necessary," Judge Stevens said. "It's probably just a   20
snake or a rat that nigger of hers killed in the yard. I'll speak to him about it."

The next day he received two more complaints, one from a man who came
in diffident deprecation. "We really must do something about it, Judge. I'd be
the last one in the world to bother Miss Emily, but we've got to do something."
That night the Board of Aldermen met — three graybeards and one younger
man, a member of the rising generation.

"It's simple enough," he said. "Send her word to have her place cleaned up.
Give her a certain time to do it in, and if she don't . . ."

"Dammit, sir," Judge Stevens said, "will you accuse a lady to her face of
smelling bad?"

So the next night, after midnight, four men crossed Miss Emily's lawn and
slunk about the house like burglars, sniffing along the base of the brickwork
and at the cellar openings while one of them performed a regular sowing motion with his hand out of a sack slung from his shoulder. They broke open the
cellar door and sprinkled lime there, and in all the outbuildings. As they re-
crossed the lawn, a window that had been dark was lighted and Miss Emily sat
in it, the light behind her, and her upright torso motionless as that of an idol.
They crept quietly across the lawn and into the shadow of the locusts that
lined the street. After a week or two the smell went away.

That was when people had begun to feel really sorry for her. People in our   25
town, remembering how old lady Wyatt, her great-aunt, had gone completely
crazy at last, believed that the Griersons held themselves a little too high for

what they really were. None of the young men were quite good enough for Miss Emily and such. We had long thought of them as a tableau, Miss Emily a slender figure in white in the background, her father a spraddled silhouette in the foreground, his back to her and clutching a horsewhip, the two of them framed by the back-flung front door. So when she got to be thirty and was still single, we were not pleased exactly, but vindicated; even with insanity in the family she wouldn't have turned down all of her chances if they had really materialized.

When her father died, it got about that the house was all that was left to her; and in a way, people were glad. At last they could pity Miss Emily. Being left alone, and a pauper, she had become humanized. Now she too would know the old thrill and the old despair of a penny more or less.

The day after his death all the ladies prepared to call at the house and offer condolence and aid, as is our custom. Miss Emily met them at the door, — dressed as usual and with no trace of grief on her face. She told them that her father was not dead. She did that for three days, with the ministers calling on her, and the doctors, trying to persuade her to let them dispose of the body. Just as they were about to resort to law and force, she broke down, and they buried her father quickly.

We did not say she was crazy then. We believed she had to do that. We remembered all the young men her father had driven away, and we knew that with nothing left, she would have to cling to that which had robbed her, as people will.

III

She was sick for a long time. When we saw her again, her hair was cut short, making her look like a girl, with a vague resemblance to those angels in colored church windows — sort of tragic and serene.

The town had just let the contracts for paving the sidewalks, and in the summer after her father's death they began the work. The construction company came with niggers and mules and machinery, and a foreman named Homer Barron, a Yankee — a big, dark, ready man, with a big voice and eyes lighter than his face. The little boys would follow in groups to hear him cuss the niggers, and the niggers singing in time to the rise and fall of picks. Pretty soon he knew everybody in town. Whenever you heard a lot of laughing anywhere about the square, Homer Barron would be in the center of the group. Presently we began to see him and Miss Emily on Sunday afternoons driving in the yellow-wheeled buggy and the matched team of bays from the livery stable.

At first we were glad that Miss Emily would have an interest, because the ladies all said, "Of course a Grierson would not think seriously of a Northerner, a day laborer." But there were still others, older people, who said that even grief could not cause a real lady to forget *noblesse oblige*° — without calling it *noblesse oblige*. They just said, "Poor Emily. Her kinsfolk should come to her." She had some kin in Alabama; but years ago her father had fallen out with them over the estate of old lady Wyatt, the crazy woman, and there was no communication between the two families. They had not even been represented at the funeral.

noblesse oblige: The obligation of people of high social position.

And as soon as the old people said, "Poor Emily," the whispering began. "Do you suppose it's really so?" they said to one another. "Of course it is. What else could . . ." This behind their hands; rustling of craned silk and satin behind jalousies closed upon the sun of Sunday afternoon as the thin, swift clop-clop-clop of the matched team passed: "Poor Emily."

She carried her head high enough — even when we believed that she was fallen. It was as if she demanded more than ever the recognition of her dignity as the last Grierson; as if it had wanted that touch of earthiness to reaffirm her imperviousness. Like when she bought the rat poison, the arsenic. That was over a year after they had begun to say "Poor Emily," and while the two female cousins were visiting her.

"I want some poison," she said to the druggist. She was over thirty then, still a slight woman, though thinner than usual, with cold, haughty black eyes in a face the flesh of which was strained across the temples and about the eye-sockets as you imagine a lighthouse-keeper's face ought to look. "I want some poison," she said.

"Yes, Miss Emily. What kind? For rats and such? I'd recom —"   35

"I want the best you have. I don't care what kind."

The druggist named several. "They'll kill anything up to an elephant. But what you want is —"

"Arsenic," Miss Emily said. "Is that a good one?"

"Is . . . arsenic? Yes, ma'am. But what you want —"

"I want arsenic."   40

The druggist looked down at her. She looked back at him, erect, her face like a strained flag. "Why, of course," the druggist said. "If that's what you want. But the law requires you to tell what you are going to use it for."

Miss Emily just stared at him, her head tilted back in order to look him eye for eye, until he looked away and went and got the arsenic and wrapped it up. The Negro delivery boy brought her the package; the druggist didn't come back. When she opened the package at home there was written on the box, under the skull and bones: "For rats."

IV

So the next day we all said, "She will kill herself"; and we said it would be the best thing. When she had first begun to be seen with Homer Barron, we had said, "She will marry him." Then we said, "She will persuade him yet," because Homer himself had remarked — he liked men, and it was known that he drank with the younger men in the Elks' Club — that he was not a marrying man. Later we said, "Poor Emily" behind the jalousies as they passed on Sunday afternoon in the glittering buggy, Miss Emily with her head high and Homer Barron with his hat cocked and a cigar in his teeth, reins and whip in a yellow glove.

Then some of the ladies began to say that it was a disgrace to the town and a bad example to the young people. The men did not want to interfere, but at last the ladies forced the Baptist minister — Miss Emily's people were Episcopal — to call upon her. He would never divulge what happened during that interview, but he refused to go back again. The next Sunday they again drove about the streets, and the following day the minister's wife wrote to Miss Emily's relations in Alabama.

So she had blood-kin under her roof again and we sat back to watch devel-   45
opments. At first nothing happened. Then we were sure that they were to be

married. We learned that Miss Emily had been to the jeweler's and ordered a man's toilet set in silver, with the letters H. B. on each piece. Two days later we learned that she had bought a complete outfit of men's clothing, including a nightshirt, and we said, "They are married." We were really glad. We were glad because the two female cousins were even more Grierson than Miss Emily had ever been.

So we were not surprised when Homer Barron—the streets had been finished some time since—was gone. We were a little disappointed that there was not a public blowing-off, but we believed that he had gone on to prepare for Miss Emily's coming, or to give her a chance to get rid of the cousins. (By that time it was a cabal, and we were all Miss Emily's allies to help circumvent the cousins.) Sure enough, after another week they departed. And, as we had expected all along, within three days Homer Barron was back in town. A neighbor saw the Negro man admit him at the kitchen door at dusk one evening.

And that was the last we saw of Homer Barron. And of Miss Emily for some time. The Negro man went in and out with the market basket, but the front door remained closed. Now and then we would see her at a window for a moment, as the men did that night when they sprinkled the lime, but for almost six months she did not appear on the streets. Then we knew that this was to be expected too; as if that quality of her father which had thwarted her woman's life so many times had been too virulent and too furious to die.

When we next saw Miss Emily, she had grown fat and her hair was turning gray. During the next few years it grew grayer and grayer until it attained an even pepper-and-salt iron-gray, when it ceased turning. Up to the day of her death at seventy-four it was still that vigorous iron-gray, like the hair of an active man.

From that time on her front door remained closed, save for a period of six or seven years, when she was about forty, during which she gave lessons in china-painting. She fitted up a studio in one of the downstairs rooms, where the daughters and granddaughters of Colonel Sartoris' contemporaries were sent to her with the same regularity and in the same spirit that they were sent to church on Sundays with a twenty-five-cent piece for the collection plate. Meanwhile her taxes had been remitted.

Then the newer generation became the backbone and the spirit of the 50 town, and the painting pupils grew up and fell away and did not send their children to her with boxes of color and tedious brushes and pictures cut from the ladies' magazines. The front door closed upon the last one and remained closed for good. When the town got free postal delivery, Miss Emily alone refused to let them fasten the metal numbers above her door and attach a mailbox to it. She would not listen to them.

Daily, monthly, yearly we watched the Negro grow grayer and more stooped, going in and out with the market basket. Each December we sent her a tax notice, which would be returned by the post office a week later, unclaimed. Now and then we would see her in one of the downstairs windows—she had evidently shut up the top floor of the house—like the carven torso of an idol in a niche, looking or not looking at us, we could never tell which. Thus she passed from generation to generation—dear, inescapable, impervious, tranquil, and perverse.

And so she died. Fell ill in the house filled with dust and shadows, with only a doddering Negro man to wait on her. We did not even know she was sick; we had long since given up trying to get information from the Negro. He talked to no one, probably not even to her, for his voice had grown harsh and rusty, as if from disuse.

She died in one of the downstairs rooms, in a heavy walnut bed with a curtain, her gray head propped on a pillow yellow and moldy with age and lack of sunlight.

V

The Negro met the first of the ladies at the front door and let them in, with their hushed, sibilant voices and their quick, curious glances, and then he disappeared. He walked right through the house and out the back and was not seen again.

The two female cousins came at once. They held the funeral on the second 55 day, with the town coming to look at Miss Emily beneath a mass of bought flowers, with the crayon face of her father musing profoundly above the bier and the ladies sibilant and macabre; and the very old men — some in their brushed Confederate uniforms — on the porch and the lawn, talking of Miss Emily as if she had been a contemporary of theirs, believing that they had danced with her and courted her perhaps, confusing time with its mathematical progression, as the old do, to whom all the past is not a diminishing road but, instead, a huge meadow which no winter ever quite touches, divided from them now by the narrow bottle-neck of the most recent decade of years.

Already we knew that there was one room in that region above stairs which no one had seen in forty years, and which would have to be forced. They waited until Miss Emily was decently in the ground before they opened it.

The violence of breaking down the door seemed to fill this room with pervading dust. A thin, acrid pall as of the tomb seemed to lie everywhere upon this room decked and furnished as for a bridal: upon the valance curtains of faded rose color, upon the rose-shaded lights, upon the dressing table, upon the delicate array of crystal and the man's toilet things backed with tarnished silver, silver so tarnished that the monogram was obscured. Among them lay a collar and tie, as if they had just been removed, which, lifted, left upon the surface a pale crescent in the dust. Upon a chair hung the suit, carefully folded; beneath it the two mute shoes and the discarded socks.

The man himself lay in the bed.

For a long while we just stood there, looking down at the profound and fleshless grin. The body had apparently once lain in the attitude of an embrace, but now the long sleep that outlasts love, that conquers even the grimace of love, had cuckolded him. What was left of him, rotted beneath what was left of the nightshirt, had become inextricable from the bed in which he lay; and upon him and upon the pillow beside him lay that even coating of the patient and biding dust.

Then we noticed that in the second pillow was the indentation of a head. 60 One of us lifted something from it, and leaning forward, that faint and invisible dust dry and acrid in the nostrils, we saw a long strand of iron-gray hair.

CONSIDERATIONS FOR CRITICAL THINKING AND WRITING

1. FIRST RESPONSE. How might this story be rewritten as a piece of formula fiction? You could write it as a romance, detective, or horror story — whatever strikes your fancy. Does Faulkner's version have elements of formulaic fiction?

2. What is the effect of the final paragraph of the story? How does it contribute to your understanding of Emily? Why is it important that we get this information last rather than at the beginning of the story?

3. What details foreshadow the conclusion of the story? Did you anticipate the ending?

4. Contrast the order of events as they happen in the story with the order in which they are told. How does this plotting create interest and suspense?

5. Faulkner uses a number of gothic elements in this plot: the imposing decrepit house, the decayed corpse, and the mysterious secret horrors connected with Emily's life. How do these elements forward the plot and establish the atmosphere?

6. How does the information provided by the exposition indicate the nature of the conflict in the story? What does Emily's southern heritage contribute to the story?

7. Who or what is the antagonist of the story? Why is it significant that Homer Barron is a construction foreman and a northerner?

8. In what sense does the narrator's telling of the story serve as "A Rose for Emily"? Why do you think the narrator uses *we* rather than *I*?

9. Explain how Emily's reasons for murdering Homer are related to her personal history and to the ways she handled previous conflicts.

10. Discuss how Faulkner's treatment of the North and South contributes to the meaning of the story.

11. Provide an alternative title and explain how the emphasis in your title is reflected in the story.

CONNECTIONS TO OTHER SELECTIONS

1. Contrast Faulkner's ordering of events with Yukio Mishima's strategy in "Patriotism" (p. 593). How does each author's arrangement of incidents create different effects on the reader?

2. To what extent do concepts of honor and tradition influence the action in "A Rose for Emily" and "Patriotism"?

3. Compare and contrast Faulkner's and Mishima's uses of death as a means of resolving conflicts having to do with love.

PERSPECTIVE

WILLIAM FAULKNER (1897–1962)

On "A Rose for Emily"   1959

Q. What is the meaning of the title "A Rose for Emily"?

A. Oh, it's simply the poor woman had had no life at all. Her father had kept her more or less locked up and then she had a lover who was about to quit her, she had to murder him. It was just "A Rose for Emily" — that's all.

Q. . . . What ever inspired you to write this story?

A. That to me was another sad and tragic manifestation of man's condition in which he dreams and hopes, in which he is in conflict with himself or with his environment or with others. In this case there was the young girl with a young girl's normal aspirations to find love and then a husband and a family, who was brow-beaten and kept down by her father, a selfish man who didn't want her to leave home because he wanted a housekeeper, and it was a natural instinct of — repressed which — you can't repress it — you can mash it down but it comes up somewhere else and very likely in a tragic form, and that was simply another manifestation of man's injustice to man, of the poor tragic human being struggling with its own heart, with others, with its environment, for the simple things which all human beings want. In that case it was a young girl that just wanted to be loved and to love and to have a husband and a family.

Q. And that purely came from your imagination?

A. Well, the story did but the condition is there. It exists. I didn't invent that condition, I didn't invent the fact that young girls dream of someone to love and children and a home, but the story of what her own particular tragedy was was invented, yes. . . .

Q. Sir, it has been argued that "A Rose for Emily" is a criticism of the North, and others have argued saying that it is a criticism of the South. Now, could this story, shall we say, be more properly classified as a criticism of the times?

A. Now that I don't know, because I was simply trying to write about people. The writer uses environment — what he knows — and if there's a symbolism in which the lover represented the North and the woman who murdered him represents the South, I don't say that's not valid and not there, but it was no intention of the writer to say, Now let's see, I'm going to write a piece in which I will use a symbolism for the North and another symbol for the South, that he was simply writing about people, a story which he thought was tragic and true, because it came out of the human heart, the human aspiration, the human — the conflict of conscience with glands, with the Old Adam. It was a conflict not between North and the South so much as between, well you might say, God and Satan.

Q. Sir, just a little more on that thing. You say it's a conflict between God and Satan. Well, I don't quite understand what you mean. Who is — did one represent the —

A. The conflict was in Miss Emily, that she knew that you do not murder people. She had been trained that you do not take a lover. You marry, you don't take a lover. She had broken all the laws of her tradition, her background, and she had finally broken the law of God too, which says you do not take human life. And she knew she was doing wrong, and that's why her own life was wrecked. Instead of murdering one lover, and then to go and take another and when she used him up to murder him, she was expiating her crime.

Q. Was the "Rose for Emily" an idea or a character? Just how did you go about it?

A. That came from a picture of the strand of hair on the pillow. It was a ghost story. Simply a picture of a strand of hair on the pillow in the abandoned house.

From *Faulkner in the University*, edited by
Frederick Gwynn and Joseph Blotner

CONSIDERATIONS FOR CRITICAL THINKING AND WRITING

1. Discuss whether you think Faulkner's explanation of the conflict between "God and Satan" limits or expands the meaning of the story for you.

2. In what sense is "A Rose for Emily" a ghost story?

3. Compare Faulkner's account of how he conceived "A Rose for Emily" with Flannery O'Connor's description of "Good Country People" in the Perspective on page 392. To what extent are their attitudes about symbolism similar?

ANDRE DUBUS (B. 1936)

Though a native of Louisiana, where he attended the Christian Brothers School and McNeese State College, Andre Dubus has lived much of his life in Massachusetts; many of his stories are set in the Merrimack Valley north of Boston. After college Dubus served as an officer for five years in the Marine Corps. He then took an M.F.A. at the University of Iowa in 1966 and began teaching at Bradford College in Massachusetts. His fiction has earned him numerous awards, and he has been both a Guggenheim and a MacArthur Fellow. Among his collections of fiction are *Separate Flights* (1975), *Adultery and Other Choices* (1977), *Finding a Girl in America* (1980), from which "Killings" is taken, *The Last Worthless Evening* (1986), *Collected Stories* (1988), and *Dancing After Hours* (1996). In 1991 he published *Broken Vessels,* a collection of autobiographical essays. His fictions are often tense with violence, anger, tenderness, and guilt; they are populated by characters who struggle to understand and survive their experiences, painful with failure and the weight of imperfect relationships. In "Killings" Dubus offers a powerful blend of intimate domestic life and shocking violence.

Killings   *1979*

On the August morning when Matt Fowler buried his youngest son, Frank, who had lived for twenty-one years, eight months, and four days, Matt's older son, Steve, turned to him as the family left the grave and walked between their friends, and said: "I should kill him." He was twenty-eight, his brown hair starting to thin in front where he used to have a cowlick. He bit his lower lip, wiped his eyes, then said it again. Ruth's arm, linked with Matt's, tightened; he looked at her. Beneath her eyes there was swelling from the three days she had suffered. At the limousine Matt stopped and looked back at the grave, the casket, and the Congregationalist minister who he thought had probably had a difficult job with the eulogy though he hadn't seemed to, and the old funeral director who was saying something to the six young pallbearers. The grave was on a hill and overlooked the Merrimack, which he could not see from where he stood; he looked at the opposite bank, at the apple orchard with its symmetrically planted trees going up a hill.

Next day Steve drove with his wife back to Baltimore where he managed the branch office of a bank, and Cathleen, the middle child, drove with her husband back to Syracuse. They had left the grandchildren with friends. A month after the funeral Matt played poker at Willis Trottier's because Ruth, who knew this was the second time he had been invited, told him to go, he couldn't sit home with her for the rest of her life, she was all right. After the game Willis went outside to tell everyone good night and, when the others had driven away, he walked with Matt to his car. Willis was a short, silver-haired man who had opened a diner after World War II, his trade then mostly very early breakfast, which he cooked, and then lunch for the men who worked at the leather and shoe factories. He now owned a large restaurant.

"He walks the Goddamn streets," Matt said.

"I know. He was in my place last night, at the bar. With a girl."

"I don't see him. I'm in the store all the time. Ruth sees him. She sees him   5 too much. She was at Sunnyhurst today getting cigarettes and aspirin, and there he was. She can't even go out for cigarettes and aspirin. It's killing her."

"Come back in for a drink."

Matt looked at his watch. Ruth would be asleep. He walked with Willis back into the house, pausing at the steps to look at the starlit sky. It was a cool summer night; he thought vaguely of the Red Sox, did not even know if they were at home tonight; since it happened he had not been able to think about any of the small pleasures he believed he had earned, as he had earned also what was shattered now forever: the quietly harried and quietly pleasurable days of fatherhood. They went inside. Willis's wife, Martha, had gone to bed hours ago, in the rear of the large house which was rigged with burglar and fire alarms. They went downstairs to the game room: the television set suspended from the ceiling, the pool table, the poker table with beer cans, cards, chips, filled ashtrays, and the six chairs where Matt and his friends had sat, the friends picking up the old banter as though he had only been away on vacation; but he could see the affection and courtesy in their eyes. Willis went behind the bar and mixed them each a Scotch and soda; he stayed behind the bar and looked at Matt sitting on the stool.

"How often have you thought about it?" Willis said.

"Every day since he got out. I didn't think about bail. I thought I wouldn't have to worry about him for years. She sees him all the time. It makes her cry."

"He was in my place a long time last night. He'll be back."   10

"Maybe he won't."

"The band. He likes the band."

"What's he doing now?"

"He's tending bar up to Hampton Beach. For a friend. Ever notice even the worst bastard always has friends? He couldn't get work in town. It's just tourists and kids up to Hampton. Nobody knows him. If they do, they don't care. They drink what he mixes."

"Nobody tells me about him."   15

"I hate him, Matt. My boys went to school with him. He was the same then. Know what he'll do? Five at the most. Remember that woman about seven years ago? Shot her husband and dropped him off the bridge in the Merrimack with a hundred-pound sack of cement and said all the way through it that nobody helped her. Know where she is now? She's in Lawrence now, a secretary. And whoever helped her, where the hell is he?"

"I've got a .38 I've had for years, I take it to the store now. I tell Ruth it's for the night deposits. I tell her things have changed: we got junkies here now too. Lots of people without jobs. She knows though."

"What does she know?"

"She knows I started carrying it after the first time she saw him in town. She knows it's in case I see him, and there's some kind of a situation —"

He stopped, looked at Willis, and finished his drink. Willis mixed him an- 20 other.

"What kind of situation?"

"Where he did something to me. Where I could get away with it."

"How does Ruth feel about that?"

"She doesn't know."

"You said she does, she's got it figured out."   25

He thought of her that afternoon: when she went into Sunnyhurst, Strout was waiting at the counter while the clerk bagged the things he had bought; she turned down an aisle and looked at soup cans until he left.

"Ruth would shoot him herself, if she thought she could hit him."

"You got a permit?"

"No."

"I do. You could get a year for that."   30

"Maybe I'll get one. Or maybe I won't. Maybe I'll just stop bringing it to the store."

Richard Strout was twenty-six years old, a high school athlete, football scholarship to the University of Massachusetts where he lasted for almost two semesters before quitting in advance of the final grades that would have forced him not to return. People then said: Dickie can do the work; he just doesn't want to. He came home and did construction work for his father but refused his father's offer to learn the business; his two older brothers had learned it, so that Strout and Sons trucks going about town, and signs on construction sites, now slashed wounds into Matt Fowler's life. Then Richard married a young girl and became a bartender, his salary and tips augmented and perhaps sometimes matched by his father, who also posted his bond. So his friends, his enemies (he had those: fist fights or, more often, boys and then young men who had not fought him when they thought they should have), and those who simply knew him by face and name, had a series of images of him which they recalled when they heard of the killing: the high school running back, the young drunk in bars, the oblivious hard-hatted young man eating lunch at a counter, the bartender who could perhaps be called courteous but not more than that: as he tended bar, his dark eyes and dark, wide-jawed face appeared less sullen, near blank.

One night he beat Frank. Frank was living at home and waiting for September, for graduate school in economics, and working as a lifeguard at Salisbury Beach, where he met Mary Ann Strout, in her first month of separation. She spent most days at the beach with her two sons. Before ten o'clock one night Frank came home; he had driven to the hospital first, and he walked into the living room with stitches over his right eye and both lips bright and swollen.

"I'm all right," he said, when Matt and Ruth stood up, and Matt turned off the television, letting Ruth get to him first: the tall, muscled but slender suntanned boy. Frank tried to smile at them but couldn't because of his lips.

"It was her husband, wasn't it?" Ruth said.   35

"Ex," Frank said. "He dropped in."

Matt gently held Frank's jaw and turned his face to the light, looked at the stitches, the blood under the white of the eye, the bruised flesh.

"Press charges," Matt said.

"No."

"What's to stop him from doing it again? Did you hit him at all? Enough 40 so he won't want to next time?"

"I don't think I touched him."

"So what are you going to do?"

"Take karate," Frank said, and tried again to smile.

"That's not the problem," Ruth said.

"You know you like her," Frank said. 45

"I like a lot of people. What about the boys? Did they see it?"

"They were asleep."

"Did you leave her alone with him?"

"He left first. She was yelling at him. I believe she had a skillet in her hand."

"Oh for God's sake," Ruth said. 50

Matt had been dealing with that too: at the dinner table on evenings when Frank wasn't home, was eating with Mary Ann; or, on the other nights — and Frank was with her every night — he talked with Ruth while they watched television, or lay in bed with the windows open and he smelled the night air and imagined, with both pride and muted sorrow, Frank in Mary Ann's arms. Ruth didn't like it because Mary Ann was in the process of divorce, because she had two children, because she was four years older than Frank, and finally — she told this in bed, where she had during all of their marriage told him of her deepest feelings: of love, of passion, of fears about one of the children, of pain Matt had caused her or she had caused him — she was against it because of what she had heard: that the marriage had gone bad early, and for most of it Richard and Mary Ann had both played around.

"That can't be true," Matt said. "Strout wouldn't have stood for it."

"Maybe he loves her."

"He's too hot-tempered. He couldn't have taken that."

But Matt knew Strout had taken it, for he had heard the stories too. He 55 wondered who had told them to Ruth; and he felt vaguely annoyed and isolated: living with her for thirty-one years and still not knowing what she talked about with her friends. On these summer nights he did not so much argue with her as try to comfort her, but finally there was no difference between the two: she had concrete objections, which he tried to overcome. And in his attempt to do this, he neglected his own objections, which were the same as hers, so that as he spoke to her he felt as disembodied as he sometimes did in the store when he helped a man choose a blouse or dress or piece of costume jewelry for his wife.

"The divorce doesn't mean anything," he said. "She was young and maybe she liked his looks and then after a while she realized she was living with a bastard. I see it as a positive thing."

"She's not divorced yet."

"It's the same thing. Massachusetts has crazy laws, that's all. Her age is no problem. What's it matter when she was born? And that other business: even if it's true, which it probably isn't, it's got nothing to do with Frank, and it's in the past. And the kids are no problem. She's been married six years; she ought to have kids. Frank likes them. He plays with them. And he's not going to marry her anyway, so it's not a problem of money."

"Then what's he doing with her?"

"She probably loves him, Ruth. Girls always have. Why can't we just leave it 60 at that?"

"He got home at six o'clock Tuesday morning."

"I didn't know you knew. I've already talked to him about it."

Which he had: since he believed almost nothing he told Ruth, he went to Frank with what he believed. The night before, he had followed Frank to the car after dinner.

"You wouldn't make much of a burglar," he said.

"How's that?"   65

Matt was looking up at him; Frank was six feet tall, an inch and a half taller than Matt, who had been proud when Frank at seventeen outgrew him; he had only felt uncomfortable when he had to reprimand or caution him. He touched Frank's bicep, thought of the young taut passionate body, believed he could sense the desire, and again he felt the pride and sorrow and envy too, not knowing whether he was envious of Frank or Mary Ann.

"When you came in yesterday morning, I woke up. One of these mornings your mother will. And I'm the one who'll have to talk to her. She won't interfere with you. Okay? I know it means —" But he stopped, thinking: I know it means getting up and leaving that suntanned girl and going sleepy to the car, I know—

"Okay," Frank said, and touched Matt's shoulder and got into the car.

There had been other talks, but the only long one was their first one: a night driving to Fenway Park, Matt having ordered the tickets so they could talk, and knowing when Frank said yes, he would go, that he knew the talk was coming too. It took them forty minutes to get to Boston, and they talked about Mary Ann until they joined the city traffic along the Charles River, blue in the late sun. Frank told him all the things that Matt would later pretend to believe when he told them to Ruth.

"It seems like a lot for a young guy to take on," Matt finally said.   70

"Sometimes it is. But she's worth it."

"Are you thinking about getting married?"

"We haven't talked about it. She can't for over a year. I've got school."

"I *do* like her," Matt said.

He did. Some evenings, when the long summer sun was still low in the sky, 75 Frank brought her home; they came into the house smelling of suntan lotion and the sea, and Matt gave them gin and tonics and started the charcoal in the backyard, and looked at Mary Ann in the lawn chair: long and very light brown hair (Matt thinking that twenty years ago she would have dyed it blonde), and the long brown legs he loved to look at; her face was pretty; she had probably never in her adult life gone unnoticed into a public place. It was in her wide brown eyes that she looked older than Frank; after a few drinks Matt thought what he saw in her eyes was something erotic, testament to the rumors about her; but he knew it wasn't that, or all that: she had, very young, been through a sort of pain that his children, and he and Ruth, had been spared. In the moments of his recognizing that pain, he wanted to tenderly touch her hair, wanted with some gesture to give her solace and hope. And he would glance at Frank, and hope they would love each other, hope Frank would soothe that pain in her heart, take it from her eyes; and her divorce, her age, and her children did not matter at all. On the first two evenings she did not bring her boys, and then Ruth asked her to bring them the next time. In bed that night Ruth said, "She hasn't brought them because she's embarrassed. She shouldn't feel embarrassed."

Richard Strout shot Frank in front of the boys. They were sitting on the living room floor watching television, Frank sitting on the couch, and Mary Ann just returning from the kitchen with a tray of sandwiches. Strout came in the front door and shot Frank twice in the chest and once in the face with a 9 mm automatic. Then he looked at the boys and Mary Ann, and went home to wait for the police.

It seemed to Matt that from the time Mary Ann called weeping to tell him until now, a Saturday night in September, sitting in the car with Willis, parked beside Strout's car, waiting for the bar to close, that he had not so much moved through his life as wandered through it, his spirits like a dazed body bumping into furniture and corners. He had always been a fearful father: when his children were young, at the start of each summer he thought of them drowning in a pond or the sea, and he was relieved when he came home in the evenings and they were there; usually that relief was his only acknowledgment of his fear, which he never spoke of, and which he controlled within his heart. As he had when they were very young and all of them in turn, Cathleen too, were drawn to the high oak in the backyard, and had to climb it. Smiling, he watched them, imagining the fall: and he was poised to catch the small body before it hit the earth. Or his legs were poised; his hands were in his pockets or his arms were folded and, for the child looking down, he appeared relaxed and confident while his heart beat with the two words he wanted to call out but did not: *Don't fall.* In winter he was less afraid: he made sure the ice would hold him before they skated, and he brought or sent them to places where they could sled without ending in the street. So he and his children had survived their childhood, and he only worried about them when he knew they were driving a long distance, and then he lost Frank in a way no father expected to lose his son, and he felt that all the fears he had borne while they were growing up, and all the grief he had been afraid of, had backed up like a huge wave and struck him on the beach and swept him out to sea. Each day he felt the same and when he was able to forget how he felt, when he was able to force himself not to feel that way, the eyes of his clerks and customers defeated him. He wished those eyes were oblivious, even cold; he felt he was withering in their tenderness. And beneath his listless wandering, every day in his soul he shot Richard Strout in the face; while Ruth, going about town on errands, kept seeing him. And at nights in bed she would hold Matt and cry, or sometimes she was silent and Matt would touch her tightening arm, her clenched fist.

As his own right fist was now, squeezing the butt of the revolver, the last of the drinkers having left the bar, talking to each other, going to their separate cars which were in the lot in front of the bar, out of Matt's vision. He heard their voices, their cars, and then the ocean again, across the street. The tide was in and sometimes it smacked the sea wall. Through the windshield he looked at the dark red side wall of the bar, and then to his left, past Willis, at Strout's car, and through its windows he could see the now-emptied parking lot, the road, the sea wall. He could smell the sea.

The front door of the bar opened and closed again and Willis looked at Matt then at the corner of the building; when Strout came around it alone Matt got out of the car, giving up the hope he had kept all night (and for the past week) that Strout would come out with friends, and Willis would simply drive away; thinking: *All right then. All right;* and he went around the front of Willis's car, and at Strout's he stopped and aimed over the hood at Strout's blue shirt ten feet away. Willis was aiming too, crouched on Matt's left, his elbow resting on the hood.

"Mr. Fowler," Strout said. He looked at each of them, and at the guns. 80 "Mr. Trottier."

Then Matt, watching the parking lot and the road, walked quickly between the car and the building and stood behind Strout. He took one leather glove from his pocket and put it on his left hand.

"Don't talk. Unlock the front and back and get in."

Strout unlocked the front door, reached in and unlocked the back, then got in, and Matt slid into the back seat, closed the door with his gloved hand, and touched Strout's head once with the muzzle.

"It's cocked. Drive to your house."

When Strout looked over his shoulder to back the car, Matt aimed at his 85 temple and did not look at his eyes.

"Drive slowly," he said. "Don't try to get stopped."

They drove across the empty front lot and onto the road, Willis's headlights shining into the car; then back through town, the sea wall on the left hiding the beach, though far out Matt could see the ocean; he uncocked the revolver; on the right were the places, most with their neon signs off, that did so much business in summer: the lounges and cafés and pizza houses, the street itself empty of traffic, the way he and Willis had known it would be when they decided to take Strout at the bar rather than knock on his door at two o'clock one morning and risk that one insomniac neighbor. Matt had not told Willis he was afraid he could not be alone with Strout for very long, smell his smells, feel the presence of his flesh, hear his voice, and then shoot him. They left the beach town and then were on the high bridge over the channel: to the left the smacking curling white at the breakwater and beyond that the dark sea and the full moon, and down to his right the small fishing boats bobbing at anchor in the cove. When they left the bridge, the sea was blocked by abandoned beach cottages, and Matt's left hand was sweating in the glove. Out here in the dark in the car he believed Ruth knew. Willis had come to his house at eleven and asked if he wanted a nightcap; Matt went to the bedroom for his wallet, put the gloves in one trouser pocket and the .38 in the other and went back to the living room, his hand in his pocket covering the bulge of the cool cylinder pressed against his fingers, the butt against his palm. When Ruth said good night she looked at his face, and he felt she could see in his eyes the gun, and the night he was going to. But he knew he couldn't trust what he saw. Willis's wife had taken her sleeping pill, which gave her eight hours — the reason, Willis had told Matt, he had the alarms installed, for nights when he was late at the restaurant — and when it was all done and Willis got home he would leave ice and a trace of Scotch and soda in two glasses in the game room and tell Martha in the morning that he had left the restaurant early and brought Matt home for a drink.

"He was making it with my wife." Strout's voice was careful, not pleading.

Matt pressed the muzzle against Strout's head, pressed it harder than he wanted to, feeling through the gun Strout's head flinching and moving forward; then he lowered the gun to his lap.

"Don't talk," he said.

Strout did not speak again. They turned west, drove past the Dairy Queen closed until spring, and the two lobster restaurants that faced each other and were crowded all summer and were now also closed, onto the short bridge crossing the tidal stream, and over the engine Matt could hear through his open window the water rushing inland under the bridge; looking to his left he saw its swift moonlit current going back into the marsh which, leaving the bridge, they entered: the salt marsh stretching out on both sides, the grass tall in patches but mostly low and leaning earthward as though windblown, a large dark rock sitting as though it rested on nothing but itself, and shallow pools reflecting the bright moon.

Beyond the marsh they drove through woods, Matt thinking now of the hole he and Willis had dug last Sunday afternoon after telling their wives they were going to Fenway Park. They listened to the game on a transistor radio, but heard none of it as they dug into the soft earth on the knoll they had chosen because elms and maples sheltered it. Already some leaves had fallen. When the hole was deep enough they covered it and the piled earth with dead branches, then cleaned their shoes and pants and went to a restaurant farther up in New Hampshire where they ate sandwiches and drank beer and watched the rest of the game on television. Looking at the back of Strout's head he thought of Frank's grave; he had not been back to it; but he would go before winter, and its second burial of snow.

He thought of Frank sitting on the couch and perhaps talking to the children as they watched television, imagined him feeling young and strong, still warmed from the sun at the beach, and feeling loved, hearing Mary Ann moving about in the kitchen, hearing her walking into the living room; maybe he looked up at her and maybe she said something, looking at him over the tray of sandwiches, smiling at him, saying something the way women do when they offer food as a gift, then the front door opening and this son of a bitch coming in and Frank seeing that he meant the gun in his hand, this son of a bitch and his gun the last person and thing Frank saw on earth.

When they drove into town the streets were nearly empty: a few slow cars, a policeman walking his beat past the darkened fronts of stores. Strout and Matt both glanced at him as they drove by. They were on the main street, and all the stoplights were blinking yellow. Willis and Matt had talked about that too: the lights changed at midnight, so there would be no place Strout had to stop and where he might try to run. Strout turned down the block where he lived and Willis's headlights were no longer with Matt in the back seat. They had planned that too, had decided it was best for just the one car to go to the house, and again Matt had said nothing about his fear of being alone with Strout, especially in his house: a duplex, dark as all the houses on the street were, the street itself lit at the corner of each block. As Strout turned into the driveway Matt thought of the one insomniac neighbor, thought of some man or woman sitting alone in the dark living room, watching the all-night channel from Boston. When Strout stopped the car near the front of the house, Matt said: "Drive it to the back."

He touched Strout's head with the muzzle.

"You wouldn't have it cocked, would you? For when I put on the brakes."

Matt cocked it, and said: "It is now."

Strout waited a moment; then he eased the car forward, the engine doing little more than idling, and as they approached the garage he gently braked. Matt opened the door, then took off the glove and put it in his pocket. He stepped out and shut the door with his hip and said: "All right."

Strout looked at the gun, then got out, and Matt followed him across the grass, and as Strout unlocked the door Matt looked quickly at the row of small backyards on either side, and scattered tall trees, some evergreens, others not, and he thought of the red and yellow leaves on the trees over the hole, saw them falling soon, probably in two weeks, dropping slowly, covering. Strout stepped into the kitchen.

"Turn on the light." 100

Strout reached to the wall switch, and in the light Matt looked at his wide back, the dark blue shirt, the white belt, the red plaid pants.

"Where's your suitcase?"

"My suitcase?"

"Where is it?"

"In the bedroom closet." 105

"That's where we're going then. When we get to a door you stop and turn on the light."

They crossed the kitchen, Matt glancing at the sink and stove and refrigerator: no dishes in the sink or even the dish rack beside it, no grease splashings on the stove, the refrigerator door clean and white. He did not want to look at any more but he looked quickly at all he could see: in the living room magazines and newspapers in a wicker basket, clean ashtrays, a record player, the records shelved next to it, then down the hall where, near the bedroom door, hung a color photograph of Mary Ann and the two boys sitting on a lawn— there was no house in the picture—Mary Ann smiling at the camera or Strout or whoever held the camera, smiling as she had on Matt's lawn this summer while he waited for the charcoal and they all talked and he looked at her brown legs and at Frank touching her arm, her shoulder, her hair; he moved down the hall with her smile in his mind, wondering: was that when they were both playing around and she was smiling like that at him and they were happy, even sometimes, making it worth it? He recalled her eyes, the pain in them, and he was conscious of the circles of love he was touching with the hand that held the revolver so tightly now as Strout stopped at the door at the end of the hall.

"There's no wall switch."

"Where's the light?"

"By the bed." 110

"Let's go."

Matt stayed a pace behind, then Strout leaned over and the room was lighted: the bed, a double one, was neatly made; the ashtray on the bedside table clean, the bureau top dustless, and no photographs; probably so the girl—who *was* she?—would not have to see Mary Ann in the bedroom she believed was theirs. But because Matt was a father and a husband, though never an ex-husband, he knew (and did not want to know) that this bedroom had never been theirs alone. Strout turned around; Matt looked at his lips, his wide jaw, and thought of Frank's doomed and fearful eyes looking up from the couch.

"Where's Mr. Trottier?"

"He's waiting. Pack clothes for warm weather."

"What's going on?" 115

"You're jumping bail."

"Mr. Fowler —"

He pointed the cocked revolver at Strout's face. The barrel trembled but not much, not as much as he had expected. Strout went to the closet and got the suitcase from the floor and opened it on the bed. As he went to the bureau, he said: "He was making it with my wife. I'd go pick up my kids and he'd be there. Sometimes he spent the night. My boys told me."

He did not look at Matt as he spoke. He opened the top drawer and Matt stepped closer so he could see Strout's hands: underwear and socks, the socks rolled, the underwear folded and stacked. He took them back to the bed, arranged them neatly in the suitcase, then from the closet he was taking shirts and trousers and a jacket; he laid them on the bed and Matt followed him to the bathroom and watched from the door while he packed those things a person accumulated and that became part of him so that at times in the store Matt felt he was selling more than clothes.

"I wanted to try to get together with her again." He was bent over the suit- 120 case. "I couldn't even talk to her. He was always with her. I'm going to jail for it; if I ever get out I'll be an old man. Isn't that enough?"

"You're not going to jail."

Strout closed the suitcase and faced Matt, looking at the gun. Matt went to his rear, so Strout was between him and the lighted hall; then using his handkerchief he turned off the lamp and said: "Let's go."

They went down the hall, Matt looking again at the photograph, and through the living room and kitchen, Matt turning off the lights and talking, frightened that he was talking, that he was telling this lie he had not planned: "It's the trial. We can't go through that, my wife and me. So you're leaving. We've got you a ticket, and a job. A friend of Mr. Trottier's. Out west. My wife keeps seeing you. We can't have that anymore."

Matt turned out the kitchen light and put the handkerchief in his pocket, and they went down the two brick steps and across the lawn. Strout put the suitcase on the floor of the back seat, then got into the front seat and Matt got in the back and put on his glove and shut the door.

"They'll catch me. They'll check passenger lists." 125

"We didn't use your name."

"They'll figure that out too. You think I wouldn't have done it myself if it was that easy?"

He backed into the street, Matt looking down the gun barrel but not at the profiled face beyond it.

"You were alone," Matt said. "We've got it worked out."

"There's no planes this time of night, Mr. Fowler." 130

"Go back through town. Then north on 125."

They came to the corner and turned, and now Willis's headlights were in the car with Matt.

"Why north, Mr. Fowler?"

"Somebody's going to keep you for a while. They'll take you to the air-port." He uncocked the hammer and lowered the revolver to his lap and said wearily: "No more talking."

As they drove back through town, Matt's body sagged, going limp with his 135 spirit and its new and false bond with Strout, the hope his lie had given Strout.

He had grown up in this town whose streets had become places of apprehension and pain for Ruth as she drove and walked, doing what she had to do; and for him too, if only in his mind as he worked and chatted six days a week in his store; he wondered now if his lie would have worked, if sending Strout away would have been enough; but then he knew that just thinking of Strout in Montana or whatever place lay at the end of the lie he had told, thinking of him walking the streets there, loving a girl there (who *was* she?) would be enough to slowly rot the rest of his days. And Ruth's. Again he was certain that she knew, that she was waiting for him.

They were in New Hampshire now, on the narrow highway, passing the shopping center at the state line, and then houses and small stores and sandwich shops. There were few cars on the road. After ten minutes he raised his trembling hand, touched Strout's neck with the gun, and said: "Turn in up here. At the dirt road."

Strout flicked on the indicator and slowed.

"Mr. Fowler?"

"They're waiting here."

Strout turned very slowly, easing his neck away from the gun. In the 140 moonlight the road was light brown, lighter and yellowed where the headlights shone; weeds and a few trees grew on either side of it, and ahead of them were the woods.

"There's nothing back here, Mr. Fowler."

"It's for your car. You don't think we'd leave it at the airport, do you?"

He watched Strout's large, big-knuckled hands tighten on the wheel, saw Frank's face that night: not the stitches and bruised eye and swollen lips, but his own hand gently touching Frank's jaw, turning his wounds to the light. They rounded a bend in the road and were out of sight of the highway: tall trees all around them now, hiding the moon. When they reached the abandoned gravel pit on the left, the bare flat earth and steep pale embankment behind it, and the black crowns of trees at its top, Matt said: "Stop here."

Strout stopped but did not turn off the engine. Matt pressed the gun hard against his neck, and he straightened in the seat and looked in the rearview mirror, Matt's eyes meeting his in the glass for an instant before looking at the hair at the end of the gun barrel.

"Turn it off."   145

Strout did, then held the wheel with two hands, and looked in the mirror.

"I'll do twenty years, Mr. Fowler; at least. I'll be forty-six years old."

"That's nine years younger than I am," Matt said, and got out and took off the glove and kicked the door shut. He aimed at Strout's ear and pulled back the hammer. Willis's headlights were off and Matt heard him walking on the soft thin layer of dust, the hard earth beneath it. Strout opened the door, sat for a moment in the interior light, then stepped out onto the road. Now his face was pleading. Matt did not look at his eyes, but he could see it in the lips.

"Just get the suitcase. They're right up the road."

Willis was beside him now, to his left. Strout looked at both guns. Then he 150 opened the back door, leaned in, and with a jerk brought the suitcase out. He was turning to face them when Matt said: "Just walk up the road. Just ahead."

Strout turned to walk, the suitcase in his right hand, and Matt and Willis followed; as Strout cleared the front of his car he dropped the suitcase and, ducking, took one step that was the beginning of a sprint to his right. The gun kicked in Matt's hand, and the explosion of the shot surrounded him, isolated him in a nimbus of sound that cut him off from all his time, all his history, isolated him standing absolutely still on the dirt road with the gun in his hand, looking down at Richard Strout squirming on his belly, kicking one leg behind him, pushing himself forward, toward the woods. Then Matt went to him and shot him once in the back of the head.

Driving south to Boston, wearing both gloves now, staying in the middle lane and looking often in the rearview mirror at Willis's headlights, he relived the suitcase dropping, the quick dip and turn of Strout's back, and the kick of the gun, the sound of the shot. When he walked to Strout, he still existed within the first shot, still trembled and breathed with it. The second shot and the burial seemed to be happening to someone else, someone he was watching. He and Willis each held an arm and pulled Strout face-down off the road and into the woods, his bouncing sliding belt white under the trees where it was so dark that when they stopped at the top of the knoll, panting and sweating, Matt could not see where Strout's blue shirt ended and the earth began. They pulled off the branches then dragged Strout to the edge of the hole and went behind him and lifted his legs and pushed him in. They stood still for a moment. The woods were quiet save for their breathing, and Matt remembered hearing the movements of birds and small animals after the first shot. Or maybe he had not heard them. Willis went down to the road. Matt could see him clearly out on the tan dirt, could see the glint of Strout's car and, beyond the road, the gravel pit. Willis came back up the knoll with the suitcase. He dropped it in the hole and took off his gloves and they went down to his car for the spades. They worked quietly. Sometimes they paused to listen to the woods. When they were finished Willis turned on his flashlight and they covered the earth with leaves and branches and then went down to the spot in front of the car, and while Matt held the light Willis crouched and sprinkled dust on the blood, backing up till he reached the grass and leaves, then he used leaves until they had worked up to the grave again. They did not stop. They walked around the grave and through the woods, using the light on the ground, looking up through the trees to where they ended at the lake. Neither of them spoke above the sounds of their heavy and clumsy strides through low brush and over fallen branches. Then they reached it: wide and dark, lapping softly at the bank, pine needles smooth under Matt's feet, moonlight on the lake, a small island near its middle, with black, tall evergreens. He took out the gun and threw for the island: taking two steps back on the pine needles, striding with the throw and going to one knee as he followed through, looking up to see the dark shapeless object arcing downward, splashing.

They left Strout's car in Boston, in front of an apartment building on Commonwealth Avenue. When they got back to town Willis drove slowly over the bridge and Matt threw the keys into the Merrimack. The sky was turning light. Willis let him out a block from his house, and walking home he listened for sounds from the houses he passed. They were quiet. A light was on in his living room. He turned it off and undressed in there, and went softly toward the bedroom; in the hall he smelled the smoke, and he stood in the bedroom doorway and looked at the orange of her cigarette in the dark. The curtains were closed. He went to the closet and put his shoes on the floor and felt for a hanger.

"Did you do it?" she said.

He went down the hall to the bathroom and in the dark he washed his 155
hands and face. Then he went to her, lay on his back, and pulled the sheet up to
his throat.

"Are you all right?" she said.

"I think so."

Now she touched him, lying on her side, her hand on his belly, his thigh.

"Tell me," she said.

He started from the beginning, in the parking lot at the bar; but soon with 160
his eyes closed and Ruth petting him, he spoke of Strout's house: the order,
the woman presence, the picture on the wall.

"The way she was smiling," he said.

"What about it?"

"I don't know. Did you ever see Strout's girl? When you saw him in town?"

"No."

"I wonder who she was." 165

Then he thought: *not was: is. Sleeping now she is his girl.* He opened his eyes,
then closed them again. There was more light beyond the curtains. With Ruth
now he left Strout's house and told again his lie to Strout, gave him again that
hope that Strout must have for a while believed, else he would have to believe
only the gun pointed at him for the last two hours of his life. And with Ruth
he saw again the dropping suitcase, the darting move to the right: and he told
of the first shot, feeling her hand on him but his heart isolated still, beating on
the road still in that explosion like thunder. He told her the rest, but the words
had no images for him, he did not see himself doing what the words said he
had done; he only saw himself on that road.

"We can't tell the other kids," she said. "It'll hurt them, thinking he got
away. But we mustn't."

"No."

She was holding him, wanting him, and he wished he could make love
with her but he could not. He saw Frank and Mary Ann making love in her
bed, their eyes closed, their bodies brown and smelling of the sea; the other girl
was faceless, bodiless, but he felt her sleeping now; and he saw Frank and
Strout, their faces alive; he saw red and yellow leaves falling on the earth, then
snow: falling and freezing and falling; and holding Ruth, his cheek touching
her breast, he shuddered with a sob that he kept silent in his heart.

CONSIDERATIONS FOR CRITICAL THINKING AND WRITING

1. FIRST RESPONSE. How do you feel about Matt's act of revenge? Trace the
   emotions his character produces in you as the plot unfolds.

2. Discuss the significance of the title. Why is "Killings" a more appropriate
   title than "Killers"?

3. What are the effects of Dubus's ordering of events in the story? How
   would the effects be different if the story were told in a chronological
   order?

4. Describe the Fowler family before Frank's murder. How does the murder
   affect Matt?

5. What is learned about Richard from the flashback in paragraphs
   32 through 75? How does this information affect your attitude toward
   him?

6. What is the effect of the description of Richard shooting Frank in paragraph 76?

7. How well planned is Matt's revenge? Why does he lie to Richard about sending him out west?

8. How do the details of the killing and the disposal of Richard's body reveal Matt's emotions? What is he thinking and feeling as he performs these actions? How did you feel reading about them?

9. Describe Matt at the end of the story when he tells his wife about the killing. How do you think this revenge killing will affect the Fowler family?

10. How might "Killings" be considered a love story as well as a murder story?

CONNECTIONS TO OTHER SELECTIONS

1. Compare and contrast Matt's motivation for murder with Emily's in "A Rose for Emily" (p. 72). Which character made you feel more empathy and sympathy for his or her actions? Why?

2. Explore the father-son relationships in "Killings" and William Faulkner's "Barn Burning" (p. 481). Read the section on psychological criticism in Chapter 37, "Critical Strategies for Reading." How do you think a psychological critic would interpret these relationships in each story?

3. In an essay discuss the respective treatments of family life in "Killings" and Gish Jen's "In the American Society" (p. 643). Do these very different stories have anything in common?

PERSPECTIVES

THOMAS E. KENNEDY (B. 1944)

On Morality and Revenge in "Killings"   1988

When Fowler fires at the younger man, "the explosion of the shot surrounded him, isolated him in a nimbus of sound that cut him off from all his time, all his history, isolated him standing absolutely still on the dirt road. . . . The second shot . . . seemed to be happening to someone else, someone he was watching." When Fowler returns home after he and his friend have buried Strout's body, his wife is waiting for him in the dark bedroom. She knows, without having been told, what he has done, and she tries to make love to him while he relates the details, but he cannot make love, for he has isolated himself by his act. The final irony occurs when they realize they will be unable to tell their other children about it, that the children will believe their brother's murderer has escaped trial and punishment and has run off. Thus, we see the first consequence of Fowler's unnatural act, the profound isolation he must suffer for it. Even his sob at the close of the story is one of isolation, "silent in his heart."

The story's point is clear: the blade of murder cuts both ways. Victim and killer are united and isolated, one in death, the other in the ultimate breach of respect for human life. Like Cain, the killer has distinguished himself from humankind and presumably must suffer that distinction for the rest of his days. An intriguing question that follows from the story is whether the act of murder affects all men equally. Will a person of inferior morality suffer equally with a person of more sensitive humanity like Matt Fowler? Throughout Fowler's abduction of Strout, he must fight to prevent himself from witnessing Strout's humanity, must forbid him from speaking lest he become too close to the sound of his voice, must prevent himself from smelling the man's smells. When, finally, he must lie to Strout to accomplish the abduction, giving the younger man hope that he is not to be killed, Fowler suffers for his cruelty. Thus, there is not even a moment's satisfaction of vengeance for Fowler; his is a rational act, an extermination to eliminate Strout from their world and end Ruth's pain. Strout, presumably, killed Fowler's son in passion. It is interesting to compare the two acts and to compare the fate of suffering attached to each.

A profound lifelong isolation awaits Fowler as a result of his act of premeditated murder. It is intriguing to consider what Strout's fate might have been had he stood trial and gone to prison for his act. The suggestion is that Strout was a man of inferior morality, the son of an affluent family who pampered him, a violent husband. Might the culmination of his weakness in murder and the suffering imposed on him for it, the experience of finally having to account for his actions, have resulted in his moral development and growth?

What then, finally, is the meaning for human society of Fowler's homicidal revenge? We understand Fowler. We follow him through his deed not without the desire for him to complete it, to succeed, to rid the world of this killer. We note his reluctance, his moral hesitation, the morality he must overcome, and we urge him, on some level, to overcome it. Once he has begun the action, abducted Strout, we know he *must* complete it, even if we share his mixed feelings about the choice he has made. Yet what is the final result for the world? Strout is eliminated, but Fowler is left morally wounded to walk the earth, and his suffering will spread, has already begun to spread to his children.

From *Andre Dubus: A Study of the Short Fiction*

CONSIDERATIONS FOR CRITICAL THINKING AND WRITING

1. Explain how you would answer the following question raised by Kennedy: "Will a person of inferior morality suffer equally with a person of more sensitive humanity like Matt Fowler?"

2. Discuss why and how profound isolation affects nearly all the characters in this story.

A. L. BADER (B. 1902)

Nothing Happens in Modern Short Stories

1945

Any teacher who has ever confronted a class with representative modern short stories will remember the disappointment, the puzzled "so-what" attitude, of certain members of the group. "Nothing happens in some of these stories," "They just end," or "They're not real stories" are frequent criticisms. . . . Sometimes the phrase "Nothing happens" seems to mean that nothing significant happens, but in a great many cases it means that the modern short story is charged with a lack of narrative structure. Readers and critics accustomed to an older type of story are baffled by a newer type. They sense the underlying and unifying design of the one, but they find nothing equivalent to it in the other. Hence they maintain that the modern short story is plotless, static, fragmentary, amorphous — frequently a mere character sketch or vignette, or a mere reporting of a transient moment, or the capturing of a mood or nuance — everything, in fact, except a story.

From "The Structure of the Modern Story" in *College English*

CONSIDERATIONS FOR CRITICAL THINKING AND WRITING

1. What is the basic objection to the "newer type" of short story? How does it differ from the "older type"?

2. Consider any one of the stories from the Album of Contemporary Stories (pp. 617-68) as an example of the newer type. Does anything "happen" in the story? How does it differ from the excerpt from Edgar Rice Burroughs's *Tarzan of the Apes* (p. 62)?

3. Read a recent story published in *The New Yorker* or the *Atlantic Monthly* and compare its narrative structure with that of Faulkner's "A Rose for Emily" (p. 72).

4

Character

Character is essential to plot. Without characters Burroughs's *Tarzan of the Apes* would be a travelogue through the jungle and Faulkner's "A Rose for Emily" little more than a faded history of a sleepy town in the South. If stories were depopulated, the plots would disappear because stories and plots are interrelated. A dangerous jungle is important only because we care what effect it has on a character. Characters are influenced by events just as events are shaped by characters. Tarzan's physical strength is the result of his growing up in the jungle, and his strength, along with his inherited intelligence, allows him to be master there.

The methods by which a writer creates people in a story so that they seem actually to exist are called *characterization.* Huck Finn never lived, yet those who have read Mark Twain's novel about his adventures along the Mississippi River feel as if they know him. A good writer gives us the illusion that a character is real, but we should also remember that a character is not an actual person but instead has been created by the author. Though we might walk out of a room in which Huck Finn's Pap talks racist nonsense, we would not throw away the book in a similar fit of anger. This illusion of reality is the magic that allows us to move beyond the circumstances of our own lives into a writer's fictional world, where we can encounter everyone from royalty to paupers, murderers, lovers, cheaters, martyrs, artists, destroyers, and, nearly always, some part of ourselves. The life that a writer breathes into a character adds to our own experiences and enlarges our view of the world.

A character is usually but not always a person. In Jack London's *Call of the Wild,* the protagonist is a devoted sled dog; in Herman Melville's *Moby-Dick,* the antagonist is an unfathomable whale. Perhaps the only possible qualification to be placed on character is that whatever it is—whether an animal or even an inanimate object, such as a robot—it must have some recognizable human qualities. The action of the plot interests us primarily because we care about what happens to people and what they do. We may identify with a character's desires and aspirations, or we may be disgusted by his or her viciousness and selfishness. To understand our response to a story, we should be able to recognize the methods of characterization the author uses.

CHARLES DICKENS (1812–1870)

Charles Dickens is well known for creating characters who have stepped off the pages of his fictions into the imaginations and memories of his readers. His characters are successful not because readers might have encountered such people in their own lives, but because his characterizations are vivid and convincing. He manages to make strange and eccentric people appear familiar. The following excerpt from *Hard Times* is the novel's entire first chapter. In it Dickens introduces and characterizes a school principal addressing a classroom full of children.

From Hard Times   *1854*

"Now, what I want is, Facts. Teach these boys and girls nothing but Facts. Facts alone are wanted in life. Plant nothing else, and root out everything else. You can only form the minds of reasoning animals upon Facts: nothing else will ever be of any service to them. This is the principle on which I bring up my own children, and this is the principle on which I bring up these children. Stick to Facts, sir!"

The scene was a plain, bare, monotonous vault of a schoolroom, and the speaker's square forefinger emphasized his observations by underscoring every sentence with a line on the schoolmaster's sleeve. The emphasis was helped by the speaker's square wall of a forehead, which had his eyebrows for its base, while his eyes found commodious cellarage in two dark caves, overshadowed by the wall. The emphasis was helped by the speaker's mouth, which was wide, thin, and hard set. The emphasis was helped by the speaker's voice, which was inflexible, dry, and dictatorial. The emphasis was helped by the speaker's hair, which bristled on the skirts of his bald head, a plantation of firs to keep the wind from its shining surface, all covered with knobs, like the crust of a plum pie, as if the head had scarcely warehouse-room for the hard facts stored inside. The speaker's obstinate carriage, square coat, square legs, square shoulders—nay, his very neckcloth, trained to take him by the throat with an unaccommodating grasp, like a stubborn fact, as it was—all helped the emphasis.

"In this life, we want nothing but Facts, sir; nothing but Facts!"

The speaker, and the schoolmaster, and the third grown person present, all backed a little, and swept with their eyes the inclined plane of little vessels then and there arranged in order, ready to have imperial gallons of facts poured into them until they were full to the brim.

Dickens withholds his character's name until the beginning of the second chapter; he calls this fact-bound educator Mr. Gradgrind. Authors sometimes put as much time and effort into naming their characters as parents invest in naming their children. Names can be used to indicate qualities that the writer associates with the characters. Mr. Gradgrind is precisely what his name suggests. The "schoolmaster" employed by Gradgrind is Mr. M'Choakumchild. Pronounce this name aloud and you have the essence of this teacher's educational philosophy. In Nathaniel Hawthorne's *The Scarlet Letter,* Chillingworth is cold and relentless in his single-minded quest for revenge. The innocent and youthful protagonist in Herman Melville's *Billy Budd* is nipped in the bud by the evil Claggart, whose name simply sounds unpleasant.

Names are also used in films to suggest a character's nature. One example that is destined to be a classic is the infamous villain Darth Vader, whose name identifies his role as an invader allied with the dark and death. On the heroic side, it makes sense that Marion Morrison decided to change his box-office name to John Wayne in order to play tough, masculine roles because both the first and last of his chosen names are unambiguously male and to the point, while his given name is androgynous. There may also be some significance to the lack of a specific identity. In Godwin's "A Sorrowful Woman" (p. 33) the woman, man, boy, and girl are reduced to a set of domestic functions, and their not being named emphasizes their roles as opposed to their individual identities. Of course, not every name is suggestive of the qualities a character may embody, but it is frequently worth determining what is in a name.

The only way to tell whether a name reveals character is to look at the other information the author supplies about the character. We evaluate fictional characters in much the same way we understand people in our own lives. By piecing together bits of information, we create a context that allows us to interpret their behavior. We can predict, for instance, that an acquaintance who is a chronic complainer is not likely to have anything good to say about a roommate. We interpret words and actions in the light of what we already know about someone, and that is why keeping track of what characters say (and how they say it) along with what they do (and don't do) is important.

Authors reveal characters by other means too. Physical descriptions can indicate important inner qualities; disheveled clothing, a crafty smile, or a blush might communicate as much as or more than what a character says. Characters can also be revealed by the words and actions of others who respond to them. In literature, moreover, we have one great advantage that life cannot offer; a work of fiction can give us access to a person's thoughts. Although in Herman Melville's "Bartleby, the Scrivener" (p. 113) we learn about Bartleby primarily through descriptive details, words, actions, and his relationships with the other characters, Melville allows us to enter the lawyer's consciousness.

Authors have two major methods of presenting characters: ***showing*** and ***telling.*** Characters shown in dramatic situations reveal themselves indirectly by what they say and do. In the first paragraph of the excerpt from *Hard Times,* Dickens shows us some of Gradgrind's utilitarian educational principles by having him speak. We can infer the kind of person he is from his reference to boys and girls as "reasoning animals," but we are not told what to think of him until the second paragraph. It would be impossible to admire Gradgrind after reading the physical description of him and the school that he oversees. The adjectives in the second paragraph make the author's evaluation of Gradgrind's values and personality clear: everything about him is rigidly "square"; his mouth is "thin, and hard set"; his voice is "inflexible, dry, and dictatorial"; and he presides over a "plain, bare, monotonous vault of a schoolroom." Dickens directly lets us know how to feel about Gradgrind, but he does so artistically. Instead of simply being presented with a statement that Gradgrind is destructively practical, we get a detailed and amusing description.

We can contrast Dickens's direct presentation in this paragraph with the indirect showing that Gail Godwin uses in "A Sorrowful Woman" (p. 33). Godwin avoids telling us how we should think about the characters. Their story includes little description and no evaluations or interpretations by the author. To determine the significance of the events, the reader must pay close attention to what the characters say and do. Like Godwin, many twentieth-century authors favor showing over telling because showing allows readers to discover the meanings, which modern authors are often reluctant to impose on an audience for whom fixed meanings and values are not as strong as they once were. However, most writers continue to reveal characters by telling as well as showing when the technique suits their purposes — when, for example, a minor character must be sketched economically or when a long time has elapsed, causing changes in a major character. Telling and showing complement each other.

Characters can be convincing whether they are presented by telling or showing, provided their actions are **motivated.** There must be reasons for how they behave and what they say. If adequate motivation is offered, we can understand and find **plausible** their actions no matter how bizarre. In "A Rose for Emily" (p. 72), Faulkner makes Emily Grierson's intimacy with a corpse credible by preparing us with information about her father's death along with her inability to leave the past and live in the present. Emily turns out to be **consistent.** Although we are surprised by the ending of the story, the behavior it reveals is compatible with her temperament.

Some kinds of fiction consciously break away from our expectations of traditional realistic stories. Consistency, plausibility, and motivation are not very useful concepts for understanding and evaluating characterizations in modern **absurdist literature,** for instance, in which characters are often alienated from themselves and their environment in an irrational world. In this world there is no possibility for traditional heroic action; instead we find an **antihero** who has little control over events. Yossarian from Joseph Heller's *Catch-22* is an example of a protagonist who is thwarted by the absurd terms on which life offers itself to many twentieth-century characters.

In most stories we expect characters to act plausibly and in ways consistent with their personalities, but that does not mean that characters cannot develop and change. A *dynamic* character undergoes some kind of change because of the action of the plot. Huck Finn's view of Jim, the runaway slave in Mark Twain's novel, develops during their experiences on the raft. Huck discovers Jim's humanity and, therefore, cannot betray him because Huck no longer sees his companion as merely the property of a white owner. On the other hand, Huck's friend, Tom Sawyer, is a *static* character because he does not change. He remains interested only in high adventure, even at the risk of Jim's life. As static characters often do, Tom serves as a foil to Huck; his frivolous concerns are contrasted with Huck's serious development. A *foil* helps to reveal by contrast the distinctive qualities of another character.

The protagonist in a story is usually a dynamic character who experiences some conflict that makes an impact on his or her life. Less commonly, static characters can also be protagonists. Rip Van Winkle wakes up from his twenty-year sleep in Washington Irving's story to discover his family dramatically changed and his country no longer a British colony, but none of these important events has an impact on his character; he continues to be the same shiftless and idle man that he was before he fell asleep. The protagonist in Faulkner's "A Rose for Emily" is also a static character; indeed, she rejects all change. Our understanding of her changes, but she does not. Ordinarily, however, a plot contains one or two dynamic characters with any number of static characters in supporting roles. This is especially true of short stories, in which brevity limits the possibilities of character development.

The extent to which a character is developed is another means by which character can be analyzed. The novelist E. M. Forster coined the terms *flat* and *round* to distinguish degrees of character development. A *flat character* embodies one or two qualities, ideas, or traits that can be readily described in a brief summary. For instance, Mr. M'Choakumchild in Dickens's *Hard Times* stifles students instead of encouraging them to grow. Flat characters tend to be one-dimensional. They are readily accessible because their characteristics are few and simple; they are not created to be psychologically complex.

Some flat characters are immediately recognizable as *stock characters.* These stereotypes are particularly popular in formula fiction, television programs, and action movies. Stock characters are types rather than individuals. The poor but dedicated writer falls in love with a hard-working understudy, who gets nowhere because the corrupt producer favors his boozy, pampered mistress for the leading role. Characters such as these — the loyal servant, the mean stepfather, the henpecked husband, the dumb blonde, the sadistic army officer, the dotty grandmother — are prepackaged; they lack individuality because their authors have, in a sense, not imaginatively created them but simply summoned them from a warehouse of clichés and social prejudices. Stock characters can become fresh if a good writer makes them vivid, interesting, or memorable, but too often a writer's use of these stereotypes is simply weak characterization.

Round characters are more complex than flat or stock characters. Round characters have more depth and require more attention. They may surprise us or puzzle us. Although they are more fully developed, round characters are also more difficult to summarize because we are aware of competing ideas, values, and possibilities in their lives. As a flat character, Huck Finn's alcoholic, bigoted father is clear to us; we know that Pap is the embodiment of racism and irrationality. But Huck is considerably less predictable because he struggles with what Twain calls a "sound heart and a deformed conscience."

In making distinctions between flat and round characters, you must understand that an author's use of a flat character—even as a protagonist—does not necessarily represent an artistic flaw. Moreover, both flat and round characters can be either dynamic or static. Each plot can be made most effective by its own special kind of characterization. Terms such as *round* and *flat* are helpful tools to use to determine what we know about a character, but they are not an infallible measurement of the quality of a story.

The next three stories—Bharati Mukherjee's "The Tenant," Herman Melville's "Bartleby, the Scrivener," and Leon Rooke's "Sweethearts"—offer character studies worthy of close analysis. As you read them, notice the methods of characterization used to bring each to life.

BHARATI MUKHERJEE (B. 1940)

Born in Calcutta, India, Bharati Mukherjee lived in London as a young girl but returned to India at the age of eleven, where she was subsequently educated at the universities of Calcutta and Baroda. After winning a scholarship to the University of Iowa Writers' Workshop, she moved to the United States and married novelist Clark Blaise in the early 1960s. Though she lived in Canada for a decade and returned to India for a year, she now lives in the United States, where she teaches and writes. Mukherjee's fiction includes four novels—*The Tiger's Daughter* (1971), *Wife* (1972), *Jasmine* (1989), and *The Holder of the World* (1993)—and two collections of short stories, *Darkness* (1985) and *The Middleman and Other Stories* (1988). Much of her work examines the stress and confusion immigrants experience as they struggle to secure identities and find a place in foreign cultures that tend to render them invisible or cast them as ethnic stereotypes. In "The Tenant," taken from *Middleman*, Mukherjee explores the conflicts an uprooted female Indian academic experiences as an immigrant in the United States.

The Tenant   *1988*

Maya Sanyal has been in Cedar Falls, Iowa, less than two weeks. She's come, books and clothes and one armchair rattling in the smallest truck that U-Haul would rent her, from New Jersey. Before that she was in North Carolina. Before that, Calcutta, India. Every place has something to give. She is sitting at the kitchen table with Fran drinking bourbon for the first time in her life. Fran Johnson found her the furnished apartment and helped her settle in. Now she's brought a bottle of bourbon which gives her the right to stay and talk for a bit. She's breaking up with someone named Vern, a pharmacist. Vern's father is also a pharmacist and owns a drugstore. Maya has seen Vern's father on TV twice already. The first time was on the local news when he spoke out against the selling of painkillers like Advil and Nuprin in supermarkets and gas stations. In the matter of painkillers, Maya is a universalist. The other time he was in a barbershop quartet. Vern gets along all right with his father. He likes the pharmacy business, as business goes, but he wants to go back to graduate school and learn to make films. Maya is drinking her first bourbon tonight because Vern left today for San Francisco State.

"I understand totally," Fran says. She teaches Utopian Fiction and a course in Women's Studies and worked hard to get Maya hired. Maya has a Ph.D. in Comparative Literature and will introduce writers like R. K. Narayan and Chinua Achebe to three sections of sophomores at the University of Northern Iowa. "A person has to leave home. Try out his wings."

Fran has to use the bathroom. "I don't feel abandoned." She pushes her chair away from the table. "Anyway, it was a sex thing totally. We were good together. It'd be different if I'd loved him."

Maya tries to remember what's in the refrigerator. They need food. She hasn't been to the supermarket in over a week. She doesn't have a car yet and so she relies on a corner store — a longish walk — for milk, cereal, and frozen dinners. Someday these exigencies will show up as bad skin and collapsed muscle tone. No folly is ever lost. Maya pictures history as a net, the kind of safety net traveling trapeze artists of her childhood fell into when they were inattentive, or clumsy. Going to circuses in Calcutta with her father is what she remembers vividly. It is a banal memory, for her father, the owner of a steel company, is a complicated man.

Fran is out in the kitchen long enough for Maya to worry. They need food. 5 Her mother believed in food. What is love, anger, inner peace, etc., her mother used to say, but the brain's biochemistry. Maya doesn't want to get into that, but she is glad she has enough stuff in the refrigerator to make an omelette. She realizes Indian women are supposed to be inventive with food, whip up exotic delights to tickle an American's palate, and she knows she should be meeting Fran's generosity and candor with some sort of bizarre and effortless countermove. If there's an exotic spice store in Cedar Falls or in neighboring Waterloo, she hasn't found it. She's looked in the phone book for common Indian names, especially Bengali, but hasn't yet struck up culinary intimacies. That will come — it always does. There's a six-pack in the fridge that her landlord, Ted Suminski, had put in because she'd be thirsty after unpacking. She was thirsty, but she doesn't drink beer. She probably should have asked him to come up and drink the beer. Except for Fran she hasn't had anyone over. Fran is more friendly and helpful than anyone Maya has known in the States since she came to North Carolina ten years ago, at nineteen. Fran is a Swede, and she is tall, with blue eyes. Her hair, however, is a dull, darkish brown.

"I don't think I can handle anything that heavy-duty," Fran says when she comes back to the room. She means the omelette. "I have to go home in any case." She lives with her mother and her aunt, two women in their mid-seventies, in a drafty farmhouse. The farmhouse now has a computer store catty-corner from it. Maya's been to the farm. She's been shown photographs of the way the corner used to be. If land values ever rebound, Fran will be worth millions.

Before Fran leaves she says, "Has Rab Chatterji called you yet?"

"No." She remembers the name, a good, reliable Bengali name, from the first night's study of the phone book. Dr. Rabindra Chatterji teaches Physics.

"He called the English office just before I left." She takes car keys out of her pocketbook. She reknots her scarf. "I bet Indian men are more sensitive than Americans. Rab's a Brahmin, that's what people say."

A Chatterji has to be a Bengali Brahmin — last names give ancestral secrets away — but Brahminness seems to mean more to Fran than it does to Maya. She was born in 1954, six full years after India became independent. Her India was Nehru's India: a charged, progressive place.

"All Indian men are wife beaters," Maya says. She means it and doesn't mean it. "That's why I married an American." Fran knows about the divorce, but nothing else. Fran is on the Hiring, Tenure, and Reappointment Committee.

Maya sees Fran down the stairs and to the car which is parked in the back in the spot reserved for Maya's car, if she had owned one. It will take her several months to save enough to buy one. She always pays cash, never borrows. She tells herself she's still recovering from the U-Haul drive halfway across the country. Ted Suminski is in his kitchen watching the women. Maya waves to him because waving to him, acknowledging him in that way, makes him seem less creepy. He seems to live alone though a sign, THE SUMINSKIS, hangs from a metal horse's head in the front yard. Maya hasn't seen Mrs. Suminski. She hasn't seen any children either. Ted always looks lonely. When she comes back from campus, he's nearly always in the back, throwing darts or shooting baskets.

"What's he like?" Fran gestures with her head as she starts up her car. "You hear these stories."

Maya doesn't want to know the stories. She has signed a year's lease. She doesn't want complications. "He's all right. I keep out of his way."

"You know what I'm thinking? Of all the people in Cedar Falls, you're the one who could understand Vern best. His wanting to try out his wings, run away, stuff like that."

"Not really." Maya is not being modest. Fran is being impulsively democratic, lumping her wayward lover and Indian friend together as headstrong adventurers. For Fran, a utopian and feminist, borders don't count. Maya's taken some big risks, made a break with her parents' ways. She's done things a woman from Ballygunge Park Road doesn't do, even in fantasies. She's not yet shared stories with Fran, apart from the divorce. She's told her nothing of men she picks up, the reputation she'd gained, before Cedar Falls, for "indiscretions." She has a job, equity, three friends she can count on for emergencies. She is an American citizen. But.

Fran's Brahmin calls her two nights later. On the phone he presents himself as Dr. Chatterji, not Rabindra or Rab. An old-fashioned Indian, she assumes. Her father still calls his closest friend, "Colonel." Dr. Chatterji asks her to tea on Sunday. She means to say no but hears herself say, "Sunday? Fiveish? I'm not doing anything special this Sunday."

Outside, Ted Suminski is throwing darts into his garage door. The door has painted-on rings: orange, purple, pink. The bull's-eye is gray. He has to be fifty at least. He is a big, thick, lonely man about whom people tell stories. Maya pulls the phone cord as far as it'll go so she can look down more directly on her landlord's large, bald head. He has his back to her as he lines up a dart. He's in black running shoes, red shorts, he's naked to the waist. He hunches his right shoulder, he pulls the arm back; a big, lonely man shouldn't have so much grace. The dart is ready to cut through the September evening. But Ted Suminski doesn't let go. He swings on worn rubber soles, catches her eye in the window (she has to have imagined this), takes aim at her shadow. Could she have imagined the noise of the dart's metal tip on her windowpane?

Dr. Chatterji is still on the phone. "You are not having any mode of transportation, is that right?"

Ted Suminski has lost interest in her. Perhaps it isn't interest, at all; per- 20 haps it's aggression. "I don't drive," she lies, knowing it sounds less shameful than not owning a car. She has said this so often she can get in the right degree of apology and Asian upper-class helplessness. "It's an awful nuisance."

"Not to worry, please." Then, "It is a great honor to be meeting Dr. Sanyal's daughter. In Calcutta business circles he is a legend."

On Sunday she is ready by four-thirty. She doesn't know what the afternoon holds; there are surely no places for "high tea" — a colonial tradition — in Cedar Falls, Iowa. If he takes her back to his place, it will mean he has invited other guests. From his voice she can tell Dr. Chatterji likes to do things correctly. She has dressed herself in a peach-colored nylon georgette sari, jade drop-earrings and a necklace. The color is good on dark skin. She is not pretty, but she does her best. Working at it is a part of self-respect. In the mid-seventies, when American women felt rather strongly about such things, Maya had been in trouble with her women's group at Duke. She was too feminine. She had tried to explain the world she came out of. Her grandmother had been married off at the age of five in a village now in Bangladesh. Her great-aunt had been burned to death over a dowry problem. She herself had been trained to speak softly, arrange flowers, sing, be pliant. If she were to seduce Ted Suminski, she thinks as she waits in the front yard for Dr. Chatterji, it would be minor heroism. She has broken with the past. But.

Dr. Chatterji drives up for her at about five ten. He is a hesitant driver. The car stalls, jumps ahead, finally slams to a stop. Maya has to tell him to back off a foot or so; it's hard to leap over two sacks of pruned branches in a sari. Ted Suminski is an obsessive pruner and gardener.

"My sincerest apologies, Mrs. Sanyal," Dr. Chatterji says. He leans across the wide front seat of his noisy, very old, very used car and unlocks the door for her. "I am late. But then, I am sure you're remembering that Indian Standard Time is not at all the same as time in the States." He laughs. He could be nervous—she often had that effect on Indian men. Or he could just be chatty. "These Americans are all the time rushing and rushing but where it gets them?" He moves his head laterally once, twice. It's the gesture made famous by Peter Sellers. When Peter Sellers did it, it had seemed hilarious. Now it suggests that Maya and Dr. Chatterji have three thousand years plus civilization, sophistication, moral virtue, over people born on this continent. Like her, Dr. Chatterji is a naturalized American.

"Call me Maya," she says. She fusses with the seat belt. She does it because 25 she needs time to look him over. He seems quite harmless. She takes in the prominent teeth, the eyebrows that run together. He's in a blue shirt and a beige cardigan with the K-Mart logo that buttons tightly over the waist. It's hard to guess his age because he has dyed his hair and his moustache. Late thirties, early forties. Older than she had expected. "Not Mrs. Sanyal."

This isn't the time to tell about ex-husbands. She doesn't know where John is these days. He should have kept up at least. John had come into her life as a graduate student at Duke, and she, mistaking the brief breathlessness of sex for love, had married him. They had stayed together two years, maybe a little less. The pain that John had inflicted all those years ago by leaving her had subsided into a cozy feeling of loss. This isn't the time, but then she doesn't want to be a legend's daughter all evening. She's not necessarily on Dr. Chatterji's side is what she wants to get across early; she's not against America and Americans. She makes the story—of marriage outside the Brahminic pale, the divorce—quick, dull. Her unsentimentality seems to shock him. His stomach sags inside the cardigan.

"We've each had our several griefs," the physicist says. "We're each required to pay our karmic debts."

"Where are we headed?"

"Mrs. Chatterji has made some Indian snacks. She is waiting to meet you because she is knowing your cousin-sister who studied in Scottish Church College. My home is okay, no?"

Fran would get a kick out of this. Maya has slept with married men, with ₃₀ nameless men, with men little more than boys, but never with an Indian man. Never.

The Chatterjis live in a small blue house on a gravelly street. There are at least five or six other houses on the street; the same size but in different colors and with different front yard treatments. More houses are going up. This is the cutting edge of suburbia.

Mrs. Chatterji stands in the driveway. She is throwing a large plastic ball to a child. The child looks about four, and is Korean or Cambodian. The child is not hers because she tells it, "Chung-Hee, ta-ta, bye-bye. Now I play with guest," as Maya gets out of the car.

Maya hasn't seen this part of town. The early September light softens the construction pits. In that light the houses too close together, the stout woman in a striped cotton sari, the child hugging a pink ball, the two plastic lawn chairs by a tender young tree, the sheets and saris on the clothesline in the back, all seem miraculously incandescent.

"Go home now, Chung-Hee. I am busy." Mrs. Chatterji points the child homeward, then turns to Maya, who has folded her hands in traditional Bengali greeting. "It is an honor. We feel very privileged." She leads Maya indoors to a front room that smells of moisture and paint.

In her new, deliquescent mood, Maya allows herself to be backed into the ₃₅ best armchair—a low-backed, boxy Goodwill item draped over with a Rajasthani bedspread—and asks after the cousin Mrs. Chatterji knows. She doesn't want to let go of Mrs. Chatterji. She doesn't want husband and wife to get into whispered conferences about their guest's misadventures in America, as they make tea in the kitchen.

The coffee table is already laid with platters of mutton croquettes, fish chops, onion pakoras, ghugni with puris, samosas, chutneys. Mrs. Chatterji has gone to too much trouble. Maya counts four kinds of sweetmeats in Corning casseroles on an end table. She looks into a see-through lid; spongy, white dumplings float in rosewater syrup. Planets contained, mysteries made visible.

"What are you waiting for, Santana?" Dr. Chatterji becomes imperious, though not unaffectionate. He pulls a dining chair up close to the coffee table.

"Make some tea." He speaks in Bengali to his wife, in English to Maya. To Maya he says, grandly, "We are having real Indian Green Label Lipton. A nephew is bringing it just one month back."

His wife ignores him. "The kettle's already on," she says. She wants to know about the Sanyal family. Is it true her great-grandfather was a member of the Star Chamber in England?

Nothing in Calcutta is ever lost. Just as her story is known to Bengalis all over America, so are the scandals of her family, the grandfather hauled up for tax evasion, the aunt who left her husband to act in films. This woman brings up the Star Chamber, the glories of the Sanyal family, her father's philanthropies, but it's a way of saying, *I know the dirt.*

The bedrooms are upstairs. In one of those bedrooms an unseen, tormented presence — Maya pictures it as a clumsy ghost that strains to shake off the body's shell — drops things on the floor. The things are heavy and they make the front room's chandelier shake. Light bulbs, shaped like tiny candle flames, flicker. The Chatterjis have said nothing about children. There are no tricycles in the hallway, no small sandals behind the doors. Maya is too polite to ask about the noise, and the Chatterjis don't explain. They talk just a little louder. They flip the embroidered cover off the stereo. What would Maya like to hear? Hemanta Kumar? Manna Dey? Oh, that young chap, Manna Dey? What sincerity, what tenderness he can convey!

Upstairs the ghost doesn't hear the music of nostalgia. The ghost throws and thumps. The ghost makes its own vehement music. Maya hears in its voice madness, self-hate.

Finally the water in the kettle comes to a boil. The whistle cuts through all fantasy and pretense. Dr. Chatterji says, "I'll see to it," and rushes out of the room. But he doesn't go to the kitchen. He shouts up the stairwell. "Poltoo, kindly stop this nonsense straightaway! We're having a brilliant and cultured lady-guest and you're creating earthquakes?" The kettle is hysterical.

Mrs. Chatterji wipes her face. The face that had seemed plump and cheery at the start of the evening is now flabby. "My sister's boy," the woman says.

So this is the nephew who has brought with him the cartons of Green Label tea, one of which will be given to Maya.

Mrs. Chatterji speaks to Maya in English as though only the alien language can keep emotions in check. "Such an intelligent boy! His father is government servant. Very highly placed."

Maya is meant to visualize a smart, clean-cut young man from south Calcutta, but all she can see is a crazy, thwarted, lost graduate student. Intelligent, proper family guarantee nothing. Even Brahmins can do self-destructive things, feel unsavory urges. Maya herself had been an excellent student.

"He was First Class in B.Sc. from Presidency College," the woman says. "Now he's getting Master's in Ag. Science at Iowa State."

The kitchen is silent. Dr. Chatterji comes back into the room with a tray. The teapot is under a tea cozy, a Kashmiri one embroidered with the usual chinar leaves, loops, and chains. "*Her* nephew," he says. The dyed hair and dyed moustache are no longer signs of a man wishing to fight the odds. He is a vain man, anxious to cut losses. "Very unfortunate business."

The nephew's story comes out slowly, over fish chops and mutton croquettes. He is in love with a student from Ghana.

"Everything was A-Okay until the Christmas break. Grades, assistantship for next semester, everything."

"I blame the college. The office for foreign students arranged a Christmas party. And now, *baapre baap!* Our poor Poltoo wants to marry a Negro Muslim."

Maya is known for her nasty, ironic one-liners. It has taken her friends weeks to overlook her malicious, un-American pleasure in others' misfortunes. Maya would like to finish Dr. Chatterji off quickly. He is pompous; he is reactionary; he wants to live and work in America but give back nothing except taxes. The confused world of the immigrant—and lostness that Maya and Poltoo feel—that's what Dr. Chatterji wants to avoid. She hates him. But.

Dr. Chatterji's horror is real. A good Brahmin boy in Iowa is in love with an African Muslim. It shouldn't be a big deal. But the more she watches the physicist, the more she realizes that "Brahmin" isn't a caste; it's a metaphor. You break one small rule, and the constellation collapses. She thinks suddenly that John Cheever—she is teaching him as a "world writer" in her classes, cheek-by-jowl with Africans and West Indians—would have understood Dr. Chatterji's dread. Cheever had been on her mind, ever since the late afternoon light slanted over Mrs. Chatterji's drying saris. She remembers now how full of a soft, Cheeverian light Durham had been the summer she had slept with John Hadwen; and how after that, her tidy graduate-student world became monstrous, lawless. All men became John Hadwen; John became all men. Outwardly, she retained her poise, her Brahminical breeding. She treated her crisis as a literary event; she lost her moral sense, her judgment, her power to distinguish. Her parents had behaved magnanimously. They had cabled from Calcutta: WHAT'S DONE IS DONE. WE ARE CONFIDENT YOU WILL HANDLE NEW SITUATIONS WELL. ALL LOVE. But she knows more than do her parents. Love is anarchy.

Poltoo is Mrs. Chatterji's favorite nephew. She looks as though it is her fault that the Sunday has turned unpleasant. She stacks the empty platters methodically. To Maya she says, "It is the goddess who pulls the strings. We are puppets. I know the goddess will fix it. Poltoo will not marry that African woman." Then she goes to the coat closet in the hall and staggers back with a harmonium, the kind sold in music stores in Calcutta, and sets it down on the carpeted floor. "We're nothing but puppets," she says again. She sits at Maya's feet, her pudgy hands on the harmonium's shiny, black bellows. She sings, beautifully, in a virgin's high voice, "Come, goddess, come, muse, come to us hapless peoples' rescue."

Maya is astonished. She has taken singing lessons at Dakshini Academy in   55
Calcutta. She plays the sitar and the tanpur, well enough to please Bengalis, to astonish Americans. But stout Mrs. Chatterji is a devotee, talking to God.

A little after eight, Dr. Chatterji drops her off. It's been an odd evening and they are both subdued.

"I want to say one thing," he says. He stops her from undoing her seat belt. The plastic sacks of pruned branches are still at the corner.

"You don't have to get out," she says.

"Please. Give me one more minute of your time."

"Sure."   60

"Maya is my favorite name."

She says nothing. She turns away from him without making her embarrassment obvious.

"Truly speaking, it is my favorite. You are sometimes lonely, no? But you are lucky. Divorced women can date, they can go to bars and discos. They can see mens, many mens. But inside marriage there is so much loneliness." A groan, low, horrible, comes out of him.

She turns back toward him, to unlatch the seat belt and run out of the car. She sees that Dr. Chatterji's pants are unzipped. One hand works hard under his Jockey shorts; the other rests, limp, penitential, on the steering wheel.

"Dr. Chatterji—*really!*" she cries.   65

The next day, Monday, instead of getting a ride home with Fran—Fran says she *likes* to give rides, she needs the chance to talk, and she won't share gas expenses, absolutely not—Maya goes to the periodicals room of the library. There are newspapers from everywhere, even from Madagascar and New Caledonia. She thinks of the periodicals room as an asylum for homesick aliens. There are two aliens already in the room, both Orientals, both absorbed in the politics and gossip of their far off homes.

She goes straight to the newspapers from India. She bunches her raincoat like a bolster to make herself more comfortable. There's so much to catch up on. A village headman, a known Congress-Indira party worker, has been shot by scooter-riding snipers. An Indian pugilist has won an international medal—in Nepal. A child drawing well water—the reporter calls the child "a neo-Buddhist, a convert from the now-outlawed untouchable caste"—has been stoned. An editorial explains that the story about stoning is not a story about caste but about failed idealism; a story about promises of green fields and clean, potable water broken, a story about bribes paid and wells not dug. But no, thinks Maya, it's about caste.

Out here, in the heartland of the new world, the India of serious newspapers unsettles. Maya longs again to feel what she had felt in the Chatterjis' living room: virtues made physical. It is a familiar feeling, a longing. Had a suitable man presented himself in the reading room at that instant, she would have seduced him. She goes on to the stack of *India Abroads*, reads through matrimonial columns, and steals an issue to take home.

Indian men want Indian brides. Married Indian men want Indian mistresses. All over America, "handsome, tall, fair" engineers, doctors, data processors—the new pioneers—cry their eerie love calls.

Maya runs a finger down the first column; her fingertip, dark with   70
newsprint, stops at random.

Hello! Hi! Yes you *are* the one I'm looking for. You are the new emancipated Indo-American woman. You have a zest for life. You are at ease in USA and yet your ethics are rooted in Indian tradition. The man of your dreams has come. Yours truly is handsome, ear-nose-throat specialist, well-settled in Connecticut. Age is 41 but never married, physically fit, sportsmanly, and strong. I adore idealism, poetry, beauty. I abhor smugness, passivity, caste system. Write with recent photo. Better still, call!!!

Maya calls. Hullo, hullo, hullo! She hears immigrant lovers cry in crowded shopping malls. Yes, you who are at ease in both worlds, you are the one. She feels she has a fair chance.

A man answers. "Ashoke Mehta speaking."

She speaks quickly into the bright-red mouthpiece of her telephone. He will be in Chicago, in transit, passing through O'Hare. United counter, Saturday, two P.M. As easy as that.

"Good," Ashoke Mehta says. "For these encounters, I, too, prefer a neutral zone."

* * *

On Saturday at exactly two o'clock the man of Maya's dreams floats to- 75
ward her as lovers used to in shampoo commercials. The United counter is a
loud, harassed place but passengers and piled-up luggage fall away from him.
Full-cheeked and fleshy-lipped, he is handsome. He hasn't lied. He is serene, assured, a Hindu god touching down in Illinois.

She can't move. She feels ugly and unworthy. Her adult life no longer
seems miraculously rebellious; it is grim, it is perverse. She has accomplished
nothing. She has changed her citizenship but she hasn't broken through into
the light, the vigor, the *hustle* of the New World. She is stuck in dead space.

"Hullo, hullo!" Their fingers touch.

Oh, the excitement! Ashoke Mehta's palm feels so right in the small of her
back. Hullo, hullo, hullo. He pushes her out of the reach of anti-Khomeini Ira-
nians, Hare Krishnas, American Fascists, men with fierce wants, and guides her
to an empty gate. They have less than an hour.

"What would you like, Maya?"

She knows he can read her mind, she knows her thoughts are open to him. 80
You, she's almost giddy with the thought, with simple desire. "From the snack
bar," he says, as though to clarify. "I'm afraid I'm starved."

Below them, where the light is strong and hurtful, a Boeing is being ser-
viced. "Nothing," she says.

He leans forward. She can feel the nap of his scarf — she recognizes the
Cambridge colors — she can smell the wool of his Icelandic sweater. She runs
her hand along the scarf, then against the flesh of his neck. "Only the impulsive ones call," he says.

The immigrant courtship proceeds. It's easy, he's good with facts. He
knows how to come across to a stranger who may end up a lover, a spouse. He
makes over a hundred thousand. He owns a house in Hartford, and two
income properties in Newark. He plays the market but he's cautious. He's
good at badminton but plays handball to keep in shape. He watches all the
sports on television. Last August he visited Copenhagen, Helsinki and
Leningrad. Once upon a time he collected stamps but now he doesn't have
hobbies, except for reading. He counts himself an intellectual, he spends too
much on books. Ludlum, Forsyth, MacInnes; other names she doesn't catch.
She suppresses a smile, she's told him only she's a graduate student. He's not
without his vices. He's a spender, not a saver. He's a sensualist: good food — all
foods, but easy on the Indian — good wine. Some temptations he doesn't try to
resist.

And I, she wants to ask, do I tempt?

"Now tell me about yourself, Maya." He makes it easy for her. "Have you 85
ever been in love?"

"No."

"But many have loved you, I can see that." He says it not unkindly. It is the
fate of women like her, and men like him. Their karmic duty, to be loved. It is
expected, not judged. She feels he can see them all, the sad parade of need and
demand. This isn't the time to reveal all.

And so the courtship enters a second phase.

When she gets back to Cedar Falls, Ted Suminski is standing on the front
porch. It's late at night, chilly. He is wearing a down vest. She's never seen him

on the porch. In fact there's no chair to sit on. He looks chilled through. He's waited around a while.

"Hi." She has her keys ready. This isn't the night to offer the six-pack in the fridge. He looks expectant, ready to pounce. 90

"Hi." He looks like a man who might have aimed the dart at her. What has he done to his wife, his kids? Why isn't there at least a dog? "Say, I left a note upstairs."

The note is written in Magic Marker and thumb-tacked to her apartment door. DUE TO PERSONAL REASONS, NAMELY REMARRIAGE, I REQUEST THAT YOU VACATE MY PLACE AT THE END OF THE SEMESTER.

Maya takes the note down and retacks it to the kitchen wall. The whole wall is like a bulletin board, made of some new, crumbly building-material. Her kitchen, Ted Suminski had told her, was once a child's bedroom. Suminski in love: the idea stuns her. She has misread her landlord. The dart at her window speaks of no twisted fantasy. The landlord wants the tenant out.

She gets a glass out of the kitchen cabinet, gets out a tray of ice, pours herself a shot of Fran's bourbon. She is happy for Ted Suminski. She is. She wants to tell someone how moved she'd been by Mrs. Chatterji's singing. How she'd felt in O'Hare, even about Dr. Rab Chatterji in the car. But Fran is not the person. No one she's ever met is the person. She can't talk about the dead space she lives in. She wishes Ashoke Mehta would call. Right now.

Weeks pass. Then two months. She finds a new room, signs another lease. 95 Her new landlord calls himself Fred. He has no arms, but he helps her move her things. He drives between Ted Suminski's place and his twice in his station wagon. He uses his toes the way Maya uses her fingers. He likes to do things. He pushes garbage sacks full of Maya's clothes up the stairs.

"It's all right to stare," Fred says. "Hell, I would."

That first afternoon in Fred's rooming house, they share a Chianti. Fred wants to cook her pork chops but he's a little shy about Indians and meat. Is it beef, or pork? Or any meat? She says it's okay, any meat, but not tonight. He has an ex-wife in Des Moines, two kids in Portland, Oregon. The kids are both normal; he's the only freak in the family. But he's self-reliant. He shops in the supermarket like anyone else, he carries out the garbage, shovels the snow off the sidewalk. He needs Maya's help with one thing. Just one thing. The box of Tide is a bit too heavy to manage. Could she get him the giant size every so often and leave it in the basement?

The dead space need not suffocate. Over the months, Fred and she will settle into companionship. She has never slept with a man without arms. Two wounded people, he will joke during their nightly contortions. It will shock her, this assumed equivalence with a man so strikingly deficient. She knows she is strange, and lonely, but being Indian is not the same, she would have thought, as being a freak.

One night in spring, Fred's phone rings. "Ashoke Mehta speaking." None of this "do you remember me?" nonsense. The god has tracked her down. He hasn't forgotten. "Hullo," he says, in their special way. And because she doesn't answer back, "Hullo, hullo, hullo." She is aware of Fred in the back of the room. He is lighting a cigarette with his toes.

"Yes," she says, "I remember." 100

"I had to take care of a problem," Ashoke Mehta says. "You know that I have my vices. That time at O'Hare I was honest with you."

She is breathless.

"Who is it, May?" asks Fred.

"You also have a problem," says the voice. His laugh echoes. "You will come to Hartford, I know."

When she moves out, she tells herself, it will not be the end of Fred's world. 105

CONSIDERATIONS FOR CRITICAL THINKING AND WRITING

1. FIRST RESPONSE. How did you feel about Maya's relationship with Fred? About her decision in the last sentence to break it off? Do those two things change the way you feel about her character?

2. What do we learn from the story's exposition that helps us to understand Maya's character?

3. What is the significance of the title "The Tenant"? How does it characterize Maya?

4. What role does Fran play in the story?

5. Consider Maya's relationship with men. What do Ted Suminski, Dr. Chatterji, her former husband John, Ashoke Mehta, and Fred reveal about Maya's values and sensibilities?

6. Maya's father and mother are barely mentioned in the story, but they are a presence even in their absence. What do they tell you about Maya?

7. How does life for Maya in the United States differ from her life in India?

8. To what extent does Maya's Indian cultural background and experiences determine her behavior?

9. What do you think Maya means at the end of the story when she says, "It will not be the end of Fred's world"?

CONNECTIONS TO OTHER SELECTIONS

1. Compare the use of exposition to reveal character in "The Tenant" and Raymond Carver's "Popular Mechanics" (p. 272). How does exposition or its relative absence affect your understanding of and response to the characters in each story?

2. Mukherjee describes Maya as having "broken with the past. But" (para. 22). How might this observation suggest a starting point for comparing "The Tenant" with Alice Munro's "Prue" (p. 454)?

3. Write an essay comparing characters' efforts to be American in "The Tenant" and Gish Jen's "In the American Society" (p. 643).

HERMAN MELVILLE (1819–1891)

Hoping to improve his distressed financial situation, Herman Melville left New York and went to sea as a young common sailor. He returned to become an uncommon writer. His experiences at sea became the basis for his early novels: *Typee* (1846), *Omoo* (1847), *Mardi* (1849), *Redburn* (1849), and *White-Jacket* (1850). Ironically, with the publication of his masterpiece,

Moby-Dick (1851), Melville lost the popular success he had enjoyed with his earlier books because his readers were not ready for its philosophical complexity. Although he wrote more, Melville's works were read less and slipped into obscurity. His final short novel, *Billy Budd*, was not published until the 1920s, when critics rediscovered him. In "Bartleby, the Scrivener," Melville presents a quiet clerk in a law office whose baffling "passive resistance" disrupts the life of his employer, a man who attempts to make sense of Bartleby's refusal to behave reasonably.

Bartleby, the Scrivener   *1853*
A Story of Wall Street

I am a rather elderly man. The nature of my avocations, for the last thirty years, has brought me into more than ordinary contact with what would seem an interesting and somewhat singular set of men, of whom, as yet, nothing, that I know of, has ever been written — I mean, the law-copyists, or scriveners. I have known very many of them, professionally and privately, and, if I pleased, could relate divers histories, at which good-natured gentlemen might smile, and sentimental souls might weep. But I waive the biographies of all other scriveners, for a few passages in the life of Bartleby, who was a scrivener, the strangest I ever saw, or heard of. While, of other law-copyists, I might write the complete life, of Bartleby nothing of that sort can be done. I believe that no materials exist, for a full and satisfactory biography of this man. It is an irreparable loss to literature. Bartleby was one of those beings of whom nothing is ascertainable, except from the original sources, and, in his case, those are very small. What my own astonished eyes saw of Bartleby, *that* is all I know of him, except, indeed, one vague report, which will appear in the sequel.

Ere introducing the scrivener, as he first appeared to me, it is fit I make some mention of myself, my *employés*, my business, my chambers, and general surroundings, because some such description is indispensable to an adequate understanding of the chief character about to be presented. Imprimis:° I am a man who, from his youth upwards, has been filled with a profound conviction that the easiest way of life is the best. Hence, though I belong to a profession proverbially energetic and nervous, even to turbulence, at times, yet nothing of that sort have I ever suffered to invade my peace. I am one of those unambitious lawyers who never address a jury, or in any way draw down public applause; but, in the cool tranquillity of a snug retreat, do a snug business among rich men's bonds, and mortgages, and title-deeds. All who know me, consider me an eminently *safe* man. The late John Jacob Astor,° a personage little given to poetic enthusiasm, had no hesitation in pronouncing my first grand point to be prudence; my next, method. I do not speak it in vanity, but simply record the fact, that I was not unemployed in my profession by the late John Jacob Astor; a name which, I admit, I love to repeat; for it hath a rounded and orbicular sound to it, and rings like unto bullion. I will freely add, that I was not insensible to the late John Jacob Astor's good opinion.

Imprimis: In the first place.
John Jacob Astor (1763–1848): An enormously wealthy American capitalist.

Some time prior to the period at which this little history begins, my avocations had been largely increased. The good old office, now extinct in the State of New York, of a Master in Chancery, had been conferred upon me. It was not a very arduous office, but very pleasantly remunerative. I seldom lose my temper; much more seldom indulge in dangerous indignation at wrongs and outrages; but I must be permitted to be rash here and declare, that I consider the sudden and violent abrogation of the office of Master in Chancery, by the new Constitution, as a —— premature act; inasmuch as I had counted upon a life-lease of the profits, whereas I only received those of a few short years. But this is by the way.

My chambers were up stairs, at No. — Wall Street. At one end, they looked upon the white wall of the interior of a spacious skylight shaft, penetrating the building from top to bottom.

This view might have been considered rather tame than otherwise, defi- 5 cient in what landscape painters call "life." But, if so, the view from the other end of my chambers offered, at least, a contrast, if nothing more. In that direction, my windows commanded an unobstructed view of a lofty brick wall, black by age and everlasting shade; which wall required no spyglass to bring out its lurking beauties, but, for the benefit of all near-sighted spectators, was pushed up to within ten feet of my window-panes. Owing to the great height of the surrounding buildings, and my chambers being on the second floor, the interval between this wall and mine not a little resembled a huge square cistern.

At the period just preceding the advent of Bartleby, I had two persons as copyists in my employment, and a promising lad as an office-boy. First, Turkey; second, Nippers; third, Ginger Nut. These may seem names, the like of which are not usually found in the Directory. In truth, they were nicknames, mutually conferred upon each other by my three clerks, and were deemed expressive of their respective persons or characters. Turkey was a short, pursy Englishman, of about my own age — that is, somewhere not far from sixty. In the morning, one might say, his face was of a fine florid hue, but after twelve o'clock, meridian — his dinner hour — it blazed like a grate full of Christmas coals; and continued blazing — but, as it were, with a gradual wane — till six o'clock, P.M., or thereabouts; after which, I saw no more of the proprietor of the face, which, gaining its meridian with the sun, seemed to set with it, to rise, culminate, and decline the following day, with the like regularity and undiminished glory. There are many singular coincidences I have known in the course of my life, not the least among which was the fact, that, exactly when Turkey displayed his fullest beams from his red and radiant countenance, just then, too, at that critical moment, began the daily period when I considered his business capacities as seriously disturbed for the remainder of the twenty-four hours. Not that he was absolutely idle, or averse to business then; far from it. The difficulty was, he was apt to be altogether too energetic. There was a strange, inflamed, flurried, flighty recklessness of activity about him. He would be incautious in dipping his pen into his inkstand. All his blots upon my documents were dropped there after twelve o'clock, meridian. Indeed, not only would he be reckless, and sadly given to making blots in the afternoon, but, some days, he went further, and was rather noisy. At such times, too, his face flamed with augmented blazonry, as if cannel coal had been heaped on anthracite. He made an unpleasant racket with his chair; spilled his sand-box;

in mending his pens, impatiently split them all to pieces, and threw them on the floor in a sudden passion; stood up, and leaned over his table, boxing his papers about in a most indecorous manner, very sad to behold in an elderly man like him. Nevertheless, as he was in many ways a most valuable person to me, and all the time before twelve o'clock, meridian, was the quickest, steadiest creature, too, accomplishing a great deal of work in a style not easily to be matched — for these reasons, I was willing to overlook his eccentricities, though, indeed, occasionally, I remonstrated with him. I did this very gently, however, because, though the civilest, nay, the blandest and most reverential of men in the morning, yet, in the afternoon, he was disposed, upon provocation, to be slightly rash with his tongue — in fact, insolent. Now, valuing his morning services as I did, and resolved not to lose them — yet, at the same time, made uncomfortable by his inflamed ways after twelve o'clock — and being a man of peace, unwilling by my admonitions to call forth unseemly retorts from him, I took upon me, one Saturday noon (he was always worse on Saturdays) to hint to him, very kindly, that, perhaps, now that he was growing old, it might be well to abridge his labors; in short, he need not come to my chambers after twelve o'clock, but, dinner over, had best go home to his lodgings, and rest himself till tea-time. But no; he insisted upon his afternoon devotions. His countenance became intolerably fervid, as he oratorically assured me — gesticulating with a long ruler at the other end of the room — that if his services in the morning were useful, how indispensable, then, in the afternoon?

"With submission, sir," said Turkey, on this occasion, "I consider myself your right-hand man. In the morning I but marshal and deploy my columns; but in the afternoon I put myself at their head, and gallantly charge the foe, thus" — and he made a violent thrust with the ruler.

"But the blots, Turkey," intimated I.

"True; but, with submission, sir, behold these hairs! I am getting old. Surely, sir, a blot or two of a warm afternoon is not to be severely urged against gray hairs. Old age — even if it blot the page — is honorable. With submission, sir, we *both* are getting old."

This appeal to my fellow-feeling was hardly to be resisted. At all events, I 10 saw that go he would not. So, I made up my mind to let him stay, resolving, nevertheless, to see to it that, during the afternoon, he had to do with my less important papers.

Nippers, the second on my list, was a whiskered, sallow, and, upon the whole, rather piratical-looking young man, of about five-and-twenty. I always deemed him the victim of two evil powers — ambition and indigestion. The ambition was evinced by a certain impatience of the duties of a mere copyist, an unwarrantable usurpation of strictly professional affairs such as the original drawing up of legal documents. The indigestion seemed betokened in an occasional nervous testiness and grinning irritability, causing the teeth to audibly grind together over mistakes committed in copying; unnecessary maledictions, hissed, rather than spoken, in the heat of business; and especially by a continual discontent with the height of the table where he worked. Though of a very ingenious mechanical turn, Nippers could never get this table to suit him. He put chips under it, blocks of various sorts, bits of pasteboard, and at last went so far as to attempt an exquisite adjustment, by final pieces of folded blotting-paper. But no invention would answer. If, for the sake of easing his back, he brought the table-lid at a sharp angle well up towards his chin, and wrote there like a man using the steep roof of a Dutch house for his desk, then he declared that it stopped the circulation in his arms. If now he lowered the table to his waistbands, and stooped over it in writing, then there was a sore aching in his back. In short, the truth of the matter was, Nippers knew not what he wanted. Or, if he wanted anything, it was to be rid of a scrivener's table altogether. Among the manifestations of his diseased ambition was a fondness he had for receiving visits from certain ambiguous-looking fellows in seedy coats, whom he called his clients. Indeed, I was aware that not only was he, at times, considerable of a ward-politician, but he occasionally did a little business at the justices' courts, and was not unknown on the steps of the Tombs.° I have good reason to believe, however, that one individual who called upon him at my chambers, and who, with a grand air, he insisted was his client, was no other than a dun, and the alleged title-deed, a bill. But, with all his failings, and the annoyances he caused me, Nippers, like his compatriot Turkey, was a very useful man to me; wrote a neat, swift hand; and, when he chose, was not deficient in a gentlemanly sort of deportment. Added to this, he always dressed in a gentlemanly sort of way; and so, incidentally, reflected credit upon my chambers. Whereas, with respect to Turkey, I had much ado to keep him from being a reproach to me. His clothes were apt to look oily, a smell of eating-houses. He wore his pantaloons very loose and baggy in summer. His coats were execrable, his hat not to be handled. But while the hat was a thing of indifference to me, inasmuch as his natural civility and deference, as a dependent Englishman, always led him to doff it the moment he entered the room, yet his coat was another matter. Concerning his coats, I reasoned with him; but with no effect. The truth was, I suppose, that a man with so small an income could not afford to sport such a lustrous face and a lustrous coat at one and the same time. As Nippers once observed, Turkey's money went chiefly for red ink. One winter day, I presented Turkey with a highly respectable-looking coat of my own — a padded gray coat, of a most comfortable warmth, and which buttoned straight up from the knee to the neck. I thought Turkey would appreciate the favor, and abate his rashness and obstreperousness of afternoons. But no; I verily believe that buttoning himself up in so downy and blanket-like a coat had a pernicious effect upon him — upon the same principle that too much oats are bad for horses. In fact, precisely as a rash, restive horse is said to feel his oats, so Turkey felt his coat. It made him insolent. He was a man whom prosperity harmed.

Though, concerning the self-indulgent habits of Turkey, I had my own private surmises, yet, touching Nippers, I was well persuaded that, whatever might be his faults in other respects, he was, at least, a temperate young man. But indeed, nature herself seemed to have been his vintner, and, at his birth, charged him so thoroughly with an irritable, brandy-like disposition, that all subsequent potations were needless. When I consider how, amid the stillness of my chambers, Nippers would sometimes impatiently rise from his seat, and stooping over his table, spread his arms wide apart, seize the whole desk, and move it, and jerk it, with a grim, grinding motion on the floor, as if the table were a perverse voluntary agent, intent on thwarting and vexing him, I plainly perceive that, for Nippers, brandy-and-water were altogether superfluous.

the Tombs: A jail in New York City.

It was fortunate for me that, owing to its peculiar cause — indigestion — the irritability and consequent nervousness of Nippers were mainly observable in the morning, while in the afternoon he was comparatively mild. So that, Turkey's paroxysms only coming on about twelve o'clock, I never had to do with their eccentricities at one time. Their fits relieved each other, like guards. When Nippers' was on, Turkey's was off; and *vice versa.* This was a good natural arrangement, under the circumstances.

Ginger Nut, the third on my list, was a lad, some twelve years old. His father was a carman, ambitious of seeing his son on the bench instead of a cart, before he died. So he sent him to my office, as student at law, errand-boy, cleaner, and sweeper, at the rate of one dollar a week. He had a little desk to himself, but he did not use it much. Upon inspection, the drawer exhibited a great array of the shells of various sorts of nuts. Indeed, to this quick-witted youth, the whole noble science of the law was contained in a nutshell. Not the least among the employments of Ginger Nut, as well as one which he discharged with the most alacrity, was his duty as cake and apple purveyor for Turkey and Nippers. Copying lawpapers being proverbially a dry, husky sort of business, my two scriveners were fain to moisten their mouths very often with Spitzenbergs, to be had at the numerous stalls nigh the Custom House and Post Office. Also, they sent Ginger Nut very frequently for that peculiar cake — small, flat, round, and very spicy — after which he had been named by them. Of a cold morning, when business was but dull, Turkey would gobble up scores of these cakes, as if they were mere wafers — indeed, they sell them at the rate of six or eight for a penny — the scrape of his pen blending with the crunching of the crisp particles in his mouth. Of all the fiery afternoon blunders and flurried rashness of Turkey, was his once moistening a ginger-cake between his lips, and clapping it on to a mortgage, for a seal. I came within an ace of dismissing him then. But he mollified me by making an oriental bow, and saying —

"With submission, sir, it was generous of me to find you in stationery on my own account." 15

Now my original business — that of a conveyancer and title hunter, and drawer-up of recondite documents of all sorts — was considerably increased by receiving the Master's office. There was now great work for scriveners. Not only must I push the clerks already with me, but I must have additional help.

In answer to my advertisement, a motionless young man one morning stood upon my office threshold, the door being open, for it was summer. I can see that figure now — pallidly neat, pitiably respectable, incurably forlorn! It was Bartleby.

After a few words touching his qualifications, I engaged him, glad to have among my corps of copyists a man of so singularly sedate an aspect, which I thought might operate beneficially upon the flighty temper of Turkey, and the fiery one of Nippers.

I should have stated before that ground-glass folding-doors divided my premises into two parts, one of which was occupied by my scriveners, the other by myself. According to my humor, I threw open these doors, or closed them. I resolved to assign Bartleby a corner by the folding-doors, but on my side of them, so as to have this quiet man within easy call, in case any trifling thing was to be done. I placed his desk close up to a small side-window in that part of the room, a window which originally had afforded a lateral view of certain grimy brickyards and bricks, but which, owing to subsequent erections, commanded at present no view at all, though it gave some light. Within three feet of the panes was a wall, and the light came down from far above, between two lofty buildings, as from a very small opening in a dome. Still further to a satisfactory arrangement, I procured a high green folding screen, which might entirely isolate Bartleby from my sight, though not remove him from my voice. And thus, in a manner, privacy and society were conjoined.

At first, Bartleby did an extraordinary quantity of writing. As if long fam- 20 ishing for something to copy, he seemed to gorge himself on my documents. There was no pause for digestion. He ran a day and night line, copying by sunlight and by candle-light. I should have been quite delighted with his application, had he been cheerfully industrious. But he wrote on silently, palely, mechanically.

It is, of course, an indispensable part of a scrivener's business to verify the accuracy of his copy, word by word. Where there are two or more scriveners in an office, they assist each other in this examination, one reading from the copy, the other holding the original. It is a very dull, wearisome, and lethargic affair. I can readily imagine that, to some sanguine temperaments, it would be altogether intolerable. For example, I cannot credit that the mettlesome poet, Byron, would have contentedly sat down with Bartleby to examine a law document of, say five hundred pages, closely written in a crimpy hand.

Now and then, in the haste of business, it had been my habit to assist in comparing some brief document myself, calling Turkey or Nippers for this purpose. One object I had, in placing Bartleby so handy to me behind the screen, was, to avail myself of his services on such trivial occasions. It was on the third day, I think, of his being with me, and before any necessity had arisen for having his own writing examined, that, being much hurried to complete a small affair I had in hand, I abruptly called to Bartleby. In my haste and natural expectancy of instant compliance, I sat with my head bent over the original on my desk, and my right hand sideways, and somewhat nervously extended with the copy, so that, immediately upon emerging from his retreat, Bartleby might snatch it and proceed to business without the least delay.

In this very attitude did I sit when I called to him, rapidly stating what it was I wanted him to do — namely, to examine a small paper with me. Imagine my surprise, nay, my consternation, when, without moving from his privacy, Bartleby, in a singularly mild, firm voice, replied, "I would prefer not to."

I sat awhile in perfect silence, rallying my stunned faculties. Immediately it occurred to me that my ears had deceived me, or Bartleby had entirely misunderstood my meaning. I repeated my request in the clearest tone I could assume; but in quite as clear a one came the previous reply, "I would prefer not to."

"Prefer not to," echoed I, rising in high excitement, and crossing the room 25 with a stride. "What do you mean? Are you moonstruck? I want you to help me compare this sheet here — take it," and I thrust it towards him.

"I would prefer not to," said he.

I looked at him steadfastly. His face was leanly composed; his gray eye dimly calm. Not a wrinkle of agitation rippled him. Had there been the least uneasiness, anger, impatience, or impertinence in his manner; in other words, had there been anything ordinarily human about him, doubtless I should have violently dismissed him from the premises. But as it was, I should have as soon thought of turning my pale plaster-of-paris bust of Cicero out of doors. I stood gazing at him awhile, as he went on with his own writing, and then reseated myself at my desk. This is very strange, thought I. What had one best do? But my business hurried me. I concluded to forget the matter for the present, reserving it for my future leisure. So, calling Nippers from the other room, the paper was speedily examined.

A few days after this, Bartleby concluded four lengthy documents, being quadruplicates of a week's testimony taken before me in my High Court of Chancery. It became necessary to examine them. It was an important suit, and great accuracy was imperative. Having all things arranged, I called Turkey, Nippers, and Ginger Nut, from the next room, meaning to place the four copies in the hands of my four clerks, while I should read from the original. Accordingly, Turkey, Nippers, and Ginger Nut had taken their seats in a row, each with his document in his hand, when I called to Bartleby to join this interesting group.

"Bartleby! quick, I am waiting."

I heard a slow scrape of his chair legs on the uncarpeted floor, and soon he 30 appeared standing at the entrance of his hermitage.

"What is wanted?" said he, mildly.

"The copies, the copies," said I, hurriedly. "We are going to examine them. There" — and I held towards him the fourth quadruplicate.

"I would prefer not to," he said, and gently disappeared behind the screen.

For a few moments I was turned into a pillar of salt, standing at the head of my seated column of clerks. Recovering myself, I advanced towards the screen, and demanded the reason for such extraordinary conduct.

"*Why* do you refuse?"   35

"I would prefer not to."

With any other man I should have flown outright into a dreadful passion, scorned all further words, and thrust him ignominiously from my presence. But there was something about Bartleby that not only strangely disarmed me, but, in a wonderful manner, touched and disconcerted me. I began to reason with him.

"These are your own copies we are about to examine. It is labor saving to you, because one examination will answer for your four papers. It is common usage. Every copyist is bound to help examine his copy. Is it not so? Will you not speak? Answer!"

"I prefer not to," he replied in a flute-like tone. It seemed to me that, while I had been addressing him, he carefully revolved every statement that I made; fully comprehended the meaning; could not gainsay the irresistible conclusion; but, at the same time, some paramount consideration prevailed with him to reply as he did.

"You are decided, then, not to comply with my request — a request made 40 according to common usage and common sense?"

He briefly gave me to understand, that on that point my judgment was sound. Yes: his decision was irreversible.

It is not seldom the case that, when a man is browbeaten in some unprecedented and violently unreasonable way, he begins to stagger in his own plainest faith. He begins, as it were, vaguely to surmise that, wonderful as it may be, all the justice and all the reason is on the other side. Accordingly, if any disinterested persons are present, he turns to them for some reinforcement for his own faltering mind.

"Turkey," said I, "what do you think of this? Am I not right?"

"With submission, sir," said Turkey, in his blandest tone, "I think that you are."

"Nippers," said I, "what do *you* think of it?" 45

"I think I should kick him out of the office."

(The reader of nice perceptions will have perceived that, it being morning, Turkey's answer is couched in polite and tranquil terms, but Nippers replies in ill-tempered ones. Or, to repeat a previous sentence, Nippers' ugly mood was on duty, and Turkey's off.)

"Ginger Nut," said I, willing to enlist the smallest suffrage in my behalf, "what do *you* think of it?"

"I think, sir, he's a little *luny,*" replied Ginger Nut, with a grin.

"You hear what they say," said I, turning towards the screen, "come forth 50 and do your duty."

But he vouchsafed no reply. I pondered a moment in sore perplexity. But once more business hurried me. I determined again to postpone the consideration of this dilemma to my future leisure. With a little trouble we made out to examine the papers without Bartleby, though at every page or two Turkey deferentially dropped his opinion, that this proceeding was quite out of the common; while Nippers, twitching in his chair with a dyspeptic nervousness, ground out, between his set teeth, occasional hissing maledictions against the stubborn oaf behind the screen. And for his (Nippers') part, this was the first and the last time he would do another man's business without pay.

Meanwhile Bartleby sat in his hermitage, oblivious to everything but his own peculiar business there.

Some days passed, the scrivener being employed upon another lengthy work. His late remarkable conduct led me to regard his ways narrowly. I observed that he never went to dinner; indeed, that he never went anywhere. As yet I had never, of my personal knowledge, known him to be outside of my office. He was a perpetual sentry in the corner. At about eleven o'clock though, in the morning, I noticed that Ginger Nut would advance toward the opening in Bartleby's screen, as if silently beckoned thither by a gesture invisible to me where I sat. The boy would then leave the office, jingling a few pence, and reappear with a handful of ginger-nuts, which he delivered in the hermitage, receiving two of the cakes for his trouble.

He lives, then, on ginger-nuts, thought I; never eats a dinner, properly speaking; he must be a vegetarian, then; but no; he never eats even vegetables, he eats nothing but ginger-nuts. My mind then ran on in reveries concerning the probable effects upon the human constitution of living entirely on ginger-nuts. Ginger-nuts are so called, because they contain ginger as one of their peculiar constituents, and the final flavoring one. Now, what was ginger? A hot, spicy thing. Was Bartleby hot and spicy? Not at all. Ginger, then, had no effect upon Bartleby. Probably he preferred it should have none.

Nothing so aggravates an earnest person as a passive resistance. If the 55 individual so resisted be of a not inhumane temper, and the resisting one perfectly harmless in his passivity, then, in the better moods of the former, he will endeavor charitably to construe to his imagination what proves impossible to be solved by his judgment. Even so, for the most part, I regarded Bartleby and his ways. Poor fellow! thought I, he means no mischief; it is plain he intends no insolence; his aspect sufficiently evinces that his eccentricities are involuntary. He is useful to me. I can get along with him. If I turn him away, the chances are he will fall in with some less indulgent employer, and then he will be rudely treated, and perhaps driven forth miserably to starve. Yes. Here I can cheaply purchase a delicious self-approval. To befriend Bartleby; to humor him in his strange wilfulness, will cost me little or nothing, while I lay up in my soul what will eventually prove a sweet morsel for my conscience. But this mood was not invariable with me. The passiveness of Bartleby sometimes irritated me. I felt strangely goaded on to encounter him in new opposition — to elicit some angry spark from him answerable to my own. But, indeed, I might as well have essayed to strike fire with my knuckles against a bit of Windsor soap. But one afternoon the evil impulse in me mastered me, and the following little scene ensued:

"Bartleby," said I, "when those papers are all copied, I will compare them with you."

"I would prefer not to."

"How? Surely you do not mean to persist in that mulish vagary?"

No answer.

I threw open the folding-doors nearby, and turning upon Turkey and Nip-   60 pers, exclaimed:

"Bartleby a second time says, he won't examine his papers. What do you think of it, Turkey?"

It was afternoon, be it remembered. Turkey sat glowing like a brass boiler; his bald head steaming; his hands reeling among his blotted papers.

"Think of it?" roared Turkey. "I think I'll just step behind his screen, and black his eyes for him!"

So saying, Turkey rose to his feet and threw his arms into a pugilistic position. He was hurrying away to make good his promise, when I detained him, alarmed at the effect of incautiously rousing Turkey's combativeness after dinner.

"Sit down, Turkey," said I, "and hear what Nippers has to say. What do you   65 think of it, Nippers? Would I not be justified in immediately dismissing Bartleby?"

"Excuse me, that is for you to decide, sir. I think his conduct quite un-usual, and, indeed, unjust, as regards Turkey and myself. But it may only be a passing whim."

"Ah," exclaimed I, "you have strangely changed your mind, then — you speak very gently of him now."

"All beer," cried Turkey; "gentleness is effects of beer — Nippers and I dined together to-day. You see how gentle I am, sir. Shall I go and black his eyes?"

"You refer to Bartleby, I suppose. No, not to-day, Turkey," I replied; "pray, put up your fists."

I closed the doors, and again advanced towards Bartleby. I felt additional   70 incentives tempting me to my fate. I burned to be rebelled against again. I re-membered that Bartleby never left the office.

"Bartleby," said I, "Ginger Nut is away; just step around to the Post Office, won't you?" (it was but a three minutes' walk) "and see if there is anything for me."

"I would prefer not to."

"You *will* not?"

"I *prefer* not."

I staggered to my desk, and sat there in a deep study. My blind inveteracy 75
returned. Was there any other thing in which I could procure myself to be ignominiously repulsed by this lean, penniless wight?—my hired clerk? What
added thing is there, perfectly reasonable, that he will be sure to refuse to do?

"Bartleby!"

No answer.

"Bartleby," in a louder tone.

No answer.

"Bartleby," I roared.   80

Like a very ghost, agreeably to the laws of magical invocation, at the third
summons, he appeared at the entrance of his hermitage.

"Go to the next room, and tell Nippers to come to me."

"I prefer not to," he respectfully and slowly said, and mildly disappeared.

"Very good, Bartleby," said I, in a quiet sort of serenely-severe self-possessed
tone, intimating the unalterable purpose of some terrible retribution very
close at hand. At the moment I half intended something of the kind. But upon
the whole, as it was drawing towards my dinner-hour, I thought it best to put
on my hat and walk home for the day, suffering much from perplexity and distress of mind.

Shall I acknowledge it? The conclusion of this whole business was, that it 85
soon became a fixed fact of my chambers, that a pale young scrivener, by the
name of Bartleby, had a desk there; that he copied for me at the usual rate of
four cents a folio (one hundred words); but he was permanently exempt from
examining the work done by him, that duty being transferred to Turkey and
Nippers, out of compliment, doubtless, to their superior acuteness; moreover,
said Bartleby was never, on any account, to be dispatched on the most trivial
errand of any sort; and that even if entreated to take upon him such a matter,
it was generally understood that he would "prefer not to"—in other words,
that he would refuse point-blank.

As days passed on, I became considerably reconciled to Bartleby. His steadi-
ness, his freedom from all dissipation, his incessant industry (except when he
chose to throw himself into a standing revery behind his screen), his great stillness, his unalterableness of demeanor under all circumstances, made him a valuable acquisition. One prime thing was this—*he was always there*—first in the
morning, continually through the day, and the last at night. I had a singular confidence in his honesty. I felt my most precious papers perfectly safe in his hands.
Sometimes, to be sure, I could not, for the very soul of me, avoid falling into sudden spasmodic passions with him. For it was exceeding difficult to bear in mind
all the time those strange peculiarities, privileges, and unheard-of exemptions,
forming the tacit stipulations on Bartleby's part under which he remained in my
office. Now and then, in the eagerness of dispatching pressing business, I would
inadvertently summon Bartleby, in a short, rapid tone, to put his finger, say, on
the incipient tie of a bit of red tape with which I was about compressing some
papers. Of course, from behind the screen the usual answer, "I prefer not to," was
sure to come; and then, how could a human creature, with the common infirmi-
ties of our nature, refrain from bitterly exclaiming upon such perverseness—
such unreasonableness? However, every added repulse of this sort which I received only tended to lessen the probability of my repeating the inadvertence.

Here it must be said, that, according to the custom of most legal gentlemen occupying chambers in densely populated law buildings, there were
several keys to my door. One was kept by a woman residing in the attic, which

person weekly scrubbed and daily swept and dusted my apartments. Another was kept by Turkey for convenience sake. The third I sometimes carried in my own pocket. The fourth I knew not who had.

Now, one Sunday morning I happened to go to Trinity Church, to hear a celebrated preacher, and finding myself rather early on the ground I thought I would walk round to my chambers for a while. Luckily I had my key with me; but upon applying it to the lock, I found it resisted by something inserted from the inside. Quite surprised, I called out; when to my consternation a key was turned from within; and thrusting his lean visage at me, and holding the door ajar, the apparition of Bartleby appeared, in his shirt-sleeves, and otherwise in a strangely tattered *deshabille,* saying quietly that he was sorry, but he was deeply engaged just then, and — preferred not admitting me at present. In a brief word or two, he moreover added, that perhaps I had better walk round the block two or three times, and by that time he would probably have concluded his affairs.

Now, the utterly unsurmised appearance of Bartleby, tenanting my lawchambers of a Sunday morning, with his cadaverously gentlemanly *nonchalance,* yet withal firm and self-possessed, had such a strange effect upon me, that incontinently I slunk away from my own door, and did as desired. But not without sundry twinges of impotent rebellion against the mild effrontery of this unaccountable scrivener. Indeed, it was his wonderful mildness chiefly, which not only disarmed me, but unmanned me, as it were. For I consider that one, for the time, is sort of unmanned when he tranquilly permits his hired clerk to dictate to him, and order him away from his own premises. Furthermore, I was full of uneasiness as to what Bartleby could possibly be doing in my office in his shirt-sleeves, and in an otherwise dismantled condition of a Sunday morning. Was anything amiss going on? Nay, that was out of the question. It was not to be thought of for a moment that Bartleby was an immoral person. But what could he be doing there? — copying? Nay again, whatever might be his eccentricities, Bartleby was an eminently decorous person. He would be the last man to sit down to his desk in any state approaching to nudity. Besides, it was Sunday; and there was something about Bartleby that forbade the supposition that he would by any secular occupation violate the proprieties of the day.

Nevertheless, my mind was not pacified; and full of a restless curiosity, at last I returned to the door. Without hindrance I inserted my key, opened it, and entered. Bartleby was not to be seen. I looked round anxiously, peeped behind his screen; but it was very plain that he was gone. Upon more closely examining the place, I surmised that for an indefinite period Bartleby must have ate, dressed, and slept in my office, and that too without plate, mirror, or bed. The cushioned seat of a rickety old sofa in one corner bore the faint impress of a lean, reclining form. Rolled away under his desk, I found a blanket; under the empty grate, a blacking box and brush; on a chair, a tin basin, with soap and a ragged towel; in a newspaper a few crumbs of ginger-nuts and a morsel of cheese. Yes, thought I, it is evident enough that Bartleby has been making his home here, keeping bachelor's hall all by himself. Immediately then the thought came sweeping across me, what miserable friendlessness and loneliness are here revealed! His poverty is great; but his solitude, how horrible! Think of it. Of a Sunday, Wall Street is deserted as Petra;° and every night of

Petra: An ancient Arabian city whose ruins were discovered in 1812.

every day it is an emptiness. This building, too, which of week-days hums with industry and life, at nightfall echoes with sheer vacancy, and all through Sunday is forlorn. And here Bartleby makes his home; sole spectator of a solitude which he has seen all populous—a sort of innocent and transformed Marius brooding among the ruins of Carthage?°

For the first time in my life a feeling of overpowering stinging melancholy seized me. Before, I had never experienced aught but a not unpleasing sadness. The bond of a common humanity now drew me irresistibly to gloom. A fraternal melancholy! For both I and Bartleby were sons of Adam. I remembered the bright silks and sparkling faces I had seen that day, in gala trim, swan-like sailing down the Mississippi of Broadway; and I contrasted them with the pallid copyist, and thought to myself, Ah, happiness courts the light, so we deem the world is gay; but misery hides aloof, so we deem that misery there is none. These sad fancyings—chimeras, doubtless, of a sick and silly brain—led on to other and more special thoughts, concerning the eccentricities of Bartleby. Presentiments of strange discoveries hovered round me. The scrivener's pale form appeared to me laid out, among uncaring strangers, in its shivering winding-sheet.

Suddenly I was attracted by Bartleby's closed desk, the key in open sight left in the lock.

I mean no mischief, seek the gratification of no heartless curiosity, thought I; besides, the desk is mine, and its contents, too, so I will make bold to look within. Everything was methodically arranged, the papers smoothly placed. The pigeon-holes were deep, and removing the files of documents, I groped into their recesses. Presently I felt something there, and dragged it out. It was an old bandanna handkerchief, heavy and knotted. I opened it, and saw it was a saving's bank.

I now recalled all the quiet mysteries which I had noted in the man. I remembered that he never spoke but to answer; that, though at intervals he had considerable time to himself, yet I had never seen him reading—no, not even a newspaper; that for long periods he would stand looking out, at his pale window behind the screen, upon the dead brick wall; I was quite sure he never visited any refectory or eating-house; while his pale face clearly indicated that he never drank beer like Turkey; or tea and coffee even, like other men; that he never went anywhere in particular that I could learn; never went out for a walk, unless, indeed, that was the case at present; that he had declined telling who he was, or whence he came, or whether he had any relatives in the world; that though so thin and pale, he never complained of ill-health. And more than all, I remembered a certain unconscious air of pallid—how shall I call it?—of pallid haughtiness, say, or rather an austere reserve about him, which had positively awed me into my tame compliance with his eccentricities, when I had feared to ask him to do the slightest incidental thing for me, even though I might know, from his long-continued motionlessness, that behind his screen he must be standing in one of those dead-wall reveries of his.

Revolving all these things, and coupling them with the recently discovered ⁹⁵ fact, that he made my office his constant abiding place and home, and not

---

Marius . . . of Carthage: Gaius Marius (157–86 B.C.), an exiled Roman general, sought refuge in the African city-state of Carthage, which was destroyed by the Romans in the Third Punic War.

forgetful of his morbid moodiness; revolving all these things, a prudential feeling began to steal over me. My first emotions had been those of pure melancholy and sincerest pity; but just in proportion as the forlornness of Bartleby grew and grew to my imagination, did that same melancholy merge into fear, that pity into repulsion. So true it is, and so terrible, too, that up to a certain point the thought or sight of misery enlists our best affections; but, in certain special cases, beyond that point it does not. They err who would assert that invariably this is owing to the inherent selfishness of the human heart. It rather proceeds from a certain hopelessness of remedying excessive and organic ill. To a sensitive being, pity is not seldom pain. And when at last it is perceived that such pity cannot lead to effectual succor, common sense bids the soul be rid of it. What I saw that morning persuaded me that the scrivener was the victim of innate and incurable disorder. I might give alms to his body; but his body did not pain him; it was his soul that suffered, and his soul I could not reach.

I did not accomplish the purpose of going to Trinity Church that morning. Somehow, the things I had seen disqualified me for the time from church-going. I walked homeward, thinking what I would do with Bartleby. Finally, I resolved upon this — I would put certain calm questions to him the next morning, touching his history, etc., and if he declined to answer them openly and unreservedly (and I supposed he would prefer not), then to give him a twenty dollar bill over and above whatever I might owe him, and tell him his services were no longer required; but that if in any other way I could assist him, I would be happy to do so, especially if he desired to return to his native place, wherever that might be, I would willingly help to defray the expenses. Moreover, if, after reaching home, he found himself at any time in want of aid, a letter from him would be sure of a reply.

The next morning came.

"Bartleby," said I, gently calling to him behind his screen.

No reply.

"Bartleby," said I, in a still gentler tone, "come here; I am not going to ask you to do anything you would prefer not to do — I simply wish to speak to you."

Upon this he noiselessly slid into view.

"Will you tell me, Bartleby, where you were born?"

"I would prefer not to."

"Will you tell me *anything* about yourself?"

"I would prefer not to."

"But what reasonable objection can you have to speak to me? I feel friendly towards you."

He did not look at me while I spoke, but kept his glance fixed upon my bust of Cicero, which, as I then sat, was directly behind me, some six inches above my head.

"What is your answer, Bartleby?" said I, after waiting a considerable time for a reply, during which his countenance remained immovable, only there was the faintest conceivable tremor of the white attenuated mouth.

"At present I prefer to give no answer," he said, and retired into his hermitage.

It was rather weak in me I confess, but his manner, on this occasion, nettled me. Not only did there seem to lurk in it a certain calm disdain, but his perverseness seemed ungrateful, considering the undeniable good usage and indulgence he had received from me.

Again I sat ruminating what I should do. Mortified as I was at his behavior, and resolved as I had been to dismiss him when I entered my office, nevertheless I strangely felt something superstitious knocking at my heart, and forbidding me to carry out my purpose, and denouncing me for a villain if I dared to breathe one bitter word against this forlornest of mankind. At last, familiarly drawing my chair behind his screen, I sat down and said: "Bartleby, never mind, then, about revealing your history; but let me entreat you, as a friend, to comply as far as may be with the usages of this office. Say now, you will help to examine papers tomorrow or next day: in short, say now, that in a day or two you will begin to be a little reasonable: — say so, Bartleby."

"At present I would prefer not to be a little reasonable," was his mildly cadaverous reply.

Just then the folding-doors opened, and Nippers approached. He seemed suffering from an unusually bad night's rest, induced by severer indigestion than common. He overheard those final words of Bartleby.

"*Prefer not,* eh?" gritted Nippers—"I'd *prefer* him, if I were you, sir," addressing me—"I'd *prefer* him; I'd give him preferences, the stubborn mule! What is it, sir, pray, that he *prefers* not to do now?"

Bartleby moved not a limb. 115

"Mr. Nippers," said I, "I'd prefer that you would withdraw for the present."

Somehow, of late, I had got into the way of involuntarily using this word "prefer" upon all sorts of not exactly suitable occasions. And I trembled to think that my contact with the scrivener had already and seriously affected me in a mental way. And what further and deeper aberration might it not yet produce? This apprehension had not been without efficacy in determining me to summary measures.

As Nippers, looking very sour and sulky, was departing, Turkey blandly and deferentially approached.

"With submission, sir," said he, "yesterday I was thinking about Bartleby here, and I think that if he would but prefer to take a quart of good ale every day, it would do much towards mending him, and enabling him to assist in examining his papers."

"So you have got the word, too," said I, slightly excited. 120

"With submission, what word, sir?" asked Turkey, respectfully crowding himself into the contracted space behind the screen, and by so doing, making me jostle the scrivener. "What word, sir?"

"I would prefer to be left alone here," said Bartleby, as if offended at being mobbed in his privacy.

"*That's* the word, Turkey," said I—"*that's* it."

"Oh, *prefer?* oh yes—queer word. I never use it myself. But, sir, as I was saying, if he would but prefer —"

"Turkey," interrupted I, "you will please withdraw." 125

"Oh certainly, sir, if you prefer that I should."

As he opened the folding-door to retire, Nippers at his desk caught a glimpse of me, and asked whether I would prefer to have a certain paper copied on blue paper or white. He did not in the least roguishly accent the word "prefer." It was plain that it involuntarily rolled from his tongue. I thought to myself, surely I must get rid of a demented man, who already has in some degree turned the tongues, if not the heads of myself and clerks. But I thought it prudent not to break the dismission at once.

The next day I noticed that Bartleby did nothing but stand at his window in his dead-wall revery. Upon asking him why he did not write, he said that he had decided upon doing no more writing.

"Why, how now? what next?" exclaimed I, "do no more writing?"

"No more." 130

"And what is the reason?"

"Do you not see the reason for yourself?" he indifferently replied.

I looked steadfastly at him, and perceived that his eyes looked dull and glazed. Instantly it occurred to me, that his unexampled diligence in copying by his dim window for the first few weeks of his stay with me might have temporarily impaired his vision.

I was touched. I said something in condolence with him. I hinted that of course he did wisely in abstaining from writing for a while; and urged him to embrace that opportunity of taking wholesome exercise in the open air. This, however, he did not do. A few days after this, my other clerks being absent, and being in a great hurry to dispatch certain letters by the mail, I thought that, having nothing else earthly to do, Bartleby would surely be less inflexible than usual, and carry these letters to the Post Office. But he blankly declined. So, much to my inconvenience, I went myself.

Still added days went by. Whether Bartleby's eyes improved or not, I could 135 not say. To all appearance, I thought they did. But when I asked him if they did, he vouchsafed no answer. At all events, he would do no copying. At last, in replying to my urgings, he informed me that he had permanently given up copying.

"What!" exclaimed I; "suppose your eyes should get entirely well—better than ever before—would you not copy then?"

"I have given up copying," he answered, and slid aside.

He remained as ever, a fixture in my chamber. Nay—if that were possible—he became still more of a fixture than before. What was to be done? He would do nothing in the office; why should he stay there? In plain fact, he had now become a millstone to me, not only useless as a necklace, but afflictive to bear. Yet I was sorry for him. I speak less than truth when I say that, on his own account, he occasioned me uneasiness. If he would but have named a single relative or friend, I would instantly have written, and urged their taking the poor fellow away to some convenient retreat. But he seemed alone, absolutely alone in the universe. A bit of wreck in the mid-Atlantic. At length, necessities connected with my business tyrannized over all other considerations. Decently as I could, I told Bartleby that in six days' time he must unconditionally leave the office. I warned him to take measures, in the interval, for procuring some other abode. I offered to assist him in this endeavor, if he himself would but take the first step towards a removal. "And when you finally quit me, Bartleby," added I, "I shall see that you go not away entirely unprovided. Six days from this hour, remember."

At the expiration of that period, I peeped behind the screen, and lo! Bartleby was there.

I buttoned up my coat, balanced myself; advanced slowly towards him, 140 touched his shoulder, and said, "The time has come; you must quit this place; I am sorry for you; here is money; but you must go."

"I would prefer not," he replied, with his back still towards me.

"You *must*."

He remained silent.

Now I had an unbounded confidence in this man's common honesty. He had frequently restored to me sixpences and shillings carelessly dropped upon the floor, for I am apt to be very reckless in such shirt-button affairs. The proceeding, then, which followed will not be deemed extraordinary.

"Bartleby," said I, "I owe you twelve dollars on account; here are thirty-two,   145 the odd twenty are yours—Will you take it?" and I handed the bills towards him.

But he made no motion.

"I will leave them here, then," putting them under a weight on the table. Then taking my hat and cane and going to the door, I tranquilly turned and added—"After you have removed your things from these offices, Bartleby, you will of course lock the door—since every one is now gone for the day but you—and if you please, slip your key underneath the mat, so that I may have it in the morning. I shall not see you again; so good-bye to you. If, hereafter, in your new place of abode, I can be of any service to you, do not fail to advise me by letter. Good-bye, Bartleby, and fare you well."

But he answered not a word; like the last column of some ruined temple, he remained standing mute and solitary in the middle of the otherwise deserted room.

As I walked home in a pensive mood, my vanity got the better of my pity. I could not but highly plume myself on my masterly management in getting rid of Bartleby. Masterly I call it, and such it must appear to any dispassionate thinker. The beauty of my procedure seemed to consist in its perfect quietness. There was no vulgar bullying, no bravado of any sort, no choleric hectoring, and striding to and fro across the apartment, jerking out vehement commands for Bartleby to bundle himself off with his beggarly traps. Nothing of the kind. Without loudly bidding Bartleby depart—as an inferior genius might have done—I *assumed* the ground that depart he must; and upon that assumption built all I had to say. The more I thought over my procedure, the more I was charmed with it. Nevertheless, next morning, upon awakening, I had my doubts—I had somehow slept off the fumes of vanity. One of the coolest and wisest hours a man has, is just after he awakes in the morning. My procedure seemed as sagacious as ever—but only in theory. How it would prove in practice—there was the rub. It was truly a beautiful thought to have assumed Bartleby's departure; but, after all, that assumption was simply my own, and none of Bartleby's. The great point was, not whether I had assumed that he would quit me, but whether he would prefer to do so. He was more a man of preferences than assumptions.

After breakfast, I walked down town, arguing the probabilities *pro* and *con*.   150 One moment I thought it would prove a miserable failure, and Bartleby would be found all alive at my office as usual; the next moment it seemed certain that I should find his chair empty. And so I kept veering about. At the corner of Broadway and Canal Street, I saw quite an excited group of people standing in earnest conversation.

"I'll take odds he doesn't," said a voice as I passed.

"Doesn't go?—done!" said I, "put up your money."

I was instinctively putting my hand in my pocket to produce my own, when I remembered that this was an election day. The words I had overheard bore no reference to Bartleby, but to the success or non-success of some candidate for the mayoralty. In my intent frame of mind, I had, as it were, imagined that all Broadway shared in my excitement, and were debating the same question with me. I passed on, very thankful that the uproar of the street screened my momentary absent-mindedness.

As I had intended, I was earlier than usual at my office door. I stood listening for a moment. All was still. He must be gone. I tried the knob. The door was locked. Yes, my procedure had worked to a charm; he indeed must be vanished. Yet a certain melancholy mixed with this: I was almost sorry for my brilliant success. I was fumbling under the door mat for the key, which Bartleby was to have left there for me, when accidentally my knee knocked against a panel, producing a summoning sound, and in response a voice came to me from within — "Not yet; I am occupied."

It was Bartleby.   155

I was thunderstruck. For an instant I stood like the man who, pipe in mouth, was killed one cloudless afternoon long ago in Virginia, by summer lightning; at his own warm open window he was killed, and remained leaning out there upon the dreamy afternoon, till some one touched him, when he fell.

"Not gone!" I murmured at last. But again obeying that wondrous ascendancy which the inscrutable scrivener had over me, and from which ascendancy, for all my chafing, I could not completely escape, I slowly went down stairs and out into the street, and while walking round the block, considered what I should next do in this unheard-of perplexity. Turn the man out by an actual thrusting I could not; to drive him away by calling him hard names would not do; calling in the police was an unpleasant idea; and yet, permit him to enjoy his cadaverous triumph over me — this, too, I could not think of. What was to be done? or, if nothing could be done, was there anything further that I could *assume* in the matter? Yes, as before I had prospectively assumed that Bartleby would depart, so now I might retrospectively assume that departed he was. In the legitimate carrying out of this assumption, I might enter my office in a great hurry, and pretending not to see Bartleby at all, walk straight against him as if he were air. Such a proceeding would in a singular degree have the appearance of a home-thrust. It was hardly possible that Bartleby could withstand such an application of the doctrine of assumption. But upon second thoughts the success of the plan seemed rather dubious. I resolved to argue the matter over with him again.

"Bartleby," said I, entering the office, with a quietly severe expression, "I am seriously displeased. I am pained, Bartleby. I had thought better of you. I had imagined you of such a gentlemanly organization, that in any delicate dilemma a slight hint would suffice — in short, an assumption. But it appears I am deceived. Why," I added, unaffectedly starting, "you have not even touched that money yet," pointing to it, just where I had left it the evening previous.

He answered nothing.

"Will you, or will you not, quit me?" I now demanded in a sudden passion,   160 advancing close to him.

"I would prefer *not* to quit you," he replied, gently emphasizing the *not*.

"What earthly right have you to stay here? Do you pay any rent? Do you pay my taxes? Or is this property yours?"

He answered nothing.

"Are you ready to go on and write now? Are your eyes recovered? Could you copy a small paper for me this morning? or help examine a few lines? or step round to the Post Office? In a word, will you do anything at all, to give a coloring to your refusal to depart the premises?"

He silently retired into his hermitage.

I was now in such a state of nervous resentment that I thought it but prudent to check myself at present from further demonstrations. Bartleby and I were alone. I remembered the tragedy of the unfortunate Adams and the still more unfortunate Colt° in the solitary office of the latter; and how poor Colt, being dreadfully incensed by Adams, and imprudently permitting himself to get wildly excited, was at unawares hurried into his fatal act — an act which certainly no man could possibly deplore more than the actor himself. Often it had occurred to me in my ponderings upon the subject that had that altercation taken place in the public street, or at a private residence, it would not have terminated as it did. It was the circumstance of being alone in a solitary office, up stairs, of a building entirely unhallowed by humanizing domestic associations — an uncarpeted office, doubtless, of a dusty, haggard sort of appearance — this it must have been, which greatly helped to enhance the irritable desperation of the hapless Colt.

But when this old Adam of resentment rose in me and tempted me concerning Bartleby, I grappled him and threw him. How? Why, simply by recalling the divine injunction: "A new commandment give I unto you, that ye love one another." Yes, this it was that saved me. Aside from higher considerations, charity often operates as a vastly wise and prudent principle — a great safeguard to its possessor. Men have committed murder for jealousy's sake, and anger's sake, and hatred's sake, and selfishness' sake, and spiritual pride's sake; but no man, that ever I heard of, ever committed a diabolical murder for sweet charity's sake. Mere self-interest, then, if no better motive can be enlisted, should, especially with high-tempered men, prompt all beings to charity and philanthropy. At any rate, upon the occasion in question, I strove to drown my exasperated feelings towards the scrivener by benevolently construing his conduct. Poor fellow, poor fellow! thought I, he don't mean anything; and besides, he has seen hard times, and ought to be indulged.

I endeavored, also, immediately to occupy myself, and at the same time to comfort my despondency. I tried to fancy, that in the course of the morning, at such time as might prove agreeable to him, Bartleby, of his own free accord, would emerge from his hermitage and take up some decided line of march in the direction of the door. But no. Half-past twelve o'clock came; Turkey began to glow in the face, overturn his inkstand, and become generally obstreperous; Nippers abated down into quietude and courtesy; Ginger Nut munched his noon apple; and Bartleby remained standing at his window in one of his profoundest dead-wall reveries. Will it be credited? Ought I to acknowledge it? That afternoon I left the office without saying one further word to him.

Some days now passed, during which, at leisure intervals I looked a little into "Edwards on the Will," and "Priestley on Necessity."° Under the circumstances,

---

Adams . . . Colt: Samuel Adams was killed by John C. Colt, brother of the gun maker, during a quarrel in 1842. After a sensational court case, Colt committed suicide just before he was to be hanged.

"Edwards . . . Necessity": Jonathan Edwards, in *Freedom of the Will* (1754), and Joseph Priestley, in *Doctrine of Philosophical Necessity* (1777), both argued that human beings do not have free will.

those books induced a salutary feeling. Gradually I slid into the persuasion that these troubles of mine, touching the scrivener, had been all predestined from eternity, and Bartleby was billeted upon me for some mysterious purpose of an all-wise Providence, which it was not for a mere mortal like me to fathom. Yes, Bartleby, stay there behind your screen, thought I; I shall persecute you no more; you are harmless and noiseless as any of these old chairs; in short, I never feel so private as when I know you are here. At last I see it, I feel it; I penetrate to the predestined purpose of my life. I am content. Others may have loftier parts to enact; but my mission in this world, Bartleby, is to furnish you with office-room for such period as you may see fit to remain.

I believe that this wise and blessed frame of mind would have continued 170 with me, had it not been for the unsolicited and uncharitable remarks obtruded upon me by my professional friends who visited the rooms. But thus it often is, that the constant friction of illiberal minds wears out at last the best resolves of the more generous. Though to be sure, when I reflected upon it, it was not strange that people entering my office should be struck by the peculiar aspect of the unaccountable Bartleby, and so be tempted to throw out some sinister observations concerning him. Sometimes an attorney, having business with me, and calling at my office, and finding no one but the scrivener there, would undertake to obtain some sort of precise information from him touching my whereabouts; but without heeding his idle talk, Bartleby would remain standing immovable in the middle of the room. So after contemplating him in that position for a time, the attorney would depart, no wiser than he came.

Also, when a reference was going on, and the room full of lawyers and witnesses, and business driving fast, some deeply-occupied legal gentleman present, seeing Bartleby wholly unemployed, would request him to run round to his (the legal gentleman's) office and fetch some papers for him. Thereupon, Bartleby would tranquilly decline, and yet remain idle as before. Then the lawyer would give a great stare, and turn to me. And what could I say? At last I was made aware that all through the circle of my professional acquaintance, a whisper of wonder was running round, having reference to the strange creature I kept at my office. This worried me very much. And as the idea came upon me of his possibly turning out a long-lived man, and keeping occupying my chambers, and denying my authority; and perplexing my visitors; and scandalizing my professional reputation; and casting a general gloom over the premises; keeping soul and body together to the last upon his savings (for doubtless he spent but half a dime a day), and in the end perhaps outlive me, and claim possession of my office by right of his perpetual occupancy: as all these dark anticipations crowded upon me more and more, and my friends continually intruded their relentless remarks upon the apparition in my room; a great change was wrought in me. I resolved to gather all my faculties together, and forever rid me of this intolerable incubus.

Ere revolving any complicated project, however, adapted to this end, I first simply suggested to Bartleby the propriety of his permanent departure. In a calm and serious tone, I commended the idea to his careful and mature consideration. But, having taken three days to meditate upon it, he apprised me, that his original determination remained the same; in short, that he still preferred to abide with me.

What shall I do? I now said to myself, buttoning up my coat to the last button. What shall I do? what ought I to do? what does conscience say I *should* do with this man, or, rather, ghost. Rid myself of him, I must; go, he shall. But how? You will not thrust him, the poor, pale, passive mortal—you will not thrust such a helpless creature out of your door? you will not dishonor yourself by such cruelty? No, I will not, I cannot do that. Rather would I let him live and die here, and then mason up his remains in the wall. What, then, will you do? For all your coaxing, he will not budge. Bribes he leaves under your own paper-weight on your table; in short, it is quite plain that he prefers to cling to you.

Then something severe, something unusual must be done. What! surely you will not have him collared by a constable, and commit his innocent pallor to the common jail? And upon what ground could you procure such a thing to be done?—a vagrant, is he? What! he a vagrant, a wanderer, who refuses to budge? It is because he will *not* be a vagrant, then, that you seek to count him *as* a vagrant. That is too absurd. No visible means of support: there I have him. Wrong again: for indubitably he *does* support himself, and that is the only unanswerable proof that any man can show of his possessing the means so to do. No more, then. Since he will not quit me, I must quit him. I will change my offices; I will move elsewhere, and give him fair notice, that if I find him on my new premises I will then proceed against him as a common trespasser.

Acting accordingly, next day I thus addressed him: "I find these chambers 175 too far from the City Hall; the air is unwholesome. In a word, I propose to remove my offices next week, and shall no longer require your services. I tell you this now, in order that you may seek another place."

He made no reply, and nothing more was said.

On the appointed day I engaged carts and men, proceeded to my chambers, and having but little furniture, everything was removed in a few hours. Throughout, the scrivener remained standing behind the screen, which I directed to be removed the last thing. It was withdrawn; and, being folded up like a huge folio, left him the motionless occupant of a naked room. I stood in the entry watching him a moment, while something from within me upbraided me.

I re-entered, with my hand in my pocket—and—and my heart in my mouth.

"Good-bye, Bartleby; I am going—good-bye, and God some way bless you; and take that," slipping something in his hand. But it dropped upon the floor, and then—strange to say—I tore myself from him whom I had so longed to be rid of.

Established in my new quarters, for a day or two I kept the door locked, 180 and started at every footfall in the passages. When I returned to my rooms, after any little absence, I would pause at the threshold for an instant, and attentively listen, ere applying my key. But these fears were needless. Bartleby never came nigh me.

I thought all was going well, when a perturbed-looking stranger visited me, inquiring whether I was the person who had recently occupied rooms at No. — Wall Street.

Full of forebodings, I replied that I was.

"Then, sir," said the stranger, who proved a lawyer, "you are responsible for the man you left there. He refuses to do any copying; he refuses to do anything; he says he prefers not to; and he refuses to quit the premises."

"I am very sorry, sir," said I, with assumed tranquillity, but an inward tremor, "but, really, the man you allude to is nothing to me — he is no relation or apprentice of mine, that you should hold me responsible for him."

"In mercy's name, who is he?"   185

"I certainly cannot inform you. I know nothing about him. Formerly I employed him as a copyist; but he has done nothing for me now for some time past."

"I shall settle him, then — good morning, sir."

Several days passed, and I heard nothing more; and, though I often felt a charitable prompting to call at the place and see poor Bartleby, yet a certain squeamishness, of I know not what, withheld me.

All is over with him, by this time, thought I, at last, when, through another week, no further intelligence reached me. But, coming to my room the day after, I found several persons waiting at my door in a high state of nervous excitement.

"That's the man — here he comes," cried the foremost one, whom I recog-   190
nized as the lawyer who had previously called upon me alone.

"You must take him away, sir, at once," cried a portly person among them, advancing upon me, and whom I knew to be the landlord of No. — Wall Street. "These gentlemen, my tenants, cannot stand it any longer; Mr. B——," pointing to the lawyer, "has turned him out of his room, and he now persists in haunting the building generally, sitting upon the banisters of the stairs by day, and sleeping in the entry by night. Everybody is concerned; clients are leaving the offices; some fears are entertained of a mob; something you must do, and that without delay."

Aghast at this torrent, I fell back before it, and would fain have locked myself in my new quarters. In vain I persisted that Bartleby was nothing to me — no more than to any one else. In vain — I was the last person known to have anything to do with him, and they held me to the terrible account. Fearful, then, of being exposed in the papers (as one person present obscurely threatened), I considered the matter, and, at length, said, that if the lawyer would give me a confidential interview with the scrivener, in his (the lawyer's) own room, I would, that afternoon, strive my best to rid them of the nuisance they complained of.

Going up stairs to my old haunt, there was Bartleby silently sitting upon the banister at the landing.

"What are you doing here, Bartleby?" said I.

"Sitting upon the banister," he mildly replied.   195

I motioned him into the lawyer's room, who then left us.

"Bartleby," said I, "are you aware that you are the cause of great tribulation to me, by persisting in occupying the entry after being dismissed from the office?"

No answer.

"Now one of two things must take place. Either you must do something, or something must be done to you. Now what sort of business would you like to engage in? Would you like to re-engage in copying for some one?"

"No; I would prefer not to make any change."   200

"Would you like a clerkship in a dry-goods store?"

"There is too much confinement about that. No, I would not like a clerkship; but I am not particular."

"Too much confinement," I cried, "why, you keep yourself confined all the time!"

"I would prefer not to take a clerkship," he rejoined, as if to settle that little item at once.

"How would a bar-tender's business suit you? There is no trying of the eye-sight in that." 205

"I would not like it at all; though, as I said before, I am not particular."

His unwonted wordiness inspirited me. I returned to the charge.

"Well, then, would you like to travel through the country collecting bills for the merchants? That would improve your health."

"No, I would prefer to be doing something else."

"How, then, would going as a companion to Europe, to entertain some young gentleman with your conversation — how would that suit you?" 210

"Not at all. It does not strike me that there is anything definite about that. I like to be stationary. But I am not particular."

"Stationary you shall be, then," I cried, now losing all patience, and, for the first time in all my exasperating connection with him, fairly flying into a passion. "If you do not go away from these premises before night, I shall feel bound — indeed, I *am* bound — to — to quit the premises myself!" I rather absurdly concluded, knowing not with what possible threat to try to frighten his immobility into compliance. Despairing of all further efforts, I was precipitately leaving him, when a final thought occurred to me — one which had not been wholly unindulged before.

"Bartleby," said I, in the kindest tone I could assume under such exciting circumstances, "will you go home with me now — not to my office, but my dwelling — and remain there till we can conclude upon some convenient arrangement for you at our leisure? Come, let us start now, right away."

"No: at present I would prefer not to make any change at all."

I answered nothing; but, effectually dodging every one by the suddenness and rapidity of my flight, rushed from the building, ran up Wall Street towards Broadway, and, jumping into the first omnibus, was soon removed from pursuit. As soon as tranquillity returned, I distinctly perceived that I had now done all that I possibly could, both in respect to the demands of the landlord and his tenants, and with regard to my own desire and sense of duty, to benefit Bartleby, and shield him from rude persecution. I now strove to be entirely care-free and quiescent; and my conscience justified me in the attempt; though, indeed, it was not so successful as I could have wished. So fearful was I of being again hunted out by the incensed landlord and his exasperated tenants, that, surrendering my business to Nippers, for a few days, I drove about the upper part of the town and through the suburbs, in my rockaway; crossed over to Jersey City and Hoboken, and paid fugitive visits to Manhattanville and Astoria. In fact, I almost lived in my rockaway for the time.

When again I entered my office, lo, a note from the landlord lay upon the desk. I opened it with trembling hands. It informed me that the writer had sent to the police, and had Bartleby removed to the Tombs as a vagrant. Moreover, since I knew more about him than any one else, he wished me to appear at that place, and make a suitable statement of the facts. These tidings had a conflicting effect upon me. At first I was indignant; but, at last, almost approved. The landlord's energetic, summary disposition, had led him to adopt a procedure which I do not think I would have decided upon myself; and yet, as a last resort, under such peculiar circumstances, it seemed the only plan.

As I afterwards learned, the poor scrivener, when told that he must be conducted to the Tombs, offered not the slightest obstacle, but, in his pale, unmoving way, silently acquiesced.

Some of the compassionate and curious by-standers joined the party; and
headed by one of the constables arm-in-arm with Bartleby, the silent procession filed its way through all the noise, and heat, and joy of the roaring thor-
oughfares at noon.

The same day I received the note, I went to the Tombs, or, to speak more
properly, the Halls of Justice. Seeking the right officer, I stated the purpose
of my call, and was informed that the individual I described was, indeed,
within. I then assured the functionary that Bartleby was a perfectly honest
man, and greatly to be compassionated, however unaccountably eccentric. I
narrated all I knew, and closed by suggesting the idea of letting him remain in
as indulgent confinement as possible, till something less harsh might be
done — though, indeed, I hardly knew what. At all events, if nothing else could
be decided upon, the almshouse must receive him. I then begged to have an
interview.

Being under no disgraceful charge, and quite serene and harmless in all 220
his ways, they had permitted him freely to wander about the prison, and, especially, in the inclosed grass-platted yards thereof. And so I found him there,
standing all alone in the quietest of the yards, his face towards a high wall,
while all around, from the narrow slits of the jail windows, I thought I saw
peering out upon him the eyes of murderers and thieves.

"Bartleby!"

"I know you," he said, without looking round — "and I want nothing to say
to you."

"It was not I that brought you here, Bartleby," said I, keenly pained at his
implied suspicion. "And to you, this should not be so vile a place. Nothing reproachful attaches to you by being here. And see, it is not so sad a place as one
might think. Look, there is the sky, and here is the grass."

"I know where I am," he replied, but would say nothing more, and so I
left him.

As I entered the corridor again, a broad meat-like man, in an apron, accosted 225
me, and, jerking his thumb over his shoulder, said — "Is that your friend?"

"Yes."

"Does he want to starve? If he does, let him live on the prison fare, that's all."

"Who are you?" asked I, not knowing what to make of such an unofficially
speaking person in such a place.

"I am the grub-man. Such gentlemen as have friends here, hire me to provide them with something good to eat."

"Is this so?" said I, turning the turnkey.   230

He said it was.

"Well, then," said I, slipping some silver into the grub-man's hands (for
so they called him), "I want you to give particular attention to my friend there;
let him have the best dinner you can get. And you must be as polite to him as
possible."

"Introduce me, will you?" said the grub-man, looking at me with an expression which seemed to say he was all impatience for an opportunity to give
a specimen of his breeding.

Thinking it would prove of benefit to the scrivener, I acquiesced; and, asking the grub-man his name, went up with him to Bartleby.

"Bartleby, this is a friend; you will find him very useful to you."   235

"Your sarvant, sir, your sarvant," said the grub-man, making a low salutation behind his apron. "Hope you find it pleasant here, sir; nice grounds — cool
apartments — hope you'll stay with us some time — try to make it agreeable.
What will you have for dinner to-day?"

"I prefer not to dine to-day," said Bartleby, turning away. "It would disagree with me; I am unused to dinners." So saying, he slowly moved to the
other side of the inclosure, and took up a position fronting the deadwall.

"How's this?" said the grub-man, addressing me with a stare of astonishment. "He's odd, ain't he?"

"I think he is a little deranged," said I, sadly.

"Deranged? deranged is it? Well, now, upon my word, I thought that   240
friend of yourn was a gentleman forger; they are always pale and genteel-like,
them forgers. I can't help pity 'em — can't help it, sir. Did you know Monroe
Edwards?" he added, touchingly, and paused. Then, laying his hand piteously
on my shoulder, sighed, "he died of consumption at Sing-Sing. So you weren't
acquainted with Monroe?"

"No, I was never socially acquainted with any forgers. But I cannot stop
longer. Look to my friend yonder. You will not lose by it. I will see you again."

Some few days after this, I again obtained admission to the Tombs, and
went through the corridors in quest of Bartleby; but without finding him.

"I saw him coming from his cell not long ago," said a turnkey, "may be he's
gone to loiter in the yards."

So I went in that direction.

"Are you looking for the silent man?" said another turnkey, passing me.   245
"Yonder he lies — sleeping in the yard there. 'Tis not twenty minutes since I saw
him lie down."

The yard was entirely quiet. It was not accessible to the common prisoners. The surrounding walls, of amazing thickness, kept off all sounds behind
them. The Egyptian character of the masonry weighed upon me with its
gloom. But a soft imprisoned turf grew under foot. The heart of the eternal
pyramids, it seemed, wherein, by some strange magic, through the clefts, grass-
seed, dropped by birds, had sprung.

Strangely huddled at the base of the wall, his knees drawn up, and lying
on his side, his head touching the cold stones, I saw the wasted Bartleby. But
nothing stirred. I paused; then went close up to him; stooped over, and saw
that his dim eyes were open; otherwise he seemed profoundly sleeping. Something prompted me to touch him. I felt his hand, when a tingling shiver ran up
my arm and down my spine to my feet.

The round face of the grub-man peered upon me now. "His dinner is
ready. Won't he dine to-day, either? Or does he live without dining?"

"Lives without dining," said I, and closed the eyes.

"Eh! — He's asleep, ain't he?"   250

"With kings and counselors,"° murmured I.

There would seem little need for proceeding further in this history. Imagination will readily supply the meagre recital of poor Bartleby's interment.
But, ere parting with the reader, let me say, that if this little narrative has

---

"*With kings and counselors*": From Job 3:13–14: "then had I been at rest, / With kings and counselors of the earth, / which built desolate places for themselves."

sufficiently interested him, to awaken curiosity as to who Bartleby was, and what manner of life he led prior to the present narrator's making his acquaintance, I can only reply, that in such curiosity I fully share, but am wholly unable to gratify it. Yet here I hardly know whether I should divulge one little item of rumor, which came to my ear a few months after the scrivener's decease. Upon what basis it rested, I could never ascertain; and hence, how true it is I cannot now tell. But, inasmuch as this vague report has not been without a certain suggestive interest to me, however sad, it may prove the same with some others; and so I will briefly mention it. The report was this: that Bartleby had been a subordinate clerk in the Dead Letter Office at Washington, from which he had been suddenly removed by a change in the administration. When I think over this rumor, hardly can I express the emotions which seize me. Dead letters! does it not sound like dead men? Conceive a man by nature and misfortune prone to a pallid hopelessness, can any business seem more fitted to heighten it than that of continually handling these dead letters, and assorting them for the flames? For by the cart-load they are annually burned. Sometimes from out the folded paper the pale clerk takes a ring — the finger it was meant for, perhaps, moulders in the grave; a bank-note sent in swiftest charity — he whom it would relieve, nor eats nor hungers any more; pardon for those who died despairing; hope for those who died unhoping; good tidings for those who died stifled by unrelieved calamities. On errands of life, these letters speed to death.

Ah, Bartleby! Ah, humanity!

CONSIDERATIONS FOR CRITICAL THINKING AND WRITING

1. FIRST RESPONSE. How does the lawyer's description of himself serve to characterize him? Why is it significant that he is a lawyer? Are his understandings and judgments about Bartleby and himself always sound?

2. Why do you think Turkey, Nippers, and Ginger Nut are introduced to the reader before Bartleby?

3. Describe Bartleby's physical characteristics. How is his physical description a foreshadowing of what happens to him?

4. How does Bartleby's "I would prefer not to" affect the routine of the lawyer and his employees?

5. What is the significance of the subtitle: "A Story of Wall Street"?

6. Who is the protagonist? Whose story is it?

7. Does the lawyer change during the story? Does Bartleby? Who is the antagonist?

8. What motivates Bartleby's behavior? Why do you think Melville withholds the information about the Dead Letter Office until the end of the story? Does this background adequately explain Bartleby?

9. Does Bartleby have any lasting impact on the lawyer?

10. Do you think Melville sympathizes more with Bartleby or with the lawyer?

11. Describe the lawyer's changing attitudes toward Bartleby.

12. Consider how this story could be regarded as a kind of protest with nonnegotiable demands.

13. Discuss the story's humor and how it affects your response to Bartleby.

14. Trace your emotional reaction to Bartleby as he is revealed in the story.

1. Compare Bartleby's withdrawal from life with that of the protagonist in Gail Godwin's "A Sorrowful Woman" (p. 33). Why does each character choose death?

2. How is Melville's use of Bartleby's experience in the Dead Letter Office similar to Nathaniel Hawthorne's use of Brown's forest encounter with the devil in "Young Goodman Brown" (p. 310)? Why is each experience crucial to an understanding of what informs the behavior of these characters?

3. Discuss the significant parallels between "Bartleby, the Scrivener" and Franz Kafka's "A Hunger Artist" (p. 528), both stories about self-denial and isolation. Explain whether you think Bartleby's and the hunger artist's responses to their environments are similar or different.

PERSPECTIVES ON MELVILLE

NATHANIEL HAWTHORNE (1804–1864)

On Herman Melville's Philosophic Stance   *1856*

[Melville] stayed with us from Tuesday till Thursday; and, on the intervening day, we took a pretty long walk together, and sat down in a hollow among the sand hills (sheltering ourselves from the high, cool wind) and smoked a cigar. Melville, as he always does, began to reason of Providence and futurity, and of everything that lies beyond human ken, and informed me that he had "pretty much made up his mind to be annihilated"; but still he does not seem to rest in that anticipation; and, I think, will never rest until he gets hold of a definite belief. It is strange how he persists — and has persisted ever since I knew him, and probably long before — in wandering to-and-fro over these deserts, as dismal and monotonous as the sand hills amid which we were sitting. He can neither believe, nor be comfortable in his unbelief; and he is too honest and courageous not to try to do one or the other. If he were a religious man, he would be one of the most truly religious and reverential; he has a very high and noble nature, and better worth immortality than most of us.

                                                        From *The American Notebooks*

1. How does this description of Melville shed light on the central concerns of "Bartleby, the Scrivener"?

2. Which side does Hawthorne seem to be on — "belief" or "unbelief"? Why?

3. Compare Hawthorne's description with Melville's view of Hawthorne (p. 364). What attitudes about life do they share?

4. Write an essay about the issue of "belief" and "unbelief" in "Bartleby, the Scrivener" and Ernest Hemingway's "Soldier's Home" (p. 145).

DAN MCCALL (B. 1940)
On the Lawyer's Character
in "Bartleby, the Scrivener"   1989

The overwhelming majority of the Bartleby Industry reads the narrator of the story in a way that is not only different from mine but quite incompatible with mine. Every virtue I see in the man, they see as a vice; where I see his strength, they see his weakness; what I see as his genuine responsiveness, they see as his cold self-absorption. Some critics read the story as I do, but we are in a distinct minority. There are several reasons this should be so, and I think I understand at least some of them, but first I should like to present as fairly as I can the majority opinion.

Robert Weisbuch, who has said the Lawyer is Charles Dickens, refers to the Lawyer as "unnatural," "anti-natural," "lifeless," "self-satisfied," "pompous," and "rationalizing." The Lawyer "investigates Bartleby but refuses authentic emotional commitment in so doing," and "Bartleby rightly refuses to credit the Lawyer's false commitment." The Lawyer is guilty of "toadyism" and his final heartbroken outburst, "Ah, Bartleby! Ah, humanity!" is no more than "a someways hollow and unfeeling exclamation."[1] Another critic calls the Lawyer a "smug fool" who is "terribly unkind to a very sick man."[2] I had always thought of the Lawyer as a kind of stand-in for us, a figure we could identify with as we struggled to understand Bartleby. On the contrary, the narrator is "deficient in humanity and quite obtuse towards human beings." I must have had it backwards, for "surely this was Melville's intention: to have his reader *not* sympathize with the Lawyer, *not* to identify with him, *not* to put himself in the Lawyer's place" (*his* italics, not mine).[3] Another critic says, "The narrator attains new heights of vague sentimentality rather than a peak of awareness in his climactic and highly revealing sigh: 'Ah, Bartleby! Ah, humanity!'" This reader provides dismissive certainty in answering the question

> Who then is Melville's narrator? He is the sort of man one tends to find in high places: the snug man whose worldly success has convinced him that this is the "best of all possible worlds," and whose virtues cluster around a "prudential" concern for maintaining his own situation. The narrator can never fully understand or truly befriend Bartleby because the narrator is simply too complacent, both philosophically and morally, to sympathize with human dissatisfaction and despair.[4]

Still another reader tells us the Lawyer's commentary "rings with blasphemy" and demonstrates "grotesque manifestations of diseased conscience."[5]

---

[1] Robert Weisbuch, "Melville's 'Bartleby' and the Dead Letter of Charles Dickens," *Atlantic Double-Cross: American Literature and British Influence in the Age of Emerson* (Chicago: University of Chicago Press, 1986), pp. 44, 45–47.
[2] David Shusterman, "The 'Reader Fallacy' and 'Bartleby, the Scrivener,'" *New England Quarterly*, 45 (March 1972), 118–24, pp. 122–23.
[3] Ibid., p. 121.
[4] Allan Emery, "The Alternatives of Melville's 'Bartleby,'" *Nineteenth-Century Fiction*, 31 (1976), 170–87, pp. 186–87.
[5] William Bysshe Stein, "Bartleby: The Christian Conscience," in *Melville Annual 1965, A Symposium: "Bartleby, the Scrivener,"* ed. Howard P. Vincent (Kent, Ohio: Kent State University Press, 1966), p. 107.

Authority is the enemy here. In the extended quotation just above it is taken for granted that the "sort of man one tends to find in high places" is superficial and selfish. Worldly success is bad for the character. The Lawyer has to be bad, or he wouldn't be in an office on Wall Street. Hershel Parker tells us that "our ultimate opinion" of the Lawyer "is not contempt so much as bleak astonishment at his secure blindness. With a bitterer irony than the narrator is capable of, we murmur something like 'Ah, narrator! Ah, humanity!' In his self-consciously eloquent sequel, after all, the lawyer has merely made his last cheap purchase of a 'delicious self-approval.'" Parker maintains that when "this easy-conscienced" man speaks of kings and counselors, "he is experiencing a comfortable, self-indulgent variety of melancholy"; when he quotes words from the Book of Job he does so "with prideful aptness," and "characteristically perverts them from profound lament to sonorous urbanity."[6]

This last feature of Parker's argument is interesting to me because it reminds me of the first time I read the story, at eighteen. I was overwhelmed by the discovery that Bartleby had died, and I didn't know that "With kings and counselors" was a quotation from the Book of Job. The phrase "With kings and counselors" seemed to me majestic and solemn and final. That "murmured I" put a deep hush around it. But it never occurred to me that the man who said those words was "easy-conscienced" or "self-indulgent" or the sort of man who "characteristically perverts" a "profound lament to sonorous urbanity." The figure of Bartleby seemed so weird and funny and painful, his death at once inevitable and shocking, that I did not see it as an occasion for the man who was telling me about it to make a "last cheap purchase" of "delicious self-approval." I trusted that Lawyer.

Thirty years later, I still do. He seems to me extremely intelligent, whimsical and ironic, generous, self-aware, passionate, and thoroughly competent.

From *The Silence of Bartleby*

[6] Hershel Parker, "The Sequel in 'Bartleby,'" in *Bartleby the Inscrutable: A Collection of Commentary on Herman Melville's Tale "Bartleby, the Scrivener,"* ed. M. Thomas Inge (Hamden, Conn.: Archon Books, 1979), 159–65, pp. 163–64.

CONSIDERATIONS FOR CRITICAL THINKING AND WRITING

1. How does McCall characterize the "majority opinion" on the lawyer's character? What is his opinion of the lawyer?

2. How does McCall's opinion of the lawyer compare with Hawthorne's opinion of Herman Melville in the preceding Perspective (p. 138)?

3. Write an essay explaining whether you find the "majority opinion" or McCall's view of the lawyer more convincing.

LEON ROOKE (B. 1934)

Born in North Carolina, Leon Rooke earned a B.A. at the University of North Carolina and was a writer in residence there in 1965. In 1969 he moved to Victoria, British Columbia, where his career has flourished. Among his awards are the Canada-Australia Literary Prize and the Governor General's Award for fiction. In 1984 he was writer-in-residence at the University of Toronto. The author of more than ten books, his novels include *Fat Woman* (1980), *The Magician in Love* (1981), and *Shakespeare's Dog* (1983). Among his collections of short stories are *The Broad Back of the Angel* (1977), *The Love Parlour* (1977), *Death Suite* (1981), *A Bolt of White Cloth* (1984), and *Who Do You Love?* (1992). Rooke is particularly well known for his rich use of language, strong female characters, and ironic humor.

Sweethearts   1996

Hey, Sweetheart, come on over. She calls me on the phone, that's what she says. Hey, Sweetheart, come on over. I say, It's late, baby, you come over here. So we argue about it. She says, But I was over there last week. I was over there last night. Wasn't I over there last night? We argue about that. I say, Was it last night? Are you sure it was last night? She says, Wait now, I could be wrong. I could be. What's your name anyhow? That's what she says: What's your name anyhow? And we argue about my name. We argue about her name. We argue about everything under the sun. She says, If you are going to argue I don't want to talk to you. I say, Talk to me. I've got to talk to someone. She says, Sweetheart, now you're talking. I'll be right over. I'll hop into a cab. Okay, I think, that settles it. She's coming. Don't get in a sweat. She'll be here pronto. Then I say, Will you spend all night? Will you? Can I count on that? And she says, Are you kidding? All night? Have you lost your senses? What about my kids? What about my toothbrush? What about all the nights I did spend all night and nothing ever happened? What about that? I say, Hold on. Hold on, I say, I think you've got the wrong party. Let's check that number again. Do we know each other? She says, If that's how you feel I'm not coming. She says, If that's how you feel you can call somebody else. I say, what I say, is who called who? What I say is I don't recall ringing your number. What I say is, Sweetheart, this isn't working out. She says, Whose fault is that, if I may ask you? Who started this? You always want to argue. Why do you always want to argue? You'd better get straight with yourself before you want to start making time with a woman like me. Am I making time? I say, Is that what I'm doing? I say, How much time am I making if you come over and nothing happens? She says, Did I say that? Did I? So we argue about what happens and what does not happen. We argue at considerable length about that. We are shouting into the phone and she says, Why are you shouting? Stop shouting, get a grip on yourself. But things have gone too far, I can't get a grip on myself. I can't get straight with myself. She says, I know. I know, that has always been your trouble. I say, What trouble? I wasn't in any trouble until I met you. She says, You're right. I don't doubt that for a minute. She says, I'm always trouble, I've been trouble for every man I've ever known. What I say is, No, you haven't. I say, You're a life saver, that's what you are. Thank you, she says. Thank you. It is very nice of you to say that. Even if you don't mean it, it is nice of you to say so. I mean it, I say. You've saved my life a thousand times. She says, If only I could believe that. If only we could start over. I say, Every time I see you is a new start, every time, even if nothing happens. She says, Oh God, what can I do? What can I say? When I say nothing happens I don't mean it the way you think I mean it. My head's in a whirl, that's what she says. I say, Tell me about it. She says, I can't talk now. She says, I've got to see you, what I want to say can't be said on the phone. We're in deep water, she says. How did we get in such deep water? I say, Let's talk about it. Okay, she says, okay. I'll be right over and we can talk about it, although that's all we do, is talk about it. Do you really think we should? What I say is, Yes, yes, we owe it to each other. Fine, she says, I'm on my way. Shall I pack my toothbrush? Shall I stay the night? Can we have a nice friendly dinner somewhere? The truth is I haven't eaten, I haven't eaten in days and days. I say, Same here. I say, God, I'm starving let's do that, let's eat somewhere. She says, Good, good, I can't wait to see you. I think to myself, God, what a shot, what a woman! I can't wait to see her, that's what I think. Wear a jacket, she says, it's cold, it's very cold out there. You too, I say. Dress warmly, don't let the cold get next to your bones. She says, You know what I want next to my bones, don't you, don't you, you've always known. I say, Hurry, let's not waste any time, why have we been wasting all this time? I'm on my way, she says, I'm flying out of the door. Me, too, I say, goodbye for now. Goodbye, she says, kiss-kiss, she says, into the phone. What a woman, I think, why are you always fighting with her? No fighting, I say, any more. Get straight with yourself, Jack, go to a nice restaurant, hold her hands, look into her eyes, get lost inside her eyes. That's the ticket, son, you're in good shape now, you're trim and fit and ready for anything. So I go down and I wait for her cab, I wait for it. She's my sweetheart, I am hers. We are sweethearts to each other, we are lovers through thick and thin. She'll be here soon, any minute now, any second now. You believe me, don't you? Accept it, every word is true. There's her cab now, turning the corner, a nice yellow one. I can see the driver, I can see her in the back seat, black coat up around her ears. Come on now, hurry, hurry it up. We've got everything, we've got all we need. What you have here, in this neighborhood, on this freezing night, are two people, two sweethearts, who utterly understand each other.

CONSIDERATIONS FOR CRITICAL THINKING AND WRITING

1. FIRST RESPONSE. What effect does this long unconventional paragraph have on you? How does the format make your reading experience different than it would be in conventional dialogue and paragraphs?

2. Characterize the two "sweethearts." Are they like each other? Different? Likable? Irritating?

3. At the end the narrator says, "We are sweethearts to each other, we are lovers through thick and thin" and then adds "You believe me, don't you?" What effect does this sudden direct address of the reader have on your view of their relationship?

4. Does "Sweethearts" have a conflict? Is there a resolution?

5. Explain whether you think this story ends happily or unhappily.

6. Try writing physical descriptions of these characters that you think reflect their sensibilities.

CONNECTIONS TO OTHER SELECTIONS

1. Read A. L. Bader's "Nothing Happens in Modern Short Stories" (p. 95). To what extent are Bader's comments relevant to "Sweethearts"?

2. In an essay compare the narrator's tone in "Sweethearts" with that in Fae Myenne Ng's "A Red Sweater" (p. 235).

5

Setting

Setting is the context in which the action of a story occurs. The major elements of setting are time, place, and social environment that frame the characters. These elements establish the world in which the characters act. In most stories they also serve as more than backgrounds and furnishings. If we are sensitive to the contexts provided by setting, we are better able to understand the behavior of the characters and the significance of their actions. It may be tempting to read quickly through a writer's descriptions and ignore the details of the setting once a geographic location and a historic period are established. But if you read a story so impatiently, the significance of the setting may slip by you. That kind of reading is similar to traveling on interstate highways: a lot of ground gets covered, but very little is seen along the way.

Settings can be used to evoke a mood or atmosphere that will prepare the reader for what is to come. In "Young Goodman Brown" (p. 310), Nathaniel Hawthorne has his pious protagonist leave his wife and village one night to keep an appointment in a New England forest near the site of the seventeenth-century witch trials. This is Hawthorne's description of Brown entering the forest:

> He had taken a dreary road, darkened by all the gloomiest trees of the forest, which barely stood aside to let the narrow path creep through, and closed immediately behind. It was all as lonely as could be; and there is this peculiarity in such a solitude, that the traveler knows not who may be concealed by the innumerable trunks and the thick boughs overhead; so that with lonely footsteps he may yet be passing through an unseen multitude.

The atmosphere established in this descriptive setting is somber and threatening. Careful reading reveals that the forest is not simply the woods; it is a moral wilderness, where anything can happen.

If we ask why a writer chooses to include certain details in a work, then we are likely to make connections that relate the details to some larger purpose, such as the story's meaning. The final scene in Godwin's "A Sorrowful Woman" (p. 33) occurs in the spring, an ironic time for the action to be set because instead of rebirth for the protagonist there is only death. There is usually a reason for placing a story in a particular time or location. Katherine Mansfield has the protagonist in "Miss Brill" (p. 258) discover her loneliness and old age in a French vacation town, a lively atmosphere that serves as a cruel contrast to an elderly (and foreign) lady's painful realization.

Melville's "Bartleby, the Scrivener" (p. 113) takes on meaning as Bartleby's "dead-wall reveries" begin to reflect his shattered vision of life. He is surrounded by walls. A folding screen separates him from others in the office; he is isolated. The office window faces walls; there is no view to relieve the deadening work. Bartleby faces a wall at the prison where he dies; the final wall is death. As the subtitle indicates, this is "A Story of Wall Street." Unless the geographic location or the physical details of a story are used merely as necessary props, they frequently shed light on character and action. All offices have walls, but Melville transforms the walls into an antagonist that represents the limitations Bartleby sees and feels all around him but does not speak of.

Time, location, and the physical features of a setting can all be relevant to the overall purpose of a story. So too is the social environment in which the characters are developed. In Faulkner's "A Rose for Emily" (p. 72) the changes in her southern town serve as a foil for Emily's tenacious hold on a lost past. She is regarded as a "fallen monument," as old-fashioned and peculiar as the "stubborn and coquettish decay" of her house. Neither she nor her house fits into the modern changes that are paving and transforming the town. Without the social context, this story would be mostly an account of a bizarre murder rather than an exploration of the conflicts Faulkner associated with the changing South. Setting enlarges the meaning of Emily's actions.

Some settings have traditional associations that are closely related to the action of a story. Adventure and romance, for example, flourish in the fertile soil of most exotic settings: the film version of Isak Dinesen's novel *Out of Africa* is a lush visual demonstration of how setting can play a significant role in generating the audience's expectations of love and excitement.

Sometimes, writers reverse traditional expectations. When a tranquil garden is the scene for a horrendously bloody murder, we are as much taken by surprise as the victim is. In John Updike's "A & P" (p. 576) there seems to be little possibility for heroic action in so mundane a place as a supermarket, but the setting turns out to be appropriate for the important, unexpected decision the protagonist makes about life. Traditional associations are also disrupted in "A Sorrowful Woman," in which Godwin disassociates home from the safety, security, and comfort usually connected with it by presenting the protagonist's home as a deadly trap. By drawing on traditional associations, a writer can fulfill or disrupt a reader's expectations about a setting in order to complement the elements of the story.

Not every story uses setting as a means of revealing mood, idea, meaning, or characters' actions. Some stories have no particularly significant setting. It is entirely possible to envision a story in which two characters speak to each other about a conflict between them and little or no mention is made of the time or place they inhabit. If, however, a shift in setting would make a serious difference to our understanding of a story, then the setting is probably an important element in the work. Consider how different "Bartleby, the Scrivener" would be if it were set in a relaxed, pleasant, sunny town in the South rather than in the grinding, limiting materialism of Wall Street. Bartleby's withdrawal from life would be less comprehensible and meaningful in such a setting. The setting is integral to that story.

The following four stories — Ernest Hemingway's "Soldier's Home," Fay Weldon's "IND AFF, or Out of Love in Sarajevo," Ruth Prawer Jhabvala's "The Englishwoman," and David Updike's "Summer" — include settings that serve to shape their meanings.

ERNEST HEMINGWAY (1899–1961)

In 1918, a year after graduating from high school in Oak Park, Illinois, Ernest Hemingway volunteered as an ambulance driver in World War I. At the Italian front, he was seriously wounded. This experience haunted him and many of the characters in his short stories and novels. *In Our Time* (1925) is a collection of short stories, including "Soldier's Home," that reflect some of Hemingway's own attempts to readjust to life back home after the war. *The Sun Also Rises* (1926), *A Farewell to Arms* (1929), and *For Whom the Bell Tolls* (1940) are also about war and its impact on people's lives. Hemingway courted violence all his life in war, the bullring, the boxing ring, and big game hunting. When he was sixty-two years old and terminally ill with cancer, he committed suicide by shooting himself with a shotgun. "Soldier's Home" takes place in a small town in Oklahoma; the war, however, is never distant from the protagonist's mind as he struggles to come home again.

Soldier's Home   *1925*

Krebs went to the war from a Methodist college in Kansas. There is a picture which shows him among his fraternity brothers, all of them wearing exactly the same height and style collar. He enlisted in the Marines in 1917 and did not return to the United States until the second division returned from the Rhine in the summer of 1919.

There is a picture which shows him on the Rhine with two German girls and another corporal. Krebs and the corporal look too big for their uniforms. The German girls are not beautiful. The Rhine does not show in the picture.

By the time Krebs returned to his home town in Oklahoma the greeting of heroes was over. He came back much too late. The men from the town who had been drafted had all been welcomed elaborately on their return. There had been a great deal of hysteria. Now the reaction had set in. People seemed to think it was rather ridiculous for Krebs to be getting back so late, years after the war was over.

At first Krebs, who had been at Belleau Wood, Soissons, the Champagne, St. Mihiel, and in the Argonne° did not want to talk about the war at all. Later he felt the need to talk but no one wanted to hear about it. His town had heard too many atrocity stories to be thrilled by actualities. Krebs found that to be listened to at all he had to lie, and after he had done this twice he, too, had a reaction against the war and against talking about it. A distaste for everything that had happened to him in the war set in because of the lies he had told. All of the times that had been able to make him feel cool and clear inside himself when he thought of them; the times so long back when he had done the one thing, the only thing for a man to do, easily and naturally, when he might have done something else, now lost their cool, valuable quality and then were lost themselves.

His lies were quite unimportant lies and consisted in attributing to himself 5 things other men had seen, done, or heard of, and stating as facts certain apocryphal incidents familiar to all soldiers. Even his lies were not sensational at the pool room. His acquaintances, who had heard detailed accounts of German women found chained to machine guns in the Argonne forest and who could not comprehend, or were barred by their patriotism from interest in, any German machine gunners who were not chained, were not thrilled by his stories.

Krebs acquired the nausea in regard to experience that is the result of untruth or exaggeration, and when he occasionally met another man who had really been a soldier and they talked a few minutes in the dressing room at a dance he fell into the easy pose of the old soldier among other soldiers: that he had been badly, sickeningly frightened all the time. In this way he lost everything.

During this time, it was late summer, he was sleeping late in bed, getting up to walk down town to the library to get a book, eating lunch at home, reading on the front porch until he became bored, and then walking down through the town to spend the hottest hours of the day in the cool dark of the pool room. He loved to play pool.

In the evening he practiced on his clarinet, strolled down town, read, and went to bed. He was still a hero to his two young sisters. His mother would have given him breakfast in bed if he had wanted it. She often came in when he was in bed and asked him to tell her about the war, but her attention always wandered. His father was noncommittal.

Before Krebs went away to the war he had never been allowed to drive the family motor car. His father was in the real estate business and always wanted the car to be at his command when he required it to take clients out into the

Belleau Wood . . . Argonne: Sites of battles in World War I in which American troops were instrumental in pushing back the Germans.

country to show them a piece of farm property. The car always stood outside the First National Bank building where his father had an office on the second floor. Now, after the war, it was still the same car.

Nothing was changed in the town except that the young girls had grown 10 up. But they lived in such a complicated world of already defined alliances and shifting feuds that Krebs did not feel the energy or the courage to break into it. He liked to look at them, though. There were so many good-looking young girls. Most of them had their hair cut short. When he went away only little girls wore their hair like that or girls that were fast. They all wore sweaters and shirt waists with round Dutch collars. It was a pattern. He liked to look at them from the front porch as they walked on the other side of the street. He liked to watch them walking under the shade of the trees. He liked the round Dutch collars above their sweaters. He liked their silk stockings and flat shoes. He liked their bobbed hair and the way they walked.

When he was in town their appeal to him was not very strong. He did not like them when he saw them in the Greek's ice cream parlor. He did not want them themselves really. They were too complicated. There was something else. Vaguely he wanted a girl but he did not want to have to work to get her. He would have liked to have a girl but he did not want to have to spend a long time getting her. He did not want to get into the intrigue and the politics. He did not want to have to do any courting. He did not want to tell any more lies. It wasn't worth it.

He did not want any consequences. He did not want any consequences ever again. He wanted to live along without consequences. Besides he did not really need a girl. The army had taught him that. It was all right to pose as though you had to have a girl. Nearly everybody did that. But it wasn't true. You did not need a girl. That was the funny thing. First a fellow boasted how girls mean nothing to him, that he never thought of them, that they could not touch him. Then a fellow boasted that he could not get along without girls, that he had to have them all the time, that he could not go to sleep without them.

That was all a lie. It was all a lie both ways. You did not need a girl unless you thought about them. He learned that in the army. Then sooner or later you always got one. When you were really ripe for a girl you always got one. You did not have to think about it. Sooner or later it would come. He had learned that in the army.

Now he would have liked a girl if she had come to him and not wanted to talk. But here at home it was all too complicated. He knew he could never get through it all again. It was not worth the trouble. That was the thing about French girls and German girls. There was not all this talking. You couldn't talk much and you did not need to talk. It was simple and you were friends. He thought about France and then he began to think about Germany. On the whole he had liked Germany better. He did not want to leave Germany. He did not want to come home. Still, he had come home. He sat on the front porch.

He liked the girls that were walking along the other side of the street. He 15 liked the look of them much better than the French girls or the German girls. But the world they were in was not the world he was in. He would like to have one of them. But it was not worth it. They were such a nice pattern. He liked the pattern. It was exciting. But he would not go through all the talking. He did not want one badly enough. He liked to look at them all, though. It was not worth it. Not now when things were getting good again.

He sat there on the porch reading a book on the war. It was a history and he was reading about all the engagements he had been in. It was the most interesting reading he had ever done. He wished there were more maps. He looked forward with a good feeling to reading all the really good histories when they would come out with good detail maps. Now he was really learning about the war. He had been a good soldier. That made a difference.

One morning after he had been home about a month his mother came into his bedroom and sat on the bed. She smoothed her apron.

"I had a talk with your father last night, Harold," she said, "and he is willing for you to take the car out in the evenings."

"Yeah?" said Krebs, who was not fully awake. "Take the car out? Yeah?"

"Yes. Your father has felt for some time that you should be able to take the car out in the evenings whenever you wished but we only talked it over last night." 20

"I'll bet you made him," Krebs said.

"No. It was your father's suggestion that we talk the matter over."

"Yeah. I'll bet you made him," Krebs sat up in bed.

"Will you come down to breakfast, Harold?" his mother said.

"As soon as I get my clothes on," Krebs said. 25

His mother went out of the room and he could hear her frying something downstairs while he washed, shaved, and dressed to go down into the dining-room for breakfast. While he was eating breakfast his sister brought in the mail.

"Well, Hare," she said. "You old sleepyhead. What do you ever get up for?"

Krebs looked at her. He liked her. She was his best sister.

"Have you got the paper?" he asked.

She handed him the Kansas City *Star* and he shucked off its brown wrapper and opened it to the sporting page. He folded the *Star* open and propped it against the water pitcher with his cereal dish to steady it, so he could read while he ate. 30

"Harold," his mother stood in the kitchen doorway, "Harold, please don't muss up the paper. Your father can't read his *Star* if it's been mussed."

"I won't muss it," Krebs said.

His sister sat down at the table and watched him while he read.

"We're playing indoor over at school this afternoon," she said. "I'm going to pitch."

"Good," said Krebs. "How's the old wing?" 35

"I can pitch better than lots of the boys. I tell them all you taught me. The other girls aren't much good."

"Yeah?" said Krebs.

"I tell them all you're my beau. Aren't you my beau, Hare?"

"You bet."

"Couldn't your brother really be your beau just because he's your brother?" 40

"I don't know."

"Sure you know. Couldn't you be my beau, Hare, if I was old enough and if you wanted to?"

"Sure. You're my girl now."

"Am I really your girl?"

"Sure." 45

"Do you love me?"

"Uh, huh."

"Will you love me always?"

"Sure."

"Will you come over and watch me play indoor?" 50

"Maybe."

"Aw, Hare, you don't love me. If you loved me, you'd want to come over and watch me play indoor."

Krebs's mother came into the dining-room from the kitchen. She carried a plate with two fried eggs and some crisp bacon on it and a plate of buckwheat cakes.

"You run along, Helen," she said. "I want to talk to Harold."

She put the eggs and bacon down in front of him and brought in a jug of 55 maple syrup for the buckwheat cakes. Then she sat down across the table from Krebs.

"I wish you'd put down the paper a minute, Harold," she said.

Krebs took down the paper and folded it.

"Have you decided what you are going to do yet, Harold?" his mother said, taking off her glasses.

"No," said Krebs.

"Don't you think it's about time?" His mother did not say this in a mean 60 way. She seemed worried.

"I hadn't thought about it," Krebs said.

"God has some work for everyone to do," his mother said. "There can be no idle hands in His Kingdom."

"I'm not in His Kingdom," Krebs said.

"We are all of us in His Kingdom."

Krebs felt embarrassed and resentful as always. 65

"I've worried about you so much, Harold," his mother went on. "I know the temptations you must have been exposed to. I know how weak men are. I know what your own dear grandfather, my own father, told us about the Civil War and I have prayed for you. I pray for you all day long, Harold."

Krebs looked at the bacon fat hardening on his plate.

"Your father is worried, too," his mother went on. "He thinks you have lost your ambition, that you haven't got a definite aim in life. Charley Simmons, who is just your age, has a good job and is going to be married. The boys are all settling down; they're all determined to get somewhere; you can see that boys like Charley Simmons are on their way to being really a credit to the community."

Krebs said nothing.

"Don't look that way, Harold," his mother said. "You know we love you 70 and I want to tell you for your own good how matters stand. Your father does not want to hamper your freedom. He thinks you should be allowed to drive the car. If you want to take some of the nice girls out riding with you, we are only too pleased. We want you to enjoy yourself. But you are going to have to settle down to work, Harold. Your father doesn't care what you start in at. All work is honorable as he says. But you've got to make a start at something. He asked me to speak to you this morning and then you can stop in and see him at his office."

"Is that all?" Krebs said.

"Yes. Don't you love your mother, dear boy?"

"No," Krebs said.

His mother looked at him across the table. Her eyes were shiny. She started crying.

"I don't love anybody," Krebs said.   75

It wasn't any good. He couldn't tell her, he couldn't make her see it. It was silly to have said it. He had only hurt her. He went over and took hold of her arm. She was crying with her head in her hands.

"I didn't mean it," he said. "I was just angry at something. I didn't mean I didn't love you."

His mother went on crying. Krebs put his arm on her shoulder.

"Can't you believe me, mother?"

His mother shook her head.   80

"Please, please, mother. Please believe me."

"All right," his mother said chokily. She looked up at him. "I believe you, Harold."

Krebs kissed her hair. She put her face up to him.

"I'm your mother," she said. "I held you next to my heart when you were a tiny baby."

Krebs felt sick and vaguely nauseated.   85

"I know, Mummy," he said. "I'll try and be a good boy for you."

"Would you kneel and pray with me, Harold?" his mother asked.

They knelt down beside the dining-room table and Krebs's mother prayed.

"Now, you pray, Harold," she said.

"I can't," Krebs said.   90

"Try, Harold."

"I can't."

"Do you want me to pray for you?"

"Yes."

So his mother prayed for him and then they stood up and Krebs kissed his 95
mother and went out of the house. He had tried so to keep his life from being complicated. Still, none of it had touched him. He had felt sorry for his mother and she had made him lie. He would go to Kansas City and get a job and she would feel all right about it. There would be one more scene maybe before he got away. He would not go down to his father's office. He would miss that one. He wanted his life to go smoothly. It had just gotten going that way. Well, that was all over now, anyway. He would go over to the schoolyard and watch Helen play indoor baseball.

Considerations for Critical Thinking and Writing

1. FIRST RESPONSE. The title, "Soldier's Home," focuses on the setting. Do you have a clear picture of Krebs's home? Describe it, filling in missing details from your associations of home, Krebs's routine, or anything else you can use.

2. What does the photograph of Krebs, the corporal, and the German girls reveal?

3. Belleau Wood, Soissons, the Champagne, St. Mihiel, and the Argonne were the sites of fierce and bloody fighting. What effect have these battles had

on Krebs? Why do you think he won't talk about them to the people at home?

4. Why does Krebs avoid complications and consequences? How has the war changed his attitudes toward work and women? How is his hometown different from Germany and France? What is the conflict in the story?

5. Why do you think Hemingway refers to the protagonist as Krebs rather than Harold? What is the significance of his sister calling him "Hare"?

6. How does Krebs's mother embody the community's values? What does Krebs think of those values?

7. Why can't Krebs pray with his mother?

8. What is the resolution to Krebs's conflict?

9. Comment on the appropriateness of the story's title.

10. Explain how Krebs's war experiences are present throughout the story even though we get no details about them.

11. Perhaps, after having been away from home for a time, you have returned to find yourself feeling alienated from your family or friends. Describe your experience. What caused the change?

CONNECTIONS TO OTHER SELECTIONS

1. Contrast the attitudes toward patriotism implicit in this story with those in Yukio Mishima's "Patriotism" (p. 593). How do the stories' settings help to account for the differences between them?

2. How might Krebs's rejection of his community's values be related to Sammy's relationship to his supermarket job in John Updike's "A & P" (p. 576)? What details does Updike use to make the setting in "A & P" a comic, though nonetheless serious, version of Krebs's hometown?

3. Explain how the violent details that Tim O'Brien uses to establish the setting in "How to Tell a True War Story" (p. 555) can be considered representative of the kinds of horrors that haunt Krebs after he returns home.

PERSPECTIVES

E. E. CUMMINGS (1894–1962)
my sweet old etcetera   *1926*

my sweet old etcetera
aunt lucy during the recent

war could and what
is more did tell you just
what everybody was fighting   5

for,
my sister

isabel created hundreds
(and

hundreds) of socks not to   10
mention shirts fleaproof earwarmers

etcetera wristers etcetera, my

mother hoped that

i would die etcetera
bravely of course my father used   15
to become hoarse talking about how it was
a privilege and if only he
could meanwhile my

self etcetera lay quietly
in the deep mud et   20

cetera
(dreaming,
et
   cetera,of
Your smile
eyes knees and of your Etcetera)   25

CONSIDERATIONS FOR CRITICAL THINKING AND WRITING

1. Compare and contrast the narrator's view of the home front with Krebs's in "Soldier's Home." To what extent does he sound like Krebs? Are there any significant differences between the narrator's voice and Krebs's?

2. Write an essay on images of home in "my sweet old etcetera" and "Soldier's Home." Consider how the setting is used in each work to suggest the nature of the conflict.

ERNEST HEMINGWAY (1899–1961)
On What Every Writer Needs   *1954*

The most essential gift for a good writer is a built-in, shock-proof, shit detector. This is the writer's radar and all great writers have had it.

    From *Writers at Work: The Paris Review Interviews* (Second Series)

CONSIDERATIONS FOR CRITICAL THINKING AND WRITING

1. Hemingway is typically forthright here, but it is tempting to dismiss his point as simply humorous. Take him seriously. What does he insist a good writer must be able to do?

2. How might Krebs in Hemingway's "Soldier's Home" (p. 145) be seen as having a similar kind of "shit detector" and "radar"?

3. Try writing a pithy, quotable statement that makes an observation about reading or writing.

Fay Weldon (b. 1933)

Born in England and raised in New Zealand, Fay Weldon graduated from St. Andrew's University in Scotland. She wrote advertising copy for various companies and was a propaganda writer for the British Foreign Office before turning to fiction. She has written novels, short stories, plays, and radio scripts. In 1971 her script for an episode of "Upstairs, Downstairs" won an award from the Society of Film and Television Arts. She has written more than a score of novels, including *The Fat Woman's Joke* (1967), *Down Among the Women* (1971), *Praxis* (1978), *The Life and Loves of a She-Devil* (1983), and *Life Force* (1991), and an equal number of plays and scripts. Her collections of short stories include *Moon Over Minneapolis* (1992) and *Wicked Women* (American edition, 1997). Weldon often uses ironic humor to portray carefully drawn female characters coming to terms with the facts of their lives.

IND AFF   1988
or Out of Love in Sarajevo

This is a sad story. It has to be. It rained in Sarajevo, and we had expected fine weather.

The rain filled up Sarajevo's pride, two footprints set into a pavement which mark the spot where the young assassin Princip stood to shoot the Archduke Franz Ferdinand and his wife. (Don't forget his wife: everyone forgets his wife, the archduchess.) That was in the summer of 1914. Sarajevo is a pretty town, Balkan style, mountain-rimmed. A broad, swift, shallow river runs through its center, carrying the mountain snow away, arched by many bridges. The one nearest the two footprints has been named the Princip Bridge. The young man is a hero in these parts. Not only does he bring in the tourists — look, look, the spot, the very spot! — but by his action, as everyone knows, he lit a spark which fired the timber which caused World War I which crumbled the Austro-Hungarian Empire, the crumbling of which made modern Yugoslavia possible. Forty million dead (or was it thirty?) but who cares? So long as he loved his country.

The river, they say, can run so shallow in the summer it's known derisively as "the wet road." Today, from what I could see through the sheets of falling rain, it seemed full enough. Yugoslavian streets are always busy — no one stays home if they can help it (thus can an indecent shortage of housing space create a sociable nation) and it seemed as if by common consent a shield of bobbing umbrellas had been erected two meters high to keep the rain off the streets. It just hadn't worked around Princip's corner.

"Come all this way," said Peter, who was a professor of classical history, "and you can't even see the footprints properly, just two undistinguished puddles." Ah, but I loved him. I shivered for his disappointment. He was supervising my thesis on varying concepts of morality and duty in the early Greek States as evidenced in their poetry and drama. I was dependent upon him for my academic future. He said I had a good mind but not a first-class mind and somehow I didn't take it as an insult. I had a feeling first-class minds weren't all that good in bed.

Sarajevo is in Bosnia, in the center of Yugoslavia, that grouping of un- 5 likely states, that distillation of languages into the phonetic reasonableness of Serbo-Croatian. We'd sheltered from the rain in an ancient mosque in Serbian Belgrade; done the same in a monastery in Croatia; now we spent a wet couple of days in Sarajevo beneath other people's umbrellas. We planned to go on to Montenegro, on the coast, where the fish and the artists come from, to swim and lie in the sun, and recover from the exhaustion caused by the sexual and moral torments of the last year. It couldn't possibly go on raining forever. Could it? Satellite pictures showed black clouds swishing gently all over Europe, over the Balkans, into Asia—practically all the way from Moscow to London, in fact. It wasn't that Peter and myself were being singled out. No. It was raining on his wife, too, back in Cambridge.

Peter was trying to decide, as he had been for the past year, between his wife and myself as his permanent life partner. To this end we had gone away, off the beaten track, for a holiday; if not with his wife's blessing, at least with her knowledge. Were we really, truly suited? We had to be sure, you see, that this was more than just any old professor-student romance; that it was the Real Thing, because the longer the indecision went on the longer Mrs. Piper would be left dangling in uncertainty and distress. They had been married for twenty-four years; they had stopped loving each other a long time ago, of course—but there would be a fearful personal and practical upheaval entailed if he decided to leave permanently and shack up, as he put it, with me. Which I certainly wanted him to do. I loved him. And so far I was winning hands down. It didn't seem much of a contest at all, in fact. I'd been cool and thin and informed on the seat next to him in a Zagreb theater (Mrs. Piper was sweaty and only liked telly); was now eager and anxious for social and political instruction in Sarajevo (Mrs. Piper spat in the face of knowledge, he'd once told me); and planned to be lissome (and I thought topless but I hadn't quite decided: this might be the area where the age difference showed) while I splashed and shrieked like a bathing belle in the shallows of the Montenegrin coast. (Mrs. Piper was a swimming coach: I imagined she smelt permanently of chlorine.)

In fact so far as I could see, it was no contest at all between his wife and myself. But Peter liked to luxuriate in guilt and indecision. And I loved him with an inordinate affection.

Princip's prints are a meter apart, placed as a modern cop on a training shoot-out would place his feet—the left in front at a slight outward angle, the right behind, facing forward. There seemed great energy focused here. Both hands on the gun, run, stop, plant the feet, aim, fire! I could see the footprints well enough, in spite of Peter's complaint. They were clear enough to me.

We went to a restaurant for lunch, since it was too wet to do what we loved to do: that is, buy bread, cheese, sausage, wine, and go off somewhere in our hired car, into the woods or the hills, and picnic and make love. It was a private restaurant—Yugoslavia went over to a mixed capitalist-communist economy years back, so you get either the best or worst of both systems, depending on your mood—that is to say, we knew we would pay more but be given a choice. We chose the wild boar.

"Probably ordinary pork soaked in red cabbage water to darken it," said   10
Peter. He was not in a good mood.

Cucumber salad was served first.

"Everything in this country comes with cucumber salad," complained
Peter. I noticed I had become used to his complaining. I supposed that when
you had been married a little you simply wouldn't hear it. He was forty-six and
I was twenty-five.

"They grow a lot of cucumber," I said.

"If they can grow cucumbers," Peter then asked, "why can't they grow
mange-tout?"° It seemed a why-can't-they-eat-cake sort of argument to me, but
not knowing enough about horticulture not to be outflanked if I debated the
point, I moved the subject on to safer ground.

"I suppose Princip's action couldn't really have started World War I," I re-   15
marked. "Otherwise, what a thing to have on your conscience! One little shot
and the deaths of thirty million."

"Forty," he corrected me. Though how they reckon these things and get
them right I can't imagine. "Of course he didn't start the war. That's just a
simple tale to keep the children quiet. It takes more than an assassination to
start a war. What happened was that the buildup of political and economic
tensions in the Balkans was such that it had to find some release."

"So it was merely the shot that lit the spark that fired the timber that
started the war, et cetera?"

"Quite," he said. "World War I would have had to have started sooner or
later."

"A bit later or a bit sooner," I said, "might have made the difference of a
million or so; if it was you on the battlefield in the mud and the rain you'd notice; exactly when they fired the starting-pistol; exactly when they blew the
final whistle. Is that what they do when a war ends; blow a whistle? So that
everyone just comes in from the trenches."

But he wasn't listening. He was parting the flesh of the soft collapsed   20
orangey-red pepper which sat in the middle of his cucumber salad; he was
carefully extracting the pips. His nan had once told him they could never be digested, would stick inside and do terrible damage. I loved him for his dexterity
and patience with his knife and fork. I'd finished my salad yonks ago, pips and
all. I was hungry. I wanted my wild boar.

Peter might be forty-six, but he was six foot two and grizzled and muscled
with it, in a dark-eyed, intelligent, broad-jawed kind of way. I adored him. I
loved to be seen with him. "Muscular academic, not weedy academic" as my
younger sister Clare once said. "Muscular academic is just a generally superior
human being: everything works well from the brain to the toes. Weedy academic is when there isn't enough vital energy in the person, and the brain
drains all the strength from the other parts." Well, Clare should know. Clare is
only twenty-three, but of the superior human variety kind herself, vividly
pretty, bright and competent — somewhere behind a heavy curtain of vibrant
red hair, which she only parts for effect. She had her first degree at twenty. Now
she's married to a Harvard professor of economics seconded to the United Nations. She can even cook. I gave up competing yonks ago. Though she too is capable of self-deception. I would say her husband was definitely of the weedy

mange-tout: A sugar pea or bean (French).

academic rather than the muscular academic type. And they have to live in Brussels.

The archduke's chauffeur had lost his way, and was parked on the corner trying to recover his nerve when Princip came running out of a café, planted his feet, aimed, and fired. Princip was nineteen — too young to hang. But they sent him to prison for life and, since he had TB to begin with, he only lasted three years. He died in 1918, in an Austrian prison. Or perhaps it was more than TB: perhaps they gave him a hard time, not learning till later, when the Austro-Hungarian Empire collapsed, that he was a hero. Poor Princip, too young to die — like so many other millions. Dying for love of a country.

"I love you," I said to Peter, my living man, progenitor already of three children by his chlorinated, swimming-coach wife.

"How much do you love me?"

"Inordinately! I love you with inordinate affection." It was a joke between us. Ind Aff!   25

"Inordinate affection is a sin," he'd told me. "According to the Wesleyans John Wesley° himself worried about it to such a degree he ended up abbreviating it in his diaries, Ind Aff. He maintained that what he felt for young Sophy, the eighteen-year-old in his congregation, was not Ind Aff, which bears the spirit away from God towards the flesh: he insisted that what he felt was a pure and spiritual, if passionate, concern for her soul."

Peter said now, as we waited for our wild boar, and he picked over his pepper, "Your Ind Aff is my wife's sorrow, that's the trouble." He wanted, I knew, one of the long half-wrangles, half soul-sharings that we could keep going for hours, and led to piercing pains in the heart which could only be made better in bed. But our bedroom at the Hotel Europa was small and dark and looked out into the well of the building — a punishment room if ever there was one. (Reception staff did sometimes take against us.) When Peter had tried to change it in his quasi-Serbo-Croatian, they'd shrugged their Bosnian shoulders and pretended not to understand, so we'd decided to put up with it. I did not fancy pushing hard single beds together — it seemed easier not to have the pain in the heart in the first place. "Look," I said, "this holiday is supposed to be just the two of us, not Mrs. Piper as well. Shall we talk about something else?"

Do not think that the archduke's chauffeur was merely careless, an inefficient chauffeur, when he took the wrong turning. He was, I imagine, in a state of shock, fright, and confusion. There had been two previous attempts on the archduke's life since the cavalcade had entered town. The first was a bomb which got the car in front and killed its driver. The second was a shot fired by none other than young Princip, which had missed. Princip had vanished into the crowd and gone to sit down in a corner café and ordered coffee to calm his nerves. I expect his hand trembled at the best of times — he did have TB. (Not the best choice of assassin, but no doubt those who arrange these things have to make do with what they can get.) The archduke's chauffeur panicked, took the wrong road, realized what he'd done, and stopped to await rescue and instructions just outside the café where Princip sat drinking his coffee.

"What shall we talk about?" asked Peter, in even less of a good mood.

John Wesley (1703–1791): English religious leader and founder of Methodism.

"The collapse of the Austro-Hungarian Empire?" I suggested. "How does 30 an empire collapse? Is there no money to pay the military or the police, so everyone goes home? Or what?" He liked to be asked questions.

"The Hungro-Austrarian Empire," said Peter to me, "didn't so much collapse as fail to exist any more. War destroys social organizations. The same thing happened after World War II. There being no organized bodies left between Moscow and London—and for London read Washington, then as now—it was left to these two to put in their own puppet governments. Yalta, 1944. It's taken the best part of forty-five years for nations of West and East Europe to remember who they are."

"Austro-Hungarian," I said, "not Hungro-Austrarian."

"I didn't say Hungro-Austrarian," he said.

"You did," I said.

"Didn't," he said. "What the hell are they doing about our wild boar? Are 35 they out in the hills shooting it?"

My sister Clare had been surprisingly understanding about Peter. When I worried about him being older, she pooh-poohed it; when I worried about him being married, she said, "Just go for it, sister. If you can unhinge a marriage, it's ripe for unhinging, it would happen sooner or later, it might as well be you. See a catch, go ahead and catch! Go for it!"

Princip saw the archduke's car parked outside, and went for it. Second chances are rare in life: they must be responded to. Except perhaps his second chance was missing in the first place? Should he have taken his cue from fate, and just sat and finished his coffee, and gone home to his mother? But what's a man to do when he loves his country? Fate delivered the archduke into his hands: how could he resist it? A parked car, a uniformed and medaled chest, the persecutor of his country—how could Princip not, believing God to be on his side, but see this as His intervention, push his coffee aside and leap to his feet?

Two waiters stood idly by and watched us waiting for our wild boar. One was young and handsome in a mountainous Bosnian way—flashing eyes, hooked nose, luxuriant black hair, sensuous mouth. He was about my age. He smiled. His teeth were even and white. I smiled back, and instead of the pain in the heart I'd become accustomed to as an erotic sensation, now felt, quite violently, an associated yet different pang which got my lower stomach. The true, the real pain of Ind Aff!

"Fancy him?" asked Peter.

"No," I said. "I just thought if I smiled the wild boar might come quicker." 40

The other waiter was older and gentler: his eyes were soft and kind. I thought he looked at me reproachfully. I could see why. In a world which for once, after centuries of savagery, was finally full of young men, unslaughtered, what was I doing with this man with thinning hair?

"What are you thinking of?" Professor Piper asked me. He liked to be in my head.

"How much I love you," I said automatically, and was finally aware how much I lied. "And about the archduke's assassination," I went on, to cover the kind of tremble in my head as I came to my senses, "and let's not forget his wife, she died too—how can you say World War I would have happened anyway. If Princip hadn't shot the archduke, something else, some undisclosed, unsuspected variable, might have come along and defused the whole political/military situation, and neither World War I nor II ever happened. We'll just never know, will we?"

I had my passport and my travelers' checks with me. (Peter felt it was less confusing if we each paid our own way.) I stood up, and took my raincoat from the peg.

"Where are you going?" he asked, startled.

45

"Home," I said. I kissed the top of his head, where it was balding. It smelt gently of chlorine, which may have come from thinking about his wife so much, but might merely have been that he'd taken a shower that morning. ("The water all over Yugoslavia, though safe to drink, is unusually chlorinated": Guide Book.) As I left to catch a taxi to the airport the younger of the two waiters emerged from the kitchen with two piled plates of roasted wild boar, potatoes duchesse, and stewed peppers. ("Yugoslavian diet is unusually rich in proteins and fats": Guide Book.) I could tell from the glisten of oil that the food was no longer hot, and I was not tempted to stay, hungry though I was. Thus fate — or was it Bosnian willfulness? — confirmed the wisdom of my intent.

And that was how I fell out of love with my professor, in Sarajevo, a city to which I am grateful to this day, though I never got to see very much of it, because of the rain.

It was a silly sad thing to do, in the first place, to confuse mere passing academic ambition with love: to try and outdo my sister Clare. (Professor Piper was spiteful, as it happened, and did his best to have my thesis refused, but I went to appeal, which he never thought I'd dare, and won. I had a first-class mind after all.) A silly sad episode, which I regret. As silly and sad as Princip, poor young man, with his feverish mind, his bright tubercular cheeks, and his inordinate affection for his country, pushing aside his cup of coffee, leaping to his feet, taking his gun in both hands, planting his feet, aiming, and firing — one, two, three shots — and starting World War I. The first one missed, the second got the wife (never forget the wife), and the third got the archduke and a whole generation, and their children, and their children's children, and on and on forever. If he'd just hung on a bit, there in Sarajevo, that June day, he might have come to his senses. People do, sometimes quite quickly.

CONSIDERATIONS FOR CRITICAL THINKING AND WRITING

1. FIRST RESPONSE. Do you agree with Weldon's first line, "This is a sad story"? Explain why or why not.

2. How does the rain establish the mood for the story in the first five paragraphs?

3. Characterize Peter. What details concerning him reveal his personality?

4. Describe the narrator's relationship with Peter. How do you think he regards her? Why is she attracted to him?

5. Why is Sarajevo important for the story's setting? What is the effect of having the story of Princip's assassination of the Archduke Franz Ferdinand and his wife woven through the plot?

6. Describe Mrs. Piper. Though she doesn't appear in the story, she does have an important role. What do you think her role is?

7. What is "Ind Aff"? Why is it an important element of this story?

8. What is the significance of the two waiters (paras. 38–40)? How do they affect the narrator?

9. Why does the narrator decide to go home (para. 46)? Do you think she makes a reasoned or an impulsive decision? Explain why you think so.

10. Discuss the relationship between the personal history and the public history recounted in the story. How are the two interconnected? Explain whether you think it is necessary to be familiar with the assassinations in Sarajevo before reading the story.

CONNECTIONS TO OTHER SELECTIONS

1. Compare and contrast "IND AFF" and Joyce Carol Oates's "The Lady with the Pet Dog" (p. 200) as love stories. Do you think that the stories end happily, or the way you would want them to end? Are the endings problematic?

2. Explain how Weldon's concept of "Ind Aff" — "inordinate affection" — can be used to make sense of the relationship between Georgiana and Aylmer in Nathaniel Hawthorne's "The Birthmark" (p. 329).

3. How does passion figure in "IND AFF" and in D. H. Lawrence's "The Horse Dealer's Daughter" (p. 543)? Explain how Weldon's and Lawrence's perspectives on passion suggest differing views of love and human relationships.

PERSPECTIVE

FAY WELDON (B. 1933)

On the Importance of Place in "IND AFF"   1997

I'm the kind of writer who lives mostly in her head, looking inwards not outwards, more sensitive to people than places, unless the place turns out to be some useful metaphor. In Sarajevo, on a book tour, brooding about Ind. Aff., inordinate affection, these days more unkindly known as neurotic dependency, I was taken to see Princip's footsteps in the sidewalk. Fancy fell away. Here was the metaphor taken physical form — chance and death, so like chance and love. Then later we went up into the hills to eat wild boar and the intellectual Englishmen I was with seemed so pallid and absurd compared to the here-and-now mountain men: people came into perspective inside a landscape. I have a kind of rule of thumb: three preoccupations make a story. I interweaved them, delivered them into paper, and fell back into jet-lagged torpor.

From an interview with Michael Meyer, November 15, 1997

CONSIDERATIONS FOR CRITICAL THINKING AND WRITING

1. Weldon's description of how she began "IND AFF" draws on her personal experience in Sarajevo. How does that experience make its way into the story?

2. Consider Weldon's observation that "Here was the metaphor taken physical form — chance and death, so like chance and love." Do you think her observation works as a summary of the story?

3. Choose any other story in this anthology that can serve as an example of how "people come into perspective inside a landscape," and write an essay about it.

RUTH PRAWER JHABVALA (B. 1927)

Born in Cologne, Germany, Ruth Prawer Jhabvala fled with her family in 1939 to England and became a British citizen in 1948. In 1951 she completed a master's degree at London University and married an architect from India, where the couple subsequently lived for nearly a quarter of a century. Currently, she lives in New York and continues to visit her husband's native land. Jhabvala's writings include many novels, such as *Amrita* (1956), *The Householder* (1960), *Three Continents* (1988), and *Shards of Memory* (1995). Among her volumes of collected stories is *Out Of India: Selected Stories* (1986). She has also written many popular screenplays including *A Passage to India*, *A Room with a View*, *Howards End*, and *Remains of the Day*. "The Englishwoman" reflects a topic frequently found in her writings: a person living in an adopted culture.

The Englishwoman   1972

The Englishwoman — her name is Sadie — was fifty-two years old when she decided to leave India. She could hardly believe it. She felt young and free. At fifty-two! Her bag is packed and she is running away. She is eloping, leaving everything behind her — husband, children, grandchildren, thirty years of married life. Her heart is light and so is her luggage. It is surprising how few things she has to take with her. Most of her clothes are not worth taking. These last years she has been mostly wearing dowdy cotton frocks sewn by a little turbaned tailor. She still has a few saris, but she is not taking them with her. She doesn't ever intend to wear those again.

The person who is crying the most at her impending departure is Annapurna, her husband's mistress. Annapurna has a very emotional nature. She looks into the packed bag; like Sadie, she is surprised by its meager contents. "Is that all you are taking with you?" she asks. Sadie answers, "It's all I've got." Annapurna breaks into a new storm of tears.

"But that's good," Sadie urges. "Not to accumulate things, to travel light, what could be better?"

"Oh, you're so spiritual," Annapurna tells her, wiping her eyes on the other's sleeve. "Really, you are far more Indian than I am."

"Nonsense," Sadie says, and she means it. What nonsense.   5

But it is true that if Indian means "spiritual" — as so many people like to believe — then Annapurna is an exception. She is a very, very physical sort of person. She is stout, with a tight glowing skin, and shining eyes and teeth, and hair glossy with black dye. She loves clothes and jewelry and rich food. Although she is about the same age as the Englishwoman, she is far more vigorous, and when she moves, her sari rustles and her bracelets jingle.

"But are you really going?"

Annapurna keeps asking this question. And Sadie keeps asking it of herself too. But they ask it in two very different ways. Annapurna is shocked and grieved (yes, grieved — she loves the Englishwoman). But Sadie is incredulous with happiness. Can it really be true? she keeps asking herself: I'm going? I'm leaving India? Her heart skips with joy and she has difficulty in repressing her smiles. She doesn't want anyone to suspect her feelings. She is ashamed of her own callousness — and yet she goes on smiling, more and more, and happiness wells up in her like a spring.

Last week she went to say good-bye to the children. They are both settled in Bombay now with their families. Dev, her son, has been married for two years and has a baby girl; Monica, the daughter, has three boys. Dev has a fine job with an advertising company; and Monica is working too, for she has too much drive to be content with just staying at home. She calls herself a go-go girl and that is what she is, charging around town interviewing people for the articles she writes for a women's magazine, talking in the latest slang current in Bombay, throwing parties of which she herself is the life and soul. Monica looks quite Indian — her eyes are black, her skin glows; she is really more like Annapurna than like the Englishwoman, who is gaunt and pale.

Although so gay, Monica also likes to have serious discussions. She attempted to have such a discussion with her mother. She said, "But, Mummy, *why* are you going?" and she looked at her with the special serious face she has for serious moments.

Sadie didn't know what to answer. What could she say? But she had to say something, or Monica would be hurt. So she too became solemn, and she explained to her daughter that when people get older they begin to get very homesick for the place in which they were born and grew up and that this homesickness becomes worse and worse till in the end life becomes almost unbearable. Monica understood what she said and sympathized with it. She made plans how they would all come and visit her in England. She promised that when the boys became bigger, she would send them to her for long holidays. She was now in full agreement with her mother's departure, so Sadie was glad she told her what she did. She was prepared to tell Dev the same thing if he asked her, but he didn't ask. He and his wife were rather worried in those days because there was an outbreak of chicken pox in their apartment building and they were afraid Baby might catch it. But they too promised frequent visits to her in England.

Only Annapurna is still crying. She looks at Sadie's little suitcase and cries, and then she looks at Sadie and cries. She keeps asking, "But why, *why?*" Sadie tries to tell her what she told Monica, but Annapurna waves her aside; for her it is not a good enough reason, and she is right. Sadie herself knows it isn't. She asks wouldn't Sadie miss all of them and their love for her, and wouldn't she miss the life she has lived and the place in which she has lived it, her whole past, everything she has been and done for thirty years? Thirty years!

she cries, again and again, appalled—and Sadie too is appalled, it is such a long time. Annapurna says that an Indian wife also yearns for her father's house, and at the beginning of her marriage she is always waiting to go off there to visit; but as the years progress and she becomes deeper and deeper embedded in her husband's home, these early memories fade till they are nothing more but a sweet sensation enshrined in the heart. Sadie knows that what Annapurna is saying is true, but also that it does not in the least apply in her own case, because her feelings are not ones of gentle nostalgia.

The Englishwoman doesn't like to remember the early years when she first came to live here. It is as if she wished to disown her happiness then. How she loved everything! She never gave a backward glance to home or England. Her husband's family enjoyed and abetted her attempts to become Indian. A whole lot of them—mother-in-law, sisters-in-law, aunts, cousins, and friends—would cram into the family car (with blue silk curtains discreetly drawn to shield them from view) and drive to the bazaar to buy saris for Sadie. She was never much consulted about their choice, and when they got home, she was tugged this way and that while they argued with each other about the best way to drape it round her. When they had finished, they stood back to admire, only instead of admiring they often could not help smiling at her appearance. She didn't care. Yes, she knew she was too tall for the sari, and too thin, and too English, but she loved wearing it and to feel herself Indian. She also made attempts to learn Hindi, and this too amused everyone, and they never tired of making her repeat certain words and going into peals of laughter at her pronunciation. Everyone, all the ladies of the household, had a lot of fun. They were healthy, rich, and gay. They were by no means a tradition-bound family, and although their life in the house did have something of the enclosed, languorous quality of purdah living, the minds flowering within it were full of energy and curiosity. The mother-in-law herself, at that time well over sixty, spent a lot of her time reading vernacular novels, and she also attempted to write some biographical sketches of her own, describing life in a high-caste household of the 1880s. She took to smoking cigarettes quite late in life and liked them so much that she ended up as a chain-smoker. When Sadie thinks of her, it is as if she can still see her reclining on an embroidered mat spread on the floor, one elbow supported on a bolster, some cushions at her back, reading a brown tattered little volume through her glasses and enveloping herself in clouds of scented cigarette smoke.

Annapurna often speaks about those days. Annapurna was a relative, some sort of cousin. She had run away from her husband (who drank and, it was whispered, went in for unnatural practices) and had come to live with them in the house. When Annapurna speaks about those distant times, she does so as if everyone were still alive and all of them as young and gay as they were then. Often she says, "If only Srilata"—or Radhika—or Raksha—or Chandralekha—"were here now, how she would laugh!" But Srilata died of typhoid twenty years ago; Raksha married a Nepalese general and has gone to live in Katmandu; Chandralekha poisoned herself over an unhappy love affair. To Annapurna, however, it is as if everyone is still there, and she recalls and brings to life every detail of a distant event so that to Sadie too it begins to appear that she can hear the voices of those days. Till Annapurna returns to the present and—with an outstretched hand, her plump palm turned up to heaven — she acknowledges that they are all gone and many of them are dead; and she turns and looks at the Englishwoman and says, "And now you are going too," and her eyes are full of reproach.

It may seem strange that the mistress should reproach the wife, but Anna- 15 purna is within her rights to do so. For so many years now it is she who has taken over from the Englishwoman all the duties of a wife. There has never been any bitterness or jealousy between them. On the contrary, Sadie has always been grateful to her. She knows that before her husband became intimate with Annapurna, he used to go to other women. He *had* to go, he was such a healthy man and needed women as strong and healthy as he was; these were often young prostitutes. But for a long time now he has been content with Annapurna. He has put on an enormous amount of weight in these last years. It is Annapurna's fault, she feeds him too well and panders to his passion for good food. His meals are frequent and so heavy that, in between them, he is not capable of moving. He lies on a couch arranged for him on a veranda and breathes heavily. Sometimes he puffs at a hookah which stands within easy reach. He lies there for hours while Annapurna sits on the other end of the couch and entertains him with lively gossip. He enjoys that, but doesn't mind at all if she has no time for him. When he feels like talking, he summons one of the servants to come and squat on the carpet near his couch.

When Sadie first knew him, as a student at Oxford, he was a slim boy with burning eyes and a lock of hair on his forehead. He was always smiling and always on the go. He loved being a student, and though he never managed to graduate, got a lot out of it. He gave breakfast parties and had his own wine merchant and a red car in which he drove up to London several times a week; he was always discovering new pleasures, like hampers from Fortnum and Mason's and champagne parties on the river. Sadie had grown up in rather an austere atmosphere. Her family were comfortably off but had high principles of self-restraint and preferred lofty thought to lavish living. Sadie herself — a serious girl, a spare, stringent, high-bred English beauty — thought she had the same principles, but the young Indian made her see another side to her nature. When he went back to India, it was impossible to stay behind. She followed him, married him, and loved him even more than she had done in England. He belonged here so completely. Sometimes Sadie didn't see him for days on end — when he went on shooting parties and other expeditions with his friends — but she didn't mind. She stayed at home with the other women and enjoyed life as much as he did. There were summer nights when they all sat out in the garden by the fountain, and Chandralekha, who had a very sweet voice, sang sad songs from the hills while Radhika accompanied her on a lutelike instrument; and the moon shone, and Annapurna cut up mangoes for all of them, and the smell of these mangoes mingled with that exuding from the flowering bushes in a mixture so pungent, so heady that when the Englishwoman recalls those nights now, it is always by their scent that they become physical and present to her.

Annapurna and Sadie's husband play cards every evening. They play for money and Annapurna usually loses and then she gets cross; she always refuses to pay up, and the next evening they conveniently forget her debt and start again from scratch. But if he loses, then she insists on immediate payment: she laughs in triumph and, holding out her hand, opens and shuts it greedily and shouts, "Come on, pay up!" She also calls to Sadie and the servants to witness his discomfiture: those evenings are always merry. But sooner or later, and often in the middle of a game, she falls asleep. Once Annapurna is asleep, everything is very quiet. The servants turn off the lights and go to their quarters; the husband sits on his couch and looks out into the garden and takes a few puffs at his hookah; Sadie is upstairs in her bedroom. Nothing stirs, there isn't a sound, until the husband gives a loud sigh as he heaves himself up. He wakes Annapurna and they support each other up the stairs to their bedroom, where they sink onto their large soft bed and are asleep immediately and totally until it is morning. It is a long time before Sadie can get to sleep. She walks up and down the room. She argues with herself to and fro, and her mind heaves in turmoil like a sea in storm. The fact that everything else is calm and sleeping exacerbates her restlessness. She longs for some response, for something or someone other than herself to be affected by what is going on within her. But there is only silence and sleep. She steps out of her room and onto the veranda. The garden is in imperfect darkness, dimly and fitfully lit by the moon. Occasionally — very, very occasionally — a bird wakes up and rustles in a tree.

It was during these hours of solitude that she came to her decision to leave. To others — and, at the actual moment of making it, even to herself — it seemed like a sudden decision, but in fact, looking back, she realizes that she has been preparing for it for twenty years. She can even mark the exact day, twenty years ago, when first she knew that she did not want to go on living here. It was when her son was sick with one of those sudden mysterious illnesses that so often attack children in India. He lay burning in the middle of a great bed, with his eyes full of fever; he was very quiet except for an occasional groan. All the women in the house had gathered round his bedside and all were giving advice and different remedies. Some sat on chairs, some on the floor; the mother-in-law squatted cross-legged on the end of his bed, her spectacles on her nose, smoking cigarettes and turning the pages of a novel; from time to time she made soothing noises at Dev and squeezed his ankles. Annapurna sat by his side and rubbed ice on his head. Every time Dev groaned they all said, "Oh, poor Baba, poor Baba." The servants moved in and out; they too said, "Oh, poor Baba" and looked at him pityingly. The Englishwoman remembered the sickbeds of her own childhood, how she lay for hours comfortable and bored with nothing to do except watch the tree outside the window and the fat wet raindrops squashing against and sliding down the windowpane. The only person who ever came in was her mother when it was time for her medicine. But Dev wouldn't have liked that. He wanted everyone with him, and if one of the aunts was out of the room for too long a time, he would ask for her in a weak voice and someone would have to go and fetch her.

Sadie went out onto the veranda. But it was no better there. The day was one of those murky yellow ones when the sun is stifled in vapors of dust. She felt full of fears, for Dev and for herself, as if they were both being sucked down by — what was it? The heat? The loving women inside? The air, thick as a swamp in which fevers breed? She longed to be alone with her sick child in some cool place. But she knew this was not possible and that they belonged here in this house crammed full of relatives and choking under a yellow sky. She could never forget the despair of that moment, though in the succeeding years there were many like it. But that was the first.

As she stood there on the veranda, she saw her husband arrive home. 20
He was a very bright spot in that murky day. He was dressed in a starched
white kurta with little jewels for buttons, and his face was raised towards her as
she stood up on the veranda and he was smiling. He was no longer the slim boy
she had first known but neither was he as fat as he is today: no, he was in the
prime of life then, and what a prime! He came bounding up the outside staircase towards her and said, "How is he?"

"How can he be," she answered, "with all of them in there."

Surprised at her tone, he stopped smiling and looked at her anxiously. Her
anger mounted, and there were other things mixed in with it now: not only the
heat and the overcrowded room but also that he was so sleek and smiling and
young while she — oh, she felt worn-out, wrung-out, and knew she looked it.
She thought of the prostitutes he went to. It seemed to her that she could see
and smell their plump, brown, wriggling young bodies, greasy with scented oil.

In a shaking voice she said, "They're stifling that poor boy — they won't let
him breathe. No one seems to have the least idea of hygiene."

He knew it was more than she was saying and continued to look at her
anxiously. "Are you ill?" he asked, and put out his hand to feel her forehead.
When she drew back, he asked, "What is it?" full of sympathy.

They had been speaking in low voices, but all the same, from inside the 25
crowded room, Annapurna had sensed that something was wrong. She left the
bedside and came out to join them. She looked inquiringly at Sadie's husband.
They were not yet lovers at that time, but there was that instinctive understanding between them that there was between all the members of that household.

"She is not well," he said.

"I *am* well! I'm perfectly well!" Sadie burst into tears. She had no control
over this. Furiously she wiped the foolish tears from her cheeks.

Both of them melted with tenderness. Annapurna folded her in an embrace; the husband stroked her back. When she struggled to get free, they
thought it was a new outbreak of anguish and redoubled their attentions. At
last she cried, "It's so *hot!*" and indeed she could hardly breathe, and perspiration ran down her in runnels from being squashed against fat Annapurna.
Then Annapurna let her go. They both stood and looked at her full of anxiety
for her; and these two round, healthy, shining faces looking at her with love,
pitying her, were so unbearable to her that, to prevent herself from bursting
into the tears that she despised but that they, she knew, not only awaited but
even expected, she turned, and, hurrying along the veranda that ran like a
gallery all round the house, she hid herself in her bedroom and locked the
door. They followed and knocked urgently and begged to be allowed to enter.
She refused to open. She could hear them discussing her outside the door:
they were full of understanding, they realized that people did get upset like
this and that then it was the duty of others to soothe and help them.

She was always being soothed and helped. She is still being soothed and
helped. Annapurna has taken everything out of her suitcase and is repacking it
in what she considers is a better way. She has had special shoe bags sewn. As a
matter of fact, she would like to have a completely new outfit of clothes made
for her. She says how will it look if Sadie arrives with nothing better than those
few shabby rags in that little suitcase. Sadie thinks to herself, look to whom?
She knows almost no one there: a few distant relatives, one old school friend;

she hasn't been there for thirty years, she has no contacts, no correspondence — and yet she is going home! Home! And again happiness rushes over her in waves, and she takes a deep breath to be able to bear it.

"And not a single piece of jewelry," Annapurna grumbles.   30

Sadie laughs. She has given it all away long ago to Monica and to Dev's wife, and very glad she was to get rid of all those heavy costly gold ornaments. They were her share of the family jewels, but she never knew what to do with them. Certainly she couldn't wear them — she was always too thin and pale to be able to carry off these pieces fit for a barbarian queen; so she had left them lying around for years in a cupboard till Annapurna had taken them away from her to lock up in a safe.

"At least *one* piece you could have let me keep for you," Annapurna now says. "Then you would have had something to show them. What will they think of us?"

"What will *who* think?" Sadie asks, and the idea of the distant relatives and her poor school friend (Clare, still unmarried and still teaching) having any thoughts on the subject of what properties she has brought back with her from India makes her laugh again. And there is a lightheartedness in her laughter that hasn't been there for a long time, and Annapurna hears it and is hurt by it.

They are both hurt by her attitude. It has been years since Sadie saw her husband so upset; but then it has been years since anything really upset him. He has led a very calm life lately. Not that his life was not always calm and comfortable, but there were times in his younger days when he, like everyone else in the house, had his outbursts. She particularly remembers one he had with his sister Chandralekha. Actually, at that time, the whole house was in upheaval. Chandralekha had formed an unfortunate attachment to a man nobody approved of. They were not a rigid family that way — there had been several love matches — but it seemed Chandralekha's choice was entirely unsuitable. Sadie had met the man, who struck her as intelligent and of a strong character. In fact, she thought Chandralekha had shown excellent taste. But when she told her husband so, he waved her aside and said she didn't understand. And it was true, she didn't, everything that went on in the house during those days was a mystery to her. Oh, she understood vaguely what it was all about — the man was of *low birth*, and all his virtues of character and self-made position could not wipe that stain away — but the passions that were aroused, the issues that were thought to be at stake, were beyond her comprehension. Yet she could see that all of them were suffering deeply, and Chandralekha was in a torment of inner conflict (indeed, she later committed suicide).

One day Chandralekha came in carrying a dish of sweet rice which she had   35
made herself. She said, "Just wait till you taste this," and she lovingly ladled a spoonful onto her brother's plate. He began to eat with relish, but quite suddenly he pushed the plate away and began to cry out loud. Everyone at once knew why, of course. The only person who was surprised was Sadie — both at the suddenness of the outburst and at the lengths to which he went. He banged his head against the wall, flung himself on the ground at Chandralekha's feet, and at one point he snatched up a knife and held it at his own throat and had to have it wrested away from him by all the women there surrounding him. "The children, the children!" he kept crying, and at first Sadie thought he meant their own children, Monica and Dev, and she couldn't understand what was

threatening them; but everyone else knew he meant Chandralekha's children who were yet unborn but who would be born, and, if she married this man, born with polluted blood. Sadie didn't know how that scene ended; she went away and locked herself up in her bedroom. She covered her ears with her hands to shut out the noise and cries that echoed through the house.

When he learned of her decision to leave, Sadie's husband begged and pleaded with her in the same way he had done with Chandralekha all those years ago. The Englishwoman felt embarrassed and ashamed for him. He looked so ridiculous, being so heavy and fat, with his great bulk heaving and emitting cries like those of an hysterical woman. No one else found him ridiculous — on the contrary, the servants and Annapurna were deeply affected by his strong emotions and tried to comfort him. But he wouldn't be comforted till in the end his passion spent itself. Then he became resigned and even quite practical and sent for his lawyer to make a settlement. He was very generous toward his wife, and indeed keeps pressing her to accept more and is distressed because she doesn't need it. So now she feels ashamed not of him but of herself and her own lack of feeling.

It is her last night in India. As usual, her husband and Annapurna are playing cards together. When she joins them, they look at her affectionately and treat her like a guest. Annapurna offers tea, sherbet, limewater, and is distressed when she declines all these suggestions. She is always distressed by the fact that Sadie needs less food than she does. She says, "How can you live like that?" After a moment's thought, she adds, "How will you live *there?* Who will look after you and see that you don't starve yourself to death?" When Sadie looks at her, it is as she feared: tears are again flowing down Annapurna's cheeks. A sob also breaks from out of her bosom. It is echoed by another sob: Sadie looks up and sees that tears are also trickling down her husband's face. Neither of them speaks, and in fact they go on playing cards. The Englishwoman lowers her eyes away from them; she sits there, silent, prim, showing no emotion. She hopes they think she *has* no emotion; she does her best to hide it — the happiness that will not be suppressed, even at the sight of their tears.

Annapurna has had enough of playing. She flings down the cards (she has been losing). She wipes her tears away with her forearm, like a child, yawns, sighs, says, "Well, time to go to bed" in resignation. He says, "Yes, it's time," with the same sigh and the same resignation. They have accepted the Englishwoman's departure; it grieves them, but they submit to it, as human beings have to submit to everything, such as old age and disease and loss of every kind. They walk upstairs slowly, leaning on each other.

When Sadie goes up to her own room, she is almost running in her excitement. She looks in the mirror and is surprised at the drained face that looks back at her. She doesn't feel like that at all — no, she feels the way she used to, so that now she expects her bright eyes back again and her pink cheeks. She turns away from the mirror, laughing at her own foolishness; and she can hear her own laughter and it is just the way it used to be. She knows she won't sleep tonight. She doesn't want to sleep. She loves this feeling of excitement and youth and pacing the room with her heart beating and wild thoughts storming in her head. The servants have turned out the lights downstairs and gone to bed. The lights are out in her husband's and Annapurna's room too; they must be fast asleep side by side on their bed.

The Englishwoman can't see the moon, but the garden is lit up by some 40
sort of faint silver light. She can make out the fountain with the stone statue,
and the lime trees, and the great flowering bush of queen of the night; there is
the bench where they used to sit in the evenings when Chandralekha sang in
her sweet voice. But as she goes on looking, the moonlit scene brightens until
it is no longer that silver garden but English downs spreading as far as the eye
can see, yellow on one side, green on another. The green side is being rained
upon by mild soft rain coming down like a curtain, and the yellow side is being
shone upon by a sun as mild and soft as that rain. On a raised knoll in the foreground there is an oak tree with leaves and acorns, and she is standing by this
tree; and as she stands there, on that eminence overlooking the downs, strong
winds blow right through her. They are as cold and fresh as the waters of a
mountain torrent. They threaten to sweep her off her feet so that she has to
plant herself down very firmly and put out her hand to support herself against
the trunk of the tree (she can feel the rough texture of its bark). She raises her
face, and her hair — not *her* hair but the shining hair of her youth — flies wild
and free in that strong wind.

CONSIDERATIONS FOR CRITICAL THINKING AND WRITING

1. FIRST RESPONSE. Why do you think Sadie feels elated about leaving India?
   Is it the country, her family, or something else she wants to leave behind?

2. What qualities do you associate with Indian culture? The narrator suggests that many people think "Indian means 'spiritual'" (para. 6). Explain
   why you agree or disagree with this popular assumption. How do your
   ideas about India affect your reading of the story?

3. How does Annapurna serve as a foil to Sadie?

4. How does Sadie explain her reasons for leaving India to her daughter? Why
   isn't Sadie's explanation adequate for Annapurna?

5. Describe Sadie's early years in India. Why doesn't she like to recall those
   years?

6. Characterize Sadie's husband. What attracted her to him? How does she
   feel about him now?

7. Why does Sadie feel uncomfortable in her husband's household? What
   causes her to change her attitude toward her husband and Indian culture?
   Where is this turning point for Sadie in the story?

8. What does Chandralekha's story reveal about life in India? How does her
   story affect Sadie?

9. What is the effect of the narrator's referring to Sadie as "the Englishwoman"? Discuss the significance of the title.

10. How does Sadie think life in England will contrast with her life in India?
    Do you think her expectations about England are realistic? Explain your
    response.

11. Given the sense of England provided by Sadie, how do you think Anna-
    purna would experience life there?

CONNECTIONS TO OTHER SELECTIONS

1. How is the meaning of "home" essential to the meanings of "The
   Englishwoman" and Hemingway's "Soldier's Home" (p. 145)?

2. To what extent is the husband's assumption that his wife is "ill" in "The Englishwoman" (paras. 24-29) similar to the situation described in Gail Godwin's "A Sorrowful Woman" (p. 33)?

3. Write an essay that discusses how the protagonists in "The Englishwoman"
   and James Joyce's "Eveline" (p. 512) are affected by the cultures in which
   they live.

DAVID UPDIKE (B. 1957)

Born in Ipswich, Massachusetts, David Updike is the son of John Updike. David received his B.A. in art history at Harvard and his M.A. from
Teachers College, Columbia University. His acclaimed children's books include *An Autumn Tale* (1988), *A Spring Story* (1989), *Seven Times Eight* (1990),
The Sounds of Summer (1993), and *A Helpful Alphabet of Friendly Objects* (1998),
which he co-authored with his father. "Summer," a poignant tale for
adults, is part of *Out on the Marsh: Stories* (1988), a collection of his short fiction; his short stories have also appeared in *The New Yorker.* Updike resides
in Cambridge, Massachusetts.

Summer   1985

It was the first week in August, the time when summer briefly pauses, shifting
between its beginning and its end: the light had not yet begun to change, the
leaves were still full and green on the trees, the nights were still warm. From
the woods and fields came the hiss of crickets; the line of distant mountains
was still dulled by the edge of summer haze, the echo of fireworks was replaced
by the rumble of thunder and the hollow premonition of school, too far off to
imagine though dimly, dully felt. His senses were consumed by the joy of their
own fulfillment: the satisfying swat of a tennis ball, the dappled damp and
light of the dirt road after rain, the alternating sensations of sand, mossy
stone, and pine needles under bare feet. His days were spent in the adolescent
pursuit of childhood pleasures: tennis, a haphazard round of golf, a variant of
baseball adapted to the local geography: two pine trees as foul poles, a broomstick as the bat, the apex of the small, secluded house the dividing line between
home runs and outs. On rainy days they swatted bottle tops across the living
room floor, and at night vented budding cerebral energy with games of chess
thoughtfully played over glasses of iced tea. After dinner they would paddle
the canoe to the middle of the lake, and drift beneath the vast, blue-black
dome of sky, looking at the stars and speaking softly in tones which, with the
waning summer, became increasingly philosophical: the sky's blue vastness,
the distance and magnitude of stars, an endless succession of numbers, gave
way to a rising sensation of infinity, eternity, an imagined universe with no
bounds. But the sound of the paddle hitting against the side of the canoe, the
faint shadow of surrounding mountains, the cry of a nocturnal bird brought
them back to the happy, cloistered finity of their world, and they paddled
slowly home and went to bed.

Homer woke to the slant and shadow of a summer morning, dressed in their shared cabin, and went into the house where Mrs. Thyme sat alone, looking out across the flat blue stillness of the lake. She poured him a cup of coffee and they quietly talked, and it was then that his happiness seemed most tangible. In this summer month with the Thymes, freed from the complications of his own family, he had released himself to them and, as interim member — friend, brother, surrogate son — he lived in a blessed realm between two worlds.

From the cool darkness of the porch, smelling faintly of moldy books and kerosene and the tobacco of burning pipes, he sat looking through the screen to the lake, shimmering beneath the heat of a summer afternoon: a dog lay sleeping in the sun, a bird hopped along a swaying branch, sunlight came in through the trees and collapsed on the sandy soil beside a patch of moss, or mimicked the shade and cadence of stones as they stepped to the edge of a lake where small waves lapped a damp rock and washed onto a sandy shore. An inverted boat lay decaying under a tree, a drooping American flag hung from its gnarled pole, a haphazard dock started out across the cove toward distant islands through which the white triangle of a sail silently moved.

The yellowed pages of the book from which he occasionally read swam before him: ". . . Holmes clapped the hat upon his head. It came right over the forehead and settled on the bridge of his nose. 'It is a question of cubic capacity' said he . . ." Homer looked up. The texture of the smooth, unbroken air was cleanly divided by the sound of a slamming door, echoing up into the woods around him. Through the screen he watched Fred's sister Sandra as she came ambling down the path, stepping lightly between the stones in her bare feet. She held a towel in one hand, a book in the other, and wore a pair of pale blue shorts — faded relics of another era. At the end of the dock she stopped, raised her hands above her head, stretching, and then sat down. She rolled over onto her stomach and, using the book as a pillow, fell asleep.

Homer was amused by the fact, that although she did this every day, she 5 didn't get any tanner. When she first came in her face was faintly flushed, and there was a pinkish line around the snowy band where her bathing suit strap had been, but the back of her legs remained an endearing, pale white, the color of eggshells, and her back acquired only the softest, brownish blur. Sometimes she kept her shoes on, other times a shirt, or sweater, or just collapsed onto the seat of the boat, her pale eyelids turned upward toward the pale sun; and as silently as she arrived, she would leave, walking back through the stones with the same, casual sway of indifference. He would watch her, hear the distant door slam, the shower running in the far corner of the house. Other times he would just look up and she would be gone.

On the tennis court she was strangely indifferent to his heroics. When the crucial moment arrived — Homer serving in the final game of the final set — the match would pause while she left, walking across the court, stopping to call the dog, swaying out through the gate. Homer watched her as she went down the path, and, impetus suddenly lost, he double faulted, stroked a routine backhand over the back fence, and the match was over.

When he arrived back at the house she asked him who won, but didn't seem to hear his answer. "I wish I could go sailing," she said, looking distractedly out over the lake.

At night, when he went out to the cottage where he and Fred slept, he could see her through the window as she lay on her bed, reading, her arm folded beneath her head like a leaf. Her nightgown, pulled and buttoned to her chin, pierced him with a regret that had no source or resolution, and its imagined texture floated in the air above him as he lay in bed at night, suspended in the surrounding darkness, the scent of pine, the hypnotic cadence of his best friend's breathing.

Was it that he had known her all his life, and as such had grown up in the shadow of her subtle beauty? Was it the condensed world of the lake, the silent reverence of surrounding woods, mountains, which heightened his sense of her and brought the warm glow of her presence into soft, amorous focus? She had the hair of a baby, the freckles of a child, and the sway of motherhood. Like his love, her beauty rose up in the world which spawned and nurtured it, and found in the family the medium in which it thrived, and in Homer distilled to a pure distant longing for something he had never had.

One day they climbed a mountain, and as the components of family and friends strung out along the path on their laborious upward hike, he found himself tromping along through the woods with her with nobody else in sight. Now and then they would stop by a stream, or sit on a stump, or stone, and he would speak to her, and then they would set off again, he following her. But in the end this day exhausted him, following her pale legs and tripping sneakers over the ruts and stones and a thousand roots, all the while trying to suppress a wordless, inarticulate passion, and the last mile or so he left her, sprinting down the path in a reckless, solitary release, howling into the woods around him. He was lying on the grass, staring up into the patterns of drifting clouds when she came ambling down. "Wher'd you go? I thought I'd lost you," she said, and sat heavily down in the seat of the car. On the ride home, his elbow hopelessly held in the warm crook of her arm, he resolved to release his love, give it up, on the grounds that it was too disruptive to his otherwise placid life. But in the days to follow he discovered that his resolution had done little to change her, and her life went on its oblivious, happy course without him.

His friendship with Fred, meanwhile, continued on its course of athletic and boyhood fulfillment. Alcohol seeped into their diet, and an occasional cigarette, and at night they would drive into town, buy two enormous cans of Australian beer and sit at a small cove by the lake, talking. One night on the ride home Fred accelerated over a small bridge, and as the family station wagon left the ground their heads floated up to the ceiling, touched, and then came crashing down as the car landed and Fred wrestled the car back onto course. Other times they would take the motorboat out onto the lake and make sudden racing turns around buoys, sending a plume of water into the air and everything in the boat crashing to one side. But always with these adventures Homer felt a pang of absence, and was always relieved when they headed back toward the familiar cove, and home.

As August ran its merciless succession of beautiful days, Sandra drifted in and out of his presence in rising oscillations of sorrow and desire. She worked at a bowling alley on the other side of the lake, and in the evening Homer and Fred would drive the boat over, bowl a couple of strings, and wait for her to get off work. Homer sat at the counter and watched her serve up sloshing cups of coffee, secretly loathing the leering gazes of whiskered truck drivers, and loving her oblivious, vacant stare in answer, hip cocked, hand on counter, gazing

10

up into the neon air above their heads. When she was finished, they would pile into the boat and skim through darkness the four or five miles home, and it was then, bundled beneath sweaters and blankets, the white hem of her waitressing dress showing through the darkness, their hair swept in the wind and their voices swallowed by the engine's slow, steady growl, that he felt most powerless to her attraction. As the boat rounded corners he would close his eyes and release himself to gravity, his body's warmth swaying into hers, guising his attraction in the thin veil of centrifugal force. Now and then he would lean into the floating strands of her hair and speak into her fragrance, watching her smile swell in the pale half-light of the moon, the umber glow of the boat's rear light, her laughter spilling backward over the swirling "V" of wake.

Into the humid days of August a sudden rain fell, leaving the sky a hard, unbroken blue and the nights clear and cool. In the morning when he woke, leaving Fred a heap of sighing covers in his bed, he stepped out into the first rays of sunlight that came through the branches of the trees and sensed, in the cool vapor that rose from damp pine needles, the piercing cry of a blue jay, that something had changed. That night as they ate dinner — hamburgers and squash and corn-on-the-cob — everyone wore sweaters, and as the sun set behind the undulating line of distant mountains — burnt, like a filament of summer into his blinking eyes — it was with an autumnal tint, a reddish glow. Several days later the tree at the end of the point bloomed with a sprig of russet leaves, one or two of which occasionally fell, and their lives became filled with an unspoken urgency. Life of summer went on in the silent knowledge that, with the slow, inexorable seepage of an hourglass, it was turning into fall. Another mountain was climbed, annual tennis matches were arranged and played. Homer and Fred became unofficial champions of the lake by trouncing the elder Dewitt boys, unbeaten in several years. "Youth, youth," glum Billy Dewitt kept saying over iced tea afterward, in jest, though Homer could tell he was hiding some greater sense of loss.

And the moment, the conjunction of circumstance that, through the steady exertion of will, minor adjustments of time and place, he had often tried to induce, never happened. She received his veiled attentions with a kind of amused curiosity, as if smiling back on innocence. One night they had been the last ones up, and there was a fleeting, shuddering moment before he stepped through the woods to his cabin and she went to her bed that he recognized, in a distant sort of way, as the moment of truth. But to touch her, or kiss her, seemed suddenly incongruous, absurd, contrary to something he could not put his finger on. He looked down at the floor and softly said goodnight. The screen door shut quietly behind him and he went out into the darkness and made his way through the unseen sticks and stones, and it was only then, tripping drunkenly on a fallen branch, that he realized he had never been able to imagine the moment he distantly longed for.

The Preacher gave a familiar sermon about another summer having run its course, the harvest of friendship reaped, and a concluding prayer that, "God willing, we will all meet again in June." That afternoon Homer and Fred went sailing, and as they swept past a neighboring cove Homer saw in its sullen shadows a girl sitting alone in a canoe, and in an eternal, melancholy signal of parting, she waved to them as they passed. And there was something in the way that she raised her arm which, when added to the distant impression of her fullness, beauty, youth, filled him with longing as their boat moved inexorably past, slapping the waves, and she disappeared behind a crop of trees.

The night before they were to leave they were all sitting in the living room after dinner — Mrs. Thyme sewing, Fred folded up with the morning paper, Homer reading on the other end of the couch where Sandra was lying — when the dog leapt up and things shifted in such a way that Sandra's bare foot was lightly touching Homer's back. Mrs. Thyme came over with a roll of newspaper, hit the dog on the head and he leapt off. But to Homer's surprise Sandra's foot remained, and he felt, in the faint sensation of exerted pressure, the passive emanation of its warmth, a distant signal of acquiescence. And as the family scene continued as before it was with the accompanying drama of Homer's hand, shielded from the family by a haphazard wall of pillows, migrating over the couch to where, in a moment of breathless abandon, settled softly on the cool hollow of her arch. She laughed at something her mother had said, her toe twitched, but her foot remained. It was only then, in the presence of the family, that he realized she was his accomplice, and that, though this was as far as it would ever go, his love had been returned.

CONSIDERATIONS FOR CRITICAL THINKING AND WRITING

1. FIRST RESPONSE. How do you respond to this love story? Would the story be more satisfying if Homer and Sandra openly acknowledged their feelings for each other and kissed at the end? Why or why not?

2. What details in the first paragraph evoke particular feelings about August? What sort of mood is created by these details?

3. How is Homer's attraction to Sandra made evident in paragraphs 5 through 9?

4. Why do you think August is described as a "merciless succession of beautiful days" (para. 12)?

5. Analyze the images in paragraph 13 that evoke the impending autumn. What does Billy Dewitt's lament about "youth, youth" add to this description?

6. Discuss the transition between paragraphs 14 and 15. How is the mood effectively changed between the night and the next day?

7. What effect does Homer's friendship with Fred and his relationship with the Thyme family have on your understanding of his reticent attraction to Sandra?

8. What, if any, significance can you attach to the names of Homer, Sandra, Thyme, and the Dewitt boys?

9. How successful do you think Updike is in evoking youthful feeling about summer in this story? Explain why you responded positively or negatively to this evocation of summer.

CONNECTIONS TO OTHER SELECTIONS

1. Compare David Updike's treatment of summer as the setting of his story with John Updike's use of summer as the setting in "A & P" (p. 576).

2. Discuss "Summer" and Dagoberto Gilb's "Love in L.A." (p. 265) as love stories. Explain why you might prefer one over the other.

3. Write an essay comparing how August is represented in "Summer" and in Sophie Cabot Black's poem "August" (p. 785).

6

Point of View

Because one of the pleasures of reading fiction consists of seeing the world through someone else's eyes, it is easy to overlook the eyes that control our view of the plot, characters, and setting. *Point of view* refers to who tells us the story and how it is told. What we know and how we feel about the events in a story are shaped by the author's choice of a point of view. The teller of a story, the *narrator,* inevitably affects our understanding of the characters' actions by filtering what is told through his or her own perspective. The narrator should not be confused with the author who has created the narrative voice because the two are usually distinct (more on this point later).

If the narrative voice is changed, the story will change. Consider, for example, how different "Bartleby, the Scrivener" (p. 113) would be if Melville had chosen to tell the story from Bartleby's point of view instead of the lawyer's. With Bartleby as narrator, much of the mystery concerning his behavior would be lost. The peculiar force of his saying "I would prefer not to" would be lessened amid all the other things he would have to say as narrator. Moreover, the lawyer's reaction — puzzled, upset, outraged, and finally sympathetic to Bartleby — would be lost too. It would be entirely possible, of course, to write a story from Bartleby's point of view, but it would not be the story Melville wrote.

The possible ways of telling a story are many, and more than one point of view can be worked into a single story. However, the various points of view that storytellers draw on can be conveniently grouped into two broad categories: (1) the third-person narrator and (2) the first-person narrator. The third-person narrator uses *he, she,* or *they* to tell the story and does not participate in the action. The first-person narrator uses *I* and is a major or minor participant in the action. A second-person narrator, *you,* is possible but rarely used because of the awkwardness in thrusting the reader into the story, as in "You are minding your own business on a park bench when a drunk steps out of the bushes and demands your lunch bag."

Let's look now at the most important and most often used variations within first- and third-person narrations.

THIRD-PERSON NARRATOR (Nonparticipant)

1. Omniscient (the narrator takes us inside the character[s])
2. Limited omniscient (the narrator takes us inside one or two characters)
3. Objective (the narrator is outside the characters)

No type of third-person narrator appears as a character in a story. The **omniscient narrator** is all-knowing. From this point of view, the narrator can move from place to place and pass back and forth through time, slipping into and out of characters as no human being possibly could in real life. This narrator can report the characters' thoughts and feelings as well as what they say and do. In the excerpt from *Tarzan of the Apes* (p. 62), Burroughs's narrator tells us about events concerning Terkoz in another part of the jungle that long preceded the battle between Terkoz and Tarzan. We also learn Tarzan's and Jane's inner thoughts and emotions during the episode. And Burroughs's narrator describes Terkoz as "an arrant coward" and a bully, thereby evaluating the character for the reader. This kind of intrusion is called **editorial omniscience.** In contrast, narration that allows characters' actions and thoughts to speak for themselves is known as **neutral omniscience.** Most modern writers use neutral omniscience so that readers can reach their own conclusions.

The **limited omniscient narrator** is much more confined than the omniscient narrator. With limited omniscience the author very often restricts the narrator to the single perspective of either a major or a minor character. Sometimes a narrator can see into more than one character, particularly in a longer work that focuses, for example, on two characters alternately from one chapter to the next. Short stories, however, frequently are restricted by length to a single character's point of view. The way people, places, and events appear to that character is the way they appear to the reader. The reader has access to the thoughts and feelings of the characters revealed by the narrator, but neither the reader nor the character has access to the inner lives of any of the other characters in the story. The events in Katherine Mansfield's "Miss Brill" (p. 258) are viewed entirely through the protagonist's eyes; we see a French vacation town as an elderly woman does. Miss Brill represents the central consciousness of the story. She unifies the story by being present through all the action. We are not told of anything that happens away from the character because the narration is based on her perception of things.

The most intense use of a central consciousness in narration can be seen in the **stream-of-consciousness technique** developed by modern writers such as James Joyce, Virginia Woolf, and William Faulkner. This technique takes a reader inside a character's mind to reveal perceptions, thoughts, and feelings on a conscious or unconscious level. A stream of consciousness suggests the flow of thought as well as its content; hence, complete sentences may give way to fragments as the character's mind makes rapid associations free of conventional logic or transitions.

The following passage is from Joyce's *Ulysses,* a novel famous for its extended use of this technique. In this paragraph Joyce takes us inside the mind of a character who is describing a funeral:

> Coffin now. Got here before us, dead as he is. Horse looking round at it with his plume skeowways [askew]. Dull eye: collar tight on his neck, pressing on a bloodvessel or something. Do they know what they cart out of here every day? Must be twenty or thirty funerals every day. Then Mount Jerome for the protestants. Funerals all over the world everywhere every minute. Shovelling them under by the cartload doublequick. Thousands every hour. Too many in the world.

The character's thoughts range from specific observations to speculations about death. Joyce creates the illusion that we are reading the character's thoughts as they occur. The stream-of-consciousness technique provides an intimate perspective on a character's thoughts.

In contrast, the ***objective point of view*** employs a narrator who does not see into the mind of any character. From this detached and impersonal perspective, the narrator reports action and dialogue without telling us directly what the character feels and thinks. We observe the characters in much the same way we would perceive events in a film or play: we supply the meanings; no analysis or interpretation is provided by the narrator. This point of view places a heavy premium on dialogue, actions, and details to reveal character.

In Hemingway's "Soldier's Home" (p. 145), a limited omniscient narration is the predominant point of view. Krebs's thoughts and reaction to being home from the war are made available to the reader by the narrator, who tells us that Krebs "felt embarrassed and resentful" or "sick and vaguely nauseated" by the small-town life he has reentered. Occasionally, however, Hemingway uses an objective point of view when he dramatizes particularly tense moments between Krebs and his mother. In the following excerpt, Hemingway's narrator shows us Krebs's feelings instead of telling us what they are. Krebs's response to his mother's concerns is presented without comment. The external details of the scene reveal his inner feelings.

> "I've worried about you so much, Harold," his mother went on. "I know the temptations you must have been exposed to. I know how weak men are. I know what your own dear grandfather, my own father, told us about the Civil War and I have prayed for you. I pray for you all day long, Harold."
>
> Krebs looked at the bacon fat hardening on his plate.
>
> "Your father is worried, too," his mother went on. "He thinks you have lost your ambition, that you haven't got a definite aim in life. Charley Simmons,

who is just your age, has a good job and is going to be married. The boys are all settling down; they're all determined to get somewhere; you can see that boys like Charley Simmons are on their way to being really a credit to the community."

Krebs said nothing.

"Don't look that way, Harold. . . ."

When Krebs looks at the bacon fat we can see him cooling and hardening too. Hemingway does not describe the expression on Krebs's face, yet we know it is a look that disturbs his mother as she goes on about what she thinks she knows. Krebs and his mother are clearly tense and upset; the details, action, and dialogue reveal that without the narrator telling the reader how each character feels.

FIRST-PERSON NARRATOR (Participant)

1. Major character
2. Minor character

With a *first-person narrator,* the *I* presents the point of view of only one character's consciousness. The reader is restricted to the perceptions, thoughts, and feelings of that single character. This is Melville's technique with the lawyer in "Bartleby, the Scrivener" (p. 113). Everything learned about the characters, action, and plot comes from the unnamed lawyer. Bartleby remains a mystery because we are limited to what the lawyer knows and reports. The lawyer cannot explain what Bartleby means because he does not entirely know himself. Melville's use of the first person encourages us to identify with the lawyer's confused reaction to Bartleby so that we pay attention not only to the scrivener but to the lawyer's response to him. We are as perplexed as the lawyer and share his effort to make sense of Bartleby.

The lawyer is a major character in Melville's story; indeed, many readers take him to be the protagonist. A first-person narrator can, however, also be a minor character (imagine how different the story would be if it were told by, say, Ginger Nut or by an observer who had little or nothing to do with the action). Faulkner uses an observer in "A Rose for Emily" (p. 72). His *we,* though plural and representative of the town's view of Emily, is nonetheless a first-person narrator.

One of the primary reasons for identifying the point of view in a story is to determine where the author stands in relation to the story. Behind the narrative voice of any story is the author, manipulating events and providing or withholding information. It is a mistake to assume that the narrative voice of a story is the author. The narrator, whether a first-person participant or a third-person nonparticipant, is a creation of the writer. A narrator's perceptions may be accepted, rejected, or modified by an author, depending on how the narrative voice is articulated.

Faulkner seems to have shared the fascination, sympathy, and horror of the narrator in "A Rose for Emily," but Melville must not be so readily identified with the lawyer in "Bartleby, the Scrivener." The lawyer's description of himself as "an eminently *safe* man," convinced "that the easiest way of life is the best," raises the question of how well equipped he is to fathom Bartleby's protest. To make sense of Bartleby, it is also necessary to understand the lawyer's point of view. Until the conclusion of the story, this "*safe* man" is too self-serving, defensive, and obtuse to comprehend the despair embodied in Bartleby and the deadening meaninglessness of Wall Street life.

The lawyer is an **unreliable narrator,** whose interpretation of events is different from the author's. We cannot entirely accept the lawyer's assessment of Bartleby because we see that the lawyer's perceptions are not totally to be trusted. Melville does not expect us, for example, to agree with the lawyer's suggestion that the solution to Bartleby's situation might be to "entertain some young gentleman with your conversation" on a trip to Europe. Given Bartleby's awful silences, this absurd suggestion reveals the lawyer's superficial understanding. The lawyer's perceptions frequently do not coincide with those Melville expects his readers to share. Hence, the lawyer's unreliability preserves Bartleby's mysterious nature while revealing the lawyer's sensibilities. The point of view is artistically appropriate for Melville's purposes because the eyes through which we perceive the plot, characters, and setting are also the subject of the story.

Narrators can be unreliable for a variety of reasons: they might lack self-knowledge, like Melville's lawyer, or they might be innocent and inexperienced, like Ralph Ellison's young narrator in "Battle Royal" (p. 223). Youthful innocence frequently characterizes a **naive narrator** such as Mark Twain's Huck Finn or Holden Caulfield, J. D. Salinger's twentieth-century version of Huck in *The Catcher in the Rye*. These narrators lack the sophistication to interpret accurately what they see; they are unreliable because the reader must go beyond their understanding of events to comprehend the situations described. Huck and Holden describe their respective social environments, but the reader, with more experience, supplies the critical perspective that each boy lacks. In "Battle Royal" that perspective is supplemented by Ellison's dividing the narration between the young man who experiences events and the mature man who reflects back on those events.

Few generalizations can be made about the advantages or disadvantages of using a specific point of view. What can be said with confidence, however, is that writers choose a point of view to achieve particular effects because point of view determines what we know about the characters and events in a story. We should, therefore, be aware of who is telling the story and whether the narrator sees things clearly and reliably.

The next three works warrant a careful examination of their points of view. In Toni Cade Bambara's "The Lesson," we hear the voice of a streetwise young black girl who resists instruction. In Anton Chekhov's and Joyce Carol Oates's versions of "The Lady with the Pet Dog," we are presented with similar stories told from two different perspectives that make for intriguing comparisons and contrasts.

TONI CADE BAMBARA (1939–1995)

Raised in New York City's Harlem and Bedford-Stuyvesant communities, Toni Cade Bambara graduated from Queens College in 1959, studied in Florence and Paris, and earned her M.A. at City College of New York in 1964. She also studied dance, linguistics, and filmmaking and worked a variety of jobs in welfare, recreation, and community housing, in addition to teaching at various schools, including Rutgers University and Spelman College. She described her writing as "straight-up fiction . . . 'cause I value my family and friends, and mostly 'cause I lie a lot anyway." Her fiction has been collected in *Gorilla, My Love* (1972) and *The Sea Birds Are Still Alive* (1977), and in 1980 she published her first novel, *Salt Eaters,* followed by *If Blessing Comes* (1987). A number of her screenplays have been produced, including *Epitaph for Willie* and *Tar Baby.* In the following story a serious lesson is prescribed with a healthy dose of humor.

The Lesson   1972

Back in the days when everyone was old and stupid or young and foolish and me and Sugar were the only ones just right, this lady moved on our block with nappy hair and proper speech and no makeup. And quite naturally we laughed at her, laughed the way we did at the junk man who went about his business like he was some big-time president and his sorry-ass horse his secretary. And we kinda hated her too, hated the way we did the winos who cluttered up our parks and pissed on our handball walls and stank up our hallways and stairs so you couldn't halfway play hide-and-seek without a goddamn gas mask. Miss Moore was her name. The only woman on the block with no first name. And she was black as hell, cept for her feet, which were fish-white and spooky. And she was always planning these boring-ass things for us to do, us being my cousin, mostly, who lived on the block cause we all moved North the same time and to the same apartment then spread out gradual to breathe. And our parents would yank our heads into some kinda shape and crisp up our clothes so we'd be presentable for travel with Miss Moore, who always looked like she was going to church, though she never did. Which is just one of the things the grownups talked about when they talked behind her back like a dog. But when she came calling with some sachet she'd sewed up or some gingerbread she'd made or some book, why then they'd all be too embarrassed to turn her down and we'd get handed over all spruced up. She'd been to college and said it was only right that she should take responsibility for the young ones' education, and she not even related by marriage or blood. So they'd go for it. Specially Aunt Gretchen. She was the main gofer in the family. You got some ole dumb shit foolishness you want somebody to go for, you send for Aunt Gretchen. She been screwed into the go-along for so long, it's a blood-deep natural thing with her. Which is how she got saddled with me and Sugar and Junior in the first place while our mothers were in a la-de-da apartment up the block having a good ole time.

So this one day Miss Moore rounds us all up at the mailbox and it's puredee hot and she's knockin herself out about arithmetic. And school suppose to let up in summer I heard, but she don't never let up. And the starch in my pinafore scratching the shit outta me and I'm really hating this nappy-head bitch and her goddamn college degree. I'd much rather go to the pool or to the show where it's cool. So me and Sugar leaning on the mailbox being surly, which is a Miss Moore word. And Flyboy checking out what everybody brought for lunch. And Fat Butt already wasting his peanut-butter-and-jelly sandwich like the pig he is. And Junebug punchin on Q.T.'s arm for potato chips. And Rosie Giraffe shifting from one hip to the other waiting for somebody to step on her foot or ask her if she from Georgia so she can kick ass, preferably Mercedes'. And Miss Moore asking us do we know what money is, like we a bunch of retards. I mean real money, she say, like it's only poker chips or monopoly papers we lay on the grocer. So right away I'm tired of this and say so. And would much rather snatch Sugar and go to the Sunset and terrorize the West Indian kids and take their hair ribbons and their money too. And Miss Moore files that remark away for next week's lesson on brotherhood, I can tell. And finally I say we oughta get to the subway cause it's cooler and besides we might meet some cute boys. Sugar done swiped her mama's lipstick, so we ready.

So we heading down the street and she's boring us silly about what things cost and what our parents make and how much goes for rent and how money ain't divided up right in this country. And then she gets to the part about we all poor and live in the slums, which I don't feature. And I'm ready to speak on that, but she steps out in the street and hails two cabs just like that. Then she hustles half the crew in with her and hands me a five-dollar bill and tells me to calculate 10 percent tip for the driver. And we're off. Me and Sugar and Junebug and Flyboy hangin out the window and hollering to everybody, putting lipstick on each other cause Flyboy a faggot anyway, and making farts with our sweaty armpits. But I'm mostly trying to figure how to spend this money. But they all fascinated with the meter ticking and Junebug starts laying bets as to how much it'll read when Flyboy can't hold his breath no more. Then Sugar lays bets as to how much it'll be when we get there. So I'm stuck. Don't nobody want to go for my plan, which is to jump out at the next light and run off to the first bar-b-que we can find. Then the driver tells us to get the hell out cause we there already. And the meter reads eighty-five cents. And I'm stalling to figure out the tip and Sugar say give him a dime. And I decide he don't need it bad as I do, so later for him. But then he tries to take off with Junebug foot still in the door so we talk about his mama something ferocious. Then we check out that we on Fifth Avenue and everybody dressed up in stockings. One lady in a fur coat, hot as it is. White folks crazy.

"This is the place," Miss Moore say, presenting it to us in the voice she uses at the museum. "Let's look in the windows before we go in."

"Can we steal?" Sugar asks very serious like she's getting the ground rules 5 squared away before she plays. "I beg your pardon," say Miss Moore, and we fall out. So she leads us around the windows of the toy store and me and Sugar screamin, "This is mine, that's mine, I gotta have that, that was made for me, I was born for that," till Big Butt drowns us out.

"Hey, I'm goin to buy that there."

"That there? You don't even know what it is, stupid."

"I do so," he say punchin on Rosie Giraffe. "It's a microscope."

"Whatcha gonna do with a microscope, fool?"

"Look at things."   10

"Like what, Ronald?" ask Miss Moore. And Big Butt ain't got the first notion. So here go Miss Moore gabbing about the thousands of bacteria in a drop of water and the somethinorother in a speck of blood and the million and one living things in the air around us is invisible to the naked eye. And what she say that for? Junebug go to town on that "naked" and we rolling. Then Miss Moore ask what it cost. So we all jam into the window smudgin it up and the price tag say $300. So then she ask how long'd take for Big Butt and Junebug to save up their allowances. "Too long," I say. "Yeh," adds Sugar, "outgrown it by that time." And Miss Moore say no, you never outgrow learning instruments. "Why, even medical students and interns and," blah, blah, blah. And we ready to choke Big Butt for bringing it up in the first damn place.

"This here costs four hundred eighty dollars," says Rosie Giraffe. So we pile up all over her to see what she pointin out. My eyes tell me it's a chunk of glass cracked with something heavy, and different-color inks dripped into the splits, then the whole thing put into a oven or something. But for $480 it don't make sense.

"That's a paperweight made of semi-precious stones fused together under tremendous pressure," she explains slowly, with her hands doing the mining and all the factory work.

"So what's a paperweight?" asks Rosie Giraffe.

"To weigh paper with, dumbbell," say Flyboy, the wise man from the East.   15

"Not exactly," say Miss Moore, which is what she say when you warm or way off too. "It's to weigh paper down so it won't scatter and make your desk untidy." So right away me and Sugar curtsy to each other and then to Mercedes who is more the tidy type.

"We don't keep paper on top of the desk in my class," say Junebug, figuring Miss Moore crazy or lyin one.

"At home, then," she say. "Don't you have a calendar and pencil case and a blotter and a letter-opener on your desk at home where you do your homework?" And she know damn well what our homes look like cause she nosys around in them every chance she gets.

"I don't even have a desk," say Junebug. "Do we?"

"No. And I don't get no homework neither," says Big Butt.   20

"And I don't even have a home," say Flyboy like he do at school to keep the white folks off his back and sorry for him. Send this poor kid to camp posters, is his specialty.

"I do," says Mercedes. "I have a box of stationery on my desk and a picture of my cat. My godmother bought the stationery and the desk. There's a big rose on each sheet and the envelopes smell like roses."

"Who wants to know about your smelly-ass stationery," say Rosie Giraffe fore I can get my two cents in.

"It's important to have a work area all your own so that . . ."

"Will you look at this sailboat, please," say Flyboy, cuttin her off and 25 pointin to the thing like it was his. So once again we tumble all over each other to gaze at this magnificent thing in the toy store which is just big enough to maybe sail two kittens across the pond if you strap them to the posts tight. We all start reciting the price tag like we in assembly. "Handcrafted sailboat of fiberglass at one thousand one hundred ninety-five dollars."

"Unbelievable," I hear myself say and am really stunned. I read it again for myself just in case the group recitation put me in a trance. Same thing. For some reason this pisses me off. We look at Miss Moore and she lookin at us, waiting for I dunno what.

"Who'd pay all that when you can buy a sailboat set for a quarter at Pop's, a tube of glue for a dime, and a ball of string for eight cents? It must have a motor and a whole lot else besides," I say. "My sailboat cost me about fifty cents."

"But will it take water?" say Mercedes with her smart ass.

"Took mine to Alley Pond Park once," say Flyboy. "String broke. Lost it. Pity."

"Sailed mine in Central Park and it keeled over and sank. Had to ask my 30 father for another dollar."

"And you got the strap," laugh Big Butt. "The jerk didn't even have a string on it. My old man wailed on his behind."

Little Q.T. was staring hard at the sailboat and you could see he wanted it bad. But he too little and somebody'd just take it from him. So what the hell. "This boat for kids, Miss Moore?"

"Parents silly to buy something like that just to get all broke up," say Rosie Giraffe.

"That much money it should last forever," I figure.

"My father'd buy it for me if I wanted it." 35

"Your father, my ass," say Rosie Giraffe getting a chance to finally push Mercedes.

"Must be rich people shop here," say Q.T.

"You are a very bright boy," say Flyboy. "What was your first clue?" And he rap him on the head with the back of his knuckles, since Q.T. the only one he could get away with. Though Q.T. liable to come up behind you years later and get his licks in when you half expect it.

"What I want to know is," I says to Miss Moore though I never talk to her, I wouldn't give the bitch that satisfaction, "is how much a real boat costs? I figure a thousand'd get you a yacht any day."

"Why don't you check that out," she says, "and report back to the group?" 40 Which really pains my ass. If you gonna mess up a perfectly good swim day least you could do is have some answers. "Let's go in," she say like she got something up her sleeve. Only she don't lead the way. So me and Sugar turn the corner to where the entrance is, but when we get there I kinda hang back. Not that I'm scared, what's there to be afraid of, just a toy store. But I feel funny, shame. But what I got to be shamed about? Got as much right to go in as anybody. But somehow I can't seem to get hold of the door, so I step away from Sugar to lead. But she hangs back too. And I look at her and she looks at me and this is ridiculous. I mean, damn, I have never ever been shy about doing nothing or going nowhere. But then Mercedes steps up and then Rosie Giraffe and Big Butt crowd in behind and shove, and next thing we all stuffed into the doorway with only Mercedes squeezing past us, smoothing out her jumper and walking right down the aisle. Then the rest of us tumble in like a glued-together jigsaw done all wrong. And people lookin at us. And it's like the time me and Sugar crashed into the Catholic church on a dare. But once we got in there and everything so hushed and holy and the candles and the bowin and the handkerchiefs on all the drooping heads, I just couldn't go through with the plan. Which was for me to run up to the altar and do a tap dance while Sugar played the nose flute and messed around in the holy water. And Sugar kept givin me the elbow. Then later teased me so bad I tied her up in the shower and turned it on and locked her in. And she'd be there till this day if Aunt Gretchen hadn't finally figured I was lyin about the boarder takin a shower.

Same thing in the store. We all walkin on tiptoe and hardly touchin the games and puzzles and things. And I watched Miss Moore who is steady watchin us like she waitin for a sign. Like Mama Drewery watches the sky and sniffs the air and takes note of just how much slant is in the bird formation. Then me and Sugar bump smack into each other, so busy gazing at the toys, specially the sailboat. But we don't laugh and go into our fat-lady bump-stomach routine. We just stare at that price tag. Then Sugar run a finger over the whole boat. And I'm jealous and want to hit her. Maybe not her, but I sure want to punch somebody in the mouth.

"Watcha bring us here for, Miss Moore?"

"You sound angry, Sylvia. Are you mad about something?" Givin me one of them grins like she tellin a grown-up joke that never turns out to be funny. And she's lookin very closely at me like maybe she planning to do my portrait from memory. I'm mad, but I won't give her that satisfaction. So I slouch around the store bein very bored and say, "Let's go."

Me and Sugar at the back of the train watchin the tracks whizzin by large then small then getting gobbled up in the dark. I'm thinkin about this tricky toy I saw in the store. A clown that somersaults on a bar then does chin-ups just cause you yank lightly at his leg. Cost $35. I could see me askin my mother for a $35 birthday clown. "You wanna who that costs what?" she'd say, cocking her head to the side to get a better view of the hole in my head. Thirty-five dollars could buy new bunk beds for Junior and Gretchen's boy. Thirty-five dollars and the whole household could go visit Granddaddy Nelson in the country. Thirty-five dollars would pay for the rent and the piano bill too. Who are these people that spend that much for performing clowns and $1000 for toy sail-boats? What kinda work they do and how they live and how come we ain't in on it? Where we are is who we are, Miss Moore always pointin out. But it don't necessarily have to be that way, she always adds then waits for somebody to say that poor people have to wake up and demand their share of the pie and don't none of us know what kind of pie she talking about in the first damn place. But she ain't so smart cause I still got her four dollars from the taxi and she sure ain't gettin it. Messin up my day with this shit. Sugar nudges me in my pocket and winks.

Miss Moore lines us up in front of the mailbox where we started from, 45 seem like years ago, and I got a headache for thinkin so hard. And we lean all over each other so we can hold up under the draggy-ass lecture she always finishes us off with at the end before we thank her for borin us to tears. But she just looks at us like she readin tea leaves. Finally she say, "Well, what did you think of F. A. O. Schwarz?"

Rosie Giraffe mumbles, "White folks crazy."

"I'd like to go there again when I get my birthday money," says Mercedes, and we shove her out the pack so she has to lean on the mailbox by herself.

"I'd like a shower. Tiring day," say Flyboy.

Then Sugar surprises me by sayin, "You know, Miss Moore, I don't think all of us here put together eat in a year what that sailboat costs." And Miss Moore lights up like somebody goosed her. "And?" she say, urging Sugar on. Only I'm standin on her foot so she don't continue.

"Imagine for a minute what kind of society it is in which some people can 50 spend on a toy what it would cost to feed a family of six or seven. What do you think?"

"I think," say Sugar pushing me off her feet like she never done before, cause I whip her ass in a minute, "that this is not much of a democracy if you ask me. Equal chance to pursue happiness means an equal crack at the dough, don't it?" Miss Moore is beside herself and I am disgusted with Sugar's treachery. So I stand on her foot one more time to see if she'll shove me. She shuts up, and Miss Moore looks at me, sorrowfully I'm thinkin. And somethin weird is goin on, I can feel it in my chest.

"Anybody else learn anything today?" lookin dead at me. I walk away and Sugar has to run to catch up and don't even seem to notice when I shrug her arm off my shoulder.

"Well, we got four dollars anyway," she says.

"Uh hunh."

"We could go to Hascombs and get half a chocolate layer and then go to 55 the Sunset and still have plenty money for potato chips and ice cream sodas."

"Un hunh."

"Race you to Hascombs," she say.

We start down the block and she gets ahead which is O.K. by me cause I'm going to the West End and then over to the Drive to think this day through. She can run if she want to and even run faster. But ain't nobody gonna beat me at nuthin.

CONSIDERATIONS FOR CRITICAL THINKING AND WRITING

1. FIRST RESPONSE. How did you react to Bambara's serious social commentary in this story? Is it convincing? Preachy? Does it make you feel guilty?

2. What is the lesson Miss Moore tries to teach Sylvia? Is she successful? Invent an alternative title that captures for you the central meaning of the story.

3. What is the conflict in this story? Is there more than one? How are these conflicts resolved?

4. Write a paragraph characterizing Miss Moore's point of view about herself. Then write a descriptive paragraph of Miss Moore from Sylvia's point of view. Try to capture their voices in your descriptions.

5. The story begins with an adult narrator recalling her youth: "Back in the days when . . ." Although that adult perspective is quickly replaced by the young girl's point of view, what do you think the adult narrator thinks of herself as a young girl?

6. Explain why the use of an editorial omniscient point of view in this story would be inappropriate.

7. How does Sylvia's use of language serve to characterize her?

8. How do you feel about Miss Moore at the end of the story compared with your feelings about her at the beginning? Why?

9. How do Sylvia and Sugar get along? What does this relationship reveal about Sylvia?

10. What do you think the last line of the story means? Does Sylvia think Sugar is smarter than she is because Sugar knew the answer to Miss Moore's question and she didn't? Who else could the "nobody" in that line refer to besides Sugar?

CONNECTIONS TO OTHER SELECTIONS

1. Compare the treatment of youth and age in "The Lesson" with the treatment in Katherine Mansfield's "Miss Brill" (p. 258).

2. Discuss Bambara's characterization of children with Flannery O'Connor's in "A Good Man Is Hard to Find" (p. 381). Which author's treatment of children seems more convincing to you? Why?

3. Write an essay comparing the lessons learned by the protagonists in "The Lesson" and in Ralph Ellison's "Battle Royal" (p. 223).

ANTON CHEKHOV (1860–1904)

Born in a small town in Russia, Anton Chekhov gave up the career his medical degree prepared him for in order to devote himself to writing. His concentration on realistic detail in the hundreds of short stories he published has had an important influence on fiction writing. Modern drama has also been strengthened by his plays, among them these classics: *The Seagull* (1896), *Uncle Vanya* (1899), *The Three Sisters* (1901), and *The Cherry Orchard* (1904). Chekhov was a close observer of people in ordinary situations who struggle to live their lives as best they can. They are not very often completely successful. Chekhov's compassion, however, makes their failures less significant than their humanity. In "The Lady with the Pet Dog," love is at the heart of a struggle that begins in Yalta, a resort town on the Black Sea.

The Lady with the Pet Dog   1899

TRANSLATED BY AVRAHM YARMOLINSKY (1947)

I

A new person, it was said, had appeared on the esplanade: a lady with a pet dog. Dmitry Dmitrich Gurov, who had spent a fortnight at Yalta and had got used to the place, had also begun to take an interest in new arrivals. As he sat in Vernet's confectionery shop, he saw, walking on the esplanade, a fair-haired young woman of medium height, wearing a beret; a white Pomeranian was trotting behind her.

And afterwards he met her in the public garden and in the square several times a day. She walked alone, always wearing the same beret and always with the white dog; no one knew who she was and everyone called her simply "the lady with the pet dog."

"If she is here alone without husband or friends," Gurov reflected, "it wouldn't be a bad thing to make her acquaintance."

He was under forty, but he already had a daughter twelve years old, and two sons at school. They had found a wife for him when he was very young, a student in his second year, and by now she seemed half as old again as he. She was a tall, erect woman with dark eyebrows, stately and dignified and, as she said of herself, intellectual. She read a great deal, used simplified spelling in her letters, called her husband, not Dmitry, but Dimitry, while he privately considered her of limited intelligence, narrow-minded, dowdy, was afraid of her, and did not like to be at home. He had begun being unfaithful to her long ago — had been unfaithful to her often and, probably for that reason, almost always spoke ill of women, and when they were talked of in his presence used to call them "the inferior race."

It seemed to him that he had been sufficiently tutored by bitter experience to call them what he pleased, and yet he could not have lived without "the inferior race" for two days together. In the company of men he was bored and ill at ease, he was chilly and uncommunicative with them; but when he was among women he felt free, and knew what to speak to them about and how to comport himself; and even to be silent with them was no strain on him. In his appearance, in his character, in his whole makeup there was something attractive and elusive that disposed women in his favor and allured them. He knew that, and some force seemed to draw him to them, too.

Oft-repeated and really bitter experience had taught him long ago that with decent people — particularly Moscow people — who are irresolute and slow to move, every affair which at first seems a light and charming adventure inevitably grows into a whole problem of extreme complexity, and in the end a painful situation is created. But at every new meeting with an interesting woman this lesson of experience seemed to slip from his memory, and he was eager for life, and everything seemed so simple and diverting.

One evening while he was dining in the public garden the lady in the beret walked up without haste to take the next table. Her expression, her gait, her dress, and the way she did her hair told him that she belonged to the upper class, that she was married, that she was in Yalta for the first time and alone, and that she was bored there. The stories told of the immorality in Yalta are to a great extent untrue; he despised them, and knew that such stories were made up for the most part by persons who would have been glad to sin themselves if they had had the chance; but when the lady sat down at the next table three paces from him, he recalled these stories of easy conquests, of trips to the mountains, and the tempting thought of swift, fleeting liaison, a romance with an unknown woman of whose very name he was ignorant suddenly took hold of him.

He beckoned invitingly to the Pomeranian, and when the dog approached him, shook his finger at it. The Pomeranian growled; Gurov threatened it again.

The lady glanced at him and at once dropped her eyes.

"He doesn't bite," she said and blushed.

"May I give him a bone?" he asked; and when she nodded he inquired affably, "Have you been in Yalta long?"

"About five days."

"And I am dragging out the second week here."

There was a short silence.

"Time passes quickly, and yet it is so dull here!" she said, not looking at him.

"It's only the fashion to say it's dull here. A provincial will live in Belyov or Zhizdra and not be bored, but when he comes here it's 'Oh, the dullness! Oh, the dust!' One would think he came from Granada."

She laughed. Then both continued eating in silence, like strangers, but after dinner they walked together and there sprang up between them the light banter of people who are free and contented, to whom it does not matter where they go or what they talk about. They walked and talked of the strange light on the sea: the water was a soft, warm, lilac color, and there was a golden band of moonlight upon it. They talked of how sultry it was after a hot day. Gurov told her that he was a native of Moscow, that he had studied languages and literature at the university, but had a post in a bank; that at one time he had trained to become an opera singer but had given it up, that he owned two houses in Moscow. And he learned from her that she had grown up in Petersburg, but had lived in S— since her marriage two years previously, that she was going to stay in Yalta for about another month, and that her husband, who needed a rest, too, might perhaps come to fetch her. She was not certain whether her husband was a member of a Government Board or served on a Zemstvo Council,° and this amused her. And Gurov learned too that her name was Anna Sergeyevna.

Afterwards in his room at the hotel he thought about her—and was certain that he would meet her the next day. It was bound to happen. Getting into bed he recalled that she had been a schoolgirl only recently, doing lessons like his own daughter; he thought how much timidity and angularity there was still in her laugh and her manner of talking with a stranger. It must have been the first time in her life that she was alone in a setting in which she was followed, looked at, and spoken to for one secret purpose alone, which she could hardly fail to guess. He thought of her slim, delicate throat, her lovely gray eyes.

"There's something pathetic about her, though," he thought, and dropped off.

II

A week had passed since they had struck up an acquaintance. It was a holiday. It was close indoors, while in the street the wind whirled the dust about and blew people's hats off. One was thirsty all day, and Gurov often went into the restaurant and offered Anna Sergeyevna a soft drink or ice cream. One did not know what to do with oneself.

In the evening when the wind had abated they went out on the pier to watch the steamer come in. There were a great many people walking about the dock; they had come to welcome someone and they were carrying bunches of

Zemstvo Council: A district council.

flowers. And two peculiarities of a festive Yalta crowd stood out: the elderly ladies were dressed like young ones and there were many generals.

Owing to the choppy sea, the steamer arrived late, after sunset, and it was a long time tacking about before it put in at the pier. Anna Sergeyevna peered at the steamer and the passengers through her lorgnette as though looking for acquaintances, and whenever she turned to Gurov her eyes were shining. She talked a great deal and asked questions jerkily, forgetting the next moment what she had asked; then she lost her lorgnette in the crush.

The festive crowd began to disperse; it was now too dark to see people's faces; there was no wind any more, but Gurov and Anna Sergeyevna still stood as though waiting to see someone else come off the steamer. Anna Sergeyevna was silent now, and sniffed her flowers without looking at Gurov.

"The weather has improved this evening," he said. "Where shall we go now? Shall we drive somewhere?"

She did not reply.   25

Then he looked at her intently, and suddenly embraced her and kissed her on the lips, and the moist fragrance of her flowers enveloped him; and at once he looked round him anxiously, wondering if anyone had seen them.

"Let us go to your place," he said softly. And they walked off together rapidly.

The air in her room was close and there was the smell of the perfume she had bought at the Japanese shop. Looking at her, Gurov thought: "What encounters life offers!" From the past he preserved the memory of carefree, good-natured women whom love made gay and who were grateful to him for the happiness he gave them, however brief it might be; and of women like his wife who loved without sincerity, with too many words, affectedly, hysterically, with an expression that it was not love or passion that engaged them but something more significant; and of two or three others, very beautiful, frigid women, across whose faces would suddenly flit a rapacious expression — an obstinate desire to take from life more than it could give, and these were women no longer young, capricious, unreflecting, domineering, unintelligent, and when Gurov grew cold to them their beauty aroused his hatred, and the lace on their lingerie seemed to him to resemble scales.

But here there was the timidity, the angularity of inexperienced youth, a feeling of awkwardness; and there was a sense of embarrassment, as though someone had suddenly knocked at the door. Anna Sergeyevna, "the lady with the pet dog," treated what had happened in a peculiar way, very seriously, as though it were her fall — so it seemed, and this was odd and inappropriate. Her features drooped and faded, and her long hair hung down sadly on either side of her face; she grew pensive and her dejected pose was that of a Magdalene in a picture by an old master.

"It's not right," she said. "You don't respect me now, you first of all."   30

There was a watermelon on the table. Gurov cut himself a slice and began eating it without haste. They were silent for at least half an hour.

There was something touching about Anna Sergeyevna; she had the purity of a well-bred, naive woman who has seen little of life. The single candle burning on the table barely illumined her face, yet it was clear that she was unhappy.

"Why should I stop respecting you, darling?" asked Gurov. "You don't know what you're saying."

"God forgive me," she said, and her eyes filled with tears. "It's terrible."

"It's as though you were trying to exonerate yourself." 35

"How can I exonerate myself? No. I am a bad, low woman; I despise myself and I have no thought of exonerating myself. It's not my husband but myself I have deceived. And not only just now; I have been deceiving myself for a long time. My husband may be a good, honest man, but he is a flunkey! I don't know what he does, what his work is, but I know he is a flunkey! I was twenty when I married him. I was tormented by curiosity; I wanted something better. 'There must be a different sort of life,' I said to myself. I wanted to live! To live, to live! Curiosity kept eating at me—you don't understand it, but I swear to God I could no longer control myself; something was going on in me: I could not be held back. I told my husband I was ill, and came here. And here I have been walking about as though in a daze, as though I were mad; and now I have become a vulgar, vile woman whom anyone may despise."

Gurov was already bored with her; he was irritated by her naive tone, by her repentance, so unexpected and so out of place; but for the tears in her eyes he might have thought she was joking or play-acting.

"I don't understand, my dear," he said softly. "What do you want?"

She hid her face on his breast and pressed close to him.

"Believe me, believe me, I beg you," she said, "I love honesty and purity, 40 and sin is loathsome to me; I don't know what I'm doing. Simple people say, 'The Evil One has led me astray.' And I may say of myself now that the Evil One has led me astray."

"Quiet, quiet," he murmured.

He looked into her fixed, frightened eyes, kissed her, spoke to her softly and affectionately, and by degrees she calmed down, and her gaiety returned; both began laughing.

Afterwards when they went out there was not a soul on the esplanade. The town with its cypresses looked quite dead, but the sea was still sounding as it broke upon the beach; a single launch was rocking on the waves and on it a lantern was blinking sleepily.

They found a cab and drove to Oreanda.

"I found out your surname in the hall just now: it was written on the 45 board—von Dideritz," said Gurov. "Is your husband German?"

"No; I believe his grandfather was German, but he is Greek Orthodox himself."

At Oreanda they sat on a bench not far from the church, looked down at the sea, and were silent. Yalta was barely visible through the morning mist; white clouds rested motionlessly on the mountaintops. The leaves did not stir on the trees, cicadas twanged, and the monotonous muffled sound of the sea that rose from below spoke of the peace, the eternal sleep awaiting us. So it rumbled below when there was no Yalta, no Oreanda here; so it rumbles now, and it will rumble as indifferently and as hollowly when we are no more. And in this constancy, in this complete indifference to the life and death of each of us, there lies, perhaps, a pledge of our eternal salvation, of the unceasing advance of life upon earth, of unceasing movement towards perfection. Sitting beside a young woman who in the dawn seemed so lovely, Gurov, soothed and spellbound by these magical surroundings—the sea, the mountains, the clouds, the wide sky—thought how everything is really beautiful in this world when one reflects: everything except what we think or do ourselves when we forget the higher aims of life and our own human dignity.

A man strolled up to them — probably a guard — looked at them and walked away. And this detail, too, seemed so mysterious and beautiful. They saw a steamer arrive from Feodosia, its lights extinguished in the glow of dawn.

"There is dew on the grass," said Anna Sergeyevna, after a silence.

"Yes, it's time to go home."   50

They returned to the city.

Then they met every day at twelve o'clock on the esplanade, lunched and dined together, took walks, admired the sea. She complained that she slept badly, that she had palpitations, asked the same questions, troubled now by jealousy and now by the fear that he did not respect her sufficiently. And often in the square or the public garden, when there was no one near them, he suddenly drew her to him and kissed her passionately. Complete idleness, these kisses in broad daylight exchanged furtively in dread of someone's seeing them, the heat, the smell of the sea, and the continual flitting before his eyes of idle, well-dressed, well-fed people, worked a complete change in him; he kept telling Anna Sergeyevna how beautiful she was, how seductive, was urgently passionate; he would not move a step away from her, while she was often pensive and continually pressed him to confess that he did not respect her, did not love her in the least, and saw in her nothing but a common woman. Almost every evening rather late they drove somewhere out of town, to Oreanda or to the waterfall; and the excursion was always a success, the scenery invariably impressed them as beautiful and magnificent.

They were expecting her husband, but a letter came from him saying that he had eye-trouble, and begging his wife to return home as soon as possible. Anna Sergeyevna made haste to go.

"It's a good thing I am leaving," she said to Gurov. "It's the hand of Fate!"

She took a carriage to the railway station, and he went with her. They were   55 driving the whole day. When she had taken her place in the express, and when the second bell had rung, she said, "Let me look at you once more — let me look at you again. Like this."

She was not crying but was so sad that she seemed ill, and her face was quivering.

"I shall be thinking of you — remembering you," she said. "God bless you; be happy. Don't remember evil against me. We are parting forever — it has to be, for we ought never to have met. Well, God bless you."

The train moved off rapidly, its lights soon vanished, and a minute later there was no sound of it, as though everything had conspired to end as quickly as possible that sweet trance, that madness. Left alone on the platform, and gazing into the dark distance, Gurov listened to the twang of the grasshoppers and the hum of the telegraph wires, feeling as though he had just waked up. And he reflected, musing, that there had now been another episode or adventure in his life, and it, too, was at an end, and nothing was left of it but a memory. He was moved, sad, and slightly remorseful: this young woman whom he would never meet again had not been happy with him; he had been warm and affectionate with her, but yet in his manner, his tone, and his caresses there had been a shade of light irony, the slightly coarse arrogance of a happy male who was, besides, almost twice her age. She had constantly called him kind, exceptional, high-minded; obviously he had seemed to her different from what he really was, so he had involuntarily deceived her.

Here at the station there was already a scent of autumn in the air; it was a chilly evening.

"It is time for me to go north, too," thought Gurov as he left the platform. 60 "High time!"

III

At home in Moscow the winter routine was already established: the stoves were heated, and in the morning it was still dark when the children were having breakfast and getting ready for school, and the nurse would light the lamp for a short time. There were frosts already. When the first snow falls, on the first day the sleighs are out, it is pleasant to see the white earth, the white roofs; one draws easy, delicious breaths, and the season brings back the days of one's youth. The old limes and birches, white with hoar-frost, have a good-natured look; they are closer to one's heart than cypresses and palms, and near them one no longer wants to think of mountains and the sea.

Gurov, a native of Moscow, arrived there on a fine frosty day, and when he put on his fur coat and warm gloves and took a walk along Petrovka, and when on Saturday night he heard the bells ringing, his recent trip and the places he had visited lost all charm for him. Little by little he became immersed in Moscow life, greedily read three newspapers a day, and declared that he did not read the Moscow papers on principle. He already felt a longing for restaurants, clubs, formal dinners, anniversary celebrations, and it flattered him to entertain distinguished lawyers and actors, and to play cards with a professor at the physicians' club. He could eat a whole portion of meat stewed with pickled cabbage and served in a pan, Moscow style.

A month or so would pass and the image of Anna Sergeyevna, it seemed to him, would become misty in his memory, and only from time to time he would dream of her with her touching smile as he dreamed of others. But more than a month went by, winter came into its own, and everything was still clear in his memory as though he had parted from Anna Sergeyevna only yesterday. And his memories glowed more and more vividly. When in the evening stillness the voices of his children preparing their lessons reached his study, or when he listened to a song or to an organ playing in a restaurant, or when the storm howled in the chimney, suddenly everything would rise up in his memory: what had happened on the pier and the early morning with the mist on the mountains, and the steamer coming from Feodosia, and the kisses. He would pace about his room a long time, remembering and smiling; then his memories passed into reveries, and in his imagination the past would mingle with what was to come. He did not dream of Anna Sergeyevna, but she followed him about everywhere and watched him. When he shut his eyes he saw her before him as though she were there in the flesh; and she seemed to him lovelier, younger, tenderer than she had been, and he imagined himself a finer man than he had been in Yalta. Of evenings she peered out at him from the bookcase, from the fireplace, from the corner — he heard her breathing, the caressing rustle of her clothes. In the street he followed the women with his eyes, looking for someone who resembled her.

Already he was tormented by a strong desire to share his memories with someone. But in his home it was impossible to talk of his love, and he had no

one to talk to outside; certainly he could not confide in his tenants or in anyone at the bank. And what was there to talk about? He hadn't loved her then,
had he? Had there been anything beautiful, poetical, edifying, or simply interesting in his relations with Anna Sergeyevna? And he was forced to talk vaguely
of love, of women, and no one guessed what he meant; only his wife would
twitch her black eyebrows and say, "The part of a philanderer does not suit you
at all, Dimitry."

One evening, coming out of the physicians' club with an official with   65
whom he had been playing cards, he could not resist saying:

"If you only knew what a fascinating woman I became acquainted with at
Yalta!"

The official got into his sledge and was driving away, but turned suddenly
and shouted: "Dmitry Dmitrich!"

"What is it?"

"You were right this evening: the sturgeon was a bit high."

These words, so commonplace, for some reason moved Gurov to indigna-   70
tion, and struck him as degrading and unclean. What savage manners, what
mugs! What stupid nights, what dull, humdrum days! Frenzied gambling,
gluttony, drunkenness, continual talk always about the same things! Futile
pursuits and conversations always about the same topics take up the better
part of one's time, the better part of one's strength, and in the end there is left
a life clipped and wingless, an absurd mess, and there is no escaping or getting
away from it—just as though one were in a madhouse or a prison.

Gurov, boiling with indignation, did not sleep all night. And he had a
headache all the next day. And the following nights too he slept badly; he sat up in
bed, thinking, or paced up and down his room. He was fed up with his children,
fed up with the bank; he had no desire to go anywhere or to talk of anything.

In December during the holidays he prepared to take a trip and told his
wife he was going to Petersburg to do what he could for a young friend—and
he set off for S——. What for? He did not know, himself. He wanted to see Anna
Sergeyevna and talk with her, to arrange a rendezvous if possible.

He arrived at S—— in the morning, and at the hotel took the best room, in
which the floor was covered with gray army cloth, and on the table there was
an inkstand, gray with dust and topped by a figure on horseback, its hat in its
raised hand and its head broken off. The porter gave him the necessary information: von Dideritz lived in a house of his own on Staro-Goncharnaya Street,
not far from the hotel: he was rich and lived well and kept his own horses;
everyone in the town knew him. The porter pronounced the name: "Dridiritz."

Without haste Gurov made his way to Staro-Goncharnaya Street and
found the house. Directly opposite the house stretched a long gray fence stud-
ded with nails.

"A fence like that would make one run away," thought Gurov, looking now   75
at the fence, now at the windows of the house.

He reflected: this was a holiday, and the husband was apt to be at home.
And in any case, it would be tactless to go into the house and disturb her. If he
were to send her a note, it might fall into her husband's hands, and that might
spoil everything. The best thing was to rely on chance. And he kept walking up
and down the street and along the fence, waiting for the chance. He saw a beggar go in at the gate and heard the dogs attack him; then an hour later he
heard a piano, and the sound came to him faintly and indistinctly. Probably it

was Anna Sergeyevna playing. The front door opened suddenly, and an old woman came out, followed by the familiar white Pomeranian. Gurov was on the point of calling to the dog, but his heart began beating violently, and in his excitement he could not remember the Pomeranian's name.

He kept walking up and down, and hated the gray fence more and more, and by now he thought irritably that Anna Sergeyevna had forgotten him, and was perhaps already diverting herself with another man, and that that was very natural in a young woman who from morning till night had to look at that damn fence. He went back to his hotel room and sat on the couch for a long while, not knowing what to do, then he had dinner and a long nap.

"How stupid and annoying all this is!" he thought when he woke and looked at the dark windows: it was already evening. "Here I've had a good sleep for some reason. What am I going to do at night?"

He sat on the bed, which was covered with a cheap gray blanket of the kind seen in hospitals, and he twitted himself in his vexation:

"So there's your lady with the pet dog. There's your adventure. A nice 80 place to cool your heels in."

That morning at the station a playbill in large letters had caught his eye. *The Geisha* was to be given for the first time. He thought of this and drove to the theater.

"It's quite possible that she goes to first nights," he thought.

The theater was full. As in all provincial theaters, there was a haze above the chandelier, the gallery was noisy and restless; in the front row, before the beginning of the performance the local dandies were standing with their hands clasped behind their backs; in the Governor's box the Governor's daughter, wearing a boa, occupied the front seat, while the Governor himself hid modestly behind the portiere and only his hands were visible; the curtain swayed; the orchestra was a long time tuning up. While the audience were coming in and taking their seats, Gurov scanned the faces eagerly.

Anna Sergeyevna, too, came in. She sat down in the third row, and when Gurov looked at her his heart contracted, and he understood clearly that in the whole world there was no human being so near, so precious, and so important to him; she, this little, undistinguished woman, lost in a provincial crowd, with a vulgar lorgnette in her hand, filled his whole life now, was his sorrow and his joy, the only happiness that he now desired for himself, and to the sounds of the bad orchestra, of the miserable local violins, he thought how lovely she was. He thought and dreamed.

A young man with small side-whiskers, very tall and stooped, came in with 85 Anna Sergeyevna and sat down beside her; he nodded his head at every step and seemed to be bowing continually. Probably this was the husband whom at Yalta, in an excess of bitter feeling, she had called a flunkey. And there really was in his lanky figure, his side-whiskers, his small bald patch, something of a flunkey's retiring manner; his smile was mawkish, and in his buttonhole there was an academic badge like a waiter's number.

During the first intermission the husband went out to have a smoke; she remained in her seat. Gurov, who was also sitting in the orchestra, went up to her and said in a shaky voice, with a forced smile:

"Good evening!"

She glanced at him and turned pale, then looked at him again in horror, unable to believe her eyes, and gripped the fan and the lorgnette tightly together in her hands, evidently trying to keep herself from fainting. Both were silent. She was sitting, he was standing, frightened by her distress and not daring to take a seat beside her. The violins and the flute that were being tuned up sang out. He suddenly felt frightened: it seemed as if all the people in the boxes were looking at them. She got up and went hurriedly to the exit; he followed her, and both of them walked blindly along the corridors and up and down stairs, and figures in the uniforms prescribed for magistrates, teachers, and officials of the Department of Crown Lands, all wearing badges, flitted before their eyes, as did also ladies, and fur coats on hangers; they were conscious of drafts and the smell of stale tobacco. And Gurov, whose heart was beating violently, thought:

"Oh, Lord! Why are these people here and this orchestra!"

And at that instant he suddenly recalled how when he had seen Anna   90
Sergeyevna off at the station he had said to himself that all was over between them and that they would never meet again. But how distant the end still was!

On the narrow, gloomy staircase over which it said "To the Amphitheatre," she stopped.

"How you frightened me!" she said, breathing hard, still pale and stunned. "Oh, how you frightened me! I am barely alive. Why did you come? Why?"

"But do understand, Anna, do understand—" he said hurriedly, under his breath. "I implore you, do understand—"

She looked at him with fear, with entreaty, with love; she looked at him intently, to keep his features more distinctly in her memory.

"I suffer so," she went on, not listening to him. "All this time I have been   95
thinking of nothing but you; I live only by the thought of you. And I wanted to forget, to forget; but why, oh, why have you come?"

On the landing above them two high school boys were looking down and smoking, but it was all the same to Gurov; he drew Anna Sergeyevna to him and began kissing her face and her hands.

"What are you doing, what are you doing!" she was saying in horror, pushing him away. "We have lost our senses. Go away today; go away at once—I conjure you by all that is sacred, I implore you—People are coming this way!"

Someone was walking up the stairs.

"You must leave," Anna Sergeyevna went on in a whisper. "Do you hear, Dmitry Dmitrich? I will come and see you in Moscow. I have never been happy; I am unhappy now, and I never, never shall be happy, never! So don't make me suffer still more! I swear I'll come to Moscow. But now let us part. My dear, good, precious one, let us part!"

She pressed his hand and walked rapidly downstairs, turning to look   100
round at him, and from her eyes he could see that she really was unhappy. Gurov stood for a while, listening, then when all grew quiet, he found his coat and left the theater.

IV

And Anna Sergeyevna began coming to see him in Moscow. Once every two or three months she left S——, telling her husband that she was going to consult a doctor about a woman's ailment from which she was suffering—and her husband did and did not believe her. When she arrived in Moscow she would stop at the Slavyansky Bazar Hotel, and at once send a man in a red cap to Gurov. Gurov came to see her, and no one in Moscow knew of it.

Once he was going to see her in this way on a winter morning (the messenger had come the evening before and not found him in). With him walked his daughter, whom he wanted to take to school: it was on the way. Snow was coming down in big wet flakes.

"It's three degrees above zero,° and yet it's snowing," Gurov was saying to his daughter. "But this temperature prevails only on the surface of the earth; in the upper layers of the atmosphere there is quite a different temperature."

"And why doesn't it thunder in winter, papa?"

He explained that, too. He talked, thinking all the while that he was on his way to a rendezvous, and no living soul knew of it, and probably no one would ever know. He had two lives: an open one, seen and known by all who needed to know it, full of conventional truth and conventional falsehood, exactly like the lives of his friends and acquaintances; and another life that went on in secret. And through some strange, perhaps accidental, combination of circumstances, everything that was of interest and importance to him, everything that was essential to him, everything about which he felt sincerely and did not deceive himself, everything that constituted the core of his life, was going on concealed from others; while all that was false, the shell in which he hid to cover the truth — his work at the bank, for instance, his discussions at the club, his references to the "inferior race," his appearances at anniversary celebrations with his wife — all that went on in the open. Judging others by himself, he did not believe what he saw, and always fancied that every man led his real, most interesting life under cover of secrecy as under cover of night. The personal life of every individual is based on secrecy, and perhaps it is partly for that reason that civilized man is so nervously anxious that personal privacy should be respected.

Having taken his daughter to school, Gurov went on to the Slavyansky Bazar Hotel. He took off his fur coat in the lobby, went upstairs, and knocked gently at the door. Anna Sergeyevna, wearing his favorite gray dress, exhausted by the journey and by waiting, had been expecting him since the previous evening. She was pale, and looked at him without a smile, and he had hardly entered when she flung herself on his breast. Their kiss was a long, lingering one, as though they had not seen one another for two years.

"Well, darling, how are you getting on there?" he asked. "What news?"

"Wait; I'll tell you in a moment — I can't speak."

She could not speak; she was crying. She turned away from him, and pressed her handkerchief to her eyes.

"Let her have her cry; meanwhile I'll sit down," he thought, and he seated himself in an armchair.

Then he rang and ordered tea, and while he was having his tea she remained standing at the window with her back to him. She was crying out of sheer agitation, in the sorrowful consciousness that their life was so sad; that they could only see each other in secret and had to hide from people like thieves! Was it not a broken life?

"Come, stop now, dear!" he said.

It was plain to him that this love of theirs would not be over soon, that the end of it was not in sight. Anna Sergeyevna was growing more and more attached to him. She adored him, and it was unthinkable to tell her that their

three degrees above zero: On the Celsius scale; about thirty-eight degrees Fahrenheit.

love was bound to come to an end some day; besides, she would not have believed it!

He went up to her and took her by the shoulders, to fondle her and say something diverting, and at that moment he caught sight of himself in the mirror.

His hair was already beginning to turn gray. And it seemed odd to him that 115 he had grown so much older in the last few years, and lost his looks. The shoulders on which his hands rested were warm and heaving. He felt compassion for this life, still so warm and lovely, but probably already about to begin to fade and wither like his own. Why did she love him so much? He always seemed to women different from what he was, and they loved in him not himself, but the man whom their imagination created and whom they had been eagerly seeking all their lives; and afterwards, when they saw their mistake, they loved him nevertheless. And not one of them had been happy with him. In the past he had met women, come together with them, parted from them, but he had never once loved; it was anything you please, but not love. And only now when his head was gray he had fallen in love, really, truly — for the first time in his life.

Anna Sergeyevna and he loved each other as people do who are very close and intimate, like man and wife, like tender friends; it seemed to them that Fate itself had meant them for one another, and they could not understand why he had a wife and she a husband; and it was as though they were a pair of migratory birds, male and female, caught and forced to live in different cages. They forgave each other what they were ashamed of in their past, they forgave everything in the present, and felt that this love of theirs had altered them both.

Formerly in moments of sadness he had soothed himself with whatever logical arguments came into his head, but now he no longer cared for logic; he felt profound compassion, he wanted to be sincere and tender.

"Give it up now, my darling," he said. "You've had your cry; that's enough. Let us have a talk now, we'll think up something."

Then they spent a long time taking counsel together, they talked of how to avoid the necessity for secrecy, for deception, for living in different cities, and not seeing one another for long stretches of time. How could they free themselves from these intolerable fetters?

"How? How?" he asked, clutching his head. "How?"   120

And it seemed as though in a little while the solution would be found, and then a new and glorious life would begin; and it was clear to both of them that the end was still far off, and that what was to be most complicated and difficult for them was only just beginning.

CONSIDERATIONS FOR CRITICAL THINKING AND WRITING

1. FIRST RESPONSE. Consider the following assessment of the story: "No excuses can be made for the lovers' adulterous affair. They behave selfishly and irresponsibly. They are immoral — and so is the story." Explain what you think Chekhov's response to this view would be, given his treatment of the lovers. How does this compare with your own views?

2. Why is it significant that the setting of this story is a resort town? How does the vacation atmosphere affect the action?

3. What does Gurov's view of women reveal about him? Why does he regard them as an "inferior race"?

4. What do we learn about Gurov's wife and Anna's husband? Why do you think Chekhov includes this exposition? How does it affect our view of the lovers?

5. When and why do Gurov's feelings about Anna begin to change? Is he really in love with her?

6. Who or what is the antagonist in this story? What is the nature of the conflict?

7. What is the effect of having Gurov as the central consciousness? How would the story be different if it were told from Anna's perspective?

8. Why do you think Chekhov does not report what ultimately becomes of the lovers? Is there a resolution to the conflict? Is the ending of the story effective?

9. Discuss the validity of Gurov's belief that people lead their real lives in private rather than in public: "The personal life of every individual is based on secrecy, and perhaps it is partly for that reason that civilized man is so nervously anxious that personal privacy should be respected."

10. Describe your response to Gurov in Parts I and II, and discuss how your judgment of him changes in the last two parts of the story.

11. Based on your understanding of the characterizations of Gurov and Anna, consider the final paragraph of the story and summarize what you think will happen to them.

PERSPECTIVE
Two Additional Translations of the Final Paragraphs of Anton Chekhov's "The Lady with the Pet Dog"

"A Note on Reading Translations" appears on page 746. Because different translators of the same work make various choices in diction, phrasing, images, and tone as they interpret both the language and the work, they often produce subtly different translations. Compare the following two versions of the final six paragraphs of Chekhov's story with Avrahm Yarmolinsky's 1947 translation, reprinted in this anthology on pages 185 to 196.

ANTON CHEKHOV (1860–1904)

From "The Lady and the Dog"   *1899*

TRANSLATED BY CONSTANCE GARNETT (1963)

Anna Sergeyevna and he loved each other like people very close and akin, like husband and wife, like tender friends; it seemed to them that fate itself had meant them for one another, and they could not understand why he had a wife and she a husband; and it was as though they were a pair of birds of passage, caught and forced to live in different cages. They forgave each other for what they were ashamed of in their past, they forgave everything in the present, and felt that this love of theirs had changed them both.

In moments of depression in the past he had comforted himself with any arguments that came into his mind, but now he no longer cared for arguments; he felt profound compassion, he wanted to be sincere and tender. . . .

"Don't cry, my darling," he said. "You've had your cry; that's enough. . . . Let us talk now, let us think of some plan."

Then they spent a long while taking counsel together, talked of how to avoid the necessity for secrecy, for deception, for living in different towns and not seeing each other for long at a time. How could they be free from this intolerable bondage?

"How? How?" he asked, clutching his head. "How?"

And it seemed as though in a little while the solution would be found, and then a new and splendid life would begin; and it was clear to both of them that they had still a long, long way to go, and that the most complicated and difficult part of it was only just beginning.

From *My Life and Other Stories*

ANTON CHEKHOV (1860–1904)

From *"A Lady with a Dog"*   *1899*

TRANSLATED BY RONALD HINGLEY (1975)

Anne and he loved each other very, very dearly, like man and wife or bosom friends. They felt themselves predestined for each other. That he should have a wife, and she a husband . . . it seemed to make no sense. They were like two migratory birds, a male and a female, caught and put in separate cages. They had forgiven each other the shameful episodes of their past, they forgave each other for the present too, and they felt that their love had transformed them both.

Once, in moments of depression, he had tried to console himself with any argument which came into his head—but now he had no use for arguments. His deepest sympathies were stirred, he only wanted to be sincere and tender.

"Stop, darling," he said. "You've had your cry—that's enough. Now let's talk, let's think of something."

Then they consulted at length about avoiding the need for concealment and deception, for living in different towns, for meeting only at rare intervals. How could they break these intolerable bonds? How, how, how?

He clutched his head and asked the question again and again.

Soon, it seemed, the solution would be found and a wonderful new life would begin. But both could see that they still had a long, long way to travel—and that the most complicated and difficult part was only just beginning.

From *The Oxford Chekhov*, Vol. IX

PERSPECTIVE

ANTON CHEKHOV (1860–1904)

On Morality in Fiction   *1890*

You abuse me for objectivity, calling it indifference to good and evil, lack of ideals and ideas, and so on. You would have me, when I describe horse-thieves, say: "Stealing horses is an evil." But that has been known for ages without my saying so. Let the jury judge them; it's my job simply to show what sort of people they are. I write: You are dealing with horse-thieves, so let me tell you that they are not beggars but well-fed people, that they are people of a special cult, and that horse-stealing is not simply theft but a passion. Of course it would be pleasant to combine art with a sermon, but for me personally it is extremely difficult and almost impossible, owing to the conditions of technique. You see, to depict horse-thieves in seven hundred lines I must all the time speak and think in their tone and feel in their spirit, otherwise, if I introduce subjectivity, the image becomes blurred and the story will not be as compact as all short stories ought to be. When I write, I reckon entirely upon the reader to add for himself the subjective elements that are lacking in the story.

From a letter to Aleksey S. Suvorin in *Letters on the Short Story, the Drama, and Other Literary Topics by Anton Chekhov*

CONSIDERATIONS FOR CRITICAL THINKING AND WRITING

1. Why does Chekhov reject sermonizing in his fiction?
2. How does his "objectivity" affect your reading of "The Lady with the Pet Dog"?
3. Compare and contrast Chekhov's views with Thomas Jefferson's belief that fiction should offer "sound morality" (p. 39).

JOYCE CAROL OATES (B. 1938)

Raised in upstate New York, Joyce Carol Oates earned degrees at Syracuse University and the University of Wisconsin. Both the range and volume of her writing are extensive. A writer of novels, plays, short stories, poetry, and literary criticism, she has published some eighty books. Oates has described the subject matter of her fiction as "real people in a real society," but her method of expression ranges from the realistic to the experimental. Her novels include *them* (1969), *Do with Me What You Will* (1973), *Childwold* (1976), *Bellefleur* (1980), *A Bloodsmoor Romance* (1982), *Marya: A Life* (1986), *You Must Remember This* (1987), and *Black Water* (1992). Among her collections of short stories are *Marriages and Infidelities* (1972), which includes "The Lady with the Pet Dog," *Raven's Wing* (1986), *The Assignation* (1988), *Heat* (1991), and *Haunted: Tales of the Grotesque* (1994). This story is her modern version of the Chekhov story of the same name, this time told from the woman's perspective.

The Lady with the Pet Dog

1972

I

Strangers parted as if to make way for him.

There he stood. He was there in the aisle, a few yards away, watching her.

She leaned forward at once in her seat, her hand jerked up to her face as if to ward off a blow — but then the crowd in the aisle hid him, he was gone. She pressed both hands against her cheeks. He was not here, she had imagined him.

"My God," she whispered.

She was alone. Her husband had gone out to the foyer to make a tele- 5 phone call; it was intermission at the concert, a Thursday evening.

Now she saw him again, clearly. He was standing there. He was staring at her. Her blood rocked in her body, draining out of her head . . . she was going to faint . . . They stared at each other. They gave no sign of recognition. Only when he took a step forward did she shake her head *no — no — keep away*. It was not possible.

When her husband returned, she was staring at the place in the aisle where her lover had been standing. Her husband leaned forward to interrupt that stare.

"What's wrong?" he said. "Are you sick?"

Panic rose in her in long shuddering waves. She tried to get to her feet, panicked at the thought of fainting here, and her husband took hold of her. She stood like an aged woman, clutching the seat before her.

At home he helped her up the stairs and she lay down. Her head was like a 10 large piece of crockery that had to be held still, it was so heavy. She was still panicked. She felt it in the shallows of her face, behind her knees, in the pit of her stomach. It sickened her, it made her think of mucus, of something thick and gray congested inside her, stuck to her, that was herself and yet not herself — a poison.

She lay with her knees drawn up toward her chest, her eyes hotly open, while her husband spoke to her. She imagined that other man saying, *Why did you run away from me?* Her husband was saying other words. She tried to listen to them. He was going to call the doctor, he said, and she tried to sit up. "No, I'm all right now," she said quickly. The panic was like lead inside her, so thickly congested. How slow love was to drain out of her, how fluid and sticky it was inside her head!

Her husband believed her. No doctor. No threat. Grateful, she drew her husband down to her. They embraced, not comfortably. For years now they had not been comfortable together, in their intimacy and at a distance, and now they struggled gently as if the paces of this dance were too rigorous for them. It was something they might have known once, but had now outgrown.

The panic in her thickened at this double betrayal: she drew her husband to her, she caressed him wildly, she shut her eyes to think about that other man.

A crowd of men and women parting, unexpectedly, and there he stood — there he stood — she kept seeing him, and yet her vision blotched at the memory. It had been finished between them, six months before, but he had come out here . . . and she had escaped him, now she was lying in her husband's arms, in his embrace, her face pressed against his. It was a kind of sleep, this love-making. She felt herself falling asleep, her body falling from her. Her eyes shut.

"I love you," her husband said fiercely, angrily.

She shut her eyes and thought of that other man, as if betraying him 15 would give her life a center.

"Did I hurt you? Are you — ?" Her husband whispered.

Always this hot flashing of shame between them, the shame of her husband's near failure, the clumsiness of his love —

"You didn't hurt me," she said.

II

They had said good-by six months before. He drove her from Nantucket, where they had met, to Albany, New York, where she visited her sister. The hours of intimacy in the car had sealed something between them, a vow of silence and impersonality: she recalled the movement of the highways, the passing of other cars, the natural rhythms of the day hypnotizing her toward sleep while he drove. She trusted him, she could sleep in his presence. Yet she could not really fall asleep in spite of her exhaustion, and she kept jerking awake, frightened, to discover that nothing had changed — still the stranger who was driving her to Albany, still the highway, the sky, the antiseptic odor of the rented car, the sense of a rhythm behind the rhythm of the air that might unleash itself at any second. Everywhere on this highway, at this moment, there were men and women driving together, bonded together — what did that mean, to be together? What did it mean to enter into a bond with another person?

No, she did not really trust him; she did not really trust men. He would 20 glance at her with his small cautious smile and she felt a declaration of shame between them.

Shame.

In her head she rehearsed conversations. She said bitterly, "You'll be relieved when we get to Albany. Relieved to get rid of me." They had spent so many days talking, confessing too much, driven to a pitch of childish excitement, laughing together on the beach, breaking into that pose of laughter that seems to eradicate the soul, so many days of this that the silence of the trip was like the silence of a hospital — all these surface noises, these rattles and hums, but an interior silence, a befuddlement. She said to him in her imagination, "One of us should die." Then she leaned over to touch him. She caressed the back of his neck. She said, aloud, "Would you like me to drive for a while?"

They stopped at a picnic area where other cars were stopped — couples, families — and walked together, smiling at their good luck. He put his arm around her shoulders and she sensed how they were in a posture together, a man and a woman forming a posture, a figure, that someone might sketch and show to them. She said slowly, "I don't want to go back. . . ."

Silence. She looked up at him. His face was heavy with her words, as if she had pulled at his skin with her fingers. Children ran nearby and distracted him — yes, he was a father too, his children ran like that, they tugged at his skin with their light, busy fingers.

"Are you so unhappy?" he said.   25

"I'm not unhappy, back there. I'm nothing. There's nothing to me," she said.

They stared at each other. The sensation between them was intense, exhausting. She thought that this man was her savior, that he had come to her at a time in her life when her life demanded completion, an end, a permanent fixing of all that was troubled and shifting and deadly. And yet it was absurd to think this. No person could save another. So she drew back from him and released him.

A few hours later they stopped at a gas station in a small city. She went to the women's rest room, having to ask the attendant for a key, and when she came back her eye jumped nervously onto the rented car — why? did she think he might have driven off without her? — onto the man, her friend, standing in conversation with the young attendant. Her friend was as old as her husband, over forty, with lanky, sloping shoulders, a full body, his hair thick, a dark, burnished brown, a festive color that made her eye twitch a little — and his hands were always moving, always those rapid conversational circles, going nowhere, gestures that were at once a little aggressive and apologetic.

She put her hand on his arm, a claim. He turned to her and smiled and she felt that she loved him, that everything in her life had forced her to this moment and that she had no choice about it.

They sat in the car for two hours, in Albany, in the parking lot of a Howard   30 Johnson's restaurant, talking, trying to figure out their past. There was no future. They concentrated on the past, the several days behind them, lit up with a hot, dazzling August sun, like explosions that already belonged to other people, to strangers. Her face was faintly reflected in the green-tinted curve of the windshield, but she could not have recognized that face. She began to cry; she told herself: *I am not here, this will pass, this is nothing.* Still, she could not stop crying. The muscles of her face were springy, like a child's, unpredictable muscles. He stroked her arms, her shoulders, trying to comfort her. "This is so hard . . . this is impossible . . ." he said. She felt panic for the world outside this car, all that was not herself and this man, and at the same time she understood that she was free of him, as people are free of other people, she would leave him soon, safely, and within a few days he would have fallen into the past, the impersonal past. . . .

"I'm so ashamed of myself!" she said finally.

She returned to her husband and saw that another woman, a shadow-woman, had taken her place — noiseless and convincing, like a dancer performing certain difficult steps. Her husband folded her in his arms and talked to her of his own loneliness, his worries about his business, his health, his mother, kept tranquilized and mute in a nursing home, and her spirit detached itself from her and drifted about the rooms of the large house she lived in with her husband, a shadow-woman delicate and imprecise. There was no boundary to her, no edge. Alone, she took hot baths and sat exhausted in the steaming water, wondering at her perpetual exhaustion. All that winter she noticed the limp, languid weight of her arms, her veins bulging slightly with the pressure of her extreme weariness. *This is fate,* she thought, to be here and not there, to be one person and not another, a certain man's wife and not the wife of another man. The long, slow pain of this certainty rose in her, but it never became clear, it was baffling and imprecise. She could not be serious about it; she kept congratulating herself on her own good luck, to have escaped so easily, to have freed herself. So much love had gone into the first several years of her marriage that there wasn't much left, now, for another man. . . . She was certain of that. But the bath water made her dizzy, all that perpetual heat, and one day in January she drew a razor blade lightly across the inside of her arm, near the elbow, to see what would happen.

Afterward she wrapped a small towel around it, to stop the bleeding. The towel soaked through. She wrapped a bath towel around that and walked through the empty rooms of her home, lightheaded, hardly aware of the stubborn seeping of blood. There was no boundary to her in this house, no precise limit. She could flow out like her own blood and come to no end.

She sat for a while on a blue love seat, her mind empty. Her husband telephoned her when he would be staying late at the plant. He talked to her always about his plans, his problems, his business friends, his future. It was obvious that he had a future. As he spoke she nodded to encourage him, and her heartbeat quickened with the memory of her own, personal shame, the shame of this man's particular, private wife. One evening at dinner he leaned forward and put his head in his arms and fell asleep, like a child. She sat at the table with him for a while, watching him. His hair had gone gray, almost white, at the temples — no one would guess that he was so quick, so careful a man, still fairly young about the eyes. She put her hand on his head, lightly, as if to prove to herself that he was real. He slept, exhausted.

One evening they went to a concert and she looked up to see her lover 35 there, in the crowded aisle, in this city, watching her. He was standing there, with his overcoat on, watching her. She went cold. That morning the telephone had rung while her husband was still home, and she had heard him answer it, heard him hang up — it must have been a wrong number — and when the telephone rang again, at 9:30, she had been afraid to answer it. She had left home to be out of the range of that ringing, but now, in this public place, in this busy auditorium, she found herself staring at that man, unable to make any sign to him, any gesture of recognition. . . .

He would have come to her but she shook her head. *No. Stay away.*

Her husband helped her out of the row of seats, saying, "Excuse us, please. Excuse us," so that strangers got to their feet, quickly, alarmed, to let them pass. Was that woman about to faint? What was wrong?

At home she felt the blood drain slowly back into her head. Her husband embraced her hips, pressing his face against her, in that silence that belonged to the earliest days of their marriage. She thought, *He will drive it out of me.* He made love to her and she was back in the auditorium again, sitting alone, now that the concert was over. The stage was empty; the heavy velvet curtains had not been drawn; the musicians' chairs were empty, everything was silent and expectant; in the aisle her lover stood and smiled at her — Her husband was impatient. He was apart from her, working on her, operating on her; and then, stricken, he whispered, "Did I hurt you?"

The telephone rang the next morning. Dully, sluggishly, she answered it. She recognized his voice at once — that "Anna?" with its lifting of the second syllable, questioning and apologetic and making its claim — "Yes, what do you want?" she said.

"Just to see you. Please —" 40

"I can't."

"Anna, I'm sorry, I didn't mean to upset you —"

"I can't see you."

"Just for a few minutes — I have to talk to you —"

"But why, why now? Why now?" she said. 45

She heard her voice rising, but she could not stop it. He began to talk again, drowning her out. She remembered his rapid conversation. She remembered his gestures, the witty energetic circling of his hands.

"Please don't hang up!" he cried.

"I can't — I don't want to go through it again —"

"I'm not going to hurt you. Just tell me how you are."

"Everything is the same." 50

"Everything is the same with me."

She looked up at the ceiling, shyly. "Your wife? Your children?"

"The same."

"Your son?"

"He's fine —" 55

"I'm so glad to hear that. I —"

"Is it still the same with you, your marriage? Tell me what you feel. What are you thinking?"

"I don't know. . . ."

She remembered his intense, eager words, the movement of his hands, that impatient precise fixing of the air by his hands, the jabbing of his fingers.

"Do you love me?" he said. 60

She could not answer.

"I'll come over to see you," he said.

"No," she said.

What will come next, what will happen?

Flesh hardening on his body, aging. Shrinking. He will grow old, but not 65 soft like her husband. They are two different types: he is nervous, lean, energetic, wise. She will grow thinner, as the tension radiates out from her backbone, wearing down her flesh. Her collarbones will jut out of her skin. Her husband, caressing her in their bed, will discover that she is another woman — she is not there with him — instead she is rising in an elevator in a downtown hotel, carrying a book as a prop, or walking quickly away from that hotel, her head bent and filled with secrets. Love, what to do with it? . . . Useless as moths' wings, as moths' fluttering. . . . She feels the flutterings of silky, crazy wings in her chest.

He flew out to visit her every several weeks, staying at a different hotel each time. He telephoned her, and she drove down to park in an underground garage at the very center of the city.

She lay in his arms while her husband talked to her, miles away, one body fading into another. He will grow old, his body will change, she thought, pressing her cheek against the back of one of these men. If it was her lover, they were in a hotel room: always the propped-up little booklet describing the hotel's many services, with color photographs of its cocktail lounge and dining room and coffee shop. Grow old, leave me, die, go back to your neurotic wife and your sad, ordinary children, she thought, but still her eyes closed gratefully against his skin and she felt how complete their silence was, how they had come to rest in each other.

"Tell me about your life here. The people who love you," he said, as he always did.

One afternoon they lay together for four hours. It was her birthday and she was intoxicated with her good fortune, this prize of the afternoon, this man in her arms! She was a little giddy, she talked too much. She told him about her parents, about her husband. . . . "They were all people I believed in, but it turned out wrong. Now, I believe in you. . . ." He laughed as if shocked by her words. She did not understand. Then she understood. "But I believe truly in you. I can't think of myself without you," she said. . . . He spoke of his wife, her ambitions, her intelligence, her use of the children against him, her use of his younger son's blindness, all of his words gentle and hypnotic and convincing in the late afternoon peace of this hotel room . . . and she felt the terror of laughter, threatening laughter. Their words, like their bodies, were aging.

She dressed quickly in the bathroom, drawing her long hair up around the 70 back of her head, fixing it as always, anxious that everything be the same. Her face was slightly raw, from his face. The rubbing of his skin. Her eyes were too bright, wearily bright. Her hair was blond but not so blond as it had been that summer in the white Nantucket air.

She ran water and splashed it on her face. She blinked at the water. Blind. Drowning. She thought with satisfaction that soon, soon, he would be back home, in that house on Long Island she had never seen, with that woman she had never seen, sitting on the edge of another bed, putting on his shoes. She wanted nothing except to be free of him. Why not be free? *Oh*, she thought suddenly, *I will follow you back and kill you. You and her and the little boy. What is there to stop me?*

She left him. Everyone on the street pitied her, that look of absolute zero.

III

A man and a child, approaching her. The sharp acrid smell of fish. The crashing of waves. Anna pretended not to notice the father with his son — there was something strange about them. That frank, silent intimacy, too gentle, the man's bare feet in the water and the boy a few feet away, leaning away from his father. He was about nine years old and still his father held his hand.

A small yipping dog, a golden dog, bounded near them.

Anna turned shyly back to her reading; she did not want to have to speak 75 to these neighbors. She saw the man's shadow falling over her legs, then over the pages of her book, and she had the idea that he wanted to see what she was reading. The dog nuzzled her; the man called him away.

She watched them walk down the beach. She was relieved that the man had not spoken to her.

She saw them in town later that day, the two of them brown-haired and patient, now wearing sandals, walking with that same look of care. The man's white shorts were soiled and a little baggy. His pullover shirt was a faded green. His face was broad, the cheekbones wide, spaced widely apart, the eyes stark in their sockets, as if they fastened onto objects for no reason, ponderous and edgy. The little boy's face was pale and sharp; his lips were perpetually parted.

Anna realized that the child was blind.

The next morning, early, she caught sight of them again. For some reason she went to the back door of her cottage. She faced the sea breeze eagerly. Her heart hammered. . . . She had been here, in her family's old house, for three days, alone, bitterly satisfied at being alone, and now it was a puzzle to her how her soul strained to fly outward, to meet with another person. She watched the man with his son, his cautious, rather stooped shoulders above the child's small shoulders.

The man was carrying something, it looked like a notebook. He sat on the sand, not far from Anna's spot of the day before, and the dog rushed up to them. The child approached the edge of the ocean, timidly. He moved in short jerky steps, his legs stiff. The dog ran around him. Anna heard the child crying out a word that sounded like "Ty"—it must have been the dog's name—and then the man joined in, his voice heavy and firm. 80

"Ty—"

Anna tied her hair back with a yellow scarf and went down to the beach.

The man glanced around at her. He smiled. She stared past him at the waves. To talk to him or not to talk—she had the freedom of that choice. For a moment she felt that she had made a mistake, that the child and the dog would not protect her, that behind this man's ordinary, friendly face there was a certain arrogant maleness—then she relented, she smiled shyly.

"A nice house you've got there," the man said.

She nodded her thanks. 85

The man pushed his sunglasses up on his forehead. Yes, she recognized the eyes of the day before—intelligent and nervous, the sockets pale, untanned.

"Is that your telephone ringing?" he said.

She did not bother to listen. "It's a wrong number," she said.

Her husband calling: she had left home for a few days, to be alone.

But the man, settling himself on the sand, seemed to misinterpret this. He smiled in surprise, one corner of his mouth higher than the other. He said nothing. Anna wondered: *What is he thinking?* The dog was leaping about her, panting against her legs, and she laughed in embarrassment. She bent to pet it, grateful for its busyness. "Don't let him jump up on you," the man said. "He's a nuisance." 90

The dog was a small golden retriever, a young dog. The blind child, standing now in the water, turned to call the dog to him. His voice was shrill and impatient.

"Our house is the third one down—the white one," the man said.

She turned, startled. "Oh, did you buy it from Dr. Patrick? Did he die?"

"Yes, finally. . . ."

Her eyes wandered nervously over the child and the dog. She felt the nervous beat of her heart out to the very tips of her fingers, the fleshy tips of her fingers: little hearts were there, pulsing. *What is he thinking?* The man had opened his notebook. He had a piece of charcoal and he began to sketch something. 95

Anna looked down at him. She saw the top of his head, his thick brown hair, the freckles on his shoulders, the quick, deft movement of his hand. Upside down, Anna herself being drawn. She smiled in surprise.

"Let me draw you. Sit down," he said.

She knelt awkwardly a few yards away. He turned the page of the sketch pad. The dog ran to her and she sat, straightening out her skirt beneath her, flinching from the dog's tongue. "Ty!" cried the child. Anna sat, and slowly the pleasure of the moment began to glow in her; her skin flushed with gratitude.

She sat there for nearly an hour. The man did not talk much. Back and forth the dog bounded, shaking itself. The child came to sit near them, in silence. Anna felt that she was drifting into a kind of trance while the man sketched her, half a dozen rapid sketches, the surface of her face given up to him. "Where are you from?" the man asked.

"Ohio. My husband lives in Ohio."   100

She wore no wedding band.

"Your wife —" Anna began.

"Yes?"

"Is she here?"

"Not right now."   105

She was silent, ashamed. She had asked an improper question. But the man did not seem to notice. He continued drawing her, bent over the sketch pad. When Anna said she had to go, he showed her the drawings — one after another of her, Anna, recognizably Anna, a woman in her early thirties, her hair smooth and flat across the top of her head, tied behind by a scarf. "Take the one you like best," he said, and she picked one of her with the dog in her lap, sitting very straight, her brows and eyes clearly defined, her lips girlishly pursed, the dog and her dress suggested by a few quick irregular lines.

"Lady with pet dog," the man said.

She spent the rest of that day reading, nearer her cottage. It was not really a cottage — it was a two-story house, large and ungainly and weathered. It was mixed up in her mind with her family, her own childhood, and she glanced up from her book, perplexed, as if waiting for one of her parents or her sister to come up to her. Then she thought of that man, the man with the blind child, the man with the dog, and she could not concentrate on her reading. Someone — probably her father — had marked a passage that must be important, but she kept reading and rereading it: *We try to discover in things, endeared to us on that account, the spiritual glamour which we ourselves have cast upon them; we are disillusioned, and learn that they are in themselves barren and devoid of the charm that they owed, in our minds, to the association of certain ideas. . . .*

She thought again of the man on the beach. She lay the book aside and thought of him: his eyes, his aloneness, his drawings of her.

They began seeing each other after that. He came to her front door in the   110
evening, without the child; he drove her into town for dinner. She was shy and extremely pleased. The darkness of the expensive restaurant released her; she heard herself chatter; she leaned forward and seemed to be offering her face up to him, listening to him. He talked about his work on a Long Island newspaper and she seemed to be listening to him, as she stared at his face, arranging her own face into the expression she had seen in that charcoal drawing. Did he see her like that, then? — girlish and withdrawn and patrician? She felt the weight of his interest in her, a force that fell upon her like a blow. A repeated blow. Of course he was married, he had children — of course she was married, permanently married. This flight from her husband was not important. She had left him before, to be alone, it was not important. Everything in her was slender and delicate and not important.

They walked for hours after dinner, looking at the other strollers, the weekend visitors, the tourists, the couples like themselves. Surely they were mistaken for a couple, a married couple. *This is the hour in which everything is decided,* Anna thought. They had both had several drinks and they talked a great deal. Anna found herself saying too much, stopping and starting giddily. She put her hand to her forehead, feeling faint.

"It's from the sun — you've had too much sun —" he said.

At the door to her cottage, on the front porch, she heard herself asking him if he would like to come in. She allowed him to lead her inside, to close the door. *This is not important,* she thought clearly, *he doesn't mean it, he doesn't love me, nothing will come of it.* She was frightened, yet it seemed to her necessary to give in; she had to leave Nantucket with that act completed, an act of adultery, an accomplishment she would take back to Ohio and to her marriage.

Later, incredibly, she heard herself asking: "Do you . . . do you love me?"

"You're so beautiful!" he said, amazed.   115

She felt this beauty, shy and glowing and centered in her eyes. He stared at her. In this large, drafty house, alone together, they were like accomplices, conspirators. She could not think: how old was she? which year was this? They had done something unforgivable together, and the knowledge of it was tugging at their faces. A cloud seemed to pass over her. She felt herself smiling shrilly.

Afterward, a peculiar raspiness, a dryness of breath. He was silent. She felt a strange, idle fear, a sense of the danger outside this room and this old comfortable bed — a danger that would not recognize her as the lady in that drawing, the lady with the pet dog. There was nothing to say to this man, this stranger. She felt the beauty draining out of her face, her eyes fading.

"I've got to be alone," she told him.

He left, and she understood that she would not see him again. She stood by the window of the room, watching the ocean. A sense of shame overpowered her: it was smeared everywhere on her body, the smell of it, the richness of it. She tried to recall him, and his face was confused in her memory: she would have to shout to him across a jumbled space, she would have to wave her arms wildly. *You love me! You must love me!* But she knew he did not love her, and she did not love him; he was a man who drew everything up into himself, like all men, walking away, free to walk away, free to have his own thoughts, free to envision her body, all the secrets of her body. . . . And she lay down again in the bed, feeling how heavy this body had become, her insides heavy with shame, the very backs of her eyelids coated with shame.

"This is the end of one part of my life," she thought.   120

But in the morning the telephone rang. She answered it. It was her lover: they talked brightly and happily. She could hear the eagerness in his voice, the love in his voice, that same still, sad amazement — she understood how simple life was, there were no problems.

They spent most of their time on the beach, with the child and the dog. He joked and was serious at the same time. He said, once, "You have defined my soul for me," and she laughed to hide her alarm. In a few days it was time for her to leave. He got a sitter for the boy and took the ferry with her to the mainland, then rented a car to drive her up to Albany. She kept thinking: *Now something will happen. It will come to an end.* But most of the drive was silent and hypnotic. She wanted him to joke with her, to say again that she had defined his soul for him, but he drove fast, he was serious, she distrusted the hawkish look of his profile — she did not know him at all. At a gas station she splashed her face with cold water. Alone in the grubby little rest room, shaky and very much alone. In such places are women totally alone with their bodies. The body grows heavier, more evil, in such silence. . . . On the beach everything had been noisy with sunlight and gulls and waves; here, as if run to earth, everything was cramped and silent and dead.

She went outside, squinting. There he was, talking with the station attendant. She could not think as she returned to him whether she wanted to live or not.

She stayed in Albany for a few days, then flew home to her husband. He met her at the airport, near the luggage counter, where her three pieces of pale-brown luggage were brought to him on a conveyor belt, to be claimed by him. He kissed her on the cheek. They shook hands, a little embarrassed. She had come home again.

"How will I live out the rest of my life?" she wondered.   125

In January her lover spied on her: she glanced up and saw him, in a public place, in the DeRoy Symphony Hall. She was paralyzed with fear. She nearly fainted. In this faint she felt her husband's body, loving her, working its love upon her, and she shut her eyes harder to keep out the certainty of his love — sometimes he failed at loving her, sometimes he succeeded, it had nothing to do with her or her pity or her ten years of love for him, it had nothing to do with a woman at all. It was a private act accomplished by a man, a husband, or a lover, in communion with his own soul, his manhood.

Her husband was forty-two years old now, growing slowly into middle age, getting heavier, softer. Her lover was about the same age, narrower in the shoulders, with a full, solid chest, yet lean, nervous. She thought, in her paralysis, of men and how they love freely and eagerly so long as their bodies are capable of love, love for a woman; and then, as love fades in their bodies, it fades from their souls and they become immune and immortal and ready to die.

Her husband was a little rough with her, as if impatient with himself. "I love you," he said fiercely, angrily. And then, ashamed, he said, "Did I hurt you? . . ."

"You didn't hurt me," she said.

Her voice was too shrill for their embrace.   130

While he was in the bathroom she went to her closet and took out that drawing of the summer before. There she was, on the beach at Nantucket, a lady with a pet dog, her eyes large and defined, the dog in her lap hardly more than a few snarls, a few coarse soft lines of charcoal . . . her dress smeared, her arms oddly limp . . . her hands not well drawn at all. . . . She tried to think: did she love the man who had drawn this? did he love her? The fever in her husband's body had touched her and driven her temperature up, and now she stared at the drawing with a kind of lust, fearful of seeing an ugly soul in that woman's face, fearful of seeing the face suddenly through her lover's eyes. She breathed quickly and harshly, staring at the drawing.

And so, the next day, she went to him at his hotel. She wept, pressing against him, demanding of him, "What do you want? Why are you here? Why don't you let me alone?" He told her that he wanted nothing. He expected nothing. He would not cause trouble.

"I want to talk about last August," he said.

"Don't —" she said.

She was hypnotized by his gesturing hands, his nervousness, his obvious 135
agitation. He kept saying, "I understand. I'm making no claims upon you."

They became lovers again.

He called room service for something to drink and they sat side by side on
his bed, looking through a copy of *The New Yorker*, laughing at the cartoons. It
was so peaceful in this room, so complete. They were on a holiday. It was a secret holiday. Four-thirty in the afternoon, on a Friday, an ordinary Friday: a secret holiday.

"I won't bother you again," he said.

He flew back to see her again in March, and in late April. He telephoned
her from his hotel — a different hotel each time — and she came down to him at
once. She rose to him in various elevators, she knocked on the doors of various
rooms, she stepped into his embrace, breathless and guilty and already angry
with him, pleading with him. One morning in May, when he telephoned, she
pressed her forehead against the doorframe and could not speak. He kept saying, "What's wrong? Can't you talk? Aren't you alone?" She felt that she was
going insane. Her head would burst. Why, why did he love her, why did he pursue her? Why did he want her to die?

She went to him in the hotel room. A familiar room: had they been here 140
before? "Everything is repeating itself. Everything is stuck," she said. He
framed her face in his hands and said that she looked thinner — was she
sick? — what was wrong? She shook herself free. He, her lover, looked about
the same. There was a small, angry pimple on his neck. He stared at her, eagerly
and suspiciously. Did she bring bad news?

"So you love me? You love me?" she asked.

"Why are you so angry?"

"I want to be free of you. The two of us free of each other."

"That isn't true — you don't want that —"

He embraced her. She was wild with that old, familiar passion for him, her 145
body clinging to his, her arms not strong enough to hold him. Ah, what despair! — what bitter hatred she felt! — she needed this man for her salvation, he
was all she had to live for, and yet she could not believe in him. He embraced
her thighs, her hips, kissing her, pressing his warm face against her, and yet she
could not believe in him, not really. She needed him in order to live, but he was
not worth her love, he was not worth her dying. . . . She promised herself this:
when she got back home, when she was alone, she would draw the razor more
deeply across her arm.

The telephone rang and he answered it: a wrong number.

"Jesus," he said.

They lay together, still. She imagined their posture like this, the two of
them one figure, one substance; and outside this room and this bed there was
a universe of disjointed, separate things, blank things, that had nothing to do
with them. She would not be Anna out there, the lady in the drawing. He
would not be her lover.

"I love you so much . . ." she whispered.

"Please don't cry! We have only a few hours, please. . . ." 150

It was absurd, their clinging together like this. She saw them as a single
figure in a drawing, their arms and legs entwined, their heads pressing mutely
together. Helpless substance, so heavy and warm and doomed. It was absurd

that any human being should be so important to another human being. She wanted to laugh: a laugh might free them both.

She could not laugh.

Sometime later he said, as if they had been arguing, "Look. It's you. You're the one who doesn't want to get married. You lie to me —"

"Lie to you?"

"You love me but you won't marry me, because you want something left over — Something not finished — All your life you can attribute your misery to me, to our not being married — you are using me —"

"Stop it! You'll make me hate you!" she cried.

"You can say to yourself that you're miserable because of *me*. We will never be married, you will never be happy, neither one of us will ever be happy —"

"I don't want to hear this!" she said.

She pressed her hands flatly against her face.

She went to the bathroom to get dressed. She washed her face and part of her body, quickly. The fever was in her, in the pit of her belly. She would rush home and strike a razor across the inside of her arm and free that pressure, that fever.

The impatient bulging of the veins: an ordeal over.

The demand of the telephone's ringing: that ordeal over.

The nuisance of getting the car and driving home in all that five o'clock traffic: an ordeal too much for a woman.

The movement of this stranger's body in hers: over, finished.

Now, dressed, a little calmer, they held hands and talked. They had to talk swiftly, to get all their news in: he did not trust the people who worked for him, he had faith in no one, his wife had moved to a textbook publishing company and was doing well, she had inherited a Ben Shahn painting from her father and wanted to "touch it up a little" — she was crazy! — his blind son was at another school, doing fairly well, in fact his children were all doing fairly well in spite of the stupid mistake of their parents' marriage — and what about her? what about her life? She told him in a rush the one thing he wanted to hear: that she lived with her husband lovelessly, the two of them polite strangers, sharing a bed, lying side by side in the night in that bed, bodies out of which souls had fled. There was no longer even any shame between them.

"And what about me? Do you feel shame with me still?" he asked.

She did not answer. She moved away from him and prepared to leave.

Then, a minute later, she happened to catch sight of his reflection in the bureau mirror — he was glancing down at himself, checking himself mechanically, impersonally, preparing also to leave. He too would leave this room: he too was headed somewhere else.

She stared at him. It seemed to her that in this instant he was breaking from her, the image of her lover fell free of her, breaking from her . . . and she realized that he existed in a dimension quite apart from her, a mysterious being. And suddenly, joyfully, she felt a miraculous calm. This man was her husband, truly — they were truly married, here in this room — they had been married haphazardly and accidentally for a long time. In another part of the city she had another husband, a "husband," but she had not betrayed that man, not really. This man, whom she loved above any other person in the world, above even her own self-pitying sorrow and her own life, was her truest lover, her destiny. And she did not hate him, she did not hate herself any longer; she did not wish to die; she was flooded with a strange certainty, a sense of gratitude, of pure selfless energy. It was obvious to her that she had, all along, been behaving correctly; out of instinct.

What triumph, to love like this in any room, anywhere, risking even the   170 craziest of accidents!

"Why are you so happy? What's wrong?" he asked, startled. He stared at her. She felt the abrupt concentration in him, the focusing of his vision on her, almost a bitterness in his face, as if he feared her. What, was it beginning all over again? Their love beginning again, in spite of them? "How can you look so happy?" he asked. "We don't have any right to it. Is it because . . . ?"

"Yes," she said.

CONSIDERATIONS FOR CRITICAL THINKING AND WRITING

1. FIRST RESPONSE. Which version do you like better — Chekhov's story or Oates's? What's the point of retelling the story?

2. How would this story be different if it were told only in chronological order as it is in Part III? What do Parts I and II contribute to the details and information provided in Part III?

3. Why are Anna and her lover drawn to each other? What do we learn about their spouses that helps explain their attraction? Are there any other explanations?

4. Why is Anna so unhappy after the affair on Nantucket begins? Why does she think of suicide?

5. What is Anna's attitude toward men? Does it change during the story?

6. What details in the story make the narration particularly convincing from a woman's perspective? How might a man tell the story differently?

7. "What triumph, to love like this in any room, anywhere, risking even the craziest of accidents!" Explain this reflection of Anna's (para. 170) and relate it to her character.

8. How does Oates's arrangement of incidents validate Anna's feeling that "everything is repeating itself. Everything is stuck" (para. 140)?

9. Consider whether Anna reaches any kind of resolution to her problems by the end of the story. Is she merely "repeating" herself, or do you think she develops?

10. At the end of paragraph 19, Oates has Anna ask herself the question "What did it mean to enter into a bond with another person?" Write an essay explaining how the story answers that question.

CONNECTIONS TO ANOTHER SELECTION

1. What similarities in setting, plot, and character are there between Oates's version and Chekhov's story? Are there any significant differences?

2. Describe how a familiarity with Chekhov's story affected your reading and expectations of Oates's version. Choose one version of the story and write an essay explaining why you prefer it over the other.

PERSPECTIVE

MATTHEW C. BRENNAN (B. 1955)
Point of View and Plotting in Chekhov's and Oates's "The Lady with the Pet Dog"   *1985*

Oates . . . retains Chekhov's third-person point of view. But unlike Chekhov, who focuses on the male lover, Gurov, Oates makes Anna S., the female lover, the center of consciousness. Because Chekhov privileges Gurov, he represents Anna's feelings only when she speaks to Gurov. In fact, when Anna S. expresses her shame to Gurov, Chekhov says, "The solitary candle on the table scarcely lit up her face"; and rather than reveal her inner thoughts he merely tells us, "it was obvious that her heart was heavy." So, by subordinating Anna S. to Gurov, Chekhov gives readers no way to understand the feminine side of a masculine story. In contrast, Oates presents what Chekhov leaves out — the female's experience — and so relegates the male lover (who in her version is nameless) to the limited status Chekhov relegates Anna S.: Oates privileges the point of view of Anna. Furthermore, because Anna S. says she feels "like a madwoman," Oates fragments Chekhov's traditionally chronological plot, which becomes a subtext against which Oates can foreground Anna's confusion, doubt, and struggle to find an identity. . . .

Chekhov develops a conventional, sequential plot. He spreads the five-step plot through the four formal divisions of his story. Part I consists of the exposition, during which Gurov and Anna S. meet at the resort, Yalta. Part II continues the exposition, as the characters become lovers, and it also introduces the rising action as they separate at the train station, Anna S. returning to her home in the town of S——, Gurov to his in Moscow. Then, in Part III, the action continues to rise as Gurov misses Anna and eventually goes to the town of S——. Here, at a concert, the two climactically meet again, and, as Part III ends, Anna S. agrees to come to Moscow. Finally, in Part IV, the action falls as Chekhov describes their affair and dramatizes it in a scene that forms the resolution, through which Gurov realizes, after looking in a mirror, that he is in love for the first time: he and Anna S. really are "as husband and wife" though separated by law.

Oates borrows all these events for her plot, but if Chekhov's is linear, hers is circular. Oates breaks her story into three parts. Part I depicts the climax, immediately giving her version the intensity that the high-strung center of consciousness, Anna, is experiencing. We are with her at the concert hall, where her lover appears and she faints, and then with her back home, where her husband clumsily makes love to her while she thinks of her lover. Part II opens with a flashback to the rising action — when the lover drives Anna to Albany where they separate, just as Chekhov's lovers separate at the train station; next, Part II both repeats the climax (at the concert and in the bedroom) and relates, for the first time, the falling action in which the lovers continue the affair. Part I, then, presents only the climax, and Part II widens the plot to record not just the center, the climax, but also the rising and falling actions that surround it. Part III, however, widens the circular plot still further. Expanding outward from the climactic center, first the plot regresses to embrace the exposition (in which the lovers meet and make love at the resort, in this version Nantucket); then it moves inward again, retracing chronologically the rising action, climax, and falling action; and finally, as Part III concludes, the plot introduces the resolution, rounding out its pattern.

Before the resolution, however, as we witness the falling action (the resumption of the affair) for the second time, Oates stresses the lack of development: Anna says, "'Everything is repeating itself. Everything is stuck.'" By having the plot repeat itself, and so fail to progress toward resolution, Oates conveys Anna's lack of identity: Anna is trapped between two relationships, two "husbands," and hence wavers throughout this version between feeling like "nothing" in her legal husband's house where "there was no boundary to her," "no precise limit," and feeling defined — as "recognizably Anna" — by her illicit lover, her true "husband," who has sketched her portrait, to which she continually refers as if grasping for a rope.

Here, then, with the climax repeated three times and the rising and falling actions twice, the plot finally progresses from this impasse to its resolution. And, appropriately, as the plot finally achieves its completion, so too does Anna, discovering as she symbolically looks into the mirror,

> this man was her husband, truly — they were truly married, here in this room — they had been married haphazardly and accidentally for a long time. In another part of the city she had another husband, a "husband," but she had not betrayed that man, not really. This man, whom she loved above any other person in the world . . . was her truest lover, her destiny.

Oates allows the plot to progress sequentially to the resolution — to integrity — only as Anna's consciousness discovers its true identity, its integration.

From *Notes on Modern American Literature*

CONSIDERATIONS FOR CRITICAL THINKING AND WRITING

1. What does Brennan mean by characterizing Chekhov's story as "masculine" and Oates's as "feminine"? How is each writer's use of point of view related to this question?

2. Brennan describes Chekhov's plot as "linear" and Oates's as "circular." How is this contrast influenced by the writer's use of point of view?

3. Brennan asserts that in Oates's story, "Anna's consciousness discovers its true identity, its integration." Write an essay explaining whether you agree or disagree with this assessment. In your response, consider how Oates's use of point of view affects your reading of Anna's character.

7

Symbolism

A *symbol* is a person, object, or event that suggests more than its literal meaning. This basic definition is simple enough, but the use of symbol in literature makes some students slightly nervous because they tend to regard it as a booby trap, a hidden device that can go off during a seemingly harmless class discussion. "I didn't see that when I was reading the story" is a frequently heard comment. This sort of surprise and recognition is both natural and common. Most readers go through a story for the first time getting their bearings, figuring out what is happening to whom and so on. Patterns and significant details often require a second or third reading before they become evident — before a symbol sheds light on a story. Then the details of a work may suddenly fit together, and its meaning may be reinforced, clarified, or enlarged by the symbol. Symbolic meanings are usually embedded in the texture of a story, but they are not "hidden"; instead, they are carefully placed. Reading between the lines (where there is only space) is unnecessary. What is needed is a careful consideration of the elements of the story, a sensitivity to its language, and some common sense.

Common sense is a good place to begin. Symbols appear all around us; anything can be given symbolic significance. Without symbols our lives would be stark and vacant. Awareness of a writer's use of symbols is not all that different from the kinds of perceptions and interpretations that allow us to make sense of our daily lives. We know, for example, that a ring used in a wedding is more than just a piece of jewelry because it suggests the unity and intimacy of a closed circle. The bride's gown may be white because we tend to associate innocence and purity with that color. Or consider the meaning of a small alligator sewn on a shirt or some other article of clothing. What started as a company trademark has gathered around it a range of meanings suggesting everything from quality and money to preppiness and silliness. The ring, the white gown, and the alligator trademark are symbolic because each has meanings that go beyond its specific qualities and functions.

Symbols such as these that are widely recognized by a society or culture are called *conventional symbols.* The Christian cross, the Star of David, a swastika, or a nation's flag all have meanings understood by large groups of people. Certain kinds of experiences also have traditional meanings in Western cultures. Winter, the setting sun, and the color black suggest death, while spring, the rising sun, and the color green evoke images of youth and new beginnings. (It is worth noting, however, that individual cultures sometimes have their own conventions; some Oriental countries associate white rather than black with death and mourning. And obviously the polo player trademark would mean nothing to anyone totally unfamiliar with American culture.) These broadly shared symbolic meanings are second nature to us.

Writers use conventional symbols to reinforce meanings. Kate Chopin, for example, emphasizes the spring setting in "The Story of an Hour" (p. 10) as a way of suggesting the renewed sense of life that Mrs. Mallard feels when she thinks herself free from her husband.

A *literary symbol* can include traditional, conventional, or public meanings, but it may also be established internally by the total context of the work in which it appears. In "Soldier's Home" (p. 145), Hemingway does not use Krebs's family home as a conventional symbol of safety, comfort, and refuge from the war. Instead, Krebs's home becomes symbolic of provincial, erroneous presuppositions compounded by blind innocence, sentimentality, and smug middle-class respectability. The symbolic meaning of his home reveals that Krebs no longer shares his family's and town's view of the world. Their notions of love, the value of a respectable job, and a belief in God seem to him petty, complicated, and meaningless. The significance of Krebs's home is determined by the events within the story, which reverse and subvert the traditional associations readers might bring to it. Krebs's interactions with his family and the people in town reveal what home has come to mean to him.

A literary symbol can be a setting, character, action, object, name, or anything else in a work that maintains its literal significance while suggesting other meanings. Symbols cannot be restricted to a single meaning; they are suggestive rather than definitive. Their evocation of multiple meanings allows a writer to say more with less. Symbols are economical devices for evoking complex ideas without having to resort to painstaking explanations that would make a story more like an essay than an experience. The many walls in Melville's "Bartleby, the Scrivener" (p. 113) cannot be reduced to one idea. They have multiple meanings that unify the story. The walls are symbols of the deadening, dehumanizing, restrictive repetitiveness of the office routine, as well as of the confining, materialistic sensibilities of Wall Street. They suggest whatever limits and thwarts human aspirations, including death itself. We don't know precisely what shatters Bartleby's will to live, but the walls in the story, through their symbolic suggestiveness, indicate the nature of the limitations that cause the scrivener to slip into hopelessness and his "dead-wall reveries."

When a character, object, or incident indicates a single, fixed meaning, the writer is using *allegory* rather than symbol. Whereas symbols have literal functions as well as multiple meanings, the primary focus in allegory is on the abstract idea called forth by the concrete object. John Bunyan's *Pilgrim's Progress,* published during the seventeenth century, is a classic example of allegory because the characters, action, and setting have no existence beyond their abstract meanings. Bunyan's purpose is to teach his readers the exemplary way to salvation and heaven. The protagonist, named Christian, flees the City of Destruction in search of the Celestial City. Along the way he encounters characters who either help or hinder his spiritual journey. Among them are Mr. Worldly Wiseman, Faithful, Prudence, Piety, and a host of others named after the virtues or vices they display. These characters, places, and actions exist solely to illustrate religious doctrine. Allegory tends to be definitive rather than suggestive. It drives meaning into a corner and keeps it there. Most modern writers prefer the exploratory nature of symbol to the reductive nature of pure allegory.

Stories often include symbols that you may or may not perceive on a first reading. Their subtle use is a sign of a writer's skill in weaving symbols into the fabric of the characters' lives. Symbols may sometimes escape you, but that is probably better than finding symbols where only literal meanings are intended. Allow the text to help you determine whether a symbolic reading is appropriate. Once you are clear about what literally happens, read carefully and notice the placement of details that are emphasized. The pervasive references to time in Faulkner's "A Rose for Emily" (p. 79) and the many kinds of walls that appear throughout "Bartleby, the Scrivener" call attention to themselves and warrant symbolic readings. A symbol, however, need not be repeated to have an important purpose in a story. We don't learn until the very end of "Bartleby, the Scrivener" that Bartleby once worked as a clerk in the Dead Letter Office in Washington, D.C. This information is offered as merely an offhand rumor by the narrator, but its symbolic value is essential for understanding what motivates Bartleby's behavior. Indeed, Bartleby's experiences in the Dead Letter Office suggest enough about the nature of his thwarted hopes and desires to account for Bartleby's rejection of life.

By keeping track of the total context of the story, you should be able to decide whether your reading is reasonable and consistent with the other facts; plenty of lemons in literature yield no symbolic meaning even if they are squeezed. Be sensitive to the meanings that the author associates with people, places, objects, and actions. You may not associate home with provincial innocence as Hemingway does in "Soldier's Home," but a close reading of the story will permit you to see how and why he constructs that symbolic meaning. If you treat stories like people — with tact and care — they ordinarily are accessible and enjoyable.

The next three stories — Sandra Cisneros's "Barbie-Q," Colette's "The Hand," and Ralph Ellison's "Battle Royal" — rely on symbols to convey meanings that go far beyond the specific incidents described in their plots.

SANDRA CISNEROS (B. 1954)

Born to a Mexican father and a Mexican American mother, Sandra Cisneros grew up in Chicago along with her six brothers. Before teaching as a writer-in-residence at California State University at Chico, the University of California at Berkeley and at Irvine, and the University of Michigan, she taught high school, served as a college admissions officer, and worked as an arts administrator. Her poetry and fiction have earned her two National Endowment for the Arts fellowships. She is the author of two collections of fiction: *The House on Mango Street* (1989), about growing up in the Hispanic section of Chicago, and *Woman Hollering Creek* (1991), from which "Barbie-Q" is taken. Cisneros's fiction explores the difficulties of living in poor neighborhoods where issues of race, class, and gender complicate her characters' lives. In "Barbie-Q" a young girl's description of her dolls suggests significant parallels to her own life.

Barbie-Q   *1991*

Yours is the one with mean eyes and a ponytail. Striped swimsuit, stilettos, sunglasses, and gold hoop earrings. Mine is the one with bubble hair. Red swimsuit, stilettos, pearl earrings, and a wire stand. But that's all we can afford, besides one extra outfit apiece. Yours, "Red Flair," sophisticated A-line coatdress with a Jackie Kennedy pillbox hat, white gloves, handbag, and heels included. Mine, "Solo in the Spotlight," evening elegance in black glitter strapless gown with a puffy skirt at the bottom like a mermaid tail, formal-length gloves, pink chiffon scarf, and mike included. From so much dressing and undressing, the black glitter wears off where her titties stick out. This and a dress invented from an old sock when we cut holes here and here and here, the cuff rolled over for the glamorous, fancy-free, off-the-shoulder look.

Every time the same story. Your Barbie is roommates with my Barbie, and my Barbie's boyfriend comes over and your Barbie steals him, okay? Kiss kiss kiss. Then the two Barbies fight. You dumbbell! He's mine. On no he's not, you stinky! Only Ken's invisible, right? Because we don't have money for a stupid-looking boy doll when we'd both rather ask for a new Barbie outfit next Christmas. We have to make do with your mean-eyed Barbie and my bubblehead Barbie and our one outfit apiece not including the sock dress.

Until next Sunday when we are walking through the flea market on Maxwell Street and *there!* Lying on the street next to some tool bits, and platform shoes with the heels all squashed, and a fluorescent green wicker wastebasket, and aluminum foil, and hubcaps, and a pink shag rug, and windshield wiper blades, and dusty mason jars, and a coffee can full of rusty nails. *There!* Where? Two Mattel boxes. One with the "Career Gal" ensemble, snappy black-and-white business suit, three-quarter-length sleeve jacket with kick-pleat skirt, red sleeveless shell, gloves, pumps, and matching hat included. The other, "Sweet Dreams," dreamy pink-and-white plaid nightgown and matching robe, lace-trimmed slippers, hairbrush and hand mirror included. How much? Please, please, please, please, please, please, please, until they say okay.

On the outside you and me skipping and humming but inside we are doing loopity-loops and pirouetting. Until at the next vendor's stand, next to boxed pies, and bright orange toilet brushes, and rubber gloves, and wrench sets, and bouquets of feather flowers, and glass towel racks, and steel wool, and Alvin and the Chipmunks records, *there!* And *there!* And *there!* And *there!* and *there!* and *there!* and *there!* Bendable Legs Barbie with her new page-boy hairdo. Midge, Barbie's best friend. Ken, Barbie's boyfriend. Skipper, Barbie's little sister. Tutti and Todd, Barbie and Skipper's tiny twin sister and brother. Skipper's friends, Scooter and Ricky. Alan, Ken's buddy. And Francie, Barbie's MOD'ern cousin.

Everybody today selling toys, all of them damaged with water and smelling 5 of smoke. Because a big toy warehouse on Halsted Street burned down yesterday — see there? — the smoke still rising and drifting across the Dan Ryan expressway. And now there is a big fire sale at Maxwell Street, today only.

So what if we didn't get our new Bendable Legs Barbie and Midge and Ken and Skipper and Tutti and Todd and Scooter and Ricky and Alan and Francie in nice clean boxes and had to buy them on Maxwell Street, all water-soaked and sooty. So what if our Barbies smell like smoke when you hold them up to your nose even after you wash and wash and wash them. And if the prettiest doll, Barbie's MOD'ern cousin Francie with real eyelashes, eyelash brush included, has a left foot that's melted a little — so? If you dress her in her new "Prom Pinks" outfit, satin splendor with matching coat, gold belt, clutch, and hair bow included, so long as you don't lift her dress, right? — who's to know.

CONSIDERATIONS FOR CRITICAL THINKING AND WRITING

1. FIRST RESPONSE. In a short essay, try to use a favorite childhood toy as an example of how you or your generation grew up.
2. What kinds of values, assumptions, and lifestyles do Barbie dolls evoke for you? Why do the dolls play so central a role in this story?
3. Describe the protagonist. How does the protagonist's language reveal her character?
4. What is the significance of the "same story" the girls play all the time?
5. What sort of place is Maxwell Street? How important is the story's setting?
6. Is there a conflict in this story? Is there a resolution?
7. What, if any, social commentary is there in the story?
8. Discuss the significance of the title.
9. What emotions does the story inspire in you? How do you think the protagonist feels at the end when she says "who's to know"?

CONNECTIONS TO OTHER SELECTIONS

1. Compare and contrast the symbolic purpose of the dolls in "Barbie-Q" with that of the dancer described as "a circus kewpie doll" in Ralph Ellison's "Battle Royal" (p. 223, paras. 7–9).

2. "Barbie-Q" and Raymond Carver's "Popular Mechanics" (p. 272) are very brief short stories. Which one is — for you — the more effective story? Explain why.

3. Write an essay that considers the ending of "Barbie-Q" and Colette's "The Hand" (p. 220). Is either conclusion a "happy ending"?

COLETTE (SIDONIE-GABRIELLE COLETTE / 1873–1954)

Born in Burgundy, France, Sidonie-Gabrielle Colette lived a long and remarkably diverse life. At various points during her career she supported herself as a novelist, music hall performer, and journalist. Her professional life and three marriages helped to shape her keen insights into modern love and women's lives. She is regarded as a significant feminist voice in the twentieth century, and her reputation is firmly fixed by her having been the first woman admitted to the Goncourt Academy and by the continued popularity of her work among readers internationally. Her best-known works include *Mitsou, or, How Girls Grow Wise* (1919), *Chéri* (1920), *Claudine's House* (1922), and *Gigi* (1944). "The Hand" signals a telling moment in the life of a young bride.

The Hand   1924

He had fallen asleep on his young wife's shoulder, and she proudly bore the weight of the man's head, blond, ruddy-complexioned, eyes closed. He had slipped his big arm under the small of her slim, adolescent back, and his strong hand lay on the sheet next to the young woman's right elbow. She smiled to see the man's hand emerging there, all by itself and far away from its owner. Then she let her eyes wander over the half-lit room. A veiled conch shed a light across the bed the color of periwinkle.

"Too happy to sleep," she thought.

Too excited also, and often surprised by her new state. It had been only two weeks since she had begun to live the scandalous life of a newlywed who tastes the joys of living with someone unknown and with whom she is in love. To meet a handsome, blond young man, recently widowed, good at tennis and rowing, to marry him a month later: her conjugal adventure had been little more than a kidnapping. So that whenever she lay awake beside her husband, like tonight, she still kept her eyes closed for a long time, then opened them again in order to savor, with astonishment, the blue of the brand-new curtains, instead of the apricot-pink through which the first light of day filtered into the room where she had slept as a little girl.

A quiver ran through the sleeping body lying next to her, and she tightened her left arm around her husband's neck with the charming authority exercised by weak creatures. He did not wake up.

"His eyelashes are so long," she said to herself.   5

To herself she also praised his mouth, full and likable, his skin the color of pink brick, and even his forehead, neither noble nor broad, but still smooth and unwrinkled.

Her husband's right hand, lying beside her, quivered in turn, and beneath the curve of her back she felt the right arm, on which her whole weight was resting, come to life.

"I'm so heavy . . . I wish I could get up and turn the light off. But he's sleeping so well . . ."

The arm twisted again, feebly, and she arched her back to make herself lighter.

"It's as if I were lying on some animal," she thought.   10

She turned her head a little on the pillow and looked at the hand lying there next to her.

"It's so big! It really is bigger than my whole head."

The light, flowing out from under the edge of a parasol of bluish crystal, spilled up against the hand, and made every contour of the skin apparent, exaggerating the powerful knuckles and the veins engorged by the pressure on the arm. A few red hairs, at the base of the fingers, all curved in the same direction, like ears of wheat in the wind, and the flat nails, whose ridges the nail buffer had not smoothed out, gleamed, coated with pink varnish.

"I'll tell him not to varnish his nails," thought the young wife. "Varnish and pink polish don't go with a hand so . . . a hand that's so . . ."

An electric jolt ran through the hand and spared the young woman from   15
having to find the right adjective. The thumb stiffened itself out, horribly long and spatulate, and pressed tightly against the index finger, so that the hand suddenly took on a vile, apelike appearance.

"Oh!" whispered the young woman, as though faced with something slightly indecent.

The sound of a passing car pierced the silence with a shrillness that seemed luminous. The sleeping man did not wake, but the hand, offended, reared back and tensed up in the shape of a crab and waited, ready for battle. The screeching sound died down and the hand, relaxing gradually, lowered its claws, and became a pliant beast, awkwardly bent, shaken by faint jerks which resembled some sort of agony. The flat, cruel nail of the overlong thumb glistened. A curve in the little finger, which the young woman had never noticed, appeared, and the wallowing hand revealed its fleshy palm like a red belly.

"And I've kissed that hand! . . . How horrible! Haven't I ever looked at it?"

The hand, disturbed by a bad dream, appeared to respond to this startling discovery, this disgust. It regrouped its forces, opened wide, and splayed its tendons, lumps, and red fur like battle dress, then slowly drawing itself in again, grabbed a fistful of the sheet, dug into it with its curved fingers, and squeezed, squeezed with the methodical pleasure of a strangler.

"Oh!" cried the young woman.   20

The hand disappeared and a moment later the big arm, relieved of its burden, became a protective belt, a warm bulwark against all the terrors of night.

But the next morning, when it was time for breakfast in bed — hot chocolate and toast — she saw the hand again, with its red hair and red skin, and the ghastly thumb curving out over the handle of a knife.

"Do you want this slice, darling? I'll butter it for you."

She shuddered and felt her skin crawl on the back of her arms and down her back.

"Oh, no . . . no . . ."

Then she concealed her fear, bravely subdued herself, and, beginning her life of duplicity, of resignation, and of a lowly, delicate diplomacy, she leaned over and humbly kissed the monstrous hand. 25

Considerations for Critical Thinking and Writing

1. FIRST RESPONSE. Where is "The Hand" set? How significant is the setting of the story?

2. How well did the young woman know her husband before she married him? What attracted her to him?

3. How does the wife regard the hand at the very beginning of the story? At what point does she begin to change her attitude?

4. Explain how the wife's description of the hand affects your own response to it. What prompts her "Oh!" in paragraphs 16 and 20? What do you suppose the wife is thinking at these moments?

5. What powerful feelings does the hand evoke in the wife? How do her descriptions of the hand suggest symbolic readings of it?

6. Describe the conflict in the story. Explain whether there is a resolution to this conflict.

7. Do you think the story is more about the husband or about the wife? Who is the central character? Explain your choice. Consider also whether the characters are static or dynamic.

8. Why do you think the narrator mentions that the husband was "recently widowed"?

9. Why do you think the wife kisses her husband's hand in the final paragraph? Write an essay explaining how the kiss symbolizes the nature of their relationship.

10. Describe the point of view in the story. Why do you suppose Colette doesn't use a first-person perspective that would reveal more intimately the wife's perceptions and concerns?

Connections to Other Selections

1. In "The Birthmark" (p. 329) Nathaniel Hawthorne also uses a hand for symbolic purposes. Compare the meanings he associates with the hand in his story with Colette's. How does each writer invest meanings in a central symbol? What are the significant similarities and differences in meanings? Write an essay explaining why you find one story more effective than the other.

2. Compare the use of settings in "The Hand" and in John Updike's "A & P" (p. 576). To what extent does each story attach meaning to its setting?

3. How might Gail Godwin's "A Sorrowful Woman" (p. 33) be read as a kind of sequel to "The Hand"?

RALPH ELLISON (1914–1994)

Born in Oklahoma and educated at the Tuskegee Institute in Alabama, where he studied music, Ralph Ellison gained his reputation as a writer on the strength of his only published novel, *Invisible Man* (1952). He also published some scattered short stories and two collections of essays, *Shadow and Act* (1964) and *Going to the Territory* (1986). Although his writing was not extensive, it is important because Ellison wrote about race relations in the context of universal human concerns. *Invisible Man* is the story of a young black man who moves from the South to the North and discovers what it means to be black in America. "Battle Royal," published in 1947 as a short story, became the first chapter of *Invisible Man*. It concerns the beginning of the protagonist's long struggle for an adult identity in a world made corrupt by racial prejudice.

Battle Royal   *1947*

It goes a long way back, some twenty years. All my life I had been looking for something, and everywhere I turned someone tried to tell me what it was. I accepted their answers too, though they were often in contradiction and even self-contradictory. I was naive. I was looking for myself and asking everyone except myself questions which I, and only I, could answer. It took me a long time and much painful boomeranging of my expectations to achieve a realization everyone else appears to have been born with: That I am nobody but myself. But first I had to discover that I am an invisible man!

And yet I am no freak of nature, nor of history. I was in the cards, other things having been equal (or unequal) eighty-five years ago. I am not ashamed of my grandparents for having been slaves. I am only ashamed of myself for having at one time been ashamed. About eighty-five years ago they were told that they were free, united with others of our country in everything pertaining to the common good, and, in everything social, separate like the fingers of the hand. And they believed it. They exulted in it. They stayed in their place, worked hard, and brought up my father to do the same. But my grandfather is the one. He was an odd old guy, my grandfather, and I am told I take after him. It was he who caused the trouble. On his deathbed he called my father to him and said, "Son, after I'm gone I want you to keep up the good fight. I never told you, but our life is a war and I have been a traitor all my born days, a spy in the enemy's country ever since I gave up my gun back in the Reconstruction. Live with your head in the lion's mouth. I want you to overcome 'em with yeses, undermine 'em with grins, agree 'em to death and destruction, let 'em swoller you till they vomit or bust wide open." They thought the old man had gone out of his mind. He had been the meekest of men. The younger children were rushed from the room, the shades drawn and the flame of the lamp turned so low that it sputtered on the wick like the old man's breathing. "Learn it to the young-uns," he whispered fiercely; then he died.

But my folks were more alarmed over his last words than over his dying. It was as though he had not died at all, his words caused so much anxiety. I was warned emphatically to forget what he had said and, indeed, this is the first time it has been mentioned outside the family circle. It had a tremendous effect upon me, however. I could never be sure of what he meant. Grandfather had been a quiet old man who never made any trouble, yet on his deathbed he had called himself a traitor and a spy, and he had spoken of his meekness as a dangerous activity. It became a constant puzzle which lay unanswered in the back of my mind. And whenever things went well for me I remembered my grandfather and felt guilty and uncomfortable. It was as though I was carrying out his advice in spite of myself. And to make it worse, everyone loved me for it. I was praised by the most lily-white men of the town. I was considered an example of desirable conduct — just as my grandfather had been. And what puzzled me was that the old man had defined it as *treachery*. When I was praised for my conduct I felt a guilt that in some way I was doing something that was really against the wishes of the white folks, that if they had understood they would have desired me to act just the opposite, that I should have been sulky and mean, and that that really would have been what they wanted, even though they were fooled and thought they wanted me to act as I did. It made me afraid that some day they would look upon me as a traitor and I would be lost. Still I was more afraid to act any other way because they didn't like that at all. The old man's words were like a curse. On my graduation day I delivered an oration in which I showed that humility was the secret, indeed, the very essence of progress. (Not that I believed this — how could I, remembering my grandfather? — I only believed that it worked.) It was a great success. Everyone praised me and I was invited to give the speech at a gathering of the town's leading white citizens. It was a triumph for our whole community.

It was in the main ballroom of the leading hotel. When I got there I discovered that it was on the occasion of a smoker, and I was told that since I was to be there anyway I might as well take part in the battle royal to be fought by some of my schoolmates as part of the entertainment. The battle royal came first.

All of the town's big shots were there in their tuxedoes, wolfing down the buffet foods, drinking beer and whiskey and smoking black cigars. It was a large room with a high ceiling. Chairs were arranged in neat rows around three sides of a portable boxing ring. The fourth side was clear, revealing a gleaming space of polished floor. I had some misgivings over the battle royal, by the way. Not from a distaste for fighting, but because I didn't care too much for the other fellows who were to take part. They were tough guys who seemed to have no grandfather's curse worrying their minds. No one could mistake their toughness. And besides, I suspected that fighting a battle royal might detract from the dignity of my speech. In those pre-invisible days I visualized myself as a potential Booker T. Washington. But the other fellows didn't care too much for me either, and there were nine of them. I felt superior to them in my way, and I didn't like the manner in which we were all crowded together into the servants' elevator. Nor did they like my being there. In fact, as the warmly lighted floors flashed past the elevator we had words over the fact that I, by taking part in the fight, had knocked one of their friends out of a night's work.

We were led out of the elevator through a rococo hall into an anteroom and told to get into our fighting togs. Each of us was issued a pair of boxing gloves and ushered out into the big mirrored hall, which we entered looking cautiously about us and whispering, lest we might accidentally be heard above the noise of the room. It was foggy with cigar smoke. And already the whiskey was taking effect. I was shocked to see some of the most important men of the town quite tipsy. They were all there — bankers, lawyers, judges, doctors, fire chiefs, teachers, merchants. Even one of the more fashionable pastors. Something we could not see was going on up front. A clarinet was vibrating sensuously and the men were standing up and moving eagerly forward. We were a small tight group, clustered together, our bare upper bodies touching and shining with anticipatory sweat; while up front the big shots were becoming increasingly excited over something we still could not see. Suddenly I heard the school superintendent, who had told me to come, yell, "Bring up the shines, gentlemen! Bring up the little shines!"

We were rushed up to the front of the ballroom, where it smelled even more strongly of tobacco and whiskey. Then we were pushed into place. I almost wet my pants. A sea of faces, some hostile, some amused, ringed around us, and in the center, facing us, stood a magnificent blonde — stark naked. There was dead silence. I felt a blast of cold air chill me. I tried to back away, but they were behind me and around me. Some of the boys stood with lowered heads, trembling. I felt a wave of irrational guilt and fear. My teeth chattered, my skin turned to goose flesh, my knees knocked. Yet I was strongly attracted and looked in spite of myself. Had the price of looking been blindness, I would have looked. The hair was yellow like that of a circus kewpie doll, the face heavily powdered and rouged, as though to form an abstract mask, the eyes hollow and smeared a cool blue, the color of a baboon's butt. I felt a desire to spit upon her as my eyes brushed slowly over her body. Her breasts were firm and round as the domes of East Indian temples, and I stood so close as to see the fine skin texture and beads of pearly perspiration glistening like dew around the pink and erected buds of her nipples. I wanted at one and the same time to run from the room, to sink through the floor, or go to her and cover her from my eyes and the eyes of the others with my body; to feel the soft thighs, to caress her and destroy her, to love her and murder her, to hide from her, and yet to stroke where below the small American flag tattooed upon her belly her thighs formed a capital V. I had a notion that of all in the room she saw only me with her impersonal eyes.

And then she began to dance, a slow sensuous movement; the smoke of a hundred cigars clinging to her like the thinnest of veils. She seemed like a fair bird-girl girdled in veils calling to me from the angry surface of some gray and threatening sea. I was transported. Then I became aware of the clarinet playing and the big shots yelling at us. Some threatened us if we looked and others if we did not. On my right I saw one boy faint. And now a man grabbed a silver pitcher from a table and stepped close as he dashed ice water upon him and stood him up and forced two of us to support him as his head hung and moans issued from his thick bluish lips. Another boy began to plead to go home. He was the largest of the group, wearing dark red fighting trunks much too small to conceal the erection which projected from him as though in answer to the insinuating low-registered moaning of the clarinet. He tried to hide himself with his boxing gloves.

And all the while the blonde continued dancing, smiling faintly at the big shots who watched her with fascination, and faintly smiling at our fear. I noticed a certain merchant who followed her hungrily, his lips loose and drooling. He was a large man who wore diamond studs in a shirtfront which swelled with the ample paunch underneath, and each time the blonde swayed her undulating hips he ran his hand through the thin hair of his bald head and, with his arms upheld, his posture clumsy like that of an intoxicated panda, wound his belly in a slow and obscene grind. This creature was completely hypnotized. The music had quickened. As the dancer flung herself about with a detached expression on her face, the men began reaching out to touch her. I could see their beefy fingers sink into the soft flesh. Some of the others tried to stop them as she began to move around the floor in graceful circles, as they gave chase, slipping and sliding over the polished floor. It was mad. Chairs went crashing, drinks were spilt, as they ran laughing and howling after her. They caught her just as she reached a door, raised her from the floor, and tossed her as college boys are tossed at a hazing, and above her red, fixed-smiling lips I saw the terror and disgust in her eyes, almost like my own terror and that which I saw in some of the other boys. As I watched, they tossed her twice and her soft breasts seemed to flatten against the air and her legs flung wildly as she spun. Some of the more sober ones helped her to escape. And I started off the floor, heading for the anteroom with the rest of the boys.

Some were still crying in hysteria. But as we tried to leave we were stopped 10
and ordered to get into the ring. There was nothing to do but what we were told. All ten of us climbed under the ropes and allowed ourselves to be blindfolded with broad bands of white cloth. One of the men seemed to feel a bit sympathetic and tried to cheer us up as we stood with our backs against the ropes. Some of us tried to grin. "See that boy over there?" one of the men said. "I want you to run across at the bell and give it to him right in the belly. If you don't get him, I'm going to get you. I don't like his looks." Each of us was told the same. The blindfolds were put on. Yet even then I had been going over my speech. In my mind each word was as bright as flame. I felt the cloth pressed into place, and frowned so that it would be loosened when I relaxed.

But now I felt a sudden fit of blind terror. I was unused to darkness. It was as though I had suddenly found myself in a dark room filled with poisonous cottonmouths. I could hear the bleary voices yelling insistently for the battle royal to begin.

"Get going in there!"

"Let me at that big nigger!"

I strained to pick up the school superintendent's voice, as though to squeeze some security out of that slightly more familiar sound.

"Let me at those black sonsabitches!" someone yelled. 15

"No, Jackson, no!" another voice yelled. "Here, somebody, help me hold Jack."

"I want to get at that ginger-colored nigger. Tear him limb from limb," the first voice yelled.

I stood against the ropes trembling. For in those days I was what they called ginger-colored, and he sounded as though he might crunch me between his teeth like a crisp ginger cookie.

Quite a struggle was going on. Chairs were being kicked about and I could hear voices grunting as with a terrific effort. I wanted to see, to see more desperately than ever before. But the blindfold was tight as a thick skin-puckering scab and when I raised my gloved hands to push the layers of white aside a voice yelled, "Oh, no you don't, black bastard! Leave that alone!"

"Ring the bell before Jackson kills him a coon!" someone boomed in the   20 sudden silence. And I heard the bell clang and the sound of the feet scuffling forward.

A glove smacked against my head. I pivoted, striking out stiffly as someone went past, and felt the jar ripple along the length of my arm to my shoulder. Then it seemed as though all nine of the boys had turned upon me at once. Blows pounded me from all sides while I struck out as best I could. So many blows landed upon me that I wondered if I were not the only blindfolded fighter in the ring, or if the man called Jackson hadn't succeeded in getting me after all.

Blindfolded, I could no longer control my motions. I had no dignity. I stumbled about like a baby or a drunken man. The smoke had become thicker and with each new blow it seemed to sear and further restrict my lungs. My saliva became like hot bitter glue. A glove connected with my head, filling my mouth with warm blood. It was everywhere. I could not tell if the moisture I felt upon my body was sweat or blood. A blow landed hard against the nape of my neck. I felt myself going over, my head hitting the floor. Streaks of blue light filled the black world behind the blindfold. I lay prone, pretending that I was knocked out, but felt myself seized by hands and yanked to my feet. "Get going, black boy! Mix it up!" My arms were like lead, my head smarting from blows. I managed to feel my way to the ropes and held on, trying to catch my breath. A glove landed in my mid-section and I went over again, feeling as though the smoke had become a knife jabbed into my guts. Pushed this way and that by the legs milling around me, I finally pulled erect and discovered that I could see the black, sweat-washed forms weaving in the smoky-blue atmosphere like drunken dancers weaving to the rapid drumlike thuds of blows.

Everyone fought hysterically. It was complete anarchy. Everybody fought everybody else. No group fought together for long. Two, three, four, fought one, then turned to fight each other, were themselves attacked. Blows landed below the belt and in the kidney, with the gloves open as well as closed, and with my eye partly opened now there was not so much terror. I moved carefully, avoiding blows, although not too many to attract attention, fighting from group to group. The boys groped about like blind, cautious crabs crouching to protect their mid-sections, their heads pulled in short against their shoulders, their arms stretched nervously before them, with their fists testing the smoke-filled air like the knobbed feelers of hypersensitive snails. In one corner I glimpsed a boy violently punching the air and heard him scream in pain as he smashed his hand against a ring post. For a second I saw him bent over holding his hand, then going down as a blow caught his unprotected head. I played one group against the other, slipping in and throwing a punch then stepping out of range while pushing the others into the melee to take the blows blindly aimed at me. The smoke was agonizing and there were no rounds, no bells at three minute intervals to relieve our exhaustion. The room spun round me, a swirl of lights, smoke, sweating bodies surrounded by tense white faces. I bled from both nose and mouth, the blood spattering upon my chest.

The men kept yelling, "Slug him, black boy! Knock his guts out!"

"Uppercut him! Kill him! Kill that big boy!"   25

Taking a fake fall, I saw a boy going down heavily beside me as though we were felled by a single blow, saw a sneaker-clad foot shoot into his groin as the two who had knocked him down stumbled upon him. I rolled out of range, feeling a twinge of nausea.

The harder we fought the more threatening the men became. And yet, I had begun to worry about my speech again. How would it go? Would they recognize my ability? What would they give me?

I was fighting automatically when suddenly I noticed that one after another of the boys was leaving the ring. I was surprised, filled with panic, as though I had been left alone with an unknown danger. Then I understood. The boys had arranged it among themselves. It was the custom for the two men left in the ring to slug it out for the winner's prize. I discovered this too late. When the bell sounded two men in tuxedoes leaped into the ring and removed the blindfold. I found myself facing Tatlock, the biggest of the gang. I felt sick at my stomach. Hardly had the bell stopped ringing in my ears than it clanged again and I saw him moving swiftly toward me. Thinking of nothing else to do I hit him smash on the nose. He kept coming, bringing the rank sharp violence of stale sweat. His face was a black blank of a face, only his eyes alive — with hate of me and aglow with a feverish terror from what had happened to us all. I became anxious. I wanted to deliver my speech and he came at me as though he meant to beat it out of me. I smashed him again and again, taking his blows as they came. Then on a sudden impulse I struck him lightly and as we clinched, I whispered, "Fake like I knocked you out, you can have the prize."

"I'll break your behind," he whispered hoarsely.

"For *them?*"

"For *me*, sonofabitch!"   30

They were yelling for us to break it up and Tatlock spun me half around with a blow, and as a joggled camera sweeps in a reeling scene, I saw the howling red faces crouching tense beneath the cloud of blue-gray smoke. For a moment the world wavered, unraveled, flowed, then my head cleared and Tatlock bounced before me. That fluttering shadow before my eyes was his jabbing left hand. Then falling forward, my head against his damp shoulder, I whispered,

"I'll make it five dollars more."

"Go to hell!"

But his muscles relaxed a trifle beneath my pressure and I breathed,   35
"Seven?"

"Give it to your ma," he said, ripping me beneath the heart.

And while I still held him I butted him and moved away. I felt myself bombarded with punches. I fought back with hopeless desperation. I wanted to deliver my speech more than anything else in the world, because I felt that only these men could judge truly my ability, and now this stupid clown was ruining my chances. I began fighting carefully now, moving in to punch him and out again with my greater speed. A lucky blow to his chin and I had him going too — until I heard a loud voice yell, "I got my money on the big boy."

Hearing this, I almost dropped my guard. I was confused: Should I try to win against the voice out there? Would not this go against my speech, and was not this a moment for humility, for nonresistance? A blow to my head as I danced about sent my right eye popping like a jack-in-the-box and settled my dilemma. The room went red as I fell. It was a dream fall, my body languid and fastidious as to where to land, until the floor became impatient and smashed up to meet me. A moment later I came to. An hypnotic voice said FIVE emphatically. And I lay there, hazily watching a dark red spot of my own blood shaping itself into a butterfly, glistening and soaking into the soiled gray world of the canvas.

When the voice drawled TEN I was lifted up and dragged to a chair. I sat dazed. My eye pained and swelled with each throb of my pounding heart and I wondered if now I would be allowed to speak. I was wringing wet, my mouth still bleeding. We were grouped along the wall now. The other boys ignored me as they congratulated Tatlock and speculated as to how much they would be paid. One boy whimpered over his smashed hand. Looking up front, I saw attendants in white jackets rolling the portable ring away and placing a small square rug in the vacant space surrounded by chairs. Perhaps, I thought, I will stand on the rug to deliver my speech.

Then the M.C. called to us, "Come on up here boys and get your money." 40 We ran forward to where the men laughed and talked in their chairs, waiting. Everyone seemed friendly now.

"There it is on the rug," the man said. I saw the rug covered with coins of all dimensions and a few crumpled bills. But what excited me, scattered here and there, were the gold pieces.

"Boys, it's all yours," the man said. "You get all you grab."

"That's right, Sambo," a blond man said, winking at me confidentially.

I trembled with excitement, forgetting my pain. I would get the gold and the bills, I thought. I would use both hands. I would throw my body against the boys nearest me to block them from the gold.

"Get down around the rug now," the man commanded, "and don't anyone 45 touch it until I give the signal."

"This ought to be good," I heard.

As told, we got around the square rug on our knees. Slowly the man raised his freckled hand as we followed it upward with our eyes.

I heard, "These niggers look like they're about to pray!"

Then, "Ready," the man said. "Go!"

I lunged for a yellow coin lying on the blue design of the carpet, touching 50 it and sending a surprised shriek to join those rising around me. I tried frantically to remove my hand but could not let go. A hot, violent force tore through my body, shaking me like a wet rat. The rug was electrified. The hair bristled up on my head as I shook myself free. My muscles jumped, my nerves jangled, writhed. But I saw that this was not stopping the other boys. Laughing in fear and embarrassment, some were holding back and scooping up the coins knocked off by the painful contortions of the others. The men roared above us as we struggled.

"Pick it up, goddamnit, pick it up!" someone called like a bass-voiced parrot. "Go on, get it!"

I crawled rapidly around the floor, picking up the coins, trying to avoid the coppers and to get greenbacks and the gold. Ignoring the shock by laughing, as I brushed the coins off quickly, I discovered that I could contain the electricity—a contradiction, but it works. Then the men began to push us onto the rug. Laughing embarrassedly, we struggled out of their hands and kept after the coins. We were all wet and slippery and hard to hold. Suddenly I saw a boy lifted into the air, glistening with sweat like a circus seal, and dropped, his wet back landing flush upon the charged rug, heard him yell and saw him literally dance upon his back, his elbows beating a frenzied tattoo upon the floor, his muscles twitching like the flesh of a horse stung by many flies. When he finally rolled off, his face was gray and no one stopped him when he ran from the floor amid booming laughter.

"Get the money," the M.C. called. "That's good hard American cash!"

And we snatched and grabbed, snatched and grabbed. I was careful not to come too close to the rug now, and when I felt the hot whiskey breath descend upon me like a cloud of foul air I reached out and grabbed the leg of a chair. It was occupied and I held on desperately.

"Leggo, nigger! Leggo!"   55

The huge face wavered down to mine as he tried to push me free. But my body was slippery and he was too drunk. It was Mr. Colcord, who owned a chain of movie houses and "entertainment palaces." Each time he grabbed me I slipped out of his hands. It became a real struggle. I feared the rug more than I did the drunk, so I held on, surprising myself for a moment by trying to topple *him* upon the rug. It was such an enormous idea that I found myself actually carrying it out. I tried not to be obvious, yet when I grabbed his leg, trying to tumble him out of the chair, he raised up roaring with laughter, and, looking at me with soberness dead in the eye, kicked me viciously in the chest. The chair leg flew out of my hand and I felt myself going and rolled. It was as though I had rolled through a bed of hot coals. It seemed a whole century would pass before I would roll free, a century in which I was seared through the deepest levels of my body to the fearful breath within me and the breath seared and heated to the point of explosion. It'll all be over in a flash, I thought as I rolled clear. It'll all be over in a flash.

But not yet, the men on the other side were waiting, red faces swollen as though from apoplexy as they bent forward in their chairs. Seeing their fingers coming toward me I rolled away as a fumbled football rolls off the receiver's fingertips, back into the coals. That time I luckily sent the rug sliding out of place and heard the coins ringing against the floor and the boys scuffling to pick them up and the M.C. calling, "All right, boys, that's all. Go get dressed and get your money."

I was limp as a dish rag. My back felt as though it had been beaten with wires.

When we had dressed the M.C. came in and gave us each five dollars, except Tatlock, who got ten for being last in the ring. Then he told us to leave. I was not to get a chance to deliver my speech, I thought. I was going out into the dim alley in despair when I was stopped and told to go back. I returned to the ballroom, where the men were pushing back their chairs and gathering in groups to talk.

The M.C. knocked on a table for quiet. "Gentlemen," he said, "we almost   60
forgot an important part of the program. A most serious part, gentlemen. This boy was brought here to deliver a speech which he made at his graduation yesterday . . ."

"Bravo!"

"I'm told that he is the smartest boy we've got out there in Greenwood. I'm told that he knows more big words than a pocket-sized dictionary."

Much applause and laughter.

"So now, gentlemen, I want you to give him your attention."

There was still laughter as I faced them, my mouth dry, my eye throbbing. 65
I began slowly, but evidently my throat was tense, because they began shouting, "Louder! Louder!"

"We of the younger generation extol the wisdom of that great leader and
educator," I shouted, "who first spoke these flaming words of wisdom: 'A ship
lost at sea for many days suddenly sighted a friendly vessel. From the mast of
the unfortunate vessel was seen a signal: "Water, water; we die of thirst!" The
answer from the friendly vessel came back: "Cast down your bucket where you
are." The captain of the distressed vessel, at last heeding the injunction, cast
down his bucket, and it came up full of fresh sparkling water from the mouth
of the Amazon River.' And like him I say, and in his words, 'To those of my race
who depend upon bettering their condition in a foreign land, or who underestimate the importance of cultivating friendly relations with the Southern
white man, who is his next-door neighbor, I would say: "Cast down your
bucket where you are" — cast it down in making friends in every manly way of
the people of all races by whom we are surrounded . . .'"

I spoke automatically and with such fervor that I did not realize that the
men were still talking and laughing until my dry mouth, filling up with blood
from the cut, almost strangled me. I coughed, wanting to stop and go to one of
the tall brass, sand-filled spittoons to relieve myself, but a few of the men, especially the superintendent, were listening and I was afraid. So I gulped it
down, blood, saliva, and all, and continued. (What powers of endurance I had
during those days! What enthusiasm! What a belief in the rightness of
things!) I spoke even louder in spite of the pain. But still they talked and still
they laughed, as though deaf with cotton in dirty ears. So I spoke with greater
emotional emphasis. I closed my ears and swallowed blood until I was nauseated. The speech seemed a hundred times as long as before, but I could not
leave out a single word. All had to be said, each memorized nuance considered,
rendered. Nor was that all. Whenever I uttered a word of three or more syllables a group of voices would yell for me to repeat it. I used the phrase "social
responsibility" and they yelled:

"What's that word you say, boy?"

"Social responsibility," I said.

"What?" 70

"Social . . ."

"Louder."

". . . responsibility."

"More!"

"Respon —" 75

"Repeat!"

"— sibility."

The room filled with the uproar of laughter until, no doubt, distracted by
having to gulp down my blood, I made a mistake and yelled a phrase I had
often seen denounced in newspaper editorials, heard debated in private.

"Social . . ."

"What?" they yelled. 80

". . . equality —"

The laughter hung smokelike in the sudden stillness. I opened my eyes,
puzzled. Sounds of displeasure filled the room. The M.C. rushed forward.
They shouted hostile phrases at me. But I did not understand.

A small dry mustached man in the front row blared out, "Say that slowly, son!"

"What, sir?"

"What you just said!"   85

"Social responsibility, sir," I said.

"You weren't being smart, were you, boy?" he said, not unkindly.

"No, sir!"

"You sure that about 'equality' was a mistake?"

"Oh, yes, sir," I said. "I was swallowing blood."   90

"Well, you had better speak more slowly so we can understand. We mean to do right by you, but you've got to know your place at all times. All right, now, go on with your speech."

I was afraid. I wanted to leave but I wanted also to speak and I was afraid they'd snatch me down.

"Thank you, sir," I said, beginning where I had left off, and having them ignore me as before.

Yet when I finished there was a thunderous applause. I was surprised to see the superintendent come forth with a package wrapped in white tissue paper, and, gesturing for quiet, address the men.

"Gentlemen, you see that I did not overpraise this boy. He makes a good   95 speech and some day he'll lead his people in the proper paths. And I don't have to tell you that that is important in these days and times. This is a good, smart boy, and so to encourage him in the right direction, in the name of the Board of Education I wish to present him a prize in the form of this . . ."

He paused, removing the tissue paper and revealing a gleaming calfskin brief case.

". . . in the form of this first-class article from Shad Whitmore's shop."

"Boy," he said, addressing me, "take this prize and keep it well. Consider it a badge of office. Prize it. Keep developing as you are and some day it will be filled with important papers that will help shape the destiny of your people."

I was so moved that I could hardly express my thanks. A rope of bloody saliva forming a shape like an undiscovered continent drooled upon the leather and I wiped it quickly away. I felt an importance that I had never dreamed.

"Open it and see what's inside," I was told.   100

My fingers a-tremble, I complied, smelling the fresh leather and finding an official-looking document inside. It was a scholarship to the state college for Negroes. My eyes filled with tears and I ran awkwardly off the floor.

I was overjoyed; I did not even mind when I discovered that the gold pieces I had scrambled for were brass pocket tokens advertising a certain make of automobile.

When I reached home everyone was excited. Next day the neighbors came to congratulate me. I even felt safe from grandfather, whose deathbed curse usually spoiled my triumphs. I stood beneath his photograph with my brief case in hand and smiled triumphantly into his stolid black peasant's face. It was a face that fascinated me. The eyes seemed to follow everywhere I went.

That night I dreamed I was at a circus with him and that he refused to laugh at the clowns no matter what they did. Then later he told me to open my brief case and read what was inside and I did, finding an official envelope stamped with the state seal; and inside the envelope I found another and another, endlessly, and I thought I would fall of weariness. "Them's years," he said. "Now open that one." And I did and in it I found an engraved document containing a short message in letters of gold. "Read it," my grandfather said. "Out loud!"

"To Whom It May Concern," I intoned. "Keep This Nigger-Boy Running."   105 I awoke with the old man's laughter ringing in my ears.

(It was a dream I was to remember and dream again for many years after. But at that time I had no insight into its meaning. First I had to attend college.)

Considerations for Critical Thinking and Writing

1. FIRST RESPONSE. Discuss how the protagonist's expectations are similar to what has come to be known as the American dream — the assumption that ambition, hard work, perseverance, intelligence, and virtue always lead to success. Do you believe in the American dream?

2. How does the first paragraph of the story sum up the conflict that the narrator confronts? In what sense is he "invisible"?

3. Why do his grandfather's last words cause so much anxiety in the family? What does his grandfather mean when he says, "I want you to overcome 'em with yeses, undermine 'em with grins, agree 'em to death"?

4. What is the symbolic significance of the naked blonde? What details reveal that she represents more than a sexual tease in the story?

5. How does the battle in the boxing ring and the scramble for money afterward suggest the kind of control whites have over blacks in the story?

6. Why is it significant that the town is named Greenwood and that the briefcase award comes from Shad Whitmore's shop? Can you find any other details that serve to reinforce the meaning of the story?

7. What is the narrator's perspective as an educated adult telling the story, in contrast to his assumptions and beliefs as a recent high school graduate? How is this contrast especially evident in the speech before the "leading white citizens" of the town?

8. How can the dream at the end of the story be related to the major incidents that precede it?

9. Given the grandfather's advice, explain how "meekness" can be a "dangerous activity" and a weapon against oppression.

10. Imagine the story as told from a third-person point of view. How would this change the story? Do you think the story would be more or less effective told from a third-person point of view? Explain your answer.

Connections to Other Selections

1. Compare and contrast Ellison's view of the South with William Faulkner's in "A Rose for Emily" (p. 79).

2. Write an essay comparing and contrasting "Battle Royal" and Mark Halliday's, "Young Man on Sixth Avenue" (p. 70) as symbolic stories that focus on their respective protagonists' illusions and disillusions about life.

3. Compare and contrast this story with M. Carl Holman's poem "Mr. Z" (p. 1098).

PERSPECTIVE

MORDECAI MARCUS (B. 1925)

What Is an Initiation Story?   *1960*

An initiation story may be said to show its young protagonist experiencing a significant change of knowledge about the world or himself, or a change of character, or of both, and this change must point or lead him toward an adult world. It may or may not contain some form of ritual, but it should give some evidence that the change is at least likely to have permanent effects.

Initiation stories obviously center on a variety of experiences and the initiations vary in effect. It will be useful, therefore, to divide initiations into types according to their power and effect. First, some initiations lead only to the threshold of maturity and understanding but do not definitely cross it. Such stories emphasize the shocking effect of experience, and their protagonists tend to be distinctly young. Second, some initiations take their protagonists across a threshold of maturity and understanding but leave them enmeshed in a struggle for certainty. These initiations sometimes involve self-discovery. Third, the most decisive initiations carry their protagonists firmly into maturity and understanding, or at least show them decisively embarked toward maturity. These initiations usually center on self-discovery. For convenience, I will call these types tentative, uncompleted, and decisive initiations.

From "What Is an Initiation Story?" in *The Journal
of Aesthetics and Art Criticism*

CONSIDERATIONS FOR CRITICAL THINKING AND WRITING

1. For a work to be classified as an initiation story, why should it "give some evidence that the change [in the protagonist] is at least likely to have permanent effects"?

2. Marcus divides initiations into three broad types: tentative, uncompleted, and decisive. Explain how you would categorize the initiation in Ellison's "Battle Royal" (p. 223).

FAE MYENNE NG (B. 1957)

The daughter of a seamstress and a laborer, Fae Myenne Ng (her last name is pronounced "Ing") was born in San Francisco. She attended the University of California-Berkeley, and received her M.F.A. at Columbia University. Ng has supported herself by working as a waitress and at other temporary jobs. *Bone* (1993), her first novel, is a story about a Chinese American family. Her short stories have appeared in the *American Voice, Calyx, City Lights Review, Crescent Review, Harper's,* and in a number of anthologies. She was awarded a grant by the National Endowment for the Arts. She currently lives in New York City.

A Red Sweater   *1987*

I chose red for my sister. Fierce, dark red. Made in Hong Kong. Hand Wash Only because it's got that skin of fuzz. She'll look happy. That's good. Everything's perfect, for a minute. That seems enough.

Red. For Good Luck. Of course. This fire-red sweater is swollen with good cheer. Wear it, I will tell her. You'll look lucky.

We're a family of three girls. By Chinese standards, that's not lucky. "Too bad," outsiders whisper, ". . . nothing but daughters. A failed family."

First, Middle, and End girl. Our order of birth marked us. That came to tell more than our given names.

My eldest sister, Lisa, lives at home. She quit San Francisco State, one se- 5
mester short of a psychology degree. One day she said, "Forget about it, I'm tired." She's working full time at Pacific Bell now. Nine hundred a month with benefits. Mah and Deh think it's a great deal. They tell everybody, "Yes, our Number One makes good pay, but that's not even counting the discount. If we call Hong Kong, China even, there's forty percent off!" As if anyone in their part of China had a telephone.

Number Two, the in-between, jumped off the "M" floor three years ago. Not true! What happened? Why? Too sad! All we say about that is, "It was her choice."

We sent Mah to Hong Kong. When she left Hong Kong thirty years ago, she was the envy of all: "Lucky girl! You'll never have to work." To marry a so-journer was to have a future. Thirty years in the land of gold and good fortune, and then she returned to tell the story: three daughters, one dead, one unmarried, another who-cares-where, the thirty years in sweatshops, and the prince of the Golden Mountain turned into a toad. I'm glad I didn't have to go with her. I felt her shame and regret. To return, seeking solace and comfort, instead of offering banquets and stories of the good life.

I'm the youngest. I started flying with American the year Mah returned to Hong Kong, so I got her a good discount. She thought I was good for something then. But when she returned, I was pregnant.

"Get an abortion," she said. "Drop the baby," she screamed.

"No."   10

"Then get married."

"No. I don't want to."

I was going to get an abortion all along. I just didn't like the way they talked about the whole thing. They made me feel like dirt, that I was a disgrace. Now I can see how I used it as an opportunity. Sometimes I wonder if there wasn't another way. Everything about those years was so steamy and angry. There didn't seem to be any answers.

"I have no eyes for you," Mah said.

"Don't call us," Deh said.   15

They wouldn't talk to me. They ranted idioms to each other for days. The apartment was filled with images and curses I couldn't perceive. I got the general idea: I was a rotten, no-good, dead thing. I would die in a gutter without rice in my belly. My spirit — if I had one — wouldn't be fed. I wouldn't see good days in this life or the next.

My parents always had a special way of saying things.

Now I'm based in Honolulu. When our middle sister jumped, she kind of closed the world. The family just sort of fell apart. I left. Now, I try to make up for it; the folks still won't see me, but I try to keep in touch with them through Lisa. Flying cuts up your life, hits hardest during the holidays. I'm always sensitive then. I feel like I'm missing something, that people are doing something really important while I'm up in the sky, flying through time zones.

So I like to see Lisa around the beginning of the year. January, New Year's, and February, New Year's again, double luckiness with our birthdays in between. With so much going on, there's always something to talk about.

"You pick the place this year," I tell her.   20

"Around here?"

"No," I say. "Around here" means the food is good and the living hard. You eat a steaming rice plate, and then you feel like rushing home to sew garments or assemble radio parts or something. We eat together only once a year, so I feel we should splurge. Besides, at the Chinatown places, you have nothing to talk about except the bare issues. In American restaurants, the atmosphere helps you along. I want nice light and a view and handsome waiters.

"Let's go somewhere with a view," I say.

We decide to go to Following Sea, a new place on the Pier 39 track. We're early, the restaurant isn't crowded. It's been clear all day, so I think the sunset will be nice. I ask for a window table. I turn to talk to my sister, but she's already talking to a waiter. He's got that dark island tone that she likes. He's looking her up and down. My sister does not blink at it. She holds his look and orders two Johnny Walkers. I pick up a fork, turn it around in my hand. I seldom use chopsticks now. At home, I eat my rice in a plate, with a fork. The only chopsticks I own, I wear in my hair. For a moment, I feel strange sitting here at this unfamiliar table. I don't know this tablecloth, this linen, these candles. Everything seems foreign. It feels like we should be different people. But each time I look up, she's the same. I know this person. She's my sister. We sat together with chopsticks, mismatched bowls, braids, and braces, across the formica tabletop.

"I like three-pronged forks," I say, pressing my thumb against the sharp   25
points.

My sister rolls her eyes. She lights a cigarette.

I ask for one.

I finally say, "So, what's new?"

"Not much." Her voice is sullen. She doesn't look at me. Once a year, I come in, asking questions. She's got the answers, but she hates them. For me, I think she's got the peace of heart, knowing that she's done her share for Mah and Deh. She thinks I have the peace, not caring. Her life is full of questions, too, but I have no answers.

I look around the restaurant. The sunset is not spectacular, and we don't   30
comment on it. The waiters are lighting candles. Ours is bringing the drinks.

He stops very close to my sister, seems to breathe her in. She raises her face toward him. "Ready?" he asks. My sister orders for us. The waiter struts off.

"Tight ass," I say.

"The best," she says.

My scotch tastes good. It reminds me of Deh. Johnny Walker or Seagrams 7, that's what they served at Chinese banquets. Nine courses and a bottle. No ice. We learned to drink it Chinese style, in teacups. Deh drank from his rice bowl, sipping it like hot soup. By the end of the meal, he took it like cool tea, in bold mouthfuls. We sat watching, our teacups in our laps, his three giggly girls.

Relaxed, I'm thinking there's a connection. Johnny Walker then and Johnny Walker now. I ask for another cigarette and this one I enjoy. Now my Johnny Walker pops with ice. I twirl the glass to make the ice tinkle.

We clink glasses. Three times for good luck. She giggles. I feel better.   35

"Nice sweater," I say.

"Michael Owyang," she says. She laughs. The light from the candle makes her eyes shimmer. She's got Mah's eyes. Eyes that make you want to talk. Lisa is reed-thin and tall. She's got a body that clothes look good on. My sister slips something on, and it wraps her like skin. Fabric has pulse on her.

"Happy birthday, soon," I say.

"Thanks, and to yours too, just as soon."

"Here's to Johnny Walker in shark's fin soup," I say.   40

"And squab dinners."

"'I Love Lucy,'" I say.

We laugh. It makes us feel like children again. We remember how to be sisters.

I raise my glass, "To 'I Love Lucy,' squab dinners, and brown bags."

"To bones," she says.   45

"Bones," I repeat. This is a funny story that gets sad, and knowing it, I keep laughing. I am surprised how much memory there is in one word. Pigeons. Only recently did I learn they're called squab. Our word for them was pigeon — on a plate or flying over Portsmouth Square. A good meal at forty cents a bird. In line by dawn, we waited at the butcher's listening for the slow churning motor of the trucks. We watched the live fish flushing out of the tanks into the garbage pails. We smelled the honey-crushed cha sui bows baking. When the white laundry truck turned into Wentworth, there was a puffing trail of feathers following it. A stench filled the alley. The crowd squeezed in around the truck. Old ladies reached into the crates, squeezing and tugging for the plumpest pigeons.

My sister and I picked the white ones, those with the most expressive eyes. Dove birds, we called them. We fed them leftover rice in water, and as long as they stayed plump, they were our pets, our baby dove birds. And then one day we'd come home from school and find them cooked. They were a special, nutritious treat. Mah let us fill our bowls high with little pigeon parts: legs, breasts, and wings, and take them out to the front room to watch "I Love Lucy." We took brown bags for the bones. We balanced our bowls on our laps and laughed at Lucy. We leaned forward, our chopsticks crossed in mid-air, and called out, "Mah! Mah! Come watch! Watch Lucy cry!"

But she always sat alone in the kitchen sucking out the sweetness of the lesser parts: necks, backs, and the head. "Bones are sweeter than you know," she always said. She came out to check the bags. "Clean bones," she said, shaking the bags. "No waste," she said.

Our dinners come with a warning. "Plate's hot. Don't touch." My sister orders a carafe of house white. "Enjoy," he says, smiling at my sister. She doesn't look up.

I can't remember how to say scallops in Chinese. I ask my sister, she 50
doesn't know either. The food isn't great. Or maybe we just don't have the taste buds in us to go crazy over it. Sometimes I get very hungry for Chinese flavors: black beans, garlic and ginger, shrimp paste and sesame oil. These are tastes we grew up with, still dream about. Crave. Run around town after. Duck liver sausage, bean curd, jook, salted fish, and fried dace with black beans. Western flavors don't stand out, the surroundings do. Three pronged forks. Pink tablecloths. Fresh flowers. Cute waiters. An odd difference.

"Maybe we should have gone to Sun Hung Heung. At least the vegetables are real," I say.

"Hung toh-yee-foo-won-tun!" she says.

"Yeah, yum!" I say.

I remember Deh teaching us how to pick bok choy, his favorite vegetable. "Stick your fingernail into the stem. Juicy and firm, good. Limp and tough, no good." The three of us followed Deh, punching our thumbnails into every stem of bok choy we saw.

"Deh still eating bok choy?" 55

"Breakfast, lunch, and dinner." My sister throws her head back, and laughs. It is Deh's motion. She recites in a mimic tone. "Your Deh, all he needs is a good hot bowl of rice and a plate full of greens. A good monk."

There was always bok choy. Even though it was nonstop for Mah — rushing to the sweatshop in the morning, out to shop on break, and then home to cook by evening — she did this for him. A plate of bok choy, steaming with the taste of ginger and garlic. He said she made good rice. Timed full-fire until the first boil, medium until the grains formed a crust along the sides of the pot, and then low-flamed to let the rice steam. Firm, that's how Deh liked his rice.

The waiter brings the wine, asks if everything is all right.

"Everything," my sister says.

There's something else about this meeting. I can hear it in the edge of her 60
voice. She doesn't say anything and I don't ask. Her lips make a contorting line; her face looks sour. She lets out a breath. It sounds like she's been holding it in too long.

"Another fight. The bank line," she says. "He waited four times in the bank line. Mah ran around outside shopping. He was doing her a favor. She was doing him a favor. Mah wouldn't stop yelling. 'Get out and go die! Useless Thing! Stinking Corpse!'"

I know he answered. His voice must have had that fortune teller's tone to it. You listened because you knew it was a warning.

He always threatened to disappear, jump off the Golden Gate. His thousand-year-old threat. I've heard it all before. "I will go. Even when dead, I won't be far enough away. Curse the good will that blinded me into taking you as wife!"

I give Lisa some of my scallops. "Eat," I tell her.

She keeps talking. "Of course, you know how Mah thinks, that nobody 65
should complain because she's been the one working all these years."

I nod. I start eating, hoping she'll follow.

One bite and she's talking again. "You know what shopping with Mah is like, either you stand outside with the bags like a servant, or inside like a marker, holding a place in line. You know how she gets into being frugal — saving time because it's the one free thing in her life. Well, they're at the bank and she had him hold her place in line while she runs up and down Stockton doing her quick shopping maneuvers. So he's in line, and it's his turn, but she's not back. So he has to start all over at the back again. Then it's his turn but she's still not back. When she finally comes in, she's got bags in both hands, and he's going through the line for the fourth time. Of course she doesn't say sorry or anything."

I interrupt. "How do you know all this?" I tell myself not to come back next year. I tell myself to apply for another transfer, to the East Coast.

"She told me. Word for word." Lisa spears a scallop, puts it in her mouth. I know it's cold by now. "Word for word," she repeats. She cuts a piece of chicken. "Try," she says.

I think about how we're sisters. We eat slowly, chewing carefully like old 70 people. A way to make things last, to fool the stomach.

Mah and Deh both worked too hard; it's as if their marriage was a marriage of toil — of toiling together. The idea is that the next generation can marry for love.

In the old country, matches were made, strangers were wedded, and that was fate. Those days, sojourners like Deh were considered princes. To become the wife to such a man was to be saved from the war-torn villages.

Saved to work. After dinner, with the rice still in between her teeth, Mah sat down at her Singer. When we pulled out the wall-bed, she was still there, sewing. The street noises stopped long before she did. The hot lamp made all the stitches blur together. And in the mornings, long before any of us awoke, she was already there, sewing again.

His work was hard, too. He ran a laundry on Polk Street. He sailed with the American President Lines. Things started to look up when he owned the take-out place in Vallejo, and then his partner ran off. So he went to Alaska and worked the canneries.

She was good to him, too. We remember. How else would we have known 75 him all those years he worked in Guam, in the Fiji Islands, in Alaska? Mah always gave him majestic welcomes home. It was her excitement that made us remember him.

I look around. The restaurant is full. The waiters move quickly.

I know Deh. His words are ugly. I've heard him. I've listened. And I've always wished for the street noises, as if in the traffic of sound, I believe I can escape. I know the hard color of his eyes and the tightness of his jaw. I can almost hear his teeth grind. I know this. Years of it.

Their lives weren't easy. So is their discontent without reason?

What about the first one? You didn't even think to come to the hospital. The first one, I say! Son or daughter, dead or alive, you didn't even come!

What about living or dying? Which did you want for me that time you pushed me 80 *back to work before my back brace was off?*

Money! Money! Money to eat with, to buy clothes with, to pass this life with!

Don't start that again! Everything I make at that dead place I hand . . .

How come . . .
What about . . .
So . . .   85

It was obvious. The stories themselves mean little. It was how hot and furious they could become.

Is there no end to it? What makes their ugliness so alive, so thick and impossible to let go of?

"I don't want to think about it anymore." The way she says it surprises me.
This time I listen. I imagine what it would be like to take her place. It will be my
turn one day.

"Ron," she says, wiggling her fingers above the candle. "A fun thing."

The opal flickers above the flame. I tell her that I want to get her something   90
special for her birthday, ". . . next trip I get abroad." She looks up at me, smiles.

For a minute, my sister seems happy. But she won't be able to hold onto it.
She grabs at things out of despair, out of fear. Gifts grow old for her. Emotions
never ripen, they sour. Everything slips away from her. Nothing sustains her.
Her beauty has made her fragile.

We should have eaten in Chinatown. We could have gone for coffee in
North Beach, then for jook at Sam Wo's.

"No work, it's been like that for months, just odd jobs," she says.

I'm thinking, it's not like I haven't done my share. I was a kid once, I did
things because I felt I should. I helped fill out forms at the Chinatown employment agencies. I went with him to the Seaman's Union. I waited too, listening
and hoping for those calls: "Busboy! Presser! Prep Man!" His bags were
packed, he was always ready to go. "On standby," he said.

Every week. All the same. Quitting and looking to start all over again. In   95
the end, it was like never having gone anywhere. It was like the bank line, waiting for nothing.

How many times did my sister and I have to hold them apart? The flat *ting!*
sound as the blade slapped onto the linoleum floor, the wooden handle of the
knife slamming into the corner. Was it she or I who screamed, repeating all of
their ugliest words? Who shook them? Who made them stop?

The waiter comes to take the plates. He stands by my sister for a moment.
I raise my glass to the waiter.

"You two Chinese?" he asks.

"No," I say, finishing off my wine. I roll my eyes. I wish I had another
Johnny Walker. Suddenly I don't care.

"We're two sisters," I say. I laugh. I ask for the check, leave a good tip. I see   100
him slip my sister a box of matches.

Outside, the air is cool and brisk. My sister links her arm into mine. We
walk up Bay onto Chestnut. We pass Galileo High School and then turn down
Van Ness to head toward the pier. The bay is black. The foghorns sound far
away. We walk the whole length of the pier without talking.

The water is white where it slaps against the wooden stakes.

For a long time Lisa's wanted out. She can stay at that point of endurance forever. Desire that becomes old feels too good, it's seductive. I know how hard it is to go.

The heart never travels. You have to be heartless. My sister holds that heart, too close and for too long. This is her weakness, and I like to think, used to be mine. Lisa endures too much.

We're lucky, not like the bondmaids growing up in service, or the newborn 105 daughters whose mouths were stuffed with ashes. Courtesans with the three-inch feet, beardless, soft-shouldered eunuchs, and the frightened child-brides, they're all stories to us. We're the lucky generation. Our parents forced themselves to live through the humiliation in this country so that we could have it better. We know so little of the old country. We repeat names of Grandfathers and Uncles, but they will always be strangers to us. Family exists only because somebody has a story, and knowing the story connects us to a history. To us, the deformed man is oddly compelling, the forgotten man is a good story. A beautiful woman suffers.

I want her beauty to buy her out.

The sweater cost two weeks' pay. Like the forty-cent birds that are now a delicacy, this is a special treat. The money doesn't mean anything. It is, if anything, time. Time is what I would like to give her.

A red sweater. One hundred percent angora. The skin of fuzz will be a fierce rouge on her naked breasts.

Red. Lucky. Wear it. Find that man. The new one. Wrap yourself around him. Feel the pulsing between you. Fuck him and think about it. One hundred percent. Hand Wash Only. Worn Once.

CONSIDERATIONS FOR CRITICAL THINKING AND WRITING

1. FIRST RESPONSE. How do you read this story's final paragraph? What emotions is the narrator revealing? Does it change the way you've thought of her up to the end?

2. Describe the narrator. What details of her personal life reveal her values and sensibilities?

3. Why is the narrator concerned about the quality of her older sister's life? Why does Lisa live with her parents?

4. How does knowing that the middle sister committed suicide affect your understanding of the family?

5. How is Chinese immigrant life portrayed in the story? How do Mah and Deh cope with their everyday lives?

6. Toward the end of the story, the narrator says, "Family exists only because somebody has a story, and knowing the story connects us to a history" (para. 105). Is this idea true of this family?

7. How does the memory of her family life affect the narrator's present life? How does she feel about her sister?

8. Which of the narrator's stories about family life seem to have significant symbolic value? Choose one to analyze in detail.

9. The red sweater frames the story. How does it function as a symbol? Does its meaning evolve over the course of the narration?

CONNECTIONS TO OTHER SELECTIONS

1. Compare the narrator in "A Red Sweater" with the narrator of Bharati Mukherjee's "The Tenant" (p. 102). In what sense might each narrator be described as a tenant?

2. Discuss the ways in which Chinese immigrant life is presented in "A Red Sweater" and Gish Jen's "In the American Society" (p. 643). What significant similarities and differences do you find?

3. Write an essay that compares issues of family loyalty in "A Red Sweater" and in William Faulkner's "Barn Burning" (p. 481).

8

Theme

Theme is the central idea or meaning of a story. It provides a unifying point around which the plot, characters, setting, point of view, symbols, and other elements of a story are organized. In some works the theme is explicitly stated. Nathaniel Hawthorne's "Wakefield," for example, begins with the author telling the reader that the point of his story is "done up neatly, and condensed into the final sentence." Most modern writers, however, present their themes implicitly (as Hawthorne does in the majority of his stories), so determining the underlying meaning of a work often requires more effort than it does from the reader of "Wakefield." One reason for the difficulty is that the theme is fused into the elements of the story, and these must be carefully examined in relation to one another as well as to the work as a whole. But then that's the value of determining the theme, for it requires a close analysis of all the elements of a work. Such a close reading often results in sharper insights into this overlooked character or that seemingly unrelated incident. Accounting for the details and seeing how they fit together result in greater understanding of the story. Such familiarity creates pleasure in much the same way that a musical piece heard more than once becomes a rich experience rather than simply a repetitive one.

Themes are not always easy to express, but some principles can aid you in articulating the central meaning of a work. First distinguish between the theme of a story and its subject. They are not equivalents. Many stories share identical subjects, such as fate, death, innocence, youth, loneliness, racial prejudice, and disillusionment. Yet each story usually makes its own statement about the subject and expresses some view of life. Hemingway's "Soldier's Home" (p. 145) and Faulkner's "Barn Burning" (p. 481) both describe young men who are unhappy at home and decide that they must leave, but the meaning of each story is quite different. A thematic generalization about "Soldier's Home" could be something like this: "The brutal experience of war can alienate a person from those — even family and friends — who are innocent of war's reality." The theme of Faulkner's story could be stated this way: "No matter how much one might love one's father, there comes a time when family loyalties must be left behind in order to be true to one's self."

These two statements of theme do not definitively sum up each story — there is no single, absolute way of expressing a work's theme — but they do describe a central idea in each. Furthermore, the emphasis in each of these themes could be modified or expanded because interpretations of interesting, complex works are always subject to revision. People have different responses to life, and so it is hardly surprising that responses to literature are not identical. When theme is considered, the possibilities for meaning are usually expanded and not reduced to categories such as "right" or "wrong."

Although readers may differ in their interpretations of a story, that does not mean that *any* interpretation is valid. If we were to assert that the soldier's dissatisfactions in Hemingway's story could be readily eliminated by his settling down to marriage and a decent job (his mother's solution), we would have missed Hemingway's purposes in writing the story; we would have failed to see how Krebs's war experiences have caused him to reexamine the assumptions and beliefs that previously nurtured him but now seem unreal to him. We would have to ignore much in the story in order to arrive at such a reading. To be valid, the statement of the theme should be responsive to the details of the story. It must be based on evidence within the story rather than solely on experiences, attitudes, or values the reader brings to the work — such as personally knowing a war veteran who successfully adjusted to civilian life after getting a good job and marrying. Familiarity with the subject matter of a story can certainly be an aid to interpretation, but it should not get in the way of seeing the author's perspective.

Sometimes readers too hastily conclude that a story's theme always consists of a moral, some kind of lesson that is dramatized by the various elements of the work. There are stories that do this — Hawthorne's "Wakefield," for example. Here are the final sentences in his story about a middle-aged man who drops out of life for twenty years:

> He has left us much food for thought, a portion of which shall lend its wisdom to a moral, and be shaped into a figure. Amid the seeming confusion of our mysterious world, individuals are so nicely adjusted to a system, and systems to one another and to a whole, that, by stepping aside for a moment, a man exposes himself to a fearful risk of losing his place forever. Like Wakefield, he may become, as it were, the Outcast of the Universe.

Most stories, however, do not include such direct caveats about the conduct of life. A tendency to look for a lesson in a story can produce a reductive and inaccurate formulation of its theme. Consider the damage done to Colette's "The Hand" (p. 220) if its theme is described as this:

"Adolescents are too young to cope with the responsibilities of marriage." Colette's focus in this story is on the young woman's response to her husband's powerful sexuality and dominance rather than on her inability to be a good wife.

In fact, a good many stories go beyond traditional moral values to explore human behavior instead of condemning or endorsing it. Chekhov's treatment of the adulterous affair between Gurov and Anna in "The Lady with the Pet Dog" (p. 185) portrays a love that is valuable and true despite the conventional moral codes it violates. That is not to say that the reader must agree with Chekhov's attitude that such love has a validity of its own. We are obligated to see that Chekhov is sympathetic to the lovers but not necessarily obligated to approve of their actions. All that is required is our willingness to explore with the author the issues set before us. The themes we encounter in literature may challenge as well as reassure us.

Determining the theme of a story can be a difficult task because all the story's elements may contribute to its central idea. Indeed, you may discover that finding the theme is more challenging than coming to grips with the author's values as they are revealed in the story. There is no precise formula that can take you to the center of a story's meaning and help you to articulate it. However, several strategies are practical and useful once you have read the story. Apply these pointers during a second or third reading:

1. Pay attention to the title of the story. It often provides a lead to a major symbol (Faulkner's "Barn Burning," p. 481) or to the subject around which the theme develops (Godwin's "A Sorrowful Woman," p. 33).

2. Look for details in the story that have potential for symbolic meanings. Careful consideration of names, places, objects, minor characters, and incidents can lead you to the central meaning — for example, think of the stripper in Ellison's "Battle Royal" (p. 223). Be especially attentive to elements you did not understand on the first reading.

3. Decide whether the protagonist changes or develops some important insight as a result of the action. Carefully examine any generalizations the protagonist or narrator makes about the events in the story.

4. When you formulate the theme of the story in your own words, write it down in one or two complete sentences that make some point about the subject matter. Revenge may be the subject of a story, but its theme should make a statement about revenge: "Instead of providing satisfaction, revenge defeats the best in one's self" is one possibility.

5. Be certain that your expression of the theme is a generalized statement rather than a specific description of particular people, places, and incidents in the story. Contrast the preceding statement of a theme on revenge with this too-specific one: "In Nathaniel Hawthorne's *The Scarlet Letter*, Roger Chillingworth loses his humanity owing to his single-minded attempts to punish Arthur Dimmesdale for fathering a child

with Chillingworth's wife, Hester." Hawthorne's theme is not re- stricted to a single fictional character named Chillingworth but to any- one whose life is ruined by revenge. Be certain that your statement of theme does not focus on only part of the story. The theme just cited for *The Scarlet Letter,* for example, relegates Hester to the status of a minor character. What it says about Chillingworth is true, but the statement is incomplete as a generalization about the novel.

6. Be wary of using clichés as a way of stating theme. They tend to short- circuit ideas instead of generating them. It may be tempting to resort to something like "Love conquers all" as a statement of the theme of Chekhov's "The Lady with the Pet Dog" (p. 185); however, even the slightest second thought reveals how much more ambiguous the end- ing of that story is.

7. Be aware that some stories emphasize theme less than others. Stories that have as their major purpose adventure, humor, mystery, or terror may have little or no theme. In Edgar Allan Poe's "The Pit and the Pen- dulum," for example, the protagonist is not used to condemn torture; instead, he becomes a sensitive gauge to measure the pain and horror he endures at the hands of his captors.

What is most valuable about articulating the theme of a work is the process by which the theme is determined. Ultimately, the theme is ex- pressed by the story itself and is inseparable from the experience of read- ing the story. Tim O'Brien's explanation of "How to Tell a True War Story" (p. 555) is probably true of most kinds of stories: "In a true war story, if there's a moral [or theme] at all, it's like the thread that makes the cloth. You can't tease it out. You can't extract the meaning without unraveling the deeper meaning." Describing the theme should not be a way to con- sume a story, to be done with it. It is a means of clarifying our thinking about what we've read and probably felt intuitively.

Margaret Atwood's "There Was Once," Stephen Crane's "The Bride Comes to Yellow Sky," Katherine Mansfield's "Miss Brill," and Dagoberto Gilb's "Love in L.A." are four stories whose respective themes emerge from the authors' skillful use of plot, character, setting, and symbol.

MARGARET ATWOOD (b. 1939)

Born in Ottawa, Ontario, Margaret Atwood was educated at the Univer- sity of Toronto and Harvard University. She has been writing fiction and poetry since she was a child; along the way she has done odd jobs and been a screenwriter and a teacher. Among her collections of short stories are *Danc- ing Girls* (1977), *Bluebird's Egg* (1983), and *Wilderness Tips* (1991). Her highly suc- cessful novels include *Surfacing* (1972), *The Handmaid's Tale* (1986), *Cat's Eye* (1989), and *The Robber Bride* (1993). She has also written twelve books of po- etry. Atwood has enhanced the appreciation of Canadian literature through her editing of *The New Oxford Book of Canadian Verse in English* (1982) and *The Oxford Book of Canadian Short Stories in English* (1986). Her own work closely examines the weight of the complex human relationships that complicate her characters' lives. In "There Was Once," taken from her collection of short works, *Good Bones and Simple Murders* (1994), Atwood has fun with some of the demands placed on contemporary writers.

There Was Once   *1992*

— There was once a poor girl, as beautiful as she was good, who lived with her wicked stepmother in a house in the forest.

— Forest? *Forest* is passé, I mean, I've had it with all this wilderness stuff. It's not the right image of our society, today. Let's have some *urban* for a change.

— There was once a poor girl, as beautiful as she was good, who lived with her wicked stepmother in a house in the suburbs.

— That's better. But I have to seriously query this word *poor.*

— But she *was* poor!   5

— Poor is relative. She lived in a house, didn't she?

— Yes.

— Then socioeconomically speaking, she was not poor.

— But none of the money was *hers!* The whole point of the story is that the wicked stepmother makes her wear old clothes and sleep in the fireplace —

— Aha! They had a *fireplace!* With *poor,* let me tell you, there's no fireplace. 10 Come down to the park, come to the subway stations after dark, come down to where they sleep in cardboard boxes, and I'll show you *poor!*

— There was once a middle-class girl, as beautiful as she was good —

— Stop right there. I think we can cut the *beautiful,* don't you? Women these days have to deal with too many intimidating physical role models as it is, what with those bimbos in the ads. Can't you make her, well, more average?

— There was once a girl who was a little overweight and whose front teeth stuck out, who —

— I don't think it's nice to make fun of people's appearances. Plus, you're encouraging anorexia.

—I wasn't making fun! I was just describing—   15

—Skip the description. Description oppresses. But you can say what color she
  was.

— What color?

— You know. Black, white, red, brown, yellow. Those are the choices. And I'm
  telling you right now, I've had enough of white. Dominant culture this,
  dominant culture that—

—I don't know what color.

—Well, it would probably be *your* color, wouldn't it?   20

— But this isn't *about* me! It's about this girl—

— Everything is about you.

— Sounds to me like you don't want to hear this story at all.

— Oh well, go on. You could make her ethnic. That might help.

—There was once a girl of indeterminate descent, as average-looking as she 25
  was good, who lived with her wicked—

—Another thing. *Good* and *wicked.* Don't you think you should transcend
  those puritanical judgmental moralistic epithets? I mean, so much of that is
  conditioning, isn't it?

—There was once a girl, as average-looking as she was well-adjusted, who lived
  with her stepmother, who was not a very open and loving person because she
  herself had been abused in childhood.

— Better. But I am so *tired* of negative female images! And stepmothers—they
  always get it in the neck! Change it to step*father,* why don't you? That would
  make more sense anyway, considering the bad behavior you're about to describe. And throw in some whips and chains. We all know what those
  twisted, repressed, middle-aged men are like—

— *Hey, just a minute!* I'm *a middle-aged*—

— Stuff it, Mister Nosy Parker. Nobody asked you to stick in your oar, or what- 30
  ever you want to call that thing. This is between the two of us. Go on.

— There was once a girl—

— How old was she?

—I don't know. She was young.

— This ends with a marriage, right?

— Well, not to blow the plot, but — yes.   35

— Then you can scratch the condescending paternalistic terminology. It's *woman*, pal. *Woman*.

— There was once —

— What's this *was, once*? Enough of the dead past. Tell me about *now*.

— There —

— So?   40

— So, what?

— So, why not *here*?

CONSIDERATIONS FOR CRITICAL THINKING AND WRITING

1. FIRST RESPONSE. Atwood plays with the conventions of the fairy tale in "There Was Once." Pick a familiar fairy tale and critique it as the second speaker might. Are such tales enjoyable, do you think? Or can they harm the children they're meant to entertain?

2. Describe the two speakers. How does Atwood individualize them even though she provides no physical descriptions of the two characters?

3. What does the second speaker object to in how the story writer tells the tale? Do you agree with any of the objections? Why or why not?

4. What does Atwood satirize in this story?

5. What is the theme of "There Was Once"? How does the title contribute to the theme?

6. Try writing a one-paragraph version of the story as you think the second speaker would want it to be.

CONNECTIONS TO OTHER SELECTIONS

1. Discuss the use of satire in "There Was Once" and in T. Coraghessan Boyle's "Carnal Knowledge" (p. 276). Though these are very different types of stories, how are the themes somewhat similar?

2. Write an essay that compares the treatment of fiction writing in "There Was Once" and in George Bowering's "A Short Story" (p. 298).

STEPHEN CRANE (1871–1900)

Born in Newark, New Jersey, Stephen Crane attended Lafayette College and Syracuse University and then worked as a free-lance journalist in New York City. He wrote newspaper pieces, short stories, poems, and novels for his entire, brief adult life. His first book, *Maggie: A Girl of the Streets* (1893), is a story about New York slum life and prostitution. His most famous novel, *The Red Badge of Courage* (1895), gives readers a vivid, convincing re-creation of Civil War battles, even though Crane had never been to war. However, Crane was personally familiar with the American West, where he traveled as a reporter. "The Bride Comes to Yellow Sky" includes some of the ingredients of a typical popular western — a confrontation between a marshal and a drunk who shoots up the town — but the story's theme is less predictable and more serious than the plot seems to suggest.

The Bride Comes to Yellow Sky   *1898*

I

The great Pullman was whirling onward with such dignity of motion that a glance from the window seemed simply to prove that the plains of Texas were pouring eastward. Vast flats of green grass, dull-hued spaces of mesquit and cactus, little groups of frame houses, woods of light and tender trees, all were sweeping into the east, sweeping over the horizon, a precipice.

A newly married pair had boarded this coach at San Antonio. The man's face was reddened from many days in the wind and sun, and a direct result of his new black clothes was that his brick-colored hands were constantly performing in a most conscious fashion. From time to time he looked down respectfully at his attire. He sat with a hand on each knee, like a man waiting in a barber's shop. The glances he devoted to other passengers were furtive and shy.

The bride was not pretty, nor was she very young. She wore a dress of blue cashmere, with small reservations of velvet here and there, and with steel buttons abounding. She continually twisted her head to regard her puff sleeves, very stiff, straight, and high. They embarrassed her. It was quite apparent that she had cooked, and that she expected to cook, dutifully. The blushes caused by the careless scrutiny of some passengers as she had entered the car were strange to see upon this plain, under-class countenance, which was drawn in placid, almost emotionless lines.

They were evidently very happy. "Ever been in a parlor-car before?" he asked, smiling with delight.

"No," she answered; "I never was. It's fine, ain't it?"   5

"Great! And then after a while we'll go forward to the diner, and get a big lay-out. Finest meal in the world. Charge a dollar."

"Oh, do they?" cried the bride. "Charge a dollar? Why, that's too much — for us — ain't it, Jack?"

"Not this trip, anyhow," he answered bravely. "We're going to go the whole thing."

Later he explained to her about the trains. "You see, it's a thousand miles from one end of Texas to the other; and this train runs right across it, and never stops but four times." He had the pride of an owner. He pointed out to her the dazzling fittings of the coach; and in truth her eyes opened wider as she contemplated the sea-green figured velvet, the shining brass, silver, and glass, the wood that gleamed as darkly brilliant as the surface of a pool of oil.

At one end a bronze figure sturdily held a support for a separated chamber, and at convenient places on the ceiling were frescoes in olive and silver.

To the minds of the pair, their surroundings reflected the glory of their 10 marriage that morning in San Antonio; this was the environment of their new estate; and the man's face in particular beamed with an elation that made him appear ridiculous to the negro porter. This individual at times surveyed them from afar with an amused and superior grin. On other occasions he bullied them with skill in ways that did not make it exactly plain to them that they were being bullied. He subtly used all the manners of the most unconquerable kind of snobbery. He oppressed them; but of this oppression they had small knowledge, and they speedily forgot that infrequently a number of travelers covered them with stares of derisive enjoyment. Historically there was supposed to be something infinitely humorous in their situation.

"We are due in Yellow Sky at 3:42," he said, looking tenderly into her eyes.

"Oh, are we?" she said, as if she had not been aware of it. To evince surprise at her husband's statement was part of her wifely amiability. She took from a pocket a little silver watch; and as she held it before her, and stared at it with a frown of attention, the new husband's face shone.

"I bought it in San Anton' from a friend of mine," he told her gleefully.

"It's seventeen minutes past twelve," she said, looking up at him with a kind of shy and clumsy coquetry. A passenger, noting this play, grew excessively sardonic, and winked at himself in one of the numerous mirrors.

At last they went to the dining-car. Two rows of negro waiters, in glowing 15 white suits, surveyed their entrance with the interest, and also the equanimity, of men who had been forewarned. The pair fell to the lot of a waiter who happened to feel pleasure in steering them through their meal. He viewed them with the manner of a fatherly pilot, his countenance radiant with benevolence. The patronage, entwined with the ordinary deference, was not plain to them. And yet, as they returned to their coach, they showed in their faces a sense of escape.

To the left, miles down a long purple slope, was a little ribbon of mist where moved the keening Rio Grande. The train was approaching it at an angle, and the apex was Yellow Sky. Presently it was apparent that, as the distance from Yellow Sky grew shorter, the husband became commensurately restless. His brick-red hands were more insistent in their prominence. Occasionally he was even rather absent-minded and far-away when the bride leaned forward and addressed him.

As a matter of truth, Jack Potter was beginning to find the shadow of a deed weigh upon him like a leaden slab. He, the town marshal of Yellow Sky, a man known, liked, and feared in his corner, a prominent person, had gone to San Antonio to meet a girl he believed he loved, and there, after the usual prayers, had actually induced her to marry him, without consulting Yellow Sky for any part of the transaction. He was now bringing his bride before an innocent and unsuspecting community.

Of course people in Yellow Sky married as it pleased them in accordance with a general custom; but such was Potter's thought of his duty to his friends, or of their idea of his duty, or of an unspoken form which does not control men in these matters, that he felt he was heinous. He had committed an extraordinary crime. Face to face with this girl in San Antonio, and spurred by his sharp impulse, he had gone headlong over all the social hedges. At San

Antonio he was like a man hidden in the dark. A knife to sever any friendly duty, any form, was easy to his hand in that remote city. But the hour of Yellow Sky—the hour of daylight—was approaching.

He knew full well that his marriage was an important thing to his town. It could only be exceeded by the burning of the new hotel. His friends could not forgive him. Frequently he had reflected on the advisability of telling them by telegraph, but a new cowardice had been upon him. He feared to do it. And now the train was hurrying him toward a scene of amazement, glee, and reproach. He glanced out of the window at the line of haze swinging slowly in toward the train.

Yellow Sky had a kind of brass band, which played painfully, to the delight 20
of the populace. He laughed without heart as he thought of it. If the citizens could dream of his prospective arrival with his bride, they would parade the band at the station and escort them, amid cheers and laughing congratulations, to his adobe home.

He resolved that he would use all the devices of speed and plainscraft in making the journey from the station to his house. Once within that safe citadel, he could issue some sort of vocal bulletin, and then not go among the citizens until they had time to wear off a little of their enthusiasm.

The bride looked anxiously at him. "What's worrying you, Jack?"

He laughed again. "I'm not worrying, girl; I'm only thinking of Yellow Sky."

She flushed in comprehension.

A sense of mutual guilt invaded their minds and developed a finer tender- 25
ness. They looked at each other with eyes softly aglow. But Potter often laughed the same nervous laugh; the flush upon the bride's face seemed quite permanent.

The traitor to the feelings of Yellow Sky narrowly watched the speeding landscape. "We're nearly there," he said.

Presently the porter came and announced the proximity of Potter's home. He held a brush in his hand, and, with all his airy superiority gone, he brushed Potter's new clothes as the latter slowly turned this way and that way. Potter fumbled out a coin and gave it to the porter, as he had seen others do. It was a heavy and muscle-bound business, as that of a man shoeing his first horse.

The porter took their bag, and as the train began to slow they moved forward to the hooded platform of the car. Presently the two engines and their long string of coaches rushed into the station of Yellow Sky.

"They have to take water here," said Potter, from a constricted throat and in mournful cadence, as one announcing death. Before the train stopped his eye had swept the length of the platform, and he was glad and astonished to see there was none upon it but the station-agent, who, with a slightly hurried and anxious air, was walking toward the water-tanks. When the train had halted, the porter alighted first, and placed in position a little temporary step.

"Come on, girl," said Potter, hoarsely. As he helped her down they each 30
laughed on a false note. He took the bag from the negro, and bade his wife cling to his arm. As they slunk rapidly away, his hang-dog glance perceived that they were unloading the two trunks, and also that the station-agent, far ahead near the baggage-car, had turned and was running toward him, making gestures. He laughed, and groaned as he laughed, when he noted the first effect of his marital bliss upon Yellow Sky. He gripped his wife's arm firmly to his side, and they fled. Behind them the porter stood, chuckling fatuously.

II

The California express on the Southern Railway was due at Yellow Sky in twenty-one minutes. There were six men at the bar of the Weary Gentleman saloon. One was a drummer° who talked a great deal and rapidly; three were Texans who did not care to talk at that time; and two were Mexican sheepherders, who did not talk as a general practice in the Weary Gentleman saloon. The barkeeper's dog lay on the board walk that crossed in front of the door. His head was on his paws, and he glanced drowsily here and there with the constant vigilance of a dog that is kicked on occasion. Across the sandy street were some vivid green grass-plots, so wonderful in appearance, amid the sands that burned near them in a blazing sun, that they caused a doubt in the mind. They exactly resembled the grass mats used to represent lawns on the stage. At the cooler end of the railway station, a man without a coat sat in a tilted chair and smoked his pipe. The fresh-cut bank of the Rio Grande circled near the town, and there could be seen beyond it a great plum-colored plain of mesquit.

Save for the busy drummer and his companions in the saloon, Yellow Sky was dozing. The new-comer leaned gracefully upon the bar, and recited many tales with the confidence of a bard who has come upon a new field.

"— and at the moment that the old man fell downstairs with the bureau in his arms, the old woman was coming up with two scuttles of coal, and of course —"

The drummer's tale was interrupted by a young man who suddenly appeared in the open door. He cried: "Scratchy Wilson's drunk, and has turned loose with both hands." The two Mexicans at once set down their glasses and faded out of the rear entrance of the saloon.

The drummer, innocent and jocular, answered: "All right, old man. S'pose 35 he has? Come in and have a drink, anyhow."

But the information had made such an obvious cleft in every skull in the room that the drummer was obliged to see its importance. All had become instantly solemn. "Say," said he, mystified, "what is this?" His three companions made the introductory gesture of eloquent speech; but the young man at the door forestalled them.

"It means, my friend," he answered, as he came into the saloon, "that for the next two hours this town won't be a health resort."

The barkeeper went to the door, and locked and barred it; reaching out of the window, he pulled in heavy wooden shutters, and barred them. Immediately a solemn, chapel-like gloom was upon the place. The drummer was looking from one to another.

"But, say," he cried, "what is this, anyhow? You don't mean there is going to be a gun-fight?"

"Don't know whether there'll be a fight or not," answered one man, 40 grimly; "but there'll be some shootin' — some good shootin'."

The young man who had warned them waved his hand. "Oh, there'll be a fight fast enough, if any one wants it. Anybody can get a fight out there in the street. There's a fight just waiting."

The drummer seemed to be swayed between the interest of a foreigner and a perception of personal danger.

drummer: Traveling salesman.

"What did you say his name was?" he asked.

"Scratchy Wilson," they answered in chorus.

"And will he kill anybody? What are you going to do? Does this happen often? Does he rampage around like this once a week or so? Can he break in that door?" 45

"No; he can't break down that door," replied the barkeeper. "He's tried it three times. But when he comes you'd better lay down on the floor, stranger. He's dead sure to shoot at it, and a bullet may come through."

Thereafter the drummer kept a strict eye upon the door. The time had not yet called for him to hug the floor, but, as a minor precaution, he sidled near the wall. "Will he kill anybody?" he said again.

The men laughed low and scornfully at the question.

"He's out to shoot, and he's out for trouble. Don't see any good in experimentin' with him."

"But what do you do in a case like this? What do you do?" 50

A man responded: "Why, he and Jack Potter—"

"But," in chorus the other men interrupted, "Jack Potter's in San Anton'."

"Well, who is he? What's he got to do with it?"

"Oh, he's the town marshal. He goes out and fights Scratchy when he gets on one of these tears."

"Wow!" said the drummer, mopping his brow. "Nice job he's got." 55

The voices had toned away to mere whisperings. The drummer wished to ask further questions, which were born of an increasing anxiety and bewilderment; but when he attempted them, the men merely looked at him in irritation and motioned him to remain silent. A tense waiting hush was upon them. In the deep shadows of the room their eyes shone as they listened for sounds from the street. One man made three gestures at the barkeeper; and the latter, moving like a ghost, handed him a glass and a bottle. The man poured a full glass of whisky, and set down the bottle noiselessly. He gulped the whisky in a swallow, and turned again toward the door in immovable silence. The drummer saw that the barkeeper, without a sound, had taken a Winchester from beneath the bar. Later he saw this individual beckoning to him, so he tiptoed across the room.

"You better come with me back of the bar."

"No thanks," said the drummer, perspiring; "I'd rather be where I can make a break for the back door."

Whereupon the man of bottles made a kindly but peremptory gesture. The drummer obeyed it, and, finding himself seated on a box with his head below the level of the bar, balm was laid upon his soul at sight of various zinc and copper fittings that bore a resemblance to armor-plate. The barkeeper took a seat comfortably upon an adjacent box.

"You see," he whispered, "this here Scratchy Wilson is a wonder with a gun—a perfect wonder; and when he goes on the war-trail, we hunt our holes—naturally. He's about the last one of the old gang that used to hang out along the river here. He's a terror when he's drunk. When he's sober he's all right—kind of simple—wouldn't hurt a fly—nicest fellow in town. But when he's drunk—whoo!" 60

There were periods of stillness. "I wish Jack Potter was back from San Anton'," said the barkeeper. "He shot Wilson up once—in the leg—and he would sail in and pull out the kinks in this thing."

Presently they heard from a distance the sound of a shot, followed by three wild yowls. It instantly removed a bond from the men in the darkened saloon. There was a shuffling of feet. They looked at each other. "Here he comes," they said.

III

A man in a maroon-colored flannel shirt, which had been purchased for purposes of decoration, and made principally by some Jewish women on the East Side of New York, rounded a corner and walked into the middle of the main street of Yellow Sky. In either hand the man held a long, heavy, blue-black revolver. Often he yelled, and these cries rang through a semblance of a deserted village, shrilly flying over the roofs in a volume that seemed to have no relation to the ordinary vocal strength of a man. It was as if the surrounding stillness formed the arch of a tomb over him. These cries of ferocious challenge rang against walls of silence. And his boots had red tops with gilded imprints, of the kind beloved in winter by little sledding boys on the hillsides of New England.

The man's face flamed in a rage begot of whisky. His eyes, rolling, and yet keen for ambush, hunted the still doorways and windows. He walked with the creeping movement of the midnight cat. As it occurred to him, he roared menacing information. The long revolvers in his hands were as easy as straws; they were removed with an electric swiftness. The little fingers of each hand played sometimes in a musician's way. Plain from the low collar of the shirt, the cords of his neck straightened and sank, straightened and sank, as passion moved him. The only sounds were his terrible invitations. The calm adobes preserved their demeanor at the passing of this small thing in the middle of the street.

There was no offer of fight — no offer of fight. The man called to the sky. 65 There were no attractions. He bellowed and fumed and swayed his revolvers here and everywhere.

The dog of the barkeeper of the Weary Gentleman saloon had not appreciated the advance of events. He yet lay dozing in front of his master's door. At sight of the dog, the man paused and raised his revolver humorously. At sight of the man, the dog sprang up and walked diagonally away, with a sullen head, and growling. The man yelled, and the dog broke into a gallop. As it was about to enter the alley, there was a loud noise, a whistling, and something spat the ground directly before it. The dog screamed, and, wheeling in terror, galloped headlong in a new direction. Again there was a noise, a whistling, and sand was kicked viciously before it. Fear-stricken, the dog turned and flurried like an animal in a pen. The man stood laughing, his weapons at his hips.

Ultimately the man was attracted by the closed door of the Weary Gentleman saloon. He went to it and, hammering with a revolver, demanded drink.

The door remaining imperturbable, he picked a bit of paper from the walk, and nailed it to the framework with a knife. He then turned his back contemptuously upon this popular resort and, walking to the opposite side of the street and spinning there on his heel quickly and lithely, fired at the bit of paper. He missed it by a half inch. He swore at himself, and went away. Later he comfortably fusilladed the windows of his most intimate friend. The man was playing with this town; it was a toy for him.

But still there was no offer of fight. The name of Jack Potter, his ancient antagonist, entered his mind, and he concluded that it would be a glad thing if he should go to Potter's house, and by bombardment induce him to come out and fight. He moved in the direction of his desire, chanting Apache scalp-music.

When he arrived at it, Potter's house presented the same still front as had the other adobes. Taking up a strategic position, the man howled a challenge. But this house regarded him as might a great stone god. It gave no sign. After a decent wait, the man howled further challenges, mingling with them wonderful epithets.

Presently there came the spectacle of a man churning himself into deepest rage over the immobility of a house. He fumed at it as the winter wind attacks a prairie cabin in the North. To the distance there should have gone the sound of a tumult like the fighting of two hundred Mexicans. As necessity bade him, he paused for breath or to reload his revolvers.

IV

Potter and his bride walked sheepishly and with speed. Sometimes they laughed together shamefacedly and low.

"Next corner, dear," he said finally.

They put forth the efforts of a pair walking bowed against a strong wind. Potter was about to raise a finger to point the first appearance of the new home when, as they circled the corner, they came face to face with a man in a maroon-colored shirt, who was feverishly pushing cartridges into a large revolver. Upon the instant the man dropped his revolver to the ground and, like lightning, whipped another from its holster. The second weapon was aimed at the bridegroom's chest.

There was a silence. Potter's mouth seemed to be merely a grave for his tongue. He exhibited an instinct to at once loosen his arm from the woman's grip, and he dropped the bag to the sand. As for the bride, her face had gone as yellow as old cloth. She was a slave to hideous rites, gazing at the apparitional snake.

The two men faced each other at a distance of three paces. He of the revolver smiled with a new and quiet ferocity.

"Tried to sneak up on me," he said. "Tried to sneak up on me!" His eyes grew more baleful. As Potter made a slight movement, the man thrust his revolver venomously forward. "No, don't you do it, Jack Potter. Don't you move a finger toward a gun just yet. Don't you move an eyelash. The time has come for me to settle with you and I'm goin' to do it my own way, and loaf along with no interferin'. So if you don't want a gun bent on you, just mind what I tell you."

Potter looked at his enemy. "I ain't got a gun on me, Scratchy," he said. "Honest, I ain't." He was stiffening and steadying, but yet somewhere at the back of his mind a vision of the Pullman floated: the sea-green figured velvet, the shining brass, silver, and glass, the wood that gleamed as darkly brilliant as the surface of a pool of oil — all the glory of marriage, the environment of the new estate. "You know I fight when it comes to fighting, Scratchy Wilson; but I ain't got a gun on me. You'll have to do all the shootin' yourself."

His enemy's face went livid. He stepped forward, and lashed his weapon to and fro before Potter's chest. "Don't you tell me you ain't got no gun on you, you whelp. Don't tell me no lie like that. There ain't a man in Texas ever seen you without no gun. Don't take me for no kid." His eyes blazed with light, and his throat worked like a pump.

"I ain't takin' you for no kid," answered Potter. His heels had not moved an inch backward. "I'm takin' you for a damn fool. I tell you I ain't got a gun, and I ain't. If you're goin' to shoot me up, you better begin now; you'll never get a chance like this again." 80

So much enforced reasoning had told on Wilson's rage; he was calmer. "If you ain't got a gun, why ain't you got a gun?" he sneered. "Been to Sunday-school?"

"I ain't got a gun because I've just come from San Anton' with my wife. I'm married," said Potter. "And if I'd thought there was going to be any galoots like you prowling around when I brought my wife home, I'd had a gun, and don't you forget it."

"Married!" said Scratchy, not at all comprehending.

"Yes, married. I'm married," said Potter, distinctly.

"Married?" said Scratchy. Seemingly for the first time, he saw the droop- 85 ing, drowning woman at the other man's side. "No!" he said. He was like a creature allowed a glimpse of another world. He moved a pace backward, and his arm, with the revolver, dropped to his side. "Is this the lady?" he asked.

"Yes; this is the lady," answered Potter.

There was another period of silence.

"Well," said Wilson at last, slowly, "I s'pose it's all off now."

"It's all off if you say so, Scratchy. You know I didn't make the trouble." Potter lifted his valise.

"Well, I 'low it's off, Jack," said Wilson. He was looking at the ground. 90 "Married!" He was not a student of chivalry; it was merely that in the presence of this foreign condition he was a simple child of the earlier plains. He picked up his starboard revolver, and, placing both weapons in their holsters, he went away. His feet made funnel-shaped tracks in the heavy sand.

CONSIDERATIONS FOR CRITICAL THINKING AND WRITING

1. FIRST RESPONSE. Think of a western you've read or seen: any of Larry McMurtry's books would work, such as *Lonesome Dove* or *Evening Star.* Compare and contrast the setting, characters, action, and theme in Crane's story with your western.

2. What is the nature of the conflict Marshal Potter feels on the train in Part I? Why does he feel that he committed a "crime" in bringing home a bride to Yellow Sky?

3. What is the function of the "drummer," the traveling salesman, in Part II?

4. How do Mrs. Potter and Scratchy Wilson serve as foils for each other? What does each represent in the story?

5. What is the significance of the setting?

6. How does Crane create suspense about what will happen when Marshal Potter meets Scratchy Wilson? Is suspense the major point of the story?

7. Is Scratchy Wilson too drunk, comical, and ineffective to be a sympathetic character? What is the meaning of his conceding that "I s'pose it's all off now" at the end of Part IV? Is he a dynamic or a static character?

8. What details seem to support the story's theme? Consider, for example, the descriptions of the bride's clothes and Scratchy Wilson's shirt and boots.

9. Explain why the heroes in western stories are rarely married and why Crane's use of marriage is central to his theme.

CONNECTIONS TO OTHER SELECTIONS

1. Although Scratchy Wilson and Katherine Mansfield's "Miss Brill" (p. 258) are radically different kinds of people, they share a painful recognition at the end of their stories. What does each of them learn? Discuss whether you think what each of them learns is of equal importance in changing his or her life.

2. Write an essay comparing Crane's use of suspense with William Faulkner's in "A Rose for Emily" (p. 72).

KATHERINE MANSFIELD (1888–1923)

Born in New Zealand, Katherine Mansfield moved to London when she was a young woman and began writing short stories. Her first collection, *In a German Pension,* appeared in 1911. Subsequent publications, which include *Bliss and Other Stories* (1920) and *The Garden Party* (1922), secured her reputation as an important writer. The full range of her short stories is available in *The Collected Short Stories of Katherine Mansfield* (1945). Mansfield tends to focus her stories on intelligent, sensitive protagonists who undergo subtle but important changes in their lives. In "Miss Brill," an aging Englishwoman spends the afternoon in a park located in an unnamed French vacation town watching the activities of the people around her. Through those observations, Mansfield characterizes Miss Brill and permits us to see her experience a moment that changes her view of the world as well as of herself.

Miss Brill   *1922*

Although it was so brilliantly fine — the blue sky powdered with gold and great spots of light like white wine splashed over the Jardins Publiques — Miss Brill was glad that she had decided on her fur. The air was motionless, but when you opened your mouth there was just a faint chill, like a chill from a glass of iced water before you sip, and now and again a leaf came drifting — from nowhere, from the sky. Miss Brill put up her hand and touched her fur. Dear little thing! It was nice to feel it again. She had taken it out of its box that afternoon, shaken out the moth-powder, given it a good brush, and rubbed the life back into the dim little eyes. "What has been happening to me?" said the sad little eyes. Oh, how sweet it was to see them snap at her again from the red eiderdown! . . . But the nose, which was of some black composition, wasn't at all firm. It must have had a knock, somehow. Never mind — a little dab of black sealing-wax when the time came — when it was absolutely necessary. . . . Little rogue! Yes, she really felt like that about it. Little rogue biting its tail just by her left ear. She could have taken it off and laid it on her lap and stroked it. She felt a tingling in her hands and arms, but that came from walking, she supposed. And when she breathed, something light and sad — no, not sad, exactly — something gentle seemed to move in her bosom.

There were a number of people out this afternoon, far more than last Sunday. And the band sounded louder and gayer. That was because the Season had begun. For although the band played all the year round on Sundays, out of season it was never the same. It was like some one playing with only the family to listen; it didn't care how it played if there weren't any strangers present. Wasn't the conductor wearing a new coat, too? She was sure it was new. He scraped with his foot and flapped his arms like a rooster about to crow, and the bandsmen sitting in the green rotunda blew out their cheeks and glared at the music. Now there came a little "flutey" bit — very pretty! — a little chain of bright drops. She was sure it would be repeated. It was; she lifted her head and smiled.

Only two people shared her "special" seat: a fine old man in a velvet coat, his hands clasped over a huge carved walking-stick, and a big old woman, sitting upright, with a roll of knitting on her embroidered apron. They did not speak. This was disappointing, for Miss Brill always looked forward to the conversation. She had become really quite expert, she thought, at listening as though she didn't listen, at sitting in other people's lives just for a minute while they talked around her.

She glanced, sideways, at the old couple. Perhaps they would go soon. Last Sunday, too, hadn't been as interesting as usual. An Englishman and his wife, he wearing a dreadful Panama hat and she button boots. And she'd gone on the whole time about how she ought to wear spectacles; she knew she needed them; but that it was no good getting any; they'd be sure to break and they'd never keep on. And he'd been so patient. He'd suggested everything — gold rims, the kind that curved round your ears, little pads inside the bridge. No, nothing would please her. "They'll always be sliding down my nose!" Miss Brill had wanted to shake her.

The old people sat on the bench, still as statues. Never mind, there was al- 5 ways the crowd to watch. To and fro, in front of the flower-beds and the band rotunda, the couples and groups paraded, stopped to talk, to greet, to buy a handful of flowers from the old beggar who had his tray fixed to the railings. Little children ran among them, swooping and laughing; little boys with big white silk bows under their chins, little girls, little French dolls, dressed up in velvet and lace. And sometimes a tiny staggerer came suddenly rocking into the open from under the trees, stopped, stared, as suddenly sat down "flop," until its small high-stepping mother, like a young hen, rushed scolding to its rescue. Other people sat on the benches and green chairs, but they were nearly always the same, Sunday after Sunday, and — Miss Brill had often noticed — there was something funny about nearly all of them. They were odd, silent, nearly all old, and from the way they stared they looked as though they'd just come from dark little rooms or even — even cupboards!

Behind the rotunda the slender trees with yellow leaves down drooping, and through them just a line of sea, and beyond the blue sky with gold-veined clouds.

Tum-tum-tum tiddle-um! tiddle-um! tum tiddley-um tum ta! blew the band.

Two young girls in red came by and two young soldiers in blue met them, and they laughed and paired and went off arm-in-arm. Two peasant women with funny straw hats passed, gravely, leading beautiful smoke-colored donkeys. A cold, pale nun hurried by. A beautiful woman came along and dropped her bunch of violets, and a little boy ran after to hand them to her, and she took them and threw them away as if they'd been poisoned. Dear me! Miss Brill didn't know whether to admire that or not! And now an ermine toque and a gentleman in grey met just in front of her. He was tall, stiff, dignified, and she was wearing the ermine toque she'd bought when her hair was yellow. Now everything, her hair, her face, even her eyes, was the same color as the shabby ermine, and her hand, in its cleaned glove, lifted to dab her lips, was a tiny yellowish paw. Oh, she was so pleased to see him — delighted! She rather thought they were going to meet that afternoon. She described where she'd been — everywhere, here, there, along by the sea. The day was so charming — didn't he agree? And wouldn't he, perhaps? . . . But he shook his head, lighted a cigarette, slowly breathed a great deep puff into her face, and, even while she was still talking and laughing, flicked the match away and walked on. The ermine toque was alone; she smiled more brightly than ever. But even the band seemed to know what she was feeling and played more softly, played tenderly, and the drum beat, "The Brute! The Brute!" over and over. What would she do? What was going to happen now? But as Miss Brill wondered, the ermine toque turned, raised her hand as though she'd seen some one else, much nicer, just over there, and pattered away. And the band changed again and played more quickly, more gaily than ever, and the old couple on Miss Brill's seat got up and marched away, and such a funny old man with long whiskers hobbled along in time to the music and was nearly knocked over by four girls walking abreast.

Oh, how fascinating it was! How she enjoyed it! How she loved sitting here, watching it all! It was like a play. It was exactly like a play. Who could believe the sky at the back wasn't painted? But it wasn't till a little brown dog trotted on solemn and then slowly trotted off, like a little "theatre" dog, a little dog that had been drugged, that Miss Brill discovered what it was that made it so exciting. They were all on the stage. They weren't only the audience, not only looking on; they were acting. Even she had a part and came every Sunday. No doubt somebody would have noticed if she hadn't been there; she was part of the performance after all. How strange she'd never thought of it like that before! And yet it explained why she made such a point of starting from home at just the same time each week — so as not to be late for the performance — and it also explained why she had quite a queer, shy feeling at telling her English pupils how she spent her Sunday afternoons. No wonder! Miss Brill nearly laughed out loud. She was on the stage. She thought of the old invalid gentleman to whom she read the newspaper four afternoons a week while he slept in the garden. She had got quite used to the frail head on the cotton pillow, the hollowed eyes, the open mouth, and the high pinched nose. If he'd been dead she mightn't have noticed for weeks; she wouldn't have minded. But suddenly he knew he was having the paper read to him by an actress! "An actress!" The old head lifted; two points of light quivered in the old eyes. "An actress — are ye?" And Miss Brill smoothed the newspaper as though it were the manuscript of her part and said gently: "Yes, I have been an actress for a long time."

The band had been having a rest. Now they started again. And what they played was warm, sunny, yet there was just a faint chill — a something, what was it? — not sadness — no, not sadness — a something that made you want to sing. The tune lifted, lifted, the light shone; and it seemed to Miss Brill that in another moment all of them, all the whole company, would begin singing. The young ones, the laughing ones who were moving together, they would begin, and the men's voices, very resolute and brave, would join them. And then she too, she too, and the others on the benches — they would come in with a kind of accompaniment — something low, that scarcely rose or fell, something so beautiful — moving. . . . And Miss Brill's eyes filled with tears and she looked smiling at all the other members of the company. Yes, we understand, we understand, she thought — though what they understood she didn't know.

Just at that moment a boy and a girl came and sat down where the old couple had been. They were beautifully dressed; they were in love. The hero and heroine, of course, just arrived from his father's yacht. And still soundlessly singing, still with that trembling smile, Miss Brill prepared to listen.

"No, not now," said the girl. "Not here, I can't."

"But why? Because of that stupid old thing at the end there?" asked the boy. "Why does she come here at all — who wants her? Why doesn't she keep her silly old mug at home?"

"It's her fu-fur which is so funny," giggled the girl. "It's exactly like a fried whiting."

"Ah, be off with you!" said the boy in an angry whisper. Then: "Tell me, ma petite chère — "

"No, not here," said the girl. "Not *yet*."

On her way home she usually bought a slice of honey-cake at the baker's. It was her Sunday treat. Sometimes there was an almond in her slice, sometimes not. It made a great difference. If there was an almond it was like carrying home a tiny present — a surprise — something that might very well not have been there. She hurried on the almond Sundays and struck the match for the kettle in quite a dashing way.

But today she passed the baker's by, climbed the stairs, went into the little dark room — her room like a cupboard — and sat down on the red eiderdown. She sat there for a long time. The box that the fur came out of was on the bed. She unclasped the necklet quickly; quickly, without looking, laid it inside. But when she put the lid on she thought she heard something crying.

CONSIDERATIONS FOR CRITICAL THINKING AND WRITING

1. FIRST RESPONSE. There is almost no physical description of Miss Brill in the story. What do you think she looks like? Develop a detailed description that would be consistent with her behavior.

2. How does the calculated omission of Miss Brill's first name contribute to her characterization?

3. What details make Miss Brill more than a stock characterization of a frail old lady?
4. What do Miss Brill's observations about the people she encounters reveal about her?
5. What is the conflict in the story? Who or what is the antagonist?
6. Locate the climax of the story. How is it resolved?
7. What is the purpose of the fur piece? What is the source of the crying in the final sentence of the story?
8. Is Miss Brill a static or a dynamic character?
9. Describe Miss Brill's sense of herself at the end of the story.
10. Discuss the function of the minor characters mentioned in the story. Analyze how Katherine Mansfield used them to reveal Miss Brill's character.

CONNECTIONS TO OTHER SELECTIONS

1. Compare Miss Brill's recognition with that of the narrator in Fay Weldon's "IND AFF, or Out of Love in Sarajevo" (p. 153).
2. Write an essay comparing the themes in "Miss Brill" and James Joyce's "Eveline" (p. 512).

PERSPECTIVE

EUDORA WELTY (B. 1909)

On the Plots of "The Bride Comes to Yellow Sky" and "Miss Brill"

1949

Stephen Crane's "The Bride Comes to Yellow Sky" tells a story of situation; it is a playful story, using two situations, like counters.

Jack Potter, the town marshal of Yellow Sky, has gone to San Anton' and gotten married and is bringing his bride home in a Pullman — the whole errand to be a complete surprise to the town of Yellow Sky. "He knew full well that his marriage was an important thing to his town. It could only be exceeded by the burning of the new hotel."

And in Yellow Sky another situation is building up in matching tempo with the running wheels. A messenger appears in the door of the Weary Gentleman saloon crying "Scratchy Wilson's drunk, and has turned loose with both hands." "Immediately a solemn, chapel-like gloom was upon the place. . . . 'Scratchy Wilson is a wonder with a gun — a perfect wonder; and when he goes on the war-trail, we hunt our holes — naturally.'" Scratchy enters town, pistols in both hands. His "cries of ferocious challenge rang against walls of silence. And his boots had red tops with gilded imprints, of the kind beloved in winter by little sledding boys on the hillsides of New England. . . . He walked with the creeping movement of the midnight cat. As it occurred to him, he roared menacing information. . . . The little fingers of each hand played sometimes in a musician's way. . . . The only sounds were his terrible invitations."

All this is delightful to us not only for itself but for its function of play, of assuring our anticipation; the more ferocious Scratchy is, the more we are charmed. Our sense of the fairness, the proportion of things is gratified when he "comfortably fusilladed the windows of his most intimate friend. The man was playing with this town; it was a toy for him." This plot of situation gives us a kind of kinetic pleasure; just as being on a seesaw is pleasant not only for where we are but for where the other person is.

The train arrives, Jack Potter and bride get off, and Jack's emotion-charged 5 meeting with Yellow Sky is due; and Scratchy Wilson turns out to be its protagonist. They come face to face, and Potter, who says, "I ain't got a gun on me, Scratchy," takes only a minute to make up his mind to be shot on his wedding day.

"'If you ain't got a gun, why ain't you got a gun?'" Scratchy sneers at the marshal. And Potter says, "'I ain't got a gun because I've just come from San Anton' with my wife. I'm married.'. . . 'Married?'" asks Scratchy—he has to ask it several times, uncomprehending. "'Married?'. . ."

"Seemingly for the first time, he saw the drooping, drowning woman at the other man's side. 'No!' he said. He was like a creature allowed a glimpse of another world. . . . 'Is this the lady?'. . .

"'Yes; this is the lady,' answered Potter. . . .

"'Well,' said Wilson at last, slowly, 'I s'pose it's all off now.'

". . . He was not a student of chivalry; it was merely that in the presence of 10 this foreign condition he was a simple child of the earlier plains. He picked up his starboard revolver, and, placing both weapons in their holsters, he went away. His feet made funnel-shaped tracks in the heavy sand."

So, in Crane's story, two situations, two forces, gather, meet — or rather are magnetized toward one another, almost — and collide. One is vanquished — the unexpected one — with neatness and absurdity, and the vanquished one exits; all equivalents of comedy.

In Katherine Mansfield's "Miss Brill," there is only one character and only one situation. The narrative is simple, Miss Brill's action consists nearly altogether in sitting down; she does nothing but go and sit in the park, return home, and sit on her bed in her little room. Yet considerably more of a story is attempted by this lesser to-do than Crane attempted in "Yellow Sky"; its plot is all implication.

"Miss Brill" is set on a stage of delight. "Although it was so brilliantly fine — the blue sky powdered with gold and great spots of light like white wine splashed over the Jardins Publiques — Miss Brill was glad that she had decided on her fur. . . . [She] put up her hand and touched her fur. Dear little thing!" We see right off that for Miss Brill delight is a kind of coziness. She sits listening to the band, her Sunday habit, and "Now there came a little 'flutey' bit — very pretty! — a little chain of bright drops. She was sure it would be repeated. It was; she lifted her head and smiled."

Miss Brill has confidence in her world — anticipation: what will happen next? Ah, but she knows. She's delighted but safe. She sees the others from her little perch, her distance — the gay ones and then those on benches: "Miss Brill had often noticed there was something funny about nearly all of *them*. They

were odd, silent, nearly all old, and from the way they stared they looked as
though they'd just come from dark little rooms or even—even cupboards!"
For she hasn't identified herself at all.

The drama is slight in this story. There is no collision. Rather the forces meet- 15
ing in the Jardins Publiques have, at the story's end, passed through each other
and come out the other side; there has not been a collision, but a change—something much more significant. This is because, though there is one small situation
going on, a very large and complex one is implied—the outside world, in fact.

One of the forces in the story is life itself, corresponding to the part of
Scratchy Wilson, so to speak. Not violent life—life in the setting of a park on
Sunday afternoon in Paris. All it usually does for Miss Brill is promenade stylishly while the band plays, form little tableaux, separate momentarily into
minor, rather darker encounters, and keep in general motion with bright colors
and light touches—there are no waving pistols at all, to storm and threaten.

Yet, being life, it does threaten. In what way, at last? Well, how much more
deadly to Miss Brill than a flourished pistol is an overheard remark—about *her*.
Miss Brill's vision—a vision of love—is brought abruptly face to face with another, ruder vision of love. The boy and girl in love sit down on her bench, but
they cannot go on with what they have been saying because of her, though "still
soundlessly singing, still with that trembling smile, Miss Brill prepared to listen.

"'No, not now,' said the girl. 'Not here, I can't.'

"'But why? Because of that stupid old thing at the end there? . . . Why
does she come here at all—who wants her? Why doesn't she keep her silly old
mug at home?'

"'It's her fu-fur which is so funny,' giggled the girl. 'It's exactly like a fried 20
whiting.'

"'Ah, be off with you!' said the boy in an angry whisper."

So Miss Brill, she who could spare even pity for this world, in her innocence—pity, the spectator's emotion—is defeated. She had allowed herself occasional glimpses of lives not too happy, here in the park, which had moved
her to little flutters of sadness. But that too had been coziness—coziness, a
remedy visitors seek to take the chill off a strange place with. She hadn't
known it wasn't good enough. All through the story she has sat in her "special
seat"—another little prop of endurance—and all unknown to her she sat in
mortal danger. This is the story. The danger nears, a word is spoken, the blow
falls—and Miss Brill retires, ridiculously easy to mow down, as the man with
the pistols was easy to stare down in "Yellow Sky," for comedy's sake. But Miss
Brill was from the first defenseless and on the losing side, and her defeat is the
deeper for it, and one feels sure it is for ever.

From "The Reading and Writing of Short Stories" in the *Atlantic Monthly*

CONSIDERATIONS FOR CRITICAL THINKING AND WRITING

1. What does Welty see as the essential difference between the plots of these
   two stories? Why does she describe Mansfield in "Miss Brill" as attempting
   "considerably more of a story" than Crane does in "Yellow Sky"?

2. Write an essay that compares and contrasts the plots of Faulkner's "A Rose
   for Emily" (p. 72) and Cisneros's "Barbie-Q" (p. 218). Which is "considerably
   more of a story" in the sense that Welty uses this phrase? Do you agree with
   her assessment of what makes a good story?

DAGOBERTO GILB (B. 1950)

Born in Los Angeles, Dagoberto Gilb is a journeyman carpenter who considers both Los Angeles and El Paso to be home. He has been a visiting writer at the University of Texas and the University of Arizona. Among his literary prizes are the James D. Phelan Award in literature and the Whiting Award; he has also won a National Endowment for the Arts Creative Writing Fellowship. Gilb's fiction has been published in a variety of journals including the *Threepenny Review, ZYZZYVA,* and *American Short Fiction.* His stories, collected in *The Magic of Blood* (1993), from which "Love in L.A." is taken, often reflect his experiences as a worker moving between Los Angeles and El Paso. In 1994 he published his first novel, *The Last Known Residence of Mickey Acuna.*

Love in L.A. 1993

Jake slouched in a clot of near motionless traffic, in the peculiar gray of concrete, smog, and early morning beneath the overpass of the Hollywood Freeway on Alvarado Street. He didn't really mind because he knew how much worse it could be trying to make a left onto the onramp. He certainly didn't do that every day of his life, and he'd assure anyone who'd ask that he never would either. A steady occupation had its advantages and he couldn't deny thinking about that too. He needed an FM radio in something better than this '58 Buick he drove. It would have crushed velvet interior with electric controls for the L.A. summer, a nice warm heater and defroster for the winter drives at the beach, a cruise control for those longer trips, mellow speakers front and rear of course, windows that hum closed, snuffing out that nasty exterior noise of freeways. The fact was that he'd probably have to change his whole style. Exotic colognes, plush, dark nightclubs, maitais and daiquiris, necklaced ladies in satin gowns, misty and sexy like in a tequila ad. Jake could imagine lots of possibilities when he let himself, but none that ended up with him pressed onto a stalled freeway.

Jake was thinking about this freedom of his so much that when he glimpsed its green light he just went ahead and stared bye bye to the steadily employed. When he turned his head the same direction his windshield faced, it was maybe one second too late. He pounced the brake pedal and steered the front wheels away from the tiny brakelights but the smack was unavoidable. Just one second sooner and it would only have been close. One second more and he'd be crawling up the Toyota's trunk. As it was, it seemed like only a harmless smack, much less solid than the one against his back bumper.

Jake considered driving past the Toyota but was afraid the traffic ahead would make it too difficult. As he pulled up against the curb a few carlengths ahead, it occurred to him that the traffic might have helped him get away too. He slammed the car door twice to make sure it was closed fully and to give himself another second more, then toured front and rear of his Buick for damage on or near the bumpers. Not an impressionable scratch even in the chrome. He perked up. Though the car's beauty was secondary to its ability to start and move, the body and paint were clean except for a few minor dings. This stood out as one of his few clearcut accomplishments over the years.

Before he spoke to the driver of the Toyota, whose looks he could see might present him with an added complication, he signaled to the driver of the car that hit him, still in his car and stopped behind the Toyota, and waved his hands and shook his head to let the man know there was no problem as far as he was concerned. The driver waved back and started his engine.

"It didn't even scratch my paint," Jake told her in that way of his. "So how 5 you doin? Any damage to the car? I'm kinda hoping so, just so it takes a little more time and we can talk some. Or else you can give me your phone number now and I won't have to lay my regular b.s. on you to get it later."

He took her smile as a good sign and relaxed. He inhaled her scent like it was clean air and straightened out his less than new but not unhip clothes.

"You've got Florida plates. You look like you must be Cuban."

"My parents are from Venezuela."

"My name's Jake." He held out his hand.

"Mariana." 10

They shook hands like she'd never done it before in her life.

"I really am sorry about hitting you like that." He sounded genuine. He fondled the wide dimple near the cracked taillight. "It's amazing how easy it is to put a dent in these new cars. They're so soft they might replace waterbeds soon." Jake was confused about how to proceed with this. So much seemed so unlikely, but there was always possibility. "So maybe we should go out to breakfast somewhere and talk it over."

"I don't eat breakfast."

"Some coffee then."

"Thanks, but I really can't." 15

"You're not married, are you? Not that that would matter that much to me. I'm an openminded kinda guy."

She was smiling. "I have to get to work."

"That sounds boring."

"I better get your driver's license," she said.

Jake nodded, disappointed. "One little problem," he said. "I didn't bring 20 it. I just forgot it this morning. I'm a musician," he exaggerated greatly, "and, well, I dunno, I left my wallet in the pants I was wearing last night. If you have some paper and a pen I'll give you my address and all that."

He followed her to the glove compartment side of her car.

"What if we don't report it to the insurance companies? I'll just get it fixed for you."

"I don't think my dad would let me do that."

"Your dad? It's not your car?"

"He bought it for me. And I live at home." 25

"Right." She was slipping away from him. He went back around to the back of her new Toyota and looked over the damage again. There was the trunk lid, the bumper, a rear panel, a taillight.

"You do have insurance?" she asked, suspicious, as she came around the back of the car.

"Oh yeah," he lied.

"I guess you better write the name of that down too."

He made up a last name and address and wrote down the name of an in- 30 surance company an old girlfriend once belonged to. He considered giving a real phone number but went against that idea and made one up.

"I act too," he lied to enhance the effect more. "Been in a couple of movies." She smiled like a fan.

"So how about your phone number?" He was rebounding maturely. She gave it to him.

"Mariana, you are beautiful," he said in his most sincere voice.   35

"Call me," she said timidly.

Jake beamed. "We'll see you, Mariana," he said holding out his hand. Her hand felt so warm and soft he felt like he'd been kissed.

Back in his car he took a moment or two to feel both proud and sad about his performance. Then he watched the rear view mirror as Mariana pulled up behind him. She was writing down the license plate numbers on his Buick, ones that he'd taken off a junk because the ones that belonged to his had expired so long ago. He turned the ignition key and revved the big engine and clicked into drive. His sense of freedom swelled as he drove into the now moving street traffic, though he couldn't stop the thought about that FM stereo radio and crushed velvet interior and the new car smell that would even make it better.

Considerations for Critical Thinking and Writing

1. FIRST RESPONSE. Is "Love in L.A." a love story? Try to argue that it is. (If the story ended with paragraph 37, how would your interpretation of the story be affected?)

2. What is the effect of setting the story's action in a Los Angeles traffic jam on the Hollywood Freeway?

3. Characterize Jake. What do his thoughts in the first two paragraphs reveal about him? About how old do you think he is?

4. There is little physical description of Jake in the story, but given what you learn about him, how would you describe his physical features and the way he dresses?

5. What causes Jake to smack into the back of Mariana's car? What is revealed about his character by the manner in which he has the accident?

6. Describe how Jake responds to Mariana when he introduces himself to her, especially in paragraph 12. What does his behavior reveal about his character?

7. How does Mariana respond to Jake? Explain whether you think she is a round or flat character.

8. Explain how their respective cars serve to characterize Jake and Mariana.

9. What does the final paragraph reveal about each character?

10. In a sentence or two write down what you think the story's theme is. How does the title contribute to that theme?

Connections to Other Selections

1. Compare and contrast the themes in "Love in L.A." and Leon Rooke's "Sweethearts" (p. 141).

2. Consider Jake's relationship with his car and the narrator's relationship with her Barbie in Sandra Cisneros's "Barbie-Q" (p. 218). In an essay explore how the car and the doll reveal each character's aspirations.

9

Style, Tone, and Irony

STYLE

Style is a concept that everyone understands on some level because in its broadest sense it refers to the particular way in which anything is made or done. Style is everywhere around us. The world is saturated with styles in cars, clothing, buildings, teaching, dancing, music, politics — in anything that reflects a distinctive manner of expression or design. Consider, for example, how a tune sung by the Beatles differs from the same tune performed by a string orchestra. There's no mistaking the two styles.

Authors also have different characteristic styles. *Style* refers to the distinctive manner in which a writer arranges words to achieve particular effects. That arrangement includes individual word choices and matters such as the length of sentences, their structure and tone, and the use of irony.

Diction refers to a writer's choice of words. Because different words evoke different associations in a reader's mind, the writer's choice of words is crucial in controlling a reader's response. The diction must be appropriate for the characters and the situations in which the author places them. Consider how inappropriate it would have been if Melville had had Bartleby respond to the lawyer's requests with "Hell no!" instead of "I would prefer not to." The word *prefer* and the tentativeness of *would* help reinforce the scrivener's mildness, his dignity, and even his seeming reasonableness — all of which frustrate the lawyer's efforts to get rid of him. Bartleby, despite his passivity, seems to be in control of the situation. If he were to shout "Hell no!" he would appear angry, aggressive, desperate, and too informal, none of which would fit with his solemn, conscious decision to die. Melville makes the lawyer the desperate party by carefully choosing Bartleby's words.

Sentence structure is another element of a writer's style. Hemingway's terse, economical sentences are frequently noted and readily perceived.

Here are the concluding sentences of Hemingway's "Soldier's Home" (p. 145), in which Krebs decides to leave home:

> He had tried so to keep his life from being complicated. Still, none of it had touched him. He had felt sorry for his mother and she had made him lie. He would go to Kansas City and get a job and she would feel all right about it. There would be one more scene maybe before he got away. He would not go down to his father's office. He would miss that one. He wanted his life to go smoothly. It had just gotten going that way. Well, that was all over now, anyway. He would go over to the schoolyard and watch Helen play indoor baseball.

Hemingway expresses Krebs's thought the way Krebs thinks. The style avoids any "complicated" sentence structures. Seven of the eleven sentences begin with the word *He*. There are no abstractions or qualifications. We feel as if we are listening not only to *what* Krebs thinks but to *how* he thinks. The style reflects his firm determination to make, one step at a time, a clean, unobstructed break from his family and the entangling complications they would impose on him.

Contrast this straightforward style with Vladimir Nabokov's description of a woman in his short story "The Vane Sisters." The sophisticated narrator teaches French literature at a women's college and is as observant as he is icily critical of the woman he describes in this passage:

> Her fingernails were gaudily painted, but badly bitten and not clean. Her lovers were a silent young photographer with a sudden laugh and two older men, brothers, who owned a small printing establishment across the street. I wondered at their tastes whenever I glimpsed, with a secret shudder, the higgledy-piggledy striation of black hairs that showed all along her pale shins through the nylon of her stockings with the scientific distinctness of a preparation flattened under glass; or when I felt, at her every movement, the dullish, stalish, not particularly conspicuous but all-pervading and depressing emanation that her seldom bathed flesh spread from under weary perfumes and creams.

This portrait — etched with a razor blade — is restrained but devastating. The woman's fingernails are "gaudily painted." She has no taste in men either. One of her lovers is "silent" except for a "sudden laugh," a telling detail that suggests a strikingly odd personality. Her other lovers, the two brothers (!), run a "small" business. We are invited to "shudder" along with the narrator as he vividly describes the "striation of black hairs" on her legs; we see the woman as if she were displayed under a microscope, an appropriate perspective given the narrator's close inspection. His scrutiny is relentless, and its object smells as awful as it looks (notice the difference in the language between this blunt description and the narrator's elegant distaste). He finds the woman "depressing" because the weight of her unpleasantness oppresses him.

The narrator reveals nearly as much about himself as about the woman, but Nabokov leaves the reader with the task of assessing the narrator's fastidious reactions. The formal style of this description is appropriately that of an educated, highly critical, close observer of life who knows how to convey the "dullish, stalish" essence of this woman. But, you might ask, what about the curious informality of "higgledy-piggledy"? Does that fit the formal professorial voice? Given Nabokov's well-known fascination with wit and, more important, the narrator's obvious relish for verbally slicing this woman into a slide specimen, the term is revealed as appropriately chosen once the reader sees the subtle, if brutal, pun on *piggledy*.

Hemingway's and Nabokov's uses of language are very different, yet each style successfully fuses what is said with how it is said. We could write summaries of both passages, but our summaries, owing to their styles, would not have the same effect as the originals. And that makes all the difference.

TONE

Style reveals ***tone,*** the author's implicit attitude toward the people, places, and events in a story. When we speak, tone is conveyed by our voice inflections, our wink of an eye, or some other gesture. A professor who says "You're going to fail the next exam" may be indicating concern, frustration, sympathy, alarm, humor, or indifference, depending on the tone of voice. In a literary work that spoken voice is unavailable; instead we must rely on the context in which a statement appears to interpret it correctly.

In Chopin's "The Story of an Hour" (p. 10), for example, we can determine that the author sympathizes with Mrs. Mallard despite the fact that her grief over her husband's assumed death is mixed with joy. Though Mrs. Mallard thinks she's lost her husband, she experiences relief because she feels liberated from an oppressive male-dominated life. That's why she collapses when she sees her husband alive at the end of the story. Chopin makes clear by the tone of the final line ("When the doctors came they said she had died of heart disease — of joy that kills") that the men misinterpret both her grief and joy, for in the larger context of Mrs. Mallard's emotions we see, unlike the doctors, that her death may well have been caused not by a shock of joy but by an overwhelming recognition of her lost freedom.

If we are sensitive to tone, we can get behind a character and see him or her from the author's perspective. In Melville's "Bartleby, the Scrivener" (p. 113) everything is told from the lawyer's point of view, but the tone of his remarks often separates him from the author's values and attitudes. When the lawyer characterizes himself at the beginning of the story, his use of language effectively allows us to see Melville disapproving of what the lawyer takes pride in:

> The late John Jacob Astor, a personage little given to poetic enthusiasm, had no hesitation in pronouncing my first grand point to be prudence; my next, method. I do not speak it in vanity.

But, of course, he is vain and a name-dropper as well. He likes the "rounded and orbicular sound" of Astor's name because it "rings like unto bullion." Tone, here, helps to characterize the lawyer. Melville doesn't tell us that the lawyer is status conscious and materialistic; instead, we discover that through the tone. This stylistic technique is frequently an important element for interpreting a story. An insensitivity to tone can lead a reader astray in determining the theme of a work. Regardless of who is speaking in a story, it is wise to listen for the author's voice too.

IRONY

One of the enduring themes in literature is that things are not always what they seem to be. What we see — or think we see — is not always what we get. The unexpected complexity that often surprises us in life — what Herman Melville in *Moby-Dick* called the "universal thump" — is fertile ground for writers of imaginative literature. They cultivate that ground through the use of *irony,* a device that reveals a reality different from what appears to be true.

Verbal irony consists of a person saying one thing but meaning the opposite. If a student driver smashes into a parked car and the angry instructor turns to say "You sure did well today," the statement is an example of verbal irony. What is meant is not what is said. Verbal irony that is calculated to hurt someone by false praise is commonly known as *sarcasm.* In literature, however, verbal irony is usually not openly aggressive; instead, it is more subtle and restrained though no less intense.

In Godwin's "A Sorrowful Woman" (p. 33), a woman retreats from her family because she cannot live in the traditional role that her husband and son expect of her. When the husband tries to be sympathetic about her withdrawal from family life, the narrator tells us three times that "he understood such things" and that in "understanding these things" he tried to be patient by "[s]till understanding these things." The narrator's repetition of these phrases constitutes verbal irony because they call attention to the fact that the husband doesn't understand his wife at all. His "understanding" is really only a form of condescension that represents part of her problem rather than a solution.

Situational irony exists when there is an incongruity between what is expected to happen and what actually happens. For instance, at the climactic showdown between Marshal Potter and Scratchy Wilson in Crane's "The Bride Comes to Yellow Sky" (p. 250), there are no gunshots, only talk — and what subdues Wilson is not Potter's strength and heroism but the fact that the marshal is now married. To take one more example, the protagonist in Godwin's "A Sorrowful Woman" seems, by traditional societal standards, to have all that a wife and mother could desire in a family, but, given her needs, that turns out not to be enough to sustain even her life, let alone her happiness. In each of these instances the ironic situation creates a distinction between appearances and realities and brings the reader closer to the central meaning of the story.

Another form of irony occurs when an author allows the reader to know more about a situation than a character knows. **Dramatic irony** creates a discrepancy between what a character believes or says and what the reader understands to be true. In Flannery O'Connor's "Revelation" (p. 407) the insecure Mrs. Turpin, as a member of "the home-and-land owner" class, believes herself to be superior to "niggers," "white-trash," and mere "home owners." She takes pride in her position in the community and in what she perceives to be her privileged position in relation to God. The reader, however, knows that her remarks underscore her failings rather than any superiority. Dramatic irony can be an effective way for an author to have a character unwittingly reveal himself or herself.

As you read Raymond Carver's "Popular Mechanics," T. Coraghessan Boyle's "Carnal Knowledge," Susan Minot's "Lust," and George Bowering's "A Short Story," pay attention to the authors' artful use of style, tone, and irony to convey meanings.

RAYMOND CARVER (1938–1988)

Born in 1938 in Clatskanie, Oregon, to working-class parents, Carver grew up in Yakima, Washington, was educated at Humboldt State College in California, and did graduate work at the University of Iowa. He married at age nineteen and during his college years worked at a series of low-paying jobs to help support his family. These difficult years eventually ended in divorce. He taught at a number of universities, among them the University of California at Berkeley, the University of Iowa, the University of Texas at El Paso, and Syracuse University. Carver's collections of stories include *Will You Please Be Quiet, Please?* (1976), *What We Talk about When We Talk about Love* (1981), from which "Popular Mechanics" is taken, *Cathedral* (1984), and *Where I'm Calling From: New and Selected Stories* (1988). Though extremely brief, "Popular Mechanics" describes a stark domestic situation with a startling conclusion.

Popular Mechanics 1981

Early that day the weather turned and the snow was melting into dirty water. Streaks of it ran down from the little shoulder-high window that faced the backyard. Cars slushed by on the street outside, where it was getting dark. But it was getting dark on the inside too.

He was in the bedroom pushing clothes into a suitcase when she came to the door.

I'm glad you're leaving! I'm glad you're leaving! she said. Do you hear?

He kept on putting his things into the suitcase.

Son of a bitch! I'm so glad you're leaving! She began to cry. You can't even 5 look me in the face, can you?

Then she noticed the baby's picture on the bed and picked it up.

He looked at her and she wiped her eyes and stared at him before turning and going back to the living room.

Bring that back, he said.

Just get your things and get out, she said.

He did not answer. He fastened the suitcase, put on his coat, looked 10 around the bedroom before turning off the light. Then he went out to the living room.

She stood in the doorway of the little kitchen, holding the baby.

I want the baby, he said.

Are you crazy?

No, but I want the baby. I'll get someone to come by for his things.

You're not touching this baby, she said. 15

The baby had begun to cry and she uncovered the blanket from around his head.

Oh, oh, she said, looking at the baby.

He moved toward her.

For God's sake! she said. She took a step back into the kitchen.

I want the baby. 20

Get out of here!

She turned and tried to hold the baby over in a corner behind the stove.

But he came up. He reached across the stove and tightened his hands on the baby.

Let go of him, he said.

Get away, get away! she cried. 25

The baby was red-faced and screaming. In the scuffle they knocked down a flowerpot that hung behind the stove.

He crowded her into the wall then, trying to break her grip. He held on to the baby and pushed with all his weight.

Let go of him, he said.

Don't, she said. You're hurting the baby, she said.

I'm not hurting the baby, he said. 30

The kitchen window gave no light. In the near-dark he worked on her fisted fingers with one hand and with the other hand he gripped the screaming baby up under an arm near the shoulder.

She felt her fingers being forced open. She felt the baby going from her.

No! she screamed just as her hands came loose.

She would have it, this baby. She grabbed for the baby's other arm. She caught the baby around the wrist and leaned back.

But he would not let go. He felt the baby slipping out of his hands and he 35 pulled back very hard.

In this manner, the issue was decided.

CONSIDERATIONS FOR CRITICAL THINKING AND WRITING

1. FIRST RESPONSE. Discuss the story's final lines. What is the "issue" that is "decided"?

2. Though there is little description of the setting in this story, how do the few details that are provided help to establish the tone?

3. How do small actions take on larger significance in the story? Consider the woman picking up the baby's picture and the knocked-down flowerpot.

4. Why is this couple splitting up? Do we know? Does it matter? Explain your response.

5. Discuss the title of the story. The original title was "Mine." Which do you think is more effective?

6. What is the conflict? How is it resolved?

7. Read I Kings 3 in the Bible for the story of Solomon. How might "Popular Mechanics" be read as a retelling of this story? What significant differences do you find in the endings of each?

8. Explain how Carver uses irony to convey theme.

CONNECTIONS TO OTHER SELECTIONS

1. Compare Carver's style with Ernest Hemingway's in "Soldier's Home" (p. 145).

2. How is the ending of "Popular Mechanics" similar to the ending of Nathaniel Hawthorne's "The Birthmark" (p. 329)?

PERSPECTIVE

JOHN BARTH (B. 1930)

On Minimalist Fiction   1987

Minimalism (of one sort or another) is the principle (one of the principles, anyhow) underlying (what I and many another interested observer consider to be perhaps) the most impressive phenomenon on the current (North American, especially the United States) literary scene (the gringo equivalent of *el boom* in the Latin American novel): I mean the new flowering of the (North) American short story (in particular the kind of terse, oblique, realistic or hyperrealistic, slightly plotted, extrospective, cool-surfaced fiction associated in the last five or ten years with such excellent writers as Frederick Barthelme, Ann Beattie, Raymond Carver, Bobbie Ann Mason, James Robison, Mary Robison, and Tobias Wolff, and both praised and damned under such labels as "K-Mart realism," "hick chic," "Diet-Pepsi minimalism" and "post-Vietnam, post-literary, postmodernist blue-collar neo-early-Hemingwayism"). . . .

The genre of the short story, as Poe distinguished it from the traditional tale in his 1842 review of Hawthorne's first collection of stories, is an early manifesto of modern narrative minimalism: "In the whole composition there should be no word written, of which the tendency . . . is not to the pre-established design. . . . Undue length is . . . to be avoided." Poe's codification informs such later nineteenth-century masters of terseness, selectivity, and implicitness (as opposed to leisurely once-upon-a-timelessness, luxuriant abundance, explicit and extended analysis) as Guy de Maupassant and Anton Chekhov. Show, don't tell, said Henry James in effect and at length in his prefaces to the 1908 New York edition of his novels. And don't tell a word more than you absolutely need to, added young Ernest Hemingway, who thus described his "new theory" in the early 1920's: "You could omit anything if you knew that you omitted, and the omitted part would strengthen the story and make people feel something more than they understood. . . ."

Old or new, fiction can be minimalist in any or all of several ways. There are minimalisms of unit, form, and scale: short words, short sentences and paragraphs, [and] super-short stories. . . . There are minimalisms of style: a stripped-down vocabulary; a stripped-down syntax that avoids periodic sentences, serial predications, and complex subordinating constructions; a stripped-down rhetoric that may eschew figurative language altogether; a stripped-down, non-emotive tone. And there are minimalisms of material: minimal characters, minimal exposition ("all that David Copperfield kind of crap," says J. D. Salinger's catcher in the rye), minimal *mises en scène*, minimal action, minimal plot.

From *Weber Studies*

CONSIDERATIONS FOR CRITICAL THINKING AND WRITING

1. To what extent do Ernest Hemingway's "Soldier's Home" (p. 145) and Raymond Carver's "Popular Mechanics" (p. 272) fulfill Barth's description of minimalist fiction? How does each story suggest that less is more?

2. Write an essay explaining why one of the short stories by Nathaniel Hawthorne, Flannery O'Connor, or Alice Munro in this anthology is not a minimalist story.

T. CORAGHESSAN BOYLE (B. 1948)

Born in Peekskill, New York, T. Coraghessan Boyle earned a doctorate at the University of Iowa and has taught at the University of Southern California. Among his literary awards is a National Endowment for the Arts Creative Writing Fellowship and the PEN/Faulkner Award for fiction. His fiction has appeared in a variety of periodicals including the *North American Review*, *The New Yorker*, *Harper's*, the *Atlantic Monthly*, and *Playboy*. His novels include *Water Music* (1981), *Budding Projects* (1984), *World's End* (1987), *East Is East* (1990), and *The Road to Wellville* (1993), recently made into a film. His short stories are collected in *Descent of Man* (1979), *Greasy Lake and Other Stories* (1985), *If the River Was Whiskey* (1989), and *Without a Hero and Other Stories* (1994), from which "Carnal Knowledge," a story characteristic of Boyle's ironic humor, is reprinted.

Carnal Knowledge 1994

I'd never really thought much about meat. It was there in the supermarket in a plastic wrapper; it came between slices of bread with mayo and mustard and a dill pickle on the side; it sputtered and smoked on the grill till somebody flipped it over, and then it appeared on the plate, between the baked potato and the julienne carrots, neatly cross-hatched and floating in a puddle of red juice. Beef, mutton, pork, venison, dripping burgers, and greasy ribs — it was all the same to me, food, the body's fuel, something to savor a moment on the tongue before the digestive system went to work on it. Which is not to say I was totally unconscious of the deeper implications. Every once in a while I'd eat at home, a quartered chicken, a package of Shake 'n Bake, Stove Top stuffing, and frozen peas, and as I hacked away at the stippled yellow skin and pink flesh of the sanitized bird I'd wonder at the darkish bits of organ clinging to the ribs — what was that, liver? kidney? — but in the end it didn't make me any less fond of Kentucky Fried or Chicken McNuggets. I saw those ads in the magazines, too, the ones that showed the veal calves penned up in their own waste, their limbs atrophied and their veins so pumped full of antibiotics they couldn't control their bowels, but when I took a date to Anna Maria's, I could never resist the veal scallopini.

And then I met Alena Jorgensen.

It was a year ago, two weeks before Thanksgiving — I remember the date because it was my birthday, my thirtieth, and I'd called in sick and gone to the beach to warm my face, read a book, and feel a little sorry for myself. The Santa Anas were blowing and it was clear all the way to Catalina, but there was an edge to the air, a scent of winter hanging over Utah, and as far as I could see in either direction I had the beach pretty much to myself. I found a sheltered spot in a tumble of boulders, spread a blanket, and settled down to attack the pastrami on rye I'd brought along for nourishment. Then I turned to my book — a comfortingly apocalyptic tract about the demise of the planet — and let the sun warm me as I read about the denuding of the rain forest, the poisoning of the atmosphere, and the swift silent eradication of species. Gulls coasted by overhead. I saw the distant glint of jetliners.

I must have dozed, my head thrown back, the book spread open in my lap, because the next thing I remember, a strange dog was hovering over me and the sun had dipped behind the rocks. The dog was big, wild-haired, with one staring blue eye, and it just looked at me, ears slightly cocked, as if it expected a Milk-Bone or something. I was startled — not that I don't like dogs, but here was this woolly thing poking its snout in my face — and I guess that I must have made some sort of defensive gesture, because the dog staggered back a step and froze. Even in the confusion of the moment I could see that there was something wrong with this dog, an unsteadiness, a gimp, a wobble to its legs. I felt a mixture of pity and revulsion — had it been hit by a car, was that it? — when all at once I became aware of a wetness on the breast of my windbreaker, and an unmistakable odor rose to my nostrils: I'd been pissed on.

Pissed on. As I lay there unsuspecting, enjoying the sun, the beach, the soli- 5 tude, this stupid beast had lifted its leg and used me as a pissoir — and now it was poised there on the edge of the blanket as if it expected a reward. A sudden rage seized me. I came up off the blanket with a curse, and it was only then that a dim apprehension seemed to seep into the dog's other eye, the brown one, and it lurched back and fell on its face, just out of reach. And then it lurched and fell again, bobbing and weaving across the sand like a seal out of water. I was on my feet now, murderous, glad to see that the thing was hobbled—it would simplify the task of running it down and beating it to death.

"Alf!" a voice called, and as the dog floundered in the sand, I turned and saw Alena Jorgensen poised on the boulder behind me. I don't want to make too much of the moment, don't want to mythologize it or clutter the scene with allusions to Aphrodite rising from the waves or accepting the golden apple from Paris, but she was a pretty impressive sight. Bare-legged, fluid, as tall and uncompromising as her Nordic ancestors, and dressed in a Gore-Tex bikini and hooded sweatshirt unzipped to the waist, she blew me away, in any event. Piss-spattered and stupified, I could only gape up at her.

"You bad boy," she said, scolding, "you get out of there." She glanced from the dog to me and back again. "Oh, you bad boy, what have you done?" she demanded, and I was ready to admit to anything, but it was the dog she was addressing, and the dog flopped over in the sand as if it had been shot. Alena skipped lightly down from the rock, and in the next moment, before I could protest, she was rubbing at the stain on my windbreaker with the wadded-up hem of her sweatshirt.

I tried to stop her—"It's all right," I said, "it's nothing," as if dogs routinely pissed on my wardrobe—but she wouldn't hear of it.

"No," she said, rubbing, her hair flying in my face, the naked skin of her thigh pressing unconsciously to my own, "no, this is terrible, I'm so embarrassed—Alf, you bad boy—I'll clean it for you, I will, it's the least—oh, look at that, it's stained right through to your T-shirt—"

I could smell her, the mousse she used in her hair, a lilac soap or perfume, 10 the salt-sweet odor of her sweat—she'd been jogging, that was it. I murmured something about taking it to the cleaner's myself.

She stopped rubbing and straightened up. She was my height, maybe even a fraction taller, and her eyes were ever so slightly mismatched, like the dog's: a deep earnest blue in the right iris, shading to sea-green and turquoise in the left. We were so close we might have been dancing. "Tell you what," she said, and her face lit with a smile, "since you're so nice about the whole thing, and most people wouldn't be, even if they knew what poor Alf has been through, why don't you let me wash it for you—and the T-shirt too?"

I was a little disconcerted at this point—I was the one who'd been pissed on, after all—but my anger was gone. I felt weightless, adrift, like a piece of fluff floating on the breeze. "Listen," I said, and for the moment I couldn't look her in the eye, "I don't want to put you to any trouble . . ."

"I'm ten minutes up the beach, and I've got a washer and dryer. Come on, it's no trouble at all. Or do you have plans? I mean, I could just pay for the cleaner's if you want . . ."

I was between relationships—the person I'd been seeing off and on for the past year wouldn't even return my calls—and my plans consisted of taking a solitary late-afternoon movie as a birthday treat, then heading over to my mother's for dinner and the cake with the candles. My Aunt Irene would be there, and so would my grandmother. They would exclaim over how big I was and how handsome and then they would begin to contrast my present self with my previous, more diminutive incarnations, and finally work themselves up to a spate of reminiscence that would continue unabated till my mother drove them home. And then, if I was lucky, I'd go out to a singles bar and make the acquaintance of a divorced computer programmer in her mid-thirties with three kids and bad breath.

I shrugged. "Plans? No, not really. I mean, nothing in particular." 15

Alena was housesitting a one-room bungalow that rose stumplike from the sand, no more than fifty feet from the tide line. There were trees in the yard behind it and the place was sandwiched between glass fortresses with crenellated decks, whipping flags, and great hulking concrete pylons. Sitting on the couch inside, you could feel the dull reverberation of each wave hitting the shore, a slow steady pulse that forever defined the place for me. Alena gave me a faded UC Davis sweatshirt that nearly fit, sprayed a stain remover on my T-shirt and windbreaker, and in a single fluid motion flipped down the lid of the washer and extracted two beers from the refrigerator beside it.

There was an awkward moment as she settled into the chair opposite me and we concentrated on our beers. I didn't know what to say. I was disoriented, giddy, still struggling to grasp what had happened. Fifteen minutes earlier I'd been dozing on the beach, alone on my birthday and feeling sorry for myself, and now I was ensconced in a cozy beach house, in the presence of Alena Jorgensen and her naked spill of leg, drinking a beer. "So what do you do?" she said, setting her beer down on the coffee table.

I was grateful for the question, too grateful maybe. I described to her at length how dull my job was, nearly ten years with the same agency, writing ad copy, my brain gone numb with disuse. I was somewhere in the middle of a blow-by-blow account of our current campaign for a Ghanian vodka distilled from calabash husks when she said, "I know what you mean," and told me she'd dropped out of veterinary school herself. "After I saw what they did to the animals. I mean, can you see neutering a dog just for our convenience, just because it's easier for us if they don't have a sex life?" Her voice grew hot. "It's the same old story, species fascism at its worst."

Alf was lying at my feet, grunting softly and looking up mournfully out of his staring blue eye, as blameless a creature as ever lived. I made a small noise of agreement and then focused on Alf. "And your dog," I said, "he's arthritic? Or is it hip dysplasia or what?" I was pleased with myself for the question — aside from "tapeworm," "hip dysplasia" was the only veterinary term I could dredge up from the memory bank, and I could see that Alf's problems ran deeper than worms.

Alena looked angry suddenly. "Don't I wish," she said. She paused to draw 20 a bitter breath. "There's nothing wrong with Alf that wasn't inflicted on him. They tortured him, maimed him, mutilated him."

"Tortured him?" I echoed, feeling the indignation rise in me — this beautiful girl, this innocent beast. "Who?"

Alena leaned forward and there was real hate in her eyes. She mentioned a prominent shoe company — spat out the name, actually. It was an ordinary name, a familiar one, and it hung in the air between us, suddenly sinister. Alf had been part of an experiment to market booties for dogs — suede, cordovan, patent leather, the works. The dogs were made to pace a treadmill in their booties, to assess wear; Alf was part of the control group.

"Control group?" I could feel the hackles rising on the back of my neck.

"They used eighty-grit sandpaper on the treads, to accelerate the process." Alena shot a glance out the window to where the surf pounded the shore; she bit her lip. "Alf was one of the dogs without booties."

I was stunned. I wanted to get up and comfort her, but I might as well have been grafted to the chair. "I don't believe it," I said. "How could anybody—" 25

"Believe it," she said. She studied me a moment, then set down her beer and crossed the room to dig through a cardboard box in the corner. If I was moved by the emotion she'd called up, I was moved even more by the sight of her bending over the box in her Gore-Tex bikini; I clung to the edge of the chair as if it were a plunging roller coaster. A moment later she dropped a dozen file folders in my lap. The uppermost bore the name of the shoe company, and it was crammed with news clippings, several pages of a diary relating to plant operations and workers' shifts at the Grand Rapids facility, and a floor plan of the laboratories. The folders beneath it were inscribed with the names of cosmetics firms, biomedical research centers, furriers, tanners, meatpackers. Alena perched on the edge of the coffee table and watched as I shuffled through them.

"You know the Draize test?"

I gave her a blank look.

"They inject chemicals into rabbits' eyes to see how much it'll take before they go blind. The rabbits are in cages, thousands of them, and they take a needle and jab it into their eyes—and you know why, you know in the name of what great humanitarian cause this is going on, even as we speak?"

I didn't know. The surf pounded at my feet. I glanced at Alf and then back 30 into her angry eyes.

"Mascara, that's what. Mascara. They torture countless thousands of rabbits so women can look like sluts."

I thought the characterization a bit harsh, but when I studied her pale lashes and tight lipstickless mouth, I saw that she meant it. At any rate, the notion set her off, and she launched into a two-hour lecture, gesturing with her flawless hands, quoting figures, digging through her files for the odd photo of legless mice or morphine-addicted gerbils. She told me how she'd rescued Alf herself, raiding the laboratory with six other members of the Animal Liberation Front, the militant group in honor of which Alf had been named. At first, she'd been content to write letters and carry placards, but now, with the lives of so many animals at stake, she'd turned to more direct action: harassment, vandalism, sabotage. She described how she'd spiked trees with Earth-First!ers in Oregon, cut miles of barbed-wire fence on cattle ranches in Nevada, destroyed records in biomedical research labs up and down the coast and insinuated herself between the hunters and the bighorn sheep in the mountains of Arizona. I could only nod and exclaim, smile ruefully and whistle in a low "holy cow!" sort of way. Finally, she paused to level her unsettling eyes on me. "You know what Isaac Bashevis Singer said?"

We were on our third beer. The sun was gone. I didn't have a clue.

Alena leaned forward. "'Every day is Auschwitz for the animals.'"

I looked down into the amber aperture of my beer bottle and nodded my 35 head sadly. The dryer had stopped an hour and a half ago. I wondered if she'd go out to dinner with me, and what she could eat if she did. "Uh, I was wondering," I said, "if . . . if you might want to go out for something to eat—"

Alf chose that moment to heave himself up from the floor and urinate on the wall behind me. My dinner proposal hung in the balance as Alena shot up off the edge of the table to scold him and then gently usher him out the door. "Poor Alf," she sighed, turning back to me with a shrug. "But listen, I'm sorry if I talked your head off—I didn't mean to, but it's rare to find somebody on your own wavelength."

She smiled. *On your own wavelength:* the words illuminated me, excited me, sent up a tremor I could feel all the way down in the deepest nodes of my reproductive tract. "So how about dinner?" I persisted. Restaurants were running through my head—would it have to be veggie? Could there be even a whiff of grilled flesh on the air? Curdled goat's milk and tabbouleh, tofu, lentil soup, sprouts: *Every day is Auschwitz for the animals.* "No place with meat, of course."

She just looked at me.

"I mean, I don't eat meat myself," I lied, "or actually, not anymore"—since the pastrami sandwich, that is—"but I don't really know any place that . . ." I trailed off lamely.

"I'm a Vegan," she said.   40

After two hours of blind bunnies, butchered calves and mutilated pups, I couldn't resist the joke. "I'm from Venus myself."

She laughed, but I could see she didn't find it all that funny. Vegans didn't eat meat or fish, she explained, or milk or cheese or eggs, and they didn't wear wool or leather—or fur, of course.

"Of course," I said. We were both standing there, hovering over the coffee table. I was beginning to feel a little foolish.

"Why don't we just eat here," she said.

The deep throb of the ocean seemed to settle in my bones as we lay there   45
in bed that night, Alena and I, and I learned all about the fluency of her limbs and the sweetness of her vegetable tongue. Alf sprawled on the floor beneath us, wheezing and groaning in his sleep, and I blessed him for his incontinence and his doggy stupidity. Something was happening to me—I could feel it in the way the boards shifted under me, feel it with each beat of the surf—and I was ready to go along with it. In the morning, I called in sick again.

Alena was watching me from bed as I dialed the office and described how the flu had migrated from my head to my gut and beyond, and there was a look in her eye that told me I would spend the rest of the day right there beside her, peeling grapes and dropping them one by one between her parted and expectant lips. I was wrong. Half an hour later, after a breakfast of brewer's yeast and what appeared to be some sort of bark marinated in yogurt, I found myself marching up and down the sidewalk in front of a fur emporium in Beverly Hills, waving a placard that read HOW DOES IT FEEL TO WEAR A CORPSE? in letters that dripped like blood.

It was a shock. I'd seen protest marches on TV, antiwar rallies and civil rights demonstrations and all that, but I'd never warmed my heels on the pavement or chanted slogans or felt the naked stick in my hand. There were maybe forty of us in all, mostly women, and we waved our placards at passing cars and blocked traffic on the sidewalk. One woman had smeared her face and hands with cold cream steeped in red dye, and Alena had found a ratty mink stole somewhere—the kind that features whole animals sewed together, snout to tail, their miniature limbs dangling—and she'd taken a can of crimson spray paint to their muzzles so that they looked freshly killed. She brandished this grisly banner on a stick high above her head, whooping like a savage and chanting, "Fur is death, fur is death," over and over again till it became a mantra for the crowd. The day was unseasonably warm, the Jaguars glinted in the sun and the palms nodded in the breeze, and no one, but for a single tight-lipped salesman glowering from behind the store's immaculate windows, paid the slightest bit of attention to us.

I marched out there on the street, feeling exposed and conspicuous, but marching nonetheless — for Alena's sake and for the sake of the foxes and martens and all the rest, and for my own sake too: with each step I took I could feel my consciousness expanding like a balloon, the breath of saintliness seeping steadily into me. Up to this point I'd worn suede and leather like anybody else, ankle boots and Air Jordans, a bombardier jacket I'd had since high school. If I'd drawn the line with fur, it was only because I'd never had any use for it. If I lived in the Yukon — and sometimes, drowsing through a meeting at work, I found myself fantasizing about it — I would have worn fur, no compunction, no second thoughts.

But not anymore. Now I was the protestor, a placard waver, now I was fighting for the right of every last weasel and lynx to grow old and die gracefully, now I was Alena Jorgensen's lover and a force to be reckoned with. Of course, my feet hurt and I was running sweat and praying that no one from work would drive by and see me there on the sidewalk with my crazy cohorts and denunciatory sign.

We marched for hours, back and forth, till I thought we'd wear a groove in 50 the pavement. We chanted and jeered and nobody so much as looked at us twice. We could have been Hare Krishnas, bums, antiabortionists, or lepers, what did it matter? To the rest of the world, to the uninitiated masses to whose sorry number I'd belonged just twenty-four hours earlier, we were invisible. I was hungry, tired, discouraged. Alena was ignoring me. Even the woman in red-face was slowing down, her chant a hoarse whisper that was sucked up and obliterated in the roar of traffic. And then, as the afternoon faded toward rush hour, a wizened silvery old woman who might have been an aging star or a star's mother or even the first dimly remembered wife of a studio exec got out of a long white car at the curb and strode fearlessly toward us. Despite the heat — it must have been eighty degrees at this point — she was wearing an ankle-length silver fox coat, a bristling shouldery wafting mass of peltry that must have decimated every burrow on the tundra. It was the moment we'd been waiting for.

A cry went up, shrill and ululating, and we converged on the lone old woman like a Cheyenne war party scouring the plains. The man beside me went down on all fours and howled like a dog. Alena slashed the air with her limp mink, and the blood sang in my ears. "Murderer!" I screamed, getting into it. "Torturer! Nazi!" The strings in my neck were tight. I didn't know what I was saying. The crowd gibbered. The placards danced. I was so close to the old woman I could smell her — her perfume, a whiff of mothballs from the coat — and it intoxicated me, maddened me, and I stepped in front of her to block her path with all the seething militant bulk of my one hundred eighty-five pounds of sinew and muscle.

I never saw the chauffeur. Alena told me afterward that he was a former kickboxing champion who'd been banned from the sport for excessive brutality.

The first blow seemed to drop down from above, a shell lobbed from deep within enemy territory; the others came at me like a windmill churning in a storm. Someone screamed. I remember focusing on the flawless rigid pleats of the chauffeur's trousers, and then things got a bit hazy.

I woke to the dull thump of the surf slamming at the shore and the touch of Alena's lips on my own. I felt as if I'd been broken on the wheel, dismantled, and put back together again. "Lie still," she said, and her tongue moved against my swollen cheek. Stricken, I could only drag my head across the pillow and gaze into the depths of her parti-colored eyes. "You're one of us now," she whispered.

Next morning I didn't even bother to call in sick.

By the end of the week I'd recovered enough to crave meat, for which I felt 55 deeply ashamed, and to wear out a pair of vinyl huaraches on the picket line. Together, and with various coalitions of antivivisectionists, militant Vegans, and cat lovers, Alena and I tramped a hundred miles of sidewalk, spray-painted inflammatory slogans across the windows of supermarkets and burger stands, denounced tanners, furriers, poulterers, and sausage makers, and somehow found time to break up a cockfight in Pacoima. It was exhilarating, heady, dangerous. If I'd been disconnected in the past, I was plugged in now. I felt righteous — for the first time in my life I had a cause — and I had Alena, Alena above all. She fascinated me, fixated me, made me feel like a tomcat leaping in and out of second-story windows, oblivious to the free-fall and the picket fence below. There was her beauty, of course, a triumph of evolution and the happy interchange of genes going all the way back to the cavemen, but it was more than that — it was her commitment to animals, to the righting of wrongs, to morality that made her irresistible. Was it love? The term is something I've always had difficulty with, but I suppose it was. Sure it was. Love, pure and simple. I had it, it had me.

"You know what?" Alena said one night as she stood over the miniature stove, searing tofu in oil and garlic. We'd spent the afternoon demonstrating out front of a tortilla factory that used rendered animal fat as a congealing agent, after which we'd been chased three blocks by an overweight assistant manager at Von's who objected to Alena's spray-painting MEAT IS DEATH over the specials in the front window. I was giddy with the adolescent joy of it. I sank into the couch with a beer and watched Alf limp across the floor to fling himself down and lick at a suspicious spot on the floor. The surf boomed like thunder.

"What?" I said.

"Thanksgiving's coming."

I let it ride a moment, wondering if I should invite Alena to my mother's for the big basted bird stuffed with canned oysters and buttered bread crumbs, and then realized it probably wouldn't be such a great idea. I said nothing.

She glanced over her shoulder. "The animals don't have a whole lot to be 60 thankful for, that's for sure. It's just an excuse for the meat industry to butcher a couple million turkeys, is all it is." She paused; hot safflower oil popped in the pan. "I think it's time for a little road trip," she said. "Can we take your car?"

"Sure, but where are we going?"

She gave me her Gioconda smile. "To liberate some turkeys."

* * *

In the morning I called my boss to tell him I had pancreatic cancer and wouldn't be in for a while, then we threw some things in the car, helped Alf scrabble into the back seat, and headed up Route 5 for the San Joaquin Valley. We drove for three hours through a fog so dense the windows might as well have been packed with cotton. Alena was secretive, but I could see she was excited. I knew only that we were on our way to rendezvous with a certain "Rolfe," a longtime friend of hers and a big name in the world of ecotage and animal rights, after which we would commit some desperate and illegal act, for which the turkeys would be eternally grateful.

There was a truck stalled in front of the sign for our exit at Calpurnia Springs, and I had to brake hard and jerk the wheel around twice to keep the tires on the pavement. Alena came up out of her seat and Alf slammed into the armrest like a sack of meal, but we made it. A few minutes later we were gliding through the ghostly vacancy of the town itself, lights drifting past in a nimbus of fog, glowing pink, yellow, and white, and then there was only the blacktop road and the pale void that engulfed it. We'd gone ten miles or so when Alena instructed me to slow down and began to study the right-hand shoulder with a keen, unwavering eye.

The earth breathed in and out. I squinted hard into the soft drifting glow   65 of the headlights. "There, there!" she cried and I swung the wheel to the right, and suddenly we were lurching along a pitted dirt road that rose up from the blacktop like a goat path worn into the side of a mountain. Five minutes later Alf sat up in the back seat and began to whine, and then a crude unpainted shack began to detach itself from the vagueness around us.

Rolfe met us on the porch. He was tall and leathery, in his fifties, I guessed, with a shock of hair and rutted features that brought Samuel Beckett to mind. He was wearing gumboots and jeans and a faded lumberjack shirt that looked as if it had been washed a hundred times. Alf took a quick pee against the side of the house, then fumbled up the steps to roll over and fawn at his feet.

"Rolfe!" Alena called, and there was too much animation in her voice, too much familiarity, for my taste. She took the steps in a bound and threw herself in his arms. I watched them kiss, and it wasn't a fatherly-daughterly sort of kiss, not at all. It was a kiss with some meaning behind it, and I didn't like it. Rolfe, I thought: What kind of name is that?

"Rolfe," Alena gasped, still a little breathless from bouncing up the steps like a cheerleader, "I'd like you to meet Jim."

That was my signal. I ascended the porch steps and held out my hand. Rolfe gave me a look out of the hooded depths of his eyes and then took my hand in a hard calloused grip, the grip of the wood splitter, the fence mender, the liberator of hothouse turkeys and laboratory mice. "A pleasure," he said, and his voice rasped like sandpaper.

There was a fire going inside, and Alena and I sat before it and warmed our   70 hands while Alf whined and sniffed and Rolfe served Red Zinger tea in Japanese cups the size of thimbles. Alena hadn't stopped chattering since we stepped through the door, and Rolfe came right back at her in his woodsy rasp, the two of them exchanging names and news and gossip as if they were talking in code. I studied the reproductions of teal and widgeon that hung from the peeling walls, noted the case of Heinz vegetarian beans in the corner and the half-gallon of Jack Daniel's on the mantel. Finally, after the third cup of tea, Alena settled back in her chair — a huge old Salvation Army sort of thing with a soiled antimacassar — and said, "So what's the plan?"

Rolfe gave me another look, a quick predatory darting of the eyes, as if he weren't sure I could be trusted, and then turned back to Alena. "Hedda Gabler's Range-Fed Turkey Ranch," he said. "And no, I don't find the name cute, not at all." He looked at me now, a long steady assay. "They grind up the heads for cat food, and the neck, the organs, and the rest, that they wrap up in paper and stuff back in the body cavity like it was a war atrocity or something. Whatever did a turkey go and do to us to deserve a fate like that?"

The question was rhetorical, even if it seemed to have been aimed at me, and I made no response other than to compose my face in a look that wedded grief, outrage, and resolve. I was thinking of all the turkeys I'd sent to their doom, of the plucked wishbones, the pope's noses,° and the crisp browned skin I used to relish as a kid. It brought a lump to my throat, and something more: I realized I was hungry.

"Ben Franklin wanted to make them our national symbol," Alena chimed in, "did you know that? But the meat eaters won out."

"Fifty thousand birds," Rolfe said, glancing at Alena and bringing his incendiary gaze back to rest on me. "I have information they're going to start slaughtering them tomorrow, for the fresh-not-frozen market."

"Yuppie poultry," Alena's voice was drenched in disgust.   75

For a moment, no one spoke. I became aware of the crackling of the fire. The fog pressed at the windows. It was getting dark.

"You can see the place from the highway," Rolfe said finally, "but the only access is through Calpurnia Springs. It's about twenty miles — twenty-two point three, to be exact."

Alena's eyes were bright. She was gazing on Rolfe as if he'd just dropped down from heaven. I felt something heave in my stomach.

"We strike tonight."

Rolfe insisted that we take my car — "Everybody around here knows my   80
pickup, and I can't take any chances on a little operation like this" — but we did mask the plates, front and back, with an inch-thick smear of mud. We blackened our faces like commandos and collected our tools from the shed out back — tin snips, a crowbar, and two five-gallon cans of gasoline. "Gasoline?" I said, trying the heft of the can. Rolfe gave me a craggy look. "To create a diversion," he said. Alf, for obvious reasons, stayed behind in the shack.

If the fog had been thick in daylight, it was impenetrable now, the sky collapsed upon the earth. It took hold of the headlights and threw them back at me till my eyes began to water from the effort of keeping the car on the road. But for the ruts and bumps we might have been floating in space. Alena sat up front between Rolfe and me, curiously silent. Rolfe didn't have much to say either, save for the occasional grunted command: "Hang a right here"; "Hard left"; "Easy, easy." I thought about meat and jail and the heroic proportions to which I was about to swell in Alena's eyes and what I intended to do to her when we finally got to bed. It was 2:00 A.M. by the dashboard clock.

pope's noses: Slang for the fleshy tail sections of turkeys and other poultry.

"Okay," Rolfe said, and his voice came at me so suddenly it startled me, "pull over here — and kill the lights."

We stepped out into the hush of night and eased the doors shut behind us. I couldn't see a thing, but I could hear the not-so-distant hiss of traffic on the highway, and another sound, too, muffled and indistinct, the gentle unconscious suspiration of thousands upon thousands of my fellow creatures. And I could smell them, a seething rancid odor of feces and feathers and naked scaly feet that crawled down my throat and burned my nostrils. "Whew," I said in a whisper, "I can smell them."

Rolfe and Alena were vague presences at my side. Rolfe flipped open the trunk and in the next moment I felt the heft of a crowbar and a pair of tin snips in my hand. "Listen, you, Jim," Rolfe whispered, taking me by the wrist in his iron grip and leading me half-a-dozen steps forward. "Feel this?"

I felt a grid of wire, which he promptly cut: *snip, snip, snip.*   85

"This is their enclosure — they're out there in the day, scratching around in the dirt. You get lost, you follow this wire. Now, you're going to take a section out of this side, Alena's got the west side and I've got the south. Once that's done I signal with the flashlight and we bust open the doors to the turkey houses — they're these big low white buildings, you'll see them when you get close — and flush the birds out. Don't worry about me or Alena. Just worry about getting as many birds out as you can."

I was worried. Worried about everything, from some half-crazed farmer with a shotgun or AK-47 or whatever they carried these days, to losing Alena in the fog, to the turkeys themselves: How big were they? Were they violent? They had claws and beaks, didn't they? And how were they going to feel about me bursting into their bedroom in the middle of the night?

"And when the gas cans go up, you hightail it back to the car, got it?"

I could hear the turkeys tossing in their sleep. A truck shifted gears out on the highway. "I think so," I whispered.

"And one more thing — be sure to leave the keys in the ignition."   90

This gave me pause. "But —"

"The getaway." Alena was so close I could feel her breath on my ear. "I mean, we don't want to be fumbling around for the keys when all hell is breaking loose out there, do we?"

I eased open the door and reinserted the keys in the ignition, even though the automatic buzzer warned me against it. "Okay," I murmured, but they were already gone, soaked up in the shadows and the mist. At this point my heart was hammering so loudly I could barely hear the rustling of the turkeys — this is crazy, I told myself, it's hurtful and wrong, not to mention illegal. Spray-painting slogans was one thing, but this was something else altogether. I thought of the turkey farmer asleep in his bed, an entrepreneur working to make America strong, a man with a wife and kids and a mortgage . . . but then I thought of all those innocent turkeys consigned to death, and finally I thought of Alena, long-legged and loving, and the way she came to me out of the darkness of the bathroom and the boom of the surf. I took the tin snips to the wire.

I must have been at it half an hour, forty-five minutes, gradually working my way toward the big white sheds that had begun to emerge from the gloom up ahead, when I saw Rolfe's flashlight blinking off to my left. This was my signal to head to the nearest shed, snap off the padlock with my crowbar, fling open the doors, and herd a bunch of cranky suspicious gobblers out into the night. It was now or never. I looked twice round me and then broke for the near shed in an awkward crouching gait. The turkeys must have sensed that something was up — from behind the long white windowless wall there arose a watchful gabbling, a soughing of feathers that fanned up like a breeze in the treetops. *Hold on, you toms and hens,* I thought, *freedom is at hand.* A jerk of the wrist, and the padlock fell to the ground. Blood pounded in my ears, I took hold of the sliding door and jerked it open with a great dull booming reverberation — and suddenly, there they were, turkeys, thousands upon thousands of them, cloaked in white feathers under a string of dim yellow bulbs. The light glinted in their reptilian eyes. Somewhere a dog began to bark.

I steeled myself and sprang through the door with a shout, whirling the 95 crowbar over my head, "All right!" I boomed, and the echo gave it back to me a hundred times over, "this is it! Turkeys, on your feet!" Nothing. No response. But for the whisper of rustling feathers and the alertly cocked heads, they might have been sculptures, throw pillows, they might as well have been dead and butchered and served up with yams and onions and all the trimmings. The barking of the dog went up a notch. I thought I heard voices.

The turkeys crouched on the concrete floor, wave upon wave of them, stupid and immovable; they perched in the rafters, on shelves and platforms, huddled in wooden stalls. Desperate, I rushed into the front rank of them, swinging my crowbar, stamping my feet, and howling like the wishbone plucker I once was. That did it. There was a shriek from the nearest bird and the others took it up till an unholy racket filled the place, and now they were moving, tumbling down from their perches, flapping their wings in a storm of dried excrement and pecked-over grain, pouring across the concrete floor till it vanished beneath them. Encouraged, I screamed again — "Yeeee-ha-ha-ha-ha!" — and beat at the aluminum walls with the crowbar as the turkeys shot through the doorway and out into the night.

It was then that the black mouth of the doorway erupted with light and the *ka-boom!* of the gas cans sent a tremor through the earth. *Run!* a voice screamed in my head, and the adrenaline kicked in and all of a sudden I was scrambling for the door in a hurricane of turkeys. They were everywhere, flapping their wings, gobbling and screeching, loosing their bowels in panic. Something hit the back of my legs and all at once I was down amongst them, on the floor, in the dirt and feathers and wet turkey shit. I was a roadbed, a turkey expressway. Their claws dug at my back, my shoulders, the crown of my head. Panicked now, choking on feathers and dust and worse, I fought to my feet as the big screeching birds launched themselves round me, and staggered out into the barnyard. "There! Who's that there?" a voice roared, and I was off and running.

What can I say? I vaulted turkeys, kicked them aside like so many footballs, slashed and tore at them as they sailed through the air. I ran till my lungs felt as if they were burning right through my chest, disoriented, bewildered, terrified of the shotgun blast I was sure would cut me down at any moment. Behind me the fire raged and lit the fog till it glowed blood-red and hellish. But where was the fence? And where the car?

I got control of my feet then and stood stock-still in a flurry of turkeys, squinting into the wall of fog. Was that it? Was that the car over there? At that moment I heard an engine start up somewhere behind me — a familiar engine with a familiar coughing gurgle in the throat of the carburetor—and then the lights blinked on briefly three hundred yards away. I heard the engine race and listened, helpless, as the car roared off in the opposite direction. I stood there a moment longer, forlorn and forsaken, and then I ran blindly off into the night, putting the fire and the shouts and the barking and the incessant mindless squawking of the turkeys as far behind me as I could.

When dawn finally broke, it was only just perceptibly, so thick was the fog. I'd made my way to a blacktop road—which road and where it led I didn't know—and sat crouched and shivering in a clump of weed just off the shoulder. Alena wouldn't desert me, I was sure of that—she loved me, as I loved her; needed me, as I needed her—and I was sure she'd be cruising along the back roads looking for me. My pride was wounded, of course, and if I never laid eyes on Rolfe again I felt I wouldn't be missing much, but at least I hadn't been drilled full of shot, savaged by farm dogs, or pecked to death by irate turkeys. I was sore all over, my shin throbbed where I'd slammed into something substantial while vaulting through the night, there were feathers in my hair, and my face and arms were a mosaic of cuts and scratches and long trailing fissures of dirt. I'd been sitting there for what seemed like hours, cursing Rolfe, developing suspicions about Alena and unflattering theories about environmentalists in general, when finally I heard the familiar slurp and roar of my Chevy Citation cutting through the mist ahead of me.

Rolfe was driving, his face impassive. I flung myself into the road like a tattered beggar, waving my arms over my head and giving vent to my joy, and he very nearly ran me down. Alena was out of the car before it stopped, wrapping me up in her arms, and then she was bundling me into the rear seat with Alf and we were on our way back to the hideaway. "What happened?" she cried, as if she couldn't have guessed. "Where were you? We waited as long as we could."

I was feeling sulky, betrayed, feeling as if I was owed a whole lot more than a perfunctory hug and a string of insipid questions. Still, as I told my tale I began to warm to it—they'd got away in the car with the heater going, and I'd stayed behind to fight the turkeys, the farmers, and the elements, too, and if that wasn't heroic, I'd like to know what was. I looked into Alena's admiring eyes and pictured Rolfe's shack, a nip or two from the bottle of Jack Daniel's, maybe a peanut-butter-and-tofu sandwich, and then the bed, with Alena in it. Rolfe said nothing.

Back at Rolfe's, I took a shower and scrubbed the turkey droppings from my pores, then helped myself to the bourbon. It was ten in the morning and the house was dark—if the world had ever been without fog, there was no sign of it here. When Rolfe stepped out on the porch to fetch an armload of firewood, I pulled Alena down into my lap. "Hey," she murmured, "I thought you were an invalid."

She was wearing a pair of too-tight jeans and an oversize sweater with nothing underneath it. I slipped my hand inside the sweater and found something to hold on to. "Invalid?" I said, nuzzling at her sleeve. "Hell, I'm a turkey liberator, an ecoguerrilla, a friend of the animals and the environment, too."

She laughed, but she pushed herself up and crossed the room to stare out the occluded window. "Listen, Jim," she said, "what we did last night was great, really great, but it's just the beginning." Alf looked up at her expectantly. I heard Rolfe fumbling around on the porch, the thump of wood on wood. She turned around to face me now. "What I mean is, Rolfe wants me to go up to Wyoming for a little bit, just outside of Yellowstone —"

Me? *Rolfe wants me?* There was no invitation in that, no plurality, no acknowledgment of all we'd done and meant to each other. "For what?" I said. "What do you mean?"

"There's this grizzly — a pair of them, actually — and they've been raiding places outside the park. One of them made off with the mayor's Doberman the other night and the people are up in arms. We — I mean Rolfe and me and some other people from the old Bolt Weevils in Minnesota? — we're going to go up there and make sure the Park Service — or the local yahoos — don't eliminate them. The bears, I mean."

My tone was corrosive. "You and Rolfe?"

"There's nothing between us, if that's what you're thinking. This has to do with animals, that's all."

"Like us?"   110

She shook her head slowly. "Not like us, no. We're the plague on this planet, don't you know that?"

Suddenly I was angry. Seething. Here I'd crouched in the bushes all night, covered in turkey crap, and now I was part of a plague. I was on my feet. "No, I don't know that."

She gave me a look that let me know it didn't matter, that she was already gone, that her agenda, at least for the moment, didn't include me and there was no use arguing about it. "Look," she said, her voice dropping as Rolfe slammed back through the door with a load of wood, "I'll see you in L.A. in a month or so, okay?" She gave me an apologetic smile. "Water the plants for me?"

An hour later I was on the road again. I'd helped Rolfe stack the wood beside the fireplace, allowed Alena to brush my lips with a good-bye kiss, and then stood there on the porch while Rolfe locked up, lifted Alf into the bed of his pickup, and rumbled down the rutted dirt road with Alena at his side. I watched till their brake lights dissolved in the drifting gray mist, then fired up the Citation and lurched down the road behind them. *A month or so:* I felt hollow inside. I pictured her with Rolfe, eating yogurt and wheat germ, stopping at motels, wrestling grizzlies, and spiking trees. The hollowness opened up, cored me out till I felt as if I'd been plucked and gutted and served up on a platter myself.

I found my way back through Calpurnia Springs without incident — there   115
were no roadblocks, no flashing lights and grim-looking troopers searching trunks and back seats for a tallish thirty-year-old ecoterrorist with turkey tracks down his back — but after I turned onto the highway for Los Angeles, I had a shock. Ten miles up the road my nightmare materialized out of the gloom: red lights everywhere, signal flares and police cars lined up on the shoulder. I was on the very edge of panicking, a beat away from cutting across the median and giving them a run for it, when I saw the truck jackknifed up ahead. I slowed to forty, thirty, and then hit the brakes again. In a moment I was stalled in a line of cars and there was something all over the road, ghostly and white in the fog. At first I thought it must have been flung from the truck, rolls of toilet paper or crates of soap powder ruptured on the pavement. It was neither. As I inched closer, the tires creeping now, the pulse of the lights in my

face, I saw that the road was coated in feathers, turkey feathers. A storm of them. A blizzard. And more: there was flesh there too, slick and greasy, a red pulp ground into the surface of the road, thrown up like slush from the tires of the car ahead of me, ground beneath the massive wheels of the truck. Turkeys. Turkeys everywhere.

The car crept forward. I flicked on the windshield wipers, hit the washer button, and for a moment a scrim of diluted blood obscured the windows and the hollowness opened up inside of me till I thought it would suck me inside out. Behind me, someone was leaning on his horn. A trooper loomed up out of the gloom, waving me on with the dead yellow eye of his flashlight. I thought of Alena and felt sick. All there was between us had come to this, expectations gone sour, a smear on the road. I wanted to get out and shoot myself, turn myself in, close my eyes, and wake up in jail, in a hair shirt, in a straitjacket, anything. It went on. Time passed. Nothing moved. And then, miraculously, a vision began to emerge from behind the smeared glass and the gray belly of the fog, lights glowing golden in the waste. I saw the sign, Gas/Food/Lodging, and my hand was on the blinker.

It took me a moment, picturing the place, the generic tile, the false cheer of the lights, the odor of charred flesh hanging heavy on the air, Big Mac, three-piece dark meat, carne asada, cheeseburger. The engine coughed. The lights glowed. I didn't think of Alena then, didn't think of Rolfe or grizzlies or the doomed bleating flocks and herds, or of the blind bunnies and cancerous mice—I thought only of the cavern opening inside me and how to fill it. "Meat," and I spoke the word aloud, talking to calm myself as if I'd awakened from a bad dream, "it's only meat."

Considerations for Critical Thinking and Writing

1. FIRST RESPONSE. How do your own views of vegetarianism and animal rights' groups influence your response to this story?

2. Comment on how Boyle achieves humorous effects through his first-person narrator in the story's first paragraph.

3. Describe the tone of the first-person narrator. How does he regard the world—the people, situations, and events—he encounters? Why is it especially appropriate that he has a job writing copy for an advertising agency?

4. How does Boyle's style reveal the narrator's character? Select several paragraphs to illustrate your points.

5. How does the narrator use irony? Select three instances of his use of irony, and discuss their effects and what they reveal about him.

6. How does Boyle create a genuinely comic character with Alf? What is the narrator's relationship with Alf?

7. Characterize Alena. Why is the narrator both attracted to her and puzzled by her?

8. How do you think the story would differ if it were told from Alena's point of view?

9. What is your response to Alena's descriptions of commercial experiments on animals? How does the narrator respond to them?

10. What is the narrator's view of the protests he engages in with Alena? Discuss specific passages to support your answer.

11. How does paragraph 93 explain the narrator's willingness to go along with the raid on the turkey farm?

12. Describe the narrator's response to Rolfe. How does Boyle make Rolfe into a comic figure?

13. What is the major conflict in the story? How is it resolved in the story's final paragraphs?

14. How do the story's last words, "it's only meat," shed light on the significance of the title? What does a dictionary tell you about possible readings of the title?

CONNECTIONS TO OTHER SELECTIONS

1. What do Alena and Nathaniel Hawthorne's Young Goodman Brown (p. 310) have in common as reformers? Are there also significant differences?

2. Read the discussion of new historicist criticism in Chapter 37, "Critical Strategies for Reading," and describe how a new historicist might use "Carnal Knowledge" to describe aspects of American life in the early 1990s.

3. Write an essay comparing Boyle's humorous treatment of animal rights issues with Alison Baker's humorous approach to sex and gender issues in "Better Be Ready 'Bout Half Past Eight" (p. 617).

SUSAN MINOT (B. 1956)

Born and raised in Massachusetts, Susan Minot earned a B.A. at Brown University and an M.F.A. at Columbia University. Before devoting herself full-time to writing, Minot worked as an assistant editor at *Grand Street* magazine. Her stories have appeared in the *Atlantic Monthly, Harper's, The New Yorker, Mademoiselle,* and *Paris Review.* Her short stories have been collected in *Lust and Other Stories* (1989), and she has published two novels — *Monkeys* (1986) and *Folly* (1992).

Lust   *1984*

Leo was from a long time ago, the first one I ever saw nude. In the spring before the Hellmans filled their pool, we'd go down there in the deep end, with baby oil, and like that. I met him the first month away at boarding school. He had a halo from the campus light behind him. I flipped.

Roger was fast. In his illegal car, we drove to the reservoir, the radio blaring, talking fast, fast, fast. He was always going for my zipper. He got kicked out sophomore year.

By the time the band got around to playing "Wild Horses," I had tasted Bruce's tongue. We were clicking in the shadows on the other side of the amplifier, out of Mrs. Donovan's line of vision. It tasted like salt, with my neck bent back, because we had been dancing so hard before.

Tim's line: "I'd like to see you in a bathing suit." I knew it was his line when he said the exact same thing to Annie Hines.

You'd go on walks to get off campus. It was raining like hell, my sweater as ₅ sopped as a wet sheep. Tim pinned me to a tree, the woods light brown and dark brown, a white house half hidden with the lights already on. The water was as loud as a crowd hissing. He made certain comments about my forehead, about my cheeks.

We started off sitting at one end of the couch and then our feet were squished against the armrest and then he went over to turn off the TV and came back after he had taken off his shirt and then we slid onto the floor and he got up again to close the door, then came back to me, a body waiting on the rug.

You'd try to wipe off the table or to do the dishes and Willie would untuck your shirt and get his hands up under in front, standing behind you, making puffy noises in your ear.

He likes it when I wash my hair. He covers his face with it and if I start to say something, he goes, "Shush."

For a long time, I had Philip on the brain. The less they noticed you, the more you got them on the brain.

My parents had no idea. Parents never really know what's going on, espe- ₁₀ cially when you're away at school most of the time. If she met them, my mother might say, "Oliver seems nice" or "I like that one" without much of an opinion. If she didn't like them, "He's a funny fellow, isn't he?" or "Johnny's perfectly nice but a drink of water." My father was too shy to talk to them at all unless they played sports and he'd ask them about that.

The sand was almost cold underneath because the sun was long gone. Eben piled a mound over my feet, patting around my ankles, the ghostly surf rumbling behind him in the dark. He was the first person I ever knew who died, later that summer, in a car crash. I thought about it for a long time.

"Come here," he says on the porch.
I go over to the hammock and he takes my wrist with two fingers.
"What?"
He kisses my palm then directs my hand to his fly. ₁₅

Songs went with whichever boy it was. "Sugar Magnolia" was Tim, with the line "Rolling in the rushes/down by the riverside." With "Darkness Darkness," I'd picture Philip with his long hair. Hearing "Under My Thumb" there'd be the smell of Jamie's suede jacket.

We hid in the listening rooms during study hall. With a record cover over the door's window, the teacher on duty couldn't look in. I came out flushed and heady and back at the dorm was surprised how red my lips were in the mirror.

One weekend at Simon's brother's, we stayed inside all day with the shades down, in bed, then went out to Store 24 to get some ice cream. He stood at the magazine rack and read through *MAD* while I got butterscotch sauce, craving something sweet.

I could do some things well. Some things I was good at, like math or painting or even sports, but the second a boy put his arm around me, I forgot about wanting to do anything else, which felt like a relief at first until it became like sinking into a muck.

It was different for a girl.   20

When we were little, the brothers next door tied up our ankles. They held the door of the goat house and wouldn't let us out till we showed them our underpants. Then they'd forget about being after us and when we played whiffle ball, I'd be just as good as they were.

Then it got to be different. Just because you have on a short skirt, they yell from the cars, slowing down for a while, and if you don't look, they screech off and call you a bitch.

"What's the matter with me?" they say, point-blank.

Or else, "Why won't you go out with me? I'm not asking you to get married," about to get mad.

Or it'd be, trying to be reasonable, in a regular voice, "Listen, I just want to   25 have a good time."

So I'd go because I couldn't think of something to say back that wouldn't be obvious, and if you go out with them, you sort of have to do something.

I sat between Mack and Eddie in the front seat of the pickup. They were having a fight about something. I've a feeling about me.

Certain nights you'd feel a certain surrender, maybe if you'd had wine. The surrender would be forgetting yourself and you'd put your nose to his neck and feel like a squirrel, safe, at rest, in a restful dream. But then you'd start to slip from that and the dark would come in and there'd be a cave. You make out the dim shape of the windows and feel yourself become a cave, filled absolutely with air, or with a sadness that wouldn't stop.

Teenage years. You know just what you're doing and don't see the things that start to get in the way.

Lots of boys, but never two at the same time. One was plenty to keep you   30 in a state. You'd start to see a boy and something would rush over you like a fast storm cloud and you couldn't possibly think of anyone else. Boys took it differently. Their eyes perked up at any little number that walked by. You'd act like you weren't noticing.

The joke was that the school doctor gave out the pill like aspirin. He didn't ask you anything. I was fifteen. We had a picture of him in assembly, holding up an IUD shaped like a T. Most girls were on the pill, if anything, because they couldn't handle a diaphragm. I kept the dial in my top drawer like my mother and thought of her each time I tipped out the yellow tablets in the morning before chapel.

If they were too shy, I'd be more so. Andrew was nervous. We stayed up with his family album, sharing a pack of Old Golds. Before it got light, we turned on the TV. A man was explaining how to plant seedlings. His mouth jerked to the side in a tic. Andrew thought it was a riot and kept imitating him. I laughed to be polite. When we finally dozed off, he dared to put his arm around me, but that was it.

You wait till they come to you. With half fright, half swagger, they stand one step down. They dare to touch the button on your coat then lose their nerve and quickly drop their hand so you — you'd do anything for them. You touch their cheek.

The girls sit around in the common room and talk about boys, smoking their heads off.
"What are you complaining about?" says Jill to me when we talk about problems.
"Yeah," says Giddy. "You always have a boyfriend."
I look at them and think, As if.

I thought the worst thing anyone could call you was a cock-teaser. So, if you flirted, you had to be prepared to go through with it. Sleeping with someone was perfectly normal once you had done it. You didn't really worry about it. But there were other problems. The problems had to do with something else entirely.

Mack was during the hottest summer ever recorded. We were renting a house on an island with all sorts of other people. No one slept during the heat wave, walking around the house with nothing on which we were used to because of the nude beach. In the living room, Eddie lay on top of a coffee table to cool off. Mack and I, with the bedroom door open for air, sweated and sweated all night.
"I can't take this," he said at three A.M. "I'm going for a swim." He and some guys down the hall went to the beach. The heat put me on edge. I sat on a cracked chest by the open window and smoked and smoked till I felt even worse, waiting for something — I guess for him to get back.

One was on a camping trip in Colorado. We zipped our sleeping bags together, the coyotes' hysterical chatter far away. Other couples murmured in other tents. Paul was up before sunrise, starting a fire for breakfast. He wasn't much of a talker in the daytime. At night, his hand leafed about in the hair at my neck.

There'd be times when you overdid it. You'd get carried away. All the next day, you'd be in a total fog, delirious, absent-minded, crossing the street and nearly getting run over.

The more girls a boy has, the better. He has a bright look, having reaped fruits, blooming. He stalks around, sure-shouldered, and you have the feeling he's got more in him, a fatter heart, more stories to tell. For a girl, with each boy it's as though a petal gets plucked each time.

Then you start to get tired. You begin to feel diluted, like watered-down stew.

Oliver came skiing with us. We lolled by the fire after everyone had gone to   45
bed. Each creak you'd think was someone coming downstairs. The silver loop bracelet he gave me had been a present from his girlfriend before.

On vacations, we went skiing, or you'd go south if someone invited you. Some people had apartments in New York that their families hardly ever used. Or summer houses, or older sisters. We always managed to find someplace to go.

We made the plan at coffee hour. Simon snuck out and met me at Main Gate after lights-out. We crept to the chapel and spent the night in the balcony. He tasted like onions from a submarine sandwich.

The boys are one of two ways: either they can't sit still or they don't move. In front of the TV, they won't budge. On weekends they play touch football while we sit on the sidelines, picking blades of grass to chew on, and watch. We're always watching them run around. We shiver in the stands, knocking our boots together to keep our toes warm, and they whizz across the ice, chopping their sticks around the puck. When they're in the rink, they refuse to look at you, only eyeing each other beneath low helmets. You cheer for them but they don't look up, even if it's a face-off when nothing's happening, even if they're doing drills before any game has started at all.

Dancing under the pick tent, he bent down and whispered in my ear. We slipped away to the lawn on the other side of the hedge. Much later, as he was leaving the buffet with two plates of eggs and sausage, I saw the grass stains on the knees of his white pants.

Tim's was shaped like a banana, with a graceful curve to it. They're all   50
different. Willie's like a bunch of walnuts when nothing was happening, another's as thin as a thin hot dog. But it's like faces; you're never really surprised.

Still, you're not sure what to expect.

I look into his face and he looks back. I look into his eyes and they look back at mine. Then they look down at my mouth so I look at his mouth, then back to his eyes then, backing up, at his whole face. I think, Who? Who are you? His head tilts to one side.

I say, "Who are you?"

"What do you mean?"

"Nothing." 55

I look at his eyes again, deeper. Can't tell who he is, what he thinks.

"What?" he says. I look at his mouth.

"I'm just wondering," I say and go wandering across his face. Study the chin line. It's shaped like a persimmon.

"Who are you? What are you thinking?"

He says, "What the hell are you talking about?" 60

Then they get mad after, when you say enough is enough. After, when it's easier to explain that you don't want to. You wouldn't dream of saying that maybe you weren't really ready to in the first place.

Gentle Eddie. We waded into the sea, the waves round and plowing in, buffalo-headed, slapping our thighs. I put my arms around his freckled shoulders and he held me up, buoyed by the water, and rocked me like a sea shell.

I had no idea whose party it was, the apartment jam-packed, stepping over people in the hallway. The room with the music was practically empty, the bare floor, me in red shoes. This fellow slides onto one knee and takes me around the waist and we rock to jazzy tunes, with my toes pointing heavenward, and waltz and spin and dip to "Smoke Gets in Your Eyes" or "I'll Love You Just for Now." He puts his head to my chest, runs a sweeping hand down my inside thigh and we go loose-limbed and sultry and as smooth as silk and I stamp my red heels and he takes me into a swoon. I never saw him again after that but I thought, I could have loved that one.

You wonder how long you can keep it up. You begin to feel as if you're showing through, like a bathroom window that only lets in grey light, the kind you can't see out of.

They keep coming around. Johnny drives up at Easter vacation from Balti- 65 more and I let him in the kitchen with everyone sound asleep. He has friends waiting in the car.

"What are you, crazy? It's pouring out there," I say.

"It's okay," he says. "They understand."

So he gets some long kisses from me, against the refrigerator, before he goes because I hate those girls who push away a boy's face as if she were made out of Ivory soap, as if she's that much greater than he is.

The note on my cubby told me to see the headmaster. I had no idea for what. He had received complaints about my amorous displays on the town green. It was Willie that spring. The headmaster told me he didn't care what I did but that Casey Academy had a reputation to uphold in the town. He lowered his glasses on his nose. "We've got twenty acres of woods on this campus," he said. "If you want to smooch with your boyfriend, there are twenty acres for you to do it out of the public eye. You read me?"

Everybody'd get weekend permissions for different places, then we'd all go   70
to someone's house whose parents were away. Usually there'd be more boys than girls. We raided the liquor closet and smoked pot at the kitchen table and you'd never know who would end up where, or with whom. There were always disasters. Ceci got bombed and cracked her head open on the banister and needed stitches. Then there was the time Wendel Blair walked through the picture window at the Lowes' and got slashed to ribbons.

He scared me. In bed, I didn't dare look at him. I lay back with my eyes closed, luxuriating because he knew all sorts of expert angles, his hands never fumbling, going over my whole body, pressing the hair up and off the back of my head, giving an extra hip shove, as if to say *There.* I parted my eyes slightly, keeping the screen of my lashes low because it was too much to look at him, his mouth loose and pink and parted, his eyes looking through my forehead, or kneeling up, looking through my throat. I was ashamed but couldn't look him in the eye.

You wonder about things feeling a little off-kilter. You begin to feel like a piece of pounded veal.

At boarding school, everyone gets depressed. We go in and see the housemother, Mrs. Gunther. She got married when she was eighteen. Mr. Gunther was her high school sweetheart, the only boyfriend she ever had.
"And you knew you wanted to marry him right off?" we ask her.
She smiles and says, "Yes."   75
"They always want something from you," says Jill, complaining about her boyfriend.
"Yeah," says Giddy. "You always feel like you have to deliver something."
"You do," says Mrs. Gunther. "Babies."

After sex, you curl up like a shrimp, something deep inside you ruined, slammed in a place that sickens at slamming, and slowly you fill up with an overwhelming sadness, an elusive gaping worry. You don't try to explain it, filled with the knowledge that it's nothing after all, everything filling up finally and absolutely with death. After the briskness of loving, loving stops. And you roll over with death stretched out alongside you like a feather boa, or a snake, light as air, and you . . . you don't even ask for anything or try to say something to him because it's obviously your own damn fault. You haven't been able to — to what? To open your heart. You open your legs but can't, or don't dare anymore, to open your heart.

It starts this way: 80
You stare into their eyes. They flash like all the stars are out. They look at you seriously, their eyes at a low burn and their hands no matter what starting off shy and with such a gentle touch that the only thing you can do is take that tenderness and let yourself be swept away. When, with one attentive finger they tuck the hair behind your ear, you —

You do everything they want. Then comes after. After when they don't look at you. They scratch their balls, stare at the ceiling. Or if they do turn, their gaze is altogether changed. They are surprised. They turn casually to look at you, distracted, and get a mild distracted surprise. You're gone. Their blank look tells you that the girl they were fucking is not there anymore. You seem to have disappeared.

Considerations for Critical Thinking and Writing

1. FIRST RESPONSE. What do you think of the narrator? Why? Do you agree with the definition the story offers for *lust*?
2. Do you think that the narrator's depiction of male and female responses to sex are accurate? Explain why or why not.
3. How effective is the narrator's description of teenage sex? What do you think she means when she says "You know just what you're doing and don't see the things that start to get in the way" (para. 29)?
4. What is the story's conflict? Explain whether you think the conflict is resolved.
5. Discuss the story's tone. Is it what you expected from the title?
6. What do you think is the theme of "Lust"? Does its style carry its theme?
7. What is the primary setting for the story? What does it reveal about the nature of the narrator's economic and social class?
8. In a *Publisher's Weekly* interview (November 6, 1992), Minot observed, "There's more fictional material in unhappiness and disappointment and frustration than there is in happiness. Who was it said, 'Happiness is like a blank page'?" What do you think of this observation?

Connections to Other Selections

1. Compare the treatments of youthful sexuality in "Lust" and David Updike's "Summer" (p. 169). Do you prefer one story over the other? Why?
2. Compare the narrators of "Lust" and Alice Munro's "An Ounce of Cure" (p. 434). What significant similarities and differences do you see between the narrators?
3. Write an essay explaining the sort of advice the narrator of Fay Weldon's "IND AFF, or Out of Love in Sarajevo" (p. 153) might give to the narrator of "Lust." You might try writing this in the form of a letter.

GEORGE BOWERING (B. 1935)

Born in Penticon, British Columbia, George Bowering earned degrees at the University of British Columbia and has taught at Simon Fraser University. A poet, fiction writer, and literary critic, he is a two-time winner of the Governor General's Award — for poetry (1969) and fiction (1980). Among his collections of poems are *Touch: Selected Poems 1960–1970* (1971), *Particular Accidents: Selected Poems* (1980), and *West Window: Selected Poetry by George Bowering* (1982). His novels include *Burning Water* (1980), *Shoot!*

(1984), and *Caprice* (1988). He has also published a collection of critical pieces, *The Mask in Place: Essays on Fiction in North America* (1983).

A Short Story   1983

Setting

It was that slightly disappointing moment in the year when the cherry blossoms have been blown off the trees, or shrunken to brown lace out of which little hard green pebbles are beginning to appear. The orchardists were running tractors between the rows of trees, disking the late spring weeds into the precious topsoil left there by the glacier that long ago receded from the desert valley.

Starlings were growing impatient with the season, tired of competing for scraps behind the Safeway store in town, eager for those high blue days when the cherries would be plump & pink, when they could laugh at the sunburnt men in high gum boots, who would again try to deceive them with fake cannons & old shirts stretcht between the branches.

High over Dog Lake a jet contrail was widening & drifting south. The orchards on the west bank were in shadow already, & sunlight sparkled off windows of the new housing development on the other shore. The lake was spotted with brown weeds dying underwater, where the newest poison had been dumpt by the government two weeks before.

Evening swallows were already dipping & soaring around the Jacobsen house, nabbing insects in their first minutes of activity after a warm day's sleep. The house was like many of the remodelled orchard homes in the southern part of the valley, its shiplap sides now covered with pastel aluminum, metallic screen doors here & there, a stone chimney marking the outside end of the living-room. Fifteen years ago the living-room had been used only when relatives from other valley towns came to visit. Now it was panelled with knotty cedar, animal heads looking across at one another from the walls, & the Jacobsens sat there after all the evening chores were done, watching Spokane television in color, and reading this week's paper, or perhaps having some toast & raspberry jam.

The rug was a pastel shade fairly close to that of the outside surface. The 5 Jacobsens lived with it, though neither of them particularly liked it. One of them had, once, when it was new; the other never thought of offering an opinion, or holding one.

Characters

The Jacobsens did not discuss things. They spoke short sentences to one another in the course of a card game, or while deciding which re-run was more worth watching on the mammoth television set parkt under a deer head on the west wall of the living-room.

"We haven't seen this Carol show, have we?" suggested Mrs Jacobsen. "I think it must have been on the night we played bridge with Stu & Ronnie."

"No, we saw it," said Mr Jacobsen from behind his sixteen-page newspaper. "This is the one where her & Harvey are on that jet plane that gets highjackt to South America."

"Sky-jackt."

"The same thing. But if you want to watch it again, go ahead."   10

"I cant remember a sky-jack one."

"Go ahead. I'll probably fall asleep in the middle, anyway," said Mr Jacobsen.

Art Jacobsen was tired every night. As soon as the after-supper card game was over, & his short legs were up on the aquamarine hassock, his eyes would begin to droop. He was 61 years old, & still working eleven hours a day in the orchard. Like most valley orchardists, he wore a shirt only during the early hours of the morning, when the dew was still on every leaf. His body was tanned & muscled, but it was getting more rectangular every year.

Audrey Jacobsen was ten years younger. She had only recently taken to coloring her hair, often a kind of brownish-red she mistakenly remembered from her youth. Her first husband used to tease her about having red hair, though it wasnt true. By the time that Ordie Michaels had died & Art Jacobsen had started courting her on rainy days, her hair was a good plain brown, usually under a kerchief.

She'd taken to wearing the kerchief, as all the women did, while sorting   15 fruit at the Coop packing-house. By the time Donna was five, Audrey had assumed the habit of wearing it all the time, except when she went for drives with Art Jacobsen.

They had been watching Carol on television for five years now, & she didn't know whether she liked the show.

It is not that I know all about the Jacobsens & Donna Michaels before I start telling you about them. I am what they call omniscient, all right, but there isnt any Jacobsen family until I commit them to this medium. I have some hazy ideas or images, rather, of their story, a sort of past & a present, I suppose, but really, for me the story is waiting somewhere in the future. Or I should say that I'm waiting for a time in the future when I will have the time to come to it, here. As a matter of fact, you dont have to, now, wait as long for it as I do.

So I am in the position ascribed to the narrator with the totally omniscient point of view. A know-it-all. Dont you believe it! "God-like." Dont you believe it!

For instance, I've been thinking about writing this story for two years. Just a month ago I began to imagine a woman visiting her mother & stepfather at their orchard home, & that common emotional violence later on. But I just got the names while I was writing the first parts of the story, & I didn't imagine the Jacobsen house near the lake — I thought it would be 40 kilometers farther south.

Do I have to mention that there is something difficult to explain about a   20 third-person omniscient narrative having all these "I's" in it? Point of view dictates distance. Well, I would like to keep you closer than your usual "god" will allow (except for people such as yourself, Leda) (no, that's not what I'm trying to do to you, reader: dont be so suspicious).

From up here I can see the Jacobsen house as a little square surrounded by trees that have nearly lost their blossoms & are just producing leaves. I have good eyes; I need them to see all that thru the drifting jet contrail.

By the way, have you noticed that when the narrator speaks in the first person, he makes you the second person? When he speaks of others in the third person, you are perhaps standing beside him, only the parallax preventing your seeing exactly what he is seeing. That makes for a greater distance produced by the first-person narrative. You must have noticed that.

Protagonist

Donna Michaels, an attractive honey-blonde in her early twenties, was about four kilometers from the Jacobsen house, driving along the lakeside road in her dented Morris Minor convertible. She had already gone thru her rite of passage between innocent childhood & knowledgeable maturity, involving strong Freudian implications. Now she was driving thru a warm valley evening, wishing that she had come a week ago, when the cherry blossoms were still at the beginning of their decline.

She had not been home during blossom time for seven years, & perhaps this more than anything else told her that she had really ceast to be a valley kid, that she was a Coast person. Looking to her right she could see, even in the shadows made by the hills over the water, splotches of brown weeds under the surface of the lake. A part of her that still wanted to be a valley person was hurt by that.

She thought about taking a Valium before she got there, only two kilome- 25 ters to go now. It was not really the time to appear. She should have arrived while Art was still out in the orchard, so she could have a calm talk with her mother. When Art was there, making his blustery remarks or criticisms about her language, her mother could be depended on to remain silent, just as she had always done during family hassles, just as she had done then.

"I love him, Donna. What am I supposed to do?" she had said.

"More than you love me?" That newcomer.

"I *chose* him."

That was the last time her mother had ever said anything so devastatingly open.

She got out of the car & took a Valium. One gets adept at swallowing 30 them without water. She was mildly surprised that she was walking slowly toward the single little ponderosa pine that used to be her going-to-be-alone place in the far corner of their orchard. It had perhaps grown four inches taller. Looking, farther up, she could see Star Bright. She made a trivial wish & walkt slowly back to the dusty car.

What a beautiful sight she was, with her long legs & summer dress, sunglasses percht on top of her short feathery blondish hair.

Symbolism

Donna got back into the dented Morris Minor, & before she let the clutch out, she unaccountably thought about the animal heads protruding from her stepfather's walls. The first time she had seen one, she had gone to the room next door, to see whether the elk's body stuck out from that side. What had ever been done with the bodies, she wondered now. Were they discarded, left on the forest floor for the delectation of ants? Did the family eat them? She couldn't remember eating mountain goat or moose, & she had been a picky eater as a child.

She decided that whatever had been done with the torso & legs, Art was only really interested in the trophy. He talkt about nature a lot, but he was quite comfortable under the stare of the big glass eyes.

Her dog Bridey passed away after a fit when she was twelve. Quickly, before he would have a chance to take her to the taxidermist, Donna put the heavy & limp body along with an adult's shovel into a wheelbarrow & pusht it for half an hour thru the crumbling earth, to the ponderosa. There she wasted no time looking at Bridey's fur & tight-closed eyes. She dug a deep hole & dropt her in & covered her up, without looking. She left no marker. She knew where Bridey was, & that was all that was necessary.

Now, she reflected, looking at the sagebrush growing around her tree, they probably knew too, he probably saw the wheel tracks the next morning. 35

She let out the clutch & drove the last kilometer slowly, having pulled on the lights. Just in time, a mother quail & her five little ones raced in a line to the safety of the roadside weeds. She smiled as she imagined the mother there, counting them.

Then she was at the turn just before their driveway, where the truck & the new Toyota were parkt in a sharp vee. People here along Rawleigh Road never pulled their drapes. Thru the window she could see Mr & Mrs Jacobsen, an over-coloured Carol, & a deer she used to call Bambi, first childishly, then later to needle her stepfather.

Her car's wheels crruncht over the driveway. Before she got out she did up her two top buttons.

Conflict

Donna had driven 400 kilometers to be there, but she didn't want to go inside the house. Of course in a setting such as this, they would know that somebody had driven up the gravel driveway, & one of them, probably her mother, would be walking to the door at this moment.

Donna wanted to be with her mother, & especially because she never wrote letters home. She did not even imagine writing "Mrs A. Jacobsen" on an envelope. She felt as if, yes, she still loved her mother, that strange older woman in polyester slacks, though they had not once spoken to each other on the telephone since Jacobsen had mounted her as his casual season's trophy. What ambiguity in the delivery of the thought. When it was accomplisht, & all three knew, what depressing decisions & solitudes. 40

Donna could not stay in that family where her first love, her first world face, lost all hope & fell in, decided to stay with the bringer of death. What polluted language in the formerly unchallenged eden. Why? How, rather.

"But I chose him. I made my choice."

"Do you love him? Can you?"

"I chose him."

She was not a woman then, but she was not a valley girl, either. She left Dog Lake, she had to, & there was no question but the city on the coast, several ruinous jobs & some solitary education. 45

Now the door opened & it was Audrey who was illuminated by the porch light. Donna was momentarily ashamed with disappointment that her mother, Mrs Michaels, was not the picture of a defeated lustreless farm wife, the sensitive buffeted by life, such as one expected to find in the Canadian novels she had been reading.

"Donna! For the Lord's sake! Why didnt you tell us you were coming? Come in, you rascal," the woman said, her arms outstretcht as if offering the red knitting she had been doing while watching television.

Donna held her mother's elbows & kissed her nose as she felt the screen door bat against her rear. Her mother chattered with a little confusion as the pretty blonde deposited her purse & a book & something wrapt in party paper on the telephone table.

"Well, well," said Art Jacobsen, looking up from his paper, his feet still stretcht out on the hassock.

Dialogue

"I wish I'd gotten here while the blossoms were in full bloom," said 50 Donna. It was the perfect little bit of business to get thru the awkwardness of their surprise.

"Oh, we had a wonderful year for blossoms," said her mother. "When a breeze came up the whole valley smelled like a garden."

"It *is* a garden," said Donna, getting herself a cup of coffee from the pot on the stove. She came back thru the arch into the living-room, where her mother was still standing with the knitting in her hands. "At least that's how we Coast people think of it."

Art shook his paper to a new page.

"It's not the blossoms that count. It's the bees."

"The workers, you mean," said Donna, a little edge on her voice. She sat 55 down with her coffee, not looking at him.

"Yeah, the queen sits at home, getting fatter & fatter, while the workers bring her the honey," said Art, his eyes looking at a news photo of the local skeet-shooting champs.

"Have you had any supper, dear?" Audrey piped in.

"Yes, I stopt at the Princeton bus station cafe, for old times sake," said Donna.

That was a nice shot. It was there that she had abandoned Art's truck that night, with the keys in the dash. She'd taken the bus to Vancouver with no baggage, not even clean underwear. Just two apples & her purse.

Art didn't say a word now. 60

"Well, well," said Audrey Jacobsen.

There was a silence. Even the knitting-needles crost & opened without a sound. It was pitch dark outside. A mirrored deer lookt in from between two young Lombardy poplars.

"How are all your aches & pains, Mom?" Donna askt at last, idly looking at snapshots from a glass bowl on the table beside her chair. Carol was over, & Art raised his remote control & shot the set off.

"Oh, the osteopath in Penticton said I did something to my lower spine when I was a girl, & I can never expect to be a hundred percent."

"Does that mean you're not all there?" askt Art. 65

Flashback

When he seemed absolutely ready to give it up, give up on it, to settle for some costly talk then, she offered him a cigarette, which he took politely, & lit one herself. It was the only sort of occasion upon which she smoked, anything. They were always grateful, the talkers, when she by her gestures allowed them a certain comfort, a freedom from embarrassment.

"Thank you," he said, & lay on his back beside her, carefully sharing the ashtray she kept on her belly.

"You needn't feel badly." Her voice was soft & sure, caring & casual, it seemed. "You might be surprised how often it happens. You had a lot to drink, I would imagine, it was only enough to make you think you wanted me. Happens quite a lot."

"No, that's not it. Well, it might be a little, but that's not really it. It's . . ."

She did not offer the interruption he was waiting for. She just smoked her cigarette. She butted it out in the ashtray, & handed the ashtray to him. So he had something to do with his free hand.

"It's just that you are about exactly the age of my daughter," he said.

"No kidding," she said, with a twiggy edge to her voice, & that was his first hint that it was time to go back to his hotel.

Foreshadowing

After he had left, she got the scissors & clipped her toenails. Having done five, she lay back & imagined the john walking back to his hotel. He did not seem like the taxi-taking kind.

She pictured him lying on her, brought by her to the margin of success. Then she yanked the scissors toward her, fetching a jolt as they sank into the flesh of his back. It was not an old movie on midnight television. The points of her scissors were just below the joining of her ribcage, forcing the skin a little.

I wonder whether I could just throw a few clothes into the car & drive to Montreal, she thought.

Maybe you could work your way across the country, she replied.

She clipped five toenails again. They were the same ones.

Plot

The spare bedroom of the Jacobsen house was also a kind of store-room. It contained a gun-rack in which one could find a pump-action shotgun, a .22 caliber repeater rifle, an old .303 that once belonged to the Canadian Army, a .44 handgun in a tooled holster, a 30-30 with a scope sight, & a collector's .30 caliber machine-gun with a plugged barrel. This is where Donna was, taking off her light cardigan & shoes, finding the toothbrush & dental floss in the bottom of her big-city street bag, looking at herself, untanned, in the vanity mirror. A severed goat head lookt over her shoulder.

Thru two walls she could hear the Jacobsens disputing. Art's voice rose & rose, & at the end of a declarative sentence fragment it uttered the word "slut," followed by an exclamation point.

One would expect the ammunition to be lockt up, & it was, in a cabinet with glass-panel doors. Donna shook the pillow out of one of the pillowcases, wrapt the pillowcase around her fist, & puncht one of the glass panels three times, each time with greater force.

The male voice rose to the word "hell!" & stopt. A door banged against a wall, & heavy footsteps approacht. Donna threw the pillowcase onto the bed beside her sweater. When Art propelled the bedroom door open, Donna was pointing a loaded shotgun at his head.

Art backt out of the bedroom & walkt backward all the way to the living-room. There he observed a slight movement of the dark holes he had wiped clean just the night before, & sat down in his favorite chair. He was on top of Audrey's knitting, but he felt convinced that he should not bring attention to such a minor problem.

Audrey Jacobsen, usually a chatterbox, found it hard to find the words she should say.

She said, "Donna . . ."

It was very frightening that Donna did not say a word. Art looked de- 85
pressed. He was a heavy man in his chair. Donna blew out her breath.

"For God's sake, girl, that's my husband!"

Donna did not breathe in.

"He's my husband, he's all I have!"

Donna turned a smooth quick arc, & shot her mother's face off.

Theme

Donna walkt from the house & into the orchard, the shotgun still dan- 90
gling. She had no shoes on. No-one followed her, & she did not look behind. She was walking between two rows of cherry trees, so that when a quick hard breeze came around a rock outface it blew a snow of exhausted blossoms over her head.

Donna walkt down the slope, not flinching when a clacking sprinkler spun slowly & soakt her dress from the waist down. It was really dark out now, & she could see the lights of the retirement village on the far side of the lake.

The gun had made a dreadful noise. But now the night life was speaking again, crickets nearby & frogs from down by the lake. They were calling each other to come & do it.

Donna walkt till she came to the dirt road with the row of couchgrass down the middle, & followed it till she arrived at her ponderosa. There she sat down with her back to its narrow trunk, & dropt the shotgun to the dry ground. The sky was filled with bright stars that seemed to have edges, & black behind them. One never saw anything like that from the streets in Vancouver. She thought of the universality speaking thru her condition.

Nearby, her dog lay curled, waiting for her to signal something to her. But she ignored her, as she fought to remember what had happened in the last hour, or was it some years? An airline jet with powerful landing lights appeared from the other side of the hills & descended over the lake, heavily pulling back on its fall toward the airstrip at the end.

Now that her eyes were adjusted to the late spring darkness of the valley, 95
she saw a bat flipping from direction to direction above her. She remembered the fear that it might get caught in your hair. Bats dont get caught in your hair.

I'm not very old, Donna thought, I'm not very old & here I am already. She pickt up the shotgun & fired the other barrel, & threw it over the side of the hill.

CONSIDERATIONS FOR CRITICAL THINKING AND WRITING

1. FIRST RESPONSE. Why do you suppose Bowering arranges the story in sections under headings such as Setting, Characters, Protagonist, and so on? What is the effect of this organizing principle on your reading?

2. If you were to go beyond the generic title of "A Short Story," what would you title it? Why?

3. What information do you get from the Setting section that is useful in understanding the story?

4. What do you make of the narrator's discussion of point of view in the Characters section? How does it affect your reading of the story?

5. Describe the Jacobsens' marriage. Do you think they are happy together? Explain your response.

6. Characterize Donna's past. What sort of life has she lived?

7. What is symbolic in the Symbolism section? Are there any other important symbols in the story?

8. What is the conflict in the Conflict section? Is it also the major conflict in the story?

9. What do the Flashback and Foreshadowing sections tell you about Donna?

10. Why does Donna shoot her mother? Explain why you think the shooting is ironic or not.

11. What do you think is the theme of the story? Can it be found tidily wrapped up in the Theme section?

CONNECTIONS TO OTHER SELECTIONS

1. Compare the motives for the killings in this story and in Andre Dubus's "Killings" (p. 81).

2. Write an essay on the narration of "A Short Story" and Tim O'Brien's "How to Tell a True War Story" (p. 555). In what sense is each story, in part, about telling stories?

10

A Study of Three Authors: Nathaniel Hawthorne, Flannery O'Connor, and Alice Munro

The twelve short stories by Nathaniel Hawthorne, Flannery O'Connor, and Alice Munro included in this chapter provide an opportunity to study three major fiction writers in some depth. Getting to know an author's work is similar to developing a friendship with someone: the more encounters, the more intimate the relationship becomes. Familiarity with a writer's concerns and methods in one story can help to illuminate another story. As we become accustomed to someone's voice—a friend's or a writer's—we become attuned to nuances in tone and meaning.

The nuances in Hawthorne's, O'Connor's, and Munro's fiction warrant close analysis. Each of the following works is a unique and absorbing story that rewards additional readings. Although the stories included are not wholly representative of the writer's work, they suggest some of the techniques and concerns that characterize their work. Each grouping of four stories provides a useful context for reading individual stories. Moreover, the works of all three authors invite comparisons and contrasts in their styles and themes. Following each set of four stories are some brief commentaries by and about Hawthorne, O'Connor, and Munro that establish additional contexts for understanding their fiction.

NATHANIEL HAWTHORNE (1804–1864)

Nathaniel Hawthorne once described himself as "the obscurest man of letters in America." During the early years of his career, this self-assessment was mostly accurate, but the publication of *The Scarlet Letter* in 1850 marked the beginning of Hawthorne's reputation as a major American writer. His novels and short stories have entertained and challenged generations of

readers; they have wide appeal because they can be read on many levels. Hawthorne skillfully creates an atmosphere of complexity and ambiguity that makes it difficult to reduce his stories to a simple view of life. The moral and psychological issues that he examines through the conflicts his characters experience are often intricate and mysterious. Readers are frequently made to feel that in exploring Hawthorne's characters they are also encountering some part of themselves.

Hawthorne achieved success as a writer only after a steady and intense struggle. His personal history was hardly conducive to producing a professional writer. Born in Salem, Massachusetts, Hawthorne came from a Puritan family of declining fortunes that prided itself on an energetic pursuit of practical matters such as law and commerce. He never knew his father, a sea captain who died in Dutch Guiana when Hawthorne was only four years old, but he did have a strong imaginative sense of an early ancestor, who as a Puritan judge persecuted Quakers, and of a later ancestor, who was a judge during the Salem witchcraft trials. His forebears seemed to haunt Hawthorne, so that in some ways he felt more involved in the past than in the present.

In "The Custom-House," the introduction to *The Scarlet Letter,* Hawthorne considers himself in relation to his severe Puritan ancestors:

> No aim, that I have ever cherished, would they recognize as laudable; no success of mine . . . would they deem otherwise than worthless, if not positively disgraceful. "What is he?" murmurs one gray shadow of my forefathers to the other. "A writer of story-books! What kind of a business in life, — what mode of glorifying God, or being serviceable to mankind in his day and generation, — may that be? Why, the degenerate fellow might as well have been a fiddler!" Such are the compliments bandied between my great-grandsires and myself, across the gulf of time! And yet, let them scorn me as they will, strong traits of their nature have intertwined with mine.

Hawthorne's sense of what his forebears might think of his work caused him to worry that the utilitarian world was more real and important than his imaginative creations. This issue became a recurring theme in his work.

Despite the Puritan strain in Hawthorne's sensibilities and his own deep suspicion that a literary vocation was not serious or productive work, Hawthorne was determined to become a writer. He found encouragement at Bowdoin College in Maine and graduated in 1825 with a class that included the poet Henry Wadsworth Longfellow and Franklin Pierce, who would be elected president of the United States in the early 1850s. After graduation

PHOTO ABOVE: *Nathaniel Hawthorne in an undated photograph, probably taken — judging from his hollow cheeks and gray hair — near the end of his life.*

Hawthorne returned to his mother's house in Salem, where for the next twelve years he read New England history as well as writers such as John Milton, William Shakespeare, and John Bunyan. During this time he lived a relatively withdrawn life devoted to developing his literary art. Hawthorne wrote and revised stories as he sought a style that would express his creative energies. Many of these early efforts were destroyed when they did not meet his high standards. His first novel, *Fanshawe*, was published anonymously in 1828; it concerns a solitary young man who fails to realize his potential and dies young. Hawthorne very nearly succeeded in reclaiming and destroying all the published copies of this work. It was not attributed to the author until after his death; not even his wife was aware that he had written it. The stories eventually published as *Twice-Told Tales* (1837) represent work that was carefully revised and survived Hawthorne's critical judgments.

Writing did not provide an adequate income, so like nearly all nineteenth-century American writers, Hawthorne had to take on other employment. He worked in the Boston Custom House from 1839 through 1840 to save money to marry Sophia Peabody, but he lost that politically appointed job when administrations changed. In 1841 he lived at Brook Farm, a utopian community founded by idealists who hoped to combine manual labor with art and philosophy. Finding that monotonous physical labor left little time for thinking and writing, Hawthorne departed after seven months. The experience failed to improve his financial situation, but it did eventually serve as the basis for a novel, *The Blithedale Romance* (1852).

Married in the summer of 1842, Hawthorne and his wife moved to the Old Manse in Concord, Massachusetts, where their neighbors included Ralph Waldo Emerson, Henry David Thoreau, Amos Bronson Alcott, and other writers and thinkers who contributed to the lively literary environment of that small town. Although Hawthorne was on friendly terms with these men, his skepticism concerning human nature prevented him from sharing either their optimism or their faith in radical reform of individuals or society. Hawthorne's view of life was chastened by a sense of what he called in "Wakefield" the "iron tissue of necessity." His sensibilities were more akin to Herman Melville's. When Melville and Hawthorne met while Hawthorne was living in the Berkshires of western Massachusetts, they responded to each other intensely. Melville admired the "power of blackness" he discovered in Hawthorne's writings and dedicated *Moby-Dick* to him.

During the several years he lived in the Old Manse, Hawthorne published a second collection of *Twice-Told Tales* (1842) and additional stories in *Mosses from an Old Manse* (1846). To keep afloat financially, he worked in the Salem Custom House from 1846 until 1849, when he again lost his job through a change in administrations. This time, however, he discovered that by leaving the oppressive materialism of the Custom House he found more energy to write: "So little adapted is the atmosphere of a Custom House to the delicate harvest of fancy and sensibility, that, had I remained there through ten Presidencies yet to come, I doubt whether the tale of

'The Scarlet Letter' would ever have been brought before the public. My imagination was a tarnished mirror [there.]" Free of the Custom House, Hawthorne was at the height of his creativity and productivity during the early 1850s. In addition to *The Scarlet Letter* and *The Blithedale Romance,* he wrote *The House of the Seven Gables* (1851); *The Snow-Image, and Other Twice-Told Tales* (1852); a campaign biography of his Bowdoin classmate, *The Life of Franklin Pierce* (1852); and two collections of stories for children, *A Wonder Book* (1852) and *Tanglewood Tales* (1853).

Hawthorne's financial situation improved during the final decade of his life. In 1853 his friend President Pierce appointed him to the U.S. consulship in Liverpool, where he remained for the next four years. Following a tour of Europe from 1858 to 1860, Hawthorne and his family returned to Concord, and he published *The Marble Faun* (1860), his final completed work of fiction. He died while traveling through New Hampshire with ex-President Pierce.

Hawthorne's stories are much more complex than the melodramatic but usually optimistic fiction published in many magazines contemporary to him. Instead of cheerfully confirming public values and attitudes, his work tends to be dark and brooding. Modern readers remain responsive to Hawthorne's work — despite the fact that his nineteenth-century style takes some getting used to — because his psychological themes are as fascinating as they are disturbing. The range of his themes is not broad, but their treatment is remarkable for its insights.

Hawthorne wrote about individuals who suffer from inner conflicts caused by sin, pride, untested innocence, hidden guilt, perverse secrecy, cold intellectuality, and isolation. His characters are often consumed by their own passions, whether those passions are motivated by an obsession with goodness or evil. He looks inside his characters and reveals to us that portion of their hearts, minds, and souls that they keep from the world and even from themselves. This emphasis accounts for the private, interior, and sometimes gloomy atmosphere in Hawthorne's works. His stories rarely end on a happy note because the questions his characters raise are almost never completely answered. Rather than positing solutions to the problems and issues his characters encounter, Hawthorne leaves us with ambiguities suggesting that experience cannot always be fully understood and controlled. Beneath the surface appearances in his stories lurk ironies and shifting meanings that point to many complex truths instead of a single simple moral.

The following four Hawthorne stories provide an opportunity to study this writer in some depth. These stories are not intended to be entirely representative of the 120 or so that Hawthorne wrote, but they do offer some sense of the range of his techniques and themes. Hawthorne's fictional world of mysterious incidents and sometimes bizarre characters increases in meaning the more his stories are read in the context of one another.

CHRONOLOGY

1804	Born on July 4 in Salem, Massachusetts.
1808	Hawthorne's father, a sea captain, dies in Surinam, Dutch Guiana, leaving the family dependent on relatives.
1821–25	Attends Bowdoin College in Maine. Franklin Pierce (later to become president) and Henry Wadsworth Longfellow are classmates. Graduates eighteenth in a class of thirty-eight.
1828	Publishes *Fanshawe: A Tale* anonymously at his own expense.
1830–37	Publishes numerous stories in periodicals anonymously or pseudonymously, collected in *Twice-Told Tales*.
1838	Becomes engaged to Sophia Peabody.
1839–40	Works in Boston Custom House.
1841	From April to November, lives at the utopian Brook Farm Community.
1842–45	Marries (eventually has three children) and lives at the Old Manse in Concord, Massachusetts, where he meets Ralph Waldo Emerson and Henry David Thoreau.
1844	Publishes his second collection of stories, *Mosses from an Old Manse*.
1846–49	Works as a surveyor in the Salem Custom House.
1850	Publishes *The Scarlet Letter*; becomes a friend of Herman Melville.
1851	Publishes *The House of the Seven Gables; The Snow-Image, and Other Twice-Told Tales;* and *True Stories from History and Biography*.
1852	Publishes *The Blithedale Romance; A Wonder Book for Girls and Boys;* and *The Life of Franklin Pierce*, a campaign biography.
1853–57	Serves as United States Consul at Liverpool on appointment by President Pierce.
1857–59	Lives in Rome and Florence.
1860	Publishes *The Marble Faun*; returns to Concord.
1863	Publishes *Our Old Home: A Series of English Sketches*.
1864	Dies on May 19 at Plymouth, New Hampshire.

Young Goodman Brown — 1835

Young Goodman Brown came forth at sunset into the street at Salem village; but put his head back, after crossing the threshold, to exchange a parting kiss with his young wife. And Faith, as the wife was aptly named, thrust her own pretty head into the street, letting the wind play with the pink ribbons of her cap while she called to Goodman Brown.

"Dearest heart," whispered she, softly and rather sadly, when her lips were close to his ear, "prithee put off your journey until sunrise and sleep in your own bed tonight. A lone woman is troubled with such dreams and such thoughts that she's afeared of herself sometimes. Pray tarry with me this night, dear husband, of all nights in the year."

"My love and my Faith," replied young Goodman Brown, "of all nights in the year, this one night must I tarry away from thee. My journey, as thou callest it, forth and back again, must needs be done 'twixt now and sunrise. What, my sweet, pretty wife, dost thou doubt me already, and we but three months married?"

"Then God bless you!" said Faith, with the pink ribbons; "and may you find all well when you come back."

"Amen!" cried Goodman Brown. "Say thy prayers, dear Faith, and go to 5 bed at dusk, and no harm will come to thee."

So they parted; and the young man pursued his way until, being about to turn the corner by the meeting-house, he looked back and saw the head of Faith still peeping after him with a melancholy air, in spite of her pink ribbons.

"Poor little Faith!" thought he, for his heart smote him. "What a wretch am I to leave her on such an errand! She talks of dreams, too. Methought as she spoke there was trouble in her face, as if a dream had warned her what work is to be done tonight. But no, no; 't would kill her to think it. Well, she's a blessed angel on earth; and after this one night I'll cling to her skirts and follow her to heaven."

With this excellent resolve for the future, Goodman Brown felt himself justified in making more haste on his present evil purpose. He had taken a dreary road, darkened by all the gloomiest trees of the forest, which barely stood aside to let the narrow path creep through, and closed immediately behind. It was all as lonely as could be; and there is this peculiarity in such a solitude, that the traveler knows not who may be concealed by the innumerable trunks and the thick boughs overhead; so that with lonely footsteps he may yet be passing through an unseen multitude.

"There may be a devilish Indian behind every tree," said Goodman Brown to himself; and he glanced fearfully behind him as he added, "What if the devil himself should be at my very elbow!"

His head being turned back, he passed a crook of the road, and, looking 10 forward again, beheld the figure of a man, in grave and decent attire, seated at the foot of an old tree. He arose at Goodman Brown's approach and walked onward side by side with him.

"You are late, Goodman Brown," said he. "The clock of the Old South was striking as I came through Boston, and that is full fifteen minutes agone."

"Faith kept me back a while," replied the young man, with a tremor in his voice, caused by the sudden appearance of his companion, though not wholly unexpected.

It was now deep dusk in the forest, and deepest in that part of it where these two were journeying. As nearly as could be discerned, the second traveler was about fifty years old, apparently in the same rank of life as Goodman Brown, and bearing a considerable resemblance to him, though perhaps more in expression than features. Still they might have been taken for father and son. And yet, though the elder person was as simply clad as the younger, and as simple in manner too, he had an indescribable air of one who knew the world, and who would not have felt abashed at the governor's dinner table or in King

William's court, were it possible that his affairs should call him thither. But the only thing about him that could be fixed upon as remarkable was his staff, which bore the likeness of a great black snake, so curiously wrought that it might almost be seen to twist and wriggle itself like a living serpent. This, of course, must have been an ocular deception, assisted by the uncertain light.

"Come, Goodman Brown," cried his fellow-traveler, "this is a dull pace for the beginning of a journey. Take my staff, if you are so soon weary."

"Friend," said the other, exchanging his slow pace for a full stop, "having kept covenant by meeting thee here, it is my purpose now to return whence I came. I have scruples touching the matter thou wot'st° of." 15

"Sayest thou so?" replied he of the serpent, smiling apart. "Let us walk on, nevertheless, reasoning as we go; and if I convince thee not thou shalt turn back. We are but a little way in the forest yet."

"Too far! too far!" exclaimed the goodman, unconsciously resuming his walk. "My father never went into the woods on such an errand, nor his father before him. We have been a race of honest men and good Christians since the days of the martyrs; and shall I be the first of the name of Brown that ever took this path and kept" —

"Such company, thou wouldst say," observed the elder person, interpreting his pause. "Well said, Goodman Brown! I have been as well acquainted with your family as with ever a one among the Puritans; and that's no trifle to say. I helped your grandfather, the constable, when he lashed the Quaker woman so smartly through the streets of Salem; and it was I that brought your father a pitch-pine knot, kindled at my own hearth, to set fire to an Indian village, in King Philip's war.° They were my good friends, both; and many a pleasant walk have we had along this path, and returned merrily after midnight. I would fain be friends with you for their sake."

"If it be as thou sayest," replied Goodman Brown, "I marvel they never spoke of these matters; or, verily, I marvel not, seeing that the least rumor of the sort would have driven them from New England. We are a people of prayer, and good works to boot, and abide no such wickedness."

"Wickedness or not," said the traveler with the twisted staff, "I have a very general acquaintance here in New England. The deacons of many a church have drunk the communion wine with me; the selectmen of divers towns make me their chairman; and a majority of the Great and General Court are firm supporters of my interest. The governor and I, too — But these are state secrets." 20

"Can this be so?" cried Goodman Brown, with a stare of amazement at his undisturbed companion. "Howbeit, I have nothing to do with the governor and council; they have their own ways, and are no rule for a simple husbandman like me. But, were I to go on with thee, how should I meet the eye of that good old man, our minister, at Salem village? Oh, his voice would make me tremble both Sabbath day and lecture day."

Thus far the elder traveler had listened with due gravity; but now burst into a fit of irrepressible mirth, shaking himself so violently that his snakelike staff actually seemed to wriggle in sympathy.

wot'st: Know.
King Philip's war (1675–76): War between the colonists and an alliance of Indian tribes led by Metacan (also known as Metacomet), leader of the Wampanoags, who was called King Philip by the colonists.

"Ha! ha! ha!" shouted he again and again; then composing himself, "Well, go on, Goodman Brown, go on; but, prithee, don't kill me with laughing."

"Well, then, to end the matter at once," said Goodman Brown, considerably nettled, "there is my wife, Faith. It would break her dear little heart; and I'd rather break my own."

"Nay, if that be the case," answered the other, "e'en go thy ways, Goodman 25 Brown. I would not for twenty old women like the one hobbling before us that Faith should come to any harm."

As he spoke he pointed his staff at a female figure on the path, in whom Goodman Brown recognized a very pious and exemplary dame, who had taught him his catechism in youth, and was still his moral and spiritual adviser, jointly with the minister and Deacon Gookin.

"A marvel, truly that Goody Cloyse should be so far in the wilderness at nightfall," said he. "But with your leave, friend, I shall take a cut through the woods until we have left this Christian woman behind. Being a stranger to you, she might ask whom I was consorting with and whither I was going."

"Be it so," said his fellow-traveler. "Betake you to the woods, and let me keep the path."

Accordingly the young man turned aside, but took care to watch his companion, who advanced softly along the road until he had come within a staff's length of the old dame. She, meanwhile, was making the best of her way, with singular speed for so aged a woman, and mumbling some indistinct words—a prayer, doubtless—as she went. The traveler put forth his staff and touched her withered neck with what seemed the serpent's tail.

"The devil!" screamed the pious old lady. 30

"Then Goody Cloyse knows her old friend?" observed the traveler, confronting her and leaning on his writhing stick.

"Ah, forsooth, and is it your worship indeed?" cried the good dame. "Yea, truly is it, and in the very image of my old gossip, Goodman Brown, the grandfather of the silly fellow that now is. But—would your worship believe it?—my broomstick hath strangely disappeared, stolen, as I suspect, by that unhanged witch, Goody Cory, and that, too, when I was all anointed with the juice of smallage, and cinquefoil, and wolfsbane"—

"Mingled with fine wheat and the fat of a newborn babe," said the shape of old Goodman Brown.

"Ah, your worship knows the recipe," cried the old lady, cackling aloud. "So, as I was saying, being all ready for the meeting, and no horse to ride on, I made up my mind to foot it; for they tell me there is a nice young man to be taken into communion tonight. But now your good worship will lend me your arm, and we shall be there in a twinkling."

"That can hardly be," answered her friend. "I may not spare you my arm, 35 Goody Cloyse; but here is my staff, if you will."

So saying, he threw it down at her feet, where, perhaps, it assumed life, being one of the rods which its owner had formerly lent to the Egyptian magi. Of this fact, however, Goodman Brown could not take cognizance. He had cast up his eyes in astonishment, and, looking down again, beheld neither Goody Cloyse nor the serpentine staff, but his fellow-traveler alone, who waited for him as calmly as if nothing had happened.

"That old woman taught me my catechism," said the young man; and there was a world of meaning in this simple comment.

They continued to walk onward, while the elder traveler exhorted his companion to make good speed and persevere in the path, discoursing so aptly that his arguments seemed rather to spring up in the bosom of his auditor than to be suggested by himself. As they went, he plucked a branch of maple to serve for a walking stick, and began to strip it of the twigs and little boughs, which were wet with evening dew. The moment his fingers touched them they became strangely withered and dried up as with a week's sunshine. Thus the pair proceeded, at a good free pace, until suddenly, in a gloomy hollow of the road, Goodman Brown sat himself down on the stump of a tree and refused to go any farther.

"Friend," he said, stubbornly, "my mind is made up. Not another step will I budge on this errand. What if a wretched old woman do choose to go to the devil when I thought she was going to heaven: is that any reason why I should quit my dear Faith and go after her?"

"You will think better of this by and by," said his acquaintance, composedly. "Sit here and rest yourself a while; and when you feel like moving again, there is my staff to help you along." 40

Without more words, he threw his companion the maple stick, and was as speedily out of sight as if he had vanished into the deepening gloom. The young man sat a few moments by the roadside, applauding himself greatly, and thinking with how clear a conscience he should meet the minister in his morning walk, nor shrink from the eye of good old Deacon Gookin. And what calm sleep would be his that very night, which was to have been spent so wickedly, but so purely and sweetly now, in the arms of Faith! Amidst these pleasant and praiseworthy meditations, Goodman Brown heard the tramp of horses along the road, and deemed it advisable to conceal himself within the verge of the forest, conscious of the guilty purpose that had brought him thither, though now so happily turned from it.

On came the hoof tramps and the voices of the riders, two grave old voices, conversing soberly as they drew near. These mingled sounds appeared to pass along the road, within a few yards of the young man's hiding-place; but, owing doubtless to the depth of the gloom at that particular spot, neither the travelers nor their steeds were visible. Though their figures brushed the small boughs by the wayside, it could not be seen that they intercepted, even for a moment, the faint gleam from the strip of bright sky athwart which they must have passed. Goodman Brown alternately crouched and stood on tiptoe, pulling aside the branches and thrusting forth his head as far as he durst without discerning so much as a shadow. It vexed him the more, because he could have sworn, were such a thing possible, that he recognized the voices of the minister and Deacon Gookin, jogging along quietly, as they were wont to do, when bound to some ordination or ecclesiastical council. While yet within hearing, one of the riders stopped to pluck a switch.

"Of the two, reverend sir," said the voice like the deacon's, "I had rather miss an ordination dinner than tonight's meeting. They tell me that some of our community are to be here from Falmouth and beyond, and others from Connecticut and Rhode Island, besides several of the Indian powwows, who, after their fashion, know almost as much deviltry as the best of us. Moreover, there is a goodly young woman to be taken into communion."

"Mighty well, Deacon Gookin!" replied the solemn old tones of the minister. "Spur up, or we shall be late. Nothing can be done, you know, until I get on the ground."

The hoofs clattered again; and the voices, talking so strangely in the empty 45
air, passed on through the forest, where no church had ever been gathered or
solitary Christian prayed. Whither, then, could these holy men be journeying
so deep into the heathen wilderness? Young Goodman Brown caught hold of a
tree for support, being ready to sink down on the ground, faint and overburdened with the heavy sickness of his heart. He looked up to the sky, doubting
whether there really was a heaven above him. Yet there was the blue arch, and
the stars brightening in it.

"With heaven above and Faith below, I will yet stand firm against the
devil!" cried Goodman Brown.

While he still gazed upward into the deep arch of the firmament and had
lifted his hands to pray, a cloud, though no wind was stirring, hurried across
the zenith and hid the brightening stars. The blue sky was still visible, except
directly overhead, where this black mass of cloud was sweeping swiftly northward. Aloft in the air, as if from the depths of the cloud, came a confused and
doubtful sound of voices. Once the listener fancied that he could distinguish
the accents of townspeople of his own, men and women, both pious and un-
godly, many of whom he had met at the communion table, and had seen others rioting at the tavern. The next moment, so indistinct were the sounds, he
doubted whether he had heard aught but the murmur of the old forest, whispering without a wind. Then came a stronger swell of those familiar tones,
heard daily in the sunshine at Salem village, but never until now from a cloud
of night. There was one voice, of a young woman, uttering lamentations, yet
with an uncertain sorrow, and entreating for some favor, which, perhaps, it
would grieve her to obtain; and all the unseen multitude, both saints and sinners, seemed to encourage her onward.

"Faith!" shouted Goodman Brown, in a voice of agony and desperation;
and the echoes of the forest mocked him, crying, "Faith! Faith!" as if bewildered wretches were seeking her all through the wilderness.

The cry of grief, rage, and terror was yet piercing the night, when the unhappy husband held his breath for a response. There was a scream, drowned
immediately in a louder murmur of voices, fading into far-off laughter, as the
dark cloud swept away, leaving the clear and silent sky above Goodman Brown.
But something fluttered lightly down through the air and caught on the
branch of a tree. The young man seized it, and beheld a pink ribbon.

"My Faith is gone!" cried he after one stupefied moment. "There is no 50
good on earth; and sin is but a name. Come, devil; for to thee is this world
given."

And, maddened with despair, so that he laughed loud and long, did Goodman Brown grasp his staff and set forth again, at such a rate that he seemed to
fly along the forest path rather than to walk or run. The road grew wilder and
drearier and more faintly traced, and vanished at length, leaving him in the heart
of the dark wilderness, still rushing onward with the instinct that guides mortal
man to evil. The whole forest was peopled with frightful sounds — the creaking
of the trees, the howling of wild beasts, and the yell of Indians; while sometimes
the wind tolled like a distant church bell, and sometimes gave a broad roar
around the traveler, as if all Nature were laughing him to scorn. But he was himself the chief horror of the scene, and shrank not from its other horrors.

"Ha! ha! ha!" roared Goodman Brown when the wind laughed at him.
"Let us hear which will laugh loudest. Think not to frighten me with your

deviltry. Come witch, come wizard, come Indian powwow, come devil himself, and here comes Goodman Brown. You may as well fear him as he fear you."

In truth, all through the haunted forest there could be nothing more frightful than the figure of Goodman Brown. On he flew among the black pines, brandishing his staff with frenzied gestures, now giving vent to an inspiration of horrid blasphemy, and now shouting forth such laughter as set all the echoes of the forest laughing like demons around him. The fiend in his own shape is less hideous than when he rages in the breast of man. Thus sped the demoniac on his course, until, quivering among the trees, he saw a red light before him, as when the felled trunks and branches of a clearing have been set on fire, and throw up their lurid blaze against the sky, at the hour of midnight. He paused, in a lull of the tempest that had driven him onward, and heard the swell of what seemed a hymn, rolling solemnly from a distance with the weight of many voices. He knew the tune; it was a familiar one in the choir of the village meeting-house. The verse died heavily away, and was lengthened by a chorus, not of human voices, but of all the sounds of the benighted wilderness pealing in awful harmony together. Goodman Brown cried out, and his cry was lost to his own ear by its unison with the cry of the desert.

In the interval of silence he stole forward until the light glared full upon his eyes. At one extremity of an open space, hemmed in by the dark wall of the forest, arose a rock, bearing some rude, natural resemblance either to an altar or a pulpit, and surrounded by four blazing pines, their tops aflame, their stems untouched, like candles at an evening meeting. The mass of foliage that had overgrown the summit of the rock was all on fire, blazing high into the night and fitfully illuminating the whole field. Each pendent twig and leafy festoon was in a blaze. As the red light arose and fell, a numerous congregation alternately shone forth, then disappeared in shadow, and again grew, as it were, out of the darkness, peopling the heart of the solitary woods at once.

"A grave and dark-clad company," quoth Goodman Brown.

In truth they were such. Among them, quivering to and fro between gloom and splendor, appeared faces that would be seen next day at the council board of the province, and others which, Sabbath after Sabbath, looked devoutly heavenward, and benignantly over the crowded pews, from the holiest pulpits in the land. Some affirm that the lady of the governor was there. At least there were high dames well known to her, and wives of honored husbands, and widows, a great multitude, and ancient maidens, all of excellent repute, and fair young girls, who trembled lest their mothers should espy them. Either the sudden gleams of light flashing over the obscure field bedazzled Goodman Brown, or he recognized a score of the church members of Salem village famous for their especial sanctity. Good old Deacon Gookin had arrived, and waited at the skirts of that venerable saint, his revered pastor. But, irreverently consorting with these grave, reputable, and pious people, these elders of the church, these chaste dames and dewy virgins, there were men of dissolute lives and women of spotted fame, wretches given over to all mean and filthy vice, and suspected even of horrid crimes. It was strange to see that the good shrank not from the wicked, nor were the sinners abashed by the saints. Scattered also among their pale-faced enemies were the Indian priests, or powwows, who had often scared their native forest with more hideous incantations than any known to English witchcraft.

55

"But where is Faith?" thought Goodman Brown; and, as hope came into his heart, he trembled.

Another verse of the hymn arose, a slow and mournful strain, such as the pious love, but joined to words which expressed all that our nature can conceive of sin, and darkly hinted at far more. Unfathomable to mere mortals is the lore of fiends. Verse after verse was sung; and still the chorus of the desert swelled between like the deepest tone of a mighty organ; and with the final peal of that dreadful anthem there came a sound, as if the roaring wind, the rushing streams, the howling beasts, and every other voice of the unconcerted wilderness were mingling and according with the voice of guilty man in homage to the prince of all. The four blazing pines threw up a loftier flame, and obscurely discovered shapes and visages of horror on the smoke wreaths above the impious assembly. At the same moment the fire on the rock shot redly forth and formed a glowing arch above its base, where now appeared a figure. With reverence be it spoken, the figure bore no slight similitude, both in garb and manner, to some grave divine of the New England churches.

"Bring forth the converts!" cried a voice that echoed through the field and rolled into the forest.

At the word, Goodman Brown stepped forth from the shadow of the trees 60 and approached the congregation, with whom he felt a loathful brotherhood by the sympathy of all that was wicked in his heart. He could have well-nigh sworn that the shape of his own dead father beckoned him to advance, looking downward from a smoke wreath, while a woman, with dim features of despair, threw out her hand to warn him back. Was it his mother? But he had no power to retreat one step, nor to resist, even in thought, when the minister and good old Deacon Gookin seized his arms and led him to the blazing rock. Thither came also the slender form of a veiled female, led between Goody Cloyse, that pious teacher of the catechism, and Martha Carrier, who had received the devil's promise to be queen of hell. A rampant hag was she. And there stood the proselytes beneath the canopy of fire.

"Welcome, my children," said the dark figure, "to the communion of your race. Ye have found thus young your nature and your destiny. My children, look behind you!"

They turned; and flashing forth, as it were, in a sheet of flame, the fiend worshipers were seen; the smile of welcome gleamed darkly on every visage.

"There," resumed the sable form, "are all whom ye have reverenced from youth. Ye deemed them holier than yourselves and shrank from your own sin, contrasting it with their lives of righteousness and prayerful aspirations heavenward. Yet here are they all in my worshiping assembly. This night it shall be granted you to know their secret deeds: how hoary-bearded elders of the church have whispered wanton words to the young maids of their households; how many a woman, eager for widows' weeds, has given her husband a drink at bedtime and let him sleep his last sleep in her bosom; how beardless youths have made haste to inherit their fathers' wealth; and how fair damsels — blush not, sweet ones — have dug little graves in the garden, and bidden me, the sole guest, to an infant's funeral. By the sympathy of your human hearts for sin ye shall scent out all the places — whether in church, bedchamber, street, field, or forest — where crime has been committed, and shall exult to behold the whole earth one stain of guilt, one mighty blood spot. Far more than this. It shall be yours to penetrate, in every bosom, the deep mystery of sin, the fountain of all wicked arts, and which inexhaustibly supplies more evil impulses than human power — than my power at its utmost — can make manifest in deeds. And now, my children, look upon each other."

They did so; and, by the blaze of the hell-kindled torches, the wretched man beheld his Faith, and the wife her husband, trembling before that unhallowed altar.

"Lo, there ye stand, my children," said the figure, in a deep and solemn 65 tone, almost sad with its despairing awfulness, as if his once angelic nature could yet mourn for our miserable race. "Depending upon one another's hearts, ye had still hoped that virtue were not all a dream. Now are ye undeceived. Evil is the nature of mankind. Evil must be your only happiness. Welcome again, my children, to the communion of your race."

"Welcome," repeated the fiend worshipers; in one cry of despair and triumph.

And there they stood, the only pair, as it seemed, who were yet hesitating on the verge of wickedness in this dark world. A basin was hollowed, naturally, in the rock. Did it contain water, reddened by the lurid light? or was it blood? or, perchance, a liquid flame? Herein did the shape of evil dip his hand and prepare to lay the mark of baptism upon their foreheads, that they might be partakers of the mystery of sin, more conscious of the secret guilt of others, both in deed and thought, than they could now be of their own. The husband cast one look at his pale wife, and Faith at him. What polluted wretches would the next glance show them to each other, shuddering alike at what they disclosed and what they saw!

"Faith! Faith!" cried the husband, "look up to heaven, and resist the wicked one."

Whether Faith obeyed he knew not. Hardly had he spoken when he found himself amid calm night and solitude, listening to a roar of the wind which died heavily away through the forest. He staggered against the rock, and felt it chill and damp; while a hanging twig, that had been all on fire, besprinkled his cheek with the coldest dew.

The next morning young Goodman Brown came slowly into the street of 70 Salem village, staring around him like a bewildered man. The good old minister was taking a walk along the graveyard to get an appetite for breakfast and meditate his sermon, and bestowed a blessing, as he passed, on Goodman Brown. He shrank from the venerable saint as if to avoid an anathema. Old Deacon Gookin was at domestic worship, and the holy words of his prayer were heard through the open window. "What God doth the wizard pray to?" quoth Goodman Brown. Goody Cloyse, that excellent old Christian, stood in the early sunshine at her own lattice, catechizing a little girl who had brought her a pint of morning's milk. Goodman Brown snatched away the child as from the grasp of the fiend himself. Turning the corner by the meeting-house, he spied the head of Faith, with the pink ribbons, gazing anxiously forth, and bursting into such joy at sight of him that she skipped along the street and almost kissed her husband before the whole village. But Goodman Brown looked sternly and sadly into her face, and passed on without a greeting.

Had Goodman Brown fallen asleep in the forest and only dreamed a wild dream of a witch-meeting?

Be it so if you will; but, alas! it was a dream of evil omen for young Goodman Brown. A stern, a sad, a darkly meditative, a distrustful, if not a desperate man did he become from the night of that fearful dream. On the Sabbath day, when the congregation were singing a holy psalm, he could not listen because an anthem of sin rushed loudly upon his ear and drowned all the blessed strain. When the minister spoke from the pulpit with power and fervid eloquence, and, with his hand on the open Bible, of the sacred truths of our religion, and of saintlike lives and triumphant deaths, and of future bliss or misery unutterable, then did Goodman Brown turn pale, dreading lest the roof should thunder down upon the gray blasphemer and his hearers. Often, awaking suddenly at midnight, he shrank from the bosom of Faith; and at morning or eventide, when the family knelt down at prayer, he scowled and muttered to himself, and gazed sternly at his wife, and turned away. And when he had lived long, and was borne to his grave a hoary corpse, followed by Faith, an aged woman, and children and grandchildren, a goodly procession, besides neighbors not a few, they carved no hopeful verse upon his tombstone, for his dying hour was gloom.

CONSIDERATIONS FOR CRITICAL THINKING AND WRITING

1. FIRST RESPONSE. Try to summarize "Young Goodman Brown" with a tidy moral. Is it possible? What makes this story complex?

2. What is the significance of Young Goodman Brown's name?

3. What is the symbolic value of the forest in this story? How are the descriptions of the forest contrasted with those of Salem village?

4. Characterize Young Goodman Brown at the beginning of the story. Why does he go into the forest? What does he mean when he says "Faith kept me back a while" (para. 12)?

5. What function do Faith's ribbons have in the story?

6. What foreshadows Young Goodman Brown's meeting with his "fellow-traveler" (para. 14)? Who is he? How do we know that Brown is keeping an appointment with a supernatural being?

7. The narrator describes the fellow-traveler's staff wriggling like a snake but then says, "This, of course, must have been an ocular deception, assisted by the uncertain light" (para. 13). What is the effect of this and other instances of ambiguity in the story?

8. What does Young Goodman Brown discover in the forest? What does he come to think of his ancestors, the church and state, Goody Cloyse, and even his wife?

9. Is Salem populated by hypocrites who cover hideous crimes with a veneer of piety and respectability? Do Faith and the other characters Brown sees when he returns from the forest appear corrupt to you?

10. Near the end of the story the narrator asks, "Had Goodman Brown fallen asleep in the forest and only dreamed a wild dream of a witch-meeting?" (para. 71). Was it a dream, or did the meeting actually happen? How does the answer to this question affect your reading of the story? Write an essay giving an answer to the narrator's question.

11. How is Young Goodman Brown changed by his experience in the forest? Does the narrator endorse Brown's unwillingness to trust anyone?

12. Discuss this story as an inward, psychological journey in which Young Goodman Brown discovers the power of blackness in himself but refuses to acknowledge that dimension of his personality.

13. Consider the story as a criticism of the village's hypocrisy.

CONNECTIONS TO OTHER SELECTIONS

1. Compare and contrast Young Goodman Brown's reasons for withdrawal with those of Melville's Bartleby, the Scrivener (p. 113). Do you find yourself more sympathetic with one character than the other? Explain.

2. To what extent is Hawthorne's use of dreams crucial in this story and in "The Birthmark" (p. 329)? Explain how Hawthorne uses dreams as a means to complicate our view of his characters.

3. What does Young Goodman Brown's pursuit of sin have in common with Aylmer's quest for perfection in "The Birthmark" (p. 329)? How do these pursuits reveal the characters' personalities and shed light on the theme of each story?

The Minister's Black Veil   1836
A Parable°

The sexton stood in the porch of Milford meeting-house, pulling lustily at the bell-rope. The old people of the village came stooping along the street. Children, with bright faces, tript merrily beside their parents, or mimicked a graver gait, in the conscious dignity of their Sunday clothes. Spruce bachelors looked sidelong at the pretty maidens, and fancied that the Sabbath sunshine made them prettier than on weekdays. When the throng had mostly streamed into the porch, the sexton began to toll the bell, keeping his eye on the Reverend Mr. Hooper's door. The first glimpse of the clergyman's figure was the signal for the bell to cease its summons.

"But what has good Parson Hooper got upon his face?" cried the sexton in astonishment.

All within hearing immediately turned about, and beheld the semblance of Mr. Hooper, pacing slowly his meditative way towards the meeting-house. With one accord they started, expressing more wonder than if some strange minister were coming to dust the cushions of Mr. Hooper's pulpit.

"Are you sure it is our parson?" inquired Goodman Gray of the sexton.

"Of a certainty it is good Mr. Hooper," replied the sexton. "He was to have 5 exchanged pulpits with Parson Shute of Westbury; but Parson Shute sent to excuse himself yesterday, being to preach a funeral sermon."

The cause of so much amazement may appear sufficiently slight. Mr. Hooper, a gentlemanly person of about thirty, though still a bachelor, was

---

Another clergyman in New England, Mr. Joseph Moody, of York, Maine, who died about eighty years since, made himself remarkable by the same eccentricity that is here related of the Reverend Mr. Hooper. In his case, however, the symbol had a different import. In early life he had accidentally killed a beloved friend; and from that day till the hour of his own death, he hid his face from men. [Hawthorne's note.]

dressed with due clerical neatness, as if a careful wife had starched his band, and brushed the weekly dust from his Sunday's garb. There was but one thing remarkable in his appearance. Swathed about his forehead, and hanging down over his face, so low as to be shaken by his breath, Mr. Hooper had on a black veil. On a nearer view, it seemed to consist of two folds of crape, which entirely concealed his features, except the mouth and chin, but probably did not intercept his sight, farther than to give a darkened aspect to all living and inanimate things. With this gloomy shade before him, good Mr. Hooper walked onward, at a slow and quiet pace, stooping somewhat and looking on the ground, as is customary with abstracted men, yet nodding kindly to those of his parishioners who still waited on the meeting-house steps. But so wonder-struck were they, that his greeting hardly met with a return.

"I can't really feel as if good Mr. Hooper's face was behind that piece of crape," said the sexton.

"I don't like it," muttered an old woman, as she hobbled into the meeting-house. "He has changed himself into something awful, only by hiding his face."

"Our parson has gone mad!" cried Goodman Gray, following him across the threshold.

A rumor of some unaccountable phenomenon had preceded Mr. Hooper 10 into the meeting-house, and set all the congregation astir. Few could refrain from twisting their heads towards the door; many stood upright, and turned directly about; while several little boys clambered upon the seats, and came down again with a terrible racket. There was a general bustle, a rustling of the women's gowns and shuffling of the men's feet, greatly at variance with that hushed repose which should attend the entrance of the minister. But Mr. Hooper appeared not to notice the perturbation of his people. He entered with an almost noiseless step, bent his head mildly to the pews on each side, and bowed as he passed his oldest parishioner, a white-haired great-grandsire, who occupied an arm-chair in the center of the aisle. It was strange to observe, how slowly this venerable man became conscious of something singular in the appearance of his pastor. He seemed not fully to partake of the prevailing wonder, till Mr. Hooper had ascended the stairs, and showed himself in the pulpit, face to face with his congregation, except for the black veil. That mysterious emblem was never once withdrawn. It shook with his measured breath as he gave out the psalm; it threw its obscurity between him and the holy page, as he read the Scriptures; and while he prayed, the veil lay heavily on his uplifted countenance. Did he seek to hide it from the dread Being whom he was addressing?

Such was the effect of this simple piece of crape, that more than one woman of delicate nerves was forced to leave the meeting-house. Yet perhaps the pale-faced congregation was almost as fearful a sight to the minister, as his black veil to them.

Mr. Hooper had the reputation of a good preacher, but not an energetic one: he strove to win his people heavenward, by mild persuasive influences, rather than to drive them thither, by the thunders of the Word. The sermon which he now delivered, was marked by the same characteristics of style and manner, as the general series of his pulpit oratory. But there was something, either in the sentiment of the discourse itself, or in the imagination of the auditors, which made it greatly the most powerful effort that they had ever heard from their pastor's lips. It was tinged, rather more darkly than usual, with the gentle gloom of Mr. Hooper's temperament. The subject had reference to secret sin, and those sad mysteries which we hide from our nearest and dearest, and would fain conceal from our own consciousness, even forgetting that the Omniscient can detect them. A subtle power was breathed into his words. Each member of the congregation, the most innocent girl, and the man of hardened breast, felt as if the preacher had crept upon them, behind his awful veil, and discovered their hoarded iniquity of deed or thought. Many spread their clasped hands on their bosoms. There was nothing terrible in what Mr. Hooper said; at least, no violence; and yet, with every tremor of his melancholy voice, the hearers quaked. An unsought pathos came hand in hand with awe. So sensible were the audience of some unwonted attribute in their minister, that they longed for a breath of wind to blow aside the veil, almost believing that a stranger's visage would be discovered, though the form, gesture, and voice were those of Mr. Hooper.

At the close of the services, the people hurried out with indecorous confusion, eager to communicate their pent-up amazement, and conscious of lighter spirits, the moment they lost sight of the black veil. Some gathered in little circles, huddled closely together, with their mouths all whispering in the center; some went homeward alone, wrapt in silent meditation; some talked loudly, and profaned the Sabbath-day with ostentatious laughter. A few shook their sagacious heads, intimating that they could penetrate the mystery; while one or two affirmed that there was no mystery at all, but only that Mr. Hooper's eyes were so weakened by the midnight lamp, as to require a shade. After a brief interval, forth came good Mr. Hooper also, in the rear of his flock. Turning his veiled face from one group to another, he paid due reverence to the hoary heads, saluted the middle-aged with kind dignity, as their friend and spiritual guide, greeted the young with mingled authority and love, and laid his hands on the little children's heads to bless them. Such was always his custom on the Sabbath-day. Strange and bewildered looks repaid him for his courtesy. None, as on former occasions, aspired to the honor of walking by their pastor's side. Old Squire Saunders, doubtless by an accidental lapse of memory, neglected to invite Mr. Hooper to his table, where the good clergyman had been wont to bless the food, almost every Sunday since his settlement. He returned, therefore, to the parsonage, and, at the moment of closing the door, was observed to look back upon the people, all of whom had their eyes fixed upon the minister. A sad smile gleamed faintly from beneath the black veil, and flickered about his mouth, glimmering as he disappeared.

"How strange," said a lady, "that a simple black veil, such as any woman might wear on her bonnet, should become such a terrible thing on Mr. Hooper's face!"

"Something must surely be amiss with Mr. Hooper's intellects," observed 15 her husband, the physician of the village. "But the strangest part of the affair is the effect of this vagary, even on a sober-minded man like myself. The black veil, though it covers only our pastor's face, throws its influence over his whole person, and makes him ghost-like from head to foot. Do you not feel it so?"

"Truly do I," replied the lady; "and I would not be alone with him for the world. I wonder he is not afraid to be alone with himself!"

"Men sometimes are so," said her husband.

That afternoon service was attended with similar circumstances. At its conclusion, the bell tolled for the funeral of a young lady. The relatives and friends were assembled in the house, and the more distant acquaintances stood about the door, speaking of the good qualities of the deceased, when their talk was interrupted by the appearance of Mr. Hooper, still covered with his black veil. It was now an appropriate emblem. The clergyman stepped into the room where the corpse was laid, and bent over the coffin, to take a last farewell of his deceased parishioner. As he stooped, the veil hung straight down from his forehead, so that, if her eye-lids had not been closed for ever, the dead maiden might have seen his face. Could Mr. Hooper be fearful of her glance, that he so hastily caught back the black veil? A person, who watched the interview between the dead and living, scrupled not to affirm, that, at the instant when the clergyman's features were disclosed, the corpse had slightly shuddered, rustling the shroud and muslin cap, though the countenance retained the composure of death. A superstitious old woman was the only witness of this prodigy. From the coffin, Mr. Hooper passed into the chamber of the mourners, and thence to the head of the staircase, to make the funeral prayer. It was a tender and heart-dissolving prayer, full of sorrow, yet so imbued with celestial hopes, that the music of a heavenly harp, swept by the fingers of the dead, seemed faintly to be heard among the saddest accents of the minister. The people trembled, though they but darkly understood him, when he prayed that they, and himself, and all of mortal race, might be ready, as he trusted this young maiden had been, for the dreadful hour that should snatch the veil from their faces. The bearers went heavily forth, and the mourners followed, saddening all the street, with the dead before them, and Mr. Hooper in his black veil behind.

"Why do you look back?" said one in the procession to his partner.

"I had a fancy," replied she, "that the minister and the maiden's spirit were walking hand in hand." 20

"And so had I, at the same moment," said the other.

That night, the handsomest couple in Milford village were to be joined in wedlock. Though reckoned a melancholy man, Mr. Hooper had a placid cheerfulness for such occasions, which often excited a sympathetic smile, where livelier merriment would have been thrown away. There was no quality of his disposition which made him more beloved than this. The company at the wedding awaited his arrival with impatience, trusting that the strange awe, which had gathered over him throughout the day, would now be dispelled. But such was not the result. When Mr. Hooper came, the first thing that their eyes rested on was the same horrible black veil, which had added deeper gloom to the funeral, and could portend nothing but evil to the wedding. Such was its immediate effect on the guests, that a cloud seemed to have rolled duskily from beneath the black crape, and dimmed the light of the candles. The bridal pair stood up before the minister. But the bride's cold fingers quivered in the tremulous hand of the bridegroom, and her death-like paleness caused a whisper, that the maiden who had been buried a few hours before, was come from her grave to be married. If ever another wedding were so dismal, it was that famous one, where they tolled the wedding-knell. After performing the ceremony, Mr. Hooper raised a glass of wine to his lips, wishing happiness to the new-married couple, in a strain of mild pleasantry that ought to have brightened the features of the guests, like a cheerful gleam from the hearth. At that instant, catching a glimpse of his figure in the looking-glass, the black veil involved his own spirit in the horror with which it overwhelmed all others. His frame shuddered—his lips grew white—he spilt the untasted wine upon the carpet—and rushed forth into the darkness. For the Earth, too, had on her Black Veil.

The next day, the whole village of Milford talked of little else than Parson Hooper's black veil. That, and the mystery concealed behind it, supplied a topic for discussion between acquaintances meeting in the street, and good women gossiping at their open windows. It was the first item of news that the tavernkeeper told to his guests. The children babbled of it on their way to school. One imitative little imp covered his face with an old black handkerchief, thereby so affrighting his playmates, that the panic seized himself, and he well nigh lost his wits by his own waggery.

It was remarkable, that, of all the busy-bodies and impertinent people in the parish, not one ventured to put the plain question to Mr. Hooper, wherefore he did this thing. Hitherto, whenever there appeared the slightest call for such interference, he had never lacked advisers, nor shown himself averse to be guided by their judgment. If he erred at all, it was by so painful a degree of self-distrust, that even the mildest censure would lead him to consider an indifferent action as a crime. Yet, though so well acquainted with this amiable weakness, no individual among his parishioners chose to make the black veil a subject of friendly remonstrance. There was a feeling of dread, neither plainly confessed nor carefully concealed, which caused each to shift the responsibility upon another, till at length it was found expedient to send a deputation of the church, in order to deal with Mr. Hooper about the mystery, before it should grow into a scandal. Never did an embassy so ill discharge its duties. The minister received them with friendly courtesy, but became silent, after they were seated, leaving to his visitors the whole burthen of introducing their important business. The topic, it might be supposed, was obvious enough. There was the black veil, swathed round Mr. Hooper's forehead, and concealing every feature above his placid mouth, on which, at times, they could perceive the glimmering of a melancholy smile. But that piece of crape, to their imagination, seemed to hang down before his heart, the symbol of a fearful secret between him and them. Were the veil but cast aside, they might speak freely of it, but not till then. Thus they sat a considerable time, speechless, confused, and shrinking uneasily from Mr. Hooper's eye, which they felt to be fixed upon them with an invisible glance. Finally, the deputies returned abashed to their constituents, pronouncing the matter too weighty to be handled, except by a council of the churches, if, indeed, it might not require a general synod.

But there was one person in the village, unappalled by the awe with which 25 the black veil had impressed all beside herself. When the deputies returned without an explanation, or even venturing to demand one, she, with the calm energy of her character, determined to chase away the strange cloud that appeared to be settling round Mr. Hooper, every moment more darkly than before. As his plighted wife, it should be her privilege to know what the black veil concealed. At the minister's first visit, therefore, she entered upon the subject, with a direct simplicity, which made the task easier both for him and her. After he had seated himself, she fixed her eyes steadfastly upon the veil, but could discern nothing of the dreadful gloom that had so overawed the multitude: it was but a double fold of crape, hanging down from his forehead to his mouth, and slightly stirring with his breath.

"No," said she aloud, and smiling, "there is nothing terrible in this piece of crape, except that it hides a face which I am always glad to look upon. Come, good sir, let the sun shine from behind the cloud. First lay aside your black veil: then tell me why you put it on."

Mr. Hooper's smile glimmered faintly.

"There is an hour to come," said he, "when all of us shall cast aside our veils. Take it not amiss, beloved friend, if I wear this piece of crape till then."

"Your words are a mystery too," returned the young lady. "Take away the veil for them, at least."

"Elizabeth, I will," said he, "so far as my vow may suffer me. Know, then, 30 this veil is a type and a symbol, and I am bound to wear it ever, both in light and darkness, in solitude and before the gaze of multitudes, and as with strangers, so with my familiar friends. No mortal eye will see it withdrawn. This dismal shade must separate me from the world: even you, Elizabeth, can never come behind it!"

"What grievous affliction hath befallen you," she earnestly inquired, "that you should thus darken your eyes for ever?"

"If it be a sign of mourning," replied Mr. Hooper, "I, perhaps, like most other mortals, have sorrows dark enough to be typified by a black veil."

"But what if the world will not believe that it is the type of an innocent sorrow?" urged Elizabeth. "Beloved and respected as you are, there may be whispers, that you hide your face under the consciousness of secret sin. For the sake of your holy office, do away this scandal!"

The color rose into her cheeks, as she intimated the nature of the rumors that were already abroad in the village. But Mr. Hooper's mildness did not forsake him. He even smiled again—that same sad smile, which always appeared like a faint glimmering of light, proceeding from the obscurity beneath the veil.

"If I hide my face for sorrow, there is cause enough," he merely replied; 35 "and if I cover it for secret sin, what mortal might not do the same?"

And with this gentle, but unconquerable obstinacy, did he resist all her entreaties. At length Elizabeth sat silent. For a few moments she appeared lost in thought, considering, probably, what new methods might be tried, to withdraw her lover from so dark a fantasy, which, if it had no other meaning, was perhaps a symptom of mental disease. Though of a firmer character than his own, the tears rolled down her cheeks. But, in an instant, as it were, a new feeling took the place of sorrow: her eyes were fixed insensibly on the black veil, when, like a sudden twilight in the air, its terrors fell around her. She arose, and stood trembling before him.

"And do you feel it then at last?" said he mournfully.

She made no reply, but covered her eyes with her hand, and turned to leave the room. He rushed forward and caught her arm.

"Have patience with me, Elizabeth!" cried he passionately. "Do not desert me, though this veil must be between us here on earth. Be mine, and hereafter there shall be no veil over my face, no darkness between our souls! It is but a mortal veil—it is not for eternity! Oh! you know not how lonely I am, and how frightened to be alone behind my black veil. Do not leave me in this miserable obscurity for ever!"

"Lift the veil but once, and look me in the face," said she.   40
"Never! It cannot be!" replied Mr. Hooper.
"Then, farewell!" said Elizabeth.

She withdrew her arm from his grasp, and slowly departed, pausing at the door, to give one long, shuddering gaze, that seemed almost to penetrate the mystery of the black veil. But, even amid his grief, Mr. Hooper smiled to think that only a material emblem had separated him from happiness, though the horrors which it shadowed forth, must be drawn darkly between the fondest of lovers.

From that time no attempts were made to remove Mr. Hooper's black veil, or, by a direct appeal, to discover the secret which it was supposed to hide. By persons who claimed a superiority to popular prejudice, it was reckoned merely an eccentric whim, such as often mingles with the sober actions of men otherwise rational, and tinges them all with its own semblance of insanity. But with the multitude, good Mr. Hooper was irreparably a bugbear. He could not walk the streets with any peace of mind, so conscious was he that the gentle and timid would turn aside to avoid him, and that others would make it a point of hardihood to throw themselves in his way. The impertinence of the latter class compelled him to give up his customary walk, at sunset, to the burial ground, for when he leaned pensively over the gate, there would always be faces behind the grave-stones, peeping at his black veil. A fable went the rounds that the stare of the dead people drove him thence. It grieved him, to the very depth of his kind heart, to observe how the children fled from his approach, breaking up their merriest sports, while his melancholy figure was yet afar off. Their instinctive dread caused him to feel, more strongly than aught else, that a preternatural horror was interwoven with the threads of the black crape. In truth, his own antipathy to the veil was known to be so great, that he never willingly passed before a mirror, nor stooped to drink at a still fountain, lest, in its peaceful bosom, he should be affrighted by himself. This was what gave plausibility to the whispers, that Mr. Hooper's conscience tortured him for some great crime, too horrible to be entirely concealed, or otherwise than so obscurely intimated. Thus, from beneath the black veil, there rolled a cloud into the sunshine, an ambiguity of sin or sorrow, which enveloped the poor minister, so that love or sympathy could never reach him. It was said, that ghost and fiend consorted with him there. With self-shudderings and outward terrors, he walked continually in its shadow, groping darkly within his own soul, or gazing through a medium that saddened the whole world. Even the lawless wind, it was believed, respected his dreadful secret, and never blew aside the veil. But still good Mr. Hooper sadly smiled, at the pale visages of the worldly throng as he passed by.

Among all its bad influences, the black veil had the one desirable effect, of   45
making its wearer a very efficient clergyman. By the aid of his mysterious emblem—for there was no other apparent cause—he became a man of awful power, over souls that were in agony for sin. His converts always regarded him with a dread peculiar to themselves, affirming, though but figuratively, that, before he brought them to celestial light, they had been with him behind the black veil. Its gloom, indeed, enabled him to sympathize with all dark affections. Dying sinners cried aloud for Mr. Hooper, and would not yield their breath till he appeared; though ever, as he stooped to whisper consolation, they shuddered at the veiled face so near their own. Such were the terrors of

the black veil, even when Death had bared his visage! Strangers came long distances to attend service at his church, with the mere idle purpose of gazing at his figure, because it was forbidden them to behold his face. But many were made to quake ere they departed! Once, during Governor Belcher's administration, Mr. Hooper was appointed to preach the election sermon. Covered with his black veil, he stood before the chief magistrate, the council, and the representatives, and wrought so deep an impression, that the legislative measures of that year were characterized by all the gloom and piety of our earliest ancestral sway.

In this manner Mr. Hooper spent a long life, irreproachable in outward act, yet shrouded in dismal suspicions; kind and loving, though unloved, and dimly feared; a man apart from men, shunned in their health and joy, but ever summoned to their aid in mortal anguish. As years wore on, shedding their snows above his sable veil, he acquired a name throughout the New-England churches, and they called him Father Hooper. Nearly all his parishioners, who were of mature age when he was settled, had been borne away by many a funeral: he had one congregation in the church, and a more crowded one in the churchyard; and having wrought so late into the evening, and done his work so well, it was now good Father Hooper's turn to rest.

Several persons were visible by the shaded candlelight, in the death-chamber of the old clergyman. Natural connections he had none. But there was the decorously grave, though unmoved physician, seeking only to mitigate the last pangs of the patient whom he could not save. There were the deacons, and other eminently pious members of his church. There, also, was the Reverend Mr. Clark, of Westbury, a young and zealous divine, who had ridden in haste to pray by the bedside of the expiring minister. There was the nurse, no hired handmaiden of death, but one whose calm affection had endured thus long, in secrecy, in solitude, amid the chill of age, and would not perish, even at the dying hour. Who, but Elizabeth! And there lay the hoary head of good Father Hooper upon the death-pillow, with the black veil still swathed about his brow and reaching down over his face, so that each more difficult gasp of his faint breath caused it to stir. All through life that piece of crape had hung between him and the world: it had separated him from cheerful brotherhood and woman's love, and kept him in that saddest of all prisons, his own heart; and still it lay upon his face, as if to deepen the gloom of his darksome chamber, and shade him from the sunshine of eternity.

For some time previous, his mind had been confused, wavering doubtfully between the past and the present, and hovering forward, as it were, at intervals, into the indistinctness of the world to come. There had been feverish turns, which tossed him from side to side, and wore away what little strength he had. But in his most convulsive struggles, and in the wildest vagaries of his intellect, when no other thought retained its sober influence, he still showed an awful solicitude lest the black veil should slip aside. Even if his bewildered soul could have forgotten, there was a faithful woman at his pillow, who, with averted eyes, would have covered that aged face, which she had last beheld in the comeliness of manhood. At length the death-stricken old man lay quietly in the torpor of mental and bodily exhaustion, with an imperceptible pulse, and breath that grew fainter and fainter, except when a long, deep, and irregular inspiration seemed to prelude the flight of his spirit.

The minister of Westbury approached the bedside.

"Venerable Father Hooper," said he, "the moment of your release is at 50
hand. Are you ready for the lifting of the veil, that shuts in time from eternity?"

Father Hooper at first replied merely by a feeble motion of his head; then,
apprehensive, perhaps, that his meaning might be doubtful, he exerted himself to speak.

"Yea," said he, in faint accents, "my soul hath a patient weariness until
that veil be lifted."

"And is it fitting," resumed the Reverend Mr. Clark, "that a man so given
to prayer, of such a blameless example, holy in deed and thought, so far as
mortal judgment may pronounce; is it fitting that a father in the church
should leave a shadow on his memory, that may seem to blacken a life so pure?
I pray you, my venerable brother, let not this thing be! Suffer us to be glad-
dened by your triumphant aspect, as you go to your reward. Before the veil of
eternity be lifted, let me cast aside this black veil from your face!"

And thus speaking, the Reverend Mr. Clark bent forward to reveal the
mystery of so many years. But, exerting a sudden energy, that made all the beholders stand aghast, Father Hooper snatched both his hands from beneath
the bedclothes, and pressed them strongly on the black veil, resolute to struggle,
if the minister of Westbury would contend with a dying man.

"Never!" cried the veiled clergyman. "On earth, never!"   55

"Dark old man!" exclaimed the affrighted minister, "with what horrible
crime upon your soul are you now passing to the judgment?"

Father Hooper's breath heaved; it rattled in his throat; but, with a mighty
effort, grasping forward with his hands, he caught hold of life, and held it
back till he should speak. He even raised himself in bed; and there he sat, shivering with the arms of death around him, while the black veil hung down,
awful, at that last moment, in the gathered terrors of a life-time. And yet the
faint, sad smile, so often there, now seemed to glimmer from its obscurity, and
linger on Father Hooper's lips.

"Why do you tremble at me alone?" cried he, turning his veiled face round
the circle of pale spectators. "Tremble also at each other! Have men avoided
me, and women shown no pity, and children screamed and fled, only for my
black veil? What, but the mystery which it obscurely typifies, has made this
piece of crape so awful? When the friend shows his inmost heart to his friend;
the lover to his best-beloved; when man does not vainly shrink from the eye of
his Creator, loathsomely treasuring up the secret of his sin; then deem me a
monster, for the symbol beneath which I have lived, and die! I look around me,
and, lo! on every visage a Black Veil!"

While his auditors shrank from one another, in mutual affright, Father
Hooper fell back upon his pillow, a veiled corpse, with a faint smile lingering
on the lips. Still veiled, they laid him in his coffin, and a veiled corpse they bore
him to the grave. The grass of many years has sprung up and withered on that
grave, the burial-stone is moss-grown, and good Mr. Hooper's face is dust; but
awful is still the thought, that it moldered beneath the Black Veil!

CONSIDERATIONS FOR CRITICAL THINKING AND WRITING

1. FIRST RESPONSE. Why do you think Hooper wears the veil? Explain
   whether you think Hooper is right or wrong to wear it.
2. Describe the veil Hooper wears. How does it affect his vision?

3. Characterize the townspeople. How does the community react to the veil?

4. What is Hooper's explanation for why he wears the veil? Is he more or less effective as a minister because he wears it?

5. What is the one feature of Hooper's face that we see? What does that feature reveal about him?

6. Describe what happens at the funeral and wedding ceremonies at which Hooper officiates. How are the incidents at these events organized around the veil?

7. Why does Elizabeth think "it should be her privilege to know what the black veil concealed" (para. 25)? Why doesn't Hooper remove it at her request?

8. How does Elizabeth react to Hooper's refusal to take off the veil? Why is her response especially significant?

9. How do others in town explain why Hooper wears the veil? Do these explanations seem adequate to you? Why or why not?

10. Why is Hooper buried with the veil? Of what significance is it that grass "withered" on his grave (para. 59)?

11. Describe the story's point of view. How would a first-person narrative change the story dramatically?

CONNECTIONS TO OTHER SELECTIONS

1. How might this story be regarded as a sequel to "Young Goodman Brown"? How are the themes similar?

2. Explain how Faith in "Young Goodman Brown" (p. 310), Georgiana in "The Birthmark" (below), and Elizabeth in "The Minister's Black Veil" are used to reveal the central male characters in each story. Describe the similarities that you see among these women characters.

3. Compare Hawthorne's use of symbol in "The Minister's Black Veil" and "The Birthmark" (below). Write an essay explaining which symbol you think works more effectively to evoke the theme of its story.

The Birthmark   1843

In the latter part of the last century there lived a man of science, an eminent proficient in every branch of natural philosophy, who not long before our story opens had made experience of a spiritual affinity more attractive than any chemical one. He had left his laboratory to the care of an assistant, cleared his fine countenance from the furnace smoke, washed the stain of acids from his fingers, and persuaded a beautiful woman to become his wife. In those days when the comparatively recent discovery of electricity and other kindred mysteries of Nature seemed to open paths into the region of miracle, it was not unusual for the love of science to rival the love of woman in its depth and absorbing energy. The higher intellect, the imagination, the spirit, and even the heart might all find their congenial ailment in pursuits which, as some of their ardent votaries believed, would ascend from one step of powerful intelligence to another, until the philosopher should lay his hand on the secret of creative force and perhaps make new worlds for himself. We know not whether Aylmer possessed this degree of faith in man's ultimate control over Nature. He had devoted himself, however, too unreservedly to scientific studies ever to be weaned from them by any second passion. His love for his young wife might prove the stronger of the two; but it could only be by intertwining itself with his love of science, and uniting the strength of the latter to his own.

Such a union accordingly took place, and was attended with truly remarkable consequences and a deeply impressive moral. One day, very soon after their marriage, Aylmer sat gazing at his wife with a trouble in his countenance that grew stronger until he spoke.

"Georgiana," said he, "has it never occurred to you that the mark upon your cheek might be removed?"

"No, indeed," said she, smiling; but perceiving the seriousness of his manner, she blushed deeply. "To tell you the truth it has been so often called a charm that I was simple enough to imagine it might be so."

"Ah, upon another face perhaps it might," replied her husband; "but never 5 on yours. No, dearest Georgiana, you came so nearly perfect from the hand of Nature that this slightest possible defect, which we hesitate whether to term a defect or a beauty, shocks me, as being the visible mark of earthly imperfection."

"Shocks you, my husband!" cried Georgiana, deeply hurt; at first reddening with momentary anger, but then bursting into tears. "Then why did you take me from my mother's side? You cannot love what shocks you!"

To explain this conversation it must be mentioned that in the center of Georgiana's left cheek there was a singular mark, deeply interwoven, as it were, with the texture and substance of her face. In the usual state of her complexion — a healthy though delicate bloom — the mark wore a tint of deeper crimson, which imperfectly defined its shape amid the surrounding rosiness. When she blushed it gradually became more indistinct, and finally vanished amid the triumphant rush of blood that bathed the whole cheek with its brilliant glow. But if any shifting motion caused her to turn pale, there was the mark again, a crimson stain upon the snow, in what Aylmer sometimes deemed an almost fearful distinctness. Its shape bore not a little similarity to the human hand, though of the smallest pygmy size. Georgiana's lovers were wont to say that some fairy at her birth hour had laid her tiny hand upon the infant's cheek, and left this impress there in token of the magic endowments that were to give her such sway over all hearts. Many a desperate swain would have risked life for the privilege of pressing his lips to the mysterious hand. It must not be concealed, however, that the impression wrought by this fairy sign manual varied exceedingly, according to the difference of temperament in the beholders. Some fastidious persons — but they were exclusively of her own sex — affirmed that the bloody hand, as they chose to call it, quite destroyed the effect of Georgiana's beauty, and rendered her countenance even hideous. But it would be as reasonable to say that one of those small blue stains which sometimes occur in the purest statuary marble would convert the Eve of Powers to a monster. Masculine observers, if the birthmark did not heighten their admiration, contented themselves with wishing it away, that the world might possess one living specimen of ideal loveliness without the semblance of a flaw.

After his marriage, — for he thought little or nothing of the matter before, — Aylmer discovered that this was the case with himself.

Had she been less beautiful, — if Envy's self could have found aught else to sneer at, — he might have felt his affection heightened by the prettiness of this mimic hand, now vaguely portrayed, now lost, now stealing forth again and glimmering to and fro with every pulse of emotion that throbbed within her heart; but seeing her otherwise so perfect, he found this one defect grow more and more intolerable with every moment of their united lives. It was the fatal flaw of humanity which Nature, in one shape or another, stamps ineffaceably on all her productions, either to imply that they are temporary and finite, or that their perfection must be wrought by toil and pain. The crimson hand expressed the ineludible gripe° in which mortality clutches the highest and purest of earthly mold, degrading them into kindred with the lowest, and even with the very brutes, like whom their visible frames return to dust. In this manner, selecting it as the symbol of his wife's liability to sin, sorrow, decay, and death, Aylmer's somber imagination was not long in rendering the birthmark a frightful object, causing him more trouble and horror than ever Georgiana's beauty, whether of soul or sense, had given him delight.

At all the seasons which should have been their happiest, he invariably and without intending it, nay, in spite of a purpose to the contrary, reverted to this one disastrous topic. Trifling as it at first appeared, it so connected itself with innumerable trains of thought and modes of feeling that it became the central point of all. With the morning twilight Aylmer opened his eyes upon his wife's face and recognized the symbol of imperfection; and when they sat together at the evening hearth his eyes wandered stealthily to her cheek, and beheld, flickering with the blaze of the wood fire, the spectral hand that wrote mortality where he would fain have worshiped. Georgiana soon learned to shudder at his gaze. It needed but a glance with the peculiar expression that his face often wore to change the roses of her cheek into a deathlike paleness, amid which the crimson hand was brought strongly out, like a bas-relief of ruby on the whitest marble.

Late one night when the lights were growing dim, so as hardly to betray 10 the stain on the poor wife's cheek, she herself, for the first time, voluntarily took up the subject.

"Do you remember, my dear Aylmer," said she, with a feeble attempt at a smile, "have you any recollection of a dream last night about this odious hand?"

"None! none whatever!" replied Aylmer, starting; but then he added, in a dry, cold tone, affected for the sake of concealing the real depth of his emotion, "I might well dream of it; for before I fell asleep it had taken a pretty firm hold of my fancy."

"And you did dream of it?" continued Georgiana hastily, for she dreaded lest a gush of tears should interrupt what she had to say. "A terrible dream! I wonder that you can forget it. Is it possible to forget this one expression? — 'It is in her heart now; we must have it out!' Reflect, my husband; for by all means I would have you recall that dream."

gripe: Grip.

The mind is in a sad state when Sleep, the all-involving, cannot confine her specters within the dim region of her sway, but suffers them to break forth, affrighting this actual life with secrets that perchance belong to a deeper one. Aylmer now remembered his dream. He had fancied himself with his servant Aminadab, attempting an operation for the removal of the birthmark; but the deeper went the knife, the deeper sank the hand, until at length its tiny grasp appeared to have caught hold of Georgiana's heart; whence, however, her husband was inexorably resolved to cut or wrench it away.

When the dream had shaped itself perfectly in his memory, Aylmer sat in 15 his wife's presence with a guilty feeling. Truth often finds its way to the mind close muffled in robes of sleep, and then speaks with uncompromising direct-ness of matters in regard to which we practice an unconscious self-deception during our waking moments. Until now he had not been aware of the tyran-nizing influence acquired by one idea over his mind, and of the lengths which he might find in his heart to go for the sake of giving himself peace.

"Aylmer," resumed Georgiana solemnly, "I know not what may be the cost to both of us to rid me of this fatal birthmark. Perhaps its removal may cause cureless deformity; or it may be the stain goes as deep as life itself. Again: do we know that there is a possibility, on any terms, of unclasping the firm grip of this little hand which was laid upon me before I came into the world?"

"Dearest Georgiana, I have spent much thought upon the subject," hastily interrupted Aylmer. "I am convinced of the perfect practicability of its re-moval."

"If there be the remotest possibility of it," continued Georgiana, "let the attempt be made at whatever risk. Danger is nothing to me; for life, while this hateful mark makes me the object of your horror and disgust, — life is a bur-den which I would fling down with joy. Either remove this dreadful hand, or take my wretched life! You have deep science. All the world bears witness of it. You have achieved great wonders. Cannot you remove this little, little mark, which I cover with the tips of two small fingers? Is this beyond your power, for the sake of your own peace, and to save your poor wife from madness?"

"Noblest, dearest, tenderest wife," cried Aylmer rapturously, "doubt not my power. I have already given this matter the deepest thought — thought which might almost have enlightened me to create a being less perfect than yourself. Georgiana, you have led me deeper than ever into the heart of science. I feel myself fully competent to render this dear cheek as faultless as its fellow; and then, most beloved, what will be my triumph when I shall have corrected what Nature left imperfect in her fairest work! Even Pygmalion, when his sculptured woman assumed life, felt not greater ecstasy than mine will be."

"It is resolved, then," said Georgiana, faintly smiling. "And, Aylmer, spare 20 me not, though you should find the birthmark take refuge in my heart at last."

Her husband tenderly kissed her cheek — her right cheek — not that which bore the impress of the crimson hand.

The next day Aylmer apprised his wife of a plan that he had formed whereby he might have opportunity for the intense thought and constant watchfulness which the proposed operation would require; while Georgiana, likewise, would enjoy the perfect repose essential to its success. They were to seclude themselves in the extensive apartments occupied by Aylmer as a labo-ratory, and where, during his toilsome youth, he had made discoveries in the elemental powers of Nature that had roused the admiration of all the learned societies in Europe. Seated calmly in this laboratory, the pale philosopher had investigated the secrets of the highest cloud region and of the profoundest mines; he had satisfied himself of the causes that kindled and kept alive the fires of the volcano; and had explained the mystery of fountains, and how it is that they gush forth, some so bright and pure, and others with such rich medicinal virtues, from the dark bosom of the earth. Here, too, at an earlier period, he had studied the wonders of the human frame, and attempted to fathom the very process by which Nature assimilates all her precious influences from earth and air, and from the spiritual world, to create and foster man, her masterpiece. The latter pursuit, however, Aylmer had long laid aside in unwilling recognition of the truth — against which all seekers sooner or later stumble — that our great creative Mother, while she amuses us with apparently working in the broadest sunshine, is yet severely careful to keep her own secrets, and, in spite of her pretended openness, shows us nothing but results. She permits us, indeed, to mar, but seldom to mend, and, like a jealous patentee, on no account to make. Now, however, Aylmer resumed these half-forgotten investigations, — not, of course, with such hopes or wishes as first suggested them, but because they involved much physiological truth and lay in the path of his proposed scheme for the treatment of Georgiana.

As he led her over the threshold of the laboratory, Georgiana was cold and tremulous. Aylmer looked cheerfully into her face, with intent to reassure her, but was so startled with the intense glow of the birthmark upon the whiteness of her cheek that he could not restrain a strong convulsive shudder. His wife fainted.

"Aminadab! Aminadab!" shouted Aylmer, stamping violently on the floor.

Forthwith there issued from an inner apartment a man of low stature, but 25 bulky frame, with shaggy hair hanging about his visage, which was grimed with the vapors of the furnace. This personage had been Aylmer's underworker during his whole scientific career, and was admirably fitted for that office by his great mechanical readiness, and the skill with which, while incapable of comprehending a single principle, he executed all the details of his master's experiments. With his vast strength, his shaggy hair, his smoky aspect, and the indescribable earthiness that encrusted him, he seemed to represent man's physical nature; while Aylmer's slender figure, and pale, intellectual face, were no less apt a type of the spiritual element.

"Throw open the door of the boudoir, Aminadab," said Aylmer, "and burn a pastille."

"Yes, master," answered Aminadab, looking intently at the lifeless form of Georgiana; and then he muttered to himself, "If she were my wife, I'd never part with that birthmark."

When Georgiana recovered consciousness she found herself breathing an atmosphere of penetrating fragrance, the gentle potency of which had recalled her from her deathlike faintness. The scene around her looked like enchantment. Aylmer had converted those smoky, dingy, somber rooms, where he had spent his brightest years in recondite pursuits, into a series of beautiful apartments not unfit to be the secluded abode of a lovely woman. The walls were hung with gorgeous curtains, which imparted the combination of grandeur and grace that no other species of adornment can achieve; and as they fell from the ceiling to the floor, their rich and ponderous folds, concealing all angles and straight lines, appeared to shut in the scene from infinite space. For aught Georgiana knew, it might be a pavilion among the clouds. And Aylmer, excluding the sunshine, which would have interfered with his chemical processes, had supplied its place with perfumed lamps, emitting flames of various hue, but all uniting in a soft, empurpled radiance. He now knelt by his wife's side, watching her earnestly, but without alarm; for he was confident in his science, and felt that he could draw a magic circle round her within which no evil might intrude.

"Where am I? Ah, I remember," said Georgiana faintly; and she placed her hand over her cheek to hide the terrible mark from her husband's eyes.

"Fear not, dearest!" exclaimed he. "Do not shrink from me! Believe me,   30 Georgiana, I even rejoice in this single imperfection, since it will be such a rapture to remove it."

"Oh, spare me!" sadly replied his wife. "Pray do not look at it again. I never can forget that convulsive shudder."

In order to soothe Georgiana, and, as it were, to release her mind from the burden of actual things, Aylmer now put in practice some of the light and playful secrets which science had taught him among its profounder lore. Airy figures, absolutely bodiless ideas, and forms of unsubstantial beauty came and danced before her, imprinting their momentary footsteps on beams of light. Though she had some indistinct idea of the method of these optical phenomena, still the illusion was almost perfect enough to warrant the belief that her husband possessed sway over the spiritual world. Then again, when she felt a wish to look forth from her seclusion, immediately, as if her thoughts were answered, the procession of external existence flitted across a screen. The scenery and the figures of actual life were perfectly represented, but with that bewitching, yet indescribable difference which always makes a picture, an image, or a shadow so much more attractive than the original. When wearied of this, Aylmer bade her cast her eyes upon a vessel containing a quantity of earth. She did so, with little interest at first; but was soon startled to perceive the germ of a plant shooting upward from the soil. Then came the slender stalk; the leaves gradually unfolded themselves; and amid them was a perfect and lovely flower.

"It is magical!" cried Georgiana. "I dare not touch it."

"Nay, pluck it," answered Aylmer: "pluck it, and inhale its brief perfume while you may. The flower will wither in a few moments and leave nothing save its brown seed vessels; but thence may be perpetuated a race as ephemeral as itself."

But Georgiana had no sooner touched the flower than the whole plant   35 suffered a blight, its leaves turning coal-black as if by the agency of fire.

"There was too powerful a stimulus," said Aylmer thoughtfully.

To make up for this abortive experiment, he proposed to take her portrait by a scientific process of his own invention. It was to be effected by rays of light striking upon a polished plate of metal. Georgiana assented; but, on looking at the result, was affrighted to find the features of the portrait blurred and indefinable; while the minute figure of a hand appeared where the cheek should have been. Aylmer snatched the metallic plate and threw it into a jar of corrosive acid.

Soon, however, he forgot these mortifying failures. In the intervals of study and chemical experiment he came to her flushed and exhausted, but seemed invigorated by her presence, and spoke in glowing language of the resources of his art. He gave a history of the long dynasty of the alchemists, who spent so many ages in quest of the universal solvent by which the golden principle might be elicited from all things vile and base. Aylmer appeared to believe that, by the plainest scientific logic, it was altogether within the limits of possibility to discover this long-sought medium; "but," he added, "a philosopher who should go deep enough to acquire the power would attain too lofty a wisdom to stoop to the exercise of it." Not less singular were his opinions in regard to the elixir vitae. He more than intimated that it was at his option to concoct a liquid that should prolong life for years, perhaps interminably; but that it would produce a discord in Nature which all the world, and chiefly the quaffer of the immortal nostrum, would find cause to curse.

"Aylmer, are you in earnest?" asked Georgiana, looking at him with amazement and fear. "It is terrible to possess such power, or even to dream of possessing it."

"Oh, do not tremble, my love," said her husband. "I would not wrong either 40 you or myself by working such inharmonious effects upon our lives; but I would have you consider how trifling, in comparison, is the skill requisite to remove this little hand."

At the mention of the birthmark, Georgiana, as usual, shrank as if a red-hot iron had touched her cheek.

Again Aylmer applied himself to his labors. She could hear his voice in the distant furnace-room giving directions to Aminadab, whose harsh, uncouth, misshapen tones were audible in response, more like the grunt or growl of a brute than human speech. After hours of absence, Aylmer reappeared and proposed that she should now examine his cabinet of chemical products and natural treasures of the earth. Among the former he showed her a small vial, in which, he remarked, was contained a gentle yet most powerful fragrance, capable of impregnating all the breezes that blow across a kingdom. They were of inestimable value, the contents of that little vial; and, as he said so, he threw some of the perfume into the air and filled the room with piercing and invigorating delight.

"And what is this?" asked Georgiana, pointing to a small crystal globe containing a gold-colored liquid. "It is so beautiful to the eye that I could imagine it the elixir of life."

"In one sense it is," replied Aylmer; "or rather, the elixir of immortality. It is the most precious poison that ever was concocted in this world. By its aid I could apportion the lifetime of any mortal at whom you might point your finger. The strength of the dose would determine whether he were to linger out years, or drop dead in the midst of a breath. No king on his guarded throne could keep his life if I, in my private station, should deem that the welfare of millions justified me in depriving him of it."

"Why do you keep such a terrific drug?" inquired Georgiana in horror. 45

"Do not mistrust me, dearest," said her husband, smiling; "its virtuous potency is yet greater than its harmful one. But see! here is a powerful cosmetic. With a few drops of this in a vase of water, freckles may be washed away as easily as the hands are cleansed. A stronger infusion would take the blood out of the cheek, and leave the rosiest beauty a pale ghost."

"Is it with this lotion that you intend to bathe my cheek?" asked Georgiana, anxiously.

"Oh, no," hastily replied her husband; "this is merely superficial. Your case demands a remedy that shall go deeper."

In his interviews with Georgiana, Aylmer generally made minute inquiries as to her sensations and whether the confinement of the rooms and the temperature of the atmosphere agreed with her. These questions had such a particular drift that Georgiana began to conjecture that she was already subjected to certain physical influences, either breathed in with the fragrant air or taken with her food. She fancied likewise, but it might be altogether fancy, that there was a stirring up of her system — a strange, indefinite sensation creeping through her veins, and tingling, half painfully, half pleasurably, at her heart. Still, whenever she dared to look into the mirror, there she beheld herself pale as a white rose and with the crimson birthmark stamped upon her cheek. Not even Aylmer now hated it so much as she.

To dispel the tedium of the hours which her husband found it necessary 50 to devote to the processes of combination and analysis, Georgiana turned over the volumes of his scientific library. In many dark old tomes she met with chapters full of romance and poetry. They were the works of the philosophers of the middle ages, such as Albertus Magnus, Cornelius Agrippa, Paracelsus, and the famous friar who created the prophetic Brazen Head. All these antique naturalists stood in advance of their centuries, yet were imbued with some of their credulity, and therefore were believed, and perhaps imagined themselves to have acquired from the investigation of Nature a power above Nature, and from physics a sway over the spiritual world. Hardly less curious and imaginative were the early volumes of the Transactions of the Royal Society, in which the members, knowing little of the limits of natural possibility, were continually recording wonders or proposing methods whereby wonders might be wrought.

But to Georgiana the most engrossing volume was a large folio from her husband's own hand, in which he had recorded every experiment of his scientific career, its original aim, the methods adopted for its development, and its final success or failure, with the circumstances to which either event was attributable. The book, in truth, was both the history and emblem of his ardent, ambitious, imaginative, yet practical and laborious life. He handled physical details as if there were nothing beyond them; yet spiritualized them all, and redeemed himself from materialism by his strong and eager aspiration towards the infinite. In his grasp the veriest clod of earth assumed a soul. Georgiana, as she read, reverenced Aylmer and loved him more profoundly than ever, but with a less entire dependence on his judgment than heretofore. Much as he had accomplished, she could not but observe that his most splendid successes were almost invariably failures, if compared with the ideal at which he aimed. His brightest diamonds were the merest pebbles, and felt to be so by himself, in comparison with the inestimable gems which lay hidden beyond his reach. The volume, rich with achievements that had won renown for its author, was yet as melancholy a record as ever mortal hand had penned. It was the sad confession and continual exemplification of the shortcomings of the composite man, the spirit burdened with clay and working in matter, and of the despair that assails the higher nature at finding itself so miserably thwarted by the earthly part. Perhaps every man of genius in whatever sphere might recognize the image of his own experience in Aylmer's journal.

So deeply did these reflections affect Georgiana that she laid her face upon the open volume and burst into tears. In this situation she was found by her husband.

"It is dangerous to read in a sorcerer's books," said he with a smile, though his countenance was uneasy and displeased. "Georgiana, there are pages in that volume which I can scarcely glance over and keep my senses. Take heed lest it prove as detrimental to you."

"It has made me worship you more than ever," said she.

"Ah, wait for this one success," rejoined he, "then worship me if you will. I 55 shall deem myself hardly unworthy of it. But come, I have sought you for the luxury of your voice. Sing to me, dearest."

So she poured out the liquid music of her voice to quench the thirst of his spirit. He then took his leave with a boyish exuberance of gaiety, assuring her that her seclusion would endure but a little longer, and that the result was already certain. Scarcely had he departed when Georgiana felt irresistibly impelled to follow him. She had forgotten to inform Aylmer of a symptom which for two or three hours past had begun to excite her attention. It was a sensation in the fatal birthmark, not painful, but which induced a restlessness throughout her system. Hastening after her husband, she intruded for the first time into the laboratory.

The first thing that struck her eye was the furnace, that hot and feverish worker, with the intense glow of its fire, which by the quantities of soot clustered above it seemed to have been burning for ages. There was a distilling apparatus in full operation. Around the room were retorts, tubes, cylinders, crucibles, and other apparatus of chemical research. An electrical machine stood ready for immediate use. The atmosphere felt oppressively close, and was tainted with gaseous odors which had been tormented forth by the processes of science. The severe and homely simplicity of the apartment, with its naked walls and brick pavement, looked strange, accustomed as Georgiana had become to the fantastic elegance of her boudoir. But what chiefly, indeed almost solely, drew her attention, was the aspect of Aylmer himself.

He was pale as death, anxious and absorbed, and hung over the furnace as if it depended upon his utmost watchfulness whether the liquid which it was distilling should be the draught of immortal happiness or misery. How different from the sanguine and joyous mien that he had assumed for Georgiana's encouragement!

"Carefully now, Aminadab; carefully, thou human machine; carefully, thou man of clay!" muttered Aylmer, more to himself than his assistant. "Now, if there be a thought too much or too little, it is all over."

"Ho! ho!" mumbled Aminadab. "Look, master! look!" 60

Aylmer raised his eyes hastily, and at first reddened, then grew paler than ever, on beholding Georgiana. He rushed towards her and seized her arm with a gripe that left the print of his fingers upon it.

"Why do you come hither? Have you no trust in your husband?" cried he impetuously. "Would you throw the blight of that fatal birthmark over my labors? It is not well done. Go, prying woman, go!"

"Nay, Aylmer," said Georgiana with the firmness of which she possessed no stinted endowment, "it is not you that have a right to complain. You mistrust your wife; you have concealed the anxiety with which you watch the development of this experiment. Think not so unworthily of me, my husband. Tell me all the risk we run, and fear not that I shall shrink; for my share in it is far less than your own."

"No, no, Georgiana!" said Aylmer impatiently; "it must not be."

"I submit," replied she calmly. "And, Aylmer, I shall quaff whatever 65 draught you bring me; but it will be on the same principle that would induce me to take a dose of poison if offered by your hand."

"My noble wife," said Aylmer, deeply moved, "I knew not the height and depth of your nature until now. Nothing shall be concealed. Know, then, that this crimson hand, superficial as it seems, has clutched its grasp into your being with a strength of which I had no previous conception. I have already administered agents powerful enough to do aught except to change your entire physical system. Only one thing remains to be tried. If that fails us we are ruined."

"Why did you hesitate to tell me this?" asked she.

"Because, Georgiana," said Aylmer in a low voice, "there is danger."

"Danger? There is but one danger — that this horrible stigma shall be left upon my cheek!" cried Georgiana. "Remove it, remove it, whatever be the cost, or we shall both go mad!"

"Heaven knows your words are too true," said Aylmer sadly. "And now, 70 dearest, return to your boudoir. In a little while all will be tested."

He conducted her back and took leave of her with a solemn tenderness which spoke far more than his words how much was now at stake. After his departure Georgiana became rapt in musings. She considered the character of Aylmer, and did it completer justice than at any previous moment. Her heart exulted, while it trembled, at his honorable love — so pure and lofty that it would accept nothing less than perfection nor miserably make itself contented with an earthlier nature than he had dreamed of. She felt how much more precious was such a sentiment than that meaner kind which would have borne with the imperfection for her sake, and have been guilty of treason to holy love by degrading its perfect idea to the level of the actual; and with her whole spirit she prayed that, for a single moment, she might satisfy his highest and deepest conception. Longer than one moment she well knew it could not be; for his spirit was ever on the march, ever ascending, and each instant required something that was beyond the scope of the instant before.

The sound of her husband's footsteps aroused her. He bore a crystal goblet containing a liquor colorless as water, but bright enough to be the draught of immortality. Aylmer was pale; but it seemed rather the consequence of a highly wrought state of mind and tension of spirit than of fear or doubt.

"The concoction of the draught has been perfect," said he, in answer to Georgiana's look. "Unless all my science have deceived me, it cannot fail."

"Save on your account, my dearest Aylmer," observed his wife, "I might wish to put off this birthmark of mortality by relinquishing mortality itself in preference to any other mode. Life is but a sad possession to those who have attained precisely the degree of moral advancement at which I stand. Were I weaker and blinder it might be happiness. Were I stronger, it might be endured hopefully. But, being what I find myself, methinks I am of all mortals the most fit to die."

"You are fit for heaven without tasting death!" replied her husband. "But 75 why do we speak of dying? The draught cannot fail. Behold its effect upon this plant."

On the window seat there stood a geranium diseased with yellow blotches, which had overspread all its leaves. Aylmer poured a small quantity of the liquid upon the soil in which it grew. In a little time, when the roots of the plant had taken up the moisture, the unsightly blotches began to be extinguished in a living verdure.

"There needed no proof," said Georgiana quietly. "Give me the goblet. I joyfully stake all upon your word."

"Drink, then, thou lofty creature!" exclaimed Aylmer, with fervid admiration. "There is no taint of imperfection on thy spirit. Thy sensible frame, too, shall soon be all perfect."

She quaffed the liquid and returned the goblet to his hand.

"It is grateful," said she, with a placid smile. "Methinks it is like water 80 from a heavenly fountain; for it contains I know not what of unobtrusive fragrance and deliciousness. It allays a feverish thirst that had parched me for many days. Now, dearest, let me sleep. My earthly senses are closing over my spirit like the leaves around the heart of a rose at sunset."

She spoke the last words with a gentle reluctance, as if it required almost more energy than she could command to pronounce the faint and lingering syllables. Scarcely had they loitered through her lips ere she was lost in slumber. Aylmer sat by her side, watching her aspect with the emotions proper to a man the whole value of whose existence was involved in the process now to be tested. Mingled with this mood, however, was the philosophic investigation characteristic of the man of science. Not the minutest symptom escaped him. A heightened flush of the cheek, a slight irregularity of breath, a quiver of the eyelid, a hardly perceptible tremor through the frame, — such were the details which, as the moments passed, he wrote down in his folio volume. Intense thought had set its stamp upon every previous page of that volume, but the thoughts of years were all concentrated upon the last.

While thus employed, he failed not to gaze often at the fatal hand, and not without a shudder. Yet once, by a strange and unaccountable impulse, he pressed it with his lips. His spirit recoiled, however, in the very act; and Georgiana, out of the midst of her deep sleep, moved uneasily and murmured as if in remonstrance. Again Aylmer resumed his watch. Nor was it without avail. The crimson hand, which at first had been strongly visible upon the marble paleness of Georgiana's cheek, now grew more faintly outlined. She remained not less pale than ever; but the birthmark, with every breath that came and went, lost somewhat of its former distinctness. Its presence had been awful; its departure was more awful still. Watch the stain of the rainbow fading out of the sky, and you will know how that mysterious symbol passed away.

"By Heaven! it is well-nigh gone!" said Aylmer to himself, in almost irrepressible ecstasy. "I can scarcely trace it now. Success! success! And now it is like the faintest rose color. The lightest flush of blood across her cheek would overcome it. But she is so pale!"

He drew aside the window curtain and suffered the light of natural day to fall into the room and rest upon her cheek. At the same time he heard a gross, hoarse chuckle, which he had long known as his servant Aminadab's expression of delight.

"Ah, clod! ah, earthly mass!" cried Aylmer, laughing in a sort of frenzy, 85 "you have served me well! Matter and spirit — earth and heaven — have both done their part in this! Laugh, thing of the senses! You have earned the right to laugh."

These exclamations broke Georgiana's sleep. She slowly unclosed her eyes and gazed into the mirror which her husband had arranged for that purpose. A faint smile flitted over her lips when she recognized how barely perceptible was now that crimson hand which had once blazed forth with such disastrous brilliancy as to scare away all their happiness. But then her eyes sought Aylmer's face with a trouble and anxiety that he could by no means account for.

"My poor Aylmer!" murmured she.

"Poor? Nay, richest, happiest, most favored!" exclaimed he. "My peerless bride, it is successful! You are perfect!"

"My poor Aylmer," she repeated, with a more than human tenderness, "you have aimed loftily; you have done nobly. Do not repent that with so high and pure a feeling, you have rejected the best the earth could offer. Aylmer, dearest Aylmer, I am dying!"

Alas! it was too true! The fatal hand had grappled with the mystery of life, 90 and was the bond by which an angelic spirit kept itself in union with a mortal frame. As the last crimson tint of the birthmark — that sole token of human imperfection — faded from her cheek, the parting breath of the now perfect woman passed into the atmosphere, and her soul, lingering a moment near her husband, took its heavenward flight. Then a hoarse, chuckling laugh was heard again! Thus ever does the gross fatality of earth exult in its invariable triumph over the immortal essence which, in this dim sphere of half development, demands the completeness of a higher state. Yet, had Aylmer reached a profounder wisdom, he need not thus have flung away the happiness which would have woven his mortal life of the selfsame texture with the celestial. The momentary circumstance was too strong for him; he failed to look beyond the shadowy scope of time, and, living once for all in eternity, to find the perfect future in the present.

CONSIDERATIONS FOR CRITICAL THINKING AND WRITING

1. FIRST RESPONSE. Consider this story as an early version of our contemporary obsession with physical perfection. What significant similarities — and differences — do you find?

2. Is Aylmer evil? Is he simply a stock version of a mad scientist? In what sense might he be regarded as an idealist?

3. What does the birthmark symbolize? How does Aylmer's view of it differ from the other perspectives provided in the story? What is the significance of its handlike shape?

4. Does Aylmer love Georgiana? Why does she allow him to risk her life to remove the birthmark?

5. In what sense can Aylmer be characterized as guilty of the sin of pride?

6. How is Aminadab a foil for Aylmer?

7. What is the significance of the descriptions of Aylmer's laboratory?

8. What do Aylmer's other experiments reveal about the nature of his work? How do they constitute foreshadowings of what will happen to Georgiana?

9. What is the theme of the story? What point is made about what it means to be a human being?

10. Despite the risks to Georgiana, Aylmer conducts his experiments in the hope and expectation of achieving a higher good. He devotes his life to science, and yet he is an egotist. Explain.

11. Discuss the extent to which Georgiana is responsible for her own death.

CONNECTIONS TO OTHER SELECTIONS

1. Compare Aylmer's unwillingness to accept things as they are with Young Goodman Brown's refusal to be a part of a community he regards as fallen.

2. Consider the devotion Georgiana expresses toward Aylmer along with Reiko's commitment to her soldier-husband in Yukio Mishima's "Patriotism" (p. 593). How might a feminist critic (see the brief discussion concerning this type of approach in Chapter 37) assess these relationships? Do Georgiana and Reiko have more or less in common as devoted, self-sacrificing wives?

3. What similarities do you see in Aylmer's growing feelings about the "crimson hand" on Georgiana's cheek and the young wife's feelings about her husband's hand in Colette's "The Hand" (p. 220)? How do Aylmer and the young wife cope with these feelings? How do you account for the differences between them?

Rappaccini's Daughter 1844

A young man, named Giovanni Guasconti, came, very long ago, from the more southern region of Italy, to pursue his studies at the University of Padua. Giovanni, who had but a scanty supply of gold ducats in his pocket, took lodgings in a high and gloomy chamber of an old edifice, which looked not unworthy to have been the palace of a Paduan noble, and which, in fact, exhibited over its entrance the armorial bearings of a family long since extinct. The young stranger, who was not unstudied in the great poem of his country, recollected that one of the ancestors of this family, and perhaps an occupant of this very mansion, had been pictured by Dante as a partaker of the immortal agonies of his Inferno. These reminiscences and associations, together with the tendency to heartbreak natural to a young man for the first time out of his native sphere, caused Giovanni to sigh heavily, as he looked around the desolate and ill-furnished apartment.

"Holy Virgin, signor," cried old dame Lisabetta, who, won by the youth's remarkable beauty of person, was kindly endeavoring to give the chamber a habitable air, "what a sigh was that to come out of a young man's heart! Do you find this old mansion gloomy? For the love of heaven, then, put your head out of the window, and you will see as bright sunshine as you have left in Naples."

Guasconti mechanically did as the old woman advised, but could not quite agree with her that the Lombard sunshine was as cheerful as that of southern Italy. Such as it was, however, it fell upon a garden beneath the window, and expended its fostering influences on a variety of plants, which seemed to have been cultivated with exceeding care.

"Does this garden belong to the house?" asked Giovanni.

"Heaven forbid, signor! — unless it were fruitful of better pot-herbs than 5 any that grow there now," answered old Lisabetta. "No: that garden is cultivated by the own hands of Signor Giacomo Rappaccini, the famous Doctor, who, I warrant him, has been heard of as far as Naples. It is said he distills these plants into medicines that are as potent as a charm. Oftentimes you may see the signor Doctor at work, and perchance the signora his daughter, too, gathering the strange flowers that grow in the garden."

The old woman had now done what she could for the aspect of the chamber, and, commending the young man to the protection of the saints, took her departure.

Giovanni still found no better occupation than to look down into the garden beneath his window. From its appearance, he judged it to be one of those botanic gardens, which were of earlier date in Padua than elsewhere in Italy, or in the world. Or, not improbably, it might once have been the pleasure-place of an opulent family; for there was the ruin of a marble fountain in the center, sculptured with rare art, but so woefully shattered that it was impossible to trace the original design from the chaos of remaining fragments. The water, however, continued to gush and sparkle into the sunbeams as cheerfully as ever. A little gurgling sound ascended to the young man's window, and made him feel as if the fountain were an immortal spirit, that sung its song unceasingly, and without heeding the vicissitudes around it; while one century embodied it in marble, and another scattered the garniture on the soil. All about the pool into which the water subsided, grew various plants, that seemed to require a plentiful supply of moisture for the nourishment of gigantic leaves, and, in some instances, flowers gorgeously magnificent. There was one shrub in particular, set in a marble vase in the midst of the pool, that bore a profusion of purple blossoms, each of which had the luster and richness of a gem; and the whole together made a show so resplendent that it seemed enough to illuminate the garden, even had there been no sunshine. Every portion of the soil was peopled with plants and herbs, which, if less beautiful, still bore tokens of assiduous care; as if all had their individual virtues, known to the scientific mind that fostered them. Some were placed in urns, rich with old carving, and others in common garden-pots; some crept serpent-like along the ground, or climbed on high, using whatever means of ascent was offered them. One plant had wreathed itself round a statue of Vertumnus,° which was thus quite veiled and shrouded in a drapery of hanging foliage, so happily arranged that it might have served a sculptor for a study.

While Giovanni stood at the window, he heard a rustling behind a screen of leaves, and became aware that a person was at work in the garden. His figure soon emerged into view, and showed itself to be that of no common laborer, but a tall, emaciated, sallow, and sickly-looking man, dressed in a scholar's garb of black. He was beyond the middle term of life, with gray hair, a thin gray beard, and a face singularly marked with intellect and cultivation, but which could never, even in his more youthful days, have expressed much warmth of heart.

Nothing could exceed the intentness with which this scientific gardener examined every shrub which grew in his path; it seemed as if he was looking into their inmost nature, making observations in regard to their creative essence, and discovering why one leaf grew in this shape, and another in that, and wherefore such and such flowers differed among themselves in hue and perfume. Nevertheless, in spite of the deep intelligence on his part, there was

---

Vertumnus: The Roman god of the seasons; the vegetation produced during the changing seasons.

no approach to intimacy between himself and these vegetable existences. On the contrary, he avoided their actual touch, or the direct inhaling of their odors, with a caution that impressed Giovanni most disagreeably; for the man's demeanor was that of one walking among malignant influences, such as savage beasts, or deadly snakes, or evil spirits, which, should he allow them one moment of license, would wreak upon him some terrible fatality. It was strangely frightful to the young man's imagination, to see this air of insecurity in a person cultivating a garden, that most simple and innocent of human toils, and which had been alike the joy and labor of the unfallen parents of the race. Was this garden, then, the Eden of the present world? — and this man, with such a perception of harm in what his own hands caused to grow, was he the Adam?

The distrustful gardener, while plucking away the dead leaves or pruning 10 the too luxuriant growth of the shrubs, defended his hands with a pair of thick gloves. Nor were these his only armor. When, in his walk through the garden, he came to the magnificent plant that hung its purple gems beside the marble fountain, he placed a kind of mask over his mouth and nostrils, as if all this beauty did but conceal a deadlier malice. But finding his task still too dangerous, he drew back, removed the mask, and called loudly, but in the infirm voice of a person affected with inward disease:

"Beatrice! — Beatrice!"

"Here am I, my father! What would you?" cried a rich and youthful voice from the window of the opposite house; a voice as rich as a tropical sunset, and which made Giovanni, though he knew not why, think of deep hues of purple or crimson, and of perfumes heavily delectable. — "Are you in the garden?"

"Yes, Beatrice," answered the gardener, "and I need your help."

Soon there emerged from under a sculptured portal the figure of a young girl, arrayed with as much richness of taste as the most splendid of the flowers, beautiful as the day, and with a bloom so deep and vivid that one shade more would have been too much. She looked redundant with life, health, and energy; all of which attributes were bound down and compressed, as it were, and girdled tensely, in their luxuriance, by her virgin zone.° Yet Giovanni's fancy must have grown morbid, while he looked down into the garden; for the impression which the fair stranger made upon him was as if here were another flower, the human sister of those vegetable ones, as beautiful as they — more beautiful than the richest of them — but still to be touched only with a glove, nor to be approached without a mask. As Beatrice came down the garden path, it was observable that she handled and inhaled the odor of several of the plants, which her father had most sedulously avoided.

"Here, Beatrice," said the latter, — "see how many needful offices require to 15 be done to our chief treasure. Yet, shattered as I am, my life might pay the penalty of approaching it so closely as circumstances demand. Henceforth, I fear, this plant must be consigned to your sole charge."

"And gladly will I undertake it," cried again the rich tones of the young lady, as she bent towards the magnificent plant, and opened her arms as if to embrace it. "Yes, my sister, my splendor, it shall be Beatrice's task to nurse and serve thee; and thou shalt reward her with thy kisses and perfumed breath, which to her is as the breath of life!"

virgin zone: A wide belt worn by an unmarried woman.

Then, with all the tenderness in her manner that was so strikingly expressed in her words, she busied herself with such attentions as the plant seemed to require; and Giovanni, at his lofty window, rubbed his eyes, and almost doubted whether it were a girl tending her favorite flower, or one sister performing the duties of affection to another. The scene soon terminated. Whether Doctor Rappaccini had finished his labors in the garden, or that his watchful eye had caught the stranger's face, he now took his daughter's arm and retired. Night was already closing in; oppressive exhalations seemed to proceed from the plants, and steal upward past the open window; and Giovanni, closing the lattice, went to his couch, and dreamed of a rich flower and beautiful girl. Flower and maiden were different and yet the same, and fraught with some strange peril in either shape.

But there is an influence in the light of morning that tends to rectify whatever errors of fancy, or even of judgment, we may have incurred during the sun's decline, or among the shadows of the night, or in the less wholesome glow of moonshine. Giovanni's first movement on starting from sleep, was to throw open the window, and gaze down into the garden which his dreams had made so fertile of mysteries. He was surprised, and a little ashamed, to find how real and matter-of-fact an affair it proved to be, in the first rays of the sun, which gilded the dew-drops that hung upon leaf and blossom, and, while giving a brighter beauty to each rare flower, brought everything within the limits of ordinary experience. The young man rejoiced, that, in the heart of the barren city, he had the privilege of overlooking this spot of lovely and luxuriant vegetation. It would serve, he said to himself, as a symbolic language, to keep him in communion with nature. Neither the sickly and thought-worn Doctor Giacomo Rappaccini, it is true, nor his brilliant daughter were now visible; so that Giovanni could not determine how much of the singularity which he attributed to both, was due to their own qualities, and how much to his wonder-working fancy. But he was inclined to take a most rational view of the whole matter.

In the course of the day, he paid his respects to Signor Pietro Baglioni, professor of medicine in the University, a physician of eminent repute, to whom Giovanni had brought a letter of introduction. The professor was an elderly personage, apparently of genial nature, and habits that might almost be called jovial; he kept the young man to dinner, and made himself very agreeable by the freedom and liveliness of his conversation, especially when warmed by a flask or two of Tuscan wine. Giovanni, conceiving that men of science, inhabitants of the same city, must needs be on familiar terms with one another, took an opportunity to mention the name of Dr. Rappaccini. But the professor did not respond with so much cordiality as he had anticipated.

"Ill would it become a teacher of the divine art of medicine," said Professor Pietro Baglioni, in answer to a question of Giovanni, "to withhold due and well-considered praise of a physician so eminently skilled as Rappaccini. But, on the other hand, I should answer it but scantily to my conscience, were I to permit a worthy youth like yourself, Signor Giovanni, the son of an ancient friend, to imbibe erroneous ideas respecting a man who might hereafter chance to hold your life and death in his hands. The truth is, our worshipful Doctor Rappaccini has as much science as any member of the faculty — with perhaps one single exception — in Padua, or all Italy. But there are certain grave objections to his professional character." 20

"And what are they?" asked the young man.

"Has my friend Giovanni any disease of body or heart, that he is so inquisitive about physicians?" said the Professor, with a smile. "But as for Rappaccini, it is said of him — and I, who know the man well, can answer for its truth — that he cares infinitely more for science than for mankind. His patients are interesting to him only as subjects for some new experiment. He would sacrifice human life, his own among the rest, or whatever else was dearest to him, for the sake of adding so much as a grain of mustard-seed to the great heap of his accumulated knowledge."

"Methinks he is an awful man, indeed," remarked Guasconti, mentally recalling the cold and purely intellectual aspect of Rappaccini. "And yet, worshipful Professor, is it not a noble spirit? Are there many men capable of so spiritual a love of science?"

"God forbid," answered the Professor, somewhat testily — "at least, unless they take sounder views of the healing art than those adopted by Rappaccini. It is his theory, that all medicinal virtues are comprised within those substances which we term vegetable poisons. These he cultivates with his own hands, and is said even to have produced new varieties of poison, more horribly deleterious than Nature, without the assistance of this learned person, would ever have plagued the world with. That the signor Doctor does less mischief than might be expected, with such dangerous substances, is undeniable. Now and then, it must be owned, he has effected — or seemed to effect — a marvellous cure. But, to tell you my private mind, Signor Giovanni, he should receive little credit for such instances of success — they being probably the work of chance — but should be held strictly accountable for his failures, which may justly be considered his own work."

The youth might have taken Baglioni's opinions with many grains of allowance, had he known that there was a professional warfare of long continuance between him and Doctor Rappaccini, in which the latter was generally thought to have gained the advantage. If the reader be inclined to judge for himself, we refer him to certain black-letter tracts on both sides, preserved in the medical department of the University of Padua.

"I know not, most learned Professor," returned Giovanni, after musing on what had been said of Rappaccini's exclusive zeal for science — "I know not how dearly this physician may love his art; but surely there is one object more dear to him. He has a daughter."

"Aha!" cries the Professor with a laugh. "So now our friend Giovanni's secret is out. You have heard of his daughter, whom all the young men in Padua are wild about, though not half a dozen have ever had the good hap to see her face. I know little of the Signora Beatrice, save that Rappaccini is said to have instructed her deeply in his science, and that, young and beautiful as fame reports her, she is already qualified to fill a professor's chair. Perchance her father destines her for mine! Other absurd rumors there be, not worth talking about, or listening to. So now, Signor Giovanni, drink of your glass of Lacryma."°

Guasconti returned to his lodgings somewhat heated with the wine he had quaffed, and which caused his brain to swim with strange fantasies in reference to Doctor Rappaccini and the beautiful Beatrice. On his way, happening to pass by a florist's, he bought a fresh bouquet of flowers.

Lacryma: An Italian wine; in Latin *lacrima* means tear.

Ascending to his chamber, he seated himself near the window, but within the shadow thrown by the depth of the wall, so that he could look down into the garden with little risk of being discovered. All beneath his eye was a solitude. The strange plants were basking in the sunshine, and now and then nodding gently to one another, as if in acknowledgment of sympathy and kindred. In the midst, by the shattered fountain, grew the magnificent shrub, with its purple gems clustering all over it; they glowed in the air, and gleamed back again out of the depths of the pool, which thus seemed to overflow with colored radiance from the rich reflection that was steeped in it. At first, as we have said, the garden was a solitude. Soon, however, — as Giovanni had half-hoped, half-feared, would be the case, — a figure appeared beneath the antique sculptured portal, and came down between the rows of plants, inhaling their various perfumes, as if she were one of those beings of old classic fable, that lived upon sweet odors. On again beholding Beatrice, the young man was even startled to perceive how much her beauty exceeded his recollection of it; so brilliant, so vivid in its character, that she glowed amid the sunlight, and, as Giovanni whispered to himself, positively illuminated the more shadowy intervals of the garden path. Her face being now more revealed than on the former occasion, he was struck by its expression of simplicity and sweetness; qualities that had not entered into his idea of her character, and which made him ask anew, what manner of mortal she might be. Nor did he fail again to observe, or imagine, an analogy between the beautiful girl and the gorgeous shrub that hung its gem-like flowers over the fountain; a resemblance which Beatrice seemed to have indulged a fantastic humor in heightening, both by the arrangement of her dress and the selection of its hues.

Approaching the shrub, she threw upon her arms, as with a passionate 30 ardor, and drew its branches into an intimate embrace; so intimate, that her features were hidden in its leafy bosom, and her glistening ringlets all intermingled with the flowers.

"Give me thy breath, my sister," exclaimed Beatrice; "for I am faint with common air! And give me this flower of thine, which I separate with gentlest fingers from the stem, and place it close beside my heart."

With these words, the beautiful daughter of Rappaccini plucked one of the richest blossoms of the shrub, and was about to fasten it in her bosom. But now, unless Giovanni's draughts of wine had bewildered his senses, a singular incident occurred. A small orange-colored reptile of the lizard or chameleon species, chanced to be creeping along the path, just at the feet of Beatrice. It appeared to Giovanni — but, at the distance from which he gazed, he could scarcely have seen anything so minute — it appeared to him, however, that a drop or two of moisture from the broken stem of the flower descended upon the lizard's head. For an instant, the reptile contorted itself violently, and then lay motionless in the sunshine. Beatrice observed this remarkable phenomenon, and crossed herself, sadly, but without surprise; nor did she therefore hesitate to arrange the fatal flower in her bosom. There it blushed, and almost glimmered with the dazzling effect of a precious stone, adding to her dress and aspect the one appropriate charm, which nothing else in the world could have supplied. But Giovanni, out of the shadow of his window bent forward and shrank back, and murmured and trembled.

"Am I awake? Have I my senses?" said he to himself. "What is this being? — beautiful, shall I call her? — or inexpressibly terrible?"

Beatrice now strayed carelessly through the garden, approaching closer beneath Giovanni's window, so that he was compelled to thrust his head quite out of its concealment in order to gratify the intense and painful curiosity which she excited. At this moment, there came a beautiful insect over the garden wall; it had perhaps wandered through the city and found no flowers nor verdure among those antique haunts of men, until the heavy perfumes of Doctor Rappaccini's shrubs had lured it from afar. Without alighting on the flowers, this winged brightness seemed to be attracted by Beatrice, and lingered in the air and fluttered about her head. Now here it could not be but that Giovanni Guasconti's eyes deceived him. Be that as it might, he fancied that while Beatrice was gazing at the insect with childish delight, it grew faint and fell at her feet! — its bright wings shivered! it was dead! — from no cause that he could discern, unless it were the atmosphere of her breath. Again Beatrice crossed herself and sighed heavily, as she bent over the dead insect.

An impulsive movement of Giovanni drew her eyes to the window. There 35 she beheld the beautiful head of the young man — rather a Grecian than an Italian head, with fair, regular features, and a glistening of gold among his ringlets — gazing down upon her like a being that hovered in mid-air. Scarcely knowing what he did, Giovanni threw down the bouquet which he had hitherto held in his hand.

"Signora," said he, "there are pure and healthful flowers. Wear them for the sake of Giovanni Guasconti!"

"Thanks, Signor," replied Beatrice, with her rich voice, that came forth as it were like a gush of music; and with a mirthful expression half childish and half woman-like. "I accept your gift, and would fain recompense it with this precious purple flower; but if I toss it into the air, it will not reach you. So Signor Guasconti must even content himself with my thanks."

She lifted the bouquet from the ground, and then as if inwardly ashamed at having stepped aside from her maidenly reserve to respond to a stranger's greeting, passed swiftly homeward through the garden. But, few as the moments were, it seemed to Giovanni when she was on the point of vanishing beneath the sculptured portal, that his beautiful bouquet was already beginning to wither in her grasp. It was an idle thought; there could be no possibility of distinguishing a faded flower from a fresh one at so great a distance.

For many days after the incident, the young man avoided the window that looked into Doctor Rappaccini's garden, as if something ugly and monstrous would have blasted his eye-sight, had he been betrayed into a glance. He felt conscious of having put himself, to a certain extent, within the influence of an unintelligible power, by the communication which he had opened with Beatrice. The wisest course would have been, if his heart were in any real danger, to quit his lodgings and Padua itself, at once; the next wiser, to have accustomed himself, as far as possible, to the familiar and daylight view of Beatrice; thus bringing her rigidly and systematically within the limits of ordinary experience. Least of all, while avoiding her sight, should Giovanni have remained so near this extraordinary being, that the proximity and possibility even of intercourse, should give a kind of substance and reality to the wild vagaries which his imagination ran riot continually in producing. Guasconti had not a deep heart — or at all events, its depths were not sounded now — but he had a quick fancy, and an ardent southern temperament, which rose every instant to a higher fever-pitch. Whether or no Beatrice possessed those terrible attributes — that fatal breath — the affinity with those so beautiful and deadly flowers — which were indicated by what Giovanni had witnessed, she had at least instilled a fierce and subtle poison into his system. It was not love, although her rich beauty was a madness to him; nor horror, even while he fancied her spirit to be imbued with the same baneful essence that seemed to pervade her physical frame; but a wild offspring of both love and horror that had each parent in it, and burned like one and shivered like the other. Giovanni knew not what to dread; still less did he know what to hope; *hope* and *dread* kept a continual warfare in his breast, alternately vanquishing one another and starting up afresh to renew the contest. Blessed are all simple emotions, be they dark or bright! It is the lurid intermixture of the two that produces the illuminating blaze of the infernal regions.

Sometimes he endeavored to assuage the fever of his spirit by a rapid walk   40
through the streets of Padua, or beyond its gates; his footsteps kept time with the throbbings of his brain, so that the walk was apt to accelerate itself to a race. One day, he found himself arrested; his arm was seized by a portly personage who had turned back on recognizing the young man, and expended much breath in overtaking him.

"Signor Giovanni! — stay, my young friend!" cried he. "Have you forgotten me? That might well be the case, if I were as much altered as yourself."

It was Baglioni, whom Giovanni had avoided, ever since their first meeting, from a doubt that the professor's sagacity would look too deeply into his secrets. Endeavoring to recover himself, he stared forth wildly from his inner world into the outer one, and spoke like a man in a dream:

"Yes; I am Giovanni Guasconti. You are Professor Pietro Baglioni. Now let me pass!"

"Not yet — not yet, Signor Giovanni Guasconti," said the Professor, smiling, but at the same time scrutinizing the youth with an earnest glance. — "What; did I grow up side by side with your father, and shall his son pass me like a stranger, in these old streets of Padua? Stand still, Signor Giovanni; for we must have a word or two, before we part."

"Speedily, then, most worshipful Professor, speedily!" said Giovanni, with   45
feverish impatience. "Does not your worship see that I am in haste?"

Now, while he was speaking, there came a man in black along the street, stooping and moving feebly, like a person in inferior health. His face was all overspread with a most sickly and sallow hue, but yet so pervaded with an expression of piercing and active intellect, that an observer might easily have overlooked the merely physical attributes, and have seen only this wonderful energy. As he passed, this person exchanged a cold and distant salutation with Baglioni, but fixed his eyes upon Giovanni with an intentness that seemed to bring out whatever was within him worthy of notice. Nevertheless, there was a peculiar quietness in the look, as if taking merely a speculative, not a human interest, in the young man.

"It is Doctor Rappaccini!" whispered the Professor, when the stranger had passed. — "Has he ever seen your face before?"

"Not that I know," answered Giovanni, starting at the name.

"He *has* seen you! — he must have seen you!" said Baglioni, hastily. "For some purpose or other, this man of science is making a study of you. I know that look of his! It is the same that coldly illuminates his face, as he bends over a bird, a mouse, or a butterfly, which, in pursuance of some experiment, he has killed by the perfume of a flower; — a look as deep as nature itself, but without nature's warmth of love. Signor Giovanni, I will stake my life upon it, you are the subject of one of Rappaccini's experiments!"

"Will you make a fool of me?" cried Giovanni, passionately. "*That,* Signor 50 Professor, were an untoward experiment."

"Patience, patience!" replied the imperturbable Professor. — "I tell thee, my poor Giovanni, that Rappaccini has a scientific interest in thee. Thou hast fallen into fearful hands! And the Signora Beatrice? What part does she act in this mystery?"

But Guasconti, finding Baglioni's pertinacity intolerable, here broke away, and was gone before the Professor could again seize his arm. He looked after the young man intently, and shook his head.

"This must not be," said Baglioni to himself. "The youth is the son of my old friend, and should not come to any harm from which the arcana of medical science can preserve him. Besides, it is too insufferable an impertinence in Rappaccini, thus to snatch the bud out of my own hands, as I may say, and make use of him for his infernal experiments. This daughter of his! It shall be looked to. Perchance, most learned Rappaccini, I may foil you where you little dream of it!"

Meanwhile, Giovanni had pursued a circuitous route, and at length found himself at the door of his lodgings. As he crossed the threshold, he was met by old Lisabetta, who smirked and smiled, and was evidently desirous to attract his attention; vainly, however, as the ebullition of his feelings had momentarily subsided into a cold and dull vacuity. He turned his eyes full upon the withered face that was puckering itself into a smile, but seemed to behold it not. The old dame, therefore, laid her grasp upon his cloak.

"Signor! — Signor!" whispered she, still with a smile over the whole 55 breadth of her visage, so that it looked not unlike a grotesque carving in wood, darkened by centuries — "Listen, Signor! There is a private entrance into the garden!"

"What do you say?" exclaimed Giovanni, turning quickly about, as if an inanimate thing should start into feverish life. — "A private entrance into Doctor Rappaccini's garden!"

"Hush! hush! — not so loud!" whispered Lisabetta, putting her hand over his mouth. "Yes; into the worshipful Doctor's garden, where you may see all his fine shrubbery. Many a young man in Padua would give gold to be admitted among those flowers."

Giovanni put a piece of gold into her hand.

"Show me the way," said he.

A surmise, probably excited by his conversation with Baglioni crossed his 60 mind, that this interposition of old Lisabetta might perchance be connected with the intrigue, whatever were its nature, in which the Professor seemed to suppose that Doctor Rappaccini was involving him. But such a suspicion, though it disturbed Giovanni, was inadequate to restrain him. The instant he was aware of the possibility of approaching Beatrice, it seemed an absolute necessity of his existence to do so. It mattered not whether she were angel or demon; he was irrevocably within her sphere, and must obey the law that whirled him onward, in ever lessening circles, towards a result which he did not attempt to foreshadow. And yet, strange to say, there came across him a sudden doubt, whether this intense interest on his part were not delusory — whether it were really of so deep and positive a nature as to justify him in now thrusting himself into an incalculable position – whether it were not merely the fantasy of a young man's brain, only slightly, or not at all, connected with his heart!

He paused – hesitated – turned half about – but again went on. His withered guide led him along several obscure passages, and finally undid a door, through which, as it was opened, there came the sight and sound of rustling leaves, with the broken sunshine glimmering among them. Giovanni stepped forth, and forcing himself through the entanglement of a shrub that wreathed its tendrils over the hidden entrance, he stood beneath his own window, in the open area of Doctor Rappaccini's garden.

How often is it the case, that, when impossibilities have come to pass, and dreams have condensed their misty substance into tangible realities, we find ourselves calm, and even coldly self-possessed, amid circumstances which it would have been a delirium of joy or agony to anticipate! Fate delights to thwart us thus. Passion will choose his own time to rush upon the scene, and lingers sluggishly behind, when an appropriate adjustment of events would seem to summon his appearance. So was it now with Giovanni. Day after day, his pulses had throbbed with feverish blood, at the improbable idea of an interview with Beatrice, and of standing with her, face to face, in this very garden, basking in the oriental sunshine of her beauty, and snatching from her full gaze the mystery which he deemed the riddle of his own existence. But now there was a singular and untimely equanimity within his breast. He threw a glance around the garden to discover if Beatrice or her father were present, and perceiving that he was alone, began a critical observation of the plants.

The aspect of one and all of them dissatisfied him; their gorgeousness seemed fierce, passionate, and even unnatural. There was hardly an individual shrub which a wanderer, straying by himself through a forest, would not have been startled to find growing wild, as if an unearthly face had glared at him out of the thicket. Several, also, would have shocked a delicate instinct by an appearance of artificiality, indicating that there had been such commixture, and, as it were, adultery of various vegetable species, that the production was no longer of God's making, but the monstrous offspring of man's depraved fancy, glowing with only an evil mockery of beauty. They were probably the result of experiment, which, in one or two cases, had succeeded in mingling plants individually lovely into a compound possessing the questionable and ominous character that distinguished the whole growth of the garden. In fine, Giovanni recognized but two or three plants in the collection, and those of a kind that he well knew to be poisonous. While busy with these contemplations, he heard the rustling of a silken garment, and turning, beheld Beatrice emerging from beneath the sculptured portal.

Giovanni had not considered with himself what should be his deportment; whether he should apologize for his intrusion into the garden, or assume that he was there with the privity, at least, if not the desire of Doctor Rappaccini or his daughter. But Beatrice's manner placed him at his ease, though leaving him still in doubt by what agency he had gained admittance. She came lightly along the path, and met him near the broken fountain. There was surprise in her face, but brightened by a simple and kind expression of pleasure.

"You are a connoisseur in flowers, Signor," said Beatrice with a smile, 65 alluding to the bouquet which he had flung her from the window. "It is no marvel, therefore, if the sight of my father's rare collection has tempted you to take a nearer view. If he were here, he could tell you many strange and interesting facts as to the nature and habits of these shrubs, for he has spent a lifetime in such studies, and this garden is his world."

"And yourself, lady" — observed Giovanni — "if fame says true — you, likewise, are deeply skilled in the virtues indicated by these rich blossoms, and these spicy perfumes. Would you deign to be my instructress, I should prove an apter scholar than under Signor Rappaccini himself."

"Are there such idle rumors?" asked Beatrice, with the music of a pleasant laugh. "Do people say that I am skilled in my father's science of plants? What a jest is there! No; though I have grown up among these flowers, I know no more of them than their hues and perfume; and sometimes, methinks I would fain rid myself of even that small knowledge. There are many flowers here, and those not the least brilliant, that shock and offend me, when they meet my eye. But, pray, Signor, do not believe these stories about my science. Believe nothing of me save what you see with your own eyes."

"And must I believe all that I have seen with my own eyes?" asked Giovanni pointedly, while the recollection of former scenes made him shrink. "No, Signora, you demand too little of me. Bid me believe nothing, save what comes from your own lips."

It would appear that Beatrice understood him. There came a deep flush to her cheek; but she looked full into Giovanni's eyes, and responded to his gaze of uneasy suspicion with a queen-like haughtiness.

"I do so bid you, Signor!" she replied. "Forget whatever you may have fancied in regard to me. If true to the outward senses, still it may be false in its essence. But the words of Beatrice Rappaccini's lips are true from the heart outward. Those you may believe!" 70

A fervor glowed in her whole aspect, and beamed upon Giovanni's consciousness like the light of truth itself. But while she spoke, there was a fragrance in the atmosphere around her, rich and delightful, though evanescent, yet which the young man, from an indefinable reluctance, scarcely dared to draw into his lungs. It might be the odor of the flowers. Could it be Beatrice's breath, which thus embalmed her words with a strange richness, as if by steeping them in her heart? A faintness passed like a shadow over Giovanni, and flitted away; he seemed to gaze through the beautiful girl's eyes into her transparent soul, and felt no more doubt or fear.

The tinge of passion that had colored Beatrice's manner vanished; she became gay, and appeared to derive a pure delight from her communion with the youth, not unlike what the maiden of a lonely island might have felt, conversing with a voyager from the civilized world. Evidently her experience of life had been confined within the limits of that garden. She talked now about matters as simple as the day-light or summer-clouds, and now asked questions in reference to the city, or Giovanni's distant home, his friends, his mother, and his sisters; questions indicating such seclusion, and such lack of familiarity with modes and forms, that Giovanni responded as if to an infant. Her spirit gushed out before him like a fresh rill, that was just catching its first glimpse of the sunlight, and wondering at the reflections of earth and sky which were flung into its bosom. There came thoughts, too, from a deep source, and fantasies of a gem-like brilliancy, as if diamonds and rubies sparkled upward among the bubbles of the fountain. Ever and anon, there gleamed across the young man's mind a sense of wonder, that he should be walking side by side with the being who had so wrought upon his imagination — whom he had idealized in such hues of terror — in whom he had positively witnessed such manifestations of dreadful attributes — that he should be conversing with Beatrice like a brother, and should find her so human and so maiden-like. But such reflections were only momentary; the effect of her character was too real, not to make itself familiar at once.

In this free intercourse, they had strayed through the garden, and now, after many turns among its avenues, were come to the shattered fountain, beside which grew the magnificent shrub with its treasury of glowing blossoms. A fragrance was diffused from it, which Giovanni recognized as identical with that which he had attributed to Beatrice's breath, but incomparably more powerful. As her eyes fell upon it, Giovanni beheld her press her hand to her bosom, as if her heart were throbbing suddenly and painfully.

"For the first time in my life," murmured she, addressing the shrub, "I had forgotten thee!"

"I remember, Signora," said Giovanni, "that you once promised to reward 75 me with one of these living gems for the bouquet, which I had the happy boldness to fling to your feet. Permit me now to pluck it as a memorial of this interview."

He made a step towards the shrub, with extended hand. But Beatrice darted forward, uttering a shriek that went through his heart like a dagger. She caught his hand, and drew it back with the whole force of her slender figure. Giovanni felt her touch thrilling through his fibers.

"Touch it not!" exclaimed she, in a voice of agony. "Not for thy life! It is fatal!"

Then, hiding her face, she fled from him, and vanished beneath the sculptured portal. As Giovanni followed her with his eyes, he beheld the emaciated figure and pale intelligence of Doctor Rappaccini, who had been watching the scene, he knew not how long, within the shadow of the entrance.

No sooner was Guasconti alone in his chamber, than the image of Beatrice came back to his passionate musings, invested with all the witchery that had been gathering around it ever since his first glimpse of her, and now likewise-imbued with a tender warmth of girlish womanhood. She was human: her nature was endowed with all gentle and feminine qualities; she was worthiest to be worshipped; she was capable, surely, on her part, of the height and heroism of love. Those tokens, which he had hitherto considered as proofs of a frightful peculiarity in her physical and moral system, were now either forgotten, or, by the subtle sophistry of passion, transmuted into a golden crown of enchantment, rendering Beatrice the more admirable, by so much as she was the more unique. Whatever had looked ugly, was now beautiful; or, if incapable of such a change, it stole away and hid itself among those shapeless half-ideas, which throng the dim region beyond the day-light of our perfect consciousness. Thus did Giovanni spend the night, nor fell asleep, until the dawn had begun to awake the slumbering flowers in Doctor Rappaccini's garden, whither his dreams doubtless led him. Up rose the sun in his due season, and flinging his beams upon the young man's eyelids, awoke him to a sense of pain. When thoroughly aroused, he became sensible of a burning and tingling agony in his hand — in his right hand — the very hand which Beatrice had grasped in her own, when he was on the point of plucking one of the gem-like flowers. On the back of that hand there was now a purple print, like that of four small fingers, and the likeness of a slender thumb upon his wrist.

Oh, how stubbornly does love — or even that cunning semblance of love 80 which flourishes in the imagination, but strikes no depth of root into the heart — how stubbornly does it hold its faith, until the moment come, when it is doomed to vanish into thin mist! Giovanni wrapt a handkerchief about his head, and wondered what evil thing had stung him, and soon forgot his pain in a reverie of Beatrice.

After the first interview, a second was in the inevitable course of what we call fate. A third; a fourth; and a meeting with Beatrice in the garden was no longer an incident in Giovanni's daily life, but the whole space in which he might be said to live; for the anticipation and memory of that ecstatic hour made up the remainder. Nor was it otherwise with the daughter of Rappaccini. She watched for the youth's appearance, and flew to his side with confidence as unreserved as if they had been playmates from early infancy — as if they were such playmates still. If, by any unwonted chance, he failed to come at the appointed moment, she stood beneath the window, and sent up the rich sweetness of her tones to float around him in his chamber, and echo and reverberate throughout his heart — "Giovanni! Giovanni! Why tarriest thou? Come down!" — And down he hastened into that Eden of poisonous flowers.

But, with all this intimate familiarity, there was still a reserve in Beatrice's demeanor, so rigidly and invariably sustained, that the idea of infringing it scarcely occurred to his imagination. By all appreciable signs, they loved; they had looked love, with eyes that conveyed the holy secret from the depths of one soul into the depths of the other, as if it were too sacred to be whispered by the way; they had even spoken love, in those gushes of passion when their spirits darted forth in articulated breath, like tongues of long-hidden flame; and yet there had been no seal of lips, no clasp of hands, nor any slightest caress, such as love claims and hallows. He had never touched one of the gleaming ringlets of her hair; her garment — so marked was the physical barrier between them — had never been waved against him by a breeze. On the few occasions when Giovanni had seemed tempted to overstep the limit, Beatrice grew so sad, so stern, and withal wore such a look of desolate separation, shuddering at itself, that not a spoken word was requisite to repel him. At such times, he was startled at the horrible suspicions that rose, monster-like, out of the caverns of his heart, and stared him in the face; his love grew thin and faint as the morning-mist; his doubts alone had substance. But when Beatrice's face brightened again, after the momentary shadow, she was transformed at once from the mysterious, questionable being, whom he had watched with so much awe and horror; she was now the beautiful and unsophisticated girl, whom he felt that his spirit knew with a certainty beyond all other knowledge.

A considerable time had now passed since Giovanni's last meeting with Baglioni. One morning, however, he was disagreeably surprised by a visit from the Professor, whom he had scarcely thought of for whole weeks, and would willingly have forgotten still longer. Given up, as he had long been, to a pervading excitement, he could tolerate no companions, except upon condition of their perfect sympathy with his present state of feeling. Such sympathy was not to be expected from Professor Baglioni.

The visitor chatted carelessly, for a few moments, about the gossip of the city and the University, and then took up another topic.

"I have been reading an old classic author lately," said he, "and met with a 85 story that strangely interested me. Possibly you may remember it. It is of an Indian prince, who sent a beautiful woman as a present to Alexander the Great. She was as lovely as the dawn, and gorgeous as the sunset; but what especially distinguished her was a certain rich perfume in her breath — richer than a garden of Persian roses. Alexander, as was natural to a youthful conqueror, fell in love at first sight with this magnificent stranger. But a certain sage physician, happening to be present, discovered a terrible secret in regard to her."

"And what was that?" asked Giovanni, turning his eyes downward to avoid those of the Professor.

"That this lovely woman," continued Baglioni, with emphasis, "had been nourished with poisons from her birth upward, until her whole nature was so imbued with them, that she herself had become the deadliest poison in existence. Poison was her element of life. With that rich perfume of her breath, she blasted the very air. Her love would have been poison! — her embrace death! Is not this a marvellous tale?"

"A childish fable," answered Giovanni, nervously starting from his chair. "I marvel how your worship finds time to read such nonsense, among your graver studies."

"By the by," said the Professor, looking uneasily about him, "what singular fragrance is this in your apartment? Is it the perfume of your gloves? It is faint, but delicious, and yet, after all, by no means agreeable. Were I to breathe it long, methinks it would make me ill. It is like the breath of a flower — but I see no flowers in the chamber."

"Nor are there any," replied Giovanni, who had turned pale as the Profes- 90 sor spoke; "nor, I think, is there any fragrance, except in your worship's imagination. Odors, being a sort of element combined of the sensual and the spiritual, are apt to deceive us in this manner. The recollection of a perfume — the bare idea of it — may easily be mistaken for a present reality."

"Aye; but my sober imagination does not often play such tricks," said Baglioni; "and were I to fancy any kind of odor, it would be that of some vile apothecary drug, wherewith my fingers are likely enough to be imbued. Our worshipful friend Rappaccini, as I have heard, tinctures his medicaments with odors richer than those of Araby. Doubtless, likewise, the fair and learned Signora Beatrice would minister to her patients with draughts as sweet as a maiden's breath. But woe to him that sips them!"

Giovanni's face evinced many contending emotions. The tone in which the Professor alluded to the pure and lovely daughter of Rappaccini was a torture to his soul; and yet, the intimation of a view of her character, opposite to his own, gave instantaneous distinctness to a thousand dim suspicions, which now grinned at him like so many demons. But he strove hard to quell them, and to respond to Baglioni with a true lover's perfect faith.

"Signor Professor," said he, "you were my father's friend — perchance, too, it is your purpose to act a friendly part towards his son. I would fain feel nothing towards you, save respect and deference. But I pray you to observe, Signor, that there is one subject on which we must not speak. You know not the Signora Beatrice. You cannot, therefore, estimate the wrong — the blasphemy, I may even say — that is offered to her character by a light or injurious word."

"Giovanni! — my poor Giovanni!" answered the Professor, with a calm expression of pity, "I know this wretched girl far better than yourself. You shall hear the truth in respect to the poisoner Rappaccini, and his poisonous daughter. Yes; poisonous as she is beautiful! Listen; for even should you do violence to my gray hairs, it shall not silence me. That old fable of the Indian woman has become a truth, by the deep and deadly science of Rappaccini, and in the person of the lovely Beatrice!"

Giovanni groaned and hid his face.   95

"Her father," continued Baglioni, "was not restrained by natural affection from offering up his child, in this horrible manner, as the victim of his insane zeal for science. For — let us do him justice — he is as true a man of science as ever distilled his own heart in an alembic. What, then, will be your fate? Beyond a doubt, you are selected as the material of some new experiment. Perhaps the result is to be death — perhaps a fate more awful still! Rappaccini, with what he calls the interest of science before his eyes, will hesitate at nothing."

"It is a dream!" muttered Giovanni to himself, "surely it is a dream!"

"But," resumed the Professor, "be of good cheer, son of my friend! It is not yet too late for the rescue. Possibly, we may even succeed in bringing back this miserable child within the limits of ordinary nature, from which her father's madness has estranged her. Behold this little silver vase! It was wrought by the hands of the renowned Benvenuto Cellini,° and is well worthy to be a love-gift to the fairest dame in Italy. But its contents are invaluable. One little sip of this antidote would have rendered the most virulent poisons of the Borgias° innocuous. Doubt not that it will be as efficacious against those of Rappaccini. Bestow the vase, and the precious liquid within it, on your Beatrice, and hopefully await the result."

Baglioni laid a small, exquisitely wrought silver phial on the table, and withdrew, leaving what he had said to produce its effect upon the young man's mind.

"We will thwart Rappaccini yet!" thought he, chuckling to himself, as he   100 descended the stairs. "But, let us confess the truth of him, he is a wonderful man! — a wonderful man indeed! A vile empiric, however, in his practice, and therefore not to be tolerated by those who respect the good old rules of the medical profession!"

Throughout Giovanni's whole acquaintance with Beatrice, he had occasionally, as we have said, been haunted by dark surmises as to her character. Yet, so thoroughly had she made herself felt by him as a simple, natural, most affectionate and guileless creature, that the image now held up by Professor Baglioni, looked as strange and incredible, as if it were not in accordance with his own original conception. True, there were ugly recollections connected with his first glimpses of the beautiful girl; he could not quite forget the bouquet that withered in her grasp, and the insect that perished amid the sunny air, by no ostensible agency, save the fragrance of her breath. These incidents, however, dissolving in the pure light of her character, had no longer the efficacy of facts, but were acknowledged as mistaken fantasies, by whatever testimony of the senses they might appear to be substantiated. There is something truer and more real, than what we can see with the eyes, and touch with the finger. On such better evidence, had Giovanni founded his confidence in Beatrice, though

Benvenuto Cellini (1500-1571): A famous Italian goldsmith and sculptor.
Borgias: A Renaissance Italian family notorious for corruption and cruelty.

rather by the necessary force of her high attributes, than by any deep and generous faith, on his part. But, now, his spirit was incapable of sustaining itself at the height to which the early enthusiasm of passion had exalted it; he fell down, groveling among earthly doubts, and defiled therewith the pure whiteness of Beatrice's image. Not that he gave her up; he did but distrust. He resolved to institute some decisive test that should satisfy him, once for all, whether there were those dreadful peculiarities in her physical nature, which could not be supposed to exist without some corresponding monstrosity of soul. His eyes, gazing down afar, might have deceived him as to the lizard, the insect, and the flowers. But if he could witness, at the distance of a few paces, the sudden blight of one fresh and healthful flower in Beatrice's hand, there would be room for no further question. With this idea, he hastened to the florist's, and purchased a bouquet that was still gemmed with the morning dew-drops.

It was now the customary hour of his daily interview with Beatrice. Before descending into the garden, Giovanni failed not to look at his figure in the mirror; a vanity to be expected in a beautiful young man, yet, as displaying itself at that troubled and feverish moment, the token of a certain shallowness of feeling and insincerity of character. He did gaze, however, and said to himself, that his features had never before possessed so rich a grace, nor his eyes such vivacity, nor his cheeks so warm a hue of superabundant life.

"At least," thought he, "her poison has not yet insinuated itself into my system. I am no flower to perish in her grasp!"

With that thought, he turned his eyes on the bouquet, which he had never once laid aside from his hand. A thrill of indefinable horror shot through his frame, on perceiving that those dewy flowers were already beginning to droop; they wore the aspect of things that had been fresh and lovely, yesterday. Giovanni grew white as marble, and stood motionless before the mirror, staring at his own reflection there, as at the likeness of something frightful. He remembered Baglioni's remark about the fragrance that seemed to pervade the chamber. It must have been the poison in his breath! Then he shuddered— shuddered at himself! Recovering from his stupor, he began to watch, with curious eye, a spider that was busily at work, hanging its web from the antique cornice of the apartment, crossing and re-crossing the artful system of interwoven lines, as vigorous and active a spider as ever dangled from an old ceiling. Giovanni bent towards the insect, and emitted a deep, long breath. The spider suddenly ceased its toil; the web vibrated with a tremor originating in the body of the small artizan. Again Giovanni sent forth a breath, deeper, longer, and imbued with a venomous feeling out of his heart; he knew not whether he were wicked or only desperate. The spider made a convulsive gripe with his limbs, and hung dead across the window.

"Accursed! Accursed!" muttered Giovanni, addressing himself. "Hast thou 105 grown so poisonous, that this deadly insect perishes by thy breath?"

At that moment, a rich, sweet voice came floating up from the garden:—

"Giovanni! Giovanni! It is past the hour! Why tarriest thou! Come down!"

"Yes," muttered Giovanni again. "She is the only being whom my breath may not slay! Would that it might!"

He rushed down, and in an instant, was standing before the bright and loving eyes of Beatrice. A moment ago, his wrath and despair had been so fierce that he could have desired nothing so much as to wither her by a glance. But, with her actual presence, there came influences which had too real an existence to be at once shaken off; recollections of the delicate and benign power of her feminine nature, which had so often enveloped him in a religious calm; recollections of many a holy and passionate outgush of her heart, when the pure fountain had been unsealed from its depths, and made visible in its transparency to his mental eye; recollections which, had Giovanni known how to estimate them, would have assured him that all this ugly mystery was but an earthly illusion, and that, whatever mist of evil might seem to have gathered over her, the real Beatrice was a heavenly angel. Incapable as he was of such high faith, still her presence had not utterly lost its magic. Giovanni's rage was quelled into an aspect of sullen insensibility. Beatrice, with a quick spiritual sense, immediately felt that there was a gulf of blackness between them, which neither he nor she could pass. They walked on together, sad and silent, and came thus to the marble fountain, and to its pool of water on the ground, in the midst of which grew the shrub that bore gem-like blossoms. Giovanni was affrighted at the eager enjoyment — the appetite, as it were — with which he found himself inhaling the fragrance of the flowers.

"Beatrice," asked he abruptly, "whence came this shrub?" 110

"My father created it," answered she, with simplicity.

"Created it! created it!" repeated Giovanni. "What mean you, Beatrice?"

"He is a man fearfully acquainted with the secrets of nature," replied Beatrice; "and, at the hour when I first drew breath, this plant sprang from the soil, the offspring of his science, of his intellect, while I was but his earthly child. Approach it not!" continued she, observing with terror that Giovanni was drawing nearer to the shrub. "It has qualities that you little dream of. But I, dearest Giovanni, — I grew up and blossomed with the plant, and was nourished with its breath. It was my sister, and I loved it with a human affection: for — alas! hast thou not suspected it? there was an awful doom."

Here Giovanni frowned so darkly upon her that Beatrice paused and trembled. But her faith in his tenderness re-assured her, and made her blush that she had doubted for an instant.

"There was an awful doom," she continued, — "the effect of my father's 115 fatal love of science — which estranged me from all society of any kind. Until Heaven sent thee, dearest Giovanni, Oh! how lonely was thy poor Beatrice!"

"Was it a hard doom?" asked Giovanni, fixing his eyes upon her.

"Only of late have I known how hard it was," answered she tenderly. "Oh, yes; but my heart was torpid, and therefore quiet."

Giovanni's rage broke forth from his sullen gloom like a lightning-flash out of a dark cloud.

"Accursed one!" cried he, with venomous scorn and anger. "And finding thy solitude wearisome, thou hast severed me, likewise, from all the warmth of life, and enticed me into thy region of unspeakable horror!"

"Giovanni!" exclaimed Beatrice, turning her large bright eyes upon his 120 face. The force of his words had not found its way into her mind; she was merely wonder-struck.

"Yes, poisonous thing!" repeated Giovanni, beside himself with passion. "Thou has done it! Thou has blasted me! Thou hast filled my veins with poison! Thou hast made me as hateful, as ugly, as loathsome and deadly a creature as thyself, — a world's wonder of hideous monstrosity! Now — if our breath be happily as fatal to ourselves as to all others — let us join our lips in one kiss of unutterable hatred, and so die!"

"What has befallen me?" murmured Beatrice, with a low moan out of her heart. "Holy Virgin pity me, a poor heart-broken child!"

"Thou! Dost thou pray?" cried Giovanni, still with the same fiendish scorn. "Thy very prayers, as they come from thy lips, taint the atmosphere with death. Yes, yes; let us pray! Let us to church, and dip our fingers in the holy water at the portal! They that come after us will perish as by a pestilence. Let us sign crosses in the air! It will be scattering curses abroad in the likeness of holy symbols!"

"Giovanni," said Beatrice calmly, for her grief was beyond passion, "why dost thou join thyself with me thus in those terrible words? I, it is true, am the horrible thing thou namest me. But thou! — what hast thou to do, save with one other shudder at my hideous misery, to go forth out of the garden and mingle with thy race, and forget that there ever crawled on earth such a monster as poor Beatrice?"

"Dost thou pretend ignorance?" asked Giovanni, scowling upon her. "Behold! This power have I gained from the pure daughter of Rappaccini!"   125

There was a swarm of summer-insects flitting through the air, in search of the food promised by the flower-odors of the fatal garden. They circled round Giovanni's head, and were evidently attracted towards him by the same influence which had drawn them, for an instant, within the sphere of several of the shrubs. He sent forth a breath among them, and smiled bitterly at Beatrice, as at least a score of insects fell dead upon the ground.

"I see it! I see it!" shrieked Beatrice. "It is my father's fatal science? No, no, Giovanni; it was not I! Never, never! I dreamed only to love thee, and be with thee a little time, and so to let thee pass away, leaving but thine image in mine heart. For, Giovanni — believe it — though my body be nourished with poison, my spirit is God's creature, and craves love as its daily food. But my father! — he has united us in this fearful sympathy. Yes; spurn me! — tread upon me! — kill me! Oh, what is death, after such words as thine? But it was not I! Not for a world of bliss would I have done it!"

Giovanni's passion had exhausted itself in its outburst from his lips. There now came across a sense, mournful, and not without tenderness, of the intimate and peculiar relationship between Beatrice and himself. They stood, as it were, in an utter solitude, which would be made none the less solitary by the densest throng of human life. Ought not, then, the desert of humanity around them to press this insulated pair close together? If they should be cruel to one another, who was there to be kind to them? Besides, thought Giovanni, might there not still be a hope of his returning within the limits of ordinary nature, and leading Beatrice — the redeemed Beatrice — by the hand? Oh, weak, and selfish, and unworthy spirit, that could dream of an earthly union and earthly happiness as possible, after such deep love had been so bitterly wronged as was Beatrice's love by Giovanni's blighting words! No, no; there could be no such hope. She must pass heavily, with that broken heart, across the borders — she must bathe her hurts in some fount of Paradise, and forget her grief in the light of immortality — and *there* be well!

But Giovanni did not know it.

"Dear Beatrice," said he, approaching her, while she shrank away, as always   130 at his approach, but now with a different impulse — "dearest Beatrice, our fate is not yet so desperate. Behold! There is a medicine, potent, as a wise physician has assured me, and almost divine in its efficacy. It is composed of ingredients the most opposite to those by which thy awful father has brought this calamity upon thee and me. It is distilled of blessed herbs. Shall we not quaff it together, and thus be purified from evil?"

"Give it me!" said Beatrice, extending her hand to receive the little silver phial which Giovanni took from his bosom. She added, with a peculiar emphasis; "I will drink — but do thou await the result."

She put Baglioni's antidote to her lips; and, at the same moment the figure of Rappaccini emerged from the portal, and came slowly towards the marble fountain. As he drew near, the pale man of science seemed to gaze with a triumphant expression at the beautiful youth and maiden, as might an artist who should spend his life in achieving a picture or a group of statuary, and finally be satisfied with his success. He paused — his bent form grew erect with conscious power, he spread out his hand over them, in the attitude of a father imploring a blessing upon his children. But those were the same hands that had thrown poison into the stream of their lives! Giovanni trembled. Beatrice shuddered nervously, and pressed her hand upon her heart.

"My daughter," said Rappaccini, "thou are no longer lonely in the world! Pluck one of those precious gems from thy sister shrub, and bid thy bridegroom wear it in his bosom. It will not harm him now! My science, and the sympathy between thee and him, have so wrought within his system, that he now stands apart from common men, as thou dost, daughter of my pride and triumph, from ordinary women. Pass on, then, through the world, most dear to one another, and dreadful to all besides!"

"My father," said Beatrice, feebly — and still, as she spoke, she kept her hand upon her heart — "wherefore didst thou inflict this miserable doom upon thy child?"

"Miserable!" exclaimed Rappaccini. "What mean you, foolish girl? Dost 135 thou deem it misery to be endowed with marvellous gifts, against which no power nor strength could avail an enemy? Misery, to be able to quell the mightiest with a breath? Misery, to be as terrible as thou art beautiful? Wouldst thou, then, have preferred the condition of a weak woman, exposed to all evil, and capable of none?"

"I would fain have been loved, not feared," murmured Beatrice, sinking down upon the ground. — "But now it matters not; I am going, father, where the evil, which thou hast striven to mingle with my being, will pass away like a dream — like the fragrance of these poisonous flowers, which will no longer taint my breath among the flowers of Eden. Farewell, Giovanni! Thy words of hatred are like lead within my heart — but they, too, will fall away as I ascend. Oh, was there not, from the first, more poison in thy nature than in mine?"

To Beatrice — so radically had her earthly part been wrought upon by Rappaccini's skill — as poison had been life, so the powerful antidote was death. And thus the poor victim of man's ingenuity and of thwarted nature, and of the fatality that attends all such efforts of perverted wisdom, perished there, at the feet of her father and Giovanni. Just at that moment, Professor Pietro Baglioni looked forth from the window, and called loudly, in a tone of triumph mixed with horror, to the thunder-stricken man of science:

"Rappaccini! Rappaccini! And is *this* the upshot of your experiment?"

CONSIDERATIONS FOR CRITICAL THINKING AND WRITING

1. FIRST RESPONSE. Is Giovanni a sympathetic character? Explain why you think he does or doesn't love Beatrice.

2. Why is Padua, Italy, a particularly appropriate setting for this story? How does Padua differ from Giovanni's Naples? Why wouldn't Young Goodman Brown's Salem be equally appropriate?

3. Why does Rappaccini poison Beatrice? How does he justify his actions?

4. How does Pietro Baglioni serve as a foil to Rappaccini? What kind of professional relationship do they have?

5. How does the narrator's description of the garden — and particularly of the purple flower — connect the garden with Beatrice? What is the significance of the similarities?

6. Write an essay that responds to the question Giovanni raises in paragraph 9 about Rappaccini's garden: "Was this garden, then, the Eden of the present world? — and this man [Rappaccini], with such a perception of harm in what his own hands caused to grow, was he the Adam?" How do the allusions to Adam, Eve, and the Garden of Eden amplify the meanings of the story?

7. How does the narrator cast doubts on Giovanni's accounts of the death of the lizard and insect and the withering of the bouquet he gives Beatrice? What is the effect of these doubts? Why do you think Hawthorne includes them in the story?

8. What is the purpose of Baglioni's description of the "old classic" he summarizes for Giovanni in paragraphs 85 to 87?

9. How do you answer Beatrice's final question to Giovanni: "Oh, was there not, from the first, more poison in thy nature than in mine?" In what ways is Giovanni poisoned? What do you think is the most deadly "poison" in the story?

10. Why do you suppose Hawthorne gives Baglioni the story's last words?

11. Write an essay explaining what you think happens to Giovanni after the final scene.

CONNECTIONS TO OTHER SELECTIONS

1. Compare Rappaccini's devotion to science with Alymer's in "The Birthmark" (p. 329). Explain the similarities and differences in the plots.

2. Write an essay comparing the themes of isolation in "Rappaccini's Daughter" and "The Minister's Black Veil" (p. 320). Are there any positive effects produced by isolation in each story?

3. In an essay explore ideas about innocence and guilt in "Rappaccini's Daughter" and Joyce Carol Oates's "The Night Nurse" (p. 653).

PERSPECTIVES ON HAWTHORNE

Hawthorne on Solitude   1837

Dear Sir,

Not to burthen you with my correspondence, I have delayed a rejoinder to your very kind and cordial letter, until now. It gratifies me to find that you have occasionally felt an interest in my situation. . . . You would have been nearer the truth if you had pictured me as dwelling in an owl's nest; for mine is about as dismal; and, like the owl I seldom venture abroad till after dark. By some witchcraft or other — for I really cannot assign any reasonable why and wherefore — I have been carried apart from the main current of life, and find it impossible to get back again. Since we last met . . . I have secluded myself from society; and yet I never meant any such thing, nor dreamed what sort of life I was going to lead. I have made a captive of myself and put me into a dungeon, and now I cannot find the key to let myself out — and if the door were open, I should be almost afraid to come out. You tell me that you have met with troubles and changes. I know not what they may have been; but I can assure you that trouble is the next best thing to enjoyment, and that there is no fate in this world so horrible as to have no share in either its joys or sorrows. For the last ten years, I have not lived, but only dreamed about living. It may be true that there have been some unsubstantial pleasures here in the shade, which I should have missed in the sunshine, but you cannot conceive how utterly devoid of satisfaction all my retrospects are. I have laid up no treasure of pleasant remembrances, against old age; but there is some comfort in thinking that my future years can hardly fail to be more varied, and therefore more tolerable, than the past.

You give me more credit than I deserve, in supposing that I have led a studious life. I have, indeed, turned over a good many books, but in so desultory a way that it cannot be called study, nor has it left me the fruits of study. As to my literary efforts, I do not think much of them — neither is it worth while to be ashamed of them. They would have been better, I trust, if written under more favorable circumstances. I have had no external excitement — no consciousness that the public would like what I wrote, nor much hope nor a very passionate desire that they should do so. Nevertheless, having nothing else to be ambitious of, I have felt considerably interested in literature; and if my writings had made any decided impression, I should probably have been stimulated to greater exertions; but there has been no warmth of approbation, so that I have always written with benumbed fingers. I have another great difficulty, in the lack of materials; for I have seen so little of the world, that I have nothing but thin air to concoct my stories of, and it is not easy to give a lifelike semblance to such shadowy stuff. Sometimes, through a peep-hole, I have caught a glimpse of the real world; and the two or three articles, in which I have portrayed such glimpses, please me better than the others. I have now, or shall soon have, one sharp spur to exertion, which I lacked at an earlier period; for I see little prospect but that I must scribble for a living. But this troubles me much less than you would suppose. I can turn my pen to all sorts of drudgery, such as children's books, etc., and by and by, I shall get some editorship that will answer my purpose. Frank Pierce, who was with us at college, offered me his influence to obtain an office in the Exploring Expedition; but I believe that he was mistaken in supposing that a vacancy existed. If such a post were attainable, I should certainly accept it; for, though fixed so long to one spot, I have always had a desire to run around the world.

The copy of my Tales was sent to Mr. Owen's, the bookseller's in Cambridge. I am glad to find that you had read and liked some of the stories. To be sure, you could not well help flattering me a little; but I value your praise too highly not to have faith in its sincerity. When I last heard from the publisher — which was not very recently — the book was doing pretty well. Six or seven hundred copies had been sold. I suppose, however, these awful times have now stopped the sale.

I intend in a week or two to come out of my owl's nest, and not return to it till late in the summer — employing the interval in making a tour somewhere in New England. You, who have the dust of distant countries on your "sandal-shoon," cannot imagine how much enjoyment I shall have in this little excursion. Whenever I get abroad, I feel just as young as I did, ten years ago. What a letter I am inflicting on you! I trust you will answer it.

Yours sincerely,

Nath. Hawthorne.

From a letter to Henry Wadsworth Longfellow, June 4, 1837

CONSIDERATIONS FOR CRITICAL THINKING AND WRITING

1. How does Hawthorne regard his solitude? How does he feel it has affected his life and writing?

2. Hawthorne explains to Longfellow, one of his Bowdoin classmates, that "there is no fate in this world so horrible as to have no share in either its joys or sorrows" (para. 1). Explain how this idea is worked into "Young Goodman Brown" (p. 310).

3. Does Hawthorne indicate any positive results for having lived in his "owl's nest" (para. 1)? Consider how "The Minister's Black Veil" (p. 320) and this letter shed light on each other.

Hawthorne on the Power of the Writer's Imagination   *1850*

. . . Moonlight, in a familiar room, falling so white upon the carpet, and show-ing all its figures so distinctly — making every object so minutely visible, yet so unlike a morning or noontide visibility — is a medium the most suitable for a romance-writer° to get acquainted with his illusive guests. There is the little domestic scenery of the well-known apartment; the chairs, with each its sep-arate individuality; the center-table, sustaining a work-basket, a volume or two, and an extinguished lamp; the sofa; the book-case; the picture on the wall — all these details, so completely seen, are so spiritualized by the unusual light, that they seem to lose their actual substance, and become things of in-tellect. Nothing is too small or too trifling to undergo this change, and ac-quire dignity thereby. A child's shoe; the doll, seated in her little wicker car-riage; the hobbyhorse — whatever, in a word, has been used or played with, during the day, is now invested with a quality of strangeness and remoteness, though still almost as vividly present as by daylight. Thus, therefore, the floor

romance-writer: Hawthorne distinguished romance writing from novel writing. In the pref-ace to *The House of the Seven Gables* he writes:

> The latter form of composition is presumed to aim at a very minute fidelity, not merely to the possible, but to the probable and ordinary course of man's experience. The for-mer — while, as a work of art, it must rigidly subject itself to laws, and while it sins un-pardonably so far as it may swerve aside from the truth of the human heart — has fairly a right to present that truth under circumstances, to a great extent, of the writer's own choosing or creation.

of our familiar room has become a neutral territory, somewhere between the real world and fairyland, where the Actual and the Imaginary may meet, and each imbue itself with the nature of the other. Ghosts might enter here, without affrighting us. It would be too much in keeping with the scene to excite surprise, were we to look about us and discover a form, beloved, but gone hence, now sitting quietly in a streak of this magic moonshine, with an aspect that would make us doubt whether it had returned from afar, or had never once stirred from our fireside.

The somewhat dim coal-fire has an essential influence in producing the effect which I would describe. It throws its unobtrusive tinge throughout the room, with a faint ruddiness upon the walls and ceiling, and a reflected gleam from the polish of the furniture. This warmer light mingles itself with the cold spirituality of the moonbeams, and communicates, as it were, a heart and sensibilities of human tenderness to the forms which fancy summons up. It converts them from snow-images into men and women. Glancing at the looking-glass, we behold — deep within its haunted verge — the smouldering glow of the half-extinguished anthracite, the white moonbeams on the floor, and a repetition of all the gleam and shadow of the picture, with one remove farther from the actual, and nearer to the imaginative. Then, at such an hour, and with this scene before him, if a man, sitting all alone, cannot dream strange things, and make them look like truth, he need never try to write romances.

From *The Scarlet Letter*

CONSIDERATIONS FOR CRITICAL THINKING AND WRITING

1. Explain how Hawthorne uses light as a means of invoking the transforming powers of the imagination.

2. How do Hawthorne's stories fulfill his definition of romance writing? Why can't they be regarded as realistic?

3. Choose one story and discuss it as an attempt to evoke "the truth of the human heart."

Hawthorne on His Short Stories   1851

[These stories] have the pale tint of flowers that blossomed in too retired a shade — the coolness of a meditative habit, which diffuses itself through the feeling and observation of every sketch. Instead of passion there is sentiment; and, even in what purport to be pictures of actual life, we have allegory, not always warmly dressed in its habiliments of flesh and blood as to be taken into the reader's mind without a shiver. Whether from lack of power, or an unconquerable reserve, the Author's touches have often an effect of tameness; the merriest man can hardly contrive to laugh at his broadest humor; the tenderest woman, one would suppose, will hardly shed warm tears at his deepest pathos. The book, if you would see anything in it, requires to be read in the clear brown, twilight atmosphere in which it was written; if opened in the sunshine, it is apt to look exceedingly like a volume of blank pages.

From the preface to the 1851 edition of *Twice-Told Tales*

CONSIDERATIONS FOR CRITICAL THINKING AND WRITING

1. How does Hawthorne characterize his stories? Does his assessment accurately describe the stories you've read?

2. Why is a "twilight atmosphere" more conducive to an appreciation of Hawthorne's art than "sunshine"?

3. Write a one-page description of Hawthorne's stories in which you generalize about his characteristic approach to one of these elements: plot, character, setting, symbol, theme, tone.

HERMAN MELVILLE (1819–1891)

On Nathaniel Hawthorne's Tragic Vision   *1851*

There is a certain tragic phase of humanity which, in our opinion, was never more powerfully embodied than by Hawthorne. We mean the tragicalness of human thought in its own unbiased, native, and profounder workings. We think that in no recorded mind has the intense feeling of the visable truth ever entered more deeply than into this man's. By visable truth, we mean the apprehension of the absolute condition of present things as they strike the eye of the man who fears them not, though they do their worst to him — the man who, like Russia or the British Empire, declares himself a sovereign nature (in himself) amid the powers of heaven, hell, and earth. He may perish; but so long as he exists he insists upon treating with all Powers upon an equal basis. If any of those other Powers choose to withhold certain secrets, let them; that does not impair my sovereignty in myself; that does not make me tributary. And perhaps, after all, there is *no* secret. We incline to think that the Problem of the Universe is like the Freemason's° mighty secret, so terrible to all children. It turns out, at last, to consist in a triangle, a mallet, and an apron — nothing more! . . . There is the grand truth about Nathaniel Hawthorne. He says NO! in thunder; but the Devil himself cannot make him say *yes.* For all men who say *yes,* lie; and all men who say *no* — why, they are in the happy condition of judicious, unincumbered travelers in Europe; they cross the frontiers into Eternity with nothing but a carpetbag — that is to say, the Ego. Whereas those *yes*-gentry, they travel with heaps of baggage, and, damn them! they will never get through the Custom House. What's the reason, Mr. Hawthorne, that in the last stages of metaphysics a fellow always falls to *swearing* so? I could rip an hour.

From a letter to Hawthorne, April 16(?), 1851

Freemasons: A member of the secret fraternity of Freemasonry.

CONSIDERATIONS FOR CRITICAL THINKING AND WRITING

1. What qualities in Hawthorne does Melville admire?

2. Explain how these qualities are embodied in one of the Hawthorne stories.

3. How might Melville's lawyer in "Bartleby, the Scrivener" (p. 113) be characterized as one of "those *yes*-gentry"?

TWO COMPLEMENTARY
CRITICAL READINGS

JUDITH FETTERLEY (B. 1938)

A Feminist Reading of "The Birthmark" 1978

It is testimony at once to Hawthorne's ambivalence, his seeking to cover with one hand what he uncovers with the other; and to the pervasive sexism of our culture that most readers would describe "The Birthmark" as a story of failure rather than as the success story it really is — the demonstration of how to murder your wife and get away with it. It is, of course, possible to read "The Birthmark" as a story of misguided idealism, a tale of the unhappy consequences of man's nevertheless worthy passion for perfecting and transcending nature; and this is the reading usually given it. This reading, however, ignores the significance of the form idealism takes in the story. It is not irrelevant that "The Birthmark" is about a man's desire to perfect his wife, nor is it accidental that the consequence of this idealism is the wife's death. In fact, "The Birthmark" provides a brilliant analysis of the sexual politics of idealization and a brilliant exposure of the mechanisms whereby hatred can be disguised as love, neurosis can be disguised as science, murder can be disguised as idealization, and success can be disguised as failure. Thus, Hawthorne's insistence in his story on the metaphor of disguise serves as both warning and clue to a feminist reading. . . .

One cannot imagine this story in reverse — that is, a woman's discovering an obsessive need to perfect her husband and deciding to perform experiments on him — nor can one imagine the story being about a man's conceiving such an obsession for another man. It is woman, and specifically woman as wife, who elicits the obsession with imperfection and the compulsion to achieve perfection, just as it is man, and specifically man as husband, who is thus obsessed and compelled. In addition, it is clear from the summary that the imagined perfection is purely physical. Aylmer is not concerned with the quality of Georgiana's character or with the state of her soul, for he considers her "fit for heaven without tasting death." Rather, he is absorbed in her physical appearance, and perfection for him is equivalent to physical beauty. Georgiana is an exemplum of woman as beautiful object, reduced to and defined by her body. . . . "The Birthmark" demonstrates the fact that the idealization of women has its source in a profound hostility toward women and that it is at once a disguise for this hostility and the fullest expression of it. . . .

. . . Unable to accept himself for what he is, Aylmer constructs a mythology of science and adopts the character of a scientist to disguise his true nature and to hide his real motives, from himself as well as others. As a consequence, he acquires a way of acting out these motives without in fact having to be aware of them. One might describe "The Birthmark" as an exposé of science because it demonstrates the ease with which science can be invoked to conceal highly subjective motives. "The Birthmark" is an exposure of the realities that underlie the scientist's posture of objectivity and rationality and the claims of science to operate in an amoral and value-free world. Pale Aylmer, the intellectual scientist, is a mask for the brutish, earthy, soot-smeared Aminadab, just as the mythology of scientific research and objectivity finally masks murder, disguising Georgiana's death as just one more experiment that failed. . . .

The implicit feminism in "The Birthmark" is considerable. On one level the story is a study of sexual politics, of the powerlessness of women and of the psychology which results from that powerlessness. Hawthorne dramatizes the fact that woman's identity is a product of men's responses to her: "It must not be concealed, however, that the impression wrought by this fairy sign manual varied exceedingly, according to the difference of temperament in the beholders." To those who love Georgiana, her birthmark is evidence of her beauty; to those who envy or hate her, it is an object of disgust. It is Aylmer's repugnance for the birthmark that makes Georgiana blanch, thus causing the mark to emerge as a sharply defined blemish against the whiteness of her cheek. Clearly, the birthmark takes on its character from the eye of the beholder. And just as clearly Georgiana's attitude toward her birthmark varies in response to different observers and definers. Her self-image derives from internalizing the attitudes toward her of the man or men around her. Since what surrounds Georgiana is an obsessional attraction expressed as a total revulsion, the result is not surprising: continual self-consciousness that leads to a pervasive sense of shame and a self-hatred that terminates in an utter readiness to be killed. "The Birthmark" demonstrates the consequences to women of being trapped in the laboratory of man's mind, the object of unrelenting scrutiny, examination, and experimentation.

From The Resisting Reader: A Feminist Approach to American Fiction

CONSIDERATIONS FOR CRITICAL THINKING AND WRITING

1. In what sense does Fetterley regard "The Birthmark" as a "success story" (para. 1)? How does her feminist perspective inform this view?

2. Why do you think Fetterley argues that it is impossible to imagine reversing the male-female roles in this story?

3. How does Fetterley make a case for reading the story as an "exposé of science" (para. 3)? Explain why science is described as an essentially male activity.

4. Although Fetterley does not include "The Minister's Black Veil" (p. 320) in her discussion, might it not be argued that it too harbors an "implicit feminism" (para. 4)? Write an analysis of the Reverend Mr. Hooper from a feminist perspective.

JAMES QUINN (B. 1937) AND ROSS BALDESSARINI (B. 1937)

A Psychological Reading of "The Birthmark"   1981

Hawthorne's art in the creation of character in many ways anticipates modern psychoanalytic psychology. As a literary psychologist, he excels at revealing unconscious sources of obsessed behavior. In "The Birthmark," Aylmer, a scientist whose ambition may be to control nature, provides an exceptionally good example of an obsessive character. He is obsessed with imperfection in human nature and is unable to achieve a mature human relationship. . . .

. . . What has happened to make Aylmer feel this way? What indeed ails him? The question is a natural one, but useless. Hawthorne does not supply an answer and by this omission seems to suggest that insights into human behavior are likely to be subjective, imperfect, unsatisfying. What is important is not the cause of obsessive thought or compulsive behavior but the effects.

The dramatic situation here is that Aylmer, by marrying Georgiana, is forced to deal with a conflict between his earlier, somewhat distant view of her as an intellectualized feminine ideal and her present tangible reality. Clearly one meaning of the red hand is a mark of her accessibility to touch, that is, of her sexuality. It also includes conflict between personal idealization and reality — a classical and ubiquitous obsessional neurotic conflict. While Aylmer's struggle is virtually universal, his fixation on Georgiana's blemish approaches a symptom that is considered characteristic of obsessive-compulsive neurosis in modern-day psychopathological terms.[1] The function of such neurotic symptoms in the psychic economy is to inhibit intolerable anxiety by focusing on an isolated and somewhat concrete representation so as to avoid a larger emotional conflict.

The psychoanalytic theorist Fenichel has written, "Many compulsive neurotics have to worry very much about small and apparently insignificant things. In analysis, these small things turn out to be substitutes for important ones."[2] And further: "Compulsive neurotics try to use external objects for the solution or relief of their inner conflicts" (p. 293). As "the compulsive neurotic tends . . . to extend the range of his symptoms . . ." (p. 294), so Aylmer's reaction to the birthmark grew "more and more intolerable with every moment of their . . . lives," presumably as a result of Georgiana's unavoidable presence. What at first seemed a trifling matter "so connected itself with innumerable trains of thought and modes of feeling that it became the *central point of all*" [stress added]. Like Parson Hooper [in "The Minister's Black Veil"], Aylmer is another Hawthornian victim of morbid forces, largely internal, beyond his control. Surely Aylmer's aversion owes its intensity and its obsessive character precisely to the fact that it is not accessible to conscious examination.[3] . . .

[1] Most of the characteristics of the illness can be found in the official definition of obsessive-compulsive disorder stated in the third edition of the American Psychiatric Association's (1980) *Diagnostic and Statistical Manual of Mental Disorders* (DSM-III):

> The essential features are recurrent obsessions and/or compulsions. Obsessions are defined as recurrent, persistent ideas, thoughts, images, or impulses which are ego-alien; that is, they are not experienced as voluntarily produced, but rather as ideas that invade the field of consciousness. Attempts are made to ignore or suppress them. Compulsions are behaviors which are not experienced as the outcome of the individual's own volition, but are accompanied by both a sense of subjective compulsion and a desire to resist (at least initially). (p. 234)

[2] Otto Fenichel, *The Psychoanalytic Theory of Neurosis* (New York, 1945), p. 290.

[3] In Freudian theory, certain ideas heavily charged or invested with affect or emotion constantly press toward conscious recognition or awareness, and certain impulses toward overt satisfaction or fulfillment. What we note in this tale is something close to "isolation of affect" or suppression and limitation or restriction of a highly charged emotion. The feeling and its source seem to be a form of anxiety, fear of being harmed through intimacy — metaphorically a problem in the category of castration anxiety or fear of being found wanting (already castrated). The idea that the birthmark is a castration symbol has already been suggested by Simon Lesser, *Fiction and the Unconscious*, p. 88.

* * *

He draws distinct lines between good and bad as does . . . Young Goodman Brown, who must see Faith, indeed all women, as Madonna or whore and who therefore remains immature and uncommitted. Aylmer, too, is like an adolescent, unable to find a point of equilibrium between two poles of thought, not realizing that "to be is to be imperfect, that the price of human existence is imperfection."[4]

An ironic aspect of such obsessed and morbid behavior so often seen in Hawthorne's works is that the more one struggles to attain perfection or to retain an unreasonable fixed idea, the more one is caught up in dealing with its opposite — imperfection and destruction. . . .

Up to this point we have been concerned with Hawthorne's presentation of Aylmer as one more neurotic and troubled obsessional soul. More important, however, is Aylmer's dramatically exaggerated representation of a more general struggle to adjust the ideal and the real. Likewise the birthmark can be viewed on more than one level. It is a mark of Georgiana's accessibility to touch, of her sexuality. It is suggestive of the scarlet letter — another public sign of secret and lustful sin, of "putting hands upon" in a sexual sense, of being touched, tainted, having sexuality and womanly characteristics. And, within the Judeo-Christian tradition . . . it seems to Hawthorne to symbolize the fallen and sinful nature of man. In an even wider application, it symbolizes the mortality of all mankind.

We miss the point, however, if we connect the birthmark solely with neurotic conflicts of atypical individuals or even with the hold death has on everyone, for the mark is also connected with sexuality and new life, indeed with aspiration to beauty and achievement and with the joy and energy for living. The importance of Hawthorne's psychological symbol is not the susceptibility of man to sin and death, but the special manner in which the marked woman suffers her fate: it is Aylmer who kills her. When the inward life concentrates narcissistically on self, demonic violence flares up in the lust to control and possess another person. Yet the first to be destroyed is Aylmer himself, who steps out of the procession of life, suffering from an incapacity to accept and integrate human emotions.

From *University of Hartford Studies in Literature:*
A Journal of Interdisciplinary Criticism

[4] Terence Martin, *Nathaniel Hawthorne* (New Haven, 1965), p. 70.

CONSIDERATIONS FOR CRITICAL THINKING AND WRITING

1. According to Quinn and Baldessarini, why isn't it fruitful to inquire into the causes of Aylmer's obsession? Explain why you agree or disagree with their assessment.

2. How might Aylmer, Parson Hooper, Young Goodman Brown, and Giovanni Guasconti all be regarded as exhibiting obsessive behavior?

3. Write an essay that discusses how and why this psychoanalytic reading leads to a focus on Aylmer while Judith Fetterley's feminist reading (p. 365)

leads to an emphasis on Georgiana. For a discussion of psychological and feminist readings see Chapter 37, "Critical Strategies for Reading."

4. Explain what you think a psychological reading of Georgiana would make of her character.

FLANNERY O'CONNOR (1925–1964)

When Flannery O'Connor died of lupus before her fortieth birthday, her work was cruelly cut short. Nevertheless, she had completed two novels, *Wise Blood* (1952) and *The Violent Bear It Away* (1960), as well as thirty-one short stories. Despite her brief life and relatively modest output, her work is regarded as among the most distinguished American fiction of the mid-twentieth century. Her two collections of short stories, *A Good Man Is Hard to Find* (1955) and *Everything That Rises Must Converge* (1965), were included in *The Complete Stories of Flannery O'Connor* (1971), which won the National Book Award.

Flannery O'Connor (undated photograph) in front of an accurate, if rather fierce self-portrait with one of her beloved peacocks.

O'Connor's fiction grapples with living a spiritual life in a secular world. Although this major concern is worked into each of her stories, she takes a broad approach to spiritual issues by providing moral, social, and psychological contexts that offer a wealth of insights and passion that her readers have found both startling and absorbing. Her stories are challenging because her characters, who initially seem radically different from people we know, turn out to be, by the end of each story, somehow familiar — somehow connected to us.

O'Connor inhabited simultaneously two radically different worlds. The world she created in her stories is populated with bratty children, malcontents, incompetents, pious frauds, bewildered intellectuals, deformed cynics, rednecks, hucksters, racists, perverts, and murderers who experience dramatically intense moments that surprise and shock readers. Her personal life, however, was largely uneventful. She humorously acknowledged its quiet nature in 1958 when she claimed that "there won't be any biographies of me because, for only one reason, lives spent between the house and the chicken yard do not make exciting copy."

A broad outline of O'Connor's life may not offer very much "exciting copy," but it does provide clues about why she wrote such powerful fiction. The only child of Catholic parents, O'Connor was born in Savannah, Georgia, where she attended a parochial grammar school and high school. When she was thirteen, her father became ill with disseminated lupus, a rare, incurable blood disease, and had to abandon his real-estate business. The family moved to Milledgeville in central Georgia, where her mother's family had lived for generations. Because there were no Catholic schools in Milledgeville, O'Connor attended a public high school. In 1942, the year after her father died of lupus, O'Connor graduated from high school and enrolled in Georgia State College for Women. There she wrote for the literary magazine until receiving her diploma in 1945. Her stories earned her a fellowship to the Writers' Workshop at the University of Iowa, and for two years she learned to write steadily and seriously. She sold her first story to *Accent* in 1946 and earned her master of fine arts degree in 1947. She wrote stories about life in the rural South, and this subject matter, along with her devout Catholic perspective, became central to her fiction.

With her formal education behind her, O'Connor was ready to begin her professional career at the age of twenty-two. Equipped with determination ("No one can convince me that I shouldn't rewrite as much as I do") and offered the opportunity to be around other practicing writers, she moved to New York, where she worked on her first novel, *Wise Blood*. In 1950, however, she was diagnosed as having lupus, and, returning to Georgia for treatment, she took up permanent residence on her mother's farm in Milledgeville. There she lived a severely restricted but productive life, writing stories and raising peacocks.

With the exception of O'Connor's early years in Iowa and New York and some short lecture trips to other states, she traveled little. Although she made a pilgrimage to Lourdes (apparently more for her mother's sake than for her own) and then to Rome for an audience with the pope, her life was centered in the South. Like those of William Faulkner and many other southern writers, O'Connor's stories evoke the rhythms of rural southern speech and manners in insulated settings where widely diverse characters mingle. Also like Faulkner, she created works whose meanings go beyond their settings. She did not want her fiction to be seen in the context of narrowly defined regionalism: she complained that "in almost every hamlet you'll find at least one old lady writing epics in Negro dialect and probably two or three old gentlemen who have impossible historical novels on the way." Refusing to be caricatured, she knew that "the woods are full of regional writers, and it is the great horror of every serious Southern writer that he will become one of them." O'Connor's stories are rooted in rural southern culture, but in a larger sense they are set within the psychological and spiritual landscapes of the human soul. This interior setting universalizes local materials in much the same way that Nathaniel Hawthorne's New England stories do. Indeed, O'Connor once described herself as "one of his descendants": "I feel more of a kinship with him than any other American."

O'Connor's deep spiritual convictions coincide with the traditional emphasis on religion in the South, where, she said, there is still the belief "that man has fallen and that he is only perfectible by God's grace, not by his own unaided efforts." Although O'Connor's Catholicism differs from the prevailing Protestant fundamentalism of the South, the religious ethos so pervasive even in rural southern areas provided fertile ground for the spiritual crises her characters experience. In a posthumous collection of her articles, essays, and reviews aptly titled *Mystery and Manners* (1969), she summarized her basic religious convictions:

> I am no disbeliever in spiritual purpose and no vague believer. I see from the standpoint of Christian orthodoxy. This means that for me the meaning of life is centered in our Redemption by Christ and what I see in the world I see in its relation to that. I don't think that this is a position that can be taken halfway or one that is particularly easy in these times to make transparent in fiction.

O'Connor realized that she was writing against the grain of the readers who discovered her stories in the *Partisan Review, Sewanee Review, Mademoiselle,* or *Harper's Bazaar.* Many readers thought that Christian dogma would make her writing doctrinaire, but she insisted that the perspective of Christianity allowed her to interpret the details of life and guaranteed her "respect for [life's] mystery." O'Connor's stories contain no prepackaged prescriptions for living, no catechisms that lay out all the answers. Instead, her characters struggle with spiritual questions in bizarre, incongruous situations. Their lives are grotesque — even comic — precisely because they do not understand their own spiritual natures. Their actions are extreme and abnormal. O'Connor explains the reasons for this in *Mystery and Manners;* she says she sought to expose the "distortions" of "modern life" that appear "normal" to her audience. Hence, she used "violent means" to convey her vision to a "hostile audience." "When you can assume that your audience holds the same beliefs you do, you can relax a little and use more normal means of talking to it." But when the audience holds different values, "you have to make your vision apparent by shock — to the hard of hearing you shout, and for the almost-blind you draw large and startling figures." O'Connor's characters lose or find their soul-saving grace in painful, chaotic circumstances that bear little or no resemblance to the slow but sure progress to the Celestial City of repentant pilgrims in traditional religious stories.

Because her characters are powerful creations who live convincing, even if ugly, lives, O'Connor's religious beliefs never supersede her storytelling. One need not be either Christian or Catholic to appreciate her concerns about human failure and degradation and her artistic ability to render fictional lives that are alternately absurdly comic and tragic. The ironies that abound in her work leave plenty of room for readers of all persuasions. O'Connor's work is narrow in the sense that her concerns are emphatically spiritual, but her compassion and her belief in human possibilities — even among the most unlikely characters — afford her fictions a capacity for wonder that is exhilarating. Her precise, deft use of language always reveals more than it seems to tell.

Like Hawthorne's fiction, O'Connor's stories present complex experiences that cannot be tidily summarized; it takes the entire story to suggest the meanings. Read the following four stories for the pleasure of entering the remarkable world O'Connor creates. You're in for some surprises.

CHRONOLOGY

1925	Born on March 25 in Savannah, Georgia.
1938	Moves with family to Milledgeville, Georgia; enters the public Peabody High School.
1941	Father dies of lupus.
1942	Graduates from Peabody High School; enters Georgia State College for Women.
1943–45	Writes stories and poems for college literary magazine; graduates from Georgia State with an undergraduate degree in English.
1945–47	Enters writing program at the University of Iowa and earns a master of fine arts degree in creative writing.
1948–49	Attends Yaddo artists' colony near Saratoga Springs, New York, for several months; lives in New York and Connecticut.
1950	After an illness, returns to Milledgeville and is diagnosed as suffering from lupus, an incurable disease. Lives on her family's dairy farm the rest of her life.

The Turkey   *1947*

His guns glinted sun steel in the ribs of the tree and, half-aloud through a crack in his mouth, he growled, "All right, Mason, this is as far as you go. The jig's up." The six-shooters in Mason's belt stuck out like waiting rattlers but he flipped them into the air and when they fell at his feet, kicked them behind him like so many dried steer skulls. "You varmint," he muttered, drawing his rope tight around the captured man's ankles, "this is the last rustlin' you'll do." He took three steps backward and leveled one gun to his eye. "Okay," he said with cold, slow precision, "This is. . . ." And then he saw it, just moving slightly through the bushes farther over, a touch of bronze and a rustle and then, through another gap in the leaves, the eye, set in red folds that covered the head and hung down along the neck, trembling slightly. He stood perfectly still and the turkey took another step, then stopped, with one foot lifted, and listened.

If he only had a gun, if he only had a gun! He could level aim and shoot it right where it was. In a second, it would slide through the bushes and be up in a tree before he could tell which direction it had gone in. Without moving his head, he strained his eyes to the ground to see if there were a stone near, but the ground looked as if it might just have been swept. The turkey moved again. The foot that had been poised half way up went down and the wing dropped over it, spreading so that Ruller could see the long single feathers, pointed at the end. He wondered if he dived into the bush on top of it. . . . It moved again and the wing came up, again and it went down.

It's limping, he thought quickly. He moved a little nearer, trying to make his motion imperceptible. Suddenly its head pierced out of the bush—he was about ten feet from it—and drew back and then abruptly back into the bush.

He began edging nearer with his arms rigid and his fingers ready to clutch. It was lame he could tell. It might not be able to fly. It shot its head out once more and saw him and shuttled back into the bushes and out again on the other side. Its motion was half-lopsided and the left wing was dragging. He was going to get it. He was going to get it if he had to chase it out of the county. He crawled through the brush and saw it about twenty feet away, watching him warily, moving its neck up and down. It stooped and tried to spread its wings and stooped again and went a little way to the side and stooped again, trying to make itself go up; but, he could tell, it couldn't fly. He was going to have it. He was going to have it if he had to run it out of the state. He saw himself going in the front door with it slung over his shoulder, and them all screaming, "Look at Ruller with that wild turkey! Ruller! where did you get that wild turkey!"

Oh, he had caught it in the woods; he had thought they might like to have him catch them one.

"You crazy bird," he muttered, "you can't fly. I've already got you." He 5
was walking in a wide circle, trying to get behind it. For a second, he almost thought he could go pick it up. It had dropped down and one foot was sprawled, but when he got near enough to pounce, it shot off in a heavy speed that made him start. He tore after it, straight out in the open for a half acre of dead cotton; then it went under a fence and into some woods again and he had to get on his hands and knees to get under the fence but still keep his eye on the turkey but not tear his shirt; and then dash after it again with his head a little dizzy, but faster to catch up with it. If he lost it in the woods, it would be lost for good; it was going for the bushes on the other side. It would go on out in the road. He was going to have it. He saw it dart through a thicket and he headed for the thicket and when he got there it darted out again and in a second disappeared under a hedge. He went through the hedge fast and heard his shirt rip and felt cool streaks on his arms where they were getting scratched. He stopped a second and looked down at his torn shirt sleeves but the turkey was only a little ahead of him and he could see it go over the edge of the hill and down again into an open space and he darted on. If he came in with the turkey, they wouldn't pay any attention to his shirt. Hane hadn't ever got a turkey. Hane hadn't ever caught anything. He guessed they'd be knocked out when they saw him; he guessed they'd talk about it in bed. That's what they did about him and Hane. Hane didn't know; he never woke up. Ruller woke up every night exactly at the time they started talking. He and Hane slept in one room and their mother and father in the next and the door was left open between and every night Ruller listened. His father would say finally, "How are the boys doing?" and their mother would say, Lord, they were wearing her to a frazzle, Lord, she guessed she shouldn't worry but how could she help worrying about Hane, the way he was now? Hane had always been an unusual boy, she said. She said he would grow up to be an unusual man too; and their father said, yes if he didn't get put in the penitentiary first, and their mother said how could he talk that way? and they argued just like Ruller and Hane and sometimes Ruller couldn't get back to sleep for thinking. He always felt tired when he got through listening but he woke up every night and listened just the same and whenever they started talking about him, he sat up in bed so he could hear better. Once his father asked why Ruller played by himself so much and his

mother said how was she to know? if he wanted to play by himself, she didn't see any reason he shouldn't; and his father said that worried him and she said well, if that was all he had to worry about, he'd do well to stop; someone told her, she said, that they had seen Hane at the Ever-Ready; hadn't they told him he couldn't go there?

His father asked Ruller the next day what he had been doing lately and Ruller said, "playing by himself," and walked off sort of like he had a limp. He guessed his father had looked pretty worried. He guessed he'd think it was something when he came home with the turkey slung over his shoulder. The turkey was heading out into a road and for a gutter along the side of it. It ran along the gutter and Ruller was gaining on it all the time until he fell over a root sticking up and spilled the things out his pockets and had to snatch them up. When he got up, it was out of sight.

"Bill, you take a posse and go down South Canyon; Joe, you cut around by the gorge and head him off," he shouted to his men. "I'll follow him this way." And he dashed off again along the ditch.

The turkey was in the ditch, not thirty feet from him, lying almost on its neck panting, and he was nearly a yard from it before it darted off again. He chased it straight until the ditch ended and then it went out in the road and slid under a hedge on the other side. He had to stop at the hedge and catch his breath and he could see the turkey on the other side through the leaves, lying on its neck, its whole body moving up and down with the panting. He could see the tip of its tongue going up and down in its opened bill. If he could stick his arm through, he might could get it while it was still too tired to move. He pushed up closer to the hedge and eased his hand through and then gripped it quickly around the turkey's tail. There was no movement from the other side. Maybe the turkey had dropped dead. He put his face close to the leaves to look through. He pushed the twigs aside with one hand but they would not stay. He let go the turkey and pulled his other hand through to hold them. Through the hole he had made, he saw the bird wobbling off drunkenly. He ran back to where the hedge began and got on the other side. He'd get it yet. It needn't think it was so smart, he muttered.

It zigged across the middle of the field and toward the woods again. It couldn't go into the woods! He'd never get it! He dashed behind it, keeping his eyes sharp on it until suddenly something hit his chest and knocked the breath black out of him. He fell back on the ground and forgot the turkey for the cutting in his chest. He lay there for a while with things rocking on either side of him. Finally he sat up. He was facing the tree he had run into. He rubbed his hands over his face and arms and the long scratches began to sting. He would have taken it in slung over his shoulder and they would have jumped up and yelled, "Good Lord look at Ruller! Ruller! Where did you get that wild turkey!" and his father would have said, "Man! That's a bird if I ever saw one!" He kicked a stone away from his foot. He'd never see the turkey now. He wondered why he had seen it in the first place if he wasn't going to be able to get it.

It was like somebody had played a dirty trick on him.   10

All that running for nothing. He sat there looking sullenly at his white ankles sticking out of his trouser legs and into his shoes. "Nuts," he muttered. He turned over on his stomach and let his cheek rest right on the ground dirty or not. He had torn his shirt and scratched his arms and got a knot on his forehead — he could feel it rising just a little, it was going to be a big one all right — all for nothing. The ground was cool to his face, but the grit bruised it and he had to turn over. Oh hell, he thought.

"Oh hell," he said cautiously.

Then in a minute he said just, "hell."

Then he said it like Hane said it, pulling the e-ull out and trying to get the look in his eye that Hane got. Once Hane said, "God!" and his mother stomped after him and said, "I don't want to hear you say that again. Thou shalt not take the name of the Lord, Thy God, in vain. Do you hear me?" and he guessed that shut Hane up. Ha! He guessed she dressed him off that time.

"God," he said. 15

He looked studiedly at the ground, making circles in the dust with his finger. "God!" he repeated.

"God dammit," he said softly. He could feel his face getting hot and his chest thumping all of a sudden inside. "God dammit to hell," he said almost inaudibly. He looked over his shoulder but no one was there.

"God dammit to hell, good Lord from Jerusalem," he said. His uncle said, "good Lord from Jerusalem."

"Good Father, good God, sweep the chickens out the yard," he said and began to giggle. His face was very red. He sat up and looked at his white ankles sticking out of his pants legs into his shoes. They looked like they didn't belong to him. He gripped a hand around each ankle and bent his knees up and rested his chin on a knee. "Our Father Who art in heaven, shoot 'em six and roll 'em seven," he said, giggling again. Boy, she'd smack his head in if she could hear him. God dammit, she'd smack his goddam head in. He rolled over in a fit of laughter. God dammit, she'd dress him off and wring his goddam neck like a goddam chicken. The laughing cut his side and he tried to hold it in but every time he thought of his goddam neck, he shook again. He lay back on the ground, red and weak with laughter, not able not to think of her smacking his goddam head in. He said the words over and over to himself and after a while he stopped laughing. He said them again but the laughing had gone out. He said them again but it wouldn't start back up. All that chasing for nothing, he thought again. He might as well go home. What did he want to be sitting around here for? He felt suddenly like he would if people had been laughing at him. Aw, go to hell, he told them. He got up and kicked his foot sharply into somebody's leg and said, "take that, sucker," and turned into the woods to take the short trail home.

And as soon as he got in the door, they would holler, "How did you tear 20 your clothes and where did you get that knot on your forehead?" He was going to say he fell in a hole. What difference would it make? Yeah, God, what difference would it make?

He almost stopped. He had never heard himself think that tone before. He wondered should he take the thought back. He guessed it was pretty bad; but heck, it was the way he felt. He couldn't help feeling that way. Heck . . . hell, it was the way he felt. He guessed he couldn't help that. He walked on a little way, thinking about it. He wondered suddenly if he were going "bad." That's what Hane had done. Hane played pool and smoked cigarettes and sneaked in at twelve-thirty and boy he thought he was something. "There's nothing you can do about it," their grandmother had told their father, "he's at that age." What age? Ruller wondered. I'm eleven, he thought. That's pretty young. Hane hadn't started until he was fifteen. I guess it's worse in me, he thought. He wondered would he fight it. Their grandmother had talked to Hane and told him the only way to conquer the devil was to fight him — if he didn't, he couldn't be her boy anymore — Ruller sat down on a stump — and she said she'd give him one more chance, did he want it? and he yelled at her, no! and would she leave him alone? and she told him, well, she loved him even if he didn't love her and he was her boy anyway and so was Ruller. Oh no I ain't Ruller thought quickly. Oh no. She's not pinning any of that stuff on me.

Boy, he could shock the pants off her. He could make her teeth fall in her soup. He started giggling. The next time she asked him if he wanted to play a game of Parcheesi, he'd say, hellno, goddammit, didn't she know any good games? Get out her goddam cards and he'd show her a few. He rolled over on the ground, choking with laughter. "Let's have some booze, kid," he'd say. "Let's get stinky." Boy, he'd knock her out of her socks! He sat on the ground, red and grinning to himself, bursting every now and then into a fresh spasm of giggles. He remembered the minister had said young men were going to the devil by the dozens this day and age; forsaking gentle ways; walking in the tracks of Satan. They would rue the day, he said. There would be weeping and gnashing of teeth. "Weeping," Ruller muttered. Men didn't weep.

How do you gnash your teeth? he wondered. He grated his jaws together and made an ugly face. He did it several times.

He bet he could steal.

He thought about chasing the turkey for nothing. It was a dirty trick. He 25
bet he could be a jewel thief. They were smart. He bet he could have all Scotland Yard on his tail. Hell.

He got up. God could go around sticking things in your face and making you chase them all afternoon for nothing.

You shouldn't think that way about God though.

But that was the way he felt. If that was the way he felt, could he help it? He looked around quickly as if someone might be hiding in the bushes; then suddenly he started.

It was rolled over at the edge of a thicket — a pile of ruffled bronze with a red head lying limp along the ground. Ruller stared at it, unable to think; then he leaned forward suspiciously. He wasn't going to touch it. Why was it there now for him to take? He wasn't going to touch it. It could just lie there. The picture of himself walking in the room with it slung over his shoulder came back to him. Look at Ruller with that turkey! Lord look at Ruller! He squatted down beside it and looked without touching it. He wondered what had been wrong with its wing. He lifted it up by the tip and looked under. The feathers were blood-soaked. It had been shot. It must weigh ten pounds, he figured.

Lord, Ruller! It's a huge turkey! He wondered how it would feel slung over 30
his shoulder. Maybe, he considered, he was supposed to take it.

Ruller gets our turkeys for us. Ruller got it in the woods, chased it dead. Yes, he's a very unusual child.

Ruller wondered suddenly if he were an unusual child.

It came down on him in an instant: he was . . . an . . . unusual . . . child.

He reckoned he was more unusual than Hane.

He had to worry more than Hane because he knew more how things were. 35

Sometimes when he was listening at night, he heard them arguing like they were going to kill each other; and the next day his father would go out early and his mother would have the blue veins out on her forehead and look like she was expecting a snake to jump from the ceiling any minute. He guessed he was one of the most unusual children ever. Maybe that was why the turkey was there. He rubbed his hand along the neck. Maybe it was to keep him from going bad. Maybe God wanted to keep him from that.

Maybe God had knocked it out right there where he'd see it when he got up.

Maybe God was in the bush now, waiting for him to make up his mind. Ruller blushed. He wondered if God could think he was a very unusual child. He must. He found himself suddenly blushing and grinning and he rubbed his hand over his face quick to make himself stop. If You want me to take it, he said, I'll be glad to. Maybe finding the turkey was a sign. Maybe God wanted him to be a preacher. He thought of Bing Crosby and Spencer Tracy. He might found a place to stay for boys who were going bad. He lifted the turkey up — it was heavy all right — and fitted it over his shoulder. He wished he could see how he looked with it slung over like that. It occurred to him that he might as well go home the long way — through town. He had plenty of time. He started off slowly, shifting the turkey until it fit comfortably over his shoulder. He remembered the things he had thought before he found the turkey. They were pretty bad, he guessed.

He guessed God had stopped him before it was too late. He should be very thankful. Thank You, he said.

Come on, boys, he said, we will take this turkey back for our dinner. We   40
certainly are much obliged to You, he said to God. This turkey weighs ten pounds. You were mighty generous.

That's okay, God said. And listen, we ought to have a talk about these boys. They're entirely in your hands, see? I'm leaving the job strictly up to you. I have confidence in you, McFarney.

You can trust me, Ruller said. I'll come through with the goods.

He went into town with the turkey over his shoulder. He wanted to do something for God but he didn't know what he could do. If anybody was playing the accordian on the street today, he'd give them his dime. He only had one dime, but he'd give it to them. Maybe he could think of something better, though. He had been going to keep the dime for something. He might could get another one from his grandmother. How about a goddam dime, kid? He pulled his mouth piously out of the grin. He wasn't going to think that way anymore. He couldn't get a dime from her anyway. His mother was going to whip him if he asked his grandmother for money again. Maybe something would turn up that he could do. If God wanted him to do something, he'd turn something up.

He was getting into the business block and through the corner of his eye he noticed people looking at him. There were eight thousand people in Mulrose County and on Saturday every one of them was in Tilford on the business block. They turned as Ruller passed and looked at him. He glanced at himself reflected in a store window, shifted the turkey slightly, and walked quickly ahead. He heard someone call, but he walked on, pretending he was deaf. It was his mother's friend, Alice Gilhard, and if she wanted him, let her catch up with him.

"Ruller!" she cried, "my goodness, where did you get that turkey?" She   45
came up behind him fast and put her hand on his shoulder. "That's some bird," she said. "You must be a good shot."

"I didn't shoot it," Ruller said coldly. "I captured it. I chased it dead."

"Heavens," she said. "You wouldn't capture me one sometime would you?"

"I might if I ever have time," Ruller said. She thought she was so cute.

Two men came over and whistled at the turkey. They yelled at some other men on the corner to look. Another of his mother's friends stopped and some country boys who had been sitting on the curb got up and tried to see the turkey without showing they were interested. A man with a hunting suit and gun stopped and looked at Ruller and walked around behind him and looked at the turkey.

"How much do you think it weighs?" a lady asked.   50

"At least ten pounds," Ruller said.

"How long did you chase it?"

"About an hour," Ruller said.

"The goddam imp," the man in the hunting suit muttered.

"That's really amazing," a lady commented.   55

"About that long," Ruller said.

"You must be very tired."

"No," Ruller said. "I have to go. I'm in a hurry." He worked his face to look as if he were thinking something out and hurried down the street until he was out of their view. He felt warm all over and nice as if something very fine were going to be or had been. He looked back once and saw that the country boys were following him. He hoped they would come up and ask to look at the turkey. God must be wonderful, he felt suddenly. He wanted to do something for God. He hadn't seen anyone playing the accordian though or selling pencils and he was just past the business block. He might see one before he really got to the streets where people lived at. If he did, he'd give away the dime — even while he knew he couldn't get another one any time soon. He began to wish he would see somebody begging.

Those country kids were still trailing along behind him. He thought he might stop and ask them did they want to see the turkey; but they might just stare at him. They were tenants' children and sometimes tenant's children just stared at you. He might found a home for tenant's children. He thought about going back through town to see if he had passed a beggar without seeing him, but he decided people might think he was showing off with the turkey.

Lord, send me a beggar, he prayed suddenly. Send me one before I get home. 60 He had never thought before of praying on his own, but it was a good idea. God had put the turkey there. He'd send him a beggar. He knew for a fact God would send him one. He was on Hill Street now and there were nothing but houses on Hill Street. It would be strange to find a beggar here. The sidewalks were empty except for a few children and some tricycles. Ruller looked back; the country boys were still following him. He decided to slow down. It might make them catch up with him and it might give a beggar more time to get to him. If one were coming. He wondered if one were coming. If one came, it would mean God had gone out of His way to get one. It would mean God was really interested. He had a sudden fear one wouldn't come; it was a whole fear quick.

One will come, he told himself. God was interested in him because he was a very unusual child. He went on. The streets were deserted now. He guessed one wouldn't come. Maybe God didn't have confidence in — no, God did. Lord, please send me a beggar! he implored. He squinched his face rigid and strained his muscles in a knot and said, "please! one right now;" and the minute he said it — the minute — Hetty Gilman turned around the corner before him, heading straight to where he was.

He felt almost like he had when he ran into the tree.

She was walking down the street right toward him. It was just like the turkey lying there. It was just as if she had been hiding behind a house until he came by. She was an old woman whom everybody said had more money than anybody in town because she had been begging for twenty years. She sneaked into people's houses and sat until they gave her something. If they didn't, she cursed them. Nevertheless, she was a beggar. Ruller walked faster. He took the dime out of his pocket so it would be ready. His heart was stomping up and down in his chest. He made a noise to see if he could talk. As they neared each other, he stuck out his hand. "Here!" he shouted. "Here!"

She was a tall, longfaced old woman in an antique black cloak. Her face was the color of a dead chicken's skin. When she saw him, she looked as if she suddenly smelled something bad. He darted at her and thrust the dime into her hand and dashed on without looking back.

Slowly his heart calmed and he began to feel full of a new feeling — like 65 being happy and embarrassed at the same time. Maybe, he thought, blushing, he would give all his money to her. He felt as if the ground did not need to be under him any longer. He noticed suddenly that the country boys' feet were shuffling just behind him and almost without thinking, he turned and asked graciously, "You all wanta see this turkey?"

They stopped where they were and stared at him. One in front spit. Ruller looked down at it quickly. There was real tobacco juice in it! "Wheered you git that turkey?" the spitter asked.

"I found it in the woods," Ruller said. "I chased it dead. See, it's been shot under the wing." He took the turkey off his shoulder and held it down where they could see. "I think it was shot twice," he went on excitedly, pulling the wing up.

"Lemme see it here," the spitter said.

Ruller handed him the turkey. "You see down there where the bullet hole is?" he asked. "Well, I think it was shot twice in the same hole, I think it was. . . ." The turkey's head flew in his face as the spitter slung it up in the air and over his own shoulder and turned. The others turned with him and together, they sauntered off in the direction they had come, the turkey sticking stiff out on the spitter's back and its head swinging slowly in a circle as he walked away.

They were in the next block before Ruller moved. Finally, he realized that 70 he could not even see them any longer they were so far away. He turned toward home, almost creeping. He walked four blocks and then suddenly, noticing that it was dark, he began to run. He ran faster and faster, and as he turned up the road to his house, his heart was running as fast as his legs and he was certain that Something Awful was tearing behind him with its arms rigid and its fingers ready to clutch.

CONSIDERATIONS FOR CRITICAL THINKING AND WRITING

1. FIRST RESPONSE. Do you think Ruller is a fairly typical eleven-year-old boy, or do you agree with his assessment of himself as "an unusual child" (para. 33)?

2. Comment on Ruller's imagination. What sorts of fantasies about himself does he have? What do they reveal about him?

3. Why does Ruller's father worry about him?

4. What does Ruller think of his brother Hane? What function does Hane serve in the story?

5. Why is Ruller eager to capture the turkey? Do you think that the turkey has any symbolic value? Explain why or why not.

6. When the turkey momentarily escapes, Ruller "wondered why he had seen it in the first place if he wasn't going to be able to get it" (para. 9). What do you make of Ruller's thinking?

7. Why do you think Ruller experiments with swearing and laughs about fantasies of cursing at his grandmother?

8. How does Ruller interpret his finally catching the turkey in terms of his relationship to God?

9. How does Ruller respond when the country boy—"the spitter"—takes away the turkey?

10. What do you think is the story's theme?

11. Discuss the humor in the story.

CONNECTIONS TO OTHER SELECTIONS

1. Compare the endings of "Turkey" and "Revelation" (p. 407). What sort of revelation, if any, does Ruller experience?

2. Compare Ruller's problems concerning religious faith with Hulga's in "Good Country People" (p. 392).

3. Write an essay comparing Ruller's relationship with his family and Sarty's with his in William Faulkner's "Barn Burning" (p. 481). How do these relationships help to identify the themes in each story?

A Good Man Is Hard to Find   1953

The dragon is by the side of the road, watching those who pass. Beware lest he devour you. We go to the Father of Souls, but it is necessary to pass by the dragon.
                                                                    —*St. Cyril of Jerusalem*°

The grandmother didn't want to go to Florida. She wanted to visit some of her connections in east Tennessee and she was seizing at every chance to change Bailey's mind. Bailey was the son she lived with, her only boy. He was sitting on the edge of his chair at the table, bent over the orange sports section of the *Journal.* "Now look here, Bailey," she said, "see here, read this," and she stood with one hand on her thin hip and the other rattling the newspaper at his bald head. "Here this fellow that calls himself The Misfit is aloose from the Federal Pen and headed toward Florida and you read here what it says he did to these people. Just you read it. I wouldn't take my children in any direction with a criminal like that aloose in it. I couldn't answer to my conscience if I did."

Bailey didn't look up from his reading so she wheeled around then and faced the children's mother, a young woman in slacks, whose face was as broad

---

St. Cyril of Jerusalem (315?–386): Roman Catholic ecclesiastic and bishop of Jerusalem.

and innocent as a cabbage and was tied around with a green headkerchief that had two points on the top like a rabbit's ears. She was sitting on the sofa, feeding the baby his apricots out of a jar. "The children have been to Florida before," the old lady said. "You all ought to take them somewhere else for a change so they would see different parts of the world and be broad. They never have been to east Tennessee."

The children's mother didn't seem to hear her but the eight-year-old boy, John Wesley, a stocky child with glasses, said, "If you don't want to go to Florida, why dontcha stay at home?" He and the little girl, June Star, were reading the funny papers on the floor.

"She wouldn't stay at home to be queen for a day," June Star said without raising her yellow head.

"Yes and what would you do if this fellow, The Misfit, caught you?" the 5 grandmother asked.

"I'd smack his face," John Wesley said.

"She wouldn't stay at home for a million bucks," June Star said. "Afraid she'd miss something. She has to go everywhere we go."

"All right, Miss," the grandmother said. "Just remember that the next time you want me to curl your hair."

June Star said her hair was naturally curly.

The next morning the grandmother was the first one in the car, ready to 10 go. She had her big black valise that looked like the head of a hippopotamus in one corner, and underneath it she was hiding a basket with Pitty Sing, the cat, in it. She didn't intend for the cat to be left alone in the house for three days because he would miss her too much and she was afraid he might brush against one of the gas burners and accidentally asphyxiate himself. Her son, Bailey, didn't like to arrive at a motel with a cat.

She sat in the middle of the back seat with John Wesley and June Star on either side of her. Bailey and the children's mother and the baby sat in front and they left Atlanta at eight forty-five with the mileage on the car at 55890. The grandmother wrote this down because she thought it would be interesting to say how many miles they had been when they got back. It took them twenty minutes to reach the outskirts of the city.

The old lady settled herself comfortably, removing her white cotton gloves and putting them up with her purse on the shelf in front of the back window. The children's mother still had on slacks and still had her head tied up in a green kerchief, but the grandmother had on a navy blue straw sailor hat with a bunch of white violets on the brim and a navy blue dress with a small white dot in the print. Her collars and cuffs were white organdy trimmed with lace and at her neckline she had pinned a purple spray of cloth violets containing a sachet. In case of an accident, anyone seeing her dead on the highway would know at once that she was a lady.

She said she thought it was going to be a good day for driving, neither too hot nor too cold, and she cautioned Bailey that the speed limit was fifty-five miles an hour and that the patrolmen hid themselves behind billboards and small clumps of trees and sped out after you before you had a chance to slow down. She pointed out interesting details of the scenery: Stone Mountain; the blue granite that in some places came up to both sides of the highway; the brilliant red clay banks slightly streaked with purple; and the various crops that made rows of green lace-work on the ground. The trees were full of silver-white sunlight and the meanest of them sparkled. The children were reading comic magazines and their mother had gone back to sleep.

"Let's go through Georgia fast so we won't have to look at it much," John Wesley said.

"If I were a little boy," said the grandmother, "I wouldn't talk about my na- 15 tive state that way. Tennessee has the mountains and Georgia has the hills."

"Tennessee is just a hillbilly dumping ground," John Wesley said, "and Georgia is a lousy state too."

"You said it," June Star said.

"In my time," said the grandmother, folding her thin veined fingers, "children were more respectful of their native states and their parents and everything else. People did right then. Oh look at the cute little pickaninny!" she said and pointed to a Negro child standing in the door of a shack. "Wouldn't that make a picture, now?" she asked and they all turned and looked at the little Negro out of the back window. He waved.

"He didn't have any britches on," June Star said.

"He probably didn't have any," the grandmother explained. "Little niggers 20 in the country don't have things like we do. If I could paint, I'd paint that picture," she said.

The children exchanged comic books.

The grandmother offered to hold the baby and the children's mother passed him over the front seat to her. She set him on her knee and bounced him and told him about the things they were passing. She rolled her eyes and screwed up her mouth and stuck her leathery thin face into his smooth bland one. Occasionally he gave her a faraway smile. They passed a large cotton field with five or six graves fenced in the middle of it, like a small island. "Look at the graveyard!" the grandmother said, pointing it out. "That was the old family burying ground. That belonged to the plantation."

"Where's the plantation?" John Wesley asked.

"Gone With the Wind," said the grandmother. "Ha. Ha."

When the children finished all the comic books they had brought, they 25 opened the lunch and ate it. The grandmother ate a peanut butter sandwich and an olive and would not let the children throw the box and the paper napkins out the window. When there was nothing else to do they played a game by choosing a cloud and making the other two guess what shape it suggested. John Wesley took one the shape of a cow and June Star guessed a cow and John Wesley said, no, an automobile, and June Star said he didn't play fair, and they began to slap each other over the grandmother.

The grandmother said she would tell them a story if they would keep quiet. When she told a story, she rolled her eyes and waved her head and was very dramatic. She said once when she was a maiden lady she had been courted by a Mr. Edgar Atkins Teagarden from Jasper, Georgia. She said he was a very goodlooking man and a gentleman and that he brought her a watermelon every Saturday afternoon with his initials cut in it, E.A.T. Well, one Saturday, she said, Mr. Teagarden brought the watermelon and there was nobody at home and he left it on the front porch and returned in his buggy to Jasper, but she never got the watermelon, she said, because a nigger boy ate it when he saw the initials, E.A.T.! This story tickled John Wesley's funny bone and he giggled and giggled but June Star didn't think it was any good. She said she wouldn't marry a man that just brought her a watermelon on Saturday. The grandmother said she would have done well to marry Mr. Teagarden because he was a gentleman and had bought Coca-Cola stock when it first came out and that he had died only a few years ago, a very wealthy man.

They stopped at The Tower for barbecued sandwiches. The Tower was a part stucco and part wood filling station and dance hall set in a clearing outside of Timothy. A fat man named Red Sammy Butts ran it and there were signs stuck here and there on the building and for miles up and down the highway saying, TRY RED SAMMY'S FAMOUS BARBECUE. NONE LIKE FAMOUS RED SAMMY'S! RED SAM! THE FAT BOY WITH THE HAPPY LAUGH. A VETERAN! RED SAMMY'S YOUR MAN!

Red Sammy was lying on the bare ground outside The Tower with his head under a truck while a gray monkey about a foot high, chained to a small chinaberry tree, chattered nearby. The monkey sprang back into the tree and got on the highest limb as soon as he saw the children jump out of the car and run toward him.

Inside, The Tower was a long dark room with a counter at one end and tables at the other and dancing space in the middle. They all sat down at a board table next to the nickelodeon and Red Sam's wife, a tall burnt-brown woman with hair and eyes lighter than her skin, came and took their order. The children's mother put a dime in the machine and played "The Tennessee Waltz," and the grandmother said that tune always made her want to dance. She asked Bailey if he would like to dance but he only glared at her. He didn't have a naturally sunny disposition like she did and trips made him nervous. The grandmother's brown eyes were very bright. She swayed her head from side to side and pretended she was dancing in her chair. June Star said play something she could tap to so the children's mother put in another dime and played a fast number and June Star stepped out onto the dance floor and did her tap routine.

"Ain't she cute?" Red Sam's wife said, leaning over the counter. "Would you like to come be my little girl?" 30

"No I certainly wouldn't," June Star said. "I wouldn't live in a broken-down place like this for a million bucks!" and she ran back to the table.

"Ain't she cute?" the woman repeated, stretching her mouth politely.

"Aren't you ashamed?" hissed the grandmother.

Red Sam came in and told his wife to quit lounging on the counter and hurry up with these people's order. His khaki trousers reached just to his hip bones and his stomach hung over them like a sack of meal swaying under his shirt. He came over and sat down at a table nearby and let out a combination sigh and yodel. "You can't win," he said. "You can't win," and he wiped his sweating red face off with a gray handkerchief. "These days you don't know who to trust," he said. "Ain't that the truth?"

"People are certainly not nice like they used to be," said the grandmother. 35

"Two fellers come in here last week," Red Sammy said, "driving a Chrysler. It was a old beat-up car but it was a good one and these boys looked all right to me. Said they worked at the mill and you know I let them fellers charge the gas they bought? Now why did I do that?"

"Because you're a good man!" the grandmother said at once.

"Yes'm, I suppose so," Red Sam said as if he were struck with this answer.

His wife brought the orders, carrying the five plates all at once without a tray, two in each hand and one balanced on her arm. "It isn't a soul in this

green world of God's that you can trust," she said. "And I don't count nobody
out of that, not nobody," she repeated, looking at Red Sammy.

"Did you read about that criminal, The Misfit, that's escaped?" asked the 40
grandmother.

"I wouldn't be a bit surprised if he didn't attack this place right here," said
the woman. "If he hears about it being here, I wouldn't be none surprised to
see him. If he hears it's two cent in the cash register, I wouldn't be a tall surprised if he. . . ."

"That'll do," Red Sam said. "Go bring these people their Co'-Colas," and
the woman went off to get the rest of the order.

"A good man is hard to find," Red Sammy said. "Everything is getting terrible. I remember the day you could go off and leave your screen door un-
latched. Not no more."

He and the grandmother discussed better times. The old lady said that in
her opinion Europe was entirely to blame for the way things were now. She said
the way Europe acted you would think we were made of money and Red Sam
said it was no use talking about it, she was exactly right. The children ran outside into the white sunlight and looked at the monkey in the lacy chinaberry
tree. He was busy catching fleas on himself and biting each one carefully between his teeth as if it were a delicacy.

They drove off again into the hot afternoon. The grandmother took cat 45
naps and woke up every few minutes with her own snoring. Outside of Toombs-
boro she woke up and recalled an old plantation that she had visited in this
neighborhood once when she was a young lady. She said the house had six
white columns across the front and that there was an avenue of oaks leading up
to it and two little wooden trellis arbors on either side in front where you sat
down with your suitor after a stroll in the garden. She recalled exactly which
road to turn off to get to it. She knew that Bailey would not be willing to lose
any time looking at an old house, but the more she talked about it, the more
she wanted to see it once again and find out if the little twin arbors were still
standing. "There was a secret panel in this house," she said craftily, not telling
the truth but wishing that she were, "and the story went that all the family silver was hidden in it when Sherman° came through but it was never found. . . ."

"Hey!" John Wesley said. "Let's go see it! We'll find it! We'll poke all the
woodwork and find it! Who lives there? Where do you turn off at? Hey Pop,
can't we turn off there?"

"We never have seen a house with a secret panel!" June Star shrieked. "Let's
go to the house with the secret panel! Hey Pop, can't we go see the house with
the secret panel!"

"It's not far from here, I know," the grandmother said. "It won't take over
twenty minutes."

Bailey was looking straight ahead. His jaw was as rigid as a horseshoe.
"No," he said.

The children began to yell and scream that they wanted to see the house 50
with the secret panel. John Wesley kicked the back of the front seat and June
Star hung over her mother's shoulder and whined desperately into her ear that
they never had any fun even on their vacation, that they could never do what

Sherman: William Tecumseh Sherman (1820–1891), Union Army commander who led infamous marches through the South during the Civil War.

THEY wanted to do. The baby began to scream and John Wesley kicked the back of the seat so hard that his father could feel the blows in his kidney.

"All right!" he shouted and drew the car to a stop at the side of the road. "Will you all shut up? Will you all just shut up for one second? If you don't shut up, we won't go anywhere."

"It would be very educational for them," the grandmother murmured.

"All right," Bailey said, "but get this: this is the only time we're going to stop for anything like this. This is the one and only time."

"The dirt road that you have to turn down is about a mile back," the grandmother directed. "I marked it when we passed."

"A dirt road," Bailey groaned. 55

After they had turned around and were headed toward the dirt road, the grandmother recalled other points about the house, the beautiful glass over the front doorway and the candle-lamp in the hall. John Wesley said that the secret panel was probably in the fireplace.

"You can't go inside this house," Bailey said. "You don't know who lives there."

"While you all talk to the people in front, I'll run around behind and get in a window," John Wesley suggested.

"We'll all stay in the car," his mother said.

They turned onto the dirt road and the car raced roughly along in a swirl 60 of pink dust. The grandmother recalled the times when there were no paved roads and thirty miles was a day's journey. The dirt road was hilly and there were sudden washes in it and sharp curves on dangerous embankments. All at once they would be on a hill, looking down over the blue tops of trees for miles around, then the next minute, they would be in a red depression with the dust-coated trees looking down on them.

"This place had better turn up in a minute," Bailey said, "or I'm going to turn around."

The road looked as if no one had traveled on it for months.

"It's not much farther," the grandmother said and just as she said it, a horrible thought came to her. The thought was so embarrassing that she turned red in the face and her eyes dilated and her feet jumped up, upsetting her valise in the corner. The instant the valise moved, the newspaper top she had over the basket under it rose with a snarl and Pitty Sing, the cat, sprang onto Bailey's shoulder.

The children were thrown to the floor and their mother, clutching the baby, was thrown out the door onto the ground; the old lady was thrown into the front seat. The car turned over once and landed right-side-up in a gulch off the side of the road. Bailey remained in the driver's seat with the cat — gray-striped with a broad white face and an orange nose — clinging to his neck like a caterpillar.

As soon as the children saw they could move their arms and legs, they 65 scrambled out of the car, shouting, "We've had an ACCIDENT!" The grandmother was curled up under the dashboard, hoping she was injured so that Bailey's wrath would not come down on her all at once. The horrible thought she had before the accident was that the house she had remembered so vividly was not in Georgia but in Tennessee.

Bailey removed the cat from his neck with both hands and flung it out the window against the side of a pine tree. Then he got out of the car and started looking for the children's mother. She was sitting against the side of the red gutted ditch, holding the screaming baby, but she only had a cut down her face and a broken shoulder. "We've had an ACCIDENT!" the children screamed in a frenzy of delight.

"But nobody's killed," June Star said with disappointment as the grandmother limped out of the car, her hat still pinned to her head but the broken front brim standing up at a jaunty angle and the violet spray hanging off the side. They all sat down in the ditch, except the children, to recover from the shock. They were all shaking.

"Maybe a car will come along," said the children's mother hoarsely.

"I believe I have injured an organ," said the grandmother, pressing her side, but no one answered her. Bailey's teeth were clattering. He had on a yellow sport shirt with bright blue parrots designed in it and his face was as yellow as the shirt. The grandmother decided that she would not mention that the house was in Tennessee.

The road was about ten feet above and they could see only the tops of the trees on the other side of it. Behind the ditch they were sitting in there were more woods, tall and dark and deep. In a few minutes they saw a car some distance away on top of a hill, coming slowly as if the occupants were watching them. The grandmother stood up and waved both arms dramatically to attract their attention. The car continued to come on slowly, disappeared around a bend and appeared again, moving even slower, on top of the hill they had gone over. It was a big black battered hearse-like automobile. There were three men in it.

It came to a stop just over them and for some minutes, the driver looked down with a steady expressionless gaze to where they were sitting, and didn't speak. Then he turned his head and muttered something to the other two and they got out. One was a fat boy in black trousers and a red sweat shirt with a silver stallion embossed on the front of it. He moved around on the right side of them and stood staring, his mouth partly open in a kind of loose grin. The other had on khaki pants and a blue striped coat and a gray hat pulled down very low, hiding most of his face. He came around slowly on the left side. Neither spoke.

The driver got out of the car and stood by the side of it, looking down at them. He was an older man than the other two. His hair was just beginning to gray and he wore silver-rimmed spectacles that gave him a scholarly look. He had a long creased face and didn't have on any shirt or undershirt. He had on blue jeans that were too tight for him and was holding a black hat and a gun. The two boys also had guns.

"We've had an ACCIDENT!" the children screamed.

The grandmother had the peculiar feeling that the bespectacled man was someone she knew. His face was as familiar to her as if she had known him all her life but she could not recall who he was. He moved away from the car and began to come down the embankment, placing his feet carefully so that he wouldn't slip. He had on tan and white shoes and no socks, and his ankles were red and thin. "Good afternoon," he said. "I see you all had you a little spill."

"We turned over twice!" said the grandmother.

"Oncet," he corrected. "We seen it happen. Try their car and see will it run, Hiram," he said quietly to the boy with the gray hat.

"What you got that gun for?" John Wesley asked. "Whatcha gonna do with that gun?"

"Lady," the man said to the children's mother, "would you mind calling them children to sit down by you? Children make me nervous. I want all you all to sit down right together there where you're at."

"What are you telling US what to do for?" June Star asked.

Behind them the line of woods gaped like a dark open mouth. "Come here," said their mother.

"Look here now," Bailey said suddenly, "we're in a predicament! We're in. . . ."

The grandmother shrieked. She scrambled to her feet and stood staring. "You're The Misfit!" she said. "I recognized you at once!"

"Yes'm," the man said, smiling slightly as if he were pleased in spite of himself to be known, "but it would have been better for all of you, lady, if you hadn't of reckernized me."

Bailey turned his head sharply and said something to his mother that shocked even the children. The old lady began to cry and The Misfit reddened.

"Lady," he said, "don't you get upset. Sometimes a man says things he don't mean. I don't reckon he meant to talk to you thataway."

"You wouldn't shoot a lady, would you?" the grandmother said and removed a clean handkerchief from her cuff and began to slap at her eyes with it.

The Misfit pointed the toe of his shoe into the ground and made a little hole and then covered it up again. "I would hate to have to," he said.

"Listen," the grandmother almost screamed, "I know you're a good man. You don't look a bit like you have common blood. I know you must come from nice people!"

"Yes mam," he said, "finest people in the world." When he smiled he showed a row of strong white teeth. "God never made a finer woman than my mother and my daddy's heart was pure gold," he said. The boy with the red sweat shirt had come around behind them and was standing with his gun at his hip. The Misfit squatted down on the ground. "Watch them children, Bobby Lee," he said. "You know they make me nervous." He looked at the six of them huddled together in front of him and he seemed to be embarrassed as if he couldn't think of anything to say. "Ain't a cloud in the sky," he remarked, looking up at it. "Don't see no sun but don't see no cloud neither."

"Yes, it's a beautiful day," said the grandmother. "Listen," she said, "you shouldn't call yourself The Misfit because I know you're a good man at heart. I can just look at you and tell."

"Hush!" Bailey yelled. "Hush! Everybody shut up and let me handle this!" He was squatting in the position of a runner about to sprint forward but he didn't move.

"I pre-chate that, lady," The Misfit said and drew a little circle in the ground with the butt of his gun.

"It'll take a half a hour to fix this here car," Hiram called, looking over the raised hood of it.

"Well, first you and Bobby Lee get him and that little boy to step over yonder with you," The Misfit said, pointing to Bailey and John Wesley. "The boys want to ast you something," he said to Bailey. "Would you mind stepping back in them woods there with them?"

"Listen," Bailey began, "we're in a terrible predicament! Nobody realizes what this is," and his voice cracked. His eyes were as blue and intense as the parrots in his shirt and he remained perfectly still.

The grandmother reached up to adjust her hat brim as if she were going to the woods with him but it came off in her hand. She stood staring at it and after a second she let it fall to the ground. Hiram pulled Bailey up by the arm as if he were assisting an old man. John Wesley caught hold of his father's hand and Bobby Lee followed. They went off toward the woods and just as they reached the dark edge, Bailey turned and supporting himself against a gray naked pine trunk, he shouted, "I'll be back in a minute, Mamma, wait on me!"

"Come back this instant!" his mother shrilled but they all disappeared into the woods.

"Bailey Boy!" the grandmother called in a tragic voice but she found she was looking at The Misfit squatting on the ground in front of her. "I just know you're a good man," she said desperately. "You're not a bit common!"

"Nome, I ain't a good man," The Misfit said after a second as if he had considered her statement carefully, "but I ain't the worst in the world neither. My daddy said I was a different breed of dog from my brothers and sisters. 'You know,' Daddy said, 'it's some that can live their whole life out without asking about it and it's others has to know why it is, and this boy is one of the latters. He's going to be into everything!'" He put on his black hat and looked up suddenly and then away deep into the woods as if he were embarrassed again. "I'm sorry I don't have on a shirt before you ladies," he said, hunching his shoulders slightly. "We buried our clothes that we had on when we escaped and we're just making do until we can get better. We borrowed these from some folks we met," he explained.

"That's perfectly all right," the grandmother said. "Maybe Bailey has an extra shirt in his suitcase." 100

"I'll look and see terrectly," The Misfit said.

"Where are they taking him?" the children's mother screamed.

"Daddy was a card himself," The Misfit said. "You couldn't put anything over on him. He never got in trouble with the Authorities though. Just had the knack of handling them."

"You could be honest too if you'd only try," said the grandmother. "Think how wonderful it would be to settle down and live a comfortable life and not have to think about somebody chasing you all the time."

The Misfit kept scratching in the ground with the butt of his gun as if he were thinking about it. "Yes'm, somebody is always after you," he murmured. 105

The grandmother noticed how thin his shoulder blades were just behind his hat because she was standing up looking down on him. "Do you ever pray?" she asked.

He shook his head. All she saw was the black hat wiggle between his shoulder blades. "Nome," he said.

There was a pistol shot from the woods, followed closely by another. Then silence. The old lady's head jerked around. She could hear the wind move through the tree tops like a long satisfied insuck of breath. "Bailey Boy!" she called.

"I was a gospel singer for a while," The Misfit said. "I been most everything. Been in the arm service, both land and sea, at home and abroad, been twict married, been an undertaker, been with the railroads, plowed Mother Earth, been in a tornado, seen a man burnt alive oncet," and he looked up at the children's mother and the little girl who were sitting close together, their faces white and their eyes glassy; "I even seen a woman flogged," he said.

"Pray, pray," the grandmother began, "pray, pray. . . ." 110

"I never was a bad boy that I remember of," The Misfit said in an almost dreamy voice, "but somewheres along the line I done something wrong and got sent to the penitentiary. I was buried alive," and he looked up and held her attention to him by a steady stare.

"That's when you should have started to pray," she said. "What did you do to get sent to the penitentiary that first time?"

"Turn to the right, it was a wall," The Misfit said, looking up again at the cloudless sky. "Turn to the left, it was a wall. Look up it was a ceiling, look down it was a floor. I forget what I done, lady. I set there and set there, trying to remember what it was I done and I ain't recalled it to this day. Oncet in a while, I would think it was coming to me, but it never come."

"Maybe they put you in by mistake," the old lady said vaguely.

"Nome," he said. "It wasn't no mistake. They had the papers on me." 115

"You must have stolen something," she said.

The Misfit sneered slightly. "Nobody had nothing I wanted," he said. "It was a head-doctor at the penitentiary said what I had done was kill my daddy but I known that for a lie. My daddy died in nineteen ought nineteen of the epidemic flu and I never had a thing to do with it. He was buried in the Mount Hopewell Baptist churchyard and you can see for yourself."

"If you would pray," the old lady said, "Jesus would help you."

"That's right," The Misfit said.

"Well then, why don't you pray?" she asked trembling with delight suddenly. 120

"I don't want no hep," he said. "I'm doing all right by myself."

Bobby Lee and Hiram came ambling back from the woods. Bobby Lee was dragging a yellow shirt with bright blue parrots in it.

"Throw me that shirt, Bobby Lee," The Misfit said. The shirt came flying at him and landed on his shoulder and he put it on. The grandmother couldn't name what the shirt reminded her of. "No, lady," The Misfit said while he was buttoning it up, "I found out the crime don't matter. You can do one thing or you can do another, kill a man or take a tire off his car, because sooner or later you're going to forget what it was you done and just be punished for it."

The children's mother had begun to make heaving noises as if she couldn't get her breath. "Lady," he asked, "would you and that little girl like to step off yonder with Bobby Lee and Hiram and join your husband?"

"Yes, thank you," the mother said faintly. Her left arm dangled helplessly 125 and she was holding the baby, who had gone to sleep, in the other. "Hep that lady up, Hiram," The Misfit said as she struggled to climb out of the ditch, "and Bobby Lee, you hold onto that little girl's hand."

"I don't want to hold hands with him," June Star said. "He reminds me of a pig."

The fat boy blushed and laughed and caught her by the arm and pulled her off into the woods after Hiram and her mother.

Alone with The Misfit, the grandmother found that she had lost her voice. There was not a cloud in the sky nor any sun. There was nothing around her but woods. She wanted to tell him that he must pray. She opened and closed her mouth several times before anything came out. Finally she found herself saying, "Jesus, Jesus," meaning Jesus will help you, but the way she was saying it, it sounded as if she might be cursing.

"Yes'm," The Misfit said as if he agreed. "Jesus thown everything off balance. It was the same case with Him as with me except He hadn't committed any crime and they could prove I had committed one because they had the papers on me. Of course," he said, "they never shown me my papers. That's why I sign myself now. I said long ago, you get your signature and sign everything you do and keep a copy of it. Then you'll know what you done and you can hold up the crime to the punishment and see do they match and in the end you'll have something to prove you ain't been treated right. I call myself The Misfit," he said, "because I can't make what all I done wrong fit what all I gone through in punishment."

There was a piercing scream from the woods, followed closely by a pistol 130 report. "Does it seem right to you, lady, that one is punished a heap and another ain't punished at all?"

"Jesus!" the old lady cried. "You've got good blood! I know you wouldn't shoot a lady! I know you come from nice people! Pray! Jesus, you ought not to shoot a lady. I'll give you all the money I've got!"

"Lady," The Misfit said, looking beyond her far into the woods, "there never was a body that give the undertaker a tip."

There were two more pistol reports and the grandmother raised her head like a parched old turkey hen crying for water and called, "Bailey Boy, Bailey Boy!" as if her heart would break.

"Jesus was the only One that ever raised the dead," The Misfit continued, "and He shouldn't have done it. He thown everything off balance. If He did what He said, then it's nothing for you to do but thow away everything and follow Him, and if He didn't, then it's nothing for you to do but enjoy the few minutes you got left the best way you can—by killing somebody or burning down his house or doing some other meanness to him. No pleasure but meanness," he said and his voice had become almost a snarl.

"Maybe He didn't raise the dead," the old lady mumbled, not knowing 135 what she was saying and feeling so dizzy that she sank down in the ditch with her legs twisted under her.

"I wasn't there so I can't say He didn't," The Misfit said. "I wisht I had of been there," he said, hitting the ground with his fist. "It ain't right I wasn't there because if I had of been there I would of known. Listen lady," he said in a high voice, "if I had of been there I would of known and I wouldn't be like I am now." His voice seemed about to crack and the grandmother's head cleared for an instant. She saw the man's face twisted close to her own as if he were going to cry and she murmured, "Why you're one of my babies. You're one of my own children!" She reached out and touched him on the shoulder. The Misfit sprang back as if a snake had bitten him and shot her three times through the chest. Then he put his gun down on the ground and took off his glasses and began to clean them.

Hiram and Bobby Lee returned from the woods and stood over the ditch, looking down at the grandmother who half sat and half lay in a puddle of blood with her legs crossed under her like a child's and her face smiling up at the cloudless sky.

Without his glasses, The Misfit's eyes were red-rimmed and pale and defenseless-looking. "Take her off and thow her where you thown the others," he said, picking up the cat that was rubbing itself against his leg.

"She was a talker, wasn't she?" Bobby Lee said, sliding down the ditch with a yodel.

"She would of been a good woman," The Misfit said, "if it had been some- 140 body there to shoot her every minute of her life."

"Some fun!" Bobby Lee said.

"Shut up, Bobby Lee," The Misfit said. "It's no real pleasure in life."

CONSIDERATIONS FOR CRITICAL THINKING AND WRITING

1. FIRST RESPONSE. How does O'Connor portray the family? What is comic about them? What qualities about them are we meant to take seriously? Are you shocked by what happens to them? Does your attitude toward them remain constant during the course of the story?

2. How do the grandmother's concerns about the trip to Florida foreshadow events in the story?

3. Describe the grandmother. How does O'Connor make her the central character?

4. What is Red Sammy's purpose in the story? Relate his view of life to the story's conflicts.

5. Characterize The Misfit. What makes him so? Can he be written off as simply insane? How does the grandmother respond to him?

6. Why does The Misfit say that "Jesus thown everything off balance" (para. 134)? What does religion have to do with the brutal action of this story?

7. What does The Misfit mean at the end when he says about the grandmother "She would of been a good woman . . . if it had been somebody there to shoot her every minute of her life"?

8. Describe the story's tone. Is it consistent? What is the effect of O'Connor's use of tone?

9. How is coincidence used to advance the plot? How do coincidences lead to ironies in the story?

10. Explain how the title points to the story's theme.

CONNECTIONS TO OTHER SELECTIONS

1. What makes "A Good Man Is Hard to Find" so difficult to interpret in contrast, say, to reading Hawthorne's "The Birthmark" (p. 329)?

2. How does this family compare with the Snopeses in Faulkner's "Barn Burning" (p. 481)? Which family are you more sympathetic to?

3. Consider the criminal behavior of The Misfit and Abner Snopes. What motivates each character? Explain the significant similarities and differences between them.

Good Country People   1955

Besides the neutral expression that she wore when she was alone, Mrs. Freeman had two others, forward and reverse, that she used for all her human dealings. Her forward expression was steady and driving like the advance of a heavy truck. Her eyes never swerved to left or right but turned as the story turned as if they followed a yellow line down the center of it. She seldom used the other expression because it was not often necessary for her to retract a statement, but when she did, her face came to a complete stop, there was an almost imperceptible movement of her black eyes, during which they seemed to be receding, and then the observer would see that Mrs. Freeman, though she might stand there as real as several grain sacks thrown on top of each other, was no longer there in spirit. As for getting anything across to her when this was the case, Mrs. Hopewell had given it up. She might talk her head off. Mrs. Freeman could never be brought to admit herself wrong on any point. She would stand there and if she could be brought to say anything, it was something like, "Well, I wouldn't of said it was and I wouldn't of said it wasn't," or letting her gaze range over the top kitchen shelf where there was an assortment of dusty bottles, she might remark, "I see you ain't ate many of them figs you put up last summer."

They carried on their most important business in the kitchen at breakfast. Every morning Mrs. Hopewell got up at seven o'clock and lit her gas heater and Joy's. Joy was her daughter, a large blonde girl who had an artificial leg. Mrs. Hopewell thought of her as a child though she was thirty-two years old and highly educated. Joy would get up while her mother was eating and lumber into the bathroom and slam the door, and before long, Mrs. Freeman would arrive at the back door. Joy would hear her mother call, "Come on in," and then they would talk for a while in low voices that were indistinguishable in the bathroom. By the time Joy came in, they had usually finished the weather report and were on one or the other of Mrs. Freeman's daughters, Glynese or Carramae, Joy called them Glycerin and Caramel. Glynese, a redhead, was eighteen and had many admirers; Carramae, a blonde, was only fifteen but already married and pregnant. She could not keep anything in her stomach. Every morning Mrs. Freeman told Mrs. Hopewell how many times she had vomited since the last report.

Mrs. Hopewell liked to tell people that Glynese and Carramae were two of the finest girls she knew and that Mrs. Freeman was a *lady* and that she was never ashamed to take her anywhere or introduce her to anybody they might meet. Then she would tell how she had happened to hire the Freemans in the first place and how they were a godsend to her and how she had had them four years. The reason for her keeping them so long was that they were not trash. They were good country people. She had telephoned the man whose name they had given as a reference and he had told her that Mr. Freeman was a good farmer but that his wife was the nosiest woman ever to walk the earth. "She's got to be into everything," the man said. "If she don't get there before the dust settles, you can bet she's dead, that's all. She'll want to know all your business. I can stand him real good," he had said, "but me nor my wife neither could have stood that woman one more minute on this place." That had put Mrs. Hopewell off for a few days.

She had hired them in the end because there were no other applicants but she had made up her mind beforehand exactly how she would handle the woman. Since she was the type who had to be into everything, then, Mrs. Hopewell decided, she would not only let her be into everything, she would *see to it* that she was into everything — she would give her the responsibility of everything, she would put her in charge. Mrs. Hopewell had no bad qualities of her own but she was able to use other people's in such a constructive way that she never felt the lack. She had hired the Freemans and she had kept them four years.

Nothing is perfect. This was one of Mrs. Hopewell's favorite sayings. Another was: that is life! And still another, the most important, was: well, other people have their opinions too. She would make these statements, usually at the table, in a tone of gentle insistence as if no one held them but her, and the large hulking Joy, whose constant outrage had obliterated every expression from her face, would stare just a little to the side of her, her eyes icy blue, with the look of someone who has achieved blindness by an act of will and means to keep it.

When Mrs. Hopewell said to Mrs. Freeman that life was like that, Mrs. Freeman would say, "I always said so myself." Nothing had been arrived at by anyone that had not first been arrived at by her. She was quicker than Mr. Freeman. When Mrs. Hopewell said to her after they had been on the place a while, "You know, you're the wheel behind the wheel," and winked, Mrs. Freeman had said, "I know it. I've always been quick. It's some that are quicker than others."

"Everybody is different," Mrs. Hopewell said.

"Yes, most people is," Mrs. Freeman said.

"It takes all kinds to make the world."

"I always said it did myself."

The girl was used to this kind of dialogue for breakfast and more of it for dinner; sometimes they had it for supper too. When they had no guest they ate in the kitchen because that was easier. Mrs. Freeman always managed to arrive at some point during the meal and to watch them finish it. She would stand in the doorway if it were summer but in the winter she would stand with one elbow on top of the refrigerator and look down on them, or she would stand by the gas heater, lifting the back of her skirt slightly. Occasionally she would stand against the wall and roll her head from side to side. At no time was she in any hurry to leave. All this was very trying on Mrs. Hopewell but she was a woman of great patience. She realized that nothing is perfect and that in the Freemans she had good country people and that if, in this day and age, you get good country people, you had better hang onto them.

She had had plenty of experience with trash. Before the Freemans she had averaged one tenant family a year. The wives of these farmers were not the kind you would want to be around you for very long. Mrs. Hopewell, who had divorced her husband long ago, needed someone to walk over the fields with her; and when Joy had to be impressed for these services, her remarks were usually so ugly and her face so glum that Mrs. Hopewell would say, "If you can't come pleasantly, I don't want you at all," to which the girl, standing square and rigid-shouldered with her neck thrust slightly forward, would reply, "If you want me, here I am — LIKE I AM."

Mrs. Hopewell excused this attitude because of the leg (which had been shot off in a hunting accident when Joy was ten). It was hard for Mrs. Hopewell to realize that her child was thirty-two now and that for more than twenty years she had had only one leg. She thought of her still as a child because it tore her heart to think instead of the poor stout girl in her thirties who had never danced a step or had any *normal* good times. Her name was really Joy but as soon as she was twenty-one and away from home, she had had it legally changed. Mrs. Hopewell was certain that she had thought and thought until she had hit upon the ugliest name in any language. Then she had gone and had the beautiful name, Joy, changed without telling her mother until after she had done it. Her legal name was Hulga.

When Mrs. Hopewell thought the name, Hulga, she thought of the broad blank hull of a battleship. She would not use it. She continued to call her Joy to which the girl responded but in a purely mechanical way.

Hulga had learned to tolerate Mrs. Freeman who saved her from taking 15 walks with her mother. Even Glynese and Carramae were useful when they occupied attention that might otherwise have been directed at her. At first she had thought she could not stand Mrs. Freeman for she had found that it was not possible to be rude to her. Mrs. Freeman would take on strange resentments and for days together she would be sullen but the source of her displeasure was always obscure; a direct attack, a positive leer, blatant ugliness to her face — these never touched her. And without warning one day, she began calling her Hulga.

She did not call her that in front of Mrs. Hopewell who would have been incensed but when she and the girl happened to be out of the house together, she would say something and add the name Hulga to the end of it, and the big spectacled Joy-Hulga would scowl and redden as if her privacy had been intruded upon. She considered the name her personal affair. She had arrived at it first purely on the basis of its ugly sound and then the full genius of its fitness had struck her. She had a vision of the name working like the ugly sweating Vulcan° who stayed in the furnace and to whom, presumably, the goddess had to come when called. She saw it as the name of her highest creative act. One of her major triumphs was that her mother had not been able to turn her dust into Joy, but the greater one was that she had been able to turn it herself into Hulga. However, Mrs. Freeman's relish for using the name only irritated her. It was as if Mrs. Freeman's beady steel-pointed eyes had penetrated far enough behind her face to reach some secret fact. Something about her seemed to fascinate Mrs. Freeman and then one day Hulga realized that it was the artificial leg. Mrs. Freeman had a special fondness for the details of secret infections, hidden deformities, assaults upon children. Of diseases, she preferred the lingering or incurable. Hulga had heard Mrs. Hopewell give her the details of the hunting accident, how the leg had been literally blasted off, how she had never lost consciousness. Mrs. Freeman could listen to it any time as if it had happened an hour ago.

When Hulga stumped into the kitchen in the morning (she could walk without making the awful noise but she made it — Mrs. Hopewell was certain — because it was ugly-sounding), she glanced at them and did not speak. Mrs. Hopewell would be in her red kimono with her hair tied around her head in rags. She would be sitting at the table, finishing her breakfast and Mrs. Freeman would be hanging by her elbow outward from the refrigerator, looking down at the table. Hulga always put her eggs on the stove to boil and then stood over them with her arms folded, and Mrs. Hopewell would look at her — a kind of indirect gaze divided between her and Mrs. Freeman — and would think that if she would only keep herself up a little, she wouldn't be so bad looking. There was nothing wrong with her face that a pleasant expression

---

Vulcan: Roman god of fire.

wouldn't help. Mrs. Hopewell said that people who looked on the bright side of things would be beautiful even if they were not.

Whenever she looked at Joy this way, she could not help but feel that it would have been better if the child had not taken the Ph.D. It had certainly not brought her out any and now that she had it, there was no more excuse for her to go to school again. Mrs. Hopewell thought it was nice for girls to go to school to have a good time but Joy had "gone through." Anyhow, she would not have been strong enough to go again. The doctors had told Mrs. Hopewell that with the best of care, Joy might see forty-five. She had a weak heart. Joy had made it plain that if it had not been for this condition, she would be far from these red hills and good country people. She would be in a university lecturing to people who knew what she was talking about. And Mrs. Hopewell could very well picture her there, looking like a scarecrow and lecturing to more of the same. Here she went about all day in a six-year-old skirt and a yellow sweat shirt with a faded cowboy on a horse embossed on it. She thought this was funny; Mrs. Hopewell thought it was idiotic and showed simply that she was still a child. She was brilliant but she didn't have a grain of sense. It seemed to Mrs. Hopewell that every year she grew less like other people and more like herself—bloated, rude, and squint-eyed. And she said such strange things! To her own mother she had said—without warning, without excuse, standing up in the middle of a meal with her face purple and her mouth half full—"Woman! do you ever look inside? Do you ever look inside and see what you are *not*? God!" she had cried sinking down again and staring at her plate, "Malebranche° was right: we are not our own light. We are not our own light!" Mrs. Hopewell had no idea to this day what brought that on. She had only made the remark, hoping Joy would take it in, that a smile never hurt anyone.

The girl had taken the Ph.D. in philosophy and this left Mrs. Hopewell at a complete loss. You could say, "My daughter is a nurse," or "My daughter is a schoolteacher," or even, "My daughter is a chemical engineer." You could not say, "My daughter is a philosopher." That was something that had ended with the Greeks and Romans. All day Joy sat on her neck in a deep chair, reading. Sometimes she went for walks but she didn't like dogs or cats or birds or flowers or nature or nice young men. She looked at nice young men as if she could smell their stupidity.

One day Mrs. Hopewell had picked up one of the books the girl had just 20 put down and opening it at random, she read, "Science, on the other hand, has to assert its soberness and seriousness afresh and declare that it is concerned solely with what-is. Nothing—how can it be for science anything but a horror and a phantasm? If science is right, then one thing stands firm: science wishes to know nothing of nothing. Such is after all the strictly scientific approach to Nothing. We know it by wishing to know nothing of Nothing." These words had been underlined with a blue pencil and they worked on Mrs. Hopewell like some evil incantation in gibberish. She shut the book quickly and went out of the room as if she were having a chill.

This morning when the girl came in, Mrs. Freeman was on Carramae. "She thrown up four times after supper," she said, "and was up twict in the night

Malebranche: Nicolas Malebranche (1638–1715), a French philosopher.

after three o'clock. Yesterday she didn't do nothing but ramble in the bureau drawer. All she did. Stand up there and see what she could run up on."

"She's got to eat," Mrs. Hopewell muttered, sipping her coffee, while she watched Joy's back at the stove. She was wondering what the child had said to the Bible salesman. She could not imagine what kind of a conversation she could possibly have had with him.

He was a tall gaunt hatless youth who had called yesterday to sell them a Bible. He had appeared at the door, carrying a large black suitcase that weighted him so heavily on one side that he had to brace himself against the door facing. He seemed on the point of collapse but he said in a cheerful voice, "Good morning, Mrs. Cedars!" and set the suitcase down on the mat. He was not a bad-looking young man though he had on a bright blue suit and yellow socks that were not pulled up far enough. He had prominent face bones and a streak of sticky-looking brown hair falling across his forehead.

"I'm Mrs. Hopewell," she said.

"Oh!" he said, pretending to look puzzled but with his eyes sparkling, "I 25 saw it said 'The Cedars' on the mailbox so I thought you was Mrs. Cedars!" and he burst out in a pleasant laugh. He picked up the satchel and under cover of a pant, he fell forward into her hall. It was rather as if the suitcase had moved first, jerking him after it. "Mrs. Hopewell!" he said and grabbed her hand. "I hope you are well!" and he laughed again and then all at once his face sobered completely. He paused and gave her a straight earnest look and said, "Lady, I've come to speak of serious things."

"Well, come in," she muttered, none too pleased because her dinner was almost ready. He came into the parlor and sat down on the edge of a straight chair and put the suitcase between his feet and glanced around the room as if he were sizing her up by it. Her silver gleamed on the two sideboards; she decided he had never been in a room as elegant as this.

"Mrs. Hopewell," he began, using her name in a way that sounded almost intimate, "I know you believe in Chrustian service."

"Well yes," she murmured.

"I know," he said and paused, looking very wise with his head cocked on one side, "that you're a good woman. Friends have told me."

Mrs. Hopewell never liked to be taken for a fool. "What are you selling?" 30 she asked.

"Bibles," the young man said and his eye raced around the room before he added, "I see you have no family Bible in your parlor, I see that is the one lack you got!"

Mrs. Hopewell could not say, "My daughter is an atheist and won't let me keep the Bible in the parlor." She said, stiffening slightly, "I keep my Bible by my bedside." This was not the truth. It was in the attic somewhere.

"Lady," he said, "the word of God ought to be in the parlor."

"Well, I think that's a matter of taste," she began. "I think . . ."

"Lady," he said, "for a Chrustian, the word of God ought to be in every 35 room in the house besides in his heart. I know you're a Chrustian because I can see it in every line of your face."

She stood up and said, "Well, young man, I don't want to buy a Bible and I smell my dinner burning."

He didn't get up. He began to twist his hands and looking down at them, he said softly, "Well lady, I'll tell you the truth — not many people want to buy one nowadays and besides, I know I'm real simple. I don't know how to say a thing but to say it. I'm just a country boy." He glanced up into her unfriendly face. "People like you don't like to fool with country people like me!"

"Why!" she cried, "good country people are the salt of the earth! Besides, we all have different ways of doing, it takes all kinds to make the world go 'round. That's life!"

"You said a mouthful," he said.

"Why, I think there aren't enough good people in the world!" she said, 40 stirred. "I think that's what's wrong with it!"

His face had brightened. "I didn't introduce myself," he said. "I'm Manley Pointer from out in the country around Willohobie, not even from a place, just from near a place."

"You wait a minute," she said. "I have to see about my dinner." She went out to the kitchen and found Joy standing near the door where she had been listening.

"Get rid of the salt of the earth," she said, "and let's eat."

Mrs. Hopewell gave her a pained look and turned the heat down under the vegetables. "*I* can't be rude to anybody," she murmured and went back into the parlor.

He had opened the suitcase and was sitting with a Bible on each knee. 45

"You might as well put those up," she told him. "I don't want one."

"I appreciate your honesty," he said. "You don't see any more real honest people unless you go way out in the country."

"I know," she said, "real genuine folks!" Through the crack in the door she heard a groan.

"I guess a lot of boys come telling you they're working their way through college," he said, "but I'm not going to tell you that. Somehow," he said, "I don't want to go to college. I want to devote my life to Chrustian service. See," he said, lowering his voice, "I got this heart condition. I may not live long. When you know it's something wrong with you and you may not live long, well then, lady . . ." He paused, with his mouth open, and stared at her.

He and Joy had the same condition! She knew that her eyes were filling 50 with tears but she collected herself quickly and murmured, "Won't you stay for dinner? We'd love to have you!" and was sorry the instant she heard herself say it.

"Yes mam," he said in an abashed voice, "I would sher love to do that!"

Joy had given him one look on being introduced to him and then throughout the meal had not glanced at him again. He had addressed several remarks to her, which she had pretended not to hear. Mrs. Hopewell could not understand deliberate rudeness, although she lived with it, and she felt she had always to overflow with hospitality to make up for Joy's lack of courtesy. She urged him to talk about himself and he did. He said he was the seventh child of twelve and that his father had been crushed under a tree when he himself was eight years old. He had been crushed very badly, in fact, almost cut in two and was practically not recognizable. His mother had got along the best she could by hard working and she had always seen that her children went to Sunday School and that they read the Bible every evening. He was now nineteen years old and he had been selling Bibles for four months. In that time he had sold seventy-seven Bibles and had the promise of two more sales. He wanted to become a missionary because he thought that was the way you could do most for people. "He who losest his life shall find it," he said simply and he was so sincere, so genuine and earnest that Mrs. Hopewell would not for the world have smiled. He prevented his peas from sliding onto the table by blocking them with a piece of bread which he later cleaned his plate with. She could see Joy observing sidewise how he handled his knife and fork and she saw too that every few minutes, the boy would dart a keen appraising glance at the girl as if he were trying to attract her attention.

After dinner Joy cleared the dishes off the table and disappeared and Mrs. Hopewell was left to talk with him. He told her again about his childhood and his father's accident and about various things that had happened to him. Every five minutes or so she would stifle a yawn. He sat for two hours until finally she told him she must go because she had an appointment in town. He packed his Bibles and thanked her and prepared to leave, but in the doorway he stopped and wrung her hand and said that not on any of his trips had he met a lady as nice as her and he asked if he could come again. She had said she would always be happy to see him.

Joy had been standing in the road, apparently looking at something in the distance, when he came down the steps toward her, bent to the side with his heavy valise. He stopped where she was standing and confronted her directly. Mrs. Hopewell could not hear what he said but she trembled to think what Joy would say to him. She could see that after a minute Joy said something and that then the boy began to speak again, making an excited gesture with his free hand. After a minute Joy said something else at which the boy began to speak once more. Then to her amazement, Mrs. Hopewell saw the two of them walk off together, toward the gate. Joy had walked all the way to the gate with him and Mrs. Hopewell could not imagine what they had said to each other, and she had not yet dared to ask.

Mrs. Freeman was insisting upon her attention. She had moved from the 55 refrigerator to the heater so that Mrs. Hopewell had to turn and face her in order to seem to be listening. "Glynese gone out with Harvey Hill again last night," she said. "She had this sty."

"Hill," Mrs. Hopewell said absently, "is the one who works in the garage?"

"Nome, he's the one that goes to chiropracter school," Mrs. Freeman said. "She had this sty. Been had it two days. So she says when he brought her in the other night he says, 'Lemme get rid of that sty for you,' and she says, 'How?' and he says, 'You just lay yourself down acrost the seat of that car and I'll show you.' So she done it and he popped her neck. Kept on a-popping it several times until she made him quit. This morning," Mrs. Freeman said, "she ain't got no sty. She ain't got no traces of a sty."

"I never heard of that before," Mrs. Hopewell said.

"He ast her to marry him before the Ordinary,"° Mrs. Freeman went on, "and she told him she wasn't going to be married in no *office*."

"Well, Glynese is a fine girl," Mrs. Hopewell said. "Glynese and Carramae 60 are both fine girls."

"Carramae said when her and Lyman was married Lyman said it sure felt sacred to him. She said he said he wouldn't take five hundred dollars for being married by a preacher."

"How much would he take?" the girl asked from the stove.

Ordinary: Justice of the peace.

"He said he wouldn't take five hundred dollars," Mrs. Freeman repeated.
"Well we all have work to do," Mrs. Hopewell said.
"Lyman said it just felt more sacred to him," Mrs. Freeman said. "The doc- 65
tor wants Carramae to eat prunes. Says instead of medicine. Says them cramps
is coming from pressure. You know where I think it is?"
"She'll be better in a few weeks," Mrs. Hopewell said.
"In the tube," Mrs. Freeman said. "Else she wouldn't be as sick as she is."

Hulga had cracked her two eggs into a saucer and was bringing them to
the table along with a cup of coffee that she had filled too full. She sat down
carefully and began to eat, meaning to keep Mrs. Freeman there by questions if
for any reason she showed an inclination to leave. She could perceive her
mother's eye on her. The first round-about question would be about the Bible
salesman and she did not wish to bring it on. "How did he pop her neck?" she
asked.

Mrs. Freeman went into a description of how he had popped her neck. She
said he owned a '55 Mercury but that Glynese said she would rather marry a
man with only a '36 Plymouth who would be married by a preacher. The girl
asked what if he had a '32 Plymouth and Mrs. Freeman said what Glynese had
said was a '36 Plymouth.

Mrs. Hopewell said there were not many girls with Glynese's common 70
sense. She said what she admired in those girls was their common sense. She
said that reminded her that they had had a nice visitor yesterday, a young man
selling Bibles. "Lord," she said, "he bored me to death but he was so sincere
and genuine I couldn't be rude to him. He was just good country people, you
know," she said, " — just the salt of the earth."

"I seen him walk up," Mrs. Freeman said, "and then later — I seen him walk
off," and Hulga could feel the slight shift in her voice, the slight insinuation,
that he had not walked off alone, had he? Her face remained expressionless
but the color rose into her neck and she seemed to swallow it down with the
next spoonful of egg. Mrs. Freeman was looking at her as if they had a secret
together.

"Well, it takes all kinds of people to make the world go 'round," Mrs.
Hopewell said. "It's very good we aren't all alike."

"Some people are more alike than others," Mrs. Freeman said.

Hulga got up and stumped, with about twice the noise that was necessary,
into her room and locked the door. She was to meet the Bible salesman at ten
o'clock at the gate. She had thought about it half the night. She had started
thinking of it as a great joke and then she had begun to see profound implications in it. She had lain in bed imagining dialogues for them that were insane
on the surface but that reached below to depths that no Bible salesman would
be aware of. Their conversation yesterday had been of this kind.

He had stopped in front of her and had simply stood there. His face was 75
bony and sweaty and bright, with a little pointed nose in the center of it, and
his look was different from what it had been at the dinner table. He was gazing
at her with open curiosity, with fascination, like a child watching a new fantastic animal at the zoo, and he was breathing as if he had run a great distance to
reach her. His gaze seemed somehow familiar but she could not think where
she had been regarded with it before. For almost a minute he didn't say anything. Then on what seemed an insuck of breath, he whispered, "You ever ate a
chicken that was two days old?"

The girl looked at him stonily. He might have just put this question up for consideration at the meeting of a philosophical association. "Yes," she presently replied as if she had considered it from all angles.

"It must have been mighty small!" he said triumphantly and shook all over with little nervous giggles, getting very red in the face, and subsiding finally into his gaze of complete admiration, while the girl's expression remained exactly the same.

"How old are you?" he asked softly.

She waited some time before she answered. Then in a flat voice she said, "Seventeen."

His smiles came in succession like waves breaking on the surface of a little lake. "I see you got a wooden leg," he said. "I think you're brave. I think you're real sweet."

The girl stood blank and solid and silent.

"Walk to the gate with me," he said. "You're a brave sweet little thing and I liked you the minute I seen you walk in the door."

Hulga began to move forward.

"What's your name?" he asked, smiling down on the top of her head.

"Hulga," she said.

"Hulga," he murmured, "Hulga. Hulga. I never heard of anybody name Hulga before. You're shy, aren't you, Hulga?" he asked.

She nodded, watching his large red hand on the handle of the giant valise.

"I like girls that wear glasses," he said. "I think a lot. I'm not like these people that a serious thought don't ever enter their heads. It's because I may die."

"I may die too," she said suddenly and looked up at him. His eyes were very small and brown, glittering feverishly.

"Listen," he said, "don't you think some people was meant to meet on account of what all they got in common and all? Like they both think serious thoughts and all?" He shifted the valise to his other hand so that the hand nearest her was free. He caught hold of her elbow and shook it a little. "I don't work on Saturday," he said. "I like to walk in the woods and see what Mother Nature is wearing. O'er the hills and far away. Pic-nics and things. Couldn't we go on a pic-nic tomorrow? Say yes, Hulga," he said and gave her a dying look as if he felt his insides about to drop out of him. He had even seemed to sway slightly toward her.

During the night she had imagined that she seduced him. She imagined that the two of them walked on the place until they came to the storage barn beyond the two back fields and there, she imagined, that things came to such a pass that she very easily seduced him and that then, of course, she had to reckon with his remorse. True genius can get an idea across even to an inferior mind. She imagined that she took his remorse in hand and changed it into a deeper understanding of life. She took all his shame away and turned it into something useful.

She set off for the gate at exactly ten o'clock, escaping without drawing Mrs. Hopewell's attention. She didn't take anything to eat, forgetting that food is usually taken on a picnic. She wore a pair of slacks and a dirty white shirt, and as an afterthought, she had put some Vapex° on the collar of it since she did not own any perfume. When she reached the gate no one was there.

Vapex: Trade name for a nasal spray.

She looked up and down the empty highway and had the furious feeling that she had been tricked, that he had only meant to make her walk to the gate after the idea of him. Then suddenly he stood up, very tall, from behind a bush on the opposite embankment. Smiling, he lifted his hat which was new and wide-brimmed. He had not worn it yesterday and she wondered if he had bought it for the occasion. It was toast-colored with a red and white band around it and was slightly too large for him. He stepped from behind the bush still carrying the black valise. He had on the same suit and the same yellow socks sucked down in his shoes from walking. He crossed the highway and said, "I knew you'd come!"

The girl wondered acidly how he had known this. She pointed to the valise and asked, "Why did you bring your Bibles?"

He took her elbow, smiling down on her as if he could not stop. "You can never tell when you'll need the word of God, Hulga," he said. She had a moment in which she doubted that this was actually happening and then they began to climb the embankment. They went down into the pasture toward the woods. The boy walked lightly by her side, bouncing on his toes. The valise did not seem to be heavy today; he even swung it. They crossed half the pasture without saying anything and then, putting his hand easily on the small of her back, he asked softly, "Where does your wooden leg join on?" 95

She turned an ugly red and glared at him and for an instant the boy looked abashed. "I didn't mean you no harm," he said. "I only meant you're so brave and all. I guess God takes care of you."

"No," she said, looking forward and walking fast, "I don't even believe in God."

At this he stopped and whistled. "No!" he exclaimed as if he were too astonished to say anything else.

She walked on and in a second he was bouncing at her side, fanning with his hat. "That's very unusual for a girl," he remarked, watching her out of the corner of his eye. When they reached the edge of the wood, he put his hand on her back again and drew her against him without a word and kissed her heavily.

The kiss, which had more pressure than feeling behind it, produced that 100 extra surge of adrenaline in the girl that enables one to carry a packed trunk out of a burning house, but in her, the power went at once to the brain. Even before he released her, her mind, clear and detached and ironic anyway, was regarding him from a great distance, with amusement but with pity. She had never been kissed before and she was pleased to discover that it was an unexceptional experience and all a matter of the mind's control. Some people might enjoy drain water if they were told it was vodka. When the boy, looking expectant but uncertain, pushed her gently away, she turned and walked on, saying nothing as if such business, for her, were common enough.

He came along panting at her side, trying to help her when he saw a root that she might trip over. He caught and held back the long swaying blades of thorn vine until she had passed beyond them. She led the way and he came breathing heavily behind her. Then they came out on a sunlit hillside, sloping softly into another one a little smaller. Beyond, they could see the rusted top of the old barn where the extra hay was stored.

The hill was sprinkled with small pink weeds. "Then you ain't saved?" he asked suddenly, stopping.

The girl smiled. It was the first time she had smiled at him at all. "In my economy," she said, "I'm saved and you are damned but I told you I didn't believe in God."

Nothing seemed to destroy the boy's look of admiration. He gazed at her now as if the fantastic animal at the zoo had put its paw through the bars and given him a loving poke. She thought he looked as if he wanted to kiss her again and she walked on before he had the chance.

"Ain't there somewheres we can sit down sometime?" he murmured, his 105 voice softening toward the end of the sentence.

"In that barn," she said.

They made for it rapidly as if it might slide away like a train. It was a large two-story barn, cool and dark inside. The boy pointed up the ladder that led into the loft and said, "It's too bad we can't go up there."

"Why can't we?" she asked.

"Yer leg," he said reverently.

The girl gave him a contemptuous look and putting both hands on the 110 ladder, she climbed it while he stood below, apparently awestruck. She pulled herself expertly through the opening and then looked down at him and said, "Well, come on if you're coming," and he began to climb the ladder, awkwardly bringing the suitcase with him.

"We won't need the Bible," she observed.

"You never can tell," he said, panting. After he had got into the loft, he was a few seconds catching his breath. She had sat down in a pile of straw. A wide sheath of sunlight, filled with dust particles, slanted over her. She lay back against a bale, her face turned away, looking out the front opening of the barn where hay was thrown from a wagon into the loft. The two pink-speckled hillsides lay back against a dark ridge of woods. The sky was cloudless and cold blue. The boy dropped down by her side and put one arm under her and the other over her and began methodically kissing her face, making little noises like a fish. He did not remove his hat but it was pushed far enough back not to interfere. When her glasses got in his way, he took them off of her and slipped them into his pocket.

The girl at first did not return any of the kisses but presently she began to and after she had put several on his cheek, she reached his lips and remained there, kissing him again and again as if she were trying to draw all the breath out of him. His breath was clear and sweet like a child's and the kisses were sticky like a child's. He mumbled about loving her and about knowing when he first seen her that he loved her, but the mumbling was like the sleepy fretting of a child being put to sleep by his mother. Her mind, throughout this, never stopped or lost itself for a second to her feelings. "You ain't said you loved me none," he whispered finally, pulling back from her. "You got to say that."

She looked away from him off into the hollow sky and then down at a black ridge and then down farther into what appeared to be two green swelling lakes. She didn't realize he had taken her glasses but this landscape could not seem exceptional to her for she seldom paid any close attention to her surroundings.

"You got to say it," he repeated. "You got to say you love me." 115

She was always careful how she committed herself. "In a sense," she began, "if you use the word loosely, you might say that. But it's not a word I use. I don't have illusions. I'm one of those people who see *through* to nothing."

The boy was frowning. "You got to say it. I said it and you got to say it," he said.

The girl looked at him almost tenderly. "You poor baby," she murmured. "It's just as well you don't understand," and she pulled him by the neck, face-down, against her. "We are all damned," she said, "but some of us have taken off our blindfolds and see that there's nothing to see. It's a kind of salvation."

The boy's astonished eyes looked blankly through the ends of her hair. "Okay," he almost whined, "but do you love me or don'tcher?"

"Yes," she said and added, "in a sense. But I must tell you something. There mustn't be anything dishonest between us." She lifted his head and looked him in the eye. "I am thirty years old," she said. "I have a number of degrees." 120

The boy's look was irritated but dogged. "I don't care," he said. "I don't care a thing about what all you done. I just want to know if you love me or don'tcher?" and he caught her to him and wildly planted her face with kisses until she said, "Yes, yes."

"Okay then," he said, letting her go. "Prove it."

She smiled, looking dreamily out on the shifty landscape. She had se-duced him without even making up her mind to try. "How?" she asked, feeling that he should be delayed a little.

He leaned over and put his lips to her ear. "Show me where your wooden leg joins on," he whispered.

The girl uttered a sharp little cry and her face instantly drained of color. The obscenity of the suggestion was not what shocked her. As a child she had sometimes been subject to feelings of shame but education had removed the last traces of that as a good surgeon scrapes for cancer; she would no more have felt it over what he was asking than she would have believed in his Bible. But she was as sensitive about the artificial leg as a peacock about his tail. No one ever touched it but her. She took care of it as someone else would his soul, in private and almost with her own eyes turned away. "No," she said. 125

"I known it," he muttered, sitting up. "You're just playing me for a sucker."

"Oh no no!" she cried. "It joins on at the knee. Only at the knee. Why do you want to see it?"

The boy gave her a long penetrating look. "Because," he said, "it's what makes you different. You ain't like anybody else."

She sat staring at him. There was nothing about her face or her round freezing-blue eyes to indicate that this had moved her; but she felt as if her heart had stopped and left her mind to pump her blood. She decided that for the first time in her life she was face to face with real innocence. This boy, with an instinct that came from beyond wisdom, had touched the truth about her. When after a minute, she said in a hoarse high voice, "All right," it was like sur-rendering to him completely. It was like losing her own life and finding it again, miraculously, in his.

Very gently he began to roll the slack leg up. The artificial limb, in a white sock and brown flat shoe, was bound in a heavy material like canvas and ended in an ugly jointure where it was attached to the stump. The boy's face and his voice were entirely reverent as he uncovered it and said, "Now show me how to take it off and on." 130

She took it off for him and put it back on again and then he took it off himself, handling it as tenderly as if it were a real one. "See!" he said with a de-lighted child's face. "Now I can do it myself!"

"Put it back on," she said. She was thinking that she would run away with him and that every night he would take the leg off and every morning put it back on again. "Put it back on," she said.

"Not yet," he murmured, setting it on its foot out of her reach. "Leave it off for a while. You got me instead."

She gave a little cry of alarm but he pushed her down and began to kiss her again. Without the leg she felt entirely dependent on him. Her brain seemed to have stopped thinking altogether and to be about some other function that it was not very good at. Different expressions raced back and forth over her face. Every now and then the boy, his eyes like two steel spikes, would glance behind him where the leg stood. Finally she pushed him off and said, "Put it back on me now."

"Wait," he said. He leaned the other way and pulled the valise toward him 135 and opened it. It had a pale blue spotted lining and there were only two Bibles in it. He took one of these out and opened the cover of it. It was hollow and contained a pocket flask of whiskey, a pack of cards, and a small blue box with printing on it. He laid these out in front of her one at a time in an evenly-spaced row, like one presenting offerings at the shrine of a goddess. He put the blue box in her hand. THIS PRODUCT TO BE USED ONLY FOR THE PRE-VENTION OF DISEASE, she read, and dropped it. The boy was unscrewing the top of the flask. He stopped and pointed, with a smile, to the deck of cards. It was not an ordinary deck but one with an obscene picture on the back of each card. "Take a swig," he said, offering her the bottle first. He held it in front of her, but like one mesmerized, she did not move.

Her voice when she spoke had an almost pleading sound. "Aren't you," she murmured, "aren't you just good country people?"

The boy cocked his head. He looked as if he were just beginning to understand that she might be trying to insult him. "Yeah," he said, curling his lip slightly, "but it ain't held me back none. I'm as good as you any day in the week."

"Give me my leg," she said.

He pushed it farther away with his foot. "Come on now, let's begin to have us a good time," he said coaxingly. "We ain't got to know one another good yet."

"Give me my leg!" she screamed and tried to lunge for it but he pushed her 140 down easily.

"What's the matter with you all of a sudden?" he asked, frowning as he screwed the top on the flask and put it quickly back inside the Bible. "You just a while ago said you didn't believe in nothing. I thought you was some girl!"

Her face was almost purple. "You're a Christian!" she hissed. "You're a fine Christian! You're just like them all—say one thing and do another. You're a perfect Christian, you're . . ."

The boy's mouth was set angrily. "I hope you don't think," he said in a lofty indignant tone, "that I believe in that crap! I may sell Bibles but I know which end is up and I wasn't born yesterday and I know where I'm going!"

"Give me my leg!" she screeched. He jumped up so quickly that she barely saw him sweep the cards and the blue box into the Bible and throw the Bible into his valise. She saw him grab the leg and then she saw it for an instant slanted forlornly across the inside of the suitcase with a Bible at either side of its opposite ends. He slammed the lid shut and snatched up the valise and swung it down the hole and then stepped through himself.

When all of him had passed but his head, he turned and regarded her with 145 a look that no longer had any admiration in it. "I've gotten a lot of interesting things," he said. "One time I got a woman's glass eye this way. And you needn't to think you'll catch me because Pointer ain't really my name. I use a different name at every house I call at and don't stay nowhere long. And I'll tell you another thing, Hulga," he said, using the name as if he didn't think much of it, "you ain't so smart. I been believing in nothing ever since I was born!" and then the toast-colored hat disappeared down the hole and the girl was left, sitting on the straw in the dusty sunlight. When she turned her churning face toward the opening, she saw his blue figure struggling successfully over the green speckled lake.

Mrs. Hopewell and Mrs. Freeman, who were in the back pasture, digging up onions, saw him emerge a little later from the woods and head across the meadow toward the highway. "Why, that looks like that nice dull young man that tried to sell me a Bible yesterday," Mrs. Hopewell said, squinting. "He must have been selling them to the Negroes back in there. He was so simple," she said, "but I guess the world would be better off if we were all that simple."

Mrs. Freeman's gaze drove forward and just touched him before he disappeared under the hill. Then she returned her attention to the evil-smelling onion shoot she was lifting from the ground. "Some can't be that simple," she said. "I know I never could."

CONSIDERATIONS FOR CRITICAL THINKING AND WRITING

1. FIRST RESPONSE. What do you think of Hulga's conviction that intelligence and education are incompatible with religious faith?

2. Why is it significant that Mrs. Hopewell's daughter has two names? How do the other characters' names serve to characterize them?

3. Why do you think Mrs. Freeman and Mrs. Hopewell are introduced before Hulga? What do they contribute to Hulga's story?

4. Identify the conflict in this story. How is it resolved?

5. Hulga and the Bible salesman play a series of jokes on each other. How are these deceptions related to the theme?

6. What is the effect of O'Connor's use of the phrase "good country people" throughout the story? Why is it an appropriate title?

7. The Bible salesman's final words to Hulga are "You ain't so smart. I been believing in nothing ever since I was born!" What religious values are expressed in the story?

8. After the Bible salesman leaves Hulga at the end of the story, O'Connor adds two more paragraphs concerning Mrs. Hopewell and Mrs. Freeman. What is the purpose of these final paragraphs?

9. Hulga's perspective on life is ironic, but she is also the subject of O'Connor's irony. Explain how O'Connor uses irony to reveal Hulga's character.

10. This story would be different if told from Hulga's point of view. Describe how the use of a limited omniscient narrator contributes to the story's effects.

CONNECTIONS TO OTHER SELECTIONS

1. How do Mrs. Hopewell's assumptions about life compare with those of Krebs's mother in Hemingway's "Soldier's Home" (p. 145)? Explain how the conflict in each story is related to what the mothers come to represent in the eyes of the central characters.

2. How are country people portrayed in this story and in "The Turkey" (p. 373)? In general, does O'Connor treat them positively or negatively?

Revelation   1964

The doctor's waiting room, which was very small, was almost full when the Turpins entered and Mrs. Turpin, who was very large, made it look even smaller by her presence. She stood looming at the head of the magazine table set in the center of it, a living demonstration that the room was inadequate and ridiculous. Her little bright black eyes took in all the patients as she sized up the seating situation. There was one vacant chair and a place on the sofa occupied by a blond child in a dirty blue romper who should have been told to move over and make room for the lady. He was five or six, but Mrs. Turpin saw at once that no one was going to tell him to move over. He was slumped down in the seat, his arms idle at his sides and his eyes idle in his head; his nose ran unchecked.

Mrs. Turpin put a firm hand on Claud's shoulder and said in a voice that included anyone who wanted to listen, "Claud, you sit in that chair there," and gave him a push down into the vacant one. Claud was florid and bald and sturdy, somewhat shorter than Mrs. Turpin, but he sat down as if he were accustomed to doing what she told him to.

Mrs. Turpin remained standing. The only man in the room besides Claud was a lean stringy old fellow with a rusty hand spread out on each knee, whose eyes were closed as if he were asleep or dead or pretending to be so as not to get up and offer her his seat. Her gaze settled agreeably on a well-dressed gray-haired lady whose eyes met hers and whose expression said: if that child belonged to me, he would have some manners and move over — there's plenty of room there for you and him too.

Claud looked up with a sigh and made as if to rise.

"Sit down," Mrs. Turpin said. "You know you're not supposed to stand on   5 that leg. He has an ulcer on his leg," she explained.

Claud lifted his foot onto the magazine table and rolled his trouser leg up to reveal a purple swelling on a plump marble-white calf.

"My!" the pleasant lady said. "How did you do that?"

"A cow kicked him," Mrs. Turpin said.

"Goodness!" said the lady.

Claud rolled his trouser leg down.   10

"Maybe the little boy would move over," the lady suggested, but the child did not stir.

"Somebody will be leaving in a minute," Mrs. Turpin said. She could not understand why a doctor — with as much money as they made charging five dollars a day to just stick their head in the hospital door and look at you — couldn't afford a decent-sized waiting room. This one was hardly bigger than a garage. The table was cluttered with limp-looking magazines and at one end of it there was a big green glass ash tray full of cigarette butts and cotton wads with little blood spots on them. If she had had anything to do with the running of the place, that would have been emptied every so often. There were no chairs against the wall at the head of the room. It had a rectangular-shaped panel in it that permitted a view of the office where the nurse came and went and the secretary listened to the radio. A plastic fern in a gold pot sat in the opening and trailed its fronds down almost to the floor. The radio was softly playing gospel music.

Just then the inner door opened and a nurse with the highest stack of yellow hair Mrs. Turpin had ever seen put her face in the crack and called for the next patient. The woman sitting beside Claud grasped the two arms of her chair and hoisted herself up; she pulled her dress free from her legs and lumbered through the door where the nurse had disappeared.

Mrs. Turpin eased into the vacant chair, which held her tight as a corset. "I wish I could reduce," she said, and rolled her eyes and gave a comic sigh.

"Oh, *you* aren't fat," the stylish lady said.   15

"Ooooo I am too," Mrs. Turpin said. "Claud he eats all he wants to and never weighs over one hundred and seventy-five pounds, but me I just look at something good to eat and I gain some weight," and her stomach and shoulders shook with laughter. "You can eat all you want to, can't you, Claud?" she asked, turning to him.

Claud only grinned.

"Well, as long as you have such a good disposition," the stylish lady said, "I don't think it makes a bit of difference what size you are. You just can't beat a good disposition."

Next to her was a fat girl of eighteen or nineteen, scowling into a thick blue book which Mrs. Turpin saw was entitled *Human Development*. The girl raised her head and directed her scowl at Mrs. Turpin as if she did not like her looks. She appeared annoyed that anyone should speak while she tried to read. The poor girl's face was blue with acne and Mrs. Turpin thought how pitiful it was to have a face like that at that age. She gave the girl a friendly smile but the girl only scowled the harder. Mrs. Turpin herself was fat but she had always had good skin, and though she was forty-seven years old, there was not a wrinkle in her face except around her eyes from laughing too much.

Next to the ugly girl was the child, still in exactly the same position, and   20
next to him was a thin leathery old woman in a cotton print dress. She and Claud had three sacks of chicken feed in their pump house that was in the same print. She had seen from the first that the child belonged with the old woman. She could tell by the way they sat — kind of vacant and white-trashy, as if they would sit there until Doomsday if nobody called and told them to get up. And at right angles but next to the well-dressed pleasant lady was a lank-faced woman who was certainly the child's mother. She had on a yellow sweat shirt and wine-colored slacks, both gritty-looking, and the rims of her lips were stained with snuff. Her dirty yellow hair was tied behind with a little piece of red paper ribbon. Worse than niggers any day, Mrs. Turpin thought.

The gospel hymn playing was, "When I looked up and He looked down," and Mrs. Turpin, who knew it, supplied the last line mentally, "And wona these days I know I'll we-eara crown."

Without appearing to, Mrs. Turpin always noticed people's feet. The well-dressed lady had on red and gray suede shoes to match her dress. Mrs. Turpin had on her good black patent leather pumps. The ugly girl had on Girl Scout shoes and heavy socks. The old woman had on tennis shoes and the white-trashy mother had on what appeared to be bedroom slippers, black straw with gold braid threaded through them — exactly what you would have expected her to have on.

Sometimes at night when she couldn't go to sleep, Mrs. Turpin would occupy herself with the question of who she would have chosen to be if she couldn't have been herself. If Jesus had said to her before he made her, "There's only two places available for you. You can either be a nigger or white-trash," what would she have said? "Please, Jesus, please," she would have said, "just let me wait until there's another place available," and he would have said, "No, you have to go right now and I have only those two places so make up your mind." She would have wiggled and squirmed and begged and pleaded but it would have been no use and finally she would have said, "All right, make me a nigger then — but that don't mean a trashy one." And he would have made her a neat clean respectable Negro woman, herself but black.

Next to the child's mother was a red-headed youngish woman, reading one of the magazines and working a piece of chewing gum, hell for leather, as Claud would say. Mrs. Turpin could not see the woman's feet. She was not white-trash, just common. Sometimes Mrs. Turpin occupied herself at night naming the classes of people. On the bottom of the heap were most colored people, not the kind she would have been if she had been one, but most of them; then next to them — not above, just away from — were the white-trash; then above them were the homeowners, and above them the home-and-land owners, to which she and Claud belonged. Above she and Claud were people with a lot of money and much bigger houses and much more land. But here the complexity of it would begin to bear in on her, for some of the people with a lot of money were common and ought to be below she and Claud and some of the people who had good blood had lost their money and had to rent and then there were colored people who owned their homes and land as well. There was a colored dentist in town who had two red Lincolns and a swimming pool and a farm with registered white-face cattle on it. Usually by the time she had fallen asleep all the classes of people were moiling and roiling around in her head, and she would dream they were all crammed in together in a box car, being ridden off to be put in a gas oven.

"That's a beautiful clock," she said and nodded to her right. It was a big 25 wall clock, the face encased in a brass sunburst.

"Yes, it's very pretty," the stylish lady said agreeably. "And right on the dot too," she added, glancing at her watch.

The ugly girl beside her cast an eye upward at the clock, smirked, then looked directly at Mrs. Turpin and smirked again. Then she returned her eyes to her book. She was obviously the lady's daughter because, although they didn't look anything alike as to disposition, they both had the same shape of face and the same blue eyes. On the lady they sparkled pleasantly but in the girl's seared face they appeared alternately to smolder and to blaze.

What if Jesus had said, "All right, you can be white-trash or a nigger or ugly"!

Mrs. Turpin felt an awful pity for the girl, though she thought it was one thing to be ugly and another to act ugly.

The woman with the snuff-stained lips turned around in her chair and 30 looked up at the clock. Then she turned back and appeared to look a little to the side of Mrs. Turpin. There was a cast in one of her eyes. "You want to know wher you can get you one of themther clocks?" she asked in a loud voice.

"No, I already have a nice clock," Mrs. Turpin said. Once somebody like her got a leg in the conversation, she would be all over it.

"You can get you one with green stamps," the woman said. "That's most likely wher he got hisn. Save you up enough, you can get you most anythang. I got me some joo'ry."

Ought to have got you a wash rag and some soap, Mrs. Turpin thought.

"I get contour sheets with mine," the pleasant lady said.

The daughter slammed her book shut. She looked straight in front of her, 35 directly through Mrs. Turpin and on through the yellow curtain and the plate glass window which made the wall behind her. The girl's eyes seemed lit all of a sudden with a peculiar light, an unnatural light like night road signs give. Mrs. Turpin turned her head to see if there was anything going on outside that she should see, but she could not see anything. Figures passing cast only a pale shadow through the curtain. There was no reason the girl should single her out for her ugly looks.

"Miss Finley," the nurse said, cracking the door. The gum-chewing woman got up and passed in front of her and Claud and went into the office. She had on red high-heeled shoes.

Directly across the table, the ugly girl's eyes were fixed on Mrs. Turpin as if she had some very special reason for disliking her.

"This is wonderful weather, isn't it?" the girl's mother said.

"It's good weather for cotton if you can get the niggers to pick it," Mrs. Turpin said, "but niggers don't want to pick cotton any more. You can't get the white folks to pick it and now you can't get the niggers—because they got to be right up there with the white folks."

"They gonna *try* anyways," the white-trash woman said, leaning forward. 40

"Do you have one of the cotton-picking machines?" the pleasant lady asked.

"No," Mrs. Turpin said, "they leave half the cotton in the field. We don't have much cotton anyway. If you want to make it farming now, you have to have a little of everything. We got a couple of acres of cotton and a few hogs and chickens and just enough white-face that Claud can look after them himself."

"One thang I don't want," the white-trash woman said, wiping her mouth with the back of her hand. "Hogs. Nasty stinking things, a-gruntin and a-rootin all over the place."

Mrs. Turpin gave her the merest edge of her attention. "Our hogs are not dirty and they don't stink," she said. "They're cleaner than some children I've seen. Their feet never touch the ground. We have a pig parlor—that's where you raise them on concrete," she explained to the pleasant lady, "and Claud scoots them down with the hose every afternoon and washes off the floor." Cleaner by far than that child right there, she thought. Poor nasty little thing. He had not moved except to put the thumb of his dirty hand into his mouth.

The woman turned her face away from Mrs. Turpin. "I know I wouldn't 45 scoot down no hog with no hose," she said to the wall.

You wouldn't have no hog to scoot down, Mrs. Turpin said to herself.

"A-gruntin and a-rootin and a-groanin," the woman muttered.

"We got a little of everything," Mrs. Turpin said to the pleasant lady. "It's no use in having more than you can handle yourself with help like it is. We found enough niggers to pick our cotton this year but Claud he has to go after them and take them home again in the evening. They can't walk that half a mile. No they can't. I tell you," she said and laughed merrily, "I sure am tired of buttering up niggers, but you got to love em if you want em to work for you. When they come in the morning, I run out and I say, 'Hi yawl this morning?'

and when Claud drives them off to the field I just wave to beat the band and they just wave back." And she waved her hand rapidly to illustrate.

"Like you read out of the same book," the lady said, showing she understood perfectly.

"Child, yes," Mrs. Turpin said. "And when they come in from the field, I 50 run out with a bucket of icewater. That's the way it's going to be from now on," she said. "You may as well face it."

"One thang I know," the white-trash woman said. "Two thangs I ain't going to do: love no niggers or scoot down no hog with no hose." And she let out a bark of contempt.

The look that Mrs. Turpin and the pleasant lady exchanged indicated they both understood that you had to *have* certain things before you could *know* certain things. But every time Mrs. Turpin exchanged a look with the lady, she was aware that the ugly girl's peculiar eyes were still on her, and she had trouble bringing her attention back to the conversation.

"When you got something," she said, "you got to look after it." And when you ain't got a thing but breath and britches, she added to herself, you can afford to come to town every morning and just sit on the Court House coping and spit.

A grotesque revolving shadow passed across the curtain behind her and was thrown palely on the opposite wall. Then a bicycle clattered down against the outside of the building. The door opened and a colored boy glided in with a tray from the drugstore. It had two large red and white paper cups on it with tops on them. He was a tall, very black boy in discolored white pants and a green nylon shirt. He was chewing gum slowly, as if to music. He set the tray down in the office opening next to the fern and stuck his head through to look for the secretary. She was not in there. He rested his arms on the ledge and waited, his narrow bottom stuck out, swaying to the left and right. He raised a hand over his head and scratched the base of his skull.

"You see that button there, boy?" Mrs. Turpin said. "You can punch that 55 and she'll come. She's probably in the back somewhere."

"Is that right?" the boy said agreeably, as if he had never seen the button before. He leaned to the right and put his finger on it. "She sometime out," he said and twisted around to face his audience, his elbows behind him on the counter. The nurse appeared and he twisted back again. She handed him a dollar and he rooted in his pocket and made the change and counted it out to her. She gave him fifteen cents for a tip and he went out with the empty tray. The heavy door swung to slowly and closed at length with the sound of suction. For a moment no one spoke.

"They ought to send all them niggers back to Africa," the white-trash woman said. "That's wher they come from in the first place."

"Oh, I couldn't do without my good colored friends," the pleasant lady said.

"There's a heap of things worse than a nigger," Mrs. Turpin agreed. "It's all kinds of them just like it's all kinds of us."

"Yes, and it takes all kinds to make the world go round," the lady said in 60 her musical voice.

As she said it, the raw-complexioned girl snapped her teeth together. Her lower lip turned downwards and inside out, revealing the pale pink inside of her mouth. After a second it rolled back up. It was the ugliest face Mrs. Turpin had ever seen anyone make and for a moment she was certain that the girl had made it at her. She was looking at her as if she had known and disliked her all her life—all of Mrs. Turpin's life, it seemed too, not just all the girl's life. Why, girl, I don't even know you, Mrs. Turpin said silently.

She forced her attention back to the discussion. "It wouldn't be practical to send them back to Africa," she said. "They wouldn't want to go. They got it too good here."

"Wouldn't be what they wanted—if I had anythang to do with it," the woman said.

"It wouldn't be a way in the world you could get all the niggers back over there," Mrs. Turpin said. "They'd be hiding out and lying down and turning sick on you and wailing and hollering and raring and pitching. It wouldn't be a way in the world to get them over there."

"They got over here," the trashy woman said. "Get back like they got over." 65

"It wasn't so many of them then," Mrs. Turpin explained.

The woman looked at Mrs. Turpin as if here was an idiot indeed but Mrs. Turpin was not bothered by the look, considering where it came from.

"Nooo," she said, "they're going to stay here where they can go to New York and marry white folks and improve their color. That's what they all want to do, every one of them, improve their color."

"You know what comes of that, don't you?" Claud asked.

"No, Claud, what?" Mrs. Turpin said. 70

Claud's eyes twinkled. "White-faced niggers," he said with never a smile.

Everybody in the office laughed except the white-trash and the ugly girl. The girl gripped the book in her lap with white fingers. The trashy woman looked around her from face to face as if she thought they were all idiots. The old woman in the feed sack dress continued to gaze expressionless across the floor at the high-top shoes of the man opposite her, the one who had been pretending to be asleep when the Turpins came in. He was laughing heartily, his hands still spread out on his knees. The child had fallen to the side and was lying now almost face down in the old woman's lap.

While they recovered from their laughter, the nasal chorus on the radio kept the room from silence.

> "You go to blank blank
> And I'll go to mine
> But we'll all blank along
> To-geth-ther,
> And all along the blank
> We'll hep each other out
> Smile-ling in any kind of
> Weath-ther!"

Mrs. Turpin didn't catch every word but she caught enough to agree with the spirit of the song and it turned her thoughts sober. To help anybody out that needed it was her philosophy of life. She never spared herself when she found somebody in need, whether they were white or black, trash or decent. And of all she had to be thankful for, she was most thankful that this was so. If Jesus had said, "You can be high society and have all the money you want and be thin and svelte-like, but you can't be a good woman with it," she would have had to say, "Well don't make me that then. Make me a good woman and it don't matter what else, how fat or how ugly or how poor!" Her heart rose. He had not made her a nigger or white-trash or ugly! He had made her herself and given her a little of everything. Jesus, thank you! she said. Thank you thank you thank you! Whenever she counted her blessings she felt as buoyant as if she weighed one hundred and twenty-five pounds instead of one hundred and eighty.

"What's wrong with your little boy?" the pleasant lady asked the white- 75 trashy woman.

"He has a ulcer," the woman said proudly. "He ain't give me a minute's peace since he was born. Him and her are just alike," she said, nodding at the old woman, who was running her leathery fingers through the child's pale hair. "Look like I can't get nothing down them two but Co' Cola and candy."

That's all you try to get down em, Mrs. Turpin said to herself. Too lazy to light the fire. There was nothing you could tell her about people like them that she didn't know already. And it was not just that they didn't have anything. Because if you gave them everything, in two weeks it would all be broken or filthy or they would have chopped it up for lightwood. She knew all this from her own experience. Help them you must, but help them you couldn't.

All at once the ugly girl turned her lips inside out again. Her eyes fixed like two drills on Mrs. Turpin. This time there was no mistaking that there was something urgent behind them.

Girl, Mrs. Turpin exclaimed silently, I haven't done a thing to you! The girl might be confusing her with somebody else. There was no need to sit by and let herself be intimidated. "You must be in college," she said boldly, looking directly at the girl. "I see you reading a book there."

The girl continued to stare and pointedly did not answer.   80

Her mother blushed at this rudeness. "The lady asked you a question, Mary Grace," she said under her breath.

"I have ears," Mary Grace said.

The poor mother blushed again. "Mary Grace goes to Wellesley College," she explained. She twisted one of the buttons on her dress. "In Massachusetts," she added with a grimace. "And in the summer she just keeps right on studying. Just reads all the time, a real book worm. She's done real well at Wellesley; she's taking English and Math and History and Psychology and Social Studies," she rattled on, "and I think it's too much. I think she ought to get out and have fun."

The girl looked as if she would like to hurl them all through the plate glass window.

"Way up north," Mrs. Turpin murmured and thought, well, it hasn't done 85 much for her manners.

"I'd almost rather to have him sick," the white-trash woman said, wrenching the attention back to herself. "He's so mean when he ain't. Look like some children just take natural to meanness. It's some gets bad when they get sick but he was the opposite. Took sick and turned good. He don't give me no trouble now. It's me waitin to see the doctor," she said.

If I was going to send anybody back to Africa, Mrs. Turpin thought, it would be your kind, woman. "Yes, indeed," she said aloud, but looking up at the ceiling, "it's a heap of things worse than a nigger." And dirtier than a hog, she added to herself.

"I think people with bad dispositions are more to be pitied than anyone on earth," the pleasant lady said in a voice that was decidedly thin.

"I thank the Lord he has blessed me with a good one," Mrs. Turpin said. "The day has never dawned that I couldn't find something to laugh at."

"Not since she married me anyways," Claud said with a comical straight 90 face.

Everybody laughed except the girl and the white-trash.

Mrs. Turpin's stomach shook. "He's such a caution," she said, "that I can't help but laugh at him."

The girl made a loud ugly noise through her teeth.

Her mother's mouth grew thin and tight. "I think the worst thing in the world," she said, "is an ungrateful person. To have everything and not appreciate it. I know a girl," she said, "who has parents who would give her anything, a little brother who loves her dearly, who is getting a good education, who wears the best clothes, but who can never say a kind word to anyone, who never smiles, who just criticizes and complains all day long."

"Is she too old to paddle?" Claud asked.   95

The girl's face was almost purple.

"Yes," the lady said, "I'm afraid there's nothing to do but leave her to her folly. Some day she'll wake up and it'll be too late."

"It never hurt anyone to smile," Mrs. Turpin said. "It just makes you feel better all over."

"Of course," the lady said sadly, "but there are just some people you can't tell anything to. They can't take criticism."

"If it's one thing I am," Mrs. Turpin said with feeling, "it's grateful. When 100 I think who all I could have been besides myself and what all I got, a little of everything, and a good disposition besides, I just feel like shouting, 'Thank you, Jesus, for making everything the way it is!' It could have been different!" For one thing, somebody else could have got Claud. At the thought of this, she was flooded with gratitude and a terrible pang of joy ran through her. "Oh thank you, Jesus, Jesus, thank you!" she cried aloud.

The book struck her directly over her left eye. It struck almost at the same instant that she realized the girl was about to hurl it. Before she could utter a sound, the raw face came crashing across the table toward her, howling. The girl's fingers sank like clamps into the soft flesh of her neck. She heard the mother cry out and Claud shout, "Whoa!" There was an instant when she was certain that she was about to be in an earthquake.

All at once her vision narrowed and she saw everything as if it were happening in a small room far away, or as if she were looking at it through the wrong end of a telescope. Claud's face crumpled and fell out of sight. The nurse ran in, then out, then in again. Then the gangling figure of the doctor rushed out of the inner door. Magazines flew this way and that as the table turned over. The girl fell with a thud and Mrs. Turpin's vision suddenly reversed itself and she saw everything large instead of small. The eyes of the white-trashy woman were staring hugely at the floor. There the girl, held down on one side by the nurse and on the other by her mother, was wrenching and turning in their grasp. The doctor was kneeling astride her, trying to hold her arm down. He managed after a second to sink a long needle into it.

Mrs. Turpin felt entirely hollow except for her heart which swung from side to side as if it were agitated in a great empty drum of flesh.

"Somebody that's not busy call for the ambulance," the doctor said in the off-hand voice young doctors adopt for terrible occasions.

Mrs. Turpin could not have moved a finger. The old man who had been sit- 105
ting next to her skipped nimbly into the office and made the call, for the secretary still seemed to be gone.

"Claud!" Mrs. Turpin called.

He was not in his chair. She knew she must jump up and find him but she felt like some one trying to catch a train in a dream, when everything moves in slow motion and the faster you try to run the slower you go.

"Here I am," a suffocated voice, very unlike Claud's, said.

He was doubled up in the corner on the floor, pale as paper, holding his leg. She wanted to get up and go to him but she could not move. Instead, her gaze was drawn slowly downward to the churning face on the floor, which she could see over the doctor's shoulder.

The girl's eyes stopped rolling and focused on her. They seemed a much 110
lighter blue than before, as if a door that had been tightly closed behind them was now open to admit light and air.

Mrs. Turpin's head cleared and her power of motion returned. She leaned forward until she was looking directly into the fierce brilliant eyes. There was no doubt in her mind that the girl did know her, knew her in some intense and personal way, beyond time and place and condition. "What you got to say to me?" she asked hoarsely and held her breath, waiting, as for a revelation.

The girl raised her head. Her gaze locked with Mrs. Turpin's. "Go back to hell where you came from, you old wart hog," she whispered. Her voice was low but clear. Her eyes burned for a moment as if she saw with pleasure that her message had struck its target.

Mrs. Turpin sank back in her chair.

After a moment the girl's eyes closed and she turned her head wearily to the side.

The doctor rose and handed the nurse the empty syringe. He leaned over 115
and put both hands for a moment on the mother's shoulders, which were shaking. She was sitting on the floor, her lips pressed together, holding Mary Grace's hand in her lap. The girl's fingers were gripped like a baby's around her thumb. "Go on to the hospital," he said. "I'll call and make the arrangements."

"Now let's see that neck," he said in a jovial voice to Mrs. Turpin. He began to inspect her neck with his first two fingers. Two little moon-shaped lines like pink fish bones were indented over her windpipe. There was the beginning of an angry red swelling above her eye. His fingers passed over this also.

"Lea' me be," she said thickly and shook him off. "See about Claud. She kicked him."

"I'll see about him in a minute," he said and felt her pulse. He was a thin gray-haired man, given to pleasantries. "Go home and have yourself a vacation the rest of the day," he said and patted her on the shoulder.

Quit your pattin me, Mrs. Turpin growled to herself.

"And put an ice pack over that eye," he said. Then he went and squatted 120
down beside Claud and looked at his leg. After a moment he pulled him up and Claud limped after him into the office.

Until the ambulance came, the only sounds in the room were the tremulous moans of the girl's mother, who continued to sit on the floor. The whitetrash woman did not take her eyes off the girl. Mrs. Turpin looked straight ahead at nothing. Presently the ambulance drew up, a long dark shadow, behind the curtain. The attendants came in and set the stretcher down beside the girl and lifted her expertly onto it and carried her out. The nurse helped the mother gather up her things. The shadow of the ambulance moved silently away and the nurse came back in the office.

"That ther girl is going to be a lunatic, ain't she?" the white-trash woman asked the nurse, but the nurse kept on to the back and never answered her.

"Yes, she's going to be a lunatic," the white-trash woman said to the rest of them.

"Po' critter," the old woman murmured. The child's face was still in her lap. His eyes looked idly out over her knees. He had not moved during the disturbance except to draw one leg up under him.

"I thank Gawd," the white-trash woman said fervently, "I ain't a lunatic."   125

Claud came limping out and the Turpins went home.

As their pick-up truck turned into their own dirt road and made the crest of the hill, Mrs. Turpin gripped the window ledge and looked out suspiciously. The land sloped gracefully down through a field dotted with lavender weeds and at the start of the rise their small yellow frame house, with its little flower beds spread out around it like a fancy apron, sat primly in its accustomed place between two giant hickory trees. She would not have been startled to see a burnt wound between two blackened chimneys.

Neither of them felt like eating so they put on their house clothes and lowered the shade in the bedroom and lay down, Claud with his leg on a pillow and herself with a damp washcloth over her eye. The instant she was flat on her back, the image of a razor-backed hog with warts on its face and horns coming out behind its ears snorted into her head. She moaned, a low quiet moan.

"I am not," she said tearfully, "a wart hog. From hell." But the denial had no force. The girl's eyes and her words, even the tone of her voice, low but clear, directed only to her, brooked no repudiation. She had been singled out for the message, though there was trash in the room to whom it might justly have been applied. The full force of this fact struck her only now. There was a woman there who was neglecting her own child but she had been overlooked. The message had been given to Ruby Turpin, a respectable, hard-working, church-going woman. The tears dried. Her eyes began to burn instead with wrath.

She rose on her elbow and the washcloth fell into her hand. Claud was   130
lying on his back, snoring. She wanted to tell him what the girl had said. At the same time, she did not wish to put the image of herself as a wart hog from hell into his mind.

"Hey, Claud," she muttered and pushed his shoulder.

Claud opened one pale baby blue eye.

She looked into it warily. He did not think about anything. He just went his way.

"Wha, whasit?" he said and closed the eye again.

"Nothing," she said. "Does your leg pain you?"   135

"Hurts like hell," Claud said.

"It'll quit terreckly," she said and lay back down. In a moment Claud was snoring again. For the rest of the afternoon they lay there. Claud slept. She scowled at the ceiling. Occasionally she raised her fist and made a small stabbing motion over her chest as if she was defending her innocence to invisible guests who were like the comforters of Job, reasonable-seeming but wrong.

About five-thirty Claud stirred. "Got to go after those niggers," he sighed, not moving.

She was looking straight up as if there were unintelligible handwriting on the ceiling. The protuberance over her eye had turned a greenish-blue. "Listen here," she said.

"What?" 140

"Kiss me."

Claud leaned over and kissed her loudly on the mouth. He pinched her side and their hands interlocked. Her expression of ferocious concentration did not change. Claud got up, groaning and growling, and limped off. She continued to study the ceiling.

She did not get up until she heard the pick-up truck coming back with the Negroes. Then she rose and thrust her feet in her brown oxfords, which she did not bother to lace, and stumped out onto the back porch and got her red plastic bucket. She emptied a tray of ice cubes into it and filled it half full of water and went out into the back yard. Every afternoon after Claud brought the hands in, one of the boys helped him put out hay and the rest waited in the back of the truck until he was ready to take them home. The truck was parked in the shade under one of the hickory trees.

"Hi yawl this morning?" Mrs. Turpin asked grimly, appearing with the bucket and the dipper. There were three women and a boy in the truck.

"Us doin nicely," the oldest woman said. "Hi you doin?" and her gaze 145 struck immediately on the dark lump on Mrs. Turpin's forehead. "You done fell down, ain't you?" she asked in a solicitous voice. The old woman was dark and almost toothless. She had on an old felt hat of Claud's set back on her head. The other two women were younger and lighter and they both had new bright green sunhats. One of them had hers on her head; the other had taken hers off and the boy was grinning beneath it.

Mrs. Turpin set the bucket down on the floor of the truck. "Yawl hep yourselves," she said. She looked around to make sure Claud had gone. "No, I didn't fall down," she said, folding her arms. "It was something worse than that."

"Ain't nothing bad happen to you!" the old woman said. She said it as if they all knew that Mrs. Turpin was protected in some special way by Divine Providence. "You just had you a little fall."

"We were in town at the doctor's office for where the cow kicked Mr. Turpin," Mrs. Turpin said in a flat tone that indicated they could leave off their foolishness. "And there was this girl there. A big fat girl with her face all broke out. I could look at that girl and tell she was peculiar but I couldn't tell how. And me and her mama was just talking and going along and all of a sudden WHAM! She throws this big book she was reading at me and . . ."

"Naw!" the old woman cried out.

"And then she jumps over the table and commences to choke me." 150

"Naw!" they all exclaimed, "naw!"

"Hi come she do that?" the old woman asked. "What ail her?"

Mrs. Turpin only glared in front of her.

"Somethin ail her," the old woman said.

"They carried her off in an ambulance," Mrs. Turpin continued, "but be- 155 fore she went she was rolling on the floor and they were trying to hold her down to give her a shot and she said something to me." She paused. "You know what she said to me?"

"What she say?" they asked.

"She said," Mrs. Turpin began, and stopped, her face very dark and heavy. The sun was getting whiter and whiter, blanching the sky overhead so that the leaves of the hickory tree were black in the face of it. She could not bring forth the words. "Something real ugly," she muttered.

"She sho shouldn't said nothin ugly to you," the old woman said. "You so sweet. You the sweetest lady I know."

"She pretty too," the one with the hat on said.

"And stout," the other one said. "I never knowed no sweeter white lady." 160

"That's the truth befo' Jesus," the old woman said. "Amen! You des as sweet and pretty as you can be."

Mrs. Turpin knew exactly how much Negro flattery was worth and it added to her rage. "She said," she began again and finished this time with a fierce rush of breath, "that I was an old wart hog from hell."

There was an astounded silence.

"Where she at?" the youngest woman cried in a piercing voice.

"Lemme see her. I'll kill her!" 165

"I'll kill her with you!" the other one cried.

"She b'long in the sylum," the old woman said emphatically. "You the sweetest white lady I know."

"She pretty too," the other two said. "Stout as she can be and sweet. Jesus satisfied with her!"

"Deed he is," the woman declared.

Idiots! Mrs. Turpin growled to herself. You could never say anything intel- 170 ligent to a nigger. You could talk at them but not with them. "Yawl ain't drunk your water," she said shortly. "Leave the bucket in the truck when you're finished with it. I got more to do than just stand around and pass the time of day," and she moved off and into the house.

She stood for a moment in the middle of the kitchen. The dark protuberance over her eye looked like a miniature tornado cloud which might any moment sweep across the horizon of her brow. Her lower lip protruded dangerously. She squared her massive shoulders. Then she marched into the front of the house and out the side door and started down the road to the pig parlor. She had the look of a woman going single-handed, weaponless, into battle.

The sun was deep yellow now like a harvest moon and was riding westward very fast over the far tree line as if it meant to reach the hogs before she did. The road was rutted and she kicked several good-sized stones out of her path as she strode along. The pig parlor was on a little knoll at the end of a lane that ran off from the side of the barn. It was a square of concrete as large as a small room, with a board fence about four feet high around it. The concrete floor sloped slightly so that the hog wash could drain off into a trench where it was carried to the field for fertilizer. Claud was standing on the outside, on the edge of the concrete, hanging onto the top board, hosing down the floor inside. The hose was connected to the faucet of a water trough nearby.

Mrs. Turpin climbed up beside him and glowered down at the hogs inside. There were seven long-snouted bristly shoats in it—tan with liver-colored spots—and an old sow a few weeks off from farrowing. She was lying on her side grunting. The shoats were running about shaking themselves like idiot children, their little slit pig eyes searching the floor for anything left. She had read that pigs were the most intelligent animal. She doubted it. They were supposed to be smarter than dogs. There had even been a pig astronaut. He had performed his assignment perfectly but died of a heart attack afterwards because they left him in his electric suit, sitting upright throughout his examination when naturally a hog should be on all fours.

A-gruntin and a-rootin and a-groanin.

"Gimme that hose," she said, yanking it away from Claud. "Go on and 175 carry them niggers home and then get off that leg."

"You look like you might have swallowed a mad dog," Claud observed, but he got down and limped off. He paid no attention to her humors.

Until he was out of earshot, Mrs. Turpin stood on the side of the pen, holding the hose and pointing the stream of water at the hind quarters of any shoat that looked as if it might try to lie down. When he had had time to get over the hill, she turned her head slightly and her wrathful eyes scanned the path. He was nowhere in sight. She turned back again and seemed to gather herself up. Her shoulders rose and she drew in her breath.

"What do you send me a message like that for?" she said in a low fierce voice, barely above a whisper but with the force of a shout in its concentrated fury. "How am I a hog and me both? How am I saved and from hell too?" Her free fist was knotted and with the other she gripped the hose, blindly pointing the stream of water in and out of the eye of the old sow whose outraged squeal she did not hear.

The pig parlor commanded a view of the back pasture where their twenty beef cows were gathered around the hay-bales Claud and the boy had put out. The freshly cut pasture sloped down to the highway. Across it was their cotton field and beyond that a dark green dusty wood which they owned as well. The sun was behind the wood, very red, looking over the paling of the trees like a farmer inspecting his own hogs.

"Why me?" she rumbled. "It's no trash around here, black or white, that I 180 haven't given to. And break my back to the bone every day working. And do for the church."

She appeared to be the right size woman to command the arena before her. "How am I a hog?" she demanded. "Exactly how am I like them?" and she jabbed the stream of water at the shoats. "There was plenty of trash there. It didn't have to be me.

"If you like trash better, go get yourself some trash then," she railed. "You could have made me trash. Or a nigger. If trash is what you wanted why didn't you make me trash?" She shook her fist with the hose in it and a watery snake appeared momentarily in the air. "I could quit working and take it easy and be filthy," she growled. "Lounge about the sidewalks all day drinking root beer. Dip snuff and spit in every puddle and have it all over my face. I could be nasty.

"Or you could have made me a nigger. It's too late for me to be a nigger," she said with deep sarcasm, "but I could act like one. Lay down in the middle of the road and stop traffic. Roll on the ground."

In the deepening light everything was taking on a mysterious hue. The pasture was growing a peculiar glassy green and the streak of highway had turned lavender. She braced herself for a final assault and this time her voice rolled out over the pasture. "Go on," she yelled, "call me a hog! Call me a hog again. From hell. Call me a wart hog from hell. Put that bottom rail on top. There'll still be a top and bottom!"

A garbled echo returned to her.   185

A final surge of fury shook her and she roared, "Who do you think you are?"

The color of everything, field and crimson sky, burned for a moment with a transparent intensity. The question carried over the pasture and across the highway and the cotton field and returned to her clearly like an answer from beyond the wood.

She opened her mouth but no sound came out of it.

A tiny truck, Claud's, appeared on the highway, heading rapidly out of sight. Its gears scraped thinly. It looked like a child's toy. At any moment a bigger truck might smash into it and scatter Claud's and the niggers' brains all over the road.

Mrs. Turpin stood there, her gaze fixed on the highway, all her muscles   190 rigid, until in five or six minutes the truck reappeared, returning. She waited until it had had time to turn into their own road. Then like a monumental statue coming to life, she bent her head slowly and gazed, as if through the very heart of mystery, down into the pig parlor at the hogs. They had settled all in one corner around the old sow who was grunting softly. A red glow suffused them. They appeared to pant with a secret life.

Until the sun slipped finally behind the tree line, Mrs. Turpin remained there with her gaze bent to them as if she were absorbing some abysmal life-giving knowledge. At last she lifted her head. There was only a purple streak in the sky, cutting through a field of crimson and leading, like an extension of the highway, into the descending dusk. She raised her hands from the side of the pen in a gesture hieratic and profound. A visionary light settled in her eyes. She saw the streak as a vast swinging bridge extending upward from the earth through a field of living fire. Upon it a vast horde of souls were rumbling toward heaven. There were whole companies of white-trash, clean for the first time in their lives, and bands of black niggers in white robes, and battalions of freaks and lunatics shouting and clapping and leaping like frogs. And bringing up the end of the procession was a tribe of people whom she recognized at once as those who, like herself and Claud, had always had a little of everything and the God-given wit to use it right. She leaned forward to observe them closer. They were marching behind the others with great dignity, accountable as they had always been for good order and common sense and respectable behavior. They alone were on key. Yet she could see by their shocked and altered faces that even their virtues were being burned away. She lowered her hands and gripped the rail of the hog pen, her eyes small but fixed unblinkingly on what lay ahead. In a moment the vision faded but she remained where she was, immobile.

At length she got down and turned off the faucet and made her slow way on the darkening path to the house. In the woods around her the invisible cricket choruses had struck up, but what she heard were the voices of the souls climbing upward into the starry field and shouting hallelujah.

CONSIDERATIONS FOR CRITICAL THINKING AND WRITING

1. FIRST RESPONSE. Does your attitude toward Mrs. Turpin change or remain the same during the story? Do you *like* her more at some points than at others? Explain why.

2. Why is it appropriate that the two major settings for the action in this story are a doctor's waiting room and a "pig parlor"?

3. How does Mrs. Turpin's treatment of her husband help to characterize her?
4. Mrs. Turpin notices people's shoes. What does this and her thoughts about "classes of people" (para. 24) reveal about her? How does she see herself in relation to other people?
5. Why does Mary Grace attack Mrs. Turpin?
6. Why is it significant that the book Mary Grace reads is *Human Development*? What is the significance of her name?
7. What does the background music played on the radio contribute to the story?
8. To whom does Mrs. Turpin address this anguished question: "What do you send me a message [Mary Grace's whispered words telling her "Go back to hell where you came from, you old wart hog"] like that for?" (para. 178). Why is Mrs. Turpin so angry and bewildered?
9. What is the "abysmal life-giving knowledge" that Mrs. Turpin discovers in the next to the last paragraph? Why is it "abysmal"? How is it "life-giving"?
10. Given the serious theme, consider whether the story's humor is appropriate.
11. When Mrs. Turpin returns home bruised, a hired African American woman tells her that nothing really "bad" happened: "You just had you a little fall" (para. 147). Pay particular attention to the suggestive language of this sentence, and discuss its significance in relation to the rest of the story.

CONNECTIONS TO OTHER SELECTIONS

1. Compare and contrast Mary Grace with Hulga of "Good Country People" (p. 392).
2. Explain how "Revelation" could be used as a title for any of the O'Connor stories you have read.
3. Discuss Mrs. Turpin's prideful hypocrisy in connection with the racial attitudes expressed by the white men at the "smoker" in Ellison's "Battle Royal" (p. 223). How do pride and personal illusions inform these characters' racial attitudes?
4. Explore the nature of the "revelation" in O'Connor's story and in John Updike's "A & P" (p. 576).

PERSPECTIVES ON O'CONNOR

O'Connor on Faith 1955

I write the way I do because (not though) I am a Catholic. This is a fact and nothing covers it like the bald statement. However, I am a Catholic peculiarly possessed of the modern consciousness, the thing Jung° describes as unhistorical, solitary, and guilty. To possess this within the Church is to bear a burden, the necessary burden for the conscious Catholic. It's to feel the contemporary situation at the ultimate level. I think that the Church is the only thing that is

Jung: Carl Jung (1875–1961), a Swiss psychiatrist.

going to make the terrible world we are coming to endurable; the only thing that makes the Church endurable is that it is somehow the body of Christ and that on this we are fed. It seems to be a fact that you suffer as much from the Church as for it but if you believe in the divinity of Christ, you have to cherish the world at the same time that you struggle to endure it. This may explain the lack of bitterness in the stories.

From a letter to "A," July 20, 1955, in The Habit of Being

CONSIDERATIONS FOR CRITICAL THINKING AND WRITING

1. Consider how O'Connor's fiction expresses her belief that "you have to cherish the world at the same time that you struggle to endure it."

2. Do you agree that "bitterness" is absent from O'Connor's stories? Explain why or why not.

O'Connor on the Materials of Fiction   1969

The beginning of human knowledge is through the senses, and the fiction writer begins where human perception begins. He appeals through the senses, and you cannot appeal to the senses with abstractions. It is a good deal easier for most people to state an abstract idea than to describe and thus re-create some object that they actually see. But the world of the fiction writer is full of matter, and this is what the beginning fiction writers are very loath to create. They are concerned primarily with unfleshed ideas and emotions. They are apt to be reformers and to want to write because they are possessed not by a story but by the bare bones of some abstract notion. They are conscious of problems, not of people, of questions and issues, not of the texture of existence, of case histories and of everything that has a sociological smack, instead of with all those concrete details of life that make actual the mystery of our position on earth. . . .

One of the most common and saddest spectacles is that of a person of really fine sensibility and acute psychological perception trying to write fiction by using these [abstract] qualities alone. This type of writer will put down one intensely emotional or keenly perceptive sentence after the other, and the result will be complete dullness. The fact is that the materials of the fiction writer are the humblest. Fiction is about everything human and we are made out of dust, and if you scorn getting yourself dusty, then you shouldn't try to write fiction. It's not a grand enough job for you.

From "The Nature and Aim of Fiction" in Mystery and Manners

CONSIDERATIONS FOR CRITICAL THINKING AND WRITING

1. Explain O'Connor's idea that "the materials of the fiction writer are the humblest" (para. 2) by reference to the materials and details of her stories.

2. Choose a substantial paragraph from an O'Connor story and describe how it "appeals through the senses" (para. 1).

3. Write an essay in which you agree or disagree with the following statement: Hawthorne's fiction is a good example of the kinds of mistakes that O'Connor attributes to a beginning fiction writer.

O'Connor on the Use of Exaggeration and Distortion 1969

When I write a novel in which the central action is a baptism, I am very well aware that for a majority of my readers, baptism is a meaningless rite, and so in my novel I have to see that this baptism carries enough awe and mystery to jar the reader into some kind of emotional recognition of its significance. To this end I have to bend the whole novel—its language, its structure, its action. I have to make the reader feel, in his bones if nowhere else, that something is going on here that counts. Distortion in this case is an instrument; exaggeration has a purpose, and the whole structure of the story or novel has been made what it is because of belief. This is not the kind of distortion that destroys; it is the kind that reveals, or should reveal.

From "Novelist and Believer" in *Mystery and Manners*

CONSIDERATIONS FOR CRITICAL THINKING AND WRITING

1. It has been observed that in many of O'Connor's works the central action takes the form of some kind of "baptism" that initiates, tests, or purifies a character. Select a story that illustrates this generalization, and explain how the conflict results in a kind of baptism.

2. O'Connor says that exaggeration and distortion reveal something in her stories. What is the effect of such exaggeration and distortion? Typically, what is revealed by it? Focus your comments on a single story to illustrate your points.

3. Do you think that O'Connor's stories have anything to offer a reader who has no religious faith? Explain why or why not.

O'Connor on Theme and Symbol 1969

When you can state the theme of a story, when you can separate it from the story itself, then you can be sure the story is not a very good one. The meaning of a story has to be embodied in it, has to be made concrete in it. A story is a way to say something that can't be said any other way, and it takes every word in the story to say what the meaning is. You tell a story because a statement would be inadequate. When anybody asks what a story is about, the only proper thing is to tell him to read the story. The meaning of fiction is not abstract meaning but experienced meaning, and the purpose of making statements about the meaning of a story is only to help you to experience that meaning more fully.

The peculiar problem of the short-story writer is how to make the action he describes reveal as much of the mystery of existence as possible. He has only a short space to do it in and he can't do it by statement. He has to do it by showing, not by saying, and by showing the concrete — so that his problem is really how to make the concrete work double time for him.

In good fiction, certain of the details will tend to accumulate meaning from the action of the story itself, and when this happens they become symbolic in the way they work. I once wrote a story called "Good Country People," in which a lady Ph.D. has her wooden leg stolen by a Bible salesman whom she has tried to seduce. Now I'll admit that, paraphrased in this way, the situation is simply a low joke. The average reader is pleased to observe anybody's wooden leg being stolen. But without ceasing to appeal to him and without making any statements of high intention, this story does manage to operate at another level of experience, by letting the wooden leg accumulate meaning. Early in the story, we're presented with the fact that the Ph.D. is spiritually as well as physically crippled. She believes in nothing but her own belief in nothing, and we perceive that there is a wooden part of her soul that corresponds to her wooden leg. Now of course this is never stated. The fiction writer states as little as possible. The reader makes this connection from things he is shown. He may not even know that he makes the connection, but the connection is there nevertheless and it has its effect on him. As the story goes on, the wooden leg continues to accumulate meaning. The reader learns how the girl feels about her leg, how her mother feels about it, and how the country woman on the place feels about it; and finally, by the time the Bible salesman comes along, the leg has accumulated so much meaning that it is, as the saying goes, loaded. And when the Bible salesman steals it, the reader realizes that he has taken away part of the girl's personality and has revealed her deeper affliction to her for the first time.

If you want to say that the wooden leg is a symbol, you can say that. But it is a wooden leg first, and as a wooden leg it is absolutely necessary to the story. It has its place on the literal level of the story, but it operates in depth as well as on the surface. It increases the story in every direction, and this is essentially the way a story escapes being short.

Now a little might be said about the way in which this happens. I wouldn't want you to think that in that story I sat down and said, "I am now going to write a story about a Ph.D. with a wooden leg, using the wooden leg as a symbol for another kind of affliction." I doubt myself if many writers know what they are going to do when they start out. When I started writing that story, I didn't know there was going to be a Ph.D. with a wooden leg in it. I merely found myself one morning writing a description of two women that I knew something about, and before I realized it, I had equipped one of them with a daughter with a wooden leg. As the story progressed, I brought in the Bible salesman, but I had no idea what I was going to do with him. I didn't know he was going to steal that wooden leg until ten or twelve lines before he did it, but when I found out that this was what was going to happen, I realized that it was inevitable. This is a story that produces a shock for the reader, and I think one reason for this is that it produced a shock for the writer.

Now despite the fact that this story came about in this seemingly mindless fashion, it is a story that almost no rewriting was done on. It is a story that was under control throughout the writing of it, and it might be asked how this kind of control comes about, since it is not entirely conscious.

From "Writing Short Stories" in *Mystery and Manners*

CONSIDERATIONS FOR CRITICAL THINKING AND WRITING

1. Why is a "statement" (para. 1) inadequate to convey the meaning of a story?

2. O'Connor describes how the wooden leg "continues to accumulate meaning" (para. 3) in "Good Country People" (p. 392). Choose another story by O'Connor and explain how something specific and concrete is invested with symbolic meaning.

JOSEPHINE HENDIN (B. 1946)
On O'Connor's Refusal to "Do Pretty"   1970

There is, in the memory of one Milledgeville matron, the image of O'Connor at nineteen or twenty who, when invited to a wedding shower for an old family friend, remained standing, her back pressed against the wall, scowling at the group of women who had sat down to lunch. Neither the devil nor her mother could make her say yes to this fiercely gracious female society, but Flannery O'Connor could not say no even in a whisper. She could not refuse the invitation but she would not accept it either. She did not exactly "fuss" but neither did she "do pretty."

From *The World of Flannery O'Connor*

CONSIDERATIONS FOR CRITICAL THINKING AND WRITING

1. How is O'Connor's personality revealed in this anecdote about her ambivalent response to society? Allow the description to be suggestive for you, and flesh out a brief portrait of her.

2. Consider how this personality makes itself apparent in any one of O'Connor's stories you have read. How does the anecdote help to characterize the narrator's voice in the story?

3. To what extent do you think biographical details such as this — assuming the Milledgeville matron's memory to be accurate — can shed light on a writer's works?

CLAIRE KAHANE (B. 1935)
The Function of Violence in O'Connor's Fiction   1974

From the moment the reader enters O'Connor's backwoods, he is poised on the edge of a pervasive violence. Characters barely contain their rage; images reflect a hostile nature; and even the Christ to whom the characters are ultimately driven is a threatening figure . . . full of the apocalyptic wrath of the Old Testament.

O'Connor's conscious purpose is evident enough . . . : to reveal the need for grace in a world grotesque without a transcendent context. "I have found that my subject in fiction is the action of grace in territory largely held by the devil," she wrote [in *Mystery and Manners*], and she was not vague about what the devil is: "an evil intelligence determined on its own supremacy." It would seem that for O'Connor, given the fact of original Sin, any intelligence deter-mined on its own supremacy was intrinsically evil. For in each work, it is the impulse toward secular autonomy, the smug confidence that human nature is perfectible by its own efforts, that she sets out to destroy, through an act of vi-olence so intense that the character is rendered helpless, a passive victim of a superior power. Again and again she creates a fiction in which a character at-tempts to live autonomously, to define himself and his values, only to be jarred back to what she calls "reality" — the recognition of helplessness in the face of contingency, and the need for absolute submission to the power of Christ.

From "Flannery O'Connor's Rage of Vision" in *American Literature*

CONSIDERATIONS FOR CRITICAL THINKING AND WRITING

1. Choose an O'Connor story, and explain how grace — the divine influence from God that redeems a person — is used in it to transform a character.

2. Which O'Connor characters can be accurately described as having an "evil intelligence determined on its own supremacy" (para. 2)? Choose one char-acter, and write an essay explaining how this description is central to the conflict of the story.

3. Compare an O'Connor story with one of Hawthorne's "in which a charac-ter attempts to live autonomously, to define himself and his values, only to be jarred back to . . . 'reality' — the recognition of helplessness in the face of contingency . . ." (para. 2).

EDWARD KESSLER (B. 1927)

On O'Connor's Use of History   *1986*

In company with other Southern writers . . . who aspire to embrace a lost tra-dition and look on history as a repository of value, Flannery O'Connor seems a curious anomaly. She wrote of herself: "I am a Catholic peculiarly possessed of the modern consciousness . . . unhistorical, solitary, and guilty." Likewise her characters comprise a gallery of misfits isolated in a present and sentenced to a lifetime of exile from the human community. In O'Connor's fiction, the past neither justifies nor even explains what is happening. If she believed, for example, in the importance of the past accident that maimed Joy in "Good Country People," she could have demonstrated how the event predetermined her present rejection of both human and external nature; but Joy's past is par-enthetical: "Mrs. Hopewell excused this attitude because of the leg (which had been shot off in a hunting accident when Joy was ten)." Believing that hu-mankind is fundamentally flawed, O'Connor spends very little time construct-ing a past for her characters. The cure is neither behind us nor before us but within us; therefore, the past — even historical time itself — supplies only a lim-ited base for self-discovery.

From *Flannery O'Connor and the Language of Apocalypse*

CONSIDERATIONS FOR CRITICAL THINKING AND WRITING

1. Consider how O'Connor uses history in any one of her stories in this an-thology and compare that "unhistorical" vision with Hawthorne's in "Young Goodman Brown" (p. 310) or "The Minister's Black Veil" (p. 320).

2. Write an essay in which you discuss Kessler's assertion that for O'Connor the "past is parenthetical," in contrast to most southern writers, who "embrace a lost tradition and look on history as a repository of value." For your point of comparison choose either William Faulkner's "A Rose for Emily" (p. 72) or "Barn Burning" (p. 481).

TWO COMPLEMENTARY CRITICAL READINGS

A. R. COULTHARD (B. 1940)
On the Visionary Ending of "Revelation"   *1983*

The second part of the story does not keep pace with its rollicking opening, but its psychological realism gives Mrs. Turpin's ultimate redemption a hard-edged credibility. When the protagonist returns home, her first impulse is, quite naturally, to resist the message of grace brought by the girl: " 'I am not,' she said tearfully, 'a wart hog. From hell.' But the denial had no force." Unable to reject the charge, Mrs. Turpin turns to resentment: "The message had been given to Ruby Turpin, a respectable, hard-working, church-going woman. The tears dried. Her eyes began to burn instead with wrath." Next she attempts to exorcise the girl's demonic words by confessing them to her black fieldhands:

> "She said," she began again and finished this time with a fierce rush of breath, "that I was an old wart hog from hell."
> There was an astounded silence.
> "Where she at?" the youngest woman cried in a piercing voice.
> "Lemme see her. I'll kill her!"
> "I'll kill her with you!" the other one cried.
> "She b'long in the sylum," the old woman said emphatically. "You the sweetest white lady I know."
> "She pretty too," the other two said. "Stout as she can be and sweet. Jesus satisfied with her!"
> "Deed he is," the woman declared.
> Idiots! Mrs. Turpin growled to herself.

This little scene is both funny and thematically significant. Mrs. Turpin's refusal to accept the phony image of herself as a good woman offered by the blacks is a step toward facing the truth.

Mrs. Turpin's next step is literal. She climbs the hill to the hogpen, apparently considering it the appropriate place to reason out the meaning of being called a wart hog from hell. Once there, Ruby gets right down to business: "What do you send me a message like that for?" she demands. "How am I a hog and me both?" Then she yells, "Go on, call me a hog! Call me a hog again. From hell. Call me a wart hog from hell." She ends her harangue by hilariously roaring at God, "Who do you think you are?" In this scene, Ruby begins to grow into a sympathetic, even lovable, character. As O'Connor said, "You got to be a very big woman to shout at the Lord across a hogpen." You also got to believe.

God answers Mrs. Turpin by sending her an epiphany which is so unobtrusively presented that at first it seems to be only description: "A tiny truck,

Claud's, appeared on the highway, heading rapidly out of sight. Its gears scraped thinly. It looked like a child's toy. At any moment a bigger truck might smash into it and scatter Claud's and the niggers' brains all over the road." The answer to Ruby's question is that God is omnipotent and that Ruby, like all mortals, is an insignificant, vulnerable creature whose life can end at any moment. Her response to this new knowledge is immediate: "Then like a monumental statue coming to life, she bent her head slowly and gazed, as if through the very heart of mystery, down into the pig parlor at the hogs."

The story originally ended at this point, but O'Connor decided that "something else was needed." Fortunately, what she added is not a concluding mini-sermon but a supernatural vision which is perfectly in keeping with the seriocomic tone of the story:

> A visionary light settled in her eyes . . . a vast horde of souls were rumbling toward heaven. There were whole companies of white-trash, clean for the first time in their lives, and bands of black niggers in white robes, and battalions of freaks and lunatics shouting and clapping and leaping like frogs. And bringing up the end of the procession was a tribe of people whom she recognized at once as those . . . like herself and Claud. . . . They were marching behind the others with great dignity. . . . They alone were on key. Yet she could see by their shocked and altered faces that even their virtues were being burned away.

This vision demolishes Ruby's earlier neat ranking of people, and its concluding sentence, which could have quotation marks around "virtues," completes her education by telling her that no one deserves grace and that we receive it only because of God's mysterious mercy. The epiphany takes, and the story ends with Ruby, "her eyes small but fixed unblinkingly on what lay ahead," prepared to face a humbler and more demanding life.

Though at least one reader whom O'Connor respected found "Revelation" pessimistic and considered the protagonist evil, O'Connor's main worry was that the story would "be taken to be one designed to make fun of Ruby," probably because her weaknesses are so vividly shown. But the great achievement of the protagonist's characterization is that Ruby Turpin retains her humanity to the end and does not, upon receiving grace, turn into an inspirational symbol. At the same time, O'Connor has made her conversion believable by dramatizing it in action and dialogue consistent with both Mrs. Turpin's humorous traits and her serious role in the story. "Revelation" is not only a delightful comedy but a profound dramatization of redemption as well.

From *American Literature*

Considerations for Critical Thinking and Writing

1. According to Coulthard, how does O'Connor avoid turning the end of the story into a "mini-sermon" (para. 5)?

2. How would your response to the story be different if it ended as O'Connor first intended it to — without the concluding paragraph? How would you regard Mrs. Turpin if this paragraph did not appear in the story?

3. Write an essay in response to this judgment of "Revelation": "Religion and comedy don't mix; therefore, the comic tone of 'Revelation' is inappropriate to the concluding religious epiphany."

MARSHALL BRUCE GENTRY (B. 1953)
On the Revised Ending of "Revelation"   1986

The precise significance of Mrs. Turpin's vision of hordes on a fiery bridge is not altogether a matter of critical agreement. And O'Connor's letters show her to have been inconsistent in her opinion of "Revelation" while she was writing it. It was the ending of the story that most troubled her, and the sequence of versions shows O'Connor trying to make clear that Ruby is not entirely corrupt. In a letter dated 25 December 1963, O'Connor mentioned that a friend who had read a draft of "Revelation" had called Mrs. Turpin "evil" and had suggested that O'Connor omit the final vision, which the friend considered to be a confirmation of Mrs. Turpin's evilness. O'Connor's reaction was, "I am not going to leave it out. I am going to deepen it so that there'll be no mistaking Ruby is not just an evil Glad Annie." As she finished revising the story, O'Connor made the final vision less obviously of Mrs. Turpin's making. One late draft, for example, contains the statement that the Turpins, "marching behind the others" toward heaven "with great dignity," were "driving them, in fact, ahead of themselves, still responsible as they had always been for good order and common sense and respectable behavior." In the published text, the Turpins are still at the end of the procession, but there is no mention of them "driving" the others on, and they are "accountable" rather than "still responsible." Another significant difference between the draft and the published text is the addition in the final version of the fact that Mrs. Turpin sees that her "virtues" are "being burned away." In both these revisions there is less emphasis on Mrs. Turpin's smug perspective, more emphasis on what shocks her.

The final version makes the vision more clearly redemptive, and one apparent implication of the revisions is that Mrs. Turpin's revelation is supernatural in origin. This implication is misleading, however; there is still much in Mrs. Turpin's vision to suggest that she produces it, and the primary effect of O'Connor's revisions is to make Mrs. Turpin's unconscious more clearly responsible for her vision of entry into a heavenly community. This view may seem peculiar when one considers Mrs. Turpin's bigotry and banality, but one's impression of that bigotry and banality is the result of the narrator's emphasis in describing Mrs. Turpin. The narrator emphasizes the ridiculous aspects of Mrs. Turpin rather than making fully apparent the tracks she has laid to carry herself to the oven in which individuality is renounced and the ideal of heavenly community achieved.

From *Flannery O'Connor's Religion of the Grotesque*

CONSIDERATIONS FOR CRITICAL THINKING AND WRITING

1. What reservations, according to Gentry, did O'Connor have about the story's ending? For what purpose did O'Connor revise the manuscript?

2. How does Gentry's reading of the ending compare with Coulthard's? Which reading do you find closer to your own? Why?

3. Write an essay that considers Gentry's final charge that Mrs. Turpin appears "ridiculous" at the end of the story in contrast to Coulthard's assessment that she "retains her humanity."

ALICE MUNRO (B. 1931)

Nearly all of Alice Munro's fiction is set in southwestern Ontario, but her reputation as a brilliant short-story writer goes far beyond the borders of her native Canada. Bharati Mukherjee, the novelist and short-story writer, echoes many writers' opinions in noting that "Munro ranks among the finest short-story writers in the English language." Her accessible and moving stories offer immediate pleasures while simultaneously exploring human complexities in what appear to be effortless anecdotal re-creations of everyday life. In one novel and seven collections of stories she has established herself as a major voice among fiction writers.

Munro began writing in her teens in the small rural town of Wingham, Ontario. She published her first story in 1950 while a student at Western Ontario University, but she left school to marry and moved to British Columbia, where she had three children and helped her husband establish a bookstore. This marriage broke up in 1972 when she returned to Ontario, and she remarried in 1976. Her first collection of stories, *Dance of the Happy Shades,* was not published until 1968, but it was highly acclaimed and won that year's Governor General's Award, Canada's highest literary prize. This success was followed by *Lives of Girls and Women* (1971), a collection of interlinked stories that was published as a novel and won the Canadian Booksellers Association International Book Year Award. This is the only novel Munro has published because she prefers the compression and brevity of short story writing. As she explains in a 1982 interview with Geoff Hancock for *Canadian Fiction Magazine,* she likes catching people in "snapshots": "I think this is why I'm not drawn to writing novels. Because I don't see that people develop and arrive somewhere. I just see people living in flashes." The form of the short story captures for Munro the fragmentary nature of her characters' experiences.

Her remaining six books are all short story collections, two of which also won the Governor General's Award in 1978 and 1986: *Something I've Been Meaning to Tell You* (1974); *Who Do You Think You Are?* (1978, titled *The Beggar Maid* in English and American editions); *The Moons of Jupiter* (1982); *The Progress of Love* (1986); *Friend of My Youth* (1990); and *Open Secrets* (1994). In addition, her stories are regularly printed in such publications as *The New Yorker,* the *Atlantic Monthly, Grand Street, Mademoiselle,* and *The Paris Review.*

The subject matter of Munro's stories has clearly developed from her own experience. She has explained in various interviews that her stories are not autobiographical, but she does claim an "emotional reality" for her characters that is drawn from her own life. Munro's experience of growing up in a relatively poor provincial southwestern Ontario town during the depression, negotiating the rebelliousness and idealism of adolescence, discovering sex, leaving home, testing herself at university, falling in love, getting married, having children, getting divorced, making a living, and getting along in a variety of complicated relationships all inform the fiction she creates.

Munro's fictional world ranges across the breadth of Canada from Ontario to British Columbia, but most readers agree that her Ontario stories, rooted as they are in her own formative past, represent more evocative settings experienced in childhood and recollected by a perceptive adult memory. Munro is repeatedly drawn back in her stories to rural Ontario despite the provincial and crabbed atmosphere of its small towns: "It's just that it's so basic like my own flesh or something that I can't be separated from." Many commentators compare Munro's interest in small-town settings to the use that American regional writers make of the rural South. Her admiration for American writers such as William Faulkner, Flannery O'Connor, Eudora Welty, and Carson McCullers has been frequently noted, and, as she has pointed out, "If I'm a regional writer, the region I'm writing about has many things in common with the American South." Munro's version of small-town Ontario, like O'Connor's version of the rural South, is one of a "closed rural society with a pretty homogeneous Scotch-Irish racial strain going slowly to decay."

Munro's characters, like Faulkner's or O'Connor's, often find themselves confronting entrenched customs and traditions, but their behavior is usually less overtly desperate and violently intense than that of their southern counterparts. To be sure there are drunks, suicides, molesters, lunatics, and bizarre eccentrics in Munro's stories, but Faulkner's Emily Grierson (p. 72) and Abner Snopes (p. 481) or O'Connor's Misfit (p. 381) represent more extreme character types than the more ordinary men and women who populate Munro's fictions. Perhaps Munro's description of the protagonist in "Prue" (p. 454) best describes her own strategies as a short story writer:

> She presents her life in anecdotes, and though it is the point of most of her anecdotes that hopes are dashed, dreams ridiculed, things never turn out as expected, everything is altered in a bizarre way and there is no explanation ever, people always feel cheered up after listening to her; they say of her that it is a relief to meet somebody who doesn't take herself too seriously, who is so unintense, and civilized, and never makes any real demands or complaints.

Given the intricacies and subtleties of Munro's stories, this description may seem overly simplistic, but it does suggest the modest and quiet wisdom to be found in her fiction. Good readers take Munro seriously.

Munro's realistic style is comfortably familiar. As she has noted, "I've never been an innovator or an experimental writer. I'm not very clever that way. I'm never ahead of what's being done at the time." Her prose is not informed by elaborate theoretical principles; instead she remembers and invents details that create a vivid character, moment, or setting that suggests larger meanings. Consider, for example the following passage from "How I Met My Husband" (p. 442), in which Munro's protagonist, a fifteen-year-old live-in cleaning girl, admires the bathroom in the house where she works:

> I had a bath in there once a week. They wouldn't have minded if I took one oftener, but to me it seemed like asking too much, or maybe risking making it less wonderful. The basin and the tub and the toilet were all pink, and there were glass doors with flamingos painted on them, to shut off the tub. The light had a rosy cast and the mat sank under your feet like snow, except that it was warm. The mirror was three-way. With the mirror all steamed up and the air like a perfume cloud, from things I was allowed to use, I stood up on the side of the tub and admired myself naked, from three directions. Sometimes I thought about the way we lived out at home and the way we lived here and how one way was so hard to imagine when you were living the other way. But I thought it was still a lot easier, living the way we lived at home, to picture something like this, the painted flamingos and the warmth and the soft mat, than it was anybody knowing only things like this to picture how it was the other way. And why was that?

Although Munro has described her own realistic sensibilities as being "very excited by what you might call the surface of life," in this passage she moves us beyond the pink surfaces of a bathroom toward an exploration of her protagonist's complex response to those surfaces. Her vivid description of the bathroom through her use of detail also works to reveal character.

In *Lives of Girls and Women* Munro has a character, Del Jordon, explain what she hopes to achieve in writing a work of fiction about small-town life in Ontario. Del works hard to portray not only what is actually "real" about the town, but what is meaningfully "true," and in order to do so she must capture the dull, ordinary simplicity of her neighbors' daily lives. Del's description of her efforts has often — and rightly — been used by critics to describe Munro's own intentions as a writer: "What I wanted was every last thing, every layer of speech and thought, stroke of light on bark or walls, every smell, pothole, pain, crack, delusion, held still and held together — radiant, everlasting." And that's really the point to be made about Munro's realistic technique: what is "everlasting," what is remembered and transformed into meaning, are details made "radiant," details that have been arranged and illuminated with meaning.

Like O'Connor's fiction, Munro's stories are filled with glimpses of what she describes in "An Ounce of Cure" (below) as the "shameless, marvelous, shattering absurdity" of life. Although Munro's fictional world is easily distinguished from O'Connor's owing to its realistic texture and everyday qualities, hovering among the quotidian details of Munro's depiction of small-town life and commonplace relationships are explorations of uncertainties, illusions, and indeterminacies.

The following four stories are characteristic of much of Munro's fiction in their treatment of female characters who both long to be part of a relationship or community and need to stand on their own in order to discover what is truly valuable to them. While reading these stories, you may find yourself surprised and puzzled by the protagonist's experiences, and you may feel, like them, that you are on the threshold of making some discovery.

CHRONOLOGY

1931   Born on July 10 in Wingham, Ontario.

1949   Graduates from Wingham and District High School.

1949–51   Attends University of Western Ontario.

1950   Publishes her first short story, "The Dimensions of a Shadow."

1951   Marries James Munro and moves to Vancouver, British Columbia.

1953   Daughter Sheila born.

1957   Daughter Jenny born.

1963   Moves to Victoria and establishes Munro Books.

1966   Daughter Sarah born.

1968   Publishes first collection of stories, *Dance of the Happy Shades;* wins Governor General's Literary Award.

1971   *Lives of Girls and Women* is published.

1972   Divorces James Munro; writer-in-residence, University of Western Ontario.

1973   *Something I've Been Meaning to Tell You* is published.

1976   Marries Gerald Fremlin and moves to a farm outside Clinton, Ontario.

1978   *Who Do You Think You Are?* (titled *Beggar Maid* in American editions) is published; wins Governor General's Literary Award.

1979–82   Tours in Australia, China, and Scandinavia.

1980   Writer-in-residence at University of British Columbia and University of Queensland.

1982   *Moons of Jupiter* is published.

1986   *The Progress of Love* is published; wins Governor General's Literary Award and Marian Engel Prize.

1990   *Friend of My Youth* is published; wins Canada Council Molson Prize.

1994   *Open Secrets* is published.

1996   *Selected Stories* is published.

An Ounce of Cure 1968

My parents didn't drink. They weren't rabid about it, and in fact I remember that when I signed the pledge in grade seven, with the rest of that superbly if impermanently indoctrinated class, my mother said, "It's just nonsense and fanaticism, children of that age." My father would drink a beer on a hot day, but my mother did not join him, and—whether accidentally or symbolically—this drink was always consumed *outside* the house. Most of the people we knew were the same way, in the small town where we lived. I ought not to say that it was this which got me into difficulties, because the difficulties I got into were a faithful expression of my own incommodious nature—the same nature that caused my mother to look at me, on any occasion which traditionally calls for feelings of pride and maternal accomplishment (my departure for my first formal dance, I mean, or my hellbent preparations for a descent on college) with an expression of brooding and fascinated despair, as if she could not possibly expect, did not ask, that it should go with me as it did with other girls; the dreamed-of spoils of daughters—orchids, nice boys, diamond rings—would be borne home in due course by the daughters of her friends, but not by me; all she could do was hope for a lesser rather than a greater disaster—an elopement, say, with a boy who could never earn his living, rather than an abduction into the White Slave trade.

But ignorance, my mother said, ignorance, or innocence if you like, is not always such a fine thing as people think and I am not sure it may not be dangerous for a girl like you; then she emphasized her point, as she had a habit of doing, with some quotation which had an innocent pomposity and odor of mothballs. I didn't even wince at it, knowing full well how it must have worked wonders with Mr. Berryman.

The evening I baby-sat for the Berrymans must have been in April. I had been in love all year, or at least since the first week in September, when a boy named Martin Collingwood had given me a surprised, appreciative, and rather ominously complacent smile in the school assembly. I never knew what surprised him; I was not looking like anybody but me; I had an old blouse on and my home-permanent had turned out badly. A few weeks after that he took me out for the first time, and kissed me on the dark side of the porch—also, I ought to say, on the mouth; I am sure it was the first time anybody had ever kissed me effectively, and I know that I did not wash my face that night or the next morning, in order to keep the imprint of those kisses intact. (I showed the most painful banality in the conduct of this whole affair, as you will see.) Two months, and a few amatory stages later, he dropped me. He had fallen for the girl who played opposite him in the Christmas production of *Pride and Prejudice*.

I said I was not going to have anything to do with that play, and I got another girl to work on Makeup in my place, but of course I went to it after all, and sat down in front with my girl friend Joyce, who pressed my hand when I was overcome with pain and delight at the sight of Mr. Darcy° in white breeches, silk waistcoat, and sideburns. It was surely seeing Martin as Darcy that did it for me; every girl is in love with Darcy anyway, and the part gave Martin an arrogance and male splendor in my eyes which made it impossible

Darcy: The hero of Jane Austen's (1775–1817) *Pride and Prejudice*.

to remember that he was simply a high-school senior, passably good-looking and of medium intelligence (and with a reputation slightly tainted, at that, by such preferences as the Drama Club and the Cadet *Band*) who happened to be the first boy, the first really presentable boy, to take an interest in me. In the last act they gave him a chance to embrace Elizabeth (Mary Bishop, with a sallow complexion and no figure, but big vivacious eyes) and during this realistic encounter I dug my nails bitterly into Joyce's sympathetic palm.

That night was the beginning of months of real, if more or less self-inflicted, misery for me. Why is it a temptation to refer to this sort of thing lightly, with irony, with amazement even, at finding oneself involved with such preposterous emotions in the unaccountable past? That is what we are apt to do, speaking of love; with adolescent love, of course, it's practically obligatory; you would think we sat around, dull afternoons, amusing ourselves with these tidbit recollections of pain. But it really doesn't make me feel very gay—worse still, it doesn't really surprise me—to remember all the stupid, sad, half-ashamed things I did, that people in love always do. I hung around the places where he might be seen, and then pretended not to see him; I made absurdly roundabout approaches, in conversation, to the bitter pleasure of casually mentioning his name. I daydreamed endlessly; in fact if you want to put it mathematically, I spent perhaps ten times as many hours thinking about Martin Collingwood—yes, pining and weeping for him—as I ever spent with him; the idea of him dominated my mind relentlessly and, after a while, against my will. For if at first I had dramatized my feelings, the time came when I would have been glad to escape them; my well-worn daydreams had become depressing and not even temporarily consoling. As I worked my math problems I would torture myself, quite mechanically and helplessly, with an exact recollection of Martin kissing my throat. I had an exact recollection of *everything*. One night I had an impulse to swallow all the aspirins in the bathroom cabinet, but stopped after I had taken six.

My mother noticed that something was wrong and got me some iron pills. She said, "Are you sure everything is going all right at school?" *School!* When I told her that Martin and I had broken up all she said was, "Well so much the better for that. I never saw a boy so stuck on himself." "Martin has enough conceit to sink a battleship," I said morosely and went upstairs and cried.

The night I went to the Berrymans was a Saturday night. I baby-sat for them quite often on Saturday nights because they liked to drive over to Baileyville, a much bigger, livelier town about twenty miles away, and perhaps have supper and go to a show. They had been living in our town only two or three years—Mr. Berryman had been brought in as plant manager of the new door-factory—and they remained, I suppose by choice, on the fringes of its society; most of their friends were youngish couples like themselves, born in other places, who lived in new ranch-style houses on a hill outside town where we used to go tobogganing. This Saturday night they had two other couples in for drinks before they all drove over to Baileyville for the opening of a new supper-club; they were all rather festive. I sat in the kitchen and pretended to do Latin. Last night had been the Spring Dance at the high school. I had not gone, since the only boy who had asked me was Millerd Crompton, who asked so many girls that he was suspected of working his way through the whole class alphabetically. But the dance was held in the Armories, which was only half a block away from our house; I had been able to see the boys in dark suits, the girls in long pale formals under their coats, passing gravely under the street-lights, stepping around the last patches of snow. I could even hear the music and I have not forgotten to this day that they played "Ballerina," and — oh, song of my aching heart — "Slow Boat to China." Joyce had phoned me up this morning and told me in her hushed way (we might have been discussing an incurable disease I had) that yes, M.C. *had* been there with M.B., and she had on a formal that must have been made out of somebody's old lace tablecloth, it just *hung*.

When the Berrymans and their friends had gone I went into the living room and read a magazine. I was mortally depressed. The big softly lit room, with its green and leaf-brown colors, made an uncluttered setting for the development of the emotions, such as you would get on a stage. At home the life of the emotions went on all right, but it always seemed to get buried under the piles of mending to be done, the ironing, the children's jigsaw puzzles and rock collections. It was the sort of house where people were always colliding with one another on the stairs and listening to hockey games and Superman on the radio.

I got up and found the Berrymans' "Danse Macabre" and put it on the record player and turned out the living-room lights. The curtains were only partly drawn. A street light shone obliquely on the windowpane, making a rectangle of thin dusty gold, in which the shadows of bare branches moved, caught in the huge sweet winds of spring. It was a mild black night when the last snow was melting. A year ago all this — the music, the wind and darkness, the shadows of the branches — would have given me tremendous happiness; when they did not do so now, but only called up tediously familiar, somehow humiliatingly personal thoughts, I gave up my soul for dead and walked into the kitchen and decided to get drunk.

No, it was not like that. I walked into the kitchen to look for a coke or 10 something in the refrigerator, and there on the front of the counter were three tall beautiful bottles, all about half full of gold. But even after I had looked at them and lifted them to feel their weight I had not decided to get drunk; I had decided to have a drink.

Now here is where my ignorance, my disastrous innocence, comes in. It is true that I had seen the Berrymans and their friends drinking their highballs as casually as I would drink a coke, but I did not apply this attitude to myself. No; I thought of hard liquor as something to be taken in extremities, and relied upon for extravagant results, one way or another. My approach could not have been less casual if I had been the Little Mermaid drinking the witch's crystal potion. Gravely, with a glance at my set face in the black window above the sink, I poured a little whisky from each of the bottles (I think now there were two brands of rye and an expensive Scotch) until I had my glass full. For I had never in my life seen anyone pour a drink and I had no idea that people frequently diluted their liquor with water, soda, et cetera, and I had seen that the glasses the Berrymans' guests were holding when I came through the living room were nearly full.

I drank it off as quickly as possible. I set the glass down and stood looking at my face in the window, half expecting to see it altered. My throat was burning, but I felt nothing else. It was very disappointing, when I had worked myself up to it. But I was not going to let it go at that. I poured another full glass, then filled each of the bottles with water to approximately the level I had seen when I came in. I drank the second glass only a little more slowly than the first. I put the empty glass down on the counter with care, perhaps feeling in my head a rustle of things to come, and went and sat down on a chair in the living room. I reached up and turned on a floor lamp beside the chair, and the room jumped on me.

When I say I was expecting extravagant results I do not mean that I was expecting this. I had thought of some sweeping emotional change, an upsurge of gaiety and irresponsibility, a feeling of lawlessness and escape, accompanied by a little dizziness and perhaps a tendency to giggle out loud. I did not have in mind the ceiling spinning like a great plate somebody had thrown at me, nor the pale green blobs of the chairs swelling, converging, disintegrating, playing with me a game full of enormous senseless inanimate malice. My head sank back; I closed my eyes. And at once opened them, opened them wide, threw myself out of the chair and down the hall and reached—thank God, thank God!—the Berrymans' bathroom, where I was sick everywhere, everywhere, and dropped like a stone.

From this point on I have no continuous picture of what happened; my memories of the next hour or two are split into vivid and improbable segments, with nothing but murk and uncertainty between. I do remember lying on the bathroom floor looking sideways at the little six-sided white tiles, which lay together in such an admirable and logical pattern, seeing them with the brief broken gratitude and sanity of one who has just been torn to pieces with vomiting. Then I remember sitting on the stool in front of the hall phone, asking weakly for Joyce's number. Joyce was not home. I was told by her mother (a rather rattlebrained woman, who didn't seem to notice a thing the matter—for which I felt weakly, mechanically grateful) that she was at Kay Stringer's house. I didn't know Kay's number so I just asked the operator; I felt I couldn't risk looking down at the telephone book.

Kay Stringer was not a friend of mine but a new friend of Joyce's. She had a vague reputation for wildness and a long switch of hair, very oddly, though naturally, colored—from soap-yellow to caramel-brown. She knew a lot of boys more exciting than Martin Collingwood, boys who had quit school or been imported into town to play on the hockey team. She and Joyce rode around in these boys' cars, and sometimes went with them—having lied of course to their mothers—to the Gay-la dance hall on the highway north of town.

I got Joyce on the phone. She was very keyed-up, as she always was with boys around, and she hardly seemed to hear what I was saying.

"Oh, I can't tonight," she said. "Some kids are here. We're going to play cards. You know Bill Kline? He's here. Ross Armour—"

"I'm *sick*," I said trying to speak distinctly; it came out an inhuman croak. "I'm *drunk* Joyce!" Then I fell off the stool and the receiver dropped out of my hand and banged for a while dismally against the wall.

I had not told Joyce where I was, so after thinking about it for a moment she phoned my mother, and using the elaborate and unnecessary subterfuge that young girls delight in, she found out. She and Kay and the boys—there were three of them—told some story about where they were going to Kay's mother, and got into the car and drove out. They found me still lying on the broadloom carpet in the hall; I had been sick again, and this time I had not made it to the bathroom.

It turned out that Kay Stringer, who arrived on this scene only by acci-   20
dent, was exactly the person I needed. She loved a crisis, particularly one like this, which had a shady and scandalous aspect and which must be kept secret from the adult world. She became excited, aggressive, efficient; that energy which was termed wildness was simply the overflow of a great female instinct to manage, comfort, and control. I could hear her voice coming at me from all directions, telling me not to worry, telling Joyce to find the biggest coffeepot they had and make it full of coffee (*strong* coffee, she said), telling the boys to pick me up and carry me to the sofa. Later, in the fog beyond my reach, she was calling for a scrub-brush.

Then I was lying on the sofa, covered with some kind of crocheted throw they had found in the bedroom. I didn't want to lift my head. The house was full of the smell of coffee. Joyce came in, looking very pale; she said that the Berryman kids had wakened up but she had given them a cookie and told them to go back to bed, it was all right; she hadn't let them out of their room and she didn't believe they'd remember. She said that she and Kay had cleaned up the bathroom and the hall though she was afraid there was still a spot on the rug. The coffee was ready. I didn't understand anything very well. The boys had turned on the radio and were going through the Berrymans' record collection; they had it out on the floor. I felt there was something odd about this but I could not think what it was.

Kay brought me a huge breakfast mug full of coffee.

"I don't know if I can," I said. "Thanks."

"Sit up," she said briskly, as if dealing with drunks was an everyday business for her, I had no need to feel myself important. (I met, and recognized, that tone of voice years later, in the maternity ward.) "Now drink," she said. I drank and at the same time realized that I was wearing only my slip. Joyce and Kay had taken off my blouse and skirt. They had brushed off the skirt and washed out the blouse, since it was nylon; it was hanging in the bathroom. I pulled the throw up under my arms and Kay laughed. She got everybody coffee. Joyce brought in the coffeepot and on Kay's instruction she kept filling my cup whenever I drank from it. Somebody said to me with interest. "You must have really wanted to tie one on."

"No," I said rather sulkily, obediently drinking my coffee. "I only had two   25
drinks."

Kay laughed, "Well it certainly gets to you, I'll say that. What time do you expect *they'll* be back?" she said.

"Late. After one I think."

"You should be all right by that time. Have some more coffee."

Kay and one of the boys began dancing to the radio. Kay danced very sexily, but her face had the gently superior and indulgent, rather cold look it had when she was lifting me up to drink the coffee. The boy was whispering to her and she was smiling, shaking her head. Joyce said she was hungry, and she went out to the kitchen to see what there was — potato chips or crackers, or something like that, that you could eat without making too noticeable a dint. Bill Kline came over and sat on the sofa beside me and patted my legs through the crocheted throw. He didn't say anything to me, just patted my legs and looked at me with what seemed to me a very stupid, half-sick, absurd, and alarming expression. I felt very uncomfortable; I wondered how it had ever got around that Bill Kline was so good looking, with an expression like that. I moved my legs nervously and he gave me a look of contempt, not ceasing to pat me. Then I scrambled off the sofa, pulling the throw around me, with the idea of going to the bathroom to see if my blouse was dry. I lurched a little when I started to walk, and for some reason — probably to show Bill Kline that he had not panicked me — I immediately exaggerated this, and calling out, "Watch me walk a straight line!" I lurched and stumbled, to the accompaniment of everyone's laughter, towards the hall. I was standing in the archway between the hall and the living room when the knob of the front door turned with a small matter-of-fact click and everything became silent behind me except the radio of course and the crocheted throw inspired by some delicate malice of its own slithered down around my feet and there — oh, delicious moment in a well-organized farce! — there stood the Berrymans, Mr. and Mrs., with expressions on their faces as appropriate to the occasion as any old-fashioned director of farces could wish. They must have been preparing those expressions, of course; they could not have produced them in the first moment of shock; with the noise we were making, they had no doubt heard us as soon as they got out of the car; for the same reason, we had not heard them. I don't think I ever knew what brought them home so early — a headache, an argument — and I was not really in a position to ask.

Mr. Berryman drove me home. I don't remember how I got into that car, or   30
how I found my clothes and put them on, or what kind of a good-night, if any, I said to Mrs. Berryman. I don't remember what happened to my friends, though I imagine they gathered up their coats and fled, covering up the ignominy of their departure with a mechanical roar of defiance. I remember Joyce with a box of crackers in her hand, saying that I had become terribly sick from eating — I think she said *sauerkraut* — for supper, and that I had called them for help. (When I asked her later what they made of this she said, "It wasn't any use. You *reeked*.") I remember also her saying, "Oh, no, Mr. Berryman I beg of you, my mother is a terribly nervous person I don't know what the shock might do to her. I will go down on my knees to you if you like but *you must not phone my mother.*" I have no picture of her down on her knees — and she would have done it in a minute — so it seems this threat was not carried out.

Mr. Berryman said to me, "Well I guess you know your behavior tonight is a pretty serious thing." He made it sound as if I might be charged with criminal negligence or something worse. "It would be very wrong of me to overlook it," he said. I suppose that besides being angry and disgusted with *me*, he was worried about taking me home in this condition to my strait-laced parents, who could always say I got the liquor in his house. Plenty of Temperance people would think that enough to hold him responsible, and the town was full of Temperance people. Good relations with the town were very important to him from a business point of view.

"I have an idea it wasn't the first time," he said. "If it was the first time, would a girl be smart enough to fill three bottles up with water? No. Well in this case, she *was* smart enough, but not smart enough to know I could spot it. What do you say to that?" I opened my mouth to answer and although I was feeling quite sober the only sound that came out was a loud, desolate-sounding giggle. He stopped in front of our house. "Light's on," he said. "Now go in and tell your parents the straight truth. And if you don't, remember I will." He did not mention paying me for my baby-sitting services of the evening and the subject did not occur to me either.

I went into the house and tried to go straight upstairs but my mother called to me. She came into the front hall, where I had not turned on the light, and she must have smelled me at once for she ran forward with a cry of pure amazement, as if she had seen somebody falling, and caught me by the shoulders, as I did indeed fall down against the banister, overwhelmed by my fantastic lucklessness, and I told her everything from the start, not omitting even the name of Martin Collingwood and my flirtation with the aspirin bottle, which was a mistake.

On Monday morning my mother took the bus over to Baileyville and found the liquor store and bought a bottle of Scotch whisky. Then she had to wait for a bus back, and she met some people she knew and she was not quite able to hide the bottle in her bag; she was furious with herself for not bringing a proper shopping-bag. As soon as she got back she walked out to the Berrymans'; she had not even had lunch. Mr. Berryman had not gone back to the factory. My mother went in and had a talk with both of them and made an excellent impression and then Mr. Berryman drove her home. She talked to them in the forthright and unemotional way she had, which was always agreeably surprising to people prepared to deal with a mother, and she told them that although I seemed to do well enough at school I was extremely backward — or perhaps eccentric — in my emotional development. I imagine that this analysis of my behavior was especially effective with Mrs. Berryman, a great reader of Child Guidance books. Relations between them warmed to the point where my mother brought up a specific instance of my difficulties, and disarmingly related the whole story of Martin Collingwood.

Within a few days it was all over town and the school that I had tried to 35 commit suicide over Martin Collingwood. But it was already all over school and the town that the Berrymans had come home on Saturday night to find me drunk, staggering, wearing nothing but my slip, in a room with three boys, one of whom was Bill Kline. My mother had said that I was to pay for the bottle she had taken the Berrymans out of my baby-sitting earnings, but my clients melted away like the last April snow, and it would not be paid for yet if newcomers to town had not moved in across the street in July, and needed a baby sitter before they talked to any of their neighbors.

My mother also said that it had been a great mistake to let me go out with boys and that I would not be going out again until well after my sixteenth birthday, if then. This did not prove to be a concrete hardship at all, because it was at least that long before anybody asked me. If you think that news of the Berrymans' adventure would put me in demand for whatever gambols and orgies were going on in and around that town, you could not be more mistaken. The extraordinary publicity which attended my first debauch may have made me seem marked for a special kind of ill luck, like the girl whose illegitimate baby turns out to be triplets: nobody wants to have anything to do with her. At any rate I had at the same time one of the most silent telephones and positively the most sinful reputation in the whole high school. I had to put up with this until the next fall, when a fat blonde girl in grade ten ran away with a married man and was picked up two months later, living in sin — though not with the same man — in the city of Saulte Ste. Marie. Then everybody forgot about me.

But there was a positive, a splendidly unexpected, result of this affair: I got completely over Martin Collingwood. It was not only that he at once said, publicly, that he had always thought I was a nut; where he was concerned I had no pride, and my tender fancy could have found a way around that, a month, a week, before. What was it that brought me back into the world again? It was the terrible and fascinating reality of my disaster; it was *the way things happened.* Not that I enjoyed it; I was a self-conscious girl and I suffered a good deal from all this exposure. But the development of events on that Saturday night — that fascinated me; I felt that I had had a glimpse of the shameless, marvelous, shattering absurdity with which the plots of life, though not of fiction, are improvised. I could not take my eyes off it.

And of course Martin Collingwood wrote his Senior Matric that June, and went away to the city to take a course at a school for Morticians, as I think it is called, and when he came back he went into his uncle's undertaking business. We lived in the same town and we would hear most things that happened to each other but I do not think we met face to face or saw one another, except at a distance, for years. I went to a shower for the girl he married, but then everybody went to everybody else's showers. No, I do not think I really saw him again until I came home after I had been married several years, to attend a relative's funeral. Then I saw him; not quite Mr. Darcy but still very nice-looking in those black clothes. And I saw him looking over at me with an expression as close to a reminiscent smile as the occasion would permit, and I knew that he had been surprised by a memory either of my devotion or my little buried catastrophe. I gave him a gentle, uncomprehending look in return. I am a grown-up woman now; let him unbury his own catastrophes.

CONSIDERATIONS FOR CRITICAL THINKING AND WRITING

1. FIRST RESPONSE. Would you call the protagonist a typical teenager? What details make her unique?

2. How important is the setting for this story? Describe the values the narrator associates with "the small town where we lived" (para. 1).

3. Discuss the narrator's sense of humor. How does her humor affect your attitude toward her?

4. Describe the differences in perspective and sensibilities between the teenager who experiences the events in the story and the adult who recounts them.

5. How does the narrator's drunken baby-sitting episode affect her reputation? What does this reveal about her and the town?

6. Why is the narrator "fascinated" by the "events on that Saturday night" (para. 37)? Why is the episode she recounts important to her?

7. How convincing are the narrator's descriptions of the effects of alcohol on her? Cite specific passages to illustrate your points.

8. How would you describe the conflict in the story? How is it resolved?

9. How do you think this story would be different if the protagonist/narrator were male rather than female?

10. Discuss the significance of the title.

CONNECTIONS TO OTHER SELECTIONS

1. In an essay compare the use of point of view in "An Ounce of Cure" with Ralph Ellison's strategies in "Battle Royal" (p. 223). How is the point of view from which each story is told connected to the story's themes?

2. In an essay discuss the narrators' humor in "An Ounce of Cure" and John Updike's "A & P" (p. 576). How does the humor affect your response to each narrator?

How I Met My Husband   1974

We heard the plane come over at noon, roaring through the radio news, and we were sure it was going to hit the house, so we all ran out into the yard. We saw it come over the treetops, all red and silver, the first close-up plane I ever saw. Mrs. Peebles screamed.

"Crash landing," their little boy said. Joey was his name.

"It's okay," said Dr. Peebles. "He knows what he's doing." Dr. Peebles was only an animal doctor, but had a calming way of talking, like any doctor.

This was my first job — working for Dr. and Mrs. Peebles, who had bought an old house out on the Fifth Line, about five miles out of town. It was just when the trend was starting of town people buying up old farms, not to work them but to live on them.

We watched the plane land across the road, where the fairgrounds used to 5 be. It did make a good landing field, nice and level for the old race track, and the barns and display sheds torn down now for scrap lumber so there was nothing in the way. Even the old grandstand bays had burned.

"All right," said Mrs. Peebles, snappy as she always was when she got over her nerves. "Let's go back in the house. Let's not stand here gawking like a set of farmers."

She didn't say that to hurt my feelings. It never occurred to her.

I was just setting the dessert down when Loretta Bird arrived, out of breath, at the screen door.

"I though it was going to crash into the house and kill youse all!"

She lived on the next place and the Peebleses thought she was a country- 10 woman, they didn't know the difference. She and her husband didn't farm, he worked on the roads and had a bad name for drinking. They had seven children and couldn't get credit at the HiWay Grocery. The Peebleses made her welcome, not knowing any better, as I say, and offered her dessert.

Dessert was never anything to write home about, at their place. A dish of Jell-O or sliced bananas or fruit out of a tin. "Have a house without a pie, be ashamed until you die," my mother used to say, but Mrs. Peebles operated differently.

Loretta Bird saw me getting the can of peaches.

"Oh, never mind," she said. "I haven't got the right kind of a stomach to trust what comes out of those tins, I can only eat home canning."

I could have slapped her. I bet she never put down fruit in her life.

"I know what he's landed here for," she said. "He's got permission to use 15 the fairgrounds and take people up for rides. It costs a dollar. It's the same fellow who was over at Palmerston last week and was up the lakeshore before that. I wouldn't go up, if you paid me."

"I'd jump at the chance," Dr. Peebles said. "I'd like to see this neighborhood from the air."

Mrs. Peebles said she would just as soon see it from the ground. Joey said he wanted to go and Heather did, too. Joey was nine and Heather was seven.

"Would you, Edie?" Heather said.

I said I didn't know. I was scared, but I never admitted that, especially in front of children I was taking care of.

"People are going to be coming out here in their cars raising dust and trampling your property, if I was you I would complain," Loretta said. She hooked her legs around the chair rung and I knew we were in for a lengthy visit. After Dr. Peebles went back to his office or out on his next call and Mrs. Peebles went for her nap, she would hang around me while I was trying to do the dishes. She would pass remarks about the Peebleses in their own house.

"She wouldn't find time to lay down in the middle of the day, if she had seven kids like I got."

She asked me did they fight and did they keep things in the dresser drawer not to have babies with. She said it was a sin if they did. I pretended I didn't know what she was talking about.

I was fifteen and away from home for the first time. My parents had made the effort and sent me to high school for a year, but I didn't like it. I was shy of strangers and the work was hard, they didn't make it nice for you or explain the way they do now. At the end of the year the averages were published in the paper, and mine came out at the very bottom, 37 percent. My father said that's enough and I didn't blame him. The last thing I wanted, anyway, was to go on and end up teaching school. It happened the very day the paper came out with my disgrace in it, Dr. Peebles was staying at our place for dinner, having just helped one of our cows have twins, and he said I looked smart to him and his wife was looking for a girl to help. He said she felt tied down, with the two children, out in the country. I guess she would, my mother said, being polite, though I could tell from her face she was wondering what on earth it would be like to have only two children and no barn work, and then to be complaining.

When I went home I would describe to them the work I had to do, and it made everybody laugh. Mrs. Peebles had an automatic washer and dryer, the first I ever saw. I have had those in my own home for such a long time now it's hard to remember how much of a miracle it was to me, not having to struggle with the wringer and hang up and haul down. Let alone not having to heat water. Then there was practically no baking. Mrs. Peebles said she couldn't make pie crust, the most amazing thing I ever heard a woman admit. I could, of course, and I could make light biscuits and a white cake and dark cake, but they didn't want it, she said they watched their figures. The only thing I didn't like about working there, in fact, was feeling half hungry a lot of the time. I used to bring back a box of doughnuts made out at home, and hide them under my bed. The children found out, and I didn't mind sharing, but I thought I better bind them to secrecy.

The day after the plane landed Mrs. Peebles put both children in the car and drove over to Chesley, to get their hair cut. There was a good woman then at Chesley for doing hair. She got hers done at the same place, Mrs. Peebles did, and that meant they would be gone a good while. She had to pick a day Dr.

Peebles wasn't going out into the country, she didn't have her own car. Cars were still in short supply then, after the war.

I loved being left in the house alone, to do my work at leisure. The kitchen was all white and bright yellow, with fluorescent lights. That was before they ever thought of making the appliances all different colors and doing the cupboards like dark old wood and hiding the lighting. I loved light. I loved the double sink. So would anybody new-come from washing dishes in a dishpan with a rag-plugged hole on an oilcloth-covered table by light of a coal-oil lamp. I kept everything shining.

The bathroom too. I had a bath in there once a week. They wouldn't have minded if I took one oftener, but to me it seemed like asking too much, or maybe risking making it less wonderful. The basin and the tub and the toilet were all pink, and there were glass doors with flamingos painted on them, to shut off the tub. The light had a rosy cast and the mat sank under your feet like snow, except that it was warm. The mirror was three-way. With the mirror all steamed up and the air like a perfume cloud, from things I was allowed to use, I stood up on the side of the tub and admired myself naked, from three directions. Sometimes I thought about the way we lived out at home and the way we lived here and how one way was so hard to imagine when you were living the other way. But I thought it was still a lot easier, living the way we lived at home, to picture something like this, the painted flamingos and the warmth and the soft mat, than it was anybody knowing only things like this to picture how it was the other way. And why was that?

I was through my jobs in no time, and had the vegetables peeled for supper and sitting in cold water besides. Then I went into Mrs. Peebles' bedroom. I had been in there plenty of times, cleaning, and I always took a good look in her closet, at the clothes she had hanging there. I wouldn't have looked in her drawers, but a closet is open to anybody. That's a lie. I would have looked in drawers, but I would have felt worse doing it and been more scared she could tell.

Some clothes in her closet she wore all the time, I was quite familiar with them. Others she never put on, they were pushed to the back. I was disappointed to see no wedding dress. But there was one long dress I could just see the skirt of, and I was hungering to see the rest. Now I took note of where it hung and lifted it out. It was satin, a lovely weight on my arm, light bluish-green in color, almost silvery. It had a fitted, pointed waist and a full skirt and an off-the-shoulder fold hiding the little sleeves.

Next thing was easy. I got out of my own things and slipped it on. I was 30 slimmer at fifteen than anybody would believe who knows me now and the fit was beautiful. I didn't, of course, have a strapless bra on, which was what it needed, I just had to slide my straps down my arms under the material. Then I tried pinning up my hair, to get the effect. One thing led to another. I put on rouge and lipstick and eyebrow pencil from her dresser. The heat of the day and the weight of the satin and all the excitement made me thirsty, and I went out to the kitchen, got-up as I was, to get a glass of ginger ale with ice cubes from the refrigerator. The Peebleses drank ginger ale, or fruit drinks, all day, like water, and I was getting so I did too. Also there was no limit on ice cubes, which I was so fond of I would even put them in a glass of milk.

I turned from putting the ice tray back and saw a man watching me through the screen. It was the luckiest thing in the world I didn't spill the ginger ale down the front of me then and there.

"I never meant to scare you. I knocked but you were getting the ice out, you didn't hear me."

I couldn't see what he looked like, he was dark the way somebody is pressed up against a screen door with the bright daylight behind them. I only knew he wasn't from around here.

"I'm from the plane over there. My name is Chris Watters and what I was wondering was if I could use that pump."

There was a pump in the yard. That was the way the people used to get 35 their water. Now I noticed he was carrying a pail.

"You're welcome," I said. "I can get it from the tap and save you pumping." I guess I wanted him to know we had piped water, didn't pump ourselves.

"I don't mind the exercise." He didn't move, though, and finally he said, "Were you going to a dance?"

Seeing a stranger there had made me entirely forget how I was dressed.

"Or is that the way ladies around here generally get dressed up in the afternoon?"

I didn't know how to joke back then. I was too embarrassed.   40

"You live here? Are you the lady of the house?"

"I'm the hired girl."

Some people change when they find that out, their whole way of looking at you and speaking to you changes, but his didn't.

"Well, I just wanted to tell you you look very nice. I was so surprised when I looked in the door and saw you. Just because you looked so nice and beautiful."

I wasn't even old enough then to realize how out of the common it is, for a 45 man to say something like that to a woman, or somebody he is treating like a woman. For a man to say a word like *beautiful*. I wasn't old enough to realize or to say anything back, or in fact to do anything but wish he would go away. Not that I didn't like him, but just that it upset me so, having him look at me, and me trying to think of something to say.

He must have understood. He said good-bye, and thanked me, and went and started filling his pail from the pump. I stood behind the Venetian blinds in the dining room, watching him. When he had gone, I went into the bedroom and took the dress off and put it back in the same place. I dressed in my own clothes and took my hair down and washed my face, wiping it on Kleenex, which I threw in the wastebasket.

The Peebleses asked me what kind of man he was. Young, middle-aged, short, tall? I couldn't say.

"Good-looking?" Dr. Peebles teased me.

I couldn't think a thing but that he would be coming to get his water again, he would be talking to Dr. or Mrs. Peebles, making friends with them, and he would mention seeing me that first afternoon, dressed up. Why not mention it? He would think it was funny. And no idea of the trouble it would get me into.

After supper the Peebleses drove into town to go to a movie. She wanted to 50 go somewhere with her hair fresh done. I sat in my bright kitchen wondering what to do, knowing I would never sleep. Mrs. Peebles might not fire me, when she found out, but it would give her a different feeling about me altogether. This was the first place I ever worked but I really had picked up things about the way people feel when you are working for them. They like to think you aren't curious. Not just that you aren't dishonest, that isn't enough. They like to feel you don't notice things, that you don't think or wonder about anything but what they liked to eat and how they liked things ironed, and so on. I don't mean they weren't kind to me, because they were. They had me eat my meals with them (to tell the truth I expected to, I didn't know there were families who don't) and sometimes they took me along in the car. But all the same.

I went up and checked on the children being asleep and then I went out. I had to do it. I crossed the road and went in the old fairgrounds gate. The plane looked unnatural sitting there, and shining with the moon. Off at the far side of the fairgrounds, where the bush was taking over, I saw his tent.

He was sitting outside it smoking a cigarette. He saw me coming.

"Hello, were you looking for a plane ride? I don't start taking people up till tomorrow." Then he looked again and said, "Oh, it's you. I didn't know you without your long dress on."

My heart was knocking away, my tongue was dried up. I had to say something. But I couldn't. My throat was closed and I was like a deaf-and-dumb.

"Did you want to ride? Sit down. Have a cigarette."   55

I couldn't even shake my head to say no, so he gave me one.

"Put it in your mouth or I can't light it. It's a good thing I'm used to shy ladies."

I did. It wasn't the first time I had smoked a cigarette, actually. My girl friend out home, Muriel Lowe, used to steal them from her brother.

"Look at your hand shaking. Did you just want to have a chat, or what?"

In one burst I said, "I wisht you wouldn't say anything about that dress."   60

"What dress? Oh, the long dress."

"It's Mrs. Peebles'."

"Whose? Oh, the lady you work for? Is that it? She wasn't home so you got dressed up in her dress, eh? You got dressed up and played queen. I don't blame you. You're not smoking the cigarette right. Don't just puff. Draw it in. Did anybody ever show you how to inhale? Are you scared I'll tell on you? Is that it?"

I was so ashamed at having to ask him to connive this way I couldn't nod. I just looked at him and he saw *yes*.

"Well I won't. I won't in the slightest way mention it or embarrass you. I   65
give you my word of honor."

Then he changed the subject, to help me out, seeing I couldn't even thank him.

"What do you think of this sign?"

It was a board sign lying practically at my feet.

SEE THE WORLD FROM THE SKY. ADULTS $1.00, CHILDREN 50¢. QUALIFIED PILOT.

"My old sign was getting pretty beat up, I thought I'd make a new one.   70
That's what I've been doing with my time today."

The lettering wasn't all that handsome, I thought. I could have done a better one in half an hour.

"I'm not an expert at sign making."

"It's very good," I said.

"I don't need it for publicity, word of mouth is usually enough. I turned away two carloads tonight. I felt like taking it easy. I didn't tell them ladies were dropping in to visit me."

Now I remembered the children and I was scared again, in case one of 75
them had waked up and called me and I wasn't there.

"Do you have to go so soon?"

I remembered some manners. "Thank you for the cigarette."

"Don't forget. You have my word of honor."

I tore off across the fairgrounds, scared I'd see the car heading home from
town. My sense of time was mixed up, I didn't know how long I'd been out of
the house. But it was all right, it wasn't late, the children were asleep. I got in
bed myself and lay thinking what a lucky end to the day, after all, and among
things to be grateful for I could be grateful Loretta Bird hadn't been the one
who caught me.

The yard and borders didn't get trampled, it wasn't as bad as that. All the 80
same it seemed very public, around the house. The sign was on the fairgrounds
gate. People came mostly after supper but a good many in the afternoon, too.
The Bird children all came without fifty cents between them and hung on the
gate. We got used to the excitement of the plane coming in and taking off, it
wasn't excitement anymore. I never went over, after that one time, but would
see him when he came to get his water. I would be out on the steps doing sitting-
down work, like preparing vegetables, if I could.

"Why don't you come over? I'll take you up in my plane."

"I'm saving my money," I said, because I couldn't think of anything else.

"For what? For getting married?"

I shook my head.

"I'll take you up for free if you come sometime when it's slack. I thought 85
you would come, and have another cigarette."

I made a face to hush him, because you never could tell when the children
would be sneaking around the porch, or Mrs. Peebles herself listening in the
house. Sometimes she came out and had a conversation with him. He told her
things he hadn't bothered to tell me. But then I hadn't thought to ask. He told
her he had been in the war, that was where he learned to fly a plane, and now he
couldn't settle down to ordinary life, this was what he liked. She said she
couldn't imagine anybody liking such a thing. Though sometimes, she said,
she was almost bored enough to try anything herself, she wasn't brought up to
living in the country. It's all my husband's idea, she said. This was news to me.

"Maybe you ought to give flying lessons," she said.

"Would you take them?"

She just laughed.

Sunday was a busy flying day in spite of it being preached against from 90
two pulpits. We were all sitting out watching. Joey and Heather were over on
the fence with the Bird kids. Their father had said they could go, after their
mother saying all week they couldn't.

A car came down the road past the parked cars and pulled up right in the
drive. It was Loretta Bird who got out, all importance, and on the driver's side
another woman got out, more sedately. She was wearing sunglasses.

"This is a lady looking for the man that flies the plane," Loretta Bird said.
"I heard her inquire in the hotel coffee shop where I was having a Coke and I
brought her out."

"I'm sorry to bother you," the lady said. "I'm Alice Kelling, Mr. Watters' fiancée."

This Alice Kelling had on a pair of brown and white checked slacks and a yellow top. Her bust looked to me rather low and bumpy. She had a worried face. Her hair had had a permanent, but had grown out, and she wore a yellow band to keep it off her face. Nothing in the least pretty or even young-looking about her. But you could tell from how she talked she was from the city, or educated, or both.

Dr. Peebles stood up and introduced himself and his wife and me and   95
asked her to be seated.

"He's up in the air right now, but you're welcome to sit and wait. He gets his water here and he hasn't been yet. He'll probably take his break about five."

"That is him, then?" said Alice Kelling, wrinkling and straining at the sky.

"He's not in the habit of running out on you, taking a different name?" Dr. Peebles laughed. He was the one, not his wife, to offer iced tea. Then she sent me into the kitchen to fix it. She smiled. She was wearing sunglasses too.

"He never mentioned his fiancée," she said.

I loved fixing iced tea with lots of ice and slices of lemon in tall glasses. I   100
ought to have mentioned before, Dr. Peebles was an abstainer, at least around the house, or I wouldn't have been allowed to take the place. I had to fix a glass for Loretta Bird too, though it galled me, and when I went out she had settled in my lawn chair, leaving me the steps.

"I knew you was a nurse when I first heard you in that coffee shop."

"How would you know a thing like that?"

"I get my hunches about people. Was that how you met him, nursing?"

"Chris? Well yes. Yes, it was."

"Oh, were you overseas?" said Mrs. Peebles.   105

"No, it was before he went overseas. I nursed him when he was stationed at Centralia and had a ruptured appendix. We got engaged and then he went overseas. My, this is refreshing, after a long drive."

"He'll be glad to see you," Dr. Peebles said. "It's a rackety kind of life, isn't it, not staying one place long enough to really make friends."

"Youse've had a long engagement," Loretta Bird said.

Alice Kelling passed that over. "I was going to get a room at the hotel, but when I was offered directions I came on out. Do you think I could phone them?"

"No need," Dr. Peebles said. "You're five miles away from him if you stay at   110
the hotel. Here, you're right across the road. Stay with us. We've got rooms on rooms, look at this big house."

Asking people to stay, just like that, is certainly a country thing, and maybe seemed natural to him now, but not to Mrs. Peebles, from the way she said, oh yes, we have plenty of room. Or to Alice Kelling, who kept protesting, but let herself be worn down. I got the feeling it was a temptation to her, to be that close. I was trying for a look at her ring. Her nails were painted red, her fingers were freckled and wrinkled. It was a tiny stone. Muriel Lowe's cousin had one twice as big.

Chris came to get his water, late in the afternoon just as Dr. Peebles had predicted. He must have recognized the car from a way off. He came smiling.

"Here I am chasing after you to see what you're up to," called Alice Kelling. She got up and went to meet him and they kissed, just touched, in front of us.

"You're going to spend a lot on gas that way," Chris said.

Dr. Peebles invited Chris to stay for supper, since he had already put up 115
the sign that said: NO MORE RIDES TILL 7 P.M. Mrs. Peebles wanted it served in
the yard, in spite of the bugs. One thing strange to anybody from the country
is this eating outside. I had made a potato salad earlier and she had made a jel-
lied salad, that was one thing she could do, so it was just a matter of getting
those out, and some sliced meat and cucumbers and fresh leaf lettuce. Loretta
Bird hung around for some time saying, "Oh, well, I guess I better get home to
those yappers," and, "It's so nice just sitting here, I sure hate to get up," but nobody invited her, I was relieved to see, and finally she had to go.

That night after rides were finished Alice Kelling and Chris went off somewhere in her car. I lay awake till they got back. When I saw the car lights sweep
my ceiling I got up to look down on them through the slats of my blind. I
don't know what I thought I was going to see. Muriel Lowe and I used to sleep
on her front veranda and watch her sister and her sister's boy friend saying
good night. Afterward we couldn't get to sleep, for longing for somebody to
kiss us and rub up against us and we would talk about suppose you were out in
a boat with a boy and he wouldn't bring you in to shore unless you did it, or
what if somebody got you trapped in a barn, you would have to, wouldn't you,
it wouldn't be your fault. Muriel said her two girl cousins used to try with a
toilet paper roll that one of them was a boy. We wouldn't do anything like that;
just lay and wondered.

All that happened was that Chris got out of the car on one side and she
got out on the other and they walked off separately — him toward the fairgrounds and her toward the house. I got back in bed and imagined about me
coming home with him, not like that.

Next morning Alice Kelling got up late and I fixed a grapefruit for her the
way I had learned and Mrs. Peebles sat down with her to visit and have another
cup of coffee. Mrs. Peebles seemed pleased enough now, having company. Alice
Kelling said she guessed she better get used to putting in a day just watching
Chris take off and come down, and Mrs. Peebles said she didn't know if she
should suggest it because Alice Kelling was the one with the car, but the lake
was only twenty-five miles away and what a good day for a picnic.

Alice Kelling took her up on the idea and by eleven o'clock they were in the
car, with Joey and Heather and a sandwich lunch I had made. The only thing
was that Chris hadn't come down, and she wanted to tell him where they were
going.

"Edie'll go over and tell him," Mrs. Peebles said. "There's no problem." 120

Alice Kelling wrinkled her face and agreed.

"Be sure and tell him we'll be back by five!"

I didn't see that he would be concerned about knowing this right away, and
I thought of him eating whatever he ate over there, alone, cooking on his camp
stove, so I got to work and mixed up a crumb cake and baked it, in between the
other work I had to do; then, when it was a bit cooled, wrapped it in a tea towel.
I didn't do anything to myself but take off my apron and comb my hair. I would
like to have put some makeup on, but I was too afraid it would remind him of
the way he first saw me, and that would humiliate me all over again.

He had come and put another sign on the gate: NO RIDES THIS P.M. APOLO-
GIES. I worried that he wasn't feeling well. No sign of him outside and the tent
flap was down. I knocked on the pole.

"Come in," he said, in a voice that would just as soon have said *Stay out.*   125
I lifted the flap.

"Oh, it's you. I'm sorry. I didn't know it was you."

He had been just sitting on the side of the bed, smoking. Why not at least sit and smoke in the fresh air?

"I brought a cake and hope you're not sick," I said.

"Why would I be sick? Oh — that sign. That's all right. I'm just tired of   130
talking to people. I don't mean you. Have a seat." He pinned back the tent flap. "Get some fresh air in here."

I sat on the edge of the bed, there was no place else. It was one of those fold-up cots, really: I remembered and gave him his fiancée's message.

He ate some of the cake. "Good."

"Put the rest away for when you're hungry later."

"I'll tell you a secret. I won't be around here much longer."

"Are you getting married?"   135

"Ha ha. What time did you say they'd be back?"

"Five o'clock."

"Well, by that time, this place will have seen the last of me. A plane can get further than a car." He unwrapped the cake and ate another piece of it, absent-mindedly.

"Now you'll be thirsty."

"There's some water in the pail."   140

"It won't be very cold. I could bring some fresh. I could bring some ice from the refrigerator."

"No," he said. "I don't want you to go. I want a nice long time of saying good-bye to you."

He put the cake away carefully and sat beside me and started those little kisses, so soft, I can't ever let myself think about them, such kindness in his face and lovely kisses, all over my eyelids and neck and ears, all over, then me kissing back as well as I could (I had only kissed a boy on a dare before, and kissed my own arms for practice) and we lay back on the cot and pressed together, just gently, and he did some other things, not bad things or not in a bad way. It was lovely in the tent, that smell of grass and hot tent cloth with the sun beating down on it, and he said, "I wouldn't do you any harm for the world." Once, when he had rolled on top of me and we were sort of rocking together on the cot, he said softly, "Oh, no," and freed himself and jumped up and got the water pail. He splashed some of it on his neck and face, and the little bit left, on me lying there.

"That's to cool us off, miss."

When we said good-bye I wasn't at all sad, because he held my face and   145
said, "I'm going to write you a letter. I'll tell you where I am and maybe you can come and see me. Would you like that? Okay then. You wait." I was really glad I think to get away from him, it was like he was piling presents on me I couldn't get the pleasure of till I considered them alone.

No consternation at first about the plane being gone. They thought he had taken somebody up, and I didn't enlighten them. Dr. Peebles had phoned he had to go to the country, so there was just us having supper, and then Loretta Bird thrusting her head in the door and saying, "I see he's took off."

"What?" said Alice Kelling, and pushed back her chair.

"The kids come and told me this afternoon he was taking down his tent. Did he think he'd run through all the business there was round here? He didn't take off without letting you know, did he?"

"He'll send me word," Alice Kelling said. "He'll probably phone tonight. He's terribly restless, since the war."

"Edie, he didn't mention to you, did he?" Mrs. Peebles said. "When you took over the message?" 150

"Yes," I said. So far so true.

"Well why didn't you say?" All of them were looking at me. "Did he say where he was going?"

"He said he might try Bayfield," I said. What made me tell such a lie? I didn't intend it.

"Bayfield, how far is that?" said Alice Kelling.

Mrs. Peebles said. "Thirty, thirty-five miles." 155

"That's not far. Oh, well, that's really not far at all. It's on the lake, isn't it?"

You'd think I'd be ashamed of myself, setting her on the wrong track. I did it to give him more time, whatever time he needed. I lied for him, and also, I have to admit, for me. Women should stick together and not do things like that. I see that now, but didn't then. I never thought of myself as being in any way like her, or coming to the same troubles, ever.

She hadn't taken her eyes off me. I thought she suspected my lie.

"When did he mention this to you?"

"Earlier." 160

"When you were over at the plane?"

"Yes."

"You must've stayed and had a chat." She smiled at me, not a nice smile. "You must've stayed and had a little visit with him."

"I took a cake," I said, thinking that telling some truth would spare me telling the rest.

"We didn't have a cake," said Mrs. Peebles rather sharply. 165

"I baked one."

Alice Kelling said, "That was very friendly of you."

"Did you get permission," said Loretta Bird. "You never know what these girls'll do next," she said. "It's not they mean harm so much, as they're ignorant."

"The cake is neither here nor there," Mrs. Peebles broke in. "Edie, I wasn't aware you knew Chris that well."

I didn't know what to say. 170

"I'm not surprised," Alice Kelling said in a high voice. "I knew by the look of her as soon as I saw her. We get them at the hospital all the time." She looked hard at me with her stretched smile. "Having their babies. We have to put them in a special ward because of their diseases. Little country tramps. Fourteen and fifteen years old. You should see the babies they have, too."

"There was a bad woman here in town had a baby that pus was running out of its eyes," Loretta Bird put in.

"Wait a minute," said Mrs. Peebles. "What is this talk? Edie. What about you and Mr. Watters? Were you intimate with him?"

"Yes," I said. I was thinking of us lying on the cot and kissing, wasn't that intimate? And I would never deny it.

They were all one minute quiet, even Loretta Bird.   175

"Well," said Mrs. Peebles. "I am surprised. I think I need a cigarette. This is the first of any such tendencies I've seen in her," she said, speaking to Alice Kelling, but Alice Kelling was looking at me.

"Loose little bitch." Tears ran down her face. "Loose little bitch, aren't you? I knew as soon as I saw you. Men despise girls like you. He just made use of you and went off, you know that, don't you? Girls like you are just nothing, they're just public conveniences, just filthy little rags!"

"Oh, now," said Mrs. Peebles.

"Filthy," Alice Kelling sobbed. "Filthy little rags!"

"Don't get yourself upset," Loretta Bird said. She was swollen up with   180
pleasure at being in on this scene. "Men are all the same."

"Edie, I'm very surprised," Mrs. Peebles said. "I thought your parents were so strict. You don't want to have a baby, do you?"

I'm still ashamed of what happened next. I lost control, just like a six-year-old, I started howling. "You don't get a baby from just doing that!"

"You see. Some of them are that ignorant," Loretta Bird said.

But Mrs. Peebles jumped up and caught my arms and shook me.

"Calm down. Don't get hysterical. Calm down. Stop crying. Listen to me.   185
Listen. I'm wondering, if you know what being intimate means. Now tell me. What did you think it meant?"

"Kissing," I howled.

She let go. "Oh, Edie. Stop it. Don't be silly. It's all right. It's all a misunderstanding. Being intimate means a lot more than that. Oh, I *wondered*."

"She's trying to cover up, now," said Alice Kelling. "Yes. She's not so stupid. She sees she got herself in trouble."

"I believe her," Mrs. Peebles said. "This is an awful scene."

"Well there is one way to find out," said Alice Kelling, getting up. "After all,   190
I am a nurse."

Mrs. Peebles drew a breath and said, "No. No. Go to your room, Edie. And stop that noise. This is too disgusting."

I heard the car start in a little while. I tried to stop crying, pulling back each wave as it started over me. Finally I succeeded, and lay heaving on the bed.

Mrs. Peebles came and stood in the doorway.

"She's gone," she said. "That Bird woman too. Of course, you know you should never have gone near that man and that is the cause of all this trouble. I have a headache. As soon as you can, go and wash your face in cold water and get at the dishes and we will not say any more about this."

Nor we didn't. I didn't figure out till years later the extent of what I had   195
been saved from. Mrs. Peebles was not very friendly to me afterward, but she was fair. Not very friendly is the wrong way of describing what she was. She had never been very friendly. It was just that now she had to see me all the time and it got on her nerves, a little.

As for me, I put it all out of my mind like a bad dream and concentrated on waiting for my letter. The mail came every day except Sunday, between one-thirty and two in the afternoon, a good time for me because Mrs. Peebles was always having her nap. I would get the kitchen all cleaned and then go up to the mailbox and sit in the grass, waiting. I was perfectly happy, waiting,

I forgot all about Alice Kelling and her misery and awful talk and Mrs. Peebles and her chilliness and the embarrassment of whether she had told Dr. Peebles and the face of Loretta Bird, getting her fill of other people's troubles. I was always smiling when the mailman got there, and continued smiling even after he gave me the mail and I saw today wasn't the day. The mailman was a Carmichael. I knew by his face because there are a lot of Carmichaels living out by us and so many of them have a sort of sticking-out top lip. So I asked his name (he was a young man, shy, but good-humored, anybody could ask him anything) and then I said, "I knew by your face!" He was pleased by that and always glad to see me and got a little less shy. "You've got the smile I've been waiting on all day!" he used to holler out the car window.

It never crossed my mind for a long time a letter might not come. I believed in it coming just like I believed the sun would rise in the morning. I just put off my hope from day to day, and there was the goldenrod out around the mailbox and the children gone back to school, and the leaves turning, and I was wearing a sweater when I went to wait. One day walking back with the hydro bill stuck in my hand, that was all, looking across at the fairgrounds with the full-blown milkweed and dark teasels, so much like fall, it just struck me: *No letter was ever going to come.* It was an impossible idea to get used to. No, not impossible. If I thought about Chris's face when he said he was going to write to me, it was impossible, but if I forgot that and thought about the actual tin mailbox, empty, it was plain and true. I kept on going to meet the mail, but my heart was heavy now like a lump of lead. I only smiled because I thought of the mailman counting on it, and he didn't have an easy life, with the winter driving ahead.

Till it came to me one day there were women doing this with their lives, all over. There were women just waiting and waiting by mailboxes for one letter or another. I imagined me making this journey day after day and year after year, and my hair starting to go gray, and I thought, I was never made to go on like that. So I stopped meeting the mail. If there were women all through life waiting, and women busy and not waiting, I knew which I had to be. Even though there might be things the second kind of women have to pass up and never know about, it still is better.

I was surprised when the mailman phoned the Peebleses' place in the evening and asked for me. He said he missed me. He asked if I would like to go to Goderich, where some well-known movie was on, I forget now what. So I said yes, and I went out with him for two years and he asked me to marry him, and we were engaged a year more while I got my things together, and then we did marry. He always tells the children the story of how I went after him by sitting by the mailbox every day, and naturally I laugh and let him, because I like for people to think what pleases them and makes them happy.

CONSIDERATIONS FOR CRITICAL THINKING AND WRITING

1. FIRST RESPONSE. Are you surprised by the husband Edie ends up with? Why do you think Munro centers the story around Edie and the man with the plane?

2. Describe the point of view used in the story. When does Edie sound more like a fifteen-year-old than like a married woman?

3. How does the married Edie differ from the girl she was at age fifteen? What attitudes and values reveal these differences? What is the effect of Munro's use of these two voices?

4. How does the story's point of view help to establish the mood of the setting?

5. How would this story be changed if it were told from Mrs. Peebles's point of view?

6. Explain why the use of an editorial omniscient point of view in this story would be inappropriate.

7. How do the women — Mrs. Peebles, Loretta Bird, and Alice Kelling — help to reveal Edie's character? How does Edie's perspective on life differ from theirs?

8. How do Chris Watters and Carmichael compare as potential husbands? What attracts Edie to them?

9. What does Edie learn about men in the story? Consider whether she made the right choice in marrying Carmichael.

10. Reread the story's next-to-last paragraph. What does Edie learn about herself here?

11. Discuss the appropriateness of the story's title. Do you consider it misleading or accurate? Invent an alternative title that captures the central meaning of the story for you.

CONNECTIONS TO OTHER SELECTIONS

1. In an essay discuss the use of irony in "How I Met My Husband" and "An Ounce of Cure" (p. 434). In your discussion consider important similarities and differences between the narrators.

2. Write an essay that compares the Peebles family in "How I Met My Husband" with the Berryman family in "An Ounce of Cure" (p. 434). How does Munro's characterization of each family contribute to each story's theme?

Prue   1983

Prue used to live with Gordon. This was after Gordon had left his wife and before he went back to her — a year and four months in all. Some time later, he and his wife were divorced. After that came a period of indecision, of living together off and on; then the wife went away to New Zealand, most likely for good.

Prue did not go back to Vancouver Island, where Gordon had met her when she was working as a dining-room hostess in a resort hotel. She got a job in Toronto, working in a plant shop. She had many friends in Toronto by that time, most of them Gordon's friends and his wife's friends. They liked Prue and were ready to feel sorry for her, but she laughed them out of it. She is very likable. She has what eastern Canadians call an English accent, though she was born in Canada — in Duncan, on Vancouver Island. This accent helps her to say the most cynical things in a winning and lighthearted way. She presents her life in anecdotes, and though it is the point of most of her anecdotes that hopes are dashed, dreams ridiculed, things never turn out as expected, everything is altered in a bizarre way and there is no explanation ever, people always feel cheered up after listening to her; they say of her that it is a relief to meet somebody who doesn't take herself too seriously, who is so unintense, and civilized, and never makes any real demands or complaints.

The only thing she complains about readily is her name. Prue is a schoolgirl, she says, and Prudence is an old virgin; the parents who gave her that name must have been too shortsighted even to take account of puberty. What if she had grown a great bosom, she says, or developed a sultry look? Or was the name itself a guarantee that she wouldn't? In her late forties now, slight and fair, attending to customers with a dutiful vivacity, giving pleasure to dinner guests, she might not be far from what those parents had in mind: bright and thoughtful, a cheerful spectator. It is hard to grant her maturity, maternity, real troubles.

Her grownup children, the products of an early Vancouver Island marriage she calls a cosmic disaster, come to see her, and instead of wanting money, like other people's children, they bring presents, try to do her accounts, arrange to have her house insulated. She is delighted with their presents, listens to their advice, and, like a flighty daughter, neglects to answer their letters.

Her children hope she is not staying on in Toronto because of Gordon. Everybody hopes that. She would laugh at the idea. She gives parties and goes to 5 parties; she goes out sometimes with other men. Her attitude toward sex is very comforting to those of her friends who get into terrible states of passion and jealousy, and feel cut loose from their moorings. She seems to regard sex as a wholesome, slightly silly indulgence, like dancing and nice dinners — something that shouldn't interfere with people's being kind and cheerful to each other.

Now that his wife is gone for good, Gordon comes to see Prue occasionally, and sometimes asks her out for dinner. They may not go to a restaurant; they may go to his house. Gordon is a good cook. When Prue or his wife lived with him he couldn't cook at all, but as soon as he put his mind to it he became — he says truthfully — better than either of them.

Recently he and Prue were having dinner at his house. He had made Chicken Kiev, and crème brûlée for dessert. Like most new, serious cooks, he talked about food.

Gordon is rich, by Prue's — and most people's — standards. He is a neurologist. His house is new, built on a hillside north of the city, where there used to be picturesque, unprofitable farms. Now there are one-of-a-kind, architect-designed, very expensive houses on half-acre lots. Prue, describing Gordon's house, will say, "Do you know there are four bathrooms? So that if four people want to have baths at the same time there's no problem. It seems a bit much, but it's very nice, really, and you'd never have to go through the hall."

Gordon's house has a raised dining area — a sort of platform, surrounded by a conversation pit, a music pit, and a bank of heavy greenery under sloping glass. You can't see the entrance area from the dining area, but there are no intervening walls, so that from one area you can hear something of what is going on in the other.

During dinner the doorbell rang. Gordon excused himself and went down the steps. Prue heard a female voice. The person it belonged to was still outside, 10 so she could not hear the words. She heard Gordon's voice, pitched low, cautioning. The door didn't close — it seemed the person had not been invited in—but the voices went on, muted and angry. Suddenly there was a cry from Gordon, and he appeared halfway up the steps, waving his arms.

"The crème brûlée," he said. "Could you?" He ran back down as Prue got up and went into the kitchen to save the dessert. When she returned he was climbing the stairs more slowly, looking both agitated and tired.

"A friend," he said gloomily. "Was it all right?"

Prue realized he was speaking of the crème brûlée, and she said yes, it was perfect, she had got it just in time. He thanked her but did not cheer up. It seemed it was not the dessert he was troubled over but whatever had happened at the door. To take his mind off it, Prue started asking him professional questions about the plants.

"I don't know a thing about them," he said. "You know that."

"I thought you might have picked it up. Like the cooking." 15

"She takes care of them."

"Mrs. Carr?" said Prue, naming his housekeeper.

"Who did you think?"

Prue blushed. She hated to be thought suspicious.

"The problem is that I think I would like to marry you," said Gordon, with 20 no noticeable lightening of his spirits. Gordon is a large man, with heavy features. He likes to wear thick clothing, bulky sweaters. His blue eyes are often bloodshot, and their expression indicates that there is a helpless, baffled soul squirming around inside this doughty fortress.

"What a problem," said Prue lightly, though she knew Gordon well enough to know that it was.

The doorbell rang again, rang twice, three times, before Gordon could get to it. This time there was a crash, as of something flung and landing hard. The door slammed and Gordon was immediately back in view. He staggered on the steps and held his hand to his head, meanwhile making a gesture with the other hand to signify that nothing serious had happened, Prue was to sit down.

"Bloody overnight bag," he said. "She threw it at me."

"Did it hit you?"

"Glancing." 25

"It made a hard sound for an overnight bag. Were there rocks in it?"

"Probably cans. Her deodorant and so forth."

"Oh."

Prue watched him pour himself a drink. "I'd like some coffee, if I might," she said. She went to the kitchen to put the water on, and Gordon followed her.

"I think I'm in love with this person," he said. 30

"Who is she?"

"You don't know her. She's quite young."

"Oh."

"But I do think I want to marry you, in a few years' time."

"After you get over being in love?" 35

"Yes."

"Well. I guess nobody knows what can happen in a few years' time."

When Prue tells about this, she says, "I think he was afraid I was going to laugh. He doesn't know why people laugh or throw their overnight bags at him, but he's noticed they do. He's such a proper person, really. The lovely dinner. Then she comes and throws her overnight bag. And it's quite reasonable to think of marrying me in a few years' time, when he gets over being in love. I think he first thought of telling me to sort of put my mind at rest."

She doesn't mention that the next morning she picked up one of Gordon's cufflinks from his dresser. The cufflinks are made of amber and he bought them in Russia, on the holiday he and wife took when they got back together again. They look like squares of candy, golden, translucent, and this one warms quickly in her hand. She drops it into the pocket of her jacket. Taking one is not a real theft. It could be a reminder, an intimate prank, a piece of nonsense.

She is alone in Gordon's house; he has gone off early, as he always does.   40
The housekeeper does not come till nine. Prue doesn't have to be at the shop until ten; she could make herself breakfast, stay and have coffee with the housekeeper, who is her friend from olden times. But once she has the cufflink in her pocket she doesn't linger. The house seems too bleak a place to spend an extra moment in. It was Prue, actually, who helped choose the building lot. But she's not responsible for approving the plans — the wife was back by that time.

When she gets home she puts the cufflink in an old tobacco tin. The children bought this tobacco tin in a junk shop years ago, and gave it to her for a present. She used to smoke, in those days, and the children were worried about her, so they gave her this tin full of toffees, jelly beans, and gumdrops, with a note saying, "Please get fat instead." That was for her birthday. Now the tin has in it several things besides the cufflink — all small things, not of great value but not worthless, either. A little enameled dish, a sterling-silver spoon for salt, a crystal fish. These are not sentimental keepsakes. She never looks at them, and often forgets what she has there. They are not booty, they don't have ritualistic significance. She does not take something every time she goes to Gordon's house, or every time she stays over, or to mark what she might call memorable visits. She doesn't do it in a daze and she doesn't seem to be under a compulsion. She just takes something, every now and then, and puts it away in the dark of the old tobacco tin, and more or less forgets about it.

CONSIDERATIONS FOR CRITICAL THINKING AND WRITING

1. FIRST RESPONSE. Do you think Gordon and Prue will get married? Explain your answer.
2. Characterize Gordon. Why do you think Prue is attracted to him?
3. Do you think the description of Prue in the second paragraph adequately characterizes her? Explain why or why not.
4. What does Prue's response to Gordon's two encounters with the woman at the door reveal about Prue?
5. Reread paragraph 3 and discuss the appropriateness of Prue's name.
6. Discuss what you think is the conflict of this story. How do Gordon and Prue handle conflict?
7. Describe what you take to be the story's theme.
8. Why do you think Prue takes Gordon's cufflink? Why do you suppose she takes only one?
9. Consider the symbolic significance of the "old tobacco tin" by carefully analyzing the final paragraph of the story.

CONNECTIONS TO OTHER SELECTIONS

1. In an essay compare the themes of "Prue" and Katherine Mansfield's "Miss Brill" (p. 258).

2. Write an essay that compares the endings of "Prue" and Collette's "The Hand" (p. 220). What significant differences and similarities do you see between the central relationships portrayed in each story?

Miles City, Montana   *1985*

My father came across the field carrying the body of the boy who had been drowned. There were several men together, returning from the search, but he was the one carrying the body. The men were muddy and exhausted, and walked with their heads down, as if they were ashamed. Even the dogs were dispirited, dripping from the cold river. When they all set out, hours before, the dogs were nervy and yelping, the men tense and determined, and there was a constrained, unspeakable excitement about the whole scene. It was understood that they might find something horrible.

The boy's name was Steve Gauley. He was eight years old. His hair and clothes were mud-colored now and carried some bits of dead leaves, twigs, and grass. He was like a heap of refuse that had been left out all winter. His face was turned in to my father's chest, but I could see a nostril, an ear, plugged up with greenish mud.

I don't think so. I don't think I really saw all this. Perhaps I saw my father carrying him, and the other men following along, and the dogs, but I would not have been allowed to get close enough to see something like mud in his nostril. I must have heard someone talking about that and imagined that I saw it. I see his face unaltered except for the mud — Steve Gauley's familiar, sharp-honed, sneaky-looking face — and it wouldn't have been like that; it would have been bloated and changed and perhaps muddied all over after so many hours in the water.

To have to bring back such news, such evidence, to a waiting family, particularly a mother, would have made searchers move heavily, but what was happening here was worse. It seemed a worse shame (to hear people talk) that there was no mother, no woman at all — no grandmother or aunt, or even a sister — to receive Steve Gauley and give him his due of grief. His father was a hired man, a drinker but not a drunk, an erratic man without being entertaining, not friendly but not exactly a troublemaker. His fatherhood seemed accidental, and the fact that the child had been left with him when the mother went away, and that they continued living together, seemed accidental. They lived in a steep-roofed, gray-shingled hillbilly sort of house that was just a bit better than a shack — the father fixed the roof and put supports under the porch, just enough and just in time — and their life was held together in a similar manner; that is, just well enough to keep the Children's Aid at bay. They didn't eat meals together or cook for each other, but there was food. Sometimes the father would give Steve money to buy food at the store, and Steve was seen to buy quite sensible things, such as pancake mix and macaroni dinner.

I had known Steve Gauley fairly well. I had not liked him more often than 5
I had liked him. He was two years older than I was. He would hang around
our place on Saturdays, scornful of whatever I was doing but unable to leave
me alone. I couldn't be on the swing without him wanting to try it, and if I
wouldn't give it up he came and pushed me so that I went crooked. He teased
the dog. He got me into trouble — deliberately and maliciously, it seemed to me
afterward — by daring me to do things I wouldn't have thought of on my own:
digging up the potatoes to see how big they were when they were still only the
size of marbles, and pushing over the stacked firewood to make a pile we could
jump off. At school, we never spoke to each other. He was solitary, though not
tormented. But on Saturday mornings, when I saw his thin, self-possessed figure sliding through the cedar hedge, I knew I was in for something and he
would decide what. Sometimes it was all right. We pretended we were cowboys
who had to tame wild horses. We played in the pasture by the river, not far
from the place where Steve drowned. We were horses and riders both, screaming and neighing and bucking and waving whips of tree branches beside a
little nameless river that flows into the Saugeen in southern Ontario.

The funeral was held in our house. There was not enough room at Steve's
father's place for the large crowd that was expected because of the circumstances. I have a memory of the crowded room but no picture of Steve in his
coffin, or of the minister, or of wreaths of flowers. I remember that I was holding one flower, a white narcissus, which must have come from a pot somebody
forced indoors, because it was too early for even the forsythia bush or the trilli-
ums and marsh marigolds in the woods. I stood in a row of children, each of
us holding a narcissus. We sang a children's hymn, which somebody played
on our piano: "When He Cometh, When He Cometh, to Make Up His Jewels."
I was wearing white ribbed stockings, which were disgustingly itchy, and
wrinkled at the knees and ankles. The feeling of these stockings on my legs is
mixed up with another feeling in my memory. It is hard to describe. It had to
do with my parents. Adults in general but my parents in particular. My father,
who had carried Steve's body from the river, and my mother, who must have
done most of the arranging of this funeral. My father in his dark-blue suit and
my mother in her brown velvet dress with the creamy satin collar. They stood
side by side opening and closing their mouths for the hymn, and I stood removed from them, in the row of children, watching. I felt a furious and sickening disgust. Children sometimes have an access of disgust concerning adults.
The size, the lumpy shapes, the bloated power. The breath, the coarseness, the
hairiness, the horrid secretions. But this was more. And the accompanying
anger had nothing sharp and self-respecting about it. There was no release, as
when I would finally bend and pick up a stone and throw it at Steve Gauley. It
could not be understood or expressed, though it died down after a while into a
heaviness, then just a taste, an occasional taste — a thin, familiar misgiving.

Twenty years or so later, in 1961, my husband, Andrew, and I got a brand-new
car, our first — that is, our first brand-new. It was a Morris Oxford, oyster-colored
(the dealer had some fancier name for the color) — a big small car, with plenty of
room for us and our two children. Cynthia was six and Meg three and a half.

Andrew took a picture of me standing beside the car. I was wearing white
pants, a black turtleneck, and sunglasses. I lounged against the car door, cant-
ing my hips to make myself look slim.

"Wonderful," Andrew said. "Great. You look like Jackie Kennedy." All over this continent probably, dark-haired, reasonably slender young women were told, when they were stylishly dressed or getting their pictures taken, that they looked like Jackie Kennedy.

Andrew took a lot of pictures of me, and of the children, our house, our garden, our excursions and possessions. He got copies made, labeled them carefully, and sent them back to his mother and his aunt and uncle in Ontario. He got copies for me to send to my father, who also lived in Ontario, and I did so, but less regularly than he sent his. When he saw pictures he thought I had already sent lying around the house, Andrew was perplexed and annoyed. He liked to have this record go forth.

That summer, we were presenting ourselves, not pictures. We were driving back from Vancouver, where we lived, to Ontario, which we still called "home," in our new car. Five days to get there, ten days there, five days back. For the first time, Andrew had three weeks' holiday. He worked in the legal department at B. C. Hydro.

On a Saturday morning, we loaded suitcases, two thermos bottles — one filled with coffee and one with lemonade — some fruit and sandwiches, picture books and coloring books, crayons, drawing pads, insect repellent, sweaters (in case it got cold in the mountains), and our two children into the car. Andrew locked the house, and Cynthia said ceremoniously, "Good-bye, house."

Meg said, "Goodbye, house." Then she said, "Where will we live now?"

"It's not goodbye forever," said Cynthia. "We're coming back. Mother! Meg thought we weren't ever coming back!"

"I did not," said Meg, kicking the back of my seat.

Andrew and I put on our sunglasses, and we drove away, over the Lions Gate Bridge and through the main part of Vancouver. We shed our house, the neighborhood, the city, and — at the crossing point between Washington and British Columbia — our country. We were driving east across the United States, taking the most northerly route, and would cross into Canada again at Sarnia, Ontario. I don't know if we chose this route because the Trans-Canada Highway was not completely finished at the time or if we just wanted the feeling of driving through a foreign, a very slightly foreign, country — that extra bit of interest and adventure.

We were both in high spirits. Andrew congratulated the car several times. He said he felt so much better driving it than our old car, a 1951 Austin that slowed down dismally on the hills and had a fussy-old-lady image. So Andrew said now.

"What kind of image does this one have?" said Cynthia. She listened to us carefully and liked to try out new words such as *image*. Usually she got them right.

"Lively," I said. "Slightly sporty. It's not show-off."

"It's sensible, but it has class," Andrew said. "Like my image."

Cynthia thought that over and said with a cautious pride, "That means like you think you want to be, Daddy?"

As for me, I was happy because of the shedding. I loved taking off. In my own house, I seemed to be often looking for a place to hide — sometimes from the children but more often from the jobs to be done and the phone ringing and the sociability of the neighborhood. I wanted to hide so that I could get busy at my real work, which was a sort of wooing of distant parts of myself.

I lived in a state of siege, always losing just what I wanted to hold on to. But on trips there was no difficulty. I could be talking to Andrew, talking to the children and looking at whatever they wanted me to look at — a pig on a sign, a pony in a field, a Volkswagen on a revolving stand — and pouring lemonade into plastic cups, and all the time those bits and pieces would be flying together inside me. The essential composition would be achieved. This made me hopeful and lighthearted. It was being a watcher that did it. A watcher, not a keeper.

We turned east at Everett and climbed into the Cascades. I showed Cynthia our route on the map. First I showed her the map of the whole United States, which showed also the bottom part of Canada. Then I turned to the separate maps of each of the states we were going to pass through. Washington, Idaho, Montana, North Dakota, Minnesota, Wisconsin. I showed her the dotted line across Lake Michigan, which was the route of the ferry we would take. Then we would drive across Michigan to the bridge that linked the United States and Canada at Sarnia, Ontario. Home.

Meg wanted to see too.

"You won't understand," said Cynthia. But she took the road atlas into 25 the back seat.

"Sit back," she said to Meg. "Sit still. I'll show you."

I could hear her tracing the route for Meg, very accurately, just as I had done it for her. She looked up all the states' maps, knowing how to find them in alphabetical order.

"You know what that line is?" she said. "It's the road. That line is the road we're driving on. We're going right along this line."

Meg did not say anything.

"Mother, show me where we are right this minute," said Cynthia. 30

I took the atlas and pointed out the road through the mountains, and she took it back and showed it to Meg. "See where the road is all wiggly?" she said. "It's wiggly because there are so many turns in it. The wiggles are the turns." She flipped some pages and waited a moment. "Now," she said, "show me where we are." Then she called to me, "Mother, she understands! She pointed to it! Meg understands maps!"

It seems to me now that we invented characters for our children. We had them firmly set to play their parts. Cynthia was bright and diligent, sensitive, courteous, watchful. Sometimes we teased her for being too conscientious, too eager to be what we in fact depended on her to be. Any reproach or failure, any rebuff, went terribly deep with her. She was fair-haired, fair-skinned, easily showing the effects of the sun, raw winds, pride, or humiliation. Meg was more solidly built, more reticent — not rebellious but stubborn sometimes, mysterious. Her silences seemed to us to show her strength of character, and her negatives were taken as signs of an imperturbable independence. Her hair was brown, and we cut it in straight bangs. Her eyes were a light hazel, clear and dazzling.

We were entirely pleased with these characters, enjoying their contradictions as well as the confirmations of them. We disliked the heavy, the uninventive, approach to being parents. I had a dread of turning into a certain kind of mother — the kind whose body sagged, who moved in a woolly-smelling, milky-smelling fog, solemn with trivial burdens. I believed that all the attention these mothers paid, their need to be burdened, was the cause of colic, bed-wetting, asthma. I favored another approach — the mock desperation, the inflated irony of the professional mothers who wrote for magazines. In those magazine pieces, the children were splendidly self-willed, hard-edged, perverse, indomitable. So were the mothers, through their wit, indomitable. The real-life mothers I warmed to were the sort who would phone up and say, "Is my embryo Hitler by any chance over at your house?" They cackled clear above the milky fog.

We saw a dead deer strapped across the front of a pickup truck.

"Somebody shot it," Cynthia said. "Hunters shoot the deer."   35

"It's not hunting season yet," Andrew said. "They may have hit it on the road. See the sign for deer crossing?"

"I would cry if we hit one," Cynthia said sternly.

I had made peanut-butter-and-marmalade sandwiches for the children and salmon-and-mayonnaise for us. But I had not put any lettuce in, and Andrew was disappointed.

"I didn't have any," I said.

"Couldn't you have got some?"   40

"I'd have had to buy a whole head of lettuce just to get enough for sandwiches, and I decided it wasn't worth it."

This was a lie. I had forgotten.

"They're a lot better with lettuce."

"I didn't think it made that much difference." After a silence, I said, "Don't be mad."

"I'm not mad. I like lettuce on sandwiches."   45

"I just didn't think it mattered that much."

"How would it be if I didn't bother to fill up the gas tank?"

"That's not the same thing."

"Sing a song," said Cynthia. She started to sing:

> *"Five little ducks went out one day,*
> *Over the hills and far away.*
> *One little duck went*
> *'Quack-quack-quack.'*
> *Four little ducks came swimming back."*

Andrew squeezed my hand and said, "Let's not fight."

"You're right. I should have got lettuce."   50

"It doesn't matter that much."

I wished that I could get my feelings about Andrew to come together into a serviceable and dependable feeling. I had even tried writing two lists, one of things I liked about him, one of things I disliked — in the cauldron of intimate life, things I loved and things I hated — as if I hoped by this to prove something, to come to a conclusion one way or the other. But I gave it up when I saw that all it proved was what I already knew — that I had violent contradictions. Sometimes the very sound of his footsteps seemed to me tyrannical, the set of his mouth smug and mean, his hard, straight body a barrier interposed — quite consciously, even dutifully, and with a nasty pleasure in its masculine authority — between me and whatever joy or lightness I could get in life. Then, with not much warning, he became my good friend and most essential companion. I felt the sweetness of his light bones and serious ideas, the vulnerability of his love, which I imagined to be much purer and more straightforward than my own. I could be greatly moved by an inflexibility, a harsh propriety, that at other times I scorned. I would think how humble he was, really, taking on such a ready-made role of husband, father, breadwinner, and how I myself in comparison was really a secret monster of egotism. Not so secret, either — not from him.

At the bottom of our fights, we served up what we thought were the ugliest truths. "I know there is something basically selfish and basically untrustworthy about you," Andrew once said. "I've always known it. I also know that that is why I fell in love with you."

"Yes," I said, feeling sorrowful but complacent.

"I know that I'd be better off without you." 55

"Yes. You would."

"You'd be happier without me."

"Yes."

And finally — finally — wracked and purged, we clasped hands and laughed, laughed at those two benighted people, ourselves. Their grudges, their grievances, their self-justification. We leapfrogged over them. We declared them liars. We would have wine with dinner, or decide to give a party.

I haven't seen Andrew for years, don't know if he is still thin, has gone 60 completely gray, insists on lettuce, tells the truth, or is hearty and disappointed.

We stayed the night in Wenatchee, Washington, where it hadn't rained for weeks. We ate dinner in a restaurant built about a tree — not a sapling in a tub but a tall, sturdy cottonwood. In the early-morning light, we climbed out of the irrigated valley, up dry, rocky, very steep hillsides that would seem to lead to more hills, and there on the top was a wide plateau, cut by the great Spokane and Columbia rivers. Grainland and grassland, mile after mile. There were straight roads here, and little farming towns with grain elevators. In fact, there was a sign announcing that this county we were going through, Douglas County, had the second-highest wheat yield of any county in the United States. The towns had planted shade trees. At least, I thought they had been planted, because there were no such big trees in the countryside.

All this was marvelously welcome to me. "Why do I love it so much?" I said to Andrew. "Is it because it isn't scenery?"

"It reminds you of home," said Andrew. "A bout of severe nostalgia." But he said this kindly.

When we said "home" and meant Ontario, we had very different places in mind. My home was a turkey farm, where my father lived as a widower, and though it was the same house my mother had lived in, had papered, painted, cleaned, furnished, it showed the effects now of neglect and of some wild sociability. A life went on in it that my mother could not have predicted or condoned. There were parties for the turkey crew, the gutters and pluckers, and sometimes one or two of the young men would be living there temporarily, inviting their own friends and having their own impromptu parties. This life, I thought, was better for my father than being lonely, and I did not disapprove, had certainly no right to disapprove. Andrew did not like to go there, naturally enough, because he was not the sort who could sit around the kitchen table with the turkey crew, telling jokes. They were intimidated by him and contemptuous of him, and it seemed to me that my father, when they were around, had to be on their side. And it wasn't only Andrew who had trouble. I could manage those jokes, but it was an effort.

I wished for the days when I was little, before we had the turkeys. We had 65 cows, and sold the milk to the cheese factory. A turkey farm is nothing like as pretty as a dairy farm or a sheep farm. You can see that the turkeys are on a straight path to becoming frozen carcasses and table meat. They don't have the pretense of a life of their own, a browsing idyll, that cattle have, or pigs in the dappled orchard. Turkey barns are long, efficient buildings — tin sheds. No beams or hay or warm stables. Even the smell of guano seems thinner and more offensive than the usual smell of stable manure. No hints there of hay coils and rail fences and songbirds and the flowering hawthorn. The turkeys were all let out into one long field, which they picked clean. They didn't look like great birds there but like fluttering laundry.

Once, shortly after my mother died, and after I was married — in fact, I was packing to join Andrew in Vancouver — I was at home alone for a couple of days with my father. There was a freakishly heavy rain all night. In the early light, we saw that the turkey field was flooded. At least, the low-lying parts of it were flooded — it was like a lake with many islands. The turkeys were huddled on these islands. Turkeys are very stupid. (My father would say, "You know a chicken? You know how stupid a chicken is? Well, a chicken is an Einstein compared with a turkey.") But they had managed to crowd to higher ground and avoid drowning. Now they might push each other off, suffocate each other, get cold and die. We couldn't wait for the water to go down. We went out in an old rowboat we had. I rowed and my father pulled the heavy, wet turkeys into the boat and we took them to the barn. It was still raining a little. The job was difficult and absurd and very uncomfortable. We were laughing. I was happy to be working with my father. I felt close to all hard, repetitive, appalling work, in which the body is finally worn out, the mind sunk (though sometimes the spirit can stay marvelously light), and I was homesick in advance for this life and this place. I thought that if Andrew could see me there in the rain, red-handed, muddy, trying to hold on to turkey legs and row the boat at the same time, he would only want to get me out of there and make me forget about it. This raw life angered him. My attachment to it angered him. I thought that I shouldn't have married him. But who else? One of the turkey crew?

And I didn't want to stay there. I might feel bad about leaving, but I would feel worse if somebody made me stay.

Andrew's mother lived in Toronto, in an apartment building looking out on Muir Park. When Andrew and his sister were both at home, his mother slept in the living room. Her husband, a doctor, had died when the children were still too young to go to school. She took a secretarial course and sold her house at Depression prices, moved to this apartment, managed to raise her children, with some help from relatives — her sister Caroline, her brother-in-law Roger. Andrew and his sister went to private schools and to camp in the summer.

"I suppose that was courtesy of the Fresh Air Fund?" I said once, scornful of his claim that he had been poor. To my mind, Andrew's urban life had been sheltered and fussy. His mother came home with a headache from working all day in the noise, the harsh light of a department-store office, but it did not occur to me that hers was a hard or admirable life. I don't think she herself believed that she was admirable — only unlucky. She worried about her work in the office, her clothes, her cooking, her children. She worried most of all about what Roger and Caroline would think.

Caroline and Roger lived on the east side of the park, in a handsome stone house. Roger was a tall man with a bald, freckled head, a fat, firm stomach. Some operation on his throat had deprived him of his voice—he spoke in a rough whisper. But everybody paid attention. At dinner once in the stone house—where all the dining-room furniture was enormous, darkly glowing, palatial—I asked him a question. I think it had to do with Whittaker Chambers, whose story was then appearing in the *Saturday Evening Post.* The question was mild in tone, but he guessed its subversive intent and took to calling me Mrs. Gromyko, referring to what he alleged to be my "sympathies." Perhaps he really craved an adversary, and could not find one. At that dinner, I saw Andrew's hand tremble as he lit his mother's cigarette. His Uncle Roger had paid for Andrew's education, and was on the board of directors of several companies.

"He is just an opinionated old man," Andrew said to me later. "What is the point of arguing with him?"

Before we left Vancouver, Andrew's mother had written, *Roger seems quite intrigued by the idea of your buying a small car!* Her exclamation mark showed apprehension. At that time, particularly in Ontario, the choice of a small European car over a large American car could be seen as some sort of declaration—a declaration of tendencies Roger had been sniffing after all along.

"It isn't that small a car," said Andrew huffily.

"That's not the point," I said. "The point is, it isn't any of his business!"

We spent the second night in Missoula. We had been told in Spokane, at a gas station, that there was a lot of repair work going on along Highway 2, and that we were in for a very hot, dusty drive, with long waits, so we turned onto the interstate and drove through Coeur d'Alene and Kellogg into Montana. After Missoula, we turned south toward Butte, but detoured to see Helena, the state capital. In the car, we played Who Am I?

Cynthia was somebody dead, and an American, and a girl. Possibly a lady. She was not in a story. She had not been seen on television. Cynthia had not read about her in a book. She was not anybody who had come to the kindergarten, or a relative of any of Cynthia's friends.

"Is she human?" said Andrew, with a sudden shrewdness.

"No! That's what you forgot to ask!"

"An animal," I said reflectively.

"Is that a question? Sixteen questions!"

"No, it is not a question. I'm thinking. A dead animal."

"It's the deer," said Meg, who hadn't been playing.

"That's not fair!" said Cynthia. "She's not playing!"

"What deer?" said Andrew.

I said, "Yesterday."

"The day before," said Cynthia. "Meg wasn't playing. Nobody got it."

"The deer on the truck," said Andrew.

"It was a lady deer, because it didn't have antlers, and it was an American and it was dead," Cynthia said.

Andrew said, "I think it's kind of morbid, being a dead deer."

"I got it," said Meg.

Cynthia said, "I think I know what morbid is. It's depressing."

Helena, an old silver-mining town, looked forlorn to us even in the morning sunlight. Then Bozeman and Billings, not forlorn in the slightest — energetic, strung-out towns, with miles of blinding tinsel fluttering over used-car lots. We got too tired and hot even to play Who Am I? These busy, prosaic cities reminded me of similar places in Ontario, and I thought about what was really waiting there — the great tombstone furniture of Roger and Caroline's dining room, the dinners for which I must iron the children's dresses and warn them about forks, and then the other table a hundred miles away, the jokes of my father's crew. The pleasures I had been thinking of — looking at the countryside or drinking a Coke in an old-fashioned drugstore with fans and a high, pressed-tin ceiling — would have to be snatched in between.

"Meg's asleep," Cynthia said. "She's so hot. She makes me hot in the same seat with her."

"I hope she isn't feverish," I said, not turning around.

What are we doing this for, I thought, and the answer came — to show off. To give Andrew's mother and my father the pleasure of seeing their grandchildren. That was our duty. But beyond that we wanted to show them something. What strenuous children we were, Andrew and I, what relentless seekers of approbation. It was as if at some point we had received an unforgettable, indigestible message — that we were far from satisfactory, and that the most commonplace success in life was probably beyond us. Roger dealt out such messages, of course — that was his style — but Andrew's mother, my own mother and father couldn't have meant to do so. All they meant to tell us was "Watch out. Get along." My father, when I was in high school, teased me that I was getting to think I was so smart I would never find a boyfriend. He would have forgotten that in a week. I never forgot it. Andrew and I didn't forget things. We took umbrage.

"I wish there was a beach," said Cynthia.

"There probably is one," Andrew said. "Right around the next curve."

"There isn't any curve," she said, sounding insulted.

"That's what I mean."

"I wish there was some more lemonade."

"I will just wave my magic wand and produce some," I said. "Okay, Cynthia? Would you rather have grape juice? Will I do a beach while I'm at it?"

She was silent, and soon I felt repentant. "Maybe in the next town there might be a pool," I said. I looked at the map. "In Miles City. Anyway, there'll be something cool to drink."

"How far is it?" Andrew said.

"Not so far," I said. "Thirty miles, about."

"In Miles City," said Cynthia, in the tones of an incantation, "there is a beautiful blue swimming pool for children, and a park with lovely trees."

Andrew said to me, "You could have started something."

But there was a pool. There was a park too, though not quite the oasis of Cynthia's fantasy. Prairie trees with thin leaves — cottonwoods and poplars — worn grass, and a high wire fence around the pool. Within this fence, a wall, not yet completed, of cement blocks. There were no shouts or splashes; over the entrance I saw a sign that said the pool was closed every day from noon until two o'clock. It was then twenty-five after twelve.

Nevertheless I called out, "Is anybody there?" I thought somebody must be around, because there was a small truck parked near the entrance. On the side of the truck were these words: *We have Brains, to fix your Drains. (We have Roto-Rooter too.)*

A girl came out, wearing a red lifeguard's shirt over her bathing suit. "Sorry, we're closed."

"We were just driving through," I said.   110

"We close every day from twelve until two. It's on the sign." She was eating a sandwich.

"I saw the sign," I said. "But this is the first water we've seen for so long, and the children are awfully hot, and I wondered if they could just dip in and out — just five minutes. We'd watch them."

A boy came into sight behind her. He was wearing jeans and a T-shirt with the words *Roto-Rooter* on it.

I was going to say that we were driving from British Columbia to Ontario, but I remembered that Canadian place names usually meant nothing to Americans. "We're driving right across the country," I said. "We haven't time to wait for the pool to open. We were just hoping the children could get cooled off."

Cynthia came running up barefoot behind me. "Mother. Mother, where is   115
my bathing suit?" Then she stopped, sensing the serious adult negotiations. Meg was climbing out of the car — just wakened, with her top pulled up and her shorts pulled down, showing her pink stomach.

"Is it just those two?" the girl said.

"Just the two. We'll watch them."

"I can't let any adults in. If it's just the two, I guess I could watch them. I'm having my lunch." She said to Cynthia, "Do you want to come in the pool?"

"Yes, please," said Cynthia firmly.

Meg looked at the ground.   120

"Just a short time, because the pool is really closed," I said. "We appreciate this very much," I said to the girl.

"Well, I can eat my lunch out there, if it's just the two of them." She looked toward the car as if she thought I might try to spring some more children on her.

When I found Cynthia's bathing suit, she took it into the changing room. She would not permit anybody, even Meg, to see her naked. I changed Meg, who stood on the front seat of the car. She had a pink cotton bathing suit with straps that crossed and buttoned. There were ruffles across the bottom.

"She *is* hot," I said. "But I don't think she's feverish."

I loved helping Meg to dress or undress, because her body still had the   125
solid unself-consciousness, the sweet indifference, something of the milky smell, of a baby's body. Cynthia's body had long ago been pared down, shaped and altered, into Cynthia. We all liked to hug Meg, press and nuzzle her. Sometimes she would scowl and beat us off, and this forthright independence, this ferocious bashfulness, simply made her more appealing, more apt to be tormented and tickled in the way of family love.

Andrew and I sat in the car with the windows open. I could hear a radio playing, and thought it must belong to the girl or her boyfriend. I was thirsty, and got out of the car to look for a concession stand, or perhaps a soft-drink machine, somewhere in the park. I was wearing shorts, and the backs of my legs were slick with sweat. I saw a drinking fountain at the other side of the park and was walking toward it in a roundabout way, keeping to the shade of the trees. No place became real till you got out of the car. Dazed with the heat, with the sun on the blistered houses, the pavement, the burnt grass, I walked slowly. I paid attention to a squashed leaf, ground a Popsicle stick under the heel of my sandal, squinted at a trash can strapped to a tree. This is the way you look at the poorest details of the world resurfaced, after you've been driving for a long time — you feel their singleness and precise location and the forlorn coincidence of your being there to see them.

Where are the children?

I turned around and moved quickly, not quite running, to a part of the fence beyond which the cement wall was not completed. I could see some of the pool. I saw Cynthia, standing about waist-deep in the water, fluttering her hands on the surface and discreetly watching something at the end of the pool, which I could not see. I thought by her pose, her discretion, the look on her face, that she must be watching some byplay between the lifeguard and her boyfriend. I couldn't see Meg. But I thought she must be playing in the shallow water — both the shallow and deep ends of the pool were out of my sight.

"Cynthia!" I had to call twice before she knew where my voice was coming from. "Cynthia! Where's Meg?"

It always seems to me, when I recall this scene, that Cynthia turns very grace- 130
fully toward me, then turns all around in the water — making me think of a ballerina on pointe — and spreads her arms in a gesture of the stage. "Dis-ap-peared!"

Cynthia was naturally graceful, and she did take dancing lessons, so these movements may have been as I have described. She did say "Disappeared" after looking all around the pool, but the strangely artificial style of speech and gesture, the lack of urgency, is more likely my invention. The fear I felt instantly when I couldn't see Meg — even while I was telling myself she must be in the shallower water — must have made Cynthia's movements seem unbearably slow and inappropriate to me, and the tone in which she could say "Disappeared" before the implications struck her (or was she covering, at once, some ever-ready guilt?) was heard by me as quite exquisitely, monstrously self-possessed.

I cried out for Andrew, and the lifeguard came into view. She was pointing toward the deep end of the pool, saying, "What's that?"

There, just within my view, a cluster of pink ruffles appeared, a bouquet, beneath the surface of the water. Why would a lifeguard stop and point, why would she ask what that was, why didn't she just dive into the water and swim to it? She didn't swim; she ran all the way around the edge of the pool. But by that time Andrew was over the fence. So many things seemed not quite plausible — Cynthia's behavior, then the lifeguard's — and now I had the impression that Andrew jumped with one bound over this fence, which seemed about seven feet high. He must have climbed it very quickly, getting a grip on the wire.

I could not jump or climb it, so I ran to the entrance, where there was a sort of lattice gate, locked. It was not very high, and I did pull myself over it. I ran through the cement corridors, through the disinfectant pool for your feet, and came out on the edge of the pool.

The drama was over. 135

Andrew had got to Meg first, and had pulled her out of the water. He just had to reach over and grab her, because she was swimming somehow, with her head underwater — she was moving toward the edge of the pool. He was carrying her now, and the lifeguard was trotting along behind. Cynthia had climbed out of the water and was running to meet them. The only person aloof from the situation was the boyfriend, who had stayed on the bench at the shallow end, drinking a milkshake. He smiled at me, and I thought that unfeeling of him, even though the danger was past. He may have meant it kindly. I noticed that he had not turned the radio off, just down.

Meg had not swallowed any water. She hadn't even scared herself. Her hair was plastered to her head and her eyes were wide open, golden with amazement. "I was getting the comb," she said. "I didn't know it was deep."

Andrew said, "She was swimming! She was swimming by herself. I saw her bathing suit in the water and then I saw her swimming."

"She nearly drowned," Cynthia said. "Didn't she? Meg nearly drowned."   140

"I don't know how it could have happened," said the lifeguard. "One moment she was there, and the next she wasn't."

What had happened was that Meg had climbed out of the water at the shallow end and run along the edge of the pool toward the deep end. She saw a comb that somebody had dropped lying on the bottom. She crouched down and reached in to pick it up, quite deceived about the depth of the water. She went over the edge and slipped into the pool, making such a light splash that nobody heard — not the lifeguard, who was kissing her boyfriend, or Cynthia, who was watching them. That must have been the moment under the trees when I thought, Where are the children? It must have been the same moment. At that moment, Meg was slipping, surprised, into the treacherously clear blue water.

"It's okay," I said to the lifeguard, who was nearly crying. "She can move pretty fast." (Though that wasn't what we usually said about Meg at all. We said she thought everything over and took her time.)

"You swam, Meg," said Cynthia, in a congratulatory way. (She told us about the kissing later.)

"I didn't know it was deep," Meg said. "I didn't drown."   145

We had lunch at a takeout place, eating hamburgers and fries at a picnic table not far from the highway. In my excitement, I forgot to get Meg a plain hamburger, and had to scrape off the relish and mustard with plastic spoons, then wipe the meat with a paper napkin, before she would eat it. I took advantage of the trash can there to clean out the car. Then we resumed driving east, with the car windows open in front. Cynthia and Meg fell asleep in the back seat.

Andrew and I talked quietly about what had happened. Suppose I hadn't had the impulse just at that moment to check on the children? Suppose we had gone uptown to get drinks, as we had thought of doing? How had Andrew got over the fence? Did he jump or climb? (He couldn't remember.) How had he reached Meg so quickly? And think of the lifeguard not watching. And Cynthia, taken up with the kissing. Not seeing anything else. Not seeing Meg drop over the edge.

Disappeared.

But she swam. She held her breath and came up swimming.

What a chain of lucky links.   150

That was all we spoke about — luck. But I was compelled to picture the opposite. At this moment, we could have been filling out forms. Meg removed from us, Meg's body being prepared for shipment. To Vancouver — where we had never noticed such a thing as a graveyard — or to Ontario? The scribbled drawings she had made this morning would still be in the back seat of the car.

How could this be borne all at once, how did people bear it? The plump, sweet shoulders and hands and feet, the fine brown hair, the rather satisfied, secretive expression — all exactly the same as when she had been alive. The most ordinary tragedy. A child drowned in a swimming pool at noon on a sunny day. Things tidied up quickly. The pool opens as usual at two o'clock. The lifeguard is a bit shaken up and gets the afternoon off. She drives away with her boyfriend in the Roto-Rooter truck. The body sealed away in some kind of shipping coffin. Sedatives, phone calls, arrangements. Such a sudden vacancy, a blind sinking and shifting. Waking up groggy from the pills, thinking for a moment it wasn't true. Thinking if only we hadn't stopped, if only we hadn't taken this route, if only they hadn't let us use the pool. Probably no one would ever have known about the comb.

There's something trashy about this kind of imagining, isn't there? Something shameful. Laying your finger on the wire to get the safe shock, feeling a bit of what it's like, then pulling back. I believed that Andrew was more scrupulous than I about such things, and that at this moment he was really trying to think about something else.

When I stood apart from my parents at Steve Gauley's funeral and watched them, and had this new, unpleasant feeling about them, I thought that I was understanding something about them for the first time. It was a deadly serious thing. I was understanding that they were implicated. Their big, stiff, dressed-up bodies did not stand between me and sudden death, or any kind of death. They gave consent. So it seemed. They gave consent to the death of children and to my death not by anything they said or thought but by the very fact that they had made children — they had made me. They had made me, and for that reason my death — however grieved they were, however they carried on — would seem to them anything but impossible or unnatural. This was a fact, and even then I knew they were not to blame.

But I did blame them. I charged them with effrontery, hypocrisy. On Steve Gauley's behalf, and on behalf of all children, who knew that by rights they should have sprung up free, to live a new, superior kind of life, not to be caught in the snares of vanquished grownups, with their sex and funerals.

Steve Gauley drowned, people said, because he was next thing to an orphan and was let run free. If he had been warned enough and given chores to do and kept in check, he wouldn't have fallen from an untrustworthy tree branch into a spring pond, a full gravel pit near the river — he wouldn't have drowned. He was neglected, he was free, so he drowned. And his father took it as an accident, such as might happen to a dog. He didn't have a good suit for the funeral, and he didn't bow his head for the prayers. But he was the only grownup that I let off the hook. He was the only one I didn't see giving consent. He couldn't prevent anything, but he wasn't implicated in anything, either — not like the others, saying the Lord's Prayer in their unnaturally weighted voices, oozing religion and dishonor.

At Glendive, not far from the North Dakota border, we had a choice — either to continue on the interstate or head northeast, toward Williston, taking Route 16, then some secondary roads that would get us back to Highway 2.

We agreed that the interstate would be faster, and that it was important for us not to spend too much time — that is, money — on the road. Nevertheless we decided to cut back to Highway 2.

"I just like the idea of it better," I said.

Andrew said, "That's because it's what we planned to do in the beginning."

"We missed seeing Kalispell and Havre. And Wolf Point. I like the name." 160

"We'll see them on the way back."

Andrew's saying "on the way back" was a surprising pleasure to me. Of course, I had believed that we would be coming back, with our car and our lives and our family intact, having covered all that distance, having dealt somehow with those loyalties and problems, held ourselves up for inspection in such a foolhardy way. But it was a relief to hear him say it.

"What I can't get over," said Andrew, "is how you got the signal. It's got to be some kind of extra sense that mothers have."

Partly I wanted to believe that, to bask in my extra sense. Partly I wanted to warn him — to warn everybody — never to count on it.

"What I can't understand," I said, "is how you got over the fence." 165

"Neither can I."

So we went on, with the two in the back seat trusting us, because of no choice, and we ourselves trusting to be forgiven, in time, for everything that had first to be seen and condemned by those children: whatever was flippant, arbitrary, careless, callous — all our natural, and particular, mistakes.

Considerations for Critical Thinking and Writing

1. FIRST RESPONSE. What's the tone of "Miles City, Montana"? Did you expect the narrator to find Meg alive in the pool? How did you feel when you realized that Meg hadn't drowned?

2. How do the opening paragraphs describing Steve Gauley's death and funeral set the tone for the story? Which details of the description seem especially effective to you?

3. How does the funeral make the narrator feel? Why does she feel that way?

4. Describe the narrator's marriage to Andrew. How do they get along? How do they regard each other? How do they handle their differences? Were you surprised to learn that they no longer live together? Why or why not?

5. At one point in the story, the narrator describes herself as a "watcher, not a keeper" (para. 22). Is this an accurate self-assessment? What does this tell us about the narrator?

6. How does the car trip from Vancouver to Ontario serve as a structural device for the story?

7. What do you think is the central conflict in the story? Are additional related conflicts presented?

8. How is the theme of the story related to the narrator's response to Steve Gauley's drowning and Meg's near-drowning? What do you think is the theme?

9. Analyze the "Who Am I?" game played in the car (para. 75-91). What purpose do you think this scene serves? How is it related to the story's theme?

10. Why does the narrator not blame Steve Gauley's father for Steve's drowning? Why does she instead blame her own parents?

11. How does knowing that the narrator no longer lives with her husband affect your reading of the story's final paragraphs (162-167)?

CONNECTIONS TO OTHER SELECTIONS

1. Compare the narrator in this story with the narrator in Munro's "An Ounce of Cure." Explain why you think their retrospective narrations are different from or similar to each other.

2. How might Steve Gauley be seen as a version of Ruller in Flannery O'Connor's "The Turkey" (p. 373). How is childhood presented in each story?

3. Write an essay that compares the fathers in this story with the father in Tobias Wolff's "Powder" (p. 665). What are some significant differences and similarities in the authors' respective treatments of fatherhood?

PERSPECTIVES ON MUNRO

GRAEME GIBSON (B. 1934)

An Interview with Munro on Writing   1973

Gibson: I'll begin with a general question: do you think writers know something special, in the way physicists or anthropologists do?

Munro: You mean probably that writers are . . . have just seen something special. I don't think they *know* something special. I do think that they, perhaps, just perhaps they see things differently. Well I know to me, just things in themselves are very important. I'm not a writer who is very concerned with ideas. I'm not an intellectual writer. I'm very, very excited by what you might call the surface of life, and it must be that this seems to me meaningful in a way I can't analyze or describe.

Gibson: Now when you say it's not that they know something special but, they see something special . . . what kinds of things?

Munro: Well for me it's just things about people, the way they look, the way they sound, the way things smell, the way everything is that you go through every day. It seems to me very important to do something with this.

Gibson: Yes. I mean, perhaps one of the most exciting things I found in reading your stuff was an incredible kind of recognition of how things are.

Munro: It seems to me very important to be able to get at the exact tone or texture of how things are. I can't really claim that it is linked to any kind of a religious feeling about the world, and yet that might come closest to describing it.

Gibson: A slightly different kind of question: in what way is writing important to you?

Munro: God . . . do you mean why do I do it? I don't know if I can get at that. I always have done it. It's . . . do you mean is it important as a kind of therapy? No, that's not it. I don't know why it's important. I don't understand this. I know that I'm never not writing, so that I'm not just sort of turning out one book and then taking a rest and then turning out another book. I'll never live long enough to deal with all the ideas that are — things that are working, because I write very slowly and things, with me, things sort of jell very slowly. But there are always things there that just — well I'm thinking of a thing I'm working on now which I haven't really begun to write much of at all, and it just, it exists and so I'm going to have to put it down or forget it. If I can.

Gibson: You say it exists. So then is your writing a response to something that is simply there?

Munro: Not there in the external world. It's there in my head, this story, if you want to call it that, the characters, the relationship, the lives of these people. I can now see it in my mind, not very well, rather dimly, and things will change as I work it out, but something is there that I'm probably going to have to deal with. Though other things are also there that I have failed to deal with. Often I fail to deal with things several times before I work them out successfully. But it's all there, and of course it comes from the external world. Where else would it come from? But I'm not the kind of writer that says: Now I've got to do something, I've got to write something about this existing problem or this relationship or this experience I've had. I don't work that directly.

Gibson: It's not problem solving then?

Munro: No. . . .

Gibson: You said you've always been writing. How really did you start writing?

Munro: I started writing things down when I was about fourteen or fifteen, and earlier than that I made up stories all the time. But I think they were the things that—I think many children do this, and I don't know, maybe loneliness in adolescence is one of the things that makes it persist.

Gibson: And insisting on your own view of the world too, I guess.

Munro: Yes, perhaps it helps to grow up feeling very alienated from the environment you happen to live in, which is another thing that happened to me.

Gibson: Where did the alienation come from?

Munro: Well I grew up in a rural community, a very traditional community. I almost always felt it. I find it still when I go back. The concern of everyone else I knew was dealing with life on a very practical level, and this is very understandable, because my family are farmers and they are two or three generations away from being pioneers. In order to survive it's necessary to be very good at making things with your hands, and always to think practically, and not to see more than is obviously there, not to see what we call beauty or—oh I'm not doing very well here, but I always realized that I had a different view of the world, and one that would bring me into great trouble and ridicule if it were exposed. I learned very early to disguise everything, and perhaps the escape into making stories was necessary.

Gibson: It's an extremely impractical kind of a thing to be doing.

Munro: To most of my relatives the work I do is still a very meaningless, useless type of work.

Gibson: A frill, if anything.

Munro: Not even a frill, almost a wrong time to be doing, because it is so—if I were hooking rugs though, it would be all right, you see, because you put the rugs on the floor and people walk on them, but what do you do with books? In the community where I grew up, books were a time-waster and reading is a bad habit, and so if even reading is a bad habit, writing is an incomprehensible thing to do.

From *Eleven Canadian Novelists*

1. What do you think Munro means when she says "I'm not a writer who is very concerned with ideas" (para. 2)? Do you think this sensibility is made apparent in her fiction? Explain your response with reference to the three stories reprinted in this book.

2. What causes Munro to feel alienated from her environment? How do you think her sense of alienation is reflected in her writing?

3. Try conducting your own "interview" with Munro. Make up a few questions about some aspect of her work and attempt to write responses based on your reading of her stories.

BENJAMIN DEMOTT (B. 1924)

On Munro's Female Protagonists   1983

Shrewd, amused, self-aware, each of [Munro's] heroines is perfectly capable of recognizing and regretting a mistake or indiscretion. . . . But Mrs. Munro's women are also capable of relishing an indiscretion. They're risk takers at heart, plucky, independent, sexually vibrant. They're people one knows exist even though, for some reason, they fail to surface at parties, mixed doubles, carol sings, or during office hours. One knows they exist in number because one keeps seeing them clearly two rows ahead on airplanes, or way over in the back on the right, in somebody else's lecture room. Their intelligence beckons, not merely their recklessness; they're likable not alone for the dangers they have passed but for their alertness to the pleasures of the passage itself, both the before and after.

From *The New York Times Book Review,* March 20, 1983

1. How do the protagonists in "An Ounce of Cure" (p. 434), "How I Met My Husband" (p. 442), "Prue" (p. 454), and "Miles City, Montana" (p. 458) indicate that they know they have made a "mistake" or committed an "indiscretion"? Which protagonists, if any, seem to regret their experiences?

2. Explain how one of the four Munro stories illustrates DeMott's observation that Munro's women are capable of "relishing an indiscretion." Discuss why you agree or disagree that such relish is an appealing quality in a character.

3. In an essay discuss both the "intelligence" and the "recklessness" of the protagonist in "Prue." In your response, consider whether or not both terms apply equally to her character.

CATHERINE SHELDRICK ROSS

On the Reader's Experience in Reading Munro's Stories   1986

The reader's experience in reading Munro's stories is one of recognition. We say, yes, that is how life is; we recognize and acknowledge discoveries about our deepest selves. And this recognition is the purpose of the author's journeys into the past, undertaken with compassion and determination to "get it right," to get down the tones, textures, and appearances of things. Instead of plots, Munro's work offers arrangements of materials that shift our perceptions of ordinary events and make us see the ordinary in an extraordinary way. Her books are a demonstration of her sense that "at some level these things open; fragments, moments, suggestions, open full of power."

From "Alice Munro," in *Canadian Writers Since 1960,*
First Series, edited by W. H. New

CONSIDERATIONS FOR CRITICAL THINKING AND WRITING

1. Is your own experience in reading Munro's stories one of recognition? Explain why or why not. If not, what do you consider to be the primary experience of reading Munro's stories?

2. What does Munro's fiction offer instead of "plots," according to Ross? Choose a story and write an essay that either refutes or demonstrates Ross's perspective on Munro's fiction.

W. R. MARTIN (B. 1920)
On Prue's Suppressed Passions 1987

"Prue" is slight and cryptic. Alice Munro has described it as "a neater story than I usually write"; its neatness goes with the wry irony that informs it. Now the protagonist is well into middle-age — in her "late forties." For some years she has had a partly-on-but-mainly-off affair with Gordon, who is a shilly-shallyer, a "helpless, baffled soul, squirming around inside his doughty fortress"; it is ironical that he is a "neurologist." He seems to have allowed his interest in food and comforts — his house has four bathrooms — to supplant his sex drive. A "quite young" and vigorous woman, whom Gordon thinks he loves, denied ingress to Gordon's house on a night when Prue is his guest to dinner, hurls her overnight bag at him, apparently out of frustration.

Gordon claims that he wants to marry Prue after he has got over "being in love" with the younger woman; perhaps he is attracted to Prue because she is habitually "cynical" and "lighthearted," "doesn't take herself too seriously," is "unintense, and civilized," "bright," and a "cheerful spectator" who can speak "lightly" of important matters; above all, "she seems to regard sex as a wholesome, slightly silly indulgence."

Throughout the story the short clipped sentences generate a dry ironic humor, and the joke is largely at the expense of Prue, who is more aptly named than she admits. When Gordon leaves her alone early in the morning, she picks up a single amber cufflink from his dresser and carries it off before the arrival of Gordon's housekeeper, her "friend from olden times." She possesses herself of the cufflink not for sentimental reasons, not as "booty," nor for its "ritualistic significance"; and she drops it into an old tobacco tin, where it joins several other ambiguous trophies, and "more or less forgets about it." She does not have the passion to throw an overnight bag at Gordon, so her response takes a devious form, apparently obscure even to herself because she shows no sign of recognising it for the revenge it is. She so slenderly knows herself that her attitudes, and even her "English accent," are artificially cultivated poses: she tells their friends that Gordon's attitude is "quite reasonable," but her suppressed passions tell a quite different story.

From *Alice Munro: Paradox and Parallel*

CONSIDERATIONS FOR CRITICAL THINKING AND WRITING

1. Explain why you agree or disagree with Martin's suggestion that "Prue" is a "slight and cryptic" story (para. 1).

2. Explain whether you agree with Martin that Prue's theft of the cufflink is a sign of "suppressed passions" (para 3). Is there any other way to interpret her behavior?

3. Martin carefully works into his own writing brief quoted passages from "Prue" to make his points. Using Martin's paragraphs as a model, write a substantial one-paragraph analysis of Prue that describes something about her that you think is important for understanding her character.

GEORGE WOODCOCK (B. 1912)

On Symbolism in Munro's Fiction 1987

Alice Munro has always been rightly reluctant to offer theoretical explanations of her methods, for she is quite obviously an antidogmatic, the kind of writer who works with feeling ahead of theory. But even on the theoretical level she is shrewd in defining the perimeters of her approach, perhaps negatively rather than positively. She once, for example, in an essay written for John Metcalf's *The Narrative Voice* — entitled "The Colonel's Hash Resettled" — cautioned against attempts to read symbolism excessively into her stories. And she was right, for essentially her stories are what they say, offering their meaning with often stark directness and gaining their effect from their intense visuality, so that they are always vivid in the mind's eye, which is another way of saying that she has learnt the power of the image and how to turn it to the purposes of prose.

Her visuality is not merely a matter of rendering the surface, the realm of mere perception, for she has understood that one of the great advantages of any effective imagist technique is that the image not merely presents itself. It reverberates with the power of its associations, and even with the intensity of its own isolated and illuminated presence. Munro herself conveyed something of this when John Metcalf, remarking on the fact that she seemed to "*glory* in the surfaces and the textures," asked whether she did not in fact feel "'surfaces' not to be surfaces," and she answered that there was "a kind of magic . . . about everything . . . a feeling about the intensity of what is *there*."

From *Northern Spring: The Flowering of Canadian Literature*

CONSIDERATIONS FOR CRITICAL THINKING AND WRITING

1. Woodcock cautions readers not to real excessive symbolism into Munro's stories, and yet he also argues that "her visuality is not merely a matter of rendering the surface" (para. 2). Can these two seemingly different perspectives be reconciled? Explain why or why not.

2. In an essay, discuss Munro's use of symbolism in "Prue" (p. 454) or "Miles City, Montana" (p. 458), and explain whether you feel it supports Woodcock's arguments in the above excerpt.

ROBERT HAMPSON (B. 1948)
On the Reader's Expectations in "How I Met My Husband"
1989

[The title of] "How I Met My Husband" sets up very clear expectations: we anticipate, probably, a romance between a man and a woman, told from the woman's viewpoint and ending in marriage. Munro's story starts with the female narrator's account of herself as a fifteen-year-old girl, with the landing of an aeroplane, and with the girl's first meeting with the airman. By the end of the first section we have our man and our woman, and the beginning of some kind of relationship between them:

> I wasn't even old enough then to realize how out of the common it is, for a man to say something like that to a woman, or somebody he is treating like a woman. For a man to say a word like *beautiful*.

So far so good: the expectations set up by the title are being comfortably confirmed.

In the fourth section of the story the developing relationship between the girl and the pilot apparently meets an obstacle, when the pilot's fiancée suddenly arrives. . . . But it soon becomes clear that the fiancée is not a serious rival — in fact, the pilot is in flight from her in both senses of the word. Our expectations of a marriage between the girl and the pilot are thus reinforced, and we now settle back comfortably to wait for the "resolution."

By the end of the fifth section the situation has almost resolved itself: the pilot has taken off in his plane to escape from his fiancée; the fiancée has disappeared in pursuit; and the girl is now waiting for the letter that the pilot has promised to send her:

> The mail came every day except Sunday, between one-thirty and two in the afternoon. . . . I would get the kitchen all cleaned and then go up to the mailbox and sit in the grass, waiting. I was perfectly happy, waiting. . . . I was always smiling when the mailman got there, and continued smiling even after he gave me the mail and I saw today wasn't the day.

When we are three paragraphs from the end, we begin to realize, with the narrator's younger self, that the letter is never going to arrive. And the girl's sense of shock is, if anything, exceeded by our own. In a story called "How I Met My Husband," here we are, less than a page from the end, and the only eligible bachelor we have noticed so far in the story has just been written off.

It is not until the final paragraph that this problem is solved, when the mailman phones up to ask the girl out:

> He asked if I would like to go to Goderich where some well-known movie was on, I forget now what. So I said yes, and I went out with him for two years and he asked me to marry him, and we were engaged a year more while I got my things together, and then we did marry.

The expectations created by the title have, technically, been fulfilled, but the reader cannot help feeling cheated by this ending, since another kind of expectation has been disappointed: the expectation that a story called "How I Met My Husband" will devote most of its narrative to the relationship indicated by the title. Instead, the reader feels puzzled by the casualness of attitude taken towards the husband. In contrast to the detailed narration of her relationship with the airman, the narrator cannot even remember the title of the "well-known movie" to which her husband took her.

We might feel tempted to try and interpret this discrepancy of narrative attention as some kind of value-judgment on these two relationships—or, more sophisticatedly, as a value-judgment on the reader's expectations, but the narrator gets in first. The last sentence of the story blocks any attempt at interpretation:

> He always tells the children the story of how I went after him by sitting by the mailbox every day, and naturally I laugh and let him, because I like for people to think what pleases them and makes them happy.

The narrator's easy acceptance of her husband's interpretation of events—which we know to be a misinterpretation—makes us hesitate about offering our interpretation. This ending exposes interpretation as a fiction-making activity. More than that, it suggests that interpretation has more to do with pleasing the interpreter than with "truth." The invitation to interpret in whatever way you wish undermines any claim to value in that interpretation. Not only then is there the "unsettling" nature of the ending—where the conclusion that the reader has been encouraged to expect does not occur, and the promise of the title is fulfilled in an unexpected way; where the bond of trust between author and reader has been used to lead the reader up the garden path—but also the reader is prevented from avoiding that uneasiness by some interpretative recuperation of the disruption of expectations. "I like for people to think what pleases them and makes them happy" identifies the end of interpretation as the security and comfort of the interpreter.

From "Johnny Panic and the Pleasures of Disruption,"
Re-reading the Short Story, edited by Claire Hanson

CONSIDERATIONS FOR CRITICAL THINKING AND WRITING

1. According to Hampson, how does the title of "How I Met My Husband" (p. 442) set up expectations in the reader?

2. Explain whether you think the final paragraph of the story cheats or fulfills the reader's expectations.

3. Write an essay that considers Hampson's assertion that "the last sentence of the story blocks any attempt at interpretation" (para. 5). Explain whether you agree or disagree with Hampson.

TWO COMPLEMENTARY CRITICAL READINGS

Munro on Narration in "An Ounce of Cure"   *1970*

One thing in ["An Ounce of Cure"] I think is interesting, now that I look back on it: when the girl's circumstances become hopelessly messy, when nothing is going to go right for her, she gets out of it by looking at the way things happen—by changing from a participant to an observer. This is what I used to do myself, it is what a writer does; I think it may be one of the things that make a writer in the first place. When I started to write the dreadful things I did write when I was about fifteen, I made the glorious leap from being a victim of my own ineptness and self-conscious miseries to being a godlike arranger of patterns and destinies, even if they were all in my head; I have never leapt back.

From "Author's Commentary" in *Sixteen by Twelve:*
Short Stories by Canadian Writers, edited by John Metcalf

CONSIDERATIONS FOR CRITICAL THINKING AND WRITING

1. Discuss the narrator's shift from participant to observer in "An Ounce of Cure" (p. 434).
2. Why do you think Munro describes her movement from participant to observer as a "glorious leap"?
3. Write an essay in which you consider an additional quality, attribute, strategy, or sensibility that you think is "one of the things that make a writer in the first place."

LORRAINE MCMULLEN (B. 1926)
On Munro's Ironic Humor in "An Ounce of Cure"   *1983*

Munro is a satirist for whom disorder, chance happenings and meetings, and the bizarre characters who reveal us to ourselves are all parts of an absurd yet real world. Irony is at the core of Munro's view of humanity and events, a view she expresses with wit and humour, mixing paradoxes, startling comparisons, and unexpectedly incisive details with farcical scenes and eccentric or contradictory personalities. In her use of comic devices, Munro goes beyond the clever and the humorous. Her careful and accurate structuring of situations and juxtaposition of incidents reveal the coexistence of the bizarre with the ordinary, the genuine with the fraudulent, the immutable with the transient. Her ironically perceived characters, whether appearing to us as outlandish or ordinary, reveal to us our own contradictory impulses and ambivalent feelings, and through their weaknesses and vulnerability remind us of our own weaknesses, our own vulnerability. Challenging myths and sweeping away stereotypes, Munro induces us to recognize, with her, the "shameless, marvellous, shattering absurdity" around and within us.

From "'Shameless, Marvellous, Shattering Absurdity':
The Humour of Paradox in Alice Munro" in *Probable Fictions:*
Alice Munro's Narrative Acts, edited by Louis K. MacKendrick

CONSIDERATIONS FOR CRITICAL THINKING AND WRITING

1. Explain why you agree or disagree with McMullen's assertion that "irony is at the core of Munro's view of humanity and events."
2. Locate and describe the kinds of comic devices Munro uses in "An Ounce of Cure" (p. 434). What are the effects of those comic devices?
3. In an essay discuss how McMullen's claim that "An Ounce of Cure" "remind[s] us of our own weaknesses, our own vulnerability" can be reconciled with Munro's assertion that becoming an "observer" rather than a "participant" allowed her to feel like a "godlike arranger of patterns and destinies" instead of a victim. Explain why you think the narrator of "An Ounce of Cure" is a weak or a triumphant character.

11

Critical Case Study:
William Faulkner's
"Barn Burning"

This chapter offers several critical approaches to a well-known short story by William Faulkner. Though there are many possible critical approaches to any given work (see Chapter 37, "Critical Strategies for Reading," for a discussion of a variety of methods), and there are numerous studies of Faulkner from formalist, biographical, historical, mythological, psychological, sociological, and other perspectives, it is worth noting that each reading of a work or writer is predicated on accepting certain assumptions about literature and life. Those assumptions or premises may be complementary or mutually exclusive, and they may appeal to you or appall you. What is interesting, however, is how various approaches reveal the text (as well as its readers and critics) by calling attention to certain elements or leaving others out. The following critical excerpts suggest only a portion of the range of possibilities, but even a small representation of approaches can help you to raise new questions, develop insights, recognize problems, and suggest additional ways of reading the text.

WILLIAM FAULKNER (1897–1962)

A biographical note for William Faulkner appears on page 72, before his story "A Rose for Emily." In "Barn Burning" Faulkner portrays a young boy's love and revulsion for his father, a frightening man who lives by a "ferocious conviction in the rightness of his own actions."

William Faulkner (May 6, 1955) in the spot where he did most of his writing—his living room—bent over a glass-topped table with a pen.

Barn Burning 1939

The store in which the Justice of the Peace's court was sitting smelled of cheese. The boy, crouched on his nail keg at the back of the crowded room, knew he smelled cheese, and more: from where he sat he could see the ranked shelves close-packed with the solid, squat, dynamic shapes of tin cans whose labels his stomach read, not from the lettering which meant nothing to his mind but from the scarlet devils and the silver curve of fish — this, the cheese which he knew he smelled and the hermetic meat which his intestines believed he smelled coming in intermittent gusts momentary and brief between the other constant one, the smell and sense just a little of fear because mostly of despair and grief, the old fierce pull of blood. He could not see the table where the Justice sat and before which his father and his father's enemy (*our enemy* he thought in that despair; *ourn! mine and hisn both! He's my father!*) stood, but he could hear them, the two of them that is, because his father had said no word yet:

"But what proof have you, Mr. Harris?"

"I told you. The hog got into my corn. I caught it up and sent it back to him. He had no fence that would hold it. I told him so, warned him. The next time I put the hog in my pen. When he came to get it I gave him enough wire to patch up his pen. The next time I put the hog up and kept it. I rode down to his house and saw the wire I gave him still rolled on to the spool in his yard. I told him he could have the hog when he paid me a dollar pound fee. That evening a nigger came with the dollar and got the hog. He was a strange nigger. He said,

'He say to tell you wood and hay kin burn.' I said, 'What?' 'That whut he say to tell you,' the nigger said. 'Wood and hay kin burn.' That night my barn burned. I got the stock out but I lost the barn."

"Where is the nigger? Have you got him?"

"He was a strange nigger, I tell you. I don't know what became of him."   5

"But that's not proof. Don't you see that's not proof?"

"Get that boy up here. He knows." For a moment the boy thought too that the man meant his older brother until Harris said, "Not him. The little one. The boy," and, crouching, small for his age, small and wiry like his father, in patched and faded jeans even too small for him, with straight, uncombed, brown hair and eyes gray and wild as storm scud, he saw the men between himself and the table part and become a lane of grim faces, at the end of which he saw the Justice, a shabby, collarless, graying man in spectacles, beckoning him. He felt no floor under his bare feet; he seemed to walk beneath the palpable weight of the grim turning faces. His father, stiff in his black Sunday coat donned not for the trial but for the moving, did not even look at him. *He aims for me to lie,* he thought, again with that frantic grief and despair. *And I will have to do hit.*

"What's your name, boy?" the Justice said.

"Colonel Sartoris Snopes," the boy whispered.

"Hey?" the Justice said. "Talk louder. Colonel Sartoris? I reckon anybody   10 named for Colonel Sartoris in this country can't help but tell the truth, can they?" The boy said nothing. *Enemy! Enemy!* he thought; for a moment he could not even see, could not see that the Justice's face was kindly nor discern that his voice was troubled when he spoke to the man named Harris: "Do you want me to question this boy?" But he could hear, and during those subsequent long seconds while there was absolutely no sound in the crowded little room save that of quiet and intent breathing it was as if he had swung outward at the end of a grape vine, over a ravine, and at the top of the swing had been caught in a prolonged instant of mesmerized gravity, weightless in time.

"No!" Harris said violently, explosively. "Damnation! Send him out of here!" Now time, the fluid world, rushed beneath him again, the voices coming to him again through the smell of cheese and sealed meat, the fear and despair and the old grief of blood:

"This case is closed. I can't find against you, Snopes, but I can give you advice. Leave this country and don't come back to it."

His father spoke for the first time, his voice cold and harsh, level, without emphasis: "I aim to. I don't figure to stay in a country among people who . . ." he said something unprintable and vile, addressed to no one.

"That'll do," the Justice said. "Take your wagon and get out of this country before dark. Case dismissed."

His father turned, and he followed the stiff black coat, the wiry figure   15 walking a little stiffly from where a Confederate provost's man's musket ball had taken him in the heel on a stolen horse thirty years ago, followed the two backs now, since his older brother had appeared from somewhere in the crowd, no taller than the father but thicker, chewing tobacco steadily, between the two lines of grim-faced men and out of the store and across the worn gallery and down the sagging steps and among the dogs and half-grown boys in the mild May dust, where as he passed a voice hissed:

"Barn burner!"

Again he could not see, whirling; there was a face in a red haze, moonlike, bigger than the full moon, the owner of it half again his size, he leaping in the red haze toward the face, feeling no blow, feeling no shock when his head struck the earth, scrabbling up and leaping again, feeling no blow this time either and tasting no blood, scrabbling up to see the other boy in full flight and himself already leaping into pursuit as his father's hand jerked him back, the harsh, cold voice speaking above him: "Go get in the wagon."

It stood in a grove of locusts and mulberries across the road. His two hulking sisters in their Sunday dresses and his mother and her sister in calico and sunbonnets were already in it, sitting on or among the sorry residue of the dozen and more movings which even the boy could remember — the battered stove, the broken beds and chairs, the clock inlaid with mother-of-pearl, which would not run, stopped at some fourteen minutes past two o'clock of a dead and forgotten day and time, which had been his mother's dowry. She was crying, though when she saw him she drew her sleeve across her face and began to descend from the wagon. "Get back," the father said.

"He's hurt. I got to get some water and wash his . . ."

"Get back in the wagon," his father said. He got in too, over the tail-gate. 20 His father mounted to the seat where the older brother already sat and struck the gaunt mules two savage blows with the peeled willow, but without heat. It was not even sadistic; it was exactly that same quality which in later years would cause his descendants to over-run the engine before putting a motor car in motion, striking and reining back in the same movement. The wagon went on, the store with its quiet crowd of grimly watching men dropped behind; a curve in the road hid it. *Forever* he thought. *Maybe he's done satisfied now, now that he has* . . . stopping himself, not to say it aloud even to himself. His mother's hand touched his shoulder.

"Does hit hurt?" she said.

"Naw," he said. "Hit don't hurt. Lemme be."

"Can't you wipe some of the blood off before hit dries?"

"I'll wash to-night," he said. "Lemme be, I tell you."

The wagon went on. He did not know where they were going. None of 25 them ever did or ever asked, because it was always somewhere, always a house of sorts waiting for them a day or two days or even three days away. Likely his father had already arranged to make a crop on another farm before he . . . Again he had to stop himself. He (the father) always did. There was something about his wolflike independence and even courage when the advantage was at least neutral which impressed strangers, as if they got from his latent ravening ferocity not so much a sense of dependability as a feeling that his ferocious conviction in the rightness of his own actions would be of advantage to all whose interest lay with his.

That night they camped, in a grove of oaks and beeches where a spring ran. The nights were still cool and they had a fire against it, of a rail lifted from a nearby fence and cut into lengths — a small fire, neat, niggard almost, a shrewd fire; such fires were his father's habit and custom always, even in freezing weather. Older, the boy might have remarked this and wondered why not a big one; why should not a man who had not only seen the waste and extravagance of war, but who had in his blood an inherent voracious prodigality with material not his own, have burned everything in sight? Then he might have gone a step farther and thought that that was the reason: that niggard blaze was the living fruit of nights passed during those four years in the woods hiding from all men, blue or gray, with his strings of horses (captured horses, he called them). And older still, he might have divined the true reason: that the element of fire spoke to some deep mainspring of his father's being, as the element of steel or of powder spoke to other men, as the one weapon for the preservation of integrity, else breath were not worth the breathing, and hence to be regarded with respect and used with discretion.

But he did not think this now and he had seen those same niggard blazes all his life. He merely ate his supper beside it and was already half asleep over his iron plate when his father called him, and once more he followed the stiff back, the stiff and ruthless limp, up the slope and on to the starlit road where, turning, he could see his father against the stars but without face or depth—a shape black, flat, and bloodless as though cut from tin in the iron folds of the frockcoat which had not been made for him, the voice harsh like tin and without heat like tin:

"You were fixing to tell them. You would have told him."

He didn't answer. His father struck him with the flat of his hand on the side of the head, hard but without heat, exactly as he had struck the two mules at the store, exactly as he would strike either of them with any stick in order to kill a horse fly, his voice still without heat or anger. "You're getting to be a man. You got to learn. You got to learn to stick to your own blood or you ain't going to have any blood to stick to you. Do you think either of them, any man there this morning, would? Don't you know all they wanted was a chance to get at me because they knew I had them beat? Eh?" Later, twenty years later, he was to tell himself, "If I had said they wanted only truth, justice, he would have hit me again." But now he said nothing. He was not crying. He just stood there. "Answer me," his father said.

"Yes," he whispered. His father turned.   30

"Get on to bed. We'll be there tomorrow."

Tomorrow they were there. In the early afternoon the wagon stopped before a paintless two-room house identical almost with the dozen others it had stopped before even in the boy's ten years, and again, as on the other dozen occasions, his mother and aunt got down and began to unload the wagon, although his two sisters and his father and brother had not moved.

"Likely hit ain't fitten for hawgs," one of the sisters said.

"Nevertheless, fit it will and you'll hog it and like it," his father said. "Get out of them chairs and help your Ma unload."

The two sisters got down, big, bovine, in a flutter of cheap ribbons; one of   35
them drew from the jumbled wagon bed a battered lantern, the other a worn broom. His father handed the reins to the older son and began to climb stiffly over the wheel. "When they get unloaded, take the team to the barn and feed them." Then he said, and at first the boy thought he was still speaking to his brother: "Come with me."

"Me?" he said.

"Yes," his father said. "You."

"Abner," his mother said. His father paused and looked back—the harsh level stare beneath the shaggy, graying, irascible brows.

"I reckon I'll have a word with the man that aims to begin tomorrow owning me body and soul for the next eight months."

They went back up the road. A week ago — or before last night, that is — he 40
would have asked where they were going, but not now. His father had struck
him before last night but never before had he paused afterward to explain why;
it was as if the blow and the following calm, outrageous voice still rang, reper-
cussed, divulging nothing to him save the terrible handicap of being young,
the light weight of his few years, just heavy enough to prevent his soaring free
of the world as it seemed to be ordered but not heavy enough to keep him
footed solid in it, to resist it and try to change the course of events.

Presently he could see the grove of oaks and cedars and the other flowering trees and shrubs where the house would be, though not the house yet.
They walked beside a fence massed with honeysuckle and Cherokee roses and
came to a gate swinging open between two brick pillars, and now, beyond a
sweep of drive, he saw the house for the first time and at that instant he forgot
his father and the terror and despair both, and even when he remembered his
father again (who had not stopped) the terror and despair did not return. Because, for all the twelve movings, they had sojourned until now in a poor country, a land of small farms and fields and houses, and he had never seen a house
like this before. *Hit's big as a courthouse* he thought quietly, with a surge of peace
and joy whose reason he could not have thought into words, being too young
for that: *They are safe from him. People whose lives are a part of this peace and dignity
are beyond his touch, he no more to them than a buzzing wasp: capable of stinging for a
little moment but that's all; the spell of this peace and dignity rendering even the barns
and stable and cribs which belong to it impervious to the puny flames he might contrive* . . . this, the peace and joy, ebbing for an instant as he looked again at the
stiff black back, the stiff and implacable limp of the figure which was not
dwarfed by the house, for the reason that it had never looked big anywhere and
which now, against the serene columned backdrop, had more than ever that
impervious quality of something cut ruthlessly from tin, depthless, as though,
sidewise to the sun, it would cast no shadow. Watching him, the boy remarked
the absolutely undeviating course which his father held and saw the stiff foot
come squarely down in a pile of fresh droppings where a horse had stood in
the drive and which his father could have avoided by a simple change of stride.
But it ebbed only for a moment, though he could not have thought this into
words either, walking on in the spell of the house, which he could even want
but without envy, without sorrow, certainly never with that ravening and jealous rage which unknown to him walked in the ironlike black coat before him:
*Maybe he will feel it too. Maybe it will even change him now from what maybe he
couldn't help but be.*

They crossed the portico. Now he could hear his father's stiff foot as it
came down on the boards with clocklike finality, a sound out of all proportion
to the displacement of the body it bore and which was not dwarfed either by
the white door before it, as though it had attained to a sort of vicious and
ravening minimum not to be dwarfed by anything — the flat, wide, black hat,
the formal coat of broadcloth which had once been black but which had now
that friction-glazed greenish cast of the bodies of old house flies, the lifted
sleeve which was too large, the lifted hand like a curled claw. The door opened
so promptly that the boy knew the Negro must have been watching them all
the time, an old man with neat grizzled hair, in a linen jacket, who stood bar-
ring the door with his body, saying, "Wipe yo foots, white man, fo you come in
here. Major ain't home nohow."

"Get out of my way, nigger," his father said, without heat too, flinging the door back and the Negro also and entering, his hat still on his head. And now the boy saw the prints of the stiff foot on the doorjamb and saw them appear on the pale rug behind the machinelike deliberation of the foot which seemed to bear (or transmit) twice the weight which the body compassed. The Negro was shouting "Miss Lula! Miss Lula!" somewhere behind them, then the boy, deluged as though by a warm wave by a suave turn of the carpeted stair and a pendant glitter of chandeliers and a mute gleam of gold frames, heard the swift feet and saw her too, a lady—perhaps he had never seen her like before either—in a gray, smooth gown with lace at the throat and an apron tied at the waist and the sleeves turned back, wiping cake or biscuit dough from her hands with a towel as she came up the hall, looking not at his father at all but at the tracks on the blond rug with an expression of incredulous amazement.

"I tried," the Negro cried. "I tole him to . . ."

"Will you please go away?" she said in a shaking voice. "Major de Spain is 45 not at home. Will you please go away?"

His father had not spoken again. He did not speak again. He did not even look at her. He just stood stiff in the center of the rug, in his hat, the shaggy iron-gray brows twitching slightly above the pebble-colored eyes as he appeared to examine the house with brief deliberation. Then with the same deliberation he turned; the boy watched him pivot on the good leg and saw the stiff foot drag round the arc of the turning, leaving a final long and fading smear. His father never looked at it, he never once looked down at the rug. The Negro held the door. It closed behind them, upon the hysteric and indistinguishable woman-wail. His father stopped at the top of the steps and scraped his boot clean on the edge of it. At the gate he stopped again. He stood for a moment, planted stiffly on the stiff foot, looking back at the house. "Pretty and white, ain't it?" he said. "That's sweat. Nigger sweat. Maybe it ain't white enough yet to suit him. Maybe he wants to mix some white sweat with it."

Two hours later the boy was chopping wood behind the house within which his mother and aunt and the two sisters (the mother and aunt, not the two girls, he knew that; even at this distance and muffled by walls the flat loud voices of the two girls emanated an incorrigible idle inertia) were setting up the stove to prepare a meal; when he heard the hooves and saw the linen-clad man on a fine sorrel mare, whom he recognized even before he saw the rolled rug in front of the Negro youth following on a fat bay carriage horse—a suffused, angry face vanishing, still at full gallop, beyond the corner of the house where his father and brother were sitting in the two tilted chairs; and a moment later, almost before he could have put the axe down, he heard the hooves again and watched the sorrel mare go back out of the yard, already galloping again. Then his father began to shout one of the sisters' names, who presently emerged backward from the kitchen door dragging the rolled rug along the ground by one end while the other sister walked behind it.

"If you ain't going to tote, go on and set up the wash pot," the first said.

"You, Sarty!" the second shouted. "Set up the wash pot!" His father appeared at the door, framed against that shabbiness, as he had been against that other bland perfection, impervious to either, the mother's anxious face at his shoulder.

"Go on," the father said. "Pick it up." The two sisters stopped, broad, 50
lethargic; stooping, they presented an incredible expanse of pale cloth and a
flutter of tawdry ribbons.

"If I thought enough of a rug to have to git hit all the way from France I
wouldn't keep hit where folks coming in would have to tromp on hit," the first
said. They raised the rug.

"Abner," the mother said. "Let me do it."

"You go back and git dinner," his father said. "I'll tend to this."

From the woodpile through the rest of the afternoon the boy watched
them, the rug spread flat in the dust beside the bubbling wash pot, the two sisters stooping over it with that profound and lethargic reluctance, while the father stood over them in turn, implacable and grim, driving them though never
raising his voice again. He could smell the harsh homemade lye they were
using; he saw his mother come to the door once and look toward them with an
expression not anxious now but very like despair; he saw his father turn, and
he fell to with the axe and saw from the corner of his eye his father raise from
the ground a flattish fragment of field stone and examine it and return to the
pot, and this time his mother actually spoke: "Abner. Abner. Please don't.
Please, Abner."

Then he was done too. It was dusk; the whippoorwills had already begun. 55
He could smell coffee from the room where they would presently eat the cold
food remaining from the midafternoon meal, though when he entered the
house he realized they were having coffee again probably because there was a
fire on the hearth, before which the rug now lay spread over the backs of the
two chairs. The tracks of his father's foot were gone. Where they had been were
now long, water-cloudy scoriations resembling the sporadic course of a lil-
liputian mowing machine.

It still hung there while they ate the cold food and then went to bed, scattered without order or claim up and down the two rooms, his mother in one bed,
where his father would later lie, the older brother in the other, himself, the aunt,
and the two sisters on pallets on the floor. But his father was not in bed yet. The
last thing the boy remembered was the depthless, harsh silhouette of the hat
and coat bending over the rug and it seemed to him that he had not even closed
his eyes when the silhouette was standing over him, the fire almost dead behind
it, the stiff foot prodding him awake. "Catch up the mule," his father said.

When he returned with the mule his father was standing in the black
door, the rolled rug over his shoulder. "Ain't you going to ride?" he said.

"No. Give me your foot."

He bent his knee into his father's hand, the wiry, surprising power flowed
smoothly, rising, he rising with it, on to the mule's bare back (they had owned
a saddle once; the boy could remember it though not when or where) and with
the same effortlessness his father swung the rug up in front of him. Now in
the starlight they retraced the afternoon's path, up the dusty road rife with
honeysuckle, through the gate and up the black tunnel of the drive to the
lightless house, where he sat on the mule and felt the rough warp of the rug
drag across his thighs and vanish.

"Don't you want me to help?" he whispered. His father did not answer and 60
now he heard again that stiff foot striking the hollow portico with that
wooden and clocklike deliberation, that outrageous overstatement of the

weight it carried. The rug, hunched, not flung (the boy could tell that even in the darkness) from his father's shoulder struck the angle of wall and floor with a sound unbelievably loud, thunderous, then the foot again, unhurried and enormous; a light came on in the house and the boy sat, tense, breathing steadily and quietly and just a little fast, though the foot itself did not increase its beat at all, descending the steps now; now the boy could see him.

"Don't you want to ride now?" he whispered. "We kin both ride now," the light within the house altering now, flaring up and sinking. *He's coming down the stairs now,* he thought. He had already ridden the mule up beside the horse block; presently his father was up behind him and he doubled the reins over and slashed the mule across the neck, but before the animal could begin to trot the hard, thin arm came around him, the hard, knotted hand jerking the mule back to a walk.

In the first red rays of the sun they were in the lot, putting plow gear on the mules. This time the sorrel mare was in the lot before he heard it at all, the rider collarless and even bareheaded, trembling, speaking in a shaking voice as the woman in the house had done, his father merely looking up once before stooping again to the hame he was buckling, so that the man on the mare spoke to his stooping back:

"You must realize you have ruined that rug. Wasn't there anybody here, any of your women . . ." he ceased, shaking, the boy watching him, the older brother leaning now in the stable door, chewing, blinking slowly and steadily at nothing apparently. "It cost a hundred dollars. But you never had a hundred dollars. You never will. So I'm going to charge you twenty bushels of corn against your crop. I'll add it in your contract and when you come to the commissary you can sign it. That won't keep Mrs. de Spain quiet but maybe it will teach you to wipe your feet before you enter her house again."

Then he was gone. The boy looked at his father, who still had not spoken or even looked up again, who was now adjusting the logger-head in the hame.

"Pap," he said. His father looked at him — the inscrutable face, the shaggy   65
brows beneath which the gray eyes glinted coldly. Suddenly the boy went toward him, fast, stopping as suddenly. "You done the best you could!" he cried. "If he wanted hit done different why didn't he wait and tell you how? He won't git no twenty bushels! He won't git none! We'll gether hit and hide hit! I kin watch . . ."

"Did you put the cutter back in that straight stock like I told you?"

"No, sir," he said.

"Then go do it."

That was Wednesday. During the rest of that week he worked steadily, at what was within his scope and some which was beyond it, with an industry that did not need to be driven nor even commanded twice; he had this from his mother, with the difference that some at least of what he did he liked to do, such as splitting wood with the half-size axe which his mother and aunt had earned, or saved money somehow, to present him with at Christmas. In company with the two older women (and on one afternoon, even one of the sisters), he built pens for the shoat and the cow which were part of his father's contract with the landlord, and one afternoon, his father being absent, gone somewhere on one of the mules, he went to the field.

They were running a middle buster now, his brother holding the plow   70
straight while he handled the reins, and walking beside the straining mule, the

rich black soil shearing cool and damp against his bare ankles, he thought *Maybe this is the end of it. Maybe even that twenty bushels that seems hard to have to pay for just a rug will be a cheap price for him to stop forever and always from being what he used to be;* thinking, dreaming now, so that his brother had to speak sharply to him to mind the mule: *Maybe he even won't collect the twenty bushels. Maybe it will all add up and balance and vanish—corn, rug, fire; the terror and grief; the being pulled two ways like between two teams of horses—gone, done with for ever and ever.*

Then it was Saturday; he looked up from beneath the mule he was harnessing and saw his father in the black coat and hat. "Not that," his father said. "The wagon gear." And then, two hours later, sitting in the wagon bed behind his father and brother on the seat, the wagon accomplished a final curve, and he saw the weathered paintless store with its tattered tobacco- and patent-medicine posters and the tethered wagons and saddle animals below the gallery. He mounted the gnawed steps behind his father and brother, and there again was the lane of quiet, watching faces for the three of them to walk through. He saw the man in spectacles sitting at the plank table and he did not need to be told this was a Justice of the Peace; he sent one glare of fierce, exultant, partisan defiance at the man in collar and cravat now, whom he had seen but twice before in his life, and that on a galloping horse, who now wore on his face an expression not of rage but of amazed unbelief which the boy could not have known was at the incredible circumstance of being sued by one of his own tenants, and came and stood against his father and cried at the Justice: "He ain't done it! He aint' burnt . . ."

"Go back to the wagon," his father said.

"Burnt?" the Justice said. "Do I understand this rug was burned too?"

"Does anybody here claim it was?" his father said. "Go back to the wagon." But he did not, he merely retreated to the rear of the room, crowded as that other had been, but not to sit down this time, instead, to stand pressing among the motionless bodies, listening to the voices:

"And you claim twenty bushels of corn is too high for the damage you did 75 to the rug?"

"He brought the rug to me and said he wanted the tracks washed out of it. I washed the tracks out and took the rug back to him."

"But you didn't carry the rug back to him in the same condition it was in before you made the tracks on it."

His father did not answer, and now for perhaps half a minute there was no sound at all save that of breathing, the faint, steady suspiration of complete and intent listening.

"You decline to answer that, Mr. Snopes?" Again his father did not answer. "I'm going to find against you, Mr. Snopes. I'm going to find that you were responsible for the injury to Major de Spain's rug and hold you liable for it. But twenty bushels of corn seems a little high for a man in your circumstances to have to pay. Major de Spain claims it cost a hundred dollars. October corn will be worth about fifty cents. I figure that if Major de Spain can stand a ninety-five dollar loss on something he paid cash for, you can stand a five-dollar loss you haven't earned yet. I hold you in damages to Major de Spain to the amount of ten bushels of corn over and above your contract with him, to be paid to him out of your crop at gathering time. Court adjourned."

It had taken no time hardly, the morning was but half begun. He thought 80 they would return home and perhaps back to the field, since they were late, far behind all other farmers. But instead his father passed on behind the wagon, merely indicating with his hand for the older brother to follow with it, and crossed the road toward the blacksmith shop opposite, pressing on after his father, overtaking him, speaking, whispering up at the harsh, calm face beneath the weathered hat: "He won't git no ten bushels neither. He won't git one. We'll . . ." until his father glanced for an instant down at him, the face absolutely calm, the grizzled eyebrows tangled above the cold eyes, the voice almost pleasant, almost gentle:

"You think so? Well, we'll wait till October anyway."

The matter of the wagon — the setting of a spoke or two and the tightening of the tires — did not take long either, the business of the tires accomplished by driving the wagon into the spring branch behind the shop and letting it stand there, the mules nuzzling into the water from time to time, and the boy on the seat with the idle reins, looking up the slope and through the sooty tunnel of the shed where the slow hammer rang and where his father sat on an upended cypress bolt, easily, either talking or listening, still sitting there when the boy brought the dripping wagon up out of the branch and halted it before the door.

"Take them on to the shade and hitch," his father said. He did so and returned. His father and the smith and a third man squatting on his heels inside the door were talking, about crops and animals; the boy, squatting too in the ammoniac dust and hoof-parings and scales of rust, heard his father tell a long and unhurried story out of the time before the birth of the older brother even when he had been a professional horsetrader. And then his father came up beside him where he stood before a tattered last year's circus poster on the other side of the store, gazing rapt and quiet at the scarlet horses, the incredible poisings and convolutions of tulle and tights and the painted leers of comedians, and said, "It's time to eat."

But not at home. Squatting beside his brother against the front wall, he watched his father emerge from the store and produce from a paper sack a segment of cheese and divide it carefully and deliberately into three with his pocket knife and produce crackers from the same sack. They all three squatted on the gallery and ate, slowly, without talking; then in the store again, they drank from a tin dipper tepid water smelling of the cedar bucket and of living beech trees. And still they did not go home. It was a horse lot this time, a tall rail fence upon and along which men stood and sat and out of which one by one horses were led, to be walked and trotted and then cantered back and forth along the road while the slow swapping and buying went on and the sun began to slant westward, they — the three of them — watching and listening, the older brother with his muddy eyes and his steady, inevitable tobacco, the father commenting now and then on certain of the animals, to no one in particular.

It was after sundown when they reached home. They ate supper by lamp- 85 light, then, sitting on the doorstep, the boy watched the night fully accomplish, listening to the whippoorwills and the frogs, when he heard his mother's voice: "Abner! No! No! Oh, God. Oh, God. Abner!" and he rose, whirled, and saw the altered light through the door where a candle stub now burned in a bottle neck on the table and his father, still in the hat and coat, at once formal and burlesque as though dressed carefully for some shabby and ceremonial violence, emptying the reservoir of the lamp back into the five-gallon kerosene can from which it had been filled, while the mother tugged at his arm until he shifted the lamp to the other hand and flung her back, not savagely or viciously, just hard, into the wall, her hands flung out against the wall for balance, her mouth open and in her face the same quality of hopeless despair as had been in her voice. Then his father saw him standing in the door.

"Go to the barn and get that can of oil we were oiling the wagon with," he said. The boy did not move. Then he could speak.

"What . . ." he cried. "What are you . . ."

"Go get that oil," his father said. "Go."

Then he was moving, running, outside the house, toward the stable: this the old habit, the old blood which he had not been permitted to choose for himself, which had been bequeathed him willy nilly and which had run for so long (and who knew where, battening on what of outrage and savagery and lust) before it came to him. *I could keep on,* he thought. *I could run on and on and never look back, never need to see his face again. Only I can't. I can't,* the rusted can in his hand now, the liquid sploshing in it as he ran back to the house and into it, into the sound of his mother's weeping in the next room, and handed the can to his father.

"Ain't you going to even send a nigger?" he cried. "At least you sent a nig- 90 ger before!"

This time his father didn't strike him. The hand came even faster than the blow had, the same hand which had set the can on the table with almost excruciating care flashing from the can toward him too quick for him to follow it, gripping him by the back of his shirt and on to tiptoe before he had seen it quit the can, the face stooping at him in breathless and frozen ferocity, the cold, dead voice speaking over him to the older brother who leaned against the table, chewing with that steady, curious, sidewise motion of cows:

"Empty the can into the big one and go on. I'll catch up with you."

"Better tie him up to the bedpost," the brother said.

"Do like I told you," the father said. Then the boy was moving, his bunched shirt and the hard, bony hand between his shoulder-blades, his toes just touching the floor, across the room and into the other one, past the sisters sitting with spread heavy thighs in the two chairs over the cold hearth, and to where his mother and aunt sat side by side on the bed, the aunt's arms about his mother's shoulders.

"Hold him," the father said. The aunt made a startled movement. "Not 95 you," the father said. "Lennie. Take hold of him. I want to see you do it." His mother took him by the wrist. "You'll hold him better than that. If he gets loose don't you know what he is going to do? He will go up yonder." He jerked his head toward the road. "Maybe I'd better tie him."

"I'll hold him," his mother whispered.

"See you do then." Then his father was gone, the stiff foot heavy and measured upon the boards, ceasing at last.

Then he began to struggle. His mother caught him in both arms, he jerking and wrenching at them. He would be stronger in the end, he knew that. But he had no time to wait for it. "Lemme go!" he cried. "I don't want to have to hit you!"

"Let him go!" the aunt said. "If he don't go, before God, I am going up there myself!"

"Don't you see I can't?" his mother cried. "Sarty! Sarty! No! No! Help me, 100 Lizzie!"

Then he was free. His aunt grasped at him but it was too late. He whirled, running, his mother stumbled forward on to her knees behind him, crying to the nearer sister. "Catch him, Net! Catch him!" But that was too late too, the sister (the sisters were twins, born at the same time, yet either of them now gave the impression of being, encompassing as much living meat and volume and weight as any other two of the family) not yet having begun to rise from the chair, her head, face, alone merely turned, presenting to him in the flying instant an astonishing expanse of young female features untroubled by any surprise even, wearing only an expression of bovine interest. Then he was out of the room, out of the house, in the mild dust of the starlit road and the heavy rifeness of honeysuckle, the pale ribbon unspooling with terrific slowness under his running feet, reaching the gate at last and turning in, running, his heart and lungs drumming, on up the drive toward the lighted house, the lighted door. He did not knock, he burst in, sobbing for breath, incapable for the moment of speech; he saw the astonished face of the Negro in the linen jacket without knowing when the Negro had appeared.

"De Spain!" he cried, panted. "Where's . . ." then he saw the white man too emerging from a white door down the hall. "Barn!" he cried. "Barn!"

"What?" the white man said. "Barn?"

"Yes!" the boy cried. "Barn!"

"Catch him!" the white man shouted. 105

But it was too late this time too. The Negro grasped his shirt, but the entire sleeve, rotten with washing, carried away, and he was out that door too and in the drive again, and had actually never ceased to run even while he was screaming into the white man's face.

Behind him the white man was shouting, "My horse! Fetch my horse!" and he thought for an instant of cutting across the park and climbing the fence into the road, but he did not know the park nor how high the vine-massed fence might be and he dared not risk it. So he ran on down the drive, blood and breath roaring; presently he was in the road again though he could not see it. He could not hear either: the galloping mare was almost upon him before he heard her, and even then he held his course, as if the very urgency of his wild grief and need must in a moment more find him wings, waiting until the ultimate instant to hurl himself aside and into the weed-choked roadside ditch as the horse thundered past and on, for an instant in furious silhouette against the stars, the tranquil early summer night sky which, even before the shape of the horse and rider vanished, strained abruptly and violently upward: a long, swirling roar incredible and soundless, blotting the stars, and he springing up and into the road again, running again, knowing it was too late yet still running even after he heard the shot and, an instant later, two shots, pausing now without knowing he had ceased to run, crying "Pap! Pap!," running again before he knew he had begun to run, stumbling, tripping over something and scrabbling up again without ceasing to run, looking backward over his shoulder at the glare as he got up, running on among the invisible trees, panting, sobbing, "Father! Father!"

At midnight he was sitting on the crest of a hill. He did not know it was midnight and he did not know how far he had come. But there was no glare behind him now and he sat now, his back toward what he had called home for four days anyhow, his face toward the dark woods which he would enter when breath was strong again, small, shaking steadily in the chill darkness, hugging himself into the remainder of his thin, rotten shirt, the grief and despair now no longer terror and fear but just grief and despair. *Father. My father,* he thought. "He was brave!" he cried suddenly, aloud but not loud, no more than a whisper:

"He was! He was in the war! He was in Colonel Sartoris' cav'ry!" not knowing that his father had gone to that war a private in the fine old European sense, wearing no uniform, admitting the authority of and giving fidelity to no man or army or flag, going to war as Malbrouck° himself did: for booty—it meant nothing and less than nothing to him if it were enemy booty or his own.

The slow constellations wheeled on. It would be dawn and then sun-up after a while and he would be hungry. But that would be tomorrow and now he was only cold, and walking would cure that. His breathing was easier now and he decided to get up and go on, and then he found that he had been asleep because he knew it was almost dawn, the night almost over. He could tell that from the whippoorwills. They were everywhere now among the dark trees below him, constant and inflectioned and ceaseless, so that, as the instant for giving over to the day birds drew nearer and nearer, there was no interval at all between them. He got up. He was a little stiff, but walking would cure that too as it would the cold, and soon there would be the sun. He went on down the hill, toward the dark woods within which the liquid silver voices of the birds called unceasing—the rapid and urgent beating of the urgent and quiring heart of the late spring night. He did not look back.

Malbrouck: John Churchill, duke of Marlborough (1650–1722), English military commander who led the armies of England and Holland in the War of Spanish Succession.

CONSIDERATIONS FOR CRITICAL THINKING AND WRITING

1. FIRST RESPONSE. Who is "Barn Burning" about? Explain your choice.

2. Explain why Sarty is a dynamic or a static character. Which term best describes his father? Why?

3. Who is the central character in this story? Explain your choice.

4. How are Sarty's emotions revealed in the story's opening paragraphs? What seems to be the function of the italicized passages there and elsewhere?

5. What do we learn from the story's exposition that helps us understand Abner's character? How does his behavior reveal his character? What do other people say about him?

6. How does Faulkner's physical description of Abner further our understanding of his personality?

7. Explain how the justice of the peace, Mr. Harris, and Major de Spain serve as foils to Abner. Discuss whether you think they are round or flat characters.

8. Who are the story's stock characters? What is their purpose?

9. Explain how the description of Major de Spain's house helps to frame the main conflicts that Sarty experiences in his efforts to remain loyal to his father.

10. Write an essay describing Sarty's attitudes toward his father as they develop and change throughout the story.

11. What do you think happens to Sarty's father and brother at the end of the story? How does your response to this question affect your reading of the last paragraph?

12. How does the language of the final paragraph suggest a kind of resolution to the conflicts Sarty has experienced?

CONNECTIONS TO OTHER SELECTIONS

1. Compare and contrast Faulkner's characterizations of Abner Snopes in this story and Miss Emily in "A Rose for Emily" (p. 72). How does the author generate sympathy for each character even though both are guilty of terrible crimes? Which character do you find more sympathetic? Explain why.

2. How does Abner Snopes's motivation for revenge compare with Matt Fowler's in Andre Dubus's "Killings" (p. 81)? How do the victims of each character's revenge differ and thereby help to shape the meanings of each story?

3. Read the section on mythological criticism in Chapter 37, "Critical Strategies for Reading." How do you think a mythological critic would make sense of Sarty Snopes and Matt Fowler?

PERSPECTIVES ON FAULKNER

JANE HILES (B. 1951)

Hiles uses a biographical approach (see p. 2027 in Chapter 37, "Critical Strategies for Reading") to determine Faulkner's intentions in his characterization of how Sarty responds to the conflicts he feels about his father.

Blood Ties in "Barn Burning"   *1985*

"'You're getting to be a man. . . . You got to learn to stick to your own blood or you ain't going to have any blood to stick to you'" : Abner Snopes's admonition to his son, Colonel Sartoris (or "Sarty"), introduces a central issue in Faulkner's "Barn Burning" — the kinship bond, which the story's narrator calls the "old fierce pull of blood." The interpretive crux of the work is a conflict between determinism, represented by the blood tie that binds Sarty to his clan, and free will, dramatized by the boy's ultimate repudiation of family ties and his decampment. Dissonances between the structure and the imagery of the work develop and amplify Sarty's conflict: viewed in the light of the narrator's deterministic assumptions, the story's denouement is a red herring which only appears to resolve the complexities created by evocative language. Sarty's seeming interruption of the antisocial pattern established by his father is actually a continuation of it, and the ostensible resolution of his moral dilemma actually no resolution at all. . . .

In an interview in Japan sixteen years after the publication of "Barn Burning," Faulkner delivered an appraisal of the phenomenon of clannishness that bears considerable relevance to Abner Snopes's defensive posture in "Barn Burning":

Yes, we are country people and we have never had too much in material possessions because 60 or 70 years ago we were invaded and we were conquered. So we have been thrown back on our selves not only for entertainment but certain [sic] amount of defense. We have to be clannish just like the people in the Scottish highlands, each springing to defend his own blood whether it be right or wrong. Just a matter of custom and habit, we have to do it; interrelated that way, and usually there is hereditary head [sic] of the whole lot, as usually, the oldest son of the oldest son and each looked upon as chief of his own particular clan. That is the tone they live by. But I am sure it is because only a comparatively short time ago we were invaded by our own people — speaking in our own language which is always a pretty savage sort of warfare.

In Faulkner's estimation, the old pull of blood transcends considerations of caste, class, and occupation:

> . . . [I]t is regional. It is through what we call the "South." It doesn't matter what the people do. They can be land people, farmers, and industrialists, but there still exists the feeling of blood, of clan, blood for blood. It is pretty general through all the classes.[1]

Faulkner's explanation of the phenomenon of Southern clannishness touches upon a number of the issues that arise in "Barn Burning." In each case, alienation from the politically and economically dominant group leads to dependence upon an alternative source of security. Just as beleaguered Southerners, Faulkner suggests, have had to look to themselves for "defense" since the South was defeated, so Ab Snopes must turn to his kin for defense not only from Union troops but also from the landed Southern aristocrat who, in what Ab perceives as a failure of paternalism, "aims to begin . . . owning [him] body and soul." The clan's identifying characteristic, then, is its orientation to survival. Perhaps most interestingly, the comments made in the interview impinge upon the central issue of the morality of Sarty's choice. Faulkner's recognition here of a private code of honor suggests that Sarty's conduct is somewhat more questionable than is generally recognized, and his articulation in the interview of a necessity for clannishness suggests at least a modicum of sympathy for the "custom and habit" of "each springing to defend his own blood whether it be right or wrong."

From *Mississippi Quarterly: The Journal of Southern Culture*

[1] James B. Meriwether and Michael Millgate, eds., *Lion in the Garden* (New York: Random House, 1968), p. 191.

CONSIDERATIONS FOR CRITICAL THINKING AND WRITING

1. To what extent does Faulkner's description of clannishness in the South affect your understanding of whether Sarty resolves his dilemma at the end of the story?

2. Do you agree with Hiles that "Sarty's conduct is somewhat more questionable than is generally recognized" (para. 4)?

BENJAMIN DEMOTT (B. 1924)

DeMott pays close attention to matters of culture, race, class, and power that affect Abner Snopes, and from those perspectives Abner is seen as more than simply malevolent.

Abner Snopes as a Victim of Class   1988

We know that Ab Snopes is harsh to his wife, his sons, and his daughters, and that he is particularly cruel to his stock. We know that his hatred of the planters with whom he enters into sharecropping agreements repeatedly issues in acts of wanton destruction. We know that he's ridden with suspicion of his own closest kin, expecting them to betray him. And we know that— worse than any of this—he often behaves with fearful coldness to those who try desperately to communicate the loving respect they feel for him.

Given such a combination of racism, destructiveness, and blank insensitivity, it's tempting to imagine Ab as a figure in whom ignorance and brutality obliterate every sympathetic impulse, every normative response to peace, dignity, or beauty. Major de Spain seems to reach something close to that conclusion after the rug-laundering episode ("Wasn't there anybody here, any of your women . . ."). And although Ab's son is intensely loyal to his father and indignant at the injustice of the Major's twenty-bushel "charge" for the destruction of the rug, Sarty clearly has a conviction that "peace and dignity" are somehow *"beyond his [father's] touch, he no more to them than a buzzing wasp."* Is there anything to be made of Ab Snopes except a person whose raging malevolence has badly stunted if not crippled his humanity?

Denying the force of the malevolence is impossible—but tracing it solely to ignorance and insensitivity falsifies Ab's nature. Uneducated, probably illiterate, schooled in none of the revolutionary traditions which, in urban settings, were shaping popular protests against "economic injustice" when this story was written in the late 1930s, Ab nevertheless has managed, through the exercise of his own primitive intelligence, to make sense of his world, to arrive at a vision of the relations between labor, money, and the beautiful. It's a vision that's miles away from transforming itself into a broadly historical account of capital accumulation. Ab Snopes can't frame a theory to himself about, say, proletarian enslavement; he has no language in which to imagine a class solidarity leading to political action aimed at securing justice and truth. Indeed, he would explode at the notion that considerations of truth and justice have any pertinence either to the interests of the authorities opposing him or to his own interests in defying them. ("Later, twenty years later, [Sarty] was to tell himself, 'If I had said they wanted only truth, justice, he would have hit me again.'") For Ab Snopes the only principle lending significance to his war with the de Spains of this world is that of blood loyalty—determination to beat your personal enemy if you can and keep faith, at all costs, with your clan.

Yet despite all this, Ab does see that part of the power of the beautiful and the orderly to command our respect depends upon our refusal to remind ourselves that they have been brought into existence by other people's labor—by effort that often in history has been slave labor and has seldom been fairly recompensed. Sarty Snopes, grown up, presumably arrives finally at an understanding both that his father's situation was one of economic oppression and that the oppressors, when sitting in a court of law, are capable of attempting to reach beyond selfishness to a decent distribution of justice. But his father had, at the time, no grip on any of this.

Yet Ab is not a fool, and brutality and insensitivity are not the only features of character that we can make out in him. What we need also to summon is the terrible frustration of an undeveloped mind—aware of the weight of an immense unfairness, aware of the habit of the weak perpetually to behave as though the elegance, grace, beauty, and order found often in the neighborhoods of the rich somehow were traceable exclusively to the superior nature of the rich — and yet unable to move forward from either awareness to anything approaching rational protest. His rage cannot become a force leading toward any positive principle; it has no way to express itself except in viciousness to those closest at hand. It can't begin to make a serious bid for admiration, because whatever inclination we might have to admire it is instantly crossed by repugnance at the cruelty inherent in it.

But it remains true that, together with the ignorance and brutality in Ab Snopes, there is a ferocious, primitive undeceivedness in his reading of the terms of the relationship between rich and poor, lucky and unlucky, advantaged and disadvantaged. Ab Snopes has seen a portion of the truth of the world that many on his level, and most who are luckier, never see. We can damn him for allowing that truth to wreck his humanity, but when we fully bring him to life as a character, it's impossible not to include with our indictment a sense of pity.

From *Close Imagining: An Introduction to Literature*

CONSIDERATIONS FOR CRITICAL THINKING AND WRITING

1. DeMott acknowledges Abner's ignorance and brutality, but he also presents him as a man who suffers injustices. What are those injustices? Discuss whether you think they warrant a more balanced assessment of Abner's character.

2. Why doesn't Abner protest his "oppression" (para. 4)? Given DeMott's perspective on him, how might Abner — in another story — have been the hero rather than a terrible source of conflict?

3. To what extent can DeMott's approach to Abner's circumstances be described as a Marxist perspective? (For a discussion of Marxist criticism see p. 2033.)

GAYLE EDWARD WILSON (B. 1931)

The following analysis combines psychology and myth as a means of understanding the conflicts in "Barn Burning." The "Apollonian man" alluded to in the discussion (para. 1) refers to the myth of Apollo and implies a person who values order, community, balance, and self-knowledge to establish true relations between the individual and his world.

Conflict in "Barn Burning"   *1990*

Ruth Benedict's descriptions of two major patterns of culture provide an advantageous starting point for a discussion of the way in which Faulkner develops the content of "Barn Burning." The Paranoid way of life, she comments, has "no political organization. In a strict sense it has no legality."[1] As a consequence

---

[1] *Patterns of Culture* (New York, 1959), p. 122.

of the Paranoid man's adherence to this life-style, he is "lawless," and is feared as a warrior who will hesitate "at no treachery" (p. 121). In such a culture, "every man's hand is against every other man," and as a result each man relies upon blood ties to form social alliances and to sanction his actions (pp. 122-123). The Apollonian man, on the other hand, "keeps to the middle of the road, stays within the known map," and strives to fulfill his civic role in terms of the expectations of the community at large (p. 70). Men in such a society, although the blood tie is relatively important as a bond, turn to the community and its collected wisdom, as it is embodied in the law, for the approval of their actions and for their security. Thus the sanction for a man's "acts comes from the formal structure, not the individual" (p. 99) — from the community, not the blood kin. In "Barn Burning" Faulkner develops the ideas contained in these descriptions of dissimilar life-styles in a way which creates the central tension in the story and keeps it constantly before the reader. The reader is thus made aware of the pervasiveness of Sarty's *"terror and the grief, the being pulled two ways like between two teams of horses."*

The tension is made evident by the presence of effects which follow from actions taken in accord with the dominant characteristic of each life-style. Abner's "wolflike independence . . . his latent ravening ferocity . . . [and] conviction in the rightness of his own actions," which have frequently manifested themselves in acts of destruction against the property of an established community, clearly mark him as a follower of the Paranoid way. As such, his actions inevitably, and repeatedly, alienate him from each settled society into which he moves. His disregard for a "formal structure" of any kind is indicated by such a minor detail as that which occurs when Abner fuels his fire with "a rail lifted from a nearby fence and cut into lengths," an act which is symbolic of his rejection of any societally imposed limits. It is by burning barns, however, that Abner's Paranoid life-style and its consequences are most forcefully dramatized. At Abner's trial for barn burning, Sarty sees the men "between himself and the table part and become a lane of grim faces." Abner and Sarty then walk between the "two lines of grim-faced men" and they leave a "quiet crowd of grimly watching men." This separation of the Snopes family from the larger society as a consequence of acts motivated by Abner's "ravening ferocity" is underscored by the Justice's command to Abner: "Take your wagon and get out of this country before dark." The Snopes's wagon, containing "the sorry residue of the dozen and more movings," becomes, therefore, a symbol of the transient and nomadic way of life which the Snopes family is forced to adopt because of Abner's adherence to the Paranoid way. The de Spain tenant house and the manner in which the Snopes family lives in it are also effects of a life-style which is not concerned with permanence or order or boundaries or limits. The house is a "paintless two-room" structure "identical almost with the dozen others" in which the family has lived as a result of its nomadic existence, and the members of the family are found "scattered without order or claim up and down the two rooms."

On the other hand, the Harris and de Spain barns represent productivity and fertility, permanence and continuity, because they house the equipment, stock, and seed by which a society produces the goods to sustain and perpetuate itself. A barn and its contents are the effects of a society which is built upon the willingness of men to subordinate their unfettered desires to a communal consensus in order to develop a permanent community. The importance of a barn to the Apollonian way is illustrated by Sarty's thoughts when he sees the effect brought about by what a barn symbolizes. When he comes upon the de Spain house for the first time, he feels that *"the spell"* of *"peace and dignity"* cast by the magnificent house will render *"even the barns and stable and cribs which belong to it impervious to the puny flames he* [Abner] *might contrive."* The sight of this apotheosis of the Apollonian way has a profound effect on Sarty: he "at that instant . . . forgot his father. . . ." It is most revealing that Sartoris should compare this house which symbolizes the *"peace and dignity"* of the Apollonian way with another kind of building which, because of what it represents, embodies the very essence of an ordered society: *"Hit's big as a courthouse* he thought quietly, with a surge of peace and joy."

Essentially, it is the concept of law, as symbolized by the de Spain house, that gives Sarty his sense of "peace and joy," for it is the law that provides man with the peace necessary to develop the "formal structure" of a communal, stable society. Without law, as Hobbes tells us, "there is no place for Industry; because the fruit thereof is uncertain: and consequently no Culture of the Earth; . . . no commodius Building; . . . no Society; and which is worst of all, continuall feare, and danger of violent death; And the life of man, solitary, poore, nasty, brutish, and short."[2] At its best, the law is moderate, even, and impartial. It protects as well as punishes; it is an elaborately worked out system designed to join men together in a common purpose, to insure the presumption of innocence until guilt is proved, and to make the punishment commensurate with the crime. In "Barn Burning" the primacy of the law in an Apollonian society is made quite evident. It is represented in a minor way by the contract in which Snopes engages with de Spain to work for eight months in return for a share of the crop. It is developed in a major way in the two trials which take place. In the first trial, the law protects Abner from unwarranted conclusions. Concerning the charge that Abner burned Harris's barn, the Justice asks Harris, "But what proof have you, Mr. Harris?" Harris tells of the Negro who appeared and gave him the cryptic message, "'wood and hay kin burn,'" to which the Justice replies, "But that's not proof. Don't you see that's not proof?" In the second trial, de Spain's unreasonable assessment of twenty bushels of corn in payment for the rug Abner ruined is not allowed. Abner is fined ten bushels, not twenty, as de Spain had wanted. For the men in "Barn Burning," . . . then, the law and its equitable application to all men is the *sine qua non* of the Apollonian way. . . . It is this belief in the law and its extensions of "justice" and "civilization" which guides and controls the behavior of the Apollonian man. This is the same realization that young Sarty is only able to articulate "twenty years" after Abner strikes him for not being willing to lie in his defense at the trial. " 'If I had said they only wanted truth, justice, he would have hit me again.' "

From *Mississippi Quarterly*

[2] Chapter XIII, *"Of the NATURAL CONDITION of Mankind, as concerning their Felicity, and Misery," Leviathan . . .* (1651) in *Seventeenth-Century Verse and Prose*, ed. Helen White, Ruth Wallerstein, and Ricardo Quintana (New York, 1967), I, 223.

CONSIDERATIONS FOR CRITICAL THINKING AND WRITING

1. What distinctions are drawn between the "Paranoid man" and the "Apollonian man" (para. 1)? How do these two different types serve to frame the conflicts in "Barn Burning"?

2. How is Snopes's wagon an appropriate symbol of the "Paranoid way" (para. 1), and how are the Harris and de Spain barns fitting symbols of the "Apollonian way" (para. 3)?

3. In an essay explain why you think Sarty chooses one way of life over the other at the end of the story.

4. Compare Wilson's description of the story's conflicts with Hiles's and De-Mott's.

JAMES FERGUSON (B. 1928)

Ferguson's formalist approach (see p. 2025 in Chapter 37, "Critical Strategies for Reading") relates Faulkner's use of point of view to his thematic concerns in the story.

Narrative Strategy in "Barn Burning"   *1991*

The point of view is largely limited to the consciousness of Sarty Snopes, but in spite of his sensitivity and his intuitive sense of right and wrong, the little boy is far too young to understand his father and the complexities of the moral choice he must make. To enhance the pathos of his situation and the drama of Sarty's initiation into life, Faulkner felt the need for the occasional intrusion of an authorial voice giving the reader insights far beyond the capabilities of the youthful protagonist. A passage, for example, about the fires Abner Snopes builds affords us a sense of the rationale for the man's actions, of his strangely perverse integrity, which could not be supplied to us by the consciousness of his son:

> The nights were still cool and they had a fire against it, of a rail lifted from a nearby fence and cut into lengths — a small fire, neat, niggard almost, a shrewd fire; such fires were his father's habit and custom always, even in freezing weather. Older, the boy might have remarked this and wondered why not a big one; why should not a man who had not only seen the waste and extravagance of war, but who had in his blood an inherent voracious prodigality with material not his own, have burned everything in sight? Then he might have gone a step farther and thought that that was the reason: that niggard blaze was the living fruit of nights passed during those four years in the woods hiding from all men, blue or gray, with his strings of horses (captured horses, he called them). And older still, he might have divined the true reason: that the element of fire spoke to some deep mainspring of his father's being, as the element of steel or of powder spoke to other men, as the one weapon for the preservation of integrity, else breath were not worth the breathing, and hence to be regarded with respect and used with discretion.

Again, near the end of the story, after Sarty has betrayed his father, there is another brief shift away from the consciousness of the protagonist:

> "He was brave!" he cried suddenly, aloud but not loud, no more than a whisper: "He was! He was in the war! He was in Colonel Sartoris' cav'ry!" not knowing that his father had gone to that war a private in the fine old European sense, wearing no uniform, admitting the authority of and giving fidelity to no man or army or flag, going to war as Malbrouck himself did: for booty — it meant nothing and less than nothing to him if it were enemy booty or his own.

"Barn Burning" is incomparably richer than it would have been without such additions not only because they supply us with ironies otherwise unavailable to us but also because these manipulations of point of view dramatize *on the level of technique* the thematic matter of the story. The tensions between the awareness of the boy and the information supplied us by the authorial voice undergird and emphasize the conflicts between youth and age, innocence and sophistication, intuition and abstraction, decency and corruption, all of which lie at the core of the work.

From *Faulkner's Short Fiction*

CONSIDERATIONS FOR CRITICAL THINKING AND WRITING

1. In the first passage quoted by Ferguson how does the narrator's analysis of Abner Snopes become progressively sophisticated in explaining his reasons for building a small fire?

2. What other examples of shifts away from the consciousness of Sarty to a more informed point of view can you find in the story? Choose what you judge to be a significant example and write an essay about how Faulkner's use of point of view contributes to the story's themes.

QUESTIONS FOR WRITING
Incorporating the Critics

The following questions can help you to incorporate materials from critical essays into your own writing about a literary work. You may initially feel intimidated by the prospect of responding to the arguments of professional critics in your own paper. However, the process will not defeat you if you have clearly formulated your own response to the literary work and are able to distinguish it from the critics' perspectives. Reading the critics can help you to develop your own thesis — perhaps, to cite just two examples, by using them as supporting evidence or by arguing with them in order to clarify or qualify their points about the literary work. As you write and discover how to advance your thesis, you'll find yourself participating in a dialogue with the critics. This sort of conversation will help you to improve your thinking and hone your argument.

Keep in mind that the work of professional critics is a means of enriching your understanding of a literary work rather than a substitution for your own analysis and interpretation of that work. Quoting, paraphrasing, or summarizing a critic's perspective does not relieve you of the obligation of choosing a topic, organizing information, developing a thesis, and arguing your point of view by citing sufficient evidence from the text you are examining. These matters are discussed in further detail in Chapter 38, "Reading and Writing." You should also be familiar with the methods for documenting sources that are explained in Chapter 39, "The Literary Research Paper"; this chapter also contains important information about how to avoid plagiarism.

No doubt you won't find all literary criticism equally useful: some critics' arguments won't address your own areas of concern; some will be too difficult for you to get a handle on; and some will seem wrong-headed. However, much of the criticism you read will serve to make a literary work more accessible and interesting to you, and disagreeing with others' arguments will often help you to develop your own ideas about a work. When you use the work of critics in your own writing, you should consider the following questions. Responding to these questions will help you to ensure that you have a clear understanding of what a critic is arguing about a work, to what extent you agree with that argument, and how you plan to incorporate and respond to the critic's reading in your own paper. The more questions you can ask yourself in response to this list or as a result of your own reading, the more you'll be able to think critically about how you are approaching both the critics and the literary work under consideration.

1. Have you read the literary work carefully and taken notes of your own impressions before reading any critical perspectives so that your initial insights are not lost to the arguments made by the critics? Have you articulated your own responses to the work in a journal entry prior to reading the critics?

2. Are you sufficiently familiar with the literary work that you can determine the accuracy, fairness, and thoroughness of the critic's use of evidence from the work?

3. Have you read the critic's piece carefully? Try summarizing the critic's argument in a brief paragraph. Do you understand the nature and purpose of the critic's argument? Which passages are especially helpful to you? Which seem unclear? Why?

4. Is the critic's reading of the literary work similar to or different from your own reading? Why do you agree or disagree? What generational, historical, cultural, or biographical considerations might help to account for any differences between the critic's responses and your own?

5. How has your reading of the critic influenced your understanding of the literary work? Do issues that previously seemed unimportant now seem significant? What are these issues, and how does a consideration of them affect your reading of the work?

6. Are you too quickly revising or even discarding your own reading because the critic's perspective seems so polished and persuasive? Are you making use of your reading notes and the responses in your journal entries?

7. How would you classify the critic's approach? Through what kind of lens does the critic view the literary work? Is the critical approach formalist, biographical, psychological, sociological, mythological, reader-response, deconstructionist, or some combination of these or possibly other strategies? (For a discussion of these approaches, see Chapter 37, "Critical Strategies for Reading.")

8. What biases, if any, can you detect in the critic's approach? How might, for example, a southern critic's reading of "Barn Burning" differ from a northern critic's?

9. Can you determine how other critics have responded to the critic's work? Is the critic's work cited and taken seriously in other critics'

books and articles? Is the work dated by having been superseded by subsequent studies?

10. Are any passages or topics that you deem important left out by the critic? Do these omissions qualify or refute the critic's argument?

11. What judgments does the critic seem to make about the work? Is the work regarded, for example, as significant, unified, representative, trivial, inept, or irresponsible? Do you agree with these judgments? If not, can you develop and support a thesis about your difference of opinion?

12. What important disagreements do critics reveal in their approaches to the work? Do you find one perspective more convincing than another? Why? Is there a way of resolving their conflicting views that could serve as a thesis for your paper?

13. Can you extend or qualify the critic's argument to matters in the literary text that are not covered by the critic's perspective? Will this allow you to develop your own topic while acknowledging the critic's useful insights?

14. Have you quoted, paraphrased, or summarized the critic accurately and fairly? Have you avoided misrepresenting the critic's arguments in any way?

15. Are the critic's words, ideas, opinions, and insights adequately acknowledged and documented in the correct format? Do you understand the difference between common knowledge and plagiarism? Have you avoided quoting excessively? Are the quotations smoothly integrated into your own text?

16. Are you certain that your incorporation of the critic's work is for the purpose of developing your paper's thesis rather than for name-dropping or padding your paper? How can you explain to yourself why the critic's work is useful for your argument?

AN EXCERPT FROM A SAMPLE PAPER

The Fires of Class Conflict in "Barn Burning"

The following excerpt consists of the first few paragraphs of a sample student paper in which the student develops a thesis based on her reading of critical perspectives by Benjamin DeMott (p. 496) and Gayle Edward Wilson (p. 497). Sonia Metzger uses the two critics' different approaches to "Barn Burning" to develop a thesis that goes beyond either critic's perspective. The rest of her paper (not included) argues her thesis that a recognition of the class conflicts suppressed by Faulkner in the story makes Abner Snopes's violent response to the economic power inherent in Major de Spain's Apollonian values appear to be justifiable, rather than merely the desperate activity of a Paranoid man. Abner has good reason to fear Apollonian values because de Spain's world is carefully constructed to exclude him while simultaneously exploiting him.

Sonia Metzger

Professor Wolf

English 109

April 15, 19--

The Fires of Class Conflict in
"Barn Burning"

The central conflict in William Faulkner's "Barn Burning" concerns a young boy named Sarty Snopes who must choose between loyalty to his father and his family and loyalty to society and humanity. A first reading of the story probably leaves most readers with the sense that the boy must turn away from his father's vicious sensibilities if he is to grow into a responsible adult. Sarty faces tremendous pressure from his father to lie in court so that his father will not be convicted of barn burning. He knows his father wants him "to stick to your own blood or you ain't going to have any blood to stick to you" (484; all page references are to the class text, <u>The Bedford Introduction to Literature</u>, 5th ed.).

Unlike the selfish, mean, vengeful father who despises the wealth and gentility of the southern aristocracy and is relentless in his contempt for the upper-class world of Major de Spain, Sarty is a gentle, vulnerable character who engages our sympathy. He is divided between wanting his father's love and loving the "peace and dignity" (485) that de Spain's house evokes within him. Gayle Edward Wilson, one of the critics I've read, mostly agrees with this view of the story's conflict, but Benjamin DeMott goes beyond the focus on Sarty's conflicted conscience to examine another, more subtle dimension of the story--the reasons for Abner Snopes's ferocious rejection of the world he wants to burn down.

Our understanding of Abner and his son is, according

to Wilson, deepened by employing two concepts from Ruth
Benedict's Patterns of Culture that she calls the "Paranoid man" and the "Apollonian man." Abner is a version of
the Paranoid man. His culture consists of a lawless, clannish, fierce world in which his nomadic, lonely existence
is characterized by violence, hatred, force, and destruction. Except for blood ties, he rejects forms of any kind:
the stability created by the Apollonian man (Major de
Spain) through law and order in a community is his enemy.
He will not be bound by any societal regulations; instead,
he destroys any sense of community through his barn burning and his erratic antisocial behavior. For Wilson, Sarty
must turn away from the Paranoid man to the Apollonian man
if he is to pledge his loyalty to justice and civilization
(499). This conflict is also recognized by Benjamin DeMott,
who acknowledges Abner's harshness, cruelty, destructiveness, paranoia, and coldness but who also raises an important question that shifts some of our focus from Sarty
onto Abner: "Is there anything to be made of Ab Snopes
except a person whose raging malevolence has badly stunted
if not crippled his humanity?" (496).

By considering when "Barn Burning" was written--
during the depression of the late 1930s--DeMott suggests
a kind of defense for understanding and even sympathizing
with Abner by pointing to issues of class and power embedded in the capitalistic culture and the nearly slave-labor
conditions endured by Abner. This version of Abner is not
merely brutish but also suffering from "the terrible frustration of an undeveloped mind--aware of the weight of an
immense unfairness . . . and yet unable to move forward . . .
to anything approaching rational protest" (496-97). DeMott
suggests that Abner warrants our pity rather than total
repudiation and that he, however imperfectly, does feel

(even if he doesn't comprehend) the pain produced by the miserable gap between the rich and the poor. With this gap in mind, I want to go further than DeMott goes and argue, using Wilson's categories, that Faulkner's portrayal of Apollonian values avoids confronting the economic oppression that Abner experiences but that neither he nor Sarty can articulate. Abner may fit much of the description associated with the Paranoid man, but there are important social reasons for his rightfully fearing the economic power of the Apollonian man.

12

Cultural Case Study: James Joyce's "Eveline"

Close reading is an essential and important means of appreciating the literary art of a text. This formalist approach to literature explores the subtle, complex relationships between how a work is constructed using elements such as plot, characterization, point of view, diction, metaphor, symbol, irony, and other literary techniques to create a coherent structure that contributes to a work's meaning. (For a more detailed discussion of formalistic approaches to literary works, see Chapter 37, "Critical Strategies for Reading.") The formalist focuses on the text itself rather than the historical, political, economic, and other contexts of a text. A formalist reading of *The Scarlet Letter,* for example, is more likely to examine how the book is structured around a series of scenes in which the main characters appear on or near the town scaffold than to analyze how the text portrays the social and religious values of Nathaniel Hawthorne or of seventeenth-century Puritan New Englanders. Although recent literary criticism has continued to demonstrate the importance of close readings to discover how a text creates its effects on a reader, scholars also have made a sustained effort to place literary texts in their historical and cultural contexts.

Cultural critics, like literary historians, place literary works in the contexts of their times, but they do not restrict themselves to major historical moments or figures. Instead of focusing on, perhaps, Hawthorne's friendship with Herman Melville, a cultural critic might examine the relationship between Hawthorne's writing and popular contemporary domestic novels that are now obscure. Cultural critics might even examine the Classic Comic book version of *The Scarlet Letter* or one of its many film versions to gain insight into how our culture has reinterpreted Hawthorne's writing. The materials used by cultural critics are taken from both "high culture" and popular culture. A cultural critic's approach to James Joyce's work might include discussions of Dublin's saloons, political pamphlets, and Catholic sexual mores as well as connections to Ezra Pound or T. S. Eliot.

The documents that follow Joyce's "Eveline" in this chapter offer a glimpse of how cultural criticism can be used to provide a rich and revealing historical context for a literary work. They include an early twentieth-century photograph of Dublin, a portion of a temperance tract, a letter from an Irish woman who emigrated to Australia, and a plot synopsis of the opera *The Bohemian Girl:* all these documents figure in one way or another in "Eveline." These documents are suggestive rather than exhaustive, but they do evoke some of the culture contemporary to Joyce that informs the world he creates in "Eveline" and thereby allow readers to gain a broader and deeper understanding of the story itself.

JAMES JOYCE (1882–1941)

James Joyce was born in Dublin, Ireland, during a time of political upheaval. The country had endured nearly a century of economic depression and terrible famine and continued to suffer under what many Irish regarded as British oppression. Irish nationalism and independence movements attempted to counter British economic exploitation and cultural arrogance. Joyce, influenced by a climate in which ecclesiastical privilege and governmental authority were at once powerful and suspect, believed the Irish were also unable to free themselves from the Catholic Church's compromises and their own political ineptitude. Change was in the air, but Ireland was slow to be moved by the reform currents already rippling through the Continent.

Modernism, as it was developing on the Continent, challenged traditional attitudes about God, humanity, and society. Scientific and industrial advances created not only material progress but also tremendous social upheaval, which sometimes produced a sense of discontinuity, fragmentation, alienation, and despair. Firm certainties gave way to anxious doubts, and the past was considered more as something to be overcome than as something to revere. Heroic action seemed remote and theatrical to a writer like Joyce, who rejected the use of remarkable historic events in his fiction and instead focused on the everyday lives of ordinary people trying to make sense of themselves.

Joyce himself came from a declining middle-class family of more than a dozen children, eventually reduced to poverty by his father's drinking. Nevertheless, Joyce received a fine classical education at Jesuit schools, including University College, Dublin. His strict early education was strongly traditional in its Catholicism, but when he entered University College, he rejected both his religion and his national heritage. By the time he took his undergraduate degree in 1902, he was more comfortable casting himself as an alienated writer than as a typical citizen of Dublin, who he thought lived a life of mediocrity, sentimentality, and self-deception. While at college he studied modern languages and taught himself Norwegian so he could read the plays of Henrik Ibsen in their original language (see p. 1564 for Ibsen's *A Doll House*). Joyce responded deeply to Ibsen's dramatizations

James Joyce and Sylvia Beach, proprietor of the Parisian bookstore Shakespeare & Company, together in Paris during the "roaring twenties." In 1920 James Joyce and his family relocated to Paris, and in 1922 Beach published the first edition of Ulysses.

of troubled individuals who repudiate public morality and social values in their efforts to create lives of integrity amid stifling families, institutions, and cultures.

After graduation Joyce left Dublin for Paris to study medicine, but that career soon ended when he dropped out of the single course for which he had registered. Instead, he wrote poetry, which was eventually published in 1907 as *Chamber Music.* In 1903 he returned to Dublin to be with his mother, then dying of cancer. The next summer he met Nora Barnacle, while she was working in a Dublin boardinghouse. After leaving Dublin with Nora in 1905 to return to the Continent, he visited his native city only a few times (the final visit was in 1912), and he lived the rest of his life in Europe. From 1920 until shortly before his death, Joyce settled in Paris, where he enjoyed the stimulation of living amid writers and artists. He lived with Nora his entire life, having two children and eventually marrying her in 1931.

Joyce earned a living by teaching at a Berlitz language school, tutoring, and working in a bank, but mostly he gathered impressions of the world around him — whether in Trieste, Zurich, Rome, or Paris — that he would incorporate into his literary work. His writings, however, were always about life in Ireland rather than the European cities in which he lived. Fortunately, Joyce's talents attracted several patrons who subsidized his income and helped him to publish.

Dubliners, Joyce's first major publication in fiction, was a collection of stories that he published in 1914 and that included "Eveline." Two years later Joyce published *A Portrait of the Artist as a Young Man,* a novel. Joyce strongly identified with the protagonist, who, like Joyce, rejected custom and tradition. If the price of independence from deadening sensibilities, crass materialism, and a circumscribed life was alienation, then so be it. Joyce believed that if the artist was to see clearly and report what he saw freshly, it was necessary to stand outside the commonplace responses to experience derived from family, church, or country. His next novel, *Ulysses* (1922), is regarded by many readers as Joyce's masterpiece. This remarkably innovative novel is an account of one day in the life of an Irish Jew named Leopold Bloom, who, despite his rather ordinary life in Dublin, represents a microcosm of all human experience. Joyce's stream-of-consciousness technique revealed the characters' thoughts as they experienced them (see pp. 175–176 for a discussion of this technique). These uninhibited thoughts were censored in the United States until 1933, when a judge ruled in a celebrated court case that the book was not obscene. Though *Ulysses* is Joyce's most famous book, *Finnegans Wake* (1939) is his most challenging. Even more unconventional and experimental than *Ulysses,* it endlessly plays with language within a fluid dream world in which the characters' experiences evolve into continuously expanding meanings produced through complex allusions and elaborate puns in multiple languages. The novel's plot defies summation, but its language warrants exploration, which is perhaps best begun by hearing a recording of Joyce reading aloud from the book. His stylistic innovations in *Ulysses* and *Finnegans Wake* had as great an influence on literature as the automobile and the radio did on people's daily lives, when people started covering more ground and hearing more voices than ever before.

Dubliners is Joyce's quarrel with his native city, and his homage to it. Written between 1904 and 1907, it is the most accessible of Joyce's works. It consists of a series of fifteen stories about characters who struggle with oppressive morality, plodding routines, somber shadows, self-conscious decency, restless desires, and frail gestures toward freedom. These stories contain no conventional high drama or action-filled episodes; instead, they are made up of small, quiet moments that turn out to be important in their characters' lives. Most of the characters are on the brink of discovering something, such as loss, shame, failure, or death. Typically, the protagonist suddenly experiences a deep realization about himself or herself, a truth that is grasped in an ordinary rather than melodramatic moment. Joyce called such a moment — when a character is overcome by a flash of recognition — an **epiphany** and defined it as "sudden spiritual manifestation, whether in the vulgarity of speech or gesture or in a memorable phase of the mind itself." Even the most commonplace experience might yield a spontaneous insight into the essential nature of a person or situation. Joyce's characters may live ordinary lives cluttered with mundane details, but their lives have significance. Indeed, they seem to stumble onto significance when they least expect it.

Joyce weaves his characters' dreams and longings into the texture of Dublin life, a social fabric that appears to limit his characters' options. He once explained to his publisher that his intention in *Dubliners* "was to write a chapter of the moral history of my country," and he focused on Dublin because that city seemed to him "the center of paralysis." The major causes of his characters' paralysis are transmitted by their family life, Catholicism, economic situations, and vulnerability to political forces. His characters have lives consisting largely of self-denial and drab duties, but they also have an irrepressible desire for something more — as in "Eveline," which focuses on a dutiful daughter's efforts to run away with her lover.

CHRONOLOGY

1882	Born on February 2 in Dublin, Ireland.
1888–98	Studies at Jesuit schools in preparation for university.
1898–1902	Attends University College, Dublin, another Jesuit school, and graduates with a degree in modern languages.
1902	Studies medicine in Paris but soon abandons it for writing.
1903	Returns to be at his mother's deathbed in Dublin.
1904	Meets Nora Barnacle, with whom he will have two children and live his entire life.
1905	Moves to the Continent to teach at the Berlitz school in Trieste and write.
1907	After working in a bank for a year in Rome, he returns to Trieste; publishes *Chamber Music,* a volume of poems.
1912	Makes his final visit to Ireland.
1914	Publishes *Dubliners* after eight years of censorship battles.
1916	Publishes *A Portrait of the Artist as a Young Man.*
1917	Has the first of a series of debilitating eye operations.
1918	Publishes *Exiles,* a play.

1920	Settles in Paris with his family.
1922	Publishes *Ulysses* amid controversy concerning its alleged obscenity.
1927	Publishes *Pomes Penyeach.*
1931	Marries Nora Barnacle.
1934	Publishes *Collected Poems.*
1939	Publishes *Finnegans Wake.*
1940	After the German occupation of Paris, the Joyces move to Zurich.
1941	Dies of a perforated ulcer on January 13 at Zurich.

Eveline   1914

She sat at the window watching the evening invade the avenue. Her head was leaned against the window curtains and in her nostrils was the odor of dusty cretonne. She was tired.

Few people passed. The man out of the last house passed on his way home; she heard his footsteps clacking along the concrete pavement and afterwards crunching on the cinder path before the new red houses. One time there used to be a field there in which they used to play every evening with other people's children. Then a man from Belfast bought the field and built houses in it—not like their little brown houses but bright brick houses with shining roofs. The children of the avenue used to play together in that field—the Devines, the Waters, the Dunns, little Keogh the cripple, she and her brothers and sisters. Ernest, however, never played: he was too grown up. Her father used often to hunt them in out of the field with his blackthorn stick; but usually little Keogh used to keep *nix* and call out when he saw her father coming. Still they seemed to have been rather happy then. Her father was not so bad then; and besides, her mother was alive. That was a long time ago; she and her brothers and sisters were all grown up; her mother was dead. Tizzie Dunn was dead, too, and the Waters had gone back to England. Everything changes. Now she was going to go away like the others, to leave her home.

Home! She looked round the room, reviewing all its familiar objects which she had dusted once a week for so many years, wondering where on earth all the dust came from. Perhaps she would never see again those familiar objects from which she had never dreamed of being divided. And yet during all those years she had never found out the name of the priest whose yellowing photograph hung on the wall above the broken harmonium beside the colored print of the promises made to Blessed Margaret Mary Alacoque. He had been a school friend of her father. Whenever he showed the photograph to a visitor her father used to pass it with a casual word:

—He is in Melbourne now.

She had consented to go away, to leave her home. Was that wise? She tried ⁵ to weigh each side of the question. In her home anyway she had shelter and food; she had those whom she had known all her life about her. Of course she had to work hard both in the house and at business. What would they say of her in the Stores when they found out that she had run away with a fellow? Say she was a fool, perhaps; and her place would be filled up by advertisement. Miss Gavan would be glad. She had always had an edge on her, especially whenever there were people listening.

— Miss Hill, don't you see these ladies are waiting?

— Look lively, Miss Hill, please.

She would not cry many tears at leaving the Stores.

But in her new home, in a distant unknown country, it would not be like that. Then she would be married — she, Eveline. People would treat her with respect then. She would not be treated as her mother had been. Even now, though she was over nineteen, she sometimes felt herself in danger of her father's violence. She knew it was that that had given her the palpitations. When they were growing up he had never gone for her, like he used to go for Harry and Ernest, because she was a girl; but latterly he had begun to threaten her and say what he would do to her only for her dead mother's sake. And now she had nobody to protect her. Ernest was dead and Harry, who was in the church decorating business, was nearly always down somewhere in the country. Besides, the invariable squabble for money on Saturday nights had begun to weary her unspeakably. She always gave her entire wages — seven shillings — and Harry always sent up what he could but the trouble was to get any money from her father. He said she used to squander the money, that she had no head, that he wasn't going to give her his hard-earned money to throw about the streets, and much more, for he was usually fairly bad of a Saturday night. In the end he would give her the money and ask her had she any intention of buying Sunday's dinner. Then she had to rush out as quickly as she could and do her marketing, holding her black leather purse tightly in her hand as she elbowed her way through the crowds and returning home late under her load of provisions. She had hard work to keep the house together and to see that the two young children who had been left to her charge went to school regularly and got their meals regularly. It was hard work — a hard life — but now that she was about to leave it she did not find it a wholly undesirable life.

She was about to explore another life with Frank. Frank was very kind, manly, open-hearted. She was to go away with him by the night-boat to be his wife and to live with him in Buenos Aires where he had a home waiting for her. How well she remembered the first time she had seen him; he was lodging in a house on the main road where she used to visit. It seemed a few weeks ago. He was standing at the gate, his peaked cap pushed back on his head and his hair tumbled forward over a face of bronze. Then they had come to know each other. He used to meet her outside the Stores every evening and see her home. He took her to see *The Bohemian Girl* and she felt elated as she sat in an unaccustomed part of the theater with him. He was awfully fond of music and sang a little. People knew that they were courting and, when he sang about the lass that loves a sailor, she always felt pleasantly confused. He used to call her Poppens out of fun. First of all it had been an excitement for her to have a fellow and then she had begun to like him. He had tales of distant countries. He had started as a deck boy at a pound a month on a ship of the Allan Line going out to Canada. He told her the names of the ships he had been on and the names of the different services. He had sailed through the Straits of Magellan and he told her stories of the terrible Patagonians. He had fallen on his feet in

Buenos Aires, he said, and had come over to the old country just for a holiday. Of course, her father had found out the affair and had forbidden her to have anything to say to him.

—I know these sailor chaps, he said.

One day he had quarreled with Frank and after that she had to meet her lover secretly.

The evening deepened in the avenue. The white of two letters in her lap grew indistinct. One was to Harry; the other was to her father. Ernest had been her favorite but she liked Harry too. Her father was becoming old lately, she noticed; he would miss her. Sometimes he could be very nice. Not long before, when she had been laid up for a day, he had read her out a ghost story and made toast for her at the fire. Another day, when their mother was alive, they had all gone for a picnic to the Hill of Howth. She remembered her father putting on her mother's bonnet to make the children laugh.

Her time was running out but she continued to sit by the window, leaning her head against the window curtain, inhaling the odor of dusty cretonne. Down far in the avenue she could hear a street organ playing. She knew the air. Strange that it should come that very night to remind her of the promise to her mother, her promise to keep the home together as long as she could. She remembered the last night of her mother's illness; she was again in the close dark room at the other side of the hall and outside she heard a melancholy air of Italy. The organ-player had been ordered to go away and given sixpence. She remembered her father strutting back into the sickroom saying:

—Damned Italians! coming over here!   15

As she mused the pitiful vision of her mother's life laid its spell on the very quick of her being—that life of commonplace sacrifices closing in final craziness. She trembled as she heard again her mother's voice saying constantly with foolish insistence:

—Derevaun Seraun! Derevaun Seraun!°

She stood up in a sudden impulse of terror. Escape! She must escape! Frank would save her. He would give her life, perhaps love, too. But she wanted to live. Why should she be unhappy? She had a right to happiness. Frank would take her in his arms, fold her in his arms. He would save her.

She stood among the swaying crowd in the station at the North Wall. He held her hand and she knew that he was speaking to her, saying something about the passage over and over again. The station was full of soldiers with brown baggages. Through the wide doors of the sheds she caught a glimpse of the black mass of the boat, lying in beside the quay wall, with illumined portholes. She answered nothing. She felt her cheek pale and cold and, out of a maze of distress, she prayed to God to direct her, to show her what was her duty. The boat blew a long mournful whistle into the mist. If she went, tomorrow she would be on the sea with Frank, steaming toward Buenos Aires. Their passage had been booked. Could she still draw back after all he had done for her? Her distress awoke a nausea in her body and she kept moving her lips in silent fervent prayer.

A bell clanged upon her heart. She felt him seize her hand: 20

Derevaun Seraun!: "The end of pleasure is pain!" (Gaelic).

—Come!

All the seas of the world tumbled about her heart. He was drawing her into them: he would drown her. She gripped with both hands at the iron railing.

—Come!

No! No! No! It was impossible. Her hands clutched the iron in frenzy. Amid the seas she sent a cry of anguish!

—Eveline! Evvy!   25

He rushed beyond the barrier and called to her to follow. He was shouted at to go on but he still called to her. She set her white face to him, passive, like a helpless animal. Her eyes gave him no sign of love or farewell or recognition.

Considerations for Critical Thinking and Writing

1. FIRST RESPONSE. Explain why you agree or disagree with Eveline's decision.

2. Describe the character of Eveline. What do you think she looks like? Though there are no physical details about her in the story, write a one-page description of her as you think she would appear at the beginning of the story looking out the window.

3. Describe the physical setting of Eveline's home. How does she feel about living at home?

4. What sort of relationship does Eveline have with her father? Describe the range of her feelings toward him.

5. How is Frank characterized? Why does Eveline's father forbid them to see each other?

6. Why does thinking of her mother make Eveline want to "escape"?

7. Before she meets him at the dock, how does Eveline expect Frank to change her life?

8. Why doesn't she go with Frank to Buenos Aires?

9. What associations do you have about Buenos Aires? What symbolic value does this Argentine city have in the story?

10. Read carefully the water imagery in the final paragraphs of the story. How does this imagery help to suggest Eveline's reasons for not leaving with Frank?

11. Explain why you agree or disagree with Eveline's decision.

12. Write a one-page physical description of Eveline as you think she would be thirty years after her decision to remain at home.

Connections to Other Selections

1. How does Eveline's response to her life at home compare with that of the narrator in Gish Jen's "In the American Society" (p. 643)? Write an essay that explores the similarities and differences in their efforts to escape to something better.

2. Write an essay about the meaning of "home" to the protagonists in "Eveline" and Ernest Hemingway's "Soldier's Home" (p. 145).

DOCUMENTS

CONSIDERATIONS FOR CRITICAL THINKING AND WRITING

1. Describe what this photograph tells you. What does it tell you about life in Dublin? Explain whether you think this photograph confirms or challenges the view of Dublin presented by Joyce in "Eveline."

2. Write an essay describing the mood evoked by this photograph, and compare it with the tone associated with urban life in "Eveline."

Photograph of Poole Street in Dublin, taken during the period 1880–1914. This street gives a sense of the "little brown house" that Eveline calls home. Reproduced by permission of The National Library of Ireland.

Resources of Ireland 1910

The Alliance Temperance Almanack *was published in London. The following excerpt describes the cost of Ireland's drinking habits in economic terms.*

Much of the public attention is at this time drawn to the wants of the labouring poor of Ireland, and the great decay of her trade and manufactures. It may therefore be worth while to lay before our countrymen some calculations of the quantity of produce and employment which might arise from the whole population of that country agreeing to apply the vast sum, which, as stated below, is spent annually on whiskey in Ireland, to the encouragement of home manufactures, and the employment of the people. These advantages would follow in the most simple and natural course from the purchase of those articles of prime necessity, or of substantial comfort, the desire for which arises in the mind of every poor man whose habits do not lead him to prefer whiskey to domestic happiness. The Linen Manufacture, which *was* the staple trade of that island, the woollen trade, and the other more useful and indispensable occupations in a civilized community, are chiefly referred to; and the observer will be struck with the immense loss which that country sustains from the propensity to the use of Distilled Spirits.

"It appears from parliamentary returns, that the average quantity of Whiskey which paid excise duty in Ireland for each of the years 1826, 1827, 1828, and 1829, was Ten millions of Gallons. To this, if there be added one-sixth for reduction of strength by retailers, and also about Two Millions, Five Hundred Thousand Gallons made, but which did not pay duty, we shall have a total of upwards of *Fourteen Millions of Gallons, costing, at nine shillings per gallon, by retail, Six Millions Three Hundred Thousand Pounds sterling;* and being equal to a yearly consumption of more than Two Gallons for every man, woman, and child of our population."

* * *

The above remarks, though intended exclusively for Ireland, apply with great force to the United Kingdom generally. The ardent spirits, at full proof, on which duty was paid for home consumption in the year ending January 6, 1830, amounted to *twenty-seven millions five hundred and thirteen thousand two hundred and sixty gallons,* imperial measure. To this if we add, at a very low estimate as above, one-sixth, for the reduction of strength by retailers, without computing either the adulterations notoriously made, the spirits smuggled from the continent, or the still greater quantity produced by illicit distillation in Scotland and Ireland, we find that we have expended in one year for ardent spirits, *eighteen millions nine hundred and eleven thousand six hundred and fifty-eight pounds, ten shillings.*

Table I. Shewing that the sum of Six Millions Three Hundred Thousand Pounds, which the People of Ireland pay annually for Whiskey, if expended as follows, would provide

1. The population of Ireland, (computed at eight millions) with 2½ yards of linen each, amounting to 20,000,000 yards, at 1s. 3d. per yard	£1,250,000
2. Ten thousand men in each county in Ireland with 3½ yards of Corduroy each, amounting to 1,120,000 yards, at 1s. per yard	56,000
3. Four thousand men in each county with 3 yards of Kersey each, amounting to 384,000 yards, at 2s. 4d. per yard	44,800
4. Ten thousand men in each county with 2½ yards of Broad Cloth, amounting to 720,000 yards, at 4s. per yard	144,000
5. Four thousand men in each county with one hat each, amounting to 128,000 hats, at 5s. per hat	32,000
6. Three millions of women and children with 1¼ yard of Check, amounting to 3,750,000 yards, at 10d. per yard.	156,250
7. One million of women and children with 6 yards of stuff each, amounting to 6,000,000 yards, at 8d. per yard	200,000
8. Three millions of women and children with 6 yards of printed calico, each, amounting to 18,000,000 yards, at 8d. per yard	600,000
9. Three hundred and twenty thousand women with 2¼ yards of grey cloaking, amounting to 720,000 yards, at 2s. 8d. per yard	96,000
10. Four millions of men, women, and children, with 2½ yards of Flannel each, amounting to 10,000,000 yards, at 1s. per yard	500,000
11. Four millions of men, women, and children, with one pair of shoes each, at 5s. per pair	1,000,000
12. Four millions of men, women and children, with one pair of stockings each, at 1s. 3d. per pair	250,000
13. Ten thousand families in each county with one pair of blankets each, amounting to 320,000 pair, at 10s. per pair	160,000
14. Four hundred tons of oatmeal for each county, amounting to 12,800 tons, at £15 per ton	192,000
15. Three hundred tons of wheat meal for each county, amounting to 9,600 tons, at £18 per ton	172,800
16. Two thousand pigs for each county, amounting to 64,000 pigs at £2 per pig	128,000
17. Two thousand sheep for each county, amounting to 64,000 sheep, at £1 5s. per sheep	80,000
18. Five hundred cows for each county, amounting to 16,000 cows, at £10 per cow	160,000
19. And pay one thousand labourers in each county, (reclaiming land, &c.) amounting to 32,000 labourers, at 6s. per week each, or £15 12s. per year	499,200
20. And support 1,000 aged and infirm in each county, amounting to 32,000 at 6d. per day, or £9 per year each	288,000
21. And build fifty school-houses in each county, amounting to 1,600 at £100 each	160,000
22. And pay fifty school-masters at £50, and fifty school-mistresses at £30 per year, in each county, amounting to 3,200 teachers, at an average salary of £40 each	128,000
23. Leaving for other charitable purposes	2,950
	Total £6,300,000

Let us now see what might be done by a proper application of the money, which the most moderate habitual tippler spends on whiskey in the course of a year.

One glass of whiskey per day, commonly called by drinking men *"their morning,"* costs (at three half-pence per glass) Two pounds Five Shillings and Seven-pence Half-penny, yearly! which sum, if laid by, would provide the following clothing, viz.: —

	£	s	d
Three yards of Kersey for great coat, at 2s. 4d. per yard	£0	7	0
Two yards and a quarter of Broad Cloth for coat and waistcoat, at 5s. 4d. per yard	0	12	0
Three yards and a half of Corduroy for Trowsers, at 1s. per yard	0	3	6
Two Neck Handkerchiefs	0	1	7½
One Hat	0	5	0
One Pair of Shoes	0	7	0
Two Pair of Stockings	0	8	0
Two Shirts	0	8	6
	£2	5	7½

Six million three hundred thousand sovereigns in gold would extend in a line from the town of Roscommon to the Circular Road of Dublin, being a distance of 66¾ Irish miles, or 85 English miles, and would require 49 horses and carts to draw them, at one ton weight each draft.

The same sum, if laid down in shillings, would extend in a line of 1442 Irish miles, or 1835 English miles, and would require 669 horses and carts to draw them, at one ton weight each draft.

The same sum, if laid down in penny pieces, would extend in a line of 25,000 miles, equal to the computed distance round the globe!

The three last year's expenditure on whiskey, say £18,900,000, would afford nine guineas for each family (four persons), in Ireland, allowing the population as already stated, at eight millions of souls!

Note. — The cost of ardent spirits in the United Kingdom which exceeds *eighteen millions nine hundred and eleven thousand pounds sterling, yearly,* would, on the calculations given, afford employment to *four hundred and twenty-eight thousand seven hundred and fifty men;* circulating among them nearly *six million pounds sterling* in wages only.

Our magistrates have already publicly declared that this enormous expenditure of £18,911,658 10s. is not to be regarded as merely useless, but horribly injurious; and their testimony is amply supported by the voice of *ninety five thousand offenders* committed within the past year to the prisons of England and Wales only. On high authority it is asserted that four-fifths of the crimes, three-fourths of the beggary, and one-half of all the madness of our countrymen arise from drinking. Have we nothing to learn from America, where, by the associated efforts of the sober and intelligent for the purpose of discouraging the use of ardent spirits, their consumption is already diminished one-third throughout the whole Union?

From *The Alliance Temperance Almanack* for 1910

CONSIDERATIONS FOR CRITICAL THINKING AND WRITING

1. Describe the tone of this analysis of Ireland's consumption of alcohol. Why is it significant that this temperance publication originates from England?

2. What sort of economic argument is made here? Explain why you find it convincing or not.

3. How does this document speak to the conditions of Eveline Hill's life? Pay particular attention to paragraph 9 of the story.

A Letter Home from an Irish Emigrant in Australia   1882

The excerpt below comes from a letter written by Bridget Burke, who, at the age of twenty-one, emigrated from Galway, Ireland, to Brisbane, Australia. Though her spelling is rough, her affection for her brother John is clear.

Dear John
I am 40 Miles from My uncle. I feal Quare without a Home to goe to when on My sunday out. I often wish to Have you out Heare. I ame verry strange out Here. I cannot make free with any body. I often Have a Walk with Patt [her brother] & Has a long yarn of Home. He is verry Kind became a steady fellow since He Left Home & also I could not expect My father to be a bit better than My Uncle. His wife & children is all right it is a nice place to go but it is to [too] far away but My brother is near me & comes to see me 2 or 3 times a week. We often Have some fun talking of the Old times at Home.

Dear John you wanted to know How do I Like the Country or what sort of people are heare. John that Queston I cannot answer. There is all sortes black & white misted & married together & Living in pretty Cotages Just the same as the white people. Thire is English Irish French German Italian black Chineease and not forgetin the Juse [Jews]. There are verry rich fancy John white girls marrid to a black man & Irish girls to [too] & to Yellow Chinaman with their Hair platted down there[?] black back. Sow [so] you see that girls dont care what the do in this Country. The would do anny think [anything] before the worke & a great Lot of them does worse[?] than that same. & this is a fine Country for a Young person that can take care of himselfe.

Now John I must ask you for all my Aunts & Uncles Cousins friends & Neighbours sweet Harts & all also did Cannopy die yet. Now John I must Conclude Hoping that You will send me as Long a Letter as I have send you & Lett me know all about Home. Dirrect Your Letter as[?] Patt told you for me, I Have more[?] to say but remaning yours fond sister for ever

BDB
From David Fitzpatrick, *Oceans of Consolation: Personal Accounts of Irish Migration to Australia,*
Cornell University Press (1994)

Considerations for Critical Thinking and Writing

1. How does Bridget feel about living in Australia? How does she feel about Ireland?

2. How is Australia's social structure different from Ireland's?

3. How does this letter help to fill in Eveline's feelings about leaving Ireland for Buenos Aires?

4. Research life in Buenos Aires during the first fifteen years of the twentieth century. What would it have been like to live there then? How would it be different from Ireland?

A Plot Synopsis of The Bohemian Girl   1843

The following synopsis recounts the story of The Bohemian Girl, *a well-loved opera by Michael William Balfe that played in the principal capitals of Europe, North America, and South America. It gives a sense of the romantic narrative Eveline and Frank would have seen at the opera.*

The action of this drama commences at the chateau of Count Arnheim, in Austria. The peasantry and retainers of the Count are making preparations for the chase, when Thaddeus, a Polish exile and fugitive from the Austrian troops, arrives in search of shelter and concealment. Here he encounters a band of Gipsies, headed by one Devilshoof, who, learning from Thaddeus that he is pursued by soldiers, gives him a disguise, conceals him, and puts the pursuing troops on the wrong track. Just at this time, shouts of distress are heard, and Florestein appears surrounded by huntsmen. The Count's child and her attendant have been attacked by an infuriated stag in the forest, and are probably destroyed. Hearing this, Thaddeus seizes a rifle, and hastens to their relief, and by a well-aimed shot kills the animal, and saves them from destruction. The Count now returns in time to hear of the peril of his darling child, and to see Thaddeus bearing her wounded form in his arms. Overjoyed to find her still alive, the Count overwhelms Thaddeus with grateful thanks, and invites him to join in the festivities about to take place. Thaddeus at first declines, but being warmly entreated to remain, at length consents to do so. They seat themselves at table, and the Count proposes as a toast, "Health and long life to the Emperor!" All except Thaddeus do honor to the toast, and his silence being observed, the Count challenges him to empty his goblet as the rest have done. Thaddeus, to the surprise of all, dashes the wine to the earth; this, of course, produces a burst of indignation. The assembled guests are infuriated by such an indignity to their monarch, and threaten the life of Thaddeus. At this moment Devilshoof returns, and at once takes sides with Thaddeus. The Count orders Devilshoof to be secured. The attendants seize and carry him into the castle. Thaddeus departs, and festivities are resumed. During the *fête*, Devilshoof escapes, taking with him the Count's infant daughter, Arline; and his flight being almost immediately discovered, the greatest excitement prevails. Peasants, huntsmen, and attendants hasten in search of the daring fugitive, and he is seen bearing the child across a dangerous precipice; he escapes, and the unhappy father sinks in despair as the First Act ends.

Twelve years are supposed to elapse, and we are transported to the city of Presburg, in the suburbs of which the Gipsies are encamped with the Queen of their tribe in whose tent dwells the Count's daughter, Arline, now a fine young woman. Florestein, a foppish *attaché* to the Court, is met by Devilshoof and his companions, who relieve him of his jewelry, among which is a medallion, which Devilshoof carries off. Thaddeus, who has joined the tribe, is now enamored of Arline, and he tells her that it was he who saved her life in infancy, but he still carefully conceals from her the secret of her birth. Arline confesses her love for Thaddeus, and they are betrothed according to the custom of the Gipsy tribe.

A grand fair is in progress in the plaza of the city, and hither, of course, come all the Gipsies, who add to the gayety and life of the scene by their peculiar dances, songs, etc. Florestein appears, and is quite fascinated by the beauty of Arline. While trying to engage her attention, he perceives his medallion hanging on her neck and claims it, charging her with having stolen it. This leads to great excitement: the guard is called, Arline is arrested, and the crowd dispersed by the soldiery. The supposed culprit is brought before Count Arnheim; Florestein presses the charge, and circumstances strengthen the appearance of guilt against Arline, when the Count perceives the mark left by the wound inflicted by the deer on Arline's arm. He asks its origin. She repeats the story as related to her by Thaddeus. The Count recognizes his long-lost child, and the Act ends with an effective *tableau*.

In the Third Act we find Arline restored to her rank and the home of her father; but the change in her prospects does not diminish her love for Thaddeus. He, daring all dangers for an interview, seeks and finds her here. He comes to bid her farewell, and prays that she will, even when surrounded by other admirers, give a thought to him who saved her life, and who loves her. She promises fidelity, and declares herself his and his only. Here we find that the Gipsy Queen, who also loves Thaddeus, has been plotting to take him from Arline. By her device the medallion was discovered in the possession of Arline. Even now she is conspiring to separate the lovers, but her plots fail. Thaddeus relates his history to Count Arnheim, who, in gratitude to the preserver of his child, bestows her upon him. Desire for vengeance now fills the heart of the Gipsy Queen; she induces one of her tribe to fire at Thaddeus as he is embracing Arline, but by a timely movement of Devilshoof the bullet reaches her own heart.

From *The Bohemian Girl*, edited by Richard Aldrich (1902)

CONSIDERATIONS FOR CRITICAL THINKING AND WRITING

1. Describe the action of this opera. How does its plot compare with Eveline's life?

2. Why do you suppose Joyce has Frank take Eveline to this particular opera?

3. One of the songs of *The Bohemian Girl* is titled "Tis Sad to Leave Our Fatherland" and contains these verses: "Without / friends, and without a home, my country too! yes, I'm exiled from thee; what / fate, what fate awaits me here, now! Pity, Heav'n! oh calm my despair!" How do these lines shed light on Eveline's situation?

13

A Collection of Stories

The eighteen short stories in this chapter represent a broad variety of styles and themes. They are written by men and women from a number of countries whose lives collectively span the nineteenth and twentieth centuries. The five stories in "An Album of World Literature," by writers from Chile, Botswana, Egypt, Japan, and China, introduce themes and styles from traditions that might differ quite a bit from your own. The five stories in "An Album of Contemporary Stories" — each written within the past ten years — offer a sustained opportunity to explore the fiction being produced today. Inevitably, you will find some of the following stories more appealing than others, but every one of them is worth a careful reading, the kind of reading rewarded by pleasure and understanding.

CHARLES JOHNSON (B. 1948)
Exchange Value   *1982*

Me and my brother, Loftis, came in by the old lady's window. There was some kinda boobytrap — boxes of broken glass — that shoulda warned us Miss Bailey wasn't the easy mark we made her to be. She been living alone for twenty years in 4-B down the hall from Loftis and me, long before our folks died — a hincty, halfbald West Indian woman with a craglike face, who kept her door barricaded, shutters closed, and wore the same sorry-looking outfit — black wingtip shoes, cropfingered gloves in winter, and a man's floppy hat — like maybe she dressed half-asleep or in a dark attic. Loftis, he figured Miss Bailey had some grandtheft dough stashed inside, jim, or leastways a shoebox full of money, 'cause she never spent a nickel on herself, not even for food, and only left her place at night.

Anyway, we figured Miss Bailey was gone. Her mailbox be full, and Pookie White, who run the Thirty-ninth Street Creole restaurant, he say she ain't dropped by in days to collect the handouts he give her so she can get by. So here's me and Loftis, tipping around Miss Bailey's blackdark kitchen. The floor be littered with fruitrinds, roaches, old food furred with blue mold. Her dirty dishes be stacked in a sink feathered with cracks, and it looks like the old lady been living, lately, on Ritz crackers and Department of Agriculture (Welfare Office) peanut butter. Her toilet be stopped up, too, and, on the bathroom floor, there's five Maxwell House coffee cans full of shit. Me, I was closing her bathroom door when I whiffed this evil smell so bad, so thick, I could hardly breathe, and what air I breathed was stifling, like solid fluid in my throatpipes, like broth or soup. "Cooter," Loftis whisper, low, across the room, "you smell that?" He went right on sniffing it, like people do for some reason when something be smelling stanky, then took out his headrag and held it over his mouth. "Smells like something crawled up in here and died!" Then, head low, he slipped his long self into the living room. Me, I stayed by the window, gulping for air, and do you know why?

You oughta know, up front, that I ain't too good at this gangster stuff, and I had a real bad feeling about Miss Bailey from the get-go. Mama used to say it was Loftis, not me, who'd go places — I see her standing at the sideboard by the sink now, big as a Frigidaire, white flour to her elbows, a washtowel over her shoulder, while we ate a breakfast of cornbread and syrup. Loftis, he graduated fifth at DuSable High School, had two gigs and, like Papa, he be always wanting the things white people had out in Hyde Park, where Mama did daywork sometimes. Loftis, he be the kind of brother who buys *Esquire*, sews Hart, Schaffner & Marx labels in Robert Hall suits, talks properlike, packs his hair with Murray's; and he took classes in politics and stuff at the Black People's Topographical Library in the late 1960s. At thirty, he make his bed military-style, reads *Black Scholar* on the bus he takes to the plant, and, come hell or high water, plans to make a Big Score. Loftis, he say I'm 'bout as useful on a hustle — or when it comes to getting ahead — as a headcold, and he says he has to count my legs sometimes to make sure I ain't a mule, seeing how, for all my eighteen years, I can't keep no job and sorta stay close to home, watching TV, or reading *World's Finest* comic books, or maybe just laying dead, listening to music, imagining I see faces or foreign places in water stains on the wallpaper, 'cause some days, when I remember Papa, then Mama, killing theyselves for chump change — a pitiful li'l bowl of porridge — I get to thinking that even if I ain't had all I wanted, maybe I've had, you know, all I'm ever gonna get.

"Cooter," Loftis say from the living room. "You best get in here quick."

Loftis, he'd switched on Miss Bailey's bright, overhead living room lights, so for a second I couldn't see and started coughing — the smell be so powerful it hit my nostrils like coke — and when my eyes cleared, shapes come forward in the light, and I thought for an instant like I'd slipped in space. I seen why Loftis called me, and went back two steps. See, 4-B's so small if you ring Miss Bailey's doorbell, the toilet'd flush. But her living room, webbed in dust, be filled to the max with dollars of all denominations, stacks of stock in General Motors, Gulf Oil, and 3M Company in old White Owl cigar boxes, battered purses, or bound in pink rubber bands. It be like the kind of cubbyhole kids play in, but filled with . . . *things*: everything, like a world inside the world, you take it from me, so like picturebook scenes of plentifulness you could seal yourself off in here and settle forever. Loftis and me both drew breath suddenly. There be unopened cases of Jack Daniel's, three safes cemented to the floor, hundreds of matchbooks, unworn clothes, a fuel-burning stove, dozens of wedding rings, rubbish, World War II magazines, a carton of a hundred canned sardines, mink stoles, old rags, a birdcage, a bucket of silver dollars, thousands of books, paintings, quarters in tobacco cans, two pianos, glass jars of pennies, a set of bagpipes, an almost complete Model A Ford dappled with rust, and, I swear, three sections of a dead tree.

"Damn!" My head be light; I sat on an upended peach crate and picked up a bottle of Jack Daniel's.

"Don't you touch *anything*!" Loftis, he panting a little; he slap both hands on a table. "No until we inventory this stuff."

"Inventory? Aw, Lord, Loftis," I say, "something ain't *right* about this stash. There could be a curse on it. . . ."

"Boy, sometime you act weak-minded."

"For real, Loftis, I got a feeling. . . ." 10

Loftis, he shucked off his shoes, and sat down heavily on the lumpy arm of a stuffed chair. "Don't say *anything*." He chewed his knuckles, and for the first time Loftis looked like he didn't know his next move. "Let me think, okay?" He squeezed his nose in a way he has when thinking hard, sighed, then stood up and say, "There's something you better see in that bedroom yonder. Cover up your mouth."

"Loftis, I ain't going in there."

He look at me right funny then. "She's a miser, that's all. She saves things."

"But a tree?" I say. "Loftis, a *tree* ain't normal!"

"Cooter, I ain't gonna tell you twice." 15

Like always, I followed Loftis, who swung his flashlight from the plant — he a night watchman — into Miss Bailey's bedroom, but me, I'm thinking how trippy this thing is getting, remembering how, last year, when I had a paper route, the old lady, with her queer, crablike walk, pulled my coat for some change in the hallway, and when I give her a handful of dimes, she say, like one of them spooks on old-time radio, "Thank you, Co-o-oter," then gulped the coins down like aspirin, no lie, and scurried off like a hunchback. Me, I wanted no parts of this squirrely old broad, but Loftis, he holding my wrist now, beaming his light onto a low bed. The room had a funny, museumlike smell. Real sour. It was full of dirty laundry. And I be sure the old lady's stuff had a terrible string attached when Loftis, looking away, lifted her bedsheets and a knot of black flies rose. I stepped back and held my breath. Miss Bailey be in her long-sleeved flannel nightgown, bloated, like she'd been blown up by a bicycle pump, her old face caved in with rot, flyblown, her fingers big and colored like spoiled bananas. Her wristwatch be ticking softly beside a half-eaten hamburger. Above the bed, her wall had roaches squashed in little swirls of bloodstain. Maggots clustered in her eyes, her ears, and one fist-sized rat hissed inside her flesh. My eyes snapped shut. My knees failed; then I did a Hollywood faint. When I surfaced, Loftis, he be sitting beside me in the living room, where he'd drug me, reading a wrinkled, yellow article from the *Chicago Daily Defender*.

"Listen to this," Loftis say. "'Elnora Bailey, forty-five, a Negro housemaid in the Highland Park home of Henry Conners, is the beneficiary of her employer's will. An old American family, the Conners arrived in this country on the *Providence* shortly after the voyage of the *Mayflower*. The family flourished in the early days of the 1900s.'. . ." He went on, getting breath: "'A distinguished and wealthy industrialist, without heirs or a wife, Conners willed his entire estate to Miss Bailey of 3347 North Clark Street for her twenty years of service to his family.'. . . ." Loftis, he give that Geoffrey Holder laugh of his, low and deep; then it eased up his throat until it hit a high note and tipped his head back onto his shoulders. "Cooter, that was before we was born! Miss Bailey kept this in the Bible next to her bed."

Standing, I braced myself with one hand against the wall. "She didn't earn it?"

"Naw." Loftis, he folded the paper — "Not one penny" — and stuffed it in his shirt pocket. His jaw looked tight as a horseshoe. "Way *I* see it," he say, "this was her one shot in a lifetime to be rich, but being country, she had backward ways and blew it." Rubbing his hands, he stood up to survey the living room. "Somebody's gonna find Miss Bailey soon, but if we stay on the case — Cooter, don't square up on me now — we can tote everything to our place before daybreak. Best we start with the big stuff."

"But why didn't she *use* it, huh? Tell me that?"   20

Loftis, he don't pay me no mind. When he gets an idea in his head, you can't dig it out with a chisel. How long it took me and Loftis to inventory, then haul Miss Bailey's queer old stuff to our crib, I can't say, but that cranky old ninnyhammer's hoard come to $879,543 in cash money, thirty-two bank books (some deposits be only $5), and me, I wasn't sure I was dreaming or what, but I suddenly flashed on this feeling, once we left her flat, that all the fears Loftis and me had about the future be gone, 'cause Miss Bailey's property was the past — the power of that fellah Henry Conners trapped like a bottle spirit — which we could live off, so it was the future, too, pure potential: can *do*. Loftis got to talking on about how that piano we pushed home be equal to a thousand bills, jim, which equals, say, a bad TEAC A-3340 tape deck, or a down payment on a deuce-and-a-quarter. Its value be (Loftis say) that of a universal standard of measure, relational, unreal as number, so that tape deck could turn, magically, into two gold lamé suits, a trip to Tijuana, or twenty-five blow jobs from a ho — we had $879,543 worth of wishes, if you can deal with that. Be like Miss Bailey's stuff is raw energy, and Loftis and me, like wizards, could transform her stuff into anything else at will. All we had to do, it seemed to me, was decide exactly what to exchange it for.

While Loftis studied this over (he looked funny, like a potato trying to say something, after the inventory, and sat, real quiet, in the kitchen), I filled my pockets with fifties, grabbed me a cab downtown to grease, yum, at one of them high-hat restaurants in the Loop. . . . But then I thought better of it, you know, like I'd be out of place — just another jig putting on airs — and scarfed instead at a ribjoint till both my eyes bubbled. This fat lady making fishburgers in the back favored an old hardleg baby-sitter I once had, a Mrs. Paine who made me eat ocher, and I wanted so bad to say, "Loftis and me Got Ovuh," but I couldn't put that in the wind, could I, so I hatted up. Then I copped a boss silk necktie, cashmere socks, and a whistle-slick maxi leather jacket on State Street, took cabs *every*where, but when I got home that evening, a funny, Pandora-like feeling hit me. I took off the jacket, boxed it — it looked trifling in the hallway's weak light — and, tired, turned my key in the door. I couldn't get in. Loftis, he'd changed the lock and, when he finally let me in, looking vaguer, crabby, like something out of the Book of Revelations, I seen this elaborate, booby-trapped tunnel of cardboard and razor blades behind him, with a two-foot space just big enough for him or me to crawl through. That wasn't all. Two bags of trash from the furnace room downstairs be sitting inside the door. Loftis, he give my leather jacket this evil look, hauled me inside, and hit me upside my head.

"How much this thing set us back?"

"Two fifty." My jaws got tight; I toss him my receipt. "You want me to take it back? Maybe I can get something else. . . ."

Loftis, he say, not to me, but to the receipt, "Remember the time Mama give me that ring we had in the family for fifty years? And I took it to Merchandise Mart and sold it for a few pieces of candy?" He hitched his chair forward and sat with his elbows on his knees. "That's what you did, Cooter. You crawled into a Clark bar." He commence to rip up my receipt, then picked up his flashlight and keys. "As soon as you buy something you *lose* the power to buy something." He button up his coat with holes in the elbows, showing his blue shirt, then turned 'round at the tunnel to say, "Don't touch Miss Bailey's money, or drink her splo, or do *anything* until I get back."

"Where you going?"

"To work. It's Wednesday, ain't it?"

"You going to work?"

"Yeah."

"You got to go *really?* Loftis," I say, "what you brang them bags of trash in here for?"

"It ain't trash!" He cut his eyes at me. "There's good clothes in there. Mr. Peterson tossed them out, he don't care, but I saw some use in them, that's all."

"Loftis . . ."

"Yeah?"

"What we gonna do with all this money?"

Loftis pressed his fingers to his eyelids, and for a second he looked caged, or like somebody'd kicked him in his stomach. Then he cut me some slack: "Let me think on it tonight — it don't pay to rush — then we can TCB, okay?"

Five hours after Loftis leave for work, that old blister Mr. Peterson, our landlord, he come collecting rent, find Mrs. Bailey's body in apartment 4-B, and phoned the fire department. Me, I be folding my new jacket in tissue paper to keep it fresh, adding the box to Miss Bailey's unsunned treasures when two paramedics squeezed her on a long stretcher through a crowd in the hallway. See, I had to pin her from the stairhead, looking down one last time at this dizzy old lady, and I seen something in her face, like maybe she'd been poor as Job's turkey for thirty years, suffering that special Negro fear of using up what little we get in this life — Loftis, he call that entropy — believing in her belly, and for all her faith, jim, that there just ain't no more coming tomorrow from grace, or the Lord, or from her own labor, like she can't kill nothing, and won't nothing die . . . so when Conners will her his wealth, it put her through changes, she be spellbound, possessed by the promise of life, panicky about depletion, and locked now in the past 'cause *every* purchase, you know, has to be a poor buy: a loss of life. Me, I wasn't worried none. Loftis, he got a brain trained by years of talking trash with people in Frog Hudson's barbershop on Thirty-fifth Street. By morning, I knew, he'd have some kinda wheeze worked out.

But Loftis, he don't come home. Me, I got kinda worried. I listen to the hi-fi all day Thursday, only pawing outside to peep down the stairs, like that'd make Loftis come sooner. So Thursday go by; and come Friday the head's out of kilter — first there's an ogrelike belch from the toilet bowl, then water bursts from the bathroom into the kitchen—and me, I can't call the super (How do I explain the tunnel?), so I gave up and quit bailing. But on Saturday, I could smell greens cooking next door. Twice I almost opened Miss Bailey's sardines, even though starving be less an evil than eating up our stash, but I waited till it was dark and, with my stomach talking to me, stepped outside to Pookie White's, lay a hard-luck story on him, and Pookie, he give me some jambalaya and gumbo. Back home in the living room, finger-feeding myself, barricaded in by all that hope-made material, the Kid felt like a king in his counting room, and I copped some Zs in an armchair till I heard the door move on its hinges, then bumping in the tunnel, and a heavy-footed walk thumped into the bedroom.

"Loftis!" I rubbed my eyes. "You back?" It be Sunday morning. Six-thirty sharp. Darkness dissolved slowly into the strangeness of twilight, with the rays of sunlight surging at exactly the same angle they fall each evening, as if the hour be an island, a moment outside time. Me, I'm afraid Loftis gonna fuss 'bout my not straightening up, letting things go. I went into the bathroom, poured water in the one-spigot washstand—brown rust come bursting out in flakes—and rinsed my face. "Loftis, you supposed to be home four days ago. Hey," I say, toweling my face, "you okay?" How come he don't answer me? Wiping my hands on the seat of my trousers, I tipped into Loftis's room. He sleeping with his mouth open. His legs be drawn up, both fists clenched between his knees. He'd kicked his blanket on the floor. In his sleep, Loftis laughed, or moaned, it be hard to tell. His eyelids, not quite shut, show slits of white. I decided to wait till Loftis wake up for his decision, but turning, I seen his watch, keys, and what looked in the first stain of sunlight to be a carefully wrapped piece of newspaper on his nightstand. The sunlight swelled to a bright shimmer, focusing the bedroom slowly like solution do a photographic image in the developer. And then something so freakish went down I ain't sure it took place. Fumble-fingered, I unfolded the paper, and inside be a blemished penny. It be like suddenly somebody slapped my head from behind. Taped on the penny be a slip of paper, and on the paper be the note "Found while walking down Devon Avenue." I hear Loftis mumble like he trapped in a nightmare. "Hold tight," I whisper. "It's all right." Me, I wanted to tell Loftis how Miss Bailey looked four days ago, that maybe it didn't have to be like that for us—did it?—because we could change. Couldn't we? Me, I pull his packed sheets over him, wrap up the penny, and, when I locate Miss Bailey's glass jar in the living room, put it away carefully, for now, with the rest of our things.

Franz Kafka (1883–1924)

A Hunger Artist   1924

TRANSLATED BY EDWIN AND WILLA MUIR

During these last decades the interest in professional fasting has markedly diminished. It used to pay very well to stage such great performances under one's own management, but today that is quite impossible. We live in a different world now. At one time the whole town took a lively interest in the hunger artist; from day to day of his fast the excitement mounted; everybody wanted to see him at least once a day; there were people who bought season tickets for the last few days and sat from morning till night in front of his small barred cage; even in the nighttime there were visiting hours, when the whole effect was heightened by torch flares; on fine days the cage was set out in the open air, and then it was the children's special treat to see the hunger artist; for their elders he was often just a joke that happened to be in fashion, but the children stood open-mouthed, holding each other's hands for greater security, marveling at him as he sat there pallid in black tights, with his ribs sticking out so prominently, not even on a seat but down among straw on the ground, sometimes giving a courteous nod, answering questions with a constrained smile, or perhaps stretching an arm through the bars so that one might feel how thin it was, and then again withdrawing deep into himself, paying no attention to anyone or anything, not even to the all-important striking of the clock that was the only piece of furniture in his cage, but merely staring into vacancy with half shut eyes, now and then taking a sip from a tiny glass of water to moisten his lips.

Besides casual onlookers there were also relays of permanent watchers selected by the public, usually butchers, strangely enough, and it was their task to watch the hunger artist day and night, three of them at a time, in case he should have some secret recourse to nourishment. This was nothing but a formality, instituted to reassure the masses, for the initiates knew well enough that during his fast the artist would never in any circumstances, not even under forcible compulsion, swallow the smallest morsel of food; the honor of his profession forbade it. Not every watcher, of course, was capable of understanding this; there were often groups of night watchers who were very lax in carrying out their duties and deliberately huddled together in a retired corner to play cards with great absorption, obviously intending to give the hunger artist the chance of a little refreshment, which they supposed he could draw from some private hoard. Nothing annoyed the artist more than such watchers; they made him miserable; they made his fast seem unendurable; sometimes he mastered his feebleness sufficiently to sing during their watch for as long as he could keep going, to show them how unjust their suspicions were. But that was of little use; they only wondered at his cleverness in being able to fill his mouth even while singing. Much more to his taste were the watchers who sat close up to the bars, who were not content with the dim night lighting of the hall but focused him in the full glare of the electric pocket torch given them by the impresario. The harsh light did not trouble him at all, in any case he could never sleep properly, and he could always drowse a little, whatever the light, at any hour, even when the hall was thronged with noisy onlookers. He was quite happy at the prospect of spending a sleepless night with such watchers; he was ready to exchange jokes with them, to tell them stories out of his nomadic life, anything at all to keep them awake and demonstrate to them again that he had no eatables in his cage and that he was fasting as not one of them could fast. But his happiest moment was when the morning came and an enormous breakfast was brought them, at his expense, on which they flung themselves with the keen appetite of healthy men after a weary night of wakefulness. Of course there were people who argued that this breakfast was an unfair attempt to bribe the watchers, but that was going rather too far, and when they were invited to take on a night's vigil without a breakfast, merely for the sake of the cause, they made themselves scarce, although they stuck stubbornly to their suspicions.

Such suspicions, anyhow, were a necessary accompaniment to the profession of fasting. No one could possibly watch the hunger artist continuously, day and night, and so no one could produce first-hand evidence that the fast had really been rigorous and continuous; only the artist himself could know that, he was therefore bound to be the sole completely satisfied spectator of his own fast. Yet for other reasons he was never satisfied; it was not perhaps mere fasting that had brought him to such skeleton thinness that many people had regretfully to keep away from his exhibitions, because the sight of him was too much for them, perhaps it was dissatisfaction with himself that had worn him down. For he alone knew, what no other initiate knew, how easy it was to fast. It was the easiest thing in the world. He made no secret of this, yet people did not believe him, at the best they set him down as modest; most of them, however, thought he was out for publicity or else was some kind of cheat who found it easy to fast because he had discovered a way of making it easy, and then had the impudence to admit the fact, more or less. He had to put up with all that, and in the course of time had got used to it, but his inner dissatisfaction always rankled, and never yet, after any term of fasting—this must be granted to his credit—had he left the cage of his own free will. The longest period of fasting was fixed by his impresario at forty days, beyond that term he was not allowed to go, not even in great cities, and there was good reason for it, too. Experience had proved that for about forty days the interest of the public could be stimulated by a steadily increasing pressure of advertisement, but after that the town began to lose interest, sympathetic support began notably to fall off; there were of course local variations as between one town and another or one country and another, but as a general rule forty days marked the limit. So on the fortieth day the flower bedecked cage was opened, enthusiastic spectators filled the hall, a military band played, two doctors entered the cage to measure the results of the fast, which were announced through a megaphone, and finally two young ladies appeared, blissful at having been selected for the honor, to help the hunger artist down the few steps leading to a small table on which was spread a carefully chosen invalid repast. And at this very moment the artist always turned stubborn. True, he would entrust his bony arms to the outstretched helping hands of the ladies bending over him, but stand up he would not. Why stop fasting at this particular moment, after forty days of it? He had held out for a long time, an illimitably long time; why stop now, when he was in his best fasting form, or rather, not yet quite in his best fasting form? Why should he be cheated of the fame he would get for fasting longer, for being not only the record hunger artist of all time, which presumably he was already, but for beating his own record by a performance beyond human imagination, since he felt that there were no limits to his capacity for fasting? His public pretended to admire him so much, why should it have so little patience with him; if he could endure fasting longer, why shouldn't the public endure it? Besides, he was tired, he was comfortable sitting in the straw, and now he was supposed to lift himself to his full height and go down to a meal the very thought of which gave him a nausea that only the presence of the ladies kept him from betraying, and even that with an effort. And he looked up into the eyes of the ladies who were apparently so friendly and in reality so cruel, and shook his head, which felt too heavy on its strengthless neck. But then there happened yet again what always happened. The impresario came forward, without a word—for the band made speech impossible—lifted his arms in the air above the artist, as if inviting Heaven to look down upon its creature here in the straw, this suffering martyr, which indeed he was, although in quite another sense; grasped him round the emaciated waist, with exaggerated caution, so that the frail condition he was in might be appreciated; and committed him to the care of the blenching ladies, not without secretly giving him a shaking so that his legs and body tottered and swayed. The artist now submitted completely; his head lolled on his breast as if it had landed there by chance; his body was hollowed out; his legs in a spasm of self-preservation clung close to each other at the knees, yet scraped on the ground as if it were not really solid ground, as if they were only trying to find solid ground; and the whole weight of his body, a feather-weight after all, relapsed onto one of the ladies, who, looking round for help and panting a little — this post of honor was not at all what she had expected it to be — first stretched her neck as far as she could to keep her face at least free from contact with the artist, when finding this impossible, and her more fortunate companion not coming to her aid but merely holding extended on her own trembling hand the little bunch of knucklebones that was the artist's, to the great delight of the spectators burst into tears and had to be replaced by an attendant who had long been stationed in readiness. Then came the food, a little of which the impresario managed to get between the artist's lips, while he sat in a kind of half-fainting trance, to the accompaniment of cheerful patter designed to distract the public's attention from the artist's condition; after that a toast was drunk to the public, supposedly prompted by a whisper from the artist in the impresario's ear; the band confirmed it with a mighty flourish, the spectators melted away, and no one had any cause to be dissatisfied with the proceedings, no one except the hunger artist himself, he only, as always.

So he lived for many years, with small regular intervals of recuperation, in visible glory, honored by the world, yet in spite of that troubled in spirit, and all the more troubled because no one would take his trouble seriously. What comfort could he possibly need? What more could he possibly wish for? And if some good-natured person, feeling sorry for him, tried to console him by pointing out that his melancholy was probably caused by fasting; it could happen, especially when he had been fasting for some time, that he reacted with an outburst of fury and to the general alarm began to shake the bars of his cage like a wild animal. Yet the impresario had a way of punishing these outbreaks which he rather enjoyed putting into operation. He would apologize publicly for the artist's behavior, which was only to be excused, he admitted, because of the irritability caused by fasting; a condition hardly to be understood by well-fed people; then by natural transition he went on to mention the artist's equally incomprehensible boast that he could fast for much longer than he was doing; he praised the high ambition, the good will, the great self-denial undoubtedly implicit in such a statement; and then quite simply countered it by bringing out photographs, which were also on sale to the public, showing the artist on the fortieth day of a fast lying in bed almost dead from exhaustion. This perversion of the truth, familiar to the artist though it was, always unnerved him afresh and proved too much for him. What was a consequence of the premature ending of his fast was here presented as the cause of it! To fight against this lack of understanding, against a whole world of nonunderstanding, was impossible. Time and again in good faith he stood by the bars listening to the impresario, but as soon as the photographs appeared he always let go and sank with a groan back on to his straw, and the reassured public could once more come close and gaze at him.

A few years later when the witnesses of such scenes called them to mind, they often failed to understand themselves at all. For meanwhile the aforementioned change in public interest had set in; it seemed to happen almost overnight; there may have been profound causes for it, but who was going to bother about that; at any rate the pampered hunger artist suddenly found himself deserted one fine day by the amusement seekers, who were streaming past him to other more favored attractions. For the last time the impresario hurried him over half Europe to discover whether the old interest might still survive here and there; all in vain; everywhere, as if by secret agreement, a positive revulsion from professional fasting was in evidence. Of course it could not really have sprung up so suddenly as all that, and many premonitory symptoms which had not been sufficiently remarked or suppressed during the rush and glitter of success now came retrospectively to mind, but it was now too late to take any countermeasures. Fasting would surely come into fashion again at some future date, yet that was no comfort for those living in the present. What, then, was the hunger artist to do? He had been applauded by thousands in his time and could hardly come down to showing himself in a street booth at village fairs, and as for adopting another profession, he was not only too old for that but too frantically devoted to fasting. So he took leave of the impresario, his partner in an unparalleled career, and hired himself to a large circus; in order to spare his own feelings he avoided reading the conditions of his contract.

A large circus with its enormous traffic in replacing and recruiting men, animals, and apparatus can always find a use for people at any time, even for a hunger artist, provided of course that he does not ask too much, and in this particular case anyhow it was not only the artist who was taken on but his famous and long-known name as well, indeed considering the peculiar nature of his performance, which was not impaired by advancing age, it could not be objected that there was an artist past his prime, no longer at the height of his professional skill, seeking a refuge in some quiet corner of a circus; on the contrary, the hunger artist averred that he could fast as well as ever, which was entirely credible; he even alleged that if he were allowed to fast as he liked, and this was at once promised him without more ado, he could astound the world by establishing a record never yet achieved, a statement which certainly provoked a smile among the other professionals, since it left out of account the change in public opinion, which the hunger artist in his zeal conveniently forgot.

He had not, however, actually lost his sense of the real situation and took it as a matter of course that he and his cage should be stationed, not in the middle of the ring as a main attraction, but outside, near the animal cages, on a site that was after all easily accessible. Large and gaily painted placards made a frame for the cage and announced what was to be seen inside it. When the public came thronging out in the intervals to see the animals, they could hardly avoid passing the hunger artist's cage and stopping there for a moment; perhaps they might even have stayed longer had not those pressing behind them in the narrow gangway, who did not understand why they should be held up on their way toward the excitements of the menagerie, made it impossible for anyone to stand gazing quietly for any length of time. And that was the reason why the hunger artist, who had of course been looking forward to these visiting hours as the main achievement of his life, began instead to shrink from them. At first he could hardly wait for the intervals; it was exhilarating to watch the crowds come streaming his way, until only too soon — not even the most obstinate self-deception, clung to almost consciously, could hold out against the fact — the conviction was borne in upon him that these people, most of them, to judge from their actions, again and again, without exception, were all on their way to the menagerie. And the first sight of them from the distance remained the best. For when they reached his cage he was at once deafened by the storm of shouting and abuse that arose from the two contending factions, which renewed themselves continuously, of those who wanted to stop and stare at him — he soon began to dislike them more than the others — not out of real interest but only out of obstinate self-assertiveness, and those who wanted to go straight on to the animals. When the first great rush was past, the stragglers came along, and these, whom nothing could have prevented from stopping to look at him as long as they had breath, raced past with long strides, hardly even glancing at him, in their haste to get to the menagerie in time. And all too rarely did it happen that he had a stroke of luck, when some father of a family fetched up before him with his children, pointed a finger at the hunger artist, and explained at length what the phenomenon meant, telling stories of earlier years when he himself had watched similar but much more thrilling performances, and the children, still rather uncomprehending, since neither inside nor outside school had they been sufficiently prepared for this lesson — what did they care about fasting? — yet showed by the brightness of their intent eyes that new and better times might be coming. Perhaps, said the hunger artist to himself many a time, things would be a little better if his cage were set not quite so near the menagerie. That made it too easy for people to make their choice, to say nothing of what he suffered from the stench of the menagerie, the animals' restlessness by night, the carrying past of raw lumps of flesh for the beasts of prey, the roaring at feeding times, which depressed him continually. But he did not dare to lodge a complaint with the management; after all, he had the animals to thank for the troops of people who passed his cage, among whom there might always be one here and there to take an interest in him, and who could tell where they might seclude him if he called attention to his existence and thereby to the fact that, strictly speaking, he was only an impediment on the way to the menagerie.

A small impediment, to be sure, one that grew steadily less. People grew familiar with the strange idea that they could be expected, in times like these, to take an interest in a hunger artist, and with this familiarity the verdict went out against him. He might fast as much as he could, and he did so; but nothing could save him now, people passed him by. Just try to explain to anyone the art of fasting! Anyone who has no feeling for it cannot be made to understand it. The fine placards grew dirty and illegible, they were torn down; the little notice board telling the number of fast days achieved, which at first was changed carefully every day, had long stayed at the same figure, for after the first few weeks even this small task seemed pointless to the staff; and so the artist simply fasted on and on, as he had once dreamed of doing, and it was no trouble to him, just as he had always foretold, but no one counted the days, no one, not even the artist himself, knew what records he was already breaking, and his heart grew heavy. And when once in a time some leisurely passerby stopped, made merry over the old figure on the board, and spoke of swindling, that was in its way the stupidest lie ever invented by indifference and inborn malice, since it was not the hunger artist who was cheating; he was working honestly, but the world was cheating him of his reward.

Many more days went by, however, and that too came to an end. An overseer's eye fell on the cage one day and asked the attendants why this perfectly good cage should be left standing there unused with dirty straw inside it; nobody knew, until one man, helped out by the notice board, remembered about the hunger artist. They poked into the straw with sticks and found him in it. "Are you still fasting?" asked the overseer. "When on earth do you mean to stop?" "Forgive me, everybody," whispered the hunger artist; only the overseer, who had his ear to the bars, understood him. "Of course," said the overseer, and tapped his forehead with a finger to let the attendants know what state the man was in, "we forgive you." "I always wanted you to admire my fasting," said the hunger artist. "We do admire it," said the overseer, affably. "But you shouldn't admire it," said the hunger artist. "Well, then we don't admire it," said the overseer, "but why shouldn't we admire it?" "Because I have to fast, I can't help it," said the hunger artist. "What a fellow you are," said the overseer, "and why can't you help it?" "Because," said the hunger artist, lifting his head a little and speaking, with his lips pursed, as if for a kiss, right into the overseer's ear, so that no syllable might be lost, "because I couldn't find the food I liked. If I had found it, believe me, I should have made no fuss and stuffed myself like you or anyone else." These were his last words, but in his dimming eyes remained the firm though no longer proud persuasion that he was still continuing to fast.

"Well, clear this out now!" said the overseer, and they buried the hunger 10 artist, straw and all. Into the cage they put a young panther. Even the most insensitive felt it refreshing to see this wild creature leaping around the cage that had so long been dreary. The panther was all right. The food he liked was brought him without hesitation by the attendants; he seemed not even to miss his freedom; his noble body, furnished almost to the bursting point with all that it needed, seemed to carry freedom around with it too; somewhere in his jaws it seemed to lurk; and the joy of life streamed with such ardent passion from his throat that for the onlookers it was not easy to stand the shock of it. But they braced themselves, crowded round the cage, and did not want ever to move away.

JAMAICA KINCAID (B. 1949)

Girl   *1978*

Wash the white clothes on Monday and put them on the stone heap; wash the color clothes on Tuesday and put them on the clothesline to dry; don't walk barehead in the hot sun; cook pumpkin fritters in very hot sweet oil; soak your little cloths right after you take them off; when buying cotton to make yourself a nice blouse, be sure that it doesn't have gum on it, because that way it won't hold up well after a wash; soak salt fish overnight before you cook it; is it true that you sing benna° in Sunday school?; always eat your food in such a way that

---

benna: Calypso music.

it won't turn someone else's stomach; on Sundays try to walk like a lady and not like the slut you are so bent on becoming; don't sing benna in Sunday school; you mustn't speak to wharf-rat boys, not even to give directions; don't eat fruits on the street — flies will follow you; *but I don't sing benna on Sundays at all and never in Sunday school;* this is how to sew on a button; this is how to make a buttonhole for the button you have just sewed on; this is how to hem a dress when you see the hem coming down and so to prevent yourself from looking like the slut I know you are so bent on becoming; this is how you iron your father's khaki shirt so that it doesn't have a crease; this is how you iron your father's khaki pants so that they don't have a crease; this is how you grow okra — far from the house, because okra tree harbors red ants; when you are growing dasheen,° make sure it gets plenty of water or else it makes your throat itch when you are eating it; this is how you sweep a corner; this is how you sweep a whole house; this is how you sweep a yard; this is how you smile to someone you don't like too much; this is how you smile to someone you don't like at all; this is how you smile to someone you like completely; this is how you set a table for tea; this is how you set a table for dinner; this is how you set a table for dinner with an important guest; this is how you set a table for lunch; this is how you set a table for breakfast; this is how to behave in the presence of men who don't know you very well, and this way they won't recognize immediately the slut I have warned you against becoming; be sure to wash every day, even if it is with your own spit; don't squat down to play marbles — you are not a boy, you know; don't pick people's flowers — you might catch something; don't throw stones at blackbirds, because it might not be a blackbird at all; this is how to make a bread pudding; this is how to make doukona;° this is how to make pepper pot;° this is how to make a good medicine for a cold; this is how to make a good medicine to throw away a child before it even becomes a child; this is how to catch a fish; this is how to throw back a fish you don't like, and that way something bad won't fall on you; this is how to bully a man; this is how a man bullies you; this is how to love a man, and if this doesn't work there are other ways, and if they don't work don't feel too bad about giving up; this is how to spit up in the air if you feel like it, and this is how to move quick so that it doesn't fall on you; this is how to make ends meet; always squeeze bread to make sure it's fresh; *but what if the baker won't let me feel the bread?;* you mean to say that after all you are really going to be the kind of woman who the baker won't let near the bread?

dasheen: The edible rootstock of taro, a tropical plant.
doukona: A spicy plantain pudding.
pepper pot: A stew.

STEPHEN KING (B. 1947)
Suffer the Little Children   1978

Miss Sidley was her name, and teaching was her game.

She was a small woman who had to stretch to write on the highest level of the blackboard, which she was doing now. Behind her, none of the children giggled or whispered or munched on secret sweets held in cupped hands. They knew Miss Sidley's deadly instincts too well. Miss Sidley could always tell who was chewing gum at the back of the room, who had a beanshooter in his pocket, who wanted to go to the bathroom to trade baseball cards rather than use the facilities. Like God, she seemed to know everything all at once.

She was graying, and the brace she wore to support her failing back was limned clearly against her print dress. Small, constantly suffering, gimlet-eyed woman. But they feared her. Her tongue was a school-yard legend. The eyes, when focused on a giggler or a whisperer, could turn the stoutest knees to water.

Now, writing the day's list of spelling words on the board, she reflected that the success of her long teaching career could be summed and checked and proven by this one everyday action: she could turn her back on her pupils with confidence.

"Vacation," she said, pronouncing the word as she wrote it in her firm, no- 5 nonsense script. "Edward, please use the word *vacation* in a sentence."

"I went on a vacation to New York City," Edward piped. Then, as Miss Sidley had taught, he repeated the word carefully. "Vay-cay-shun."

"Very good, Edward." She began on the next word.

She had her little tricks, of course; success, she firmly believed, depended as much on the little things as on the big ones. She applied the principle constantly in the classroom, and it never failed.

"Jane," she said quietly.

Jane, who had been furtively perusing her Reader, looked up guiltily. 10

"Close that book right now, please." The book shut; Jane looked with pale, hating eyes at Miss Sidley's back. "And you will remain at your desk for fifteen minutes after the final bell."

Jane's lips trembled. "Yes, Miss Sidley."

One of her little tricks was the careful use of her glasses. The whole class was reflected in their thick lenses and she had always been thinly amused by their guilty, frightened faces when she caught them at their nasty little games. Now she saw a phantomish, distorted Robert in the first row wrinkle his nose. She did not speak. Not yet. Robert would hang himself if given just a little more rope.

"Tomorrow," she pronounced clearly. "Robert, you will please use the word *tomorrow* in a sentence."

Robert frowned over the problem. The classroom was hushed and sleepy 15 in the late-September sun. The electric clock over the door buzzed a rumor of three o'clock dismissal just a half-hour away, and the only thing that kept young heads from drowsing over their spellers was the silent, ominous threat of Miss Sidley's back.

"I am waiting, Robert."

"Tomorrow a bad thing will happen," Robert said. The words were perfectly innocuous, but Miss Sidley, with the seventh sense that all strict disciplinarians have, didn't like them a bit. "Too-mor-row," Robert finished. His hands were folded neatly on the desk, and he wrinkled his nose again. He also smiled a tiny side-of-the-mouth smile. Miss Sidley was suddenly, unaccountably sure Robert knew about her little trick with the glasses.

All right; very well.

She began to write the next word with no word of commendation for Robert, letting her straight body speak its own message. She watched carefully with one eye. Soon Robert would stick out his tongue or make that disgusting finger-gesture they all knew (even the girls seemed to know it these days), just to see if she really knew what he was doing. Then he would be punished.

The reflection was small, ghostly, and distorted. And she had all but the 20
barest corner of her eye on the word she was writing.

Robert changed.

She caught just a flicker of it, just a frightening glimpse of Robert's face
changing into something . . . different.

She whirled around, face white, barely noticing the protesting stab of pain
in her back.

Robert looked at her blandly, questioningly. His hands were neatly folded.
The first signs of an afternoon cowlick showed at the back of his head. He did
not look frightened.

I imagined it, she thought. *I was looking for something, and when there was noth-* 25
ing, my mind just made something up. Very cooperative of it. However—

"Robert?" She meant to be authoritative; meant for her voice to make the
unspoken demand for confession. It did not come out that way.

"Yes, Miss Sidley?" His eyes were a very dark brown, like the mud at the
bottom of a slow-running stream.

"Nothing."

She turned back to the board. A little whisper ran through the class.

"*Be quiet!*" she snapped, and turned again to face them. "One more sound 30
and we will all stay after school with Jane!" She addressed the whole class, but
looked most directly at Robert. He looked back with childlike innocence: *Who,*
me? Not me, Miss Sidley.

She turned to the board and began to write, not looking out of the corners of her glasses. The last half-hour dragged, and it seemed that Robert gave
her a strange look on the way out. A look that said, *We have a secret, don't we?*

The look wouldn't leave her mind. It was stuck there, like a tiny string of
roast beef between two molars—a small thing, actually, but feeling as big as a
cinderblock.

She sat down to her solitary dinner at five (poached eggs on toast) still
thinking about it. She knew she was getting older and accepted the knowledge
calmly. She was not going to be one of those old-maid schoolmarms dragged
kicking and screaming from their classes at the age of retirement. They reminded her of gamblers unable to leave the tables while they were losing. But
she was not losing. She had always been a winner.

She looked down at her poached eggs.

Hadn't she? 35

She thought of the well-scrubbed faces in her third-grade classroom, and
found Robert's face most prominent among them.

She got up and switched on another light.

Later, just before she dropped off to sleep, Robert's face floated in front of
her, smiling unpleasantly in the darkness behind her lids. The face began to
change—

But before she saw exactly what it was changing into, darkness overtook her.

Miss Sidley spent an unrestful night and consequently the next day her 40
temper was short. She waited, almost hoping for a whisperer, a giggler, perhaps
a note-passer. But the class was quiet—very quiet. They all stared at her unre-
sponsively, and it seemed that she could feel the weight of their eyes on her like
blind, crawling ants.

Stop that! she told herself sternly. *You're acting like a skittish girl just out of*
teachers college!

Again the day seemed to drag, and she believed she was more relieved than the children when the last bell rang. The children lined up in orderly rows at the door, boys and girls by height, hands dutifully linked.

"Dismissed," she said, and listened sourly as they shrieked their way down the hall and into the bright sunlight.

What was it I saw when he changed? Something bulbous. Something that shimmered. Something that stared at me, yes, stared and grinned and wasn't a child at all. It was old and it was evil and—

"Miss Sidley?"   45

Her head jerked up and a little *Oh!* hiccupped involuntarily from her throat.

It was Mr. Hanning. He smiled apologetically. "Didn't mean to disturb you."

"Quite all right," she said, more curtly than she had intended. What had she been thinking? What was wrong with her?

"Would you mind checking the paper towels in the girls' lav?"

"Surely." She got up, placing her hands against the small of her back. Mr.   50
Hanning looked at her sympathetically. *Save it*, she thought. *The old maid is not amused. Or even interested.*

She brushed by Mr. Hanning and started down the hall to the girls' lavatory. A snigger of boys carrying scratched and pitted baseball equipment grew silent at the sight of her and leaked guiltily out the door, where their cries began again.

Miss Sidley frowned after them, reflecting that children had been different in her day. Not more polite—children have never had time for that—and not exactly more respectful of their elders; it was a kind of hypocrisy that had never been there before. A smiling quietness around adults that had never been there before. A kind of quiet contempt that was upsetting and unnerving. As if they were . . .

Hiding behind masks? Is that it?

She pushed the thought away and went into the lavatory. It was a small, L-shaped room. The toilets were ranged along one side of the longer bar, the sinks along both sides of the shorter one.

As she checked the paper-towel containers, she caught a glimpse of her   55
face in one of the mirrors and was startled into looking at it closely. She didn't care for what she saw—not a bit. There was a look that hadn't been there two days before, a frightened, watching look. With sudden shock she realized that the blurred reflection in her glasses of Robert's pale, respectful face had gotten inside her and was festering.

The door opened and she heard two girls come in, giggling secretly about something. She was about to turn the corner and walk out past them when she heard her own name. She turned back to the washbowls and began checking the towel holders again.

"And then he—"

Soft giggles.

"She knows, but—"

More giggles, soft and sticky as melting soap.   60

"Miss Sidley is—"

Stop it! Stop that noise!

By moving slightly she could see their shadows, made fuzzy and ill-defined by the diffuse light filtering through the frosted windows, holding onto each other with girlish glee.

Another thought crawled up out of her mind.

They knew she was there.   65

Yes. Yes they did. The little bitches knew.

She would shake them. Shake them until their teeth rattled and their giggles turned to wails, she would thump their heads against the tile walls and she would make them *admit* that they knew.

That was when the shadows changed. They seemed to elongate, to flow like dripping tallow, taking on strange hunched shapes that made Miss Sidley cringe back against the porcelain washstands, her heart swelling in her chest.

But they went on giggling.

The voices changed, no longer girlish, now sexless and soulless, and quite, quite evil. A slow, turgid sound of mindless humor that flowed around the corner to her like sewage.

She stared at the hunched shadows and suddenly screamed at them. The scream went on and on, swelling in her head until it attained a pitch of lunacy. And then she fainted. The giggling, like the laughter of demons, followed her down into darkness.

She could not, of course, tell them the truth.

Miss Sidley knew this even as she opened her eyes and looked up at the anxious faces of Mr. Hanning and Mrs. Crossen. Mrs. Crossen was holding the bottle of smelling salts from the gymnasium first-aid kit under her nose. Mr. Hanning turned around and told the two little girls who were looking curiously at Miss Sidley to go home now, please.

They both smiled at her — slow, we-have-a-secret smiles — and went out.

Very well, she would keep their secret. For awhile. She would not have people thinking her insane, or that the first feelers of senility had touched her early. She would play their game. Until she could expose their nastiness and rip it out by the roots.

"I'm afraid I slipped," she said calmly, sitting up and ignoring the excruciating pain in her back. "A patch of wetness."

"This is awful," Mr. Hanning said. "Terrible. Are you —"

"Did the fall hurt your back, Emily?" Mrs. Crossen interrupted. Mr. Hanning looked at her gratefully.

Miss Sidley got up, her spine screaming in her body.

"No," she said. "In fact, the fall seems to have worked some minor chiropractic miracle. My back hasn't felt this well in years."

"We can send for a doctor —" Mr. Hanning began.

"Not necessary." Miss Sidley smiled at him coolly.

"I'll call you a taxi from the office."

"You'll do no such thing," Miss Sidley said, walking to the door of the girls' lav and opening it. "I always take the bus."

Mr. Hanning sighed and looked at Mrs. Crossen. Mrs. Crossen rolled her eyes and said nothing.

The next day Miss Sidley kept Robert after school. He did nothing to warrant the punishment, so she simply accused him falsely. She felt no qualms; he was a monster, not a little boy. She must make him admit it.

Her back was in agony. She realized Robert knew; he expected that would help him. But it wouldn't. That was another of her little advantages. Her back had been a constant pain to her for the last twelve years, and there had been many times when it had been this bad — well, *almost* this bad.

She closed the door, shutting the two of them in.

For a moment she stood still, training her gaze on Robert. She waited for him to drop his eyes. He didn't. He looked back at her, and presently a little smile began to play around the corners of his mouth.

"Why are you smiling, Robert?" she asked softly. 90

"I don't know," Robert said, and went on smiling.

"Tell me, please."

Robert said nothing.

And went on smiling.

The outside sounds of children at play were distant, dreamy. Only the hyp- 95 notic buzz of the wall clock was real.

"There's quite a few of us," Robert said suddenly, as if he were commenting on the weather.

It was Miss Sidley's turn to be silent.

"Eleven right here in this school."

Quite evil, she thought, amazed. *Very, incredibly evil.*

"Little boys who tell stories go to hell," she said clearly. "I know many par- 100 ents no longer make their . . . their *spawn* . . . aware of that fact, but I assure you that it is a *true* fact, Robert. Little boys who tell stories go to hell. Little girls too, for that matter."

Robert's smile grew wider; it became vulpine. "Do you want to see me change, Miss Sidley? Do you want a really good look?"

Miss Sidley felt her back prickle. "Go away," she said curtly. "And bring your mother or your father to school with you tomorrow. We'll get this business straightened out." There. On solid ground again. She waited for his face to crumple, waited for the tears.

Instead, Robert's smile grew wider — wide enough to show his teeth. "It will be just like Show and Tell, won't it, Miss Sidley? Robert — the *other* Robert — he liked Show and Tell. He's still hiding way, way down in my head." The smile curled at the corners of his mouth like charring paper. "Sometimes he runs around . . . it itches. He wants me to let him out."

"Go away," Miss Sidley said numbly. The buzzing of the clock seemed very loud.

Robert changed. 105

His face suddenly ran together like melting wax, the eyes flattening and spreading like knife-struck egg yolks, nose widening and yawning, mouth disappearing. The head elongated, and the hair was suddenly not hair but straggling, twitching growths.

Robert began to chuckle.

The slow, cavernous sound came from what had been his nose, but the nose was eating into the lower half of his face, nostrils meeting and merging into a central blackness like a huge, shouting mouth.

Robert got up, still chuckling, and behind it all she could see the last shattered remains of the other Robert, the real little boy this alien thing had usurped, howling in maniac terror, screeching to be let out.

She ran. 110

She fled screaming down the corridor, and the few late-leaving pupils turned to look at her with large and uncomprehending eyes. Mr. Hanning jerked open his door and looked out just as she plunged through the wide glass front doors, a wild, waving scarecrow silhouetted against the bright September sky.

He ran after her, Adam's apple bobbing. "Miss Sidley! *Miss Sidley!*"

Robert came out of the classroom and watched curiously.

Miss Sidley neither heard nor saw. She clattered down the steps and across the sidewalk and into the street with her screams trailing behind her. There was a huge, blatting horn and then the bus was looming over her, the bus driver's face a plaster mask of fear. Air brakes whined and hissed like angry dragons.

Miss Sidley fell, and the huge wheels shuddered to a smoking stop just 115 eight inches from her frail, brace-armored body. She lay shuddering on the pavement, hearing the crowd gather around her.

She turned over and the children were staring down at her. They were ringed in a tight little circle, like mourners around an open grave. And at the head of the grave was Robert, a small sober sexton ready to shovel the first spade of dirt into her face.

From far away, the bus driver's shaken babble: " . . . crazy or somethin . . . my God, another half a foot . . ."

Miss Sidley stared at the children. Their shadows covered her. Their faces were impassive. Some of them were smiling little secret smiles, and Miss Sidley knew that soon she would begin to scream again.

Then Mr. Hanning broke their tight noose, shooed them away, and Miss Sidley began to sob weakly.

She didn't go back to her third grade for a month. She told Mr. Hanning 120 calmly that she had not been feeling herself, and Mr. Hanning suggested that she see a reputable doctor and discuss the matter with him. Miss Sidley agreed that this was the only sensible and rational course. She also said that if the school board wished for her resignation she would tender it immediately although doing so would hurt her very much. Mr. Hanning, looking uncomfortable, said he doubted if that would be necessary. The upshot was that Miss Sidley came back in late October, once again ready to play the game and now knowing how to play it.

For the first week she let things go on as ever. It seemed the whole class now regarded her with hostile, shielded eyes. Robert smiled distantly at her from his front-row seat, and she did not have the courage to take him to task.

Once, while she was on playground duty, Robert walked over to her, holding a dodgem ball, smiling. "There's so many of us now you wouldn't believe it," he said. "And neither would anyone else." He stunned her by dropping a wink of infinite slyness. "If you, you know, tried to tell em."

A girl on the swings looked across the playground into Miss Sidley's eyes and laughed at her.

Miss Sidley smiled serenely down at Robert. "Why, Robert, whatever do you mean?"

But Robert only continued smiling as he went back to his game. 125

Miss Sidley brought the gun to school in her handbag. It had been her brother's. He had taken it from a dead German shortly after the Battle of the Bulge. Jim had been gone ten years now. She hadn't opened the box that held the gun in at least five, but when she did it was still there, gleaming dully. The clips of ammunition were still there, too, and she loaded the gun carefully, just as Jim had shown her.

She smiled pleasantly at her class; at Robert in particular. Robert smiled back and she could see the murky alienness swimming just below his skin, muddy, full of filth.

She had no idea what was now living inside Robert's skin, and she didn't care; she only hoped that the real little boy was entirely gone by now. She did not wish to be a murderess. She decided the real Robert must have died or gone insane, living inside the dirty, crawling thing that had chuckled at her in the classroom and sent her screaming into the street. So even if he was still alive, putting him out of his misery would be a mercy.

"Today we're going to have a Test," Miss Sidley said.

The class did not groan or shift apprehensively; they merely looked at her. 130 She could feel their eyes, like weights. Heavy, smothering.

"It's a very special Test. I will call you down to the mimeograph room one by one and give it to you. Then you may have a candy and go home for the day. Won't that be nice?"

They smiled empty smiles and said nothing.

"Robert, will you come first?"

Robert got up, smiling his little smile. He wrinkled his nose quite openly at her. "Yes, Miss Sidley."

Miss Sidley took her bag and they went down the empty, echoing corridor 135 together, past the sleepy drone of classes reciting behind closed doors. The mimeograph room was at the far end of the hall, past the lavatories. It had been soundproofed two years ago; the big machine was very old and very noisy. Miss Sidley closed the door behind them and locked it.

"No one can hear you," she said calmly. She took the gun from her bag. "You or this."

Robert smiled innocently. "There are lots of us, though. Lots more than here." He put one small scrubbed hand on the paper-tray of the mimeograph machine. "Would you like to see me change again?"

Before she could speak, Robert's face began to shimmer into the grotesqueness beneath and Miss Sidley shot him. Once. In the head. He fell back against the paper-lined shelves and slid down to the floor, a little dead boy with a round black hole above his right eye.

He looked very pathetic.   140

Miss Sidley stood over him, panting. Her cheeks were pale.

The huddled figure didn't move.

It was human.

It was Robert.

No!   145

It was all in your mind, Emily. All in your mind.

No! No, no, *no!*

She went back up to the room and began to lead them down, one by one. She killed twelve of them and would have killed them all if Mrs. Crossen hadn't come down for a package of composition paper.

Mrs. Crossen's eyes got very big; one hand crept up and clutched her mouth. She began to scream and she was still screaming when Miss Sidley reached her and put a hand on her shoulder. "It had to be done, Margaret," she told the screaming Mrs. Crossen. "It's terrible, but it had to. They are all monsters."

Mrs. Crossen stared at the gaily clothed little bodies scattered around the 150 mimeograph and continued to scream. The little girl whose hand Miss Sidley was holding began to cry steadily and monotonously: *"Waahhh . . . waahhhh . . . waahhhh."*

"Change," Miss Sidley said. "Change for Mrs. Crossen. Show her it had to be done."

The girl continued to weep uncomprehendingly.

"Damn you, *change!*" Miss Sidley screamed. "Dirty bitch, dirty crawling, filthy unnatural *bitch!* Change! God damn you, *change!*" She raised the gun. The little girl cringed, and then Mrs. Crossen was on her like a cat, and Miss Sidley's back gave way.

No trial.

The papers screamed for one, bereaved parents swore hysterical oaths 155 against Miss Sidley, and the city sat back on its haunches in numb shock, but in the end, cooler heads prevailed and there was no trial. The State Legislature called for more stringent teacher exams, Summer Street School closed for a week of mourning, and Miss Sidley went quietly to Juniper Hill in Augusta. She was put in deep analysis, given the most modern drugs, introduced into daily work-therapy sessions. A year later, under strictly controlled conditions, Miss Sidley was put in an experimental encounter-therapy situation.

Buddy Jenkins was his name, psychiatry was his game.

He sat behind a one-way glass with a clipboard, looking into a room which had been outfitted as a nursery. On the far wall, the cow was jumping over the moon and the mouse ran up the clock. Miss Sidley sat in her wheelchair with a story book, surrounded by a group of trusting, drooling, smiling, cataclysmically retarded children. They smiled at her and drooled and touched her with small wet fingers while attendants at the next window watched for the first sign of an aggressive move.

For a time Buddy thought she responded well. She read aloud, stroked a girl's head, consoled a small boy when he fell over a toy block. Then she seemed to see something which disturbed her; a frown creased her brow and she looked away from the children.

"Take me away, please," Miss Sidley said, softly and tonelessly, to no one in particular.

And so they took her away. Buddy Jenkins watched the children watch her 160 go, their eyes wide and empty, but somehow deep. One smiled, and another put his fingers in his mouth slyly. Two little girls clutched each other and giggled.

That night Miss Sidley cut her throat with a bit of broken mirror-glass, and after that Buddy Jenkins began to watch the children more and more. In the end, he was hardly able to take his eyes off them.

D. H. LAWRENCE (1885–1930)
The Horse Dealer's Daughter 1922

"Well, Mabel, and what are you going to do with yourself?" asked Joe, with foolish flippancy. He felt quite safe himself. Without listening for an answer, he turned aside, worked a grain of tobacco to the tip of his tongue, and spat it out. He did not care about anything, since he felt safe himself.

The three brothers and the sister sat round the desolate breakfast-table, attempting some sort of desultory consultation. The morning's post had given the final tap to the family fortunes, and all was over. The dreary dining-room itself, with its heavy mahogany furniture, looked as if it were waiting to be done away with.

But the consultation amounted to nothing. There was a strange air of ineffectuality about the three men, as they sprawled at table, smoking and reflecting vaguely on their own condition. The girl was alone, a rather short, sullen-looking young woman of twenty-seven. She did not share the same life as her brothers. She would have been good-looking, save for the impressive fixity of her face, "bull-dog," as her brothers called it.

There was a confused tramping of horses' feet outside. The three men all sprawled round in their chairs to watch. Beyond the dark holly bushes that separated the strip of lawn from the high-road, they could see a cavalcade of shire horses swinging out of their own yard, being taken for exercise. This was the last time. These were the last horses that would go through their hands. The young men watched with critical, callous looks. They were all frightened at the collapse of their lives, and the sense of disaster in which they were involved left them no inner freedom.

Yet they were three fine, well-set fellows enough. Joe, the eldest, was a man 5 of thirty-three, broad and handsome in a hot, flushed way. His face was red, he twisted his black mustache over a thick finger, his eyes were shallow and restless. He had a sensual way of uncovering his teeth when he laughed, and his bearing was stupid. Now he watched the horses with a glazed look of helplessness in his eyes, a certain stupor of downfall.

The great draft-horses swung past. They were tied head to tail, four of them, and they heaved along to where a lane branched off from the high-road, planting their great hoofs floutingly in the fine black mud, swinging their great rounded haunches sumptuously, and trotting a few sudden steps as they were led into the lane, round the corner. Every movement showed a massive, slumbrous strength, and a stupidity which held them in subjection. The groom at the head looked back, jerking the leading rope. And the cavalcade moved out of sight up the lane, the tail of the last horse, bobbed up tight and stiff, held out taut from the swinging great haunches as they rocked behind the hedges in a motionlike sleep.

Joe watched with glazed hopeless eyes. The horses were almost like his own body to him. He felt he was done for now. Luckily he was engaged to a woman as old as himself, and therefore her father, who was steward of a neighboring estate, would provide him with a job. He would marry and go into harness. His life was over, he would be a subject animal now.

He turned uneasily aside, the retreating steps of the horses echoing in his ears. Then, with foolish restlessness, he reached for the scraps of bacon-rind from the plates, and making a faint whistling sound, flung them to the terrier that lay against the fender. He watched the dog swallow them, and waited till the creature looked into his eyes. Then a faint grin came on his face, and in a high, foolish voice he said:

"You won't get much more bacon, shall you, you little b——?"

The dog faintly and dismally wagged its tail, then lowered its haunches, 10 circled round, and lay down again.

There was another helpless silence at the table. Joe sprawled uneasily in his seat, not willing to go till the family conclave was dissolved. Fred Henry, the second brother, was erect, clean-limbed, alert. He had watched the passing of the horses with more *sang-froid*.° If he was an animal, like Joe, he was an animal which controls, not one which is controlled. He was master of any horse, and he carried himself with a well-tempered air of mastery. But he was not master of the situations of life. He pushed his coarse brown mustache upwards, off his lip, and glanced irritably at his sister, who sat impassive and inscrutable.

"You'll go and stop with Lucy for a bit, shan't you?" he asked. The girl did not answer.

"I don't see what else you can do," persisted Fred Henry.

"Go as a skivvy,"° Joe interpolated laconically.

The girl did not move a muscle.   15

"If I was her, I should go in for training for a nurse," said Malcolm, the youngest of them all. He was the baby of the family, a young man of twenty-two, with a fresh, jaunty *museau*.°

But Mabel did not take any notice of him. They had talked at her and round her for so many years, that she hardly heard them at all.

The marble clock on the mantelpiece softly chimed the half-hour, the dog rose uneasily from the hearth-rug and looked at the party at the breakfast-table. But still they sat on in ineffectual conclave.

"Oh, all right," said Joe suddenly, apropos of nothing. "I'll get a move on."

He pushed back his chair, straddled his knees with a downward jerk, to get   20
them free, in horsey fashion, and went to the fire. Still he did not go out of the room; he was curious to know what the others would do or say. He began to charge his pipe, looking down at the dog and saying in a high, affected voice:

"Going wi' me? Going wi' me are ter? Tha'rt goin' further than tha counts on just now, dost hear?"

The dog faintly wagged its tail, the man stuck out his jaw and covered his pipe with his hands, and puffed intently, losing himself in the tobacco, looking down all the while at the dog with an absent brown eye. The dog looked up at him in mournful distrust. Joe stood with his knees stuck out, in real horsey fashion.

"Have you had a letter from Lucy?" Fred Henry asked of his sister.

"Last week," came the neutral reply.

"And what does she say?"   25
There was no answer.

"Does she *ask* you to go and stop there?" persisted Fred Henry.

"She says I can if I like."

"Well, then, you'd better. Tell her you'll come on Monday."

This was received in silence.   30

"That's what you'll do then, is it?" said Fred Henry, in some exasperation.

But she made no answer. There was a silence of futility and irritation in the room. Malcolm grinned fatuously.

"You'll have to make up your mind between now and next Wednesday," said Joe loudly, "or else find yourself lodgings on the curbstone."

The face of the young woman darkened, but she sat on immutable.

"Here's Jack Fergusson!" exclaimed Malcolm, who was looking aimlessly   35
out of the window.

"Where?" exclaimed Joe loudly.

sang-froid: Coolness, composure.
skivvy: Domestic worker.
museau: Slang for face.

"Just gone past."

"Coming in?"

Malcolm craned his neck to see the gate.

"Yes," he said.   40

There was a silence. Mabel sat on like one condemned, at the head of the table. Then a whistle was heard from the kitchen. The dog got up and barked sharply. Joe opened the door and shouted:

"Come on."

After a moment a young man entered. He was muffled up in overcoat and a purple woolen scarf, and his tweed cap, which he did not remove, was pulled down on his head. He was of medium height, his face was rather long and pale, his eyes looked tired.

"Hello, Jack! Well, Jack!" exclaimed Malcolm and Joe. Fred Henry merely said: "Jack."

"What's doing?" asked the newcomer, evidently addressing Fred Henry.   45

"Same. We've got to be out by Wednesday. Got a cold?"

"I have — got it bad, too."

"Why don't you stop in?"

"*Me* stop in? When I can't stand on my legs, perhaps I shall have a chance," the young man spoke huskily. He had a slight Scotch accent.

"It's a knock-out, isn't it," said Joe, boisterously, "if a doctor goes round   50 croaking with a cold. Looks bad for the patients, doesn't it?"

The young doctor looked at him slowly.

"Anything the matter with *you*, then?" he asked sarcastically.

"Not as I know of. Damn your eyes, hope not. Why?"

"I thought you were very concerned about the patients, wondered if you might be one yourself."

"Damn it, no, I've never been patient to no flaming doctor, and hope I   55 never shall be," returned Joe.

At this point Mabel rose from the table, and they all seemed to become aware of her existence. She began putting the dishes together. The young doctor looked at her, but did not address her. He had not greeted her. She went out of the room with the tray, her face impassive and unchanged.

"When are you off then, all of you?" asked the doctor.

"I'm catching the eleven-forty," replied Malcolm. "Are you goin' down wi' th' trap,° Joe?"

"Yes, I've told you I'm going down wi' th' trap, haven't I?"

"We'd better be getting her in then. So long, Jack, if I don't see you before I   60 go," said Malcolm, shaking hands.

He went out, followed by Joe, who seemed to have his tail between his legs.

"Well, this is the devil's own," exclaimed the doctor, when he was left alone with Fred Henry. "Going before Wednesday, are you?"

"That's the orders," replied the other.

"Where, to Northampton?"

"That's it."   65

"The devil!" exclaimed Fergusson, with quiet chagrin.

And there was silence between the two.

"All settled up, are you?" asked Fergusson.

---

trap: A light two-wheeled carriage.

"About."

There was another pause.

"Well, I shall miss yer, Freddy, boy," said the young doctor.

"And I shall miss thee, Jack," returned the other.

"Miss you like hell," mused the doctor.

Fred Henry turned aside. There was nothing to say. Mabel came in again, to finish clearing the table.

"What are *you* going to do, then, Miss Pervin?" asked Fergusson. "Going to your sister's, are you?"

Mabel looked at him with her steady, dangerous eyes, that always made him uncomfortable, unsettling his superficial ease.

"No," she said.

"Well, what in the name of fortune *are* you going to do? Say what you mean to do," cried Fred Henry, with futile intensity.

But she only averted her head, and continued her work. She folded the white table-cloth, and put on the chenille cloth.

"The sulkiest bitch that ever trod!" muttered her brother.

But she finished her task with perfectly impassive face, the young doctor watching her interestedly all the while. Then she went out.

Fred Henry stared after her, clenching his lips, his blue eyes fixing in sharp antagonism, as he made a grimace of sour exasperation.

"You could bray her into bits, and that's all you'd get out of her," he said, in a small, narrowed tone.

The doctor smiled faintly.

"What's she *going* to do, then?" he asked.

"Strike me if *I* know!" returned the other.

There was a pause. Then the doctor stirred.

"I'll be seeing you tonight, shall I?" he said to his friend.

"Ay — where's it to be? Are we going over to Jessdale?"

"I don't know. I've got such a cold on me. I'll come round to the 'Moon and Stars,' anyway."

"Let Lizzie and May miss their night for once, eh?"

"That's it — if I feel as I do now."

"All's one — "

The two young men went through the passage and down to the back door together. The house was large, but it was servantless now, and desolate. At the back was a small bricked houseyard and beyond that a big square, graveled fine and red, and having stables on two sides. Sloping, dank, winter-dark fields stretched away on the open sides.

But the stables were empty. Joseph Pervin, the father of the family, had been a man of no education, who had become a fairly large horse dealer. The stables had been full of horses, there was a great turmoil and come-and-go of horses and of dealers and grooms. Then the kitchen was full of servants. But of late things had declined. The old man had married a second time, to re-trieve his fortunes. Now he was dead and everything was gone to the dogs, there was nothing but debt and threatening.

For months, Mabel had been servantless in the big house, keeping the home together in penury for her ineffectual brothers. She had kept house for ten years. But previously it was with unstinted means. Then, however brutal and coarse everything was, the sense of money had kept her proud, confident.

The men might be foul-mouthed, the women in the kitchen might have bad reputations, her brothers might have illegitimate children. But so long as there was money, the girl felt herself established, and brutally proud, reserved.

No company came to the house, save dealers and coarse men. Mabel had no associates of her own sex, after her sister went away. But she did not mind. She went regularly to church, she attended to her father. And she lived in the memory of her mother, who had died when she was fourteen, and whom she had loved. She had loved her father, too, in a different way, depending upon him, and feeling secure in him, until at the age of fifty-four he married again. And then she had set hard against him. Now he had died and left them all hopelessly in debt.

She had suffered badly during the period of poverty. Nothing, however, could shake the curious, sullen, animal pride that dominated each member of the family. Now, for Mabel, the end had come. Still she would not cast about her. She would follow her own way just the same. She would always hold the keys of her own situation. Mindless and persistent, she endured from day to day. Why should she think? Why should she answer anybody? It was enough that this was the end, and there was no way out. She need not pass any more darkly along the main street of the small town, avoiding every eye. She need not demean herself any more, going into the shops and buying the cheapest food. This was at an end. She thought of nobody, not even of herself. Mindless and persistent, she seemed in a sort of ecstasy to be coming nearer to her fulfillment, her own glorification, approaching her dead mother, who was glorified.

In the afternoon she took a little bag, with shears and sponge and a small scrubbing-brush, and went out. It was a gray, wintry day, with saddened, dark green fields and an atmosphere blackened by the smoke of foundries not far off. She went quickly, darkly along the causeway, heeding nobody, through the town to the churchyard.

There she always felt secure, as if no one could see her, although as a mat- 100 ter of fact she was exposed to the stare of everyone who passed along under the churchyard wall. Nevertheless, once under the shadow of the great looming church, among the graves, she felt immune from the world, reserved within the thick churchyard wall as in another country.

Carefully she clipped the grass from the grave, and arranged the pinky white, small chrysanthemums in the tin cross. When this was done, she took an empty jar from a neighboring grave, brought water, and carefully, most scrupulously sponged the marble headstone and the coping-stone.

It gave her sincere satisfaction to do this. She felt in immediate contact with the world of her mother. She took minute pains, went through the park in a state bordering on pure happiness, as if in performing this task she came into a subtle, intimate connection with her mother. For the life she followed here in the world was far less real than the world of death she inherited from her mother.

The doctor's house was just by the church. Fergusson, being a mere hired assistant, was slave to the countryside. As he hurried now to attend to the out-patients in the surgery, glancing across the graveyard with his quick eye, he saw the girl at her task at the grave. She seemed so intent and remote, it was like looking into another world. Some mystical element was touched in him. He slowed down as he walked, watching her as if spellbound.

She lifted her eyes, feeling him looking. Their eyes met. And each looked again at once, each feeling, in some way, found out by the other. He lifted his cap and passed on down the road. There remained distinct in his consciousness, like a vision, the memory of her face, lifted from the tombstone in the churchyard, and looking at him with slow, large, portentous eyes. It *was* portentous, her face. It seemed to mesmerize him. There was a heavy power in her eyes which laid hold of his whole being, as if he had drunk some powerful drug. He had been feeling weak and done before. Now the life came back into him, he felt delivered from his own fretted, daily self.

He finished his duties at the surgery as quickly as might be, hastily filling up the bottles of the waiting people with cheap drugs. Then, in perpetual haste, he set off again to visit several cases in another part of his round, before teatime. At all times he preferred to walk if he could, but particularly when he was not well. He fancied the motion restored him.

The afternoon was falling. It was gray, deadened, and wintry, with a slow, moist, heavy coldness sinking in and deadening all the faculties. But why should he think or notice? He hastily climbed the hill and turned across the dark green fields, following the black cinder-track. In the distance, across a shallow dip in the country, the small town was clustered like smoldering ash, a tower, a spire, a heap of low, raw, extinct houses. And on the nearest fringe of the town, sloping into the dip, was Oldmeadow, the Pervins' house. He could see the stables and the outbuildings distinctly, as they lay towards him on the slope. Well, he would not go there many more times! Another resource would be lost to him, another place gone: the only company he cared for in the alien, ugly little town he was losing. Nothing but work, drudgery, constant hastening from dwelling to dwelling among the colliers and the iron-workers. It wore him out, but at the same time he had a craving for it. It was a stimulant to him to be in the homes of the working people, moving, as it were, through the innermost body of their life. His nerves were excited and gratified. He could come so near, into the very lives of the rough, inarticulate, powerful emotional men and women: He grumbled, he said he hated the hellish hole. But as a matter of fact it excited him, the contact with the rough, strongly-feeling people was a stimulant applied direct to his nerves.

Below Oldmeadow, in the green, shallow, soddened hollow of fields, lay a square, deep pond. Roving across the landscape, the doctor's quick eye detected a figure in black passing through the gate of the field, down towards the pond. He looked again. It would be Mabel Pervin. His mind suddenly became alive and attentive.

Why was she going down there? He pulled up on the path on the slope above, and stood staring. He could just make sure of the small black figure moving in the hollow of the failing day. He seemed to see her in the midst of such obscurity, that he was like a clairvoyant, seeing rather with the mind's eye than with ordinary sight. Yet he could see her positively enough, whilst he kept his eye attentive. He felt, if he looked away from her, in the thick, ugly falling dusk, he would lose her altogether.

He followed her minutely as she moved, direct and intent, like something transmitted rather than stirring in voluntary activity, straight down from the field towards the pond. There she stood on the bank for a moment. She never raised her head. Then she waded slowly into the water.

He stood motionless as the small black figure walked slowly and deliber- 110
ately towards the center of the pond, very slowly, gradually moving deeper into
the motionless water, and still moving forward as the water got up to her
breast. Then he could see her no more in the dusk of the dead afternoon.

"There!" he exclaimed. "Would you believe it?"

And he hastened straight down, running over the wet, soddened fields,
pushing through the hedges, down into the depression of callous wintry obscurity. It took him several minutes to come to the pond. He stood on the
bank, breathing heavily. He could see nothing. His eyes seemed to penetrate
the dead water. Yes, perhaps that was the dark shadow of her black clothing
beneath the surface of the water.

He slowly ventured into the pond. The bottom was deep, soft clay, he sank
in, and the water clasped dead cold round his legs. As he stirred he could smell
the cold, rotten clay that fouled up into the water. It was objectionable in his
lungs. Still, repelled and yet not heeding, he moved deeper into the pond. The
cold water rose over his thighs, over his loins, upon his abdomen. The lower
part of his body was all sunk in the hideous cold element. And the bottom was
so deeply soft and uncertain, he was afraid of pitching with his mouth underneath. He could not swim, and was afraid.

He crouched a little, spreading his hands under the water and moving
them round, trying to feel for her. The dead cold pond swayed upon his chest.
He moved again, a little deeper, and again, with his hands underneath, he felt
all around under the water. And he touched her clothing. But it evaded his fingers. He made a desperate effort to grasp it.

And so doing he lost his balance and went under, horribly, suffocating in 115
the foul earthy water, struggling madly for a few moments. At last, after what
seemed an eternity, he got his footing, rose again into the air, and looked
around. He gasped, and knew he was in the world. Then he looked at the water.
She had risen near him. He grasped her clothing, and drawing her nearer,
turned to take his way to land again.

He went very slowly, carefully, absorbed in the slow progress. He rose
higher, climbing out of the pond. The water was now only about his legs; he
was thankful, full of relief to be out of the clutches of the pond. He lifted her
and staggered on to the bank, out of the horror of wet, gray clay.

He laid her down on the bank. She was quite unconscious and running
with water. He made the water come from her mouth, he worked to restore her.
He did not have to work very long before he could feel the breathing begin
again in her; she was breathing naturally. He worked a little longer. He could
feel her live beneath his hands; she was coming back. He wiped her face,
wrapped her in his overcoat, looked round into the dim, dark gray world, then
lifted her and staggered down the bank and across the fields.

It seemed an unthinkably long way, and his burden so heavy he felt he
would never get to the house. But at last he was in the stable-yard, and then in
the house-yard. He opened the door and went into the house. In the kitchen he
laid her down on the hearth-rug and called. The house was empty. But the fire
was burning in the grate.

Then again he kneeled to attend to her. She was breathing regularly,
her eyes were wide open and as if conscious, but there seemed something
missing in her look. She was conscious in herself, but unconscious of her
surroundings.

He ran upstairs, took blankets from a bed, and put them before the fire to   120
warm. Then he removed her saturated, earthy-smelling clothing, rubbed her
dry with a towel, and wrapped her naked in the blankets. Then he went into
the dining-room, to look for spirits. There was a little whiskey. He drank a gulp
himself, and put some into her mouth.

The effect was instantaneous. She looked full into his face, as if she had
been seeing him for some time, and yet had only just become conscious of
him.

"Dr. Fergusson?" she said.

"What?" he answered.

He was divesting himself of his coat, intending to find some dry clothing
upstairs. He could not bear the smell of the dead, clayey water, and he was
mortally afraid for his own health.

"What did I do?" she asked.   125

"Walked into the pond," he replied. He had begun to shudder like one
sick, and could hardly attend to her. Her eyes remained full on him, he seemed
to be going dark in his mind, looking back at her helplessly. The shuddering
became quieter in him, his life came back to him, dark and unknowing, but
strong again.

"Was I out of my mind?" she asked, while her eyes were fixed on him all the
time.

"Maybe, for the moment," he replied. He felt quiet, because his strength
had come back. The strange fretful strain had left him.

"Am I out of my mind now?" she asked.

"Are you?" he reflected a moment. "No," he answered truthfully, "I don't   130
see that you are." He turned his face aside. He was afraid now, because he felt
dazed, and felt dimly that her power was stronger than his, in this issue. And
she continued to look at him fixedly all the time. "Can you tell me where I shall
find some dry things to put on?" he asked.

"Did you dive into the pond for me?" she asked.

"No," he answered. "I walked in. But I went in overhead as well."

There was silence for a moment. He hesitated. He very much wanted to go
upstairs to get into dry clothing. But there was another desire in him. And she
seemed to hold him. His will seemed to have gone to sleep, and left him, standing there slack before her. But he felt warm inside himself. He did not shudder
at all, though his clothes were sodden on him.

"Why did you?" she asked.

"Because I didn't want you to do such a foolish thing," he said.   135

"It wasn't foolish," she said, still gazing at him as she lay on the floor, with
a sofa cushion under her head. "It was the right thing to do. *I* knew best, then."

"I'll go and shift these wet things," he said. But still he had not the power
to move out of her presence, until she sent him. It was as if she had the life of
his body in her hands, and he could not extricate himself. Or perhaps he did
not want to.

Suddenly she sat up. Then she became aware of her own immediate condition. She felt the blankets about her, she knew her own limbs. For a moment it
seemed as if her reason were going. She looked round, with wild eyes, as if seeking something. He stood still with fear. She saw her clothing lying scattered.

"Who undressed me?" she asked, her eyes resting full and inevitable on his
face.

"I did," he replied, "to bring you round."   140
For some moments she sat and gazed at him, awfully, her lips parted.
"Do you love me, then?" she asked.
He only stood and stared at her, fascinated. His soul seemed to melt.
She shuffled forward on her knees, and put her arms round him, round
his legs, as he stood there, pressing her breasts against his knees and thighs,
clutching him with strange, convulsive certainty, pressing his thighs against
her, drawing him to her face, her throat, as she looked up at him with flaring,
humble eyes of transfiguration, triumphant in first possession.
"You love me," she murmured, in strange transport, yearning and tri-   145
umphant and confident. "You love me. I know you love me, I know."
And she was passionately kissing his knees, through the wet clothing, passionately and indiscriminately kissing his knees, his legs, as if unaware of
everything.
He looked down at the tangled wet hair, the wild, bare, animal shoulders.
He was amazed, bewildered, and afraid. He had never thought of loving her.
He had never wanted to love her. When he rescued her and restored her, he was
a doctor, and she was a patient. He had had no single personal thought of her.
Nay, this introduction of the personal element was very distasteful to him, a
violation of his professional honor. It was horrible to have her there embracing his knees. It was horrible. He revolted from it, violently. And yet—and
yet—he had not the power to break away.
She looked at him again, with the same supplication of powerful love, and
that same transcendent, frightening light of triumph. In view of the delicate
flame which seemed to come from her face like a light, he was powerless. And
yet he had never intended to love her. He had never intended. And something
stubborn in him could not give way.
"You love me," she repeated, in a murmur of deep, rhapsodic assurance.
"You love me."
Her hands were drawing him, drawing him down to her. He was afraid,   150
even a little horrified. For he had, really, no intention of loving her. Yet her
hands were drawing him towards her. He put out his hand quickly to steady
himself, and grasped her bare shoulder. A flame seemed to burn the hand that
grasped her soft shoulder. He had no intention of loving her: his whole will
was against his yielding. It was horrible. And yet wonderful was the touch of
her shoulders, beautiful the shining of her face. Was she perhaps mad? He had
a horror of yielding to her. Yet something in him ached also.
He had been staring away at the door, away from her. But his hand
remained on her shoulder. She had gone suddenly very still. He looked down
at her. Her eyes were now wide with fear, with doubt, the light was dying from
her face, a shadow of terrible grayness was returning. He could not bear the
touch of her eyes' question upon him, and the look of death behind the
question.
With an inward groan he gave way, and let his heart yield towards her. A
sudden gentle smile came on his face. And her eyes, which never left his face,
slowly, slowly filled with tears. He watched the strange water rise in her eyes,
like some slow fountain coming up. And his heart seemed to burn and melt
away in his breast.
He could not bear to look at her any more. He dropped on his knees and
caught her head with his arms and pressed her face against his throat. She was

very still. His heart, which seemed to have broken, was burning with a kind of agony in his breast. And he felt her slow, hot tears wetting his throat. But he could not move.

He felt the hot tears wet his neck and the hollows of his neck, and he remained motionless, suspended through one of man's eternities. Only now it had become indispensable to him to have her face pressed close to him; he could never let her go again. He could never let her head go away from the close clutch of his arm. He wanted to remain like that for ever, with his heart hurting him in a pain that was also life to him. Without knowing, he was looking down on her damp, soft brown hair.

Then, as it were suddenly, he smelt the horrid stagnant smell of that 155 water. And at the same moment she drew away from him and looked at him. Her eyes were wistful and unfathomable. He was afraid of them, and he fell to kissing her, not knowing what he was doing. He wanted her eyes not to have that terrible, wistful, unfathomable look.

When she turned her face to him again, a faint delicate flush was glowing, and there was again dawning that terrible shining of joy in her eyes, which really terrified him, and yet which he now wanted to see, because he feared the look of doubt still more.

"You love me?" she said, rather faltering.

"Yes." The word cost him a painful effort. Not because it wasn't true. But because it was too newly true, the *saying* seemed to tear open again his newly-torn heart. And he hardly wanted it to be true, even now.

She lifted her face to him, and he bent forward and kissed her on the mouth, gently, with the one kiss that is an eternal pledge. And as he kissed her his heart strained again in his breast. He never intended to love her. But now it was over. He had crossed over the gulf to her, and all that he had left behind had shriveled and become void.

After the kiss, her eyes again slowly filled with tears. She sat still, away 160 from him, with her face drooped aside, and her hands folded in her lap. The tears fell very slowly. There was complete silence. He too sat there motionless and silent on the hearth-rug. The strange pain of his heart that was broken seemed to consume him. That he should love her? That this was love! That he should be ripped open in this way! Him, a doctor! How they would all jeer if they knew! It was agony to him to think they might know.

In the curious naked pain of the thought he looked again to her. She was still sitting there drooped into a muse. He saw a tear fall, and his heart flared hot. He saw for the first time that one of her shoulders was quite uncovered, one arm bare, he could see one of her small breasts; dimly, because it had become almost dark in the room.

"Why are you crying?" he asked, in an altered voice.

She looked up at him, and behind her tears the consciousness of her situation for the first time brought a dark look of shame to her eyes.

"I'm not crying, really," she said, watching him, half frightened.

He reached his hand, and softly closed it on her bare arm.   165

"I love you! I love you!" he said in a soft, low vibrating voice, unlike himself.

She shrank, and dropped her head. The soft, penetrating grip of his hand on her arm distressed her. She looked up at him.

"I want to go," she said. "I want to go and get you some dry things."

"Why?" he said. "I'm all right."

"But I want to go," she said. "And I want you to change your things."   170

He released her arm, and she wrapped herself in the blanket, looking at him rather frightened. And still she did not rise.

"Kiss me," she said wistfully.

He kissed her, but briefly, half in anger.

Then, after a second, she rose nervously, all mixed up in the blanket. He watched her in her confusion as she tried to extricate herself and wrap herself up so that she could walk. He watched her relentlessly, as she knew. And as she went, the blanket trailing, and as he saw a glimpse of her feet and her white leg, he tried to remember her as she was when he had wrapped her in the blanket. But then he didn't want to remember, because she had been nothing to him then, and his nature revolted from remembering her as she was when she was nothing to him.

A tumbling, muffled noise from within the dark house startled him. Then   175 he heard her voice: "There are clothes." He rose and went to the foot of the stairs, and gathered up the garments she had thrown down. Then he came back to the fire, to rub himself down and dress. He grinned at his own appearance when he had finished.

The fire was sinking, so he put on coal. The house was now quite dark, save for the light of a street-lamp that shone in faintly from beyond the holly trees. He lit the gas with matches he found on the mantelpiece. Then he emptied the pockets of his own clothes, and threw all his wet things in a heap into the scullery. After which he gathered up her sodden clothes, gently, and put them in a separate heap on the copper-top in the scullery.

It was six o'clock on the clock. His own watch had stopped. He ought to go back to the surgery. He waited, and still she did not come down. So he went to the foot of the stairs and called:

"I shall have to go."

Almost immediately he heard her coming down. She had on her best dress of black voile, and her hair was tidy, but still damp. She looked at him — and in spite of herself, smiled.

"I don't like you in those clothes," she said.   180

"Do I look a sight?" he answered.

They were shy of one another.

"I'll make you some tea," she said.

"No, I must go."

"Must you?" And she looked at him again with the wide, strained, doubt-   185 ful eyes. And again, from the pain of his breast, he knew how he loved her. He went and bent to kiss her, gently, passionately, with his heart's painful kiss.

"And my hair smells so horrible," she murmured in distraction. "And I'm so awful, I'm so awful! Oh, no, I'm too awful." And she broke into bitter, heart-broken sobbing. "You can't want to love me, I'm horrible."

"Don't be silly, don't be silly," he said, trying to comfort her, kissing her, holding her in his arms. "I want you, I want to marry you, we're going to be married, quickly, quickly — tomorrow if I can."

But she only sobbed terribly, and cried:

"I feel awful. I feel awful. I feel I'm horrible to you."

"No, I want you, I want you," was all he answered, blindly, with that ter-   190 rible intonation which frightened her almost more than her horror lest he should *not* want her.

Tɪᴍ O'Bʀɪᴇɴ   (ʙ. 1946)
How to Tell a True War Story   1987

This is true.
  I had a buddy in Vietnam. His name was Bob Kiley, but everybody called him Rat.
  A friend of his gets killed, so about a week later Rat sits down and writes a letter to the guy's sister. Rat tells her what a great brother she had, how strack° the guy was, a number one pal and comrade. A real soldier's soldier, Rat says. Then he tells a few stories to make the point, how her brother would always volunteer for stuff nobody else would volunteer for in a million years, dangerous stuff, like doing recon° or going out on these really badass night patrols. Stainless steel balls, Rat tells her. The guy was a little crazy, for sure, but crazy in a good way, a real daredevil, because he liked the challenge of it, he liked testing himself, just man against gook. A great, great guy, Rat says.
  Anyway, it's a terrific letter, very personal and touching. Rat almost bawls writing it. He gets all teary telling about the good times they had together, how her brother made the war seem almost fun, always raising hell and lighting up villes° and bringing smoke to bear every which way. A great sense of humor, too. Like the time at this river when he went fishing with a whole damn crate of hand grenades. Probably the funniest thing in world history, Rat says, all that gore, about twenty zillion dead gook fish. Her brother, he had the right attitude. He knew how to have a good time. On Halloween, this real hot spooky night, the dude paints up his body all different colors and puts on this weird mask and goes out on ambush almost stark naked, just boots and balls and an M-16. A tremendous human being, Rat says. Pretty nutso sometimes, but you could trust him with your life.
  And then the letter gets very sad and serious. Rat pours his heart out. He   5
says he loved the guy. He says the guy was his best friend in the world. They were like soul mates, he says, like twins or something, they had a whole lot in common. He tells the guy's sister he'll look her up when the war's over.
  So what happens?
  Rat mails the letter. He waits two months. The dumb cooze never writes back.

  A true war story is never moral. It does not instruct, nor encourage virtue, nor suggest models of proper human behavior, nor restrain men from doing the things they have always done. If a story seems moral, do not believe it. If at the end of a war story you feel uplifted, or if you feel that some small bit of rectitude has been salvaged from the larger waste, then you have been made the victim of a very old and terrible lie. There is no rectitude whatsover. There is no virtue. As a first rule of thumb, therefore, you can tell a true war story by its absolute and uncompromising allegiance to obscenity and evil. Listen to Rat Kiley. *Cooze*, he says. He does not say *bitch*. He certainly does not say *woman*, or *girl*. He says *cooze*. Then he spits and stares. He's nineteen years old — it's too

---

strack: A strict military appearance.
doing recon: Reconnaissance, or exploratory survey of enemy territory.
villes: Villages.

much for him — so he looks at you with those big gentle killer eyes and says *cooze,* because his friend is dead, and because it's so incredibly sad and true: she never wrote back.

You can tell a true war story if it embarrasses you. If you don't care for obscenity, you don't care for the truth; if you don't care for the truth, watch how you vote. Send guys to war, they come home talking dirty.

Listen to Rat: "Jesus Christ, man, I write this beautiful fucking letter, I slave over it, and what happens? The dumb cooze never writes back." 10

The dead guy's name was Curt Lemon. What happened was, we crossed a muddy river and marched west into the mountains, and on the third day we took a break along a trail junction in deep jungle. Right away, Lemon and Rat Kiley started goofing off. They didn't understand about the spookiness. They were kids; they just didn't know. A nature hike, they thought, not even a war, so they went off into the shade of some giant trees — quadruple canopy, no sunlight at all — and they were giggling and calling each other motherfucker and playing a silly game they'd invented. The game involved smoke grenades, which were harmless unless you did stupid things, and what they did was pull out the pin and stand a few feet apart and play catch under the shade of those huge trees. Whoever chickened out was a motherfucker. And if nobody chickened out, the grenade would make a light popping sound and they'd be covered with smoke and they'd laugh and dance around and then do it again.

It's all exactly true.

It happened nearly twenty years ago, but I still remember that trail junction and the giant trees and a soft dripping sound somewhere beyond the trees. I remember the smell of moss. Up in the canopy there were tiny white blossoms, but no sunlight at all, and I remember the shadows spreading out under the trees where Lemon and Rat Kiley were playing catch with smoke grenades. Mitchell Sanders sat flipping his yo-yo. Norman Bowker and Kiowa and Dave Jensen were dozing, or half-dozing, and all around us were those ragged green mountains.

Except for the laughter things were quiet.

At one point, I remember, Mitchell Sanders turned and looked at me, not quite nodding, then after a while he rolled up his yo-yo and moved away. 15

It's hard to tell what happened next.

They were just goofing. There was a noise, I suppose, which must've been the detonator, so I glanced behind me and watched Lemon step from the shade into bright sunlight. His face was suddenly brown and shining. A handsome kid, really. Sharp gray eyes, lean and narrow-waisted, and when he died it was almost beautiful, the way the sunlight came around him and lifted him up and sucked him high into a tree full of moss and vines and white blossoms.

In any war story, but especially a true one, it's difficult to separate what happened from what seemed to happen. What seems to happen becomes its own happening and has to be told that way. The angles of vision are skewed. When a booby trap explodes, you close your eyes and duck and float outside yourself. When a guy dies, like Lemon, you look away and then look back for a moment and then look away again. The pictures get jumbled; you tend to miss a lot. And then afterward, when you go to tell about it, there is always that surreal seemingness, which makes the story seem untrue, but which in fact represents the hard and exact truth as it seemed.

In many cases a true war story cannot be believed. If you believe it, be skeptical. It's a question of credibility. Often the crazy stuff is true and the normal stuff isn't because the normal stuff is necessary to make you believe the truly incredible craziness.

In other cases you can't even tell a true war story. Sometimes it's just be-   20
yond telling.

I heard this one, for example, from Mitchell Sanders. It was near dusk and we were sitting at my foxhole along a wide, muddy river north of Quang Ngai. I remember how peaceful the twilight was. A deep pinkish red spilled out on the river, which moved without sound, and in the morning we would cross the river and march west into the mountains. The occasion was right for a good story.

"God's truth," Mitchell Sanders said. "A six-man patrol goes up into the mountains on a basic listening-post operation. The idea's to spend a week up there, just lie low and listen for enemy movement. They've got a radio along, so if they hear anything suspicious — anything — they're supposed to call in artillery or gunships, whatever it takes. Otherwise they keep strict field discipline. Absolute silence. They just listen."

He glanced at me to make sure I had the scenario. He was playing with his yo-yo, making it dance with short, tight little strokes of the wrist.

His face was blank in the dusk.

"We're talking hardass LP.° These six guys, they don't say boo for a solid   25
week. They don't got tongues. *All* ears."

"Right," I said.

"Understand me?"

"Invisible."

Sanders nodded.

"Affirm," he said. "Invisible. So what happens is, these guys get themselves   30
deep in the bush, all camouflaged up, and they lie down and wait and that's all they do, nothing else, they lie there for seven straight days and just listen. And man, I'll tell you — it's spooky. This is mountains. You don't *know* spooky till you been there. Jungle, sort of, except it's way up in the clouds and there's always this fog — like rain, except it's not raining — everything's all wet and swirly and tangled up and you can't see jack, you can't find your own pecker to piss with. Like you don't even have a body. Serious spooky. You just go with the vapors — the fog sort of takes you in. . . . And the sounds, man. The sounds carry forever. You hear shit nobody should *ever* hear."

Sanders was quiet for a second, just working the yo-yo, then he smiled at me. "So, after a couple days the guys start hearing this real soft, kind of wacked-out music. Weird echoes and stuff. Like a radio or something, but it's not a radio, it's this strange gook music that comes right out of the rocks. Faraway, sort of, but right up close, too. They try to ignore it. But it's a listening post, right? So they listen. And every night they keep hearing this crazyass gook concert. All kinds of chimes and xylophones. I mean, this is wilderness — no way, it

LP: Listening post.

can't be real—but there it *is,* like the mountains are tuned in to Radio Fucking Hanoi. Naturally they get nervous. One guy sticks Juicy Fruit in his ears. Another guy almost flips. Thing is, though, they can't report music. They can't get on the horn and call back to base and say, 'Hey, listen, we need some firepower, we got to blow away this weirdo gook rock band.' They can't do that. It wouldn't go down. So they lie there in the fog and keep their mouths shut. And what makes it extra bad, see, is the poor dudes can't horse around like normal. Can't joke it away. Can't even talk to each other except maybe in whispers, all hush-hush, and that just revs up the willies. All they do is listen."

Again there was some silence as Mitchell Sanders looked out on the river. The dark was coming on hard now, and off to the west I could see the mountains rising in silhouette, all the mysteries and unknowns.

"This next part," Sanders said quietly, "you won't believe."

"Probably not," I said.

"You won't. And you know why?"   35

"Why?"

He gave me a tired smile. "Because it happened. Because every word is absolutely dead-on true."

Sanders made a little sound in his throat, like a sigh, as if to say he didn't care if I believed it or not. But he did care. He wanted me to believe, I could tell. He seemed sad, in a way.

"These six guys, they're pretty fried out by now, and one night they start hearing voices. Like at a cocktail party. That's what it sounds like, this big swank gook cocktail party somewhere out there in the fog. Music and chitchat and stuff. It's crazy, I know, but they hear the champagne corks. They hear the actual martini glasses. Real hoity-toity, all very civilized, except this isn't civilization. This is Nam.

"Anyway, the guys try to be cool. They just lie there and groove, but after a   40
while they start hearing—you won't believe this—they hear chamber music. They hear violins and shit. They hear this terrific mama-san soprano. Then after a while they hear gook opera and a glee club and the Haiphong Boys Choir and a barbershop quartet and all kinds of weird chanting and Buddha-Buddha stuff. The whole time, in the background, there's still that cocktail party going on. All these different voices. Not human voices, though. Because it's the mountains. Follow me? The rock—it's *talking.* And the fog, too, and the grass and the goddamn mongooses. Everything talks. The trees talk politics, the monkeys talk religion. The whole country. Vietnam, the place talks.

"The guys can't cope. They lose it. They get on the radio and report enemy movement—a whole army, they say—and they order up the firepower. They get arty° and gunships. They call in air strikes. And I'll tell you, they fuckin' crash that cocktail party. All night long, they just smoke those mountains. They make jungle juice. They blow away trees and glee clubs and whatever else there is to blow away. Scorch time. They walk napalm up and down the ridges. They bring in the Cobras and F-4s, they use Willie Peter and HE° and incendiaries. It's all fire. They make those mountains burn.

---

arty: Artillery.
Willie Peter and HE: White phosphorus, an incendiary substance, and high explosives.

"Around dawn things finally get quiet. Like you never even *heard* quiet before. One of those real thick, real misty days—just clouds and fog, they're off in this special zone—and the mountains are absolutely dead-flat silent. Like Brigadoon°—pure vapor, you know? Everything's all sucked up inside the fog. Not a single sound, except they still *hear* it.

"So they pack up and start humping. They head down the mountain, back to base camp, and when they get there they don't say diddly. They don't talk. Not a word, like they're deaf and dumb. Later on this fat bird colonel comes up and asks what the hell happened out there. What'd they hear? Why all the ordnance? The man's ragged out, he gets down tight on their case. I mean, they spent six trillion dollars on firepower, and this fatass colonel wants answers, he wants to know what the fuckin' story is.

"But the guys don't say zip. They just look at him for a while, sort of funny-like, sort of amazed, and the whole war is right there in that stare. It says everything you can't ever say. It says, man, you got *wax* in your ears. It says, poor bastard, you'll never know—wrong frequency—you don't *even* want to hear this. Then they salute the fucker and walk away, because certain stories you don't ever tell."

You can tell a true war story by the way it never seems to end. Not then, 45 not ever. Not when Mitchell Sanders stood up and moved off into the dark.

It all happened.

Even now I remember that yo-yo. In a way, I suppose, you had to be there, you had to hear it, but I could tell how desperately Sanders wanted me to believe him, his frustration at not quite getting the details right, not quite pinning down the final and definitive truth.

And I remember sitting at my foxhole that night, watching the shadows of Quang Ngai, thinking about the coming day and how we would cross the river and march west into the mountains, all the ways I might die, all the things I did not understand.

Late in the night Mitchell Sanders touched my shoulder.

"Just came to me," he whispered. "The moral, I mean. Nobody listens. No- 50 body hears nothing. Like that fatass colonel. The politicians, all the civilian types, what they need is to go out on LP. The vapors, man. Trees and rocks—you got to *listen* to your enemy."

And then again, in the morning, Sanders came up to me. The platoon was preparing to move out, checking weapons, going through all the little rituals that preceded a day's march. Already the lead squad had crossed the river and was filing off toward the west.

"I got a confession to make," Sanders said. "Last night, man, I had to make up a few things."

"I know that."

"The glee club. There wasn't any glee club."

"Right." 55

"No opera."

"Forget it, I understand."

Brigadoon: A fictional village in Scotland that only appears once every one hundred years; subject of a popular American musical (1947).

"Yeah, but listen, it's still true. Those six guys, they heard wicked sound out there. They heard sound you just plain won't believe."

Sanders pulled on his rucksack, closed his eyes for a moment, then almost smiled at me.

I knew what was coming but I beat him to it.   60

"All right," I said, "what's the moral?"

"Forget it."

"No, go ahead."

For a long while he was quiet, looking away, and the silence kept stretching out until it was almost embarrassing. Then he shrugged and gave me a stare that lasted all day.

"Hear that quiet, man?" he said. "There's your moral."   65

In a true war story, if there's a moral at all, it's like the thread that makes the cloth. You can't tease it out. You can't extract the meaning without unraveling the deeper meaning. And in the end, really, there's nothing much to say about a true war story, except maybe "Oh."

True war stories do not generalize. They do not indulge in abstraction or analysis.

For example: War is hell. As a moral declaration the old truism seems perfectly true, and yet because it abstracts, because it generalizes, I can't believe it with my stomach. Nothing turns inside.

It comes down to gut instinct. A true war story, if truly told, makes the stomach believe.

This one does it for me. I've told it before — many times, many versions —   70
but here's what actually happened.

We crossed the river and marched west into the mountains. On the third day, Curt Lemon stepped on a booby-trapped 105 round. He was playing catch with Rat Kiley, laughing, and then he was dead. The trees were thick; it took nearly an hour to cut an LZ for the dustoff.°

Later, higher in the mountains, we came across a baby VC° water buffalo. What it was doing there I don't know — no farms or paddies — but we chased it down and got a rope around it and led it along to a deserted village where we set for the night. After supper Rat Kiley went over and stroked its nose.

He opened up a can of C rations, pork and beans, but the baby buffalo wasn't interested.

Rat shrugged.

He stepped back and shot it through the right front knee. The animal did   75
not make a sound. It went down hard, then got up again, and Rat took careful aim and shot off an ear. He shot it in the hindquarters and in the little hump at its back. He shot it twice in the flanks. It wasn't to kill; it was just to hurt. He put the rifle muzzle up against the mouth and shot the mouth away. Nobody said much. The whole platoon stood there watching, feeling all kinds of things, but there wasn't a great deal of pity for the baby water buffalo. Lemon was dead. Rat Kiley had lost his best friend in the world. Later in the week he would write a long personal letter to the guy's sister, who would not write

LZ for the dustoff: Landing zone for a helicopter evacuation of a casualty.
VC: Vietcong (North Vietnamese).

back, but for now it was a question of pain. He shot off the tail. He shot away chunks of meat below the ribs. All around us there was the smell of smoke and filth, and deep greenery, and the evening was humid and very hot. Rat went to automatic. He shot randomly, almost casually, quick little spurts in the belly and butt. Then he reloaded, squatted down, and shot it in the left front knee. Again the animal fell hard and tried to get up, but this time it couldn't quite make it. It wobbled and went down sideways. Rat shot it in the nose. He bent forward and whispered something, as if talking to a pet, then he shot it in the throat. All the while the baby buffalo was silent, or almost silent, just a light bubbling sound where the nose had been. It lay very still. Nothing moved except the eyes, which were enormous, the pupils shiny black and dumb.

Rat Kiley was crying. He tried to say something, but then cradled his rifle and went off by himself.

The rest of us stood in a ragged circle around the baby buffalo. For a time no one spoke. We had witnessed something essential, something brand-new and profound, a piece of the world so startling there was not yet a name for it.

Somebody kicked the baby buffalo.

It was still alive, though just barely, just in the eyes.

"Amazing," Dave Jensen said. "My whole life, I never seen anything like it." 80

"Never?"

"Not hardly. Not once."

Kiowa and Mitchell Sanders picked up the baby buffalo. They hauled it across the open square, hoisted it up, and dumped it in the village well.

Afterward, we sat waiting for Rat to get himself together.

"Amazing," Dave Jensen kept saying. 85

"For sure."

"A new wrinkle. I never seen it before."

Mitchell Sanders took out his yo-yo.

"Well, that's Nam," he said. "Garden of Evil. Over here, man, every sin's real fresh and original."

How do you generalize? 90

War is hell, but that's not the half of it, because war is also mystery and terror and adventure and courage and discovery and holiness and pity and despair and longing and love. War is nasty; war is fun. War is thrilling; war is drudgery. War makes you a man; war makes you dead.

The truths are contradictory. It can be argued, for instance, that war is grotesque. But in truth war is also beauty. For all its horror, you can't help but gape at the awful majesty of combat. You stare out at tracer rounds unwinding through the dark like brilliant red ribbons. You crouch in ambush as a cool, impassive moon rises over the nighttime paddies. You admire the fluid symmetries of troops on the move, the harmonies of sound and shape and proportion, the great sheets of metal-fire streaming down from a gunship, the illumination rounds, the white phosphorous, the purply black glow of napalm, the rocket's red glare. It's not pretty, exactly. It's astonishing. It fills the eye. It commands you. You hate it, yes, but your eyes do not. Like a killer forest fire, like cancer under a microscope, any battle or bombing raid or artillery barrage has the aesthetic purity of absolute moral indifference — a powerful, implacable beauty — and a true war story will tell the truth about this, though the truth is ugly.

To generalize about war is like generalizing about peace. Almost everything is true. Almost nothing is true. At its core, perhaps, war is just another name for death, and yet any soldier will tell you, if he tells the truth, that proximity to death brings with it a corresponding proximity to life. After a fire fight, there is always the immense pleasure of aliveness. The trees are alive. The grass, the soil—everything. All around you things are purely living, and you among them, and the aliveness makes you tremble. You feel an intense, out-of-the-skin awareness of your living self—your truest self, the human being you want to be and then become by the force of wanting it. In the midst of evil you want to be a good man. You want decency. You want justice and courtesy and human concord, things you never knew you wanted. There is a kind of largeness to it; a kind of godliness. Though it's odd, you're never more alive than when you're almost dead. You recognize what's valuable. Freshly, as if for the first time, you love what's best in yourself and in the world, all that might be lost. At the hour of dusk you sit at your foxhole and look out on a wide river turning pinkish red, and at the mountains beyond, and although in the morning you must cross the river and go into the mountains and do terrible things and maybe die, even so, you find yourself studying the fine colors on the river, you feel wonder and awe at the setting of the sun, and you are filled with a hard, aching love for how the world could be and always should be, but now is not.

Mitchell Sanders was right. For the common soldier, at least, war has the feel—the spiritual texture—of a great ghostly fog, thick and permanent. There is no clarity. Everything swirls. The old rules are no longer binding, the old truths no longer true. Right spills over into wrong. Order blends into chaos, love into hate, ugliness into beauty, law into anarchy, civility into savagery. The vapors suck you in. You can't tell where you are, or why you're there, and the only certainty is absolute ambiguity.

In war you lose your sense of the definite, hence your sense of truth itself, 95 and therefore it's safe to say that in a true war story nothing much is ever very true.

Often in a true war story there is not even a point, or else the point doesn't hit you until twenty years later, in your sleep, and you wake up and shake your wife and start telling the story to her, except when you get to the end you've forgotten the point again. And then for a long time you lie there watching the story happen in your head. You listen to your wife's breathing. The war's over. You close your eyes. You smile and think, Christ, what's the *point*?

This one wakes me up.

In the mountains that day, I watched Lemon turn sideways. He laughed and said something to Rat Kiley. Then he took a peculiar half step, moving from shade into bright sunlight, and the booby-trapped 105 round blew him into a tree. The parts were just hanging there, so Norman Bowker and I were ordered to shinny up and peel him off. I remember the white bone of an arm. I remember pieces of skin and something wet and yellow that must've been the intestines. The gore was horrible, and stays with me, but what wakes me up twenty years later is Norman Bowker singing "Lemon Tree" as we threw down the parts.

You can tell a true war story by the questions you ask. Somebody tells a story, let's say, and afterward you ask, "Is it true?" and if the answer matters, you've got your answer.

For example, we've all heard this one. Four guys go down a trail. A grenade sails out. One guy jumps on it and takes the blast and saves his three buddies.

Is it true?

The answer matters.

You'd feel cheated if it never happened. Without the grounding reality, it's just a trite bit of puffery, pure Hollywood, untrue in the way all such stories are untrue. Yet even if it did happen—and maybe it did, anything's possible—even then you know it can't be true, because a true war story does not depend upon that kind of truth. Happeningness is irrelevant. A thing may happen and be a total lie; another thing may not happen and be truer than the truth. For example: four guys go down a trail. A grenade sails out. One guy jumps on it and takes the blast, but it's a killer grenade and everybody dies anyway. Before they die, though, one of the dead guys says, "The fuck you do *that* for?" and the jumper says, "Story of my life, man," and the other guy starts to smile but he's dead.

That's a true story that never happened.

Twenty years later, I can still see the sunlight on Lemon's face. I can see him turning, looking back at Rat Kiley, then he laughed and took that curious half step from shade into sunlight, his face suddenly brown and shining, and when his foot touched down, in that instant, he must've thought it was the sunlight that was killing him. It was not the sunlight. It was a rigged 105 round. But if I could ever get the story right, how the sun seemed to gather around him and pick him up and lift him into a tree, if I could somehow recreate the fatal whiteness of that light, the quick glare, the obvious cause and effect, then you would believe the last thing Lemon believed, which for him must've been the final truth.

Now and then, when I tell this story, someone will come up to me afterward and say she liked it. It's always a woman. Usually it's an older woman of kindly temperament and humane politics. She'll explain that as a rule she hates war stories, she can't understand why people want to wallow in blood and gore. But this one she liked. Sometimes, even, there are little tears. What I should do, she'll say, is put it all behind me. Find new stories to tell.

I won't say it but I'll think it.

I'll picture Rat Kiley's face, his grief, and I'll think, *You dumb cooze.*

Because she wasn't listening.

It wasn't a war story. It was a love story. It was a ghost story.

But you can't say that. All you can do is tell it one more time, patiently, adding and subtracting, making up a few things to get at the real truth. No Mitchell Sanders, you tell her. No Lemon, no Rat Kiley. And it didn't happen in the mountains, it happened in this little village on the Batangan Peninsula, and it was raining like crazy, and one night a guy named Stink Harris woke up screaming with a leech on his tongue. You can tell a true war story if you just keep on telling it.

In the end, of course, a true war story is never about war. It's about the special way that dawn spreads out on a river when you know you must cross the river and march into the mountains and do things you are afraid to do. It's about love and memory. It's about sorrow. It's about sisters who never write back and people who never listen.

EDGAR ALLAN POE (1809–1849)

The Purloined Letter 1845

Nil sapientiae odiosius acumine nimio.°
— *Seneca*

At Paris, just after dark one gusty evening in the autumn of 18—, I was enjoying the twofold luxury of meditation and a meerschaum, in company with my friend C. Auguste Dupin, in his little back library, or bookcloset, *au troisième, No. 33, Rue Dunôt Faubourg St. Germain.* For one hour at least we had maintained a profound silence; while each, to any casual observer, might have seemed intently and exclusively occupied with the curling eddies of smoke that oppressed the atmosphere of the chamber. For myself, however, I was mentally discussing certain topics which had formed matter for conversation between us at an earlier period of the evening; I mean the affair of the Rue Morgue, and the mystery attending the murder of Marie Rogêt.° I looked upon it, therefore, as something of a coincidence, when the door of our apartment was thrown open and admitted our old acquaintance, Monsieur G——, the Prefect of the Parisian police.

We gave him a hearty welcome; for there was nearly half as much of the entertaining as of the contemptible about the man, and we had not seen him for several years. We had been sitting in the dark, and Dupin now arose for the purpose of lighting a lamp, but sat down again, without doing so, upon G.'s saying that he had called to consult us, or rather to ask the opinion of my friend, about some official business which had occasioned a great deal of trouble.

"If it is any point requiring reflection," observed Dupin, as he forbore to enkindle the wick, "we shall examine it to better purpose in the dark."

"That is another of your odd notions," said the Prefect, who had a fashion of calling every thing "odd" that was beyond his comprehension, and thus lived amid an absolute legion of "oddities."

"Very true," said Dupin, as he supplied his visitor with a pipe, and rolled towards him a comfortable chair.

"And what is the difficulty now?" I asked. "Nothing more in the assassination way, I hope?"

"Oh no; nothing of that nature. The fact is, the business is *very* simple indeed, and I make no doubt that we can manage it sufficiently well ourselves; but then I thought Dupin would like to hear the details of it, because it is so excessively *odd.*"

"Simple and odd," said Dupin.

5

Nil . . . nimio: "Nothing is more hateful to wisdom than too much cunning."
Rue Morgue . . . Marie Rogêt: Poe's first two detective stories, "The Murders in the Rue Morgue (1841) and "The Mystery of Marie Rogêt" (1842).

"Why, yes; and not exactly that, either. The fact is, we have all been a good deal puzzled because the affair *is* so simple, and yet baffles us altogether."

"Perhaps it is the very simplicity of the thing which puts you at fault," said 10 my friend.

"What nonsense you *do* talk!" replied the Prefect, laughing heartily.

"Perhaps the mystery is a little *too* plain," said Dupin.

"Oh, good heavens! who ever heard of such an idea?"

"A little *too* self-evident."

"Ha! ha! ha! — ha! ha! ha! — ho! ho! ho!" — roared our visitor, profoundly 15 amused, "oh, Dupin, you will be the death of me yet!"

"And what, after all, *is* the matter on hand?" I asked.

"Why, I will tell you," replied the Prefect, as he gave a long, steady, and contemplative puff, and settled himself in his chair. "I will tell you in a few words; but, before I begin, let me caution you that this is an affair demanding the greatest secrecy, and that I should most probably lose the position I now hold, were it known that I confided it to any one."

"Proceed," said I.

"Or not," said Dupin.

"Well, then; I have received personal information, from a very high quar- 20 ter, that a certain document of the last importance, has been purloined from the royal apartments. The individual who purloined it is known; this beyond a doubt; he was seen to take it. It is known, also, that it still remains in his possession."

"How is this known?" asked Dupin.

"It is clearly inferred," replied the Prefect, "from the nature of the document, and from the non-appearance of certain results which would at once arise from its passing *out* of the robber's possession; — that is to say, from his employing it as he must design in the end to employ it."

"Be a little more explicit," I said.

"Well, I may venture so far as to say that the paper gives its holder a certain power in a certain quarter where such power is immensely valuable." The Prefect was fond of the cant of diplomacy.

"Still I do not quite understand," said Dupin. 25

"No? Well; the disclosure of the document to a third person, who shall be nameless, would bring in question the honor of a personage of most exalted station; and this fact gives the holder of the document an ascendancy over the illustrious personage whose honor and peace are so jeopardized."

"But this ascendancy," I interposed, "would depend upon the robber's knowledge of the loser's knowledge of the robber. Who would dare —"

"The thief," said G——, "is the Minister D——, who dares all things, those unbecoming as well as those becoming a man. The method of the theft was not less ingenious than bold. The document in question — a letter, to be frank — had been received by the personage robbed while alone in the royal *boudoir*. During its perusal she was suddenly interrupted by the entrance of the other exalted personage from whom especially it was her wish to conceal it. After a hurried and vain endeavor to thrust it in a drawer, she was forced to place it, open as it was, upon a table. The address, however, was uppermost, and, the contents thus unexposed, the letter escaped notice. At this juncture enters the Minister D——. His lynx eye immediately perceives the paper, recognizes the handwriting of the address, observes the confusion of the personage addressed, and fathoms her secret. After some business transactions, hurried through in his ordinary manner, he produces a letter somewhat similar to the one in question, opens it, pretends to read it, and then places it in close juxtaposition to the other. Again he converses, for some fifteen minutes, upon the public affairs. At length, in taking leave, he takes also from the table the letter to which he had no claim. Its rightful owner saw, but, of course, dared not call attention to the act, in the presence of the third personage who stood at her elbow. The minister decamped; leaving his own letter — one of no importance — upon the table."

"Here, then," said Dupin to me, "you have precisely what you demand to make the ascendancy complete — the robber's knowledge of the loser's knowledge of the robber."

"Yes," replied the Prefect; "and the power thus attained has, for some 30 months past, been wielded, for political purposes, to a very dangerous extent. The personage robbed is more thoroughly convinced, every day, of the necessity of reclaiming her letter. But this, of course, cannot be done openly. In fine, driven to despair, she has committed the matter to me."

"Than whom," said Dupin, amid a perfect whirlwind of smoke, "no more sagacious agent could, I suppose, be desired or even imagined."

"You flatter me," replied the Prefect; "but it is possible that some such opinion may have been entertained."

"It is clear," said I, "as you observe, that the letter is still in possession of the minister; since it is in this possession, and not any employment of the letter, which bestows the power. With the employment the power departs."

"True," said G.; "and upon this conviction I proceeded. My first care was to make thorough search of the minister's hotel;° and here my chief embarrassment lay in the necessity of searching without his knowledge. Beyond all things, I have been warned of the danger which would result from giving him reason to suspect our design."

"But," said I, "you are quite *au fait*° in these investigations. The Parisian 35 police have done this thing often before."

"O yes; and for this reason I did not despair. The habits of the minister gave me, too, a great advantage. He is frequently absent from home all night. His servants are by no means numerous. They sleep at a distance from their master's apartment, and, being chiefly Neapolitans, are readily made drunk. I have keys, as you know, with which I can open any chamber or cabinet in Paris. For three months a night has not passed, during the greater part of which I have not been engaged, personally, in ransacking the D—— Hôtel. My honor is interested, and, to mention a great secret, the reward is enormous. So I did not abandon the search until I had become fully satisfied that the thief is a more astute man than myself. I fancy that I have investigated every nook and corner of the premises in which it is possible that the paper can be concealed."

"But is it not possible," I suggested, "that although the letter may be in possession of the minister, as it unquestionably is, he may have concealed it elsewhere than upon his own premises?"

"This is barely possible," said Dupin. "The present peculiar condition of affairs at court, and especially of those intrigues in which D—— is known to be

---

hotel: Mansion.
au fait: Accomplished.

involved, would render the instant availability of the document — its susceptibility of being produced at a moment's notice — a point of nearly equal importance with its possession."

"Its susceptibility of being produced?" said I.

"That is to say, of being *destroyed,*" said Dupin. 40

"True," I observed; "the paper is clearly then upon the premises. As for its
being upon the person of the minister, we may consider that as out of the
question."

"Entirely," said the Prefect. "He has been twice waylaid, as if by footpads,°
and his person rigorously searched under my own inspection."

"You might have spared yourself this trouble," said Dupin. "D——, I presume, is not altogether a fool, and, if not, must have anticipated these waylayings, as a matter of course."

"Not *altogether* a fool," said G., "but then he's a poet, which I take to be
only one remove from a fool."

"True," said Dupin, after a long and thoughtful whiff from his meer- 45
schaum, "although I have been guilty of certain doggerel myself."

"Suppose you detail," said I, "the particulars of your search."

"Why the fact is, we took our time, and we searched *every where*. I have had
long experience in these affairs. I took the entire building, room by room; devoting the nights of a whole week to each. We examined, first, the furniture of
each apartment. We opened every possible drawer; and I presume you know
that, to a properly trained police agent, such a thing as a *secret drawer* is impossible. Any man is a dolt who permits a 'secret' drawer to escape him in a search
of this kind. The thing is *so* plain. There is a certain amount of bulk — of
space — to be accounted for in every cabinet. Then we have accurate rules. The
fiftieth part of a line could not escape us. After the cabinets we took the chairs.
The cushions we probed with the fine long needles you have seen me employ.
From the tables we removed the tops."

"Why so?"

"Sometimes the top of a table, or other similarly arranged piece of furniture, is removed by the person wishing to conceal an article; then the leg is ex-
cavated, the article deposited within the cavity, and the top replaced. The bottoms and tops of bed-posts are employed in the same way."

"But could not the cavity be detected by sounding?" I asked. 50

"By no means, if, when the article is deposited, a sufficient wadding of cotton be placed around it. Besides, in our case, we were obliged to proceed without noise."

"But you could not have removed — you could not have taken to pieces *all*
articles of furniture in which it would have been possible to make a deposit in
the manner you mention. A letter may be compressed into a thin spiral roll,
not differing much in shape or bulk from a large knitting-needle, and in this
form it might be inserted into the rung of a chair, for example. You did not
take to pieces all the chairs?"

"Certainly not; but we did better — we examined the rungs of every chair
in the hotel, and, indeed, the jointings of every description of furniture, by
the aid of a most powerful microscope. Had there been any traces of recent
disturbance we should not have failed to detect it instantly. A single grain of

footpads: Robbers.

gimlet-dust, for example, would have been as obvious as an apple. Any disorder in the gluing — any unusual gaping in the joints — would have sufficed to insure detection."

"I presume you looked to the mirrors, between the boards and the plates, and you probed the beds and the bed-clothes, as well as the curtains and carpets."

"That of course; and when we had absolutely completed every article of the furniture in this way, then we examined the house itself. We divided its entire surface into compartments, which we numbered, so that none might be missed; then we scrutinized each individual square inch throughout the premises, including the two houses immediately adjoining, with the microscope, as before."

"The two houses adjoining!" I exclaimed; "you must have had a great deal of trouble."

"We had; but the reward offered is prodigious."

"You include the *grounds* about the houses?"

"All the grounds are paved with brick. They gave us comparatively little trouble. We examined the moss between the bricks, and found it undisturbed."

"You looked among D——'s papers, of course, and into the books of the library?"

"Certainly; we opened every package and parcel; we not only opened every book, but we turned over every leaf in each volume, not contenting ourselves with a mere shake, according to the fashion of some of our police officers. We also measured the thickness of every book-*cover,* with the most accurate admeasurement, and applied to each the most jealous scrutiny of the microscope. Had any of the bindings been recently meddled with, it would have been utterly impossible that the fact should have escaped observation. Some five or six volumes, just from the hands of the binder, we carefully probed, longitudinally, with the needles."

"You explored the floors beneath the carpets?"

"Beyond doubt. We removed every carpet, and examined the boards with the microscope."

"And the paper on the walls?"

"Yes."

"You looked into the cellars?"

"We did."

"Then," I said, "you have been making a miscalculation, and the letter is *not* upon the premises, as you suppose."

"I fear you are right there," said the Prefect. "And now, Dupin, what would you advise me to do?"

"To make a thorough re-search of the premises."

"That is absolutely needless," replied G——. "I am not more sure that I breathe than I am that the letter is not at the Hôtel."

"I have no better advice to give you," said Dupin. "You have, of course, an accurate description of the letter?"

"Oh yes!" — And here the Prefect, producing a memorandum-book, proceeded to read aloud a minute account of the internal, and especially of the external appearance of the missing document. Soon after finishing the perusal of this description, he took his departure, more entirely depressed in spirits than I had ever known the good gentleman before.

In about a month afterwards he paid us another visit, and found us occupied very nearly as before. He took a pipe and a chair and entered into some

ordinary conversation. At length I said, — "Well, but G——, what of the purloined letter? I presume you have at last made up your mind that there is no
such thing as overreaching the Minister?"

"Confound him, say I — yes; I made the re-examination, however, as Dupin 75
suggested — but it was all labor lost, as I knew it would be."

"How much was the reward offered, did you say?" asked Dupin.

"Why, a very great deal — a *very* liberal reward — I don't like to say how
much, precisely; but one thing I *will* say, that I wouldn't mind giving my individual check for fifty thousand francs to any one who could obtain me that letter. The fact is, it is becoming of more and more importance every day; and the
reward has been lately doubled. If it were trebled, however, I could do no more
than I have done."

"Why, yes," said Dupin, drawlingly, between the whiffs of his meerschaum, "I really — think, G——, you have not exerted yourself — to the utmost
in this matter. You might — do a little more, I think, eh?"

"How? — in what way?"

"Why — puff, puff — you might — puff, puff — employ counsel in the mat- 80
ter, eh? — puff, puff, puff. Do you remember the story they tell of Abernethy?"°

"No; hang Abernethy!"

"To be sure! hang him and welcome. But, once upon a time, a certain rich
miser conceived the design of spunging upon this Abernethy for a medical
opinion. Getting up, for this purpose, an ordinary conversation in a private
company, he insinuated his case to the physician, as that of an imaginary
individual.

"'We will suppose,' said the miser, 'that his symptoms are such and such;
now, doctor, what would *you* have directed him to take?'"

"'Take!' said Abernethy, 'why, take advice, to be sure.'"

"But," said the Prefect, a little discomposed, "I am *perfectly* willing to take 85
advice, and to pay for it. I would *really* give fifty thousand francs to any one
who would aid me in the matter."

"In that case," replied Dupin, opening a drawer, and producing a check-
book, "you may as well fill me up a check for the amount mentioned. When
you have signed it, I will hand you the letter."

I was astounded. The Prefect appeared absolutely thunder-stricken. For
some minutes he remained speechless and motionless, looking incredulously
at my friend with open mouth, and eyes that seemed starting from their sockets; then, apparently recovering himself in some measure, he seized a pen, and
after several pauses and vacant stares, finally filled up and signed a check for
fifty thousand francs, and handed it across the table to Dupin. The latter
examined it carefully and deposited it in his pocketbook; then, unlocking an
escritoire,° took thence a letter and gave it to the Prefect. This functionary
grasped it in a perfect agony of joy, opened it with a trembling hand, cast a
rapid glance at its contents, and then, scrambling and struggling to the door,
rushed at length unceremoniously from the room and from the house, without having uttered a syllable since Dupin had requested him to fill up the
check.

When he had gone, my friend entered into some explanations.

Abernethy: John Abernethy, a famous English surgeon (1764-1831).
escritoire: A writing desk.

"The Parisian police," he said, "are exceedingly able in their way. They are persevering, ingenious, cunning, and thoroughly versed in the knowledge which their duties seem chiefly to demand. Thus, when G—— detailed to us his mode of searching the premises at the Hôtel D——, I felt entire confidence in his having made a satisfactory investigation — so far as his labors extended."

"So far as his labors extended?" said I.

"Yes," said Dupin. "The measures adopted were not only the best of their kind, but carried out to absolute perfection. Had the letter been deposited within the range of their search, these fellows would, beyond a question, have found it."

I merely laughed — but he seemed quite serious in all that he said.

"The measures, then," he continued, "were good in their kind, and well executed; their defect lay in their being inapplicable to the case, and to the man. A certain set of highly ingenious resources are, with the Prefect, a sort of Procrustean bed, to which he forcibly adapts his designs. But he perpetually errs by being too deep or too shallow for the matter in hand; and many a schoolboy is a better reasoner than he. I knew one about eight years of age, whose success at guessing in the game of 'even and odd' attracted universal admiration. This game is simple, and is played with marbles. One player holds in his hand a number of these toys, and demands of another whether that number is even or odd. If the guess is right, the guesser wins one; if wrong, he loses one. The boy to whom I allude won all the marbles of the school. Of course he had some principle of guessing; and this lay in mere observation and admeasurement of the astuteness of his opponents. For example, an arrant simpleton is his opponent, and, holding up his closed hand, asks, 'are they even or odd?' Our schoolboy replies, 'odd,' and loses; but upon the second trial he wins, for he then says to himself, 'the simpleton had them even upon the first trial, and his amount of cunning is just sufficient to make him have them odd upon the second; I will therefore guess odd;' — he guesses odd, and wins. Now, with a simpleton a degree above the first, he would have reasoned thus: 'This fellow finds that in the first instance I guessed odd, and, in the second, he will propose to himself, upon the first impulse, a simple variation from even to odd, as did the first simpleton; but then a second thought will suggest that this is too simple a variation, and finally he will decide upon putting it even as before. I will therefore guess even', — he guesses even, and wins. Now this mode of reasoning in the schoolboy, whom his fellows termed 'lucky,' — what, in its last analysis, is it?"

"It is merely," I said, "an identification of the reasoner's intellect with that of his opponent."

"It is," said Dupin; "and, upon inquiring of the boy by what means he effected the *thorough* identification in which his success consisted, I received answer as follows: 'When I wish to find out how wise, or how stupid, or how good, or how wicked is any one, or what are his thoughts at the moment, I fashion the expression of my face, as accurately as possible, in accordance with the expression of his, and then wait to see what thoughts or sentiments arise in my mind or heart, as if to match or correspond with the expression.' This response of the school-boy lies at the bottom of all the spurious profundity which has been attributed to Rochefoucault, to La Bougive, to Machiavelli, and to Campanella."

"And the identification," I said, "of the reasoner's intellect with that of his opponent, depends, if I understand you aright, upon the accuracy with which the opponent's intellect is admeasured."

"For its practical value it depends upon this," replied Dupin; "and the Prefect and his cohort fail so frequently, first, by default of this identification, and, secondly, by ill-admeasurement, or rather through non-admeasurement, of the intellect with which they are engaged. They consider only their *own* ideas of ingenuity; and, in searching for any thing hidden, advert only to the modes in which *they* would have hidden it. They are right in this much — that their own ingenuity is a faithful representative of that of *the mass;* but when the cunning of the individual felon is diverse in character from their own, the felon foils them, of course. This always happens when it is above their own, and very usually when it is below. They have no variation of principle in their investigations; at best, when urged by some unusual emergency — by some extraordinary reward — they extend or exaggerate their old modes of *practice,* without touching their principles. What, for example, in this case of D——, has been done to vary the principle of action? What is all this boring, and probing, and sounding, and scrutinizing with the microscope, and dividing the surface of the building into registered square inches — what is it all but an exaggeration *of the application* of the one principle or set of principles of search, which are based upon the set of notions regarding human ingenuity, to which the Prefect, in the long routine of his duty, has been accustomed? Do you not see he has taken it for granted that *all* men proceed to conceal a letter, not exactly in a gimlet-hole bored in a chair-leg, but, at least, in *some* out-of-the-way hole or corner suggested by the same tenor of thought which would urge a man to secrete a letter in a gimlet-hole bored in a chair-leg? And do you not see also, that such *recherchés* nooks for concealment are adapted only for ordinary occasions, and would be adopted only by ordinary intellects; for, in all cases of concealment, a disposal of the article concealed — a disposal of it in this *recherché* manner, — is, in the very first instance, presumable and presumed; and thus its discovery depends, not at all upon the acumen, but altogether upon the mere care, patience, and determination of the seekers; and where the case is of importance — or, what amounts to the same thing in the policial eyes, when the reward is of magnitude, — the qualities in question have *never* been known to fail. You will now understand what I meant in suggesting that, had the purloined letter been hidden anywhere within the limits of the Prefect's examination — in other words, had the principle of its concealment been comprehended within the principles of the Prefect — its discovery would have been a matter altogether beyond question. This functionary, however, has been thoroughly mystified; and the remote source of his defeat lies in the supposition that the Minister is a fool, because he has acquired renown as a poet. All fools are poets; this the Prefect *feels;* and he is merely guilty of a *non distributio medii*° in thence inferring that all poets are fools."

"But is this really the poet?" I asked. "There are two brothers, I know; and both have attained reputation in letters. The Minister I believe has written learnedly on the Differential Calculus. He is a mathematician, and no poet."

"You are mistaken; I know him well; he is both. And poet *and* mathematician, he would reason well; as mere mathematician, he could not have reasoned at all, and thus would have been at the mercy of the Prefect."

---

non distributio medii: Latin term in logic for the "undistributed middle," a syllogistic fallacy indicating false reasoning.

"You surprise me," I said, "by these opinions, which have been contradicted 100 by the voice of the world. You do not mean to set at naught the well-digested idea of centuries. The mathematical reason has long been regarded as *the* reason *par excellence.*"

"'*Il y a parier,*'" replied Dupin, quoting from Chamfort,° "'*que toute idée publique, toute convention reçue, est une sottise, car elle a convenue au plus grand nombre.*'° The mathematicians, I grant you, have done their best to promulgate the popular error to which you allude, and which is none the less an error for its promulgation as truth. With an art worthy a better cause, for example, they have insinuated the term, 'analysis' into application to algebra. The French are the originators of this particular deception; but if a term is of any importance — if words derive any value from applicability — then 'analysis' conveys 'algebra' about as much as, in Latin, '*ambitus*' implies 'ambition,' '*religio*' 'religion,' or '*homines honesti,*' 'a set of *honorable* men'."

"You have a quarrel on hand, I see," said I, "with some of the algebraists of Paris; but proceed."

"I dispute the availability, and thus the value, of that reason which is cultivated in any especial form other than the abstractly logical. I dispute, in particular, the reason educed by mathematical study. The mathematics are the science of form and quantity; mathematical reasoning is merely logic applied to observation upon form and quantity. The great error lies in supposing that even the truths of what is called *pure* algebra, are abstract or general truths. And this error is so egregious that I am confounded at the universality with which it has been received. Mathematical axioms are *not* axioms of general truth. What is true of *relation* — of form and quantity — is often grossly false in regard to morals, for example. In this latter science it is very usually *un*true that the aggregated parts are equal to the whole. In chemistry also the axiom fails. In the consideration of motive it fails; for two motives, each of a given value, have not, necessarily, a value when united, equal to the sum of their values apart. There are numerous other mathematical truths which are only truths within the limits of *relation.* But the mathematician argues, from his *finite truths,* through habit, as if they were of an absolutely general applicability — as the world indeed imagines them to be. Bryant, in his very learned 'Mythology,'° mentions an analogous source of error, when he says that 'although the Pagan fables are not believed, yet we forget ourselves continually, and make inferences from them as existing realities.' With the algebraists, however, who are Pagans themselves, the 'Pagan fables' *are* believed, and the inferences are made, not so much through lapse of memory, as through an unaccountable addling of the brains. In short, I never yet encountered the mere mathematician who could be trusted out of equal roots, or one who did not clandestinely hold it as a point of his faith that $x^2 + px$ was absolutely and unconditionally equal to q. Say to one of these gentlemen, by way of experiment, if you please, that you believe occasions may occur where $x^2 + px$ is *not*

Chamfort: Sébastien Roch Nicolas Chamfort (1740–1794), French playwright and writer.
Il . . . nombre: The chances are that every popular idea, every accepted convention, is foolishness, because it is convenient to the majority.
Bryant . . . 'Mythology': Jacob Bryant (1715–1804), English author of *A New System or Analysis of Ancient Mythology* (1774–1776).

altogether equal to *q*, and, having made him understand what you mean, get out of his reach as speedily as convenient, for, beyond doubt, he will endeavor to knock you down.

"I mean to say," continued Dupin, while I merely laughed at his last observations, "that if the Minister had been no more than a mathematician, the Prefect would have been under no necessity of giving me this check. I knew him, however, as both mathematician and poet, and my measures were adapted to his capacity, with reference to the circumstances by which he was surrounded. I knew him as a courtier, too, and as a bold *intriguant*. Such a man, I considered, could not fail to be aware of the ordinary policial modes of action. He could not have failed to anticipate — and events have proved that he did not fail to anticipate — the waylayings to which he was subjected. He must have foreseen, I reflected, the secret investigations of his premises. His frequent absences from home at night, which were hailed by the Prefect as certain aids to his success, I regarded only as *ruses*, to afford opportunity for thorough search to the police, and thus the sooner to impress them with the conviction to which G——, in fact, did finally arrive — the conviction that the letter was not upon the premises. I felt, also, that the whole train of thought, which I was at some pains in detailing to you just now, concerning the invariable principle of political action in searches for articles concealed — I felt that this whole train of thought would necessarily pass through the mind of the Minister. It would imperatively lead him to despise all the ordinary *nooks* of concealment. *He* could not, I reflected, be so weak as not to see that the most intricate and remote recess of his hotel would be as open as his commonest closets to the eyes, to the probes, to the gimlets, and to the microscopes of the Prefect. I saw, in fine, that he would be driven, as a matter of course, to *simplicity*, if not deliberately induced to it as a matter of choice. You will remember, perhaps, how desperately the Prefect laughed when I suggested, upon our first interview, that it was just possible this mystery troubled him so much on account of its being so *very* self-evident."

"Yes," said I, "I remember his merriment well. I really thought he would have fallen into convulsions." 105

"The material world," continued Dupin, "abounds with very strict analogies to the immaterial; and thus some color of truth has been given to the rhetorical dogma, that metaphor, or simile, may be made to strengthen an argument, as well as to embellish a description. The principle of the *vis inertiae*,° for example, seems to be identical in physics and metaphysics. It is not more true in the former, that a large body is with more difficulty set in motion than a smaller one, and that its subsequent *momentum* is commensurate with this difficulty, than it is, in the latter, that intellects of the vaster capacity, while more forcible, more constant, and more eventful in their movements than those of inferior grade, are yet the less readily moved, and more embarrassed and full of hesitation in the first few steps of their progress. Again: have you ever noticed which of the street signs, over the shop doors, are the most attractive of attention?"

"I have never given the matter a thought," I said.

"There is a game of puzzles," he resumed, "which is played upon a map. One party playing requires another to find a given word — the name of town,

vis inertiae: The power of inertia.

river, state or empire—any word, in short, upon the motley and perplexed surface of the chart. A novice in the game generally seeks to embarrass his opponents by giving them the most minutely lettered names; but the adept selects such words as stretch, in large characters, from one end of the chart to the other. These, like the over-largely lettered signs and placards of the street, escape observation by dint of being excessively obvious; and here the physical oversight is precisely analogous with the moral inapprehension by which the intellect suffers to pass unnoticed those considerations which are too obtrusively and too palpably self-evident. But this is a point, it appears, somewhat above or beneath the understanding of the Prefect. He never once thought it probable, or possible, that the Minister had deposited the letter immediately beneath the nose of the whole world, by way of best preventing any portion of that world from perceiving it.

"But the more I reflected upon the daring, dashing, and discriminating ingenuity of D——; upon the fact that the document must always have been *at hand*, if he intended to use it to good purpose; and upon the decisive evidence, obtained by the Prefect, that it was not hidden within the limits of that dignitary's ordinary search—the more satisfied I became that, to conceal this letter, the Minister had resorted to the comprehensive and sagacious expedient of not attempting to conceal it at all.

"Full of these ideas, I prepared myself with a pair of green spectacles, 110 and called one fine morning, quite by accident, at the Ministerial hotel. I found D—— at home, yawning, lounging, and dawdling, as usual, and pretending to be in the last extremity of *ennui*. He is, perhaps, the most really energetic human being now alive—but that is only when nobody sees him.

"To be even with him, I complained of my weak eyes, and lamented the necessity of the spectacles, under cover of which I cautiously and thoroughly surveyed the apartment, while seemingly intent only upon the conversation of my host.

"I paid special attention to a large writing-table near which he sat, and upon which lay confusedly, some miscellaneous letters and other papers, with one or two musical instruments and a few books. Here, however, after a long and very deliberate scrutiny, I saw nothing to excite particular suspicion.

"At length my eyes, in going the circuit of the room, fell upon a trumpery filigree card-rack of paste-board, that hung dangling by a dirty blue ribbon, from a little brass knob just beneath the middle of the mantel-piece. In this rack, which had three or four compartments, were five or six visiting cards and a solitary letter. This last was much soiled and crumpled. It was torn nearly in two, across the middle—as if a design, in the first instance, to tear it entirely up as worthless, had been altered, or stayed, in the second. It had a large black seal, bearing the D—— cipher *very* conspicuously, and was addressed, in a diminutive female hand, to D——, the minister, himself. It was thrust carelessly, and even, as it seemed, contemptuously, into one of the upper divisions of the rack.

"No sooner had I glanced at this letter, than I concluded it to be that of which I was in search. To be sure, it was, to all appearance, radically different from the one of which the Prefect had read us so minute a description. Here the seal was large and black, with the D—— cipher; there it was small and red, with the ducal arms of the S—— family. Here, the address, to the Minister, was diminutive and feminine; there the superscription, to a certain royal personage, was markedly bold and decided; the size alone formed a point of correspondence. But, then, the *radicalness* of these differences, which was excessive; the dirt; the soiled and torn condition of the paper, so inconsistent with the *true* methodical habits of D—— and so suggestive of a design to delude the beholder into an idea of the worthlessness of the document; these things, together with the hyper-obtrusive situation of this document, full in the view of every visitor, and thus exactly in accordance with the conclusions to which I had previously arrived; these things, I say, were strongly corroborative of suspicion, in one who came with the intention to suspect.

"I protracted my visit as long as possible, and, while I maintained a most 115 animated discussion with the Minister, on a topic which I knew well had never failed to interest and excite him, I kept my attention really riveted upon the letter. In this examination, I committed to memory its external appearance and arrangement in the rack; and also fell, at length, upon a discovery which set at rest whatever trivial doubt I might have entertained. In scrutinizing the edges of the paper, I observed them to be more *chafed* than seemed necessary. They presented the *broken* appearance which is manifested when a stiff paper, having been once folded and pressed with a folder, is refolded in a reversed direction, in the same creases or edges which had formed the original fold. This discovery was sufficient. It was clear to me that the letter had been turned, as a glove, inside out, re-directed, and re-sealed. I bade the Minister good morning, and took my departure at once, leaving a gold snuff-box upon the table.

"The next morning I called for the snuff-box, when we resumed, quite eagerly, the conversation of the preceding day. While thus engaged, however, a loud report, as if of a pistol, was heard immediately beneath the windows of the hotel, and was succeeded by a series of fearful screams, and the shoutings of a mob. D—— rushed to a casement, threw it open, and looked out. In the meantime, I stepped to the card-rack, took the letter, put it in my pocket, and replaced it by a *facsimile* (so far as regards externals), which I had carefully prepared at my lodgings; imitating the D—— cipher, very readily, by means of a seal formed of bread.

"The disturbance in the street had been occasioned by the frantic behavior of a man with a musket. He had fired it among a crowd of women and children. It proved, however, to have been without ball, and the fellow was suffered to go his way as a lunatic or a drunkard. When he had gone, D—— came from the window, whither I had followed him immediately upon securing the object in view. Soon afterwards I bade him farewell. The pretended lunatic was a man in my own pay."

"But what purpose had you," I asked, "in replacing the letter by a *facsimile*? Would it not have been better, at the first visit, to have seized it openly, and departed?"

"D——," replied Dupin, "is a desperate man, and a man of nerve. His hotel, too, is not without attendants devoted to his interests. Had I made the wild attempt you suggest, I might never have left the Ministerial presence alive. The good people of Paris might have heard of me no more. But I had an object apart from these considerations. You know my political prepossessions. In this matter, I act as a partisan of the lady concerned. For eighteen months the Minister has had her in his power. She has now him in hers; since, being unaware that the letter is not in his possession, he will proceed with his exactions as if it was. Thus will he inevitably commit himself, at once, to his political destruction.

His downfall, too, will not be more precipitate than awkward. It is all very well to talk about the *facilis descensus Averni;*° but in all kinds of climbing, as Catalani° said of singing, it is far more easy to get up than to come down. In the present instance I have no sympathy — at least no pity — for him who descends. He is that *monstrum horrendum,* an unprincipled man of genius. I confess, however, that I should like very well to know the precise character of his thoughts, when, being defied by her whom the Prefect terms 'a certain personage,' he is reduced to opening the letter which I left for him in the card-rack."

"How? did you put any thing particular in it?" 120

"Why — it did not seem altogether right to leave the interior blank — that would have been insulting. D——, at Vienna once, did me an evil turn, which I told him, quite good-humoredly, that I should remember. So, as I knew he would feel some curiosity in regard to the identity of the person who had outwitted him, I thought it a pity not to give him a clue. He is well acquainted with my MS., and I just copied into the middle of the blank sheet the words —

> —Un dessein si funeste,
> S'il n'est digne d'Atrée, est digne de
> Thyeste.°

They are to be found in Crébillon's 'Atrée.'"

facilis . . . Averni: "Easy is the descent into the Hell." Virgil's *Aeneid.*
Catalini: Angelica Catalini (1780–1849), a famous Italian opera singer.
Un . . . Thyeste: "A design so deadly, if not worthy of Atreus, is quite worthy of Thyestes." The wife of King Atreus was seduced by Thyestes, and so Atreus murdered Thyestes' sons and served them in a meal to their father.

JOHN UPDIKE (B. 1932)

A & P 1961

In walks these three girls in nothing but bathing suits. I'm in the third check-out slot, with my back to the door, so I don't see them until they're over by the bread. The one that caught my eye first was the one in the plaid green two-piece. She was a chunky kid, with a good tan and a sweet broad soft-looking can with those two crescents of white just under it, where the sun never seems to hit, at the top of the backs of her legs. I stood there with my hand on a box of HiHo crackers trying to remember if I rang it up or not. I ring it up again and the customer starts giving me hell. She's one of these cash-register-watchers, a witch about fifty with rouge on her cheekbones and no eyebrows, and I know it made her day to trip me up. She'd been watching cash registers for fifty years and probably never seen a mistake before.

By the time I got her feathers smoothed and her goodies into a bag — she gives me a little snort in passing, if she'd been born at the right time they would have burned her over in Salem — by the time I get her on her way the girls had circled around the bread and were coming back, without a pushcart, back my way along the counters, in the aisle between the checkouts and the Special bins. They didn't even have shoes on. There was this chunky one, with the two-piece — it was bright green and the seams on the bra were still sharp and her belly was still pretty pale so I guessed she just got it (the suit) — there was this one, with one of those chubby berry-faces, the lips all bunched together under her nose, this one, and a tall one, with black hair that hadn't quite frizzed right, and one of these sunburns right across under the eyes, and a chin that was too long — you know, the kind of girl other girls think is very "striking" and "attractive" but never quite makes it, as they very well know, which is why they like her so much — and then the third one, that wasn't quite so tall. She was the queen. She kind of led them, the other two peeking around and making their shoulders round. She didn't look around, not this queen, she just walked straight on slowly, on these long white prima-donna legs. She came down a little hard on her heels, as if she didn't walk in her bare feet that much, putting down her heels and then letting the weight move along to her toes as if she was testing the floor with every step, putting a little deliberate extra action into it. You never know for sure how girls' minds work (do you really think it's a mind in there or just a little buzz like a bee in a glass jar?) but you got the idea she had talked the other two into coming in here with her, and now she was showing them how to do it, walk slow and hold yourself straight.

She had on a kind of dirty-pink — beige maybe, I don't know — bathing suit with a little nubble all over it and, what got me, the straps were down. They were off her shoulders looped loose around the cool tops of her arms, and I guess as a result the suit had slipped a little on her, so all around the top of the cloth there was this shining rim. If it hadn't been there you wouldn't have known there could have been anything whiter than those shoulders. With the straps pushed off, there was nothing between the top of the suit and the top of her head except just *her*, this clean bare plane of the top of her chest down from the shoulder bones like a dented sheet of metal tilted in the light. I mean, it was more than pretty.

She had sort of oaky hair that the sun and salt had bleached, done up in a bun that was unraveling, and a kind of prim face. Walking into the A & P with your straps down, I suppose it's the only kind of face you *can* have. She held her head so high her neck, coming up out of those white shoulders, looked kind of stretched, but I didn't mind. The longer her neck was, the more of her there was.

She must have felt in the corner of her eye me and over my shoulder Stoke-   5
sie in the second slot watching, but she didn't tip. Not this queen. She kept her eyes moving across the racks, and stopped, and turned so slow it made my stomach rub the inside of my apron, and buzzed to the other two, who kind of huddled against her for relief, and then they all three of them went up the cat-and-dog-food-breakfast-cereal-macaroni-rice-raisins-seasonings-spreads-spaghetti-soft-drinks-crackers-and-cookies aisle. From the third slot I look straight up this aisle to the meat counter, and I watched them all the way. The fat one with the tan sort of fumbled with the cookies, but on second thought she put the package back. The sheep pushing their carts down the aisle — the girls were walking against the usual traffic (not that we have one-way signs or anything) — were pretty hilarious. You could see them, when Queenie's white shoulders dawned on them, kind of jerk, or hop, or hiccup, but their eyes snapped back to their own baskets and on they pushed. I bet you could set off dynamite in an A & P and the people would by and large keep reaching and checking oatmeal off their lists and muttering "Let me see, there was a third thing, began with A, asparagus, no, ah, yes, applesauce!" or whatever it is they do mutter. But there was no doubt, this jiggled them. A few houseslaves in pin

curlers even looked around after pushing their carts past to make sure what they had seen was correct.

You know, it's one thing to have a girl in a bathing suit down on the beach, where what with the glare nobody can look at each other much anyway, and another thing in the cool of the A & P, under the fluorescent lights, against all those stacked packages, with her feet paddling along naked over our checkerboard green-and-cream rubber-tile floor.

"Oh Daddy," Stokesie said beside me. "I feel so faint."

"Darling," I said. "Hold me tight." Stokesie's married, with two babies chalked up on his fuselage already, but as far as I can tell that's the only difference. He's twenty-two, and I was nineteen this April.

"Is it done?" he asks, the responsible married man finding his voice. I forgot to say he thinks he's going to be manager some sunny day, maybe in 1990 when it's called the Great Alexandrov and Petrooshki Tea Company or something.

What he meant was, our town is five miles from a beach, with a big sum- 10 mer colony out on the Point, but we're right in the middle of town, and the women generally put on a shirt or shorts or something before they get out of the car into the street. And anyway these are usually women with six children and varicose veins mapping their legs and nobody, including them, could care less. As I say, we're right in the middle of town, and if you stand at our front doors you can see two banks and the Congregational church and the newspaper store and three real-estate offices and about twenty-seven old freeloaders tearing up Central Street because the sewer broke again. It's not as if we're on the Cape, we're north of Boston and there's people in this town haven't seen the ocean for twenty years.

The girls had reached the meat counter and were asking McMahon something. He pointed, they pointed, and they shuffled out of sight behind a pyramid of Diet Delight peaches. All that was left for us to see was old McMahon patting his mouth and looking after them sizing up their joints. Poor kids, I began to feel sorry for them, they couldn't help it.

Now here comes the sad part of the story, at least my family says it's sad, but I don't think it's so sad myself. The store's pretty empty, it being Thursday afternoon, so there was nothing much to do except lean on the register and wait for the girls to show up again. The whole store was like a pinball machine and I didn't know which tunnel they'd come out of. After a while they come around out of the far aisle, around the light bulbs, records at discount of the Caribbean Six or Tony Martin Sings or some such gunk you wonder they waste the wax on, sixpacks of candy bars, and plastic toys done up in cellophane that fall apart when a kid looks at them anyway. Around they come, Queenie still leading the way, and holding a little gray jar in her hands. Slots Three through Seven are unmanned and I could see her wondering between Stokes and me, but Stokesie with his usual luck draws an old party in baggy gray pants who stumbles up with four giant cans of pineapple juice (what do these bums *do* with all that pineapple juice? I've often asked myself). So the girls come to me. Queenie puts down the jar and I take it into my fingers icy cold. Kingfish Fancy Herring Snacks in Pure Sour Cream: 49¢. Now her hands are empty, not a ring or a bracelet, bare as God made them, and I wonder where the money's coming from. Still with that prim look she lifts a folded dollar bill out of the hollow at the center of her nubbled pink top. The jar went heavy in my hand. Really, I thought that was so cute.

Then everybody's luck begins to run out. Lengel comes in from haggling with a truck full of cabbages on the lot and is about to scuttle into that door marked MANAGER behind which he hides all day when the girls touch his eye. Lengel's pretty dreary, teaches Sunday school and the rest, but he doesn't miss that much. He comes over and says, "Girls, this isn't the beach."

Queenie blushes, though maybe it's just a brush of sunburn I was noticing for the first time, now that she was so close. "My mother asked me to pick up a jar of herring snacks." Her voice kind of startled me, the way voices do when you see the people first, coming out so flat and dumb yet kind of tony, too, the way it ticked over "pick up" and "snacks." All of a sudden I slid right down her voice into the living room. Her father and the other men were standing around in ice-cream coats and bow ties and the women were in sandals picking up herring snacks on toothpicks off a big glass plate and they were all holding drinks the color of water with olives and sprigs of mint in them. When my parents have somebody over they get lemonade and if it's a real racy affair Schlitz in tall glasses with "They'll Do It Every Time" cartoons stenciled on.

"That's all right," Lengel said. "But this isn't the beach." His repeating this 15 struck me as funny, as if it had just occurred to him, and he had been thinking all these years the A & P was a great big dune and he was the head lifeguard. He didn't like my smiling — as I say he doesn't miss much — but he concentrates on giving the girls that sad Sunday-school-superintendent stare.

Queenie's blush is no sunburn now, and the plump one in plaid, that I liked better from the back — a really sweet can — pipes up, "We weren't doing any shopping. We just came in for the one thing."

"That makes no difference," Lengel tells her, and I could see from the way his eyes went that he hadn't noticed she was wearing a two-piece before. "We want you decently dressed when you come in here."

"We *are* decent," Queenie says suddenly, her lower lip pushing, getting sore now that she remembers her place, a place from which the crowd that runs the A & P must look pretty crummy. Fancy Herring Snacks flashed in her very blue eyes.

"Girls, I don't want to argue with you. After this come in here with your shoulders covered. It's our policy." He turns his back. That's policy for you. Policy is what the kingpins want. What the others want is juvenile delinquency.

All this while, the customers had been showing up with their carts but, 20 you know, sheep, seeing a scene, they had all bunched up on Stokesie, who shook open a paper bag as gently as peeling a peach, not wanting to miss a word. I could feel in the silence everybody getting nervous, most of all Lengel, who asks me, "Sammy, have you rung up their purchase?"

I thought and said "No" but it wasn't about that I was thinking. I go through the punches, 4, 9, GROC. TOT — it's more complicated than you think, and after you do it often enough, it begins to make a little song, that you hear words to, in my case "Hello (*bing*) there, you (*gung*) hap-py *pee*-pul (*splat*)!" — the *splat* being the drawer flying out. I uncrease the bill, tenderly as you may imagine, it just having come from between the two smoothest scoops of vanilla I had ever known were there, and pass a half and a penny into her narrow pink palm, and nestle the herrings in a bag and twist its neck and hand it over, all the time thinking.

The girls, and who'd blame them, are in a hurry to get out, so I say "I quit" to Lengel quick enough for them to hear, hoping they'll stop and watch me, their unsuspected hero. They keep right on going, into the electric eye; the door flies open and they flicker across the lot to their car, Queenie and Plaid and Big Tall Goony-Goony (not that as raw material she was so bad), leaving me with Lengel and a kink in his eyebrow.

"Did you say something, Sammy?"

"I said I quit."

"I thought you did." 25

"You didn't have to embarrass them."

"It was they who were embarrassing us."

I started to say something that came out "Fiddle-de-doo." It's a saying of my grandmother's, and I know she would have been pleased.

"I don't think you know what you're saying," Lengel said.

"I know you don't," I said. "But I do." I pull the bow at the back of my apron 30 and start shrugging it off my shoulders. A couple customers that had been heading for my slot begin to knock against each other, like scared pigs in a chute.

Lengel sighs and begins to look very patient and old and gray. He's been a friend of my parents for years. "Sammy, you don't want to do this to your Mom and Dad," he tells me. It's true, I don't. But it seems to me that once you begin a gesture it's fatal not to go through with it. I fold the apron, "Sammy" stitched in red on the pocket, and put it on the counter, and drop the bow tie on top of it. The bow tie is theirs, if you've ever wondered. "You'll feel this for the rest of your life," Lengel says, and I know that's true, too, but remembering how he made the pretty girl blush makes me so scrunchy inside I punch the No Sale tab and the machine whirs "pee-pul" and the drawer splats out. One advantage to this scene taking place in summer, I can follow this up with a clean exit, there's no fumbling around getting your coat and galoshes, I just saunter into the electric eye in my white shirt that my mother ironed the night before, and the door heaves itself open, and outside the sunshine is skating around on the asphalt.

I look around for my girls, but they're gone, of course. There wasn't anybody but some young married screaming with her children about some candy they didn't get by the door of a powder-blue Falcon station wagon. Looking back in the big windows, over the bags of peat moss and aluminum lawn furniture stacked on the pavement, I could see Lengel in my place in the slot, checking the sheep through. His face was dark gray and his back stiff, as if he'd just had an injection of iron, and my stomach kind of fell as I felt how hard the world was going to be to me hereafter.

AN ALBUM OF WORLD LITERATURE

Isabel Allende (Chile / b. 1942)

Isabel Allende was born in Peru to an intensely political family. Her father, a Chilean diplomat, suddenly and mysteriously disappeared when she was very young. After high school she worked as a secretary in the Department of Information of the United Nations Food and Agriculture organization in Chile. She subsequently developed a weekly television program and wrote for magazines. In 1973 her father's first cousin Salvadore Allende, the president of Chile, was assassinated. To escape the repressive political climate, she moved to Venezuela in 1975, where she worked as a journalist, taught school, and began writing her first novel based on her exile. An English translation of *House of Spirits* appeared in 1985 and made her one of the most internationally popular women writers from Latin America. Her two other translated novels, *Of Love and Shadows* (1987) and *Eva Luna* (1989), also center on the political instability in Latin America. Her most recent novel, *The Infinite Plan* (1993), takes place in the United States. Though her characters are often faced with terrible choices generated by repressive social conditions, Allende creates strong characters — particularly women — who take courageous risks.

The Judge's Wife   1989
TRANSLATED BY NICK CAISTOR

Nicolas Vidal always knew he would lose his head over a woman. So it was foretold on the day of his birth, and later confirmed by the Turkish woman in the corner shop the one time he allowed her to read his fortune in the coffee grounds. Little did he imagine though that it would be on account of Casilda, Judge Hidalgo's wife. It was on her wedding day that he first glimpsed her. He was not impressed, preferring his women dark-haired and brazen. This ethereal slip of a girl in her wedding gown, eyes filled with wonder, and fingers obviously unskilled in the art of rousing a man to pleasure, seemed to him almost ugly. Mindful of his destiny, he had always been wary of any emotional contact with women, hardening his heart and restricting himself to the briefest of encounters whenever the demands of manhood needed satisfying. Casilda, however, appeared so insubstantial, so distant, that he cast aside all precaution and, when the fateful moment arrived, forgot the prediction that usually weighed in all his decisions. From the roof of the bank, where he was crouching with two of his men, Nicolas Vidal peered down at this young lady from the capital. She had a dozen equally pale and dainty relatives with her, who spent the whole of the ceremony fanning themselves with an air of utter bewilderment, then departed straight away, never to return. Along with everyone else in the town, Vidal was convinced the young bride would not withstand the climate, and that within a few months the old women would be dressing her up again, this time for her funeral. Even if she did survive the heat and the dust that filtered in through every pore to lodge itself in the soul, she would be bound to succumb to the fussy habits of her confirmed bachelor of a husband. Judge Hidalgo was twice her age, and had slept alone for so many years he didn't have the slightest notion of how to go about pleasing a woman. The severity and stubbornness with which he executed the law even at the expense of justice had made him feared throughout the province. He refused to apply any common sense in the exercise of his profession, and was equally harsh in his condemnation of the theft of a chicken as of a premeditated murder. He dressed formally in black, and, despite the all-pervading dust in this godforsaken town, his boots always shone with beeswax. A man such as he was never meant to be a husband, and yet not only did the gloomy wedding-day prophecies

remain unfulfilled, but Casilda emerged happy and smiling from three preg-
nancies in rapid succession. Every Sunday at noon she would go to mass with
her husband, cool and collected beneath her Spanish mantilla, seemingly untouched by our pitiless summer, as wan and frail-looking as on the day of her
arrival: a perfect example of delicacy and refinement. Her loudest words were a
soft-spoken greeting; her most expressive gesture was a graceful nod of the
head. She was such an airy, diaphanous creature that a moment's carelessness
might mean she disappeared altogether. So slight an impression did she make
that the changes noticeable in the Judge were all the more remarkable. Though
outwardly he remained the same — he still dressed as black as a crow and was as
stiff-necked and brusque as ever — his judgments in court altered dramatically.
To general amazement, he found the youngster who robbed the Turkish shopkeeper innocent, on the grounds that she had been selling him short for years,
and the money he had taken could therefore be seen as compensation. He also
refused to punish an adulterous wife, arguing that since her husband himself
kept a mistress he did not have the moral authority to demand fidelity. Word
in the town had it that the Judge was transformed the minute he crossed the
threshold at home: that he flung off his gloomy apparel, rollicked with his
children, chuckled as he sat Casilda on his lap. Though no one ever succeeded
in confirming these rumors, his wife got the credit for his newfound kindness,
and her reputation grew accordingly. None of this was of the slightest interest
to Nicolas Vidal, who as a wanted man was sure there would be no mercy
shown him the day he was brought in chains before the Judge. He paid no heed
to the talk about Doña Casilda, and the rare occasions he glimpsed her from
afar only confirmed his first impression of her as a lifeless ghost.

　　Born thirty years earlier in a windowless room in the town's only brothel,
Vidal was the son of Juana the Forlorn and an unknown father. The world had
no place for him. His mother knew it, and so tried to wrench him from her
womb with sprigs of parsley, candle butts, douches of ashes, and other violent
purgatives, but the child clung to life. Once, years later, Juana was looking at
her mysterious son and realized that, while all her infallible methods of abort-
ing might have failed to dislodge him, they had none the less tempered his soul
to the hardness of iron. As soon as he came into the world, he was lifted in the
air by the midwife who examined him by the light of an oil lamp. She saw he
had four nipples.
　　"Poor creature: he'll lose his head over a woman," she predicted, drawing
on her wealth of experience.
　　Her words rested on the boy like a deformity. Perhaps a woman's love
would have made his existence less wretched. To atone for all her attempts to
kill him before birth, his mother chose him a beautiful first name, and an imposing family name picked at random. But the lofty name of Nicolas Vidal was
no protection against the fateful cast of his destiny. His face was scarred from
knife fights before he reached his teens, so it came as no surprise to decent folk
that he ended up a bandit. By the age of twenty, he had become the leader of a
band of desperadoes. The habit of violence toughened his sinews. The solitude
he was condemned to for fear of falling prey to a woman lent his face a doleful
expression. As soon as they saw him, everyone in the town knew from his eyes,
clouded by tears he would never allow to fall, that he was the son of Juana the
Forlorn. Whenever there was an outcry after a crime had been committed in

the region, the police set out with dogs to track him down, but after scouring the hills invariably returned empty-handed. In all honesty they preferred it that way, because they could never have fought him. His gang gained such a fearsome reputation that the surrounding villages and estates paid to keep them away. This money would have been plenty for his men, but Nicolas Vidal kept them constantly on horseback in a whirlwind of death and destruction so they would not lose their taste for battle. Nobody dared take them on. More than once, Judge Hidalgo had asked the government to send troops to reinforce the police, but after several useless forays the soldiers returned to their barracks and Nicolas Vidal's gang to their exploits. On one occasion only did Vidal come close to falling into the hands of justice, and then he was saved by his hardened heart.

Weary of seeing the laws flouted, Judge Hidalgo resolved to forget his 5 scruples and set a trap for the outlaw. He realized that to defend justice he was committing an injustice, but chose the lesser of two evils. The only bait he could find was Juana the Forlorn, as she was Vidal's sole known relative. He had her dragged from the brothel where by now, since no clients were willing to pay for her exhausted charms, she scrubbed floors and cleaned out the lavatories. He put her in a specially made cage which was set up in the middle of the Plaza de Armas, with only a jug of water to meet her needs.

"As soon as the water's finished, she'll start to squawk. Then her son will come running, and I'll be waiting for him with the soldiers," Judge Hidalgo said.

News of this torture, unheard of since the days of slavery, reached Nicolas Vidal's ears shortly before his mother drank the last of the water. His men watched as he received the report in silence, without so much as a flicker of emotion on his blank lone wolf's face, or a pause in the sharpening of his dagger blade on a leather strap. Though for many years he had had no contact with Juana, and retained few happy childhood memories, this was a question of honor. No man can accept such an insult, his gang reasoned as they got guns and horses ready to rush into the ambush and, if need be, lay down their lives. Their chief showed no sign of being in a hurry. As the hours went by tension mounted in the camp. The perspiring, impatient men stared at each other, not daring to speak. Fretful, they caressed the butts of their revolvers and their horses' manes, or busied themselves coiling their lassos. Night fell. Nicolas Vidal was the only one in the camp who slept. At dawn, opinions were divided. Some of the men reckoned he was even more heartless than they had ever imagined, while others maintained their leader was planning a spectacular ruse to free his mother. The one thing that never crossed any of their minds was that his courage might have failed him, for he had always proved he had more than enough to spare. By noon, they could bear the suspense no longer, and went to ask him what he planned to do.

"I'm not going to fall into his trap like an idiot," he said.

"What about your mother?"

"We'll see who's got more balls, the Judge or me," Nicolas Vidal coolly replied. 10

By the third day, Juana the Forlorn's cries for water had ceased. She lay curled on the cage floor, with wildly staring eyes and swollen lips, moaning softly whenever she regained consciousness, and the rest of the time dreaming she was in hell. Four armed guards stood watch to make sure nobody brought her water. Her groans penetrated the entire town, filtering through closed shutters or being carried by the wind through the cracks in doors. They got stuck in corners, where dogs worried at them, and passed them on in their howls to the newly born, so that whoever heard them was driven to distraction. The Judge couldn't prevent a steady stream of people filing through the square to show their sympathy for the old woman, and was powerless to stop the prostitutes going on a sympathy strike just as the miners' fortnight holiday was beginning. That Saturday, the streets were thronged with lusty workmen desperate to unload their savings, who now found nothing in town apart from the spectacle of the cage and this universal wailing carried mouth to mouth down from the river to the coast road. The priest headed a group of Catholic ladies to plead with Judge Hidalgo for Christian mercy and to beg him to spare the poor old innocent woman such a frightful death, but the man of the law bolted his door and refused to listen to them. It was then they decided to turn to Doña Casilda.

The Judge's wife received them in her shady living room. She listened to their pleas looking, as always, bashfully down at the floor. Her husband had not been home for three days, having locked himself in his office to wait for Nicolas Vidal to fall into his trap. Without so much as glancing out of the window, she was aware of what was going on, for Juana's long-drawn-out agony had forced its way even into the vast rooms of her residence. Doña Casilda waited until her visitors had left, dressed her children in their Sunday best, tied a black ribbon round their arms as a token of mourning, then strode out with them in the direction of the square. She carried a food hamper and a bottle of fresh water for Juana the Forlorn. When the guards spotted her turning the corner, they realized what she was up to, but they had strict orders, and barred her way with their rifles. When, watched now by a small crowd, she persisted, they grabbed her by the arms. Her children began to cry.

Judge Hidalgo sat in his office overlooking the square. He was the only person in the town who had not stuffed wax in his ears, because his mind was intent on the ambush and he was straining to catch the sound of horses' hoofs, the signal for action. For three long days and nights he put up with Juana's groans and the insults of the townspeople gathered outside the courtroom, but when he heard his own children start to wail he knew he had reached the bounds of his endurance. Vanquished, he walked out of the office with his three days' beard, his eyes bloodshot from keeping watch, and the weight of a thousand years on his back. He crossed the street, turned into the square and came face to face with his wife. They gazed at each other sadly. In seven years, this was the first time she had gone against him, and she had chosen to do so in front of the whole town. Easing the hamper and the bottle from Casilda's grasp, Judge Hidalgo himself opened the cage to release the prisoner.

"Didn't I tell you he wouldn't have the balls?" laughed Nicolas Vidal when the news reached him.

His laughter turned sour the next day, when he heard that Juana the Forlorn had hanged herself from the chandelier in the brothel where she had spent her life, overwhelmed by the shame of her only son leaving her to fester in a cage in the middle of the Plaza de Armas.

"That Judge's hour has come," said Vidal.

He planned to take the Judge by surprise, put him to a horrible death, then dump him in the accursed cage for all to see. The Turkish shopkeeper sent him word that the Hidalgo family had left that same night for a seaside resort to rid themselves of the bitter taste of defeat.

The Judge learned he was being pursued when he stopped to rest at a wayside inn. There was little protection for him there until an army patrol could arrive, but he had a few hours' start, and his motor car could outrun the gang's horses. He calculated he could make it to the next town and summon help there. He ordered his wife and children into the car, put his foot down on the accelerator, and sped off along the road. He ought to have arrived with time to spare, but it had been ordained that Nicolas Vidal was that day to meet the woman who would lead him to his doom.

Overburdened by the sleepless nights, the townspeople's hostility, the blow to his pride, and the stress of this race to save his family, Judge Hidalgo's heart gave a massive jolt, then split like a pomegranate. The car ran out of control, turned several somersaults and finally came to a halt in the ditch. It took Doña Casilda some minutes to work out what had happened. Her husband's advancing years had often led her to think what it would be like to be left a widow, yet she had never imagined he would leave her at the mercy of his enemies. She wasted little time dwelling on her situation, knowing she must act at once to get her children to safety. When she gazed around her, she almost burst into tears. There was no sign of life in the vast plain baked by a scorching sun, only barren cliffs beneath an unbounded sky bleached colorless by the fierce light. A second look revealed the dark shadow of a passage or cave on a distant slope, so she ran towards it with two children in her arms and the third clutching her skirts.

One by one she carried her children up the cliff. The cave was a natural 20 one, typical of many in the region. She peered inside to be certain it wasn't the den of some wild animal, sat her children against its back wall, then, dry-eyed, kissed them good-bye.

"The troops will come to find you a few hours from now. Until then, don't for any reason whatsoever come out of here, even if you hear me screaming — do you understand?"

Their mother gave one final glance at the terrified children clinging to each other, then clambered back down to the road. She reached the car, closed her husband's eyes, smoothed back her hair and settled down to wait. She had no idea how many men were in Nicolas Vidal's gang, but prayed there were a lot of them so it would take them all the more time to have their way with her. She gathered strength pondering on how long it would take her to die if she determined to do it as slowly as possible. She willed herself to be desirable, luscious, to create more work for them and thus gain time for her children.

Casilda did not have long to wait. She soon saw a cloud of dust on the horizon and heard the gallop of horses' hoofs. She clenched her teeth. Then, to her astonishment, she saw there was only one rider, who stopped a few yards from her, gun at the ready. By the scar on his face she recognized Nicolas Vidal, who had set out all alone in pursuit of Judge Hidalgo, as this was a private matter between the two men. The Judge's wife understood she was going to have to endure something far worse than a lingering death.

A quick glance at her husband was enough to convince Vidal that the Judge was safely out of his reach in the peaceful sleep of death. But there was his wife, a shimmering presence in the plain's glare. He leapt from his horse and strode over to her. She did not flinch or lower her gaze, and to his amazement he realized that for the first time in his life another person was facing him without fear. For several seconds that stretched to eternity, they sized each other up, trying to gauge the other's strength, and their own powers of resistance. It gradually dawned on both of them that they were up against a formidable opponent. He lowered his gun. She smiled.

Casilda won each moment of the ensuing hours. To all the wiles of seduc- 25 tion known since the beginning of time she added new ones born of necessity to bring this man to the heights of rapture. Not only did she work on his body like an artist, stimulating his every fiber to pleasure, but she brought all the delicacy of her spirit into play on her side. Both knew their lives were at stake, and this added a new and terrifying dimension to their meeting. Nicolas Vidal had fled from love since birth, and knew nothing of intimacy, tenderness, secret laughter, the riot of the senses, the joy of shared passion. Each minute brought the detachment of troops and the noose that much nearer, but he gladly accepted this in return for her prodigious gifts. Casilda was a passive, demure, timid woman who had been married to an austere old man in front of whom she had never even dared appear naked. Not once during that unforgettable afternoon did she forget that her aim was to win time for her children, and yet at some point, marveling at her own possibilities, she gave herself completely, and felt something akin to gratitude towards him. That was why, when she heard the soldiers in the distance, she begged him to flee to the hills. Instead, Nicolas Vidal chose to fold her in a last embrace, thus fulfilling the prophecy that had sealed his fate from the start.

CONNECTIONS TO OTHER SELECTIONS

1. Discuss Allende's treatment of justice with that of Andre Dubus in "Killings" (p. 81).

2. Write an essay comparing Allende's use of irony with T. Coraghessan Boyle's in "Carnal Knowledge" (p. 276).

BESSIE HEAD (BOTSWANA / 1937–1986)

Born in Pietermaritzburg, South Africa, Bessie Head was the daughter of a black father and a white mother. After growing up in a foster home and orphanage, she taught grammar school and wrote fiction for a local paper. In her twenties she moved to a farm commune in Botswana to avoid the apartheid of her homeland. Her first novel, *When Rain Clouds Gather,* was published in 1969. Her collection of stories, *The Collector of Treasures and Other Botswana Village Tales* (1977), was followed by two other novels, *Serowe: Village of the Rain Wind* (1981) and *A Bewitched Crossroad* (1984). Head's familiarity with oppression and the daily difficulties endured by its victims produced in her work a heightened sensitivity to the necessity for human decency. In "The Prisoner Who Wore Glasses," oppression and decency turn out to be complex matters.

The Prisoner Who Wore Glasses   1974

Scarcely a breath of wind disturbed the stillness of the day and the long rows of cabbages were bright green in the sunlight. Large white clouds drifted slowly across the deep blue sky. Now and then they obscured the sun and caused a chill on the backs of the prisoners who had to work all day long in the cabbage field. This trick the clouds were playing with the sun eventually caused one of the prisoners who wore glasses to stop work, straighten up, and peer shortsightedly at them. He was a thin little fellow with a hollowed-out chest and comic knobbly knees. He also had a lot of fanciful ideas because he smiled at the clouds.

"Perhaps they want me to send a message to the children," he thought, tenderly, noting that the clouds were drifting in the direction of his home some hundred miles away. But before he could frame the message, the warder in charge of his work span° shouted: "Hey, what you tink you're doing, Brille?"

The prisoner swung round, blinking rapidly, yet at the same time sizing up the enemy. He was a new warder, named Jacobus Stephanus Hannetjie. His eyes were the color of the sky but they were frightening. A simple, primitive, brutal soul gazed out of them. The prisoner bent down quickly and a message was quietly passed down the line: "We're in for trouble this time, comrades."

"Why?" rippled back up the line.

"Because he's not human," the reply rippled down and yet only the   5
crunching of the spades as they turned over the earth disturbed the stillness.

This particular work span was known as Span One. It was composed of ten men and they were all political prisoners. They were grouped together for convenience as it was one of the prison regulations that no black warder should be in charge of a political prisoner lest this prisoner convert him to his views. It never seemed to occur to the authorities that this very reasoning was the strength of Span One and a clue to the strange terror they aroused in the warders. As political prisoners they were unlike the other prisoners in the sense that they felt no guilt nor were they outcasts of society. All guilty men instinctively cower, which was why it was the kind of prison where men got knocked out cold with a blow at the back of the head from an iron bar. Up until the arrival of Warder Hannetjie, no warder had dared beat any member of Span One and no warder had lasted more than a week with them. The battle was entirely psychological. Span One was assertive and it was beyond the scope of white warders to handle assertive black men. Thus, Span One had got out of control. They were the best thieves and liars in the camp. They lived all day on raw cabbages. They chatted and smoked tobacco. And since they moved, thought, and acted as one, they had perfected every technique of group concealment.

Trouble began that very day between Span One and Warder Hannetjie. It was because of the shortsightedness of Brille. That was the nickname he was given in prison and is the Afrikaans word for someone who wears glasses. Brille could never judge the approach of the prison gates and on several previous occasions he had munched on cabbages and dropped them almost at the feet of the warder and all previous warders had overlooked this. Not so Warder Hannetjie.

"Who dropped that cabbage?" he thundered.

Brille stepped out of line.

span: Squad.

"I did," he said meekly.

"Alright," said Hannetjie. "The whole Span goes three meals off."

"But I told you I did it," Brille protested.

The blood rushed to Warder Hannetjie's face.

"Look 'ere," he said. "I don't take orders from a kaffir.° I don't know what kind of kaffir you tink you are. Why don't you say Baas? I'm your Baas. Why don't you say Baas, hey?"

Brille blinked his eyes rapidly but by contrast his voice was strangely calm. 15

"I'm twenty years older than you," he said. It was the first thing that came to mind but the comrades seemed to think it a huge joke. A titter swept up the line. The next thing Warder Hannetjie whipped out a knobkerrie° and gave Brille several blows about the head. What surprised his comrades was the speed with which Brille had removed his glasses or else they would have been smashed to pieces on the ground.

That evening in the cell Brille was very apologetic.

"I'm sorry, comrades," he said. "I've put you into a hell of a mess."

"Never mind, brother," they said. "What happens to one of us, happens to all."

"I'll try to make up for it, comrades," he said. "I'll steal something so that 20 you don't go hungry."

Privately, Brille was very philosophical about his head wounds. It was the first time an act of violence had been perpetrated against him but he had long been a witness of extreme, almost unbelievable human brutality. He had twelve children and his mind traveled back that evening through the sixteen years of bedlam in which he had lived. It had all happened in a small drab little three-bedroomed house in a small drab little street in the Eastern Cape and the children kept coming year after year because neither he nor Martha ever managed the contraceptives the right way and a teacher's salary never allowed moving to a bigger house and he was always taking exams to improve his salary only to have it all eaten up by hungry mouths. Everything was pretty horrible, especially the way the children fought. They'd get hold of each other's heads and give them a good bashing against the wall. Martha gave up somewhere along the line so they worked out a thing between them. The bashings, biting, and blood were to operate in full swing until he came home. He was to be the bogey-man and when it worked he never failed to have a sense of godhead at the way in which his presence could change savages into fairly reasonable human beings.

Yet somehow it was this chaos and mismanagement at the center of his life that drove him into politics. It was really an ordered beautiful world with just a few basic slogans to learn along with the rights of mankind. At one stage, before things became very bad, there were conferences to attend, all very far away from home.

"Let's face it," he thought ruefully. "I'm only learning right now what it means to be a politician. All this while I've been running away from Martha and the kids."

And the pain in his head brought a hard lump to his throat. That was what the children did to each other daily and Martha wasn't managing and if Warder Hannetjie had not interrupted him that morning he would have sent

kaffir: A black South African; often used as a disparaging term.
knobkerrie: A club.

the following message: "Be good comrades, my children. Cooperate, then life will run smoothly."

The next day Warder Hannetjie caught this old man of twelve children stealing grapes from the farm shed. They were an enormous quantity of grapes in a ten-gallon tin and for this misdeed the old man spent a week in the isolation cell. In fact, Span One as a whole was in constant trouble. Warder Hannetjie seemed to have eyes at the back of his head. He uncovered the trick about the cabbages, how they were split in two with the spade and immediately covered with earth and then unearthed again and eaten with split-second timing. He found out how tobacco smoke was beaten into the ground and he found out how conversations were whispered down the wind.

For about two weeks Span One lived in acute misery. The cabbages, tobacco, and conversations had been the pivot of jail life to them. Then one evening they noticed that their good old comrade who wore the glasses was looking rather pleased with himself. He pulled out a four-ounce packet of tobacco by way of explanation and the comrades fell upon it with great greed. Brille merely smiled. After all, he was the father of many children. But when the last shred had disappeared, it occurred to the comrades that they ought to be puzzled. Someone said: "I say, brother. We're watched like hawks these days. Where did you get the tobacco?"

"Hannetjie gave it to me," said Brille.

There was a long silence. Into it dropped a quiet bombshell.

"I saw Hannetjie in the shed today," and the failing eyesight blinked rapidly. "I caught him in the act of stealing five bags of fertilizer and he bribed me to keep my mouth shut."

There was another long silence.

"Prison is an evil life," Brille continued, apparently discussing some irrelevant matter. "It makes a man contemplate all kinds of evil deeds."

He held out his hand and closed it.

"You know, comrades," he said. "I've got Hannetjie. I'll betray him tomorrow."

Everyone began talking at once.

"Forget it, brother. You'll get shot."

Brille laughed.

"I won't," he said. "That is what I mean about evil. I am a father of children and I saw today that Hannetjie is just a child and stupidly truthful. I'm going to punish him severely because we need a good warder."

The following day, with Brille as witness, Hannetjie confessed to the theft of the fertilizer and was fined a large sum of money. From then on Span One did very much as they pleased while Warder Hannetjie stood by and said nothing. But it was Brille who carried this to extremes. One day, at the close of work Warder Hannetjie said: "Brille, pick up my jacket and carry it back to the camp."

"But nothing in the regulations say I'm your servant, Hannetjie," Brille replied coolly.

"I've told you not to call me Hannetjie. You must say, 'Baas,'" but Warder Hannetjie's voice lacked conviction. In turn, Brille squinted up at him.

"I'll tell you something about this Baas business, Hannetjie," he said. "One of these days we are going to run the country. You are going to clean my car. Now I have a fifteen-year-old son and I'd die of shame if you had to tell him that I ever called you Baas."

Warder Hannetjie went red in the face and picked up his coat.

On another occasion Brille was seen to be walking about the prison yard, openly smoking tobacco. On being taken before the prison commander he claimed to have received the tobacco from Warder Hannetjie. All throughout the tirade from his chief, Warder Hannetjie failed to defend himself but his nerve broke completely. He called Brille to one side.

"Brille," he said. "This thing between you and me must end. You may not know it but I have a wife and children and you're driving me to suicide."

"Why don't you like your own medicine, Hannetjie?" Brille asked quietly.   45

"I can give you anything you want," Warder Hannetjie said in desperation.

"It's not only me but the whole of Span One," said Brille, cunningly. "The whole of Span One wants something from you."

Warder Hannetjie brightened with relief.

"I tink I can manage if it's tobacco you want," he said.

Brille looked at him, for the first time struck with pity, and guilt.   50

He wondered if he had carried the whole business too far. The man was really a child.

"It's not tobacco we want, but you," he said. "We want you on our side. We want a good warder because without a good warder we won't be able to manage the long stretch ahead."

Warder Hannetjie interpreted this request in his own fashion and his interpretation of what was good and human often left the prisoners of Span One speechless with surprise. He had a way of slipping off his revolver and picking up a spade and digging alongside Span One. He had a way of producing unheard-of luxuries like boiled eggs from his farm nearby and things like cigarettes, and Span One responded nobly and got the reputation of being the best work span in the camp. And it wasn't only take from their side. They were awfully good at stealing certain commodities like fertilizer which were needed on the farm of Warder Hannetjie.

Connections to Other Selections

1. Discuss how the issue of race relations is presented in "The Prisoner Who Wore Glasses" and Ralph Ellison's "Battle Royal" (p. 223). Compare Brille's strategy of dealing with racial issues with the strategy suggested by the last words from the grandfather in "Battle Royal" (para. 2).

2. Compare Brille's character with Abner Snopes's in William Faulkner's "Barn Burning" (p. 481). How does each character cope with oppression?

3. Write an essay about the effect of the final sentence in Head's story and in Isabel Allende's "The Judge's Wife" (p. 581). How does the last sentence of each story affect your response to what has come before it?

Naguib Mahfouz (Egypt / b. 1911)

Born in Cairo, Egypt, Naguib Mahfouz graduated from Cairo University in 1934 and spent most of his life writing while working as a government employee in the Ministry of Islamic Affairs until his retirement in 1971. He continues to write fiction and has published nearly forty novels along with fourteen collections of short stories. His reputation in the Arab world is secure, and he has been celebrated internationally since 1988, when he was awarded the Nobel Prize in literature. Among his most popular novels translated into English are *Miramar* (1978), *Children of Gebelawi* (1981), and *Sugar Street: The Cairo Trilogy* (1992). "The Answer Is No" is reprinted from *The Time and the Place and Other Stories* (1991).

The Answer Is No   *1991*

TRANSLATED BY DENYS JOHNSON-DAVIES

The important piece of news that the new headmaster had arrived spread through the school. She heard of it in the women teachers' common room as she was casting a final glance at the day's lessons. There was no getting away from joining the other teachers in congratulating him, and from shaking him by the hand too. A shudder passed through her body, but it was unavoidable.

"They speak highly of his ability," said a colleague of hers. "And they talk too of his strictness."

It had always been a possibility that might occur, and now it had. Her pretty face paled, and a staring look came to her wide black eyes.

When the time came, the teachers went in single file, decorously attired, to his open room. He stood behind his desk as he received the men and women. He was of medium height, with a tendency to portliness, and had a spherical face, hooked nose, and bulging eyes; the first thing that could be seen of him was a thick, puffed-up mustache, arched like a foam-laden wave. She advanced with her eyes fixed on his chest. Avoiding his gaze, she stretched out her hand. What was she to say? Just what the others had said? However, she kept silent, uttered not a word. What, she wondered, did his eyes express? His rough hand shook hers, and he said in a gruff voice, "Thanks." She turned elegantly and moved off.

She forgot her worries through her daily tasks, though she did not look in 5 good shape. Several of the girls remarked, "Miss is in a bad mood." When she returned to her home at the beginning of the Pyramids Road, she changed her clothes and sat down to eat with her mother. "Everything all right?'" inquired her mother, looking her in the face.

"Badran, Badran Badawi," she said briefly. "Do you remember him? He's been appointed our headmaster."

"Really!"

Then, after a moment of silence, she said, "It's of no importance at all — it's an old and long-forgotten story."

After eating, she took herself off to her study to rest for a while before correcting some exercise books. She had forgotten him completely. No, not completely. How could he be forgotten completely? When he had first come to give her a private lesson in mathematics, she was fourteen years of age. In fact not quite fourteen. He had been twenty-five years older, the same age as her father. She had said to her mother, "His appearance is a mess, but he explains things well." And her mother had said, "We're not concerned with what he looks like; what's important is how he explains things."

He was an amusing person, and she got on well with him and benefited 10 from his knowledge. How, then, had it happened? In her innocence she had not noticed any change in his behavior to put her on her guard. Then one day he had been left on his own with her, her father having gone to her aunt's clinic. She had not the slightest doubts about a man she regarded as a second father. How, then, had it happened? Without love or desire on her part the thing had happened. She had asked in terror about what had occurred, and he had told her, "Don't be frightened or sad. Keep it to yourself and I'll come and propose to you the day you come of age."

And he had kept his promise and had come to ask for her hand. By then she had attained a degree of maturity that gave her an understanding of the dimensions of their tragic position. She had found that she had no love or respect for him and that he was as far as he could be from her dreams and from the ideas she had formed of what constituted an ideal and moral person. But what was to be done? Her father had passed away two years ago, and her mother had been taken aback by the forwardness of the man. However, she had said to her, "I know your attachment to your personal independence, so I leave the decision to you."

She had been conscious of the critical position she was in. She had either to accept or to close the door forever. It was the sort of situation that could force her into something she detested. She was the rich, beautiful girl, a by-word in Abbasiyya for her nobility of character, and now here she was struggling helplessly in a well-sprung trap, while he looked down at her with rapacious eyes. Just as she had hated his strength, so too did she hate her own weakness. To have abused her innocence was one thing, but for him to have the upper hand now that she was fully in possession of her faculties was something else. He had said, "So here I am, making good my promise because I love you." He had also said, "I know of your love of teaching, and you will complete your studies at the College of Science."

She had felt such anger as she had never felt before. She had rejected coercion in the same way as she rejected ugliness. It had meant little to her to sacrifice marriage. She had welcomed being on her own, for solitude accompanied by self-respect was not loneliness. She had also guessed he was after her money. She had told her mother quiet straightforwardly, "No," to which her mother had replied, "I am astonished you did not make this decision from the first moment."

The man had blocked her way outside and said, "How can you refuse? Don't you realize the outcome?" And she had replied with an asperity he had not expected, "For me any outcome is preferable to being married to you."

After finishing her studies, she had wanted something to do to fill her 15
spare time, so she had worked as a teacher. Chances to marry had come time after time, but she had turned her back on them all.

"Does no one please you?" her mother asked her.

"I know what I'm doing," she had said gently.

"But time is going by."

"Let it go as it pleases, I am content."

Day by day she becomes older. She avoids love, fears it. With all her strength 20
she hopes that life will pass calmly, peacefully, rather than happily. She goes on persuading herself that happiness is not confined to love and motherhood. Never has she regretted her firm decision. Who knows what the morrow holds? But she was certainly unhappy that he should again make his appearance in her life, that she would be making of the past a living and painful present.

Then, the first time he was alone with her in his room, he asked her, "How are you?"

She answered coldly, "I'm fine."

He hesitated slightly before inquiring, "Have you not . . . I mean, did you get married?"

In the time of someone intent on cutting short a conversation, she said, "I told you, I'm fine."

CONNECTIONS TO OTHER SELECTIONS

1. Discuss the similarities and differences between the older men in "The Answer Is No" and Fay Weldon's "IND AFF, or Out of Love in Sarajevo" (p. 153).

2. In an essay compare the protagonists' decisions not to marry in "The Answer Is No" and James Joyce's "Eveline" (p. 512).

YUKIO MISHIMA (JAPAN / 1925–1970)

Yukio Mishima is the pseudonym of Kimitake Hiraoka. He was born in Tokyo and educated at an elite private school and Tokyo Imperial University. Because he failed an army physical, he did not serve in World War II. After the war, he attended law school and worked for a short time at the Finance Ministry. *Confessions of a Mask,* his first novel, was published in 1949. He wrote poetry, stories, plays, novels, travel books, articles, and he translated a number of No dramas. Some of his best-known works in English translation are *Temple of the Golden Pavilion* (1956), *The Sailor Who Fell from Grace with the Sea* (1963), *The Sea of Fertility* (1975), and *Acts of Worship* (1989). In addition to writing, acting, singing, and modeling, he also became an expert in martial arts. Indeed, he formed his own private army. In 1970 he took over an army headquarters because he felt Japan was drifting too far from its classic samurai traditions. When his ultraconservative demands were unmet by the government, he committed ritual suicide, *seppuku.* In "Patriotism" Mishima's devotion to ancient traditions and honor are strikingly evident.

Patriotism 1966

TRANSLATED BY GEOFFREY W. SARGENT

I

On the twenty-eighth of February, 1936 (on the third day, that is, of the February 26 Incident°), Lieutenant Shinji Takeyama of the Konoe Transport Battalion — profoundly disturbed by the knowledge that his closest colleagues had been with the mutineers from the beginning, and indignant at the imminent

---

the February 26 Incident: When right-wing officers killed several moderate officials in an effort to establish a more militant Japan.

prospect of Imperial troops attacking Imperial troops — took his officer's sword and ceremoniously disemboweled himself in the eight-mat room of his private residence in the sixth block of Aoba-chō, in Yotsuya Ward. His wife, Reiko, followed him, stabbing herself to death. The lieutenant's farewell note consisted of one sentence: "Long live the Imperial Forces." His wife's, after apologies for her unfilial conduct in thus preceding her parents to the grave, concluded: "The day which, for a soldier's wife, had to come, has come. . . ." The last moments of this heroic and dedicated couple were such as to make the gods themselves weep. The lieutenant's age, it should be noted, was thirty-one, his wife's twenty-three; and it was not half a year since the celebration of their marriage.

II

Those who saw the bride and bridegroom in the commemorative photograph — perhaps no less than those actually present at the lieutenant's wedding — had exclaimed in wonder at the bearing of this handsome couple. The lieutenant, majestic in military uniform, stood protectively beside his bride, his right hand resting upon his sword, his officer's cap held at his left side. His expression was severe, and his dark brows and wide-gazing eyes well conveyed the clear integrity of youth. For the beauty of the bride in her white over-robe no comparisons were adequate. In the eyes, round beneath soft brows, in the slender, finely shaped nose, and in the full lips, there was both sensuousness and refinement. One hand, emerging shyly from a sleeve of the over-robe, held a fan, and the tips of the fingers, clustering delicately, were like the bud of a moon-flower.

After the suicide, people would take out this photograph and examine it, and sadly reflect that too often there was a curse on these seemingly flawless unions. Perhaps it was no more than imagination, but looking at the picture after the tragedy it almost seemed as if the two young people before the gold-lacquered screen were gazing, each with equal clarity, at the deaths which lay before them.

Thanks to the good offices of their go-between, Lieutenant General Ozeki, they had been able to set themselves up in a new home at Aoba-chō in Yotsuya. "New home" is perhaps misleading. It was an old three-room rented house backing onto a small garden. As neither the six- nor the four-and-a-half-mat room downstairs was favored by the sun, they used the upstairs eight-mat room as both bedroom and guest room. There was no maid, so Reiko was left alone to guard the house in her husband's absence.

The honeymoon trip was dispensed with on the grounds that these were times of national emergency. The two of them had spent the first night of their marriage at this house. Before going to bed, Shinji, sitting erect on the floor with his sword laid before him, had bestowed upon his wife a soldierly lecture. A woman who had become the wife of a soldier should know and resolutely accept that her husband's death might come at any moment. It could be tomorrow. It could be the day after. But, no matter when it came — he asked — was she steadfast in her resolve to accept it? Reiko rose to her feet, pulled open a drawer of the cabinet, and took out what was the most prized of her new possessions, the dagger her mother had given her. Returning to her place, she laid the dagger without a word on the mat before her, just as her husband had laid his sword. A silent understanding was achieved at once, and the lieutenant never again sought to test his wife's resolve.

In the first few months of her marriage Reiko's beauty grew daily more radiant, shining serene like the moon after rain.

As both were possessed of young, vigorous bodies, their relationship was passionate. Nor was this merely a matter of the night. On more than one occasion, returning home straight from maneuvers, and begrudging even the time it took to remove his mud-splashed uniform, the lieutenant had pushed his wife to the floor almost as soon as he had entered the house. Reiko was equally ardent in her response. For a little more or a little less than a month, from the first night of their marriage Reiko knew happiness, and the lieutenant, seeing this, was happy too.

Reiko's body was white and pure, and her swelling breasts conveyed a firm and chaste refusal; but, upon consent, those breasts were lavish with their intimate, welcoming warmth. Even in bed these two were frighteningly and awesomely serious. In the very midst of wild, intoxicating passions, their hearts were sober and serious.

By day the lieutenant would think of his wife in the brief rest periods between training; and all day long, at home, Reiko would recall the image of her husband. Even when apart, however, they had only to look at the wedding photograph for their happiness to be once more confirmed. Reiko felt not the slightest surprise that a man who had been a complete stranger until a few months ago should now have become the sun about which her whole world revolved.

All these things had a moral basis, and were in accordance with the Education Rescript's injunction that "husband and wife should be harmonious." Not once did Reiko contradict her husband, nor did the lieutenant ever find reason to scold his wife. On the god shelf below the stairway, alongside the tablet from the Great Ise Shrine, were set photographs of their Imperial Majesties, and regularly every morning, before leaving for duty, the lieutenant would stand with his wife at this hallowed place and together they would bow their heads low. The offering water was renewed each morning, and the sacred sprig of *sasaki* was always green and fresh. Their lives were lived beneath the solemn protection of the gods and were filled with an intense happiness, which set every fiber in their bodies trembling.

III

Although Lord Privy Seal Saitō's house was in their neighborhood, neither of them heard any noise of gunfire on the morning of February 26. It was a bugle, sounding muster in the dim, snowy dawn, when the ten-minute tragedy had already ended, which first disrupted the lieutenant's slumbers. Leaping at once from his bed, and without speaking a word, the lieutenant donned his uniform, buckled on the sword held ready for him by his wife, and hurried swiftly out into the snow-covered streets of the still darkened morning. He did not return until the evening of the twenty-eighth.

Later, from the radio news, Reiko learned the full extent of this sudden eruption of violence. Her life throughout the subsequent two days was lived alone, in complete tranquillity, and behind locked doors.

In the lieutenant's face, as he hurried silently out into the snowy morning, Reiko had read the determination to die. If her husband did not return, her own decision was made: she too would die. Quietly she attended to the disposition of her personal possessions. She chose her sets of visiting kimonos as keepsakes for friends of her schooldays, and she wrote a name and address on the stiff paper wrapping in which each was folded. Constantly admonished by her husband never to think of the morrow, Reiko had not even kept a diary and was now denied the pleasure of assiduously rereading her record of the happiness of the past few months and consigning each page to the fire as she did so. Ranged across the top of the radio were a small china dog, a rabbit, a squirrel, a bear, and a fox. There were also a small vase and a water pitcher. These comprised Reiko's one and only collection. But it would hardly do, she imagined, to give such things as keepsakes. Nor again would it be quite proper to ask specifically for them to be included in the coffin. It seemed to Reiko, as these thoughts passed through her mind, that the expression on the small animals' faces grew even more lost and forlorn.

Reiko took the squirrel in her hand and looked at it. And then, her thoughts turning to a realm far beyond these childlike affections, she gazed up into the distance at the great sunlike principle which her husband embodied. She was ready, and happy, to be hurtled along to her destruction in that gleaming sun chariot—but now, for these few moments of solitude, she allowed herself to luxuriate in this innocent attachment to trifles. The time when she had genuinely loved these things, however, was long past. Now she merely loved the memory of having once loved them, and their place in her heart had been filled by more intense passions, by a more frenzied happiness. . . . For Reiko had never, even to herself, thought of those soaring joys of the flesh as a mere pleasure. The February cold, and the icy touch of the china squirrel, had numbed Reiko's slender fingers; yet, even so, in her lower limbs, beneath the ordered repetition of the pattern which crossed the skirt of her trim *meisen* kimono, she could feel now, as she thought of the lieutenant's powerful arms reaching out toward her, a hot moistness of the flesh which defied the snows.

She was not in the least afraid of the death hovering in her mind. Waiting ₁₅ alone at home, Reiko firmly believed that everything her husband was feeling or thinking now, his anguish and distress, was leading her—just as surely as the power in his flesh—to a welcome death. She felt as if her body could melt away with ease and be transformed to the merest fraction of her husband's thought.

Listening to the frequent announcements on the radio, she heard the names of several of her husband's colleagues mentioned among those of the insurgents. This was news of death. She followed the developments closely, wondering anxiously, as the situation became daily more irrevocable, why no Imperial ordinance was sent down, and watching what had at first been taken as a movement to restore the nation's honor come gradually to be branded with the infamous name of mutiny. There was no communication from the regiment. At any moment, it seemed, fighting might commence in the city streets, where the remains of the snow still lay.

Toward sundown on the twenty-eighth Reiko was startled by a furious pounding on the front door. She hurried downstairs. As she pulled with fumbling fingers at the bolt, the shape dimly outlined beyond the frosted-glass panel made no sound, but she knew it was her husband. Reiko had never known the bolt on the sliding door to be so stiff. Still it resisted. The door just would not open.

In a moment, almost before she knew she had succeeded, the lieutenant was standing before her on the cement floor inside the porch, muffled in a khaki greatcoat, his top boots heavy with slush from the street. Closing the door behind him, he returned the bolt once more to its socket. With what significance, Reiko did not understand.

"Welcome home."

Reiko bowed deeply, but her husband made no response. As he had already unfastened his sword and was about to remove his greatcoat, Reiko moved around behind to assist. The coat, which was cold and damp and had lost the odor of horse dung it normally exuded when exposed to the sun, weighed heavily upon her arm. Draping it across a hanger, and cradling the sword and leather belt in her sleeves, she waited while her husband removed his top boots and then followed behind him into the "living room." This was the six-mat room downstairs.

Seen in the clear light from the lamp, her husband's face, covered with a heavy growth of bristle, was almost unrecognizably wasted and thin. The cheeks were hollow, their luster and resilience gone. In his normal good spirits he would have changed into old clothes as soon as he was home and have pressed her to get supper at once, but now he sat before the table still in his uniform, his head drooping dejectedly. Reiko refrained from asking whether she should prepare the supper.

After an interval the lieutenant spoke.

"I knew nothing. They hadn't asked me to join. Perhaps out of consideration, because I was newly married. Kano, and Homma too, and Yamaguchi."

Reiko recalled momentarily the faces of high-spirited officers, friends of her husband, who had come to the house occasionally as guests.

"There may be an Imperial ordinance sent down tomorrow. They'll be posted as rebels, I imagine. I shall be in command of a unit with orders to attack them. . . . I can't do it. It's impossible to do a thing like that."

He spoke again.

"They've taken me off guard duty, and I have permission to return home for one night. Tomorrow morning, without question, I must leave to join the attack. I can't do it, Reiko."

Reiko sat erect with lowered eyes. She understood clearly that her husband had spoken of his death. The lieutenant was resolved. Each word, being rooted in death, emerged sharply and with powerful significance against this dark, unmovable background. Although the lieutenant was speaking of his dilemma, already there was no room in his mind for vacillation.

However, there was a clarity, like the clarity of a stream fed from melting snows, in the silence which rested between them. Sitting in his own home after the long two-day ordeal, and looking across at the face of his beautiful wife, the lieutenant was for the first time experiencing true peace of mind. For he had at once known, though she said nothing, that his wife divined the resolve which lay beneath his words.

"Well, then . . ." The lieutenant's eyes opened wide. Despite his exhaustion they were strong and clear, and now for the first time they looked straight into the eyes of his wife. "Tonight I shall cut my stomach."

Reiko did not flinch.

Her round eyes showed tension, as taut as the clang of a bell.

"I am ready," she said. "I ask permission to accompany you."

The lieutenant felt almost mesmerized by the strength of those eyes. His words flowed swiftly and easily, like the utterances of a man in delirium, and it was beyond his understanding how permission in a matter of such weight could be expressed so casually.

"Good. We'll go together. But I want you as a witness, first, for my own sui- 35 cide. Agreed?"

When this was said a sudden release of abundant happiness welled up in both their hearts. Reiko was deeply affected by the greatness of her husband's trust in her. It was vital for the lieutenant, whatever else might happen, that there should be no irregularity in his death. For that reason there had to be a witness. The fact that he had chosen his wife for this was the first mark of his trust. The second, and even greater mark, was that though he had pledged that they should die together he did not intend to kill his wife first—he had deferred her death to a time when he would no longer be there to verify it. If the lieutenant had been a suspicious husband, he would doubtless, as in the usual suicide pact, have chosen to kill his wife first.

When Reiko said, "I ask permission to accompany you," the lieutenant felt these words to be the final fruit of the education which he had himself given his wife, starting on the first night of their marriage, and which had schooled her, when the moment came, to say what had to be said without a shadow of hesitation. This flattered the lieutenant's opinion of himself as a self-reliant man. He was not so romantic or conceited as to imagine that the words were spoken spontaneously, out of love for her husband.

With happiness welling almost too abundantly in their hearts, they could not help smiling at each other. Reiko felt as if she had returned to her wedding night.

Before her eyes was neither pain nor death. She seemed to see only a free and limitless expanse opening out into vast distances.

"The water is hot. Will you take your bath now?" 40

"Ah yes, of course."

"And supper . . . ?"

The words were delivered in such level, domestic tones that the lieutenant came near to thinking, for the fraction of a second, that everything had been a hallucination.

"I don't think we'll need supper. But perhaps you could warm some sake?"

"As you wish." 45

As Reiko rose and took a *tanzen* gown from the cabinet for after the bath, she purposely directed her husband's attention to the opened drawer. The lieutenant rose, crossed to the cabinet, and looked inside. From the ordered array of paper wrappings he read, one by one, the addresses of the keepsakes. There was no grief in the lieutenant's response to this demonstration of heroic resolve. His heart was filled with tenderness. Like a husband who is proudly shown the childish purchases of a young wife, the lieutenant, overwhelmed by affection, lovingly embraced his wife from behind and implanted a kiss upon her neck.

Reiko felt the roughness of the lieutenant's unshaven skin against her neck. This sensation, more than being just a thing of this world, was for Reiko almost the world itself, but now—with the feeling that it was soon to be lost forever—it had freshness beyond all her experience. Each moment had its own vital strength, and the senses in every corner of her body were reawakened. Accepting her husband's caresses from behind, Reiko raised herself on the tips of her toes, letting the vitality seep through her entire body.

"First the bath, and then, after some sake . . . lay out the bedding upstairs, will you?"

The lieutenant whispered the words into his wife's ear. Reiko silently nodded.

Flinging off his uniform, the lieutenant went to the bath. To faint back- 50 ground noises of slopping water Reiko tended the charcoal brazier in the living room and began the preparations for warming the sake.

Taking the *tanzen*, a sash, and some underclothes, she went to the bathroom to ask how the water was. In the midst of a coiling cloud of steam the lieutenant was sitting cross-legged on the floor, shaving, and she could dimly discern the rippling movements of the muscles on his damp, powerful back as they responded to the movement of his arms.

There was nothing to suggest a time of any special significance. Reiko, going busily about her tasks, was preparing side dishes from odds and ends in stock. Her hands did not tremble. If anything, she managed even more efficiently and smoothly than usual. From time to time, it is true, there was a strange throbbing deep within her breast. Like distant lightning, it had a moment of sharp intensity and then vanished without trace. Apart from that, nothing was in any way out of the ordinary.

The lieutenant, shaving in the bathroom, felt his warmed body miraculously healed at last of the desperate tiredness of the days of indecision and filled — in spite of the death which lay ahead — with pleasurable anticipation. The sound of his wife going about her work came to him faintly. A healthy physical craving, submerged for two days, reasserted itself.

The lieutenant was confident there had been no impurity in that joy they had experienced when resolving upon death. They had both sensed at that moment — though not, of course, in any clear and conscious way — that those permissible pleasures which they shared in private were once more beneath the protection of Righteousness and Divine Power, and of a complete and unassailable morality. On looking into each other's eyes and discovering there an honorable death, they had felt themselves safe once more behind steel walls which none could destroy, encased in an impenetrable armor of Beauty and Truth. Thus, so far from seeing any inconsistency or conflict between the urges of his flesh and the sincerity of his patriotism, the lieutenant was even able to regard the two as parts of the same thing.

Thrusting his face close to the dark, cracked, misted wall mirror, the lieu- 55 tenant shaved himself with great care. This would be his death face. There must be no unsightly blemishes. The clean-shaven face gleamed once more with a youthful luster, seeming to brighten the darkness of the mirror. There was a certain elegance, he even felt, in the association of death with this radiantly healthy face.

Just as it looked now, this would become his death face! Already, in fact, it had half departed from the lieutenant's personal possession and had become the bust above a dead soldier's memorial. As an experiment he closed his eyes tight. Everything was wrapped in blackness, and he was no longer a living, seeing creature.

Returning from the bath, the traces of the shave glowing faintly blue beneath his smooth cheeks, he seated himself beside the now well-kindled charcoal brazier. Busy though Reiko was, he noticed, she had found time lightly to touch up her face. Her cheeks were gay and her lips moist. There was no shadow of sadness to be seen. Truly, the lieutenant felt, as he saw this mark of his young wife's passionate nature, he had chosen the wife he ought to have chosen.

As soon as the lieutenant had drained his sake cup he offered it to Reiko. Reiko had never before tasted sake, but she accepted without hesitation and sipped timidly.

"Come here," the lieutenant said.

Reiko moved to her husband's side and was embraced as she leaned back- 60 ward across his lap. Her breast was in violent commotion, as if sadness, joy, and the potent sake were mingling and reacting within her. The lieutenant looked down into his wife's face. It was the last face he would see in this world, the last face he would see of his wife. The lieutenant scrutinized the face minutely, with the eyes of a traveler bidding farewell to splendid vistas which he will never revisit. It was a face he could not tire of looking at—the features regular yet not cold, the lips lightly closed with a soft strength. The lieutenant kissed those lips, unthinkingly. And suddenly, though there was not the slightest distortion of the face into the unsightliness of sobbing, he noticed that tears were welling slowly from beneath the long lashes of the closed eyes and brimming over into the glistening stream.

When, a little later, the lieutenant urged that they should move to the upstairs bedroom, his wife replied that she would follow after taking a bath. Climbing the stairs alone to the bedroom, where the air was already warmed by the gas heater, the lieutenant lay down on the bedding with arms outstretched and legs apart. Even the time at which he lay waiting for his wife to join him was no later and no earlier than usual.

He folded his hands beneath his head and gazed at the dark boards of the ceiling in the dimness beyond the range of the standard lamp. Was it death he was now waiting for? Or a wild ecstasy of the senses? The two seemed to overlap, almost as if the object of this bodily desire was death itself. But, however that might be, it was certain that never before had the lieutenant tasted such total freedom.

There was the sound of a car outside the window. He could hear the screech of its tires skidding in the snow piled at the side of the street. The sound of its horn reechoed from nearby walls. . . . Listening to these noises he had the feeling that the house rose like a solitary island in the ocean of a society going as restlessly about its business as ever. All around, vastly and untidily, stretched the country for which he grieved. He was to give his life for it. But would that great country, with which he was prepared to remonstrate to the extent of destroying himself, take the slightest heed of his death? He did not know; and it did not matter. His was a battlefield without glory, a battlefield where none could display deeds of valor: it was the front line of the spirit.

Reiko's footsteps sounded on the stairway. The steep stairs in this old house creaked badly. There were fond memories in that creaking, and many a time, while waiting in bed, the lieutenant had listened to its welcome sound. At the thought that he would hear it no more he listened with intense concentration, striving for every corner of every moment of this precious time to be filled with the sound of those soft footfalls on the creaking stairway. The moments seemed transformed to jewels, sparkling with inner light.

Reiko wore a Nagoya sash about the waist of her *yukata,* but as the lieu- 65 tenant reached toward it, its redness sobered by the dimness of the light,

Reiko's hand moved to his assistance and the sash fell away, slithering swiftly to the floor. As she stood before him, still in her *yukata*, the lieutenant inserted his hands through the side slits beneath each sleeve, intending to embrace her as she was; but at the touch of his finger tips upon the warm naked flesh, and as the armpits closed gently about his hands, his whole body was suddenly aflame.

In a few moments the two lay naked before the glowing gas heater.

Neither spoke the thought, but their hearts, their bodies, and their pounding breasts blazed with the knowledge that this was the very last time. It was as if the words "The Last Time" were spelled out, in invisible brushstrokes, across every inch of their bodies.

The lieutenant drew his wife close and kissed her vehemently. As their tongues explored each other's mouths, reaching out into the smooth, moist interior, they felt as if the still-unknown agonies of death had tempered their senses to the keenness of red-hot steel. The agonies they could not yet feel, the distant pains of death, had refined their awareness of pleasure.

"This is the last time I shall see your body," said the lieutenant. "Let me look at it closely." And, tilting the shade on the lampstand to one side, he directed the rays along the full length of Reiko's outstretched form.

Reiko lay still with her eyes closed. The light from the low lamp clearly re- 70 vealed the majestic sweep of her white flesh. The lieutenant, not without a touch of egocentricity, rejoiced that he would never see this beauty crumble in death.

At his leisure, the lieutenant allowed the unforgettable spectacle to engrave itself upon his mind. With one hand he fondled the hair, with the other he softly stroked the magnificent face, implanting kisses here and there where his eyes lingered. The quiet coldness of the high, tapering forehead, the closed eyes with their long lashes beneath faintly etched brows, the set of the finely shaped nose, the gleam of teeth glimpsed between full, regular lips, the soft cheeks and the small, wise chin . . . these things conjured up in the lieutenant's mind the vision of a truly radiant death face, and again and again he pressed his lips tight against the white throat—where Reiko's own hand was soon to strike—and the throat reddened faintly beneath his kisses. Returning to the mouth he laid his lips against it with the gentlest of pressures, and moved them rhythmically over Reiko's with the light rolling motion of a small boat. If he closed his eyes, the world became a rocking cradle.

Wherever the lieutenant's eyes moved his lips faithfully followed. The high, swelling breasts, surmounted by nipples like the buds of a wild cherry, hardened as the lieutenant's lips closed about them. The arms flowed smoothly downward from each side of the breast, tapering toward the wrists, yet losing nothing of their roundness or symmetry, and at their tips were those delicate fingers which had held the fan at the wedding ceremony. One by one, as the lieutenant kissed them, the fingers withdrew behind their neighbor as if in shame. . . . The natural hollow curving between the bosom and the stomach carried in its lines a suggestion not only of softness but of resilient strength, and while it gave forewarning of the rich curves spreading outward from here to the hips it had, in itself, an appearance only of restraint and proper discipline. The whiteness and richness of the stomach and hips was like milk brimming in a great bowl, and the sharply shadowed dip of the navel could have been the fresh impress of a raindrop, fallen there that very moment. Where the shadows gathered more thickly, hair clustered, gentle and sensitive, and as the agitation mounted in the now no longer passive body there hung over this region a scent like the smoldering of fragrant blossoms, growing steadily more pervasive.

At length, in a tremendous voice, Reiko spoke.

"Show me. . . . Let me look too, for the last time."

Never before had he heard from his wife's lips so strong and unequivocal a 75 request. It was as if something which her modesty had wished to keep hidden to the end had suddenly burst its bonds of constraint. The lieutenant obediently lay back and surrendered himself to his wife. Lithely she raised her white, trembling body, and — burning with an innocent desire to return to her husband what he had done for her — placed two white fingers on the lieutenant's eyes, which gazed fixedly up at her, and gently stroked them shut.

Suddenly overwhelmed by tenderness, her cheeks flushed by a dizzying uprush of emotion, Reiko threw her arms about the lieutenant's close-cropped head. The bristly hairs rubbed painfully against her breast, the prominent nose was cold as it dug into her flesh, and his breath was hot. Relaxing her embrace, she gazed down at her husband's masculine face. The severe brows, the closed eyes, the splendid bridge of the nose, the shapely lips drawn firmly together . . . the blue, clean-shaven cheeks reflecting the light and gleaming smoothly. Reiko kissed each of these. She kissed the broad nape of the neck, the strong, erect shoulders, the powerful chest with its twin circles like shields and its russet nipples. In the armpits, deeply shadowed by the ample flesh of the shoulders and chest, a sweet and melancholy odor emanated from the growth of hair, and in the sweetness of this odor was contained, somehow, the essence of young death. The lieutenant's naked skin glowed like a field of barley, and everywhere the muscles showed in sharp relief, converging on the lower abdomen about the small, unassuming navel. Gazing at the youthful, firm stomach, modestly covered by a vigorous growth of hair, Reiko thought of it as it was soon to be, cruelly cut by the sword, and she laid her head upon it, sobbing in pity, and bathed it with kisses.

At the touch of his wife's tears upon his stomach the lieutenant felt ready to endure with courage the cruelest agonies of his suicide.

What ecstasies they experienced after these tender exchanges may well be imagined. The lieutenant raised himself and enfolded his wife in a powerful embrace, her body now limp with exhaustion after her grief and tears. Passionately they held their faces close, rubbing cheek against cheek. Reiko's body was trembling. Their breasts, moist with sweat, were tightly joined, and every inch of the young and beautiful bodies had become so much one with the other that it seemed impossible there should ever again be a separation. Reiko cried out. From the heights they plunged into the abyss, and from the abyss they took wing and soared once more to dizzying heights. The lieutenant panted like the regimental standard-bearer on a route march. . . . As one cycle ended, almost immediately a new wave of passion would be generated, and together — with no trace of fatigue — they would climb again in a single breathless movement to the very summit.

IV

When the lieutenant at last turned away, it was not from weariness. For one thing, he was anxious not to undermine the considerable strength he would need in carrying out his suicide. For another, he would have been sorry to mar the sweetness of these last memories by overindulgence.

Since the lieutenant had clearly desisted, Reiko too, with her usual com- 80
pliance, followed his example. The two lay naked on their backs, with fingers
interlaced, staring fixedly at the dark ceiling. The room was warm from the
heater, and even when the sweat had ceased to pour from their bodies they felt
no cold. Outside, in the hushed night, the sounds of passing traffic had
ceased. Even the noises of the trains and streetcars around Yotsuya Station did
not penetrate this far. After echoing through the region bounded by the moat,
they were lost in the heavily wooded park fronting the broad driveway before
Akasaka Palace. It was hard to believe in the tension gripping this whole quarter, where the two factions of the bitterly divided Imperial Army now confronted each other, poised for battle.

Savoring the warmth glowing within themselves, they lay still and recalled
the ecstasies they had just known. Each moment of the experience was relived.
They remembered the taste of kisses which had never wearied, the touch of
naked flesh, episode after episode of dizzying bliss. But already, from the dark
boards of the ceiling, the face of death was peering down. These joys had been
final, and their bodies would never know them again. Not that joy of this intensity—and the same thought had occurred to them both—was ever likely to
be reexperienced, even if they should live on to old age.

The feel of their fingers intertwined—this too would soon be lost. Even
the wood-grain patterns they now gazed at on the dark ceiling boards would
be taken from them. They could feel death edging in, nearer and nearer. There
could be no hesitation now. They must have the courage to reach out to death
themselves, and to seize it.

"Well, let's make our preparations," said the lieutenant. The note of determination in the words was unmistakable, but at the same time Reiko had
never heard her husband's voice so warm and tender.

After they had risen, a variety of tasks awaited them.

The lieutenant, who had never once before helped with the bedding, now 85
cheerfully slid back the door of the closet, lifted the mattress across the room
by himself, and stowed it away inside.

Reiko turned off the gas heater and put away the lamp standard. During
the lieutenant's absence she had arranged this room carefully, sweeping and
dusting it to a fresh cleanness, and now—if one overlooked the rosewood table
drawn into one corner—the eight-mat room gave all the appearance of a reception room ready to welcome an important guest.

"We've seen some drinking here, haven't we? With Kano and Homma and
Noguchi . . ."

"Yes, they were great drinkers, all of them."

"We'll be meeting them before long, in the other world. They'll tease us, I
imagine, when they find I've brought you with me."

Descending the stairs, the lieutenant turned to look back into this calm, 90
clean room, now brightly illuminated by the ceiling lamp. There floated across
his mind the faces of the young officers who had drunk there, and laughed,
and innocently bragged. He had never dreamed then that he would one day cut
open his stomach in this room.

In the two rooms downstairs husband and wife busied themselves
smoothly and serenely with their respective preparations. The lieutenant went
to the toilet, and then to the bathroom to wash. Meanwhile Reiko folded away
her husband's padded robe, placed his uniform tunic, his trousers, and a newly
cut bleached loincloth in the bathroom, and set out sheets of paper on the

living-room table for the farewell notes. Then she removed the lid from the writing box and began rubbing ink from the ink tablet. She had already decided upon the wording of her own note.

Reiko's fingers pressed hard upon the cold gilt letters of the ink tablet, and the water in the shallow well at once darkened, as if a black cloud had spread across it. She stopped thinking that this repeated action, this pressure from her fingers, this rise and fall of faint sound, was all and solely for death. It was a routine domestic task, a simple paring away of time until death should finally stand before her. But somehow, in the increasingly smooth motion of the tablet rubbing on the stone, and in the scent from the thickening ink, there was unspeakable darkness.

Neat in his uniform, which he now wore next to his skin, the lieutenant emerged from the bathroom. Without a word he seated himself at the table, bolt upright, took a brush in his hand, and stared undecidedly at the paper before him.

Reiko took a white silk kimono with her and entered the bathroom. When she reappeared in the living room, clad in the white kimono and with her face lightly made up, the farewell note lay completed on the table beneath the lamp. The thick black brushstrokes said simply:

"Long Live the Imperial Forces—Army Lieutenant Takeyama Shinji."   95

While Reiko sat opposite him writing her own note, the lieutenant gazed in silence, intensely serious, at the controlled movement of his wife's pale fingers as they manipulated the brush.

With their respective notes in their hands—the lieutenant's sword strapped to his side, Reiko's small dagger thrust into the sash of her white kimono—the two of them stood before the god shelf and silently prayed. Then they put out all the downstairs lights. As he mounted the stairs the lieutenant turned his head and gazed back at the striking, white-clad figure of his wife, climbing behind him, with lowered eyes, from the darkness beneath.

The farewell notes were laid side by side in the alcove of the upstairs room. They wondered whether they ought not to remove the hanging scroll, but since it had been written by their go-between, Lieutenant General Ozeki, and consisted, moreover, of two Chinese characters signifying "Sincerity," they left it where it was. Even if it were to become stained with splashes of blood, they felt that the lieutenant general would understand.

The lieutenant, sitting erect with his back to the alcove, laid his sword on the floor before him.

Reiko sat facing him, a mat's width away. With the rest of her so severely   100
white the touch of rouge on her lips seemed remarkably seductive.

Across the dividing mat they gazed intently into each other's eyes. The lieutenant's sword lay before his knees. Seeing it, Reiko recalled their first night and was overwhelmed with sadness. The lieutenant spoke, in a hoarse voice:

"As I have no second to help me I shall cut deep. It may look unpleasant, but please do not panic. Death of any sort is a fearful thing to watch. You must not be discouraged by what you see. Is that all right?"

"Yes."

Reiko nodded deeply.

Looking at the slender white figure of his wife the lieutenant experienced   105
a bizarre excitement. What he was about to perform was an act in his public capacity as a soldier, something he had never previously shown his wife. It

called for a resolution equal to the courage to enter battle; it was a death of no less degree and quality than death in the front line. It was his conduct on the battlefield that he was now to display.

Momentarily the thought led the lieutenant to a strange fantasy. A lonely death on the battlefield, a death beneath the eyes of his beautiful wife . . . in the sensation that he was now to die in these two dimensions, realizing an impossible union of them both, there was sweetness beyond words. This must be the very pinnacle of good fortune, he thought. To have every moment of his death observed by those beautiful eyes—it was like being borne to death on a gentle, fragrant breeze. There was some special favor here. He did not understand precisely what it was, but it was a domain unknown to others: a dispensation granted to no one else had been permitted to himself. In the radiant, bridelike figure of his white-robed wife the lieutenant seemed to see a vision of all those things he had loved and for which he was to lay down his life—the Imperial Household, the Nation, the Army Flag. All these, no less than the wife who sat before him, were presences observing him closely with clear and never-faltering eyes.

Reiko too was gazing intently at her husband, so soon to die, and she thought that never in this world had she seen anything so beautiful. The lieutenant always looked well in uniform, but now, as he contemplated death with severe brows and firmly closed lips, he revealed what was perhaps masculine beauty at its most superb.

"It's time to go," the lieutenant said at last.

Reiko bent her body low to the mat in a deep bow. She could not raise her face. She did not wish to spoil her makeup with tears, but the tears could not be held back.

When at length she looked up she saw hazily through the tears that her husband had wound a white bandage around the blade of his now unsheathed sword, leaving five or six inches of naked steel showing at the point.

Resting the sword in its cloth wrapping on the mat before him, the lieutenant rose from his knees, resettled himself cross-legged, and unfastened the hooks of his uniform collar. His eyes no longer saw his wife. Slowly, one by one, he undid the flat brass buttons. The dusky brown chest was revealed, and then the stomach. He unclasped his belt and undid the buttons of his trousers. The pure whiteness of the thickly coiled loincloth showed itself. The lieutenant pushed the cloth down with both hands, further to ease his stomach, and then reached for the white-bandaged blade of his sword. With his left hand he massaged his abdomen, glancing downward as he did so.

To reassure himself on the sharpness of his sword's cutting edge the lieutenant folded back the left trouser flap, exposing a little of his thigh, and lightly drew the blade across the skin. Blood welled up in the wound at once, and several streaks of red trickled downward, glistening in the strong light.

It was the first time Reiko had ever seen her husband's blood, and she felt a violent throbbing in her chest. She looked at her husband's face. The lieutenant was looking at the blood with calm appraisal. For a moment—though thinking at the same time that it was hollow comfort—Reiko experienced a sense of relief.

The lieutenant's eyes fixed his wife with an intense, hawklike stare. Moving the sword around to his front, he raised himself slightly on his hips and let the upper half of his body lean over the sword point. That he was mustering his whole strength was apparent from the angry tension of the uniform at his shoulders. The lieutenant aimed to strike deep into the left of his stomach. His sharp eye pierced the silence of the room.

Despite the effort he had himself put into the blow, the lieutenant had the impression that someone else had struck the side of his stomach agonizingly with a thick rod of iron. For a second or so his head reeled and he had no idea what had happened. The five or six inches of naked point had vanished completely into his flesh, and the white bandage, gripped in his clenched fist, pressed directly against his stomach.

He returned to consciousness. The blade had certainly pierced the wall of the stomach, he thought. His breathing was difficult, his chest thumped violently, and in some far deep region, which he could hardly believe was a part of himself, a fearful and excruciating pain came welling up as if the ground had split open to disgorge a boiling stream of molten rock. The pain came suddenly nearer, with terrifying speed. The lieutenant bit his lower lip and stifled an instinctive moan.

Was this *seppuku?* — he was thinking. It was a sensation of utter chaos, as if the sky had fallen on his head and the world was reeling drunkenly. His willpower and courage, which had seemed so robust before he made the incision, had now dwindled to something like a single hairlike thread of steel, and he was assailed by the uneasy feeling that he must advance along this thread, clinging to it with desperation. His clenched fist had grown moist. Looking down, he saw that both his hand and the cloth about the blade were drenched in blood. His loincloth too was dyed a deep red. It struck him as incredible that, amidst this terrible agony, things which could be seen could still be seen, and existing things existed still.

The moment the lieutenant thrust the sword into his left side and she saw the deathly pallor fall across his face, like an abruptly lowered curtain, Reiko had to struggle to prevent herself from rushing to his side. Whatever happened, she must watch. She must be a witness. That was the duty her husband had laid upon her. Opposite her, a mat's space away, she could clearly see her husband biting his lip to stifle the pain. The pain was there, with absolute certainty, before her eyes. And Reiko had no means of rescuing him from it.

The sweat glistened on her husband's forehead. The lieutenant closed his eyes, and then opened them again, as if experimenting. The eyes had lost their luster, and seemed innocent and empty like the eyes of a small animal.

The agony before Reiko's eyes burned as strong as the summer sun, utterly remote from the grief which seemed to be tearing herself apart within. The pain grew steadily in stature, stretching upward. Reiko felt that her husband had already become a man in a separate world, a man whose whole being had been resolved into pain, a prisoner in a cage of pain where no hand could reach out to him. But Reiko felt no pain at all. Her grief was not pain. As she thought about this, Reiko began to feel as if someone had raised a cruel wall of glass high between herself and her husband.

Ever since her marriage her husband's existence had been her own existence, and every breath of his had been a breath drawn by herself. But now, while her husband's existence in pain was a vivid reality, Reiko could find in this grief of hers no certain proof at all of her own existence.

With only his right hand on the sword the lieutenant began to cut sideways across his stomach. But as the blade became entangled with the entrails it was pushed constantly outward by their soft resilience; and the lieutenant realized that it would be necessary, as he cut, to use both hands to keep the point pressed deep into his stomach. He pulled the blade across. It did not cut as easily as he had expected. He directed the strength of his whole body into his right hand and pulled again. There was a cut of three or four inches.

The pain spread slowly outward from the inner depths until the whole stomach reverberated. It was like the wild clanging of a bell. Or like a thousand bells which jangled simultaneously at every breath he breathed and every throb of his pulse, rocking his whole being. The lieutenant could no longer stop himself from moaning. But by now the blade had cut its way through to below the navel, and when he noticed this he felt a sense of satisfaction, and a renewal of courage.

The volume of blood had steadily increased, and now it spurted from the wound as if propelled by the beat of the pulse. The mat before the lieutenant was drenched red with splattered blood, and more blood overflowed onto it from pools which gathered in the folds of the lieutenant's khaki trousers. A spot, like a bird, came flying across to Reiko and settled on the lap of her white kimono.

By the time the lieutenant had at last drawn the sword across to the right side of his stomach, the blade was already cutting shallow and had revealed its naked tip, slippery with blood and grease. But, suddenly stricken by a fit of vomiting, the lieutenant cried out hoarsely. The vomiting made the fierce pain fiercer still, and the stomach, which had thus far remained firm and compact, now abruptly heaved, opening wide its wound, and the entrails burst through, as if the wound too were vomiting. Seemingly ignorant of their master's suffering, the entrails gave an impression of robust health and almost disagreeable vitality as they slipped smoothly out and spilled over into the crotch. The lieutenant's head drooped, his shoulders heaved, his eyes opened to narrow slits, and a thin trickle of saliva dribbled from his mouth. The gold markings on his epaulets caught the light and glinted.

Blood was scattered everywhere. The lieutenant was soaked in it to his knees, and he sat now in a crumpled and listless posture, one hand on the floor. A raw smell filled the room. The lieutenant, his head drooping, retched repeatedly, and the movement showed vividly in his shoulders. The blade of the sword, now pushed back by the entrails and exposed to its tip, was still in the lieutenant's right hand.

It would be difficult to imagine a more heroic sight than that of the lieutenant at this moment, as he mustered his strength and flung back his head. The movement was performed with sudden violence, and the back of his head struck with a sharp crack against the alcove pillar. Reiko had been sitting until now with her face lowered, gazing in fascination at the tide of blood advancing toward her knees, but the sound took her by surprise and she looked up.

The lieutenant's face was not the face of a living man. The eyes were hollow, the skin parched, the once so lustrous cheeks and lips the color of dried mud. The right hand alone was moving. Laboriously gripping the sword, it hovered shakily in the air like the hand of a marionette and strove to direct the point at the base of the lieutenant's throat. Reiko watched her husband make this last, most heartrending, futile exertion. Glistening with blood and grease, the point was thrust at the throat again and again. And each time it missed its aim. The strength to guide it was no longer there. The straying point struck the collar and the collar badges. Although its hooks had been unfastened, the stiff military collar had closed together again and was protecting the throat.

Reiko could bear the sight no longer. She tried to go to her husband's help, but she could not stand. She moved through the blood on her knees, and her white skirts grew deep red. Moving to the rear of her husband, she helped no more than by loosening the collar. The quivering blade at last contacted the naked flesh of the throat. At that moment Reiko's impression was that she herself had propelled her husband forward; but that was not the case. It was a movement planned by the lieutenant himself, his last exertion of strength. Abruptly he threw his body at the blade, and the blade pierced his neck, emerging at the nape. There was a tremendous spurt of blood and the lieutenant lay still, cold blue-tinged steel protruding from his neck at the back.

V

Slowly, her socks slippery with blood, Reiko descended the stairway. The upstairs room was now completely still. 130

Switching on the ground-floor lights, she checked the gas jet and the main gas plug and poured water over the smoldering, half-buried charcoal in the brazier. She stood before the upright mirror in the four-and-a-half mat room and held up her skirts. The bloodstains made it seem as if a bold, vivid pattern was printed across the lower half of her white kimono. When she sat down before the mirror, she was conscious of the dampness and coldness of her husband's blood in the region of her thighs, and she shivered. Then, for a long while, she lingered over her toilet preparations. She applied the rouge generously to her cheeks, and her lips too she painted heavily. This was no longer makeup to please her husband. It was makeup for the world which she would leave behind, and there was a touch of the magnificent and the spectacular in her brushwork. When she rose, the mat before the mirror was wet with blood. Reiko was not concerned about this.

Returning from the toilet, Reiko stood finally on the cement floor of the porchway. When her husband had bolted the door here last night it had been in preparation for death. For a while she stood immersed in the consideration of a simple problem. Should she now leave the bolt drawn? If she were to lock the door, it could be that the neighbors might not notice their suicide for several days. Reiko did not relish the thought of their two corpses putrefying before discovery. After all, it seemed, it would be best to leave it open. . . . She released the bolt, and also drew open the frosted-glass door a fraction. . . . At once a chill wind blew in. There was no sign of anyone in the midnight streets, and stars glittered ice-cold through the trees in the large house opposite.

Leaving the door as it was, Reiko mounted the stairs. She had walked here and there for some time and her socks were no longer slippery. About halfway up, her nostrils were already assailed by a peculiar smell.

The lieutenant was lying on his face in a sea of blood. The point protruding from his neck seemed to have grown even more prominent than before. Reiko walked heedlessly across the blood. Sitting beside the lieutenant's corpse, she stared intently at the face, which lay on one cheek on the mat. The eyes were opened wide, as if the lieutenant's attention had been attracted by something. She raised the head, folding it in her sleeve, wiped the blood from the lips, and bestowed a last kiss.

Then she rose and took from the closet a new white blanket and a waist cord. To prevent any derangement of her skirts, she wrapped the blanket about her waist and bound it there firmly with the cord. 135

Reiko sat herself on a spot about one foot distant from the lieutenant's body. Drawing the dagger from her sash, she examined its dully gleaming blade intently, and held it to her tongue. The taste of the polished steel was slightly sweet.

Reiko did not linger. When she thought how the pain which had previously opened such a gulf between herself and her dying husband was now to become a part of her own experience, she saw before her only the joy of herself entering a realm her husband had already made his own. In her husband's agonized face there had been something inexplicable which she was seeing for the first time. Now she would solve that riddle. Reiko sensed that at last she too would be able to taste the true bitterness and sweetness of that great moral principle in which her husband believed. What had until now been tasted only faintly through her husband's example she was about to savor directly with her own tongue.

Reiko rested the point of the blade against the base of her throat. She thrust hard. The wound was only shallow. Her head blazed, and her hands shook uncontrollably. She gave the blade a strong pull sideways. A warm substance flooded into her mouth, and everything before her eyes reddened, in a vision of spouting blood. She gathered her strength and plunged the point of the blade deep into her throat.

CONNECTIONS TO OTHER SELECTIONS

1. Contrast Reiko's response to her husband's death in this story with Mrs. Mallard's in Chopin's "The Story of an Hour" (p. 10). How do the differences indicate different sensibilities in the culture of each story?

2. Compare and contrast Mishima's description of the couple's suicides with Tim O'Brien's descriptions of a soldier being blown up and a water buffalo being shot in "How to Tell a True War Story" (p. 555). How do these descriptions of violent actions support the theme of each story?

3. How does Reiko's suicide provide meaning to her life in contrast to Mabel's suicide attempt in Lawrence's "The Horse Dealer's Daughter" (p. 543)? How is human passion a central concern in both stories?

BI SHUMIN (CHINA / B. 1952)

Born in Shandong, China, Bi Shumin attended middle school and then served in the army. She is a professional writer whose work focuses on life in the army. Her works include *Kunlun Mountains, A Red Carpet,* and *Flying Northward.*

Broken Transformers   1992

TRANSLATED BY SHI JUNBAO

"Mum, let's go. I don't want a Transformer," said my ten-year-old son.

We were standing in a newly opened department store. As mother of a low-income family I was used to steering my son firmly away from toy counters; but this store had taken me by surprise; its manager had shrewdly filled the entrance hall with brightly colored playthings instead of the usual dull array of cosmetics.

I stood in the doorway, debating whether or not to leave. There had been a sign outside saying the store sold wool, and I desperately needed to knit myself a new hat and scarf. Still, wool could be bought elsewhere.

I gripped my son's hand and drew him towards me intending to make up some excuse to get him out of the store, and thus out of temptation's way. Ten was an age, after all, at which innocence gradually begins to give way to questioning, and I didn't want him to become conscious too early of the power of money and thus of our limited supply. At the same time I hated the thought of his disappointment at not being able to have the toy he so adored. I felt like covering his eyes with my palm!

The last thing I expected him to say was, "Mum, let's leave. I don't want a 5 Transformer." I was at a loss to know how to express my gratitude.

I hated the monstrous cartoon family which had my son glued to the TV set every Saturday and Sunday night; not only did it prevent me watching the news, but it had so captured the imagination of thousands of children that the toy replicas now pouring into the stores were sucking money from parents like locusts devouring crops.

If we hadn't been in the crowded store I would have bent down and kissed his smooth brow, now covered with beads of salty sweet sweat. But it immediately became clear to me that my sense of relief was premature, for his feet were as though rooted to the spot. His neck twisted towards the counter and he stared, through long dark eyelashes, at the colorful range of robots which stared back at him in disdain.

My heart bled as I looked admiringly at his lithe young neck which, like the branch of a willow tree, seemed able to twist back endlessly without incurring discomfort. Was it only a matter of a hat and a scarf?

A perfect example of the trend towards "late marriage and late birth" characteristic of the time, I had now passed the age of forty while my son was only ten. I had been through all the turmoil and confusion, whereas his was still to come. My troubles tended to be physical, like the fact that the first northern winter winds had nearly frozen my head off and, worse, I had discovered I was beginning to lose my hair which was, moreover, turning grey. This was not only thoroughly unattractive, but meant I was even less well insulated than before. I considered myself pretty good with my hands; as well as lathing machine parts I could also knit and sew. For some time now I had been planning to knit myself a really good hat and scarf and had even told my husband about it. He had, as a gesture towards financing the project, stubbed out his cigarette. I knew he wouldn't give up permanently, of that I had been convinced from the very first day I met him, no matter what other money-saving hobbies he might dispense with. We also saved by eating less meat at dinner, concentrating our chopsticks on vegetables and hoping our son wouldn't notice the decline.

Despite the fact that since the boy's birth cold winds tended to cause a 10 painful throbbing in my head, I could still do without a hat; my old square scarf would suffice, though no doubt I would look odd, like a solemn Arab woman or Mother Hen from the children's cartoon series. But so what? As long as my son could get his beloved robot.

I glanced at the Transformers. They were so expensive that the price of a hat and scarf would be enough to cover maybe the leg of one of the larger models.

And what would my husband say? He had always maintained that I spoiled the child and warned me that ours was just an ordinary "blue-collar family" which shouldn't aspire to the same heights of those better-off.

But was it to be the case that no "blue-collar" worker should ever own a Transformer?

I had enough money with me for one of the smallest models available, and knew I could make up a story about the hat and scarf which would satisfy my husband and indicate that I didn't need them.

It was at this point, just as I had made up my mind to buy it, that my son 15 suddenly turned towards the exit, saying resolutely, "Mum, let's go. The paper says Transformers are only foreign kids' cast-offs. They move them into China to get our money."

He tugged my hand with his little damp one and glanced back at the toys as though taking a last look at a corpse. Then he quickened his short legs and made for the door as if fearful the Transformers might otherwise snatch him back.

He sounded like an adult, the logic of his argument certainly exceeded anything I might have come up with and it occurred to me that in comparison with our boy, who was, moreover, a model student at school, my husband and I were selfish.

Spurred by this revelation I strode back to the counter and, without giving a second's thought as to who profited by my action, whether foreigners or Hong Kong Chinese, I impulsively took possession of the smallest Transformer money could buy. Suddenly I no longer cared about the pains I would get in my head and neck. This purchase was a token of appreciation for my son's understanding and an expression of our mutual love.

That evening he skipped dinner in order to play with his robot. He put a black toy pistol into its hand and the creature, with a twist and a turn, obligingly turned into an exquisite streamlined bomber. The thermo-colored American trademark turned from red to blue and back to red in his warm little hands.

"Convertible Transformer fights for justice and freedom with an iron 20 will . . ." he sang sweetly. It was the theme song from the TV series.

Although my husband had grumbled, I felt the purchase had been a wise one. True, Transformers were expensive, but the moments of happiness they gave were priceless. In the event of my son growing up to be an important public figure, I didn't want to have to read in his autobiography: I liked toys when I was little but my family was too poor to afford them, so I could only watch the other children playing with theirs. . . .

Of course he might also simply turn out to be a blue-collar worker; either way I was loath to leave him with any regrets about his childhood. Children are, after all, easy to satisfy: the smallest Transformer intoxicates them.

"Don't neglect your homework now," I cautioned in an unusually serious, perhaps overcompensatory, tone of voice. He earnestly promised not to.

Over the next few days I carried out spot checks on his homework and was satisfied to find that he had lost none of his willpower; he allowed himself to play with his toy only after finishing his work.

Winter finally arrived with a vengeance. 25

My husband prolonged his prohibition on cigarettes, and though I tried to reassure him that my old scarf was perfectly adequate, his response was gloomy. "You should have a pair of warm boots," he said.

I gave him a grateful smile and made a face indicating that it was indeed cold down there.

One evening I suddenly found my son playing with a different Transformer: this one was yellow, and much larger and fiercer than his own.

"What's this?" I asked, almost severely. All the guidebooks on "parenting" warned us not to ignore any new tangents a child went off on.

"Transformer Giant," he answered calmly, as though discussing a close   30 relative.

Thanks to the protracted TV series, I was equipped with basic knowledge of the Transformer family and I knew that the Giant was one of the principal characters.

Be that as it may, its name was not important to me — its owner was. Without softening my voice I demanded to know whose it was. His reply was matter-of-fact. "One of my classmates," he said, without registering my suspicion. "Almost everybody has one and they're all different, so we trade to play."

Although I felt a slight twinge of guilt about my tone of voice, I couldn't guarantee I wouldn't react in the same way in the future. Dishonesty was above all others the thing I feared most in children and I was constantly on the lookout for it.

The kids were clever. They traded like primitive tribes. It was a new phenomenon, and I wasn't sure whether to oppose or support it. "Giant or not," I said to my elated son, "don't let it ruin your school work, and be careful with other people's toys."

He nodded his assent. I could always rely on him to listen.   35

Somebody was tapping at the door.

My son ran over and hospitably pulled it wide open. But the visitor slowly closed it again as if he wished to remain outside. Presently a round head hesitantly pushed its way through the crack. It was my son's classmate, one who seemed to go by the name of Fatty and who regularly dropped by to get my son to help him with his homework. Only this time Fatty hadn't come for help. He neither entered nor retreated but remained hovering on the threshold facing my son and glancing up at me with a miserable expression on his face. Finally he stammered out in embarrassment, "I'm so sorry . . . I broke your toy . . ."

The blood drained from my son's cheeks. I had never seen such an agonized look pass across his face. He took the dismantled toy from Fatty, held it before his eyes and blew on it softly, as though it were a wounded pigeon.

After the initial shock had subsided, my son looked at me to rescue him. For one bitter moment the sacrificed hat and scarf flashed across my mind, but there was nothing we could do except face it. Trying to avoid my son's eye, I said, "It's up to you. It's your toy, what do you think we should do?"

Perhaps inhibited by my presence, he remained silent. I therefore dis-   40 creetly moved into the inner room and listened intently. I could hear Fatty wheezing in the silence and longed to put an end to his misery by running out and saying, "Fatty, you may leave now." But the verdict, whatever it was, had to come from my son.

"How did you smash it?" I heard him ask, with anger in his voice.

"I just . . . then, flop . . ." Fatty must have been gesticulating. An exasperated gurgle appeared to be my son's stifled response.

What was I to do? Maybe I should go out and intervene. Transformers cost money, but magnanimity is something that no amount of money can buy; and although I believed my son had absorbed the moral principles I had instilled in him over the years, I nevertheless recognized that to him a small Transformer was the equivalent of a color TV set or a deluxe camera to an adult. The prolonged silence was agony, for him and for Fatty as well as for me.

Finally he spoke. He seemed to have covered a great deal of mental ground and his voice, though weak, was none the less clear: "Don't worry . . . ."

Fatty grasped the opportunity and fled, as though afraid that my son 45 might otherwise change his mind.

I heaved a long sigh of relief, as if I too had just returned from a long journey. Emerging, I kissed my son's sweaty forehead.

"It's dead," he said as his eyes filled with tears.

"I'll try and glue it together," I said comfortingly, though with little hope of success.

I duly went flat out to fix it, drawing on all my resources of skill and ingenuity. After spending a great deal more time and effort on it than I would have spent knitting a hat, it finally became recognizable again as a toy. But though it looked all right, it was too delicate to touch and it could no longer change shapes.

My son, meanwhile, devoted himself to the Giant. A Transformer should 50 change shape, he said, otherwise it was just a trinket. So saying, he deftly changed the shape of the toy he had in his hand. One has to admire the Americans. Who else would come up with the idea of turning the belly of a fighter into a robot's head and then proceed to create a machine that executes the transition so flawlessly?

A good toy attracts both children and grown-ups, but no sooner had I begun to move closer to watch him play than I heard an ominous crash and saw the toy collapse in pieces.

What had happened? We looked at each other in horror.

Unfortunately, though we could hardly believe it, the truth was all too painfully clear: he had broken the Giant.

For a while my son tried to fix it, but only ended up with more pieces than he had started with. Realizing the situation was hopeless, he gathered the pieces together, wrapped them in a sheet of paper and prepared to leave the house.

"Where are you going?" I asked, still in a state of shock. 55

"To return the toy and apologize," he said, looking calm and prepared.

"Is it Fatty's?" I asked, with a glimmer of hope.

"No." He then mentioned a name.

Hers! My heart plunged, then leapt into my throat.

The only impression I had ever been able to gain of this girl was that she 60 was like a delicate flower and had a very arrogant mother. The family was well heeled — my husband would call them "wealthy" — and it was entirely natural that they should have bought such a large and ferocious-looking toy for their daughter.

"You're going . . . like this?" I stammered.

"Should I take something with me?" he asked, confused.

I looked at his limpid eyes and refrained from further comment.

"OK, mum, I'm off." He disappeared out the door.

"Come home soon," I called after him apprehensively. 65

I knew he wouldn't dawdle, but he didn't return soon, and when he hadn't returned later either my heart began to flutter like fish on a hook.

I should have warned him that people were all different, that he might not be pardoned, even though he himself had forgiven a similar accident. I should have prepared him better for the possibility of an unpleasant scene, otherwise he might cry.

On the other hand things might turn out OK. His classmate might have asked him hospitably to stay a little, while her mother peeled him an orange, which my son would naturally push back politely. He is a lovable boy. They would surely forgive him in the same manner in which we had forgiven little Fatty.

The more I thought about it the more I convinced myself that that could be the only possible outcome. Moreover I congratulated myself now on not having filled his heart with my own cynical suspicions.

But as time passed, no matter how I tried to reassure myself, I grew in-   70
creasingly concerned.

At last he returned, his footstep so light that, deep in thought as I was, I didn't even notice he was there until he was standing right in front of me.

One look at him was enough to convince me that he had undergone a profound inner trauma. I could also tell that he had been crying and that he had already dried his tears in the cold wind so that I wouldn't notice. A child often reveals more when he is hiding something.

I did not have the heart to get him to go into details; it would have been too painful.

"Mum, they want us . . . to compensate . . ." he said finally, as large, cold teardrops rolled down his cheeks and on to my hand.

I now had to deal not only with a broken toy but with a broken heart.   75

"It's only natural," I said, wiping away his tears, "that they'd want to be compensated for their loss."

"Then let me go and find Fatty and ask him to compensate me for mine. All he said was 'I'm sorry.' Next time I go shopping I won't take my money, I'll just say, 'I'm sorry.' Will that do?" he asked, jumping up to leave.

"Don't go!" I pulled him back. He struggled wildly, suddenly seeming to have acquired the strength of a calf.

"Why, mum? Tell me!" he demanded, lifting his head.

I didn't know how to respond. Sometimes principles are all very well and,   80
like beautiful clothes can be very attractive, but they are not the stuff from which clothes are actually made.

I had to give him an answer. It is a cat's responsibility to teach her kitten how to catch mice. I had to provide my son with an explanation, no matter how impractical it might be.

"The words 'I'm sorry' mean you are being courteous. Their value ought not to be counted in terms of money."

He nodded quietly. I probably sounded like one of his teachers, so he forced himself to listen.

"You forgave Fatty when he broke your Transformer," I continued, patiently trying to explain things in terms he would understand. "He was relieved. That was a nice thing to do."

"But, mum, I haven't been forgiven for a similar mistake!" he protested.   85
His sense of shame seemed to override my reasoned arguments.

"Well, son, there are many ways of solving a problem. Problems are like Transformers: they can either be a robot, a plane or a car . . . Understand?"

"Yeah." He nodded reluctantly. I knew he was unconvinced, and just wanted to placate me.

I let go of his hand, exhausted.

He relaxed and stood aside.

The large broken toy was going to involve a hideous amount of money, 90 and though we hadn't yet reached the stage where we needed to go to the pawn shop — which our street didn't have anyway — we were still pretty broke.

Sitting on the bad news, we waited for my husband to come home. My son looked at me pitifully. Was he hoping I would not tell him about the incident at all, or hoping I would do it quickly?

I dreaded the prospect, but knew it had to be done, and despite my inclination to postpone the reckoning I knew it would be better in the long run to get it over and done with immediately.

On hearing the news, my husband managed temporarily to retain his composure.

"Tell me," he said calmly, "how did you come to break the thing?" He couldn't bring himself to give it a name.

"I just twisted it, and 'flop,' it broke . . ." stammered my son, looking at 95 me appealingly for support. I'd seen it happen, certainly, but I couldn't have said how.

But describing how it broke was in any event unimportant. The consequence was that our son would never again be able to play with such a costly toy.

My husband's eyebrows locked and the ferocity of his expression sent my son scurrying behind me for protection. Suddenly he exploded.

"Tell me," he said, his voice rising in a crescendo, "did you break it on purpose or deliberately?"

I frankly couldn't see what the difference was between "on purpose" and "deliberately," but didn't dare interfere.

"I did it . . . on purpose. No, dad, I did it deliberately . . ." Desperately 100 searching for whichever seemed the less incriminating, he lurched from one to the other, shrinking beneath his father's glare.

"You little wretch! A whole month's salary won't pay for this thing, yet you think you can go around lording it like the master of some grand mansion. I'll give you a hiding you'll never forget."

With that he raised his arm, and as it came crashing down I lifted my own to intercept the blow. A blinding pain instantly spread from my side down to my fingers. He was a strong man, a laborer, and it was fortunate I had blocked him.

For a few moments my son was stunned, then he let out a sharp cry, as if it had been he who had been hit.

"You've got a nerve to blubber like that!" shouted my husband, breathing heavily. "That damn thing your mother bought you already cost her her wool hat, and now that! That's our fuel and cabbage for the whole winter gone!" Then he turned to me and added, "It's your fault for spoiling him."

I let him rant. As long as he didn't resort to violence again I could cope. 105 My son had never been beaten before.

That winter, on one particularly freezing day when the sun seemed to be emanating blasts of cold air instead of warmth, I arrived home to find that the stove was barely alight. My son was waiting for me, his face burning red and his eyes glittering like stars reflected in a pool. I was afraid he had a fever.

"Close your eyes, mum," he said. That sweet tone of his voice reassured me that he was not ill.

I closed my eyes quietly. I thought he must have a little surprise for me: a perfect exam paper perhaps, or a toy he might have made out of paper and bottles.

"You can open your eyes now, mum."

I kept my eyes closed, savoring the happy moment that only a mother can 110 experience.

"Quick, mum!" he urged.

I opened my eyes on to what seemed at first like a meadow in springtime. It took me a moment to register that what my son was, in fact, holding in front of me was a bundle of green knitting wool.

"Do you like the color, mum?" he asked, looking at me expectantly.

Green was my favorite.

"Yes, very much! How did you know I like it?" 115

"You must have forgotten. You've always knitted me green clothes ever since I was little. I would be able to pick out the color among a thousand others." He must have wondered how I could even ask such a question.

"Did dad take you there?"

"No, I went by myself," he said proudly.

"Where did you get the money?" I asked in surprise.

He didn't answer, but stared at me motionlessly. 120

He could not have stolen it. The very thought of stealing was anathema to my young son. He must have got the money by recycling used paper or toothpaste tubes, but I hadn't noticed him returning home late with blackened fingers. Well, I'd have to ask him again.

"Tell me, where did you get the money?" I persisted, almost pleading with him to give me a satisfactory answer.

"I asked Fatty for it," he answered clearly.

"You asked who?" I couldn't believe my ears. It was impossible that he could have done something like that. He had always been so obedient.

"Fatty!" he repeated, staring at me resolutely. 125

A loud buzzing sounded in my head. His bold expression seemed to come from a boy I didn't know.

"How did you get it from him?" I asked in a weak voice.

"The way those other people asked us for it," he said dismissively, as though I was being pernickety.

He saw my hand rise and, thinking I was about to stroke his head, moved in closer. But I slapped him. Remembering, in the split second before my arm descended, an article I had read somewhere warning parents never to hit their children on the head. But it was too late. My hand slanted at an angle and landed on his neck.

He didn't flinch, but merely looked at me in astonishment. 130

I had never really hit him before, but now I felt certain that this would not be the last time.

Since then, every time a gust of wind pushes open the front door, I expect to see a little fellow with a round head appear. But Fatty has never been back. He paid for our Transformer and left it with us.

I fixed the big one with glue. Its bold appearance added a sense of wealth to our house.

Now we have two Transformers that do not transform.

My son has never touched them again. 135

CONNECTIONS TO OTHER SELECTIONS

1. Compare the significance of the Transformer in this story with the Barbie doll in Sandra Cisneros's "Barbie-Q" (p. 218).
2. Compare the conflict in "Broken Transformers" and in Charles Johnson's "Exchange Value" (p. 523).
3. Write an essay comparing the characterization of the mothers in "Broken Transformers" and Alice Munro's "Miles City, Montana" (p. 458). Are the mothers more alike than different? Explain. How do cultural differences shed light on the mothers' behavior toward their children?

AN ALBUM OF CONTEMPORARY STORIES

ALISON BAKER (B. 1953)

Born in Pennsylvania, Alison Baker was raised in Indiana and has subsequently lived in Chicago, Maine, and Utah. After graduating from Reed College, she worked in a hospital as a library assistant and earned a master's degree in library science. She now lives and writes in Oregon. Her stories are collected in *How I Came West and Why I Stayed* (1993) and in *Loving Wanda Beaver: Novella and Stories* (1995). "Better Be Ready 'Bout Half Past Eight" originally appeared in the *Atlantic Monthly* and was awarded first prize in the 1994 competition for the O. Henry Awards. Baker describes her fiction writing as "a comforting way of revising both my own past and the apparent present, as well as foretelling the unlikeliest of much-to-be-desired futures."

Better Be Ready 'Bout Half Past Eight   1993

"I'm changing sex," Zach said.

Byron looked up from his lab notebook. "For the better, I hope."

"This is something I've never discussed with you," Zach said, stepping back and leaning against the office door. "I need to. Do you want to get a beer or something?"

"I have to transcribe this data," Byron said. "What do you need to discuss?"

"My sexuality," Zach said. "The way I feel trapped in the wrong body."   5

"Well, I suppose you were right," Byron said.

"Right?" Zach said.

"Not to discuss it with me," Byron said. "It's none of my business, is it?"

"We've been friends a long time," Zach said.

"Have you always felt this way?" Byron said.   10

Zach nodded. "I didn't know it was this I was feeling," he said. "But I've been in therapy for over a year now, and I'm sure."

"You've been seeing Terry about *this?*"

Byron had given Zach the name of Terry Wu, whom he himself had once consulted professionally.

Zach nodded again.

"He's terrific. He knew the first time he met me what I was." 15

"What were you?" Byron said.

"A woman," Zach said.

Had he missed any signs? Byron sat frowning at the computer screen. Then he stood, shoved his hands into his pockets, and stared out the window. He could see the sky and the top of the snow-covered hills. On this floor all the windows started at chin level, so you couldn't see the parking lot or the ground outside; you could see only distances, clouds, and sections of sunrise.

He walked up and down the hall for a while. The surrounding labs buzzed with action, students leaning intently over whirring equipment, technicians laughing over coffee. Secretaries clopped through the hall and said, "Hi, Dr. Glass," when they passed him. He could ignore them, because he had a reputation for being absentminded; he was absorbed in his research, or perhaps in a new poem. He was well known, particularly in scientific circles, for his poetry. He edited the poetry column of a major scientific research journal. He judged many poetry-writing competitions, and he had edited anthologies.

What had he missed? 20

Worrying about it was useless. Zach's sexuality wasn't his concern. "Just as long as it doesn't interfere with work," he would say. "I can't have people's personal lives taking over the lab."

But in fact he didn't believe in the separation of work and home. "If your love life's screwed up, you're probably going to screw up the science," he'd said more than once when he sent a sobbing technician home, or gave a distraught graduate student the name of a counselor. As a result, his workers did sacrifice, to some extent, their personal lives; they came in on weekends or at night to see to an experiment. The dictum, even if artificial, seemed to work.

"Go on home," he imagined himself saying to Zach, patting him on the shoulder. "Come back when it's all over."

But that wouldn't work. For one thing, the fretting wouldn't end. For another thing, Zach wouldn't be Zach when he came back. He would be a woman Byron had never met.

"He's putting you on," Emily said. She was sitting at the table, ostensibly 25 editing a paper on the synthesis of mRNA at the transcriptional level in the Drosophila Per protein, but whenever the spoon Byron held approached Toby's mouth, her own mouth opened in anticipation.

"Nope," Byron said, spooning more applesauce from the jar. "He wanted to tell me before he started wearing makeup."

"If Zach thinks that's the definition of women, he's headed for trouble," Emily said. "I suppose he's shaving his legs and getting silicone implants too."

"Not to mention waxing his bikini line," Byron said.

"Oh, God," Emily said, laughing. "I don't want to hear any more." She handed Byron a washcloth, and Byron carefully wiped applesauce off Toby's chin. "How would you know you were the wrong sex?"

"Women's intuition?" Byron said.   30

"Very attractive," he said the next morning, when Zach walked into the lab wearing eye shadow.

"Don't make fun of me, okay?" Zach said.

Byron felt embarrassed. "I didn't mean anything," he said. "I mean, it's subtle and everything."

Zach looked pleased. "I've been practicing," he said. "You know what? My younger brother wears more makeup than I do. Is this a crazy world or what?"

"Yeah," Byron said. He'd met Zach's brother, whose makeup was usually 35 black. "Are you doing this gradually? Or are you sort of going cold turkey? I mean, will you come in in nylons and spike heels some morning?"

"Babe," Zach said, "I've been getting hormones for six months. Don't you notice anything different?"

He put his hands on his hips and turned slowly around, and Byron saw discernible breasts pushing up the cloth of Zach's rugby shirt. Byron felt a little faint, but he managed to say, "You're wearing a bra."

Zach went over to look in the mirror behind the door. He stood on tiptoe, staring intently at his breasts for a moment, and then, as he took his lab coat off the hook, he said, "God, I'm starting to feel good."

"You are?" was all Byron could manage. He was wondering how to say, without hurting Zach's new feelings, *Don't call me babe.*

All day he tried not to look at Zach's breasts, but there they were, right in 40 front of him, as Zach bent over the bench, or peered into the microscope, or leaned back with his hands behind his neck, staring at the ceiling, thinking.

"I'm heading out," Byron said to Sarah in midafternoon.

"Are you okay?" she said, looking up from the bench. "You look a little peaked."

"I'm fine," Byron said. "I'll be back in the morning."

But once out in the parking lot, sitting in his car, he could think of no place he wanted to go. He hung on to the steering wheel and stared at the Mercedes in front of him, which had a Utah license plate that read IMAQT. A woman, of course.

Well, it's not *my* life, he thought. Nothing has changed for me.   45

"I haven't had this much trouble with breasts since I was sixteen," he said to Emily as they sat at the kitchen table watching the sunset.

"How big are they?" Emily said.

"Jesus, I don't know," Byron said.

"Bigger than mine?" she said.

Byron looked at Emily's breasts, which were bigger since she'd had Toby. 50 "No," he said. "But I think they've just started."

"You mean he'll keep taking hormones till they're the size he wants?" Emily said. "I should do that."

"You know," Byron said, "what I don't understand is why it bothers me so much. You'd think he's doing it to spite me."

"Going to meetings will be more expensive," she said.

"What do you mean?" Byron said.

"Honey," Emily said, "if Zach's a woman, you won't be sharing a room. 55 Will you?"

"Oh," Byron said. "Do you think it will make that much difference?"

"You're already obsessed with his breasts," Emily said. "Wait till he's fully equipped."

Byron leaned his head on his hand. He hadn't even *thought* about the surgical procedure.

"I think you're letting this come between us," Zach said the next day.

"What?" Byron said. 60

"We've been friends a long time. I don't want to lose that."

"Zach," Byron said, "I don't see how things can stay the same."

"But I'm still the same person," Zach said.

Byron was not at all sure of that. "Well, how's it going?" he finally said.

Zach seemed pleased to be asked. He sat down on the desk and folded his 65 arms. "Really well," he said. "The surgeon says the physiological changes are right on schedule. I'm scheduled for surgery starting next month."

"Starting?" Byron said.

"I'm going to have a series of operations," Zach said. "Over several months. Cosmetic surgery for the most part."

"Zach," Byron said, "maybe it's none of my business, but don't you feel —" He cast about for the right way to say it. "Won't the operations make you feel, uh, mutilated?"

Zach shook his head. "That's what it's all about," he said. "They won't. To tell you the truth, in the past year or two I've come to feel as if my penis is an alien growth on my body. It's my *enemy*, Byron. This surgery's going to liberate me."

Byron crossed his legs. "I don't think I can relate to that," he said. 70

"I know," Zach said. "My support group says nobody really understands."

"Your support group?" Byron said.

"Women who've had the operation," Zach said, "or are in the process. We meet every week."

"How many are there?"

"More than you'd think," Zach said. 75

"So," Byron said. "Are you — I mean, should I call you 'she' now?"

Zach grinned. "I've been calling myself 'she' for a while. But so far nobody outside my group has."

"Well," Byron said. He tried to look at Zach and smile, but he couldn't do both at once. He smiled first, and then looked. "I'll work on it," he said. "But it's not exactly easy for me either, you know."

"I know," Zach said. "I really appreciate your trying to understand." He stood up. "Back to work," he said. "Oh." He turned around with his hand on the doorknob. "I'm changing my name, too. As of next month I'll be Zoe."

"Zoe," Byron said. 80

"It means 'life,'" Zach said. "Mine is finally beginning."

"It means 'life,'" Byron said mincingly to Toby as he pulled the soggy diaper out from under him. "'Life,' for Christ's sake."

Toby smiled.

"What's he been for thirty-eight years — dead?" Byron said. He dried Toby and sprinkled him with powder, smoothing it into the soft creases. As he lifted Toby's feet to slide a clean diaper underneath him, a stream of pee arced gracefully into the air and hit Byron in the chest, leaving a trail of droplets across Toby's powdered thighs.

"Oh, geez," Byron said. "Couldn't you wait ten seconds?" He reached for 85 the washcloth and wiped the baby off. Then he wiggled the little penis between his thumb and forefinger. "You know what you are, don't you?" he said, leaning over and peering into Toby's face. "A little man. No question about that."

Toby laughed.

After he'd put Toby into the crib, Byron went into the bathroom, pulling his T-shirt off. He caught sight of himself in the mirror and stood still. With the neckband of the shirt stuck on his head, framing his face, the shirt hung from his head like a wig of green hair.

He took his glasses off to blur the details and moved close to the mirror, looking at the line of his jaw. Was his jaw strong? Some women who had what were called "strong features" were quite attractive. Byron's mother used to say that Emily was built like a football player, but Byron had always thought she was sexy.

He put his glasses on and stepped back, bending his knees so that only his shoulders showed in the glass. With long hair around his face, and a few hormones to change his shape a little, he'd make a terrific woman.

He opened the medicine cabinet and took out one of Emily's lipsticks. He 90 leaned forward and spread it on his mouth, and as he pressed his lips together, a woman's face materialized in the mirror. Byron's heart came to a standstill.

It was his mother.

"It was the weirdest thing," he said. "I never looked like her before. Never."

"You never cross-dressed before," Zach said, continuing to stare at the computer screen. "What's going on with this data?"

"Of course I never cross-dressed," Byron said. "I still don't cross-dress. I just happened to look in the mirror when my shirt was on my head."

Zach looked up at him and grinned. "And there she was," he said. "You 95 would be amazed what we find out about ourselves when we come to terms with our sexuality."

"Oh, for God's sake," Byron said. "I was taking my shirt off. I wasn't coming to terms with anything."

"That's fairly obvious," Zach said, tapping at the keyboard.

"Jesus!" Byron said. "Do those hormones come complete with bitchiness? Or is your period starting?"

Zach stared at him. "I can't believe you said that," he said.

Byron couldn't believe he'd said it either, but he went on. "Everything's 100 sexuality with you these days," he said crossly. "I'm trying to tell you about my mother and you tell me it's my goddamn sexuality."

Zach stood up and stepped away from the desk. "Look," he said, folding his arms, "it's called the Tiresias° syndrome. You're jealous because I understand both sexes. By cross-dressing — whether you go around in Emily's underwear or just pretend you've got a wig on — you're trying to identify with me."

Tiresias: A blind prophet from Greek legend.

For a long moment Byron was unable to move. "What?" he finally said.

"You can't handle talking about the things that really matter, can you?" Zach said. "As soon as we get close to personal feelings, you back off."

"Feelings," Byron said.

"You're a typical man when it comes to emotions," Zach said.   105

"And you're a typical woman," Byron said.

Zach shook his head. "You are in trouble, boy."

"*I'm* in trouble?" Byron said. "Looks to me like you're the one with the problem."

"That's the difference between us," Zach said. "I'm taking steps to correct my problem. You won't even admit yours."

"My problem is you," Byron said. "You are a fucking prick."   110

"Not for long," Zach said.

"Once a prick, always a prick," Byron shouted.

After Zach walked out the door, Byron sat down at his desk and stared at the data Zach had pulled up on the screen, but its sense eluded him. Finally he spun his chair around and put his feet up on the bookcase behind him, and reached for a legal pad.

He always wrote his poetry on long yellow legal pads. He had once tried to jot down some poetic thoughts on the computer, but they had slipped out of his poem and insinuated themselves into a new idea for a research project, which in fact developed into a grant proposal that was later funded. The experience had scared him.

He stared up at the slice of sky that was visible from where he sat, and held   115 the legal pad on his lap for more than an hour, during which time he wrote down thirteen words. When Sarah stuck her head into the office and said, "See you tomorrow," he put the pad down and left work for the day.

Driving home, he thought about his dead mother, Melba Glass. She had never liked Emily, but once Byron was married, his mother stopped saying snide things about her. She asked them instead. "Honey," she'd say, "isn't Emily a little *strident?*"

"What do you mean, 'strident'?" Byron would snarl, and she would say she'd meant nothing at all, really, young women were just *different* these days. Byron would narrow his eyes at her, but later, when he'd driven his mother to the train station and waved her off, the idea would come back to him. Emily *was* vociferous in her opinions. And not particularly tolerant of her mother-in-law's old-fashioned tendencies.

"Why doesn't your mother *drive?*" she'd say.

"Why should she?" he'd say. "She never needed to."

"She needs to now, doesn't she?" Emily would say.   120

"Why should she?" Byron would repeat, and for a couple of days he would react to everything Emily said as if she were being highly unreasonable, and *strident.*

What would Emily say if he told her that his dead mother had appeared to him? Worse, that he had appeared to himself as his dead mother?

Emily would lean over Toby's crib in the dark. "I'll be Don Ameche in a taxi, honey," she'd sing. "Better be ready 'bout half past eight."

"How are you? Three of you now. Ha!" Terry Wu said.

"Three of me?" Byron said.   125

"You have a little baby?" Terry said.

"Oh! Toby! Terrific! And Emily. I see. Sure, we're fine. Really. Everything's terrific."

A concerned look seized Terry Wu's face. "Do you protest too much?" he said, and he leaned forward, pressing his fingertips together.

"Protest?" Byron said. "That's not why I'm here."

"Maybe no, maybe yes," Terry said, but he leaned back again.   130

"No, it's my, uh, colleague. You know, Zach."

"Ah," Terry said.

"I seem obsessed," Byron said weakly.

"You are obsessed with your colleague?"

"With his sex," Byron said.   135

"*His* sex?" Terry said.

Byron felt himself blushing. "I can't get used to the idea that he's a woman."

Terry nodded again. "Each one is a mystery."

"No, it's just—why didn't I know?"

"Did you know your wife was pregnant when she conceived?"   140

"What does that have to do with it?" Byron said.

"Well," Terry said, "you were there when it happened, in fact you did the deed, and yet you didn't know about it."

"Terry, I think that's something else."

Terry shrugged. "Are you in love with your colleague?"

"Of course not." He was becoming angry. "What are you getting at?"   145

"I am trying to elicit a coherent statement from you," Terry said. "So far all you have managed to tell me is that you are obsessed with your colleague and are not in love with her. I am having trouble following your flight of ideas."

"Look." Byron stared down at his feet. "Someone whom I have known for more than twenty years has overnight turned into a woman. It's shaken my understanding of reality. I can no longer trust what I see before my eyes."

"Yet you call yourself a scientist," Terry said thoughtfully. "It is simply a matter of surgery and hormonal therapy, isn't it? Changing one form into another by a well-documented protocol?"

Byron stared at him. "That's not what I mean," he said.

Terry clasped his hands together happily. "Yet a magical process is in-   150
volved as well! An invisible and powerful force! Something that is beyond our understanding! But"—he put his hands on his desk and stared into Byron's eyes—"even your poetic license will not allow you to accept it?"

"My poetic license?" Byron said.

"Are man and woman so different, so unrelated, that no transformation is possible? It's this Western culture," Terry said in disgust. "In my country, people exchange sexes every day."

Byron wondered if he had understood Terry correctly.

"Suppose your little baby comes to you in twenty years and says, 'Daddy, I am now Chinese.' Will you disown the child, after twenty years of paternity? No! He will still be the son you love."

"Chinese?" Byron said.   155

"I fear our time is up," Terry said. He stood up and held his hand out. Byron stood too, and shook it. "Good to see you again. Would you like to resume these discussions on a regular basis? I can see you at this time every week."

"I don't think so," Byron said. "I just wanted this one consultation."

"Glad to be of service," Terry said. "No charge, no charge. Professional courtesy. Someday I may need an experiment!" He chuckled. "Or a poem."

"A shower?" Byron said.

"Isn't it a kick?" Emily said. "Gifts like garter belts and strawberry douches." 160

"That's sick," he said.

"Oh, come on, honey. His men friends are invited too." She put down the screwdriver she'd been using to put together Toby's Baby Bouncer and leaned over to kiss Byron's knee. "It'll be fun."

"Why don't we just play red rover?" Byron said. "All the girls can stand on one side and yell, 'Let Zach come on over.'"

"You act as if you've lost your best friend," Emily said.

"I *am* losing him. I've known him for twenty years and suddenly I find out 165 he's the opposite of what I thought he was."

"Ah," Emily said, and she sat back against the sofa. "Here we go. Men and women are the exact opposite."

"Don't you start," he said. "I don't need an attack on the home front."

"I'm supposed to comfort you, I suppose," Emily said. "Sympathize with you because your good buddy's going over to the enemy."

"Well?" Byron said. "Aren't you secretly glad? Having a celebration? Letting him in on all your girlish secrets?"

Emily shook her head. "We're talking about a human being who has suf- 170 fered for forty years, and you're jealous because we're giving him some lacy underpants? You're welcome to some of mine, if that's what you want." She smiled at him.

"Suffered?" Byron said. "The dire fate of living in a male body? A fate worse than death, clearly."

"Why are you attacking *me?*" Emily said.

"I'm not attacking you," he said. "I'm just upset." He scooted closer to her and put his arms around her, laying his head against her breasts. "What if I lost you, too?"

"Sweetheart," Emily said, "you're stuck with me for the duration."

"I hope so," Byron said. He turned his head and pressed his face against 175 her. "I certainly hope so." His voice, caught in her cleavage, sounded very far away.

"Nearly twenty years ago," Byron said softly, holding Toby in his arms as he rocked in the dark, "when Daddy and Uncle Zach were very young—"

Toby, who was gazing at his eyes as he spoke, flung out a fist.

"He was still Uncle Zach at the time," Byron said. He tucked the fist into his armpit. "Anyway, we used to ride out to the quarries outside Bloomington to go swimming. You've never been swimming, but it's a lot like bobbing around in Mummy's uterus."

Toby's eyes closed.

"We used to ride our bikes out there after we'd finished our lab work," 180 Byron said. "Riding a bike in the summertime in southern Indiana is a lot like swimming too. The air is so full of humidity you can hardly push the sweat out your pores.

"So we would ride out there in the late afternoon, and hide our bikes in the trees, and go out to our favorite jumping-off place," Byron said. "And

Daddy and Uncle Zach would take off all their clothes, and get a running start, and jump right off the edge of the cliff into space!"

Toby made a sound.

"Yes, the final frontier," Byron said. "And we would hit the water at the same instant, and sink nearly to the bottom of the bottomless pit, and bob up without any breath. It was so cold."

He frowned. What kind of story was this to tell his son? Toby was asleep now, but in a few years he'd complain. He'd want plot, and character development.

"That was poetry, son," Byron whispered. He stood up and laid the sleep- 185 ing baby on his stomach in the crib. Tomorrow morning Emily would put Toby in his new Baby Bouncer, and Toby Glass would begin to move through the world on his own.

"What are you giving her?" Sarah said.

"Who?" Byron said, looking up from his calculations.

"Zoe," Sarah said. "We're giving her silk underwear from Frederick's of Hollywood. Do you know her bra size?"

"Sarah," Byron said, pushing his chair back and crossing his arms, "why on earth would I know Zach's bra size?"

"Oooh," Sarah said. "Touchy, aren't we? You *are* friends." She stood there 190 watching him as if, Byron thought, she was daring him to deny it.

"There are some things you just don't discuss in the locker room," he said.

"Oh," Sarah said. "Well, what are you getting her?"

"I haven't thought about it," Byron said.

"Don't you think you *ought* to think about it?"

It was his mother's voice, and for a moment Byron thought his mother 195 had spoken, there in his office. It was just what she would have said. She would look at him over her glasses, a long, questioning look. "Why not something personal? Intimate? You two have known each other a long time."

"Mom, you don't get something intimate for another guy," he would say.

"Oh, Byron, Byron. You should be more flexible, dear. You sound like your father." Every time she had said it she meant it as a reproach, but Byron was always rather pleased.

He wished sadly that he *could* talk to his mother. She never even knew that he had a son of his own. He looked at the picture of Toby on the desk and thought, she would be disappointed to see how much he looks like Emily's father.

He pictured her sitting in the chair beside his desk, her legs crossed. She had had very nice legs. She always insisted on buying expensive stockings at Dellekamps'. "When I worked at Du Pont," she told him more than once, holding out her foot and gazing at her delicately pointed toes, "they gave us all the stockings we wanted, but they were nylon."

"Mom," Byron said aloud, "I don't want to give him anything." 200

And as if he had disappointed her again, he saw her sadly pick up her purse from the floor and stand up.

"Just let me tell you this, Byron," she said. "If you don't support Zoe at this time in her life, you'll regret it forever."

She stepped toward him, shaking her finger at him.

"Forever, Byron."

He sighed, and looked at the legal pad lying in wait on the desk. His mother 205
had once told him she used to write poetry, but he had never read any of it.

"I wonder what happened to all my mother's poems," Byron said.

Emily looked up from the paper she was reading and stared at him
thoughtfully, chewing on the end of her red pencil. "It wasn't very *good* poetry,"
she said.

"How do you know?" he said.

She frowned. "Byron, sometimes I think you live in a cocoon."

"You read it?" Byron said in amazement. 210

"Sure," she said. "You know, little poems about love, flowers, the moon."
She shook her head, looking at the paper in her lap. "This guy should try poetry," she said.

"Why didn't she let me read it?" Byron said. He glanced at the television
screen, where a woman was talking about teenage reproductive strategies in
abusive households. "Em. What happened to it?"

"She threw it away," Emily said. "She thought it was too embarrassing to
keep."

"Why did she talk to *you* about it?" Byron said.

"We had to talk about something," Emily said. 215

"Maybe your mother is right," Byron said. "Maybe I have no idea what's
going on in the world." He peered into the rearview mirror at Toby, who was
snoring softly in his car seat and paying no attention.

Byron had thought in the beginning that being a scientist would increase
his understanding of the world, and the world's understanding of itself. But
instead, as his work grew more specialized over the years and his expertise became narrower, his brain seemed to be purging its data banks of extraneous information and shutting down, one after another, his receptors for external
stimuli. He had been so caught up in chronicling the minuscule changes taking place in the gels and tubes of his laboratory that the universe had changed
its very nature without his even noticing. The world had a new arrangement
that everyone else seemed to understand very well; even his poetry had simply
served to keep him self-absorbed, oblivious of what must be reality.

Actually, he rather liked the idea of living in a cocoon while the world became a wilder and more exotic place. Sirens wailed, cars throbbing with bass
notes roared past him with mere children at the wheel, dead women appeared
in mirrors, and men changed into women; but Byron and Toby Glass putted
across town safe and snug inside a cocoon.

"What do *I* know?" Byron thought. "What *do* I know?"

"Can I help you?" said a heavily scented woman with beige hair. Her lips 220
were a carnivorous shade of red, and her eyelids were a remarkable magenta.

"I'm looking for a gift," Byron said.

"For Baby's mother?" the woman said.

"Who?" Byron said.

"Baby's mother," she said, and with a long scarlet fingernail she poked at
the Snugli where Toby Glass was sleeping peacefully against Byron's stomach.

"Oh," Byron said. "No. This is for a shower." 225

"Oh, I love showers!" the woman said. "What kind?"

"Sort of a coming-out shower."

"We don't see many of those," she said. She turned to survey her wares. "Are you close to the young lady?"

"I used to be," Byron said. "But she's changed."

"*Plus ça change,*" the woman said. "Something to remember you by. Some-   230
thing in leather?"

"Well, I don't know," Byron said, nervously stroking the warm curve of Toby's back. "I thought maybe stockings?"   •

The woman frowned. "You mean like pantyhose?"

"I guess not," he said.

"I know." The woman tapped Byron's lower lip with the red fingernail. "Follow me." She led him to the back of the store and leaned down to pull open a drawer. "For our discerning customers. A Merry Widow." She held up a lacy black item covered with ribbons and zippers.

"Wow," Byron said. "I didn't know they still made those."   235

"They are *hot,*" the saleswoman said. She held it up against her body. "Imagine your friend in this!"

"I can't," Byron said.

"Do you know her bra size?" the woman asked.

"I'm not sure it's final yet," Byron said.

"Oh," the woman said. "Well. Maybe some perfume." Byron followed   240
her back to the front of the store, where she waved her hand grandly at a locked glass cabinet. "These are very fine perfumes, from the perfume capitals of the world. Paris, Hong Kong, Aspen. This one is very popular — La Différence."

"That's good," Byron said. "I'll take some of that."

"Oh, excellent choice!" The woman patted his cheek before she reached into her cleavage and drew out a golden key to unlock the perfume cabinet.

"While Ginny rings that up, would you like to try on some of our makeup?" said another salesperson.

"No, thanks," Byron said.

The woman pouted at him. "You *should,*" she said. "Lots of men wear it.   245
Girls go crazy for it." She patted a stool in front of the counter. "Sit down."

Byron sat, and she removed his glasses. "You'll look *terrific,*" she said. She leaned toward him, her lips parted, and gently massaged his eyelid with a colorful finger. "'Scuse me while I kiss the sky," she sang softly, stroking the other one. Then she drew on his eyelid with a long black instrument. "This is Creem-So-Soft," she told him. "It is *so* easy to put on." She drew it across the other eyelid, and finally she brushed his eyelashes with a little brush and stood back. "There," she said. "You are a *killer.*"

Toby began to gasp into Byron's shirt. The makeup woman swooped down. "Oooh," she said. "Little booper's making hungry noises." She lifted her eyes to Byron. "Bet I can stall him."

"You can?" Byron said.

"Babies *love* this," she said. She maneuvered Toby out of the Snugli and sat him down facing her on Byron's lap. She began to sketch on his face with the Creem-So-Soft while Toby stared silently at her nose. "There!" She picked Toby up and held him for Byron to examine.

Toby beamed and waved his limbs. He was adorned with a black mous-   250
tache and a pointy black goatee.

"Oh, how darling," Ginny said, coming back from the cash register. "Will this be cash or charge?"

Byron looked at the bill she handed him. "Charge," he said. "I thought this store went out of business a long time ago."

"Lots of people say that," Ginny said.

"What have you done to the baby?" Emily said when Byron walked in the door.

"Babies like this," Byron said. "It's a preview of what he'll look like in 255 twenty years."

"He's going to be a beatnik?" Emily said. She took Toby from Byron's arms. "Don't you think you're rushing things a little?"

Byron sighed. "They grow up so fast," he said. He kissed the top of Toby's head, and then kissed Emily. "How do you like the new me?"

Emily looked at him. "Did you get your hair cut?" she said.

"Em, I'm wearing makeup," Byron said.

"Oh," she said. "So you are." She held Toby up and sniffed at his bottom. 260 "Daddy didn't change your dipes," she said, and she carried him off to his room.

Byron went into the bathroom to look at himself. His eyelids were a very bright purple. He picked up Emily's Barn Red lipstick and carefully covered his lips with it. Then he took off his glasses.

"You know who you look like?" Emily said, appearing beside him in the mirror. "Your mother. Honest to God. If you had one of those curly little perms, you could pass for your own mother." She peered into the mirror, stretching her upper lip with her forefinger. "Do you think I should shave my moustache?"

"No," Byron said. "It's sexy." He slid his hands under her arms and over her breasts. "Let's go to bed."

"No, thanks," Emily said. She picked up her Creem-So-Soft and started to outline her eyes. "I have no desire to sleep with your mother."

"You never did like my mother," Byron said. 265

"Not a lot," Emily said.

"I think I'll go over to the lab," Byron said. He kissed her cheek, leaving a large red lip print.

"Hold still," Emily said. She wet a washcloth, and as she scrubbed his lips he had a sudden vision of his mother scrubbing at grape juice the same way thirty-five years ago. "There. Now you look like my husband again."

He looked in the mirror. His stinging lips were still pinker than normal. "Is wearing makeup always so painful?"

"Always," she said. "We do it for love." 270

Byron liked weekends at the lab. He liked weekdays, too, when students and technicians wandered in and out of one another's labs borrowing chemicals, and all the world seemed engaged in analyzing the structures and chemical interactions of various tissues. But weekends, when the offices were empty and the halls were quiet, and only the odd student padded back and forth from the bathroom, had a cozy, private feeling. Byron could think better in the silence, and he felt close to other scientists, who had given up time in the outside world to bend lovingly over their benches and peer into microscopes, hoping to add to the world's slim store of truth. Both the lab work he did and the poetry he wrote on weekends seemed to spring from a deeper level: a place of intuition and hope that was inaccessible when he was distracted by bustle. On weekends he caught glimpses of the world he hoped to find, where poetry and science were one, and could explain the meaning of life.

"The meaning of life," he said aloud, and wrote it down on his legal pad. Then he turned and typed it on the keyboard, and it appeared in amber letters on the screen in front of him. He smiled and pushed back in his chair, and put his feet on the desk. Poem or experiment? Either one!

He felt that he was on the threshold of an important discovery.

"Why are you doing this?"

Byron opened his eyes. It was Zoe, leaning against the doorjamb. It was   275
definitely and absolutely Zoe; she could no longer be mistaken for a man. He stared at her; what *was* it? The hair, the clothes, the jaw, the way the arms were folded: all were utterly familiar. What had happened?

"The makeup," Zoe said. She shook her head. "You're trying to be something you're not."

He had forgotten about the purple eye shadow and the mascara, but he said, "How do you know what I'm not?"

"It's just that you're so conservative," Zoe said.

"No," he said. "I'm really quite wild. I'm just handicapped by my many fears."

"You?" Zoe said.   280

He nodded. "But you're wild through and through."

Zoe shook her head. "I'm conservative at the core. That's always been my major problem." She gazed out the window at the white hills. "You know the only thing I regret? I'll never have any children now."

"You could adopt."

She shook her head. "They won't have my genes."

"You never really know your children anyway," Byron said.   285

Zoe sighed. "Tell me honestly. Did Emily teach you how to put that eyeliner on?"

Byron smiled. "No," he said. "In fact she learned from me."

Zoe narrowed her eyes and stared at him for a moment, and then sat down on a stool. "I'm thinking of going to law school."

"Are you serious?" he said. "You'd leave the lab?"

"Sure. Patents is the way to go."   290

"You'd leave me?"

Zoe reached over and seized the tablet. "Poetry, poetry, poetry," she said. "Always with you it's the poetry. Anyone would think you're too distracted to work."

"You think any of this is easy?" Byron said.

"None of it," she said, and they sat together for a while without talking. "Are you coming to my shower?"

"Aren't showers supposed to be a surprise?" Byron said.   295

Zoe shrugged. "I hate surprises. I told Sarah she could give me a shower only if she invited men, too."

"I got you a gift." Byron was surprised to feel suddenly shy. "But is there anything you'd really like?"

"Will you come see me in the hospital?"

Byron nodded.

Zoe smiled. "Actually, you look good in makeup," she said. "It redefines 300 your features. You look stronger."

"It's the same old me, though," Byron said. "I'm not any stronger than before."

"I really am thinking of law school," Zoe said. "I need to change my life."

"Changing your sex isn't enough?"

"No. That's who I've been all along."

"Oh," Byron said, and all at once he felt very sad, and exhausted. He put 305 his feet up on the desk, and they sat there in silence, gazing at the part of the world they could see through the window.

After a while he told Zoe about Toby's trip to Dellekamps'. "And then," he said, "I'm sitting on a bench in the mall giving him his bottle, and I look up and these two old ladies are staring at him. 'That is dis*gust*ing,' one of them says. And then the other one gasps and grabs her arm and points at me. And they both back away looking horrified."

Zoe began to laugh.

"And then a man and a little girl walk by, and the little girl says, 'Daddy, is that a homeless person?' And the father says, 'No, dear, that's a man with problems.'"

"Oh," Zoe gasped, holding her ribs.

Byron wiped the tears from his own cheeks, and when he looked at his 310 hand, he saw that it was smeared with mascara. "I had no idea," he said, "no idea why these people were saying these things. I'd forgotten about my makeup. And Toby just looked normal to me."

"Stop," Zoe said, bending over and clutching her stomach.

"And finally a man comes up to me with his hands on his hips and says, 'You ought to be ashamed.'"

"I'm dying," Zoe croaked. "I can't breathe. Oh." She jumped from the stool and ran through the door. "I have to pee."

"You," Byron called after her, "should be ashamed." He listened to the squeegeeing of her sneakers as she ran down the empty hall, and to the familiar creak of the hinges as she pushed open the door to the men's room.

"Glad you could make it, glad you could make it," Terry Wu said, shaking 315 Byron's hand vigorously.

"Did you doubt that I would?" Byron said.

"You're a busy man," Terry said. "So often the cells can't wait." He leaned forward and whispered, "I am giving her a vibrator." Aloud, he said, "The muscles of the calves ache when one first wears high heels."

"That is so true," Emily said. She smiled at Terry Wu and pulled Byron away. "That guy gives me the creeps," she said.

"Honey, you're being xenophobic," Byron said. "Things are different in his country."

They pushed their way through the crowd, Byron cupping one hand pro- 320 tectively around Toby's head to keep him from being squashed in his Snugli.

"There you are!" Sarah appeared in front of them. "Isn't the turnout great?" She waved her arm at the crowd.

Emily hugged her. "Did you get it?" she said.

Sarah nodded. "I never spent that much on a bra in my life."

"How did you know what size to get?" Byron asked.

"I asked her," Sarah said. She led them over to where Zoe stood beside a 325 gift-covered table. "Here are the Glasses!"

"I'm so glad you could come," Zoe said. She kissed Emily on the cheek and prodded Toby's bottom with a glistening red-tipped forefinger. "How's my little beatnik godbaby?"

"Zoe, you look gorgeous," Emily said. "Really. You look so — you."

"Next I'm going to have electrolysis on my facial hair," Zoe said.

"You look pretty good as you are," Byron said. He wondered when the time would come that Zoe would kiss *his* cheek. "I bought you some perfume, but I ended up giving it to Emily."

"Thank goodness," Zoe said. "I'm allergic to everything but La Différence, 330 anyway."

"One of these days," Byron said, "I'll write you a poem."

"He's never done that for me." Emily waved her hand at the table in front of them. "Look at all this loot."

They stared at the pile of presents. "I can't wait to open them," Zoe said. "I've always wanted a shower."

"Isn't it wonderful to get what you always wanted?" Byron put his arm through hers and squeezed it, and he could feel her breast against his triceps as she squeezed back, her muscles hardening briefly against his own.

He felt a rush of pleasure. On his left Emily reached for a bacon-wrapped 335 chicken liver; on his right his oldest friend in the world gently disengaged her arm from his to touch the hands of the dozens of people who had come to wish her well; and from his shoulders, like a newly discovered organ of delight, hung the little bag full of Toby Glass.

Toby Glass, who could grow up to be anything!

The musicians in the string quartet hired for the occasion began to tune their instruments, leaning toward each other, listening, nodding gravely. The cellist moved her stool a little closer to the violinist; the violinist held her instrument away from her neck as she shook back her long red hair, and then replaced it firmly under her chin. Suddenly, as if spontaneously, each player lifted her bow and held it poised in the air for a long moment, until at some prearranged and invisible signal they plunged their bows toward the strings of their various instruments and began to play.

CONNECTIONS TO OTHER SELECTIONS

1. Compare the opening line of this story with several others in this anthology. Discuss how their respective writers immediately engage their readers' interest.

2. Discuss how the endings of Baker's story and Andre Dubus's "Killings" (p. 81) affect your understanding of and emotional response to the events in each story.

3. "You would be amazed what we find out about ourselves when we come to terms with our sexuality" (para. 95). Reflect on this observation made by Zach/Zoe in "Better Be Ready 'Bout Half Past Eight," and write a comparative analysis of Baker's story and David Henry Hwang's play *M. Butterfly* (p. 1675).

RICHARD FORD (B. 1944)

Born in Jackson, Mississippi, Richard Ford grew up in Arkansas and was educated at Michigan State University, the University of California at Irvine, and Washington University Law School. He has won awards from the Guggeheim Foundation and the National Endowment for the Arts. In addition to a collection of short stories, *Rock Springs* (1987), he has published five novels — *A Piece of My Heart* (1976), *The Ultimate Good Luck* (1981), *The Sports Writer* (1986), *Wildlife* (1990), and *Independence Day* (1995), for which he won the Pulitzer Prize — and three novellas in *Women with Men* (1997).

Bascombe, in Realty   *1993*

In Haddam, summer floats over tree-softened streets like a sweet lotion balm from a careless, languorous god, and the world falls in tune with its own mysterious anthems.

Outside on peaceful Jefferson Street I hear the footfalls of a jogger slipping down the hill toward Taft Lane and the Choir College to run a ways in the damp grass. I hear a car door close across the street and the soft voice of Skip McPherson, returning from his summer hockey league in East Windsor. A street away somone begins to bounce a driveway ball: squeak . . . breathing . . . a coughing laugh. And far out on the main line the breeze is right to hear the Amtrak hurtle past for Philly — the Merchants Special.

Elsewhere, the morning marriage-enrichment class has let out at the high school, its members sleepy-eyed and dazed, bound for bed again. In our Negro trace, men sit on stoops, pant legs rolled above their sock tops, sipping cool coffee in the growing, easeful heat. And along on the breeze, a sea-salt smell floats from miles and miles, mingling shadowy rhododendron aromas with the last of the summer's stalwart azaleas, while the varsity band begins its drills, two a day, on the cropped gridiron, revving up for the midsummer classic: "Boom-ta-ta, boom-ta-ta, boom-boom-boom. Haddam! Haddam! Up 'nnnnn at-'em! Ba-boom."

Though all is not exactly kosher here, in spite of a good beginning (when is anything *exactly* kosher?). I, myself, was mugged a street over, in late May, legging it back from the realty office on Carnegie Street just before dark, a list of facts and figures in my head. Three young boys, one of whom I might've seen before but couldn't name, came careening down the sidewalk on minibikes and conked me in the head with a Pepsi bottle, then rode off howling. Later, the Zumbros' house, two doors down, was burgled twice in the same week ("they" missed something the first time and came back to get it). And then, to all our dismay, a realtor from our office, Clair Devane, our one black agent, was murdered in a condo she was showing in the country lanes out beyond Penn's Neck: roped and tied, raped and stabbed. No good clues left, only a pink WHILE YOU WERE OUT left lying on the floor, saying, in her own hand, "Luther Family. Just started looking. Mid-2's or lower. 3 P.M. Get key. Dinner with Eddie." Eddie is her boyfriend.

And all around, our summer swoon notwithstanding, there's a feeling of a 5 wild world being just beyond our perimeter, a new and untallied feeling among our residents, one they'll never adjust to — or that's my guess — one they'll die before accommodating. A sad fact about adult life is that you can see the very things you'll never adapt to coming up on the horizon. You see them as the problems they are, you worry like hell about them, you tell yourself you'll have to change your way of doing things. Only then you don't. You can't. Somehow it's too late. And maybe it's worse than even that: maybe the thing you see coming is not even the real thing, the thing that scares you, but its aftermath.

Haddam does not seem like a town in the throes of a price decline. It looks, in fact, pretty prosperous — uppity and singleminded about its various expectations and agendas. The housing stock has plenty of big nineteenth-century Second Empires and bracketed villas (mostly owned by high-priced lawyers and software CEOs) with cupolas and belvederes and oriels to spice up the basic lingua franca, which is Greek with Federalist detail elements, and postrevolutionary stone houses with fan lights, columned entries, and Roman flutings. All these houses, both in the village and out into the surrounding woods, were big-ticket items the day the last door was hung a hundred and fifty years ago and hardly ever come on the market, except in extremely vicious divorce proceedings in which one vindictive spouse wants a FOR SALE sign stuck in front of a former love nest to get under the skin of the party of the second part. Even the few "village-in" Georgian row houses have now become high-dollar and are mostly all owned by rich widows, privacy-hungry gay husbands, and well-heeled M.D.'s from Philadelphia who keep them as country places to hie off to with their receptionists during the color season.

But looks can be deceiving. Property values are decidedly down (though asking prices have yet to reflect it), and houses aren't moving in the prime selling season between March 21 and the first of October — now, in other words. Banks are ratcheting up on the price of money and coming back to us realtors with problematic news about appraisals. Sellers who'd made retirement plans for Lake-of-the-Ozarks or for a smaller house scaled-down-to-practical-needs-now-that-the-kids-are-finished-at-UVA are retrenching and taking a wait/see attitude toward the next expected upswing, finding Haddam a better place to live than they'd been thinking when they thought their house was worth a fortune.

For the first time since I moved here in 1970, there are two businesses on Bank Street that have left their stores standing empty, the management getting out of town under cover of darkness owing a lot of people money and merchandise (one has relocated to the Mahwah Mall; the other hasn't been heard from). In the early Eighties, when things were clicking and whirring along and I was still writing for a sports magazine, all our weekenders were suave New Yorkers — rich SoHo residents and well-heeled East-Siders down to "the country" for the day. Now all those people are either staying at home in their cement and barred enclaves and getting into "urban pioneering" or whatever their checkbooks allow for a weekend splurge, or else they've sold out and gone back to Kansas, or decided to forge a new start in the Twin Cities, where life's slower (and cheaper). Plenty, I'm sure, are lonely and bored silly wherever they are, wishing someone would try to rob them.

Yet like most people I am optimistic about the foreseeable future, though cautious; in most ways the boom of the Eighties has paid off no matter what things feel like at the moment. So that my only real concern is with the long run, something that progress American-style doesn't take much of an interest in. And maybe it's just a factor of my own flat-footed stage of life, or my off-again, on-again sense of urgency, or my anxiety about physical disappearance (when you're forty-five your queasy, mid-life crises are all back in the road someplace). It's true that at forty-five you commence to factor in the grinding issue of your age. It becomes a function of damn-near everything: how your colon works; the millimeters of useful enamel left on your choppers; your performance on the treadmill and in bed. For everything you do reasonably well, there's somebody wearing a white cotton smock with a blue-and-white name tag on the front to comment, "that is, at your age": "Your toes look just fine to me, Mr. Bascombe, for a man your age." Or, "For a man your age the amount of slag built up in your abdominal aortic artery is nothing I'd even worry about. You'll be dead from something else before your heart gives out."

Nothing good is *really* good, in other words, when you're forty-five. It's not 10 bad enough to drive you to a twelve-step program or to run your car off Bryce Canyon or to miss a curve on Mulholland Drive, or into a Catholic Church or an ashram. But it's a truth — there is your life like a great winged bird of uncertain temper (maybe vicious, maybe cold, maybe blind) that keeps flying over you and over you, casting its shadow on your person. For some human situations there is no twelve-step program.

It's true, of course, that I *feel* the same way I felt when I was twenty-five. Everything still works okay (I wear glasses to read, have a little arthritis in my fingers from my years as a sports reporter; my hair's not all where it once was). But I am still able to feel "purely pleased," as when I am taking the train through some rough industrial wasteland in mid-October and chance to see a willow stranded lone as a sentinel amid canals and tracks and rusted car carcasses, a tree full of autumn fires, burning with some mysterious bright light, and feel for a flashing moment *just good about it.* Nothing epic or religious, nothing lasting. Just good. That trick's still mine. It is when I lose that ability, if that's what it is, that I'll think about life in a different light. A less bright one, when the shadow doesn't move, but stays.

Though strictly speaking about my town — Haddam — I am bemused, and find myself missing it (missing the very town I live in!) even as I go on living in it. Some odd, evasive quality it has now it didn't have the year Ann and I showed up here as sturdy young-marrieds from NYC, our firstborn not yet born, some new quality related to newcomers, to refurbished landmarks, a new post office, new pavement, smoother sidewalks — a function of the "boom" and the postcoital triste of after-boom-life's slow resumption.

And practically speaking, it must mean *something* to a town, to the local *esprit,* for its value on the open market to signify less. If some otherwise healthy charcoal-briquette company's stock takes a nose dive, the company responds ASAP: Its "people" stay at their desks an extra hour (unless they're fired outright); men go home a lot more dog-tired and carrying no flowers; citizens stand staring up at the tree limbs in need of trimming a little longer in the hazy evening hours, opt for an extra Pimm's before the next candlelight dinner alone with the wife, wake oddly at 4:00 A.M. with nothing much in mind, just restless.

Likewise in Haddam, where falling property values ride like an odorless, colorless mist through the trees, and all breathe it in, all sense it. Though, because no one's truly responsible for anybody else, because a town's not to blame for having done all it can but less than enough, because your next-door neighbor is new and seems too young and not too social—because of all these "conditions" and more—the signs are subtle and largely withheld: worried words get passed at breakfast, not at dinner when there'd be time for a real discussion or a fight; the feeling of what's any hour really worth lingers as you bend to adjust the sweep of the sprinkler; the anxiety of selling stays with you like a worrisome EKG, though you've never thought of selling, never once—meant this house to be the last you owned, the one you're buried out of, the one the town might eventually put a plaque on to commemorate your having lived there.

Privately, I have begun wondering—and not in an alarmist's or a gloomy, fugueish way, but more in an archaeological spirit, as if in the practice of realty I were each day at the job of unearthing the ongoing stelae and mysterious petroglyphs of my time, fitting pieces together, deciphering partial inscriptions, discovering how the whole site is shaped and lies upon the hilltop, and which way it faced—wondering: Where is all this heading? Where will buying a new house get anybody that staying put and having cancer won't get them just as fast? How would I feel, what would I need to learn? How would the view be if I woke up in Haddam like Rip van Winkle in a hundred years? It's a question I often think about while I stuff envelopes with updates—"Price reduced for qualified clients"; "Motivated seller"; "Act now!" And the answer is much like the answer to the question of what happens to us when we die. Either it'll be exactly the same as this (not my guess) or it'll be so different I can't imagine it, in which case I'm not that interested.

These days I am living happily in a bachelor's buttoned-down way in my ex-wife's house on Jefferson, or I should say, the house formerly owned by formerly my wife, Ann Leurtsma Bascombe, now Mrs. Charley O'Dell, 86 Swallow Lane, Deep River, CT, the shetland sweater, shiitake mushroom, Swedish food processor, good Brie, and Laura Ashley capital of North America (she has reactivated her maiden name and now is just Ann Leurtsma, formerly of Grosse Pointe Woods). My children live there, too, though I am not so sure how blissful they are or even should be under the circumstances, especially my son, Paul, who is not having an easy time of it now, has been arrested for shoplifting in a mall near O'Dell's house, and is in need of real fatherly assistance.

I have lived here now for three years, slightly longer than I have been in my new profession of house-selling for the Lauren-Schwindell Firm—offices on Carnegie Street across from the Theological Institute, as well as in Ocean Grove, and Hopatcong in the New Jersey lake district. The configuration of life events that led me to this profession and to this very house might seem unusual if your model for human existence is based on a family-professional Kinsey report from the late Forties, or the ideal American family-life profile from some right-wing think tank—one of whose directors actually lives in Haddam and who are usually apologists for a model life no one can actually live without resorting to mind-numbing, impulse-suppressing, memory-clotting drugs they also don't want you to have (though I'm sure *they* have 'em by the tractor-trailer loads). To anyone else, though, my life will seem more or less normal-under-the-microscope, full of oddities and incongruities none of us escapes but which do little harm.

Not long after coming back from an extended trip to Europe, during which I came to grips with some of life's abstracter facts and resolved to turn over some bright, new leaves (get chummier with my children before it was too late, take trips to Yellowstone and Banff to teach them respect for nature's bounty, drive them to Atlantic City to see Mel Tormé at Trop World — all of which I did), not long after all this, Ann called up to say she and Charley O'Dell, the architect she'd been having a six-month-long "your-place-or-mine" relationship with, were planning marriage. She was, she said, selling her house and moving kit and caboodle up to O'Dell's in Deep River, where Charley captained his one-man design firm, housed predictably in a converted seaman's chapel situated on stilts at the marsh edge (tall, hygienically clean clerestories, cantilevered cathedral ceilings, plenty of imported blond wood from Norway and Outer Mongolia, everything built-in, dovetailed, and rabbeted, classical music going day and night, *ya-ta-ta, ya-ta-ta*), all of it just downwind of "the Knoll," his equally pretentious hand-hewn, post-and-beam Nantucket Cottage adaptation (fifty more windows, solar panels, heated floor tiles, Finnish sauna, et cetera. Charley, I hardly need say, attended Yale, hails from New Canaan, and sails his own twenty-five-foot Alerion, built with his own methodical, well-calloused fingers, using sails he sewed himself at night listening to Sibelius). She hoped I wouldn't be too upset.

I, of course, didn't know what in the hell to think and was for several seconds totally dumb struck, just sat holding the receiver to my ear as if the line were dead. There was no clause in our divorce decree, she reminded me in the perplexed ticking silence, to keep her from hauling the kids out of town — though that was only because nothing so outlandish had ever occurred to me way back when.

My first thought, though, once the words themselves were swallowed, was that I (as well as Paul and Clarissa) had been scaldingly and unfairly betrayed at a critical point in our lives — and just when I was getting things nicely turned around for the long, leisurely canter back to the barn — a life's point of sovereign amelioration — sins forgiven, all lesions healed. 20

I had met architect Charley (tall, rangy, tan-skinned, loose-hipped pseudoaesthete, given to clean white T-shirts, canvas walking shorts, and expensive deck shoes sans socks) on several occasions having to do with the delivery and pickup of children, and had officially declared him a "no-threat." Though Ann wouldn't agree, wouldn't finally break down on the evenings we stood out by my car in the silent dark of divorced friends who still love each other and dream up cagey, smirky jokes at O'Dell's expense the way she had with all her other suitors — jokes about the custom seat covers in the cars they drove, or their taste in suits, or the personality of their ex-spouses. Mum was uncomfortably the word where O'Dell was concerned, and I suppose now I should've seen it coming and torpedoed him the way any sane man would.

Though as a result, when she told me on the phone one Friday evening just at cocktail hour, just as the sun had cleared the yardarm all over town and trays of ice cubes were being cracked and tumbled into clean crystal buckets and leaded tumblers and slim pitchers, the vermouth hauled ritually out from the butler's pantry, the smell of juniper rising into the nostrils of many a bushed but dutiful hubby standing musing out onto a mottled summery lawn, wondering if he oughtn't sprinkle one more time where he'd worked the new super-sun zoysia seed into the bare spot where the neighbors' dog had dug, or ought he to trust a heavy dew to keep the ground moist till morning when he could slip out before work with the hose and the fine spray attachment — as a result I was hit amidships.

"Frank," Ann said very firmly, "I'm calling to tell you that I'm getting married."

"Married?" My heart made one possibly loud but absolutely palpable clunk deep toward the bottom of my chest. "Who to?"

"To Charley," she said calmly. 25

"The bricklayer?"

"Right," Ann said. "The bricklayer. The architect."

"Why?" I said.

"Why? Because I want somebody to make love to me more than eight times and then never get to see them again. Because I want a nicer house. Because I want the kids to live someplace besides the suburbs. Because I want to get away from here and live where I can see the Connecticut in the morning mist and go sailing in a skiff with my children. In more traditional terminology, I guess I'm in love with him. What'd you think?"

"Those seem like good enough reasons," I said. 30

"I'm happy you agree."

"I don't agree," I said. "I think it's goddamn awful."

"Then I'm sorry you don't agree. But it's not awful."

"What do the children think about it?" I felt my heart thunk-a-thunk again. This is a serious issue, of course, one in which the father almost never fares well and is usually seen either as a stooge or else as a betrayer who's forced Mom into marrying a hairy outsider. Either way insult is glommed onto injury.

"They think it's wonderful," Ann said. "Or I guess they will. I think they 35 expect me to be happy, too."

"Sure," I said, "why not?"

"Why not? Right." And then there was a long and cold silence, a silence we both knew to be the silence of the millennium, the silence of divorce, the silence of love lost where something could've made it not be lost but somehow didn't, the silence of death, long before death might even be winked at, the silence of fatigue over love being parceled out the way it had been.

"That's all I really have to say," Ann said crisply. A curtain had been parted and then closed.

I was in *fact* standing in the butler's pantry, staring out the little round nautically paned window into the yard, where the big copper beech cast an ominous predark shadow over the soft green grasses of a middle-spring evening. "When's all this happening?" I asked in a hopeful voice. I put my hand to my cheek and my cheek was cold.

"In a month. I guess." 40

"Not wasting any time."

"Why should I? I've done that already." An unmistakable jab at me. I almost said "ouch!" but didn't.

"What about the club?" Ann had stayed on as a part-time teaching pro at Cranberry Hills. Once, briefly, she had been an aspirant to the ladies' tour. I suspected she had met Charley there, on the cadge with his reciprocating membership.

"It's fine," she said. "I've taught enough women to play golf. I put the house on the market this morning with Lauren-Schwindell. I priced it to sell."

"Maybe *I'll* buy it," I said for no reason but to have something bold and 45
unexpected that was mine to say. All my lines in these terrible moments
seemed to be written for me.

"That'd be novel," she said.

"Maybe what I'll do is buy it and sell this place and move into your house."
I of course had no earthly idea why I would say anything so ridiculous.
Though as soon as the words left my mouth I had the dead-eyed conviction
that I was going to do exactly that, and in a hurry, too — perhaps so she could
never get rid of me, not that you ever get rid of anybody, ever, and especially
somebody you've been married to! That may be, in fact, what marriage means
in layman's terms: it is the institution you share with the one person in all the
earth you can't get rid of except by dying. (Why, one wonders, would anyone do
it twice?)

"I'll leave the real estate ideas to you," Ann said, and I knew she wanted to get
off the phone. I bleakly imagined Frank Lloyd O'Dell lounging on the couch beside her, big feet up, browsing with a big smirk through a *Sailing* magazine.

"Is Charley there now?" I said irritably, since it was conceivable I would just
go over there right then and bust him up. Bloody up his Safari World pullover.

"No, he's not here," Ann said. "And don't you come over here, please. This 50
isn't easy for me. I'm crying, and you don't get to see that." I, however, couldn't
hear her crying and assumed she was lying to make me feel like a louse, which
is how I felt though I hadn't done anything. It was she who was getting married — I who was getting left behind.

"I won't come over there," I said glumly. For a silent moment I watched a
small gray bunny hop out from under a big rhododendron Ann and I had
planted together for privacy's sake by the Deffeyes' property line back in '76.
And then suddenly, while I was holding the phone to my ear, another completely inert silence filled the optic lines connecting Ann and me. And for no
reason at all I had the sharpest pang that Ann was going to die. Not immediately. Not even soon, necessarily. But not so long from then either, at the end of
a period of time, which, because she was leaving town on the arm of another
man, would pass by me almost imperceptibly — her life's extinguishment playing out beyond my knowing via a series of small but exquisite noticings, won-
derings, anxieties, appointments, dismays, unhappy lab reports, gloomy X rays,
struggles, tiny victories, reprieves, then failures — life's lists of distracting hap-
penstance — at the sudden, misty conclusion of which a call would come, or a
voice mail, or a fax or a mailgram saying, "Ann Leurtsma died Tuesday. Services
today. Thought you'd want to know. Condolences. C. O'Dell."

After which my own life would be ruined and over with big-time! All the
marbles, no tomorrow, no coming back for seconds, the whole cake gone. (It is
another matter of my age, I know, that all new events seem to threaten to ruin
my precious remaining years. Nothing like that feeling exists when you're
thirty-two.)

And it's cheap, of course — a kind of sentimentalism the gods on Olympus frown on, sending down avengers to punish the small-time con men of
emotion. Only sometimes you can't feel anything about a subject without hy-
pothesizing its extinction. Which is how I did feel: full of emotion that Ann
was going away now to start the part of her life (she was forty-two) that would
end in her death. And I would play no part in it. I would be elsewhere, piddling
around at nothing very important, as I'd been — depending on your point of

view — for either three years or twenty. And worse, I would be unthought-of; or thought-of only as "a man I was once married to . . . I'm not sure where he is now. No. He was strange." (This, from her sickbed.)

So if I was to have a part in it at all, it would have had to be spoken now — on the phone, streets away, different neighborhoods (the geography of divorce), at cocktail hour, she alone in her house, me alone in mine, feeling as recently as ten minutes previous pretty good about my unruined prospects, then suddenly feeling as divorced as a man can be.

"Don't marry him, sweetheart! Marry me! Marry me again! Let's sell *both* our shitty houses and move to Quoddy Head, where I'll buy a small newspaper from the proceeds. You can learn to sail a skiff on the Grand Manan, and the kids can become (in the time they have left as kids) skeptical little mariners, learn to print by hand, become clever with lobster pots, trade their Jersey accents, go to Bowdoin and Bates." These are words I *didn't* say into the dense millennial silence. They would've been laughed at and ignored and should've been. Suffice it to say that I wanted to say them and didn't, which psychologists will tell you means I didn't really want to.

"I understand all of this" is what I said in a convinced voice as I poured myself a convincing amount of gin, bypassing the vermouth. "And I love you, by the way."

"Please," Ann said, annoyed. "Just please. How can that be true? And even if it is, what difference does that make? Anyway, I'm finished with what I had to tell you." Ann is the kind of bedrock literalist who simply doesn't take an interest in the unreasonable and farfetched — the things I sometimes feel I'm *only* interested in and suited for. It's as if she only believes in stale facts.

"But sweetheart, to say that some important truths are founded on flimsy evidence isn't to complain about very much," I said runically.

"That's your philosophy, Frank," Ann said coldly. "It just matters to you how long the farfetched things hold up, right?"

"Right." I took a sip of not quite glacially cold gin (nothing is better under the circumstances). "For some people the farfetched can last long enough to become true. For some people it can't, unfortunately."

"I'm in group two," Ann said. "And if you were about to ask me to marry you instead of Charley, don't. I won't. I don't want to."

"I wasn't," I said. "I was just trying to speak an ephemeral truth and trudge on beyond it."

"Trudge on, then," she said. "I've got to cook dinner for the children. I did always think, though, it'd be you who'd get married as soon as we got divorced. Some bimbo."

"Maybe you didn't know me very well."

"Maybe not. Sorry. My fault."

"Thanks for calling me," I said. "Congratulations."

"Sure. It was nothing," Ann said glumly, then she said "goodbye" and hung up.

Nothing! It was something! I bolted back the rest of my gin in one shuddering gulp to wash down a frothing bitterness. Nothing? It was epochal! (I didn't actually care if it was blue-blood Charley O'Dell from Yale/New Canaan, or pencil-necked, breast-pocket-penholder, screw-loose Fred from Bell Labs, or Lonnie from down at High Tide Seafood — I'd have felt the same: like shit.)

Ann and I had had a nice system worked out, one by which we lived separate lives in separate houses in one small, tidy, and peril-free town; we'd had flings, woes, despairs, joys, a whole gearbox full of life's meshings and unmeshings, on and on, but fundamentally we were the same two people — only in a different equipoise: same planets, different orbits, same solar system. In a pinch, a real pinch, say a head-on car crash requiring life-support, or a prolonged and ravaging bout with corrosive chemo, no one but the other would've been "in attendance," consulting the docs, chatting up the nurses, judiciously closing and opening curtains, monitoring the game shows through the long afternoons, shooing away unwanted neighbors and long-ignored relatives, former boyfriends, girlfriends, old nemeses, old roomies — shepherding them all back down the long, empty, softly lit corridors, speaking in whispers, saying he/she had "had a good day but was resting now," all this while the other — the patient — dozed and the machines clicked and whirred and sighed, and all just so we could be alone. Eventually, after a long recovery during which one or the other would have to relearn some basic life functions up to now taken for granted (walking, breathing, pissing) certain "key conversations" would've taken place, certain dour admissions offered or would already have been offered in moments of extremis, certain truths would've been reconciled so that a new and (this time) *really* binding union of spirits could've been forged. Or maybe not. Maybe we would simply have parted again, though with new strengths and insights and respects achieved through the fragile life experiences of the other.

All of that was gone like a fart in a skillet. And jeez Louise! If I'd known 70 Ann would get remarried (knowing it as demonstrated by actually thinking it) I'd have fought like a Viking instead of giving in to divorce years ago like a queasy, uninspired saint. And I'd have fought it for a good reason: because no matter where she holds the mortgage papers, she completely supposes my existence. My life was and still is at a stage in which she is continually in its audience (whether she's paying attention or not). All my decent, reasonable, patient, loving components were developed in the laboratory of our life together, and I realized that by moving house up to Deep River, she was at that moment taking most of those components with her to lavish on a surrogate, leaving me with only worn-out costumes to play myself with.

I, of course, fell into a sulfurous funk for the next week. I stayed at home, called no one, spoke briefly to both my children, who seemed to calculate their mother's marriage with the alacrity of seeing a small gain in a stock they'd bought too high and realized they would probably lose money on in the long term.

Paul declared Charley to be an "okay guy" and admitted to having gone to a Giants game with him the November before — something I hadn't heard about because I was away in Europe. Charley had season tickets through some Yale cronies who were in thick with the team owners, which didn't impress Paul, who'd been in plenty of press boxes when his old man was a sports hack.

Clarissa seemed more interested in the wedding than in the conception of remarriage. The event itself was to be an intimate but elegant lawn party affair of close friends, all taking place at the Knoll. Ann's mother was flying in from Newport Beach (her father having since passed on to a happier world), and Charley's parents were motoring down from Blue Hill or Northeast Harbor.

"Since I missed you guys' wedding, I'll get to see this one," Clary said cheerily on the phone one afternoon. "When you get married I'll come to it, too."

"Will you be the best man?" I said, uncheerily.   75

"I'll be a bridesmaid if I like who you marry," she said. "Paul has to be the best man."

"When you're up there in Connecticut you'll have to find somebody for me to marry," I said. "Maybe there'll be more girls up there than there are here."

"You don't want a girl, Daddy," Clarissa said very solemn, "you want a woman."

"That's right. I forgot."

"*I'm* a girl," she said. "You can't marry someone like me. You're weird."   80

"That's right," I said. "I forget the details."

"You're weird," she said and laughed famously.

"I *am* weird," I said. "I don't know what happened to me when I was younger, sweetheart. I just got weird. I'm sorry."

Some quality, some keening spirit in my human voice seemed to bemuse her then, and she began to talk about the dress she was going to wear, and where everyone was staying — the Griswold Inn in Old Saybrook, the groom's party at the Susse Chalet in Lyme. We talked a minute more, then parted company, never to speak under those same circumstances or in those same voices again. Gone. Poof.

But no sooner had Ann solemnized her rethreaded vows with Charley "the   85
master builder" than I began to plunge forward with new plans of my own — to purchase her house on Jefferson (she was asking $495), and to get loose from my big old soffit-sagging half-timber on Hoving Road, where I'd lived every minute of my life in Haddam, N.J., and where for a few blissful years I mistakenly thought I could live forever.

Ann's house was a crisp, plainspoken, freestanding Greek Revival In-town of a style typical to our Central Jersey area, a place she'd bought on the cheap after our divorce, done some modernizing work on — opening out the back, spanking up the bathrooms and the kitchen, repointing some basement piers, adding skylights and crown moldings for effect, and finishing off the third floor to be Paul's lair, then giving the whole place a new white paint job.

And setting aside the preliminary strangeness of moving into your ex-wife's ex-house, the place actually seemed like a natural for me, having spent a long collection of sleepless nights there when a child was sick, or when in the early days of our divorced life I'd had the jimjams so bad Ann would sometimes feel sorry for me and let me come sleep on the couch.

It felt like home, in other words. And if not my home, at least my kids' home — someone's home. Whereas our old place had begun to feel barny and murmurous and queer, and myself strangely outdistanced as an owner, around in the yard Saturdays, raking my leaves or cranking away diligently on my lawnmower, or standing in my driveway, hands-on-hips, overseeing from below the patching by two Greek swindlers from Trenton of a new squirrel hole under the roof flashing. *Outdistanced,* meaning I had no business doing it anymore since I wasn't preserving anything *for* anything, just going through the motions, joining life's rough timbers end to end.

So the day Charley and Ann flew off to St. Barts for a week of what I hoped could possibly be arguments, sad realizations, and finally frantic phone calls to be met at Newark and the beginning movements of the annulment waltz, I got myself over to Lauren-Schwindell and threw my hat in both rings at once — hers to buy, mine to sell.

And before the lovebirds had even turned to home (no annulment pend- 90 ing, though I detected a stony grimness in Ann the moment I talked to her on the phone about my bid) I had made a full-price cash offer on 33 Jefferson, and through a realtor's connections arranged an extremely advantageous deal with the Theological Institute to take over my house for the purpose of converting it into a conference center where guests like Bishop Tutu and the Dalai Lama and the head of the Icelandic Federation of Churches could hold private meetings about the fate of the world and still find it homey enough to slip down after midnight for a snack. The institute was unusually sensitive to my tax situation (my house appraised out at a million-two at the peak) and set up a complex annuity that allowed me to donate the house as an outright gift, claim the deduction, and also receive a special "consultant's" fee in what must've been temporal affairs. The rest was small print.

I simply walked out of my house one bright May morning, leaving all my furniture except for books and nostalgic attachments, drove to Ann's house on Jefferson with all her old-new furniture sitting exactly where she'd left it, and took up residence. I got to keep my phone number.

And truth to tell, I hardly noticed a difference, so often had I lain awake nights in my old house, or roamed the rooms and halls of hers when all were sleeping, searching, I suppose, for where I fit in or where I'd gone wrong, or how I could breathe air into my ghostly self and become a recognizable if changed figure in their sweet, lost lives. One house is as good as another for that kind of enterprise. The poet was right again. "Let the winged Fancy roam/Pleasure never is at home."

CONNECTIONS TO OTHER SELECTIONS

1. Discuss the significance of the small-town settings in "Bascombe, in Realty" and Alice Munro's "An Ounce of Cure" (p. 434).
2. Compare the protagonist of Ford's story with that of Mark Halliday's in "Young Man on Sixth Avenue" (p. 70). To what extent does life meet their expectations?
3. Write an essay about how family life in late twentieth-century America is represented in this story and in Tobias Wolff's "Powder" (p. 665).

GISH JEN (B. 1956)

The daughter of Chinese immigrants, Gish Jen grew up in Yonkers and Scarsdale, New York, and was educated at Harvard, Stanford, and the Iowa Writers' Workshop. A fellowship at Radcliffe's Bunting Institute led to her first novel, *Typical American* (1991), which describes how Chinese immigrants in the United States are transformed by their efforts to pursue the American dream. Her second novel, *Mona*, appeared in 1996. Of her own family's experience as immigrants she says, "My parents were born into a culture that puts society first," but "I was born into a culture that puts the individual first. This forced me to carve out a balance for myself." Jen's concern about her characters' identities is close to her own heart: her real name is Lillian but in high school she adopted Gish—after the actress Lillian Gish—because that "was part of becoming a writer" rather than "becoming the person I was supposed to be." Jen's fiction enlarges her readers' sense of what constitutes a "typical American." "In the American Society," which first appeared in the *Sewanee Review*, is collected in *Imagining America: Stories from the Promised Land* (1991); it explores both the difficulties and the humor associated with her characters' struggles with their identities.

In the American Society   *1991*

I. His Own Society

When my father took over the pancake house, it was to send my little sister Mona and me to college. We were only in junior high at the time, but my father believed in getting a jump on things. "Those Americans always saying it," he told us. "Smart guys thinking in advance." My mother elaborated, explaining that businesses took bringing up, like children. They could take years to get going, she said, years.

In this case, though, we got rich right away. At two months we were breaking even, and at four, those same hotcakes that could barely withstand the weight of butter and syrup were supporting our family with ease. My mother bought a station wagon with air conditioning, my father an oversized, red vinyl recliner for the back room; and as time went on and the business continued to thrive, my father started to talk about his grandfather and the village he had reigned over in China—things my father had never talked about when he worked for other people. He told us about the bags of rice his family would give out to the poor at New Year's, and about the people who came to beg, on their hands and knees, for his grandfather to intercede for the more wayward of their relatives. "Like that Godfather in the movie," he would tell us as, his feet up, he distributed paychecks. Sometimes an employee would get two green envelopes instead of one, which meant that Jimmy needed a tooth pulled, say, or that Tiffany's husband was in the clinker again.

"It's nothing, nothing," he would insist, sinking back into his chair. "Who else is going to take care of you people?"

My mother would mostly just sigh about it. "Your father thinks this is China," she would say, and then she would go back to her mending. Once in a while, though, when my father had given away a particularly large sum, she would exclaim, outraged, "But this here is the U—S—of—A!"—this apparently having been what she used to tell immigrant stock boys when they came in late.

She didn't work at the supermarket anymore; but she had made it to the rank of manager before she left, and this had given her not only new words 5 and phrases, but new ideas about herself, and about America, and about what was what in general. She had opinions, now, on how downtown should be zoned; she could pump her own gas and check her own oil; and for all she used to chide Mona and me for being "copycats," she herself was now interested in espadrilles, and wallpaper, and most recently, the town country club.

"So join already," said Mona, flicking a fly off her knee.

My mother enumerated the problems as she sliced up a quarter round of watermelon: there was the cost. There was the waiting list. There was the fact that no one in our family played either tennis or golf.

"So what?" said Mona.

"It would be waste," said my mother.

"Me and Callie can swim in the pool."   10

"Plus you need that recommendation letter from a member."

"Come *on*," said Mona. "Annie's mom'd write you a letter in a *sec*."

My mother's knife glinted in the early summer sun. I spread some more newspaper on the picnic table.

"*Plus* you have to eat there twice a month. You know what that means." My mother cut another, enormous slice of fruit.

"No, I *don't* know what that means," said Mona.   15

"It means Dad would have to wear a jacket, dummy," I said.

"Oh! Oh! Oh!" said Mona, clasping her hand to her breast. "Oh! Oh! Oh! Oh! Oh!"

We all laughed: my father had no use for nice clothes, and would wear only ten-year-old shirts, with grease-spotted pants, to show how little he cared what anyone thought.

"Your father doesn't believe in joining the American society," said my mother. "He wants to have his own society."

"So go to dinner without him." Mona shot her seeds out in long arcs over   20
the lawn. "Who cares what he thinks?"

But of course we all did care, and knew my mother could not simply up and do as she pleased. For in my father's mind, a family owed its head a degree of loyalty that left no room for dissent. To embrace what he embraced was to love; and to embrace something else was to betray him.

He demanded a similar sort of loyalty of his workers, whom he treated more like servants than employees. Not in the beginning, of course. In the beginning all he wanted was for them to keep on doing what they used to do, and to that end he concentrated mostly on leaving them alone. As the months passed, though, he expected more and more of them, with the result that for all his largesse, he began to have trouble keeping help. The cooks and busboys complained that he asked them to fix radiators and trim hedges, not only at the restaurant, but at our house; the waitresses that he sent them on errands and made them chauffeur him around. Our head waitress, Gertrude, claimed that he once even asked her to scratch his back.

"It's not just the blacks don't believe in slavery," she said when she quit.

My father never quite registered her complaint, though, nor those of the others who left. Even after Eleanor quit, then Tiffany, then Gerald, and Jimmy, and even his best cook, Eureka Andy, for whom he had bought new glasses, he remained mostly convinced that the fault lay with them.

"All they understand is that assembly line," he lamented. "Robots, they   25
are. They want to be robots."

There *were* occasions when the clear running truth seemed to eddy, when he would pinch the vinyl of his chair up into little peaks and wonder if he was doing things right. But with time he would always smooth the peaks back down; and when business started to slide in the spring, he kept on like a horse in his ways.

By the summer our dishboy was overwhelmed with scraping. It was no longer just the hashbrowns that people were leaving for trash, and the service was as bad as the food. The waitresses served up French pancakes instead of German, apple juice instead of orange, spilt things on laps, on coats. On the Fourth of July some greenhorn sent an entire side of fries slaloming down a lady's *massif centrale*. Meanwhile in the back room, my father labored through articles on the economy.

"What is housing starts?" he puzzled. "What is GNP?"

Mona and I did what we could, filling in as busgirls and bookkeepers and, one afternoon, stuffing the comments box that hung by the cashier's desk. That was Mona's idea. We rustled up a variety of pens and pencils, checked boxes for an hour, smeared the cards up with coffee and grease, and waited. It took a few days for my father to notice that the box was full, and he didn't say anything about it for a few days more. Finally, though, he started to complain of fatigue; and then he began to complain that the staff was not what it could be. We encouraged him in this — pointing out, for instance, how many dishes got chipped — but in the end all that happened was that, for the first time since we took over the restaurant, my father got it into his head to fire someone. Skip, a skinny busboy who was saving up for a sportscar, said nothing as my father mumbled on about the price of dishes. My father's hands shook as he wrote out the severance check; and he spent the rest of the day napping in his chair once it was over.

As it was going on midsummer, Skip wasn't easy to replace. We hung a 30 sign in the window and advertised in the paper, but no one called the first week, and the person who called the second didn't show up for his interview. The third week, my father phoned Skip to see if he would come back, but a friend of his had already sold him a Corvette for cheap.

Finally a Chinese guy named Booker turned up. He couldn't have been more than thirty, and was wearing a lighthearted seersucker suit, but he looked as though life had him pinned: his eyes were bloodshot and his chest sunken, and the muscles of his neck seemed to strain with the effort of holding his head up. In a single dry breath he told us that he had never bussed tables but was willing to learn, and that he was on the lam from the deportation authorities.

"I do not want to lie to you," he kept saying. He had come to the United States on a student visa, had run out of money, and was now in a bind. He was loath to go back to Taiwan, as it happened — he looked up at this point, to be sure my father wasn't pro-KMT — but all he had was a phony social security card and a willingness to absorb all blame, should anything untoward come to pass.

"I do not think, anyway, that it is against law to hire me, only to be me," he said, smiling faintly.

Anyone else would have examined him on this, but my father conceived of laws as speed bumps rather than curbs. He wiped the counter with his sleeve, and told Booker to report the next morning.

"I will be good worker," said Booker. 35

"Good," said my father.

"Anything you want me to do, I will do."

My father nodded.

Booker seemed to sink into himself for a moment. "Thank you," he said finally. "I am appreciate your help. I am very, very appreciate for everything." He reached out to shake my father's hand.

My father looked at him. "Did you eat today?" he asked in Mandarin.　　40

Booker pulled at the hem of his jacket.

"Sit down," said my father. "Please, have a seat."

My father didn't tell my mother about Booker, and my mother didn't tell my father about the country club. She would never have applied, except that Mona, while over at Annie's, had let it drop that our mother wanted to join. Mrs. Lardner came by the very next day.

"Why, I'd be honored and delighted to write you people a letter," she said. Her skirt billowed around her.

"Thank you so much," said my mother. "But it's too much trouble for you,　45 and also my husband is . . ."

"Oh, it's no trouble at all, no trouble at all. I tell you." She leaned forward so that her chest freckles showed. "I know just how it is. It's a secret of course, but you know, my natural father was Jewish. Can you see it? Just look at my skin."

"My husband," said my mother.

"I'd be honored and delighted," said Mrs. Lardner with a little wave of her hands. "Just honored and delighted."

Mona was triumphant. "See, Mom," she said, waltzing around the kitchen when Mrs. Lardner left. "What did I tell you? 'I'm just honored and delighted, just honored and delighted.'" She waved her hands in the air.

"You know, the Chinese have a saying," said my mother. "To do nothing is　50 better than to overdo. You mean well, but you tell me now what will happen."

"I'll talk Dad into it," said Mona, still waltzing. "Or I bet Callie can. He'll do anything Callie says."

"I can try, anyway," I said.

"Did you hear what I said?" said my mother. Mona bumped into the broom closet door. "You're not going to talk anything; you've already made enough trouble." She started on the dishes with a clatter.

Mona poked diffidently at a mop.

I sponged off the counter. "Anyway," I ventured, "I bet our name'll never　55 even come up."

"That's if we're lucky," said my mother.

"There's all these people waiting," I said.

"Good," she said. She started on a pot.

I looked over at Mona, who was still cowering in the broom closet. "In fact, there's some black family's been waiting so long, they're going to sue," I said.

My mother turned off the water. "Where'd you hear that?"　　60

"Patty told me."

She turned the water back on, started to wash a dish, then put it back down and shut the faucet.

"I'm sorry," said Mona.

"Forget it," said my mother. "Just forget it."

Booker turned out to be a model worker, whose boundless gratitude　65 translated into a willingness to do anything. As he also learned quickly, he soon knew not only how to bus, but how to cook, and how to wait table, and how to keep the books. He fixed the walk-in door so that it stayed shut, re-upholstered the torn seats in the dining room, and devised a system for track-ing inventory. The only stone in the rice was that he tended to be sickly; but, reliable even in illness, he would always send a friend to take his place. In this way we got to know Ronald, Lynn, Dirk, and Cedric, all of whom, like Booker, had problems with their legal status and were anxious to please. They weren't all as capable as Booker, though, with the exception of Cedric, whom my fa-ther often hired even when Booker was well. A round wag of a man who called Mona and me *shou hou* — skinny monkeys — he was a professed nonsmoker who was nevertheless always begging drags off of other people's cigarettes. This last habit drove our head cook, Fernando, crazy, especially since, when refused a hit, Cedric would occasionally snitch one. Winking impishly at Mona and me, he would steal up to an ashtray, take a quick puff, and then break out laughing so that the smoke came rolling out of his mouth in a great incrimi-natory cloud. Fernando accused him of stealing fresh cigarettes too, even whole packs.

"Why else do you think he's weaseling around in the back of the store all the time," he said. His face was blotchy with anger. "The man is a frigging thief."

Other members of the staff supported him in this contention and joined in on an "Operation Identification," which involved numbering and initialing their cigarettes — even though what they seemed to fear for wasn't so much their cigarettes as their jobs. Then one of the cooks quit; and rather than pro-mote someone, my father hired Cedric for the position. Rumors flew that he was taking only half the normal salary, that Alex had been pressured to resign, and that my father was looking for a position with which to placate Booker, who had been bypassed because of his health.

The result was that Fernando categorically refused to work with Cedric.

"The only way I'll cook with that piece of slime," he said, shaking his huge tattooed fist, "is if it's his ass frying on the grill."

My father cajoled and cajoled, to no avail, and in the end was simply 70 forced to put them on different schedules.

The next week Fernando got caught stealing a carton of minute steaks. My father would not tell even Mona and me how he knew to be standing by the back door when Fernando was on his way out, but everyone suspected Booker. Everyone but Fernando, that is, who was sure Cedric had been the tip-off. My father held a staff meeting in which he tried to reassure everyone that Alex had left on his own, and that he had no intention of firing anyone. But though he was careful not to mention Fernando, everyone was so amazed that he was being allowed to stay that Fernando was incensed nonetheless.

"Don't you all be putting your bug eyes on me," he said. "*He's* the frigging crook." He grabbed Cedric by the collar.

Cedric raised an eyebrow. "Cook, you mean," he said.

At this Fernando punched Cedric in the mouth; and the words he had just uttered notwithstanding, my father fired him on the spot.

With everything that was happening, Mona and I were ready to be getting 75 out of the restaurant. It was almost time: the days were still stuffy with sum-mer, but our window shade had started flapping in the evening as if gearing up to go out. That year the breezes were full of salt, as they sometimes were when they came in from the East, and they blew anchors and docks through my mind like so many tumbleweeds, filling my dreams with wherries and lobsters and grainyfaced men who squinted, day in and day out, at the sky.

It was time for a change, you could feel it; and yet the pancake house was the same as ever. The day before school started my father came home with bad news.

"Fernando called police," he said, wiping his hand on his pant leg.

My mother naturally wanted to know what police; and so with much coughing and hawing, the long story began, the latest installment of which had the police calling immigration, and immigration sending an investigator. My mother sat stiff as whalebone as my father described how the man summarily refused lunch on the house and how my father had admitted, under pressure, that he knew there were "things" about his workers.

"So now what happens?"

My father didn't know. "Booker and Cedric went with him to the jail," he said. "But me, here I am." He laughed uncomfortably.

The next day my father posted bail for "his boys" and waited apprehensively for something to happen. The day after that he waited again, and the day after that he called our neighbor's law student son, who suggested my father call the immigration department under an alias. My father took his advice; and it was thus that he discovered that Booker was right: it was illegal for aliens to work, but it wasn't to hire them.

In the happy interval that ensued, my father apologized to my mother, who in turn confessed about the country club, for which my father had no choice but to forgive her. Then he turned his attention back to "his boys."

My mother didn't see that there was anything to do.

"I like to talking to the judge," said my father.

"This is not China," said my mother.

"I'm only talking to him. I'm not give him money unless he wants it."

"You're going to land up in jail."

"So what else I should do?" My father threw up his hands. "Those are my boys."

"Your boys!" exploded my mother. "What about your family? What about your wife?"

My father took a long sip of tea. "You know," he said finally, "in the war my father sent our cook to the soldiers to use. He always said it—the province comes before the town, the town comes before the family."

"A restaurant is not a town," said my mother.

My father sipped at his tea again. "You know, when I first come to the United States, I also had to hide-and-seek with those deportation guys. If people did not helping me, I'm not here today."

My mother scrutinized her hem.

After a minute I volunteered that before seeing a judge, he might try a lawyer.

He turned. "Since when did you become so afraid like your mother?"

I started to say that it wasn't a matter of fear, but he cut me off.

"What I need today," he said, "is a son."

My father and I spent the better part of the next day standing in lines at the immigration office. He did not get to speak to a judge, but with much persistence he managed to speak to a judge's clerk, who tried to persuade him that it was not her place to extend him advice. My father, though, shamelessly plied her with compliments and offers of free pancakes until she finally conceded that she personally doubted anything would happen to either Cedric or Booker.

"Especially if they're 'needed workers,'" she said, rubbing at the red marks her glasses left on her nose. She yawned. "Have you thought about sponsoring them to become permanent residents?"

Could he do that? My father was overjoyed. And what if he saw to it right away? Would she perhaps put in a good word with the judge? 100

She yawned again, her nostrils flaring. "Don't worry," she said. "They'll get a fair hearing."

My father returned jubilant. Booker and Cedric hailed him as their savior, their Buddha incarnate. He was like a father to them, they said; and laughing and clapping, they made him tell the story over and over, sorting over the details like jewels. And how old was the assistant judge? And what did she say?

That evening my father tipped the paperboy a dollar and bought a pot of mums for my mother, who suffered them to be placed on the dining room table. The next night he took us all out to dinner. Then on Saturday, Mona found a letter on my father's chair at the restaurant.

Dear Mr. Chang,
     You are the grat boss. But, we do not like to trial, so will runing away now. Plese to excus us. People saying the law in America is fears like dragon. Here is only $140. We hope some day we can pay back the rest bale. You will getting intrest, as you diserving, so grat a boss you are. Thank you for every thing. In next life you will be burn in rich family, with no more pancaks.
                                        Yours truley,
                                        Booker + Cedric

In the weeks that followed my father went to the pancake house for crises, but otherwise hung around our house, fiddling idly with the sump pump and boiler in an effort, he said, to get ready for winter. It was as though he had gone into retirement, except that instead of moving South, he had moved to the basement. He even took to showering my mother with little attentions, and to calling her "old girl," and when we finally heard that the club had entertained all the applications it could for the year, he was so sympathetic that he seemed more disappointed than my mother.

II. In the American Society

Mrs. Lardner tempered the bad news with an invitation to a bon voyage "bash" she was throwing for a friend of hers who was going to Greece for six months. 105

"Do come," she urged. "You'll meet everyone, and then, you know, if things open up in the spring . . ." She waved her hands.

My mother wondered if it would be appropriate to show up at a party for someone they didn't know, but "the honest truth" was that this was an annual affair. "If it's not Greece, it's Antibes," sighed Mrs. Lardner. "We really just do it because his wife left him and his daughter doesn't speak to him, and poor Jeremy just feels so *unloved*."

She also invited Mona and me to the goings on, as "*demi*-guests" to keep Annie out of the champagne. I wasn't too keen on the idea, but before I could say anything, she had already thanked us for so generously agreeing to honor her with our presence.

"A pair of little princesses, you are!" she told us. "A pair of princesses!"

The party was that Sunday. On Saturday, my mother took my father out shopping for a suit. As it was the end of September, she insisted that he buy a worsted rather than a seersucker, even though it was only ten, rather than fifty percent off. My father protested that it was as hot out as ever, which was true — a thick Indian summer had cozied murderously up to us — but to no avail. Summer clothes, said my mother, were not properly worn after Labor Day.

The suit was unfortunately as extravagant in length as it was in price, which posed an additional quandary, since the tailor wouldn't be in until Monday. The salesgirl, though, found a way of tacking it up temporarily.

"Maybe this suit not fit me," fretted my father.

"Just don't take your jacket off," said the salesgirl.

He gave her a tip before they left, but when he got home refused to remove the price tag.

"I like to asking the tailor about the size," he insisted.

"You mean you're going to *wear* it and then return it?" Mona rolled her eyes.

"I didn't say I'm return it," said my father stiffly. "I like to asking the tailor, that's all."

The party started off swimmingly, except that most people were wearing bermudas or wrap skirts. Still, my parents carried on, sharing with great feeling the complaints about the heat. Of course my father tried to eat a cracker full of shallots and burnt himself in an attempt to help Mr. Lardner turn the coals of the barbecue; but on the whole he seemed to be doing all right. Not nearly so well as my mother, though, who had accepted an entire cupful of Mrs. Lardner's magic punch, and seemed indeed to be under some spell. As Mona and Annie skirmished over whether some boy in their class inhaled when he smoked, I watched my mother take off her shoes, laughing and laughing as a man with a beard regaled her with navy stories by the pool. Apparently he had been stationed in the Orient and remembered a few words of Chinese, which made my mother laugh still more. My father excused himself to go to the men's room then drifted back and "dropped" anchor at the hors d'oeuvre table, while my mother sailed on to a group of women, who tinkled at length over the clarity of her complexion. I dug out a book I had brought.

Just when I'd cracked the spine, though, Mrs. Lardner came by to bewail her shortage of servers. Her caterers were criminals, I agreed; and the next thing I knew I was handing out bits of marine life, making the rounds as amicably as I could.

"Here you go, Dad," I said when I got to the hors d'oeuvre table.

"Everything is fine," he said.

I hesitated to leave him alone; but then the man with the beard zeroed in on him, and though he talked of nothing but my mother, I thought it would be okay to get back to work. Just that moment, though, Jeremy Brothers lurched our way, an empty, albeit corked, wine bottle in hand. He was a slim, well-proportioned man, with a Roman nose and small eyes and a nice manly jaw that he allowed to hang agape.

"Hello," he said drunkenly. "Pleased to meet you."

"Pleased to meeting you," said my father.

"Right," said Jeremy. "Right. Listen. I have this bottle here, this most recal- 125
citrant bottle. You see that it refuses to do my bidding. I bid it open sesame,
please, and it does nothing." He pulled the cork out with his teeth, then
turned the bottle upside down.

My father nodded.

"Would you have a word with it please?" said Jeremy. The man with the
beard excused himself. "Would you please have a god-damned word with it?"

My father laughed uncomfortably.

"Ah!" Jeremy bowed a little. "Excuse me, excuse me, excuse me. You are not
my man, not my man at all." He bowed again and started to leave, but then
circled back. "Viticulture is not your forte, yes I can see that, see that plainly.
But may I trouble you on another matter? Forget the damned bottle." He
threw it into the pool, and winked at the people he splashed. "I have another
matter. Do you speak Chinese?"

My father said he did not, but Jeremy pulled out a handkerchief with 130
some characters on it anyway, saying that his daughter had sent it from Hong
Kong and that he thought the characters might be some secret message.

"Long life," said my father.

"But you haven't looked at it yet."

"I know what it says without looking." My father winked at me.

"You do?"

"Yes, I do." 135

"You're making fun of me, aren't you?"

"No, no, no," said my father, winking again.

"Who are you anyway?" said Jeremy.

His smile fading, my father shrugged.

"Who are you?" 140

My father shrugged again.

Jeremy began to roar. "This is my party, *my party,* and I've never seen you
before in my life." My father backed up as Jeremy came toward him. *"Who are
you? WHO ARE YOU?"*

Just as my father was going to step back into the pool, Mrs. Lardner came
running up. Jeremy informed her that there was a man crashing his party.

"Nonsense," said Mrs. Lardner. "This is Ralph Chang, who I invited extra
especially so he could meet you." She straightened the collar of Jeremy's peach-
colored polo shirt for him.

"Yes, well we've had a chance to chat," said Jeremy. 145

She whispered in his ear; he mumbled something; she whispered something more.

"I do apologize," he said finally.

My father didn't say anything.

"I do." Jeremy seemed genuinely contrite. "Doubtless you've seen drunks
before, haven't you? You must have them in China."

"Okay," said my father. 150

As Mrs. Lardner glided off, Jeremy clapped his arm over my father's shoulders. "You know, I really am quite sorry, quite sorry."

My father nodded.

"What can I do, how can I make it up to you?"

"No thank you."

"No, tell me, tell me," wheedled Jeremy. "Tickets to casino night?" My fa- 155
ther shook his head. "You don't gamble. Dinner at Bartholomew's?" My father
shook his head again. "You don't eat." Jeremy scratched his chin. "You know,
my wife was like you. Old Annabelle could never let me make things up —
never, never, never, never, never."

My father wriggled out from under his arm.

"How about sport clothes? You are rather overdressed, you know, excuse
me for saying so. But here." He took off his polo shirt and folded it up. "You
can have this with my most profound apologies." He ruffled his chest hairs
with his free hand.

"No thank you," said my father.

"No, take it, take it. Accept my apologies." He thrust the shirt into my father's arms. "I'm so very sorry, so very sorry. Please, try it on."

Helplessly holding the shirt, my father searched the crowd for my mother. 160

"Here, I'll help you off with your coat."

My father froze.

Jeremy reached over and took his jacket off. "Milton's, one hundred
twenty-five dollars reduced to one hundred twelve-fifty," he read. "What a bargain, what a bargain!"

"Please give it back," pleaded my father. "Please."

"Now for your shirt," ordered Jeremy. 165

Heads began to turn.

"Take off your shirt."

"I do not take orders like a servant," announced my father.

"Take off your shirt, or I'm going to throw this jacket right into the pool,
just right into this little pool here." Jeremy held it over the water.

"Go ahead." 170

"One hundred twelve-fifty," taunted Jeremy. "One hundred twelve . . ."

My father flung the polo shirt into the water with such force that part of it
bounced back up into the air like a fluorescent fountain. Then it settled into a
soft heap on top of the water. My mother hurried up.

"You're a sport!" said Jeremy, suddenly breaking into a smile and slapping
my father on the back. "You're a sport! I like that. A man with spirit, that's
what you are. A man with panache. Allow me to return to you your jacket." He
handed it back to my father. "Good value you got on that, good value."

My father hurled the coat into the pool too. "We're leaving," he said
grimly. "Leaving!"

"Now, Ralphie," said Mrs. Lardner, bustling up; but my father was already 175
stomping off.

"Get your sister," he told me. To my mother: "Get your shoes."

"That was *great*, Dad," said Mona as we walked down to the car. "You were
stupendous."

"Way to show 'em," I said.

"What?" said my father offhandedly.

Although it was only just dusk, we were in a gulch, which made it hard to 180
see anything except the gleam of his white shirt moving up the hill ahead of us.

"It was all my fault," began my mother.

"Forget it," said my father grandly. Then he said, "The only trouble is I left those keys in my jacket pocket."

"Oh *no*," said Mona.

"Oh no is right," said my mother.

"So we'll walk home," I said.   185

"But how're we going to get into the *house*," said Mona.

The noise of the party churned through the silence.

"Someone has to going back," said my father.

"Let's go to the pancake house first," suggested my mother. "We can wait there until the party is finished, and then call Mrs. Lardner."

Having all agreed that that was a good plan, we started walking again.   190

"God, just think," said Mona. "We're going to have to *dive* for them."

My father stopped a moment. We waited.

"You girls are good swimmers," he said finally. "Not like me."

Then his shirt started moving again, and we trooped up the hill after it, into the dark.

CONNECTIONS TO OTHER SELECTIONS

1. Discuss the role of cultural tradition in Jen's story and Mishima's "Patriotism" (p. 593).

2. Compare the purpose of humor in Jen's story with its purpose in O'Connor's "A Good Man Is Hard to Find" (p. 381).

3. Write an essay on the role of fathers in Jen's story and Hemingway's "Soldier's Home" (p. 145).

JOYCE CAROL OATES (B. 1938)

A biographical note for Joyce Carol Oates appears on page 199, before her story "The Lady with the Pet Dog." In "The Night Nurse" Oates presents a tense encounter during an unexpected medical emergency.

The Night Nurse   *1993*

Don't doubt there's a future. Rushing toward you.

It was flat pavement, a busy pedestrian mall between downtown streets where she was walking in the tattered sunshine of a moist April morning when without warning the sidewalk tilted to her left, and a sharp pain like a wasp's stinging attacked the calf of her left leg. Wide-eyed and astonished, too surprised at this time to be frightened, she did not scream. She was not the kind of person to scream, especially in a public place.

She fell heavily on her side. Her glasses went flying, her handsome leather handbag dropped from her fingers, the side of her face struck concrete. Her immediate thought was *I've been shot*. The pain was so sudden and so absolute.

Strangers hurried to help. They seemed, to the stricken woman, to be materializing out of the air, with remarkable swiftness and kindness. Afterward she would count herself lucky that she was a well-dressed, well-groomed Caucasian woman stricken in this particular pedestrian mall with its Bonwit's, its Waldenbooks, its gourmet food store and pricey boutiques, and not elsewhere on the fringes of downtown. She was lucky that her handbag wasn't taken from her in the confusion of her fall and that strangers perceived her as one of their kind and not someone diseased, homeless, threatening.

She would remember little of her collapse afterward except its suddenness. And the terrible helplessness of her body fallen to the pavement. An ambulance arrived, its deafening siren translating to her confused brain as a lurid neon-red color. White-clad youngish medics examined her, lifted her onto a stretcher. As in a dream she was being borne aloft. A crowd of curious, snatching eyes parted for her. Alive? Dead? Dying? No one, least of all the stricken woman, seemed to know. 5

And in the speeding ambulance delirious with pain and mounting terror, an incandescent bulb of pain in her left leg just below the knee but still she did not scream biting her lips to keep from screaming and thinking even at this time *I am behaving well, look how calm and civilized.* Then she was being carried into a room glaring with laser-lights, again the quick purposeful hands of strangers probed her, her blood pressure was taken and blood extracted from her limp arm and her voice faltered trying to explain to someone she could not see what had happened to her, the pain in her leg more terrible than any pain she'd known, and a tightness in her chest and shortness of breath but she did not break down sobbing nor did she ask *Am I dying? Will I die?* nor did she beg *Save me!* Her name was Grace Burkhardt and she was forty-four years old and she was a woman accustomed, as the chief administrator of a state arts council, to exercising authority but she seemed to remember none of these external facts as if they applied not to her but to another person and that person a stranger to her. She wanted to explain *I am in good health, I can't believe this has happened to me* as if to repudiate responsibility but she was fainting and could not speak. They would check her identification, they would contact her nearest-of-kin, they would rush her into surgery and all this would be done apart from her volition and so there was a perverse comfort in that—in knowing that, if she died, now, it would not be her fault.

Of course they saved her. Emergency surgery for a "massive" blood clot in her leg which, had it broken free and been carried to her heart, would have resulted in a pulmonary embolism. Grace Burkhardt, dead at the age of forty-four never regaining consciousness even to realize the future had been condensed into the present tense and all was over.

By degrees she woke moaning in the post-op room not knowing where she was but knowing that this was a place strange and frightening to her. And so cold! — she was shivering, her teeth chattering. She experienced a sensation of utter sick helplessness as if she were paralyzed. She could not recall the surgery, or having collapsed. She could not recall if she had been saved from death or was even now being prepared for death. Her vision was blurred as if she were underwater. A face floated near, a stranger's face that was at the same time familiar as a lost sister's.

Help me! she begged the face. *I'm so cold, I'm so frightened!*

The face was a woman's. The features were indistinct but the skin was strangely flushed and shiny, like something not quite fully hatched. There was 10 a smile, thin-lipped and tentative. No-color eyes. *Don't leave me, help! I'm so frightened!* Grace Burkhardt begged as like a large bubble playful and elusive the face rose, lifted lighter than air to disappear through the invisible ceiling.

Her nearest-of-kin was a married, older sister who drove forty miles from Rochester to be with her, staying through much of the day. As news of her "emergency surgery" spread among friends, acquaintances, colleagues at the arts council, there were telephone calls and the first of the floral deliveries. The public self, the self that was Grace Burkhardt, and not this woman in a hospital bed hooked to an IV gurney, her left leg raised and immobile swathed in bandages, struggled to emerge. You could not have guessed that Grace Burkhardt had survived a life-threatening collapse for, on the phone, she was wry, ironic, slightly embarrassed, determined to minimalize her condition. Her eyes were ringed with fatigue, her skin waxy-white, yet her voice maintained its usual timbre, or almost. Nothing meant more to her than to take back the control she'd lost back there in the pedestrian mall, to tell her story as if it were her own. For it was her own. *You wouldn't believe it! So suddenly. Yes, this morning. Yes, downtown. By ambulance. No, no warning. Yes, vascular surgery. A Dr. Rodman, do you know him? Yes, I'm lucky. I know. If it had to happen at all.*

Her sister finally took the telephone from her. She was protesting but too weak to prevail. Her head rang like the interior of a giant seashell. The pain in her leg was a balloon floating at a little distance from her — recognizable as her own, yet not *her. My name is Grace Burkhardt, my name is Grace Burkhardt* believing that this fact would save her. If anything would save her.

A powerful anti-coagulant drug was dripping into her veins to forestall more blood clots — that would save her.

The telephone messages. Daffodils, hyacinth, narcissus from the arts council staff, a potted pink azalea from a woman friend, another potted azalea so vividly crimson she could not look directly at it — these would save her. And the vascular surgeon who'd operated on her and saved her life, who came by the room to speak with her and with her sister. And her own doctor, an internist associated with the hospital who also dropped by on his rounds. And medical insurance forms, with which her sister helped her, and which, in a frail spidery hand, she signed. *You see? I'm fine, my mind hasn't been affected at all.*

And abruptly then, the day ended. This day that stretched dreamlike behind Grace Burkhardt as if to the very horizon to a region she could not see, nor even recall. It was evening, and she was alone. A nurse came to examine her and to give her a barbituate, a nurse's aide, a young cocoa-skinned woman, came to take away her bedpan discreetly covered with an aluminum lid, the light in her room was switched off. She called her sister's name not seeming to recall her sister's actual departure. Now alone, with no witness to admire her bravery, she tasted panic. Her left leg was swollen and stiff encased in bandages and elevated above the bed to reduce the condition the surgeon called "thrombophlebitis" which was the way, she understood, that death would enter her. The crepey-soft interior of her right elbow stung with a mysterious IV fluid dripping into a vein. Death would come as a lethal blood clot or death would come as a sudden massive hemorrhage that was the result of anti-coagulant medication. Though the stricken woman had not prayed in more than thirty years her parched lips moved silently *Help me through the night. Help me through the night.*

She felt a moment's rage at the injustice — that she, a good person, a woman known for her intelligence and her graciousness and her dependability in all things, a woman so widely liked, yes and respected, should be in this position, a life-threatening position. And trapped.

Help me through the night dear God, oh please!

As mercifully the contours of the room melted, the floor sank into darkness as into a pit, the powerful sleeping pill took her.

But then she woke, agitated and open-eyed as if she hadn't slept at all. As if someone had called her name — "Grace Burkhardt." 20

There was a pinching sensation in her bladder, an urgent need to urinate. And such cold, why was the room so cold? — she woke shivering beneath a freezing sheet, a single-ply flannel blanket. The hospital by night was perceptibly cooler than by day. A ventilator rumbled, drafts of cold air passed over her. She'd been dreaming strangely and hadn't there been birds' wings flapping overhead stirring the air against her face . . .

"Grace Burkhardt."

The door had opened, now the door was closed. Someone had been in the room? — Grace tried to sit up, frightened, but was nearly immobilized. A sudden movement awakened pain, her heart's panicked throbbing that was pain, a sharp stinging in her right arm. Her eyes, mildly myopic, dulled with medication, moved blinking in the dark, this was an unfamiliar dark, she understood it was not her bedroom in her home nor any bedroom in her memory. The smell of disinfectant, the ventilator smell. The compression of space that was the size of a cell. She stared at the door a few yards away seeing a rim of light beneath it. For some moments she tried to remember where she was, and why such discomfort and pain, her leg elevated and held fast, her heartbeat so accelerated. As if pulling out of the dark a tangled dream of such complexity, the very effort was exhausting. She heard herself moan but the sound seemed to come from another part of the room. It was self-pity, it was terror and animal pain, it was not *her. I almost died, I'm in the hospital. I'm alone.* Struggling to sit up, to raise her head which swayed dangerously heavy on her shoulders, in a sudden mad terror of choking on her own tears and saliva and the mucus rapidly forming in her sinuses.

She fumbled to switch on her bedside light. Her sister had bought a traveler's digital clock in the gift shop downstairs — it was 2:55 A.M. She would never get through the night.

Yet she tried to calm herself. She was a patient in an excellent suburban 25 hospital, she could not possibly be in danger of dying. *Help me! Help me I'm alone* but she rang the bedside buzzer because she desperately needed a bedpan. The barbituate had apparently knocked her out so completely, at 8:30 P.M., she hadn't wakened until the need to urinate was painful. And she needed an extra blanket. She rang the buzzer as she'd been instructed earlier to ring it and waited and there was no reply over the intercom so she rang it again and still there was no reply and so she counted twenty before ringing it again *Where are you? Isn't anyone there? Please help me* and this time a voice, a female voice, sounded over the intercom asking curtly what did she want and she explained her needs as clearly and politely as possible and the voice mumbled what sounded like *Yes ma'am* and was gone.

And now she waited. Waited and waited. It was three A.M., it was 3:10 A.M., it was 3:16 A.M. She could not get a comfortable position in the bed, her bladder so stricken, her leg at such an angle. Each second was agony. She tried to contract her lower body, her loins, as, as a small child, she'd tried to hold in the warm pee by pressing her thighs as tightly together as possible and not moving, hardly breathing. If she had an accident, urinating in the bed! — if that happened! All her life's history, all the striving of her very soul — to come to *that*. She felt a helpless child-anxiety she hadn't recalled for nearly forty years. The child-anxiety deep in the body of the adult. Remembering the agony of being trapped in some place (in the car, her father driving and unwilling to stop; in school assembly where she would have had to push her way out over the legs of her classmates enduring their jeering attention and the annoyance of her teacher) unable to get to a bathroom. The shame of it. The helplessness.

She rang the buzzer another, protracted time. Just as, thank God, the door was pushed open, and a nurse entered carrying a bedpan.

The night nurse, so short as to seem almost dwarfish. Hardly five feet tall. But round-bodied, with a moon face, peculiar flushed skin that was smooth and shiny as scar tissue; small close-set damp eyes; a thin pursed mouth. At a first glance the nurse might appear young but closer up she was obviously middle-aged, her eyes bracketed by fine white creases. "Here, lift up, like this, come *on* —" she issued instructions to the patient not so much coldly as mechanically, shoving the enamel bedpan beneath her buttocks, pulling down but not replacing the covers. Her manner was brisk and on the edge of impatience as if she and the patient had gone through this routine many times already and there was no need for coyness.

Grace's teeth were chattering with cold. She whispered, flinching under the nurse's unsmiling stare, "Thank you — very much." She could not help herself but began urinating immediately, as soon as the receptacle was in place, while the nurse was still in the room, though on her way out, turning away from Grace as if in disgust. No further words, no questioning of the patient if she needed anything else, no backwards glance. But Grace Burkhardt trapped in the bed was so grateful for this awkward receptacle, this adult-size potty, in which to empty her bursting bladder, she scarcely noticed the nurse's rudeness. If it was rudeness.

Her eyes smarted with the tears of gratitude and humility. Even the pain 30 in her leg seemed to subside. The panicky numbness in her brain. But how long she urinated, in a gush of scalding liquid, then a thinning stream, ceasing and beginning again, she did not know. Minutes? Actual minutes? Looking at the clock finally, when the last of the urine dripped from her, she saw it was 3:38 A.M.

Outside the room's single window it was night. Yet not true night for the room, being lighted now, was reflected in the glass; not as in a mirror but dimly, shapes without substance or color.

I could die here in this room. Others have died here.

She'd had a lover once who had been terrified of hospitals. An intelligent man, a reasonable man, yet, on the subject of hospitals, adamantly irrational. Hospitals are seething with germs, hospitals are where you die. Hospitals are where you have to entrust strangers with your life and you pay for the privilege.

A lover, and not a husband. So many years later, Grace could not clearly remember which of them had loved more deeply, which had been more hurt.

Now they lived a thousand miles apart, and kept in touch by telephone, a   35
few times a year. Thank God they no longer had any mutual friends who might
tell him of her collapse, her emergency surgery. *Massive blood clot. Risk of embolism.* He knew her as a healthy, independent woman. Not the kind of woman
you feel sorry for.

Now Grace was finished with the bedpan, and the sharp smell of urine
pinched her nostrils, she waited for the night nurse, or an attendant, to come
take it away. Surely they knew, at the nurses' station? — she hesitated to ring
the buzzer again.

So she waited. It was 3:40 A.M., it was 3:50 A.M. Finally, shyly, she rang the
buzzer. There was no reply over the intercom.

Maybe the night nurse was making rounds. Giving medication, checking
patients. Maybe, routinely, she would be back in a few minutes. Maybe she
would bring an extra blanket.

At four A.M. Grace rang the buzzer again. There was a sound of static or
shrill voices, then silence. "Hello? Hello —" her voice was plaintive, faltering.

Could die here in this room. Others have died here.   40

The enamel bedpan was pressing into the soft flesh of her buttocks. The
elevation of her leg, and its stiffness, made the pressure more intense.

And how cold the room was — freezing. A continual draft from the window and another, smelling of something dank, metallic, unclean, from the air
vent overhead.

In desperation she wondered if she could remove the damned bedpan herself. But set it where? On the bedside table, only a few inches away? And what if
she spilled it, as certainly she would? — it was impossible to lift herself and to
remove the bedpan at the same time. And now her leg, the entire left side of
her body, was throbbing with pain.

She rang the buzzer again, trying not to panic. Though the intercom was
dead she begged for help — "Please, can you come? I need medication, I'm in
pain. I need a blanket —"

If the night nurse withheld the painkiller from her, what would she do?   45

Don't be absurd. Why would a complete stranger want to hurt you resolved not to
give in to panic though she was trapped in this cell of a room in this bed at the
mercy of the nursing staff. Whom she knew it would be a mistake to antagonize,
especially so early in her hospitalization — Dr. Rodman had told her she might
have to be here a week or more, thrombophlebitis is a serious condition. And her
sister, meaning well, had told her alarming tales of negligent and even hostile
nurses and attendants at big-city hospitals as a way of assuring Grace that here,
by contrast, in this suburban hospital, she would receive better treatment.

At night, the hospital seemed very different than it did by day. It was
closed to visitors until 8:30 A.M. In a panicked fantasy, Grace imagined a fire, at
once she could smell smoke, and she, here, trapped, crippled with pain, paralyzed. If she wrenched her leg free, would its wound be torn open? — would she
begin to bleed? She shuddered, whimpering to herself. Trapped! Trapped on a
bedpan! It was ludicrous, it was laughable! Her own urine sloshing beneath
her, threatening to spill and soak the bed.

She thought she heard the door being opened, the doorknob turning —
but no. If there were footsteps out in the corridor they were gone now.

Strange how the hospital was not much quieter at night. A different and more mysterious kind of sound prevailed—a ceaseless churning like a motor turning over, never quite starting; a deeper throbbing like a jazz downbeat, but arhythmic, irregular. Beyond the vibrating of the ventilator there were distant voices. Pleading, crying. *Help me. Help. Me. Help me.* The voices overlapped, drowning one another out.

When she stopped breathing to listen more closely, the voices faded.

Grace did not want to think whose voices these were.

It seemed to her that she could feel tiny blood clots forming in her afflicted leg, like rain at the point at which it turns to sleet. If a single one of these clots broke free into her bloodstream it would be carried to her heart, to her pulmonary artery, and kill her.

What it is, what finality—to fall to the ground, on dirty pavement, at the feet of strangers. Grace Burkhardt now knew.

She pressed the buzzer another time. The intercom remained dead.

"Help me! Where are you!"

She was agitated, on the brink of hysteria and yet, somehow, she was falling asleep. The room began to shift and lose its contours; the light rapidly fading as if sucked down a drain. The bedpan filled with cooling piss, *her* piss, began to melt, too, its hard enamel warmed by her body. She'd drawn the inadequate covers up to her chin and her eyes were starkly open waiting for the night nurse to return and suddenly she saw—was it possible?—the night nurse *was* back, had been back for some time, evidently?—standing motionless, watching her, just inside the door.

"Grace Burkhardt."

The nurse enunciated these syllables in a flat, nasal, ironic voice.

"Grace Burkhardt."

Grace whispered, frightened, "Yes? Do you know me?"

It was as if she'd never heard her own name before. Never heard its strangeness before.

The nurse's thin lips stretched in a smile. Her small close-set eyes shone with the opacity of glass marbles. "Do you know *me*, Grace Burkhardt?"

Grace stared. Quick as a thread pulled through the eye of a needle and out again she *knew*—knew the woman, or knew the girl the woman had been; but she remembered no name; and did not remember that face. She heard herself saying, quickly, "No. I've never been in this hospital before. I've never—" Her voice trailed off weakly.

There was an awkward pause. The nurse continued to stand motionless, arms folded tight across her breasts. Her peculiar shiny-smooth skin that looked like scar tissue, or like something incompletely hatched, was the color of spoiled cantaloupe. Her lips were bemused, childish in derision. "You wouldn't remember, Grace Burkhardt. No, not *you*."

The stricken woman lay trapped in bed. Her stiff throbbing leg, her arm hooked to an IV apparatus. *She's mad, she's come to injure me* though smiling at the nurse, trying to smile. As if this was an ordinary exchange. Or might become so, if she smiled the right way, if she spoke the right words. "I—can't see very well. My glasses—my eyes— *Do* I know you?"

The nurse made a derisive laughing sound though her eyes showed no mirth. She jerked her chin at the bed—"You're finished there, eh? Grace Burkhardt? So you want *me* to take it away?"

Quickly, apologetically, Grace said, "If you would, please —"

"Registered nurses aren't required to touch bedpans."

"Then — an attendant? Could you call one?"

The nurse shook her head slowly. Bemused, disgusted. Still she stood ⁷⁰ without moving, arms folded across her breasts. In that face, in those eyes, Grace saw — who? It had been years. Half her lifetime. *No! No I don't know you!* She whispered, pleading, "Please, I'm helpless. I need medication, I'm in pain. And this bedpan —"

"*You're* helpless. *You* need help. So what? 'Grace Burkhardt.'"

"Why do you keep saying my name? Do you know me?"

"Why don't you say *my* name? Don't you know *me?*"

Grace stared, and swallowed hard. *I am a good person, I am well-liked, respected.* Recalling how through the years of her career, in her several administrative positions at Wells College, and at the State University at Buffalo, and more recently on the New York State Council of the Arts, she'd been praised for her industry, her fair-mindedness, her diplomacy; her intelligence, her warmth, her inconspicuous competency. Hadn't she overheard, to her embarrassment, just the other day, two young women staff members at the arts council speaking of Grace Burkhardt warmly, comparing her favorably to her male predecessor. *I am an adult now, I am a professional woman, I am no one you know.* Grace heard herself saying in a voice of forced surprise, with a forced smile, "Harriet — ? Is it — Zimmer?"

The nurse said curtly, "*Zink.* Harriet *Zink.*" ⁷⁵

"Of course. Harriet *Zink.*"

Grace should have exclaimed what a coincidence, after so many years, twenty-five? twenty-six? so you became a nurse after all, you didn't give up, how wonderful, Harriet, I'm happy for you — remembering vaguely that Harriet Zink, one of her roommates for part of her freshman year at the State University at Albany had been enrolled in nursing school. But when she drew breath to speak a wave of nausea swept over her. She whispered, "— Please, I need help. My leg — the pain. And the bedpan —"

As if aroused by the word *pain,* the night nurse became more animated. She came closer to Grace, peering at her curiously, almost hungrily. Grace had not given Harriet Zink a thought, or hardly a thought, in twenty-six years, and now — what an irony! The mere face of Harriet Zink, with that childish moon face, now middle-aged — how repulsive! Grace recalled her ex-roommate's prominent front teeth, the peculiar blush of her skin, her unnerving manner that was both groveling and insolent — oh, unmistakable.

They'd lived on the fourth, top floor of Ailey Hall, one of the older residences south of campus near the university hospital. Entering freshman, class of 1967. They were of the same generation glancing at the other's third finger, left hand, to see if there was a wedding band. Neither wore one.

Harriet Zink was asking in a bright, mock-earnest voice, "How is Jilly Her- ⁸⁰ man?" and Grace Burkhardt had to stop to think, "— Jilly Herman?" and Harriet Zink said impatiently, "Grace Burkhardt's roomie Jilly Herman — how is she?" Grace stared at her, perplexed. *I am dreaming this, am I dreaming this* trying not to show the fear she felt as Harriet Zink went on derisively, "The one with the cute blond curls, Jilly Herman," gesturing at her own steely-gray hair with exaggerated wriggly fingers, "— the one with the cute *ass.*"

Grace said, in a faltering voice, "— I haven't seen or heard from Jill Herman in twenty years." Though this was true it sounded weak, like a lie.

Harriet Zink said suspiciously, "You haven't? You expect me to believe that?" When Grace began to protest she cut her off with childish vehemence, "Oh no! I don't believe that! Gracie Burkhardt and Jilly Herman were *best friends*. I bet you still *are*."

These words were mocking, singsong. Grace tried to maintain her smile which was strained and ghastly against her bared teeth. She explained that, after freshman year, she and Jill went their separate ways, speaking earnestly as if this exchange in the middle of the night in such circumstances was not at all extraordinary but normal, and no occasion for alarm. But Harriet Zink interrupted, "And what about Linda Mecky, and Sandy McGuire, and Dolly Slosson," spitting out these names Grace scarcely recalled, and had hardly given a thought to since graduation, " — Barbara West, Sue Ferguson — " the names of freshman girls who'd roomed on the fourth floor of the old sandstone residence hall in the fall of 1963.

There had been six rooms on the floor, all doubles except for the largest which was a triple to which Grace Burkhardt and Jill Herman and Harriet Zink were assigned. But Harriet Zink didn't arrive on campus until October, twelve days late; there'd been an "emergency crisis" in her family. (The residence advisor hinted that Harriet's mother had died, and there'd been other trouble besides. She warned the girls not to bring up the subject unless Harriet initiated it herself—which she was never to do.) By the time the mysterious Harriet Zink arrived at Ailey Hall, friendships and alliances had been formed among the fourth-floor girls in that quick, desperate way in which such relationships are formed in new, disorienting surroundings. There had not seemed space enough for another girl. There had not seemed any need for another girl. And there was the problem, too, of Harriet Zink.

I tried to be nice to you. I did what I could. How am I to blame.   85

Harriet Zink was demanding to know what of these other girls, and Grace Burkhardt was trying to explain she really knew nothing of them, she wasn't in contact with any of them, but Harriet Zink seemed not to believe her, and angry that she should be lying. Grace tried to explain that most of them had only been friends during freshman year and that had been a kind of accident, stuck away on the top floor of Ailey Hall so far from the center of campus life, she tried to evoke the shabby comedy of Ailey Hall with its falling plaster and its leaky windows and its cockroaches, but Harriet Zink kept interrupting, pursuing her own line of inquiry. "Do you remember what you did to me? You, and your friends?" Her face was heated and her small eyes brightly moist. There were half-moons of perspiration beneath the arms of her snug-fitting white nylon uniform and Grace remembered across the abyss of twenty-six years a snug-fitting clumsily homemade red plaid jumper of Harriet Zink's whose underarms were permanently stained. "Don't say you don't remember, Grace Burkhardt!"

Grace frowned, innocently perplexed. She was miserable in her bed, her leg pounding in pain, her head pounding, and, dear God, the sharp smell of urine penetrating the covers, had she spilled some of the urine into the bed, she bit her lip to keep from sobbing *I must not let her see I'm afraid of her, I must stay calm* shaking her head saying, "No, please, Harriet, I don't—" which brought the angry little woman closer to the bed, how like a dwarf she was, so short, and stouter now than she'd been at the age of eighteen, her face rounder, puffier, and that mouth made you think of a slug, always moving, working. Harriet

Zink said in a tone of near-dignity, "*I remember. I still dream about it some-times.*"

Grace said softly, "Harriet, I'm sorry."

"Huh! How can you be sorry, if you don't remember?"

"Please, I'm in pain. If you could help me—"   90

"*I was in pain. You didn't help me.*"

"—I need medication. Painkiller. Please. And this bedpan—please could you take it away—"

"I told you: registered nurses aren't required to take away bedpans. That's not our job."

You never took showers or baths. You wore your clothes until they were filthy. You smelled. You stank. You cried yourself to sleep every night. How am I to blame! Grace knew, yet didn't know: couldn't quite remember. It was so long ago, it was like a bad dream, not her own dream but another's. What exactly had happened be-tween the time Harriet Zink, who like Grace Burkhardt was from a farming family in the central part of the state, and the weekend before Thanksgiving when she moved out of Ailey Hall, dropped out of nursing school. Disap-peared. *I tried to be nice to you. I did what I could. How am I to blame!*

In a lowered, quavering voice Harriet Zink was saying, "You and Jill Her-   95
man, you wouldn't talk to me. I'd be there in the room and you'd send each other signals. Look right through me. Like I was dirt. If I came into the lounge you'd all stop talking and make like there was a bad smell. If I came into the cafeteria where you were all sitting you'd look away and freeze me out. You knew about my mother and how I cried at night and that was funny to you wasn't it. Everything about me was funny to you wasn't it. I was late starting classes and behind on all my work and you could see how scared I was, I couldn't sleep and I couldn't keep food down and all of you knew it, all twelve of you, but it was just a joke to you wasn't it—that I wanted to die."

Grace Burkhardt could not believe what she was hearing. She said, weakly, "Not me, Harriet. Not me. I tried—"

"Oh sure! You'd say to them sometimes, 'Let her alone.' Once in the down-stairs lounge when they were laughing together you said to them, 'That's enough, it isn't funny, let her alone.' But you wouldn't say my name. You wouldn't ever say my name. It was like I was *it* to you. You wouldn't look at me even when we were alone together and if I talked to you, you'd just mumble something back and walk away. I could see in your face you felt sorry for me, sure, you pitied me like a leper, you thought you were so much better than me, you, 'Grace Burkhardt'! You tried to stop them from the worst of what they did but you didn't try hard *enough.*"

"Harriet, I'm sorry. We were so young, then—so ignorant."

"You weren't ignorant. *You* were a scholarship student."

"We didn't mean to be cruel—"   100

"Yes you did! You meant to be cruel," Harriet Zink said, with angry satis-faction. "It made you happy, all of you, to be cruel."

"Harriet, no—"

Harriet Zink continued speaking in her low, accusing voice, her face now brightly flushed, recounting incidents Grace Burkhardt had long since forgot-ten, if indeed she'd ever known. She tried to remember how long pathetic Har-riet Zink had actually roomed with her and Jill Herman before moving down-stairs to a single room near the resident advisor's suite—that room kept in readiness for just such an emergency. *Yes, it's so. It made us happy. Our cruelty. Our loathing for the true freak among us.* After Harriet Zink dropped out of school, having failed more of her midterms, the girls of the fourth floor, including several nursing students to whom she'd been a particular embarrassment, had not missed her. Or, if they missed her, they did not dwell upon her absence. They did not consider its significance. It had nothing to do with them, did it? — *they* were normal, *they* were adjusting to college life. After Harriet Zink moved out of their room Grace and Jill cleaned it as they'd never cleaned it before, exhilarated, singing along with the Kingston Trio whose hit record Jill played repeatedly on her turntable, airing out the room, windows open to a bright dry autumn day, a breeze lifting papers on their desks. Gaily they vacuumed, they scrubbed. Their door was wide open to welcome their friends. *Sad to say, I'm on my way, won't be back for many a day* but their lifted voices, their shining eyes, were anything but sad. The third desk, in the corner, was bare. The third bed, beneath the tilt of the eave, was bare. Later, Grace would cover the bed with a beautiful afghan quilt knitted by her grandmother. The third desk was used by both girls. They were particularly grateful for the extra closet space.

Now Harriet Zink, middle-aged, squat body in her nurse's uniform solid as a little barrel, was leaning over Grace Burkhardt in her bed, saying, in disgust, "'Grace Burkhardt' — you were the evil one among them because you were the one who *knew.* I could see it in your face. And right now! You knew, but you wouldn't help me, you wouldn't be my friend."

Grace said stammering, "Harriet, I'm — I didn't —" her eyes brimming ₁₀₅ with tears of shame, " — forgive me!" She was so frightened she'd leaned away from the angry woman and caused the IV needle to pop out of her vein.

There was a pause. Harriet Zink stared at Grace, leaning so close over her that Grace could see specks of hazel in the iris of her eyes; a glimmer of gold fillings in her mouth. Harriet was breathing harshly, like an overweight woman who has climbed a stairs too quickly. Yet her expression shifted suddenly, turned unexpectedly thoughtful. She said, with the air of one making a discovery, "Yes, I can forgive you, Grace Burkhardt. I'm a Christian woman. In my heart I'm empowered to forgive." She nodded gravely, as if, not knowing until this instant what she'd intended, what she would do, she was taking pleasure in it. "When I saw you here, Grace Burkhardt, and I thought, 'Am I strong enough to forgive that woman? Even with Jesus' help, am I strong enough?' I didn't know. But now I know. I *am* strong enough, I *can* forgive." She spoke with such sudden pride, it was as if sunshine flooded the room.

In this way, as a terrified Grace Burkhardt would not have anticipated, the siege ended.

For a long time after the night nurse left the room Grace lay unmoving too shocked to think even *How am I to blame! I tried, I did try* incredulous thinking *Evil — me? Of all people — me? The woman is a religious maniac.* She was too agitated to sleep yet somehow must have slept if only briefly and then waking opening her eyes wide and amazed that it was still night? still night? when in her dream she'd been staring into the sun as if in penance and her eyes were seared and aching.

She struggled to sit up. She could breathe better, sitting up. Her leg throbbed with pain, pain was like a wave that washed over her and through her leaving her exhausted but wakeful. The bedside lamp was still on. She'd thought the night nurse had turned it off. In the room's single window flat, ghostly reflections floated. She could not identify her own among them.

The night nurse, after her mad outburst, had treated Grace Burkhardt 110 kindly. Or, if not kindly, with a brisk businesslike efficiency. She'd replaced the needle in Grace's bruised right arm, and saw that the IV fluid was dripping into her vein. She called an aide, a young black girl, to bring an extra blanket and to carry away, at last, the bedpan. But, as she explained, she could not give Grace any of the painkiller Oxycodone prescribed for her by Dr. Rodman because the next dosage was scheduled for seven A.M. By that time the day staff would be on duty and another nurse would take care of her. Thank you, Grace murmured, thank you so much, Harriet, humbled and grateful as a chastened child but the night nurse merely shrugged as if embarrassed and then she was gone.

It was only 4:54 A.M. The extra blanket seemed not to make much difference—Grace was still shivering, the room was still very cold. There was a smell of something close, damp, unclean like mold. There was a faint smell of urine. *Help me, help* but Grace had already rung the buzzer and she understood that she'd already been helped and that there was no more help. She decided to sit up sleepless through the remainder of this terrible night though believing, with the resigned half-humor of the damned, that it would never end. Never would it be dawn and never the miraculous hour of seven A.M. and a respite from pain. Thinking, *I am not that strong. I am not evil, but I am not that strong. In her place, I could not forgive.* When she looked at the little digital clock her sister had brought her she saw it was 4:56 A.M.

CONNECTIONS TO OTHER SELECTIONS

1. How is fear made central in "The Night Nurse" and Stephen King's "Suffer the Little Children" (p. 535)? What do you think is the purpose for evoking fear in each story?

2. Discuss the effects of the settings in "The Night Nurse" and Hawthorne's "Young Goodman Brown" (p. 310). Pay particular attention to how the night is treated.

3. Write an essay comparing the protagonist's sense of herself as a human being in "The Night Nurse" and in Susan Minot's "Lust" (p. 290).

TOBIAS WOLFF (B. 1945)

Born in Alabama, Tobias Wolff grew up in the state of Washington. After quitting high school he worked on a ship and for a carnival. In the army he served four years as a paratrooper, after which he studied to pass the entrance exams for Oxford University, from which he graduated with honors. He has published two memoirs—*This Boy's Life* (1989) and *In Pharoah's Army: Memories of the Lost War* (1994). His fiction includes a novel, *The Barracks Thief* (1984) and three collections of stories—*In the Garden of North American Martyrs* (1981), *Back in the World* (1985), and *The Night in Question* (1996). "Powder" was included in *The Best American Short Stories* for 1997.

Powder   *1996*

Just before Christmas my father took me skiing at Mount Baker. He's had to fight for the privilege of my company, because my mother was still angry with him for sneaking me into a night-club during our last visit, to see Thelonious Monk.

He wouldn't give up. He promised, hand on heart, to take good care of me and have me home for dinner on Christmas Eve, and she relented. But as we were checking out of the lodge that morning it began to snow, and in this snow he observed some quality that made it necessary for us to get in one last run. We got in several last runs. He was indifferent to my fretting. Snow whirled around us in bitter, blinding squalls, hissing like sand, and still we skied. As the lift bore us to the peak yet again, my father looked at his watch and said, "Criminey. This'll have to be a fast one."

By now I couldn't see the trail. There was no point in trying. I stuck to him like white on rice and did what he did and somehow made it to the bottom without sailing off a cliff. We returned our skis and my father put chains on the Austin-Healy while I swayed from foot to foot, clapping my mittens and wishing I were home. I could see everything. The green tablecloth, the plates with the holly pattern, the red candles waiting to be lit.

We passed a diner on our way out. "You want some soup?" my father asked. I shook my head. "Buck up," he said. "I'll get you there. Right, doctor?"

I was supposed to say, "Right, doctor," but I didn't say anything.   5

A state trooper waved us down outside the resort. A pair of sawhorses were blocking the road. The trooper came up to our car and bent down to my father's window. His face was bleached by the cold. Snowflakes clung to his eyebrows and to the fur trim of his jacket and cap.

"Don't tell me," my father said.

The trooper told him. The road was closed. It might get cleared, it might not. Storm took everyone by surprise. So much, so fast. Hard to get people moving. Christmas Eve. What can you do?

My father said, "Look. We're talking about four, five inches. I've taken this car through worse than that."

The trooper straightened up, boots creaking. His face was out of sight but   10
I could hear him. "The road is closed."

My father sat with both hands on the wheel, rubbing the wood with his thumbs. He looked at the barricade for a long time. He seemed to be trying to master the idea of it. Then he thanked the trooper, and with a weird, old-maidy show of caution turned the car around. "Your mother will never forgive me for this," he said.

"We should have left before," I said. "Doctor."

He didn't speak to me again until we were both in a booth at the diner, waiting for our burgers. "She won't forgive me," he said. "Do you understand? Never."

"I guess," I said, but no guesswork was required; she wouldn't forgive him.

"I can't let that happen." He bent toward me. "I'll tell you what I want. I   15
want us to be together again. Is that what you want?"

I wasn't sure, but I said, "Yes, sir."

He bumped my chin with his knuckles. "That's all I needed to hear."

When we finished eating he went to the pay phone in the back of the diner, then joined me in the booth again. I figured he'd called my mother, but he didn't give a report. He sipped at his coffee and stared out the window at the empty road. "Come on!" When the trooper's car went past, lights flashing, he got up and dropped some money on the check. "Okay. *Vamanos.*"

The wind had died. The snow was falling straight down, less of it now; lighter. We drove away from the resort, right up to the barricade. "Move it," my father told me. When I looked at him he said, "What are you waiting for?" I got out and dragged one of the sawhorses aside, then pushed it back after he drove through. When I got inside the car he said, "Now you're an accomplice. We go down together." He put the car in gear and looked at me. "Joke, doctor."

"Funny, doctor."   20

Down the first long stretch I watched the road behind us, to see if the trooper was on our tail. The barricade vanished. Then there was nothing but snow: snow on the road, snow kicking up from the chains, snow on the trees, snow in the sky; and our trail in the snow. I faced around and had a shock. The lie of the road behind us had been marked by our own tracks, but there were no tracks ahead of us. My father was breaking virgin snow between a line of tall trees. He was humming "Stars Fell on Alabama." I felt snow brush along the floorboards under my feet. To keep my hands from shaking I clamped them between my knees.

My father grunted in a thoughtful way and said, "Don't ever try this your-self."

"I won't."

"That's what you say now, but someday you'll get your license and then you'll think you can do anything. Only you won't be able to do this. You need, I don't know—a certain instinct."

"Maybe I have it."   25

"You don't. You have your strong points, but not . . . you know. I only mention it because I don't want you to get the idea this is something just any-body can do. I'm a great driver. That's not a virtue, okay? It's just a fact, and one you should be aware of. Of course you have to give the old heap some credit, too—there aren't many cars I'd try this with. Listen!"

I listened. I heard the slap of the chains, the stiff, jerky rasp of the wipers, the purr of the engine. It really did purr. The car was almost new. My father couldn't afford it, and kept promising to sell it, but here it was.

I said, "Where do you think that policeman went to?"

"Are you warm enough?" He reached over and cranked up the blower. Then he turned off the wipers. We didn't need them. The clouds had bright-ened. A few sparse, feathery flakes drifted into our slipstream and were swept away. We left the trees and entered a broad field of snow that ran level for a while and then tilted sharply downward. Orange stakes had been planted at intervals in two parallel lines and my father ran a course between them, though they were far enough apart to leave considerable doubt in my mind as to where exactly the road lay. He was humming again, doing little scat riffs around the melody.

"Okay, then. What are my strong points?"   30

"Don't get me started," he said. "It'd take all day."

"Oh, right. Name one."

"Easy. You always think ahead."

True. I always thought ahead. I was a boy who kept his clothes on num-bered hangers to ensure proper rotation. I bothered my teachers for homework assignments far ahead of their due dates so I could make up schedules. I thought ahead, and that was why I knew that there would be other troopers waiting for us at the end of our ride, if we got there. What I did not know was that my father would wheedle and plead his way past them — he didn't sing "O Tannenbaum" but just about — and get me home for dinner, buying a little more time before my mother decided to make the split final. I knew we'd get caught; I was resigned to it. And maybe for this reason I stopped moping and began to enjoy myself.

Why not? This was one for the books. Like being in a speedboat, only bet- 35 ter. You can't go downhill in a boat. And it was all ours. And it kept coming, the laden trees, the unbroken surface of snow, the sudden white vistas. Here and there I saw hints of the road, ditches, fences, stakes, but not so many that I could have found my way. But then I didn't have to. My father in his forty-eighth year, rumpled, kind, bankrupt of honor, flushed with certainty. He was a great driver. All persuasion, no coercion. Such subtlety at the wheel, such tactful pedalwork. I actually trusted him. And the best was yet to come — switchbacks and hairpins impossible to describe. Except maybe to say this: if you haven't driven fresh powder, you haven't driven.

CONNECTIONS TO OTHER SELECTIONS

1. Compare the relationship between the father and son in "Powder" and in Faulkner's "Barn Burning" (p. 481). How is loyalty an issue in each story?

2. Consider the significance of the titles of "Powder" and of David Updike's "Summer" (p. 169). What alternative titles for these two stories can you think of to help evoke their meaning?

3. Write an essay on the first-person narration of "Powder" and John Updike's "A & P" (p. 576). How does the voice of each narrator affect your view of him? Explain why you prefer one narrator to the other.

POETRY

POETRY

14

Reading Poetry

READING POETRY RESPONSIVELY

Perhaps the best way to begin reading poetry responsively is not to allow yourself to be intimidated by it. Come to it, initially at least, the way you might listen to a song on the radio. You probably listen to a song several times before you hear it all, before you have a sense of how it works, where it's going, and how it gets there. You don't worry about analyzing a song when you listen to it, even though after repeated experiences with it you know and anticipate a favorite part and know, on some level, why it works for you. Give yourself a chance to respond to poetry. The hardest work has already been done by the poet, so all you need to do at the start is listen for the pleasure produced by the poet's arrangement of words.

Try reading the following poem aloud. Read it aloud before you read it silently. You may stumble once or twice, but you'll make sense of it if you pay attention to its punctuation and don't stop at the end of every line where there is no punctuation. The title gives you an initial sense of what the poem is about.

MARGE PIERCY (B. 1936)

The Secretary Chant   *1973*

My hips are a desk.
From my ears hang
chains of paper clips.
Rubber bands form my hair.
My breasts are wells of mimeograph ink.   5
My feet bear casters.
Buzz. Click.
My head is a badly organized file.

My head is a switchboard
where crossed lines crackle.   10
Press my fingers
and in my eyes appear
credit and debit.
Zing. Tinkle.
My navel is a reject button.   15
From my mouth issue canceled reams.
Swollen, heavy, rectangular
I am about to be delivered
of a baby
Xerox machine.   20
File me under W
because I wonce
was
a woman.

What is your response to this secretary's chant? The point is simple
enough — she feels dehumanized by her office functions — but the pleasures are manifold. Piercy makes the speaker's voice sound mechanical by
using short bursts of sound and by having her make repetitive, flat, matter-
of-fact statements ("My breasts . . . My feet . . . My head . . . My navel").
"The Secretary Chant" makes a serious statement about how such women
are reduced to functionaries. The point is made, however, with humor
since we are asked to visualize the misappropriation of the secretary's
body — her identity — as it is transformed into little more than a piece of
office equipment, which seems to be breaking down in the final lines, when
we learn that she "wonce / was / a woman." Is there the slightest hint of
something subversive in this misspelling of "wonce"? Maybe so, but the
humor is clear enough, particularly if you try to make a drawing of what
this dehumanized secretary has become.

The next poem creates a different kind of mood. Think about the title,
"Those Winter Sundays," before you begin reading the poem. What associations do you have with winter Sundays? What emotions does the phrase
evoke in you?

ROBERT HAYDEN (1913–1980)

Those Winter Sundays   1962

Sundays too my father got up early
and put his clothes on in the blueblack cold,
then with cracked hands that ached
from labor in the weekday weather made
banked fires blaze. No one ever thanked him.   5

I'd wake and hear the cold splintering, breaking.
When the rooms were warm, he'd call,
and slowly I would rise and dress,
fearing the chronic angers of that house,

Speaking indifferently to him,   10
who had driven out the cold
and polished my good shoes as well.
What did I know, what did I know
of love's austere and lonely offices?

Does the poem match the feelings you have about winter Sundays? Either way your response can be useful in reading the poem. For most of us Sundays are days at home; they might be cozy and pleasant experiences or they might be dull and depressing. Whatever they are, Sundays are more evocative than, say, Tuesdays. Hayden uses that response to call forth a sense of missed opportunity in the poem. The person who reflects on those winter Sundays didn't know until much later how much he had to thank his father for "love's austere and lonely offices." This is a poem about a cold past and a present reverence for his father — elements brought together by the phrase "Winter Sundays." *His* father? You may have noticed that the poem doesn't use a masculine pronoun; hence the voice could be a woman's. Does the sex of the voice make any difference to your reading? Would it make any difference about which details are included or what language is used?

What is most important about your initial readings of a poem is that you ask questions. If you read responsively, you'll find yourself asking all kinds of questions about the words, descriptions, sounds, and structures of a poem. The specifics of those questions will be generated by the particular poem. We don't, for example, ask how humor is achieved in "Those Winter Sundays" because there is none, but it is worth asking what kind of tone is established by the description of "the chronic angers of that house." The remaining chapters in this part will help you to formulate and answer questions about a variety of specific elements in poetry, such as speaker, image, metaphor, symbol, rhyme, and rhythm. For the moment, however, read the following poem several times and note your response at different points in the poem. Then write down a half dozen or so questions about what produces your response to the poem. To answer questions, it's best to know first what the questions are, and that's what the rest of this chapter is about.

JOHN UPDIKE (B. 1932)

Dog's Death   1969

She must have been kicked unseen or brushed by a car.
Too young to know much, she was beginning to learn
To use the newspapers spread on the kitchen floor
And to win, wetting there, the words, "Good dog! Good dog!"

We thought her shy malaise was a shot reaction.   5
The autopsy disclosed a rupture in her liver.
As we teased her with play, blood was filling her skin
And her heart was learning to lie down forever.

Monday morning, as the children were noisily fed
And sent to school, she crawled beneath the youngest's bed.   10

We found her twisted and limp but still alive.
In the car to the vet's, on my lap, she tried

To bite my hand and died. I stroked her warm fur
And my wife called in a voice imperious with tears.
Though surrounded by love that would have upheld her,   15
Nevertheless she sank and, stiffening, disappeared.

Back home, we found that in the night her frame,
Drawing near to dissolution, had endured the shame
Of diarrhoea and had dragged across the floor
To a newspaper carelessly left there. *Good dog.*   20

Here's a simple question to get started with your own questions: what would its effect have been if Updike had titled the poem "Good Dog" instead of "Dog's Death"?

THE PLEASURE OF WORDS

The impulse to create and appreciate poetry is as basic to human experience as language itself. Although no one can point to the precise origins of poetry, it is one of the most ancient of the arts, because it has existed ever since human beings discovered pleasure in language. The tribal ceremonies of peoples without written languages suggest that the earliest primitive cultures incorporated rhythmic patterns of words into their rituals. These chants, very likely accompanied by the music of a simple beat and the dance of a measured step, expressed what people regarded as significant and memorable in their lives. They echoed the concerns of the chanters and the listeners by chronicling acts of bravery, fearsome foes, natural disasters, mysterious events, births, deaths, and whatever else brought people pain or pleasure, bewilderment or revelation. Later cultures, such as the ancient Greeks, made poetry an integral part of religion.

Thus, from its very beginnings, poetry has been associated with what has mattered most to people. These concerns — whether natural or supernatural — can, of course, be expressed without vivid images, rhythmic patterns, and pleasing sounds, but human beings have always sensed a magic in words that goes beyond rational, logical understanding. Poetry is not simply a method of communication; it is a unique experience in itself.

What is special about poetry? What makes it valuable? Why should we read it? How is reading it different from reading prose? To begin with, poetry pervades our world in a variety of forms, ranging from advertising jingles to song lyrics. These may seem to be a long way from the chants heard around a primitive campfire, but they serve some of the same purposes. Like poems printed in a magazine or book, primitive chants, catchy jingles, and popular songs attempt to stir the imagination through the carefully measured use of words.

Although reading poetry usually makes more demands than does the kind of reading used to skim a magazine or newspaper, the appreciation of poetry comes naturally enough to anyone who enjoys playing with words. Play is an important element of poetry. Consider, for example, how the following words appeal to the children who gleefully chant them in playgrounds:

> I scream, you scream
> We all scream
> For ice cream.

These lines are an exuberant evocation of the joy of ice cream. Indeed, chanting the words turns out to be as pleasurable as eating ice cream. In poetry, the expression of the idea is as important as the idea expressed.

But is "I scream . . ." poetry? Some poets and literary critics would say that it certainly is one kind of poem because the children who chant it experience some of the pleasures of poetry in its measured beat and repeated sounds. However, other poets and critics would define poetry more narrowly and insist, for a variety of reasons, that this isn't true poetry but merely *doggerel,* a term used for lines whose subject matter is trite and whose rhythm and sounds are monotonously heavy-handed.

Although probably no one would argue that "I scream . . ." is a great poem, it does contain some poetic elements that appeal, at the very least, to children. Does that make it poetry? The answer depends on one's definition, but poetry has a way of breaking loose from definitions. Because there are nearly as many definitions of poetry as there are poets, Edwin Arlington Robinson's succinct observations are useful: "poetry has two outstanding characteristics. One is that it is undefinable. The other is that it is eventually unmistakable."

This comment places more emphasis on how a poem affects a reader than on how a poem is defined. By characterizing poetry as "undefinable," Robinson acknowledges that it can include many different purposes, subjects, emotions, styles, and forms. What effect does the following poem have on you?

WILLIAM HATHAWAY (b. 1944)
Oh, Oh
1982

My girl and I amble a country lane,
moo cows chomping daisies, our own
sweet saliva green with grass stems.
"Look, look," she says at the crossing,
"the choo-choo's light is on." And sure   5
enough, right smack dab in the middle
of maple dappled summer sunlight
is the lit headlight — so funny.
An arm waves to us from the black window.
We wave gaily to the arm. "When I hear   10
trains at night I dream of being president,"

I say dreamily. "And me first lady," she
says loyally. So when the last boxcars,
named after wonderful, faraway places,
and the caboose chuckle by we look   15
eagerly to the road ahead. And there,
poised and growling, are fifty Hell's Angels.

Hathaway's poem serves as a convenient reminder that poetry can be full of surprises. Even on a first reading there is no mistaking the emotional reversal created by the last few words of this poem. With the exception of the final line, the poem's language conjures up an idyllic picture of a young couple taking a pleasant walk down a country lane. Contented as "moo cows," they taste the sweetness of the grass, hear peaceful country sounds, and are dazzled by "dappled summer sunlight." Their future together seems to be all optimism as they anticipate "wonderful, faraway places" and the "road ahead." Full of confidence, this couple, like the reader, is unprepared for the shock to come. When we see those "fifty Hell's Angels," we are confronted with something like a bucket of cold water in the face.

But even though our expectations are abruptly and powerfully reversed, we are finally invited to view the entire episode from a safe distance — the distance provided by the delightful humor in this poem. After all, how seriously can we take a poem that is titled "Oh, Oh"? The poet has his way with us, but we are brought in on the joke too. The terror takes on comic proportions as the innocent couple is confronted by no fewer than *fifty* Hell's Angels. This is the kind of raucous overkill that informs a short animated film produced some years ago titled *Bambi Meets Godzilla:* you might not have seen it, but you know how it ends. The poem's good humor comes through when we realize how pathetically inadequate the response of "Oh, Oh" is to the circumstances.

As you can see, reading a description of what happens in a poem is not the same as experiencing a poem. The exuberance of "I scream . . ." and the surprise of Hathaway's "Oh, Oh" are in the hearing or reading rather than in the retelling. A *paraphrase* is a prose restatement of the central ideas of a poem in your own language. Consider the difference between the following poem and the paraphrase that follows it. What is missing from the paraphrase?

ROBERT FRANCIS (1901–1987)

Catch   *1950*

Two boys uncoached are tossing a poem together,
Overhand, underhand, backhand, sleight of hand, every hand,
Teasing with attitudes, latitudes, interludes, altitudes,
High, make him fly off the ground for it, low, make him stoop,
Make him scoop it up, make him as-almost-as-possible miss it,   5
Fast, let him sting from it, now, now fool him slowly,
Anything, everything tricky, risky, nonchalant,

Anything under the sun to outwit the prosy,
Over the tree and the long sweet cadence down,
Over his head, make him scramble to pick up the meaning,   10
And now, like a posy, a pretty one plump in his hands.

Paraphrase: A poet's relationship to a reader is similar to a game of catch. The poem, like a ball, should be pitched in a variety of ways to challenge and create interest. Boredom and predictability must be avoided if the game is to be engaging and satisfying.

A paraphrase can help us achieve a clearer understanding of a poem, but, unlike a poem, it misses all the sport and fun. It is the poem that "outwit[s] the prosy" because the poem serves as an example of what it suggests poetry should be. Moreover, the two players — the poet and the reader — are "uncoached." They know how the game is played, but their expectations do not preclude spontaneity and creativity or their ability to surprise and be surprised. The solid pleasure of the workout — of reading poetry — is the satisfaction derived from exercising your imagination and intellect.

That pleasure is worth emphasizing. Poetry uses language to move and delight even when it includes a cast of fifty Hell's Angels. The pleasure is in having the poem work its spell on us. For that to happen, it is best to relax and enjoy poetry rather than worry about definitions of it. Pay attention to what the poet throws you. We read poems for emotional and intellectual discovery — to feel and to experience something about the world and ourselves. The ideas in poetry — what can be paraphrased in prose — are important, but the real value of a poem consists in the words that work their magic by allowing us to feel, see, and be more than we were before. Perhaps the best way to approach a poem is similar to what Francis's "Catch" implies: expect to be surprised; stay on your toes; and concentrate on the delivery.

A SAMPLE ANALYSIS

Tossing Metaphors Together in "Catch"

The following sample paper on Robert Francis's "Catch" was written in response to an assignment that asked the students to discuss the use of metaphor in the poem. Notice that Chris Leggett's paper is clearly focused and well organized. His discussion of the use of metaphor in the poem stays on track from beginning to end without any detours concerning unrelated topics (for a definition of *metaphor,* see p. 777). His title draws on the central metaphor of the poem, and he organizes the paper around four key words used in the poem: "attitudes, latitudes, interludes, altitudes." These constitute the heart of the paper's four substantive paragraphs, and they are effectively framed by introductory and concluding paragraphs. Moreover, the transitions between paragraphs clearly indicate that the author was not merely tossing a paper together.

Chris Leggett
Professor Lyles
English 203-1
November 9, 19--

Tossing Metaphors Together in "Catch"

The word "catch" is an attention getter. It usually
means something is about to be hurled at someone and that
he or she is expected to catch it. "Catch" can also signal
a challenge to another player if the toss is purposefully
difficult. Robert Francis, in his poem "Catch," uses the
extended metaphor of two boys playing catch to explore
the considerations a poet makes when "tossing a poem together." Line 3 of "Catch" enumerates these considerations
metaphorically as "attitudes, latitudes, interludes, [and]
altitudes." While regular prose is typically straightforward and easily understood, poetry usually takes great
effort to understand and appreciate. To exemplify this,
Francis presents the reader not with a normal game of
catch with the ball flying back and forth in a repetitive
and predictable fashion, but with a physically challenging
game in which one must concentrate, scramble, and exert
oneself to catch the ball, as one must stretch the intellect to truly grasp a poem.

The first consideration mentioned by Francis is attitude. Attitude, when applied to the game of catch, indicates the ball's pitch in flight, upward, downward, or
straight. It could also describe the players' attitudes
toward each other or toward the game in general. Below
this literal level lies attitude's meaning in relation to
poetry. Attitude in this case represents a poem's tone. A
poet may "teas[e] with attitude" by experimenting with
different tones to achieve the desired mood. The underlying tone of "Catch" is a playful one, set and reinforced

by the use of a game. This playfulness is further reinforced by such words and phrases as "teasing," "outwit,"
and "fool him."

Considered also in the metaphorical game of catch is
latitude, which, when applied to the game, suggests the
range the object may be thrown--how high, how low, or how
far. Poetic latitude, along similar lines, concerns a
poem's breadth, or the scope of topic. Taken one level
further, latitude suggests freedom from normal restraints
or limitations, indicating the ability to go outside the
norm to find originality of expression. The entire game of
catch described in Francis's poem reaches outside the normal expectations of something being merely tossed back and
forth in a predictable manner. The ball is thrown in almost every conceivable fashion, "overhand, underhand . . .
every hand." Other terms describing the throws--such as
"tricky," "risky," "fast," "slowly," and "Anything under
the sun"--express endless latitude for avoiding predictability in Francis's game of catch and metaphorically in
writing poetry.

During a game of catch the ball may be thrown at different intervals, establishing a steady rhythm or a broken, irregular one. Other intervening features, such as
the field being played on or the weather, could also affect the game. These features of the game are alluded to
in the poem by the use of the word "interludes." "Interlude" in the poetic sense represents the poem's form,
which can similarly establish or diminish rhythm or enhance meaning. Lines 6 and 9 respectively show a broken
and a flowing rhythm. Line 6 begins rapidly as a hard toss
that stings the catcher's hand is described. The rhythm of
the line is immediately slowed, however, by the word "now"
followed by a comma, followed by the rest of the line. In

contrast, line 9 flows smoothly as the reader visualizes the ball flying over the tree and sailing downward. The words chosen for this line function perfectly. The phrase "the long sweet cadence down" establishes a sweet rhythm that reads smoothly and rolls off the tongue easily. The choice of diction not only affects the poem's rhythmic flow but also establishes through connotative language the various levels at which the poem can be understood, represented in "Catch" as altitude.

While "altitudes" when referring to the game of catch means how high an object is thrown, in poetry it could refer to the level of diction, lofty or down-to-earth, formal or informal. It suggests also the levels at which a poem can be comprehended, the literal as well as the interpretive. In Francis's game of catch the ball is thrown either high to make the player reach, low to make him stoop, or over his head to make him scramble, implying that the player should have to exert himself to catch it. So too, then, should the reader of poetry put great effort into understanding the full meaning of a poem. Francis exemplifies this consideration in writing poetry by giving "Catch" not only an enjoyable literal meaning concerning the game of catch but also a rich metaphorical meaning--reflecting the process of writing poetry. Francis uses several phrases and words with multiple meanings. The phrase "tossing a poem together" can be understood as tossing something back and forth or the process of constructing a poem. While "prosy" suggests prose itself, it also means the mundane or the ordinary. In the poem's final line the word "posy" of course represents a flower, while it is also a variant of the word "poesy," meaning poetry, or the practice of composing poetry.

```
                                                Leggett 4
     Francis effectively describes several considerations
to be taken in writing poetry in order to "outwit the
prosy." His use of the extended metaphor in "Catch" shows
that a poem must be unique, able to be comprehended on
multiple levels, and a challenge to the reader. The vari-
ous rhythms in the lines of "Catch" exemplify the ideas
they express. While achieving an enjoyable poem on the
literal level, Francis has also achieved a rich metaphori-
cal meaning. The poem offers a good workout both physi-
cally and intellectually.
```

Before beginning your own writing assignment on poetry, you should review Chapter 15, "Writing about Poetry," and Chapter 38, "Reading and Writing," which provides a step-by-step overview of how to choose a topic, develop a thesis, and organize various types of writing assignments. If you are using outside sources in your paper, you should make sure that you are familiar with the conventional documentation procedures described in Chapter 39, "The Literary Research Paper."

WOLE SOYINKA (B. 1934)

Telephone Conversation   *1960*

The price seemed reasonable, location
Indifferent. The landlady swore she lived
Off premises. Nothing remained
But self-confession. "Madam," I warned,
"I hate a wasted journey — I am African."   5
Silence. Silenced transmission of
Pressurized good-breeding. Voice, when it came,
Lipstick coated, long gold-rolled
Cigarette-holder pipped. Caught I was, foully.
"HOW DARK?" . . . I had not misheard . . . "ARE YOU LIGHT   10
OR VERY DARK?" Button B. Button A. Stench
Of rancid breath of public hide-and-speak.
Red booth. Red pillar-box. Red double-tiered
Omnibus squelching tar. It *was* real! Shamed
By ill-mannered silence, surrender   15

Pushed dumbfoundment to beg simplification.
Considerate she was, varying the emphasis —
"ARE YOU DARK? OR VERY LIGHT?" Revelation came.
"You mean — like plain or milk chocolate?"
Her assent was clinical, crushing in its light   20
Impersonality. Rapidly, wave-length adjusted,
I chose. "West African sepia" — and as afterthought,
"Down in my passport." Silence for spectroscopic
Flight of fancy, till truthfulness clanged her accent
Hard on the mouthpiece. "WHAT'S THAT?" conceding   25
"DON'T KNOW WHAT THAT IS." "Like brunette."
"THAT'S DARK, ISN'T IT?" "Not altogether.
Facially, I am brunette, but madam, you should see
The rest of me. Palm of my hand, soles of my feet
Are a peroxide blonde. Friction, caused —   30
Foolishly madam — by sitting down, has turned
My bottom raven black — One moment madam!" — sensing
Her receiver rearing on the thunderclap
About my ears — "Madam," I pleaded, "wouldn't you rather
See for yourself?"   35

   The conversation that we hear in this traditional English telephone
box evokes serious racial tensions as well as a humorous treatment of
them; the benighted tradition represented by the landlady seems to be no
match for the speaker's satiric wit.
   Poets often remind us that beauty can be found in unexpected places.
What is it that Elizabeth Bishop finds so beautiful about the "battered"
fish she describes in the following poem?

ELIZABETH BISHOP (1911–1979)

The Fish   *1946*

I caught a tremendous fish
and held him beside the boat
half out of water, with my hook
fast in a corner of his mouth.
He didn't fight.   5
He hadn't fought at all.
He hung a grunting weight,
battered and venerable
and homely. Here and there
his brown skin hung in strips   10
like ancient wall-paper,
and its pattern of darker brown
was like wall-paper:
shapes like full-blown roses
stained and lost through age.   15

He was speckled with barnacles,
fine rosettes of lime,
and infested
with tiny white sea-lice,
and underneath two or three   20
rags of green weed hung down.
While his gills were breathing in
the terrible oxygen
— the frightening gills,
fresh and crisp with blood,   25
that can cut so badly —
I thought of the coarse white flesh
packed in like feathers,
the big bones and the little bones,
the dramatic reds and blacks   30
of his shiny entrails,
and the pink swim-bladder
like a big peony.
I looked into his eyes
which were far larger than mine   35
but shallower, and yellowed,
the irises backed and packed
with tarnished tinfoil
seen through the lenses
of old scratched isinglass.   40
They shifted a little, but not
to return my stare.
— It was more like the tipping
of an object toward the light.
I admired his sullen face,   45
the mechanism of his jaw,
and then I saw
that from his lower lip
— if you could call it a lip —
grim, wet, and weapon-like,   50
hung five old pieces of fish-line,
or four and a wire leader
with the swivel still attached,
with all their five big hooks
grown firmly in his mouth.   55
A green line, frayed at the end
where he broke it, two heavier lines,
and a fine black thread
still crimped from the strain and snap
when it broke and he got away.   60
Like medals with their ribbons
frayed and wavering,
a five-haired beard of wisdom
trailing from his aching jaw.
I stared and stared   65

and victory filled up
the little rented boat,
from the pool of bilge
where oil had spread a rainbow
around the rusted engine   70
to the bailer rusted orange,
the sun-cracked thwarts,
the oarlocks on their strings,
the gunnels — until everything
was rainbow, rainbow, rainbow!   75
And I let the fish go.

CONSIDERATIONS FOR CRITICAL THINKING AND WRITING

1. FIRST RESPONSE. Which lines in this poem provide especially vivid details of
   the fish? What makes these descriptions effective?
2. How is the fish characterized? Is it simply a weak victim because it "didn't
   fight"?
3. Comment on lines 65–76. In what sense has "victory filled up" the boat,
   given that the speaker finally lets the fish go?

The speaker in Bishop's "The Fish" ends on a triumphantly joyful
note. The *speaker* is the voice used by the author in the poem; like the narrator in a work of fiction, the speaker is often a created identity rather than
the author's actual self. The two should not automatically be equated.
Contrast the attitude toward life of the speaker in "The Fish" with that of
the speaker in the following poem.

PHILIP LARKIN (1922–1985)
A Study of Reading Habits   *1964*

When getting my nose in a book
Cured most things short of school,
It was worth ruining my eyes
To know I could still keep cool,
And deal out the old right hook   5
To dirty dogs twice my size.

Later, with inch-thick specs,
Evil was just my lark:
Me and my cloak and fangs
Had ripping times in the dark.   10
The women I clubbed with sex!
I broke them up like meringues.

Don't read much now: the dude
Who lets the girl down before
The hero arrives, the chap   15

Who's yellow and keeps the store,
Seem far too familiar. Get stewed:
Books are a load of crap.

What the speaker sees and describes in "The Fish" is close if not identical to Bishop's own vision and voice. The joyful response to the fish is clearly shared by the speaker and the poet, between whom there is little or no distance. In "A Study of Reading Habits," however, Larkin distances himself from a speaker whose sensibilities he does not wholly share. The poet — and many readers — might identify with the reading habits described by the speaker in the first twelve lines, but Larkin uses the last six lines to criticize the speaker's attitude toward life as well as reading. The speaker recalls in lines 1-6 how as a schoolboy he identified with the hero, whose virtuous strength always triumphed over "dirty dogs," and in lines 7-12 he recounts how his schoolboy fantasies were transformed by adolescence into a fascination with violence and sex. This description of early reading habits is pleasantly amusing, because many readers of popular fiction will probably recall having moved through similar stages, but at the end of the poem the speaker provides more information about himself than he intends to.

As an adult the speaker has lost interest in reading because it is no longer an escape from his own disappointed life. Instead of identifying with heroes or villains, he finds himself identifying with minor characters who are irresponsible and cowardly. Reading is now a reminder of his failures, so he turns to alcohol. His solution, to "Get stewed" because "Books are a load of crap," is obviously self-destructive. The speaker is ultimately exposed by Larkin as someone who never grew beyond fantasies. Getting drunk is consistent with the speaker's immature reading habits. Unlike the speaker, the poet understands that life is often distorted by escapist fantasies, whether through a steady diet of popular fiction or through alcohol. The speaker in this poem, then, is not Larkin but a created identity whose voice is filled with disillusionment and delusion.

The problem with Larkin's speaker is that he misreads books as well as his own life. Reading means nothing to him unless it serves as an escape from himself. It is not surprising that Larkin has him read fiction rather than poetry because poetry places an especially heavy emphasis on language. Fiction, indeed any kind of writing, including essays and drama, relies on carefully chosen and arranged words, but poetry does so to an even greater extent. Notice, for example, how Larkin's deft use of trite expressions and slang characterizes the speaker so that his language reveals nearly as much about his dreary life as what he says. Larkin's speaker would have no use for poetry.

What is "unmistakable" in poetry (to use Robinson's term again) is its intense, concentrated use of language — its emphasis on individual words to convey meanings, experiences, emotions, and effects. Poets never simply process words; they savor them. Words in poems frequently create their own tastes, textures, scents, sounds, and shapes. They often seem more sensuous than ordinary language, and readers usually sense that a word has been hefted before making its way into a poem. Although poems are crafted differently from the ways a painting, sculpture, or musical composition is created, in each form of art the creator delights in the medium. Poetry is carefully orchestrated so that the words work together as elements in a structure to sustain close, repeated readings. The words are chosen to interact with one another to create the maximum desired effect, whether the purpose is to capture a mood or feeling, create a vivid experience, express a point of view, narrate a story, or portray a character.

Here is a poem that looks quite different from most *verse,* a term used for lines composed in a measured rhythmical pattern, which are often, but not necessarily, rhymed.

ROBERT MORGAN (B. 1944)

Mountain Graveyard   1979

for the author of "Slow Owls"

Spore Prose

stone	notes
slate	tales
sacred	cedars
heart	earth
asleep	please
hated	death

Though unconventional in its appearance, this is unmistakably poetry because of its concentrated use of language. The poem demonstrates how serious play with words can lead to some remarkable discoveries. At first glance "Mountain Graveyard" may seem intimidating. What, after all, does this list of words add up to? How is it in any sense a poetic use of language? But if the words are examined closely, it is not difficult to see how they work. The wordplay here is literally in the form of a game. Morgan uses a series of *anagrams* (words made from the letters of other words, such as *read* and *dare*) to evoke feelings about death. "Mountain Graveyard" is one of several poems that Morgan has called "Spore Prose" (another anagram) because he finds in individual words the seeds of poetry. He wrote the poem in honor of the fiftieth birthday of another poet, Jonathan Williams, the author of "Slow Owls," whose title is also an anagram.

The title, "Mountain Graveyard," indicates the poem's setting, which is also the context in which the individual words in the poem interact to provide a larger meaning. Morgan's discovery of the words on the stones of a graveyard is more than just clever. The observations he makes among the silent graves go beyond the curious pleasure a reader experiences in finding the words *sacred cedars,* referring to evergreens common in cemeteries, to

consist of the same letters. The surprise and delight of realizing the connection between heart and earth is tempered by the more sober recognition that everyone's story ultimately ends in the ground. The hope that the
dead are merely asleep is expressed with a plea that is answered grimly by a
hatred of death's finality.

Little is told in this poem. There is no way of knowing who is buried or
who is looking at the graves, but the emotions of sadness, hope, and pain
are unmistakable — and are conveyed in fewer than half the words of this
sentence. Morgan takes words that initially appear to be a dead, prosaic list
and energizes their meanings through imaginative juxtapositions.

The following poem also involves a startling discovery about words.
With the peculiar title "l(a," the poem cannot be read aloud, so there is no
sound, but is there sense, a *theme,* a central idea or meaning, in the poem?

E. E. CUMMINGS (1894–1962)
l(a   1958

l(a

le

af

fa

ll

s)

one

l

iness

CONSIDERATIONS FOR CRITICAL THINKING AND WRITING

1. FIRST RESPONSE. Discuss the connection between what appears inside and
   outside the parentheses in this poem.

2. What does Cummings draw attention to by breaking up the words? How
   do this strategy and the poem's overall shape contribute to its theme?

3. Which seems more important in this poem — what is expressed, or the way
   it is expressed?

Although "Mountain Graveyard" and "l(a" do not resemble the kind
of verse that readers might recognize immediately as poetry on a page,
both are actually a very common type of poem, called the *lyric,* usually a
brief poem that expresses the personal emotions and thoughts of a single
speaker. Lyrics are often written in the first person but sometimes — as in
"Spore Prose" and "l(a" — no speaker is specified. Lyrics present a subjective
mood, emotion, or idea. Very often they are about love or death, but
almost any subject or experience that evokes some intense emotional
response can be found in lyrics. In addition to brevity and emotional intensity, lyrics are also frequently characterized by their musical qualities. The

word *lyric* derives from the Greek word *lyre*, meaning a musical instrument that originally accompanied the singing of a lyric. Lyric poems can be organized in a variety of ways, such as the sonnet, elegy, and ode (see Chapter 22), but it is enough to point out here that lyrics are an extremely popular kind of poetry with writers and readers.

The following anonymous lyric was found in a sixteenth-century manuscript.

ANONYMOUS

Western Wind

c. 1500

Western wind, when wilt thou blow,
The small rain down can rain?
Christ, if my love were in my arms,
And I in my bed again!

This speaker's intense longing for his lover is characteristic of lyric poetry. He impatiently addresses the western wind that brings spring to England and could make it possible for him to be reunited with the woman he loves. We do not know the details of these lovers' lives because this poem focuses on the speaker's emotion. We do not learn why the lovers are apart or if they will be together again. We don't even know if the speaker is a man. But those issues are not really important. The poetry gives us a feeling rather than a story.

A poem that tells a story is called a ***narrative poem.*** Narrative poetry may be short or very long. An ***epic,*** for example, is a long narrative poem on a serious subject chronicling heroic deeds and important events. Among the most famous epics are Homer's *Iliad* and *Odyssey,* the Old English *Beowulf,* Dante's *Divine Comedy,* and John Milton's *Paradise Lost.* More typically, however, narrative poems are considerably shorter, such as the following poem, which tells the story of a child's memory of her father.

REGINA BARRECA (B. 1957)

Nighttime Fires

1986

When I was five in Louisville
we drove to see nighttime fires. Piled seven of us,
all pajamas and running noses, into the Olds,
drove fast toward smoke. It was after my father
lost his job, so not getting up in the morning   5
gave him time: awake past midnight, he read old newspapers
with no news, tried crosswords until he split the pencil
between his teeth, mad. When he heard
the wolf whine of the siren, he woke my mother,
and she pushed and shoved   10

us all into waking. Once roused we longed for burnt wood
and a smell of flames high into the pines. My old man liked
driving to rich neighborhoods best, swearing in a good mood
as he followed fire engines that snaked like dragons
and split the silent streets. It was festival, carnival. 15

If there were a Cadillac or any car
in a curved driveway, my father smiled a smile
from a secret, brittle heart.
His face lit up in the heat given off by destruction
like something was being made, or was being set right. 20
I bent my head back to see where sparks
ate up the sky. My father who never held us
would take my hand and point to falling cinders that
covered the ground like snow, or, excited, show us
the swollen collapse of a staircase. My mother 25
watched my father, not the house. She was happy
only when we were ready to go, when it was finally over
and nothing else could burn.
Driving home, she would sleep in the front seat
as we huddled behind. I could see his quiet face in the 30
rearview mirror, eyes like hallways filled with smoke.

This narrative poem could have been a short story if the poet had wanted to say more about the "brittle heart" of this unemployed man whose daughter so vividly remembers the desperate pleasure he took in watching fire consume other people's property. Indeed, a reading of Faulkner's short story "Barn Burning" suggests how such a character can be further developed and how his child responds to him. The similarities between Faulkner's angry character and the poem's father, whose "eyes [are] like hallways filled with smoke," are coincidental, but the characters' sense of "something . . . being set right" by flames is worth comparing. Although we do not know everything about this man and his family, we have a much firmer sense of their story than we do of the story of the couple in "Western Wind."

Although narrative poetry is still written, short stories and novels have largely replaced the long narrative poem. Lyric poems tend to be the predominant type of poetry today. Regardless of whether a poem is a narrative or a lyric, however, the strategies for reading it are somewhat different from those for reading prose. Try these suggestions for approaching poetry.

SUGGESTIONS FOR APPROACHING POETRY

1. Assume that it will be necessary to read a poem more than once. Give yourself a chance to become familiar with what the poem has to offer. Like a piece of music, a poem becomes more pleasurable with each encounter.

2. Pay attention to the title; it will often provide a helpful context for the poem and serve as an introduction to it. Larkin's "A Study of Reading Habits" is precisely what its title describes.

3. As you read the poem for the first time, avoid becoming entangled in words or lines that you don't understand. Instead, give yourself a chance to take in the entire poem before attempting to resolve problems encountered along the way.

4. On a second reading, identify any words or passages that you don't understand. Look up words you don't know; these might include names, places, historical and mythical references, or anything else that is unfamiliar to you.

5. Read the poem aloud (or perhaps have a friend read it to you). You'll probably discover that some puzzling passages suddenly fall into place when you hear them. You'll find that nothing helps, though, if the poem is read in an artificial, exaggerated manner. Read in as natural a voice as possible, with slight pauses at line breaks. Silent reading is preferable to imposing a te-tumpty-te-tum reading on a good poem.

6. Read the punctuation. Poems use punctuation marks — in addition to the space on the page — as signals for readers. Be especially careful not to assume that the end of a line marks the end of a sentence, unless it is concluded by punctuation. Consider, for example, the opening lines of Hathaway's "Oh, Oh":

> My girl and I amble a country lane,
> moo cows chomping daisies, our own
> sweet saliva green with grass stems.

Line 2 makes little or no sense if a reader stops after "own." Keeping track of the subjects and verbs will help you find your way among the sentences.

7. Paraphrase the poem to determine whether you understand what happens in it. As you work through each line of the poem, a paraphrase will help you to see which words or passages need further attention.

8. Try to get a sense of who is speaking and what the setting or situation is. Don't assume that the speaker is the author; often it is a created character.

9. Assume that each element in the poem has a purpose. Try to explain how the elements of the poem work together.

10. Be generous. Be willing to entertain perspectives, values, experiences, and subjects that you might not agree with or approve. Even if baseball bores you, you should be able to comprehend its imaginative use in Francis's "Catch."

11. Try developing a coherent approach to the poem that helps you to shape a discussion of the text. See Chapter 37, "Critical Strategies for Reading," to review formalist, biographical, historical, psychological, feminist, and other possible critical approaches.

12. Don't expect to produce a definitive reading. Many poems do not resolve all the ideas, issues, or tensions in them, and so it is not always

possible to drive their meaning into an absolute corner. Your reading will explore rather than define the poem. Poems are not trophies to be stuffed and mounted. They're usually more elusive. And don't be afraid that a close reading will damage the poem. Poems aren't hurt when we analyze them; instead, they come alive as we experience them and put into words what we discover through them.

A list of more specific questions using the literary terms and concepts discussed in the following chapters begins on page 711. That list, like the suggestions just made, raises issues and questions that can help you to read just about any poem closely. These strategies should be a useful means for getting inside poems to understand how they work. Furthermore, because reading poetry inevitably increases sensitivity to language, you're likely to find yourself a better reader of words in any form—whether in a novel, a newspaper editorial, an advertisement, a political speech, or a conversation—after having studied poetry. In short, many of the reading skills that make poetry accessible also open up the world you inhabit.

You'll probably find some poems amusing or sad, some fierce or tender, and some fascinating or dull. You may find, too, some poems that will get inside you. Their kinds of insights—the poet's and yours—are what Emily Dickinson had in mind when she defined poetry this way: "If I read a book and it makes my whole body so cold no fire can ever warm me, I know that it is poetry. If I feel physically as if the top of my head were taken off, I know that it is poetry." Dickinson's response may be more intense than most—poetry was, after all, at the center of her life—but you too might find yourself moved by poems in unexpected ways. In any case, as Edwin Arlington Robinson knew, poetry is, to an alert and sensitive reader, "eventually unmistakable."

POETRY IN POPULAR FORMS

Before you try out these strategies for reading on a few more poems, it is worth acknowledging that the verse that enjoys the widest readership appears not in collections, magazines, or even anthologies for students, but in greeting cards. A significant amount of the personal daily mail delivered in the United States consists of greeting cards. That represents millions of lines of verse going by us on the street and in planes over our heads. These verses share some similarities with the poetry included in this anthology, but there are also important differences that indicate the need for reading serious poetry closely rather than casually.

The popularity of greeting cards is easy to explain: just as many of us have neither the time nor the talent to make gifts for birthdays, weddings, anniversaries, graduations, Valentine's Day, Mother's Day, and other holidays, we are unlikely to write personal messages when cards conveniently say them for us. Although impersonal, cards are efficient and convey an important message no matter what the occasion for them: I care. These greetings are rarely serious poetry; they are not written to be. Nevertheless, they demonstrate the impulse in our culture to generate and receive poetry.

In a handbook for greeting-card free-lancers, a writer and past editor of such verse began with this advice:

> Once you determine what you want to say—and in this regard it is best to stick to one basic idea—you must choose your words to do several things at the same time:
>
> 1. Your idea must be expressed as a complete idea; it must have a beginning, a middle, and an end.
> 2. There must be coherence in your verse. Every line must be linked logically and smoothly with its neighbors.
> 3. Your expressions . . . must be conversational. High-flown language rarely comes off successfully in greeting card writing.
> 4. You must write with emphasis—and something else: enthusiasm. It's necessary to create interest in that all-important first line. From that point on, writing your verse is a matter of developing your idea and bringing it to a peak of emphasis in the last line. Occasionally you will find that you have shot your wad too early in the verse, and whatever you say after that point sounds like an afterthought.
> 5. You must do all of the above and at the same time make everything come out right in the meter-and-rhyme department.[1]

This advice is followed by a list of approximately fifty of the most frequently used rhyme sounds accompanied by rhyming words, such as *love, of, above* for the sound *uv*. The point of these prescriptions is that the verse must be written so that it is immediately accessible—consumable—by both the buyer and the recipient. Writers of these cards are expected to avoid any complexity.

Compare the following greeting-card verse with the poem that comes after it. "Magic of Love," by Helen Farries, has been a longtime favorite in a major greeting-card company's "wedding line"; with different endings it has been used also in valentines and friendship cards.

Helen Farries

Magic of Love   *date unknown*

There's a wonderful gift that can give you a lift,
It's a blessing from heaven above!
It can comfort and bless, it can bring happiness—
It's the wonderful MAGIC OF LOVE!

Like a star in the night, it can keep your faith bright,   5
Like the sun, it can warm your hearts, too—

---

[1]Chris Fitzgerald, "Conventional Verse: The Sentimental Favorite," *The Greeting Card Writer's Handbook,* ed. H. Joseph Chadwick (Cincinnati: Writer's Digest, 1975): 13, 17.

It's a gift you can give every day that you live,
And when given, it comes back to you!

When love lights the way, there is joy in the day
And all troubles are lighter to bear,   10
Love is gentle and kind, and through love you will find
There's an answer to your every prayer!

May it never depart from your two loving hearts,
May you treasure this gift from above —
You will find if you do, all your dreams will come true,   15
In the wonderful MAGIC OF LOVE!

JOHN FREDERICK NIMS (B. 1913)

Love Poem   1947

My clumsiest dear, whose hands shipwreck vases,
At whose quick touch all glasses chip and ring,
Whose palms are bulls in china, burs in linen,
And have no cunning with any soft thing

Except all ill-at-ease fidgeting people: 5
The refugee uncertain at the door
You make at home; deftly you steady
The drunk clambering on his undulant floor.

Unpredictable dear, the taxi drivers' terror,
Shrinking from far headlights pale as a dime   10
Yet leaping before red apoplectic streetcars —
Misfit in any space. And never on time.

A wrench in clocks and the solar system. Only
With words and people and love you move at ease.
In traffic of wit expertly maneuver   15
And keep us, all devotion, at your knees.

Forgetting your coffee spreading on our flannel,
Your lipstick grinning on our coat,
So gaily in love's unbreakable heaven
Our souls on glory of spilt bourbon float.   20

Be with me, darling, early and late. Smash glasses —
I will study wry music for your sake.
For should your hands drop white and empty
All the toys of the world would break.

CONSIDERATIONS FOR CRITICAL THINKING AND WRITING

1. FIRST RESPONSE. Read these two works aloud. How are they different? How
   the same?
2. To what extent does the advice to would-be greeting-card writers apply to
   each work?

3. Compare the two speakers. Which do you find more appealing? Why?
4. How does Nims's description of love differ from Farries's?

In contrast to poetry, which transfigures and expresses an emotion or experience through an original use of language, the verse in "Magic of Love" relies on *clichés,* ideas or expressions that have become tired and trite from overuse, such as describing love as "a blessing from heaven above." Clichés anesthetize readers instead of alerting them to the possibility of fresh perceptions. They are used to draw out *stock responses,* predictable, conventional reactions to language, characters, symbols, or situations; God, heaven, the flag, motherhood, hearts, puppies, and peace are some often-used objects of stock responses. Advertisers manufacture careers from this sort of business.

Clichés and stock responses are two of the major ingredients of sentimentality in literature. *Sentimentality* exploits the reader by inducing responses that exceed what the situation warrants. This pejorative term should not be confused with *sentiment,* which is synonymous with *emotion* or *feeling.* Sentimentality cons readers into falling for the mass murderer who is devoted to stray cats, and it requires that we not think twice about what we're feeling because those tears shed for the little old lady, the rage aimed at the vicious enemy soldier, and the longing for the simple virtues of poverty might disappear under the slightest scrutiny. The experience of sentimentality is not unlike biting into a swirl of cotton candy; it's momentarily sweet but wholly insubstantial.

Clichés, stock responses, and sentimentality are generally the hallmarks of weak writing. Poetry — the kind that is unmistakable — achieves freshness, vitality, and genuine emotion that sharpen our perceptions of life.

Although the most widely read verse is found in greeting cards, the most widely *heard* poetry appears in song lyrics. Not all songs are poetic, but a good many share the same effects and qualities as poems. Consider these lyrics by Bruce Springsteen about Philadelphia, the City of Brotherly Love.

BRUCE SPRINGSTEEN (B. 1949)

Streets of Philadelphia   *1993*

I was bruised and battered and I couldn't tell
What I felt
I was unrecognizable to myself
I saw my reflection in a window I didn't know
My own face   5
Oh brother are you gonna leave me
Wastin' away
On the streets of Philadelphia

I walked the avenue till my legs felt like stone
I heard the voices of friends vanished and gone   10

At night I could hear the blood in my veins
Black and whispering as the rain
On the streets of Philadelphia

Ain't no angel gonna greet me
It's just you and I my friend   15
My clothes don't fit me no more
I walked a thousand miles
Just to slip this skin

The night has fallen, I'm lyin' awake
I can feel myself fading away   20
So receive me brother with your faithless kiss
Or will we leave each other alone like this
On the streets of Philadelphia

CONSIDERATIONS FOR CRITICAL THINKING AND WRITING

1. FIRST RESPONSE. Characterize Philadelphia in this song lyric. What sort of life is described by the speaker? Which images seem especially evocative to you?

2. Why is there almost no punctuation in these lines? How do you make sense of the lines in the absence of conventional punctuation?

3. What kind of mood is evoked by the language of this song? How does your reading of "Streets of Philadelphia" compare with listening to Springsteen singing it (available on his *Greatest Hits,* a Columbia CD)?

4. Explain whether you think this song can be accurately called a narrative poem.

QUEEN LATIFAH (B. 1970)

The Evil That Men Do   *1989*

You asked, I came
So behold the Queen
Let's add a little sense to the scene
I'm livin' positive
Not out here knocked up   5
But the lines are so dangerous
I oughta be locked up
This rhyme doesn't require prime time
I'm just sharin' thoughts in mind
Back again because I knew you wanted it   10
From the Latifah with the Queen in front of it
Droppin' bombs, you're up in arms and puzzled
The lines will flow like fluid while you guzzle
You slip, I'll drop you on a BDP-produced track
From KRS to be exact   15
It's a Flavor Unit quest that today has me speakin'
'Cause it's knowledge I'm seekin'

Enough about myself, I think it's time that I tell you
About the Evil That Men Do

Situations, reality, what a concept   20
Nothin' ever seems to stay in step
So today here is a message for my sisters and brothers
Here are some things I want to cover
A woman strives for a better life
But who the hell cares   25
Because she's livin' on welfare
The government can't come up with a decent housin' plan
So she's in no man's land
It's a sucker who tells you you're equal
(You don't need 'em   30
Johannesburg cries for freedom)
We the people hold these truths to be self-evident
(But there's no response from the president)
Someone's livin' the good life tax-free
'Cause some poor girl can't find   35
A way to be crack-free
And that's just part of the message
I thought I had to send you
About the Evil That Men Do

Tell me, don't you think it's a shame   40
When someone can put a quarter in a video game
But when a homeless person approaches you on the street
You can't treat him the same
It's time to teach the deaf, the dumb, the blind
That black on black crime only shackles and binds   45
You to a doom, a fate worse than death
But there's still time left
To stop puttin' your conscience on cease
And bring about some type of peace
Not only in your heart but also in your mind   50
It will benefit all mankind
Then there will be one thing
That will never stop you
And it's the Evil That Men Do

CONSIDERATIONS FOR CRITICAL THINKING AND WRITING

1. FIRST RESPONSE. Describe the "message for my sisters and brothers" in this
   rap song (line 22).

2. Comment on the effects of the rhymes. How do they help the lines "flow
   like fluid" (line 13)?

3. This song's title is taken from III. ii. of Shakespeare's play *Julius Caesar*:

   Friends, Romans, countrymen, lend me your ears;
   I come to bury Caesar, not to praise him.

The evil that men do lives after them,
The good is oft interred with their bones.

How does knowing the context of Queen Latifah's title enrich your under-standing of the poem?

CONNECTION TO ANOTHER SELECTION

1. Compare the world described in this song with that presented in "Streets of Philadelphia" (p. 694).

PERSPECTIVE

ROBERT FRANCIS (1901–1987)

On "Hard" Poetry   *1965*

When Robert Frost said he liked poems hard he could scarcely have meant he liked them difficult. If he had meant difficult he would have said he didn't like them easy. What he said was that he didn't like them soft.

Poems can be soft in several ways. They can be soft in form (invertebrate). They can be soft in thought and feeling (sentimental). They can be soft with excess verbiage. Frost used to advise [writers] to squeeze the water out of a poem. He liked poems dry. What is dry tends to be hard, and what is hard is al-ways dry, except perhaps on the outside.

Yet though hardness here does not mean difficulty, some difficulty natu-rally goes with hardness. A hard poem may not be hard to read but is hard to write. Not too hard, preferably. Not so hard to write that there is no flow in the writer. But hard enough for the growing poem to meet with some healthy re-sistance. Frost often found this healthy resistance in a tight rhyme scheme and strict meter. There are other ways of getting good resistance, of course.

And in the reader too, a hard poem will bring some difficulty. Preferably not too much. Not enough difficulty to completely baffle him. Ideally a hard poem should not be too hard to make sense of, but hard to exhaust its mean-ing and its beauty.

"What I care about is the hardness of the poems. I don't like them soft, I want them to be little pebbles, but placed where they won't dislodge easily. And I'd like them to be little pebbles of precious stone—precious, or semi-precious" (interview with John Ciardi, *Saturday Review,* March 21, 1959).

Here is hard prose talking about hard poetry. Frost was never shrewder or more illuminating. Here, as well as in anything else he ever said, is his flavor.

What contemporary of his can you imagine saying this or anything like it?

In 1843 Emerson jotted in his journal: "Hard clouds and hard expressions, and hard manners, I love."

From *The Satirical Rogue on Poetry*

CONSIDERATIONS FOR CRITICAL THINKING AND WRITING

1. What is the distinction between "hard" and "soft" poetry?

2. Given Francis's brief essay and his poem "Catch" (p. 676), write a review of Helen Farries's "Magic of Love" (p. 692) as you think Francis would.

3. Explain whether you would characterize Bruce Springsteen's "Streets of Philadelphia" (p. 694) as hard or soft.

POEMS FOR FURTHER STUDY

MICHAEL ONDAATJE (B. 1943)

To a Sad Daughter   *1984*

All night long the hockey pictures
gaze down at you
sleeping in your tracksuit.
Belligerent goalies are your ideal.
Threats of being traded   5
cuts and wounds
— all this pleases you.
O my god! you say at breakfast
reading the sports page over the Alpen
as another player breaks his ankle   10
or assaults the coach.

When I thought of daughters
I wasn't expecting this
but I like this more.
I like all your faults   15
even your purple moods
when you retreat from everyone
to sit in bed under a quilt.
And when I say "like"
I mean of course "love"   20
but that embarrasses you.
You who feel superior to black and white movies
(coaxed for hours to see *Casablanca*)
though you were moved
by *Creature from the Black Lagoon.*   25

One day I'll come swimming
beside your ship or someone will
and if you hear the siren
listen to it. For if you close your ears
only nothing happens. You will never change.   30
I don't care if you risk
your life to angry goalies

creatures with webbed feet.
You can enter their caves and castles
their glass laboratories. Just   35
don't be fooled by anyone but yourself.

This is the first lecture I've given you.
You're "sweet sixteen" you said.
I'd rather be your closest friend
than your father. I'm not good at advice   40
you know that, but ride
the ceremonies
until they grow dark.

Sometimes you are so busy
discovering your friends   45
I ache with a loss
— but that is greed.
And sometimes I've gone
into *my* purple world
and lost you.   50

One afternoon I stepped
into your room. You were sitting
at the desk where I now write this.
Forsythia outside the window
and sun spilled over you   55
like a thick yellow miracle
as if another planet
was coaxing you out of the house
— all those possible worlds! —
and you, meanwhile, busy with mathematics.   60

I cannot look at forsythia now
without loss, or joy for you.
You step delicately
into the wild world
and your real prize will be   65
the frantic search.
Want everything. If you break
break going out not in.
How you live your life I don't care
but I'll sell my arms for you,   70
hold your secrets for ever.

If I speak of death
which you fear now, greatly,
it is without answers,
except that each   75
one we know is
in our blood.
Don't recall graves.
Memory is permanent.
Remember the afternoon's   80

yellow suburban annunciation.
Your goalie
in his frightening mask
dreams perhaps
of gentleness.   85

CONSIDERATIONS FOR CRITICAL THINKING AND WRITING

1. FIRST RESPONSE. What sort of relationship does this father have with his daughter?

2. Consider the appropriateness of the title. In what sense is the daughter "sad"?

3. Discuss the references to hockey in the poem. What purpose do they serve?

CONNECTION TO ANOTHER SELECTION

1. Write an essay comparing the father in this poem with the father in Sylvia Plath's "Daddy" (p. 1113).

ALICE WALKER (B. 1944)

a woman is not a potted plant   *1991*

A WOMAN IS NOT
A POTTED PLANT

her roots bound
to the confines
of her house   5

a woman is not
a potted plant
her leaves trimmed
to the contours
of her sex   10

a woman is not
a potted plant
her branches
espaliered
against the fences   15
of her race
her country
her mother
her man

her trained blossom   20
turning
this way
& that
to follow
the sun   25

of whoever feeds
and waters
her

a woman
is wilderness   30
unbounded
holding the future
between each breath
walking the earth
only because   35
she is free
and not creepervine
or tree.

Nor even honeysuckle
or bee.   40

CONSIDERATIONS FOR CRITICAL THINKING AND WRITING

1. FIRST RESPONSE. According to the speaker, how do the properties of a pot-
    ted plant inappropriately describe a woman? (Have you ever considered a
    woman to be *like* a potted plant?)

2. What *is* a woman, according to the speaker? What is the effect of defining
    her primarily by what she is not?

3. Describe the meaning and effect of the poem's final two lines.

CONNECTION TO ANOTHER SELECTION

1. Compare Walker's take on female identity in this poem with Piercy's in "The
    Secretary Chant" (p. 671). How are their conceptions similar? Different?

WYATT PRUNTY (B. 1947)

Elderly Lady Crossing on Green   1993

And give her no scouts doing their one good deed
Or sentimental cards to wish her well
During Christmas time or gallstone time —
Because there was a time, she'd like to tell,

She drove a loaded V8 powerglide   5
And would have run you flat as paint
To make the light before it turned on her,
Make it as she watched you faint

When looking up you saw her bearing down
Eyes locking you between the wheel and dash,   10
And you either scrambled back where you belonged
Or jaywalked to eternity, blown out like trash

Behind the grease spot where she braked on you. . . .
Never widow, wife, mother, or a bride,

And nothing up ahead she's looking for   15
But asphalt, the dotted line, the other side,

The way she's done a million times before,
With nothing in her brief to tell you more
Than she's a small tug on the tidal swell
Of her own sustaining notion that she's doing well.   20

CONSIDERATIONS FOR CRITICAL THINKING AND WRITING

1. FIRST RESPONSE. Does the description of the elderly lady in the poem undercut your expectations about her created by the title? Is this poem sentimental, ironic, or something else?

2. In what ways is this elderly woman "doing well" (line 20)? Does the poem
   suggest any ways in which she's not?

3. Describe the effect produced by the first line's beginning with "And . . . ."
   Why is this a fitting introduction to this elderly lady?

CONNECTION TO ANOTHER SELECTION

1. Write an essay comparing the humor in this poem with that of Hathaway's
   "Oh, Oh" (p. 675).

ALBERTO RÍOS (B. 1952)

Seniors   *1985*

William cut a hole in his Levi's pocket
so he could flop himself out in class
behind the girls so the other guys
could see and shit what guts we all said.
All Konga wanted to do over and over   5
was the rubber band trick, but he showed
everyone how, so nobody wanted to see
anymore and one day he cried, just cried
until his parents took him away forever.
Maya had a Hotpoint refrigerator standing   10
in his living room, just for his family to show
anybody who came that they could afford it.

Me, I got a French kiss, finally, in the catholic
darkness, my tongue's farthest half vacationing
loudly in another mouth like a man in Bermudas,   15
and my body jumped against a flagstone wall,
I could feel it through her thin, almost
nonexistent body: I had, at that moment, that moment,
a hot girl on a summer night, the best of all
the things we tried to do. Well, she   20
let me kiss her, anyway, all over.

Or it was just a flagstone wall
with a flaw in the stone, an understanding cavity

for burning young men with smooth dreams—
the true circumstance is gone, the true   25
circumstances about us all then
are gone. But when I kissed her, all water,
she would close her eyes, and they into somewhere
would disappear. Whether she was there
or not, I remember her, clearly, and she moves   30
around the room, sometimes, until I sleep.

I have lain on the desert in watch
low in the back of a pick-up truck
for nothing in particular, for stars, for
the things behind stars, and nothing comes   35
more than the moment: always now, here in a truck,
the moment again to dream of making love and sweat,
this time to a woman, or even to all of them
in some allowable way, to those boys, then,
who couldn't cry, to the girls before they were   40
women, to friends, me on my back, the sky over me
pressing its simple weight into her body
on me, into the bodies of them all, on me.

CONSIDERATIONS FOR CRITICAL THINKING AND WRITING

1. FIRST RESPONSE. Comment on the use of slang in the poem. Does it surprise you? How does it characterize the speaker?

2. How does the language of the final stanza differ from that of the first stanza? To what purpose?

3. Write an essay that discusses the speaker's attitudes toward sex and life. How are they related?

CONNECTIONS TO OTHER SELECTIONS

1. Compare the treatment of sex in this poem with that in Sharon Olds's "Sex without Love" (p. 740).

2. Think about "Seniors" as a kind of love poem and compare the speaker's voice here with the one in T. S. Eliot's "The Love Song of J. Alfred Prufrock" (p. 1045). How are these two voices used to evoke different cultures? Of what value is love in these cultures?

MARY JO SALTER (B. 1954)

Welcome to Hiroshima   *1985*

is what you first see, stepping off the train:
a billboard brought to you in living English
by Toshiba Electric. While a channel
silent in the TV of the brain

projects those flickering re-runs of a cloud   5
that brims its risen columnful like beer

and, spilling over, hangs its foamy head,
you feel a thirst for history: what year

it started to be safe to breathe the air,
and when to drink the blood and scum afloat   10
on the Ohta River. But no, the water's clear,
they pour it for your morning cup of tea

in one of the countless sunny coffee shops
whose plastic dioramas advertise
mutations of cuisine behind the glass: 15
a pancake sandwich; a pizza someone tops

with a maraschino cherry. Passing by
the Peace Park's floral hypocenter (where
how bravely, or with what mistaken cheer,
humanity erased its own erasure),   20

you enter the memorial museum
and through more glass are served, as on a dish
of blistered grass, three mannequins. Like gloves
a mother clips to coatsleeves, strings of flesh

hang from their fingertips; or as if tied   25
to recall a duty for us, *Reverence*
the dead whose mourners too shall soon be dead,
but all commemoration's swallowed up

in questions of bad taste, how re-created
horror mocks the grim original,   30
and thinking at last *They should have left it all*
you stop. This is the wristwatch of a child.

Jammed on the moment's impact, resolute
to communicate some message, although mute,
it gestures with its hands at eight-fifteen   35
and eight-fifteen and eight-fifteen again

while tables of statistics on the wall
update the news by calling on a roll
of tape, death gummed on death, and in the case
adjacent, an exhibit under glass   40

is glass itself: a shard the bomb slammed in
a woman's arm at eight-fifteen, but some
three decades on — as if to make it plain
hope's only as renewable as pain,

and as if all the unsung   45
debasements of the past may one day come
rising to the surface once again —
worked its filthy way out like a tongue.

CONSIDERATIONS FOR CRITICAL THINKING AND WRITING

1. FIRST RESPONSE. Describe the tone of the poem's final line. How does it make you feel?

2. Describe the scene set by the first five stanzas. Is the speaker in "Welcome to Hiroshima" feeling welcome? Welcoming the reader?

3. How is the commemoration of the atomic bombing of Hiroshima "swallowed up in questions of bad taste" (lines 28–29) in this poem? Pick out specific images, and describe your reaction to them.

4. Do the speaker's emotions change through the course of the poem? Explain whether or not you think this is a hopeful or pessimistic poem.

CONNECTION TO ANOTHER SELECTION

1. Write an essay comparing Salter's treatment of the commemoration of Hiroshima with Denise Levertov's in "Gathered at the River" (p. 907).

JOHN DONNE (1572–1631)

The Sun Rising   *c. 1633*

      Busy old fool, unruly sun,
        Why dost thou thus,
Through windows, and through curtains, call on us?
Must to thy motions lovers' seasons run?
        Saucy pedantic wretch, go chide   5
        Late schoolboys, and sour prentices,
   Go tell court-huntsmen that the king will ride,
   Call country ants° to harvest offices;   *farm workers*
Love, all alike, no season knows, nor clime,
Nor hours, days, months, which are the rags of time.   10

      Thy beams, so reverend and strong
        Why shouldst thou think?
I could eclipse and cloud them with a wink,
But that I would not lose her sight so long:
        If her eyes have not blinded thine,   15
        Look, and tomorrow late, tell me
   Whether both the Indias° of spice and mine   *East and West Indies*
   Be where thou left'st them, or lie here with me.
Ask for those kings whom thou saw'st yesterday,
And thou shalt hear, all here in one bed lay.   20

      She is all states, and all princes I,
        Nothing else is.
Princes do but play us; compared to this,
All honor's mimic, all wealth alchemy.
        Thou, sun, art half as happy as we,   25
        In that the world's contracted thus;
   Thine age asks ease, and since thy duties be
To warm the world, that's done in warming us.

Shine here to us, and thou art every where;
This bed thy center° is, these walls thy sphere.   *of orbit*   30

CONSIDERATIONS FOR CRITICAL THINKING AND WRITING

1. FIRST RESPONSE. What is the situation in this poem? Why is the speaker angry with the sun? What does he urge the sun to do in the first stanza?

2. What claims does the speaker make about the power of love in stanzas 2 and 3? What does he mean when he says, "Shine here to us, and thou art every where"?

3. Are any of the speaker's exaggerations in any sense true? How?

CONNECTION TO ANOTHER SELECTION

1. Compare this lyric poem with Richard Wilbur's "A Late Aubade" (p. 732). What similarities do you find in the ideas and emotions expressed in each?

LI HO (791–817)

A Beautiful Girl Combs Her Hair   *date unknown*

TRANSLATED BY DAVID YOUNG

Awake at dawn
she's dreaming
by cool silk curtains

fragrance of spilling hair
half sandalwood, half aloes   5

windlass creaking at the well
singing jade

the lotus blossom wakes, refreshed

her mirror
two phoenixes   10
a pool of autumn light

standing on the ivory bed
loosening her hair
watching the mirror

one long coil, aromatic silk   15
a cloud down to the floor

drop the jade comb — no sound

delicate fingers
pushing the coils into place
color of raven feathers   20

shining blue-black stuff
the jewelled comb will hardly hold it

spring wind makes me restless
her slovenly beauty upsets me

eighteen and her hair's so thick   25
she wears herself out fixing it!

she's finished now
the whole arrangement in place

in a cloud-patterned skirt
she walks with even steps   30
a wild goose on the sand

turns away without a word
where is she off to?

down the steps to break a spray of
    cherry blossoms   35

CONSIDERATIONS FOR CRITICAL THINKING AND WRITING

1. FIRST RESPONSE. Try to paraphrase the poem. What is lost by rewording?
2. How does the speaker use sensuous language to create a vivid picture of the girl?
3. What are the speaker's feelings toward the girl? Do they remain the same throughout the poem?

CONNECTIONS TO OTHER SELECTIONS

1. Compare the description of hair in this poem with that in Cathy Song's "The White Porch" (p. 772). What significant similarities do you find?
2. Write an essay that explores the differing portraits in this poem and in Sylvia Plath's "Mirror" (p. 786). Which portrait is more interesting to you? Explain why.

ROBERT HASS (B. 1941)
Happiness   1996

Because yesterday morning from the steamy window
we saw a pair of red foxes across the creek
eating the last windfall apples in the rain—
they looked up at us with their green eyes
long enough to symbolize the wakefulness of living things   5
and then went back to eating—

and because this morning
when she went into the gazebo with her black pen and yellow pad
to coax an inquisitive soul
from what she thinks of as the reluctance of matter,   10
I drove into town to drink tea in the cafe
and write notes in a journal—mist rose from the bay

like the luminous and indefinite aspect of intention,
and a small flock of tundra swans
for the second winter in a row were feeding on new grass   15
in the soaked fields; they symbolize mystery, I suppose,
they are also called whistling swans, are very white,
and their eyes are black —

and because the tea steamed in front of me,
and the notebook, turned to a new page,   20
was blank except for a faint blue idea of order,
I wrote: *happiness! it is December, very cold,*
we woke early this morning,
and lay in bed kissing,
our eyes squinched up like bats.   25

CONSIDERATIONS FOR CRITICAL THINKING AND WRITING

1. FIRST RESPONSE. What kinds of experiences contribute to the speaker's happiness? Describe the person speaking.

2. Try writing a paraphrase of "Happiness." What happens to the poem when it's changed to prose? What accounts for these changes?

3. As Hass has done, define happiness or a moment in which you felt that emotion, in poetry or prose.

CONNECTION TO ANOTHER SELECTION

1. Write an essay that compares and contrasts "Happiness" with Emily Dickinson's "I like a look of Agony" (p. 938). Do they both succeed in capturing an emotion? What message do you take away from each?

MILLER WILLIAMS (B. 1930)

Excuse Me   *1992*

Give me just a second before you start.
Let's agree on what you're reading here.
Let's call it a poem, a poem being an act
of language meant to hold its own exceptions,
which you therefore read with a double mind,   5
accepting and rejecting what you find.

If part of what you find is what you brought,
let's call this reading a poem, one of the games
imaginations play when they meet.
If you suspect you may not have the wit   10
to face the other player, one to one,
then you can be a deconstructionist
and make believe the other doesn't exist,
though that will be like sitting on one end
of a seesaw in summer, wishing you had a friend.   15

CONSIDERATIONS FOR CRITICAL THINKING AND WRITING

1. FIRST RESPONSE. How do you feel about being directly addressed by the speaker? How does it change your reading of the poem?

2. How does the speaker define a poem (lines 3–6)? Do you agree?

3. What is a deconstructionist (line 12)? Read the section on deconstructionist criticism (p. 2041). What do you think is the speaker's attitude toward deconstructionists?

4. Discuss the significance of the title. How does it affect the tone of the poem?

15

Writing about Poetry

FROM READING TO WRITING

Writing about poetry can be a rigorous means of testing the validity of your own reading of a poem. Anyone who has been asked to write several pages about a fourteen-line poem knows how intellectually challenging this exercise is, because it means paying close attention to language. Such scrutiny of words, however, not only sensitizes you to the poet's use of language, but to your own use of language as well. At first you may feel intimidated by having to compose a paper that is longer than the poem you're writing about, but a careful reading will reveal that there's plenty to write about what the poem says and how it says it. Keep in mind that your job is not to produce a definitive reading of the poem — even Carl Sandburg once confessed that "I've written some poetry I don't understand myself." It is enough to develop an interesting thesis and to present it clearly and persuasively.

An interesting thesis will come to you if you read and reread, take notes, annotate the text, and generate ideas (for a discussion of this process see Chapter 38, "Reading and Writing"). Although it requires energy to read closely and to write convincingly about the charged language found in poery, there is nothing mysterious about such reading and writing. This chapter provides a set of questions designed to sharpen your reading and writing about poetry. Following these questions is a sample paper that offers a clear and well-developed thesis concerning Elizabeth Bishop's "Manners."

QUESTIONS FOR RESPONSIVE READING AND WRITING

The following questions can help you respond to important elements that reveal a poem's effects and meanings. The questions are general, so not all of them will necessarily be relevant to a particular poem. Many, however, should prove useful for thinking, talking, and writing about each poem in this collection. If you are uncertain about the meaning of a term used in a question, consult the Glossary of Literary Terms beginning on page 2123.

Before addressing these questions, read the poem you are studying in its entirety. Don't worry about interpretation on a first reading; allow yourself the pleasure of enjoying whatever makes itself apparent to you. Then on subsequent readings, use the questions to understand and appreciate how the poem works.

1. Who is the speaker? Is it possible to determine the speaker's age, sex, sensibilities, level of awareness, and values?
2. Is the speaker addressing anyone in particular?
3. How do you respond to the speaker? Favorably? Negatively? What is the situation? Are there any special circumstances that inform what the speaker says?
4. Is there a specific setting of time and place?
5. Does reading the poem aloud help you to understand it?
6. Does a paraphrase reveal the basic purpose of the poem?
7. What does the title emphasize?
8. Is the theme presented directly or indirectly?
9. Do any allusions enrich the poem's meaning?
10. How does the diction reveal meaning? Are any words repeated? Do any carry evocative connotative meanings? Are there any puns or other forms of verbal wit?
11. Are figures of speech used? How does the figurative language contribute to the poem's vividness and meaning?
12. Do any objects, persons, places, events, or actions have allegorical or symbolic meanings? What other details in the poem support your interpretation?
13. Is irony used? Are there any examples of situational irony, verbal irony, or dramatic irony? Is understatement or paradox used?
14. What is the tone of the poem? Is the tone consistent?
15. Does the poem use onomatopoeia, assonance, consonance, or alliteration? How do these sounds affect you?
16. What sounds are repeated? If there are rhymes, what is their effect? Do they seem forced or natural? Is there a rhyme scheme? Do the rhymes contribute to the poem's meaning?
17. Do the lines have a regular meter? What is the predominant meter? Are there significant variations? Does the rhythm seem appropriate for the tone of the poem?

18. Does the poem's form — its overall structure — follow an established pattern? Do you think the form is a suitable vehicle for the poem's meaning and effects?
19. Is the language of the poem intense and concentrated? Do you think it warrants more than one or two close readings?
20. Did you enjoy the poem? What, specifically, pleased or displeased you about what was expressed and how it was expressed?
21. Is there a particular critical approach that seems especially appropriate for this poem? (See the discussion of "Critical Strategies for Reading" beginning on p. 2021.)
22. How might biographical information about the author help to determine the central concerns of the poem?
23. How might historical information about the poem provide a useful context for interpretation?
24. To what extent do your own experiences, values, beliefs, and assumptions inform your interpretation?
25. What kinds of evidence from the poem are you focusing on to support your interpretation? Does your interpretation leave out any important elements that might undercut or qualify your interpretation?
26. Given that there are a variety of ways to interpret the poem, which one seems the most useful to you?

A SAMPLE ANALYSIS

Memory in Elizabeth Bishop's "Manners"

The following sample paper on Elizabeth Bishop's "Manners" was written in response to an assignment that called for a 750-word discussion of the ways in which at least five of the following elements work to develop and reinforce the poem's themes:

diction and tone	irony	form
images	sound and rhyme	speaker
figures of speech	rhythm and meter	setting and situation
symbols		

In her paper, Debra Epstein discusses the ways in which a number of these elements contribute to what she sees as a central theme of "Manners": the loss of a way of life that Bishop associates with the end of World War I. Not all of the elements of poetry are covered equally in Epstein's paper because some, such as the speaker and setting, are more important to her argument than others. Notice how rather than merely listing each of the elements, Epstein mentions them in her discussion as she needs to in order to develop the thesis that she clearly and succinctly expresses in her opening paragraph.

Elizabeth Bishop (1911–1979)

Manners

1965

for a Child of 1918

My grandfather said to me
as we sat on the wagon seat,
"Be sure to remember to always
speak to everyone you meet."

We met a stranger on foot.   5
My grandfather's whip tapped his hat.
"Good day, sir. Good day. A fine day."
And I said it and bowed where I sat.

Then we overtook a boy we knew
with his big pet crow on his shoulder.   10
"Always offer everyone a ride;
don't forget that when you get older,"

my grandfather said. So Willy
climbed up with us, but the crow
gave a "Caw!" and flew off. I was worried.   15
How would he know where to go?

But he flew a little way at a time
from fence post to fence post, ahead;
and when Willy whistled he answered.
"A fine bird," my grandfather said,   20

"and he's well brought up. See, he answers
nicely when he's spoken to.
Man or beast, that's good manners.
Be sure that you both always do."

When automobiles went by,   25
the dust hid the people's faces,
but we shouted "Good day! Good day!
Fine day!" at the top of our voices.

When we came to Hustler Hill,
he said that the mare was tired,   30
so we all got down and walked,
as our good manners required.

Debra Epstein

Professor Brown

English 210

May 1, 19--

              Memory in Elizabeth Bishop's "Manners"

       The subject of Elizabeth Bishop's "Manners" has to do with behaving well, but the theme of the poem has more to do with a way of life than with etiquette. The poem suggests that modern society has lost something important-- a friendly openness, a generosity of spirit, a sense of decency and consideration--in its race toward progress. Although the narrative is simply told, Bishop enriches this poem about manners by developing an implicit theme through her subtle use of such elements of poetry as speaker, setting, rhyme, meter, symbol, and images.

       The dedication suggests that the speaker is "a Child of 1918" who accompanies his or her grandfather on a wagon ride and who is urged to practice good manners by greeting people, offering everyone a ride, and speaking when spoken to by anyone. During the ride they say hello to a stranger, give a ride to a boy with a pet crow, shout greetings to a passing automobile, and get down from the wagon when they reach a hill because the horse is tired. They walk because "good manners required" (line 32) such consideration, even for a horse. This summary indicates what goes on in the poem but not its significance. That requires a closer look at some of the poem's elements.

       Given the speaker's simple language (there are no metaphors or similes and only a few words out of thirty-two lines are more than two syllables), it seems likely that he or she is a fairly young child, rather than an adult reminiscing. (It is interesting to note that Bishop herself, though not identical with the speaker, would have been seven in 1918.) Because the speaker is a young child who uses simple diction, Bishop has to show us the ride's significance indirectly rather than having the speaker explicitly state it.

The setting for the speaker's narrative is important because 1918 was the year World War I ended, and it marked the beginning of a new era of technology that was the result of rapid industrialization during the war. Horses and wagons would soon be put out to pasture. The grandfather's manners emphasize a time gone by; the child must be told to "remember" what the grandfather says because he or she will take that advice into a new and very different world.

The grandfather's world of the horse and wagon is uncomplicated, and this is reflected in both the simple quatrains that move predictably along in an abcb rhyme scheme and the frequent anapestic meter (ăs wĕ sát ŏn thĕ wágŏn [2]) that pulls the lines rapidly and lightly. The one moment Bishop breaks the set rhyme scheme is in the seventh stanza when the automobile (the single four-syllable word in the poem) rushes by in a cloud of dust so that people cannot see or hear each other. The only off rhymes in the poem--"faces" (26) and "voices" (28)--are also in this stanza, which suggests that the automobile and the people in it are somehow off or out of sync with what goes on in the other stanzas. The automobile is a symbol of a way of life in which people--their faces hidden--and manners take a back seat to speed and noise. The people in the car don't wave, don't offer a ride, and don't speak when spoken to.

Maybe the image of the crow's noisy cawing and flying from post to post is a foreshadowing that should prepare readers for the automobile. The speaker feels "worried" about the crow's apparent directionlessness: "How would

he know where to go?" (16). However, neither the child
nor the grandfather (nor the reader on a first reading)
clearly sees the two worlds that Bishop contrasts in the
final stanza.

"Hustler Hill" is the perfect name for what finally
tires out the mare. There is no hurry for the grandfather
and child, but there is for those people in the car and
the postwar hustle and bustle they represent. The fast-
paced future overtakes the tired symbol of the past in the
poem. The pace slows as the wagon passengers get down to
walk, but the reader recognizes that the grandfather's
way has been lost to a world in which good manners are
not required.

16

Word Choice,
Word Order, and Tone

DICTION

Like all good writers, poets are keenly aware of *diction,* their choice of words. Poets, however, choose words especially carefully because the words in poems call attention to themselves. Characters, actions, settings, and symbols may appear in a poem, but in the foreground, before all else, is the poem's language. Also, poems are usually briefer than other forms of writing. A few inappropriate words in a 200-page novel (which would have about 100,000 words) create fewer problems than they would in a 100-word poem. Functioning in a compressed atmosphere, the words in a poem must convey meanings gracefully and economically. Readers therefore have to be alert to the ways in which those meanings are released.

Although poetic language is often more intensely charged than ordinary speech, the words used in poetry are not necessarily different from everyday speech. Inexperienced readers may sometimes assume that language must be high-flown and out of date to be included in a poem: instead of reading about a boy "enjoying a swim," they expect to read about a boy "disporting with pliant arm o'er a glassy wave." During the eighteenth century this kind of *poetic diction* — the use of elevated language over ordinary language — was highly valued in English poetry, but since the nineteenth century poets have generally overridden the distinctions that were once made between words used in everyday speech and those used in poetry. Today all levels of diction can be found in poetry.

A poet, like any writer, has several levels of diction from which to choose; they range from formal to middle to informal. *Formal diction* consists of a dignified, impersonal, and elevated use of language. Notice, for example, the formality of Thomas Hardy's description of the sunken luxury liner *Titanic* in this stanza from "The Convergence of the Twain" (the entire poem appears on p. 738):

> In a solitude of the sea
> Deep from human vanity,
> And the Pride of Life that planned her, stilly couches she.

There is nothing casual or relaxed about these lines. Hardy's use of "stilly," meaning "quietly" or "calmly," is purely literary; the word rarely, if ever, turns up in everyday English.

The language used in Richard Wilbur's "A Late Aubade" (p. 732) represents a less formal level of diction; the speaker uses a *middle diction* spoken by most educated people. Consider how Wilbur's speaker tells his lover what she might be doing instead of being with him:

> You could be sitting now in a carrel
> Turning some liver-spotted page,
> Or rising in an elevator-cage
> Toward Ladies' Apparel.

The speaker elegantly enumerates his lover's unattractive alternatives to being with him — reading old books in a library or shopping in a department store — but the wit of his description lessens its formality.

Informal diction is evident in Larkin's "A Study of Reading Habits" (p. 684). The speaker's account of his early reading is presented *colloquially*, in a conversational manner that in this instance includes slang expressions not used by the culture at large:

> When getting my nose in a book
> Cured most things short of school,
> It was worth ruining my eyes
> To know I could still keep cool,
> And deal out the old right hook
> To dirty dogs twice my size.

This level of diction is clearly not that of Hardy's or Wilbur's speakers.

Poets may also draw on another form of informal diction, called *dialect.* Dialects are spoken by definable groups of people from a particular geographic region, economic group, or social class. New England dialects are often heard in Robert Frost's poems, for example. Gwendolyn Brooks employs a black dialect in "We Real Cool" (p. 743) to characterize a group of pool players. Another form of diction related to particular groups is *jargon,* a category of language defined by a trade or profession. Sociologists, photographers, carpenters, baseball players, and dentists, for example, all use words that are specific to their fields. E. E. Cummings manages to get quite a lot of mileage out of automobile jargon in "she being Brand" (p. 721).

Many levels of diction are available to poets. The variety of diction to be found in poetry is enormous, and that is how it should be. No language is foreign to poetry because it is possible to imagine any human voice as the speaker of a poem. When we say a poem is formal, informal, or somewhere in between, we are making a descriptive statement rather than an evaluative one. What matters in a poem is not only which words are used but how they are used.

DENOTATIONS AND CONNOTATIONS

One important way that the meaning of a word is communicated in a poem is through sound: snakes *hiss*, saws *buzz*. This and other matters related to sound are discussed in Chapter 20. Individual words also convey meanings through denotations and connotations. **Denotations** are the literal, dictionary meanings of a word. For example, *bird* denotes a feathered animal with wings (other denotations for the same word include a shuttlecock, an airplane, or an odd person), but in addition to its denotative meanings, *bird* also carries **connotations**, associations and implications that go beyond a word's literal meanings. Connotations derive from how the word has been used and the associations people make with it. Therefore, the connotations of *bird* might include fragility, vulnerability, altitude, the sky, or freedom, depending on the context in which the word is used. Consider also how different the connotations are for the following types of birds: hawk, dove, penguin, pigeon, chicken, peacock, duck, crow, turkey, gull, owl, goose, coot, and vulture. These words have long been used to refer to types of people as well as birds. They are rich in connotative meanings.

Connotations derive their resonance from a person's experiences with a word. Those experiences may not always be the same, especially when the people having them are in different times and places. *Theater*, for instance, was once associated with depravity, disease, and sin, whereas today the word usually evokes some sense of high culture and perhaps visions of elegant opulence. In several ethnic communities in the United States many people would find *squid* appetizing, but elsewhere the word is likely to produce negative connotations. Readers must recognize, then, that words written in other times and places may have unexpected connotations. Annotations usually help in these matters, which is why it makes sense to pay attention to them when they are available.

Ordinarily, though, the language of poetry is accessible, even when the circumstances of the reader and the poet are different. Although connotative language may be used subtly, it mostly draws on associations experienced by many people. Poets rely on widely shared associations rather than the idiosyncratic response that an individual might have to a word. Someone who has received a severe burn from a fireplace accident may associate the word *hearth* with intense pain instead of home and family life, but that reader must not allow a personal experience to undermine the response the poet intends to evoke. Connotative meanings are usually public meanings.

Perhaps this can be seen most clearly in advertising, where language is also used primarily to convey moods and feelings rather than information. For instance, nearly three decades of increasing interest in nutrition and general fitness have created a collective consciousness that advertisers have capitalized on successfully. Knowing that we want to be slender or lean or slim (not spare or scrawny and certainly not gaunt), advertisers have created a new word to describe beers, wines, sodas, cheeses, canned fruits, and other products that tend to overload what used to be called sweatclothes and sneakers. The word is *lite*. The assumed denotative meaning of *lite* is low in calories, but as close readers of ingredient labels know, some *lites* are heavier than regularly prepared products. There can be no doubt about the connotative meaning of *lite*, however. Whatever is *lite* cannot hurt you; less is more. Even the word is lighter than *light;* there is no unnecessary droopy *g* or plump *h*. *Lite* is a brilliantly manufactured use of connotation.

Connotative meanings are valuable because they allow poets to be economical and suggestive simultaneously. In this way emotions and attitudes are carefully woven into the texture of the poem's language. Read the following poem and pay close attention to the connotative meanings of its words.

RANDALL JARRELL (1914–1965)

The Death of the Ball Turret Gunner 1945

From my mother's sleep I fell into the State
And I hunched in its belly till my wet fur froze.
Six miles from earth, loosed from its dream of life,
I woke to black flack and the nightmare fighters.
When I died they washed me out of the turret with a hose.

The title of this poem establishes the setting and the speaker's situation. Like the setting of a short story, the setting of a poem is important when the time and place influence what happens. "The Death of the Ball Turret Gunner" is set in the midst of a war and, more specifically, in a ball turret—a Plexiglas sphere housing machine guns on the underside of a bomber. The speaker's situation obviously places him in extreme danger; indeed, his fate is announced in the title.

Although the poem is written in the first-person singular, its speaker is clearly not the poet. Jarrell uses a *persona,* a speaker created by the poet. In this poem the persona is a disembodied voice that makes the gunner's story all the more powerful. What is his story? A paraphrase might read something like this:

> After I was born, I grew up to find myself at war, cramped into the turret of a bomber's belly some 31,000 feet above the ground. Below me were exploding shells from antiaircraft guns and attacking fighter planes. I was killed, but the bomber returned to base, where my remains were cleaned out of the turret so the next man could take my place.

This paraphrase is accurate, but its language is much less suggestive than the poem's. The first line of the poem has the speaker emerge from his "mother's sleep," the anesthetized sleep of her giving birth. The phrase also suggests the comfort, warmth, and security he knew as a child. This safety was left behind when he "fell," a verb that evokes the danger and involuntary movement associated with his subsequent "State" (*fell* also echoes, perhaps, the fall from innocence to experience related in the Bible).

Several dictionary definitions appear for the noun *state;* it can denote a territorial unit, the power and authority of a government, a person's social status, or a person's emotional or physical condition. The context provided by the rest of the poem makes clear that "State" has several denotative meanings here: because it is capitalized, it certainly refers to the violent world of a government at war, but it also refers to the gunner's vulnerable status as well as his physical and emotional condition. By having "State" carry more than one meaning, Jarrell has created an intentional ambiguity. *Ambiguity* allows for two or more simultaneous interpretations of a word, phrase, action, or situation, all of which can be supported by the context of a work. Through his ambiguous use of "State," Jarrell connects the horrors of war not just to bombers and gunners but to the governments that control them.

Related to this ambiguity is the connotative meaning of "State" in the poem. The context demands that the word be read with a negative charge. The word is not used with patriotic pride but to suggest an anonymous, impersonal "State" that kills rather than nurtures the life in its "belly." The state's "belly" is a bomber, and the gunner is "hunched" like a fetus in the cramped turret, where, in contrast to the warmth of his mother's womb, everything is frozen, even the "wet fur" of his flight jacket (newborn infants have wet fur too). The gunner is not just 31,000 feet from the ground but "Six miles from earth." *Six miles* has roughly the same denotative meaning as 31,000 feet, but Jarrell knew that the connotative meaning of *six miles* makes the speaker's position seem even more remote and frightening.

When the gunner is born into the violent world of war, he finds himself waking up to a "nightmare" that is all too real. The poem's final line is grimly understated, but it hits the reader with the force of an exploding shell: what the State-bomber-turret gives birth to is a gruesome death that is merely one of an endless series. It may be tempting to reduce the theme of this poem to the idea that "war is hell," but Jarrell's target is more specific. He implicates the "State," which routinely executes such violence, and he does so without preaching or hysterical denunciations. Instead, his use of language conveys his theme subtly and powerfully. Consider how this next poem uses connotative meanings to express its theme.

E. E. CUMMINGS (1894–1962)

she being Brand   *1926*

she being Brand

-new;and you
know consequently a
little stiff i was
careful of her and(having   5

thoroughly oiled the universal
joint tested my gas felt of
her radiator made sure her springs were O.

K.)i went right to it flooded-the-carburetor cranked her

up,slipped the   10
clutch(and then somehow got into reverse she
kicked what
the hell)next
minute i was back in neutral tried and

again slo-wly;bare,ly nudg. ing (my   15
lev-er Right-
oh and her gears being in
A 1 shape passed
from low through
second-in-to-high like   20
greasedlightning) just as we turned the corner of Divinity

avenue i touched the accelerator and give
her the juice,good

                              (it
was the first ride and believe i we was   25
happy to see how nice she acted right up to
the last minute coming back down by the Public
Gardens i slammed on

the
internalexpanding   30
&
externalcontracting
brakes Bothatonce and

brought allofher tremB
-ling   35
to a:dead.

stand-
;Still)

CONSIDERATIONS FOR CRITICAL THINKING AND WRITING

1. FIRST RESPONSE. How does Cummings's arrangement of the words on the
   page help you to read this poem aloud? What does the poem describe?

2. What ambiguities in language does the poem ride on? At what point were
   you first aware of these double meanings?

3. Explain why you think the poem is primarily serious or humorous.

4. Find some advertisements for convertibles or sports cars in magazines and
   read them closely. What similarities do you find in the use of connotative
   language in them and in Cummings's poem? Write a brief essay explaining
   how language is used to convey the theme of one of the advertisements and
   the poem.

WORD ORDER

Meanings in poems are conveyed not only by denotations and connotations but also by the poet's arrangement of words into phrases, clauses, and sentences to achieve particular effects. The ordering of words into meaningful verbal patterns is called *syntax*. A poet can manipulate the syntax of a line to place emphasis on a word; this is especially apparent when a poet varies normal word order. In Dickinson's "A narrow Fellow in the Grass" (p. 2), for example, the speaker says about the snake that "His notice sudden is." Ordinarily, that would be expressed as "his notice is sudden." By placing the verb *is* unexpectedly at the end of the line, Dickinson creates the sense of surprise we feel when we suddenly come upon a snake. Dickinson's inversion of the standard word order also makes the final sound of the line a hissing *is*.

Cummings uses one long sentence in "she being Brand" to take the reader on a ride that begins with a false start but accelerates quickly before coming to a halt. The jargon creates an exuberantly humorous mood that is helped along by the poem's syntax. How do Cummings's ordering of words and sentence structure reinforce the meaning of the lines?

TONE

Tone is the writer's attitude toward the subject, the mood created by all the elements in the poem. Writing, like speech, may be characterized as serious or light, sad or happy, private or public, angry or affectionate, bitter or nostalgic, or any other attitudes and feelings that human beings experience. In Jarrell's "The Death of the Ball Turret Gunner," the tone is clearly serious; the voice in the poem even sounds dead. Listen again to the persona's final words: "When I died they washed me out of the turret with a hose." The brutal, restrained matter-of-factness of this line is effective because the reader is called on to supply the appropriate anger and despair, a strategy that makes those emotions all the more convincing.

Consider how tone is used to convey meaning in the next poem, inspired by the poet's contemplating how island life has changed.

Derek Walcott (b. 1930)
The Virgins   1976

Down the dead streets of sun-stoned Frederiksted,°
the first free port to die for tourism,
strolling at funeral pace, I am reminded
of life not lost to the American dream;

1 *Frederiksted:* A duty-free port in St. Croix, one of the American Virgin Islands.

but my small-islander's simplicities   5
can't better our new empire's civilized
exchange of cameras, watches, perfumes, brandies
for the good life, so cheaply underpriced
that only the crime rate is on the rise
in streets blighted with sun, stone arches   10
and plazas blown dry by the hysteria
of rumor. A condominium drowns
in vacancy; its bargains are dusted,
but only a jeweled housefly drones
over the bargains. The roulettes spin   15
rustily to the wind — the vigorous trade
that every morning would begin afresh
by revving up green water round the pierhead
heading for where the banks of silver thresh.

CONSIDERATIONS FOR CRITICAL THINKING AND WRITING

1. FIRST RESPONSE. What is the speaker's attitude toward the "American
   dream"? How is it defined?
2. In what sense are the streets of Frederiksted dead? In what sense alive? Pick
   out the images of death and life and discuss how they work together.
3. Discuss the diction of lines 16–19. (You might want to look up "trade
   wind.") How do the last four lines contrast with the first fifteen? What is
   your final impression of trade?

RUTH FAINLIGHT (B. 1931)

Flower Feet   *1989*

(SILK SHOES IN THE WHITWORTH ART GALLERY,
MANCHESTER, ENGLAND)

Real women's feet wore these objects
that look like toys or spectacle cases stitched
from bands of coral, jade, and apricot silk
embroidered with twined sprays of flowers.
Those hearts, tongues, crescents, and disks, leather   5
shapes an inch across, are the soles of shoes
no wider or longer than the span of my ankle.

If the feet had been cut off and the raw stumps
thrust inside the openings, surely
it could not hurt more than broken toes, twisted   10
back and bandaged tight. An old woman,
leaning on a cane outside her door
in a Chinese village, smiled to tell how
she fought and cried, how when she stood on points
of pain that gnawed like fire, nurse and mother   15
praised her tottering walk on flower feet.
Her friends nodded, glad the times had changed.
Otherwise, they would have crippled their daughters.

CONSIDERATIONS FOR CRITICAL THINKING AND WRITING

1. FIRST RESPONSE. Why did the Chinese bind girls' and women's feet? Are there any contemporary equivalents in other cultures?

2. How is the speaker's description of the process of binding feet in lines 8 to 16 different from the description of the shoes in lines 1 to 7?

3. Describe the poem's tone. Does it remain the same throughout the poem or does it change? Explain your response.

CONNECTIONS TO OTHER SELECTIONS

1. How is the speaker's perspective on tradition and custom in this poem similar to that in Robert Frost's "Mending Wall" (p. 979)?

2. The final line of this poem is startling. Why? How is it similar in its strategy to James Merrill's "Casual Wear" (p. 817)?

The next work is a ***dramatic monologue,*** a type of poem in which a character — the speaker — addresses a silent audience in such a way as to reveal unintentionally some aspect of his or her temperament or personality. What tone is created by Machan's use of a persona?

KATHARYN HOWD MACHAN (B. 1952)

Hazel Tells LaVerne   1976

last night
im cleanin out my
howard johnsons ladies room
when all of a sudden
up pops this frog   5
musta come from the sewer
swimmin aroun an tryin ta
climb up the sida the bowl
so i goes ta flushm down
but sohelpmegod he starts talkin   10
bout a golden ball
an how i can be a princess
me a princess
well my mouth drops
all the way to the floor   15
an he says
kiss me just kiss me
once on the nose
well i screams
ya little green pervert   20
an i hitsm with my mop
an has ta flush
the toilet down three times
me
a princess   25

CONSIDERATIONS FOR CRITICAL THINKING AND WRITING

1. FIRST RESPONSE. What do you imagine the situation and setting are for this poem? Do you like this revision of the fairy tale "The Frog Prince"?

2. What creates the poem's humor? How does Hazel's use of language reveal her personality? Is her treatment of the frog consistent with her character?

3. Although it has no punctuation, this poem is easy to follow. How does the arrangement of the lines organize Hazel's speech for clarity and emphasis?

4. What is the theme? Is it conveyed through denotative or connotative language?

5. Write what you think might be LaVerne's reply to Hazel. First, write LaVerne's response as a series of ordinary sentences, and then try editing and organizing them into poetic lines.

CONNECTION TO ANOTHER SELECTION

1. Although Robert Browning's "My Last Duchess" (p. 821) is a more complex poem than Machan's, both use dramatic monologues to reveal character. How are the strategies in each poem similar?

MARTÍN ESPADA (B. 1957)
Latin Night at the Pawnshop   1987

Chelsea, Massachusetts
Christmas, 1987

The apparition of a salsa band
gleaming in the Liberty Loan
pawnshop window:

Golden trumpet,
silver trombone,
congas, maracas, tambourine,
all with price tags dangling
like the city morgue ticket
on a dead man's toe.

CONSIDERATIONS FOR CRITICAL THINKING AND WRITING

1. FIRST RESPONSE. What is "Latin" about this night at the pawnshop?

2. What kind of tone is created by the poet's word choice and by the rhythm of the poem?

3. Does it matter that this apparition occurs on Christmas night? Why or why not?

4. What do you think is the central point of this poem?

How do the speaker's attitude and tone change during the course of this next poem?

MAXINE KUMIN (B. 1925)

Woodchucks   1972

Gassing the woodchucks didn't turn out right.
The knockout bomb from the Feed and Grain Exchange
was featured as merciful, quick at the bone
and the case we had against them was airtight,
both exits shoehorned shut with puddingstone,°   5
but they had a sub-sub-basement out of range.

Next morning they turned up again, no worse
for the cyanide than we for our cigarettes
and state-store Scotch, all of us up to scratch.
They brought down the marigolds as a matter of course   10
and then took over the vegetable patch
nipping the broccoli shoots, beheading the carrots.

The food from our mouths, I said, righteously thrilling
to the feel of the .22, the bullets' neat noses.
I, a lapsed pacifist fallen from grace   15
puffed with Darwinian° pieties for killing,
now drew a bead on the littlest woodchuck's face.
He died down in the everbearing roses.

Ten minutes later I dropped the mother. She
flipflopped in the air and fell, her needle teeth   20
still hooked in a leaf of early Swiss chard.
Another baby next. O one-two-three
the murderer inside me rose up hard,
the hawkeye killer came on stage forthwith.

There's one chuck left. Old wily fellow, he keeps   25
me cocked and ready day after day after day.
All night I hunt his humped-up form. I dream
I sight along the barrel in my sleep.
If only they'd all consented to die unseen
gassed underground the quiet Nazi way.   30

5 *puddingstone:* Pebbles cemented together.   16 *Darwinian:* Charles Darwin (1809–1882),
an English naturalist associated with the ideas of evolution and natural selection.

CONSIDERATIONS FOR CRITICAL THINKING AND WRITING

1. FIRST RESPONSE. To what extent is this poem about woodchucks? What else
   is it about?

2. How does the word *airtight* help create the tone of the first stanza?

3. How does the speaker's attitude toward the woodchucks change in the second stanza? How does that affect the tone in lines 13–24?

4. What competing emotions are present in the speaker's descriptions of the
   woodchucks' activities and the descriptions of killing them?

5. Given that "Gassing" begins the poem, why does the speaker withhold the description of the woodchucks being "gassed underground the quiet Nazi way" until the final line?

6. Explain how line 15 suggests, along with the final stanza, the theme of the poem.

DICTION AND TONE IN FOUR LOVE POEMS

The first three of these love poems share the same basic situation and theme: a male speaker addresses a female (in the first poem it is a type of female) urging that love should not be delayed because time is short. This theme is as familiar in poetry as it is in life. In Latin this tradition is known as *carpe diem,* "seize the day." Notice how the poets' diction helps create a distinctive tone in each poem, even though the subject matter and central ideas are similar (although not identical) in all three.

ROBERT HERRICK (1591–1674)

To the Virgins, to Make Much of Time   *1648*

Gather ye rose-buds while ye may,
 Old Time is still a-flying;
And this same flower that smiles today,
 Tomorrow will be dying.

The glorious lamp of heaven, the sun,   5
 The higher he's a-getting,
The sooner will his race be run,
 And nearer he's to setting.

That age is best which is the first,
 When youth and blood are warmer;   10
But being spent, the worse, and worst
 Times still succeed the former.

Then be not coy, but use your time,
 And while ye may, go marry;
For having lost but once your prime,   15
 You may for ever tarry.

CONSIDERATIONS FOR CRITICAL THINKING AND WRITING

1. FIRST RESPONSE. Would there be any change in meaning if the title of this poem were "To Young Women, to Make Much of Time"? Do you think the poem can apply to young men too?

2. What do the virgins have in common with the flowers (lines 1–4) and the course of the day (5–8)?

3. How does the speaker develop his argument? What will happen to the virgins if they don't "marry"? Paraphrase the poem.
4. What is the tone of the speaker's advice?

The next poem was also written in the seventeenth century, but it includes some words that have changed in usage and meaning over the past three hundred years. The title of Marvell's "To His Coy Mistress" requires some explanation. "Mistress" does not refer to a married man's illicit lover but to a woman who is loved and courted — a sweetheart. Marvell uses "coy" to describe a woman who is reserved and shy rather than coquettish or flirtatious. Often such shifts in meanings over time are explained in the notes that accompany reprintings of poems. You should keep in mind, however, that it is helpful to have a reasonably thick dictionary available when you are reading poetry. The most thorough is the *Oxford English Dictionary (OED)*, which provides histories of words. The *OED* is a multivolume leviathan, but there are other useful unabridged dictionaries and desk dictionaries.

Knowing its original meaning can also enrich your understanding of why a contemporary poet chooses a particular word. Elizabeth Bishop begins "The Fish" (p. 682) this way: "I caught a tremendous fish." We know immediately in this context that "tremendous" means very large. In addition, given that the speaker clearly admires the fish in the lines that follow, we might even understand "tremendous" in the colloquial sense of wonderful and extraordinary. But a dictionary gives us some further relevant insights. Because, by the end of the poem, we see the speaker thoroughly moved as a result of the encounter with the fish ("everything / was rainbow, rainbow, rainbow!"), the dictionary's additional information about the history of *tremendous* shows why it is the perfect adjective to introduce the fish. The word comes from the Latin *tremere* (to tremble) and therefore once meant "such as to make one tremble." That is precisely how the speaker is at the end of the poem: deeply affected and trembling. Knowing the origin of *tremendous* gives us the full heft of the poet's word choice.

Although some of the language in "To His Coy Mistress" requires annotations for the modern reader, this poem continues to serve as a powerful reminder that time is a formidable foe, even for lovers.

ANDREW MARVELL (1621–1678)

To His Coy Mistress   *1681*

Had we but world enough, and time,
This coyness, lady, were no crime.
We would sit down, and think which way
To walk, and pass our long love's day.
Thou by the Indian Ganges'° side   5
Shouldst rubies find; I by the tide

5 *Ganges:* A river in India sacred to the Hindus.

Of Humber° would complain.° I would   *write love songs*
Love you ten years before the Flood,
And you should, if you please, refuse
Till the conversion of the Jews.   10
My vegetable love should grow°
Vaster than empires, and more slow;
An hundred years should go to praise
Thine eyes and on thy forehead gaze,
Two hundred to adore each breast,   15
But thirty thousand to the rest:
An age at least to every part,
And the last age should show your heart.
For, lady, you deserve this state,
Nor would I love at lower rate.   20
   But at my back I always hear
Time's wingèd chariot hurrying near;
And yonder all before us lie
Deserts of vast eternity.
Thy beauty shall no more be found,   25
Nor in thy marble vault shall sound
My echoing song; then worms shall try
That long preserved virginity,
And your quaint honor turn to dust,
And into ashes all my lust.   30
The grave's a fine and private place,
But none, I think, do there embrace.
   Now, therefore, while the youthful hue
Sits on thy skin like morning dew,
And while thy willing soul transpires°   *breathes forth* 35
At every pore with instant fires,
Now let us sport us while we may,
And now, like amorous birds of prey,
Rather at once our time devour
Than languish in his slow-chapped° power.   *slow-jawed* 40
Let us roll all our strength and all
Our sweetness up into one ball,
And tear our pleasures with rough strife
Thorough° the iron gates of life.   *through*
Thus, though we cannot make our sun   45
Stand still, yet we will make him run.

7 *Humber:* A river that flows through Marvell's native town, Hull.   11 *My vegetable love . . .
grow:* A slow, unconscious growth.

CONSIDERATIONS FOR CRITICAL THINKING AND WRITING

1. FIRST RESPONSE. Do you think this *carpe diem* poem is hopelessly dated or
   does it speak to our contemporary concerns?
2. This poem is divided into a three-part argument. Briefly summarize each
   section: if (lines 1–20), but (21–32), therefore (33–46).

3. What is the speaker's tone in lines 1–20? How much time would he spend adoring his mistress? Is he sincere? How does he expect his mistress to respond to these lines?

4. How does the speaker's tone change beginning with line 21? What is his view of time in lines 21–32? What does this description do to the lush and leisurely sense of time in lines 1–20? How do you think his mistress would react to lines 21–32?

5. In the final lines of Herrick's "To the Virgins, to Make Much of Time" (p. 728), the speaker urges the virgins to "go marry." What does Marvell's speaker urge in lines 33–46? How is the pace of these lines (notice the verbs) different from that of the first twenty lines of the poem?

6. This poem is sometimes read as a vigorous but simple celebration of flesh. Is there more to the theme than that?

PERSPECTIVE

BERNARD DUYFHUIZEN (B. 1953)

"To His Coy Mistress": On How a Female Might Respond   1988

Clearly a female reader of "To His Coy Mistress" might have trouble identifying with the poem's speaker; therefore, her first response would be to identify with the listener-in-the-poem, the eternally silent Coy Mistress. In such a reading she is likely to recognize that she has heard this kind of line before although maybe not with the same intensity and insistence. Moreover, she is likely to (re)experience the unsettling emotions that such an egoistic assault on her virginal autonomy would provoke. She will also see differently, even by contemporary standards, the plot beyond closure, the possible consequences — both physical and social — that the Mistress will encounter. Lastly, she is likely to be angered by this poem, by her marginalization in an argument that seeks to overpower the core of her being.

From "Textual Harassment of Marvell's Coy Mistress:
The Institutionalization of Masculine Criticism,"
College English, April 1988

CONSIDERATIONS FOR CRITICAL THINKING AND WRITING

1. Explain whether you find convincing Duyfhuizen's description of a female's potential response to the poem. How does his description compare with your own response?

2. Characterize the silent mistress of the poem. How do you think the speaker treats her? What do his language and tone suggest about his relationship to her?

3. Does the fact that this description of a female response is written by a man make any difference in your assessment of it? Explain why or why not.

The third in this series of *carpe diem* poems is a twentieth-century work. The language of Wilbur's "A Late Aubade" is more immediately accessible than that of Marvell's "To His Coy Mistress"; a dictionary will quickly identify any words unfamiliar to a reader, including the allusion to Arnold Schoenberg, the composer, in line 11. An ***allusion*** is a brief reference to a person, place, thing, event, or idea in history or literature. Allusive words, like connotative words, are both suggestive and economical; poets use allusions to conjure up biblical authority, scenes from Shakespeare's plays, historic figures, wars, great love stories, and anything else that might serve to deepen and enrich their own work. The speaker in "A Late Aubade" makes an allusion that an ordinary dictionary won't explain. He tells his lover: "I need not rehearse / The rosebuds-theme of centuries of verse." True to his word, he says no more about this for her or the reader. The lines refer, of course, to the *carpe diem* theme as found familiarly in Herrick's "To the Virgins, to Make Much of Time." Wilbur assumes that his reader will understand the allusion.

Allusions imply reading and cultural experiences shared by the poet and reader. Literate audiences once had more in common than they do today because more people had similar economic, social, and educational backgrounds. But a judicious use of specialized dictionaries, encyclopedias, and other reference tools can help you decipher allusions that grow out of this body of experience. (See page 2100 for a list of useful reference works for students of literature.) As you read more, you'll be able to make connections based on your own experiences with literature. In a sense, allusions make available what other human beings have deemed worth remembering, and that is certainly an economical way of supplementing and enhancing your own experience.

Wilbur's version of the *carpe diem* theme follows. What strikes you as particularly modern about it?

RICHARD WILBUR (B. 1921)

A Late Aubade   *1968*

You could be sitting now in a carrel
Turning some liver-spotted page,
Or rising in an elevator-cage
Toward Ladies' Apparel.

You could be planting a raucous bed   5
Of salvia, in rubber gloves,
Or lunching through a screed of someone's loves
With pitying head,

Or making some unhappy setter
Heel, or listening to a bleak   10

Lecture on Schoenberg's serial technique.
Isn't this better?

Think of all the time you are not
Wasting, and would not care to waste,
Such things, thank God, not being to your taste.   15
Think what a lot

Of time, by woman's reckoning,
You've saved, and so may spend on this,
You who had rather lie in bed and kiss
Than anything.   20

It's almost noon, you say? If so,
Time flies, and I need not rehearse
The rosebuds-theme of centuries of verse.
If you *must* go,

Wait for a while, then slip downstairs   25
And bring us up some chilled white wine,
And some blue cheese, and crackers, and some fine
Ruddy-skinned pears.

Considerations for Critical Thinking and Writing

1. FIRST RESPONSE. Explain whether or not you find the speaker appealing.

2. An *aubade* is a song about lovers parting at dawn, but in this "late aubade," "It's almost noon." Is there another way of reading the adjective *late* in the title?

3. How does the speaker's diction characterize both him and his lover? What sort of lives do they live? What does the casual allusion to Herrick's poem (line 23) reveal about them?

4. What is the effect of using "liver-spotted page," "elevator-cage," "raucous bed," "screed," "unhappy setter," and "bleak / Lecture" to describe the woman's activities?

Connections to Other Selections

1. How does the man's argument in "A Late Aubade" differ from the speakers' in Herrick's and Marvell's poems? Which of the three arguments do you find most convincing?

2. Explain how the tone of each poem is suited to its theme.

This fourth love poem is by a woman. Listen to the speaker's voice. Does it sound different from the way the men speak in the previous three poems?

DIANE ACKERMAN (B. 1948)

A Fine, a Private Place

1983

He took her one day
under the blue horizon
where long sea fingers
parted like beads
hitched in the doorway   5
of an opium den,
and canyons mazed the deep
reef with hollows,
cul-de-sacs, and narrow boudoirs,
and had to ask twice   10
before she understood
his stroking her arm
with a marine feather
slobbery as aloe pulp
was wooing, or saw the octopus   15
in his swimsuit
stretch one tentacle
and ripple its silky bag.

While bubbles rose
like globs of mercury,   20
they made love
mask to mask, floating
with oceans of air between them,
she his sea-geisha
in an orange kimono   25
of belts and vests,
her lacquered hair waving,
as Indigo Hamlets
tattooed the vista,
and sunlight   30
cut through the water,
twisting its knives
into corridors of light.

His sandy hair
and sea-blue eyes,   35
his kelp-thin waist
and chest ribbed wider
than a sandbar
where muscles domed
clear and taut as shells   40
(freckled cowries,
flat, brawny scallops
the color of dawn),
his sea-battered hands

gripping her thighs   45
like tawny starfish
and drawing her close
as a pirate vessel
to let her board:
who was this she loved?   50

Overhead, sponges
sweating raw color
jutted from a coral arch,
Clown Wrasses°   *brightly colored tropical fish*
hovered like fireworks,   55
and somewhere an abalone opened
its silver wings.
Part of a lusty dream
under aspic, her hips rolled
like a Spanish galleon,   60
her eyes swam
and chest began to heave.
Gasps melted on the tide.
Knowing she would soon be
breathless as her tank,   65
he pumped his brine
deep within her,
letting sea water drive it
through petals
delicate as anemone veils   70
to the dark purpose
of a conch-shaped womb.
An ear to her loins
would have heard the sea roar.

When panting ebbed,   75
and he signaled *Okay?*
as lovers have asked,
land or waterbound
since time heaved ho,
he led her to safety: 80
shallower realms,
heading back toward
the boat's even keel,
though ocean still petted her
cell by cell, murmuring   85
along her legs and neck,
caressing her
with pale, endless arms.

Later, she thought often
of that blue boudoir,   90
pillow-soft and filled
with cascading light,

where together
they'd made a bell
that dumbly clanged   95
beneath the waves
and minutes lurched
like mountain goats.
She could still see
the quilted mosaics   100
that were fish
twitching spangles overhead,
still feel the ocean
inside and out, turning her
evolution around.   105

She thought of it miles
and fathoms away, often,
at odd moments: watching
the minnow snowflakes
dip against the windowframe,   110
holding a sponge
idly under tap-gush,
sinking her teeth
into the cleft
of a voluptuous peach.   115

CONSIDERATIONS FOR CRITICAL THINKING AND WRITING

1. FIRST RESPONSE. How is your response to this poem affected by the fact that the speaker is female?

2. Read Marvell's "To His Coy Mistress" (p. 729). To what in Marvell's poem does Ackerman's title allude? Explain how the allusion to Marvell is crucial to understanding Ackerman's poem.

3. Comment on the descriptive passages of "A Fine, a Private Place." Which images seem especially vivid to you? How do they contribute to the poem's meanings?

4. What are the speaker's reflections on her experience in lines 106–115? What echoes of Marvell do you hear in these lines?

CONNECTIONS TO OTHER SELECTIONS

1. Write an essay comparing the tone of Ackerman's poem with that of Marvell's "To His Coy Mistress" (p. 729). To what extent are the central ideas in the poems similar?

2. Compare the speaker's voice in Ackerman's poem with the voice you imagine for the coy mistress in Marvell's poem.

POEMS FOR FURTHER STUDY

MARGARET ATWOOD (B. 1939)

Bored
1995

All those times I was bored
out of my mind. Holding the log
while he sawed it. Holding
the string while he measured, boards,
distances between things, or pounded   5
stakes into the ground for rows and rows
of lettuces and beets, which I then (bored)
weeded. Or sat in the back
of the car, or sat still in boats,
sat, sat, while at the prow, stern, wheel   10
he drove, steered, paddled. It
wasn't even boredom, it was looking,
looking hard and up close at the small
details. Myopia. The worn gunwales,
the intricate twill of the seat   15
cover. The acid crumbs of loam, the granular
pink rock, its igneous veins, the sea-fans
of dry moss, the blackish and then the greying
bristles on the back of his neck.
Sometimes he would whistle, sometimes   20
I would. The boring rhythm of doing
things over and over, carrying
the wood, drying
the dishes. Such minutiae. It's what
the animals spend most of their time at,   25
ferrying the sand, grain by grain, from their tunnels,
shuffling the leaves in their burrows. He pointed
such things out, and I would look
at the whorled texture of his square finger, earth under
the nail. Why do I remember it as sunnier   30
all the time then, although it more often
rained, and more birdsong?
I could hardly wait to get
the hell out of there to
anywhere else. Perhaps though   35
boredom is happier. It is for dogs or
groundhogs. Now I wouldn't be bored.
Now I would know too much.
Now I would know.

CONSIDERATIONS FOR CRITICAL THINKING AND WRITING

1. FIRST RESPONSE. Atwood has described this poem as one of several about
   her father and his death. Is it possible to determine that "he" is the

speaker's father from the details of the poem? Explain whether or not you think it matters who "he" is.

2. Play with the possible meanings of the word "bored" and its variations in the poem. What function does the repetition of the word serve?

3. What does the speaker "know" at the end of the poem that she didn't before?

Connection to Another Selection

1. Write an essay on the speaker's attitude toward the father in this poem and in Hayden's "Those Winter Sundays" (p. 672).

Thomas Hardy (1840–1928)
The Convergence of the Twain   *1912*

Lines on the Loss of the "Titanic" °

I

    In a solitude of the sea
    Deep from human vanity,
And the Pride of Life that planned her, stilly couches she.

II

    Steel chambers, late the pyres
    Of her salamandrine fires,°   5
Cold currents thrid,° and turn to rhythmic tidal lyres.   *thread*

III

    Over the mirrors meant
    To glass the opulent
The sea-worm crawls — grotesque, slimed, dumb, indifferent.

IV

    Jewels in joy designed   10
    To ravish the sensuous mind
Lie lightless, all their sparkles bleared and black and blind.

V

    Dim moon-eyed fishes near
    Gaze at the gilded gear
And query: "What does this vaingloriousness down here?"   15

VI

    Well: while was fashioning
    This creature of cleaving wing,
The Immanent Will that stirs and urges everything

Titanic: A luxurious ocean liner, reputed to be unsinkable, which sank after hitting an iceberg on its maiden voyage in 1912. Only a third of the 2,200 passengers survived.
5 *salamandrine fires:* Salamanders were, according to legend, able to survive fire; hence, the ship's fires burned even though under water.

VII

Prepared a sinister mate
For her — so gaily great —
A Shape of Ice, for the time far and dissociate.

20

VIII

And as the smart ship grew
In stature, grace, and hue,
In shadowy silent distance grew the Iceberg too.

IX

Alien they seemed to be:
No mortal eye could see
The intimate welding of their later history,

25

X

Or sign that they were bent
By paths coincident
On being anon twin halves of one august event,

30

XI

Till the Spinner of the Years
Said "Now!" And each one hears,
And consummation comes, and jars two hemispheres.

CONSIDERATIONS FOR CRITICAL THINKING AND WRITING

1. FIRST RESPONSE. Describe a contemporary disaster comparable to the *Titanic*. How was your response to it similar to or different from the speaker's response to the *Titanic*?
2. How do the words used to describe the ship in this poem reveal the speaker's attitude toward the *Titanic*?
3. The diction of the poem suggests that the *Titanic* and the iceberg participate in something like an arranged marriage. What specific words imply this?
4. Who or what causes the disaster? Does the speaker assign responsibility?

DAVID R. SLAVITT (B. 1935)

Titanic

1983

Who does not love the *Titanic*?
If they sold passage tomorrow for that same crossing,
who would not buy?

To go down . . . We all go down, mostly
alone. But with crowds of people, friends, servants,
well fed, with music, with lights! Ah!

5

And the world, shocked, mourns, as it ought to do
and almost never does. There will be the books and movies

to remind our grandchildren who we were
and how we died, and give them a good cry.   10

Not so bad, after all. The cold
water is anesthetic and very quick.
The cries on all sides must be a comfort.

We all go: only a few, first-class.

CONSIDERATIONS FOR CRITICAL THINKING AND WRITING

1. FIRST RESPONSE. What, according to the speaker in this poem, is so compelling about the *Titanic*? Do you agree?

2. Discuss the speaker's tone. Why would it be inaccurate to describe it as solemn and mournful?

3. What is the effect of the poem's final line? What emotions does it produce in you?

CONNECTIONS TO OTHER SELECTIONS

1. How does "Titanic" differ in its attitude toward opulence from "The Convergence of the Twain" (p. 738)?

2. Which poem, "Titanic" or "The Convergence of the Twain," is more emotionally satisfying to you? Explain why.

3. Compare the speakers' tones in "Titanic" and "The Convergence of the Twain."

4. Hardy wrote his poem in 1912, the year the *Titanic* went down, but Slavitt wrote his more than seventy years later. How do you think Slavitt's poem would have been received if it had been published in 1912? Write an essay explaining why you think what you do.

SHARON OLDS (B. 1942)
Sex without Love   1984

How do they do it, the ones who make love
without love? Beautiful as dancers,
gliding over each other like ice skaters
over the ice, fingers hooked
inside each other's bodies, faces   5
red as steak, wine, wet as the
children at birth whose mothers are going to
give them away. How do they come to the
come to the   come to the   God   come to the
still waters, and not love   10
the one who came there with them, light
rising slowly as steam off their joined
skin? These are the true religious,
the purists, the pros, the ones who will not
accept a false Messiah, love the   15
priest instead of the God. They do not
mistake the lover for their own pleasure,

they are like great runners: they know they are alone
with the road surface, the cold, the wind,
the fit of their shoes, their over-all cardio-   20
vascular health — just factors, like the partner
in the bed, and not the truth, which is the
single body alone in the universe
against its own best time.

CONSIDERATIONS FOR CRITICAL THINKING AND WRITING

1. FIRST RESPONSE. What is the nature of the question asked by the speaker in
   the poem's first two lines? What is being asked here?

2. What is the effect of describing the lovers as athletes? How do these descriptions and phrases reveal the speaker's tone toward the lovers?

3. To what extent does the title suggest the central meaning of this poem? Try
   to create some alternative titles that are equally descriptive.

CONNECTIONS TO OTHER SELECTIONS

1. How does the treatment of sex and love in Olds's poem compare with that
   in Cummings's "she being Brand" (p. 721)?

2. Just as Olds describes sex without love, she implies a definition of love in
   this poem. Consider whether the lovers in Wilbur's "A Late Aubade" (p. 732)
   fall within Olds's definition.

JOHN KEATS (1795–1821)

Ode on a Grecian Urn   *1819*

I
Thou still unravished bride of quietness,
    Thou foster-child of silence and slow time,
Sylvan° historian, who canst thus express
    A flowery tale more sweetly than our rhyme:
What leaf-fringed legend haunts about thy shape   5
    Of deities or mortals, or of both,
        In Tempe or the dales of Arcady?°
What men or gods are these? What maidens loath?
    What mad pursuit? What struggle to escape?
        What pipes and timbrels? What wild ecstasy?   10

II
Heard melodies are sweet, but those unheard
    Are sweeter; therefore, ye soft pipes, play on;
Not to the sensual ear, but, more endeared,
    Pipe to the spirit ditties of no tone:
Fair youth, beneath the trees, thou canst not leave   15
    Thy song, nor ever can those trees be bare;

3 *Sylvan:* Rustic. The urn is decorated with a forest scene.   7 *Tempe, Arcady:* Beautiful
rural valleys in Greece.

Bold Lover, never, never canst thou kiss,
Though winning near the goal — yet, do not grieve;
  She cannot fade, though thou hast not thy bliss,
    For ever wilt thou love, and she be fair!   20

III
Ah, happy, happy boughs! that cannot shed
  Your leaves, nor ever bid the Spring adieu;
And, happy melodist, unwearièd,
  For ever piping songs for ever new;
More happy love! more happy, happy love!   25
  For ever warm and still to be enjoyed,
    For ever panting, and for ever young;
All breathing human passion far above,
  That leaves a heart high-sorrowful and cloyed,
    A burning forehead, and a parching tongue.   30

IV
Who are these coming to the sacrifice?
  To what green altar, O mysterious priest,
Lead'st thou that heifer lowing at the skies,
  And all her silken flanks with garlands drest?
What little town by river or sea shore,   35
  Or mountain-built with peaceful citadel,
    Is emptied of this folk, this pious morn?
And, little town, thy streets for evermore
  Will silent be; and not a soul to tell
    Why thou art desolate, can e'er return.   40

V
O Attic° shape! Fair attitude! with brede°
  Of marble men and maidens overwrought,
With forest branches and the trodden weed;
  Thou, silent form, dost tease us out of thought
As doth eternity: Cold Pastoral!   45
  When old age shall this generation waste,
    Thou shalt remain, in midst of other woe
Than ours, a friend to man, to whom thou say'st,
  Beauty is truth, truth beauty — that is all
    Ye know on earth, and all ye need to know.   50

41 *Attic:* Possessing classic Athenian simplicity;   *brede:* Design.

CONSIDERATIONS FOR CRITICAL THINKING AND WRITING

1. FIRST RESPONSE. What does the speaker's diction reveal about his attitude toward the urn in this ode? Does his view develop or change?

2. How is the happiness in stanza III related to the assertion in lines 11–12 that "Heard melodies are sweet, but those unheard / Are sweeter"?

3. What is the difference between the world depicted on the urn and the speaker's world?

4. What do lines 49 and 50 suggest about the relation of art to life? Why is the urn described as a "Cold Pastoral" (line 45)?

5. Which world does the speaker seem to prefer, the urn's or his own?

6. Describe the overall tone of the poem.

CONNECTIONS TO OTHER SELECTIONS

1. Write an essay comparing the view of time in this ode with that in Marvell's "To His Coy Mistress" (p. 729). Pay particular attention to the connotative language in each poem.

2. Discuss the treatment and meaning of love in this ode and in Richard Wilbur's "Love Calls Us to the Things of This World" (p. 1124).

3. Compare the tone and attitude toward life in this ode with those in John Keats's "To Autumn" (p. 771).

GWENDOLYN BROOKS (B. 1917)

We Real Cool   *1960*

The Pool Players.
Seven at the Golden Shovel.

We real cool. We
Left school. We

Lurk late. We   5
Strike straight. We

Sing sin. We
Thin gin. We

Jazz June. We
Die soon.   10

CONSIDERATIONS FOR CRITICAL THINKING AND WRITING

1. FIRST RESPONSE. How does the speech of the pool players in this poem help to characterize them? What is the effect of the pronouns coming at the ends of the lines? How would the poem sound if the pronouns came at the beginnings of lines?

2. What is the author's attitude toward the players? Is there a change in tone in the last line?

3. How is the pool hall's name related to the rest of the poem and its theme?

MARILYN BOWERING (B. 1949)

Wishing Africa   *1980*

There's never enough whiskey or rain
when the blood is thin and white,
but oh it was beautiful,
the wind delicate as Queen Anne's lace,

only wild with insects   5
breeding the sponge-green veldt,
and bands of white butterflies
slapping the acacia.
The women's bodies were variable as coral
and men carried snakes on staves.   10

It would do me no good
to go back,
I am threaded
with pale veins,
I am full with dying   15
and ordinary;
but oh if there was a way
of wishing Africa.

When there was planting,
when there was harvesting,   20
I was not far behind
those who first
opened the ground.
I stitched in seed,
I grew meat in the earth's blond side.   25
I did it all with little bloody stitches.
What red there was in me
I let out there.
The sun stayed forever
then was gone.   30

I am scented with virus,
I breed flowers for the ochre
my skin was.
There is no sex in it.
I am white as a geisha,   35
my roots indiscriminate
since my bones gave way.
It is a small, personal pruning
that keeps me.
I had a soul,   40
and remember how it hurt
to be greedy and eat.

CONSIDERATIONS FOR CRITICAL THINKING AND WRITING

1. FIRST RESPONSE. What values does the speaker associate with Africa? How are those values contrasted with the speaker's present life?

2. Explain how the word choice in this poem creates a sensual tone.

3. Trace the connotative meanings (both traditional and untraditional) of the color white throughout the poem.

CONNECTIONS TO OTHER SELECTIONS

1. What does the use of sensuality in this poem and in Ackerman's "A Fine, a Private Place" (p. 734) reveal about the speaker in each poem?

2. In an essay compare the themes of "Wishing Africa" and Rainer Maria Rilke's "The Panther" (p. 767).

D. H. LAWRENCE (1885–1930)

The English Are So Nice!   *1932*

The English are so nice
So awfully nice
They are the nicest people in the world.

And what's more, they're very nice about being nice
About your being nice as well!   5
If you're not nice they soon make you feel it.

Americans and French and Germans and so on
They're all very well
But they're not *really* nice, you know.
They're not nice in *our* sense of the word, are they now?   10

That's why one doesn't have to take them seriously.
We must be nice to them, of course,
Of course, naturally.
But it doesn't really matter what you say to them,
They don't really understand   15
You can just say anything to them:
Be nice, you know, just nice
But you must never take them seriously, they wouldn't understand,
Just be nice, you know! oh, fairly nice,
Not too nice of course, they take advantage   20
But nice enough, just nice enough
To let them feel they're not quite as nice as they might be.

CONSIDERATIONS FOR CRITICAL THINKING AND WRITING

1. FIRST RESPONSE. What is the effect of the repetition of the word "nice"?

2. What does "nice" ordinarily mean? What does it come to mean in this poem?

3. Describe the speaker's tone and style. What does he really think of the English? Does he deliver his message in a nice way?

CONNECTION TO ANOTHER SELECTION

1. Write an essay that compares and contrasts the English in this poem with the way they're presented in Langston Hughes's "The English" (p. 1024).

LOUIS SIMPSON (B. 1923)

In the Suburbs

1963

There's no way out.
You were born to waste your life.
You were born to this middleclass life

As others before you
Were born to walk in procession
To the temple, singing.

CONSIDERATIONS FOR CRITICAL THINKING AND WRITING

1. FIRST RESPONSE. Is the title of this poem especially significant? What images does it conjure up for you?
2. What does the repetition in lines 2–3 suggest?
3. Discuss the possible connotative meanings of lines 5 and 6. Who are the "others before you"?

CONNECTION TO ANOTHER SELECTION

1. Write an essay on suburban life based on this poem and John Ciardi's "Suburban" (p. 818).

A NOTE ON READING TRANSLATIONS

Sometimes translation can inadvertently be a comic business. Consider, for example, the discovery made by John Steinbeck's wife, Elaine, when in a Yokohama bookstore she asked for a copy of her husband's famous novel *The Grapes of Wrath* and learned that it had been translated into Japanese as *Angry Raisins.* Close but no cigar (perhaps translated as: Nearby, yet no smoke). As amusing as that *Angry Raisins* title is, it teaches an important lesson about the significance of a poet's or a translator's choices when crafting a poem: a powerful piece moves us through diction and tone, both built word by careful word. Translations are frequently regarded as merely vehicular, a way to arrive at the original work. It is, of course, the original work — its spirit, style, and meaning — that most readers expect to find in a translation. Even so, it is important to understand that a translation is *by nature* different from the original — and that despite that difference, a fine translation can be an important part of the journey and become part of the literary landscape itself. Reading a translation of a poem is not the same as reading the original, but neither is watching two different performances of *Hamlet.* The translator provides a reading of the poem in much the same way that a director shapes the play. Each interprets the text from a unique perspective.

Basically, there are two distinct approaches to translation: literal translations and adaptations. A literal translation sets out to create a word-for-word equivalent that is absolutely faithful to the original. As simple and direct as this method may sound, literal translations are nearly impossible over extended passages because of the structural differences between languages. Moreover, the meaning of a single word in one language may not exist in another language, or it may require a phrase, clause, or entire sentence to capture its implications. Adaptations of works offer broader, more open-ended approaches to translation. Unlike a literal translation, an adaptation moves beyond denotative meanings in an attempt to capture the spirit of a work so that its idioms, dialects, slang, and other conventions are recreated in the language of the translation.

The question we ask of an adaptation should not be "Is this exactly how the original reads?" Instead, we ask "Is this an insightful, graceful rendering worth reading?" To translate poetry it is not enough to know the language of the original; it is also necessary that the translator be a poet. A translated poem is more than a collation of decisions based on dictionaries and grammars; it must also be poetry. However undefinable poetry may be, it is unmistakable in its intense use of language. Poems are not merely translated; they are savored.

Two Translations of Neruda's "Juventud"

Here are the original and two translations of "Juventud" written by the Chilean poet Pablo Neruda. Read through the Spanish version first even if you don't know Spanish so that you have a sense of what the translators worked through to create their poems. Pay particular attention to the way in which diction and word order help to create the tone in each of the translations.

PABLO NERUDA (1904–1973)

Juventud   *1942*

Un perfume como una ácida espada
de ciruelas en un camino,
los besos del azúcar en los dientes,
las gotas vitales resbalando en los dedos,
la dulce pulpa erótica,   5
las eras, los pajares, los incitantes
sitios secretos de las casas anchas,
los colchones dormidos en el pasado, el agrio valle verde
mirado desde arriba, desde el vidrio escondido:
toda la adolescencia mojándose y ardiendo   10
como una lámpara derribada en la lluvia.

Youth   *1942*

TRANSLATED BY ROBERT BLY (1971)

An odor like an acid sword made
of plum branches along the road,
the kisses like sugar in the teeth,
the drops of life slipping on the fingertips,
the sweet sexual fruit,   5
the yards, the haystacks, the inviting
rooms hidden in the deep houses,
the mattresses sleeping in the past, the savage green valley
seen from above, from the hidden window:
adolescence all sputtering and burning   10
like a lamp turned over in the rain.

Youth   *1942*

TRANSLATED BY JACK SCHMITT (1991)

A perfume like an acid plum
sword on a road,
sugary kisses on the teeth,
vital drops trickling down the fingers,
sweet erotic pulp,   5
threshing floors, haystacks, inciting
secret hideaways in spacious houses,
mattresses asleep in the past, the pungent green valley
seen from above, from the hidden window:
all adolescence becoming wet and burning   10
like a lantern tipped in the rain.

CONSIDERATIONS FOR CRITICAL THINKING AND WRITING

1. FIRST RESPONSE. How are the Bly and Schmitt translations similar in their
   treatment of youth?

2. Consult a Spanish dictionary and write a word-for-word translation of "Juventud" into English. Which lines are particularly difficult to translate?
   How does your translation compare with Bly's and Schmitt's? Explain why
   one of the two translations is closest to the original Spanish.

3. Compare the diction and images in the Bly and Schmitt translations and explain which you think is more effective. Explain why, for example, you find
   Bly's "sweet sexual fruit" or Schmitt's "sweet erotic pulp" more effective.

Four Translations of a Poem by Sappho

Sappho, born about 630 B.C. and a native of the Greek island of
Lesbos, is the author of a hymn to Aphrodite, the goddess of love and
beauty in Greek myth. The four translations that follow suggest how

widely translations can differ from one another. The first, by Henry T. Wharton, is intended to be a literal prose translation of the original Greek.

SAPPHO (C. 630 B.C.–C. 570 B.C.)

Immortal Aphrodite of the broidered throne date unknown

TRANSLATED BY HENRY T. WHARTON (1885)

Immortal Aphrodite of the broidered throne, daughter of Zeus, weaver of wiles, I pray thee break not my spirit with anguish and distress, O Queen. But come hither, if ever before thou didst hear my voice afar, and listen, and leaving thy father's golden house camest with chariot yoked, and fair fleet sparrows drew thee, flapping fast their wings around the dark earth, from heaven through mid sky. Quickly arrived they; and thou, blessed one, smiling with immortal countenance, didst ask What now is befallen me, and Why now I call, and What I in my mad heart most desire to see. 'What Beauty now wouldst thou draw to love thee? Who wrongs thee, Sappho? For even if she flies she shall soon follow, and if she rejects gifts shall yet give, and if she loves not shall soon love, however loth.' Come, I pray thee, now too, and release me from cruel cares; and all that my heart desires to accomplish, accomplish thou, and be thyself my ally.

Beautiful-throned, immortal Aphrodite

TRANSLATED BY T. W. HIGGINSON (1871)

Beautiful-throned, immortal Aphrodite,
Daughter of Zeus, beguiler, I implore thee,
Weigh me not down with weariness and anguish
    O Thou most holy!

Come to me now, if ever thou in kindness 5
Hearkenedst my words, — and often hast thou
    hearkened —
Heeding, and coming from the mansions golden
    Of thy great Father,

Yoking thy chariot, borne by the most lovely 10
Consecrated birds, with dusky-tinted pinions,
Waving swift wings from utmost heights of
    heaven
    Through the mid-ether;

Swiftly they vanished, leaving thee, O goddess, 15
Smiling, with face immortal in its beauty,
Asking why I grieved, and why in utter longing
    I had dared call thee;

Asking what I sought, thus hopeless in desiring,
Wildered in brain, and spreading nets of 20
    passion —

Alas, for whom? and saidst thou, "Who has
    harmed thee?
       "O my poor Sappho!

"Though now he flies, ere long he shall pursue   25
    thee;
"Fearing thy gifts, he too in turn shall bring
    them;
"Loveless to-day, to-morrow he shall woo thee,
       "Though thou shouldst spurn him."   30

Thus seek me now, O holy Aphrodite!
Save me from anguish; give me all I ask for,
Gifts at thy hand; and thine shall be the glory,
    Sacred protector!

Invocation to Aphrodite

TRANSLATED BY RICHARD LATTIMORE (1955)

Throned in splendor, deathless, O Aphrodite,
child of Zeus, charm-fashioner, I entreat you
not with griefs and bitternesses to break my
    spirit, O goddess;

standing by me rather, if once before now   5
far away you heard, when I called upon you,
left your father's dwelling place and descended,
    yoking the golden

chariot to sparrows, who fairly drew you
down in speed aslant the black world, the bright   10
trembling at the heart to the pulse of countless
    fluttering wingbeats.

Swiftly then they came, and you, blessed lady,
smiling on me out of immortal beauty,
asked me what affliction was on me, why I   15
    called thus upon you,

what beyond all else I would have befall my
tortured heart: "Whom then would you have Per-
    suasion
force to serve desire in your heart? Who is it,   20
    Sappho, that hurt you?

Though she now escape you, she soon will follow;
though she take not gifts from you, she will give
    them:
though she love not, yet she will surely love you   25
    even unwilling."

In such guise come even again and set me
free from doubt and sorrow; accomplish all those

things my heart desires to be done; appear and
     stand at my shoulder.   30

Artfully adorned Aphrodite, deathless

TRANSLATED BY JIM POWELL (1993)

Artfully adorned Aphrodite, deathless
child of Zeus and weaver of wiles I beg you
please don't hurt me, don't overcome my spirit,
     goddess, with longing,

but come here, if ever at other moments   5
hearing these my words from afar you listened
and responded: leaving your father's house, all
     golden, you came then,

hitching up your chariot: lovely sparrows
drew you quickly over the dark earth, whirling   10
on fine beating wings from the heights of heaven
     down through the sky and

instantly arrived — and then O my blessed
goddess with a smile on your deathless face you
asked me what the matter was *this* time, what I   15
     called you for this time,

what I now most wanted to happen in my
raving heart: "Whom *this* time should I persuade to
lead you back again to her love? Who *now*, oh
     Sappho, who wrongs you?   20

If she flees you now, she will soon pursue you;
if she won't accept what you give, she'll give it;
if she doesn't love you, she'll love you soon now,
     even unwilling."

Come to me again, and release me from this   25
want past bearing. All that my heart desires to
happen — make it happen. And stand beside me,
     goddess, my ally.

CONSIDERATIONS FOR CRITICAL THINKING AND WRITING

1. FIRST RESPONSE. Try rewriting Wharton's prose version in contemporary language. How does your prose version differ in tone from Wharton's?
2. Explain which translation seems closest to Wharton's prose version.
3. Discuss the images and metaphors in Higginson's and Lattimore's versions. Which version is more appealing to you? Explain why.
4. How does Powell's use of language clearly make his version the most contemporary of the translations?

17

Images

POETRY'S APPEAL TO THE SENSES

A poet, to borrow a phrase from Henry James, is one of those on whom nothing is lost. Poets take in the world and give us impressions of what they experience through images. An *image* is language that addresses the senses. The most common images in poetry are visual; they provide verbal pictures of the poets' encounters — real or imagined — with the world. But poets also create images that appeal to our other senses. Richard Wilbur arouses several senses when he has the speaker in "A Late Aubade" gently urge his lover to linger in bed with him instead of getting on with her daily routines and obligations:

> Wait for a while, then slip downstairs
> And bring us up some chilled white wine,
> And some blue cheese, and crackers, and some fine
> Ruddy-skinned pears.

These images are simultaneously tempting and satisfying. We don't have to literally touch that cold, clear glass of wine (or will it come in a green bottle beaded with moisture?) or smell the cheese or taste the crackers to appreciate this vivid blend of colors, textures, tastes, and fragrances.

Images give us the physical world to experience in our imaginations. Some poems, like the following one, are written to do just that; they make no comment about what they describe.

WILLIAM CARLOS WILLIAMS (1883–1963)

Poem   1934

As the cat
climbed over
the top of

the jamcloset
first the right   5
forefoot

carefully
then the hind
stepped down

into the pit of   10
the empty
flowerpot

This poem defies paraphrase because it is all an image of agile move-ment. No statement is made about the movement; the title, "Poem" — really no title — signals Williams's refusal to comment on the movements. To impose a meaning on the poem, we'd probably have to knock over the flowerpot.

We experience the image in Williams's "Poem" more clearly because of how the sentence is organized into lines and groups of lines, or stanzas. Consider how differently the sentence is read if it is arranged as prose:

> As the cat climbed over the top of the jamcloset, first the right forefoot care-fully then the hind stepped down into the pit of the empty flowerpot.

The poem's line and stanza division transforms what is essentially an awk-ward prose sentence into a rhythmic verbal picture. Especially when the poem is read aloud, this line and stanza division allows us to feel the image we see. Even the lack of a period at the end suggests that the cat is only pausing.

Images frequently do more than offer only sensory impressions, how-ever. They also convey emotions and moods, as in the following lyric.

BONNIE JACOBSON (B. 1933)

On Being Served Apples   1989

Apples in a deep blue dish
        are the shadows of nuns
Apples in a basket
        are warm red moons on Indian women
Apples in a white bowl
        are virgins waiting in snow

Beware of apples on an orange plate:
        they are the anger of wives

The four images of apples in this poem suggest a range of emotions. How would you describe these emotions? How does the meaning of the apples change depending on the context in which they are served? In this poem we are given more than just images of the world selected by the poet; we are also given her feelings about them.

What mood is established in this next poem's view of Civil War troops moving across a river?

WALT WHITMAN (1819–1892)

Cavalry Crossing a Ford   *1865*

A line in long array where they wind betwixt green islands,
They take a serpentine course, their arms flash in the sun — hark to the
      musical clank,
Behold the silvery river, in it the splashing horses loitering stop to drink,
Behold the brown-faced men, each group, each person, a picture, the
      negligent rest on the saddles,
Some emerge on the opposite bank, others are just entering the ford — while,
Scarlet and blue and snowy white,
The guidon flags flutter gaily in the wind.

CONSIDERATIONS FOR CRITICAL THINKING AND WRITING

1. FIRST RESPONSE. Do the colors and sounds establish the mood of this poem? What *is* the mood?
2. How would the poem's mood have been changed if Whitman had used "look" or "see" instead of "behold" (lines 3–4)?
3. Where is the speaker as he observes this troop movement?
4. Does "serpentine" in line 2 have an evil connotation in this poem? Explain your answer.

Whitman seems to capture momentarily all the troop's actions, and through carefully chosen, suggestive details — really very few — he succeeds in making "each group, each person, a picture." Specific details, even when few are provided, give us the impression that we see the entire picture; it is as if those are the details we would remember if we had viewed the scene ourselves. Notice too that the movement of the "line in long array" is emphasized by the continuous winding syntax of the poem's lengthy lines.

Movement is also central to the next poem, in which action and motion are created through carefully chosen verbs.

DAVID SOLWAY (B. 1941)

Windsurfing

1993

It rides upon the wrinkled hide
of water, like the upturned hull
of a small canoe or kayak
waiting to be righted — yet its law
is opposite to that of boats,   5
it floats upon its breastbone and
brings whatever spine there is to light.
A thin shaft is slotted into place.
Then a puffed right-angle of wind
pushes it forward, out into the bay,   10
where suddenly it glitters into speed,
tilts, knifes up, and for the moment's
nothing but a slim projectile
of cambered fiberglass,
peeling the crests.   15

        The man's
clamped to the mast, taut as a guywire.
Part of the sleek apparatus
he controls, immaculate nerve
of balance, plunge and curvet,   20
he clinches all component movements
into single motion.
It bucks, stalls, shudders, yaws, and dips
its hissing sides beneath the surface
that sustains it, tensing   25
into muscle that nude ellipse
of lunging appetite and power.

And now the mechanism's wholly
dolphin, springing toward its prey
of spume and beaded sunlight,   30
tossing spray, and hits the vertex
of the wide, salt glare of distance,
and reverses.

        Back it comes through
a screen of particles,   35
scalloped out of water, shimmer
and reflection, the wind snapping
and lashing it homeward,
shearing the curve of the wave,
breaking the spell of the caught breath   40
and articulate play of sinew, to enter
the haven of the breakwater
and settle in a rush of silence.

Now the crossing drifts
in the husk of its wake   45

and nothing's the same again
as, gliding elegantly on a film of water,
the man guides
his brash, obedient legend
into shore.   50

CONSIDERATIONS FOR CRITICAL THINKING AND WRITING

1. FIRST RESPONSE. Draw a circle around the verbs that seem especially effective
   in conveying a strong sense of motion, and explain why they are effective.
2. How is the man made to seem to be one with his board and sail?
3. How does the rhythm of the poem change beginning with line 45?

CONNECTIONS TO OTHER SELECTIONS

1. Consider the effects of the images in "Windsurfing" and Ho's "A Beautiful
   Girl Combs Her Hair" (p. 706). In an essay explain how these images produce emotional responses in you.
2. Compare the descriptions in "Windsurfing" and Bishop's "The Fish"
   (p. 682). How does each poet appeal to your senses to describe windsurfing
   and fishing?

"Windsurfing" is awash with images of speed, fluidity, and power. Even
the calming aftermath of the breakwater is described as a "rush of silence,"
adding to the sense of motion that is detailed and expanded throughout
the poem.

Poets choose details the way they choose the words to present those
details: only telling ones will do. Consider the images Theodore Roethke
uses in "Root Cellar."

THEODORE ROETHKE (1908–1963)

Root Cellar   1948

Nothing would sleep in that cellar, dank as a ditch,
Bulbs broke out of boxes hunting for chinks in the dark,
Shoots dangled and drooped,
Lolling obscenely from mildewed crates,
Hung down long yellow evil necks, like tropical snakes.   5
And what a congress of stinks!
Roots ripe as old bait,
Pulpy stems, rank, silo-rich,
Leaf-mold, manure, lime, piled against slippery planks.
Nothing would give up life: 10
Even the dirt kept breathing a small breath.

CONSIDERATIONS FOR CRITICAL THINKING AND WRITING

1. FIRST RESPONSE. Explain why you think this is a positive or negative rendition of a root cellar.

2. What senses are engaged by the images in this poem? Is the poem simply a series of sensations, or do the detailed images make some kind of point about the root cellar?

3. What controls the choice of details in the poem? Why isn't there, for example, a rusty shovel leaning against a dirt wall or a worn gardener's glove atop one of the crates?

4. Look up *congress* in a dictionary for its denotative meanings. Explain why "congress of stinks" is especially appropriate given the nature of the rest of the poem's imagery.

5. What single line in the poem suggests a theme?

The tone of the images and mood of the speaker are consistent in Roethke's "Root Cellar." In Matthew Arnold's "Dover Beach," however, they shift as the theme is developed.

MATTHEW ARNOLD (1822–1888)

Dover Beach   *1867*

The sea is calm tonight.
The tide is full, the moon lies fair
Upon the straits; — on the French coast the light
Gleams and is gone; the cliffs of England stand,
Glimmering and vast, out in the tranquil bay.   5
Come to the window, sweet is the night-air!
Only, from the long line of spray
Where the sea meets the moon-blanched land,
Listen! you hear the grating roar
Of pebbles which the waves draw back, and fling,   10
At their return, up the high strand,
Begin, and cease, and then again begin,
With tremulous cadence slow, and bring
The eternal note of sadness in.

Sophocles long ago   15
Heard it on the Aegean, and it brought
Into his mind the turbid ebb and flow
Of human misery;° we
Find also in the sound a thought,
Hearing it by this distant northern sea.   20

The Sea of Faith
Was once, too, at the full, and round earth's shore
Lay like the folds of a bright girdle furled.
But now I only hear
Its melancholy, long, withdrawing roar,   25
Retreating, to the breath

15–18 *Sophocles . . . misery:* In *Antigone* (lines 656–677), Sophocles likens the disasters that beset the house of Oedipus to a "mounting tide."

Of the night-wind, down the vast edges drear
And naked shingles° of the world.   *pebble beaches*

Ah, love, let us be true
To one another! for the world, which seems   30
To lie before us like a land of dreams,
So various, so beautiful, so new,
Hath really neither joy, nor love, nor light,
Nor certitude, nor peace, nor help for pain;
And we are here as on a darkling plain   35
Swept with confused alarms of struggle and flight,
Where ignorant armies clash by night.

CONSIDERATIONS FOR CRITICAL THINKING AND WRITING

1. FIRST RESPONSE. Discuss what you consider to be this poem's central point. How do the speaker's descriptions of the ocean work toward making that point?

2. Contrast the images in lines 4–8 and 9–13. How do they reveal the speaker's mood? To whom is he speaking?

3. What is the cause of the "sadness" in line 14? What is the speaker's response to the ebbing "Sea of Faith"? Is there anything to replace his sense of loss?

4. What details of the beach seem related to the ideas in the poem? How is the sea used differently in lines 1–14 and lines 21–28?

5. Describe the differences in tone between lines 1–8 and 35–37. What has caused the change?

CONNECTIONS TO OTHER SELECTIONS

1. Explain how the images in Wilfred Owen's "Dulce et Decorum Est" (p. 763) develop further the ideas and sentiments suggested by Arnold's final line concerning "ignorant armies clash[ing] by night."

2. Contrast Arnold's images with those of Anthony Hecht in his parody "The Dover Bitch" (p. 1096). How do Hecht's images create a very different mood from that of "Dover Beach"?

Consider the poetic appetite for images displayed in the celebration of chile peppers in the following passionate poem.

JIMMY SANTIAGO BACA (B. 1952)

Green Chile   *1989*

I prefer red chile over my eggs
and potatoes for breakfast.
Red chile *ristras*° decorate my door,   *a braided string of peppers*
dry on my roof, and hang from eaves.
They lend open-air vegetable stands   5
historical grandeur, and gently swing

with an air of festive welcome.
I can hear them talking in the wind,
haggard, yellowing, crisp, rasping
tongues of old men, licking the breeze.   10

But grandmother loves green chile.
When I visit her,
she holds the green chile pepper
in her wrinkled hands.
Ah, voluptuous, masculine,   15
an air of authority and youth simmers
from its swan-neck stem, tapering to a flowery
collar, fermenting resinous spice.
A well-dressed gentleman at the door
my grandmother takes sensuously in her hand,   20
rubbing its firm glossed sides,
caressing the oily rubbery serpent,
with mouth-watering fulfillment,
fondling its curves with gentle fingers.
Its bearing magnificent and taut   25
as flanks of a tiger in mid-leap,
she thrusts her blade into
and cuts it open, with lust
on her hot mouth, sweating over the stove,
bandanna round her forehead,   30
mysterious passion on her face
and she serves me green chile con carne
between soft warm leaves of corn tortillas,
with beans and rice — her sacrifice
to her little prince.   35
I slurp from my plate
with last bit of tortilla, my mouth burns
and I hiss and drink a tall glass of cold water.

All over New Mexico, sunburned men and women
drive rickety trucks stuffed with gunny-sacks   40
of green chile, from Belen, Veguita, Willard, Estancia,
San Antonio y Socorro, from fields
to roadside stands, you see them roasting green chile
in screen-sided homemade barrels, and for a dollar a bag,
we relive this old, beautiful ritual again and again.   45

CONSIDERATIONS FOR CRITICAL THINKING AND WRITING

1. FIRST RESPONSE. What's the difference between red and green chiles in this poem? Find the different images the speaker uses to draw a distinction between the two.

2. What kinds of images are used to describe the grandmother's preparation of green chile? What is the effect of those images?

3. Try writing a description — in poetry or prose — that uses vivid images to evoke a powerful response (either positive or negative) to a particular food.

POEMS FOR FURTHER STUDY

Seamus Heaney (b. 1939)

The Pitchfork

1991

Of all implements, the pitchfork was the one
That came near to an imagined perfection:
When he tightened his raised hand and aimed with it,
It felt like a javelin, accurate and light.

So whether he played the warrior or the athlete   5
Or worked in earnest in the chaff and sweat,
He loved its grain of tapering, dark-flecked ash
Grown satiny from its own natural polish.

Riveted steel, turned timber, burnish, grain,
Smoothness, straightness, roundness, length and sheen.   10
Sweat-cured, sharpened, balanced, tested, fitted.
The springiness, the clip and dart of it.

And then when he thought of probes that reached the
    farthest,
He would see the shaft of a pitchfork sailing past   15
Evenly, imperturbably through space,
Its prongs starlit and absolutely soundless —

But has learned at last to follow that simple lead
Past its own aim, out to an other side
Where perfection — or nearness to it — is imagined   20
Not in the aiming but the opening hand.

Considerations for Critical Thinking and Writing

1. FIRST RESPONSE. Provide an alternate title that you think captures the poem's meaning.

2. How do the images make this pitchfork more than merely one of many "implements"?

3. In what ways does the pitchfork change through the course of the poem?

4. Explain what the speaker means by "imagined perfection" (lines 2 and 20).

5. What does the thrower of the pitchfork learn in lines 13-16?

Connection to Another Selection

1. Pitchforks and green chile do not have much in common, but the images used to describe the pitchfork in this poem and the chile in Jimmy Santiago Baca's "Green Chile" (p. 758) invest significance in these otherwise ordinary objects. Write an essay that discusses how the images in these two poems give these objects qualities that are not inherent in either pitchforks or chile.

H. D. (HILDA DOOLITTLE/1886–1961)

Heat   *1916*

O wind, rend open the heat,
cut apart the heat,
rend it to tatters.

Fruit cannot drop
through this thick air —   5
fruit cannot fall into heat
that presses up and blunts
the points of pears
and rounds the grapes.

Cut the heat —   10
plough through it,
turning it on either side
of your path.

CONSIDERATIONS FOR CRITICAL THINKING AND WRITING

1. FIRST RESPONSE. Is this poem more about heat or fruit? Explain your answer.
2. What physical properties are associated with heat in this poem?
3. Explain the effect of the description of fruit in lines 4–9.
4. Why is the image of the cutting plow especially effective in lines 10–13?

TIMOTHY STEELE (B. 1948)

An Aubade   *1986*

As she is showering, I wake to see
A shine of earrings on the bedside stand,
A single yellow sheet which, over me,
Has folds as intricate as drapery
In paintings from some fine old master's hand.   5

The pillow which, in dozing, I embraced
Retains the salty sweetness of her skin;
I sense her smooth back, buttocks, belly, waist,
The leggy warmth which spread and gently laced
Around my legs and loins, and drew me in.   10

I stretch and curl about a bit and hear her
Singing among the water's hiss and race.
Gradually the early light makes clearer
The perfume bottles by the dresser's mirror,
The silver flashlight, standing on its face,   15

Which shares the corner of the dresser with
An ivy spilling tendrils from a cup.
And so content am I, I can forgive

Pleasure for being brief and fugitive.
I'll stretch some more, but postpone getting up   20

Until she finishes her shower and dries
(Now this and now that foot placed on a chair)
Her fineboned ankles, and her calves and thighs,
The pink full nipples of her breasts, and ties
Her towel up, turban-style, about her hair.   25

Considerations for Critical Thinking and Writing

1. FIRST RESPONSE. Characterize the poem's speaker. What does his language reveal about him?
2. How does this poem fit the definition of an aubade?
3. What do you think is the central point of this poem?
4. Is this a *carpe diem* poem? Explain why or why not.

Connections to Other Selections

1. How does the tone of Steele's poem compare with Wilbur's "A Late Aubade" (p. 732)? Explain why you prefer one over the other.
2. Write an essay that compares and contrasts the speaker/observer in "An Aubade" with that of Joan Murray's in "Play-By-Play" (p. 1163).

WILLIAM BLAKE (1757–1827)

London   *1794*

I wander through each chartered° street,   *defined by law*
Near where the chartered Thames does flow,
And mark in every face I meet
Marks of weakness, marks of woe.

In every cry of every man,   5
In every Infant's cry of fear,
In every voice, in every ban,
The mind-forged manacles I hear.

How the Chimney-sweeper's cry
Every black'ning Church appalls;   10
And the hapless Soldier's sigh
Runs in blood down Palace walls.

But most through midnight streets I hear
How the youthful Harlot's curse
Blasts the new-born Infant's tear,   15
And blights with plagues the Marriage hearse.

Considerations for Critical Thinking and Writing

1. FIRST RESPONSE. What feelings do the visual images in this poem suggest to you?

2. What is the predominant sound heard in the poem?

3. What is the meaning of line 8? What is the cause of the problems that the speaker sees and hears in London? Does the speaker suggest additional causes?

4. The image in lines 11 and 12 cannot be read literally. Comment on its effectiveness.

5. How does Blake's use of denotative and connotative language enrich this poem's meaning?

6. An earlier version of Blake's last stanza appeared this way:

> But most the midnight harlot's curse
> From every dismal street I hear,
> Weaves around the marriage hearse
> And blasts the new-born infant's tear.

Examine carefully the differences between the two versions. How do Blake's revisions affect his picture of London life? Which version do you think is more effective? Why?

WILFRED OWEN (1893–1918)

Dulce et Decorum Est   *1920*

Bent double, like old beggars under sacks,
Knock-kneed, coughing like hags, we cursed through sludge,
Till on the haunting flares we turned our backs,
And towards our distant rest began to trudge.

Men marched asleep. Many had lost their boots,   5
But limped on, blood-shod. All went lame, all blind;
Drunk with fatigue; deaf even to the hoots
Of gas-shells dropping softly behind.

Gas! GAS! Quick, boys! — An ecstasy of fumbling,
Fitting the clumsy helmets just in time,   10
But someone still was yelling out and stumbling
And flound'ring like a man in fire or lime. —
Dim through the misty panes and thick green light,
As under a green sea, I saw him drowning.

In all my dreams before my helpless sight   15
He plunges at me, guttering, choking, drowning.

If in some smothering dreams, you too could pace
Behind the wagon that we flung him in,
And watch the white eyes writhing in his face,
His hanging face, like a devil's sick of sin,   20
If you could hear, at every jolt, the blood
Come gargling from the froth-corrupted lungs
Bitter as the cud
Obscene as cancer,
Of vile, incurable sores on innocent tongues, —   25
My friend, you would not tell with such high zest

To children ardent for some desperate glory,
The old lie: *Dulce et decorum est*
Pro patria mori.

CONSIDERATIONS FOR CRITICAL THINKING AND WRITING

1. FIRST RESPONSE. The Latin quotation in lines 27 and 28 is from Horace: "It is sweet and fitting to die for one's country." Owen served as a British soldier during World War I and was killed. Is this poem unpatriotic? What is its purpose?

2. Which images in the poem are most vivid? To which senses do they speak?

3. Describe the speaker's tone. What is his relationship to his audience?

4. How are the images of the soldiers in this poem different from the images that typically appear in recruiting posters?

MARGARET HOLLEY (B. 1944)

Peepers   *1992*

One amber inch
of blinking berry-eyed
amphibian,

four fetal fingers
on each hand,
a honey and mud-brown   5

pulse of appetite
surprised into stillness,
folded in a momentary lump

of flying bat-fish   10
ready to jump
full-tilt into anything

— the whole strength
of its struggling length
you can hold in your hand.   15

Its poetry, a raucous
refrain of pleasure
in the April-warm pools

of rain, the insistent
chorus of whistles   20
jingles through night woods,

Females! It's time!
that confident come-on
to a whole wet population

of embraces, eggs, tadpoles   25
— all head and tail,
mind darting in every direction

until the articulating torso,
Ovidian bag of bones,
results in the "mature adult":   30

a rumpled face in the mirror
still sleeping through Basho's°
awakening plop,

re-enchanted daily
by the comforting slop   35
of burgeoning spring woods

and all this sexual chatter,
doing its best to make
the wet and silky season

last forever. Yet   40
as you lie dreaming mid-leap,
splayed in the sheets,

the future as a kind
but relentless scientist
feels around in your flesh   45

for the nerve of surprise;
he just loves
the look of wonder on your face,

the world on your open lips
for the immensity   50
that grips you,

Oh.

32 *Basho:* Matsuo Bashō (1644–1694), a Japanese poet most famous for his haiku. See
"Under cherry trees" (p. 891).

CONSIDERATIONS FOR CRITICAL THINKING AND WRITING

1. FIRST RESPONSE. What is the speaker's attitude toward what is described in
   this poem?
2. What is being described in lines 1–40? How does the subject shift in lines
   40–52? What is the relationship between these two groups of lines?
3. The word "Peepers" only appears in the title, but are there images in the
   poem that connect to the title? What does the title mean?
4. What is the effect and significance of the final line?

ELIZABETH BARRETT BROWNING (1806–1861)

Grief   *1844*

I tell you, hopeless grief is passionless;
That only men incredulous of despair,
Half-taught in anguish, through the midnight air
Beat upward to God's throne in loud access

Of shrieking and reproach. Full desertness,   5
In souls as countries, lieth silent-bare
Under the blanching, vertical eye-glare
Of the absolute Heavens. Deep-hearted man, express
Grief for thy Dead in silence like to death —
Most like a monumental statue set   10
In everlasting watch and moveless woe
Till itself crumble to the dust beneath.
Touch it; the marble eyelids are not wet.
If it could weep, it could arise and go.

CONSIDERATIONS FOR CRITICAL THINKING AND WRITING

1. FIRST RESPONSE. What is the effect of the poem's first words, "I tell you"?
   How do they serve to characterize the speaker?
2. What images does Browning use to describe grief?
3. Describe the emotional tone of this poem.

JAMES DICKEY (1923–1997)

Deer Among Cattle   *1981*

Here and there in the searing beam
Of my hand going through the night meadow
They all are grazing

With pins of human light in their eyes.
A wild one also is eating   5
The human grass,

Slender, graceful, domesticated
By darkness, among the bred-
for-slaughter,

Having bounded their paralyzed fence   10
And inclined his branched forehead onto
Their green frosted table,

The only live thing in this flashlight
Who can leave whenever he wishes,
Turn grass into forest,   15

Foreclose inhuman brightness from his eyes
But stands here still, unperturbed,
In their wide-open country,

The sparks from my hand in his pupils
Unmatched anywhere among cattle,   20

Grazing with them the night of the hammer
As one of their own who shall rise.

CONSIDERATIONS FOR CRITICAL THINKING AND WRITING

1. FIRST RESPONSE. What images distinguish the deer from the cattle?

2. Do the words "domesticated" and "human" have positive or negative connotations in this poem? Explain your answer.

3. Discuss the possible implications of the last two lines. You may want to
   consider the speaker and his role in this tableau.

CONNECTION TO ANOTHER SELECTION

1. Discuss the idea of confinement in "Deer Among Cattle" and Rainer Maria
   Rilke's "The Panther" (below).

RAINER MARIA RILKE (1875–1926)

The Panther   *1927*

TRANSLATED BY STEPHEN MITCHELL

His vision, from the constantly passing bars,
has grown so weary that it cannot hold
anything else. It seems to him there are
a thousand bars; and behind the bars, no world.

As he paces in cramped circles, over and over,   5
the movement of his powerful soft strides
is like a ritual dance around a center
in which a mighty will stands paralyzed.

Only at times, the curtain of the pupils
lifts, quietly — . An image enters in,   10
rushes down through the tensed, arrested muscles,
plunges into the heart and is gone.

CONSIDERATIONS FOR CRITICAL THINKING AND WRITING

1. FIRST RESPONSE. Why do you think Rilke chooses a panther rather than,
   say, a lion as the subject of the poem's images?

2. What kind of "image enters in" the heart of the panther in the final stanza?

3. How are images of confinement achieved in the poem? Why doesn't Rilke
   describe the final image in lines 10–12?

CONNECTION TO ANOTHER SELECTION

1. Write an essay explaining how a sense of movement is achieved by the images and rhythms in this poem and in Dickinson's "A Bird came down the
   Walk —" (p. 829).

JANE KENYON (1947–1995)

The Blue Bowl

1990

Like primitives we buried the cat
with his bowl. Bare-handed
we scraped sand and gravel
back into the hole.
                They fell with a hiss   5

and thud on his side,
on his long red fur, the white feathers
between his toes, and his
long, not to say aquiline, nose.

We stood and brushed each other off.   10
There are sorrows keener than these.

Silent the rest of the day, we worked,
ate, stared, and slept. It stormed
all night; now it clears, and a robin
burbles from a dripping bush   15
like the neighbor who means well
but always says the wrong thing.

CONSIDERATIONS FOR CRITICAL THINKING AND WRITING

1. FIRST RESPONSE. How do the descriptions of the cat—"the white feathers/between his toes"—affect your reading of the poem?
2. Why do you think Kenyon titles the poem "The Blue Bowl" rather than, perhaps, "The Cat's Bowl"?
3. What is the effect of being reminded that "There are sorrows keener than these"?
4. Why is the robin's song "the wrong thing"?

CONNECTION TO ANOTHER SELECTION

1. Write an essay comparing the death of this cat with the death of the dog in Updike's "Dog's Death" (p. 673). Which poem draws a more powerful response from you? Explain why.

SALLY CROFT (B. 1935)

Home-Baked Bread

1981

Nothing gives a household a greater sense of stability and common comfort than the aroma of cooling bread. Begin, if you like, with a loaf of whole wheat, which requires neither sifting nor kneading, and go on from there to more cunning triumphs.
                                        — The Joy of Cooking

What is it she is not saying?
Cunning triumphs. It rings

of insinuation. Step into my kitchen,
I have prepared a cunning triumph
for you. Spices and herbs   5
sealed in this porcelain jar,

a treasure of my great-aunt
who sat up past midnight
in her Massachusetts bedroom
when the moon was dark. Come,   10
rest your feet. I'll make
you tea with honey and slices

of warm bread spread with peach butter.
I picked the fruit this morning
still fresh with dew. The fragrance   15
is seductive? I hoped you would say that.
See how the heat rises
when the bread opens. Come,

we'll eat together, the small flakes
have scarcely any flavor. What cunning   20
triumphs we can discover in my upstairs room
where peach trees breathe their sweetness
beside the open window and
sun lies like honey on the floor.

CONSIDERATIONS FOR CRITICAL THINKING AND WRITING

1. FIRST RESPONSE. Why does the speaker in this poem seize on the phrase "cunning triumphs" from the *Joy of Cooking* excerpt?

2. Distinguish between the voice we hear in lines 1–3 and the second voice in lines 3–24. Who is the "you" in the poem?

3. Why is "insinuation" an especially appropriate word choice in line 3?

4. How do the images in lines 20–24 bring together all the senses evoked in the preceding lines?

5. Write a paragraph that describes the sensuous (and perhaps sensual) qualities of a food you enjoy.

CAROLYN KIZER (B. 1925)
Food for Love   1984

Eating is touch carried to the bitter end.
— *Samuel Butler II*

I'm going to murder you with love;
I'm going to suffocate you with embraces;
I'm going to hug you, bone by bone,

Till you're dead all over.
Then I will dine on your delectable marrow.   5

You will become my personal Sahara;
I'll sun myself in you, then with one swallow
Drain your remaining brackish well.
With my female blade I'll carve my name
In your most aspiring palm   10
Before I chop it down.
Then I'll inhale your last oasis whole.

But in the total desert you become
You'll see me stretch, horizon to horizon,
Opulent mirage!   15
Wisteria balconies dripping cyclamen.
Vistas ablaze with crystal, laced in gold.

So you will summon each dry grain of sand
And move towards me in undulating dunes
Till you arrive at sudden ultramarine: 20
A Mediterranean to stroke your dusty shores;
Obstinate verdure, creeping inland, fast renudes
Your barrens; succulents spring up everywhere,
Surprising life! And I will be that green.

When you are fed and watered, flourishing   25
With shoots entwining trellis, dome and spire,
Till you are resurrected field in bloom,
I will devour you, my natural food,
My host, my final supper on the earth,
And you'll begin to die again.   30

Considerations for Critical Thinking and Writing

1. FIRST RESPONSE. What's going on here? Is this a love poem? Explain why or why not.

2. What does the epigraph from Samuel Butler contribute to your understanding of the poem?

3. Contrast the speaker's relationship with her "personal Sahara" in lines 1–12 and in lines 13–30.

Connections to Other Selections

1. Write a reply to this poem — in poetry or prose — as you think the speaker of Marvell's "To His Coy Mistress" (p. 729) would respond.

2. Discuss the relationship between food and love in Kizer's poem and in "Home-Baked Bread."

3. Write an essay comparing the tone of "Food for Love" and Elaine Magarrell's "The Joy of Cooking" (p. 792).

JOHN KEATS (1795–1821)

To Autumn   *1819*

I
Season of mists and mellow fruitfulness,
　　Close bosom-friend of the maturing sun;
Conspiring with him how to load and bless
　　With fruit the vines that round the thatch-eves run;
To bend with apples the mossed cottage-trees,   5
　　And fill all fruit with ripeness to the core;
　　　　To swell the gourd, and plump the hazel shells
　　With a sweet kernel; to set budding more,
And still more, later flowers for the bees,
Until they think warm days will never cease,   10
　　　　For summer has o'er-brimmed their clammy cells.

II
Who hath not seen thee oft amid thy store?
　　Sometimes whoever seeks abroad may find
Thee sitting careless on a granary floor,
　　Thy hair soft-lifted by the winnowing wind;   15
Or on a half-reaped furrow sound asleep,
　　Drowsed with the fume of poppies, while thy hook°   *scythe*
　　　　Spares the next swath and all its twinèd flowers:
And sometimes like a gleaner thou dost keep
　　Steady thy laden head across a brook;   20
　　Or by a cider-press, with patient look,
　　　　Thou watchest the last oozings hours by hours.

III
Where are the songs of spring? Ay, where are they?
　　Think not of them, thou hast thy music too, —
While barred clouds bloom the soft-dying day,   25
　　And touch the stubble-plains with rosy hue;
Then in a wailful choir the small gnats mourn
　　Among the river swallows,° borne aloft   *willows*
　　　　Or sinking as the light wind lives or dies;
And full-grown lambs loud bleat from hilly bourn;°   *territory* 30
　　Hedge-crickets sing; and now with treble soft
　　The redbreast whistles from a garden-croft,
　　　　And gathering swallows twitter in the skies.

CONSIDERATIONS FOR CRITICAL THINKING AND WRITING

1. FIRST RESPONSE. How is autumn made to seem like a person in each stanza
   of this ode?
2. Which senses are most emphasized in each stanza?
3. How is the progression of time expressed in the ode?
4. How does the imagery convey tone? Which words have particularly strong
   connotative values?
5. What is the speaker's view of death?

CONNECTIONS TO OTHER SELECTIONS

1. Compare this poem's tone and its perspective on death with those of Robert Frost's "After Apple-Picking" (p. 983).

2. Write an essay comparing the significance of the images of "mellow fruit-fulness" (line 1) in "To Autumn" with that of the images of ripeness in Roethke's "Root Cellar" (p. 756). Explain how the images in each poem lead to very different feelings about the same phenomenon.

EZRA POUND (1885–1972)

In a Station of the Metro°   1913

The apparition of these faces in the crowd;
Petals on a wet, black bough.

Metro: Underground railroad in Paris.

CONSIDERATIONS FOR CRITICAL THINKING AND WRITING

1. FIRST RESPONSE. Why is the title essential for this poem?

2. What kind of mood does the image in the second line convey?

3. Why is "apparition" a better word choice than, say, "appearance" or "sight"?

CATHY SONG (B. 1955)

The White Porch   1983

I wrap the blue towel
after washing,
around the damp
weight of hair, bulky
as a sleeping cat,   5
and sit out on the porch.
Still dripping water,
it'll be dry by supper,
by the time the dust
settles off your shoes,   10
though it's only five
past noon. Think
of the luxury: how to use
the afternoon like the stretch
of lawn spread before me.   15
There's the laundry,
sun-warm clothes at twilight,
and the mountain of beans
in my lap. Each one,

I'll break and snap 20
thoughtfully in half.

But there is this slow arousal.
The small buttons
of my cotton blouse
are pulling away from my body. 25
I feel the strain of threads,
the swollen magnolias
heavy as a flock of birds
in the tree. Already,
the orange sponge cake 30
is rising in the oven.
I know you'll say it makes
your mouth dry
and I'll watch you
drench your slice of it 35
in canned peaches
and lick the plate clean.

So much hair, my mother
used to say, grabbing
the thick braided rope 40
in her hands while we washed
the breakfast dishes, discussing
dresses and pastries.
My mind often elsewhere
as we did the morning chores together. 45
Sometimes, a few strands
would catch in her gold ring.
I worked hard then,
anticipating the hour
when I would let the rope down 50
at night, strips of sheets,
knotted and tied,
while she slept in tight blankets.
My hair, freshly washed
like a measure of wealth, 55
like a bridal veil.
Crouching in the grass,
you would wait for the signal,
for the movement of curtains
before releasing yourself 60
from the shadow of moths.
Cloth, hair and hands,
smuggling you in.

CONSIDERATIONS FOR CRITICAL THINKING AND WRITING

1. FIRST RESPONSE. How is hair made erotic in this poem? Discuss the images
   that you deem especially effective.

2. Who is the "you" that the speaker refers to in each stanza?

3. What role does the mother play in this poem about desire?

4. Why do you think the poem is titled "The White Porch"?

CONNECTIONS TO OTHER SELECTIONS

1. Compare the images used to describe the speaker's "slow arousal" (line 22) in this poem with Croft's images in "Home-Baked Bread" (p. 768). What similarities do you see? What makes each description so effective?

2. Write an essay comparing the images of sensuality in this poem with those in Ho's "A Beautiful Girl Combs Her Hair" (p. 706). Which poem seems more erotic to you? Why?

PERSPECTIVE

T. E. HULME (1883–1917)

On the Differences between Poetry and Prose 1924

In prose as in algebra concrete things are embodied in signs or counters which are moved about according to rules, without being visualized at all in the process. There are in prose certain type situations and arrangements of words, which move as automatically into certain other arrangements as do functions in algebra. One only changes the X's and the Y's back into physical things at the end of the process. Poetry, in one aspect at any rate, may be considered as an effort to avoid this characteristic of prose. It is not a counter language, but a visual concrete one. It is a compromise for a language of intuition which would hand over sensations bodily. It always endeavors to arrest you, and to make you continuously see a physical thing, to prevent you gliding through an abstract process. It chooses fresh epithets and fresh metaphors, not so much because they are new, and we are tired of the old, but because the old cease to convey a physical thing and become abstract counters. A poet says a ship "coursed the seas" to get a physical image, instead of the counter word "sailed." Visual meanings can only be transferred by the new bowl of metaphor; prose is an old pot that lets them leak out. Images in verse are not mere decoration, but the very essence of an intuitive language. Verse is a pedestrian taking you over the ground, prose — a train which delivers you at a destination.

From "Romanticism and Classicism," in *Speculations*,
edited by Herbert Read

CONSIDERATIONS FOR CRITICAL THINKING AND WRITING

1. What distinctions does Hulme make between poetry and prose? Which seems to be the most important difference?

2. Write an essay that discusses Hulme's claim that poetry "is a compromise for a language of intuition which would hand over sensations bodily."

18

Figures of Speech

Figures of speech are broadly defined as a way of saying one thing in terms of something else. An overeager funeral director might, for example, be described as a vulture. Although figures of speech are indirect, they are designed to clarify, not obscure, our understanding of what they describe. Poets frequently use them because, as Emily Dickinson said, the poet's work is to "Tell all the truth but tell it slant" to capture the reader's interest and imagination. But figures of speech are not limited to poetry. Hearing them, reading them, or using them is as natural as using language itself.

Suppose that in the middle of a class discussion concerning the economic causes of World War II your history instructor introduces a series of statistics by saying, "Let's get down to brass tacks." Would anyone be likely to expect a display of brass tacks for students to examine? Of course not. To interpret the statement literally would be to wholly misunderstand the instructor's point that the time has come for a close look at the economic circumstances leading to the war. A literal response transforms the statement into the sort of hilariously bizarre material often found in a sketch by Woody Allen.

The class does not look for brass tacks because, to put it in a nutshell, they understand that the instructor is speaking figuratively. They would understand, too, that in the preceding sentence "in a nutshell" refers to brevity and conciseness rather than to the covering of a kernel of a nut. Figurative language makes its way into our everyday speech and writing as well as into literature because it is a means of achieving color, vividness, and intensity.

Consider the difference, for example, between these two statements:

Literal: The diner strongly expressed anger at the waiter.
Figurative: The diner leaped from his table and roared at the waiter.

The second statement is more vivid because it creates a picture of ferocious anger by likening the diner to some kind of wild animal, such as a lion or tiger. By comparison, "strongly expressed anger" is neither especially strong nor especially expressive; it is flat. Not all figurative language avoids this kind of flatness, however. Figures of speech such as "getting down to brass tacks" and "in a nutshell" are clichés because they lack originality and freshness. Still, they suggest how these devices are commonly used to give language some color, even if that color is sometimes a bit faded.

There is nothing weak about William Shakespeare's use of figurative language in the following passage from *Macbeth*. Macbeth has just learned that his wife is dead, and he laments her loss as well as the course of his own life.

WILLLIAM SHAKESPEARE (1564–1616)

From Macbeth *(Act V, Scene v)*   *1605–1606*

Tomorrow, and tomorrow, and tomorrow
Creeps in this petty pace from day to day
To the last syllable of recorded time;
And all our yesterdays have lighted fools
The way to dusty death. Out, out, brief candle!   5
Life's but a walking shadow, a poor player,
That struts and frets his hour upon the stage,
And then is heard no more. It is a tale
Told by an idiot, full of sound and fury,
Signifying nothing.   10

This passage might be summarized as "life has no meaning," but such a brief paraphrase does not take into account the figurative language that reveals the depth of Macbeth's despair and his view of the absolute meaninglessness of life. By comparing life to a "brief candle," Macbeth emphasizes the darkness and death that surround human beings. The light of life is too brief and unpredictable to be of any comfort. Indeed, life for Macbeth is a "walking shadow," futilely playing a role that is more farcical than dramatic, because life is, ultimately, a desperate story filled with pain and devoid of significance. What the figurative language provides, then, is the emotional force of Macbeth's assertion; his comparisons are disturbing because they are so apt.

The remainder of this chapter discusses some of the most important figures of speech used in poetry. A familiarity with them will help you to understand how poetry achieves its effects.

SIMILE AND METAPHOR

The two most common figures of speech are simile and metaphor. Both compare things that are ordinarily considered unlike each other. A *simile* makes an explicit comparison between two things by using words such as *like, as, than, appears,* or *seems:* "A sip of Mrs. Cook's coffee is like a punch in the stomach." The force of the simile is created by the differences between the two things compared. There would be no simile if the comparison were stated this way: "Mrs. Cook's coffee is as strong as the cafeteria's coffee." This is a literal comparison because Mrs. Cook's coffee is compared with something like it, another kind of coffee. Consider how simile is used in this poem.

MARGARET ATWOOD (B. 1939)

you fit into me   1971

you fit into me
like a hook into an eye

a fish hook
an open eye

If you blinked on a second reading, you got the point of this poem because you recognized that the simile "like a hook into an eye" gives way to a play on words in the final two lines. There the hook and eye, no longer a pleasant domestic image of fitting closely together, become a literal, sharp fishhook and a human eye. The wordplay qualifies the simile and drastically alters the tone of this poem by creating a strong and unpleasant surprise.

A *metaphor*, like a simile, makes a comparison between two unlike things, but it does so implicitly, without words such as *like* or *as:* "Mrs. Cook's coffee is a punch in the stomach." Metaphor asserts the identity of dissimilar things. Macbeth tells us that life *is* a "brief candle," life *is* "a walking shadow," life *is* "a poor player," life *is* "a tale / Told by an idiot." Metaphor transforms people, places, objects, and ideas into whatever the poet imagines them to be, and if metaphors are effective, the reader's experience, understanding, and appreciation of what is described are enhanced. Metaphors are frequently more demanding than similes because they are not signaled by particular words. They are both subtle and powerful.

Here is a poem about presentiment, a foreboding that something terrible is about to happen.

EMILY DICKINSON (1830–1886)

Presentiment — is that long Shadow —
on the lawn —   *c. 1863*

Presentiment — is that long Shadow — on the lawn —
Indicative that Suns go down —

The notice to the startled Grass
That Darkness — is about to pass —

The metaphors in this poem define the abstraction "Presentiment." The sense of foreboding that Dickinson expresses is identified with a particular moment, the moment when darkness is just about to envelop an otherwise tranquil ordinary scene. The speaker projects that fear onto the "startled Grass" so that it seems any life must be frightened by the approaching "Shadow" and "Darkness" — two richly connotative words associated with death. The metaphors obliquely tell us ("tell it slant" was Dickinson's motto, remember) that presentiment is related to a fear of death, and, more important, the metaphors convey the feelings that attend that idea.

Some metaphors are more subtle than others because their comparison of terms is less explicit. Notice the difference between the following two metaphors, both of which describe a shaggy derelict refusing to leave the warmth of a hotel lobby: "He was a mule standing his ground" is a quite explicit comparison. The man is a mule; X is Y. But this metaphor is much more covert: "He brayed his refusal to leave." This second version is an *implied metaphor* because it does not explicitly identify the man with a mule. Instead, it hints at or alludes to the mule. Braying is associated with mules and is especially appropriate in this context because of those animals' reputation for stubbornness. Implied metaphors can slip by readers, but they offer the alert reader the energy and resonance of carefully chosen, highly concentrated language.

Some poets write extended comparisons in which part or all of the poem consists of a series of related metaphors or similes. Extended metaphors are more common than extended similes. In "Catch" (p. 676), Francis creates an *extended metaphor* that compares poetry to a game of catch. The entire poem is organized around this comparison, just as all of the elements in Cummings's "she being Brand" (p. 721) are clustered around the extended comparison of a car and a woman. Because these comparisons are at work throughout the entire poem, they are called *controlling metaphors*. Extended comparisons can serve as a poem's organizing principle; they are also a reminder that in good poems metaphor and simile are not merely decorative but inseparable from what is expressed.

Notice the controlling metaphor in this poem, written by a woman whose contemporaries identified her more as a wife and mother than as a poet. Bradstreet's first volume of poetry, *The Tenth Muse*, was published by her brother-in-law in 1650 without her prior knowledge.

ANNE BRADSTREET (c. 1612–1672)

The Author to Her Book 1678

Thou ill-formed offspring of my feeble brain,
Who after birth did'st by my side remain,
Till snatched from thence by friends, less wise than true,
Who thee abroad exposed to public view;
Made thee in rags, halting, to the press to trudge,   5

Where errors were not lessened, all may judge.
At thy return my blushing was not small,
My rambling brat (in print) should mother call;
I cast thee by as one unfit for light,
Thy visage was so irksome in my sight;   10
Yet being mine own, at length affection would
Thy blemishes amend, if so I could:
I washed thy face, but more defects I saw,
And rubbing off a spot, still made a flaw.
I stretched thy joints to make thee even feet,   15
Yet still thou run'st more hobbling than is meet;
In better dress to trim thee was my mind,
But nought save homespun cloth in the house I find.
In this array, 'mongst vulgars may'st thou roam;
In critics' hands beware thou dost not come;   20
And take thy way where yet thou are not known.
If for thy Father asked, say thou had'st none;
And for thy Mother, she alas is poor,
Which caused her thus to send thee out of door.

     The extended metaphor likening her book to a child came naturally to Bradstreet and allowed her to regard her work both critically and affectionately. Her conception of the book as her child creates just the right tone of amusement, self-deprecation, and concern.

     The controlling metaphor in the following poem is identified by the title. The game of chess these two players are engaged in is simultaneously literal and metaphoric.

ROSARIO CASTELLANOS (1925–1974)

Chess   *1988*

TRANSLATED BY MAUREEN AHERN

Because we were friends and sometimes loved each other,
perhaps to add one more tie
to the many that already bound us,
we decided to play games of the mind.

We set up a board between us;   5
equally divided into pieces, values,
and possible moves.
We learned the rules, we swore to respect them,
and the match began.

We've been sitting here for centuries, meditating   10
ferociously
how to deal the one last blow that will finally
annihilate the other one forever.

CONSIDERATIONS FOR CRITICAL THINKING AND WRITING

1. FIRST RESPONSE. Why do the players decide to play chess? Are you surprised by the effect the game has on their relationship?

2. Why is chess a particularly resonant controlling metaphor? Explain why chess is more evocative than, say, cards or checkers.

3. How does the poem's diction suggest tensions between the two players that go beyond a literal game of chess? Which lines are especially suggestive to you?

4. Do you think the players are men, women, or a man and a woman? Explain your response. How does the sex of the players affect your reading of the poem?

OTHER FIGURES

Perhaps the humblest figure of speech — if not one of the most familiar — is the pun. A *pun* is a play on words that relies on a word having more than one meaning or sounding like another word. For example, "A fad is in one era and out the other" is the sort of pun that produces obligatory groans. But most of us find pleasant and interesting surprises in puns. Here's one that has a slight edge to its humor.

EDMUND CONTI (B. 1929)

Pragmatist   1985

Apocalypse soon
Coming our way
Ground zero at noon
Halve a nice day.

Grimly practical under the circumstances, the pragmatist divides the familiar cheerful cliché by half. As simple as this poem is, its tone is mixed because it makes us laugh and wince at the same time.

Puns can be used to achieve serious effects as well as humorous ones. Although we may have learned to underrate puns as figures of speech, it is a mistake to underestimate their power and the frequency with which they appear in poetry. A close examination, for example, of Henry Reed's "Naming of Parts" (p. 817), Robert Frost's "Design" (p. 993), or almost any lengthy passage from a Shakespeare play will confirm the value of puns.

Synecdoche is a figure of speech in which part of something is used to signify the whole: a neighbor is a "wagging tongue" (a gossip); a criminal is placed "behind bars" (in prison). Less typically, synecdoche refers to the whole used to signify the part: "Germany invaded Poland"; "Princeton won the fencing match." Clearly, certain individuals participated in these activities, not all of Germany or Princeton. Another related figure of speech is *metonymy,* in which something closely associated with a subject is substituted for it: "She preferred the silver screen [motion pictures] to reading." "At precisely ten o'clock the paper shufflers [office workers] stopped for coffee."

Synecdoche and metonymy may overlap and are therefore sometimes difficult to distinguish. Consider this description of a disapproving minister entering a noisy tavern: "As those pursed lips came through the swinging door, the atmosphere was suddenly soured." The pursed lips signal the presence of the minister and are therefore a synecdoche, but they additionally suggest an inhibiting sense of sin and guilt that makes the bar patrons feel uncomfortable. Hence, the pursed lips are also a metonymy, since they are in this context so closely connected with religion. Although the distinction between synecdoche and metonymy can be useful, when a figure of speech overlaps categories, it is usually labeled a metonymy.

Knowing the precise term for a figure of speech is, finally, less important than responding to its use in a poem. Consider how metonymy and synecdoche convey the tone and meaning of the following poem.

DYLAN THOMAS (1914–1953)

The Hand That Signed the Paper 1936

The hand that signed the paper felled a city;
Five sovereign fingers taxed the breath,
Doubled the globe of dead and halved a country;
These five kings did a king to death.

The mighty hand leads to a sloping shoulder,   5
The finger joints are cramped with chalk;
A goose's quill has put an end to murder
That put an end to talk.

The hand that signed the treaty bred a fever,
And famine grew, and locusts came;   10
Great is the hand that holds dominion over
Man by a scribbled name.

The five kings count the dead but do not soften
The crusted wound nor stroke the brow;
A hand rules pity as a hand rules heaven;   15
Hands have no tears to flow.

The "hand" in this poem is a synecdoche for a powerful ruler because it is a part of someone used to signify the entire person. The "goose's quill" is a metonymy that also refers to the power associated with the ruler's hand. By using these figures of speech, Thomas depersonalizes and ultimately dehumanizes the ruler. The final synecdoche tells us that "Hands have no tears to flow." It makes us see the political power behind the hand as remote and inhuman. How is the meaning of the poem enlarged when the speaker says, "A hand rules pity as a hand rules heaven"?

One of the ways writers energize the abstractions, ideas, objects, and animals that constitute their created worlds is through **personification,** the attribution of human characteristics to nonhuman things: temptation pursues the innocent; trees scream in the raging wind; mice conspire in the cupboard. We are not explicitly told that these things are people; instead, we are invited to see that they behave like people. Perhaps it is human vanity that makes personification a frequently used figure of speech. Whatever the reason, personification, a form of metaphor that connects the nonhuman with the human, makes the world understandable in human terms. Consider this concise example from William Blake's *The Marriage of Heaven and Hell,* a long poem that takes delight in attacking conventional morality: "Prudence is a rich ugly old maid courted by Incapacity." By personifying prudence, Blake transforms what is usually considered a virtue into a comic figure hardly worth emulating.

Often related to personification is another rhetorical figure called **apostrophe,** an address either to someone who is absent and therefore cannot hear the speaker or to something nonhuman that cannot comprehend. Apostrophe provides an opportunity for the speaker of a poem to think aloud, and often the thoughts expressed are in a formal tone. John Keats, for example, begins "Ode on a Grecian Urn" (p. 741) this way: "Thou still unravished bride of quietness." Apostrophe is frequently accompanied by intense emotion that is signaled by phrasing such as "O Life." In the right hands — such as Keats's — apostrophe can provide an intense and immediate voice in a poem, but when it is overdone or extravagant it can be ludicrous. Modern poets are more wary of apostrophe than their predecessors because apostrophizing strikes many self-conscious twentieth-century sensibilities as too theatrical. Thus modern poets tend to avoid exaggerated situations in favor of less charged though equally meditative moments, as in this next poem, with its amusing, half-serious cosmic twist.

JANICE TOWNLEY MOORE (B. 1939)

To a Wasp 1984

You must have chortled
finding that tiny hole
in the kitchen screen. Right
into my cheese cake batter
you dived, 5
no chance to swim ashore,
no saving spoon,
the mixer whirring
your legs, wings, stinger,
churning you into such 10

delicious death.
Never mind the bright April day.
Did you not see
rising out of cumulus clouds
That fist aimed at both of us?   15

Moore's apostrophe "To a Wasp" is based on the simplest of domestic circumstances; there is almost nothing theatrical or exaggerated in the poem's
tone until "That fist" in the last line, when exaggeration takes center stage. As
a figure of speech exaggeration is known as **overstatement** or *hyperbole* and
adds emphasis without intending to be literally true: "The teenage boy ate
everything in the house." Notice how the speaker of Marvell's "To His Coy
Mistress" (p. 729) exaggerates his devotion in the following overstatement:

> An hundred years should go to praise
> Thine eyes and on thy forehead gaze,
> Two hundred to adore each breast,
> But thirty thousand to the rest:

That comes to 30,500 years. What is expressed here is heightened emotion, not deception.

The speaker also uses the opposite figure of speech, **understatement,**
which says less than is intended. In the next section he sums up why he
cannot take 30,500 years to express his love:

> The grave's a fine and private place,
> But none, I think, do there embrace.

The speaker is correct, of course, but by deliberately understating—
saying "I think" when he is actually certain—he makes his point, that
death will overtake their love, all the more emphatic. Another powerful example of understatement appears in the final line of Randall Jarrell's "The
Death of the Ball Turret Gunner" (p. 720), when the disembodied voice of
the machine-gunner describes his death in a bomber: "When I died they
washed me out of the turret with a hose."

Paradox is a statement that initially appears to be self-contradictory
but that, on closer inspection, turns out to make sense: "The pen is mightier than the sword." In a fencing match, anyone would prefer the sword,
but if the goal is to win the hearts and minds of people, the art of persuasion can be more compelling than swordplay. To resolve the paradox, it is
necessary to discover the sense that underlies the statement. If we see that
"pen" and "sword" are used as metonymies for writing and violence, then
the paradox rings true. **Oxymoron** is a condensed form of paradox in
which two contradictory words are used together. Combinations such as
"sweet sorrow," "silent scream," "sad joy," and "cold fire" indicate the kinds
of startling effects that oxymorons can produce. Paradox is useful in poetry because it arrests a reader's attention by its seemingly stubborn refusal
to make sense, and once a reader has penetrated the paradox, it is difficult

to resist a perception so well earned. Good paradoxes are knotty pleasures. Here is a simple but effective one.

J. PATRICK LEWIS (B. 1942)

The Unkindest Cut   1993

Knives can harm you, heaven forbid;
Axes may disarm you, kid;
Guillotines are painful, but
There's nothing like a paper cut!

This quatrain is a humorous version of "the pen is mightier than the sword." The wounds escalate to the paper cut, which paradoxically is more damaging than even the broad blade of a guillotine. "The unkindest cut" of all (an allusion to Shakespeare's *Julius Caesar,* III.ii.188) is produced by chilling words on a page rather than cold steel, but it is more painfully fatal nonetheless.

The following poems are rich in figurative language. As you read and study them, notice how their figures of speech vivify situations, clarify ideas, intensify emotions, and engage your imagination. Although the terms for the various figures discussed in this chapter are useful for labeling the particular devices used in poetry, they should not be allowed to get in the way of your response to a poem. Don't worry about rounding up examples of figurative language. First relax and let the figures work their effects on you. Use the terms as a means of taking you further into poetry, and they will serve your reading well.

POEMS FOR FURTHER STUDY

MARGARET ATWOOD (B. 1939)

February   1995

Winter. Time to eat fat
and watch hockey. In the pewter mornings, the cat,
a black fur sausage with yellow
Houdini eyes, jumps up on the bed and tries
to get onto my head. It's his   5
way of telling whether or not I'm dead.
If I'm not, he wants to be scratched; if I am
he'll think of something. He settles
on my chest, breathing his breath
of burped-up meat and musty sofas,   10
purring like a washboard. Some other tomcat,

not yet a capon, has been spraying our front door,
declaring war. It's all about sex and territory,
which are what will finish us off
in the long run. Some cat owners around here   15
should snip a few testicles. If we wise
hominids were sensible, we'd do that too,
or eat our young, like sharks.
But it's love that does us in. Over and over
again, *He shoots, he scores!* and famine   20
crouches in the bedsheets, ambushing the pulsing
eiderdown, and the windchill factor hits
thirty below, and pollution pours
out of our chimneys to keep us warm.
February, month of despair,   25
with a skewered heart in the centre.
I think dire thoughts, and lust for French fries
with a splash of vinegar.
Cat, enough of your greedy whining
and your small pink bumhole.   30
Off my face! You're the life principle,
more or less, so get going
on a little optimism around here.
Get rid of death. Celebrate increase. Make it be spring.

CONSIDERATIONS FOR CRITICAL THINKING AND WRITING

1. FIRST RESPONSE. How do your own associations with February compare with the speaker's?

2. Explain how the poem is organized around an extended metaphor that defines winter as a "Time to eat fat / and watch hockey" (lines 1–2).

3. Explain the paradox in "it's love that does us in" (line 19).

4. What theme(s) do you find in the poem? How is the cat central to them?

SOPHIE CABOT BLACK (B. 1958)

August   1994

A doe puts her nose to sky: stark hub
Around which the second cut of hay spins
Into one direction. A man rests
Against the fence, waiting

For the last minute to turn home. By heart   5
He knows the tilt and decline of each field,
His own faulty predictions. The well
Hoards its shadow while a raw haze gluts

With harvest, with guessing rains, presses
At the temple and wrist. The pastures, tired   10

Of abiding, begin to burn. Gold takes over,
Loose, unguarded. Cows stay deep

In the chafe of underbush; reckless leaves shawl
The edges, unaware of the sap that will send them down.

CONSIDERATIONS FOR CRITICAL THINKING AND WRITING

1. FIRST RESPONSE. How does the final line affect your understanding of the poem?
2. What tone is created by the poem's images of August?
3. How does Black's use of personification contribute to the tone?
4. Discuss what you think is the poem's theme.

CONNECTION TO ANOTHER SELECTION

1. Discuss the moods created in "August" and Atwood's "February." To what extent do you think each poem is successful in capturing the essence of the title's subject?

ERNEST SLYMAN (B. 1946)

Lightning Bugs   *1988*

In my backyard,
They burn peepholes in the night
And take snapshots of my house.

CONSIDERATIONS FOR CRITICAL THINKING AND WRITING

1. FIRST RESPONSE. Explain why the title is essential to this poem.
2. What makes the description of the lightning bugs effective? How do the second and third lines complement each other?
3. As Slyman has done, take a simple, common fact of nature and make it vivid by using a figure of speech to describe it.

SYLVIA PLATH (1932–1963)

Mirror   *1963*

I am silver and exact. I have no preconceptions.
Whatever I see I swallow immediately
Just as it is, unmisted by love or dislike.
I am not cruel, only truthful —
The eye of a little god, four-cornered.   5
Most of the time I meditate on the opposite wall.
It is pink, with speckles. I have looked at it so long

I think it is a part of my heart. But it flickers.
Faces and darkness separate us over and over.

Now I am a lake. A woman bends over me,   10
Searching my reaches for what she really is.
Then she turns to those liars, the candles or the moon.
I see her back, and reflect it faithfully.
She rewards me with tears and an agitation of hands.
I am important to her. She comes and goes.   15
Each morning it is her face that replaces the darkness.
In me she has drowned a young girl, and in me an old woman
Rises toward her day after day, like a terrible fish.

CONSIDERATIONS FOR CRITICAL THINKING AND WRITING

1. FIRST RESPONSE. What is the effect of the personification in this poem?
   How would our view of the aging woman be different if she, rather than
   the mirror, told her story?

2. What is the mythical allusion in "Now I am a lake" (line 10)?

3. In what sense can "candles or the moon" be regarded as "liars"? Explain
   this metaphor.

4. Discuss the effectiveness of the simile in the final line of the poem.

WILLIAM WORDSWORTH (1770–1850)

London, 1802   *1802*

Milton!° thou should'st be living at this hour:
England hath need of thee: she is a fen
Of stagnant waters: altar, sword, and pen,
Fireside, the heroic wealth of hall and bower,
Have forfeited their ancient English dower   5
Of inward happiness. We are selfish men;
Oh! raise us up, return to us again;
And give us manners, virtue, freedom, power.
Thy soul was like a star, and dwelt apart:
Thou hadst a voice whose sound was like the sea: 10
Pure as the naked heavens, majestic, free,
So didst thou travel on life's common way,
In cheerful godliness; and yet thy heart
The lowliest duties on herself did lay.

1 *Milton:* John Milton (1608–1674), poet, famous especially for his religious epic *Paradise Lost*
and his defense of political freedom.

CONSIDERATIONS FOR CRITICAL THINKING AND WRITING

1. FIRST RESPONSE. Describe the poem's tone. Is it nostalgic, angry, or something else?

2. Explain the metonymies in lines 3–6 of this poem. What is the speaker's assessment of England?

3. How would the effect of the poem be different if it were in the form of an address to Wordsworth's contemporaries rather than an apostrophe to Milton? What qualities does Wordsworth attribute to Milton by the use of figurative language?

JIM STEVENS (B. 1922)

Schizophrenia   1992

It was the house that suffered most.

It had begun with slamming doors, angry feet scuffing the carpets,
dishes slammed onto the table,
greasy stains spreading on the cloth.

Certain doors were locked at night,   5
feet stood for hours outside them,
dishes were left unwashed, the cloth
disappeared under a hardened crust.

The house came to miss the shouting voices,
the threats, the half-apologies, noisy   10
reconciliations, the sobbing that followed.

Then lines were drawn, borders established,
some rooms declared their loyalties,
keeping to themselves, keeping out the other.
The house divided against itself.   15

Seeing cracking paint, broken windows,
the front door banging in the wind,
the roof tiles flying off, one by one,
the neighbors said it was a madhouse.

It was the house that suffered most.   20

CONSIDERATIONS FOR CRITICAL THINKING AND WRITING

1. FIRST RESPONSE. What is the effect of personifying the house in this poem?

2. How are the people who live in the house characterized? What does their behavior reveal about them? How does the house respond to them?

3. Comment on the title. If the title were missing, what, if anything, would be missing from the poem? Explain your answer.

WALT WHITMAN (1819–1892)

A Noiseless Patient Spider   1868

A noiseless patient spider,
I mark'd where on a little promontory it stood isolated,
Mark'd how to explore the vacant vast surrounding,

It launch'd forth filament, filament, filament, out of itself,
Ever unreeling them, ever tirelessly speeding them.   5

And you O my soul where you stand,
Surrounded, detached, in measureless oceans of space,
Ceaselessly musing, venturing, throwing, seeking the spheres to connect
    them,
Till the bridge you will need be form'd, till the ductile anchor hold,
Till the gossamer thread you fling catch somewhere, O my soul.   10

CONSIDERATIONS FOR CRITICAL THINKING AND WRITING

1. FIRST RESPONSE. Spiders are not usually regarded as pleasant creatures.
   Why does the speaker in this poem liken his soul to one? What similarities
   are there in the poem between spider and soul? Are there any significant
   differences?

2. How do the images of space relate to the connections made between the
   speaker's soul and the spider?

CONNECTION TO ANOTHER SELECTION

1. Read the early version of "A Noiseless Patient Spider" printed below. Which
   version is more unified by its metaphors? Which do you prefer? Why? Write
   an essay about the change of focus from the early version to the final one.

WALT WHITMAN (1819–1892)

The Soul, reaching, throwing out for love   *c. 1862*

The Soul, reaching, throwing out for love,
As the spider, from some little promontory, throwing out filament after filament,
    tirelessly out of itself, that one at least may catch and form a link, a bridge,
    a connection
O I saw one passing along, saying hardly a word — yet full of love I detected
    him, by certain signs
O eyes wishfully turning! O silent eyes!
For then I thought of you o'er the world,
O latent oceans, fathomless oceans of love!
O waiting oceans of love! yearning and fervid! and of you sweet souls perhaps
    in the future, delicious and long:
But Death, unknown on the earth — ungiven, dark here, unspoken, never born:
You fathomless latent souls of love — you pent and unknown oceans of love!

JOHN DONNE (1572–1631)

A Valediction: Forbidding Mourning   1611

As virtuous men pass mildly away,
   And whisper to their souls to go,
While some of their sad friends do say,
   The breath goes now, and some say, no:

So let us melt, and make no noise,   5
   No tear-floods, nor sigh-tempests move;
'Twere profanation of our joys
   To tell the laity our love.

Moving of th' earth° brings harms and fears,   *earthquakes*
   Men reckon what it did and meant,   10
But trepidation of the spheres,°
   Though greater far, is innocent.

Dull sublunary° lovers' love
   (Whose soul is sense) cannot admit
Absence, because it doth remove   15
   Those things which elemented° it.   *composed*

But we by a love so much refined,
   That ourselves know not what it is,
Inter-assured of the mind,
   Care less, eyes, lips, and hands to miss.   20

Our two souls therefore, which are one,
   Though I must go, endure not yet
A breach, but an expansion,
   Like gold to airy thinness beat.

If they be two, they are two so   25
   As stiff twin compasses are two;
Thy soul the fixed foot, makes no show
   To move, but doth, if th' other do.

And though it in the center sit,
   Yet when the other far doth roam,   30
It leans, and hearkens after it,
   And grows erect, as that comes home.

Such wilt thou be to me, who must
   Like th' other foot, obliquely run;
Thy firmness makes my circle just,°   35
   And makes me end, where I begun.

---

11 *trepidation of the spheres:* According to Ptolemaic astronomy, the planets sometimes moved violently, like earthquakes, but these movements were not felt by people on earth. 13 *sublunary:* Under the moon; hence, mortal and subject to change. 35 *circle just:* The circle is a traditional symbol of perfection.

CONSIDERATIONS FOR CRITICAL THINKING AND WRITING

1. FIRST RESPONSE. A valediction is a farewell. Donne wrote this poem for his wife before leaving on a trip to France. What kind of "mourning" is the speaker forbidding?
2. Explain how the simile in lines 1–4 is related to the couple in lines 5–8. Who is described as dying?
3. How does the speaker contrast the couple's love to "sublunary lovers' love" (line 13)?
4. Explain the similes in lines 24 and 25–36.

LINDA PASTAN (B. 1932)

Marks   *1978*

My husband gives me an A
for last night's supper,
an incomplete for my ironing,
a B plus in bed.
My son says I am average,   5
an average mother, but if
I put my mind to it
I could improve.
My daughter believes
in Pass/Fail and tells me   10
I pass. Wait 'til they learn
I'm dropping out.

CONSIDERATIONS FOR CRITICAL THINKING AND WRITING

1. FIRST RESPONSE. Explain the appropriateness of the controlling metaphor in this poem. How does it reveal the woman's relationship to her family?
2. Discuss the meaning of the title.
3. How does the last line serve as both the climax of the woman's story and the controlling metaphor of the poem?

LUCILLE CLIFTON (B. 1936)

come home from the movies   *1974*

come home from the movies,
black girls and boys,
the picture be over and the screen
be cold as our neighborhood.
come home from the show,   5
don't be the show.
take off some flowers and plant them,
pick us some papers and read them,

stop making some babies and raise them.
come home from the movies   10
black girls and boys,
show our fathers how to walk like men,
they already know how to dance.

CONSIDERATIONS FOR CRITICAL THINKING AND WRITING

1. FIRST RESPONSE. What are the "movies" a metaphor for?
2. What advice does the speaker urge upon "black girls and boys"?
3. Explain the final two lines. Why do they come last?

ELAINE MAGARRELL (B. 1928)

The Joy of Cooking   1988

I have prepared my sister's tongue,
scrubbed and skinned it,
trimmed the roots, small bones, and gristle.
Carved through the hump it slices thin and neat.
Best with horseradish   5
and economical — it probably will grow back.
Next time perhaps a creole sauce
or mold of aspic?

I will have my brother's heart,
which is firm and rather dry,
slow cooked. It resembles muscle   10
more than organ meat
and needs an apple-onion stuffing
to make it interesting at all.
Although beef heart serves six   15
my brother's heart barely feeds two.
I could also have it braised
and served in sour sauce.

CONSIDERATIONS FOR CRITICAL THINKING AND WRITING

1. FIRST RESPONSE. Describe the poem's tone. Do you find it amusing, bitter,
   or something else?
2. How are the tongue and heart used to characterize the sister and brother in
   this poem?
3. Describe the speaker's tone. What effect does the title have on your determining the tone?

CONNECTION TO ANOTHER SELECTION

1. Write an essay that explains how cooking becomes a way of talking about
   something else in this poem and in Croft's "Home-Baked Bread" (p. 768).

STEPHEN PERRY (B. 1947)

Blue Spruce   *1991*

My grandfather worked in a barbershop
smelling of lotions he'd slap on your face,
hair and talc. The black razor strop

hung like the penis of an ox. He'd draw
the sharp blade in quick strokes over   5
the smooth-rough hide, and then carefully

over your face. The tiny hairs would gather
on the blade, a congregation singing
under blue spruce in winter,

a bandstand in the center of town   10
bright with instruments, alto sax, tenor
sax, tuba or sousaphone — the bright

oompah-pahs shaving the town somehow,
a bright cloth shaking the air
into flakes of silvering hair   15

floating down past the houses, the horses
pulling carriages past the town fountain,
which had frozen into a coiffure

of curly glass. My grandfather had an affair
with the girl who did their nails   20
bright pink, bright red, never blue,

perhaps as the horses clip-clopped on ice
outside his shop, his kisses
smelling of lather and new skin —

when she grew too big and round   25
with his child, with his oompah love,
with his bandstand love, with his brassy love,

and the town dropped its grace notes
of gossip and whispered hiss,
he bundled her out of town   30

with the savings which should have gone
to my mom. But how could you hate him?
My mother did, my father did,

and my grandmother, who bore his neglect.
When she was covered in sheets   35
at her last death,

he flirted with the nurses, bright
as winter birds in spruces
above a bandstand —

I'll always remember him in snow, a deep lather   40
of laughter, the picture
where he took me from my mother

and raised me high, a baby, into the bell
of his sousaphone, as if I were a note
he'd play into light —   45

CONSIDERATIONS FOR CRITICAL THINKING AND WRITING

1. FIRST RESPONSE. The grandfather is presented as an outrageous figure, "But how could you hate him?" (line 32). Do you think the speaker is successful in preventing the reader from hating his grandfather? Explain.

2. What are the controlling metaphors in "Blue Spruce"? How do they help to characterize the grandfather?

3. Write a paragraph detailing what you think the speaker means by his grandfather's "oompah love" (line 26).

ROBIN BECKER (B. 1951)

Shopping   *1996*

If things don't work out
I'll buy the belt
with the fashionable silver buckle
we saw on Canyon Road.
If we can't make peace   5
I'll order the leather duster and swagger
across the plaza in Santa Fe,
cross-dressing for the girls.

If you leave I'll go back
for the Navaho blanket   10
and the pawn ring, bargain
with the old woman who will know
I intend to buy.
If you pack your things,
if you undress in the bathroom,   15
if you see me for what I am,
I'll invest in the folk art mirror
with the leaping rabbits
on either side, I'll spring
for the Anasazi pot with the hole   20
in the bottom where the spirit
of the potter is said to escape
after her death.

If you say you never intended
to share your life, I'll haunt the museum   25

shops and flea markets,
I'll don the Spanish riding hat,
the buckskin gloves with fringe at the wrists,
I'll step into the cowboy boots
tanned crimson and designed to make   30
any woman feel like she owns the street.
If you never touch me again,
I'll do what my mother did
after she buried my sister:
outfitted herself in an elegant suit   35
for the rest of her life.

Considerations for Critical Thinking and Writing

1. FIRST RESPONSE. Is shopping an extended metaphor in this poem? For what, do you think?
2. What purpose does the speaker's imagined shopping serve for her?
3. Describe the shift in tone in lines 32–36.

Connection to Another Selection

1. In an essay examine the relationship between love and death in "Shopping" and Emily Dickinson's "The Bustle in a House" (p. 950).

PERSPECTIVE

John R. Searle (b. 1932)

Figuring Out Metaphors   *1979*

If you hear somebody say, "Sally is a block of ice," or, "Sam is a pig," you are likely to assume that the speaker does not mean what he says literally, but that he is speaking metaphorically. Furthermore, you are not likely to have very much trouble figuring out what he means. If he says, "Sally is a prime number between 17 and 23," or "Bill is a barn door," you might still assume he is speaking metaphorically, but it is much harder to figure out what he means. The existence of such utterances—utterances in which the speaker means metaphorically something different from what the sentence means literally—poses a series of questions for any theory of language and communication: What is metaphor, and how does it differ from both literal and other forms of figurative utterances? Why do we use expressions metaphorically instead of saying exactly and literally what we mean? How do metaphorical utterances work, that is, how is it possible for speakers to communicate to hearers when speaking metaphorically inasmuch as they do not say what they mean? And why do some metaphors work and others do not?

From Expression and Meaning

CONSIDERATIONS FOR CRITICAL THINKING AND WRITING

1. Searle poses a series of important questions. Write an essay that explores one of these questions, basing your discussion on the poems in this chapter.

2. Try writing a brief poem that provides a context for the line "Sally is a prime number between 17 and 23" or the line "Bill is a barn door." Your task is to create a context so that either one of these metaphoric statements is as readily understandable as "Sally is a block of ice" or "Sam is a pig." Share your poem with your classmates and explain how the line generated the poem you built around it.

19

Symbol, Allegory, and Irony

SYMBOL

A *symbol* is something that represents something else. An object, person, place, event, or action can suggest more than its literal meaning. A handshake between two world leaders might be simply a greeting, but if it is done ceremoniously before cameras, it could be a symbolic gesture signifying unity, issues resolved, and joint policies that will be followed. We live surrounded by symbols. When an $80,000 Mercedes-Benz comes roaring by in the fast lane, we get a quick glimpse of not only an expensive car but an entire life-style that suggests opulence, broad lawns, executive offices, and power. One of the reasons some buyers are willing to spend roughly the cost of five Chevrolets for a single Mercedes-Benz is that they are aware of the car's symbolic value. A symbol is a vehicle for two things at once: it functions as itself, and it implies meanings beyond itself.

The meanings suggested by a symbol are determined by the context in which they appear. The Mercedes could symbolize very different things depending on where it was parked. Would an American political candidate be likely to appear in a Detroit blue-collar neighborhood with such a car? Probably not. Although a candidate might be able to afford the car, it would be an inappropriate symbol for someone seeking votes from all the people. As a symbol, the German-built Mercedes would backfire if voters perceived it as representing an entity partially responsible for layoffs of automobile workers or, worse, as a sign of decadence and corruption. Similarly, a huge portrait of Mao Tse-tung conveys different meanings to residents of Beijing than it would to farmers in Prairie Center, Illinois. Because symbols depend on contexts for their meaning, literary artists provide those contexts so that the reader has enough information to determine the probable range of meanings suggested by a symbol.

In the following poem the speaker describes walking at night. How is the night used symbolically?

ROBERT FROST (1874–1963)
Acquainted with the Night   *1928*

I have been one acquainted with the night.
I have walked out in rain — and back in rain.
I have outwalked the furthest city light.

I have looked down the saddest city lane.
I have passed by the watchman on his beat   5
And dropped my eyes, unwilling to explain.

I have stood still and stopped the sound of feet
When far away an interrupted cry
Came over houses from another street,

But not to call me back or say good-by;   10
And further still at an unearthly height
One luminary clock against the sky

Proclaimed the time was neither wrong nor right.
I have been one acquainted with the night.

In approaching this or any poem, you should read for literal meanings first and then allow the elements of the poem to invite you to symbolic readings, if they are appropriate. Here the somber tone suggests that the lines have symbolic meaning too. The flat matter-of-factness created by the repetition of "I have" (lines 1–5, 7, 14) understates the symbolic subject matter of the poem, which is, finally, more about the "night" located in the speaker's mind or soul than it is about walking away from a city and back again. The speaker is "acquainted with the night." The importance of this phrase is emphasized by Frost's title and by the fact that he begins and ends the poem with it. Poets frequently use this kind of repetition to alert readers to details that carry more than literal meanings.

The speaker in this poem has personal knowledge of the night but does not indicate specifically what the night means. To arrive at the potential meanings of the night in this context, it is necessary to look closely at its connotations, along with the images provided in the poem. The connotative meanings of night suggest, for example, darkness, death, and grief. By drawing on these connotations, Frost uses a *conventional symbol,* something that is recognized by many people to represent certain ideas. Roses conventionally symbolize love or beauty; laurels, fame; spring, growth; the moon, romance. Poets often use conventional symbols to convey tone and meaning.

Frost uses the night as a conventional symbol, but he also develops it into a *literary* or *contextual symbol* that goes beyond traditional, public meanings. A literary symbol cannot be summarized in a word or two. It tends to be as elusive as experience itself. The night cannot be reduced to or equated with darkness or death or grief, but it evokes those associations and more. Frost took what perhaps initially appears to be an overworked, conventional symbol and prevented it from becoming a cliché by deepening and extending its meaning.

The images in "Acquainted with the Night" lead to the poem's symbolic meaning. Unwilling, and perhaps unable, to explain explicitly to the watchman (and to the reader) what the night means, the speaker nevertheless conveys feelings about it. The brief images of darkness, rain, sad city lanes, the necessity for guards, the eerie sound of a distressing cry coming over rooftops, and the "luminary clock against the sky" proclaiming "the time was neither wrong nor right" all help to create a sense of anxiety in this tight-lipped speaker. Although we cannot know what unnamed personal experiences have acquainted the speaker with the night, the images suggest that whatever the night means, it is somehow associated with insomnia, loneliness, isolation, coldness, darkness, death, fear, and a sense of alienation from humanity and even time. Daylight—ordinary daytime thoughts and life itself—seems remote and unavailable in this poem. The night is literally the period from sunset to sunrise, but, more important, it is an internal state of being felt by the speaker and revealed through the images.

Frost used symbols rather than an expository essay that would explain the conditions that cause these feelings because most readers can provide their own list of sorrows and terrors that evoke similar emotions. Through symbol, the speaker's experience is compressed and simultaneously expanded by the personal darkness that each reader brings to the poem. The suggestive nature of symbols makes them valuable for poets and evocative for readers.

ALLEGORY

Unlike expansive, suggestive symbols, *allegory* is a narration or description usually restricted to a single meaning because its events, actions, characters, settings, and objects represent specific abstractions or ideas. Although the elements in an allegory may be interesting in themselves, the emphasis tends to be on what they ultimately mean. Characters may be given names such as Hope, Pride, Youth, and Charity; they have few, if any, personal qualities beyond their abstract meanings. These personifications are a form of extended metaphor, but their meanings are severely restricted. They are not symbols because, for instance, the meaning of a character named Charity is precisely that virtue.

There is little or no room for broad speculation and exploration in allegories. If Frost had written "Acquainted with the Night" as an allegory, he

might have named his speaker Loneliness and had him leave the City of
Despair to walk the Streets of Emptiness, where Crime, Poverty, Fear, and
other characters would define the nature of city life. The literal elements in
an allegory tend to be de-emphasized in favor of the message. Symbols, however, function both literally and symbolically, so that "Acquainted with the
Night" is about both a walk and a sense that something is terribly wrong.

Allegory especially lends itself to ***didactic poetry,*** which is designed to
teach an ethical, moral, or religious lesson. Many stories, poems, and plays
are concerned with values, but didactic literature is specifically created to
convey a message. "Acquainted with the Night" does not impart advice or
offer guidance. If the poem argued that city life is self-destructive or sinful,
it would be didactic; instead, it is a lyric poem that expresses the emotions
and thoughts of a single speaker.

Although allegory is often enlisted in didactic causes because it can so
readily communicate abstract ideas through physical representations, not
all allegories teach a lesson. Here is a poem describing a haunted palace
while also establishing a consistent pattern that reveals another meaning.

EDGAR ALLAN POE (1809–1849)

The Haunted Palace   *1839*

I
In the greenest of our valleys,
    By good angels tenanted,
Once a fair and stately palace —
    Radiant palace — reared its head.
In the monarch Thought's dominion —   5
    It stood there!
Never seraph spread a pinion
    Over fabric half so fair.

II
Banners yellow, glorious, golden,
    On its roof did float and flow;   10
(This — all this — was in the olden
    Time long ago)
And every gentle air that dallied,
    In that sweet day,
Along the ramparts plumed and pallid,   15
    A wingèd odor went away.

III
Wanderers in that happy valley
    Through two luminous windows saw
Spirits moving musically
    To a lute's well-tunèd law,   20
Round about a throne, where sitting

(Porphyrogene!)°   *born to purple, royal*
In state his glory well befitting,
  The ruler of the realm was seen.

IV
And all with pearl and ruby glowing   25
  Was the fair palace door,
Through which came flowing, flowing, flowing
  And sparkling evermore,
A troop of Echoes whose sweet duty
  Was but to sing,   30
In voices of surpassing beauty,
  The wit and wisdom of their king.

V
But evil things, in robes of sorrow,
  Assailed the monarch's high estate;
(Ah, let us mourn, for never morrow   35
  Shall dawn upon him, desolate!)
And, round about his home, the glory
  That blushed and bloomed
Is but a dim-remembered story
  Of the old time entombed.   40

VI
And travelers now within that valley,
  Through the red-litten windows see
Vast forms that move fantastically
  To a discordant melody;
While, like a rapid ghastly river,   45
  Through the pale door,
A hideous throng rush out forever,
  And laugh — but smile no more.

On one level this poem describes how a once happy palace is desolated
by "evil things" (line 33). If the reader pays close attention to the diction,
however, an allegorical meaning becomes apparent on a second reading. A
systematic pattern develops in the choice of words used to describe the
palace, so that it comes to stand for a human mind. The palace, banners,
windows, door, echoes, and throng are equated with a person's head, hair,
eyes, mouth, voice, and laughter. That mind, once harmoniously ordered, is
overthrown by evil, haunting thoughts that lead to the mad laughter in the
poem's final lines. Once the general pattern is seen, the rest of the details
fall neatly into place to strengthen the parallels between the surface description of a palace and the allegorical representation of a disordered mind.

Modern writers generally prefer symbol over allegory because they
tend to be more interested in opening up the potential meanings of an experience instead of transforming it into a closed pattern of meaning. Perhaps the major difference is that while allegory may delight a reader's
imagination, symbol challenges and enriches it.

IRONY

Another important resource writers use to take readers beyond literal meanings is *irony*, a technique that reveals a discrepancy between what appears to be and what is actually true. Here is a classic example in which appearances give way to the underlying reality.

EDWIN ARLINGTON ROBINSON (1869–1935)

Richard Cory   *1897*

Whenever Richard Cory went down town,
We people on the pavement looked at him:
He was a gentleman from sole to crown,
Clean favored, and imperially slim.

And he was always quietly arrayed,   5
And he was always human when he talked;
But still he fluttered pulses when he said,
"Good-morning," and he glittered when he walked.

And he was rich — yes, richer than a king —
And admirably schooled in every grace: 10
In fine, we thought that he was everything
To make us wish that we were in his place.

So on we worked, and waited for the light,
And went without the meat, and cursed the bread;
And Richard Cory, one calm summer night,   15
Went home and put a bullet through his head.

Richard Cory seems to have it all. Those less fortunate, the "people on the pavement," regard him as well-bred, handsome, tasteful, and richly endowed with both money and grace. Until the final line of the poem, the reader, like the speaker, is charmed by Cory's good fortune, so quietly expressed in his decent, easy manner. That final, shocking line, however, shatters the appearances of Cory's life and reveals him to have been a desperately unhappy man. While everyone else assumes that Cory represented "everything" to which they aspire, the reality is that he could escape his miserable life only as a suicide. This discrepancy between what appears to be true and what actually exists is known as *situational irony:* what happens is entirely different from what is expected. We are not told why Cory shoots himself; instead, the irony in the poem shocks us into the recognition that appearances do not always reflect realities.

Words are also sometimes intended to be taken at other than face value. *Verbal irony* is saying something different from what is meant. After reading "Richard Cory," to say "That rich gentleman sure was happy" is ironic. The tone of voice would indicate that just the opposite was meant; hence, verbal irony is usually easy to detect in spoken language. In literature, however, a reader can sometimes take literally what a writer intends ironically. The remedy for this kind of misreading is to pay close attention to the poem's context. There is no formula that can detect verbal irony, but contradictory actions and statements as well as the use of understatement and overstatement can often be signals that verbal irony is present.

Consider how verbal irony is used in this poem.

KENNETH FEARING (1902–1961)

AD   *1938*

Wanted: Men;
Millions of men are *wanted at once* in a big new field;
New, tremendous, thrilling, great.
If you've ever been a figure in the chamber of horrors,
If you've ever escaped from a psychiatric ward,   5
If you thrill at the thought of throwing poison into wells, have heavenly
    visions of people, by the thousands, dying in flames —

You are the very man we want
We mean business and our business is *you*
Wanted: A race of brand-new men.   10

Apply: Middle Europe;
No skill needed;
No ambition required; no brains wanted and no character allowed;

Take a permanent job in the coming profession
Wages: *Death.*   15

This poem was written as Nazi troops stormed across Europe at the start of World War II. The advertisement suggests on the surface that killing is just an ordinary job, but the speaker indicates through understatement that there is nothing ordinary about the "business" of this "*coming profession.*" Fearing uses verbal irony to indicate how casually and mindlessly people are prepared to accept the horrors of war.

Consider how the next poem, by Janice Mirikitani, a third-generation Japanese American, uses a similar ironic strategy in a different context.

JANICE MIRIKITANI (B. 1942)

Recipe   *1987*

Round Eyes

Ingredients: scissors, Scotch magic transparent tape,
                eyeliner — water based, black.
                Optional: false eyelashes.

Cleanse face thoroughly. 5

For best results, powder entire face, including eyelids.
   (lighter shades suited to total effect desired)

With scissors, cut magic tape 1/16" wide, 3/4"–1/2" long —
depending on length of eyelid.

Stick firmly onto mid–upper eyelid area 10
   (looking down into handmirror facilitates finding
   adequate surface)

If using false eyelashes, affix first on lid, folding any
excess lid over the base of eyelash with glue.

Paint black eyeliner on tape and entire lid. 15

Do not cry.

CONSIDERATIONS FOR CRITICAL THINKING AND WRITING

1. FIRST RESPONSE. Discuss your response to the poem's final line.
2. What is the effect of the very specific details of this recipe?
3. Why is "false eyelashes" a particularly resonant phrase in the context of this poem?
4. Try writing your own "recipe" in poetic lines — one that makes a commentary concerning a social issue that you feel strongly about.

CONNECTIONS TO OTHER SELECTIONS

1. Why are the formulas for an advertisement and a recipe especially suited for Fearing's and Mirikitani's respective purposes? To what extent do the ironic strategies lead to a similar tone and theme?
2. Write an essay comparing the themes in "Recipe" to those in Fainlight's "Flower Feet" (p. 724).

Like "AD," "Recipe" is a *satire,* an example of the literary art of ridiculing a folly or vice in an effort to expose or correct it. The object of satire is usually some human frailty; people, institutions, ideas, and things are all fair game for satirists. Fearing satirizes the insanity of a world mobilizing itself for war: His irony reveals the speaker's knowledge that there is nothing *"New, tremendous, thrilling,* [or] *great"* about going off to kill and be killed. The implication of the poem is that no one should respond to advertisements for war. The poem serves as a satiric corrective to those who would troop off armed with unrealistic expectations; wage war and the wages consist of death.

Dramatic irony is used when a writer allows a reader to know more about a situation than a character does. This creates a discrepancy between what a character says or thinks and what the reader knows to be true. Dramatic irony is often used to reveal character. In the following poem the speaker delivers a public speech that ironically tells us more about him than it does about the patriotic holiday he is commemorating.

E. E. CUMMINGS (1894–1962)
next to of course god america i 1926

"next to of course god america i
love you land of the pilgrims' and so forth oh
say can you see by the dawn's early my
country 'tis of centuries come and go
and are no more what of it we should worry 5
in every language even deafanddumb
thy sons acclaim your glorious name by gorry
by jingo by gee by gosh by gum
why talk of beauty what could be more beautiful than these heroic happy dead 10
who rushed like lions to the roaring slaughter
they did not stop to think they died instead
then shall the voice of liberty be mute?"

He spoke. And drank rapidly a glass of water

This verbal debauch of chauvinistic clichés (notice the run-on phrases and lines) reveals that the speaker's relationship to God and country is not, as he claims, one of love. His public address suggests a hearty mindlessness that leads to "roaring slaughter" rather than to reverence or patriotism. Cummings allows the reader to see through the speaker's words to their dangerous emptiness. What the speaker means and what Cummings means are entirely different. Like Fearing's "AD," this poem is a satire that invites the reader's laughter and contempt in order to deflate the benighted attitudes expressed in it.

When a writer uses God, destiny, or fate to dash the hopes and expectations of a character or humankind in general, it is called **cosmic irony.** In "The Convergence of the Twain" (p. 738), for example, Hardy describes how "The Immanent Will" brought together the *Titanic* and a deadly iceberg. Technology and pride are no match for "the Spinner of the Years." Here's a painfully terse version of cosmic irony.

STEPHEN CRANE (1871–1900)
A Man Said to the Universe 1899

A man said to the universe:
"Sir, I exist!"
"However," replied the universe,
"The fact has not created in me
A sense of obligation."

Unlike in "The Convergence of the Twain," there is the slightest bit of humor in Crane's poem, but the joke is on us.

Irony is an important technique that allows a writer to distinguish between appearances and realities. In situational irony a discrepancy exists between what we expect to happen and what actually happens; in verbal irony a discrepancy exists between what is said and what is meant; in dramatic irony a discrepancy exists between what a character believes and what the reader knows to be true; and in cosmic irony a discrepancy exists between what a character aspires to and what universal forces provide. With each form of irony, we are invited to move beyond surface appearances and sentimental assumptions to see the complexity of experience. Irony is often used in literature to reveal a writer's perspective on matters that previously seemed settled.

POEMS FOR FURTHER STUDY

JANE KENYON (1947–1995)

Surprise   *1996*

He suggests pancakes at the local diner,
followed by a walk in search of mayflowers,
while friends convene at the house
bearing casseroles and a cake, their cars
pulled close along the sandy shoulders   5
of the road, where tender ferns unfurl
in the ditches, and this year's budding leaves
push last year's spectral leaves from the tips
of the twigs of the ash trees. The gathering
itself is not what astounds her, but the casual   10
accomplishment with which he has lied.

CONSIDERATIONS FOR CRITICAL THINKING AND WRITING

1. FIRST RESPONSE. Does it matter that this poem is set in the spring?
2. Consider the connotative meaning of "ash trees." Why are they particularly appropriate?
3. Why do you suppose Kenyon uses "astounds" rather than "surprises" in line 10? Use a dictionary to help you determine the possible reasons for this choice.
4. Discuss the irony in the poem.

CONNECTIONS TO OTHER SELECTIONS

1. Write an essay on the nature of the surprises in Kenyon's poem and in Hathaway's "Oh, Oh" (p. 675). Include in your discussion a comparison of the tone and irony in each poem.
2. Compare and contrast in an essay the irony associated with the birthday parties in "Surprise" and Sharon Olds's "Rite of Passage" (p. 915).

CONRAD HILBERRY (B. 1928)
The Frying Pan   *1978*

My mark is my confusion.
If I believe it, I am
another long-necked girl
with the same face.
I am emptiness reflected   5
in a looking glass, a head
kept by a collar and leash,
a round belly with something
knocking to get in.

But cross the handle   10
with a short stroke
and I am Venus, the old
beauty. I am both the egg
and the pan it cooks in,
the slow heat, the miraculous   15
sun rising.

CONSIDERATIONS FOR CRITICAL THINKING AND WRITING

1. FIRST RESPONSE. Discuss the meanings of the "mark" in the first line. Can
   you think of any potential readings not mentioned by the speaker?
2. How is the pan transformed into an entirely different kind of symbol in the
   second stanza? How do the images of lines 13-16 create powerful symbolic
   values?
3. Discuss the significance of the poem's title.
4. The speaker of this poem is a woman, but the author is a man. Write an
   essay explaining whether knowing this makes any difference in your appreciation or understanding of the poem.

WILLIAM BLAKE (1757-1827)
The Sick Rose   *1794*

O Rose, thou art sick!
The invisible worm
That flies in the night,
In the howling storm,

Has found out thy bed
Of crimson joy,
And his dark secret love
Does thy life destroy.

CONSIDERATIONS FOR CRITICAL THINKING AND WRITING

1. FIRST RESPONSE. Discuss some of the possible meanings of the rose. How does the description of the worm help to explain the rose?
2. How does the use of personification in this poem indicate that the speaker laments the fate of more than a rose?
3. Is this poem to be read allegorically or symbolically? Can it be read literally?

PAUL LAURENCE DUNBAR (1872–1906)
We Wear the Mask   1896

We wear the mask that grins and lies,
It hides our cheeks and shades our eyes, —
This debt we pay to human guile;
With torn and bleeding hearts we smile,
And mouth with myriad subtleties.   5

Why should the world be overwise,
In counting all our tears and sighs?
Nay, let them only see us, while
      We wear the mask.

We smile, but, O great Christ, our cries   10
To thee from tortured souls arise.
We sing, but oh the clay is vile
Beneath our feet, and long the mile;
But let the world dream otherwise,
      We wear the mask!   15

CONSIDERATIONS FOR CRITICAL THINKING AND WRITING

1. FIRST RESPONSE. What does the mask symbolize? What kind of behavior does it represent?
2. Dunbar was a black man. Does awareness of that fact affect your reading of the poem? Explain why or why not.

CONNECTIONS TO OTHER SELECTIONS

1. How might the first line of this poem be used to describe the theme of Langston Hughes's "Dinner Guest: Me" (p. 1033)?
2. Write an essay on oppression as explored in "We Wear the Mask" and William Blake's "The Chimney Sweeper" (p. 822).

ROBERT BLY (b. 1926)

Snowbanks North of the House

1975

Those great sweeps of snow that stop suddenly six feet
    from the house . . .
Thoughts that go so far.

The boy gets out of high school and reads no more books;
    the son stops calling home.
The mother puts down her rolling pin and makes no more
    bread.   5
And the wife looks at her husband one night at a party
    and loves him no more.
The energy leaves the wine, and the minister falls leaving
    the church.
It will not come closer —
the one inside moves back, and the hands touch nothing,
    and are safe.

And the father grieves for his son, and will not leave the
    room where the coffin stands;   10
he turns away from his wife, and she sleeps alone.

And the sea lifts and falls all night; the moon goes on
    through the unattached heavens alone.
And the toe of the shoe pivots
in the dust. . . .
The man in the black coat turns, and goes back down the
    hill.   15
No one knows why he came, or why he turned away, and
    did not climb the hill.

CONSIDERATIONS FOR CRITICAL THINKING AND WRITING

1. FIRST RESPONSE. How can the varying images in the poem be related to one
   another? What do they have in common?

2. Describe the tone produced by the images. What emotions do you experience after carefully considering the images?

3. What symbolic meanings do you think are associated with the poem's images? Describe in a paragraph what you think the poem's themes are.

CONNECTIONS TO OTHER SELECTIONS

1. "Snowbanks North of the House" is the first poem in Bly's collection titled
   The Man in the Black Coat Turns (1981), a title drawn from line 15 of the poem.
   In *Selected Poems* (1986) Bly explains that

   > I wanted the poems in *The Man in the Black Coat Turns* to rise out of some
   > darkness beneath us, as when the old Norse poets fished with an ox head
   > as bait in the ocean. We know that the poem will break water only for a
   > moment before it sinks again, but just seeing it rise beneath the boat is

enough pleasure for one day; and to know that a large thing lives down there puts us in a calm mood, lets us endure our deprived lives with more grace.

How does Bly's observation that such a poem "lets us endure our deprived lives with more grace" shed light on "Snowbanks North of the House" and Bly's "Snowfall in the Afternoon" (p. 1078)? Write an essay that details your response.

2. Compare and contrast the symbolic images in "Snowbanks North of the House" and Robert Frost's "Stopping by Woods on a Snowy Evening" (p. 989).

PERSPECTIVE

ROBERT BLY (B. 1926)

On "Snowbanks North of the House"   1996

William Stafford has spoken so beautifully about what an assertion means in a poem, and how early you can make one. In one of his books, maybe *Writing the Australian Crawl*, he says if you make strong assertions too early in the poem, you can lose the reader. The reader needs to receive a couple of assertions first that it can agree with, such as "It's summer," or "Animals own a fur world," or "Those lines on your palm, they can be read," or "There was a river under First and Main." The reader needs to experience rather mild assertions so that he or she can begin to trust your mind; then when you make a wilder assertion later, the reader is more likely to climb up with you into that intense place from which the assertion came. My first assertion is

Those great sweeps of snow that stop suddenly six feet from the house.

Some snow blows all the way down from Canada and then stops six feet from the house. For people who've never lived on the prairie and have experienced only gently falling snow or snow interrupted by woods, my first line may seem a risky assertion. So my second line is mild.

Thoughts that go so far.

I want my poem to continue, but not to ascend, so I need an ordinary event, something we've all known a thousand times:

The boy gets out of high school and reads no more books.

I can stay with that ordinariness for a little while:

The son stops calling home.

I experienced that refusal to call home when I lived in New York during my late twenties. Certain ways of living come to an end:

The mother puts down her rolling pin and makes no more bread.

I was thinking of my grandmother making Norwegian flat bread; readers correctly told me that ordinary bread these days is not made with rolling pins. But the child in me wrote that line. The adult in me wrote the next line:

And the wife looks at her husband one night at a party and loves him no more.

I'm not conscious that that line happened to me, but it's possible. I do recall seeing both halves of the line at one instant in the wife's glance. It's another sadness. It's just an ordinary sadness. It doesn't happen only to special people.

The energy leaves the wine, and the minister falls leaving the church.

My father always had a particular tenderness for the old Lutheran minister in our town, and made sure that he received game such as pheasants in the fall, and geese at Christmas; I had some sympathy for the way a minister has to hold himself up and perform his role no matter what is happening in his private life. He has to keep giving the Communion.

A month or two after I wrote the poem, I read it to a friend who was an Episcopal priest of great spirit; he told me that I had described exactly what had happened to him a month before. He couldn't say the Communion words wholeheartedly on that particular Sunday, and he fell on the steps outside. One could say that for many ordinary people — and I am one of those — a fine energy sometimes refuses to become friends with us, or perhaps we refuse to make the courtly gesture that would welcome that energy. When we fall, it's an ordinary sadness.

It will not come closer —
the one inside moves back, and the hands touch nothing, and are safe.

I think a lot of my childhood is alive in that last half-sentence. And I spent in my mid-twenties two years alone in New York, talking to people barely once a month. It was all right. I felt safe: "The hands touch nothing, and are safe."

I must have felt that grief during the poem. The poem is moving away from sadness now and toward grief. And I recalled a scene from Abraham Lincoln's life. He loved his son Tad so much, and when the boy was eight, he died of tuberculosis or some such thing. They put the coffin into a room by itself in that kind of home visitation that people did at that time. Lincoln went into the room and didn't come out. He stayed all afternoon, and then he stayed there all night, and then he stayed there the next day. Around noon people started pounding on the door and telling him to come out, but he paid no attention. There was something a little extraordinary in that, but the general situation is not unusual, it's something we've all noticed or heard about many times. Sometimes after the death of a child, the husband and wife never do come back to each other.

The father grieves for his son, and will not leave the room where the coffin stands.
He turns away from his wife, and she sleeps alone.

Now what to do? Now we've arrived at a really ordinary place, in which life and its motions go on, but the shocked man or woman doesn't pay much informed attention to those motions anymore. Donald Hall has written about this place in his poem called "Mr. Wakeville on Interstate 90":

I will work forty hours a week clerking at the paintstore. . . .
I will watch my neighbors' daughters grow up, marry,
raise children. The joints of my fingers will stiffen.

The way such a life moves mechanically is a form of depression. At the beginning of *A Farewell to Arms*, Hemingway says, "That fall the war was still there, but we didn't go to it anymore."

And the sea lifts and falls all night; the moon goes on through the unattached heavens alone.

I loved that word "unattached" when I saw it on the page. It brought together the son who stops calling home and the man who lives alone in New York for two years.

Then I saw the toe of a black shoe. It seemed like an ordinary shoe, not standing on marble or red carpet, but on ordinary dust. Some elegant movement as of a hinge suddenly arrived, breaking all these long forward motions:

> The toe of the shoe pivots
> in the dust . . .
> and the man in the black coat turns, and goes back down the hill.

The first time I read the poem to an audience, there was some silence afterwards, and a woman asked, "Who is the man in the black coat?" I said, "I don't know." She said, "That's outrageous; you wrote the poem." I didn't answer. It was only when I got back to the farm that I thought of the proper answer: "If I had known who the man in the black coat was, I could have written an essay." I don't mean to demean essays with such a sentence, but it's good to think clearly in an essay, which can be a series of really clear and interlocking thoughts that are luminous. But sometimes a poem amounts to the creation of some sort of nourishing mud pond in which partly developed tadpoles can live for a while, and certain images can receive enough sustenance from the darkness around them to keep breathing without being forced into some early adulthood or job or retirement. It's possible the man in the black coat is Lincoln. He did turn and go back down the hill, and his face got sadder every year that the war went on. I also noticed in a family album a photograph of my father about 25 years old, standing by the windmill holding a baby rather awkwardly couched in his right arm; it's possible the baby was myself. He was wearing a large black coat. I don't know exactly why the last line closes the poem. I didn't intend it. It just came along. Perhaps it's the most ordinary thing of all. Our mother, or our grandmother, or grandfather, or our father, goes through incredible labors, keeping despite turbulent winds and strong blows the chosen direction forward, following some route. But why? What was the aim of Lincoln's life? What was the aim of my father's life? Or my life? We know a little bit of the story — what's the rest of the story? Why don't we know that?

> No one knows why he came, or why he turned away, and did not climb the hill.

From a typed manuscript sent to Michael Meyer, 1997

CONSIDERATIONS FOR CRITICAL THINKING AND WRITING

1. What do you think Bly means when he says he begins with "mild assertions" and "ordinariness" to help readers "climb up" to "wilder assertion[s]"? How does "Snowbanks North of the House" (p. 809) proceed this way?

2. Why do you think the woman in the audience thinks it "outrageous" that the poet doesn't know the identity of "the man in the black coat"? Explain why you agree or disagree with her response.

3. Discuss Bly's idea that "sometimes a poem amounts to the creation of some sort of nourishing mud pond in which partly developed tadpoles can live for a while." What does this description (and the rest of the sentence in which it appears) suggest about the nature of meaning in this poem?

4. How does Bly's reading and explanation of the poem compare with your own experience of it? Do you think his essay limits or expands your interpretation of the poem? Explain your response.

WILLIAM STAFFORD (B. 1914)

Traveling through the Dark

1962

Traveling through the dark I found a deer
dead on the edge of the Wilson River road.
It is usually best to roll them into the canyon:
that road is narrow; to swerve might make more dead.

By glow of the tail-light I stumbled back of the car   5
and stood by the heap, a doe, a recent killing;
she had stiffened already, almost cold.
I dragged her off; she was large in the belly.

My fingers touching her side brought me the reason —
her side was warm; her fawn lay there waiting,   10
alive, still, never to be born.
Beside that mountain road I hesitated.

The car aimed ahead its lowered parking lights;
under the hood purred the steady engine.
I stood in the glare of the warm exhaust turning red;   15
around our group I could hear the wilderness listen.

I thought hard for us all — my only swerving —
then pushed her over the edge into the river.

CONSIDERATIONS FOR CRITICAL THINKING AND WRITING

1. FIRST RESPONSE. Notice the description of the car in this poem: the "glow
   of the tail-light," the "lowered parking lights," and how the engine
   "purred." How do these and other details suggest symbolic meanings for
   the car and the "recent killing"?

2. Discuss the speaker's tone. Does the speaker seem, for example, tough, callous, kind, sentimental, confused, or confident?

3. What is the effect of the last stanza's having only two lines rather than the
   established four lines of the previous stanzas?

4. Discuss the appropriateness of this poem's title. In what sense has the
   speaker "thought hard for us all"? What are those thoughts?

5. Is this a didactic poem?

ANDREW HUDGINS (B. 1951)

Seventeen

1991

Ahead of me, the dog reared on its rope,
and swayed. The pickup took a hard left turn,
and the dog tipped off the side. He scrambled, fell,
and scraped along the hot asphalt
before he tumbled back into the air.   5
I pounded on my horn and yelled. The rope
snapped and the brown dog hurtled into the weeds.

I braked, still pounding on my horn. The truck
stopped too.

　　　　　　　　We met halfway, and stared　　　　　　　　10
down at the shivering dog, which flinched
and moaned and tried to flick its tail.
Most of one haunch was scraped away
and both hind legs were twisted. *You stupid shit!*
I said. He squinted at me. "Well now, bud—　　　　　　15
you best watch what you say to me."
I'd never cussed a grown-up man before.
I nodded. I figured on a beating. He grinned.
"You so damn worried about that ole dog,
he's yours." He strolled back to his truck,　　　　　　20
gunned it, and slewed off, spraying gravel.
The dog whined harshly.

　　　　　　　　By the road,
gnats rose waist-high as I waded through
the dry weeds, looking for a rock.　　　　　　　　25
I knelt down by the dog—tail flick—
and slammed the rock down twice. The first
blow did the job, but I had planned for two.
My hands swept up and down again. I grabbed
the hind legs, swung twice, and heaved the dog　　　30
into a clump of butterfly weed and vetch.
But then I didn't know that they had names,
those roadside weeds. His truck was a blue Ford,
the dog a beagle. I was seventeen.
The gnats rose, gathered to one loose cloud,　　　　35
then scattered through coarse orange and purple weeds.

Considerations for Critical Thinking and Writing

1. FIRST RESPONSE. Hudgins has described "Seventeen" as a "rite of passage." How does the title focus this idea?

2. What kind of language does Hudgins use to describe the injured dog (lines 1–14)? What is its effect?

3. Characterize the speaker and the driver of the pickup. What clues does the poem provide to the way each perceives the other?

4. Might killing the dog be understood as a symbolic action? Try to come up with more than one interpretation for the speaker's actions.

Connections to Other Selections

1. Write an essay that compares the speakers and themes of "Seventeen" and "Traveling through the Dark."

2. In an essay discuss the speakers' attitudes toward dogs in "Seventeen" and Ronald Wallace's "Dogs" (p. 1164). What do these attitudes reveal about the speakers?

ALDEN NOWLAN (1933–1983)

The Bull Moose 1962

Down from the purple mist of trees on the mountain,
lurching through forests of white spruce and cedar,
stumbling through tamarack swamps,
came the bull moose
to be stopped at last by a pole-fenced pasture. 5

Too tired to turn or, perhaps, aware
there was no place left to go, he stood with the cattle.
They, scenting the musk of death, seeing his great head
like the ritual mask of a blood god, moved to the other end
of the field, and waited. 10

The neighbors heard of it, and by afternoon
cars lined the road. The children teased him
with alder switches and he gazed at them
like an old, tolerant collie. The women asked
if he could have escaped from a Fair. 15

The oldest man in the parish remembered seeing
a gelded moose yoked with an ox for plowing.
The young men snickered and tried to pour beer
down his throat, while their girl friends took their pictures.

The bull moose let them stroke his tick-ravaged flanks, 20
let them pry open his jaws with bottles, let a giggling girl
plant a little purple cap
of thistles on his head.

When the wardens came, everyone agreed it was a shame
to shoot anything so shaggy and cuddlesome. 25
He looked like the kind of pet
women put to bed with their sons.

So they held their fire. But just as the sun dropped in the river
the bull moose gathered his strength
like a scaffolded king, straightened and lifted his horns 30
so that even the wardens backed away as they raised their rifles.
When he roared, people ran to their cars. All the young men
leaned on their automobile horns as he toppled.

CONSIDERATIONS FOR CRITICAL THINKING AND WRITING

1. FIRST RESPONSE. How does the speaker present the moose and the townspeople? How are the moose and townspeople contrasted? Discuss specific
   lines to support your response.

2. Explain how the symbols in this poem point to a conflict between humanity
   and nature. What do you think the speaker's attitude toward this conflict is?

3. Read the section on mythological criticism in Chapter 37, "Critical Strategies for Reading," and write an essay on "The Bull Moose" that approaches
   the poem from a mythological perspective.

CONNECTION TO ANOTHER SELECTION

1. In an essay compare and contrast how the animals portrayed in "The Bull Moose" and in Stafford's "Traveling through the Dark" (p. 813) are used as symbols.

JULIO MARZÁN (B. 1946)

Ethnic Poetry 1994

The ethnic poet said: "The earth is maybe
a huge maraca / and the sun a trombone /
and life / is to move your ass / to slow beats."
The ethnic audience roasted a suckling pig.

The ethnic poet said: "Oh thank Goddy, Goddy /   5
I be me, my toenails curled downward /
deep, deep, deep into Mama earth."
The ethnic audience shook strands of sea shells.

The ethnic poet said: "The sun was created black /
so we should imagine light / and also dream /   10
a walrus emerging from the broken ice."
The ethnic audience beat on sealskin drums.

The ethnic poet said: "Reproductive organs /
Eagles nesting California redwoods /
Shut up and listen to my ancestors."   15
The ethnic audience ate fried bread and honey.

The ethnic poet said: "Something there is that
doesn't love a wall / That sends
the frozen-ground-swell under it."
The ethnic audience deeply understood humanity.   20

CONSIDERATIONS FOR CRITICAL THINKING AND WRITING

1. FIRST RESPONSE. What is the implicit definition of ethnic poetry in this poem?

2. The final stanza quotes lines from Robert Frost's "Mending Wall" (p. 979). Read the entire poem. Why do you think Marzán chooses these lines and this particular poem as one kind of ethnic poetry?

3. What is the poem's central irony? Pay particular attention to the final line. What is being satirized here?

CONNECTION TO ANOTHER SELECTION

1. Write an essay that discusses the speaker's ideas about what poetry should be in "Ethnic Poetry" and in Langston Hughes's "Formula" (p. 1021).

JAMES MERRILL (1926–1995)

Casual Wear

Your average tourist: Fifty. 2.3
Times married. Dressed, this year, in Ferdi Plinthbower
Originals. Odds 1 to 9
Against her strolling past the Embassy

Today at noon. Your average terrorist: 5
Twenty-five. Celibate. No use for trends,
At least in clothing. Mark, though, where it ends.
People have come forth made of colored mist

Unsmiling on one hundred million screens
To tell of his prompt phone call to the station,   10
"Claiming responsibility" — devastation
Signed with a flourish, like the dead wife's jeans.

CONSIDERATIONS FOR CRITICAL THINKING AND WRITING

1. FIRST RESPONSE. What is the effect of the statistics in this poem?

2. Describe the speaker's tone. Is it appropriate for the subject matter? Explain why or why not.

3. Comment on the ironies that emerge from the final two lines. How are the tourist and terrorist linked by the speaker's description? Explain why you think the speaker sympathizes more with the tourist or the terrorist — or with neither.

CONNECTION TO ANOTHER SELECTION

1. Compare the satire in this poem with that in Peter Meinke's "The ABC of Aerobics" (p. 922). What is satirized in each poem? Which satire is more pointed from your perspective?

HENRY REED (1914–1986)

Naming of Parts

Today we have naming of parts. Yesterday,
We had daily cleaning. And tomorrow morning,
We shall have what to do after firing. But today,
Today we have naming of parts. Japonica
Glistens like coral in all of the neighboring gardens,   5
        And today we have naming of parts.

This is the lower sling swivel. And this
Is the upper sling swivel, whose use you will see,
When you are given your slings. And this is the piling swivel,
Which in your case you have not got. The branches   10

Hold in the gardens their silent, eloquent gestures,
        Which in our case we have not got.

This is the safety-catch, which is always released
With an easy flick of the thumb. And please do not let me
See anyone using his finger. You can do it quite easy   15
If you have any strength in your thumb. The blossoms
Are fragile and motionless, never letting anyone see
        Any of them using their finger.

And this you can see is the bolt. The purpose of this
Is to open the breech, as you see. We can slide it   20
Rapidly backwards and forwards: we call this
Easing the spring. And rapidly backwards and forwards
The early bees are assaulting and fumbling the flowers:
        They call it easing the Spring.

They call it easing the Spring: it is perfectly easy   25
If you have any strength in your thumb: like the bolt,
And the breech, and the cocking-piece, and the point of balance,
Which in our case we have not got; and the almond-blossom
Silent in all of the gardens and the bees going backwards and forwards,
        For today we have naming of parts.   30

CONSIDERATIONS FOR CRITICAL THINKING AND WRITING

1. FIRST RESPONSE. Characterize the two speakers in this poem. Identify the lines spoken by each. How do their respective lines differ in tone?

2. What is the effect of the last line of each stanza?

3. How do ambiguities and puns contribute to the poem's meaning?

4. What symbolic contrast is made between the rifle instruction and the gardens? How is this contrast ironic?

JOHN CIARDI (1916–1986)

Suburban   *1978*

Yesterday Mrs. Friar phoned. "Mr. Ciardi,
    how do you do?" she said. "I am sorry to say
this isn't exactly a social call. The fact is
    your dog has just deposited — forgive me —
a large repulsive object in my petunias."   5

I thought to ask, "Have you checked the rectal grooving
    for a positive I.D.?" My dog, as it happened,
was in Vermont with my son, who had gone fishing —
    if that's what one does with a girl, two cases of beer,
and a borrowed camper. I guessed I'd get no trout.   10

But why lose out on organic gold for a wise crack?
    "Yes, Mrs. Friar," I said, "I understand."

"Most kind of you," she said. "Not at all," I said.
    I went with a spade. She pointed, looking away.
"I always have loved dogs," she said, "but really!"   15

I scooped it up and bowed. "The animal of it.
    I hope this hasn't upset you, Mrs. Friar."
"Not really," she said, "but really!" I bore the turd
    across the line to my own petunias
and buried it till the glorious resurrection   20

when even these suburbs shall give up their dead.

CONSIDERATIONS FOR CRITICAL THINKING AND WRITING

1. FIRST RESPONSE. How does the speaker transform Mrs. Friar into a symbolic figure of the suburbs?

2. Why do you suppose Ciardi focuses on this particular incident to make a comment upon the suburbs? What is the speaker's attitude toward suburban life?

3. Write a one-paragraph physical description of Mrs. Friar that captures her character for you.

CONNECTION TO ANOTHER SELECTION

1. Compare the speakers' voices in "Suburban" and in Updike's "Dog's Death" (p. 673).

CHITRA BANERJEE DIVAKARUNI (B. 1956)

Indian Movie, New Jersey   *1990*

Not like the white filmstars, all rib
and gaunt cheekbone, the Indian sex-goddess
smiles plumply from behind a flowery
branch. Below her brief red skirt, her thighs
are satisfying-solid, redeeming   5
as tree trunks. She swings her hips
and the men-viewers whistle. The lover-hero
dances in to a song, his lip-sync
a little off, but no matter, we
know the words already and sing along.   10
It is safe here, the day
golden and cool so no one sweats,
roses on every bush and the Dal Lake
clean again.
                 The sex-goddess switches   15
to thickened English to emphasize
a joke. We laugh and clap. Here
we need not be embarrassed by words
dropping like lead pellets into foreign ears.

The flickering movie-light   20
wipes from our faces years of America, sons
who want mohawks and refuse to run
the family store, daughters who date
on the sly.
        When at the end the hero   25
dies for his friend who also
loves the sex-goddess and now can marry her,
we weep, understanding. Even the men
clear their throats to say, "What *qurbani!*°   *sacrifice*
What *dosti!*"° After, we mill around   *friendship* 30
unwilling to leave, exchange greetings
and good news: a new gold chain, a trip
to India. We do not speak
of motel raids, canceled permits, stones
thrown through glass windows, daughters and sons   35
raped by Dotbusters.°
        In this dim foyer
we can pull around us the faint, comforting smell
of incense and *pakoras,*° can arrange   *fried appetizers*
our children's marriages with hometown boys and girls, 40
open a franchise, win a million
in the mail. We can retire
in India, a yellow two-storied house
with wrought-iron gates, our own
Ambassador car. Or at least   45
move to a rich white suburb, Summerfield
or Fort Lee, with neighbors that will
talk to us. Here while the film-songs still echo
in the corridors and restrooms, we can trust
in movie truths: sacrifice, success, love and luck,   50
the America that was supposed to be.

36 *Dotbusters:* New Jersey gangs that attack Indians.

CONSIDERATIONS FOR CRITICAL THINKING AND WRITING

1. FIRST RESPONSE. Why does the speaker feel comfortable at the movies? How is the world inside the theater different from life outside in New Jersey?

2. Explain the differences portrayed by the speaker between life in India and life in New Jersey. What connotative values are associated with each location in the poem?

3. Discuss the irony in the final two lines.

ROBERT BROWNING (1812–1889)
My Last Duchess

1842

Ferrara°

That's my last Duchess painted on the wall,
Looking as if she were alive. I call
That piece a wonder, now: Frà Pandolf's° hands
Worked busily a day, and there she stands.
Will't please you sit and look at her? I said   5
"Frà Pandolf" by design, for never read
Strangers like you that pictured countenance,
The depth and passion of its earnest glance,
But to myself they turned (since none puts by
The curtain I have drawn for you, but I)   10
And seemed as they would ask me, if they durst,
How such a glance came there; so, not the first
Are you to turn and ask thus. Sir, 'twas not
Her husband's presence only, called that spot
Of joy into the Duchess' cheek: perhaps   15
Frà Pandolf chanced to say "Her mantle laps
Over my lady's wrist too much," or "Paint
Must never hope to reproduce the faint
Half-flush that dies along her throat": such stuff
Was courtesy, she thought, and cause enough   20
For calling up that spot of joy. She had
A heart — how shall I say? — too soon made glad,
Too easily impressed; she liked whate'er
She looked on, and her looks went everywhere.
Sir, 'twas all one! My favor at her breast,   25
The dropping of the daylight in the West,
The bough of cherries some officious fool
Broke in the orchard for her, the white mule
She rode with round the terrace — all and each
Would draw from her alike the approving speech,   30
Or blush, at least. She thanked men, — good! but thanked
Somehow — I know not how — as if she ranked
My gift of a nine-hundred-years-old name
With anybody's gift. Who'd stoop to blame
This sort of trifling? Even had you skill   35
In speech — which I have not — to make your will
Quite clear to such an one, and say, "Just this
Or that in you disgusts me; here you miss,
Or there exceed the mark" — and if she let
Herself be lessoned so, nor plainly set   40

Ferrara: In the sixteenth century, the duke of this Italian city arranged to marry a second time after the mysterious death of his very young first wife.   3 *Frà Pandolf:* A fictitious artist.

Her wits to yours, forsooth, and made excuse,
— E'en then would be some stooping; and I choose
Never to stoop. Oh sir, she smiled, no doubt,
Whene'er I passed her; but who passed without
Much the same smile? This grew; I gave commands;   45
Then all smiles stopped together. There she stands
As if alive. Will't please you rise? We'll meet
The company below, then. I repeat,
The Count your master's known munificence
Is ample warrant that no just pretense   50
Of mine for dowry will be disallowed;
Though his fair daughter's self, as I avowed
At starting, is my object. Nay, we'll go
Together down, sir. Notice Neptune, though,
Taming a sea-horse, thought a rarity,   55
Which Claus of Innsbruck° cast in bronze for me!

56 *Claus of Innsbruck:* Also a fictitious artist.

CONSIDERATIONS FOR CRITICAL THINKING AND WRITING

1. FIRST RESPONSE. What do you think happened to the duchess?
2. To whom is the duke addressing his remarks about the duchess in this poem? What is ironic about the situation?
3. Why was the duke unhappy with his first wife? What does this reveal about the duke? What does the poem's title suggest about his attitude toward women in general?
4. What seems to be the visitor's response (lines 53–54) to the duke's account of his first wife?

CONNECTION TO ANOTHER SELECTION

1. Write an essay describing the ways in which the speakers of "My Last Duchess" and "Hazel Tells LaVerne" (p. 725) by Katharyn Howd Machan inadvertently reveal themselves.

WILLIAM BLAKE (1757–1827)
The Chimney Sweeper   *1789*

When my mother died I was very young,
And my father sold me while yet my tongue
Could scarcely cry "'weep! 'weep! 'weep! 'weep!"
So your chimneys I sweep, and in soot I sleep.

There's little Tom Dacre, who cried when his head,   5
That curled like a lamb's back, was shaved: so I said

"Hush, Tom! never mind it, for when your head's bare
You know that the soot cannot spoil your white hair."

And so he was quiet, and that very night,
As Tom was a-sleeping, he had such a sight!   10
That thousands of sweepers, Dick, Joe, Ned, and Jack,
Were all of them locked up in coffins of black.

And by came an Angel who had a bright key,
And he opened the coffins and set them all free;
Then down a green plain leaping, laughing, they run,   15
And wash in a river, and shine in the sun.

Then naked and white, all their bags left behind,
They rise upon clouds and sport in the wind;
And the Angel told Tom, if he'd be a good boy,
He'd have God for his father, and never want joy.   20

And so Tom awoke; and we rose in the dark,
And got with our bags and our brushes to work.
Though the morning was cold, Tom was happy and warm;
So if all do their duty they need not fear harm.

Considerations for Critical Thinking and Writing

1. FIRST RESPONSE. Discuss the validity of this statement: "'The Chimney Sweeper' is a sentimental poem about a shameful eighteenth-century social problem; such a treatment of child abuse cannot be taken seriously."

2. Characterize the speaker in this poem, and describe his tone. Is his tone the same as the poet's? Consider especially lines 7, 8, and 24.

3. What is the symbolic value of the dream in lines 11 to 20?

4. Why is irony central to the meaning of this poem?

GARY SOTO (B. 1952)

Behind Grandma's House   *1985*

At ten I wanted fame. I had a comb
And two Coke bottles, a tube of Bryl-creem.
I borrowed a dog, one with
Mismatched eyes and a happy tongue,
And wanted to prove I was tough   5
In the alley, kicking over trash cans,
A dull chime of tuna cans falling.
I hurled light bulbs like grenades
And men teachers held their heads,
Fingers of blood lengthening   10
On the ground. I flicked rocks at cats,

Their goofy faces spurred with foxtails.
I kicked fences. I shooed pigeons.
I broke a branch from a flowering peach
And frightened ants with a stream of spit.   15
I said *"Chale,"* "In your face," and "No way
Daddy-O" to an imaginary priest
Until grandma came into the alley,
Her apron flapping in a breeze,
Her hair mussed, and said, "Let me help you,"   20
And punched me between the eyes.

CONSIDERATIONS FOR CRITICAL THINKING AND WRITING

1. FIRST RESPONSE. What is the central irony of this poem?
2. How does the speaker characterize himself at ten?
3. Though the "grandma" appears only briefly, she seems, in a sense, fully characterized. How would you describe her? Why do you think she says, "Let me help you"?

CONNECTION TO ANOTHER SELECTION

1. Write an essay comparing the themes of "Behind Grandma's House" and Sharon Olds's "Rite of Passage" (p. 915).

ROBERT BLY (B. 1927)

Sitting Down to Dinner   *1988*

Suppose a man can't find what is his.
Suppose as a boy he imagined that some demon
Forced him to live in "his room,"
And sit on "his chair" and be a child of "his parents."

That would happen each time he sat down to dinner.   5
His own birthday party belonged to someone else.
And — was it sweet potatoes that he liked? —
He should resist them. Whose plate is this?

That man would be like a lean-to attached
To a house. It doesn't have a foundation.   10
He would be helpful and hostile at the same time.
Such a person leans toward you and leans away.

Do you feel me leaning?

CONSIDERATIONS FOR CRITICAL THINKING AND WRITING

1. FIRST RESPONSE. Do you feel the speaker leaning toward you or away from you? Explain your response.
2. What kind of "demon" is described in line 2?

3. How do the boy's experiences serve to shape the man, according to the speaker?

4. Discuss the symbolic values associated with "dinner" in this poem.

CONNECTION TO ANOTHER SELECTION

1. In an essay consider how early childhood experiences affect adult identities in "Sitting Down to Dinner" and in Judy Page Heitzman's "The School-room on the Second Floor of the Knitting Mill" (p. 1158).

PERSPECTIVE

EZRA POUND (1885–1972)

On Symbols 1912

I believe that the proper and perfect symbol is the natural object, that if a man uses "symbols" he must so use them that their symbolic function does not obtrude; so that *a* sense, and the poetic quality of the passage, is not lost to those who do not understand the symbol as such, to whom, for instance, a hawk is a hawk.

From "Prolegomena," *Poetry Review*, February 1912

CONSIDERATIONS FOR CRITICAL THINKING AND WRITING

1. Discuss whether you agree with Pound that the "perfect symbol" is a "natural object" that does not insist on being read as a symbol.

2. Write an essay in which you discuss Alden Nowlan's "The Bull Moose" (p. 815) as an example of the "perfect symbol" Pound proposes.

20

Sounds

Poems yearn to be read aloud. Much of their energy, charm, and beauty comes to life only when they are heard. Poets choose and arrange words for their sounds as well as for their meanings. Most poetry is best read with your lips, teeth, and tongue because they serve to articulate the effects that sound may have in a poem. When a voice is breathed into a good poem, there is pleasure in the reading, the saying, and the hearing.

LISTENING TO POETRY

The earliest poetry—before writing and painting—was chanted or sung. The rhythmic quality of such oral performances served two purposes: it helped the chanting bard remember the lines, and it entertained audiences with patterned sounds of language, which were sometimes accompanied by musical instruments. Poetry has always been closely related to music. Indeed, as the word suggests, lyric poetry evolved from songs. "Western Wind" (p. 688), an anonymous Middle English lyric, survived as song long before it was written down. Had Robert Frost lived in a nonliterate society, he probably would have sung some version—a very different version to be sure—of "Acquainted with the Night" (p. 798) instead of writing it down. Even though Frost creates a speaking rather than a singing voice, the speaker's anxious tone is distinctly heard in any careful reading of the poem.

Like lyrics, early narrative poems were originally part of an anonymous oral folk tradition. A *ballad* such as "Bonny Barbara Allan" (p. 1074) told a story that was sung from one generation to the next until it was finally transcribed. Since the eighteenth century, this narrative form has sometimes been imitated by poets who write *literary ballads.* John Keats's "La Belle Dame sans Merci" (p. 1103) is, for example, a more complex and sophisticated nineteenth-century reflection of the original ballad traditions that developed in the fifteenth century and earlier. In considering poetry as sound, we should not forget that poetry traces its beginnings to song.

These next lines exemplify poetry's continuing relation to song. What poetic elements can you find in this ballad, which was adapted by Simon and Garfunkel and became a popular antiwar song in the 1960s?

ANONYMOUS

Scarborough Fair   *date unknown*

Where are you going? To Scarborough Fair?
Parsley, sage, rosemary, and thyme,
Remember me to a bonny lass there,
For once she was a true lover of mine.

Tell her to make me a cambric shirt,   5
Parsley, sage, rosemary, and thyme,
Without any needle or thread work'd in it,
And she shall be a true lover of mine.

Tell her to wash it in yonder well,
Parsley, sage, rosemary, and thyme,   10
Where water ne'er sprung nor a drop of rain fell,
And she shall be a true lover of mine.

Tell her to plough me an acre of land,
Parsley, sage, rosemary, and thyme,
Between the sea and the salt sea strand,   15
And she shall be a true lover of mine.

Tell her to plough it with one ram's horn,
Parsley, sage, rosemary, and thyme,
And sow it all over with one peppercorn,
And she shall be a true lover of mine.   20

Tell her to reap it with a sickle of leather,
Parsley, sage, rosemary, and thyme,
And tie it all up with a tom tit's feather,
And she shall be a true lover of mine.

Tell her to gather it all in a sack,   25
Parsley, sage, rosemary, and thyme,
And carry it home on a butterfly's back,
And then she shall be a true lover of mine.

CONSIDERATIONS FOR CRITICAL THINKING AND WRITING

1. FIRST RESPONSE. What do you associate with "Parsley, sage, rosemary, and thyme"? What images does this poem evoke? How?
2. What kinds of demands does the speaker make on his former lover? What do these demands have in common?
3. What is the tone of this ballad?

4. Choose a contemporary song that you especially like and examine the lyrics. Write an essay explaining whether or not you consider the lyrics poetic.

Of course, reading "Scarborough Fair" is not the same as hearing it. Like the lyrics of a song, many poems must be heard — or at least read with listening eyes — before they can be fully understood and enjoyed. The sounds of words are a universal source of music for human beings. This has been so from ancient tribes to bards to the two-year-old child in a bakery gleefully chanting "Cuppitycake, cuppitycake!"

Listen to the sound of this poem as you read it aloud. How do the words provide, in a sense, their own musical accompaniment?

JOHN UPDIKE (B. 1932)

Player Piano   1958

My stick fingers click with a snicker
And, chuckling, they knuckle the keys;
Light-footed, my steel feelers flicker
And pluck from these keys melodies.

My paper can caper; abandon   5
Is broadcast by dint of my din,
And no man or band has a hand in
The tones I turn on from within.

At times I'm a jumble of rumbles,
At others I'm light like the moon,   10
But never my numb plunker fumbles,
Misstrums me, or tries a new tune.

The speaker in this poem is a piano that can play automatically by means of a mechanism that depresses keys in response to signals on a perforated roll. Notice how the speaker's voice approximates the sounds of a piano. In each stanza a predominant sound emerges from the carefully chosen words. How is the sound of each stanza tuned to its sense?

Like Updike's "Player Piano," this next poem is also primarily about sounds.

MAY SWENSON (B. 1919)

A Nosty Fright   1984

The roldengod and the soneyhuckle,
the sack eyed blusan and the wistle theed
are all tangled with the oison pivy,
the fallen nine peedles and the wumbleteed.

A mipchunk caught in a wobceb tried   5
to hip and skide in a dandy sune

but a stobler put up a EEP KOFF sign.
Then the unfucky lellow met a phytoon

and was sept out to swea. He difted for drays
till a hassgropper flying happened to spot   10
the boolish feast all debraggled and wet,
covered with snears and tot.

Loonmight shone through the winey poods
where rushmooms grew among risted twoots.
Back blats flew betreen the twees   15
and orned howls hounded their soots.

A kumkpin stood with tooked creeth
on the sindow will of a house
where a icked wold itch lived all alone
except for her stoombrick, a mitten and a kouse.   20

"Here we part," said hassgropper.
"Pere we hart," said mipchunk, too.
They purried away on opposite haths,
both scared of some "Bat!" or "Scoo!"

October was ending on a nosty fright   25
with scroans and greeches and chanking clains,
with oblins and gelfs, coaths and urses,
skinning grulls and stoodblains.

Will it ever be morning, Nofember virst,
skue bly and the sappy hun, our friend?   30
With light breaves of wall by the fayside?
I sope ho, so that this oem can pend.

At just the right moments Swenson transposes letters to create amusing
sound effects and wild wordplays. Although there is a story lurking in "A
Nosty Fright," any serious attempt to interpret its meaning is confronted
with "a EEP KOFF sign." Instead, we are invited to enjoy the delicious
sounds the poet has cooked up.

Few poems revel in sound so completely. More typically, the sounds of
a poem contribute to its meaning rather than become its meaning. Consider how sound is used in the next poem.

EMILY DICKINSON (1830–1886)

A Bird came down the Walk —   *c. 1862*

A Bird came down the Walk —
He did not know I saw —
He bit an Angleworm in halves
And ate the fellow, raw,

And then he drank a Dew   5
From a convenient Grass —

And then hopped sidewise to the Wall
To let a Beetle pass —

He glanced with rapid eyes
That hurried all around —   10
They looked like frightened Beads, I thought —
He stirred his Velvet Head

Like one in danger, Cautious,
I offered him a Crumb
And he unrolled his feathers   15
And rowed him softer home —

Than Oars divide the Ocean,
Too silver for a seam —
Or Butterflies, off Banks of Noon
Leap, plashless as they swim.   20

    This description of a bird offers a close look at how differently a bird moves when it hops on the ground than when it flies in the air. On the ground the bird moves quickly, awkwardly, and irregularly as it plucks up a worm, washes it down with dew, and then hops aside to avoid a passing beetle. The speaker recounts the bird's rapid, abrupt actions from a somewhat superior, amused perspective. By describing the bird in human terms (as if, for example, it chose to eat the worm "raw"), the speaker is almost condescending. But when the attempt to offer a crumb fails and the frightened bird flies off, the speaker is left looking up instead of down at the bird.

    With that shift in perspective the tone shifts from amusement to awe in response to the bird's graceful flight. The jerky movements of lines 1 to 13 give way to the smooth motion of lines 15 to 20. The pace of the first three stanzas is fast and discontinuous. We tend to pause at the end of each line, and this reinforces a sense of disconnected movements. In contrast, the final six lines are to be read as a single sentence in one flowing movement, lubricated by various sounds.

    Read again the description of the bird flying away. Several *o*-sounds contribute to the image of the serene, expansive, confident flight, just as the *s*-sounds serve as smooth transitions from one line to the next. Notice how these sounds are grouped in the following vertical columns:

unr*o*lled	*so*fter	*too*	his	*O*cean	Banks
r*o*wed	*O*ars	N*oo*n	feather*s*	*s*ilver	plashle*ss*
h*o*me	*O*r		*s*ofter	*s*eam	a*s*
*O*cean	*o*ff		*O*ar*s*	Butterflie*s*	*s*wim

This blending of sounds (notice how "Leap, plashless" brings together the *p*- and *l*-sounds without a ripple) helps convey the bird's smooth grace in the air. Like a feathered oar, the bird moves seamlessly in its element.

    The repetition of sounds in poetry is similar to the function of the tones and melodies that are repeated, with variations, in music. Just as the patterned sounds in music unify a work, so do the words in poems, which have been carefully chosen for the combinations of sounds they create. These sounds are produced in a number of ways.

The most direct way in which the sound of a word suggests its meaning is through **onomatopoeia,** which is the use of a word that resembles the sound it denotes: *quack, buzz, rattle, bang, squeak, bowwow, burp, choo-choo, ding-a-ling, sizzle.* The sound and sense of these words are closely related, but they represent a very small percentage of the words available to us. Poets usually employ more subtle means for echoing meanings.

Onomatopoeia can consist of more than just single words. In its broadest meaning the term refers to lines or passages in which sounds help to convey meanings, as in these lines from Updike's "Player Piano":

> My stick fingers click with a snicker
> And, chuckling, they knuckle the keys.

The sharp, crisp sounds of these two lines approximate the sounds of a piano; the syllables seem to "click" against one another. Contrast Updike's rendition with the following lines:

> My long fingers play with abandon
> And, laughing, they cover the keys.

The original version is more interesting and alive because the sounds of the words are pleasurable and they reinforce the meaning through a careful blending of consonants and vowels.

Alliteration is the repetition of the same consonant sounds at the beginnings of nearby words: "*d*escending *d*ewdrops"; "*l*uscious *l*emons." Sometimes the term is also used to describe the consonant sounds within words: "trespasser's reproach"; "wedded lady." Alliteration is based on sound rather than spelling. "*K*een" and "*c*ar" alliterate, but "*c*ar" does not alliterate with "*c*ite." Rarely is heavy-handed alliteration effective. Used too self-consciously, it can be distracting instead of strengthening meaning or emphasizing a relation between words. Consider the relentless *h*'s in this line: "Horrendous horrors haunted Helen's happiness." Those *h*'s certainly suggest that Helen is being pursued, but they have a more comic than serious effect because they are overdone.

Assonance is the repetition of the same vowel sound in nearby words: "asl*ee*p under a tr*ee*"; "t*i*me and t*i*de"; "h*au*nt" and "*aw*esome"; "*ea*ch *e*vening." Both alliteration and assonance help to establish relations among words in a line or a series of lines. Whether the effect is **euphony** (lines that are musically pleasant to the ear and smooth, like the final lines of Dickinson's "A Bird came down the Walk—") or the effect is **cacophony** (lines that are discordant and difficult to pronounce, like the claim that "never my numb plunker fumbles" in Updike's "Player Piano"), the sounds of words in poetry can be as significant as the words' denotative or connotative meanings.

This next poem provides a feast of sounds. Read the poem aloud and try to determine the effects of its sounds.

Galway Kinnell (b. 1927)

Blackberry Eating 1980

I love to go out in late September
among the fat, overripe, icy, black blackberries
to eat blackberries for breakfast,
the stalks very prickly, a penalty
they earn for knowing the black art   5
of blackberry-making; and as I stand among them
lifting the stalks to my mouth, the ripest berries
fall almost unbidden to my tongue,
as words sometimes do, certain peculiar words
like *strengths* or *squinched*,   10
many-lettered, one-syllabled lumps,
which I squeeze, squinch open, and splurge well
in the silent, startled, icy, black language
of blackberry-eating in late September.

Considerations for Critical Thinking and Writing

1. FIRST RESPONSE. What types of sounds does Kinnell use throughout this
   poem? What categories can you place them in? What is the effect of these
   sounds?

2. How do lines 4–6 fit into the poem? What does this prickly image add to
   the poem?

3. Explain what you think the poem's theme is.

4. Write an essay that considers the speaker's love of blackberry eating along
   with the speaker's appetite for words. How are the two blended in the
   poem?

RHYME

Like alliteration and assonance, **rhyme** is a way of creating sound patterns. Rhyme, broadly defined, consists of two or more words or phrases
that repeat the same sounds: *happy* and *snappy*. Rhyme words often have
similar spellings, but that is not a requirement of rhyme; what matters is
that the words sound alike: *vain* rhymes with *reign* as well as *rain*. Moreover,
words may look alike but not rhyme at all. In **eye rhyme** the spellings are
similar, but the pronunciations are not, as with *bough* and *cough*, or *brow*
and *blow*.

Not all poems employ rhyme. Many great poems have no rhymes, and
many weak verses use rhyme as a substitute for poetry. These are especially
apparent in commercial messages and greeting-card lines. At its worst,
rhyme is merely a distracting decoration that can lead to dullness and predictability. But used skillfully, rhyme creates lines that are memorable and
musical.

Following is a poem using rhyme that you might remember the next time you are in a restaurant.

RICHARD ARMOUR (1906–1989)

Going to Extremes   *1954*

Shake and shake
  The catsup bottle
None'll come —
  And then a lot'll.

The experience recounted in Armour's poem is common enough, but the rhyme's humor is special. The final line clicks the poem shut, an effect that is often achieved by the use of rhyme. That click provides a sense of a satisfying and fulfilled form. Rhymes have a number of uses: they can emphasize words, direct a reader's attention to relations between words, and provide an overall structure for a poem.

Rhyme is used in the following poem to imitate the sound of cascading water.

ROBERT SOUTHEY (1774–1843)

From "The Cataract of Lodore"   *1820*

    "How does the water

    Come down at Lodore?"
. . . .
From its sources which well
  In the tarn on the fell;
    From its fountains   5
    In the mountains,
  Its rills and its gills;
Through moss and through brake,
    It runs and it creeps
    For awhile, till it sleeps   10
    In its own little lake.
And thence at departing,
Awakening and starting,
    It runs through the reeds
    And away it proceeds,   15
Through meadow and glade,
    In sun and in shade,
And through the wood-shelter,
    Among crags in its flurry,
      Helter-skelter,   20
      Hurry-scurry.

Here it comes sparkling,
And there it lies darkling;
Now smoking and frothing
  Its tumult and wrath in,   25
    Till in this rapid race
      On which it is bent,
    It reaches the place
    Of its steep descent.

    The cataract strong   30
    Then plunges along,
  Striking and raging
    As if a war waging
Its caverns and rocks among:
    Rising and leaping,   35
    Sinking and creeping,
    Swelling and sweeping,
  Showering and springing,
    Flying and flinging,
    Writhing and ringing,   40
Eddying and whisking,
Spouting and frisking,
Turning and twisting,
    Around and around
    With endless rebound!   45
  Smiting and fighting,
    A sight to delight in;
Confounding, astounding,
Dizzying and deafening the ear with its sound.
. . . .
Dividing and gliding and sliding,   50
And falling and brawling and spawling,
And driving and riving and striving,
And sprinkling and twinkling and wrinkling,
And sounding and bounding and rounding,
And bubbling and troubling and doubling,   55
And grumbling and rumbling and tumbling,
And clattering and battering and shattering;
Retreating and beating and meeting and sheeting,
Delaying and straying and playing and spraying,
Advancing and prancing and glancing and dancing,   60
Recoiling, turmoiling and toiling and boiling,
And gleaming and streaming and steaming and beaming,
And rushing and flushing and brushing and gushing,
And flapping and rapping and clapping and slapping,
And curling and whirling and purling and twirling,   65
And thumping and plumping and bumping and jumping,
And dashing and flashing and splashing and clashing;
And so never ending, but always descending,
Sounds and motions forever and ever are blending,

All at once and all o'er, with a mighty uproar;   70
And this way the water comes down at Lodore.

This deluge of rhymes consists of "Sounds and motions forever and ever . . . blending" (line 69). The pace quickens as the water creeps from its mountain source and then descends in rushing cataracts. As the speed of the water increases, so do the number of rhymes, until they run in fours: "dashing and flashing and splashing and clashing" (line 67). Most rhymes meander through poems instead of flooding them; nevertheless, Southey's use of rhyme suggests how sounds can flow with meanings. "The Cataract of Lodore" has been criticized, however, for overusing onomatopoeia. Some readers find the poem silly; others regard it as a brilliant example of sound effects. What do you think?

A variety of types of rhyme is available to poets. The most common form, *end rhyme,* comes at the ends of lines (lines 14–17).

> It runs through the reeds
>   And away it proceeds,
> Through meadow and glade,
>   In sun and in shade.

Internal rhyme places at least one of the rhymed words within the line, as in "Dividing and gliding and sliding" (line 50) or, more subtly, in the fourth and final words of "In mist or cloud, on mast or shroud."

The rhyming of single-syllable words such as *glade* and *shade* is known as *masculine rhyme:*

> Loveliest of trees, the cherry now
> Is hung with bloom along the bough.
>   — A. E. Housman

Rhymes using words of more than one syllable are also called masculine when the same sound occurs in a final stressed syllable, as in *defend, contend; betray, away.* A *feminine rhyme* consists of a rhymed stressed syllable followed by one or more rhymed unstressed syllables, as in *butter, clutter; gratitude, attitude; quivering, shivering:*

> Lord confound this surly sister,
> Blight her brow and blotch and blister.
>   — John Millington Synge

All the examples so far have been *exact rhymes* because they share the same stressed vowel sounds as well as any sounds that follow the vowel. In *near rhyme* (also called *off rhyme, slant rhyme,* and *approximate rhyme*), the sounds are almost but not exactly alike. There are several kinds of near rhyme. One of the most common is *consonance,* an identical consonant sound preceded by a different vowel sound: *home, same; worth, breath; trophy, daffy.* Near rhyme can also be achieved by using different vowel sounds with identical consonant sounds: *sound, sand; kind, conned; fellow, fallow.* The dissonance of *blade* and *blood* in the following lines helps to reinforce their grim tone:

> Let the boy try along this bayonet-blade
> How cold steel is, and keen with hunger of blood.
> — Wilfred Owen

Near rhymes greatly broaden the possibility for musical effects in English, a language that, compared with Spanish or Italian, contains few exact rhymes. Do not assume, however, that a near rhyme represents a failed attempt at exact rhyme. Near rhymes allow a musical subtlety and variety and can avoid the sometimes overpowering jingling effects that exact rhymes may create.

These basic terms hardly exhaust the ways in which the sounds in poems can be labeled and discussed, but the terms can help you to describe how poets manipulate sounds for effect. Read "God's Grandeur" (p. 837) aloud and try to determine how the sounds of the lines contribute to their sense.

PERSPECTIVE

DAVID LENSON (B. 1945)

On the Contemporary Use of Rhyme   *1988*

One impediment to a respectable return to rhyme is the popular survival of "functional" verse: greeting cards, pedagogical and mnemonic devices ("Thirty days hath September"), nursery rhymes, advertising jingles, and of course song lyrics. Pentameters, irregular rhymes, and free verse aren't much use in songwriting, where the meter has to be governed by the time signature of the music.

Far from universities, there has been a revival of rhymed couplets in rap music, in which, to the accompaniment of synthesizers, vocalists deliver lengthy first-person narratives in tetrameter. While most writing teachers would dismiss such lyrics as doggerel, the aim of the songs is really not so far from that of Alexander Pope: to use rhyme to sharpen social insight, in the hope that the world may be reordered.

From *The Chronicle of Higher Education,* February 24, 1988

CONSIDERATIONS FOR CRITICAL THINKING AND WRITING

1. Read some contemporary song lyrics from a wide range of groups or vocalists. Is Lenson correct in his assessment that irregular rhyme is not much use in songwriting?

2. Examine the rhymed couplets of some rap music. Discuss whether they are used "to sharpen social insight." What is the effect of using rhymes in rap music?

3. What is your own response to rhymed poetry? Do you like yours with or without? What do you think informs your preference?

SOUND AND MEANING

Gerard Manley Hopkins (1844–1889)

God's Grandeur 1877

The world is charged with the grandeur of God
  It will flame out, like shining from shook foil;°   *shaken gold foil*
  It gathers to a greatness, like the ooze of oil
Crushed.° Why do men then now not reck his rod?°
Generations have trod, have trod, have trod;   5
  And all is seared with trade; bleared, smeared with toil;
  And wears man's smudge and shares man's smell: the soil
Is bare now, nor can foot feel, being shod.
And for all this, nature is never spent;
  There lives the dearest freshness deep down things;   10
And though the last lights off the black West went
  Oh, morning, at the brown brink eastward, springs —
Because the Holy Ghost over the bent
  World broods with warm breast and with ah! bright wings.

    The subject of this poem is announced in the title and the first line: "The world is charged with the grandeur of God." The poem is a celebration of the power and greatness of God's presence in the world, but the speaker is also perplexed and dismayed by people who refuse to recognize God's authority and grandeur as they are manifested in the creation. Instead of glorifying God, "men" have degraded the earth through meaningless toil and cut themselves off from the spiritual renewal inherent in the beauty of nature. The relentless demands of commerce and industry have blinded people to the earth's natural and spiritual resources. In spite of this abuse and insensitivity to God's grandeur, however, "nature is never spent"; the morning light that "springs" in the east redeems the "black West" of the night and is a sign that the spirit of the Holy Ghost is ever present in the world. This summary of the poem sketches some of the thematic significance of the lines, but it does not do justice to how they are organized around the use of sound. Hopkins's poem, unlike Southey's "The Cataract of Lodore," employs sounds in a subtle and complex way.

    In the opening line Hopkins uses alliteration — a device apparent in almost every line of the poem — to connect "Go*d*" to the "worl*d*," which is "charge*d*" with his "gran*d*eur." These consonants unify the line as well. The alliteration in lines 2 and 3 suggests a harmony in the creation: the *f*'s in

---

4 *Crushed:* Olives crushed in their oil;   *reck his rod:* Obey God.

"*f*lame" and "*f*oil," the *sh*'s in "*sh*ining" and "*sh*ook," the *g*'s in "*g*athers" and "*g*reatness," and the visual (not alliterative) similarities of "*ooze* of *oil*" emphasize a world that is held together by God's will.

That harmony is abruptly interrupted by the speaker's angry question in line 4: "Why do men then now not reck his rod?" The question is as painful to the speaker as it is difficult to pronounce. The arrangement of the alliteration ("*n*ow," "*n*ot"; "*r*eck," "*r*od"), the assonance ("n*o*t," "r*o*d"; "m*e*n," "th*e*n," "r*e*ck"), and the internal rhyme ("m*en*," "th*en*") contribute to the difficulty in saying the line, a difficulty associated with human behavior. That behavior is introduced in line 5 by the repetition of "have trod" to emphasize the repeated mistakes — sins — committed by human beings. The tone is dirgelike because humanity persists in its mistaken path rather than progressing. The speaker's horror at humanity is evident in the cacophonous sounds of lines 6 to 8. Here the alliteration of "*sm*eared," "*sm*udge," and "*sm*ell" along with the internal rhymes of "s*eared*," "bl*eared*," and "sm*eared*" echo the disgust with which the speaker views humanity's "toil" with the "soil," an end rhyme that calls attention to our mistaken equation of nature with production rather than with spirituality.

In contrast to this cacophony, the final six lines build toward the joyful recognition of the new possibilities that accompany the rising sun. This recognition leads to the euphonic description of the "H*o*ly Gh*o*st *o*ver" (notice the reassuring consistency of the assonance) the world. Traditionally represented as a dove, the Holy Ghost brings love and peace to the "*w*orld," and "*b*roods *w*ith *w*arm *b*reast and *w*ith ah! *b*right *w*ings." The effect of this alliteration is mellifluous: the sound bespeaks the harmony that prevails at the end of the poem resulting from the speaker's recognition that "nature is never spent" because God loves and protects the world.

The sounds of "God's Grandeur" enhance the poem's theme; more can be said about its sounds, but it is enough to point out here that for this poem the sound strongly echoes the theme in nearly every line. Here are some more poems in which sound plays a significant role.

POEMS FOR FURTHER STUDY

EDGAR ALLAN POE (1809–1849)
The Bells   1849

I
Hear the sledges with the bells —
    Silver bells!
What a world of merriment their melody foretells!
How they tinkle, tinkle, tinkle,
    In the icy air of night!   5
While the stars that oversprinkle
All the heavens, seem to twinkle

With a crystalline delight;
   Keeping time, time, time,
   In a sort of Runic rhyme,   10
To the tintinnabulation that so musically wells
   From the bells, bells, bells, bells,
     Bells, bells, bells —
From the jingling and the tinkling of the bells

          II
Hear the mellow wedding bells —   15
    Golden bells!
What a world of happiness their harmony foretells!
   Through the balmy air of night
   How they ring out their delight! —
    From the molten-golden notes,   20
     And all in tune,
    What a liquid ditty floats
To the turtle-dove that listens, while she gloats
     On the moon!
    Oh, from out the sounding cells,   25
What a gush of euphony voluminously wells!
    How it swells!
    How it dwells
   On the Future! — how it tells
    Of the rapture that impels   30
   To the swinging and the ringing
    Of the bells, bells, bells —
Of the bells, bells, bells, bells,
    Bells, bells, bells —
To the rhyming and the chiming of the bells!   35

         III
Hear the loud alarum bells —
    Brazen bells!
What a tale of terror, now, their turbulency tells!
   In the startled ear of night
   How they scream out their affright!   40
    Too much horrified to speak,
    They can only shriek, shriek,
     Out of tune,
In a clamorous appealing to the mercy of the fire,
In a mad expostulation with the deaf and frantic fire,   45
     Leaping higher, higher, higher,
    With a desperate desire,
    And a resolute endeavor
    Now — now to sit, or never,
By the side of the pale-faced moon.   50
     Oh, the bells, bells, bells!
    What a tale their terror tells
     Of Despair!
   How they clang, and clash, and roar!
   What a horror they outpour   55

On the bosom of the palpitating air!
    Yet the ear, it fully knows,
       By the twanging
       And the clanging,
      How the danger ebbs and flows;   60
    Yet the ear distinctly tells,
       In the jangling
       And the wrangling,
    How the danger sinks and swells,
By the sinking or the swelling in the anger of the bells —   65
       Of the bells, —
  Of the bells, bells, bells, bells,
      Bells, bells, bells —
In the clamor and the clangor of the bells!

              IV
Hear the tolling of the bells —   70
      Iron bells!
What a world of solemn thought their monody compels!
    In the silence of the night,
    How we shiver with affright
At the melancholy menace of their tone!   75
    For every sound that floats
    From the rust within their throats
        Is a groan.
      And the people — ah, the people —
      They that dwell up in the steeple,   80
        All alone,
  And who tolling, tolling, tolling,
    In that muffled monotone,
Feel a glory in so rolling
      On the human heart a stone —   85
They are neither man nor woman —
They are neither brute nor human —
       They are Ghouls: —
  And their king it is who tolls: —
  And he rolls, rolls, rolls,
      Rolls   90
      A pæan from the bells!
  And his merry bosom swells
      With the pæan of the bells!
    And he dances, and he yells;   95
Keeping time, time, time,
In a sort of Runic rhyme,
      To the pæan of the bells —
      Of the bells:
Keeping time, time, time,   100
In a sort of Runic rhyme,
       To the throbbing of the bells —
    Of the bells, bells, bells —
       To the sobbing of the bells;

Keeping time, time, time,   105
   As he knells, knells, knells.
In a happy Runic rhyme,
   To the rolling of the bells —
Of the bells, bells, bells: —
   To the tolling of the bells —   110
Of the bells, bells, bells, bells,
      Bells, bells, bells —
To the moaning and the groaning of the bells.

CONSIDERATIONS FOR CRITICAL THINKING AND WRITING

1. FIRST RESPONSE. How does Poe create the sounds of each kind of bell in
   each of the poem's four sections?
2. How is onomatopoeia used in each section to echo meanings?
3. What is the effect of the many repetitions of the word "bells"?
4. How do the length of the lines in the poem create musical rhythms?
5. What kinds of rhymes are used to achieve sound effects?
6. What do you think is the theme of "The Bells"?

CONNECTION TO ANOTHER SELECTION

1. Compare Poe's sound effects with Southey's in "The Cataract of Lodore"
   (p. 833). Which poem do you find more effective in its use of sound? Explain why.

LEWIS CARROLL (CHARLES LUTWIDGE DODGSON/1832–1898)

Jabberwocky   1871

'Twas brillig, and the slithy toves
   Did gyre and gimble in the wabe:
All mimsy were the borogoves,
   And the mome raths outgrabe.

"Beware the Jabberwock, my son!   5
   The jaws that bite, the claws that catch!
Beware the Jubjub bird, and shun
   The frumious Bandersnatch!"

He took his vorpal sword in hand;
   Long time the manxome foe he sought —   10
So rested he by the Tumtum tree,
   And stood awhile in thought.

And, as in uffish thought he stood,
   The Jabberwock, with eyes of flame,
Came whiffling through the tulgey wood,   15
   And burbled as it came!

One, two! One, two! And through and through
   The vorpal blade went snicker-snack!

He left it dead, and with its head
   He went galumphing back.   20

"And hast thou slain the Jabberwock?
   Come to my arms, my beamish boy!
O frabjous day! Callooh, Callay!"
   He chortled in his joy.

'Twas brillig, and the slithy toves   25
   Did gyre and gimble in the wabe:
All mimsy were the borogoves,
   And the mome raths outgrabe.

Considerations for Critical Thinking and Writing

1. FIRST RESPONSE. What happens in this poem? Does it have any meaning?

2. Not all the words used in this poem appear in dictionaries. In *Through the Looking Glass,* Humpty Dumpty explains to Alice that "'slithy' means 'lithe and slimy.' 'Lithe' is the same as 'active.' You see it's like a portmanteau — there are two meanings packed up into one word." Are there any other portmanteau words in the poem?

3. Which words in the poem sound especially meaningful, even if they are devoid of any denotative meanings?

Connection to Another Selection

1. Compare Carroll's strategies for creating sound and meaning with those used by Swenson in "A Nosty Fright" (p. 828).

Sylvia Plath (1932–1963)

Mushrooms   *1960*

Overnight, very
Whitely, discreetly,
Very quietly

Our toes, our noses
Take hold on the loam,   5
Acquire the air.

Nobody sees us,
Stops us, betrays us;
The small grains make room.

Soft fists insist on   10
Heaving the needles,
The leafy bedding,

Even the paving.
Our hammers, our rams,
Earless and eyeless,   15

Perfectly voiceless,
Widen the crannies,
Shoulder through holes. We

Diet on water,
On crumbs of shadow,   20
Bland-mannered, asking

Little or nothing.
So many of us!
So many of us!

We are shelves, we are   25
Tables, we are meek,
We are edible,

Nudgers and shovers
In spite of ourselves.
Our kind multiplies: 30

We shall by morning
Inherit the earth.
Our foot's in the door.

CONSIDERATIONS FOR CRITICAL THINKING AND WRITING

1. FIRST RESPONSE. Is the tone of this poem serious or comic? What effects do alliteration and assonance have on your reading of the tone?
2. How important is the title?
3. Discuss what you take to be the poem's theme.

WILLIAM HEYEN (B. 1940)

The Trains   *1984*

Signed by Franz Paul Stangl, Commandant,
there is in Berlin a document,
an order of transmittal from Treblinka:

248 freight cars of clothing,
400,000 gold watches,   5
25 freight cars of women's hair.

Some clothing was kept, some pulped for paper.
The finest watches were never melted down.
All the women's hair was used for mattresses, or dolls.

Would these words like to use some of that same paper?   10
One of those watches may pulse in your own wrist.
Does someone you know collect dolls, or sleep on human hair?

He is dead at last, Commandant Stangl of Treblinka,
but the camp's three syllables still sound like freight cars
straining around a curve, Treblinka,   15

Treblinka. Clothing, time in gold watches,
women's hair for mattresses and dolls' heads.
Treblinka. The trains from Treblinka.

CONSIDERATIONS FOR CRITICAL THINKING AND WRITING

1. FIRST RESPONSE. How does the sound of the word *Treblinka* inform your understanding of the poem?

2. Why does the place name of Treblinka continue to resonate over time? If you don't know why Treblinka is infamous, use the library to find out.

3. Why do you suppose Heyen uses the word *in* instead of *on* in line 11?

4. Why is sound so important for establishing the tone of this poem? In what sense do the "camp's three syllables still sound like freight cars"?

5. How does this poem make you feel? Why?

JEAN TOOMER (1894–1967)

Reapers   1923

Black reapers with the sound of steel on stones
Are sharpening scythes. I see them place the hones
In their hip-pockets as a thing that's done,
And start their silent swinging, one by one.
Black horses drive a mower through the weeds,
And there, a field rat, startled, squealing bleeds,
His belly close to ground. I see the blade,
Blood-stained, continue cutting weeds and shade.

CONSIDERATIONS FOR CRITICAL THINKING AND WRITING

1. FIRST RESPONSE. Is this poem primarily about harvesting or does it suggest something else? How do the sounds, particularly the rhyme, contribute to the meaning?

2. What is the poem's tone?

3. The reapers' work is described alliteratively as "silent swinging." How are the alliteration and assonance of lines 1–2 and 6 related to their meaning?

4. Why is Toomer's version of line 6 more effective than this one: "And there a startled, squealing field rat bleeds"?

JOHN DONNE (1572–1631)

Song   1633

Go and catch a falling star
    Get with child a mandrake root,°
Tell me where all past years are,
    Or who cleft the Devil's foot,

---

2 *mandrake root:* This V-shaped root resembles the lower half of the human body.

Teach me to hear mermaids singing,   5
  Or to keep off envy's stinging,
      And find
      What wind
Serves to advance an honest mind.

If thou be'st borne to strange sights,   10
  Things invisible to see,
Ride ten thousand days and nights,
  Till age snow white hairs on thee,
Thou, when thou return'st, wilt tell me
  All strange wonders that befell thee,   15
      And swear
      Nowhere
Lives a woman true, and fair.

If thou findst one, let me know,
  Such a pilgrimage were sweet —   20
Yet do not, I would not go,
  Though at next door we might meet;
Though she were true, when you met her,
  And last, till you write your letter,
      Yet she   25
      Will be
False, ere I come, to two or three.

CONSIDERATIONS FOR CRITICAL THINKING AND WRITING

1. FIRST RESPONSE. What is the speaker's tone in this poem? What is his view
   of a woman's love? What does the speaker's use of hyperbole reveal about
   his emotional state?

2. Do you think Donne wants the speaker's argument to be taken seriously?
   Is there any humor in the poem?

3. Most of these lines end with masculine rhymes. What other kinds of
   rhymes are used for end rhymes?

JOSEPH BRODSKY (1940–1996)

Love Song   *1996*

If you were drowning, I'd come to the rescue,
  wrap you in my blanket and pour hot tea.
If I were a sheriff, I'd arrest you
  and keep you in the cell under lock and key.

If you were a bird, I'd cut a record   5
  and listen all night long to your high-pitched trill.
If I were a sergeant, you'd be my recruit,
  and boy I can assure you you'd love the drill.

If you were Chinese, I'd learn the language,
  burn a lot of incense, wear funny clothes.   10

If you were a mirror, I'd storm the Ladies,
  give you my red lipstick and puff your nose.

If you loved volcanoes, I'd be lava
  relentlessly erupting from my hidden source.
And if you were my wife, I'd be your lover   15
  because the church is firmly against divorce.

CONSIDERATIONS FOR CRITICAL THINKING AND WRITING

1. FIRST RESPONSE. Describe the poem's tone. Is it consistent throughout? How does the rhyme scheme contribute to the tone?

2. How do the rhymes contribute to the tone?

3. What is this poem finally about? How do you interpret the last line?

THOMAS HARDY (1840–1928)

The Oxen   *1915*

Christmas Eve, and twelve of the clock.
  "Now they are all on their knees,"
An elder said as we sat in a flock
  By the embers in hearthside ease.

We pictured the meek mild creatures where   5
  They dwelt in their strawy pen,
Nor did it occur to one of us there
  To doubt they were kneeling then.

So fair a fancy few would weave
  In these years! Yet, I feel,   10
If someone said on Christmas Eve,
  "Come; see the oxen kneel

"In the lonely barton° by yonder coomb°   *farmyard; ravine*
  Our childhood used to know,"
I should go with him in the gloom,   15
  Hoping it might be so.

CONSIDERATIONS FOR CRITICAL THINKING AND WRITING

1. FIRST RESPONSE. Traditionally, European peasants believed that animals worship God on Christmas Eve. How does the speaker feel about this belief? What is the difference between the speaker's attitude as a child and, "In these years," as an adult?

2. The speaker seems to feel nostalgic about his lost childhood. Does he feel the loss of anything more than that?

3. How do the sounds in the final stanza reinforce the tone and theme of the poem?

ALEXANDER POPE (1688–1774)

From An Essay on Criticism   1711

But most by numbers° judge a poet's song;   *versification*
And smooth or rough, with them, is right or wrong;
In the bright muse though thousand charms conspire,
Her voice is all these tuneful fools admire;
Who haunt Parnassus° but to please their ear,   5
Not mend their minds; as some to church repair,
Not for the doctrine, but the music there.
These equal syllables alone require,
Though oft the ear the open vowels tire;
While expletives° their feeble aid do join;   10
And ten low words oft creep in one dull line;
While they ring round the same unvaried chimes,
With sure returns of still expected rhymes;
Where'er you find "the cooling western breeze,"
In the next line, it "whispers through the trees":   15
If crystal streams "with pleasing murmurs creep,"
The reader's threatened (not in vain) with "sleep":
Then, at the last and only couplet fraught
With some unmeaning thing they call a thought,
A needless Alexandrine° ends the song,   20
That, like a wounded snake, drags its slow length along.
Leave such to tune their own dull rhymes, and know
What's roundly smooth, or languishingly slow;
And praise the easy vigor of a line,
Where Denham's strength, and Waller's° sweetness join.   25
True ease in writing comes from art, not chance,
As those move easiest who have learned to dance.
'Tis not enough no harshness gives offense,
The sound must seem an echo to the sense:
Soft is the strain when Zephyr° gently blows,   *the west wind* 30
And the smooth stream in smoother numbers flows;
But when loud surges lash the sounding shore,
The hoarse, rough verse should like the torrent roar:
When Ajax° strives some rock's vast weight to throw,
The line too labors, and the words move slow;   35
Not so, when swift Camilla° scours the plain,
Flies o'er th' unbending corn, and skims along the main.

5 *Parnassus:* A Greek mountain sacred to the Muses.   10 *expletives:* Unnecessary words
used to fill a line, as the *do* in this line.   20 *Alexandrine:* A twelve-syllable line, as line 21.
25 *Denham's . . . Waller's:* Sir John Denham (1615–1669) and Edmund Waller (1606–1687) were
poets who used heroic couplets.   34 *Ajax:* A Greek warrior famous for his strength in the
Trojan War.   36 *Camilla:* A goddess famous for her delicate speed.

CONSIDERATIONS FOR CRITICAL THINKING AND WRITING

1. FIRST RESPONSE. In these lines Pope describes some faults he finds in poems and illustrates those faults within the lines that describe them. How do the sounds in lines 4, 9, 10, 11, and 21 illustrate what they describe?

2. What is the objection to the "expected rhymes" in lines 12–17? How do they differ from Pope's end rhymes?

3. Some lines discuss how to write successful poetry. How do lines 23, 24, 32–33, 35, 36, and 37 illustrate what they describe?

4. Do you agree that in a good poem "The sound must seem an echo to the sense"?

MARILYN HACKER (B. 1942)

Groves of Academe   *1984*

The hour dragged on, and I was badly needing
coffee; that encouraged my perversity.
I asked the students of Poetry Writing,
"Tell me about the poetry you're reading."
There was some hair chewing and some nail biting.   5
Snowdrifts piled up around the university.
"I've really gotten into science fiction."
"I don't read much — it breaks my concentration.
I wouldn't want to influence my style."
"We taped some Sound Poems for the college station."   10
"When *I* give readings, should I work on diction?"
"Is it true that no really worthwhile
contemporary poets write in rhyme?"
"Do you think it would be a waste of time
to send my poems to *Vanity Fair*?   15
I mean — could they relate to my work there?"

CONSIDERATIONS FOR CRITICAL THINKING AND WRITING

1. FIRST RESPONSE. Characterize the speaker. How do the students compare?

2. What do the students' comments and questions in response to their teacher's request (line 4) reveal about themselves?

3. How does the speaker implicitly answer the question about poetic rhyme in lines 12 and 13?

CONNECTION TO ANOTHER SELECTION

1. Write an essay that compares the teachers in "Groves of Academe" and in Mark Halliday's "Graded Paper" (p. 1156). Which teacher would you rather have teach you? Explain why.

MAXINE HONG KINGSTON   (B. 1940)

Restaurant   1981

for Lilah Kan

The main cook lies sick on a banquette, and his assistant
has cut his thumb. So the quiche cook takes
their places at the eight-burner range, and you and I
get to roll out twenty-three rounds of pie
dough and break a hundred eggs, four at a crack,   5
and sift out shell with a China cap, pack
spinach in the steel sink, squish and squeeze
the water out, and grate a full moon of cheese.
Pam, the pastry chef, who is baking Choco-
late Globs (once called Mulattos) complains about the disco,   10
which Lewis, the salad man, turns up louder out of spite.
"Black so-called musician," "Broads. Whites."
The porters, who speak French, from the Ivory Coast,
sweep up droppings and wash the pans without soap.
We won't be out of here until three A.M. In this basement,   15
I lose my size. I am a bent-over
child, Gretel or Jill, and I can
lift a pot as big as a tub with both hands.
Using a pitchfork, you stoke the broccoli and bacon.
Then I find you in the freezer, taking   20
a nibble of a slab of chocolate as big as a table.
We put the quiches in the oven, then we are able
to stick our heads up out of the sidewalk into the night
and wonder at the clean diners behind glass in candlelight.

CONSIDERATIONS FOR CRITICAL THINKING AND WRITING

1. FIRST RESPONSE. How do the sounds of this poem contribute to the descriptions of what goes on in the restaurant kitchen? How do they contribute to the diners?

2. In what sense does the speaker "lose [her] size" in the kitchen? How would
   you describe her?

3. Examine the poem's rhymes. What effect do they have on your reading?

4. Describe the tone of the final line. How does it differ from the rest of the
   poem?

CONNECTION TO ANOTHER SELECTION

1. Write an essay analyzing how the kitchen activities described in "Restaurant," Kizer's "Food for Love" (p. 769), and Magarrell's "The Joy of Cooking" (p. 792) are used to convey the themes of these poems.

PAUL HUMPHREY (B. 1915)

Blow   *1983*

Her skirt was lofted by the gale;
When I, with gesture deft,
Essayed to stay her frisky sail
She luffed, and laughed, and left.

CONSIDERATIONS FOR CRITICAL THINKING AND WRITING

1. FIRST RESPONSE. How do alliteration and assonance contribute to the euphonic effects in this poem?
2. What is the poem's controlling metaphor? Why is it especially appropriate?
3. Explain the ambiguity of the title.

ROBERT FRANCIS (1901–1987)

The Pitcher   *1953*

His art is eccentricity, his aim
How not to hit the mark he seems to aim at,

His passion how to avoid the obvious,
His technique how to vary the avoidance.

The others throw to be comprehended. He   5
Throws to be a moment misunderstood.

Yet not too much. Not errant, arrant, wild,
But every seeming aberration willed.

Not to, yet still, still to communicate
Making the batter understand too late.   10

CONSIDERATIONS FOR CRITICAL THINKING AND WRITING

1. FIRST RESPONSE. Explain how each pair of lines in this poem works together to describe the pitcher's art.
2. Consider how the poem itself works the way a good pitcher does. Which lines illustrate what they describe?
3. Comment on the effects of the poem's rhymes. How are the final two lines different in their rhyme from the previous lines? How does sound echo sense in lines 9–10?
4. Write an essay that considers "The Pitcher" as an extended metaphor for talking about poetry. How well does the poem characterize strategies for writing poetry as well as pitching?
5. Write an essay that develops an extended comparison between writing or reading poetry and playing or watching another sport.

1. Compare this poem with Robert Wallace's "The Double-Play" (p. 1122), another poem that explores the relation of baseball to poetry.
2. Write an essay comparing "The Pitcher" with Francis's "Catch" (p. 676). One poem defines poetry implicitly, the other defines it explicitly. Which poem do you prefer? Why?

HELEN CHASIN (B. 1938)

The Word Plum   *1968*

The word *plum* is delicious

pout and push, luxury of
self-love, and savoring murmur
full in the mouth and falling
like fruit   5

taut skin
pierced, bitten, provoked into
juice, and tart flesh

question
and reply, lip and tongue   10
of pleasure.

CONSIDERATIONS FOR CRITICAL THINKING AND WRITING

1. FIRST RESPONSE. What is the effect of the repetitions of the alliteration and assonance throughout the poem? How does it contribute to the poem's meaning?
2. Which sounds in the poem are like the sounds one makes while eating a plum?
3. Discuss the title. Explain whether you think this poem is more about the word *plum* or about the plum itself. Consider whether the two can be separated in the poem.

CONNECTION TO ANOTHER SELECTION

1. How is Kinnell's "Blackberry Eating" (p. 832) similar in technique to Chasin's poem? Try writing such a poem yourself: choose a food to describe that allows you to evoke its sensuousness in sounds.

JOHN KEATS (1795–1821)

Ode to a Nightingale   *1819*

I
My heart aches, and a drowsy numbness pains
   My sense, as though of hemlock° I had drunk,   *a poison*
Or emptied some dull opiate to the drains

One minute past, and Lethe-wards° had sunk:
'Tis not through envy of thy happy lot,   5
But being too happy in thine happiness —
    That thou, light-wingèd Dryad° of the trees,   *wood nymph*
        In some melodious plot
Of beechen green, and shadows numberless,
    Singest of summer in full-throated ease.   10

II
O, for a draught of vintage! that hath been
    Cooled a long age in the deep-delved earth,
Tasting of Flora° and the country green,   *goddess of flowers*
    Dance, and Provençal song,° and sunburnt mirth!
O for a beaker full of the warm South,   15
    Full of the true, the blushful Hippocrene,°
        With beaded bubbles winking at the brim,
            And purple-stainèd mouth;
    That I might drink, and leave the world unseen,
        And with thee fade away into the forest dim.   20

III
Fade far away, dissolve, and quite forget
    What thou among the leaves hast never known,
The weariness, the fever, and the fret
    Here, where men sit and hear each other groan;
Where palsy shakes a few, sad, last gray hairs,   25
    Where youth grows pale, and specter-thin, and dies,
        Where but to think is to be full of sorrow
            And leaden-eyed despairs,
    Where Beauty cannot keep her lustrous eyes;
        Or new Love pine at them beyond tomorrow.   30

IV
Away! away! for I will fly to thee,
    Not charioted by Bacchus and his pards,°
But on the viewless wings of Poesy,
    Though the dull brain perplexes and retards:
Already with thee! tender is the night,   35
    And haply the Queen-Moon is on her throne,
        Clustered around by all her starry Fays;
            But here there is no light,
    Save what from heaven is with the breezes blown
        Through verdurous glooms and winding mossy ways.   40

V
I cannot see what flowers are at my feet,
    Nor what soft incense hangs upon the boughs,
But, in embalmèd° darkness, guess each sweet   *perfumed*

---

4 *Lethe-wards:* Toward Lethe, the river of forgetfulness in the Hades of Greek mythology.
14 *Provençal song:* The medieval troubadours of Provence, France, were known for their
singing.   16 *Hippocrene:* The fountain of the Muses in Greek mythology.   32 *Bacchus
and his pards:* The Greek god of wine traveled in a chariot drawn by leopards.

Wherewith the seasonable month endows
The grass, the thicket, and the fruit-tree wild;   45
    What hawthorn, and the pastoral eglantine;
        Fast fading violets covered up in leaves;
            And mid-May's eldest child,
    The coming musk-rose, full of dewy wine,
        The murmurous haunt of flies on summer eves.   50

VI

Darkling° I listen; and for many a time   *in the dark*
    I have been half in love with easeful Death,
Called him soft names in many a musèd rhyme,
    To take into the air my quiet breath;
Now more than ever seems it rich to die,   55
    To cease upon the midnight with no pain,
        While thou art pouring forth thy soul abroad
            In such an ecstasy!
    Still wouldst thou sing, and I have ears in vain —
        To thy high requiem become a sod.   60

VII

Thou wast not born for death, immortal Bird!
    No hungry generations tread thee down;
The voice I hear this passing night was heard
    In ancient days by emperor and clown:
Perhaps the selfsame song that found a path   65
    Through the sad heart of Ruth,° when, sick for home,
        She stood in tears amid the alien corn:
            The same that oft-times hath
    Charmed magic casements, opening on the foam
        Of perilous seas, in faery lands forlorn.   70

VIII

Forlorn! the very word is like a bell
    To toll me back from thee to my sole self!
Adieu! the fancy cannot cheat so well
    As she is famed to do, deceiving elf.
Adieu! adieu! thy plaintive anthem fades   75
    Past the near meadows, over the still stream,
        Up the hill side; and now 'tis buried deep
            In the next valley-glades:
    Was it a vision, or a waking dream?
        Fled is that music: — Do I wake or sleep?   80

66 *Ruth:* A young widow in the Bible (see the Book of Ruth).

CONSIDERATIONS FOR CRITICAL THINKING AND WRITING

1. FIRST RESPONSE. Why does the speaker in this ode want to leave his world for the nightingale's? What might the nightingale symbolize?

2. How does the speaker attempt to escape his world? Is he successful?

3. What changes the speaker's view of death at the end of stanza VI?

4. What does the allusion to Ruth (line 66) contribute to the ode's meaning?
5. In which lines is the imagery especially sensuous? How does this effect add to the conflict presented?
6. What calls the speaker back to himself at the end of stanza VII and the beginning of stanza VIII?
7. Choose a stanza and explain how sound is related to its meaning.
8. How regular is the stanza form of this ode?

PERSPECTIVE

DYLAN THOMAS (1914–1953)

On the Words in Poetry   *1961*

You want to know why and how I just began to write poetry. . . .

To answer . . . this question, I should say I wanted to write poetry in the beginning because I had fallen in love with words. The first poems I knew were nursery rhymes, and before I could read them for myself I had come to love just the words of them, the words alone. What the words stood for, symbolized, or meant, was of very secondary importance. What mattered was the *sound* of them as I heard them for the first time on the lips of the remote and incomprehensible grown-ups who seemed, for some reason, to be living in my world. And these words were, to me, as the notes of bells, the sounds of musical instruments, the noises of wind, sea, and rain, the rattle of milkcarts, the clopping of hooves on cobbles, the fingering of branches on a window pane, might be to someone, deaf from birth, who has miraculously found his hearing. I did not care what the words said, overmuch, not what happened to Jack and Jill and the Mother Goose rest of them; I cared for the shapes of sound that their names, and the words describing their actions, made in my ears; I cared for the colors the words cast on my eyes. I realize that I may be, as I think back all that way, romanticizing my reactions to the simple and beautiful words of those pure poems; but that is all I can honestly remember, however much time might have falsified my memory. I fell in love—that is the only expression I can think of, at once, and am still at the mercy of words, though sometimes now, knowing a little of their behavior very well, I think I can influence them slightly and have even learned to beat them now and then, which they appear to enjoy. I tumbled for words at once. And, when I began to read the nursery rhymes for myself, and, later, to read other verses and ballads, I knew that I had discovered the most important things, to me, that could be ever. There they were, seemingly lifeless, made only of black and white, but out of them, out of their own being, came love and terror and pity and pain and wonder and all the other vague abstractions that make our ephemeral lives dangerous, great, and bearable. Out of them came the gusts and grunts and hiccups and heehaws of the common fun of the earth; and though what the words meant was, in its own way, often deliciously funny enough, so much funnier seemed to me, at that almost forgotten time, the shape and shade and size and noise of the words as they hummed, strummed, jugged, and galloped along. That was the time of innocence; words burst upon me, unencumbered by trivial or portentous association; words were their springlike selves, fresh with Eden's dew, as they flew out of the air. They made their own original associations as they sprang and shone. The words "Ride a cock-horse to Banbury Cross" were as haunting to me, who did not know then what a cock-horse was nor cared a damn where Banbury Cross might be, as, much later, were such lines as John Donne's "Go and catch a falling star, Get with child a mandrake root," which also I could not understand when I first read them. And as I read more and more, and it was not all verse, by any means, my love for the real life of words increased until I knew that I must live *with* them and *in* them always. I knew, in fact, that I must be a writer of words, and nothing else. The first thing was to feel and know their sound and substance; what I was going to do with those words, what use I was going to make of them, what I was going to *say* through them, would come later. I knew I had to know them most intimately in all their forms and moods, their ups and downs, their chops and changes, their needs and demands. (Here, I am afraid, I am beginning to talk too vaguely. I do not like writing *about* words, because then I often use bad and wrong and stale and wooly words. What I like to do is treat words as a craftsman does his wood or stone or what-have-you, to hew, carve, mold, coil, polish, and plane them into patterns, sequences, sculptures, fugues of sound expressing some lyrical impulse, some spiritual doubt or conviction, some dimly-realized truth I must try to reach and realize.)

From *Early Prose Writings*

CONSIDERATIONS FOR CRITICAL THINKING AND WRITING

1. Why does Thomas value nursery rhymes so highly? What nursery rhyme was your favorite as a child? Why were you enchanted by it?

2. Explain what you think Thomas would have to say about Carroll's "Jabberwocky" (p. 841) or Swenson's "A Nosty Fright" (p. 828).

3. Consider Thomas's comparison at the end of this passage, in which he likens a poet's work to a craftsman's. In what sense is making poetry similar to sculpting, painting, or composing music? What are some of the significant differences?

21

Patterns of Rhythm

The rhythms of everyday life surround us in regularly recurring movements and sounds. As you read these words, your heart pulsates while somewhere else a clock ticks, a cradle rocks, a drum beats, a dancer sways, a foghorn blasts, a wave recedes, or a child skips. We may tend to overlook rhythm since it is so tightly woven into the fabric of our experience, but it is there nonetheless, one of the conditions of life. Rhythm is also one of the conditions of speech because the voice alternately rises and falls as words are stressed or unstressed and as the pace quickens or slackens. In poetry *rhythm* refers to the recurrence of stressed and unstressed sounds. Depending on how the sounds are arranged, this can result in a pace that is fast or slow, choppy or smooth.

SOME PRINCIPLES OF METER

Poets use rhythm to create pleasurable sound patterns and to reinforce meanings. "Rhythm," Edith Sitwell once observed, "might be described as, to the world of sound, what light is to the world of sight. It shapes and gives new meaning." Prose can use rhythm effectively too, but prose that does so tends to be an exception. The following exceptional lines are from a speech by Winston Churchill to the House of Commons after Allied forces lost a great battle to German forces at Dunkirk during World War II:

> We shall not flag or fail. We shall go on to the end. We shall fight in France, we shall fight on the seas and oceans, we shall fight with growing confidence and growing strength in the air, we shall defend our island, whatever the cost may be, we shall fight on the beaches, we shall fight on the landing grounds, we shall fight in the fields and in the streets, we shall fight in the hills; we shall never surrender.

The stressed repetition of "we shall" bespeaks the resolute singleness of purpose that Churchill had to convey to the British people if they were to win the war. Repetition is also one of the devices used in poetry to create rhythmic effects. In the following excerpt from "Song of the Open Road," Walt Whitman urges the pleasures of limitless freedom on his reader:

> Allons!° the road is before us!   *Let's go!*
> It is safe — I have tried it — my own feet have tried it well — be not detain'd!
> Let the paper remain on the desk unwritten, and the book on the
>   shelf unopen'd!
> Let the tools remain in the workshop! Let the money remain unearn'd!
> Let the school stand! mind not the cry of the teacher!   5
> Let the preacher preach in his pulpit! Let the lawyer plead in the
>   court, and the judge expound the law.
>
> Camerado,° I give you my hand!   *friend*
> I give you my love more precious than money,
> I give you myself before preaching or law;
> Will you give me yourself? will you come travel with me?   10
> Shall we stick by each other as long as we live?

These rhythmic lines quickly move away from conventional values to the open road of shared experiences. Their recurring sounds are not created by rhyme or alliteration and assonance (see Chapter 20) but by the repetition of words and phrases.

Although the repetition of words and phrases can be an effective means of creating rhythm in poetry, the more typical method consists of patterns of accented or unaccented syllables. Words contain syllables that are either stressed or unstressed. A **stress** (or **accent**) places more emphasis on one syllable than on another. We say "*syl*lable" not "syl*la*ble," "*em*phasis" not "em*pha*sis." We routinely stress syllables when we speak: "*Is* she con*tent* with the *con*tents of the *yel*low *pack*age?" To distinguish between two people we might say "Is *she* content. . . ?" In this way stress can be used to emphasize a particular word in a sentence. Poets often arrange words so that the desired meaning is suggested by the rhythm; hence, emphasis is controlled by the poet rather than left entirely to the reader.

When a rhythmic pattern of stresses recurs in a poem, the result is **meter**. Taken together, all the metrical elements in a poem make up what is called the poem's **prosody**. **Scansion** consists of measuring the stresses in a line to determine its metrical pattern. Several methods can be used to mark lines. One widely used system employs ´ for a stressed syllable and ˘ for an unstressed syllable. In a sense, the stress mark represents the equivalent of tapping one's foot to a beat:

> Híckŏrў, dĭckŏrў, dóck,
> The móuse răn úp thĕ clóck.
> The clóck strŭck óne,
> Ănd dówn hĕ rún,
> Híckŏrў, dĭckŏrў, dóck.

In the first two lines and the final line of this familiar nursery rhyme we hear three stressed syllables. In lines 3 and 4, where the meter changes for variety, we hear just two stressed syllables. The combination of stresses provides the pleasure of the rhythm we hear.

To hear the rhythms of "Hickory, dickory, dock" does not require a formal study of meter. Nevertheless, an awareness of the basic kinds of meter that appear in English poetry can enhance your understanding of how a poem achieves its effects. Understanding the sound effects of a poem and having a vocabulary with which to discuss those effects can intensify your pleasure in poetry. Although the study of meter can be extremely technical, the terms used to describe the basic meters of English poetry are relatively easy to comprehend.

The *foot* is the metrical unit by which a line of poetry is measured. A foot usually consists of one stressed and one or two unstressed syllables. A vertical line is used to separate the feet: "The clock | struck one" consists of two feet. A foot of poetry can be arranged in a variety of patterns; here are five of the chief ones:

Foot	Pattern	Example
iamb	˘ ´	awáy
trochee	´ ˘	Lóvely
anapest	˘ ˘ ´	understánd
dactyl	´ ˘ ˘	désperate
spondee	´ ´	déad sét

The most common lines in English poetry contain meters based on iambic feet. However, even lines that are predominantly iambic will often include variations to create particular effects. Other important patterns include trochaic, anapestic, and dactylic feet. The spondee is not a sustained meter but occurs for variety or emphasis.

Iambic
    What képt | his eyés | from gív | ing báck | the gáze

Trochaic
    Hé was | loúder | thán the | préacher

Anapestic
    I am called | to the frónt | of the room

Dactylic
    Síng it all | mérrily

These meters have different rhythms and can create different effects. Iambic and anapestic are known as *rising meters* because they move from unstressed to stressed sounds, while trochaic and dactylic are known as *falling meters.* Anapests and dactyls tend to move more lightly and rapidly than iambs or trochees. Although no single kind of meter can be considered always better than another for a given subject, it is possible to determine whether the meter of a specific poem is appropriate for its subject. A serious poem about a tragic death would most likely not be well served by lilting rhythms. Keep in mind too that though one or another of these four basic meters might constitute the predominant rhythm of a poem, variations can occur within lines to change the pace or call attention to a particular word.

A *line* is measured by the number of feet it contains. Here, for example, is an iambic line with three feet: "If she | should write | a note." These are the names for line lengths:

monometer: one foot	pentameter: five feet
dimeter: two feet	hexameter: six feet
trimeter: three feet	heptameter: seven feet
tetrameter: four feet	octameter: eight feet

By combining the name of a line length with the name of a foot, we can describe the metrical qualities of a line concisely. Consider, for example, the pattern of feet and length of this line:

I didn't want the boy to hit the dog.

The iambic rhythm of this line falls into five feet; hence it is called *iambic pentameter.* Iambic is the most common pattern in English poetry because its rhythm appears so naturally in English speech and writing. Unrhymed iambic pentameter is called *blank verse;* Shakespeare's plays are built on such lines.

Less common than the iamb, trochee, anapest, or dactyl is the *spondee,* a two-syllable foot in which both syllables are stressed (´´). Note the effect of the spondaic foot at the beginning of this line:

Dead set | against | the plan | he went | away.

Spondees can slow a rhythm and provide variety and emphasis, particularly in iambic and trochaic lines. A line that ends with a stressed syllable is said to have a *masculine ending,* whereas a line that ends with an extra unstressed syllable is said to have a *feminine ending.* Consider, for example, these two lines from Timothy Steel's "Waiting for the Storm" (the entire poem appears on p. 861):

feminine: The sand | at my feet | grow cold | er,
masculine: The damp | air chill | and spread.

The effects of English meters are easily seen in the following lines by Samuel Taylor Coleridge, in which the rhythm of each line illustrates the meter described in it:

Trochee trips from long to short;
From long to long in solemn sort
Slow Spondee stalks; strong foot yet ill able
Ever to come up with Dactylic trisyllable.
Iambics march from short to long—
With a leap and a bound the swift Anapests throng.

The speed of a line is also affected by the number of pauses in it. A pause within a line is called a *caesura* and is indicated by a double vertical line (‖). A caesura can occur anywhere within a line and need not be indicated by punctuation:

> Camerado, ‖ I give you my hand!
> I give you my love ‖ more precious than money.

A slight pause occurs within each of these lines and at its end. Both kinds of pauses contribute to the lines' rhythm.

When a line has a pause at its end, it is called an *end-stopped line.* Such pauses reflect normal speech patterns and are often marked by punctuation. A line that ends without a pause and continues into the next line for its meaning is called a *run-on line.* Running over from one line to another is also called *enjambment.* The first and eighth lines of the following poem are run-on lines; the rest are end-stopped.

WILLIAM WORDSWORTH (1770–1850)

My Heart Leaps Up   *1807*

My heart leaps up when I behold
  A rainbow in the sky:
So was it when my life began;
So is it now I am a man;
So be it when I shall grow old,
  Or let me die!
The child is father of the Man;
And I could wish my days to be
Bound each to each by natural piety.

Run-on lines have a different rhythm from end-stopped lines. Lines 3 and 4 and lines 8 and 9 are iambic, but the effect of their two rhythms is very different when we read these lines aloud. The enjambment of lines 8 and 9 reinforces their meaning; just as the "days" are bound together, so are the lines.

The rhythm of a poem can be affected by several devices: the kind and number of stresses within lines, the length of lines, and the kinds of pauses that appear within lines or at their ends. In addition, as we saw in Chapter 20, the sound of a poem is affected by alliteration, assonance, rhyme, and consonance. These sounds help to create rhythms by controlling our pronunciations, as in the following lines by Alexander Pope:

> Soft is the strain when Zephyr gently blows,
> And the smooth stream in smoother numbers flows;
> But when loud surges lash the sounding shore,
> The hoarse, rough verse should like the torrent roar.

These lines are effective because their rhythm and sound work with their meaning.

SUGGESTIONS FOR SCANNING A POEM

These suggestions should help you in talking about a poem's meter.

1. After reading the poem through, read it aloud and mark the stressed syllables in each line. Then mark the unstressed syllables.
2. From your markings, identify what kind of foot is dominant (iambic, trochaic, dactylic, or anapestic) and divide the lines into feet, keeping in mind that the vertical line marking a foot may come in the middle of a word as well as at its beginning or end.
3. Determine the number of feet in each line. Remember that there may be variations; some lines may be shorter or longer than the predominant meter. What is important is the overall pattern. Do not assume that variations represent the poet's inability to fulfill the overall pattern. Notice the effects of variations and whether they emphasize words and phrases or disrupt your expectation for some other purpose.
4. Listen for pauses within lines and mark the caesuras; many times there will be no punctuation to indicate them.
5. Recognize that scansion does not always yield a definitive measurement of a line. Even experienced readers may differ over the scansion of a given line. What is important is not a precise description of the line but an awareness of how a poem's rhythms contribute to its effects.

The following poem demonstrates how you can use an understanding of meter and rhythm to gain a greater appreciation for what a poem is saying.

TIMOTHY STEELE (B. 1948)

Waiting for the Storm

1986

Breeze sent | a wrink | ling dark | ness
Across | the bay. || I knelt
Beneath | an up | turned boat,
And, mo | ment by mo | ment, felt

The sand | at my feet | grow cold | er,
The damp | air chill | and spread.
Then the | first rain | drops sound | ed
On the hull | above | my head.

    The predominant meter of this poem is iambic trimeter, but there is plenty of variation as the storm rapidly approaches and finally begins to pelt the sheltered speaker. The emphatic spondee ("Breeze sent") pushes the darkness quickly across the bay while the caesura at the end of the sentence in line 2 creates a pause that sets up a feeling of suspense and expectation that is measured in the ticking rhythm of line 4, a run-on line that brings us into the chilly sand and air of the second stanza. Perhaps the most impressive sound effect used in the poem appears in the second syllable of "sounded" in line 7. That "ed" precedes the sound of the poem's final word "head" just as if it were the first drop of rain hitting the hull above the speaker. The visual, tactile, and auditory images make "Waiting for the Storm" an intense sensory experience.

This next poem also reinforces meanings through its use of meter and rhythm.

WILLIAM BUTLER YEATS (1865–1939)

That the Night Come   1912

She lived | in storm | and strife,
Her soul | had such | desire
For what | proud death | may bring
That it | could not | endure
The com | mon good | of life,
But lived | as 'twere | a king
That packed | his mar | riage day
With ban | neret | and pen | non,
Trumpet | and ket | tledrum,
And the | outrag | eous can | non,
To bun | dle time | away
That the | night come.

Scansion reveals that the predominant meter here is iambic trimeter. Each line contains three stressed and unstressed syllables that form a regular, predictable rhythm through line 7. That rhythm is disrupted, however, when the speaker compares the woman's longing for what death brings to a king's eager anticipation of his wedding night. The king packs the day with noisy fanfares and celebrations to fill up time and distract himself. Unable to accept "The common good of life," the woman fills her days with "storm and strife." In a determined effort "To bundle time away," she, like the king, impatiently awaits the night.

Lines 8–10 break the regular pattern established in the first seven lines. The extra unstressed syllable in lines 8 and 10 along with the trochaic feet in lines 9 ("trumpet") and 10 ("And the") interrupt the basic iambic trimeter and parallel the woman's and the king's frenetic activity. These lines thus echo the inability of the woman and king to "endure" regular or normal time. The last line is the most irregular in the poem. The final two accented syllables sound like the deep resonant beats of a kettledrum or a cannon firing. The words "night come" dramatically remind us that what the woman anticipates is not a lover but the mysterious finality of death.

The meter serves, then, in both its regularity and variations to reinforce the poem's meaning and tone.

The following poems are especially rich in their rhythms and sounds. As you read and study them, notice how patterns of rhythm and the sounds of words reinforce meanings and contribute to the poems' effects. And, perhaps most important, read the poems aloud so that you can hear them.

POEMS FOR FURTHER STUDY

ALICE JONES (B. 1949)

The Foot 1993

Our improbable support, erected
on the osseous architecture
of the calcaneus, talus, cuboid,
navicular, cuneiforms, metatarsals,
phalanges, a plethora of hinges,   5

all strung together by gliding
tendons, covered by the pearly
plantar fascia, then fat-padded
to form the sole, humble surface
of our contact with earth.   10

Here the body's broadest tendon
anchors the heel's fleshy base,
the finely wrinkled skin stretches
forward across the capillaried arch,
to the ball, a balance point.   15

A wide web of flexor tendons
and branched veins maps the dorsum,
fades into the stub-laden bone
splay, the stuffed sausage sacks
of toes, each with a tuft   20

of proximal hairs to introduce
the distal nail, whose useless
curve remembers an ancestor,
the vanished creature's wild
and necessary claw.   25

CONSIDERATIONS FOR CRITICAL THINKING AND WRITING

I. FIRST RESPONSE. What is the effect of the diction? What sort of tone is established by the use of anatomical terms? How do the terms affect the rhythm?

2. Alice Jones has described the form of "The Foot" as "five stubby stanzas." Explain why the lines of this poem may or may not warrant this description of the stanzas.

3. Describe the effect of the final stanza. How would your reading be affected if the poem ended after the comma in the middle of line 22?

A. E. HOUSMAN (1859–1936)

When I was one-and-twenty   *1896*

When I was one-and-twenty
  I heard a wise man say,
"Give crowns and pounds and guineas
  But not your heart away;
Give pearls away and rubies   5
  But keep your fancy free."
But I was one-and-twenty,
  No use to talk to me.

When I was one-and-twenty
  I heard him say again,   10
"The heart out of the bosom
  Was never given in vain;
'Tis paid with sighs a plenty
  And sold for endless rue."
And I am two-and-twenty,   15
  And oh, 'tis true, 'tis true.

CONSIDERATIONS FOR CRITICAL THINKING AND WRITING

1. FIRST RESPONSE. How does the basic metrical pattern affect your understanding of the speaker?

2. How do lines 1–8 parallel lines 9–16 in their use of rhyme and metaphor? Are there any significant differences between the stanzas?

3. What do you think has happened to change the speaker's attitude toward love?

4. Explain why you agree or disagree with the advice given by the "wise man."

5. What is the effect of the repetition in line 16?

RACHEL HADAS (B. 1948)

The Red Hat   *1995*

It started before Christmas. Now our son
officially walks to school alone.
Semi-alone, it's accurate to say:
I or his father track him on the way.
He walks up on the east side of West End,   5

we on the west side. Glances can extend
(and do) across the street; not eye contact.
Already ties are feeling and not fact.
Straus Park is where these parallel paths part;
he goes alone from there. The watcher's heart   10
stretches, elastic in its love and fear,
toward him as we see him disappear,
striding briskly. Where two weeks ago,
holding a hand, he'd dawdle, dreamy, slow,
he now is hustled forward by the pull   15
of something far more powerful than school.

The mornings we turn back to are no more
than forty minutes longer than before,
but they feel vastly different — flimsy, strange,
wavering in the eddies of this change,   20
empty, unanchored, perilously light
since the red hat vanished from our sight.

CONSIDERATIONS FOR CRITICAL THINKING AND WRITING

1. FIRST RESPONSE. What emotions do the parents experience throughout the
   poem? How do you think the boy feels? Does the metrical pattern affect
   your understanding of the parents or the boy?

2. What prevents the rhymed couplets in this poem from sounding sing-
   songy? What is the predominant meter?

3. What is it that "pull[s]" the boy along in lines 15-16?

4. Why do you think Hadas titled the poem "The Red Hat" rather than, for example, "Paths Part" (line 9)?

CONNECTION TO ANOTHER SELECTION

1. In an essay discuss the themes of "The Red Hat" and Bly's "Sitting Down to
   Dinner" (p. 824). Pay particular attention to the way parents are presented
   in each poem.

ROBERT HERRICK (1591–1674)
Delight in Disorder   *1648*

A sweet disorder in the dress
Kindles in clothes a wantonness.
A lawn° about the shoulders thrown   *linen scarf*
Into a fine distraction;
An erring lace, which here and there   5
Enthralls the crimson stomacher,
A cuff neglectful, and thereby
Ribbons to flow confusedly;
A winning wave, deserving note,
In the tempestuous petticoat;   10

A careless shoestring, in whose tie
I see a wild civility;
Do more bewitch me than when art
Is too precise in every part.

CONSIDERATIONS FOR CRITICAL THINKING AND WRITING

1. FIRST RESPONSE. Why does the speaker in this poem value "disorder" so highly? How do the poem's organization and rhythmic order relate to its theme? Are they "precise in every part"?

2. Which words in the poem indicate disorder? Which words indicate the speaker's response to that disorder? What are the connotative meanings of each set of words? Why are they appropriate? What do they suggest about the woman and the speaker?

3. Write a short essay in which you agree or disagree with the speaker's views on dress.

BEN JONSON (1573–1637)

Still to Be Neat

1609

Still° to be neat, still to be dressed,   *continually*
As you were going to a feast;
Still to be powdered, still perfumed;
Lady, it is to be presumed,
Though art's hid causes are not found,   5
All is not sweet, all is not sound.

Give me a look, give me a face
That makes simplicity a grace;
Robes loosely flowing, hair as free;
Such sweet neglect more taketh me   10
Then all th' adulteries of art.
They strike mine eyes, but not my heart.

CONSIDERATIONS FOR CRITICAL THINKING AND WRITING

1. FIRST RESPONSE. What are the speaker's reservations about the lady in the first stanza? What do you think "sweet" means in line 6?

2. What does the speaker want from the lady in the second stanza? How has the meaning of "sweet" shifted from line 6 to line 10? What other words in the poem are especially charged with connotative meanings?

3. How do the rhythms of Jonson's lines help to reinforce meanings? Pay particular attention to lines 6 and 12.

CONNECTIONS TO OTHER SELECTIONS

1. Write an essay comparing the themes of "Still to Be Neat" and Herrick's preceding poem, "Delight in Disorder." How do the speakers make similar points but from different perspectives?

2. How does the rhythm of "Still to Be Neat" compare with that of "Delight in Disorder"? Which do you find more effective? Explain why.

CHARLES MARTIN (B. 1942)

Victoria's Secret   *1994*

Victorian mothers instructed their daughters, ahem,
That whenever their husbands were getting it on them,
The only thing for it was just to lie perfectly flat
And try to imagine themselves out buying a new hat;
So, night after night, expeditions grimly set off   5
Each leaving a corpse in its wake to service the toff°   *dandy*
With the whiskers and whiskey, the lecherous ogre bent
Over her, thrashing and thrusting until he was spent.
Or so we imagine, persuaded that our ancestors
Couldn't have been as free from repression as we are,   10
As our descendants will no doubt mock any passion
They think we were prone to, if thinking comes back into fashion.
And here is *Victoria's Secret*, which fondly supposes
That the young women depicted in various poses
Of complaisant negligence somehow or other reveal   15
More than we see of them: we're intended to feel
That this isn't simply a matter of sheer lingerie,
But rather the baring of something long hidden away
Behind an outmoded conception of rectitude:
Liberation appears to us, not entirely nude,   20
In the form of a fullbreasted nymph, impeccably slim,
Airbrushed at each conjunction of torso and limb,
Who looks up from the page with large and curious eyes
That never close: and in their depths lie frozen
The wordless dreams shared by all merchandise,   25
Even the hats that wait in the dark to be chosen.

CONSIDERATIONS FOR CRITICAL THINKING AND WRITING

1. FIRST RESPONSE. Describe the speaker. How does the metrical pattern affect your understanding of the speaker? What reflections does he (and is it a he?) have about past and future generations?

2. Does the speaker's description of *Victoria's Secret* models ring true to you? Explain why or why not.

3. What is the effect of the changed rhyme scheme in lines 23–26?

4. Comment on the title. How is it related to the poem's theme?

CONNECTION TO ANOTHER SELECTION

1. Write an essay on the social criticism aimed at advertising in this poem and in Fearing's "AD" (p. 803).

William Blake (1757–1827)

The Lamb   1789

      Little Lamb, who made thee?
      Dost thou know who made thee?
Gave thee life, and bid thee feed
By the stream and o'er the mead;
Gave thee clothing of delight,   5
Softest clothing, wooly, bright;
Gave thee such a tender voice,
Making all the vales rejoice?
      Little Lamb, who made thee?
      Dost thou know who made thee?   10

      Little Lamb, I'll tell thee,
      Little Lamb, I'll tell thee:
He is callèd by thy name,
For he calls himself a Lamb.
He is meek, and he is mild;   15
He became a little child.
I a child, and thou a lamb,
We are callèd by his name.
      Little Lamb, God bless thee!
      Little Lamb, God bless thee!   20

Considerations for Critical Thinking and Writing

1. FIRST RESPONSE. This poem is from Blake's *Songs of Innocence*. Describe its tone. How do the meter, rhyme, and repetition help to characterize the speaker's voice?

2. Why is it significant that the animal addressed by the speaker is a lamb? What symbolic value would be lost if the animal were, for example, a doe?

3. How does the second stanza answer the question raised in the first? What is the speaker's view of the creation?

William Blake (1757–1827)

The Tyger   1794

Tyger! Tyger! burning bright
In the forests of the night,
What immortal hand or eye
Could frame thy fearful symmetry?

In what distant deeps or skies   5
Burnt the fire of thine eyes?
On what wings dare he aspire?
What the hand dare seize the fire?

And what shoulder, and what art,
Could twist the sinews of thy heart?   10

And when thy heart began to beat,
What dread hand? and what dread feet?

What the hammer? what the chain?
In what furnace was thy brain?
What the anvil? what dread grasp   15
Dare its deadly terrors clasp?

When the stars threw down their spears,
And watered heaven with their tears,
Did he smile his work to see?
Did he who made the Lamb make thee?   20

Tyger! Tyger! burning bright
In the forests of the night,
What immortal hand or eye
Dare frame thy fearful symmetry?

CONSIDERATIONS FOR CRITICAL THINKING AND WRITING

1. FIRST RESPONSE. This poem from Blake's *Songs of Experience* is often paired
   with "The Lamb." Describe the poem's tone. Is the speaker's voice the same
   here as in "The Lamb"? Which words are repeated, and how do they contribute to the tone?

2. What is revealed about the nature of the tiger by the words used to describe
   its creation? What do you think the tiger symbolizes?

3. Unlike in "The Lamb," more than one question is raised in "The Tyger."
   What are these questions? Are they answered?

4. Compare the rhythms in "The Lamb" and "The Tyger." Each basically uses
   a seven-syllable line, but the effects are very different. Why?

5. Using these two poems as the basis of your discussion, describe what distinguishes innocence from experience.

DOROTHY PARKER (1893–1967)

One Perfect Rose   *1926*

A single flow'r he sent me, since we met.
    All tenderly his messenger he chose;
Deep-hearted, pure, with scented dew still wet —
    One perfect rose.

I knew the language of the floweret;   5
    "My fragile leaves," it said, "his heart enclose."
Love long has taken for his amulet
    One perfect rose.

Why is it no one ever sent me yet
    One perfect limousine, do you suppose?   10
Ah no, it's always just my luck to get
    One perfect rose.

CONSIDERATIONS FOR CRITICAL THINKING AND WRITING

1. FIRST RESPONSE. Describe the tone of the first two stanzas. How do rhyme and meter help to establish the tone?

2. How does the meaning of "One perfect rose" in line 12 compare with the way you read it in lines 4 and 8?

3. Describe the speaker. What sort of woman is she? How do you respond to her?

ALFRED, LORD TENNYSON (1809–1892)

The Charge of the Light Brigade   *1855*

I
Half a league, half a league,
    Half a league onward,
All in the valley of Death
    Rode the six hundred.
"Forward, the Light Brigade!   5
Charge for the guns!" he said:
Into the valley of Death
    Rode the six hundred.

2
"Forward, the Light Brigade!"
Was there a man dismayed?   10
Not though the soldier knew
    Some one had blundered:
Their's not to make reply,
Their's not to reason why,
Their's but to do and die: 15
Into the valley of Death
    Rode the six hundred.

3
Cannon to right of them,
Cannon to left of them,
Cannon in front of them   20
    Volleyed and thundered;
Stormed at with shot and shell,
Boldly they rode and well,
Into the jaws of Death,
Into the mouth of Hell   25
    Rode the six hundred.

4
Flashed all their sabers bare,
Flashed as they turned in air
Sabring the gunners there,
Charging an army, while   30
    All the world wondered:
Plunged in the battery-smoke

Right through the line they broke;
Cossack and Russian
Reeled from the saber-stroke   35
    Shattered and sundered.
Then they rode back, but not
    Not the six hundred.

                5
Cannon to right of them,
Cannon to left of them,   40
Cannon behind them
    Volleyed and thundered;
Stormed at with shot and shell,
While horse and hero fell,
They that had fought so well   45
Came through the jaws of Death,
Back from the mouth of Hell,
All that was left of them,
    Left of six hundred.

                6
When can their glory fade?   50
O the wild charge they made!
    All the world wondered.
Honor the charge they made!
Honor the Light Brigade,
    Noble six hundred!   55

Considerations for Critical Thinking and Writing

1. FIRST RESPONSE. How do the meter and rhyme contribute to the meaning of this poem's lines?

2. What is the speaker's attitude toward war?

3. Describe the tone, paying particular attention to stanza 2.

Connection to Another Selection

1. Compare the theme of "The Charge of the Light Brigade" with Owen's "*Dulce et Decorum Est*" (p. 763).

Theodore Roethke (1908–1963)
My Papa's Waltz   *1948*

The whiskey on your breath
Could make a small boy dizzy;
But I hung on like death:
Such waltzing was not easy.

We romped until the pans   5
Slid from the kitchen shelf;

My mother's countenance
Could not unfrown itself.

The hand that held my wrist
Was battered on one knuckle;   10
At every step you missed
My right ear scraped a buckle.

You beat time on my head
With a palm caked hard by dirt,
Then waltzed me off to bed   15
Still clinging to your shirt.

CONSIDERATIONS FOR CRITICAL THINKING AND WRITING

1. FIRST RESPONSE. What details characterize the father in this poem? How
   does the speaker's choice of words reveal his feeling about his father? Is the
   remembering speaker still a boy?

2. Characterize the rhythm of the poem. Does it move "like death," or is it
   more like a waltz? Is the rhythm regular throughout the poem? What is its
   effect?

3. Comment on the appropriateness of the title. Why do you suppose
   Roethke didn't use "My Father's Waltz"?

ARON KEESBURY (B. 1971)

Song to a Waitress   1997

Yes. I want a big fat cup of coffee and
I want it hot. I want a big hot cup
of coffee in a big fat mug. And bring
it here and put it down and get the hell

away from me. And I want sugar in   5
a jar. A glass jar. Big, fat, glass jar with
a metal top and none of them pink, pansy
sugar packets in dainty little cups.

And come back every now and then and fill
my big fat mug and keep it hot and full.   10
And I don't want to hear your waitress talk
and I don't want to see you smile. So fill

my big fat mug and get the hell away.
I don't want to see your face today.

CONSIDERATIONS FOR CRITICAL THINKING AND WRITING

1. FIRST RESPONSE. What does this speaker want?

2. What is the predominant metrical pattern in the poem? Where does the
   poem deviate from that pattern? How do these deviations affect the
   speaker's tone?

3. In what ways does this poem resemble a sonnet? How does it differ? (See p. 879 for a description of a sonnet.) What do the similarities and differences to the form add to your understanding of the speaker's intent?

4. What is the effect of the repetition of "big," "fat," and "mug" throughout the poem? What other patterns of repetition can you find? Why does the speaker repeat those specific words when he does?

CONNECTION TO ANOTHER SELECTION

1. Write a reply to the speaker in "Song to a Waitress" from the point of view of the waitress. You might begin by writing a prose paragraph and then try organizing it into lines of poetry. Read Machan's "Hazel Tells LaVerne" (p. 725) for a source of inspiration.

EDWARD HIRSCH (B. 1950)

Fast Break   1985

(In Memory of Dennis Turner, 1946–1984)

A hook shot kisses the rim and
hangs there, helplessly, but doesn't drop

and for once our gangly starting center
boxes out his man and times his jump

perfectly, gathering the orange leather   5
from the air like a cherished possession

and spinning around to throw a strike
to the outlet who is already shoveling

an underhand pass toward the other guard
scissoring past a flat-footed defender   10

who looks stunned and nailed to the floor
in the wrong direction, turning to catch sight

of a high, gliding dribble and a man
letting the play develop in front of him

in slow motion, almost exactly   15
like a coach's drawing on the blackboard,

both forwards racing down the court
the way that forwards should, fanning out

and filling the lanes in tandem, moving
together as brothers passing the ball   20

between them without a dribble, without
a single bounce hitting the hardwood

until the guard finally lunges out
and commits to the wrong man

while the power-forward explodes past them   25
in a fury, taking the ball into the air

by himself now and laying it gently
against the glass for a layup,

but losing his balance in the process,
inexplicably falling, hitting the floor   30

with a wild, headlong motion
for the game he loved like a country

and swiveling back to see an orange blur
floating perfectly through the net.

Considerations for Critical Thinking and Writing

1. FIRST RESPONSE. How might this poem — to borrow a phrase from Robert
   Frost — represent a "momentary stay against confusion"?

2. Why are run-on lines especially appropriate for this poem? How do they
   affect its sound and sense? Do the lines have a regular meter? What is the
   effect of the poem being one long sentence?

3. In addition to accurately describing a fast break, this poem is a tribute to a
   dead friend. How are the two purposes related in the poem?

GREG WILLIAMSON (B. 1964)

Waterfall   *1995*

In still transparency, the water pools
    High in a mountain stream, then spills
Over the lip and in a sheet cascades
Across the shoal, obeying hidden rules,
        So that the pleats and braids,   5
The feather-stitched white water, little rills
    And divots seem to ride in place
    Above the crevices and sills,
Although the water runs along the race.

What makes these rapids, this little waterfall,   10
    Cascading like a chandelier
Of frosted glass or like a willow tree,
Is not the water only nor the fall
        But some complicity
Of both, so that these similes appear   15
    Inaccurate and limited,
    Neglecting that the bed will steer
The water as the water steers the bed.

So too with language, so even with this verse.
    From a pool of syllables, words hover   20
With rich potential, then spill across the lip

And riffle down the page, for better or worse,
    Making their chancy trip,
Becoming sentences as they discover
    (Now flowing, now seeming to stammer)   25
    Their English channels, trickling over
The periodic pauses of its grammar.

CONSIDERATIONS FOR CRITICAL THINKING AND WRITING

1. FIRST RESPONSE. Comment on the rhythm of the lines. How do the varying meters flow with the movements described?

2. Is this poem primarily about a waterfall or writing poetry — or both? Explain your answer.

3. In what ways can stanza 2 be considered a transitional device between stanzas 1 and 3?

4. How well does stanza 3 explain how poetry is created?

PERSPECTIVE

LOUISE BOGAN (1897–1970)

On Formal Poetry   *1953*

What is formal poetry? It is poetry written in form. And what is *form?* The elements of form, so far as poetry is concerned, are meter and rhyme. Are these elements merely mold and ornaments that have been impressed upon poetry from without? Are they indeed restrictions which bind and fetter language and the thought and emotion behind, under, within language in a repressive way? Are they arbitrary rules which have lost all validity since they have been broken to good purpose by "experimental poets," ancient and modern? Does the breaking up of form, or its total elimination, always result in an increase of power and of effect; and is any return to form a sort of relinquishment of freedom, or retreat to old fogeyism?

                                 From *A Poet's Alphabet*

CONSIDERATIONS FOR CRITICAL THINKING AND WRITING

1. Choose one of the questions Bogan raises and write an essay in response to it using two or three poems from this chapter to illustrate your answer.

2. Try writing a poem in meter and rhyme. Does the experience make your writing feel limited or not?

22

Poetic Forms

Poems come in a variety of shapes. Although the best poems always have their own unique qualities, many of them also conform to traditional patterns. Frequently the *form* of a poem — its overall structure or shape — follows an already established design. A poem that can be categorized by the patterns of its lines, meter, rhymes, and stanzas is considered a *fixed form* because it follows a prescribed model such as a sonnet. However, poems written in a fixed form do not always fit models precisely; writers sometimes work variations on traditional forms to create innovative effects.

Not all poets are content with variations on traditional forms. Some prefer to create their own structures and shapes. Poems that do not conform to established patterns of meter, rhyme, and stanza are called *free verse* or *open form* poetry. (See Chapter 23 for further discussion of open forms.) This kind of poetry creates its own ordering principles through the careful arrangement of words and phrases in line lengths that embody rhythms appropriate to the meaning. Modern and contemporary poets in particular have learned to use the blank space on the page as a significant functional element (for a striking example, see Cummings's "l(a," p. 687). Good poetry of this kind is structured in ways that can be as demanding, interesting, and satisfying as fixed forms. Open and fixed forms represent different poetic styles, but they are identical in the sense that both use language in concentrated ways to convey meanings, experiences, emotions, and effects.

SOME COMMON POETIC FORMS

A familiarity with some of the most frequently used fixed forms of poetry is useful because it allows for a better understanding of how a poem works. Classifying patterns allows us to talk about the effects of established rhythm and rhyme and recognize how significant variations from them affect the pace and meaning of the lines. An awareness of form also allows us to anticipate how a poem is likely to proceed. As we shall see, a sonnet creates a different set of expectations in a reader from those of, say, a limerick. A reader isn't likely to find in limericks the kind of serious themes that often make their way into sonnets. The discussion that follows identifies some of the important poetic forms frequently encountered in English poetry.

The shape of a fixed form poem is often determined by the way in which the lines are organized into stanzas. A *stanza* consists of a grouping of lines, set off by a space, that usually has a set pattern of meter and rhyme. This pattern is ordinarily repeated in other stanzas throughout the poem. What is usual is not obligatory, however; some poems may use a different pattern for each stanza, somewhat like paragraphs in prose.

Traditionally, though, stanzas do share a common *rhyme scheme,* the pattern of end rhymes. We can map out rhyme schemes by noting patterns of rhyme with lowercase letters: the first rhyme sound is designated *a,* the second becomes *b,* the third *c,* and so on. Using this system, we can describe the rhyme scheme in the following poem this way: *aabb, ccdd, eeff.*

A. E. HOUSMAN (1859–1936)

Loveliest of trees, the cherry now   1896

Loveliest of trees, the cherry now	*a*
Is hung with bloom along the bough,	*a*
And stands about the woodland ride	*b*
Wearing white for Eastertide.	*b*
Now, of my threescore years and ten,	*c*
Twenty will not come again,	*c*
And take from seventy springs a score,	*d*
It only leaves me fifty more.	*d*
And since to look at things in bloom	*e*
Fifty springs are little room,	*e*
About the woodlands I will go	*f*
To see the cherry hung with snow.	*f*

(Line numbers: 5 at "Now, of my threescore years and ten,"; 10 at "Fifty springs are little room,")

CONSIDERATIONS FOR CRITICAL THINKING AND WRITING

1. FIRST RESPONSE. What is the speaker's attitude in this poem toward time and life?

2. Why is spring an appropriate season for the setting rather than, say, winter?

3. Paraphrase each stanza. How do the images in each reinforce the poem's themes?

4. Lines 1 and 12 are not intended to rhyme, but they are close. What is the effect of the near rhyme of "now" and "snow"? How does the rhyme enhance the theme?

Poets often create their own stanzaic patterns; hence there is an infinite number of kinds of stanzas. One way of talking about stanzaic forms is to describe a given stanza by how many lines it contains.

A *couplet* consists of two lines that usually rhyme and have the same meter; couplets are frequently not separated from each other by space on the page. A *heroic couplet* consists of rhymed iambic pentameter. Here is an example from Pope's "An Essay on Criticism":

One science only will one genius fit;	*a*
So vast is art, so narrow human wit:	*a*
Not only bounded to peculiar arts,	*b*
But oft in those confined to single parts.	*b*

A *tercet* is a three-line stanza. When all three lines rhyme they are called a *triplet*. Two triplets make up this captivating poem.

ROBERT HERRICK (1591–1674)

Upon Julia's Clothes 1648

Whenas in silks my Julia goes,	*a*
Then, then, methinks, how sweetly flows	*a*
That liquefaction of her clothes.	*a*
Next, when I cast mine eyes, and see	*b*
That brave vibration, each way free,	*b*
O, how that glittering taketh me!	*b*

CONSIDERATIONS FOR CRITICAL THINKING AND WRITING

1. FIRST RESPONSE. What purpose does alliteration serve in this poem?
2. Comment on the effect of the meter. How is it related to the speaker's description of Julia's clothes?
3. Look up the word *brave* in the *Oxford English Dictionary*. Which of its meanings is appropriate to describe Julia's movement? Some readers interpret lines 4–6 to mean that Julia has no clothes on. What do you think?

CONNECTION TO ANOTHER SELECTION

1. Compare the tone of this poem with that of Humphrey's "Blow" (p. 850). Are the situations and speakers similar? Is there any difference in tone between these two poems?

Terza rima consists of an interlocking three-line rhyme scheme: *aba, bcb, cdc, ded,* and so on. Dante's *The Divine Comedy* uses this pattern, as does Frost's "Acquainted with the Night" (p. 798) and Percy Bysshe Shelley's "Ode to the West Wind" (p. 894).

A *quatrain,* or four-line stanza, is the most common stanzaic form in the English language and can have various meters and rhyme schemes (if any). The most common rhyme schemes are *aabb, abba, aaba,* and *abcb.* This last pattern is especially characteristic of the popular **ballad stanza,** which consists of alternating eight- and six-syllable lines. Samuel Taylor Coleridge adopted this pattern in "The Rime of the Ancient Mariner"; here is one representative stanza:

> All in a hot and copper sky
> The bloody Sun, at noon,
> Right up above the mast did stand,
> No bigger than the Moon.

There are a number of longer stanzaic forms and the list of types of stanzas could be extended considerably, but knowing these three most basic patterns should prove helpful to you in talking about the form of a great many poems. In addition to stanzaic forms, there are fixed forms that characterize entire poems. Lyric poems can be, for example, sonnets, villanelles, sestinas, or epigrams.

Sonnet

The **sonnet** has been a popular literary form in English since the sixteenth century, when it was adopted from the Italian *sonnetto,* meaning "little song." A sonnet consists of fourteen lines, usually written in iambic pentameter. Because the sonnet has been such a favorite form, writers have experimented with many variations on its essential structure. Nevertheless, there are two basic types of sonnets: the Italian and the English.

The **Italian sonnet** (also known as the **Petrarchan sonnet,** from the fourteenth-century Italian poet Petrarch) divides into two parts. The first eight lines (the **octave**) typically rhyme *abbaabba.* The final six lines (the **sestet**) may vary; common patterns are *cdecde, cdcdcd,* and *cdccdc.* Very often the octave presents a situation, attitude, or problem that the sestet comments upon or resolves, as in John Keats's "On First Looking into Chapman's Homer."

JOHN KEATS (1795–1821)

On First Looking into Chapman's Homer°   1816

Much have I traveled in the realms of gold,
   And many goodly states and kingdoms seen;
   Round many western islands have I been
Which bards in fealty to Apollo° hold.
Oft of one wide expanse had I been told   5

Chapman's Homer: Before reading George Chapman's (c. 1560–1634) poetic Elizabethan translations of Homer's *Iliad* and *Odyssey,* Keats had known only stilted and pedestrian eighteenth-century translations.   4 *Apollo:* Greek god of poetry.

That deep-browed Homer ruled as his demesne;
  Yet did I never breathe its pure serene°   *atmosphere*
Till I heard Chapman speak out loud and bold:
Then felt I like some watcher of the skies
  When a new planet swims into his ken;   10
Or like stout Cortez° when with eagle eyes
  He stared at the Pacific — and all his men
Looked at each other with a wild surmise —
  Silent, upon a peak in Darien.

11 *Cortez:* Vasco Núñez de Balboa, not Hernando Cortés, was the first European to sight the Pacific from Darien, a peak in Panama.

CONSIDERATIONS FOR CRITICAL THINKING AND WRITING

1. FIRST RESPONSE. How do the images shift from the octave to the sestet? How does the tone change? Does the meaning?
2. What is the controlling metaphor of this poem?
3. What is it that the speaker discovers?
4. How does the rhythm of the lines change between the octave and the sestet? How does that change reflect the tones of both the octave and the sestet?
5. Does Keats's mistake concerning Cortés and Balboa affect your reading of the poem? Explain why or why not.

The Italian sonnet pattern is also used in the next sonnet, but notice that the thematic break between octave and sestet comes within line 9 rather than between lines 8 and 9. This unconventional break helps to reinforce the speaker's impatience with the conventional attitudes he describes.

WILLIAM WORDSWORTH (1770–1850)

The World Is Too Much with Us   *1807*

The world is too much with us; late and soon,
Getting and spending, we lay waste our powers;
Little we see in Nature that is ours;
We have given our hearts away, a sordid boon!
This Sea that bares her bosom to the moon;   5
The winds that will be howling at all hours,
And are up-gathered now like sleeping flowers;
For this, for everything, we are out of tune;
It moves us not. — Great God! I'd rather be
A Pagan suckled in a creed outworn;   10
So might I, standing on this pleasant lea,
Have glimpses that would make me less forlorn;
Have sight of Proteus rising from the sea;
Or hear old Triton blow his wreathèd horn.

CONSIDERATIONS FOR CRITICAL THINKING AND WRITING

1. FIRST RESPONSE. What is the speaker's complaint in this sonnet? How do the conditions described affect him?

2. Look up "Proteus" and "Triton." What do these mythological allusions contribute to the sonnet's tone?

3. What is the effect of the personification of the sea and wind in the octave?

CONNECTION TO ANOTHER SELECTION

1. Compare the theme of this sonnet with that of Hopkins's "God's Grandeur" (p. 837).

The **English sonnet,** more commonly known as the **Shakespearean sonnet,** is organized into three quatrains and a couplet, which typically rhyme *abab cdcd efef gg.* This rhyme scheme is more suited to English poetry because English has fewer rhyming words than Italian. English sonnets, because of their four-part organization, also have more flexibility about where thematic breaks can occur. Frequently, however, the most pronounced break or turn comes with the concluding couplet.

In the following Shakespearean sonnet, the three quatrains compare the speaker's loved one to a summer's day and explain why the loved one is even more lovely. The couplet bestows eternal beauty and love upon both the loved one and the sonnet.

WILLIAM SHAKESPEARE (1564–1616)

Shall I compare thee to a summer's day?   1609

Shall I compare thee to a summer's day?
Thou art more lovely and more temperate:
Rough winds do shake the darling buds of May,
And summer's lease hath all too short a date.
Sometime too hot the eye of heaven shines,   5
And often is his gold complexion dimmed;
And every fair from fair sometime declines,
By chance, or nature's changing course, untrimmed.
But thy eternal summer shall not fade,
Nor lose possession of that fair thou ow'st°   *possess* 10
Nor shall death brag thou wand'rest in his shade,
When in eternal lines to time thou grow'st.
        So long as men can breathe or eyes can see,
        So long lives this, and this gives life to thee.

CONSIDERATIONS FOR CRITICAL THINKING AND WRITING

1. FIRST RESPONSE. Describe the shift in tone and subject matter that begins in line 9.

2. Why is the speaker's loved one more lovely than a summer's day? What qualities does he admire in the loved one?
3. What does the couplet say about the relation between art and love?
4. Which syllables are stressed in the final line? How do these syllables relate to the meaning of the line?

Sonnets have been the vehicles for all kinds of subjects, including love, death, politics, and cosmic questions. Although most sonnets tend to treat their subjects seriously, this fixed form does not mean a fixed expression; humor is also possible in it. Compare this next Shakespearean sonnet with "Shall I compare thee to a summer's day?" They are, finally, both love poems, but their tones are markedly different.

WILLIAM SHAKESPEARE (1564–1616)
My mistress' eyes are nothing like the sun   1609

My mistress' eyes are nothing like the sun;
Coral is far more red than her lips' red;
If snow be white, why then her breasts are dun;
If hairs be wires, black wires grow on her head.
I have seen roses damasked red and white,   5
But no such roses see I in her cheeks;
And in some perfumes is there more delight
Than in the breath that from my mistress reeks.
I love to hear her speak, yet well I know
That music hath a far more pleasing sound;   10
I grant I never saw a goddess go:
My mistress, when she walks, treads on the ground.
      And yet, by heaven, I think my love as rare
      As any she,° belied with false compare.   *lady*

CONSIDERATIONS FOR CRITICAL THINKING AND WRITING

1. FIRST RESPONSE. What does "mistress" mean in this sonnet? Write a description of this particular mistress based on the images used in the sonnet.
2. What sort of person is the speaker? Does he truly love the woman he describes?
3. In what sense are this sonnet and "Shall I compare thee" about poetry as well as love?

EDNA ST. VINCENT MILLAY (1892–1950)
I will put Chaos into fourteen lines   1954

I will put Chaos into fourteen lines
And keep him there; and let him thence escape
If he be lucky; let him twist, and ape
Flood, fire, and demon — his adroit designs

Will strain to nothing in the strict confines   5
Of this sweet Order, where, in pious rape,
I hold his essence and amorphous shape,
Till he with Order mingles and combines.
Past are the hours, the years, of our duress,
His arrogance, our awful servitude: 10
I have him. He is nothing more nor less
Than something simple not yet understood;
I shall not even force him to confess;
Or answer. I will only make him good.

CONSIDERATIONS FOR CRITICAL THINKING AND WRITING

1. FIRST RESPONSE. Does the poem contain "Chaos"? If so, how? If not, why not?
2. What properties of a sonnet does this poem possess?
3. What do you think is meant by the phrase "pious rape" in line 6?
4. What is the effect of the personification in the poem?

CONNECTION TO ANOTHER SELECTION

1. Compare the theme of this poem with that of Robert Frost's "Design" (p. 993).

MOLLY PEACOCK (B. 1947)

Desire   *1984*

It doesn't speak and it isn't schooled,
like a small foetal animal with wettened fur.
It is the blind instinct for life unruled,
visceral frankincense and animal myrrh.
It is what babies bring to kings,   5
an eyes-shut, ears-shut medicine of the heart
that smells and touches endings and beginnings
without the details of time's experienced *part-*
fit-into-part-fit-into-part. Like a paw,
it is blunt; like a pet who knows you   10
and nudges your knee with its snout — but more raw
and blinder and younger and more divine, too,
than the tamed wild — it's the drive for what is real,
deeper than the brain's detail: the drive to feel.

CONSIDERATIONS FOR CRITICAL THINKING AND WRITING

1. FIRST RESPONSE. Taken together, what do all the metaphors that appear in this poem reveal about the speaker's conception of desire?
2. What is the "it" being described in lines 3–5? How do the allusions to the three wise men relate to the other metaphors used to define desire?
3. How is this English sonnet structured? What is the effect of its irregular meter?

1. Compare the treatment of desire in this poem with that of Ackerman's "A Fine, a Private Place" (p. 734). In an essay, identify the theme of each poem and compare their conceptions of desire. How alike are these two poems?

MARK JARMAN (B. 1952)

Unholy Sonnet   *1993*

After the praying, after the hymn-singing,
After the sermon's trenchant commentary
On the world's ills, which make ours secondary,
After communion, after the hand-wringing,
And after peace descends upon us, bringing   5
Our eyes up to regard the sanctuary
And how the light swords through it, and how, scary
In their sheer numbers, motes of dust ride, clinging—
There is, as doctors say about some pain,
Discomfort knowing that despite your prayers,   10
Your listening and rejoicing, your small part
In this communal stab at coming clean,
There is one stubborn remnant of your cares
Intact. There is still murder in your heart.

CONSIDERATIONS FOR CRITICAL THINKING AND WRITING

1. FIRST RESPONSE. Describe the rhyme scheme and structure of this sonnet. Explain why it is an English or Italian sonnet.

2. What are the effects of the use of "after" in lines 1, 2, 4, and 5 and "there" in lines 9, 13, and 14?

3. In what sense might this poem be summed up as a "communal stab" (line 12)? Discuss the accuracy of this assessment.

4. Try writing a reply to the theme of Jarman's poem using the same sonnet form that he uses.

CONNECTIONS TO OTHER SELECTIONS

1. Jarman has said that his "Unholy Sonnets" (there are about twenty of them) are modeled after John Donne's *Holy Sonnets* but that he does not share the same Christian assumptions about faith and mercy that inform Donne's sonnets. Instead, Jarman says, he "work[s] against any assumption or shared expression of faith, to write a devotional poetry against the grain." Keeping this statement in mind, write an essay comparing and contrasting the tone and theme of Jarman's sonnet with John Donne's "Batter My Heart" (p. 1089) or "Death Be Not Proud" (p. 1090).

Villanelle

The *villanelle* is a fixed form consisting of nineteen lines of any length divided into six stanzas: five tercets and a concluding quatrain. The first and third lines of the initial tercet rhyme; these rhymes are repeated in each subsequent tercet (*aba*) and in the final two lines of the quatrain (*abaa*). Moreover, line 1 appears in its entirety as lines 6, 12, and 18, while line 3 appears as lines 9, 15, and 19. This form may seem to risk monotony, but in competent hands a villanelle can create haunting echoes, as in Dylan Thomas's "Do not go gentle into that good night."

DYLAN THOMAS (1914–1953)

Do not go gentle into that good night   *1952*

Do not go gentle into that good night,
Old age should burn and rave at close of day;
Rage, rage against the dying of the light.

Though wise men at their end know dark is right,
Because their words had forked no lightning they   5
Do not go gentle into that good night.

Good men, the last wave by, crying how bright
Their frail deeds might have danced in a green bay,
Rage, rage against the dying of the light.

Wild men who caught and sang the sun in flight,   10
And learn, too late, they grieved it on its way,
Do not go gentle into that good night.

Grave men, near death, who see with blinding sight
Blind eyes could blaze like meteors and be gay,
Rage, rage against the dying of the light.   15

And you, my father, there on the sad height,
Curse, bless, me now with your fierce tears, I pray.
Do not go gentle into that good night.
Rage, rage against the dying of the light.

CONSIDERATIONS FOR CRITICAL THINKING AND WRITING

1. FIRST RESPONSE. How does Thomas vary the meanings of the poem's two refrains: "Do not go gentle into that good night," and "Rage, rage against the dying of the light"?

2. Thomas's father was close to death when this poem was written. How does the tone contribute to the poem's theme?

3. How is "good" used in line 1?

4. Characterize the men who are "wise" (line 4), "Good" (7), "Wild" (10), and "Grave" (13).

5. What do figures of speech contribute to this poem?

6. Discuss this villanelle's sound effects.

CONNECTION TO ANOTHER SELECTION

1. In Thomas's poem we experience "rage against the dying of the light." Contrast this with the rage you find in Sylvia Plath's "Daddy" (p. 1113). What produces the emotion in Plath's poem?

Julia Alvarez (b. 1950)

Woman's Work   *1996*

Who says a woman's work isn't high art?
She'd challenge as she scrubbed the bathroom tiles.
Keep house as if the address were your heart.

We'd clean the whole upstairs before we'd start
downstairs. I'd sigh, hearing my friends outside.   5
Doing her woman's work was a hard art

to practice when the summer sun would bar
the floor I swept till she was satisfied.
She kept me prisoner in her housebound heart.

She'd shine the tines of forks, the wheels of carts,   10
cut lacy lattices for all her pies.
Her woman's work was nothing less than art.

And, I, her masterpiece since I was smart,
was primed, praised, polished, scolded and advised
to keep a house much better than my heart.   15

I did not want to be her counterpart!
I struck out . . . but became my mother's child:
a woman working at home on her art,
housekeeping paper as if it were her heart.

Considerations for Critical Thinking and Writing

1. FIRST RESPONSE. Characterize the mother and daughter. How are they similar to one another?

2. How is the structure of this poem different from a conventional villanelle? How do these differences contribute to the speaker's description of "woman's work"?

3. How does the concluding quatrain make an important distinction between the mother and daughter while redefining "woman's work"?

Connection to Another Selection

1. Compare and contrast the themes and tone of "Woman's Work" and Thomas's "Do not go gentle into that good night." Will the speaker in Alvarez's poem "go gentle into that good night"? Would the speaker in Thomas's call woman's work, as described above, "high art"?

Sestina

Although the *sestina* usually does not rhyme, it is perhaps an even more demanding fixed form than the villanelle. A sestina consists of thirty-nine lines of any length divided into six, six-line stanzas and a three-line concluding stanza called an *envoy*. The difficulty is in repeating the six words at the ends of the first stanza's lines at the ends of the lines in the other five, six-line stanzas as well. Those words must also appear in the final three lines, where they often resonate important themes. The sestina originated in the Middle Ages, but contemporary poets continue to find it a fascinating and challenging form.

ELIZABETH BISHOP (1911–1979)

Sestina   1965

September rain falls on the house.
In the failing light, the old grandmother
sits in the kitchen with the child
beside the Little Marvel Stove,
reading the jokes from the almanac,   5
laughing and talking to hide her tears.

She thinks that her equinoctial tears
and the rain that beats on the roof of the house
were both foretold by the almanac,
but only known to a grandmother.   10
The iron kettle sings on the stove.
She cuts some bread and says to the child,

It's time for tea now; but the child
is watching the teakettle's small hard tears
dance like mad on the hot black stove,   15
the way the rain must dance on the house.
Tidying up, the old grandmother
hangs up the clever almanac

on its string. Birdlike, the almanac
hovers half open above the child,   20
hovers above the old grandmother
and her teacup full of dark brown tears.
She shivers and says she thinks the house
feels chilly, and puts more wood in the stove.

It was to be, says the Marvel Stove.   25
I know what I know, says the almanac.
With crayons the child draws a rigid house
and a winding pathway. Then the child
puts in a man with buttons like tears
and shows it proudly to the grandmother.   30

But secretly, while the grandmother
busies herself about the stove,
the little moons fall down like tears
from between the pages of the almanac
into the flower bed the child   35
has carefully placed in the front of the house.

Time to plant tears, says the almanac.
The grandmother sings to the marvelous stove
and the child draws another inscrutable house.

CONSIDERATIONS FOR CRITICAL THINKING AND WRITING

1. FIRST RESPONSE. How are the six end words — "house," "grandmother," "child," "stove," "almanac," and "tears" — central to the sestina's meaning?

2. Number the end words of the first stanza 1, 2, 3, 4, 5, and 6, and then use those numbers for the corresponding end words in the remaining five stanzas to see how the pattern of the line-end words is worked out in this sestina. Also locate the six end words in the envoy.

3. What happens in this sestina? Why is the grandmother "laughing and talking to hide her tears" (line 6)?

4. Underline the images that seem especially vivid to you. What effects do they create? What is the tone of the sestina?

5. How is the almanac used symbolically? Does Bishop use any other symbols to convey meanings?

6. Write a brief essay explaining why you think a poet might derive pleasure from writing in a fixed form such as a villanelle or sestina. Can you think of similar activities outside the field of writing in which discipline and restraint give pleasure?

FLORENCE CASSEN MAYERS (B. 1940)

All-American Sestina   1996

One nation, indivisible
two-car garage
three strikes you're out
four-minute mile
five-cent cigar
six-string guitar   5

six-pack Bud
one-day sale
five-year warranty
two-way street
fourscore and seven years ago   10
three cheers

three-star restaurant
sixty-
four-dollar question   15
one-night stand
two-pound lobster
five-star general

five-course meal
three sheets to the wind   20
two bits
six-shooter
one-armed bandit
four-poster

four-wheel drive   25
five-and-dime

hole in one
three-alarm fire
sweet sixteen
two-wheeler   30

two-tone Chevy
four rms, hi flr, w/vu
six-footer
high five
three-ring circus   35
one-room schoolhouse

two thumbs up, five-karat diamond
Fourth of July, three-piece suit
six feet under, one-horse town

Considerations for Critical Thinking and Writing

1. FIRST RESPONSE. Discuss the significance of the title; what is "All-American"? Why a sestina?

2. How is the structure of this poem different from a conventional sestina? (What structural requirement does Mayers add for this sestina?)

3. Do you think important themes are raised by this poem, as is traditional for a sestina? If so, what are they? If not, what is being played with by using this convention?

Connection to Another Selection

1. Describe and compare the strategy used to create meaning in "All-American Sestina" with that used by Cummings in "next to of course god america i" (p. 805).

Epigram

An *epigram* is a brief, pointed, and witty poem. Although most rhyme and often are written in couplets, epigrams take no prescribed form. Instead, they are typically polished bits of compressed irony, satire, or paradox. Here is an epigram that defines itself.

Samuel Taylor Coleridge (1772–1834)

What Is an Epigram?   1802

What is an epigram? A dwarfish whole;
Its body brevity, and wit its soul.

These additional examples by A. R. Ammons, David McCord, and Paul Laurence Dunbar satisfy Coleridge's definition.

A. R. AMMONS (B. 1926)

Coward

1975

Bravery runs in my family.

DAVID MCCORD (1897–1997)

Epitaph on a Waiter

1954

By and by
God caught his eye.

PAUL LAURENCE DUNBAR (1872–1906)

Theology

1896

There is a heaven, for ever, day by day,
The upward longing of my soul doth tell me so.
There is a hell, I'm quite as sure; for pray,
If there were not, where would my neighbors go?

CONSIDERATIONS FOR CRITICAL THINKING AND WRITING

1. FIRST RESPONSE. In what sense is each of these epigrams, as Coleridge puts it, a "dwarfish whole"?

2. Explain which of these epigrams, in addition to being witty, makes a serious point.

3. Try writing a few epigrams that say something memorable about whatever you choose to focus upon.

Limerick

The *limerick* is always light and humorous. Its usual form consists of five predominantly anapestic lines rhyming *aabba;* lines 1, 2, and 5 contain three feet, while lines 3 and 4 contain two. Limericks have delighted everyone from schoolchildren to sophisticated adults, and they range in subject matter from the simply innocent and silly to the satiric or obscene. The sexual humor helps to explain why so many limericks are written anonymously. Here is one that is anonymous but more concerned with physics than physiology:

There was a young lady named Bright,
Who traveled much faster than light,
     She started one day
     In a relative way,
And returned on the previous night.

This next one is a particularly clever definition of a limerick.

LAURENCE PERRINE (B. 1915)

The limerick's never averse   *1982*

The limerick's never averse
To expressing itself in a terse
   Economical style,
   And yet, all the while,
The limerick's *always* a verse.

CONSIDERATIONS FOR CRITICAL THINKING AND WRITING

1. FIRST RESPONSE. How does this limerick differ from others you know? How is it similar?

2. Scan Perrine's limerick. How do the lines measure up to the traditional fixed metrical pattern?

3. Try writing a limerick. Use the following basic pattern.

You might begin with a friend's name or the name of your school or town. Your instructor is, of course, fair game, too, provided your tact matches your wit.

Haiku

Another brief fixed poetic form, borrowed from the Japanese, is the *haiku*. A haiku is usually described as consisting of seventeen syllables organized into three unrhymed lines of five, seven, and five syllables. Owing to language difference, however, English translations of haiku are often only approximated, because a Japanese haiku exists in time (Japanese syllables have duration). The number of syllables in our sense is not as significant as the duration. These poems typically present an intense emotion or vivid image of nature, which, in the Japanese, are also designed to lead to a spiritual insight.

MATSUO BASHŌ (1644–1694)

Under cherry trees   *date unknown*

Under cherry trees
Soup, the salad, fish and all . . .
Seasoned with petals.

ETHERIDGE KNIGHT (B. 1931)

Eastern Guard Tower   1968

Eastern guard tower
glints in sunset; convicts rest
like lizards on rocks.

CONSIDERATIONS FOR CRITICAL THINKING AND WRITING

1. FIRST RESPONSE. What different emotions do these two haiku evoke?
2. What differences and similarities are there between the effects of a haiku and those of an epigram?
3. Compose a haiku. Try to make it as allusive and suggestive as possible.

Elegy

An elegy in classical Greek and Roman literature was written in alternating hexameter and pentameter lines. Since the seventeenth century, however, the term *elegy* has been used to describe a lyric poem written to commemorate someone who is dead. The word is also used to refer to a serious meditative poem produced to express the speaker's melancholy thoughts. Elegies no longer conform to a fixed pattern of lines and stanzas, but their characteristic subject is related to death and their tone is mournfully contemplative.

SEAMUS HEANEY (B. 1939)

Mid-term Break   1966

I sat all morning in the college sick bay
Counting bells knelling classes to a close.
At two o'clock our neighbors drove me home.

In the porch I met my father crying—
He had always taken funerals in his stride—   5
And Big Jim Evans saying it was a hard blow.

The baby cooed and laughed and rocked the pram
When I came in, and I was embarrassed
By old men standing up to shake my hand

And tell me they were "sorry for my trouble,"   10
Whispers informed strangers I was the eldest,
Away at school, as my mother held my hand

In hers and coughed out angry tearless sighs.
At ten o'clock the ambulance arrived
With the corpse, stanched and bandaged by the nurses.   15

Next morning I went up into the room. Snowdrops
And candles soothed the bedside; I saw him
For the first time in six weeks. Paler now,

Wearing a poppy bruise on his left temple,
He lay in the four foot box as in his cot.   20
No gaudy scars, the bumper knocked him clear.

A four foot box, a foot for every year.

CONSIDERATIONS FOR CRITICAL THINKING AND WRITING

1. FIRST RESPONSE. What effect does the title have on your understanding of
   the speaker? What else does the title imply?

2. How do simple details contribute to the effects of this elegy?

3. Does this elegy use any kind of formal pattern for its structure? What is the
   effect of the last line standing by itself?

4. Another spelling for *stanched* (line 15) is *staunched*. Usage is about evenly divided between the two in the United States. What is the effect of Heaney's
   choosing the former spelling rather than the latter?

CONNECTIONS TO OTHER SELECTIONS

1. Compare Heaney's elegy with A. E. Housman's "To an Athlete Dying
   Young" (p. 1101). Which do you find more moving? Explain why.

2. Write an essay comparing this story of a boy's death with Updike's "Dog's
   Death" (p. 673). Do you think either of the poems is sentimental? Explain
   why or why not.

ANDREW HUDGINS (B. 1951)
Elegy for My Father, Who Is Not Dead   *1991*

One day I'll lift the telephone
and be told my father's dead. He's ready.
In the sureness of his faith, he talks
about the world beyond this world
as though his reservations have   5
been made. I think he wants to go,
a little bit — a new desire
to travel building up, an itch
to see fresh worlds. Or older ones.
He thinks that when I follow him   10
he'll wrap me in his arms and laugh,
the way he did when I arrived
on earth. I do not think he's right.
He's ready. I am not. I can't
just say good-bye as cheerfully   15
as if he were embarking on a trip

to make my later trip go well.
I see myself on deck, convinced
his ship's gone down, while he's convinced
I'll see him standing on the dock   20
and waving, shouting, Welcome back.

CONSIDERATIONS FOR CRITICAL THINKING AND WRITING

1. FIRST RESPONSE. Why does this speaker elegize his father if the father "is not dead"?
2. How does the speaker's view of immortality differ from his father's?
3. Explain why you think this is an optimistic or pessimistic poem — or explain why these two categories fail to describe the poem.
4. In what sense can this poem be regarded as an elegy?

CONNECTION TO ANOTHER SELECTION

1. Write an essay comparing attitudes toward death in this poem and in Thomas's "Do not go gentle into that good night" (p. 885). Both speakers invoke their fathers, nearer to death than they are; what impact does this have?

Ode

An **ode** is characterized by a serious topic and formal tone, but no prescribed formal pattern describes all odes. In some odes the pattern of each stanza is repeated throughout, while in others each stanza introduces a new pattern. Odes are lengthy lyrics that often include lofty emotions conveyed by a dignified style. Typical topics include truth, art, freedom, justice, and the meaning of life. Frequently such lyrics tend to be more public than private, and their speakers often employ apostrophe.

PERCY BYSSHE SHELLEY (1792–1822)
Ode to the West Wind   *1820*

I
O wild West Wind, thou breath of Autumn's being,
Thou, from whose unseen presence the leaves dead
Are driven, like ghosts from an enchanter fleeing,

Yellow, and black, and pale, and hectic red,
Pestilence-stricken multitudes: O thou,   5
Who chariotest to their dark wintry bed

The wingèd seeds, where they lie cold and low,
Each like a corpse within its grave, until
Thine azure sister of the Spring shall blow

Her clarion o'er the dreaming earth, and fill   10
(Driving sweet buds like flocks to feed in air)
With living hues and odors plain and hill:

Wild Spirit, which art moving everywhere;
Destroyer and preserver; hear, oh, hear!

II
Thou on whose stream, mid the steep sky's commotion,   15
Loose clouds like earth's decaying leaves are shed,
Shook from the tangled boughs of Heaven and Ocean,

Angels° of rain and lightning: there are spread   *messengers*
On the blue surface of thine airy surge,
Like the bright hair uplifted from the head   20

Of some fierce Maenad,° even from the dim verge
Of the horizon to the zenith's height,
The locks of the approaching storm. Thou dirge

Of the dying year, to which this closing night
Will be the dome of a vast sepulcher,   25
Vaulted with all thy congregated might

Of vapors, from whose solid atmosphere
Black rain, and fire, and hail will burst: oh, hear!

III
Thou who didst waken from his summer dreams
The blue Mediterranean, where he lay,   30
Lulled by the coil of his crystálline streams,

Beside a pumice isle in Baiae's bay,°
And saw in sleep old palaces and towers
Quivering within the wave's intenser day,

All overgrown with azure moss and flowers   35
So sweet, the sense faints picturing them! Thou
For whose path the Atlantic's level powers

Cleave themselves into chasms, while far below
The sea-blooms and the oozy woods which wear
The sapless foliage of the ocean, know   40

Thy voice, and suddenly grow gray with fear,
And tremble and despoil themselves: oh, hear!

IV
If I were a dead leaf thou mightest bear;
If I were a swift cloud to fly with thee;
A wave to pant beneath thy power, and share   45

---

21 *Maenad:* In Greek mythology, a frenzied worshiper of Dionysus, god of wine and fertility.
32 *Baiae's bay:* A bay in the Mediterranean Sea.

The impulse of thy strength, only less free
Than thou, O uncontrollable! If even
I were as in my boyhood, and could be

The comrade by thy wanderings over Heaven,
As then, when to outstrip thy skyey speed   50
Scarce seemed a vision; I would ne'er have striven

As thus with thee in prayer in my sore need.
Oh, lift me as a wave, a leaf, a cloud!
I fall upon the thorns of life! I bleed!

A heavy weight of hours has chained and bowed   55
One too like thee: tameless, and swift, and proud.

V
Make me thy lyre,° even as the forest is:
What if my leaves are falling like its own!
The tumult of thy mighty harmonies

Will take from both a deep, autumnal tone,   60
Sweet though in sadness. Be thou, Spirit fierce,
My spirit! Be thou me, impetuous one!

Drive my dead thoughts over the universe
Like withered leaves to quicken a new birth!
And, by the incantation of this verse,   65

Scatter, as from an unextinguished hearth
Ashes and sparks, my words among mankind!
Be through my lips to unawakened earth

The trumpet of a prophecy! O Wind,
If Winter comes, can Spring be far behind?   70

57 *Make me thy lyre:* Sound is produced on an Aeolian lyre, or wind harp, by wind blowing
across its strings.

CONSIDERATIONS FOR CRITICAL THINKING AND WRITING

1. FIRST RESPONSE. Write a summary of each of this ode's five sections.
2. What is the speaker's situation? What is his "sore need" (line 52)? What does the speaker ask of the wind in lines 57–70?
3. What does the wind signify in this ode? How is it used symbolically?
4. Determine the meter and rhyme of the first five stanzas. How do these elements contribute to the ode's movement? Is this pattern continued in the other four sections?

Picture Poem

By arranging lines into particular shapes, poets can sometimes organize typography into *picture poems* of what they describe. Words have been arranged into all kinds of shapes, from apples to light bulbs. Notice how the shape of this next poem embodies its meaning.

MICHAEL MCFEE (B. 1954)

In Medias Res°   *1985*

His waist
like the plot
thickens, wedding
pants now breathtaking,
belt no longer the cinch   5
it once was, belly's cambium
expanding to match each birthday,
his body a wad of anonymous tissue
swung in the same centrifuge of years
that separates a house from its foundation,   10
undermining sidewalks grim with joggers
and loose-filled graves and families
and stars collapsing on themselves,
no preservation society capable
of plugging entropy's dike,   15
under his zipper's sneer
a belly hibernation-
soft, ready for
the kill.

In Medias Res: A Latin term for a story that begins "in the middle of things."

CONSIDERATIONS FOR CRITICAL THINKING AND WRITING

1. FIRST RESPONSE. Explain how the title is related to this poem's shape. How is the meaning related?
2. Identify the puns. How do they work in the poem?
3. What is "cambium" (line 6)? Why is the phrase "belly's cambium" especially appropriate?
4. What is the tone of this poem? Is it consistent throughout?

Parody

A *parody* is a humorous imitation of another, usually serious, work. It can take any fixed or open form because parodists imitate the tone, language, and shape of the original. While a parody may be teasingly close to a work's style, it typically deflates the subject matter to make the original seem absurd. Parody can be used as a kind of literary criticism to expose the defects in a work, but it is also very often an affectionate acknowledgment that a well-known work has become both institutionalized in our culture and fair game for some fun. Read Marvell's "To His Coy Mistress" (p. 729) and then study this parody.

PETER DE VRIES (B. 1910)

To His Importunate Mistress   *1986*

Andrew Marvell Updated

Had we but world enough, and time,
My coyness, lady, were a crime,
But at my back I always hear
Time's wingèd chariot, striking fear
The hour is nigh when creditors   5
Will prove to be my predators.
As wages of our picaresque,
Bag lunches bolted at my desk
Must stand as fealty to you
For each expensive rendezvous.   10
Obeisance at your marble feet
Deserves the best-appointed suite,
And would have, lacked I not the pelf
To pleasure also thus myself;
But aptly sumptuous amorous scenes   15
Rule out the rake of modest means.

Since mistress presupposes wife,
It means a doubly costly life;
For fools by second passion fired
A second income is required,   20
The earning which consumes the hours
They'd hoped to spend in rented bowers.
To hostelries the worst of fates
That weekly raise their daily rates!
I gather, lady, from your scoffing   25
A bloke more solvent in the offing.
So revels thus to rivals go
For want of monetary flow.
How vexing that inconstant cash
The constant suitor must abash,   30
Who with excuses vainly pled
Must rue the undisheveled bed,
And that for paltry reasons given
His conscience may remain unriven.

CONSIDERATIONS FOR CRITICAL THINKING AND WRITING

1. FIRST RESPONSE. To what extent does this poem duplicate Marvell's style? How does it differ?

2. How is De Vries's use of "mistress" different from Marvell's (p. 729)? How does the speaker's complaint in this poem differ from that in "To His Coy Mistress"?

3. Explain how "picaresque" is used in line 7.

4. Choose a poet whose work you know reasonably well or would like to know better and determine what is characteristic about his or her style. Then choose a poem to parody. It's probably best to attempt a short poem or a section of a long work. If you have difficulty selecting an author, you might consider Herrick, Blake, Keats, Dickinson, Whitman, or Frost, since a number of their works are included in this book.

CONNECTION TO ANOTHER SELECTION

1. Read Anthony Hecht's "The Dover Bitch" (p. 1096), a parody of Arnold's "Dover Beach" (p. 757). Write an essay comparing the effectiveness of Hecht's parody with that of De Vries's "To His Importunate Mistress." Which parody do you prefer? Explain why.

Here's a parody for all seasons — not just Christmas — that brings together two popular icons of our culture.

X. J. KENNEDY (B. 1929)
A Visit from St. Sigmund   1993

Freud is just an old Santa Claus.
        — Margaret Mead°

'Twas the night before Christmas, when all through each kid
Not an Ego was stirring, not even an Id.
The hangups were hung by the chimney with care
In hopes that St. Sigmund Freud soon would be there.
The children in scream class had knocked off their screams,   5
Letting Jungian archetypes dance through their dreams,
And Mamma with her bra off and I on her lap
Had just snuggled down when a vast thunderclap
Boomed and from my unconscious arose such a chatter
As Baptist John's teeth made on Salome's platter.   10
Away from my darling I flew like a flash,
Tore straight to the bathroom and threw up, and — *smash!*
Through the windowpane hurtled and bounced on the floor
A big brick — holy smoke, it was hard to ignore.
As I heard further thunderclaps — lo and behold —   15
Came a little psychiatrist eighty years old.
He drove a wheeled couch pulled by five fat psychoses
And the gleam in his eye might induce a hypnosis.
Like subliminal meanings his coursers they came
And, consulting his notebook, he called them by name: 20
"Now Schizo, now Fetish, now Fear of Castration!
On Paranoia! on Penis-fixation!
Ach, yes, that big brick through your glass I should mention:
Just a simple device to compel your attention.

Margaret Mead (1901–1978): Noted American anthropologist.

You need, boy, to be in an analyst's power: 25
You talk, I take notes — fifty schillings an hour."
A bag full of symbols he'd slung on his back;
He looked smug as a junk-peddler laden with smack
Or a shrewd politician soliciting votes
And his chinbeard was stiff as a starched billygoat's.   30
Then laying one finger aside of his nose,
He chortled, "What means this? Mein Gott, I suppose
There's a meaning in fingers, in candles und wicks,
In mouseholes und doughnut holes, steeples und sticks.
You see, it's the imminent prospect of sex   35
That makes all us humans run round till we're wrecks,
Und each innocent infant since people began
Wants to bed with his momma und kill his old man;
So never you fear that you're sick as a swine —
Your hangups are every sane person's und mine.   40
Even Hamlet was hot for his mom — there's the rub;
Even Oedipus Clubfoot was one of the club.
Hmmm, that's humor unconscious." He gave me rib-pokes
And for almost two hours explained phallic jokes.
Then he sprang to his couch, to his crew gave a nod,   45
And away they all flew like the concept of God.
In the worst of my dreams I can hear him shout still,
"Merry Christmas to all! In the mail comes my bill."

CONSIDERATIONS FOR CRITICAL THINKING AND WRITING

1. FIRST RESPONSE. What makes Freud a particularly appropriate substitute
   for Santa Claus? How does this substitute facilitate the poem's humor?

2. What is the tone of this parody? How does the quotation from Margaret
   Mead help to establish the poem's tone?

3. What do you think is the poet's attitude toward Freud? Cite specific lines to
   support your point.

4. Is the focus of this parody the Christmas story or Freud? Explain your response.

PERSPECTIVES

ROBERT MORGAN (B. 1944)

On the Shape of a Poem   1983

In the body of the poem, lineation is part flesh and part skeleton, as form is
the towpath along which the burden of content, floating on the formless, is
pulled. All language is both mental and sacramental, is not "real" but is the
working of lip and tongue to subvert the "real." Poems empearl irritating facts

until they become opalescent spheres of moment, not so much résumés of history as of human faculties working with pain. Every poem is necessarily a fragment empowered by its implicitness. We sing to charm the snake in our spines, to make it sway with the pulse of the world, balancing the weight of consciousness on the topmost vertebra.

From *Epoch,* Fall/Winter 1983

CONSIDERATIONS FOR CRITICAL THINKING AND WRITING

1. Explain Morgan's metaphors for describing lineation and form in a poem. Why are these metaphors useful?
2. Choose one of the poems in this chapter that makes use of a particular form and explain how it is "a fragment empowered by its implicitness."

ELAINE MITCHELL (B. 1924)

Form   1994

Is it a corset
or primal wave?
Don't try to force it.

Even endorse it
to shape and deceive.   5
Ouch, too tight a corset.

Take it off. No remorse. It
's an ace up your sleeve.
No need to force it.

Can you make a horse knit?   10
Who would believe?
Consider. Of course, it

might be a resource. Wit,
your grateful slave.
Form. Sometimes you force it,   15

sometimes divorce it
to make it behave.
So don't try to force it.
Respect a good corset.

CONSIDERATIONS FOR CRITICAL THINKING AND WRITING

1. FIRST RESPONSE. What is the speaker's attitude toward form?
2. Explain why you think the form of this poem does or does not conform to the advice of the speaker.
3. Why is the metaphor of a corset a particularly apt image for this poem?

23

Open Form

Many poems, especially those written in the twentieth century, are composed of lines that cannot be scanned for a fixed or predominant meter. Moreover, very often these poems do not rhyme. Known as *free verse* (from the French, *vers libre*), such lines can derive their rhythmic qualities from the repetition of words, phrases, or grammatical structures; the arrangement of words on the printed page; or some other means. In recent years the term *open form* has been used in place of *free verse* to avoid the erroneous suggestion that this kind of poetry lacks all discipline and shape.

Although the following two poems do not use measurable meters, they do have rhythm.

E. E. CUMMINGS (1894–1962)

in Just- 1923

in Just-
spring   when the world is mud-
luscious the little
lame balloonman

whistles   far   and wee   5

and eddieandbill come
running from marbles and
piracies and it's
spring

when the world is puddle-wonderful   10

the queer
old balloonman whistles
far   and   wee

and bettyandisbel come dancing

from hop-scotch and jump-rope and   15

it's

spring

and

    the

        goat-footed   20

balloonMan   whistles
far
and
wee

CONSIDERATIONS FOR CRITICAL THINKING AND WRITING

1. FIRST RESPONSE. What is the effect of this poem's arrangement of words and use of space on the page? How would the effect differ if it was written out in prose?

2. What is the effect of Cummings's combining the names "eddieandbill" and "bettyandisbel"?

3. The allusion in line 20 refers to Pan, a Greek god associated with nature. How does this allusion add to the meaning of the poem?

WALT WHITMAN (1819–1892)

From "I Sing the Body Electric"   *1855*

O my body! I dare not desert the likes of you in other men and women,
    nor the likes of the parts of you,
I believe the likes of you are to stand or fall with the likes of the soul, (and
    that they are the soul,)
I believe the likes of you shall stand or fall with my poems, and that they
    are my poems.
Man's, woman's, child's, youth's, wife's, husband's, mother's, father's,
    young man's, young woman's poems.
Head, neck, hair, ears, drop and tympan of the ears.   5
Eyes, eye-fringes, iris of the eye, eyebrows, and the waking or sleeping of
    the lids,
Mouth, tongue, lips, teeth, roof of the mouth, jaws, and the jaw-hinges,
Nose, nostrils of the nose, and the partition,
Cheeks, temples, forehead, chin, throat, back of the neck, neck-slue,
Strong shoulders, manly beard, scapula, hind-shoulders, and the ample
    side-round of the chest,   10
Upper-arm, armpit, elbow-socket, lower-arm, arm-sinews, arm-bones,
Wrist and wrist-joints, hand, palm, knuckles, thumb, forefinger, finger-
    joints, finger-nails,
Broad breast-front, curling hair of the breast, breast-bone, breast-side,
Ribs, belly, backbone, joints of the backbone,

Hips, hip-sockets, hip-strength, inward and outward round, man-balls, 15
    man-root,
Strong set of thighs, well carrying the trunk above,
Leg-fibers, knee, knee-pan, upper-leg, under-leg,
Ankles, instep, foot-ball, toes, toe-joints, the heel;
All attitudes, all the shapeliness, all the belongings of my or your body or
    of any one's body, male or female,
The lung-sponges, the stomach-sac, the bowels sweet and clean, 20
The brain in its folds inside the skull-frame,
Sympathies, heart-valves, palate-valves, sexuality, maternity,
Womanhood, and all that is a woman, and the man that comes from woman,
The womb, the teats, nipples, breast-milk, tears, laughter, weeping, love-
    looks, love-perturbations and risings,
The voice, articulation, language, whispering, shouting aloud, 25
Food, drink, pulse, digestion, sweat, sleep, walking, swimming,
Poise on the hips, leaping, reclining, embracing, arm-curving and tightening,
The continual changes of the flex of the mouth, and around the eyes,
The skin, the sunburnt shade, freckles, hair,
The curious sympathy one feels when feeling with the hand the naked
    meat of the body, 30
The circling rivers the breath, and breathing it in and out,
The beauty of the waist, and thence of the hips, and thence downward
    toward the knees,
The thin red jellies within you or within me, the bones and the marrow
    in the bones,
The exquisite realization of health;
O I say these are not the parts and poems of the body only, but of the soul, 35
O I say now these are the soul!

Considerations for Critical Thinking and Writing

1. FIRST RESPONSE. What informs this speaker's attitude toward the human body?

2. Read the poem aloud. Is it simply a tedious enumeration of body parts, or do the lines achieve some kind of rhythmic cadence?

PERSPECTIVE

Walt Whitman (1819–1892)

On Rhyme and Meter   *1855*

The poetic quality is not marshaled in rhyme or uniformity or abstract addresses to things nor in melancholy complaints or good precepts, but is the life of these and much else and is in the soul. The profit of rhyme is that it drops seeds of a sweeter and more luxuriant rhyme, and of uniformity that it conveys itself into its own roots in the ground out of sight. The rhyme and uniformity of perfect poems show the free growth of metrical laws and bud from them as unerringly and loosely as lilacs or roses on a bush, and take shapes as compact as the shapes of chestnuts and oranges and melons and pears, and shed the perfume impalpable to form. The fluency and ornaments of the finest poems or music or orations or recitations are not independent but dependent. All beauty comes from beautiful blood and a beautiful brain. If the greatnesses are in conjunction in a man or woman it is enough . . . the fact will prevail through the universe . . . but the gaggery and gilt of a million years will not prevail. Who troubles himself about his ornaments or fluency is lost.

From the preface to the 1855 edition of *Leaves of Grass*

CONSIDERATIONS FOR CRITICAL THINKING AND WRITING

1. According to Whitman, what determines the shape of a poem?
2. Why does Whitman prefer open forms over fixed forms such as the sonnet?
3. Is Whitman's poetry devoid of any structure or shape? Choose one of his poems (listed in the index) to illustrate your answer.

Open form poetry is sometimes regarded as formless because it is unlike the strict fixed forms of a sonnet, villanelle, or sestina. But even though open form poems may not employ traditional meters and rhymes, they still rely on an intense use of language to establish rhythms and relations between meaning and form. Open form poems use the arrangement of words and phrases on the printed page, pauses, line lengths, and other means to create unique forms that express their particular meaning and tone.

Cummings's "in Just-" and the excerpt from Whitman's "I Sing the Body Electric" demonstrate how the white space on a page and rhythmic cadences can be aligned with meaning, but there is one kind of open form poetry that doesn't even look like poetry on a page. A *prose poem* is printed as prose and represents, perhaps, the most clear opposite of fixed forms. Here is a brief example.

GALWAY KINNELL (B. 1927)

After Making Love We Hear Footsteps   1980

For I can snore like a bullhorn
or play loud music
or sit up talking with any reasonably sober Irishman
and Fergus will only sink deeper
into his dreamless sleep, which goes by all in one flash,   5
but let there be that heavy breathing
or a stifled come-cry anywhere in the house
and he will wrench himself awake
and make for it on the run — as now, we lie together,
after making love, quiet, touching along the length of our bodies,   10
familiar touch of the long-married,
and he appears — in his baseball pajamas, it happens,

the neck opening so small
he has to screw them on, which one day may make him wonder
about the mental capacity of baseball players —   15
and says, "Are you loving and snuggling? May I join?"
He flops down between us and hugs us and snuggles himself to sleep,
his face gleaming with satisfaction at being this very child.

In the half darkness we look at each other
and smile   20
and touch arms across his little, startlingly muscled body —
this one whom habit of memory propels to the ground of his making,
sleeper only the mortal sounds can sing awake,
this blessing love gives again into our arms.

CONSIDERATIONS FOR CRITICAL THINKING AND WRITING

1. FIRST RESPONSE. Explore Kinnell's line endings. Why does he break the lines where he does?
2. How does the speaker's language reveal his character?
3. Describe the shift in tone between lines 18 and 19 with the shift in focus from child to adult. How does the use of space here emphasize this shift?
4. Do you think this poem is sentimental? Explain why or why not.

CONNECTIONS TO OTHER SELECTIONS

1. Discuss how this poem helps to bring into focus the sense of loss Robert Frost evokes in "Home Burial" (p. 980).
2. Write an essay comparing the tone and theme of this poem with those of Donald Hall's "My Son, My Executioner" (p. 1093), paying particular attention to the treatment of the child in each poem.

WILLIAM CARLOS WILLIAMS (1883–1963)
The Red Wheelbarrow   *1923*

so much depends
upon

a red wheel
barrow

glazed with rain
water

beside the white
chickens.

CONSIDERATIONS FOR CRITICAL THINKING AND WRITING

1. FIRST RESPONSE. What "depends upon" the things mentioned in the poem? What is the effect of these images? Do they have a particular meaning?
2. Do these lines have any kind of rhythm?
3. How does this poem resemble a haiku? How is it different?

Denise Levertov (1923–1997)
Gathered at the River   *1983*

For Beatrice Hawley and John Jagel

As if the trees were not indifferent . . .

A breeze flutters the candles but the trees give off
a sense of listening, of hush.

The dust of August on their leaves.
But it grows dark. Their dark green   5
is something known about, not seen.

But summer twilight takes away
only color, not form. The tree-forms,
massive trunks and the great domed heads,
leaning in towards us, are visible,   10

a half-circle of attention.

They listen because the war
we speak of, the human war with ourselves,

the war against earth,
against nature,   15
is a war against them.

The words are spoken
of those who survived a while,
living shadowgraphs, eyes fixed forever
on witnessed horror,   20
who survived to give
testimony, that no-one
may plead ignorance.
Contra naturam.° The trees,   *Against nature (Latin)*
the trees are not indifferent.   25

We intone together, *Never again,*

we stand in a circle,
singing, speaking, making vows,

remembering the dead
of Hiroshima,   30
of Nagasaki.

We are holding candles: we kneel to set them
afloat on the dark river
as they do
there in Hiroshima. We are invoking   35

saints and prophets,
heroes and heroines of justice and peace,

to be with us, to help us
stop the torment of our evil dreams . . .

Windthreatened flames bob on the current . . .   40

They don't get far from shore. But none capsizes
even in the swell of a boat's wake.

The waxy paper cups sheltering them
catch fire. But still the candles
sail their gold downstream.   45

And still the trees ponder our strange doings, as if
well aware that if we fail,
we fail for them:
if our resolves and prayers are weak and fail

there will be nothing left of their slow and innocent wisdom,   50

no roots,
no bole nor branch,
no memory
of shade,
of leaf,   55

no pollen.

Considerations for Critical Thinking and Writing

1. FIRST RESPONSE. How does Levertov use images of light and darkness throughout the poem? How do these images especially contribute to the meaning of the poem?

2. The first line is a fragment that is initially puzzling. Why is it nonetheless an appropriate beginning to this poem?

3. Why do you think the speaker focuses more on the trees than the human victims of the atomic bombings?

4. Discuss the symbolic significance of the trees, paying particular attention to lines 51–56.

Connections to Other Selections

1. In her comments on "Gathered at the River," Levertov affirms her "underlying belief in a great design, a potential harmony which can be violated or be sustained." How does Robert Frost's "Design" (p. 993) comment on Levertov's beliefs? Explain whether you agree with Levertov or not.

2. Levertov also expresses a concern in her essay for the necessity of having "a sense of the sacredness of the earthly creation" and mentions that Gerard Manley Hopkins has always been one of her favorite poets. Write an essay comparing "Gathered at the River" with Hopkins's "God's Grandeur" (p. 837) or "Pied Beauty" (p. 1099). What significant similarities do you find?

PERSPECTIVE

DENISE LEVERTOV (1923–1997)

On "Gathered at the River"   1985

This is the prose of it: Each year on August 6 (and sometimes on August 9 as well) some kind of memorial observance of the bombing of Hiroshima and Nagasaki is held in the Boston/Cambridge area, as in so many other locations. Some years this has consisted of a silent vigil held near Faneuil Hall and other monuments of the American Revolution. Participants stand in a circle facing outward to display signs explaining the theme of the vigil, or pace slowly round, sometimes accompanied by the drums and chanting of attendant Buddhist monks. People stay for varying periods — there may be a constant presence for three days and nights. In 1982 the poet Suzanne Belote (of the Catholic radical peace group Ailanthus) and some others created a variation on this event. Participants (with the usual age range — babes in arms to white-haired old men and women) came to the Cambridge Friends' Meeting House for a brief preparatory assembly, then filed out to receive a candle apiece — thick Jahrzeit candles nailed to pieces of wood and shielded by paper cups — and proceeded to walk in a hushed column along Memorial Drive, beside the Charles River. The sun was low; a long summer day was ending. When we got to the wide grassy area near the Lars Anderson Bridge, where our ceremony was to take place, it was twilight. Shielding flickering flames from the evening breeze, we formed a large circle, into the center of which stepped successive readers of portions from the descriptions recorded (as in the book *Unforgettable Fire*) by survivors of the atomic bombings. A period of silence followed. And then "saints and prophets, heroes and heroines of justice and peace" — including Gandhi, Martin Luther King, A. J. Muste, Emma Goldman, Archbishop Romero, Eugene Debs, Pope John XXIII, Dorothy Day, Saint Francis of Assisi, Saint Thomas More, Prince Kropotkin, Ammon Hennacy, the Prophet Isaiah, and many others I can't remember — were invoked. A form of ritual — an ecumenical liturgy — had been devised for the occasion, and as each such name was uttered by some member of the circle, the rest responded with a phrase that said essentially, "Be with us, great spirits, in this time of great need." The persons conducting the continuum of the liturgy turned slowly as they read the survivors' testimony, or statements of dedication to the cause of peace, so that all could hear at least part of each passage: for we had no microphones, preferring to depend on the unaided human voice for an occasion which had a personal, intimate character for each participant rather than being a PR event. Some music was interspersed among the verbal antiphonies, and the human atmosphere was solemn, harmonious, truly dedicated: from within it I began to feel the strong presence of the trees which half encircled us. Cars passed along Memorial Drive — slowed as drivers craned to see what was happening — passed on. A few blinked their lights in a friendly way, guessing from the date, I suppose, why we were there.

While we earnestly committed — or recommitted — ourselves to do all in our power to prevent nuclear war from ever taking place, it was growing dark. In the soft summer darkness details stood out: hands cupping wicks, small children's gold-illumined faces gazing up in wonder at the crouch and leap of flames, adults' heads bent close to one another as they clustered in twos and threes to relight candles blown out. And now the first part of the ritual was over and it was time to set our candles afloat, as they are set on the river in Hiroshima each year, that river where many drowned in the vain attempt to escape the burning of their own flesh.

People scrambled and helped each other down the short slope of the riverbank to launch the little candle-boats. Oblivious, a motorboat or two sped upriver, and minutes after a big slow wave would reach the shore. The water was black; the candle-boats seemed so fragile, and so tenacious. And all the time the large plane trees (saved from a road-widening project years before, incidentally, by citizens who chained themselves to their trunks in protest), and the other trees and bushes near them, were intensely, watchfully present. I have been asked if I really believe trees can listen. I've always thought our scientific knowledge has made us very arrogant in our assumptions. Wiser and older individuals and cultures have believed other kinds of consciousness and feeling could and did exist alongside of ours; I see no reason to disagree. It is not that I don't know trees have no "gray matter." It is possible that there are other routes to sentience than those with which we consider ourselves familiar.

The form of the poem: The title came from the literal sense of our being gathered there on the shore of the Charles, and also with the cognizance of the Quaker sense of gathering—a *"gathered meeting"* being, to my understanding, one which has not merely acquired the full complement of those who are going to attend it but which has attained a certain level, or quality, of attunement. Then, too, I had a vague memory of the song or hymn from which James Wright took the title of one of his books, and which I presumed must refer to the river of Jordan—"one more river, one more river to cross," as another song says. And though the symbolism there is of heaven lying upon the far shore, yet there is also, in the implication of *lastness,* of a final ordeal, the clear sense of a catastrophic alternative to attaining that shore. (No doubt *Pilgrim's Progress* was in the back of my mind too.) The analogy is obviously not a very close one, since survival of life on earth is a more modest goal than eternal bliss. Yet, relative to the hell proposed by our twentieth-century compound of the ancient vices of greed and love of power with nuclear and other "advanced" technology, mere survival would be a kind of heaven—especially since survival is not a static condition but offers the opportunity, and therefore the hope, of positive change. (For if one hopes for the survival of life on earth, one must logically hope and *intend* also the reshaping of those forces and factors which, unchanged, will only continue to threaten annihilation by one means or another.)

The structure of the poem stems as directly as the title from my experience of the event. The first line stands alone because that perception of the trees as animate and not uninterested presences—witnesses—was the discrete first in a series of heightened perceptions, most of which came in clusters. The following two-line stanza expands the first, more tentative observation, and places the trees' air of attention in the context of a breeze (which does not seem to distract them) and of the fluttering candles, which are thus introduced right at the start. Looking more closely at the trees, I see their late-summer color, but then recognize I am no longer seeing it, for dusk is falling—literally, but also metaphorically. The next stanza notes the largeness (and implied gravity, in both senses) of the trees, which it is not too dark to see, then again in a single line reasserts with more assurance the focus of my own attention: the trees' attentiveness. Following that comes the recognition of why, and for what, they are listening. The Latin words introduced here (echoing Pound's use of them) express the idea that "sin" occurs when humans violate the well-being of their own species and other living things, denying the natural law, the interdependence of all. (That usury belongs in this category, as Pound reemphasized, is not irrelevant to the subject of this poem, recalling the economic underpinning of the arms race and of war itself.)

My underlying belief in a great design, a potential harmony which can be violated or be sustained, probably strikes some people as quaint; but I would be dishonest, as person and artist, if I disowned it. I don't at this stage of my life feel ready for a public discussion of my religious concepts: but I think it must be clear from my writings that I have never been an atheist, and that — given my background and the fact that all my life George Herbert, Henry Vaughan, Thomas Traherne, and Gerard Manley Hopkins have been on my "short list" of favorite poets — whatever degree of belief I might attain would have a Christian context. This in turn implies a concern with the osmosis of "faith and works" and a sense of the sacredness of the earthly creation. That sense, not exclusive to Christianity, and deeply experienced and expressed by, for instance, Native Americans, is linked to Christians to the mystery of the Incarnation. To violate ourselves and our world is to violate the Divine.

The trees' concern, proposed with a tentative "as if" at the beginning, and then as an impression they "give off," is now asserted unequivocally. Once more comes a single line, "We intone together, *Never again*," focused on the purpose of our gathering; and the words "never again" bring together the thought of the Nazi Holocaust with that of the crime committed by the U.S. against Japanese civilians, a crime advocates of the arms race prepare to commit again on a scale vaster than that of any massacre in all of history. This association might carry with it, I would hope, the sense that those who vow to work for prevention of war also are dedicated to political, economic, and racial justice, and understand something of the connections between long-standing oppression, major and "minor" massacres, and the giant shadow of global war and annihilation.

The narration continues, up to the launching of the candle-boats; pauses — a pause indicated by the ellipsis — as we hold our breath to watch them go; and continues as they "bob on the current" and, though close to shore, begin to move downstream. Like ourselves, they are few and pitifully small. But at least they don't sink. Like all candles lit for the dead or in prayer, they combine remembrance with aspiration.

Finally the poem returns its regard to the trees, with the feeling that they know what we know — a knowledge those lines state and which it would be silly to paraphrase. The single lines again center on the primary realizations. Indeed, I see that a kind of précis of the entire poem could be extracted by reading the isolated lines alone:

As if the trees were not indifferent . . .

. . . .

a half-circle of attention.

. . . .

We intone together, *Never again.*

. . . .

Windthreatened flames bob on the current . . .

. . . .

there will be nothing left of their slow and innocent wisdom,

. . . .

no pollen,

except that one absolutely essential bone would be missing from that skeleton: the "if" of "if we fail." The poem, like the ceremony it narrates, and which gives it its slow, serious *pace* and, I hope, tone, is about interconnection, about dread, and about hope; that word, *if,* is its core.

> "'Gathered at the River': Background and Form" in *Singular Voices:*
> *American Poetry Today,* edited by Stephen Berg (Levertov's essay
> was written in response to a request from Berg)

CONSIDERATIONS FOR CRITICAL THINKING AND WRITING

1. In this essay, Levertov describes why and how she wrote "Gathered at the River" (p. 907). Does her account of the memorial observance help you to appreciate the poem more? Why or why not? Is the background information to the poem ("the prose of it") essential for an understanding of it?

2. Why is the word "if" (line 1) essential to the poem's meaning?

3. Does Levertov exhaust the possibilities for discussing the poem? What can you add to her comments?

4. Poets are usually extremely reluctant to comment on their own poetry. Why do you think they frequently refuse to talk about the background and form of their poems?

MARILYN NELSON WANIEK (B. 1946)
Emily Dickinson's Defunct   1978

She used to
pack poems
in her hip pocket.
Under all the
gray old lady   5
clothes she was
dressed for action.
She had hair,
imagine,
in certain places, and   10
believe me
she smelled human
on a hot summer day.
Stalking snakes
or counting   15
the thousand motes

in sunlight
she walked just
like an Indian.
She was New England's   20
favorite daughter,
she could pray
like the devil.
She was a
two-fisted woman,   25
this babe.
All the flies
just stood around
and buzzed
when she died.   30

CONSIDERATIONS FOR CRITICAL THINKING AND WRITING

1. FIRST RESPONSE. How does the speaker characterize Dickinson? Explain why this characterization is different from the popular view of Dickinson.

2. How does the diction of the poem serve to characterize the speaker?

3. Discuss the function of the poem's title.

CONNECTIONS TO ANOTHER SELECTION

1. Waniek alludes to at least two other poems in "Emily Dickinson's Defunct." The title refers to E. E. Cummings's "Buffalo Bill 's" (p. 1087), and the final lines (27–30) refer to Dickinson's "I heard a Fly buzz — when I died —" (p. 946). Read those poems and write an essay discussing how they affect your reading of Waniek's poem.

JIM DANIELS (B. 1956)

Short-order Cook   *1985*

An average joe comes in
and orders thirty cheeseburgers and thirty fries.

I wait for him to pay before I start cooking.
He pays.
He ain't no average joe.   5

The grill is just big enough for ten rows of three.
I slap the burgers down
throw two buckets of fries in the deep frier
and they pop pop spit spit . . .
psss . . .   10
The counter girls laugh.
I concentrate.
It is the crucial point —
they are ready for the cheese:
my fingers shake as I tear off slices   15

toss them on the burgers/fries done/dump/
refill buckets/burgers ready/flip into buns/
beat that melting cheese/wrap burgers in plastic/
into paper bags/fries done/dump/fill thirty bags/
bring them to the counter/wipe sweat on sleeve   20
and smile at the counter girls.
I puff my chest out and bellow:
"Thirty cheeseburgers, thirty fries!"
They look at me funny.
I grab a handful of ice, toss it in my mouth   25
do a little dance and walk back to the grill.
Pressure, responsibility, success,
thirty cheeseburgers, thirty fries.

Considerations for Critical Thinking and Writing

1. FIRST RESPONSE. What motivates this speaker?
2. What function do the three stanzas serve?
3. How do the varying line lengths contribute to the poem's meaning?
4. What is the effect of the slashes in lines 16–20?
5. What role do the counter girls play in the poem?

Connection to Another Selection

1. Write a narrative poem or prose poem in which you imagine an encounter
   between this short-order cook and the speaker of Keesbury's "Song to a
   Waitress" (p. 872).

Carolyn Forché (b. 1950)

The Colonel   *May 1978*

What you have heard is true. I was in his house. His wife carried a
tray of coffee and sugar. His daughter filed her nails, his son went
out for the night. There were daily papers, pet dogs, a pistol on the
cushion beside him. The moon swung bare on its black cord over
the house. On the television was a cop show. It was in English. Bro-   5
ken bottles were embedded in the walls around the house to scoop
the kneecaps from a man's legs or cut his hands to lace. On the
windows there were gratings like those in liquor stores. We had
dinner, rack of lamb, good wine, a gold bell was on the table for
calling the maid. The maid brought green mangoes, salt, a type of   10
bread. I was asked how I enjoyed the country. There was a brief
commercial in Spanish. His wife took everything away. There was
some talk then of how difficult it had become to govern. The parrot said hello on the terrace. The colonel told it to shut up, and
pushed himself from the table. My friend said to me with his eyes: 15
say nothing. The colonel returned with a sack used to bring
groceries home. He spilled many human ears on the table. They

were like dried peach halves. There is no other way to say this. He
took one of them in his hands, shook it in our faces, dropped it
into a water glass. It came alive there. I am tired of fooling around   20
he said. As for the rights of anyone, tell your people they can go
fuck themselves. He swept the ears to the floor with his arm and
held the last of his wine in the air. Something for your poetry, no?
he said. Some of the ears on the floor caught this scrap of his voice.
Some of the ears on the floor were pressed to the ground.   25

CONSIDERATIONS FOR CRITICAL THINKING AND WRITING

1. FIRST RESPONSE. How does this poem make you feel? Is it consistent
   throughout? How do the images contribute to its effects?

2. What kind of horror is described here? Characterize the colonel.

3. What makes this prose poem not a typical prose passage? How is it organized differently?

4. What poetic elements can you find in it?

5. What is the tone of the final two sentences?

SHARON OLDS (B. 1942)

Rite of Passage   *1983*

As the guests arrive at my son's party
they gather in the living room —
short men, men in first grade
with smooth jaws and chins.
Hands in pockets, they stand around   5
jostling, jockeying for place, small fights
breaking out and calming. One says to another
How old are you? Six. I'm seven. So?
They eye each other, seeing themselves
tiny in the other's pupils. They clear their   10
throats a lot, a room of small bankers,
they fold their arms and frown. *I could beat you
up*, a seven says to a six,
the dark cake, round and heavy as a
turret, behind them on the table. My son,   15
freckles like specks of nutmeg on his cheeks,
chest narrow as the balsa keel of a
model boat, long hands
cool and thin as the day they guided him
out of me, speaks up as a host   20
for the sake of the group.
We could easily kill a two-year-old,
he says in his clear voice. The other
men agree, they clear their throats
like Generals, they relax and get down to   25
playing war, celebrating my son's life.

1. FIRST RESPONSE. In what sense is this birthday party a "Rite of Passage"?
2. How does the speaker transform these six- and seven-year-old boys into men? What is the point of doing so?
3. Comment on the appropriateness of the image of the cake in lines 14–15.
4. Why does the son's claim that "We could easily kill a two-year-old" (line 22) come as such a shock at that point in the poem?

CONNECTIONS TO OTHER SELECTIONS

1. In an essay discuss the treatment of violence in "Rite of Passage" and Forché's "The Colonel" (p. 914). To what extent might the colonel be regarded as an adult version of the generals in Olds's poem?
2. Discuss the use of irony in "Rite of Passage" and Owen's "Dulce et Decorum Est" (p. 763). Which do you think is a more effective antiwar poem? Explain why.

CAROLYNN HOY (B. 1947)

In the Summer Kitchen   1993

We speared long wooden spoons
into steaming galvanized tubs
churning and scooping the checked cotton
to feed back and forth
through a wringer   5
from her hand to mine.

And there, on that Monday,
she mentioned Harry, her first born,
my uncle, who died at three months.
That was all,   10
a slip of the tongue
as she hastily turned away.

On the stoop by the clothesline
beyond the screen door,
she snapped our flattened   15
shirts to attention,
shoulders as straight and squared
as her chiselled headstone
I now visit.

That silence.   20

The dignity of it all.

1. FIRST RESPONSE. Explain how the details about doing the wash take on more than a literal significance.

2. How do the grouping of stanzas and the spacing of lines affect your reading?

3. How do you think the speaker feels about her grandmother?

4. How might the poem be regarded as a kind of elegy for the grandmother?

CONNECTION TO ANOTHER SELECTION

1. Compare the tone of this poem with that of Emily Dickinson's "The Bustle in a House" (p. 950).

ALLEN GINSBERG (1926–1997)

First Party at Ken Kesey's with Hell's Angels   1965

Cool black night thru the redwoods
cars parked outside in shade
behind the gate, stars dim above
the ravine, a fire burning by the side
porch and a few tired souls hunched over   5
in black leather jackets. In the huge
wooden house, a yellow chandelier
at 3 A.M. the blast of loudspeakers
hi-fi Rolling Stones Ray Charles Beatles
Jumping Joe Jackson and twenty youths   10
dancing to the vibration thru the floor,
a little weed in the bathroom, girls in scarlet
tights, one muscular smooth skinned man
sweating dancing for hours, beer cans
bent littering the yard, a hanged man   15
sculpture dangling from a high creek branch,
children sleeping softly in their bedroom bunks.
And 4 police cars parked outside the painted
gate, red lights revolving in the leaves.

CONSIDERATIONS FOR CRITICAL THINKING AND WRITING

1. FIRST RESPONSE. How does the list of images help to set the poem's scene? What is the effect of the poem's last two lines (18–19) on the overall tone?

2. Who is Ken Kesey? Use the library to find out the kinds of books he writes. How does his name help to establish the poem's setting?

3. How does the absence of commas in lines 8–10 indicate how to read these lines aloud?

CONNECTION TO ANOTHER SELECTION

1. Write an essay that compares the impact of this poem's ending with that of Hathaway's "Oh, Oh" (p. 675).

ANONYMOUS

The Frog

date unknown

What a wonderful bird the frog are!
When he stand he sit almost;
When he hop he fly almost.
He ain't got no sense hardly;
He ain't got no tail hardly either.
When he sit, he sit on what he ain't got almost.

CONSIDERATIONS FOR CRITICAL THINKING AND WRITING

1. FIRST RESPONSE. How is the poem a description of the speaker as well as of a frog?

2. Though this poem is ungrammatical, it does have a patterned structure. How does the pattern of sentences create a formal structure?

TATO LAVIERA (B. 1951)

AmeRícan

1985

we gave birth to a new generation,
AmeRícan, broader than lost gold
never touched, hidden inside the
puerto rican mountains.

we gave birth to a new generation,   5
AmeRícan, it includes everything
imaginable you-name-it-we-got-it
society.

we gave birth to a new generation,
AmeRícan salutes all folklores,   10
european, indian, black, spanish,
and anything else compatible:

AmeRícan,   singing to composer pedro flores'° palm
            trees high up in the universal sky!

AmeRícan,   sweet soft spanish danzas gypsies   15
            moving lyrics la *española*° cascabelling   *Spanish*
            presence always singing at our side!

AmeRícan,   beating jíbaro° modern troubadours
            crying guitars romantic continental
            bolero love songs!   20

AmeRícan,   across forth and across back
            back across and forth back

---

13 *Pedro Flores:* Puerto Rican composer of popular romantic songs.   18 *jíbaro:* A particular style of music played by Puerto Rican mountain farmers.

        forth across and back and forth
        our trips are walking bridges!

        it all dissolved into itself, the attempt   25
        was truly made, the attempt was truly
        absorbed, digested, we spit out
        the poison, we spit out the malice,
        we stand, affirmative in action,
        to reproduce a broader answer to the   30
        marginality that gobbled us up abruptly!

AmeRícan,   walking plena- rhythms° in new york,
        strutting beautifully alert, alive,
        many turning eyes wondering,
        admiring!   35

AmeRícan,   defining myself my own way any way many
        ways Am e Rícan, with the big R and the
        accent on the í!

AmeRícan,   like the soul gliding talk of gospel
        boogie music!   40

AmeRícan,   speaking new words in spanglish tenements,
        fast tongue moving street corner *"que
        corta"*° talk being invented at the insistence   *that cuts*
        of a smile!

AmeRícan,   abounding inside so many ethnic english   45
        people, and out of humanity, we blend
        and mix all that is good!

AmeRícan,   integrating in new york and defining our
        own *destino,*° our own way of life,   *destiny*

AmeRícan,   defining the new america, humane america,   50
        admired america, loved america, harmonious
        america, the world in peace, our energies
        collectively invested to find other civili-
        zations, to touch God, further and further,
        to dwell in the spirit of divinity!   55

AmeRícan,   yes, for now, for i love this, my second
        land, and i dream to take the accent from
        the altercation, and be proud to call
        myself american, in the u.s. sense of the
        word, AmeRícan, America!   60

32 *plena- rhythms:* African–Puerto Rican folklore, music, and dance.

CONSIDERATIONS FOR CRITICAL THINKING AND WRITING

1. FIRST RESPONSE. How does the arrangement of lines communicate a sense
   of energy and vitality?

2. How does the speaker portray Puerto Ricans living in the United States?

3. How does the poet describe the United States?

CONNECTION TO ANOTHER SELECTION

1. In an essay consider the themes, styles, and tones of "AmeRícan" and Divakaruni's "Indian Movie, New Jersey" (p. 819).

THOM WARD (B. 1963)

Vasectomy   *1996*

for Adam Smith°

No one's notified the workers
special dividends have been issued,
the factory sold. Frames
are still being welded, transmissions
bolted to engines, acetylene torches lit   5
gold like the light from miners' helmets
on groaning timber. Coal
is still chiseled and dust
spun into lungs. No one's posted signs:
Road Out. Bridge Out. Danger Ahead.   10
Fingers black with dye, young girls
disappear in looms. Women
boil metal, pour it steaming into molds.
Day fused to night, millions of laborers,
backs crooked and hands cracked,   15
manufacture bottles, canisters and cogs,
replicating product
that will never reach foreign markets.
Soldiers turn semis back at the border.
Executives charter planes,   20
shift funds into Swiss accounts.
How long before word of this
hits the factories, the mines, the wicked
textile mills? What good, what possible good,
is supply without demand?   25

Adam Smith (1723-1790): Scottish political economist and philosopher.

CONSIDERATIONS FOR CRITICAL THINKING AND WRITING

1. FIRST RESPONSE. What does the title have to do with the poem's meaning?
2. What is this poem about? What is its tone?
3. Why is the dedication of the poem relevant to its theme?

JOSEPH BRUCHAC (B. 1942)
Ellis Island 1979

Beyond the red brick of Ellis Island
where the two Slovak children
who became my grandparents
waited the long days of quarantine,
after leaving the sickness, 5
the old Empires of Europe,
a Circle Line° ship slips easily *a tour boat*
on its way to the island
of the tall woman,° green *Statue of Liberty*
as dreams of forests and meadows 10
waiting for those who'd worked
a thousand years
yet never owned their own.

Like millions of others,
I too come to this island, 15
nine decades the answerer
of dreams.

Yet only one part of my blood loves that memory.
Another voice speaks
of native lands 20
within this nation.
Lands invaded
when the earth became owned.
Lands of those who followed
the changing Moon, 25
knowledge of the seasons
in their veins.

CONSIDERATIONS FOR CRITICAL THINKING AND WRITING

1. FIRST RESPONSE. What chains of past events are evident in this poem? How do they affect your reading of the poem?

2. Joseph Bruchac is part Slovakian and part Native American (Abenaki) in heritage. How does this information affect your reading of the poem? Do you think the speaker values one part of his heritage more than another? Why or why not?

3. Discuss the rhythm of lines 1–13 and 18–27. How does the rhythm of the lines reinforce their meaning?

4. How do you regard your own relationship to America? How does it compare with the speaker's in "Ellis Island"?

CONNECTION TO ANOTHER SELECTION

1. Write an essay that discusses the speakers' attitudes toward immigration in "Ellis Island" and in Laviera's "AmeRícan."

PETER MEINKE (B. 1932)

The ABC of Aerobics

1983

Air seeps through alleys and our diaphragms
balloon blackly with this mix of
carbon monoxide and the thousand corrosives a city
doles out free to its constituents;
everyone's jogging through Edgemont Park,   5
frightened by death and fatty tissue,
gasping at the maximal heart rate,
hoping to outlive all the others streaming
in the lanes like lemmings lurching toward their last
jump. I join in despair   10
knowing my arteries jammed with
lint and tobacco, lard and bourbon — my
medical history a noxious marsh:
newts and moles slink through the sodden veins,
owls hoot in the lungs' dark branches;   15
probably I shall keel off the john like
queer Uncle George and lie on the bathroom floor
raging about Shirley Clark, my true love in
seventh grade, God bless her wherever she lives
tied to that turkey who hugely   20
undervalues the beauty of her tiny earlobes, one
view of which (either one: they are both perfect)
would add years to my life and I could skip these
x-rays, turn in my insurance card, and trade
yoga and treadmills and jogging and zen and   25
zucchini for drinking and dreaming of her, breathing hard.

CONSIDERATIONS FOR CRITICAL THINKING AND WRITING

1. FIRST RESPONSE. How does the title help to establish a pattern throughout the poem? How does the pattern contribute to the poem's meaning?

2. How does the speaker feel about exercise? How do his descriptions of his physical condition serve to characterize him?

3. A primer is a book that teaches children to read or introduces them, in an elementary way, to the basics of a subject. The title "The ABC of Aerobics" indicates that this poem is meant to be a primer. What is it trying to teach us? Is its final lesson serious or ironic?

4. Discuss Meinke's use of humor. Is it effective?

CONNECTIONS TO OTHER SELECTIONS

1. Write an essay comparing the way Olds connects sex and exercise in "Sex without Love" (p. 740) with Meinke's treatment here.

2. Compare the voice in this poem with that in Kinnell's "After Making Love We Hear Footsteps" (p. 905). Which do you find more appealing? Why?

GARY SOTO (B. 1952)

Mexicans Begin Jogging   *1995*

At the factory I worked
In the fleck of rubber, under the press
Of an oven yellow with flame,
Until the border patrol opened
Their vans and my boss waved for us to run.   5
"Over the fence, Soto," he shouted,
And I shouted that I was American.
"No time for lies," he said, and pressed
A dollar in my palm, hurrying me
Through the back door.   10

Since I was on his time, I ran
And became the wag to a short tail of Mexicans —
Ran past the amazed crowds that lined
The street and blurred like photographs, in rain.
I ran from that industrial road to the soft   15
Houses where people paled at the turn of an autumn sky.
What could I do but yell *vivas*
To baseball, milkshakes, and those sociologists
Who would clock me
As I jog into the next century   20
On the power of a great, silly grin.

CONSIDERATIONS FOR CRITICAL THINKING AND WRITING

1. FIRST RESPONSE. What ironies are present in this poem?
2. Soto was born and raised in Fresno, California. How does this fact affect your reading of the first stanza?
3. In what different ways does the speaker become "the wag" (line 12) in this poem? (You may want to look up the word to consider all possible meanings.)
4. Explain lines 17-21. What serious point is being made in these humorous lines?

CONNECTION TO ANOTHER SELECTION

1. Compare the speakers' ironic attitudes toward exercise in this poem and in Meinke's "The ABC of Aerobics" (p. 922).

Found Poem

This next poem is a *found poem,* an unintentional poem discovered in a nonpoetic context, such as a conversation, news story, or an advertisement. Found poems are playful reminders that the words in poems are very often the language we use every day. Whether such found language should be regarded as a poem is an issue left for you to consider.

DONALD JUSTICE (B. 1925)

Order in the Streets   *1969*

*(From instructions printed on a child's toy, Christmas 1968, as reported in
the* New York Times*)*

1. 2. 3.
Switch on.

Jeep rushes
to the scene
of riot   5

Jeep goes
in all directions
by mystery action.

Jeep stops periodically
to turn hood over   10

machine gun appears
with realistic
shooting noise.

After putting down riot,
jeep goes   15
back to the headquarters.

CONSIDERATIONS FOR CRITICAL THINKING AND WRITING

1. FIRST RESPONSE. What is the effect of arranging these instructions in lines?
   How are the language and meaning enhanced by this arrangement?

2. Look for phrases or sentences in ads, textbooks, labels, or directions — in
   anything that might inadvertently contain provocative material that would
   be revealed by arranging the words in lines. You may even discover some
   patterns of rhyme and rhythm. After arranging the lines, explain why you
   organized them as you did.

24

A Study of Three Poets: Emily Dickinson, Robert Frost, and Langston Hughes

This chapter includes poems by Emily Dickinson, Robert Frost, and Langston Hughes in order to provide an opportunity to study three major poets in some depth. None of the collections is wholly representative of the poet's work, but each offers enough poems to suggest some of the techniques and concerns that characterize the poet's writings. The poems within each group speak not only to readers but also to one another. That's natural enough: the more familiar you are with a writer's work, the easier it is to perceive and enjoy the strategies and themes he or she employs. If you are asked to write about these authors, you may find useful the Questions for Writing about an Author in Depth (p. 965) and the sample paper on Emily Dickinson's attitudes toward religious faith in four of her poems (pp. 966–971).

EMILY DICKINSON (1830–1886)

Emily Dickinson grew up in a prominent and prosperous household in Amherst, Massachusetts. Along with her younger sister Lavinia and older brother Austin, she experienced a quiet and reserved family life headed by her father, Edward Dickinson. In a letter to Austin at law school, she once described the atmosphere in her father's house as "pretty much all sobriety." Her mother, Emily Norcross Dickinson, was not as powerful a presence in her life; she seems not to have been as emotionally accessible as Dickinson would have liked. Her daughter is said to have characterized her as not the sort of mother "to whom you hurry when you are troubled." Both parents raised Dickinson to be a cultured Christian woman who would one day be responsible for a family of her own. Her father attempted to protect her from reading books that might "joggle" her mind, particularly her religious faith, but Dickinson's individualistic instincts and irreverent sensibilities created conflicts that did not allow her to fall into step with the conventional piety, domesticity, and social duty prescribed by her father and the orthodox Congregationalism of Amherst.

The Dickinsons were well known in Massachusetts. Her father was a lawyer and served as the treasurer of Amherst College (a position Austin eventually took up as well), and her grandfather was one of the college's founders. Although nineteenth-century politics, economics, and social issues do not appear in the foreground of her poetry, Dickinson lived in a family environment that was steeped in them: her father was an active town official and served in the General Court of Massachusetts, the state senate, and the United States House of Representatives.

Dickinson, however, withdrew not only from her father's public world but also from almost all social life in Amherst. She refused to see most people, and aside from a single year at South Hadley Female Seminary (now Mount Holyoke College), one excursion to Philadelphia and Washington, and several brief trips to Boston to see a doctor about eye problems, she lived all her life in her father's house. She dressed only in white and developed a reputation as a reclusive eccentric. Dickinson selected her own society carefully and frugally. Like her poetry, her relationship to the world was intensely reticent. Indeed, during the last twenty years of her life she rarely left the house.

Though Dickinson never married, she had significant relationships with several men who were friends, confidantes, and mentors. She also enjoyed an intimate relationship with her friend Susan Huntington Gilbert, who became her sister-in-law by marrying Austin. Susan and her husband lived next door and were extremely close with Dickinson. Biographers have attempted to find in a number of her relationships the source for the passion of some of her love poems and letters. Several possibilities have been put forward as the person she addressed in three letters as "Dear Master": Benjamin Newton, a clerk in her father's office who talked about books with her; Samuel Bowles, editor of the *Springfield Republican* and friend of the family; the Reverend Charles Wadsworth, a Presbyterian preacher with a reputation for powerful sermons; and an old friend and widower, Judge Otis P. Lord. Despite these speculations, no biographer has been able to identify definitively the object of Dickinson's love. What matters, of course, is not with whom she was in love — if, in fact, there was any single person — but that she wrote about such passions so intensely and convincingly in her poetry.

Choosing to live life internally within the confines of her home, Dickinson brought her life into sharp focus. For she also chose to live within the limitless expanses of her imagination, a choice she was keenly aware of and which she described in one of her poems this way: "I dwell in Possibility—" (p. 943). Her small circle of domestic life did not impinge on her creative sensibilities. Like Henry David Thoreau, she simplified her life so that doing without was a means of being within. In a sense she redefined the meaning of deprivation because being denied something—whether it was faith, love, literary recognition, or some other desire—provided a sharper, more intense understanding than she would have experienced had she achieved what she wanted: "'Heaven,'" she wrote, "is what I cannot reach!" This poem (p. 936), along with many others, such as "Water, is taught by thirst" (p. 933) and "Success is counted sweetest / By those who ne'er succeed" (p. 932), suggests just how persistently she saw deprivation as a way of sensitizing herself to the value of what she was missing. For Dickinson hopeful expectation was always more satisfying than achieving a golden moment. Perhaps that's one reason she was so attracted to John Keats's poetry (see, for example, his "Ode on a Grecian Urn," p. 741).

Dickinson enjoyed reading Keats as well as Emily and Charlotte Brontë; Robert and Elizabeth Barrett Browning; Alfred, Lord Tennyson; and George Eliot. Even so, these writers had little or no effect on the style of her writing. In her own work she was original and innovative, but she did draw on her knowledge of the Bible, classical myths, and Shakespeare for allusions and references in her poetry. She also used contemporary popular church hymns, transforming their standard rhythms into free-form hymn meters. Among American writers she appreciated Ralph Waldo Emerson and Thoreau, but she apparently felt Walt Whitman was better left unread. She once mentioned to Thomas Wentworth Higginson, a leading critic with whom she corresponded about her poetry, that as for Whitman "I never read his Book—but was told that he was disgraceful" (for the kind of Whitman poetry she had been warned against, see his "I Sing the Body Electric," p. 903). Nathaniel Hawthorne, however, intrigued her with his faith in the imagination and his dark themes: "Hawthorne appals—entices," a remark that might be used to describe her own themes and techniques.

Today, Dickinson is regarded as one of America's greatest poets, but when she died at the age of fifty-six after devoting most of her life to writing poetry, her nearly two thousand poems—only a dozen of which were published, anonymously, during her lifetime—were unknown except to a small number of friends and relatives. Dickinson was not recognized as a major poet until the twentieth century, when modern readers ranked her as a major new voice whose literary innovations were unmatched by any other nineteenth-century poet in the United States.

Dickinson neither completed many poems nor prepared them for publication. She wrote her drafts on scraps of paper, grocery lists, and the backs of recipes and used envelopes. Early editors of her poems took the liberty of making them more accessible to nineteenth-century readers when several volumes of selected poems were published in the 1890s. The poems were made to appear like traditional nineteenth-century verse by assigning them titles, rearranging their syntax, normalizing their grammar, and regularizing

Manuscript page for "What Soft—Cherubic Creatures—" (p. 940), taken from one of Dickinson's forty fascicles—small booklets hand-sewn with white string that contained her poetry as well as other miscellaneous writings. These fascicles are important for Dickinson scholars, as this manuscript page makes clear: her style to some extent resists translation into the conventions of print. Reprinted by permission of the Robert Frost Library.

their capitalizations. Instead of dashes editors used standard punctuation; instead of the highly elliptical telegraphic lines so characteristic of her poems editors added articles, conjunctions, and prepositions to make them more readable and in line with conventional expectations. In addition, the poems were made more predictable by organizing them into categories such as friendship, nature, love, and death. Not until 1955, when Thomas Johnson published Dickinson's complete works in a form that attempted to be true to her manuscript versions, did readers have the opportunity to see the full range of her style and themes.

Like that of Robert Frost, Dickinson's popular reputation has sometimes relegated her to the role of a New England regionalist who writes quaint uplifting verses that touch the heart. In 1971 that image was mailed first class all over the country by the United States Postal Service. In addition to issuing a commemorative stamp featuring a portrait of Dickinson, the Postal Service affixed the stamp to a first-day-of-issue envelope that included an engraved rose and one of her poems. Here's the poem chosen from among the nearly two thousand she wrote:

If I can stop one Heart from breaking
c. 1864

If I can stop one Heart from breaking
I shall not live in vain
If I can ease one Life the Aching
or cool one Pain

Or help one fainting Robin
Unto his Nest again
I shall not live in Vain.

This is typical not only of many nineteenth-century popular poems but of the kind of verse that can be found in contemporary greeting cards. The speaker tells us what we imagine we should think about and makes the point simply with a sentimental image of a "fainting Robin." To point out that robins don't faint or that altruism isn't necessarily the only rule of conduct by which one should live one's life is to make trouble for this poem. Moreover, its use of language is unexceptional; the metaphors used, like that robin, are a bit weary. If this poem were characteristic of Dickinson's poetry, the U.S. Postal Service probably would not have been urged to issue a stamp in her honor, nor would you be reading her poems in this anthology or many others. Here's a poem by Dickinson that is more typical of her writing:

If I shouldn't be alive
c. 1860

If I shouldn't be alive
When the Robins come,
Give the one in Red Cravat,
A Memorial crumb.

If I couldn't thank you,
Being fast asleep,

You will know I'm trying
With my Granite lip!

This poem is more representative of Dickinson's sensibilities and techniques. Although the first stanza sets up a rather mild concern that the speaker might not survive the winter (a not uncommon fear for those who fell prey to pneumonia, for example, during Dickinson's time), the concern can't be taken too seriously—a gentle humor lightens the poem when we realize that all robins have red cravats and are therefore the speaker's favorite. Furthermore, the euphemism that describes the speaker "Being fast asleep" in line 6 makes death seem not so threatening after all. But the sentimental expectations of the first six lines—lines that could have been written by any number of popular nineteenth-century writers—are dashed by the penultimate word of the last line. "Granite" is the perfect word here because it forces us to reread the poem and to recognize that it's not about feeding robins or offering a cosmetic treatment of death; rather, it's a bone-chilling description of a corpse's lip that evokes the cold, hard texture and grayish color of tombstones. These lips will never say "thank you" or anything else.

Instead of the predictable rhymes and sentiments of "If I can stop one Heart from breaking," this poem is unnervingly precise in its use of language and tidily points out how much emphasis Dickinson places on an individual word. Her use of near rhyme with "asleep" and "lip" brilliantly mocks a euphemistic approach to death by its jarring dissonance. This is a better poem, not because it's grim or about death, but because it demonstrates Dickinson's skillful use of language to produce a shocking irony.

Dickinson found irony, ambiguity, and paradox lurking in the simplest and commonest experiences. The materials and subject matter of her poetry are quite conventional. Her poems are filled with robins, bees, winter light, household items, and domestic duties. These materials represent the range of what she experienced in and around her father's house. She used them because they constituted so much of her life and, more important, because she found meanings latent in them. Though her world was simple, it was also complex in its beauties and its terrors. Her lyric poems capture impressions of particular moments, scenes, or moods, and she characteristically focuses on topics such as nature, love, immortality, death, faith, doubt, pain, and the self.

Though her materials were conventional, her treatment of them was innovative because she was willing to break whatever poetic conventions stood in the way of the intensity of her thought and images. Her conciseness, brevity, and wit are tightly packed. Typically she offers her observations via one or two images that reveal her thought in a powerful manner. She once characterized her literary art by writing "My business is circumference." Her method is to reveal the inadequacy of declarative statements by evoking qualifications and questions with images that complicate firm assertions and affirmations. In one of her poems she describes her strategies this way: "Tell all the Truth but tell it slant—/ Success in Circuit lies." This might well stand as a working definition of Dickinson's aesthetics and is embodied in the following poem:

The Thought beneath so slight a film —   *c. 1860*

The Thought beneath so slight a film —
Is more distinctly seen —
As laces just reveal the surge —
Or Mists — the Apennine°   *Italian mountain range*

    Paradoxically, "Thought" is more clearly understood precisely because a slight "film" — in this case language — covers it. Language, like lace, enhances what it covers and reveals it all the more — just as a mountain range is more engaging to the imagination if it is covered in mists rather than starkly presenting itself. Poetry for Dickinson intensifies, clarifies, and organizes experience.

    Dickinson's poetry is challenging because it is radical and original in its rejection of most traditional nineteenth-century themes and techniques. Her poems require active engagement from the reader because she seems to leave out so much with her elliptical style and remarkable contracting metaphors. But these apparent gaps are filled with meaning if we are sensitive to her use of devices such as personification, allusion, symbolism, and startling syntax and grammar. Since her use of dashes is sometimes puzzling, it helps to read her poems aloud to hear how carefully the words are arranged. What might initially seem intimidating on a silent page can surprise the reader with meaning when heard. It's also worth keeping in mind that Dickinson was not always consistent in her views and that they can change from poem to poem, depending on how she felt at a given moment. For example, her definition of religious belief in "'Faith' is a fine invention" (p. 966) reflects an ironically detached wariness in contrast to the faith embraced in "I never saw a Moor —" (p. 967). Dickinson was less interested in absolute answers to questions than she was in examining and exploring their "circumference."

    Because Dickinson's poems are all relatively brief (none is longer than fifty lines), they invite browsing and sampling, but perhaps a useful way into their highly metaphoric and witty world is this "how to" poem that reads almost like a recipe:

To make a prairie it takes a clover and one bee   *date unknown*

To make a prairie it takes a clover and one bee,
One clover, and a bee,
And revery.
The revery alone will do,
If bees are few.

    This quiet but infinite claim for a writer's imagination brings together the range of ingredients in Dickinson's world of domestic and ordinary natural details. Not surprisingly, she deletes rather than adds to the recipe, because the one essential ingredient is the writer's creative imagination. *Bon appétit.*

CHRONOLOGY

1830	Born December 10 in Amherst, Massachusetts.
1840	Starts her first year at Amherst Academy.
1847–48	Graduates from Amherst Academy and enters South Hadley Female Seminary (now Mount Holyoke College).
1855	Visits Philadelphia and Washington, D.C.
1857	Emerson lectures in Amherst.
1862	Starts corresponding with Thomas Wentworth Higginson, asking for advice about her poems.
1864	Visits Boston for eye treatments.
1870	Higginson visits her in Amherst.
1873	Higginson visits her for a second and final time.
1874	Her father dies in Boston.
1875	Her mother suffers from paralysis.
1882	Her mother dies.
1886	Dies on May 15 in Amherst, Massachusetts.
1890	First edition of her poetry, edited by Mabel Loomis Todd and Thomas Wentworth Higginson, is published.
1955	Thomas H. Johnson publishes *The Poems of Emily Dickinson* in three volumes, thereby making available her poetry known to that date.

Success is counted sweetest   *c. 1859*

Success is counted sweetest
By those who ne'er succeed.
To comprehend a nectar
Requires sorest need.

Not one of all the purple Host   5
Who took the Flag today
Can tell the definition
So clear of Victory

As he defeated — dying —
On whose forbidden ear   10
The distant strains of triumph
Burst agonized and clear!

CONSIDERATIONS FOR CRITICAL THINKING AND WRITING

1. FIRST RESPONSE. How is "success" defined in this poem? To what extent does that definition agree with your own understanding of the word?

2. What do you think is meant by the use of "comprehend" in line 3? How can a nectar be comprehended?

3. Why do the defeated understand victory better than the victorious?

4. Discuss the effect of the poem's final line.

CONNECTION TO ANOTHER SELECTION

1. In an essay compare the themes of this poem with those of John Keats's "Ode on a Grecian Urn" (p. 741).

Water, is taught by thirst   *c. 1859*

Water, is taught by thirst.
Land — by the Oceans passed.
Transport — by throe —
Peace — by its battles told —
Love, by Memorial Mold —
Birds, by the Snow.

CONSIDERATIONS FOR CRITICAL THINKING AND WRITING

1. FIRST RESPONSE. Which image do you find most powerful? Explain why.

2. How is the paradox of each line of the poem resolved? How is the first word of each line "taught" by the phrase that follows it?

3. Try your hand at writing similar lines in which something is "taught."

CONNECTIONS TO OTHER SELECTIONS

1. What does this poem have in common with the preceding poem, "Success is counted sweetest"? Which poem do you think is more effective? Explain why.

2. How is the crucial point of this poem related to "I like a look of Agony," (p. 938)?

Safe in their Alabaster Chambers —   *1859 version*

Safe in their Alabaster Chambers —
Untouched by Morning
And untouched by Noon —
Sleep the meek members of the Resurrection —
Rafter of satin,   5
And Roof of stone.

Light laughs the breeze
In her Castle above them —

Babbles the Bee in a stolid Ear,
Pipe the Sweet Birds in ignorant cadence —   10
Ah, what sagacity perished here!

Safe in their Alabaster Chambers —   *1861 version*

Safe in their Alabaster Chambers —
Untouched by Morning —
And untouched by Noon —
Lie the meek members of the Resurrection —
Rafter of Satin — and Roof of Stone!   5

Grand go the Years — in the Crescent — above them —
Worlds scoop their arcs —
And Firmaments — row —
Diadems — drop — and Doges° — surrender —
Soundless as dots — on a Disc of Snow —   10

9 *Doges:* Chief magistrates of Venice from the twelfth to the sixteenth centuries.

CONSIDERATIONS FOR CRITICAL THINKING AND WRITING

1. FIRST RESPONSE. Dickinson permitted the 1859 version of this poem, entitled "The Sleeping," to be printed in the *Springfield Republican*. The second version she sent privately to Thomas Wentworth Higginson. Why do you suppose she would agree to publish the first but not the second version?

2. Are there any significant changes in the first stanzas of the two versions? If you answered yes, explain the significance of the changes.

3. Describe the different kinds of images used in the two second stanzas. How do those images affect the tones and meanings of those stanzas?

4. Discuss why you prefer one version of the poem to the other.

CONNECTIONS TO OTHER SELECTIONS

1. Compare the theme in the 1861 version with the theme of Robert Frost's "Design" (p. 993).

2. In an essay discuss the attitude toward death in the 1859 version and in "Apparently with no surprise" (p. 967).

Portraits are to daily faces   *c. 1860*

Portraits are to daily faces
As an Evening West,
To a fine, pedantic sunshine —
In a satin Vest!

Considerations for Critical Thinking and Writing

1. FIRST RESPONSE. Dickinson once described her literary art this way: "My business is circumference." Does this poem fit her characterization of her poetry?

2. How is the basic strategy of this poem similar to the following statement: "Doorknob is to door as button is to sweater"?

3. Identify the four metonymies in the poem. Pay close attention to their connotative meanings.

4. If you don't know the meaning of "pedantic," look it up in a dictionary. How does its meaning affect your reading of "fine"?

Connections to Other Selections

1. Compare Dickinson's view of poetry in this poem with Francis's perspective in "Catch" (p. 676). What important similarities and differences do you find?

2. Write an essay describing Robert Frost's strategy in "Mending Wall" (p. 979) or "Birches" (p. 986) as the business of circumference.

3. How is the theme of this poem related to the central idea in "The Thought beneath so slight a film —" (p. 931)?

4. Compare the use of the word "fine" here with its use in "'Faith' is a fine invention" (p. 966).

Some keep the Sabbath going to Church —   c. 1860

Some keep the Sabbath going to Church —
I keep it, staying at Home —
With a Bobolink for a Chorister —
And an Orchard, for a Dome —

Some keep the Sabbath in Surplice°   *holy robes*   5
I just wear my Wings —
And instead of tolling the Bell, for Church,
Our little Sexton — sings.

God preaches, a noted Clergyman —
And the sermon is never long,   10
So instead of getting to Heaven, at last —
I'm going, all along.

Considerations for Critical Thinking and Writing

1. FIRST RESPONSE. What is the effect of referring to "Some" people?

2. Characterize the speaker's tone.

3. How does the speaker distinguish himself or herself from those who go to church?

4. How might "Surplice" be read as a pun?

5. According to the speaker, how should the Sabbath be observed?

CONNECTION TO ANOTHER SELECTION

1. Write an essay that discusses nature in this poem and in Walt Whitman's "When I Heard the Learn'd Astronomer" (p. 1124).

I taste a liquor never brewed —

1861

I taste a liquor never brewed —
From Tankards scooped in Pearl —
Not all the Vats upon the Rhine
Yield such an Alcohol!

Inebriate of Air — am I —   5
And Debauchee of Dew —
Reeling — thro endless summer days —
From inns of Molten Blue —

When "Landlords" turn the drunken Bee
Out of the Foxglove's door —   10
When Butterflies — renounce their "drams" —
I shall but drink the more!

Till Seraphs° swing their snowy Hats —   *angels*
And Saints — to windows run —
To see the little Tippler   15
Leaning against the — Sun —

CONSIDERATIONS FOR CRITICAL THINKING AND WRITING

1. FIRST RESPONSE. What is this poem about? How is its central metaphor developed in each stanza?
2. Which images suggest the causes of the speaker's intoxication?
3. Characterize the speaker's relationship to nature.

CONNECTIONS TO OTHER SELECTIONS

1. In an essay compare this speaker's relationship with nature to that in "A narrow Fellow in the Grass" (p. 2).
2. Discuss the tone created by the images in this poem and in Kinnell's "Blackberry Eating" (p. 832).

"Heaven" — is what I cannot reach!

c. 1861

"Heaven" — is what I cannot reach!
The Apple on the Tree —
Provided it do hopeless — hang —
That — "Heaven" is — to Me!

The Color, on the Cruising Cloud —   5
The interdicted Land —

Behind the Hill — the House behind —
There — Paradise — is found!

Her teasing Purples — Afternoons —
The credulous — decoy —   10
Enamored — of the Conjuror —
That spurned us — Yesterday!

CONSIDERATIONS FOR CRITICAL THINKING AND WRITING

1. FIRST RESPONSE. How does the speaker define heaven? How does that definition compare with conventional views of heaven?

2. Look up the myth of Tantalus and explain the allusion in line 3.

3. Given the speaker's definition of heaven, how do you think the speaker
   would describe hell?

CONNECTIONS TO OTHER SELECTIONS

1. Write an essay that discusses desire in this poem and in "Water, is taught by
   thirst" (p. 933).

2. Discuss the speakers' attitudes toward pleasure in this poem and in Ackerman's "A Fine, a Private Place" (p. 734).

Of Bronze — and Blaze —   *c. 1861*

Of Bronze — and Blaze —
The North — Tonight —
So adequate — it forms —
So preconcerted with itself —
So distant — to alarms —   5
An Unconcern so sovereign
To Universe, or me —
Infects my simple spirit
With Taints of Majesty —
Till I take vaster attitudes —   10
And strut upon my stem —
Disdaining Men, and Oxygen,
For Arrogance of them —

My Splendors, are Menagerie —
But their Competeless Show   15
Will entertain the Centuries
When I, am long ago,
An Island in dishonored Grass —
Whom none but Beetles — know.

CONSIDERATIONS FOR CRITICAL THINKING AND WRITING

1. FIRST RESPONSE. What is the tone of this description of northern lights in
   the sky?

2. How does the rhythm of lines 1–5 help to convey their meaning?

3. How does the speaker feel about ordinary life as a result of viewing the sky (lines 6–13)?

4. What comparison is made between human life and the "Competeless Show" (line 15) in the sky?

CONNECTIONS TO OTHER SELECTIONS

1. Compare the theme of this poem with that of Crane's "A Man Said to the Universe" (p. 805).

2. In an essay compare the sense of wonder expressed in "Of Bronze — and Blaze —" and in Keats's "On First Looking into Chapman's Homer" (p. 879).

I like a look of Agony,   c. 1861

I like a look of Agony,
Because I know it's true —
Men do not sham Convulsion,
Nor simulate, a Throe —

The Eyes glaze once — and that is Death —
Impossible to feign
The Beads upon the Forehead
By homely Anguish strung.

CONSIDERATIONS FOR CRITICAL THINKING AND WRITING

1. FIRST RESPONSE. Why does the speaker "like a look of Agony"? How do you respond to her appreciation of "Convulsion"?

2. Discuss the image of "The Eyes glaze once —." Why is that a particularly effective metaphor for death?

3. Characterize the speaker. One critic once described the voice in this poem as "almost a hysterical shriek." Explain why you agree or disagree.

CONNECTION TO ANOTHER SELECTION

1. Write an essay on Dickinson's attitudes toward pain and deprivation, using this poem, "'Heaven' — is what I cannot reach!" (p. 936), and "Success is counted sweetest" (p. 932) as the basis for your discussion.

I'm Nobody! Who are you?   c. 1861

I'm Nobody! Who are you?
Are you — Nobody — too?
Then there's a pair of us!
Don't tell! they'd advertise — you know!

How dreary — to be — Somebody!
How public — like a Frog —

To tell your name — the livelong June —
To an admiring Bog!

CONSIDERATIONS FOR CRITICAL THINKING AND WRITING

1. FIRST RESPONSE. What does the speaker wish to have in common with the reader? Explain whether you feel it is better to be "Nobody" or "Somebody."
2. Explain why it is "dreary — to be — Somebody!"
3. Discuss the simile in line 6. Why does it work so well?
4. What does the speaker think of most people?

CONNECTION TO ANOTHER SELECTION

1. Contrast the sense of self in this poem and Walt Whitman's "One's-Self I Sing" (p. 1124).

Wild Nights — Wild Nights!   *c. 1861*

Wild Nights — Wild Nights!
Were I with thee
Wild Nights should be
Our luxury!

Futile — the Winds —   5
To a Heart in port —
Done with the Compass —
Done with the Chart!

Rowing in Eden —
Ah, the Sea!   10
Might I but moor — Tonight —
In Thee!

CONSIDERATIONS FOR CRITICAL THINKING AND WRITING

1. FIRST RESPONSE. Thomas Wentworth Higginson, Dickinson's mentor, once said he was afraid that some "malignant" readers might "read into [a poem like this] more than that virgin recluse ever dreamed of putting there." What do you think?
2. Look up the meaning of "luxury" in a dictionary. Why does this word work especially well here?
3. Given the imagery of the final stanza, do you think the speaker is a man or woman? Explain why.

CONNECTION TO ANOTHER SELECTION

1. Write an essay that compares the voice, figures of speech, and theme of this poem with those of Atwood's "you fit into me" (p. 777).

I cannot dance upon my Toes —

c. 1862

I cannot dance upon my Toes —
No Man instructed me —
But oftentimes, among my mind,
A Glee possesseth me,

That had I Ballet knowledge —   5
Would put itself abroad
In Pirouette to blanch a Troupe —
Or lay a Prima, mad,

And though I had no Gown of Gauze —
No Ringlet, to my Hair,   10
Nor hopped to Audiences — like Birds,
One Claw upon the Air,

Nor tossed my shape in Eider Balls,
Nor rolled on wheels of snow
Till I was out of sight, in sound,   15
The House encore me so —

Nor any know I know the Art
I mention — easy — Here —
Nor any Placard boast me —
It's full as Opera —   20

CONSIDERATIONS FOR CRITICAL THINKING AND WRITING

1. FIRST RESPONSE. What can the speaker do, though she "cannot dance"?
2. Why is the speaker possessed by "Glee" (line 4)?
3. Discuss the images of dancing in lines 6–15 and explain their effects. What is the speaker's attitude toward dance, do you think?
4. Paraphrase the final stanza and explain how it relates to the poem's theme.

CONNECTION TO ANOTHER SELECTION

1. Consider the power of "mind" in this poem and in "To make a prairie it takes a clover and one bee" (p. 931).

What Soft — Cherubic Creatures —

1862

What Soft — Cherubic Creatures —
These Gentlewomen are —
One would as soon assault a Plush —
Or violate a Star —

Such Dimity° Convictions —   *sheer cotton fabric* 5
A Horror so refined

Of freckled Human Nature —
Of Deity — ashamed —

It's such a common — Glory —
A Fisherman's — Degree —   10
Redemption — Brittle Lady —
Be so — ashamed of Thee —

CONSIDERATIONS FOR CRITICAL THINKING AND WRITING

1. FIRST RESPONSE. Characterize the "Gentlewomen" in this poem.
2. How do the sounds produced in the first line help to reinforce their meaning?
3. What are "Dimity Convictions," and what do they make "Of freckled Human Nature"?
4. Discuss the irony in the final stanza.

CONNECTION TO ANOTHER SELECTION

1. How are the "Gentlewomen" in this poem similar to the "Gentlemen" in "'Faith' is a fine invention" (p. 966)?

The Soul selects her own Society —   *c. 1862*

The Soul selects her own Society —
Then — shuts the Door —
To her divine Majority —
Present no more —

Unmoved — she notes the Chariots — pausing —   5
At her low Gate —
Unmoved — an Emperor be kneeling
Upon her Mat —

I've known her — from an ample nation —
Choose One —
Then — close the Valves of her attention —   10
Like Stone —

CONSIDERATIONS FOR CRITICAL THINKING AND WRITING

1. FIRST RESPONSE. Characterize the speaker. Is she self-reliant and self-sufficient? Cold? Angry?
2. Why do you suppose the "Soul" in this poem is female? Would it make any difference if it were male?
3. Discuss the effect of the images in the final two lines. Pay particular attention to the meanings of "Valves" in line 11.

This is my letter to the World   c. 1862

This is my letter to the World
That never wrote to Me —
The simple News that Nature told —
With tender Majesty

Her Message is committed
To Hands I cannot see —
For love of Her — Sweet — countrymen —
Judge tenderly — of Me

CONSIDERATIONS FOR CRITICAL THINKING AND WRITING

1. FIRST RESPONSE. In what sense did the world not write to the speaker?
2. Read the section on biographical criticism in Chapter 37, "Critical Strategies for Reading" (p. 2027). Why and how is biographical criticism especially useful for interpreting this poem?

CONNECTIONS TO OTHER SELECTIONS

1. In an essay compare the tone of this poem with that of "The Soul selects her own Society —" (p. 941).
2. Consider in an essay how "This is my letter to the World" might be explained using the themes in "'Heaven' — is what I cannot reach!" (p. 936).

Much Madness is divinest Sense —   c. 1862

Much Madness is divinest Sense —
To a discerning Eye —
Much Sense — the starkest Madness —
'Tis the Majority
In this, as All, prevail —
Assent — and you are sane —
Demur — you're straightway dangerous —
And handled with a Chain —

CONSIDERATIONS FOR CRITICAL THINKING AND WRITING

1. FIRST RESPONSE. Thomas Wentworth Higginson's wife once referred to Dickinson as the "partially cracked poetess of Amherst." Assuming that Dickinson had some idea of how she was regarded by the "Majority," how might this poem be seen as an insight into her life?
2. Discuss the conflict between the individual and society in this poem. Which images are used to describe each? How do these images affect your attitudes about them?
3. Comment on the effectiveness of the poem's final line.

1. Discuss the theme of self-reliance in this poem and in "The Soul selects her own Society—" (p. 941).

I dwell in Possibility —   c. 1862

I dwell in Possibility—
A fairer House than Prose—
More numerous of Windows—
Superior—for Doors—

Of Chambers as the Cedars—   5
Impregnable of Eye—
And for an Everlasting Roof
The Gambrels° of the Sky—   *angled roofs*

Of Visitors—the fairest—
For Occupation—This—   10
The spreading wide my narrow Hands
To gather Paradise—

CONSIDERATIONS FOR CRITICAL THINKING AND WRITING

1. FIRST RESPONSE. What distinction is made between poetry and prose in this poem? Explain why you agree or disagree with the speaker's distinctions.

2. What is the poem's central metaphor in the second and third stanzas?

3. How does the use of metaphor in this poem become a means for the speaker to envision and create a world beyond the circumstances of the speaker's actual life?

CONNECTIONS TO OTHER SELECTIONS

1. Compare what this poem says about poetry and prose with Hulme's comments in the perspective "On the Differences between Poetry and Prose" (p. 774).

2. How can the speaker's sense of expansiveness in this poem be reconciled with the speaker's insistence on contraction in "The Soul selects her own Society—" (p. 941)? Are these poems contradictory? Explain why or why not.

This was a Poet — It is That   c. 1862

This was a Poet—It is That
Distills amazing sense
From ordinary Meanings—
And Attar so immense

From the familiar species   5
That perished by the Door—

We wonder it was not Ourselves
Arrested it — before —

Of Pictures, the Discloser —
The Poet — it is He —   10
Entitles Us — by Contrast —
To ceaseless Poverty —

Of Portion — so unconscious —
The Robbing — could not harm —
Himself — to Him — a Fortune —   15
Exterior — to Time —

CONSIDERATIONS FOR CRITICAL THINKING AND WRITING

1. FIRST RESPONSE. According to the speaker, what powers does a poet have?
   Why are these powers important?

2. Explain the metaphors of "Poverty" (line 12) and "Fortune" (line 15) and
   how they contribute to the poem's theme.

CONNECTIONS TO OTHER SELECTIONS

1. Write an essay about a life lived in imagination as depicted in this poem
   and in "I dwell in Possibility —" (p. 943).

2. Discuss "A Bird came down the Walk" (p. 829) as an example of a poem that
   "Distills amazing sense / From ordinary Meanings —" (lines 2-3).

I read my sentence — steadily —   *c. 1862*

I read my sentence — steadily —
Reviewed it with my eyes,
To see that I made no mistake
In its extremest clause —
The Date, and manner, of the shame —   5
And then the Pious Form
That "God have mercy" on the Soul
The Jury voted Him —
I made my soul familiar — with her extremity —
That at the last, it should not be a novel Agony —   10
But she, and Death, acquainted —
Meet tranquilly, as friends —
Salute, and pass, without a Hint —
And there, the Matter ends —

CONSIDERATIONS FOR CRITICAL THINKING AND WRITING

1. FIRST RESPONSE. What is the speaker's "sentence"? What do you think of
   the tone of the poem, considering its subject?

2. What is the central metaphor? Why is it appropriate for this poem's subject matter?

3. How does the speaker regard death in lines 9–14?

CONNECTIONS TO OTHER SELECTIONS

1. Compare the treatment of death in this poem and in "Because I could not stop for Death —" (p. 948).

2. In an essay discuss the "Agony" in this poem and in "I like a look of Agony" (p. 938).

The Grass so little has to do —

c. 1862

The Grass so little has to do —
A Sphere of simple Green —
With only Butterflies to brood
And Bees to entertain —

And stir all day to pretty Tunes   5
The Breezes fetch along —
And hold the Sunshine in its lap
And bow to everything —

And thread the Dews, all night, like Pearls —
And make itself so fine   10
A Duchess were too common
For such a noticing —

And even when it dies — to pass
In Odors so divine —
Like Lowly spices, lain to sleep —   15
Or Spikenards, perishing —

And then, in Sovereign Barns to dwell —
And dream the Days away,
The Grass so little has to do
I wish I were a Hay —   20

CONSIDERATIONS FOR CRITICAL THINKING AND WRITING

1. FIRST RESPONSE. Do you think this is a sentimental poem? Explain your response.

2. What is the effect of the repeated use of "And"?

3. How is the grass described? Which images seem especially effective to you?

CONNECTIONS TO OTHER SELECTIONS

1. Discuss the tone of this poem and "Presentiment — is that long Shadow — on the lawn —" (p. 777).

2. In an essay compare the speaker's contemplation of death in this poem and in Robert Frost's "Stopping by Woods on a Snowy Evening" (p. 989).

After great pain, a formal feeling comes —

c. 1862

After great pain, a formal feeling comes —
The Nerves sit ceremonious, like Tombs —
The stiff Heart questions was it He, that bore,
And Yesterday, or Centuries before?

The Feet, mechanical, go round — 5
Of Ground, or Air, or Ought —
A Wooden way
Regardless grown,
A Quartz contentment, like a stone —

This is the Hour of Lead — 10
Remembered, if outlived,
As Freezing persons, recollect the Snow —
First — Chill — then Stupor — then the letting go —

CONSIDERATIONS FOR CRITICAL THINKING AND WRITING

1. FIRST RESPONSE. What do you think has caused the speaker's pain?
2. How does the rhythm of the lines create a slow, somber pace?
3. Discuss why "the Hour of Lead" (line 10) could serve as a useful title for this poem.

CONNECTIONS TO OTHER SELECTIONS

1. How might this poem be read as a kind of sequel to "The Bustle in a House" (p. 950).
2. Write an essay that discusses this poem in relation to Robert Frost's "Home Burial" (p. 980).

I heard a Fly buzz — when I died —

c. 1862

I heard a Fly buzz — when I died —
The Stillness in the Room
Was like the Stillness in the Air —
Between the Heaves of Storm —

The Eyes around — had wrung them dry — 5
And Breaths were gathering firm
For that last Onset — when the King
Be witnessed — in the Room —

I willed my Keepsakes — Signed away
What portion of me be 10
Assignable — and then it was
There interposed a Fly —

With Blue — uncertain stumbling Buzz —
Between the light — and me —

And then the Windows failed — and then   15
I could not see to see —

CONSIDERATIONS FOR CRITICAL THINKING AND WRITING

1. FIRST RESPONSE. What was expected to happen "when the King" was "witnessed"? What happened instead?
2. Why do you think Dickinson chooses a fly rather than perhaps a bee or gnat?
3. What is the effect of the last line? Why not end the poem with "I could not see" instead of the additional "to see"?
4. Discuss the sounds in the poem. Are there any instances of onomatopoeia?

CONNECTIONS TO OTHER SELECTIONS

1. Contrast the symbolic significance of the fly with the spider in Whitman's "A Noiseless Patient Spider" (p. 788).
2. Consider the meaning of "light" in this poem and in "There's a certain Slant of light" (p. 2082).

One need not be a Chamber — to be Haunted —   *c. 1863*

One need not be a Chamber — to be Haunted —
One need not be a House —
The Brain has Corridors — surpassing
Material Place —

Far safer, of a Midnight Meeting   5
External Ghost
Than its interior Confronting —
That Cooler Host.

Far safer, through an Abbey gallop,
The Stones a'chase —   10
Than Unarmed, one's a'self encounter —
In lonesome Place —

Ourself behind ourself, concealed —
Should startle most —
Assassin hid in our Apartment   15
Be Horror's least.

The Body — borrows a Revolver —
He bolts the Door —
O'erlooking a superior spectre —
Or More —   20

CONSIDERATIONS FOR CRITICAL THINKING AND WRITING

1. FIRST RESPONSE. Paraphrase the poem. Which stanza is most difficult to paraphrase? Why?

2. What is the controlling metaphor? Explain why you think it is effective or not.

3. What is the "superior spectre" in line 19?

CONNECTIONS TO OTHER SELECTIONS

1. Compare and contrast this poem with Poe's "The Haunted Palace" (p. 800) and Stevens's "Schizophrenia" (p. 788). In an essay explain which poem you find the most frightening.

Because I could not stop for Death —   *c. 1863*

Because I could not stop for Death —
He kindly stopped for me —
The Carriage held but just Ourselves —
And Immortality.

We slowly drove — He knew no haste   5
And I had put away
My labor and my leisure too,
For His Civility —

We passed the School, where Children strove
At Recess — in the Ring —   10
We passed the Fields of Gazing Grain —
We passed the Setting Sun —

Or rather — He passed Us —
The Dews drew quivering and chill —
For only Gossamer, my Gown —   15
My Tippet° — only Tulle —   *shawl*

We paused before a House that seemed
A Swelling of the Ground —
The Roof was scarcely visible —
The Cornice — in the Ground —   20

Since then — 'tis Centuries — and yet
Feels shorter than the Day
I first surmised the Horses' Heads
Were toward Eternity —

CONSIDERATIONS FOR CRITICAL THINKING AND WRITING

1. FIRST RESPONSE. Why couldn't the speaker "stop for Death"?

2. How is death personified in this poem? How does the speaker respond to him? Why are they accompanied by immortality?

3. What is the significance of the things they "passed" in the third stanza?

4. What is the "House" in lines 17–20?

5. Discuss the rhythm of the lines. How, for example, is the rhythm of line 14 related to its meaning?

CONNECTIONS TO OTHER SELECTIONS

1. Compare the tone of this poem with that of Dickinson's "Apparently with no surprise" (p. 967).
2. Write an essay comparing Dickinson's view of death in this poem and in "If I shouldn't be alive" (p. 929). Which poem is more powerful for you? Explain why.

A Light exists in Spring   *c. 1864*

A Light exists in Spring
Not present on the Year
At any other period —
When March is scarcely here

A Color stands abroad   5
On Solitary Fields
That Science cannot overtake
But Human Nature feels.

It waits upon the Lawn,
It shows the furthest Tree   10
Upon the furthest Slope you know
It almost speaks to you.

Then as Horizons step
Or Noons report away
Without the Formula of sound   15
It passes and we stay —

A quality of loss
Affecting our Content
As Trade had suddenly encroached
Upon a Sacrament.   20

CONSIDERATIONS FOR CRITICAL THINKING AND WRITING

1. FIRST RESPONSE. Describe the poem's tone. Does it change from the beginning to the end?
2. What does the speaker associate with the spring light of March? Paraphrase each stanza. Which one reveals most clearly the nature of this light for you?
3. Discuss the meaning of the speaker's use of "Trade."

CONNECTIONS TO OTHER SELECTIONS

1. Discuss the treatment of spring in this poem and in Cummings's "in Just-" (p. 902).
2. In an essay compare Dickinson's use of "light" in this poem, in "I heard a Fly buzz — when I died —" (p. 946), and in "There's a certain Slant of light" (p. 2082).

I felt a Cleaving in my Mind —   c. 1864

I felt a Cleaving in my Mind —
As if my Brain had split —
I tried to match it — Seam by Seam —
But could not make them fit.

The thought behind, I strove to join
Unto the thought before —
But Sequence ravelled out of Sound
Like Balls — upon a Floor.

CONSIDERATIONS FOR CRITICAL THINKING AND WRITING

1. FIRST RESPONSE. What is going on in the speaker's mind?
2. What is the poem's controlling metaphor? Describe the simile in lines 7 and 8. How does it clarify further the first stanza?
3. Discuss the rhymes. How do they reinforce meaning?

CONNECTION TO ANOTHER SELECTION

1. Compare the power of the speaker's mind described here with the power of imagination described in "To make a prairie it takes a clover and one bee" (p. 931).

The Bustle in a House   c. 1866

The Bustle in a House
The Morning after Death
Is solemnest of industries
Enacted upon Earth —

The Sweeping up the Heart
And putting Love away
We shall not want to use again
Until Eternity.

CONSIDERATIONS FOR CRITICAL THINKING AND WRITING

1. FIRST RESPONSE. What is the relationship between love and death in this poem?
2. Why do you think mourning (notice the pun in line 2) is described as an industry?
3. Discuss the tone of the ending of the poem. Consider whether you think it is hopeful, sad, resigned, or some other mood.

CONNECTIONS TO OTHER SELECTIONS

1. Compare this poem with "After great pain, a formal feeling comes —" (p. 946). Which poem is, for you, a more powerful treatment of mourning?

2. How does this poem qualify "I like a look of Agony," (p. 938)? Does it contradict the latter poem? Explain why or why not.

Tell all the Truth but tell it slant —

c. 1868

Tell all the Truth but tell it slant —
Success in Circuit lies
Too bright for our infirm Delight
The Truth's superb surprise

As Lightning to the Children eased
With explanation kind
The Truth must dazzle gradually
Or every man be blind —

CONSIDERATIONS FOR CRITICAL THINKING AND WRITING

1. FIRST RESPONSE. What do you think the first line means? Why should truth be told "slant" and circuitously?
2. How does the second stanza explain the first?
3. How is this poem an example of its own theme?

CONNECTIONS TO OTHER SELECTIONS

1. How does the first stanza of "I know that He exists" (p. 967) suggest an idea similar to this poem's? Why do you think the last eight lines of the former aren't similar in theme to this poem?
2. Write an essay on Dickinson's attitudes about the purpose and strategies of poetry by considering this poem as well as "The Thought beneath so slight a film —" (p. 931) and "Portraits are to daily faces" (p. 934).

From all the Jails the Boys and Girls

c. 1881

From all the Jails the Boys and Girls
Ecstatically leap —
Beloved only Afternoon
That Prison doesn't keep

They storm the Earth and stun the Air,
A Mob of solid Bliss —
Alas — that Frowns should lie in wait
For such a Foe as this —

CONSIDERATIONS FOR CRITICAL THINKING AND WRITING

1. FIRST RESPONSE. What are the "Jails"? How are children characterized in this poem?

2. Comment on the effectiveness of the description in lines 5 and 6.

3. How might "Frowns" be read symbolically?

CONNECTIONS TO OTHER SELECTIONS

1. Compare the theme of this poem with that of William Blake's "The Garden of Love" (p. 1078).

2. In an essay discuss the treatment of childhood in this poem and in Robert Frost's "Out, Out—" (p. 987).

PERSPECTIVES ON DICKINSON

Dickinson's Description of Herself   *1862*

Mr Higginson,

Your kindness claimed earlier gratitude—but I was ill—and write today, from my pillow.

Thank you for the surgery—it was not so painful as I supposed. I bring you others°—as you ask—though they might not differ—

While my thought is undressed—I can make the distinction, but when I put them in the Gown—they look alike, and numb.

You asked how old I was? I made no verse — but one or two° — until this winter — Sir —

I had a terror—since September—I could tell to none—and so I sing, as the Boy does by the Burying Ground—because I am afraid—You inquire my Books—For Poets—I have Keats—and Mr and Mrs Browning. For Prose—Mr Ruskin—Sir Thomas Browne—and the Revelations. I went to school—but in your manner of the phrase—had no education. When a little Girl, I had a friend, who taught me Immortality—but venturing too near, himself—he never returned—Soon after, my Tutor, died—and for several years, my Lexicon—was my only companion—Then I found one more—but he was not contented I be his scholar—so he left the Land.

You ask of my Companions Hills—Sir—and the Sundown—and a Dog—large as myself, that my Father bought me—They are better than Beings—because they know—but do not tell—and the noise in the Pool, at Noon—excels my Piano. I have a Brother and Sister—My Mother does not care for thought—and Father, too busy with his Briefs—to notice what we do—He buys me many Books—but begs me not to read them—because he fears they joggle the Mind. They are religious—except me—and address an Eclipse, every morning—whom they call their "Father." But I fear my story fatigues you—I would like to learn—Could you tell me how to grow—or is it unconveyed—like Melody—or Witchcraft?

From a letter to Thomas Wentworth Higginson, April 25, 1862

others: Dickinson had sent poems to Higginson for his opinions and enclosed more with this letter.
one or two: Actually she had written almost 300 poems.

CONSIDERATIONS FOR CRITICAL THINKING AND WRITING

1. What impression does this letter give you of Dickinson?
2. What kinds of thoughts are there in the foreground of her thinking?
3. To what extent is the style of her letter writing like that of her poetry?

THOMAS WENTWORTH HIGGINSON (1823–1911)
On Meeting Dickinson for the First Time   *1870*

A large county lawyer's house, brown brick, with great trees & a garden — I sent up my card. A parlor dark & cool & stiffish, a few books & engravings & an open piano. . . .

A step like a pattering child's in entry & in glided a little plain woman with two smooth bands of reddish hair & a face a little like Belle Dove's; not plainer — with no good feature — in a very plain & exquisitely clean white pique & a blue net worsted shawl. She came to me with two day lilies which she put in a sort of childlike way into my hand & said "These are my introduction" in a soft frightened breathless childlike voice — & added under her breath Forgive me if I am frightened; I never see strangers & hardly know what I say — but she talked soon & thenceforward continuously — & deferentially — sometimes stopping to ask me to talk instead of her — but readily recommencing . . . thoroughly ingenuous & simple . . . & saying many things which you would have thought foolish & I wise — & some things you wd. hv. liked. I add a few over the page. . . .

"Women talk; men are silent; that is why I dread women."

"My father only reads on Sunday — he reads *lonely* & *rigorous* books."

"If I read a book [and] it makes my whole body so cold no fire ever can warm me I know *that* is poetry. If I feel physically as if the top of my head were taken off, I know *that* is poetry. These are the only ways I know it. Is there any other way."

"How do most people live without any thoughts. There are many people in the world (you must have noticed them in the street) How do they live. How do they get strength to put on their clothes in the morning"

"When I lost the use of my Eyes it was a comfort to think there were so few real *books* that I could easily find some one to read me all of them"

"Truth is such a *rare* thing it is delightful to tell it."

"I find ecstasy in living — the mere sense of living is joy enough"

I asked if she never felt want of employment, never going off the place & never seeing any visitor "I never thought of conceiving that I could ever have the slightest approach to such a want in all future time" (& added) "I feel that I have not expressed myself strongly enough."

From a letter to his wife, August 16, 1870

CONSIDERATIONS FOR CRITICAL THINKING AND WRITING

1. How old is Dickinson when Higginson meets her? Does this description seem commensurate with her age? Explain why or why not.

2. Choose one of the quotations from Dickinson that Higginson includes and write an essay about what it reveals about her.

MABEL LOOMIS TODD (1856–1932)
The Character *of Amherst*   *1881*

I must tell you about the *character* of Amherst. It is a lady whom the people call the *Myth.* She is a sister of Mr. Dickinson, & seems to be the climax of all the family oddity. She has not been outside of her own house in fifteen years, except once to see a new church, when she crept out at night, & viewed it by moonlight. No one who calls upon her mother & sister ever see her, but she allows little children once in a great while, & one at a time, to come in, when she gives them cake or candy, or some nicety, for she is very fond of little ones. But more often she lets down the sweetmeat by a string, out of a window, to them. She dresses wholly in white, & her mind is said to be perfectly wonderful. She writes finely, but no one *ever* sees her. Her sister, who was at Mrs. Dickinson's party, invited me to come & sing to her mother sometime. . . . People tell me the *myth* will hear every note—she will be near, but unseen. . . . Isn't that like a book? So interesting.

From a letter to her parents, November 6, 1881

CONSIDERATIONS FOR CRITICAL THINKING AND WRITING

1. Todd, who in the 1890s would edit Dickinson's poems and letters, had known her for only two months when she wrote this letter. How does Todd characterize Dickinson?
2. Does this description seem positive or negative to you? Explain your answer.
3. A few of Dickinson's poems, such as "Much Madness is divinest Sense—" (p. 942) suggest that she was aware of this perception of her. Refer to her poems in discussing Dickinson's response to this perception.

RICHARD WILBUR (B. 1921)
On Dickinson's Sense of Privation   *1960*

What did Emily Dickinson do, as a poet, with her sense of privation? One thing she quite often did was to pose as the laureate and attorney of the empty-handed, and question God about the economy of His creation. Why, she asked, is a fatherly God so sparing of His presence? Why is there never a sign that prayers are heard? Why does Nature tell us no comforting news of its Maker? Why do some receive a whole loaf, while others must starve on a crumb? Where is the benevolence in shipwreck and earthquake? By asking such questions as these, she turned complaint into critique, and used her own sufferings as experiential evidence about the nature of the deity. The God who emerges from these poems is a God who does not answer, an unrevealed God whom one cannot confidently approach through Nature or through doctrine.

But there was another way in which Emily Dickinson dealt with her sentiment of lack—another emotional strategy which was both more frequent and more fruitful. I refer to her repeated assertion of the paradox that privation is more plentiful than plenty; that to renounce is to possess the more; that "The Banquet of abstemiousness / Defaces that of wine." We all know how the poet illustrated this ascetic paradox in her behavior—how in her latter years she chose to live in relative retirement, keeping the world, even in its dearest aspects, at a physical remove. She would write her friends, telling them how she missed them, then flee upstairs when they came to see her; afterward, she might send a note of apology, offering the odd explanation that "We shun because we prize." Any reader of Dickinson biographies can furnish other examples, dramatic or homely, of this prizing and shunning, this yearning and renouncing: in my own mind's eye is a picture of Emily Dickinson watching a gay circus caravan from the distance of her chamber window.

> From "Sumptuous Destitution" in *Emily Dickinson: Three Views,*
> by Richard Wilbur, Louise Bogan, and Archibald MacLeish

CONSIDERATIONS FOR CRITICAL THINKING AND WRITING

1. Which poems by Dickinson reprinted in this anthology suggest that she was "the laureate and attorney of the empty-handed"?
2. Which poems suggest that "privation is more plentiful"?
3. Of these two types of poems, which do you prefer? Write an essay that explains your preference.

SANDRA M. GILBERT (B. 1936) AND
SUSAN GUBAR (B. 1944)

On Dickinson's White Dress   1979

Today a dress that the Amherst Historical Society assures us is *the* white dress Dickinson wore—or at least one of her "Uniforms of Snow"—hangs in a drycleaner's plastic bag in the closet of the Dickinson homestead. Perfectly preserved, beautifully flounced and tucked, it is larger than most readers would have expected this self-consciously small poet's dress to be, and thus reminds visiting scholars of the enduring enigma of Dickinson's central metaphor, even while it draws gasps from more practical visitors, who reflect with awe upon the difficulties of maintaining such a costume. But what exactly did the literal and figurative whiteness of this costume represent? What rewards did it offer that would cause an intelligent woman to overlook those practical difficulties? Comparing Dickinson's obsession with whiteness to Melville's, William R. Sherwood suggests that "it reflected in her case the Christian mystery and not a Christian enigma . . . a decision to announce . . . the assumption of a worldly death that paradoxically involved regeneration." This, he adds, her gown—"a typically slant demonstration of truth"—should have revealed "to anyone with the wit to catch on."[1]

We might reasonably wonder, however, if Dickinson herself consciously intended her wardrobe to convey any one message. The range of associations

[1] *Circumference and Circumstance: Stages in the Mind and Art of Emily Dickinson* (New York: Columbia UP, 1968) 152, 231.

her white poems imply suggests, on the contrary, that for her, as for Melville, white is the ultimate symbol of enigma, paradox, and irony, "not so much a color as the visible absence of color, and at the same time the concrete of all colors." Melville's question [in *Moby-Dick*] might, therefore, also be hers: "is it for these reasons that there is such a dumb blankness, full of meaning, in a wide landscape of snows — a colorless, all-color of atheism from which we shrink?" And his concluding speculation might be hers too, his remark "that the mystical cosmetic which produces every one of [Nature's] hues, the great principle of light, for ever remains white or colorless in itself, and if operating without medium upon matter, would touch all objects . . . with its own blank tinge." For white, in Dickinson's poetry, frequently represents both the energy (the white heat) of Romantic creativity, and the loneliness (the polar cold) of the renunciation or tribulation Romantic creativity may demand, both the white radiance of eternity — or Revelation — and the white terror of a shroud.

From *The Madwoman in the Attic: The Woman Writer and the Nineteenth-Century Literary Imagination*

CONSIDERATIONS FOR CRITICAL THINKING AND WRITING

1. What meanings do Gilbert and Gubar attribute to Dickinson's white dress?

2. Discuss the meaning of the implicit whiteness in "Safe in their Alabaster Chambers —" (pp. 933–934) and "After great pain, a formal feeling comes —" (p. 946). To what extent do these poems incorporate the meanings of whiteness that Gilbert and Gubar suggest?

3. What other possible reasons can you think of that would account for Dickinson's wearing only white?

KARL KELLER (B. 1933)

Robert Frost on Dickinson   1979

Frost lived in Amherst for quite a number of years — 1917–20, 1923–25, 1926–38, and then intermittently in the late 1940s and throughout the 1950s when he taught regularly at Amherst College. He often recited her poems from memory, and he conversed with students, friends, and townspeople about her poetry; his concern was almost always over her ability to contain/limit an open-ended universe. He felt this was "what Emily Dickinson surely intends," as he put it, "when she contends: 'In insecurity to lie / Is Joy's insuring quality.'"

It appears that Frost had a one-track mind about Emily Dickinson — her doggedness. For him she was an example of the poet "whose 'state,'" as he put it himself, "never gets sidetracked."

> Since she wrote without thought of publication and was not under the necessity of revamping and polishing, it was easy for her to go right to the point and say precisely what she thought and felt. Her technical irregularities give her poems strength as if she were saying, "Look out, Rhyme and Meter, here I come."

Frost apparently liked this willfulness, the unmanageability of the thought by the poetic form, and yet he thought she arrived at it a little too easily and that it was therefore sometimes indistinguishable from carelessness. He felt she had given up the technical struggle too easily. For Frost, to use a general state-ment of his about poetic rhythm, she was a little too "easy in [her] harness."[1]

Emily Dickinson succeeded, Frost was forced to admit, by flouting poetic systems, by playing freely with the form.

> I try to make good sentences fit the meter. That is important. Good grammar. I don't like to twist the order around in order to fit a form. I try to keep to regu-lar structure and good rhymes. Though I admit that Emily Dickinson, for one, didn't do this always. When she started a poem, it was "Here I come!" and she came plunging through. The meter and rhyme often had to take care of itself.[2]

Though envious of this carefree energy, Frost was also critical of her when she did not achieve regular forms.

> Emily Dickinson didn't study technique. But she should have been more care-ful. She was more interested in getting the poem down and writing a new one. I feel that she left some to be revised later, and she never revised them. And those two ladies at Amherst printed a lot of her slipshod work which she might not have liked to see printed. She has all kinds of off rhymes. Some that do not rhyme. Her meter does not always go together.[3]

She was therefore substantially different from him; her ability to be conscious of poetic conventions and yet to rise above them surprised him. He generously yielded her his highest admiration for the heresy.

> One of the great things in life is being true within the conventions. I deny in a good poem or a good life that there is compromise. When there is, it is an at-tempt to so flex the lines that no suspicion can be cast upon what the poet does. Emily Dickinson's poems are examples of this. When the rhyme begins to bother, she says, "Here I come with my truth. Let the rhyme take care of it-self." This makes me feel her strength.[4]

For him the large strain of poetry was "a little shifted from the straight-out, a little curved from the straight." Emily Dickinson's poems were, for him, the best examples of this liberty, this flawing. "Can you imagine some people taking that? Can't you imagine some people not accepting that kind of play at all?"[5]

It was this factor of play in Emily Dickinson's poetry that consistently at-tracted Frost. "Rime reminds you that poetry is play," he said on one occasion, after reciting a Dickinson poem ("The Mountains — grow unnoticed") and calling it "particularly fine," "and that is one of its chief importances. You shouldn't be too sincere to play or you'll be a fraud."[6] Her mischief with poetic form was an indication to him that she was serious about what she was saying and would bend conventions to get it said, and also that she was having a good time trying to say it, but more important than that, that with her poetry (and her ideas) she was *at play*. He appears to have marveled at that in her. "Poetry," Frost used to exclaim to his friends, "is fooling."[7]

From *The Only Kangaroo Among the Beauty: Emily Dickinson in America*

---

[1] Robert Francis, *Frost: A Time to Talk* (Amherst, 1972) 53-54.
[2] Daniel Smythe, *Robert Frost Speaks* (New York, np, 1964) 140.
[3] Smythe, 140.
[4] Reginald Lansing Cook, *The Dimensions of Robert Frost* (New York: Barnes and Noble, 1968) 57-58.
[5] Cook, 99.
[6] Cook, 180.
[7] Cook, 181.

CONSIDERATIONS FOR CRITICAL THINKING AND WRITING

1. According to Keller, how did Frost respond to Dickinson's "poetic systems" of rhyme and meter?

2. Explain why you agree or disagree with Frost's assessment of Dickinson's poetry as being "slipshod."

3. Choose a poem from each poet and demonstrate how both are versions of "play."

CYNTHIA GRIFFIN WOLFF (B. 1935)

On the Many Voices in Dickinson's Poetry   1986

There were many "Voices." This fact has sometimes puzzled Dickinson's readers. One poem may be delivered in a child's Voice; another in the Voice of a young woman scrutinizing nature and the society in which she makes her place. Sometimes the Voice is that of a woman self-confidently addressing her lover in a language of passion and sexual desire. At still other times, the Voice of the verse seems so precariously balanced at the edge of hysteria that even its calmest observations grate like the shriek of dementia. There is the Voice of the housewife and the Voice that has recourse to the occasionally agonizing, occasionally regal language of the conversion experience of latter-day New England Puritanism. In some poems the Voice is distinctive principally because it speaks in the aftermath of wounding and can comprehend extremities of pain. Moreover, these Voices are not always entirely distinct from one another: the child's Voice that opens a poem may yield to the Voice of a young woman speaking the idiom of ardent love; in a different poem, the speaker may fall into a mood of almost religious contemplation in an attempt to analyze or define such abstract entities as loneliness or madness or eternity; the diction of the housewife may be conflated with the sovereign language of the New Jerusalem, and taken together, they may render some aspect of the wordsmith's labor. No manageable set of discrete categories suffices to capture the diversity of discourse, and any attempt to simplify Dickinson's methods does violence to the verse.

Yet there is a paradox here. This is, by no stretch of the imagination, a body of poetry that might be construed as a series of lyrics spoken by many different people. Disparate as these many Voices are, somehow they all appear to issue from the same "self." . . . It is the enigmatic "Emily Dickinson" readers suppose themselves to have found in this poetry, even in the extreme case when Dickinson's supposed speaker is male. One explanation for this sense of intrinsic unity in the midst of diversity is the persistence with which Dickinson addresses the same set of problems, using a remarkably durable repertoire of linguistic modes. Evocations of injury and wounding — threats to the coherence of the self — appear in the earliest poems and continue until the end; ways of rendering face-to-face encounters change, but this preoccupation with "interview" is sustained by metaphors of "confrontation" that weave throughout. The summoning of one or another Voice in a given poem, then, is not an unselfconscious emotive reflection of Emily Dickinson's mood at the moment of creation. Rather, each different Voice is a calculated tactic, an attempt to touch her readers and engage them intimately with the poetry. Each Voice had its unique advantages; each its limitations. A poet self-conscious in her craft, she calculated this element as carefully as every other.

From *Emily Dickinson*

CONSIDERATIONS FOR CRITICAL THINKING AND WRITING

1. From the poems in this anthology, try adding to the list of voices Wolff cites.
2. Despite the many voices in Dickinson's poetry, why, according to Wolff, is there still a "sense of intrinsic unity" in her poetry?
3. Choose a Dickinson poem and describe how the choice of voice is a "calculated tactic."

PAULA BENNETT (B. 1936)
On "I heard a Fly buzz — when I died —"   *1990*

Dickinson's rage against death, a rage that led her at times to hate both life and death, might have been alleviated, had she been able to gather hard evidence about an afterlife. But, of course, she could not. "The *Bareheaded life* — under the grass — ," she wrote to Samuel Bowles in c. 1860, "worries one like a Wasp." If death was the gate to a better life in "the childhood of the kingdom of Heaven," as the sentimentalists — and Christ — claimed, then, perhaps, there was compensation and healing for life's woes. . . . But how do we know? What can we know? In "I heard a Fly buzz — when I died," Dickinson concludes that we do not know much. . . .

Like many people in her period, Dickinson was fascinated by death-bed scenes. How, she asked various correspondents, did this or that person die? In particular, she wanted to know if their deaths revealed any information about the nature of the afterlife. In this poem, however, she imagines her own deathbed scene, and the answer she provides is grim, as grim (and, at the same time, as ironically mocking), as anything she ever wrote.

In the narrowing focus of death, the fly's insignificant buzz, magnified tenfold by the stillness in the room, is all that the speaker hears. This kind of distortion in scale is common. It is one of the "illusions" of perception. But here it is horrifying because it defeats every expectation we have. Death is supposed to be an experience of awe. It is the moment when the soul, departing the body, is taken up by God. Hence the watchers at the bedside wait for the moment when the "King" (whether God or death) "be witnessed" in the room. And hence the speaker assigns away everything but that which she expects God (her soul) or death (her body) to take.

What arrives instead, however, is neither God nor death but a fly, "[w]ith Blue — uncertain — stumbling Buzz," a fly, that is, no more secure, no more sure, than we are. Dickinson had associated flies with death once before in the exquisite lament, "How many times these low feet / staggered." In this poem, they buzz "on the / chamber window," and speckle it with dirt, reminding us that the housewife, who once protected us from such intrusions, will protect us no longer. Their presence is threatening but only in a minor way, "dull" like themselves. They are a background noise we do not have to deal with yet.

In "I heard a Fly buzz," on the other hand, there is only one fly and its buzz is not only foregrounded. Before the poem is over, the buzz takes up the entire field of perception, coming between the speaker and the "light" (of day, of life, of knowledge). It is then that the "Windows" (the eyes that are the windows of the soul as well as, metonymically, the light that passes through the panes of glass) "fail" and the speaker is left in darkness — in death, in ignorance. She cannot "see" to "see" (understand).

Given that the only sure thing we know about "life after death" is that flies — in their adult form and more particularly, as maggots — devour us, the poem is at the very least a grim joke. In projecting her death-bed scene, Dickinson confronts her ignorance and gives back the only answer human knowledge can with any certainty give. While we may hope for an afterlife, no one, not even the dying, can prove it exists.

From *Emily Dickinson: Woman Poet*

CONSIDERATIONS FOR CRITICAL THINKING AND WRITING

1. According to Bennett, what is the symbolic value of the fly?
2. Does Bennett leave out any significant elements of the poem in her analysis? Explain why you think she did or did not.
3. Choose a Dickinson poem and write a detailed analysis that attempts to account for all its major elements.

JOAN KIRKBY
On the Fragility of Language in Dickinson's Poetry   *1991*

The abyss between one meaning and another — when the mind experiences the world bereft of articulation — was for Dickinson an exhilarating if dangerous moment of expanse. In [a] prose fragment this experience becomes her definition of life: "Emerging from an Abyss and entering it again — that is Life, is it not?" It is an experience that she courted daily in the poetry, referring in Poem 1323, to "the Daily mind . . . tilling its abyss." She found power and expanse in the moment of transition between an old meaning and a new one.

If language is the tool of thought and gives access to power in the world, it is also a flawed instrument and much of Dickinson's effort is to make us aware of the way language structures and familiarizes the world and makes us blind to it in the process. There are a number of abyss poems which suggest the precarious nature of language performing its trapeze acts over the void. The difficulty of the poems, their frequent resistance to interpretation, is a function of the poet's determination to problematize the fitting of language to experience. The fractures of syntax and diction call attention to the very processes of signification by which we structure the world and challenge familiar and comfortable assumptions. By altering the grammar she alters perception.

The method varies; sometimes she takes a familiar word and shows just how frightening its meaning might be; sometimes she takes an experience and shows up the inadequacy of any word to contain it. In a letter written to Thomas Higginson shortly after he had enlisted in the Civil War, Dickinson wrote: "I should have liked to see you, before you became improbable."

"Improbable" used in this context has the impact of a rifle shot. The friend is turned into a statistic, something not likely to be true or to happen; authenticity and agency are despatched in a word. . . .

Dickinson's poems constantly remind us of the fragility of our worded world. Daily life rests upon the articulation of a significant and coherent world, but Dickinson reminds us that this articulation is but a plank over the abyss.

From *Emily Dickinson*

CONSIDERATIONS FOR CRITICAL THINKING AND WRITING

1. How does Kirkby define the "abyss" in Dickinson's poetry?

2. The brief discussion following Dickinson's "Presentiment — is that long Shadow — on the lawn —" in this textbook (p. 777) uses that poem to suggest how Dickinson, to quote Kirkby, "takes a familiar word and shows just how frightening its meaning might be." First read this discussion and then write about either "Success is counted sweetest" (p. 932) or "'Heaven' — is what I cannot reach!" (p. 936) as yet another example that illustrates Kirkby's point.

3. In an essay discuss several Dickinson poems from this anthology that can be used to illustrate Kirkby's observation that "fractures of syntax and diction call attention to the very processes of signification by which we structure the world and challenge familiar and comfortable assumptions" (para. 2).

GALWAY KINNELL (B. 1927)

The Deconstruction of Emily Dickinson   *1994*

The lecture had ended when I came in,
and the professor was answering questions.
I do not know what he had been doing with her
poetry, but now he was speaking of her
as a victim of reluctant male publishers.   5
When the questions dwindled, I put up my hand.
I said the ignorant meddling of the Springfield *Daily Republican*
and the hidebound response of literary men,
and the gulf between the poetic wishfulness
then admired and her own harsh knowledge,   10
had let her see that her poems
would not be understood in her time;
and therefore, passionate to publish,
she vowed not to publish again. I said
I would recite a version of her vow,   15

> Publication — is the Auction
> Of the mind of Man —

But before I could, the professor broke in.
"Yes," he said, "'the Auction' — 'auction,' from *augere, auctum,* to augment,
    to author . . ."

"Let's hear the poem!" "The poem!" several women,   20
who at such a moment are more outspoken than men, shouted,
but I kept still and he kept going.
"In *auctum* the economy of the signifier is split, revealing an unconscious
          collusion in the bourgeois commodification of consciousness. While
          our author says 'no,' the unreified text says 'yes,' yes?"
He kissed his lips together and turned to me
saying, "Now, may we hear the poem?"   25
I waited a moment for full effect.
Without rising to my feet, I said,
"Professor, to understand Dickinson
it may not always be necessary to uproot her words.
Why not, first, try *listening* to her?   30
Loyalty forbids me to recite her poem now."
No, I didn't say that — I realized
she would want me to finish him off with one wallop.
So I said, "Professor, I thought you
would welcome the words of your author.   35
I see you prefer to hear yourself speak."
No, I held back — for I could hear her
urging me to put outrage into my voice
and substance into my argument.
I stood up so that everyone might see   40
the derision in my smile. "Professor," I said,
"you live in Amherst at the end of the twentieth century.
For you 'auction' means a quaint event
where somebody coaxes out the bids
on butter churns on a summer Saturday.   45
Forget etymology, this is history.
In Amherst in 1860 'auction' meant
the slave auction, you dope!"
Well, I didn't say that either,
although I have said them all,   50
many times, in the middle of the night.
In reality, I stood up and recited
like a schoolboy called upon in class.
My voice gradually weakened, and the women
who had called out for the poem   55
now looked as though they were thinking
of errands to be done on the way home.
When I finished, the professor smiled.
"Thank you. So, what at first some of us may have taken as
          a simple outcry, we all now see is an ambivalent,
          self-subversive text."
As people got up to go, I moved   60
into that sanctum within me where Emily
sometimes speaks a verse, and listened
for a sign of how she felt, such as,
"Thanks — Sweet — countryman —
for wanting — to Sing out — of Me —   65
after all that Humbug." But she was silent.

1. Describe the professor's critical approach to Dickinson's poetry (for information about deconstructionist criticism, see p. 2041). How does it compare to the speaker's approach? What does he value in Dickinson's poetry?

2. Discuss the use of irony in the poem.

3. Do you think it inevitable that a poet's response to poetry will be different from a critic's? Explain your answer.

TWO COMPLEMENTARY CRITICAL READINGS

CHARLES R. ANDERSON (B. 1902)

Eroticism in "Wild Nights — Wild Nights!"   1960

The frank eroticism of this poem might puzzle the biographer of a spinster, but the critic can only be concerned with its effectiveness as a poem. Unless one insists on taking the "I" to mean Emily Dickinson, there is not even any reversal of the lovers' roles (which has been charged, curiously enough, as a fault in this poem). The opening declaration — "Wild Nights should be / Our luxury!" — sets the key of her song, for *luxuria* included the meaning of lust as well as lavishness of sensuous enjoyment, as she was Latinist enough to know. This is echoed at the end in "Eden," her recurring image, in letters and poems, for the paradise of earthly love. The theme here is that of sexual passion which is lawless, outside the rule of "Chart" and "Compass." But it lives by a law of its own, the law of Eden, which protects it from mundane wind and wave.

This is what gives the magic to her climactic vision, "Rowing in Eden," sheltered luxuriously in those paradisiac waters while the wild storms of this world break about them. Such love was only possible before the Fall. Since then the bower of bliss is frugal of her leases, limiting each occupant to "an instant" she says in another poem, for "Adam taught her Thrift / Bankrupt once through his excesses." In the present poem she limits her yearning to the mortal term, just "Tonight." But this echoes the surge of ecstasy that initiated her song and gives the reiterated "Wild Nights!" a double reference, to the passionate experience in Eden as well as to the tumult of the world shut out by it. So she avoids the chief pitfall of the love lyric, the tendency to exploit emotion for its own sake. Instead she generates out of the conflicting aspects of love, its ecstasy and its brevity, the symbol that contains the poem's meaning.

From *Emily Dickinson's Poetry: Stairway of Surprise*

1. According to Anderson what is the theme of "Wild Nights — Wild Nights!"?

2. How does Anderson discuss the "frank eroticism" of the poem? How detailed is his discussion?

3. If there is a "reversal of the lovers' roles" in this poem, do you think it represents, as some critics have charged, "a fault in this poem"? Explain why or why not.

4. Compare Anderson's treatment of this poem with David S. Reynolds's reading that follows. Discuss which one you find more useful and explain why.

DAVID S. REYNOLDS (B. 1949)

Popular Literature and "Wild Nights — Wild Nights!"   1988

It is not known whether Dickinson had read any of the erotic literature of the day or if she knew of the stereotype of the sensual woman. Given her fascination with sensational journalism and with popular literature in general, it is hard to believe she would not have had at least some exposure to erotic literature. At any rate, her treatment of the daring theme of woman's sexual fantasy in this deservedly famous poem bears comparison with erotic themes as they appeared in popular sensational writings. The first stanza of the poem provides an uplifting or purification of sexual fantasy not distant from the effect of Whitman's cleansing rhetoric, which, as we have seen, was consciously designed to counteract the prurience of the popular "love plot." Dickinson's repeated phrase "Wild Nights" is a simple but dazzling metaphor that communicates wild passion — even lust — but simultaneously lifts sexual desire out of the scabrous by fusing it with the natural image of the night. The second verse introduces a second nature image, the turbulent sea and the contrasting quiet port, which at once universalizes the passion and purifies it further by distancing it through a more abstract metaphor. Also, the second verse makes clear that this is not a poem of sexual consummation but rather of pure fantasy and sexual impossibility. Unlike popular erotic literature, the poem portrays neither a consummated seduction nor the heartless deception that it involves. There is instead a pure, fervent fantasy whose frustration is figured forth in the contrasting images of the ocean (the longed-for-but-never-achieved consummation) and the port (the reality of the poet's isolation). The third verse begins with an image, "Rowing in Eden," that further uplifts sexual passion by yoking it with a religious archetype. Here as elsewhere, Dickinson capitalizes nicely on the new religious style, which made possible such fusions of the divine and the earthly. The persona's concluding wish to "moor" in the sea expresses the sustained intense sexual longing and the simultaneous frustration of that longing. In the course of the poem, Dickinson has communicated great erotic passion, and yet, by effectively projecting this passion through unusual nature and religious images, has rid it of even the tiniest residue of sensationalism.

From *Beneath the American Renaissance: The Subversive Imagination in the Age of Emerson and Melville*

CONSIDERATIONS FOR CRITICAL THINKING AND WRITING

1. According to Reynolds, how do Dickinson's images provide a "cleansing" effect in the poem?
2. Explain whether you agree that the poem portrays a "pure, fervent fantasy" or something else.
3. Does Reynolds's reading of the poem compete with Anderson's or complement it? Explain your answer.

4. Given the types of critical strategies described in Chapter 37, how would you characterize Anderson's and Reynolds's approaches?

QUESTIONS FOR WRITING
ABOUT AN AUTHOR IN DEPTH

This section includes four poems by Emily Dickinson as the subject of a sample in-depth study of her poetry. The following questions can help you to respond to multiple works by the same author. You're likely to be struck by the similarities and differences in works by the same author. Previous knowledge of a writer's work can set up useful expectations in a reader. By being familiar with a number of works by the same writer you can begin to discern particular kinds of concerns and techniques that characterize and help to shed light on a writer's work.

As you read multiple works by the same author you'll begin to recognize situations, events, characters, issues, perspectives, styles, and strategies — even recurring words or phrases — that provide a kind of signature, making the poem in some way identifiable with that particular writer. In the case of the four Dickinson poems included in this section, religion emerges as a central topic linked to a number of issues including faith, immortality, skepticism, and the nature of God. The student selected these poems because he noticed Dickinson's intense interest in religious faith owing to the many poems that explore a variety of religious attitudes in her work. He chose these four because they were closely related, but he also might have found equally useful clusters of poems about love, nature, domestic life, or writing as well as other topics. What especially intrigued him was some of the information he read about Dickinson's sternly religious father and the orthodox nature of the religious values of her hometown of Amherst, Massachusetts. Since this paper was not a research paper, he did not pursue these issues beyond the level of the general remarks provided in an introduction to her poetry (though he might have). He did, however, use this biographical and historical information as a means of framing his search for poems that were related to one another. In doing so he discovered consistent concerns along with contradictory themes that became the basis of his paper.

The questions provided below should help you to listen to how a writer's works can speak to each other and to you. Additional useful questions will be found in other chapters of this book. See Writing about Poetry (p. 710) and Arguing about Literature (p. 2071).

1. What topics reappear in the writer's work? What seem to be the major concerns of the author?
2. Does the author have a definable world view that can be discerned from work to work? Is, for example, the writer liberal, conservative, apolitical, or religious?

3. What social values come through in the author's work? Does he or she seem to identify with a particular group or social class?
4. Is there a consistent voice or point of view from work to work? Is it a persona or the author's actual self?
5. How much of the author's own life experiences and historical moment make their way into the works?
6. Does the author experiment with style from work to work, or are the works mostly consistent with one another?
7. Can the author's work be identified with a literary tradition, such as *carpe diem* poetry, that aligns his or her work with that of other writers?
8. What is distinctive about the author's writing? Is the language innovative? Are the themes challenging? Are the voices conventional? Is the tone characteristic?
9. Could you identify another work by the same author without a name being attached to it? What are the distinctive features that allow you to do so?
10. Do any of the writer's works seem *not* to be by that writer? Why?
11. What other writers are most like this author in style and content? Why?
12. Has the writer's work evolved over time? Are there significant changes or developments? Are there new ideas and styles, or do the works remain largely the same?
13. How would you characterize the writing habits of the writer? Is it possible to anticipate what goes on in different works, or are you surprised by their content or style?
14. Can difficult or ambiguous passages in a work be resolved by referring to a similar passage in another work?
15. What does the writer say about his or her own work? Do you trust the teller or the tale? Which do you think is more reliable?

A SAMPLE IN-DEPTH STUDY

Religious Faith in Four Poems by Emily Dickinson

The following paper was written for an assignment that called for an analysis (about 750 words) on any topic that could be traced in three or four poems by Dickinson. The student chose "'Faith' is a fine invention," "I know that He exists," "I never saw a Moor —," and "Apparently with no surprise."

"Faith" is a fine invention   c. 1860

"Faith" is a fine invention
When Gentlemen can *see* —
But *Microscopes* are prudent
In an Emergency.

I know that He exists

c. 1862

I know that He exists.
Somewhere — in Silence —
He has hid his rare life
From our gross eyes.

'Tis an instant's play.   5
'Tis a fond Ambush —
Just to make Bliss
Earn her own surprise!

But — should the play
Prove piercing earnest —   10
Should the glee-glaze —
In Death's — stiff — stare —

Would not the fun
Look too expensive!
Would not the jest —   15
Have crawled too far!

I never saw a Moor —

c. 1865

I never saw a Moor —
I never saw the Sea —
Yet know I how the Heather looks
And what a Billow be.

I never spoke with God
Nor visited in Heaven —
Yet certain am I of the spot
As if the Checks were given —

Apparently with no surprise

c. 1884

Apparently with no surprise
To any happy Flower
The Frost beheads it at its play —
In accidental power —
The blond Assassin passes on —
The Sun proceeds unmoved
To measure off another Day
For an Approving God.

Michael Weitz

Professor Pearl

English 270

May 5, 19- -

Religious Faith in Four Poems by Emily Dickinson

Throughout much of her poetry, Emily Dickinson wrestles with complex notions of God, faith, and religious
devotion. She adheres to no consistent view of religion:
rather, her poetry reveals a vision of God and faith that
is constantly evolving. Dickinson's gods range from the
strict and powerful Old Testament father to a loving spiritual guide to an irrational and ridiculous imaginary
figure. Through these varying images of God, Dickinson
portrays contrasting images of the meaning and validity of
religious faith. Her work reveals competing attitudes
toward religious devotion as conventional religious piety
struggles with a more cynical perception of God and religious worship.

Dickinson's "I never saw a Moor- -" reveals a vision of
traditional religious sensibilities. Although the speaker
readily admits that "I never spoke with God / Nor visited
in Heaven," her devout faith in a supreme being does not
waver. The poem appears to be a straightforward profession
of true faith stemming from the argument that the proof of
God's existence is the universe's existence. Dickinson's
imagery therefore evolves from the natural to the supernatural, first establishing her convictions that Moors and
Seas exist, in spite of her lack of personal contact with
either. This leads to the foundation of her religious
faith, again based not on physical experience but on intellectual convictions. The speaker professes that she
believes in the existence of Heaven even without conclusive evidence: "Yet certain am I of the spot / As if the

Checks were given--" But the appearance of such idealistic views of God and faith in "I never saw a Moor--" are transformed in Dickinson's other poems into a much more skeptical vision of the validity of religious piety.

While faith is portrayed as an authentic and deeply important quality in "I never saw a Moor--," Dickinson's "'Faith' is a fine invention" portrays faith as much less essential. Faith is defined in the poem as "a fine invention" suggesting that it is created by man for man and therefore is not a crucial aspect of the natural universe. Thus the strong idealistic faith of "I never saw a Moor--" becomes discredited in the face of scientific rationalism. The speaker compares religious faith with actual microscopes, both of which are meant to enhance one's vision in some way. But "Faith" is useful only "When Gentlemen can see--" already; "In an Emergency," when one ostensibly cannot see, "Microscopes are prudent." Dickinson pits religion against science, suggesting that science, with its tangible evidence and rational attitude, is a more reliable lens through which to view the world. Faith is irreverently reduced to a mere invention and one that is ultimately less useful than microscopes or other scientific instruments.

Rational, scientific observations are not the only contributing factor to the portrayal of religious skepticism in Dickinson's poems; nature itself is seen to be incompatible in some ways with conventional religious ideology. In "Apparently with no surprise," the speaker recognizes the inexorable cycle of natural life and death as a morning frost kills a flower. But the tension in this poem stems not from the "happy Flower" struck down by the frost's "accidental power" but from the apparent indifference of the "Approving God" who condones this seemingly

cruel and unnecessary death. God is seen as remote and
uncompromising, and it is this perceived distance between
the speaker and God that reveals the increasing absurdity
of traditional religious faith. The speaker understands
that praying to God or believing in religion cannot change
the course of nature, and as a result feels so helplessly
distanced from God that religious faith becomes virtually
meaningless.

Dickinson's religious skepticism becomes even more
explicit in "I know that He exists," in which the speaker
attempts to understand the connection between seeing God
and facing death. In this poem Dickinson characterizes God
as a remote and mysterious figure; the speaker mockingly
asserts, "I know that He exists," even though "He has hid
his rare life / From our gross eyes." The skepticism
toward religious faith revealed in this poem stems from
the speaker's recognition of the paradoxical quest that
people undertake to know and to see God. A successful attempt to see God, to win the game of hide-and-seek that He
apparently is orchestrating, results inevitably in death.
With this recognition the speaker comes to view religion
as an absurd and reckless game in which the prize may be
"Bliss" but more likely is "Death's--stiff--stare--" For
to see God and to meet one's death as a result certainly
suggests that the game of trying to see God (the so-called
"fun") is much "too expensive" and that religion itself is
a "jest" that, like the serpent in Genesis, has "crawled
too far."

Ultimately, the vision of religious faith that Dickinson describes in her poems is one of suspicion and cyni-
cism. She cannot reconcile the physical world to the
spiritual existence that Christian doctrine teaches, and
as a result the traditional perception of God becomes

ludicrous. "I never saw a Moor--" does attempt to sustain
a conventional vision of religious devotion, but Dickinson's poems overall are far more likely to suggest that
God is elusive, indifferent, and often cruel, thus undermining the traditional vision of God as a loving father
worthy of devout worship. Thus, not only religious faith
but also those who are religiously faithful become targets
for Dickinson's irreverent criticism of conventional
belief.

ROBERT FROST (1874–1963)

Few poets have enjoyed the popular success that Robert Frost achieved during his lifetime, and no twentieth-century American poet has had his or her work as widely read and honored. Frost is as much associated with New England as the stone walls that help define its landscape; his reputation, however, transcends regional boundaries. Although he was named poet laureate of Vermont only two years before his death, he was for many years the nation's unofficial poet laureate. Frost collected honors the way some people pick up burrs on country walks. Among his awards were four Pulitzer Prizes, the Bollingen Prize, a Congressional Medal, and dozens of honorary degrees. Perhaps his most moving appearance was his recitation of "The Gift Outright" for millions of Americans at the inauguration of John F. Kennedy in 1961.

Frost's recognition as a poet is especially remarkable because his career as a writer did not attract any significant attention until he was nearly forty years old. He taught himself to write while he labored at odd jobs, taught school, or farmed.

Frost's early identity seems very remote from the New England soil. Although his parents were descended from generations of New Englanders, he was born in San Francisco and was named Robert Lee Frost after the Confederate general. After his father died in 1885, his mother moved the family back to Massachusetts to live with relatives. Frost graduated from high school sharing valedictorian honors with the classmate who would become his wife three years later. Between high school and marriage, he

Robert Frost at his writing desk in Franconia, New Hampshire, 1915. Reprinted by permission of The Jones Library.

attended Dartmouth College for a few months and then taught. His teaching prompted him to enroll in Harvard in 1897, but after less than two years he withdrew without a degree (though Harvard would eventually award him an honorary doctorate in 1937, four years after Dartmouth conferred its honorary degree on him). For the next decade, Frost read and wrote poems when he was not chicken farming or teaching. In 1912, he sold his farm and moved his family to England, where he hoped to find the audience that his poetry did not have in America.

Three years in England made it possible for Frost to return home as a poet. His first two volumes of poetry, *A Boy's Will* (1913) and *North of Boston* (1914), were published in England. During the next twenty years, honors and awards were conferred on collections such as *Mountain Interval* (1916), *New Hampshire* (1923), *West-Running Brook* (1928), and *A Further Range* (1936). These are the volumes on which most of Frost's popular and critical reputation rests. Later collections include *A Witness Tree* (1942), *A Masque of Reason* (1945), *Steeple Bush* (1947), *A Masque of Mercy* (1947), *Complete Poems* (1949), and *In the Clearing* (1962). In addition to publishing his works, Frost endeared himself to audiences throughout the country by presenting his poetry almost as conversations. He also taught at a number of schools, including Amherst College, the University of Michigan, Harvard University, Dartmouth College, and Middlebury College.

Frost's countless poetry readings generated wide audiences eager to claim him as their poet. The image he cultivated resembled closely what the public likes to think a poet should be. Frost was seen as a lovable, wise old man; his simple wisdom and cracker-barrel sayings appeared comforting and homey. From this Yankee rustic, audiences learned that "There's a lot yet that isn't understood" or "We love the things we love for what they are" or "Good fences make good neighbors."

In a sense, Frost packaged himself for public consumption. "I am . . . my own salesman," he said. When asked direct questions about the meanings of his poems, he often winked or scratched his head to give the impression that the customer was always right. To be sure, there is a simplicity in Frost's language, but that simplicity does not fully reflect the depth of the man, the complexity of his themes, or the richness of his art.

The folksy optimist behind the public lectern did not reveal his private troubles to his audiences, although he did address those problems at his writing desk. Frost suffered from professional jealousies, anger, and depression. His family life was especially painful. Three of his four children died: a son at the age of four, a daughter in her late twenties from tuberculosis, and another son by suicide. His marriage was filled with tension. Although Frost's work is landscaped with sunlight, snow, birches, birds, blueberries, and squirrels, it is important to recognize that he was also intimately "acquainted with the night," a phrase that serves as the haunting title of one of his poems (see p. 798).

As a corrective to Frost's popular reputation, one critic, Lionel Trilling, described the world Frost creates in his poems as a "terrifying universe," characterized by loneliness, anguish, frustration, doubts, disappointment, and despair (see p. 1001 for an excerpt from this essay). To point this out is not to annihilate the pleasantness and even good-natured cheerfulness that can be enjoyed in Frost's poetry, but it is to say that Frost is not so one-dimensional as he is sometimes assumed to be. Frost's poetry requires readers who are alert and willing to penetrate the simplicity of its language to see the elusive and ambiguous meanings that lie below the surface.

Frost's treatment of nature helps to explain the various levels of meaning in his poetry. The familiar natural world his poems evoke is sharply detailed. We hear icy branches clicking against themselves, we see the snow-white trunks of birches, we feel the smarting pain of a twig lashing across a face. The aspects of the natural world Frost describes are designated to give pleasure, but they are also frequently calculated to provoke thought. His use of nature tends to be symbolic. Complex meanings are derived from simple facts, such as a spider killing a moth or the difference between fire and ice (see "Design," p. 993, and "Fire and Ice," p. 988). Although Frost's strategy is to talk about particular events and individual experiences, his poems evoke universal issues.

Frost's poetry has strong regional roots and is "versed in country things," but it flourishes in any receptive imagination because, in the final analysis, it is concerned with human beings. Frost's New England landscapes

Neither Out Far nor In Deep
The people along the sand
All turn and look one way.
They turn their backs on the land;
They look at the sea all day.

As long as it takes to pass
A ship keeps raising its hull.
The wetter ground like glass
Reflects a standing gull.

The land may vary more,
But wherever the truth may be —
The water comes ashore
And the people look at the sea.

They cannot look out far;
They cannot look in deep;
But when was that ever a bar
To any watch they keep.

Robert Frost

With the permission of The Yale Review.

Manuscript page for Robert Frost's "Neither Out Far nor In Deep" (p. 993), which was first published in The Yale Review in 1934 and later, with a few punctuation changes, in A Further Range in 1936. Reprinted by permission of the Robert Frost Library.

are the occasion rather than the ultimate focus of his poems. Like the rural voices he creates in his poems, Frost typically approaches his themes indirectly. He explained the reason for this in a talk titled "Education by Poetry":

> Poetry provides the one permissible way of saying one thing and meaning another. People say, "Why don't you say what you mean?" We never do that, do

we, being all of us too much poets. We like to talk in parables and in hints and in indirections — whether from diffidence or some other instinct.

The result is that the settings, characters, and situations that make up the subject matter of Frost's poems are vehicles for his perceptions about life.

In "Stopping by Woods on a Snowy Evening" (p. 989), for example, Frost uses the kind of familiar New England details that constitute his poetry for more than descriptive purposes. He shapes them into a meditation on the tension we sometimes feel between life's responsibilities and the "lovely, dark, and deep" attraction that death offers. When the speaker's horse "gives his harness bells a shake," we are reminded that we are confronting a universal theme as well as a quiet moment of natural beauty.

Among the major concerns that appear in Frost's poetry are the fragility of life, the consequences of rejecting or accepting the conditions of one's life, the passion of inconsolable grief, the difficulty of sustaining intimacy, the fear of loneliness and isolation, the inevitability of change, the tensions between the individual and society, and the place of tradition and custom.

Whatever theme is encountered in a poem by Frost, a reader is likely to agree with him that "the initial delight is in the surprise of remembering something I didn't know." To achieve that fresh sense of discovery, Frost allowed himself to follow his instincts; his poetry

> inclines to the impulse, it assumes direction with the first line laid down, it runs a course of lucky events, and ends in a clarification of life — not necessarily a great clarification, such as sects and cults are founded on, but in a momentary stay against confusion.

This description from "The Figure a Poem Makes" (see p. 998 for the complete essay), Frost's brief introduction to *Complete Poems,* may sound as if his poetry is formless and merely "lucky," but his poems tend to be more conventional than experimental: "The artist in me," as he put the matter in one of his poems, "cries out for design."

From Frost's perspective, "free verse is like playing tennis with the net down." He exercised his own freedom in meeting the challenges of rhyme and meter. His use of fixed forms such as couplets, tercets, quatrains, blank verse, and sonnets was not slavish because he enjoyed working them into the natural English speech patterns — especially the rhythms, idioms, and tones of speakers living north of Boston — that give voice to his themes. Frost often liked to use "Stopping by Woods on a Snowy Evening" as an example of his graceful way of making conventions appear natural and inevitable. He explored "the old ways to be new."

Frost's eye for strong, telling details was matched by his ear for natural speech rhythms. His flexible use of what he called "iambic and loose iambic" enabled him to create moving lyric poems that reveal the personal thoughts of a speaker and dramatic poems that convincingly characterize people caught in intense emotional situations. The language in his poems appears to be little more than a transcription of casual and even rambling speech, but it is in actuality Frost's poetic creation, carefully crafted to reveal the joys and sorrows that are woven into people's daily lives. What is missing from Frost's poems is artificiality, not art. Consider this poem.

The Road Not Taken

1916

Two roads diverged in a yellow wood,
And sorry I could not travel both
And be one traveler, long I stood
And looked down one as far as I could
To where it bent in the undergrowth;   5

Then took the other, as just as fair,
And having perhaps the better claim,
Because it was grassy and wanted wear;
Though as for that the passing there
Had worn them really about the same,   10

And both that morning equally lay
In leaves no step had trodden black.
Oh, I kept the first for another day!
Yet knowing how way leads on to way,
I doubted if I should ever come back.   15

I shall be telling this with a sigh
Somewhere ages and ages hence:
Two roads diverged in a wood, and I —
I took the one less traveled by,
And that has made all the difference.   20

This poem intrigues readers because it is at once so simple and so deeply resonant. Recalling a walk in the woods, the speaker describes how he came to a fork in the road, which forced him to choose one path over another. Though "sorry" that he "could not travel both," he made a choice after carefully weighing his two options. This, essentially, is what happens in the poem; there is no other action. However, the incident is charged with symbolic significance by the speaker's reflections on the necessity and consequences of his decision.

The final stanza indicates that the choice concerns more than simply walking down a road, for the speaker says that choosing the "less traveled" path has affected his entire life — that "that has made all the difference." Frost draws on a familiar enough metaphor when he compares life to a journey, but he is also calling attention to a less commonly noted problem: despite our expectations, aspirations, appetites, hopes, and desires, we can't have it all. Making one choice precludes another. It is impossible to determine what particular decision the speaker refers to: perhaps he had to choose a college, a career, a spouse; perhaps he was confronted with mutually exclusive ideas, beliefs, or values. There is no way to know because Frost wisely creates a symbolic choice and implicitly invites us to supply our own circumstances.

The speaker's reflections about his choice are as central to an understanding of the poem as the choice itself; indeed, they may be more central. He describes the road taken as "having perhaps the better claim, / Because it was grassy and wanted wear"; he prefers the "less traveled" path. This seems to be an expression of individualism, which would account for "the difference" his choice made in his life. But Frost complicates matters by having the speaker also acknowledge that there was no significant difference between the two roads; one was "just as fair" as the other; each was "worn . . . really about the same"; and "both that morning equally lay / In leaves no step had trodden black."

The speaker imagines that in the future, "ages and ages hence," he will recount his choice with "a sigh" that will satisfactorily explain the course of his life, but Frost seems to be having a little fun here by showing us how the speaker will embellish his past decision to make it appear more dramatic. What we hear is someone trying to convince himself that the choice he made significantly changed his life. When he recalls what happened in the "yellow wood," a color that gives a glow to that irretrievable moment when his life seemed to be on verge of a momentous change, he appears more concerned with the path he did not choose than with the one he took. Frost shrewdly titles the poem to suggest the speaker's sense of loss at not being able to "travel both" roads. When the speaker's reflections about his choice are examined, the poem reveals his nostalgia instead of affirming his decision to travel a self-reliant path in life.

The rhymed stanzas of "The Road Not Taken" follow a pattern established in the first five lines (*abaab*). This rhyme scheme reflects, perhaps, the speaker's efforts to shape his life into a pleasing and coherent form. The natural speech rhythms Frost uses allow him to integrate the rhymes unobtrusively, but there is a slight shift in lines 19 and 20, when the speaker asserts self-consciously that the "less traveled" road — which we already know to be basically the same as the other road — "made all the difference." Unlike all the other rhymes in the poem, "difference" does not rhyme precisely with "hence." The emphasis that must be placed on "differ*ence*" to make it rhyme perfectly with "hence" may suggest that the speaker is trying just a little too hard to pattern his life on his earlier choice in the woods.

Perhaps the best way to begin reading Frost's poetry is to accept the invitation he placed at the beginning of many volumes of his poems. "The Pasture" means what it says of course; it is about taking care of some farm chores, but it is also a means of "saying one thing in terms of another."

The Pasture   1913

I'm going out to clean the pasture spring;
I'll only stop to rake the leaves away
(And wait to watch the water clear, I may):
I shan't be gone long. — You come too.

I'm going out to fetch the little calf
That's standing by the mother. It's so young
It totters when she licks it with her tongue.
I shan't be gone long. — You come too.

"The Pasture" is a simple but irresistible songlike invitation to the pleasure of looking at the world through the eyes of a poet.

CHRONOLOGY

1874	Born on March 26 in San Francisco, California.
1885	Father dies and family moves to Lawrence, Massachusetts.
1892	Graduates from Lawrence High School.
1893–94	Studies at Dartmouth College.
1895	Marries his high school sweetheart, Elinor White.
1897–99	Studies at Harvard College.
1900	Moves to a farm in West Derry, New Hampshire.
1912	Moves to England, where he farms and writes.
1913	*A Boy's Will* is published in London.
1914	*North of Boston* is published in London.
1915	Moves to a farm near Franconia, New Hampshire.
1916	Elected to National Institute of Letters.
1917–20	Teaches at Amherst College.
1919	Moves to South Shaftsbury, Vermont.
1921–23	Teaches at the University of Michigan.
1923	*Selected Poems* and *New Hampshire* are published; the latter is awarded a Pulitzer Prize.
1928	*West-Running Brook* is published.
1930	*Collected Poems* is published.
1936	*A Further Range* is published; teaches at Harvard.
1938	Wife dies.
1939–42	Teaches at Harvard.
1942	*A Witness Tree* is published, which is awarded a Pulitzer Prize.

Mending Wall   *1914*

Something there is that doesn't love a wall,
That sends the frozen-ground-swell under it,
And spills the upper boulders in the sun;
And makes gaps even two can pass abreast.
The work of hunters is another thing: 5
I have come after them and made repair
Where they have left not one stone on a stone,
But they would have the rabbit out of hiding,
To please the yelping dogs. The gaps I mean,
No one has seen them made or heard them made,   10
But at spring mending-time we find them there.
I let my neighbor know beyond the hill;
And on a day we meet to walk the line
And set the wall between us once again.
We keep the wall between us as we go.   15
To each the boulders that have fallen to each.
And some are loaves and some so nearly balls
We have to use a spell to make them balance:
"Stay where you are until our backs are turned!"
We wear our fingers rough with handling them.   20
Oh, just another kind of outdoor game,
One on a side. It comes to little more:
There where it is we do not need the wall:
He is all pine and I am apple orchard.
My apple trees will never get across   25
And eat the cones under his pines, I tell him.
He only says, "Good fences make good neighbors."
Spring is the mischief in me, and I wonder
If I could put a notion in his head:
"Why do they make good neighbors? Isn't it   30
Where there are cows? But here there are no cows.
Before I built a wall I'd ask to know
What I was walling in or walling out,
And to whom I was like to give offense.

Something there is that doesn't love a wall, 35
That wants it down." I could say "Elves" to him,
But it's not elves exactly, and I'd rather
He said it for himself. I see him there
Bringing a stone grasped firmly by the top
In each hand, like an old-stone savage armed. 40
He moves in darkness as it seems to me,
Not of woods only and the shade of trees.
He will not go behind his father's saying,
And he likes having thought of it so well
He says again, "Good fences make good neighbors." 45

CONSIDERATIONS FOR CRITICAL THINKING AND WRITING

1. FIRST RESPONSE. What might the "Something" be that "doesn't love a wall"? Why does the speaker remind his neighbor each spring that the wall needs to be repaired? Is it ironic that the *speaker* initiates the mending? Is there anything good about the wall?

2. How do the speaker and his neighbor in this poem differ in sensibilities? What is suggested about the neighbor in lines 41 and 42?

3. The neighbor likes the saying "Good fences make good neighbors" so well that he repeats it (lines 27, 45). Does the speaker also say something twice? What else suggests that the speaker's attitude toward the wall is not necessarily Frost's?

4. Although the speaker's language is colloquial, what is poetic about the sounds and rhythms he uses?

5. This poem was first published in 1914; Frost read it to an audience when he visited Russia in 1962. What do these facts suggest about the symbolic value of "Mending Wall"?

CONNECTIONS TO OTHER SELECTIONS

1. How do you think the neighbor in this poem would respond to Dickinson's idea of imagination in "To make a prairie it takes a clover and one bee" (p. 931)?

2. What similarities and differences does the neighbor have with the people Frost describes in "Neither Out Far nor In Deep" (p. 993)?

Home Burial 1914

He saw her from the bottom of the stairs
Before she saw him. She was starting down,
Looking back over her shoulder at some fear.
She took a doubtful step and then undid it
To raise herself and look again. He spoke 5
Advancing toward her: "What is it you see
From up there always — for I want to know."
She turned and sank upon her skirts at that,

And her face changed from terrified to dull.
He said to gain time: "What is it you see,"   10
Mounting until she cowered under him.
"I will find out now — you must tell me, dear."
She, in her place, refused him any help
With the least stiffening of her neck and silence.
She let him look, sure that he wouldn't see,   15
Blind creature; and awhile he didn't see.
But at last he murmured, "Oh," and again, "Oh."

"What is it — what?" she said.

                   "Just that I see."

"You don't," she challenged. "Tell me what it is."   20

"The wonder is I didn't see at once.
I never noticed it from here before.
I must be wonted° to it — that's the reason.
The little graveyard where my people are!
So small the window frames the whole of it.   25
Not so much larger than a bedroom, is it?
There are three stones of slate and one of marble,
Broad-shouldered little slabs there in the sunlight
On the sidehill. We haven't to mind *those*.
But I understand: it is not the stones,   30
But the child's mound —"

           "Don't, don't, don't, don't," she cried.

She withdrew, shrinking from beneath his arm
That rested on the banister, and slid downstairs;
And turned on him with such a daunting look,   35
He said twice over before he knew himself:
"Can't a man speak of his own child he's lost?"

"Not you! — Oh, where's my hat? Oh, I don't need it!
I must get out of here. I must get air.
I don't know rightly whether any man can."   40

"Amy! Don't go to someone else this time.
Listen to me. I won't come down the stairs."
He sat and fixed his chin between his fists.
"There's something I should like to ask you, dear."

"You don't know how to ask it."   45

                 "Help me, then."
Her fingers moved the latch for all reply.

"My words are nearly always an offense.
I don't know how to speak of anything
So as to please you. But I might be taught,   50
I should suppose. I can't say I see how.

23 *wonted:* Accustomed.

A man must partly give up being a man
With women-folk. We could have some arrangement
By which I'd bind myself to keep hands off
Anything special you're a-mind to name.   55
Though I don't like such things 'twixt those that love.
Two that don't love can't live together without them.
But two that do can't live together with them."
She moved the latch a little. "Don't — don't go.
Don't carry it to someone else this time.   60
Tell me about it if it's something human.
Let me into your grief. I'm not so much
Unlike other folks as your standing there
Apart would make me out. Give me my chance.
I do think, though, you overdo it a little.   65
What was it brought you up to think it the thing
To take your mother-loss of a first child
So inconsolably — in the face of love.
You'd think his memory might be satisfied —"

"There you go sneering now!"   70

                    "I'm not, I'm not!
You make me angry. I'll come down to you.
God, what a woman! And it's come to this,
A man can't speak of his own child that's dead."

"You can't because you don't know how to speak.   75
If you had any feelings, you that dug
With your own hand — how could you? — his little grave;
I saw you from that very window there,
Making the gravel leap and leap in air,
Leap up, like that, like that, and land so lightly   80
And roll back down the mound beside the hole.
I thought, Who is that man? I didn't know you.
And I crept down the stairs and up the stairs
To look again, and still your spade kept lifting.
Then you came in. I heard your rumbling voice   85
Out in the kitchen, and I don't know why,
But I went near to see with my own eyes.
You could sit there with the stains on your shoes
Of the fresh earth from your own baby's grave
And talk about your everyday concerns.   90
You had stood the spade up against the wall
Outside there in the entry, for I saw it."

"I shall laugh the worst laugh I ever laughed.
I'm cursed. God, if I don't believe I'm cursed."

"I can repeat the very words you were saying.   95
'Three foggy mornings and one rainy day
Will rot the best birch fence a man can build.'
Think of it, talk like that at such a time!
What had how long it takes a birch to rot

To do with what was in the darkened parlor 100
You *couldn't* care! The nearest friends can go
With anyone to death, comes so far short
They might as well not try to go at all.
No, from the time when one is sick to death,
One is alone, and he dies more alone. 105
Friends make pretense of following to the grave.
But before one is in it, their minds are turned
And making the best of their way back to life
And living people, and things they understand.
But the world's evil. I won't have grief so 110
If I can change it. Oh, I won't, I won't!"

"There, you have said it all and you feel better.
You won't go now. You're crying. Close the door.
The heart's gone out of it: why keep it up.
Amy! There's someone coming down the road!" 115

"*You* — oh, you think the talk is all. I must go —
Somewhere out of this house. How can I make you —"

"If — you — do!" She was opening the door wider.
"Where do you mean to go? First tell me that.
I'll follow and bring you back by force. I *will!* —" 120

CONSIDERATIONS FOR CRITICAL THINKING AND WRITING

1. FIRST RESPONSE. This poem tells a story of a relationship. Is the husband insensitive and indifferent to his wife's grief? Characterize the wife. Has Frost invited us to sympathize with one character more than with the other?

2. How has the burial of the child within sight of the stairway window affected the relationship of the couple in this poem? Is the child's grave a symptom or a cause of the conflict between them?

3. What is the effect of splitting the iambic pentameter pattern in lines 18 and 19, 31 and 32, 45 and 46, and 70 and 71?

4. Is the conflict resolved at the conclusion of the poem? Do you think the husband and wife will overcome their differences?

After Apple-Picking 1914

My long two-pointed ladder's sticking through a tree
Toward heaven still,
And there's a barrel that I didn't fill
Beside it, and there may be two or three
Apples I didn't pick upon some bough. 5
But I am done with apple-picking now.
Essence of winter sleep is on the night,
The scent of apples: I am drowsing off.
I cannot rub the strangeness from my sight
I got from looking through a pane of glass 10

I skimmed this morning from the drinking trough
And held against the world of hoary grass.
It melted, and I let it fall and break.
But I was well
Upon my way to sleep before it fell, 15
And I could tell
What form my dreaming was about to take.
Magnified apples appear and disappear,
Stem end and blossom end,
And every fleck of russet showing clear. 20
My instep arch not only keeps the ache,
It keeps the pressure of a ladder-round.
I feel the ladder sway as the boughs bend.
And I keep hearing from the cellar bin
The rumbling sound 25
Of load on load of apples coming in.
For I have had too much
Of apple-picking: I am overtired
Of the great harvest I myself desired.
There were ten thousand thousand fruit to touch, 30
Cherish in hand, lift down, and not let fall.
For all
That struck the earth,
No matter if not bruised or spiked with stubble,
Went surely to the cider-apple heap 35
As of no worth.
One can see what will trouble
This sleep of mine, whatever sleep it is.
Were he not gone,
The woodchuck could say whether it's like his 40
Long sleep, as I describe its coming on,
Or just some human sleep.

CONSIDERATIONS FOR CRITICAL THINKING AND WRITING

1. FIRST RESPONSE. How does this poem illustrate Frost's view that "Poetry provides the one permissible way of saying one thing and meaning another"? When do you first sense that the detailed description of apple picking is being used that way?

2. What comes after apple picking? What does the speaker worry about in the dream beginning in line 18?

3. Why do you suppose Frost uses apples rather than, say, pears or squash?

The Wood-Pile   *1914*

Out walking in the frozen swamp one gray day,
I paused and said, "I will turn back from here.
No, I will go on farther—and we shall see."
The hard snow held me, save where now and then
One foot went through. The view was all in lines 5

Straight up and down of tall slim trees
Too much alike to mark or name a place by
So as to say for certain I was here
Or somewhere else: I was just far from home.
A small bird flew before me. He was careful   10
To put a tree between us when he lighted,
And say no word to tell me who he was
Who was so foolish as to think what *he* thought.
He thought that I was after him for a feather —
The white one in his tail; like one who takes   15
Everything said as personal to himself.
One flight out sideways would have undeceived him.
And then there was a pile of wood for which
I forgot him and let his little fear
Carry him off the way I might have gone,   20
Without so much as wishing him good-night.
He went behind it to make his last stand.
It was a cord of maple, cut and split
And piled — and measured, four by four by eight.
And not another like it could I see.   25
No runner tracks in this year's snow looped near it.
And it was older sure than this year's cutting,
Or even last year's or the year's before.
The wood was gray and the bark warping off it
And the pile somewhat sunken. Clematis   30
Had wound strings round and round it like a bundle.
What held it though on one side was a tree
Still growing, and on one a stake and prop,
These latter about to fall. I thought that only
Someone who lived in turning to fresh tasks   35
Could so forget his handiwork on which
He spent himself, the labor of his ax,
And leave it there far from a useful fireplace
To warm the frozen swamp as best it could
With the slow smokeless burning of decay.   40

Considerations for Critical Thinking and Writing

1. FIRST RESPONSE. Write a paraphrase of the poem. What do you think it's about?

2. How does the "small bird" (line 10) figure in the poem? Why do you think it's there? How is it related to the woodpile?

3. What symbolic value can you find in the speaker's account of his discovery of the woodpile?

4. Characterize the speaker's tone. How does the rhythm of the poem's lines help to create the tone?

Connections to Other Selections

1. Write an essay comparing the speaker in this poem to the speaker in "Stopping by Woods on a Snowy Evening" (p. 989). How, in each poem, do simple activities reveal something important about the speaker?

2. Discuss the speaker's sense of time in "The Wood-Pile" and in "Nothing Gold Can Stay" (p. 989).

Birches

1916

When I see birches bend to left and right
Across the lines of straighter darker trees,
I like to think some boy's been swinging them.
But swinging doesn't bend them down to stay
As ice-storms do. Often you must have seen them   5
Loaded with ice a sunny winter morning
After a rain. They click upon themselves
As the breeze rises, and turn many-colored
As the stir cracks and crazes their enamel.
Soon the sun's warmth makes them shed crystal shells   10
Shattering and avalanching on the snow-crust—
Such heaps of broken glass to sweep away
You'd think the inner dome of heaven had fallen.
They are dragged to the withered bracken by the load,
And they seem not to break; though once they are bowed   15
So low for long, they never right themselves:
You may see their trunks arching in the woods
Years afterwards, trailing their leaves on the ground
Like girls on hands and knees that throw their hair
Before them over their heads to dry in the sun.   20
But I was going to say when Truth broke in
With all her matter-of-fact about the ice-storm,
I should prefer to have some boy bend them
As he went out and in to fetch the cows—
Some boy too far from town to learn baseball,   25
Whose only play was what he found himself,
Summer or winter, and could play alone.
One by one he subdued his father's trees
By riding them down over and over again
Until he took the stiffness out of them,   30
And not one but hung limp, not one was left
For him to conquer. He learned all there was
To learn about not launching out too soon
And so not carrying the tree away
Clear to the ground. He always kept his poise   35
To the top branches, climbing carefully
With the same pains you use to fill a cup
Up to the brim, and even above the brim.
Then he flung outward, feet first, with a swish,
Kicking his way down through the air to the ground.   40
So was I once myself a swinger of birches.
And so I dream of going back to be.
It's when I'm weary of considerations,

And life is too much like a pathless wood
Where your face burns and tickles with the cobwebs   45
Broken across it, and one eye is weeping
From a twig's having lashed across it open.
I'd like to get away from earth awhile
And then come back to it and begin over.
May no fate willfully misunderstand me   50
And half grant what I wish and snatch me away
Not to return. Earth's the right place for love:
I don't know where it's likely to go better.
I'd like to go by climbing a birch tree,
And climb black branches up a snow-white trunk,   55
Toward heaven, till the tree could bear no more,
But dipped its top and set me down again.
That would be good both going and coming back.
One could do worse than be a swinger of birches.

CONSIDERATIONS FOR CRITICAL THINKING AND WRITING

1. FIRST RESPONSE. What do you think the swinging of birches symbolizes?

2. Why does the speaker in this poem prefer the birches to have been bent by boys instead of ice storms?

3. How is "earth" (line 52) described in the poem? Why does the speaker choose it over "heaven" (line 56)?

4. How might the effect of this poem be changed if it were written in heroic couplets instead of blank verse?

"Out, Out —"°   1916

The buzz-saw snarled and rattled in the yard
And made dust and dropped stove-length sticks of wood,
Sweet-scented stuff when the breeze drew across it.
And from there those that lifted eyes could count
Five mountain ranges one behind the other   5
Under the sunset far into Vermont.
And the saw snarled and rattled, snarled and rattled,
As it ran light, or had to bear a load.
And nothing happened: day was all but done.
Call it a day, I wish they might have said   10
To please the boy by giving him the half hour
That a boy counts so much when saved from work.
His sister stood beside them in her apron
To tell them "Supper." At the word, the saw,
As if to prove saws knew what supper meant,   15
Leaped out at the boy's hand, or seemed to leap —

"*Out, Out* —": From Act V, Scene v, of Shakespeare's *Macbeth*. The passage appears on page 776.

He must have given the hand. However it was,
Neither refused the meeting. But the hand!
The boy's first outcry was a rueful laugh,
As he swung toward them holding up the hand   20
Half in appeal, but half as if to keep
The life from spilling. Then the boy saw all—
Since he was old enough to know, big boy
Doing a man's work, though a child at heart—
He saw all spoiled. "Don't let him cut my hand off—   25
The doctor, when he comes. Don't let him, sister!"
So. But the hand was gone already.
The doctor put him in the dark of ether.
He lay and puffed his lips out with his breath.
And then—the watcher at his pulse took fright.   30
No one believed. They listened at his heart.
Little—less—nothing!—and that ended it.
No more to build on there. And they, since they
Were not the one dead, turned to their affairs.

CONSIDERATIONS FOR CRITICAL THINKING AND WRITING

1. FIRST RESPONSE. This narrative poem is about the accidental death of a Vermont boy. What is the purpose of the story? Some readers have argued that the final lines reveal the speaker's callousness and indifference. What do you think?

2. How does Frost's allusion to *Macbeth* contribute to the meaning of this poem? Does the speaker seem to agree with the view of life expressed in Macbeth's lines?

CONNECTIONS TO OTHER SELECTIONS

1. What are the similarities and differences in theme between this poem and Frost's "Nothing Gold Can Stay" (p. 989)?

2. Write an essay comparing how grief is handled by the boy's family in this poem and the couple in "Home Burial" (p. 980).

3. Compare the tone and theme of "'Out, Out—'" and those of Crane's "A Man Said to the Universe" (p. 805).

Fire and Ice   *1923*

Some say the world will end in fire,
Some say in ice.
From what I've tasted of desire
I hold with those who favor fire.
But if it had to perish twice,
I think I know enough of hate
To say that for destruction ice
Is also great
And would suffice.

CONSIDERATIONS FOR CRITICAL THINKING AND WRITING

1. FIRST RESPONSE. What characteristics of human behavior does the speaker associate with fire and ice?
2. What theories about the end of the world are alluded to in lines 1 and 2?
3. How does the speaker's use of understatement and rhyme affect the tone of this poem?

Stopping by Woods on a Snowy Evening   1923

Whose woods these are I think I know.
His house is in the village, though;
He will not see me stopping here
To watch his woods fill up with snow.

My little horse must think it queer   5
To stop without a farmhouse near
Between the woods and frozen lake
The darkest evening of the year.

He gives his harness bells a shake
To ask if there is some mistake.   10
The only other sound's the sweep
Of easy wind and downy flake.

The woods are lovely, dark and deep,
But I have promises to keep,
And miles to go before I sleep,   15
And miles to go before I sleep.

CONSIDERATIONS FOR CRITICAL THINKING AND WRITING

1. FIRST RESPONSE. What is the significance of the setting in this poem? How is tone conveyed by the images?
2. What does the speaker find appealing about the woods? What is the purpose of the horse in the poem?
3. Although the last two lines are identical, they are not read at the same speed. Why the difference? What is achieved by the repetition?
4. What is the rhyme scheme of this poem? What is the effect of the rhyme in the final stanza?

Nothing Gold Can Stay   1923

Nature's first green is gold,
Her hardest hue to hold.
Her early leaf's a flower;
But only so an hour.

The leaf subsides to leaf.
So Eden sank to grief.
So dawn goes down to day.
Nothing gold can stay.

CONSIDERATIONS FOR CRITICAL THINKING AND WRITING

1. FIRST RESPONSE. What is meant by "gold" in the poem? Why can't it "stay"?
2. What do the leaf, humanity, and a day have in common?

CONNECTION TO ANOTHER SELECTION

1. Write an essay comparing the tone and theme of "Nothing Gold Can Stay" with Herrick's "To the Virgins, to Make Much of Time" (p. 728).

Once by the Pacific

1928

The shattered water made a misty din.
Great waves looked over others coming in,
And thought of doing something to the shore
That water never did to land before.
The clouds were low and hairy in the skies,   5
Like locks blown forward in the gleam of eyes.
You could not tell, and yet it looked as if
The shore was lucky in being backed by cliff,
The cliff in being backed by continent;
It looked as if a night of dark intent   10
Was coming, and not only a night, an age.
Someone had better be prepared for rage.
There would be more than ocean-water broken
Before God's last *Put out the Light* was spoken.

CONSIDERATIONS FOR CRITICAL THINKING AND WRITING

1. FIRST RESPONSE. Is this poem about more than an approaching storm? What tells you so?
2. What kind of sonnet is this poem? Does its form seem suited to the subject matter? Why or why not?
3. Comment on the title. What purpose does it serve?
4. Write an alternative line for line 14 and explain how your line changes the poem's effect and meaning.

CONNECTION TO ANOTHER SELECTION

1. Write an essay that discusses Frost's use of the ocean in "Once by the Pacific" and in "Neither Out Far nor In Deep" (p. 993).

Two Tramps in Mud Time 1936

Out of the mud two strangers came
And caught me splitting wood in the yard.
And one of them put me off my aim
By hailing cheerily 'Hit them hard!'
I knew pretty well why he dropped behind   5
And let the other go on a way.
I knew pretty well what he had in mind:
He wanted to take my job for pay.

Good blocks of oak it was I split,
As large around as the chopping block;   10
And every piece I squarely hit
Fell splinterless as a cloven rock.
The blows that a life of self-control
Spares to strike for the common good
That day, giving a loose to my soul,   15
I spent on the unimportant wood.

The sun was warm but the wind was chill.
You know how it is with an April day
When the sun is out and the wind is still,
You're one month on in the middle of May.   20
But if you so much as dare to speak,
A cloud comes over the sunlit arch,
A wind comes off a frozen peak,
And you're two months back in the middle of March.

A bluebird comes tenderly up to alight   25
And turns to the wind to unruffle a plume
His song so pitched as not to excite
A single flower as yet to bloom.
It is snowing a flake: and he half knew
Winter was only playing possum.   30
Except in color he isn't blue,
But he wouldn't advise a thing to blossom.

The water for which we may have to look
In summertime with a witching-wand,
In every wheelrut's now a brook,   35
In every print of a hoof a pond.
Be glad of water, but don't forget
The lurking frost in the earth beneath
That will steal forth after the sun is set
And show on the water its crystal teeth.   40

The time when most I loved my task
These two must make me love it more
By coming with what they came to ask.
You'd think I never had felt before
The weight of an ax-head poised aloft,   45

The grip on earth of outspread feet.
The life of muscles rocking soft
And smooth and moist in vernal heat.

Out of the woods two hulking tramps
(From sleeping God knows where last night,   50
But not long since in the lumber camps).
They thought all chopping was theirs of right
Men of the woods and lumberjacks,
They judged me by their appropriate tool.
Except as a fellow handled an ax,   55
They had no way of knowing a fool.

Nothing on either side was said.
They knew they had but to stay their stay
And all their logic would fill my head:
As that I had no right to play   60
With what was another man's work for gain.
My right might be love but theirs was need.
And where the two exist in twain
Theirs was the better right — agreed.

But yield who will to their separation,   65
My object in living is to unite
My avocation and my vocation
As my two eyes make one in sight.
Only where love and need are one,
And the work is play for mortal stakes,   70
Is the deed ever really done
For Heaven and the future's sakes.

CONSIDERATIONS FOR CRITICAL THINKING AND WRITING

1. FIRST RESPONSE. What happens in this poem? Does the speaker offer to pay the tramp to chop his wood? Explain.

2. Explain lines 13-16. How do they serve to characterize the speaker?

3. Make a list of all the images related to nature and the changing seasons. How would you characterize "Mud Time"? Is there a relationship between this time between seasons and the speaker's "object in living" (lines 65-72)?

4. Describe the poem's rhythm and rhyme. How do they contribute to its meaning?

CONNECTION TO ANOTHER SELECTION

1. In an essay discuss attitudes toward work in this poem and in "After Apple-Picking" (p. 983).

Design

I found a dimpled spider, fat and white,
On a white heal-all,° holding up a moth
Like a white piece of rigid satin cloth —
Assorted characters of death and blight
Mixed ready to begin the morning right,   5
Like the ingredients of a witches' broth —
A snow-drop spider, a flower like a froth,
And dead wings carried like a paper kite.

What had the flower to do with being white,
The wayside blue and innocent heal-all?   10
What brought the kindred spider to that height,
Then steered the white moth thither in the night?
What but design of darkness to appall? —
If design govern in a thing so small.

2 *heal-all:* A common flower, usually blue, once used for medicinal purposes.

CONSIDERATIONS FOR CRITICAL THINKING AND WRITING

1. FIRST RESPONSE. What kinds of speculations are raised in the final two lines? Consider the meaning of the title. Is there more than one way to read it?

2. How does the division of the octave and sestet in this sonnet serve to organize the speaker's thoughts and feelings? What is the predominant rhyme? How does that rhyme relate to the poem's meaning?

3. Which words seem especially rich in connotative meanings? Explain how they function in the sonnet.

CONNECTIONS TO OTHER SELECTIONS

1. Compare the ironic tone of "Design" with the tone of Hathaway's "Oh, Oh" (p. 675). What would you have to change in Hathaway's poem to make it more like Frost's?

2. In an essay discuss Frost's view of God in this poem and Dickinson's perspective in "I know that He exists" (p. 967).

3. Compare "Design" with "In White," Frost's early version of it (p. 996).

Neither Out Far nor In Deep

The people along the sand
All turn and look one way.
They turn their back on the land.
They look at the sea all day.

As long as it takes to pass   5
A ship keeps raising its hull;

The wetter ground like glass
Reflects a standing gull.

The land may vary more;
But wherever the truth may be —   10
The water comes ashore,
And the people look at the sea.

They cannot look out far.
They cannot look in deep.
But when was that ever a bar   15
To any watch they keep?

CONSIDERATIONS FOR CRITICAL THINKING AND WRITING

1. FIRST RESPONSE. Frost built this poem around a simple observation that raises some questions. Why do people at the beach almost always face the ocean? What feelings and thoughts are evoked by looking at the ocean?

2. Notice how the verb "look" takes on added meaning as the poem progresses. What are the people looking for?

3. How does the final stanza extend the poem's significance?

4. Does the speaker identify with the people described, or does he ironically distance himself from them?

Come In   *1942*

As I came to the edge of the woods,
Thrush music — hark!
Now if it was dusk outside,
Inside it was dark.

Too dark in the woods for a bird   5
By sleight of wing
To better its perch for the night,
Though it still could sing.

The last of the light of the sun
That had died in the west   10
Still lived for one song more
In a thrush's breast.

Far in the pillared dark
Thrush music went —
Almost like a call to come in   15
To the dark and lament.

But no, I was out for stars:
I would not come in.
I meant not even if asked,
And I hadn't been.   20

CONSIDERATIONS FOR CRITICAL THINKING AND WRITING

1. FIRST RESPONSE. What does "dark" mean in this poem? Can it be read as more than simply literal darkness?

2. How does the bird's song affect the poem's tone?

3. In what sense is the speaker "out for stars"? Why won't the speaker "come in"?

CONNECTION TO ANOTHER SELECTION

1. Write an essay comparing the themes of "Come In" with those of "The Pasture" (p. 978). How might each poem be regarded as a kind of invitation?

The Silken Tent   1942

She is as in a field a silken tent
At midday when a sunny summer breeze
Has dried the dew and all its ropes relent,
So that in guys° it gently sways at ease,   *ropes that steady a tent*
And its supporting central cedar pole,   5
That is its pinnacle to heavenward
And signifies the sureness of the soul,
Seems to owe naught to any single cord,
But strictly held by none, is loosely bound
By countless silken ties of love and thought   10
To everything on earth the compass round,
And only by one's going slightly taut
In the capriciousness of summer air
Is of the slightest bondage made aware.

CONSIDERATIONS FOR CRITICAL THINKING AND WRITING

1. FIRST RESPONSE. What is being compared in this sonnet? How does the detail accurately describe both elements of the comparison?

2. How does the form of this one-sentence sonnet help to express its theme? Pay particular attention to the final three lines.

3. How do the sonnet's sounds contribute to its meaning?

The Most of It   1942

He thought he kept the universe alone;
For all the voice in answer he could wake
Was but the mocking echo of his own
From some tree-hidden cliff across the lake.
Some morning from the boulder-broken beach   5

He would cry out on life, that what it wants
Is not its own love back in copy speech,
But counter-love, original response.
And nothing ever came of what he cried
Unless it was the embodiment that crashed 10
In the cliff's talus on the other side,
And then in the far distant water splashed.
But after a time allowed for it to swim,
Instead of proving human when it neared
And someone else additional to him, 15
As a great buck it powerfully appeared,
Pushing the crumpled water up ahead,
And landed pouring like a waterfall,
And stumbled through the rocks with horny tread,
And forced the underbrush — and that was all. 20

CONSIDERATIONS FOR CRITICAL THINKING AND WRITING

1. FIRST RESPONSE. Discuss the meaning of the title, "The Most of It." What is the "It," do you think?

2. What does the voice "cry out" for (line 6)? What does he want?

3. Comment on the effects of the sounds in this poem.

4. Does the description of the buck have any symbolic meaning? Explain, paying special attention to the language describing it.

CONNECTIONS TO OTHER SELECTIONS

1. Write an essay that compares the images of nature in "The Most of It" with those in "Two Tramps in Mud Time" (p. 991). Is nature presented the same way by the two poems? What ideas about nature are expressed by their imagery?

2. Compare and contrast ideas about solitude in this poem and in Emily Dickinson's "The Soul selects her own Society —" (p. 941).

PERSPECTIVES ON FROST

"In White": Frost's Early Version of "Design" 1912

A dented spider like a snow drop white
On a white Heal-all, holding up a moth
Like a white piece of lifeless satin cloth —
Saw ever curious eye so strange a sight? —
Portent in little, assorted death and blight 5
Like the ingredients of a witches' broth? —

The beady spider, the flower like a froth,
And the moth carried like a paper kite.

What had that flower to do with being white,
The blue prunella every child's delight.   10
What brought the kindred spider to that height?
(Make we no thesis of the miller's° plight.)   *miller moth*
What but design of darkness and of night?
Design, design! Do I use the word aright?

CONSIDERATIONS FOR CRITICAL THINKING AND WRITING

1. Read "In White" and "Design" (p. 993) aloud. Which version sounds better to you? Why?

2. Compare these versions line for line, paying particular attention to word choice. List the differences, and try to explain why you think Frost revised the lines.

3. How does the change in titles reflect a shift in emphasis in the poem?

Frost on the Living Part of a Poem   1914

The living part of a poem is the intonation entangled somehow in the syntax, idiom, and meaning of a sentence. It is only there for those who have heard it previously in conversation. . . . It is the most volatile and at the same time important part of poetry. It goes and the language becomes dead language, the poetry dead poetry. With it go the accents, the stresses, the delays that are not the property of vowels and syllables but that are shifted at will with the sense. Vowels have length there is no denying. But the accent of sense supersedes all other accent, overrides it and sweeps it away. I will find you the word *come* variously used in various passages, a whole, half, third, fourth, fifth, and sixth note. It is as long as the sense makes it. When men no longer know the intonations on which we string our words they will fall back on what I may call the absolute length of our syllables, which is the length we would give them in passages that meant nothing. . . . I say you can't read a single good sentence with the salt in it unless you have previously heard it spoken. Neither can you with the help of all the characters and diacritical marks pronounce a single word unless you have previously heard it actually pronounced. Words exist in the mouth not books.

From a letter to Sidney Cox in *A Swinger of Birches: A Portrait of Robert Frost*

CONSIDERATIONS FOR CRITICAL THINKING AND WRITING

1. Why does Frost place so much emphasis on hearing poetry spoken?

2. Choose a passage from "Home Burial" (p. 980) or "After Apple-Picking" (p. 983) and read it aloud. How does Frost's description of his emphasis on intonation help explain the effects he achieves in the passage you have selected?

3. Do you think it is true that all poetry must be heard? Do "Words exist in the mouth not books"?

AMY LOWELL (1874–1925)

On Frost's Realistic Technique

1915

I have said that Mr. Frost's work is almost photographic. The qualification was unnecessary, it is photographic. The pictures, the characters, are reproduced directly from life, they are burnt into his mind as though it were a sensitive plate. He gives out what has been put in unchanged by any personal mental process. His imagination is bounded by what he has seen, he is confined within the limits of his experience (or at least what might have been his experience) and bent all one way like the windblown trees of New England hillsides.

From a review of *North of Boston, The New Republic,* February 20, 1915

CONSIDERATIONS FOR CRITICAL THINKING AND WRITING

1. Consider the "photographic" qualities of Frost's poetry by discussing particular passages that strike you as having been "reproduced directly from life."

2. Write an essay that supports or refutes Lowell's assertion that "He gives out what has been put in unchanged by any personal mental process."

Frost on the Figure a Poem Makes

1939

Abstraction is an old story with the philosophers, but it has been like a new toy in the hands of the artists of our day. Why can't we have any one quality of poetry we choose by itself? We can have in thought. Then it will go hard if we can't in practice. Our lives for it.

Granted no one but a humanist much cares how sound a poem is if it is only *a* sound. The sound is the gold in the ore. Then we will have the sound out alone and dispense with the inessential. We do till we make the discovery that the object in writing poetry is to make all poems sound as different as possible from each other, and the resources for that of vowels, consonants, punctuation, syntax, words, sentences, meter are not enough. We need the help of context — meaning — subject matter. That is the greatest help towards variety. All that can be done with words is soon told. So also with meters — particularly in our language where there are virtually but two, strict iambic and loose iambic. The ancients with many were still poor if they depended on meters for all tune. It is painful to watch our sprung-rhythmists straining at the point of omitting one short from a foot for relief from monotony. The possibilities for tune from the dramatic tones of meaning struck across the rigidity of a limited meter are endless. And we are back in poetry as merely one more art of having something to say, sound or unsound. Probably better if sound, because deeper and from wider experience.

Then there is this wildness whereof it is spoken. Granted again that it has an equal claim with sound to being a poem's better half. If it is a wild tune, it is a poem. Our problem then is, as modern abstractionists, to have the wildness pure; to be wild with nothing to be wild about. We bring up as aberrationists, giving way to undirected associations and kicking ourselves from one chance suggestion to another in all directions as of a hot afternoon in the life of a grasshopper.

Theme alone can steady us down. Just as the first mystery was how a poem could have a tune in such a straightness as meter, so the second mystery is how a poem can have wildness and at the same time a subject that shall be fulfilled.

It should be of the pleasure of a poem itself to tell how it can. The figure a poem makes. It begins in delight and ends in wisdom. The figure is the same as for love. No one can really hold that the ecstasy should be static and stand still in one place. It begins in delight, it inclines to the impulse, it assumes direction with the first line laid down, it runs a course of lucky events, and ends in a clarification of life — not necessarily a great clarification, such as sects and cults are founded on, but in a momentary stay against confusion. It has denouement. It has an outcome that though unforeseen was predestined from the first image of the original mood — and indeed from the very mood. It is but a trick poem and no poem at all if the best of it was thought of first and saved for the last. It finds its own name as it goes and discovers the best waiting for it in some final phrase at once wise and sad — the happy-sad blend of the drinking song.

No tears in the writer, no tears in the reader. No surprise for the writer, no surprise for the reader. For me the initial delight is in the surprise of remembering something I didn't know I knew. I am in a place, in a situation, as if I had materialized from cloud or risen out of the ground. There is a glad recognition of the long lost and the rest follows. Step by step the wonder of unexpected supply keeps going. The impressions most useful to my purpose seem always those I was unaware of and so made no note of at the time when taken, and the conclusion is come to that like giants we are always hurling experience ahead of us to pave the future with against the day when we may want to strike a line of purpose across it for somewhere. The line will have the more charm for not being mechanically straight. We enjoy the straight crookedness of a good walking stick. Modern instruments of precision are being used to make things crooked as if by eye and hand in the old days.

I tell how there may be a better wildness of logic than of inconsequence. But the logic is backward, in retrospect, after the act. It must be more felt than seen ahead like prophecy. It must be a revelation, or a series of revelations, as much for the poet as for the reader. For it to be that there must have been the greatest freedom of the material to move about in it and to establish relations in it regardless of time and space, previous relation, and everything but affinity. We prate of freedom. We call our schools free because we are not free to stay away from them till we are sixteen years of age. I have given up my democratic prejudices and now willingly set the lower classes free to be completely taken care of by the upper classes. Political freedom is nothing to me. I bestow it right and left. All I would keep for myself is the freedom of my material — the condition of body and mind now and then to summons aptly from the vast chaos of all I have lived through.

Scholars and artists thrown together are often annoyed at the puzzle of where they differ. Both work for knowledge; but I suspect they differ most importantly in the way their knowledge is come by. Scholars get theirs with conscientious thoroughness along projected lines of logic; poets theirs cavalierly and as it happens in and out of books. They stick to nothing deliberately, but let what will stick to them like burrs where they walk in the fields. No acquirement is on assignment, or even self-assignment. Knowledge of the second kind is much more available in the wild free ways of wit and art. A school boy may be defined as one who can tell you what he knows in the order in which he learned it. The artist must value himself as he snatches a thing from some previous order in time and space into a new order with not so much as a ligature clinging to it of the old place where it was organic.

More than once I should have lost my soul to radicalism if it had been the originality it was mistaken for by its young converts. Originality and initiative are what I ask for my country. For myself the originality need be no more than the freshness of a poem run in the way I have described: from delight to wisdom. The figure is the same as for love. Like a piece of ice on a hot stove the poem must ride on its own melting. A poem may be worked over once it is in being, but may not be worried into being. Its most precious quality will remain its having run itself and carried away the poet with it. Read it a hundred times: it will forever keep its freshness as a metal keeps its fragrance. It can never lose its sense of a meaning that once unfolded by surprise as it went.

From *Complete Poems of Robert Frost*

CONSIDERATIONS FOR CRITICAL THINKING AND WRITING

1. Frost places a high premium on sound in his poetry because it "is the gold in the ore." Choose one of Frost's poems in this book and explain the effects of its sounds and how they contribute to its meaning.

2. Discuss Frost's explanation of how his poems are written. In what sense is the process both spontaneous and "predestined"?

3. What do you think Frost means when he says he's given up his "democratic prejudices"? Why is "political freedom" nothing to him?

4. Write an essay that examines in more detail the ways scholars and artists "come by" knowledge.

5. Explain what you think Frost means when he writes that "Like a piece of ice on a hot stove the poem must ride on its own melting."

Frost on the Way to Read a Poem   1951

The way to read a poem in prose or verse is in the light of all the other poems ever written. We may begin anywhere. We *duff* into our first. We read that imperfectly (thoroughness with it would be fatal), but the better to read the second. We read the second the better to read the third, the third the better to read the fourth, the fourth better to read the fifth, the fifth the better to read the first again, or the second if it so happens. For poems are not meant to be read in course any more than they are to be made a study of. I once made a resolve never to put any book to any use it wasn't intended for by its author. Improvement will not be a progression but a widening circulation. Our instinct is to settle down like a revolving dog and make ourselves at home among the poems, completely at our ease as to how they should be taken. The same people will be apt to take poems right as know how to take a hint when there is one and not to take a hint when none is intended. Theirs is the ultimate refinement.

From "Poetry and School," *Atlantic Monthly*, June 1951

CONSIDERATIONS FOR CRITICAL THINKING AND WRITING

1. Given your own experience, how good is Frost's advice about reading in general and his poems in particular?

2. In what sense is a good reader like a "revolving dog" and a person who knows "how to take a hint"?

3. Frost elsewhere in this piece writes, "One of the dangers of college to any-one who wants to stay a human reader (that is to say a humanist) is that he will become a specialist and lose his sensitive fear of landing on the lovely too hard. (With beak and talon.)" Write an essay in response to this concern. Do you agree with Frost's distinction between a "human reader" and a "specialist"?

LIONEL TRILLING (1905-1975)
On Frost as a Terrifying Poet   *1959*

I have to say that my Frost — *my Frost*: what airs we give ourselves when once we believe that we have come into possession of a poet! — I have to say that my Frost is not the Frost I seem to perceive existing in the minds of so many of his admirers. He is not the Frost who confounds the characteristically modern practice of poetry by his notable democratic simplicity of utterance: on the contrary. He is not the Frost who controverts the bitter modern astonishment at the nature of human life: the opposite is so. He is not the Frost who reassures us by his affirmation of old virtues, simplicities, pieties, and ways of feeling: anything but. I will not go so far as to say that my Frost is not essentially an American poet at all: I believe that he is quite as American as everyone thinks he is, but not in the way that everyone thinks he is.

In the matter of the Americanism of American literature one of my chief guides is that very remarkable critic, D. H. Lawrence. Here are the opening sentences of Lawrence's great outrageous book about classic American literature. "We like to think of the old fashioned American classics as children's books. Just childishness on our part. The old American art speech contains an alien quality which belongs to the American continent and to nowhere else." And this unique alien quality, Lawrence goes on to say, the world has missed. "It is hard to hear a new voice," he says, "as hard as to listen to an unknown language. . . . Why? Out of fear. The world fears a new experience more than it fears anything. It can pigeonhole any idea. But it can't pigeonhole a real new experience. It can only dodge. The world is a great dodger, and the Americans the greatest. Because they dodge their own very selves." I should like to pick up a few more of Lawrence's sentences, feeling the freer to do so because they have an affinity to Mr. Frost's prose manner and substance: "An artist is usually a damned liar, but his art, if it be art, will tell you the truth of his day. And that is all that matters. Away with eternal truth. Truth lives from day to day. . . . The old American artists were hopeless liars. . . . Never trust the artist. Trust the tale. The proper function of the critic is to save the tale from the artist who created it. . . . Now listen to me, don't listen to him. He'll tell you the lie you expect, which is partly your fault for expecting it."

Now in point of fact Robert Frost is *not* a liar. I would not hesitate to say that he was if I thought he was. But no, he is not. In certain of his poems — I shall mention one or two in a moment — he makes it perfectly plain what he is doing; and if we are not aware of what he is doing in other of his poems, where he is not quite so plain, that is not his fault but our own. It is not from him that the tale needs to be saved.

I conceive that Robert Frost is doing in his poems what Lawrence says the great writers of the classic American tradition did. That enterprise of theirs was of an ultimate radicalism. It consisted, Lawrence says, of two things: a disintegration and sloughing off of the old consciousness, by which Lawrence means the old European consciousness, and the forming of a new consciousness underneath.

So radical a work, I need scarcely say, is not carried out by reassurance, nor by the affirmation of old virtues and pieties. It is carried out by the representation of the terrible actualities of life in a new way. I think of Robert Frost as a terrifying poet. Call him, if it makes things any easier, a tragic poet, but it might be useful every now and then to come out from under the shelter of that literary word. The universe that he conceives is a terrifying universe. Read the poem called "Design" and see if you sleep the better for it. Read "Neither Out Far nor In Deep," which often seems to me the most perfect poem of our time, and see if you are warmed by anything in it except the energy with which emptiness is perceived.

But the *people*, it will be objected, the *people* who inhabit this possibly terrifying universe! About them there is nothing that can terrify; surely the people in Mr. Frost's poems can only reassure us by their integrity and solidity. Perhaps so. But I cannot make the disjunction. It may well be that ultimately they reassure us in some sense, but first they terrify us, or should. We must not be misled about them by the curious tenderness with which they are represented, a tenderness which extends to a recognition of the tenderness which they themselves can often give. But when ever have people been so isolated, so lightning-blasted, so tied down and calcined by life, so reduced, each in his own way, to some last irreducible core of being. Talk of the disintegration and sloughing off of the old consciousness! The people of Robert Frost's poems have done that with a vengeance. Lawrence says that what the Americans refused to accept was "the post-Renaissance humanism of Europe," "the old European spontaneity," "the flowing easy humor of Europe" and that seems to me a good way to describe the people who inhabit Robert Frost's America. In the interests of what great other thing these people have made this rejection we cannot know for certain. But we can guess that it was in the interest of truth, of some truth of the self. This is what they all affirm by their humor (which is so *not* "the easy flowing humor of Europe"), by their irony, by their separateness and isolateness. They affirm *this* of themselves: that they are what they are, that this is their truth, and that if the truth be bare, as the truth often is, it is far better than a lie. For me the process by which they arrive at that truth is always terrifying. The manifest America of Mr. Frost's poems may be pastoral; the actual America is tragic.

From "A Speech on Robert Frost: A Cultural Episode,"
Partisan Review, Summer 1959

CONSIDERATIONS FOR CRITICAL THINKING AND WRITING

1. How does Trilling distinguish *"my Frost"* from other readers'?

2. Read the section on biographical criticism in Chapter 37 (p. 2027) and familiarize yourself with Frost's life. How does a knowledge of Frost's biography influence your reading of his poems?

3. Write an essay indicating whether you agree or disagree with Trilling's assessment of Frost "as a Terrifying Poet." Use evidence from the poems to support your view.

HERBERT R. COURSEN JR. (B. 1932)

A Parodic Interpretation of "Stopping by Woods on a Snowy Evening" 1962

Much ink has spilled on many pages in exegesis of this little poem. Actually, critical jottings have only obscured what has lain beneath critical noses all these years. To say that the poem means merely that a man stops one night to observe a snowfall, or that the poem contrasts the mundane desire for creature comfort with the sweep of aesthetic appreciation, or that it renders worldly responsibilities paramount, or that it reveals the speaker's latent death-wish is to miss the point rather badly. Lacking has been that mind simple enough to see what is *really* there. . . .

The "darkest evening of the year" in New England is December 21st, a date near that on which the western world celebrates Christmas. It may be that December 21st *is* the date of the poem, or (and with poets this seems more likely) that this is the closest the poet can come to Christmas without giving it all away. Who has "promises to keep" at or near this date, and who must traverse much territory to fulfill these promises? Yes, and who but St. Nick would know the location of *each* home? Only he would know who had "just settled down for a long winter's nap" (the poem's third line — "He will not see me stopping here" — is clearly a veiled allusion) and would not be out inspecting his acreage this night. The unusual phrase "fill up with snow," in the poem's fourth line, is a transfer of Santa's occupational preoccupation to the countryside; he is mulling the filling of countless stockings hung above countless fireplaces by countless careful children. "Harness bells," of course, allude to "Sleighing Song," a popular Christmas tune of the time the poem was written in which the refrain "Jingle Bells! Jingle Bells!" appears; thus again are we put on the Christmas track. The "little horse," like the date, is another attempt at poetic obfuscation. Although the "rein-reindeer" ambiguity has been eliminated from the poem's final version,[1] probably because too obvious, we may speculate that the animal is really a reindeer disguised as a horse by the poet's desire for obscurity, a desire which we must concede has been fulfilled up to now.

The animal is clearly concerned, like the faithful Rudolph — another possible allusion (post facto, hence unconscious) — lest his master fail to complete his mission. Seeing no farmhouse in the second quatrain, but pulling a load of presents, no wonder the little beast wonders! It takes him a full two quatrains to rouse his driver to remember all the empty stockings which hang ahead. And Santa does so reluctantly at that, poor soul, as he ponders the myriad farmhouses and villages which spread between him and his own "winter's nap." The modern St. Nick, lonely and overworked, tosses no "Happy Christmas to all and to all a good night!" into the precipitation. He merely shrugs his shoulders and resignedly plods away.

From "The Ghost of Christmas Past: 'Stopping by Woods on a Snowy Evening,'" *College English*, December 1962

---

[1]The original draft contained the following line: "That bid me give the reins a shake" (Stageberg-Anderson, *Poetry as Experience* [New York, 1952], p. 457). [Coursen's note]

CONSIDERATIONS FOR CRITICAL THINKING AND WRITING

1. Is this critical spoof at all credible? Does the interpretation hold any water? Is the evidence reasonable? Why or why not? Which of the poem's details are accounted for and which are ignored?

2. Choose a Frost poem and try writing a parodic interpretation of it.

3. What criteria do you use to distinguish between a sensible interpretation of a poem and an absurd one? In an essay compare and contrast your criteria with the criteria suggested by Peter Rabinowitz in his perspective "On Close Readings" (p. 2055).

DONALD J. GREINER (B. 1940)

On What Comes "After Apple-Picking"   1982

"After Apple-Picking" was first published in *North of Boston* (1914), and it is my nomination for Frost's greatest poem. In the letter to John Cournos (27 July 1914), Frost explains that "After Apple-Picking" is the only poem in his second book that "will intone." Although he does not elaborate, he means that the rest of the poems sound like human speech whereas "After Apple-Picking" is a lyrical meditation on the tension between a job well done and the uncertainties accompanying the end of something significant. Note that the first word in the title is "After." Frost's refusal to specify what has ended, other than apple picking, is one of the glories of the poem.

The other glories are the examples of technical brilliance. The rhymes alone are worth the reading. Every one of the forty-two lines is rhymed, but Frost eschews the tradition of rhyme scheme altogether. The result is a beautiful, even haunting, rendering of the natural progression of a person's meditation as he uneasily ponders the ambiguities which suddenly well up before him now that his job is done. Similarly, the brilliant use of irregular iambic pentameter . . . to suggest the uncertain balance between the poet figure's need to maintain form in the face of confusion and the threat to his effort cast in the form of truncated lines illustrates the union of technique and theme when Frost is at his best. Although the poem begins with its longest line, the iambic heptameter "My long two-pointed ladder's sticking through a tree," and includes a line as short as "For all," the meter invariably returns to the predominant rhythm of iambic pentameter as the meditator struggles to keep his balance in uncertainty as he has kept it on the ladder of his life.

Nuances of aspiration, satisfaction, completion, rest, and death echo throughout "After Apple-Picking" beginning with the title. Like the speaker, the reader never knows how far to pursue the mythical association between apples and man's expulsion from Eden. If such associations are to be dismissed, then the speaker has safely and satisfactorily completed his task — whatever it literally is — of harvesting the "ten thousand thousand fruit." The phrase "after apple-picking" thus suggests rest. But the genius of the poem is that the speaker is never sure. If the associations between apples and Eden are not to be dismissed, then the poet figure has finished his life's work only to be confronted with an overwhelming uncertainty about what awaits him now. "After Apple-Picking" thus suggests death.

The imagery of hazy speculation is precise. The phrase "toward heaven" indicates the speaker's ultimate aspiration, and the line "Essence of winter sleep is on the night" reverberates with suggestions of termination and the question of rebirth. The point is that the poet figure needs answers to questions he will not pose, and he can only see as through a glass darkly:

> I cannot rub the strangeness from my sight
> I got from looking through a pane of glass
> I skimmed this morning from the drinking trough. . . .

The woodchuck, so unthinkingly confident of rebirth from its winter hibernation, cannot help him. "After Apple-Picking" is a poem of encroaching fear because it is a poem of uncertainty. Although the religious connotations are never obtrusive, this great poem is another of Frost's explorations of what he considered to be man's greatest terror: that our best may not be good enough in Heaven's sight.

From "The Indispensable Robert Frost," in *Critical Essays on Robert Frost*, edited by Philip L. Gerber

CONSIDERATIONS FOR CRITICAL THINKING AND WRITING

1. How far do you think "the mythical association between apples and man's expulsion from Eden" should be pursued by readers of this poem?

2. Greiner cites several examples of the poem's "technical brilliance." What other examples can you find?

3. Write an essay that explores as the theme of the poem Greiner's idea that "our best may not be good enough in Heaven's sight."

BLANCHE FARLEY (B. 1937)

The Lover Not Taken   *1984*

Committed to one, she wanted both
And, mulling it over, long she stood,
Alone on the road, loath
To leave, wanting to hide in the undergrowth.
This new guy, smooth as a yellow wood   5

Really turned her on. She liked his hair,
His smile. But the other, Jack, had a claim
On her already and she had to admit, he did wear
Well. In fact, to be perfectly fair,
He understood her. His long, lithe frame   10

Beside hers in the evening tenderly lay.
Still, if this blond guy dropped by someday,
Couldn't way just lead on to way?
No. For if way led on and Jack
Found out, she doubted if he would ever come back.   15

Oh, she turned with a sigh.
Somewhere ages and ages hence,

She might be telling this. "And I—"
She would say, "stood faithfully by."
But by then who would know the difference?   20

With that in mind, she took the fast way home,
The road by the pond, and phoned the blond.

CONSIDERATIONS FOR CRITICAL THINKING AND WRITING

1. Which Frost poem is the object of this parody?
2. Describe how the stylistic elements mirror Frost's poem.
3. Does this parody seem successful to you? Explain what makes a successful parody.
4. Choose a Frost poem — or a portion of one if it is long — and try writing a parody of it.

DEREK WALCOTT (B. 1930)

The Road Taken   *1996*

Robert Frost: the icon of Yankee values, the smell of wood smoke, the sparkle of dew, the reality of farmhouse dung, the jocular honesty of an uncle.

Why is the favorite figure of American patriotism not paternal but avuncular? Because uncles are wiser than fathers. They have humor, they keep their distance, they are bachelors, they can't be fooled by rhetoric. Frost loved playing the uncle, relishing the dry enchantment of his own voice, the homely gravel in the throat, the keep-your-distance pseudo-rusticity that suspected every stranger, meaning every reader. The voice is like its weather. It tells you to stay away until you are invited. Its first lines, in the epigraph to Frost's 1949 *Complete Poems,* are not so much invitations as warnings.

I'm going out to clean the pasture spring;
I'll only stop to rake the leaves away
(And wait to watch the water clear, I may):
I sha'n't be gone long. — You come too.

From the very epigraph, then, the surly ambiguities slide in. Why "I may"? Not for the rhyme, the desperation of doggerel, but because of this truth: that it would take too long to watch the agitated clouded water settle, that is, for as long as patience allows the poet to proceed to the next line. (Note that the parentheses function as a kind of container, or bank, or vessel, of the churned spring.) The refrain, "You come too." An invitation? An order? And how sincere is either? That is the point of Frost's tone, the authoritative but ambiguous distance of a master ironist.

Frost is an autocratic poet rather than a democratic poet. His invitations are close-lipped, wry, quiet; neither the voice nor the metrical line has the open-armed municipal mural expansion of the other democratic poet, Whitman. The people in Frost's dramas occupy a tight and taciturn locale. They are not part of Whitman's parade of blacksmiths, wheelwrights made communal by work. Besieged and threatened, their virtues are as cautious and measured as the scansion by which they are portrayed.

From Joseph Brodsky, Seamus Heaney, and Derek Walcott,
Homage to Robert Frost

CONSIDERATIONS FOR CRITICAL THINKING AND WRITING

1. Why does Walcott characterize Frost as more an uncle than a father? Explain why you agree or disagree.

2. Choose one of Frost's poems in this anthology and use it to demonstrate that he is a "master ironist."

3. Write an essay that fleshes out Walcott's observation that the people in Frost's poems are "Besieged and threatened, their virtues . . . as cautious and measured as the scansion by which they are portrayed."

TWO COMPLEMENTARY CRITICAL READINGS

RICHARD POIRIER (B. 1925)

On Emotional Suffocation in "Home Burial" 1977

Frost's poetry recurrently dramatizes the discovery that the sharing of a "home" can produce imaginations of uncontrollable threat inside or outside. "Home" can become the source of those fears from which it is supposed to protect us; it can become the habitation of that death whose anguish it is supposed to ameliorate. And this brings us to one of Frost's greatest poetic dramatizations of the theme, "Home Burial." [T]he pressure is shared by a husband and wife, but . . . the role of the husband is ambiguous. Though he does his best to comprehend the wife's difficulties, he is only partly able to do so. The very title of the poem means something about the couple as well as about the dead child buried in back of the house. It is as if "home" were a burial plot for all of them.

The opening lines of Frost's dramatic narratives are usually wonderfully deft in suggesting the metaphoric nature of "home," the human opportunities or imperatives which certain details represent for a husband or a wife. . . . [I]n "Home Burial," the couple are trapped inside the house, which is described as a kind of prison, or perhaps more aptly, a mental hospital. Even the wife's glance out the window can suggest to the husband the desperation she feels within the confines of what has always been his family's "home"; it looks directly on the family graveyard which now holds the body of their recently dead child: [lines 1–30 of "Home Burial" are quoted here].

The remarkable achievement here is that the husband and wife have become so nearly inarticulate in their animosities that the feelings have been transferred to a vision of household arrangements and to their own bodily movements. They and the house conspire together to create an aura of suffocation. . . . Frost's special genius is in the placement of words. The first line poses the husband as a kind of spy; the opening of the second line suggests a habituated wariness on her part, but from that point to line 5 we are shifted back to his glimpse of her as she moves obsessively again, as yet unaware of being watched, to the window. Suggestions of alienation, secretiveness, male intimidation ("advancing toward her") within a situation of mutual distrust, a miasmic fear inside as well as outside the house — we are made to sense this before anyone speaks. Initially the fault seems to lie mostly with the husband.

But as soon as she catches him watching her, and as soon as he begins to talk, it is the grim mutuality of their dilemma and the shared responsibilities for it that sustain the dramatic intelligence and power of the poem.

From *Robert Frost: The Work of Knowing*

CONSIDERATIONS FOR CRITICAL THINKING AND WRITING

1. According to Poirier, how can the couple's home be regarded as a kind of "mental hospital"? Compare Poirier's view with Kearns's description in the following perspective on the house as a "marital asylum."

2. Explain why you agree or disagree that the husband's behavior is a form of "male intimidation."

3. Write an essay that discusses the "grim mutuality" of the couple's "dilemma."

KATHERINE KEARNS (B. 1949)
On the Symbolic Setting of "Home Burial"   1987

"Home Burial" may be used to clarify Frost's intimate relationships between sex, death, and madness. The physical iconography is familiar — a stairwell, a window, a doorway, and a grave — elements which Frost reiterates throughout his poetry. The marriage in "Home Burial" has been destroyed by the death of a first and only son. The wife is in the process of leaving the house, crossing the threshold from marital asylum into freedom. The house is suffocating her. Her window view of the graveyard is not enough and is, in fact, a maddening reminder that she could not enter the earth with her son. With its transparent barrier, the window is a mockery of a widened vision throughout Frost's poetry and seems to incite escape rather than quelling it; in "Home Burial" the woman can "see" through the window and into the grave in a way her husband cannot, and the fear is driving her down the steps toward the door — "She was starting down — / Looking back over her shoulder at some fear" — even before she sees her husband. He threatens to follow his wife and bring her back by force, as if he is the cause of her leaving, but his gesture will be futile because it is based on the mistaken assumption that she is escaping him. Pathetically, he is merely an obstacle toward which she reacts at first dully and then with angry impatience. He is an inanimate part of the embattled household, her real impetus for movement comes from the grave.

The house itself, reduced symbolically and literally to a womblike passageway between the bedroom and the threshold, is a correlative for the sexual tension generated by the man's insistence on his marital rights. He offers to "give up being a man" by binding himself "to keep hands off," but their marriage is already sexually damaged and empty. The man and woman move in an intricate dance, she coming downward and then retracing a step, he "Mounting until she cower[s] under him," she "shrinking from beneath his arm" to slide downstairs. Randall Jarrell examines the image of the woman sinking into "a modest, compact, feminine bundle" upon her skirts;[1] it might be further observed that this childlike posture is also very much a gesture of sexual denial, body bent, knees drawn up protectively against the breasts, all encompassed by

[1] "Robert Frost's 'Home Burial,'" in *The Moment of Poetry*, ed. Don Cameron Allen (Baltimore: Johns Hopkins UP, 1962), p. 104.

voluminous skirts. The two are in profound imbalance, and Frost makes the wife's speech and movements the poetic equivalent of stumbling and resistance; her lines are frequently eleven syllables, and often are punctuated by spondees whose forceful but awkward slowness embodies the woman's vacillations "from terrified to dull," and from frozen and silent immobility to anger. Her egress from the house will be symbolic verification of her husband's impotence, and if she leaves it and does not come back, the house will rot as the best birch fence will rot. Unfilled, without a woman with child, it will fall into itself, an image that recurs throughout Frost's poetry. Thus the child's grave predicts the dissolution of household, . . . almost a literal "home burial."

From "'The Place Is the Asylum': Women and Nature in Robert Frost's Poetry," *American Literature*, May 1987

Considerations for Critical Thinking and Writing

1. How does Kearns's discussion of the stairwell, window, doorway, and grave shed light on your reading of "Home Burial"?

2. Discuss whether Kearns sympathizes more with the wife or the husband. Which character do you feel more sympathetic toward? Do you think Frost sides with one or the other? Explain your response.

3. Write an essay in which you agree or disagree with Kearns's assessment that "The wife is in the process of crossing the threshold from marital asylum into freedom."

LANGSTON HUGHES (1902–1967)

Even as a child, Langston Hughes was wrapped in an important African American legacy. He was raised by his maternal grandmother, who was the widow of Lewis Sheridan Leary, one of the band of men who participated in John Brown's raid on the federal arsenal at Harpers Ferry in 1859. The raid was a desperate attempt to ignite an insurrection that would ultimately liberate slaves in the South. It was a failure. Leary was killed, but the shawl he wore, which was returned to his wife bloodstained and riddled with bullet holes, was proudly worn by Hughes's grandmother fifty years after the raid, and she used it to cover her grandson at night when he was a young boy.

Throughout his long career as a professional writer, Hughes remained true to the African American heritage he celebrated in his writings, which

Photo Above: *Langston Hughes testifying before the Senate Investigations Subcommittee — Senator Joseph McCarthy's subcommittee on subversive activities — on March 27, 1953. (See "Un-American Investigators," p. 1030.) Reprinted by permission of UPI/Corbis-Bettmann.*

were frankly "racial in theme and treatment, derived from the life I know." In an influential essay published in *The Nation*, "The Negro Artist and the Racial Mountain" (1926), he insisted on the need for black artists to draw on their heritage rather than "to run away spiritually from . . . race":

> We younger Negro artists who create now intend to express our individual dark-skinned selves without fear or shame. If white people are pleased, we are glad. If they are not, it doesn't matter. We know we are beautiful. And ugly too. The tom-tom cries and the tom-tom laughs. If colored people are pleased we are glad. If they are not, their displeasure doesn't matter either. We build our temples for tomorrow, strong as we know how, and we stand on top of the mountain, free within ourselves.

That freedom was hard won for Hughes. His father, James Nathaniel Hughes, could not accommodate the racial prejudice and economic frustration that were the result of James's black and white racial ancestry. James abandoned his wife, Carrie Langston Hughes, only one year after their son was born in Joplin, Missouri, and went to find work in Mexico, where he hoped the color of his skin would be less of an issue than in the United States. During the periods when Hughes's mother shuttled from city to city in the Midwest looking for work, she sent her son to live with his grandmother.

Hughes's spotty relationship with his father—a connection he developed in his late teens and maintained only sporadically thereafter—consisted mostly of arguments about his becoming a writer rather than an engineer and businessman as his father wished. Hughes's father could not appreciate or even tolerate his son's ambition to write about the black experience, and Hughes (whose given name was also James but who refused to be identified by it) could not abide his father's contempt for blacks. Consequently, his determination, as he put it in "The Negro Artist," "to express our individual dark-skinned selves without fear or shame" was not only a profound response to African American culture but also an intensely personal commitment that made a relationship with his own father impossible. Though Hughes had been abandoned by his father, he nevertheless felt an early and deep connection to his ancestors, as he reveals in the following poem, written while crossing over the Mississippi River by train as he traveled to visit his father in Mexico, just a month after his high-school graduation.

The Negro Speaks of Rivers   1921

I've known rivers:
I've known rivers ancient as the world and older than the
    flow of human blood in human veins.

My soul has grown deep like the rivers.

I bathed in Euphrates when dawns were young.   5
I built my hut near the Congo and it lulled me to sleep.

I looked upon the Nile and raised the pyramids above it.
I heard the singing of the Mississippi when Abe Lincoln
    went down to New Orleans, and I've seen its muddy
    bosom turn all golden in the sunset.   10

I've known rivers:
Ancient, dusky rivers.

My soul has grown deep like the rivers.

This poem appeared in *The Crisis*, the official publication of the National Association for the Advancement of Colored People, which eventually published more of Hughes's poems than any other magazine or journal. This famous poem's simple and direct free verse makes clear that Africa's "dusky rivers" run concurrently with the poet's soul as he draws spiritual strength as well as individual identity from the collective experience of his ancestors. The themes of racial pride and personal dignity work their way through some forty books that Hughes wrote, edited, or compiled during his forty-five years of writing.

His works include volumes of poetry, novels, short stories, essays, plays, opera librettos, histories, documentaries, autobiographies, biographies, anthologies, children's books, and translations, as well as radio and television scripts. This impressive body of work makes him an important literary artist and a leading African American voice of the twentieth century. First and foremost, he considered himself a poet. He set out to be a poet who could address himself to the concerns of his people in poems that could be read with no formal training or extensive literary background. He wanted his poetry to be "direct, comprehensible, and the epitome of simplicity."

His poetry echoes the voices of ordinary African Americans and the rhythms of their music. Hughes drew on an oral tradition of working-class folk poetry that embraced black vernacular language at a time when some middle-class blacks of the 1920s felt that the use of the vernacular was an embarrassing handicap and an impediment to social progress. Hughes's response to such concerns was unequivocal; at his readings, some of which were accompanied by jazz musicians or singers, his innovative voice found an appreciative audience. As Hughes very well knew, much of the pleasure associated with his poetry comes from reading it aloud; his many recorded readings give testimony to that pleasure.

The blues can be heard moving through Hughes's poetry as well as in the works of many of his contemporaries associated with the Harlem Renaissance, a movement of African American artists — writers, painters, sculptors, actors, and musicians — who were active in New York City's Harlem of the 1920s. Hughes's introduction to the "laughter and pain, hunger and heartache" of blues music began the year he spent at Columbia University. He dropped out after only two semesters because he preferred the night life and culture of Harlem to academic life. The sweet, sad blues songs captured for Hughes the intense pain and yearning that he saw around him and that he incorporated into poems such as "The Weary

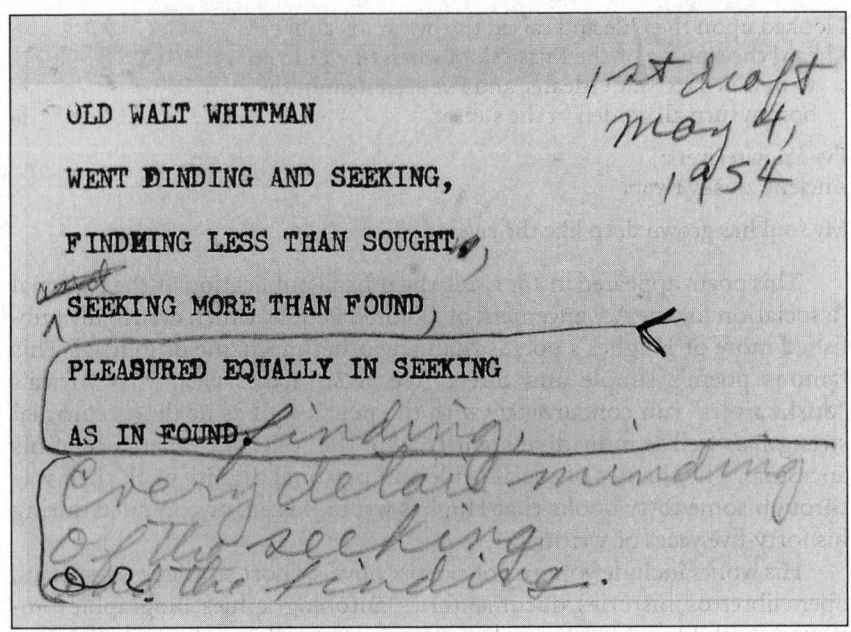

OLD WALT WHITMAN

WENT ƉINDING AND SEEKING,

FINDﻙING LESS THAN SOUGHT,

SEEKING MORE THAN FOUND,

PLEAƉURED EQUALLY IN SEEKING

AS IN FOUND.

1st draft
May 4,
1954

finding,
Every detail minding
of the seeking
or the finding.

Manuscript page for "Old Walt" (1954) showing an earlier stage of the poem than the one published here (p. 1031) and Hughes's revisions.

Blues" (p. 1019). He also reveled in the jazz music of Harlem and discovered in its open forms and improvisations an energy and freedom that significantly influenced the style of his poetry.

Hughes's life, like the jazz music that influenced his work, was characterized by improvisation and openness. After leaving Columbia, he worked a series of odd jobs and then traveled as a merchant seaman to Africa and Europe from 1923 to 1924. He jumped ship to work for several months in the kitchen of a Paris nightclub. As he broadened his experience through travel, he continued to write poetry. After his return to the United States in 1925 he published poems in two black magazines, *The Crisis* and *Opportunity,* and met the critic Carl Van Vechten, who sent his poems to the publisher Alfred A. Knopf. He also—as a busboy in a Washington, D.C., hotel—met the poet Vachel Lindsay, who was instrumental in advancing Hughes's reputation as a poet. In 1926 Hughes published his first volume of poems, *The Weary Blues,* and enrolled in Lincoln University in Pennsylvania, his education funded by a generous patron. His second volume of verse, *Fine Clothes to the Jew,* appeared in 1927, and by the time he graduated from Lincoln in 1929 he was on a book tour of the South giving poetry readings. Hughes ended the decade as more than a promising poet; as Countee Cullen pronounced in a mixed review of *The Weary Blues* (mixed because Cullen believed that African American poets should embrace universal themes rather than racial themes), Hughes had "arrived."

Hughes wrote more prose than poetry during the 1930s, publishing his first novel, *Not Without Laughter* (1930), and a collection of stories, *The Ways of White Folks* (1934). In addition to writing a variety of magazine articles, he also worked on a number of plays and screenplays. Many of his poems from this period reflect proletarian issues. During this decade Hughes's travels took him to all points of the compass — Cuba, Haiti, the Soviet Union, China, Japan, Mexico, France, and Spain — but his general intellectual movement was decidedly toward the left. Hughes was attracted to the American Communist Party, owing to its insistence on equality for all working-class people regardless of race. Like many other Americans of the thirties, he turned his attention away from the exotic twenties and focused on the economic and political issues attending the Great Depression that challenged the freedom and dignity of common humanity.

During World War II, Hughes helped the war effort by writing jingles and catchy verses to sell war bonds and to bolster morale. His protest poems of the thirties were largely replaced by poems that returned to earlier themes centered on the everyday lives of African Americans. In 1942 Hughes described his new collection of poems, *Shakespeare in Harlem*, as "light verse. Afro-American in the blues mood . . . to be read aloud, crooned, shouted, recited, and sung. Some with gestures, some not — as you like." Soon after this collection appeared, the character of Jesse B. Simple emerged from Hughes's 1943 newspaper column for the Chicago *Defender.* Hughes developed this popular urban African American character in five humorous books published over a fifteen-year period: *Simple Speaks His Mind* (1950), *Simple Takes a Wife* (1953), *Simple Stakes a Claim* (1957), *The Best of Simple* (1961), and *Simple's Uncle Sam* (1965). Two more poetry collections appeared in the forties: *Fields of Wonder* (1947) and *One-Way Ticket* (1949).

In the 1950s and 1960s Hughes's poetry again revealed the strong influence of black music, especially in the rhythms of *Montage of a Dream Deferred* (1951) and *Ask Your Mama: 12 Moods for Jazz* (1961). From the poem "Harlem" (p. 1030) in *Montage of a Dream Deferred,* Lorraine Hansberry derived the title of her 1959 play *A Raisin in the Sun.* This is only a small measure of Hughes's influence on his fellow African American writers, but it is suggestive nonetheless. For some in the 1950s, however, Hughes and his influence occasioned suspicion. He was watched closely by the FBI and the Special Committee on Un-American Activities of the House of Representatives because of his alleged communist activities in the 1930s. Hughes denied that he was ever a member of the Communist Party, but he and others, including Albert Einstein and Paul Robeson, were characterized as "dupes and fellow travelers" by *Life* magazine in 1949. Hughes was subpoenaed to appear before Senator Joseph McCarthy's subcommittee on subversive activities in 1953 and listed by the FBI as a security risk until 1959. His anger and indignation over these attacks from the right can be seen in his poem "Un-American Investigators" (p. 1030), published posthumously in *The Panther and the Lash* (1967).

Despite the tremendous amount that Hughes published, including two autobiographies, *The Big Sea* (1940) and *I Wonder as I Wander* (1956), he remains somewhat elusive. He never married or had friends who can lay claim to truly knowing him beyond what he wanted them to know (even though there are several biographies). And yet Hughes is well known — not for his personal life but for his treatment of the possibilities of African American experiences and identities. Like Walt Whitman, one of his fa-vorite writers, Hughes created a persona that spoke for more than himself. Consider Hughes's voice in the following poem.

I, Too   *1925*

I, too, sing America.

I am the darker brother.
They send me to eat in the kitchen
When company comes,
But I laugh,   5
And eat well,
And grow strong.

Tomorrow,
I'll be at the table
When company comes.   10
Nobody'll dare
Say to me,
"Eat in the kitchen,"
Then.

Besides,   15
They'll see how beautiful I am
And be ashamed —

I, too, am America.

The "darker brother" who celebrates America is certain of a better future when he will no longer be shunted aside by "company." The poem is charac-teristic of Hughes's faith in the racial consciousness of African Americans, a consciousness that reflects their integrity and beauty while simultane-ously demanding respect and acceptance from others: "Nobody'll dare / Say to me, / 'Eat in the kitchen,' / Then."

Hughes's poetry reveals his hearty appetite for all humanity, his insis-tence on justice for all, and his faith in the transcendent possibilities of joy and hope that make room for everyone at America's table.

CHRONOLOGY

1902	Born on February 1, in Joplin, Missouri.
1903–14	Lives primarily with his grandmother in Lawrence, Kansas.
1920	Graduates from high school in Cleveland, Ohio.
1921–22	Attends Columbia University for one year but then drops out to work odd jobs and discover Harlem.
1923–24	Travels to Africa and Europe while working on a merchant ship.
1926	Publishes his first collection of poems, *The Weary Blues,* and enters Lincoln University in Pennsylvania.
1929	Graduates from Lincoln University.
1930	Publishes his first novel, *Not without Laughter.*
1932	Travels to the Soviet Union.
1934	Publishes his first collection of short stories, *The Ways of White Folks.*
1935	His play *Mulatto* is produced on Broadway.
1937	Covers the Spanish Civil War for the Baltimore *Afro-American.*
1938–39	Founds African American theaters in Harlem and Los Angeles.
1940	Publishes his first autobiography, *The Big Sea.*
1943	Creates the character of Simple in columns for the Chicago *Defender.*
1947	Is poet-in-residence at Atlanta University.
1949	Teaches at University of Chicago's Laboratory School.
1950	Publishes his first volume of Simple sketches, *Simple Speaks His Mind.*
1951	Publishes a translation of Federico García Lorca's *Gypsy Ballads.*
1953	Is subpoenaed to appear before Senator Joseph McCarthy's subcommittee on subversive activities in Washington, D.C.
1954–55	Publishes a number of books for young readers including *The First Book of Jazz* and *Famous American Negroes.*
1956	Publishes his second autobiography, *I Wonder as I Wander.*
1958	Publishes *The Langston Hughes Reader.*
1960	Publishes *An African Treasury: Articles, Essays, Stories, Poems by Black Africans.*
1961	Is inducted into the National Institute of Arts and Letters.
1962	Publishes *Fight for Freedom: The Story of the NAACP.*
1963	Publishes *Five Plays by Langston Hughes.*
1964	Publishes *New Negro Poets: U.S.A.*
1965	Defends Martin Luther King, Jr., from attacks by militant blacks.
1966	Is appointed by President Johnson to lead the American delegation to the First World Festival of Negro Arts in Dakar.

1967   Dies on May 22 in New York City; his last volume of poems, *The Panther and the Lash*, is published posthumously.

1994   *The Collected Poems of Langston Hughes*, edited by Arnold Rampersad and David Roessel, published posthumously.

Negro   1922

I am a Negro:
  Black as the night is black,
  Black like the depths of my Africa.

I've been a slave:
  Caesar told me to keep his door-steps clean.   5
  I brushed the boots of Washington.

I've been a worker:
  Under my hand the pyramids arose.
  I made mortar for the Woolworth Building.

I've been a singer: 10
  All the way from Africa to Georgia
  I carried my sorrow songs.
  I made ragtime.

I've been a victim:
  The Belgians cut off my hands in the Congo.   15
  They lynch me still in Mississippi.

I am a Negro:
  Black as the night is black,
  Black like the depths of my Africa.

CONSIDERATIONS FOR CRITICAL THINKING AND WRITING

1. FIRST RESPONSE. What sort of identity does the speaker claim for the "Negro"? What is the effect of the litany of roles?

2. What is the effect of the repetition of the first and last stanzas?

3. What kind of history of black people does the speaker describe?

CONNECTIONS TO OTHER SELECTIONS

1. How does Hughes's use of night and blackness in "Negro" help to explain their meaning in the poem "Dream Variations" (p. 1018)?

2. Write an essay comparing the treatment of oppression in "Negro" with that in Blake's "The Chimney Sweeper" (p. 822).

Danse Africaine   1922

The low beating of the tom-toms,
The slow beating of the tom-toms,
    Low . . . slow
    Slow . . . low —
    Stirs your blood.   5
      Dance!
A night-veiled girl
    Whirls softly into a
    Circle of light.
    Whirls softly . . . slowly,   10
Like a wisp of smoke around the fire —
    And the tom-toms beat,
    And the tom-toms beat,
And the low beating of the tom-toms
    Stirs your blood.   15

CONSIDERATIONS FOR CRITICAL THINKING AND WRITING

1. FIRST RESPONSE. How do the sounds of this poem build its meaning? (What *is* its meaning?)
2. What effect do the repeated rhythms have? You may need to read the poem aloud to answer.

CONNECTION TO ANOTHER SELECTION

1. Try rewriting this poem based on the prescription for poetry in "Formula" (p. 1021).

Jazzonia   1923

Oh, silver tree!
Oh, shining rivers of the soul!

In a Harlem cabaret
Six long-headed jazzers play.
A dancing girl whose eyes are bold   5
Lifts high a dress of silken gold.

Oh, singing tree!
Oh, shining rivers of the soul!

Were Eve's eyes
In the first garden
Just a bit too bold?   10
Was Cleopatra gorgeous
In a gown of gold?

Oh, shining tree!
Oh, silver rivers of the soul!   15

In a whirling cabaret
Six long-headed jazzers play.

CONSIDERATIONS FOR CRITICAL THINKING AND WRITING

1. FIRST RESPONSE. Does "Jazzonia" capture what you imagine a Harlem cabaret to have been like? Discuss the importance of the setting.

2. What is the effect of the variations in lines 1–2, 7–8, and 14–15?

3. What do the allusions to Eve and Cleopatra add to the poem's meaning? Are the questions raised about them answered?

CONNECTION TO ANOTHER SELECTION

1. Compare in an essay the rhythms of "Jazzonia" and "Danse Africaine."

Dream Variations   *1924*

To fling my arms wide
In some place of the sun,
To whirl and to dance
Till the white day is done.
Then rest at cool evening   5
Beneath a tall tree
While night comes on gently,
    Dark like me —
That is my dream!

To fling my arms wide   10
In the face of the sun,
Dance! Whirl! Whirl!
Till the quick day is done.
Rest at pale evening . . .
A tall, slim tree . . .   15
Night coming tenderly
    Black like me.

CONSIDERATIONS FOR CRITICAL THINKING AND WRITING

1. FIRST RESPONSE. What distinctions are made in the poem between night and day? Which is the dream?

2. Describe the speaker's "Dream." How might the dream be understood metaphorically?

3. How do the rhythms of the lines contribute to the effects of the poem?

CONNECTIONS TO OTHER SELECTIONS

1. In an essay compare and contrast the meanings of darkness and the night in this poem and in Stafford's "Traveling through the Dark" (p. 813).
2. Discuss the significance of the dream in this poem and in "Dream Boogie" (p. 1029).

Johannesburg Mines   1925

In the Johannesburg mines
There are 240,000
Native Africans working.
What kind of poem
Would you
Make out of that?
240,000 natives
Working in the
Johannesburg mines.

CONSIDERATIONS FOR CRITICAL THINKING AND WRITING

1. FIRST RESPONSE. What "kind of poem" does the speaker make out of the fact that 240,000 natives work in the mines of Johannesburg, South Africa? How do you respond to the speaker's direct address of you, the reader?
2. Describe the poem's tone.
3. What do you think is the poem's theme?

CONNECTION TO ANOTHER SELECTION

1. Read the perspective by Hulme, "On the Differences between Poetry and Prose" (p. 774), and write an essay on why you think "Johannesburg Mines" is best described as poetry or prose.

The Weary Blues   1925

Droning a drowsy syncopated tune,
Rocking back and forth to a mellow croon,
    I heard a Negro play.
Down on Lenox Avenue° the other night   *street in Harlem*
By the pale dull pallor of an old gas light   5
    He did a lazy sway. . . .
    He did a lazy sway. . . .
To the tune o' those Weary Blues.
With his ebony hands on each ivory key
He made that poor piano moan with melody.   10
    O Blues!
Swaying to and fro on his rickety stool

He played that sad raggy tune like a musical fool.
    Sweet Blues!
Coming from a black man's soul.   15
    O Blues!
In a deep song voice with a melancholy tone
I heard that Negro sing, that old piano moan —
    "Ain't got nobody in all this world,
        Ain't got nobody but ma self.   20
        I's gwine to quit ma frownin'
        And put ma troubles on the shelf."

Thump, thump, thump, went his foot on the floor.
He played a few chords then he sang some more —
    "I got the Weary Blues   25
        And I can't be satisfied.
    Got the Weary Blues
        And can't be satisfied —
    I ain't happy no mo'
    And I wish that I had died."   30
And far into the night he crooned that tune.
The stars went out and so did the moon.
The singer stopped playing and went to bed
While the Weary Blues echoed through his head.
He slept like a rock or a man that's dead.   35

CONSIDERATIONS FOR CRITICAL THINKING AND WRITING

1. FIRST RESPONSE. Write a one-paragraph description of the blues based on how the poem presents blues music.
2. How does the rhythm of the lines reflect their meaning?
3. How does the speaker's voice compare with the singer's?
4. Comment on the effects of the rhymes.

CONNECTION TO ANOTHER SELECTION

1. Discuss "The Weary Blues" and "Lenox Avenue: Midnight" (p. 1022) as vignettes of urban life in America. Do you think that, though written more than seventy years ago, they are still credible descriptions of city life? Explain why or why not.

Cross   *1925*

My old man's a white old man
And my old mother's black.
If ever I cursed my white old man
I take my curses back.

If ever I cursed my black old mother   5
And wished she were in hell,

I'm sorry for that evil wish
And now I wish her well.

My old man died in a fine big house.
My ma died in a shack.   10
I wonder where I'm gonna die,
Being neither white nor black?

CONSIDERATIONS FOR CRITICAL THINKING AND WRITING

1. FIRST RESPONSE. What do you think has caused the speaker to retract his
   hard feelings about his parents?
2. Discuss the possible meaning of the title.
3. Why do you think the speaker regrets having "cursed" his or her father and
   mother? Is it possible to determine if the speaker is male or female? Why or
   why not?
4. What informs the speaker's attitude toward life?

CONNECTION TO ANOTHER SELECTION

1. Read the perspective by Francis, "On 'Hard' Poetry" (p. 697), and write an
   essay explaining why you would characterize "Cross" as "hard" or "soft"
   poetry.

Formula   *1926*

Poetry should treat
    Of lofty things
Soaring thoughts
    And birds with wings.

The Muse of Poetry   5
    Should not know
That roses
    In manure grow.

The Muse of Poetry
    Should not care   10
That earthly pain
    Is everywhere.

Poetry!
    Treats of lofty things:
Soaring thoughts   15
    And birds with wings.

CONSIDERATIONS FOR CRITICAL THINKING AND WRITING

1. FIRST RESPONSE. What makes this poem a parody? What assumptions
   about poetry are being made fun of in the poem?
2. How does "Formula" fit the prescriptions offered in the advice to greeting-
   card free-lancers (p. 692)?

1. Choose any two poems by Hughes in this collection and explain why they do not fit the "Formula."
2. Write an essay that explains how Farries's "Magic of Love" (p. 692) conforms to the ideas about poetry presented in "Formula."

Lenox Avenue: Midnight   *1926*

The rhythm of life
Is a jazz rhythm,
Honey.
The gods are laughing at us.

The broken heart of love,   5
The weary, weary heart of pain, —
     Overtones,
     Undertones,
To the rumble of street cars,
To the swish of rain.   10

Lenox Avenue,
Honey.
Midnight,
And the gods are laughing at us.

CONSIDERATIONS FOR CRITICAL THINKING AND WRITING

1. FIRST RESPONSE. What, in your own experience, is the equivalent of Lenox Avenue for the speaker?
2. For so brief a poem there are many sounds in these fourteen lines. What are they? How do they reinforce the poem's meanings?
3. What do you think is the poem's theme?

CONNECTIONS TO OTHER SELECTIONS

1. In an essay compare the theme of this poem with that of Emily Dickinson's "I know that He exists" (p. 967).
2. Compare and contrast the speaker's tone in this poem with the tone of the speaker in Thomas Hardy's "Hap" (p. 1093).

Red Silk Stockings   *1927*

Put on yo' red silk stockings,
Black gal.
Go out an' let de white boys
Look at yo' legs.

Ain't nothin' to do for you, nohow,   5
Round this town, —
You's too pretty.

Put on yo' red silk stockings, gal,
An' tomorrow's chile'll
Be a high yaller.   10

Go out an' let de white boys
Look at yo' legs.

CONSIDERATIONS FOR CRITICAL THINKING AND WRITING

1. FIRST RESPONSE. Who do you think is speaking? Describe his or her tone.
2. Discuss the racial dimensions of this poem.
3. Write a response from the girl — does she put on the red silk stockings? Explain why you imagine her reacting in a certain way.

CONNECTION TO ANOTHER SELECTION

1. Write an essay that compares relations between whites and blacks in this poem and in "Dinner Guest: Me" (p. 1033).

Rent-Party° Shout: For a Lady Dancer   *1930*

Whip it to a jelly!
Too bad Jim!
Mamie's got ma man —
An' I can't find him.
Shake that thing! O!   5
Shake it slow!
That man I love is
Mean an' low.
Pistol an' razor!
Razor an' gun!   10
If I sees ma man he'd
Better run —
For I'll shoot him in de shoulder,
Else I'll cut him down,
Cause I knows I can find him   15
When he's in de ground —
Then can't no other women
Have him layin' round.
So play it, Mr. Nappy!
Yo' music's fine!   20
I'm gonna kill that
Man o' mine!

Rent-Party: In Harlem during the 1920s, parties were given that charged admission to raise money for rent.

CONSIDERATIONS FOR CRITICAL THINKING AND WRITING

1. FIRST RESPONSE. Describe the type of music you think might be played at this party today.
2. In what sense is this poem a kind of "Shout"?

3. How is the speaker's personality characterized by her use of language?
4. How does Hughes's use of short lines affect your reading of the poem?

The English   1930

In ships all over the world
The English comb their hair for dinner,
Stand watch on the bridge,
Guide by strange stars,
Take on passengers,   5
Slip up hot rivers,
Nose across lagoons,
Bargain for trade,
Buy, sell or rob,
Load oil, load fruit,   10
Load cocoa beans, load gold
In ships all over the world,
Comb their hair for dinner.

CONSIDERATIONS FOR CRITICAL THINKING AND WRITING

1. FIRST RESPONSE. What do you think the symbolic significance is of combing one's hair in the poem? Who do you think the speaker is?
2. What is the speaker's attitude toward the English?
3. Which words reveal the speaker's attitudes?

CONNECTION TO ANOTHER SELECTION

1. Write an essay that discusses hair combing as symbolic action in this poem and in Ho's "A Beautiful Girl Combs Her Hair" (p. 706).

Note on Commercial Theatre   1940

You've taken my blues and gone—
You sing 'em on Broadway
And you sing 'em in Hollywood Bowl,
And you mixed 'em up with symphonies
And you fixed 'em   5
So they don't sound like me.
Yep, you done taken my blues and gone.

You also took my spirituals and gone.
You put me in Macbeth and Carmen Jones
And all kinds of Swing Mikados   10
And in everything but what's about me—

But someday somebody'll
Stand up and talk about me,
And write about me —
Black and beautiful — 15
And sing about me,
And put on plays about me!
I reckon it'll be
Me myself!

Yes, it'll be me. 20

CONSIDERATIONS FOR CRITICAL THINKING AND WRITING

1. FIRST RESPONSE. What is the speaker's complaint? Does it remain valid today?
2. Compare the tone of the title with that of the poem. Are they consistent?
3. Do you think the speaker is male or female? Explain your response.

CONNECTION TO ANOTHER SELECTION

1. Compare in an essay the tone and theme of this poem and "Frederick Douglass: 1817–1895" (p. 1034).

Ballad of the Landlord 1940

Landlord, landlord,
My roof has sprung a leak.
Don't you 'member I told you about it
Way last week?

Landlord, landlord, 5
These steps is broken down.
When you come up yourself
It's a wonder you don't fall down.

Ten Bucks you say I owe you?
Ten Bucks you say is due? 10
Well, that's Ten Bucks more'n I'll pay you
Till you fix this house up new.

What? You gonna get eviction orders?
You gonna cut off my heat?
You gonna take my furniture and 15
Throw it in the street?

Um-huh! You talking high and mighty.
Talk on — till you get through.
You ain't gonna be able to say a word
If I land my fist on you. 20

Police! Police!
Come and get this man!

He's trying to ruin the government
And overturn the land!

Copper's whistle!   25
Patrol bell!
Arrest.

Precinct Station.
Iron cell.
Headlines in press: 30

MAN THREATENS LANDLORD
TENANT HELD NO BAIL
JUDGE GIVES NEGRO 90 DAYS IN COUNTY JAIL

CONSIDERATIONS FOR CRITICAL THINKING AND WRITING

1. FIRST RESPONSE. The poem incorporates both humor and serious social commentary. Which do you think is dominant? Explain.

2. Why is the literary ballad an especially appropriate form for the content of this poem?

3. How does the speaker's language simultaneously characterize him and the landlord?

CONNECTION TO ANOTHER SELECTION

1. Write an essay on landlords based on this poem and Soyinka's "Telephone Conversation" (p. 681).

Midnight Raffle   1949

I put my nickel
In the raffle of the night.
Somehow that raffle
Didn't turn out right.

I lost my nickel.   5
I lost my time.
I got back home
Without a dime.

When I dropped that nickel
In the subway slot,   10
I wouldn't have dropped it,
Knowing what I got.

I could just as well've
Stayed home inside:
My bread wasn't buttered   15
On neither side.

CONSIDERATIONS FOR CRITICAL THINKING AND WRITING

1. FIRST RESPONSE. What has the speaker lost, do you think? A nickel, or something else? And what do you think the prize of the raffle might have been?

2. How is the phrase "raffle of the night" different from "Midnight Raffle"? Which seems more suggestive to you? Explain why.

3. Discuss the meaning and tone of the last stanza.

CONNECTION TO ANOTHER SELECTION

1. Compare in an essay the meaning of home in "Midnight Raffle" and "door-knobs" (p. 1032).

Theme for English B   1949

The instructor said,

> Go home and write
> a page tonight.
> And let that page come out of you —
> Then, it will be true.   5

I wonder if it's that simple?
I am twenty-two, colored, born in Winston-Salem.
I went to school there, then Durham, then here
to this college on the hill above Harlem.
I am the only colored student in my class.   10
The steps from the hill lead down into Harlem,
through a park, then I cross St. Nicholas,
Eighth Avenue, Seventh, and I come to the Y,
the Harlem Branch Y, where I take the elevator
up to my room, sit down, and write this page: 15

It's not easy to know what is true for you or me
at twenty-two, my age. But I guess I'm what
I feel and see and hear, Harlem, I hear you:
hear you, hear me — we two — you, me, talk on this page.
(I hear New York, too.) Me — who?   20
Well, I like to eat, sleep, drink, and be in love.
I like to work, read, learn, and understand life.
I like a pipe for a Christmas present,
or records — Bessie,° bop, or Bach.
I guess being colored doesn't make me *not* like   25
the same things other folks like who are other races.
So will my page be colored that I write?
Being me, it will not be white.
But it will be

24 *Bessie:* Bessie Smith (1898?–1937), a famous blues singer.

a part of you, instructor. 30
You are white —
yet a part of me, as I am part of you.
That's American.
Sometimes perhaps you don't want to be a part of me.
Nor do I often want to be a part of you. 35
But we are, that's true!
As I learn from you,
I guess you learn from me —
although you're older — and white —
and somewhat more free. 40

This is my page for English B.

CONSIDERATIONS FOR CRITICAL THINKING AND WRITING

1. FIRST RESPONSE. Try to write "a page" in response to the instructor that, like the speaker's, captures who you are.

2. What complicates the writing assignment for the speaker? Does he fulfill the assignment? Explain why or why not.

3. What are the circumstances of the speaker's life? How does the speaker respond to the question "So will my page be colored that I write?" (line 27). Discuss the tone of lines 27–40.

4. Write a one-paragraph response to this poem as you think the speaker's instructor would in grading it.

CONNECTIONS TO OTHER SELECTIONS

1. Use your imagination and write about an encounter between the student-speaker in this poem and the instructor-speaker of Mark Halliday's "Graded Paper" (p. 1156). Choose a form (such as an essay, a dialogue, or a short story) that will allow you to explore their responses to one another.

2. Discuss the attitudes expressed toward the United States in this poem and in Divakaruni's "Indian Movie, New Jersey" (p. 819).

Juke Box Love Song 1950

I could take the Harlem night
and wrap around you,
Take the neon lights and make a crown,
Take the Lenox Avenue busses,
Taxis, subways,
And for your love song tone their rumble down. 5
Take Harlem's heartbeat,
Make a drumbeat,
Put it on a record, let it whirl,
And while we listen to it play,
Dance with you till day — 10
Dance with you, my sweet brown Harlem girl.

CONSIDERATIONS FOR CRITICAL THINKING AND WRITING

1. FIRST RESPONSE. What kinds of songs do you associate with juke boxes? What kind of song do you think this poem would be?

2. Discuss the images in the poem. Are they effective? What makes them work or fail?

CONNECTION TO ANOTHER SELECTION

1. Compare the tone of this poem with "Red Silk Stockings" (p. 1022). Which poem do you prefer? Explain why.

Dream Boogie   1951

Good morning, daddy!
Ain't you heard
The boogie-woogie rumble
Of a dream deferred?
Listen closely: 5
You'll hear their feet
Beating out and beating out a —

    You think
    It's a happy beat?

Listen to it closely: 10
Ain't you heard
something underneath
like a —

    What did I say?

Sure,   15
I'm happy!
Take it away!

    Hey, pop!
    Re-bop!
    Mop!   20

    Y-e-a-h!

CONSIDERATIONS FOR CRITICAL THINKING AND WRITING

1. FIRST RESPONSE. Answer the question, *"You think / It's a happy beat?"*

2. Discuss the poem's musical qualities. Which lines are most musical?

3. Describe the competing tones in the poem. Which do you think is predominant?

CONNECTIONS TO OTHER SELECTIONS

1. In an essay compare and contrast the thematic tensions in this poem and in "Harlem" (p. 1030).

2. How are the "dreams" different in "Dream Boogie" and "Dream Variations" (p. 1018)?

Harlem   1951

What happens to a dream deferred?

Does it dry up
like a raisin in the sun?
Or fester like a sore —
And then run?   5
Does it stink like rotten meat?
Or crust and sugar over —
like a syrupy sweet?

Maybe it just sags
like a heavy load.   10

Or does it explode?

CONSIDERATIONS FOR CRITICAL THINKING AND WRITING

1. How might the question asked in this poem be raised by any individual or group whose dreams and aspirations are thwarted?

2. In some editions of Hughes's poetry the title of this poem is "Dream Deferred." What would the effect of this change be on your reading of the poem's symbolic significance?

3. How might the final line be completed as a simile? What is the effect of the speaker not completing the simile? Why is this an especially useful strategy?

CONNECTION TO ANOTHER SELECTION

1. Write an essay on the themes of "Harlem" and Merrill's "Casual Wear" (p. 817).

Un-American Investigators   1953

The committee's fat,
Smug, almost secure
Co-religionists
Shiver with delight
In warm manure   5
As those investigated —
Too brave to name a name —
Have pseudonyms revealed
In Gentile game

Of who,   10
Born Jew,
Is who?
Is not your name Lipshitz?
Yes.
Did you not change it   15
For subversive purposes?
No.
For nefarious gain?
Not so.
Are you sure?   20
The committee shivers
With delight in
Its manure.

CONSIDERATIONS FOR CRITICAL THINKING AND WRITING

1. FIRST RESPONSE. What are the politics of the speaker, do you think? What in the poem suggests this?

2. Research in the library the hearings and investigations of the House of Representatives' Special Committee on Un-American Activities. How is this background information relevant to an understanding of this poem?

3. How does the speaker characterize the investigators?

4. Given the images in the poem, what might serve as a substitute for its ironic title?

CONNECTION TO ANOTHER SELECTION

1. Write an essay that connects the committee described in this poem with the speaker in E. E. Cummings's "next to of course god america i" (p. 805). What do they have in common?

Old Walt   1954

Old Walt Whitman
Went finding and seeking,
Finding less than sought
Seeking more than found,
Every detail minding   5
Of the seeking or the finding.

Pleasured equally
In seeking as in finding,
Each detail minding,
Old Walt went seeking   10
And finding.

CONSIDERATIONS FOR CRITICAL THINKING AND WRITING

1. FIRST RESPONSE. Read any poem by Whitman in this book. Do you agree with the speaker's take on Whitman's poetry?

2. Write an explication of "Old Walt." (For a discussion of how to explicate a poem, see the sample explication on p. 2082.)

3. What is the effect of the poem's repeated sounds?

4. To what extent do you think lines 3 and 4 could be used to describe Hughes's poetry as well as Whitman's?

CONNECTION TO ANOTHER SELECTION

1. How does Hughes's tribute to Whitman compare with his tribute to Frederick Douglass (p. 1034)?

doorknobs 1961

The simple silly terror
of a doorknob on a door
that turns to let in life
on two feet standing,
walking, talking, 5
wearing dress or trousers,
maybe drunk or maybe sober,
maybe smiling, laughing, happy,
maybe tangled in the terror
of a yesterday past grandpa 10
when the door from out there opened
into here where I, antenna,
recipient of your coming,
received the talking image
of the simple silly terror 15
of a door that opens
at the turning of a knob
to let in life
walking, talking, standing
wearing dress or trousers, 20
drunk or maybe sober,
smiling, laughing, happy,
or tangled in the terror
of a yesterday past grandpa
not of our own doing. 25

CONSIDERATIONS FOR CRITICAL THINKING AND WRITING

1. FIRST RESPONSE. Why is the doorknob associated with "terror"? Does it have any symbolic value or should it be read literally?

2. How do the style and content of this poem differ from those of the other poems by Hughes in this anthology?

3. The final eight lines repeat much of the first part of the poem. What is repeated and what is changed? What is the effect of this repetition?

CONNECTION TO ANOTHER SELECTION

1. Write an essay comparing the theme of this poem with that of Stevens's "Schizophrenia" (p. 788).

Dinner Guest: Me

1965

I know I am
The Negro Problem
Being wined and dined,
Answering the usual questions
That come to white mind   5
Which seeks demurely
To probe in polite way
The why and wherewithal
Of darkness U.S.A.—
Wondering how things got this way   10
In current democratic night,
Murmuring gently
Over *fraises du bois,*
"I'm so ashamed of being white."

The lobster is delicious,   15
The wine divine,
And center of attention
At the damask table, mine.
To be a Problem on
Park Avenue at eight   20
Is not so bad.
Solutions to the Problem,
Of course, wait.

CONSIDERATIONS FOR CRITICAL THINKING AND WRITING

1. FIRST RESPONSE. What does the speaker satirize in this description of a dinner party? Do you think this "Problem" exists today?
2. Why is line 9, "Of darkness U.S.A.—," especially resonant?
3. What effects are created by the speaker's diction?
4. Discuss the effects of the rhymes in lines 15–23.

CONNECTION TO ANOTHER SELECTION

1. Write an essay on the speaker's treatment of the diners in this poem and in Kingston's "Restaurant" (p. 849).

Frederick Douglass: 1817–1895°   1966

Douglass was someone who,
Had he walked with wary foot
And frightened tread,
From very indecision
Might be dead,   5
Might have lost his soul,
But instead decided to be bold
And capture every street
On which he set his feet,
To route each path   10
Toward freedom's goal,
To make each highway
Choose *his* compass' choice,
To all the world cried,
Hear my voice! . . .   15
Oh, to be a beast, a bird,
Anything but a slave! he said.

Who would be free
Themselves must strike
The first blow, he said.   20

       He died in 1895.
       He is not dead.

1817–1895: Douglass was actually born in 1818; as a slave, he did not know his true birth date.

CONSIDERATIONS FOR CRITICAL THINKING AND WRITING

1. FIRST RESPONSE. This poem was published when the civil rights movement
   was very active in America. Does that information affect your reading of it?
2. What does Hughes celebrate about the life of Douglass, author of *Narrative
   of the Life of Frederick Douglass, an American Slave, Written by Himself* (1845)?

CONNECTION TO ANOTHER SELECTION

1. How is the speaker's attitude toward violence in this poem similar to that
   of the speaker in "Harlem" (p. 1030)?

PERSPECTIVES ON HUGHES

Hughes on Racial Shame and Pride   1926

[J]azz to me is one of the inherent expressions of Negro life in America: the eternal tom-tom beating in the Negro soul — the tom-tom of revolt against weariness in a white world, a world of subway trains, and work, work, work; the tom-
tom of joy and laughter, and pain swallowed in a smile. Yet the Philadelphia

clubwoman is ashamed to say that her race created it and she does not like me to write about it. The old subconscious "white is best" runs through her mind. Years of study under white teachers, a lifetime of white books, pictures, and papers, and white manners, morals, and Puritan standards made her dislike the spirituals. And now she turns up her nose at jazz and all its manifestations — likewise almost everything else distinctly racial. She doesn't care for the Winold Reiss° portraits of Negroes because they are "too Negro." She does not want a true picture of herself from anybody. She wants the artist to flatter her, to make the white world believe that all Negroes are as smug and as near white in soul as she wants to be. But, to my mind, it is the duty of the younger Negro artist, if he accepts any duties at all from outsiders, to change through the force of his art that old whispering "I want to be white," hidden in the aspirations of his people, to "Why should I want to be white? I am a Negro — and beautiful!"

From "The Negro Artist and the Racial Mountain," *The Nation*, June 23, 1926

Winold Reiss (1887–1953): A white painter whose work emphasized the individuality of blacks.

CONSIDERATIONS FOR CRITICAL THINKING AND WRITING

1. Why does the Philadelphia clubwoman refuse to accept jazz as part of her heritage?
2. Compare and contrast Hughes's description of the Philadelphia clubwoman with M. Carl Holman's "Mr. Z" (p. 1098). In what sense are these two characters made for each other?

Hughes on Harlem Rent Parties   *1940*

Then [in the late twenties and early thirties] it was that house-rent parties began to flourish — and not always to raise the rent either. But, as often as not, to have a get-together of one's own, where you could do the black-bottom with no stranger behind you trying to do it, too. Non-theatrical, non-intellectual Harlem was an unwilling victim of its own vogue. It didn't like to be stared at by white folks. But perhaps the downtowners never knew this — for the cabaret owners, the entertainers, and the speakeasy proprietors treated them fine — as long as they paid.

The Saturday night rent parties that I attended were often more amusing than any night club, in small apartments where God knows who lived — because the guests seldom did — but where the piano would often be augmented by a guitar, or an odd cornet, or somebody with a pair of drums walking in off the street. And where awful bootleg whiskey and good fried fish or steaming chitterling were sold at very low prices. And the dancing and singing and impromptu entertaining went on until dawn came in at the windows.

These parties, often termed whist parties or dances, were usually announced by brightly colored cards stuck in the grille of apartment house elevators. Some of the cards were highly entertaining in themselves:

> We got yellow girls, we've got black and tan
> Will you have a good time? - YEAH MAN !
>
> # A Social Whist Party
> —GIVEN BY—
> MARY WINSTON
> 147 West 145th Street   Apt. 5
>
> ## SATURDAY EVE., MARCH 19th, 1932
>
> GOOD MUSIC   REFRESHMENTS

Almost every Saturday night when I was in Harlem I went to a house-rent party. I wrote lots of poems about house-rent parties, and ate thereat many a fried fish and pig's foot—with liquid refreshments on the side. I met ladies' maids and truck drivers, laundry workers and shoe shine boys, seamstresses and porters. I can still hear their laughter in my ears, hear the soft slow music, and feel the floor shaking as the dancers danced.

From "When the Negro Was in Vogue," in *The Big Sea*

CONSIDERATIONS FOR CRITICAL THINKING AND WRITING

1. What, according to Hughes, was the appeal of the rent parties in contrast to the nightclubs?
2. Describe the tone in which Hughes recounts his memory of these parties.

DONALD B. GIBSON (B. 1933)

The Essential Optimism of Hughes and Whitman   1971

As optimists generally do, Langston Hughes and Walt Whitman lacked a sense of evil. This (and all it implies) puts Hughes in a tradition with other American writers. He stands with Whitman, Emerson, Thoreau, and later Sandburg, Lindsay, and Steinbeck, as opposed to Hawthorne, Poe, Melville, James, Faulkner, and Eliot. This is not to say that he did not recognize the existence of evil, but, as Yeats says of Emerson and Whitman, he lacked the "Vision of Evil." He did not see evil as inherent in the character of nature and man, hence he felt that the evil (small *e*) about which he wrote so frequently in his poems (lynchings, segregation, discrimination of all kinds) would be eradicated with the passage of time. Of course the Hughes of *The Panther and the Lash* (1967) is not as easily optimistic as the poet was twenty or twenty-five years before. Hughes could not have written "I, Too," or even "The Negro Speaks of Rivers" in the sixties. But the evidence as I see it has it that though he does not speak so readily about the fulfillment of the American ideal for black people, and though something of the spirit of having waited too long prevails, still the optimism remains. . . .

Montage of a Dream Deferred (1951), included in *Selected Poems,* describes the dream as deferred, not dead nor incapable of fulfillment. There is a certain grimness in the poem, for example in its most famous section, "Harlem," which begins, "What happens to a dream deferred? / Does it dry up / like a raisin in the sun?" but the grimness is by no means unrelieved. There is, as a matter of fact, a lightness of tone throughout the poem which could not exist did the poet see the ravages of racial discrimination as manifestations of Evil. . . . The whole tone of *Montage of a Dream Deferred* is characterized by the well-known "Ballad of the Landlord." There the bitter-sweet quality of Hughes's attitude toward his subject is clear.

> From "The Good Black Poet and the Good Grey Poet: The Poetry of
> Hughes and Whitman," in *Langston Hughes: Black Genius: A Critical*
> *Evaluation,* edited by Therman B. O'Daniel

CONSIDERATIONS FOR CRITICAL THINKING AND WRITING

1. What distinction does Gibson make between "Evil" and "evil"?
2. Discuss whether you agree or disagree that Hughes lacked a "Vision of Evil."
3. Why do you think Gibson writes that Hughes couldn't have written "The Negro Speaks of Rivers" (p. 1010) or "I, Too" (p. 1014) in the 1960s?
4. What aspects of Whitman does Hughes seem to admire in "Old Walt" (p. 1031)?

JAMES A. EMANUEL (B. 1921)
Hughes's Attitudes toward Religion   1973

Religion, because of its historical importance during and after slavery, is an undeniably useful theme in the work of any major black writer. In a writer whose special province for almost forty-five years was more recent black experience, the theme is doubly vital. Hughes's personal religious orientation is pertinent. Asked about it by the Reverend Dana F. Kennedy of the "Viewpoint" radio and television show (on December 10, 1960), the poet responded:

> I grew up in a not very religious family, but I had a foster aunt who saw that I went to church and Sunday school . . . and I was very much moved, always, by the, shall I say, the rhythms of the Negro church . . . of the spirituals, . . . of those wonderful old-time sermons. . . . There's great beauty in the mysticism of much religious writing, and great help there — but I also think that we live in a world . . . of solid earth and vegetables and a need for jobs and a need for housing. . . .

Two years earlier, the poet had told John Kirkwood of British Columbia's *Vancouver Sun* (December 3, 1958): "I'm not anti-Christian. I'm not against anyone's religion. Religion is one of the innate needs of mankind. What I am against is the misuse of religion. But I won't ridicule it. . . . Whatever part of God is in anybody is not to be played with, and everybody has got a part of God in them."

These typical public protestations by Hughes boil down to his insistence that religion is naturally sacred and beautiful, and that its needed sustenance must not be exploited.

From "Christ in Alabama: Religion in the Poetry of Langston Hughes," in *Modern Black Poets,* edited by Donald B. Gibson

CONSIDERATIONS FOR CRITICAL THINKING AND WRITING

1. Why do you think Emanuel asserts that, owing to slavery, religion "is an undeniably useful theme in the work of any major Black writer"?

2. How does Hughes's concern for the "solid earth and vegetables and a need for jobs and a need for housing" qualify his attitudes toward religion?

RICHARD K. BARKSDALE (B. 1915)

On Censoring "Ballad of the Landlord" 1977

In 1940, ["Ballad of the Landlord"] was a rather innocuous rendering of an imaginary dialogue between a disgruntled tenant and a tight-fisted landlord. In creating a poem about two such social archetypes, the poet was by no means taking any new steps in dramatic poetry. The literature of most capitalist and noncapitalist societies often pits the haves against the have-nots, and not infrequently the haves are wealthy men of property who "lord" it over improvident men who own nothing. So the confrontation between tenant and landlord was in 1940 just another instance of the social malevolence of a system that punished the powerless and excused the powerful. In fact, Hughes's tone of dry irony throughout the poem leads one to suspect that the poet deliberately overstated a situation and that some sardonic humor was supposed to be squeezed out of the incident. . . .

Ironically, this poem, which in 1940 depicted a highly probable incident in American urban life and was certainly not written to incite an economic revolt or promote social unrest, became, by the mid-1960s, a verboten assignment in a literature class in a Boston high school. In his Langston Hughes headnote in *Black Voices* (1967), Abraham Chapman reported that a Boston high school English teacher named Jonathan Kozol was fired for assigning it to his students. By the mid-sixties, Boston and many other American cities had become riottorn, racial tinderboxes, and their ghettos seethed with tenant anger and discontent. So the poem gathered new meanings reflecting the times, and the word of its tenant persona bespoke the collective anger of thousands of black have-nots.

From *Langston Hughes: The Poet and His Critics*

CONSIDERATIONS FOR CRITICAL THINKING AND WRITING

1. Why do you think the Boston School Committee believed the "Ballad of the Landlord" (p. 1025) should be censored?

2. Do you agree with Barksdale that the poem is a "rather innocuous rendering" of economic and social issues? Explain your answer.

3. How did the poem acquire "new meanings reflecting the times" between the 1940s and 1960s? What new meanings might it have for readers today?

STEVEN C. TRACY (b. 1954)
A Reading of "The Weary Blues"   1988

Clearly in this poem the blues unite the speaker and the performer in some way. There is an immediate implied relationship between the two because of the ambiguous syntax. The "droning" and "rocking" can refer either to the "I" or to the "Negro," immediately suggesting that the music invites, even requires, the participation of the speaker. Further, the words suggest that the speaker's poem is a "drowsy syncopated tune" as well, connecting speaker and performer even further by having them working in the same tradition. The performer remains anonymous . . . because he is not a famous, celebrated performer; he is one of the main practitioners living the unglamorous life that is far more common than the kinds of lives the most successful blues stars lived. His "drowsy syncopated tune," which at once implies both rest and activity (a tune with shifting accents), signals the tension between the romantic image and the reality, and very likely influences the speaker to explore the source of the tension between the singer's stoicism and his resignation to his fate as expressed in his blues lyrics. Significantly, the eight-bar blues stanza, the one with no repeat line, is his hopeful stanza. Its presence as an eight-bar stanza works by passing more quickly, reinforcing both his loneliness *and* the fleeting nature of the kind of hope expressed. This is especially true since the singer's next stanza, a twelve-bar blues, uses the repeat line to emphasize his weariness and lack of satisfaction, and his wish to die.

All the singer seems to have is his moaning blues, the revelation of "a black man's soul," and those blues are what helps keep him alive. Part of that ability to sustain is apparently the way the blues help him keep his identity. Even in singing the blues, he is singing about his life, about the way that he and other blacks have to deal with white society. As his black hands touch the white keys, the accepted Western sound of the piano and the form of Western music are changed. The piano itself comes to life as an extension of the singer, and moans, transformed by the black tradition to a mirror of black sorrow that also reflects the transforming power and beauty of the black tradition. Finally, it is that tradition that helps keep the singer alive and gives him his identity, since when he is done and goes to bed he sleeps like an inanimate or de-animated object, with the blues echoing beyond his playing, beyond the daily cycles, and through both conscious and unconscious states.

Another source of the melancholy aura of the poem is the lack of an actual connection between the performer and the speaker. They do not strike up a conversation, share a drink, or anything else. The speaker observes, helpless to do anything about the performer and his weariness save to write the poem and try to understand the performer's experiences and how they relate to his own. Ultimately he finds the man and his songs wistfully compelling; and he hears in his song the collective weary blues of blacks in America and tries to reconcile the sadness with the sweetness of the form and expression.

From *Langston Hughes and the Blues*

CONSIDERATIONS FOR CRITICAL THINKING AND WRITING

1. How does Tracy use the blues form to inform his reading of "The Weary Blues" (p. 1019)?

2. What is the relationship between the speaker and the performer, according to Tracy?

3. How is the performer's playing of the piano different from "the accepted Western sound . . . and the form of Western music"?

DAVID CHINITZ (B. 1962)
The Romanticization of Africa in the 1920s   1997

In Europe black culture was an exotic import; in America it was domestic and increasingly mass-produced. If postwar [World War I] disillusionment judged the majority culture mannered, neurotic, and repressive, Americans had an easily accessible alternative. The need for such an Other produced a discourse in which black Americans figured as barely civilized exiles from the jungle, with — so the clichés ran — tom-toms beating in their blood and dark laughter in their souls. The African American became a model of "natural" human behavior to contrast with the falsified, constrained and impotent modes of the "civilized."

Far from being immune to the lure of this discourse, for the better part of the 1920s Hughes asserted an open pride in the supposed primitive qualities of his race, the atavistic legacy of the African motherland. Unlike most of those who romanticized Africa, Hughes had at least some firsthand experience of the continent; yet he processed what he saw there in images conditioned by European primitivism, rendering "[the land] wild and lovely, the people dark and beautiful, the palm trees tall, the sun bright, and the rivers deep."[1] His short story "Luani of the Jungle," in attempting to glorify aboriginal African vigor as against European anemia, shows how predictable and unextraordinary even Hughes's primitivism could be. To discover in the descendents of idealized Africans the same qualities of innate health, spontaneity, and naturalness requires no great leap; one has only to identify the African American as a displaced primitive, as Hughes does repeatedly in his first book, *The Weary Blues:*

> They drove me out of the forest.
> They took me away from the jungles.
> I lost my trees.
> I lost my silver moons.
>
> Now they've caged me
> In the circus of civilization.[2]

Hughes depicts black atavism vividly and often gracefully, yet in a way that is entirely consistent with the popular iconography of the time. His African Americans retain "among the skyscrapers" the primal fears and instincts of their ancestors "among the palms in Africa."[3] The scion of Africa is still more than half primitive: "All the tom-toms of the jungles beat in my blood, / And all the wild hot moons of the jungles shine in my soul."[4]

From "Rejuvenation through Joy: Langston Hughes, Primitivism and Jazz," in *American Literary History,* Spring 1997

---

[1] *The Big Sea.* 1940. N.Y.: Thunder's Mouth, 1986, 11.
[2] *The Weary Blues.* N.Y.: Knopf, 1926, 100.
[3] *Ibid.* 101.
[4] *Ibid.* 102.

CONSIDERATIONS FOR CRITICAL THINKING AND WRITING

1. According to Chinitz, why did Europeans and Americans romanticize African culture?

2. Consider the poems published by Hughes in the 1920s reprinted in this anthology. Explain whether you find any "primitivism" in these poems.

3. Later in this essay, Chinitz points out that Hughes eventually rejected the "reductive mischaracterizations of black culture, the commercialism, the sham sociology, and the downright silliness of the primitivist fad." Choose and discuss a poem from this anthology that you think reflects Hughes's later views of primitivism.

TWO COMPLEMENTARY CRITICAL READINGS

COUNTEE CULLEN (1903–1946)

On Racial Poetry 1926

Here is a poet with whom to reckon, to experience, and here and there, with that apologetic feeling of presumption that should companion all criticism, to quarrel.

What has always struck me most forcibly in reading Mr. Hughes' poems has been their utter spontaneity and expression of a unique personality. . . . This poet represents a transcendently emancipated spirit among a class of young writers whose particular battle-cry is freedom. With the enthusiasm of a zealot, he pursues his way, scornful, in subject matter, in photography, and rhythmical treatment, of whatever obstructions time and tradition have placed before him. To him it is essential that he be himself. Essential and commendable surely; yet the thought persists that some of these poems would have been better had Mr. Hughes held himself a bit in check. . . .

If I have the least powers of prediction, the first section of this book, *The Weary Blues,* will be most admired, even if less from intrinsic poetical worth than because of its dissociation from the traditionally poetic. Never having been one to think all subjects and forms proper for poetic consideration, I regard these jazz poems as interlopers in the company of the truly beautiful poems in other sections of the book. They move along with the frenzy and electric heat of a Methodist or Baptist revival meeting, and affect me in much the same manner. The revival meeting excites me, cooling and flushing me with alternate chills and fevers of emotion; so do these poems. But when the storm is over, I wonder if the quiet way of communing is not more spiritual for the God-seeking heart; and in the light of reflection I wonder if jazz poems really belong to that dignified company, that select and austere circle of high literary expression which we call poetry. . . .

Taken as a group the selections in this book seem one-sided to me. They tend to hurl this poet into the gaping pit that lies before all Negro writers, in the confines of which they become racial artists instead of artists pure and simple. There is too much emphasis here on strictly Negro themes; and this is probably an added reason for my coldness toward the jazz poems — they seem to set a too definite limit upon an already limited field.

From *Opportunity: A Journal of Negro Life*

CONSIDERATIONS FOR CRITICAL THINKING AND WRITING

1. In Cullen's review of *The Weary Blues,* what is his "quarrel" (para. 1) with Hughes?

2. Given the tenor of Hughes's comments on racial pride in the excerpt from "The Negro Artist and the Racial Mountain" (p. 1034), what do you think his response to Cullen would be?

3. Explain why you agree or disagree with Cullen's view that Hughes's poems are "one-sided" (para. 4).

4. Do you think his argument is dated, or is it relevant to today's social climate?

ONWUCHEKWA JEMIE (B. 1940)
On Universal Poetry   1976

Hughes entertained no doubts as to the sufficiency and greatness of the molds provided by black music, nor of black life as subject matter. On the question of whether such black matter and manner could attain "universality," Hughes in his Spingarn Speech issued a definitive answer:

> There is so much richness in Negro humor, so much beauty in black dreams, so much dignity in our struggle, and so much universality in our problems, in us — in each living human being of color — that I do not understand the tendency today that some American Negro artists have of seeking to run away from themselves, of running away from us, of being afraid to sing our own songs, paint our own pictures, write about ourselves — when it is our music that has given America its greatest music, our humor that has enriched its entertainment media, our rhythm that has guided its dancing feet from plantation days to the Charleston, the Lindy Hop, and currently the Madison. . . .
>
> Could you possibly be afraid that the rest of the world will not accept it? Our spirituals are sung and loved in the great concert halls of the whole world. Our blues are played from Topeka to Tokyo. Harlem's jive talk delights Hong Kong. Those of our writers who have concerned themselves with our very special problems are translated and read around the world. The local, the regional can — and does — become universal. Sean O'Casey's Irishmen are an example. So I would say to young Negro writers, do not be afraid of yourselves. You are the world.[1]

Hughes's confidence in blackness is a major part of his legacy, for the questions he had to answer have had to be answered over again by subsequent generations of black artists. Black culture is still embattled; and Hughes provides a model for answering the questions and making the choices. Whether they say so or not, those who, like Cullen, . . . plead the need to be "universal" as an excuse for avoiding racial material, or for treating such material from

[1]See Hughes, Letter to the Editor, *The Crisis,* 35:9 (September 1928), 302.

perspectives rooted in alien sensibilities, invariably equate "white" or "Western" with "universal," and "black" or "non-Western" with its opposite, forgetting that the truly universal — that is, the foundation elements of human experience, the circumstances attending birth, growth, decline, and death, the emotions of joy and grief, love and hate, fear and guilt, anger and pain — are common to all humanity. The multiplicity of nations and cultures in the world makes it inevitable that the details and particulars of human experience will vary according to time, place, and circumstance, and it follows that the majority of writers will dramatize and interpret human life according to the usages of their particular nation and epoch. Indeed, the question whether a writer's work is universal or not rarely arises when that writer is European or white American. It arises so frequently in discussions of black writers for no other reason than that the long-standing myth of white superiority and black inferiority has led so many to believe that in literature, and in other areas of life as well, the black particular of universal human experience is less appropriate than the white particular.

From *Langston Hughes: An Introduction to Poetry*

CONSIDERATIONS FOR CRITICAL THINKING AND WRITING

1. How does Jemie go beyond Hughes's own argument to make a case for the universality of poetry about black experience?

2. How might Jemie's argument be extended to other minority groups or to women?

3. Do you think that Jemie's or Cullen's argument is more persuasive? Explain.

25

Critical Case Study:
T. S. Eliot's "The Love Song
of J. Alfred Prufrock"

This chapter provides several critical approaches to a challenging but highly rewarding poem by T. S. Eliot. After studying this poem, you're likely to find yourself quoting bits of its striking imagery. At the very least, you'll recognize the lines when you hear other people fold them into their own conversations. There have been numerous critical approaches to this poem because it raises so many issues relating to matters such as history and biography as well as imagery, symbolism, irony, and myth. The following critical excerpts offer a small and partial sample of the possible formalist, biographical, historical, mythological, psychological, sociological, and other perspectives that have attempted to shed light on the poem (see Chapter 37, "Critical Strategies for Reading," for a discussion of a variety of critical methods). They should help you to enjoy the poem more by raising questions, providing insights, and inviting you further into the text.

T. S. ELIOT (1888–1965)

Born into a prominent New England family that had moved to St. Louis, Missouri, Thomas Stearns Eliot was a major in English literature between the two world wars. He studied literature and philosophy at Harvard and on the Continent, subsequently choosing to live in England for most of his life and becoming a citizen of that country in 1927. His allusive and challenging poetry had a powerful influence on other writers, particularly his treatment of postwar life in *The Waste Land* (1922) and his exploration of religious questions in *The Four Quartets* (1943). In addition, he wrote plays, including *Murder in the Cathedral* (1935) and *The Cocktail Party* (1950). He was awarded the Nobel Prize for literature in 1948. In "The Love Song of J. Alfred Prufrock," Eliot presents a comic but serious figure who expresses through

T. S. Eliot (November 10, 1959), in a pose that suggests the Prufrock persona, holding a book containing some of his earlier work during a press conference at the University of Chicago.

a series of fragmented images the futility, boredom, and meaninglessness associated with much of modern life.

The Love Song of J. Alfred Prufrock   1917

S'io credesse che mia risposta fosse
A persona che mai tornasse al mondo,
Questa fiamma staria senza più scosse.
Ma perciocchè giammai di questo fondo
Non tornò vivo alcun, s'i'odo il vero,
Senza tema d'infamia ti rispondo. °

Epigraph: *S'io credesse . . . rispondo:* Dante's *Inferno,* XXVII, 58–63. In the Eighth Chasm of the Inferno, Dante and Virgil meet Guido da Montefeltro, one of the False Counselors, who is punished by being enveloped in an eternal flame. When Dante asks Guido to tell his life story, the spirit replies: "If I thought that my answer were to one who might ever return to the world, this flame would shake no more; but since from this depth none ever returned alive, if what I hear is true, I answer you without fear of infamy."

Let us go then, you and I,
When the evening is spread out against the sky
Like a patient etherized upon a table;
Let us go, through certain half-deserted streets,
The muttering retreats
Of restless nights in one-night cheap hotels   5
And sawdust restaurants with oyster-shells:
Streets that follow like a tedious argument
Of insidious intent
To lead you to an overwhelming question . . .   10

Oh, do not ask, "What is it?"
Let us go and make our visit.

In the room the women come and go
Talking of Michelangelo.

    The yellow fog that rubs its back upon the window panes,   15
The yellow smoke that rubs its muzzle on the window panes
Licked its tongue into the corners of the evening,
Lingered upon the pools that stand in drains,
Let fall upon its back the soot that falls from chimneys,
Slipped by the terrace, made a sudden leap,   20
And seeing that it was a soft October night,
Curled once about the house, and fell asleep.

    And indeed there will be time°
For the yellow smoke that slides along the street,
Rubbing its back upon the window panes;   25
There will be time, there will be time
To prepare a face to meet the faces that you meet;
There will be time to murder and create,
And time for all the works and days° of hands
That lift and drop a question on your plate: 30
Time for you and time for me,
And time yet for a hundred indecisions,
And for a hundred visions and revisions,
Before the taking of a toast and tea.

In the room the women come and go   35
Talking of Michelangelo.

    And indeed there will be time
To wonder, "Do I dare?" and, "Do I dare?" —
Time to turn back and descend the stair,
With a bald spot in the middle of my hair —   40
(They will say: "How his hair is growing thin!")
My morning coat, my collar mounting firmly to the chin,
My necktie rich and modest, but asserted by a simple pin —
(They will say: "But how his arms and legs are thin!")

23 *there will be time:* An allusion to Ecclesiastes 3:1–8: "To everything there is a season, and a time to every purpose under heaven. . . ." 29 *works and days:* Hesiod's eighth century B.C. poem *Works and Days* gave practical advice on how to conduct one's life in accordance with the seasons.

Do I dare 45
Disturb the universe?
In a minute there is time
For decisions and revisions which a minute will reverse.

    For I have known them all already, known them all:
Have known the evenings, mornings, afternoons, 50
I have measured out my life with coffee spoons;
I know the voices dying with a dying fall
Beneath the music from a farther room.
    So how should I presume?

    And I have known the eyes already, known them all — 55
The eyes that fix you in a formulated phrase.
And when I am formulated, sprawling on a pin,
When I am pinned and wriggling on the wall,
Then how should I begin
To spit out all the butt-ends of my days and ways? 60
    And how should I presume?

    And I have known the arms already, known them all —
Arms that are braceleted and white and bare
(But in the lamplight, downed with light brown hair!)
    Is it perfume from a dress 65
    That makes me so digress?
Arms that lie along a table, or wrap about a shawl.
    And should I then presume?
    And how should I begin?

    Shall I say, I have gone at dusk through narrow streets, 70
And watched the smoke that rises from the pipes
Of lonely men in shirtsleeves, leaning out of windows? . . .

I should have been a pair of ragged claws
Scuttling across the floors of silent seas.

    And the afternoon, the evening, sleeps so peacefully! 75
Smoothed by long fingers,
Asleep . . . tired . . . or it malingers,
Stretched on the floor, here beside you and me.
Should I, after tea and cakes and ices,
Have the strength to force the moment to its crisis? 80
But though I have wept and fasted, wept and prayed,
Though I have seen my head (grown slightly bald) brought in upon a platter,°
I am no prophet — and here's no great matter;
I have seen the moment of my greatness flicker,
And I have seen the eternal Footman hold my coat, and snicker, 85
    And in short, I was afraid.

    And would it have been worth it, after all,
After the cups, the marmalade, the tea,
Among the porcelain, among some talk of you and me,

---

82 *head . . . upon a platter:* At Salome's request, Herod had John the Baptist decapitated and
had the severed head delivered to her on a platter (see Matt. 14:1–12 and Mark 6:17–29).

Would it have been worth while   90
To have bitten off the matter with a smile,
To have squeezed the universe into a ball°
To roll it toward some overwhelming question,
To say: "I am Lazarus,° come from the dead,
Come back to tell you all, I shall tell you all" —   95
If one, settling a pillow by her head,
    Should say: "That is not what I meant at all;
      That is not it, at all."

    And would it have been worth it, after all,
Would it have been worth while,   100
After the sunsets and the dooryards and the sprinkled streets,
After the novels, after the teacups, after the skirts that trail along the floor —
And this, and so much more? —
It is impossible to say just what I mean!
But as if a magic lantern threw the nerves in patterns on a screen: 105
Would it have been worth while
If one, settling a pillow or throwing off a shawl,
And turning toward the window, should say:
    "That is not it at all,
    That is not what I meant, at all."   110

No! I am not Prince Hamlet, nor was meant to be;
Am an attendant lord,° one that will do
To swell a progress,° start a scene or two   *state procession*
Advise the prince: withal, an easy tool,
Deferential, glad to be of use,   115
Politic, cautious, and meticulous;
Full of high sentence, but a bit obtuse;
At times, indeed, almost ridiculous —
Almost, at times, the Fool.

I grow old . . . I grow old . . .   120
I shall wear the bottoms of my trowsers rolled.

    Shall I part my hair behind? Do I dare to eat a peach?
I shall wear white flannel trowsers, and walk upon the beach.
I have heard the mermaids singing, each to each.

I do not think that they will sing to me.   125

I have seen them riding seaward on the waves,
Combing the white hair of the waves blown back
When the wind blows the water white and black.

We have lingered in the chambers of the sea
By seagirls wreathed with seaweed red and brown,   130
Till human voices wake us, and we drown.

92 *squeezed the universe into a ball:* See Marvell's "To His Coy Mistress" (p. 729), lines 41–42:
"Let us roll all our strength and all / Our sweetness up into one ball."   94 *Lazarus:* The
brother of Mary and Martha who was raised from the dead by Jesus (John 11:1–44). In Luke
16:19–31, a rich man asks that another Lazarus return from the dead to warn the living about
their treatment of the poor.   112 *attendant lord:* Like Polonius in Shakespeare's *Hamlet.*

CONSIDERATIONS FOR CRITICAL THINKING AND WRITING

1. What does J. Alfred Prufrock's name connote? How would you characterize him?

2. What do you think is the purpose of the epigraph from Dante's *Inferno*?

3. What is it that Prufrock wants to do? How does he behave? What does he think of himself? Which parts of the poem answer these questions?

4. Who is the "you" of line 1 and the "we" in the final lines?

5. Discuss the imagery in the poem. How does the imagery reveal Prufrock's character? Which images seem especially striking to you?

CONNECTIONS TO OTHER SELECTIONS

1. Write an essay comparing Prufrock's sense of himself as an individual with that of Walt Whitman's speaker in "One's-Self I Sing" (p. 1124).

2. Discuss in an essay the tone of "The Love Song of J. Alfred Prufrock" and Frost's "Acquainted with the Night" (p. 798).

PERSPECTIVES ON ELIOT

ELISABETH SCHNEIDER (1897–1984)

Schneider uses a biographical approach to the poem to suggest that part of what went into the characterization of Prufrock were some of Eliot's own sensibilities.

Hints of Eliot in Prufrock 1952

Perhaps never again did Eliot find an epigraph quite so happily suited to his use as the passage from the *Inferno* which sets the underlying serious tone for *Prufrock* and conveys more than one level of its meaning: "S'io credesse che mia risposta . . . ," lines in which Guido da Montefeltro consents to tell his story to Dante only because he believes that none ever returns to the world of the living from his depth. One in Hell can bear to expose his shame only to another of the damned; Prufrock speaks to, will be understood only by, other Prufrocks (the "you and I" of the opening, perhaps), and, I imagine the epigraph also hints, Eliot himself is speaking to those who know this kind of hell. The poem, I need hardly say, is not in a literal sense autobiographical: for one thing, though it is clear that Prufrock will never marry, the poem was published in the year of Eliot's own first marriage. Nevertheless, friends who knew the young Eliot almost all describe him, retrospectively but convincingly, in Prufrockian terms; and Eliot himself once said of dramatic monologue in general that what we normally hear in it "is the voice of the poet, who has put on the costume and make-up either of some historical character, or of one out of fiction." . . . I suppose it to be one of the many indirect clues to his own poetry planted with evident deliberation throughout his prose. "What every poet starts from," he also once said, "is his own emotions," and, writing of Dante, he asserted that the *Vita nuova* "could only have been written around a personal experience," a statement that, under the circumstances, must be equally applicable to Prufrock; Prufrock was Eliot, though Eliot was much more than Prufrock. We miss the whole tone of the poem, however, if we read it as social satire only. Eliot was not either the dedicated apostle in theory, or the great exemplar in practice, of complete "depersonalization" in poetry that one influential early essay of his for a time led readers to suppose.

From "Prufrock and After: The Theme of Change," *PMLA*, October 1952

CONSIDERATIONS FOR CRITICAL THINKING AND WRITING

1. Though Schneider concedes that the poem is not literally autobiographical, she does assert that "Prufrock was Eliot." How does she argue this point? Explain why you find her argument convincing or unconvincing.

2. Find information in the library about Eliot's early career when he was writing this poem. To what extent does the poem reveal his circumstances and concerns at that point in his life?

BARBARA EVERETT

Everett's discussion of tone is used to make a distinction between Eliot and his characterization of Prufrock.

The Problem of Tone in Prufrock   *1974*

Eliot's poetry presents a peculiar problem as far as tone is concerned. *Tone* really means the way the attitude of a speaker is manifested by the inflections of his speaking voice. Many critics have already recognized that for a mixture of reasons it is difficult, sometimes almost impossible, to ascertain Eliot's tone in this way. It is not that the poetry lacks "voice," for in fact Eliot has an extraordinarily recognizable poetic voice, often imitated and justifying his own comment in the . . . *Paris Review* that "in a poem you're writing for your own voice, which is very important. You're thinking in terms of your own voice." It is this authoritative, idiosyncratic, and exact voice that holds our complete attention in poem after poem, however uninterested we are in what opinions it may seem or happen to be expressing. But Eliot too seems uninterested in what opinions it may happen to be expressing, for he invariably dissociates himself from his poems before they are even finished — before they are hardly begun — by balancing a derisory name or title against an "I," by reminding us that there is always going to be a moment at which detachment will take place or has taken place, a retrospective angle from which, far in the future, critical judgment alters the scene, and the speaking voice of the past has fallen silent. "I have known them all already, known them all." Thus whatever started to take place in the beginning of a poem by Eliot cannot truly be said to be

Eliot's opinion because at some extremely early stage he began that process of dissociation to be loosely called "dramatization," a process reflected in the peculiar distances of the tone, as though everything spoken was in inverted commas.

From "In Search of Prufrock," *Critical Quarterly,* Summer 1974

CONSIDERATIONS FOR CRITICAL THINKING AND WRITING

1. According to Everett, why is it difficult to describe Eliot's tone in his poetry?
2. How does Eliot's tone make it difficult to make an autobiographical connection between Prufrock and Eliot?
3. How does Everett's reading of the relationship between Prufrock and Eliot differ from Schneider's in the preceding perspective?

MICHAEL L. BAUMANN (B. 1926)

Baumann takes a close look at the poem's images in his formalist efforts to make a point about Prufrock's character.

The "Overwhelming Question" for Prufrock   *1981*

Most critics . . . have seen the overwhelming question related to sex. . . . They have implicitly assumed—and given their readers to understand—that Prufrock's is the male's basic question: Can I?

Delmore Schwartz once said that "J. Alfred Prufrock is unable to make love to women of his own class and kind because of shyness, self-consciousness, and fear of rejection."[1] This is undoubtedly true, but Prufrock's inability to *feel* love has something to do with his inability to *make* love, too. . . . A simple desire, lust, is more than honest Prufrock can cope with as he mounts the stairs.

But Prufrock is coping with another, less simple desire as well. . . . If birth, copulation, and death is all there is, then, once we are born, once we have copulated, only death remains (for the male of the species, at least). Prufrock, having "known them all already, known them all," having "known the evenings, mornings, afternoons," having "measured out" his life "with coffee spoons," desires death. The "overwhelming question" that assails him would no longer be the romantic rhetorical "Is life worth living?" (to which the answer is obviously No), but the more immediate shocker: "Should one commit suicide?" which is to say: "Should I?" . . .

. . . The poem makes clear that Prufrock wants more than the "entire destruction of consciousness as we understand it," a notion Prufrock expresses

[1] "T. S. Eliot as the International Hero," *Partisan Review,* 12 (1945), 202; rpt in *T. S. Eliot: A Selected Critique,* ed. Leonard Unger (New York: Rinehart & Company, Inc., 1948), 46.

by wishing he were "a pair of ragged claws, / Scuttling across the floors of silent seas." Prufrock wants death itself, physical death, and the poem, I believe, is explicit about this desire.

Not only does Prufrock seem to be tired of time — "time yet for a hundred indecisions" — a tiredness that goes far beyond the acedia Prufrock is generally credited with feeling, if only because "there will be time to murder and create," time, in other words (in one sense at least) to copulate, but Prufrock is also tired of his own endless vanities, from feeling he must "prepare a face to meet the faces that you meet," to having to summon up those ironies with which to contemplate his own thin arms and legs, and, indeed, to asking if, in the rather tedious enterprise of preparing for copulation, the moment is worth "forcing to its crisis." No wonder Prufrock compares himself to John the Baptist and, in conjuring up this first concrete image of his own death, sees his head brought in upon a platter. That would be the easy way out. He had, after all, "wept and fasted, wept and prayed," but he realizes he is no prophet — and no Salome will burst into passion, will ignite for him. When the eternal Footman, Death, who holds his coat, snickers, he does so because Prufrock has let "the moment" of his "greatness" flicker, because Prufrock was unable to comply with the one imperative greatness would have thrust upon him: to kill himself. Prufrock explains: "I was afraid." Yet the achievement of his vision at the end of the poem, his being able to linger "in the chambers of the sea / By sea-girls wreathed with seaweed red and brown," is an act of the imagination that only physical death can complete, unless Prufrock wants human voices to wake him, and drown him. His romantic vision demands the voluntary act: suicide. It is to be expected that he will fail in this too, as he has failed in everything else.

From "Let Us Ask 'What Is It,'" *Arizona Quarterly*, Spring 1981

CONSIDERATIONS FOR CRITICAL THINKING AND WRITING

1. Describe the evidence used by Baumann to argue that Prufrock contemplates suicide.

2. Explain in an essay why you do or do not find Baumann's argument convincing.

3. Later in his essay Baumann connects Prufrock's insistence that "No, I am not Prince Hamlet" with Hamlet's "To be or not to be" speech. How do you think this reference might be used to support Baumann's argument?

FREDERIK L. RUSCH (B. 1938)

Rusch makes use of the insights developed by Erich Fromm, a social psychologist who believed "psychic forces [are] a process of constant interaction between man's needs and the social and historical reality in which he participates."

Society and Character in
"The Love Song of J. Alfred Prufrock"   1984

In looking at fiction, drama, and poetry from the Frommian point of view, the critic understands literature to be social portrayal as well as character portrayal or personal statement. Society and character are inextricably joined. The Frommian approach opens up the study of literary work, giving a social context to its characters, which suggests why those characters behave as they do. The Frommian approach recognizes human beings for what they are — basically gregarious individuals who are interdependent upon each other, in need of each other, and thus, to a certain degree, products of their social environments, although those environments may be inimical to their mental well-being. That is, as stated earlier, the individual's needs and drives have a social component and are not purely biological. The Frommian approach to literature assumes that a writer is — at least by implication — analyzing society and its setting as well as character. . . .

In T. S. Eliot's "The Love Song of J. Alfred Prufrock," Prufrock is talking to himself, expressing a fantasy or daydream. In his monologue, Prufrock, as noted by Grover Smith, "is addressing, as if looking into a mirror, his whole public personality."[1] Throughout the poem, Prufrock is extremely self-conscious, believing that the people in his imaginary drawing room will examine him as a specimen insect, "sprawling on a pin, / . . . pinned and wriggling on the wall. . . ." Of course, self-consciousness — being conscious of one's self — is not necessarily neurotic. Indeed, it is part of being a human being. It is only when self-consciousness, which has always led man to feel a separation from nature, becomes obsessive that we have a problem. Prufrock is certainly obsessed with his self-consciousness, convinced that everyone notices his balding head, his clothes (his prudent frocks), his thin arms and legs.

On one level, however, Prufrock is merely expressing the pain that all human beings must feel. Although his problem is extreme, he is quite representative of the human race:

> Self-awareness, reason, and imagination have disrupted the "harmony" that characterizes animal existence. Their emergence has made man into an anomaly, the freak of the universe. He is part of nature, subject to her physical laws and unable to change them, yet he transcends nature. He is set apart while being a part; he is homeless, yet chained to the home he shares with all creatures. . . . Being aware of himself, he realizes his powerlessness and the limitations of his existence. He is never free from the dichotomy of his existence: he cannot rid himself of his mind, even if he would want to; he cannot rid himself of his body as long as he is alive — and his body makes him want to be alive.[2]

This is the predicament of the human being. His self-awareness has made him feel separate from nature. This causes pain and sorrow. What, then, is the solution to the predicament? Fromm believed that mankind filled the void of alienation from nature with the creation of a culture, a society: "Man's existential,

[1] Grover Smith, *T. S. Eliot's Poetry and Plays: A Study in Sources and Meaning* (Chicago: U of Chicago P, 1962), 16.
[2] Erich Fromm, *The Anatomy of Human Destructiveness* (New York: Holt, Rinehart & Winston, 1973), 225.

and hence unavoidable disequilibrium can be relatively stable when he has found, with the support of his culture, a more or less adequate way of coping with his existential problems" (*Destructiveness* 225). But, unfortunately for Prufrock, his culture and society do not allow him to overcome his existential predicament. The fact is, he is bored by his modern, urban society.

In image after image, Prufrock's mind projects boredom:

> For I have known them all already, known them all:
> Have known the evenings, mornings, afternoons,
> I have measured out my life with coffee spoons. . . .
> . . . .
>
> And I have known the eyes already, known them all —
> . . . .
>
> Then how should I begin
> To spit out all the butt-ends of my days and ways?
> . . . .
>
> And I have known the arms already, known them all — . . . .

Prufrock is completely unstimulated by his social environment, to the point of near death. The evening in which he proposes to himself to make a social visit is "etherized upon a table." The fog, as a cat, falls asleep; it is "tired . . . or it malingers, / Stretched on the floor. . . ."

Prufrock, living in a city of "half-deserted streets, / . . . one-night cheap hotels/ And sawdust restaurants with oyster-shells," gets no comfort, no nurturing from his environment. He is, in the words of Erich Fromm, a "modern mass man . . . isolated and lonely" (*Destructiveness* 107). He lives in a destructive environment. Instead of providing communion with fellow human beings, it alienates him through boredom. Such boredom leads to "a state of chronic depression" that can cause the pathology of "insufficient inner productivity" in the individual (*Destructiveness* 243). Such a lack of productivity is voiced by Prufrock when he confesses that he is neither Hamlet nor John the Baptist.

An interesting tension in "The Love Song of J. Alfred Prufrock" is caused by the reader's knowledge that Prufrock understands his own predicament quite well. Although he calls himself a fool, he has wisdom about himself and his predicament. This, however, only reinforces his depression and frustration. In his daydream, he is able to reveal truths about himself that, while they lead to self-understanding, apparently cannot alleviate his problems in his waking life. The poem suggests no positive movement out of the predicament. Prufrock is like a patient cited by Fromm, who under hypnosis envisioned "a black barren place with many masks," and when asked what the vision meant said "that everything was dull, dull, dull; that the masks represent the different roles he takes to fool people into thinking he is feeling well" (*Destructiveness* 246). Likewise, Prufrock understands that "There will be time, there will be time / To prepare a face to meet the faces that you meet. . . ." But despite his understanding of the nature of his existence, he cannot attain a more productive life.

It was Fromm's belief that with boredom "the decisive conditions are to be found in the overall environmental situation. . . . It is highly probable that even cases of severe depression-boredom would be less frequent and less intense . . . in a society where a mood of hope and love of life predominated. But in recent decades the opposite is increasingly the case, and thus a fertile soil for the development of individual depressive states is provided" (*Destructiveness* 251). There is no "mood of hope and love of life" in Prufrock's society. Prufrock is a lonely man, as lonely as "the lonely men in shirt-sleeves, leaning out of windows" of his fantasy. His only solution is to return to the animal state that his race was in before evolving into human beings.

Animals are one with nature, not alienated from their environments. They *are* nature, unselfconscious. Prufrock would return to a preconscious existence in the extreme: "I should have been a pair of ragged claws / Scuttling across the floors of silent seas." Claws *without a head* surely would not be alienated, bored, or depressed. They would seek and would need no psychological nurturing from their environment. And in the end Prufrock's fantasy of becoming claws is definitely more positive for him than his life as a human being. He completes his monologue with depressing irony, to say the least: it is with human voices waking us, bringing us back to human society, that we drown.

From "Approaching Literature through the Social Psychology of
Erich Fromm," in *Psychological Perspectives on Literature:
Freudian Dissidents and Non-Freudians*, edited by Joseph Natoli

CONSIDERATIONS FOR CRITICAL THINKING AND WRITING

1. According to Rusch, why is Fromm's approach useful for understanding Prufrock's character as well as his social context?

2. In what ways is Prufrock "representative of the human race" (para. 3)? Is he like any other characters you have read about in this anthology? Explain your response.

3. In an essay consider how Rusch's analysis of Prufrock might be used to support Baumann's argument that Prufrock's "overwhelming question" is whether or not he should kill himself (p. 1051).

ROBERT SWARD (B. 1933)

Sward, a poet, provides a detailed explication, framed by his own personal experiences during the war in Korea.

A Personal Analysis of
"The Love Song of J. Alfred Prufrock"   *1996*

In 1952, sailing to Korea as a U.S. Navy librarian for Landing Ship Tank 914, I read T. S. Eliot's "The Love Song of J. Alfred Prufrock." Ill-educated, a product of Chicago's public-school system, I was nineteen-years-old and, awakened by Whitman, Eliot, and Williams, had just begun writing poetry. I was also reading all the books I could get my hands on.

Eliot had won the Nobel Prize in 1948 and, curious, I was trying to make sense of poems like "Prufrock" and "The Waste Land."

"What do you know about T. S. Eliot?" I asked a young officer who'd been to college and studied English literature. I knew from earlier conversations that we shared an interest in what he called "modern poetry." A yeoman third class, two weeks at sea and bored, I longed for someone to talk to. "T. S. Eliot was born in St. Louis, Missouri, but he lives now in England and is studying to become an Englishman," the officer said, tapping tobacco into his pipe. "The 'T. S.' stands for 'tough shit.' You read Eliot's 'Love Song of J. Alfred Prufrock,' what one English prof called 'the first poem of the modern movement,' and if you don't understand it, 'tough shit.' All I can say is that's some love song."

An anthology of poetry open before us, we were sitting in the ship's all-metal, eight by eight-foot library eating bologna sandwiches and drinking coffee. Fortunately, the captain kept out of sight and life on the slow-moving (eight to ten knots), flat-bottomed amphibious ship was unhurried and anything but formal.

"Then why does Eliot bother calling it a love song?" I asked, as the ship rolled and the coffee sloshed onto a steel table. The tight metal room smelled like a cross between a diesel engine and a New York deli.

"Eliot's being ironic, sailor. 'Prufrock' is the love song of a sexually repressed and horny man who has no one but himself to sing to." Drawing on his pipe, the officer scratched his head. "Like you and I, Mr. Prufrock is a lonely man on his way to a war zone. We're sailing to Korea and we know the truth, don't we? We may never make it back. Prufrock marches like a brave soldier to a British drawing room that, he tells us, may be the death of him. He's a mock heroic figure who sings of mermaids and peaches and drowning."

Pointing to lines 129–31, the officer read aloud:

> We have lingered in the chambers of the sea
> By sea-girls wreathed with seaweed red and brown
> Till human voices wake us and we drown.

"Prufrock is also singing because he's a poet. Prufrock *is* T. S. Eliot and, the truth is, Eliot is so much like Prufrock that he has to distance himself from his creation. That's why he gives the man that pompous name. Did you know 'Tough Shit,' as a young man, sometimes signed himself 'T. Stearns Eliot'? You have to see the humor — the irony — in 'Prufrock' to understand the poem."

"I read it, I hear it in my head, but I still don't get it," I confessed. "What is 'Prufrock' about?"

"'Birth, death and copulation, that's all there is.' That's what Eliot himself says. Of course the poem also touches on aging, social status, and fashion."

"Aging and fashion?" I asked.

The officer threw back his head and recited:

> (They will say: "How his hair is growing thin!")
> My morning coat, my collar mounting firmly to the chin,
> My necktie rich and modest, but asserted by a simple pin.

He paused, then went on:

> I grow old . . . I grow old . . .
> I shall wear the bottoms of my trousers rolled.

"At the time the poem was written it was fashionable for young men to roll their trousers. In lines 120–21, Thomas Stearns Prufrock is laughing at himself for being middle-aged and vain.

"Anyway, 'The Love Song of J. Alfred Prufrock' is an interior monologue," said the officer, finishing his bologna sandwich and washing it down with dark rum. Wiping mustard from his mouth, he continued. "The whole thing takes place in J. Alfred Prufrock's head. That's clear, isn't it?"

I had read Browning's "My Last Duchess" and understood about interior monologues.

"Listen, sailor: Prufrock thinks about drawing rooms, but he never actually sets foot in one. Am I right?"

"Yeah," I said after rereading the first ten lines. "I think so."

"The poem is about what goes through Prufrock's mind on his way to some upper-class drawing room. It's a foggy evening in October, and what Mr. Prufrock really needs is a drink. He's a tightass Victorian, a lonely teetotaling intellectual. Anyone else would forget the toast and marmalade and step into a pub and ask for a pint of beer."

Setting down his pipe, the naval officer opened the flask and refilled our coffee mugs.

"Every time I think I know what 'Prufrock' means it turns out to mean something else," I said. "Eliot uses too many symbols. Why doesn't he just say what he means?"

"The city—'the lonely men in shirt-sleeves' and the 'one-night cheap hotels'—are masculine," said the officer. "That's what cities are like, aren't they: ugly and oppressive. What's symbolic—or should I say, what's obscure—about that?"

"Nothing," I said. "That's the easy part—Prufrock walking along like that."

"Okay," said the officer. "And in contrast to city streets, you've got the oppressive drawing room that, in Prufrock's mind, is feminine—'Arms that are braceleted and white and bare' and 'the marmalade, the tea, / Among the porcelain, among some talk of you and me.'" Using a pencil, the officer underlined those images in the paperback anthology.

"You ever been to a tea party, Sward?"

"No, sir, I haven't. Not like Prufrock's."

"Well," said the officer, "I have and I have a theory about that 'overwhelming question' Prufrock wants to ask in line 10—and again in line 93. Twice in the poem we hear about an 'overwhelming question.' What do you think he's getting at with that 'overwhelming question,' sailor?"

"Prufrock wants to ask the women what they're doing with their lives, but he's afraid they'll laugh at him," I said.

"Guess again, Sward," he said leaning back in his chair, stretching his arms.

"What's your theory, sir?"

"Sex," said the officer. "On the one hand, it's true, he wants to fit in and play the game because, after all, he's privileged. He belongs in the drawing room with the clever Englishwomen. At the same time he fantasizes. If he could, I think he'd like to shock them. Prufrock longs to put down his dainty porcelain teacup and shout, 'I am Lazarus, come from the dead, / Come back to tell you all, I shall tell you all.'"

"Why doesn't he do it?" I asked.

"Because Prufrock is convinced no matter what he says he won't reach them. He feels the English gentlewomen he's dealing with are unreachable. He believes his situation is as hopeless as theirs. He's dead and they're dead, too. That's why the poem begins with an image of sickness, 'a patient etherized upon a table,' and ends with people drowning. Prufrock is tough shit, man."

"You said you think there's a connection between Eliot the poet and J. Alfred Prufrock," I said.

"Of course there's a connection. Tommy Eliot from St. Louis, Missouri," said the officer. "Try as he will, he doesn't fit in. His English friends call him 'The American' and laugh. Tom Eliot the outsider with his rolled umbrella. T. S. Eliot is a self-conscious, make-believe Englishman and you have to understand that to understand 'Prufrock.'

"The poem is dark and funny at the same time. It's filled with humor and Prufrock is capable of laughing at himself. Just read those lines, 'Is it perfume from a dress / That makes me so digress?'"

"You were talking about Prufrock being sexually attracted to the women. How could that be if he is, as you say, 'dead.'" I asked.

"By 'dead' I mean desolate, inwardly barren, godforsaken. Inwardly, spiritually, Prufrock is a desolate creature. He's a moral man, he's a civilized man, but he's also hollow. But there's hope for him. In spite of himself, Prufrock is drawn to women.

"Look at line 64. He's attracted and repelled. Prufrock attends these teas, notices the women's arms 'downed with light brown hair!' and it scares the hell out of him because what he longs to do is to get them onto a drawing-room floor or a beach somewhere and bury his face in that same wonderfully tantalizing 'light brown hair.' What do you think of that, sailor?"

"I think you're right, sir."

"Then tell me this, Mr. Sward: Why doesn't he ask the overwhelming question? Hell, man, maybe it's not sexual. Maybe I'm wrong. Maybe what he wants to do is to ask some question like what you yourself suggested: 'What's the point in going on living when, in some sense, we're all already dead?'"

"I think he doesn't ask the question because he's so repressed, sir. He longs for physical contact, like you say, but he also wants another kind of intimacy, and he's afraid to ask for it and it's making him crazy."

"That's right, sailor. He's afraid. Eliot wrote the poem in 1911 when women were beginning to break free."

"Break free of what?" I asked.

"Of the prim and proper Victorian ideal. Suffragettes, feminists they called themselves. At the time Eliot wrote 'Prufrock,' women in England and America were catching on to the fact that they were disfranchised and had begun fighting for the right to vote, among other things, and for liberation, equality with men.

"Of course Prufrock is more prim and proper than the bored, overcivilized women in the poem. And it's ironic, isn't it, that he doesn't understand that the women are one step ahead of him. What you have in Prufrock is a man who tries to reconcile the image of real women with 'light brown hair' on their arms with some ideal, women who are a cross between the goddess Juno and a sweet Victorian maiden."

"Prufrock seems to know pretty well what he's feeling," I said. "He's not a liar and he's not a coward. To be honest, sir, I identify with Prufrock. He may try on one mask or another, but he ends up removing the mask and exposing himself."

"Now, about interior monologues: to understand 'Prufrock' you have to understand that most poems have one or more speakers and an audience, implied or otherwise. Let's go back to line 1. Who is this 'you and I' Eliot writes about?"

"Prufrock is talking to both his inner self and the reader," I said.

"How do you interpret the first ten lines?" the officer asked, pointing with his pencil.

"'Let us go then, you and I,' he's saying, let us stroll, somnolent and numb as a sedated patient, through these seedy 'half-deserted streets, / The muttering retreats / Of restless nights in one-night cheap hotels.'"

"That's it, sailor. And while one might argue that Prufrock 'wakes' at the end of the poem, he is for the most part a ghostly inhabitant of a world that is, for him, a sort of hell. He is like the speaker in the Italian epigraph from Dante's *Inferno*, who says, essentially, 'Like you, reader, I'm in purgatory and there is no way out. Nobody ever escapes from this pit and, for that reason, I can speak the truth without fear of ill fame.'

"Despairing and sick of heart, Prufrock is a prisoner. Trapped in himself and trapped in society, he attends another and another in an endless series of effete, decorous teas.

In the room the women come and go
Talking of Michelangelo.

"Do you get it now? Do you see what I mean when I say 'tough shit'?" said the officer.

"Yeah, I'm beginning to," I said.

"T. S. Eliot's 'Prufrock' has become so much a part of the English language that people who have never read the poem are familiar with phrases like 'I have measured out my life with coffee spoons' and 'I grow old . . . I grow old . . . / I shall wear the bottoms of my trousers rolled' and 'Do I dare to eat a peach?' and 'In the room the women come and go.'

"Do you get it now? Eliot's irregularly rhymed, 131-line interior monologue has become part of the monologue all of us carry on in our heads. We are all of us, whether we know it or not, love-hungry, sex-crazed soldiers and sailors, brave, bored and lonely. At some level in our hearts, we are all J. Alfred Prufrock, every one of us, and we are all sailing into a war zone from which, as the last line of the poem implies, we may never return."

From "T. S. Eliot's 'Love Song of J. Alfred Prufrock'" in *Touchstones: American Poets on a Favorite Poem*, edited by Robert Pack and Jay Parini

CONSIDERATIONS FOR CRITICAL THINKING AND WRITING

1. How satisfactory is this reading of the poem? Are any significant portions of the poem left out of this reading?

2. Compare the tone of this critical approach to any other in this chapter. Explain why you prefer one over another.

3. Using Sward's personal approach, write an analysis of a poem of your choice in this anthology.

26

Cultural Case Study:
Julia Alvarez's "Queens, 1963"

Close readings allow us to appreciate and understand the literary art of a text. These formalist approaches to literature study the intrinsic elements of a work to determine how it is constructed, emphasizing how various elements such as diction, image, figures of speech, tone, symbol, irony, sound, rhythm, and other literary techniques provide patterns related to the work's meaning. Instead of examining extrinsic matters such as social, political, and economic contexts related to a poem, formalist critics focus on the intrinsic qualities of the text itself. A formalist might, for example, approach Thomas Hardy's 1912 poem "The Convergence of the Twain" (p. 738) by placing significant emphasis on the form of this poem — its rhyming three-line stanzas — rather than the historical contexts around the sinking of the *Titanic*. A formalist would be more concerned with the effects produced by these triplets rather than the identities of some of the enormously wealthy people who went down with the ship. In more recent literary criticism, however, there has been a renewed interest in the historical and cultural contexts of works that go beyond close readings of the text.

Cultural critics pay close attention to the historical contexts of a work, but unlike literary historians, they do not limit themselves to major historical events or famous people. A cultural critic might, for example, approach "The Convergence of the Twain" not only as an opportunity to examine the "vaingloriousness" of the rich who put their faith in the technology that produced the *Titanic,* but also as an occasion to investigate how poor people made jokes about the sinking to deflate the pretensions of the rich. The ironies that go unsuspected by "human vanity" can be seen to go even deeper in the nervous jokes that infiltrate popular culture when such a catastrophe occurs. Hardy's dignified, if pessimistic, poetic response can be illuminated in radically different ways such as by advertising before the voyage or the jokes and sentimental poetic eulogies published after the disaster. Cultural critics study material drawn from a broad spectrum that includes "high" culture and popular culture. A cultural critic's approach to Hardy's treatment of the *Titanic*'s fate — captained by what Hardy calls the "Spinner of the Years" — might include discussions of everything from the actual construction plans of the ship, to passenger cabin accommodations, to manuals for lifeboat drills, as well as connections to Hardy's contemporaries, who also wrote about the *Titanic*.

The documents that follow Alvarez's "Queens, 1963" are provided to suggest how cultural criticism can be used to contextualize a literary work historically. The documents include an excerpt from an interview with Alvarez on growing up as an immigrant in New York City; an advertisement showing typical row houses; a newspaper article that summarizes the Chamber of Commerce's perspective of Queens in 1963; an excerpt from a television script for *All in the Family* (set in Queens); and a photograph of a civil rights demonstration at a Queens construction site. These documents offer some possible approaches to understanding the culture contemporary to "Queens, 1963." A variety of such approaches can create a wider and more informed understanding of the poem while deepening one's appreciation of Alvarez's achievement in writing it.

JULIA ALVAREZ (B. 1950)

Although Julia Alvarez was born in New York City, she lived in the Dominican Republic until she was ten-years-old. She returned to New York after her father, a physician, was connected to a plot to overthrow the dictatorship of Rafael Trujillo, and the family had to flee. Growing up in Queens was radically different from the Latino Caribbean world she experienced during her early childhood. A new culture and new language sensitized Alvarez to her surroundings and her use of language so that emigration from the Dominican Republic to Queens was the beginning of her movement toward becoming a writer. Alvarez quotes the Polish poet Czeslow Milosz's assertion that "Language is the only homeland" to explain her own sense that what she really settled into was not so much the United States as the English language.

Her fascination with English continued into high school and took shape in college as she became a serious writer — first at Connecticut College from 1967 to 1969 and then at Middlebury College, where she earned her B.A. in 1971. At Syracuse University she was awarded the American Academy of Poetry Prize and, in 1975, earned an M.A. in creative writing. Since then she has worked as a writer-in-residence for the Kentucky Arts

Commission, the Delaware Arts Council, and the Arts Council of Fayetteville, North Carolina, working in schools and community organizations. She has taught at California State College, College of Sequoias, Phillips Andover Academy, the University of Vermont, George Washington University, the University of Illinois, and, since 1988, at Middlebury College where she is a professor of literature and creative writing.

Alvarez's poetry has been widely published in journals and magazines ranging from *The New Yorker* to *Mirabella* to *The Kenyon Review*. Her book of poems, *Homecoming* (1984; second edition, 1986), uses simple — yet incisive — language to explore issues related to love, domestic life, and work (see, for example, "Woman's Work" [p. 886]). Her second book of poetry, *The Other Side/El Otro Lado* (1995), is a bilingual collection of meditations on her childhood memories of immigrant life that served to shape her adult identity and sensibilities.

In addition to her two volumes of poetry, Alvarez has also published three novels. The first, *How the García Girls Lost Their Accents* (1991), is a collection of fifteen separate but interrelated stories that cover thirty years of the lives of the García sisters from the late 1950s to the late 1980s. Drawing upon her own experiences, Alvarez describes the sisters fleeing the Dominican Republic and growing up as Latinas in the United States as well as their relationship to the country they left behind. Alvarez's second novel, *In the Time of the Butterflies* (1994), is a fictional account of a true story concerning four sisters who opposed Trujillo's dictatorship. Three of the sisters were murdered in 1960 by the government, and the fourth surviving sister recounts the events of their personal and political lives that led up to her sisters' deaths. Shaped by the history of Dominican freedom and tyranny, the novel also explores the sisters' relationships to each other and their country.

In *¡Yo!* (1997), her third novel, Alvarez focuses on Yolanda, one of the García sisters from her first novel, who is now a writer. Written in the different voices of Yo's friends and family members, this fractured narrative constructs a complete picture of a woman who uses her relationships as fodder for fiction; a woman who is selfish, aggravating, and finally lovable — and who is deeply embedded in American culture while remaining aware of her Dominican roots.

In "Queens, 1963" Alvarez remembers the neighborhood she lived in when she was thirteen-years-old and how "Everyone seemed more American/than we, newly arrived." The tensions that arose when new immigrants and ethnic groups moved onto the block were mirrored in many American neighborhoods in 1963. Indeed, the entire nation was made keenly aware of such issues as antisegregation when demonstrations were organized across the South and a massive march on Washington in support of civil rights for African Americans drew hundreds of thousands of demonstrators who listened to Martin Luther King deliver his electrifying "I have a dream" speech. But the issues were hardly resolved, as evidenced by 1963's two best-selling books: *Happiness Is a Warm Puppy* and *Security Is a Thumb and a Blanket*, by Charles M. Schulz of "Peanuts" cartoon fame. The popularity of these books is, perhaps, understandable given the tensions that moved across the country and which seemed to culminate on November 22, 1963, when President Kennedy was assassinated in Dallas, Texas. These events are not mentioned in "Queens, 1963," but they are certainly part of the context that helps us to understand Alvarez's particular neighborhood.

CHRONOLOGY

1950	Born on March 27 in New York City.
1950–60	Raised in the Dominican Republic.
1960	Alvarez family flees the Dominican Republic for New York City after her father joins efforts to overthrow the dictatorship of Rafael Trujillo.
1961	Rafael Trujillo is assassinated.
1967–69	Attends Connecticut College.
1971	Graduates from Middlebury College with a B.A.
1975	Graduates from Syracuse University with an M.F.A.
1979–80	Attends Bread Loaf School of English.
1979–81	Instructor at Phillips Andover Academy.
1981–83	Visiting assistant professor at University of Vermont.
1984	Publishes *Homecoming*, a volume of poems.
1984–85	Visiting writer-in-residence at George Washington University.
1985–88	Assistant professor of English at University of Illinois.
1987–88	Awarded a National Endowment for the Arts fellowship.
1988–present	Professor of English at Middlebury College.
1991	Publishes *How the García Girls Lost Their Accents*, a novel.
1994	Publishes *In the Time of Butterflies*, a novel.
1995	Publishes *The Other Side/El Otro Lado*, a volume of poems.
1997	Publishes *¡Yo!*, a novel.

Queens, 1963   *1995*

Everyone seemed more American
than we, newly arrived,
foreign dirt still on our soles.
By year's end, a sprinkler waving

like a flag on our mowed lawn,   5
we were melted into the block,
owned our own mock Tudor house.
Then the house across the street
sold to a black family.
Cop cars patrolled our block   10
from the Castellucci's at one end
to the Balakian's on the other.
We heard rumors of bomb threats,
a burning cross on their lawn.
(It turned out to be a sprinkler.)   15
Still the neighborhood buzzed.
The barber's family, Haralambides,
our left side neighbors, didn't want trouble.
They'd come a long way to be free!
Mr. Scott, the retired plumber,   20
and his plump midwestern wife,
considered moving back home
where white and black got along
by staying where they belonged.
They had cultivated our street   25
like the garden she'd given up
on account of her ailing back,
bad knees, poor eyes, arthritic hands.
She went through her litany daily.
Politely, my mother listened—   30
¡Ay, Mrs. Scott, qué pena!°
— her Dominican good manners
still running on automatic.
The Jewish counselor next door,
had a practice in her house;   35
clients hurried up her walk
ashamed to be seen needing.
(I watched from my upstairs window,
gloomy with adolescence,
and guessed how they too must have   40
hypocritical old world parents.)
Mrs. Bernstein said it was time
the neighborhood opened up.
As the first Jew on the block,
she remembered the snubbing she got   45
a few years back from Mrs. Scott.
But real estate worried her,
our houses' plummeting value.
She shook her head as she might
at a client's grim disclosures.   50
Too bad the world works this way.
The German girl playing the piano

31 *qué pena:* What a shame!

down the street abruptly stopped
in the middle of a note.
I completed the tune in my head   55
as I watched *their* front door open.
A dark man in a suit
with a girl about my age
walked quickly into a car.
My hand lifted but fell   60
before I made a welcoming gesture.
On her face I had seen a look
from the days before we had melted
into the United States of America.
It was hardness mixed with hurt.   65
It was knowing she never could be
the right kind of American.
A police car followed their car.
Down the street, curtains fell back.
Mrs. Scott swept her walk   70
as if it had just been dirtied.
Then the German piano commenced
downward scales as if tracking
the plummeting real estate.
One by one I imagined the houses   75
sinking into their lawns,
the grass grown wild and tall
in the past tense of this continent
before the first foreigners owned
any of this free country.   80

CONSIDERATIONS FOR CRITICAL THINKING AND WRITING

1. FIRST RESPONSE. What nationalities live in this neighborhood in the New York City borough of Queens? Are they neighborly to each other?

2. In line 3, why do you suppose Alvarez writes "foreign dirt still on our soles" rather than "foreign soil still on our shoes"? What does Alvarez's particular word choice suggest about her feelings for her native country?

3. Characterize the speaker. How old is she? How does she feel about having come from the Dominican Republic? About living in the United States?

4. Do you think this poem is optimistic or pessimistic about racial relations in the United States? Explain your answer by referring to specific details in the poem.

CONNECTIONS TO OTHER SELECTIONS

1. Compare the use of irony in "Queens, 1963" with that in John Ciardi's "Suburban" (p. 818). How does irony contribute to each poem?

2. Discuss the problems immigrants encounter in this poem and in Chitra Banerjee Divakaruni's "Indian Movie, New Jersey" (p. 819).

3. Write an essay comparing and contrasting the tone and theme in "Queens, 1963" and in Tato Laviera's "AmeRícan" (p. 918).

DOCUMENTS

Marny Requa (b. 1971)

From an Interview with Julia Alvarez   *1997*

M.R. What was it like when you came to the United States?

J.A. When we got to Queens, it was really a shock to go from a totally Latino, *familia* Caribbean world into this very cold and kind of forbidding one in which we didn't speak the language. I didn't grow up with a tradition of writing or reading books at all. People were always telling stories but it wasn't a tradition of literary . . . reading a book or doing something solitary like that. Coming to this country I discovered books, I discovered that it was a way to enter into a portable homeland that you could carry around in your head. You didn't have to suffer what was going on around you. I found in books a place to go. I became interested in language because I was learning a language intentionally at the age of ten. I was wondering, "Why is it that word and not another?" which any writer has to do with their language. I always say I came to English late but to the profession early. By high school I was pretty set: that's what I want to do, be a writer.

M.R. Did you have culture shock returning to the Dominican Republic as you were growing up?

J.A. The culture here had an effect on me — at the time this country was coming undone with protests and flower children and drugs. Here I was back in the Dominican Republic and I wouldn't keep my mouth shut. I had my own ideas and I had my own politics, and it, I just didn't gel anymore with the family. I didn't quite feel I ever belonged in this North American culture and I always had this nostalgia that when I went back I'd belong, and then I found out I didn't belong there either.

M.R. Was it a source of inspiration to have a foot in both cultures?

J.A. I only came to that later. [Then], it was a burden because I felt torn. I wanted to be part of one culture and then part of the other. It was a time when the model for the immigrant was that you came and you became an American and you cut off your ties and that was that. My parents had that frame of mind, because they were so afraid, and they were "Learn your English" and "Become one of them," and that left out so much. Now I see the richness. Part of what I want to do with my work is that complexity, that richness. I don't want it to be simplistic and either/or.

From "The Politics of Fiction," *Frontera* magazine 5 (1997)

Considerations for Critical Thinking and Writing

1. What do you think Alvarez means when she describes books as "a portable homeland that you could carry around in your head"?

2. Why is it difficult for Alvarez to feel that she belongs in either the Dominican or the North American culture?

3. Alvarez says that in the 1960s "the model for the immigrant was that you came and you became an American and you cut off your ties and that was

that." Do you think this model has changed in the 1990s in the United States? Explain your response.

4. How might this interview alter your understanding of "Queens, 1963"? What light is shed, for example, on the speaker's feeling that her family "melted into the block" in line 6?

An Advertisement for Tudor Row Houses   *1920*

From *Queen's Borough New York City, 1910–1920*

CONSIDERATIONS FOR CRITICAL THINKING AND WRITING

1. This advertisement from a publication of the Queens Chamber of Commerce shows row houses as the "Ideal Home Place." Write a paragraph describing how the details in the photograph make you feel about living there.

2. Compare the neighborhood in this picture with the neighborhood Alvarez describes in "Queens, 1963." How might the physical characteristics of such a neighborhood have changed between 1920 and 1963? What factors might have influenced such a change?

3. How does this advertisement shed light on "Queens, 1963"?

Queens: "The 'Fair' Borough"   1963

This newspaper account anticipates the opening of the 1964 World's Fair in Queens.

Cariello Glorifies Queens as Example of Gracious Living

The borough of Queens "truly represents the full flowering of advanced urban living," Borough President Mario J. Cariello says.

His encomium is in a brightly colored eight-page brochure entitled "The 'Fair' Borough." Mr. Cariello's foreword says the brochure was prepared "to reacquaint our residents" with the borough's history and present stature when they play host to "millions of visitors to the World's Fair."

Twenty-five thousand copies have been printed by photo-offset at a competitive bid cost of $1,600. The money came from the Borough President's special expense fund for proclamations, certificates and the like, a spokesman said yesterday.

A section on current "Data about Queens," compiled by the Queens Chamber of Commerce, says the borough has "such beautiful rural home communities as Forest Hills, Jamaica Estates, Kew Gardens, Jackson Heights, Flushing and Douglaston."

The booklet includes a map of 44 communities, a list of bus routes, a description of the Borough President's functions, the text of the 1657 Flushing Remonstrance as "the first declaration of religious freedom by a group of free citizens in America," a picture of the borough flag, and a brief history.

From the *New York Times*, July 18, 1963

CONSIDERATIONS FOR CRITICAL THINKING AND WRITING

1. Based on the newspaper article, how would you describe the probable tone of the eight-page brochure about Queens?

2. After reading Alvarez's poem about Queens, do you see any irony in the title of the brochure, "The 'Fair' Borough"? Explain why or why not.

3. What is left out of Borough President Cariello's account of Queens? Why do you suppose its focus is very different from that of "Queens, 1963"?

4. Try writing a dialogue between the Borough President and Alvarez on the subject of Queens as a representation of "the full flowering of advanced urban living." If you prefer, write an essay on this topic instead.

"Talkin' about Prejudice" in Queens

All in the Family, created by Norman Lear, was produced for nine seasons from 1971 to 1979, and at the height of its popularity, an estimated one-third of all Americans regularly viewed the program. Although this famous series has ceased production, reruns have preserved its popularity. The show's main character, Archie Bunker — a resident of a row house in a working-class Queens neighborhood — is so well known that his name has been used to describe anyone who is loud, stubborn, and blindly prejudiced. The basic conflict of the series centers on the verbal skirmishes that occur when Archie's middle-aged, working-class biases are challenged by his son-in-law Mike's liberal views. One reason for the show's popularity during its original run was that it mirrored so many issues of its time, such as racism, sexism, politics, religion, and alternative life-styles. The following excerpt is from the first episode of *All in the Family*.

NORMAN LEAR (B. 1922)

Meet the Bunkers 1971

CHARACTERS

Archie Bunker
Edith Bunker, Archie's wife
Michael Stivic, the Bunkers' son-in-law
Gloria Stivic, the Bunkers' daughter
Lionel, a neighbor

In this scene, Lionel, a black neighbor of the Bunkers, appears at the door on the heels of a dinner conversation in which Archie has fervently denied but amply demonstrated his prejudices. Earlier we learn from Lionel that Archie likes to ask him what he wants to study when he goes to college so that Lionel will say, "Ahm gwana be a 'lectical ingineer." Lionel obliges Archie because he believes that by giving "people what they want," he indeed can become an electrical engineer. He also enjoys watching Archie fall for his put-ons.

Mike: Hey, Lionel. How you doin'? Come on in. You know, in a way we were just talking about you.
Gloria: Michael!
Archie: Talkin' about prejudice, I'm glad you're here Lionel. (*Gets up and goes to living room.*)
Lionel: Yes, sir. Mr. Bunker, sir. (*Hands flowers to Edith.*) These are for you, Mrs. Bunker. A present from an admirer.
Edith (overwhelmed): For me? Oh my goodness, I ain't had a present for ten years.
Gloria: I wonder who it's from.
Archie (coming back to table): There's something I want to ask you, Lionel.
Gloria: Wait a minute, Daddy. Let her open her gift first.

Archie: She waited ten years; another minute ain't gonna kill her! (*Puts gift on table, takes Lionel to living room.*) Come here, Lionel. Let me ask your opinion of somethin' there, Lionel. When you started doin' odd jobs in the neighborhood, wasn't I one of the first guys to throw a little work your way — by the way, didya fix the TV up in the bedroom?

Lionel: Sure did, Mr. Bunker. (*Lionel nods. Archie slips him some change.*)

Archie: Swell. Good boy . . . Here, put this in your pocket.

Edith: Cheaper than a repairman, believe me.

Archie: Is anybody talkin' to you . . . Now, Lionel you could say by throwin' you these little jobs, in a way I was helpin' you get some money so you can get through college so's you can become . . .

Lionel: A 'lectical ingineer.

Archie (loves it): Yeah. Ya hear that?

Mike (impatient): Archie, ask your question already!

Archie: Will you keep your drawers on? Hey, by the way, that's a pretty nice looking suit you got on there. I mean it's classy, it's quiet. Where'd you get it?

Lionel: Up in Harlem.

Archie (looks): Nah.

Lionel: Now I got two more, but one's in yellow with stripes, the other one's in purple with checks. You know, for when I'm with *my* people.

Archie: Well, anyway Lionel, I'd say you know me pretty good, wouldn't you?

Lionel: Oh, yes, sir. I got a bead on you, all right. I know you real good.

Archie: Good, good.

Mike (crossing to living room): Alright, alright, let's get to the point. Lionel, what he wants to know, is if you think he's prejudiced.

Lionel (feigning innocence): Prejudiced?

Archie: Yeah.

Lionel: Prejudiced against who?

Mike: Against Black People.

Lionel: Against Black People! Mr. Bunker! That's the most ridiculous thing I ever heard!

    Archie turns proudly to the others.

Archie: There, you see that, wise guy. (*Turns to Mike.*) You thought you knew him. You thought you knew me. Oh these liberals — they're supposed to be so sensitive, ya know. I'll tell you where this guy's sensitive, Lionel — right in his tochas. (*Archie goes to dining room table.*)

Lionel (surprise): Where?

Mike: It's a Yiddish word. It means — (*points to buttocks*).

Lionel: Oh, I know where it's at. I was just wonderin', Mr. Bunker — what's with the Jewish word?

Archie: I hear them. We got a couple of Hebes working down the building.

Lionel: Does he use words like that very often?

Mike: Now and then.

Archie: I told ya, I work with a couple of Jews.

Lionel: Beggin' your pardon, Mr. Bunker, but you wouldn't happen to be one of them, would you?

Archie (no humor about this): What??

Lionel: I mean people don't use Jewish words just like that, do they, Mike?

Mike (crossing to table, sits): No, not in my experience.

Archie: Maybe people don't but *I* do! And I ain't no Yid!

Mike: Come to think of it . . . when your father was visiting last year . . . wasn't his name Davie, or somethin'?

Archie: David, my father's name is David.

Mike: Yeah, David. And your mother's name . . . uh . . . Sarah, wasn't it?

Archie (to Lionel): Sarah, my mother's name is Sarah — So what?

Lionel: David and Sarah, two Jewish names.

Archie: David and Sarah. Two names right out of the Bible — which is got nothin' to do with the Jews.

Lionel: You don't wanna get up tight about it, Mr. Bunker. There's nothing to be ashamed of being Jewish.

Archie: But I ain't Jewish!

Mike: Look at that — see the way he uses his hands when he argues. A very Semitic gesture.

Archie: What do you know about it, you dumb Polack.

Mike: All right, I'm a Polack.

Archie: You sure are! You're a Polack Joke!

Mike: Okay, I don't mind, so I'm Polish. I don't mind. I'm proud of it!

Lionel: There you are, Mr. Bunker. Now you oughta be proud that you're Jewish.

Archie (whining): But I ain't Jewish.

Edith: I didn't know you was Jewish.

Archie: What the hell are you talking about? You, of all people, should *know* that I ain't Jewish.

Edith: You *are* talking with your hands.

Lionel: See, the Jews tend to be emotional.

Archie (blowing): Now listen to me, Lionel. I'm going to give it to you just once more and that's all. I am not Jewish.

Lionel: Yes, Sir, Mr. Bunker. But even if you are, it doesn't change things between you and me. I mean I'm not gonna throw away nine years of friendship over a little thing like that. So long, everybody. (*He exits.*)

All: Bye, Lionel!

Archie watches him go and turns to others. They resume eating quickly.

Archie: Well, I hate a smart aleck kid, and I don't care what color he is!

Applause. Fade to black.

CONSIDERATIONS FOR CRITICAL THINKING AND WRITING

1. What kinds of assumptions does Archie make about Lionel because he is black? How does Lionel use Archie's prejudices to satirize him?

2. Some critics have insisted that *All in the Family* negatively affected society because the series presents a bigot who is likable, thereby characterizing his racial prejudices as funny and acceptable rather than harmful and repugnant. Do you think Archie is a dangerous character because his prejudices are presented humorously? Explain why or why not.

3. Compare and contrast how racial prejudice is treated in this script and in "Queens, 1963." Which treatment do you find more effective? Explain why.

4. How do the script and the poem suggest what it was like to be Jewish in Queens in the 1960s? Write an essay that explores how each work treats Jewishness. Consider whether these treatments are simplistic and reductive or complex and subtle.

A Civil Rights Demonstration   *1963*

In this photograph police remove a Congress of Racial Equality (CORE) demonstrator from a Queens construction site. Demonstrators blocked the delivery entrance to the site because they wanted more African Americans and Puerto Ricans hired in the building-trade industry.

Considerations for Critical Thinking and Writing

1. Discuss the role played by the police in this photograph and in "Queens, 1963." What attitudes toward the police do the photograph and the poem display?

2. How do you think the Scotts and Mrs. Bernstein would have responded to this photograph in 1963?

3. Compare the tensions in "Queens, 1963" to those depicted in this picture. How do the speaker's private reflections relate to this public protest?

27

A Collection of Poems

MAYA ANGELOU (B. 1924)

Africa 1975

Thus she had lain
sugar cane sweet
deserts her hair
golden her feet
mountains her breasts   5
two Niles her tears
Thus she has lain
Black through the years.

Over the white seas
rime white and cold   10
brigands ungentled
icicle bold
took her young daughters
sold her strong sons
churched her with Jesus   15
bled her with guns.
Thus she has lain.

Now she is rising
remember her pain
remember the losses   20
her screams loud and vain
remember her riches
her history slain
now she is striding
although she had lain.   25

ANONYMOUS (TRADITIONAL SCOTTISH BALLAD)

Bonny Barbara Allan

date unknown

It was in and about the Martinmas° time,
    When the green leaves were afalling,
That Sir John Graeme, in the West Country,
    Fell in love with Barbara Allan.

He sent his men down through the town,   5
    To the place where she was dwelling:
"Oh haste and come to my master dear,
    Gin° ye be Barbara Allan."   *if*

O hooly,° hooly rose she up,   *slowly*
    To the place where he was lying,   10
And when she drew the curtain by:
    "Young man, I think you're dying."

"O it's I'm sick, and very, very sick,
    And 'tis a' for Barbara Allan."—
"O the better for me ye's never be,   15
    Tho your heart's blood were aspilling."

"O dinna ye mind,° young man," she said,   *don't you remember*
    "When ye was in the tavern adrinking,
That ye made the health° gae round and round,   *toasts*
    And slighted Barbara Allan?"   20

He turned his face unto the wall,
    And death was with him dealing:
"Adieu, adieu, my dear friends all,
    And be kind to Barbara Allan."

And slowly, slowly raise her up,   25
    And slowly, slowly left him,
And sighing said she could not stay,
    Since death of life had reft him.

She had not gane a mile but twa,
    When she heard the dead-bell ringing,   30
And every jow° that the dead-bell geid,   *stroke*
    It cried, "Woe to Barbara Allan!"

"O mother, mother, make my bed!
    O make it saft and narrow!
Since my love died for me today,   35
    I'll die for him tomorrow."

---

1 *Martinmas:* St. Martin's Day, November 11.

ANONYMOUS

Lord Randal   1500s

"Oh, where have you been, Lord Randal, my son?
Oh, where have you been, my handsome young man?"
"Oh, I've been to the wildwood; mother, make my bed soon,
I'm weary of hunting and I fain° would lie down."   *gladly*

"And whom did you meet there, Lord Randal, my son?   5
And whom did you meet there, my handsome young man?"
"Oh, I met with my true love; mother, make my bed soon,
I'm weary of hunting and I fain would lie down."

"What got you for supper, Lord Randal, my son?
What got you for supper, my handsome young man?"   10
"I got eels boiled in broth; mother, make my bed soon,
I'm weary of hunting and I fain would lie down."

"And who got your leavings, Lord Randal, my son?
And who got your leavings, my handsome young man?"
"I gave them to my dogs; mother, make my bed soon,   15
I'm weary of hunting and I fain would lie down."

"And what did your dogs do, Lord Randal, my son?
And what did your dogs do, my handsome young man?"
"Oh, they stretched out and died; mother, make my bed soon,
I'm weary of hunting and I fain would lie down."   20

"Oh, I fear you are poisoned, Lord Randal, my son,
Oh, I fear you are poisoned, my handsome young man."
"Oh, yes, I am poisoned; mother, make my bed soon,
For I'm sick at my heart and I fain would lie down."

"What will you leave your mother, Lord Randal, my son?   25
What will you leave your mother, my handsome young man?"
"My house and my lands; mother, make my bed soon,
For I'm sick at my heart and I fain would lie down."

"What will you leave your sister, Lord Randal, my son?
What will you leave your sister, my handsome young man?"   30
"My gold and my silver; mother, make my bed soon,
For I'm sick at my heart and I fain would lie down."

"What will you leave your brother, Lord Randal, my son?
What will you leave your brother, my handsome young man?"
"My horse and my saddle; mother, make my bed soon,   35
For I'm sick at my heart and I fain would lie down."

"What will you leave your true-love, Lord Randal, my son?
What will you leave your true-love, my handsome young man?"
"A halter to hang her; mother, make my bed soon,
For I'm sick at my heart and I want to lie down."   40

ANONYMOUS

Scottsboro°   *1936*

Paper come out — done strewed de news
Seven po' chillun moan deat' house blues,
Seven po' chillun moanin' deat' house blues.
Seven nappy heads wit' big shiny eye
All boun' in jail and framed to die,   5
All boun' in jail and framed to die.

Messin' white woman — snake lyin' tale
Hang and burn and jail wit' no bail.
Dat hang and burn and jail wit' no bail.
Worse ol' crime in white folks' lan'   10
Black skin coverin' po' workin' man,
Black skin coverin' po' workin' man.

Judge and jury — all in de stan'
Lawd, biggety name for same lynchin' ban'
Lawd, biggety name for same lynchin' ban'.   15
White folks and nigger in great co't house
Like cat down cellar wit' nohole mouse.
Like cat down cellar wit' nohole mouse.

Scottsboro: This blues song refers to the 1931 arrest of nine black youths in Scottsboro, Alabama, who were charged with raping two white women. All nine were acquitted after several
trials, but a few of them had already been sentenced to death when this song was written.

W. H. AUDEN (1907–1973)

The Unknown Citizen   *1940*

(To JS/07/M/378
This Marble Monument
Is Erected by the State)

He was found by the Bureau of Statistics to be
One against whom there was no official complaint,
And all the reports on his conduct agree
That, in the modern sense of an old-fashioned word, he was a saint,
For in everything he did he served the Greater Community.   5
Except for the War till the day he retired
He worked in a factory and never got fired,
But satisfied his employers, Fudge Motors Inc.
Yet he wasn't a scab or odd in his views,
For his Union reports that he paid his dues,   10
(Our report on his Union shows it was sound)
And our Social Psychology workers found
That he was popular with his mates and liked a drink.
The Press are convinced that he bought a paper every day

And that his reactions to advertisements were normal in every way.   15
Policies taken out in his name prove that he was fully insured,
And his Health-card shows he was once in hospital but left it cured.
Both Producers Research and High-Grade Living declare
He was fully sensible to the advantages of the Installment Plan
And had everything necessary to the Modern Man,   20
A phonograph, radio, car and a frigidaire.
Our researchers into Public Opinion are content
That he held the proper opinions for the time of year;
When there was peace, he was for peace; when there was war, he went.
He was married and added five children to the population,   25
Which our Eugenist says was the right number for a parent of his generation,
And our teachers report that he never interfered with their education.
Was he free? Was he happy? The question is absurd:
Had anything been wrong, we should certainly have heard.

MARGARET AVISON (B. 1918)

Tennis   *1996*

Service is joy, to see or swing. Allow
All tumult to subside. Then tensest winds
Buffet, brace, viol° and sweeping bow.
Courts are for love and volley. No one minds
The cruel ellipse of service and return,   5
Dancing white galliardes° at tape or net
Till point, on the wire's tip, or the long burn-
ing arc to nethercourt° marks game and set.
Purpose apart, perched like an umpire, dozes,
Dreams golden balls whirring through indigo.   10
Clay blurs the whitewash but day still encloses
The albinos, bonded in their flick and flow.
Playing in musicked gravity, the pair
Score liquid Euclids° in foolscaps of air.

3 *viol:* A stringed musical instrument.   6 *galliardes:* Spirited dance movements.   8 *nether-court:* Down court.   14 *Euclids:* Geometric shapes.

AMIRI BARAKA (B. 1934)

SOS   *1969*

Calling black people
Calling all black people, man woman child
Wherever you are, calling you, urgent, come in
Black People, come in, wherever you are, urgent, calling
you, calling all black people
calling all black people, come in, black people, come
on in.

WILLIAM BLAKE (1757–1827)
The Garden of Love
1794

I went to the Garden of Love,
And saw what I never had seen:
A Chapel was built in the midst,
Where I used to play on the green.

And the gates of this Chapel were shut, 5
And "Thou shalt not" writ over the door;
So I turned to the Garden of Love
That so many sweet flowers bore;

And I saw it was filled with graves,
And tomb-stones where flowers should be; 10
And Priests in black gowns were walking their rounds,
And binding with briars my joys and desires.

WILLIAM BLAKE (1757–1827)
Ah Sun-flower
1794

Ah Sun-flower, weary of time,
Who countest the steps of the Sun,
Seeking after that sweet golden clime
Where the traveller's journey is done:

Where the Youth pined away with desire,
And the pale Virgin shrouded in snow
Arise from their graves and aspire
Where my Sun-flower wishes to go.

ROBERT BLY (B. 1926)
Snowfall in the Afternoon
1962

1
The grass is half-covered with snow.
It was the sort of snowfall that starts in late afternoon.
And now the little houses of the grass are growing dark.

2
If I reached my hands down, near the earth,
I could take handfuls of darkness! 5
A darkness was always there, which we never noticed.

3
As the snow grows heavier, the cornstalks fade farther away,
And the barn moves nearer to the house.
The barn moves all alone in the growing storm.

4
The barn is full of corn, and moving toward us now,   10
Like a hulk blown toward us in a storm at sea;
All the sailors on deck have been blind for many years.

ROBERT BLY (B. 1926)

Waking from Sleep   1962

Inside the veins there are navies setting forth,
Tiny explosions at the water lines,
And seagulls weaving in the wind of the salty blood.

It is the morning. The country has slept the whole winter.
Window seats were covered with fur skins, the yard was full   5
Of stiff dogs, and hands that clumsily held heavy books.

Now we wake, and rise from bed, and eat breakfast! —
Shouts rise from the harbor of the blood,
Mist, and masts rising, the knock of wooden tackle in the sunlight.

Now we sing, and do tiny dances on the kitchen floor.   10
Our whole body is like a harbor at dawn;
We know that our master has left us for the day.

ROO BORSON (B. 1952)

Talk   1981

The shops, the streets are full of old men
who can't think of a thing to say anymore.
Sometimes, looking at a girl, it
almost occurs to them, but they can't make it out,
they go pawing toward it through the fog.   5

The young men are still jostling shoulders
as they walk along, tussling at one another with words.
They're excited by talk, they can still see the danger.
The old women, thrifty with words,
haggling for oranges, their mouths   10
take bites out of the air. They know the value of oranges.
They had to learn everything
on their own.

The young women are the worst off, no one has bothered
to show them things.
You can see their minds on their faces,   15
they are like little lakes before a storm.
They don't know it's confusion that makes them sad.
It's lucky in a way though, because the young men take
a look of confusion for inscrutability, and this   20

excites them and makes them want to own
this face they don't understand,
something to be tinkered with at their leisure.

ANNE BRADSTREET (c. 1612–1672)

Before the Birth of One of Her Children   1678

All things within this fading world hath end,
Adversity doth still our joys attend;
No ties so strong, no friends so dear and sweet,
But with death's parting blow is sure to meet.
The sentence past is most irrevocable,   5
A common thing, yet oh, inevitable.
How soon, my Dear, death may my steps attend,
How soon't may be thy lot to lose thy friend,
We both are ignorant, yet love bids me
These farewell lines to recommend to thee,   10
That when that knot's untied that made us one,
I may seem thine, who is effect am none.
And if I see not half my days that's due,
What nature would, God grant to yours and you;
The many faults that well you know I have   15
Let be interred in my oblivious grave;
If any worth or virtue were in me,
Let that live freshly in thy memory
And when thou feel'st no grief, as I no harms,
Yet love thy dead, who long lay in thine arms,   20
And when thy loss shall be repaid with gains
Look to my little babes, my dear remains.
And if thou love thyself, or loved'st me,
These O protect from stepdame's° injury.   *stepmother's*
And if chance to thine eyes shall bring this verse,   25
With some sad sighs honor my absent hearse;
And kiss this paper for thy love's dear sake,
Who with salt tears this last farewell did take.

ANNE BRADSTREET (c. 1612–1672)

To My Dear and Loving Husband   1678

If ever two were one, then surely we.
If ever man were loved by wife, then thee;
If ever wife was happy in a man,
Compare with me, ye women, if you can.
I prize thy love more than whole mines of gold   5
Or all the riches that the East doth hold.
My love is such that rivers cannot quench,

Nor ought but love from thee, give recompense.
Thy love is such I can no way repay,
The heavens reward thee manifold, I pray.   10
Then while we live, in love let's so persevere
That when we live no more, we may live ever.

GWENDOLYN BROOKS (B. 1917)

The Mother   *1945*

Abortions will not let you forget.
You remember the children you got that you did not get,
The damp small pulps with a little or with no hair,
The singers and workers that never handled the air.
You will never neglect or beat   5
Them, or silence or buy with a sweet.
You will never wind up the sucking-thumb
Or scuttle off ghosts that come.
You will never leave them, controlling your luscious sigh,
Return for a snack of them, with gobbling mother-eye.   10

I have heard in the voices of the wind the voices of my dim
        killed children
I have contracted. I have eased
My dim dears at the breasts they could never suck.
I have said, Sweets, if I sinned, if I seized
Your luck   15
And your lives from your unfinished reach,
If I stole your births and your names,
Your straight baby tears and your games,
Your stilted or lovely loves, your tumults, your marriages, aches,
        and your deaths,
If I poisoned the beginnings of your breaths,   20
Believe that even in my deliberateness I was not deliberate.
Though why should I whine,
Whine that the crime was other than mine? —
Since anyhow you are dead.
Or rather, or instead,   25
You were never made.

But that too, I am afraid,
Is faulty: oh, what shall I say, how is the truth to be said?
You were born, you had body, you died.
It is just that you never giggled or planned or cried.   30

Believe me, I loved you all.
Believe me, I knew you, though faintly, and I loved, I loved you
All.

ROBERT BROWNING (1812–1889)
Meeting at Night

1845

The gray sea and the long black land;
And the yellow half-moon large and low;
And the startled little waves that leap
In firey ringlets from their sleep,
As I gain the cove with pushing prow,
And quench its speed i' the slushy sand.

5

Then a mile of warm sea-scented beach;
Three fields to cross till a farm appears;
A tap at the pane, the quick sharp scratch
And blue spurt of a lighted match,
And a voice less loud, through its joys and fears,
Than the two hearts beating each to each!

10

ROBERT BROWNING (1812–1889)
Parting at Morning

1845

Round the cape of a sudden came the sea,
And the sun looked over the mountain's rim:
And straight was a path of gold for him,
And the need of a world of men for me.

GEORGE GORDON, LORD BYRON (1788–1824)
She Walks in Beauty

1814

From Hebrew Melodies

I
She walks in Beauty, like the night
    Of cloudless climes and starry skies;
And all that's best of dark and bright
    Meet in her aspect and her eyes:
Thus mellowed to that tender light
    Which Heaven to gaudy day denies.

5

II
One shade the more, one ray the less,
    Had half impaired the nameless grace
Which waves in every raven tress,
    Or softly lightens o'er her face;
Where thoughts serenely sweet express,
    How pure, how dear their dwelling-place.

10

III
And on that cheek, and o'er that brow,
    So soft, so calm, yet eloquent,
The smiles that win, the tints that glow,   15
    But tell of days in goodness spent,
A mind at peace with all below,
    A heart whose love is innocent!

LUCILLE CLIFTON (B. 1936)
for deLawd   *1969*

people say they have a hard time
understanding how I
go on about my business
playing my Ray Charles
hollering at the kids —   5
seem like my Afro
cut off in some old image
would show I got a long memory
and I come from a line
of black and going on women   10
who got used to making it through murdered sons
and who grief kept on pushing
who fried chicken
ironed
swept off the back steps   15
who grief kept
for their still alive sons
for their sons coming
for their sons gone
just pushing   20

SAMUEL TAYLOR COLERIDGE (1772–1834)
Kubla Khan: or, a Vision in a Dream °   *1798*

In Xanadu did Kubla Khan°
    A stately pleasure-dome decree:
Where Alph, the sacred river, ran
Through caverns measureless to man
    Down to a sunless sea.   5

So twice five miles of fertile ground
With walls and towers were girdled round:

Vision in a Dream: This poem came to Coleridge in an opium-induced dream, but he was interrupted by a visitor while writing it down. He was later unable to remember the rest of the poem.   1 *Kubla Khan:* The historical Kublai Khan (1216–1294, grandson of Genghis Khan) was the founder of the Mongol dynasty in China.

And here were gardens bright with sinuous rills
Where blossomed many an incense-bearing tree;
And there were forests ancient as the hills,   10
Enfolding sunny spots of greenery.

But oh! that deep romantic chasm which slanted
Down the green hill athwart a cedarn cover!°
A savage place! as holy and enchanted
As e'er beneath a waning moon was haunted   15
By woman wailing for her demon-lover!
And from this chasm, with ceaseless turmoil seething,
As if this earth in fast thick pants were breathing,
A mighty fountain momently was forced,
Amid whose swift half-intermitted burst   20
Huge fragments vaulted like rebounding hail,
Of chaffy grain beneath the thresher's flail:
And 'mid these dancing rocks at once and ever
It flung up momently the sacred river.
Five miles meandering with a mazy motion   25
Through wood and dale the sacred river ran,
Then reached the caverns measureless to man,
And sank in tumult to a lifeless ocean:
And 'mid this tumult Kubla heard from far
Ancestral voices prophesying war!   30
    The shadow of the dome of pleasure
    Floated midway on the waves;
    Where was heard the mingled measure
    From the fountain and the caves.
It was a miracle of rare device,   35
A sunny pleasure-dome with caves of ice!

    A damsel with a dulcimer
    In a vision once I saw:
    It was an Abyssinian maid,
    And on her dulcimer she played,   40
    Singing of Mount Abora.
    Could I revive within me
    Her symphony and song,
    To such a deep delight 'twould win me,
That with music loud and long,   45
I would build that dome in air,
That sunny dome! those caves of ice!
And all who heard should see them there,
And all should cry, Beware! Beware!
His flashing eyes, his floating hair!   50
Weave a circle round him thrice,
And close your eyes with holy dread,
For he on honey-dew hath fed,
And drunk the milk of Paradise.

13 *athwart . . . cover:* Spanning a grove of cedar trees.

WILLIAM COWPER (1731–1800)

Epitaph on a Hare   1784

Here lies, whom hound did ne'er pursue,
   Nor swifter greyhound follow,
Whose foot ne'er tainted° morning dew,   *left a scent on*
   Nor ear heard huntsman's hallo',

Old Tiney, surliest of his kind,   5
   Who, nursed with tender care,
And to domestic bounds confined,
   Was still a wild jack-hare.

Though duly from my hand he took
   His pittance every night,   10
He did it with a jealous look,
   And, when he could, would bite.

His diet was of wheaten bread,
   And milk, and oats, and straw,
Thistles, or lettuces instead,   15
   With sand to scour his maw.

On twigs of hawthorn he regaled,°   *feasted*
   On pippins'° russet peel;   *apples'*
And, when his juicy salads failed,
   Sliced carrot pleased him well.   20

A Turkey carpet was his lawn,
   Whereon he loved to bound,
To skip and gambol like a fawn,
   And swing his rump around.

His frisking was at evening hours,   25
   For then he lost his fear;
But most before approaching showers,
   Or when a storm drew near.

Eight years and five round-rolling moons
   He thus saw steal away,   30
Dozing out all his idle noons,
   And every night at play.

I kept him for his humor's sake,
   For he would oft beguile
My heart of thoughts that made it ache,   35
   And force me to a smile.

But now, beneath this walnut-shade
   He finds his long, last home,
And waits in snug concealment laid,
   Till gentler Puss shall come.   40

He, still more agèd, feels the shocks
   From which no care can save,

And, partner once of Tiney's box,
  Must soon partake his grave.

VICTOR HERNÁNDEZ CRUZ (B. 1949)

Anonymous   1982

And if I lived in those olden times
With a funny name like Choicer or
Henry Howard, Earl of Surrey, what chimes!
I would spend my time in search of rhymes
Make sure the measurement termination surprise   5
In the court of kings snapping till woo sunrise
Plus always be using the words *alas* and *hath*
And not even knowing that that was my path
Just think on the Lower East Side of Manhattan
It would have been like living in satin   10
Alas! The projects hath not covered the river
Thou see-est vision to make thee quiver
Hath I been delivered to that "wildernesse"
So past
I would have been the last one in the   15
Dance to go
Taking note the minuet so slow
All admire my taste
Within thou *mambo* of much more haste.

COUNTEE CULLEN (1903–1946)

Yet Do I Marvel   1925

I doubt not God is good, well-meaning, kind,
And did He stoop to quibble could tell why
The little buried mole continues blind,
Why flesh that mirrors Him must some day die,
Make plain the reason tortured Tantalus   5
Is baited by the fickle fruit, declare
If merely brute caprice dooms Sisyphus
To struggle up a never-ending stair.
Inscrutable His ways are, and immune
To catechism by a mind too strewn   10
With petty cares to slightly understand
What awful brain compels His awful hand.
Yet do I marvel at this curious thing:
To make a poet black, and bid him sing!

E. E. CUMMINGS (1894–1962)
Buffalo Bill 's° 1923

Buffalo Bill 's
defunct
  who used to
  ride a watersmooth-silver
          stallion 5
and break onetwothreefourfive pigeonsjustlikethat
           Jesus
he was a handsome man
      and what i want to know is
how do you like your blueeyed boy 10
Mister Death

Buffalo Bill: William Frederick Cody (1846–1917) was an American frontier scout and Indian killer turned international circus showman with his Wild West show, which employed Sitting Bull and Annie Oakley.

E. E. CUMMINGS (1894–1962)
since feeling is first 1926

since feeling is first
who pays any attention
to the syntax of things
will never wholly kiss you;

wholly to be a fool 5
while Spring is in the world

my blood approves,
and kisses are a better fate
than wisdom
lady i swear by all flowers. Don't cry 10
— the best gesture of my brain is less than
your eyelids' flutter which says

we are for each other: then
laugh, leaning back in my arms
for life's not a paragraph 15

And death i think is no parenthesis

MARY DI MICHELE (B. 1949)
As in the Beginning 1983

A man has two hands and when one
gets caught on the belt and his fingers
are amputated and then patched
he cannot work. His hands are insured

however so he gets some money 5
for the work his hands have done before.
If he loses a finger he gets a flat sum
of $250 for each digit &/or $100 for a joint
missing for the rest of his stay on earth,
like an empty stool at a beggar's banquet. 10
When the hands are my father's hands
it makes me cry although my pen must keep scratching
its head across the page of another night.
To you my father is a stranger
and perhaps you think the insurance paid is enough. 15

Give me my father's hands when they are not broken
and swollen,
give me my father's hands, young again,
and holding the hands of my mother,
give me my father's hands still brown and uncallused, 20
beautiful hands that broke bread for us at table,
hands as smooth as marble and naked as the morning,
give me hands without a number tattooed at the wrist,
without the copper sweat of clinging change,
give my father's hands as they were in the beginning, 25
whole,
open,
warm
and without fear.

GREGORY DJANIKIAN (B. 1949)

When I First Saw Snow 1989

Tarrytown, N.Y.

Bing Crosby was singing "White Christmas"
    on the radio, we were staying at my aunt's house
    waiting for papers, my father was looking for a job.
We had trimmed the tree the night before,
    sap had run on my fingers and for the first time 5
    I was smelling pine wherever I went.
Anais, my cousin, was upstairs in her room
    listening to Danny and the Juniors.
Haigo was playing Monopoly with Lucy, his sister,
    Buzzy, the boy next door, had eyes for her 10
    and there was a rattle of dice, a shuffling
    of Boardwalk, Park Place, Marvin Gardens.
There were red bows on the Christmas tree.
It had snowed all night.
My boot buckles were clinking like small bells 15
    as I thumped to the door and out
    onto the gray planks of the porch dusted with snow.

The world was immaculate, new,
    even the trees had changed color,
    and when I touched the snow on the railing   20
    I didn't know what I had touched, ice or fire.
I heard, "I'm dreaming . . ."
I heard, "At the hop, hop, hop . . . oh, baby."
I heard "B & O" and the train in my imagination
    was whistling through the great plains.   25
And I was stepping off,
I was falling deeply into America.

JOHN DONNE (1572–1631)

The Apparition   *c. 1600*

When by thy scorn, O murderess, I am dead,
    And that thou thinkst thee free
From all solicitation from me,
Then shall my ghost come to thy bed,
And thee, feigned vestal, in worse arms shall see;   5
Then thy sick taper° will begin to wink,   *candle*
And he, whose thou art then, being tired before,
Will, if thou stir, or pinch to wake him, think
    Thou call'st for more,
And in false sleep will from thee shrink.   10
And then, poor aspen wretch, neglected, thou,
Bathed in a cold quicksilver sweat, wilt lie
    A verier° ghost than I.   *truer*
What I will say, I will not tell thee now,
Lest that preserve thee; and since my love is spent,   15
I had rather thou shouldst painfully repent,
Than by my threatenings rest still innocent.

JOHN DONNE (1572–1631)

Batter My Heart   *1610*

Batter my heart, three-personed God; for You
As yet but knock, breathe, shine, and seek to mend;
That I may rise and stand, o'erthrow me, and bend
Your force, to break, blow, burn, and make me new.
I, like an usurped town, to another due,   5
Labor to admit You, but Oh, to no end!
Reason, Your viceroy in me, me should defend,
But is captived, and proves weak or untrue.
Yet dearly I love You, and would be loved fain.
But am betrothed unto Your enemy: 10
Divorce me, untie, or break that knot again,
Take me to You, imprison me, for I,

Except You enthrall me, never shall be free,
Nor ever chaste, except You ravish me.

JOHN DONNE (1572–1631)
Death Be Not Proud   *1611*

Death be not proud, though some have callèd thee
Mighty and dreadful, for thou art not so;
For those whom thou think'st thou dost overthrow
Die not, poor Death, nor yet canst thou kill me.
From rest and sleep, which but thy pictures° be,   *images* 5
Much pleasure; then from thee much more must flow,
And soonest our best men with thee do go,
Rest of their bones, and soul's delivery.°   *deliverance*
Thou art slave to Fate, Chance, kings, and desperate men,
And dost with Poison, War, and Sickness dwell;   10
And poppy or charms can make us sleep as well,
And better than thy stroke; why swell'st° thou then?   *swell with pride*
One short sleep past, we wake eternally
And death shall be no more; Death, thou shalt die.

JOHN DONNE (1572–1631)
The Flea   *1633*

Mark but this flea, and mark in this°
How little that which thou deny'st me is;
It sucked me first, and now sucks thee,
And in this flea our two bloods mingled be;
Thou know'st that this cannot be said   5
A sin, nor shame, nor loss of maidenhead,
        Yet this enjoys before it woo,
        And pampered swells with one blood made of two,
        And this, alas, is more than we would do.°

Oh stay, three lives in one flea spare,   10
Where we almost, yea more than, married are.
This flea is you and I, and this
Our marriage bed, and marriage temple is;
Though parents grudge, and you, we're met
And cloistered in these living walls of jet.   15
        Though use° make you apt to kill me,   *habit*
        Let not to that, self-murder added be,
        And sacrilege, three sins in killing three.

Cruel and sudden, hast thou since
Purpled thy nail in blood of innocence?   20

1 *mark in this:* Take note of the moral lesson in this object.   9 *more than we would do:* That
is, if we do not join our blood in conceiving a child.

Wherein could this flea guilty be,
Except in that drop which it sucked from thee?
Yet thou triumph'st, and say'st that thou
Find'st not thyself, nor me, the weaker now;
    'Tis true; then learn how false, fears be;   25
    Just so much honor, when thou yield'st to me,
    Will waste, as this flea's death took life from thee.

DAVID DONNELL (B. 1939)

The Canadian Prairies View of Literature   *1983*

First of all it has to be anecdotal; ideas don't exist;
themes struggle dimly out of accrued material like the shadow
of a slow caterpillar struggling out of a large cocoon;
even this image itself is somewhat urban inasmuch is it suggests
the tree-bordered streets of small southern Ontario towns;   5
towns are alright; Ontario towns are urban; French towns are European;
the action should take place on a farm between April and October;
nature is quiet during winter; when it snows, there's a lot of it;
the poem shimmers in the school-teacher's head like an image
of being somewhere else without a railway ticket to return;   10
the novel shifts its haunches in the hot reporter's head
and surveys the possible relationship between different farms;
sometimes the action happens in the beverage rooms and cheap
hotels area of a small town that has boomed into a new city;
Indians and Metis appear in the novel wearing the marks   15
of their alienation like a sullen confusion of the weather;
the town drunk appears looking haggard and the town mayor
out ward-heeling and smelling women's hands buys him a drink;
a woman gets married and another woman has a child;
the child is not old enough to plow a field and therefore   20
does not become a focus of interest except as another mouth;
they sit around with corn shucks in the head and wonder
who they should vote for, the question puzzles them,
vote for the one with the cracked shoes, he's a good boy,
or the one who jumped over six barrels at a local dance;   25
the fewer buildings they have, the more nationalistic they become
like a man who has stolen all his life accused of cheating;
above all, they dislike the east which at least gives them form
and allows their musings and discontents to flower into rancour;
musing and rancorous, I turn down the small side streets of Galt,   30
Ontario, afternoon light, aged twelve, past South Water Street,
not quite like Rimbaud leaving Charleville,
my hands in my windbreaker pockets like white stones,
and promise myself once again that when I get to the city
everything will happen, I will learn all of its history   35
and become the best writer they have ever dreamed of,
I'll make them laugh and I'll even make them cry,
I'll drink their whiskey and make love to all their wives,

the words tumbling out of my mouth as articulate as the young Hector,
the corn under my shirt awkward a little rough light brown dry   40
and making me itch at times

GEORGE ELIOT (MARY ANN EVANS / 1819–1880)

In a London Drawingroom   1865

The sky is cloudy, yellowed by the smoke.
For view there are the houses opposite,
Cutting the sky with one long line of wall
Like solid fog: far as the eye can stretch
Monotony of surface and of form   5
Without a break to hang a guess upon.
No bird can make a shadow as it flies,
For all its shadow, as in ways o'erhung
By thickest canvas, where the golden rays
Are clothed in hemp. No figure lingering   10
Pauses to feed the hunger of the eye
Or rest a little on the lap of life.
All hurry on and look upon the ground
Or glance unmarking at the passersby.
The wheels are hurrying, too, cabs, carriages   15
All closed, in multiplied identity.
The world seems one huge prison-house and court
Where men are punished at the slightest cost,
With lowest rate of color, warmth, and joy.

LOUISE GLÜCK (B. 1943)

The School Children   1975

The children go forward with their little satchels.
And all morning the mothers have labored
to gather the late apples, red and gold,
like words of another language.

And on the other shore   5
are those who wait behind great desks
to receive these offerings.

How orderly they are — the nails
on which the children hang
their overcoats of blue or yellow wool.   10

And the teachers shall instruct them in silence
and the mothers shall scour the orchards for a way out,
drawing to themselves the gray limbs of the fruit trees
bearing so little ammunition.

DONALD HALL (B. 1928)
My Son, My Executioner   1955

My son, my executioner,
   I take you in my arms,
Quiet and small and just astir,
   And whom my body warms.

Sweet death, small son, our instrument   5
   Of immortality,
Your cries and hungers document
   Our bodily decay.

We twenty-five and twenty-two,
   Who seemed to live forever,   10
Observe enduring life in you
   And start to die together.

THOMAS HARDY (1840–1928)
Hap   1866

If but some vengeful god would call to me
From up the sky, and laugh: "Thou suffering thing,
Know that thy sorrow is my ecstasy,
That thy love's loss is my hate's profiting!"

Then would I bear it, clench myself, and die,   5
Steeled by the sense of ire unmerited;
Half-eased in that a Powerfuller than I
Had willed and meted me the tears I shed.

But not so. How arrives it joy lies slain,
And why unblooms the best hope ever sown?   10
— Crass Casualty obstructs the sun and rain,
And dicing Time for gladness casts a moan. . . .
These purblind Doomsters had as readily strown
Blisses about my pilgrimage as pain.

THOMAS HARDY (1840–1928)
The Ruined Maid   1902

"O'Melia, my dear, this does everything crown!
Who could have supposed I should meet you in Town?
And whence such fair garments, such prosperi-ty?"
"O didn't you know I'd been ruined?" said she.

"You left us in tatters, without shoes or socks,   5
Tired of digging potatoes, and spudding up docks;

And now you've gay bracelets and bright feathers three!"
"Yes: that's how we dress when we're ruined," said she.

"At home in the barton° you said 'thee' and 'thou,'   *farm*
And 'thik oon,' and 'theäs oon,' and 't'other'; but now   10
Your talking quite fits 'ee for high compa-ny!"
"Some polish is gained with one's ruin," said she.

Your hands were like paws then, your face blue and bleak
But now I'm bewitched by your delicate cheek,
And your little gloves fit as on any la-dy!"   15
"We never do work when we're ruined," said she.

"You used to call home-life a hag-ridden dream,
And you'd sigh, and you'd sock; but at present you seem
To know not of megrims° or melancho-ly!"   *depressions*
"True. One's pretty lively when ruined," said she.   20

"I wish I had feathers, a fine sweeping gown,
And a delicate face, and could strut about Town!"
"My dear — a raw country girl, such as you be,
Cannot quite expect that. You ain't ruined," said she.

Joy Harjo (b. 1951)

Fishing   *1991*

This is the longest day of the year, on the Illinois River or a similar river in
the same place. Cicadas are part of the song as they praise their invisible
ancestors while fish blinking back the relentless sun in Oklahoma circle in
the muggy river of life. They dare the fisher to come and get them. Fish too
anticipate the game of fishing. Their ancestors perfected the moves, sent   5
down stories that appear as electrical impulse when sunlight hits water.
The hook carries great symbology in the coming of age, and is crucial to
the making of warriors. The greatest warriors are those who dangle a
human for hours on a string, break sacred water for the profanity of air
then snap fiercely back into pearly molecules that describe fishness. They   10
smell me as I walk the banks with fishing pole, nightcrawlers and a
promise I made to that old friend Louis to fish with him this summer. This
is the only place I can keep that promise, inside a poem as familiar to him
as the banks of his favorite fishing place. I try not to let the fish see me see
them as they look for his tracks on the soft earth made of fossils and ashes.   15
I hear the burble of fish talk: When is that old Creek coming back? He
was the one we loved to tease most, we liked his songs and once in awhile
he gave us a good run. Last night I dreamed I tried to die, I was going to
look for Louis. It was rather comical. I worked hard to muster my last
breath, then lay down in the summer, along the banks of the last mythic   20
river, my pole and tackle box next to me. What I thought was my last
breath floated off as a cloud making an umbrella of grief over my relatives.
How embarrassing when the next breath came, and then the next. I reeled
in one after another, as if I'd caught a bucket of suckers instead of bass. I
guess it wasn't my time, I explained, and went fishing anyway as a liar   25

and I know most fishers to be liars most of the time. Even Louis when it
came to fishing, or even dying. The leap between the sacred and profane is
as thin as a fishing line, and is part of the mystery on this river of life, as is
the way our people continue to make warriors in the strangest of times. I
save this part of the poem for the fish camp next to the oldest spirits whose 30
dogs bark to greet visitors. It's near Louis's favorite spot where the
wisest and fattest fish laze. I'll meet him there.

MICHAEL S. HARPER (B. 1938)

Grandfather   *1975*

In 1915 my grandfather's
neighbors surrounded his house
near the dayline he ran
on the Hudson
in Catskill, NY   5
and thought they'd burn
his family out
in a movie they'd just seen
and be rid of his kind:
the death of a lone black   10
family is *the Birth
of a Nation,*°
or so they thought.
His 5'4" waiter gait
quenched the white jacket smile   15
he'd brought back from watered
polish of my father
on the turning seats,
and he asked his neighbors
up on his thatched porch   20
for the first blossom of fire
that would burn him down.

They went away, his nation,
spittooning their torched necks
in the shadows of the riverboat   25
they'd seen, posse decomposing;
and I see him on Sutter
with white bag from your
restaurant, challenged by his first
grandson to a foot-race   30
he will win in white clothes.

I see him as he buys galoshes
for his railed yard near Mineo's

11-12 *Birth of a Nation:* A 1915 film directed by D. W. Griffith that praises the rise of the Ku
Klux Klan in the South during Reconstruction.

metal shop, where roses jump
as the el circles his house   35
toward Brooklyn, where his rain fell;
and I see cigar smoke in his eyes,
chocolate Madison Square Garden chews
he breaks on his set teeth,
stitched up after cancer,   40
the great white nation immovable
as his weight wilts
and he is on a porch
that won't hold my arms,
or the legs of the race run   45
forwards, or the film
played backwards on his grandson's eyes.

ANTHONY HECHT (B. 1923)

The Dover Bitch °   *1968*

A Criticism of Life

So there stood Matthew Arnold and this girl
With the cliffs of England crumbling away behind them,
And he said to her, "Try to be true to me,
And I'll do the same for you, for things are bad
All over, etc., etc."   5
Well now, I knew this girl. It's true she had read
Sophocles in a fairly good translation
And caught that bitter allusion to the sea,°
But all the time he was talking she had in mind
The notion of what his whiskers would feel like   10
On the back of her neck. She told me later on
That after a while she got to looking out
At the lights across the channel, and really felt sad,
Thinking of all the wine and enormous beds
And blandishments in French and the perfumes.   15
And then she got really angry. To have been brought
All the way down from London, and then be addressed
As a sort of mournful cosmic last resort
Is really tough on a girl, and she was pretty.
Anyway, she watched him pace the room   20
And finger his watch-chain and seem to sweat a bit,
And then she said one or two unprintable things.
But you mustn't judge her by that. What I mean to say is,
She's really all right. I still see her once in a while

The Dover Bitch: A parody of Arnold's poem "Dover Beach" (see p. 757).   8 *allusion to the sea:*
Lines 9–18 in "Dover Beach" refer to Sophocles' *Antigone*, lines 583–591.

And she always treats me right. We have a drink 25
And I give her a good time, and perhaps it's a year
Before I see her again, but there she is,
Running to fat, but dependable as they come.
And sometimes I bring her a bottle of *Nuit d'Amour*.

GEORGE HERBERT (1593–1633)

The Collar   *1633*

I struck the board° and cried, "No more;   *table*
       I will abroad!
What? shall I ever sigh and pine?
My lines and life are free, free as the road,
   Loose as the wind, as large as store.°   5
       Shall I be still in suit?°   *serving another*
   Have I no harvest but a thorn
   To let me blood, and not restore
What I have lost with cordial° fruit?   *restorative*
       Sure there was wine   10
Before my sighs did dry it; there was corn
       Before my tears did drown it.
Is the year only lost to me?
       Have I no bays° to crown it,   *triumphal wreaths*
No flowers, no garlands gay? All blasted?   15
       All wasted?
   Not so, my heart; but there is fruit,
       And thou hast hands.
   Recover all thy sigh-blown age
On double pleasures: leave thy cold dispute   20
Of what is fit, and not. Forsake thy cage,
       Thy rope of sands,
Which petty thoughts have made, and made to thee
   Good cable, to enforce and draw,
       And be thy law,   25
   While thou didst wink and wouldst not see.
       Away! take heed;
       I will abroad.
Call in thy death's-head° there; tie up thy fears.
       He that forbears   30
       To suit and serve his need,
       Deserves his load."
But as I raved and grew more fierce and wild
       At every word,
Methought I heard one calling, *Child!*   35
       And I replied, *My Lord.*

---

5 *store:* A storehouse or warehouse.   29 *death's-head:* A skull, reminder of mortality.

LINDA HOGAN (B. 1947)

Song for My Name

1979

Before sunrise
think of brushing out an old woman's
dark braids.
Think of your hands,
fingertips on the soft hair.   5

If you have this name,
your grandfather's dark hands
lead horses toward the wagon
and a cloud of dust follows,
ghost of silence.   10

That name is full of women
with black hair
and men with eyes like night.
It means no money
tomorrow.   15

Such a name my mother loves
while she works gently
in the small house.
She is a white dove
and in her own land   20
the mornings are pale,
birds sing into the white curtains
and show off their soft breasts.

If you have a name like this,
there's never enough water.   25
There is too much heat.
When lightning strikes, rain
refuses to follow.
It's my name,
that of a woman living   30
between the white moon
and the red sun, waiting to leave.
It's the name that goes with me
back to earth
no one else can touch.   35

M. CARL HOLMAN (1919–1988)

Mr. Z

1967

Taught early that his mother's skin was the sign of error,
He dressed and spoke the perfect part of honor;
Won scholarships, attended the best schools,
Disclaimed kinship with jazz and spirituals;

Chose prudent, raceless views for each situation,   5
Or when he could not cleanly skirt dissension,
Faced up to the dilemma, firmly seized
Whatever ground was Anglo-Saxonized.

In diet, too, his practice was exemplary:
Of pork in its profane forms he was wary;   10
Expert in vintage wines, sauces and salads,
His palate shrank from cornbread, yams and collards.

He was as careful whom he chose to kiss:
His bride had somewhere lost her Jewishness,
But kept her blue eyes; an Episcopalian   15
Prelate proclaimed them matched chameleon.
Choosing the right addresses, here, abroad,
They shunned those places where they might be barred;
Even less anxious to be asked to dine
Where hosts catered to kosher accent or exotic skin.   20

And so he climbed, unclogged by ethnic weights,
An airborne plant, flourishing without roots.
Not one false note was struck — until he died:
His subtly grieving widow could have flayed
The obit writers, ringing crude changes on a clumsy phrase: 25
"One of the most distinguished members of his race."

GERARD MANLEY HOPKINS   (1844–1889)

Pied Beauty   *1877*

Glory be to God for dappled things —
        For skies of couple-color as a brinded cow;
                For rose-moles all in stipple upon trout that swim;
Fresh-firecoal chestnut-falls;° finches' wings;   *fallen chestnut*
        Landscape plotted and pieced — fold, fallow, and plow;   5
                And all trades, their gear and tackle and trim.

All things counter, original, spare, strange;
        Whatever is fickle, freckled (who knows how?)
                With swift, slow; sweet, sour; adazzle, dim;
He fathers-forth whose beauty is past change: 10
                Praise him.

GERARD MANLEY HOPKINS (1844–1889)

The Windhover°

1877

To Christ Our Lord

I caught this morning morning's minion,° king-   *favorite*
    dom of daylight's dauphin, dapple-dawn-drawn Falcon, in his riding
      Of the rolling level underneath him steady air, and striding
High there, how he rung upon the rein of a wimpling wing
In his ecstasy! then off, off forth on swing,   5
    As a skate's heel sweeps smooth on a bow-bend: the hurl and gliding
    Rebuffed the big wind. My heart in hiding
Stirred for a bird, — the achieve of, the mastery of the thing!

Brute beauty and valour and act, oh, air, pride, plume, here
    Buckle!° AND the fire that breaks from thee then, a billion   10
Times told lovelier, more dangerous, O my chevalier!

    No wonder of it: shéer plód makes plough down sillion°   *furrow*
Shine, and blue-bleak embers, ah my dear,
    Fall, gall themselves, and gash gold-vermilion.

The Windhover: "A name for the kestrel [a kind of small hawk], from its habit of hovering or hanging with its head to the wind" [*OED*].   10 *Buckle:* To join, to equip for battle, to crumple.

A. E. HOUSMAN (1859–1936)

Is my team ploughing

1896

"Is my team ploughing,
    That I was used to drive
And hear the harness jingle
    When I was man alive?"

Ay, the horses trample,   5
    The harness jingles now;
No change though you lie under
    The land you used to plough.

"Is football playing
    Along the river shore,
With lads to chase the leather,   10
    Now I stand up no more?"

Ay, the ball is flying,
    The lads play heart and soul;
The goal stands up, the keeper
    Stands up to keep the goal.   15

"Is my girl happy,
    That I thought hard to leave,

And has she tired of weeping
    As she lies down at eve?"   20

Ay, she lies down lightly,
    She lies not down to weep:
Your girl is well contented.
    Be still, my lad, and sleep.

"Is my friend hearty,   25
    Now I am thin and pine,
And has he found to sleep in
    A better bed than mine?"

Yes, lad, I lie easy,
    I lie as lads would choose;   30
I cheer a dead man's sweetheart,
    Never ask me whose.

A. E. HOUSMAN (1859–1936)

To an Athlete Dying Young   *1896*

The time you won your town the race
We chaired° you through the marketplace;
Man and boy stood cheering by,
And home we brought you shoulder-high.

Today, the road all runners come,   5
Shoulder-high we bring you home,
And set you at your threshold down,
Townsman of a stiller town.

Smart lad, to slip betimes away
From fields where glory does not stay,   10
And early though the laurel° grows
It withers quicker than the rose.

Eyes the shady night has shut
Cannot see the record cut,
And silence sounds no worse than cheers   15
After earth has stopped the ears:

Now you will not swell the rout
Of lads that wore their honors out,
Runners whom renown outran
And the name died before the man.   20

To set, before its echoes fade,
The fleet foot on the sill of shade,

---

2 *chaired:* Carried on the shoulders in triumphal parade.   11 *laurel:* Flowering shrub traditionally used to fashion wreaths of honor.

And hold to the low lintel up
The still-defended challenge-cup.

And round that early-laureled head   25
Will flock to gaze the strengthless dead,
And find unwithered on its curls
The garland briefer than a girl's.

BEN JONSON (1573–1637)

On My First Son   *1603*

Farewell, thou child of my right hand,° and joy.
My sin was too much hope of thee, loved boy;
Seven years thou wert lent to me, and I thee pay,
Exacted by thy fate, on the just day.°   *his birthday*
Oh, could I lose all father° now. For why   *fatherhood* 5
Will man lament the state he should envỳ? —
To have so soon 'scaped world's and flesh's rage,
And, if no other misery, yet age.
Rest in soft peace, and asked, say, "Here doth lie
Ben Jonson his best piece of poetry,"   10
For whose sake henceforth all his vows be such
As what he loves may never like too much.

    1 *child of my right hand:* This phrase translates the Hebrew name "Benjamin," Jonson's son.

BEN JONSON (1573–1637)

To Celia   *1616*

Drink to me only with thine eyes,
    And I will pledge with mine;
Or leave a kiss but in the cup,
    And I'll not ask for wine.
The thirst that from the soul doth rise   5
    Doth ask a drink divine;
But might I of Jove's nectar sup,
    I would not change for thine.

I sent thee late a rosy wreath,
    Not so much honoring thee   10
As giving it a hope that there
    It could not withered be.
But thou thereon didst only breathe,
    And sent'st it back to me;
Since when it grows, and smells, I swear,   15
    Not of itself but thee.

JOHN KEATS (1795–1821)

When I have fears that I may cease to be   *1818*

When I have fears that I may cease to be
    Before my pen has gleaned my teeming brain,
Before high-piled books, in charactery,°   *print*
    Hold like rich garners the full ripened grain;
When I behold, upon the night's starred face,   5
    Huge cloudy symbols of a high romance,
And think that I may never live to trace
    Their shadows, with the magic hand of chance;
And when I feel, fair creature of an hour,
    That I shall never look upon thee more,   10
Never have relish in the faery° power   *magic*
    Of unreflecting love;—then on the shore
Of the wide world I stand alone, and think
Till love and fame to nothingness do sink.

JOHN KEATS (1795–1821)

La Belle Dame sans Merci °   *1819*

O what can ail thee, knight-at-arms,
    Alone and palely loitering?
The sedge has withered from the lake,
    And no birds sing.

O what can ail thee, knight-at-arms,   5
    So haggard and so woe-begone?
The squirrel's granary is full,
    And the harvest's done.

I see a lily on thy brow,
    With anguish moist and fever dew,   10
And on thy cheeks a fading rose
    Fast withereth too.

I met a lady in the meads,
    Full beautiful—a faery's child,
Her hair was long, her foot was light,   15
    And her eyes were wild.

I made a garland for her head,
    And bracelets too, and fragrant zone;°   *belt*
She looked at me as she did love,
    And made sweet moan.   20

I set her on my pacing steed,
    And nothing else saw all day long,

La Belle Dame sans Merci: This title is borrowed from a medieval poem and means "The Beautiful Lady without Mercy."

For sidelong would she bend, and sing
    A faery's song.

She found me roots of relish sweet,   25
    And honey wild, and manna dew,
And sure in language strange she said,
    "I love thee true."

She took me to her elfin grot,
    And there she wept, and sighed full sore,   30
And there I shut her wild wild eyes
    With kisses four.

And there she lullèd me asleep,
    And there I dreamed — Ah! woe betide!
The latest° dream I ever dreamed   *last* 35
    On the cold hill side.

I saw pale kings and princes too,
    Pale warriors, death-pale were they all;
They cried — "La Belle Dame sans Merci
    Hath thee in thrall!"   40

I saw their starved lips in the gloam,
    With horrid warning gapèd wide,
And I awoke and found me here,
    On the cold hill's side.

And this is why I sojourn here,   45
    Alone and palely loitering,
Though the sedge has withered from the lake,
    And no birds sing.

ETHERIDGE KNIGHT (B. 1931)

A Watts Mother Mourns While Boiling Beans   *1973*

The blooming flower of my life is roaming
in the night, and I think surely
that never since he was born
have I been free from fright.
My boy is bold, and his blood   5
grows quickly hot/ even now
he could be crawling in the street
bleeding out his life, likely as not.
Come home, my bold and restless son. — Stop
my heart's yearning! But I must quit   10
this thinking — my husband is coming
and the beans are burning.

PHILIP LARKIN (1922–1985)

This Be the Verse

1974

They fuck you up, your mum and dad.
    They may not mean to, but they do.
They fill you with the faults they had
    And add some extras, just for you.

But they were fucked up in their turn   5
    By fools in old-style hats and coats,
Who half the time were soppy-stern
    And half at one another's throats.

Man hands on misery to man.
    It deepens like a coastal shelf.   10
Get out as early as you can,
    And don't have any kids yourself.

LI-YOUNG LEE (B. 1957)

Eating Together

1986

In the steamer is the trout
seasoned with slivers of ginger,
two sprigs of green onion, and sesame oil.
We shall eat it with rice for lunch,
brothers, sister, my mother who will   5
taste the sweetest meat of the head,
holding it between her fingers
deftly, the way my father did
weeks ago. Then he lay down
to sleep like a snow-covered road   10
winding through pines older than him,
without any travelers, and lonely for no one.

PHILIP LEVINE (B. 1928)

The Simple Truth

1995

I bought a dollar and a half's worth of small red potatoes,
took them home, boiled them in their jackets
and ate them for dinner with a little butter and salt.
Then I walked through the dried fields
on the edge of town. In middle June the light   5
hung on in the dark furrows at my feet,
and in the mountain oaks overhead the birds
were gathering for the night, the jays and mockers
squawking back and forth, the finches still darting

into the dusty light. The woman who sold me   10
the potatoes was from Poland; she was someone
out of my childhood in a pink spangled sweater and sunglasses
praising the perfection of all her fruits and vegetables
at the road-side stand and urging me to taste
even the pale, raw sweet corn trucked all the way,   15
she swore, from New Jersey. "Eat, eat," she said,
"Even if you don't I'll say you did."
                              Some things
you know all your life. They are so simple and true
they must be said without elegance, meter and rhyme,   20
they must be laid on the table beside the salt shaker,
the glass of water, the absence of light gathering
in the shadows of picture frames, they must be
naked and alone, they must stand for themselves.
My friend Henri and I arrived at this together in 1965   25
before I went away, before he began to kill himself,
and the two of us to betray our love. Can you taste
what I'm saying? It is onions or potatoes, a pinch
of simple salt, the wealth of melting butter, it is obvious,
it stays in the back of your throat like a truth   30
you never uttered because the time was always wrong,
it stays there for the rest of your life, unspoken,
made of that dirt we call earth, the metal we call salt,
in a form we have no words for, and you live on it.

HENRY WADSWORTH LONGFELLOW (1807–1882)

Snow-Flakes   *1863*

Out of the bosom of the Air,
    Out of the cloud-folds of her garments shaken,
Over the woodlands brown and bare
    Over the harvest-fields forsaken,
        Silent, and soft, and slow   5
        Descends the snow.

Even as our cloudy fancies take
    Suddenly shape in some divine expression,
Even as the troubled heart doth make
In the white countenance confession,   10
    The troubled sky reveals
    The grief it feels.

This is the poem of the air,
    Slowly in silent syllables recorded;
This is the secret of despair,
    Long in its cloudy bosom hoarded,   15
        Now whispered and revealed
        To wood and field.

AUDRE LORDE (1934–1992)

Hanging Fire

1978

I am fourteen
and my skin has betrayed me
the boy I cannot live without
still sucks his thumb
in secret   5
how come my knees are
always so ashy
what if I die
before morning
and mamma's in the bedroom   10
with the door closed.

I have to learn how to dance
in time for the next party
my room is too small for me
suppose I die before graduation   15
they will sing sad melodies
but finally
tell the truth about me
There is nothing I want to do
and too much   20
that has to be done
and momma's in the bedroom
with the door closed.

Nobody even stops to think
about my side of it   25
I should have been on Math Team
my marks were better than his
why do I have to be
the one
wearing braces   30
I have nothing to wear tomorrow
will I live long enough
to grow up
and momma's in the bedroom
with the door closed.   35

ARCHIBALD MACLEISH (1892–1982)

Ars Poetica

1926

A poem should be palpable and mute
As a globed fruit,

Dumb
As old medallions to the thumb,

Silent as the sleeve-worn stone 5
Of casement ledges where the moss has grown —

A poem should be wordless
As the flight of birds.

A poem should be motionless in time
As the moon climbs, 10

Leaving, as the moon releases
Twig by twig the night-entangled trees,

Leaving, as the moon behind the winter leaves,
Memory by memory the mind —

A poem should be motionless in time 15
As the moon climbs.

A poem should be equal to:
Not true.

For all the history of grief
An empty doorway and a maple leaf. 20

For love
The leaning grasses and two lights above the sea —

A poem should not mean
But be.

CHRISTOPHER MARLOWE (1564–1593)

The Passionate Shepherd to His Love 1599?

Come live with me and be my love,
And we will all the pleasure prove
That valleys, groves, hills, and fields,
Woods, or steepy mountain yields.

And we will sit upon the rocks, 5
Seeing the shepherds feed their flocks,
By shallow rivers to whose falls
Melodious birds sing madrigals.

And I will make thee beds of roses
And a thousand fragrant posies, 10
A cap of flowers, and a kirtle°
Embroidered all with leaves of myrtle;

A gown made of the finest wool
Which from our pretty lambs we pull;
Fair lined slippers for the cold, 15
With buckles of the purest gold;

A belt of straw and ivy buds,
With coral clasps and amber studs:

11 *kirtle:* Dress or skirt.

And if these pleasures may thee move,
Come live with me, and be my love. 20

The shepherd swains shall dance and sing
For thy delight each May morning:
If these delights thy mind may move,
Then live with me and be my love.

HERMAN MELVILLE (1819–1891)

The Maldive Shark 1888

About the Shark, phlegmatical one,
Pale sot of the Maldive sea,
The sleek little pilot-fish, azure and slim,
How alert in attendance be.
From his saw-pit of mouth, from his charnel of maw 5
They have nothing of harm to dread,
But liquidly glide on his ghastly flank
Or before his Gorgonian head;
Or lurk in the port of serrated teeth
In white triple tiers of glittering gates, 10
And there find a haven when peril's abroad,
An asylum in jaws of the Fates!

They are friends; and friendly they guide him to prey,
Yet never partake of the treat—
Eyes and brains to the dotard lethargic and dull, 15
Pale ravener of horrible meat.

JOHN MILTON (1608–1674)

On the Late Massacre in Piedmont° 1655

Avenge, O Lord, thy slaughtered saints, whose bones
        Lie scattered on the Alpine mountains cold;
        Even them who kept thy truth so pure of old,
When all our fathers worshiped stocks and stones,°
Forget not: in thy book record their groans 5
        Who were thy sheep, and in their ancient fold
        Slain by the bloody Piedmontese, that rolled
Mother with infant down the rocks.° Their moans

On the Late Massacre . . . : Milton's protest against the treatment of the Waldenses, members of a Puritan sect living in the Piedmont region of northwest Italy, was not limited to this sonnet. It is thought that he wrote Cromwell's appeals to the duke of Savoy and to others to end the persecution. 4 *When . . . stones:* In Milton's Protestant view, English Catholics had worshiped their stone and wooden statues in the twelfth century, when the Waldensian sect was formed. 5-8 *in thy book . . . rocks:* On Easter Day, 1655, 1,700 members of the Waldensian sect were massacred in Piedmont by the duke of Savoy's forces.

The vales redoubled to the hills, and they
    To heaven. Their martyred blood and ashes sow   10
O'er all the Italian fields, where still doth sway
    The triple Tyrant;° that from these may grow
    A hundredfold, who, having learnt thy way,
    Early may fly the Babylonian woe.°

12 *triple Tyrant:* The Pope, with his three-crowned tiara, has authority on earth and in Heaven and Hell.   14 *Babylonian woe:* The destruction of Babylon, symbol of vice and corruption, at the end of the world (see Rev. 17–18). Protestants interpreted the "Whore of Babylon" as the Roman Catholic Church.

JOHN MILTON (1608–1674)

When I consider how my light is spent   *c. 1655*

When I consider how my light is spent,°
    Ere half my days in this dark world and wide,
    And that one talent° which is death to hide
Lodged with me useless, though my soul more bent
To serve therewith my Maker, and present   5
    My true account, lest He returning chide;
    "Doth God exact day-labor, light denied?"
I fondly° ask. But Patience, to prevent   *foolishly*
That murmur, soon replies, "God doth not need
    Either man's work or His own gifts. Who best   10
    Bear His mild yoke, they serve Him best. His state
Is kingly: thousands at His bidding speed,
    And post o'er land and ocean without rest;
    They also serve who only stand and wait."

1 *how my light is spent:* Milton had been totally blind since 1651.   3 *that one talent:* Refers to Jesus' parable of the talents (units of money), in which a servant entrusted with a talent buries it rather than invests it and is punished on his master's return (Matt. 25:14–30).

N. SCOTT MOMADAY (B. 1934)

The Bear   *1992*

    What ruse of vision,
escarping the wall of leaves,
    rending incision
into countless surfaces,

    would cull and color   5
his somnolence, whose old age
    has outworn valor,
all but the fact of courage?

    Seen, he does not come,
move, but seems forever there,   10

dimensionless, dumb,
in the windless noon's hot glare.

More scarred than others
these years since the trap maimed him,
   pain slants his withers,   15
drawing up the crooked limb.

Then he is gone, whole,
without urgency, from sight,
   as buzzards control,
imperceptibly, their flight.   20

MARIANNE MOORE (1887–1972)

Poetry   1921

I, too, dislike it: there are things that are important beyond all this fiddle.
   Reading it, however, with a perfect contempt for it, one discovers in it
   after all, a place for the genuine.
      Hands that can grasp, eyes
         that can dilate, hair that can rise   5
            if it must, these things are important not because a

high-sounding interpretation can be put upon them but because they are
   useful. When they become so derivative as to become unintelligible,
   the same thing may be said for all of us, that we
      do not admire what   10
         we cannot understand: the bat
            holding on upside down or in quest of something to

eat, elephants pushing, a wild horse taking a roll, a tireless wolf under
   a tree, the immovable critic twitching his skin like a horse that feels a
      flea, the base-
         ball fan, the statistician —   15
            nor is it valid
               to discriminate against "business documents and

school-books"; all these phenomena are important. One must make a
      distinction
however: when dragged into prominence by half poets, the result is
      not poetry,
         nor till the poets among us can be   20
            "literalists of
               the imagination" — above
                  insolence and triviality and can present

for inspection, "imaginary gardens with real toads in them," shall we have
   it. In the meantime, if you demand on the one hand,   25
      the raw material of poetry in
         all its rawness and
            that which is on the other hand
               genuine, you are interested in poetry.

WILFRED OWEN (1893–1918)

Arms and The Boy°   1917

Let the boy try along this bayonet-blade
How cold steel is, and keen with hunger of blood;
Blue with all malice, like a madman's flash;
And thinly drawn with famishing for flesh.

Lend him to stroke these blind, blunt bullet-leads,   5
Which long to nuzzle in the hearts of lads,
Or give him cartridges whose fine zinc teeth
Are sharp with sharpness of grief and death.

For his teeth seem for laughing round an apple.
There lurk no claws behind his fingers supple;   10
And God will grow no talons at his heels,
Nor antlers through the thickness of his curls.

Arms and The Boy: A variation on Virgil's *The Aeneid:* "Of arms and the man I sing."

MARGE PIERCY (B. 1936)

Barbie Doll   1969

This girlchild was born as usual
and presented dolls that did pee-pee
and miniature GE stoves and irons
and wee lipsticks the color of cherry candy.
Then in the magic of puberty, a classmate said: 5
You have a great big nose and fat legs.

She was healthy, tested intelligent,
possessed strong arms and back,
abundant sexual drive and manual dexterity.
She went to and fro apologizing.   10
Everyone saw a fat nose on thick legs.

She was advised to play coy,
exhorted to come on hearty,
exercise, diet, smile and wheedle.
Her good nature wore out   15
like a fan belt.

So she cut off her nose and her legs
and offered them up.
In the casket displayed on satin she lay
with the undertaker's cosmetics painted on,   20
a turned-up putty nose,
dressed in a pink and white nightie.
Doesn't she look pretty? everyone said.
Consummation at last.
To every woman a happy ending.   25

SYLVIA PLATH (1932–1963)

Daddy   1962

You do not do, you do not do
Any more, black shoe
In which I have lived like a foot
For thirty years, poor and white,
Barely daring to breathe or Achoo.   5

Daddy, I have had to kill you.
You died before I had time —
Marble-heavy, a bag full of God,
Ghastly statue with one gray toe
Big as a Frisco seal   10

And a head in the freakish Atlantic
Where it pours bean green over blue
In the waters off beautiful Nauset.°   *Cape Cod inlet*
I used to pray to recover you.
Ach, du.°   *Oh, you*   15

In the German tongue, in the Polish Town°
Scraped flat by the roller
Of wars, wars, wars.
But the name of the town is common.
My Polack friend   20

Says there are a dozen or two.
So I never could tell where you
Put your foot, your root,
I never could talk to you.
The tongue stuck in my jaw.   25

It stuck in a barb wire snare.
Ich, ich, ich, ich,°   *I, I, I, I,*
I could hardly speak.
I thought every German was you.
And the language obscene   30

An engine, an engine
Chuffing me off like a Jew.
A Jew to Dachau, Auschwitz, Belsen.°
I began to talk like a Jew.
I think I may well be a Jew.   35

The snows of the Tyrol, the clear beer of Vienna
Are not very pure or true.
With my gypsy-ancestress and my weird luck
And my Taroc° pack and my Taroc pack

---

16 *Polish Town:* Refers to Otto Plath's birthplace, Granbow.   33 *Dachau . . . Belsen:* Nazi
death camps in World War II.   39 *Taroc:* Or *Tarot,* a pack of cards used to tell fortunes. It is
said to have originated among the early Jewish Cabalists and to have been transmitted to European Gypsies during the Middle Ages.

I may be a bit of a Jew.   40

I have always been scared of *you*,
With your Luftwaffe,° your gobbledygoo.
And your neat mustache
And your Aryan eye, bright blue.
Panzer-man, panzer-man,° O You —   45

Not God but a swastika
So black no sky could squeak through.
Every woman adores a Fascist,
The boot in the face, the brute
Brute heart of a brute like you.   50

You stand at the blackboard, daddy,
In the picture I have of you,
A cleft in your chin instead of your foot
But no less a devil for that, no not
Any less the black man who   55

Bit my pretty red heart in two.
I was ten when they buried you.
At twenty I tried to die
And get back, back, back to you.
I thought even the bones would do.   60

But they pulled me out of the sack,
And they stuck me together with glue.
And then I knew what to do.
I made a model of you,
A man in black with a Meinkampf° look   65

And a love of the rack and the screw.
And I said I do, I do.
So daddy, I'm finally through.
The black telephone's off at the root,
The voices just can't worm through.   70

If I've killed one man, I've killed two —
The vampire who said he was you
And drank my blood for a year,
Seven years, if you want to know.
Daddy, you can lie back now.   75

There's a stake in your fat black heart
And the villagers never liked you.
They are dancing and stamping on you.
They always *knew* it was you.
Daddy, daddy, you bastard, I'm through.   80

---

42 *Luftwaffe:* World War II German air force.   45 *panzer-man:* A member of the panzer division of the German army in World War II, which used armored vehicles and was organized for rapid attack.   65 *Meinkampf:* An allusion to Hitler's autobiography (*My Struggle*).

SYLVIA PLATH (1932–1963)
Metaphors 1960

I'm a riddle in nine syllables,
An elephant, a ponderous house,
A melon strolling on two tendrils.
O red fruit, ivory, fine timbers!
This loaf's big with its yeasty rising.
Money's new-minted in this fat purse.
I'm a means, a stage, a cow in calf.
I've eaten a bag of green apples,
Boarded the train there's no getting off.

EDGAR ALLAN POE (1809–1849)
Alone 1875

From childhood's hour I have not been
As others were — I have not seen
As others saw — I could not bring
My passions from a common spring —
From the same source I have not taken   5
My sorrow — I could not awaken
My heart to joy at the same tone —
And all I lov'd — *I* lov'd alone —
Then — in my childhood — in the dawn
Of a most stormy life — was drawn   10
From ev'ry depth of good and ill
The mystery which binds me still —
From the torrent, or the fountain —
From the red cliff of the mountain —
From the sun that round me roll'd   15
In its autumn tint of gold —
From the lightning in the sky
As it pass'd me flying by —
From the thunder, and the storm —
And the cloud that took the form   20
(When the rest of Heaven was blue)
Of a demon in my view —

ADRIENNE RICH (B. 1929)
Living in Sin 1955

She had thought the studio would keep itself,
no dust upon the furniture of love.
Half heresy, to wish the taps less vocal,
the panes relieved of grime. A plate of pears,

a piano with a Persian shawl, a cat   5
stalking the picturesque amusing mouse
had risen at his urging.
Not that at five each separate stair would writhe
under the milkman's tramp; that morning light
so coldly would delineate the scraps   10
of last night's cheese and three sepulchral bottles;
that on the kitchen shelf among the saucers
a pair of beetle-eyes would fix her own —
envoy from some black village in the mouldings . . .
Meanwhile, he, with a yawn,   15
sounded a dozen notes upon the keyboard,
declared it out of tune, shrugged at the mirror,
rubbed at his beard, went out for cigarettes;
while she, jeered by the minor demons,
pulled back the sheets and made the bed and found   20
a towel to dust the table-top,
and let the coffee-pot boil over on the stove.
By evening she was back in love again,
though not so wholly but throughout the night
she woke sometimes to feel the daylight coming   25
like a relentless milkman up the stairs.

CHRISTINA GEORGINA ROSSETTI (1830–1894)

Some Ladies Dress in Muslin Full and White   *c. 1848*

Some ladies dress in muslin full and white,
Some gentlemen in cloth succinct and black;
Some patronise a dog-cart, some a hack,
    Some think a painted clarence only right.
    Youth is not always such a pleasing sight: 5
Witness a man with tassels on his back;
Or woman in a great-coat like a sack,
    Towering above her sex with horrid height.
If all the world were water fit to drown,
    There are some whom you would not teach to swim,   10
    Rather enjoying if you saw them sink:
    Certain old ladies dressed in girlish pink,
With roses and geraniums on their gown.
    Go to the basin, poke them o'er the rim —

WILLIAM SHAKESPEARE (1564–1616)

Not marble, nor the gilded monuments   *1609*

Not marble, nor the gilded monuments
Of princes, shall outlive this powerful rhyme;
But you shall shine more bright in these conténts

Than unswept stone, besmeared with sluttish time.
When wasteful war shall statues overturn,   5
And broils root out the work of masonry,
Nor Mars his° swords nor war's quick fire shall burn   *possessive of Mars*
The living record of your memory.
'Gainst death and all-oblivious enmity
Shall you pace forth; your praise shall still find room   10
Even in the eyes of all posterity
That wear this world out to the ending doom.
   So, till the judgment that yourself arise,
   You live in this, and dwell in lovers' eyes.

WILLIAM SHAKESPEARE (1564–1616)

That time of year thou mayst in me behold   *1609*

That time of year thou mayst in me behold
When yellow leaves, or none, or few, do hang
Upon those boughs which shake against the cold,
Bare ruined choirs, where late the sweet birds sang.
In me thou see'st the twilight of such day   5
As after sunset fadeth in the west;
Which by and by black night doth take away,
Death's second self,° that seals up all in rest.   *sleep*
In me thou see'st the glowing of such fire,
That on the ashes of his youth doth lie,   10
As the deathbed whereon it must expire,
Consumed with that which it was nourished by.
   This thou perceiv'st, which makes thy love more strong,
   To love that well which thou must leave ere long.

WILLIAM SHAKESPEARE (1564–1616)

When forty winters shall besiege thy brow   *1609*

When forty winters shall besiege thy brow
And dig deep trenches in thy beauty's field,
Thy youth's proud livery, so gazed on now,
Will be a tattered weed,° of small worth held.   *garment*
Then being asked where all thy beauty lies,   5
Where all the treasure of thy lusty days,
To say within thine own deep-sunken eyes
Were an all-eating shame and thriftless praise.
How much more praise deserved thy beauty's use
If thou couldst answer, "This fair child of mine   10
Shall sum my count and make my old excuse,"
Proving his beauty by succession thine.
   This were to be new made when thou art old,
   And see thy blood warm when thou feel'st it cold.

WILLIAM SHAKESPEARE (1564–1616)
When, in disgrace with Fortune and men's eyes   1609

When, in disgrace with Fortune and men's eyes,
I all alone beweep my outcast state,
And trouble deaf heaven with my bootless cries,
And look upon myself and curse my fate,
Wishing me like to one more rich in hope,   5
Featured like him, like him with friends possessed,
Desiring this man's art, and that man's scope,
With what I most enjoy contented least,
Yet in these thoughts myself almost despising,
Haply I think on thee, and then my state,   10
Like to the lark at break of day arising
From sullen earth, sings hymns at heaven's gate;
    For thy sweet love remembered such wealth brings
    That then I scorn to change my state with kings.

PERCY BYSSHE SHELLEY (1792–1822)
Ozymandias°   1818

I met a traveler from an antique land
Who said: Two vast and trunkless legs of stone
Stand in the desert. . . . Near them, on the sand,
Half sunk, a shattered visage lies, whose frown,
And wrinkled lip, and sneer of cold command,   5
Tell that its sculptor well those passions read
Which yet survive, stamped on these lifeless things,
The hand that mocked them, and the heart that fed:
And on the pedestal these words appear:
"My name is Ozymandias, King of Kings: 10
Look on my works, ye Mighty, and despair!"
Nothing beside remains. Round the decay
Of that colossal wreck, boundless and bare
The lone and level sands stretch far away.

Ozymandias: Greek name for Ramses II, pharaoh of Egypt for sixty-seven years during the thirteenth century B.C. His colossal statue lies prostrate in the sands of Luxor. Napoleon's soldiers measured it (56 feet long, ear 3¾ feet long, weight 1,000 tons). Its inscription, according to the Greek historian Diodorus Siculus, was "I am Ozymandias, King of Kings; if anyone wishes to know what I am and where I lie, let him surpass me in some of my exploits."

SIR PHILIP SIDNEY (1554–1586)

Loving in Truth, and Fain in Verse My Love to Show   1591

Loving in truth, and fain in verse my love to show,
That she, dear she, might take some pleasure of my pain,
Pleasure might cause her read, reading might make her know,
Knowledge might pity win, and pity grace obtain,
I sought fit words to paint the blackest face of woe,   5
Studying inventions fine, her wits to entertain,
Oft turning others' leaves, to see if thence would flow
Some fresh and fruitful showers upon my sunburnt brain.
But words came halting forth, wanting Invention's stay;
Invention, Nature's child, fled step-dame° Study's blows;   *stepmother*   10
And others' feet still seemed but strangers in my way.
Thus great with child to speak, and helpless in my throes,
Biting my truant pen, beating myself for spite:
"Fool," said my Muse to me, "look in thy heart and write."

GARY SOTO (B. 1952)

Black Hair   1985

At eight I was brilliant with my body.
In July, that ring of heat
We all jumped through, I sat in the bleachers
Of Romain Playground, in the lengthening
Shade that rose from our dirty feet.   5
The game before us was more than baseball.
It was a figure — Hector Moreno
Quick and hard with turned muscles,
His crouch the one I assumed before an altar
Of worn baseball cards, in my room.   10
I came here because I was Mexican, a stick
Of brown light in love with those
Who could do it — the triple and hard slide,
The gloves eating balls into double plays.
What could I do with 50 pounds, my shyness,   15
My black torch of hair, about to go out?
Father was dead, his face no longer
Hanging over the table or our sleep,
And mother was the terror of mouths
Twisting hurt by butter knives.   20

In the bleachers I was brilliant with my body,
Waving players in and stomping my feet,
Growing sweaty in the presence of white shirts.
I chewed sunflower seeds. I drank water
And bit my arm through the late innings.   25

When Hector lined balls into deep
Center, in my mind I rounded the bases
With him, my face flared, my hair lifting
Beautifully, because we were coming home
To the arms of brown people.   30

WALLACE STEVENS (1879–1955)
The Emperor of Ice-Cream   *1923*

Call the roller of big cigars,
The muscular one, and bid him whip
In kitchen cups concupiscent curds.°
Let the wenches dawdle in such dress
As they are used to wear, and let the boys   5
Bring flowers in last month's newspapers.
Let be be finale of seem.°
The only emperor is the emperor of ice-cream.

Take from the dresser of deal,
Lacking the three glass knobs, that sheet   10
On which she embroidered fantails once
And spread it so as to cover her face.
If her horny feet protrude, they come
To show how cold she is, and dumb.
Let the lamp affix its beam.   15
The only emperor is the emperor of ice-cream.

3 *concupiscent curds:* "The words 'concupiscent curds' have no genealogy; they are merely expressive: at least, I hope they are expressive. They express the concupiscence of life, but, by
contrast with the things in relation in the poem, they express or accentuate life's destitution,
and it is this that gives them something more than a cheap lustre" (Wallace Stevens, *Letters*
[New York: Knopf, 1960], p. 500).   7 *Let . . . seem:* "The true sense of 'Let be be finale of
seem' is let being become the conclusion or denouement of appearing to be: in short, ice
cream is an absolute good. The poem is obviously not about ice cream, but about being as
distinguished from seeming to be" (*Letters,* p. 341).

ALFRED, LORD TENNYSON (1809–1892)
Ulysses °   *1833*

   It little profits that an idle king,
By this still hearth, among these barren crags,
Matched with an agèd wife,° I mete and dole   *Penelope*
Unequal laws unto a savage race,
That hoard, and sleep, and feed, and know not me.   5
   I cannot rest from travel; I will drink
Life to the lees. All times I have enjoyed
Greatly, have suffered greatly, both with those

Ulysses: Ulysses, the hero of Homer's epic poem the *Odyssey,* is presented by Dante in *The Inferno,* XXVI, as restless after his return to Ithaca, and eager for new adventures.

That loved me, and alone; on shore, and when
Through scudding drifts the rainy Hyades°   10
Vexed the dim sea. I am become a name;
For always roaming with a hungry heart
Much have I seen and known—cities of men
And manners, climates, councils, governments,
Myself not least, but honored of them all—   15
And drunk delight of battle with my peers,
Far on the ringing plains of windy Troy.
I am a part of all that I have met;
Yet all experience is an arch wherethrough
Gleams that untraveled world, whose margin fades   20
For ever and for ever when I move.
How dull it is to pause, to make an end,
To rust unburnished, not to shine in use!
As though to breathe were life. Life piled on life
Were all too little, and of one to me   25
Little remains; but every hour is saved
From that eternal silence, something more,
A bringer of new things; and vile it were
For some three suns to store and hoard myself,
And this gray spirit yearning in desire   30
To follow knowledge like a sinking star,
Beyond the utmost bound of human thought.

　　This is my son, mine own Telemachus,
To whom I leave the scepter and the isle—
Well-loved of me, discerning to fulfill   35
This labor, by slow prudence to make mild
A rugged people, and through soft degrees
Subdue them to the useful and the good.
Most blameless is he, centered in the sphere
Of common duties, decent not to fail   40
In offices of tenderness, and pay
Meet adoration to my household gods,
When I am gone. He works his work, I mine.

　　There lies the port; the vessel puffs her sail:
There gloom the dark, broad seas. My mariners,   45
Souls that have toiled, and wrought, and thought with me—
That ever with a frolic welcome took
The thunder and the sunshine, and opposed
Free hearts, free foreheads—you and I are old;
Old age hath yet his honor and his toil.   50
Death closes all; but something ere the end,
Some work of noble note, may yet be done,
Not unbecoming men that strove with Gods.
The lights begin to twinkle from the rocks;
The long day wanes; the slow moon climbs; the deep   55

10 *Hyades:* Five stars in the constellation Taurus, supposed by the ancients to predict rain
when they rose with the sun.

Moans round with many voices. Come, my friends.
'Tis not too late to seek a newer world.
Push off, and sitting well in order smite
The sounding furrows; for my purpose holds
To sail beyond the sunset, and the baths   60
Of all the western stars, until I die.
It may be that the gulfs will wash us down;
It may be we shall touch the Happy Isles,°
And see the great Achilles,° whom we knew.
Though much is taken, much abides; and though   65
We are not now that strength which in old days
Moved earth and heaven, that which we are, we are:
One equal temper of heroic hearts,
Made weak by time and fate, but strong in will
To strive, to seek, to find, and not to yield.   70

63 *Happy Isles:* Elysium, the home after death of heroes and others favored by the gods. It
was thought by the ancients to lie beyond the sunset in the uncharted Atlantic.   64 *Achilles:*
The hero of Homer's *Iliad.*

ROBERT WALLACE (B. 1932)

The Double-Play   *1961*

In his sea lit
distance, the pitcher winding
like a clock about to chime comes down with

the ball, hit
sharply, under the artificial   5
banks of arc-lights, bounds like a vanishing string

over the green
to the shortstop magically
scoops to his right whirling above his invisible

shadows   10
in the dust redirects
its flight to the running poised second baseman

pirouettes
leaping, above the slide, to throw
from mid-air, across the colored tightened interval,   15

to the leaning-
out first baseman ends the dance
drawing it disappearing into his long brown glove

stretches. What
is too swift for deception   20
is final, lost, among the loosened figures

jogging off the field
(the pitcher walks), casual
in the space where the poem has happened.

EDMUND WALLER (1606–1687)

Go, Lovely Rose

1645

Go, lovely rose,
Tell her that wastes her time and me
That now she knows,
When I resemble° her to thee,   compare
How sweet and fair she seems to be.   5

Tell her that's young
And shuns to have her graces spied,
That hadst thou sprung
In deserts where no men abide,
Thou must have uncommended died.   10

Small is the worth
Of beauty from the light retired:
Bid her come forth,
Suffer herself to be desired,
And not blush so to be admired.   15

Then die, that she
The common fate of all things rare
May read in thee,
How small a part of time they share
That are so wondrous sweet and fair.   20

WALT WHITMAN (1819–1892)

One Hour to Madness and Joy

1860

One hour to madness and joy! O furious! O confine me not!
(What is this that frees me so in storms?
What do my shouts amid lightnings and raging winds mean?)

O to drink the mystic deliria deeper than any other man!
O savage and tender achings! (I bequeath them to you my children,   5
I tell them to you, for reasons, O bridegroom and bride.)
O to be yielded to you whoever you are, and you to be yielded to me in
    defiance of the world!
O to return to Paradise! O bashful and feminine!
O to draw you to me, to plant on you for the first time the lips of a
    determin'd man.
O the puzzle, the thrice-tied knot, the deep and dark pool, all untied and   10
    illumin'd!
O to speed where there is space enough and air enough at last!
To be absolv'd from previous ties and conventions, I from mine and you
    from yours!
To find a new unthought-of nonchalance with the best of Nature!
To have the gag remov'd from one's mouth!
To have the feeling to-day or any day I am sufficient as I am.   15

O something unprov'd! something in a trance!
To escape utterly from others' anchors and holds!
To drive free! to love free! to dash reckless and dangerous!
To court destruction with taunts, with invitations!
To ascend, to leap to the heavens of the love indicated to me!   20
To rise thither with my inebriate soul!
To be lost if it must be so!
To feed the remainder of life with one hour of fulness and freedom!
With one brief hour of madness and joy.

WALT WHITMAN (1819–1892)

One's-Self I Sing   *1867*

One's-Self I sing, a simple separate person,
Yet utter the word Democratic, the word En-Masse.

Of physiology from top to toe I sing,
Not physiognomy alone nor brain alone is worthy for the Muse, I say the
       Form complete is worthier far,
The Female equally with the Male I sing.

Of Life immense in passion, pulse, and power,
Cheerful, for freest action formed under the laws divine,
The Modern Man I sing.

WALT WHITMAN (1819–1892)

When I Heard the Learn'd Astronomer   *1865*

When I heard the learn'd astronomer,
When the proofs, the figures, were ranged in columns before me,
When I was shown the charts and diagrams, to add, divide, and measure them,
When I sitting heard the astronomer where he lectured with much applause
       in the lecture-room,
How soon unaccountable I became tired and sick,
Till rising and gliding out I wandered off by myself,
In the mystical moist night-air, and from time to time,
Looked up in perfect silence at the stars.

RICHARD WILBUR (B. 1921)

Love Calls Us to the Things of This World°   *1956*

       The eyes open to a cry of pulleys,°
And spirited from sleep, the astounded soul
Hangs for a moment bodiless and simple

Loves Calls Us . . . : From St. Augustine's *Commentary on the Psalms.* 1 *pulleys:* Grooved
wheels at each end of a laundry line; clothes are hung on the line and advance as the line is
moved.

As false dawn.
              Outside the open window   5
The morning air is all awash with angels.
Some are in bed-sheets, some are in blouses,
Some are in smocks: but truly there they are.
Now they are rising together in calm swells
Of halcyon feeling, filling whatever they wear   10
With the deep joy of their impersonal breathing;
Now they are flying in place, conveying
The terrible speed of their omnipresence, moving
And staying like white water; and now of a sudden
They swoon down into so rapt a quiet   15
That nobody seems to be there.
                   The soul shrinks

             From all that it is about to remember,
From the punctual rape of every blessèd day,
And cries,   20
        "Oh, let there be nothing on earth but laundry,
Nothing but rosy hands in the rising steam
And clear dances done in the sight of heaven."

Yet, as the sun acknowledges
With a warm look the world's hunks and colors,   25
The soul descends once more in bitter love
To accept the waking body, saying now
In a changed voice as the man yawns and rises,

"Bring them down from their ruddy gallows;
Let there be clean linen for the backs of thieves;   30
Let lovers go fresh and sweet to be undone,
And the heaviest nuns walk in a pure floating
Of dark habits,
        keeping their difficult balance."

MILLER WILLIAMS (B. 1930)

Thinking about Bill, Dead of AIDS   *1989*

We did not know the first thing about
how blood surrenders to even the smallest threat
when old allergies turn inside out,

the body rescinding all its normal orders
to all defenders of flesh, betraying the head,   5
pulling its guards back from all its borders.

Thinking of friends afraid to shake your hand,
we think of your hand shaking, your mouth set,
your eyes drained of any reprimand.

Loving, we kissed you, partly to persuade   10
both you and us, seeing what eyes had said,
that we were loving and we were not afraid.

If we had had more, we would have given more.
As it was we stood next to your bed,
stopping, though, to set our smiles at the door.   15

Not because we were less sure at the last.
Only because, not knowing anything yet,
we didn't know what look would hurt you least.

WILLIAM CARLOS WILLIAMS (1883–1963)

Spring and All   *1923*

By the road to the contagious hospital
under the surge of the blue
mottled clouds driven from the
northeast — a cold wind. Beyond, the
waste of broad, muddy fields   5
brown with dried weeds, standing and fallen

patches of standing water
and scattering of tall trees

All along the road the reddish
purplish, forked, upstanding, twiggy   10
stuff of bushes and small trees
with dead, brown leaves under them
leafless vines —

Lifeless in appearance, sluggish
dazed spring approaches —   15

They enter the new world naked,
cold, uncertain of all
save that they enter. All about them
the cold, familiar wind —

Now the grass, tomorrow   20
the stiff curl of wildcarrot leaf
One by one objects are defined —
It quickens: clarity, outline of leaf

But now the stark dignity of
entrance — Still, the profound change   25
has come upon them: rooted, they
grip down and begin to awaken

WILLIAM CARLOS WILLIAMS (1883–1963)

This Is Just to Say

1934

I have eaten
the plums
that were in
the icebox

and which   5
you were probably
saving
for breakfast

Forgive me
they were delicious   10
so sweet
and so cold

WILLIAM WORDSWORTH (1770–1850)

I Wandered Lonely as a Cloud

1807

I wandered lonely as a cloud
That floats on high o'er vales and hills,
When all at once I saw a crowd,
A host, of golden daffodils,
Beside the lake, beneath the trees,   5
Fluttering and dancing in the breeze.

Continuous as the stars that shine
And twinkle on the milky way,
They stretched in never-ending line
Along the margin of a bay;   10
Ten thousand saw I at a glance,
Tossing their heads in sprightly dance.

The waves beside them danced, but they
Outdid the sparkling waves in glee;
A poet could not but be gay,   15
In such a jocund company;
I gazed—and gazed—but little thought
What wealth the show to me had brought:

For oft, when on my couch I lie
In vacant or in pensive mood,   20
They flash upon that inward eye
Which is the bliss of solitude;
And then my heart with pleasure fills,
And dances with the daffodils.

WILLIAM WORDSWORTH (1770–1850)

A Slumber Did My Spirit Seal

1800

A slumber did my spirit seal;
    I had no human fears —
She seemed a thing that could not feel
    The touch of earthly years.

No motion has she now, no force;
    She neither hears nor sees;
Rolled round in earth's diurnal course.
    With rocks, and stones, and trees.

WILLIAM WORDSWORTH (1770–1850)

The Solitary Reaper °

1807

Behold her, single in the field,
Yon solitary Highland lass!
Reaping and singing by herself;
Stop here, or gently pass!
Alone she cuts and binds the grain,   5
And sings a melancholy strain;
O listen! for the vale profound
Is overflowing with the sound.

No nightingale did ever chaunt
More welcome notes to weary bands   10
Of travelers in some shady haunt
Among Arabian sands.
A voice so thrilling ne'er was heard
In springtime from the cuckoo-bird,
Breaking the silence of the seas   15
Among the farthest Hebrides.

Will no one tell me what she sings? —
Perhaps the plaintive numbers flow
For old, unhappy, far-off things,
And battles long ago.   20
Or is it some more humble lay,
Familiar matter of today?
Some natural sorrow, loss, or pain,
That has been, and may be again?

Whate'er the theme, the maiden sang   25
As if her song could have no ending;

The Solitary Reaper: Dorothy Wordsworth (William's sister) writes that the poem was suggested by this sentence in Thomas Wilkinson's *Tour of Scotland:* "Passed a female who was reaping alone; she sung in Erse, as she bended over her sickle; the sweetest human voice I ever heard;
her strains were tenderly melancholy, and felt delicious, long after they were heard no more."

I saw her singing at her work,
And o'er the sickle bending —
I listened, motionless and still;
And, as I mounted up the hill,   30
The music in my heart I bore
Long after it was heard no more.

JAMES WRIGHT (1927–1980)

A Blessing   *1961*

Just off the highway to Rochester, Minnesota,
Twilight bounds softly forth on the grass.
And the eyes of those two Indian ponies
Darken with kindness.
They have come gladly out of the willows   5
To welcome my friend and me.
We step over the barbed wire into the pasture
Where they have been grazing all day, alone.
They ripple tensely, they can hardly contain their happiness
That we have come.   10
They bow shyly as wet swans. They love each other.
There is no loneliness like theirs.
At home once more,
They begin munching the young tufts of spring in the darkness.
I would like to hold the slenderer one in my arms,   15
For she has walked over to me
And nuzzled my left hand.
She is black and white,
Her mane falls wild on her forehead,
And the light breeze moves me to caress her long ear   20
That is delicate as the skin over a girl's wrist.
Suddenly I realize
That if I stepped out of my body I would break
Into blossom.

MITSUYE YAMADA (B. 1923)

A Bedtime Story   *1976*

Once upon a time,
an old Japanese legend
goes as told
by Papa,
an old woman traveled through   5
many small villages
seeking refuge
for the night.

Each door opened
a sliver
in answer to her knock   10
then closed.
Unable to walk
any further
she wearily climbed a hill   15
found a clearing
and there lay down to rest
a few moments to catch
her breath.

The village town below   20
lay asleep except
for a few starlike lights.
Suddenly the clouds opened
and a full moon came into view
over the town.   25

The old woman sat up
turned toward
the village town
and in supplication
called out   30
Thank you people
of the village,
If it had not been for your
kindness
in refusing me a bed   35
for the night
these humble eyes would never
have seen this
memorable sight.

Papa paused, I waited.   40
In the comfort of our
hilltop home in Seattle
overlooking the valley,
I shouted
"That's the *end?*"   45

WILLIAM BUTLER YEATS (1865–1939)

Adam's Curse°   *1903*

We sat together at one summer's end,
That beautiful mild woman, your close friend,
And you and I, and talked of poetry.
I said, "A line will take us hours maybe;

Adam's Curse: After his fall from grace and eviction from Eden, Adam was cursed with hard work, pain, and death.

Yet if it does not seem a moment's thought, 5
Our stitching and unstitching has been naught.
Better go down upon your marrow-bones
And scrub a kitchen pavement, or break stones
Like an old pauper, in all kinds of weather;
For to articulate sweet sounds together 10
Is to work harder than all these, and yet
Be thought an idler by the noisy set
Of banker, schoolmasters, and clergymen
The martyrs call the world!"
                     And thereupon 15
That beautiful mild woman for whose sake
There's many a one shall find out all heartache
On finding that her voice is sweet and low
Replied, "To be born woman is to know —
Although they do not talk of it at school — 20
That we must labor to be beautiful."

I said, "It's certain there is no fine thing
Since Adam's fall but needs much laboring.
There have been lovers who thought love should be
So much compounded of high courtesy 25
That they would sigh and quote with learned looks
Precedents out of beautiful old books;
Yet now it seems an idle trade enough."

We sat grown quiet at the name of love;
We saw the last embers of daylight die, 30
And in the trembling blue-green of the sky
A moon, worn as if it had been a shell
Washed by time's waters as they rose and fell
About the stars and broke in days and years.

I had a thought for no one's but your ears: 35
That you were beautiful, and that I strove
To love you in the old high way of love;
That it had all seemed happy; and yet we'd grown
As weary-hearted as that hollow moon.

WILLIAM BUTLER YEATS (1865–1939)

Crazy Jane Talks with the Bishop 1933

I met the Bishop on the road
And much said he and I.
"Those breasts are flat and fallen now,
Those veins must soon be dry;
Live in a heavenly mansion, 5
Not in some foul sty."

"Fair and foul are near of kin,
And fair needs foul," I cried.
"My friends are gone, but that's a truth

Nor grave nor bed denied,   10
Learned in bodily lowliness
And in the heart's pride.

"A woman can be proud and stiff
When on love intent;
But Love has pitched his mansion in   15
The place of excrement;
For nothing can be sole or whole
That has not been rent."

WILLIAM BUTLER YEATS (1865–1939)
Leda and the Swan °   *1924*

A sudden blow: the great wings beating still
Above the staggering girl, her thighs caressed
By the dark webs, her nape caught in his bill,
He holds her helpless breast upon his breast.

How can those terrified vague fingers push   5
The feathered glory from her loosening thighs?
And how can body, laid in that white rush,
But feel the strange heart beating where it lies?

A shudder in the loins engenders there
The broken wall, the burning roof and tower   10
And Agamemnon dead.
                              Being so caught up,
So mastered by the brute blood of the air,
Did she put on his knowledge with his power
Before the indifferent beak could let her drop?   15

Leda and the Swan: In Greek myth, Zeus in the form of a swan seduced Leda and fathered
Helen of Troy (whose abduction started the Trojan War) and Clytemnestra, Agamemnon's
wife and murderer. Yeats thought of Zeus's appearance to Leda as a type of annunciation,
like the angel appearing to Mary.

WILLIAM BUTLER YEATS (1865–1939)
Sailing to Byzantium °   *1927*

I
That is no country for old men. ° The young
In one another's arms, birds in the trees
— Those dying generations — at their song,
The salmon-falls, the mackerel-crowded seas

Byzantium: Old name for the modern city of Istanbul, capital of the Eastern Roman Empire, ancient artistic and intellectual center. Yeats uses Byzantium as a symbol for "artificial"
(and therefore, deathless) art and beauty, as opposed to the beauty of the natural world,
which is bound to time and death.   1 *That . . . men:* Ireland, part of the time-bound world.

Fish, flesh, or fowl, commend all summer long   5
Whatever is begotten, born and dies.
Caught in that sensual music all neglect
Monuments of unaging intellect.

II
An aged man is but a paltry thing,
A tattered coat upon a stick, unless   10
Soul clap its hands and sing, and louder sing
For every tatter in its mortal dress,
Nor is there singing school but studying
Monuments of its own magnificence;
And therefore I have sailed the seas and come   15
To the holy city of Byzantium.

III
O sages standing in God's holy fire
As in the gold mosaic of a wall,
Come from the holy fire, perne in a gyre,°
And be the singing-masters of my soul.   20
Consume my heart away; sick with desire
And fastened to a dying animal
It knows not what it is; and gather me
Into the artifice of eternity.

IV
Once out of nature I shall never take   25
My bodily form from any natural thing,
But such a form as Grecian goldsmiths make
Of hammered gold and gold enameling
To keep a drowsy Emperor awake;°
Or set upon a golden bough° to sing   30
To lords and ladies of Byzantium
Of what is past, or passing, or to come.

19 *perne in a gyre:* Bobbin making a spiral pattern.   27–29 *such . . . awake:* "I have read somewhere that in the Emperor's palace at Byzantium was a tree made of gold and silver, and artificial birds that sang." [Yeats's note.]   30 *golden bough:* In Greek legend, Aeneas had to pluck a golden bough from a tree in order to descend into Hades. As soon as the bough was plucked, another grew in its place.

WILLIAM BUTLER YEATS (1865–1939)

The Second Coming°   *1921*

Turning and turning in the widening gyre°
The falcon cannot hear the falconer;
Things fall apart; the center cannot hold;

The Second Coming: According to Matthew 24:29–44, Christ will return to earth after a time of tribulation to reward the righteous and establish the millennium of heaven on earth. Yeats saw his troubled time as the end of the Christian era and feared the portents of the new cycle. 1 *gyre:* Widening spiral of a falcon's flight, used by Yeats to describe the cycling of history.

Mere anarchy is loosed upon the world,
The blood-dimmed tide is loosed, and everywhere   5
The ceremony of innocence is drowned;
The best lack all conviction, while the worst
Are full of passionate intensity.

Surely some revelation is at hand;
Surely the Second Coming is at hand.   10
The Second Coming! Hardly are those words out
When a vast image out of *Spiritus Mundi*°   Soul of the world
Troubles my sight: somewhere in sands of the desert
A shape with lion body and the head of a man,
A gaze blank and pitiless as the sun,   15
Is moving its slow thighs, while all about it
Reel shadows of the indignant desert birds.
The darkness drops again; but now I know
That twenty centuries of stony sleep
Were vexed to nightmare by a rocking cradle,   20
And what rough beast, its hour come round at last,
Slouches towards Bethlehem to be born?

DAVID ZIEROTH (B. 1946)

Time over Earth   1993

Above bank after bank of cloud
and the sudden open hole for rock or snow,
his seat partner
wrestles newspaper into a fold,
and in the cockpit the first officer   5
fights ennui and gazes into the round faces
of his instruments as they cast upon him
their evening glow, their eagerness
to serve. The steward from first class
offers comments from the passengers   10
on the delicacy of the flight,
the sureness of the surge, the persuasiveness
of their arc in and out of heaven.

Meanwhile in seat 16A
the view slips   15
into darkness once more,
forcing the eyes back from the vista.
His worries resurface
in this airy world
of alloy and wine, foam seats and hard-eyed   20
understanding focused in the one-brain
of the crew. A beam, he thinks, will soon
pick them up and lead them down,

and they will stay fastened
to this hope.   25

They rush to smell the new city — or the same one
returned to, which he re-enters
unchanged by time over earth; he knew
the thin light reaching into black
had not touched him   30
when he swept through revolving doors
in no less hurry
than other earthling friends.
Now asleep in his bed
his body still floats   35
across space, trying to arrive
on time, not caught
by the trees reaching up
to tear and throw him open.
Motionless under quilt, on pillow,   40
his eyes repeat all he has seen
and feared to see, each breath
hanging out of his body
in the worst kind of silent air.

AN ALBUM OF WORLD LITERATURE

ANNA AKHMATOVA (RUSSIA / 1888–1966)

Born in Russia, Anna Akhmatova was a poet and translator who was regarded as a major modern poet in Russia. Although she was expelled from the Union of Soviet Writers during Stalin's rule, she was reclaimed by her country in the 1960s. Her poetry is characterized by its clarity, precision, and simplicity. Her work is translated in *Complete Poems of Anna Akhmatova* (1990).

Dedication   *1940*

TRANSLATED BY RICHARD MCKANE

Such grief might make the mountains stoop,
reverse the waters where they flow,
but cannot burst these ponderous bolts
that block us from the prison cells
crowded with mortal woe. . . .   5

For some the wind can freshly blow,
for some the sunlight fade at ease,
but we, made partners in our dread,
hear but the grating of the keys,
and heavy-booted soldiers' tread.   10
As if for early mass, we rose
and each day walked the wilderness,
trudging through silent street and square,
to congregate, less live than dead.
The sun declined, the Neva blurred,   15
and hope sang always from afar.
Whose sentence is decreed? . . . That moan,
that sudden spurt of woman's tears,
shows one distinguished from the rest,
as if they'd knocked her to the ground   20
and wrenched the heart out of her breast,
then let her go, reeling, alone.
Where are they now, my nameless friends
from those two years I spent in hell?
What specters mock them now, amid   25
the fury of Siberian snows,
or in the blighted circle of the moon?
To them I cry, Hail and Farewell!

CONNECTIONS TO OTHER SELECTIONS

1. Compare the metaphors of imprisonment in "Dedication" and Faiz
   Ahmed Faiz's "If You Look at the City from Here" (p. 1139).
2. Write an essay on the "sentence" decreed in this poem and in Dickinson's
   "I read my sentence — steadily —" (p. 944).

CLARIBEL ALEGRÍA (EL SALVADOR / B. 1924)

Born in Estelí, Nicaragua, Claribel Alegría moved with her family to El
Salvador within a year of her birth. A 1948 graduate of George Washington
University, she considers herself a Salvadoran, and much of her writing reflects the political upheaval of recent Latin American history. In 1978 she was
awarded the Casa de las Americas Prize for her book *I Survive*. A bilingual edition of her major works, *Flowers from the Volcano*, was published in 1982.

I Am Mirror   *1978*

TRANSLATED BY ELECTA ARENAL AND MARSHA GABRIELA DREYER

Water sparkles
on my skin
and I don't feel it
water streams

down my back   5
I don't feel it
I rub myself with a towel
I pinch myself in the arm
I don't feel
frightened I look at myself in the mirror   10
she also pricks herself
I begin to get dressed
stumbling
from the corners
shouts like lightning bolts   15
tortured eyes
scurrying rats
and teeth shoot forth
although I feel nothing
I wander through the streets: 20
children with dirty faces
ask me for charity
child prostitutes
who are not yet fifteen
the streets are paved with pain   25
tanks that approach
raised bayonets
bodies that fall
weeping
finally I feel my arm   30
I am no longer a phantom
I hurt
therefore I exist
I return to watch the scene:
children who run   35
bleeding
women with panic
in their faces
this time it hurts me less
I pinch myself again   40
and already I feel nothing
I simply reflect
what happens at my side
the tanks
are not tanks   45
nor are the shouts
shouts
I am a blank mirror
that nothing penetrates
my surface   50
is hard
is brilliant
is polished
I became a mirror

and I am fleshless   55
scarcely preserving
a vague memory
of pain.

CONNECTIONS TO OTHER SELECTIONS

1. Compare the ways Alegría uses mirror images to reflect life in El Salvador
    with Plath's concerns in "Mirror" (p. 786).
2. Write an essay comparing the speaker's voice in this poem and that in
    Blake's "London" (p. 762). How do the speakers evoke emotional responses
    to what they describe?

KATERINA ANGHELÁKI-ROOKE (GREECE / B. 1939)

Born in Athens, Katerina Angheláki-Rooke graduated from the University of Geneva in 1962. She has been awarded Ford Foundation and Ful-
bright grants and has taught at the universities of Iowa and Utah as well as
San Francisco State University and Harvard University. Her works include
Wolves and Clouds (1963); *Magdalene the Vast Mammal* (1974); *Counter Love*
(1982), which was reprinted as *Being and Things on Their Own;* and *Wind Dialogue* (1990).

Jealousy   *1990*

TRANSLATED BY RAE DALVEN

On Sundays he goes out with that woman
together they enjoy the rural
landscapes in ruins.
Here they are now, passing in front of the farms;
two dead pigs against the fence   5
stretch their hoofs in the afternoon;
light frost covers the mud
the snows have melted
but the earth is still mute
and alone before it becomes a butterfly.   10
Is their love peace,
is it tyranny?
The sun is a lemon color.
Who is she?
What is her face like?   15
Her breast?
The countryside gluts itself slowly with night
this geography has nothing
exotic; and he

holds the woman with so much passion 20
and they slip as one body into the room.
He removes his shirt
his tormented breast
smells of sweat and fresh air
little by little the dry branches retreat 25
in memory
and the landscape starts anew within them
in full spring.

CONNECTIONS TO OTHER SELECTIONS

1. Compare the speaker's attitude toward desire in "Jealousy" with that of the speaker in Dickinson's "'Heaven'—is what I cannot reach!" (p. 936).
2. In an essay discuss the treatment of love in "Jealousy" and in Olds's "Sex without Love" (p. 740).

FAIZ AHMED FAIZ (PAKISTAN / 1911–1984)

Born in Pakistan, Faiz Ahmed Faiz served in the British Indian Army during World War II. After the war he became a spokesman for Pakistani and Indian rights by editing the *Pakistani Times* and writing poetry in Urdu. Faiz served several jail sentences for his political activism, spending a considerable amount of time in solitary confinement. His poetry is widely known in India and the subcontinent; a translation of some is available as *Poems by Faiz* (1971).

If You Look at the City from Here 1971

TRANSLATED BY NAOMI LAZARD

If you look at the city from here
you see it is laid out in concentric circles,
each circle surrounded by a wall
        exactly like a prison.
Each street is a dog-run for prisoners, 5
no milestones, no destinations, no way out.

If anyone moves too quickly you wonder
why he hasn't been stopped by a shout.
If someone raises his arm
you expect to hear the jangling of chains. 10

If you look at the city from here
there is no one with dignity,
no one fully in control of his senses.

Every young man bears the brand of a criminal,
every young woman the emblem of a slave.   15

You cannot tell whether you see
            a group of revelers or mourners
in the shadows dancing around the distant lamps,
and from here you cannot tell
whether the color streaming down the walls   20
is that of blood or roses.

CONNECTIONS TO OTHER SELECTIONS

1. Compare the treatment of the city in this poem and in Blake's "London" (p. 762).
2. Write an essay on the meaning of confinement in Faiz's poem and in Rilke's "The Panther" (p. 767).

XU GANG (CHINA / B. 1945)

Born in Shanghai, China, Xu Gang served in the army after being drafted in 1962 and began writing poetry in support of the Cultural Revolution. However, after graduating from Beijing University in 1974, he questioned the principles and brutally disruptive consequences of the Cultural Revolution, a disillusionment suggested by "Red Azalea on the Cliff." His collections of poems include *The Flower of Rain, Songs for the Far Away,* and *One Hundred Lyrics.*

Red Azalea on the Cliff   *1982*

TRANSLATED BY FANG DAI, DENNIS DING, AND EDWARD MORIN

Red azalea, smiling
From the cliffside at me,
You make my heart shudder with fear!
A body could smash and bones splinter in the canyon—
Beauty, always looking on at disaster.   5

But red azalea on the cliff,
That you comb your twigs even in a mountain gale
Calms me down a bit.
Of course you're not wilfully courting danger,
Nor are you at ease with whatever happens to you.   10
You're merely telling me: beauty is nature.

Would anyone like to pick a flower
To give to his love
Or pin to his own lapel?
On the cliff there is no road   15
And no azalea grows where there is a road.

If someone actually reached that azalea,
Then an azalea would surely bloom in his heart.

Red azalea on the cliff,
You smile like the Yellow Mountains,   20
Whose sweetness encloses slyness,
Whose intimacy embraces distance.
You remind us all of our first love.
Sometimes the past years look
Just like the azalea on the cliff.   25

MAY 1982
Yellow Mountain
Revised at Hangzhou

CONNECTIONS TO OTHER SELECTIONS

1. Compare the significance of the flower in "Red Azalea on the Cliff" with
   that of the flower in Blake's "The Sick Rose" (p. 807).
2. In an essay explain how beauty is associated with danger in Xu Gang's
   poem and in Keats's "La Belle Dame sans Merci" (p. 1103).

PABLO NERUDA (CHILE / 1904–1973)

Born in Chile, Pablo Neruda insisted all his life on the connection between poetry and politics. He was an activist and a Chilean diplomat in a
number of countries during the 1920s and 1930s and remained politically
active until his death. Neruda was regarded as a great and influential poet
(he was awarded the Nobel Prize in 1971) whose poetry ranged from specific
political issues to the yearnings of romantic love. Among his many works
are *Twenty Love Poems and a Song of Despair* (1924), *Residence on Earth* (three
series, 1925–45), *Spain in the Heart* (1937), *The Captain's Verses* (1952), and
Memorial of Isla Negra (1964).

Sweetness, Always   *1958*

TRANSLATED BY ALASTAIR REID

Why such harsh machinery?
Why, to write down the stuff
and people of every day,
must poems be dressed up in gold,
in old and fearful stone?   5
I want verses of felt or feather
which scarcely weigh, mild verses
with the intimacy of beds
where people have loved and dreamed.

I want poems stained
by hands and everydayness.

Verses of pastry which melt
into milk and sugar in the mouth,
air and water to drink,
the bites and kisses of love.
I long for eatable sonnets,
poems of honey and flour.

Vanity keeps prodding us
to lift ourselves skyward
or to make deep and useless
tunnels underground.
So we forget the joyous
love-needs of our bodies.
We forget about pastries.
We are not feeding the world.

In Madras a long time since,
I saw a sugary pyramid,
a tower of confectionery —
one level after another,
and in the construction, rubies,
and other blushing delights,
medieval and yellow.

Someone dirtied his hands
to cook up so much sweetness.

Brother poets from here
and there, from earth and sky,
from Medellín, from Veracruz,
Abyssinia, Antofagasta,
do you know the recipe for honeycombs?

Let's forget all about that stone.

Let your poetry fill up
the equinoctial pastry shop
our mouths long to devour —
all the children's mouths
and the poor adults' also.
Don't go on without seeing,
relishing, understanding
all these hearts of sugar.

Don't be afraid of sweetness.

With us or without us,
sweetness will go on living
and is infinitely alive,
forever being revived,
for it's in a man's mouth,
whether he's eating or singing,
that sweetness has its place.

10

15

20

25

30

35

40

45

50

55

CONNECTIONS TO OTHER SELECTIONS

1. Compare the view of life offered in this poem with that in Frost's "Birches" (p. 986).
2. Write an essay that discusses Kinnell's "Blackberry Eating" (p. 832) and Chasin's "The Word *Plum*" (p. 851) as the sort of "eatable" poetry the speaker calls for in this poem.

OCTAVIO PAZ (MEXICO / 1914–1998)

Born in Mexico City, Octavio Paz studied at the National Autonomous University and in 1943 helped found one of Mexico's most important literary reviews, the *Prodigal Son*. He served in the Mexican diplomatic corps in Paris, New Delhi, and New York. Much of Paz's poetry reflects Hispanic traditions and European modernism as well as Buddhism. In 1990 he received the Nobel Prize for Literature. Paz's major works include *Sun Stone* (1958), *The Violent Season* (1958), *Salamander* (1962), *Blanco* (1966), *Eastern Rampart* (1968), *Renga* (1971), and *Collected Poems, 1957–1987* (1987).

The Street   1963

A long silent street.
I walk in blackness and I stumble and fall
and rise, and I walk blind, my feet
stepping on silent stones and dry leaves.
Someone behind me also stepping on stones, leaves: 5
if I slow down, he slows;
if I run, he runs. I turn: nobody.
Everything dark and doorless.
Turning and turning among these corners
which lead forever to the street   10
where nobody waits for, nobody follows me,
where I pursue a man who stumbles
and rises and says when he sees me: nobody.

CONNECTIONS TO OTHER SELECTIONS

1. How does the speaker's anxiety in this poem compare with that in Frost's "Acquainted with the Night" (p. 798)?
2. Write an essay comparing the tone of this poem and that of Hughes's "Lenox Avenue: Midnight" (p. 1022).

INDIRA SANT (INDIA / B. 1914)

Born in Pune in the state of Maharashtra, India, Indira Sant began her career as a teacher and a writer of children's fiction. In the 1950s she focused her talent on writing feminist poetry that sympathetically described the hardships endured by Indian mothers, wives, and daughters.

Her work has not been widely translated, but the following poem appeared in the journal *Daedalus*.

Household Fires   1989

TRANSLATED BY VINAY DHARWADKER

The daughter's job: without a murmur
to do the chores piling up around the house
until she leaves for work,
to pay her younger brother's fees,
to buy her sister ribbons,   5
to get her father's spectacles changed.
To take the others to the movies on holidays,
to keep back a little and hand over the rest
on payday.

The son's job: fresh savory snacks   10
for the whole household to eat:
to bring back the clothes from the washerman,
to clean and put away the bicycle,
to sing out of key while packing his father's lunch
at the stroke of the hour,   15
to open the door sulkily
whenever someone comes home from the movies,
to wrinkle his brow
when he puts out his hand for money
and is asked instead, "How much? For what?"   20

The younger daughter's job:
to savor the joys of shyness,
to shrink back minute by minute.
The younger son's job:
to choke all the while, grow up slowly   25
in states of wet and dry.

Four children learning in her fold,
her body drained by hardship,
what's left of her? A mass of tatters,
five tongues of flame   30
licking and licking at her on every side,
fanning and fanning the fire in her eyes
till her mind boils over,
gets burned.

CONNECTIONS TO OTHER SELECTIONS

1. Implicit in this poem is the father's presence. Compare the treatment of the father in "Household Fires" and Plath's "Daddy" (p. 1113).

2. Write an essay that compares the life described in this poem with Divakaruni's "Indian Movie, New Jersey" (p. 819).

WOLE SOYINKA (NIGERIA / B. 1934)

Born Oluwole Akinwande Soyinka, in the western Nigerian town of Akinwande, Wole Soyinka has embodied in his life and art the contradictions and tensions that can often seem inevitable for the European-educated, English-speaking African writers. Although he has written and published novels and poetry (the following poem is from *A Shuttle in the Crypt* [1972]), Soyinka is most renowned as a playwright whose work embodies his concerns as a political reformer and social critic. His many plays include *The Lion and the Jewel* (1959), *The Strong Bond* (1963), and *Death of the King's Horseman* (1976). His autobiography *The Man Died* (1973) records his experiences as a political prisoner in Nigeria. In 1986 he was awarded the Nobel Prize for Literature.

Future Plans   1972

The meeting is called
To odium: Forgers, framers
Fabricators Inter-
national. Chairman,
A dark horse, a circus nag turned blinkered sprinter   5

Mach Three°
We rate him — one for the Knife°
Two for 'iavelli,° Three —
Breaking speed
Of the truth barrier by a swooping detention decree   10
Projects in view:
Mao Tse Tung° in league
With Chiang Kai. Nkrumah°
Makes a secret
Pact with Verwood, sworn by Hastings Banda.°   15
Proven: Arafat°
In flagrante cum
Golda Meir. Castro° drunk
With Richard Nixon°
Contraceptives stacked beneath the papal bunk . . .   20
           . . . and more to come

6 *Mach Three:* An air speed of three times the speed of sound.   7 *Knife:* Mack the Knife, an unsavory character from *The Threepenny Opera* (1933), by Bertolt Brecht and Kurt Weill. 8 *'iavelli:* Niccolò Machiavelli (1469–1527), an Italian political theorist who described ruthless strategies for gaining power in *The Prince* (1532).   12 *Mao Tse Tung:* Mao Tse-tung (1893–1975), Chinese Communist leader.   13 *Chiang Kai, Nkrumah:* Chiang Kai-shek (1887–1975), Chinese Nationalist leader exiled in Taiwan by Mao Tse-tung; Kwame Nkrumah (1909–1972), first president of Ghana.   15 *Verwood, Hastings Banda:* Hendrick Verwoerd (1901–1966), former prime minister of South Africa, assassinated in 1966; Hastings Banda (b. 1905), African political leader and first president of Malawi.   16 *Arafat:* Yasir Arafat (b. 1929), Palestinian leader.   18 *Golda Meir, Castro:* Golda Meir (1898–1978), former prime minister of Israel; Fidel Castro (b. 1927), Cuban premier since 1959.   19 *Richard Nixon* (1913–1994): Former U.S. president forced to resign in 1974 due to political scandal.

CONNECTIONS TO OTHER SELECTIONS

1. Discuss the political satire in "Future Plans" and in Fearing's "AD" (p. 803).
2. Write an essay on whether the leaders alluded to in "Future Plans" are manifestations of the type of leader described in Thomas's "The Hand That Signed the Paper" (p. 781).

WISLAWA SZYMBORSKA (POLAND / B. 1923)

Born in Poland, Wislawa Szymborska has lived in Cracow since the age of eight. She steadfastly refuses to reveal biographical details of her life, insisting that her poems should speak for themselves. With the exception of *Sounds, Feelings, Thoughts: Seventy Poems by Wislawa Szymborska* (1981), translated and introduced by Magnus J. Krynski and Robert A. Maguire, and *View with a Grain of Sand: Selected Poems* (1995), translated by Stanislaw Barańczak and Clare Cavanagh, only some of Szymborska's poems have been translated into English. Three of her later poetry collections — as yet untranslated — are *There But for the Grace* (1972), *A Great Number* (1976), and *The People of the Bridge* (1986). She was awarded the Nobel Prize in Literature in 1996.

End and Beginning   *1993*

TRANSLATED BY JOSEPH BRODSKY

After each war
somebody has to clear up
put things in order
by itself it won't happen.

Somebody's got to push   5
rubble to the highway shoulder
making way
for the carts filled up with corpses.

Someone might trudge
through muck and ashes,   10
sofa springs,
splintered glass
and blood-soaked rugs.

Somebody has to haul
beams for propping a wall,   15
another put glass in a window
and hang the door on hinges.

This is not photogenic
and takes years.

All the cameras have left already   20
for another war.

Bridges are needed
also new railroad stations.
Tatters turn into sleeves
for rolling up.   25

Somebody, broom in hand,
still recalls how it was,
Someone whose head was not
torn away listens nodding.
But nearby already   30
begin to bustle those
who'll need persuasion.

Somebody still at times
digs up from under the bushes
some rusty quibble   35
to add it to burning refuse.

Those who knew
what this was all about
must yield to those
who know little   40
or less than little
essentially nothing.

In the grass that has covered
effects in causes
somebody must recline,   45
a stalk of rye in the teeth,
ogling the clouds.

CONNECTIONS TO OTHER SELECTIONS

1. Discuss the treatment of war in this poem and in Arnold's "Dover Beach" (p. 757).
2. Write an essay comparing the themes of this poem and Levertov's "Gathered at the River" (p. 907).

TOMAS TRANSTROMER (SWEDEN / B. 1931)

Born in Stockholm, Sweden, Tomas Transtromer's work is translated more than any other contemporary Scandinavian poet's. He has worked as a psychologist with juvenile offenders and handicapped persons. His collections of poetry include *Night Vision* (1971), *Windows and Stones: Selected Poems* (1972), *Truth Barriers* (1978), and *Selected Poems* (1981). Among his awards are the Petrarch Prize (1981) and a lifetime subsidy from the government of Sweden.

April and Silence

1991

TRANSLATED BY ROBIN FULTON

Spring lies desolate.
The velvet-dark ditch
crawls by my side
without reflections.

The only thing that shines   5
is yellow flowers.

I am carried in my shadow
like a violin
in its black box.

The only thing I want to say   10
glitters out of reach
like the silver
in a pawnbroker's.

CONNECTIONS TO OTHER SELECTIONS

1. Discuss the description of spring in this poem and in Williams's "Spring and All" (p. 1126).

2. In an essay explain how the dictions used in "April and Silence" and Espada's "Latin Night at the Pawnshop" (p. 726) contribute to the poems' meanings and tone.

AN ALBUM OF CONTEMPORARY POEMS

ELIZABETH ALEXANDER (B. 1962)

Born in New York City, Elizabeth Alexander has taught at the University of Chicago and Yale University. She has published two collections of poetry: *The Venus Hottentot* (1990) and *Body of Life* (1996).

Harlem Birthday Party

1996

When my grandfather turned ninety we had a party
in a restaurant in Harlem called Copeland's.
Harlem restaurants are always dim to dark and this
was no exception. Daddy would have gone downtown

but Baba, as we called him, wanted to stay   5
in the neighborhood, and this place was "swanky."
We picked him up in his house on Hamilton Terrace.
His wife, "poor Minnette," had Alzheimer's disease
and thought Hordgie, who was not dead, was dead. She kept
cluck-clucking, "Poor Hordgie," and filling with tears.   10
They had organized a block watch on Hamilton
Terrace, which I was glad of; I worried always
about old people getting mugged; I was afraid
of getting old myself and knocked down in the street;
I was afraid it would happen to my grandfather.   15

My father moves fast always but in Harlem
something clicks into his walk which I love watching.
We argued about taking a car, about parking;
in the end some walked, some drove, and the restaurant
parked the car for us. They treated my grandfather   20
like a Pope or like Duke Ellington. We ate salad,
fried chicken, mashed potatoes, broccoli, chocolate
cake, and Gustavo, who was then my boyfriend, cut Minnette's
meat for her and that became one of the things I would cite
forever when people asked me, How did you know   25
you wanted to marry him? I remember looking
at all the people at the party I had never seen,
and thinking, My grandfather has a whole life
we know nothing about, like at his funeral,
two years later, when a dreadlocked man about my age   30
went on and on about coming to Harlem
from Jamaica, they all said, talk to Mister Alexander, and they talked, and my grandfather scolded,
advised, and today the young brother owns a patty stand
in Brooklyn. Who ever knew this young man, or all the rest?   35

The star appearance at Copeland's, besides my father, was
my grandfather's wife's cousin, Jane Tillman Irving,
who broadcast on WCBS all-news radio.
What is a Harlem birthday party without a star?
What is a black family without someone   40
who's related to someone else who is a little
bit famous, if only to other black people?

And then goodbye, and then goodbye, and back
to New Haven, Washington, and Philadelphia,
where I lived with Gustavo. We walked downtown   45
after the party to Macy's to get feather pillows
on sale, and then we took Amtrak home. I cannot think
about this party without thinking how glad I am
we had it, that he lived long and healthy, that two years
later he was gone. He was born in Jamaica,   50
West Indies, and he died in Harlem, New York.

CONNECTIONS TO OTHER SELECTIONS

1. Compare the speaker's tone in this poem with that in Harper's "Grandfather" (p. 1095).
2. Write an essay that compares the grandfather's identity in "Harlem Birthday Party" with the man described in Holman's "Mr. Z" (p. 1098).

CORNELIUS EADY (B. 1954)

Cornelius Eady, born in Rochester, New York, has taught poetry at several colleges and universities; he is currently director of the Poetry Center at the State University of New York at Stony Brook. The recipient of many fellowships and awards, he has published five books of poetry including *Victims of the Latest Dance Craze* (1986) and *The Gathering of My Name* (1991).

The Supremes   *1991*

We were born to be gray. We went to school,
Sat in rows, ate white bread,
Looked at the floor a lot. In the back
Of our small heads

A long scream. We did what we could,   5
And all we could do was
Turn on each other. How the fat kids suffered!
Not even being jolly could save them.

And then there were the anal retentives,
The terrified brown-noses, the desperately   10
Athletic or popular. This, of course,
Was training. At home

Our parents shook their heads and waited.
We learned of the industrial revolution,
The sectioning of the clock into pie slices.   15
We drank cokes and twiddled our thumbs. In the
Back of our minds

A long scream. We snapped butts in the showers,
Froze out shy girls on the dance floor,
Pin-pointed flaws like radar.   20
Slowly we understood: this was to be the world.

We were born insurance salesmen and secretaries,
Housewives and short order cooks,
Stock room boys and repairmen,
And it wouldn't be a bad life, they promised,   25
In a tone of voice that would force some of us
To reach in self-defense for wigs,
Lipstick,

Sequins.

CONNECTIONS TO OTHER SELECTIONS

1. Discuss the speakers' memories of school in "The Supremes" and in Judy Page Heitzman's "The Schoolroom on the Second Floor of the Knitting Mill" (p. 1158).
2. In an essay compare the themes of "The Supremes" and Dickinson's "From all the Jails the Boys and Girls" (p. 951).

MARTÍN ESPADA (B. 1957)

Martín Espada was born in Brooklyn, New York. He has worked as a tenant lawyer in Boston and now teaches in the English Department at the University of Massachusetts at Amherst. He has been awarded several fellowships including two from the National Endowment for the Arts. His books of poetry include *Rebellion Is the Circle of a Lover's Hand* (1990), *City of Coughing and Dead Radiators* (1993), and *Imagine the Angels of Bread* (1996).

Coca-Cola and Coco Frío   1993

On his first visit to Puerto Rico,
island of family folklore,
the fat boy wandered
from table to table
with his mouth open.   5
At every table, some great-aunt
would steer him with cool spotted hands
to a glass of Coca-Cola.
One even sang to him, in all the English
she could remember, a Coca-Cola jingle   10
from the forties. He drank obediently, though
he was bored with this potion, familiar
from soda fountains in Brooklyn.

Then, at a roadside stand off the beach, the fat boy
opened his mouth to coco frío, a coconut   15
chilled, then scalped by a machete
so that a straw could inhale the clear milk.
The boy tilted the green shell overhead
and drooled coconut milk down his chin;
suddenly, Puerto Rico was not Coca-Cola   20
or Brooklyn, and neither was he.

For years afterward, the boy marveled at an island
where the people drank Coca-Cola
and sang jingles from World War II
in a language they did not speak,   25
while so many coconuts in the trees
sagged heavy with milk, swollen
and unsuckled.

1. Compare what the boy in this poem discovers about Puerto Rico with what the speaker learns in Hughes's "Theme for English B" (p. 1027).
2. Write an essay discussing the images used to describe Puerto Rico and the United States in this poem and in Laviera's "AmeRícan" (p. 918).

DEBORAH GARRISON (B. 1965)

Raised in Ann Arbor, Michigan, Deborah Garrison graduated from Brown University and currently lives in New York City, where she works on the editorial staff of *The New Yorker*. She has not published a collection of poems to date, but her poetry appears regularly in *The New Yorker*.

She Was Waiting to Be Told   *1990*

For you she learned to wear a short black slip
and red lipstick,
how to order a glass of red wine
and finish it. She learned to reach out
as if to touch your arm and then not   5
touch it, changing the subject
Didn't you think, she'd begin, or
Weren't you sorry. . . .

To call your best friends
by their schoolboy names   10
and give them kisses good-bye,
to turn her head away when they say
Your wife! So your confidence grows.
She doesn't ask what you want
because she knows.   15

Isn't that what you think?

When actually she was only waiting
to be told *Take off your dress* —
to be stunned, and then do this,
never rehearsed, but perfectly obvious: 20
in one motion up, over, and gone,
the X of her arms crossing and uncrossing,
her face flashing away from you in the fabric
so that you couldn't say if she was
appearing or disappearing.   25

1. Write an essay comparing the women in Garrison's "She Was Waiting to Be Told" and Keats's "La Belle Dame sans Merci" (p. 1103).

2. Discuss the relationship between the man and woman in Garrison's poem and the lovers in Wilbur's "A Late Aubade" (p. 732).

DONALD HALL (B. 1928)

Born in New Haven, Connecticut, Donald Hall taught at the University of Michigan and for years has made his living in New Hampshire as a freelance writer of numerous books of poetry as well as literary criticism, essays, and children's books. His collections of poems include *The One Day* (1988), winner of the National Book Critics Award, *The Museum of Clear Ideas* (1993), and *Without* (1998).

Letter with No Address   1996

Your daffodils rose up
and collapsed in their yellow
bodies on the hillside
garden above the bricks
you laid out in sand, squatting   5
with pants pegged and face
masked like a beekeeper's
against the black flies.
Buttercups circle the planks
of the old wellhead   10
this May while your silken
gardener's body withers or moulds
in the Proctor graveyard.
I drive and talk to you crying
and come back to this house   15
to talk to your photographs.

There's news to tell you:
Maggie Fisher's pregnant.
I carried myself like an egg
at Abigail's birthday party   20
a week after you died,
as three-year-olds bounced
uproarious on a mattress.
Joyce and I met for lunch
at the mall and strolled weepily   25
through Sears and B. Dalton.

Today it's four weeks
since you lay on our painted bed
and I closed your eyes.
Yesterday I cut irises to set   30
in a pitcher on your grave;

today I brought a carafe
to fill it with fresh water.
I remember the bone-pain,
vomiting, and delirium. I remember   35
the pond afternoons.

          My routine
is established: coffee;
the *Globe;* breakfast;
writing you this letter   40
at my desk. When I go to bed
to sleep after baseball,
Gus follows me into the bedroom
as he used to follow us.
Most of the time he flops   45
down in the parlor
with his head on his paws.

Once a week I drive to Tilton
to see Dick and Nan.
Nan doesn't understand much   50
but she knows you're dead;
I feel her fretting. The tune
of Dick and me talking
seems to console her.

          You know now   55
whether the soul survives death.
Or you don't. When you were dying
you said you didn't fear
punishment. We never dared
to speak of Paradise.   60

At five a.m., when I walk outside,
mist lies thick on hayfields.
By eight, the air is clear,
cool, sunny with the pale yellow
light of mid-May. Kearsarge   65
rises huge and distinct,
each birch and balsam visible.
To the west the waters
of Eagle Pond waver
and flash through popples just   70
leafing out.

          Always the weather,
writing its book of the world,
returns you to me.
Ordinary days were best,   75
when we worked over poems
in our separate rooms.
I remember watching you gaze

out the January window
into the garden of snow
and ice, your face rapt
as you imagined burgundy lilies.

Your presence in this house
is almost as enormous
and painful as your absence.
Driving home from Tilton,
I remember how you cherished
that vista with its center
the red door of a farmhouse
against green fields.
Are you past pity?
If you have consciousness now,
if something I can call
"you" has something
like "consciousness," I doubt
you remember the last days.
I play them over and over:
I lift your wasted body
onto the commode, your arms
looped around my neck, aiming
your bony bottom so that
it will not bruise on a rail.
Faintly you repeat,
"Momma, Momma."

                        You lay
astonishing in the long box
while Alice Ling prayed
and sang "Amazing Grace"
a capella. Three times today
I drove to your grave.
Sometimes, coming back home
to our circular driveway,
I imagine you've returned
before me, bags of groceries upright
in the back of the Saab,
its trunklid delicately raised
as if proposing an encounter,
dog-fashion, with the Honda.

CONNECTIONS TO OTHER SELECTIONS

1. Compare how the speaker copes with grief in "Letter with No Address" with the speaker in Dickinson's "The Bustle in a House" (p. 950).
2. Write an essay on the tone of this poem and Frost's "Home Burial" (p. 980).

MARK HALLIDAY (B. 1949)

Born in Ann Arbor, Michigan, Mark Halliday earned a B.A. and an M.A. from Brown University and a Ph.D. from Brandeis University. A teacher at the University of Pennsylvania, his poems have appeared in a variety of periodicals, including the *Massachusetts Review, Michigan Quarterly Review,* and the *New Republic.* His collection of poems, *Little Star,* was selected by The National Poetry Series for publication in 1987. He has also written a critical study on poet Wallace Stevens titled *Stevens and the Interpersonal* (1991).

Graded Paper   *1991*

On the whole this is quite successful work:
your main argument about the poet's ambivalence —
how he loves the very things he attacks —
is mostly persuasive and always engaging.
At the same time,   5
                    there are spots
where your thinking becomes, for me,
alarmingly opaque, and your syntax seems to jump
backwards through unnecessary hoops,
as on p. 2 where you speak of "precognitive awareness   10
not yet disestablished by the shell that encrusts
each thing that a person actually says"
or at the top of p. 5 where your discussion of
"subverbal undertow miming the subversion of self-belief
woven counter to desire's outreach"   15
leaves me groping for firmer footholds.
(I'd have said it differently,
or rather, said something else.)
And when you say that women "could not fulfill themselves" (p. 6)
"in that era" (only forty years ago, after all!)   20
are you so sure that the situation is so different today?
Also, how does Whitman bluff his way into
your penultimate paragraph? He is the *last* poet
I would have quoted in this context!
What plausible way of behaving   25
does the passage you quote represent? Don't you think
literature should ultimately reveal possibilities for *action?*

Please notice how I've repaired your use of semicolons.

And yet, despite what may seem my cranky response,
I do admire the freshness of   30
your thinking and your style; there is
a vitality here; your sentences thrust themselves forward
with a confidence as impressive as it is cheeky. . . .

You are not
      me, finally,
and though this is an awkward problem, involving
the inescapable fact that you are so young, so young
it is also a delightful provocation.

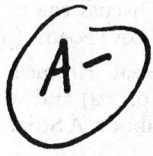

35

CONNECTIONS TO OTHER SELECTIONS

1. Compare the ways in which Halliday reveals the speaker's character in this poem with the strategies used by Browning in "My Last Duchess" (p. 821).

2. Write an essay on the teacher in this poem and the one in Judy Page Heitzman's "The Schoolroom on the Second Floor of the Knitting Mill" (p. 1158). What are the significant similarities and differences between them?

ROBERT HASS (B. 1941)

Born and raised in San Francisco, Robert Hass was educated at St. Mary's College and Stanford University. He has taught at the State University of New York at Buffalo, St. Mary's College, and the University of California at Berkeley. His first collection of poems, *Field Guide* (1973), was awarded the Yale Series of Younger Poets Award; this collection was followed by three more: *Praise* (1978), *Human Wishes* (1989), and *Sun Under Wood* (1996). He has also published a collection of essays, *Twentieth-Century Pleasures* (1984), and been the recipient of the National Book Circle Critics Award for criticism as well as the John D. and Catherine T. MacArthur Fellowship. In 1995 he was named the nation's Poet Laureate to the Library of Congress.

A Story About the Body   *1989*

The young composer, working that summer at an artists' colony, had watched her for a week. She was Japanese, a painter, almost sixty, and he thought he was in love with her. He loved her work, and her work was like the way she moved her body, used her hands, looked at him directly when she made amused and considered answers to his questions. One night, walking back from a concert, they came to her door and she turned to him and said, "I think you would like to have me. I would like that too, but I must tell you that I have had a double mastectomy," and when he didn't understand, "I've lost both my breasts." The radiance that he had carried around in his belly and chest cavity—like music—withered very quickly, and he made himself look at her when he said, "I'm sorry. I don't think I could." He walked back to his own cabin through the pines, and in the morning he found a small blue bowl on the porch outside his door. It looked to be full of rose petals, but he found when he picked it up that the rose petals were on top; the rest of the bowl—she must have swept them from the corners of her studio—was full of dead bees.

CONNECTIONS TO OTHER SELECTIONS

1. Discuss the treatments of love in "A Story About the Body" and Nims's "Love Poem" (p. 693).
2. Read Hulme's remarks "On the Differences between Poetry and Prose" (p. 774) and write an essay on what you think Hulme would have to say about "A Story About the Body."

JUDY PAGE HEITZMAN (B. 1952)

Judy Page Heitzman lives in Marshfield, Massachusetts, and teaches English at Duxbury High School. She has not published a collection of poems to date, but her poetry has appeared in *The New Yorker, Yankee Magazine, Wind, Yarro,* and *Three Rivers Poetry Journal.*

The Schoolroom on the Second Floor of the Knitting Mill   *1991*

While most of us copied letters out of books,
Mrs. Lawrence carved and cleaned her nails.
Now the red and buff cardinals at my back-room window
make me miss her, her room, her hallway,
even the chimney outside   5
that broke up the sky.

In my memory it is afternoon.
Sun streams in through the door
next to the fire escape where we are lined up
getting our coats on to go out to the playground,   10
the tether ball, its towering height, the swings.
She tells me to make sure the line
does not move up over the threshold.
That would be dangerous.
So I stand guard at the door.   15
Somehow it happens
the way things seem to happen when we're not really looking,
or we are looking, just not the right way.
Kids crush up like cattle, pushing me over the line.

Judy is not a good leader is all Mrs. Lawrence says.   20
She says it quietly. Still, everybody hears.
Her arms hang down like sausages.
I hear her every time I fail.

CONNECTIONS TO OTHER SELECTIONS

1. Compare the representations and meanings of being a schoolchild in this poem with those in Dickinson's "From all the Jails the Boys and Girls" (p. 951).

2. Discuss how the past impinges on the present in Heitzman's poem and in Larkin's "This Be The Verse" (p. 1105).

JANE HIRSHFIELD (B. 1953)

Born in New York City, Jane Hirshfield is the author of four books of poetry, most recently *The Lives of the Heart* (1997), and a collection of essays, *Nine Gates: Entering the Mind of Poetry* (1997). She has also edited and co-translated two collections of poetry by women from the past, *Women in Praise of the Sacred: Forty-three Centuries of Spiritual Poetry by Women* (1995) and *The Ink Dark Moon: Poems by Ono no Komachi and Izumi Shikibu, Women of the Ancient Court of Japan* (1990). Hirshfield's awards include the Poetry Center Book Award, the Bay Area Book Reviewers Award, Columbia University's Translation Center Award, and fellowships from the Guggenheim and Rockefeller Foundations.

The Lives of the Heart   *1997*

Are ligneous, muscular, chemical.
Wear birch-colored feathers,
green tunnels of horse-tail reed.
Wear calcified spirals, Fibonnacian° spheres.
Are edible; are glassy; are clay; blue schist.   5
Can be burned as tallow, as coal,
can be skinned for garnets, for shoes.
Cast shadows or light;
shuffle; snort; cry out in passion.
Are salt, are bitter,   10
tear sweet grass with their teeth.
Step silently into blue needle-fall at dawn.
Thrash in the net until hit.
Rise up as cities, as serpentined magma, as maples,
hiss lava-red into the sea.   15
Leave the strange kiss of their bodies
in Burgess Shale. Can be found, can be lost,
can be carried, broken, sung.
Lie dormant until they are opened by ice,
by drought. Go blind in the service of lace.   20

---

4 *Fibonnacian:* An apparent reference to Leonardo Fibonacci (1170-1240), a famous Italian mathematician.

Are starving, are sated, indifferent, curious, mad.
Are stamped out in plastic, in tin.
Are stubborn, are careful, are slipshod,
are strung on the blue backs of flies
on the black backs of cows.   25
Wander the vacant whale-roads, the white thickets
heavy with slaughter.
Wander the fragrant carpets of alpine flowers.
Not one is not held in the arms of the rest, to blossom.
Not one is not given to ecstasy's lions.   30
Not one does not grieve.
Each of them opens and closes, closes and opens
the heavy gate — violent, serene, consenting, suffering it all.

CONNECTIONS TO OTHER SELECTIONS

1. Discuss the use of personification in this poem and Steven's "Schizophrenia" (p. 788).
2. Write an essay that compares the diction and images of "The Lives of the Heart" and Alice Jones's "The Foot" (p. 863).

LINDA HOGAN (B. 1947)

Born in Denver, Colorado, and raised in Oklahoma, Linda Hogan is a member of the Chickasaw tribe. She was educated at the University of Colorado, where she now teaches creative writing. She has been awarded fellowships from the Guggenheim Foundation and the National Endowment for the Arts and has received an American Book Award. In addition to publishing fiction — her novel *Mean Spirit* appeared in 1989 — she has published several volumes of poetry including *Eclipse* (1985), *Seeing through the Sun* (1985), *Savings* (1988), and *The Book of Medicines* (1993).

Hunger   *1993*

Hunger crosses oceans.
It loses its milk teeth.
It sits on the ship and cries.

Thin, afraid,
it fashioned hooks to catch   5
the passing songs of whales so large
the men grew small
as distant, shrinking lands.
They sat on the ship and cried.

Hunger was the fisherman   10
who said dolphins are like women,

we took them from the sea
and had our way
with them.

Hunger knows we have not yet reached   15
the black and raging depths of anything.

It is the old man
who comes in the night

to cast a line
and wait at the luminous shore.   20
He knows the sea is pregnant
with clear fish
and their shallow pools of eggs
and that the ocean has hidden
signs of its own hunger,   25
lost men and boats
and squid that flew
toward churning light.

Hunger lives in the town
whose walls are made of shells   30
white and shining in the moon,
where people live surrounded
by what they've eaten
to forget that hunger
sits on a ship and cries.   35

And it is a kind of hunger
that brings us to love,
to rocking currents of a secret wave
and the body that wants to live beyond itself
like the destitute men   40
who took the shining dolphins from the sea.
They were like women,
they said,
and had their way
with them,   45
wanting to be inside,
to drink
and be held in
the thin, clear milk of the gods.

CONNECTIONS TO OTHER SELECTIONS

1. Write an essay comparing Hogan's definition of hunger with Dickinson's definition of heaven in "'Heaven' — is what I cannot reach!" (p. 936). Which definition do you find more complete and satisfying? Explain why.

2. Discuss the relation between love and hunger in this poem and in Croft's "Home-Baked Bread" (p. 768).

YUSEF KOMUNYAKAA (B. 1947)

Yusef Komunyakaa, born in Bogalusa, Louisiana, a Vietnam veteran, earned an M.F.A. from the University of California and now teaches creative writing and African American studies at Indiana University. Among his awards is a National Endowment for the Arts fellowship. His volumes of poetry include *Copacetic* (1984), *I Apologize for the Eyes in My Head* (1986), *Dien Cai Dau* (1989), and *Magic City* (1992). In 1994 *Neon Vernacular* was awarded a Pulitzer Prize.

Facing It   *1988*

My black face fades,
hiding inside the black granite.
I said I wouldn't,
dammit: No tears.
I'm stone. I'm flesh.   5
My clouded reflection eyes me
like a bird of prey, the profile of night
slanted against morning. I turn
this way — the stone lets me go.
I turn that way — I'm inside   10
the Vietnam Veterans Memorial
again, depending on the light
to make a difference.
I go down the 58,022 names,
half-expecting to find   15
my own in letters like smoke.
I touch the name Andrew Johnson;
I see the booby trap's white flash.
Names shimmer on a woman's blouse
but when she walks away   20
the names stay on the wall.
Brushstrokes flash, a red bird's
wings cutting across my stare.
The sky. A plane in the sky.
A white vet's image floats   25
closer to me, then his pale eyes
look through mine. I'm a window.
He's lost his right arm
inside the stone. In the black mirror
a woman's trying to erase names: 30
No, she's brushing a boy's hair.

CONNECTIONS TO OTHER SELECTIONS

1. Discuss the speakers' attitudes toward war in "Facing It" and Cummings's "next to of course god america i" (p. 805).

2. In an essay compare the treatment of memory and sorrow in "Facing It" and Hall's "Letter with No Address" (p. 1153).

JOAN MURRAY (B. 1945)

Born and raised in New York City, Joan Murray was educated at Hunter College and New York University. She has taught at Lehman College of the City University of New York. Among her awards for poetry are the National Endowment for the Arts and a Pushcart Prize. Her published volumes of poetry include *Egg Tooth* (1975) and *The Same Water* (1990).

Play-By-Play   *1997*

Yaddo°

Would it surprise the young men
playing softball on the hill to hear the women
on the terrace admiring their bodies:
the slim waist of the pitcher, the strength
of the runner's legs, the torso of the catcher   5
rising off his knees to toss the ball back to the mound?
Would it embarrass them
to hear two women, sitting together after dinner,
praising even their futile motions:
the flex of a batter's hips   10
before his missed swing, the wide-spread stride
of a man picked off his base, the intensity
on the new man's face
as he waits on deck and fans the air?

Would it annoy them, the way some women   15
take offense when men caress them with their eyes?
And why should it surprise me that these women,
well past sixty, haven't put aside desire
but sit at ease and in pleasure,
watching the young men move above the rose garden   20
where the marble Naiads
pose and yawn in their fountain?
Who better than these women, with their sweaters
draped across their shoulders, their perspectives
honed from years of lovers, to recognize   25
the beauty that would otherwise
go unnoticed on this hill?

Yaddo: An artist's colony in Saratoga Springs, New York.

And will it compromise their pleasure
if I sit down at their table to listen
to the play-by-play and see it through their eyes? 30

Would it distract the young men if they realized
that three women laughing softly on the terrace
above closed books and half-filled wineglasses
are moving beside them on the field?
Would they want to know how they've been 35
held to the light till some motion or expression
showed the unsuspected loveliness
in a common shape or face?
Wouldn't they have liked to see how they looked
down there, as they stood for a moment at the plate, 40
bathed in the light of perfect expectation,
before their shadows lengthened, before they
walked together up the darkened hill,
so beautiful they would not have
recognized themselves? 45

Connections to Other Selections

1. Compare the voice of the speaker in "Play-By-Play" with that of Acker-man's "A Fine, a Private Place" (p. 734).

2. Write an essay on the speaker's gaze in this poem and Steele's "An Aubade" (p. 761).

Ronald Wallace (b. 1945)

Born in Cedar Rapids, Iowa, Ronald Wallace earned a B.A. at the College of Wooster, and an M.A. and a Ph.D. at the University of Michigan. He has taught in the Department of English at the University of Wisconsin, Madison, since 1972. Among his awards are a Rackham Prize Fellowship and several American Council of Learned Society fellowships. His collections of poems include *People and Dog in the Sun* (1987), *The Makings of Happiness* (1991), and *Time's Fancy* (1994).

Dogs 1997

When I was six years old I hit one with
a baseball bat. An accident, of course,
and broke his jaw. They put that dog to sleep,
a euphemism even then I knew
could not excuse me from the lasting wrath 5

of memory's flagellation. My remorse
could dog me as it would, it wouldn't keep
me from the life sentence that I drew:

For I've been barked at, bitten, nipped, knocked flat,
slobbered over, humped, sprayed, beshat,   10
by spaniel, terrier, retriever, bull, and Dane.
But through the years what's given me most pain
of all the dogs I've been the victim of
are those whose slow eyes gazed at me, in love.

Connections to Other Selections

1. Compare this poem's theme with Updike's "Dog's Death" (p. 673).
2. In an essay discuss the strategies used in this sonnet and Shakespeare's "My mistress' eyes are nothing like the sun" (p. 882) to create emotion in the reader.

DRAMA

28

Reading Drama

READING DRAMA RESPONSIVELY

The publication of a short story, novel, or poem represents for most writers the final step in a long creative process that might have begun with an idea, issue, emotion, or question that demanded expression. *Playwrights* — writers who make plays — may begin a work in the same way as other writers, but rarely are they satisfied with only its publication because most dramatic literature — what we call *plays* — is written to be performed by actors on a stage before an audience. Playwrights typically create a play keeping in mind not only readers but also actors, producers, directors, costumers, designers, technicians, and a theater full of other support staff who have a hand in presenting the play to a live audience.

Drama is literature equipped with arms, legs, tears, laughs, whispers, shouts, and gestures that are alive and immediate. Indeed, the word *drama* derives from the Greek word *dran*, meaning "to do" or "to perform." The text of many plays — the *script* — may come to life fully only when the written words are transformed into a performance. Although there are plays that do not invite production, they are relatively few. Such plays, written to be read rather than performed, are called *closet dramas.* In this kind of work (primarily associated with nineteenth-century English literature), literary art outweighs all other considerations. The majority of playwrights, however, view the written word as the beginning of a larger creation and hope that a producer will deem their scripts worthy of production.

Given that most playwrights intend their works to be performed, it might be argued that reading a play is a poor substitute for seeing it acted on a stage — perhaps something like reading a recipe without having access to the ingredients and a kitchen. This analogy is tempting, but it overlooks the literary dimensions of a script; the words we hear on a stage were written first. Read from a page, these words can feed an imagination in ways that a recipe cannot satisfy a hungry cook. We can fill in a play's missing faces, voices, actions, and settings in much the same way that we imagine these elements in a short story or novel. Like any play director, we are free to include as many ingredients as we have an appetite for.

This imaginative collaboration with the playwright creates a mental world that can be nearly as real and vivid as a live performance. Sometimes readers find that they prefer their own reading of a play to a director's interpretation. Shakespeare's Hamlet, for instance, has been presented as a whining son, but you may read him as a strong prince. Rich plays often accommodate a wide range of imaginative responses to their texts. Reading, then, is an excellent way to appreciate and evaluate a production of a play. Moreover, reading is valuable in its own right because it allows us to enter the playwright's created world even when a theatrical production is unavailable.

Reading a play, however, requires more creative imagining than sitting in an audience watching actors on a stage presenting lines and actions before you. As a reader you become the play's director; you construct an interpretation based on the playwright's use of language, development of character, arrangement of incidents, description of settings, and directions for staging. Keeping track of the playwright's handling of these elements will help you to organize your response to the play. You may experience suspense, fear, horror, sympathy, or humor, but whatever experience a play evokes, ask yourself why you respond to it as you do. You may discover that your assessment of Hamlet's character is different from someone else's, but whether you find him heroic, indecisive, neurotic, or a complex of competing qualities, you'll be better equipped to articulate your interpretation of him if you pay attention to your responses and ask yourself questions as you read. Consider, for example, how his reactions might be similar to or different from your own. How does his language reveal his character? Does his behavior seem justified? How would you play the role yourself? What actor do you think might best play the Hamlet that you have created in your imagination? Why would he or she (women have also played Hamlet onstage) fill the role best?

These kinds of questions (see Questions for Responsive Reading and Writing, p. 1211) can help you to think and talk about your responses to a play. Happily, such questions needn't — and often can't — be fully answered as you read the play. Frequently you must experience the entire play before you can determine how its elements work together. That's why reading a play can be such a satisfying experience. You wouldn't think of asking a live actor onstage to repeat her lines because you didn't quite comprehend their significance, but you can certainly reread a page in a book. Rereading allows you to replay language, characters, and incidents carefully and thoroughly to your own satisfaction.

Trifles

In the following play, Susan Glaspell skillfully draws on many dramatic elements and creates an intense story that is as effective on the page as it is in the theater. Glaspell wrote *Trifles* in 1916 for the Provincetown Players on Cape Cod, in Massachusetts. Their performance of the work helped her develop a reputation as a writer sensitive to feminist issues. The year after *Trifles* was produced, Glaspell transformed the play into a short story titled "A Jury of Her Peers." (A passage from the story appears on p. 1182 for comparison.)

Glaspell's life in the Midwest provided her with the setting for *Trifles*. Born and raised in Davenport, Iowa, she graduated from Drake University in 1899 and then worked for a short time as a reporter on the *Des Moines News,* until her short stories were accepted in magazines such as *Harper's* and *Ladies' Home Journal.* Glaspell moved to the Northeast when she was in her early thirties to continue writing fiction and drama. She published some twenty plays, novels, and more than forty short stories. *Alison's House,* based on Emily Dickinson's life, earned her a Pulitzer Prize for drama in 1931. *Trifles* and "A Jury of Her Peers" remain, however, Glaspell's best-known works.

Glaspell wrote *Trifles* to complete a bill that was to feature several one-act plays by Eugene O'Neill. In *The Road to the Temple* (1926) she recalls how the play came to her as she sat in the theater looking at a bare stage. First, "the stage became a kitchen. . . . Then the door at the back opened, and people all bundled up came in — two or three men. I wasn't sure which, but sure enough about the two women, who hung back, reluctant to enter that kitchen. When I was a newspaper reporter out in Iowa, I was sent downstate to do a murder trial, and I never forgot going to the kitchen of a woman who had been locked up in town."

Trifles is about a murder committed in a midwestern farmhouse, but the play goes beyond the kinds of questions raised by most whodunit stories. The murder is the occasion instead of the focus. The play's major concerns are the moral, social, and psychological aspects of the assumptions and perceptions of the men and women who search for the murderer's motive. Glaspell is finally more interested in the meaning of Mrs. Wright's life than in the details of Mr. Wright's death.

As you read the play keep track of your responses to the characters and note in the margin the moments when Glaspell reveals how men and women respond differently to the evidence before them. What do those moments suggest about the kinds of assumptions these men and women make about themselves and each other? How do their assumptions compare with your own?

Susan Glaspell (1882–1948)

Trifles   *1916*

CHARACTERS

George Henderson, county attorney
Henry Peters, sheriff
Lewis Hale, a neighboring farmer
Mrs. Peters
Mrs. Hale

SCENE: *The kitchen in the now abandoned farmhouse of John Wright, a gloomy kitchen, and left without having been put in order—the walls covered with a faded wall paper. Down right is a door leading to the parlor. On the right wall above this door is a built-in kitchen cupboard with shelves in the upper portion and drawers below. In the rear wall at right, up two steps is a door opening onto stairs leading to the second floor. In the rear wall at left is a door to the shed and from there to the outside. Between these two doors is an old-fashioned black iron stove. Running along the left wall from the shed door is an old iron sink and sink shelf, in which is set a hand pump. Downstage of the sink is an uncurtained window. Near the window is an old wooden rocker. Center stage is an unpainted wooden kitchen table with straight chairs on either side. There is a small chair down right. Unwashed pans under the sink, a loaf of bread outside the breadbox, a dish towel on the table—other signs of incompleted work. At the rear the shed door opens and the Sheriff comes in followed by the County Attorney and Hale. The Sheriff and Hale are men in middle life, the County Attorney is a young man; all are much bundled up and go at once to the stove. They are followed by the two women—the Sheriff's wife, Mrs. Peters, first; she is a slight wiry woman, a thin nervous face. Mrs. Hale is larger and would ordinarily be called more comfortable looking, but she is disturbed now and looks fearfully about as she enters. The women have come in slowly, and stand close together near the door.*

County Attorney *(at stove rubbing his hands):* This feels good. Come up to the fire, ladies.

Mrs. Peters *(after taking a step forward):* I'm not—cold.

Sheriff *(unbuttoning his overcoat and stepping away from the stove to right of table as if to mark the beginning of official business):* Now, Mr. Hale, before we move things about, you explain to Mr. Henderson just what you saw when you came here yesterday morning.

County Attorney *(crossing down to left of the table):* By the way, has anything been moved? Are things just as you left them yesterday?

Sheriff *(looking about):* It's just about the same. When it dropped below zero last night I thought I'd better send Frank out this morning to make a fire for us—*(sits right of center table)* no use getting pneumonia with a big case on, but I told him not to touch anything except the stove—and you know Frank.

County Attorney: Somebody should have been left here yesterday.

Sheriff: Oh—yesterday. When I had to send Frank to Morris Center for that man who went crazy—I want you to know I had my hands full yesterday. I knew you could get back from Omaha by today and as long as I went over everything here myself——

County Attorney: Well, Mr. Hale, tell just what happened when you came here yesterday morning.

Hale (crossing down to above table): Harry and I had started to town with a load of potatoes. We came along the road from my place and as I got here I said, "I'm going to see if I can't get John Wright to go in with me on a party telephone." I spoke to Wright about it once before and he put me off, saying folks talked too much anyway, and all he asked was peace and quiet— I guess you know about how much he talked himself; but I thought maybe if I went to the house and talked about it before his wife, though I said to Harry that I didn't know as what his wife wanted made much difference to John——

County Attorney: Let's talk about that later, Mr. Hale. I do want to talk about that, but tell now just what happened when you got to the house.

Hale: I didn't hear or see anything; I knocked at the door, and still it was all quiet inside. I knew they must be up, it was past eight o'clock. So I knocked again, and I thought I heard somebody say, "Come in." I wasn't sure, I'm not sure yet, but I opened the door—this door *(indicating the door by which the two women are still standing)* and there in that rocker—*(pointing to it)* sat Mrs. Wright. *(They all look at the rocker down left.)*

County Attorney: What—was she doing?

Hale: She was rockin' back and forth. She had her apron in her hand and was kind of—pleating it.

County Attorney: And how did she—look?

Hale: Well, she looked queer.

County Attorney: How do you mean—queer?

Hale: Well, as if she didn't know what she was going to do next. And kind of done up.

County Attorney (takes out notebook and pencil and sits left of center table): How did she seem to feel about your coming?

Hale: Why, I don't think she minded—one way or other. She didn't pay much attention. I said, "How do, Mrs. Wright, it's cold, ain't it?" And she said, "Is it?"—and went on kind of pleating at her apron. Well, I was surprised; she didn't ask me to come up to the stove, or to set down, but just sat there, not even looking at me, so I said, "I want to see John." And then she—laughed. I guess you would call it a laugh. I thought of Harry and the team outside, so I said a little sharp: "Can't I see John?" "No," she says, kind o' dull like. "Ain't he home?" says I. "Yes," says she, "he's home." "Then why can't I see him?" I asked her, out of patience. "'Cause he's dead," says she. "*Dead?*" says I. She just nodded her head, not getting a bit excited, but rockin' back and forth. "Why—where is he?" says I, not knowing what to say. She just pointed upstairs—like that. *(Himself pointing to the room above.)* I started for the stairs, with the idea of going up there. I walked from there to here—then I says, "Why, what did he die of?" "He died of a rope round his neck," says she, and just went on pleatin' at her apron. Well, I went out and called Harry. I thought I might—need help. We went upstairs and there he was lyin'——

County Attorney: I think I'd rather have you go into that upstairs, where you can point it all out. Just go on now with the rest of the story.

Hale: Well, my first thought was to get that rope off. It looked . . . *(stops; his face twitches)* . . . but Harry, he went up to him, and he said, "No, he's dead all right, and we'd better not touch anything." So we went back downstairs. She was still sitting that same way. "Has anybody been notified?" I asked. "No," says she, unconcerned. "Who did this, Mrs. Wright?" said Harry. He said it businesslike — and she stopped pleatin' of her apron. "I don't know," she says. "You don't *know?*" says Harry. "No," says she. "Weren't you sleepin' in the bed with him?" says Harry. "Yes," says she, "but I was on the inside." "Somebody slipped a rope round his neck and strangled him and you didn't wake up?" says Harry. "I didn't wake up," she said after him. We must 'a' looked as if we didn't see how that could be, for after a minute she said, "I sleep sound." Harry was going to ask her more questions but I said maybe we ought to let her tell her story first to the coroner, or the sheriff, so Harry went fast as he could to Rivers' place, where there's a telephone.

County Attorney: And what did Mrs. Wright do when she knew that you had gone for the coroner?

Hale: She moved from the rocker to that chair over there (*pointing to a small chair in the down right corner*) and just sat there with her hands held together and looking down. I got a feeling that I ought to make some conversation, so I said I had come in to see if John wanted to put in a telephone, and at that she started to laugh, and then she stopped and looked at me — scared. (*The County Attorney, who has had his notebook out, makes a note.*) I dunno, maybe it wasn't scared. I wouldn't like to say it was. Soon Harry got back, and then Dr. Lloyd came and you, Mr. Peters, and so I guess that's all I know that you don't.

County Attorney (*rising and looking around*): I guess we'll go upstairs first — and then out to the barn and around there. (*To the Sheriff.*) You're convinced that there was nothing important here — nothing that would point to any motive?

Sheriff: Nothing here but kitchen things. (*The County Attorney, after again looking around the kitchen, opens the door of a cupboard closet in right wall. He brings a small chair from right — gets on it and looks on a shelf. Pulls his hand away, sticky.*)

County Attorney: Here's a nice mess. (*The women draw nearer up center.*)

Mrs. Peters (*to the other woman*): Oh, her fruit; it did freeze. (*To the Lawyer.*) She worried about that when it turned so cold. She said the fire'd go out and her jars would break.

Sheriff (*rises*): Well, can you beat the woman! Held for murder and worryin' about her preserves.

County Attorney (*getting down from chair*): I guess before we're through she may have something more serious than preserves to worry about. (*Crosses down right center.*)

Hale: Well, women are used to worrying over trifles. (*The two women move a little closer together.*)

County Attorney (*with the gallantry of a young politician*): And yet, for all their worries, what would we do without the ladies? (*The women do not unbend. He goes below the center table to the sink, takes a dipperful of water from the pail, and pouring it into a basin, washes his hands. While he is doing this the Sheriff and Hale cross to cupboard, which they inspect. The County Attorney starts to wipe his hands on the roller towel, turns it for a cleaner place.*) Dirty towels! (*Kicks his foot against the pans under the sink.*) Not much of a housekeeper, would you say, ladies?

Mrs. Hale (*stiffly*): There's a great deal of work to be done on a farm.

County Attorney: To be sure. And yet *(with a little bow to her)* I know there are some Dickson County farmhouses which do not have such roller towels. *(He gives it a pull to expose its full-length again.)*

Mrs. Hale: Those towels get dirty awful quick. Men's hands aren't always as clean as they might be.

County Attorney: Ah, loyal to your sex, I see. But you and Mrs. Wright were neighbors. I suppose you were friends, too.

Mrs. Hale (shaking her head): I've not seen much of her of late years. I've not been in this house — it's more than a year.

County Attorney (crossing to women up center): And why was that? You didn't like her?

Mrs. Hale: I liked her all well enough. Farmers' wives have their hands full, Mr. Henderson. And then ——

County Attorney: Yes ——?

Mrs. Hale (looking about): It never seemed a very cheerful place.

County Attorney: No — it's not cheerful. I shouldn't say she had the homemaking instinct.

Mrs. Hale: Well, I don't know as Wright had, either.

County Attorney: You mean that they didn't get on very well?

Mrs. Hale: No, I don't mean anything. But I don't think a place'd be any cheerfuller for John Wright's being in it.

County Attorney: I'd like to talk more of that a little later. I want to get the lay of things upstairs now. *(He goes past the women to up right where steps lead to a stair door.)*

Sheriff: I suppose anything Mrs. Peters does'll be all right. She was to take in some clothes for her, you know, and a few little things. We left in such a hurry yesterday.

County Attorney: Yes, but I would like to see what you take, Mrs. Peters, and keep an eye out for anything that might be of use to us.

Mrs. Peters: Yes, Mr. Henderson. *(The men leave by up right door to stairs. The women listen to the men's steps on the stairs, then look about the kitchen.)*

Mrs. Hale (crossing left to sink): I'd hate to have men coming into my kitchen, snooping around and criticizing. *(She arranges the pans under sink which the lawyer had shoved out of place.)*

Mrs. Peters: Of course it's no more than their duty. *(Crosses to cupboard up right.)*

Mrs. Hale: Duty's all right, but I guess that deputy sheriff that came out to make the fire might have got a little of this on. *(Gives the roller towel a pull.)* Wish I'd thought of that sooner. Seems mean to talk about her for not having things slicked up when she had to come away in such a hurry. *(Crosses right to Mrs. Peters at cupboard.)*

Mrs. Peters (who has been looking through cupboard, lifts one end of towel that covers a pan): She had bread set. *(Stands still.)*

Mrs. Hale (eyes fixed on a loaf of bread beside the breadbox, which is on a low shelf of the cupboard): She was going to put this in there. *(Picks up loaf, abruptly drops it. In a manner of returning to familiar things.)* It's a shame about her fruit. I wonder if it's all gone. *(Gets up on the chair and looks.)* I think there's some here that's all right, Mrs. Peters. Yes — here; *(holding it toward the window)* this is cherries, too. *(Looking again.)* I declare I believe that's the only one. *(Gets down, jar in her hand. Goes to the sink and wipes it off on the outside.)* She'll feel awful bad after all her hard work in the hot weather. I remember the afternoon I put up my cherries last summer. *(She puts the jar on the big kitchen table, center of the room. With a sigh, is about to sit down in the rocking chair. Before she is seated realizes what chair it is; with a slow look at it, steps back. The chair which she has touched rocks back and forth. Mrs. Peters moves to center table and they both watch the chair rock for a moment or two.)*

Mrs. Peters *(shaking off the mood which the empty rocking chair has evoked. Now in a businesslike manner she speaks):* Well I must get those things from the front room closet. *(She goes to the door at the right but, after looking into the other room, steps back.)* You coming with me, Mrs. Hale? You could help me carry them. *(They go in the other room; reappear, Mrs. Peters carrying a dress, petticoat, and skirt, Mrs. Hale following with a pair of shoes.)* My, it's cold in there. *(She puts the clothes on the big table and hurries to the stove.)*

Mrs. Hale *(right of center table examining the skirt):* Wright was close. I think maybe that's why she kept so much to herself. She didn't even belong to the Ladies' Aid. I suppose she felt she couldn't do her part, and then you don't enjoy things when you feel shabby. I heard she used to wear pretty clothes and be lively, when she was Minnie Foster, one of the town girls singing in the choir. But that — oh, that was thirty years ago. This all you want to take in?

Mrs. Peters: She said she wanted an apron. Funny thing to want, for there isn't much to get you dirty in jail, goodness knows. But I suppose just to make her feel more natural. *(Crosses to cupboard.)* She said they was in the top drawer in this cupboard. Yes, here. And then her little shawl that always hung behind the door. *(Opens stair door and looks.)* Yes, here it is. *(Quickly shuts door leading upstairs.)*

Mrs. Hale *(abruptly moving toward her):* Mrs. Peters?

Mrs. Peters: Yes, Mrs. Hale? *(At up right door.)*

Mrs. Hale: Do you think she did it?

Mrs. Peters *(in a frightened voice):* Oh, I don't know.

Mrs. Hale: Well, I don't think she did. Asking for an apron and her little shawl. Worrying about her fruit.

Mrs. Peters *(starts to speak, glances up, where footsteps are heard in the room above. In a low voice):* Mr. Peters says it looks bad for her. Mr. Henderson is awful sarcastic in a speech and he'll make fun of her sayin' she didn't wake up.

Mrs. Hale: Well, I guess John Wright didn't wake when they was slipping that rope under his neck.

Mrs. Peters *(crossing slowly to table and placing shawl and apron on table with other clothing):* No, it's strange. It must have been done awful crafty and still. They say it was such a — funny way to kill a man, rigging it all up like that.

Mrs. Hale *(crossing to left of Mrs. Peters at table):* That's just what Mr. Hale said. There was a gun in the house. He says that's what he can't understand.

Mrs. Peters: Mr. Henderson said coming out that what was needed for the case was a motive; something to show anger, or — sudden feeling.

Mrs. Hale *(who is standing by the table):* Well, I don't see any signs of anger around here. *(She puts her hand on the dish towel, which lies on the table, stands looking down at table, one-half of which is clean, the other half messy.)* It's wiped to here. *(Makes a move as if to finish work, then turns and looks at loaf of bread outside the breadbox. Drops towel. In that voice of coming back to familiar things.)* Wonder how they are finding things upstairs. *(Crossing below table to down right.)* I hope she had it a little more red-up up there. You know, it seems kind of *sneaking*. Locking her up in town and then coming out here and trying to get her own house to turn against her!

Mrs. Peters: But, Mrs. Hale, the law is the law.

Mrs. Hale: I s'pose 'tis. *(Unbuttoning her coat.)* Better loosen up your things, Mrs. Peters. You won't feel them when you go out. *(Mrs. Peters takes off her fur tippet, goes to hang it on chair back left of table, stands looking at the work basket on floor near down left window.)*

Mrs. Peters: She was piecing a quilt. *(She brings the large sewing basket to the center table and they look at the bright pieces, Mrs. Hale above the table and Mrs. Peters left of it.)*

Mrs. Hale: It's a log cabin pattern. Pretty, isn't it? I wonder if she was goin' to quilt it or just knot it? *(Footsteps have been heard coming down the stairs. The Sheriff enters followed by Hale and the County Attorney.)*

Sheriff: They wonder if she was going to quilt it or just knot it! *(The men laugh, the women look abashed.)*

County Attorney (rubbing his hands over the stove): Frank's fire didn't do much up there, did it? Well, let's go out to the barn and get that cleared up. *(The men go outside by up left door.)*

Mrs. Hale (resentfully): I don't know as there's anything so strange, our takin' up our time with little things while we're waiting for them to get the evidence. *(She sits in chair right of table smoothing out a block with decision.)* I don't see as it's anything to laugh about.

Mrs. Peters (apologetically): Of course they've got awful important things on their minds. *(Pulls up a chair and joins Mrs. Hale at the left of the table.)*

Mrs. Hale (examining another block): Mrs. Peters, look at this one. Here, this is the one she was working on, and look at the sewing! All the rest of it has been so nice and even. And look at this! It's all over the place! Why, it looks as if she didn't know what she was about! *(After she has said this they look at each other, then start to glance back at the door. After an instant Mrs. Hale has pulled at a knot and ripped the sewing.)*

Mrs. Peters: Oh, what are you doing, Mrs. Hale?

Mrs. Hale (mildly): Just pulling out a stitch or two that's not sewed very good. *(Threading a needle.)* Bad sewing always made me fidgety.

Mrs. Peters (with a glance at door, nervously): I don't think we ought to touch things.

Mrs. Hale: I'll just finish up this end. *(Suddenly stopping and leaning forward.)* Mrs. Peters?

Mrs. Peters: Yes, Mrs. Hale?

Mrs. Hale: What do you suppose she was so nervous about?

Mrs. Peters: Oh—I don't know. I don't know as she was nervous. I sometimes sew awful queer when I'm just tired. *(Mrs. Hale starts to say something, looks at Mrs. Peters, then goes on sewing.)* Well, I must get these things wrapped up. They may be through sooner than we think. *(Putting apron and other things together.)* I wonder where I can find a piece of paper, and string. *(Rises.)*

Mrs. Hale: In that cupboard, maybe.

Mrs. Peters (crosses right looking in cupboard): Why, here's a bird-cage. *(Holds it up.)* Did she have a bird, Mrs. Hale?

Mrs. Hale: Why, I don't know whether she did or not—I've not been here for so long. There was a man around last year selling canaries cheap, but I don't know as she took one; maybe she did. She used to sing real pretty herself.

Mrs. Peters (glancing around): Seems funny to think of a bird here. But she must have had one, or why would she have a cage? I wonder what happened to it?

Mrs. Hale: I s'pose maybe the cat got it.

Mrs. Peters: No, she didn't have a cat. She's got that feeling some people have about cats — being afraid of them. My cat got in her room and she was real upset and asked me to take it out.

Mrs. Hale: My sister Bessie was like that. Queer, ain't it?

Mrs. Peters (examining the cage): Why, look at this door. It's broke. One hinge is pulled apart. *(Takes a step down to Mrs. Hale's right.)*

Mrs. Hale (looking too): Looks as if someone must have been rough with it.

Mrs. Peters: Why, yes. *(She brings the cage forward and puts it on the table.)*

Mrs. Hale (glancing toward up left door): I wish if they're going to find any evidence they'd be about it. I don't like this place.

Mrs. Peters: But I'm awful glad you came with me, Mrs. Hale. It would be lonesome for me sitting here alone.

Mrs. Hale: It would, wouldn't it? *(Dropping her sewing.)* But I tell you what I do wish, Mrs. Peters. I wish I had come over sometimes when *she* was here. I — *(looking around the room)* — wish I had.

Mrs. Peters: But of course you were awful busy, Mrs. Hale — your house and your children.

Mrs. Hale (rises and crosses left): I could've come. I stayed away because it weren't cheerful — and that's why I ought to have come. I — *(looking out left window)* — I've never liked this place. Maybe because it's down in a hollow and you don't see the road. I dunno what it is, but it's a lonesome place and always was. I wish I had come over to see Minnie Foster sometimes. I can see now — *(Shakes her head.)*

Mrs. Peters (left of table and above it): Well, you mustn't reproach yourself, Mrs. Hale. Somehow we just don't see how it is with other folks until — something turns up.

Mrs. Hale: Not having children makes less work — but it makes a quiet house, and Wright out to work all day, and no company when he did come in. *(Turning from window.)* Did you know John Wright, Mrs. Peters?

Mrs. Peters: Not to know him; I've seen him in town. They say he was a good man.

Mrs. Hale: Yes — good; he didn't drink, and kept his word as well as most, I guess, and paid his debts. But he was a hard man, Mrs. Peters. Just to pass the time of day with him — *(Shivers.)* Like a raw wind that gets to the bone. *(Pauses, her eye falling on the cage.)* I should think she would 'a' wanted a bird. But what do you suppose went with it?

Mrs. Peters: I don't know, unless it got sick and died. *(She reaches over and swings the broken door, swings it again, both women watch it.)*

Mrs. Hale: You weren't raised round here, were you? *(Mrs. Peters shakes her head.)* You didn't know — her?

Mrs. Peters: Not till they brought her yesterday.

Mrs. Hale: She — come to think of it, she was kind of like a bird herself — real sweet and pretty, but kind of timid and — fluttery. How — she — did — change. *(Silence: then as if struck by a happy thought and relieved to get back to everyday things. Crosses right above Mrs. Peters to cupboard, replaces small chair used to stand on to its original place down right.)* Tell you what, Mrs. Peters, why don't you take the quilt in with you? It might take up her mind.

Mrs. Peters: Why, I think that's a real nice idea, Mrs. Hale. There couldn't possibly be any objection to it could there? Now, just what would I take? I wonder if her patches are in here — and her things. *(They look in the sewing basket.)*

Mrs. Hale (crosses to right of table): Here's some red. I expect this has got sewing things in it. *(Brings out a fancy box.)* What a pretty box. Looks like something somebody would give you. Maybe her scissors are in here. *(Opens box. Suddenly puts her hand to her nose.)* Why —— *(Mrs. Peters bends nearer, then turns her face away.)* There's something wrapped up in this piece of silk.

Mrs. Peters: Why, this isn't her scissors.

Mrs. Hale (lifting the silk): Oh, Mrs. Peters — it's —— *(Mrs. Peters bends closer.)*

Mrs. Peters: It's the bird.

Mrs. Hale: But, Mrs. Peters — look at it! Its neck! Look at its neck! It's all — other side *to.*

Mrs. Peters: Somebody — wrung — its — neck. *(Their eyes meet. A look of growing comprehension, of horror. Steps are heard outside. Mrs. Hale slips box under quilt pieces, and sinks into her chair. Enter Sheriff and County Attorney. Mrs. Peters steps down left and stands looking out of window.)*

County Attorney (as one turning from serious things to little pleasantries): Well, ladies, have you decided whether she was going to quilt it or knot it? *(Crosses to center above table.)*

Mrs. Peters: We think she was going to — knot it. *(Sheriff crosses to right of stove, lifts stove lid, and glances at fire, then stands warming hands at stove.)*

County Attorney: Well, that's interesting, I'm sure. *(Seeing the bird-cage.)* Has the bird flown?

Mrs. Hale (putting more quilt pieces over the box): We think the — cat got it.

County Attorney (preoccupied): Is there a cat? *(Mrs. Hale glances in a quick covert way at Mrs. Peters.)*

Mrs. Peters (turning from window takes a step in): Well, not *now.* They're superstitious, you know. They leave.

County Attorney (to Sheriff Peters, continuing an interrupted conversation): No sign at all of anyone having come from the outside. Their own rope. Now let's go up again and go over it piece by piece. *(They start upstairs.)* It would have to have been someone who knew just the —— *(Mrs. Peters sits down left of table. The two women sit there not looking at one another, but as if peering into something and at the same time holding back. When they talk now it is in the manner of feeling their way over strange ground, as if afraid of what they are saying, but as if they cannot help saying it.)*

Mrs. Hale (hesitatively and in hushed voice): She liked the bird. She was going to bury it in that pretty box.

Mrs. Peters (in a whisper): When I was a girl — my kitten — there was a boy took a hatchet, and before my eyes — and before I could get there —— *(Covers her face an instant.)* If they hadn't held me back I would have — *(catches herself, looks upstairs where steps are heard, falters weakly)* — hurt him.

Mrs. Hale (with a slow look around her): I wonder how it would seem never to have had any children around. *(Pause.)* No, Wright wouldn't like the bird — a thing that sang. She used to sing. He killed that, too.

Mrs. Peters (moving uneasily): We don't know who killed the bird.

Mrs. Hale: I knew John Wright.

Mrs. Peters: It was an awful thing was done in this house that night, Mrs. Hale. Killing a man while he slept, slipping a rope around his neck that choked the life out of him.

Mrs. Hale: His neck. Choked the life out of him. *(Her hand goes out and rests on the bird-cage.)*

Mrs. Peters (with rising voice): We don't know who killed him. We don't *know.*

Mrs. Hale (her own feeling not interrupted): If there'd been years and years of nothing, then a bird to sing to you, it would be awful — still, after the bird was still.

Mrs. Peters (something within her speaking): I know what stillness is. When we homesteaded in Dakota, and my first baby died — after he was two years old, and me with no other then ——

Mrs. Hale (moving): How soon do you suppose they'll be through looking for the evidence?

Mrs. Peters: I know what stillness is. *(Pulling herself back.)* The law has got to punish crime, Mrs. Hale.

Mrs. Hale (not as if answering that): I wish you'd seen Minnie Foster when she wore a white dress with blue ribbons and stood up there in the choir and sang. *(A look around the room.)* Oh, I *wish* I'd come over here once in a while! That was a crime! That was a crime! Who's going to punish that?

Mrs. Peters (looking upstairs): We mustn't — take on.

Mrs. Hale: I might have known she needed help! I know how things can be — for women. I tell you, it's queer, Mrs. Peters. We live close together and we live far apart. We all go through the same things — it's all just a different kind of the same thing. *(Brushes her eyes, noticing the jar of fruit, reaches out for it.)* If I was you I wouldn't tell her her fruit was gone. Tell her it *ain't.* Tell her it's all right. Take this in to prove it to her. She — she may never know whether it was broke or not.

Mrs. Peters (takes the jar, looks about for something to wrap it in; takes petticoat from the clothes brought from the other room, very nervously begins winding this around the jar. In a false voice): My, it's a good thing the men couldn't hear us. Wouldn't they just laugh! Getting all stirred up over a little thing like a — dead canary. As if that could have anything to do with — with — wouldn't they *laugh!* (The men are heard coming downstairs.)*

Mrs. Hale (under her breath): Maybe they would — maybe they wouldn't.

County Attorney: No, Peters, it's all perfectly clear except a reason for doing it. But you know juries when it comes to women. If there was some definite thing. *(Crosses slowly to above table. Sheriff crosses down right. Mrs. Hale and Mrs. Peters remain seated at either side of table.)* Something to show — something to make a story about — a thing that would connect up with this strange way of doing it —— *(The women's eyes meet for an instant. Enter Hale from outer door.)*

Hale (remaining by door): Well, I've got the team around. Pretty cold out there.

County Attorney: I'm going to stay awhile by myself. *(To the Sheriff.)* You can send Frank out for me, can't you? I want to go over everything. I'm not satisfied that we can't do better.

Sheriff: Do you want to see what Mrs. Peters is going to take in? *(The Lawyer picks up the apron, laughs.)*

County Attorney: Oh, I guess they're not very dangerous things the ladies have picked out. *(Moves a few things about, disturbing the quilt pieces which cover the box. Steps back.)* No, Mrs. Peters doesn't need supervising. For that matter a sheriff's wife is married to the law. Ever think of it that way, Mrs. Peters?

Mrs. Peters: Not — just that way.

Sheriff (chuckling): Married to the law. *(Moves to down right door to the other room.)* I just want you to come in here a minute, George. We ought to take a look at these windows.

County Attorney (scoffingly): Oh, windows!

Sheriff: We'll be right out, Mr. Hale. *(Hale goes outside. The Sheriff follows the County Attorney into the room. Then Mrs. Hale rises, hands tight together, looking intensely at Mrs. Peters, whose eyes make a slow turn, finally meeting Mrs. Hale's. A moment Mrs. Hale holds her, then her own eyes point the way to where the box is concealed. Suddenly Mrs. Peters throws back quilt pieces and tries to put the box in the bag she is carrying. It is too big. She opens box, starts to take bird out, cannot touch it, goes to pieces, stands there helpless. Sound of a knob turning in the other room. Mrs. Hale snatches the box and puts it in the pocket of her big coat. Enter County Attorney and Sheriff, who remains down right.)*

County Attorney (crosses to up left door facetiously): Well, Henry, at least we found out that she was not going to quilt it. She was going to — what is it you call it, ladies?

Mrs. Hale (standing center below table facing front, her hand against her pocket): We call it — knot it, Mr. Henderson.

Curtain.

CONSIDERATIONS FOR CRITICAL THINKING AND WRITING

1. FIRST RESPONSE. Describe the setting of this play. What kind of atmosphere is established by the details in the opening scene? Does the atmosphere change through the course of the play?

2. Where are Mrs. Hale and Mrs. Peters while Mr. Hale explains to the county attorney how the murder was discovered? How does their location suggest the relationship between the men and the women in the play?

3. What kind of person was Minnie Foster before she married? How do you think her marriage affected her?

4. Characterize John Wright. Why did his wife kill him?

5. Why do the men fail to see the clues that Mrs. Hale and Mrs. Peters discover?

6. What is the significance of the birdcage and the dead bird? Why do Mrs. Hale and Mrs. Peters respond so strongly to them? How do you respond?

7. Why don't Mrs. Hale and Mrs. Peters reveal the evidence they have uncovered? What would you have done?

8. How do the men's conversations and actions reveal their attitudes toward women?

9. Why do you think Glaspell allows us only to hear about Mr. and Mrs. Wright? What is the effect of their never appearing on stage?

10. Does your impression of Mrs. Wright change during the course of the play? If so, what changes it?

11. What is the significance of the play's last line, spoken by Mrs. Hale: "We call it—knot it, Mr. Henderson"? Explain what you think the tone of Mrs. Hale's voice is when she says this line. What is she feeling? What are you feeling?

12. Several times the characters say things that they don't mean, and this creates a discrepancy between what appears to be and what is actually true. Point to instances of irony in the play and explain how they contribute to its effects and meanings. (For discussions of irony elsewhere in this book, see the Index of Terms.)

13. Explain the significance of the play's title. Do you think *Trifles* or "A Jury of Her Peers," Glaspell's title for the short story version of the play, is more appropriate? Can you think of other titles that capture the play's central concerns?

14. If possible, find a copy of "A Jury of Her Peers" in the library (reprinted in *The Best Short Stories of 1917*, ed. E. J. O'Brien [Boston: Small, Maynard, 1918], pp. 256–282), and write an essay that explores the differences between the play and the short story. (An alternative is to work with the excerpt below.)

CONNECTIONS TO OTHER SELECTIONS

1. Compare and contrast how Glaspell provides background information in *Trifles* with how Sophocles does so in *Oedipus the King* (p. 1224).

2. Write an essay comparing the views of marriage in *Trifles* and in Kate Chopin's short story "The Story of an Hour" (p. 10). What similarities do you find in the themes of these two works? Are there any significant differences between the works?

3. In an essay compare Mrs. Wright's motivation for committing murder with that of Matt Fowler, the central character from Andre Dubus's short story "Killings" (p. 81). To what extent do you think they are responsible for and guilty of these crimes?

PERSPECTIVE

SUSAN GLASPELL (1882–1948)

From the Short Story Version of Trifles   1917

When Martha Hale opened the storm-door and got a cut of the north wind, she ran back for her big woolen scarf. As she hurriedly wound that round her head her eye made a scandalized sweep of her kitchen. It was no ordinary thing that called her away—it was probably farther from ordinary than anything that had ever happened in Dickson County. But what her eye took in was that her kitchen was in no shape for leaving: her bread all ready for mixing, half the flour sifted and half unsifted.

She hated to see things half done; but she had been at that when the team from town stopped to get Mr. Hale, and then the sheriff came running in to say his wife wished Mrs. Hale would come too — adding, with a grin, that he guessed she was getting scarey and wanted another woman along. So she had dropped everything right where it was.

"Martha!" now came her husband's impatient voice. "Don't keep folks waiting out here in the cold."

She again opened the storm-door, and this time joined the three men and the one woman waiting for her in the big two-seated buggy.

After she had the robes tucked around her she took another look at the woman who sat beside her on the back seat. She had met Mrs. Peters the year before at the county fair, and the thing she remembered about her was that she didn't seem like a sheriff's wife. She was small and thin and didn't have a strong voice. Mrs. Gorman, sheriff's wife before Gorman went out and Peters came in, had a voice that somehow seemed to be backing up the law with every word. But if Mrs. Peters didn't look like a sheriff's wife, Peters made it up in looking like a sheriff. He was to a dot the kind of man who could get himself elected sheriff — a heavy man with a big voice, who was particularly genial with the law-abiding, as if to make it plain that he knew the difference between criminals and noncriminals. And right there it came into Mrs. Hale's mind, with a stab, that this man who was so pleasant and lively with all of them was going to the Wrights' now as a sheriff.

"The country's not very pleasant this time of year," Mrs. Peters at last ventured, as if she felt they ought to be talking as well as the men.

Mrs. Hale scarcely finished her reply, for they had gone up a little hill and could see the Wright place now, and seeing it did not make her feel like talking. It looked very lonesome this cold March morning. It had always been a lonesome-looking place. It was down in a hollow, and the poplar trees around it were lonesome-looking trees. The men were looking at it and talking about what had happened. The county attorney was bending to one side of the buggy, and kept looking steadily at the place as they drew up to it.

"I'm glad you came with me," Mrs. Peters said nervously, as the two women were about to follow the men in through the kitchen door.

Even after she had her foot on the door-step, her hand on the knob, Martha Hale had a moment of feeling she could not cross that threshold. And the reason it seemed she couldn't cross it now was simply because she hadn't crossed it before. Time and time again it had been in her mind, "I ought to go over and see Minnie Foster" — she still thought of her as Minnie Foster, though for twenty years she had been Mrs. Wright. And then there was always something to do and Minnie Foster would go from her mind. But *now* she could come.

The men went over to the stove. The women stood close together by the door. Young Henderson, the county attorney, turned around and said, "Come up to the fire, ladies."

Mrs. Peters took a step forward, then stopped. "I'm not — cold," she said.

And so the two women stood by the door, at first not even so much as looking around the kitchen.

The men talked for a minute about what a good thing it was the sheriff had sent his deputy out that morning to make a fire for them, and then Sheriff Peters stepped back from the stove, unbuttoned his outer coat, and leaned his hands on the kitchen table in a way that seemed to mark the beginning of official business. "Now, Mr. Hale," he said in a sort of semiofficial voice, "before we move things about, you tell Mr. Henderson just what it was you saw when you came here yesterday morning."

The county attorney was looking around the kitchen.

"By the way," he said, "has anything been moved?" He turned to the sheriff. "Are things just as you left them yesterday?"

Peters looked from cupboard to sink; from that to a small worn rocker a little to one side of the kitchen table.

"It's just the same."

"Somebody should have been left here yesterday," said the county attorney.

"Oh — yesterday," returned the sheriff, with a little gesture as if yesterday having been more than he could bear to think of. "When I had to send Frank to Morris Center for that man who went crazy — let me tell you, I had my hands full *yesterday*. I knew you could get back from Omaha by to-day, George, and as long as I went over everything here myself —"

"Well, Mr. Hale," said the county attorney, in a way of letting what was past and gone go, "tell just what happened when you came here yesterday morning."

Mrs. Hale, still leaning against the door, had that sinking feeling of the mother whose child is about to speak a piece. Lewis often wandered along and got things mixed up in a story. She hoped he would tell this straight and plain, and not say unnecessary things that would just make things harder for Minnie Foster. He didn't begin at once, and she noticed that he looked queer — as if standing in that kitchen and having to tell what he had seen there yesterday morning made him almost sick.

"Yes, Mr. Hale?" the county attorney reminded.

"Harry and I had started to town with a load of potatoes," Mrs. Hale's husband began.

Harry was Mrs. Hale's oldest boy. He wasn't with them now, for the very good reason that those potatoes never got to town yesterday and he was taking them this morning, so he hadn't been home when the sheriff stopped to say he wanted Mr. Hale to come over to the Wright place and tell the county attorney his story there, where he could point it all out. With all Mrs. Hale's other emotions came the fear that maybe Harry wasn't dressed warm enough — they hadn't any of them realized how that north wind did bite.

"We come along this road," Hale was going on, with a motion of his hand to the road over which they had just come, "and as we got in sight of the house I says to Harry, 'I'm goin' to see if I can't get John Wright to take a telephone.' You see," he explained to Henderson, "unless I can get somebody to go in with me they won't come out this branch road except for a price *I* can't pay. I'd spoke to Wright about it once before; but he put me off, saying folks talked too much anyway, and all he asked was peace and quiet — guess you know about how much he talked himself. But I thought maybe if I went to the house and talked about it before his wife, and said all the women-folks liked the telephones, and that in this lonesome stretch of road it would be a good thing — well, I said to Harry that that was what I was going to say — though I said at the same time that I didn't know as what his wife wanted made much difference to John —"

Now, there he was! — saying things he didn't need to say. Mrs. Hale tried to catch her husband's eye, but fortunately the county attorney interrupted with:

"Let's talk about that a little later, Mr. Hale. I do want to talk about that, but I'm anxious now to get along to just what happened when you got here."

From "A Jury of Her Peers"

CONSIDERATIONS FOR CRITICAL THINKING AND WRITING

1. In this opening scene from the story, how is the setting established differently from the way it is in the play (p. 1172)?

2. What kind of information is provided in the opening paragraphs of the story that is missing from the play's initial scene? What is emphasized early in the story but not in the play?

3. Which version brings us into more intimate contact with the characters? How is that achieved?

4. Does the short story's title, "A Jury of Her Peers," suggest any shift in emphasis from the play's title, *Trifles?*

5. Explain why you prefer one version over the other.

ELEMENTS OF DRAMA

Trifles is a ***one-act play;*** in other words, the entire play takes place in a single location and unfolds as one continuous action. As in a short story, the characters in a one-act play are presented economically, and the action is sharply focused. In contrast, full-length plays can include many characters as well as different settings in place and time. The main divisions of a full-length play are typically ***acts;*** their ends are indicated by lowering a curtain or turning up the houselights. Playwrights frequently employ acts to accommodate changes in time, setting, characters on stage, or mood. In many full-length plays, such as Shakespeare's *Hamlet,* acts are further divided into ***scenes;*** according to tradition a scene changes when the location of the action changes or when a new character enters. Acts and scenes are ***conventions*** that are understood and accepted by audiences because they have come, through usage and time, to be recognized as familiar techniques. The major convention of a one-act play is that it typically consists of only a single scene; nevertheless, one-act plays contain many of the elements of drama that characterize their full-length counterparts.

One-act plays create their effects through compression. They especially lend themselves to modestly budgeted productions with limited stage facilities, such as those put on by little theater groups. However, the potential of a one-act play to move audiences and readers is not related to its length. As *Trifles* shows, one-acts represent a powerful form of dramatic literature.

The single location that comprises the ***setting*** for *Trifles* is described at the very beginning of the play; it establishes an atmosphere that will later influence our judgment of Mrs. Wright. The kitchen, "gloomy" and with walls "covered with a faded wall paper," is disordered, bare, and sparsely equipped with a stove, sink, and rocker — each of them "old" — an un-painted table, some chairs, three doors, and an uncurtained window. The only color mentioned is, appropriately, black. These details are just enough to allow us to imagine the stark, uninviting place where Mrs. Wright spent most of her time. Moreover, "signs of incompleted work," coupled with the presence of the sheriff and county attorney, create an immediate tension by suggesting that something is terribly wrong. Before a single word is spoken, *suspense* is created as the characters enter. This suspenseful situation causes an anxious uncertainty about what will happen next.

The setting is further developed through the use of *exposition,* a device that provides the necessary background information about the characters and their circumstances. For example, we immediately learn through *dialogue* — the verbal exchanges between characters — that Mr. Henderson, the county attorney, is just back from Omaha. This establishes the setting as somewhere in the Midwest, where winters can be brutally cold and barren. We also find out that John Wright has been murdered and that his wife has been arrested for the crime.

Even more important, Glaspell deftly characterizes the Wrights through exposition alone. Mr. Hale's conversation with Mr. Henderson explains how Mr. Wright's body was discovered, but it also reveals that Wright was a noncommunicative man, who refused to share a "party telephone" and who did not consider "what his wife wanted." Later Mrs. Hale adds to this characterization when she tells Mrs. Peters that though Mr. Wright was an honest, good man who paid his bills and did not drink, he was a "hard man" and "Like a raw wind that gets to the bone." Mr. Hale's description of Mrs. Wright sitting in the kitchen dazed and disoriented gives us a picture of a shattered, exhausted woman. But it is Mrs. Hale who again offers further insights when she describes how Minnie Foster, a sweet, pretty, timid young woman who sang in the choir, was changed by her marriage to Mr. Wright and by her childless, isolated life on the farm.

This information about Mr. and Mrs. Wright is worked into the dialogue throughout the play in order to suggest the nature of the *conflict* or struggle between them, a motive, and, ultimately, a justification for the murder. In the hands of a skillful playwright, exposition is not merely a mechanical device; it can provide important information while simultaneously developing characterizations and moving the action forward.

The action is shaped by the *plot,* the author's arrangement of incidents in the play that gives the story a particular focus and emphasis. Plot involves more than simply what happens; it involves how and why things happen. Glaspell begins with a discussion of the murder. Why? She could have begun with the murder itself: the distraught Mrs. Wright looping the rope around her husband's neck. The moment would be dramatic and horribly vivid. We neither see the body nor hear very much about it. When Mr. Hale describes finding Mr. Wright's body, Glaspell has the county attorney cut him off by saying, "I think I'd rather have you go into that upstairs, where you can point it all out. Just go on now with the rest of the story." It is precisely the "rest of the story" that interests Glaspell. Her arrangement of incidents prevents us from sympathizing with Mr. Wright. We are, finally, invited to see Mrs. Wright instead of her husband as the victim.

Mr. Henderson's efforts to discover a motive for the murder appear initially to be the play's focus, but the real conflicts are explored in what seems to be a *subplot,* a secondary action that reinforces or contrasts with the main plot. The discussions between Mrs. Hale and Mrs. Peters and the tensions between the men and the women turn out to be the main plot because they address the issues that Glaspell chooses to explore. Those issues are not about murder but about marriage and how men and women relate to each other.

The *protagonist* of *Trifles,* the central character with whom we tend to identify, is Mrs. Hale. The *antagonist,* the character who is in some kind of opposition to the central character, is the county attorney, Mr. Henderson. These two characters embody the major conflicts presented in the play because each speaks for a different set of characters who represent disparate values. Mrs. Hale and Mr. Henderson are developed less individually than as representative types.

Mrs. Hale articulates a sensitivity to Mrs. Wright's miserable life as well as an awareness of how women are repressed in general by men; she also helps Mrs. Peters to arrive at a similar understanding. When Mrs. Hale defends Mrs. Wright's soiled towels from Mr. Henderson's criticism, Glaspell has her say more than the county attorney is capable of hearing. The *stage directions,* the playwright's instructions about how the actors are to move and behave, indicate that Mrs. Hale responds "stiffly" to Mr. Henderson's disparagements: "Men's hands aren't always as clean as they might be." Mrs. Hale eventually comes to see that the men are, in a sense, complicit because it was insensitivity like theirs that drove Mrs. Wright to murder.

Mr. Henderson, on the other hand, represents the law in a patriarchal, conventional society that blithely places a minimal value on the concerns of women. In his attempt to gather evidence against Mrs. Wright, he implicitly defends men's severe dominance over women. He also patronizes Mrs. Hale and Mrs. Peters. Like Sheriff Peters and Mr. Hale, he regards the women's world as nothing more than "kitchen things" and "trifles." Glaspell, however, patterns the plot so that the women see more about Mrs. Wright's motives than the men do and shows that the women have a deeper understanding of justice.

Many plays are plotted in what has come to be called a *pyramidal pattern,* because the plot is divided into three essential parts. Such plays begin with a *rising action,* in which complication creates conflict for the protagonist. The resulting tension builds to the second major division, known as the *climax,* when the action reaches a final *crisis,* a turning point that has a powerful effect on the protagonist. The third part consists of *falling action;* here the tensions are diminished in the *resolution* of the plot's conflicts and complications (the resolution is also referred to as the **conclusion** or **dénouement**, a French word meaning "unknotting"). These divisions may occur at different times. There are many variations to this pattern. The terms are helpful for identifying various moments and movements within a given plot, but they are less useful if seen as a means of reducing dramatic art to a formula.

Because *Trifles* is a one-act play, this pyramidal pattern is less elaborately worked out than it might be in a full-length play, but the basic elements of the pattern can still be discerned. The complication consists mostly of Mrs. Hale's refusal to assign moral or legal guilt to Mrs. Wright's murder of her husband. Mrs. Hale is able to discover the motive in the domestic details that are beneath the men's consideration. The men fail to see the significance of the fruit jars, messy kitchen, and badly sewn quilt.

At first Mrs. Peters seems to voice the attitudes associated with the men. Unlike Mrs. Hale, who is "more comfortable looking," Mrs. Peters is "a slight wiry woman" with "a thin nervous face" who sounds like her husband, the sheriff, when she insists, "the law is the law." She also defends the men's patronizing attitudes, because "they've got awful important things on their minds." But Mrs. Peters is a *foil* — a character whose behavior and values contrast with the protagonist's — only up to a point. When the most telling clue is discovered, Mrs. Peters suddenly understands, along with Mrs. Hale, the motive for the killing. Mrs. Wright's caged life was no longer tolerable to her after her husband had killed the bird (which was the one bright spot in her life and which represents her early life as the young Minnie Foster). This revelation brings about the climax, when the two women must decide whether to tell the men what they have discovered. Both women empathize with Mrs. Wright as they confront this crisis, and their sense of common experience leads them to withhold the evidence.

This resolution ends the play's immediate conflicts and complications. Presumably, without a motive the county attorney will have difficulty prosecuting Mrs. Wright — at least to the fullest extent of the law. However, the larger issues related to the **theme**, the central idea or meaning of the play, are left unresolved. The men have both missed the clues and failed to perceive the suffering that acquits Mrs. Wright in the minds of the two women. The play ends with Mrs. Hale's ironic answer to Mr. Henderson's question about quilting. When she says "knot it," she gives him part of the evidence he needs to connect Mrs. Wright's quilting with the knot used to strangle her husband. Mrs. Hale knows — and we know — that Mr. Henderson will miss the clue she offers because he is blinded by his own self-importance and assumptions.

Though brief, *Trifles* is a masterful representation of dramatic elements working together to keep both audiences and readers absorbed in its characters and situations.

Sure Thing

Sure Thing is a one-act play that's even briefer than *Trifles* but that manages to include a variety of characters and a wide range of emotions despite the fact that all the action takes place between two characters sitting in a city café. How, you might ask, can there be a "variety of characters" in a two-character play? The answer is found in the play's premise, which experiments with the intriguing question of what life would be like if we could instantly replay moments in our lives that do not go our way. Imagine how interesting an encounter with someone might be if we could immediately revise what we said until we got the response we desired and thus script our own lives. David Ives plays with this fantasy in *Sure Thing* with insight and wicked wit.

Born in Chicago and educated at Northwestern University and the Yale Drama School, David Ives writes for television, film, and opera and has created a number of one-act plays for the annual comedy festival of Manhattan Punch Line, where *Sure Thing* was first produced in 1988. As you read, notice how many elements of drama Ives works into the play, with comic effect.

DAVID IVES (B. 1950)

Sure Thing   *1988*

CHARACTERS

Bill and *Betty*, both in their late twenties

SETTING: *A café table, with a couple of chairs*

> *Betty, reading at the table. An empty chair opposite her. Bill enters.*

Bill: Excuse me. Is this chair taken?
Betty: Excuse me?
Bill: Is this taken?
Betty: Yes it is.
Bill: Oh. Sorry.
Betty: Sure thing. *(A bell rings softly.)*
Bill: Excuse me. Is this chair taken?
Betty: Excuse me?
Bill: Is this taken?
Betty: No, but I'm expecting somebody in a minute.
Bill: Oh. Thanks anyway.
Betty: Sure thing. *(A bell rings softly.)*
Bill: Excuse me. Is this chair taken?
Betty: No, but I'm expecting somebody very shortly.
Bill: Would you mind if I sit here till he or she or it comes?
Betty (glances at her watch): They seem to be pretty late. . . .

Bill: You never know who you might be turning down.

Betty: Sorry. Nice try, though.

Bill: Sure thing. *(Bell.)* Is this seat taken?

Betty: No it's not.

Bill: Would you mind if I sit here?

Betty: Yes I would.

Bill: Oh. *(Bell.)* Is this chair taken?

Betty: No it's not.

Bill: Would you mind if I sit here?

Betty: No. Go ahead.

Bill: Thanks. *(He sits. She continues reading.)* Everyplace else seems to be taken.

Betty: Mm-hm.

Bill: Great place.

Betty: Mm-hm.

Bill: What's the book?

Betty: I just wanted to read in quiet, if you don't mind.

Bill: No. Sure thing. *(Bell.)*

Bill: Everyplace else seems to be taken.

Betty: Mm-hm.

Bill: Great place for reading.

Betty: Yes, I like it.

Bill: What's the book?

Betty: *The Sound and the Fury.*

Bill: Oh. Hemingway. *(Bell.)* What's the book?

Betty: *The Sound and the Fury.*

Bill: Oh. Faulkner.

Betty: Have you read it?

Bill: Not . . . actually. I've sure read *about* . . . it, though. It's supposed to be great.

Betty: It is great.

Bill: I hear it's great. *(Small pause.)* Waiter? *(Bell.)* What's the book?

Betty: *The Sound and the Fury.*

Bill: Oh. Faulkner.

Betty: Have you read it?

Bill: I'm a Mets fan, myself. *(Bell.)*

Betty: Have you read it?

Bill: Yeah, I read it in college.

Betty: Where was college?

Bill: I went to Oral Roberts University. *(Bell.)*

Betty: Where was college?

Bill: I was lying. I never really went to college. I just like to party. *(Bell.)*

Betty: Where was college?

Bill: Harvard.

Betty: Do you like Faulkner?

Bill: I love Faulkner. I spent a whole winter reading him once.

Betty: I've just started.

Bill: I was so excited after ten pages that I went out and bought everything else he wrote. One of the greatest reading experiences of my life. I mean, all that incredible psychological understanding. Page after page of gorgeous prose. His profound grasp of the mystery of time and human existence. The smells of the earth . . . What do you think?

Betty: I think it's pretty boring. *(Bell.)*
Bill: What's the book?
Betty: The Sound and the Fury.
Bill: Oh! Faulkner!
Betty: Do you like Faulkner?
Bill: I love Faulkner.
Betty: He's incredible.
Bill: I spent a whole winter reading him once.
Betty: I was so excited after ten pages that I went out and bought everything else he wrote.
Bill: All that incredible psychological understanding.
Betty: And the prose is so gorgeous.
Bill: And the way he's grasped the mystery of time —
Betty: — and human existence. I can't believe I've waited this long to read him.
Bill: You never know. You might not have liked him before.
Betty: That's true.
Bill: You might not have been ready for him. You have to hit these things at the right moment or it's no good.
Betty: That's happening to me.
Bill: It's all in the timing. *(Small pause.)* My name's Bill, by the way.
Betty: I'm Betty.
Bill: Hi.
Betty: Hi. *(Small pause.)*
Bill: Yes I thought reading Faulkner was . . . a great experience.
Betty: Yes. *(Small pause.)*
Bill: The Sound and the Fury . . . *(Another small pause.)*
Betty: Well. Onwards and upwards. *(She goes back to her book.)*
Bill: Waiter — ? *(Bell.)* You have to hit these things at the right moment or it's no good.
Betty: That's happened to me.
Bill: It's all in the timing. My name's Bill, by the way.
Betty: I'm Betty.
Bill: Hi.
Betty: Hi.
Bill: Do you come in here a lot?
Betty: Actually I'm just in town for two days from Pakistan.
Bill: Oh. Pakistan. *(Bell.)* My name's Bill, by the way.
Betty: I'm Betty.
Bill: Hi.
Betty: Hi.
Bill: Do you come here a lot?
Betty: Every once in a while. Do you?
Bill: Not much anymore. Not as much as I used to. Before my nervous breakdown. *(Bell.)* Do you come in here a lot?
Betty: Why are you asking?
Bill: Just interested.
Betty: Are you really interested, or do you just want to pick me up?
Bill: No, I'm really interested.
Betty: Why would you be interested in whether I come in here a lot?
Bill: Just . . . getting acquainted.

Betty: Maybe you're only interested for the sake of making small talk long enough to ask me back to your place to listen to some music, or because you've just rented some great tape for your VCR, or because you've got some terrific unknown Django Reinhardt record, only all you'll really want to do is fuck—which you won't do very well—after which you'll go into the bathroom and pee very loudly, then pad into the kitchen and get yourself a beer from the refrigerator without asking me whether I'd like anything, and then you'll proceed to lie back down beside me and confess that you've got a girlfriend named Stephanie who's away at medical school in Belgium for a year, and that you've been involved with her—*off and on*—in what you'll call a very "intricate" relationship, for about *seven YEARS*. None of which *interests* me, mister!

Bill: Okay. (*Bell.*) Do you come in here a lot?

Betty: Every other day, I think.

Bill: I come in here quite a lot and I don't remember seeing you.

Betty: I guess we must be on different schedules.

Bill: Missed connections.

Betty: Yes. Different time zones.

Bill: Amazing how you can live right next door to somebody in this town and never even know it.

Betty: I know.

Bill: City life.

Betty: It's crazy.

Bill: We probably pass each other in the street every day. Right in front of this place, probably.

Betty: Yep.

Bill (looks around): Well, the waiters here sure seem to be in some different time zone. I can't seem to locate one anywhere . . . Waiter! (*He looks back.*) So what do you— (*He sees that she's gone back to her book.*)

Betty: I beg pardon?

Bill: Nothing. Sorry. (*Bell.*)

Betty: I guess we must be on different schedules.

Bill: Missed connections.

Betty: Yes. Different time zones.

Bill: Amazing how you can live right next door to somebody in this town and never even know it.

Betty: I know.

Bill: City life.

Betty: It's crazy.

Bill: You weren't waiting for somebody when I came in, were you?

Betty: Actually, I was.

Bill: Oh. Boyfriend?

Betty: Sort of.

Bill: What's a sort-of boyfriend?

Betty: My husband.

Bill: Ah-ha. (*Bell.*) You weren't waiting for somebody when I came in, were you?

Betty: Actually I was.

Bill: Oh. Boyfriend?

Betty: Sort of.

Bill: What's a sort-of boyfriend?

Betty: We were meeting here to break up.

Bill: Mm-hm . . . *(Bell.)* What's a sort-of boyfriend?

Betty: My lover. Here she comes right now! *(Bell.)*

Bill: You weren't waiting for somebody when I came in, were you?

Betty: No, just reading.

Bill: Sort of a sad occupation for a Friday night, isn't it? Reading here, all by yourself?

Betty: Do you think so?

Bill: Well sure. I mean, what's a good-looking woman like you doing out alone on a Friday night?

Betty: Trying to keep away from lines like that.

Bill: No, listen — *(Bell.)* You weren't waiting for somebody when I came in, were you?

Betty: No, just reading.

Bill: Sort of a sad occupation for a Friday night, isn't it? Reading here all by yourself?

Betty: I guess it is, in a way.

Bill: What's a good-looking woman like you doing out alone on a Friday night anyway? No offense, but . . .

Betty: I'm out alone on a Friday night for the first time in a very long time.

Bill: Oh.

Betty: You see, I just recently ended a relationship.

Bill: Oh.

Betty: Of rather long standing.

Bill: I'm sorry. *(Small pause.)* Well listen, since reading by yourself *is* such a sad occupation for a Friday night, would you like to go elsewhere?

Betty: No . . .

Bill: Do something else?

Betty: No thanks.

Bill: I was headed out to the movies in a while anyway.

Betty: I don't think so.

Bill: Big chance to let Faulkner catch his breath. All those long sentences get him pretty tired.

Betty: Thanks anyway.

Bill: Okay.

Betty: I appreciate the invitation.

Bill: Sure thing. *(Bell.)* You weren't waiting for somebody when I came in, were you?

Betty: No, just reading.

Bill: Sort of a sad occupation for a Friday night, isn't it? Reading here all by yourself?

Betty: I guess I was trying to think of it as existentially romantic. You know — cappuccino, great literature, rainy night . . .

Bill: That only works in Paris. We *could* hop the late plane to Paris. Get on a Concorde. Find a café . . .

Betty: I'm a little short on plane fare tonight.

Bill: Darn it, so am I.

Betty: To tell you the truth, I was headed to the movies after I finished this section. Would you like to come along? Since you can't locate a waiter?

Bill: That's a very nice offer, but . . .

Betty: Uh-huh. Girlfriend?

Bill: Two, actually. One of them's pregnant, and Stephanie — *(Bell.)*

Betty: Girlfriend?

Bill: No, I don't have a girlfriend. Not if you mean the castrating bitch I dumped last night. *(Bell.)*

Betty: Girlfriend?

Bill: Sort of. Sort of.

Betty: What's a sort-of girlfriend?

Bill: My mother. *(Bell.)* I just ended a relationship, actually.

Betty: Oh.

Bill: Of rather long standing.

Betty: I'm sorry to hear it.

Bill: This is my first night out alone in a long time. I feel a little bit at sea, to tell you the truth.

Betty: So you didn't stop to talk because you're a Moonie, or you have some weird political affiliation — ?

Bill: Nope. Straight-down-the-ticket Republican. *(Bell.)* Straight-down-the-ticket Democrat. *(Bell.)* Can I tell you something about politics? *(Bell.)* I like to think of myself as a citizen of the universe. *(Bell.)* I'm unaffiliated.

Betty: That's a relief. So am I.

Bill: I vote my beliefs.

Betty: Labels are not important.

Bill: Labels are not important, exactly. Like me, for example. I mean, what does it matter if I had a two-point at — *(bell)* — three-point at *(bell)* — four-point at college, or if I did come from Pittsburgh — *(bell)* — Cleveland — *(bell)* — Westchester County?

Betty: Sure.

Bill: I believe that a man is what he is. *(Bell.)* A person is what he is. *(Bell.)* A person is . . . what they are.

Betty: I think so too.

Bill: So what if I admire Trotsky? *(Bell.)* So what if I once had a total-body liposuction? *(Bell.)* So what if I don't have a penis? *(Bell.)* So what if I once spent a year in the Peace Corps? I was acting on my convictions.

Betty: Sure.

Bill: You can't just hang a sign on a person.

Betty: Absolutely. I'll bet you're a Scorpio. *(Many bells ring.)* Listen, I was headed to the movies after I finished this section. Would you like to come along?

Bill: That sounds like fun. What's playing?

Betty: A couple of the really early Woody Allen movies.

Bill: Oh.

Betty: Don't you like Woody Allen?

Bill: Sure. I like Woody Allen.

Betty: But you're not crazy about Woody Allen.

Bill: Those early ones kind of get on my nerves.

Betty: Uh-huh. *(Bell.)*

| *Bill:* Y'know I was | — *(simultaneously)* — | *Betty:* I was thinking |
| headed to the — | | about — |

Bill: I'm sorry.

Betty: No, go ahead.
Bill: I was going to say that I was headed to the movies in a little while, and . . .
Betty: So was I.
Bill: The Woody Allen festival?
Betty: Just up the street.
Bill: Do you like the early ones?
Betty: I think anybody who doesn't ought to be run off the planet.
Bill: How many times have you seen *Bananas*?
Betty: Eight times.
Bill: Twelve. So are you still interested? *(Long pause.)*
Betty: Do you like Entenmann's crumb cake . . . ?
Bill: Last night I went out at two in the morning to get one. *(Small pause.)* Did you have an Etch-a-Sketch as a child?
Betty: Yes! And do you like Brussels sprouts? *(Small pause.)*
Bill: I think they're gross.
Betty: They *are* gross!
Bill: Do you still believe in marriage in spite of current sentiments against it?
Betty: Yes.
Bill: And children?
Betty: Three of them.
Bill: Two girls and a boy.
Betty: Harvard, Vassar, and Brown.
Bill: And will you love me?
Betty: Yes.
Bill: And cherish me forever?
Betty: Yes.
Bill: Do you still want to go to the movies?
Betty: Sure thing.
Bill and Betty (together): Waiter!

   (Blackout.)

Considerations for Critical Thinking and Writing

1. FIRST RESPONSE. Very little information is provided about the play's setting. How do you envision the café? What does the setting suggest to you about the characters?

2. What is the purpose of the ringing bell?

3. Which character would you describe as the antagonist? What do you think is the play's central conflict?

4. How is the formulaic plot of "boy meets girl" complicated and made suspenseful in this play? Where would you say that the climax occurs? What is the plot's resolution?

5. How would you describe the play's theme?

6. Discuss the significance of the title. How is it related to your understanding of the play's theme?

7. At one point Bill says, "You have to hit these things at the right moment or it's no good" (p. 1191). How might this line be used to describe Ives's strategy for writing this play?

8. Try your hand at writing another scene between Betty and Bill that takes place after they come out of the movies. Write a comic scene the way you think Ives might create it.

Connections to Other Selections

1. Choose what you think is an appropriate moment in Susan Glaspell's *Trifles* (p. 1172) and rewrite the scene using Ives's ringing bell.
2. Compare and contrast Ives's treatment of romance and love with their treatment in Shakespeare's *A Midsummer Night's Dream* (p. 1327).

DRAMA IN POPULAR FORMS

Audiences for live performances of plays have been thinned by high ticket prices but perhaps even more significantly by the impact of motion pictures and television. Motion pictures, the original threat to live theater, have in turn been superseded by television (along with videocassettes), now the most popular form of entertainment in America. Television audiences are measured in the millions. Probably more people have seen a single weekly episode of a top-rated prime-time program such as *ER* in one evening than have viewed a live performance of *Hamlet* in nearly four hundred years.

Though most of us are seated more often before a television than before live actors, our limited experience with the theater presents relatively few obstacles to appreciation because many of the basic elements of drama are similar whether the performance is on videotape or on a stage. Television has undoubtedly seduced audiences that otherwise might have been attracted to the theater, but television obviously satisfies some aspects of our desire for drama and can be seen as a potential introduction to live theater rather than as its irresistible rival.

Significant differences do, of course, exist between television and theater productions. Most obviously, television's special camera effects can capture phenomena such as earthquakes, raging fires, car chases, and space travel that cannot be realistically rendered on a live stage. The presentation of characters and the plotting of action are also handled differently owing to both the possibilities and limitations of television and the theater. Television's multiple camera angles and close-ups provide a degree of intimacy that cannot be duplicated by actors on stage, yet this intimacy does not achieve the immediacy that live actors create. On commercial television the plot must accommodate itself to breaks in the action so that advertisements can be aired at regular intervals. Beyond these and many other differences, however, there are enough important similarities that the experience of watching television shows can enhance our understanding of a theater production.

Seinfeld

Seinfeld, which aired on NBC, was first produced during the summer of 1989. Although the series ended in the spring of 1998, it remains popular in syndicated reruns. No one expected the half-hour situation comedy that evolved from the pilot to draw some twenty-seven million viewers per week who avidly watched Jerry Seinfeld playing himself as a standup comic. Nominated for numerous Emmys, the show became one of the most popular programs of the 1990s. Although *Seinfeld* portrays a relatively narrow band of contemporary urban life concerning four thirty-something characters living in New York City's Upper West Side, its quirky humor and engaging characters have attracted vast numbers of devoted fans who have conferred on it a kind of cult status. If you haven't watched an episode on television, noticed the T-shirts and posters, or read *Seinlanguage* (a bestselling collection of Seinfeld's monologues), you can catch up on the Internet, where fans discuss the popularity and merits of the show.

The setting for *Seinfeld* is determined by its subject matter, which is everyday life in Manhattan. Most of the action alternates between two principal locations: Jerry's modest one-bedroom apartment on West 81st Street and the characters' favorite restaurant in the neighborhood. Viewers are often surprised to learn that the show is filmed on a soundstage before a live audience in Studio City, California, because the sights, sounds, and seemingly unmistakable texture of Manhattan appear in background shots so that the city functions almost as a major character in many episodes. If you ever find yourself on the corner of Broadway and 112th Street, you'll recognize the facade of Jerry's favorite restaurant; but don't bother to look for the building that matches the exterior shot of his apartment building because it is in Los Angeles, as are the scenes in which the characters actually appear on the street. The care with which the sets are created suggests how important the illusion of the New York City environment is to the show.

As the central character, Jerry begins and ends each episode with a standup comedy act delivered before a club audience. These monologues (played down in later episodes) are connected to the events in the episodes and demonstrate with humor and insight that ordinary experience — such as standing in line at a supermarket or getting something caught in your teeth — can be a source of genuine humor. For Jerry, life is filled with daily annoyances that he copes with by making sharp humorous observations. Here's a brief instance from "The Pitch" (not reprinted in the excerpt on p. 1199) in which Jerry is in the middle of a conversation with friends when he is interrupted by a phone call.

Jerry (into phone): Hello?
Man (v[oice] o[ver]): Hi, would you be interested in switching over to T.M.I. long distance service?

Jerry: Oh gee, I can't talk right now, why don't you give me your home number and I'll call you later?
Man (v[oice] o[ver]): Uh, well I'm sorry, we're not allowed to do that.
Jerry: Oh, I guess you don't want people calling you at home.
Man (v[oice] o[ver]): No.
Jerry: Well now you know how I feel.
Hangs up.

This combination of polite self-assertion and humor is Jerry's first line of defense in his ongoing skirmishes with the irritations of daily life. Unthreatening in his Nikes and neatly pressed jeans, Jerry nonetheless knows how to give it back when he is annoyed. Seinfeld has described his fictional character as a "nice, New York Jewish boy," but his character's bemused and pointed observations reveal a tough-mindedness that is often wittily on target.

Jerry's life and apartment are continually invaded by his three closest friends: George, Kramer, and Elaine. His refrigerator is the rallying point from which they feed each other lines over cardboard takeout cartons and containers of juice. Jerry's success as a standup comic is their cue to enjoy his groceries as well as his company, but they know their intrusions are welcome because the refrigerator is always restocked.

Jerry's closest friend is George Costanza (played by Jason Alexander), a frequently unemployed, balding, pudgy schlemiel. Any straightforward description of his behavior and sensibilities makes him sound starkly unappealing: he is hypochondriacal, usually upset and depressed, inept with women, embarrassingly stingy, and persistently demanding while simultaneously displaying a vain and cocky nature. As intolerable as he can be, he is nonetheless endearing. The pleasure of his character is in observing how he talks his way into trouble and then attempts to talk his way out of it to Jerry's amazement and amusement.

Across the hall from Jerry's apartment lives Kramer (played by Michael Richards), who is strategically located so as to be the mooch in Jerry's life. Known only as Kramer (until an episode later than "The Pitch" revealed his first name to be Cosmo), his slapstick twitching, tripping, and falling serve as a visual contrast to all the talking that goes on. His bizarre schemes and eccentric behavior have their physical counterpart in his vertical hair and his outrageous thrift-shop shirts from the 1960s.

Elaine Benes (played by Julia Louis-Dreyfus), on the other hand, is a sharp-tongued, smart, sexy woman who can hold her own and is very definitely a female member of this boy's club. As Jerry's ex-girlfriend, she provides some interesting romantic tension while serving as a sounding board for the relationship issues that George and Jerry obsess about. Employed at a book company at the time of the episode reprinted on page 1199, she, like George and Kramer, is also in the business of publishing her daily problems in Jerry's apartment.

The plots of most *Seinfeld* episodes are generated by the comical situations that Jerry and his friends encounter during the course of their daily lives. Minor irritations develop into huge conflicts that are offbeat, irreverent, or even absurd. The characters have plenty of time to create conflicts in their lives over such everyday situations as dealing with parents, finding an apartment, getting a date, riding the subway, ordering a meal, and losing a car in a mall parking garage. The show's screwball plots involve freewheeling misadventures that are played out in unremarkable but hilarious conversations.

The following scenes from *Seinfeld* are from a script titled "The Pitch" that concerns Jerry's and George's efforts to develop a television show for NBC. The script is loosely based on events that actually occurred when Jerry Seinfeld and his real-life friend Larry David (the author of "The Pitch") sat down to discuss ideas for the pilot NBC produced in 1989. As brief as these scenes are, they contain some of the dramatic elements found in a play.

LARRY DAVID

Seinfeld   *1992*

"THE PITCH"
[The following excerpted scenes do not appear one after the other in the original script but are interspersed through several subplots involving Kramer and Elaine.]

ACT ONE

SCENE A: *Int[erior] comedy club bar—night*

> *Jerry and George are talking. Suits enter, Stu and Jay.*

Stu: Excuse me, Jerry? I'm Stu Chermak. I'm with NBC.
Jerry: Hi.
Stu: Could we speak for a few moments?
Jerry: Sure, sure.
Jay: Hi, Jay Crespi.
Jerry: Hello.
George: C-R-E-S-P-I?
Jay: That's right.
George: I'm unbelievable at spelling last names. Give me a last name.
Jay: Mm, I'm not—
Jerry: George.
George (backing off): Huh? All right, fine.
Stu: First of all, that was a terrific show.
Jerry: Oh thank you very much.
Stu: And basically, I just wanted to let you know that we've been discussing you at some of our meetings and we'd be very interested in doing something.
Jerry: Really? Wow.
Stu: So, if you have an idea for like a TV show for yourself, well, we'd just love to talk about it.

Jerry: I'd be very interested in something like that.
Stu: Well, here, why don't you give us a call and maybe we can develop a series.

> *They start to exit.*

Jerry: Okay. Great. Thanks.
Stu: It was very nice meeting you.
Jerry: Thank you.
Jay: Nice meeting you.
Jerry: Nice meeting you.

> *George returns.*

George: What was that all about?
Jerry: They said they were interested in me.
George: For what?
Jerry: You know, a TV show.
George: Your own show?
Jerry: Yeah, I guess so.
George: They want you to do a TV show?
Jerry: Well, they want me to come up with an idea. I mean, I don't have any ideas.
George: Come on, how hard is that? Look at all the junk that's on TV. You want an idea? Here's an idea. You coach a gymnastics team in high school. And you're married. And your son's not interested in gymnastics and you're pushing him into gymnastics.
Jerry: Why should I care if my son's into gymnastics?
George: Because you're a gymnastics teacher. It's only natural.
Jerry: But gymnastics is not for everybody.
George: I know, but he's your son.
Jerry: So what?
George: All right, forget that idea, it's not for you. . . . Okay, okay, I got it, I got it. You run an antique store.
Jerry: Yeah and . . . ?
George: And people come in the store and you get involved in their lives.
Jerry: What person who runs an antique store gets involved in people's lives?
George: Why not?
Jerry: So someone comes in to buy an old lamp and all of a sudden I'm getting them out of a jam? I could see if I was a pharmacist because a pharmacist knows what's wrong with everybody that comes in.
George: I know, but antiques are very popular right now.
Jerry: No they're not, they used to be.
George: Oh yeah, like you know.
Jerry: Oh like you do.

> *Cut to:*

ACT ONE

SCENE B: *Int[erior] Jerry's apartment—day*

> *Jerry and Kramer.*

Kramer: . . . And you're the manager of the circus.
Jerry: A circus?

Kramer: Come on, this is a great idea. Look at the characters. You've got all these freaks on the show. A woman with a moustache? I mean, who wouldn't tune in to see a woman with a moustache? You've got the tallest man in the world; the guy who's just a head.

Jerry: I don't think so.

Kramer: Look Jerry, the show isn't about the circus, it's about watching freaks.

Jerry: I don't think the network will go for it.

Kramer: Why not?

Jerry: Look, I'm not pitching a show about freaks.

Kramer: Oh come on Jerry, you're wrong. People they want to watch freaks. This is a "can't miss."

ACT ONE

SCENE C: *Int[erior] coffee shop—lunchtime—day*

   Jerry and George enter.

George: So, what's happening with the TV show? You come up with anything?

Jerry: No, nothing.

George: Why don't they have salsa on the table?

Jerry: What do you need salsa for?

George: Salsa is now the number one condiment in America.

Jerry: You know why? Because people like to say "salsa." "Excuse me, do you have salsa?" "We need more salsa." "Where is the salsa? No salsa?"

George: You know it must be impossible for a Spanish person to order seltzer and not get salsa. *(Angry.)* "I wanted seltzer, not salsa."

Jerry: "Don't you know the difference between seltzer and salsa? You have the seltzer after the salsa!"

George: See, this should be the show. This is the show.

Jerry: What?

George: This. Just talking.

Jerry (dismissing): Yeah, right.

George: I'm really serious. I think that's a good idea.

Jerry: Just talking? What's the show about?

George: It's about nothing.

Jerry: No story?

George: No, forget the story.

Jerry: You've got to have a story.

George: Who says you gotta have a story? Remember when we were waiting for that table in that Chinese restaurant that time? That could be a TV show.

Jerry: And who is on the show? Who are the characters?

George: I could be a character.

Jerry: You?

George: You could base a character on me.

Jerry: So on the show there's a character named George Costanza?

George: Yeah. There's something wrong with that? I'm a character. People are always saying to me, "You know you're quite a character."

Jerry: And who else is on the show?

George: Elaine could be a character. Kramer.

Jerry: Now he's a character. . . . So, everyone I know is a character on the show.

George: Right.

Jerry: And it's about nothing?

George: Absolutely nothing.

Jerry: So you're saying, I go in to NBC and tell them I got this idea for a show about nothing.

George: We go into NBC.

Jerry: We? Since when are you a writer?

George: Writer. We're talking about a sit-com.

Jerry: You want to go with me to NBC?

George: Yeah, I think we really got something here.

Jerry: What do we got?

George: An idea.

Jerry: What idea?

George: An idea for the show.

Jerry: I still don't know what the idea is.

George: It's about nothing.

Jerry: Right.

George: Everybody's doing something, we'll do nothing.

Jerry: So we go into NBC, we tell them we've got an idea for a show about nothing.

George: Exactly.

Jerry: They say, "What's your show about?" I say, "Nothing."

George: There you go.

> *A beat.*

Jerry: I think you may have something there.

> *Cut to:*

ACT ONE

SCENE D: *Int[erior] Jerry's apartment—day*

> *Jerry and Kramer.*

Jerry: So it would be about my real life. And one of the characters would be based on you.

Kramer (thinks): No. I don't think so.

Jerry: What do you mean you don't think so?

Kramer: I don't like it.

Jerry: I don't understand. What don't you like about it?

Kramer: I don't like the idea of a character based on me.

Jerry: Why not?

Kramer: Doesn't sit well.

Jerry: You're my neighbor. There's got to be a character based on you.

Kramer: That's your problem, buddy.

Jerry: I don't understand what the big deal is.

Kramer: Hey I'll tell you what, you can do it on one condition.

Jerry: Whatever you want.

Kramer: I get to play Kramer.

Jerry: You can't play Kramer.
Kramer: I am Kramer.
Jerry: But you can't act.

ACT ONE

Scene G: *Int[erior] NBC reception area—day*

> *Jerry and George.*

Jerry (to himself): Salsa, seltzer. Hey excuse me, you got any salsa? No not seltzer, salsa. *(George doesn't react.)* What's the matter?
George (nervous): Nothing.
Jerry: You sure? You look a little pale.
George: No, I'm fine. I'm good. I'm fine. I'm very good.
Jerry: What are you, nervous?
George: No, not nervous. I'm good, very good. *(A beat, then: explodes.)* I can't do this! Can't do this!
Jerry: What?
George: I can't do this! I can't do it. I have tried. I'm here. It's impossible.
Jerry: This was your idea.
George: What idea? I just said something. I didn't know you'd listen to me.
Jerry: Don't worry about it. They're just TV executives.
George: They're men with jobs, Jerry! They wear suits and ties. They're married, they have secretaries.
Jerry: I told you not to come.
George: I need some water. I gotta get some water.
Jerry: They'll give us water inside.
George: Really? That's pretty good. . . .

> *Receptionist enters.*

Receptionist: They're ready for you.
George: Okay, okay, look, you do all the talking, okay?
Jerry: Relax. Who are they?
George: Yeah, they're not better than me.
Jerry: Course not.
George: Who are they?
Jerry: They're nobody.
George: What about me?
Jerry: What about you?
George: Why them? Why not me?
Jerry: Why not you?
George: I'm as good as them.
Jerry: Better.
George: You really think so?
Jerry: No.

> *Door opens, Jerry and George P.O.V., the four execs stand up.*

> *Fade out.*

ACT TWO

SCENE G: *Int[erior] NBC president's office—day*

> *The mood is jovial. Stu Chermak is there—along with Susan Ross, Jay Crespi, and Russell Dalrymple, the head of the network.*

Stu (to Jerry): The bit, the bit I really liked was where the parakeet flew into the mirror. Now that's funny.

George: The parakeet in the mirror. That is a good one, Stu.

Jerry: Yeah, it's one of my favorites.

Russell: What about you George, have you written anything we might know?

George: Well, possibly. I wrote an off-Broadway show, "La Cocina". . . . Actually it was off-off-Broadway. It was a comedy about a Mexican chef.

Jerry: Oh it was very funny. There was one great scene with the chef—what was his name?

George: Pepe.

Jerry: Oh Pepe, yeah Pepe. And, uh, he was making tamales.

Susan: Oh, he actually cooked on the stage?

George: No, no, he mimed it. That's what was so funny about it.

Russell: So what have you two come up with?

Jerry: Well we've thought about this in a variety of ways. But the basic idea is I will play myself.

George (interrupting, to Jerry): May I?

Jerry: Go ahead.

George: I think I can sum up the show for you with one word. NOTHING.

Russell: Nothing?

George: Nothing.

Russell: What does that mean?

George: The show is about nothing.

Jerry (to George): Well, it's not about nothing.

George (to Jerry): No, it's about nothing.

Jerry: Well, maybe in philosophy. But even nothing is something.

> *Jerry and George glare at each other. Receptionist sticks her head in.*

Receptionist: Mr. Dalrymple, your niece is on the phone.

Russell: I'll call back.

George: D-A-L-R-I-M-P-E-L.

Russell: Not even close.

George: Is it with a "y"?

Russell: No.

Susan: What's the premise?

Jerry: . . . Well, as I was saying, I would play myself. And as a comedian, living in New York, and I have a friend and a neighbor and an ex-girlfriend, which is all true.

George: Yeah, but nothing happens on the show. You see, it's just like life. You know, you eat, you go shopping, you read. You eat, you read, you go shopping.

Russell: You read? You read on the show?

Jerry: Well I don't know about the reading. We didn't discuss the reading.

Russell: All right, tell me, tell me about the stories. What kind of stories?

George: Oh no, no stories.

Russell: No stories? So what is it?

George: What'd you do today?

Russell: I got up and came to work.

George: There's a show. That's a show.

Russell (confused): How is that a show?

Jerry: Well, uh, maybe something happens on the way to work.

George: No, no, no. Nothing happens.

Jerry: Well, something happens.

Russell: Well why am I watching it?

George: Because it's on TV.

Russell: Not yet.

George: Okay, uh, look, if you want to just keep on doing the same old thing, then maybe this idea is not for you. I for one will not compromise my artistic integrity. And I'll tell you something else. This is the show and we're not going to change it. *(To Jerry.)* Right?

Jerry: How about this? I manage a circus . . .

CONSIDERATIONS FOR CRITICAL THINKING AND WRITING

1. FIRST RESPONSE. What does George mean when he says the proposed show should be about "nothing"? Why is George's idea both a comic and a serious proposal?

2. How does the stage direction "Suits enter" serve to characterize Stu and Jay? Write a description of how you think they would look.

3. What is revealed about George's character when he spells Crespi's and Dalrymple's names?

4. Discuss Kramer's assertion that people "want to watch freaks." Do you think this line could be used to sum up accurately audience responses to *Seinfeld?*

5. Choose a scene, and explain how humor is worked into it. What other emotions are evoked in the scene?

6. View an episode of *Seinfeld.* How does reading a script compare with watching the show? Which do you prefer? Why?

CONNECTION TO ANOTHER SELECTION

1. In an essay explain whether or not you think David Ives's play *Sure Thing* (p. 1189) fills George's prescription that a story should be about "nothing."

Like those of many plays, the settings for these scenes are not detailed. Jerry's apartment and the coffee shop are, to cite only two examples, not described at all. We are told only that it is lunchtime in the coffee shop. Even without a set designer's version of these scenes, we readily create a mental picture of these places that provides a background for the characters. In the coffee shop scene we can assume that Jerry and George are having lunch, but we must supply the food, the plates and cutlery, the tables and chairs, and the other customers. For the television show sets were used that replicated the details of a Manhattan coffee shop, right down to the menus and cash register. If the scene were presented on a stage, a set designer might use minimal sets and props to suggest the specific location. The director of such a production would rely on the viewers' imagination to create the details of the setting.

As brief as they are, these scenes include some exposition to provide the necessary background about the characters and their circumstances. We learn through dialogue, for example, that George is not a writer and that he doesn't think it takes very much talent to write a sit-com even though he's unemployed. These bits of information help to characterize George and allow an audience to place his attitudes and comments in a larger context that will be useful for understanding how other characters read them. Rather than dramatizing background information, the scriptwriter arranges incidents to create a particular focus and effect while working in the necessary exposition through dialogue.

The plot in these scenes shapes the conflicts to emphasize humor. As in any good play, incidents are carefully arranged to achieve a particular effect. In the first scene we learn that NBC executives are interested in having Jerry do his own television show. We also learn, through his habit of spelling people's last names when he meets them, that George is a potential embarrassment. The dialogue between Jerry and George quickly establishes the conflict. The NBC executives would like to produce a TV show with Jerry provided that he can come up with an idea for the series; Jerry, however, has no ideas (here's the complication of the pyramidal plot pattern discussed in Elements of Drama, p. 1185). This complication sets up a conflict for Jerry because George assumes that he can help Jerry develop an idea for the show, which, after all, shouldn't be any more difficult than spelling a stranger's name. As George says, "How hard is that? Look at all the junk that's on TV."

All of a sudden everyone is an expert on scriptwriting. George's off-the-wall suggestions that the premise for the show be Jerry's running an antique shop or teaching gymnastics are complemented by Kramer's idea that Jerry be "the manager of the circus" because "people they want to watch freaks." As unhelpful as Kramer's suggestion is, there is some truth here as well as humor, given his own freakish behavior. However, it is George who comes through with the most intriguing suggestion. As a result of the exuberantly funny riff he and Jerry do on "the difference between seltzer and salsa," George suddenly realizes that the show should be "about nothing" — that it should consist of nothing more than Jerry talking and hanging out with his friends George, Elaine, and Kramer. Jerry's initial skepticism gives way as he seriously considers George's proposal and is intrigued enough to bring George with him to the NBC offices to make the pitch. His decision to bring George to the meeting can only, of course, complicate matters further.

Before the meeting with the NBC executives, George is stricken with one of his crises of confidence when he compares himself to the "men with jobs" who are married and have secretaries. Characteristically, George's temporary lack of confidence shifts to an equally ill-timed arrogance once the meeting begins. He usurps Jerry's role and makes the pitch himself: "Nothing happens on the show. You see, it's just like life. You know, you eat, you go shopping, you read. You eat, you read, you go shopping." The climax occurs when George refuses even to consider any of the reservations the executives have about "nothing" happening on the show. George's insistence that he not compromise his "artistic integrity" creates a crisis for Jerry, a turning point that makes him realize that George's ridiculous arrogance might cost him his opportunity to have a TV show. Jerry's final lines to the executives—"How about this? I manage a circus . . ."—work two ways: he resignedly acknowledges that something—not "nothing"—has just happened and that George is, indeed, something of a freak.

The failing action and resolution typical of a pyramidal plot are not present in "The Pitch" because the main plot is not resolved until a later episode. "The Pitch" also contains several subplots not included in the scenes excerpted in this book. Like the main plot, these subplots involving Elaine, Kramer, and a few minor characters are not resolved until later episodes. Self-contained series episodes are increasingly rare on television, as programmers attempt to hook viewers week after week by creating suspense once associated with serialized stories that appeared weekly or monthly in magazines.

The theme of "The Pitch" is especially interesting because it self-reflexively comments on the basic premise of *Seinfeld* scripts: they are all essentially about "nothing" in that they focus on the seemingly trivial details of the four main characters' lives. The unspoken irony of this theme is that such details are in fact significant because it is just such small, everyday activities that constitute most people's lives.

PERSPECTIVE

GEOFFREY O'BRIEN (B. 1948)

On Seinfeld *as Sitcom Moneymaker* 1997

If *Seinfeld* is indeed, in the words of *Entertainment Weekly*, "the defining sitcom of our age" (one wonders how many such ages, each defined by its own sitcom, have already elapsed), the question remains what exactly it defines. Deliberate satire is alien to the spirit of the enterprise. *Seinfeld* has perfected a form in which anything can be invoked—masturbation, Jon Voight, death, kasha, deafness, faked orgasms, Salman Rushdie, Pez dispensers—without assuming the burden of saying anything about it (thereby avoiding the "social message" trap of programs like Norman Lear's *All in the Family* or *Maude*).

The show does not comment on anything except, famously, itself, in the series of episodes where Jerry and George create a pilot for a sitcom "about nothing," a sitcom identical to the one we are watching. This ploy—which ultimately necessitates a whole set of look-alikes to impersonate the cast of the show-within-a-show *Jerry* — ties in with the recursive, alternate-universe mode of such comedies as *The Purple Rose of Cairo* and *Groundhog Day*, while holding back just this side of the paranormal. If conspiracy theories surface from time to time, it is purely for amusement value, as in the episode where a spitting incident at the ballpark becomes the occasion for an elaborate parody — complete with Zapruder-like home movie° — of the Single Bullet Theory (figuring in this context as the ultimate joke on the idea of explanation).

The result is a vastly entertaining mosaic of observed bits and traits and frames. Imagine some future researcher trying to annotate any one of these episodes, like a Shakespearean scholar dutifully noting that "tapsters were proverbially poor at arithmetic." It would not merely be a matter of explaining jokes and cultural references and curt showbiz locutions — "He does fifteen minutes on Ovaltine" or "They cancelled Rick James" — but of explicating (always assuming that they were detected in the first place) each shrug and curtailed expostulation and deftly averted glance.

Where it might once have been asked if *Seinfeld* was a commentary on society, the question now should probably be whether society has not been reconfigured as a milieu for commenting on *Seinfeld*. If the craziness enacted on the show is nothing more than the usual business of comedy, the craziness that swirls around it in the outside world is of a less hilarious order. Comedy and money have always been around, but not always in such intimate linkage, and certainly not on so grandiose a scale. In the fifteenth century, the fate of Tudor commerce was not perceived to hinge on the traveling English players who wowed foreign audiences as far afield as Denmark.

The information-age money culture for which *Seinfeld* is only another, fatter, bargaining chip clearly lost its sense of humor a long time ago, a fact that becomes ever more apparent as we move into an economy where sit-coms replace iron and steel as principal products and where fun is not merely big business but seemingly the only business. The once-endearing razzmatazz of showbiz hype warps into a perceptible desperation that registers all too plainly how much is at stake for the merchandisers. One becomes uncomfortably aware of them looming behind the audience, running electronic analyses of the giggles, and nervously watching for the dreaded moment when the laughter begins to dry up. It all begins to seem too much like work even for the audience, who may well begin to wonder why they should be expected to care about precisely how much their amusement is worth to the ticket-sellers.

As for the actual creators of the fun, I would imagine that — allowing for difference of scale and pressure — they go about their work pretty much the same way regardless of the going price for a good laugh. Some years ago, in a dusty corner of Languedoc,° I watched a dented circus truck pull up unannounced along the roadside. The family of performers who clambered out proceeded to set up a makeshift stage, which in a few hours time was ready for their show: a display of tumbling and magic that could have been presented without significant difference in the fifteenth century. After two hours of sublime entertainment, they passed the hat around and drove away toward the

Zapruder-like home movie: A reference to the Dallas bystander who captured John F. Kennedy's assassination on film.
Languedoc: A region in southern France.

next bend in the road. It is strange to think of the fate of empires, even entertainment empires, hinging on such things.

From the *New York Review of Books,* August 14, 1997

CONSIDERATIONS FOR CRITICAL THINKING AND WRITING

1. In what sense might *Seinfeld* be described as "the defining sitcom of our age"? Do you think this is an accurate description of the show? Why or why not?

2. Explain why you agree or disagree with O'Brien's assertion that *Seinfeld* "does not comment on anything except, famously, itself."

3. Comment on O'Brien's idea that "Comedy and money have always been around, but not always in such intimate linkage." How does *Seinfeld* fit into an "information-age money culture"?

29

Writing about Drama

FROM READING TO WRITING

Because dramatic literature is written to be performed, writing about reading a play may seem twice removed from what playwrights intend the experience of drama to be: a live audience responding to live actors. Although reading a play creates distance between yourself and a performance of it, reading a play can actually bring you closer to understanding that what supports a stage production of any play is the literary dimension of a script. Writing about that script — examining carefully how the language of the stage directions, setting, exposition, dialogue, plot, and other dramatic elements serve to produce effects and meanings — can enhance an imaginative re-creation of a performance. In a sense, writing about a play gauges your own interpretative response as an audience member — the difference, of course, is that instead of applauding, you are typing.

"There's the rub," as Hamlet might say, because you're working with the precision of your fingertips rather than with the hearty response of your palms. Composing an essay about drama recor_.s more than your response to a play; writing also helps you explore, clarify, and discover dimensions of the play you may not have perceived by simply watching a performance of it. Writing is work, of course, but it's the kind of work that brings you closer to your own imagination as well as to the play. That process is more accessible if you read carefully, take notes, and annotate the text to generate ideas (for a discussion of this process see Chapter 38, "Reading and Writing"). This chapter offers a set of questions to help you read and write about drama and includes a sample paper that argues for a feminist reading of Susan Glaspell's *Trifles*.

QUESTIONS FOR RESPONSIVE READING AND WRITING

The questions in this chapter can help you consider important elements that reveal a play's effects and meanings. These questions are general and will not, therefore, always be relevant to a particular play. Many of them, however, should prove to be useful for thinking, talking, and writing about drama. If you are uncertain about the meaning of a term used in a question, consult the Glossary of Literary Terms beginning on page 2123.

1. Did you enjoy the play? What, specifically, pleased or displeased you about what was expressed and how it was expressed?
2. What is the significance of the play's title? How does it suggest the author's overall emphasis?
3. What information do the stage directions provide about the characters, action, and setting? Are these directions primarily descriptive, or are they also interpretive?
4. How is the exposition presented? What does it reveal? How does the playwright's choice *not* to dramatize certain events on stage help to determine what the focus of the play is?
5. In what ways is the setting important? Would the play be altered significantly if the setting were changed?
6. Are foreshadowings used to suggest what is to come? Are flashbacks used to dramatize what has already happened?
7. What is the major conflict the protagonist faces? What complications constitute the rising action? Where is the climax? Is the conflict resolved?
8. Are one or more subplots used to qualify or complicate the main plot? Is the plot unified so that each incident somehow has a function that relates it to some other element in the play?
9. Does the author purposely avoid a pyramidal plot structure of rising action, climax, and falling action? Is the plot experimental? Is the plot logically and chronologically organized, or is it fantastical or absurd? What effects are produced by the plot? How does it reflect the author's view of life?
10. Who is the protagonist? Who (or what) is the antagonist?
11. By what means does the playwright reveal character? What do the characters' names, physical qualities, actions, and words convey about them? What do the characters reveal about each other?
12. What is the purpose of the minor characters? Are they individualized, or do they primarily represent ideas or attitudes? Are any character foils used?
13. Do the characters all use the same kind of language, or is their speech differentiated? Is it formal or informal? How do the characters' diction and manner of speaking serve to characterize them?
14. Does your response to the characters change in the course of the play? What causes the change?

15. Are words and images repeated in the play so that they take on special meanings? Which speeches seem particularly important? Why?

16. How does the playwright's use of language contribute to the tone of the play? Is the dialogue, for example, predominantly light, humorous, relaxed, sentimental, sad, angry, intense, or violent?

17. Are any symbols used in the play? Which actions, characters, settings, objects, or words convey more than their literal meanings?

18. Are any unfamiliar theatrical conventions used that present problems in understanding the play? How does knowing more about the nature of the theater from which the play originated help to resolve these problems?

19. Is the theme stated directly, or is it developed implicitly through the plot, characters, or some other element? Does the theme confirm or challenge most people's values?

20. How does the play reflect the values of the society in which it is set and in which it was written?

21. How does the play reflect or challenge your own values?

22. Is there a recording, film, or videocassette of the play available in your library or media center? How does this version compare with your own reading?

23. How would you produce the play on a stage? Consider scenery, costumes, casting, and characterizations. What would you emphasize most in your production?

24. Is there a particular critical approach that seems especially appropriate for this play? (See Chapter 37, "Critical Strategies for Reading," which begins on p. 2021.)

25. How might biographical information about the author help the reader to grasp the central concerns of the play?

26. How might historical information about the play provide a useful context for interpretation?

27. To what extent do your own experiences, values, beliefs, and assumptions inform your interpretation?

28. What kinds of evidence from the play are you focusing on to support your interpretation? Does your interpretation leave out any important elements that might undercut or qualify your interpretation?

29. Given that there are a variety of ways to interpret the play, which one seems the most useful to you?

A SAMPLE PAPER

The Feminist Evidence in Trifles

The following paper was written in response to an assignment that required an analysis — about 750 words — of an assigned play. Chris Duffy's paper argues that although *Trifles* was written close to eighty years ago, it

should be seen as a feminist play because its treatment of the tensions between men and women deliberately reveals the oppressiveness that women
have had to cope with in their everyday lives. The paper discusses a number
of the play's elements, but the discussion is unified through its focus on
how the women characters are bound together by a set of common concerns. Notice that page numbers are provided to document quoted passages but no separate list for the work cited is included because the play
appears in the anthology assigned for the course.

Chris Duffy

Professor Barrina-Barrou

English 109-2

October 6, 19--

The Feminist Evidence in Trifles

Despite its early publication date, Susan Glaspell's
Trifles (1916) can be regarded as a work of feminist literature. The play depicts the life of a woman who has been
suppressed, oppressed, and subjugated by a patronizing,
patriarchal husband. Mrs. Wright is eventually driven to
kill her "hard" (1178) husband who has stifled every last
twitch of her identity. Trifles dramatizes the hypocrisy
and ingrained discrimination of male-dominated society
while simultaneously speaking to the dangers for women who
succumb to such hierarchies. Because Mrs. Wright follows
the role mapped by her husband and is directed by society's patriarchal expectations, her identity is lost somewhere along the way. However, Mrs. Hale and Mrs. Peters
quietly insist on preserving their own identities by protecting Mrs. Wright from the men who seek to convict her
of murder.

Mrs. Wright is described as someone who used to have
a flair for life. Her neighbor, Mrs. Hale, comments that
the last time Mrs. Wright appeared happy and vivacious was
before she was married or, more important, when she was

Minnie Foster and not Mrs. Wright. Mrs. Hale laments, "I heard she used to wear pretty clothes and be lively, when she was Minnie Foster, one of the town girls singing in the choir" (1176). But after thirty years of marriage, Mrs. Wright is now worried about her canned preserves freezing and being without an apron while she is in jail. This subservient image was so accepted in society that Mrs. Peters, the sheriff's wife, speculates that Mrs. Wright must want her apron in order to "feel more natural" (1176). Any other roles would be considered uncharacteristic.

This wifely role is predicated on the supposition that women have no ability to make complicated decisions, to think critically, or to rely on themselves. As the title suggests, the men in this story think of homemaking as much less important than a husband's breadwinning role. Mr. Hale remarks, "Well, women are used to worrying over trifles" (1174), and Sheriff Peters assumes the insignificance of "kitchen things" (1174). Hence, women are forced into a domestic, secondary role, like it or not, and are not even respected for that. Mr. Hale, Sheriff Peters, and the county attorney all dismiss the dialogue between Mrs. Peters and Mrs. Hale as feminine chitchat. Further, the county attorney allows the women to leave the Wrights' house unsupervised because he sees Mrs. Peters as merely an extension of her husband.

Even so, the domestic system the men have set up for their wives and their disregard for them after the rules and boundaries have been laid down prove to be the men's downfall. The evidence that Mrs. Wright killed her husband is woven into Mrs. Hale's and Mrs. Peters's conversations about Mrs. Wright's sewing and her pet bird. The knots in her quilt match those in the rope used to strangle Mr.

Wright, and the bird, the last symbol of Mrs. Wright's
vitality to be taken by her husband, is found dead. Unable
to play the role of subservient wife anymore, Mrs. Wright
is foreign to herself and therefore lives a lie. As Mrs.
Hale proclaims, "It looks as if she didn't know what she
was about!" (1177).

   Mrs. Hale, however, does ultimately understand what
Mrs. Wright is about. She comprehends the desperation,
loneliness, and pain that Mrs. Wright experienced, and she
instinctively knows that the roles Mrs. Wright played--
even that of murderer--are scripted by the male-dominated
circumstances of her life. As Mrs. Hale shrewdly and
covertly observes in the context of a discussion about
housecleaning with the county attorney: "Men's hands
aren't always as clean as they might be" (1175). In fact,
even Mrs. Hale feels some guilt for not having made an
effort to visit Mrs. Wright over the years to help relieve
the monotony of Mrs. Wright's life with her husband:

> I might have known she needed help! I know how
> things can be--for women. I tell you, it's
> queer, Mrs. Peters. We live close together and
> we live far apart. We all go through the same
> things--it's all just a different kind of the
> same thing. (1180)

Mrs. Hale cannot help identifying with her neighbor.

   In contrast, Mrs. Peters is initially reluctant to
support Mrs. Wright. Not only is she married to the sheriff, but, as the county attorney puts it, "a sheriff's
wife is married to the law" (1181) as well. She reminds
Mrs. Hale that "the law has got to punish crime" (1180),
even if it means revealing the existence of the dead bird
and exposing the motive that could convict Mrs. Wright
of murdering her husband. But finally Mrs. Peters also

becomes complicit in keeping information from her husband and other men. She too--owing to the loss of her first child--understands what loss means and what Mrs. Hale means when she says that women "all go through the same things" (1180).

The women in Trifles cannot, as the play reveals, be trifled with. Although Glaspell wrote the play close to eighty years ago, it continues to be relevant to contemporary relationships between men and women because its essentially feminist perspective provides a convincing case for the necessity of women to move beyond destructive stereotypes and oppressive assumptions in order to be true to their own significant--not trifling--experiences.

30

A Study of Sophocles

Sophocles lived a long, productive life (496?–406 B.C.) in Athens. During his life Athens became a dominant political and cultural power after the Persian Wars, but before he died Sophocles witnessed the decline of Athens as a result of the Peloponnesian Wars and the city's subsequent surrender to Sparta. He saw Athenian culture reach remarkable heights as well as collapse under enormous pressures.

Sophocles embodied much of the best of Athenian culture; he enjoyed success as a statesman, general, treasurer, priest, and, of course, prize-winning dramatist. Although surviving fragments indicate that he wrote over 120 plays, only a handful remain intact. Those that survive consist of the three plays he wrote about Oedipus and his children — *Oedipus the King, Oedipus at Colonus,* and *Antigone* — and four additional tragedies: *Philoctetes, Ajax, Maidens of Trachis,* and *Electra.*

His plays won numerous prizes at festival competitions because of his careful, subtle plotting and the sense of inevitability with which their action is charged. Moreover, his development of character is richly complex. Instead of relying on the extreme situations and exaggerated actions that earlier tragedians used, Sophocles created powerfully motivated characters who even today fascinate audiences with their psychological depth.

In addition to crafting sophisticated tragedies for the Greek theater, Sophocles introduced several important innovations to the stage. Most important, he broke the tradition of using only two actors; adding a third resulted in more complicated relationships and intricate dialogue among characters. As individual actors took center stage more often, Sophocles re-duced the role of the chorus (discussed on p. 1219). This shift placed even more emphasis on the actors, although the chorus remained important as a means of commenting on the action and establishing its tone. Sophocles was also the first dramatist to write plays with specific actors in mind, a de-velopment that many later playwrights, including Shakespeare, exploited usefully. But without question Sophocles' greatest contribution to drama was *Oedipus the King*, which, it has been argued, is the most influential drama ever written.

CHRONOLOGY

c. 496 B.C.	Born at Colonus.
480	Athenian victory over the Persians at Salamis. (Sophocles participates as a musician in the victory celebration.)
468	Sophocles' first triumph (over Aeschylus) in the drama competition at the Festival of Dionysus.
443–42	Serves as one of the treasurers of the league against Persia.
c. 441	Writes *Antigone*.
431	The Peloponnesian War begins. This conflict among the Greek states (including Athens and Sparta) lasts nearly thirty years.
c. 430	Writes *Oedipus the King*.
413	Athenian force defeated in Sicily. Sophocles is chosen as one of the leaders to deal with the Sicilian crisis.
406	Sophocles dies.
404	Athens capitulates to Sparta.
401	*Oedipus at Colonus* produced posthumously.

THEATRICAL CONVENTIONS OF GREEK DRAMA

More than twenty-four hundred years have passed since 430 B.C., when Sophocles' *Oedipus the King* was probably first produced on a Greek stage. We inhabit a vastly different planet than Sophocles' audience did, yet con-cerns about what it means to be human in a world that frequently runs counter to our desires and aspirations have remained relatively constant. The ancient Greeks continue to speak to us. But inexperienced readers or viewers may have some initial difficulty understanding the theatrical con-ventions used in classical Greek tragedies such as *Oedipus the King* and *Antigone*. If Sophocles were alive today, he would very likely need some sort of assistance with the conventions of an Arthur Miller play or a television production of *Seinfeld.*

Classical Greek drama developed from religious festivals that paid homage to Dionysus, the god of wine and fertility. Most of the details of these festivals have been lost, but we do know that they included dancing and singing that celebrated legends about Dionysus. From these choral songs developed stories of both Dionysus and mortal culture-heroes. These heroes became the subject of playwrights whose works were produced in contests at the festivals. The Dionysian festivals lasted more than five hundred years, but relatively few of their plays have survived. Among the works of the three great writers of tragedy, only seven plays each by Sophocles and Aeschylus (525?–456 B.C.) and nineteen plays by Euripides (480?–406 B.C.) survive.

Plays were such important events in Greek society that they were partially funded by the state. The Greeks associated drama with religious and community values as well as entertainment. In a sense, their plays celebrate their civilization; in approving the plays, audiences applauded their own culture. The enormous popularity of the plays is indicated by the size of surviving amphitheaters. Although information about these theaters is sketchy, we do know that most of them shared a common form. They were built into hillsides with rising rows of seats accommodating more than fourteen thousand people. These seats partially encircled an ***orchestra*** or "dancing place," where the ***chorus*** of a dozen or so men chanted lines and danced.

Tradition credits the Greek poet Thespis with adding an actor who was separate from the choral singing and dancing of early performances. A second actor was subsequently included by Aeschylus and a third, as noted earlier, by Sophocles. These additions made possible the conflicts and complicated relationships that evolved into the dramatic art we know today. The two or three male actors who played all the roles appeared behind the orchestra in front of the ***skene,*** a stage building that served as dressing rooms. As Greek theater evolved, a wall of the skene came to be painted to suggest a palace or some other setting, and the roof was employed to indicate, for instance, a mountain location. Sometimes gods were lowered from the roof by mechanical devices to set matters right among the mortals below. This method of rescuing characters from complications beyond their abilities to resolve was known in Latin as ***deus ex machina*** ("god from the machine"), a term now used to describe any improbable means by which an author provides a too-easy resolution for a story.

Inevitably, the conventions of the Greek theaters affected how plays were presented. Few if any scene changes occurred because the amphitheater stage was set primarily for one location. If an important event happened somewhere else, it was reported by a minor character, such as a messenger. The chorus also provided necessary background information. In *Oedipus the King* and *Antigone,* the choruses, acting as townspeople, also assess the characters' strengths and weaknesses, praising them for their virtues, chiding them for their rashness, and giving them advice. The reactions

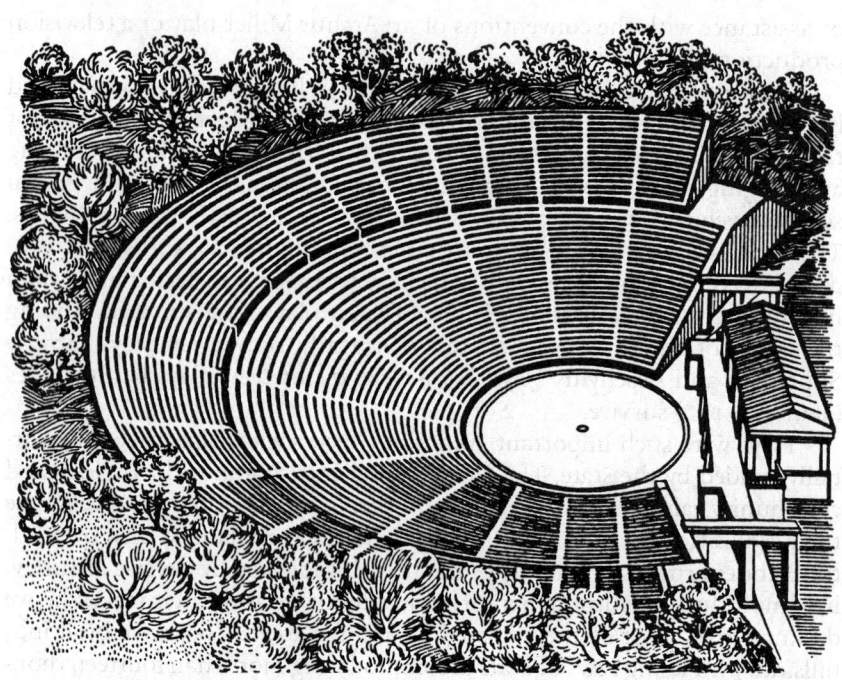

Based on scholarly sources, this drawing represents the features typical of classical Greek theater. (Drawing by Gerda Becker. From Kenneth Macgowan and William Melnitz, The Living Stage, *© 1990 by Prentice Hall/A Division of Simon & Schuster.)*

of the chorus provide a connection between the actors and audience because the chorus is at once a participant in and an observer of the action. In addition, the chorus helps structure the action by indicating changes in scene or mood. Thus the chorus could be used in a variety of ways to shape the audience's response to the play's action and characters.

Actors in classical Greek amphitheaters faced considerable challenges. An intimate relationship with the audience was impossible because many spectators would have been too far away to see a facial expression or subtle gesture. Indeed, some in the audience would have had difficulty even hearing the voices of individual actors. To compensate for these disadvantages, actors wore large masks that extravagantly expressed the major characters' emotions or identified the roles of minor characters. The masks also allowed the two or three actors in a performance to play all the characters without confusing the audience. Each mask was fitted so that the mouthpiece amplified the actor's voice. The actors were further equipped with padded costumes and elevated shoes (*cothurni* or *buskins*) that made them appear larger than life.

As a result of these adaptive conventions, Greek plays tend to emphasize words—formal, impassioned speeches—more than physical action. We are invited to ponder actions and events rather than to see all of them enacted. Although the stark simplicity of Greek theater does not offer an audience realistic detail, the classical tragedies that have survived present characters in dramatic situations that transcend theatrical conventions. Tragedy, it seems, has always been compelling for human beings, regardless of the theatrical forms it has taken.

A Greek tragedy is typically divided into five parts: prologue, parodos, episodia, stasimon, and exodus. In some translations these terms appear as headings, but in more recent translations, as those by Robert Fagles included here, the headings do not appear. Still, understanding these terms provides a sense of the overall rhythm of a Greek play. The opening speech or dialogue is known as the *prologue* and usually gives the exposition necessary to follow the subsequent action. In the *parodos* the chorus makes its first entrance and gives its perspective on what the audience has learned in the prologue. Several *episodia,* or episodes, follow, in which characters engage in dialogue that frequently consists of heated debates dramatizing the play's conflicts. Following each episode is a choral ode or *stasimon,* in which the chorus responds to and interprets the preceding dialogue. The *exodus,* or last scene, follows the final episode and stasimon; in it the resolution occurs and the characters leave the stage.

The effect of alternating dialogues and choral odes has sometimes been likened to that of opera. Greek tragedies were written in verse, and the stasima were chanted or sung as the chorus moved rhythmically, so the plays have a strong musical element that is not always apparent on the printed page. If we remember their musical qualities we are less likely to forget that no matter how terrifying or horrific the conflicts they describe, these plays are stately, measured, and dignified works that reflect a classical Greek sense of order and proportion.

TRAGEDY

Newspapers are filled with daily reports of tragedies: a child is struck and crippled by a car; an airplane plunges into a suburban neighborhood; a volcano erupts and kills thousands. These unexpected instances of suffering are commonly and accurately described as tragic, but they are not tragedies in the literary sense of the term. A literary *tragedy* presents courageous individuals who confront powerful forces within or outside themselves with a dignity that reveals the breadth and depth of the human spirit in the face of failure, defeat, and even death.

Aristotle (384–322 B.C.), in his *Poetics,* defined *tragedy* on the basis of the plays contemporary to him. His definition has generated countless variations, qualifications, and interpretations, but we still derive our literary understanding of this term from Aristotle.

The protagonist of a Greek tragedy is someone regarded as extraordinary rather than typical: a great man or woman brought from happiness to agony. The character's stature is important because it makes his or her fall

all the more terrifying. The protagonist also carries mythic significance for the audience. Oedipus and Antigone, for example, are not only human beings but legendary figures from a distant, revered past. Although the gods do not appear onstage in either *Oedipus the King* or *Antigone,* their power is ever present as the characters invoke their help or attempt to defy them. In addition, Greek tragedy tends to be public rather than private. The fate of the community—the state—is often linked with that of the protagonist, as when Thebes suffers a plague as a result of Oedipus's mistaken actions.

The protagonists of classical Greek tragedies (and of those of Shakespeare) are often rulers of noble birth who represent the monarchical values of their periods, but in modern tragedies the protagonists are more likely to reflect democratic values that make it possible for anyone to be a suitable subject. What is finally important is not so much the protagonist's social stature as a greatness of character that steadfastly confronts suffering, whether it comes from supernatural, social, or psychological forces. Although Greek tragic heroes were aristocrats, the nobility of their characters was more significant than their inherited titles and privileges.

The protagonist's eminence and determination to complete some task or goal make him or her admirable in Greek tragedy, but that does not free the protagonist from what Aristotle described as "some error or frailty" that brings about his or her misfortune. The term Aristotle used for this weakness is *hamartia.* This word has frequently been interpreted to mean that the protagonist's fall is the result of an internal *tragic flaw,* such as an excess of pride, ambition, passion, or some other character trait that leads directly to disaster.

Sometimes, however, misfortunes are not the result of a character flaw but of misunderstood events that overtake and thwart the protagonist's best intentions. Thus, virtue can lead to tragedy too. *Hamartia* has also been interpreted to mean "wrong act"—a mistake based not on a personal failure but on circumstances outside the protagonist's personality and control. Many readers find that a combination of these two interpretations sheds the most light on the causes of the tragic protagonist's fall. Both internal and external forces can lead to downfall because the protagonist's personality may determine crucial judgments that result in mistaken actions.

However the idea of tragic flaw is understood, it is best not to use it as a means of reducing the qualities of a complex character to an adjective or two that labels Oedipus as guilty of "overweening pride" (the Greek term for which is *hubris* or *hybris*) or Antigone as "fated." The protagonists of tragedies require more careful characterization than a simplistic label can provide.

Whatever the causes of the tragic protagonist's downfall, he or she accepts responsibility for it. Hence, even in his or her encounter with failure (and possibly death) the tragic protagonist displays greatness of character. Perhaps it is the witnessing of this greatness, which seems both to accept and to transcend human limitations, that makes audiences feel relief rather than hopelessness at the end of a tragedy. Aristotle described this response as a *catharsis,* or purgation of the emotions of "pity and fear." We are faced with the protagonist's misfortune, which often seems out of proportion to his or her actions, and so we are likely to feel compassionate pity. Simultaneously, we may experience fear because the failure of the protagonist, who is so great in stature and power, is a frightening reminder of our own vulnerabilities. Ultimately, however, both these negative emotions are purged because the tragic protagonist's suffering is an affirmation of human values — even if they are not always triumphant — rather than a despairing denial of them.

Nevertheless, tragedies are disturbing. Instead of coming away with the reassurance of a happy ending, we must take solace in the insight produced by the hero's suffering. And just as our expectations are changed, so are the protagonist's. Aristotle described the moment in the plot when this change occurs as a *reversal* (*peripeteia*), the point when the hero's fortunes turn in an unexpected direction. He more specifically defined this term as meaning an action performed by a character that has the opposite of its intended effect. An example cited by Aristotle is the messenger's attempts to relieve Oedipus's anxieties about his relationship to his father and mother. Instead, the messenger reveals previously unknown information that eventually results in a *recognition* (*anagnorisis*); Oedipus discovers the terrible truth that he has killed his father and married his mother.

Tragedy is typically filled with ironies because there are so many moments in the plot when what seems to be turns out to be radically different from what actually is. Because of this, a particular form of irony called *dramatic irony* is also known as *tragic irony.* In dramatic irony, the meaning of a character's words or actions is understood by the audience but not by the character. Audiences of Greek tragedy shared with the playwrights a knowledge of the stories on which many tragic plots were based. Consequently, they frequently were aware of what was going to happen before the characters were. When Oedipus declares that he will seek out the person responsible for the plague that ravishes his city, the audience already knows that the person Oedipus pursues is himself.

Oedipus the King

A familiarity with the Oedipus legend allows modern readers to appreciate the series of ironies that unfolds in Sophocles' *Oedipus the King.* In the opening scene, Oedipus appears with a "telltale limp." As an infant, he had been abandoned by his parents, Laius and Jocasta, the king and queen of Thebes, because a prophecy warned that their son would kill his father and marry his mother. They instructed a servant to leave him on a mountain to die. The infant's feet were pierced and pinned together, but he was not left on the mountain; instead the servant, out of pity, gave him to a shepherd, who in turn presented him to the king and queen of Corinth. They named him Oedipus (for "swollen foot") and raised him as their own son.

On reaching manhood, Oedipus learned from an oracle that he would kill his father and marry his mother; to avoid this horrendous fate, he left Corinth forever. In his travels, Oedipus found his way blocked by a chariot at a crossroads; in a fit of anger, he killed the servants and their passenger. That passenger, unknown to Oedipus, was his real father. In Thebes, Oedipus successfully answered the riddle of the Sphinx, a winged lion with a woman's head. The reward for defeating this dreaded monster was both the crown and the dead king's wife. Oedipus and Jocasta had four children and prospered. But when the play begins, Oedipus's rule is troubled by a plague that threatens to destroy Thebes, and he is determined to find the cause of the plague in order to save the city again.

Oedipus the King is widely recognized as the greatest of the surviving Greek tragedies. Numerous translations are available (Robert Fagles's recent highly regarded translations of *Oedipus the King* and *Antigone*, the choice here, are especially accessible to modern readers. For an excerpt from another version of *Oedipus the King*, see Perspectives on Sophocles, p. 1303). The play has absorbed readers for centuries because Oedipus's character—his intelligence, confidence, rashness, and suffering—represents powers and limitations that are both exhilarating and chastening. Although no reader or viewer is likely to identify with Oedipus's extreme circumstances, anyone can appreciate his heroic efforts to find the truth about himself. In that sense, he is one of us—at our best.

SOPHOCLES (496?–406 B.C.)

Oedipus the King

c. 430 B.C.

TRANSLATED BY ROBERT FAGLES

CHARACTERS

Oedipus, king of Thebes
A Priest of Zeus
Creon, brother of Jocasta
A Chorus of Theban citizens and their *Leader*
Tiresias, a blind prophet
Jocasta, the queen, wife of Oedipus
A Messenger from Corinth
A Shepherd
A Messenger from inside the palace
Antigone, Ismene, daughters of Oedipus and Jocasta
Guards and attendants
Priests of Thebes

TIME AND SCENE: *The royal house of Thebes. Double doors dominate the facade; a stone altar stands at the center of the stage.*

Many years have passed since Oedipus solved the riddle of the Sphinx and ascended the throne of Thebes, and now a plague has struck the city. A procession of priests enters; suppliants, broken and despondent, they carry branches wound in wool and lay them on the altar.

The doors open. Guards assemble. Oedipus comes forward, majestic but for a telltale limp, and slowly views the condition of his people.

Oedipus: Oh my children, the new blood of ancient Thebes,
    why are you here? Huddling at my altar,
    praying before me, your branches wound in wool.°
    Our city reeks with the smoke of burning incense,
    rings with cries for the Healer and wailing for the dead.   5
    I thought it wrong, my children, to hear the truth
    from others, messengers. Here I am myself—
    you all know me, the world knows my fame:
    I am Oedipus.

Helping a Priest to his feet.

                Speak up, old man. Your years,
    your dignity—you should speak for the others.   10
    Why here and kneeling, what preys upon you so?
    Some sudden fear? some strong desire?
    You can trust me; I am ready to help,
    I'll do anything. I would be blind to misery
    not to pity my people kneeling at my feet.   15
Priest: Oh Oedipus, king of the land, our greatest power!
    You see us before you, men of all ages
    clinging to your altars. Here are boys,
    still too weak to fly from the nest,
    and here the old, bowed down with the years,   20
    the holy ones—a priest of Zeus° myself—and here
    the picked, unmarried men, the young hope of Thebes.
    And all the rest, your great family gathers now,
    branches wreathed, massing in the squares,
    kneeling before the two temples of queen Athena°   25
    or the river-shrine where the embers glow and die
    and Apollo sees the future in the ashes.
                    Our city—
    look around you, see with your own eyes—
    our ship pitches wildly, cannot lift her head
    from the depths, the red waves of death . . .   30
    Thebes is dying. A blight on the fresh crops
    and the rich pastures, cattle sicken and die,
    and the women die in labor, children stillborn,
    and the plague, the fiery god of fever hurls down
    on the city, his lightning slashing through us—   35
    raging plague in all its vengeance, devastating

---

3 *wool:* Wool was used in offerings to Apollo, god of poetry, the sun, prophecy, and healing.
21 *Zeus:* The highest Olympian deity and father of Apollo.   25 *Athena:* Goddess of wisdom and protector of Greek cities.

the house of Cadmus!° And Black Death luxuriates
in the raw, wailing miseries of Thebes.

Now we pray to you. You cannot equal the gods,
your children know that, bending at your altar.   40
But we do rate you first of men,
both in the common crises of our lives
and face-to-face encounters with the gods.
You freed us from the Sphinx; you came to Thebes
and cut us loose from the bloody tribute we had paid   45
that harsh, brutal singer. We taught you nothing,
no skill, no extra knowledge, still you triumphed.
A god was with you, so they say, and we believe it —
you lifted up our lives.
                              So now again,
Oedipus, king, we bend to you, your power —   50
we implore you, all of us on our knees:
find us strength, rescue! Perhaps you've heard
the voice of a god or something from other men,
Oedipus . . . what do you know?
The man of experience — you see it every day —   55
his plans will work in a crisis, his first of all.
Act now — we beg you, best of men, raise up our city!
Act, defend yourself, your former glory!
Your country calls you savior now
for your zeal, your action years ago.   60
Never let us remember of your reign:
you helped us stand, only to fall once more.
Oh raise up our city, set us on our feet.
The omens were good that day you brought us joy —
be the same man today!   65
Rule our land, you know you have the power,
but rule a land of the living, not a wasteland.
Ship and towered city are nothing, stripped of men
alive within it, living all as one.

Oedipus: My children,
I pity you. I see — how could I fail to see   70
what longings bring you here? Well I know
you are sick to death, all of you,
but sick as you are, not one is sick as I.
Your pain strikes each of you alone, each
in the confines of himself, no other. But my spirit   75
grieves for the city, for myself and all of you.
I wasn't asleep, dreaming. You haven't wakened me —
I've wept through the nights, you must know that,
groping, laboring over many paths of thought.
After a painful search I found one cure: 80
I acted at once. I sent Creon,
my wife's own brother, to Delphi°—

---

37 *Cadmus:* The legendary founder of Thebes.   82 *Delphi:* The shrine where the oracle of
Apollo held forth.

Apollo the Prophet's oracle — to learn
what I might do or say to save our city.

Today's the day. When I count the days gone by   85
it torments me . . . what is he doing?
Strange, he's late, he's gone too long.
But once he returns, then, then I'll be a traitor
if I do not do all the god makes clear.
Priest: Timely words. The men over there   90
are signaling — Creon's just arriving.
Oedipus:

Sighting Creon, then turning to the altar.

Lord Apollo,
let him come with a lucky word of rescue,
shining like his eyes!
Priest: Welcome news, I think — he's crowned, look,
and the laurel wreath is bright with berries.   95
Oedipus: We'll soon see. He's close enough to hear —

Enter Creon from the side; his face is shaded with a wreath.

Creon, prince, my kinsman, what do you bring us?
What message from the god?
Creon: Good news.
I tell you even the hardest things to bear,
if they should turn out well, all would be well.   100
Oedipus: Of course, but what were the god's *words?* There's no hope
and nothing to fear in what you've said so far.
Creon: If you want my report in the presence of these . . .

Pointing to the priests while drawing Oedipus toward the palace.

I'm ready now, or we might go inside.
Oedipus: Speak out,
speak to us all. I grieve for these, my people,   105
far more than I fear for my own life.
Creon: Very well,
I will tell you what I heard from the god.
Apollo commands us — he was quite clear —
"Drive the corruption from the land,
don't harbor it any longer, past all cure,   110
don't nurse it in your soil — root it out!"
Oedipus: How can we cleanse ourselves — what rites?
What's the source of the trouble?
Creon: Banish the man, or pay back blood with blood.
Murder sets the plague-storm on the city.
Oedipus: Whose murder?   115
Whose fate does Apollo bring to light?
Creon: Our leader,
my lord, was once a man named Laius,
before you came and put us straight on course.
Oedipus: I know —
or so I've heard. I never saw the man myself.

Creon: Well, he was killed, and Apollo commands us now—   120
    he could not be more clear,
    "Pay the killers back—whoever is responsible."

Oedipus: Where on earth are they? Where to find it now,
    the trail of the ancient guilt so hard to trace?

Creon: "Here in Thebes," he said.   125
    Whatever is sought for can be caught, you know,
    whatever is neglected slips away.

Oedipus: But where,
    in the palace, the fields or foreign soil,
    where did Laius meet his bloody death?

Creon: He went to consult an oracle, he said,   130
    and he set out and never came home again.

Oedipus: No messenger, no fellow-traveler saw what happened?
    Someone to cross-examine?

Creon: No,
    they were all killed but one. He escaped,
    terrified, he could tell us nothing clearly,   135
    nothing of what he saw—just one thing.

Oedipus: What's that?
    One thing could hold the key to it all,
    a small beginning gives us grounds for hope.

Creon: He said thieves attacked them—a whole band,
    not single-handed, cut King Laius down.

Oedipus: A thief,   140
    so daring, wild, he'd kill a king? Impossible,
    unless conspirators paid him off in Thebes.

Creon: We suspected as much. But with Laius dead
    no leader appeared to help us in our troubles.

Oedipus: Trouble? Your *king* was murdered—royal blood!   145
    What stopped you from tracking down the killer
    then and there?

Creon: The singing, riddling Sphinx.
    She . . . persuaded us to let the mystery go
    and concentrate on what lay at our feet.

Oedipus: No,
    I'll start again—I'll bring it all to light myself!   150
    Apollo is right, and so are you, Creon,
    to turn our attention back to the murdered man.
    Now you have *me* to fight for you, you'll see:
    I am the land's avenger by all rights
    and Apollo's champion too.   155
    But not to assist some distant kinsman, no,
    for my own sake I'll rid us of this corruption.
    Whoever killed the king may decide to kill me too,
    with the same violent hand—by avenging Laius
    I defend myself.

To the priests.

                Quickly, my children.   160
Up from the steps, take up your branches now.

To the guards.

One of you summon the city here before us,
tell them I'll do everything. God help us,
we will see our triumph — or our fall.

Oedipus and Creon enter the palace, followed by the guards.

Priest: Rise, my sons. The kindness we came for   165
Oedipus volunteers himself.
Apollo has sent his word, his oracle —
Come down, Apollo, save us, stop the plague.

*The priests rise, remove their branches, and exit to the side. Enter a Chorus, the
citizens of Thebes, who have not heard the news that Creon brings. They march
around the altar, chanting.*

Chorus: Zeus!
Great welcome voice of Zeus, what do you bring?
What word from the gold vaults of Delphi   170
comes to brilliant Thebes? I'm racked with terror —
                         terror shakes my heart
and I cry your wild cries, Apollo, Healer of Delos°
I worship you in dread . . . what now, what is your price?
some new sacrifice? some ancient rite from the past   175
come round again each spring? —
                  what will you bring to birth?
Tell me, child of golden Hope
         warm voice that never dies!

You are the first I call, daughter of Zeus   180
deathless Athena — I call your sister Artemis,°
heart of the market place enthroned in glory,
                         guardian of our earth —
I call Apollo astride the thunderheads of heaven —
O triple shield against death, shine before me now!   185
If ever, once in the past, you stopped some ruin
launched against our walls
                  you hurled the flame of pain
far, far from Thebes — you gods
         come now, come down once more!

                         No, no   190
the miseries numberless, grief on grief, no end —
too much to bear, we are all dying
O my people . . .
         Thebes like a great army dying
and there is no sword of thought to save us, no   195
and the fruits of our famous earth, they will not ripen
no and the women cannot scream their pangs to birth —

---

173 *Delos:* Apollo was born on this sacred island.   181 *Artemis:* Apollo's sister, goddess of
hunting, the moon, and chastity.

screams for the Healer, children dead in the womb
      and life on life goes down
                  you can watch them go   200
    like seabirds winging west, outracing the day's fire
down the horizon, irresistibly
        streaking on to the shores of Evening
                             Death
so many deaths, numberless deaths on deaths, no end —
Thebes is dying, look, her children   205
stripped of pity . . .
      generations strewn on the ground
unburied, unwept, the dead spreading death
and the young wives and gray-haired mothers with them
cling to the altars, trailing in from all over the city —   210
Thebes, city of death, one long cortege
       and the suffering rises
               wails for mercy rise
     and the wild hymn for the Healer blazes out
clashing with our sobs our cries of mourning —   215
      O golden daughter of god, send rescue
      radiant as the kindness in your eyes!
Drive him back! — the fever, the god of death
                   that raging god of war
not armored in bronze, not shielded now, he burns me,   220
battle cries in the onslaught burning on —
O rout him from our borders!
Sail him, blast him out to the Sea-queen's chamber
                the black Atlantic gulfs
      or the northern harbor, death to all   225
where the Thracian surf comes crashing.
Now what the night spares he comes by day and kills —
the god of death.

          O lord of the stormcloud,
you who twirl the lightning, Zeus, Father,
thunder Death to nothing!   230

Apollo, lord of the light, I beg you —
        whip your longbow's golden cord
showering arrows on our enemies — shafts of power
champions strong before us rushing on!

Artemis, Huntress,   235
torches flaring over the eastern ridges —
            ride Death down in pain!

God of the headdress gleaming gold, I cry to you —
your name and ours are one, Dionysus° —

239 *Dionysus:* God of fertility and wine.

come with your face aflame with wine   240
                  your raving women's cries°
your army on the march! Come with the lightning
come with torches blazing, eyes ablaze with glory!
Burn that god of death that all gods hate!

*Oedipus enters from the palace to address the Chorus, as if addressing the
entire city of Thebes.*

Oedipus: You pray to the gods? Let me grant your prayers.   245
Come, listen to me — do what the plague demands:
you'll find relief and lift your head from the depths.

I will speak out now as a stranger to the story,
a stranger to the crime. If I'd been present then,
there would have been no mystery, no long hunt   250
without a clue in hand. So now, counted
a native Theban years after the murder,
to all of Thebes I make this proclamation:
if any one of you knows who murdered Laius,
the son of Labdacus, I order him to reveal   255
the whole truth to me. Nothing to fear,
even if he must denounce himself,
let him speak up
and so escape the brunt of the charge —
he will suffer no unbearable punishment,   260
nothing worse than exile, totally unharmed.

Oedipus pauses, waiting for a reply.

                                                       Next,
if anyone knows the murderer is a stranger,
a man from alien soil, come, speak up.
I will give him a handsome reward, and lay up
gratitude in my heart for him besides.   265

Silence again, no reply.

But if you keep silent, if anyone panicking,
trying to shield himself or friend or kin,
rejects my offer, then hear what I will do.
I order you, every citizen of the state
where I hold throne and power: banish this man —   270
whoever he may be — never shelter him, never
speak a word to him, never make him partner
to your prayers, your victims burned to the gods.
Never let the holy water touch his hands.
Drive him out, each of you, from every home.   275
He is the plague, the heart of our corruption,
as Apollo's oracle has revealed to me

---

241 *your . . . cries:* Dionysus was attended by female celebrants.

just now. So I honor my obligations:
I fight for the god and for the murdered man.

Now my curse on the murderer. Whoever he is,   280
a lone man unknown in his crime
or one among many, let that man drag out
his life in agony, step by painful step —
I curse myself as well . . . if by any chance
he proves to be an intimate of our house,   285
here at my hearth, with my full knowledge,
may the curse I just called down on him strike me!

These are your orders: perform them to the last.
I command you, for my sake, for Apollo's, for this country
blasted root and branch by the angry heavens.   290
Even if god had never urged you on to act,
how could you leave the crime uncleansed so long?
A man so noble — your king, brought down in blood —
you should have searched. But I am the king now,
I hold the throne that he held then, possess his bed   295
and a wife who shares our seed . . . why, our seed
might be the same, children born of the same mother
might have created blood-bonds between us
if his hope of offspring hadn't met disaster —
but fate swooped at his head and cut him short.   300
So I will fight for him as if he were my father,
stop at nothing, search the world
to lay my hands on the man who shed his blood,
the son of Labdacus descended of Polydorus,
Cadmus of old and Agenor, founder of the line: 305
their power and mine are one.

                              Oh dear gods,
my curse on those who disobey these orders!
Let no crops grow out of the earth for them —
shrivel their women, kill their sons,
burn them to nothing in this plague   310
that hits us now, or something even worse.
But you, loyal men of Thebes who approve my actions,
may our champion, Justice, may all the gods
be with us, fight beside us to the end!

Leader: In the grip of your curse, my king, I swear   315
I'm not the murderer, cannot point him out.
As for the search, Apollo pressed it on us —
he should name the killer.

Oedipus: Quite right,
but to force the gods to act against their will —
no man has the power.

Leader: Then if I might mention   320
the next best thing . . .

Oedipus: The third best too —
don't hold back, say it.

Leader: I still believe . . .
   Lord Tiresias sees with the eyes of Lord Apollo.
   Anyone searching for the truth, my king,
   might learn it from the prophet, clear as day.   325
Oedipus: I've not been slow with that. On Creon's cue
   I sent the escorts, twice, within the hour.
   I'm surprised he isn't here.
Leader: We need him—
   without him we have nothing but old, useless rumors.
Oedipus: Which rumors? I'll search out every word.   330
Leader: Laius was killed, they say, by certain travelers.
Oedipus: I know—but no one can find the murderer.
Leader: If the man has a trace of fear in him
   he won't stay silent long,
   not with your curses ringing in his ears.   335
Oedipus: He didn't flinch at murder,
   he'll never flinch at words.   /

*Enter Tiresias, the blind prophet, led by a boy with escorts in attendance. He
remains at a distance.*

Leader: Here is the one who will convict him, look,
   they bring him on at last, the seer, the man of god.
   The truth lives inside him, him alone.
Oedipus: O Tiresias,   340
   master of all the mysteries of our life,
   all you teach and all you dare not tell,
   signs in the heavens, signs that walk the earth!
   Blind as you are, you can feel all the more
   what sickness haunts our city. You, my lord,   345
   are the one shield, the one savior we can find.

   We asked Apollo—perhaps the messengers
   haven't told you—he sent his answer back:
   "Relief from the plague can only come one way.
   Uncover the murderers of Laius,   350
   put them to death or drive them into exile."
   So I beg you, grudge us nothing now, no voice,
   no message plucked from the birds, the embers
   or the other mantic ways within your grasp.
   Rescue yourself, your city, rescue me—   355
   rescue everything infected by the dead.
   We are in your hands. For a man to help others
   with all his gifts and native strength:
   that is the noblest work.
Tiresias: How terrible—to see the truth
   when the truth is only pain to him who sees!   360
   I knew it well, but I put it from my mind,
   else I never would have come.
Oedipus: What's this? Why so grim, so dire?
Tiresias: Just send me home. You bear your burdens,

I'll bear mine. It's better that way, 365
please believe me.
Oedipus: Strange response — unlawful,
unfriendly too to the state that bred and raised you;
you're withholding the word of god.
Tiresias: I fail to see
that your own words are so well-timed.
I'd rather not have the same thing said of me . . . 370
Oedipus: For the love of god, don't turn away,
not if you know something. We beg you,
all of us on our knees.
Tiresias: None of you knows —
and I will never reveal my dreadful secrets,
not to say your own. 375
Oedipus: What? You know and you won't tell?
You're bent on betraying us, destroying Thebes?
Tiresias: I'd rather not cause pain for you or me.
So why this . . . useless interrogation?
You'll get nothing from me.
Oedipus: Nothing! You, 380
you scum of the earth, you'd enrage a heart of stone!
You won't talk? Nothing moves you?
Out with it, once and for all!
Tiresias: You criticize my temper . . . unaware
of the one *you* live with, you revile me. 385
Oedipus: Who could restrain his anger hearing you?
What outrage — you spurn the city!
Tiresias: What will come will come.
Even if I shroud it all in silence.
Oedipus: What will come? You're bound to *tell* me that. 390
Tiresias: I'll say no more. Do as you like, build your anger
to whatever pitch you please, rage your worst —
Oedipus: Oh I'll let loose, I have such fury in me —
now I see it all. You helped hatch the plot,
you did the work, yes, short of killing him 395
with your own hands — and given eyes I'd say
you did the killing single-handed!
Tiresias: Is that so!
I charge you, then, submit to that decree
you just laid down: from this day onward
speak to no one, not these citizens, not myself. 400
You are the curse, the corruption of the land!
Oedipus: You, shameless —
aren't you appalled to start up such a story?
You think you can get away with this?
Tiresias: I have already.
The truth with all its power lives inside me.
Oedipus: Who primed you for this? Not your prophet's trade. 405
Tiresias: You did, you forced me, twisted it out of me.
Oedipus: What? Say it again — I'll understand it better.

Tiresias: Didn't you understand, just now?
    Or are you tempting me to talk?   410
Oedipus: No, I can't say I grasped your meaning.
    Out with it, again!
Tiresias: I say you are the murderer you hunt.
Oedipus: That obscenity, twice—by god, you'll pay.
Tiresias: Shall I say more, so you can really rage?   415
Oedipus: Much as you want. Your words are nothing—futile.
Tiresias: You cannot imagine . . . I tell you,
    you and your loved ones live together in infamy,
    you cannot see how far you've gone in guilt.
Oedipus: You think you can keep this up and never suffer?   420
Tiresias: Indeed, if the truth has any power.
Oedipus: It does
    but not for you, old man. You've lost your power,
    stone-blind, stone-deaf—senses, eyes blind as stone!
Tiresias: I pity you, flinging at me the very insults
    each man here will fling at you so soon.
Oedipus: Blind,   425
    lost in the night, endless night that nursed you!
    You can't hurt me or anyone else who sees the light—
    you can never touch me.
Tiresias: True, it is not your fate
    to fall at my hands. Apollo is quite enough,
    and he will take some pains to work this out.   430
Oedipus: Creon! Is this conspiracy his or yours?
Tiresias: Creon is not your downfall, no, you are your own.
Oedipus: O power—
    wealth and empire, skill outstripping skill
    in the heady rivalries of life,
    what envy lurks inside you! Just for this,   435
    the crown the city gave me—I never sought it,
    they laid it in my hands—for this alone, Creon,
    the soul of trust, my loyal friend from the start
    steals against me . . . so hungry to overthrow me
    he sets this wizard on me, this scheming quack,   440
    this fortune-teller peddling lies, eyes peeled
    for his own profit—seer blind in his craft!

    Come here, you pious fraud. Tell me,
    when did you ever prove yourself a prophet?
    When the Sphinx, that chanting Fury kept her deathwatch here,   445
    why silent then, not a word to set our people free?
    There was a riddle, not for some passer-by to solve—
    it cried out for a prophet. Where were you?
    Did you rise to the crisis? Not a word,
    you and your birds, your gods—nothing.   450
    No, but I came by, Oedipus the ignorant,
    I stopped the Sphinx! With no help from the birds,
    the flight of my own intelligence hit the mark.

And this is the man you'd try to overthrow?
You think you'll stand by Creon when he's king?   455
You and the great mastermind —
you'll pay in tears, I promise you, for this,
this witch-hunt. If you didn't look so senile
the lash would teach you what your scheming means!
Leader: I'd suggest his words were spoken in anger,   460
Oedipus . . . yours too, and it isn't what we need.
The best solution to the oracle, the riddle
posed by god — we should look for that.
Tiresias: You are the king no doubt, but in one respect,
at least, I am your equal: the right to reply.   465
I claim that privilege too.
I am not your slave. I serve Apollo.
I don't need Creon to speak for me in public.
                                                      So,
you mock my blindness? Let me tell you this.
You with your precious eyes,   470
you're blind to the corruption of your life,
to the house you live in, those you live with —
who *are* your parents? Do you know? All unknowing
you are the scourge of your own flesh and blood,
the dead below the earth and the living here above,   475
and the double lash of your mother and your father's curse
will whip you from this land one day, their footfall
treading you down in terror, darkness shrouding
your eyes that now can see the light!
                                            Soon, soon
you'll scream aloud — what haven won't reverberate?   480
What rock of Cithaeron° won't scream back in echo?
That day you learn the truth about your marriage,
the wedding-march that sang you into your halls,
the lusty voyage home to the fatal harbor!
And a load of other horrors you'd never dream   485
will level you with yourself and all your children.

There. Now smear us with insults — Creon, myself
and every word I've said. No man will ever
be rooted from the earth as brutally as you.
Oedipus: Enough! Such filth from him? Insufferable —   490
what, still alive? Get out —
faster, back where you came from — vanish!
Tiresias: I'd never have come if you hadn't called me here.
Oedipus: If I thought you'd blurt out such absurdities,
you'd have died waiting before I'd had you summoned.   495
Tiresias: Absurd, am I? To you, not to your parents:
the ones who bore you found me sane enough.
Oedipus: Parents — who? Wait . . . who is my father?
Tiresias: This day will bring your birth and your destruction.

481 *Cithaeron:* The mountains where Oedipus was abandoned as an infant.

Oedipus: Riddles—all you can say are riddles, murk and darkness.   500
Tiresias: Ah, but aren't you the best man alive at solving riddles?
Oedipus: Mock me for that, go on, and you'll reveal my greatness.
Tiresias: Your great good fortune, true, it was your ruin.
Oedipus: Not if I saved the city—what do I care?
Tiresias: Well then, I'll be going.

   To his attendant.

Take me home, boy.   505

Oedipus: Yes, take him away. You're a nuisance here.
   Out of the way, the irritation's gone.

   Turning his back on Tiresias, moving toward the palace.

Tiresias: I will go,
   once I have said what I came here to say.
   I'll never shrink from the anger in your eyes—
   you can't destroy me. Listen to me closely: 510
   the man you've sought so long, proclaiming,
   cursing up and down, the murderer of Laius—
   he is here. A stranger,
   you may think, who lives among you,
   he soon will be revealed a native Theban   515
   but he will take no joy in the revelation.
   Blind who now has eyes, beggar who now is rich,
   he will grope his way toward a foreign soil,
   a stick tapping before him step by step.

   Oedipus enters the palace.

   Revealed at last, brother and father both   520
   to the children he embraces, to his mother
   son and husband both—he sowed the loins
   his father sowed, he spilled his father's blood!

   Go in and reflect on that, solve that.
   And if you find I've lied   525
   from this day onward call the prophet blind.

   Tiresias and the boy exit to the side.

Chorus: Who—
   who is the man the voice of god denounces
   resounding out of the rocky gorge of Delphi?
      The horror too dark to tell,
   whose ruthless bloody hands have done the work?   530
   His time has come to fly
      to outrace the stallions of the storm
                his feet a streak of speed—
   Cased in armor, Apollo son of the Father
   lunges on him, lightning-bolts afire!   535
   And the grim unerring Furies°

---

536 *Furies:* Three spirits who avenged evildoers.

closing for the kill.
      Look,
the word of god has just come blazing
flashing off Parnassus'° snowy heights!
    That man who left no trace—   540
after him, hunt him down with all our strength!
Now under bristling timber
   up through rocks and caves he stalks
       like the wild mountain bull—
cut off from men, each step an agony, frenzied, racing blind 545
but he cannot outrace the dread voices of Delphi
ringing out of the heart of Earth,
   the dark wings beating around him shrieking doom
      the doom that never dies, the terror—

The skilled prophet scans the birds and shatters me with terror! 550
I can't accept him, can't deny him, don't know what to say,
I'm lost, and the wings of dark foreboding beating—
I cannot see what's come, what's still to come . . .
and what could breed a blood feud between
   Laius' house and the son of Polybus?°   555
I know of nothing, not in the past and not now,
no charge to bring against our king, no cause
to attack his fame that rings throughout Thebes—
   not without proof—not for the ghost of Laius,
   not to avenge a murder gone without a trace.   560

Zeus and Apollo know, they know, the great masters
    of all the dark and depth of human life.
But whether a mere man can know the truth,
whether a seer can fathom more than I—
there is no test, no certain proof   565
   though matching skill for skill
a man can outstrip a rival. No, not till I see
these charges proved will I side with his accusers.
We saw him then, when the she-hawk° swept against him,
saw with our own eyes his skill, his brilliant triumph— 570
   there was the test—he was the joy of Thebes!
   Never will I convict my king, never in my heart.

Enter Creon from the side.

Creon: My fellow-citizens, I hear King Oedipus
  levels terrible charges at me. I had to come.
  I resent it deeply. If, in the present crisis,   575
  he thinks he suffers any abuse from me,
  anything I've done or said that offers him
  the slightest injury, why, I've no desire
  to linger out this life, my reputation a shambles.

---

539 *Parnassus:* A mountain in Greece associated with Apollo. 555 *Polybus:* The King of Corinth, who is thought to be Oedipus's father. 569 *she-hawk:* The Sphinx.

The damage I'd face from such an accusation 580
is nothing simple. No, there's nothing worse:
branded a traitor in the city, a traitor
to all of you and my good friends.
Leader: True,
but a slur might have been forced out of him,
by anger perhaps, not any firm conviction. 585
Creon: The charge was made in public, wasn't it?
I put the prophet up to spreading lies?
Leader: Such things were said . . .
I don't know with what intent, if any.
Creon: Was his glance steady, his mind right 590
when the charge was brought against me?
Leader: I really couldn't say. I never look
to judge the ones in power.

The doors open. Oedipus enters.

                      Wait,
here's Oedipus now.
Oedipus: You — here? You have the gall
to show your face before the palace gates? 595
You, plotting to kill me, kill the king —
I see it all, the marauding thief himself
scheming to steal my crown and power!
                      Tell me,
in god's name, what did you take me for,
coward or fool, when you spun out your plot? 600
Your treachery — you think I'd never detect it
creeping against me in the dark? Or sensing it,
not defend myself ? Aren't you the fool,
you and your high adventure. Lacking numbers,
powerful friends, out for the big game of empire — 605
you need riches, armies to bring that quarry down!
Creon: Are you quite finished? It's your turn to listen
for just as long as you've . . . instructed me.
Hear me out, then judge me on the facts.
Oedipus: You've a wicked way with words, Creon, 610
but I'll be slow to learn — from you.
I find you a menace, a great burden to me.
Creon: Just one thing, hear me out in this.
Oedipus: Just one thing,
don't tell me you're not the enemy, the traitor.
Creon: Look, if you think crude, mindless stubbornness 615
such a gift, you've lost your sense of balance.
Oedipus: If you think you can abuse a kinsman,
then escape the penalty, you're insane.
Creon: Fair enough, I grant you. But this injury
you say I've done you, what is it? 620
Oedipus: Did you induce me, yes or no,
to send for that sanctimonious prophet?
Creon: I did. And I'd do the same again.

Oedipus: All right then, tell me, how long is it now
    since Laius . . .
Creon: Laius — what did *he* do?
Oedipus: Vanished,   625
    swept from sight, murdered in his tracks.
Creon: The count of the years would run you far back . . .
Oedipus: And that far back, was the prophet at his trade?
Creon: Skilled as he is today, and just as honored.
Oedipus: Did he ever refer to me then, at that time?
Creon: No,   630
    never, at least, when I was in his presence.
Oedipus: But you did investigate the murder, didn't you?
Creon: We did our best, of course, discovered nothing.
Oedipus: But the great seer never accused me then — why not?
Creon: I don't know. And when I don't, *I* keep quiet.   635
Oedipus: You do know this, you'd tell it too —
    if you had a shred of decency.
Creon: What?
    If I know, I won't hold back.
Oedipus: Simply this:
    if the two of you had never put heads together,
    we'd never have heard about *my* killing Laius.   640
Creon: If that's what he says . . . well, you know best.
    But now I have a right to learn from you
    as you just learned from me.
Oedipus: Learn your fill,
    you never will convict me of the murder.
Creon: Tell me, you're married to my sister, aren't you?   645
Oedipus: A genuine discovery — there's no denying that.
Creon: And you rule the land with her, with equal power?
Oedipus: She receives from me whatever she desires.
Creon: And I am the third, all of us are equals?
Oedipus: Yes, and it's there you show your stripes —   650
    you betray a kinsman.
Creon: Not at all.
    Not if you see things calmly, rationally,
    as I do. Look at it this way first:
    who in his right mind would rather rule
    and live in anxiety than sleep in peace?   655
    Particularly if he enjoys the same authority.
    Not I, I'm not the man to yearn for kingship,
    not with a king's power in my hands. Who would?
    No one with any sense of self-control.
    Now, as it is, you offer me all I need,   660
    not a fear in the world. But if I wore the crown . . .
    there'd be many painful duties to perform,
    hardly to my taste.
                  How could kingship
    please me more than influence, power
    without a qualm? I'm not that deluded yet,   665

to reach for anything but privilege outright,
profit free and clear.
Now all men sing my praises, all salute me,
now all who request your favors curry mine.
I'm their best hope: success rests in me.   670
Why give up that, I ask you, and borrow trouble?
A man of sense, someone who sees things clearly
would never resort to treason.
No, I've no lust for conspiracy in me,
nor could I ever suffer one who does.   675

Do you want proof? Go to Delphi yourself,
examine the oracle and see if I've reported
the message word-for-word. This too:
if you detect that I and the clairvoyant
have plotted anything in common, arrest me,   680
execute me. Not on the strength of one vote,
two in this case, mine as well as yours.
But don't convict me on sheer unverified surmise.

How wrong it is to take the good for bad,
purely at random, or take the bad for good.   685
But reject a friend, a kinsman? I would as soon
tear out the life within us, priceless life itself.
You'll learn this well, without fail, in time.
Time alone can bring the just man to light;
the criminal you can spot in one short day.
Leader: Good advice,   690
  my lord, for anyone who wants to avoid disaster.
  Those who jump to conclusions may be wrong.
Oedipus: When my enemy moves against me quickly,
  plots in secret, I move quickly too, I must,
  I plot and pay him back. Relax my guard a moment,   695
  waiting his next move — he wins his objective,
  I lose mine.
Creon: What do you want?
  You want me banished?
Oedipus: No, I want you dead.
Creon: Just to show how ugly a grudge can . . .
Oedipus: So,
  still stubborn? you don't think I'm serious?   700
Creon: I think you're insane.
Oedipus: Quite sane — in my behalf.
Creon: Not just as much in mine?
Oedipus: You — my mortal enemy?
Creon: What if you're wholly wrong?
Oedipus: No matter — I must rule.
Creon: Not if you rule unjustly.
Oedipus: Hear him, Thebes, my city!
Creon: My city too, not yours alone!   705
Leader: Please, my lords.

Enter Jocasta from the palace.

Look, Jocasta's coming,
and just in time too. With her help
you must put this fighting of yours to rest.
Jocasta: Have you no sense? Poor misguided men,
　　such shouting—why this public outburst?　　　　　　710
　　Aren't you ashamed, with the land so sick,
　　to stir up private quarrels?

To Oedipus.

Into the palace now. And Creon, you go home.
Why make such a furor over nothing?
Creon: My sister, it's dreadful . . . Oedipus, your husband,　　715
　　he's bent on a choice of punishments for me,
　　banishment from the fatherland or death.
Oedipus: Precisely. I caught him in the act, Jocasta,
　　plotting, about to stab me in the back.
Creon: Never—curse me, let me die and be damned　　720
　　if I've done you any wrong you charge me with.
Jocasta: Oh god, believe it, Oedipus,
　　honor the solemn oath he swears to heaven.
　　Do it for me, for the sake of all your people.

The Chorus begins to chant.

Chorus: Believe it, be sensible　　　　　　　　　　725
　　　　　　give way, my king, I beg you!
Oedipus: What do you want from me, concessions?
Chorus: Respect him—he's been no fool in the past
　　and now he's strong with the oath he swears to god.
Oedipus: You know what you're asking?
Chorus:　　　　　　　　　　　　　I do.
Oedipus:　　　　　　　　　　　　　　　Then out with it!　　730
Chorus: The man's your friend, your kin, he's under oath—
　　don't cast him out, disgraced
　　branded with guilt on the strength of hearsay only.
Oedipus: Know full well, if that's what you want
　　you want me dead or banished from the land.
Chorus:　　　　　　　　　　　　　　Never—　　735
　　no, by the blazing Sun, first god of the heavens!
　　　　Stripped of the gods, stripped of loved ones,
　　let me die by inches if that ever crossed my mind.
　　But the heart inside me sickens, dies as the land dies
　　and now on top of the old griefs you pile this,　　740
　　your fury—both of you!
Oedipus:　　　　　　　　Then let him go,
　　even if it does lead to my ruin, my death
　　or my disgrace, driven from Thebes for life.
　　It's you, not him I pity—your words move me.
　　He, wherever he goes, my hate goes with him.　　745
Creon: Look at you, sullen in yielding, brutal in your rage—

you'll go too far. It's perfect justice:
natures like yours are hardest on themselves.
Oedipus: Then leave me alone — get out!
Creon: I'm going.
You're wrong, so wrong. These men know I'm right.   750

Exit to the side. The Chorus turns to Jocasta.

Chorus: Why do you hesitate, my lady
              why not help him in?
Jocasta: Tell me what's happened first.
Chorus: Loose, ignorant talk started dark suspicions
and a sense of injustice cut deeply too.   755
Jocasta: On both sides?
Chorus: Oh yes.
Jocasta: What did they say?
Chorus: Enough, please, enough! The land's so racked already
or so it seems to me . . .
End the trouble here, just where they left it.
Oedipus: You see what comes of your good intentions now?   760
And all because you tried to blunt my anger.
Chorus: My king,
I've said it once, I'll say it time and again —
     I'd be insane, you know it,
senseless, ever to turn my back on you.
You who set our beloved land — storm-tossed, shattered —   765
straight on course. Now again, good helmsman,
steer us through the storm!

The Chorus draws away, leaving Oedipus and Jocasta side by side.

Jocasta: For the love of god,
Oedipus, tell me too, what is it?
Why this rage? You're so unbending.
Oedipus: I will tell you. I respect you, Jocasta,   770
much more than these . . .

Glancing at the Chorus.

Creon's to blame, Creon schemes against me.
Jocasta: Tell me clearly, how did the quarrel start?
Oedipus: He says I murdered Laius — I am guilty.
Jocasta: How does he know? Some secret knowledge   775
or simple hearsay?
Oedipus: Oh, he sent his prophet in
to do his dirty work. You know Creon,
Creon keeps his own lips clean.
Jocasta: A prophet?
Well then, free yourself of every charge!
Listen to me and learn some peace of mind: 780
no skill in the world,
nothing human can penetrate the future.
Here is proof, quick and to the point.
An oracle came to Laius one fine day

(I won't say from Apollo himself 785
but his underlings, his priests) and it said
that doom would strike him down at the hands of a son,
our son, to be born of our own flesh and blood. But Laius,
so the report goes at least, was killed by strangers,
thieves, at a place where three roads meet . . . my son — 790
he wasn't three days old and the boy's father
fastened his ankles, had a henchman fling him away
on a barren, trackless mountain.
                                    There, you see?
Apollo brought neither thing to pass. My baby
no more murdered his father than Laius suffered — 795
his wildest fear — death at his own son's hands.
That's how the seers and their revelations
mapped out the future. Brush them from your mind.
Whatever the god needs and seeks
he'll bring to light himself, with ease.
Oedipus: Strange, 800
    hearing you just now . . . my mind wandered,
    my thoughts racing back and forth.
Jocasta: What do you mean? Why so anxious, startled?
Oedipus: I thought I heard you say that Laius
    was cut down at a place where three roads meet. 805
Jocasta: That was the story. It hasn't died out yet.
Oedipus: Where did this thing happen? Be precise.
Jocasta: A place called Phocis, where two branching roads,
    one from Daulia, one from Delphi,
    come together — a crossroads. 810
Oedipus: When? How long ago?
Jocasta: The heralds no sooner reported Laius dead
    than you appeared and they hailed you king of Thebes.
Oedipus: My god, my god — what have you planned to do to me?
Jocasta: What, Oedipus? What haunts you so?
Oedipus: Not yet. 815
    Laius — how did he look? Describe him.
    Had he reached his prime?
Jocasta: He was swarthy,
    and the gray had just begun to streak his temples,
    and his build . . . wasn't far from yours.
Oedipus: Oh no no,
    I think I've just called down a dreadful curse 820
    upon myself — I simply didn't know!
Jocasta: What are you saying? I shudder to look at you.
Oedipus: I have a terrible fear the blind seer can see.
    I'll know in a moment. One thing more —
Jocasta: Anything,
    afraid as I am — ask, I'll answer, all I can. 825
Oedipus: Did he go with a light or heavy escort,
    several men-at-arms, like a lord, a king?

Jocasta: There were five in the party, a herald among them,
and a single wagon carrying Laius.
Oedipus: Ai—
now I can see it all, clear as day. 830
Who told you all this at the time, Jocasta?
Jocasta: A servant who reached home, the lone survivor.
Oedipus: So, could he still be in the palace—even now?
Jocasta: No indeed. Soon as he returned from the scene
and saw you on the throne with Laius dead and gone, 835
he knelt and clutched my hand, pleading with me
to send him into the hinterlands, to pasture,
far as possible, out of sight of Thebes.
I sent him away. Slave though he was,
he'd earned that favor—and much more. 840
Oedipus: Can we bring him back, quickly?
Jocasta: Easily. Why do you want him so?
Oedipus: I'm afraid,
Jocasta, I have said too much already.
That man—I've got to see him.
Jocasta: Then he'll come.
But even I have a right, I'd like to think, 845
to know what's torturing you, my lord.
Oedipus: And so you shall—I can hold nothing back from you,
now I've reached this pitch of dark foreboding.
Who means more to me than you? Tell me,
whom would I turn toward but you 850
as I go through all this?

My father was Polybus, king of Corinth.
My mother, a Dorian, Merope. And I was held
the prince of the realm among the people there,
till something struck me out of nowhere, 855
something strange . . . worth remarking perhaps,
hardly worth the anxiety I gave it.
Some man at a banquet who had drunk too much
shouted out—he was far gone, mind you—
that I am not my father's son. Fighting words! 860
I barely restrained myself that day
but early the next I went to mother and father,
questioned them closely, and they were enraged
at the accusation and the fool who let it fly.
So as for my parents I was satisfied, 865
but still this thing kept gnawing at me,
the slander spread—I had to make my move.
And so,
unknown to mother and father I set out for Delphi,
and the god Apollo spurned me, sent me away
denied the facts I came for, 870
but first he flashed before my eyes a future

great with pain, terror, disaster — I can hear him cry,
"You are fated to couple with your mother, you will bring
a breed of children into the light no man can bear to see —
you will kill your father, the one who gave you life!"   875
I heard all that and ran. I abandoned Corinth,
from that day on I gauged its landfall only
by the stars, running, always running
toward some place where I would never see
the shame of all those oracles come true.   880
And as I fled I reached that very spot
where the great king, you say, met his death.
Now, Jocasta, I will tell you all.
Making my way toward this triple crossroad
I began to see a herald, then a brace of colts   885
drawing a wagon, and mounted on the bench . . . a man,
just as you've described him, coming face-to-face,
and the one in the lead and the old man himself
were about to thrust me off the road — brute force —
and the one shouldering me aside, the driver,   890
I strike him in anger! — and the old man, watching me
coming up along his wheels — he brings down
his prod, two prongs straight at my head!
I paid him back with interest!
Short work, by god — with one blow of the staff   895
in this right hand I knock him out of his high seat,
roll him out of the wagon, sprawling headlong —
I killed them all — every mother's son!

Oh, but if there is any blood-tie
between Laius and this stranger . . .   900
what man alive more miserable than I?
More hated by the gods? *I* am the man
no alien, no citizen welcomes to his house,
law forbids it — not a word to me in public,
driven out of every hearth and home.   905
And all these curses I — no one but I
brought down these piling curses on myself!
And you, his wife, I've touched your body with these,
the hands that killed your husband cover you with blood.

Wasn't I born for torment? Look me in the eyes!   910
I am abomination — heart and soul!
I must be exiled, and even in exile
never see my parents, never set foot
on native earth again. Else I'm doomed
to couple with my mother and cut my father down . . .   915
Polybus who reared me, gave me life.
                              But why, why?
Wouldn't a man of judgment say — and wouldn't he be right —
some savage power has brought this down upon my head?

Oh no, not that, you pure and awesome gods,
never let me see that day! Let me slip   920
from the world of men, vanish without a trace
before I see myself stained with such corruption,
stained to the heart.
Leader: My lord, you fill our hearts with fear.
But at least until you question the witness,   925
do take hope.
Oedipus: Exactly. He is my last hope —
I'm waiting for the shepherd. He is crucial.
Jocasta: And once he appears, what then? Why so urgent?
Oedipus: I'll tell you. If it turns out that his story
matches yours, I've escaped the worst.   930
Jocasta: What did I say? What struck you so?
Oedipus: You said *thieves* —
he told you a whole band of them murdered Laius.
So, if he still holds to the same number,
I cannot be the killer. One can't equal many.
But if he refers to one man, one alone,   935
clearly the scales come down on me:
I am guilty.
Jocasta: Impossible. Trust me,
I told you precisely what he said,
and he can't retract it now;
the whole city heard it, not just I.   940
And even if he should vary his first report
by one man more or less, still, my lord,
he could never make the murder of Laius
truly fit the prophecy. Apollo was explicit:
my son was doomed to kill my husband . . . my son,   945
poor defenseless thing, he never had a chance
to kill his father. They destroyed him first.

So much for prophecy. It's neither here nor there.
From this day on, I wouldn't look right or left.
Oedipus: True, true. Still, that shepherd,   950
someone fetch him — now!
Jocasta: I'll send at once. But do let's go inside.
I'd never displease you, least of all in this.

Oedipus and Jocasta enter the palace.

Chorus: Destiny guide me always
Destiny find me filled with reverence   955
            pure in word and deed.
Great laws tower above us, reared on high
born for the brilliant vault of heaven —
        Olympian sky their only father,
nothing mortal, no man gave them birth,   960
their memory deathless, never lost in sleep:
within them lives a mighty god, the god does not grow old.

Pride breeds the tyrant
violent pride, gorging, crammed to bursting
    with all that is overripe and rich with ruin —   965
clawing up to the heights, headlong pride
crashes down the abyss — sheer doom!
    No footing helps, all foothold lost and gone,
But the healthy strife that makes the city strong —
I pray that god will never end that wrestling: 970
god, my champion, I will never let you go.

But if any man comes striding, high and mighty
    in all he says and does,
no fear of justice, no reverence
for the temples of the gods —   975
    let a rough doom tear him down,
repay his pride, breakneck, ruinous pride!
If he cannot reap his profits fairly
    cannot restrain himself from outrage —
mad, laying hands on the holy things untouchable!   980

        Can such a man, so desperate, still boast
        he can save his life from the flashing bolts of god?
          If all such violence goes with honor now
            why join the sacred dance?

Never again will I go reverent to Delphi,   985
    the inviolate heart of Earth
or Apollo's ancient oracle at Abae
or Olympia of the fires —
    unless these prophecies all come true
for all mankind to point toward in wonder.   990
King of kings, if you deserve your titles
    Zeus, remember, never forget!
You and your deathless, everlasting reign.

        They are dying, the old oracles sent to Laius,
        now our masters strike them off the rolls.   995
          Nowhere Apollo's golden glory now —
            the gods, the gods go down.

Enter Jocasta from the palace, carrying a suppliant's branch wound in wool.

Jocasta: Lords of the realm, it occurred to me,
    just now, to visit the temples of the gods,
    so I have my branch in hand and incense too.   1000

    Oedipus is beside himself. Racked with anguish,
    no longer a man of sense, he won't admit
    the latest prophecies are hollow as the old —
    he's at the mercy of every passing voice
    if the voice tells of terror.   1005
    I urge him gently, nothing seems to help,
    so I turn to you, Apollo, you are nearest.

Placing her branch on the altar, while an old herdsman enters from the side, not the one just summoned by the king but an unexpected messenger from Corinth.

I come with prayers and offerings . . . I beg you,
cleanse us, set us free of defilement!
Look at us, passengers in the grip of fear,   1010
watching the pilot of the vessel go to pieces.

Messenger:

Approaching Jocasta and the Chorus.

Strangers, please, I wonder if you could lead us
to the palace of the king . . . I think it's Oedipus.
Better, the man himself — you know where he is?

Leader: This is his palace, stranger. He's inside.   1015
But here is his queen, his wife and mother
of his children.

Messenger: Blessings on you, noble queen,
queen of Oedipus crowned with all your family —
blessings on you always!

Jocasta: And the same to you, stranger, you deserve it . . .   1020
such a greeting. But what have you come for?
Have you brought us news?

Messenger: Wonderful news —
for the house, my lady, for your husband too.

Jocasta: Really, what? Who sent you?

Messenger: Corinth.
I'll give you the message in a moment.   1025
You'll be glad of it — how could you help it? —
though it costs a little sorrow in the bargain.

Jocasta: What can it be, with such a double edge?

Messenger: The people there, they want to make your Oedipus
king of Corinth, so they're saying now.   1030

Jocasta: Why? Isn't old Polybus still in power?

Messenger: No more. Death has got him in the tomb.

Jocasta: What are you saying? Polybus, dead? — dead?

Messenger: If not,
if I'm not telling the truth, strike me dead too.

Jocasta:

To a servant.

Quickly, go to your master, tell him this!   1035

You prophecies of the gods, where are you now?
This is the man that Oedipus feared for years,
he fled him, not to kill him — and now he's dead,
quite by chance, a normal, natural death,
not murdered by his son.

Oedipus:

Emerging from the palace.

                         Dearest,   1040
what now? Why call me from the palace?

Jocasta:

> *Bringing the Messenger closer.*

> Listen to *him,* see for yourself what all
> those awful prophecies of god have come to.

Oedipus: And who is he? What can he have for me?

Jocasta: He's from Corinth, he's come to tell you   1045
> your father is no more — Polybus — he's dead!

Oedipus:

> *Wheeling on the Messenger.*

> What? Let me have it from your lips.

Messenger: Well,
> if that's what you want first, then here it is:
> make no mistake, Polybus is dead and gone.

Oedipus: How — murder? sickness? — what? what killed him?   1050

Messenger: A light tip of the scales can put old bones to rest.

Oedipus: Sickness then — poor man, it wore him down.

Messenger: That,
> and the long count of years he'd measured out.

Oedipus: So!
> Jocasta, why, why look to the Prophet's hearth,
> the fires of the future? Why scan the birds   1055
> that scream above our heads? They winged me on
> to the murder of my father, did they? That was my doom?
> Well look, he's dead and buried, hidden under the earth,
> and here I am in Thebes, I never put hand to sword —
> unless some longing for me wasted him away,   1060
> then in a sense you'd say I caused his death.
> But now, all those prophecies I feared — Polybus
> packs them off to sleep with him in hell!
> They're nothing, worthless.

Jocasta: There.
> Didn't I tell you from the start?   1065

Oedipus: So you did. I was lost in fear.

Jocasta: No more, sweep it from your mind forever.

Oedipus: But my mother's bed, surely I must fear —

Jocasta: Fear?
> What should a man fear? It's all chance,
> chance rules our lives. Not a man on earth   1070
> can see a day ahead, groping through the dark.
> Better to live at random, best we can.
> And as for this marriage with your mother —
> have no fear. Many a man before you,
> in his dreams, has shared his mother's bed.   1075
> Take such things for shadows, nothing at all —
> Live, Oedipus,
> as if there's no tomorrow!

Oedipus: Brave words,
> and you'd persuade me if mother weren't alive.

But mother lives, so for all your reassurances   1080
   I live in fear, I must.
Jocasta: But your father's death,
   that, at least, is a great blessing, joy to the eyes!
Oedipus: Great, I know . . . but I fear *her* — she's still alive.
Messenger: Wait, who is this woman, makes you so afraid?
Oedipus: Merope, old man. The wife of Polybus.   1085
Messenger: The queen? What's there to fear in her?
Oedipus: A dreadful prophecy, stranger, sent by the gods.
Messenger: Tell me, could you? Unless it's forbidden
   other ears to hear.
Oedipus: Not at all.
   Apollo told me once — it is my fate —   1090
   I must make love with my own mother,
   shed my father's blood with my own hands.
   So for years I've given Corinth a wide berth,
   and it's been my good fortune too. But still,
   to see one's parents and look into their eyes   1095
   is the greatest joy I know.
Messenger: You're afraid of that?
   That kept you out of Corinth?
Oedipus: My *father*, old man —
   so I wouldn't kill my father.
Messenger: So that's it.
   Well then, seeing I came with such good will, my king,
   why don't I rid you of that old worry now?   1100
Oedipus: What a rich reward you'd have for that.
Messenger: What do you think I came for, majesty?
   So you'd come home and I'd be better off.
Oedipus: Never, I will never go near my parents.
Messenger: My boy, it's clear, you don't know what you're doing.   1105
Oedipus: What do you mean, old man? For god's sake, explain.
Messenger: If you ran from *them*, always dodging home . . .
Oedipus: Always, terrified Apollo's oracle might come true —
Messenger: And you'd be covered with guilt, from both your parents.
Oedipus: That's right, old man, that fear is always with me.   1110
Messenger: Don't you know? You've really nothing to fear.
Oedipus: But why? If I'm their son — Merope, Polybus?
Messenger: Polybus was nothing to you, that's why, not in blood.
Oedipus: What are you saying — Polybus was not my father?
Messenger: No more than I am. He and I are equals.
Oedipus: My father —   1115
   how can my father equal nothing? You're nothing to me!
Messenger: Neither was he, no more your father than I am.
Oedipus: Then why did he call me his son?
Messenger: You were a gift,
   years ago — know for a fact he took you
   from my hands.
Oedipus: No, from another's hands?   1120
   Then how could he love me so? He loved me, deeply . . .

Messenger: True, and his early years without a child
    made him love you all the more.
Oedipus: And you, did you . . .
    buy me? find me by accident?
Messenger: I stumbled on you,
    down the woody flanks of Mount Cithaeron.
Oedipus: So close,   1125
    what were you doing here, just passing through?
Messenger: Watching over my flocks, grazing them on the slopes.
Oedipus: A herdsman, were you? A vagabond, scraping for wages?
Messenger: Your savior too, my son, in your worst hour.
Oedipus: Oh —
    when you picked me up, was I in pain? What exactly?   1130
Messenger: Your ankles . . . they tell the story. Look at them.
Oedipus: Why remind me of that, that old affliction?
Messenger: Your ankles were pinned together; I set you free.
Oedipus: That dreadful mark — I've had it from the cradle.
Messenger: And you got your name from that misfortune too,   1135
    the name's still with you.
Oedipus: Dear god, who did it? —
    mother? father? Tell me.
Messenger: I don't know.
    The one who gave you to me, he'd know more.
Oedipus: What? You took me from someone else?
    You didn't find me yourself?
Messenger: No sir,   1140
    another shepherd passed you on to me.
Oedipus: Who? Do you know? Describe him.
Messenger: He called himself a servant of . . .
    if I remember rightly — Laius.

    Jocasta turns sharply.

Oedipus: The king of the land who ruled here long ago?   1145
Messenger: That's the one. That herdsman was *his* man.
Oedipus: Is he still alive? Can I see him?
Messenger: They'd know best, the people of these parts.

    Oedipus and the Messenger turn to the Chorus.

Oedipus: Does anyone know that herdsman,
    the one he mentioned? Anyone seen him   1150
    in the fields, in town? Out with it!
    The time has come to reveal this once for all.
Leader: I think he's the very shepherd you wanted to see,
    a moment ago. But the queen, Jocasta,
    she's the one to say.
Oedipus: Jocasta,   1155
    you remember the man we just sent for?
    Is *that* the one he means?
Jocasta: That man . . .
    why ask? Old shepherd, talk, empty nonsense,
    don't give it another thought, don't even think —

Oedipus: What — give up now, with a clue like this?   1160
  Fail to solve the mystery of my birth?
  Not for all the world!
Jocasta: Stop — in the name of god,
  if you love your own life, call off this search!
  My suffering is enough.
Oedipus: Courage!
  Even if my mother turns out to be a slave,   1165
  and I a slave, three generations back,
  you would not seem common.
Jocasta: Oh no,
  listen to me, I beg you, don't do this.
Oedipus: Listen to you? No more. I must know it all,
  see the truth at last.
Jocasta: No, please —   1170
  for your sake — I want the best for you!
Oedipus: Your best is more than I can bear.
Jocasta: You're doomed —
  may you never fathom who you are!
Oedipus:

  To a servant.

  Hurry, fetch me the herdsman, now!
  Leave her to glory in her royal birth.   1175
Jocasta: Aieeeeee —
              man of agony —
  that is the only name I have for you,
  that, no other — ever, ever, ever!

  Flinging [herself] through the palace doors. A long, tense silence follows.

Leader: Where's she gone, Oedipus?
  Rushing off, such wild grief . . .   1180
  I'm afraid that from this silence
  something monstrous may come bursting forth.
Oedipus: Let it burst! Whatever will, whatever must!
  I must know my birth, no matter how common
  it may be — must see my origins face-to-face.   1185
  She perhaps, she with her woman's pride
  may well be mortified by my birth,
  but I, I count myself the son of Chance,
  the great goddess, giver of all good things —
  I'll never see myself disgraced. She is my mother!   1190
  And the moons have marked me out, my blood-brothers,
  one moon on the wane, the next moon great with power.
  That is my blood, my nature — I will never betray it,
  never fail to search and learn my birth!
Chorus: Yes — if I am a true prophet   1195
          if I can grasp the truth,
      by the boundless skies of Olympus,
  at the full moon of tomorrow, Mount Cithaeron
  you will know how Oedipus glories in you —

you, his birthplace, nurse, his mountain-mother!   1200
And we will sing you, dancing out your praise—
you lift our monarch's heart!
    Apollo, Apollo, god of the wild cry
        may our dancing please you!
                Oedipus—
        son, dear child, who bore you?   1205
Who of the nymphs who seem to live forever
mated with Pan,° the mountain-striding Father?
Who was your mother? who, some bride of Apollo
the god who loves the pastures spreading toward the sun?
    Or was it Hermes, king of the lightning ridges?   1210
Or Dionysus, lord of frenzy, lord of the barren peaks—
did he seize you in his hands, dearest of all his lucky finds?—
    found by the nymphs, their warm eyes dancing, gift
to the lord who loves them dancing out his joy!

Oedipus strains to see a figure coming from the distance. Attended by palace guards, an old Shepherd enters slowly, reluctant to approach the king.

Oedipus: I never met the man, my friends . . . still,   1215
    if I had to guess, I'd say that's the shepherd,
    the very one we've looked for all along.
    Brothers in old age, two of a kind,
    he and our guest here. At any rate
    the ones who bring him in are my own men,   1220
    I recognize them.

    Turning to the Leader.

            But you know more than I,
    you should, you've seen the man before.
Leader: I know him, definitely. One of Laius' men,
    a trusty shepherd, if there ever was one.
Oedipus: You, I ask you first, stranger,   1225
    you from Corinth—is this the one you mean?
Messenger: You're looking at him. He's your man.
Oedipus:

    To the Shepherd.

    You, old man, come over here—
    look at me. Answer all my questions.
    Did you ever serve King Laius?
Shepherd: So I did . . .   1230
    a slave, not bought on the block though,
    born and reared in the palace.
Oedipus: Your duties, your kind of work?
Shepherd: Herding the flocks, the better part of my life.
Oedipus: Where, mostly? Where did you do your grazing?

1207 *Pan:* God of shepherds, who was, like Hermes and Dionysus, associated with the wilderness.

Shepherd: Well,   1235
    Cithaeron sometimes, or the foothills round about.
Oedipus: This man — you know him? ever see him there?
Shepherd:

Confused, glancing from the Messenger to the King.

    Doing what — what man do you mean?
Oedipus:

Pointing to the Messenger.

    This one here — ever have dealings with him?
Shepherd: Not so I could say, but give me a chance,   1240
    my memory's bad . . .
Messenger: No wonder he doesn't know me, master.
    But let me refresh his memory for him.
    I'm sure he recalls old times we had
    on the slopes of Mount Cithaeron;   1245
    he and I, grazing our flocks, he with two
    and I with one — we both struck up together,
    three whole seasons, six months at a stretch
    from spring to the rising of Arcturus° in the fall,
    then with winter coming on I'd drive my herds   1250
    to my own pens, and back he'd go with his
    to Laius' folds.

    To the Shepherd.

            Now that's how it was,
    wasn't it — yes or no?
Shepherd: Yes, I suppose . . .
    it's all so long ago.
Messenger: Come, tell me,
    you gave me a child back then, a boy, remember?   1255
    A little fellow to rear, my very own.
Shepherd: What? Why rake up that again?
Messenger: Look, here he is, my fine old friend —
    the same man who was just a baby then.
Shepherd: Damn you, shut your mouth — quiet!   1260
Oedipus: Don't lash out at him, old man —
    you need lashing more than he does.
Shepherd: Why,
    master, majesty — what have I done wrong?
Oedipus: You won't answer his question about the boy.
Shepherd: He's talking nonsense, wasting his breath.   1265
Oedipus: So, you won't talk willingly —
    then you'll talk with pain.

    The guards seize the Shepherd.

Shepherd: No, dear god, don't torture an old man!
Oedipus: Twist his arms back, quickly!

1249 *Arcturus:* A star whose rising marked the end of summer.

Shepherd: God help us, why? —
   what more do you need to know?   1270
Oedipus: Did you give him that child? He's asking.
Shepherd: I did . . . I wish to god I'd died that day.
Oedipus: You've got your wish if you don't tell the truth.
Shepherd: The more I tell, the worse the death I'll die.
Oedipus: Our friend here wants to stretch things out, does he?   1275

    Motioning to his men for torture.

Shepherd: No, no, I gave it to him — I just said so.
Oedipus: Where did you get it? Your house? Someone else's?
Shepherd: It wasn't mine, no, I got it from . . . someone.
Oedipus: Which one of them?

    Looking at the citizens.

                  Whose house?
Shepherd: No —
   god's sake, master, no more questions!   1280
Oedipus: You're a dead man if I have to ask again.
Shepherd: Then — the child came from the house . . .
   of Laius.
Oedipus: A slave? or born of his own blood?
Shepherd: Oh no,
   I'm right at the edge, the horrible truth — I've got to say it!   1285
Oedipus: And I'm at the edge of hearing horrors, yes, but I must hear!
Shepherd: All right! His son, they said it was — his son!
   But the one inside, your wife,
   she'd tell it best.
Oedipus: My wife —   1290
   she gave it to you?
Shepherd: Yes, yes, my king.
Oedipus: Why, what for?
Shepherd: To kill it.
Oedipus: Her own child,   1295
   how could she?
Shepherd: She was afraid —
   frightening prophecies.
Oedipus: What?
Shepherd: They said —
   he'd kill his parents.   1300
Oedipus: But you gave him to this old man — why?
Shepherd: I pitied the little baby, master,
   hoped he'd take him off to his own country,
   far away, but he saved him for this, this fate.
   If you are the man he says you are, believe me,   1305
   you were born for pain.
Oedipus: O god —
   all come true, all burst to light!
   O light — now let me look my last on you!
   I stand revealed at last —
   cursed in my birth, cursed in marriage,   1310
   cursed in the lives I cut down with these hands!

Rushing through the doors with a great cry. The Corinthian Messenger, the
Shepherd, and attendants exit slowly to the side.

Chorus: O the generations of men
      the dying generations — adding the total
      of all your lives I find they come to nothing . . .
             does there exist, is there a man on earth   1315
      who seizes more joy than just a dream, a vision?
      And the vision no sooner dawns than dies
      blazing into oblivion.

      You are my great example, you, your life,
      your destiny, Oedipus, man of misery —   1320
      I count no man blest.

                You outranged all men!
           Bending your bow to the breaking-point
      you captured priceless glory, O dear god,
      and the Sphinx came crashing down,
              the virgin, claws hooked   1325
      like a bird of omen singing, shrieking death —
      like a fortress reared in the face of death
      you rose and saved our land.

      From that day on we called you king
      we crowned you with honors, Oedipus, towering over all —   1330
      mighty king of the seven gates of Thebes.

      But now to hear your story — is there a man more agonized?
      More wed to pain and frenzy? Not a man on earth,
      the joy of your life ground down to nothing
      O Oedipus, name for the ages —   1335
          one and the same wide harbor served you
                   son and father both
      son and father came to rest in the same bridal chamber.
      How, how could the furrows your father plowed
      bear you, your agony, harrowing on   1340
      in silence O so long?

                But now for all your power
      Time, all-seeing Time has dragged you to the light,
      judged your marriage monstrous from the start —
      the son and the father tangling, both one —
      O child of Laius, would to god   1345
          I'd never seen you, never never!
            Now I weep like a man who wails the dead
      and the dirge comes pouring forth with all my heart!
      I tell you the truth, you gave me life
      my breath leapt up in you   1350
      and now you bring down night upon my eyes.

      Enter a Messenger from the palace.

Messenger: Men of Thebes, always the first in honor,
      what horrors you will hear, what you will see,

what a heavy weight of sorrow you will shoulder . . .
if you are true to your birth, if you still have   1355
some feeling for the royal house of Thebes.
I tell you neither the waters of the Danube
nor the Nile can wash this palace clean.
Such things it hides, it soon will bring to light—
terrible things, and none done blindly now,   1360
all done with a will. The pains
we inflict upon ourselves hurt most of all.
Leader: God knows we have pains enough already.
    What can you add to them?
Messenger: The queen is dead.
Leader: Poor lady—how?   1365
Messenger: By her own hand. But you are spared the worst,
    you never had to watch . . . I saw it all,
    and with all the memory that's in me
    you will learn what that poor woman suffered.

Once she'd broken in through the gates,   1370
dashing past us, frantic, whipped to fury,
ripping her hair out with both hands—
straight to her rooms she rushed, flinging herself
across the bridal-bed, doors slamming behind her—
once inside, she wailed for Laius, dead so long,   1375
remembering how she bore his child long ago,
the life that rose up to destroy him, leaving
its mother to mother living creatures
with the very son she'd borne.
Oh how she wept, mourning the marriage-bed   1380
where she let loose that double brood—monsters—
husband by her husband, children by her child.
                      And then—
but how she died is more than I can say. Suddenly
Oedipus burst in, screaming, he stunned us so
we couldn't watch her agony to the end,   1385
our eyes were fixed on him. Circling
like a maddened beast, stalking, here, there
crying out to us—
             Give him a sword! His wife,
no wife, his mother, where can he find the mother earth
that cropped two crops at once, himself and all his children?   1390
He was raging—one of the dark powers pointing the way,
none of us mortals crowding around him, no,
with a great shattering cry—someone, something leading him on—
he hurled at the twin doors and bending the bolts back
out of their sockets, crashed through the chamber.   1395
And there we saw the woman hanging by the neck,
cradled high in a woven noose, spinning,
swinging back and forth. And when he saw her,
giving a low, wrenching sob that broke our hearts,

slipping the halter from her throat, he eased her down,   1400
in a slow embrace he laid her down, poor thing . . .
then, what came next, what horror we beheld!

He rips off her brooches, the long gold pins
holding her robes — and lifting them high,
looking straight up into the points,   1405
he digs them down the sockets of his eyes, crying, "You,
you'll see no more the pain I suffered, all the pain I caused!
Too long you looked on the ones you never should have seen,
blind to the ones you longed to see, to know! Blind
from this hour on! Blind in the darkness — blind!"   1410
His voice like a dirge, rising, over and over
raising the pins, raking them down his eyes.
And at each stroke blood spurts from the roots,
splashing his beard, a swirl of it, nerves and clots —
black hail of blood pulsing, gushing down.   1415

These are the griefs that burst upon them both,
coupling man and woman. The joy they had so lately,
the fortune of their old ancestral house
was deep joy indeed. Now, in this one day,
wailing, madness and doom, death, disgrace,   1420
all the griefs in the world that you can name,
all are theirs forever.

Leader: Oh poor man, the misery —
has he any rest from pain now?

A voice within, in torment.

Messenger: He's shouting,
    "Loose the bolts, someone, show me to all of Thebes!
My father's murderer, my mother's — "   1425
No, I can't repeat it, it's unholy.
Now he'll tear himself from his native earth,
not linger, curse the house with his own curse.
But he needs strength, and a guide to lead him on.
This is sickness more than he can bear.

The palace doors open.

                        Look,   1430
he'll show you himself. The great doors are opening —
you are about to see a sight, a horror
even his mortal enemy would pity.

*Enter Oedipus, blinded, led by a boy. He stands at the palace steps, as if
surveying his people once again.*

Chorus: O the terror —
    the suffering, for all the world to see,
the worst terror that ever met my eyes.   1435
What madness swept over you? What god,
what dark power leapt beyond all bounds,
beyond belief, to crush your wretched life? —

godforsaken, cursed by the gods!
    I pity you but I can't bear to look.   1440
    I've much to ask, so much to learn,
    so much fascinates my eyes,
    but you . . . I shudder at the sight.
Oedipus: Oh, Ohhh —
    the agony! I am agony —
    where am I going? where on earth?   1445
          where does all this agony hurl me?
    where's my voice? —
          winging, swept away on a dark tide —
    My destiny, my dark power, what a leap you made!
Chorus: To the depths of terror, too dark to hear, to see.   1450
Oedipus: Dark, horror of darkness
    my darkness, drowning, swirling around me
    crashing wave on wave — unspeakable, irresistible
         headwind, fatal harbor! Oh again,
    the misery, all at once, over and over   1455
    the stabbing daggers, stab of memory
    raking me insane.
Chorus: No wonder you suffer
    twice over, the pain of your wounds,
    the lasting grief of pain.
Oedipus: Dear friend, still here?
    Standing by me, still with a care for me,   1460
    the blind man? Such compassion,
         loyal to the last. Oh it's you,
    I know you're here, dark as it is
    I'd know you anywhere, your voice —
    it's yours, clearly yours.
Chorus: Dreadful, what you've done . . .   1465
    how could you bear it, gouging out your eyes?
    What superhuman power drove you on?
Oedipus: Apollo, friends, Apollo —
    he ordained my agonies — these, my pains on pains!
    But the hand that struck my eyes was mine,   1470
    mine alone — no one else —
        I did it all myself!
    What good were eyes to me?
    Nothing I could see could bring me joy.
Chorus: No, no, exactly as you say.
Oedipus: What can I ever see?   1475
    What love, what call of the heart
    can touch my ears with joy? Nothing, friends.
    Take me away, far, far from Thebes,
      quickly, cast me away, my friends —
    this great murderous ruin, this man cursed to heaven,   1480
    the man the deathless gods hate most of all!
Chorus: Pitiful, you suffer so, you understand so much . . .
    I wish you'd never known.

Oedipus: Die, die —
    whoever he was that day in the wilds
  who cut my ankles free of the ruthless pins,   1485
    he pulled me clear of death, he saved my life
    for this, this kindness —
                Curse him, kill him!
    If I'd died then, I'd never have dragged myself,
  my loved ones through such hell.   1490
Chorus: Oh if only . . . would to god.
Oedipus: I'd never have come to this,
    my father's murderer — never been branded
  mother's husband, all men see me now! Now,
    loathed by the gods, son of the mother I defiled
    coupling in my father's bed, spawning lives in the loins   1495
  that spawned my wretched life. What grief can crown this grief?
          It's mine alone, my destiny — I am Oedipus!
Chorus: How can I say you've chosen for the best?
  Better to die than be alive and blind.
Oedipus: What I did was best — don't lecture me,   1500
  no more advice. I, with *my* eyes,
  how could I look my father in the eyes
  when I go down to death? Or mother, so abused . . .
  I've done such things to the two of them,
  crimes too huge for hanging.
              Worse yet,   1505
  the sight of my children, born as they were born,
  how could I long to look into their eyes?
  No, not with these eyes of mine, never.
  Not this city either, her high towers,
  the sacred glittering images of her gods —   1510
  I am misery! I, her best son, reared
  as no other son of Thebes was ever reared,
  I've stripped myself, I gave the command myself.
  All men must cast away the great blasphemer,
  the curse now brought to light by the gods,   1515
  the son of Laius — I, my father's son!

  Now I've exposed my guilt, horrendous guilt,
  could I train a level glance on you, my countrymen?
  Impossible! No, if I could just block off my ears,
  the springs of hearing, I would stop at nothing —   1520
  I'd wall up my loathsome body like a prison,
  blind to the sound of life, not just the sight.
  Oblivion — what a blessing . . .
  for the mind to dwell a world away from pain.

  O Cithaeron, why did you give me shelter?   1525
  Why didn't you take me, crush my life out on the spot?
  I'd never have revealed my birth to all mankind.

  O Polybus, Corinth, the old house of my fathers,
  so I believed — what a handsome prince you raised —

under the skin, what sickness to the core.   1530
Look at me! Born of outrage, outrage to the core.

O triple roads — it all comes back, the secret,
dark ravine, and the oaks closing in
where the three roads join . . .
You drank my father's blood, my own blood   1535
spilled by my own hands — you still remember me?
What things you saw me do? Then I came here
and did them all once more!
                  Marriages! O marriage,
you gave me birth, and once you brought me into the world
you brought my sperm rising back, springing to light   1540
fathers, brothers, sons — one deadly breed —
brides, wives, mothers. The blackest things
a man can do, I have done them all!
                     No more —
it's wrong to name what's wrong to do. Quickly,
for the love of god, hide me somewhere,   1545
kill me, hurl me into the sea
where you can never look on me again.

Beckoning to the Chorus as they shrink away.

                        Closer,
it's all right. Touch the man of sorrow.
Do. Don't be afraid. My troubles are mine
and I am the only man alive who can sustain them.   1550

Enter Creon from the palace, attended by palace guards.

Leader: Put your requests to Creon. Here he is,
just when we need him. He'll have a plan, he'll act.
Now that he's the sole defense of the country
in your place.
Oedipus: Oh no, what can I say to him?
How can I ever hope to win his trust?   1555
I wronged him so, just now, in every way.
You must see that — I was so wrong, so wrong.
Creon: I haven't come to mock you, Oedipus,
or to criticize your former failings.

Turning to the guards.

                    You there,
have you lost all respect for human feeling?   1560
At least revere the Sun, the holy fire
that keeps us all alive. Never expose a thing
of guilt and holy dread so great it appalls
the earth, the rain from heaven, the light of day!
Get him into the halls — quickly as you can.   1565
Piety demands no less. Kindred alone
should see a kinsman's shame. This is obscene.
Oedipus: Please, in god's name . . . you wipe my fears away,
coming so generously to me, the worst of men.
Do one thing more, for your sake, not mine.   1570

Creon: What do you want? Why so insistent?
Oedipus: Drive me out of the land at once, far from sight,
    where I can never hear a human voice.
Creon: I'd have done that already, I promise you.
    First I wanted the god to clarify my duties.   1575
Oedipus: The god? His command was clear, every word:
    death for the father-killer, the curse—
    he said destroy me!
Creon: So he did. Still, in such a crisis
    it's better to ask precisely what to do.   1580
Oedipus: You'd ask the oracle about a man like me?
Creon: By all means. And this time, I assume,
    even you will obey the god's decrees.
Oedipus: I will,
    I will. And you, I command you—I beg you . . .
    the woman inside, bury her as you see fit.   1585
    It's the only decent thing,
    to give your own the last rites. As for me,
    never condemn the city of my fathers
    to house my body, not while I'm alive, no,
    let me live on the mountains, on Cithaeron,   1590
    my favorite haunt, I have made it famous.
    Mother and father marked out that rock
    to be my everlasting tomb—buried alive.
    Let me die there, where they tried to kill me.
    Oh but this I know: no sickness can destroy me,   1595
    nothing can. I would never have been saved
    from death—I have been saved
    for something great and terrible, something strange.
    Well let my destiny come and take me on its way!

    About my children, Creon, the boys at least,   1600
    don't burden yourself. They're men;
    wherever they go, they'll find the means to live.
    But my two daughters, my poor helpless girls,
    clustering at our table, never without me
    hovering near them . . . whatever I touched,   1605
    they always had their share. Take care of them,
    I beg you. Wait, better—permit me, would you?
    Just to touch them with my hands and take
    our fill of tears. Please . . . my king.
    Grant it, with all your noble heart.   1610
    If I could hold them, just once, I'd think
    I had them with me, like the early days
    when I could see their eyes.

Antigone and Ismene, two small children, are led in from the palace by a nurse.

                    What's that?
    O god! Do I really hear you sobbing?—
    my two children. Creon, you've pitied me?   1615
    Sent me my darling girls, my own flesh and blood!
    Am I right?

Creon: Yes, it's my doing.
    I know the joy they gave you all these years,
    the joy you must feel now.
Oedipus: Bless you, Creon!
    May god watch over you for this kindness,   1620
    better than he ever guarded me.
                         Children, where are you?
    Here, come quickly—

*Groping for Antigone and Ismene, who approach their father cautiously, then
embrace him.*

                    Come to these hands of mine,
    your brother's hands, your own father's hands
    that served his once bright eyes so well—
    that made them blind. Seeing nothing, children,   1625
    knowing nothing, I became your father,
    I fathered you in the soil that gave me life.

    How I weep for you—I cannot see you now . . .
    just thinking of all your days to come, the bitterness,
    the life that rough mankind will thrust upon you.   1630
    Where are the public gatherings you can join,
    the banquets of the clans? Home you'll come,
    in tears, cut off from the sight of it all,
    the brilliant rites unfinished.
    And when you reach perfection, ripe for marriage,   1635
    who will he be, my dear ones? Risking all
    to shoulder the curse that weighs down my parents,
    yes and you too—that wounds us all together.
    What more misery could you want?
    Your father killed his father, sowed his mother,   1640
    one, one and the selfsame womb sprang you—
    he cropped the very roots of his existence.
    Such disgrace, and you must bear it all!
    Who will marry you then? Not a man on earth.
    Your doom is clear: you'll wither away to nothing,   1645
    single, without a child.

Turning to Creon.

                    Oh Creon,
    you are the only father they have now . . .
    we who brought them into the world
    are gone, both gone at a stroke—
    Don't let them go begging, abandoned,   1650
    women without men. Your own flesh and blood!
    Never bring them down to the level of my pains.
    Pity them. Look at them, so young, so vulnerable,
    shorn of everything—you're their only hope.
    Promise me, noble Creon, touch my hand.   1655

Reaching toward Creon, who draws back.

You, little ones, if you were old enough
to understand, there is much I'd tell you.
Now, as it is, I'd have you say a prayer.
Pray for life, my children,
live where you are free to grow and season.   1660
Pray god you find a better life than mine,
the father who begot you.
Creon: Enough.
You've wept enough. Into the palace now.
Oedipus: I must, but I find it very hard.
Creon: Time is the great healer, you will see.   1665
Oedipus: I am going — you know on what condition?
Creon: Tell me. I'm listening.
Oedipus: Drive me out of Thebes, in exile.
Creon: Not I. Only the gods can give you that.
Oedipus: Surely the gods hate me so much —   1670
Creon: You'll get your wish at once.
Oedipus: You consent?
Creon: I try to say what I mean; it's my habit.
Oedipus: Then take me away. It's time.
Creon: Come along, let go of the children.
Oedipus: No —
don't take them away from me, not now! No no no!   1675

*Clutching his daughters as the guards wrench them loose and take them
through the palace doors.*

Creon: Still the king, the master of all things?
No more: here your power ends.
None of your power follows you through life.

*Exit Oedipus and Creon to the palace. The Chorus comes forward to address
the audience directly.*

Chorus: People of Thebes, my countrymen, look on Oedipus.
He solved the famous riddle with his brilliance,   1680
he rose to power, a man beyond all power.
Who could behold his greatness without envy?
Now what a black sea of terror has overwhelmed him.
Now as we keep our watch and wait the final day,
count no man happy till he dies, free of pain at last.   1685

Exit in procession.

CONSIDERATIONS FOR CRITICAL THINKING AND WRITING

1. FIRST RESPONSE. Is it possible for a twentieth-century reader to identify with Oedipus's plight? What philosophic issues does he confront?

2. In the opening scene what does the priest's speech reveal about how Oedipus has been regarded as a ruler of Thebes?

3. What do Oedipus's confrontations with Tiresias and Creon indicate about his character?

4. Aristotle defined a tragic flaw as consisting of "error and frailties." What errors does Oedipus make? What are his frailties?

5. What causes Oedipus's downfall? Is he simply a pawn in a predetermined game played by the gods? Can he be regarded as responsible for the suffering and death in the play?

6. Locate instances of dramatic irony in the play. How do they serve as foreshadowings?

7. Describe the function of the Chorus. How does the Chorus's view of life and the gods differ from Jocasta's?

8. Trace the images of vision and blindness throughout the play. How are they related to the theme? Why does Oedipus blind himself instead of joining Jocasta in suicide?

9. What is your assessment of Oedipus at the end of the play? Was he foolish? Heroic? Fated? To what extent can your emotions concerning him be described as "pity and fear"?

10. *Oedipus complex* is a well-known term used in psychoanalysis. What does it mean? Does the concept offer any insights into the conflicts dramatized in the play?

CONNECTIONS TO OTHER SELECTIONS

1. Consider the endings of *Oedipus the King* and Shakespeare's *Hamlet* (p. 1383). What feelings do you have about these endings? Are they irredeemably unhappy? Is there anything that suggests hope for the future at the ends of these plays?

2. Sophocles does not include violence in his plays; any bloodshed occurs offstage. Compare and contrast the effects of this strategy with the use of violence in either *Hamlet* (p. 1383) or *The Tempest* (p. 1483).

3. Write an essay explaining why *Oedipus the King* cannot be considered a realistic play in the way that Henrik Ibsen's *A Doll House* (p. 1564) can be.

Antigone

Antigone was actually written before Sophocles' other two plays about Oedipus and his family. *Oedipus the King* ends with Oedipus, the king of Thebes, blinding himself because he has unknowingly murdered his father and married his mother, Jocasta. Creon, his brother-in-law, becomes the ruler of Thebes and is entrusted with caring for Oedipus's two daughters, Antigone and Ismene. *Oedipus at Colonus* continues the story some twenty years later. Oedipus has been rejected by his two sons, Polynices and Eteocles, and wanders in exile, cared for by Antigone. Meanwhile, his sons struggle for power in Thebes. Polynices travels to Argos to gather a force to attack his brother as Oedipus arrives in Colonus, near Athens. There Oedipus curses his sons for their ruthless selfishness and predicts their violent deaths. Oedipus, however, dies in peace, with dignity, and bestows a blessing on Athens.

Antigone begins after the two brothers have killed each other in battle. The throne of Thebes subsequently returns to Creon, who decrees that

Polynices was traitorous and therefore must not be buried. As the play opens, Antigone tells her sister that she will defy Creon's ruling, even though the penalty for disobedience is death.

Antigone's insistence on obeying the law of the gods instead of civil laws dramatizes a conflict that continues to move audiences and readers who ponder the relation of the individual's conscience to the demands of the state. One manifestation of this concern in the twentieth century is Jean Anouilh's 1944 production of *Antigone* in Paris, when that city was occupied by German troops during World War II. Anouilh's Antigone reflects the French resistance movement, and his Creon is a representative of German authority who must preserve order in the face of unyielding opposition. (A brief excerpt of this play appears on p. 1310.) Sophocles' play — as does Anouilh's — presents an agonizing dilemma. Neither Antigone nor Creon is wholly virtuous or blameless, so the complexities they embody remain a moral and intellectual challenge.

SOPHOCLES (496?–406 B.C.)

Antigone

c. 441 B.C.

TRANSLATED BY ROBERT FAGLES

CHARACTERS

Antigone, daughter of Oedipus and Jocasta
Ismene, sister of Antigone
A *Chorus* of old Theban citizens and their *Leader*
Creon, king of Thebes, uncle of Antigone and Ismene
A *Sentry*
Haemon, son of Creon and Eurydice
Tiresias, a blind prophet
A *Messenger*
Eurydice, wife of Creon
Guards, attendants, and a boy

TIME AND SCENE: *The royal house of Thebes. It is still night, and the invading armies of Argos have just been driven from the city. Fighting on opposite sides, the sons of Oedipus, Eteocles and Polynices, have killed each other in combat. Their uncle, Creon, is now king of Thebes.*

 Enter Antigone, slipping through the central doors of the palace. She motions to her sister, Ismene, who follows her cautiously toward an altar at the center of the stage.

Antigone: My own flesh and blood — dear sister, dear Ismene,
 how many griefs our father Oedipus handed down!
 Do you know one, I ask you, one grief
 that Zeus° will not perfect for the two of us
 while we still live and breathe? There's nothing,   5
 no pain — our lives are pain — no private shame,

4 *Zeus:* The highest Olympian deity.

no public disgrace, nothing I haven't seen
in your griefs and mine. And now this:
an emergency decree, they say, the Commander
has just declared for all of Thebes.   10
What, haven't you heard? Don't you see?
The doom reserved for enemies
marches on the ones we love the most.

Ismene: Not I, I haven't heard a word, Antigone.
Nothing of loved ones,   15
no joy or pain has come my way, not since
the two of us were robbed of our two brothers,
both gone in a day, a double blow —
not since the armies of Argos vanished,
just this very night. I know nothing more,   20
whether our luck's improved or ruin's still to come.

Antigone: I thought so. That's why I brought you out here,
past the gates, so you could hear in private.

Ismene: What's the matter? Trouble, clearly . . .
you sound so dark, so grim.   25

Antigone: Why not? Our own brothers' burial!
Hasn't Creon graced one with all the rites,
disgraced the other? Eteocles, they say,
has been given full military honors,
rightly so — Creon's laid him in the earth   30
and he goes with glory down among the dead.
But the body of Polynices, who died miserably —
why, a city-wide proclamation, rumor has it,
forbids anyone to bury him, even mourn him.
He's to be left unwept, unburied, a lovely treasure   35
for birds that scan the field and feast to their heart's content.

Such, I hear, is the martial law our good Creon
lays down for you and me — yes, me, I tell you —
and he's coming here to alert the uninformed
in no uncertain terms,   40
and he won't treat the matter lightly. Whoever
disobeys in the least will die, his doom is sealed:
stoning to death inside the city walls!

There you have it. You'll soon show what you are,
worth your breeding, Ismene, or a coward —   45
for all your royal blood.

Ismene: My poor sister, if things have come to this,
who am I to make or mend them, tell me,
what good am I to you?

Antigone: Decide.
Will you share the labor, share the work?   50

Ismene: What work, what's the risk? What do you mean?

Antigone:

Raising her hands.

Will you lift up his body with these bare hands
and lower it with me?
Ismene: What? You'd bury him —
when a law forbids the city?
Antigone: Yes!
He is my brother and — deny it as you will —   55
your brother too.
No one will ever convict me for a traitor.
Ismene: So desperate, and Creon has expressly —
Antigone: No,
he has no right to keep me from my own.
Ismene: Oh my sister, think —   60
think how our own father died, hated,
his reputation in ruins, driven on
by the crimes he brought to light himself
to gouge out his eyes with his own hands —
then mother . . . his mother and wife, both in one,   65
mutilating her life in the twisted noose —
and last, our two brothers dead in a single day,
both shedding their own blood, poor suffering boys,
battling out their common destiny hand-to-hand.

Now look at the two of us, left so alone . . .   70
think what a death we'll die, the worst of all
if we violate the laws and override
the fixed decree of the throne, its power —
we must be sensible. Remember we are women,
we're not born to contend with men. Then too,   75
we're underlings, ruled by much stronger hands,
so we must submit in this, and things still worse.

I, for one, I'll beg the dead to forgive me —
I'm forced, I have no choice — I must obey
the ones who stand in power. Why rush to extremes?   80
It's madness, madness.
Antigone: I won't insist,
no, even if you should have a change of heart,
I'd never welcome you in the labor, not with me.
So, do as you like, whatever suits you best —
I'll bury him myself.   85
And even if I die in the act, that death will be a glory.
I'll lie with the one I love and loved by him —
an outrage sacred to the gods! I have longer
to please the dead than please the living here:
in the kingdom down below I'll lie forever.   90
Do as you like, dishonor the laws
the gods hold in honor.
Ismene: I'd do them no dishonor . . .
but defy the city? I have no strength for that.
Antigone: You have your excuses. I am on my way,
I'll raise a mound for him, for my dear brother.   95

Ismene: Oh Antigone, you're so rash—I'm so afraid for you!
Antigone: Don't fear for me. Set your own life in order.
Ismene: Then don't, at least, blurt this out to anyone.
    Keep it a secret. I'll join you in that, I promise.
Antigone: Dear god, shout it from the rooftops. I'll hate you   100
    all the more for silence—tell the world!
Ismene: So fiery—and it ought to chill your heart.
Antigone: I know I please where I must please the most.
Ismene: Yes, if you can, but you're in love with impossibility.
Antigone: Very well then, once my strength gives out   105
    I will be done at last.
Ismene: You're wrong from the start,
    you're off on a hopeless quest.
Antigone: If you say so, you will make me hate you,
    and the hatred of the dead, by all rights,
    will haunt you night and day.   110
    But leave me to my own absurdity, leave me
    to suffer this—dreadful thing. I'll suffer
    nothing as great as death without glory.

Exit to the side.

Ismene: Then go if you must, but rest assured,
    wild, irrational as you are, my sister,
    you are truly dear to the ones who love you.   115

*Withdrawing to the palace. Enter a Chorus, the old citizens of Thebes,
chanting as the sun begins to rise.*

Chorus: Glory!—great beam of sun, brightest of all
    that ever rose on the seven gates of Thebes,
        you burn through night at last!
              Great eye of the golden day,   120
    mounting the Dirce's° banks you throw him back—
    the enemy out of Argos, the white shield, the man of bronze—
    he's flying headlong now
        the bridle of fate stampeding him with pain!

    And he had driven against our borders,   125
    launched by the warring claims of Polynices—
    like an eagle screaming, winging havoc
    over the land, wings of armor
    shielded white as snow,
    a huge army massing,   130
    crested helmets bristling for assault.

He hovered above our roofs, his vast maw gaping
closing down around our seven gates,
    his spears thirsting for the kill
        but now he's gone, look,   135
before he could glut his jaws with Theban blood
or the god of fire put our crown of towers to the torch.

121 *the Dirce:* A river near Thebes.

He grappled the Dragon none can master — Thebes —
  the clang of our arms like thunder at his back!

Zeus hates with a vengeance all bravado,   140
the mighty boasts of men. He watched them
coming on in a rising flood, the pride
of their golden armor ringing shrill —
and brandishing his lightning
blasted the fighter just at the goal,   145
rushing to shout his triumph from our walls.

Down from the heights he crashed, pounding down on the earth!
And a moment ago, blazing torch in hand —
  mad for attack, ecstatic
he breathed his rage, the storm   150
  of his fury hurling at our heads!
But now his high hopes have laid him low
and down the enemy ranks the iron god of war
  deals his rewards, his stunning blows — Ares°
  rapture of battle, our right arm in the crisis.   155

Seven captains marshaled at seven gates
seven against their equals, gave
their brazen trophies up to Zeus,
god of the breaking rout of battle,
all but two: those blood brothers,   160
one father, one mother — matched in rage,
spears matched for the twin conquest —
clashed and won the common prize of death.

But now for Victory! Glorious in the morning,
joy in her eyes to meet our joy   165
  she is winging down to Thebes,
our fleets of chariots wheeling in her wake —
  Now let us win oblivion from the wars,
thronging the temples of the gods
in singing, dancing choirs through the night!   170
  Lord Dionysus,° god of the dance
  that shakes the land of Thebes, now lead the way!

Enter Creon from the palace, attended by his guard.

But look, the king of the realm is coming,
Creon, the new man for the new day,
whatever the gods are sending now . . .   175
what new plan will he launch?
Why this, this special session?
Why this sudden call to the old men
summoned at one command?
Creon: My countrymen,
the ship of state is safe. The gods who rocked her,   180
after a long, merciless pounding in the storm,

---

154 *Ares:* God of war.   171 *Dionysus:* God of fertility and wine.

have righted her once more.
                              Out of the whole city
I have called you here alone. Well I know,
first, your undeviating respect
for the throne and royal power of King Laius.   185
Next, while Oedipus steered the land of Thebes,
and even after he died, your loyalty was unshakable,
you still stood by their children. Now then,
since the two sons are dead — two blows of fate
in the same day, cut down by each other's hands,   190
both killers, both brothers stained with blood —
as I am next in kin to the dead,
I now possess the throne and all its powers.

Of course you cannot know a man completely,
his character, his principles, sense of judgment,   195
not till he's shown his colors, ruling the people,
making laws. Experience, there's the test.
As I see it, whoever assumes the task,
the awesome task of setting the city's course,
and refuses to adopt the soundest policies   200
but fearing someone, keeps his lips locked tight,
he's utterly worthless. So I rate him now,
I always have. And whoever places a friend
above the good of his own country, he is nothing:
I have no use for him. Zeus my witness,   205
Zeus who sees all things, always —
I could never stand by silent, watching destruction
march against our city, putting safety to rout,
nor could I ever make that man a friend of mine
who menaces our country. Remember this: 210
our country *is* our safety.
Only while she voyages true on course
can we establish friendships, truer than blood itself.
Such are my standards. They make our city great.

Closely akin to them I have proclaimed,   215
just now, the following decree to our people
concerning the two sons of Oedipus.
Eteocles, who died fighting for Thebes,
excelling all in arms: he shall be buried,
crowned with a hero's honors, the cups we pour   220
to soak the earth and reach the famous dead.

But as for his blood brother, Polynices,
who returned from exile, home to his father-city
and the gods of his race, consumed with one desire —
to burn them roof to roots — who thirsted to drink   225
his kinsmen's blood and sell the rest to slavery:
that man — a proclamation has forbidden the city
to dignify him with burial, mourn him at all.

No, he must be left unburied, his corpse
carrion for the birds and dogs to tear,   230
an obscenity for the citizens to behold!

These are my principles. Never at my hands
will the traitor be honored above the patriot.
But whoever proves his loyalty to the state:
I'll prize that man in death as well as life.   235
Leader: If this is your pleasure, Creon, treating
  our city's enemy and our friend this way . . .
  The power is yours, I suppose, to enforce it
  with the laws, both for the dead and all of us,
  the living.
Creon: Follow my orders closely then,   240
  be on your guard.
Leader: We're too old.
  Lay that burden on younger shoulders.
Creon: No, no,
  I don't mean the body — I've posted guards already.
Leader: What commands for us then? What other service?
Creon: See that you never side with those who break my orders.   245
Leader: Never. Only a fool could be in love with death.
Creon: Death is the price — you're right. But all too often
  the mere hope of money has ruined many men.

  A Sentry enters from the side.

Sentry: My lord,
  I can't say I'm winded from running, or set out
  with any spring in my legs either — no sir,   250
  I was lost in thought, and it made me stop, often,
  dead in my tracks, wheeling, turning back,
  and all the time a voice inside me muttering,
  "Idiot, why? You're going straight to your death."
  Then muttering, "Stopped again, poor fool?   255
  If somebody gets the news to Creon first,
  what's to save your neck?"
                          And so,
  mulling it over, on I trudged, dragging my feet,
  you can make a short road take forever . . .
  but at last, look, common sense won out,   260
  I'm here, and I'm all yours,
  and even though I come empty-handed
  I'll tell my story just the same, because
  I've come with a good grip on one hope,
  what will come will come, whatever fate —   265
Creon: Come to the point!
  What's wrong — why so afraid?
Sentry: First, myself, I've got to tell you,
  I didn't do it, didn't see who did —
  Be fair, don't take it out on me.   270

Creon: You're playing it safe, soldier,
    barricading yourself from any trouble.
    It's obvious, you've something strange to tell.
Sentry: Dangerous too, and danger makes you delay
    for all you're worth.   275
Creon: Out with it — then dismiss!
Sentry: All right, here it comes. The body —
    someone's just buried it, then run off . . .
    sprinkled some dry dust on the flesh,
    given it proper rites.
Creon: What?   280
    What man alive would dare —
Sentry: I've no idea, I swear it.
    There was no mark of a spade, no pickaxe there,
    no earth turned up, the ground packed hard and dry,
    unbroken, no tracks, no wheelruts, nothing,
    the workman left no trace. Just at sunup   285
    the first watch of the day points it out —
    it was a wonder! We were stunned . . .
    a terrific burden too, for all of us, listen:
    you can't see the corpse, not that it's buried,
    really, just a light cover of road-dust on it,   290
    as if someone meant to lay the dead to rest
    and keep from getting cursed.
    Not a sign in sight that dogs or wild beasts
    had worried the body, even torn the skin.

    But what came next! Rough talk flew thick and fast,   295
    guard grilling guard — we'd have come to blows
    at last, nothing to stop it; each man for himself
    and each the culprit, no one caught red-handed,
    all of us pleading ignorance, dodging the charges,
    ready to take up red-hot iron in our fists,   300
    go through fire, swear oaths to the gods —
    "I didn't do it, I had no hand in it either,
    not in the plotting, not in the work itself!"

    Finally, after all this wrangling came to nothing,
    one man spoke out and made us stare at the ground,   305
    hanging our heads in fear. No way to counter him,
    no way to take his advice and come through
    safe and sound. Here's what he said:
    "Look, we've got to report the facts to Creon,
    we can't keep this hidden." Well, that won out,   310
    and the lot fell on me, condemned me,
    unlucky as ever, I got the prize. So here I am,
    against my will and yours too, well I know —
    no one wants the man who brings bad news.
Leader: My king,
    ever since he began I've been debating in my mind,   315
    could this possibly be the work of the gods?

Creon: Stop—
    before you make me choke with anger—the gods!
    You, you're senile, must you be insane?
    You say—why it's intolerable—say the gods
    could have the slightest concern for that corpse?   320
    Tell me, was it for meritorious service
    they proceeded to bury him, prized him so? The hero
    who came to burn their temples ringed with pillars,
    their golden treasures—scorch their hallowed earth
    and fling their laws to the winds.   325
    Exactly when did you last see the gods
    celebrating traitors? Inconceivable!

    No, from the first there were certain citizens
    who could hardly stand the spirit of my regime,
    grumbling against me in the dark, heads together,   330
    tossing wildly, never keeping their necks beneath
    the yoke, loyally submitting to their king.
    These are the instigators, I'm convinced—
    they've perverted my own guard, bribed them
    to do their work.
                        Money! Nothing worse   335
    in our lives, so current, rampant, so corrupting.
    Money—you demolish cities, root men from their homes,
    you train and twist good minds and set them on
    to the most atrocious schemes. No limit,
    you make them adept at every kind of outrage,   340
    every godless crime—money!
                                Everyone—
    the whole crew bribed to commit this crime,
    they've made one thing sure at least:
    sooner or later they will pay the price.

    Wheeling on the Sentry.

    You—   345
    I swear to Zeus as I still believe in Zeus,
    if you don't find the man who buried that corpse,
    the very man, and produce him before my eyes,
    simple death won't be enough for you,
    not till we string you up alive   350
    and wring the immorality out of you.
    Then you can steal the rest of your days,
    better informed about where to make a killing.
    You'll have learned, at last, it doesn't pay
    to itch for rewards from every hand that beckons.   355
    Filthy profits wreck most men, you'll see—
    they'll never save your life.
Sentry: Please,
    may I say a word or two, or just turn and go?
Creon: Can't you tell? Everything you say offends me.
Sentry: Where does it hurt you, in the ears or in the heart? 360

Creon: And who are you to pinpoint my displeasure?
Sentry: The culprit grates on your feelings,
     I just annoy your ears.
Creon: Still talking?
     You talk too much! A born nuisance —
Sentry: Maybe so,
     but I never did this thing, so help me!
Creon: Yes you did —   365
     what's more, you squandered your life for silver!
Sentry: Oh it's terrible when the one who does the judging
     judges things all wrong.
Creon: Well now,
     you just be clever about your judgments —
     if you fail to produce the criminals for me,   370
     you'll swear your dirty money brought you pain.

     Turning sharply, reentering the palace.

Sentry: I hope he's found. Best thing by far.
     But caught or not, that's in the lap of fortune;
     I'll never come back, you've seen the last of me.
     I'm saved, even now, and I never thought,   375
     I never hoped —
     dear gods, I owe you all my thanks!

     Rushing out.

Chorus: Numberless wonders
     terrible wonders walk the world but none the match for man —
     that great wonder crossing the heaving gray sea,
                    driven on by the blasts of winter   380
     on through breakers crashing left and right,
          holds his steady course
     and the oldest of the gods he wears away —
     the Earth, the immortal, the inexhaustible —
     as his plows go back and forth, year in, year out   385
          with the breed of stallions turning up the furrows.

     And the blithe, lightheaded race of birds he snares,
     the tribes of savage beasts, the life that swarms the depths —
                    with one fling of his nets
     woven and coiled tight, he takes them all,   390
          man the skilled, the brilliant!
     He conquers all, taming with his techniques
     the prey that roams the cliffs and wild lairs,
     training the stallion, clamping the yoke across
          his shaggy neck, and the tireless mountain bull.   395

     And speech and thought, quick as the wind
     and the mood and mind for law that rules the city —
          all these he has taught himself
     and shelter from the arrows of the frost
     when there's rough lodging under the cold clear sky   400

and the shafts of lashing rain —
　　　ready, resourceful man!
　　　　　Never without resources
never an impasse as he marches on the future —
only Death, from Death alone he will find no rescue　　　405
but from desperate plagues he has plotted his escapes.

Man the master, ingenious past all measure
past all dreams, the skills within his grasp —
　　　he forges on, now to destruction
now again to greatness. When he weaves in　　　410
the laws of the land, and the justice of the gods
that binds his oaths together
　　　　　he and his city rise high —
　　　　　　　but the city casts out
that man who weds himself to inhumanity　　　415
thanks to reckless daring. Never share my hearth
never think my thoughts, whoever does such things.

Enter Antigone from the side, accompanied by the Sentry.

　　Here is a dark sign from the gods —
　　what to make of this? I know her,
　　how can I deny it? That young girl's Antigone!　　　420
　　Wretched, child of a wretched father,
　　Oedipus. Look, is it possible?
　　They bring you in like a prisoner —
　　why? did you break the king's laws?
　　Did they take you in some act of mad defiance?　　　425

Sentry: She's the one, she did it single-handed —
　　we caught her burying the body. Where's Creon?

Enter Creon from the palace.

Leader: Back again, just in time when you need him.
Creon: In time for what? What is it?
Sentry:　　　　　　　My king,
　　there's nothing you can swear you'll never do —　　　430
　　second thoughts make liars of us all.
　　I could have sworn I wouldn't hurry back
　　(what with your threats, the buffeting I just took),
　　but a stroke of luck beyond our wildest hopes,
　　what a joy, there's nothing like it. So,　　　435
　　back I've come, breaking my oath, who cares?
　　I'm bringing in our prisoner — this young girl —
　　we took her giving the dead the last rites.
　　But no casting lots this time; this is *my* luck,
　　my prize, no one else's.
　　　　　　　　Now, my lord,　　　440
　　here she is. Take her, question her,
　　cross-examine her to your heart's content.
　　But set me free, it's only right —
　　I'm rid of this dreadful business once for all.

Creon: Prisoner! Her? You took her—where, doing what?   445
Sentry: Burying the man. That's the whole story.
Creon: What?
        You mean what you say, you're telling me the truth?
Sentry: She's the one. With my own eyes I saw her
        bury the body, just what you've forbidden.
        There. Is that plain and clear?   450
Creon: What did you see? Did you catch her in the act?
Sentry: Here's what happened. We went back to our post,
        those threats of yours breathing down our necks—
        we brushed the corpse clean of the dust that covered it,
        stripped it bare . . . it was slimy, going soft,   455
        and we took to high ground, backs to the wind
        so the stink of him couldn't hit us;
        jostling, baiting each other to keep awake,
        shouting back and forth—no napping on the job,
        not this time. And so the hours dragged by   460
        until the sun stood dead above our heads,
        a huge white ball in the noon sky, beating,
        blazing down, and then it happened—
        suddenly, a whirlwind!
        Twisting a great dust-storm up from the earth,   465
        a black plague of the heavens, filling the plain,
        ripping the leaves off every tree in sight,
        choking the air and sky. We squinted hard
        and took our whipping from the gods.

        And after the storm passed—it seemed endless—   470
        there, we saw the girl!
        And she cried out a sharp, piercing cry,
        like a bird come back to an empty nest,
        peering into its bed, and all the babies gone . . .
        Just so, when she sees the corpse bare   475
        she bursts into a long, shattering wail
        and calls down withering curses on the heads
        of all who did the work. And she scoops up dry dust,
        handfuls, quickly, and lifting a fine bronze urn,
        lifting it high and pouring, she crowns the dead   480
        with three full libations.
                                Soon as we saw
        we rushed her, closed on the kill like hunters,
        and she, she didn't flinch. We interrogated her,
        charging her with offenses past and present—
        she stood up to it all, denied nothing. I tell you,   485
        it made me ache and laugh in the same breath.
        It's pure joy to escape the worst yourself,
        it hurts a man to bring down his friends.
        But all that, I'm afraid, means less to me
        than my own skin. That's the way I'm made.

Creon:

> *Wheeling on Antigone.*

You,   490
with your eyes fixed on the ground — speak up.
Do you deny you did this, yes or no?

Antigone: I did it. I don't deny a thing.

Creon:

> *To the Sentry.*

You, get out, wherever you please —
you're clear of a very heavy charge.   495

> *He leaves; Creon turns back to Antigone.*

You, tell me briefly, no long speeches —
were you aware a decree had forbidden this?

Antigone: Well aware. How could I avoid it? It was public.

Creon: And still you had the gall to break this law?

Antigone: Of course I did. It wasn't Zeus, not in the least,   500
who made this proclamation — not to me.
Nor did that Justice, dwelling with the gods
beneath the earth, ordain such laws for men.
Nor did I think your edict had such force
that you, a mere mortal, could override the gods,   505
the great unwritten, unshakable traditions.
They are alive, not just today or yesterday:
they live forever, from the first of time,
and no one knows when they first saw the light.

These laws — I was not about to break them,   510
not out of fear of some man's wounded pride,
and face the retribution of the gods.
Die I must, I've known it all my life —
how could I keep from knowing? — even without
your death-sentence ringing in my ears.   515
And if I am to die before my time
I consider that a gain. Who on earth,
alive in the midst of so much grief as I,
could fail to find his death a rich reward?
So for me, at least, to meet this doom of yours   520
is precious little pain. But if I had allowed
my own mother's son to rot, an unburied corpse —
that would have been an agony! This is nothing.
And if my present actions strike you as foolish,
let's just say I've been accused of folly   525
by a fool.

Leader: Like father like daughter,
passionate, wild . . .
she hasn't learned to bend before adversity.

Creon: No? Believe me, the stiffest stubborn wills
fall the hardest; the toughest iron,   530

tempered strong in the white-hot fire,
you'll see it crack and shatter first of all.
And I've known spirited horses you can break
with a light bit — proud, rebellious horses.
There's no room for pride, not in a slave,   535
not with the lord and master standing by.

This girl was an old hand at insolence
when she overrode the edicts we made public.
But once she'd done it — the insolence,
twice over — to glory in it, laughing,   540
mocking us to our face with what she'd done.
I'm not the man, not now: she is the man
if this victory goes to her and she goes free.

Never! Sister's child or closer in blood
than all my family clustered at my altar   545
worshiping Guardian Zeus — she'll never escape,
she and her blood sister, the most barbaric death.
Yes, I accuse her sister of an equal part
in scheming this, this burial.

To his attendants.

                                   Bring her here!
I just saw her inside, hysterical, gone to pieces.   550
It never fails: the mind convicts itself
in advance, when scoundrels are up to no good,
plotting in the dark. Oh but I hate it more
when a traitor, caught red-handed,
tries to glorify his crimes.   555
Antigone: Creon, what more do you want
     than my arrest and execution?
Creon: Nothing. Then I have it all.
Antigone: Then why delay? Your moralizing repels me,
     every word you say — pray god it always will.   560
     So naturally all I say repels you too.
                                   Enough.
     Give me glory! What greater glory could I win
     than to give my own brother decent burial?
     These citizens here would all agree,

To the Chorus.

     they'd praise me too   565
     if their lips weren't locked in fear.

Pointing to Creon.

     Lucky tyrants — the perquisites of power!
     Ruthless power to do and say whatever pleases *them.*
Creon: You alone, of all the people in Thebes,
     see things that way.
Antigone: They see it just that way   570
     but defer to you and keep their tongues in leash.

Creon: And you, aren't you ashamed to differ so from them?
    So disloyal!

Antigone: Not ashamed for a moment,
    not to honor my brother, my own flesh and blood.

Creon: Wasn't Eteocles a brother too — cut down, facing him?   575

Antigone: Brother, yes, by the same mother, the same father.

Creon: Then how can you render his enemy such honors,
    such impieties in his eyes?

Antigone: He'll never testify to that,
    Eteocles dead and buried.

Creon: He will —   580
    if you honor the traitor just as much as him.

Antigone: But it was his brother, not some slave that died —

Creon: Ravaging our country! —
    but Eteocles died fighting in our behalf.

Antigone: No matter — Death longs for the same rites for all.   585

Creon: Never the same for the patriot and the traitor.

Antigone: Who, Creon, who on earth can say the ones below
    don't find this pure and uncorrupt?

Creon: Never. Once an enemy, never a friend,
    not even after death.   590

Antigone: I was born to join in love, not hate —
    that is my nature.

Creon: Go down below and love,
    if love you must — love the dead! While I'm alive,
    no woman is going to lord it over me.

Enter Ismene from the palace, under guard.

Chorus: Look,
    Ismene's coming, weeping a sister's tears,   595
    loving sister, under a cloud . . .
    her face is flushed, her cheeks streaming.
    Sorrow puts her lovely radiance in the dark.

Creon: You —
    in my house, you viper, slinking undetected,
    sucking my life-blood! I never knew   600
    I was breeding twin disasters, the two of you
    rising up against my throne. Come, tell me,
    will you confess your part in the crime or not?
    Answer me. Swear to me.

Ismene: I did it, yes —
    if only she consents — I share the guilt,   605
    the consequences too.

Antigone: No,
    Justice will never suffer that — not you,
    you were unwilling. I never brought you in.

Ismene: But now you face such dangers . . . I'm not ashamed
    to sail through trouble with you,   610
    make your troubles mine.

Antigone: Who did the work?

Let the dead and the god of death bear witness!
I've no love for a friend who loves in words alone.
Ismene: Oh no, my sister, don't reject me, please,
    let me die beside you, consecrating   615
    the dead together.
Antigone: Never share my dying,
    don't lay claim to what you never touched.
    My death will be enough.
Ismene: What do I care for life, cut off from you?
Antigone: Ask Creon. Your concern is all for him.   620
Ismene: Why abuse me so? It doesn't help you now.
Antigone: You're right —
    if I mock you, I get no pleasure from it,
    only pain.
Ismene: Tell me, dear one,
    what can I do to help you, even now?
Antigone: Save yourself. I don't grudge you your survival.   625
Ismene: Oh no, no, denied my portion in your death?
Antigone: You chose to live, I chose to die.
Ismene: Not, at least,
    without every kind of caution I could voice.
Antigone: Your wisdom appealed to one world — mine, another.
Ismene: But look, we're both guilty, both condemned to death.   630
Antigone: Courage! Live your life. I gave myself to death,
    long ago, so I might serve the dead.
Creon: They're both mad, I tell you, the two of them.
    One's just shown it, the other's been that way
    since she was born.
Ismene: True, my king,   635
    the sense we were born with cannot last forever . . .
    commit cruelty on a person long enough
    and the mind begins to go.
Creon: Yours did,
    when you chose to commit your crimes with her.
Ismene: How can I live alone, without her?
Creon: Her?   640
    Don't even mention her — she no longer exists.
Ismene: What? You'd kill your own son's bride?
Creon: Absolutely:
    there are other fields for him to plow.
Ismene: Perhaps,
    but never as true, as close a bond as theirs.
Creon: A worthless woman for my son? It repels me.   645
Ismene: Dearest Haemon, your father wrongs you so!
Creon: Enough, enough — you and your talk of marriage!
Ismene: Creon — you're really going to rob your son of Antigone?
Creon: Death will do it for me — break their marriage off.
Leader: So, it's settled then? Antigone must die?   650
Creon: Settled, yes — we both know that.

    To the guards.

Stop wasting time. Take them in.
From now on they'll act like women.
Tie them up, no more running loose;
even the bravest will cut and run,   655
once they see Death coming for their lives.

*The guards escort Antigone and Ismene into the palace. Creon remains while
the old citizens form their chorus.*

Chorus: Blest, they are the truly blest who all their lives
have never tasted devastation. For others, once
the gods have rocked a house to its foundations
        the ruin will never cease, cresting on and on   660
from one generation on throughout the race —
like a great mounting tide
driven on by savage northern gales,
        surging over the dead black depths
roiling up from the bottom dark heaves of sand   665
and the headlands, taking the storm's onslaught full-force,
roar, and the low moaning
                        echoes on and on
                                and now
as in ancient times I see the sorrows of the house,
the living heirs of the old ancestral kings,
piling on the sorrows of the dead   670
        and one generation cannot free the next —
some god will bring them crashing down,
the race finds no release.
And now the light, the hope
        springing up from the late last root   675
in the house of Oedipus, that hope's cut down in turn
by the long, bloody knife swung by the gods of death
by a senseless word
                by fury at the heart.
                            Zeus,
yours is the power, Zeus, what man on earth
can override it, who can hold it back?   680
Power that neither Sleep, the all-ensnaring
        no, nor the tireless months of heaven
can ever overmaster — young through all time,
mighty lord of power, you hold fast
        the dazzling crystal mansions of Olympus.   685
And throughout the future, late and soon
as through the past, your law prevails:
no towering form of greatness
        enters into the lives of mortals
                free and clear of ruin.
                            True,   690
our dreams, our high hopes voyaging far and wide
bring sheer delight to many, to many others
        delusion, blithe, mindless lusts
and the fraud steals on one slowly . . . unaware

till he trips and puts his foot into the fire. 695
    He was a wise old man who coined
the famous saying: "Sooner or later
foul is fair, fair is foul
to the man the gods will ruin"—
    He goes his way for a moment only 700
        free of blinding ruin.

Enter Haemon from the palace.

    Here's Haemon now, the last of all your sons.
Does he come in tears for his bride,
his doomed bride, Antigone—
bitter at being cheated of their marriage? 705
Creon: We'll soon know, better than seers could tell us.

Turning to Haemon.

    Son, you've heard the final verdict on your bride?
Are you coming now, raving against your father?
Or do you love me, no matter what I do?
Haemon: Father, I'm your *son* . . . you in your wisdom 710
set my bearings for me—I obey you.
No marriage could ever mean more to me than you,
whatever good direction you may offer.
Creon: Fine, Haemon.
That's how you ought to feel within your heart,
subordinate to your father's will in every way. 715
That's what a man prays for: to produce good sons—
households full of them, dutiful and attentive,
so they can pay his enemy back with interest
and match the respect their father shows his friend.
But the man who rears a brood of useless children, 720
what has he brought into the world, I ask you?
Nothing but trouble for himself, and mockery
from his enemies laughing in his face.
                Oh Haemon,
never lose your sense of judgment over a woman.
The warmth, the rush of pleasure, it all goes cold 725
in your arms, I warn you . . . a worthless woman
in your house, a misery in your bed.
What wound cuts deeper than a loved one
turned against you? Spit her out,
like a mortal enemy—let the girl go. 730
Let her find a husband down among the dead.

Imagine it: I caught her in naked rebellion,
the traitor, the only one in the whole city.
I'm not about to prove myself a liar,
not to my people, no, I'm going to kill her! 735
That's right—so let her cry for mercy, sing her hymns
to Zeus who defends all bonds of kindred blood.

Why, if I bring up my own kin to be rebels,
think what I'd suffer from the world at large.
Show me the man who rules his household well: 740
I'll show you someone fit to rule the state.
That good man, my son,
I have every confidence he and he alone
can give commands and take them too. Staunch
in the storm of spears he'll stand his ground,   745
a loyal, unflinching comrade at your side.

But whoever steps out of line, violates the laws
or presumes to hand out orders to his superiors,
he'll win no praise from me. But that man
the city places in authority, his orders   750
must be obeyed, large and small,
right and wrong.
                    Anarchy—
show me a greater crime in all the earth!
She, she destroys cities, rips up houses,
breaks the ranks of spearmen into headlong rout.   755
But the ones who last it out, the great mass of them
owe their lives to discipline. Therefore
we must defend the men who live by law,
never let some woman triumph over us.
Better to fall from power, if fall we must,   760
at the hands of a man—never be rated
inferior to a woman, never.
Leader: To us,
unless old age has robbed us of our wits,
you seem to say what you have to say with sense.
Haemon: Father, only the gods endow a man with reason,   765
the finest of all their gifts, a treasure.
Far be it from me—I haven't the skill,
and certainly no desire, to tell you when,
if ever, you make a slip in speech . . . though
someone else might have a good suggestion.   770

Of course it's not for you,
in the normal run of things, to watch
whatever men say or do, or find to criticize.
The man in the street, you know, dreads your glance,
he'd never say anything displeasing to your face.   775
But it's for me to catch the murmurs in the dark,
the way the city mourns for this young girl.
"No woman," they say, "ever deserved death less,
and such a brutal death for such a glorious action.
She, with her own dear brother lying in his blood—   780
she couldn't bear to leave him dead, unburied,
food for the wild dogs or wheeling vultures.
Death? She deserves a glowing crown of gold!"
So they say, and the rumor spreads in secret,

darkly . . .

     I rejoice in your success, father —   785
nothing more precious to me in the world.
What medal of honor brighter to his children
than a father's growing glory? Or a child's
to his proud father? Now don't, please,
be quite so single-minded, self-involved,   790
or assume the world is wrong and you are right.
Whoever thinks that he alone possesses intelligence,
the gift of eloquence, he and no one else,
and character too . . . such men, I tell you,
spread them open — you will find them empty.

               No,   795
it's no disgrace for a man, even a wise man,
to learn many things and not to be too rigid.
You've seen trees by a raging winter torrent,
how many sway with the flood and salvage every twig,
but not the stubborn — they're ripped out, roots and all.   800
Bend or break. The same when a man is sailing:
haul your sheets too taut, never give an inch,
you'll capsize, go the rest of the voyage
keel up and the rowing-benches under.

Oh give way. Relax your anger — change!   805
I'm young, I know, but let me offer this:
it would be best by far, I admit,
if a man were born infallible, right by nature.
If not — and things don't often go that way,
it's best to learn from those with good advice.   810
Leader: You'd do well, my lord, if he's speaking to the point,
  to learn from him,

  Turning to Haemon.

      and you, my boy, from him.
  You both are talking sense.
Creon: So,
  men our age, we're to be lectured, are we? —
  schooled by a boy his age?   815
Haemon: Only in what is right. But if I seem young,
  look less to my years and more to what I do.
Creon: Do? Is admiring rebels an achievement?
Haemon: I'd never suggest that you admire treason.
Creon: Oh? —
  isn't that just the sickness that's attacked her?   820
Haemon: The whole city of Thebes denies it, to a man.
Creon: And is Thebes about to tell me how to rule?
Haemon: Now, you see? Who's talking like a child?
Creon: Am I to rule this land for others — or myself?
Haemon: It's no city at all, owned by one man alone.   825
Creon: What? The city *is* the king's — that's the law!

Haemon: What a splendid king you'd make of a desert island—
    you and you alone.
Creon:

    To the Chorus.

                    This boy, I do believe,
    is fighting on her side, the woman's side.
Haemon: If you are a woman, yes;   830
    my concern is all for you.
Creon: Why, you degenerate—bandying accusations,
    threatening me with justice, your own father!
Haemon: I see my father offending justice—wrong.
Creon: Wrong?
    To protect my royal rights?
Haemon: Protect your rights?   835
    When you trample down the honors of the gods?
Creon: You, you soul of corruption, rotten through—
    woman's accomplice!
Haemon: That may be,
    but you'll never find me accomplice to a criminal.
Creon: That's what *she* is,   840
    and every word you say is a blatant appeal for her—
Haemon: And you, and me, and the gods beneath the earth.
Creon: You'll never marry her, not while she's alive.
Haemon: Then she'll die . . . but her death will kill another.
Creon: What, brazen threats? You go too far!
Haemon: What threat?   845
    Combating your empty, mindless judgments with a word?
Creon: You'll suffer for your sermons, you and your empty wisdom!
Haemon: If you weren't my father, I'd say you were insane.
Creon: Don't flatter me with Father—you woman's slave!
Haemon: You really expect to fling abuse at me   850
    and not receive the same?
Creon: Is that so!
    Now, by heaven, I promise you, you'll pay—
    taunting, insulting me! Bring her out,
    that hateful—she'll die now, here,
    in front of his eyes, beside her groom!   855
Haemon: No, no, she will never die beside me—
    don't delude yourself. And you will never
    see me, never set eyes on my face again.
    Rage your heart out, rage with friends
    who can stand the sight of you.   860

    Rushing out.

Leader: Gone, my king, in a burst of anger.
    A temper young as his . . . hurt him once,
    he may do something violent.
Creon: Let him do—
    dream up something desperate, past all human limit!

Good riddance. Rest assured,   865
he'll never save those two young girls from death.
Leader: Both of them, you really intend to kill them both?
Creon: No, not her, the one whose hands are clean;
    you're quite right.
Leader: But Antigone—
what sort of death do you have in mind for her?   870
Creon: I'll take her down some wild, desolate path
never trod by men, and wall her up alive
in a rocky vault, and set out short rations,
just a gesture of piety
to keep the entire city free of defilement.   875
There let her pray to the one god she worships:
Death—who knows?—may just reprieve her from death.
Or she may learn at last, better late than never,
what a waste of breath it is to worship Death.

    Exit to the palace.

Chorus: Love, never conquered in battle   880
Love the plunderer laying waste the rich!
Love standing the night-watch
        guarding a girl's soft cheek,
you range the seas, the shepherds' steadings off in the wilds—
not even the deathless gods can flee your onset,   885
nothing human born for a day—
whoever feels your grip is driven mad.
              Love
you wrench the minds of the righteous into outrage,
swerve them to their ruin—you have ignited this,
this kindred strife, father and son at war   890
        and Love alone the victor—
warm glance of the bride triumphant, burning with desire!
Throned in power, side-by-side with the mighty laws!
Irresistible Aphrodite,° never conquered—
Love, you mock us for your sport.   895

    Antigone is brought from the palace under guard.

    But now, even I'd rebel against the king,
    I'd break all bounds when I see this—
    I fill with tears, can't hold them back,
    not any more . . . I see Antigone make her way
    to the bridal vault where all are laid to rest.   900
Antigone: Look at me, men of my fatherland,
    setting out on the last road
looking into the last light of day
the last I'll ever see . . .
the god of death who puts us all to bed   905
takes me down to the banks of Acheron° alive—
    denied my part in the wedding-songs,

---

894 *Aphrodite:* Goddess of love.   906 *Acheron:* A river in the underworld, to which the dead go.

no wedding-song in the dusk has crowned my marriage—
I go to wed the lord of the dark waters.
Chorus: Not crowned with glory, crowned with a dirge,   910
      you leave for the deep pit of the dead.
      No withering illness laid you low,
      no strokes of the sword—a law to yourself,
      alone, no mortal like you, ever, you go down
      to the halls of Death alive and breathing.   915
Antigone: But think of Niobe°—well I know her story—
    think what a living death she died,
Tantalus' daughter, stranger queen from the east:
there on the mountain heights, growing stone
binding as ivy, slowly walled her round   920
and the rains will never cease, the legends say
the snows will never leave her . . .
    wasting away, under her brows the tears
showering down her breasting ridge and slopes—
a rocky death like hers puts me to sleep.   925
Chorus: But she was a god, born of gods,
      and we are only mortals born to die.
      And yet, of course, it's a great thing
      for a dying girl to hear, just hear
      she shares a destiny equal to the gods,   930
      during life and later, once she's dead.
Antigone: O you mock me!
Why, in the name of all my fathers' gods
why can't you wait till I am gone—
    must you abuse me to my face?
O my city, all your fine rich sons!   935
And you, you springs of the Dirce,
holy grove of Thebes where the chariots gather,
      you at least, you'll bear me witness, look,
unmourned by friends and forced by such crude laws
I go to my rockbound prison, strange new tomb—   940
    always a stranger, O dear god,
I have no home on earth and none below,
    not with the living, not with the breathless dead.
Chorus: You went too far, the last limits of daring—
      smashing against the high throne of Justice!   945
      Your life's in ruins, child—I wonder . . .
      do you pay for your father's terrible ordeal?
Antigone: There—at last you've touched it, the worst pain
the worst anguish! Raking up the grief for father
    three times over, for all the doom   950
that's struck us down, the brilliant house of Laius.
O mother, your marriage-bed
the coiling horrors, the coupling there—
you with your own son, my father—doomstruck mother!

---

916 *Niobe:* A queen of Thebes who was punished by the gods for her pride and was turned into stone.

Such, such were my parents, and I their wretched child. 955
I go to them now, cursed, unwed, to share their home —
    I am a stranger! O dear brother, doomed
    in your marriage — your marriage murders mine,
        your dying drags me down to death alive!

Enter Creon.

Chorus: Reverence asks some reverence in return — 960
        but attacks on power never go unchecked,
            not by the man who holds the reins of power.
        Your own blind will, your passion has destroyed you.
Antigone: No one to weep for me, my friends,
        no wedding-song — they take me away 965
        in all my pain . . . the road lies open, waiting.
        Never again, the law forbids me to see
        the sacred eye of day. I am agony!
        No tears for the destiny that's mine,
        no loved one mourns my death.
Creon: Can't you see? 970
    If a man could wail his own dirge *before* he dies,
    he'd never finish.

To the guards.

                    Take her away, quickly!
    Wall her up in the tomb, you have your orders.
    Abandon her there, alone, and let her choose —
    death or a buried life with a good roof for shelter. 975
    As for myself, my hands are clean. This young girl —
    dead or alive, she will be stripped of her rights,
    her stranger's rights, here in the world above.
Antigone: O tomb, my bridal-bed — my house, my prison
        cut in the hollow rock, my everlasting watch! 980
        I'll soon be there, soon embrace my own,
        the great growing family of our dead
        Persephone° has received among her ghosts.
                                                    I,
        the last of them all, the most reviled by far,
        go down before my destined time's run out. 985
        But still I go, cherishing one good hope:
        my arrival may be dear to father,
        dear to you, my mother,
        dear to you, my loving brother, Eteocles —
        When you died I washed you with my hands, 990
        I dressed you all, I poured the cups
        across your tombs. But now, Polynices,
        because I laid your body out as well,
        this, this is my reward. Nevertheless
        I honored you — the decent will admit it — 995
        well and wisely too.
                        Never, I tell you,

---

983 *Persephone:* Queen of the underworld.

if I had been the mother of children
or if my husband died, exposed and rotting —
I'd never have taken this ordeal upon myself,
never defied our people's will. What law,   1000
you ask, do I satisfy with what I say?
A husband dead, there might have been another.
A child by another too, if I had lost the first.
But mother and father both lost in the halls of Death,
no brother could ever spring to light again.   1005

For this law alone I held you first in honor.
For this, Creon, the king, judges me a criminal
guilty of dreadful outrage, my dear brother!
And now he leads me off, a captive in his hands,
with no part in the bridal-song, the bridal-bed,   1010
denied all joy of marriage, raising children —
deserted so by loved ones, struck by fate,
I descend alive to the caverns of the dead.

What law of the mighty gods have I transgressed?
Why look to the heavens any more, tormented as I am?   1015
Whom to call, what comrades now? Just think,
my reverence only brands me for irreverence!
Very well: if this is the pleasure of the gods,
once I suffer I will know that I was wrong.
But if these men are wrong, let them suffer   1020
nothing worse than they mete out to me —
these masters of injustice!
Leader: Still the same rough winds, the wild passion
        raging through the girl.
Creon:

    To the guards.

                        Take her away.
    You're wasting time — you'll pay for it too.   1025
Antigone: Oh god, the voice of death. It's come, it's here.
Creon: True. Not a word of hope — your doom is sealed.
Antigone: Land of Thebes, city of all my fathers —
        O you gods, the first gods of the race!
        They drag me away, now, no more delay.   1030
        Look on me, you noble sons of Thebes —
        the last of a great line of kings,
        I alone, see what I suffer now
        at the hands of what breed of men —
        all for reverence, my reverence for the gods!   1035

    She leaves under guard; the Chorus gathers.

Chorus: Danaë, Danaë° —
        even she endured a fate like yours,
            in all her lovely strength she traded

1036 *Danaë:* Locked in a cell by her father because it was prophesied that her son would kill
him, but visited by Zeus in the form of a shower of gold. Their son was Perseus.

the light of day for the bolted brazen vault —
buried within her tomb, her bridal-chamber,   1040
wed to the yoke and broken.
    But she was of glorious birth
                 my child, my child
and treasured the seed of Zeus within her womb,
the cloudburst streaming gold!   1045
    The power of fate is a wonder,
    dark, terrible wonder —
    neither wealth nor armies
    towered walls nor ships
    black hulls lashed by the salt   1050
    can save us from that force.

The yoke tamed him too
    young Lycurgus° flaming in anger
king of Edonia, all for his mad taunts
Dionysus clamped him down, encased   1055
in the chain-mail of rock
    and there his rage
               his terrible flowering rage burst —
sobbing, dying away . . . at last that madman
came to know his god —   1060
    the power he mocked, the power
    he taunted in all his frenzy
    trying to stamp out
    the women strong with the god —
    the torch, the raving sacred cries —   1065
    enraging the Muses° who adore the flute.

And far north where the Black Rocks
    cut the sea in half
and murderous straits
split the coast of Thrace   1070
    a forbidding city stands
where once, hard by the walls
the savage Ares thrilled to watch
a king's new queen, a Fury rearing in rage
    against his two royal sons —   1075
          her bloody hands, her dagger-shuttle
stabbing out their eyes — cursed, blinding wounds —
their eyes blind sockets screaming for revenge!

They wailed in agony, cries echoing cries
    the princes doomed at birth . . .   1080
and their mother doomed to chains,
walled off in a tomb of stone —
    but she traced her own birth back
to a proud Athenian line and the high gods

1053 *Lycurgus:* Punished by Dionysus because he would not worship him. 1066 *Muses:*
Goddesses of the arts.

and off in caverns half the world away,   1085
born of the wild North Wind
    she sprang on her father's gales,
      racing stallions up the leaping cliffs —
child of the heavens. But even on her the Fates
the gray everlasting Fates rode hard   1090
my child, my child.

Enter Tiresias, the blind prophet, led by a boy.

Tiresias: Lords of Thebes,
    I and the boy have come together,
    hand in hand. Two see with the eyes of one . . .
    so the blind must go, with a guide to lead the way.
Creon: What is it, old Tiresias? What news now?   1095
Tiresias: I will teach you. And you obey the seer.
Creon: I will,
    I've never wavered from your advice before.
Tiresias: And so you kept the city straight on course.
Creon: I owe you a great deal, I swear to that.
Tiresias: Then reflect, my son: you are poised,   1100
    once more, on the razor-edge of fate.
Creon: What is it? I shudder to hear you.
Tiresias: You will learn
    when you listen to the warnings of my craft.
    As I sat on the ancient seat of augury,°
    in the sanctuary where every bird I know   1105
    will hover at my hands — suddenly I heard it,
    a strange voice in the wingbeats, unintelligible,
    barbaric, a mad scream! Talons flashing, ripping,
    they were killing each other — that much I knew —
    the murderous fury whirring in those wings   1110
    made that much clear!
                      I was afraid,
    I turned quickly, tested the burnt-sacrifice,
    ignited the altar at all points — but no fire,
    the god in the fire never blazed.
    Not from those offerings . . . over the embers   1115
    slid a heavy ooze from the long thighbones,
    smoking, sputtering out, and the bladder
    puffed and burst — spraying gall into the air —
    and the fat wrapping the bones slithered off
    and left them glistening white. No fire!   1120
    The rites failed that might have blazed the future
    with a sign. So I learned from the boy here;
    he is my guide, as I am guide to others.
                    And it's you —
    your high resolve that sets this plague on Thebes.
    The public altars and sacred hearths are fouled,   1125

1104 *seat of augury:* Where Tiresias looked for omens among birds.

one and all, by the birds and dogs with carrion
torn from the corpse, the doomstruck son of Oedipus!
And so the gods are deaf to our prayers, they spurn
the offerings in our hands, the flame of holy flesh.
No birds cry out an omen clear and true— 1130
they're gorged with the murdered victim's blood and fat.
Take these things to heart, my son, I warn you.
All men make mistakes, it is only human.
But once the wrong is done, a man
can turn his back on folly, misfortune too, 1135
if he tries to make amends, however low he's fallen,
and stops his bullnecked ways. Stubbornness
brands you for stupidity—pride is a crime.
No, yield to the dead!
Never stab the fighter when he's down. 1140
Where's the glory, killing the dead twice over?

I mean you well. I give you sound advice.
It's best to learn from a good adviser
when he speaks for your own good:
it's pure gain.
Creon: Old man—all of you! So, 1145
you shoot your arrows at my head like archers at the target—
I even have *him* loosed on me, this fortune-teller.
Oh his ilk has tried to sell me short
and ship me off for years. Well,
drive your bargains, traffic—much as you like— 1150
in the gold of India, silver-gold of Sardis.
You'll never bury that body in the grave,
not even if Zeus's eagles rip the corpse
and wing their rotten pickings off to the throne of god!
Never, not even in fear of such defilement 1155
will I tolerate his burial, that traitor.
Well I know, we can't defile the gods—
no mortal has the power.
     No,
reverend old Tiresias, all men fall,
it's only human, but the wisest fall obscenely 1160
when they glorify obscene advice with rhetoric—
all for their own gain.
Tiresias: Oh god, is there a man alive
who knows, who actually believes . . .
Creon: What now?
What earth-shattering truth are you about to utter? 1165
Tiresias: . . . just how much a sense of judgment, wisdom
is the greatest gift we have?
Creon: Just as much, I'd say,
as a twisted mind is the worst affliction going.
Tiresias: You are the one who's sick, Creon, sick to death.
Creon: I am in no mood to trade insults with a seer. 1170

Tiresias: You have already, calling my prophecies a lie.
Creon: Why not?
    You and the whole breed of seers are mad for money!
Tiresias: And the whole race of tyrants lusts to rake it in.
Creon: This slander of yours —
    are you aware you're speaking to the king?   1175
Tiresias: Well aware. Who helped you save the city?
Creon: You —
    you have your skills, old seer, but you lust for injustice!
Tiresias: You will drive me to utter the dreadful secret in my heart.
Creon: Spit it out! Just don't speak it out for profit.
Tiresias: Profit? No, not a bit of profit, not for you.   1180
Creon: Know full well, you'll never buy off my resolve.
Tiresias: Then know this too, learn this by heart!
    The chariot of the sun will not race through
    so many circuits more, before you have surrendered
    one born of your own loins, your own flesh and blood,   1185
    a corpse for corpses given in return, since you have thrust
    to the world below a child sprung for the world above,
    ruthlessly lodged a living soul within the grave —
    then you've robbed the gods below the earth,
    keeping a dead body here in the bright air,   1190
    unburied, unsung, unhallowed by the rites.

    You, you have no business with the dead,
    nor do the gods above — this is violence
    you have forced upon the heavens.
    And so the avengers, the dark destroyers late   1195
    but true to the mark, now lie in wait for you,
    the Furies sent by the gods and the god of death
    to strike you down with the pains that you perfected!

    There. Reflect on that, tell me I've been bribed.
    The day comes soon, no long test of time, not now,   1200
    that wakes the wails for men and women in your halls.
    Great hatred rises against you —
    cities in tumult, all whose mutilated sons
    the dogs have graced with burial, or the wild beasts,
    some wheeling crow that wings the ungodly stench of carrion   1205
    back to each city, each warrior's hearth and home.

    These arrows for your heart! Since you've raked me
    I loose them like an archer in my anger,
    arrows deadly true. You'll never escape
    their burning, searing force.   1210

    Motioning to his escort.

    Come, boy, take me home.
    So he can vent his rage on younger men,
    and learn to keep a gentler tongue in his head
    and better sense than what he carries now.

Exit to the side.

Leader: The old man's gone, my king —   1215
 terrible prophecies. Well I know,
 since the hair on this old head went gray,
 he's never lied to Thebes.
Creon: I know it myself — I'm shaken, torn.
 It's a dreadful thing to yield . . . but resist now?   1220
 Lay my pride bare to the blows of ruin?
 That's dreadful too.
Leader: But good advice,
 Creon, take it now, you must.
Creon: What should I do? Tell me . . . I'll obey.
Leader: Go! Free the girl from the rocky vault   1225
 and raise a mound for the body you exposed.
Creon: That's your advice? You think I should give in?
Leader: Yes, my king, quickly. Disasters sent by the gods
 cut short our follies in a flash.
Creon: Oh it's hard.
 giving up the heart's desire . . . but I will do it —   1230
 no more fighting a losing battle with necessity.
Leader: Do it now, go, don't leave it to others.
Creon: Now — I'm on my way! Come, each of you,
 take up axes, make for the high ground,
 over there, quickly! I and my better judgment   1235
 have come round to this — I shackled her,
 I'll set her free myself. I am afraid . . .
 it's best to keep the established laws
 to the very day we die.

Rushing out, followed by his entourage. The Chorus clusters around the altar.

Chorus: God of a hundred names!
        Great Dionysus —   1240
    Son and glory of Semele! Pride of Thebes —
 Child of Zeus whose thunder rocks the clouds —
 Lord of the famous lands of evening —
 King of the Mysteries!
      King of Eleusis, Demeter's plain°
 her breasting hills that welcome in the world —   1245
 Great Dionysus!
      Bacchus,° living in Thebes
 the mother-city of all your frenzied women —
            Bacchus
   living along the Ismenus'° rippling waters
 standing over the field sown with the Dragon's teeth!

 You — we have seen you through the flaring smoky fires,   1250
  your torches blazing over the twin peaks

1244 *Demeter's plain:* The goddess of grain was worshiped at Eleusis, near Athens.
1246 *Bacchus:* Another name for Dionysus. 1248 *Ismenus:* A river near Thebes where the
founders of the city were said to have sprung from a dragon's teeth.

where nymphs of the hallowed cave climb onward
            fired with you, your sacred rage —
we have seen you at Castalia's running spring°
and down from the heights of Nysa° crowned with ivy   1255
the greening shore rioting vines and grapes
      down you come in your storm of wild women
           ecstatic, mystic cries —
                      Dionysus —
down to watch and ward the roads of Thebes!

First of all cities, Thebes you honor first   1260
you and your mother, bride of the lightning —
come, Dionysus! now your people lie
in the iron grip of plague,
come in your racing, healing stride
           down Parnassus'° slopes   1265
or across the moaning straits.
                Lord of the dancing —
dance, dance the constellations breathing fire!
Great master of the voices of the night!
Child of Zeus, God's offspring, come, come forth!
Lord, king, dance with your nymphs, swirling, raving   1270
arm-in-arm in frenzy through the night
      they dance you, Iacchus° —
               Dance, Dionysus
giver of all good things!

Enter a Messenger from the side.

Messenger: Neighbors,
friends of the house of Cadmus° and the kings,
there's not a thing in this life of ours   1275
I'd praise or blame as settled once for all.
Fortune lifts and Fortune fells the lucky
and unlucky every day. No prophet on earth
can tell a man his fate. Take Creon:
there was a man to rouse your envy once,   1280
as I see it. He saved the realm from enemies;
taking power, he alone, the lord of the fatherland,
he set us true on course — flourished like a tree
with the noble line of sons he bred and reared . . .
and now it's lost, all gone.
               Believe me,   1285
when a man has squandered his true joys,
he's good as dead, I tell you, a living corpse.
Pile up riches in your house, as much as you like —
live like a king with a huge show of pomp,

1254 *Castalia's running spring:* The sacred spring of Apollo's oracle at Delphi.   1255 *Nysa:*
A mountain where Dionysus was worshiped.   1265 *Parnassus:* A mountain in Greece that
was sacred to Dionysus as well as other gods and goddesses.   1272 *Iacchus:* Dionysus.
1274 *Cadmus:* The legendary founder of Thebes.

but if real delight is missing from the lot,   1290
I wouldn't give you a wisp of smoke for it,
not compared with joy.
Leader: What now?
What new grief do you bring the house of kings?
Messenger: Dead, dead — and the living are guilty of their death!
Leader: Who's the murderer? Who is dead? Tell us.   1295
Messenger: Haemon's gone, his blood spilled by the very hand —
Leader: His father's or his own?
Messenger: His own . . .
raging mad with his father for the death —
Leader: Oh great seer,
you saw it all, you brought your word to birth!
Messenger: Those are the facts. Deal with them as you will.   1300

As he turns to go, Eurydice enters from the palace.

Leader: Look, Eurydice. Poor woman, Creon's wife,
so close at hand. By chance perhaps,
unless she's heard the news about her son.
Eurydice: My countrymen,
all of you — I caught the sound of your words
as I was leaving to do my part,   1305
to appeal to queen Athena° with my prayers.
I was just loosing the bolts, opening the doors,
when a voice filled with sorrow, family sorrow,
struck my ears, and I fell back, terrified,
into the women's arms — everything went black.   1310
Tell me the news, again, whatever it is . . .
sorrow and I are hardly strangers;
I can bear the worst.
Messenger: I — dear lady,
I'll speak as an eye-witness. I was there.
And I won't pass over one word of the truth.   1315
Why should I try to soothe you with a story,
only to prove a liar in a moment?
Truth is always best.
                So,
I escorted your lord, I guided him
to the edge of the plain where the body lay,   1320
Polynices, torn by the dogs and still unmourned.
And saying a prayer to Hecate of the Crossroads,
Pluto° too, to hold their anger and be kind,
we washed the dead in a bath of holy water
and plucking some fresh branches, gathering . . .   1325
what was left of him, we burned them all together
and raised a high mound of native earth, and then
we turned and made for that rocky vault of hers,
the hollow, empty bed of the bride of Death.

1306 *Athena:* Goddess of wisdom and protector of Greek cities.   1322–1323 *Hecate, Pluto:*
Gods of the underworld.

And far off, one of us heard a voice,   1330
a long wail rising, echoing
out of that unhallowed wedding-chamber;
he ran to alert the master and Creon pressed on,
closer — the strange, inscrutable cry came sharper,
throbbing around him now, and he let loose   1335
a cry of his own, enough to wrench the heart,
"Oh god, am I the prophet now? going down
the darkest road I've ever gone? My son —
it's *his* dear voice, he greets me! Go, men,
closer, quickly! Go through the gap,   1340
the rocks are dragged back —
right to the tomb's very mouth — and look,
see if it's Haemon's voice I think I hear,
or the gods have robbed me of my senses."

The king was shattered. We took his orders,   1345
went and searched, and there in the deepest,
dark recesses of the tomb we found her . . .
hanged by the neck in a fine linen noose,
strangled in her veils — and the boy,
his arms flung around her waist,   1350
clinging to her, wailing for his bride,
dead and down below, for his father's crimes
and the bed of his marriage blighted by misfortune.
When Creon saw him, he gave a deep sob,
he ran in, shouting, crying out to him,   1355
"Oh my child — what have you done? what seized you,
what insanity? what disaster drove you mad?
Come out, my son! I beg you on my knees!"
But the boy gave him a wild burning glance,
spat in his face, not a word in reply,   1360
he drew his sword — his father rushed out,
running as Haemon lunged and missed! —
and then, doomed, desperate with himself,
suddenly leaning his full weight on the blade,
he buried it in his body, halfway to the hilt.   1365
And still in his senses, pouring his arms around her,
he embraced the girl and breathing hard,
released a quick rush of blood,
bright red on her cheek glistening white.
And there he lies, body enfolding body . . .   1370
he has won his bride at last, poor boy,
not here but in the houses of the dead.

Creon shows the world that of all the ills
afflicting men the worst is lack of judgment.

Eurydice turns and reenters the palace.

Leader: What do you make of that? The lady's gone,   1375
         without a word, good or bad.

Messenger: I'm alarmed too
   but here's my hope — faced with her son's death,
   she finds it unbecoming to mourn in public.
   Inside, under her roof, she'll set her women
   to the task and wail the sorrow of the house.   1380
   She's too discreet. She won't do something rash.
Leader: I'm not so sure. To me, at least,
   a long heavy silence promises danger,
   just as much as a lot of empty outcries.
Messenger: We'll see if she's holding something back,   1385
   hiding some passion in her heart.
   I'm going in. You may be right — who knows?
   Even too much silence has its dangers.

   Exit to the palace. Enter Creon from the side, escorted by attendants carrying
   Haemon's body on a bier.

Leader: The king himself! Coming toward us,
         look, holding the boy's head in his hands.   1390
         Clear, damning proof, if it's right to say so —
         proof of his own madness, no one else's,
               no, his own blind wrongs.
Creon: Ohhh,
   so senseless, so insane . . . my crimes,
   my stubborn, deadly —   1395
   Look at us, the killer, the killed,
   father and son, the same blood — the misery!
   My plans, my mad fanatic heart,
   my son, cut off so young!
   Ai, dead, lost to the world,   1400
   not through your stupidity, no, my own.
Leader: Too late,
   too late, you see what justice means.
Creon: Oh I've learned
   through blood and tears! Then, it was then,
   when the god came down and struck me — a great weight
   shattering, driving me down that wild savage path,   1405
   ruining, trampling down my joy. Oh the agony,
         the heartbreaking agonies of our lives.

   Enter the Messenger from the palace.

Messenger: Master,
   what a hoard of grief you have, and you'll have more.
   The grief that lies to hand you've brought yourself —

   Pointing to Haemon's body.

   the rest, in the house, you'll see it all too soon.   1410
Creon: What now? What's worse than this?
Messenger: The queen is dead.
   The mother of this dead boy . . . mother to the end —
   poor thing, her wounds are fresh.
Creon: No, no,
         harbor of Death, so choked, so hard to cleanse! —

why me? why are you killing me?   1415
Herald of pain, more words, more grief?
I died once, you kill me again and again!
What's the report, boy . . . some news for me?
My wife dead? O dear god!
Slaughter heaped on slaughter?

The doors open; the body of Eurydice is brought out on her bier.

Messenger: See for yourself: 1420
now they bring her body from the palace.
Creon: Oh no,
another, a second loss to break the heart.
What next, what fate still waits for me?
I just held my son in my arms and now,
look, a new corpse rising before my eyes —   1425
wretched, helpless mother — O my son!
Messenger: She stabbed herself at the altar,
then her eyes went dark, after she'd raised
a cry for the noble fate of Megareus,° the hero
killed in the first assault, then for Haemon,   1430
then with her dying breath she called down
torments on your head — you killed her sons.
Creon: Oh the dread,
I shudder with dread! Why not kill me too? —
run me through with a good sharp sword?
Oh god, the misery, anguish —   1435
I, I'm churning with it, going under.
Messenger: Yes, and the dead, the woman lying there,
piles the guilt of all their deaths on you.
Creon: How did she end her life, what bloody stroke?
Messenger: She drove home to the heart with her own hand,   1440
once she learned her son was dead . . . that agony.
Creon: And the guilt is all mine —
can never be fixed on another man,
no escape for me. I killed you,
I, god help me, I admit it all!   1445

To his attendants.

Take me away, quickly, out of sight.
I don't even exist — I'm no one. Nothing.
Leader: Good advice, if there's any good in suffering.
Quickest is best when troubles block the way.
Creon:

Kneeling in prayer.

Come, let it come! — that best of fates for me   1450
that brings the final day, best fate of all.
Oh quickly, now —
so I never have to see another sunrise.
Leader: That will come when it comes;

1429 *Megareus:* A son of Creon and Eurydice; he died when Thebes was attacked.

we must deal with all that lies before us.   1455
The future rests with the ones who tend the future.
Creon: That prayer — I poured my heart into that prayer!
Leader: No more prayers now. For mortal men
there is no escape from the doom we must endure.
Creon: Take me away, I beg you, out of sight.   1460
A rash, indiscriminate fool!
I murdered you, my son, against my will —
you too, my wife . . .
Wailing wreck of a man,
whom to look to? where to lean for support?

Desperately turning from Haemon to Eurydice on their biers.

Whatever I touch goes wrong — once more   1465
a crushing fate's come down upon my head.

The Messenger and attendants lead Creon into the palace.

Chorus: Wisdom is by far the greatest part of joy,
and reverence toward the gods must be safeguarded.
The mighty words of the proud are paid in full
with mighty blows of fate, and at long last   1470
those blows will teach us wisdom.

The old citizens exit to the side.

Considerations for Critical Thinking and Writing

1. FIRST RESPONSE. What are Creon's reasons for issuing the decree forbidding Polynices' burial? What are Antigone's reasons for rejecting Creon's order? Whose arguments are more convincing?

2. What is the Chorus's position on Creon's decree? Does the Chorus see the conflict between Antigone and Creon as simply a collision between two strong-willed individuals, or does it see a larger issue at stake?

3. How does Ismene serve as a foil to Antigone? Does Ismene seem weak, or is she reasonable? Why does Antigone reject her sister's offer to martyr herself?

4. How does Haemon serve as a foil to Creon? Is Haemon's decision to commit suicide plausible?

5. What is Creon's attitude toward women? How does this affect his reaction to Antigone's disobedience to the state?

6. Who is responsible for what happens? Does Sophocles suggest that the tragedy could have been avoided if Creon or Antigone had behaved differently? Do Creon and Antigone share any similar characteristics?

7. Describe what you think Sophocles' attitudes were concerning the competing claims for the authority of the state over the individual. Explain how those views are indicated in the play and whether you agree or disagree with them.

8. How might the emphasis of the play have been changed if Sophocles had included the scene in the tomb between Haemon and Antigone? Why do you think he left out such a potentially affecting scene?

9. If you were to stage this play in a contemporary setting, describe what kinds of sets you would use and how you would costume the players.

CONNECTIONS TO OTHER SELECTIONS

1. How is Creon's reaction to Haemon's and Tiresias's pleas that he rescind the decree similar to Oedipus's reaction to Creon and Tiresias in *Oedipus the King?*

2. What similarities and differences are there in Sophocles' characterization of Creon in *Antigone* and in *Oedipus the King?*

3. Consider this assessment of Antigone by the leader of the Chorus (lines 526–528):

> Like father like daughter,
> passionate, wild . . .
> she hasn't learned to bend before adversity.

Does this accurately characterize Antigone? What similarities are there between Oedipus and his daughter? Could these lines also be used to describe Haemon and Ismene?

PERSPECTIVES ON SOPHOCLES

ARISTOTLE (384–322 B.C.)

On Tragic Character   *c. 340 B.C.*

Now since in the finest kind of tragedy the structure should be complex and not simple, and since it should also be a representation of terrible and piteous events (that being the special mark of this type of imitation), in the first place, it is evident that good men ought not to be shown passing from happiness to misfortune, for this does not inspire either pity or fear, but only revulsion; nor evil men rising from ill fortune to prosperity, for this is the most untragic plot of all — it lacks every requirement, in that it neither elicits human sympathy nor stirs pity or fear. And again, neither should an extremely wicked man be seen falling from prosperity into misfortune, for a plot so constructed might indeed call forth human sympathy, but would not excite pity or fear, since the first is felt for a person whose misfortune is undeserved and the second for someone like ourselves — pity for the man suffering undeservedly, fear for the man like ourselves — and hence neither pity nor fear would be aroused in this case. We are left with the man whose place is between these extremes. Such is the man who on the one hand is not preeminent in virtue and justice, and yet on the other hand does not fall into misfortune through vice or depravity, but falls because of some mistake; one among the number of the highly renowned and prosperous, such as Oedipus . . . and other famous men from families like [his].

It follows that the plot which achieves excellence will necessarily be single in outcome and not, as some say, double, and will consist in a change of fortune, not to prosperity from misfortune, but the opposite, from prosperity to misfortune, occasioned not by depravity, but by some great mistake on the part of one who is either such as I have described or better than this rather than worse. What actually has taken place has confirmed this; for though at first the poets accepted whatever myths came to hand, today the finest tragedies are founded upon the stories of only a few houses . . . and such . . . as have chanced to suffer terrible things or to do them. So then, tragedy having this construction is the finest kind of tragedy from an artistic point of view. And consequently those persons fall into the same error who bring it as a charge against Euripides° that this is what he does in his tragedies and that most of his plays have unhappy endings. For this is in fact the right procedure, as I have said; and the best proof is that on the stage and in the dramatic contests, plays of this kind seem the most tragic, provided they are successfully worked out, and Euripides, even if in everything else his management is faulty, seems at any rate to be the most tragic of the poets.

Second to this is the kind of plot that some persons place first, that which like the *Odyssey*° has a double structure and ends in opposite ways for the better characters and the worse. If it seems to be first, that is attributable to the weakness of the audience, since the poets only follow their lead and compose the kind of plays the spectators want. The pleasure it gives, however, is not that which comes from tragedy, but is rather the pleasure proper to comedy; for in comedy those who in the legend are the worst of enemies . . . end by leaving the scene as friends, and nobody is killed by anybody. . . .

With regard to the characters there are four things to aim at. First and foremost is that the characters be good. The personages will have character if, as aforesaid, they reveal in speech or in action what their moral choices are, and a good character will be one whose choices are good. It is possible to portray goodness in every class of persons; a woman may be good and a slave may be good, though perhaps as a class women are inferior and slaves utterly base. The second requisite is to make the character appropriate. Thus it is possible to portray any character as manly, but inappropriate for a female character to be manly or formidable in the way I mean. Third is to make the characters lifelike, which is something different from making them good and appropriate as described above. Fourth is to make them consistent. Even if the person being imitated is inconsistent and this is what the character is supposed to be, he should nevertheless be portrayed as consistently inconsistent. . . .

In the characters and in the plot-construction alike, one must strive for that which is either necessary or probable, so that whatever a character of any kind says or does may be the sort of thing such a character will inevitably or probably say or do and the events of the plot may follow one after another either inevitably or with probability. (Obviously, then, the *dénouement* of the plot should arise from the plot itself and not be brought about "from the machine." . . . The machine is to be used for matters lying outside the drama, either antecedents of the action which a human being cannot know, or things subsequent to the action that have to be prophesied and announced; for we accept it that the gods see everything. Within the events of the plot itself, however, there should be nothing unreasonable, or if there is, it should be kept outside the play proper as is done in the *Oedipus* of Sophocles.)

Inasmuch as tragedy is an imitation of persons who are better than the average, the example of good portrait-painters should be followed. These, while reproducing the distinctive appearance of their subjects in a recognizable like-

---

Euripides: Fifth century B.C. Greek playwright whose tragedies include *Electra, Medea,* and *Alcestis.*
Odyssey: The epic by the ancient Greek poet Homer that chronicles the voyage home from the Trojan War of Odysseus (also known as Ulysses).

ness, make them handsomer in the picture than they are in reality. Similarly the poet when he comes to imitate men who are irascible or easygoing or have other defects of character should depict them as such and yet as good men at the same time.

From *Poetics,* translated by James Hutton

CONSIDERATIONS FOR CRITICAL THINKING AND WRITING

1. Why does Aristotle insist that both virtuous and depraved characters are unsuitable as tragic figures? What kind of person constitutes a tragic character according to him?

2. Aristotle argues that it is "inappropriate for a female character to be manly or formidable" (para. 4). Do you think Antigone fits this negative description? Does she seem "inferior" to the men in the play?

3. Aristotle says that characters should be "lifelike" (para. 4), but he also points out that characters should be made "handsomer . . . than they are in reality" (para. 6). Is this a contradiction? Explain why or why not.

SIGMUND FREUD (1856–1939)
On the Oedipus Complex   *1900*

If *Oedipus Rex* moves a modern audience no less than it did the contemporary Greek one, the explanation can only be that its effect does not lie in the contrast between destiny and human will, but is to be looked for in the particular nature of the material on which that contrast is exemplified. There must be something which makes a voice within us ready to recognize the compelling force of destiny in the *Oedipus.* . . . His destiny moves us only because it might have been ours — because the oracle laid the same curse upon us before our birth as upon him. It is the fate of all of us, perhaps, to direct our first sexual impulse toward our mother and our first hatred and our first murderous wish against our father. Our dreams convince us that this is so. King Oedipus, who slew his father Laïus and married his mother Jocasta, merely shows us the fulfillment of our own childhood wishes. But, more fortunate than he, we have meanwhile succeeded, in so far as we have not become psychoneurotics, in detaching our sexual impulses from our mothers and in forgetting our jealousy of our fathers. Here is one in whom these primeval wishes of our childhood have been fulfilled, and we shrink back from him with the whole force of the repression by which those wishes have since that time been held down within us. While the poet, as he unravels the past, brings to light the guilt of Oedipus, he is at the same time compelling us to recognize our own inner minds, in which those same impulses, though suppressed, are still to be found. The contrast with which the closing Chorus leaves us confronted —

> . . . Fix on Oedipus your eyes,
> Who resolved the dark enigma, noblest champion and most wise.
> Like a star his envied fortune mounted beaming far and wide:
> Now he sinks in seas of anguish, whelmed beneath a raging tide . . .[1]

[1] Lewis Campbell's translation, lines 1524ff [in *The Bedford Introduction to Literature,* lines 1678–1682].

— strikes as a warning at ourselves and our pride, at us who since our childhood have grown so wise and so mighty in our own eyes. Like Oedipus, we live in ignorance of these wishes, repugnant to morality, which have been forced upon us by Nature, and after their revelation we may all of us well seek to close our eyes to the scenes of our childhood.

There is an unmistakable indication in the text of Sophocles' tragedy itself that the legend of Oedipus sprang from some primeval dream material which had as its content the distressing disturbance of a child's relation to his parents owing to the first stirrings of sexuality. At a point when Oedipus, though he is not yet enlightened, has begun to feel troubled by his recollection of the oracle, Jocasta consoles him by referring to a dream which many people dream, though, as she thinks, it has no meaning:

> Many a man ere now in dreams hath lain
> With her who bare him. He hath least annoy
> Who with such omens troubleth not his mind.[2]

Today, just as then, many men dream of having sexual relations with their mothers, and speak of the fact with indignation and astonishment. It is clearly the key to the tragedy and the complement to the dream of the dreamer's father being dead. The story of Oedipus is the reaction of the imagination to these two typical dreams. And just as these dreams, when dreamt by adults, are accompanied by feelings of repulsion, so too the legend must include horror and self-punishment. Its further modification originates once again in a misconceived secondary revision of the material, which has sought to exploit it for theological purposes. . . . The attempt to harmonize divine omnipotence with human responsibility must naturally fail in connection with this subject matter just as with any other.

From *Interpretation of Dreams,* translated by James Strachey

[2]Lewis Campbell's translation, lines 982ff [in *The Bedford Introduction to Literature,* lines 1074-1076].

CONSIDERATIONS FOR CRITICAL THINKING AND WRITING

1. Read the section on psychological criticism in Critical Strategies for Reading (p. 2029) for additional information about Freud's theory concerning the Oedipus complex. Explain whether you agree or disagree that Freud's approach offers the "key to the tragedy" of *Oedipus the King.*

2. How does Freud's view of tragic character differ from Aristotle's (p. 1303)?

SOPHOCLES (496?–406 B.C.)
Another Translation of a Scene from Oedipus the King *1920*

Enter Oedipus, blind.

Chorus: O sight for all the world to see
    Most terrible! O suffering
Of all mine eyes have seen most terrible!
    Alas! What Fury came on thee?
    What evil Spirit, from afar,

O Oedipus! O Wretched!
   Leapt on thee, to destroy?
I cannot even Alas! look
Upon thy face, though much I have
To ask of thee, and much to hear,
   Aye, and to see — I cannot!
   Such terror is in thee!

Oedipus: Alas! O Wretched! Whither go
   My steps? My voice? It seems to float
    Far, far away from me.
   Alas! Curse of my Life, how far
    Thy leap hath carried thee!

Chorus: To sorrows none can bear to see or hear.

Oedipus: Ah! The cloud!
   Visitor unspeakable! Darkness upon me horrible!
   Unconquerable! Cloud that may not ever pass away!
      Alas!
   And yet again, alas! How deep they stab —
   These throbbing pains, and all those memories.

Chorus: Where such afflictions are, I marvel not,
   If soul and body made one doubled woe.

Oedipus: Ah! My friend!
   Still remains thy friendship. Still thine is the help that comforts me,
   And kindness, that can look upon these dreadful eyes unchanged.
      Ah me!
   My friend, I feel thy presence. Though mine eyes
   Be darkened, yet I hear thy voice, and know.

Chorus: Oh, dreadful deed! How wert thou steeled to quench
   Thy vision thus? What Spirit came on thee?

Oedipus: Apollo! 'Twas Apollo, friends,
   Willed the evil, willed, and brought the agony to pass!
    And yet the hand that struck was mine, mine only, wretched.
    Why should I see, whose eyes
   Had no more any good to look upon?

Chorus: 'Twas even as thou sayest.

Oedipus: Aye. For me . . . Nothing is left for sight.
    Nor anything to love:
   Nor shall the sound of greetings any more
    Fall pleasant on my ear.
   Away! Away! Out of the land, away!
    Banishment, Banishment! Fatal am I, accursed,
    And the hate on me, as on no man else, of the gods!

Chorus: Unhappy in thy fortune and the wit
   That shows it thee. Would thou hadst never known.

Oedipus: A curse upon the hand that loosed
   In the wilderness the cruel fetters of my feet,
    Rescued me, gave me life! Ah! Cruel was his pity,
     Since, had I died, so much
   I had not harmed myself and all I love.

Chorus: Aye, even so 'twere better.

Oedipus: Aye, for life never had led me then
      To shed my father's blood;
      Men had not called me husband of the wife
      That bore me in the womb.
    But now — but now — Godless am I, the son
     Born of impurity, mate of my father's bed,
      And if worse there be, I am Oedipus! It is mine!
Chorus: In this I know not how to call thee wise,
    For better wert thou dead than living — blind.
Oedipus: Nay, give me no more counsel. Bid me not
    Believe my deed, thus done, is not well done.
    I know 'tis well. When I had passed the grave,
    How could those eyes have met my father's gaze,
    Or my unhappy mother's — since on both
    I have done wrongs beyond all other wrong?
    Or live and see my children? — Children born
    As they were born! What pleasure in that sight?
    None for these eyes of mine, for ever, none.
    Nor in the sight of Thebes, her castles, shrines
    And images of the gods, whereof, alas!
    I robbed myself — myself, I spoke that word,
    I that she bred and nurtured, I her prince,
    And bade her thrust the sinner out, the man
    Proved of the gods polluted — Laïus' son.
    When such a stain by my own evidence
    Was on me, could I raise my eyes to them?
    No! Had I means to stop my ears, and choke
    The wells of sound, I had not held my hand,
    But closed my body like a prison-house
    To hearing as to sight. Sweet for the mind
    To dwell withdrawn, where troubles could not come.
      Cithaeron! Ah, why didst thou welcome me?
    Why, when thou hadst me there, didst thou not kill,
    Never to show the world myself — my birth!
      O Polybus, and Corinth, and the home
    Men called my father's ancient house, what sores
    Festered beneath that beauty that ye reared,
    Discovered now, sin out of sin begot.
      O ye three roads, O secret mountain-glen,
    Trees, and a pathway narrowed to the place
    Where met the three, do you remember me?
    I gave you blood to drink, my father's blood,
    And so my own! Do you remember that?
    The deed I wrought for you? Then, how I passed
    Hither to other deeds?
                O Marriage-bed
    That gave me birth, and, having borne me, gave
    Fresh children to your seed, and showed the world
    Father, son, brother, mingled and confused,

Bride, mother, wife in one, and all the shame
Of deeds the foulest ever known to man.
   No. Silence for a deed so ill to do
Is better. Therefore lead me hence, away!
To hide me or to kill. Or to the sea
Cast me, where you shall look on me no more.
Come! Deign to touch me, though I am a man
Accursèd. Yield! Fear nothing! Mine are woes
That no man else, but I alone, must bear.

                            Translated by J. T. Sheppard

CONSIDERATIONS FOR CRITICAL THINKING AND WRITING

1. This excerpt from Sheppard's translation corresponds to lines 1433–1550 in Robert Fagles's translation (pp. 1224–1266). Examine both versions of the scene and describe the diction and tone of each. If you find one of the translations more effective than the other, indicate why.

2. Explain whether the different translations affect your understanding or interpretation of the scene.

MURIEL RUKEYSER (1913–1980)

On Oedipus the King   1973
Myth

Long afterward, Oedipus, old and blinded, walked the
roads.   He smelled a familiar smell.   It was
the Sphinx.   Oedipus said, "I want to ask one question.
Why didn't I recognize my mother?"   "You gave the
wrong answer," said the Sphinx.   "But that was what   5
made everything possible," said Oedipus.   "No," she said.
"When I asked, What walks on four legs in the morning,
two at noon, and three in the evening, you answered,
Man.   You didn't say anything about woman."
"When you say Man," said Oedipus, "you include women   10
too. Everyone knows that."   She said, "That's what
you think."

CONSIDERATIONS FOR CRITICAL THINKING AND WRITING

1. What elements of the Oedipus story does Rukeyser allude to in the poem?

2. To what does the title of Rukeyser's poem, "Myth," refer? How does the word *myth* carry more than one meaning?

3. This poem is amusing, but its ironic ending points to a serious theme. What is it? Does Sophocles' play address any of the issues raised in the poem?

JEAN ANOUILH (1910–1987)

A Scene from Antigone   1944

Creon: I shall save you yet. *(He goes below the table to the chair at end of table, takes off his coat, and places it on the chair.)* God knows, I have things enough to do today without wasting my time on an insect like you. There's plenty to do, I assure you, when you've just put down a revolution. But urgent things can wait. I am not going to let politics be the cause of your death. For it is a fact that this whole business is nothing but politics: the mournful shade of Polynices, the decomposing corpse, the sentimental weeping, and the hysteria that you mistake for heroism — nothing but politics.

Look here. I may not be soft, but I'm fastidious. I like things clean, ship-shape, well scrubbed. Don't think that I am not just as offended as you are by the thought of that meat rotting in the sun. In the evening, when the breeze comes in off the sea, you can smell it in the palace, and it nauseates me. But I refuse even to shut my window. It's vile; and I can tell you what I wouldn't tell anybody else: it's stupid, monstrously stupid. But the people of Thebes have got to have their noses rubbed into it a little longer. My God! If it was up to me, I should have had them bury your brother long ago as a mere matter of public hygiene. I admit that what I am doing is childish. But if the featherheaded rabble I govern are to understand what's what, that stench has got to fill the town for a month!

Antigone (turns to him): You are a loathsome man!

Creon: I agree. My trade forces me to be. We could argue whether I ought or ought not to follow my trade; but once I take on the job, I must do it properly.

Antigone: Why do you do it at all?

Creon: My dear, I woke up one morning and found myself King of Thebes. God knows, there were other things I loved in life more than power.

Antigone: Then you should have said no.

Creon: Yes, I could have done that. Only, I felt that it would have been cowardly. I should have been like a workman who turns down a job that has to be done. So I said yes.

Antigone: So much the worse for you, then. I didn't say yes. I can say no to anything I think vile, and I don't have to count the cost. But because you said yes, all that you can do, for all your crown and your trappings, and your guards — all that you can do is to have me killed.

Creon: Listen to me.

Antigone: If I want to. I don't have to listen to you if I don't want to. You've said your *yes*. There is nothing more you can tell me that I don't know. You stand there, drinking in my words. *(She moves behind chair.)* Why is it that you don't call your guards? I'll tell you why. You want to hear me out to the end; that's why.

Creon: You amuse me.

Antigone: Oh, no, I don't. I frighten you. That is why you talk about saving me. Everything would be so much easier if you had a docile, tongue-tied little Antigone living in the palace. I'll tell you something, Uncle Creon: I'll give you back one of your own words. You are too fastidious to make a good tyrant. But you are going to have to put me to death today, and you know it. And that's what frightens you. God! Is there anything uglier than a frightened man!

Creon: Very well. I am afraid, then. Does that satisfy you? I am afraid that if you insist upon it, I shall have to have you killed. And I don't want to.

Antigone: I don't have to do things that I think are wrong. If it comes to that, you didn't really want to leave my brother's body unburied, did you? Say it! Admit that you didn't.

Creon: I have said it already.

Antigone: But you did it just the same. And now, though you don't want to do it, you are going to have me killed. And you call that being a king!

Creon: Yes, I call that being a king.

Antigone: Poor Creon! My nails are broken, my fingers are bleeding, my arms are covered with the welts left by the paws of your guards — but I am a queen!

Creon: Then why not have pity on me, and live? Isn't your brother's corpse, rotting there under my windows, payment enough for peace and order in Thebes? My son loves you. Don't make me add your life to the payment. I've paid enough.

Antigone: No, Creon! You said yes, and made yourself king. Now you will never stop paying.

Creon: But God in heaven! Won't you try to understand me! I'm trying hard enough to understand you! There had to be one man who said yes. Somebody had to agree to captain the ship. She had sprung a hundred leaks; she was loaded to the water line with crime, ignorance, poverty. The wheel was swinging with the wind. The crew refused to work and were looting the cargo. The officers were building a raft, ready to slip overboard and desert the ship. The mast was splitting, the wind was howling, the sails were beginning to rip. Every man jack on board was about to drown — and only because the only thing they thought of was their own skins and their cheap little day-to-day traffic. Was that a time, do you think, for playing with words like yes and no? Was that a time for a man to be weighing the pros and cons, wondering if he wasn't going to pay too dearly later on; if he wasn't going to lose his life, or his family, or his touch with other men? You grab the wheel, you right the ship in the face of a mountain of water. You shout an order, and if one man refuses to obey, you shoot straight into the mob. Into the mob, I say! The beast as nameless as the wave that crashes down upon your deck; as nameless as the whipping wind. The thing that drops when you shoot may be someone who poured you a drink the night before; but it has no name. And you, braced at the wheel, you have no name, either. Nothing has a name — except the ship, and the storm. *(A pause as he looks at her.)* Now do you understand?

Antigone: I am not here to understand. That's all very well for you. I am here to say no to you, and die.

Creon: It is easy to say no.

Antigone: Not always.

Creon: It is easy to say no. To say yes, you have to sweat and roll up your sleeves and plunge both hands into life up to the elbows. It is easy to say no, even if saying no means death. All you have to do is to sit still and wait. Wait to go on living; wait to be killed. That is the coward's part. *No* is one of your man-made words. Can you imagine a world in which trees say *no* to the sap? In which beasts say *no* to hunger or to propagation? Animals are good, simple, tough. They move in droves, nudging one another onwards, all traveling the same road. Some of them keel over, but the rest go on; and no matter how many may fall by the wayside, there are always those few left that go on bringing their young into the world, traveling the same road with the same obstinate will, unchanged from those who went before.

Antigone: Animals, eh, Creon! What a king you could be if only men were animals!

Translated by Lewis Galantière

Considerations for Critical Thinking and Writing

1. What are Creon's reasons for not burying Polynices? How does he defend his actions as a ruler?

2. In what sense is Antigone correct when she describes Creon as "too fastidious to make a good tyrant"?

3. Do you agree with Creon that Antigone takes "the coward's part" by saying no rather than yes? With which character do you sympathize more? How might Creon's position be related to the fact that France was occupied by German troops during World War II, when Anouilh wrote this play?

4. How does Anouilh's treatment of Creon compare with Sophocles'?

Maurice Sagoff

A Humorous Distillation of Antigone   1980

Tyrant Creon's stern advice is
"Do not bury Polynices!
Thebes' defenders had to squash him—
Now we'll let the buzzards nosh him!"
But Antigone, the brave,   5
Dared to dig her brother's grave:
"Man-made laws my soul defies—
Live by laws divine!" she cries.

Creon locks her up, the demon!
Though she's pledged to marry Haemon   10
(That's his son). Now comes a seer
Prophesying woes severe:
If her brother's not entombed
And she dies, then Haemon's doomed!

Creon seeing things go screwy,   15
Wilts, and tries to bang a U-ee,
But the Gods who drive the hearse
Seldom shove it in reverse . . .
Carnage follows, sure as Fate;
Here's the body-count to date—   20
1. Antigone   2. her brother

3. young Haemon   4. his mother
(If more bodies fail to fall,
It's because the cast is small).

Strung-out Creon takes the blame.   25
Exits, croaking "Rotten shame!"
        From *Shrinklits: Seventy of the World's Towering Classics Cut Down to Size*

Considerations for Critical Thinking and Writing

1. Sagoff writes in his tongue-in-cheek introduction to *Shrinklits* that "inside
   every fat book is a skinny book trying to get out, struggling to cut through
   the mummylike wrappings of long-winded descriptions, superfluous characters, endless conversations, and turgid style." How successful is this poem
   in summarizing the plot of *Antigone*? What is left out of Sagoff's account?

2. Using Sagoff's version of *Antigone* as your inspiration, choose another play
   in the text and try writing a shrinklit that does it humorous justice.

Bernard Knox (b. 1914)
On Oedipus and Human Freedom   *1982*

Oedipus did have one freedom: he was free to find out or not find out the
truth. This was the element of Sophoclean sleight-of-hand that enabled him
to make a drama out of the situation which the philosophers used as the classic demonstration of man's subjection to fate. But it is more than a solution to
an apparently insoluble dramatic problem; it is the key to the play's tragic
theme and the protagonist's heroic stature. One freedom is allowed him: the
freedom to search for the truth, the truth about the prophecies, about the
gods, about himself. And of this freedom he makes full use. Against the advice
and appeals of others, he pushes on, searching for the truth, the whole truth,
and nothing but the truth. And in this search he shows all those great qualities
that we admire in him — courage, intelligence, perseverance, the qualities that
make human beings great. This freedom to search, and the heroic way in
which Oedipus uses it, makes the play not a picture of man's utter feebleness
caught in the toils of fate, but on the contrary, a heroic example of man's dedication to the search for truth, the truth about himself. This is perhaps the
only human freedom, the play seems to say, but there could be none more
noble.
        From the Introduction to *Three Theban Plays*, translated by Robert Fagles

Considerations for Critical Thinking and Writing

1. Do you agree with Knox that Oedipus's "freedom to search for the truth"
   represents a genuine kind of freedom, despite the outcome of his search?

2. What other qualities do you find in Oedipus besides "courage, intelligence," and "perseverance"?

3. Write an essay that considers whether Oedipus should be regarded as a
   "classic demonstration of man's subjection to fate."

TWO COMPLEMENTARY CRITICAL READINGS

R. G. A. BUXTON (B. 1948)

The Major Critical Issue in Antigone   *1984*

It seems agreed that the main critical issue is: how do we evaluate the respective moral positions of Antigone and Creon. Provided this is not asked in order to achieve "that nice apportionment of blame to which critics are so much more prone than dramatists,"[1] but rather with the aim of teasing out just what is at stake between the two principal figures, the question is worthwhile.

Defenders of Creon appear from time to time. There is no doubt that some of the sentiments he expresses, particularly in his opening programmatic speech, are laudable in themselves; nor should there be any doubt that Creon receives some measure of sympathy as he carries his son's body on stage at the end. But is his original proclamation (it is not a law) morally acceptable? Tiresias' dire warnings strongly suggest it is not. There has been much argument about how Creon's edict related to Athenian law, but certain points are clear: although there was apparently nothing abnormal in the denial of burial in his homeland to a traitor, not only was there a custom, specifically associated with Athens, according to which one should not pass a corpse by without placing some dust upon it, but also, in forbidding Polynices burial *anywhere*, in actively ensuring that his body be torn apart by dogs and birds, Creon plainly went too far.

Most critics accept the moral impropriety of Creon's proclamation and disagree only in the degree (or absence) of qualification which they allow in their approval of Antigone. For some the approval is absolute; others, believing gray to be a more interesting color than black and white, stress problematic aspects of her behavior—harshness towards Ismene, relentless concern with honor, etc. A beneficial corollary of the latter approach is that, by emphasizing the particularity of Antigone's character, it makes us less likely to reduce the play to an opposition between principles — city *versus* kin-bond, state *versus* individual, or whatever. Neither Creon nor Antigone is the vehicle for a simple idea: "the theme of . . . *Antigone* . . . [is] the tragedy of two human downfalls, separate in nature, . . . following one another as contrasting patterns."[2]

From *Sophocles*

[1]R. P. Winnington-Ingram, *Sophocles: Art Interpretation* (Cambridge, England: Cambridge UP, 1980), 75.
[2]Reinhardt, *Sophocles* (Oxford, England: Oxford UP, 1979), 65. For *Antigone* as comprising two interdependent and equally important downfalls, see J. C. Hogan, "The Protagonists of the *Antigone*," *Arethusa* 5 (1972), 93–100.

CONSIDERATIONS FOR CRITICAL THINKING AND WRITING

1. How do you think "the particularity of Antigone's character . . . makes us less likely to reduce the play to an opposition between principles" (para. 3)? How does Sophocles' characterization of her make the play more complex?

2. Write an essay in which you agree or disagree that the theme of *Antigone* is "the tragedy of two human downfalls, separate in nature . . . following one

another as contrasting patterns" (para. 3). Do you think this theme is a means of resolving critical debate about the play or a way to evade having to choose between Antigone and Creon?

CYNTHIA P. GARDINER (B. 1942)

The Function of the Chorus in Antigone   *1987*

[*Antigone* is] concerned with the topic of political morality, with philosophies of governance and the conflict of religion and law. Yet despite the immensity of these abstractions, the immediate dramatic intent of the poet is not the subject of critical dispute, in that critics do not tend to hold violently contradictory opinions about the poet's own views. Nearly everyone agrees that Sophocles intended to portray Antigone's burial of Polynices as "right" — sanctioned by the gods according to Tiresias' revelations — and Creon's opposition to the burial as "wrong," insofar as his opposition arises from tyrannical behavior. It then becomes merely a question of the degree to which one condemns Creon or approves Antigone; the latter course usually involves an appraisal of Antigone's motives and of her behavior as a woman.

The lengthy and frequent lyrics have exerted considerable influence upon the interpretation of the play's symbolism and judgment. Some of the odes are apparently so loosely connected to the action that they can be readily lifted out of context to function as independent poems. Or, when left in the play, they seem sometimes so ambiguous that their relevance to the plot is perceptible only through the most detailed and subtle analysis. It is generally agreed nowadays that the most productive approach to interpreting the choral lyrics is to assume that they arise from a distinct and consistent persona. This being accepted, it is again a question of the degree to which one believes that the chorus support either Creon or Antigone. Some say that the chorus are utterly devoted to Creon throughout the play, or right up to the last possible moment at line 1272; some, that they begin by supporting the king but change their minds at one earlier point or another during the action. Others see the chorus as vacillating between viewpoints until a decision is forced upon them by Tiresias; still others see them as Antigone's partisans, though necessarily secret ones, from the very beginning.

From *The Sophoclean Chorus: A Study of Character and Function*

CONSIDERATIONS FOR CRITICAL THINKING AND WRITING

1. Do you agree with Gardiner that Antigone was "right" and Creon "wrong" (para. 1)? Explain why. How is this issue made complicated by Antigone's character?

2. Of the various interpretations Gardiner summarizes concerning the chorus's loyalty to Creon or Antigone, which do you think is most accurate? In an essay explain why.

31

A Study of
William Shakespeare

Although relatively little is known about William Shakespeare's life, his writings reveal him to have been an extraordinary man. His vitality, compassion, and insights are evident in his broad range of characters, who have fascinated generations of audiences, and his powerful use of the English language, which has been celebrated since his death nearly four centuries ago. Ben Jonson, his contemporary, rightly claimed that "he was not of an age, but for all time!" Shakespeare's plays have been produced so often and his writings read so widely that quotations from them have woven their way into our everyday conversations. If you have ever experienced "fear and trembling" because there was "something in the wind" or discovered that it was "a foregone conclusion" that you would "make a virtue of necessity," then it wouldn't be quite accurate for you to say that Shakespeare "was Greek to me" because these phrases come, respectively, from his plays *Much Ado about Nothing, Comedy of Errors, Othello, The Two Gentlemen of Verona,* and *Julius Caesar.* Many more examples could be cited, but it is enough to say that Shakespeare's art endures. His words may give us only an oblique glimpse of his life, but they continue to give us back the experience of our own lives.

Shakespeare was born in Stratford-on-Avon on or about April 23, 1564. His father, an important citizen who held several town offices, married a

PHOTO ABOVE: *Image of William Shakespeare included on the* First Folio, *a collected edition of Shakespeare plays published seven years after his death. Reprinted by permission of The Folger Shakespeare Library.*

woman from a prominent family; however, when their son was only a teenager, the family's financial situation became precarious. Shakespeare probably attended the Stratford grammar school, but no records of either his schooling or his early youth exist. As limited as his education was, it is clear that he was for his time a learned man. At the age of eighteen, he struck out on his own and married the twenty-six-year-old Anne Hathaway, who bore him a daughter in 1583 and twins, a boy and a girl, in 1585. Before he was twenty-one, Shakespeare had a wife and three children to support.

What his life was like for the next seven years is not known, but there is firm evidence that by 1592 he was in London enjoying some success as both an actor and a playwright. By 1594 he had also established himself as a poet with two lengthy poems, *Venus and Adonis* and *The Rape of Lucrece*. But it was in the theater that he made his living and his strongest reputation. He was well connected with a successful troupe first known as the Lord Chamberlain's Men; they built the famous Globe Theatre in 1599. Later this company, because of the patronage of King James, came to be known as the King's Men. Writing plays for this company throughout his career, Shakespeare also became one of its principal shareholders, an arrangement that allowed him to prosper in London as well as in his native Stratford, where in 1597 he bought a fine house called New Place. About 1611 he retired there with his family, although he continued writing plays. He died on April 23, 1616, and was buried at Holy Trinity Church in Stratford.

The documented details of Shakespeare's life provide barely enough information for a newspaper obituary. But if his activities remain largely unknown, his writings — among them thirty-seven plays and 154 sonnets — more than compensate for that loss. Plenty of authors have produced more work, but no writer has created so much literature that has been so universally admired. Within twenty-five years Shakespeare's dramatic works included *Hamlet, Macbeth, King Lear, Othello, Julius Caesar, Richard III, 1 Henry IV, Romeo and Juliet, Love's Labour's Lost, A Midsummer Night's Dream, The Tempest, Twelfth Night,* and *Measure for Measure.* These plays represent a broad range of characters and actions conveyed in poetic language that reveals human nature as well as the author's genius.

CHRONOLOGY

1564   Born in April in Stratford-on-Avon. Shakespeare's birthday is traditionally observed on April 23.

1568   Shakespeare's father becomes bailiff (comparable to mayor).

1582   Marries Anne Hathaway.

1583   Daughter Susanna is born.

1585   Twins, Hamnet and Judith, are born.

1585–92	The "lost years." There are many myths about how Shakespeare spent this time before he became known as a playwright in London, but none can be proven and nothing definite is known.
1592	Works as an actor and playwright in London.
1592–93	Writes *Richard III,* among other plays.
1593	Narrative poem *Venus and Adonis* is published.
1594	Works as actor and playwright with the Lord Chamberlain's Company of players, a company that performs at the Globe Theatre.
c. 1594–96	Writes *Romeo and Juliet, Richard II,* and *A Midsummer Night's Dream,* among other plays.
1596	Hamnet (Shakespeare's son) dies.
1596–98	Writes *1 Henry IV* and *2 Henry IV.*
1599	Writes *Julius Caesar.*
c. 1600	Writes *Hamlet.*
1601	Shakespeare's father dies.
1603	Queen Elizabeth I of England dies.
1603–04	Writes *Othello.*
1604	King James I of England is coronated. (James patronizes Shakespeare's company, so they become known as the King's Men.)
1605–07	Writes *King Lear, Macbeth,* and *Antony and Cleopatra.*
c. 1610–11	Writes *The Tempest.*
1616	Dies on April 23.
1623	First Folio edition of Shakespeare's plays is published.

SHAKESPEARE'S THEATER

Drama languished in Europe after the fall of Rome during the fifth and sixth centuries. From about A.D. 400 to 900 almost no record of dramatic productions exists except for those of minstrels and other entertainers, such as acrobats and jugglers, who traveled through the countryside. The Catholic church was instrumental in suppressing drama because the theater — represented by the excesses of Roman productions — was seen as subversive. No state-sponsored festivals brought people together in huge theaters the way they had in Greek and Roman times.

In the tenth century, however, the church helped revive theater by incorporating dialogues into the Mass as a means of dramatizing portions of the Gospels. These brief dialogues developed into more elaborate mystery plays, miracle plays, and morality plays, anonymous works that were created primarily to inculcate religious principles rather than to entertain.

But these works also marked the reemergence of relatively large dramatic productions.

Mystery plays dramatize stories from the Bible, such as the Creation, the Fall of Adam and Eve, or the Crucifixion. The most highly regarded surviving example is *The Second Shepherd's Play* (c. 1400), which dramatizes Christ's nativity. **Miracle plays** are based on the lives of saints. An extant play of the late fifteenth century, for example, is titled *Saint Mary Magdalene*. **Morality plays** present allegorical stories in which virtues and vices are personified to teach humanity how to achieve salvation. *Everyman* (c. 1500), the most famous example, has as its central conflict every person's struggle to avoid the sins that lead to hell and practice the virtues that are rewarded in heaven.

The clergy who performed these plays gave way to trade guilds that presented them outside the church on stages featuring scenery and costumed characters. The plays' didactic content was gradually abandoned in favor of broad humor and worldly concerns. Thus by the sixteenth century religious drama had been replaced largely by secular drama.

Because theatrical productions were no longer sponsored and financed by the church or trade guilds during Shakespeare's lifetime, playwrights had to figure out ways to draw audiences willing to pay for entertainment. This necessitated some simple but important changes. Somehow, people had to be prevented from seeing a production unless they paid. Hence an enclosed space with controlled access was created. In addition, the plays had to change frequently enough to keep audiences returning, and this resulted in more experienced actors and playwrights sensitive to their audiences' tastes and interests. Plays compelling enough to attract audiences had to employ a powerful writing brought to life by convincing actors in entertaining productions. Shakespeare always wrote his dramas for the stage — for audiences who would see and hear the characters. The conventions of the theater for which he wrote are important, then, for appreciating and understanding his plays. Detailed information about Elizabethan theater (theater during the reign of Elizabeth I, from 1558 to 1603) is less than abundant, but historians have been able to piece together a good sense of what theaters were like from sources such as drawings, building contracts, and stage directions.

Early performances of various kinds took place in the courtyards of inns and taverns. These secular entertainments attracted people of all classes. To the dismay of London officials, such gatherings were also settings for the illegal activities of brawlers, thieves, and prostitutes. To avoid licensing regulations, some theaters were constructed outside the city's limits. The Globe, for instance, built by the Lord Chamberlain's Company, with which Shakespeare was closely associated, was located on the south bank of the Thames River. Regardless of the play, an Elizabethan theatergoer was likely to have an exciting time. Playwrights understood the varied nature of their audiences, so the plays appealed to a broad range of sensibilities and tastes. Philosophy and poetry rubbed shoulders with violence and sexual jokes, and somehow all were made compatible.

Physically, Elizabethan theaters resembled the courtyards where they originated, but the theaters could accommodate more people—perhaps as many as twenty-five hundred. The exterior of a theater building was many-sided or round and enclosed a yard that was only partially roofed over, to take advantage of natural light. The interior walls consisted of three galleries of seats looking onto a platform stage that extended from the rear wall. These seats were sheltered from the weather and more comfortable than the area in front of the stage, which was known as the *pit.* Here "groundlings" paid a penny to stand and watch the performance. Despite the large number of spectators, the theater created an intimate atmosphere because the audience closely surrounded the stage on three sides.

This arrangement produced two theatrical conventions: asides and soliloquies. An *aside* is a speech directed only to the audience. It makes the audience privy to a character's thoughts, allowing them to perceive ironies and intrigues that other characters know nothing about. In a large performing space, such as a Greek amphitheater, asides would be unconvincing because they would have to be declaimed loudly to be heard, but they were well suited to Elizabethan theaters. A *soliloquy* is a speech delivered while an actor is alone on the stage; like an aside, it reveals a character's state of mind. Hamlet's "To be or not to be" speech is the most famous example of a soliloquy.

The Elizabethan platform stage was large enough—approximately 25 feet deep and 40 feet wide—to allow a wide variety of actions, ranging from festive banquets to bloody battles. Sections of the floor could be opened or removed to create, for instance, the gravediggers' scene in *Hamlet* or to allow characters to exit through trapdoors. At the rear of the platform an inner stage was covered by curtains that could be drawn to reveal an interior setting, such as a bedroom or tomb. The curtains were also a natural location for a character to hide in order to overhear conversations. On each side of the curtains were doors through which characters entered and exited. An upper stage could be used as a watchtower, a castle wall, or a balcony. Although most of the action occurred on the main platform stage, there were opportunities for fluid movements from one acting area to another, providing a variety of settings.

These settings were not, however, elaborately indicated by scenery or props. A scene might change when one group of characters left the stage and another entered. A table and some chairs could be carried on quickly to suggest a tavern. But the action was not interrupted for set changes. Instead, the characters' speeches often identify the location of a scene. (In modern editions of Shakespeare's plays, editors indicate in brackets the scene breaks, settings, and movements of actors not identified in the original manuscripts to help readers keep track of things.) Today's performances of the plays frequently use more elaborate settings and props. But

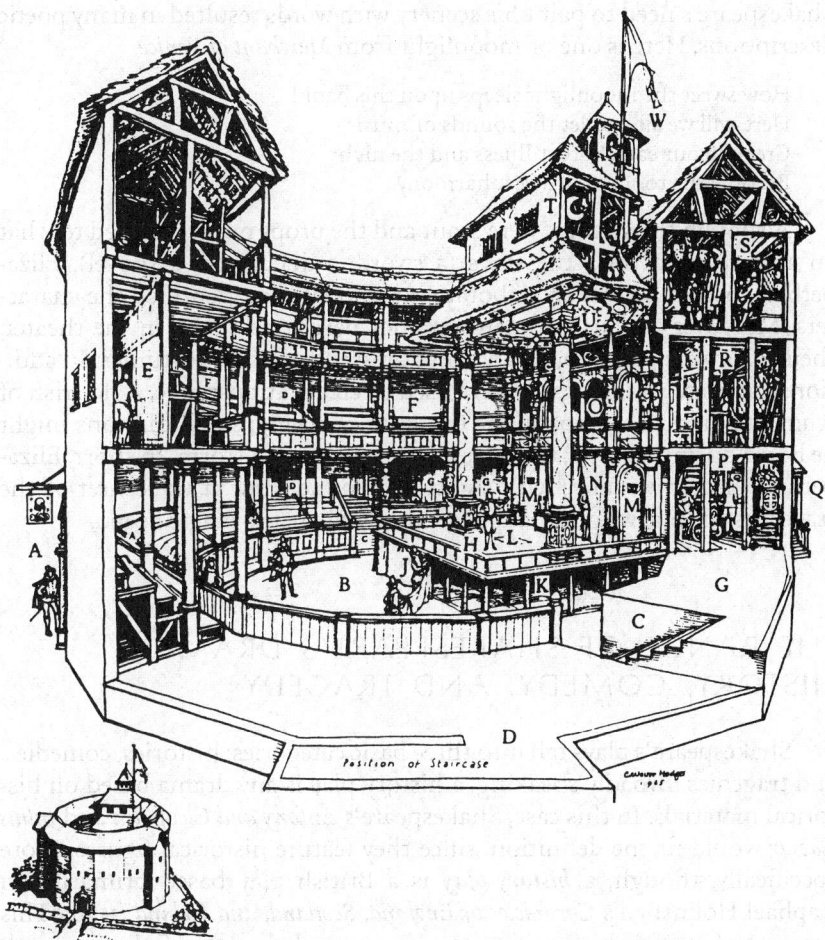

A	Main entrance
B	The yard
C	Entrances to lowest gallery
D	Position of entrances to staircase and upper galleries
E	Corridor serving the different sections of the middle gallery
F	Middle gallery ("Twopenny Rooms")
G	Position of "Gentlemen's Rooms" or "Lords' Rooms"
H	The stage
J	The hanging being put up round the stage
K	The "hell" under the stage

L	The stage trap leading down to the hell
M	Stage doors
N	Curtained "place behind the stage"
O	Gallery above the stage, used as required sometimes by musicians, sometimes by spectators, and often as part of the play
P	Backstage area (the tiring-house)
Q	Tiring-house door
R	Dressing-rooms
S	Wardrobe and storage
T	The hut housing the machine for lowering enthroned gods, etc., to the stage
U	The "heavens"
W	Hoisting the playhouse flag

A conjectural reconstruction of the Globe Theatre, 1599–1613. (Drawing by C. Walter Hodges from his The Globe Restored, *published by Oxford University Press. © 1968 C. Walter Hodges. Reprinted by permission of Oxford University Press.)*

Shakespeare's need to paint his scenery with words resulted in many poetic descriptions. Here is one of moonlight from *Merchant of Venice:*

> How sweet the moonlight sleeps upon this bank!
> Here will we sit and let the sounds of music
> Creep in our ears. Soft stillness and the night
> Become the touches of sweet harmony.

Although the settings were scant and the props mostly limited to what an actor carried onto the stage (a sword, a document, a shovel), Elizabethan costuming was an elaborate visual treat that identified the characters. Moreover, because women were not permitted to act in the theater, their roles were played by young boys dressed in female costumes. In addition, elaborate sound effects were used to create atmosphere. A flourish of trumpets might accompany the entrance of a king; small cannons might be heard during a battle; thunder might punctuate a storm. In short, Elizabethan theater was alive with sights and sounds, but at the center of the stage was the playwright's language; that's where the magic began.

THE RANGE OF SHAKESPEARE'S DRAMA: HISTORY, COMEDY, AND TRAGEDY

Shakespeare's plays fall into three basic categories: histories, comedies, and tragedies. Broadly speaking, a history play is any drama based on historical materials. In this case, Shakespeare's *Antony and Cleopatra* and *Julius Caesar* would fit the definition, since they feature historical figures. More specifically, though, a **history play** is a British play based primarily on Raphael Holinshed's *Chronicles of England, Scotland, and Ireland* (1578). This account of British history was popular toward the end of the sixteenth century because of the patriotic pride that was produced by the British defeat of the Spanish Armada in 1588, and it was an important source for a series of plays Shakespeare wrote treating the reigns of British kings from Richard II to Henry VIII. The political subject matter of these plays both entertained audiences and instructed them in virtues and vices involved in England's past efforts to overcome civil war and disorder. Ambition, deception, and treason were of more than historical interest. Shakespeare's audiences saw these plays about the fifteenth century as ways of sorting through the meanings of both the calamities of the past and the uncertainties of the present.

Although Shakespeare used Holinshed's *Chronicles* as a source, he did not hesitate to make changes for dramatic purposes. In *1 Henry IV,* for example, he ages Henry IV to contrast him with the youthful Prince Hal, and he makes Hotspur younger than he actually was to have him serve as a foil to the prince. The serious theme of Hal's growth into the kind of man who would make an ideal king is counterweighted by Shakespeare's comic creation of Falstaff, that good-humored "huge hill of flesh" filled with delightful contradictions. Falstaff had historic antecedents, but the true source of his identity is the imagination of Shakespeare, a writer who was, after all, a dramatist first.

Comedy is a strong element in *1 Henry IV,* but the play's overall tone is serious. Falstaff's behavior ultimately gives way to the measured march of English history. While Shakespeare encourages us to laugh at some of the participants, we are not invited to laugh at the history of English monarchies. Comedy even appears in Shakespeare's tragedies, as in Hamlet's jests with the gravediggers or in Emilia's biting remarks in *Othello.* This use of comedy is called *comic relief,* a humorous scene or incident that alleviates tension in an otherwise serious work. In many instances these moments enhance the thematic significance of the story in addition to providing laughter. When Hamlet jokes with the gravediggers, we laugh, but something hauntingly serious about the humor also intensifies our more serious emotions.

A true comedy, however, lacks a tragedy's sense that some great disaster will finally descend on the protagonist. There are conflicts and obstacles that must be confronted, but in comedy the characters delight us by overcoming whatever initially thwarts them. We can laugh at their misfortunes because we are confident that everything will turn out fine in the end. Shakespearean comedy tends to follow this general principle; it begins with problems and ends with their resolution.

Shakespeare's comedies are called *romantic comedies* because they typically involve lovers whose hearts are set on each other but whose lives are complicated by disapproving parents, deceptions, jealousies, illusions, confused identities, disguises, or other misunderstandings. Conflicts are present, but they are more amusing than threatening. This lightness is apparent in some of the comedies' titles: the conflict in a play such as *A Midsummer Night's Dream* is, in a sense, *Much Ado about Nothing — As You Like It* in a comedy. Shakespeare orchestrates the problems and confusion that typify the initial plotting of a romantic comedy into harmonious wedding arrangements in the final scenes. In these comedies life is a celebration, a feast that always satisfies, because the generosity of the humor leaves us with a revived appetite for life's surprising possibilities. Discord and misunderstanding give way to concord and love. Marriage symbolizes a pledge that life itself is renewable, so we are left with a sense of new beginnings.

Although a celebration of life, comedy is also frequently used as a vehicle for criticizing human affairs. *Satire* casts a critical eye on vices and follies by holding them up to ridicule — usually to point out an absurdity so that it can be avoided or corrected. In *Twelfth Night* Malvolio is satirized for his priggishness and pomposity. He thinks himself better than almost everyone around him, but Shakespeare reveals him to be comic as well as pathetic. We come to understand what Malvolio will apparently never comprehend: that no one can take him as seriously as he takes himself. Polonius is subjected to a similar kind of scrutiny in *Hamlet*.

Malvolio's ambitious efforts to attract Olivia's affections are rendered absurd by Shakespeare's use of both high and low comedy. **High comedy** consists of verbal wit, while **low comedy** is generally associated with physical action and is less intellectual. Through puns and witty exchanges, Shakespeare's high comedy displays Malvolio's inconsistencies of character. His self-importance is deflated by low comedy. We are treated to a *farce,* a form of humor based on exaggerated, improbable incongruities, when the staid Malvolio is tricked into wearing bizarre clothing and behaving like a fool to win Olivia. Our laughter is Malvolio's pain, but though he has been "notoriously abus'd" and he vows in the final scene to be "reveng'd on the whole pack" of laughing conspirators who have tricked him, the play ends on a light note. Indeed, it concludes with a song, the last line of which reminds us of the predominant tone of the play as well as the nature of comedy: "And we'll strive to please you every day."

Tragedy, in contrast, does not promise peace and contentment. The basic characteristics of tragedy have already been outlined in the context of Greek drama (see Chapter 30). Like Greek tragic heroes, Shakespeare's protagonists are exceptional human beings whose stature makes their misfortune all the more dramatic. These characters pay a high price for their actions. Oedipus's search for the killer of Laius, Antigone's and Creon's refusal to compromise their principles, Hamlet's agonized conviction that "The time is out of joint," and Othello's willingness to doubt his wife's fidelity all lead to irreversible results. Comic plots are largely free of this sense of inevitability. Instead of the festive mood that prevails once the characters in a comedy recognize their true connection to each other, tragedy gives us dark reflections that emanate from suffering. The laughter of comedy is a shared experience, a recognition of human likeness, but suffering estranges tragic heroes from the world around them.

Some of the wrenching differences between comedy and tragedy can be experienced in *Othello*. Although this play is a tragedy, Shakespeare includes in its plot many of the ingredients associated with comedy. For a time it seems possible that Othello and Desdemona will overcome the complications of a disapproving father, along with the seemingly minor deceptions, awkward misperceptions, and tender illusions that hover around them. But in *Othello* marriage is not a sign of concord displacing discord; instead, love and marriage mark the beginning of the tragic action.

Another important difference between tragedy and comedy is the way characters are presented. The tragic protagonist is portrayed as a remarkable individual whose unique qualities compel us with their power and complexity. Macbeth is not simply a murderer nor is Othello merely a jealous husband. But despite their extreme passions, behavior, and even crimes, we identify with tragic heroes in ways that we do not with comic characters. We can laugh at pretentious fools, smug hypocrites, clumsy oafs, and thwarted lovers because we see them from a distance. They are amusing precisely because their problems are not ours; we recognize them as types instead of as ourselves (or so we think). No reader of *Twelfth Night* worries about Sir Toby Belch's excessive drinking; he is a cheerful "sot" whose passion for ale is cause for celebration rather than concern. Shakespeare's comedy is sometimes disturbing— Malvolio's character certainly is—but it is never devastating. Tragic heroes do confront devastation; they command our respect and compassion because they act in spite of terrifying risks. Their triumph is not measured by the attainment of what they seek but by the wisdom that defeat imposes on them.

A NOTE ON READING SHAKESPEARE

Readers who have had no previous experience with Shakespeare's language may find it initially daunting. They might well ask whether people ever talked the way, for example, Hamlet does in his most famous soliloquy:

> To be, or not to be: that is the question:
> Whether 'tis nobler in the mind to suffer
> The slings and arrows of outrageous fortune,
> Or to take arms against a sea of troubles,
> And by opposing end them?

People did not talk like this in Elizabethan times. Hamlet speaks poetry. Shakespeare might have had him say something like this: "The most important issue one must confront is whether the pain that life inevitably creates should be passively accepted or resisted." But Shakespeare chose poetry to reveal the depth and complexity of Hamlet's experience. This heightened language is used to clarify rather than obscure his characters' thoughts. Shakespeare has Hamlet, as well as many other characters, speak in prose too, but in general his plays are written in poetry. If you keep in mind that Shakespeare's dialogue is not typically intended to imitate everyday speech, it should be easier to understand that his language is more than simply a vehicle for expressing the action of the play.

Here are a few practical suggestions to enhance your understanding of and pleasure in reading Shakespeare's plays.

1. Keep track of the characters by referring to the *dramatis personae* (characters) listed and briefly described at the beginning of each play.
2. Remember that poetic language deserves to be read slowly and carefully. A difficult passage can sometimes be better understood if it's read aloud. Don't worry if every line isn't absolutely clear to you.

3. Pay attention to the annotations, which explain unfamiliar words, phrases, and allusions in the text. These can be distracting, but they are sometimes necessary to determine the basic meaning of a passage.

4. As you read each scene, try to imagine how it would be played on a stage.

5. If you find the reading especially difficult, try listening to a recording of the play. (Most college libraries have records and tapes of Shakespeare's plays). Allowing professional actors to do the reading aloud for you can enrich your imaginative reconstruction of the action and characters. Hearing a play can help you with subsequent readings of it.

6. After reading the play, view a film or videocassette recording of a performance. It is important to view the performance *after* your reading, though, so that your own mental re-creation of the play is not short-circuited by a director's production.

And finally, to quote Hamlet, "Be not too tame . . . let your own discretion be your tutor." Read Shakespeare's work as best you can; it warrants such careful attention not because the language and characters are difficult to understand but because they offer so much to enjoy.

A Midsummer Night's Dream

A Midsummer Night's Dream, one of Shakespeare's most popular plays with readers and audiences, is a romantic comedy about the complex nature of love and marriage. Though some serious points about law and social order are made along the way, the action is propelled by the powers of youth, romance, love, passion, and the hilarious pursuits of characters turned about by fairies, illusions, and their own misunderstandings.

Shakespeare uses several sets of couples to dramatize love's tribulations and triumphs. The play opens with Theseus, Duke of Athens, making arrangements to wed Hippolyta, queen of the Amazons. Once enemies, they now seek love and peace in the harmony of marriage. Their union represents the happy necessity of order in the state and suggests a model of behavior that the other characters struggle to achieve.

In contrast to the serene plans for the royal wedding is the conflict produced by four Athenian youths who are thwarted in love: Helena loves Demetrius, but Demetrius loves Hermia, who wants to marry Lysander. This collision of passions is further complicated by Hermia's father, who insists in the Duke's presence that if she doesn't marry Demetrius, she must die or spend her life in a nunnery. Much of the play's conflict concerns how these two young couples align their love for one another so that each desires and is desired by the right person. When Hermia defies her father and refuses to marry Demetrius, she flees to the woods, followed by Lysander and Demetrius as well as Helena, who is in pursuit of Demetrius.

Once in the woods, the lovers find themselves in a supernatural world, the unpredictable kingdom of Oberon and Titania, the king and queen of the fairies. The fourth couple creates even more confusion through Oberon's impatience with Titania. Their quarrel results in Oberon ordering his servant, Puck, to cast magical spells on the lovers as well as on Titania. This gives Puck the license to reveal their foolishness while eventually saving them from their own confused passions. Their reconciliations and reunions are not achieved, however, until Puck puts them through a series of comic encounters based on their illusions and vulnerabilities.

The final act includes the play within the play, "the most lamentable comedy" of two more lovers, Pyramus and Thisbe, who misunderstand one another. This travesty of a tragedy is put on by Athenian craftsmen — who are clearly better laborers than they are actors — at the Duke's request for a wedding entertainment. This play within the play reinforces the larger play's concerns about the nature of love and, indeed, of reality itself, because it raises questions about the fluid, complex relationship between art and reality. Ultimately, however, questions, issues, and conflicts give way to a generous sense of everything working out for the best as the play ends with Puck's warm assurances to the audience and his gentle urging to "Give me your hands."

WILLIAM SHAKESPEARE (1564–1616)

A Midsummer Night's Dream

c. 1595

[DRAMATIS PERSONAE

Theseus, Duke of Athens
Hippolyta, Queen of the Amazons, betrothed to Theseus
Philostrate, Master of the Revels
Egeus, father of Hermia

Hermia, daughter of Egeus, in love with Lysander
Lysander, in love with Hermia
Demetrius, in love with Hermia and favored by Egeus
Helena, in love with Demetrius

Oberon, King of the Fairies
Titania, Queen of the Fairies
Puck, or *Robin Goodfellow*
Peaseblossom,
Cobweb,
Mote,   } fairies attending Titania
Mustardseed,
Other Fairies attending

Peter Quince, a carpenter,

Nick Bottom, a weaver,

Francis Flute, a bellows mender,

Tom Snout, a tinker,   } representing

Snug, a joiner,

Robin Starveling, a tailor,

Lords and Attendants on Theseus and Hippolyta

Prologue

Pyramus

Thisbe

Wall

Lion

Moonshine

SCENE: *Athens, and a wood near it.*]

[ACT I

SCENE I: *Athens. Theseus' court.*]

Enter Theseus, Hippolyta, [and Philostrate,] with others.

Theseus: Now, fair Hippolyta, our nuptial hour

Draws on apace. Four happy days bring in

Another moon; but, O, methinks, how slow

This old moon wanes! She lingers° my desires,

Like to a stepdame° or a dowager°   5

Long withering out° a young man's revenue.

Hippolyta: Four days will quickly steep themselves° in night;

Four nights will quickly dream away the time;

And then the moon, like to a silver bow

New bent in heaven, shall behold the night   10

Of our solemnities.°

Theseus: Go Philostrate,

Stir up the Athenian youth to merriments.

Awake the pert and nimble spirit of mirth.

Turn melancholy forth to funerals;

The pale companion° is not for our pomp.°   *[Exit Philostrate.]*   15

Hippolyta, I wooed thee with my sword°

And won thy love doing thee injuries;

But I will wed thee in another key,

With pomp, with triumph,° and with reveling.

Enter Egeus and his daughter Hermia, and Lysander, and Demetrius.

Egeus: Happy be Theseus, our renownèd duke!   20

Theseus: Thanks, good Egeus. What's the news with thee?

Egeus: Full of vexation come I, with complaint

Against my child, my daughter Hermia. —

Stand forth, Demetrius. — My noble lord,

Act I, Scene I.   4 *lingers:* Postpones, delays the fulfillment of.   5 *stepdame:* Stepmother; *a dowager:* I.e., a widow (whose right of inheritance from her dead husband is eating into her son's estate).   6 *withering out:* Causing to dwindle.   7 *steep themselves:* Saturate themselves, to be absorbed in.   11 *solemnities:* Festive ceremonies of marriage.   15 *companion:* Fellow; *pomp:* Ceremonial magnificence.   16 *with my sword:* In a military engagement against the Amazons, when Hippolyta was taken captive.   19 *triumph:* Public festivity.

This man hath my consent to marry her.—   25
Stand forth, Lysander.—And, my gracious Duke,
This man hath bewitched the bosom of my child.
Thou, thou Lysander, thou hast given her rhymes
And interchanged love tokens with my child.
Thou hast by moonlight at her window sung   30
With feigning° voice verses of feigning° love,
And stol'n the impression of her fantasy°
With bracelets of thy hair, rings, gauds,° conceits,°
Knacks,° trifles, nosegays, sweetmeats — messengers
Of strong prevailment in° unhardened youth.   35
With cunning hast thou filched my daughter's heart,
Turned her obedience, which is due to me,
To stubborn harshness. And, my gracious Duke,
Be it so° she will not here before Your Grace
Consent to marry with Demetrius,   40
I beg the ancient privilege of Athens:
As she is mine, I may dispose of her,
Which shall be either to this gentleman
Or to her death, according to our law
Immediately° provided in that case.   45
Theseus: What say you, Hermia? Be advised, fair maid.
To you your father should be as a god —
One that composed your beauties, yea, and one
To whom you are but as a form in wax
By him imprinted, and within his power   50
To leave° the figure or disfigure° it.
Demetrius is a worthy gentleman.
Hermia: So is Lysander.
Theseus: In himself he is;
But in this kind,° wanting° your father's voice,°
The other must be held the worthier.   55
Hermia: I would my father looked but with my eyes.
Theseus: Rather your eyes must with his judgment look.
Hermia: I do entreat Your Grace to pardon me.
I know not by what power I am made bold,
Nor how it may concern° my modesty   60
In such a presence here to plead my thoughts;
But I beseech Your Grace that I may know
The worst that may befall me in this case
If I refuse to wed Demetrius.
Theseus: Either to die the death° or to abjure   65
Forever the society of men.
Therefore, fair Hermia, question your desires,

---

31 *feigning:* (1) Counterfeiting (2) faining, desirous.   32 *And . . . fantasy:* And made her fall in
love with you (imprinting your image on her imagination) by stealthy and dishonest means.
33 *gauds:* Playthings; *conceits:* Fanciful trifles.   34 *Knacks:* Knickknacks.   35 *prevailment
in:* Influence on.   39 *Be it so:* If.   45 *Immediately:* Directly, with nothing intervening.
51 *leave:* Leave unaltered; *disfigure:* Obliterate.   54 *kind:* Respect; *wanting:* Lacking; *voice:*
Approval.   60 *concern:* Befit.   65 *die the death:* Be executed by legal process.

Know of your youth, examine well your blood,°
Whether, if you yield not to your father's choice,
You can endure the livery° of a nun,   70
For aye° to be in shady cloister mewed,°
To live a barren sister all your life,
Chanting faint hymns to the cold fruitless moon.
Thrice blessèd they that master so their blood
To undergo such maiden pilgrimage;   75
But earthlier happy° is the rose distilled°
Than that which, withering on the virgin thorn,
Grows, lives, and dies in single blessedness.

Hermia: So will I grow, so live, so die, my lord,
Ere I will yield my virgin patent° up   80
Unto his lordship, whose unwishèd yoke
My soul consents not to give sovereignty.

Theseus: Take time to pause, and by the next new moon —
The sealing day betwixt my love and me
For everlasting bond of fellowship —   85
Upon that day either prepare to die
For disobedience to your father's will,
Or° else to wed Demetrius, as he would,
Or on Diana's altar to protest°
For aye austerity and single life.   90

Demetrius: Relent, sweet Hermia, and, Lysander, yield
Thy crazèd° title to my certain right.

Lysander: You have her father's love, Demetrius;
Let me have Hermia's. Do you marry him.

Egeus: Scornful Lysander! True, he hath my love,   95
And what is mine my love shall render him.
And she is mine, and all my right of her
I do estate unto° Demetrius.

Lysander: I am, my lord, as well derived° as he,
As well possessed;° my love is more than his;   100
My fortunes every way as fairly° ranked,
If not with vantage,° as Demetrius';
And, which is more than all these boasts can be,
I am beloved of beauteous Hermia.
Why should not I then prosecute my right?   105
Demetrius, I'll avouch it to his head,°
Made love to Nedar's daughter, Helena,
And won her soul; and she, sweet lady, dotes,
Devoutly dotes, dotes in idolatry
Upon this spotted° and inconstant man.   110

---

68 *blood:* Passions.   70 *livery:* Habit, costume.   71 *aye:* Ever; *mewed:* Shut in (said of a hawk, poultry, etc.).   76 *earthlier happy:* Happier as respects this world; *distilled:* Separated to make perfume.   80 *patent:* Privilege.   88 *Or:* Either.   89 *protest:* Vow.   92 *crazèd:* Cracked, unsound.   98 *estate unto:* Settle or bestow upon.   99 *as well derived:* As well born and descended.   100 *possessed:* Endowed with wealth.   101 *fairly:* Handsomely.   102 *vantage:* Superiority.   106 *head:* I.e., face.   110 *spotted:* I.e., morally stained.

Theseus: I must confess that I have heard so much,
  And with Demetrius thought to have spoke thereof;
  But, being overfull of self-affairs,°
  My mind did lose it. But, Demetrius, come,
  And come, Egeus, you shall go with me;   115
  I have some private schooling° for you both.
  For you, fair Hermia, look you arm° yourself
  To fit your fancies° to your father's will,
  Or else the law of Athens yields you up—
  Which by no means we may extenuate°—   120
  To death or to a vow of single life.
  Come, my Hippolyta. What cheer, my love?
  Demetrius and Egeus, go° along.
  I must employ you in some business
  Against° our nuptial, and confer with you   125
  Of something nearly that° concerns yourselves.
Egeus: With duty and desire we follow you.
                        Exeunt [all but Lysander and Hermia].
Lysander: How now, my love, why is your cheek so pale?
  How chance the roses there do fade so fast?
Hermia: Belike° for want of rain, which I could well   130
  Beteem° them from the tempest of my eyes.
Lysander: Ay me! For aught that I could ever read,
  Could ever hear by tale or history,
  The course of true love never did run smooth;
  But either it was different in blood°—   135
Hermia: O cross!° Too high to be enthralled to low.
Lysander: Or else misgrafted° in respect of years—
Hermia: O spite! Too old to be engaged to young.
Lysander: Or else it stood upon the choice of friends°—
Hermia: O hell, to choose love by another's eyes!   140
Lysander: Or if there were a sympathy° in choice,
  War, death, or sickness did lay siege to it,
  Making it momentany° as a sound,
  Swift as a shadow, short as any dream,
  Brief as the lightning in the collied° night   145
  That in a spleen° unfolds° both heaven and earth,
  And ere a man hath power to say "Behold!"
  The jaws of darkness do devour it up.
  So quick° bright things come to confusion.°
Hermia: If then true lovers have been ever crossed,°   150

---

113 *self-affairs:* My own concerns.   116 *schooling:* Admonition.   117 *look you arm:* Take care you prepare.   118 *fancies:* Likings, thoughts of love.   120 *extenuate:* Mitigate, relax.   123 *go:* I.e., come.   125 *Against:* In preparation for.   126 *nearly that:* That closely.   130 *Belike:* Very likely.   131 *Beteem:* Grant, afford.   135 *blood:* Hereditary station.   136 *cross:* Vexation.   137 *misgrafted:* Ill grafted, badly matched.   139 *friends:* Relatives.   141 *sympathy:* Agreement.   143 *momentany:* Lasting but a moment.   145 *collied:* Blackened (as with coal dust), darkened.   146 *in a spleen:* In a swift impulse, in a violent flash; *unfolds:* Reveals.   149 *quick:* Quickly; also, living, alive; *confusion:* Ruin.   150 *ever crossed:* Always thwarted.

It stands as an edict in destiny.
Then let us teach our trial patience,°
Because it is a customary cross,
As due to love as thoughts, and dreams, and sighs,
Wishes, and tears, poor fancy's° followers.   155

Lysander: A good persuasion.° Therefore, hear me, Hermia:
I have a widow aunt, a dowager
Of great revenue, and she hath no child.
From Athens is her house remote seven leagues;
And she respects° me as her only son.   160
There, gentle Hermia, may I marry thee,
And to that place the sharp Athenian law
Cannot pursue us. If thou lovest me, then,
Steal forth thy father's house tomorrow night;
And in the wood, a league without° the town,   165
Where I did meet thee once with Helena
To do observance to a morn of May,°
There will I stay for thee.

Hermia: My good Lysander!
I swear to thee, by Cupid's strongest bow,
By his best arrow° with the golden head,   170
By the simplicity° of Venus' doves,°
By that which knitteth souls and prospers loves,
And by that fire which burned the Carthage queen°
When the false Trojan° under sail was seen,
By all the vows that ever men have broke,   175
In number more than ever women spoke,
In that same place thou hast appointed me
Tomorrow truly will I meet with thee.

Lysander: Keep promise, love. Look, here comes Helena.

  Enter Helena.

Hermia: God speed, fair° Helena! Whither away?   180
Helena: Call you me fair? That "fair" again unsay.
Demetrius loves your fair.° O happy fair!°
Your eyes are lodestars,° and your tongue's sweet air°
More tunable° than lark to shepherd's ear
When wheat is green, when hawthorn buds appear.   185
Sickness is catching. O, were favor° so,
Yours would I catch, fair Hermia, ere I go;

---

152 *teach . . . patience:* I.e., teach ourselves patience in this trial.   155 *fancy's:* Amorous passion's.   156 *persuasion:* Doctrine.   160 *respects:* Regards.   165 *without:* Outside.
167 *do . . . May:* Perform the ceremonies of May Day.   170 *best arrow:* Cupid's best gold-pointed arrows were supposed to induce love; his blunt leaden arrows, aversion.   171 *simplicity:* Innocence; *Venus's doves:* Doves that drew Venus's chariot.   173, 174 *Carthage queen,
false Trojan:* (Dido, Queen of Carthage, immolated herself on a funeral pyre after having been deserted by the Trojan hero Aeneas.)   180 *fair:* Fair-complexioned (generally regarded by the Elizabethans as more beautiful than a dark complexion).   182 *your fair:* Your beauty (even though Hermia is dark-complexioned); *happy fair:* Lucky fair one.   183 *lodestars:* Guiding stars; *air:* Music.   184 *tunable:* Tuneful, melodious.   186 *favor:* Appearance, looks.

My ear should catch your voice, my eye your eye,
My tongue should catch your tongue's sweet melody.
Were the world mine, Demetrius being bated,° 190
The rest I'd give to be to you translated.°
O, teach me how you look and with what art
You sway the motion° of Demetrius' heart.
Hermia: I frown upon him, yet he loves me still.
Helena: O, that your frowns would teach my smiles such skill! 195
Hermia: I give him curses, yet he gives me love.
Helena: O, that my prayers could such affection° move!°
Hermia: The more I hate, the more he follows me.
Helena: The more I love, the more he hateth me.
Hermia: His folly, Helena, is no fault of mine. 200
Helena: None, but your beauty. Would that fault were mine!
Hermia: Take comfort. He no more shall see my face.
  Lysander and myself will fly this place.
  Before the time I did Lysander see
  Seemed Athens as a paradise to me.° 205
  O, then, what graces in my love do dwell,
  That he hath turned a heaven unto a hell?
Lysander: Helen, to you our minds we will unfold.
  Tomorrow night, when Phoebe° doth behold
  Her silver visage in the watery glass,° 210
  Decking with liquid pearl the bladed grass,
  A time that lovers' flights doth still° conceal,
  Through Athens' gates have we devised to steal.
Hermia: And in the wood, where often you and I
  Upon faint° primrose beds were wont to lie, 215
  Emptying our bosoms of their counsel° sweet,
  There my Lysander and myself shall meet,
  And thence from Athens turn away our eyes
  To seek new friends and stranger companies.°
  Farewell, sweet playfellow. Pray thou for us, 220
  And good luck grant thee thy Demetrius!
  Keep word, Lysander. We must starve our sight
  From lovers' food till morrow deep midnight.
Lysander: I will, my Hermia. *(Exit Hermia.)* Helena, adieu.
  As you on him, Demetrius dote on you!   *Exit Lysander.* 225
Helena: How happy some o'er other some can be!°
  Through Athens I am thought as fair as she.
  But what of that? Demetrius thinks not so;
  He will not know what all but he do know.
  And as he errs, doting on Hermia's eyes, 230

---

190 *bated:* Excepted.   191 *translated:* Transformed.   193 *sway the motion:* Control the impulse.   197 *affection:* Passion; *move:* Arouse.   204-205 *Before . . . to me:* (Hermia seemingly means that love has led to complications and jealousies, making Athens hell for her.)   209 *Phoebe:* Diana, the moon.   210 *glass:* Mirror.   212 *still:* Always.   215 *faint:* Pale.   216 *counsel:* Secret thought.   219 *stranger companies:* The company of strangers.   226 *o'er . . . can be:* Can be in comparison to some others.

So I, admiring of° his qualities.
Things base and vile, holding no quantity,°
Love can transpose to form and dignity.
Love looks not with the eyes, but with the mind,
And therefore is winged Cupid painted blind.   235
Nor hath Love's mind of any judgment taste;°
Wings and no eyes figure° unheedy haste.
And therefore is Love said to be a child,
Because in choice° he is so oft beguiled.°
As waggish° boys in game° themselves forswear,   240
So the boy Love is perjured everywhere.
For ere Demetrius looked on Hermia's eyne,°
He hailed down oaths that he was only mine;
And when this hail some heat from Hermia felt,
So he dissolved, and showers of oaths did melt.   245
I will go tell him of fair Hermia's flight.
Then to the wood will he tomorrow night
Pursue her; and for this intelligence°
If I have thanks, it is a dear° expense.°
But herein mean I to enrich my pain,   250
To have his sight thither and back again.   *Exit.*

[SCENE II: *Athens.*]

*Enter Quince the carpenter, and Snug the joiner, and Bottom the weaver, and Flute
the bellows mender, and Snout the tinker, and Starveling the tailor.*

Quince: Is all our company here?

Bottom: You were best to call them generally,° man by man, according to
the scrip.°

Quince: Here is the scroll of every man's name which is thought fit,
through all Athens, to play in our interlude° before the Duke and the   5
Duchess on his wedding day at night.

Bottom: First, good Peter Quince, say what the play treats on, then read
the names of the actors, and so grow to° a point.

Quince: Marry,° our play is "The most lamentable comedy and most cruel
death of Pyramus and Thisbe."   10

Bottom: A very good piece of work, I assure you, and a merry. Now, good
Peter Quince, call forth your actors by the scroll. Masters, spread
yourselves.

Quince: Answer as I call you. Nick Bottom,° the weaver.

231 *admiring of:* Wondering at.   232 *holding no quantity:* I.e., unsubstantial, unshapely.
236 *Nor . . . taste:* I.e., nor has Love, which dwells in the fancy or imagination, any *taste* or least
bit of judgment or reason.   237 *figure:* Are a symbol of.   239 *in choice:* In choosing; *beguiled:* Self-deluded, making unaccountable choices.   240 *waggish:* Playful, mischievous;
game: Sport, jest.   242 *eyne:* Eyes (old form of plural).   248 *intelligence:* Information.
249 *a dear expense:* I.e., a trouble worth taking on my part, or a begrudging effort on his part;
dear: Costly.   **Scene II.**   2 *generally:* (Bottom's blunder for "individually.")   3 *scrip:*
Scrap (Bottom's error for "script").   5 *interlude:* Play.   8 *grow to:* Come to.   9 *Marry:*
(A mild oath; originally the name of the Virgin Mary.)   14 *Bottom:* Object around which
weavers wound thread.

Bottom: Ready. Name what part I am for, and proceed.   15
Quince: You, Nick Bottom, are set down for Pyramus.
Bottom: What is Pyramus? A lover or a tyrant?
Quince: A lover, that kills himself most gallant for love.
Bottom: That will ask some tears in the true performing of it. If I do it, let
     the audience look to their eyes. I will move storms; I will condole° in   20
     some measure. To the rest—yet my chief humor° is for a tyrant. I
     could play Ercles° rarely, or a part to tear a cat° in, to make all split.°
          "The raging rocks
          And shivering shocks
          Shall break the locks   25
               Of prison gates;
          And Phibbus' car°
          Shall shine from far
          And make and mar
               The foolish Fates."   30
     This was lofty! Now name the rest of the players. This is Ercles' vein, a
     tyrant's vein. A lover is more condoling.
Quince: Francis Flute, the bellows mender.
Flute: Here, Peter Quince.
Quince: Flute, you must take Thisbe on you.   35
Flute: What is Thisbe? A wandering knight?
Quince: It is the lady that Pyramus must love.
Flute: Nay, faith, let not me play a woman. I have a beard coming.
Quince: That's all one.° You shall play it in a mask, and you may speak as
     small° as you will.   40
Bottom: An° I may hide my face, let me play Thisbe too. I'll speak in a mon-
     strous little voice: "Thisne, Thisne!" "Ah, Pyramus, my lover dear! Thy
     Thisbe dear, and lady dear!"
Quince: No, no, you must play Pyramus, and Flute, you Thisbe.
Bottom: Well, proceed.   45
Quince: Robin Starveling, the tailor.
Starveling: Here, Peter Quince.
Quince: Robin Starveling, you must play Thisbe's mother. Tom Snout, the
     tinker.
Snout: Here, Peter Quince.   50
Quince: You, Pyramus' father; myself, Thisbe's father; Snug, the joiner,
     you, the lion's part; and I hope here is a play fitted.
Snug: Have you the lion's part written? Pray you, if it be, give it me, for I
     am slow of study.
Quince: You may do it extempore, for it is nothing but roaring.   55
Bottom: Let me play the lion too. I will roar that I will do any man's heart
     good to hear me. I will roar that I will make the Duke say, "Let him
     roar again, let him roar again."
Quince: An you should do it too terribly, you would fright the Duchess

---

20 *condole:* Lament, arouse pity.   21 *humor:* Inclination, whim.   22 *Ercles:* Hercules (the
tradition of ranting came from Seneca's *Hercules Furens*); *tear a cat:* I.e., rant; *make all split:*
I.e., cause a stir, bring the house down.   27 *Phibbus' car:* Phoebus', the sun god's, chariot.
39 *That's all one:* It makes no difference.   40 *small:* High-pitched.   41 *An:* If (also at
line 59).

and the ladies, that they would shriek; and that were enough to hang   60
us all.

All: That would hang us, every mother's son.

Bottom: I grant you, friends, if you should fright the ladies out of their
wits, they would have no more discretion but to hang us; but I will
aggravate° my voice so that I will roar you° as gently as any sucking   65
dove;° I will roar you an 'twere° any nightingale.

Quince: You can play no part but Pyramus; for Pyramus is a sweet-faced
man, a proper° man as one shall see in a summer's day, a most lovely
gentlemanlike man. Therefore you must needs play Pyramus.

Bottom: Well, I will undertake it. What beard were I best to play it in?   70

Quince: Why, what you will.

Bottom: I will discharge° it in either your° straw-color beard, your orange-
tawny beard, your purple-in-grain° beard, or your French-crown-
color° beard, your perfect yellow.

Quince: Some of your French crowns° have no hair at all, and then you   75
will play barefaced. But, masters, here are your parts. *[He distributes
parts.]* And I am to entreat you, request you, and desire you to con°
them by tomorrow night, and meet me in the palace wood, a mile
without the town, by moonlight. There will we rehearse; for if we
meet in the city, we shall be dogged with company, and our devices°   80
known. In the meantime I will draw a bill° of properties, such as our
play wants. I pray you, fail me not.

Bottom: We will meet, and there we may rehearse most obscenely° and
courageously. Take pains, be perfect.° Adieu.

Quince: At the Duke's oak we meet.   85

Bottom: Enough. Hold, or cut bowstrings.°   *Exeunt.*

[ACT II

SCENE I: *A wood near Athens.]*

Enter a Fairy at one door, and Robin Goodfellow [Puck] at another.

Puck: How now, spirit, whither wander you?

Fairy: Over hill, over dale,
         Thorough° bush, thorough brier,
      Over park, over pale,°
         Thorough flood, thorough fire,   5

65 *aggravate:* (Bottom's blunder for "moderate."); *roar you:* I.e., roar for you.   66 *sucking
dove:* (Bottom conflates *sitting dove* and *sucking lamb,* two proverbial images of innocence.); *an
'twere:* As if it were.   68 *proper:* Handsome.   72 *discharge:* Perform; *your:* I.e., you know
the kind I mean.   73 *purple-in-grain:* Dyed a very deep red (from *grain,* the name applied to
the dried insect used to make the dye).   74 *French-crown-color:* I.e., color of a French
crown, a gold coin.   75 *crowns:* Heads bald from syphilis, the "French disease."   77 *con:*
Learn by heart.   80 *devices:* Plans.   81 *draw a bill:* Draw up a list.   83 *obscenely:* (An
unintentionally funny blunder, whatever Bottom meant to say.)   84 *perfect:* I.e., letter-
perfect in memorizing your parts.   86 *Hold . . . bowstrings:* (An archer's expression, not
definitely explained, but probably meaning here "keep your promises, or give up the play.")
Act II, Scene I.   3 *Thorough:* Through.   4 *pale:* Enclosure.

      I do wander everywhere,
      Swifter than the moon's sphere;°
      And I serve the Fairy Queen,
      To dew° her orbs° upon the green.
      The cowslips tall her pensioners° be.   10
      In their gold coats spots you see;
      Those be rubies, fairy favors;°
      In those freckles live their savors.°
    I must go seek some dewdrops here
    And hang a pearl in every cowslip's ear.   15
    Farewell, thou lob° of spirits; I'll be gone.
    Our Queen and all her elves come here anon.°
Puck: The King doth keep his revels here tonight.
    Take heed the Queen come not within his sight.
    For Oberon is passing fell° and wrath,°   20
    Because that she as her attendant hath
    A lovely boy, stolen from an Indian king;
    She ne'er had so sweet a changeling.°
    And jealous Oberon would have the child
    Knight of his train, to trace° the forests wild.   25
    But she perforce° withholds the lovèd boy,
    Crowns him with flowers, and makes him all her joy.
    And now they never meet in grove or green,
    By fountain° clear, or spangled starlight sheen,°
    But they do square,° that all their elves for fear   30
    Creep into acorn cups and hide them there.
Fairy: Either I mistake your shape and making quite,
    Or else you are that shrewd° and knavish sprite°
    Called Robin Goodfellow. Are not you he
    That frights the maidens of the villagery,°   35
    Skim milk,° and sometimes labor in the quern,°
    And bootless° make the breathless huswife° churn,
    And sometimes make the drink to bear no barm,°
    Mislead night wanderers,° laughing at their harm?
    Those that "Hobgoblin" call you, and "Sweet Puck,"°   40
    You do their work, and they shall have good luck.
    Are you not he?

---

7 *sphere:* Orbit.   9 *dew:* Sprinkle with dew; *orbs:* Circles, i.e., fairy rings (circular bands of grass, darker than the surrounding area, caused by fungi enriching the soil).   10 *pensioners:* Retainers, members of the royal bodyguard.   12 *favors:* Love tokens.   13 *savors:* Sweet smells.   16 *lob:* Country bumpkin.   17 *anon:* At once.   20 *passing fell:* Exceedingly angry; *wrath:* Wrathful.   23 *changeling:* Child exchanged for another by the fairies. 25 *trace:* Range through.   26 *perforce:* Forcibly.   29 *fountain:* Spring; *starlight sheen:* Shining starlight.   30 *square:* Quarrel.   33 *shrewd:* Mischievous; *sprite:* Spirit.   35 *villagery:* Village population.   36 *Skim milk:* I.e., steal the cream; *quern:* Hand mill (where Puck presumably hampers the grinding of grain).   37 *bootless:* In vain (Puck prevents the cream from turning to butter); *huswife:* Housewife.   38 *barm:* Head on the ale (Puck prevents the barm or yeast from producing fermentation).   39 *Mislead night wanderers:* I.e., mislead with false fire those who walk abroad at night (hence earning Puck his other names of Jack o' Lantern and Will o' the Wisp).   40 *Those . . . Puck:* I.e., those who call you by the names you favor rather than those denoting the mischief you do.

Puck: Thou speakest aright;
    I am that merry wanderer of the night.
    I jest to Oberon and make him smile
    When I a fat and bean-fed° horse beguile,   45
    Neighing in likeness of a filly foal;
    And sometimes lurk I in a gossip's° bowl
    In very likeness of a roasted crab,°
    And when she drinks, against her lips I bob
    And on her withered dewlap° pour the ale.   50
    The wisest aunt,° telling the saddest° tale,
    Sometimes for three-foot stool mistaketh me;
    Then slip I from her bum, down topples she,
    And "Tailor"° cries, and falls into a cough;
    And then the whole choir° hold their hips and laugh,   55
    And waxen° in their mirth, and neeze,° and swear
    A merrier hour was never wasted° there.
    But, room,° fairy! Here comes Oberon.
Fairy: And here my mistress. Would that he were gone!

> *Enter [Oberon] the King of Fairies at one door, with his train, and [Titania]*
> *the Queen at another, with hers.*

Oberon: Ill met by moonlight, proud Titania.   60
Titania: What, jealous Oberon? Fairies, skip hence.
    I have forsworn his bed and company.
Oberon: Tarry, rash wanton.° Am not I thy lord?
Titania: Then I must be thy lady; but I know
    When thou hast stolen away from Fairyland   65
    And in the shape of Corin° sat all day,
    Playing on the pipes of corn° and versing love
    To amorous Phillida.° Why art thou here
    Come from the farthest step° of India,
    But that, forsooth, the bouncing Amazon,   70
    Your buskined° mistress and your warrior love,
    To Theseus must be wedded, and you come
    To give their bed joy and prosperity.
Oberon: How canst thou thus for shame, Titania,
    Glance at my credit with Hippolyta,°   75
    Knowing I know thy love to Theseus?
    Didst not thou lead him through the glimmering night
    From Perigenia,° whom he ravishèd?

---

45 *bean-fed:* Well fed on field beans.   47 *gossip's:* Old woman's.   48 *crab:* Crab apple.
50 *dewlap:* Loose skin on neck.   51 *aunt:* Old woman; *saddest:* Most serious.   54 *Tailor:*
(Possibly because she ends up sitting cross-legged on the floor, looking like a tailor, or else referring to the *tail* or buttocks.)   55 *choir:* Company.   56 *waxen:* Increase; *neeze:* Sneeze.
57 *wasted:* Spent.   58 *room:* Stand aside, make room.   63 *wanton:* Headstrong creature.
66, 68 *Corin, Phillida:* (Conventional names of pastoral lovers.)   67 *corn:* (Here, oat
stalks.)   69 *step:* Farthest limit of travel, or, perhaps, *steep,* "mountain range."   71 *busk-
ined:* Wearing half-boots called buskins.   75 *Glance . . . Hippolyta:* Make insinuations
about my favored relationship with Hippolyta.   78 *Perigenia:* I.e., Perigouna, one of Theseus' conquests. (This and the following women are named in Thomas North's translation
of Plutarch's "Life of Theseus.")

And make him with fair Aegles° break his faith,
With Ariadne° and Antiopa?°   80
Titania: These are the forgeries of jealousy;
And never, since the middle summer's spring,°
Met we on hill, in dale, forest, or mead,°
By pavèd° fountain or by rushy° brook,
Or in° the beachèd margent° of the sea,   85
To dance our ringlets to° the whistling wind,
But with thy brawls thou hast disturbed our sport.
Therefore the winds, piping to us in vain,
As in revenge, have sucked up from the sea
Contagious° fogs which, falling in the land,   90
Hath every pelting° river made so proud
That they have overborne their continents.°
The ox hath therefore stretched his yoke° in vain,
The plowman lost his sweat, and the green corn°
Hath rotted ere his youth attained a beard;   95
The fold° stands empty in the drownèd field,
And crows are fatted with the murrain° flock;
The nine-men's morris° is filled up with mud,
And the quaint mazes° in the wanton° green
For lack of tread are indistinguishable.   100
The human mortals want° their winter° here;
No night is now with hymn or carol blessed.
Therefore° the moon, the governess of floods,
Pale in her anger, washes° all the air,
That rheumatic diseases° do abound.   105
And thorough this distemperature° we see
The seasons alter: hoary-headed frosts
Fall in the fresh lap of the crimson rose,
And on old Hiems'° thin and icy crown
An odorous chaplet of sweet summer buds   110
Is, as in mockery, set. The spring, the summer,
The childing° autumn, angry winter, change

79 *Aegles:* I.e., Aegle, for whom Theseus deserted Ariadne according to some accounts.
80 *Ariadne:* The daughter of Minos, King of Crete, who helped Theseus to escape the
labyrinth after killing the Minotaur; later she was abandoned by Theseus; *Antiopa:* Queen of
the Amazons and wife of Theseus, elsewhere identified with Hippolyta, but here thought of
as a separate woman.   82 *middle summer's spring:* Beginning of midsummer.   83 *mead:*
Meadow.   84 *pavèd:* With pebbled bottom; *rushy:* Bordered with rushes.   85 *in:* On;
margent: Edge, border.   86 *ringlets to:* Dances in a ring (see *orbs* in II.i.9) to the sound of.
90 *Contagious:* Noxious.   91 *pelting:* Paltry.   92 *continents:* Banks that contain them.
93 *stretched his yoke:* I.e., pulled at his yoke in plowing.   94 *corn:* Grain of any kind.
96 *fold:* Pen for sheep or cattle.   97 *murrain:* Having died of the plague.   98 *nine-men's
morris:* I.e., portion of the village green marked out in a square for a game played with nine
pebbles or pegs.   99 *quaint mazes:* I.e., intricate paths marked out on the village green to
be followed rapidly on foot as a kind of contest; *wanton:* Luxuriant.   101 *want:* Lack; *winter:*
I.e., regular winter season; or, proper observances of winter, such as the *hymn* or *carol* in the
next line (?).   103 *Therefore:* I.e., as a result of our quarrel.   104 *washes:* Saturates with
moisture.   105 *rheumatic diseases:* Colds, flu, and other respiratory infections.   106 *distemperature:* Disturbance in nature.   109 *Hiems':* The winter god's.   112 *childing:* Fruitful, pregnant.

Their wonted liveries,° and the mazèd° world
By their increase° now knows not which is which.
And this same progeny of evils comes   115
From our debate,° from our dissension.
We are their parents and original.°
Oberon: Do you amend it, then. It lies in you.
Why should Titania cross her Oberon?
I do but beg a little changeling boy   120
To be my henchman.°
Titania: Set your heart at rest.
The fairy land buys not the child of me.
His mother was a vot'ress of my order,°
And in the spicèd Indian air by night
Full often hath she gossiped by my side   125
And sat with me on Neptune's yellow sands,
Marking th' embarkèd traders° on the flood,°
When we have laughed to see the sails conceive
And grow big-bellied with the wanton° wind;
Which she, with pretty and with swimming° gait,   130
Following — her womb then rich with my young squire —
Would imitate, and sail upon the land
To fetch me trifles, and return again
As from a voyage, rich with merchandise.
But she, being mortal, of that boy did die;   135
And for her sake do I rear up her boy,
And for her sake I will not part with him.
Oberon: How long within this wood intend you stay?
Titania: Perchance till after Theseus' wedding day.
If you will patiently dance in our round°   140
And see our moonlight revels, go with us;
If not, shun me, and I will spare° your haunts.
Oberon: Give me that boy, and I will go with thee.
Titania: Not for thy fairy kingdom. Fairies, away!
We shall chide downright, if I longer stay.   145

                              Exeunt [Titania with her train].

Oberon: Well, go thy way. Thou shalt not from° this grove
Till I torment thee for this injury.
My gentle Puck, come hither. Thou rememb'rest
Since° once I sat upon a promontory,
And heard a mermaid on a dolphin's back   150
Uttering such dulcet° and harmonious breath°
That the rude° sea grew civil at her song,

---

113 *wonted liveries:* Usual apparel; *mazèd:* Bewildered.   114 *their increase:* Their yield, what they produce.   116 *debate:* Quarrel.   117 *original:* Origin.   121 *henchman:* Attendant, page.   123 *was... order:* Had taken a vow to serve me.   127 *traders:* Trading vessels; *flood:* Flood tide.   129 *wanton:* (1) Playful (2) amorous.   130 *swimming:* Smooth, gliding. 140 *round:* Circular dance.   142 *spare:* Shun.   146 *from:* Go from.   149 *Since:* When. 151 *dulcet:* Sweet; *breath:* Voice, song.   152 *rude:* Rough.

And certain stars shot madly from their spheres
To hear the sea-maid's music?
Puck: I remember.
Oberon: That very time I saw, but thou couldst not,   155
    Flying between the cold moon and the earth
    Cupid, all° armed. A certain° aim he took
    At a fair vestal° thronèd by° the west,
    And loosed° his love shaft smartly from his bow
    As° it should pierce a hundred thousand hearts;   160
    But I might° see young Cupid's fiery shaft
    Quenched in the chaste beams of the watery moon,
    And the imperial vot'ress passèd on,
    In maiden meditation, fancy-free.°
    Yet marked I where the bolt° of Cupid fell: 165
    It fell upon a little western flower,
    Before milk-white, now purple with love's wound,
    And maidens call it love-in-idleness.°
    Fetch me that flower; the herb I showed thee once.
    The juice of it on sleeping eyelids laid   170
    Will make or man or° woman madly dote
    Upon the next live creature that it sees.
    Fetch me this herb, and be thou here again
    Ere the leviathan° can swim a league.
Puck: I'll put a girdle round about the earth   175
    In forty° minutes.   *[Exit.]*
Oberon: Having once this juice,
    I'll watch Titania when she is asleep
    And drop the liquor of it in her eyes.
    The next thing then she waking looks upon,
    Be it on lion, bear, or wolf, or bull,   180
    On meddling monkey, or on busy ape,
    She shall pursue it with the soul of love.
    And ere I take this charm from off her sight,
    As I can take it with another herb,
    I'll make her render up her page to me.   185
    But who comes here? I am invisible,
    And I will overhear their conference.

Enter Demetrius, Helena following him.

Demetrius: I love thee not; therefore pursue me not.
    Where is Lysander and fair Hermia?
    The one I'll slay; the other slayeth me.   190
    Thou toldst me they were stol'n unto this wood;

---

157 *all:* Fully; *certain:* Sure.   158 *vestal:* Vestal virgin (contains a complimentary allusion to Queen Elizabeth as a votaress of Diana and probably refers to an actual entertainment in her honor at Elvetham in 1591); *by:* In the region of.   159 *loosed:* Released.   160 *As:* As if. 161 *might:* Could.   164 *fancy-free:* Free of love's spell.   165 *bolt:* Arrow.   168 *love-in-idleness:* Pansy, heartsease.   171 *or . . . or:* Either . . . or.   174 *leviathan:* Sea monster, whale. 176 *forty:* (Used indefinitely.)

And here am I, and wood° within this wood
Because I cannot meet my Hermia.
Hence, get thee gone, and follow me no more.
Helena: You draw me, you hardhearted adamant!° 195
But yet you draw not iron, for my heart
Is true as steel. Leave you° your power to draw,
And I shall have no power to follow you.
Demetrius: Do I entice you? Do I speak you fair?°
Or rather do I not in plainest truth 200
Tell you I do not nor I cannot love you?
Helena: And even for that do I love you the more.
I am your spaniel; and, Demetrius,
The more you beat me I will fawn on you.
Use me but as your spaniel, spurn me, strike me, 205
Neglect me, lose me; only give me leave,
Unworthy as I am, to follow you.
What worser place can I beg in your love —
And yet a place of high respect with me —
Than to be usèd as you use your dog? 210
Demetrius: Tempt not too much the hatred of my spirit,
For I am sick when I do look on thee.
Helena: And I am sick when I look not on you.
Demetrius: You do impeach° your modesty too much
To leave° the city and commit yourself 215
Into the hands of one that loves you not,
To trust the opportunity of night
And the ill counsel of a desert° place
With the rich worth of your virginity.
Helena: Your virtue° is my privilege.° For that° 220
It is not night when I do see your face,
Therefore I think I am not in the night;
Nor doth this wood lack worlds of company,
For you, in my respect,° are all the world.
Then how can it be said I am alone 225
When all the world is here to look on me?
Demetrius: I'll run from thee and hide me in the brakes,°
And leave thee to the mercy of wild beasts.
Helena: The wildest hath not such a heart as you.
Run when you will. The story shall be changed: 230
Apollo flies and Daphne holds the chase,°

---

192 *and wood:* And mad, frantic (with an obvious wordplay on *wood,* meaning "woods"). 195 *adamant:* Lodestone, magnet (with pun on *hardhearted,* since adamant was also thought to be the hardest of all stones and was confused with the diamond). 197 *Leave you:* Give up. 199 *speak you fair:* Speak courteously to you. 214 *impeach:* Call into question. 215 *To leave:* By leaving. 218 *desert:* Deserted. 220 *virtue:* Goodness or power to attract; *privilege:* Safeguard, warrant; *For that:* Because. 224 *in my respect:* As far as I am concerned, in my esteem. 227 *brakes:* Thickets. 231 *Apollo ... chase:* (In the ancient myth, Daphne fled from Apollo and was saved from rape by being transformed into a laurel tree; here it is the female who *holds the chase,* or pursues, instead of the male.)

The dove pursues the griffin,° the mild hind°
Makes speed to catch the tiger — bootless° speed,
When cowardice pursues and valor flies!
Demetrius: I will not stay thy questions.° Let me go!   235
Or if thou follow me, do not believe
But I shall do thee mischief in the wood.
Helena: Ay, in the temple, in the town, the field,
You do me mischief. Fie, Demetrius!
Your wrongs do set a scandal on my sex.°   240
We cannot fight for love, as men may do;
We should be wooed and were not made to woo.   *[Exit Demetrius.]*
I'll follow thee and make a heaven of hell,
To die upon° the hand I love so well.   *[Exit.]*
Oberon: Fare thee well, nymph. Ere he do leave this grove   245
Thou shalt fly him, and he shall seek thy love.

Enter Puck.

Has thou the flower there? Welcome, wanderer.
Puck: Aye, there it is.   *[He offers the flower.]*
Oberon: I pray thee, give it to me.
I know a bank where the wild thyme blows,°
Where oxlips° and the nodding violet grows,   250
Quite overcanopied with luscious woodbine,°
With sweet muskroses° and with eglantine.°
There sleeps Titania sometime of° the night,
Lulled in these flowers with dances and delight;
And there the snake throws° her enameled skin,   255
Weed° wide enough to wrap a fairy in.
And with the juice of this I'll streak° her eyes
And make her full of hateful fantasies.
Take thou some of it, and seek through this grove.
                                [He gives some love juice.]
A sweet Athenian lady is in love   260
With a disdainful youth. Anoint his eyes,
But do it when the next thing he espies
May be the lady. Thou shalt know the man
By the Athenian garments he hath on.
Effect it with some care, that he may prove   265
More fond on° her than she upon her love;
And look thou meet me ere the first cock crow.
Puck: Fear not, my lord, your servant shall do so.   *Exeunt [separately].*

232 *griffin:* A fabulous monster with the head and wings of an eagle and the body of a lion;
hind: Female deer.   233 *bootless:* Fruitless.   235 *stay thy questions:* Wait for or put up with
your talk or argument.   240 *Your... sex:* I.e., the wrongs that you do me cause me to act
in a manner that disgraces my sex.   244 *upon:* By.   249 *blows:* Blooms.   250 *oxlips:*
Flowers resembling cowslip and primrose.   251 *woodbine:* Honeysuckle.   252 *muskroses:*
A kind of large, sweet-scented rose; *eglantine:* Sweetbrier, another kind of rose.   253 *sometime of:* For part of.   255 *throws:* Sloughs off, sheds.   256 *Weed:* Garment.   257 *streak:*
Anoint, touch gently.   266 *fond on:* Doting on.

[SCENE II: *The wood.*]

Enter Titania, Queen of Fairies, with her train.

Titania: Come, now a roundel° and a fairy song;
Then, for the third part of a minute,° hence—
Some to kill cankers° in the muskrose buds,
Some war with reremice° for their leathern wings
To make my small elves coats, and some keep back   5
The clamorous owl, that nightly hoots and wonders
At our quaint° spirits. Sing me now asleep.
Then to your offices, and let me rest.

Fairies sing.

First Fairy: You spotted snakes with double° tongue,
        Thorny hedgehogs, be not seen;   10
    Newts° and blindworms, do no wrong;
        Come not near our Fairy Queen.
Chorus [dancing]: Philomel,° with melody
        Sing in our sweet lullaby;
    Lulla, lulla, lullaby, lulla, lulla, lullaby.   15
        Never harm
        Nor spell nor charm
    Come our lovely lady nigh.
        So good night, with lullaby.
First Fairy: Weaving spiders, come not here;   20
        Hence, you long-legged spinners, hence!
    Beetles black, approach not near;
        Worm nor snail, do no offense.°
Chorus [dancing]: Philomel, with melody
        Sing in our sweet lullaby;   25
    Lulla, lulla, lullaby, lulla, lulla, lullaby.
        Never harm
        Nor spell nor charm
    Come our lovely lady nigh.
        So good night, with lullaby.   *[Titania sleeps.]*   30
Second Fairy: Hence, away! Now all is well.
    One aloof stand sentinel.°   *[Exeunt Fairies, leaving one sentinel.]*

Enter Oberon [and squeezes the flower on Titania's eyelids].

Oberon: What thou seest when thou dost wake,
    Do it for thy true love take;
    Love and languish for his sake.   35
    Be it ounce,° or cat, or bear,

Scene II.   1 *roundel:* Dance in a ring.   2 *the third . . . minute:* (Indicative of the fairies'
quickness.)   3 *cankers:* Cankerworms (i.e., caterpillars or grubs).   4 *reremice:* Bats.
7 *quaint:* Dainty.   9 *double:* Forked.   11 *Newts:* Water lizards (considered poisonous,
as were *blindworms* — small snakes with tiny eyes — and spiders).   13 *Philomel:* The
nightingale. (Philomela, daughter of King Pandion, was transformed into a nightingale, according to Ovid's *Metamorphoses* 6, after she had been raped by her sister Procne's husband,
Tereus.)   23 *offense:* Harm.   32 *sentinel:* (Presumably Oberon is able to outwit or intimidate this guard.)   36 *ounce:* Lynx.

Pard,° or boar with bristled hair,
In thy eye that shall appear
When thou wak'st, it is thy dear.
Wake when some vile thing is near.   *[Exit.]*   40

Enter Lysander and Hermia.

Lysander: Fair love, you faint with wandering in the wood;
    And to speak truth, I have forgot our way.
We'll rest us, Hermia, if you think it good,
    And tarry for the comfort of the day.
Hermia: Be it so, Lysander. Find you out a bed,   45
    For I upon this bank will rest my head.
Lysander: One turf shall serve as pillow for us both;
    One heart, one bed, two bosoms, and one troth.°
Hermia: Nay, good Lysander, for my sake, my dear,
    Lie further off yet. Do not lie so near.   50
Lysander: O, take the sense, sweet, of my innocence!°
    Love takes the meaning in love's conference.°
I mean that my heart unto yours is knit,
    So that but one heart we can make of it;
Two bosoms interchainèd with an oath —   55
    So then two bosoms and a single troth.
Then by your side no bed-room me deny,
    For lying so, Hermia, I do not lie.°
Hermia: Lysander riddles very prettily.
    Now much beshrew° my manners and my pride   60
If Hermia meant to say Lysander lied.
    But, gentle friend, for love and courtesy
Lie further off, in human° modesty.
    Such separation as may well be said
Becomes a virtuous bachelor and a maid,   65
    So far be distant; and, good night, sweet friend.
Thy love ne'er alter till thy sweet life end!
Lysander: Amen, amen, to that fair prayer, say I,
    And then end life when I end loyalty!
Here is my bed. Sleep give thee all his rest!   70
Hermia: With half that wish the wisher's eyes be pressed!°

               [They sleep, separated by a short distance.]

    Enter Puck.

Puck: Through the forest have I gone,
    But Athenian found I none
    On whose eyes I might approve°
    This flower's force in stirring love.
    Night and silence. — Who is here?   75

---

37 *Pard:* Leopard.   48 *troth:* Faith, trothplight.   51 *take . . . innocence:* I.e., interpret my
intention as innocent.   52 *Love . . . conference:* I.e., when lovers confer, love teaches each
lover to interpret the other's meaning lovingly.   58 *lie:* Tell a falsehood (with a riddling
pun on *lie,* "recline").   60 *beshrew:* Curse (but mildly meant).   63 *human:* Courteous
(and perhaps suggesting "humane").   71 *With . . . pressed:* I.e., may we share your wish, so
that your eyes too are *pressed,* closed, in sleep.   74 *approve:* Test.

Weeds of Athens he doth wear.
This is he, my master said,
Despisèd the Athenian maid;
And here the maiden, sleeping sound,   80
On the dank and dirty ground.
Pretty soul, she durst not lie
Near this lack-love, this kill-courtesy.
Churl, upon thy eyes I throw
All the power this charm doth owe.°   *[He applies the love juice.]*   85
When thou wak'st, let love forbid
Sleep his seat on thy eyelid.
So awake when I am gone,
For I must now to Oberon.   *Exit.*

Enter Demetrius and Helena, running.

Helena: Stay, though thou kill me, sweet Demetrius!   90
Demetrius: I charge thee, hence, and do not haunt me thus.
Helena: O, wilt thou darkling° leave me? Do not so.
Demetrius: Stay, on thy peril!° I alone will go.   *[Exit.]*
Helena: O, I am out of breath in this fond° chase!
The more my prayer, the lesser is my grace.°   95
Happy is Hermia, wheresoe'er she lies,°
For she hath blessèd and attractive eyes.
How came her eyes so bright? Not with salt tears;
If so, my eyes are oftener washed than hers.
No, no, I am as ugly as a bear,   100
For beasts that meet me run away for fear.
Therefore no marvel though Demetrius
Do, as a monster, fly my presence thus.°
What wicked and dissembling glass of mine
Made me compare° with Hermia's sphery eyne?°   105
But who is here? Lysander, on the ground?
Dead, or asleep? I see no blood, no wound.
Lysander, if you live, good sir, awake.
Lysander [awaking]: And run through fire I will for thy sweet sake.
Transparent° Helena! Nature shows art,°   110
That through thy bosom makes me see thy heart.
Where is Demetrius? O, how fit a word
Is that vile name to perish on my sword!
Helena: Do not say so, Lysander; say not so.
What though he love your Hermia? Lord, what though?   115
Yet Hermia still loves you. Then be content.
Lysander: Content with Hermia? No! I do repent
The tedious minutes I with her have spent.
Not Hermia but Helena I love.

---

85 *owe:* Own.   92 *darkling:* In the dark.   93 *on thy peril:* I.e., on pain of danger to you
if you don't obey me and stay.   94 *fond:* Doting.   95 *my grace:* The favor I obtain.
96 *lies:* Dwells.   102–103 *no marvel . . . thus:* I.e., no wonder that Demetrius flies from me
as from a monster.   105 *compare:* Vie; *sphery eyne:* Eyes as bright as stars in their spheres.
110 *Transparent:* (1) Radiant (2) able to be seen through, lacking in deceit; *art:* Skill, magic
power.

Who will not change a raven for a dove?   120
The will° of man is by his reason swayed,
And reason says you are the worthier maid.
Things growing are not ripe until their season;
So I, being young, till now ripe not° to reason.
And, touching° now the point° of human skill,°   125
Reason becomes the marshal to my will
And leads me to your eyes, where I o'erlook°
Love's stories written in love's richest book.

Helena: Wherefore° was I to this keen mockery born?
When at your hands did I deserve this scorn?   130
Is't not enough, is't not enough, young man,
That I did never — no, nor never can —
Deserve a sweet look from Demetrius' eye,
But you must flout my insufficiency?
Good troth,° you do me wrong, good sooth,° you do,   135
In such disdainful manner me to woo.
But fare you well. Perforce I must confess
I thought you lord of° more true gentleness.°
O, that a lady, of° one man refused,
Should of another therefore be abused!°   *Exit.* 140

Lysander: She sees not Hermia. Hermia, sleep thou there,
And never mayst thou come Lysander near!
For as a surfeit of the sweetest things
The deepest loathing to the stomach brings,
Or as the heresies that men do leave   145
Are hated most of those they did deceive,°
So thou, my surfeit and my heresy,
Of all be hated, but the most of° me!
And, all my powers, address° your love and might
To honor Helen and to be her knight!   *Exit.* 150

Hermia [awaking]: Help me, Lysander, help me! Do thy best
To pluck this crawling serpent from my breast!
Ay me, for pity! What a dream was here!
Lysander, look how I do quake with fear.
Methought a serpent ate my heart away,   155
And you sat smiling at his cruel prey.°
Lysander! What, removed? Lysander! Lord!
What, out of hearing? Gone? No sound, no word?
Alack, where are you? Speak, an if° you hear;
Speak, of all loves!° I swoon almost with fear.   160
No? Then I well perceive you are not nigh.
Either death, or you, I'll find immediately.
                    Exit. [The sleeping Titania remains.]

---

121 *will:* Desire.   124 *ripe not:* (Am) not ripened.   125 *touching:* Reaching; *point:* Summit; *skill:* Judgment.   127 *o'erlook:* Read.   129 *Wherefore:* Why.   135 *Good troth, good sooth:* I.e., indeed, truly.   138 *lord of:* I.e., possessor of; *gentleness:* Courtesy.   139 *of:* By.   140 *abused:* Ill treated.   145–146 *as . . . deceive:* As renounced heresies are hated most by those persons who formerly were deceived by them.   148 *Of . . . of:* By . . . by.   149 *address:* Direct, apply.   156 *prey:* Act of preying.   159 *an if:* If.   160 *of all loves:* For love's sake.

[ACT III

SCENE I: *The wood.*]

Enter the clowns° [*Quince, Snug, Bottom, Flute, Snout, and Starveling*].

Bottom: Are we all met?

Quince: Pat, pat,° and here's a marvelous convenient place for our rehearsal. This green plot shall be our stage, this hawthorn brake° our tiring-house,° and we will do it in action as we will do it before the Duke.   5

Bottom: Peter Quince?

Quince: What sayest thou, bully° Bottom?

Bottom: There are things in this comedy of Pyramus and Thisbe that will never please. First, Pyramus must draw a sword to kill himself, which the ladies cannot abide. How answer you that?   10

Snout: By 'r lakin,° a parlous° fear.

Starveling: I believe we must leave the killing out, when all is done.°

Bottom: Not a whit. I have a device to make all well. Write me° a prologue, and let the prologue seem to say, we will do no harm with our swords, and that Pyramus is not killed indeed; and for the more better   15 assurance, tell them that I, Pyramus, am not Pyramus but Bottom the weaver. This will put them out of fear.

Quince: Well, we will have such a prologue, and it shall be written in eight and six.°

Bottom: No, make it two more: let it be written in eight and eight.   20

Snout: Will not the ladies be afeard of the lion?

Starveling: I fear it, I promise you.

Bottom: Masters, you ought to consider with yourself, to bring in — God shield us! — a lion among ladies° is a most dreadful thing. For there is not a more fearful° wildfowl than your lion living, and we ought to   25 look to 't.

Snout: Therefore another prologue must tell he is not a lion.

Bottom: Nay, you must name his name, and half his face must be seen through the lion's neck, and he himself must speak through, saying thus or to the same defect:° "Ladies," or "Fair ladies, I would wish   30 you," or "I would request you," or "I would entreat you, not to fear, not to tremble; my life for yours.° If you think I come hither as a lion, it were pity of my life.° No, I am no such thing; I am a man as other men are." And there indeed let him name his name, and tell them plainly he is Snug the joiner.   35

Act III, Scene I.   *clowns:* Rustics.   2 *Pat:* On the dot, punctually.   3 *brake:* Thicket. 4 *tiring-house:* Attiring area, hence backstage.   7 *bully:* I.e., worthy, jolly, fine fellow.   11 *By 'r lakin:* By our ladykin, i.e., the Virgin Mary; *parlous:* Perilous, alarming.   12 *when all is done:* I.e., when all is said and done.   13 *Write me:* I.e., write at my suggestion (*me* is used colloquially).   19 *eight and six:* Alternate lines of eight and six syllables, a common ballad measure.   24 *lion among ladies:* (A contemporary pamphlet tells how, at the christening in 1594 of Prince Henry, eldest son of King James VI of Scotland, later James I of England, a "blackamoor" instead of a lion drew the triumphal chariot, since the lion's presence might have "brought some fear to the nearest.")   25 *fearful:* Fear-inspiring.   30 *defect:* (Bottom's blunder for "effect.")   32 *my life for yours:* I.e., I pledge my life to make your lives safe. 33 *it were . . . life:* I.e., I should be sorry, by my life; or, my life would be endangered.

Quince: Well, it shall be so. But there is two hard things: that is, to bring
the moonlight into a chamber; for, you know, Pyramus and Thisbe
meet by moonlight.

Snout: Doth the moon shine that night we play our play?

Bottom: A calendar, a calendar! Look in the almanac. Find out moon-   40
shine, find out moonshine.   *[They consult an almanac.]*

Quince: Yes, it doth shine that night.

Bottom: Why then may you leave a casement of the great chamber window where we play open, and the moon may shine in at the casement.   45

Quince: Ay; or else one must come in with a bush of thorns° and a
lantern and say he comes to disfigure,° or to present,° the person of
Moonshine. Then there is another thing: we must have a wall in
the great chamber; for Pyramus and Thisbe, says the story, did talk
through the chink of a wall.   50

Snout: You can never bring in a wall. What say you, Bottom?

Bottom: Some man or other must present Wall. And let him have some
plaster, or some loam, or some roughcast° about him, to signify wall;
or let him hold his fingers thus, and through that cranny shall
Pyramus and Thisbe whisper.   55

Quince: If that may be, then all is well. Come, sit down, every mother's
son, and rehearse your parts. Pyramus, you begin. When you have spoken your speech, enter into that brake, and so everyone according to
his cue.

Enter Robin [Puck].

Puck [aside]: What hempen homespuns° have we swaggering here   60
So near the cradle° of the Fairy Queen?
What, a play toward?° I'll be an auditor;
An actor, too, perhaps, if I see cause.

Quince: Speak, Pyramus. Thisbe, stand forth.

Bottom [as Pyramus]: "Thisbe, the flowers of odious savors sweet —" 65

Quince: Odors, odors.

Bottom: " — Odors savors sweet;
So hath thy breath, my dearest Thisbe dear.
But hark, a voice! Stay thou but here awhile,
And by and by I will to thee appear."   *Exit.*   70

Puck: A stranger Pyramus than e'er played here.°   *[Exit.]*

Flute: Must I speak now?

Quince: Ay, marry, must you; for you must understand he goes but to see a
noise that he heard, and is to come again.

Flute [as Thisbe]: "Most radiant Pyramus, most lily-white of hue,   75
Of color like the red rose on triumphant° brier,

Most brisky juvenal° and eke° most lovely Jew,°
    As true as truest horse that yet would never tire.
I'll meet thee, Pyramus, at Ninny's tomb."
Quince: "Ninus'° tomb," man. Why, you must not speak that yet. That you   80
    answer to Pyramus. You speak all your part° at once, cues and all.
    Pyramus, enter. Your cue is past; it is "never tire."
Flute: O — "As true as truest horse, that yet would never tire."

    [Enter Puck, and Bottom as Pyramus with the ass head.°]

Bottom: "If I were fair,° Thisbe, I were° only thine."
Quince: O, monstrous! O, strange! We are haunted. Pray, masters! Fly, mas-   85
    ters! Help!   *[Exeunt Quince, Snug, Flute, Snout, and Starveling.]*
Puck: I'll follow you, I'll lead you about a round,°
    Thorough bog, thorough bush, thorough brake, thorough brier.
    Sometimes a horse I'll be, sometimes a hound,
        A hog, a headless bear, sometimes a fire;°   90
    And neigh, and bark, and grunt, and roar, and burn,
    Like horse, hound, hog, bear, fire, at every turn.   *Exit.*
Bottom: Why do they run away? This is a knavery of them to make me
    afeard.

    Enter Snout.

Snout: O Bottom, thou art changed! What do I see on thee?   95
Bottom: What do you see? You see an ass head of your own, do you?
                            [Exit Snout.]

    Enter Quince.

Quince: Bless thee, Bottom, bless thee! Thou art translated.°   *Exit.*
Bottom: I see their knavery. This is to make an ass of me, to fright me, if
    they could. But I will not stir from this place, do what they can. I will
    walk up and down here, and will sing, that they shall hear I am not   100
    afraid.   *[He sings.]*
        The ouzel cock° so black of hue,
            With orange-tawny bill,
        The throstle° with his note so true,
            The wren with little quill°—   105
Titania [awaking]: What angel wakes me from my flowery bed?
Bottom [sings]:
        The finch, the sparrow, and the lark,
            The plainsong° cuckoo gray,
        Whose note full many a man doth mark,

---

77 *brisky juvenal:* Lively youth; *eke:* Also; *Jew:* (An absurd repetition of the first syllable of *ju-venal* and an indication of how desperately Quince searches for his rhymes.)   80 *Ninus':* Mythical founder of Nineveh (whose wife, Semiramis, was supposed to have built the walls of Babylon where the story of Pyramus and Thisbe takes place).   81 *part:* (An actor's *part* was a script consisting only of his speeches and their cues.)   *with the ass head:* (This stage direction presumably refers to a standard stage property.)   84 *fair:* Handsome; *were:* Would be.   87 *about a round:* Roundabout.   90 *fire:* Will-o'-the-wisp.   97 *translated:* Transformed.   102 *ouzel cock:* Male blackbird.   104 *throstle:* Song thrush.   105 *quill:* (Literally, a reed pipe; hence, the bird's piping song.)   108 *plainsong:* Singing a melody without variations.

And dares not answer nay°—   110
For indeed, who would set his wit to° so foolish a bird? Who would
give a bird the lie,° though he cry "cuckoo" never so?°
Titania: I pray thee, gentle mortal, sing again.
Mine ear is much enamored of thy note;
So is mine eye enthrallèd to thy shape;   115
And thy fair virtue's force° perforce doth move me
On the first view to say, to swear, I love thee.
Bottom: Methinks, mistress, you should have little reason for that. And
yet, to say the truth, reason and love keep little company together
nowadays—the more the pity that some honest neighbors will not   120
make them friends. Nay, I can gleek° upon occasion.
Titania: Thou art as wise as thou art beautiful.
Bottom: Not so, neither. But if I had wit enough to get out of this wood,
I have enough to serve mine own turn.°
Titania: Out of this wood do not desire to go.   125
Thou shalt remain here, whether thou wilt or no.
I am a spirit of no common rate.°
The summer still doth tend upon my state,°
And I do love thee. Therefore, go with me.
I'll give thee fairies to attend on thee,   130
And they shall fetch thee jewels from the deep,
And sing while thou on pressèd flowers dost sleep.
And I will purge thy mortal grossness° so
That thou shalt like an airy spirit go.
Peaseblossom, Cobweb, Mote,° and Mustardseed!   135

Enter four Fairies [Peaseblossom, Cobweb, Mote, and Mustardseed].

Peaseblossom: Ready.
Cobweb: And I.
Mote: And I.
Mustardseed: And I.
All: Where shall we go?
Titania: Be kind and courteous to this gentleman.
Hop in his walks and gambol in his eyes;°
Feed him with apricots and dewberries,°   140
With purple grapes, green figs, and mulberries;
The honey bags steal from the humble-bees,
And for night tapers crop their waxen thighs
And light them at the fiery glowworms' eyes,
To have my love to bed and to arise;   145
And pluck the wings from painted butterflies

---

110 *dares... nay:* I.e., cannot deny that he is a cuckold.   111 *set his wit to:* Employ his intelligence to answer.   112 *give... lie:* Call the bird a liar; *never so:* Ever so much.   116 *thy...
force:* The power of your unblemished excellence.   121 *gleek:* Jest.   124 *serve... turn:*
Answer my purpose.   127 *rate:* Rank, value.   128 *still... state:* Always waits upon me as
a part of my royal retinue.   133 *mortal grossness:* Materiality (i.e., the corporeal nature of a
mortal being).   135 *Mote:* I.e., speck. (The two words *moth* and *mote* were pronounced
alike, and both meanings may be present.)   139 *in his eyes:* In his sight (i.e., before him).
140 *dewberries:* Blackberries.

   To fan the moonbeams from his sleeping eyes.
   Nod to him, elves, and do him courtesies.
Peaseblossom: Hail, mortal!
Cobweb: Hail!   150
Mote: Hail!
Mustardseed: Hail!
Bottom: I cry your worships mercy,° heartily. I beseech your worship's name.
Cobweb: Cobweb.
Bottom: I shall desire you of more acquaintance,° good Master Cobweb. If   155
   I cut my finger, I shall make bold with you.° — Your name, honest
   gentleman?
Peaseblossom: Peaseblossom.
Bottom: I pray you, commend me to Mistress Squash,° your mother,
   and to Master Peascod,° your father. Good Master Peaseblossom, I   160
   shall desire you of more acquaintance too. — Your name, I beseech
   you, sir?
Mustardseed: Mustardseed.
Bottom: Good Master Mustardseed, I know your patience° well. That same
   cowardly, giantlike ox-beef hath devoured many a gentleman of your   165
   house. I promise you, your kindred hath made my eyes water° ere now.
   I desire you of more acquaintance, good Master Mustardseed.
Titania: Come wait upon him; lead him to my bower.
   The moon methinks looks with a watery eye;
   And when she weeps,° weeps every little flower,   170
   Lamenting some enforcèd° chastity.
   Tie up my lover's tongue;° bring him silently.   *Exeunt.*

[SCENE II: *The wood.*]

   Enter [Oberon,] King of Fairies.

Oberon: I wonder if Titania be awaked;
   Then, what it was that next came in her eye,
   Which she must dote on in extremity.

   [Enter] Robin Goodfellow [Puck].

   Here comes my messenger. How now, mad spirit?
   What night-rule° now about this haunted° grove?   5
Puck: My mistress with a monster is in love.
   Near to her close° and consecrated bower,
   While she was in her dull° and sleeping hour,

---

153 *I cry...mercy:* I beg pardon of your worships (for presuming to ask a question).
155 *I...acquaintance:* I crave to be better acquainted with you.   155-156 *If...you:* (Cobwebs were used to stanch bleeding.)   159 *Squash:* Unripe pea pod.   160 *Peascod:* Ripe pea
pod.   164 *your patience:* What you have endured (mustard is eaten with beef).   166 *water:*
(1) Weep for sympathy (2) smart, sting.   170 *she weeps:* I.e., she causes dew.   171 *enforcèd:*
Forced, violated; or, possibly, constrained (since Titania at this moment is hardly concerned about chastity).   172 *Tie...tongue:* (Presumably Bottom is braying like an ass.)
Scene II.   5 *night-rule:* Diversion or misrule for the night; *haunted:* Much frequented.
7 *close:* Secret, private.   8 *dull:* Drowsy.

A crew of patches,° rude mechanicals,°
That work for bread upon Athenian stalls,°   10
Were met together to rehearse a play
Intended for great Theseus' nuptial day.
The shallowest thickskin of that barren sort,°
Who Pyramus presented,° in their sport
Forsook his scene° and entered in a brake.   15
When I did him at this advantage take,
An ass's noll° I fixèd on his head.
Anon his Thisbe must be answerèd,
And forth my mimic° comes. When they him spy,
As wild geese that the creeping fowler° eye,   20
Or russet-pated choughs,° many in sort,°
Rising and cawing at the gun's report,
Sever° themselves and madly sweep the sky,
So, at his sight, away his fellows fly;
And, at our stamp, here o'er and o'er one falls;   25
He "Murder!" cries and help from Athens calls.
Their sense thus weak, lost with their fears thus strong,
Made senseless things begin to do them wrong,
For briers and thorns at their apparel snatch;
Some, sleeves — some, hats; from yielders all things catch.°   30
I led them on in this distracted fear
And left sweet Pyramus translated there,
When in that moment, so it came to pass,
Titania waked and straightway loved an ass.
Oberon: This falls out better than I could devise.   35
    But hast thou yet latched° the Athenian's eyes
    With the love juice, as I did bid thee do?
Puck: I took him sleeping — that is finished too —
    And the Athenian woman by his side,
    That, when he waked, of force° she must be eyed.   40

    Enter Demetrius and Hermia.

Oberon: Stand close. This is the same Athenian.
Puck: This is the woman, but not this the man.   *[They stand aside.]*
Demetrius: O, why rebuke you him that loves you so?
    Lay breath so bitter on your bitter foe.
Hermia: Now I but chide; but I should use thee worse,   45
    For thou, I fear, hast given me cause to curse.
    If thou hast slain Lysander in his sleep,
    Being o'er shoes° in blood, plunge in the deep,
    And kill me too.
    The sun was not so true unto the day   50

---

9 *patches:* Clowns, fools; *rude mechanicals:* Ignorant artisans.   10 *stalls:* Market booths.
13 *barren sort:* Stupid company or crew.   14 *presented:* Acted.   15 *scene:* Playing area.
17 *noll:* Noddle, head.   19 *mimic:* Burlesque actor.   20 *fowler:* Hunter of game birds.
21 *russet-pated choughs:* Reddish brown or gray-headed jackdaws; *in sort:* In a flock.   23 *Sever:*
I.e., scatter.   30 *from . . . catch:* I.e., everything preys on those who yield to fear.   36 *latched:*
Fastened, snared.   40 *of force:* Perforce.   48 *Being o'er shoes:* Having waded in so far.

As he to me. Would he have stolen away
From sleeping Hermia? I'll believe as soon
This whole° earth may be bored, and that the moon
May through the center creep, and so displease
Her brother's° noontide with th' Antipodes.° 55
It cannot be but thou hast murdered him;
So should a murderer look, so dead,° so grim.

Demetrius: So should the murdered look, and so should I,
Pierced through the heart with your stern cruelty.
Yet you, the murderer, look as bright, as clear 60
As yonder Venus in her glimmering sphere.

Hermia: What's this to° my Lysander? Where is he?
Ah, good Demetrius, wilt thou give him me?

Demetrius: I had rather give his carcass to my hounds.

Hermia: Out, dog! Out, cur! Thou driv'st me past the bounds 65
Of maiden's patience. Hast thou slain him, then?
Henceforth be never numbered among men.
O, once° tell true, tell true, even for my sake:
Durst thou have looked upon him being awake?
And hast thou killed him sleeping? O brave touch!° 70
Could not a worm,° an adder, do so much?
An adder did it; for with doubler° tongue
Than thine, thou serpent, never adder stung.

Demetrius: You spend your passion° on a misprised mood.°
I am not guilty of Lysander's blood, 75
Nor is he dead, for aught that I can tell.

Hermia: I pray thee, tell me then that he is well.

Demetrius: And if I could, what should I get therefor?°

Hermia: A privilege never to see me more.
And from thy hated presence part I so. 80
See me no more, whether he be dead or no. *Exit.*

Demetrius: There is no following her in this fierce vein.
Here therefore for a while I will remain.
So sorrow's heaviness doth heavier° grow
For debt that bankrupt° sleep doth sorrow owe, 85
Which now in some slight measure it will pay,
If for his tender here I make some stay.° *[He] lie[s] down [and sleeps].*

Oberon: What hast thou done? Thou hast mistaken quite
And laid the love juice on some true love's sight.
Of thy misprision° must perforce ensue 90
Some true love turned, and not a false turned true.

---

53 *whole:* Solid. 55 *Her brother's:* I.e., the sun's; *th' Antipodes:* The people on the opposite side of the earth (where the moon is imagined bringing night to noontime). 57 *dead:* Deadly, or deathly pale. 62 *to:* To do with. 68 *once:* Once and for all. 70 *brave touch!:* Fine stroke! (said ironically). 71 *worm:* Serpent. 72 *doubler:* (1) More forked (2) more deceitful. 74 *passion:* Violent feelings; *misprised mood:* Anger based on misconception. 78 *therefor:* In return for that. 84 *heavier:* (1) Harder to bear (2) more drowsy. 85 *bankrupt:* (Demetrius is saying that his sleepiness adds to the weariness caused by sorrow.) 86–87 *Which . . . stay:* I.e., to a small extent, I will be able to "pay back" and hence find some relief from sorrow, if I pause here awhile (*make some stay*) while sleep "tenders" or offers itself by way of paying the debt owed to sorrow. 90 *misprision:* Mistake.

Puck: Then fate o'errules, that, one man holding troth,°
   A million fail, confounding oath on oath.°
Oberon: About the wood go swifter than the wind,
   And Helena of Athens look° thou find.   95
   All fancy-sick° she is and pale of cheer°
   With sighs of love, that cost the fresh blood° dear.
   By some illusion see thou bring her here.
   I'll charm his eyes against she do appear.°
Puck: I go, I go, look how I go,   100
   Swifter than arrow from the Tartar's bow.°   *[Exit.]*
Oberon [applying love juice to Demetrius' eyes]: Flower of this purple dye,
   Hit with Cupid's archery,
   Sink in apple° of his eye.
   When his love he doth espy,   105
   Let her shine as gloriously
   As the Venus of the sky.
   When thou wak'st, if she be by,
   Beg of her for remedy.

   Enter Puck.

Puck: Captain of our fairy band,   110
   Helena is here at hand,
   And the youth, mistook by me,
   Pleading for a lover's fee.°
   Shall we their fond pageant° see?
   Lord, what fools these mortals be!   115
Oberon: Stand aside. The noise they make
   Will cause Demetrius to awake.
Puck: Then will two at once woo one;
   That must needs be sport alone.°
   And those things do best please me   120
   That befall preposterously.°   *[They stand aside.]*

   Enter Lysander and Helena.

Lysander: Why should you think that I should woo in scorn?
   Scorn and derision never come in tears.
   Look when° I vow, I weep; and vows so born,
   In their nativity all truth appears.°   125
   How can these things in me seem scorn to you,
   Bearing the badge° of faith to prove them true?
Helena: You do advance° your cunning more and more.

---

92 *that . . . troth:* In that, for each man keeping true faith in love.   93 *confounding . . . oath:* I.e., breaking oath after oath.   95 *look:* I.e., be sure.   96 *fancy-sick:* Lovesick; *cheer:* Face. 97 *sighs . . . blood:* (An allusion to the physiological theory that each sigh costs the heart a drop of blood.)   99 *against . . . appear:* In anticipation of her coming.   101 *Tartar's bow:* (Tartars were famed for their skill with the bow.)   104 *apple:* Pupil.   113 *fee:* Privilege, reward.   114 *fond pageant:* Foolish spectacle.   119 *alone:* Unequaled.   121 *preposterously:* Out of the natural order.   124 *Look when:* Whenever.   124–125 *vows . . . appears:* I.e., vows made by one who is weeping give evidence thereby of their sincerity.   127 *badge:* Identifying device such as that worn on the servants' livery (here, his tears).   128 *advance:* Carry forward, display.

When truth kills truth,° O, devilish-holy fray!
These vows are Hermia's. Will you give her o'er?   130
   Weigh oath with oath, and you will nothing weigh.
Your vows to her and me, put in two scales,
Will even weigh, and both as light as tales.°
Lysander: I had no judgment when to her I swore.
Helena: Nor none, in my mind, now you give her o'er.   135
Lysander: Demetrius loves her, and he loves not you.
Demetrius [awaking]: O Helen, goddess, nymph, perfect, divine!
To what, my love, shall I compare thine eyne?
Crystal is muddy. O, how ripe in show°
Thy lips, those kissing cherries, tempting grow!   140
That pure congealèd white, high Taurus'° snow,
Fanned with the eastern wind, turns to a crow°
When thou hold'st up thy hand. O, let me kiss
This princess of pure white, this seal° of bliss!
Helena: O spite! O hell! I see you all are bent   145
To set against° me for your merriment.
If you were civil and knew courtesy,
You would not do me thus much injury.
Can you not hate me, as I know you do,
But you must join in souls° to mock me too?   150
If you were men, as men you are in show,
You would not use a gentle lady so —
To vow, and swear, and superpraise° my parts,°
When I am sure you hate me with your hearts.
You both are rivals, and love Hermia,   155
And now both rivals to mock Helena.
A trim° exploit, a manly enterprise,
To conjure tears up in a poor maid's eyes
With your derision! None of noble sort°
Would so offend a virgin and extort°   160
A poor soul's patience, all to make you sport.
Lysander: You are unkind, Demetrius. Be not so.
For you love Hermia; this you know I know.
And here, with all good will, with all my heart,
In Hermia's love I yield you up my part;   165
And yours of Helena to me bequeath,
Whom I do love, and will do till my death.
Helena: Never did mockers waste more idle breath.
Demetrius: Lysander, keep thy Hermia; I will none.°
If e'er I loved her, all that love is gone.   170
My heart to her but as guestwise sojourned,°

129 *truth kills truth:* I.e., one of Lysander's vows must invalidate the other.   133 *tales:* Lies.
139 *show:* Appearance.   141 *Taurus:* A lofty mountain range in Asia Minor.   142 *turns to a crow:* I.e., seems black by contrast.   144 *seal:* Pledge.   146 *set against:* Attack.   150 *in souls:* I.e., heart and soul.   153 *superpraise:* Overpraise; *parts:* Qualities.   157 *trim:* Pretty, fine (said ironically).   159 *sort:* Character, quality.   160 *extort:* Twist, torture.   169 *will none:* I.e., want no part of her.   171 *to . . . sojourned:* Only visited with her.

And now to Helen is it home returned,
   There to remain.
Lysander: Helen, it is not so.
Demetrius: Disparage not the faith thou dost not know,
   Lest, to thy peril, thou aby° it dear.   175
   Look where thy love comes; yonder is thy dear.

   Enter Hermia.

Hermia: Dark night, that from the eye his° function takes,
   The ear more quick of apprehension makes;
   Wherein it doth impair the seeing sense,
   It pays the hearing double recompense.   180
   Thou art not by mine eye, Lysander, found;
   Mine ear, I thank it, brought me to thy sound.
   But why unkindly didst thou leave me so?
Lysander: Why should he stay, whom love doth press to go?
Hermia: What love could press Lysander from my side?   185
Lysander: Lysander's love, that would not let him bide —
   Fair Helena, who more engilds° the night
   Than all yon fiery oes° and eyes of light.
   Why seek'st thou me? Could not this make thee know
   The hate I bear thee made me leave thee so?   190
Hermia: You speak not as you think. It cannot be.
Helena: Lo, she is one of this confederacy!
   Now I perceive they have conjoined all three
   To fashion this false sport, in spite of me.°
   Injurious Hermia, most ungrateful maid!   195
   Have you conspired, have you with these contrived°
   To bait° me with this foul derision?
   Is all the counsel° that we two have shared —
   The sisters' vows, the hours that we have spent
   When we have chid the hasty-footed time   200
   For parting us — O, is all forgot?
   All schooldays' friendship, childhood innocence?
   We, Hermia, like two artificial° gods
   Have with our needles created both one flower,
   Both on one sampler, sitting on one cushion,   205
   Both warbling of one song, both in one key,
   As if our hands, our sides, voices, and minds
   Had been incorporate.° So we grew together,
   Like to a double cherry, seeming parted,
   But yet an union in partition,   210
   Two lovely° berries molded on one stem;
   So, with two seeming bodies but one heart,
   Two of the first, like coats in heraldry,

---

175 *aby:* Pay for.   177 *his:* Its.   187 *engilds:* Gilds, brightens with a golden light.   188 *oes:* Spangles (here, stars).   194 *in spite of me:* To vex me.   196 *contrived:* Plotted.   197 *bait:* Torment, as one sets on dogs to bait a bear.   198 *counsel:* Confidential talk.   203 *artificial:* Skilled in art or creation.   208 *incorporate:* Of one body.   211 *lovely:* Loving.

Due but to one and crownèd with one crest.°
And will you rend our ancient love asunder,   215
To join with men in scorning your poor friend?
It is not friendly, 'tis not maidenly.
Our sex, as well as I, may chide you for it,
Though I alone do feel the injury.

Hermia: I am amazèd at your passionate words.   220
    I scorn you not. It seems that you scorn me.

Helena: Have you not set Lysander, as in scorn,
    To follow me and praise my eyes and face?
    And made your other love, Demetrius,
    Who even but now did spurn me with his foot,   225
    To call me goddess, nymph, divine, and rare,
    Precious, celestial? Wherefore speaks he this
    To her he hates? And wherefore doth Lysander
    Deny your love, so rich within his soul,
    And tender° me, forsooth, affection,   230
    But by your setting on, by your consent?
    What though I be not so in grace° as you,
    So hung upon with love, so fortunate,
    But miserable most, to love unloved?
    This you should pity rather than despise.   235

Hermia: I understand not what you mean by this.

Helena: Ay, do! Persever, counterfeit sad° looks,
    Make mouths° upon° me when I turn my back,
    Wink each at other, hold the sweet jest up.°
    This sport, well carried,° shall be chronicled.   240
    If you have any pity, grace, or manners,
    You would not make me such an argument.°
    But fare ye well. 'Tis partly my own fault,
    Which death, or absence, soon shall remedy.

Lysander: Stay, gentle Helena; hear my excuse,   245
    My love, my life, my soul, fair Helena!

Helena: O excellent!

Hermia [to Lysander]: Sweet, do not scorn her so.

Demetrius [to Lysander]: If she cannot entreat,° I can compel.

Lysander: Thou canst compel no more than she entreat.   250
    Thy threats have no more strength than her weak prayers.
    Helen, I love thee, by my life, I do!
    I swear by that which I will lose for thee,
    To prove him false that says I love thee not.

Demetrius [to Helena]: I say I love thee more than he can do.   255

Lysander: If thou say so, withdraw, and prove it too.°

213–214 *Two . . . crest:* I.e., we have two separate bodies, just as a coat of arms in heraldry can
be represented twice on a shield but surmounted by a single crest.   230 *tender:* Offer.
232 *grace:* Favor.   237 *sad:* Grave, serious.   238 *mouths:* I.e., mows, faces, grimaces;
upon: At.   239 *hold . . . up:* Keep up the joke.   240 *carried:* Managed.   242 *argument:*
Subject for a jest.   249 *entreat:* I.e., succeed by entreaty.   256 *withdraw . . . too:* I.e., withdraw with me and prove your claim in a duel (the two gentlemen are armed).

Demetrius: Quick, come!
Hermia: Lysander, whereto tends all this?
Lysander: Away, you Ethiope!°   *[He tries to break away from Hermia.]*
Demetrius: No, no; he'll
     Seem to break loose; take on as° you would follow,
     But yet come not. You are a tame man. Go!   260
Lysander [to Hermia]: Hang off,° thou cat, thou burr! Vile thing, let loose,
     Or I will shake thee from me like a serpent!
Hermia: Why are you grown so rude? What change is this,
     Sweet love?
Lysander: Thy love? Out, tawny Tartar, out!
     Out, loathèd med'cine!° O hated potion, hence!   265
Hermia: Do you not jest?
Helena: Yes, sooth,° and so do you.
Lysander: Demetrius, I will keep my word with thee.
Demetrius: I would I had your bond, for I perceive
     A weak bond° holds you. I'll not trust your word.
Lysander: What, should I hurt her, strike her, kill her dead?   270
     Although I hate her, I'll not harm her so.
Hermia: What, can you do me greater harm than hate?
     Hate me? Wherefore? O me, what news,° my love?
     Am not I Hermia? Are not you Lysander?
     I am as fair now as I was erewhile.°   275
     Since night you loved me; yet since night you left me.
     Why, then you left me — O, the gods forbid! —
     In earnest, shall I say?
Lysander: Ay, by my life!
     And never did desire to see thee more.
     Therefore be out of hope, of question, of doubt;   280
     Be certain, nothing truer. 'Tis no jest
     That I do hate thee and love Helena.
Hermia [to Helena]: O me! You juggler! You cankerblossom!°
     You thief of love! What, have you come by night
     And stol'n my love's heart from him?
Helena: Fine, i' faith!   285
     Have you no modesty, no maiden shame,
     No touch of bashfulness? What, will you tear
     Impatient answers from my gentle tongue?
     Fie, fie! You counterfeit, you puppet,° you!
Hermia: "Puppet"? Why, so!° Ay, that way goes the game.   290
     Now I perceive that she hath made compare
     Between our statures; she hath urged her height,

---

258 *Ethiope:* (Referring to Hermia's relatively dark hair and complexion; see also *tawny Tartar* six lines later.)   259 *take on as:* Act as if, make a fuss as if.   261 *Hang off:* Let go.   265 *med'cine:* I.e., poison.   266 *sooth:* Truly.   269 *weak bond:* I.e., Hermia's arm (with a pun on *bond,* "oath," in the previous line).   273 *what news:* What is the matter.   275 *erewhile:* Just now.   283 *cankerblossom:* Worm that destroys the flower bud, or wild rose.   289 *puppet:* (1) Counterfeit (2) dwarfish woman (in reference to Hermia's smaller stature).   290 *Why, so:* I.e., Oh, so that's how it is.

And with her personage, her tall personage,
Her height, forsooth, she hath prevailed with him.
And are you grown so high in his esteem   295
Because I am so dwarfish and so low?
How low am I, thou painted maypole? Speak!
How low am I? I am not yet so low
But that my nails can reach unto thine eyes.

[She flails at Helena but is restrained.]

Helena: I pray you, though you mock me, gentlemen,   300
Let her not hurt me. I was never curst;°
I have no gift at all in shrewishness;
I am a right° maid for my cowardice.
Let her not strike me. You perhaps may think,
Because she is something° lower than myself,   305
That I can match her.

Hermia: Lower? Hark, again!

Helena: Good Hermia, do not be so bitter with me.
I evermore did love you, Hermia,
Did ever keep your counsels, never wronged you,
Save that, in love unto Demetrius,   310
I told him of your stealth° unto this wood.
He followed you; for love I followed him.
But he hath chid me hence° and threatened me
To strike me, spurn me, nay, to kill me too.
And now, so° you will let me quiet go,   315
To Athens will I bear my folly back
And follow you no further. Let me go.
You see how simple and how fond° I am.

Hermia: Why, get you gone. Who is't that hinders you?

Helena: A foolish heart, that I leave here behind.   320

Hermia: What, with Lysander?

Helena: With Demetrius.

Lysander: Be not afraid; she shall not harm thee, Helena.

Demetrius: No, sir, she shall not, though you take her part.

Helena: O, when she is angry, she is keen° and shrewd.°
She was a vixen when she went to school;   325
And though she be but little, she is fierce.

Hermia: "Little" again? Nothing but "low" and "little"?
Why will you suffer her to flout me thus?
Let me come to her.

Lysander: Get you gone, you dwarf!
You minimus,° of hindering knotgrass° made!   330
You bead, you acorn!

Demetrius: You are too officious
In her behalf that scorns your services.
Let her alone. Speak not of Helena;

---

301 *curst:* Shrewish.   303 *right:* True.   305 *something:* Somewhat.   311 *stealth:* Stealing away.   313 *chid me hence:* Driven me away with his scolding.   315 *so:* If only.   318 *fond:* Foolish.   324 *keen:* Fierce, cruel; *shrewd:* Shrewish.   330 *minimus:* Diminutive creature; *knotgrass:* A weed, an infusion of which was thought to stunt the growth.

Take not her part. For, if thou dost intend°
Never so little show of love to her,   335
Thou shalt aby° it.
Lysander: Now she holds me not.
Now follow, if thou dar'st, to try whose right,
Of thine or mine, is most in Helena.   *[Exit.]*
Demetrius: Follow? Nay, I'll go with thee, cheek by jowl.°
                              [Exit, following Lysander.]
Hermia: You, mistress, all this coil° is 'long of° you.   340
Nay, go not back.°
Helena: I will not trust you, I,
Nor longer stay in your curst company.
Your hands than mine are quicker for a fray;
My legs are longer, though, to run away.   *[Exit.]*
Hermia: I am amazed and know not what to say.   *Exit.* 345

[Oberon and Puck come forward.]

Oberon: This is thy negligence. Still thou mistak'st,
Or else committ'st thy knaveries willfully.
Puck: Believe me, king of shadows, I mistook.
Did not you tell me I should know the man
By the Athenian garments he had on?   350
And so far blameless proves my enterprise
That I have 'nointed an Athenian's eyes;
And so far° am I glad it so did sort,°
As° this their jangling I esteem a sport.
Oberon: Thou seest these lovers seek a place to fight.   355
Hie° therefore, Robin, overcast the night;
The starry welkin° cover thou anon
With drooping fog as black as Acheron,°
And lead these testy rivals so astray
As° one come not within another's way.   360
Like to Lysander sometimes frame thy tongue,
Then stir Demetrius up with bitter wrong;°
And sometimes rail thou like Demetrius.
And from each other look thou lead them thus,
Till o'er their brows death-counterfeiting sleep   365
With leaden legs and batty° wings doth creep.
Then crush this herb° into Lysander's eye,   *[giving herb]*
Whose liquor hath this virtuous° property,
To take from thence all error with his° might
And make his eyeballs roll with wonted° sight.   370
When they next wake, all this derision°
Shall seem a dream and fruitless vision,

334 *intend:* Give sign of.   336 *aby:* Pay for.   339 *cheek by jowl:* I.e., side by side.   340 *coil:* Turmoil, dissension; *'long of:* On account of.   341 *go not back:* I.e., don't retreat (Hermia is again proposing a flight).   353 *so far:* At least to this extent; *sort:* Turn out.   354 *As:* In that.   356 *Hie:* Hasten.   357 *welkin:* Sky.   358 *Acheron:* River of Hades (here representing Hades itself).   360 *As:* That.   362 *wrong:* Insults.   366 *batty:* Batlike.   367 *this herb:* I.e., the antidote (mentioned in II.i.184) to love-in-idleness.   368 *virtuous:* Efficacious.   369 *his:* Its.   370 *wonted:* Accustomed.   371 *derision:* Laughable business.

And back to Athens shall the lovers wend
With league whose date° till death shall never end.
Whiles I in this affair do thee employ,   375
I'll to my queen and beg her Indian boy;
And then I will her charmèd eye release
From monster's view, and all things shall be peace.
Puck: My fairy lord, this must be done with haste,
For night's swift dragons° cut the clouds full fast,   380
And yonder shines Aurora's harbinger,°
At whose approach ghosts, wand'ring here and there,
Troop home to churchyards. Damnèd spirits all,
That in crossways and floods have burial,°
Already to their wormy beds are gone.   385
For fear lest day should look their shames upon,
They willfully themselves exile from light
And must for aye° consort with black-browed night.
Oberon: But we are spirits of another sort.
I with the Morning's love° have oft made sport,   390
And, like a forester,° the groves may tread
Even till the eastern gate, all fiery red,
Opening on Neptune with fair blessèd beams,
Turns into yellow gold his salt green streams.
But notwithstanding, haste, make no delay.   395
We may effect this business yet ere day.   *[Exit.]*
Puck: Up and down, up and down,
I will lead them up and down.
I am feared in field and town.
Goblin,° lead them up and down.   400
Here comes one.

Enter Lysander.

Lysander: Where art thou, proud Demetrius? Speak thou now.
Puck [mimicking Demetrius]: Here, villain, drawn° and ready. Where art
thou?
Lysander: I will be with thee straight.°
Puck: Follow me, then,
To plainer° ground.   *[Lysander wanders about,° following the voice.]*

Enter Demetrius.

Demetrius: Lysander! Speak again!   405
Thou runaway, thou coward, art thou fled?
Speak! In some bush? Where dost thou hide thy head?

---

374 *date:* Term of existence.   380 *dragons:* (Supposed by Shakespeare to be yoked to the car
of the goddess of night or the moon.)   381 *Aurora's harbinger:* The morning star, precursor
of dawn.   384 *crossways . . . burial:* (Those who had committed suicide were buried at crossways, with a stake driven through them; those who intentionally or accidentally drowned
[in *floods* or deep water] would be condemned to wander disconsolately for lack of burial
rights.)   388 *for aye:* Forever.   390 *the Morning's love:* Cephalus, a beautiful youth beloved
by Aurora; or perhaps the goddess of the dawn herself.   391 *forester:* Keeper of a royal forest.   400 *Goblin:* Hobgoblin (Puck refers to himself).   403 *drawn:* With drawn sword.
404 *straight:* Immediately.   405 *plainer:* More open.   *Lysander wanders about:* (Lysander
may exit here, but perhaps not; neither exit nor reentrance is indicated in the early texts.)

Puck [mimicking Lysander]: Thou coward, art thou bragging to the stars,
  Telling the bushes that thou look'st for wars,
  And wilt not come? Come, recreant;° come, thou child,   410
  I'll whip thee with a rod. He is defiled
  That draws a sword on thee.
Demetrius: Yea, art thou there?
Puck: Follow my voice. We'll try° no manhood here.   *Exeunt.*

  [Lysander returns.]

Lysander: He goes before me and still dares me on.
  When I come where he calls, then he is gone.   415
  The villain is much lighter-heeled than I.
  I followed fast, but faster he did fly,
  That fallen am I in dark uneven way,
  And here will rest me. *[He lies down.]* Come, thou gentle day!
  For if but once thou show me thy gray light,   420
  I'll find Demetrius and revenge this spite. *[He sleeps.]*

  [Enter] Robin [Puck] and Demetrius.

Puck: Ho, ho, ho! Coward, why com'st thou not?
Demetrius: Abide° me, if thou dar'st; for well I wot°
  Thou runn'st before me, shifting every place,
  And dar'st not stand nor look me in the face.   425
  Where art thou now?
Puck: Come hither. I am here.
Demetrius: Nay, then, thou mock'st me. Thou shalt buy° this dear,°
  If ever I thy face by daylight see.
  Now go thy way. Faintness constraineth me
  To measure out my length on this cold bed.   430
  By day's approach look to be visited.   *[He lies down and sleeps.]*

  Enter Helena.

Helena: O weary night, O long and tedious night,
  Abate° thy hours! Shine comforts from the east,
  That I may back to Athens by daylight
  From these that my poor company detest;   435
  And sleep, that sometimes shuts up sorrow's eye,
  Steal me awhile from mine own company.   *[She lies down and] sleep[s].*
Puck: Yet but three? Come one more;
  Two of both kinds makes up four.
  Here she comes, curst° and sad.   440
  Cupid is a knavish lad,
  Thus to make poor females mad.

  [Enter Hermia.]

Hermia: Never so weary, never so in woe,
  Bedabbled with the dew and torn with briers,
  I can no further crawl, no further go;   445
  My legs can keep no pace with my desires.

---

410 *recreant:* Cowardly wretch.   413 *try:* Test.   423 *Abide:* Confront, face; *wot:* know.
427 *buy:* Aby, pay for; *dear:* Dearly.   433 *Abate:* Lessen, shorten.   440 *curst:* Ill-tempered.

Here will I rest me till the break of day.
Heavens shield Lysander, if they mean a fray! *[She lies down and sleeps.]*
Puck: On the ground
    Sleep sound.   450
    I'll apply
    To your eye,
    Gentle lover, remedy.   *[He squeezes the juice on Lysander's eyes.]*
    When thou wak'st,
    Thou tak'st   455
    True delight
    In the sight
Of thy former lady's eye;
And the country proverb known,
That every man should take his own,   460
In your waking shall be shown:
    Jack shall have Jill;°
    Naught shall go ill;
The man shall have his mare again, and all shall be well.
[Exit. The four sleeping lovers remain.]

[ACT IV

SCENE I: *The wood. The lovers are still asleep onstage.*]

*Enter [Titania,] Queen of Fairies, and [Bottom the] clown, and Fairies; and
[Oberon,] the King, behind them.*

Titania: Come, sit thee down upon this flowery bed,
    While I thy amiable° cheeks do coy,°
And stick muskroses in thy sleek smooth head,
    And kiss thy fair large ears, my gentle joy.   *[They recline.]*
Bottom: Where's Peaseblossom?   5
Peaseblossom: Ready.
Bottom: Scratch my head, Peaseblossom. Where's Monsieur Cobweb?
Cobweb: Ready.
Bottom: Monsieur Cobweb, good monsieur, get you your weapons in your
    hand, and kill me a red-lipped humble-bee on the top of a thistle; and,   10
    good monsieur, bring me the honey bag. Do not fret yourself too
    much in the action, monsieur; and, good monsieur, have a care the
    honey bag break not. I would be loath to have you overflown with a
    honey bag, signor. *[Exit Cobweb.]* Where's Monsieur Mustardseed?
Mustardseed: Ready.   15
Bottom: Give me your neaf,° Monsieur Mustardseed. Pray you, leave your
    courtesy,° good monsieur.
Mustardseed: What's your will?

---

462 *Jack shall have Jill:* (Proverbial for "boy gets girl.")   **Act IV, Scene I.**   2 *amiable:*
Lovely; *coy:* Caress.   16 *neaf:* Fist.   16–17 *leave your courtesy:* I.e., stop bowing, or put on
your hat.

Bottom: Nothing, good monsieur, but to help Cavalery° Cobweb° to
  scratch. I must to the barber's, monsieur, for methinks I am mar-   20
  velous hairy about the face; and I am such a tender ass, if my hair do
  but tickle me I must scratch.
Titania: What, wilt thou hear some music, my sweet love?
Bottom: I have a reasonable good ear in music. Let's have the tongs and
  the bones.°   *[Music: tongs, rural music.°]*   25
Titania: Or say, sweet love, what thou desirest to eat.
Bottom: Truly, a peck of provender.° I could munch your good dry oats.
  Methinks I have a great desire to a bottle° of hay. Good hay, sweet hay,
  hath no fellow.°
Titania: I have a venturous fairy that shall seek   30
  The squirrel's hoard, and fetch thee new nuts.
Bottom: I had rather have a handful or two of dried peas. But, I pray you,
  let none of your people stir° me. I have an exposition of° sleep come
  upon me.
Titania: Sleep thou, and I will wind thee in my arms.   35
  Fairies, begone, and be all ways° away.   *[Exeunt Fairies.]*
  So doth the woodbine° the sweet honeysuckle
  Gently entwist; the female ivy so
  Enrings the barky fingers of the elm.
  O, how I love thee! How I dote on thee!   *[They sleep.]*   40

  Enter Robin Goodfellow [Puck].

Oberon [coming forward]: Welcome, good Robin. Seest thou this sweet sight?
  Her dotage now I do begin to pity.
  For, meeting her of late behind the wood
  Seeking sweet favors° for this hateful fool,
  I did upbraid her and fall out with her.   45
  For she his hairy temples then had rounded
  With coronet of fresh and fragrant flowers;
  And that same dew, which sometime° on the buds
  Was wont to swell like round and orient pearls,°
  Stood now within the pretty flowerets' eyes   50
  Like tears that did their own disgrace bewail.
  When I had at my pleasure taunted her,
  And she in mild terms begged my patience,
  I then did ask of her her changeling child,
  Which straight she gave me, and her fairy sent   55
  To bear him to my bower in Fairyland.
  And, now I have the boy, I will undo

19 *Cavalery:* Cavalier (form of address for a gentleman); *Cobweb:* (Seemingly an error, since
Cobweb has been sent to bring honey, while Peaseblossom has been asked to scratch.)
24–25 *tongs . . . bones:* Instruments for rustic music (the tongs were played like a triangle,
whereas the bones were held between the fingers and used as clappers).   *Music . . . music:*
(This stage direction is added from the Folio.)   27 *peck of provender:* One-quarter bushel
of grain.   28 *bottle:* Bundle.   29 *fellow:* Equal.   33 *stir:* Disturb; *exposition of:* (Bottom's phrase for "disposition to.")   36 *all ways:* In all directions.   37 *woodbine:*
Bindweed, a climbing plant that twines in the opposite direction from that of honeysuckle.
44 *favors:* I.e., gifts of flowers.   48 *sometime:* Formerly.   49 *orient pearls:* I.e., the most
beautiful of all pearls, those coming from the Orient.

This hateful imperfection of her eyes.
And, gentle Puck, take this transformèd scalp
From off the head of this Athenian swain,   60
That he, awaking when the other° do,
May all to Athens back again repair,°
And think no more of this night's accidents
But as the fierce vexation of a dream.
But first I will release the Fairy Queen.   65
                 [He squeezes an herb on her eyes.]
       Be as thou wast wont to be;
       See as thou wast wont to see.
       Dian's bud° o'er Cupid's flower
       Hath such force and blessèd power.
       Now, my Titania, wake you, my sweet queen.   70
Titania [awaking]: My Oberon! What visions have I seen!
Methought I was enamored of an ass.
Oberon: There lies your love.
Titania: How came these things to pass?
O, how mine eyes do loathe his visage now!
Oberon: Silence awhile. Robin, take off this head.   75
Titania, music call, and strike more dead
Than common sleep of all these five° the sense.
Titania: Music, ho! Music, such as charmeth° sleep!   *[Music.]*
Puck [removing the ass head]: Now, when thou wak'st, with thine own fool's
     eyes peep.
Oberon: Sound, music! Come, my queen, take hands with me,   80
And rock the ground whereon these sleepers be.   *[They dance.]*
Now thou and I are new in amity,
And will tomorrow midnight solemnly°
Dance in Duke Theseus' house triumphantly,
And bless it to all fair prosperity.   85
There shall the pairs of faithful lovers be
Wedded, with Theseus, all in jollity.
Puck: Fairy King, attend, and mark:
       I do hear the morning lark.
Oberon: Then, my queen, in silence sad,°   90
       Trip we after night's shade.
       We the globe can compass soon,
       Swifter than the wandering moon.
Titania: Come, my lord, and in our flight
       Tell me how it came this night   95
       That I sleeping here was found
       With these mortals on the ground.
          Exeunt [Oberon, Titania, and Puck]. Wind horn [within].

---

61 *other:* Others.   62 *repair:* Return.   68 *Dian's bud:* (Perhaps the flower of the *agnus castus* or chaste-tree, supposed to preserve chastity; or perhaps referring simply to Oberon's herb by which he can undo the effects of "Cupid's flower," the love-in-idleness of II.i.166–168.) 77 *these five:* I.e., the four lovers and Bottom.   78 *charmeth:* Brings about, as though by a charm.   83 *solemnly:* Ceremoniously.   90 *sad:* Sober.

Enter Theseus and all his train; [Hippolyta, Egeus].

Theseus: Go, one of you, find out the forester,
For now our observation° is performed;
And since we have the vaward° of the day,   100
My love shall hear the music of my hounds.
Uncouple° in the western valley; let them go.
Dispatch, I say, and find the forester.   *[Exit an Attendant.]*
We will, fair queen, up to the mountain's top
And mark the musical confusion   105
Of hounds and echo in conjunction.

Hippolyta: I was with Hercules and Cadmus° once
When in a wood of Crete they bayed° the bear
With hounds of Sparta.° Never did I hear
Such gallant chiding;° for, besides the groves,   110
The skies, the fountains, every region near
Seemed all one mutual cry. I never heard
So musical a discord, such sweet thunder.

Theseus: My hounds are bred out of the Spartan kind,°
So flewed,° so sanded,° and their heads are hung   115
With ears that sweep away the morning dew;
Crook-kneed, and dewlapped° like Thessalian bulls;
Slow in pursuit, but matched in mouth like bells,
Each under each.° A cry° more tunable°
Was never holloed to nor cheered° with horn   120
In Crete, in Sparta, nor in Thessaly.
Judge when you hear. *[He sees the sleepers.]* But soft!° What nymphs
are these?

Egeus: My lord, this is my daughter here asleep,
And this Lysander; this Demetrius is;
This Helena, old Nedar's Helena.   125
I wonder of° their being here together.

Theseus: No doubt they rose up early to observe
The rite of May, and hearing our intent,
Came here in grace of our solemnity.°
But speak, Egeus. Is not this the day   130
That Hermia should give answer of her choice?

Egeus: It is, my lord.

Theseus: Go bid the huntsmen wake them with their horns.
                                      [Exit an Attendant.]

Shout within. Wind horns. They all start up.

---

99 *observation:* I.e., observance to a morn of May (I.i.167).   100 *vaward:* Vanguard, i.e., earliest part.   102 *Uncouple:* Set free for the hunt.   107 *Cadmus:* Mythical founder of Thebes. (This story about him is unknown.)   108 *bayed:* Brought to bay.   109 *hounds of Sparta:* (A breed famous in antiquity for their hunting skill.)   110 *chiding:* I.e., yelping.   114 *kind:* Strain, breed.   115 *So flewed:* Similarly having large hanging chaps or fleshy covering of the jaw; *sanded:* Of sandy color.   117 *dewlapped:* Having pendulous folds of skin under the neck.   118–119 *matched . . . each:* I.e., harmoniously matched in their various cries like a set of bells, from treble down to bass; *cry:* Pack of hounds; *tunable:* Well tuned, melodious.   120 *cheered:* Encouraged.   122 *soft:* I.e., gently, wait a minute.   126 *wonder of:* Wonder at.   129 *in . . . solemnity:* In honor of our wedding ceremony.

Good morrow, friends. Saint Valentine° is past.
Begin these woodbirds but to couple now?   135
Lysander: Pardon, my lord.   *[They kneel.]*
Theseus: I pray you all, stand up.   *[They stand.]*
    I know you two are rival enemies;
    How comes this gentle concord in the world,
    That hatred is so far from jealousy°
    To sleep by hate and fear no enmity?   140
Lysander: My lord, I shall reply amazedly,
    Half sleep, half waking; but as yet, I swear,
    I cannot truly say how I came here.
    But, as I think — for truly would I speak,
    And now I do bethink me, so it is —   145
    I came with Hermia hither. Our intent
    Was to be gone from Athens, where° we might,
    Without° the peril of the Athenian law —
Egeus: Enough, enough, my lord; you have enough.
    I beg the law, the law, upon his head.   150
    They would have stol'n away; they would, Demetrius,
    Thereby to have defeated° you and me,
    You of your wife and me of my consent,
    Of my consent that she should be your wife.
Demetrius: My lord, fair Helen told me of their stealth,   155
    Of this their purpose hither° to this wood,
    And I in fury hither followed them,
    Fair Helena in fancy° following me.
    But, my good lord, I wot not by what power —
    But by some power it is — my love to Hermia,   160
    Melted as the snow, seems to me now
    As the remembrance of an idle gaud°
    Which in my childhood I did dote upon;
    And all the faith, the virtue of my heart,
    The object and the pleasure of mine eye,   165
    Is only Helena. To her, my lord,
    Was I betrothed ere I saw Hermia,
    But like a sickness did I loathe this food;
    But, as in health, come to my natural taste,
    Now I do wish it, love it, long for it,   170
    And will forevermore be true to it.
Theseus: Fair lovers, you are fortunately met.
    Of this discourse we more will hear anon.
    Egeus, I will overbear your will;
    For in the temple, by and by, with us   175
    These couples shall eternally be knit.
    And, for° the morning now is something° worn,
    Our purposed hunting shall be set aside.

---

134 *Saint Valentine:* (Birds were supposed to choose their mates on Saint Valentine's Day.)
139 *jealousy:* Suspicion.   147 *where:* Wherever; or, to where.   148 *Without:* Outside of,
beyond.   152 *defeated:* Defrauded.   156 *hither:* In coming hither.   158 *in fancy:* Driven
by love.   162 *idle gaud:* Worthless trinket.   177 *for:* Since; *something:* Somewhat.

Away with us to Athens. Three and three,
We'll hold a feast in great solemnity.°   180
Come Hippolyta.   *[Exeunt Theseus, Hippolyta, Egeus, and train.]*
Demetrius: These things seem small and undistinguishable,
    Like far-off mountains turnèd into clouds.
Hermia: Methinks I see these things with parted° eye,
    When everything seems double.
Helena: So methinks;   185
    And I have found Demetrius like a jewel,
    Mine own, and not mine own.°
Demetrius: Are you sure
    That we are awake? It seems to me
    That yet we sleep, we dream. Do not you think
    The Duke was here, and bid us follow him?   190
Hermia: Yea, and my father.
Helena: And Hippolyta.
Lysander: And he did bid us follow to the temple.
Demetrius: Why, then, we are awake. Let's follow him,
    And by the way let us recount our dreams.   *[Exeunt the lovers.]*
Bottom [awaking]: When my cue comes, call me, and I will answer. My   195
    next is "Most fair Pyramus." Heigh-ho! Peter Quince! Flute, the bel-
    lows mender! Snout, the tinker! Starveling! God's° my life, stolen
    hence and left me asleep! I have had a most rare vision. I have had a
    dream, past the wit of man to say what dream it was. Man is but an
    ass if he go about° to expound this dream. Methought I was — there is   200
    no man can tell what. Methought I was — and methought I had — but
    man is but a patched° fool if he will offer° to say what methought I
    had. The eye of man hath not heard, the ear of man hath not seen,
    man's hand is not able to taste, his tongue to conceive, nor his heart
    to report° what my dream was. I will get Peter Quince to write a bal-   205
    lad° of this dream. It shall be called "Bottom's Dream," because it
    hath no bottom;° and I will sing it in the latter end of a play, before
    the Duke. Peradventure, to make it the more gracious, I shall sing it
    at her° death.   *[Exit.]*

[SCENE II: *Athens.*]

    Enter Quince, Flute, [Snout, and Starveling].

Quince: Have you sent to Bottom's house? Is he come home yet?
Starveling: He cannot be heard of. Out of doubt he is transported.°
Flute: If he come not, then the play is marred. It goes not forward. Doth it?

---

180 *in great solemnity:* With great ceremony.   184 *parted:* I.e., improperly focused.
186–187 *like ... mine own:* I.e., like a jewel that one finds by chance and therefore possesses
but cannot certainly consider one's own property.   197 *God's:* May God save.   200 *go
about:* Attempt.   202 *patched:* Wearing motley, i.e., a dress of various colors; *offer:*
Venture.   203–205 *The eye ... report:* (Bottom garbles the terms of 1 Corinthians 2:9.)
206 *ballad:* (The proper medium for relating sensational stories and preposterous events.)
207 *hath no bottom:* Is unfathomable.   209 *her:* Thisbe's (?).   **Scene II.**   2 *transported:*
Carried off by fairies; or, possibly, transformed.

Quince: It is not possible. You have not a man in all Athens able to dis-
charge° Pyramus but he.   5
Flute: No, he hath simply the best wit° of any handicraft man in Athens.
Quince: Yea, and the best person° too, and he is a very paramour for a sweet
voice.
Flute: You must say "paragon." A paramour is, God bless us, a thing of
naught.°   10

Enter Snug the joiner.

Snug: Masters, the Duke is coming from the temple, and there is two or
three lords and ladies more married. If our sport had gone forward,
we had all been made men.°
Flute: O sweet bully Bottom! Thus hath he lost sixpence a day° during his
life; he could not have scaped sixpence a day. An the Duke had not   15
given him sixpence a day for playing Pyramus, I'll be hanged. He
would have deserved it. Sixpence a day in Pyramus, or nothing.

Enter Bottom.

Bottom: Where are these lads? Where are these hearts?°
Quince: Bottom! O most courageous day! O most happy hour!
Bottom: Masters, I am to discourse wonders.° But ask me not what; for if I   20
tell you, I am no true Athenian. I will tell you everything, right as it fell
out.
Quince: Let us hear, sweet Bottom.
Bottom: Not a word of° me. All that I will tell you is that the Duke hath
dined. Get your apparel together, good strings° to your beards, new   25
ribbons to your pumps;° meet presently° at the palace; every man
look o'er his part; for the short and the long is, our play is preferred.°
In any case, let Thisbe have clean linen; and let not him that plays the
lion pare his nails, for they shall hang out for the lion's claws. And,
most dear actors, eat no onions nor garlic, for we are to utter sweet   30
breath; and I do not doubt but to hear them say it is a sweet comedy.
No more words. Away! Go, away!   *[Exeunt.]*

[ACT V

SCENE I: *Athens. The palace of Theseus.*]

Enter Theseus, Hippolyta, and Philostrate, [lords, and attendants].

Hippolyta: 'Tis strange, my Theseus, that° these lovers speak of.
Theseus: More strange than true. I never may° believe
These antique° fables nor these fairy toys.°

---

5 *discharge:* Perform.   6 *wit:* Intellect.   7 *person:* Appearance.   9–10 *a . . . naught:* A
shameful thing.   13 *we . . . men:* I.e., we would have had our fortunes made.   14 *sixpence a day:* I.e., as a royal pension.   18 *hearts:* Good fellows.   20 *am . . . wonders:* Have
wonders to relate.   24 *of:* Out of.   25 *strings:* (To attach the beards.)   26 *pumps:*
Light shoes or slippers; *presently:* Immediately.   27 *preferred:* Selected for consideration.
Act V, Scene I.   1 *that:* That which.   2 *may:* Can.   3 *antique:* Old-fashioned (punning, too, on *antic,* "strange," "grotesque"); *fairy toys:* Trifling stories about fairies.

Lovers and madmen have such seething brains,
Such shaping fantasies,° that apprehend°   5
More than cool reason ever comprehends.°
The lunatic, the lover, and the poet
Are of imagination all compact.°
One sees more devils than vast hell can hold;
That is the madman. The lover, all as frantic,   10
Sees Helen's° beauty in a brow of Egypt.°
The poet's eye, in a fine frenzy rolling,
Doth glance from heaven to earth, from earth to heaven;
And as imagination bodies forth
The forms of things unknown, the poet's pen   15
Turns them to shapes and gives to airy nothing
A local habitation and a name.
Such tricks hath strong imagination
That, if it would but apprehend some joy,
It comprehends some bringer° of that joy;   20
Or in the night, imagining some fear,°
How easy is a bush supposed a bear!
Hippolyta: But all the story of the night told over,
And all their minds transfigured so together,
More witnesseth than fancy's images°   25
And grows to something of great constancy;°
But, howsoever,° strange and admirable.°

Enter lovers: Lysander, Demetrius, Hermia, and Helena.

Theseus: Here come the lovers, full of joy and mirth.
Joy, gentle friends! Joy and fresh days of love
Accompany your hearts!
Lysander: More than to us   30
Wait in your royal walks, your board, your bed!
Theseus: Come now, what masques,° what dances shall we have,
To wear away this long age of three hours
Between our after-supper and bedtime?
Where is our usual manager of mirth?   35
What revels are in hand? Is there no play
To ease the anguish of a torturing hour?
Call Philostrate.
Philostrate: Here, mighty Theseus.
Theseus: Say, what abridgment° have you for this evening?
What masque? What music? How shall we beguile   40
The lazy time, if not with some delight?
Philostrate [giving him a paper]: There is a brief° how many sports are ripe.
Make choice of which Your Highness will see first.

---

5 *fantasies:* Imaginations; *apprehend:* Conceive, imagine.   6 *comprehends:* Understands.
8 *compact:* Formed, composed.   11 *Helen's:* I.e., of Helen of Troy, pattern of beauty; *brow of
Egypt:* I.e., face of a gypsy.   20 *bringer:* I.e., source.   21 *fear:* Object of fear.   25 *More . . .
images:* Testifies to something more substantial than mere imaginings.   26 *constancy:* Certainty.   27 *howsoever:* In any case; *admirable:* A source of wonder.   32 *masques:* Courtly
entertainments.   39 *abridgment:* Pastime (to abridge or shorten the evening).   42 *brief:*
Short written statement, summary.

Theseus [reads.]: "The battle with the Centaurs,° to be sung
    By an Athenian eunuch to the harp"?
    We'll none of that. That have I told my love,   45
    In glory of my kinsman° Hercules.
    [He reads.] "The riot of the tipsy Bacchanals,
    Tearing the Thracian singer in their rage"?°
    That is an old device;° and it was played
    When I from Thebes came last a conqueror.   50
    [He reads.] "The thrice three Muses mourning for the death
    Of Learning, late deceased in beggary"?°
    That is some satire, keen and critical,
    Not sorting with° a nuptial ceremony.
    [He reads.] "A tedious brief scene of young Pyramus   55
    And his love Thisbe; very tragical mirth"?
    Merry and tragical? Tedious and brief?
    That is, hot ice and wondrous strange° snow.
    How shall we find the concord of this discord?   60
Philostrate: A play there is, my lord, some ten words long,
    Which is as brief as I have known a play;
    But by ten words, my lord, it is too long,
    Which makes it tedious. For in all the play
    There is not one word apt, one player fitted.   65
    And tragical, my noble lord, it is,
    For Pyramus therein doth kill himself.
    Which, when I saw rehearsed, I must confess,
    Made mine eyes water; but more merry tears
    The passion of loud laughter never shed.   70
Theseus: What are they that do play it?
Philostrate: Hardhanded men that work in Athens here,
    Which never labored in their minds till now,
    And now have toiled° their unbreathed° memories
    With this same play, against° your nuptial.   75
Theseus: And we will hear it.
Philostrate: No, my noble lord,
    It is not for you. I have heard it over,
    And it is nothing, nothing in the world;
    Unless you can find sport in their intents,
    Extremely stretched° and conned° with cruel pain   80
    To do you service.

---

44 *battle . . . Centaurs:* (Probably refers to the battle of the Centaurs and the Lapithae, when the Centaurs attempted to carry off Hippodamia, bride of Theseus' friend Pirothous. The story is told in Ovid's *Metamorphoses* 12.)   47 *kinsman:* (Plutarch's "Life of Theseus" states that Hercules and Theseus were near kinsmen. Theseus is referring to a version of the battle of the Centaurs in which Hercules was said to be present.)   48–49 *The riot . . . rage:* (This was the story of the death of Orpheus, as told in *Metamorphoses* 11.)   50 *device:* Show, performance.   52–53 *The thrice . . . beggary:* (Possibly an allusion to Spenser's *Teares of the Muses,* 1591, though "satires" deploring the neglect of learning and the creative arts were commonplace.)   55 *sorting with:* Befitting.   59 *strange:* (Sometimes emended to an adjective that would contrast with *snow,* just as *hot* contrasts with *ice.*)   74 *toiled:* Taxed; *unbreathed:* Unexercised.   75 *against:* In preparation for.   80 *stretched:* Strained; *conned:* Memorized.

Theseus: I will hear that play;
    For never anything can be amiss
    When simpleness° and duty tender it.
    Go, bring them in; and take your places, ladies.
                              [Philostrate goes to summon the players.]
Hippolyta: I love not to see wretchedness o'ercharged,°   85
    And duty in his service° perishing.
Theseus: Why, gentle sweet, you shall see no such thing.
Hippolyta: He says they can do nothing in this kind.°
Theseus: The kinder we, to give them thanks for nothing.
    Our sport shall be to take what they mistake;   90
    And what poor duty cannot do, noble respect°
    Takes it in might, not merit.°
    Where I have come, great clerks° have purposèd
    To greet me with premeditated welcomes;
    Where I have seen them shiver and look pale,   95
    Make periods in the midst of sentences,
    Throttle their practiced accent° in their fears,
    And in conclusion dumbly have broke off,
    Not paying me a welcome. Trust me, sweet,
    Out of this silence yet I picked a welcome;   100
    And in the modesty of fearful duty
    I read as much as from the rattling tongue
    Of saucy and audacious eloquence.
    Love, therefore, and tongue-tied simplicity
    In least° speak most, to my capacity.°   105

[Philostrate returns.]

Philostrate: So please Your Grace, the Prologue° is addressed.°
Theseus: Let him approach.   *[A flourish of trumpets.]*

    Enter the Prologue [Quince].

Prologue: If we offend, it is with our good will.
        That you should think, we come not to offend,
        But with good will. To show our simple skill,   110
        That is the true beginning of our end.
    Consider, then, we come but in despite.
        We do not come, as minding° to content you,
    Our true intent is. All for your delight
        We are not here. That you should here repent you,   115
    The actors are at hand; and, by their show,
    You shall know all that you are like to know.

---

83 *simpleness:* Simplicity.   85 *wretchedness o'ercharged:* Social or intellectual inferiors overburdened.   86 *his service:* Its attempt to serve.   88 *kind:* Kind of thing.   91 *respect:*
Evaluation, consideration.   92 *Takes . . . merit:* Values it for the effort made rather than for
the excellence achieved.   93 *clerks:* Learned men.   97 *practiced accent:* I.e., rehearsed speech;
or, usual way of speaking.   105 *least:* I.e., saying least; *to my capacity:* In my judgment and
understanding.   106 *Prologue:* Speaker of the prologue; *addressed:* Ready.   113 *minding:*
Intending.

Theseus: This fellow doth not stand upon points.°

Lysander: He hath rid° his prologue like a rough° colt; he knows not the stop.° A good moral, my lord: it is not enough to speak, but to speak 120 true.

Hippolyta: Indeed, he hath played on his prologue like a child on a recorder:° a sound, but not in government.°

Theseus: His speech was like a tangled chain: nothing° impaired, but all disordered. Who is next? 125

Enter Pyramus [Bottom], and Thisbe [Flute], and Wall [Snout], and Moonshine [Starveling], and Lion [Snug].

Prologue: Gentles, perchance you wonder at this show;
    But wonder on, till truth make all things plain.
This man is Pyramus, if you would know;
    This beauteous lady Thisbe is, certain.
This man with lime and roughcast doth present 130
    Wall, that vile wall which did these lovers sunder;
And through Wall's chink, poor souls, they are content
    To whisper. At the which let no man wonder.
This man, with lantern, dog, and bush of thorn,
    Presenteth Moonshine; for, if you will know, 135
By moonshine did these lovers think no scorn°
    To meet at Ninus' tomb, there, there to woo.
This grisly beast, which Lion hight° by name,
    The trusty Thisbe coming first by night
Did scare away, or rather did affright; 140
    And as she fled, her mantle she did fall,°
    Which Lion vile with bloody mouth did stain.
Anon comes Pyramus, sweet youth and tall,°
    And finds his trusty Thisbe's mantle slain;
Whereat, with blade, with bloody, blameful blade, 145
    He bravely broached° his boiling bloody breast.
And Thisbe, tarrying in mulberry shade,
    His dagger drew, and died. For all the rest,
Let Lion, Moonshine, Wall, and lovers twain
    At large° discourse, while here they do remain. 150

Exeunt Lion, Thisbe, and Moonshine.

Theseus: I wonder if the lion be to speak.

Demetrius: No wonder, my lord. One lion may, when many asses do.

Wall: In this same interlude° it doth befall
    That I, one Snout by name, present a wall;
    And such a wall as I would have you think 155
    That had in it a crannied hole or chink,

---

118 *stand upon points:* (1) Heed niceties or small points (2) pay attention to punctuation in his reading. (The humor of Quince's speech is in the blunders of its punctuation.) 119 *rid:* Ridden; *rough:* unbroken. 120 *stop:* (1) Stopping of a colt by reining it in (2) punctuation mark. 123 *recorder:* Wind instrument like a flute; *government:* Control. 124 *nothing:* Not at all. 136 *think no scorn:* Think it no disgraceful matter. 138 *hight:* Is called. 141 *fall:* Let fall. 143 *tall:* Courageous. 146 *broached:* Stabbed. 150 *At large:* In full, at length. 153 *interlude:* Play.

Through which the lovers, Pyramus and Thisbe,
Did whisper often, very secretly.
This loam, this roughcast, and this stone doth show
That I am that same wall; the truth is so.   160
And this the cranny is, right and sinister,°
Through which the fearful lovers are to whisper.
Theseus: Would you desire lime and hair to speak better?
Demetrius: It is the wittiest partition° that ever I heard discourse, my lord.

   [Pyramus comes forward.]

Theseus: Pyramus draws near the wall. Silence!   165
Pyramus: O grim-looked° night! O night with hue so black!
   O night, which ever art when day is not!
   O night, O night! Alack, alack, alack,
     I fear my Thisbe's promise is forgot.
   And thou, O wall, O sweet, O lovely wall,   170
     That stand'st between her father's ground and mine,
   Thou wall, O wall, O sweet and lovely wall,
     Show me thy chink, to blink through with mine eyne.
   Thanks, courteous wall. Jove shield thee well for this.
   But what see I? No Thisbe do I see.   175
   O wicked wall, through whom I see no bliss!
   Cursed be thy stones for thus deceiving me!
Theseus: The wall, methinks, being sensible,° should curse again.°
Pyramus: No, in truth, sir, he should not. "Deceiving me" is Thisbe's cue:
   she is to enter now, and I am to spy her through the wall. You shall see, 180
   it will fall pat° as I told you. Yonder she comes.

   Enter Thisbe.

Thisbe: O wall, full often hast thou heard my moans
   For parting my fair Pyramus and me.
   My cherry lips have often kissed thy stones,
     Thy stones with lime and hair knit up in thee.   185
Pyramus: I see a voice. Now will I to the chink,
   To spy an° I can hear my Thisbe's face.
   Thisbe!
Thisbe: My love! Thou art my love, I think.
Pyramus: Think what thou wilt, I am thy lover's grace,°   190
   And like Limander° am I trusty still.
Thisbe: And I like Helen,° till the Fates me kill.
Pyramus: Not Shafalus to Procrus° was so true.
Thisbe: As Shafalus to Procrus, I to you.
Pyramus: O, kiss me through the hole of this vile wall!   195
Thisbe: I kiss the wall's hole, not your lips at all.

---

161 *right and sinister:* I.e., the right side of it and the left; or, running from right to left, horizontally.   164 *partition:* (1) Wall (2) section of a learned treatise or oration.   166 *grim-looked:* Grim-looking.   178 *sensible:* Capable of feeling; *again:* In return.   181 *pat:* Exactly.   187 *an:* If.   190 *lover's grace:* I.e., gracious lover.   191–192 *Limander, Helen:* (Blunders for "Leander" and "Hero").   193 *Shafalus, Procrus:* (Blunders for "Cephalus" and "Procris," also famous lovers.)

Pyramus: Wilt thou at Ninny's tomb meet me straightway?
Thisbe: 'Tide life, 'tide° death, I come without delay.

                      [Exeunt Pyramus and Thisbe.]

Wall: Thus have I, Wall, my part dischargèd so;
    And, being done, thus Wall away doth go.   *[Exit.]*   200
Theseus: Now is the mural down between the two neighbors.
Demetrius: No remedy, my lord, when walls are so willful° to hear without
    warning.°
Hippolyta: This is the silliest stuff that ever I heard.
Theseus: The best in this kind° are but shadows,° and the worst are no   205
    worse, if imagination amend them.
Hippolyta: It must be your imagination then, and not theirs.
Theseus: If we imagine no worse of them than they of themselves, they
    may pass for excellent men. Here come two noble beasts in, a man
    and a lion.   210

    Enter Lion and Moonshine.

Lion: You, ladies, you, whose gentle hearts do fear
      The smallest monstrous mouse that creeps on floor,
    May now perchance both quake and tremble here,
      When lion rough in wildest rage doth roar.
    Then know that I, as Snug the joiner, am   215
    A lion fell,° nor else no lion's dam;
    For, if I should as lion come in strife
    Into this place, 'twere pity on my life.
Theseus: A very gentle beast, and of a good conscience.
Demetrius: The very best at a beast, my lord, that e'er I saw.   220
Lysander: This lion is a very fox for his valor.°
Theseus: True; and a goose for his discretion.°
Demetrius: Not so, my lord, for his valor cannot carry his discretion, and
    the fox carries the goose.
Theseus: His discretion, I am sure, cannot carry his valor; for the goose car-   225
    ries not the fox. It is well. Leave it to his discretion, and let us listen
    to the moon.
Moon: This lanthorn° doth the hornèd moon present—
Demetrius: He should have worn the horns on his head.°
Theseus: He is no crescent,° and his horns are invisible within the cir-   230
    cumference.
Moon: This lanthorn doth the hornèd moon present;
    Myself the man i' the moon do seem to be.

---

198 *'tide:* Betide, come.   202 *willful:* Willing.   202–203 *without warning:* I.e., without
warning the parents. (Demetrius makes a joke on the proverb "Walls have ears.")   205 *in
this kind:* Of this sort; *shadows:* Likenesses, representations.   216 *lion fell:* Fierce lion (with
a play on the idea of "lion skin").   221 *is . . . valor:* I.e., his valor consists of craftiness and
discretion.   222 *a goose . . . discretion:* I.e., as discreet as a goose, that is, more foolish than
discreet.   228 *lanthorn:* (This original spelling, *lanthorn,* may suggest a play on the *horn* of
which lanterns were made and also on a cuckold's horns; however, the spelling *lanthorn* is not
used consistently for comic effect in this play or elsewhere. At Act V, Scene I, line 134, for example, the word is *lantern* in the original.)   229 *on his head:* (As a sign of cuckoldry.)
230 *crescent:* A waxing moon.

Theseus: This is the greatest error of all the rest. The man should be put
   into the lanthorn. How is it else the man i' the moon?   235
Demetrius: He dares not come there for° the candle, for you see it is al-
   ready in snuff.°
Hippolyta: I am weary of this moon. Would he would change!
Theseus: It appears, by his small light of discretion, that he is in the wane;
   but yet, in courtesy, in all reason, we must stay the time.   240
Lysander: Proceed, Moon.
Moon: All that I have to say is to tell you that the lanthorn is the moon, I,
   the man i' the moon, this thornbush my thornbush, and this dog my
   dog.
Demetrius: Why, all these should be in the lanthorn, for all these are in   245
   the moon. But silence! Here comes Thisbe.

      Enter Thisbe.

Thisbe: This is old Ninny's tomb. Where is my love?
Lion [roaring]: O!
Demetrius: Well roared, Lion.   *[Thisbe runs off, dropping her mantle.]*
Theseus: Well run, Thisbe.   250
Hippolyta: Well shone, Moon. Truly, the moon shines with a good grace.
                                         [The Lion worries Thisbe's mantle.]
Theseus: Well moused,° Lion.

      [Enter Pyramus; exit Lion.]

Demetrius: And then came Pyramus.
Lysander: And so the Lion vanished.
Pyramus: Sweet Moon, I thank thee for thy sunny beams;   255
   I thank thee, Moon, for shining now so bright;
   For, by thy gracious, golden, glittering gleams,
      I trust to take of truest Thisbe sight.
         But stay, O spite!
         But mark, poor knight,   260
   What dreadful dole° is here?
         Eyes, do you see?
         How can it be?
   O dainty duck! O dear!
         Thy mantle good,   265
         What, stained with blood?
   Approach, ye Furies° fell!°
         O Fates,° come, come,
         Cut thread and thrum;°
   Quail,° crush, conclude, and quell!°   270

---

236 *for:* Because of, for fear of.   237 *in snuff:* (1) Offended (2) in need of snuffing or
trimming.   252 *moused:* Shaken, torn, bitten.   261 *dole:* Grievous event.   267 *Furies:*
Avenging goddesses of Greek myth; *fell:* Fierce.   268 *Fates:* The three goddesses (Clotho,
Lachesis, Atropos) of Greek myth who spun, drew, and cut the thread of human life.
269 *thread and thrum:* I.e., everything — the good and bad alike; literally, the warp in weaving
and the loose end of the warp.   270 *Quail:* Overpower; *quell:* Kill, destroy.

Theseus: This passion, and the death of a dear friend, would go near to
  make a man look sad.°
Hippolyta: Beshrew my heart, but I pity the man.
Pyramus: O, wherefore, Nature, didst thou lions frame?
  Since lion vile hath here deflowered my dear,   275
  Which is — no, no, which was — the fairest dame
  That lived, that loved, that liked, that looked with cheer.°
     Come, tears, confound,
     Out, sword, and wound
    The pap° of Pyramus;   280
    Ay, that left pap,
    Where heart doth hop.   *[He stabs himself.]*
  Thus die I, thus, thus, thus.
     Now am I dead,
     Now am I fled;   285
    My soul is in the sky.
     Tongue, lose thy light;
     Moon, take thy flight.   *[Exit Moonshine.]*
     Now die, die, die, die, die.   *[Pyramus dies.]*
Demetrius: No die, but an ace,° for him; for he is but one.°   290
Lysander: Less than an ace, man; for he is dead, he is nothing.
Theseus: With the help of a surgeon he might yet recover, and yet prove
  an ass.°
Hippolyta: How chance Moonshine is gone before Thisbe comes back and
  finds her lover?
                                              295
Theseus: She will find him by starlight.

  [Enter Thisbe.]

  Here she comes; and her passion ends the play.
Hippolyta: Methinks she should not use a long one for such a Pyramus. I
  hope she will be brief.
Demetrius: A mote° will turn the balance, which Pyramus, which° Thisbe,   300
  is the better: he for a man, God warrant us; she for a woman, God
  bless us.
Lysander: She hath spied him already with those sweet eyes.
Demetrius: And thus she means,° videlicet:°
Thisbe: Asleep, my love?
    What, dead, my dove?   305
    O Pyramus, arise!
    Speak, speak. Quite dumb?
    Dead, dead? A tomb
    Must cover thy sweet eyes.   310

271–272 *This . . . sad:* I.e., if one had other reason to grieve, one might be sad, but not from this
absurd portrayal of passion.   277 *cheer:* Countenance.   280 *pap:* Breast.   290 *ace:*
The side of the die featuring the single pip, or spot (the pun is on *die* as a singular of *dice;*
Bottom's performance is not worth a whole *die* but rather one single face of it, one small portion); *one:* (1) An individual person (2) unique.   293 *ass:* (With a pun on *ace.*)   300 *mote:*
Small particle; *which . . . which:* Whether . . . or.   304 *means:* Moans, laments (with a pun
on the meaning "lodge a formal complaint"); *videlicet:* To wit.

These lily lips,
     This cherry nose,
These yellow cowslip cheeks,
     Are gone, are gone!
     Lovers, make moan.   315
His eyes were green as leeks.
     O Sisters Three,°
     Come, come to me,
With hands as pale as milk;
     Lay them in gore,   320
     Since you have shore°
With shears his thread of silk.
     Tongue, not a word.
     Come, trusty sword,
Come, blade, my breast imbrue!°   *[She stabs herself.]* 325
     And farewell, friends.
     Thus Thisbe ends.
     Adieu, adieu, adieu.   *[She dies.]*

Theseus: Moonshine and Lion are left to bury the dead.
Demetrius: Ay, and Wall too.   330
Bottom [starting up, as Flute does also]: No, I assure you, the wall is down
     that parted their fathers. Will it please you to see the epilogue, or to
     hear a Bergomask dance° between two of our company?

[The other players enter.]

Theseus: No epilogue, I pray you; for your play needs no excuse. Never
     excuse; for when the players are all dead, there need none to be   335
     blamed. Marry, if he that writ it had played Pyramus and hanged him-
     self in Thisbe's garter, it would have been a fine tragedy; and so it
     is, truly, and very notably discharged. But, come, your Bergomask.
     Let your epilogue alone.   *[A dance.]*
     The iron tongue° of midnight hath told° twelve.   340
     Lovers, to bed, 'tis almost fairy time.
     I fear we shall outsleep the coming morn
     As much as we this night have overwatched.°
     This palpable-gross° play hath well beguiled
     The heavy° gait of night. Sweet friends, to bed.   345
     A fortnight hold we this solemnity,
     In nightly revels and new jollity.   *Exeunt.*

Enter Puck [carrying a broom].

Puck: Now the hungry lion roars,
           And the wolf behowls the moon,
     Whilst the heavy° plowman snores,   350
           All with weary task fordone.°

---

317 *Sisters Three:* The Fates.   321 *shore:* Shorn.   325 *imbrue:* Stain with blood.
333 *Bergomask dance:* A rustic dance named from Bergamo, a province in the state of Venice.
340 *iron tongue:* Clapper of a bell; *told:* Counted, struck ("tolled").   343 *overwatched:*
Stayed up too late.   344 *palpable-gross:* Palpably gross, obviously crude.   345 *heavy:*
Drowsy, dull.   350 *heavy:* Tired.   351 *fordone:* Exhausted.

Now the wasted brands° do glow,
  Whilst the screech owl, screeching loud,
Puts the wretch that lies in woe
  In remembrance of a shroud.   355
Now it is the time of night
  That the graves, all gaping wide,
Every one lets forth his sprite,°
  In the church-way paths to glide.
And we fairies, that do run   360
  By the triple Hecate's° team
From the presence of the sun,
  Following darkness like a dream,
Now are frolic.° Not a mouse
  Shall disturb this hallowed house.   365
I am sent with broom before,
To sweep the dust behind° the door.

Enter [Oberon and Titania,] King and Queen of Fairies, with all their train.

Oberon: Through the house give glimmering light,
  By the dead and drowsy fire;
Every elf and fairy sprite   370
  Hop as light as bird from brier;
And this ditty, after me,
Sing, and dance it trippingly.
Titania: First, rehearse° your song by rote,
  To each word a warbling note.   375
Hand in hand, with fairy grace,
Will we sing, and bless this place.   *[Song and dance.]*
Oberon: Now, until the break of day,
  Through this house each fairy stray.
To the best bride-bed will we,   380
  Which by us shall blessèd be;
And the issue there create°
  Ever shall be fortunate.
So shall all the couples three
  Ever true in loving be;   385
And the blots of Nature's hand
  Shall not in their issue stand;
Never mole, harelip, nor scar,
  Nor mark prodigious,° such as are
Despisèd in nativity,   390
  Shall upon their children be.
With this field dew consecrate,°

---

352 *wasted brands:* Burned-out logs.   358 *Every...sprite:* Every grave lets forth its ghost.
361 *triple Hecate's:* (Hecate ruled in three capacities: as Luna or Cynthia in heaven, as Diana
on earth, and as Proserpina in hell.)   364 *frolic:* Merry.   367 *behind:* From behind, or
else like sweeping the dirt under the carpet (Robin Goodfellow was a household spirit
who helped good housemaids and punished lazy ones, but he could, of course, be mischievous).   374 *rehearse:* Recite.   382 *create:* Created.   389 *prodigious:* Monstrous, unnatural.   392 *consecrate:* Consecrated.

Every fairy take his gait,°
And each several° chamber bless,
Through this palace, with sweet peace;   395
And the owner of it blest
Ever shall in safety rest.
Trip away; make no stay;
Meet me all by break of day.   *Exeunt [Oberon, Titania, and train].*
Puck [to the audience]: If we shadows have offended,   400
Think but this, and all is mended,
That you have but slumbered here°
While these visions did appear.
And this weak and idle theme,
No more yielding but° a dream,   405
Gentles, do not reprehend.
If you pardon, we will mend.°
And, as I am an honest Puck,
If we have unearnèd luck
Now to scape the serpent's tongue,°   410
We will make amends ere long;
Else the Puck a liar call.
So, good night unto you all.
Give me your hands,° if we be friends,
And Robin shall restore amends.°   *[Exit.]* 415

393 *take his gait:* Go his way.   394 *several:* Separate.   402 *That...here:* I.e., that it is a
"midsummer night's dream."   405 *No...but:* Yielding no more than.   407 *mend:* Improve.   410 *serpent's tongue:* I.e., hissing.   414 *Give...hands:* Applaud.   415 *restore
amends:* Give satisfaction in return.

CONSIDERATIONS FOR CRITICAL THINKING AND WRITING

1. FIRST RESPONSE. Discuss the significance of the play's title. What expectations does it create for you?

2. Describe how the two settings, Athens and the nearby woods, reflect different social and physical environments as well as different types of behavior
   among the characters.

3. What is the symbolic function of the marriage of Theseus and Hippolyta?
   How is that function revealed in the scenes in which they appear?

4. Characterize the four young lovers. How individualized are their personalities? How does the extent of their characterizations suggest their function in the play?

5. What makes Bottom such a comic figure? How does his behavior shed
   light on the behavior of the other characters?

6. Consider how women — Hippolyta, Titania, Hermia, and Helena — are presented in the play. What characteristics do they have in common? How do
   they relate to the men in their lives?

7. Why does Puck describe "mortals" as "fools" (III.ii.115)? To what degree
   does this description fit the fairies as well?

8. How might Puck be regarded as the play's director as well as a central character?

9. How does the plot bring together the four groups of characters — Theseus and Hippolyta, the four lovers, the craftsmen, and the fairies — into a unified whole? Write a plot summary of the play that connects these four groups of characters. How does this summary resemble popular situation comedies that you've seen on television?

10. Choose a scene that you find particularly funny, and analyze how the humor is created. Describe how the scene contributes to the rest of the play.

11. What is the relationship between the play within the play, "Pyramus and Thisbe," and *A Midsummer Night's Dream*? How do the plot and theme of each serve as commentaries on each other?

12. Despite its comic scenes and happy ending, at various moments this play does raise the specter of potential tragedy. How seriously do you think we are meant to worry about the characters? What are your emotions about the young lovers as they struggle to sort things out in the woods? Discuss how this play might be transformed into a tragedy.

CONNECTIONS TO OTHER SELECTIONS

1. Write an essay concerning the problematic nature of love in *A Midsummer Night's Dream* and Anton Chekhov's *The Proposal: A Jest in One Act* (p. 1615). How is the depiction of love in each play used to create conflict?

2. Discuss Shakespeare's use of the play within the play in *A Midsummer Night's Dream* and *Hamlet* (p. 1383). What emotions does each produce? What conflicts and themes do they emphasize? What attitudes do they suggest about the nature of drama?

3. In an essay discuss the significance of marriage in *A Midsummer Night's Dream* and Henrik Ibsen's *A Doll House* (p. 1564).

4. Write an essay that explores the difficulty of distinguishing between reality and illusion in *A Midsummer Night's Dream* and a very different work, Tim O'Brien's short story "How to Tell a True War Story" (p. 555). What are the similarities and differences in their perspectives on the actual and imaginary?

Hamlet, Prince of Denmark

Hamlet, the most famous play in English literature, continues to fascinate and challenge both readers and audiences. Interpretations of Hamlet's character and actions abound, because the play has produced so many intense and varied responses. No small indication of the tragedy's power is that actors long to play its title role.

A brief summary can suggest the movement of the plot but not the depth of Hamlet's character. After learning of his father's death, Prince Hamlet returns to the Danish court from his university studies to find Claudius, the dead king's brother, ruling Denmark and married to Hamlet's mother, Gertrude. Her remarriage within two months of his father's death has left Hamlet disillusioned, confused, and suspicious of Claudius. When his father's ghost appears before Hamlet to reveal that Claudius murdered the king, Hamlet is confronted with having to avenge his father's death.

Hamlet's efforts to carry out this obligation would have been a familiar kind of plot to Elizabethan audiences. **Revenge tragedy** was a well-established type of drama that traced its antecedents to Greek and Roman plays, particularly through the Roman playwright Seneca (c. 3 B.C.–A.D. 65), whose plays were translated and produced in English in the late sixteenth century. Shakespeare's audiences knew its conventions, particularly from Thomas Kyd's popular *Spanish Tragedy* (c. 1587). Basically, this type of play consists of a murder that has to be avenged by a relative of the victim. Typically, the victim's ghost appears to demand revenge, and invariably madness of some sort is worked into subsequent events, which ultimately result in the deaths of the murderer, the avenger, and a number of other characters. Crime, madness, ghostly anguish, poison, overheard conversations, conspiracies, and a final scene littered with corpses: *Hamlet* subscribes to the basic ingredients of the formula, but it also transcends the conventions of revenge tragedy because Hamlet contemplates not merely revenge but suicide and the meaning of life itself.

Hamlet must face not only a diseased social order but also conflicts within himself when his indecisiveness becomes as agonizing as the corruption surrounding him. However, Hamlet is also a forceful and attractive character. His intelligence is repeatedly revealed in his penetrating use of language; through images and metaphors he creates a perspective on his world that is at once satiric and profoundly painful. His astonishing and sometimes shocking wit is leveled at his mother, his beloved Ophelia, and Claudius as well as himself. Nothing escapes his critical eye and divided imagination. Hamlet, no less than the people around him, is perplexed by his alienation from life.

Hamlet's limitations as well as his virtues make him one of Shakespeare's most complex characters. His keen self-awareness is both agonizing and liberating. Although he struggles throughout the play with painful issues ranging from family loyalties to matters of state, he retains his dignity as a tragic hero, whom generations of audiences have found compelling.

WILLIAM SHAKESPEARE (1564–1616)

Hamlet, Prince of Denmark   *1600*

[DRAMATIS PERSONAE

Claudius, King of Denmark
Hamlet, son to the late and nephew to the present king
Polonius, lord chamberlain
Horatio, friend to Hamlet
Laertes, son to Polonius

Voltimand ⎫
Cornelius ⎟
Rosencrantz ⎬ courtiers
Guildenstern ⎟
Osric ⎭
A Gentleman
A Priest
Marcellus ⎫ officers
Bernardo ⎭
Francisco, a soldier
Reynaldo, servant to Polonius
Players
Two Clowns, grave-diggers
Fortinbras, Prince of Norway
A Captain
English Ambassadors
Gertrude, Queen of Denmark, and mother to Hamlet
Ophelia, daughter to Polonius
Lords, Ladies, Officers, Soldiers, Sailors, Messengers, and other Attendants
Ghost of Hamlet's Father

SCENE: *Denmark.*]

[ACT I

SCENE I: *Elsinore. A platform° before the castle.*]

Enter Bernardo and Francisco, two sentinels.

Bernardo: Who's there?
Francisco: Nay, answer me:° stand, and unfold yourself.
Bernardo: Long live the king!°
Francisco: Bernardo?
Bernardo: He.
Francisco: You come most carefully upon your hour.   5
Bernardo: 'Tis now struck twelve; get thee to bed, Francisco.
Francisco: For this relief much thanks: 'tis bitter cold,
    And I am sick at heart.
Bernardo: Have you had quiet guard?
Francisco: Not a mouse stirring.   10
Bernardo: Well, good night.
    If you do meet Horatio and Marcellus,
    The rivals° of my watch, bid them make haste.

Enter Horatio and Marcellus.

Act I, Scene I.   *platform:* A level space on the battlements of the royal castle at Elsinore, a Danish seaport; now Helsingör.   2 *me:* This is emphatic, since Francisco is the sentry. 3 *Long live the king:* Either a password or greeting; Horatio and Marcellus use a different one in line 15.   13 *rivals:* Partners.

Francisco: I think I hear them. Stand, ho! Who is there?
Horatio: Friends to this ground.
Marcellus: And liegemen to the Dane.   15
Francisco: Give you° good night.
Marcellus: O, farewell, honest soldier:
    Who hath reliev'd you?
Francisco: Bernardo hath my place.
    Give you good night.   *Exit Francisco.*
Marcellus: Holla! Bernardo!
Bernardo: Say,
    What, is Horatio there?
Horatio: A piece of him.
Bernardo: Welcome, Horatio: welcome, good Marcellus.   20
Marcellus: What, has this thing appear'd again to-night?
Bernardo: I have seen nothing.
Marcellus: Horatio says 'tis but our fantasy,
    And will not let belief take hold of him
    Touching this dreaded sight, twice seen of us: 25
    Therefore I have entreated him along
    With us to watch the minutes of this night;
    That if again this apparition come,
    He may approve° our eyes and speak to it.
Horatio: Tush, tush, 'twill not appear.
Bernardo: Sit down awhile;   30
    And let us once again assail your ears,
    That are so fortified against our story
    What we have two nights seen.
Horatio: Well, sit we down,
    And let us hear Bernardo speak of this.
Bernardo: Last night of all,   35
    When yond same star that's westward from the pole°
    Had made his course t' illume that part of heaven
    Where now it burns, Marcellus and myself,
    The bell then beating one, —

    Enter Ghost.

Marcellus: Peace, break thee off; look, where it comes again!   40
Bernardo: In the same figure, like the king that's dead.
Marcellus: Thou art a scholar;° speak to it, Horatio.
Bernardo: Looks 'a not like the king? mark it, Horatio.
Horatio: Most like: it harrows° me with fear and wonder.
Bernardo: It would be spoke to.°
Marcellus: Speak to it, Horatio.   45
Horatio: What art thou that usurp'st this time of night,
    Together with that fair and warlike form

---

16 *Give you:* God give you.   29 *approve:* Corroborate.   36 *pole:* Polestar.   42 *scholar:* Exorcisms were performed in Latin, which Horatio as an educated man would be able to speak.   44 *harrows:* Lacerates the feelings.   45 *It...to:* A ghost could not speak until spoken to.

In which the majesty of buried Denmark°
Did sometimes march? by heaven I charge thee, speak!
Marcellus: It is offended.
Bernardo: See it stalks away!   50
Horatio: Stay! speak, speak! I charge thee, speak!   *Exit Ghost.*
Marcellus: 'Tis gone, and will not answer.
Bernardo: How now, Horatio! you tremble and look pale:
    Is not this something more than fantasy?
    What think you on 't?   55
Horatio: Before my God, I might not this believe
    Without the sensible and true avouch
    Of mine own eyes.
Marcellus: Is it not like the king?
Horatio: As thou art to thyself:
    Such was the very armour he had on   60
    When he the ambitious Norway combated;
    So frown'd he once, when, in an angry parle,
    He smote° the sledded Polacks° on the ice.
    'Tis strange.
Marcellus: Thus twice before, and jump° at this dead hour,   65
    With martial stalk hath he gone by our watch.
Horatio: In what particular thought to work I know not;
    But in the gross and scope° of my opinion,
    This bodes some strange eruption to our state.
Marcellus: Good now,° sit down, and tell me, he that knows,   70
    Why this same strict and most observant watch
    So nightly toils° the subject° of the land,
    And why such daily cast° of brazen cannon,
    And foreign mart° for implements of war;
    Why such impress° of shipwrights, whose sore task   75
    Does not divide the Sunday from the week;
    What might be toward, that this sweaty haste
    Doth make the night joint-labourer with the day:
    Who is't that can inform me?
Horatio: That can I;
    At least, the whisper goes so. Our last king,   80
    Whose image even but now appear'd to us,
    Was, as you know, by Fortinbras of Norway,
    Thereto prick'd on° by a most emulate° pride,
    Dar'd to the combat; in which our valiant Hamlet—
    For so this side of our known world esteem'd him—   85
    Did slay this Fortinbras; who, by a seal'd compact,
    Well ratified by law and heraldry,°

48 *buried Denmark:* The buried king of Denmark.   63 *smote:* Defeated; *sledded Polacks:* Po-
landers using sledges.   65 *jump:* Exactly.   68 *gross and scope:* General drift.   70 *Good
now:* An expression denoting entreaty or expostulation.   72 *toils:* Causes or makes to toil;
subject: People, subjects.   73 *cast:* Casting, founding.   74 *mart:* Buying and selling,
traffic.   75 *impress:* Impressment.   83 *prick'd on:* Incited; *emulate:* Rivaling.   87 *law
and heraldry:* Heraldic law, governing combat.

Did forfeit, with his life, all those his lands
Which he stood seiz'd° of, to the conqueror:
Against the which, a moiety competent°   90
Was gaged by our king; which had return'd
To the inheritance of Fortinbras,
Had he been vanquisher; as, by the same comart,°
And carriage° of the article design'd,
His fell to Hamlet. Now, sir, young Fortinbras,   95
Of unimproved° mettle hot and full,°
Hath in the skirts of Norway here and there
Shark'd up° a list of lawless resolutes,°
For food and diet,° to some enterprise
That hath a stomach in't; which is no other—   100
As it doth well appear unto our state—
But to recover of us, by strong hand
And terms compulsatory, those foresaid lands
So by his father lost: and this, I take it,
Is the main motive of our preparations,   105
The source of this our watch and the chief head
Of this post-haste and romage° in the land.
Bernardo: I think it be no other but e'en so:
    Well may it sort° that this portentous figure
    Comes armed through our watch; so like the king   110
    That was and is the question of these wars.
Horatio: A mote° it is to trouble the mind's eye.
    In the most high and palmy state° of Rome,
    A little ere the mightiest Julius fell,
    The graves stood tenantless and the sheeted dead   115
    Did squeak and gibber in the Roman streets:
    As stars with trains of fire° and dews of blood,
    Disasters° in the sun; and the moist star°
    Upon whose influence Neptune's empire° stands
    Was sick almost to doomsday with eclipse: 120
    And even the like precurse° of fear'd events,
    As harbingers preceding still the fates
    And prologue to the omen coming on,
    Have heaven and earth together demonstrated
    Unto our climatures and countrymen.—   125

Enter Ghost.

But soft, behold! lo, where it comes again!
I'll cross° it, though it blast me. Stay, illusion!
If thou hast any sound, or use of voice,

---

89 *seiz'd:* Possessed.   90 *moiety competent:* Adequate or sufficient portion.   93 *comart:* Joint bargain.   94 *carriage:* Import, bearing.   96 *unimproved:* Not turned to account; *hot and full:* Full of fight.   98 *Shark'd up:* Got together in haphazard fashion; *resolutes:* Desperadoes.   99 *food and diet:* No pay but their keep.   107 *romage:* Bustle, commotion.   109 *sort:* Suit.   112 *mote:* Speck of dust.   113 *palmy state:* Triumphant sovereignty.   117 *stars...fire:* I.e., comets.   118 *Disasters:* Unfavorable aspects; *moist star:* The moon, governing tides.   119 *Neptune's empire:* The sea.   121 *precurse:* Heralding.   127 *cross:* Meet, face, thus bringing down the evil influence on the person who crosses it.

Speak to me! *It° spreads his arms.*
If there be any good thing to be done, 130
That may to thee do ease and grace to me,
Speak to me!
If thou art privy to thy country's fate,
Which, happily, foreknowing may avoid,
O, speak! 135
Or if thou hast uphoarded in thy life
Extorted treasure in the womb of earth,
For which, they say, you spirits oft walk in death, *The cock crows.*
Speak of it:° stay, and speak! Stop it, Marcellus.
Marcellus: Shall I strike at it with my partisan?° 140
Horatio: Do, if it will not stand.
Bernardo: 'Tis here!
Horatio: 'Tis here!
Marcellus: 'Tis gone! *[Exit Ghost.]*
We do it wrong, being so majestical,
To offer it the show of violence;
For it is, as the air, invulnerable, 145
And our vain blows malicious mockery.
Bernardo: It was about to speak, when the cock crew.°
Horatio: And then it started like a guilty thing
Upon a fearful summons. I have heard,
The cock, that is the trumpet to the morn, 150
Doth with his lofty and shrill-sounding throat
Awake the god of day; and, at his warning,
Whether in sea or fire, in earth or air,
Th' extravagant and erring° spirit hies
To his confine:° and of the truth herein 155
This present object made probation.°
Marcellus: It faded on the crowing of the cock.
Some say that ever 'gainst° that season comes
Wherein our Saviour's birth is celebrated,
The bird of dawning singeth all night long: 160
And then, they say, no spirit dare stir abroad;
The nights are wholesome; then no planets strike,°
No fairy takes, nor witch hath power to charm,
So hallow'd and so gracious° is that time.
Horatio: So have I heard and do in part believe it. 165
But, look, the morn, in russet mantle clad,
Walks o'er the dew of yon high eastward hill:
Break we our watch up; and by my advice,
Let us impart what we have seen to-night

---

129 *It:* The Ghost, or perhaps Horatio.   133–139 *If...it:* Horatio recites the traditional reasons why ghosts might walk.   140 *partisan:* Long-handled spear with a blade having lateral projections.   147 *cock crew:* According to traditional ghost lore, spirits returned to their confines at cockcrow.   154 *extravagant and erring:* Wandering. Both words mean the same thing.   155 *confine:* Place of confinement.   156 *probation:* Proof, trial.   158 *'gainst:* Just before.   162 *planets strike:* It was thought that planets were malignant and might strike travelers by night.   164 *gracious:* Full of goodness.

Unto young Hamlet; for, upon my life,   170
This spirit, dumb to us, will speak to him.
Do you consent we shall acquaint him with it,
As needful in our loves, fitting our duty?
Marcellus: Let's do 't, I pray; and I this morning know
Where we shall find him most conveniently.   *Exeunt.* 175

[SCENE II: *A room of state in the castle.*]

Flourish. Enter Claudius, King of Denmark, Gertrude the Queen, Councilors,
Polonius and his Son Laertes, Hamlet, cum aliis° [including Voltimand and
Cornelius].

King: Though yet of Hamlet our dear brother's death
      The memory be green, and that it us befitted
      To bear our hearts in grief and our whole kingdom
      To be contracted in one brow of woe,
      Yet so far hath discretion fought with nature   5
      That we with wisest sorrow think on him,
      Together with remembrance of ourselves.
      Therefore our sometime sister, now our queen,
      Th' imperial jointress° to this warlike state,
      Have we, as 'twere with a defeated joy, —   10
      With an auspicious and a dropping eye,
      With mirth in funeral and with dirge in marriage,
      In equal scale weighing delight and dole, —
      Taken to wife: nor have we herein barr'd
      Your better wisdoms, which have freely gone   15
      With this affair along. For all, our thanks.
      Now follows, that° you know, young Fortinbras,
      Holding a weak supposal° of our worth,
      Or thinking by our late dear brother's death
      Our state to be disjoint° and out of frame,°   20
      Colleagued° with this dream of his advantage,°
      He hath not fail'd to pester us with message,
      Importing° the surrender of those lands
      Lost by his father, with all bands of law,
      To our most valiant brother. So much for him.   25
      Now for ourself and for this time of meeting:
      Thus much the business is: we have here writ
      To Norway, uncle of young Fortinbras, —
      Who, impotent and bed-rid, scarcely hears
      Of this his nephew's purpose, — to suppress   30
      His further gait° herein; in that the levies,
      The lists and full proportions, are all made

Scene II.   *cum aliis:* With others.   9 *jointress:* Woman possessed of a jointure, or, joint
tenancy of an estate.   17 *that:* That which.   18 *weak supposal:* Low estimate.   20 *dis-*
joint: Distracted, out of joint; *frame:* Order.   21 *Colleagued:* added to; *dream . . . advantage:*
Visionary hope of success.   23 *Importing:* Purporting, pertaining to.   31 *gait:* Proceeding.

Out of his subject:° and we here dispatch
You, good Cornelius, and you, Voltimand,
For bearers of this greeting to old Norway;   35
Giving to you no further personal power
To business with the king, more than the scope
Of these delated° articles allow.
Farewell, and let your haste commend your duty.

Cornelius: ⎫
            ⎬ In that and all things will we show our duty.   40
Voltimand: ⎭

King: We doubt it nothing: heartily farewell.

                              [Exeunt Voltimand and Cornelius.]
And now, Laertes, what's the news with you?
You told us of some suit; what is't, Laertes?
You cannot speak of reason to the Dane,°
And lose your voice:° what wouldst thou beg, Laertes,   45
That shall not be my offer, not thy asking?
The head is not more native° to the heart,
The hand more instrumental° to the mouth,
Than is the throne of Denmark to thy father.
What wouldst thou have, Laertes?

Laertes: My dread lord,   50
Your leave and favour to return to France;
From whence though willingly I came to Denmark,
To show my duty in your coronation,
Yet now, I must confess, that duty done,
My thoughts and wishes bend again toward France   55
And bow them to your gracious leave and pardon.°

King: Have you your father's leave? What says Polonius?
Polonius: He hath, my lord, wrung from me my slow leave
By laboursome petition, and at last
Upon his will I seal'd my hard consent: 60
I do beseech you, give him leave to go.
King: Take thy fair hour, Laertes; time be thine,
And thy best graces spend it at thy will!
But now, my cousin° Hamlet, and my son, —
Hamlet [aside]: A little more than kin, and less than kind!°   65
King: How is it that the clouds still hang on you?
Hamlet: Not so, my lord; I am too much in the sun.°
Queen: Good Hamlet, cast thy nighted colour off,
And let thine eye look like a friend on Denmark.
Do not for ever with thy vailed lids   70

---

33 *Out of his subject:* At the expense of Norway's subjects (collectively).   38 *delated:* Expressly stated.   44 *the Dane:* Danish king.   45 *lose your voice:* Speak in vain.   47 *native:* Closely connected, related.   48 *instrumental:* Serviceable.   56 *leave and pardon:* Permission to depart.   64 *cousin:* Any kin not of the immediate family.   65 *A little ... kind:* My relation to you has become more than kinship warrants; it has also become unnatural. 67 *I am ... sun:* (1) I am too much out of doors, (2) I am too much in the sun of your grace (ironical), (3) I am too much of a son to you. Possibly an allusion to the proverb "Out of heaven's blessing into the warm sun"; i.e., Hamlet is out of house and home in being deprived of the kingship.

      Seek for thy noble father in the dust:
      Thou know'st 'tis common; all that lives must die,
      Passing through nature to eternity.
Hamlet: Ay, madam, it is common.°
Queen: If it be,
      Why seems it so particular with thee?   75
Hamlet: Seems, madam! nay, it is; I know not "seems."
      'Tis not alone my inky cloak, good mother,
      Nor customary suits° of solemn black,
      Nor windy suspiration° of forc'd breath,
      No, nor the fruitful river in the eye,   80
      Nor the dejected 'haviour of the visage,
      Together with all forms, moods, shapes of grief,
      That can denote me truly: these indeed seem,
      For they are actions that a man might play:
      But I have that within which passeth show;   85
      These but the trappings and the suits of woe.
King: 'Tis sweet and commendable in your nature, Hamlet,
      To give these mourning duties to your father:
      But, you must know, your father lost a father;
      That father lost, lost his, and the survivor bound   90
      In filial obligation for some term
      To do obsequious° sorrow: but to persever
      In obstinate condolement° is a course
      Of impious stubbornness; 'tis unmanly grief;
      It shows a will most incorrect° to heaven,   95
      A heart unfortified, a mind impatient,
      An understanding simple and unschool'd:
      For what we know must be and is as common
      As any the most vulgar thing° to sense,
      Why should we in our peevish opposition   100
      Take it to heart? Fie! 'tis a fault to heaven,
      A fault against the dead, a fault to nature,
      To reason most absurd; whose common theme
      Is death of fathers, and who still hath cried,
      From the first corse till he that died to-day,   105
      "This must be so." We pray you, throw to earth
      This unprevailing° woe, and think of us
      As of a father: for let the world take note,
      You are the most immediate° to our throne;
      And with no less nobility° of love   110
      Than that which dearest father bears his son,
      Do I impart° toward you. For your intent

---

74 *Ay . . . common:* It is common, but it hurts nevertheless; possibly a reference to the commonplace quality of the queen's remark.   78 *customary suits:* Suits prescribed by custom for mourning.   79 *windy suspiration:* Heavy sighing.   92 *obsequious:* Dutiful.   93 *condolement:* Sorrowing.   95 *incorrect:* Untrained, uncorrected.   99 *vulgar thing:* Common experience.   107 *unprevailing:* Unavailing.   109 *most immediate:* Next in succession.   110 *nobility:* High degree.   112 *impart:* The object is apparently *love* (l. 110).

In going back to school in Wittenberg,°
It is most retrograde° to our desire:
And we beseech you, bend you° to remain   115
Here, in the cheer and comfort of our eye,
Our chiefest courtier, cousin, and our son.
Queen: Let not thy mother lose her prayers, Hamlet:
I pray thee, stay with us; go not to Wittenberg.
Hamlet: I shall in all my best obey you, madam.   120
King: Why, 'tis a loving and a fair reply:
Be as ourself in Denmark. Madam, come;
This gentle and unforc'd accord of Hamlet
Sits smiling to my heart: in grace whereof,
No jocund health that Denmark drinks to-day,   125
But the great cannon to the clouds shall tell,
And the king's rouse° the heaven shall bruit again,°
Re-speaking earthly thunder. Come away.

                              Flourish. Exeunt all but Hamlet.

Hamlet: O, that this too too sullied flesh would melt,
Thaw and resolve itself into a dew!   130
Or that the Everlasting had not fix'd
His canon 'gainst self-slaughter! O God! God!
How weary, stale, flat and unprofitable,
Seem to me all the uses of this world!
Fie on't! ah fie! 'tis an unweeded garden,   135
That grows to seed; things rank and gross in nature
Possess it merely.° That it should come to this!
But two months dead: nay, not so much, not two:
So excellent a king; that was, to this,
Hyperion° to a satyr; so loving to my mother   140
That he might not beteem° the winds of heaven
Visit her face too roughly. Heaven and earth!
Must I remember? why, she would hang on him,
As if increase of appetite had grown
By what it fed on: and yet, within a month —   145
Let me not think on't — Frailty, thy name is woman! —
A little month, or ere those shoes were old
With which she followed my poor father's body,
Like Niobe,° all tears: — why she, even she —
O God! a beast, that wants discourse of reason,°   150
Would have mourn'd longer — married with my uncle,
My father's brother, but no more like my father
Than I to Hercules: within a month:
Ere yet the salt of most unrighteous tears

113 *Wittenberg:* Famous German university founded in 1502. 114 *retrograde:* Contrary.
115 *bend you:* Incline yourself; imperative. 127 *rouse:* Draft of liquor; *bruit again:* Echo.
137 *merely:* Completely, entirely. 140 *Hyperion:* God of the sun in the older regime of ancient gods. 141 *beteem:* Allow. 149 *Niobe:* Tantalus's daughter, who boasted that she
had more sons and daughters than Leto; for this Apollo and Artemis slew her children. She
was turned into stone by Zeus on Mount Sipylus. 150 *discourse of reason:* Process or faculty of reason.

Had left the flushing in her galled° eyes,   155
She married. O, most wicked speed, to post
With such dexterity° to incestuous sheets!
It is not nor it cannot come to good:
But break, my heart; for I must hold my tongue.

Enter Horatio, Marcellus, and Bernardo.

Horatio: Hail to your lordship!
Hamlet: I am glad to see you well: 160
   Horatio! — or I do forget myself.
Horatio: The same, my lord, and your poor servant ever.
Hamlet: Sir, my good friend; I'll change that name with you:°
   And what make you from Wittenberg, Horatio?
   Marcellus?   165
Marcellus: My good lord —
Hamlet: I am very glad to see you. Good even, sir.
   But what, in faith, make you from Wittenberg?
Horatio: A truant disposition, good my lord.
Hamlet: I would not hear your enemy say so,   170
   Nor shall you do my ear that violence,
   To make it truster of your own report
   Against yourself: I know you are no truant.
   But what is your affair in Elsinore?
   We'll teach you to drink deep ere you depart.   175
Horatio: My lord, I came to see your father's funeral.
Hamlet: I prithee, do not mock me, fellow-student;
   I think it was to see my mother's wedding.
Horatio: Indeed, my lord, it follow'd hard° upon.
Hamlet: Thrift, thrift, Horatio! the funeral bak'd meats°   180
   Did coldly furnish forth the marriage tables.
   Would I had met my dearest° foe in heaven
   Or ever I had seen that day, Horatio!
   My father! — methinks I see my father.
Horatio: Where, my lord!
Hamlet: In my mind's eye, Horatio.   185
Horatio: I saw him once; 'a° was a goodly king.
Hamlet: 'A was a man, take him for all in all,
   I shall not look upon his like again.
Horatio: My lord, I think I saw him yesternight.
Hamlet: Saw? who?   190
Horatio: My lord, the king your father.
Hamlet: The king my father!
Horatio: Season your admiration° for a while
   With an attent ear, till I may deliver,

---

155 *galled:* Irritated.   157 *dexterity:* Facility.   163 *I'll . . . you:* I'll be your servant, you shall be my friend; also explained as "I'll exchange the name of friend with you."   179 *hard:* Close.   180 *bak'd meats:* Meat pies.   182 *dearest:* Direst. The adjective *dear* in Shakespeare has two different origins: O.E. *deore,* "beloved," and O.E. *deor,* "fierce." *Dearest* is the superlative of the second.   186 *'a:* He.   192 *Season your admiration:* Restrain your astonishment.

Upon the witness of these gentlemen,
This marvel to you.
Hamlet: For God's love, let me hear.   195
Horatio: Two nights together had these gentlemen,
     Marcellus and Bernardo, on their watch,
     In the dead waste and middle of the night,
     Been thus encount'red. A figure like your father,
     Armed at point exactly, cap-a-pe,°   200
     Appears before them, and with solemn march
     Goes slow and stately by them: thrice he walk'd
     By their oppress'd° and fear-surprised eyes,
     Within his truncheon's° length; whilst they, distill'd°
     Almost to jelly with the act° of fear,   205
     Stand dumb and speak not to him. This to me
     In dreadful secrecy impart they did;
     And I with them the third night kept the watch:
     Where, as they had deliver'd, both in time,
     Form of the thing, each word made true and good,   210
     The apparition comes: I knew your father;
     These hands are not more like.
Hamlet: But where was this?
Marcellus: My lord, upon the platform where we watch'd.
Hamlet: Did you not speak to it?
Horatio: My lord, I did;
     But answer made it none: yet once methought   215
     It lifted up it° head and did address
     Itself to motion, like as it would speak;
     But even then the morning cock crew loud,
     And at the sound it shrunk in haste away,
     And vanish'd from our sight.
Hamlet: 'Tis very strange.   220
Horatio: As I do live, my honour'd lord, 'tis true;
     And we did think it writ down in our duty
     To let you know of it.
Hamlet: Indeed, indeed, sirs, but this troubles me.
     Hold you the watch to-night?
Marcellus: ⎱
Bernardo: ⎰   We do, my lord.   225
Hamlet: Arm'd, say you?
Marcellus: ⎱
Bernardo: ⎰   Arm'd, my lord.
Hamlet: From top to toe?
Marcellus: ⎱
Bernardo: ⎰   My lord, from head to foot.
Hamlet: Then saw you not his face?
Horatio: O, yes, my lord; he wore his beaver° up.

---

200 *cap-a-pe:* From head to foot.   203 *oppress'd:* Distressed.   204 *truncheon:* Officer's staff; *distill'd:* Softened, weakened.   205 *act:* Action.   216 *it:* Its.   230 *beaver:* Visor on the helmet.

Hamlet: What, look'd he frowningly?
Horatio: A countenance more   230
    In sorrow than in anger.
Hamlet: Pale or red?
Horatio: Nay, very pale.
Hamlet: And fix'd his eyes upon you?
Horatio: Most constantly.
Hamlet: I would I had been there.
Horatio: It would have much amaz'd you.
Hamlet: Very like, very like. Stay'd it long?   235
Horatio: While one with moderate haste might tell a hundred.
Marcellus: ⎫
Bernardo: ⎭ Longer, longer.
Horatio: Not when I saw't.
Hamlet: His beard was grizzled,—no?
Horatio: It was, as I have seen it in his life,
    A sable° silver'd.
Hamlet: I will watch to-night;   240
    Perchance 'twill walk again.
Horatio: I warr'nt it will.
Hamlet: If it assume my noble father's person,
    I'll speak to it, though hell itself should gape
    And bid me hold my peace. I pray you all,
    If you have hitherto conceal'd this sight,   245
    Let it be tenable in your silence still;
    And whatsoever else shall hap to-night,
    Give it an understanding, but no tongue:
    I will requite your loves. So, fare you well:
    Upon the platform, 'twixt eleven and twelve,   250
    I'll visit you.
All: Our duty to your honour.
Hamlet: Your loves, as mine to you: farewell.   *Exeunt [all but Hamlet].*
    My father's spirit in arms! all is not well;
    I doubt° some foul play: would the night were come!
    Till then sit still, my soul: foul deeds will rise,   255
    Though all the earth o'erwhelm them, to men's eyes.   *Exit.*

[SCENE III: *A room in Polonius's house.*]

    Enter Laertes and Ophelia, his Sister.

Laertes: My necessaries are embark'd: farewell:
    And, sister, as the winds give benefit
    And convoy is assistant,° do not sleep,
    But let me hear from you.
Ophelia: Do you doubt that?
Laertes: For Hamlet and the trifling of his favour,   5

---

240 *sable:* Black color.   254 *doubt:* Fear.   **Scene III.**   3 *convoy is assistant:* Means of conveyance are available.

Hold it a fashion° and a toy in blood,°
A violet in the youth of primy° nature,
Forward,° not permanent, sweet, not lasting,
The perfume and suppliance of a minute;°
No more.

Ophelia: No more but so?
Laertes: Think it no more: 10
For nature, crescent,° does not grow alone
In thews° and bulk, but, as this temple° waxes,
The inward service of the mind and soul
Grows wide withal. Perhaps he loves you now,
And now no soil° nor cautel° doth besmirch   15
The virtue of his will: but you must fear,
His greatness weigh'd,° his will is not his own;
For he himself is subject to his birth:
He may not, as unvalued persons do,
Carve for himself; for on his choice depends   20
The safety and health of this whole state;
And therefore must his choice be circumscrib'd
Unto the voice and yielding° of that body
Whereof he is the head. Then if he says he loves you,
It fits your wisdom so far to believe it   25
As he in his particular act and place
May give his saying deed;° which is no further
Than the main voice of Denmark goes withal.
Then weigh what loss your honour may sustain,
If with too credent° ear you list his songs,   30
Or lose your heart, or your chaste treasure open
To his unmast'red° importunity.
Fear it, Ophelia, fear it, my dear sister,
And keep you in the rear of your affection,
Out of the shot and danger of desire.   35
The chariest° maid is prodigal enough,
If she unmask her beauty to the moon:
Virtue itself 'scapes not calumnious strokes:
The canker galls the infants of the spring,°
Too oft before their buttons° be disclos'd,°   40
And in the morn and liquid dew° of youth
Contagious blastments° are most imminent.
Be wary then; best safety lies in fear:
Youth to itself rebels, though none else near.

---

6 *fashion:* Custom, prevailing usage; *toy in blood:* Passing amorous fancy.   7 *primy:* In its
prime.   8 *Forward:* Precocious.   9 *suppliance of a minute:* Diversion to fill up a minute.
11 *crescent:* Growing, waxing.   12 *thews:* Bodily strength; *temple:* Body.   15 *soil:* Blemish; *cautel:* Crafty device.   17 *greatness weigh'd:* High position considered.   23 *voice and
yielding:* Assent, approval.   27 *deed:* Effect.   30 *credent:* Credulous.   32 *unmast'red:*
Unrestrained.   36 *chariest:* Most scrupulously modest.   39 *The canker...spring:* The
cankerworm destroys the young plants of spring.   40 *buttons:* Buds; *disclos'd:* Opened.
41 *liquid dew:* I.e., time when dew is fresh.   42 *blastments:* Blights.

Ophelia: I shall the effect of this good lesson keep,   45
    As watchman to my heart. But, good my brother,
    Do not, as some ungracious° pastors do,
    Show me the steep and thorny way to heaven;
    Whiles, like a puff'd° and reckless libertine,
    Himself the primrose path of dalliance treads,   50
    And recks° not his own rede.°

    Enter Polonius.

Laertes: O, fear me not.
    I stay too long: but here my father comes.
    A double° blessing is a double grace;
    Occasion° smiles upon a second leave.
Polonius: Yet here, Laertes? aboard, aboard, for shame!   55
    The wind sits in the shoulder of your sail,
    And you are stay'd for. There; my blessing with thee!
    And these few precepts° in thy memory
    Look thou character.° Give thy thoughts no tongue,
    Nor any unproportion'd° thought his act.   60
    Be thou familiar, but by no means vulgar.°
    Those friends thou hast, and their adoption tried,
    Grapple them to thy soul with hoops of steel;
    But do not dull thy palm with entertainment
    Of each new-hatch'd, unfledg'd° comrade. Beware   65
    Of entrance to a quarrel, but being in,
    Bear't that th' opposed may beware of thee.
    Give every man thy ear, but few thy voice;
    Take each man's censure, but reserve thy judgement.
    Costly thy habit as thy purse can buy,   70
    But not express'd in fancy;° rich, not gaudy;
    For the apparel oft proclaims the man,
    And they in France of the best rank and station
    Are of a most select and generous chief in that.°
    Neither a borrower nor a lender be;   75
    For loan oft loses both itself and friend,
    And borrowing dulleth edge of husbandry.°
    This above all: to thine own self be true,
    And it must follow, as the night the day,
    Thou canst not then be false to any man.   80
    Farewell: my blessing season° this in thee!
Laertes: Most humbly do I take my leave, my lord.
Polonius: The time invites you; go; your servants tend.

---

47 *ungracious:* Graceless.   49 *puff'd:* Bloated.   51 *recks:* Heeds; *rede:* Counsel.   53 *double:* I.e., Laertes has already bade his father good-by.   54 *Occasion:* Opportunity.   58 *precepts:* Many parallels have been found to the series of maxims which follows, one of the closer being that in Lyly's *Euphues.*   59 *character:* Inscribe.   60 *unproportion'd:* Inordinate.   61 *vulgar:* Common.   65 *unfledg'd:* Immature.   71 *express'd in fancy:* Fantastical in design.   74 *Are . . . that: Chief* is usually taken as a substantive meaning "head," "eminence."   77 *husbandry:* Thrift.   81 *season:* Mature.

Laertes: Farewell, Ophelia; and remember well
   What I have said to you.
Ophelia: 'Tis in my memory lock'd,   85
   And you yourself shall keep the key of it.
Laertes: Farewell.   *Exit Laertes.*
Polonius: What is 't, Ophelia, he hath said to you?
Ophelia: So please you, something touching the Lord Hamlet.
Polonius: Marry, well bethought: 90
   'Tis told me, he hath very oft of late
   Given private time to you; and you yourself
   Have of your audience been most free and bounteous:
   If it be so, as so't is put on° me,
   And that in way of caution, I must tell you,   95
   You do not understand yourself so clearly
   As it behooves my daughter and your honour.
   What is between you? give me up the truth.
Ophelia: He hath, my lord, of late made many tenders°
   Of his affection to me.   100
Polonius: Affection! pooh! you speak like a green girl,
   Unsifted° in such perilous circumstance.
   Do you believe his tenders, as you call them?
Ophelia: I do not know, my lord, what I should think.
Polonius: Marry, I will teach you: think yourself a baby;   105
   That you have ta'en these tenders° for true pay,
   Which are not sterling.° Tender° yourself more dearly;
   Or — not to crack the wind° of the poor phrase,
   Running it thus — you'll tender me a fool.°
Ophelia: My lord, he hath importun'd me with love   110
   In honourable fashion.
Polonius: Ay, fashion° you may call it; go to, go to.
Ophelia: And hath given countenance° to his speech, my lord,
   With almost all the holy vows of heaven.
Polonius: Ay, springes° to catch woodcocks.° I do know,   115
   When the blood burns, how prodigal the soul
   Lends the tongue vows: these blazes, daughter,
   Giving more light than heat, extinct in both,
   Even in their promise, as it is a-making,
   You must not take for fire. From this time   120
   Be somewhat scanter of your maiden presence;
   Set your entreatments° at a higher rate
   Than a command to parley.° For Lord Hamlet,
   Believe so much in him,° that he is young,
   And with a larger tether may he walk   125

---

94 *put on:* Impressed on.   99, 103 *tenders:* Offers.   102 *Unsifted:* Untried.   106 *tenders:* Promises to pay.   107 *sterling:* Legal currency; *Tender:* Hold.   108 *crack the wind:* I.e., run it until it is broken-winded.   109 *tender . . . fool:* Show me a fool (for a daughter). 112 *fashion:* Mere form, pretense.   113 *countenance:* Credit, support.   115 *springes:* Snares; *woodcocks:* Birds easily caught, type of stupidity.   122 *entreatments:* Conversations, interviews.   123 *command to parley:* Mere invitation to talk.   124 *so . . . him:* This much concerning him.

Than may be given you: in few,° Ophelia,
Do not believe his vows; for they are brokers;°
Not of that dye° which their investments° show,
But mere implorators of° unholy suits,
Breathing° like sanctified and pious bawds,   130
The better to beguile. This is for all:
I would not, in plain terms, from this time forth,
Have you so slander° any moment leisure,
As to give words or talk with the Lord Hamlet.
Look to 't, I charge you: come your ways.   135
Ophelia: I shall obey, my lord.   *Exeunt.*

[SCENE IV: *The platform.*]

Enter Hamlet, Horatio, and Marcellus.

Hamlet: The air bites shrewdly; it is very cold.
Horatio: It is a nipping and an eager air.
Hamlet: What hour now?
Horatio: I think it lacks of twelve.
Marcellus: No, it is struck.
Horatio: Indeed? I heard it not: then it draws near the season   5
Wherein the spirit held his wont to walk.

A flourish of trumpets, and two pieces go off.

What does this mean, my lord?
Hamlet: The king doth wake° to-night and takes his rouse,°
Keeps wassail,° and the swagg'ring up-spring° reels;°
And, as he drains his draughts of Rhenish° down,   10
The kettle-drum and trumpet thus bray out
The triumph of his pledge.°
Horatio: Is it a custom?
Hamlet: Ay, marry, is 't:
But to my mind, though I am native here
And to the manner born,° it is a custom   15
More honour'd in the breach than the observance.
This heavy-headed revel east and west
Makes us traduc'd and tax'd of other nations:
They clepe° us drunkards, and with swinish phrase°
Soil our addition;° and indeed it takes   20
From our achievements, though perform'd at height,
The pith and marrow of our attribute.°

---

126 *in few:* Briefly.   127 *brokers:* Go-betweens, procurers.   128 *dye:* Color or sort; *invest-ments:* Clothes.   129 *implorators of:* Solicitors of.   130 *Breathing:* Speaking.   133 *slan-der:* Bring disgrace or reproach upon.   **Scene IV.**   8 *wake:* Stay awake, hold revel; *rouse:* Carouse, drinking bout.   9 *wassail:* Carousal; *up-spring:* Last and wildest dance at German merry-makings; *reels:* Reels through.   10 *Rhenish:* Rhine wine.   12 *triumph...pledge:* His glorious achievement as a drinker.   15 *to...born:* Destined by birth to be subject to the custom in question.   19 *clepe:* Call; *with swinish phrase:* By calling us swine.   20 *addi-tion:* Reputation.   22 *attribute:* Reputation.

So, oft it chances in particular men,
That for some vicious mole of nature° in them,
As, in their birth — wherein they are not guilty, 25
Since nature cannot choose his origin —
By the o'ergrowth of some complexion,
Oft breaking down the pales° and forts of reason,
Or by some habit that too much o'er-leavens°
The form of plausive° manners, that these men, 30
Carrying, I say, the stamp of one defect,
Being nature's livery,° or fortune's star,° —
Their virtues else — be they as pure as grace,
As infinite as man may undergo —
Shall in the general censure take corruption 35
From that particular fault: the dram of eale°
Doth all the noble substance of a doubt
To his own scandal.°

Enter Ghost.

Horatio: Look, my lord, it comes!
Hamlet: Angels and ministers of grace° defend us!
Be thou a spirit of health or goblin damn'd, 40
Bring with thee airs from heaven or blasts from hell,
Be thy intents wicked or charitable,
Thou com'st in such a questionable° shape
That I will speak to thee: I'll call thee Hamlet,
King, father, royal Dane: O, answer me! 45
Let me not burst in ignorance; but tell
Why thy canoniz'd° bones, hearsed° in death,
Have burst their cerements;° why the sepulchre,
Wherein we saw thee quietly interr'd,
Hath op'd his ponderous and marble jaws, 50
To cast thee up again. What may this mean,
That thou, dead corse, again in complete steel
Revisits thus the glimpses of the moon,°
Making night hideous; and we fools of nature°
So horridly to shake our disposition 55
With thoughts beyond the reaches of our souls?
Say, why is this? wherefore? what should we do?

[Ghost] beckons [Hamlet].

---

24 *mole of nature:* Natural blemish in one's constitution.   28 *pales:* Palings (as of a fortification).   29 *o'er-leavens:* Induces a change throughout (as yeast works in bread).   30 *plausive:* Pleasing.   32 *nature's livery:* Endowment from nature; *fortune's star:* The position in which one is placed by fortune, a reference to astrology. The two phrases are aspects of the same thing.   36-38 *the dram ... scandal:* A famous crux: *dram of eale* has had various interpretations, the preferred one being probably, "a dram of evil."   39 *ministers of grace:* Messengers of God.   43 *questionable:* Inviting question or conversation.   47 *canoniz'd:* Buried according to the canons of the church; *hearsed:* Coffined.   48 *cerements:* Graveclothes.   53 *glimpses of the moon:* The earth by night.   54 *fools of nature:* Mere men, limited to natural knowledge.

Horatio: It beckons you to go away with it,
  As if it some impartment° did desire
  To you alone.
Marcellus: Look, with what courteous action   60
  It waves you to a more removed° ground:
  But do not go with it.
Horatio: No, by no means.
Hamlet: It will not speak; then I will follow it.
Horatio: Do not, my lord!
Hamlet: Why, what should be the fear?
  I do not set my life at a pin's fee;   65
  And for my soul, what can it do to that,
  Being a thing immortal as itself?
  It waves me forth again: I'll follow it.
Horatio: What if it tempt you toward the flood, my lord,
  Or to the dreadful summit of the cliff   70
  That beetles o'er° his base into the sea,
  And there assume some other horrible form,
  Which might deprive your sovereignty of reason°
  And draw you into madness? think of it:
  The very place puts toys of desperation,°   75
  Without more motive, into every brain
  That looks so many fathoms to the sea
  And hears it roar beneath.
Hamlet: It waves me still.
  Go on; I'll follow thee.
Marcellus: You shall not go, my lord.
Hamlet: Hold off your hands!   80
Horatio: Be rul'd; you shall not go.
Hamlet: My fate cries out,
  And makes each petty artere° in this body
  As hardy as the Nemean lion's° nerve.°
  Still am I call'd. Unhand me, gentlemen.
  By heaven, I'll make a ghost of him that lets° me!   85
  I say, away! Go on; I'll follow thee.   *Exeunt Ghost and Hamlet.*
Horatio: He waxes desperate with imagination.
Marcellus: Let's follow; 'tis not fit thus to obey him.
Horatio: Have after. To what issue° will this come?
Marcellus: Something is rotten in the state of Denmark.   90
Horatio: Heaven will direct it.°
Marcellus: Nay, let's follow him.   *Exeunt.*

---

59 *impartment:* Communication.   61 *removed:* Remote.   71 *beetles o'er:* Overhangs threateningly.   73 *deprive . . . reason:* Take away the sovereignty of your reason. It was thought
that evil spirits would sometimes assume the form of departed spirits in order to work madness in a human creature.   75 *toys of desperation:* Freakish notions of suicide.   82 *artere:*
Artery.   83 *Nemean lion's:* The Nemean lion was one of the monsters slain by Hercules;
nerve: Sinew, tendon. The point is that the arteries which were carrying the spirits out into
the body were functioning and were as stiff and hard as the sinews of the lion.   85 *lets:*
Hinders.   89 *issue:* Outcome.   91 *it:* I.e., the outcome.

[SCENE V: *Another part of the platform.*]

    Enter Ghost and Hamlet.

Hamlet: Whither wilt thou lead me? speak; I'll go no further.
Ghost: Mark me.
Hamlet: I will.
Ghost: My hour is almost come,
    When I to sulphurous and tormenting flames
    Must render up myself.
Hamlet: Alas, poor ghost!
Ghost: Pity me not, but lend thy serious hearing   5
    To what I shall unfold.
Hamlet: Speak; I am bound to hear.
Ghost: So art thou to revenge, when thou shalt hear.
Hamlet: What?
Ghost: I am thy father's spirit,
    Doom'd for a certain term to walk the night,   10
    And for the day confin'd to fast° in fires,
    Till the foul crimes done in my days of nature
    Are burnt and purg'd away. But that I am forbid
    To tell the secrets of my prison-house,
    I could a tale unfold whose lightest word   15
    Would harrow up thy soul, freeze thy young blood,
    Make thy two eyes, like stars, start from their spheres,°
    Thy knotted° and combined° locks to part
    And each particular hair to stand an end,
    Like quills upon the fretful porpentine:°   20
    But this eternal blazon° must not be
    To ears of flesh and blood. List, list, O, list!
    If thou didst ever thy dear father love —
Hamlet: O God!
Ghost: Revenge his foul and most unnatural° murder.   25
Hamlet: Murder!
Ghost: Murder most foul, as in the best it is;
    But this most foul, strange and unnatural.
Hamlet: Haste me to know't, that I, with wings as swift
    As meditation or the thoughts of love,   30
    May sweep to my revenge.
Ghost: I find thee apt;
    And duller shouldst thou be than the fat weed°
    That roots itself in ease on Lethe wharf,°
    Wouldst thou not stir in this. Now, Hamlet, hear:

Scene V.   11 *fast:* Probably, do without food. It has been sometimes taken in the sense of doing general penance.   17 *spheres:* Orbits.   18 *knotted:* Perhaps intricately arranged; *combined:* Tied, bound.   20 *porpentine:* Porcupine.   21 *eternal blazon:* Promulgation or proclamation of eternity, revelation of the hereafter.   25 *unnatural:* I.e., pertaining to fratricide.   32 *fat weed:* Many suggestions have been offered as to the particular plant intended, including asphodel; probably a general figure for plants growing along rotting wharves and piles.   33 *Lethe wharf:* Bank of the river of forgetfulness in Hades.

'Tis given out that, sleeping in my orchard,   35
A serpent stung me; so the whole ear of Denmark
Is by a forged process of my death
Rankly abus'd: but know, thou noble youth,
The serpent that did sting thy father's life
Now wears his crown.
Hamlet: O my prophetic soul!   40
   My uncle!
Ghost: Ay, that incestuous, that adulterate° beast,
   With witchcraft of his wit, with traitorous gifts, —
   O wicked wit and gifts, that have the power
   So to seduce! — won to his shameful lust   45
   The will of my most seeming-virtuous queen:
   O Hamlet, what a falling-off was there!
   From me, whose love was of that dignity
   That it went hand in hand even with the vow
   I made to her in marriage, and to decline   50
   Upon a wretch whose natural gifts were poor
   To those of mine!
   But virtue, as it never will be moved,
   Though lewdness court it in a shape of heaven,
   So lust, though to a radiant angel link'd,   55
   Will sate itself in a celestial bed,
   And prey on garbage.
   But, soft! methinks I scent the morning air;
   Brief let me be. Sleeping within my orchard,
   My custom always of the afternoon,   60
   Upon my secure° hour thy uncle stole,
   With juice of cursed hebona° in a vial,
   And in the porches of my ears did pour
   The leperous° distilment; whose effect
   Holds such an enmity with blood of man   65
   That swift as quicksilver it courses through
   The natural gates and alleys of the body,
   And with a sudden vigour it doth posset°
   And curd, like eager° droppings into milk,
   The thin and wholesome blood: so did it mine;   70
   And a most instant tetter bark'd about,
   Most lazar-like,° with vile and loathsome crust,
   All my smooth body.
   Thus was I, sleeping, by a brother's hand
   Of life, of crown, of queen, at once dispatch'd:°   75
   Cut off even in the blossoms of my sin,
   Unhous'led,° disappointed,° unanel'd,°

---

42 *adulterate:* Adulterous.   61 *secure:* Confident, unsuspicious.   62 *hebona:* Generally
supposed to mean henbane, conjectured *hemlock; ebenus,* meaning "yew."   64 *leperous:*
Causing leprosy.   68 *posset:* Coagulate, curdle.   69 *eager:* Sour, acid.   72 *lazar-like:*
Leperlike.   75 *dispatch'd:* Suddenly bereft.   77 *Unhous'led:* Without having received the
sacrament; *disappointed:* Unready, without equipment for the last journey; *unanel'd:* Without
having received extreme unction.

No reck'ning made, but sent to my account
With all my imperfections on my head:
O, horrible! O, horrible! most horrible!°   80
If thou hast nature in thee, bear it not;
Let not the royal bed of Denmark be
A couch for luxury° and damned incest.
But, howsomever thou pursues this act,
Taint not thy mind,° nor let thy soul contrive   85
Against thy mother aught: leave her to heaven
And to those thorns that in her bosom lodge,
To prick and sting her. Fare thee well at once!
The glow-worm shows the matin° to be near,
And 'gins to pale his uneffectual fire:°   90
Adieu, adieu, adieu! remember me.   *[Exit.]*

Hamlet: O all you host of heaven! O earth! what else?
And shall I couple° hell? O, fie! Hold, hold, my heart;
And you, my sinews, grow not instant old,
But bear me stiffly up. Remember thee!   95
Ay, thou poor ghost, whiles memory holds a seat
In this distracted globe.° Remember thee!
Yea, from the table of my memory
I'll wipe away all trivial fond records,
All saws° of books, all forms, all pressures° past,   100
That youth and observation copied there;
And thy commandment all alone shall live
Within the book and volume of my brain,
Unmix'd with baser matter: yes, by heaven!
O most pernicious woman!   105
O villain, villain, smiling, damned villain!
My tables,° — meet it is I set it down,
That one may smile, and smile, and be a villain;
At least I am sure it may be so in Denmark: *[Writing.]*
So, uncle, there you are. Now to my word;°   110
It is "Adieu, adieu! remember me,"
I have sworn't.

     Enter Horatio and Marcellus.

Horatio: My lord, my lord —
Marcellus: Lord Hamlet, —
Horatio: Heavens secure him!
Hamlet: So be it!
Marcellus: Hillo, ho, ho,° my lord!   115

---

80 *O . . . horrible:* Many editors give this line to Hamlet; Garrick and Sir Henry Irving spoke it in that part.   83 *luxury:* Lechery.   85 *Taint . . . mind:* Probably, deprave not thy character, do nothing except in the pursuit of a natural revenge.   89 *matin:* Morning. 90 *uneffectual fire:* Cold light.   93 *couple:* Add.   97 *distracted globe:* Confused head. 100 *saws:* Wise sayings; *pressures:* Impressions stamped.   107 *tables:* Probably a small portable writing-tablet carried at the belt.   110 *word:* Watchword.   115 *Hillo, ho, ho:* A falconer's call to a hawk in air.

Hamlet: Hillo, ho, ho, boy! come, bird, come.

Marcellus: How is 't, my noble lord?

Horatio: What news, my lord?

Hamlet: O, wonderful!

Horatio: Good my lord, tell it.

Hamlet: No; you will reveal it.

Horatio: Not I, my lord, by heaven.

Marcellus: Nor I, my lord.   120

Hamlet: How say you, then; would heart of man once think it?
      But you'll be secret?

Horatio: ⎱
Marcellus: ⎰   Ay, by heaven, my lord.

Hamlet: There's ne'er a villain dwelling in all Denmark
      But he's an arrant° knave.

Horatio: There needs no ghost, my lord, come from the grave   125
      To tell us this.

Hamlet: Why, right; you are in the right;
      And so, without more circumstance at all,
      I hold it fit that we shake hands and part:
      You, as your business and desire shall point you;
      For every man has business and desire,   130
      Such as it is; and for my own poor part,
      Look you, I'll go pray.

Horatio: These are but wild and whirling words, my lord.

Hamlet: I am sorry they offend you, heartily;
      Yes, 'faith, heartily.

Horatio: There's no offence, my lord.   135

Hamlet: Yes, by Saint Patrick,° but there is, Horatio,
      And much offence too. Touching this vision here,
      It is an honest° ghost, that let me tell you:
      For your desire to know what is between us,
      O'ermaster 't as you may. And now, good friends,   140
      As you are friends, scholars and soldiers,
      Give me one poor request.

Horatio: What is 't, my lord? we will.

Hamlet: Never make known what you have seen to-night.

Horatio: ⎱
Marcellus: ⎰ My lord, we will not.

Hamlet: Nay, but swear 't.

Horatio: In faith,   145
      My lord, not I.

Marcellus: Nor I, my lord, in faith.

Hamlet: Upon my sword.°

Marcellus: We have sworn, my lord, already.

---

124 *arrant:* Thoroughgoing.   136 *Saint Patrick:* St. Patrick was keeper of Purgatory and patron saint of all blunders and confusion.   138 *honest:* I.e., a real ghost and not an evil spirit.   147 *sword:* I.e., the hilt in the form of a cross.

Hamlet: Indeed, upon my sword, indeed.   *Ghost cries under the stage.*
Ghost: Swear.
Hamlet: Ah, ha, boy! say'st thou so? art thou there, truepenny?°   150
   Come on — you hear this fellow in the cellarage —
   Consent to swear.
Horatio: Propose the oath, my lord.
Hamlet: Never to speak of this that you have seen,
   Swear by my sword.
Ghost [beneath]: Swear.   155
Hamlet: Hic et ubique?° then we'll shift our ground.
   Come hither, gentlemen,
   And lay your hands again upon my sword:
   Swear by my sword,
   Never to speak of this that you have heard.   160
Ghost [beneath]: Swear by his sword.
Hamlet: Well said, old mole! canst work i' th' earth so fast?
   A worthy pioner!° Once more remove, good friends.
Horatio: O day and night, but this is wondrous strange!
Hamlet: And therefore as a stranger give it welcome.   165
   There are more things in heaven and earth, Horatio,
   Than are dreamt of in your philosophy.
   But come;
   Here, as before, never, so help you mercy,
   How strange or odd soe'er I bear myself,   170
   As I perchance hereafter shall think meet
   To put an antic° disposition on,
   That you, at such times seeing me, never shall,
   With arms encumb'red° thus, or this head-shake,
   Or by pronouncing of some doubtful phrase,   175
   As "Well, well, we know," or "We could, an if we would,"
   Or "If we list to speak," or "There be, an if they might,"
   Or such ambiguous giving out,° to note°
   That you know aught of me: this not to do,
   So grace and mercy at your most need help you,   180
   Swear.
Ghost [beneath]: Swear.
Hamlet: Rest, rest, perturbed spirit! *[They swear.]* So, gentlemen,
   With all my love I do commend me to you:
   And what so poor a man as Hamlet is   185
   May do, t' express his love and friending° to you,
   God willing, shall not lack. Let us go in together;
   And still your fingers on your lips, I pray.
   The time is out of joint: O cursed spite,
   That ever I was born to set it right!   190
   Nay, come, let's go together.   *Exeunt.*

---

150 *truepenny:* Good old boy, or the like.   156 *Hic et ubique?:* Here and everywhere?
163 *pioner:* Digger, miner.   172 *antic:* Fantastic.   174 *encumb'red:* Folded or entwined.
178 *giving out:* Profession of knowledge; *to note:* To give a sign.   186 *friending:* Friendliness.

[ACT II

SCENE I: *A room in Polonius's house.*]

Enter old Polonius with his man [Reynaldo].

Polonius: Give him this money and these notes, Reynaldo.
Reynaldo: I will, my lord.
Polonius: You shall do marvellous wisely, good Reynaldo,
  Before you visit him, to make inquire
  Of his behaviour.
Reynaldo: My lord, I did intend it.   5
Polonius: Marry, well said; very well said. Look you, sir,
  Inquire me first what Danskers° are in Paris;
  And how, and who, what means, and where they keep,°
  What company, at what expense; and finding
  By this encompassment° and drift° of question   10
  That they do know my son, come you more nearer
  Than your particular demands will touch it:°
  Take° you as 'twere, some distant knowledge of him;
  As thus, "I know his father and his friends,
  And in part him": do you mark this, Reynaldo?   15
Reynaldo: Ay, very well, my lord.
Polonius: "And in part him; but" you may say "not well:
  But, if 't be he I mean, he's very wild;
  Addicted so and so": and there put on° him
  What forgeries° you please; marry, none so rank   20
  As may dishonour him; take heed of that;
  But, sir, such wanton,° wild and usual slips
  As are companions noted and most known
  To youth and liberty.
Reynaldo: As gaming, my lord.
Polonius: Ay, or drinking, fencing,° swearing, quarrelling,   25
  Drabbing;° you may go so far.
Reynaldo: My lord, that would dishonour him.
Polonius: 'Faith, no; as you may season it in the charge.
  You must not put another scandal on him,
  That he is open to incontinency;°   30
  That's not my meaning: but breathe his faults so quaintly°
  That they may seem the taints of liberty,°
  The flash and outbreak of a fiery mind,

Act II, Scene I.   7 *Danskers:* Danke was a common variant for "Denmark"; hence "Dane."
8 *keep:* Dwell.   10 *encompassment:* Roundabout talking; *drift:* Gradual approach or course.
11–12 *come...it:* I.e., you will find out more this way than by asking pointed questions.
13 *Take:* Assume, pretend.   19 *put on:* Impute to.   20 *forgeries:* Invented tales.   22 *wanton:* Sportive, unrestrained.   25 *fencing:* Indicative of the ill repute of professional fencers
and fencing schools in Elizabethan times.   26 *Drabbing:* Associating with immoral
women.   30 *incontinency:* Habitual loose behavior.   31 *quaintly:* Delicately, ingeniously.
32 *taints of liberty:* Blemishes due to freedom.

A savageness in unreclaimed° blood,
Of general assault.°
Reynaldo: But, my good lord, —   35
Polonius: Wherefore should you do this?
Reynaldo: Ay, my lord,
I would know that.
Polonius: Marry, sir, here's my drift;
And, I believe, it is a fetch of wit:°
You laying these slight sullies on my son,
As 'twere a thing a little soil'd i' th' working,   40
Mark you,
Your party in converse, him you would sound,
Having ever° seen in the prenominate° crimes
The youth you breathe of guilty, be assur'd
He closes with you in this consequence;°   45
"Good sir," or so, or "friend," or "gentleman,"
According to the phrase or the addition
Of man and country.
Reynaldo: Very good, my lord.
Polonius: And then, sir, does 'a this — 'a does — what was I about to say? By
the mass, I was about to say something: where did I leave?   50
Reynaldo: At "closes in the consequence," at "friend or so," and "gentle-
man."
Polonius: At "closes in the consequence," ay, marry;
He closes thus: "I know the gentleman;
I saw him yesterday, or t' other day,   55
Or then, or then; with such, or such; and, as you say,
There was 'a gaming; there o'ertook in 's rouse;°
There falling out at tennis": or perchance,
"I saw him enter such a house of sale,"
Videlicet,° a brothel, or so forth.   60
See you now;
Your bait of falsehood takes this carp of truth:
And thus do we of wisdom and of reach,°
With windlasses° and with assays of bias,°
By indirections° find directions° out: 65
So by my former lecture° and advice,
Shall you my son. You have me, have you not?
Reynaldo: My lord, I have.
Polonius: God bye ye;° fare ye well.
Reynaldo: Good my lord!
Polonius: Observe his inclination in yourself.°   70

---

34 *unreclaimed:* Untamed.   36 *general assault:* Tendency that assails all untrained youth.
38 *fetch of wit:* Clever trick.   43 *ever:* At any time; *prenominate:* Before-mentioned.
45 *closes . . . consequence:* Agrees with you in this conclusion.   57 *o'ertook in 's rouse:* Overcome by drink.   60 *Videlicet:* Namely.   63 *reach:* Capacity, ability.   64 *windlasses:* I.e.,
circuitous paths; *assays of bias:* Attempts that resemble the course of the bowl, which, being
weighted on one side, has a curving motion.   65 *indirections:* Devious courses; *directions:*
Straight courses, i.e., the truth.   66 *lecture:* Admonition.   68 *bye ye:* Be with you.
70 *Observe . . . yourself:* In your own person, not by spies; or conform your own conduct to
his inclination; or test him by studying yourself.

Reynaldo: I shall, my lord.
Polonius: And let him ply his music.°
Reynaldo: Well, my lord.
Polonius: Farewell!   *Exit Reynaldo.*

    Enter Ophelia.

                How now, Ophelia! what's the matter?
Ophelia: O, my lord, my lord, I have been so affrighted!
Polonius: With what, i' th' name of God?   75
Ophelia: My lord, as I was sewing in my closet,°
    Lord Hamlet, with his doublet° all unbrac'd;°
    No hat upon his head; his stockings foul'd,
    Ungart'red, and down-gyved° to his ankle;
    Pale as his shirt; his knees knocking each other;   80
    And with a look so piteous in purport
    As if he had been loosed out of hell
    To speak of horrors,—he comes before me.
Polonius: Mad for thy love?
Ophelia: My lord, I do not know;
    But truly, I do fear it.
Polonius: What said he?   85
Ophelia: He took me by the wrist and held me hard;
    Then goes he to the length of all his arm;
    And, with his other hand thus o'er his brow,
    He falls to such perusal of my face
    As 'a would draw it. Long stay'd he so;   90
    At last, a little shaking of mine arm
    And thrice his head thus waving up and down,
    He rais'd a sigh so piteous and profound
    As it did seem to shatter all his bulk°
    And end his being: that done, he lets me go: 95
    And, with his head over his shoulder turn'd,
    He seem'd to find his way without his eyes;
    For out o' doors he went without their helps,
    And, to the last, bended their light on me.
Polonius: Come, go with me: I will go seek the king.   100
    This is the very ecstasy of love,
    Whose violent property° fordoes° itself
    And leads the will to desperate undertakings
    As oft as any passion under heaven
    That does afflict our natures. I am sorry.   105
    What, have you given him any hard words of late?
Ophelia: No, my good lord, but, as you did command,
    I did repel his letters and denied
    His access to me.
Polonius: That hath made him mad.
    I am sorry that with better heed and judgement   110

---

72 *ply his music:* Probably to be taken literally.   76 *closet:* Private chamber.   77 *doublet:*
Close-fitting coat; *unbrac'd:* Unfastened.   79 *down-gyved:* Fallen to the ankles (like gyves
or fetters).   94 *bulk:* Body.   102 *property:* Nature; *fordoes:* Destroys.

I had not quoted° him: I fear'd he did but trifle,
And meant to wrack thee; but, beshrew my jealousy!°
By heaven, it is as proper to our age
To cast beyond° ourselves in our opinions
As it is common for the younger sort   115
To lack discretion. Come, go we to the king:
This must be known; which, being kept close, might move
More grief to hide than hate to utter love.°
Come.   *Exeunt.*

[SCENE II: *A room in the castle.*]

Flourish. Enter King and Queen, Rosencrantz, and Guildenstern [with others].

King: Welcome, dear Rosencrantz and Guildenstern!
Moreover that° we much did long to see you,
The need we have to use you did provoke
Our hasty sending. Something have you heard
Of Hamlet's transformation; so call it,   5
Sith° nor th' exterior nor the inward man
Resembles that it was. What it should be,
More than his father's death, that thus hath put him
So much from th' understanding of himself,
I cannot dream of: I entreat you both,   10
That, being of so young days° brought up with him,
And sith so neighbour'd to his youth and haviour,
That you vouchsafe your rest° here in our court
Some little time: so by your companies
To draw him on to pleasures, and to gather,   15
So much as from occasion you may glean,
Whether aught, to us unknown, afflicts him thus,
That, open'd, lies within our remedy.
Queen: Good gentlemen, he hath much talk'd of you;
And sure I am two men there are not living   20
To whom he more adheres. If it will please you
To show us so much gentry° and good will
As to expend your time with us awhile,
For the supply and profit° of our hope,
Your visitation shall receive such thanks   25
As fits a king's remembrance.
Rosencrantz: Both your majesties
Might, by the sovereign power you have of us,
Put your dread pleasures more into command
Than to entreaty.

---

111 *quoted:* Observed.   112 *beshrew my jealousy:* Curse my suspicions.   114 *cast beyond:*
Overshoot, miscalculate.   117-118 *might... love:* I.e., I might cause more grief to others by
hiding the knowledge of Hamlet's love to Ophelia than hatred to me and mine by telling of it.
Scene II.   2 *Moreover that:* Besides the fact that.   6 *Sith:* Since.   11 *of... days:* From
such early youth.   13 *vouchsafe your rest:* Please to stay.   22 *gentry:* Courtesy.   24 *supply and profit:* Aid and successful outcome.

Guildenstern: But we both obey,
   And here give up ourselves, in the full bent°   30
   To lay our service freely at your feet,
   To be commanded.
King: Thanks, Rosencrantz and gentle Guildenstern.
Queen: Thanks, Guildenstern and gentle Rosencrantz:
   And I beseech you instantly to visit   35
   My too much changed son. Go, some of you,
   And bring these gentlemen where Hamlet is.
Guildenstern: Heavens make our presence and our practices
   Pleasant and helpful to him!
Queen: Ay, amen!
          Exeunt Rosencrantz and Guildenstern [with some Attendants].

   Enter Polonius.

Polonius: Th' ambassadors from Norway, my good lord,   40
   Are joyfully return'd.
King: Thou still hast been the father of good news.
Polonius: Have I, my lord? I assure my good liege,
   I hold my duty, as I hold my soul,
   Both to my God and to my gracious king: 45
   And I do think, or else this brain of mine
   Hunts not the trail of policy so sure
   As it hath us'd to do, that I have found
   The very cause of Hamlet's lunacy.
King: O, speak of that; that do I long to hear.   50
Polonius: Give first admittance to th' ambassadors;
   My news shall be the fruit to that great feast.
King: Thyself do grace to them, and bring them in.   *[Exit Polonius.]*
   He tells me, my dear Gertrude, he hath found
   The head and source of all your son's distemper.   55
Queen: I doubt° it is no other but the main;°
   His father's death, and our o'erhasty marriage.
King: Well, we shall sift him.

   Enter Ambassadors [Voltimand and Cornelius, with Polonius.]
                    Welcome, my good friends!
   Say, Voltimand, what from our brother Norway?
Voltimand: Most fair return of greetings and desires.   60
   Upon our first, he sent out to suppress
   His nephew's levies; which to him appear'd
   To be a preparation 'gainst the Polack;
   But, better look'd into, he truly found
   It was against your highness: whereat griev'd,   65
   That so his sickness, age and impotence
   Was falsely borne in hand,° sends out arrests
   On Fortinbras; which he, in brief, obeys;

---

30 *in . . . bent:* To the utmost degree of our mental capacity.   56 *doubt:* Fear; *main:* Chief
point, principal concern.   67 *borne in hand:* Deluded.

Receives rebuke from Norway, and in fine°
Makes vow before his uncle never more   70
To give th' assay° of arms against your majesty.
Whereon old Norway, overcome with joy,
Gives him three score thousand crowns in annual fee,
And his commission to employ those soldiers,
So levied as before, against the Polack: 75
With an entreaty, herein further shown,   [Giving a paper.]
That it might please you to give quiet pass
Through your dominions for this enterprise,
On such regards of safety and allowance°
As therein are set down.
King: It likes° us well;   80
And at our more consider'd° time we'll read,
Answer, and think upon this business.
Meantime we thank you for your well-took labour:
Go to your rest; at night we'll feast together:
Most welcome home!   Exeunt Ambassadors.
Polonius: This business is well ended.   85
My liege, and madam, to expostulate
What majesty should be, what duty is,
Why day is day, night night, and time is time,
Were nothing but to waste night, day and time.
Therefore, since brevity is the soul of wit,°   90
And tediousness the limbs and outward flourishes,°
I will be brief: your noble son is mad:
Mad call I it; for, to define true madness
What is 't but to be nothing else but mad?
But let that go.
Queen: More matter, with less art.   95
Polonius: Madam, I swear I use no art at all.
That he is mad, 'tis true: 'tis true 'tis pity;
And pity 'tis 'tis true: a foolish figure;°
But farewell it, for I will use no art.
Mad let us grant him, then: and now remains   100
That we find out the cause of this effect,
Or rather say, the cause of this defect,
For this effect defective comes by cause:
Thus it remains, and the remainder thus.
Perpend.°   105
I have a daughter — have while she is mine —
Who, in her duty and obedience, mark,
Hath given me this: now gather, and surmise. [Reads the letter.] "To the
celestial and my soul's idol,
the most beautified Ophelia," —   110

69 in fine: In the end.   71 assay: Assault, trial (of arms).   79 safety and allowance:
Pledges of safety to the country and terms of permission for the troops to pass.   80 likes:
Pleases.   81 consider'd: Suitable for deliberation.   90 wit: Sound sense or judgment.
91 flourishes: Ostentation, embellishments.   98 figure: Figure of speech.   105 Perpend:
Consider.

That's an ill phrase, a vile phrase; "beautified" is a vile phrase: but you
shall hear. Thus: *[Reads.]*
"In her excellent white bosom, these, & c."
Queen: Came this from Hamlet to her?
Polonius: Good madam, stay awhile; I will be faithful.   *[Reads.]*   115
        "Doubt thou the stars are fire;
          Doubt that the sun doth move;
          Doubt truth to be a liar;
          But never doubt I love.
"O dear Ophelia, I am ill at these numbers;° I have not art to reckon°   120
my groans: but that I love thee best, O most best, believe it. Adieu.
   "Thine evermore, most dear lady, whilst this machine° is to him,
                              HAMLET."
This, in obedience, hath my daughter shown me,
And more above,° hath his solicitings,   125
As they fell out° by time, by means° and place,
All given to mine ear.
King: But how hath she
Receiv'd his love?
Polonius: What do you think of me?
King: As of a man faithful and honourable.
Polonius: I would fain prove so. But what might you think,   130
When I had seen this hot love on the wing—
As I perceiv'd it, I must tell you that,
Before my daughter told me—what might you,
Or my dear majesty your queen here, think,
If I had play'd the desk or table-book,°   135
Or given my heart a winking,° mute and dumb,
Or look'd upon this love with idle sight;
What might you think? No, I went round to work,
And my young mistress thus I did bespeak:°
"Lord Hamlet is a prince, out of thy star;°   140
This must not be": and then I prescripts gave her,
That she should lock herself from his resort,
Admit no messengers, receive no tokens.
Which done, she took the fruits of my advice;
And he, repelled—a short tale to make—   145
Fell into a sadness, then into a fast,
Thence to a watch,° thence into a weakness,
Thence to a lightness,° and, by this declension,°
Into the madness wherein now he raves,
And all we mourn for.
King: Do you think 'tis this?   150
Queen: It may be, very like.

---

120 *ill . . . numbers:* Unskilled at writing verses; *reckon:* Number metrically, scan.   122 *ma-chine:* Bodily frame.   125 *more above:* Moreover.   126 *fell out:* Occurred; *means:* Oppor-tunities (of access).   135 *play'd . . . table-book:* I.e., remained shut up, concealed this in-formation.   136 *given . . . winking:* Given my heart a signal to keep silent.   139 *bespeak:* Address.   140 *out . . . star:* Above thee in position.   147 *watch:* State of sleeplessness.   148 *lightness:* Lightheadedness; *declension:* Decline, deterioration.

Polonius: Hath there been such a time — I would fain know that —
That I have positively said " 'Tis so,"
When it prov'd otherwise?
King: Not that I know.
Polonius [pointing to his head and shoulder]: Take this from this, if this be   155
    otherwise:
If circumstances lead me, I will find
Where truth is hid, though it were hid indeed
Within the centre.°
King: How may we try it further?
Polonius: You know, sometimes he walks four hours together
Here in the lobby.
Queen: So he does indeed.   160
Polonius: At such a time I'll loose my daughter to him:
Be you and I behind an arras° then;
Mark the encounter: if he love her not
And be not from his reason fall'n thereon,°
Let me be no assistant for a state,   165
But keep a farm and carters.
King: We will try it.

    Enter Hamlet [reading on a book].

Queen: But, look, where sadly the poor wretch comes reading.
Polonius: Away, I do beseech you both, away:
                          Exeunt King and Queen [with Attendants].
I'll board° him presently. O, give me leave.
How does my good Lord Hamlet?   170
Hamlet: Well, God-a-mercy.
Polonius: Do you know me, my lord?
Hamlet: Excellent well; you are a fishmonger.°
Polonius: Not I, my lord.
Hamlet: Then I would you were so honest a man.   175
Polonius: Honest, my lord!
Hamlet: Ay, sir; to be honest, as this world goes, is to be one man picked
    out of ten thousand.
Polonius: That's very true, my lord.
Hamlet: For if the sun breed maggots in a dead dog, being a good kissing   180
    carrion,° — Have you a daughter?
Polonius: I have, my lord.
Hamlet: Let her not walk i' the sun:° conception° is a blessing: but as your
    daughter may conceive — Friend, look to 't.
Polonius [aside]: How say you by° that? Still harping on my daughter: yet   185
    he knew me not at first; 'a said I was a fishmonger: 'a is far gone, far

---

158 *centre:* Middle point of the earth.   162 *arras:* Hanging, tapestry.   164 *thereon:* On
that account.   169 *board:* Accost.   173 *fishmonger:* An opprobrious expression meaning
"bawd," "procurer."   180–181 *good kissing carrion:* I.e., a good piece of flesh for kissing (?).
183 *i' the sun:* In the sunshine of princely favors; *conception:* Quibble on "understanding"
and "pregnancy."   185 *by:* Concerning.

gone: and truly in my youth I suffered much extremity for love; very near this. I'll speak to him again. What do you read, my lord?

Hamlet: Words, words, words.

Polonius: What is the matter,° my lord?   190

Hamlet: Between who?°

Polonius: I mean, the matter that you read, my lord.

Hamlet: Slanders, sir: for the satirical rogue says here that old men have grey beards, that their faces are wrinkled, their eyes purging° thick amber and plum-tree gum and that they have a plentiful lack of wit,   195 together with most weak hams: all which, sir, though I most powerfully and potently believe, yet I hold it not honesty° to have it thus set down, for yourself, sir, should be old as I am, if like a crab you could go backward.

Polonius [aside]: Though this be madness, yet there is method in 't. — Will   200 you walk out of the air, my lord?

Hamlet: Into my grave.

Polonius: Indeed, that's out of the air. *(Aside.)* How pregnant sometimes his replies are! a happiness° that often madness hits on, which reason and sanity could not so prosperously° be delivered of. I will leave   205 him, and suddenly contrive the means of meeting between him and my daughter. — My honourable lord, I will most humbly take my leave of you.

Hamlet: You cannot, sir, take from me any thing that I will more willingly part withal: except my life, except my life, except my life.   210

Enter Guildenstern and Rosencrantz.

Polonius: Fare you well, my lord.

Hamlet: These tedious old fools!

Polonius: You go to seek the Lord Hamlet; there he is.

Rosencrantz [to Polonius]: God save you, sir!   *[Exit Polonius.]*

Guildenstern: My honoured lord!   215

Rosencrantz: My most dear lord!

Hamlet: My excellent good friends! How dost thou, Guildenstern? Ah, Rosencrantz! Good lads, how do ye both?

Rosencrantz: As the indifferent° children of the earth.

Guildenstern: Happy, in that we are not over-happy;   220 On Fortune's cap we are not the very button.

Hamlet: Nor the soles of her shoe?

Rosencrantz: Neither, my lord.

Hamlet: Then you live about her waist, or in the middle of her favours?

Guildenstern: 'Faith, her privates° we.   225

Hamlet: In the secret parts of Fortune? O, most true; she is a strumpet. What's the news?

Rosencrantz: None, my lord, but that the world's grown honest.

---

190 *matter:* Substance.   191 *Between who:* Hamlet deliberately takes *matter* as meaning "basis of dispute."   194 *purging:* discharging.   197 *honesty:* Decency.   204 *happiness:* Felicity of expression.   205 *prosperously:* Successfully.   219 *indifferent:* Ordinary.   225 *privates:* I.e., ordinary men (sexual pun on *private parts*).

Hamlet: Then is doomsday near: but your news is not true. Let me question more in particular: what have you, my good friends, deserved at 230 the hands of Fortune, that she sends you to prison hither?

Guildenstern: Prison, my lord!

Hamlet: Denmark's a prison.

Rosencrantz: Then is the world one.

Hamlet: A goodly one; in which there are many confines,° wards and 235 dungeons, Denmark being one o' the worst.

Rosencrantz: We think not so, my lord.

Hamlet: Why, then, 'tis none to you; for there is nothing either good or bad, but thinking makes it so: to me it is a prison.

Rosencrantz: Why then, your ambition makes it one; 'tis too narrow for 240 your mind.

Hamlet: O God, I could be bounded in a nutshell and count myself a king of infinite space, were it not that I have bad dreams.

Guildenstern: Which dreams indeed are ambition, for the very substance of the ambitious° is merely the shadow of a dream. 245

Hamlet: A dream itself is but a shadow.

Rosencrantz: Truly, and I hold ambition of so airy and light a quality that it is but a shadow's shadow.

Hamlet: Then are our beggars bodies, and our monarchs and outstretched heroes the beggars' shadows. Shall we to the court? for, by 250 my fay,° I cannot reason.°

Rosencrantz: ⎫
Guildenstern: ⎭ We'll wait upon° you.

Hamlet: No such matter: I will not sort° you with the rest of my servants, for, to speak to you like an honest man, I am most dreadfully attended.° But, in the beaten way of friendship,° what make you at 255 Elsinore?

Rosencrantz: To visit you, my lord: no other occasion.

Hamlet: Beggar that I am, I am ever poor in thanks; but I thank you: and sure, dear friends, my thanks are too dear a° halfpenny. Were you not sent for? Is it your own inclining? Is it a free visitation? Come, come, 260 deal justly with me: come, come; nay, speak.

Guildenstern: What should we say, my lord?

Hamlet: Why, any thing, but to the purpose. You were sent for; and there is a kind of confession in your looks which your modesties have not craft enough to colour: I know the good king and queen have sent for 265 you.

Rosencrantz: To what end, my lord?

Hamlet: That you must teach me. But let me conjure° you, by the rights of our fellowship, by the consonancy of our youth,° by the obligation of our ever-preserved love, and by what more dear a better proposer° 270

---

235 *confines:* Places of confinement.   244-245 *very . . . ambitious:* That seemingly most substantial thing which the ambitious pursue.   251 *fay:* Faith; *reason:* Argue.   252 *wait upon:* Accompany.   253 *sort:* Class.   254-255 *dreadfully attended:* Poorly provided with servants.   255 *in the . . . friendship:* As a matter of course among friends.   259 *a:* I.e., at a. 268 *conjure:* Adjure, entreat.   269 *consonancy of our youth:* The fact that we are of the same age.   270 *better proposer:* One more skillful in finding proposals.

could charge you withal, be even and direct with me, whether you were sent for, or no?

Rosencrantz [aside to Guildenstern]: What say you?

Hamlet [aside]: Nay, then, I have an eye of you. — If you love me, hold not off.   275

Guildenstern: My lord, we were sent for.

Hamlet: I will tell you why; so shall my anticipation prevent your discovery,° and your secrecy to the king and queen moult no feather. I have of late — but wherefore I know not — lost all my mirth, forgone all custom of exercises; and indeed it goes so heavily with my disposition 280 that this goodly frame, the earth, seems to me a sterile promontory, this most excellent canopy, the air, look you, this brave o'erhanging firmament, this majestical roof fretted° with golden fire, why, it appeareth nothing to me but a foul and pestilent congregation of vapours. What a piece of work is a man! how noble in reason! how 285 infinite in faculties!° in form and moving how express° and admirable! in action how like an angel! in apprehension° how like a god! the beauty of the world! the paragon of animals! And yet, to me, what is this quintessence° of dust? man delights not me: no, nor woman neither, though by your smiling you seem to say so.   290

Rosencrantz: My lord, there was no such stuff in my thoughts.

Hamlet: Why did you laugh then, when I said "man delights not me"?

Rosencrantz: To think, my lord, if you delight not in man, what lenten° entertainment the players shall receive from you: we coted° them on the way; and hither are they coming, to offer you service.   295

Hamlet: He that plays the king shall be welcome; his majesty shall have tribute of me; the adventurous knight shall use his foil and target;° the lover shall not sigh gratis; the humorous man° shall end his part in peace; the clown shall make those laugh whose lungs are tickle o' the sere;° and the lady shall say her mind freely, or the blank verse 300 shall halt for 't.° What players are they?

Rosencrantz: Even those you were wont to take delight in, the tragedians of the city.

Hamlet: How chances it they travel? their residence,° both in reputation and profit, was better both ways.   305

Rosencrantz: I think their inhibition° comes by the means of the late innovation.°

Hamlet: Do they hold the same estimation they did when I was in the city? are they so followed?

Rosencrantz: No, indeed, are they not.   310

277-278 *prevent your discovery:* Forestall your disclosure.   283 *fretted:* Adorned.   286 *faculties:* Capacity; *express:* Well-framed (?), exact (?).   287 *apprehension:* Understanding. 289 *quintessence:* The fifth essence of ancient philosophy, supposed to be the substance of the heavenly bodies and to be latent in all things.   293 *lenten:* Meager.   294 *coted:* Overtook and passed beyond.   297 *foil and target:* Sword and shield.   298 *humorous man:* Actor who takes the part of the humor characters.   299-300 *tickle o' the sere:* Easy on the trigger.   300-301 *the lady . . . for 't:* The lady (fond of talking) shall have opportunity to talk, blank verse or no blank verse.   304 *residence:* Remaining in one place.   306 *inhibition:* Formal prohibition (from acting plays in the city or, possibly, at court).   307 *innovation:* The new fashion in satirical plays performed by boy actors in the "private" theaters.

Hamlet: How° comes it? do they grow rusty?

Rosencrantz: Nay, their endeavour keeps in the wonted pace: but there is, sir, an aery° of children, little eyases,° that cry out on the top of ques-tion,° and are most tyrannically° clapped for 't: these are now the fashion, and so berattle° the common stages°—so they call them— 315 that many wearing rapiers° are afraid of goose-quills° and dare scarce come thither.

Hamlet: What, are they children? who maintains 'em? how are they es-coted?° Will they pursue the quality° no longer than they can sing?° will they not say afterwards, if they should grow themselves to com- 320 mon° players—as it is most like, if their means are no better— their writers do them wrong, to make them exclaim against their own succession?°

Rosencrantz: 'Faith, there has been much to do on both sides; and the na-tion holds it no sin to tarre° them to controversy: there was, for a 325 while, no money bid for argument,° unless the poet and the player went to cuffs° in the question.°

Hamlet: Is't possible?

Guildenstern: O, there has been much throwing about of brains.

Hamlet: Do the boys carry it away?° 330

Rosencrantz: Ay, that they do, my lord; Hercules and his load° too.

Hamlet: It is not very strange; for my uncle is king of Denmark, and those that would make mows° at him while my father lived, give twenty, forty, fifty, a hundred ducats° a-piece for his picture in little.° 'Sblood, there is something in this more than natural, if philosophy could find 335 it out. *A flourish [of trumpets within].*

Guildenstern: There are the players.

Hamlet: Gentlemen, you are welcome to Elsinore. Your hands, come then: the appurtenance of welcome is fashion and ceremony: let me com-ply° with you in this garb,° lest my extent° to the players, which, I tell 340 you, must show fairly outwards, should more appear like entertain-ment than yours. You are welcome: but my uncle-father and aunt-mother are deceived.

Guildenstern: In what, my dear lord?

311–331 *How . . . load:* The passage is the famous one dealing with the War of the Theatres (1599–1602); namely, the rivalry between the children's companies and the adult actors. 313 *aery:* Nest; *eyases:* Young hawks. 313–314 *cry . . . question:* Speak in a high key domi-nating conversation; clamor forth the height of controversy; probably "excel"; perhaps intended to decry leaders of the dramatic profession. 314 *tyrannically:* Outrageously. 315 *berattle:* Berate; *common stages:* Public theaters. 316 *many wearing rapiers:* Many men of fashion, who were afraid to patronize the common players for fear of being satirized by the poets who wrote for the children; *goose-quills:* I.e., pens of satirists. 318–319 *escoted:* Maintained; *quality:* Acting profession; *no longer . . . sing:* I.e., until their voices change. 320–321 *common:* Regular, adult. 323 *succession:* Future careers. 325 *tarre:* Set on (as dogs). 326 *argument:* Probably, plot for a play. 327 *went to cuffs:* Came to blows; *ques-tion:* Controversy. 330 *carry it away:* Win the day. 331 *Hercules . . . load:* Regarded as an allusion to the sign of the Globe Theatre, which was Hercules bearing the world on his shoulder. 333 *mows:* Grimaces. 334 *ducats:* Gold coins worth 9s. 4d; *in little:* In minia-ture. 339–340 *comply:* Observe the formalities of courtesy. 340 *garb:* Manner; *extent:* Showing of kindness.

Hamlet: I am but mad north-north-west:° when the wind is southerly I   345
  know a hawk from a handsaw.°

  Enter Polonius.

Polonius: Well be with you, gentlemen!

Hamlet: Hark you, Guildenstern; and you too: at each ear a hearer: that
  great baby you see there is not yet out of his swaddling-clouts.°

Rosencrantz: Happily he is the second time come to them; for they say an   350
  old man is twice a child.

Hamlet: I will prophesy he comes to tell me of the players; mark it. — You
  say right, sir: o' Monday morning;° 'twas then indeed.

Polonius: My lord, I have news to tell you.

Hamlet: My lord, I have news to tell you. When Roscius° was an actor in   355
  Rome, —

Polonius: The actors are come hither, my lord.

Hamlet: Buz, buz!°

Polonius: Upon my honour, —

Hamlet: Then came each actor on his ass, —   360

Polonius: The best actors in the world, either for tragedy, comedy,
  history, pastoral, pastoral-comical, historical-pastoral, tragical-
  historical, tragical-comical-historical-pastoral, scene individable,° or
  poem unlimited:° Seneca° cannot be too heavy, nor Plautus° too light.
  For the law of writ and the liberty,° these are the only men.   365

Hamlet: O Jephthah, judge of Israel,° what a treasure hadst thou!

Polonius: What a treasure had he, my lord?

Hamlet: Why,
    "One fair daughter, and no more,
      The which he loved passing well."   370

Polonius [aside]: Still on my daughter.

Hamlet: Am I not i' the right, old Jephthah?

Polonius: If you call me Jephthah, my lord, I have a daughter that I love
  passing° well.

Hamlet: Nay, that follows not.   375

Polonius: What follows, then, my lord?

Hamlet: Why,
    "As by lot, God wot,"
  and then, you know,
    "It came to pass, as most like° it was," —   380

---

345 *I am ... north-north-west:* I am only partly mad, i.e., in only one point of the compass.
346 *handsaw:* A proposed reading of *hernshaw* would mean "heron"; *handsaw* may be an early
corruption of *hernshaw.* Another view regards *hawk* as the variant of *hack,* a tool of the pickax
type, and *handsaw* as a saw operated by hand.   349 *swaddling-clouts:* Cloths in which to
wrap a newborn baby.   353 *o' Monday morning:* Said to mislead Polonius.   355 *Roscius:*
A famous Roman actor.   358 *Buz, buz:* An interjection used at Oxford to denote stale
news.   363 *scene individable:* A play observing the unity of place.   364 *poem unlimited:* A
play disregarding the unities of time and place; *Seneca:* Writer of Latin tragedies, model of
early Elizabethan writers of tragedy; *Plautus:* Writer of Latin comedy.   365 *law ... liberty:*
Pieces written according to rules and without rules, i.e., "classical" and "romantic" dramas.
366 *Jephthah ... Israel:* Jephthah had to sacrifice his daughter; see Judges 11.   374 *passing:*
Surpassingly.   380 *like:* Probable.

the first row° of the pious chanson° will show you more; for look, where my abridgement comes.°

Enter the Players.

You are welcome, masters; welcome, all. I am glad to see thee well. Welcome, good friends. O, old friend! why, thy face is valanced° since I saw thee last: comest thou to beard me in Denmark? What, my 385 young lady and mistress! By'r lady, your ladyship is nearer to heaven than when I saw you last, by the altitude of a chopine.° Pray God, your voice, like a piece of uncurrent° gold, be not cracked within the ring.° Masters, you are all welcome. We'll e'en to 't like French falcon- ers, fly at any thing we see: we'll have a speech straight: come, give us 390 a taste of your quality; come, a passionate speech.

First Player: What speech, my good lord?

Hamlet: I heard thee speak me a speech once, but it was never acted; or, if it was, not above once; for the play, I remember, pleased not the mil- lion; 'twas caviary to the general:° but it was—as I received it, and 395 others, whose judgements in such matters cried in the top of° mine—an excellent play, well digested in the scenes, set down with as much modesty as cunning.° I remember, one said there were no sal- lets° in the lines to make the matter savoury, nor no matter in the phrase that might indict° the author of affectation; but called it an 400 honest method, as wholesome as sweet, and by very much more handsome than fine.° One speech in 't I chiefly loved: 'twas Æneas' tale to Dido;° and thereabout of it especially, where he speaks of Priam's slaughter: if it live in your memory, begin at this line: let me see, let me see— 405
"The rugged Pyrrhus,° like th' Hyrcanian beast,"°—
'tis not so:—it begins with Pyrrhus:—
"The rugged Pyrrhus, he whose sable arms,
Black as his purpose, did the night resemble
When he lay couched in the ominous horse,° 410
Hath now this dread and black complexion smear'd
With heraldry more dismal; head to foot
Now is he total gules;° horridly trick'd°
With blood of fathers, mothers, daughters, sons,
Bak'd and impasted° with the parching streets, 415

---

381 *row:* Stanza; *chanson:* Ballad. 382 *abridgement comes:* Opportunity comes for cutting short the conversation. 384 *valanced:* Fringed (with a beard). 387 *chopine:* Kind of shoe raised by the thickness of the heel; worn in Italy, particularly at Venice. 388 *uncur- rent:* Not passable as lawful coinage. 388-389 *cracked within the ring:* In the center of coins were rings enclosing the sovereign's head; if the coin was cracked within this ring, it was unfit for currency. 395 *caviary to the general:* Not relished by the multitude. 396 *cried in the top of:* Spoke with greater authority than. 398 *cunning:* Skill. 398-399 *sallets:* Salads: here, spicy improprieties. 400 *indict:* Convict. 401-402 *as wholesome...fine:* Its beauty was not that of elaborate ornament, but that of order and proportion. 402-403 *Æneas' tale to Dido:* The lines recited by the player are imitated from Marlowe and Nashe's *Dido Queen of Carthage* (II.i.214 ff.). They are written in such a way that the conventionality of the play within a play is raised above that of ordinary drama. 406 *Pyrrhus:* A Greek hero in the Trojan War; *Hyrcanian beast:* The tiger; see Virgil, *Aeneid*, IV.266. 410 *ominous horse:* Tro- jan horse. 413 *gules:* Red, a heraldic term; *trick'd:* Spotted, smeared. 415 *impasted:* Made into a paste.

That lend a tyrannous and a damned light
To their lord's murder: roasted in wrath and fire,
And thus o'er-sized° with coagulate gore,
With eyes like carbuncles, the hellish Pyrrhus
Old grandsire Priam seeks."   420
So, proceed you.
Polonius: 'Fore God, my lord, well spoken, with good accent and good
   discretion.
First Player: "Anon he finds him
   Striking too short at Greeks; his antique sword,   425
   Rebellious to his arm, lies where it falls,
   Repugnant° to command: unequal match'd,
   Pyrrhus at Priam drives; in rage strikes wide;
   But with the whiff and wind of his fell sword
   Th' unnerved father falls. Then senseless Ilium,°   430
   Seeming to feel this blow, with flaming top
   Stoops to his base, and with a hideous crash
   Takes prisoner Pyrrhus' ear: for, lo! his sword
   Which was declining on the milky head
   Of reverend Priam, seem'd i' th' air to stick: 435
   So, as a painted tyrant,° Pyrrhus stood,
   And like a neutral to his will and matter,°
   Did nothing.
   But, as we often see, against° some storm,
   A silence in the heavens, the rack° stand still,   440
   The bold winds speechless and the orb below
   As hush as death, anon the dreadful thunder
   Doth rend the region,° so, after Pyrrhus' pause,
   Aroused vengeance sets him new a-work;
   And never did the Cyclops' hammers fall   445
   On Mars's armour forg'd for proof eterne°
   With less remorse than Pyrrhus' bleeding sword
   Now falls on Priam.
   Out, out, thou strumpet, Fortune! All you gods,
   In general synod,° take away her power;   450
   Break all the spokes and fellies° from her wheel,
   And bowl the round nave° down the hill of heaven,
   As low as to the fiends!"
Polonius: This is too long.
Hamlet: It shall to the barber's, with your beard. Prithee, say on: he's for a 455
   jig° or a tale of bawdry,° or he sleeps: say on: come to Hecuba.°
First Player: "But who, ah woe! had seen the mobled° queen —"
Hamlet: "The mobled queen?"

---

418 *o'er-sized:* Covered as with size or glue.   427 *Repugnant:* Disobedient.   430 *Then
senseless Ilium:* Insensate Troy.   436 *painted tyrant:* Tyrant in a picture.   437 *matter:* Task.
439 *against:* Before.   440 *rack:* Mass of clouds.   443 *region:* Assembly.   446 *proof
eterne:* External resistance to assault.   450 *synod:* Assembly.   451 *fellies:* Pieces of wood
forming the rim of a wheel.   452 *nave:* Hub.   456 *jig:* Comic performance given at the
end or in an interval of a play; *bawdry:* Indecency; *Hecuba:* Wife of Priam, king of Troy.
457 *mobled:* Muffled.

Polonius: That's good; "mobled queen" is good.
First Player: "Run barefoot up and down, threat'ning the flames 460
 With bisson rheum;° a clout° upon that head
 Where late the diadem stood, and for a robe,
 About her lank and all o'er-teemed° loins,
 A blanket, in the alarm of fear caught up;
 Who this had seen, with tongue in venom steep'd, 465
 'Gainst Fortune's state would treason have pronounc'd:°
 But if the gods themselves did see her then
 When she saw Pyrrhus make malicious sport
 In mincing with his sword her husband's limbs,
 The instant burst of clamour that she made, 470
 Unless things mortal move them not at all,
 Would have made milch° the burning eyes of heaven,
 And passion in the gods."
Polonius: Look, whe'r he has not turned° his colour and has tears in 's
 eyes. Prithee, no more. 475
Hamlet: 'Tis well; I'll have thee speak out the rest soon. Good my lord,
 will you see the players well bestowed? Do you hear, let them be well
 used; for they are the abstract° and brief chronicles of the time: after
 your death you were better have a bad epitaph than their ill report
 while you live. 480
Polonius: My lord, I will use them according to their desert.
Hamlet: God's bodykins,° man, much better: use every man after his
 desert, and who shall 'scape whipping? Use them after your own honour and dignity: the less they deserve, the more merit is in your
 bounty. Take them in. 485
Polonius: Come, sirs.
Hamlet: Follow him, friends: we'll hear a play tomorrow. *[Aside to First
 Player.]* Dost thou hear me, old friend; can you play the Murder of
 Gonzago?
First Player: Ay, my lord. 490
Hamlet: We'll ha 't to-morrow night. You could, for a need, study a speech
 of some dozen or sixteen lines,° which I would set down and insert
 in 't, could you not?
First Player: Ay, my lord.
Hamlet: Very well. Follow that lord; and look you mock him not. — My 495
 good friends, I'll leave you till night: you are welcome to Elsinore.
                               Exeunt Polonius and Players.
Rosencrantz: Good my lord!   *Exeunt [Rosencrantz and Guildenstern.]*
Hamlet: Ay, so, God bye to you. — Now I am alone.
 O, what a rogue and peasant° slave am I!
 Is it not monstrous that this player here, 500
 But in a fiction, in a dream of passion,
 Could force his soul so to his own conceit

461 *bisson rheum:* Blinding tears; *clout:* Piece of cloth. 463 *o'er-teemed:* Worn out with bearing children. 466 *pronounc'd:* Proclaimed. 472 *milch:* Moist with tears. 474 *turned:* Changed. 478 *abstract:* Summary account. 482 *bodykins:* Diminutive form of the oath "by God's body." 492 *dozen or sixteen lines:* Critics have amused themselves by trying to locate Hamlet's lines. Lucianus's speech III.ii.229-234 is the best guess. 499 *peasant:* Base.

That from her working all his visage wann'd,°
Tears in his eyes, distraction in 's aspect,
A broken voice, and his whole function suiting   505
With forms to his conceit?° and all for nothing!
For Hecuba!
What's Hecuba to him, or he to Hecuba,
That he should weep for her? What would he do,
Had he the motive and the cue for passion   510
That I have? He would drown the stage with tears
And cleave the general ear with horrid speech,
Make mad the guilty and appall the free,
Confound the ignorant, and amaze indeed
The very faculties of eyes and ears.   515
Yet I,
A dull and muddy-mettled° rascal, peak,°
Like John-a-dreams,° unpregnant of° my cause,
And can say nothing; no, not for a king.
Upon whose property° and most dear life   520
A damn'd defeat was made. Am I a coward?
Who calls me villain? breaks my pate across?
Plucks off my beard, and blows it in my face?
Tweaks me by the nose? gives me the lie i' th' throat,
As deep as to the lungs? who does me this?   525
Ha!
'Swounds, I should take it: for it cannot be
But I am pigeon-liver'd° and lack gall
To make oppression bitter, or ere this
I should have fatted all the region kites°   530
With this slave's offal: bloody, bawdy villain!
Remorseless, treacherous, lecherous, kindless° villain!
O, vengeance!
Why, what an ass am I! This is most brave,
That I, the son of a dear father murder'd,   535
Prompted to my revenge by heaven and hell,
Must, like a whore, unpack my heart with words,
And fall a-cursing, like a very drab,°
A stallion!°
Fie upon 't! foh! About,° my brains! Hum, I have heard   540
That guilty creatures sitting at a play
Have by the very cunning of the scene
Been struck so to the soul that presently
They have proclaim'd their malefactions;

---

503 *wann'd:* Grew pale.   505–506 *his whole . . . conceit:* His whole being responded with forms to suit his thought.   517 *muddy-mettled:* Dull-spirited; *peak:* Mope, pine.   518 *John-a-dreams:* An expression occurring elsewhere in Elizabethan literature to indicate a dreamer; *unpregnant of:* Not quickened by.   520 *property:* Proprietorship (of crown and life). 528 *pigeon-liver'd:* The pigeon was supposed to secrete no gall; if Hamlet, so he says, had had gall, he would have felt the bitterness of oppression, and avenged it.   530 *region kites:* Kites of the air.   532 *kindless:* Unnatural.   538 *drab:* Prostitute.   539 *stallion:* Prostitute (male or female).   540 *About:* About it, or turn thou right about.

For murder, though it have no tongue, will speak   545
With most miraculous organ. I'll have these players
Play something like the murder of my father
Before mine uncle: I'll observe his looks:
I'll tent° him to the quick: if 'a do blench,°
I know my course. The spirit that I have seen   550
May be the devil:° and the devil hath power
T' assume a pleasing shape; yea, and perhaps
Out of my weakness and my melancholy,
As he is very potent with such spirits,°
Abuses me to damn me: I'll have grounds   555
More relative° than this:° the play's the thing
Wherein I'll catch the conscience of the king.   *Exit.*

[ACT III

SCENE I: *A room in the castle.*]

Enter King, Queen, Polonius, Ophelia, Rosencrantz, Guildenstern, Lords.

King: And can you, by no drift of conference,°
  Get from him why he puts on this confusion,
  Grating so harshly all his days of quiet
  With turbulent and dangerous lunacy?
Rosencrantz: He does confess he feels himself distracted;   5
  But from what cause 'a will by no means speak.
Guildenstern: Nor do we find him forward° to be sounded,
  But, with a crafty madness, keeps aloof,
  When we would bring him on to some confession
  Of his true state.
Queen: Did he receive you well?   10
Rosencrantz: Most like a gentleman.
Guildenstern: But with much forcing of his disposition.°
Rosencrantz: Niggard of question;° but, of our demands,
  Most free in his reply.
Queen: Did you assay° him
  To any pastime?   15
Rosencrantz: Madam, it so fell out, that certain players
  We o'er-raught° on the way: of these we told him;
  And there did seem in him a kind of joy
  To hear of it: they are here about the court,

---

549 *tent:* Probe; *blench:* Quail, flinch.   551 *May be the devil:* Hamlet's suspicion is properly grounded in the belief of the time.   554 *spirits:* Humors.   556 *relative:* Closely related, definite; *this:* I.e., the ghost's story.   **Act III, Scene I.**   1 *drift of conference:* Device of conversation.   7 *forward:* Willing.   12 *forcing of his disposition:* I.e., against his will.   13 *Niggard of question:* Sparing of conversation.   14 *assay:* Try to win.   17 *o'er-raught:* Overtook.

And, as I think, they have already order   20
This night to play before him.
Polonius: 'Tis most true:
And he beseech'd me to entreat your majesties
To hear and see the matter.
King: With all my heart; and it doth much content me
To hear him so inclin'd.   25
Good gentlemen, give him a further edge,°
And drive his purpose into these delights.
Rosencrantz: We shall, my lord.   *Exeunt Rosencrantz and Guildenstern.*
King: Sweet Gertrude, leave us too;
For we have closely° sent for Hamlet hither,
That he, as 'twere by accident, may here   30
Affront° Ophelia:
Her father and myself, lawful espials,°
Will so bestow ourselves that, seeing, unseen,
We may of their encounter frankly judge,
And gather by him, as he is behav'd,   35
If 't be th' affliction of his love or no
That thus he suffers for.
Queen: I shall obey you.
And for your part, Ophelia, I do wish
That your good beauties be the happy cause
Of Hamlet's wildness:° so shall I hope your virtues   40
Will bring him to his wonted way again,
To both your honours.
Ophelia: Madam, I wish it may.   *[Exit Queen.]*
Polonius: Ophelia, walk you here. Gracious,° so please you,
We will bestow ourselves. *[To Ophelia.]* Read on this book;
That show of such an exercise° may colour°   45
Your loneliness. We are oft to blame in this,—
'Tis too much prov'd—that with devotion's visage
And pious action we do sugar o'er
The devil himself.
King: *[aside]* O, 'tis too true!
How smart a lash that speech doth give my conscience!   50
The harlot's cheek, beautied with plast'ring art,
Is not more ugly to° the thing° that helps it
Than is my deed to my most painted word:
O heavy burthen!
Polonius: I hear him coming: let's withdraw, my lord.   55
                                        [Exeunt King and Polonius.]

     Enter Hamlet.

---

26 *edge:* Incitement.   29 *closely:* Secretly.   31 *Affront:* Confront.   32 *lawful espials:* Legitimate spies.   40 *wildness:* Madness.   43 *Gracious:* Your grace (addressed to the king).
45 *exercise:* Act of devotion (the book she reads is one of devotion); *colour:* Give a plausible
appearance to.   52 *to:* Compared to; *thing:* I.e., the cosmetic.

Hamlet: To be, or not to be: that is the question:
Whether 'tis nobler in the mind to suffer
The slings and arrows of outrageous fortune,
Or to take arms against a sea° of troubles,
And by opposing end them? To die: to sleep;   60
No more; and by a sleep to say we end
The heart-ache and the thousand natural shocks
That flesh is heir to, 'tis a consummation
Devoutly to be wish'd. To die, to sleep;
To sleep: perchance to dream: ay, there's the rub;   65
For in that sleep of death what dreams may come
When we have shuffled° off this mortal coil,°
Must give us pause: there's the respect°
That makes calamity of so long life;°
For who would bear the whips and scorns of time,°   70
Th' oppressor's wrong, the proud man's contumely,
The pangs of despis'd° love, the law's delay,
The insolence of office° and the spurns°
That patient merit of th' unworthy takes,
When he himself might his quietus° make   75
With a bare bodkin?° who would fardels° bear,
To grunt and sweat under a weary life,
But that the dread of something after death,
The undiscover'd country from whose bourn°
No traveller returns, puzzles the will   80
And makes us rather bear those ills we have
Than fly to others that we know not of?
Thus conscience° does make cowards of us all;
And thus the native hue° of resolution
Is sicklied o'er° with the pale cast° of thought,   85
And enterprises of great pitch° and moment°
With this regard° their currents° turn awry,
And lose the name of action — Soft you now!
The fair Ophelia! Nymph, in thy orisons°
Be all my sins rememb'red.

Ophelia: Good my lord,   90
How does your honour for this many a day?
Hamlet: I humbly thank you; well, well, well.
Ophelia: My lord, I have remembrances of yours,

---

59 *sea:* The mixed metaphor of this speech has often been commented on; a later emendation *siege* has sometimes been spoken on the stage.   67 *shuffled:* Sloughed, cast; *coil:* Usually means "turmoil"; here, possibly "body" (conceived of as wound about the soul like rope); *clay, soil, veil,* have been suggested as emendations.   68 *respect:* Consideration.   69 *of ... life:* So long-lived.   70 *time:* The world.   72 *despis'd:* Rejected.   73 *office:* Officeholders; *spurns:* Insults.   75 *quietus:* Acquittance; here, death.   76 *bare bodkin:* Mere dagger; *bare* is sometimes understood as "unsheathed"; *fardels:* Burdens.   79 *bourn:* Boundary.   83 *conscience:* Probably, inhibition by the faculty of reason restraining the will from doing wrong.   84 *native hue:* Natural color; metaphor derived from the color of the face.   85 *sicklied o'er:* Given a sickly tinge; *cast:* Shade of color.   86 *pitch:* Height (as of a falcon's flight); *moment:* Importance.   87 *regard:* Respect, consideration; *currents:* Courses.   89 *orisons:* Prayers.

That I have longed long to re-deliver;
I pray you, now receive them.
Hamlet: No, not I;   95
   I never gave you aught.
Ophelia: My honour'd lord, you know right well you did;
   And, with them, words of so sweet breath compos'd
   As made the things more rich: their perfume lost,
   Take these again; for to the noble mind   100
   Rich gifts wax poor when givers prove unkind.
   There, my lord.
Hamlet: Ha, ha! are you honest?°
Ophelia: My lord?
Hamlet: Are you fair?   105
Ophelia: What means your lordship?
Hamlet: That if you be honest and fair, your honesty° should admit no
   discourse to° your beauty.
Ophelia: Could beauty, my lord, have better commerce° than with honesty?
Hamlet: Ay, truly; for the power of beauty will sooner transform honesty   110
   from what it is to a bawd than the force of honesty can trans-
   late beauty into his likeness: this was sometime a paradox, but now
   the time° gives it proof. I did love you once.
Ophelia: Indeed, my lord, you made me believe so.
Hamlet: You should not have believed me; for virtue cannot so inoculate°   115
   our old stock but we shall relish of it:° I loved you not.
Ophelia: I was the more deceived.
Hamlet: Get thee to a nunnery: why wouldst thou be a breeder of sinners?
   I am myself indifferent honest;° but yet I could accuse me of such
   things that it were better my mother had not borne me: I am very   120
   proud, revengeful, ambitious, with more offences at my beck° than I
   have thoughts to put them in, imagination to give them shape, or
   time to act them in. What should such fellows as I do crawling be-
   tween earth and heaven? We are arrant knaves, all; believe none of us.
   Go thy ways to a nunnery. Where's your father?   125
Ophelia: At home, my lord.
Hamlet: Let the doors be shut upon him, that he may play the fool no
   where but in 's own house. Farewell.
Ophelia: O, help him, you sweet heavens!
Hamlet: If thou dost marry, I'll give thee this plague for thy dowry: be   130
   thou as chaste as ice, as pure as snow, thou shalt not escape calumny.
   Get thee to a nunnery, go: farewell. Or, if thou wilt needs marry,
   marry a fool; for wise men know well enough what monsters° you
   make of them. To a nunnery, go, and quickly too. Farewell.
Ophelia: O heavenly powers, restore him!   135

103-108 *are you honest . . . beauty: Honest* meaning "truthful" and "chaste" and *fair* meaning "just, honorable" (line 105) and "beautiful" (line 107) are not mere quibbles; the speech has the irony of a *double entendre.*   107 *your honesty:* Your chastity.   108 *discourse to:* Familiar intercourse with.   109 *commerce:* Intercourse.   113 *the time:* The present age.   115 *inoculate:* Graft (metaphorical).   116 *but . . . it:* I.e., that we do not still have about us a taste of the old stock; i.e., retain our sinfulness.   119 *indifferent honest:* Moderately virtuous.   121 *beck:* Command.   133 *monsters:* An allusion to the horns of a cuckold.

Hamlet: I have heard of your° paintings too, well enough; God hath given
  you one face, and you make yourselves another: you jig,° you amble,
  and you lisp; you nick-name God's creatures, and make your wantonness your ignorance.° Go to, I'll no more on 't; it hath made me mad. I
  say, we will have no moe marriage: those that are married already, all   140
  but one,° shall live; the rest shall keep as they are. To a nunnery, go.

Exit.

Ophelia: O, what a noble mind is here o'er-thrown!
  The courtier's, soldier's, scholar's, eye, tongue, sword;
  Th' expectancy and rose° of the fair state,
  The glass of fashion and the mould of form,°   145
  Th' observ'd of all observers,° quite, quite down!
  And I, of ladies most deject and wretched,
  That suck'd the honey of his music vows,
  Now see that noble and most sovereign reason,
  Like sweet bells jangled, out of time and harsh;   150
  That unmatch'd form and feature of blown° youth
  Blasted with ecstasy:° O, woe is me,
  T' have seen what I have seen, see what I see!

Enter King and Polonius.

King: Love! his affections do not that way tend;
  Nor what he spake, though it lack'd form a little,   155
  Was not like madness. There's something in his soul,
  O'er which his melancholy sits on brood;
  And I do doubt° the hatch and the disclose°
  Will be some danger: which for to prevent,
  I have in quick determination   160
  Thus set it down: he shall with speed to England,
  For the demand of our neglected tribute:
  Haply the seas and countries different
  With variable° objects shall expel
  This something-settled° matter in his heart,   165
  Whereon his brains still beating puts him thus
  From fashion of himself.° What think you on 't?

Polonius: It shall do well: but yet do I believe
  The origin and commencement of his grief
  Sprung from neglected love. How now, Ophelia!   170
  You need not tell us what Lord Hamlet said;
  We heard it all. My lord, do as you please;
  But, if you hold it fit, after the play
  Let his queen mother all alone entreat him

---

136 *your:* Indefinite use.   137 *jig:* Move with jerky motion; probably allusion to the *jig,* or
song and dance, of the current stage.   138–139 *make . . . ignorance:* I.e., excuse your wantonness on the ground of your ignorance.   141 *one:* I.e., the king.   144 *expectancy and rose:*
Source of hope.   145 *The glass . . . form:* The mirror of fashion and the pattern of courtly
behavior.   146 *observ'd . . . observers:* I.e., the center of attention in the court.   151 *blown:*
Blooming.   152 *ecstasy:* Madness.   158 *doubt:* Fear; *disclose:* Disclosure or revelation (by
chipping of the shell).   164 *variable:* Various.   165 *something-settled:* Somewhat settled.
167 *From . . . himself:* Out of his natural manner.

To show his grief: let her be round° with him;   175
And I'll be plac'd, so please you, in the ear
Of all their conference. If she find him not,
To England send him, or confine him where
Your wisdom best shall think.

King: It shall be so: 180
Madness in great ones must not unwatch'd go.   *Exeunt.*

[SCENE II: *A hall in the castle.*]

Enter Hamlet and three of the Players.

Hamlet: Speak the speech, I pray you, as I pronounced it to you, trippingly on the tongue: but if you mouth it, as many of your° players do, I had as lief the town-crier spoke my lines. Nor do not saw the
air too much with your hand, thus, but use all gently; for in the very
torrent, tempest, and, as I may say, whirlwind of your passion, you   5
must acquire and beget a temperance that may give it smoothness.
O, it offends me to the soul to hear a robustious° periwig-pated° fellow tear a passion to tatters, to very rags, to split the ears of the
groundlings,° who for the most part are capable of° nothing but
inexplicable° dumb-shows and noise: I would have such a fellow   10
whipped for o'er-doing Termagant;° it out-herods Herod:° pray you,
avoid it.

First Player: I warrant your honour.

Hamlet: Be not too tame neither, but let your own discretion be your
tutor: suit the action to the word, the word to the action; with this   15
special observance, that you o'er-step not the modesty of nature: for
any thing so overdone is from the purpose of playing, whose end,
both at the first and now, was and is, to hold, as 't were, the mirror up
to nature; to show virtue her own feature, scorn her own image, and
the very age and body of the time his form and pressure.° Now this   20
overdone, or come tardy off,° though it make the unskilful laugh,
cannot but make the judicious grieve; the censure of the which one°
must in your allowance o'erweigh a whole theatre of others. O, there
be players that I have seen play, and heard others praise, and that
highly, not to speak it profanely, that, neither having the accent of   25
Christians nor the gait of Christian, pagan, nor man, have so strut-
ted and bellowed that I have thought some of nature's journeymen°
had made men and not made them well, they imitated humanity so
abominably.

---

175 *round:* Blunt.   **Scene II.**   2 *your:* Indefinite use.   7 *robustious:* Violent, boisterous;
periwig-pated: Wearing a wig.   9 *groundlings:* Those who stood in the yard of the theater;
capable of: Susceptible of being influenced by.   10 *inexplicable:* Of no significance worth
explaining.   11 *Termagant:* A god of the Saracens; a character in the St. Nicholas play,
where one of his worshipers, leaving him in charge of goods, returns to find them stolen;
whereupon he beats the god (or idol), which howls vociferously; *Herod:* Herod of Jewry; a
character in *The Slaughter of the Innocents* and other cycle plays. The part was played with great
noise and fury.   20 *pressure:* Stamp, impressed character.   21 *come tardy off:* Inade-
quately done.   22 *the censure ... one:* The judgment of even one of whom.   27 *journey-
men:* Laborers not yet masters in their trade.

First Player: I hope we have reformed that indifferently° with us, sir.　30
Hamlet: O, reform it altogether. And let those that play your clowns speak
no more than is set down for them; for there be of° them that will
themselves laugh, to set on some quantity of barren° spectators to
laugh too; though, in the mean time, some necessary question of
the play be then to be considered: that's villanous, and shows a most　35
pitiful ambition in the fool that uses it. Go, make you ready.

[Exeunt Players.]

Enter Polonius, Guildenstern, and Rosencrantz.

How now, my lord! will the king hear this piece of work?
Polonius: And the queen too, and that presently.
Hamlet: Bid the players make haste.　　　*[Exit Polonius.]*
Will you two help to hasten them?　　　　　　　　　　　40

Rosencrantz:　} We will, my lord.　　　　　*Exeunt they two.*
Guildenstern:

Hamlet:　　　　　　　　　What ho! Horatio!

Enter Horatio.

Horatio: Here, sweet lord, at your service.
Hamlet: Horatio, thou art e'en as just° a man
As e'er my conversation cop'd withal.
Horatio: O, my dear lord, —
Hamlet:　　　　　　　　Nay, do not think I flatter;　45
For what advancement may I hope from thee
That no revenue hast but thy good spirits,
To feed and clothe thee? Why should the poor be flatter'd?
No, let the candied tongue lick absurd pomp,
And crook the pregnant° hinges of the knee　　　50
Where thrift° may follow fawning. Dost thou hear?
Since my dear soul was mistress of her choice
And could of men distinguish her election,
S' hath seal'd thee for herself; for thou hast been
As one, in suff'ring all, that suffers nothing,　　　55
A man that fortune's buffets and rewards
Hast ta'en with equal thanks: and blest are those
Whose blood and judgement are so well commeddled,
That they are not a pipe for fortune's finger
To sound what stop° she please. Give me that man　60
That is not passion's slave, and I will wear him
In my heart's core, ay, in my heart of heart,
As I do thee. — Something too much of this. —
There is a play to-night before the king;
One scene of it comes near the circumstance　　　65
Which I have told thee of my father's death:
I prithee, when thou seest that act afoot,

30 *indifferently:* Fairly, tolerably.　32 *of:* I.e., some among them.　33 *barren:* I.e., of wit.
43 *just:* Honest, honorable.　50 *pregnant:* Pliant.　51 *thrift:* Profit.　60 *stop:* Hole in
a wind instrument for controlling the sound.

Even with the very comment of thy soul°
Observe my uncle: if his occulted° guilt
Do not itself unkennel in one speech,   70
It is a damned° ghost that we have seen,
And my imaginations are as foul
As Vulcan's stithy.° Give him heedful note;
For I mine eyes will rivet to his face,
And after we will both our judgements join   75
In censure of his seeming.°
Horatio: Well, my lord:
If 'a steal aught the whilst this play is playing,
And 'scape detecting, I will pay the theft.

Enter trumpets and kettledrums, King, Queen, Polonius, Ophelia,
[Rosencrantz, Guildenstern, and others].

Hamlet: They are coming to the play; I must be idle:° Get you a place.
King: How fares our cousin Hamlet?   80
Hamlet: Excellent, i' faith; of the chameleon's dish:° I eat the air, promise-
   crammed: you cannot feed capons so.
King: I have nothing with° this answer, Hamlet; these words are not
   mine.°
Hamlet: No, nor mine now. *[To Polonius.]* My lord, you played once i' the   85
   university, you say?
Polonius: That did I, my lord; and was accounted a good actor.
Hamlet: What did you enact?
Polonius: I did enact Julius Cæsar: I was killed i' the Capitol; Brutus
   killed me.   90
Hamlet: It was a brute part of him to kill so capital a calf there. Be the
   players ready?
Rosencrantz: Ay, my lord; they stay upon your patience.
Queen: Come hither, my dear Hamlet, sit by me.
Hamlet: No, good mother, here's metal more attractive.   95
Polonius [to the king]: O, ho! do you mark that?
Hamlet: Lady, shall I lie in your lap?   *[Lying down at Ophelia's feet.]*
Ophelia: No, my lord.
Hamlet: I mean, my head upon your lap?
Ophelia: Ay, my lord.   100
Hamlet: Do you think I meant country° matters?
Ophelia: I think nothing, my lord.
Hamlet: That's a fair thought to lie between maids' legs.
Ophelia: What is, my lord?
Hamlet: Nothing.   105
Ophelia: You are merry, my lord.
Hamlet: Who, I?

---

68 *very ... soul:* Inward and sagacious criticism.   69 *occulted:* Hidden.   71 *damned:* In
league with Satan.   73 *stithy:* Smithy, place of *stiths* (anvils).   76 *censure ... seeming:* Judgment of his appearance or behavior.   79 *idle:* Crazy, or not attending to anything serious.
81 *chameleon's dish:* Chameleons were supposed to feed on air. (Hamlet deliberately misinter-
prets the king's "fares" as "feeds.")   83 *have ... with:* Make nothing of.   83-84 *are not
mine:* Do not respond to what I ask.   101 *country:* With a bawdy pun.

Ophelia: Ay, my lord.

Hamlet: O God, your only° jig-maker.° What should a man do but be
merry? for, look you, how cheerfully my mother looks, and my father 110
died within's two hours.

Ophelia: Nay, 'tis twice two months, my lord.

Hamlet: So long? Nay then, let the devil wear black, for I'll have a suit of
sables.° O heavens! die two months ago, and not forgotten yet? Then
there's hope a great man's memory may outlive his life half a year: 115
but, by 'r lady, 'a must build churches, then; or else shall 'a suffer not
thinking on,° with the hobbyhorse, whose epitaph is "For, O, for, O,
the hobbyhorse is forgot."°

The trumpets sound. Dumb show follows.

*Enter a King and a Queen [very lovingly]; the Queen embracing him,
and he her. [She kneels, and makes show of protestation unto him.] He takes
her up, and declines his head upon her neck: he lies him down upon a bank of
flowers: she, seeing him asleep, leaves him. Anon comes in another man, takes
off his crown, kisses it, pours poison in the sleeper's ears, and leaves him. The
Queen returns; finds the King dead, makes passionate action. The Poisoner,
with some three or four come in again, seem to condole with her. The dead
body is carried away. The Poisoner woos the Queen with gifts: she seems harsh
awhile, but in the end accepts love. [Exeunt.]*

Ophelia: What means this, my lord?

Hamlet: Marry, this is miching mallecho;° it means mischief. 120

Ophelia: Belike this show imports the argument of the play.

Enter Prologue.

Hamlet: We shall know by this fellow: the players cannot keep counsel;
they'll tell all.

Ophelia: Will 'a tell us what this show meant?

Hamlet: Ay, or any show that you'll show him: be not you ashamed to 125
show, he'll not shame to tell you what it means.

Ophelia: You are naught, you are naught:° I'll mark the play.

Prologue: For us, and for our tragedy,
Here stooping° to your clemency,
We beg your hearing patiently.   *[Exit.]* 130

Hamlet: Is this a prologue, or the posy° of a ring?

Ophelia: 'Tis brief, my lord.

Hamlet: As woman's love.

Enter [two Players as] King and Queen.

Player King: Full thirty times hath Phoebus' cart gone round
Neptune's salt wash° and Tellus'° orbed ground,   135
And thirty dozen moons with borrowed° sheen

---

109 *your only:* Only your; *jig-maker:* Composer of jigs (song and dance).   113–114 *suit of
sables:* Garments trimmed with the fur of the sable, with a quibble on *sable* meaning
"black."   116–117 *suffer...on:* Undergo oblivion.   117–118 *"For...forgot":* Verse of a song
occurring also in *Love's Labour's Lost,* III.i.30. The hobbyhorse was a character in the Morris
Dance.   120 *miching mallecho:* Sneaking mischief.   127 *naught:* Indecent.   129 *stooping:*
Bowing.   131 *posy:* Motto.   135 *salt wash:* The sea; *Tellus:* Goddess of the earth (*orbed
ground*).   136 *borrowed:* I.e., reflected.

About the world have times twelve thirties been,
Since love our hearts and Hymen° did our hands
Unite commutual° in most sacred bands.
Player Queen: So many journeys may the sun and moon   140
    Make us again count o'er ere love be done!
    But, woe is me, you are so sick of late,
    So far from cheer and from your former state,
    That I distrust° you. Yet, though I distrust,
    Discomfort you, my lord, it nothing must: 145
    For women's fear and love holds quantity;°
    In neither aught, or in extremity.
    Now, what my love is, proof hath made you know;
    And as my love is siz'd, my fear is so:
    Where love is great, the littlest doubts are fear;   150
    Where little fears grow great, great love grows there.
Player King: 'Faith, I must leave thee, love, and shortly too;
    My operant° powers their functions leave° to do:
    And thou shalt live in this fair world behind,
    Honour'd, belov'd; and haply one as kind   155
    For husband shalt thou—
Player Queen: O, confound the rest!
    Such love must needs be treason in my breast:
    In second husband let me be accurst!
    None wed the second but who kill'd the first.
Hamlet (aside): Wormwood, wormwood.   160
Player Queen: The instances that second marriage move
    Are base respects of thrift, but none of love:
    A second time I kill my husband dead,
    When second husband kisses me in bed.
Player King: I do believe you think what now you speak;   165
    But what we do determine oft we break.
    Purpose is but the slave to memory,
    Of violent birth, but poor validity:
    Which now, like fruit unripe, sticks on the tree;
    But fall, unshaken, when they mellow be.   170
    Most necessary 'tis that we forget
    To pay ourselves what to ourselves is debt:
    What to ourselves in passion we propose,
    The passion ending, doth the purpose lose.
    The violence of either grief or joy   175
    Their own enactures° with themselves destroy:
    Where joy most revels, grief doth most lament;
    Grief joys, joy grieves, on slender accident.
    This world is not for aye,° nor 'tis not strange
    That even our loves should with our fortunes change;   180
    For 'tis a question left us yet to prove,

---

138 *Hymen:* God of matrimony.   139 *commutual:* Mutually.   144 *distrust:* Am anxious
about.   146 *holds quantity:* Keeps proportion between.   153 *operant:* Active; *leave:* Cease.
176 *enactures:* Fulfillments.   179 *aye:* Ever.

Whether love lead fortune, or else fortune love.
The great man down, you mark his favourite flies;
The poor advanc'd makes friends of enemies.
And hitherto doth love on fortune tend;   185
For who° not needs shall never lack a friend,
And who in want a hollow friend doth try,
Directly seasons° him his enemy.
But, orderly to end where I begun,
Our wills and fates do so contrary run   190
That our devices still are overthrown;
Our thoughts are ours, their ends° none of our own:
So think thou wilt no second husband wed;
But die thy thoughts when thy first lord is dead.
Player Queen: Nor earth to me give food, nor heaven light!   195
Sport and repose lock from me day and night!
To desperation turn my trust and hope!
An anchor's° cheer° in prison be my scope!
Each opposite° that blanks° the face of joy
Meet what I would have well and it destroy!   200
Both here and hence pursue me lasting strife,
If, once a widow, ever I be wife!
Hamlet: If she should break it now!
Player King: 'Tis deeply sworn. Sweet, leave me here awhile;
My spirits grow dull, and fain I would beguile   205
The tedious day with sleep.   *[Sleeps.]*
Player Queen: Sleep rock thy brain;
And never come mischance between us twain!   *Exit.*
Hamlet: Madam, how like you this play?
Queen: The lady doth protest too much, methinks.
Hamlet: O, but she'll keep her word.   210
King: Have you heard the argument? Is there no offence in 't?
Hamlet: No, no, they do but jest, poison in jest; no offence i' the world.
King: What do you call the play?
Hamlet: The Mouse-trap. Marry, how? Tropically.° This play is the image
of a murder done in Vienna: Gonzago° is the duke's name; his wife,   215
Baptista: you shall see anon; 't is a knavish piece of work: but what o'
that? your majesty and we that have free souls, it touches us not: let
the galled jade° winch,° our withers° are unwrung.°

Enter Lucianus.

This is one Lucianus, nephew to the king.
Ophelia: You are as good as a chorus,° my lord.   220

---

186 *who:* Whoever.   188 *seasons:* Matures, ripens.   192 *ends:* Results.   198 *An anchor's:*
An anchorite's; *cheer:* Fare; sometimes printed as *chair.*   199 *opposite:* Adverse thing; *blanks:*
Causes to *blanch* or grow pale.   214 *Tropically:* Figuratively, *trapically* suggests a pun on *trap*
in *Mouse-trap* (l. 214).   215 *Gonzago:* In 1538 Luigi Gonzago murdered the Duke of Urbano
by pouring poisoned lotion in his ears.   218 *galled jade:* Horse whose hide is rubbed by
saddle or harness; *winch:* Wince; *withers:* The part between the horse's shoulder blades; *unwrung:* Not wrung or twisted.   220 *chorus:* In many Elizabethan plays the action was explained by an actor known as the "chorus"; at a puppet show the actor who explained the action was known as an "interpreter," as indicated by the lines following.

Hamlet: I could interpret between you and your love, if I could see the puppets dallying.°

Ophelia: You are keen, my lord, you are keen.

Hamlet: It would cost you a groaning to take off my edge.

Ophelia: Still better, and worse.°   225

Hamlet: So you mistake° your husbands. Begin, murderer; pox,° leave thy damnable faces, and begin. Come: the croaking raven doth bellow for revenge.

Lucianus: Thoughts black, hands apt, drugs fit, and time agreeing;
Confederate° season, else no creature seeing;   230
Thou mixture rank, of midnight weeds collected,
With Hecate's° ban° thrice blasted, thrice infected,
Thy natural magic and dire property,
On wholesome life usurp immediately.

                                     [Pours the poison into the sleeper's ears.]

Hamlet: 'A poisons him i' the garden for his estate. His name's Gonzago: 235
the story is extant, and written in very choice Italian: you shall see anon how the murderer gets the love of Gonzago's wife.

Ophelia: The king rises.

Hamlet: What, frighted with false fire!°

Queen: How fares my lord?   240

Polonius: Give o'er the play.

King: Give me some light: away!

Polonius: Lights, lights, lights!   *Exeunt all but Hamlet and Horatio.*

Hamlet: Why, let the strucken deer go weep,
    The hart ungalled play;   245
For some must watch, while some must sleep:
    Thus runs the world away.°
Would not this,° sir, and a forest of feathers°—if the rest of my fortunes turn Turk with° me—with two Provincial roses° on my razed°
shoes, get me a fellowship in a cry° of players,° sir?   250

Horatio: Half a share.°

Hamlet: A whole one, I.
For thou dost know, O Damon dear,
    This realm dismantled° was
Of Jove himself; and now reigns here   255
    A very, very°—pajock.°

---

222 *dallying:* With sexual suggestion, continued in *keen* (sexually aroused), *groaning* (i.e., in pregnancy), and *edge* (i.e., sexual desire or impetuosity).   225 *Still . . . worse:* More keen, less decorous.   226 *mistake:* Err in taking; *pox:* An imprecation.   230 *Confederate:* Conspiring (to assist the murderer).   232 *Hecate:* The goddess of witchcraft; *ban:* Curse.   239 *false fire:* Fireworks, or a blank discharge.   244–247 *Why . . . away:* Probably from an old ballad, with allusion to the popular belief that a wounded deer retires to weep and die. Cf. *As You Like It,* II.i.66.   248 *this:* I.e., the play; *feathers:* Allusion to the plumes which Elizabethan actors were fond of wearing.   249 *turn Turk with:* Go back on; *two Provincial roses:* Rosettes of ribbon like the roses of Provins near Paris, or else the roses of Provence; *razed:* Cut, slashed (by way of ornament).   250 *cry:* Pack (as of hounds); *fellowship . . . players:* Partnership in a theatrical company.   251 *Half a share:* Allusion to the custom in dramatic companies of dividing the ownership into a number of shares among the householders.   254 *dismantled:* Stripped, divested.   253–256 *For . . . very:* Probably from an old ballad having to do with Damon and Pythias.   256 *pajock:* Peacock (a bird with a bad reputation). Possibly the word was *patchock,* diminutive of *patch,* clown.

Horatio: You might have rhymed.

Hamlet: O good Horatio, I'll take the ghost's word for a thousand
    pound. Didst perceive?

Horatio: Very well, my lord.   260

Hamlet: Upon the talk of the poisoning?

Horatio: I did very well note him.

Hamlet: Ah, ha! Come, some music! come, the recorders!°
    For if the king like not the comedy,
    Why then, belike, he likes it not, perdy.°   265
    Come, some music!

    Enter Rosencrantz and Guildenstern.

Guildenstern: Good my lord, vouchsafe me a word with you.

Hamlet: Sir, a whole history.

Guildenstern: The king, sir, —

Hamlet: Ay, sir, what of him?   270

Guildenstern: Is in his retirement marvellous distempered.

Hamlet: With drink, sir?

Guildenstern: No, my lord, rather with choler.°

Hamlet: Your wisdom should show itself more richer to signify this to
    his doctor; for, for me to put him to his purgation would perhaps   275
    plunge him into far more choler.

Guildenstern: Good my lord, put your discourse into some frame° and
    start not so wildly from my affair.

Hamlet: I am tame, sir: pronounce.

Guildenstern: The queen, your mother, in most great affliction of spirit,   280
    hath sent me to you.

Hamlet: You are welcome.

Guildenstern: Nay, good my lord, this courtesy is not of the right breed. If
    it shall please you to make me a wholesome° answer, I will do your
    mother's commandment; if not, your pardon and my return shall be   285
    the end of my business.

Hamlet: Sir, I cannot.

Guildenstern: What, my lord?

Hamlet: Make you a wholesome answer; my wit's diseased: but, sir, such
    answer as I can make, you shall command; or, rather, as you say, my   290
    mother: therefore no more, but to the matter:° my mother, you say, —

Rosencrantz: Then thus she says; your behaviour hath struck her into
    amazement and admiration.

Hamlet: O wonderful son, that can so 'stonish a mother! But is there no
    sequel at the heels of this mother's admiration? Impart.   295

Rosencrantz: She desires to speak with you in her closet, ere you go to bed.

Hamlet: We shall obey, were she ten times our mother. Have you any fur-
    ther trade with us?

Rosencrantz: My lord, you once did love me.

Hamlet: And do still, by these pickers and stealers.°   300

---

263 *recorders:* Wind instruments of the flute kind.   265 *perdy:* Corruption of *par dieu.*
273 *choler:* Bilious disorder, with quibble on the sense "anger."   277 *frame:* Order.
284 *wholesome:* Sensible.   291 *matter:* Matter in hand.   300 *pickers and stealers:* Hands,
so called from the catechism "to keep my hands from picking and stealing."

Rosencrantz: Good my lord, what is your cause of distemper? you do, surely, bar the door upon your own liberty, if you deny your griefs to your friend.

Hamlet: Sir, I lack advancement.

Rosencrantz: How can that be, when you have the voice° of the king him- 305 self for your succession in Denmark?

Hamlet: Ay, sir, but "While the grass grows,"° — the proverb is something musty.

Enter the Players with recorders.

O, the recorders! let me see one. To withdraw° with you: — why do you go about to recover the wind° of me, as if you would drive me 310 into a toil?°

Guildenstern: O, my lord, if my duty be too bold, my love is too unman-nerly.°

Hamlet: I do not well understand that. Will you play upon this pipe?

Guildenstern: My lord, I cannot. 315

Hamlet: I pray you.

Guildenstern: Believe me, I cannot.

Hamlet: I beseech you.

Guildenstern: I know no touch of it, my lord.

Hamlet: 'Tis as easy as lying: govern these ventages° with your fingers and 320 thumb, give it breath with your mouth, and it will discourse most eloquent music. Look you, these are the stops.

Guildenstern: But these cannot I command to any utterance of harmony; I have not the skill.

Hamlet: Why, look you now, how unworthy a thing you make of me! You 325 would play upon me; you would seem to know my stops; you would pluck out the heart of my mystery; you would sound me from my lowest note to the top of my compass:° and there is much music, excellent voice, in this little organ;° yet cannot you make it speak. 'Sblood, do you think I am easier to be played on than a pipe? Call 330 me what instrument you will, though you can fret° me, you cannot play upon me.

Enter Polonius.

God bless you, sir!

Polonius: My lord, the queen would speak with you, and presently.

Hamlet: Do you see yonder cloud that's almost in shape of a camel? 335

Polonius: By the mass, and 'tis like a camel, indeed.

Hamlet: Methinks it is like a weasel.

Polonius: It is backed like a weasel.

Hamlet: Or like a whale?

Polonius: Very like a whale. 340

---

305 *voice:* Support.   307 *"While . . . grows":* The rest of the proverb is "the silly horse starves." Hamlet may be destroyed while he is waiting for the succession to the kingdom. 309 *withdraw:* Speak in private.   310 *recover the wind:* Get to the windward side.   311 *toil:* Snare.   312–313 *if . . . unmannerly:* If I am using an unmannerly boldness, it is my love which occasions it.   320 *ventages:* Stops of the recorders.   328 *compass:* Range of voice. 329 *organ:* Musical instrument, i.e., the pipe.   331 *fret:* Quibble on meaning "irritate" and the piece of wood, gut, or metal which regulates the fingering.

Hamlet: Then I will come to my mother by and by. *[Aside.]* They fool me to
    the top of my bent.° — I will come by and by.°
Polonius: I will say so.   *[Exit.]*
Hamlet: By and by is easily said.
    Leave me, friends.   *[Exeunt all but Hamlet.]* 345
    'Tis now the very witching time° of night,
    When churchyards yawn and hell itself breathes out
    Contagion to this world: now could I drink hot blood,
    And do such bitter business as the day
    Would quake to look on. Soft! now to my mother.   350
    O heart, lose not thy nature; let not ever
    The soul of Nero° enter this firm bosom:
    Let me be cruel, not unnatural:
    I will speak daggers to her, but use none;
    My tongue and soul in this be hypocrites;   355
    How in my words somever she be shent,°
    To give them seals° never, my soul, consent!   *Exit.*

[SCENE III: *A room in the castle.*]

    Enter King, Rosencrantz, and Guildenstern.

King: I like him not, nor stands it safe with us
    To let his madness range. Therefore prepare you;
    I your commission will forthwith dispatch,°
    And he to England shall along with you:
    The terms° of our estate° may not endure   5
    Hazard so near us as doth hourly grow
    Out of his brows.°
Guildenstern: We will ourselves provide:
    Most holy and religious fear it is
    To keep those many many bodies safe
    That live and feed upon your majesty.   10
Rosencrantz: The single and peculiar° life is bound,
    With all the strength and armour of the mind,
    To keep itself from noyance;° but much more
    That spirit upon whose weal depend and rest
    The lives of many. The cess° of majesty   15
    Dies not alone; but, like a gulf,° doth draw
    What's near it with it: it is a massy wheel,
    Fix'd on the summit of the highest mount,
    To whose huge spokes ten thousand lesser things
    Are mortis'd and adjoin'd; which, when it falls,   20
    Each small annexment, petty consequence,

---

342 *top of my bent:* Limit of endurance, i.e., extent to which a bow may be bent; *by and by:*
Immediately.   346 *witching time:* I.e., time when spells are cast.   352 *Nero:* Murderer of
his mother, Agrippina.   356 *shent:* Rebuked.   357 *give them seals:* Confirm with
deeds.   **Scene III.**   3 *dispatch:* Prepare.   5 *terms:* Condition, circumstances; *estate:*
State.   7 *brows:* Effronteries.   11 *single and peculiar:* Individual and private.   13 *noy-
ance:* Harm.   15 *cess:* Decease.   16 *gulf:* Whirlpool.

Attends° the boist'rous ruin. Never alone
Did the king sigh, but with a general groan.
King: Arm° you, I pray you, to this speedy voyage;
For we will fetters put about this fear,   25
Which now goes too free-footed.
Rosencrantz: We will haste us.
                    Exeunt Gentlemen [Rosencrantz and Guildenstern].

      Enter Polonius.

Polonius: My lord, he's going to his mother's closet:
Behind the arras° I'll convey° myself,
To hear the process;° I'll warrant she'll tax him home:°
And, as you said, and wisely was it said,   30
'Tis meet that some more audience than a mother,
Since nature makes them partial, should o'erhear
The speech, of vantage.° Fare you well, my liege:
I'll call upon you ere you go to bed,
And tell you what I know.
King: Thanks, dear my lord.   *Exit [Polonius].* 35
O, my offence is rank, it smells to heaven;
It hath the primal eldest curse° upon't,
A brother's murder. Pray can I not,
Though inclination be as sharp as will:°
My stronger guilt defeats my strong intent;   40
And, like a man to double business bound,
I stand in pause where I shall first begin,
And both neglect. What if this cursed hand
Were thicker than itself with brother's blood,
Is there not rain enough in the sweet heavens   45
To wash it white as snow? Whereto serves mercy
But to confront° the visage of offence?
And what's in prayer but this two-fold force,
To be forestalled° ere we come to fall,
Or pardon'd being down? Then I'll look up;   50
My fault is past. But, O, what form of prayer
Can serve my turn? "Forgive me my foul murder"?
That cannot be: since I am still possess'd
Of those effects for which I did the murder,
My crown, mine own ambition° and my queen.   55
May one be pardon'd and retain th' offence?°
In the corrupted currents° of this world
Offence's gilded hand° may shove by justice,

---

22 *Attends:* Participates in.   24 *Arm:* Prepare.   28 *arras:* Screen of tapestry placed around the walls of household apartments; *convey:* Implication of secrecy, *convey* was often used to mean "steal."   29 *process:* Proceedings; *tax him home:* Reprove him severely.   33 *of vantage:* From an advantageous place.   37 *primal eldest curse:* The curse of Cain, the first to kill his brother.   39 *sharp as will:* I.e., his desire is as strong as his determination.   47 *confront:* Oppose directly.   49 *forestalled:* Prevented.   55 *ambition:* I.e., realization of ambition.   56 *offence:* Benefit accruing from offense.   57 *currents:* Courses.   58 *gilded hand:* Hand offering gold as a bribe.

And oft 'tis seen the wicked prize° itself
Buys out the law: but 'tis not so above;   60
There is no shuffling,° there the action lies°
In his true nature; and we ourselves compell'd,
Even to the teeth and forehead° of our faults,
To give in evidence. What then? what rests?°
Try what repentance can: what can it not?   65
Yet what can it when one can not repent?
O wretched state! O bosom black as death!
O limed° soul, that, struggling to be free,
Art more engag'd!° Help, angels! Make assay!°
Bow, stubborn knees; and, heart with strings of steel,   70
Be soft as sinews of the new-born babe!
All may be well.   *[He kneels.]*

Enter Hamlet.

Hamlet: Now might I do it pat,° now he is praying;
And now I'll do't. And so 'a goes to heaven;
And so am I reveng'd. That would be scann'd:°   75
A villain kills my father; and for that,
I, his sole son, do this same villain send
To heaven.
Why, this is hire and salary, not revenge.
'A took my father grossly, full of bread;°   80
With all his crimes broad blown,° as flush° as May;
And how his audit stands who knows save heaven?
But in our circumstance and course° of thought,
'Tis heavy with him: and am I then reveng'd,
To take him in the purging of his soul,   85
When he is fit and season'd for his passage?°
No!
Up, sword; and know thou a more horrid hent:°
When he is drunk asleep,° or in his rage,
Or in th' incestuous pleasure of his bed;   90
At game, a-swearing, or about some act
That has no relish of salvation in't;
Then trip him, that his heels may kick at heaven,
And that his soul may be as damn'd and black
As hell, whereto it goes. My mother stays: 95
This physic° but prolongs thy sickly days.   *Exit.*
King: *[Rising]* My words fly up, my thoughts remain below:
Words without thoughts never to heaven go.   *Exit.*

---

59 *wicked prize:* Prize won by wickedness.   61 *shuffling:* Escape by trickery; *lies:* Is sustainable.   63 *teeth and forehead:* Very face.   64 *rests:* Remains.   68 *limed:* Caught as with birdlime.   69 *engag'd:* Embedded; *assay:* Trial.   73 *pat:* Opportunely.   75 *would be scann'd:* Needs to be looked into.   80 *full of bread:* Enjoying his worldly pleasures (see Ezekiel 16:49).   81 *broad blown:* In full bloom; *flush:* Lusty.   83 *in . . . course:* As we see it in our mortal situation.   86 *fit . . . passage:* I.e., reconciled to heaven by forgiveness of his sins.   88 *hent:* Seizing; or more probably, occasion of seizure.   89 *drunk asleep:* In a drunken sleep.   96 *physic:* Purging (by prayer).

[SCENE IV: *The Queen's closet.*]

    Enter [Queen] Gertrude and Polonius.

Polonius: 'A will come straight. Look you lay° home to him:
    Tell him his pranks have been too broad° to bear with,
    And that your grace hath screen'd and stood between
    Much heat° and him. I'll sconce° me even here.
    Pray you, be round° with him.   5
Hamlet (within): Mother, mother, mother!
Queen: I'll warrant you,
    Fear me not: withdraw, I hear him coming.
                          [Polonius hides behind the arras.]

    Enter Hamlet.

Hamlet: Now, mother, what's the matter?
Queen: Hamlet, thou hast thy father much offended.
Hamlet: Mother, you have my father° much offended.   10
Queen: Come, come, you answer with an idle tongue.
Hamlet: Go, go, you question with a wicked tongue.
Queen: Why, how now, Hamlet!
Hamlet: What's the matter now?
Queen: Have you forgot me?
Hamlet: No, by the rood,° not so:
    You are the queen, your husband's brother's wife;   15
    And — would it were not so! — you are my mother.
Queen: Nay, then, I'll set those to you that can speak.
Hamlet: Come, come, and sit you down; you shall not budge;
    You go not till I set you up a glass
    Where you may see the inmost part of you.   20
Queen: What wilt thou do? thou wilt not murder me?
    Help, help, ho!
Polonius [behind]: What, ho! help, help; help!
Hamlet [drawing]: How now! a rat? Dead, for a ducat, dead!
                      [Makes a pass through the arras.]
Polonius [behind]: O, I am slain!   *[Falls and dies.]*   25
Queen: O me, what hast thou done?
Hamlet: Nay, I know not:
    Is it the king?
Queen: O, what a rash and bloody deed is this!
Hamlet: A bloody deed! almost as bad, good mother,
    As kill a king, and marry with his brother.   30
Queen: As kill a king!
Hamlet: Ay, lady, it was my word.
          [Lifts up the arras and discovers Polonius.]
    Thou wretched, rash, intruding fool, farewell!
    I took thee for thy better: take thy fortune;

Scene IV.   1 *lay:* Thrust.   2 *broad:* Unrestrained.   4 *Much heat:* I.e., the king's anger;
sconce: Hide.   5 *round:* Blunt.   9–10 *thy father, my father:* I.e., Claudius, the elder Hamlet.
let.   14 *rood:* Cross.

Thou find'st to be too busy is some danger.
Leave wringing of your hands: peace! sit you down,   35
And let me wring your heart; for so I shall,
If it be made of penetrable stuff,
If damned custom have not braz'd° it so
That it be proof and bulwark against sense.

Queen: What have I done, that thou dar'st wag thy tongue   40
In noise so rude against me?

Hamlet: Such an act
That blurs the grace and blush of modesty,
Calls virtue hypocrite, takes off the rose
From the fair forehead of an innocent love
And sets a blister° there, makes marriage-vows   45
As false as dicers' oaths: O, such a deed
As from the body of contraction° plucks
The very soul, and sweet religion° makes
A rhapsody° of words: heaven's face does glow
O'er this solidity and compound mass   50
With heated visage, as against the doom
Is thought-sick at the act.°

Queen: Ay me, what act,
That roars so loud, and thunders in the index?°

Hamlet: Look here, upon this picture, and on this.
The counterfeit presentment° of two brothers.   55
See, what a grace was seated on this brow;
Hyperion's° curls; the front° of Jove himself;
An eye like Mars, to threaten and command;
A station° like the herald Mercury
New-lighted on a heaven-kissing hill;   60
A combination and a form indeed,
Where every god did seem to set his seal,
To give the world assurance° of a man:
This was your husband. Look you now, what follows:
Here is your husband; like a mildew'd ear,°   65
Blasting his wholesome brother. Have you eyes?
Could you on this fair mountain leave to feed,
And batten° on this moor?° Ha! have you eyes?
You cannot call it love; for at your age
The hey-day° in the blood is tame, it's humble,   70
And waits upon the judgement: and what judgement

---

38 *braz'd:* Brazened, hardened.   45 *sets a blister:* Brands as a harlot.   47 *contraction:* The marriage contract.   48 *religion:* Religious vows.   49 *rhapsody:* Senseless string. 49–52 *heaven's . . . act:* Heaven's face blushes to look down on this world, and Gertrude's marriage makes heaven feel as sick as though the day of doom were near.   53 *index:* Prelude or preface.   55 *counterfeit presentment:* Portrayed representation.   57 *Hyperion's:* The sun god's; *front:* Brow.   59 *station:* Manner of standing.   63 *assurance:* Pledge, guarantee.   65 *mildew'd ear:* See Genesis 41:5-7.   68 *batten:* Grow fat; *moor:* Barren upland.   70 *hey-day:* State of excitement.

Would step from this to this? Sense, sure, you have,
Else could you not have motion;° but sure, that sense
Is apoplex'd;° for madness would not err,
Nor sense to ecstasy was ne'er so thrall'd°   75
But it reserv'd some quantity of choice,°
To serve in such a difference. What devil was't
That thus hath cozen'd° you at hoodman-blind?°
Eyes without feeling, feeling without sight,
Ears without hands or eyes, smelling sans° all,   80
Or but a sickly part of one true sense
Could not so mope.°
O shame! where is thy blush? Rebellious hell,
If thou canst mutine° in a matron's bones,
To flaming youth let virtue be as wax,   85
And melt in her own fire: proclaim no shame
When the compulsive ardour gives the charge,°
Since frost itself as actively doth burn
And reason pandars will.°
Queen: O Hamlet, speak no more:
Thou turn'st mine eyes into my very soul;   90
And there I see such black and grained° spots
As will not leave their tinct.
Hamlet: Nay, but to live
In the rank sweat of an enseamed° bed,
Stew'd in corruption, honeying and making love
Over the nasty sty, —
Queen: O, speak to me no more;   95
These words, like daggers, enter in mine ears;
No more, sweet Hamlet!
Hamlet: A murderer and a villain;
A slave that is not twentieth part the tithe
Of your precedent lord;° a vice of kings;°
A cutpurse of the empire and the rule,   100
That from a shelf the precious diadem stole,
And put it in his pocket!
Queen: No more!

    Enter Ghost.

72–73 *Sense . . . motion:* Sense and motion are functions of the middle or sensible soul, the possession of sense being the basis of motion.   74 *apoplex'd:* Paralyzed. Mental derangement was thus of three sorts: apoplexy, ecstasy, and diabolic possession.   75 *thrall'd:* Enslaved.   76 *quantity of choice:* Fragment of the power to choose.   78 *cozen'd:* Tricked, cheated; *hoodman-blind:* Blindman's buff.   80 *sans:* Without.   82 *mope:* Be in a depressed, spiritless state, act aimlessly.   84 *mutine:* Mutiny, rebel.   87 *gives the charge:* Delivers the attack.   89 *reason pandars will:* The normal and proper situation was one in which reason guided the will in the direction of good; here, reason is perverted and leads in the direction of evil.   91 *grained:* Dyed in grain.   93 *enseamed:* Loaded with grease, greased.   99 *precedent lord:* I.e., the elder Hamlet; *vice of kings:* Buffoon of kings; a reference to the Vice, or clown, of the morality plays and interludes.

Hamlet: A king of shreds and patches,° —
     Save me, and hover o'er me with your wings,
     You heavenly guards! What would your gracious figure?   105
Queen: Alas, he's mad!
Hamlet: Do you not come your tardy son to chide,
     That, laps'd in time and passion,° lets go by
     Th' important° acting of your dread command?
     O, say!   110
Ghost: Do not forget: this visitation
     Is but to whet thy almost blunted purpose.
     But, look, amazement° on thy mother sits:
     O, step between her and her fighting soul:
     Conceit in weakest bodies strongest works: 115
     Speak to her, Hamlet.
Hamlet: How is it with you, lady?
Queen: Alas, how is 't with you,
     That you do bend your eye on vacancy
     And with th' incorporal° air do hold discourse?
     Forth at your eyes your spirits wildly peep;   120
     And, as the sleeping soldiers in th' alarm,
     Your bedded° hair, like life in excrements,°
     Start up, and stand an° end. O gentle son,
     Upon the heat and flame of thy distemper
     Sprinkle cool patience. Whereon do you look?   125
Hamlet: On him, on him! Look you, how pale he glares!
     His form and cause conjoin'd,° preaching to stones,
     Would make them capable. — Do not look upon me;
     Lest with this piteous action you convert
     My stern effects:° then what I have to do   130
     Will want true colour;° tears perchance for blood.
Queen: To whom do you speak this?
Hamlet: Do you see nothing there?
Queen: Nothing at all; yet all that is I see.
Hamlet: Nor did you nothing hear?
Queen: No, nothing but ourselves.
Hamlet: Why, look you there! look, how it steals away!   135
     My father, in his habit as he liv'd!
     Look, where he goes, even now, out at the portal!   *Exit Ghost.*
Queen: This is the very coinage of your brain:
     This bodiless creation ecstasy
     Is very cunning in.

---

103 *shreds and patches:* I.e., motley, the traditional costume of the Vice.   108 *laps'd . . . passion:* Having suffered time to slip and passion to cool; also explained as "engrossed in casual events and lapsed into mere fruitless passion, so that he no longer entertains a rational purpose."   109 *important:* Urgent.   113 *amazement:* Frenzy, distraction.   119 *incorporal:* Immaterial.   122 *bedded:* Laid in smooth layers; *excrements:* The hair was considered an excrement or voided part of the body.   123 *an:* On.   127 *conjoin'd:* United.   129-130 *convert . . . effects:* Divert me from my stern duty. For *effects,* possibly *affects* (affections of the mind).   131 *want true colour:* Lack good reason so that (with a play on the normal sense of *colour*) I shall shed tears instead of blood.

Hamlet: Ecstasy!   140
   My pulse, as yours, doth temperately keep time,
   And makes as healthful music: it is not madness
   That I have utt'red: bring me to the test,
   And I the matter will re-word,° which madness
   Would gambol° from. Mother, for love of grace,   145
   Lay not that flattering unction° to your soul,
   That not your trespass, but my madness speaks:
   It will but skin and film the ulcerous place,
   Whiles rank corruption, mining° all within,
   Infects unseen. Confess yourself to heaven;   150
   Repent what's past; avoid what is to come;°
   And do not spread the compost° on the weeds,
   To make them ranker. Forgive me this my virtue;°
   For in the fatness° of these pursy° times
   Virtue itself of vice must pardon beg,   155
   Yea, curb° and woo for leave to do him good.
Queen: O Hamlet, thou hast cleft my heart in twain.
Hamlet: O, throw away the worser part of it,
   And live the purer with the other half.
   Good night: but go not to my uncle's bed;   160
   Assume a virtue, if you have it not.
   That monster, custom, who all sense doth eat,
   Of habits devil, is angel yet in this,
   That to the use of actions fair and good
   He likewise gives a frock or livery,   165
   That aptly is put on. Refrain to-night,
   And that shall lend a kind of easiness
   To the next abstinence: the next more easy;
   For use almost can change the stamp of nature,
   And either . . . the devil, or throw him out°   170
   With wondrous potency. Once more, good night:
   And when you are desirous to be bless'd,°
   I'll blessing beg of you. For this same lord,   *[Pointing to Polonius.]*
   I do repent: but heaven hath pleas'd it so,
   To punish me with this and this with me,   175
   That I must be their scourge and minister.
   I will bestow him, and will answer well
   The death I gave him. So, again, good night.
   I must be cruel, only to be kind:
   Thus bad begins and worse remains behind.   180
   One word more, good lady.

---

144 *re-word:* Repeat in words.   145 *gambol:* Skip away.   146 *unction:* Ointment used
medicinally or as a rite; suggestion that forgiveness for sin may not be so easily achieved.
149 *mining:* Working under the surface.   151 *what is to come:* I.e., the sins of the future.
152 *compost:* Manure.   153 *this my virtue:* My virtuous talk in reproving you.   154 *fatness:*
Grossness; *pursy:* Short-winded, corpulent.   156 *curb:* Bow, bend the knee.   170 Defective line usually emended by inserting *master* after *either.*   172 *be bless'd:* Become blessed,
i.e., repentant.

Queen: What shall I do?
Hamlet: Not this, by no means, that I bid you do:
    Let the bloat° king tempt you again to bed;
    Pinch wanton on your cheek; call you his mouse;
    And let him, for a pair of reechy° kisses,   185
    Or paddling in your neck with his damn'd fingers,
    Make you to ravel all this matter out,
    That I essentially° am not in madness,
    But mad in craft. 'Twere good you let him know;
    For who, that's but a queen, fair, sober, wise,   190
    Would from a paddock,° from a bat, a gib,°
    Such dear concernings° hide? who would do so?
    No, in despite of sense and secrecy,
    Unpeg the basket on the house's top,
    Let the birds fly, and, like the famous ape,°   195
    To try conclusions,° in the basket creep,
    And break your own neck down.
Queen: Be thou assur'd, if words be made of breath,
    And breath of life, I have no life to breathe
    What thou hast said to me.   200
Hamlet: I must to England; you know that?
Queen: Alack,
    I had forgot: 'tis so concluded on.
Hamlet: There's letters seal'd: and my two schoolfellows,
    Whom I will trust as I will adders fang'd,
    They bear the mandate; they must sweep my way,°   205
    And marshal me to knavery. Let it work;
    For 'tis the sport to have the enginer°
    Hoist° with his own petar:° and 't shall go hard
    But I will delve one yard below their mines,
    And blow them at the moon: O, 'tis most sweet,   210
    When in one line two crafts° directly meet.
    This man shall set me packing:°
    I'll lug the guts into the neighbour room.
    Mother, good night. Indeed this counsellor
    Is now most still, most secret and most grave,   215
    Who was in life a foolish prating knave.
    Come, sir, to draw° toward an end with you.
    Good night, mother.   *Exeunt [severally; Hamlet dragging in Polonius.]*

---

183 *bloat:* Bloated.   185 *reechy:* Dirty, filthy.   188 *essentially:* In my essential nature.
191 *paddock:* Toad; *gib:* Tomcat.   192 *dear concernings:* Important affairs.   195 *the famous
ape:* A letter from Sir John Suckling seems to supply other details of the story, otherwise
not identified: "It is the story of the jackanapes and the partridges; thou starest after a
beauty till it be lost to thee, then let'st out another, and starest after that till it is gone too."
196 *conclusions:* Experiments.   205 *sweep my way:* Clear my path.   207 *enginer:* Con-
structor of military works, or possibly, artilleryman.   208 *Hoist:* Blown up; *petar:* Defined
as a small engine of war used to blow in a door or make a breach, and as a case filled with ex-
plosive materials.   211 *two crafts:* Two acts of guile, with quibble on the sense of "two
ships."   212 *set me packing:* Set me to making schemes, and set me to lugging (him), and,
also, send me off in a hurry.   217 *draw:* Come, with quibble on literal sense.

[ACT IV

SCENE I: *A room in the castle.*]

Enter King and Queen, with Rosencrantz and Guildenstern.

King: There's matter in these sighs, these profound heaves:
You must translate: 'tis fit we understand them.
Where is your son?
Queen: Bestow this place on us a little while.
　　　　　　　　　　[Exeunt Rosencrantz and Guildenstern.]
Ah, mine own lord, what have I seen to-night!　　　　　　5
King: What, Gertrude? How does Hamlet?
Queen: Mad as the sea and wind, when both contend
Which is the mightier: in his lawless fit,
Behind the arras hearing something stir,
Whips out his rapier, cries, "A rat, a rat!"　　　　　　10
And, in this brainish° apprehension,° kills
The unseen good old man.
King: 　　　　　　　　　O heavy deed!
It had been so with us, had we been there:
His liberty is full of threats to all;
To you yourself, to us, to every one.　　　　　　15
Alas, how shall this bloody deed be answer'd?
It will be laid to us, whose providence°
Should have kept short,° restrain'd and out of haunt,°
This mad young man: but so much was our love,
We would not understand what was most fit;　　　　　　20
But, like the owner of a foul disease,
To keep it from divulging,° let it feed
Even on the pith of life. Where is he gone?
Queen: To draw apart the body he hath kill'd:
O'er whom his very madness, like some ore　　　　　　25
Among a mineral° of metals base,
Shows itself pure; 'a weeps for what is done.
King: O Gertrude, come away!
The sun no sooner shall the mountains touch,
But we will ship him hence: and this vile deed　　　　　　30
We must, with all our majesty and skill,
Both countenance and excuse. Ho, Guildenstern!

Enter Rosencrantz and Guildenstern.

Friends both, go join you with some further aid:
Hamlet in madness hath Polonius slain,
And from his mother's closet hath he dragg'd him:　　　　　　35
Go seek him out; speak fair, and bring the body
Into the chapel. I pray you, haste in this.

Act IV, Scene I. 11 *brainish:* Headstrong, passionate; *apprehension:* Conception, imagination. 17 *providence:* Foresight. 18 *short:* I.e., on a short tether; *out of haunt:* Secluded. 22 *divulging:* Becoming evident. 26 *mineral:* Mine.

[Exeunt Rosencrantz and Guildenstern.]

Come, Gertrude, we'll call up our wisest friends;
And let them know, both what we mean to do,
And what's untimely done . . .°   40
Whose whisper o'er the world's diameter,°
As level° as the cannon to his blank,°
Transports his pois'ned shot, may miss our name,
And hit the woundless° air. O, come away!
My soul is full of discord and dismay.   *Exeunt.*   45

[SCENE II: *Another room in the castle.*]

Enter Hamlet.

Hamlet: Safely stowed.

Rosencrantz: ⎫
                      ⎬ *(within)* Hamlet! Lord Hamlet!
Guildenstern: ⎭

Hamlet: But soft, what noise? who calls on Hamlet? O, here they come.

Enter Rosencrantz and Guildenstern.

Rosencrantz: What have you done, my lord, with the dead body?

Hamlet: Compounded it with dust, whereto 'tis kin.

Rosencrantz: Tell us where 'tis, that we may take it thence   5
And bear it to the chapel.

Hamlet: Do not believe it.

Rosencrantz: Believe what?

Hamlet: That I can keep your counsel° and not mine own. Besides, to be
demanded of a sponge! what replication° should be made by the son   10
of a king?

Rosencrantz: Take you me for a sponge, my lord?

Hamlet: Ay, sir, that soaks up the king's countenance, his rewards, his
authorities.° But such officers do the king best service in the end: he
keeps them, like an ape an apple, in the corner of his jaw; first   15
mouthed, to be last swallowed: when he needs what you have gleaned,
it is but squeezing you, and, sponge, you shall be dry again.

Rosencrantz: I understand you not, my lord.

Hamlet: I am glad of it: a knavish speech sleeps in a foolish ear.

Rosencrantz: My lord, you must tell us where the body is, and go with us   20
to the king.

Hamlet: The body is with the king, but the king is not with the body.°
The king is a thing —

Guildenstern: A thing, my lord!

Hamlet: Of nothing: bring me to him. Hide fox, and all after.°   *Exeunt.*   25

40 Defective line; some editors add: *so, haply, slander;* others add: *for, haply, slander;* other
conjectures.   41 *diameter:* Extent from side to side.   42 *level:* Straight; *blank:* White
spot in the center of a target.   44 *woundless:* Invulnerable.   **Scene II.**   9 *keep your
counsel:* Hamlet is aware of their treachery but says nothing about it.   10 *replication:*
Reply.   14 *authorities:* Authoritative backing.   22 *The body . . . body:* There are many interpretations; possibly, "The body lies in death with the king, my father; but my father walks
disembodied"; or "Claudius has the bodily possession of kingship, but kingliness, or justice
of inheritance, is not with him."   25 *Hide . . . after:* An old signal cry in the game of hide-
and-seek.

[SCENE III: *Another room in the castle.*]

Enter King, and two or three.

King: I have sent to seek him, and to find the body.
  How dangerous is it that this man goes loose!
  Yet must not we put the strong law on him:
  He's lov'd of the distracted° multitude,
  Who like not in their judgement, but their eyes;   5
  And where 'tis so, th' offender's scourge° is weigh'd,°
  But never the offence. To bear all smooth and even,
  This sudden sending him away must seem
  Deliberate pause:° diseases desperate grown
  By desperate appliance are reliev'd,   10
  Or not at all.

Enter Rosencrantz, [Guildenstern,] and all the rest.

            How now! what hath befall'n?
Rosencrantz: Where the dead body is bestow'd, my lord,
  We cannot get from him.
King: But where is he?
Rosencrantz: Without, my lord; guarded, to know your pleasure.
King: Bring him before us.   15
Rosencrantz: Ho! bring in the lord.

      They enter [with Hamlet].

King: Now, Hamlet, where's Polonius?
Hamlet: At supper.
King: At supper! where?
Hamlet: Not where he eats, but where 'a is eaten: a certain convocation of   20
  politic° worms° are e'en at him. Your worm is your only emperor
  for diet: we fat all creatures else to fat us, and we fat ourselves for
  maggots: your fat king and your lean beggar is but variable service,°
  two dishes, but to one table: that's the end.
King: Alas, alas!   25
Hamlet: A man may fish with the worm that hath eat of a king, and eat of
  the fish that hath fed of that worm.
King: What dost thou mean by this?
Hamlet: Nothing but to show you how a king may go a progress° through
  the guts of a beggar.   30
King: Where is Polonius?
Hamlet: In heaven; send thither to see: if your messenger find him not
  there, seek him i' the other place yourself. But if indeed you find him
  not within this month, you shall nose him as you go up the stairs
  into the lobby.   35
King [to some Attendants]: Go seek him there.
Hamlet: 'A will stay till you come.   *[Exeunt Attendants.]*

Scene III.   4 *distracted:* I.e., without power of forming logical judgments.   6 *scourge:*
Punishment; *weigh'd:* Taken into consideration.   9 *Deliberate pause:* Considered action.
20-21 *convocation...worms:* Allusion to the Diet of Worms (1521).   21 *politic:* Crafty.
23 *variable service:* A variety of dishes.   29 *progress:* Royal journey of state.

King: Hamlet, this deed, for thine especial safety,—
    Which we do tender,° as we dearly grieve
    For that which thou hast done,—must send thee hence   40
    With fiery quickness: therefore prepare thyself;
    The bark is ready, and the wind at help,
    Th' associates tend, and everything is bent
    For England.
Hamlet: For England!
King: Ay, Hamlet.
Hamlet: Good.
King: So is it, if thou knew'st our purposes.   45
Hamlet: I see a cherub° that sees them. But, come; for England! Farewell,
    dear mother.
King: Thy loving father, Hamlet.
Hamlet: My mother: father and mother is man and wife; man and wife is
    one flesh; and so, my mother. Come, for England!   *Exit.*   50
King: Follow him at foot;° tempt him with speed aboard;
    Delay it not; I'll have him hence to-night:
    Away! for every thing is seal'd and done
    That else leans on th' affair: pray you, make haste.
                     [Exeunt all but the King.]
    And, England, if my love thou hold'st at aught—   55
    As my great power thereof may give thee sense,
    Since yet thy cicatrice° looks raw and red
    After the Danish sword, and thy free awe°
    Pays homage to us—thou mayst not coldly set
    Our sovereign process; which imports at full,   60
    By letters congruing to that effect,
    The present death of Hamlet. Do it, England;
    For like the hectic° in my blood he rages,
    And thou must cure me: till I know 'tis done,
    Howe'er my haps,° my joys were ne'er begun.   *Exit.*   65

[SCENE IV: *A plain in Denmark.*]

    Enter Fortinbras with his Army over the stage.

Fortinbras: Go, captain, from me greet the Danish king;
    Tell him that, by his license,° Fortinbras
    Craves the conveyance° of a promis'd march
    Over his kingdom. You know the rendezvous.
    If that his majesty would aught with us,   5
    We shall express our duty in his eye;°
    And let him know so.
Captain: I will do't, my lord.

---

39 *tender:* Regard, hold dear.   46 *cherub:* Cherubim are angels of knowledge.   51 *at foot:* Close behind, at heel.   57 *cicatrice:* Scar.   58 *free awe:* Voluntary show of respect. 63 *hectic:* Fever.   65 *haps:* Fortunes.   **Scene IV.**   2 *license:* Leave.   3 *conveyance:* Escort, convoy.   6 *in his eye:* In his presence.

Fortinbras: Go softly° on.   *[Exeunt all but Captain.]*

    Enter Hamlet, Rosencrantz, [Guildenstern,] &c.

Hamlet: Good sir, whose powers are these?
Captain: They are of Norway, sir.   10
Hamlet: How purpos'd, sir, I pray you?
Captain: Against some part of Poland.
Hamlet: Who commands them, sir?
Captain: The nephew to old Norway, Fortinbras.
Hamlet: Goes it against the main° of Poland, sir,   15
    Or for some frontier?
Captain: Truly to speak, and with no addition,
    We go to gain a little patch of ground
    That hath in it no profit but the name.
    To pay five ducats, five, I would not farm it;°   20
    Nor will it yield to Norway or the Pole
    A ranker rate, should it be sold in fee.°
Hamlet: Why, then the Polack never will defend it.
Captain: Yes, it is already garrison'd.
Hamlet: Two thousand souls and twenty thousand ducats   25
    Will not debate the question of this straw:°
    This is th' imposthume° of much wealth and peace,
    That inward breaks, and shows no cause without
    Why the man dies. I humbly thank you, sir.
Captain: God be wi' you, sir.   *[Exit.]*
Rosencrantz: Will 't please you go, my lord?   30
Hamlet: I'll be with you straight. Go a little before.
                        [Exeunt all except Hamlet.]
    How all occasions° do inform against° me,
    And spur my dull revenge! What is a man,
    If his chief good and market of his time°
    Be but to sleep and feed? a beast, no more.   35
    Sure, he that made us with such large discourse,
    Looking before and after, gave us not
    That capability and god-like reason
    To fust° in us unus'd. Now, whether it be
    Bestial oblivion, or some craven scruple   40
    Of thinking too precisely on th' event,
    A thought which, quarter'd, hath but one part wisdom
    And ever three parts coward, I do not know
    Why yet I live to say "This thing 's to do";
    Sith I have cause and will and strength and means   45
    To do 't. Examples gross as earth exhort me:
    Witness this army of such mass and charge

---

8 *softly:* Slowly.   15 *main:* Country itself.   20 *farm it:* Take a lease of it.   22 *fee:* Fee
simple.   26 *debate...straw:* Settle this trifling matter.   27 *imposthume:* Purulent abscess
or swelling.   32 *occasions:* Incidents, events; *inform against:* Generally defined as "show,"
"betray" (i.e., his tardiness); more probably *inform* means "take shape," as in *Macbeth,* II.i.48.
34 *market of his time:* The best use he makes of his time, or, that for which he sells his time.
39 *fust:* Grow moldy.

Led by a delicate and tender prince,
Whose spirit with divine ambition puff'd
Makes mouths at the invisible event,   50
Exposing what is mortal and unsure
To all that fortune, death and danger dare,
Even for an egg-shell. Rightly to be great
Is not to stir without great argument,
But greatly to find quarrel in a straw   55
When honour's at the stake. How stand I then,
That have a father kill'd, a mother stain'd,
Excitements of° my reason and my blood,
And let all sleep? while, to my shame, I see
The imminent death of twenty thousand men,   60
That, for a fantasy and trick° of fame,
Go to their graves like beds, fight for a plot°
Whereon the numbers cannot try the cause,
Which is not tomb enough and continent
To hide the slain? O, from this time forth,   65
My thoughts be bloody, or be nothing worth!   *Exit.*

[SCENE V: *Elsinore. A room in the castle.*]

    Enter Horatio, [Queen] Gertrude, and a Gentleman.

Queen: I will not speak with her.
Gentleman: She is importunate, indeed distract:
    Her mood will needs be pitied.
Queen: What would she have?
Gentleman: She speaks much of her father; says she hears
    There's tricks° i' th' world; and hems, and beats her heart;°   5
    Spurns enviously at straws;° speaks things in doubt,
    That carry but half sense: her speech is nothing,
    Yet the unshaped° use of it doth move
    The hearers to collection;° they yawn° at it,
    And botch° the words up fit to their own thoughts;   10
    Which, as her winks, and nods, and gestures yield° them,
    Indeed would make one think there might be thought,
    Though nothing sure, yet much unhappily.°
Horatio: 'Twere good she were spoken with: for she may strew
    Dangerous conjectures in ill-breeding minds.°   15
Queen: Let her come in.   *[Exit Gentleman.]*
    [Aside.] To my sick soul, as sin's true nature is,
    Each toy seems prologue to some great amiss:°

---

58 *Excitements of:* Incentives to.   61 *trick:* Toy, trifle.   62 *plot:* Piece of ground.   **Scene V.**
5 *tricks:* Deceptions; *heart:* I.e., breast.   6 *Spurns...straws:* Kicks spitefully at small objects in her path.   8 *unshaped:* Unformed, artless.   9 *collection:* Inference, a guess at
some sort of meaning; *yawn:* Wonder.   10 *botch:* Patch.   11 *yield:* Deliver, bring forth
(her words).   13 *much unhappily:* Expressive of much unhappiness.   15 *ill-breeding minds:*
Minds bent on mischief.   18 *great amiss:* Calamity, disaster.

So full of artless jealousy is guilt,
It spills itself in fearing to be spilt.°   20

Enter Ophelia [distracted].

Ophelia: Where is the beauteous majesty of Denmark?
Queen: How now, Ophelia!
Ophelia (she sings): How should I your true love know
    From another one?
    By his cockle hat° and staff,   25
    And his sandal shoon.°
Queen: Alas, sweet lady, what imports this song?
Ophelia: Say you? nay, pray you mark.
    (Song) He is dead and gone, lady,
      He is dead and gone;   30
    At his head a grass-green turf,
      At his heels a stone.
    O, ho!
Queen: Nay, but, Ophelia—
Ophelia: Pray you, mark   35
    [Sings.] White his shroud as the mountain snow,—

Enter King.

Queen: Alas, look here, my lord.
Ophelia (Song): Larded° all with flowers;
    Which bewept to the grave did not go
      With true-love showers.   40
King: How do you, pretty lady?
Ophelia: Well, God 'ild° you! They say the owl° was a baker's daughter.
    Lord, we know what we are, but know not what we may be. God be at
    your table!
King: Conceit upon her father.   45
Ophelia: Pray let's have no words of this; but when they ask you what it
    means, say you this:
    (Song) To-morrow is Saint Valentine's day,
      All in the morning betime,
    And I a maid at your window,   50
      To be your Valentine.°
    Then up he rose, and donn'd his clothes,
      And dupp'd° the chamber-door;
    Let in the maid, that out a maid
      Never departed more.   55
King: Pretty Ophelia!

19–20 *So . . . spilt:* Guilt is so full of suspicion that it unskillfully betrays itself in fearing to
be betrayed.   25 *cockle hat:* Hat with cockleshell stuck in it as a sign that the wearer
has been a pilgrim to the shrine of St. James of Compostella. The pilgrim's garb was a conventional disguise for lovers.   26 *shoon:* Shoes.   38 *Larded:* Decorated.   42 *God 'ild:*
God yield or reward; *owl:* Reference to a monkish legend that a baker's daughter was turned
into an owl for refusing bread to the Savior.   51 *Valentine:* This song alludes to the belief
that the first girl seen by a man on the morning of this day was his valentine or true love.
53 *dupp'd:* Opened.

Ophelia: Indeed, la, without an oath, I'll make an end on 't:
  [Sings.] By Gis° and by Saint Charity,
    Alack, and fie for shame!
  Young men will do 't, if they come to 't;   60
    By cock,° they are to blame.
  Quoth she, before you tumbled me,
    You promis'd me to wed.
  So would I ha' done, by yonder sun,
    An thou hadst not come to my bed.   65

King: How long hath she been thus?

Ophelia: I hope all will be well. We must be patient: but I cannot choose
  but weep, to think they would lay him i' the cold ground. My brother
  shall know of it: and so I thank you for your good counsel. Come, my
  coach! Good night, ladies; good night, sweet ladies; good night, good   70
  night.   *[Exit.]*

King: Follow her close; give her good watch, I pray you.   *[Exit Horatio.]*
  O, this is the poison of deep grief; it springs
  All from her father's death. O Gertrude, Gertrude,
  When sorrows come, they come not single spies,   75
  But in battalions. First, her father slain:
  Next your son gone; and he most violent author
  Of his own just remove: the people muddied,
  Thick and unwholesome in their thoughts and whispers,
  For good Polonius' death; and we have done but greenly,°   80
  In hugger-mugger° to inter him: poor Ophelia
  Divided from herself and her fair judgement,
  Without the which we are pictures, or mere beasts:
  Last, and as much containing as all these,
  Her brother is in secret come from France;   85
  Feeds on his wonder, keeps himself in clouds,°
  And wants not buzzers° to infect his ear
  With pestilent speeches of his father's death;
  Wherein necessity, of matter beggar'd,°
  Will nothing stick° our person to arraign   90
  In ear and ear.° O my dear Gertrude, this,
  Like to a murd'ring-piece,° in many places
  Gives me superfluous death.   *A noise within.*

Queen: Alack, what noise is this?

King: Where are my Switzers?° Let them guard the door.

  Enter a Messenger.

  What is the matter?

Messenger: Save yourself, my lord: 95
  The ocean, overpeering° of his list,°

---

58 *Gis:* Jesus.   61 *cock:* Perversion of "God" in oaths.   80 *greenly:* Foolishly.   81 *hugger-mugger:* Secret haste.   86 *in clouds:* Invisible.   87 *buzzers:* Gossipers.   89 *of matter beggar'd:* Unprovided with facts.   90 *nothing stick:* Not hesitate.   91 *In ear and ear:* In everybody's ears.   92 *murd'ring-piece:* Small cannon or mortar; suggestion of numerous missiles fired.   94 *Switzers:* Swiss guards, mercenaries.   96 *overpeering:* Overflowing; *list:* Shore.

Eats not the flats with more impiteous haste
Than young Laertes, in a riotous head,
O'erbears your officers. The rabble call him lord;
And, as the world were now but to begin,   100
Antiquity forgot, custom not known,
The ratifiers and props of every word,°
They cry "Choose we: Laertes shall be king":
Caps, hands, and tongues, applaud it to the clouds:
"Laertes shall be king, Laertes king!"   *A noise within.*   105
Queen: How cheerfully on the false trail they cry!
    O, this is counter,° you false Danish dogs!
King: The doors are broke.

    Enter Laertes with others.

Laertes: Where is this king? Sirs, stand you all without.
Danes: No, let's come in.
Laertes: I pray you, give me leave.   110
Danes: We will, we will.   *[They retire without the door.]*
Laertes: I thank you: keep the door. O thou vile king,
    Give me my father!
Queen: Calmly, good Laertes.
Laertes: That drop of blood that's calm proclaims me bastard,
    Cries cuckold to my father, brands the harlot   115
    Even here, between the chaste unsmirched brow
    Of my true mother.
King: What is the cause, Laertes,
    That thy rebellion looks so giant-like?
    Let him go, Gertrude; do not fear our person:
    There's such divinity doth hedge a king,   120
    That treason can but peep to° what it would,°
    Acts little of his will. Tell me, Laertes,
    Why thou art thus incens'd. Let him go, Gertrude.
    Speak, man.
Laertes: Where is my father?
King: Dead.
Queen: But not by him.   125
King: Let him demand his fill.
Laertes: How came he dead? I'll not be juggled with:
    To hell, allegiance! vows, to the blackest devil!
    Conscience and grace, to the profoundest pit!
    I dare damnation. To this point I stand,   130
    That both the worlds I give to negligence,°
    Let come what comes; only I'll be reveng'd
    Most throughly° for my father.
King: Who shall stay you?

---

102 *word:* Promise.   107 *counter:* A hunting term meaning to follow the trail in a direction opposite to that which the game has taken.   121 *peep to:* I.e., look at from afar off; *would:* Wishes to do.   131 *give to negligence:* He despises both the here and the hereafter. 133 *throughly:* thoroughly.

Laertes: My will,° not all the world's:
      And for my means, I'll husband them so well,   135
      They shall go far with little.
King: Good Laertes,
      If you desire to know the certainty
      Of your dear father, is 't writ in your revenge,
      That, swoopstake,° you will draw both friend and foe,
      Winner and loser?   140
Laertes: None but his enemies.
King: Will you know them then?
Laertes: To his good friends thus wide I'll ope my arms;
      And like the kind life-rend'ring pelican,°
      Repast° them with my blood.
King: Why, now you speak
      Like a good child and a true gentleman.   145
      That I am guiltless of your father's death,
      And am most sensibly in grief for it,
      It shall as level to your judgement 'pear
      As day does to your eye.   *A noise within: "Let her come in."*
Laertes: How now! what noise is that?   150

      Enter Ophelia.

      O heat,° dry up my brains! tears seven times salt,
      Burn out the sense and virtue of mine eye!
      By heaven, thy madness shall be paid with weight,
      Till our scale turn the beam. O rose of May!
      Dear maid, kind sister, sweet Ophelia!   155
      O heavens! is 't possible, a young maid's wits
      Should be as mortal as an old man's life?
      Nature is fine in love, and where 'tis fine,
      It sends some precious instance of itself
      After the thing it loves.   160
Ophelia (Song): They bore him barefac'd on the bier;
      Hey non nonny, nonny, hey nonny;
      And in his grave rain'd many a tear: —
      Fare you well, my dove!
Laertes: Hadst thou thy wits, and didst persuade revenge,   165
      It could not move thus.
Ophelia [sings]: You must sing a-down a-down,
            An you call him a-down-a.
      O, how the wheel° becomes it! It is the false steward,° that stole his
      master's daughter.   170
Laertes: This nothing's more than matter.

---

134 *My will:* He will not be stopped except by his own will.   139 *swoopstake:* Literally,
drawing the whole stake at once, i.e., indiscriminately.   143 *pelican:* Reference to the belief
that the pelican feeds its young with its own blood.   144 *Repast:* Feed.   151 *heat:* Probably the heat generated by the passion of grief.   169 *wheel:* Spinning wheel as accompaniment to the song refrain; *false steward:* The story is unknown.

Ophelia: There's rosemary,° that's for remembrance; pray you, love, remember: and there is pansies,° that's for thoughts.
Laertes: A document° in madness, thoughts and remembrance fitted.
Ophelia: There's fennel° for you, and columbines:° there's rue° for you;   175
   and here's some for me: we may call it herb of grace° o' Sundays: O,
   you must wear your rue with a difference. There's a daisy:° I would
   give you some violets,° but they withered all when my father died:
   they say 'a made a good end, —
   [Sings.] For bonny sweet Robin is all my joy.°   180
Laertes: Thought° and affliction, passion, hell itself,
   She turns to favour and to prettiness.
Ophelia (Song): And will 'a not come again?°
   And will 'a not come again?
      No, no, he is dead: 185
      Go to thy death-bed:
   He never will come again.

   His beard was as white as snow,
   All flaxen was his poll:°
      He is gone, he is gone,   190
      And we cast away° moan:
   God ha' mercy on his soul!
   And of all Christian souls, I pray God. God be wi' you.   *[Exit.]*
Laertes: Do you see this, O God?
King: Laertes, I must commune with your grief,   195
   Or you deny me right.° Go but apart,
   Make choice of whom your wisest friends you will,
   And they shall hear and judge 'twixt you and me:
   If by direct or by collateral° hand
   They find us touch'd,° we will our kingdom give,   200
   Our crown, our life, and all that we call ours,
   To you in satisfaction; but if not,
   Be you content to lend your patience to us,
   And we shall jointly labour with your soul
   To give it due content.
Laertes: Let this be so;   205
   His means of death, his obscure funeral —
   No trophy, sword, nor hatchment° o'er his bones,

---

172 *rosemary:* Used as a symbol of remembrance both at weddings and at funerals.
173 *pansies:* Emblems of love and courtship (from the French *pensée*).   174 *document:*
Piece of instruction or lesson.   175, 176 *fennel:* Emblem of flattery; *columbines:* Emblem of
unchastity (?) or ingratitude (?); *rue:* Emblem of repentance. It was usually mingled with
holy water and then known as *herb of grace*. Ophelia is probably playing on the two meanings
of *rue*, "repentant" and "even for ruth (pity)"; the former signification is for the queen, the latter for herself.   177 *daisy:* Emblem of dissembling, faithlessness.   178 *violets:* Emblems
of faithfulness.   180 *For...joy:* Probably a line from a Robin Hood ballad.   181 *Thought:*
Melancholy thought.   183 *And...again:* This song appeared in the songbooks as "The
Merry Milkmaids' Dumps."   189 *poll:* Head.   191 *cast away:* Shipwrecked.   196 *right:*
My rights.   199 *collateral:* Indirect.   200 *touch'd:* Implicated.   207 *hatchment:* Tablet
displaying the armorial bearings of a deceased person.

No noble rite nor formal ostentation —
Cry to be heard, as 'twere from heaven to earth,
That I must call 't in question.
King: So you shall;   210
And where th' offence is let the great axe fall.
I pray you, go with me.   *Exeunt.*

[SCENE VI: *Another room in the castle.*]

Enter Horatio and others.

Horatio: What are they that would speak with me?
Gentleman: Sea-faring men, sir: they say they have letters for you.
Horatio: Let them come in.   *[Exit Gentleman.]*
I do not know from what part of the world
I should be greeted, if not from lord Hamlet.   5

Enter Sailors.

First Sailor: God bless you, sir.
Horatio: Let him bless thee too.
First Sailor: 'A shall sir, an 't please him. There's a letter for you, sir; it
comes from the ambassador that was bound for England; if your
name be Horatio, as I am let to know it is.   10
Horatio [reads]: "Horatio, when thou shalt have overlooked this, give
these fellows some means° to the king: they have letters for him. Ere
we were two days old at sea, a pirate of very warlike appointment gave
us chase. Finding ourselves too slow of sail, we put on a compelled
valour, and in the grapple I boarded them: on the instant they got   15
clear of our ship; so I alone became their prisoner. They have dealt
with me like thieves of mercy:° but they knew what they did; I am to
do a good turn for them. Let the king have the letters I have sent; and
repair thou to me with as much speed as thou wouldest fly death. I
have words to speak in thine ear will make thee dumb; yet are they   20
much too light for the bore° of the matter. These good fellows will
bring thee where I am. Rosencrantz and Guildenstern hold their
course for England: of them I have much to tell thee. Farewell.
          "He that thou knowest thine, HAMLET."
Come, I will give you way for these your letters;   25
And do 't the speedier, that you may direct me
To him from whom you brought them.   *Exeunt.*

[SCENE VII: *Another room in the castle.*]

Enter King and Laertes.

King: Now must your conscience° my acquittance seal,
And you must put me in your heart for friend,

Scene VI. 12 *means:* Means of access.   17 *thieves of mercy:* Merciful thieves.   21 *bore:*
Caliber, importance.   **Scene VII.** 1 *conscience:* Knowledge that this is true.

Sith you have heard, and with a knowing ear,
That he which hath your noble father slain
Pursued my life.
Laertes: It well appears: but tell me   5
Why you proceeded not against these feats,
So criminal and so capital° in nature,
As by your safety, wisdom, all things else,
You mainly° were stirr'd up.
King: O, for two special reasons;
Which may to you, perhaps, seem much unsinew'd,°   10
But yet to me th' are strong. The queen his mother
Lives almost by his looks; and for myself—
My virtue or my plague, be it either which—
She's so conjunctive° to my life and soul,
That, as the star moves not but in his sphere,°   15
I could not but by her. The other motive,
Why to a public count° I might not go,
Is the great love the general gender° bear him;
Who, dipping all his faults in their affection,
Would, like the spring° that turneth wood to stone,   20
Convert his gyves° to graces; so that my arrows,
Too slightly timber'd° for so loud° a wind,
Would have reverted to my bow again,
And not where I had aim'd them.
Laertes: And so have I a noble father lost;   25
A sister driven into desp'rate terms,°
Whose worth, if praises may go back° again,
Stood challenger on mount° of all the age°
For her perfections: but my revenge will come.
King: Break not your sleeps for that: you must not think   30
That we are made of stuff so flat and dull
That we can let our beard be shook with danger
And think it pastime. You shortly shall hear more:
I lov'd your father, and we love ourself;
And that, I hope, will teach you to imagine—   35

Enter a Messenger with letters.

How now! what news?
Messenger: Letters, my lord, from Hamlet:
These to your majesty; this to the queen.°
King: From Hamlet! who brought them?

---

7 *capital:* Punishable by death.   9 *mainly:* Greatly.   10 *unsinew'd:* Weak.   14 *conjunctive:* Conformable (the next line suggesting planetary conjunction).   15 *sphere:* The hollow sphere in which, according to Ptolemaic astronomy, the planets were supposed to move.
17 *count:* Account, reckoning.   18 *general gender:* Common people.   20 *spring:* I.e., one heavily charged with lime.   21 *gyves:* Fetters; here, faults, or possibly, punishments inflicted (on him).   22 *slightly timber'd:* Light; *loud:* Strong.   26 *terms:* State, condition.
27 *go back:* Return to Ophelia's former virtues.   28 *on mount:* Set up on high, *mounted* (on horseback); *of all the age:* Qualifies *challenger* and not *mount.*   37 *to the queen:* One hears no more of the letter to the queen.

Messenger: Sailors, my lord, they say; I saw them not:
>They were given me by Claudio;° he receiv'd them 40
>Of him that brought them.

King: Laertes, you shall hear them.
>Leave us. *[Exit Messenger.]*

[Reads.] "High and mighty, You shall know I am set naked° on your
kingdom. To-morrow shall I beg leave to see your kingly eyes: when I
shall, first asking your pardon thereunto, recount the occasion of my 45
sudden and more strange return. "HAMLET."

>What should this mean? Are all the rest come back?
>Or is it some abuse, and no such thing?

Laertes: Know you the hand?

King: 'Tis Hamlet's character. "Naked!"
>And in a postscript here, he says "alone." 50
>Can you devise° me?

Laertes: I'm lost in it, my lord. But let him come;
>It warms the very sickness in my heart,
>That I shall live and tell him to his teeth,
>"Thus didst thou."

King: If it be so, Laertes — 55
>As how should it be so? how otherwise?°—
>Will you be rul'd by me?

Laertes: Ay, my lord;
>So you will not o'errule me to a peace.

King: To thine own peace. If he be now return'd,
>As checking at° his voyage, and that he means 60
>No more to undertake it, I will work him
>To an exploit, now ripe in my device,
>Under the which he shall not choose but fall:
>And for his death no wind of blame shall breathe,
>But even his mother shall uncharge the practice° 65
>And call it accident.

Laertes: My lord, I will be rul'd;
>The rather, if you could devise it so
>That I might be the organ.°

King: It falls right.
>You have been talk'd of since your travel much,
>And that in Hamlet's hearing, for a quality 70
>Wherein, they say, you shine: your sum of parts
>Did not together pluck such envy from him
>As did that one, and that, in my regard,
>Of the unworthiest siege.°

Laertes: What part is that, my lord?

---

40 *Claudio:* This character does not appear in the play. 43 *naked:* Unprovided (with retinue). 51 *devise:* Explain to. 56 *As . . . otherwise?* How can this (Hamlet's return) be true? (yet) how otherwise than true (since we have the evidence of his letter)? Some editors read *How should it not be so,* etc., making the words refer to Laertes's desire to meet with Hamlet. 60 *checking at:* Used in falconry of a hawk's leaving the quarry to fly at a chance bird; turn aside. 65 *uncharge the practice:* Acquit the stratagem of being a plot. 68 *organ:* Agent, instrument. 74 *siege:* Rank.

King: A very riband in the cap of youth, 　　　　　　　　　　　 75
　　　Yet needful too; for youth no less becomes
　　　The light and careless livery that it wears
　　　Than settled age his sables° and his weeds,
　　　Importing health and graveness. Two months since,
　　　Here was a gentleman of Normandy:— 　　　　　　　　　　　 80
　　　I have seen myself, and serv'd against, the French,
　　　And they can well° on horseback: but this gallant
　　　Had witchcraft in 't; he grew unto his seat;
　　　And to such wondrous doing brought his horse,
　　　As had he been incorps'd and demi-natur'd° 　　　　　　　　 85
　　　With the brave beast: so far he topp'd° my thought,
　　　That I, in forgery° of shapes and tricks,
　　　Come short of what he did.
Laertes: 　　　　　　　　　　　A Norman was 't?
King: A Norman.
Laertes: Upon my life, Lamord.°
King: 　　　　　　　　　　　The very same. 　　　　　　　　　 90
Laertes: I know him well: he is the brooch indeed
　　　And gem of all the nation.
King: He made confession° of you,
　　　And gave you such a masterly report
　　　For art and exercise° in your defence° 　　　　　　　　　　 95
　　　And for your rapier most especial,
　　　That he cried out, 'twould be a sight indeed,
　　　If one could match you: the scrimers° of their nation,
　　　He swore, had neither motion, guard, nor eye,
　　　If you oppos'd them. Sir, this report of his 　　　　　　　　 100
　　　Did Hamlet so envenom with his envy
　　　That he could nothing do but wish and beg
　　　Your sudden coming o'er, to play° with you.
　　　Now, out of this,—
Laertes: 　　　　　　　　　What out of this, my lord?
King: Laertes, was your father dear to you? 　　　　　　　　　 105
　　　Or are you like the painting of a sorrow,
　　　A face without a heart?
Laertes: 　　　　　　　　　Why ask you this?
King: Not that I think you did not love your father;
　　　But that I know love is begun by time;
　　　And that I see, in passages of proof,° 　　　　　　　　　　 110
　　　Time qualifies the spark and fire of it.
　　　There lives within the very flame of love
　　　A kind of wick or snuff that will abate it;
　　　And nothing is at a like goodness still;

---

78 *sables:* Rich garments.　　82 *can well:* Are skilled.　　85 *incorps'd and demi-natur'd:* Of one body and nearly of one nature (like the centaur).　　86 *topp'd:* Surpassed.　　87 *forgery:* Invention.　　90 *Lamord:* This refers possibly to Pietro Monte, instructor to Louis XII's master of the horse.　　93 *confession:* Grudging admission of superiority.　　95 *art and exercise:* Skillful exercise; *defence:* Science of defense in sword practice.　　98 *scrimers:* Fencers. 103 *play:* Fence.　　110 *passages of proof:* Proved instances.

For goodness, growing to a plurisy,°   115
Dies in his own too much:° that we would do,
We should do when we would; for this "would" changes
And hath abatements° and delays as many
As there are tongues, are hands, are accidents;°
And then this "should" is like a spendthrift° sigh,   120
That hurts by easing. But, to the quick o' th' ulcer:°—
Hamlet comes back: what would you undertake,
To show yourself your father's son in deed
More than in words?
Laertes: To cut his throat i' th' church.
King: No place, indeed, should murder sanctuarize;°   125
Revenge should have no bounds. But, good Laertes,
Will you do this, keep close within your chamber.
Hamlet return'd shall know you are come home:
We'll put on those shall praise your excellence
And set a double varnish on the fame   130
The Frenchman gave you, bring you in fine together
And wager on your heads: he, being remiss,
Most generous and free from all contriving,
Will not peruse the foils; so that, with ease,
Or with a little shuffling, you may choose   135
A sword unbated,° and in a pass of practice°
Requite him for your father.
Laertes: I will do 't:
And, for that purpose, I'll anoint my sword.
I bought an unction of a mountebank,°
So mortal that, but dip a knife in it,   140
Where it draws blood no cataplasm° so rare,
Collected from all simples° that have virtue
Under the moon,° can save the thing from death
That is but scratch'd withal: I'll touch my point
With this contagion, that, if I gall° him slightly,   145
It may be death.
King: Let's further think of this;
Weigh what convenience both of time and means
May fit us to our shape:° if this should fail,
And that our drift look through our bad performance,°
'Twere better not assay'd: therefore this project   150
Should have a back or second, that might hold,
If this should blast in proof.° Soft! let me see:

---

115 *plurisy:* Excess, plethora.   116 *in his own too much:* Of its own excess.   118 *abatements:* Diminutions.   119 *accidents:* Occurrences, incidents.   120 *spendthrift:* An allusion to the belief that each sigh cost the heart a drop of blood.   121 *quick o' th' ulcer:* Heart of the difficulty.   125 *sanctuarize:* Protect from punishment; allusion to the right of sanctuary with which certain religious places were invested.   136 *unbated:* Not blunted, having no button; *pass of practice:* Treacherous thrust.   139 *mountebank:* Quack doctor.   141 *cataplasm:* Plaster or poultice.   142 *simples:* Herbs.   143 *Under the moon:* I.e., when collected by moonlight to add to their medicinal value.   145 *gall:* Graze, wound.   148 *shape:* Part we propose to act.   149 *drift...performance:* Intention be disclosed by our bungling.   152 *blast in proof:* Burst in the test (like a cannon).

We'll make a solemn wager on your cunnings:°
I ha 't:
When in your motion you are hot and dry —   155
As make your bouts more violent to that end —
And that he calls for drink, I'll have prepar'd him
A chalice° for the nonce, whereon but sipping,
If he by chance escape your venom'd stuck,°
Our purpose may hold there. But stay, what noise?   160

Enter Queen.

Queen: One woe doth tread upon another's heel,
So fast they follow: your sister's drown'd, Laertes.
Laertes: Drown'd! O, where?
Queen: There is a willow° grows askant° the brook,
That shows his hoar° leaves in the glassy stream;   165
There with fantastic garlands did she make
Of crow-flowers,° nettles, daisies, and long purples°
That liberal° shepherds give a grosser name,
But our cold maids do dead men's fingers call them:
There, on the pendent boughs her crownet° weeds   170
Clamb'ring to hang, an envious sliver° broke;
When down her weedy° trophies and herself
Fell in the weeping brook. Her clothes spread wide;
And, mermaid-like, awhile they bore her up:
Which time she chanted snatches of old lauds;°   175
As one incapable° of her own distress,
Or like a creature native and indued°
Upon that element: but long it could not be
Till that her garments, heavy with their drink,
Pull'd the poor wretch from her melodious lay   180
To muddy death.
Laertes: Alas, then, she is drown'd?
Queen: Drown'd, drown'd.
Laertes: Too much of water hast thou, poor Ophelia,
And therefore I forbid my tears: but yet
It is our trick;° nature her custom holds,   185
Let shame say what it will: when these are gone,
The woman will be out.° Adieu, my lord:
I have a speech of fire, that fain would blaze,
But that this folly drowns it.   *Exit.*
King: Let's follow, Gertrude:
How much I had to do to calm his rage!   190
Now fear I this will give it start again;
Therefore let 's follow.   *Exeunt.*

---

153 *cunnings:* Skills.   158 *chalice:* Cup.   159 *stuck:* Thrust (from *stoccado*).   164 *willow:*
For its significance of forsaken love; *askant:* Aslant.   165 *hoar:* White (i.e., on the underside).   167 *crow-flowers:* Buttercups; *long purples:* Early purple orchids.   168 *liberal:*
Probably, free-spoken.   170 *crownet:* Coronet; made into a chaplet.   171 *sliver:* Branch.
172 *weedy:* I.e., of plants.   175 *lauds:* Hymns.   176 *incapable:* Lacking capacity to apprehend.   177 *indued:* Endowed with qualities fitting her for living in water.   185 *trick:*
Way.   186–187 *when . . . out:* When my tears are all shed, the woman in me will be satisfied.

[ACT V

SCENE I: *A churchyard.*]

Enter two Clowns° [with spades, &c.].

First Clown: Is she to be buried in Christian burial when she wilfully seeks her own salvation?

Second Clown: I tell thee she is; therefore make her grave straight:° the crowner° hath sat on her, and finds it Christian burial.

First Clown: How can that be, unless she drowned herself in her own defence?   5

Second Clown: Why, 'tis found so.

First Clown: It must be "se offendendo";° it cannot be else. For here lies the point: if I drown myself wittingly,° it argues an act: and an act hath three branches;° it is, to act, to do, and to perform: argal,° she   10
drowned herself wittingly.

Second Clown: Nay, but hear you, goodman delver,°—

First Clown: Give me leave. Here lies the water; good: here stands the man; good: if the man go to this water, and drown himself, it is, will he, nill he, he goes,—mark you that; but if the water come to him and   15
drown him, he drowns not himself: argal, he that is not guilty of his own death shortens not his own life.

Second Clown: But is this law?

First Clown: Ay, marry, is 't; crowner's quest° law.

Second Clown: Will you ha' the truth on 't? If this had not been a gentle-   20
woman, she should have been buried out o' Christian burial.

First Clown: Why, there thou say'st:° and the more pity that great folk should have countenance° in this world to drown or hang themselves, more than their even° Christian. Come, my spade. There is no ancient gentlemen but gardeners, ditchers, and grave-makers: they   25
hold up° Adam's profession.

Second Clown: Was he a gentleman?

First Clown: 'A was the first that ever bore arms.

Second Clown: Why, he had none.

First Clown: What, art a heathen? How dost thou understand the Scrip-   30
ture? The Scripture says "Adam digged": could he dig without arms?
I'll put another question to thee: if thou answerest me not to the purpose, confess thyself°—

Second Clown: Go to.°

First Clown: What is he that builds stronger than either the mason, the   35
shipwright, or the carpenter?

Act V, Scene I. *Clowns:* The word *clown* was used to denote peasants as well as humorous characters; here applied to the rustic type of clown.   3 *straight:* Straightway, immediately; some interpret "from east to west in a direct line, parallel with the church."   4 *crowner:* Coroner.   8 *"se offendendo":* For *se defendendo,* term used in verdicts of justifiable homi-
cide.   9 *wittingly:* Intentionally.   10 *three branches:* Parody of legal phraseology; *argal:* Corruption of *ergo,* therefore.   12 *delver:* Digger.   19 *quest:* Inquest.   22 *there thou say'st:* That's right.   23 *countenance:* Privilege.   24 *even:* Fellow.   26 *hold up:* Maintain, continue.   33 *confess thyself:* "And be hanged" completes the proverb.   34 *Go to:* Perhaps, "begin," or some other form of concession.

Second Clown: The gallows-maker; for that frame outlives a thousand tenants.

First Clown: I like thy wit well, in good faith: the gallows does well; but how does it well? it does well to those that do ill: now thou dost ill to say the gallows is built stronger than the church: argal, the gallows may do well to thee. To 't again, come.   40

Second Clown: "Who builds stronger than a mason, a shipwright, or a carpenter?"

First Clown: Ay, tell me that, and unyoke.°   45

Second Clown: Marry, now I can tell.

First Clown: To 't.

Second Clown: Mass,° I cannot tell.

          Enter Hamlet and Horatio [at a distance].

First Clown: Cudgel thy brains no more about it, for your dull ass will not mend his pace with beating; and, when you are asked this question   50
next, say "a grave-maker": the houses he makes lasts till doomsday.
Go, get thee in, and fetch me a stoup° of liquor.

                    [Exit Second Clown.] Song. [He digs.]

          In youth, when I did love, did love,
               Methought it was very sweet,
          To contract — O — the time, for — a — my behove,°   55
               O, methought, there — a — was nothing — a — meet.

Hamlet: Has this fellow no feeling of his business, that 'a sings at grave-making?

Horatio: Custom hath made it in him a property of easiness.°

Hamlet: 'Tis e'en so: the hand of little employment hath the daintier   60
sense.

First Clown: (*Song.*) But age, with his stealing steps,
               Hath claw'd me in his clutch,
          And hath shipped me into the land
               As if I had never been such.   *[Throws up a skull.]*   65

Hamlet: That skull had a tongue in it, and could sing once: how the knave
jowls° it to the ground, as if 'twere Cain's jaw-bone,° that did the first
murder! This might be the pate of a politician,° which this ass now
o'er-reaches;° one that would circumvent God, might it not?

Horatio: It might, my lord.   70

Hamlet: Or of a courtier; which could say "Good morrow, sweet lord! How
dost thou, sweet lord?" This might be my lord such-a-one, that
praised my lord such-a-one's horse, when he meant to beg it; might
it not?

Horatio: Ay, my lord.   75

Hamlet: Why, e'en so: and now my Lady Worm's; chapless,° and knocked
about the mazzard° with a sexton's spade: here's fine revolution, an

---

45 *unyoke:* After this great effort you may unharness the team of your wits.   48 *Mass:* By
the Mass.   52 *stoup:* Two-quart measure.   55 *behove:* Benefit.   59 *property of easiness:* A
peculiarity that now is easy.   67 *jowls:* Dashes; *Cain's jaw-bone:* Allusion to the old tradition
that Cain slew Abel with the jawbone of an ass.   68 *politician:* Schemer, plotter.   69 *o'er-
reaches:* Quibble on the literal sense and the sense "circumvent."   76 *chapless:* Having no
lower jaw.   77 *mazzard:* Head.

we had the trick to see 't. Did these bones cost no more the breeding,
but to play at loggats° with 'em? mine ache to think on 't.

First Clown: (*Song.*) A pick-axe, and a spade, a spade,   80
    For and° a shrouding sheet:
O, a pit of clay for to be made
    For such a guest is meet.   *[Throws up another skull.]*

Hamlet: There's another: why may not that be the skull of a lawyer?
Where be his quiddities° now, his quillities,° his cases, his tenures,°   85
and his tricks? why does he suffer this mad knave now to knock him
about the sconce° with a dirty shovel, and will not tell him of his action of battery? Hum! This fellow might be in 's time a great buyer
of land, with his statutes, his recognizances,° his fines, his double
vouchers,° his recoveries:° is this the fine° of his fines, and the re-   90
covery of his recoveries, to have his fine pate full of fine dirt? will
his vouchers vouch him no more of his purchases, and double ones
too, than the length and breadth of a pair of indentures?° The very
conveyances of his lands will scarcely lie in this box; and must the
inheritor° himself have no more, ha?   95

Horatio: Not a jot more, my lord.

Hamlet: Is not parchment made of sheep-skins?

Horatio: Ay, my lord, and of calf-skins° too.

Hamlet: They are sheep and calves which seek out assurance in that.°
I will speak to this fellow. Whose grave's this, sirrah?   100

First Clown: Mine, sir.

[Sings.] O, a pit of clay for to be made
    For such a guest is meet.

Hamlet: I think it be thine, indeed; for thou liest in 't.

First Clown: You lie out on 't, sir, and therefore 't is not yours: for my part,   105
I do not lie in 't, yet it is mine.

Hamlet: Thou dost lie in 't, to be in 't and say it is thine: 'tis for the dead,
not for the quick; therefore thou liest.

First Clown: 'Tis a quick lie, sir; 'twill away again, from me to you.

Hamlet: What man dost thou dig it for?   110

First Clown: For no man, sir.

Hamlet: What woman, then?

First Clown: For none, neither.

Hamlet: Who is to be buried in 't?

First Clown: One that was a woman, sir; but, rest her soul, she's dead.   115

Hamlet: How absolute° the knave is! we must speak by the card,° or
equivocation° will undo us. By the Lord, Horatio, these three years I

---

79 *loggats:* A game in which six sticks are thrown to lie as near as possible to a stake fixed
in the ground, or block of wood on a floor.   81 *For and:* And moreover.   85 *quiddities:*
Subtleties, quibbles; *quillities:* Verbal niceties, subtle distinctions; *tenures:* The holding of a
piece of property or office or the conditions or period of such holding.   87 *sconce:* Head.
89 *statutes, recognizances:* Legal terms connected with the transfer of land.   90 *vouchers:*
Persons called on to warrant a tenant's title; *recoveries:* Process for transfer of entailed estate;
fine: The four uses of this word are as follows: (1) end, (2) legal process, (3) elegant, (4) small.
93 *indentures:* Conveyances or contracts.   95 *inheritor:* Possessor, owner.   98 *calf-skins:*
Parchments.   99 *assurance in that:* Safety in legal parchments.   116 *absolute:* Positive,
decided; *by the card:* With precision, i.e., by the mariner's card on which the points of the
compass were marked.   117 *equivocation:* Ambiguity in the use of terms.

have taken note of it; the age is grown so picked° that the toe of the
peasant comes so near the heel of the courtier, he galls° his kibe.°
How long hast thou been a grave-maker?   120

First Clown: Of all the day i' the year, I came to 't that day that our last
king Hamlet overcame Fortinbras.

Hamlet: How long is that since?

First Clown: Cannot you tell that? every fool can tell that: it was the very
day that young Hamlet was born; he that is mad, and sent into   125
England.

Hamlet: Ay, marry, why was he sent into England?

First Clown: Why, because 'a was mad: 'a shall recover his wits there; or, if
'a do not, 'tis no great matter there.

Hamlet: Why?   130

First Clown: 'Twill not be seen in him there; there the men are as mad
as he.

Hamlet: How came he mad?

First Clown: Very strangely, they say.

Hamlet: How strangely?   135

First Clown: Faith, e'en with losing his wits.

Hamlet: Upon what ground?

First Clown: Why, here in Denmark: I have been sexton here, man and boy,
thirty years.°

Hamlet: How long will a man lie i' the earth ere he rot?   140

First Clown: Faith, if 'a be not rotten before 'a die — as we have many
pocky° corses now-a-days, that will scarce hold the laying in — 'a will
last you some eight year or nine year: a tanner will last you nine year.

Hamlet: Why he more than another?

First Clown: Why, sir, his hide is so tanned with his trade, that 'a will keep 145
out water a great while; and your water is a sore decayer of your
whoreson dead body. Here's a skull now hath lain you i' th' earth
three and twenty years.

Hamlet: Whose was it?

First Clown: A whoreson mad fellow's it was: whose do you think it was?   150

Hamlet: Nay, I know not.

First Clown: A pestilence on him for a mad rogue! 'a poured a flagon of
Rhenish on my head once. This same skull, sir, was Yorick's skull, the
king's jester.

Hamlet: This?   155

First Clown: E'en that.

Hamlet: Let me see. *[Takes the skull.]* Alas, poor Yorick! I knew him, Horatio: a fellow of infinite jest, of most excellent fancy: he hath borne me
on his back a thousand times; and now, how abhorred in my imagination it is! my gorge rises at it. Here hung those lips that I have   160
kissed I know not how oft. Where be your gibes now? your gambols?
your songs? your flashes of merriment, that were wont to set the
table on a roar? Not one now, to mock your own grinning? quite

---

118 *picked:* Refined, fastidious.   119 *galls:* Chafes; *kibe:* Chilblain.   139 *thirty years:* This
statement with that in line 125 shows Hamlet's age to be thirty years.   142 *pocky:* Rotten,
diseased.

chap-fallen? Now get you to my lady's chamber, and tell her, let her
paint an inch thick, to this favour she must come; make her laugh at   165
that. Prithee, Horatio, tell me one thing.

Horatio: What's that, my lord?

Hamlet: Dost thou think Alexander looked o' this fashion i' the earth?

Horatio: E'en so.

Hamlet: And smelt so? pah!   *[Puts down the skull.]*   170

Horatio: E'en so, my lord.

Hamlet: To what base uses we may return, Horatio! Why may not imagination trace the noble dust of Alexander, till 'a find it stopping a
bung-hole?

Horatio: 'Twere to consider too curiously,° to consider so.   175

Hamlet: No, faith, not a jot; but to follow him thither with modesty
enough, and likelihood to lead it: as thus: Alexander died, Alexander
was buried, Alexander returneth into dust; the dust is earth; of earth
we make loam;° and why of that loam, whereto he was converted,
might they not stop a beer-barrel?   180
     Imperious° Cæsar, dead and turn'd to clay,
     Might stop a hole to keep the wind away:
     O, that that earth, which kept the world in awe,
     Should patch a wall t'expel the winter's flaw!°
But soft! but soft awhile! here comes the king,   185

*Enter King, Queen, Laertes, and the Corse of [Ophelia, in procession, with
Priest, Lords, etc.].*

The queen, the courtiers: who is this they follow?
And with such maimed rites? This doth betoken
The corse they follow did with desp'rate hand
Fordo° it° own life: 'twas of some estate.
Couch° we awhile, and mark.   *[Retiring with Horatio.]*   190

Laertes: What ceremony else?

Hamlet: That is Laertes,
A very noble youth: mark.

Laertes: What ceremony else?

First Priest: Her obsequies have been as far enlarg'd°
     As we have warranty: her death was doubtful;   195
     And, but that great command o'ersways the order,
     She should in ground unsanctified have lodg'd
     Till the last trumpet; for charitable prayers,
     Shards,° flints and pebbles should be thrown on her:
     Yet here she is allow'd her virgin crants,°   200
     Her maiden strewments° and the bringing home
     Of bell and burial.°

175 *curiously:* Minutely.   179 *loam:* Clay paste for brickmaking.   181 *Imperious:* Imperial.   184 *flaw:* Gust of wind.   189 *Fordo:* Destroy; *it:* Its.   190 *Couch:* Hide, lurk.
194 *enlarg'd:* Extended, referring to the fact that suicides are not given full burial rites.
199 *Shards:* Broken bits of pottery.   200 *crants:* Garlands customarily hung upon the biers
of unmarried women.   201 *strewments:* Traditional strewing of flowers.   201–202 *bringing . . . burial:* The laying to rest of the body, to the sound of the bell.

Laertes: Must there no more be done?
First Priest: No more be done:
   We should profane the service of the dead
   To sing a requiem and such rest to her   205
   As to peace-parted° souls.
Laertes: Lay her i' th' earth:
   And from her fair and unpolluted flesh
   May violets spring! I tell thee, churlish priest,
   A minist'ring angel shall my sister be,
   When thou liest howling.°
Hamlet: What, the fair Ophelia!   210
Queen: Sweets to the sweet: farewell!   *[Scattering flowers.]*
   I hop'd thou shouldst have been my Hamlet's wife;
   I thought thy bride-bed to have deck'd, sweet maid,
   And not have strew'd thy grave.
Laertes: O, treble woe
   Fall ten times treble on that cursed head,   215
   Whose wicked deed thy most ingenious sense°
   Depriv'd thee of! Hold off the earth awhile,
   Till I have caught her once more in mine arms: *[Leaps into the grave.]*
   Now pile your dust upon the quick and dead,
   Till of this flat a mountain you have made,   220
   T' o'ertop old Pelion,° or the skyish head
   Of blue Olympus.
Hamlet: *[Advancing]* What is he whose grief
   Bears such an emphasis? whose phrase of sorrow
   Conjures the wand'ring stars,° and makes them stand
   Like wonder-wounded hearers? This is I,   225
   Hamlet the Dane.   *[Leaps into the grave.]*
Laertes: The devil take thy soul!   *[Grappling with him.]*
Hamlet: Thou pray'st not well.
   I prithee, take thy fingers from my throat;
   For, though I am not splenitive° and rash,
   Yet have I in me something dangerous,   230
   Which let thy wisdom fear: hold off thy hand.
King: Pluck them asunder.
Queen: Hamlet, Hamlet!
All: Gentlemen, —
Horatio: Good my lord, be quiet.

[The Attendants part them, and they come out of the grave.]

Hamlet: Why, I will fight with him upon this theme
   Until my eyelids will no longer wag.°   235
Queen: O my son, what theme?

---

206 *peace-parted:* Allusion to the text "Lord, now lettest thou thy servant depart in
peace."   210 *howling:* I.e., in hell.   216 *ingenious sense:* Mind endowed with finest qualities.   221 *Pelion:* Olympus, Pelion, and Ossa are mountains in the north of Thessaly.
224 *wand'ring stars:* Planets.   229 *splenitive:* Quick-tempered.   235 *wag:* Move (not used
ludicrously).

Hamlet: I lov'd Ophelia: forty thousand brothers
  Could not, with all their quantity° of love,
  Make up my sum. What wilt thou do for her?
King: O, he is mad, Laertes. 240
Queen: For love of God, forbear° him.
Hamlet: 'Swounds,° show me what thou 'lt do:
  Woo 't° weep? woo 't fight? woo 't fast? woo 't tear thyself?
  Woo 't drink up eisel?° eat a crocodile?
  I'll do 't. Dost thou come here to whine? 245
  To outface me with leaping in her grave?
  Be buried quick with her, and so will I:
  And, if thou prate of mountains, let them throw
  Millions of acres on us, till our ground,
  Singeing his pate against the burning zone,° 250
  Make Ossa like a wart! Nay, an thou 'lt mouth,
  I'll rant as well as thou.
Queen: This is mere madness:
  And thus awhile the fit will work on him;
  Anon, as patient as the female dove.
  When that her golden couplets° are disclos'd, 255
  His silence will sit drooping.
Hamlet: Hear you, sir;
  What is the reason that you use me thus?
  I lov'd you ever: but it is no matter;
  Let Hercules himself do what he may,
  The cat will mew and dog will have his day. 260
King: I pray thee, good Horatio, wait upon him.   *Exit Hamlet and Horatio.*
  [To Laertes.] Strengthen your patience in° our last night's speech;
  We'll put the matter to the present push.°
  Good Gertrude, set some watch over your son.
  This grave shall have a living° monument: 265
  An hour of quiet shortly shall we see;
  Till then, in patience our proceeding be.   *Exeunt.*

[SCENE II: *A hall in the castle.*]

Enter Hamlet and Horatio.

Hamlet: So much for this, sir: now shall you see the other;
  You do remember all the circumstance?
Horatio: Remember it, my lord!
Hamlet: Sir, in my heart there was a kind of fighting,
  That would not let me sleep: methought I lay 5

238 *quantity:* Some suggest that the word is used in a deprecatory sense (little bits, fragments).   241 *forbear:* Leave alone.   242 *'Swounds:* Oath, "God's wounds."   243 *Woo 't:* Wilt thou.   244 *eisel:* Vinegar. Some editors have taken this to be the name of a river, such as the Yssel, the Weissel, and the Nile.   250 *burning zone:* Sun's orbit.   255 *golden couplets:* The pigeon lays two eggs; the young when hatched are covered with golden down. 262 *in:* By recalling.   263 *present push:* Immediate test.   265 *living:* Lasting; also refers (for Laertes's benefit) to the plot against Hamlet.

Worse than the mutines in the bilboes.° Rashly,°
And prais'd be rashness for it, let us know,
Our indiscretion sometime serves us well,
When our deep plots do pall:° and that should learn us
There's a divinity that shapes our ends,   10
Rough-hew° them how we will, —
Horatio: That is most certain.
Hamlet: Up from my cabin,
    My sea-gown° scarf'd about me, in the dark
    Grop'd I to find out them; had my desire,
    Finger'd° their packet, and in fine° withdrew   15
    To mine own room again; making so bold,
    My fears forgetting manners, to unseal
    Their grand commission; where I found, Horatio, —
    O royal knavery! — an exact command,
    Larded° with many several sorts of reasons   20
    Importing Denmark's health and England's too,
    With, ho! such bugs° and goblins in my life,°
    That, on the supervise,° no leisure bated,°
    No, not to stay the grinding of the axe,
    My head should be struck off.
Horatio: Is 't possible?   25
Hamlet: Here's the commission: read it at more leisure.
    But wilt thou hear me how I did proceed?
Horatio: I beseech you.
Hamlet: Being thus be-netted round with villanies, —
    Ere I could make a prologue to my brains,   30
    They had begun the play°—I sat me down,
    Devis'd a new commission, wrote it fair:
    I once did hold it, as our statists° do,
    A baseness to write fair° and labour'd much
    How to forget that learning, but, sir, now   35
    It did me yeoman's° service: wilt thou know
    Th' effect of what I wrote?
Horatio: Ay, good my lord.
Hamlet: An earnest conjuration from the king,
    As England was his faithful tributary,
    As love between them like the palm might flourish,   40
    As peace should still her wheaten garland° wear
    And stand a comma° 'tween their amities,

Scene II.   6 *mutines in the bilboes:* Mutineers in shackles; *Rashly:* Goes with line 12.
9 *pall:* Fail.   11 *Rough-hew:* Shape roughly; it may mean "bungle."   13 *sea-gown:* "A sea-
gown, or a coarse, high-collered, and short-sleeved gowne, reaching down to the mid-leg,
and used most by seamen and saylors" (Cotgrave, quoted by Singer).   15 *Finger'd:* Pilfered,
filched; *in fine:* Finally.   20 *Larded:* Enriched.   22 *bugs:* Bugbears; *such...life:* Such
imaginary dangers if I were allowed to live.   23 *supervise:* Perusal; *leisure bated:* Delay allowed.   30-31 *prologue...play:* I.e., before I could begin to think, my mind had made its
decision.   33 *statists:* Statesmen.   34 *fair:* In a clear hand.   36 *yeoman's:* I.e., faithful.
41 *wheaten garland:* Symbol of peace.   42 *comma:* Smallest break or separation. Here
amity begins and *amity* ends the period, and *peace* stands between like a dependent clause.
The comma indicates continuity, link.

And many such-like 'As'es° of great charge,°
That, on the view and knowing of these contents,
Without debatement further, more or less,   45
He should the bearers put to sudden death,
Not shriving-time° allow'd.
Horatio: How was this seal'd?
Hamlet: Why, even in that was heaven ordinant.°
I had my father's signet in my purse,
Which was the model of that Danish seal;   50
Folded the writ up in the form of th' other,
Subscrib'd it, gave 't th' impression, plac'd it safely,
The changeling never known. Now, the next day
Was our sea-fight; and what to this was sequent°
Thou know'st already.   55
Horatio: So Guildenstern and Rosencrantz go to 't.
Hamlet: Why, man, they did make love to this employment;
They are not near my conscience; their defeat
Does by their own insinuation° grow:
'Tis dangerous when the baser nature comes   60
Between the pass° and fell incensed° points
Of mighty opposites.
Horatio: Why, what a king is this!
Hamlet: Does it not, think thee, stand° me now upon —
He that hath kill'd my king and whor'd my mother,
Popp'd in between th' election° and my hopes,   65
Thrown out his angle° for my proper life,
And with such coz'nage° — is 't not perfect conscience,
To quit° him with this arm? and is 't not to be damn'd,
To let this canker° of our nature come
In further evil?   70
Horatio: It must be shortly known to him from England
What is the issue of the business there.
Hamlet: It will be short: the interim is mine;
And a man's life's no more than to say "One."
But I am very sorry, good Horatio,   75
That to Laertes I forgot myself;
For, by the image of my cause, I see
The portraiture of his: I'll court his favours:
But, sure, the bravery° of his grief did put me
Into a tow'ring passion.
Horatio: Peace! who comes here?   80

Enter a Courtier [Osric].

---

43 *'As'es:* The "whereases" of a formal document, with play on the word *ass; charge:* Import, and
burden.   47 *shriving-time:* Time for absolution.   48 *ordinant:* Directing.   54 *sequent:*
Subsequent.   59 *insinuation:* Interference.   61 *pass:* Thrust; *fell incensed:* Fiercely angered.   63 *stand:* Become incumbent.   65 *election:* The Danish throne was filled by election.   66 *angle:* Fishing line.   67 *coz'nage:* Trickery.   68 *quit:* Repay.   69 *canker:*
Ulcer, or possibly the worm which destroys buds and leaves.   79 *bravery:* Bravado.

Osric: Your lordship is right welcome back to Denmark.

Hamlet: I humbly thank you, sir. *[To Horatio.]* Dost know this water-fly?°

Horatio: No, my good lord.

Hamlet: Thy state is the more gracious; for 'tis a vice to know him. He
    hath much land, and fertile: let a beast be lord of beasts,° and his crib   85
    shall stand at the king's mess:° 'tis a chough;° but, as I say, spacious
    in the possession of dirt.

Osric: Sweet lord, if your lordship were at leisure, I should impart a thing
    to you from his majesty.

Hamlet: I will receive it, sir, with all diligence of spirit. Put your bonnet to   90
    his right use; 'tis for the head.

Osric: I thank you lordship, it is very hot.

Hamlet: No, believe me, 'tis very cold; the wind is northerly.

Osric: It is indifferent° cold, my lord, indeed.

Hamlet: But yet methinks it is very sultry and hot for my complexion.   95

Osric: Exceedingly, my lord; it is very sultry, — as 'twere, — I cannot tell
    how. But, my lord, his majesty bade me signify to you that 'a has laid a
    great wager on your head: sir, this is the matter, —

Hamlet: I beseech you, remember°—

                             [Hamlet moves him to put on his hat.]

Osric: Nay, good my lord; for mine ease,° in good faith. Sir, here is newly   100
    come to court Laertes; believe me, an absolute gentleman, full of
    most excellent differences, of very soft° society and great showing:°
    indeed, to speak feelingly° of him, he is the card° or calendar of gen-
    try,° for you shall find in him the continent of what part a gentleman
    would see.   105

Hamlet: Sir, his definement° suffers no perdition° in you; though, I know,
    to divide him inventorially° would dozy° the arithmetic of memory,
    and yet but yaw° neither, in respect of his quick sail. But, in the verity
    of extolment, I take him to be a soul of great article;° and his infu-
    sion° of such dearth and rareness,° as, to make true diction of him,   110
    his semblable° is his mirror; and who else would trace° him, his um-
    brage,° nothing more.

Osric: Your lordship speaks most infallibly of him.

Hamlet: The concernancy,° sir? why do we wrap the gentleman in our
    more rawer breath?°   115

Osric: Sir?

---

82 *water-fly:* Vain or busily idle person.   85 *lord of beasts:* See Genesis 1:26, 28.   85–86 *his*
crib . . . mess: He shall eat at the king's table and be one of the group of persons (usually four)
constituting a *mess* at a banquet.   86 *chough:* Probably, chattering jackdaw; also explained
as *chuff,* provincial boor or churl.   94 *indifferent:* Somewhat.   99 *remember:* I.e., remember thy courtesy; conventional phrase for "Be covered."   100 *mine ease:* Conventional reply
declining the invitation of "Remember thy courtesy."   102 *soft:* Gentle; *showing:* Distinguished appearance.   103 *feelingly:* With just perception; *card:* Chart, map.   103–104 *gen-*
try: Good breeding.   106 *definement:* Definition; *perdition:* Loss, diminution.   107 *di-*
vide him inventorially: I.e., enumerate his graces; *dozy:* Dizzy.   108 *yaw:* To move unsteadily
(of a ship).   109 *article:* Moment or importance.   109–110 *infusion:* Infused temperament,
character imparted by nature.   110 *dearth and rareness:* Rarity.   111 *semblable:* True likeness; *trace:* Follow.   111–112 *umbrage:* Shadow.   114 *concernancy:* Import.   115 *breath:*
Speech.

Horatio [aside to Hamlet]: Is 't not possible to understand in another tongue?° You will do 't, sir, really.

Hamlet: What imports the nomination° of this gentleman?

Osric: Of Laertes?   120

Horatio [aside to Hamlet]: His purse is empty already; all 's golden words are spent.

Hamlet: Of him, sir.

Osric: I know you are not ignorant —

Hamlet: I would you did, sir; yet, in faith, if you did, it would not much   125
approve° me. Well, sir?

Osric: You are not ignorant of what excellence Laertes is —

Hamlet: I dare not confess that, lest I should compare with him in excellence; but, to know a man well, were to know himself.°

Osric: I mean, sir, for his weapon; but in the imputation° laid on him by   130
them, in his meed° he's unfellowed.

Hamlet: What's his weapon?

Osric: Rapier and dagger.

Hamlet: That's two of his weapons: but, well.

Osric: The king, sir, hath wagered with him six Barbary horses: against   135
the which he has impawned,° as I take it, six French rapiers and poniards, with their assigns, as girdle, hangers,° and so: three of the carriages, in faith, are very dear to fancy,° very responsive° to the hilts, most delicate° carriages, and of very liberal conceit.°

Hamlet: What call you the carriages?   140

Horatio [aside to Hamlet]: I knew you must be edified by the margent° ere you had done.

Osric: The carriages, sir, are the hangers.

Hamlet: The phrase would be more german° to the matter, if we could carry cannon by our sides: I would it might be hangers till then. But,   145
on: six Barbary horses against six French swords, their assigns, and three liberal-conceited carriages; that's the French bet against the Danish. Why is this "impawned," as you call it?

Osric: The king, sir, hath laid, that in a dozen passes between yourself and him, he shall not exceed you three hits: he hath laid on twelve for   150
nine; and it would come to immediate trial, if your lordship would vouchsafe the answer.

Hamlet: How if I answer "no"?

Osric: I mean, my lord, the opposition of your person in trial.

Hamlet: Sir, I will walk here in the hall: if it please his majesty, it is the   155
breathing time° of day with me; let the foils be brought, the gentleman willing, and the king hold his purpose, I will win for him as I can; if not, I will gain nothing but my shame and the odd hits.

117–118 *Is 't... tongue?:* I.e., can one converse with Osric only in this outlandish jargon?
119 *nomination:* Naming.   126 *approve:* Command.   129 *but... himself:* But to know a man as excellent were to know Laertes.   130 *imputation:* Reputation.   131 *meed:* Merit.
136 *he has impawned:* He has wagered.   137 *hangers:* Straps on the sword belt from which the sword hung.   138 *dear to fancy:* Fancifully made; *responsive:* Probably, well balanced, corresponding closely.   139 *delicate:* Fine in workmanship; *liberal conceit:* Elaborate design.   141 *margent:* Margin of a book, place for explanatory notes.   144 *german:* Germane, appropriate.   156 *breathing time:* Exercise period.

Osric: Shall I re-deliver you e'en so?

Hamlet: To this effect, sir; after what flourish your nature will.   160

Osric: I commend my duty to your lordship.

Hamlet: Yours, yours. *[Exit Osric.]* He does well to commend it himself; there are no tongues else for 's turn.

Horatio: This lapwing° runs away with the shell on his head.

Hamlet: 'A did comply, sir, with his dug,° before 'a sucked it. Thus has   165
hey — and many more of the same breed that I know the drossy° age
dotes on — only got the tune° of the time and out of an habit of encounter;° a kind of yesty° collection, which carries them through
and through the most fann'd and winnowed° opinions; and do but
blow them to their trial, the bubbles are out.°   170

Enter a Lord.

Lord: My lord, his majesty commended him to you by young Osric, who
brings back to him, that you attend him in the hall: he sends to know
if your pleasure hold to play with Laertes, or that you will take longer
time.

Hamlet: I am constant to my purposes; they follow the king's pleasure: if   175
his fitness speaks, mine is ready; now or whensoever, provided I be so
able as now.

Lord: The king and queen and all are coming down.

Hamlet: In happy time.°

Lord: The queen desires you to use some gentle entertainment to Laertes   180
before you fall to play.

Hamlet: She well instructs me.   *[Exit Lord.]*

Horatio: You will lose this wager, my lord.

Hamlet: I do not think so; since he went into France, I have been in continual practice; I shall win at the odds. But thou wouldst not think   185
how ill all 's here about my heart: but it is no matter.

Horatio: Nay, good my lord, —

Hamlet: It is but foolery; but it is such a kind of gain-giving,° as would
perhaps trouble a woman.

Horatio: If your mind dislike any thing, obey it: I will forestall their repair   190
hither, and say you are not fit.

Hamlet: Not a whit, we defy augury: there's a special providence in the
fall of a sparrow. If it be now, 'tis not to come; if it be not to come, it
will be now; if it be not now, yet it will come: the readiness is all:°
since no man of aught he leaves knows, what is 't to leave betimes?   195
Let be.

*A table prepared. [Enter] Trumpets, Drums, and Officers with cushions; King,
Queen, [Osric,] and all the State; foils, daggers, [and wine borne in;] and Laertes.*

---

164 *lapwing:* Peewit; noted for its wiliness in drawing a visitor away from its nest and its supposed habit of running about when newly hatched with its head in the shell; possibly an allusion to Osric's hat.   165 *did comply . . . dug:* Paid compliments to his mother's breast.
166 *drossy:* Frivolous.   167 *tune:* Temper, mood.   167–168 *habit of encounter:* Demeanor
of social intercourse.   168 *yesty:* Frothy.   169 *fann'd and winnowed:* Select and refined.
170 *blow . . . out:* I.e., put them to the test, and their ignorance is exposed.   179 *In happy
time:* A phrase of courtesy.   188 *gain-giving:* Misgiving.   194 *all:* All that matters.

King: Come, Hamlet, come, and take this hand from me.

[The King puts Laertes's hand into Hamlet's.]

Hamlet: Give me your pardon, sir: I have done you wrong;
But pardon 't as you are a gentleman.
This presence° knows,   200
And you must needs have heard, how I am punish'd
With a sore distraction. What I have done,
That might your nature, honour and exception°
Roughly awake, I here proclaim was madness.
Was 't Hamlet wrong'd Laertes? Never Hamlet: 205
If Hamlet from himself be ta'en away,
And when he's not himself does wrong Laertes,
Then Hamlet does it not, Hamlet denies it.
Who does it, then? His madness: if 't be so,
Hamlet is of the faction that is wrong'd;   210
His madness is poor Hamlet's enemy.
Sir, in this audience,
Let my disclaiming from a purpos'd evil
Free me so far in your most generous thoughts,
That I have shot mine arrow o'er the house,   215
And hurt my brother.

Laertes: I am satisfied in nature,°
Whose motive, in this case, should stir me most
To my revenge: but in my terms of honour
I stand aloof; and will no reconcilement,
Till by some elder masters, of known honour,   220
I have a voice° and precedent of peace,
To keep my name ungor'd. But till that time,
I do receive your offer'd love like love,
And will not wrong it.

Hamlet: I embrace it freely;
And will this brother's wager frankly play.   225
Give us the foils. Come on.

Laertes: Come, one for me.

Hamlet: I'll be your foil,° Laertes: in mine ignorance
Your skill shall, like a star i' th' darkest night,
Stick fiery off° indeed.

Laertes: You mock me, sir.

Hamlet: No, by this hand.   230

King: Give them the foils, young Osric. Cousin Hamlet,
You know the wager?

Hamlet: Very well, my lord;
Your grace has laid the odds o' th' weaker side.

---

200 *presence:* Royal assembly.   203 *exception:* Disapproval.   216 *nature:* I.e., he is personally satisfied, but his honor must be satisfied by the rules of the code of honor.   221 *voice:* Authoritative pronouncement.   227 *foil:* Quibble on the two senses: "background which sets something off," and "blunted rapier for fencing."   229 *Stick fiery off:* Stand out brilliantly.

King: I do not fear it; I have seen you both:
    But since he is better'd, we have therefore odds.   235
Laertes: This is too heavy, let me see another.
Hamlet: This likes me well. These foils have all a length?

    [They prepare to play.]

Osric: Ay, my good lord.
King: Set me the stoups of wine upon that table.
    If Hamlet give the first or second hit,   240
    Or quit in answer of the third exchange,
    Let all the battlements their ordnance fire;
    The king shall drink to Hamlet's better breath;
    And in the cup an union° shall he throw,
    Richer than that which four successive kings   245
    In Denmark's crown have worn. Give me the cups;
    And let the kettle° to the trumpet speak,
    The trumpet to the cannoneer without,
    The cannons to the heavens, the heavens to earth,
    "Now the king drinks to Hamlet." Come begin: *Trumpets the while.* 250
    And you, the judges, bear a wary eye.
Hamlet: Come on, sir.
Laertes: Come, my lord.   *[They play.]*
Hamlet: One.
Laertes: No.
Hamlet: Judgement.
Osric: A hit, a very palpable hit.

    Drum, trumpets, and shot. Flourish. A piece goes off.

Laertes: Well; again.
King: Stay; give me drink. Hamlet, this pearl° is thine;
    Here's to thy health. Give him the cup.   255
Hamlet: I'll play this bout first; set it by awhile.
    Come. *[They play.]* Another hit; what say you?
Laertes: A touch, a touch, I do confess 't.
King: Our son shall win.
Queen: He's fat,° and scant of breath.
    Here, Hamlet, take my napkin, rub thy brows: 260
    The queen carouses° to thy fortune, Hamlet.
Hamlet: Good madam!
King: Gertrude, do not drink.
Queen: I will, my lord; I pray you, pardon me.   *[Drinks.]*
King [aside]: It is the poison'd cup: it is too late.
Hamlet: I dare not drink yet, madam; by and by.   265
Queen: Come, let me wipe thy face.
Laertes: My lord, I'll hit him now.
King: I do not think 't.

---

244 *union:* Pearl.   247 *kettle:* Kettledrum.   254 *pearl:* I.e., the poison.   259 *fat:* Not
physically fit, out of training. Some earlier editors speculated that the term applied to the
corpulence of Richard Burbage, who originally played the part, but the allusion now appears
unlikely. *Fat* may also suggest "sweaty."   261 *carouses:* Drinks a toast.

Laertes [aside]: And yet 'tis almost 'gainst my conscience.
Hamlet: Come, for the third, Laertes: you but dally;
 I pray you, pass with your best violence;   270
 I am afeard you make a wanton° of me.
Laertes: Say you so? come on.   *[They play.]*
Osric: Nothing, neither way.
Laertes: Have at you now!

 [Laertes wounds Hamlet; then, in scuffling, they change rapiers,° and Hamlet
 wounds Laertes.]

King: Part them; they are incens'd.
Hamlet: Nay, come again.   *[The Queen falls.]*
Osric: Look to the queen there, ho!   275
Horatio: They bleed on both sides. How is it, my lord?
Osric: How is 't, Laertes?
Laertes: Why, as a woodcock° to mine own springe,° Osric;
 I am justly kill'd with mine own treachery.
Hamlet: How does the queen?
King: She swounds° to see them bleed.   280
Queen: No, no, the drink, the drink, — O my dear Hamlet, —
 The drink, the drink! I am poison'd.   *[Dies.]*
Hamlet: O villany! Ho! let the door be lock'd:
 Treachery! Seek it out.   *[Laertes falls.]*
Laertes: It is here, Hamlet: Hamlet, thou art slain;   285
 No med'cine in the world can do thee good;
 In thee there is not half an hour of life;
 The treacherous instrument is in thy hand,
 Unbated° and envenom'd: the foul practice
 Hath turn'd itself on me; lo, here I lie,   290
 Never to rise again: thy mother's poison'd:
 I can no more: the king, the king's to blame.
Hamlet: The point envenom'd too!
 Then, venom, to thy work.   *[Stabs the King.]*
All: Treason! treason!   295
King: O, yet defend me, friends; I am but hurt.
Hamlet: Here, thou incestuous, murd'rous, damned Dane,
 Drink off this potion. Is thy union here?
 Follow my mother.   *[King dies.]*
Laertes: He is justly serv'd;
 It is a poison temper'd° by himself.   300
 Exchange forgiveness with me, noble Hamlet:
 Mine and my father's death come not upon thee,
 Nor thine on me!   *[Dies.]*
Hamlet: Heaven make thee free of it! I follow thee.
 I am dead, Horatio. Wretched queen, adieu!   305
 You that look pale and tremble at this chance,

---

271 *wanton:* Spoiled child. *in scuffling, they change rapiers:* According to a widespread stage tradition, Hamlet receives a scratch, realizes that Laertes's sword is unbated, and accordingly forces an exchange. 278 *woodcock:* As type of stupidity or as decoy; *springe:* Trap, snare. 280 *swounds:* Swoons. 289 *Unbated:* Not blunted with a button. 300 *temper'd:* Mixed.

That are but mutes° or audience to this act,
Had I but time — as this fell sergeant,° Death,
Is strict in his arrest — O, I could tell you —
But let it be. Horatio, I am dead;   310
Thou livest; report me and my cause aright
To the unsatisfied.
Horatio: Never believe it:
I am more an antique Roman° than a Dane:
Here 's yet some liquor left.
Hamlet: As th' art a man,
Give me the cup: let go, by heaven, I'll ha 't.   315
O God! Horatio, what a wounded name,
Things standing thus unknown, shall live behind me!
If thou didst ever hold me in thy heart,
Absent thee from felicity awhile,
And in this harsh world draw thy breath in pain,   320
To tell my story.   *A march afar off.*
          What warlike noise is this?
Osric: Young Fortinbras, with conquest come from Poland,
To the ambassadors of England gives
This warlike volley.
Hamlet: O, I die, Horatio;
The potent poison quite o'er-crows° my spirit: 325
I cannot live to hear the news from England;
But I do prophesy th' election lights
On Fortinbras: he has my dying voice;
So tell him, with th' occurrents,° more and less,
Which have solicited.° The rest is silence.   *[Dies.]* 330
Horatio: Now cracks a noble heart. Good night, sweet prince;
And flights of angels sing thee to thy rest!
Why does the drum come hither?   *[March within.]*

Enter Fortinbras, with the [English] Ambassadors [and others].

Fortinbras: Where is this sight?
Horatio: What is it you would see?
If aught of woe or wonder, cease your search.   335
Fortinbras: This quarry° cries on havoc.° O proud Death,
What feast is toward in thine eternal cell,
That thou so many princes at a shot
So bloodily hast struck?
First Ambassador: The sight is dismal;
And our affairs from England come too late: 340
The ears are senseless that should give us hearing,
To tell him his commandment is fulfill'd,
That Rosencrantz and Guildenstern are dead:
Where should we have our thanks?

---

307 *mutes:* Performers in a play who speak no words.   308 *sergeant:* Sheriff's officer.
313 *Roman:* It was the Roman custom to follow masters in death.   325 *o'er-crows:* Triumphs
over.   329 *occurrents:* Events, incidents.   330 *solicited:* Moved, urged.   336 *quarry:*
Heap of dead; *cries on havoc:* Proclaims a general slaughter.

Horatio: Not from his mouth,°
Had it th' ability of life to thank you: 345
He never gave commandment for their death.
But since, so jump° upon this bloody question,°
You from the Polack wars, and you from England,
Are here arriv'd, give order that these bodies
High on a stage° be placed to the view;   350
And let me speak to th' yet unknowing world
How these things came about: so shall you hear
Of carnal, bloody, and unnatural acts,
Of accidental judgements, casual slaughters,
Of deaths put on by cunning and forc'd cause,   355
And, in this upshot, purposes mistook
Fall'n on th' inventors' heads: all this can I
Truly deliver.
Fortinbras: Let us haste to hear it,
And call the noblest to the audience.
For me, with sorrow I embrace my fortune: 360
I have some rights of memory° in this kingdom,
Which now to claim my vantage doth invite me.
Horatio: Of that I shall have also cause to speak,
And from his mouth whose voice will draw on more:°
But let this same be presently perform'd,   365
Even while men's minds are wild; lest more mischance,
On° plots and errors, happen.
Fortinbras: Let four captains
Bear Hamlet, like a soldier, to the stage;
For he was likely, had he been put on,
To have prov'd most royal: and, for his passage,°   370
The soldiers' music and the rites of war
Speak loudly for him.
Take up the bodies: such a sight as this
Becomes the field,° but here shows much amiss.
Go, bid the soldiers shoot.   375

*Exeunt [marching, bearing off the dead bodies; after which a peal of ordnance
is shot off].*

344 *his mouth:* I.e., the king's.   347 *jump:* Precisely; *question:* Dispute.   350 *stage:* Platform.   361 *of memory:* Traditional, remembered.   364 *voice ... more:* Vote will influence
still others.   367 *On:* On account of, or possibly, on top of, in addition to.   370 *passage:*
Death.   374 *field:* I.e., of battle.

CONSIDERATIONS FOR CRITICAL THINKING AND WRITING

1. FIRST RESPONSE. Why does Hamlet find avenging his father's death so difficult? Why doesn't he take decisive action as soon as he seems convinced
   of Claudius's guilt?

2. Claudius urges Hamlet to leave behind his "obstinate condolement" and
   give up grieving for his dead father because it represents "impious stub-

bornness" (I.ii.93–94). Consider Claudius's advice in this speech (lines 87–117). Is it sensible? Why won't Hamlet heed this advice?

3. Are Polonius's admonitions to Laertes and Ophelia good advice (I.iii.55–81, 115–135)? What does his advice suggest about life at court, given that he is the chief counselor to the king?

4. When the ghost tells Hamlet that Claudius murdered him, Hamlet cries out, "O my prophetic soul!" (I.v.40). Why? What does the ghost demand of Hamlet?

5. What is known about the kind of person Hamlet was before his father's death? Does he have the stature of a tragic hero such as Oedipus? How does news of the murder and his mother's remarriage affect his behavior and view of life? Is he mad, as Polonius assumes, or is he pretending to be mad? Is there a "method in 't" (II.ii.200)? What do we learn from Hamlet's soliloquies?

6. What is the purpose of the play within the play? How does it provide a commentary on the action of the larger play?

7. Is Ophelia connected in any way with the crime Hamlet seeks to avenge? Why is he so brutal to Ophelia in Act III, Scene i? Why does she go mad?

8. Does Hamlet think Gertrude is as guilty as Claudius? Why is Hamlet so thoroughly disgusted by her in Act III, Scene iv?

9. Why doesn't Hamlet kill Claudius as he prays (III.iii)? Do you feel any sympathy for Claudius in this scene, or is he presented as a callous murderer?

10. If Hamlet had killed Claudius in Act III and the play had ended there, what would be missing in Hamlet's perceptions of himself and the world? How does his character develop in Acts IV and V? What softens our realization that Hamlet is in various degrees responsible for the deaths of Polonius, Ophelia, Laertes, Rosencrantz, Guildenstern, Claudius, and Gertrude?

11. What purpose does Fortinbras serve in the action? Would anything be lost if he were edited out of the play?

12. Despite its tragic dimensions, *Hamlet* includes humorous scenes and many witty lines delivered by the title character himself. Locate those scenes and lines, and then determine the tone and purpose of the play's humor.

Connections to Other Selections

1. Compare in an essay Hamlet's attitudes about revenge with Matt Fowler's in Andre Dubus's short story "Killings" (p. 81).

2. What kind of king is Claudius? How does he compare with Creon in Sophocles' *Antigone* (p. 1267)? How are matters of state and the political atmosphere in the world of each play affected by the rules of Claudius and Creon?

3. Here's a long reach but a potentially interesting one: write an essay that considers Gertrude as a wife and mother alongside Nora in Henrik Ibsen's *A Doll House* (p. 1564). How responsible are they to themselves and to others? Can they be discussed in the same breath, or are they from such different worlds that nothing useful can be said about comparing them? Either way, explain your response.

The Tempest

The Tempest, one of Shakespeare's last plays, is usually associated with his three other romances — *The Winter's Tale, Cymbeline,* and *Pericles* — which are concerned with an affirmation of life by characters who endure loss but are reconciled to the good that can come from misfortune. Unlike the violent and dark world of tragedy, romance ends peacefully with the plot bringing us a sense of new beginnings and possibilities.

The play is set on an imaginary enchanted island that evoked for Shakespeare's contemporaries all the exotic strangeness and infinite possibility that explorers attested to in their travel narratives of the newly discovered world of America. This new world became an ambiguous theater for the European imagination: the dream was that paradise might be regained in unspoiled nature free of corrupt histories and sin, but the nightmare was that civilization could be lost in the base, unformed primitivism of unredeemed nature. Shakespeare explores both the powerful attractions and terrifying anxieties his contemporaries experienced concerning this "brave new world."

Twelve years before the action of the play begins, Prospero, a magician and the deposed Duke of Milan, is stranded on a nearly deserted tropical island with his young daughter, Miranda. They had been betrayed by Prospero's brother, Antonio, who usurped the dukedom with the help of Alonso, King of Naples. As the play opens, Prospero, owing to his magical powers, knows that his enemies are sailing near the island, and with the help of his supernatural servant, Ariel, he creates a tempest that forces them to abandon ship and seek refuge on the island.

Ariel divides the refugees into three groups consisting of Prince Ferdinand, the gallant son of Alonso; King Alonso and those attending him, including Sebastian, his treacherous brother, and Antonio, who betrayed Prospero; and Stephano and Trinculo, a pair of comic figures who conspire against Prospero. Shakespeare — through Prospero's magic — plots the action around these three groups as each undergoes a series of ordeals. At the center of the play's energy is Caliban, the aboriginal inhabitant of the island. A deformed savage enslaved by Prospero, Caliban is the product of a sexual union between a witch (who practiced black magic, in contrast to Prospero's white magic) and a devil. Caliban's primitivism seems at once debased and innocent, but however he is perceived, he serves as a means of measuring the characters from the civilized world who stumble onto the island. In his dealings with the other characters Caliban indirectly indicates the significance and value of civilization while simultaneously suggesting its abuses and corruptions.

In the face of usurpation, murderous conspiracies, lust, and depravity, Prospero uses magic to impose discipline and order on his island refugees, and he does so in a spirit of tolerance and forgiveness. What might have become a tragic story of revenge on those who would destroy Prospero is instead a romantic comedy. Romance ends with reconciliation and love rather than horror and death; *The Tempest* concludes with the serene anticipation of Ferdinand and Miranda's marriage, as vengeance gives merciful way to harmony. In the Epilogue, Prospero steps partially out of character and urges on his audience a prayer for mercy in all things: "As you from crimes would pardoned be, / Let your indulgence set me free." The play makes clear that more than applause is at stake here, since forgiveness is so crucial to weathering tempests in the real world off the magical island and off the stage.

WILLIAM SHAKESPEARE (1564–1616)

The Tempest

c. 1611

NAMES OF THE ACTORS

Alonso, King of Naples
Sebastian, his brother
Prospero, the right Duke of Milan
Antonio, his brother, the usurping Duke of Milan
Ferdinand, son to the King of Naples
Gonzalo, an honest old councillor
Adrian and } lords
Francisco,
Caliban, a savage and deformed slave
Trinculo, a jester
Stephano, a drunken butler
Master of a ship
Boatswain
Mariners

Miranda, daughter to Prospero

Ariel, an airy spirit
Iris,
Ceres,
Juno,   } [presented by] spirits
Nymphs,
Reapers,
[*Other Spirits attending on Prospero*]

THE SCENE: *An uninhabited island*

[ACT I

SCENE I: *On board ship, off the island's coast.*]

A tempestuous noise of thunder and lightning heard. Enter a Shipmaster and a Boatswain.

Master: Boatswain!

Boatswain: Here, Master. What cheer?

Master: Good,° speak to the mariners. Fall to 't yarely,° or we run ourselves aground. Bestir, bestir!   *Exit.*

Enter Mariners.

Boatswain: Heigh, my hearts! Cheerly, cheerly, my hearts! Yare, yare! Take   5
in the topsail. Tend° to the Master's whistle. — Blow° till thou burst
thy wind, if room enough!°

Enter Alonso, Sebastian, Antonio, Ferdinand, Gonzalo, and others.

Alonso: Good Boatswain, have care. Where's the Master? Play the men.°

Boatswain: I pray now, keep below.

Antonio: Where is the Master, Boatswain?   10

Boatswain: Do you not hear him? You mar our labor. Keep° your cabins!
You do assist the storm.

Gonzalo: Nay, good,° be patient.

Boatswain: When the sea is. Hence! What cares these roarers° for the name
of king? To cabin! Silence! Trouble us not.   15

Gonzalo: Good, yet remember whom thou hast aboard.

Boatswain: None that I more love than myself. You are a councillor; if you
can command these elements to silence and work the peace of the
present,° we will not hand° a rope more. Use your authority. If you
cannot, give thanks you have lived so long and make yourself ready in   20
your cabin for the mischance of the hours, if it so hap°—Cheerly,
good hearts! — Out of our way, I say.   *Exit.*

Gonzalo: I have great comfort from this fellow. Methinks he hath no
drowning mark upon him; his complexion is perfect gallows.° Stand
fast, good Fate, to his hanging! Make the rope of his destiny our   25
cable, for our own doth little advantage.° If he be not born to be
hanged, our case is miserable.°   *Exeunt [courtiers].*

Enter Boatswain.

Act I, Scene I.   3 *Good:* I.e., it's good you've come, or, my good fellow; *yarely:* Nimbly.
6 *Tend:* Attend; *Blow:* (Addressed to the wind.)   7 *if room enough:* As long as we have sea
room enough.   8 *Play the men:* Act like men (?) ply, urge the men to exert themselves (?).
11 *Keep:* Remain in.   13 *good:* Good fellow.   14 *roarers:* Waves or winds, or both; spoken to as though they were "bullies" or "blusterers."   18-19 *work...present:* Bring calm to
our present circumstances.   19 *hand:* Handle.   21 *hap:* Happen.   24 *complexion...
gallows:* Appearance shows he was born to be hanged (and therefore, according to the
proverb, in no danger of drowning).   26 *our...advantage:* Our own cable is of little benefit.   27 *case is miserable:* Circumstances are desperate.

Boatswain: Down with the topmast! Yare! Lower, lower! Bring her to try
  wi' the main course.° *(A cry within.)* A plague upon this howling!
  They are louder than the weather or our office.°   30

  Enter Sebastian, Antonio, and Gonzalo.

  Yet again? What do you hear? Shall we give o'er° and drown? Have you
  a mind to sink?
Sebastian: A pox o' your throat, you bawling, blasphemous, incharitable
  dog!
Boatswain: Work you, then.   35
Antonio: Hang, cur! Hang, you whoreson, insolent noisemaker! We are
  less afraid to be drowned than thou art.
Gonzalo: I'll warrant him for drowning,° though the ship were no stronger
  than a nutshell and as leaky as an unstanched° wench.
Boatswain: Lay her ahold, ahold!° Set her two courses.° Off to sea again!   40
  Lay her off!

  Enter Mariners, wet.

Mariners: All lost! To prayers, to prayers! All lost!
      [The Mariners run about in confusion, exiting at random.]
Boatswain: What, must our mouths be cold?°
Gonzalo: The King and Prince at prayers! Let's assist them,
  For our case is as theirs.
Sebastian: I am out of patience.   45
Antonio: We are merely° cheated of our lives by drunkards.
  This wide-chapped° rascal! Would thou mightst lie drowning
  The washing of ten tides!°
Gonzalo: He'll be hanged yet,
  Though every drop of water swear against it
  And gape at wid'st° to glut° him.
  (A confused noise within:)   "Mercy on us!" —   50
  "We split, we split!"° — "Farewell my wife and children!" —
  "Farewell, brother!" — "We split, we split, we split!"   *[Exit Boatswain.]*
Antonio: Let's all sink wi' the King.
Sebastian: Let's take leave of him.   *Exit [with Antonio].*
Gonzalo: Now would I give a thousand furlongs of sea for an acre of bar-   55
  ren ground: long heath,° brown furze,° anything. The wills above be
  done! But I would fain° die a dry death.   *Exit.*

28–29 *Bring . . . course:* Sail her close to the wind by means of the mainsail.   30 *our office:*
I.e., the noise we make at our work.   31 *give o'er:* Give up.   38 *warrant him for drowning:*
Guarantee that he will never be drowned.   39 *unstanched:* Insatiable, loose, unrestrained
(suggesting also "incontinent" and "menstrual").   40 *ahold:* Ahull, close to the wind;
courses: Sails, i.e., foresail as well as mainsail, set in an attempt to get the ship back out into
open water.   43 *must . . . cold:* I.e., must we drown in the cold sea, or, let us heat up our
mouths with liquor.   46 *merely:* Utterly.   47 *wide-chapped:* With mouth wide open.
47–48 *lie . . . tides:* (Pirates were hanged on the shore and left until three tides had come in.)
50 *at wid'st:* Wide open; *glut:* Swallow.   51 *split:* Break apart.   56 *heath:* Heather; *furze:*
Gorse, a weed growing on wasteland.   57 *fain:* Rather.

[SCENE II: *The island, near Prospero's cell. On the Elizabethan stage, this cell is implicitly at hand throughout the play, although in some scenes the convention of flexible distance allows us to imagine characters in other parts of the island.*]

Enter Prospero [in his magic cloak] and Miranda.

Miranda: If by your art,° my dearest father, you have
    Put the wild waters in this roar, allay° them.
    The sky, it seems, would pour down stinking pitch,
    But that the sea, mounting to th' welkin's cheek,°
    Dashes the fire out. O, I have suffered   5
    With those that I saw suffer! A brave° vessel,
    Who had, no doubt, some noble creature in her,
    Dashed all to pieces. O, the cry did knock
    Against my very heart! Poor souls, they perished.
    Had I been any god of power, I would   10
    Have sunk the sea within the earth or ere°
    It should the good ship so have swallowed and
    The freighting° souls within her.
Prospero: Be collected.°
    No more amazement.° Tell your piteous° heart
    There's no harm done.
Miranda: O, woe the day!
Prospero: No harm.   15
    I have done nothing but° in care of thee,
    Of thee, my dear one, thee, my daughter, who
    Art ignorant of what thou art, naught knowing
    Of whence I am, nor that I am more better°
    Than Prospero, master of a full° poor cell,   20
    And thy no greater father.
Miranda: More to know
    Did never meddle° with my thoughts.
Prospero: 'Tis time
    I should inform thee farther. Lend thy hand
    And pluck my magic garment from me. So,
                 [laying down his magic cloak and staff]
    Lie there, my art. — Wipe thou thine eyes. Have comfort.   25
    The direful spectacle of the wreck,° which touched
    The very virtue° of compassion in thee,
    I have with such provision° in mine art
    So safely ordered that there is no soul —
    No, not so much perdition° as an hair   30
    Betid° to any creature in the vessel
    Which° thou heard'st cry, which thou saw'st sink. Sit down,
    For thou must now know farther.

Scene II. 1 *art:* Magic. 2 *allay:* Pacify. 4 *welkin's cheek:* Sky's face. 6 *brave:* Gallant, splendid. 11 *or ere:* Before. 13 *freighting:* Forming the cargo; *collected:* Calm, composed. 14 *amazement:* Consternation; *piteous:* Pitying. 16 *but:* Except. 19 *more better:* Of higher rank. 20 *full:* Very. 22 *meddle:* Mingle. 26 *wreck:* Shipwreck. 27 *virtue:* Essence. 28 *provision:* Foresight. 30 *perdition:* Loss. 31 *Betid:* Happened. 32 *Which:* Whom.

Miranda [sitting]:   You have often
   Begun to tell me what I am, but stopped
   And left me to a bootless inquisition,°   35
   Concluding, "Stay, not yet."
Prospero: The hour's now come;
   The very minute bids thee ope thine ear.
   Obey, and be attentive. Canst thou remember
   A time before we came unto this cell?
   I do not think thou canst, for then thou wast not   40
   Out° three years old.
Miranda: Certainly, sir, I can.
Prospero: By what? By any other house or person?
   Of anything the image, tell me, that
   Hath kept with thy remembrance.
Miranda: 'Tis far off,
   And rather like a dream than an assurance   45
   That my remembrance warrants.° Had I not
   Four or five women once that tended me?
Prospero: Thou hadst, and more, Miranda. But how is it
   That this lives in thy mind? What seest thou else
   In the dark backward and abysm of time?°   50
   If thou rememberest aught° ere thou cam'st here,
   How thou cam'st here thou mayst.
Miranda: But that I do not.
Prospero: Twelve year since, Miranda, twelve year since,
   Thy father was the Duke of Milan and
   A prince of power.
Miranda: Sir, are not you my father?   55
Prospero: Thy mother was a piece° of virtue, and
   She said thou wast my daughter; and thy father
   Was Duke of Milan, and his only heir
   And princess no worse issued.°
Miranda: O the heavens!
   What foul play had we, that we came from thence?   60
   Or blessèd was't we did?
Prospero: Both, both, my girl.
   By foul play, as thou sayst, were we heaved thence,
   But blessedly holp° hither.
Miranda: O, my heart bleeds
   To think o' the teen that I have turned you to,°
   Which is from° my remembrance! Please you, farther.   65
Prospero: My brother and thy uncle, called Antonio—
   I pray thee mark me—that a brother should
   Be so perfidious!—he whom next° thyself
   Of all the world I loved, and to him put

---

35 *bootless inquisition:* Profitless inquiry.   41 *Out:* Fully.   45–46 *assurance…warrants:* Certainty that my memory guarantees.   50 *backward…time:* Abyss of the past.   51 *aught:* Anything.   56 *piece:* Masterpiece, exemplar.   59 *no worse issued:* No less nobly born, descended.   63 *holp:* Helped.   64 *teen…to:* Trouble I've caused you to remember or put you to.   65 *from:* Out of.   68 *next:* Next to.

The manage° of my state, as at that time   70
Through all the seigniories° it was the first,
And Prospero the prime° duke, being so reputed
In dignity, and for the liberal arts
Without a parallel; those being all my study,
The government I cast upon my brother   75
And to my state grew stranger,° being transported°
And rapt in secret studies. Thy false uncle —
Dost thou attend me?
Miranda: Sir, most heedfully.
Prospero: Being once perfected° how to grant suits,
How to deny them, who t' advance and who   80
To trash° for overtopping,° new created
The creatures° that were mine, I say, or changed 'em,
Or else new formed 'em;° having both the key°
Of officer and office, set all hearts i' the state
To what tune pleased his ear, that° now he was   85
The ivy which had hid my princely trunk
And sucked my verdure° out on 't.° Thou attend'st not.
Miranda: O, good sir, I do.
Prospero: I pray thee, mark me.
I, thus neglecting worldly ends, all dedicated
To closeness° and the bettering of my mind   90
With that which, but by being so retired,
O'erprized all popular rate,° in my false brother
Awaked an evil nature; and my trust,
Like a good parent,° did beget of° him
A falsehood in its contrary as great   95
As my trust was, which had indeed no limit,
A confidence sans° bound. He being thus lorded°
Not only with what my revenue yielded
But what my power might else° exact, like one
Who, having into° truth by telling of it,   100
Made such a sinner of his memory
To° credit his own lie,° he did believe
He was indeed the Duke, out o'° the substitution

70 *manage:* Management, administration.   71 *seigniories:* I.e., city-states of northern Italy.
72 *prime:* First in rank and importance.   76 *to ... stranger:* I.e., withdrew from my responsibilities as duke; *transported:* Carried away.   79 *perfected:* Grown skillful.   81 *trash:*
Check a hound by tying a cord or weight to its neck; *overtopping:* Running too far ahead of the
pack; surmounting, exceeding one's authority.   82 *creatures:* Dependents.   82–83 *or
changed ... formed 'em:* I.e., either changed their loyalties and duties or else created new ones.
83 *key:* (1) Key for unlocking (2) tool for tuning stringed instruments.   85 *that:* So that.
87 *verdure:* Vitality; *on 't:* Of it.   90 *closeness:* Retirement, seclusion.   91–92 *but ... rate:*
I.e., were it not that its private nature caused me to neglect my public responsibilities, had a
value far beyond what public opinion could appreciate, or, simply because it was done in such
seclusion, had a value not appreciated by popular opinion.   94 *good parent:* (Alludes to
the proverb that good parents often bear bad children; see also line 120); *of:* In.   97 *sans:*
Without; *lorded:* Raised to lordship, with power and wealth.   99 *else:* Otherwise, additionally.   100–102 *Who ... lie:* I.e., who, by repeatedly telling the lie (that he was indeed
Duke of Milan), made his memory such a confirmed sinner against truth that he began to
believe his own lie; *into:* Unto, against; *To:* So as to.   103 *out o':* As a result of.

And executing th' outward face of royalty°
With all prerogative. Hence his ambition growing —   105
Dost thou hear?
Miranda: Your tale, sir, would cure deafness.
Prospero: To have no screen between this part he played
And him he played it for,° he needs will be°
Absolute Milan.° Me, poor man, my library
Was dukedom large enough. Of temporal royalties°   110
He thinks me now incapable; confederates° —
So dry° he was for sway° — wi' the King of Naples
To give him annual tribute, do him° homage,
Subject his coronet to his° crown, and bend°
The dukedom yet° unbowed — alas, poor Milan! —   115
To most ignoble stooping.
Miranda: O the heavens!
Prospero: Mark his condition° and th' event,° then tell me
If this might be a brother.
Miranda: I should sin
To think but° nobly of my grandmother.
Good wombs have borne bad sons.
Prospero: Now the condition.   120
This King of Naples, being an enemy
To me inveterate, hearkens° my brother's suit,
Which was that he,° in lieu o' the premises°
Of homage and I know not how much tribute,
Should presently extirpate° me and mine   125
Out of the dukedom and confer fair Milan,
With all the honors, on my brother. Whereon,
A treacherous army levied, one midnight
Fated to th' purpose did Antonio open
The gates of Milan, and, i' the dead of darkness,   130
The ministers for the purpose° hurried thence°
Me and thy crying self.
Miranda: Alack, for pity!
I, not remembering how I cried out then,
Will cry it o'er again. It is a hint°
That wrings° mine eyes to 't.
Prospero: Hear a little further,   135
And then I'll bring thee to the present business

---

104 *And ... royalty:* And (as a result of) his carrying out all the visible functions of royalty.
107–108 *To have ... it for:* To have no separation or barrier between his role and himself.
(Antonio wanted to act in his own person, not as substitute.)   108 *needs will be:* Insisted
on becoming.   109 *Absolute Milan:* Unconditional Duke of Milan.   110 *temporal royalties:*
Practical prerogatives and responsibilities of a sovereign.   111 *confederates:* Conspires, allies
himself.   112 *dry:* Thirsty; *sway:* Power.   113 *him:* I.e., the King of Naples.   114 *his ...
his:* Antonio's ... the King of Naples'; *bend:* Make bow down.   115 *yet:* Hitherto.   117 *condition:* Pact; *event:* Outcome.   119 *but:* Other than.   122 *hearkens:* Listens to.   123 *he:*
The King of Naples; *in ... premises:* In return for the stipulation.   125 *presently extirpate:*
At once remove.   131 *ministers ... purpose:* Agents employed to do this; *thence:* From there.
134 *hint:* Occasion.   135 *wrings:* (1) Constrains (2) wrings tears from.

Which now's upon's, without the which this story
Were most impertinent.°
Miranda: Wherefore° did they not
    That hour destroy us?
Prospero: Well demanded,° wench.°
    My tale provokes that question. Dear, they durst not,   140
    So dear the love my people bore me, nor set
    A mark so bloody° on the business, but
    With colors fairer° painted their foul ends.
    In few,° they hurried us aboard a bark,°
    Bore us some leagues to sea, where they prepared   145
    A rotten carcass of a butt,° not rigged,
    Nor tackle,° sail, nor mast; the very rats
    Instinctively have quit° it. There they hoist us,
    To cry to th' sea that roared to us, to sigh
    To th' winds whose pity, sighing back again,   150
    Did us but loving wrong.°
Miranda: Alack, what trouble
    Was I then to you!
Prospero: O, a cherubin
    Thou wast that did preserve me. Thou didst smile,
    Infusèd with a fortitude from heaven,
    When I have decked° the sea with drops full salt,   155
    Under my burden groaned, which° raised in me
    An undergoing stomach,° to bear up
    Against what should ensue.
Miranda: How came we ashore?
Prospero: By Providence divine.   160
    Some food we had, and some fresh water, that
    A noble Neapolitan, Gonzalo,
    Out of his charity, who being then appointed
    Master of this design, did give us, with
    Rich garments, linens, stuffs,° and necessaries,   165
    Which since have steaded much.° So, of° his gentleness,
    Knowing I loved my books, he furnished me
    From mine own library with volumes that
    I prize above my dukedom.
Miranda: Would° I might
    But ever° see that man!
Prospero: Now I arise.   *[He puts on his magic cloak.]*   170
    Sit still, and hear the last of our sea sorrow.°

138 *impertinent:* Irrelevant; *Wherefore:* Why.   139 *demanded:* Asked; *wench:* (Here a term of
endearment.)   141–142 *set ... bloody:* I.e., make obvious their murderous intent (from
the practice of marking with the blood of the prey those who have participated in a successful hunt).   143 *fairer:* Apparently more attractive.   144 *few:* Few words; *bark:* Ship.
146 *butt:* Cask, tub.   147 *Nor tackle:* Neither rigging.   148 *quit:* Abandoned.   151 *Did ...
wrong:* (I.e., the winds pitied Prospero and Miranda, though of necessity they blew them
from shore.)   155 *decked:* Covered (with salt tears), adorned.   156 *which:* I.e., the smile.
157 *undergoing stomach:* Courage to go on.   165 *stuffs:* Supplies.   166 *steaded much:* Been
of much use; *So, of:* Similarly, out of.   169 *Would:* I wish.   170 *But ever:* I.e., someday.
171 *sea sorrow:* Sorrowful adventure at sea.

Here in this island we arrived; and here
Have I, thy schoolmaster, made thee more profit°
Than other princess'° can, that have more time
For vainer° hours and tutors not so careful.   175
Miranda: Heavens thank you for 't! And now, I pray you, sir —
For still 'tis beating in my mind — your reason
For raising this sea storm?
Prospero: Know thus far forth:
By accident most strange, bountiful Fortune,
Now my dear lady,° hath mine enemies   180
Brought to this shore; and by my prescience
I find my zenith° doth depend upon
A most auspicious star, whose influence°
If now I court not, but omit,° my fortunes
Will ever after droop. Here cease more questions.   185
Thou art inclined to sleep. 'Tis a good dullness,°
And give it way.° I know thou canst not choose.   *[Miranda sleeps.]*
Come away,° servant, come! I am ready now.
Approach, my Ariel, come.

Enter Ariel.

Ariel: All hail, great master, grave sir, hail! I come   190
To answer thy best pleasure; be 't to fly,
To swim, to dive into the fire, to ride
On the curled clouds, to thy strong bidding task°
Ariel and all his quality.°
Prospero: Hast thou, spirit,
Performed to point° the tempest that I bade thee?   195
Ariel: To every article.
I boarded the King's ship. Now on the beak,°
Now in the waist,° the deck,° in every cabin,
I flamed amazement.° Sometimes I'd divide
And burn in many places; on the topmast,   200
The yards, and bowsprit would I flame distinctly,°
Then meet and join. Jove's lightning, the precursors
O' the dreadful thunderclaps, more momentary
And sight-outrunning° were not.° The fire and cracks
Of sulfurous roaring the most mighty Neptune°   205
Seem to besiege and make his bold waves tremble,
Yea, his dread trident shake.
Prospero: My brave spirit!

173 *more profit:* Profit more.   174 *princess':* Princesses (or the word may be *princes*, referring
to royal children both male and female).   175 *vainer:* More foolishly spent.   180 *my dear
lady:* (Refers to Fortune, not Miranda.)   182 *zenith:* Height of fortune (astrological term).
183 *influence:* Astrological power.   184 *omit:* Ignore.   186 *dullness:* Drowsiness.   187 *give
it way:* Let it happen (i.e., don't fight it).   188 *Come away:* Come.   193 *task:* Make demands upon.   194 *quality:* (1) Fellow spirits (2) abilities.   195 *to point:* To the smallest detail.   197 *beak:* Prow.   198 *waist:* Midships; *deck:* Poop deck at the stern.   199 *flamed
amazement:* Struck terror in the guise of fire, i.e., Saint Elmo's fire.   201 *distinctly:* In different places.   204 *sight-outrunning:* Swifter than sight; *were not:* Could not have been.
205 *Neptune:* Roman god of the sea.

Who was so firm, so constant, that this coil°
Would not infect his reason?
Ariel: Not a soul
But felt a fever of the mad° and played   210
Some tricks of desperation. All but mariners
Plunged in the foaming brine and quit the vessel,
Then all afire with me. The King's son, Ferdinand,
With hair up-staring° — then like reeds, not hair —
Was the first man that leapt; cried, "Hell is empty,   215
And all the devils are here!"
Prospero: Why, that's my spirit!
But was not this nigh shore?
Ariel: Close by, my master.
Prospero: But are they, Ariel, safe?
Ariel: Not a hair perished.
On their sustaining garments° not a blemish,
But fresher than before; and, as thou bad'st° me,   220
In troops° I have dispersed them, 'bout the isle.
The King's son have I landed by himself,
Whom I left cooling of° the air with sighs
In an odd angle° of the isle, and sitting,
His arms in this sad knot.°   *[He folds his arms.]*
Prospero: Of the King's ship,   225
The mariners, say how thou hast disposed,
And all the rest o' the fleet.
Ariel: Safely in harbor
Is the King's ship; in the deep nook,° where once
Thou called'st me up at midnight to fetch dew°
From the still-vexed Bermudas,° there she's hid;   230
The mariners all under hatches stowed,
Who, with a charm joined to their suffered labor,°
I have left asleep. And for the rest o' the fleet,
Which I dispersed, they all have met again
And are upon the Mediterranean float°   235
Bound sadly home for Naples,
Supposing that they saw the King's ship wrecked
And his great person perish.
Prospero: Ariel, thy charge
Exactly is performed. But there's more work.
What is the time o' the day?
Ariel: Past the mid season.°   240
Prospero: At least two glasses.° The time twixt six and now
Must by us both be spent most preciously.

---

208 *coil:* Tumult.   210 *of the mad:* I.e., such as madmen feel.   214 *up-staring:* Standing
on end.   219 *sustaining garments:* Garments that buoyed them up in the sea.   220 *bad'st:*
Ordered.   221 *troops:* Groups.   223 *cooling of:* Cooling.   224 *angle:* Corner.   225 *sad
knot:* (Folded arms are indicative of melancholy.)   228 *nook:* Bay.   229 *dew:* (Collected
at midnight for magical purposes; compare with line 325.)   230 *still-vexed Bermudas:* Ever
stormy Bermudas.   232 *with . . . labor:* By means of a spell added to all the labor they have
undergone.   235 *float:* Sea.   240 *mid season:* Noon.   241 *glasses:* Hourglasses.

Ariel: Is there more toil? Since thou dost give me pains,°
    Let me remember° thee what thou hast promised,
    Which is not yet performed me.
Prospero: How now? Moody?   245
    What is 't thou canst demand?
Ariel: My liberty.
Prospero: Before the time be out? No more!
Ariel: I prithee,
    Remember I have done thee worthy service,
    Told thee no lies, made thee no mistakings, served
    Without or grudge or grumblings. Thou did promise   250
    To bate° me a full year.
Prospero: Dost thou forget
    From what a torment I did free thee?
Ariel: No.
Prospero: Thou dost, and think'st it much to tread the ooze
    Of the salt deep,
    To run upon the sharp wind of the north,   255
    To do me° business in the veins° o' the earth
    When it is baked° with frost.
Ariel: I do not, sir.
Prospero: Thou liest, malignant thing! Hast thou forgot
    The foul witch Sycorax, who with age and envy°
    Was grown into a hoop?° Hast thou forgot her?   260
Ariel: No, sir.
Prospero: Thou hast. Where was she born? Speak. Tell me.
Ariel: Sir, in Argier.°
Prospero: O, was she so? I must
    Once in a month recount what thou hast been,
    Which thou forgett'st. This damned witch Sycorax,   265
    For mischiefs manifold and sorceries terrible
    To enter human hearing, from Argier,
    Thou know'st, was banished. For one thing she did°
    They would not take her life. Is not this true?
Ariel: Ay, sir.   270
Prospero: This blue-eyed° hag was hither brought with child°
    And here was left by the sailors. Thou, my slave,
    As thou report'st thyself, was then her servant;
    And, for° thou wast a spirit too delicate
    To act her earthy and abhorred commands,   275
    Refusing her grand hests,° she did confine thee,
    By help of her more potent ministers
    And in her most unmitigable rage,

---

243 *pains:* Labors.   244 *remember:* Remind.   251 *bate:* Remit, deduct.   256 *do me:* Do
for me; *veins:* Veins of minerals, or, underground streams, thought to be analogous to the
veins of the human body.   257 *baked:* Hardened.   259 *envy:* Malice.   260 *grown into a
hoop:* I.e., so bent over with age as to resemble a hoop.   263 *Argier:* Algiers.   268 *one . . .
did:* (Perhaps a reference to her pregnancy, for which her life would be spared.)   271 *blueeyed:* With dark circles under the eyes or with blue eyelids, implying pregnancy; *with child:*
Pregnant.   274 *for:* Because.   276 *hests:* Commands.

Into a cloven pine, within which rift
Imprisoned thou didst painfully remain   280
A dozen years; within which space she died
And left thee there, where thou didst vent thy groans
As fast as mill wheels strike.° Then was this island —
Save° for the son that she did litter° here,
A freckled whelp,° hag-born° — not honored with   285
A human shape.
Ariel: Yes, Caliban her son.°
Prospero: Dull thing, I say so:° he, that Caliban
    Whom now I keep in service. Thou best know'st
    What torment I did find thee in. Thy groans
    Did make wolves howl, and penetrate the breasts   290
    Of ever-angry bears. It was a torment
    To lay upon the damned, which Sycorax
    Could not gain undo. It was mine art,
    When I arrived and heard thee, that made gape°
    The pine and let thee out.
Ariel: I thank thee, master.   295
Prospero: If thou more murmur'st, I will rend an oak
    And peg thee in his° knotty entrails till
    Thou hast howled away twelve winters.
Ariel: Pardon, master.
    I will be correspondent° to command
    And do my spriting° gently.°   300
Prospero: Do so, and after two days
    I will discharge thee.
Ariel: That's my noble master!
    What shall I do? Say what? What shall I do?
Prospero: Go make thyself like a nymph o' the sea. Be subject
    To no sight but thine and mine, invisible   305
    To every eyeball else. Go take this shape
    And hither come in 't. Go, hence with diligence!   *Exit [Ariel].*
    Awake, dear heart, awake! Thou hast slept well.
    Awake!
Miranda: The strangeness of your story put   310
    Heaviness° in me.
Prospero: Shake it off. Come on,
    We'll visit Caliban, my slave, who never
    Yields us kind answer.
Miranda: 'Tis a villain, sir,
    I do not love to look on.
Prospero: But, as 'tis,

---

283 *as mill wheels strike:* As the blades of a mill wheel strike the water.   284 *Save:* Except;
litter: Give birth to.   285 *whelp:* Offspring (used of animals); *hag-born:* Born of a female
demon.   286 *Yes . . . son:* (Ariel is probably concurring with Prospero's comment about
a "freckled whelp," not contradicting the point about "A human shape.")   287 *Dull . . .
so:* I.e., exactly, that's what I said, you dullard.   294 *gape:* Open wide.   297 *his:* Its.
299 *correspondent:* Responsive, submissive.   300 *spriting:* Duties as a spirit; *gently:* Willingly, ungrudgingly.   311 *Heaviness:* Drowsiness.

We cannot miss° him. He does make our fire,   315
Fetch in our wood, and serves in offices°
That profit us. — What ho! Slave! Caliban!
Thou earth, thou! Speak.
Caliban (within):   There's wood enough within.
Prospero: Come forth, I say! There's other business for thee.
Come, thou tortoise! When?°   320

Enter Ariel like a water nymph.

Fine apparition! My quaint° Ariel,
Hark in thine ear.   *[He whispers.]*
Ariel: My lord, it shall be done.   *Exit.*
Prospero: Thou poisonous slave, got° by the devil himself
Upon thy wicked dam,° come forth!

Enter Caliban.

Caliban: As wicked° dew as e'er my mother brushed   325
With raven's feather from unwholesome fen°
Drop on you both! A southwest° blow on ye
And blister you all o'er!
Prospero: For this, be sure, tonight thou shalt have cramps,
Side-stitches that shall pen thy breath up. Urchins°   330
Shall forth at vast° of night that they may work
All exercise on thee. Thou shalt be pinched
As thick as honeycomb,° each pinch more stinging
Than bees that made 'em.°
Caliban: I must eat my dinner.
This island's mine, by Sycorax my mother,   335
Which thou tak'st from me. When thou cam'st first,
Thou strok'st me and made much of me, wouldst give me
Water with berries in 't, and teach me how
To name the bigger light, and how the less,°
That burn by day and night. And then I loved thee   340
And showed thee all the qualities o' th' isle,
The fresh springs, brine pits, barren place and fertile.
Cursed be I that did so! All the charms°
Of Sycorax, toads, beetles, bats, light on you!
For I am all the subjects that you have,   345
Which first was mine own king; and here you sty° me
In this hard rock, whiles you do keep from me
The rest o' th' island.

---

315 *miss:* Do without.   316 *offices:* Functions, duties.   320 *When:* (An exclamation of impatience.)   321 *quaint:* Ingenious.   323 *got:* Begotten, sired.   324 *dam:* Mother (used of animals).   325 *wicked:* Mischievous, harmful.   326 *fen:* Marsh, bog.   327 *southwest:* I.e., wind thought to bring disease.   330 *Urchins:* Hedgehogs; here, suggesting goblins in the guise of hedgehogs.   331 *vast:* Lengthy, desolate time. (Malignant spirits were thought to be restricted to the hours of darkness.)   333 *As thick as honeycomb:* I.e., all over, with as many pinches as a honeycomb has cells.   334 *'em:* I.e., the honeycomb.   339 *the bigger . . . less:* I.e., the sun and the moon (see Genesis 1:16: "God then made two great lights: the greater light to rule the day, and the less light to rule the night").   343 *charms:* Spells.   346 *sty:* Confine as in a sty.

Prospero: Thou most lying slave,
     Whom stripes° may move, not kindness! I have used thee,
     Filth as thou art, with humane° care, and lodged thee   350
     In mine own cell, till thou didst seek to violate
     The honor of my child.
Caliban: Oho, oho! Would 't had been done!
     Thou didst prevent me; I had peopled else°
     This isle with Calibans.
Miranda: Abhorrèd° slave,   355
     Which any print° of goodness wilt not take,
     Being capable of all ill! I pitied thee,
     Took pains to make thee speak, taught thee each hour
     One thing or other. When thou didst not, savage,
     Know thine own meaning, but wouldst gabble like   360
     A thing most brutish, I endowed thy purposes°
     With words that made them known. But thy vile race,°
     Though thou didst learn, had that in 't which good natures
     Could not abide to be with; therefore wast thou
     Deservedly confined into this rock,   365
     Who hadst deserved more than a prison.
Caliban: You taught me language, and my profit on 't
     Is I know how to curse. The red plague° rid° you
     For learning° me your language!
Prospero: Hagseed,° hence!
     Fetch us in fuel, and be quick, thou'rt best,°   370
     To answer other business.° Shrugg'st thou, malice?
     If thou neglect'st or dost unwillingly
     What I command, I'll rack thee with old° cramps,
     Fill all thy bones with aches,° make thee roar
     That beasts shall tremble at thy din.
Caliban: No, pray thee.   375
     [Aside.] I must obey. His art is of such power
     It would control my dam's god, Setebos,°
     And make a vassal of him.
Prospero: So, slave, hence!   *Exit Caliban.*

Enter Ferdinand; and Ariel, invisible,° playing and singing. [Ferdinand does not
see Prospero and Miranda.]

          Ariel's Song.

Ariel: Come unto these yellow sands,
     And then take hands;   380

---

349 *stripes:* Lashes.   350 *humane:* (Not distinguished as word from *human.*)   354 *peo-*
pled else: Otherwise populated.   355–366 Abhorrèd . . . prison: (Sometimes assigned by
editors to Prospero.)   356 *print:* Imprint, impression.   361 *purposes:* Meanings, desires.
362 *race:* Natural disposition; species, nature.   368 *red plague:* Plague characterized by
red sores and evacuation of blood; *rid:* Destroy.   369 *learning:* Teaching; *Hagseed:* Offspring of a female demon.   370 *thou'rt best:* You'd be well advised.   371 *answer other busi-*
ness: Perform other tasks.   373 *old:* Such as old people suffer, or, plenty of.   374 *aches:*
(Pronounced "aitches.")   377 *Setebos:* (A god of the Patagonians, named in Robert Eden's
History of Travel, 1577.)   *Ariel, invisible:* (Ariel wears a garment that by convention indicates
he is invisible to the other characters.)

Curtsied when you have,° and kissed
   The wild waves whist,°
Foot it featly° here and there,
   And, sweet sprites,° bear
The burden.° Hark, hark!

Burden, dispersedly° [within]. Bow-wow.   385
   The watchdogs bark.

[Burden, dispersedly within.] Bow-wow.
Hark, hark! I hear
The strain of strutting chanticleer
   Cry Cock-a-diddle-dow.

Ferdinand: Where should this music be? I' th' air or th' earth?   390
   It sounds no more; and sure it waits upon°
Some god o' th' island. Sitting on a bank,°
Weeping again the King my father's wreck,
This music crept by me upon the waters,
Allaying both their fury and my passion°   395
With its sweet air. Thence° I have followed it,
Or it hath drawn me rather. But 'tis gone.
No, it begins again.

         Ariel's Song.

Ariel: Full fathom five thy father lies.
   Of his bones are coral made.   400
   Those are pearls that were his eyes.
      Nothing of him that doth fade
   But doth suffer a sea change
   Into something rich and strange.
   Sea nymphs hourly ring his knell.°

Burden [within]. Ding dong.   405
Hark, now I hear them, ding dong bell.
Ferdinand: The ditty does remember° my drowned father.
   This is no mortal business, nor no sound
   That the earth owes.° I hear it now above me.
Prospero [to Miranda]: The fringèd curtains of thine eye advance°   410
   And say what thou seest yond.
Miranda: What is 't? A spirit?
   Lord, how it looks about! Believe me, sir,
   It carries a brave° form. But 'tis a spirit.
Prospero: No, wench, it eats and sleeps and hath such senses
   As we have, such. This gallant which thou seest   415
   Was in the wreck; and, but° he's something stained°
   With grief, that's beauty's canker,° thou mightst call him

---

381 *Curtsied . . . have:* When you have curtsied.   381–382 *kissed . . . whist:* Kissed the waves
into silence, or, kissed while the waves are being hushed.   383 *Foot it featly:* Dance nimbly.
384 *sprites:* Spirits.   385 *burden:* Refrain, undersong; *dispersedly:* I.e., from all directions,
not in unison.   391 *waits upon:* Serves, attends.   392 *bank:* Sandbank.   395 *passion:*
Grief.   396 *Thence:* I.e., from the bank on which I sat.   405 *knell:* Announcement of a
death by the tolling of a bell.   407 *remember:* Commemorate.   409 *owes:* Owns.
410 *advance:* Raise.   413 *brave:* Excellent.   416 *but:* Except that; *something stained:*
Somewhat disfigured.   417 *canker:* Cankerworm (feeding on buds and leaves).

A goodly person. He hath lost his fellows
And strays about to find 'em.
Miranda: I might call him
A thing divine, for nothing natural   420
I ever saw so noble.
Prospero [aside]:   It goes on,° I see,
As my soul prompts it. — Spirit, fine spirit, I'll free thee
Within two days for this.
Ferdinand [seeing Miranda]: Most sure, the goddess
On whom these airs° attend! — Vouchsafe° my prayer   425
May know° if you remain° upon this island,
And that you will some good instruction give
How I may bear me° here. My prime° request,
Which I do last pronounce, is — O you wonder!° —
If you be maid or no?°
Miranda: No wonder, sir,   430
But certainly a maid.
Ferdinand: My language? Heavens!
I am the best° of them that speak this speech,
Were I but where 'tis spoken.
Prospero [coming forward]:   How? The best?
What wert thou if the King of Naples heard thee?
Ferdinand: A single° thing, as I am now, that wonders   435
To hear thee speak of Naples.° He does hear me,°
And that he does I weep.° Myself am Naples,°
Who with mine eyes, never since at ebb,° beheld
The King my father wrecked.
Miranda: Alack, for mercy!
Ferdinand: Yes, faith, and all his lords, the Duke of Milan   440
And his brave son° being twain.
Prospero [aside]:   The Duke of Milan
And his more braver° daughter could control° thee,
If now 'twere fit to do 't. At the first sight
They have changed eyes.° — Delicate Ariel,
I'll set thee free for this. *[To Ferdinand.]* A word, good sir.   445
I fear you have done yourself some wrong.° A word!
Miranda [aside]: Why speaks my father so urgently? This
Is the third man that e'er I saw, the first
That e'er I sighed for. Pity move my father
To be inclined my way!

---

421 *It goes on:* I.e., my plan works.   425 *airs:* Songs; *Vouchsafe:* Grant.   426 *May know:* I.e., that I may know; *remain:* Dwell.   428 *bear me:* Conduct myself; *prime:* Chief.   429 *wonder:* (Miranda's name means "to be wondered at.")   430 *maid or no:* I.e., a human maiden as opposed to a goddess or married woman.   432 *best:* I.e., in birth.   435 *single:* (1) Solitary, being at once King of Naples and myself (2) feeble.   436, 437 *Naples:* The King of Naples.   436 *He does hear me:* I.e., the King of Naples does hear my words, for I am King of Naples.   437 *And... weep:* I.e., and I weep at this reminder that my father is seemingly dead, leaving me heir.   438 *at ebb:* I.e., dry, not weeping.   441 *son:* (The only reference in the play to a son of Antonio.)   442 *more braver:* More splendid; *control:* Refute.   444 *changed eyes:* Exchanged amorous glances.   446 *done... wrong:* I.e., spoken falsely.

Ferdinand: O, if a virgin,   450
   And your affection not gone forth, I'll make you
   The Queen of Naples.
Prospero: Soft, sir! One word more.
   [Aside.] They are both in either's° powers; but this swift business
   I must uneasy° make, lest too light winning
   Make the prize light.° *[To Ferdinand.]* One word more: I charge thee   455
   That thou attend° me. Thou dost here usurp
   The name thou ow'st° not, and hast put thyself
   Upon this island as a spy, to win it
   From me, the lord on 't.°
Ferdinand: No, as I am a man.
Miranda: There's nothing ill can dwell in such a temple.   460
   If the ill spirit have so fair a house,
   Good things will strive to dwell with 't.°
Prospero: Follow me. —
   Speak not you for him; he's a traitor. — Come,
   I'll manacle thy neck and feet together.
   Seawater shalt thou drink; thy food shall be   465
   The fresh-brook mussels, withered roots, and husks
   Wherein the acorn cradled. Follow.
Ferdinand: No!
   I will resist such entertainment° till
   Mine enemy has more power.   *He draws, and is charmed° from moving.*
Miranda: O dear father,
   Make not too rash° a trial of him, for   470
   He's gentle,° and not fearful.°
Prospero: What, I say,
   My foot° my tutor? — Put thy sword up, traitor,
   Who mak'st a show but dar'st not strike, thy conscience
   Is so possessed with guilt. Come, from thy ward,°
   For I can here disarm thee with this stick   475
   And make thy weapon drop.   *[He brandishes his staff.]*
Miranda [trying to hinder him]: Beseech you, father!
Prospero: Hence! Hang not on my garments.
Miranda: Sir, have pity!
   I'll be his surety.°
Prospero: Silence! One word more
   Shall make me chide thee, if not hate thee. What,   480
   An advocate for an impostor? Hush!
   Thou think'st there is no more such shapes as he,
   Having seen but him and Caliban. Foolish wench,

---

453 *both in either's:* Each in the other's.   454 *uneasy:* Difficult.   454–455 *light…light:* Easy…
cheap.   456 *attend:* Follow, obey.   457 *ow'st:* Ownest.   459 *on 't:* Of it.   462 *strive…
with 't:* I.e., expel the evil and occupy the *temple,* the body.   468 *entertainment:* Treatment.
charmed: Magically prevented.   470 *rash:* Harsh.   471 *gentle:* Wellborn; *fearful:* Frightening, dangerous, or perhaps, cowardly.   472 *foot:* Subordinate (Miranda, the foot, presumes to
instruct Prospero, the head).   474 *ward:* Defensive posture (in fencing).   479 *surety:* Guarantee.

To° the most of men this is a Caliban,
And they to him are angels.
Miranda: My affections   485
Are then most humble; I have no ambition
To see a goodlier man.
Prospero [to Ferdinand]:   Come on, obey.
Thy nerves° are in their infancy again
And have no vigor in them.
Ferdinand: So they are.
My spirits,° as in a dream, are all bound up.   490
My father's loss, the weakness which I feel,
The wreck of all my friends, nor this man's threats
To whom I am subdued, are but light° to me,
Might I but through my prison once a day
Behold this maid. All corners else° o' th' earth   495
Let liberty make use of; space enough
Have I in such a prison.
Prospero [aside]: It works. [To Ferdinand.] Come on. — [To Ariel]
Thou hast done well, fine Ariel! [To Ferdinand.] Follow me.
[To Ariel.] Hark what thou else shalt do me.°
Miranda [to Ferdinand]:   Be of comfort.   500
My father's of a better nature, sir,
Than he appears by speech. This is unwonted°
Which now came from him.
Prospero [to Ariel]:   Thou shalt be as free
As mountain winds; but then° exactly do
All points of my command.
Ariel: To th' syllable.   505
Prospero [to Ferdinand]: Come, follow. [To Miranda.] Speak not for him.
                                                  Exeunt.

[ACT II

Scene I: *Another part of the island.*]

Enter Alonso, Sebastian, Antonio, Gonzalo, Adrian, Francisco, and others.

Gonzalo [to Alonso]: Beseech you, sir, be merry. You have cause,
So have we all, of joy, for our escape
Is much beyond our loss. Our hint° of woe
Is common; every day some sailor's wife,
The masters of some merchant, and the merchant,°   5
Have just our theme of woe. But for the miracle,
I mean our preservation, few in millions

---

484 *To:* Compared to.   488 *nerves:* Sinews.   490 *spirits:* Vital powers.   493 *light:* Unimportant.   495 *corners else:* Other corners, regions.   500 *me:* For me.   502 *unwonted:*
Unusual.   504 *then:* Until then, or, if that is to be so.   **Act II, Scene I.**   3 *hint:* Occasion.   5 *masters . . . the merchant:* Officers of some merchant vessel and the merchant himself, the owner.

Can speak like us. Then wisely, good sir, weigh
Our sorrow with° our comfort.
Alonso: Prithee, peace.
Sebastian [aside to Antonio]: He receives comfort like cold porridge.°   10
Antonio [aside to Sebastian]: The visitor° will not give him o'er° so.
Sebastian: Look, he's winding up the watch of his wit; by and by it will strike.
Gonzalo [to Alonso]: Sir—
Sebastian [aside to Antonio]: One. Tell.°
Gonzalo: When every grief is entertained   15
That's offered, comes to th' entertainer°—
Sebastian: A dollar.°
Gonzalo: Dolor comes to him, indeed. You have spoken truer than you
purposed.
Sebastian: You have taken it wiselier than I meant you should.   20
Gonzalo [to Alonso]: Therefore, my lord—
Antonio: Fie, what a spendthrift is he of his tongue!
Alonso [to Gonzalo]: I prithee, spare.°
Gonzalo: Well, I have done. But yet—
Sebastian [aside to Antonio]: He will be talking.   25
Antonio [aside to Sebastian]: Which, of he or Adrian, for a good wager, first
begins to crow?°
Sebastian: The old cock.°
Antonio: The cockerel.°
Sebastian: Done. The wager?   30
Antonio: A laughter.°
Sebastian: A match!°
Adrian: Though this island seem to be desert°—
Antonio: Ha, ha, ha!
Sebastian: So, you're paid.°   35
Adrian: Uninhabitable and almost inaccessible—
Sebastian: Yet—
Adrian: Yet—
Antonio: He could not miss 't.°
Adrian: It must needs be° of subtle, tender, and delicate temperance.°   40
Antonio: Temperance° was a delicate° wench.

---

9 *with:* Against.   10 *porridge:* Pun suggested by *peace* for "peas" or "pease," a common ingredient of porridge.   11 *visitor:* One taking nourishment and comfort to the sick, as Gonzalo is doing; *give him o'er:* Abandon him.   14 *Tell:* Keep count.   15-16 *When . . . entertainer:* When every sorrow that presents itself is accepted without resistance, there comes to the recipient.   17 *dollar:* Widely circulated coin, the German thaler and the Spanish piece of eight (Sebastian puns on *entertainer* in the sense of innkeeper; to Gonzalo, *dollar* suggests "dolor," grief).   23 *spare:* Forbear, cease.   26-27 *Which . . . crow:* Which of the two, Gonzalo or Adrian, do you bet will speak (crow) first?   28 *old cock:* I.e., Gonzalo. 29 *cockerel:* I.e., Adrian.   31 *laughter:* (1) Burst of laughter (2) sitting of eggs. (When Adrian, the *cockerel*, begins to speak two lines later, Sebastian loses the bet. . . .)   32 *A match:* A bargain; agreed.   33 *desert:* Uninhabited.   35 *you're paid:* I.e., you've had your laugh.   39 *miss 't:* (1) Avoid saying "Yet" (2) miss the island.   40 *must needs be:* Has to be; *temperance:* Mildness of climate.   41 *Temperance:* A girl's name; *delicate:* (Here it means "given to pleasure, voluptuous"; in line 40, "pleasant." Antonio is evidently suggesting that *tender, and delicate temperance* sounds like a Puritan phrase, which Antonio then mocks by applying the words to a woman rather than an island. He began this bawdy comparison with a double entendre on *inaccessible,* line 36.)

Sebastian: Ay, and a subtle,° as he most learnedly delivered.°
Adrian: The air breathes upon us here most sweetly.
Sebastian: As if it had lungs, and rotten ones.
Antonio: Or as 'twere perfumed by a fen.   45
Gonzalo: Here is everything advantageous to life.
Antonio: True, save° means to live.
Sebastian: Of that there's none, or little.
Gonzalo: How lush and lusty° the grass looks! How green!
Antonio: The ground indeed is tawny.°   50
Sebastian: With an eye° of green in 't.
Antonio: He misses not much.
Sebastian: No. He doth but° mistake the truth totally.
Gonzalo: But the rarity of it is — which is indeed almost beyond credit —
Sebastian: As many vouched rarities° are.   55
Gonzalo: That our garments, being, as they were, drenched in the sea, hold
    notwithstanding their freshness and glosses, being rather new-dyed
    than stained with salt water.
Antonio: If but one of his pockets° could speak, would it not say he lies?
Sebastian: Ay, or very falsely pocket up° his report.°   60
Gonzalo: Methinks our garments are now as fresh as when we put them
    on first in Afric, at the marriage of the King's fair daughter Claribel to
    the King of Tunis.
Sebastian: 'Twas a sweet marriage, and we prosper well in our return.
Adrian: Tunis was never graced before with such a paragon to° their   65
    queen.
Gonzalo: Not since widow Dido's° time.
Antonio [aside to Sebastian]: Widow? A pox o' that! How came that "widow"
    in? Widow Dido!
Sebastian: What if he had said "widower Aeneas" too? Good Lord, how   70
    you take° it!
Adrian [to Gonzalo]: "Widow Dido" said you? You make me study of° that.
    She was of Carthage, not of Tunis.
Gonzalo: This Tunis, sir, was Carthage.
Adrian: Carthage?   75
Gonzalo: I assure you, Carthage.
Antonio: His word is more than the miraculous harp.°

42 *subtle:* (Here it means "tricky, sexually crafty"; in line 40, "delicate"); *delivered:* Uttered.
(Sebastian joins Antonio in baiting the Puritans with his use of the pious cant phrase
learnedly delivered.)   47 *save:* Except.   49 *lusty:* Healthy.   50 *tawny:* Dull brown, yellowish.   51 *eye:* Tinge, or spot (perhaps with reference to Gonzalo's eye or judgment).
53 *but:* Merely.   55 *vouched rarities:* Allegedly real though strange sights.   59 *pockets:*
I.e., because they are muddy.   60 *pocket up:* I.e., conceal, suppress; often used in the sense
of "receive unprotestingly, fail to respond to a challenge"; *his report:* (Sebastian's jest is that
the evidence of Gonzalo's soggy and sea-stained pockets would confute Gonzalo's speech
and his reputation for truth telling.)   65 *to:* For.   67 *widow Dido:* Queen of Carthage,
deserted by Aeneas. (She was, in fact, a widow when Aeneas, a widower, met her, but Antonio
may be amused at Gonzalo's prudish use of the term "widow" to describe a woman deserted
by her lover.)   71 *take:* Understand, respond to, interpret.   72 *study of:* Think about.
77 *miraculous harp:* (Alludes to Amphion's harp, with which he raised the walls of Thebes;
Gonzalo has exceeded that deed by recreating ancient Carthage — *wall and houses* — mistakenly on the site of modern-day Tunis. Some Renaissance commentators believed, like Gonzalo, that the two sites were near each other.)

Sebastian: He hath raised the wall, and houses too.

Antonio: What impossible matter will he make easy next?

Sebastian: I think he will carry this island home in his pocket and give it   80
his son for an apple.

Antonio: And, sowing the kernels° of it in the sea, bring forth more islands.

Gonzalo: Ay.°

Antonio: Why, in good time.°

Gonzalo [to Alonso]: Sir, we were talking° that our garments seem now as   85
fresh as when we were at Tunis at the marriage of your daughter, who
is now queen.

Antonio: And the rarest° that e'er came there.

Sebastian: Bate,° I beseech you, widow Dido.

Antonio: O, widow Dido! Ay, widow Dido.   90

Gonzalo: Is not, sir, my doublet° as fresh as the first day I wore it? I mean,
in a sort.°

Antonio: That "sort"° was well wished for.

Gonzalo: When I wore it at your daughter's marriage.

Alonso: You cram these words into mine ears against   95
The stomach of my sense.° Would I had never
Married° my daughter there! For, coming thence,
My son is lost and, in my rate,° she too,
Who is so far from Italy removed
I ne'er again shall see her. O thou mine heir   100
Of Naples and of Milan, what strange fish
Hath made his meal on thee?

Francisco: Sir, he may live.
I saw him beat the surges° under him
And ride upon their backs. He trod the water,
Whose enmity he flung aside, and breasted   105
The surge most swoll'n that met him. His bold head
'Bove the contentious waves he kept, and oared
Himself with his good arms in lusty° stroke
To th' shore, that o'er his° wave-worn basis bowed,°
As° stooping to relieve him. I not doubt   110
He came alive to land.

Alonso: No, no, he's gone.

Sebastian [to Alonso]: Sir, you may thank yourself for this great loss,
That° would not bless our Europe with your daughter,
But rather° loose° her to an African,

---

82 *kernels:* Seeds.   83 *Ay:* (Gonzalo may be reasserting his point about Carthage, or
he may be responding ironically to Antonio, who, in turn, answers sarcastically.)   84 *in
good time:* (An expression of ironical acquiescence or amazement, i.e., "sure, right away.")
85 *talking:* Saying.   88 *rarest:* Most remarkable, beautiful.   89 *Bate:* Abate, except,
leave out (Sebastian says sardonically, surely you should allow widow Dido to be an exception).   91 *doublet:* Close-fitting jacket.   92 *in a sort:* In a way.   93 *"sort":* (Antonio
plays on the idea of drawing lots and on "fishing" for something to say.)   96 *The stomach . . . sense:* My appetite for hearing them.   97 *Married:* Given in marriage.   98 *rate:*
Estimation,   opinion.   103 *surges:* Waves.   108 *lusty:* Vigorous.   109 *that . . . bowed:*
I.e., that projected out over the base of the cliff that had been eroded by the surf, thus
seeming to bend down toward the sea; *his:* Its.   110 *As:* As if.   113 *That:* You who.
114 *rather:* Would rather; *loose:* (1) Release, let loose (2) lose.

Where she at least is banished from your eye,° 115
Who hath cause to wet the grief on 't.°
Alonso: Prithee, peace.
Sebastian: You were kneeled to and importuned° otherwise
By all of us, and the fair soul herself
Weighed between loathness and obedience at
Which end o' the beam should bow.° We have lost your son, 120
I fear, forever. Milan and Naples have
More widows in them of this business' making°
Than we bring men to comfort them.
The fault's your own.
Alonso: So is the dear'st° o' the loss. 125
Gonzalo: My lord Sebastian,
The truth you speak doth lack some gentleness
And time° to speak it in. You rub the sore
When you should bring the plaster.°
Sebastian: Very well.
Antonio: And most chirurgeonly.° 130
Gonzalo [to Alonso]: It is foul weather in us all, good sir,
When you are cloudy.
Sebastian [to Antonio]: Fowl° weather?
Antonio [to Sebastian]: Very foul.
Gonzalo: Had I plantation° of this isle, my lord —
Antonio [to Sebastian]: He'd sow 't with nettle seed.
Sebastian: Or docks, or mallows.°
Gonzalo: And were the king on 't, what would I do? 135
Sebastian: Scape° being drunk for want° of wine.
Gonzalo: I' the commonwealth I would by contraries°
Execute all things; for no kind of traffic,°
Would I admit; no name of magistrate,
Letters° should not be known; riches, poverty, 140
And use of service,° none; contract, succession,°
Bourn, bound of land, tilth,° vineyard, none;
No use of metal, corn,° or wine, or oil;

---

115 *is banished from your eye:* Is not constantly before your eye to serve as a reproachful reminder of what you have done. 116 *Who . . . on 't:* I.e., your eye, which has good reason to weep because of this, or, Claribel, who has good reason to weep for it. 117 *importuned:* Urged, implored. 118-120 *the fair . . . bow:* Claribel herself was poised uncertainly between unwillingness to marry and obedience to her father as to which end of the scales should sink, which should prevail. 122 *of . . . making:* On account of this marriage and subsequent shipwreck. 125 *dear'st:* Heaviest, most costly. 128 *time:* Appropriate time. 129 *plaster:* (A medical application.) 130 *chirurgeonly:* Like a skilled surgeon. (Antonio mocks Gonzalo's medical analogy of a *plaster* applied curatively to a wound.) 132 *Fowl:* (With a pun on *foul,* returning to the imagery of lines 26-29.) 133 *plantation:* Colonization (with subsequent wordplay on the literal meaning, "planting"). 134 *docks, mallows:* (Weeds used as antidotes for nettle stings.) 136 *Scape:* Escape; *want:* Lack. (Sebastian jokes sarcastically that this hypothetical ruler would be saved from dissipation only by the barrenness of the island.) 137 *contraries:* By what is directly opposite to usual custom. 138 *traffic:* Trade. 140 *Letters:* Learning. 141 *use of service:* Custom of employing servants; *succession:* Holding of property by right of inheritance. 142 *Bourn . . . tilth:* Boundaries, property limits, tillage of soil. 143 *corn:* Grain.

No occupation; all men idle, all,
And women too, but innocent and pure;   145
No sovereignty —
Sebastian: Yet he would be king on 't.
Antonio: The latter end of his commonwealth forgets the beginning.
Gonzalo: All things in common nature should produce
   Without sweat or endeavor. Treason, felony,
   Sword, pike,° knife, gun, or need of any engine°   150
   Would I not have; but nature should bring forth,
   Of its own kind, all foison,° all abundance,
   To feed my innocent people.
Sebastian: No marrying 'mong his subjects?
Antonio: None, man, all idle — whores and knaves.   155
Gonzalo: I would with such perfection govern, sir,
   T' excel the Golden Age.°
Sebastian: 'Save° His Majesty!
Antonio: Long live Gonzalo!
Gonzalo: And — do you mark me, sir?
Alonso: Prithee, no more. Thou dost talk nothing to me.
Gonzalo: I do well believe Your Highness, and did it to minister occasion° 160
   to these gentlemen, who are of such sensible° and nimble lungs that
   they always use° to laugh at nothing.
Antonio: 'Twas you we laughed at.
Gonzalo: Who in this kind of merry fooling am nothing to you; so you
   may continue, and laugh at nothing still.   165
Antonio: What a blow was there given!
Sebastian: An° it had not fallen flat-long.°
Gonzalo: You are gentlemen of brave mettle;° you would lift the moon
   out of her sphere° if she would continue in it five weeks without
   changing.   170

   Enter Ariel [invisible] playing solemn music.

Sebastian: We would so, and then go a-batfowling.°
Antonio: Nay, good my lord, be not angry.
Gonzalo: No, I warrant you, I will not adventure my discretion so weakly.°
   Will you laugh me asleep? For I am very heavy.°
Antonio: Go sleep, and hear us.°   175

---

150 *pike:* Lance; *engine:* Instrument of warfare.   152 *foison:* Plenty.   157 *the Golden Age:*
The age, according to Hesiod, when Cronus, or Saturn, ruled the world; an age of innocence
and abundance; *'Save:* God save.   160 *minister occasion:* Furnish opportunity.   161 *sensible:* Sensitive.   162 *use:* Are accustomed.   167 *An:* If; *flat-long:* With the flat of the
sword, i.e., ineffectually. (Compare with "fallen flat.")   168 *mettle:* Temperament, courage.
(The sense of *metal,* indistinguishable as a form from *mettle,* continues the metaphor of the
sword.)   169 *sphere:* Orbit (literally, one of the concentric zones occupied by planets in
Ptolemaic astronomy).   171 *a-batfowling:* Hunting birds at night with lantern and *bat,* or
"stick"; also, gulling a simpleton (Gonzalo is the simpleton, or fowl, and Sebastian will use the
moon as his lantern).   173 *adventure ... weakly:* Risk my reputation for discretion for so
trivial a cause (by getting angry at these sarcastic fellows).   174 *heavy:* Sleepy.   175 *Go ...
us:* I.e., get ready for sleep, and we'll do our part by laughing.

[All sleep except Alonso, Sebastian, and Antonio.]

Alonso: What, all so soon asleep? I wish mine eyes
    Would, with themselves, shut up my thoughts.° I find
    They are inclined to do so.
Sebastian: Please you, sir,
    Do not omit° the heavy° offer of it.
    It seldom visits sorrow; when it doth,   180
    It is a comforter.
Antonio: We two, my lord,
    Will guard your person while you take your rest,
    And watch your safety.
Alonso: Thank you. Wondrous heavy.
                        [Alonso sleeps. Exit Ariel.]
Sebastian: What a strange drowsiness possesses them!
Antonio: It is the quality o' the climate.
Sebastian: Why   185
    Doth it not then our eyelids sink? I find not
    Myself disposed to sleep.
Antonio: Nor I. My spirits are nimble.
    They° fell together all, as by consent;°
    They dropped, as by a thunderstroke. What might,
    Worthy Sebastian, O, what might—? No more.   190
    And yet methinks I see it in thy face,
    What thou shouldst be. Th' occasion speaks thee,° and
    My strong imagination sees a crown
    Dropping upon thy head.
Sebastian: What, art thou waking?
Antonio: Do you not hear me speak?
Sebastian: I do, and surely   195
    It is a sleepy° language, and thou speak'st
    Out of thy sleep. What is it thou didst say?
    This is a strange repose, to be asleep
    With eyes wide open—standing, speaking, moving—
    And yet so fast asleep.
Antonio: Noble Sebastian,   200
    Thou lett'st thy fortune sleep—die, rather; wink'st°
    Whiles thou art waking.
Sebastian: Thou dost snore distinctly;°
    There's meaning in thy snores.
Antonio: I am more serious than my custom. You
    Must be so too if heed° me, which to do   205
    Trebles thee o'er.°
Sebastian: Well, I am standing water.°

---

177 *Would . . . thoughts:* Would shut off my melancholy brooding when they close themselves
in sleep.   179 *omit:* Neglect; *heavy:* Drowsy.   188 *They:* The sleepers; *consent:* Common
agreement.   192 *occasion speaks thee:* Opportunity of the moment calls upon you, i.e., proclaims you usurper of Alonso's crown.   196 *sleepy:* Dreamlike, fantastic.   201 *wink'st:*
(You) shut your eyes.   202 *distinctly:* Articulately.   205 *if heed:* If you heed.   206 *Trebles
thee o'er:* Makes you three times as great and rich; *standing water:* Water that neither ebbs nor
flows, at a standstill.

Antonio: I'll teach you how to flow.
Sebastian: Do so. To ebb°
    Hereditary sloth° instructs me.
Antonio: O,
    If you but knew how you the purpose cherish
    Whiles thus you mock it!° How, in stripping it,   210
    You more invest° it!° Ebbing men, indeed,
    Most often do so near the bottom° run
    By their own fear or sloth.
Sebastian: Prithee, say on.
    The setting° of thine eye and cheek proclaim
    A matter° from thee, and a birth indeed   215
    Which throes° thee much to yield.°
Antonio: Thus, sir:
    Although this lord° of weak remembrance,° this
    Who shall be of as little memory
    When he is earthed,° hath here almost persuaded —
    For he's a spirit of persuasion, only   220
    Professes to persuade° — the King his son's alive,
    'Tis as impossible that he's undrowned
    As he that sleeps here swims.
Sebastian: I have no hope
    That he's undrowned.
Antonio: O, out of that "no hope"
    What great hope have you! No hope that way° is   225
    Another way so high a hope that even
    Ambition cannot pierce a wink° beyond,
    But doubt discovery there.° Will you grant with me
    That Ferdinand is drowned?
Sebastian: He's gone.
Antonio: Then tell me,   230
    Who's the next heir of Naples?
Sebastian: Claribel.
Antonio: She that is Queen of Tunis; she that dwells
    Ten leagues beyond man's life;° she that from Naples

---

207 *ebb:* Recede, decline.   208 *Hereditary sloth:* Natural laziness and the position of
younger brother, one who cannot inherit.   209-210 *If . . . mock it:* If you only knew how
much you really enhance the value of ambition even while your words mock your purpose.
210-211 *How . . . invest it:* I.e., how the more you speak flippantly of ambition, the more you,
in effect, affirm it; *invest:* Clothe (Antonio's paradox is that, by skeptically stripping away
illusions, Sebastian can see the essence of a situation and the opportunity it presents or
that, by disclaiming and deriding his purpose, Sebastian shows how valuable it really is).
212 *the bottom:* I.e., on which unadventurous men may go aground and miss the tide of fortune.   214 *setting:* Set expression (of earnestness).   215 *matter:* Matter of importance.
216 *throes:* Causes pain, as in giving birth; *yield:* Give forth, speak about.   217 *this lord:*
I.e., Gonzalo; *remembrance:* (1) Power of remembering (2) being remembered after his death.
219 *earthed:* Buried.   220-221 *only . . . persuade:* Whose whole function (as a privy councillor) is to persuade.   225 *that way:* I.e., in regard to Ferdinand's being saved.   227 *wink:*
Glimpse.   227-228 *Ambition . . . there:* Ambition itself cannot see any further than that
hope (of the crown), is unsure of finding anything to achieve beyond it or even there.
233 *Ten . . . life:* I.e., further than the journey of a lifetime.

Can have no note,° unless the sun were post°—
The Man i' the Moon's too slow—till newborn chins   235
Be rough and razorable;° she that from° whom
We all were sea-swallowed, though some cast° again,
And by that destiny to perform an act
Whereof what's past is prologue, what to come
In yours and my discharge.°   240

Sebastian: What stuff is this? How say you?
    'Tis true my brother's daughter's Queen of Tunis,
So is she heir of Naples, twixt which regions
There is some space.

Antonio: A space whose every cubit°
    Seems to cry out, "How shall that Claribel   245
Measure us° back to Naples? Keep° in Tunis,
And let Sebastian wake."° Say this were death
That now hath seized them, why, they were no worse
Than now they are. There be° that can rule Naples
As well as he that sleeps, lords that can prate°   250
As amply and unnecessarily
As this Gonzalo. I myself could make
A chough of as deep chat.° O, that you bore
The mind that I do! What a sleep were this
For your advancement! Do you understand me?   255

Sebastian: Methinks I do.

Antonio: And how does your content°
    Tender° your own good fortune?

Sebastian: I remember
You did supplant your brother Prospero.

Antonio: True.
And look how well my garments sit upon me,
Much feater° than before. My brother's servants   260
Were then my fellows. Now they are my men.

Sebastian: But, for your conscience?

Antonio: Ay, sir, where lies that? If 'twere a kibe,°
'Twould put me to° my slipper; but I feel not
This deity in my bosom. Twenty consciences   265
That stand twixt me and Milan,° candied° be they°
And melt ere they molest!° Here lies your brother,
No better than the earth he lies upon,
If he were that which now he's like—that's dead,

---

234 *note:* News, intimation; *post:* Messenger.   236 *razorable:* Ready for shaving; *from:* On our voyage from.   237 *cast:* Were disgorged (with a pun on *casting* of parts for a play). 240 *discharge:* Performance.   244 *cubit:* Ancient measure of length of about twenty inches. 246 *Measure us:* I.e., traverse the cubits, find her way; *Keep:* Stay (addressed to Claribel). 247 *wake:* I.e., to his good fortune.   249 *There be:* There are those.   250 *prate:* Speak foolishly.   252–253 *I . . . chat:* I could teach a jackdaw to talk as wisely, or, be such a garrulous talker myself.   256 *content:* Desire, inclination.   257 *Tender:* Regard, look after. 260 *feater:* More becomingly, fittingly.   263 *kibe:* Chilblain, here a sore on the heel. 264 *put me to:* Oblige me to wear.   266 *Milan:* The dukedom of Milan; *candied:* Frozen, congealed in crystalline form; *be they:* May they be.   267 *molest:* Interfere.

Whom I, with this obedient steel, three inches of it,   270
Can lay to bed forever; whiles you, doing thus,°
To the perpetual wink° for aye° might put
This ancient morsel, this Sir Prudence, who
Should not° upbraid our course. For all the rest,
They'll take suggestion° as a cat laps milk;   275
They'll tell the clock° to any business that
We say befits the hour.
Sebastian: Thy case, dear friend,
Shall be my precedent. As thou gott'st Milan,
I'll come by Naples. Draw thy sword. One stroke
Shall free thee from the tribute° which thou payest,   280
And I the king shall love thee.
Antonio: Draw together;
And when I rear my hand, do you the like
To fall it° on Gonzalo.   *[They draw.]*
Sebastian: O, but one word.   *[They talk apart.]*

Enter Ariel [invisible], with music and song.

Ariel [to Gonzalo]: My master through his art foresees the danger
That you, his friend, are in, and sends me forth —   285
For else his project dies — to keep them living.   *Sings in Gonzalo's ear.*
            While you here do snoring lie,
            Open-eyed conspiracy
                His time° doth take.
            If of life you keep a care,   290
            Shake off slumber, and beware.
                Awake, awake!
Antonio: Then let us both be sudden.°
Gonzalo [waking]: Now, good angels preserve the King!   *[The others wake.]*
Alonso: Why, how now, ho, awake? Why are you drawn?   295
Wherefore this ghastly looking?
Gonzalo: What's the matter?
Sebastian: Whiles we stood here securing° your repose,
Even now, we heard a hollow burst of bellowing
Like bulls, or rather lions. Did 't not wake you?
It struck mine ear most terribly.
Alonso: I heard nothing.   300
Antonio: O, 'twas a din to fright a monster's ear,
To make an earthquake! Sure it was the roar
Of a whole herd of lions.
Alonso: Heard you this, Gonzalo?
Gonzalo: Upon mine honor, sir. I heard a humming,   305
And that a strange one too, which did awake me.
I shaked you, sir, and cried.° As mine eyes opened,

271 *thus:* Similarly. (The actor makes a stabbing gesture.)   272 *wink:* Sleep, closing of eyes;
aye: Ever.   274 *Should not:* Would not then be able to.   275 *take suggestion:* Respond to
prompting.   276 *tell the clock:* I.e., agree, answer appropriately, chime.   280 *tribute:*
(See I.ii.113, 124.)   283 *fall it:* Let it fall.   289 *time:* Opportunity.   293 *sudden:* Quick.
297 *securing:* Standing guard over.   307 *cried:* Called out.

I saw their weapons drawn. There was a noise,
That's verily.° 'Tis best we stand upon our guard,
Or that we quit this place. Let's draw our weapons.   310
Alonso: Lead off this ground, and let's make further search
For my poor son.
Gonzalo: Heavens keep him from these beasts!
For he is, sure, i' th' island.
Alonso: Lead away.
Ariel [aside]: Prospero my lord shall know what I have done.
So, King, go safely on to seek thy son.   *Exeunt [separately].*   315

[Scene II: *Another part of the island.*]

Enter Caliban with a burden of wood. A noise of thunder heard.

Caliban: All the infections that the sun sucks up
From bogs, fens, flats,° on Prosper fall, and make him
By inchmeal° a disease! His spirits hear me,
And yet I needs must° curse. But they'll nor° pinch,
Fright me with urchin shows,° pitch me i' the mire,   5
Nor lead me, like a firebrand,° in the dark
Out of my way, unless he bid 'em. But
For every trifle are they set upon me,
Sometimes like apes, that mow° and chatter at me
And after bite me; then like hedgehogs, which   10
Lie tumbling in my barefoot way and mount
Their pricks at my footfall. Sometimes am I
All wound with° adders, who with cloven tongues
Do hiss me into madness.

Enter Trinculo.

                        Lo, now, lo!
Here comes a spirit of his, and to torment me   15
For bringing wood in slowly. I'll fall flat.
Perchance he will not mind° me.   *[He lies down.]*
Trinculo: Here's neither bush nor shrub to bear off° any weather at all.
And another storm brewing; I hear it sing i' the wind. Yond same
black cloud, yond huge one, looks like a foul bombard° that would   20
shed his° liquor. If it should thunder as it did before, I know not
where to hide my head. Yond same cloud cannot choose but fall by
pailfuls. *[Seeing Caliban.]* What have we here, a man or a fish? Dead or
alive? A fish, he smells like a fish; a very ancient and fishlike smell; a
kind of not-of-the-newest Poor John.° A strange fish! Were I in Eng-   25
land now, as once I was, and had but this fish painted,° not a holi-

309 *verily:* True.   **Scene II.**   2 *flats:* Swamps.   3 *By inchmeal:* Inch by inch.   4 *needs must:* Have to; *nor:* Neither.   5 *urchin shows:* Elvish apparitions shaped like hedgehogs. 6 *like a firebrand:* They in the guise of a will-o'-the-wisp.   9 *mow:* Make faces.   13 *wound with:* Entwined by.   17 *mind:* Notice.   18 *bear off:* Keep off.   20 *foul bombard:* Dirty leather jug.   21 *his:* Its.   25 *Poor John:* Salted fish, type of poor fare.   26 *painted:* I.e., painted on a sign set up outside a booth or tent at a fair.

day fool there but would give a piece of silver. There would this
monser make a man.° Any strange beast there makes a man. When
they will not give a doit° to relieve a lame beggar, they will lay out ten
to see a dead Indian. Legged like a man, and his fins like arms! Warm,   30
o' my troth!° I do now let loose my opinion, hold it° no longer: this is
no fish, but an islander, that hath lately suffered° by a thunderbolt.
[Thunder.] Alas, the storm is come again! My best way is to creep
under his gaberdine.° There is no other shelter hereabout. Misery ac-
quaints a man with strange bedfellows. I will here shroud° till the   35
dregs° of the storm be past.   *[He creeps under Caliban's garment.]*

Enter Stephano, singing, [a bottle in his hand].

Stephano: "I shall no more to sea, to sea,
         Here shall I die ashore —"
This is a very scurvy tune to sing at a man's funeral.
Well, here's my comfort.   *Drinks.* 40
(Sings.)
         "The master, the swabber,° the boatswain, and I,
            The gunner and his mate,
         Loved Mall, Meg, and Marian, and Margery,
            But none of us cared for Kate.
               For she had a tongue with a tang,°   45
               Would cry to a sailor, 'Go hang!'
         She loved not the savor of tar nor of pitch,
         Yet a tailor might scratch her where'er she did itch.°
            Then to sea, boys, and let her go hang!"
This is a scurvy tune too. But here's my comfort.   *Drinks.* 50
Caliban: Do not torment me!° O!
Stephano: What's the matter?° Have we devils here? Do you put tricks
   upon 's° with savages and men of Ind,° ha? I have not scaped drowning to be afeard now of your four legs. For it hath been said, "As
   proper° a man as ever went on four legs° cannot make him give   55
   ground"; and it shall be said so again while Stephano breathes at'°
   nostrils.
Caliban: This spirit torments me! O!
Stephano: This is some monster of the isle with four legs, who hath got,
   as I take it, an ague.° Where the devil should he learn° our language? I   60
   will give him some relief, if it be but for that.° If I can recover° him

---

28 *make a man:* (1) Make one's fortune (2) be indistinguishable from an Englishman.
29 *doit:* Small coin.   31 *o' my troth:* By my faith; *hold it:* Hold it in.   32 *suffered:* I.e.,
died.   34 *gaberdine:* Cloak, loose upper garment.   35 *shroud:* Take shelter.   36 *dregs:*
I.e., last remains (as in a *bombard* or jug, line 20).   41 *swabber:* Crew member whose job is
to wash the decks.   45 *tang:* Sting.   48 *tailor . . . itch:* (A dig at tailors for their supposed
effeminacy and a bawdy suggestion of satisfying a sexual craving.)   51 *Do . . . me:* (Caliban
assumes that one of Prospero's spirits has come to punish him.)   52 *What's the matter?:*
What's going on here?   52–53 *put tricks upon 's:* Trick us with conjuring shows.   53 *Ind:*
India.   55 *proper:* Handsome; *four legs:* (The conventional phrase would supply *two* legs,
but the creature Stephano thinks he sees has four.)   56 *at':* At the.   60 *ague:* Fever.
(Probably both Caliban and Trinculo are quaking; see lines 71 and 97.); *should he learn:* Could
he have learned.   61 *for that:* I.e., for knowing our language; *recover:* Restore.

and keep him tame and get to Naples with him, he's a present for any
emperor that ever trod on neat's leather.°
Caliban: Do not torment me, prithee. I'll bring my wood home faster.
Stephano: He's in his fit now and does not talk after the wisest.° He shall   65
taste of my bottle. If he have never drunk wine afore,° it will go near
to° remove his fit. If I can recover° him and keep him tame, I will not
take too much° for him. He shall pay for him that hath° him,° and
that soundly.
Caliban: Thou dost me yet but little hurt; thou wilt anon,° I know it by thy   70
trembling. Now Prosper works upon thee.
Stephano: Come on your ways. Open your mouth. Here is that which will
give language to you, cat. Open your mouth.° This will shake your
shaking, I can tell you, and that soundly. *[Giving Caliban a drink.]* You
cannot tell who's your friend. Open your chaps° again.   75
Trinculo: I should know that voice. It should be — but he is drowned, and
these are devils. O, defend me!
Stephano: Four legs and two voices — a most delicate° monster! His forward voice now is to speak well of his friend; his backward voice° is to
utter foul speeches and to detract. If all the wine in my bottle will re-   80
cover him,° I will help° his ague. Come. *[Giving a drink.]* Amen! I
will pour some in thy other mouth.
Trinculo: Stephano!
Stephano: Doth thy other mouth call me?° Mercy, mercy! This is a devil,
and no monster. I will leave him. I have no long spoon.°   85
Trinculo: Stephano! If thou beest Stephano, touch me and speak to me,
for I am Trinculo — be not afeard — thy good friend Trinculo.
Stephano: If thou beest Trinculo, come forth. I'll pull thee by the lesser
legs. If any be Trinculo's legs, these are they. *[Pulling him out.]* Thou
art very Trinculo indeed! How cam'st thou to be the siege° of this   90
mooncalf?° Can he vent° Trinculos?
Trinculo: I took him to be killed with a thunderstroke. But art thou not
drowned, Stephano? I hope now thou art not drowned. Is the storm
overblown?° I hid me under the dead mooncalf's gaberdine for fear
of the storm. And art thou living, Stephano? O Stephano, two   95
Neapolitans scaped!   *[He capers with Stephano.]*
Stephano: Prithee, do not turn me about. My stomach is not constant.°
Caliban: These be fine things, an if° they be not spirits.

---

63 *neat's leather:* Cowhide.   65 *after the wisest:* In the wisest fashion.   66 *afore:* Before.
66–67 *go near to:* Be in a fair way to.   67 *recover:* Restore.   67–68 *I will... much:* I.e., no
sum can be too much.   68 *He shall... hath him:* I.e., anyone who wants him will have to
pay dearly for him; *hath:* Possesses, receives.   70 *anon:* Presently.   73 *cat... mouth:* (Allusion to the proverb "Good liquor will make a cat speak.")   75 *chaps:* Jaws.   78 *delicate:*
Ingenious.   79 *backward voice:* (Trinculo and Caliban are facing in opposite directions.
Stephano supposes the monster to have a rear end that can emit *foul speeches* or foul-smelling
wind at the monster's *other mouth,* line 84.)   80–81 *If... him:* Even if it takes all the wine in
my bottle to cure him.   81 *help:* Cure.   84 *call me:* I.e., call me by name, know supernat-
urally who I am.   85 *long spoon:* (Allusion to the proverb "He that sups with the devil has
need of a long spoon.")   90 *siege:* Excrement.   91 *mooncalf:* Monstrous or misshapen
creature (whose deformity is caused by the malignant influence of the moon); *vent:* Excrete,
defecate.   94 *overblown:* Blown over.   97 *not constant:* Unsteady.   98 *an if:* If.

That's a brave° god, and bears° celestial liquor.
I will kneel to him.   100
Stephano: How didst thou scape? How cam'st thou hither? Swear by this
bottle how thou cam'st hither. I escaped upon a butt of sack° which
the sailors heaved o'erboard — by this bottle,° which I made of the
bark of a tree with mine own hands since° I was cast ashore.
Caliban [kneeling]: I'll swear upon that bottle to be thy true subject, for the   105
liquor is not earthly.
Stephano: Here. Swear then how thou escapedst.
Trinculo: Swum ashore, man, like a duck. I can swim like a duck, I'll be
sworn.
Stephano: Here, kiss the book.° Though thou canst swim like a duck, thou   110
art made like a goose.   *[Giving him a drink.]*
Trinculo: O Stephano, hast any more of this?
Stephano: The whole butt, man. My cellar is in a rock by the seaside, where
my wine is hid. — How now, mooncalf? How does thine ague?
Caliban: Hast thou not dropped from heaven?   115
Stephano: Out o' the moon, I do assure thee. I was the Man i' the Moon
when time was.°
Caliban: I have seen thee in her, and I do adore thee. My mistress showed
me thee, and thy dog, and thy bush.°
Stephano: Come, swear to that. Kiss the book. I will furnish it anon with   120
new contents. Swear.   *[Giving him a drink.]*
Trinculo: By this good light,° this is a very shallow monster! I afeard of
him? A very weak monster! The Man i' the Moon? A most poor credu-
lous monster! Well drawn,° monster, in good sooth!°
Caliban [to Stephano]: I'll show thee every fertile inch o' th' island, And I   125
will kiss thy foot. I prithee, be my god.
Trinculo: By this light, a most perfidious and drunken monster! When 's
god's asleep, he'll rob his bottle.°
Caliban: I'll kiss thy foot. I'll swear myself thy subject.
Stephano: Come on then. Down, and swear.   *[Caliban kneels.]*   130
Trinculo: I shall laugh myself to death at this puppy-headed monster. A
most scurvy monster! I could find in my heart to beat him —
Stephano: Come, kiss.
Trinculo: But that the poor monster's in drink.° An abominable monster!
Caliban: I'll show thee the best springs. I'll pluck thee berries.   135
I'll fish for thee and get thee wood enough.
A plague upon the tyrant that I serve!
I'll bear him no more sticks, but follow thee,
Thou wondrous man.

99 *brave:* Fine, magnificent; *bears:* He carries.   102 *butt of sack:* Barrel of Canary wine.
103 *by this bottle:* I.e., I swear by this bottle.   104 *since:* After.   110 *book:* I.e., bottle (but
with ironic reference to the practice of kissing the Bible in swearing an oath; see *I'll be sworn*
in lines 108–109).   117 *when time was:* Once upon a time.   119 *dog . . . bush:* (The Man
in the Moon was popularly imagined to have with him a dog and a bush of thorn.)
122 *By . . . light:* By God's light, by this good light from heaven.   124 *Well drawn:* Well
pulled (on the bottle); *in good sooth:* Truly, indeed.   127–128 *When . . . bottle:* I.e., Caliban
wouldn't even stop at robbing his god of his bottle if he could catch him asleep.   134 *in
drink:* Drunk.

Trinculo: A most ridiculous monster, to make a   140
    wonder of a poor drunkard!
Caliban: I prithee, let me bring thee where crabs° grow,
    And I with my long nails will dig thee pignuts,°
    Show thee a jay's nest, and instruct thee how
    To snare the nimble marmoset.° I'll bring thee   145
    To clustering filberts, and sometimes I'll get thee
    Young scamels° from the rock. Wilt thou go with me?
Stephano: I prithee now, lead the way without any more talking.—Trin-
    culo, the King and all our company else° being drowned, we will
    inherit° here.—Here, bear my bottle.—Fellow Trinculo, we'll fill him   150
    by and by again.
Caliban (sings drunkenly): Farewell, master, farewell, farewell!
Trinculo: A howling monster; a drunken monster!
Caliban: No more dams I'll make for fish,
    Nor fetch in firing°   155
      At requiring,
   Nor scrape trenchering,° nor wash dish.
     'Ban, 'Ban, Ca–Caliban
    Has a new master. Get a new man!°
  Freedom, high-day! High-day,° freedom! Freedom, high-day, freedom!   160
Stephano: O brave monster! Lead the way.   *Exeunt.*

[ACT III

SCENE I: *Before Prospero's cell.*]

Enter Ferdinand, bearing a log.

Ferdinand: There be some sports are painful, and their labor
    Delight in them sets off.° Some kinds of baseness°
    Are nobly undergone,° and most poor° matters
    Point to rich ends. This my mean° task
    Would be as heavy to me as odious, but°   5
    The mistress which I serve quickens° what's dead
    And makes my labors pleasures. O, she is
    Ten times more gentle than her father's crabbed,
    And he's composed of harshness. I must remove

142 *crabs:* Crab apples, or perhaps crabs.   143 *pignuts:* Earthnuts, edible tuberous roots.
145 *marmoset:* Small monkey.   147 *scamels:* (Possibly *seamews,* mentioned in Strachey's letter, or shellfish, or perhaps from *squamelle,* "furnished with little scales." Contemporary
French and Italian travel accounts report that the natives of Patagonia in South America ate
small fish described as *fort scameux* and *squame.*)   149 *else:* In addition, besides ourselves.
150 *inherit:* Take possession.   155 *firing:* Firewood.   157 *trenchering:* Trenchers, wooden
plates.   159 *Get a new man:* (Addressed to Prospero.)   160 *high-day:* Holiday.   **Act III,
Scene I.** 1-2 *There . . . sets off:* Some pastimes are laborious, but the pleasure we get from
them compensates for the effort. (Pleasure is *set off* by labor as a jewel is set off by its foil.)
2 *baseness:* Menial activity.   3 *undergone:* Undertaken; *most poor:* Poorest.   4 *mean:* Lowly.
5 *but:* Were it not that.   6 *quickens:* Gives life to.

Some thousands of these logs and pile them up,   10
Upon a sore injunction.° My sweet mistress
Weeps when she sees me work and says such baseness
Had never like executor.° I forget;°
But these sweet thoughts do even refresh my labors,
Most busy lest when I do it.°

Enter Miranda; and Prospero [at a distance, unseen].

Miranda: Alas now, pray you,   15
Work not so hard. I would the lightning had
Burnt up those logs that you are enjoined° to pile!
Pray, set it down and rest you. When this° burns,
'Twill weep° for having wearied you. My father
Is hard at study. Pray now, rest yourself.   20
He's safe for these° three hours.
Ferdinand: O most dear mistress,
The sun will set before I shall discharge°
What I must strive to do.
Miranda: If you'll sit down,
I'll bear your logs the while. Pray, give me that.
I'll carry it to the pile.
Ferdinand: No, precious creature,   25
I had rather crack my sinews, break my back,
Than you should such dishonor undergo
While I sit lazy by.
Miranda: It would become me
As well as it does you; and I should do it
With much more ease, for my good will is to it,   30
And yours it is against.
Prospero [aside]:   Poor worm, thou art infected!
This visitation° shows it.
Miranda: You look wearily.
Ferdinand: No, noble mistress, 'tis fresh morning with me
When you are by° at night. I do beseech you —
Chiefly that I might set it in my prayers —   35
What is your name?
Miranda: Miranda. — O my father,
I have broke your hest° to say so.
Ferdinand: Admired Miranda!°
Indeed the top of admiration, worth
What's dearest° to the world! Full many a lady
I have eyed with best regard,° and many a time   40

---

11 *sore injunction:* Severe command.   13 *Had . . . executor:* I.e., was never before undertaken
by so noble a being; *I forget:* I.e., I forget that I'm supposed to be working, or, I forget my
happiness, oppressed by my labor.   15 *Most . . . it:* I.e., busy at my labor but with my mind
on other things (?) (the line may be in need of emendation).   17 *enjoined:* Commanded.
18 *this:* I.e., the log.   19 *weep:* I.e., exude resin.   21 *these:* The next.   22 *discharge:* Complete.   32 *visitation:* (1) Miranda's visit to Ferdinand (2) visitation of the plague, i.e., infec-
tion of love.   34 *by:* Nearby.   37 *hest:* Command; *Admired Miranda:* (Her name means "to
be admired or wondered at.")   39 *dearest:* Most treasured.   40 *best regard:* Thoughtful
and approving attention.

    The harmony of their tongues hath into bondage
    Brought my too diligent° ear. For several° virtues
    Have I liked several women, never any
    With so full soul but some defect in her
    Did quarrel with the noblest grace she owed°   45
    And put it to the foil.° But you, O you,
    So perfect and so peerless, are created
    Of° every creature's best!
Miranda: I do not know
    One of my sex; no woman's face remember,
    Save, from my glass, mine own. Nor have I seen   50
    More that I may call men than you, good friend,
    And my dear father. How features are abroad°
    I am skilless° of; but, by my modesty,°
    The jewel in my dower, I would not wish
    Any companion in the world but you;   55
    Nor can imagination form a shape,
    Besides yourself, to like of.° But I prattle
    Something° too wildly, and my father's precepts
    I therein do forget.
Ferdinand: I am in my condition°
    A prince, Miranda; I do think, a king—   60
    I would, not so!—and would° no more endure
    This wooden slavery° than to suffer
    The flesh-fly° blow° my mouth. Hear my soul speak:
    The very instant that I saw you did
    My heart fly to your service, there resides   65
    To make me slave to it, and for your sake
    Am I this patient long-man.
Miranda: Do you love me?
Ferdinand: O heaven, O earth, bear witness to this sound,
    And crown what I profess with kind event°
    If I speak true! If hollowly,° invert°   70
    What best is boded° me to mischief!° I
    Beyond all limit of what° else i' the world
    Do love, prize, honor you.
Miranda [weeping]:   I am a fool
    To weep at what I am glad of.
Prospero [aside]:   Fair encounter
    Of two most rare affections! Heavens rain grace   75
    On that which breeds between 'em!
Ferdinand: Wherefore weep you?

---

42 *diligent:* Attentive; *several:* Various (also on line 43).   45 *owed:* Owned.   46 *put . . . foil:* (1) Overthrew it (as in wrestling) (2) served as a *foil,* or "contrast," to set it off.   48 *Of:* Out of.   52 *How . . . abroad:* What people look like in other places.   53 *skilless:* Ignorant; *modesty:* Virginity.   57 *like of:* Be pleased with, be fond of.   58 *Something:* Somewhat. 59 *condition:* Rank.   61 *would:* Wish (it were).   62 *wooden slavery:* Being compelled to carry wood.   63 *flesh-fly:* Insect that deposits its eggs in dead flesh; *blow:* Befoul with fly eggs.   69 *kind event:* Favorable outcome.   70 *hollowly:* Insincerely, falsely; *invert:* Turn. 71 *boded:* In store for; *mischief:* Harm.   72 *what:* Whatever.

Miranda: At mine unworthiness, that dare not offer
    What I desire to give, and much less take
    What I shall die° to want.° But this is trifling,
    And all the more it seeks to hide itself   80
    The bigger bulk it shows. Hence, bashful cunning,°
    And prompt me, plain and holy innocence!
    I am your wife, if you will marry me;
    If not, I'll die your maid.° To be your fellow°
    You may deny me, but I'll be your servant   85
    Whether you will° or no.
Ferdinand: My mistress,° dearest,
    And I thus humble ever.
Miranda: My husband, then?
Ferdinand: Ay, with a heart as willing°
    As bondage e'er of freedom. Here's my hand.   90
Miranda [clasping his hand]: And mine, with my heart in 't. And now farewell
    Till half an hour hence.
Ferdinand: A thousand thousand!°
                 Exeunt [Ferdinand and Miranda, separately].
Prospero: So glad of this as they I cannot be,
    Who are surprised with all;° but my rejoicing
    At nothing can be more. I'll to my book,   95
    For yet ere suppertime must I perform
    Much business appertaining.°   *Exit.*

[**Scene II**: *Another part of the island.*]

   Enter Caliban, Stephano, and Trinculo.

Stephano: Tell not me. When the butt is out,° we will drink water, not a
    drop before. Therefore bear up and board 'em.° Servant monster,
    drink to me.
Trinculo: Servant monster? The folly of° this island! They say there's but
    five upon this isle. We are three of them; if th' other two be brained°   5
    like us, the state totters.
Stephano: Drink, servant monster, when I bid thee. Thy eyes are almost
    set° in thy head.   *[Giving a drink.]*
Trinculo: Where should they be set° else? He were a brave° monster indeed
    if they were set in his tail.   10
Stephano: My man-monster hath drowned his tongue in sack. For my
    part, the sea cannot drown me. I swam, ere I could recover° the shore,

79 *die:* (Probably with an unconscious sexual meaning that underlies all of lines 77–81.); *to want:* Through lacking.   81 *bashful cunning:* Coyness.   84 *maid:* Handmaiden, servant; *fellow:* Mate, equal.   86 *will:* Desire it; *My mistress:* I.e., the woman I adore and serve (not an illicit sexual partner).   89 *willing:* Desirous.   92 *A thousand thousand:* I.e., a thousand thousand farewells.   94 *with all:* By everything that has happened, or, *withal,* "with it."   97 *appertaining:* Related to this.   **Scene II.**   1 *out:* Empty.   2 *bear . . . 'em:* (Stephano uses the terminology of maneuvering at sea and boarding a vessel under attack as a way of urging an assault on the liquor supply.)   4 *folly of:* I.e., stupidity found on.   5 *be brained:* Are endowed with intelligence.   8 *set:* Fixed in a drunken stare, or, sunk, like the sun.   9 *set:* Placed; *brave:* Fine, splendid.   12 *recover:* Gain, reach.

five and thirty leagues° off and on.° By this light,° thou shalt be my
lieutenant, monster, or my standard.°
Trinculo: Your lieutenant, if you list;° he's no standard.°   15
Stephano: We'll not run,° Monsieur Monster.
Trinculo: Nor go° neither, but you'll lie° like dogs and yet say nothing
neither.
Stephano: Mooncalf, speak once in thy life, if thou beest a good mooncalf.
Caliban: How does thy honor? Let me lick thy shoe. I'll not serve him. He   20
is not valiant.
Trinculo: Thou liest, most ignorant monster, I am in case to jostle a con-
stable.° Why, thou debauched° fish, thou, was there ever man a coward
that hath drunk so much sack° as I today? Wilt thou tell a monstrous
lie, being but half a fish and half a monster?   25
Caliban: Lo, how he mocks me! Wilt thou let him, my lord?
Trinculo: "Lord," quoth he? That a monster should be such a natural!°
Caliban: Lo, lo, again! Bite him to death, I prithee.
Stephano: Trinculo, keep a good tongue in your head. If you prove a muti-
neer — the next tree!° The poor monster's my subject, and he shall not   30
suffer indignity.
Caliban: I thank my noble lord. Wilt thou be pleased
To hearken once again to the suit I made to thee?
Stephano: Marry,° will I. Kneel and repeat it. I will stand, and so shall
Trinculo.   *[Caliban kneels.]*   35

Enter Ariel, invisible.°

Caliban: As I told thee before, I am subject to a tyrant,
A sorcerer, that by his cunning hath
Cheated me of the island.
Ariel [mimicking Trinculo]: Thou liest.
Caliban: Thou liest, thou jesting monkey, thou!
I would my valiant master would destroy thee.   40
I do not lie.
Stephano: Trinculo, if you trouble him any more in 's tale, by this hand, I
will supplant° some of your teeth.
Trinculo: Why, I said nothing.
Stephano: Mum, then, and no more. — Proceed.   45
Caliban: I say by sorcery he got this isle;
From me he got it. If thy greatness will
Revenge it on him — for I know thou dar'st,
But this thing° dare not —

---

13 *leagues:* Units of distance, each equaling about three miles; *off and on:* Intermittently;
By this light: (An oath: by the light of the sun.).   14 *standard:* Standard-bearer, ensign (as
distinguished from *lieutenant,* lines 14, 15).   15 *list:* Prefer; *no standard:* I.e., not able to
stand up.   16 *run:* (1) Retreat (2) urinate (taking Trinculo's *standard,* line 14, in the old
sense of "conduit").   17 *go:* Walk; *lie:* (1) Tell lies, (2) lie prostrate, (3) excrete.   22–23 *in
case . . . constable:* I.e., in fit condition, made valiant by drink, to taunt or challenge the police.
23 *debauched:* (1) Seduced away from proper service and allegiance (2) depraved.   24 *sack:*
Spanish white wine.   27 *natural:* (1) Idiot (2) natural as opposed to unnatural, monster-
like.   30 *the next tree:* I.e., you'll hang.   34 *Marry:* I.e., indeed (originally an oath, "by
the Virgin Mary").   *invisible:* I.e., wearing a garment to connote invisibility, as at I.ii.378.
43 *supplant:* Uproot, displace.   49 *this thing:* I.e., Trinculo.

Stephano: That's most certain.   50
Caliban: Thou shalt be lord of it, and I'll serve thee.
Stephano: How now shall this be compassed?° Canst thou bring me to the
    party?
Caliban: Yea, yea, my lord. I'll yield him thee asleep,
    Where thou mayst knock a nail into his head.   55
Ariel: Thou liest; thou canst not.
Caliban: What a pied ninny's° this! Thou scurvy patch!°—
    I do beseech thy greatness, give him blows
    And take his bottle from him. When that's gone
    He shall drink naught but brine, for I'll not show him   60
    Where the quick freshes° are.
Stephano: Trinculo, run into no further danger. Interrupt the monster one
    word further° and, by this hand, I'll turn my mercy out o' doors° and
    make a stockfish° of thee.
Trinculo: Why, what did I? I did nothing. I'll go farther off.°   65
Stephano: Didst thou not say he lied?
Ariel: Thou liest.
Stephano: Do I so? Take thou that. *[He beats Trinculo.]* As you like this, give
    me the lie° another time.
Trinculo: I did not give the lie. Out o' your wits and hearing too? A pox o'   70
    your bottle! This can sack and drinking do. A murrain° on your
    monster, and the devil take your fingers!
Caliban: Ha, ha, ha!
Stephano: Now, forward with your tale. *[To Trinculo.]* Prithee, stand fur-
    ther off.   75
Caliban: Beat him enough. After a little time
    I'll beat him too.
Stephano: Stand farther.—Come, proceed.
Caliban: Why, as I told thee, 'tis a custom with him
    I' th' afternoon to sleep. There thou mayst brain him,   80
    Having first seized his books; or with a log
    Batter his skull, or paunch° him with a stake,
    Or cut his weasand° with thy knife. Remember
    First to possess his books, for without them
    He's but a sot,° as I am, nor hath not   85
    One spirit to command. They all do hate him
    As rootedly as I. Burn but his books.
    He has brave utensils°—for so he calls them—
    Which, when he has a house, he'll deck withal.°
    And that most deeply to consider is   90
    The beauty of his daughter. He himself
    Calls her a nonpareil. I never saw a woman
    But only Sycorax my dam and she;

---

52 *compassed:* Achieved.   57 *pied ninny:* Fool in motley; *patch:* Fool.   61 *quick freshes:* Running springs.   62–63 *one word further:* I.e., one more time.   63 *turn . . . doors:* I.e., forget
about being merciful.   64 *stockfish:* Dried cod beaten before cooking.   65 *off:* Away.
68–69 *give me the lie:* Call me a liar to my face.   71 *murrain:* Plague (literally, a cattle disease).
82 *paunch:* Stab in the belly.   83 *weasand:* Windpipe.   85 *sot:* Fool.   88 *brave utensils:*
Fine furnishings.   89 *deck withal:* Furnish it with.

But she as far surpasseth Sycorax
As great'st does least.   95
Stephano: Is it so brave° a lass?
Caliban: Ay, lord. She will become° thy bed, I warrant,
And bring thee forth brave brood.
Stephano: Monster, I will kill this man. His daughter and I will be king
and queen—save Our Graces!—and Trinculo and thyself shall be   100
viceroys. Dost thou like the plot, Trinculo?
Trinculo: Excellent.
Stephano: Give me thy hand. I am sorry I beat thee; but, while thou liv'st,
keep a good tongue in thy head.
Caliban: Within this half hour will he be asleep.   105
Wilt thou destroy him then?
Stephano: Ay, on mine honor.
Ariel [aside]: This will I tell my master.
Caliban: Thou mak'st me merry; I am full of pleasure.
Let us be jocund.° Will you troll the catch°   110
You taught me but whilere?°
Stephano: At thy request, monster, I will do reason, any reason.°—Come
on, Trinculo, let us sing.   *Sings.*
"Flout° 'em and scout° 'em
And scout 'em and flout em!   115
Thought is free."
Caliban: That's not the tune.   *Ariel plays the tune on a tabor° and pipe.*
Stephano: What is this same?
Trinculo: This is the tune of our catch, played by the picture of Nobody.°
Stephano: If thou beest a man, show thyself in thy likeness. If thou beest a   120
devil, take 't as thou list.°
Trinculo: O, forgive me my sins!
Stephano: He that dies pays all debts.° I defy thee. Mercy upon us!
Caliban: Art thou afeard?
Stephano: No, monster, not I.   125
Caliban: Be not afeard. The isle is full of noises,
Sounds, and sweet airs, that give delight and hurt not.
Sometimes a thousand twangling instruments
Will hum about mine ears, and sometimes voices
That, if I then had waked after long sleep,   130
Will make me sleep again; and then, in dreaming,
The clouds methought would open and show riches
Ready to drop upon me, that when I waked
I cried to dream° again.
Stephano: This will prove a brave kingdom to me, where I shall have my   135
music for nothing.
Caliban: When Prospero is destroyed.

---

96 *brave:* Splendid, attractive.   97 *become:* Suit (sexually).   110 *jocund:* Jovial, merry; *troll
the catch:* Sing the round.   111 *but whilere:* Only a short time ago.   112 *reason, any
reason:* Anything reasonable.   114 *Flout:* Scoff at; *scout:* Deride.   117 *tabor:* Small drum.
119 *picture of Nobody:* (Refers to a familiar figure with head, arms, and legs but no trunk.)
121 *take 't . . . list:* I.e., take my defiance as you please, as best you can.   123 *He . . . debts:* I.e.,
if I have to die, at least that will be the end of all my woes and obligations.   134 *to dream:*
Desirous of dreaming.

Stephano: That shall be by and by.° I remember the story.
Trinculo: The sound is going away. Let's follow it, and after do our work.
Stephano: Lead, monster; we'll follow. I would I could see this taborer! He 140
     lays it on.°
Trinculo: Wilt come? I'll follow, Stephano.   *Exeunt [following Ariel's music].*

[SCENE III: *Another part of the island.*]

     Enter Alonso, Sebastian, Antonio, Gonzalo, Adrian, Francisco, etc.

Gonzalo: By 'r lakin,° I can go no further, sir.
     My old bones aches. Here's a maze trod indeed
     Through forthrights and meanders!° By your patience,
     I needs must° rest me.
Alonso: Old lord, I cannot blame thee,
     Who am myself attached° with weariness,   5
     To th' dulling of my spirits.° Sit down and rest.
     Even here I will put off my hope, and keep it
     No longer for° my flatterer. He is drowned
     Whom thus we stray to find, and the sea mocks
     Our frustrate° search on land. Well, let him go. *[Alonso and Gonzalo sit.]* 10
Antonio [aside to Sebastian]: I am right° glad that he's so out of hope.
     Do not, for° one repulse, forgo the purpose
     That you resolved t' effect.
Sebastian [to Antonio]:   The next advantage
     Will we take throughly.°
Antonio [to Sebastian]:   Let it be tonight,
     For, now° they are oppressed with travel,° they   15
     Will not, nor cannot, use° such vigilance
     As when they are fresh.
Sebastian [to Antonio]:   I say tonight. No more.

     Solemn and strange music; and Prospero on the top,° invisible.

Alonso: What harmony is this? My good friends, hark!
Gonzalo: Marvelous sweet music!

     *Enter several strange shapes, bringing in a banquet, and dance about it with
     gentle actions of salutations; and, inviting the King, etc., to eat, they depart.*

Alonso: Give us kind keepers,° heavens! What were these?   20
Sebastian: A living° drollery.° Now I will believe
     That there are unicorns; that in Arabia
     There is one tree, the phoenix' throne, one phoenix°

138 *by and by:* Very soon.   141 *lays it on:* I.e., plays the drum vigorously.   **Scene III.**   1 *By
'r lakin:* By our Ladykin, by our Lady.   3 *forthrights and meanders:* Paths straight and
crooked.   4 *needs must:* Have to.   5 *attached:* Seized.   6 *To . . . spirits:* To the point of
being dull-spirited.   8 *for:* As.   10 *frustrate:* Frustrated.   11 *right:* Very.   12 *for:* Because of.   14 *throughly:* Thoroughly.   15 *now:* Now that; *travel:* Carrying the sense of labor
as well as traveling.   16 *use:* Apply; *on the top:* At some high point of the tiring-house or
the theater, on a third level above the gallery.   20 *kind keepers:* Guardian angels.   21 *living:* With live actors; *drollery:* Comic entertainment, caricature, puppet show.   23 *phoenix:*
Mythical bird consumed to ashes every five hundred to six hundred years, only to be renewed
into another cycle.

At this hour reigning there.

Antonio: I'll believe both;
And what does else want credit,° come to me   25
And I'll be sworn 'tis true. Travelers ne'er did lie,
Though fools at home condemn 'em.

Gonzalo: If in Naples
I should report this now, would they believe me
If I should say I saw such islanders?
For, certes,° these are people of the island,   30
Who, though they are of monstrous° shape, yet note,
Their manners are more gentle, kind, than of
Our human generation you shall find
Many, nay, almost any.

Prospero [aside]:   Honest lord,
Thou hast said well, for some of you there present   35
Are worse than devils.

Alonso: I cannot too much muse°
Such shapes, such gesture, and such sound, expressing—
Although they want° the use of tongue—a kind
Of excellent dumb discourse.

Prospero [aside]:   Praise in departing.°

Francisco: They vanished strangely.

Sebastian: No matter, since   40
They have left their viands° behind, for we have stomachs.°
Will 't please you taste of what is here?

Alonso: Not I.

Gonzalo: Faith, sir, you need not fear. When we were boys,
Who would believe that there were mountaineers°
Dewlapped° like bulls, whose throats had hanging at 'em   45
Wallets° of flesh? Or that there were such men
Whose heads stood in their breasts? Which now we find
Each putter-out of five for one° will bring us
Good warrant° of.

Alonso: I will stand to° and feed,
Although my last°—no matter, since I feel   50
The best° is past. Brother, my lord the Duke,
Stand to, and do as we.   *[They approach the table.]*

*Thunder and lightning. Enter Ariel, like a harpy,° claps his wings upon the
table, and with a quaint device° the banquet vanishes.°*

25 *want credit:* Lack credence.   30 *certes:* Certainly.   31 *monstrous:* Unnatural.   36 *muse:*
Wonder at.   38 *want:* Lack.   39 *Praise in departing:* I.e., save your praise until the end of
the performance (proverbial).   41 *viands:* Provisions; *stomachs:* Appetites.   44 *moun-
taineers:* Mountain dwellers.   45 *Dewlapped:* Having a dewlap, or fold of skin hanging
from the neck, like cattle.   46 *Wallets:* Pendent folds of skin, wattles.   48 *putter-out…
one:* One who invests money or gambles on the risks of travel on the condition that the traveler who returns safely is to receive five times the amount deposited; hence, any traveler.
49 *Good warrant:* Assurance; *stand to:* Fall to, take the risk.   50 *Although my last:* Even if
this were to be my last meal.   51 *best:* Best part of life.   *harpy:* A fabulous monster with
a woman's face and breasts and a vulture's body, supposed to be a minister of divine
vengeance; *quaint device:* Ingenious stage contrivance; *the banquet vanishes:* I.e., the food vanishes; the table remains until line 82.

Ariel: You are three men of sin, whom Destiny —
　　That hath to instrument this lower world
　　And what is in 't — the never-surfeited sea   55
　　Hath caused to belch up you,° and on this island
　　Where man doth not inhabit, you 'mongst men
　　Being most unfit to life. I have made you mad;
　　And even with suchlike valor° men hang and drown
　　Their proper° selves.   *[Alonso, Sebastian, and Antonio draw their swords.]*
　　　　　　　　　　　　You fools! I and my fellows   60
　　Are ministers of Fate. The elements
　　Of whom° your swords are tempered° may as well
　　Wound the loud winds, or with bemocked-at° stabs
　　Kill the still-closing° waters, as diminish
　　One dowl° that's in my plume. My fellow ministers   65
　　Are like° invulnerable. If° you could hurt,
　　Your swords are now too massy° for your strengths
　　And will not be uplifted. But remember —
　　For that's my business to you — that you three
　　From Milan did supplant good Prospero;   70
　　Exposed unto the sea, which hath requit° it,
　　Him and his innocent child; for which foul deed
　　The powers, delaying, not forgetting, have
　　Incensed the seas and shores, yea, all the creatures,
　　Against your peace. Thee of thy son, Alonso,   75
　　They have bereft; and to pronounce by me
　　Ling'ring perdition,° worse than any death
　　Can be at once, shall step by step attend
　　You and your ways; whose° wraths to guard you from —
　　Which here, in this most desolate isle, else° falls   80
　　Upon your heads — is nothing° but heart's sorrow
　　And a clear° life ensuing.

　　He vanishes in thunder; then, to soft music, enter the shapes again, and dance,
　　with mocks and mows,° and carrying out the table.

Prospero: Bravely° the figure of this harpy hast thou
　　Performed, my Ariel; a grace it had devouring.°
　　Of my instruction hast thou nothing bated°   85
　　In what thou hadst to say. So,° with good life°

53–56 *whom . . . up you:* You whom Destiny, controller of the sublunary world as its instrument, has caused the ever hungry sea to belch up.   59 *suchlike valor:* I.e., the reckless valor derived from madness.   60 *proper:* Own.   62 *whom:* Which; *tempered:* Composed and hardened.   63 *bemocked-at:* Scorned.   64 *still-closing:* Always closing again when parted. 65 *dowl:* Soft, fine feather.   66 *like:* Likewise, similarly; *If:* Even if.   67 *massy:* Heavy. 71 *requit:* Requited, avenged.   77 *perdition:* Ruin, destruction.   79 *whose:* (Refers to the heavenly powers.)   80 *else:* Otherwise.   81 *is nothing:* There is no way.   82 *clear:* Unspotted, innocent; *mocks and mows:* Mocking gestures and grimaces.   83 *Bravely:* Finely, dashingly.   84 *a grace . . . devouring:* I.e., you gracefully caused the banquet to disappear as if you had consumed it (with puns on *grace,* meaning "gracefulness" and "a blessing on the meal," and on *devouring,* meaning "a literal eating" and "an all-consuming or ravishing grace").   85 *bated:* Abated, omitted.   86 *So:* In the same fashion; *good life:* Faithful reproduction.

And observation strange,° my meaner° ministers
Their several kinds° have done. My high charms work,
And these mine enemies are all knit up
In their distractions.° They now are in my power;   90
And in these fits I leave them, while I visit
Young Ferdinand, whom they suppose is drowned,
And his and mine loved darling.   *[Exit above.]*
Gonzalo: I' the name of something holy, sir, why° stand you
In this strange stare?
Alonso: O, it° is monstrous, monstrous!   95
Methought the billows° spoke and told me of it;
The winds did sing it to me, and the thunder,
That deep and dreadful organ pipe, pronounced
The name of Prosper; it did bass my trespass.°
Therefor° my son i' th' ooze is bedded; and   100
I'll seek him deeper than e'er plummet° sounded,°
And with him there lie mudded.   *Exit.*
Sebastian: But one fiend at a time,
I'll fight their legions o'er.°
Antonio: I'll be thy second.
                    Exeunt [Sebastian and Antonio].
Gonzalo: All three of them are desperate.° Their great guilt,   105
Like poison given to work a great time after,
Now 'gins to bite the spirits.° I do beseech you,
That are of suppler joints, follow them swiftly
And hinder them from what this ecstasy°
May now provoke them to.
Adrian: Follow, I pray you.   *Exeunt omnes.* 110

[ACT IV

SCENE I: *Before Prospero's cell.*]

Enter Prospero, Ferdinand, and Miranda.

Prospero: If I have too austerely punished you,
Your companion makes amends, for I
Have given you here a third° of mine own life,

---

87 *observation strange:* Exceptional attention to detail; *meaner:* I.e., subordinate to Ariel.
88 *several kinds:* Individual parts.   90 *distractions:* Trancelike state.   94 *why:* (Gonzalo
was not addressed in Ariel's speech to the *three men of sin,* line 53, and is not, as they are, in a
maddened state; see lines 105–107.)   95 *it:* I.e., my sin (also in line 96).   96 *billows:*
Waves.   99 *bass my trespass:* Proclaim my trespass like a bass note in music.   100 *Therefor:* In consequence of that.   101 *plummet:* A lead weight attached to a line for testing
depth; *sounded:* Probed, tested the depth of.   104 *o'er:* One after another.   105 *desperate:*
Despairing and reckless.   107 *bite the spirits:* Sap their vital powers through anguish.
109 *ecstasy:* Mad frenzy.   **Act IV, Scene I.**   3 *a third:* I.e., Miranda, into whose education Prospero has put a third of his life (?) or who represents a large part of what he cares
about, along with his dukedom and his learned study (?).

Or that for which I live; who once again
I tender° to thy hand. All thy vexations   5
Were but my trials of thy love, and thou
Hast strangely° stood the test. Here, afore heaven,
I ratify this my rich gift. O Ferdinand,
Do not smile at me that I boast her off,°
For thou shalt find she will outstrip all praise   10
And make it halt° behind her.
Ferdinand: I do believe it.
Against an oracle.°
Prospero: Then, as my gift and thine own acquisition
Worthily purchased, take my daughter. But
If thou dost break her virgin-knot before   15
All sanctimonious° ceremonies may
With full and holy rite be ministered,
No sweet aspersion° shall the heavens let fall
To make this contract grow; but barren hate,
Sour-eyed disdain, and discord shall bestrew   20
The union of your bed with weeds° so loathly
That you shall hate it both. Therefore take heed,
As Hymen's lamps shall light you.°
Ferdinand: As I hope
For quiet days, fair issue,° and long life,
With such love as 'tis now, the murkiest den,   25
The most opportune place, the strong'st suggestion°
Our worser genius° can,° shall never melt
Mine honor into lust, to° take away
The edge° of that day's celebration
When I shall think or° Phoebus' steeds are foundered°   30
Or Night kept chained below.
Prospero: Fairly spoke.
Sit then and talk with her. She is thine own.
                    [Ferdinand and Miranda sit and talk together.]
What,° Ariel! My industrious servant, Ariel!

        Enter Ariel.

Ariel: What would my potent master? Here I am.
Prospero: Thou and thy meaner fellows° your last service   35
        Did worthily perform, and I must use you

---

5 *tender:* Offer.   7 *strangely:* Extraordinarily.   9 *boast her off:* I.e., praise her so, or, perhaps an error for "boast of her."   11 *halt:* Limp.   12 *Against an oracle:* Even if an oracle should declare otherwise.   16 *sanctimonious:* Sacred.   18 *aspersion:* Dew, shower. 21 *weeds:* (In place of the flowers customarily strewn on the marriage bed.)   23 *As . . . you:* I.e., as you long for happiness and concord in your marriage. (Hymen was the Greek and Roman god of marriage; his symbolic torches, the wedding torches, were supposed to burn brightly for a happy marriage and smokily for a troubled one.)   24 *issue:* Offspring. 26 *suggestion:* Temptation.   27 *worser genius:* Evil genius, or, evil attendant spirit; *can:* Is capable of.   28 *to:* So as to.   29 *edge:* Keen enjoyment, sexual ardor.   30 *or:* Either; *foundered:* Broken down, made lame. (Ferdinand will wait impatiently for the bridal night.) 33 *What:* Now then.   35 *meaner fellows:* Subordinates.

In such another trick.° Go bring the rabble,°
O'er whom I give thee power, here to this place.
Incite them to quick motion, for I must
Bestow upon the eyes of this young couple
Some vanity° of mine art. It is my promise,   40
And they expect it from me.
Ariel: Presently?°
Prospero: Ay, with a twink.°
Ariel: Before you can say "Come" and "Go,"
     And breathe twice, and cry "So, so,"   45
     Each one, tripping on his toe,
     Will be here with mop and mow.°
     Do you love me, master? No?
Prospero: Dearly, my delicate Ariel. Do not approach
     Till thou dost hear me call.
Ariel: Well; I conceive.°   *Exit.*   50
Prospero: Look thou be true;° do not give dalliance
     Too much the rein. The strongest oaths are straw
     To the fire i' the blood. Be more abstemious,
     Or else good night° your vow!
Ferdinand: I warrant° you, sir,
     The white cold virgin snow upon my heart°   55
     Abates the ardor of my liver.°
Prospero: Well.
     Now come, my Ariel! Bring a corollary,°
     Rather than want° a spirit. Appear, and pertly!°—
     No tongue!° All eyes! Be silent.   *Soft music.*

     Enter Iris.°

Iris: Ceres,° most bounteous lady, thy rich leas°   60
     Of wheat, rye, barley, vetches,° oats, and peas;
     Thy turfy mountains, where live nibbling sheep,
     And flat meads° thatched with stover,° them to keep;
     Thy banks with pionèd and twillèd° brims,
     Which spongy° April at thy hest° betrims   65
     To make cold nymphs chaste crowns; and thy broom groves,°
     Whose shadow the dismissèd bachelor° loves,
     Being lass-lorn; thy poll-clipped° vineyard;

---

37 *trick:* Device; *rabble:* Band, i.e., the *meaner fellows* of line 35.   41 *vanity:* (1) Illusion, (2) trifle, (3) desire for admiration, conceit.   42 *Presently:* Immediately.   43 *with a twink:* In the twinkling of an eye.   47 *mop and mow:* Gestures and grimaces.   50 *conceive:* Understand.   51 *true:* True to your promise.   54 *good night:* I.e., say good-bye to; *warrant:* Guarantee.   55 *The white . . . heart:* I.e., the ideal of chastity and consciousness of Miranda's chaste innocence enshrined in my heart.   56 *liver:* (As the presumed seat of the passions.)   57 *corollary:* Surplus, extra supply.   58 *want:* Lack; *pertly:* Briskly.   59 *No tongue:* All the beholders are to be silent (lest the spirits vanish).   *Iris:* Goddess of the rainbow and Juno's messenger.   60 *Ceres:* Goddess of the generative power of nature; *leas:* Meadows.   61 *vetches:* Plants for forage, fodder.   63 *meads:* Meadows; *stover:* Winter fodder for cattle.   64 *pionèd and twillèd:* Undercut by the swift current and protected by roots and branches that tangle to form a barricade.   65 *spongy:* Wet; *hest:* Command.   66 *broom groves:* Clumps of broom, gorse, yellow-flowered shrub.   67 *dismissèd bachelor:* Rejected male lover.   68 *poll-clipped:* Pruned, lopped at the top, or *pole-clipped,* "hedged in with poles."

And thy sea marge,° sterile and rocky hard,
Where thou thyself dost air:° the queen o' the sky,°   70
Whose watery arch° and messenger am I,
Bids thee leave these, and with her sovereign grace,
                              Juno descends° [slowly in her car].
Here on this grass plot, in this very place,
To come and sport. Her peacocks° fly amain.°
Approach, rich Ceres, her to entertain.°   75

Enter Ceres.

Ceres: Hail, many-colored messenger, that ne'er
Dost disobey the wife of Jupiter,
Who with thy saffron° wings upon my flowers
Diffusest honeydrops, refreshing showers,
And with each end of thy blue bow° dost crown   80
My bosky° acres and my unshrubbed down,°
Rich scarf° to my proud earth. Why hath thy queen
Summoned me hither to this short-grassed green?
Iris: A contract of true love to celebrate,
And some donation freely to estate°   85
On the blest lovers.
Ceres: Tell me, heavenly bow,
If Venus or her son,° as° thou dost know,
Do now attend the Queen? Since they did plot
The means that° dusky° Dis my daughter got,°
Her° and her blind boy's scandaled° company   90
I have forsworn.
Iris: Of her society°
Be not afraid. I met her deity°
Cutting the clouds towards Paphos,° and her son
Dove-drawn° with her. Here thought they to have done°
Some wanton charm° upon this man and maid,   95
Whose vows are that no bed-right shall be paid
Till Hymen's torch be lighted; but in vain.
Mars's hot minion° is returned° again;
Her waspish-headed° son has broke his arrows,
Swears he will shoot no more, but play with sparrows°   100
And be a boy right out.°

69 *sea marge:* Shore.   70 *thou . . . air:* You take the air, go for walks; *queen o' the sky:* I.e.,
Juno.   71 *watery arch:* Rainbow.   *Juno descends:* I.e., starts her descent from the "heavens" above the stage (?).   74 *peacocks:* Birds sacred to Juno and used to pull her chariot;
amain: With full speed.   75 *entertain:* Receive.   78 *saffron:* Yellow.   80 *bow:* I.e.,
rainbow.   81 *bosky:* Wooded; *unshrubbed down:* Open upland.   82 *scarf:* (The rainbow
is like a colored silk band adorning the earth.)   85 *estate:* Bestow.   87 *son:* I.e., Cupid;
as: As far as.   89 *that:* Whereby; *dusky:* Dark; *Dis . . . got:* (Pluto, or *Dis,* god of the infernal
regions, carried off Proserpina, daughter of Ceres, to be his bride in Hades.)   90 *Her:* I.e.,
Venus's; *scandaled:* Scandalous.   91 *society:* Company.   92 *her deity:* I.e., Her Highness.
93 *Paphos:* Place on the island of Cyprus, sacred to Venus.   94 *Dove-drawn:* (Venus's chariot was drawn by doves); *done:* Placed.   95 *wanton charm:* Lustful spell.   98 *Mars's hot
minion:* I.e., Venus, the beloved of Mars; *returned:* I.e., returned to Paphos.   99 *waspish-
headed:* Hotheaded, peevish.   100 *sparrows:* (Supposed lustful, and sacred to Venus.)
101 *right out:* Outright.

[Juno alights.]

Ceres: Highest Queen of state,°
   Great Juno, comes; I know her by her gait.°
Juno: How does my bounteous sister?° Go with me
   To bless this twain, that they may prosperous be,
   And honored in their issue.°   *They sing:* 105
Juno: Honor, riches, marriage blessing,
   Long continuance, and increasing,
   Hourly joys be still° upon you!
   Juno sings her blessings on you.
Ceres: Earth's increase, foison plenty,°   110
   Barns and garners° never empty,
   Vines with clustering bunches growing,
   Plants with goodly burden bowing;

   Spring come to you at the farthest
   In the very end of harvest!°   115
   Scarcity and want shall shun you;
   Ceres' blessing so is on you.
Ferdinand: This is a most majestic vision, and
   Harmonious charmingly.° May I be bold
   To think these spirits?
Prospero: Spirits, which by mine art   120
   I have from their confines called to enact
   My present fancies.
Ferdinand: Let me live here ever!
   So rare a wondered° father and a wife
   Makes this place Paradise.

                    Juno and Ceres whisper, and send Iris on employment.

Prospero: Sweet now, silence!
   Juno and Ceres whisper seriously;   125
   There's something else to do. Hush and be mute,
   Or else our spell is marred.
Iris [calling offstage]: You nymphs, called naiads,° of the windring° brooks,
   With your sedged° crowns and ever-harmless° looks,
   Leave your crisp° channels, and on this green land   130
   Answer your summons; Juno does command.
   Come, temperate° nymphs, and help to celebrate
   A contract of true love. Be not too late.

   Enter certain nymphs.

   You sunburned sicklemen,° of August weary,°
   Come hither from the furrow° and be merry.   135

---

101 *Highest...state:* Most majestic Queen.   102 *gait:* I.e., majestic bearing.   103 *sister:* I.e.,
fellow goddess (?).   105 *issue:* Offspring.   108 *still:* Always.   110 *foison plenty:* Plentiful harvest.   111 *garners:* Granaries.   115 *In...harvest:* I.e., with no winter in between.
119 *charmingly:* Enchantingly.   123 *wondered:* Wonder-performing, wondrous.   128 *naiads:* Nymphs of springs, rivers, or lakes; *windring:* Wandering, winding (?).   129 *sedged:*
Made of reeds; *ever-harmless:* Ever innocent.   130 *crisp:* Curled, rippled.   132 *temperate:*
Chaste.   134 *sicklemen:* Harvesters, field workers who cut down grain and grass; *of August
weary:* I.e., weary of the hard work of the harvest.   135 *furrow:* I.e., plowed fields.

Make holiday; your rye-straw hats put on,
And these fresh nymphs encounter° every one
In country footing.°

Enter certain reapers, properly° habited. They join with the nymphs in a graceful
dance, towards the end whereof Prospero starts suddenly, and speaks; after which,
to a strange, hollow, and confused noise, they heavily° vanish.

Prospero [aside]: I had forgot that foul conspiracy
  Of the beast Caliban and his confederates   140
  Against my life. The minute of their plot
  Is almost come. *[To the Spirits.]* Well done! Avoid;° no more!
Ferdinand [to Miranda]: This is strange. Your father's in some passion
  That works° him strongly.
Miranda: Never till this day
  Saw I him touched with anger so distempered.   145
Prospero: You do look, my son, in a moved sort,°
  As if you were dismayed. Be cheerful, sir.
  Our revels° now are ended. These our actors,
  As I foretold you, were all spirits and
  Are melted into air, into thin air;   150
  And, like the baseless fabric° of this vision,
  The cloud-capped towers, the gorgeous palaces,
  The solemn temples, the great globe° itself,
  Yea, all which it inherit,° shall dissolve,
  And, like this insubstantial pageant faded,   155
  Leave not a rack° behind. We are such stuff
  As dreams are made on,° and our little life
  Is rounded° with a sleep. Sir, I am vexed.
  Bear with my weakness. My old brain is troubled.
  Be not disturbed with° my infirmity.   160
  If you be pleased, retire° into my cell
  And there repose. A turn or two I'll walk
  To still my beating° mind.
Ferdinand, Miranda: We wish your peace.
                          Exeunt [Ferdinand and Miranda].
Prospero: Come with a thought!° I thank thee, Ariel. Come.

Enter Ariel.

Ariel: Thy thoughts I cleave° to. What's thy pleasure?
Prospero: Spirit,   165
  We must prepare to meet with Caliban.

---

137 *encounter:* Join.   138 *country footing:* Country dancing.   *properly:* Suitably; *heavily:*
Slowly, dejectedly.   142 *Avoid:* Withdraw.   144 *works:* Affects, agitates.   146 *moved*
sort: Troubled state, condition.   148 *revels:* Entertainment, pageant.   151 *baseless fabric:*
Unsubstantial theatrical edifice or contrivance.   153 *great globe:* (With a glance at the
Globe Theatre.)   154 *which it inherit:* Who subsequently occupy it.   156 *rack:* Wisp of
cloud.   157 *on:* Of.   158 *rounded:* Surrounded (before birth and after death), or
crowned, rounded off.   160 *with:* By.   161 *retire:* Withdraw, go.   163 *beating:* Agitated.   164 *with a thought:* I.e., on the instant, or, summoned by my thought, no sooner
thought of than here.   165 *cleave:* Cling, adhere.

Ariel: Ay, my commander. When I presented° Ceres,
    I thought to have told thee of it, but I feared
    Lest I might anger thee.
Prospero: Say again, where didst thou leave these varlets?   170
Ariel: I told you, sir, they were red-hot with drinking;
    So full of valor that they smote the air
    For breathing in their faces, beat the ground
    For kissing of their feet; yet always bending°
    Towards their project. Then I beat my tabor,   175
    At which, like unbacked° colts, they pricked their ears,
    Advanced° their eyelids, lifted up their noses
    As° they smelt music. So I charmed their ears
    That calflike they my lowing° followed through
    Toothed briers, sharp furzes, pricking gorse,° and thorns,   180
    Which entered their frail shins. At last I left them
    I' the filthy-mantled° pool beyond your cell,
    There dancing up to the chins, that the foul lake
    O'erstunk° their feet.
Prospero: This was well done, my bird.
    Thy shape invisible retain thou still.   185
    The trumpery° in my house, go bring it hither,
    For stale° to catch these thieves.
Ariel: I go, I go.   *Exit.*
Prospero: A devil, a born devil, on whose nature
    Nurture can never stick; on whom my pains,
    Humanely taken, all, all lost, quite lost!   190
    And as with age his body uglier grows,
    So his mind cankers.° I will plague them all,
    Even to roaring.

Enter Ariel, loaden with glistering apparel, etc.

                    Come, hang them on this line.°

[Ariel hangs up the showy finery; Prospero and Ariel remain,° invisible.]
Enter Caliban, Stephano, and Trinculo, all wet.

Caliban: Pray you, tread softly, that the blind mole may
    Not hear a foot fall. We now are near his cell.   195
Stephano: Monster, your fairy, which you say is a harmless fairy, has done
    little better than played the jack° with us.
Trinculo: Monster, I do smell all horse piss, at which my nose is in great in-
    dignation.

---

167 *presented:* Acted the part of, or, introduced.   174 *bending:* Aiming.   176 *unbacked:*
Unbroken, unridden.   177 *Advanced:* Lifted up.   178 *As:* As if.   179 *lowing:* Moo-
ing.   180 *furzes, gorse:* Prickly shrubs.   182 *filthy-mantled:* Covered with a slimy coating.
184 *O'erstunk:* Smelled worse than, or, caused to stink terribly.   186 *trumpery:* Cheap
goods, the *glistering apparel* mentioned in the following stage direction.   187 *stale:*
(1) Decoy (2) out-of-fashion garments (with possible further suggestions of "horse piss," as
in line 198, and "steal," pronounced like *stale*). *For stale* could also mean "fit for a prostitute."
192 *cankers:* Festers, grows malignant.   193 *line:* Lime tree or linden.   *Prospero and Ariel*
remain: (The staging is uncertain. They may instead exit here and return with the spirits at
line 248.)   197 *jack:* (1) Knave (2) will-o'-the-wisp.

Stephano: So is mine. Do you hear, monster? If I should take a dis-   200
   pleasure against you, look you —
Trinculo: Thou wert but a lost monster.
Caliban: Good my lord, give me thy favor still.
   Be patient, for the prize I'll bring thee to
   Shall hoodwink this mischance.° Therefore speak softly.   205
   All's hushed as midnight yet.
Trinculo: Ay, but to lose our bottles in the pool —
Stephano: There is not only disgrace and dishonor in that, monster, but
   an infinite loss.
Trinculo: That's more to me than my wetting. Yet this is your harmless   210
   fairy, monster!
Stephano: I will fetch off my bottle, though I be o'er ears° for my labor.
Caliban: Prithee, my king, be quiet. Seest thou here,
   This is the mouth o' the cell. No noise, and enter.
   Do that good mischief which may make this island   215
   Thine own forever, and I thy Caliban
   For aye thy footlicker.
Stephano: Give me thy hand. I do begin to have bloody thoughts.
Trinculo [seeing the finery]: O King Stephano! O peer!° O worthy Stephano!
   Look what a wardrobe here is for thee!   220
Caliban: Let it alone, thou fool, it is but trash.
Trinculo: Oho, monster! We know what belongs to a frippery.° O King
   Stephano!   *[He puts on a gown.]*
Stephano: Put off° that gown, Trinculo. By this hand, I'll have that gown.
Trinculo: Thy Grace shall have it.   225
Caliban: The dropsy° drown this fool! What do you mean
   To dote thus on such luggage?° Let 't alone
   And do the murder first. If he awake,
   From toe to crown° he'll fill our skins with pinches,
   Make us strange stuff.   230
Stephano: Be you quiet, monster. — Mistress line,° is not this my jerkin?°
   [He takes it down.] Now is the jerkin under the line.° Now, jerkin, you
   are like° to lose your hair and prove a bald° jerkin.
Trinculo: Do, do!° We steal by line and level,° an 't like° Your Grace.
Stephano: I thank thee for that jest. Here's a garment for 't. *[He gives a*   235

---

205 *hoodwink this mischance:* (Misfortune is to be prevented from doing further harm by
being hooded like a hawk and also put out of remembrance.)   212 *o'er ears:* I.e., totally
submerged and perhaps drowned.   219 *King...peer:* (Alludes to the old ballad beginning,
"King Stephen was a worthy peer.")   222 *frippery:* Place where cast-off clothes are sold.
224 *Put off:* Put down, or, take off.   226 *dropsy:* Disease characterized by the accumulation of fluid in the connective tissue of the body.   227 *luggage:* Cumbersome trash.
229 *crown:* Head.   231 *Mistress line:* (Addressed to the linden or lime tree upon which, at
line 193, Ariel hung the *glistering apparel*); *jerkin:* Jacket made of leather.   232 *under the line:*
Under the lime tree (with punning sense of being south of the equinoctial line or equator;
sailors on long voyages to the southern regions were popularly supposed to lose their hair
from scurvy or other diseases. Stephano also quibbles bawdily on losing hair through
syphilis, and in *Mistress* and *jerkin*).   233 *like:* Likely; *bald:* (1) Hairless, napless (2) meager.
234 *Do, do:* I.e., bravo (said in response to the jesting or to the taking of the jerkin, or both);
by line and level: I.e., by means of plumb line and carpenter's level, methodically (with pun on
line, "lime tree," line 232, and *steal*, pronounced like *stale*, i.e., prostitute, continuing
Stephano's bawdy quibble); *an 't like:* If it please.

garment.] Wit shall not go unrewarded while I am king of this country. "Steal by line and level" is an excellent pass of pate.° There's another garment for 't.

Trinculo: Monster, come, put some lime° upon your fingers, and away
with the rest.   240

Caliban: I will have none on 't. We shall lose our time,
And all be turned to barnacles,° or to apes
With foreheads villainous° low.

Stephano: Monster, lay to° your fingers. Help to bear this° away where my
hogshead° of wine is, or I'll turn you out of my kingdom. Go to,° 245
carry this.

Trinculo: And this.

Stephano: Ay, and this.   *[They load Caliban with more and more garments.]*

*A noise of hunters heard. Enter divers spirits, in shape of dogs and hounds,
hunting them about, Prospero and Ariel setting them on.*

Prospero: Hey, Mountain, hey!

Ariel: Silver! There it goes, Silver!   250

Prospero: Fury, Fury! There, Tyrant, there! Hark! Hark!
[Caliban, Stephano, and Trinculo are driven out.]
Go, charge my goblins that they grind their joints
With dry° convulsions,° shorten up their sinews
With agèd° cramps, and more pinch-spotted make them
Than pard° or cat o' mountain.°

Ariel: Hark, they roar!   255

Prospero: Let them be hunted soundly.° At this hour
Lies at my mercy all mine enemies.
Shortly shall all my labors end, and thou
Shalt have the air at freedom. For a little°
Follow, and do me service.   *Exeunt.* 260

[ACT V

SCENE I: *Before Prospero's cell.]*

Enter Prospero in his magic robes, [with his staff,] and Ariel.

Prospero: Now does my project gather to a head.
My charms crack° not, my spirits obey, and Time
Goes upright with his carriage.° How's the day?

237 *pass of pate:* Sally of wit. (The metaphor is from fencing.)   239 *lime:* Birdlime, sticky substance (to give Caliban sticky fingers).   242 *barnacles:* Barnacle geese, formerly supposed to be hatched from barnacles attached to trees or to rotting timber; here, evidently used, like *apes,* as types of simpletons.   243 *villainous:* Miserably.   244 *lay to:* Start using; *this:* I.e., the *glistering apparel.*   245 *hogshead:* Large cask; *Go to:* (An expression of exhortation or remonstrance.)   253 *dry:* Associated with age, arthritic (?); *convulsions:* Cramps. 254 *agèd:* Characteristic of old age.   255 *pard:* Panther or leopard; *cat o' mountain:* Wildcat.   256 *soundly:* Thoroughly (and suggesting the sounds of the hunt).   259 *little:* Little while longer.   **Act V, Scene I.** 2 *crack:* Collapse, fail. (The metaphor is probably alchemical, as in *project* and *gather to a head,* line 1.)   3 *his carriage:* Its burden (time is no longer heavily burdened and so can go *upright,* "standing straight and unimpeded").

Ariel: On° the sixth hour, at which time, my lord,
　　You said our work should cease.
Prospero:　　　　　　　　　　　I did say so,　　　　　　　　　5
　　When first I raised the tempest. Say, my spirit,
　　How fares the King and 's followers?
Ariel:　　　　　　　　　　　　　Confined together
　　In the same fashion as you gave in charge,
　　Just as you left them; all prisoners, sir,
　　In the line grove° which weather-fends° your cell.　　　　　10
　　They cannot budge till your release.° The King,
　　His brother, and yours abide all three distracted,°
　　And the remainder mourning over them,
　　Brim full of sorrow and dismay; but chiefly
　　Him that you termed, sir, the good old lord, Gonzalo.　　　15
　　His tears runs down his beard like winter's drops
　　From eaves of reeds.° Your charm so strongly works 'em
　　That if you now beheld them your affections°
　　Would become tender.
Prospero:　　　　　　　　Dost thou think so, spirit?
Ariel: Mine would, sir, were I human.°
Prospero:　　　　　　　　　　And mine shall.　　　　　　　20
　　Hast thou, which art but air, a touch,° a feeling
　　Of their afflictions, and shall not myself,
　　One of their kind, that relish all as sharply
　　Passion as they,° be kindlier° moved than thou art?
　　Though with their high wrongs I am struck to the quick,　　25
　　Yet with my nobler reason 'gainst my fury
　　Do I take part. The rarer° action is
　　In virtue than in vengeance. They being penitent,
　　The sole drift of my purpose doth extend
　　Not a frown further. Go release them, Ariel.　　　　　　　30
　　My charms I'll break, their senses I'll restore,
　　And they shall be themselves.
Ariel:　　　　　　　　　I'll fetch them, sir.　　　　*Exit.*
　　　　　　　　　[Prospero traces a charmed circle with his staff.]
Prospero: Ye elves of hills, brooks, standing lakes, and groves,
　　And ye that on the sands with printless foot
　　Do chase the ebbing Neptune, and do fly him　　　　　　35
　　When he comes back; you demi-puppets° that
　　By moonshine do the green sour ringlets° make,
　　Whereof the ewe not bites; and you whose pastime

---

4 *On:* Approaching.　10 *line grove:* Grove of lime trees; *weather-fends:* Protects from the weather.　11 *your release:* You release them.　12 *distracted:* Out of their wits.　17 *eaves of reeds:* Thatched roofs.　18 *affections:* Disposition, feelings.　20 *human:* Humane [as well as human].　21 *touch:* Sense, apprehension.　23-24 *that . . . they:* I who experience human passions as acutely as they.　24 *kindlier:* (1) More sympathetically (2) more naturally, humanly.　27 *rarer:* Nobler.　33-50 *Ye . . . art:* (This famous passage is an embellished paraphrase of Golding's translation of Ovid's *Metamorphoses,* Book VII, lines 197–219.)　36 *demi-puppets:* Puppets of half size, i.e., elves and fairies.　37 *green sour ringlets:* Fairy rings, circles in grass (actually produced by mushrooms).

Is to make midnight mushrooms,° that rejoice
To hear the solemn curfew;° by whose aid,   40
Weak masters° though ye be, I have bedimmed
The noontide sun, called forth the mutinous winds,
And twixt the green sea and the azured vault°
Set roaring war; to the dread rattling thunder
Have I given fire,° and rifted° Jove's stout oak°   45
With his own bolt;° the strong-based promontory
Have I made shake, and by the spurs° plucked up
The pine and cedar; graves at my command
Have waked their sleepers, oped, and let 'em forth
By my so potent art. But this rough° magic   50
I here abjure, and when I have required°
Some heavenly music—which even now I do—
To work mine end upon their senses that°
This airy charm° is for, I'll break my staff,
Bury it certain fathoms in the earth,   55
And deeper than did ever plummet sound
I'll drown my book.   *Solemn music.*

Here enters Ariel before; then Alonso, with a frantic gesture, attended by Gonzalo; Sebastian and Antonio in like manner, attended by Adrian and Francisco. They all enter the circle which Prospero had made, and there stand charmed; which Prospero observing, speaks:

[To Alonso.] A solemn air,° and° the best comforter
To an unsettled fancy,° cure thy brains,
Now useless, boiled° within thy skull! *[To Sebastian and Antonio.]*
   There stand,   60
For you are spell-stopped.—
Holy Gonzalo, honorable man,
Mine eyes, e'en sociable° to the show° of thine,
Fall° fellowly drops. *[Aside.]* The charm dissolves apace,
And as the morning steals upon the night,   65
Melting the darkness, so their rising senses
Begin to chase the ignorant fumes° that mantle°
Their clearer° reason.—O good Gonzalo,
My true preserver, and a loyal sir
To him thou follow'st! I will pay thy graces°   70
Home° both in word and deed.—Most cruelly
Didst thou, Alonso, use me and my daughter.

39 *midnight mushrooms:* Mushrooms appearing overnight.   40 *curfew:* Evening bell, usually rung at nine o'clock, ushering in the time when spirits are abroad.   41 *Weak masters:* I.e., subordinate spirits, as in IV.i.35 (?).   43 *the azured vault:* I.e., the sky.   44–45 *to . . . fire:* I have discharged the dread rattling thunderbolt.   45 *rifted:* Riven, split; *oak:* A tree that was sacred to Jove.   46 *bolt:* Lightning bolt.   47 *spurs:* Roots.   50 *rough:* Violent.   51 *required:* Requested.   53 *their senses that:* The senses of those whom.   54 *airy charm:* I.e., music.   58 *air:* Song; *and:* I.e., which is.   59 *fancy:* Imagination.   60 *boiled:* I.e., extremely agitated.   63 *sociable:* Sympathetic; *show:* Appearance.   64 *Fall:* Let fall.   67 *ignorant fumes:* Fumes that render them incapable of comprehension; *mantle:* Envelop.   68 *clearer:* Growing clearer.   70 *pay thy graces:* Requite your favors and virtues.   71 *Home:* Fully.

Thy brother was a furtherer° in the act. —
Thou art pinched° for 't now, Sebastian. *[To Antonio.]* Flesh and blood,
You, brother mine, that entertained ambition,   75
Expelled remorse° and nature,° whom,° with Sebastian,
Whose inward pinches therefore are most strong,
Would here have killed your king, I do forgive thee,
Unnatural though thou art. — Their understanding
Begins to swell, and the approaching tide   80
Will shortly fill the reasonable shore°
That now lies foul and muddy. Not one of them
That yet looks on me, or would know me. — Ariel,
Fetch me the hat and rapier in my cell.
                      [Ariel goes to the cell and returns immediately.]
I will discase° me and myself present   85
As I was sometime Milan.° Quickly, spirit!
Thou shalt ere long be free.   *Ariel sings and helps to attire him.*
Ariel: Where the bee sucks, there suck I.
    In a cowslip's bell I lie;
    There I couch° when owls do cry.   90
    On the bat's back I do fly
    After° summer merrily.
    Merrily, merrily shall I live now
    Under the blossom that hangs on the bough.
Prospero: Why, that's my dainty Ariel! I shall miss thee,   95
But yet thou shalt have freedom. So, so, so.°
To the King's ship, invisible as thou art!
There shalt thou find the mariners asleep
Under the hatches. The Master and the Boatswain
Being awake, enforce them to this place,   100
And presently,° I prithee.
Ariel: I drink the air before me and return
    Or ere° your pulse twice beat.   *Exit.*
Gonzalo: All torment, trouble, wonder, and amazement
Inhabits here. Some heavenly power guide us   105
Out of this fearful° country!
Prospero: Behold, sir King,
The wrongèd Duke of Milan, Prospero.
For more assurance that a living prince
Does now speak to thee, I embrace thy body;
And to thee and thy company I bid   110
A hearty welcome.   *[Embracing him.]*
Alonso: Whe'er thou be'st he or no,
Or some enchanted trifle° to abuse° me,

---

73 *furtherer:* Accomplice.   74 *pinched:* Punished, afflicted.   76 *remorse:* Pity; *nature:* Natural feeling; *whom:* I.e., who.   81 *reasonable shore:* Shores of reason, i.e., minds (their reason returns, like the incoming tide).   85 *discase:* Disrobe.   86 *As . . . Milan:* In my former appearance as Duke of Milan.   90 *couch:* Lie.   92 *After:* I.e., pursuing.   96 *So, so, so:* (Expresses approval of Ariel's help as valet.)   101 *presently:* Immediately.   103 *Or ere:* Before.   106 *fearful:* Frightening.   112 *trifle:* Trick of magic; *abuse:* Deceive.

As late° I have been, I not know. Thy pulse
Beats as of flesh and blood; and, since I saw thee,
Th' affliction of my mind amends, with which   115
I fear a madness held me. This must crave°—
An if this be at all°—a most strange story.°
Thy dukedom I resign,° and do entreat
Thou pardon me my wrongs.° But how should Prospero
Be living, and be here?
Prospero [to Gonzalo]:   First, noble friend,   120
Let me embrace thine age,° whose honor cannot
Be measured or confined.   *[Embracing him.]*
Gonzalo: Whether this be
Or be not, I'll not swear.
Prospero: You do yet taste
Some subtleties° o' th' isle, that will not let you
Believe things certain. Welcome, my friends all!   125
[Aside to Sebastian and Antonio.] But you, my brace° of lords, were I so
    minded,
I here could pluck His Highness' frown upon you
And justify you° traitors. At this time
I will tell no tales.
Sebastian: The devil speaks in him.
Prospero: No.
[To Antonio.] For you, most wicked sir, whom to call brother   130
Would even infect my mouth, I do forgive
Thy rankest fault—all of them; and require
My dukedom of thee, which perforce° I know
Thou must restore.
Alonso: If thou be'st Prospero,
Give us particulars of thy preservation,   135
How thou hast met us here, whom° three hours since
Were wrecked upon this shore, where I have lost—
How sharp the point of this remembrance is!—
My dear son Ferdinand.
Prospero: I am woe° for 't, sir.
Alonso: Irreparable is the loss, and Patience   140
Says it is past her cure.
Prospero: I rather think
You have not sought her help, of whose soft grace°
For the like loss I have her sovereign° aid
And rest myself content.
Alonso: You the like loss?

---

113 *late:* Lately.   116 *crave:* Require.   117 *An...all:* If this is actually happening; *story:*
I.e., explanation.   118 *Thy...resign:* (Alonso made arrangements with Antonio at the time
of Prospero's banishment for Milan to pay tribute to Naples; see I.ii.113-127.)   119 *wrongs:*
Wrongdoings.   121 *thine age:* Your venerable self.   124 *subtleties:* Illusions, magical powers (playing on the idea of "pastries, concoctions").   126 *brace:* Pair.   128 *justify you:*
Prove you to be.   133 *perforce:* Necessarily.   136 *whom:* I.e., who.   139 *woe:* Sorry.
142 *of...grace:* By whose mercy.   143 *sovereign:* Efficacious.

Prospero: As great to me as late,° and supportable   145
    To make the dear loss, have I° means much weaker
    Than you may call to comfort you; for I
    Have lost my daughter.
Alonso: A daughter?
    O heavens, that they were living both in Naples,   150
    The king and queen there! That° they were, I wish
    Myself were mudded° in that oozy bed
    Where my son lies. When did you lose your daughter?
Prospero: In this last tempest. I perceive these lords
    At this encounter do so much admire°   155
    That they devour their reason° and scarce think
    Their eyes do offices of truth, their words
    Are natural breath.° But, howsoever you have
    Been jostled from your senses, know for certain
    That I am Prospero and that very duke   160
    Which was thrust forth of° Milan, who most strangely
    Upon this shore, where you were wrecked, was landed
    To be the lord on 't. No more yet of this,
    For 'tis a chronicle of day by day,°
    Not a relation for a breakfast nor   165
    Befitting this first meeting. Welcome, sir.
    This cell's my court. Here have I few attendants,
    And subjects none abroad.° Pray you, look in.
    My dukedom since you have given me again,
    I will requite° you with as good a thing,   170
    At least bring forth a wonder to content ye
    As much as me my dukedom.

    Here Prospero discovers° Ferdinand and Miranda, playing at chess.

Miranda: Sweet lord, you play me false.°
Ferdinand: No, my dearest love,
    I would not for the world.   175
Miranda: Yes, for a score of kingdoms you should wrangle,
    And I would call it fair play.°
Alonso: If this prove
    A vision° of the island, one dear son
    Shall I twice lose.
Sebastian: A most high miracle!

---

145 *late:* Recent.   145–146 *supportable... have I:* To make the deeply felt loss bearable, I have.
151 *That:* So that.   152 *mudded:* Buried in the mud.   155 *admire:* Wonder.   156 *devour their reason:* I.e., are openmouthed, dumbfounded.   156–158 *scarce... breath:* Scarcely believe that their eyes inform them accurately as to what they see or that their words are naturally spoken.   161 *of:* From.   164 *of day by day:* Requiring days to tell.   168 *abroad:* Away from here, anywhere else.   170 *requite:* Repay; *discovers:* I.e., by opening a curtain, presumably rearstage.   173 *play me false:* I.e., press your advantage.   176–177 *Yes... play:* Yes, even if we were playing for only twenty kingdoms, you would still press your advantage against me, and I would lovingly let you do it as though it were fair play, or if you were to play not just for stakes but literally for kingdoms, my complaint would be out of order in that your "wrangling" would be proper.   178 *vision:* Illusion.

Ferdinand [approaching his father]:
    Though the seas threaten, they are merciful;   180
    I have cursed them without cause.   *[He kneels.]*
Alonso: Now all the blessings
    Of a glad father compass° thee about!
    Arise, and say how thou cam'st here.   *[Ferdinand rises.]*
Miranda: O, wonder!
    How many goodly creatures are there here!
    How beauteous mankind is! O brave° new world   185
    That has such people in 't!
Prospero: 'Tis new to thee.
Alonso: What is this maid with whom thou wast at play?
    Your eld'st° acquaintance cannot be three hours.
    Is she the goddess that hath severed us,
    And brought us thus together?
Ferdinand: Sir, she is mortal;   190
    But by immortal Providence she's mine.
    I chose her when I could not ask my father
    For his advice, nor thought I had one. She
    Is daughter to this famous Duke of Milan,
    Of whom so often I have heard renown,   195
    But never saw before; of whom I have
    Received a second life; and second father
    This lady makes him to me.
Alonso: I am hers.
    But O, how oddly will it sound that I
    Must ask my child forgiveness!
Prospero: There, sir, stop.   200
    Let us not burden our remembrances with
    A heaviness° that's gone.
Gonzalo: I have inly° wept,
    Or should have spoke ere this. Look down, you gods,
    And on this couple drop a blessèd crown!
    For it is you that have chalked forth the way°   205
    Which brought us hither.
Alonso: I say amen, Gonzalo!
Gonzalo: Was Milan° thrust from Milan, that his issue
    Should become kings of Naples? O, rejoice
    Beyond a common joy, and set it down
    With gold on lasting pillars: In one voyage   210
    Did Claribel her husband find at Tunis,
    And Ferdinand, her brother, found a wife
    Where he himself was lost; Prospero his dukedom
    In a poor isle; and all of us ourselves
    When no man was his own.°

---

182 *compass:* Encompass, embrace.   185 *brave:* Splendid, gorgeously appareled, handsome.   188 *eld'st:* Longest.   202 *heaviness:* Sadness;   *inly:* Inwardly.   205 *chalked . . . way:* Marked as with a piece of chalk the pathway.   207 *Was Milan:* Was the Duke of Milan.   214–215 *all . . . own:* All of us have found ourselves and our sanity when we all had lost our senses.

Alonso [to Ferdinand and Miranda]: Give me your hands.   215
   Let grief and sorrow still° embrace his° heart
   That° doth not wish you joy!
Gonzalo: Be it so! Amen!

   Enter Ariel, with the Master and Boatswain amazedly following.

   O, look, sir, look, sir! Here is more of us.
   I prophesied, if a gallows were on land,
   This fellow could not drown. — Now, blasphemy,°   220
   That swear'st grace o'erboard,° not an oath° on shore?
   Hast thou no mouth by land? What is the news?
Boatswain: The best news is that we have safely found
   Our King and company; the next, our ship —
   Which, but three glasses° since, we gave out° split —   225
   Is tight and yare° and bravely° rigged as when
   We first put out to sea.
Ariel [aside to Prospero]:   Sir, all this service
   Have I done since I went.
Prospero [aside to Ariel]:   My tricksy° spirit!
Alonso: These are not natural events; they strengthen°
   From strange to stranger. Say, how came you hither?   230
Boatswain: If I did think, sir, I were well awake,
   I'd strive to tell you. We were dead of sleep,°
   And — how we know not — all clapped under hatches,
   Where but even now, with strange and several° noises
   Of roaring, shrieking, howling, jingling chains,   235
   And more diversity of sounds, all horrible,
   We were awaked; straightway at liberty;
   Where we, in all her trim, freshly beheld
   Our royal, good, and gallant ship, our Master
   Cap'ring to eye° her. On a trice,° so please you,   240
   Even in a dream, were we divided from them°
   And were brought moping° hither.
Ariel [aside to Prospero]:   Was 't well done?
Prospero [aside to Ariel]: Bravely, my diligence. Thou shalt be free.
Alonso: This is as strange a maze as e'er men trod,
   And there is in this business more than nature   245
   Was ever conduct° of. Some oracle
   Must rectify our knowledge.
Prospero: Sir, my liege,
   Do not infest° your mind with beating on°
   The strangeness of this business. At picked° leisure,

---

216 *still:* Always; *his:* That person's.   217 *That:* Who.   220 *blasphemy:* I.e., blasphemer.
221 *That swear'st grace o'erboard:* I.e., you who banish heavenly grace from the ship by your
blasphemies; *not an oath:* Aren't you going to swear an oath.   225 *glasses:* I.e., hours; *gave out:*
Reported, professed to be.   226 *yare:* Ready; *bravely:* Splendidly.   228 *tricksy:* Ingenious,
sportive.   229 *strengthen:* Increase.   232 *dead of sleep:* Deep in sleep.   234 *several:* Diverse.   240 *Cap'ring to eye:* Dancing for joy to see; *On a trice:* In an instant.   241 *them:*
I.e., the other crew members.   242 *moping:* In a daze.   246 *conduct:* Guide.   248 *in-
fest:* Harass, disturb; *beating on:* Worrying about.   249 *picked:* Chosen, convenient.

Which shall be shortly, single° I'll resolve° you,   250
Which to you shall seem probable,° of every
These° happened accidents;° till when, be cheerful
And think of each thing well.° *[Aside to Ariel.]* Come hither, spirit.
Set Caliban and his companions free.
Untie the spell. *[Exit Ariel.]* How fares my gracious sir?   255
There are yet missing of your company
Some few odd° lads that you remember not.

Enter Ariel, driving in Caliban, Stephano, and Trinculo, in their stolen apparel.

Stephano: Every man shift° for all the rest,° and let no man take care for
himself; for all is but fortune. Coragio,° bully monster,° coragio!
Trinculo: If these be true spies° which I wear in my head, here's a goodly 260
sight.
Caliban: O Setebos, these be brave° spirits indeed!
How fine° my master is! I am afraid
He will chastise me.
Sebastian: Ha, ha!   265
What things are these, my lord Antonio?
Will money buy 'em?
Antonio: Very like. One of them
Is a plain fish, and no doubt marketable.
Prospero: Mark but the badges° of these men, my lords,
Then say if they be true.° This misshapen knave,   270
His mother was a witch, and one so strong
That could control the moon, make flows and ebbs,
And deal in her command without her power.°
These three have robbed me, and this demidevil —
For he's a bastard° one — had plotted with them   275
To take my life. Two of these fellows you
Must know and own.° This thing of darkness I
Acknowledge mine.
Caliban: I shall be pinched to death.
Alonso: Is not this Stephano, my drunken butler?
Sebastian: He is drunk now. Where had he wine?
Alonso: And Trinculo is reeling ripe.° Where should they   280
Find this grand liquor that hath gilded° em?
[To Trinculo.] How cam'st thou in this pickle?°

---

250 *single:* Privately, by my own human powers; *resolve:* Satisfy, explain to.   251 *probable:*
Plausible.   251–252 *of every These:* About every one of these.   252 *accidents:* Occurrences.   253 *well:* Favorably.   257 *odd:* Unaccounted for.   258 *shift:* Provide; *for all the
rest:* (Stephano drunkenly gets wrong the saying "Every man for himself.")   259 *Coragio:*
Courage; *bully monster:* Gallant monster (ironical).   260 *true spies:* Accurate observers (i.e.,
sharp eyes).   262 *brave:* Handsome.   263 *fine:* Splendidly attired.   269 *badges:* Emblems of cloth or silver worn by retainers to indicate whom they serve. (Prospero refers here
to the stolen clothes as emblems of their villainy.)   270 *true:* Honest.   273 *deal . . .
power:* Wield the moon's power, either without her authority or beyond her influence, or, even
though to do so was beyond Sycorax's own power.   275 *bastard:* Counterfeit.   277 *own:*
Recognize, admit as belonging to you.   281 *reeling ripe:* Stumbling drunk.   282 *gilded:*
(1) Flushed, made drunk (2) covered with gilt (suggesting the horse urine).   283 *pickle:*
(1) Fix, predicament (2) pickling brine (in this case, horse urine).

Trinculo: I have been in such a pickle since I saw you last that, I fear me,
    will never out of my bones. I shall not fear flyblowing.°   285
Sebastian: Why, how now, Stephano?
Stephano: O, touch me not! I am not Stephano, but a cramp.
Prospero: You'd be king o' the isle, sirrah?°
Stephano: I should have been a sore° one, then.
Alonso [pointing to Caliban]: This is a strange thing as e'er I looked on.   290
Prospero: He is as disproportioned in his manners
    As in his shape. — Go, sirrah, to my cell.
    Take with you your companions. As you look
    To have my pardon, trim° it handsomely.
Caliban: Ay, that I will; and I'll be wise hereafter   295
    And seek for grace.° What a thrice-double ass
    Was I to take this drunkard for a god
    And worship this dull fool!
Prospero: Go to. Away!
Alonso: Hence, and bestow your luggage where you found it.
Sebastian: Or stole it, rather.   *[Exeunt Caliban, Stephano, and Trinculo.]*   300
Prospero: Sir, I invite Your Highness and your train
    To my poor cell, where you shall take your rest
    For this one night; which, part of it, I'll waste°
    With such discourse as, I not doubt, shall make it
    Go quick away: the story of my life,   305
    And the particular accidents° gone by
    Since I came to this isle. And in the morn
    I'll bring you to your ship, and so to Naples,
    Where I have hope to see the nuptial
    Of these our dear-belovèd solemnized;   310
    And thence retire me° to my Milan, where
    Every third thought shall be my grave.
Alonso: I long
    To hear the story of your life, which must
    Take° the ear strangely.
Prospero: I'll deliver° all;
    And promise you calm seas, auspicious gales,   315
    And sail so expeditious that shall catch
    Your royal fleet far off.° *[Aside to Ariel.]* My Ariel, chick,
    That is thy charge. Then to the elements
    Be free, and fare thou well! — Please you, draw near.°
                             Exeunt omnes [except Prospero].

---

285 *flyblowing:* I.e., being fouled by fly eggs (from which he is saved by being pickled).
288 *sirrah:* (Standard form of address to an inferior, here expressing reprimand.)   289 *sore:*
(1) Tyrannical (2) sorry, inept (3) wracked by pain.   294 *trim:* Prepare, decorate.   296 *grace:*
Pardon, favor.   303 *waste:* Spend.   306 *accidents:* Occurrences.   311 *retire me:* Return.   314 *Take:* Take effect upon, enchant; *deliver:* Declare, relate.   316–317 *catch . . . far
off:* Enable you to catch up with the main part of your royal fleet, now afar off en route to
Naples (see I.ii.233–236).   319 *draw near:* I.e., enter my cell.

EPILOGUE

Spoken by Prospero.

Now my charms are all o'erthrown,
And what strength I have 's mine own,
Which is most faint. Now, 'tis true,
I must be here confined by you
Or sent to Naples. Let me not,   5
Since I have my dukedom got
And pardoned the deceiver, dwell
In this bare island by your spell,
But release me from my bands°
With the help of your good hands.°   10
Gentle breath° of yours my sails
Must fill, or else my project fails,
Which was to please. Now I want°
Spirits to enforce,° art to enchant,
And my ending is despair,   15
Unless I be relieved by prayer,°
Which pierces so that it assaults°
Mercy itself, and frees° all faults.
As you from crimes° would pardoned be,
Let your indulgence° set me free.   *Exit.* 20

Epilogue.   9 *bands:* Bonds.   10 *hands:* I.e., applause (the noise of which would break the spell of silence).   11 *Gentle breath:* Favorable breeze (produced by hands clapping or favorable comment).   13 *want:* Lack.   14 *enforce:* Control.   16 *prayer:* I.e., Prospero's petition to the audience.   17 *assaults:* Rightfully gains the attention of.   18 *frees:* Obtains forgiveness for.   19 *crimes:* Sins.   20 *indulgence:* (1) Humoring, lenient approval (2) remission of punishment for sin.

Considerations for Critical Thinking and Writing

1. FIRST RESPONSE. Though Caliban is presented as a depraved savage, does he have any dignity or redeeming features? Why isn't he merely a flat character?

2. Explain how Ariel and Caliban serve as character foils for each other. Consider their physical appearances and their roles as servants to Prospero.

3. Describe Miranda. How is she a product of "nurture" rather than nature? What values does she represent in the play?

4. Why does Prospero initially want to make difficult the relationship between Miranda and Ferdinand? How does this complicate the plot?

5. How does Ferdinand's love for Miranda differ from Caliban's attraction to her? How do their responses to her reveal the character of each?

6. Describe how Sebastian and Antonio's plan to kill King Alonso parallels the plan of Caliban, Stephano, and Trinculo to kill Prospero. How do these parallel plots serve as commentaries on each other?

7. Prospero has been criticized by some readers as an overbearing patriarchal figure, a colonist, and even a racist. Consider these assertions, and deter-

mine through your own perspective on him whether you agree or disagree with these charges.

8. According to Gonzalo, what constitutes an ideal commonwealth (II.i.137–157)? How does Gonzalo's vision of a ruler's power compare with Prospero's? How does it compare with Sebastian's and Stephano's ambitions for power?

9. Stephano, King Alonso's drunken butler, says to Caliban, "You cannot tell who's your friend" (II.ii.74–75). How does this warning represent an important element in the plot of the play?

10. Discuss Prospero's comparison of life to the stage (IV.i.148–158). How is the theme of reality and illusion made an issue throughout the play?

11. How does Prospero's magic differ from that of Sycorax? Why do you think Prospero gives up his magic (V.i.50–57)?

12. Describe the natural world depicted on the island. Is it innocent or corrupt? Is it redeemed by contact with civilization or corrupted by it?

CONNECTIONS TO OTHER SELECTIONS

1. In an essay compare *The Tempest*'s island setting with the forest in *A Midsummer Night's Dream* (p. 1327). Describe each setting, and explain how it represents a state of mind as well as a physical location.

2. Compare Prospero's attitudes about revenge against those who conspire against him with Hamlet's attitudes. Why can't Hamlet agree with Prospero's conviction that "The rarer action is / In virtue than in vengeance" (V. i.27–28)?

3. Write an essay on the function of illusion in *The Tempest* and *The Glass Menagerie* (p. 1864). How do the characters' illusions indicate the thematic concerns of each play?

4. Discuss in an essay the father-daughter relationships in *The Tempest* and in Nathaniel Hawthorne's short story "Rappaccini's Daughter" (p. 341). In particular consider the degree to which Miranda and Beatrice are protected, victimized, or both by their fathers.

PERSPECTIVES ON SHAKESPEARE

Objections to the Elizabethan Theater by the Mayor of London
1597

The inconueniences that grow by Stage playes abowt the Citie of London.

1. They are a speaciall cause of corrupting their Youth, conteninge nothinge but vnchast matters, lascivious devices, shiftes of Coozenage,° & other lewd & vngodly practizes, being so as that they impresse the very qualitie & corruption of manners which they represent, Contrary to the rules & art prescribed for the making of Comedies eauen amonge the Heathen, who vsd

shiftes of Coozenage: Perverse behavior.

them seldom & at certen sett tymes, and not all the year longe as our manner is. Whearby such as frequent them, beinge of the base & refuze sort of people or such young gentlemen as haue small regard of credit or conscience, drawe the same into imitacion and not to the avoidinge the like vices which they represent.

2. They are the ordinary places for vagrant persons, Maisterles men, thieves, horse stealers, whoremongers, Coozeners, Conycatchers,° contrivers of treason, and other idele and daungerous persons to meet together & to make theire matches to the great displeasure of Almightie God & the hurt & annoyance of her Maiesties people, which cannot be prevented nor discovered by the Gouernours of the Citie for that they are owt of the Citiees iurisdiction.

3. They maintaine idlenes in such persons as haue no vocation & draw apprentices and other seruantes from theire ordinary workes and all sortes of people from the resort vnto sermons and other Christian exercises, to the great hinderance of traides & prophanation of religion established by her highnes within this Realm.

4. In the time of sickness it is fownd by experience, that many hauing sores and yet not hart sicke take occasion hearby to walk abroad & to recreat themselves by heareinge a play Whearby others are infected, and them selves also many things miscarry.

From Edmund K. Chambers, The Elizabethan Stage

Conycatchers: Tricksters.

CONSIDERATIONS FOR CRITICAL THINKING AND WRITING

1. Summarize the mayor's objections to the theater. Do any of his reasons for protesting theatrical productions seem reasonable to you? Why or why not?

2. Are any of these concerns reflected in attitudes about the theater today? Why or why not?

3. How would you defend *Hamlet* or *A Midsummer Night's Dream* against charges that they draw some people into "imitacion and not to the avoidinge the like vices which they represent"?

LISA JARDINE (B. 1944)

On Boy Actors in Female Roles   *1989*

Every schoolchild knows that there were no women actors on the Elizabethan stage; the female parts were taken by young male actors. But every schoolchild also learns that this fact is of little consequence for the twentieth-century reader of Shakespeare's plays. Because the taking of female parts by boys was universal and commonplace, we are told, it was accepted as "verisimilitude" by the Elizabethan audience, who simply disregarded it, as we would disregard the creaking of stage scenery and accept the backcloth forest as "real" for the duration of the play.

Conventional or no, the taking of female parts by boy players actually occasioned a good deal of contemporary comment and created considerable moral uneasiness, even amongst those who patronized and supported the theaters. Amongst those who opposed them, transvestism on stage was a main plank in the anti-stage polemic. "The appareil of wemen is a great provocation of men to lust and leacherie," wrote Dr. John Rainoldes, a leading Oxford divine (quoting the Bishop of Paris), in *Th' Overthrow of Stage-Playes* (Middleburgh, 1599). And he continues with an unhealthy interest which infuses the entire pamphlet: "A womans garment beeing put on a man doeth vehemently touch and moue him with the remembrance and imagination of a woman; and the imagination of a thing desirable doth stirr up the desire."

According to Rainoldes, and the authorities with whose independent testimony he lards his polemic, the wearing of female dress by boy players "is an occasion of wantonnes and lust." Sexuality, misdirected toward the boy masquerading in female dress, is "stirred" by attire and gesture; male prostitution and perverted sexual activity is the inevitable accompaniment of female impersonation.

From *Still Harping on Daughters*, Second Edition

CONSIDERATIONS FOR CRITICAL THINKING AND WRITING

1. How does Jardine complicate the Elizabethan convention of boy actors assuming female roles? To what extent does it add to the representation of Elizabethan theater put forward by the Mayor of London (p. 1543)?

2. What do you think would be your own response to a boy actor playing a female role? Consider, for example, Hippolyta in *A Midsummer Night's Dream*, Ophelia in *Hamlet*, or Miranda in *The Tempest*.

SAMUEL JOHNSON (1709–1784)

On Shakespeare's Characters   1765

Shakespeare is above all writers, at least above all modern writers, the poet of nature: the poet that holds up to his readers a faithful mirror of manners and life. His characters are not modified by the customs of particular places, unpracticed by the rest of the world; by the peculiarities of studies or professions, which can operate but upon small numbers; or by the accidents of transient fashions or temporary opinions: they are the genuine progeny of common humanity, such as the world will always supply, and observation will always find. His persons act and speak by the influence of those general passions and principles by which all minds are agitated, and the whole system of life is continued in motion. In the writings of other poets a character is too often an individual; in those of Shakespeare it is commonly a species.

From the preface to Johnson's edition of Shakespeare's works

CONSIDERATIONS FOR CRITICAL THINKING AND WRITING

1. Johnson made this famous assessment of Shakespeare's ability to portray "common humanity" in the eighteenth century. As a twentieth-century reader, explain why you agree or disagree with Johnson's view that Shakespeare's characters have universal appeal.

2. Write an essay discussing whether you think it is desirable or necessary for characters to be "a faithful mirror of manners and life." Along the way consider whether you encountered any characters in *Hamlet* or *The Tempest* that do not provide what you consider to be an accurate mirror of human life.

SIGMUND FREUD (1856–1939)

On Repression in Hamlet

1900

Another of the great creations of tragic poetry, Shakespeare's *Hamlet,* has its roots in the same soil as *Oedipus Rex.* But the changed treatment of the same material reveals the whole difference in the mental life of these two widely separated epochs of civilization: the secular advance of repression in the emotional life of mankind. In the *Oedipus* the child's wishful fantasy that underlies it is brought into the open and realized as it would be in a dream. In *Hamlet* it remains repressed; and — just as in the case of a neurosis — we only learn of its existence from its inhibiting consequences. Strangely enough, the overwhelming effect produced by the more modern tragedy has turned out to be compatible with the fact that people have remained completely in the dark as to the hero's character. The play is built up on Hamlet's hesitations over fulfilling the task of revenge that is assigned to him; but its text offers no reasons or motives for these hesitations and an immense variety of attempts at interpreting them have failed to produce a result. According to the view which was originated by Goethe and is still the prevailing one today, Hamlet represents the type of man whose power of direct action is paralyzed by an excessive development of his intellect. (He is "sicklied o'er with the pale cast of thought.") According to another view, the dramatist has tried to portray a pathologically irresolute character which might be classed as neurasthenic. The plot of the drama shows us, however, that Hamlet is far from being represented as a person incapable of taking any action. We see him doing so on two occasions: first in a sudden outburst of temper, when he runs his sword through the eavesdropper behind the arras, and secondly, in a premeditated and even crafty fashion, when, with all the callousness of a Renaissance prince, he sends the two courtiers to the death that had been planned for himself. What is it, then, that inhibits him in fulfilling the task set him by his father's ghost? The answer, once again, is that it is the peculiar nature of the task. Hamlet is able to do anything — except take vengeance on the man who did away with his father and took that father's place with his mother, the man who shows him the repressed wishes of his own childhood realized. Thus the loathing which should drive him on to revenge is replaced in him by self-reproaches, by scruples of conscience, which remind him that he himself is literally no better than the sinner whom he is to punish. Here I have translated into conscious terms what was bound to remain unconscious in Hamlet's mind; and if anyone is inclined to call him a hysteric, I can only accept the fact as one that is implied by my interpretation. The distaste for sexuality expressed by Hamlet in his conversation with Ophelia fits in very well with this: the same distaste which was destined to take possession of the poet's mind more and more during the years that followed, and which reached its extreme expression in *Timon of Athens*. For it can of course only be the poet's own mind which confronts us in Hamlet. I observe in a book on Shakespeare by Georg Brandes (1896) a statement that *Hamlet* was written immediately after the death of Shakespeare's father (in 1601), that is, under the immediate impact of his bereavement and, as we may well assume, while his childhood feelings about his father had been freshly revived. It is known, too, that Shakespeare's own son who died at an early age bore the name "Hamnet," which is identical with "Hamlet." Just as *Hamlet* deals with the relation of a son to his parents, so *Macbeth* (written at approximately the same period) is concerned with the subject of childlessness. But just as all neurotic symptoms, and, for that matter, dreams, are capable of being "overinterpreted" and indeed need to be, if they are to be fully understood, so all genuinely creative writings are the product of more than a single motive and more than a single impulse in the poet's mind, and are open to more than a single interpretation. In what I have written I have only attempted to interpret the deepest layer of impulses in the mind of the creative writer.

From *The Interpretation of Dreams*, translated by James Strachey

CONSIDERATIONS FOR CRITICAL THINKING AND WRITING

1. What reason does Freud offer for Hamlet's inability to avenge his father's death? Explain whether you find Freud's reasoning convincing.

2. Read the section on psychological criticism (p. 2029) in Chapter 37, "Critical Strategies for Reading," and then discuss Freud's assertion that "it can of course only be the poet's mind which confronts us in Hamlet." Explain why you agree or disagree.

3. Write an essay discussing whether you think Freud's approach to *Hamlet* opens up perspectives on the play or narrowly limits them.

JAN KOTT (B. 1914)
On Producing Hamlet   1964

No Dane of flesh and blood has been written about so extensively as Hamlet. Shakespeare's prince is certainly the best known representative of his nation. Innumerable glossaries and commentaries have grown round Hamlet, and he is one of the few literary heroes who live apart from the text, apart from the theater. His name means something even to those who have never seen or read Shakespeare's play. In this respect he is rather like Leonardo's Mona Lisa. We know she is smiling even before we have seen the picture, as it were. It contains not only what Leonardo expressed in it but also everything that has been written about it. Too many people — girls, women, poets, painters — have tried to solve the mystery of that smile. It is not just Mona Lisa that is smiling at us now, but all those who have tried to analyze, or imitate, that smile.

This is also the case with *Hamlet*, or rather — with *Hamlet* in the theater. For we have been separated from the text not only by Hamlet's "independent life" in our culture, but simply by the size of the play. *Hamlet* cannot be performed in its entirety, because the performance would last nearly six hours. One has to select, curtail, and cut. One can perform only one of several *Hamlet*s potentially existing in this arch-play. It will always be a poorer *Hamlet* than Shakespeare's *Hamlet* is; but it may also be a *Hamlet* enriched by being of our time. It may, but I would rather say — it must be so.

For *Hamlet* cannot be played simply. This may be the reason why it is so tempting to producers and actors. Many generations have seen their own reflections in this play. The genius of *Hamlet* consists, perhaps, in the fact that the play can serve as a mirror. An ideal *Hamlet* would be one most true to Shakespeare and most modern at the same time. Is this possible? I do not know. But we can only appraise any Shakespearean production by asking how much there is of Shakespeare in it, and how much of us.

What I have in mind is not a forced topicality, a *Hamlet* that would be set in a cellar of young existentialists. *Hamlet* has been performed for that matter in evening dress and in circus tights; in medieval armor and in Renaissance costume. Costumes do not matter. What matters is that through Shakespeare's text we ought to get at our modern experience, anxiety, and sensibility.

There are many subjects in *Hamlet*. There is politics, force opposed to morality; there is discussion of the divergence between the theory and practice, of the ultimate purpose of life; there is tragedy of love, as well as family drama, political, eschatological, and metaphysical problems are considered. There is everything you want, including deep psychological analysis, a bloody story, a duel, and general slaughter. One can select at will. But one must know what one selects, and why.

From *"Hamlet* of the Mid-Century" in *Shakespeare Our Contemporary*,
translated by Boleslaw Taborski

CONSIDERATIONS FOR CRITICAL THINKING AND WRITING

1. "Many generations have seen their own reflections in this play." Use this statement as a basis for researching productions of *Hamlet*. How have events contemporary to the play's performances influenced the ways it has been presented?

2. Explain why you think it is good or bad for a producer to interpret a play in light of events contemporary to it.

3. If you were to produce *Hamlet* today, what would you emphasize? Consider how you would handle the setting, costuming, casting, and theme.

4. What do you think a reader-response critic would have to say about Kott's comments on producing *Hamlet*? Base your answer on the discussion of reader-response criticism (p. 2039) in Chapter 37, "Critical Strategies for Reading."

COPPÉLIA KAHN (B. 1939)
On Cuckoldry in Hamlet   *1981*

The Ghost in *Hamlet* is so poignantly powerful in his injured majesty that it seems ungracious to remember that he is also a cuckold. He himself obliquely notes it when he calls Claudius "that incestuous, that adulterate beast," distinguishing incest, the fact of his brother's sexual liaison with Gertrude, from its timing, which made it adultery (I.v.42). Hamlet's awareness of this ignominious aspect of his father's grievance, though only indirectly revealed to us, shapes his attitude toward the great task of revenge by complicating his identification with his father.[1] A mighty wrong has been done to a noble king; as he is noble, so must his anger and his cause be great. But insofar as part of that wrong is cuckoldry, his nobility is diminished, his anger impotent, and his cause an embarrassment. Viewed in this context, Hamlet's well-known misogyny and preoccupation with Gertrude's faults are an outlet for the rage mingled with shame he feels at his father's situation. He must bury or disguise his awareness of it, because to admit it would damage severely his idealized image of that father. So long as he can blame a woman's frailty for the indignity his father suffers, as the conventions of cuckoldry enable him to do, that image can be saved. But at the same time, his concern with his mother's crime diverts him from revenge and inevitably reminds him of his father's weakness: King Hamlet, like the most ordinary cuckold, was hoodwinked by his own wife. Thus to the extent that Hamlet sees his father as a cuckold, his anxiety and propensity to delay revenge are increased by a paralyzing ambivalence.[2]

. . . I do not suggest that cuckoldry is a major issue in *Hamlet*, or for Hamlet himself. Rather, I merely wish to show that it is one aspect of Hamlet's dilemma, largely ignored by critics, and that if taken into account it deepens the tragic complications of his task. Much of the evidence I offer for the importance of cuckoldry has been presented before as evidence of the oedipal situation in the play.[3] In a longer study, it could be shown how cuckoldry

[1] Cf. Avi Erlich's interesting argument in *Hamlet's Absent Father* (Princeton: Princeton UP, 1978). He contends that Hamlet delays his revenge because he is waiting for his absent, ghostly father to prove his strength by returning to kill Claudius himself. The source of Hamlet's perception of his father as weak and absent, Erlich holds, is his unconscious fantasy that his father was castrated by Gertrude in a primal scene. I see evidence of a different kind of castration, in the fact rather than the fantasy of King Hamlet's cuckoldry.

[2] Richard Flatter, in his *Hamlet's Father* (New Haven: Yale UP, 1949), argues that Hamlet's delay is largely caused by the Ghost's prohibition against harming his mother, for Hamlet cannot properly revenge his father's murder until he discovers whether his mother was complicit in it. Flatter dismisses the question of Gertrude's adultery, saying that it has been partly absolved by time and her subsequent marriage, and stresses the problem of her complicity. But he does show, in a penetrating analysis of the closet scene, how obsessed Hamlet is with the connection between the adultery and the murder, and how the purposes of the father, to conceal this connection, and of the son, to discover it, diverge.

[3] Ernest Jones's *Hamlet and Oedipus* (Garden City, NY: Doubleday Anchor, 1955) remains the classic oedipal interpretation. For a useful review of similar interpretations from Freud to 1965, see Norman Holland, *Psychoanalysis and Shakespeare* (New York: McGraw-Hill, 1964), especially pp. 164-178 and pp. 180-184. In the oedipal situation, the son's feelings toward his mother are at least as complicated and ambivalent as those toward his father. Not only does he desire her, he also feels that she has betrayed him, because he once thought her the virginal object solely of his affections—a feeling that would powerfully reinforce Hamlet's resentment at Gertrude's betrayal of his father. Incestuous desire also goes hand in hand with matricidal impulses, as Frederic C. Wertham believes, in "The Matricidal Impulse: Critique of Freud's Interpretation of *Hamlet*," in *The Design Within: Psychoanalytic Approaches to Shakespeare*, ed. Melvin D. Faber (New York: Science House, 1970), pp. 113-120, arguing that "The basis of Hamlet's hostility against his mother is his overattachment to her," a reaction-formation sparked by fear of the castrating father. Hamlet's sexual disgust at Gertrude and women in general can be read both in oedipal terms and in terms of cuckoldry without conflict. In both contexts, Hamlet as son shares his father's sense of shame at having been sexually betrayed by a woman he loved.

participates in that situation, but here I am only concerned with isolating cuckoldry somewhat artificially from the play's other concerns so as to demonstrate its presence and its importance.

From *Man's Estate: Masculine Identity in Shakespeare*

CONSIDERATIONS FOR CRITICAL THINKING AND WRITING

1. According to Kahn, why is cuckoldry important for understanding Hamlet's "propensity to delay revenge"?
2. In an essay compare Sigmund Freud's analysis (p. 1546) of why Hamlet delays his revenge with Kahn's analysis.

RUSSELL JACKSON (B. 1949)
A Film Diary of the Shooting of Kenneth Branagh's Hamlet   *1996*

Wednesday 3 January
Rehearsals Begin

First morning in Shepperton. This may be one of the major British studios but it's not, on first sight, impressive. Located in a semi-suburban hinterland southwest of London, it seems at first like an industrial estate, a jumble of sheds, hangars, workshops, and what look like builders' yards, with a mansion trapped in the middle of it all like a genteel hostage from Edwardian England. . . .

We're in the elegant boardroom of the old house, round a long green-baize covered table. First session is with Derek Jacobi (Claudius) and Julie Christie (Gertrude), plus Ken, Orlando Seale (his "acting double"), Annie Wotton (Script Supervisor), Simon Mosley (First A.D.), and Hugh Cruttwell.

Ken distributes phials [vials] of a herbal "Rescue Remedy" (only half a joke, admitting nervous apprehension). Everyone has read the screenplay, and the actors have already had some discussion of their roles with Ken, but these days of rehearsal before we begin shooting will give everyone time for reappraisal, adjustments, and (most important) finding out how the story will be told by *this* company of actors, in *these* circumstances. We won't start with a read-through: better to edge toward the play. We discuss royal families (including the current one), privacy, politics, and draw toward a reading of the scenes when Claudius and Gertrude are together. There's talk about the issue of complicity between them (not at all, so far as murder is concerned) and the "essential" Claudius, which she took (and part of him still takes) as loving, kind, a "good" man. Derek goes along with this, though he and Hugh Cruttwell remind us of Hamlet's very different point of view. Gertrude and Claudius feel responsible for Hamlet but Claudius has another agenda she knows nothing about — concerning the potential threat posed by her son.

After lunch the Polonius family join us, with Horatio. By now we feel able to discuss frankly and simply (and off the record) our own experiences of family, bereavement, grief. (This is not just to canvass ideas about the emotions of the play to draw on them in performance: it also establishes common ground among us.) Then we try to imagine an "ideal" family, successful and well-balanced according to current middle-class notions, professional but not competitive, materially well-off but not showy—which (we agree) turns out quite repulsive. Then on to the Polonius family.

Polonius (Richard Briers) was promoted by new king. Laertes (Michael Maloney) is in Paris getting the gentlemanly accomplishments (N.B. not at Wittenberg). Ophelia (Kate Winslett) and Hamlet have been having an affair (yes, they have been to bed together, because we want this relationship to be as serious as possible) since the death of Hamlet senior. (Effect of a surge of feeling in time of bereavement and crisis?)

Thursday 4 — Monday 8 January

We work through scenes, trying various approaches, finding snags, problems, opportunities. Ophelia's motivations in returning Hamlet's love tokens are considered: she is going further than Polonius suggested in any instructions we have heard, and whatever her father and the king expect from this confrontation, she has her own agenda (perhaps to find out why Hamlet is behaving this way to her, to put him on the spot?). The kinder and more circumspect Polonius seems, the harder it will be for her to betray him—hence her lying to Hamlet ("Where's your father?—At home, my lord"). In "To be or not to be" Ken wants to show Hamlet alone with his mirror image(s) in the vast space of the mirrored hall. He has to be careful not to give the soliloquy an energy or momentum that it does not need—those qualities are coming soon enough in what follows when he encounters Ophelia. Ken steers Derek toward seeming even more vulnerable as Claudius, "quietly anxious" about Hamlet after "nunnery" scene, rarely openly angry, even when Rosencrantz and Guildenstern have screwed up. So, when he does flare up, becomes desperate, it will be more shocking.

On 8 January we go over each actor's list of their character's priorities. Claudius has specific aims: inspiring confidence and trust in himself; loving Gertrude; making Hamlet look indulgent and neurotic (and thus defusing him); creating a new, strong, triumphalist Denmark (a military regime). Gertrude's aims are more general: decorum, sense of behaving properly in public; *noblesse oblige*, etiquette; sense of culture, confidence; loving Hamlet. Old Hamlet (Brian Blessed) points out that when he was alive he never let Claudius see how little he mattered—there has to be an underlying bitterness in what Claudius has done to get the crown as well as intense love for Gertrude. We consider different ways of showing these relationships in a short flashback—perhaps Old Hamlet and his son playing chess while Gertrude and Claudius watch, or some other activity (perhaps outdoors) that will focus their various feelings for each other.

From *Hamlet*. Screenplay and Introduction by
Kenneth Branagh. Film diary by Russell Jackson

Considerations for Critical Thinking and Writing

1. In what sense can the actors' discussions of character motivation and background be considered an interpretation of *Hamlet*? Why do you suppose the actors find these kinds of discussions useful?

2. Create a list of "priorities" for characters *not* already discussed by the actors on Branagh's set. Consider, for example, Horatio, Laertes, Rosencrantz, Guildenstern, Marcellus, or Bernardo.

3. How does Jackson's comment that it was essential for the actors to determine "how the story will be told by *this* company of actors, in *these* circumstances" compare with Jan Kott's observations on producing *Hamlet* (p. 1547)?

4. Rent a videotape of Branagh's *Hamlet* and write an essay that focuses on a single character or scene that you find especially effective (or not).

LOUIS ADRIAN MONTROSE (B. 1946)

On Amazonian Mythology
in A Midsummer Night's Dream   1983

The beginning of *A Midsummer Night's Dream* coincides with the end of a struggle in which Theseus has been victorious over the Amazon warrior:

> Hippolyta, I woo'd thee with my sword,
> And won thy love doing thee injuries;
> But I will wed thee in another key,
> With pomp, with triumph, and with revelling.
>   (I.i.16–19)

Descriptions of the Amazons are ubiquitous in Elizabethan texts. . . .
Sixteenth-century travel narratives often recreate the ancient Amazons of Scythia in South America or in Africa. Invariably, the Amazons are relocated just beyond the receding boundary of *terra incognita.*° Thus, in Sierra Leone in 1582, the chaplain of an English expedition to the Spice Islands recorded the report of a Portuguese trader that "near the mountains of the moon there is a queen, empress of all these Amazons, a witch and a cannibal who daily feeds on the flesh of boys. She ever remains unmarried, but she has intercourse with a great number of men by whom she begets offspring. The kingdom, however, remains hereditary to the daughters, not to the sons."[1] This cultural fantasy assimilates Amazonian myth, witchcraft, and cannibalism into an anticulture which precisely inverts European norms of political authority, sexual license, marriage practices, and inheritance rules.[2] The attitude toward the Amazons

terra incognita: Unknown land.

[1]*An Elizabethan in 1582: The Diary of Richard Madox, Fellow of All Souls,* ed. Elizabeth Story Donno, Hakluyt Society, second ser., no. 47 (London, 1977), p. 183. I owe this reference to Stephen Greenblatt, *Renaissance Self-Fashioning: From More to Shakespeare* (Chicago, 1980), p. 181.

[2]The linkage of Amazon, witch, and cannibal exemplifies a logic of inversion ingrained in European categories of thought. It has been suggested recently that sixteenth- and seventeenth-century witchcraft beliefs were a coherent, meaningful, and indeed necessary component of a larger intellectual system based upon principles of hierarchy, opposition, and inversion. This system linked together demonism, political sedition and rebellion, and female misrule as inversions of the divinely sanctioned order in the cosmos, state, and family. See Stuart Clark, "Inversion, Misrule and the Meaning of Witchcraft," *Past & Present,* no. 87 (May 1980), 98–127. . . .

expressed in such Renaissance texts is a mixture of fascination and horror. Amazonian mythology seems symbolically to embody and to control a collective anxiety about the power of the female not only to dominate or reject the male but to create and destroy him. It is an ironic acknowledgment by an androcentric° culture of the degree to which men are in fact dependent upon women: upon mothers and nurses, for their birth and nurture; upon mistresses and wives, for the validation of their manhood.

Shakespeare engages his wedding play in a dialectic with this mythological formation. The Amazons have been defeated before the play begins; and nuptial rites are to be celebrated when it ends. *A Midsummer Night's Dream* focuses upon different crucial transitions in the male and female life cycles: the fairy plot, upon taking "a little changeling boy" from childhood into youth, from the world of the mother into the world of the father; the Athenian plot, upon taking a maiden from youth into maturity, from the world of the father into the world of the husband. The pairing of the four Athenian lovers is made possible by the magical powers of Oberon and made lawful by the political authority of Theseus. Each of these rulers is preoccupied with the fulfillment of his own desires in the possession or repossession of a wife. Only after Hippolyta has been mastered by Theseus may marriage seal them "in everlasting bond of fellowship" (I.i.85). And only after "proud Titania" has been degraded by "jealous Oberon" (II.i.60, 61), has "in mild terms begg'd" (IV.i.53) his patience, and has readily yielded the changeling boy to him, may they be "new in amity" (IV.i.82).

The . . . structure of *A Midsummer Night's Dream* eventually restores the inverted Amazonian system of gender and nurture to a patriarchal norm.

From "'Shaping Fantasies': Figurations of Gender and Power in Elizabethan Culture," *Representations,* Spring 1983

androcentric: Male-centered.

CONSIDERATIONS FOR CRITICAL THINKING AND WRITING

1. How does Montrose use "Amazonian mythology" to account for the plot elements in the play?

2. In an essay use the insights provided in Montrose's perspective to explore how order is associated with masculinity and rebellion is associated with femininity in *A Midsummer Night's Dream.*

JAMES KINCAID (B. 1937)
On the Value of Comedy in the Face of Tragedy 1991

[O]ur current hierarchical arrangement (tragedy high — comedy low) betrays an acquiescence in the most smothering of political conservatisms. Put another way, by coupling tragedy with the sublime, the ineffable, the metaphysical and by aligning comedy with the mundane, the quotidian, and the material we manage to muffle, even to erase, the most powerful narratives of illumination and liberation we have. . . .

The point is comic relief, the *concept* of comic relief and who it relieves. Now we usually refer to comic relief in the same tone we use for academic deans, other people's children, Melanie Griffith, the new criticism, jogging, Big Macs, the *New York Times Book Review,* leisure suits, people who go on cruises, realtors, and the MLA: bemused contempt. (Which is what we think about comic relief.) Comedy is that which attends on, offers relaxation from, prepares us for more of—something else, something serious and demanding. Comedy is not demanding—it does not demand or take, it gives. And we know that any agency which gives cannot be worth much. Tragedy's seriousness is guaranteed by its bullying greed, its insistence on having things its own way and pulling from us not only our tears, which we value little, but our attention, which we hate to give. Comedy, on the other hand, doesn't care if we attend closely. Tragedy is sleek and single-minded, comedy rumpled and hospitable to any idea or agency. Tragedy stares us out of countenance; comedy winks and leers and drools. Tragedy is all dressed up; comedy is always taking things off, mooning us. We find it inevitable that we associate tragedy with the high, comedy with the low. What is at issue here is the nature of that inevitability, our willingness to conspire in a discourse which pays homage to tragic grandeur and reduces comedy to release, authorized license, periodic relief—like a sneeze or yawn or belch. By allowing such discourse to flow through us, we add our bit of cement to the cultural edifice that sits on top of comedy, mashes it down into a mere adjunct to tragedy, its reverse and inferior half, its silly little carnival. By cooperating in this move, we relieve orthodox and conservative power structures of any pressure that might be exercised against them. Comic relief relieves the status quo, in other words, contains the power of comedy. . . .

Let's put it this way, comedy is not a mode that stands in opposition to tragedy. Comedy is the *whole* story, the narrative which refuses to leave things out. Tragedy insists on a formal structure that is unified and coherent, formally balanced and elegantly tight. Only that which is coordinate is allowed to adorn the tragic body. With comedy, nothing is sacrificed, nothing lost; the discoordinate and the discontinuous are especially welcome. Tragedy protects itself by its linearity, its tight conclusiveness; comedy's generosity and ability never to end make it gloriously vulnerable. Pitting tragedy against comedy is running up algebra against recess. . . .

From a paper read at the 1991 meeting of the Modern Language Association, "Who Is Relieved by the Idea of Comic Relief?"

CONSIDERATIONS FOR CRITICAL THINKING AND WRITING

1. What distinctions does Kincaid make between comedy and tragedy? How does his description of tragedy compare with Aristotle's (see p. 1303)?

2. How does Kincaid's description of comedy fit *A Midsummer Night's Dream*?

3. According to Kincaid, why is the denigration of comedy a conservative impulse? In an essay explain why you agree or disagree with the argument.

TWO COMPLEMENTARY CRITICAL READINGS

G. WILSON KNIGHT (1897–1985)

Prospero's Civilizing Influence   1947

The Tempest at no point contradicts the essence of English history, widely viewed; and can, very generally, be considered as reflecting the destiny of Shakespeare's land, then young.

The background action is, as usual with Shakespeare, political. This strong political reference distinguishes the Shakespearian statement from our other examples of visionary literature, whilst also enabling it to reflect the wider history of Great Britain, itself so largely concerned with the attempt to fuse Christianity and politics. Prospero is Plato's philosopher-king betrayed by a Machiavellian "policy"; and Ariel's denunciation of his betrayers is an indictment of the second-rate or third-rate, in government, so criminally opposed against the first-rate, arduous, idealism. Prospero himself, against whom magic swords are futile, is now at least no impractical dreamer. He curtly dismisses his masque to meet Caliban's revolution; which, though it seems trivial, is yet, its implications understood, far otherwise, symbolizing that bestial retrogression and drunken worship of a Stephano as "wondrous man" (II.ii.136) in place of a Prospero, that utter miscarriage of all true valuation, which lurks within every denial of highest sovereignty. Prospero's story is set between an impractical idealism on the one side and political villainy and lust on the other; while dramatizing the attainment of a practical idealism negatively pointed by the satire on Gonzalo's Utopian dream. *The Tempest* accordingly falls into alignment with Shakespeare's massed statements elsewhere in definition of true sovereignty and, directly or indirectly, of British destiny; the "liberal arts" (I.ii.73) of Renaissance Europe are here shaped firmly into an Elizabethan mold; while Britain has, since Shakespeare's day, labored with varying success towards the middle course suggested.

The inclusiveness of Prospero's art illustrates a British tendency. The building up of our island population by continental invasion produced a blend of unbending integrity and wide catholicity properly reflected in Prospero. Since Shakespeare's day the drawing to our island of other peoples has, as was prophesied in Queen Elizabeth's prayer before the Armada, more than once characterized our history. The implied equation of Prospero's island with Great Britain remains, however, a momentary analogy that could bear no stress.

Prospero's magic is largely a sea-magic; his island story is sea-rooted . . . and ends with a voyage home; in the interim, he has been gradually mastering the sea-powers. Similarly Great Britain has labored at ocean-mastery; the "ocean" being both the actual ocean and those oceanic instincts, or forces, within man which it so consistently throughout the ages symbolizes. British colonization from the start went hand in hand with Puritanism; the early colonizers, not unlike Prospero, being impelled by political or religious tyrannies to follow their soul-cravings across the sea and there work out the controlled magic of personal integration.

Suppose that Britain's contribution were being assessed some ten thousand years hence by an enlightened historian. He would probably point to (1) her in-ruling severe, yet inclusive and tolerant, religious and political instincts, of which her first colonial adventures and the Puritan revolution were active examples; (2) her inventive and poetic genius variously concerned with the tapping and use of natural energy; and (3) her colonizing, especially her will to raise savage peoples from superstition and blood-sacrifice, taboos and witchcraft and the attendant fears and slaveries, to a more enlightened existence. Little ingenuity is needed to find correspondences with Prospero, Ariel, and Caliban. Especially we may equate the king who is yet no tyrant, the student-prince un-at-home with forceful action, who yet, under pressure of his island existence, gains power to control armed opposition, with the dimly apprehended pacifism inspiring Great Britain's history and the implied liberalism of her constitutional monarchy; only gestures as yet, but gestures that speak "an excellent dumb discourse." As for Miranda, what of her? Without her, perhaps, our ten-thousand-years-hence historian would not have been born; or, at least, been in no position to write his book.

It is, perhaps, inevitable that Shakespeare, whose work . . . is so saturated with the spirit of his land, should, in such a summation of that work in *The Tempest*, have outlined, among much else, a myth of the national soul.

From *The Crown of Life: Essays in Interpretation of Shakespeare's Final Plays*

CONSIDERATIONS FOR CRITICAL THINKING AND WRITING

1. How does Knight describe Prospero as a ruler? Explain why you agree or disagree.

2. What connection does Knight make between the play and the history of Great Britain? How is Britain's history of colonization regarded by Knight? What assumptions does he make about civilization and "savage peoples" (para. 5)?

3. Compare the views expressed about colonization here with the issues raised in the perspective that follows by Alden T. Vaughan.

ALDEN T. VAUGHAN (B. 1929)
Caliban as a Sociopolitical Symbol   *1988*

For nearly four centuries, writers, speakers, and casual commentators have ransacked Shakespeare's works for useful metaphors. Often the purpose has been less literary than ideological — to signify a social or political position by invoking a familiar Shakespearean phrase or character. During the past century, probably the most frequent and malleable Shakespearean sociopolitical symbol has been *The Tempest*'s Caliban, for the "savage and deformed slave" has played varied metaphoric roles in response to changing national and international ideologies. This essay explores Caliban's adoption by late-nineteenth- and twentieth-century writers, especially in Latin America and Africa, as a potent symbol of either Western imperialism or imperialism's victims.

Beginning in the 1890s, and especially since 1950, many writers from Third World nations have contended that *The Tempest* embodies heretofore neglected meanings for their societies and that Caliban conveys a very different message than traditional scholarship has allowed. Such authors—few are Shakespearean scholars but many are distinguished in other fields—argue that Caliban is no mere fish or monster or even, as has often been argued, a North American Indian. His true significance lies instead in emblematic identifications with modern men and women, especially Latin Americans and Africans, no matter how anachronistic those identifications may seem to *Tempest* specialists.

Authors who invoke Caliban as an image of Latin Americans or Africans agree that he is a palpable and poignant symbol, but they disagree, sometimes vehemently, about who or what he symbolizes. Diametrical opposites are proposed: Caliban as exemplar of imperialist oppressors (the prevalent view in the late nineteenth and early twentieth centuries) or Caliban as emblem of oppressed natives (prevalent in recent decades). Advocates of the first approach find Shakespeare's monster a handy image for everything gross and vicious in a domineering nation or social class—Yankee imperialism, for example, or European racism. The second and now more widespread view stresses Caliban's implicit virtues—his innate sensitivity, rough dignity, articulateness, and intelligence—rather than his cruder characteristics. Thus recast, Caliban stands for the countless victims of European imperialism and colonization. Like Caliban (so the argument goes), colonized peoples are disinherited, exploited, and subjugated. Like he, they learned a conqueror's language and perhaps his values. Like he, they endured enslavement and contempt by European usurpers and eventually rebelled. . . .

Either approach—Caliban as oppressor or Caliban as oppressed—differs fundamentally from traditional interpretive modes. Whereas traditional scholarship is at least partly concerned with the probable prototypes for Shakespeare's characters, most Third World authors who borrow emblems from *The Tempest* ignore, as irrelevant, Shakespeare's sources and intentions. The Third World interpretation of Caliban is symbolic, not historic; it adopts Caliban for what he represents to the observer, not for what Shakespeare may have had in mind. Few Third World authors who apply *Tempest* images contend that Shakespeare expected his audience to see Caliban as a black African, brown mestizo, or white American; instead, they want modern readers to accept Shakespeare's dramatic symbols because, retrospectively, they fit. New situations give the play's characters new meanings. As one exponent of Caliban metaphors explains, "*The Tempest* is a Masque, an art form strongly dependent on symbolism. It presents figures that are suggestive, evocative, and allusive; and it often relies on mythopoetic references for full effect. If we accept this, . . . we may . . . come out with applications appropriate for a present cultural dilemma."

From *Massachusetts Review,* Summer 1988

CONSIDERATIONS FOR CRITICAL THINKING AND WRITING

1. According to Vaughan, how has Caliban been read as a sociopolitical symbol? How have these readings conflicted?

2. What do you think of appropriating a literary character for the purpose of clarifying "a present cultural dilemma" (para. 4)?

3. Explain in an essay how G. Wilson Knight's approach to Prospero (in the preceding perspective) is similar to the uses to which Caliban has been put by the Third World interpretations described by Vaughan.

32

Modern Drama

REALISM

Realism is a literary technique that attempts to create the appearance of life as it is actually experienced. Characters in modern realistic plays (written during and after the last quarter of the nineteenth century) speak dialogue that we might hear in our daily lives. These characters are not larger than life but representative of it; they seem to speak the way we do rather than in highly poetic language, formal declarations, asides, or soliloquies. It is impossible to imagine a heroic figure such as Oedipus inhabiting a comfortably furnished living room and chatting about his wife's household budget the way Torvald Helmer does in Henrik Ibsen's *A Doll House.* Realism brings into focus commonplace, everyday life rather than the extraordinary kinds of events that make up Sophocles' *Oedipus the King* or Shakespeare's *Hamlet.*

Realistic characters can certainly be heroic, but like Nora Helmer, they find that their strength and courage are tested in the context of events ordinary people might experience. Work, love, marriage, children, and death are often the focus of realistic dramas. These subjects can also constitute much of the material in nonrealistic plays, but modern realistic dramas present such material in the realm of the probable. Conflicts in realistic plays are likely to reflect problems in our own lives. Hence, making ends meet takes precedence over saving a kingdom; middle- and lower-class individuals take center stage as primary characters in main plots rather than being secondary characters in subplots. Thus we can see why the nineteenth-century movement toward realism paralleled the rise of a middle class eagerly seeking representations of its concerns in the theater.

Before the end of the nineteenth century, however, few attempts were made in the theater to present life as it is actually lived. The chorus's role in

Sophocles' *Oedipus the King,* the allegorical figures in morality plays, the remarkable mistaken identities in Shakespeare's comedies, or the rhymed couplets spoken in seventeenth-century plays such as Molière's *Tartuffe* represent theatrical conventions rather than life. Theatergoers have understood and appreciated these conventions for centuries — and still do — but in the nineteenth century social, political, and industrial revolutions helped create an atmosphere in which some playwrights found it necessary to create works that more directly reflected their audiences' lives.

Playwrights such as Henrik Ibsen and Anton Chekhov refused to join the ranks of their romantic contemporaries, who they felt falsely idealized life. The most popular plays immediately preceding the works of these realistic writers consisted primarily of love stories and action-packed plots. Such **melodramas** offer audiences thrills and chills as well as happy endings. They typically include a virtuous individual struggling under the tyranny of a wicked oppressor, who is defeated only at the last moment. Suspense is reinforced by a series of pursuits, captures, and escapes that move the plot quickly and de-emphasize character or theme. These representations of extreme conflicts enjoyed wide popularity in the nineteenth century — indeed, they still do — because their formula was varied enough to be entertaining yet their outcomes were always comforting to the audience's sense of justice. From the realists' perspective, melodramas were merely escape fantasies that distorted life by refusing to examine the real world closely and objectively. But an indication of the popularity of such happy endings can be seen in Chekhov's farcical comedies, such as *The Proposal* (see p. 1615), a one-act play filled with exaggerated characters and action. Despite his realist's values, Chekhov was also sometimes eager to please audiences.

Realists attempted to open their audiences' eyes; to their minds, the only genuine comfort was in knowing the truth. Many of their plays concern controversial issues of the day and focus on people who fall prey to indifferent societal institutions. English dramatist John Galsworthy (1867–1933) examined social values in *Strife* (1909) and *Justice* (1910), two plays whose titles broadly suggest the nature of his concerns. British playwright George Bernard Shaw (1856–1950) often used comedy and irony as means of awakening his audiences to contemporary problems: *Arms and the Man* (1894) satirizes romantic attitudes toward war, and *Mrs. Warren's Profession* (1898) indicts a social and economic system that drives a woman to prostitution. Chekhov's major plays are populated by characters frustrated by their social situations and their own sensibilities; they are ordinary people who long for happiness but become entangled in everyday circumstances that limit their lives. Ibsen also took a close look at his characters' daily lives. His plays attack social conventions and challenge popular attitudes toward marriage; he stunned audiences by dramatizing the suffering of a man dying of syphilis.

With these kinds of materials, Ibsen and his contemporaries popularized the **problem play,** a drama that represents a social issue in order to awaken the audience to it. These plays usually reject romantic plots in favor of holding up a mirror that reflects not simply what audiences want to see but what the playwright sees in them. Nineteenth-century realistic theater was no refuge from the social, economic, and psychological problems that melodrama ignored or sentimentalized.

NATURALISM

Related to realism is another movement, called **naturalism**. Essentially more of a philosophical attitude than a literary technique, naturalism derives its name from the idea that human beings are part of nature and subject to its laws. According to naturalists, heredity and environment shape and control people's lives; their behavior is determined more by instinct than by reason. This deterministic view argues that human beings have no transcendent identity because there is no soul or spiritual world that ultimately distinguishes humanity from any other form of life. Characters in naturalistic plays are generally portrayed as victims overwhelmed by internal and external forces. Thus literary naturalism tends to include not only the commonplace but the sordid, destructive, and chaotic aspects of life. Naturalism, then, is an extreme form of realism.

The earliest and most articulate voice of naturalism was that of French author Émile Zola (1840–1902), who urged artists to draw their characters from life and present their histories as faithfully as scientists report laboratory findings. Zola's best-known naturalistic play, *Thérèse Raquin* (1873), is a dramatization of an earlier novel involving a woman whose passion causes her to take a lover and plot with him to kill her husband. In his preface to the novel, Zola explains that his purpose is to take "a strong man and unsatisfied woman," "throw them into a violent drama and note scrupulously the sensations and acts of these creatures." The diction of Zola's statement reveals his nearly clinical approach, which becomes even more explicit when Zola likens his method of revealing character to that of an autopsy: "I have simply done on two living bodies the work which surgeons do on corpses."

Although some naturalistic plays have been successfully produced and admired (notably Maxim Gorky's *The Lower Depths* [1902], set in a grim boardinghouse occupied by characters who suffer poverty, crime, betrayal, disease, and suicide), few important dramatists fully subscribed to naturalism's extreme methods and values. Nevertheless, the movement significantly influenced playwrights. Because of its insistence on the necessity of closely observing characters' environment, playwrights placed a new emphasis on detailed settings and natural acting. This verisimilitude became a significant feature of realistic drama.

THEATRICAL CONVENTIONS
OF MODERN DRAMA

The picture-frame stage that is often used for realistic plays typically reproduces the setting of a room in some detail. Within the stage, framed by a proscenium arch (from which the curtain hangs), scenery and props are used to create an illusion of reality. Whether the "small bookcase with richly bound books" described in the opening scene of Ibsen's *A Doll House* is only painted scenery or an actual case with books, it will probably look real to the audience. Removing the fourth wall of a room so that an audience can look in fosters the illusion that the actions onstage are real events happening before unseen spectators. The texture of Nora's life is communicated by the set as well as by what she says and does. That doesn't happen in a play like Sophocles' *Oedipus the King*. Technical effects can make us believe there is wood burning in a fireplace or snow falling outside a window. Outdoor settings are made similarly realistic by props and painted sets. In one of Chekhov's full-length plays, for example, the second act opens in a meadow with the faint outline of a city on the horizon.

In addition to lifelike sets, a particular method of acting is used to create a realistic atmosphere. Actors address each other instead of directing formal speeches toward the audience; they act within the setting, not merely before it. At the beginning of the twentieth century Konstantin Stanislavsky (1863–1938), a Russian director, teacher, and actor, developed a system of acting that was an important influence in realistic theater. He trained actors to identify with the inner emotions of the characters they played. They were encouraged to recall from their own lives emotional responses similar to those they were portraying. The goal was to present a role truthfully by first feeling and then projecting the character's situation. Among Stanislavsky's early successes in this method were the plays of Chekhov.

There are, however, degrees of realism on the stage. Tennessee Williams's *The Glass Menagerie* (p. 1864), for example, is a partially realistic portrayal of characters whose fragile lives are founded on illusions. Williams's dialogue rings true, and individual scenes resemble the kind of real-life action we would imagine such vulnerable characters engaging in, but other elements of the play are nonrealistic. For instance, Williams uses Tom as a major character in the play as well as a narrator and a stage manager. Here is part of Williams's stage directions: "The narrator is an undisguised convention of the play. He takes whatever license with dramatic convention as is convenient to his purposes." Although this play can be accurately described as including realistic elements, Williams, like many other contemporary playwrights, does not attempt an absolute fidelity to reality. He uses flashbacks — as does Arthur Miller in *Death of a Salesman* (p. 1795) — to present incidents that occurred before the opening scene because the past impinges so heavily on the present. Most playwrights don't attempt to duplicate reality, since that can now be done so well by motion pictures.

Realism needn't lock a playwright into a futile attempt to make everything appear as it is in life. There is no way to avoid theatrical conventions: actors impersonate characters in a setting that is, after all, a stage. Indeed, even the dialogue in a realistic play is quite different from the pauses, sentence fragments, repetitions, silences, and incoherencies that characterize the way people usually speak. Realistic dialogue may seem like ordinary speech, but it, like Shakespeare's poetic language, is constructed. If we remember that realistic drama represents only the appearance of reality and that what we read on a page or see and hear onstage is the result of careful selecting, editing, and even distortion, then we are more likely to appreciate the playwright's art.

A Doll House

Henrik Ibsen was born in Skien, Norway, to wealthy parents, who lost their money while he was a young boy. His early experiences with small-town life and genteel poverty sensitized him to the problems that he subsequently dramatized in a number of his plays. At age sixteen he was apprenticed to a druggist; he later thought about studying medicine, but by his early twenties he was earning a living writing and directing plays in various Norwegian cities. By the time of his death he enjoyed an international reputation for his treatment of social issues related to middle-class life.

Ibsen's earliest dramatic works were historical and romantic plays, some in verse. His first truly realistic work was *The Pillars of Society* (1877), whose title ironically hints at the corruption and hypocrisy exposed in it. The realistic social-problem plays for which he is best known followed. These dramas at once fascinated and shocked international audiences. Among his most produced and admired works are *A Doll House* (1879), *Ghosts* (1881), *An Enemy of the People* (1882), *The Wild Duck* (1884), and *Hedda Gabler* (1890). The common denominator in many of Ibsen's dramas is his interest in individuals struggling for an authentic identity in the face of tyrannical social conventions. This conflict often results in his characters' being divided between a sense of duty to themselves and their responsibility to others.

Ibsen used such external and internal conflicts to propel his plays' action. Like many of his contemporaries who wrote realistic plays, he adopted the form of the well-made play. A dramatic structure popularized in France by Eugène Scribe (1791-1861) and Victorien Sardou (1831-1908), the *well-made play* employs conventions including plenty of suspense created by meticulous plotting. Extensive exposition explains past events that ultimately lead to an inevitable climax. Tension is released when a secret that reverses the protagonist's fortunes is revealed. Ibsen, having directed a number of Scribe's plays in Norway, knew their cause-to-effect plot arrangements and used them for his own purposes in his problem plays.

A *Doll House* dramatizes the tensions of a nineteenth-century middle-class marriage in which a wife struggles to step beyond the limited identity imposed on her by her husband and society. Although the Helmers' pleasant apartment seems an unlikely setting for the fierce conflicts that develop, the issues raised in the play are unmistakably real. *A Doll House* affirms the necessity to reject hypocrisy, complacency, cowardice, and stifling conventions if life is to have dignity and meaning. Several critical approaches to the play can be found in Chapter 33, "Critical Case Study: Henrik Ibsen's *A Doll House.*"

HENRIK IBSEN (1828–1906)

A Doll House   1879

TRANSLATED BY ROLF FJELDE

THE CHARACTERS

Torvald Helmer, a lawyer
Nora, his wife
Dr. Rank
Mrs. Linde
Nils Krogstad, a bank clerk
The Helmers' three small children
Anne-Marie, their nurse
Helene, a maid
A Delivery Boy

SCENE: *The action takes place in Helmer's residence.*

ACT I

A comfortable room, tastefully but not expensively furnished. A door to the right in the back wall leads to the entryway; another to the left leads to Helmer's study. Between these doors, a piano. Midway in the left-hand wall a door, and further back a window. Near the window a round table with an armchair and a small sofa. In the right-hand wall, toward the rear, a door, and nearer the foreground a porcelain stove with two armchairs and a rocking chair beside it. Between the stove and the side door, a small table. Engravings on the walls. An etagère with china figures and other small art objects; a small bookcase with richly bound books; the floor carpeted; a fire burning in the stove. It is a winter day.

A bell rings in the entryway; shortly after we hear the door being unlocked. Nora comes into the room, humming happily to herself; she is wearing street clothes and carries an armload of packages, which she puts down on the table to the right. She has left the hall door open; and through it a Delivery Boy is seen, holding a Christmas tree and a basket, which he gives to the Maid who let them in.

Nora: Hide the tree well, Helene. The children mustn't get a glimpse of it till this evening, after it's trimmed. *(To the Delivery Boy, taking out her purse.)* How much?

Delivery Boy: Fifty, ma'am.

Nora: There's a crown. No, keep the change. *(The Boy thanks her and leaves. Nora shuts the door. She laughs softly to herself while taking off her street things. Drawing a bag of macaroons from her pocket, she eats a couple, then steals over and listens at her husband's study door.)* Yes, he's home. *(Hums again as she moves to the table right.)*

Helmer (from the study): Is that my little lark twittering out there?

Nora (busy opening some packages): Yes, it is.

Helmer: Is that my squirrel rummaging around?

Nora: Yes!

Helmer: When did my squirrel get in?

Nora: Just now. *(Putting the macaroon bag in her pocket and wiping her mouth.)* Do come in, Torvald, and see what I've bought.

Helmer: Can't be disturbed. *(After a moment he opens the door and peers in, pen in hand.)* Bought, you say? All that there? Has the little spendthrift been out throwing money around again?

Nora: Oh, but Torvald, this year we really should let ourselves go a bit. It's the first Christmas we haven't had to economize.

Helmer: But you know we can't go squandering.

Nora: Oh yes, Torvald, we can squander a little now. Can't we? Just a tiny, wee bit. Now that you've got a big salary and are going to make piles and piles of money.

Helmer: Yes—starting New Year's. But then it's a full three months till the raise comes through.

Nora: Pooh! We can borrow that long.

Helmer: Nora! *(Goes over and playfully takes her by the ear.)* Are your scatterbrains off again? What if today I borrowed a thousand crowns, and you squandered them over Christmas week, and then on New Year's Eve a roof tile fell on my head and I lay there—

Nora (putting her hand on his mouth): Oh! Don't say such things!

Helmer: Yes, but what if it happened—then what?

Nora: If anything so awful happened, then it just wouldn't matter if I had debts or not.

Helmer: Well, but the people I'd borrowed from?

Nora: Them? Who cares about them! They're strangers.

Helmer: Nora, Nora, how like a woman! No, but seriously, Nora, you know what I think about that. No debts! Never borrow! Something of freedom's lost—and something of beauty, too—from a home that's founded on borrowing and debt. We've made a brave stand up to now, the two of us; and we'll go right on like that the little while we have to.

Nora (going toward the stove): Yes, whatever you say, Torvald.

Helmer (following her): Now, now, the little lark's wings mustn't droop. Come on, don't be a sulky squirrel. *(Taking out his wallet.)* Nora, guess what I have here.

Nora (turning quickly): Money!

Helmer: There, see. *(Hands her some notes.)* Good grief, I know how costs go up in a house at Christmastime.

Nora: Ten — twenty — thirty — forty. Oh, thank you, Torvald; I can manage no end on this.

Helmer: You really will have to.

Nora: Oh yes, I promise I will! But come here so I can show you everything I bought. And so cheap! Look, new clothes for Ivar here — and a sword. Here a horse and a trumpet for Bob. And a doll and a doll's bed here for Emmy; they're nothing much, but she'll tear them to bits in no time anyway. And here I have dress material and handkerchiefs for the maids. Old Anne-Marie really deserves something more.

Helmer: And what's in that package there?

Nora (with a cry): Torvald, no! You can't see that till tonight!

Helmer: I see. But tell me now, you little prodigal, what have you thought of for yourself?

Nora: For myself? Oh, I don't want anything at all.

Helmer: Of course you do. Tell me just what — within reason — you'd most like to have.

Nora: I honestly don't know. Oh, listen, Torvald —

Helmer: Well?

Nora (fumbling at his coat buttons, without looking at him): If you want to give me something, then maybe you could — you could —

Helmer: Come on, out with it.

Nora (hurriedly): You could give me money, Torvald. No more than you think you can spare; then one of these days I'll buy something with it.

Helmer: But Nora —

Nora: Oh please, Torvald darling, do that! I beg you, please. Then I could hang the bills in pretty gilt paper on the Christmas tree. Wouldn't that be fun?

Helmer: What are those little birds called that always fly through their fortunes?

Nora: Oh yes, spendthrifts: I know all that. But let's do as I say, Torvald; then I'll have time to decide what I really need most. That's very sensible, isn't it?

Helmer (smiling): Yes, very — that is, if you actually hung onto the money I give you, and you actually used it to buy yourself something. But it goes for the house and for all sorts of foolish things, and then I only have to lay out some more.

Nora: Oh, but Torvald —

Helmer: Don't deny it, my dear little Nora. *(Putting his arm around her waist.)* Spendthrifts are sweet, but they use up a frightful amount of money. It's incredible what it costs a man to feed such birds.

Nora: Oh, how can you say that! Really, I save everything I can.

Helmer (laughing): Yes, that's the truth. Everything you can. But that's nothing at all.

Nora (humming, with a smile of quiet satisfaction): Hm, if you only knew what expenses we larks and squirrels have, Torvald.

Helmer: You're an odd little one. Exactly the way your father was. You're never at a loss for scaring up money; but the moment you have it, it runs right out through your fingers; you never know what you've done with it. Well, one takes you as you are. It's deep in your blood. Yes, these things are hereditary, Nora.

Nora: Ah, I could wish I'd inherited many of Papa's qualities.

Helmer: And I couldn't wish you anything but just what you are, my sweet little lark. But wait; it seems to me you have a very—what should I call it?—a very suspicious look today—

Nora: I do?

Helmer: You certainly do. Look me straight in the eye.

Nora (looking at him): Well?

Helmer (shaking an admonitory finger): Surely my sweet tooth hasn't been running riot in town today, has she?

Nora: No. Why do you imagine that?

Helmer: My sweet tooth really didn't make a little detour through the confectioner's?

Nora: No, I assure you, Torvald—

Helmer: Hasn't nibbled some pastry?

Nora: No, not at all.

Helmer: Not even munched a macaroon or two?

Nora: No, Torvald, I assure you, really—

Helmer: There, there now. Of course I'm only joking.

Nora (going to the table, right): You know I could never think of going against you.

Helmer: No, I understand that; and you *have* given me your word. *(Going over to her.)* Well, you keep your little Christmas secrets to yourself, Nora darling. I expect they'll come to light this evening, when the tree is lit.

Nora: Did you remember to ask Dr. Rank?

Helmer: No. But there's no need for that; it's assumed he'll be dining with us. All the same, I'll ask him when he stops by here this morning. I've ordered some fine wine. Nora, you can't imagine how I'm looking forward to this evening.

Nora: So am I. And what fun for the children, Torvald!

Helmer: Ah, it's so gratifying to know that one's gotten a safe, secure job, and with a comfortable salary. It's a great satisfaction, isn't it?

Nora: Oh, it's wonderful!

Helmer: Remember last Christmas? Three whole weeks before, you shut yourself in every evening till long after midnight, making flowers for the Christmas tree, and all the other decorations to surprise us. Ugh, that was the dullest time I've ever lived through.

Nora: It wasn't at all dull for me.

Helmer (smiling): But the outcome *was* pretty sorry, Nora.

Nora: Oh, don't tease me with that again. How could I help it that the cat came in and tore everything to shreds.

Helmer: No, poor thing, you certainly couldn't. You wanted so much to please us all, and that's what counts. But it's just as well that the hard times are past.

Nora: Yes, it's really wonderful.

Helmer: Now I don't have to sit here alone, boring myself, and you don't have to tire your precious eyes and your fair little delicate hands—

Nora (clapping her hands): No, is it really true, Torvald, I don't have to? Oh, how wonderfully lovely to hear! *(Taking his arm.)* Now I'll tell you just how I've thought we should plan things. Right after Christmas—*(The doorbell rings.)* Oh, the bell. *(Straightening the room up a bit.)* Somebody would have to come. What a bore!

Helmer: I'm not home to visitors, don't forget.

Maid (from the hall doorway): Ma'am, a lady to see you —

Nora: All right, let her come in.

Maid (to Helmer): And the doctor's just come too.

Helmer: Did he go right to my study?

Maid: Yes, he did.

> *Helmer goes into his room. The Maid shows in Mrs. Linde, dressed in traveling clothes, and shuts the door after her.*

Mrs. Linde (in a dispirited and somewhat hesitant voice): Hello, Nora.

Nora (uncertain): Hello —

Mrs. Linde: You don't recognize me.

Nora: No, I don't know — but wait, I think — *(Exclaiming.)* What! Kristine! Is it really you?

Mrs. Linde: Yes, it's me.

Nora: Kristine! To think I didn't recognize you. But then, how could I? *(More quietly.)* How you've changed, Kristine!

Mrs. Linde: Yes, no doubt I have. In nine — ten long years.

Nora: Is it so long since we met! Yes, it's all of that. Oh, these last eight years have been a happy time, believe me. And so now you've come in to town, too. Made the long trip in the winter. That took courage.

Mrs. Linde: I just got here by ship this morning.

Nora: To enjoy yourself over Christmas, of course. Oh, how lovely! Yes, enjoy ourselves, we'll do that. But take your coat off. You're not still cold? *(Helping her.)* There now, let's get cozy here by the stove. No, the easy chair there! I'll take the rocker here. *(Seizing her hands.)* Yes, now you have your old look again; it was only in that first moment. You're a bit more pale, Kristine — and maybe a bit thinner.

Mrs. Linde: And much, much older, Nora.

Nora: Yes, perhaps a bit older: a tiny, tiny bit; not much at all. *(Stopping short; suddenly serious.)* Oh, but thoughtless me, to sit here, chattering away. Sweet, good Kristine, can you forgive me?

Mrs. Linde: What do you mean, Nora?

Nora (softly): Poor Kristine, you've become a widow.

Mrs. Linde: Yes, three years ago.

Nora: Oh, I knew it, of course: I read it in the papers. Oh, Kristine, you must believe me; I often thought of writing you then, but I kept postponing it, and something always interfered.

Mrs. Linde: Nora dear, I understand completely.

Nora: No, it was awful of me, Kristine. You poor thing, how much you must have gone through. And he left you nothing?

Mrs. Linde: No.

Nora: And no children?

Mrs. Linde: No.

Nora: Nothing at all, then?

Mrs. Linde: Not even a sense of loss to feed on.

Nora (looking incredulously at her): But Kristine, how could that be?

Mrs. Linde (smiling wearily and smoothing her hair): Oh, sometimes it happens, Nora.

Nora: So completely alone. How terribly hard that must be for you. I have three lovely children. You can't see them now; they're out with the maid. But now you must tell me everything—

Mrs. Linde: No, no, no, tell me about yourself.

Nora: No, you begin. Today I don't want to be selfish. I want to think only of you today. But there *is* something I must tell you. Did you hear of the wonderful luck we had recently?

Mrs. Linde: No, what's that?

Nora: My husband's been made manager in the bank, just think!

Mrs. Linde: Your husband? How marvelous!

Nora: Isn't it? Being a lawyer is such an uncertain living, you know, especially if one won't touch any cases that aren't clean and decent. And of course Torvald would never do that, and I'm with him completely there. Oh, we're simply delighted, believe me! He'll join the bank right after New Year's and start getting a huge salary and lots of commissions. From now on we can live quite differently—just as we want. Oh, Kristine, I feel so light and happy! Won't it be lovely to have stacks of money and not a care in the world?

Mrs. Linde: Well, anyway, it would be lovely to have enough for necessities.

Nora: No, not just for necessities, but stacks and stacks of money!

Mrs. Linde (smiling): Nora, Nora, aren't you sensible yet? Back in school you were such a free spender.

Nora (with a quiet laugh): Yes, that's what Torvald still says. (*Shaking her finger.*) But "Nora, Nora" isn't as silly as you all think. Really, we've been in no position for me to go squandering. We've had to work, both of us.

Mrs. Linde: You too?

Nora: Yes, at odd jobs—needlework, crocheting, embroidery, and such—(*Casually.*) and other things too. You remember that Torvald left the department when we were married? There was no chance of promotion in his office, and of course he needed to earn more money. But that first year he drove himself terribly. He took on all kinds of extra work that kept him going morning and night. It wore him down, and then he fell deathly ill. The doctors said it was essential for him to travel south.

Mrs. Linde: Yes, didn't you spend a whole year in Italy?

Nora: That's right. It wasn't easy to get away, you know. Ivar had just been born. But of course we had to go. Oh, that was a beautiful trip, and it saved Torvald's life. But it cost a frightful sum, Kristine.

Mrs. Linde: I can well imagine.

Nora: Four thousand, eight hundred crowns it cost. That's really a lot of money.

Mrs. Linde: But it's lucky you had it when you needed it.

Nora: Well, as it was, we got it from Papa.

Mrs. Linde: I see. It was just about the time your father died.

Nora: Yes, just about then. And, you know, I couldn't make that trip out to nurse him. I had to stay here, expecting Ivar any moment, and with my poor sick Torvald to care for. Dearest Papa, I never saw him again, Kristine. Oh, that was the worst time I've known in all my marriage.

Mrs. Linde: I know how you loved him. And then you went off to Italy?

Nora: Yes. We had the means now, and the doctors urged us. So we left a month after.

Mrs. Linde: And your husband came back completely cured?

Nora: Sound as a drum!

Mrs. Linde: But—the doctor?

Nora: Who?

Mrs. Linde: I thought the maid said he was a doctor, the man who came in with me.

Nora: Yes, that was Dr. Rank—but he's not making a sick call. He's our closest friend, and he stops by at least once a day. No, Torvald hasn't had a sick moment since, and the children are fit and strong, and I am, too. (*Jumping up and clapping her hands.*) Oh, dear God, Kristine, what a lovely thing to live and be happy! But how disgusting of me—I'm talking of nothing but my own affairs. (*Sits on a stool close by Kristine, arms resting across her knees.*) Oh, don't be angry with me! Tell me, is it really true that you weren't in love with your husband? Why did you marry him, then?

Mrs. Linde: My mother was still alive, but bedridden and helpless—and I had my two younger brothers to look after. In all conscience, I didn't think I could turn him down.

Nora: No, you were right there. But was he rich at the time?

Mrs. Linde: He was very well off, I'd say. But the business was shaky, Nora. When he died, it all fell apart, and nothing was left.

Nora: And then—?

Mrs. Linde: Yes, so I had to scrape up a living with a little shop and a little teaching and whatever else I could find. The last three years have been like one endless workday without a rest for me. Now it's over, Nora. My poor mother doesn't need me, for she's passed on. Nor the boys, either; they're working now and can take care of themselves.

Nora: How free you must feel—

Mrs. Linde: No—only unspeakably empty. Nothing to live for now. (*Standing up anxiously.*) That's why I couldn't take it any longer out in that desolate hole. Maybe here it'll be easier to find something to do and keep my mind occupied. If I could only be lucky enough to get a steady job, some office work—

Nora: Oh, but Kristine, that's so dreadfully tiring, and you already look so tired. It would be much better for you if you could go off to a bathing resort.

Mrs. Linde (going toward the window): I have no father to give me travel money, Nora.

Nora (rising): Oh, don't be angry with me.

Mrs. Linde (going to her): Nora dear, don't you be angry with me. The worst of my kind of situation is all the bitterness that's stored away. No one to work for, and yet you're always having to snap up your opportunities. You have to live; and so you grow selfish. When you told me the happy change in your lot, do you know I was delighted less for your sakes than for mine?

Nora: How so? Oh, I see. You think maybe Torvald could do something for you.

Mrs. Linde: Yes, that's what I thought.

Nora: And he will, Kristine! Just leave it to me; I'll bring it up so delicately—find something attractive to humor him with. Oh, I'm so eager to help you.

Mrs. Linde: How very kind of you, Nora, to be so concerned over me—doubly kind, considering you really know so little of life's burdens yourself.

Nora: I —? I know so little —?

Mrs. Linde (smiling): Well, my heavens — a little needlework and such — Nora, you're just a child.

Nora (tossing her head and pacing the floor): You don't have to act so superior.

Mrs. Linde: Oh?

Nora: You're just like the others. You all think I'm incapable of anything serious —

Mrs. Linde: Come now —

Nora: That I've never had to face the raw world.

Mrs. Linde: Nora dear, you've just been telling me all your troubles.

Nora: Hm! Trivia! *(Quietly.)* I haven't told you the big thing.

Mrs. Linde: Big thing? What do you mean?

Nora: You look down on me so, Kristine, but you shouldn't. You're proud that you worked so long and hard for your mother.

Mrs. Linde: I don't look down on a soul. But it *is* true: I'm proud — and happy, too — to think it was given to me to make my mother's last days almost free of care.

Nora: And you're also proud thinking of what you've done for your brothers.

Mrs. Linde: I feel I've a right to be.

Nora: I agree. But listen to this, Kristine — I've also got something to be proud and happy for.

Mrs. Linde: I don't doubt it. But whatever do you mean?

Nora: Not so loud. What if Torvald heard! He mustn't, not for anything in the world. Nobody must know, Kristine. No one but you.

Mrs. Linde: But what is it, then?

Nora: Come here. *(Drawing her down beside her on the sofa.)* It's true — I've also got something to be proud and happy for. I'm the one who saved Torvald's life.

Mrs. Linde: Saved —? Saved how?

Nora: I told you about the trip to Italy. Torvald never would have lived if he hadn't gone south —

Mrs. Linde: Of course; your father gave you the means —

Nora (smiling): That's what Torvald and all the rest think, but —

Mrs. Linde: But —?

Nora: Papa didn't give us a pin. I was the one who raised the money.

Mrs. Linde: You? That whole amount?

Nora: Four thousand, eight hundred crowns. What do you say to that?

Mrs. Linde: But Nora, how was it possible? Did you win the lottery?

Nora (disdainfully): The lottery? Pooh! No art to that.

Mrs. Linde: But where did you get it from then?

Nora (humming, with a mysterious smile): Hmm, tra-la-la-la.

Mrs. Linde: Because you couldn't have borrowed it.

Nora: No? Why not?

Mrs. Linde: A wife can't borrow without her husband's consent.

Nora (tossing her head): Oh, but a wife with a little business sense, a wife who knows how to manage —

Mrs. Linde: Nora, I simply don't understand —

Nora: You don't have to. Whoever said I *borrowed* the money? I could have gotten it other ways. *(Throwing herself back on the sofa.)* I could have gotten it from some admirer or other. After all, a girl with my ravishing appeal —

Mrs. Linde: You lunatic.

Nora: I'll bet you're eaten up with curiosity, Kristine.

Mrs. Linde: Now listen here, Nora — you haven't done something indiscreet?

Nora (sitting up again): Is it indiscreet to save your husband's life?

Mrs. Linde: I think it's indiscreet that without his knowledge you —

Nora: But that's the point: he mustn't know! My Lord, can't you understand? He mustn't ever know the close call he had. It was to *me* the doctors came to say his life was in danger — that nothing could save him but a stay in the south. Didn't I try strategy then! I began talking about how lovely it would be for me to travel abroad like other young wives; I begged and I cried; I told him please to remember my condition, to be kind and indulge me; and then I dropped a hint that he could easily take out a loan. But at that, Kristine, he nearly exploded. He said I was frivolous, and it was his duty as man of the house not to indulge me in whims and fancies — as I think he called them. Aha, I thought, now you'll just have to be saved — and that's when I saw my chance.

Mrs. Linde: And your father never told Torvald the money wasn't from him?

Nora: No, never. Papa died right about then. I'd considered bringing him into my secret and begging him never to tell. But he was too sick at the time — and then, sadly, it didn't matter.

Mrs. Linde: And you've never confided in your husband since?

Nora: For heaven's sake, no! Are you serious? He's so strict on that subject. Besides — Torvald, with all his masculine pride — how painfully humiliating for him if he ever found out he was in debt to me. That would just ruin our relationship. Our beautiful, happy home would never be the same.

Mrs. Linde: Won't you ever tell him?

Nora (thoughtfully, half smiling): Yes — maybe sometime, years from now, when I'm no longer so attractive. Don't laugh! I only mean when Torvald loves me less than now, when he stops enjoying my dancing and dressing up and reciting for him. Then it might be wise to have something in reserve — *(Breaking off.)* How ridiculous! That'll never happen — Well, Kristine, what do you think of my big secret? I'm capable of something too, hm? You can imagine, of course, how this thing hangs over me. It really hasn't been easy meeting the payments on time. In the business world there's what they call quarterly interest and what they call amortization, and these are always so terribly hard to manage. I've had to skimp a little here and there, wherever I could, you know. I could hardly spare anything from my house allowance, because Torvald has to live well. I couldn't let the children go poorly dressed; whatever I got for them, I felt I had to use up completely — the darlings!

Mrs. Linde: Poor Nora, so it had to come out of your own budget, then?

Nora: Yes, of course. But I was the one most responsible, too. Every time Torvald gave me money for new clothes and such, I never used more than half; always bought the simplest, cheapest outfits. It was a godsend that everything looks so well on me that Torvald never noticed. But it did weigh me down at times, Kristine. It *is* such a joy to wear fine things. You understand.

Mrs. Linde: Oh, of course.

Nora: And then I found other ways of making money. Last winter I was lucky enough to get a lot of copying to do. I locked myself in and sat writing every evening till late in the night. Ah, I was tired so often, dead tired. But still it was wonderful fun, sitting and working like that, earning money. It was almost like being a man.

Mrs. Linde: But how much have you paid off this way so far?

Nora: That's hard to say, exactly. These accounts, you know, aren't easy to figure. I only know that I've paid out all I could scrape together. Time and again I haven't known where to turn. *(Smiling.)* Then I'd sit here dreaming of a rich old gentleman who had fallen in love with me —

Mrs. Linde: What! Who is he?

Nora: Oh, really! And that he'd died, and when his will was opened, there in big letters it said, "All my fortune shall be paid over in cash, immediately, to that enchanting Mrs. Nora Helmer."

Mrs. Linde: But Nora dear — who *was* this gentleman?

Nora: Good grief, can't you understand? The old man never existed; that was only something I'd dream up time and again whenever I was at my wits' end for money. But it makes no difference now; the old fossil can go where he pleases for all I care; I don't need him or his will — because now I'm free. *(Jumping up.)* Oh, how lovely to think of that, Kristine! Carefree! To know you're carefree, utterly carefree; to be able to romp and play with the children, and to keep up a beautiful, charming home — everything just the way Torvald likes it! And think, spring is coming, with big blue skies. Maybe we can travel a little then. Maybe I'll see the ocean again. Oh yes, it *is* so marvelous to live and be happy!

The front doorbell rings.

Mrs. Linde (rising): There's the bell. It's probably best that I go.

Nora: No, stay. No one's expected. It must be for Torvald.

Maid (from the hall doorway): Excuse me, ma'am — there's a gentleman here to see Mr. Helmer, but I didn't know — since the doctor's with him —

Nora: Who is the gentleman?

Krogstad (from the doorway): It's me, Mrs. Helmer.

Mrs. Linde starts and turns away toward the window.

Nora (stepping toward him, tense, her voice a whisper): You? What is it? Why do you want to speak to my husband?

Krogstad: Bank business — after a fashion. I have a small job in the investment bank, and I hear now your husband is going to be our chief —

Nora: In other words, it's —

Krogstad: Just dry business, Mrs. Helmer. Nothing but that.

Nora: Yes, then please be good enough to step into the study. *(She nods indifferently as she sees him out by the hall door, then returns and begins stirring up the stove.)*

Mrs. Linde: Nora — who was that man?

Nora: That was a Mr. Krogstad — a lawyer.

Mrs. Linde: Then it really was him.

Nora: Do you know that person?

Mrs. Linde: I did once — many years ago. For a time he was a law clerk in our town.

Nora: Yes, he's been that.

Mrs. Linde: How he's changed.

Nora: I understand he had a very unhappy marriage.

Mrs. Linde: He's a widower now.

Nora: With a number of children. There now, it's burning. *(She closes the stove door and moves the rocker a bit to one side.)*

Mrs. Linde: They say he has a hand in all kinds of business.

Nora: Oh? That may be true; I wouldn't know. But let's not think about business. It's so dull.

> *Dr. Rank enters from Helmer's study.*

Rank (still in the doorway): No, no really—I don't want to intrude, I'd just as soon talk a little while with your wife. *(Shuts the door, then notices Mrs. Linde.)* Oh, beg pardon. I'm intruding here too.

Nora: No, not at all. *(Introducing him.)* Dr. Rank, Mrs. Linde.

Rank: Well now, that's a name much heard in this house. I believe I passed the lady on the stairs as I came.

Mrs. Linde: Yes, I take the stairs very slowly. They're rather hard on me.

Rank: Uh-hm, some touch of internal weakness?

Mrs. Linde: More overexertion, I'd say.

Rank: Nothing else? Then you're probably here in town to rest up in a round of parties?

Mrs. Linde: I'm here to look for work.

Rank: Is that the best cure for overexertion?

Mrs. Linde: One has to live, Doctor.

Rank: Yes, there's a common prejudice to that effect.

Nora: Oh, come on, Dr. Rank—you really do want to live yourself.

Rank: Yes, I really do. Wretched as I am, I'll gladly prolong my torment indefinitely. All my patients feel like that. And it's quite the same, too, with the morally sick. Right at this moment there's one of those moral invalids in there with Helmer—

Mrs. Linde (softly): Ah!

Nora: Who do you mean?

Rank: Oh, it's a lawyer, Krogstad, a type you wouldn't know. His character is rotten to the root—but even he began chattering all-importantly about how he had to *live.*

Nora: Oh? What did he want to talk to Torvald about?

Rank: I really don't know. I only heard something about the bank.

Nora: I didn't know that Krog—that this man Krogstad had anything to do with the bank.

Rank: Yes, he's gotten some kind of berth down there. *(To Mrs. Linde.)* I don't know if you also have, in your neck of the woods, a type of person who scuttles about breathlessly, sniffing out hints of moral corruption, and then maneuvers his victim into some sort of key position where he can keep an eye on him. It's the healthy these days that are out in the cold.

Mrs. Linde: All the same, it's the sick who most need to be taken in.

Rank (with a shrug): Yes, there we have it. That's the concept that's turning society into a sanatorium.

> *Nora, lost in her thoughts, breaks out into quiet laughter and claps her hands.*

Rank: Why do you laugh at that? Do you have any real idea of what society is?

Nora: What do I care about dreary old society? I was laughing at something
quite different — something terribly funny. Tell me, Doctor — is everyone
who works in the bank dependent now on Torvald?

Rank: Is that what you find so terribly funny?

Nora (smiling and humming): Never mind, never mind! *(Pacing the floor.)* Yes,
that's really immensely amusing: that we — that Torvald has so much
power now over all those people. *(Taking the bag out of her pocket.)* Dr. Rank,
a little macaroon on that?

Rank: See here, macaroons! I thought they were contraband here.

Nora: Yes, but these are some that Kristine gave me.

Mrs. Linde: What? I — ?

Nora: Now, now, don't be afraid. You couldn't possibly know that Torvald had
forbidden them. You see, he's worried they'll ruin my teeth. But hmp! Just
this once! Isn't that so, Dr. Rank? Help yourself! *(Puts a macaroon in his
mouth.)* And you too, Kristine. And I'll also have one, only a little one — or
two, at the most. *(Walking about again.)* Now I'm really tremendously happy.
Now there's just one last thing in the world that I have an enormous desire
to do.

Rank: Well! And what's that?

Nora: It's something I have such a consuming desire to say so Torvald could
hear.

Rank: And why can't you say it?

Nora: I don't dare. It's quite shocking.

Mrs. Linde: Shocking?

Rank: Well, then it isn't advisable. But in front of us you certainly can. What
do you have such a desire to say so Torvald could hear?

Nora: I have such a huge desire to say — to hell and be damned!

Rank: Are you crazy?

Mrs. Linde: My goodness, Nora!

Rank: Go on, say it. Here he is.

Nora (hiding the macaroon bag): Shh, shh, shh!

Helmer comes in from his study, hat in hand, overcoat over his arm.

Nora (going toward him): Well, Torvald dear, are you through with him?

Helmer: Yes, he just left.

Nora: Let me introduce you — this is Kristine, who's arrived here in town.

Helmer: Kristine — ? I'm sorry, but I don't know —

Nora: Mrs. Linde, Torvald dear. Mrs. Kristine Linde.

Helmer: Of course. A childhood friend of my wife's, no doubt?

Mrs. Linde: Yes, we knew each other in those days.

Nora: And just think, she made the long trip down here in order to talk with
you.

Helmer: What's this?

Mrs. Linde: Well, not exactly —

Nora: You see, Kristine is remarkably clever in office work, and so she's terribly
eager to come under a capable man's supervision and add more to what
she already knows —

Helmer: Very wise, Mrs. Linde.

Nora: And then when she heard that you'd become a bank manager — the story
was wired out to the papers — then she came in as fast as she could and —

Really, Torvald, for my sake you can do a little something for Kristine, can't you?

Helmer: Yes, it's not at all impossible. Mrs. Linde, I suppose you're a widow?

Mrs. Linde: Yes.

Helmer: Any experience in office work?

Mrs. Linde: Yes, a good deal.

Helmer: Well, it's quite likely that I can make an opening for you —

Nora (clapping her hands): You see, you see!

Helmer: You've come at a lucky moment, Mrs. Linde.

Mrs. Linde: Oh, how can I thank you?

Helmer: Not necessary. *(Putting his overcoat on.)* But today you'll have to excuse me —

Rank: Wait, I'll go with you. *(He fetches his coat from the hall and warms it at the stove.)*

Nora: Don't stay out long, dear.

Helmer: An hour; no more.

Nora: Are you going too, Kristine?

Mrs. Linde (putting on her winter garments): Yes, I have to see about a room now.

Helmer: Then perhaps we can all walk together.

Nora (helping her): What a shame we're so cramped here, but it's quite impossible for us to —

Mrs. Linde: Oh, don't even think of it! Good-bye, Nora dear, and thanks for everything.

Nora: Good-bye for now. Of course you'll be back this evening. And you too, Dr. Rank. What? If you're well enough? Oh, you've got to be! Wrap up tight now.

In a ripple of small talk the company moves out into the hall; children's voices are heard outside on the steps.

Nora: There they are! There they are! *(She runs to open the door. The children come in with their nurse, Anne-Marie.)* Come in, come in! *(Bends down and kisses them.)* Oh, you darlings — ! Look at them, Kristine. Aren't they lovely!

Rank: No loitering in the draft here.

Helmer: Come, Mrs. Linde — this place is unbearable now for anyone but mothers.

Dr. Rank, Helmer, and Mrs. Linde go down the stairs. Anne-Marie goes into the living room with the children. Nora follows, after closing the hall door.

Nora: How fresh and strong you look. Oh, such red cheeks you have! Like apples and roses. *(The children interrupt her throughout the following.)* And it was so much fun? That's wonderful. Really? You pulled both Emmy and Bob on the sled? Imagine, all together! Yes, you're a clever boy, Ivar. Oh, let me hold her a bit, Anne-Marie. My sweet little doll baby! *(Takes the smallest from the nurse and dances with her.)* Yes, yes, Mama will dance with Bob as well. What? Did you throw snowballs? Oh, if I'd only been there! No, don't bother, Anne-Marie — I'll undress them myself. Oh yes, let me. It's such fun. Go in and rest; you look half frozen. There's hot coffee waiting for you on the stove. *(The nurse goes into the room to the left. Nora takes the children's winter things off, throwing them about, while the children talk to her all at once.)* Is that so? A big dog chased you? But it didn't bite? No, dogs never bite little, lovely doll babies. Don't peek in the packages, Ivar! What is it? Yes, wouldn't you like to know. No, no, it's an ugly something. Well? Shall we play? What shall we play? Hide-and-seek? Yes, let's play hide-and-seek. Bob must hide first. I must? Yes, let me hide first. *(Laughing and shouting, she and the children play in and out of the living room and the adjoining room to the right. At last Nora hides under the table. The children come storming in, search, but cannot find her, then hear her muffled laughter, dash over to the table, lift the cloth up and find her. Wild shouting. She creeps forward as if to scare them. More shouts. Meanwhile, a knock at the hall door; no one has noticed it. Now the door half opens, and Krogstad appears. He waits a moment; the game goes on.)*

Krogstad: Beg pardon, Mrs. Helmer —

Nora (with a strangled cry, turning and scrambling to her knees): Oh! What do you want?

Krogstad: Excuse me. The outer door was ajar; it must be someone forgot to shut it —

Nora (rising): My husband isn't home, Mr. Krogstad.

Krogstad: I know that.

Nora: Yes — then what do you want here?

Krogstad: A word with you.

Nora: With —? *(To the children, quietly.)* Go in to Anne-Marie. What? No, the strange man won't hurt Mama. When he's gone, we'll play some more. *(She leads the children into the room to the left and shuts the door after them. Then, tense and nervous:)* You want to speak to me?

Krogstad: Yes, I want to.

Nora: Today? But it's not yet the first of the month —

Krogstad: No, it's Christmas Eve. It's going to be up to you how merry a Christmas you have.

Nora: What is it you want? Today I absolutely can't —

Krogstad: We won't talk about that till later. This is something else. You do have a moment to spare, I suppose?

Nora: Oh yes, of course — I do, except —

Krogstad: Good. I was sitting over at Olsen's Restaurant when I saw your husband go down the street —

Nora: Yes?

Krogstad: With a lady.

Nora: Yes. So?

Krogstad: If you'll pardon my asking: wasn't that lady a Mrs. Linde?

Nora: Yes.

Krogstad: Just now come into town?

Nora: Yes, today.

Krogstad: She's a good friend of yours?

Nora: Yes, she is. But I don't see —

Krogstad: I also knew her once.

Nora: I'm aware of that.

Krogstad: Oh? You know all about it. I thought so. Well, then let me ask you short and sweet: is Mrs. Linde getting a job in the bank?

Nora: What makes you think you can cross-examine me, Mr. Krogstad — you, one of my husband's employees? But since you ask, you might as well know — yes, Mrs. Linde's going to be taken on at the bank. And I'm the one who spoke for her, Mr. Krogstad. Now you know.

Krogstad: So I guessed right.

Nora (pacing up and down): Oh, one does have a tiny bit of influence, I should hope. Just because I am a woman, don't think it means that — When one has a subordinate position, Mr. Krogstad, one really ought to be careful about pushing somebody who — hm —

Krogstad: Who has influence?

Nora: That's right.

Krogstad (in a different tone): Mrs. Helmer, would you be good enough to use your influence on my behalf?

Nora: What? What do you mean?

Krogstad: Would you please make sure that I keep my subordinate position in the bank?

Nora: What does that mean? Who's thinking of taking away your position?

Krogstad: Oh, don't play the innocent with me. I'm quite aware that your friend would hardly relish the chance of running into me again; and I'm also aware now whom I can thank for being turned out.

Nora: But I promise you —

Krogstad: Yes, yes, yes, to the point: there's still time, and I'm advising you to use your influence to prevent it.

Nora: But Mr. Krogstad, I have absolutely no influence.

Krogstad: You haven't? I thought you were just saying —

Nora: You shouldn't take me so literally. I! How can you believe that I have any such influence over my husband?

Krogstad: Oh, I've known your husband from our student days. I don't think the great bank manager's more steadfast than any other married man.

Nora: You speak insolently about my husband, and I'll show you the door.

Krogstad: The lady has spirit.

Nora: I'm not afraid of you any longer. After New Year's, I'll soon be done with the whole business.

Krogstad (restraining himself): Now listen to me, Mrs. Helmer. If necessary, I'll fight for my little job in the bank as if it were life itself.

Nora: Yes, so it seems.

Krogstad: It's not just a matter of income; that's the least of it. It's something else — All right, out with it! Look, this is the thing. You know, just like all the others, of course, that once, a good many years ago, I did something rather rash.

Nora: I've heard rumors to that effect.

Krogstad: The case never got into court; but all the same, every door was closed in my face from then on. So I took up those various activities you know about. I had to grab hold somewhere; and I dare say I haven't been among the worst. But now I want to drop all that. My boys are growing up. For their sakes, I'll have to win back as much respect as possible here in town. That job in the bank was like the first rung in my ladder. And now your husband wants to kick me right back down in the mud again.

Nora: But for heaven's sake, Mr. Krogstad, it's simply not in my power to help you.

Krogstad: That's because you haven't the will to — but I have the means to make you.

Nora: You certainly won't tell my husband that I owe you money?

Krogstad: Hm — what if I told him that?

Nora: That would be shameful of you. *(Nearly in tears.)* This secret — my joy and my pride — that he should learn it in such a crude and disgusting way — learn it from you. You'd expose me to the most horrible unpleasantness —

Krogstad: Only unpleasantness?

Nora (vehemently): But go on and try. It'll turn out the worse for you, because then my husband will really see what a crook you are, and then you'll *never* be able to hold your job.

Krogstad: I asked if it was just domestic unpleasantness you were afraid of?

Nora: If my husband finds out, then of course he'll pay what I owe at once, and then we'd be through with you for good.

Krogstad (a step closer): Listen, Mrs. Helmer — you've either got a very bad memory, or else no head at all for business. I'd better put you a little more in touch with the facts.

Nora: What do you mean?

Krogstad: When your husband was sick, you came to me for a loan of four thousand, eight hundred crowns.

Nora: Where else could I go?

Krogstad: I promised to get you that sum —

Nora: And you got it.

Krogstad: I promised to get you that sum, on certain conditions. You were so involved in your husband's illness, and so eager to finance your trip, that I guess you didn't think out all the details. It might just be a good idea to remind you. I promised you the money on the strength of a note I drew up.

Nora: Yes, and that I signed.

Krogstad: Right. But at the bottom I added some lines for your father to guarantee the loan. He was supposed to sign down there.

Nora: Supposed to? He did sign.

Krogstad: I left the date blank. In other words, your father would have dated his signature himself. Do you remember that?

Nora: Yes, I think —

Krogstad: Then I gave you the note for you to mail to your father. Isn't that so?

Nora: Yes.

Krogstad: And naturally you sent it at once — because only some five, six days later you brought me the note, properly signed. And with that, the money was yours.

Nora: Well, then; I've made my payments regularly, haven't I?

Krogstad: More or less. But — getting back to the point — those were hard times for you then, Mrs. Helmer.

Nora: Yes, they were.

Krogstad: Your father was very ill, I believe.

Nora: He was near the end.

Krogstad: He died soon after?

Nora: Yes.

Krogstad: Tell me, Mrs. Helmer, do you happen to recall the date of your father's death? The day of the month, I mean.

Nora: Papa died the twenty-ninth of September.

Krogstad: That's quite correct; I've already looked into that. And now we come to a curious thing — *(Taking out a paper.)* which I simply cannot comprehend.

Nora: Curious thing? I don't know —

Krogstad: This is the curious thing: that your father co-signed the note for your loan three days after his death.

Nora: How — ? I don't understand.

Krogstad: Your father died the twenty-ninth of September. But look. Here your father dated his signature October second. Isn't that curious, Mrs. Helmer? *(Nora is silent.)* Can you explain it to me? *(Nora remains silent.)* It's also remarkable that the words "October second" and the year aren't written in your father's hand, but rather in one that I think I know. Well, it's easy to understand. Your father forgot perhaps to date his signature, and then someone or other added it, a bit sloppily, before anyone knew of his death. There's nothing wrong in that. It all comes down to the signature. And there's no question about *that*, Mrs. Helmer. It really *was* your father who signed his own name here, wasn't it?

Nora (after a short silence, throwing her head back and looking squarely at him): No, it wasn't. *I* signed Papa's name.

Krogstad: Wait, now — are you fully aware that this is a dangerous confession?

Nora: Why? You'll soon get your money.

Krogstad: Let me ask you a question — why didn't you send the paper to your father?

Nora: That was impossible. Papa was so sick. If I'd asked him for his signature, I also would have had to tell him what the money was for. But I couldn't tell him, sick as he was, that my husband's life was in danger. That was just impossible.

Krogstad: Then it would have been better if you'd given up the trip abroad.

Nora: I couldn't possibly. The trip was to save my husband's life. I couldn't give that up.

Krogstad: But didn't you ever consider that this was a fraud against me?

Nora: I couldn't let myself be bothered by that. You weren't any concern of mine. I couldn't stand you, with all those cold complications you made, even though you knew how badly off my husband was.

Krogstad: Mrs. Helmer, obviously you haven't the vaguest idea of what you've involved yourself in. But I can tell you this: it was nothing more and nothing worse that I once did — and it wrecked my whole reputation.

Nora: You? Do you expect me to believe that you ever acted bravely to save your wife's life?

Krogstad: Laws don't inquire into motives.

Nora: Then they must be very poor laws.

Krogstad: Poor or not — if I introduce this paper in court, you'll be judged according to law.

Nora: This I refuse to believe. A daughter hasn't a right to protect her dying father from anxiety and care? A wife hasn't a right to save her husband's life? I don't know much about laws, but I'm sure that somewhere in the books these things are allowed. And you don't know anything about it — you who practice the law? You must be an awful lawyer, Mr. Krogstad.

Krogstad: Could be. But business — the kind of business we two are mixed up in — don't you think I know about that? All right. Do what you want now. But I'm telling you *this*: if I get shoved down a second time, you're going to keep me company. *(He bows and goes out through the hall.)*

Nora (pensive for a moment, then tossing her head): Oh, really! Trying to frighten me! I'm not so silly as all that. *(Begins gathering up the children's clothes, but soon stops.)* But—? No, but that's impossible! I did it out of love.

The Children (in the doorway, left): Mama, that strange man's gone out the door.

Nora: Yes, yes, I know it. But don't tell anyone about the strange man. Do you hear? Not even Papa!

The Children: No, Mama. But now will you play again?

Nora: No, not now.

The Children: Oh, but Mama, you promised.

Nora: Yes, but I can't now. Go inside; I have too much to do. Go in, go in, my sweet darlings. *(She herds them gently back in the room and shuts the door after them. Settling on the sofa, she takes up a piece of embroidery and makes some stitches, but soon stops abruptly.)* No! *(Throws the work aside, rises, goes to the hall door and calls out.)* Helene! Let me have the tree in here. *(Goes to the table, left, opens the table drawer, and stops again.)* No, but that's utterly impossible!

Maid (with the Christmas tree): Where should I put it, ma'am?

Nora: There. The middle of the floor.

Maid: Should I bring anything else?

Nora: No, thanks. I have what I need.

The Maid, who has set the tree down, goes out.

Nora (absorbed in trimming the tree): Candles here—and flowers here. That terrible creature! Talk, talk, talk! There's nothing to it at all. The tree's going to be lovely. I'll do anything to please you, Torvald. I'll sing for you, dance for you—

Helmer comes in from the hall, with a sheaf of papers under his arm.

Nora: Oh! You're back so soon?

Helmer: Yes. Has anyone been here?

Nora: Here? No.

Helmer: That's odd. I saw Krogstad leaving the front door.

Nora: So? Oh yes, that's true. Krogstad was here a moment.

Helmer: Nora, I can see by your face that he's been here, begging you to put in a good word for him.

Nora: Yes.

Helmer: And it was supposed to seem like your own idea? You were to hide it from me that he'd been here. He asked you that, too, didn't he?

Nora: Yes, Torvald, but—

Helmer: Nora, Nora, and you could fall for that? Talk with that sort of person and promise him anything? And then in the bargain, tell me an untruth.

Nora: An untruth—?

Helmer: Didn't you say that no one had been here? *(Wagging his finger.)* My little songbird must never do that again. A songbird needs a clean beak to warble with. No false notes. *(Putting his arm about her waist.)* That's the way it should be, isn't it? Yes, I'm sure of it. *(Releasing her.)* And so, enough of that. *(Sitting by the stove.)* Ah, how snug and cozy it is here. *(Leafing among his papers.)*

Nora (busy with the tree, after a short pause): Torvald!

Helmer: Yes.

Nora: I'm so much looking forward to the Stenborgs' costume party, day after tomorrow.

Helmer: And I can't wait to see what you'll surprise me with.

Nora: Oh, that stupid business!

Helmer: What?

Nora: I can't find anything that's right. Everything seems so ridiculous, so inane.

Helmer: So my little Nora's come to *that* recognition?

Nora (going behind his chair, her arms resting on its back): Are you very busy, Torvald?

Helmer: Oh—

Nora: What papers are those?

Helmer: Bank matters.

Nora: Already?

Helmer: I've gotten full authority from the retiring management to make all necessary changes in personnel and procedure. I'll need Christmas week for that. I want to have everything in order by New Year's.

Nora: So that was the reason this poor Krogstad—

Helmer: Hm.

Nora (still leaning on the chair and slowly stroking the nape of his neck): If you weren't so very busy, I would have asked you an enormous favor, Torvald.

Helmer: Let's hear. What is it?

Nora: You know, there isn't anyone who has your good taste—and I want so much to look well at the costume party. Torvald, couldn't you take over and decide what I should be and plan my costume?

Helmer: Ah, is my stubborn little creature calling for a lifeguard?

Nora: Yes, Torvald, I can't get anywhere without your help.

Helmer: All right—I'll think it over. We'll hit on something.

Nora: Oh, how sweet of you. *(Goes to the tree again. Pause.)* Aren't the red flowers pretty—? But tell me, was it really such a crime that this Krogstad committed?

Helmer: Forgery. Do you have any idea what that means?

Nora: Couldn't he have done it out of need?

Helmer: Yes, or thoughtlessness, like so many others. I'm not so heartless that I'd condemn a man categorically for just one mistake.

Nora: No, of course not, Torvald!

Helmer: Plenty of men have redeemed themselves by openly confessing their crimes and taking their punishment.

Nora: Punishment—?

Helmer: But now Krogstad didn't go that way. He got himself out by sharp practices, and that's the real cause of his moral breakdown.

Nora: Do you really think that would—?

Helmer: Just imagine how a man with that sort of guilt in him has to lie and cheat and deceive on all sides, has to wear a mask even with the nearest and dearest he has, even with his own wife and children. And with the children, Nora—that's where it's most horrible.

Nora: Why?

Helmer: Because that kind of atmosphere of lies infects the whole life of a home. Every breath the children take in is filled with the germs of something degenerate.

Nora (coming closer behind him): Are you sure of that?

Helmer: Oh, I've seen it often enough as a lawyer. Almost everyone who goes bad early in life has a mother who's a chronic liar.

Nora: Why just — the mother?

Helmer: It's usually the mother's influence that's dominant, but the father's works in the same way, of course. Every lawyer is quite familiar with it. And still this Krogstad's been going home year in, year out, poisoning his own children with lies and pretense; that's why I call him morally lost. *(Reaching his hands out toward her.)* So my sweet little Nora must promise me never to plead his cause. Your hand on it. Come, come, what's this? Give me your hand. There, now. All settled. I can tell you it'd be impossible for me to work alongside of him. I literally feel physically revolted when I'm anywhere near such a person.

Nora (withdraws her hand and goes to the other side of the Christmas tree): How hot it is here! And I've got so much to do.

Helmer (getting up and gathering his papers): Yes, and I have to think about getting some of these read through before dinner. I'll think about your costume, too. And something to hang on the tree in gilt paper, I may even see about that. *(Putting his hand on her head.)* Oh you, my darling little songbird. *(He goes into his study and closes the door after him.)*

Nora (softly, after a silence): Oh, really! It isn't so. It's impossible. It must be impossible.

Anne-Marie (in the doorway, left): The children are begging so hard to come in to Mama.

Nora: No, no, no, don't let them in to me! You stay with them, Anne-Marie.

Anne-Marie: Of course, ma'am. *(Closes the door.)*

Nora (pale with terror): Hurt my children —! Poison my home? *(A moment's pause; then she tosses her head.)* That's not true. Never. Never in all the world.

ACT II

Same room. Beside the piano the Christmas tree now stands stripped of ornament, burned-down candle stubs on its ragged branches. Nora's street clothes lie on the sofa. Nora, alone in the room, moves restlessly about; at last she stops at the sofa and picks up her coat.

Nora (dropping the coat again): Someone's coming! *(Goes toward the door, listens.)* No — there's no one. Of course — nobody's coming today, Christmas Day — or tomorrow, either. But maybe — *(Opens the door and looks out.)* No, nothing in the mailbox. Quite empty. *(Coming forward.)* What nonsense! He won't do anything serious. Nothing terrible could happen. It's impossible. Why, I have three small children.

Anne-Marie, with a large carton, comes in from the room to the left.

Anne-Marie: Well, at last I found the box with the masquerade clothes.

Nora: Thanks. Put it on the table.

Anne-Marie (does so): But they're all pretty much of a mess.

Nora: Ahh! I'd love to rip them in a million pieces!

Anne-Marie: Oh, mercy, they can be fixed right up. Just a little patience.

Nora: Yes, I'll go get Mrs. Linde to help me.

Anne-Marie: Out again now? In this nasty weather? Miss Nora will catch cold — get sick.

Nora: Oh, worse things could happen. How are the children?

Anne-Marie: The poor mites are playing with their Christmas presents, but —

Nora: Do they ask for me much?

Anne-Marie: They're so used to having Mama around, you know.

Nora: Yes, but Anne-Marie, I *can't* be together with them as much as I was.

Anne-Marie: Well, small children get used to anything.

Nora: You think so? Do you think they'd forget their mother if she was gone for good?

Anne-Marie: Oh, mercy — gone for good!

Nora: Wait, tell me, Anne-Marie — I've wondered so often — how could you ever have the heart to give your child over to strangers?

Anne-Marie: But I had to, you know, to become little Nora's nurse.

Nora: Yes, but how could you *do* it?

Anne-Marie: When I could get such a good place? A girl who's poor and who's gotten in trouble is glad enough for that. Because that slippery fish, he didn't do a thing for me, you know.

Nora: But your daughter's surely forgotten you.

Anne-Marie: Oh, she certainly has not. She's written to me, both when she was confirmed and when she was married.

Nora (clasping her about the neck): You old Anne-Marie, you were a good mother for me when I was little.

Anne-Marie: Poor little Nora, with no other mother but me.

Nora: And if the babies didn't have one, then I know that you'd — What silly talk! *(Opening the carton.)* Go in to them. Now I'll have to — Tomorrow you can see how lovely I'll look.

Anne-Marie: Oh, there won't be anyone at the party as lovely as Miss Nora. *(She goes off into the room, left.)*

Nora (begins unpacking the box, but soon throws it aside): Oh, if I dared to go out. If only nobody would come. If only nothing would happen here while I'm out. What craziness — nobody's coming. Just don't think. This muff — needs a brushing. Beautiful gloves, beautiful gloves. Let it go. Let it go! One, two, three, four, five, six — *(With a cry.)* Oh, there they are! *(Poises to move toward the door, but remains irresolutely standing. Mrs. Linde enters from the hall, where she has removed her street clothes.)*

Nora: Oh, it's you, Kristine. There's no one else out there? How good that you've come.

Mrs. Linde: I hear you were up asking for me.

Nora: Yes, I just stopped by. There's something you really can help me with. Let's get settled on the sofa. Look, there's going to be a costume party tomorrow evening at the Stenborgs' right above us, and now Torvald wants me to go as a Neapolitan peasant girl and dance the tarantella that I learned in Capri.

Mrs. Linde: Really, are you giving a whole performance?

Nora: Torvald says yes, I should. See, here's the dress. Torvald had it made for me down there; but now it's all so tattered that I just don't know —

Mrs. Linde: Oh, we'll fix that up in no time. It's nothing more than the trimmings — they're a bit loose here and there. Needle and thread? Good, now we have what we need.

Nora: Oh, how sweet of you!

Mrs. Linde (sewing): So you'll be in disguise tomorrow, Nora. You know what? I'll stop by then for a moment and have a look at you all dressed up. But listen, I've absolutely forgotten to thank you for that pleasant evening yesterday.

Nora (getting up and walking about): I don't think it was as pleasant as usual yesterday. You should have come to town a bit sooner, Kristine — Yes, Torvald really knows how to give a home elegance and charm.

Mrs. Linde: And you do, too, if you ask me. You're not your father's daughter for nothing. But tell me, is Dr. Rank always so down in the mouth as yesterday?

Nora: No, that was quite an exception. But he goes around critically ill all the time — tuberculosis of the spine, poor man. You know, his father was a disgusting thing who kept mistresses and so on — and that's why the son's been sickly from birth.

Mrs. Linde (lets her sewing fall to her lap): But my dearest Nora, how do you know about such things?

Nora (walking more jauntily): Hmp! When you've had three children, then you've had a few visits from — from women who know something of medicine, and they tell you this and that.

Mrs. Linde (resumes sewing; a short pause): Does Dr. Rank come here every day?

Nora: Every blessed day. He's Torvald's best friend from childhood, and *my* good friend, too. Dr. Rank almost belongs to this house.

Mrs. Linde: But tell me — is he quite sincere? I mean, doesn't he rather enjoy flattering people?

Nora: Just the opposite. Why do you think that?

Mrs. Linde: When you introduced us yesterday, he was proclaiming that he'd often heard my name in this house; but later I noticed that your husband hadn't the slightest idea who I really was. So how could Dr. Rank — ?

Nora: But it's all true, Kristine. You see, Torvald loves me beyond words, and, as he puts it, he'd like to keep me all to himself. For a long time he'd almost be jealous if I even mentioned any of my old friends back home. So of course I dropped that. But with Dr. Rank I talk a lot about such things, because he likes hearing about them.

Mrs. Linde: Now listen, Nora; in many ways you're still like a child. I'm a good deal older than you, with a little more experience. I'll tell you something: you ought to put an end to all this with Dr. Rank.

Nora: What should I put an end to?

Mrs. Linde: Both parts of it, I think. Yesterday you said something about a rich admirer who'd provide you with money —

Nora: Yes, one who doesn't exist — worse luck. So?

Mrs. Linde: Is Dr. Rank well off?

Nora: Yes, he is.

Mrs. Linde: With no dependents?

Nora: No, no one. But —

Mrs. Linde: And he's over here every day?

Nora: Yes, I told you that.

Mrs. Linde: How can a man of such refinement be so grasping?

Nora: I don't follow you at all.

Mrs. Linde: Now don't try to hide it, Nora. You think I can't guess who loaned you the forty-eight hundred crowns?

Nora: Are you out of your mind? How could you think such a thing! A friend of ours, who comes here every single day. What an intolerable situation that would have been!

Mrs. Linde: Then it really wasn't him.

Nora: No, absolutely not. It never even crossed my mind for a moment—And he had nothing to lend in those days; his inheritance came later.

Mrs. Linde: Well, I think that was a stroke of luck for you, Nora dear.

Nora: No, it never would have occurred to me to ask Dr. Rank—Still, I'm quite sure that if I had asked him—

Mrs. Linde: Which you won't, of course.

Nora: No, of course not. I can't see that I'd ever need to. But I'm quite positive that if I talked to Dr. Rank—

Mrs. Linde: Behind your husband's back?

Nora: I've got to clear up this other thing; *that's* also behind his back. I've *got* to clear it all up.

Mrs. Linde: Yes, I was saying that yesterday, but—

Nora (pacing up and down): A man handles these problems so much better than a woman—

Mrs. Linde: One's husband does, yes.

Nora: Nonsense. *(Stopping.)* When you pay everything you owe, then you get your note back, right?

Mrs. Linde: Yes, naturally.

Nora: And can rip it into a million pieces and burn it up—that filthy scrap of paper!

Mrs. Linde (looking hard at her, laying her sewing aside, and rising slowly): Nora, you're hiding something from me.

Nora: You can see it in my face?

Mrs. Linde: Something's happened to you since yesterday morning. Nora, what is it?

Nora (hurrying toward her): Kristine! *(Listening.)* Shh! Torvald's home. Look, go in with the children a while. Torvald can't bear all this snipping and stitching. Let Anne-Marie help you.

Mrs. Linde (gathering up some of the things): All right, but I'm not leaving here until we've talked this out. *(She disappears into the room, left, as Torvald enters from the hall.)*

Nora: Oh, how I've been waiting for you, Torvald dear.

Helmer: Was that the dressmaker?

Nora: No, that was Kristine. She's helping me fix up my costume. You know, it's going to be quite attractive.

Helmer: Yes, wasn't that a bright idea I had?

Nora: Brilliant! But then wasn't I good as well to give in to you?

Helmer: Good—because you give in to your husband's judgment? All right, you little goose, I know you didn't mean it like that. But I won't disturb you. You'll want to have a fitting, I suppose.

Nora: And you'll be working?

Helmer: Yes. *(Indicating a bundle of papers.)* See. I've been down to the bank. *(Starts toward his study.)*

Nora: Torvald.

Helmer (stops): Yes.

Nora: If your little squirrel begged you, with all her heart and soul, for something—?

Helmer: What's that?

Nora: Then would you do it?

Helmer: First, naturally, I'd have to know what it was.

Nora: Your squirrel would scamper about and do tricks, if you'd only be sweet and give in.

Helmer: Out with it.

Nora: Your lark would be singing high and low in every room —

Helmer: Come on, she does that anyway.

Nora: I'd be a wood nymph and dance for you in the moonlight.

Helmer: Nora — don't tell me it's that same business from this morning?

Nora (coming closer): Yes, Torvald, I beg you, please!

Helmer: And you actually have the nerve to drag that up again?

Nora: Yes, yes, you've got to give in to me; you *have* to let Krogstad keep his job in the bank.

Helmer: My dear Nora, I've slated his job for Mrs. Linde.

Nora: That's awfully kind of you. But you could just fire another clerk instead of Krogstad.

Helmer: This is the most incredible stubbornness! Because you go and give an impulsive promise to speak up for him, I'm expected to —

Nora: That's not the reason, Torvald. It's for your own sake. That man does writing for the worst papers; you said it yourself. He could do you any amount of harm. I'm scared to death of him —

Helmer: Ah, I understand. It's the old memories haunting you.

Nora: What do you mean by that?

Helmer: Of course, you're thinking about your father.

Nora: Yes, all right. Just remember how those nasty gossips wrote in the papers about Papa and slandered him so cruelly. I think they'd have had him dismissed if the department hadn't sent you up to investigate, and if you hadn't been so kind and open-minded toward him.

Helmer: My dear Nora, there's a notable difference between your father and me. Your father's official career was hardly above reproach. But mine is; and I hope it'll stay that way as long as I hold my position.

Nora: Oh, who can ever tell what vicious minds can invent? We could be so snug and happy now in our quiet, carefree home — you and I and the children, Torvald! That's why I'm pleading with you so —

Helmer: And just by pleading for him you make it impossible for me to keep him on. It's already known at the bank that I'm firing Krogstad. What if it's rumored around now that the new bank manager was vetoed by his wife —

Nora: Yes, what then — ?

Helmer: Oh yes — as long as our little bundle of stubbornness gets her way —! I should go and make myself ridiculous in front of the whole office — give people the idea I can be swayed by all kinds of outside pressure. Oh, you can bet I'd feel the effects of that soon enough! Besides — there's something that rules Krogstad right out at the bank as long as I'm the manager.

Nora: What's that?

Helmer: His moral failings I could maybe overlook if I had to —

Nora: Yes, Torvald, why not?

Helmer: And I hear he's quite efficient on the job. But he was a crony of mine back in my teens — one of those rash friendships that crop up again and again to embarrass you later in life. Well, I might as well say it straight out: we're on a first-name basis. And that tactless fool makes no effort at all to hide it in front of others. Quite the contrary—he thinks that entitles him to take a familiar air around me, and so every other second he comes booming out with his "Yes, Torvald!" and "Sure thing, Torvald!" I tell you, it's been excruciating for me. He's out to make my place in the bank unbearable.

Nora: Torvald, you can't be serious about all this.

Helmer: Oh no? Why not?

Nora: Because these are such petty considerations.

Helmer: What are you saying? Petty? You think I'm petty!

Nora: No, just the opposite, Torvald dear. That's exactly why—

Helmer: Never mind. You call my motives petty; then I might as well be just that. Petty! All right! We'll put a stop to this for good. *(Goes to the hall door and calls.)* Helene!

Nora: What do you want?

Helmer (searching among his papers): A decision. *(The maid comes in.)* Look here; take this letter; go out with it at once. Get hold of a messenger and have him deliver it. Quick now. It's already addressed. Wait, here's some money.

Maid: Yes, sir. *(She leaves with the letter.)*

Helmer (straightening his papers): There, now, little Miss Willful.

Nora (breathlessly): Torvald, what was that letter?

Helmer: Krogstad's notice.

Nora: Call it back, Torvald! There's still time. Oh, Torvald, call it back! Do it for my sake—for your sake, for the children's sake! Do you hear, Torvald; do it! You don't know how this can harm us.

Helmer: Too late.

Nora: Yes, too late.

Helmer: Nora dear, I can forgive you this panic, even though basically you're insulting me. Yes, you are! Or isn't it an insult to think that *I* should be afraid of a courtroom hack's revenge? But I forgive you anyway, because this shows so beautifully how much you love me. *(Takes her in his arms.)* This is the way it should be, my darling Nora. Whatever comes, you'll see; when it really counts, I have strength and courage enough as a man to take on the whole weight myself.

Nora (terrified): What do you mean by that?

Helmer: The whole weight, I said.

Nora (resolutely): No, never in all the world.

Helmer: Good. So we'll share it, Nora, as man and wife. That's as it should be. *(Fondling her.)* Are you happy now? There, there, there—not these frightened dove's eyes. It's nothing at all but empty fantasies—Now you should run through your tarantella and practice your tambourine. I'll go to the inner office and shut both doors, so I won't hear a thing; you can make all the noise you like. *(Turning in the doorway.)* And when Rank comes, just tell him where he can find me. *(He nods to her and goes with his papers into the study, closing the door.)*

Nora (standing as though rooted, dazed with fright, in a whisper): He really could do it. He will do it. He'll do it in spite of everything. No, not that, never, never! Anything but that! Escape! A way out—*(The doorbell rings.)* Dr. Rank! Anything but that! *Anything,* whatever it is! *(Her hands pass over her face, smoothing it; she pulls herself together, goes over and opens the hall door. Dr. Rank stands outside, hanging his fur coat up. During the following scene, it begins getting dark.)*

Nora: Hello, Dr. Rank. I recognized your ring. But you mustn't go in to Torvald yet; I believe he's working.

Rank: And you?

Nora: For you, I always have an hour to spare — you know that. *(He has entered, and she shuts the door after him.)*

Rank: Many thanks. I'll make use of these hours while I can.

Nora: What do you mean by that? While you can?

Rank: Does that disturb you?

Nora: Well, it's such an odd phrase. Is anything going to happen?

Rank: What's going to happen is what I've been expecting so long — but I honestly didn't think it would come so soon.

Nora (gripping his arm): What is it you've found out? Dr. Rank, you have to tell me!

Rank (sitting by the stove): It's all over for me. There's nothing to be done about it.

Nora (breathing easier): Is it you — then — ?

Rank: Who else? There's no point in lying to one's self. I'm the most miserable of all my patients, Mrs. Helmer. These past few days I've been auditing my internal accounts. Bankrupt! Within a month I'll probably be laid out and rotting in the churchyard.

Nora: Oh, what a horrible thing to say.

Rank: The thing itself is horrible. But the worst of it is all the other horror before it's over. There's only one final examination left; when I'm finished with that, I'll know about when my disintegration will begin. There's something I want to say. Helmer with his sensitivity has such a sharp distaste for anything ugly. I don't want him near my sickroom.

Nora: Oh, but Dr. Rank —

Rank: I won't have him in there. Under no condition. I'll lock my door to him — As soon as I'm completely sure of the worst, I'll send you my calling card marked with a black cross, and you'll know then the wreck has started to come apart.

Nora: No, today you're completely unreasonable. And I wanted you so much to be in a really good humor.

Rank: With death up my sleeve? And then to suffer this way for somebody else's sins. Is there any justice in that? And in every single family, in some way or another, this inevitable retribution of nature goes on —

Nora (her hands pressed over her ears): Oh, stuff! Cheer up! Please — be gay!

Rank: Yes, I'd just as soon laugh at it all. My poor, innocent spine, serving time for my father's gay army days.

Nora (by the table, left): He was so infatuated with asparagus tips and pâté de foie gras, wasn't that it?

Rank: Yes — and with truffles.

Nora: Truffles, yes. And then with oysters, I suppose?

Rank: Yes, tons of oysters, naturally.

Nora: And then the port and champagne to go with it. It's so sad that all these delectable things have to strike at our bones.

Rank: Especially when they strike at the unhappy bones that never shared in the fun.

Nora: Ah, that's the saddest of all.

Rank (looks searchingly at her): Hm.

Nora (after a moment): Why did you smile?

Rank: No, it was you who laughed.

Nora: No, it was you who smiled, Dr. Rank!

Rank (getting up): You're even a bigger tease than I'd thought.

Nora: I'm full of wild ideas today.

Rank: That's obvious.

Nora (putting both hands on his shoulders): Dear, dear Dr. Rank, you'll never die for Torvald and me.

Rank: Oh, that loss you'll easily get over. Those who go away are soon forgotten.

Nora (looks fearfully at him): You believe that?

Rank: One makes new connections, and then—

Nora: Who makes new connections?

Rank: Both you and Torvald will when I'm gone. I'd say you're well under way already. What was that Mrs. Linde doing here last evening?

Nora: Oh, come—you can't be jealous of poor Kristine?

Rank: Oh yes, I am. She'll be my successor here in the house. When I'm down under, that woman will probably—

Nora: Shh! Not so loud. She's right in there.

Rank: Today as well. So you see.

Nora: Only to sew on my dress. Good gracious, how unreasonable you are. *(Sitting on the sofa.)* Be nice now, Dr. Rank. Tomorrow you'll see how beautifully I'll dance; and you can imagine then that I'm dancing only for you—yes, and of course for Torvald, too—that's understood. *(Takes various items out of the carton.)* Dr. Rank, sit over here and I'll show you something.

Rank (sitting): What's that?

Nora: Look here. Look.

Rank: Silk stockings.

Nora: Flesh-colored. Aren't they lovely? Now it's so dark here, but tomorrow— No, no, no, just look at the feet. Oh well, you might as well look at the rest.

Rank: Hm—

Nora: Why do you look so critical? Don't you believe they'll fit?

Rank: I've never had any chance to form an opinion on that.

Nora (glancing at him a moment): Shame on you. *(Hits him lightly on the ear with the stockings.)* That's for you. *(Puts them away again.)*

Rank: And what other splendors am I going to see now?

Nora: Not the least bit more, because you've been naughty. *(She hums a little and rummages among her things.)*

Rank (after a short silence): When I sit here together with you like this, completely easy and open, then I don't know—I simply can't imagine—whatever would have become of me if I'd never come into this house.

Nora (smiling): Yes, I really think you feel completely at ease with us.

Rank (more quietly, staring straight ahead): And then to have to go away from it all—

Nora: Nonsense, you're not going away.

Rank (his voice unchanged): —and not even be able to leave some poor show of gratitude behind, scarcely a fleeting regret—no more than a vacant place that anyone can fill.

Nora: And if I asked you now for—? No—
Rank: For what?
Nora: For a great proof of your friendship—
Rank: Yes, yes?
Nora: No, I mean—for an exceptionally big favor—
Rank: Would you really, for once, make me so happy?
Nora: Oh, you haven't the vaguest idea what it is.
Rank: All right, then tell me.
Nora: No, but I can't, Dr. Rank—it's all out of reason. It's advice and help, too—and a favor—
Rank: So much the better. I can't fathom what you're hinting at. Just speak out. Don't you trust me?
Nora: Of course. More than anyone else. You're my best and truest friend, I'm sure. That's why I want to talk to you. All right, then, Dr. Rank: there's something you can help me prevent. You know how deeply, how inexpressibly dearly Torvald loves me; he'd never hesitate a second to give up his life for me.
Rank (leaning close to her): Nora—do you think he's the only one—
Nora (with a slight start): Who—?
Rank: Who'd gladly give up his life for you.
Nora (heavily): I see.
Rank: I swore to myself you should know this before I'm gone. I'll never find a better chance. Yes, Nora, now you know. And also you know now that you can trust me beyond anyone else.
Nora (rising, natural and calm): Let me by.
Rank (making room for her, but still sitting): Nora—
Nora (in the hall doorway): Helene, bring the lamp in. *(Goes over to the stove.)* Ah, dear Dr. Rank, that was really mean of you.
Rank (getting up): That I've loved you just as deeply as somebody else? Was *that* mean?
Nora: No, but that you came out and told me. That was quite unnecessary—
Rank: What do you mean? Have you known—?

The Maid comes in with the lamp, sets it on the table, and goes out again.

Rank: Nora—Mrs. Helmer—I'm asking you: have you known about it?
Nora: Oh, how can I tell what I know or don't know? Really, I don't know what to say—Why did you have to be so clumsy, Dr. Rank! Everything was so good.
Rank: Well, in any case, you now have the knowledge that my body and soul are at your command. So won't you speak out?
Nora (looking at him): After that?
Rank: Please, just let me know what it is.
Nora: You can't know anything now.
Rank: I have to. You mustn't punish me like this. Give me the chance to do whatever is humanly possible for you.
Nora: Now there's nothing you can do for me. Besides, actually, I don't need any help. You'll see—it's only my fantasies. That's what it is. Of course! *(Sits in the rocker, looks at him, and smiles.)* What a nice one you are, Dr. Rank. Aren't you a little bit ashamed, now that the lamp is here?
Rank: No, not exactly. But perhaps I'd better go—for good?
Nora: No, you certainly can't do that. You must come here just as you always have. You know Torvald can't do without you.

Rank: Yes, but *you?*

Nora: You know how much I enjoy it when you're here.

Rank: That's precisely what threw me off. You're a mystery to me. So many times I've felt you'd almost rather be with me than with Helmer.

Nora: Yes—you see, there are some people that one loves most and other people that one would almost prefer being with.

Rank: Yes, there's something to that.

Nora: When I was back home, of course I loved Papa most. But I always thought it was so much fun when I could sneak down to the maids' quarters, because they never tried to improve me, and it was always so amusing, the way they talked to each other.

Rank: Aha, so it's *their* place that I've filled.

Nora (jumping up and going to him): Oh, dear, sweet Dr. Rank, that's not what I meant at all. But you can understand that with Torvald it's just the same as with Papa—

The Maid enters from the hall.

Maid: Ma'am—please! *(She whispers to Nora and hands her a calling card.)*

Nora (glancing at the card): Ah! *(Slips it into her pocket.)*

Rank: Anything wrong?

Nora: No, no, not at all. It's only some—it's my new dress—

Rank: Really? But—there's your dress.

Nora: Oh, that. But this is another one—I ordered it—Torvald mustn't know—

Rank: Ah, now we have the big secret.

Nora: That's right. Just go in with him—he's back in the inner study. Keep him there as long as—

Rank: Don't worry. He won't get away. *(Goes into the study.)*

Nora (to the Maid): And he's standing waiting in the kitchen?

Maid: Yes, he came up by the back stairs.

Nora: But didn't you tell him somebody was here?

Maid: Yes, but that didn't do any good.

Nora: He won't leave?

Maid: No, he won't go till he's talked with you, ma'am.

Nora: Let him come in, then—but quietly. Helene, don't breathe a word about this. It's a surprise for my husband.

Maid: Yes, yes, I understand—*(Goes out.)*

Nora: This horror—it's going to happen. No, no, no, it can't happen, it mustn't. *(She goes and bolts Helmer's door. The Maid opens the hall door for Krogstad and shuts it behind him. He is dressed for travel in a fur coat, boots, and a fur cap.)*

Nora (going toward him): Talk softly. My husband's home.

Krogstad: Well, good for him.

Nora: What do you want?

Krogstad: Some information.

Nora: Hurry up, then. What is it?

Krogstad: You know, of course, that I got my notice.

Nora: I couldn't prevent it, Mr. Krogstad. I fought for you to the bitter end, but nothing worked.

Krogstad: Does your husband's love for you run so thin? He knows everything I can expose you to, and all the same he dares to—

Nora: How can you imagine he knows anything about this?

Krogstad: Ah, no — I can't imagine it either, now. It's not at all like my fine Torvald Helmer to have so much guts —

Nora: Mr. Krogstad, I demand respect for my husband!

Krogstad: Why, of course — all due respect. But since the lady's keeping it so carefully hidden, may I presume to ask if you're also a bit better informed than yesterday about what you've actually done?

Nora: More than you could ever teach me.

Krogstad: Yes, I *am* such an awful lawyer.

Nora: What is it you want from me?

Krogstad: Just a glimpse of how you are, Mrs. Helmer. I've been thinking about you all day long. A cashier, a night-court scribbler, a — well, a type like me also has a little of what they call a heart, you know.

Nora: Then show it. Think of my children.

Krogstad: Did you or your husband ever think of mine? But never mind. I simply wanted to tell you that you don't need to take this thing too seriously. For the present, I'm not proceeding with any action.

Nora: Oh no, really! Well — I knew that.

Krogstad: Everything can be settled in a friendly spirit. It doesn't have to get around town at all; it can stay just among us three.

Nora: My husband must never know anything of this.

Krogstad: How can you manage that? Perhaps you can pay me the balance?

Nora: No, not right now.

Krogstad: Or you know some way of raising the money in a day or two?

Nora: No way that I'm willing to use.

Krogstad: Well, it wouldn't have done you any good, anyway. If you stood in front of me with a fistful of bills, you still couldn't buy your signature back.

Nora: Then tell me what you're going to do with it.

Krogstad: I'll just hold onto it — keep it on file. There's no outsider who'll even get wind of it. So if you've been thinking of taking some desperate step —

Nora: I have.

Krogstad: Been thinking of running away from home —

Nora: I have!

Krogstad: Or even of something worse —

Nora: How could you guess that?

Krogstad: You can drop those thoughts.

Nora: How could you guess I was thinking of *that*?

Krogstad: Most of us think about *that* at first. I thought about it too, but I discovered I hadn't the courage —

Nora (lifelessly): I don't either.

Krogstad (relieved): That's true, you haven't the courage? You too?

Nora: I don't have it — I don't have it.

Krogstad: It would be terribly stupid, anyway. After that first storm at home blows out, why, then — I have here in my pocket a letter for your husband —

Nora: Telling everything?

Krogstad: As charitably as possible.

Nora (quickly): He mustn't ever get that letter. Tear it up. I'll find some way to get money.

Krogstad: Beg pardon, Mrs. Helmer, but I think I just told you —

Nora: Oh, I don't mean the money I owe you. Let me know how much you want from my husband, and I'll manage it.

Krogstad: I don't want money from your husband.

Nora: What do you want, then?

Krogstad: I'll tell you what. I want to recoup, Mrs. Helmer; I want to get on in the world — and there's where your husband can help me. For a year and a half I've kept myself clean of anything disreputable — all that time struggling with the worst conditions; but I was satisfied, working my way up step by step. Now I've been written right off, and I'm just not in the mood to come crawling back. I tell you, I want to move on. I want to get back in the bank — in a better position. Your husband can set up a job for me —

Nora: He'll never do that!

Krogstad: He'll do it. I know him. He won't dare breathe a word of protest. And once I'm in there together with him, you just wait and see! Inside of a year, I'll be the manager's right-hand man. It'll be Nils Krogstad, not Torvald Helmer, who runs the bank.

Nora: You'll never see the day!

Krogstad: Maybe you think you can —

Nora: I have the courage now — for *that*.

Krogstad: Oh, you don't scare me. A smart, spoiled lady like you —

Nora: You'll see; you'll see!

Krogstad: Under the ice, maybe? Down in the freezing coal-black water? There, till you float up in the spring, ugly, unrecognizable, with your hair falling out —

Nora: You don't frighten me.

Krogstad: Nor do you frighten me. One doesn't do these things, Mrs. Helmer. Besides, what good would it be? I'd still have him safe in my pocket.

Nora: Afterwards? When I'm no longer — ?

Krogstad: Are you forgetting that *I'll* be in control then over your final reputation? *(Nora stands speechless, staring at him.)* Good; now I've warned you. Don't do anything stupid. When Helmer's read my letter, I'll be waiting for his reply. And bear in mind that it's your husband himself who's forced me back to my old ways. I'll never forgive him for that. Good-bye, Mrs. Helmer. *(He goes out through the hall.)*

Nora (goes to the hall door, opens it a crack, and listens): He's gone. Didn't leave the letter. Oh no, no, that's impossible too! *(Opening the door more and more.)* What's that? He's standing outside — not going downstairs. He's thinking it over? Maybe he'll — ? *(A letter falls in the mailbox; then Krogstad's footsteps are heard, dying away down a flight of stairs. Nora gives a muffled cry and runs over toward the sofa table. A short pause.)* In the mailbox. *(Slips warily over to the hall door.)* It's lying there. Torvald, Torvald — now we're lost!

Mrs. Linde (entering with costume from the room, left): There now, I can't see anything else to mend. Perhaps you'd like to try —

Nora (in a hoarse whisper): Kristine, come here.

Mrs. Linde (tossing the dress on the sofa): What's wrong? You look upset.

Nora: Come here. See that letter? *There!* Look — through the glass in the mailbox.

Mrs. Linde: Yes, yes, I see it.

Nora: That letter's from Krogstad —

Mrs. Linde: Nora — it's Krogstad who loaned you the money!

Nora: Yes, and now Torvald will find out everything.

Mrs. Linde: Believe me, Nora, it's best for both of you.

Nora: There's more you don't know. I forged a name.

Mrs. Linde: But for heaven's sake — ?

Nora: I only want to tell you that, Kristine, so that you can be my witness.

Mrs. Linde: Witness? Why should I — ?

Nora: If I should go out of my mind — it could easily happen —

Mrs. Linde: Nora!

Nora: Or anything else occurred — so I couldn't be present here —

Mrs. Linde: Nora, Nora, you aren't yourself at all!

Nora: And someone should try to take on the whole weight, all of the guilt, you follow me —

Mrs. Linde: Yes, of course, but why do you think — ?

Nora: Then you're the witness that it isn't true, Kristine. I'm very much myself; my mind right now is perfectly clear; and I'm telling you: nobody else has known about this; I alone did everything. Remember that.

Mrs. Linde: I will. But I don't understand all this.

Nora: Oh, how could you ever understand it? It's the miracle now that's going to take place.

Mrs. Linde: The miracle?

Nora: Yes, the miracle. But it's so awful, Kristine. It mustn't take place, not for anything in the world.

Mrs. Linde: I'm going right over and talk with Krogstad.

Nora: Don't go near him; he'll do you some terrible harm!

Mrs. Linde: There was a time once when he'd gladly have done anything for me.

Nora: He?

Mrs. Linde: Where does he live?

Nora: Oh, how do I know? Yes. *(Searches in her pocket.)* Here's his card. But the letter, the letter — !

Helmer (from the study, knocking on the door): Nora!

Nora (with a cry of fear): Oh! What is it? What do you want?

Helmer: Now, now, don't be so frightened. We're not coming in. You locked the door — are you trying on the dress?

Nora: Yes, I'm trying it. I'll look just beautiful, Torvald.

Mrs. Linde (who has read the card): He's living right around the corner.

Nora: Yes, but what's the use? We're lost. The letter's in the box.

Mrs. Linde: And your husband has the key?

Nora: Yes, always.

Mrs. Linde: Krogstad can ask for his letter back unread; he can find some excuse —

Nora: But it's just this time that Torvald usually —

Mrs. Linde: Stall him. Keep him in there. I'll be back as quick as I can. *(She hurries out through the hall entrance.)*

Nora (goes to Helmer's door, opens it, and peers in): Torvald!

Helmer (from the inner study): Well — does one dare set foot in one's own living room at last? Come on, Rank, now we'll get a look — *(In the doorway.)* But what's this?

Nora: What, Torvald dear?

Helmer: Rank had me expecting some grand masquerade.

Rank (in the doorway): That was my impression, but I must have been wrong.

Nora: No one can admire me in my splendor — not till tomorrow.

Helmer: But Nora dear, you look so exhausted. Have you practiced too hard?

Nora: No, I haven't practiced at all yet.

Helmer: You know, it's necessary —

Nora: Oh, it's absolutely necessary, Torvald. But I can't get anywhere without your help. I've forgotten the whole thing completely.

Helmer: Ah, we'll soon take care of that.

Nora: Yes, take care of me, Torvald, please! Promise me that? Oh, I'm so nervous. That big party — You must give up everything this evening for me. No business — don't even touch your pen. Yes? Dear Torvald, promise?

Helmer: It's a promise. Tonight I'm totally at your service — you little helpless thing. Hm — but first there's one thing I want to — *(Goes toward the hall door.)*

Nora: What are you looking for?

Helmer: Just to see if there's any mail.

Nora: No, no, don't do that, Torvald!

Helmer: Now what?

Nora: Torvald, please. There isn't any.

Helmer: Let me look, though. *(Starts out. Nora, at the piano, strikes the first notes of the tarantella. Helmer, at the door, stops.)* Aha!

Nora: I can't dance tomorrow if I don't practice with you.

Helmer (going over to her): Nora dear, are you really so frightened?

Nora: Yes, so terribly frightened. Let me practice right now; there's still time before dinner. Oh, sit down and play for me, Torvald. Direct me. Teach me, the way you always have.

Helmer: Gladly, if it's what you want. *(Sits at the piano.)*

Nora (snatches the tambourine up from the box, then a long, varicolored shawl, which she throws around herself, whereupon she springs forward and cries out): Play for me now! Now I'll dance!

> *Helmer plays and Nora dances. Rank stands behind Helmer at the piano and looks on.*

Helmer (as he plays): Slower. Slow down.

Nora: Can't change it.

Helmer: Not so violent, Nora!

Nora: Has to be just like this.

Helmer (stopping): No, no, that won't do at all.

Nora (laughing and swinging her tambourine): Isn't that what I told you?

Rank: Let me play for her.

Helmer (getting up): Yes, go on. I can teach her more easily then.

> *Rank sits at the piano and plays; Nora dances more and more wildly. Helmer has stationed himself by the stove and repeatedly gives her directions; she seems not to hear them; her hair loosens and falls over her shoulders; she does not notice, but goes on dancing. Mrs. Linde enters.*

Mrs. Linde (standing dumbfounded at the door): Ah — !

Nora (still dancing): See what fun, Kristine!

Helmer: But Nora darling, you dance as if your life were at stake.

Nora: And it is.

Helmer: Rank, stop! This is pure madness. Stop it, I say!

   Rank breaks off playing, and Nora halts abruptly.

Helmer (going over to her): I never would have believed it. You've forgotten everything I taught you.

Nora (throwing away the tambourine): You see for yourself.

Helmer: Well, there's certainly room for instruction here.

Nora: Yes, you see how important it is. You've got to teach me to the very last minute. Promise me that, Torvald?

Helmer: You can bet on it.

Nora: You mustn't, either today or tomorrow, think about anything else but me; you mustn't open any letters — or the mailbox —

Helmer: Ah, it's still the fear of that man —

Nora: Oh yes, yes, that too.

Helmer: Nora, it's written all over you — there's already a letter from him out there.

Nora: I don't know. I guess so. But you mustn't read such things now; there mustn't be anything ugly between us before it's all over.

Rank (quietly to Helmer): You shouldn't deny her.

Helmer (putting his arms around her): The child can have her way. But tomorrow night, after you've danced —

Nora: Then you'll be free.

Maid (in the doorway, right): Ma'am, dinner is served.

Nora: We'll be wanting champagne, Helene.

Maid: Very good, ma'am. *(Goes out.)*

Helmer: So — a regular banquet, hm?

Nora: Yes, a banquet — champagne till daybreak! *(Calling out.)* And some macaroons, Helene. Heaps of them — just this once.

Helmer (taking her hands): Now, now, now — no hysterics. Be my own little lark again.

Nora: Oh, I will soon enough. But go on in — and you, Dr. Rank. Kristine, help me put up my hair.

Rank (whispering, as they go): There's nothing wrong — really wrong, is there?

Helmer: Oh, of course not. It's nothing more than this childish anxiety I was telling you about. *(They go out, right.)*

Nora: Well?

Mrs. Linde: Left town.

Nora: I could see by your face.

Mrs. Linde: He'll be home tomorrow evening. I wrote him a note.

Nora: You shouldn't have. Don't try to stop anything now. After all, it's a wonderful joy, this waiting here for the miracle.

Mrs. Linde: What is it you're waiting for?

Nora: Oh, you can't understand that. Go in to them; I'll be along in a moment.

   Mrs. Linde goes into the dining room. Nora stands a short while as if composing herself; then she looks at her watch.

Nora: Five. Seven hours to midnight. Twenty-four hours to the midnight after, and then the tarantella's done. Seven and twenty-four? Thirty-one hours to live.

Helmer (in the doorway, right): What's become of the little lark?
Nora (going toward him with open arms): Here's your lark!

ACT III

> *Same scene. The table, with chairs around it, has been moved to the center of the room. A lamp on the table is lit. The hall door stands open. Dance music drifts down from the floor above. Mrs. Linde sits at the table, absently paging through a book, trying to read, but apparently unable to focus her thoughts. Once or twice she pauses, tensely listening for a sound at the outer entrance.*

Mrs. Linde (glancing at her watch): Not yet — and there's hardly any time left. If only he's not — *(Listening again.)* Ah, there he is. *(She goes out in the hall and cautiously opens the outer door. Quiet footsteps are heard on the stairs. She whispers:)* Come in. Nobody's here.

Krogstad (in the doorway): I found a note from you at home. What's back of all this?

Mrs. Linde: I just *had* to talk to you.

Krogstad: Oh? And it just *had* to be here in this house?

Mrs. Linde: At my place it was impossible; my room hasn't a private entrance. Come in; we're all alone. The maid's asleep, and the Helmers are at the dance upstairs.

Krogstad (entering the room): Well, well, the Helmers are dancing tonight? Really?

Mrs. Linde: Yes, why not?

Krogstad: How true — why not?

Mrs. Linde: All right, Krogstad, let's talk.

Krogstad: Do we two have anything more to talk about?

Mrs. Linde: We have a great deal to talk about.

Krogstad: I wouldn't have thought so.

Mrs. Linde: No, because you've never understood me, really.

Krogstad: Was there anything more to understand — except what's all too common in life? A calculating woman throws over a man the moment a better catch comes by.

Mrs. Linde: You think I'm so thoroughly calculating? You think I broke it off lightly?

Krogstad: Didn't you?

Mrs. Linde: Nils — is that what you really thought?

Krogstad: If you cared, then why did you write me the way you did?

Mrs. Linde: What else could I do? If I had to break off with you, then it was my job as well to root out everything you felt for me.

Krogstad (wringing his hands): So that was it. And this — all this, simply for money!

Mrs. Linde: Don't forget I had a helpless mother and two small brothers. We couldn't wait for you, Nils; you had such a long road ahead of you then.

Krogstad: That may be; but you still hadn't the right to abandon me for somebody else's sake.

Mrs. Linde: Yes—I don't know. So many, many times I've asked myself if I did have that right.

Krogstad (more softly): When I lost you, it was as if all the solid ground dissolved from under my feet. Look at me; I'm a half-drowned man now, hanging onto a wreck.

Mrs. Linde: Help may be near.

Krogstad: It was near—but then you came and blocked it off.

Mrs. Linde: Without my knowing it, Nils. Today for the first time I learned that it's you I'm replacing at the bank.

Krogstad: All right—I believe you. But now that you know, will you step aside?

Mrs. Linde: No, because that wouldn't benefit you in the slightest.

Krogstad: Not "benefit" me, hm! I'd step aside anyway.

Mrs. Linde: I've learned to be realistic. Life and hard, bitter necessity have taught me that.

Krogstad: And life's taught me never to trust fine phrases.

Mrs. Linde: Then life's taught you a very sound thing. But you do have to trust in actions, don't you?

Krogstad: What does that mean?

Mrs. Linde: You said you were hanging on like a half-drowned man to a wreck.

Krogstad: I've good reason to say that.

Mrs. Linde: I'm also like a half-drowned woman on a wreck. No one to suffer with; no one to care for.

Krogstad: You made your choice.

Mrs. Linde: There wasn't any choice then.

Krogstad: So—what of it?

Mrs. Linde: Nils, if only we two shipwrecked people could reach across to each other.

Krogstad: What are you saying?

Mrs. Linde: Two on one wreck are at least better off than each on his own.

Krogstad: Kristine!

Mrs. Linde: Why do you think I came into town?

Krogstad: Did you really have some thought of me?

Mrs. Linde: I have to work to go on living. All my born days, as long as I can remember, I've worked, and it's been my best and my only joy. But now I'm completely alone in the world; it frightens me to be so empty and lost. To work for yourself—there's no joy in that. Nils, give me something—someone to work for.

Krogstad: I don't believe all this. It's just some hysterical feminine urge to go out and make a noble sacrifice.

Mrs. Linde: Have you ever found me to be hysterical?

Krogstad: Can you honestly mean this? Tell me—do you know everything about my past?

Mrs. Linde: Yes.

Krogstad: And you know what they think I'm worth around here.

Mrs. Linde: From what you were saying before, it would seem that with me you could have been another person.

Krogstad: I'm positive of that.

Mrs. Linde: Couldn't it happen still?

Krogstad: Kristine—you're saying this in all seriousness? Yes, you are! I can see it in you. And do you really have the courage, then—?

Mrs. Linde: I need to have someone to care for; and your children need a mother. We both need each other. Nils, I have faith that you're good at heart — I'll risk everything together with you.

Krogstad (gripping her hands): Kristine, thank you, thank you — Now I know I can win back a place in their eyes. Yes — but I forgot —

Mrs. Linde (listening): Shh! The tarantella. Go now! Go on!

Krogstad: Why? What is it?

Mrs. Linde: Hear the dance up there? When that's over, they'll be coming down.

Krogstad: Oh, then I'll go. But — it's all pointless. Of course, you don't know the move I made against the Helmers.

Mrs. Linde: Yes, Nils, I know.

Krogstad: And all the same, you have the courage to — ?

Mrs. Linde: I know how far despair can drive a man like you.

Krogstad: Oh, if I only could take it all back.

Mrs. Linde: You easily could — your letter's still lying in the mailbox.

Krogstad: Are you sure of that?

Mrs. Linde: Positive. But —

Krogstad (looks at her searchingly): Is that the meaning of it, then? You'll save your friend at any price. Tell me straight out. Is that it?

Mrs. Linde: Nils — anyone who's sold herself for somebody else once isn't going to do it again.

Krogstad: I'll demand my letter back.

Mrs. Linde: No, no.

Krogstad: Yes, of course. I'll stay here till Helmer comes down; I'll tell him to give me my letter again — that it only involves my dismissal — that he shouldn't read it —

Mrs. Linde: No, Nils, don't call the letter back.

Krogstad: But wasn't that exactly why you wrote me to come here?

Mrs. Linde: Yes, in that first panic. But it's been a whole day and night since then, and in that time I've seen such incredible things in this house. Helmer's got to learn everything; this dreadful secret has to be aired; those two have to come to a full understanding; all these lies and evasions can't go on.

Krogstad: Well, then, if you want to chance it. But at least there's one thing I can do, and do right away —

Mrs. Linde (listening): Go now, go quick! The dance is over. We're not safe another second.

Krogstad: I'll wait for you downstairs.

Mrs. Linde: Yes, please do; take me home.

Krogstad: I can't believe it; I've never been so happy. (*He leaves by way of the outer door; the door between the room and the hall stays open.*)

Mrs. Linde (straightening up a bit and getting together her street clothes): How different now! How different! Someone to work for, to live for — a home to build. Well, it is worth the try! Oh, if they'd only come! (*Listening.*) Ah, there they are. Bundle up. (*She picks up her hat and coat. Nora's and Helmer's voices can be heard outside; a key turns in the lock, and Helmer brings Nora into the hall almost by force. She is wearing the Italian costume with a large black shawl about her; he has on evening dress, with a black domino open over it.*)

Nora (struggling in the doorway): No, no, no, not inside! I'm going up again. I don't want to leave so soon.

Helmer: But Nora dear—

Nora: Oh, I beg you, please, Torvald. From the bottom of my heart, *please*—only an hour more!

Helmer: Not a single minute, Nora darling. You know our agreement. Come on, in we go; you'll catch cold out here. *(In spite of her resistance, he gently draws her into the room.)*

Mrs. Linde: Good evening.

Nora: Kristine!

Helmer: Why, Mrs. Linde—are you here so late?

Mrs. Linde: Yes, I'm sorry, but I did want to see Nora in costume.

Nora: Have you been sitting here, waiting for me?

Mrs. Linde: Yes. I didn't come early enough; you were all upstairs; and then I thought I really couldn't leave without seeing you.

Helmer (removing Nora's shawl): Yes, take a good look. She's worth looking at, I can tell you that, Mrs. Linde. Isn't she lovely?

Mrs. Linde: Yes, I should say—

Helmer: A dream of loveliness, isn't she? That's what everyone thought at the party, too. But she's horribly stubborn—this sweet little thing. What's to be done with her? Can you imagine, I almost had to use force to pry her away.

Nora: Oh, Torvald, you're going to regret you didn't indulge me, even for just a half hour more.

Helmer: There, you see. She danced her tarantella and got a tumultuous hand—which was well earned, although the performance may have been a bit too naturalistic—I mean it rather overstepped the proprieties of art. But never mind—what's important is, she made a success, an overwhelming success. You think I could let her stay on after that and spoil the effect? Oh no; I took my lovely little Capri girl—my capricious little Capri girl, I should say—took her under my arm; one quick tour of the ballroom, a curtsy to every side, and then—as they say in novels—the beautiful vision disappeared. An exit should always be effective, Mrs. Linde, but that's what I can't get Nora to grasp. Phew, it's hot in here. *(Flings the domino on a chair and opens the door to his room.)* Why's it dark in here? Oh yes, of course. Excuse me. *(He goes in and lights a couple of candles.)*

Nora (in a sharp, breathless whisper): So?

Mrs. Linde (quietly): I talked with him.

Nora: And—?

Mrs. Linde: Nora—you must tell your husband everything.

Nora (dully): I knew it.

Mrs. Linde: You've got nothing to fear from Krogstad, but you have to speak out.

Nora: I won't tell.

Mrs. Linde: Then the letter will.

Nora: Thanks, Kristine. I know now what's to be done. Shh!

Helmer (reentering): Well, then, Mrs. Linde—have you admired her?

Mrs. Linde: Yes, and now I'll say good night.

Helmer: Oh, come, so soon? Is this yours, this knitting?

Mrs. Linde: Yes, thanks. I nearly forgot it.

Helmer: Do you knit, then?

Mrs. Linde: Oh yes.

Helmer: You know what? You should embroider instead.

Mrs. Linde: Really? Why?

Helmer: Yes, because it's a lot prettier. See here, one holds the embroidery so, in the left hand, and then one guides the needle with the right — so — in an easy, sweeping curve — right?

Mrs. Linde: Yes, I guess that's —

Helmer: But, on the other hand, knitting — it can never be anything but ugly. Look, see here, the arms tucked in, the knitting needles going up and down — there's something Chinese about it. Ah, that was really a glorious champagne they served.

Mrs. Linde: Yes, good night, Nora, and don't be stubborn anymore.

Helmer: Well put, Mrs. Linde!

Mrs. Linde: Good night, Mr. Helmer.

Helmer (accompanying her to the door): Good night, good night. I hope you get home all right. I'd be very happy to — but you don't have far to go. Good night, good night. *(She leaves. He shuts the door after her and returns.)* There, now, at last we got her out the door. She's a deadly bore, that creature.

Nora: Aren't you pretty tired, Torvald?

Helmer: No, not a bit.

Nora: You're not sleepy?

Helmer: Not at all. On the contrary, I'm feeling quite exhilarated. But you? Yes, you really look tired and sleepy.

Nora: Yes, I'm very tired. Soon now I'll sleep.

Helmer: See! You see! I was right all along that we shouldn't stay longer.

Nora: Whatever you do is always right.

Helmer (kissing her brow): Now my little lark talks sense. Say, did you notice what a time Rank was having tonight?

Nora: Oh, was he? I didn't get to speak with him.

Helmer: I scarcely did either, but it's a long time since I've seen him in such high spirits. *(Gazes at her a moment, then comes nearer her.)* Hm — it's marvelous, though, to be back home again — to be completely alone with you. Oh, you bewitchingly lovely young woman!

Nora: Torvald, don't look at me like that!

Helmer: Can't I look at my richest treasure? At all that beauty that's mine, mine alone — completely and utterly.

Nora (moving around to the other side of the table): You mustn't talk to me that way tonight.

Helmer (following her): The tarantella is still in your blood, I can see — and it makes you even more enticing. Listen. The guests are beginning to go. *(Dropping his voice.)* Nora — it'll soon be quiet through this whole house.

Nora: Yes, I hope so.

Helmer: You do, don't you, my love? Do you realize — when I'm out at a party like this with you — do you know why I talk to you so little, and keep such a distance away; just send you a stolen look now and then — you know why I do it? It's because I'm imagining then that you're my secret darling, my secret bride-to-be, and that no one suspects there's anything between us.

Nora: Yes, yes; oh, yes, I know you're always thinking of me.

Helmer: And then when we leave and I place the shawl over those fine young rounded shoulders — over that wonderful curving neck — then I pretend that you're my young bride, that we're just coming from the wedding, that for the first time I'm bringing you into my house—that for the first time I'm alone with you—completely alone with you, your trembling young beauty! All this evening I've longed for nothing but you. When I saw you turn and sway in the tarantella—my blood was pounding till I couldn't stand it—that's why I brought you down here so early—

Nora: Go away, Torvald! Leave me alone. I don't want all this.

Helmer: What do you mean? Nora, you're teasing me. You will, won't you? Aren't I your husband—?

A knock at the outside door.

Nora (startled): What's that?

Helmer (going toward the hall): Who is it?

Rank (outside): It's me. May I come in a moment?

Helmer (with quiet irritation): Oh, what does he want now? *(Aloud.)* Hold on. *(Goes and opens the door.)* Oh, how nice that you didn't just pass us by!

Rank: I thought I heard your voice, and then I wanted so badly to have a look in. *(Lightly glancing about.)* Ah, me, these old familiar haunts. You have it snug and cozy in here, you two.

Helmer: You seemed to be having it pretty cozy upstairs, too.

Rank: Absolutely. Why shouldn't I? Why not take in everything in life? As much as you can, anyway, and as long as you can. The wine was superb—

Helmer: The champagne especially.

Rank: You noticed that too? It's amazing how much I could guzzle down.

Nora: Torvald also drank a lot of champagne this evening.

Rank: Oh?

Nora: Yes, and that always makes him so entertaining.

Rank: Well, why shouldn't one have a pleasant evening after a well-spent day?

Helmer: Well spent? I'm afraid I can't claim that.

Rank (slapping him on the back): But I can, you see!

Nora: Dr. Rank, you must have done some scientific research today.

Rank: Quite so.

Helmer: Come now—little Nora talking about scientific research!

Nora: And can I congratulate you on the results?

Rank: Indeed you may.

Nora: Then they were good?

Rank: The best possible for both doctor and patient—certainty.

Nora (quickly and searchingly): Certainty?

Rank: Complete certainty. So don't I owe myself a gay evening afterwards?

Nora: Yes, you're right, Dr. Rank.

Helmer: I'm with you—just so long as you don't have to suffer for it in the morning.

Rank: Well, one never gets something for nothing in life.

Nora: Dr. Rank—are you very fond of masquerade parties?

Rank: Yes, if there's a good array of odd disguises—

Nora: Tell me, what should we two go as at the next masquerade?

Helmer: You little featherhead—already thinking of the next!

Rank: We two? I'll tell you what: you must go as Charmed Life—

Helmer: Yes, but find a costume for *that!*

Rank: Your wife can appear just as she looks every day.

Helmer: That was nicely put. But don't you know what you're going to be?

Rank: Yes, Helmer, I've made up my mind.

Helmer: Well?

Rank: At the next masquerade I'm going to be invisible.

Helmer: That's a funny idea.

Rank: They say there's a hat — black, huge — have you never heard of the hat that makes you invisible? You put it on, and then no one on earth can see you.

Helmer (suppressing a smile): Ah, of course.

Rank: But I'm quite forgetting what I came for. Helmer, give me a cigar, one of the dark Havanas.

Helmer: With the greatest pleasure. *(Holds out his case.)*

Rank: Thanks. *(Takes one and cuts off the tip.)*

Nora (striking a match): Let me give you a light.

Rank: Thank you. *(She holds the match for him; he lights the cigar.)* And now good-bye.

Helmer: Good-bye, good-bye, old friend.

Nora: Sleep well, Doctor.

Rank: Thanks for that wish.

Nora: Wish me the same.

Rank: You? All right, if you like — Sleep well. And thanks for the light. *(He nods to them both and leaves.)*

Helmer (his voice subdued): He's been drinking heavily.

Nora (absently): Could be. *(Helmer takes his keys from his pocket and goes out in the hall.)* Torvald — what are you after?

Helmer: Got to empty the mailbox; it's nearly full. There won't be room for the morning papers.

Nora: Are you working tonight?

Helmer: You know I'm not. Why — what's this? Someone's been at the lock.

Nora: At the lock — ?

Helmer: Yes, I'm positive. What do you suppose — ? I can't imagine one of the maids — ? Here's a broken hairpin. Nora, it's yours —

Nora (quickly): Then it must be the children —

Helmer: You'd better break them of that. Hm, hm — well, opened it after all. *(Takes the contents out and calls into the kitchen.)* Helene! Helene, would you put out the lamp in the hall. *(He returns to the room shutting the hall door, then displays the handful of mail.)* Look how it's piled up. *(Sorting through them.)* Now what's this?

Nora (at the window): The letter! Oh, Torvald, no!

Helmer: Two calling cards — from Rank.

Nora: From Dr. Rank?

Helmer (examining them): "Dr. Rank, Consulting Physician." They were on top. He must have dropped them in as he left.

Nora: Is there anything on them?

Helmer: There's a black cross over the name. See? That's a gruesome notion. He could almost be announcing his own death.

Nora: That's just what he's doing.

Helmer: What! You've heard something? Something he's told you?

Nora: Yes. That when those cards came, he'd be taking his leave of us. He'll shut himself in now and die.

Helmer: Ah, my poor friend! Of course I knew he wouldn't be here much longer. But so soon — And then to hide himself away like a wounded animal.

Nora: If it has to happen, then it's best it happens in silence — don't you think so, Torvald?

Helmer (pacing up and down): He'd grown right into our lives. I simply can't imagine him gone. He with his suffering and loneliness — like a dark cloud setting off our sunlit happiness. Well, maybe it's best this way. For him, at least. *(Standing still.)* And maybe for us too, Nora. Now we're thrown back on each other, completely. *(Embracing her.)* Oh you, my darling wife, how can I hold you close enough? You know what, Nora — time and again I've wished you were in some terrible danger, just so I could stake my life and soul and everything, for your sake.

Nora (tearing herself away, her voice firm and decisive): Now you must read your mail, Torvald.

Helmer: No, no, not tonight. I want to stay with you, dearest.

Nora: With a dying friend on your mind?

Helmer: You're right. We've both had a shock. There's ugliness between us — these thoughts of death and corruption. We'll have to get free of them first. Until then — we'll stay apart.

Nora (clinging about his neck): Torvald — good night! Good night!

Helmer (kissing her on the cheek): Good night, little songbird. Sleep well, Nora. I'll be reading my mail now. *(He takes the letters into his room and shuts the door after him.)*

Nora (with bewildered glances, groping about, seizing Helmer's domino, throwing it around her, and speaking in short, hoarse, broken whispers): Never see him again. Never, never. *(Putting her shawl over her head.)* Never see the children either — them, too. Never, never. Oh, the freezing black water! The depths — down — Oh, I wish it were over — He has it now; he's reading it — now. Oh no, no, not yet. Torvald, good-bye, you and the children — *(She starts for the hall; as she does, Helmer throws open his door and stands with an open letter in his hand.)*

Helmer: Nora!

Nora (screams): Oh — !

Helmer: What is this? You know what's in this letter?

Nora: Yes, I know. Let me go! Let me out!

Helmer (holding her back): Where are you going?

Nora (struggling to break loose): You can't save me, Torvald!

Helmer (slumping back): True! Then it's true what he writes? How horrible! No, no, it's impossible — it can't be true.

Nora: It *is* true. I've loved you more than all this world.

Helmer: Ah, none of your slippery tricks.

Nora (taking one step toward him): Torvald — !

Helmer: What *is* this you've blundered into!

Nora: Just let me loose. You're not going to suffer for my sake. You're not going to take on my guilt.

Helmer: No more play-acting. *(Locks the hall door.)* You stay right here and give me a reckoning. You understand what you've done? Answer! You understand?

Nora (looking squarely at him, her face hardening): Yes. I'm beginning to understand everything now.

Helmer (striding about): Oh, what an awful awakening! In all these eight years — she who was my pride and joy — a hypocrite, a liar — worse, worse — a criminal! How infinitely disgusting it all is! The shame! *(Nora says nothing and goes on looking straight at him. He stops in front of her.)* I should have suspected something of the kind. I should have known. All your father's flimsy values — Be still! All your father's flimsy values have come out in you. No religion, no morals, no sense of duty — Oh, how I'm punished for letting him off! I did it for your sake, and you repay me like this.

Nora: Yes, like this.

Helmer: Now you've wrecked all my happiness — ruined my whole future. Oh, it's awful to think of. I'm in a cheap little grafter's hands; he can do anything he wants with me, ask for anything, play with me like a puppet — and I can't breathe a word. I'll be swept down miserably into the depths on account of a featherbrained woman.

Nora: When I'm gone from this world, you'll be free.

Helmer: Oh, quit posing. Your father had a mess of those speeches too. What good would that ever do me if you were gone from this world, as you say? Not the slightest. He can still make the whole thing known; and if he does, I could be falsely suspected as your accomplice. They might even think that I was behind it — that I put you up to it. And all that I can thank you for — you that I've coddled the whole of our marriage. Can you see now what you've done to me?

Nora (icily calm): Yes.

Helmer: It's so incredible, I just can't grasp it. But we'll have to patch up whatever we can. Take off the shawl. I said, take if off! I've got to appease him somehow or other. The thing has to be hushed up at any cost. And as for you and me, it's got to seem like everything between us is just as it was — to the outside world, that is. You'll go right on living in this house, of course. But you can't be allowed to bring up the children; I don't dare trust you with them — Oh, to have to say this to someone I've loved so much! Well, that's done with. From now on happiness doesn't matter; all that matters is saving the bits and pieces, the appearance — *(The doorbell rings. Helmer starts.)* What's that? And so late. Maybe the worst —? You think he'd —? Hide, Nora! Say you're sick. *(Nora remains standing motionless. Helmer goes and opens the door.)*

Maid (half dressed, in the hall): A letter for Mrs. Helmer.

Helmer: I'll take it. *(Snatches the letter and shuts the door.)* Yes, it's from him. You don't get it; I'm reading it myself.

Nora: Then read it.

Helmer (by the lamp): I hardly dare. We may be ruined, you and I. But — I've got to know. *(Rips open the letter, skims through a few lines, glances at an enclosure, then cries out joyfully.)* Nora! *(Nora looks inquiringly at him.)* Nora! Wait — better check it again — Yes, yes, it's true. I'm saved. Nora, I'm saved!

Nora: And I?

Helmer: You too, of course. We're both saved, both of us. Look. He's sent back your note. He says he's sorry and ashamed — that a happy development in his life — oh, who cares what he says! Nora, we're saved! No one can hurt

you. Oh, Nora, Nora—but first, this ugliness all has to go. Let me see—
(Takes a look at the note.) No, I don't want to see it; I want the whole thing to
fade like a dream. *(Tears the note and both letters to pieces, throws them into the
stove and watches them burn.)* There—now there's nothing left—He wrote
that since Christmas Eve you—Oh, they must have been three terrible
days for you, Nora.

Nora: I fought a hard fight.

Helmer: And suffered pain and saw no escape but—No, we're not going to
dwell on anything unpleasant. We'll just be grateful and keep on repeating: it's over now, it's over! You hear me, Nora? You don't seem to realize—it's over. What's it mean—that frozen look? Oh, poor little Nora, I
understand. You can't believe I've forgiven you. But I have, Nora; I swear I
have. I know that what you did, you did out of love for me.

Nora: That's true.

Helmer: You loved me the way a wife ought to love her husband. It's simply the
means that you couldn't judge. But you think I love you any the less for
not knowing how to handle your affairs? No, no—just lean on me; I'll
guide you and teach you. I wouldn't be a man if this feminine helplessness
didn't make you twice as attractive to me. You mustn't mind those sharp
words I said—that was all in the first confusion of thinking my world had
collapsed. I've forgiven you, Nora; I swear I've forgiven you.

Nora: My thanks for your forgiveness. *(She goes out through the door, right.)*

Helmer: No, wait—*(Peers in.)* What are you doing in there?

Nora (inside): Getting out of my costume.

Helmer (by the open door): Yes, do that. Try to calm yourself and collect your
thoughts again, my frightened little songbird. You can rest easy now; I've
got wide wings to shelter you with. *(Walking about close by the door.)* How
snug and nice our home is, Nora. You're safe here; I'll keep you like a
hunted dove I've rescued out of a hawk's claws. I'll bring peace to your
poor, shuddering heart. Gradually it'll happen, Nora; you'll see. Tomorrow all this will look different to you; then everything will be as it was. I
won't have to go on repeating I forgive you; you'll feel it for yourself. How
can you imagine I'd ever conceivably want to disown you—or even blame
you in any way? Ah, you don't know a man's heart, Nora. For a man there's
something indescribably sweet and satisfying in knowing he's forgiven his
wife—and forgiven her out of a full and open heart. It's as if she belongs
to him in two ways now: in a sense he's given her fresh into the world
again, and she's become his wife and his child as well. From now on that's
what you'll be to me—you little, bewildered, helpless thing. Don't be
afraid of anything, Nora; just open your heart to me, and I'll be conscience
and will to you both—*(Nora enters in her regular clothes.)* What's this? Not in
bed? You've changed your dress?

Nora: Yes, Torvald, I've changed my dress.

Helmer: But why now, so late?

Nora: Tonight I'm not sleeping.

Helmer: But Nora dear—

Nora (looking at her watch): It's still not so very late. Sit down, Torvald; we have a
lot to talk over. *(She sits at one side of the table.)*

Helmer: Nora—what is this? That hard expression—

Nora: Sit down. This'll take some time. I have a lot to say.

Helmer (sitting at the table directly opposite her): You worry me, Nora. And I don't understand you.

Nora: No, that's exactly it. You don't understand me. And I've never understood you either — until tonight. No, don't interrupt. You can just listen to what I say. We're closing out accounts, Torvald.

Helmer: How do you mean that?

Nora (after a short pause): Doesn't anything strike you about our sitting here like this?

Helmer: What's that?

Nora: We've been married now eight years. Doesn't it occur to you that this is the first time we two, you and I, man and wife, have ever talked seriously together?

Helmer: What do you mean — seriously?

Nora: In eight whole years — longer even — right from our first acquaintance, we've never exchanged a serious word on any serious thing.

Helmer: You mean I should constantly go and involve you in problems you couldn't possibly help me with?

Nora: I'm not talking of problems. I'm saying that we've never sat down seriously together and tried to get to the bottom of anything.

Helmer: But dearest, what good would that ever do you?

Nora: That's the point right there: you've never understood me. I've been wronged greatly, Torvald — first by Papa, and then by you.

Helmer: What! By us — the two people who've loved you more than anyone else?

Nora (shaking her head): You never loved me. You've thought it fun to be in love with me, that's all.

Helmer: Nora, what a thing to say!

Nora: Yes, it's true now, Torvald. When I lived at home with Papa, he told me all his opinions, so I had the same ones too; or if they were different I hid them, since he wouldn't have cared for that. He used to call me his doll-child, and he played with me the way I played with my dolls. Then I came into your house —

Helmer: How can you speak of our marriage like that?

Nora (unperturbed): I mean, then I went from Papa's hands into yours. You arranged everything to your own taste, and so I got the same taste as you — or I pretended to; I can't remember. I guess a little of both, first one, then the other. Now when I look back, it seems as if I'd lived here like a beggar — just from hand to mouth. I've lived by doing tricks for you, Torvald. But that's the way you wanted it. It's a great sin what you and Papa did to me. You're to blame that nothing's become of me.

Helmer: Nora, how unfair and ungrateful you are! Haven't you been happy here?

Nora: No, never. I thought so — but I never have.

Helmer: Not — not happy!

Nora: No, only lighthearted. And you've always been so kind to me. But our home's been nothing but a playpen. I've been your doll-wife here, just as at home I was Papa's doll-child. And in turn the children have been my dolls. I thought it was fun when you played with me, just as they thought it fun when I played with them. That's been our marriage, Torvald.

Helmer: There's some truth in what you're saying—under all the raving exaggeration. But it'll all be different after this. Playtime's over; now for the schooling.

Nora: Whose schooling—mine or the children's?

Helmer: Both yours and the children's, dearest.

Nora: Oh, Torvald, you're not the man to teach me to be a good wife to you.

Helmer: And you can say that?

Nora: And I—how am I equipped to bring up children?

Helmer: Nora!

Nora: Didn't you say a moment ago that that was no job to trust me with?

Helmer: In a flare of temper! Why fasten on that?

Nora: Yes, but you were so very right. I'm not up to the job. There's another job I have to do first. I have to try to educate myself. You can't help me with that. I've got to do it alone. And that's why I'm leaving you now.

Helmer (jumping up): What's that?

Nora: I have to stand completely alone, if I'm ever going to discover myself and the world out there. So I can't go on living with you.

Helmer: Nora, Nora!

Nora: I want to leave right away. Kristine should put me up for the night—

Helmer: You're insane! You've no right! I forbid you!

Nora: From here on, there's no use forbidding me anything. I'll take with me whatever is mine. I don't want a thing from you, either now or later.

Helmer: What kind of madness is this!

Nora: Tomorrow I'm going home—I mean, home where I came from. It'll be easier up there to find something to do.

Helmer: Oh, you blind, incompetent child!

Nora: I must learn to be competent, Torvald.

Helmer: Abandon your home, your husband, your children! And you're not even thinking what people will say.

Nora: I can't be concerned about that. I only know how essential this is.

Helmer: Oh, it's outrageous. So you'll run out like this on your most sacred vows.

Nora: What do you think are my most sacred vows?

Helmer: And I have to tell you that! Aren't they your duties to your husband and children?

Nora: I have other duties equally sacred.

Helmer: That isn't true. What duties are they?

Nora: Duties to myself.

Helmer: Before all else, you're a wife and mother.

Nora: I don't believe in that anymore. I believe that, before all else, I'm a human being, no less than you—or anyway, I ought to try to become one. I know the majority thinks you're right, Torvald, and plenty of books agree with you, too. But I can't go on believing what the majority says, or what's written in books. I have to think over these things myself and try to understand them.

Helmer: Why can't you understand your place in your own home? On a point like that, isn't there one everlasting guide you can turn to? Where's your religion?

Nora: Oh, Torvald, I'm really not sure what religion is.

Helmer: What—?

Nora: I only know what the minister said when I was confirmed. He told me religion was this thing and that. When I get clear and away by myself, I'll go
   into that problem too. I'll see if what the minister said was right, or, in any
   case, if it's right for me.

Helmer: A young woman your age shouldn't talk like that. If religion can't
   move you, I can try to rouse your conscience. You do have some moral feeling? Or, tell me — has that gone too?

Nora: It's not easy to answer that, Torvald. I simply don't know. I'm all confused about these things. I just know I see them so differently from you. I
   find out, for one thing, that the law's not at all what I'd thought — but I
   can't get it through my head that the law is fair. A woman hasn't a right to
   protect her dying father or save her husband's life! I can't believe that.

Helmer: You talk like a child. You don't know anything of the world you live in.

Nora: No, I don't. But now I'll begin to learn for myself. I'll try to discover
   who's right, the world or I.

Helmer: Nora, you're sick; you've got a fever. I almost think you're out of your
   head.

Nora: I've never felt more clearheaded and sure in my life.

Helmer: And — clearheaded and sure — you're leaving your husband and children?

Nora: Yes.

Helmer: Then there's only one possible reason.

Nora: What?

Helmer: You no longer love me.

Nora: No. That's exactly it.

Helmer: Nora! You can't be serious!

Nora: Oh, this is so hard, Torvald — you've been so kind to me always. But I
   can't help it. I don't love you anymore.

Helmer (struggling for composure): Are you also clearheaded and sure about that?

Nora: Yes, completely. That's why I can't go on staying here.

Helmer: Can you tell me what I did to lose your love?

Nora: Yes, I can tell you. It was this evening when the miraculous thing didn't
   come — then I knew you weren't the man I'd imagined.

Helmer: Be more explicit; I don't follow you.

Nora: I've waited now so patiently eight long years — for, my Lord, I know miracles don't come every day. Then this crisis broke over me, and such a certainty filled me: *now* the miraculous event would occur. While Krogstad's
   letter was lying out there, I never for an instant dreamed that you could
   give in to his terms. I was so utterly sure you'd say to him: go on, tell your
   tale to the whole wide world. And when he'd done that —

Helmer: Yes, what then? When I'd delivered my own wife into shame and disgrace —

Nora: When he'd done that, I was so utterly sure that you'd step forward, take
   the blame on yourself and say: I am the guilty one.

Helmer: Nora — !

Nora: You're thinking I'd never accept such a sacrifice from you? No, of course
   not. But what good would my protests be against you? That was the miracle I was waiting for, in terror and hope. And to stave that off, I would have
   taken my life.

Helmer: I'd gladly work for you day and night, Nora—and take on pain and deprivation. But there's no one who gives up honor for love.

Nora: Millions of women have done just that.

Helmer: Oh, you think and talk like a silly child.

Nora: Perhaps. But you neither think nor talk like the man I could join myself to. When your big fright was over—and it wasn't from any threat against me, only for what might damage you—when all the danger was past, for you it was just as if nothing had happened. I was exactly the same, your little lark, your doll, that you'd have to handle with double care now that I'd turned out so brittle and frail. *(Gets up.)* Torvald—in that instant it dawned on me that for eight years I've been living here with a stranger, and that I've even conceived three children—oh, I can't stand the thought of it! I could tear myself to bits.

Helmer (heavily): I see. There's a gulf that's opened between us—that's clear. Oh, but Nora, can't we bridge it somehow?

Nora: The way I am now, I'm no wife for you.

Helmer: I have the strength to make myself over.

Nora: Maybe—if your doll gets taken away.

Helmer: But to part! To part from you! No, Nora no—I can't imagine it.

Nora (going out, right): All the more reason why it has to be. *(She reenters with her coat and a small overnight bag, which she puts on a chair by the table.)*

Helmer: Nora, Nora, not now! Wait till tomorrow.

Nora: I can't spend the night in a strange man's room.

Helmer: But couldn't we live here like brother and sister—

Nora: You know very well how long that would last. *(Throws her shawl about her.)* Good-bye, Torvald. I won't look in on the children. I know they're in better hands than mine. The way I am now, I'm no use to them.

Helmer: But someday, Nora—someday—?

Nora: How can I tell? I haven't the least idea what'll become of me.

Helmer: But you're my wife, now and wherever you go.

Nora: Listen, Torvald—I've heard that when a wife deserts her husband's house just as I'm doing, then the law frees him from all responsibility. In any case, I'm freeing you from being responsible. Don't feel yourself bound, any more than I will. There has to be absolute freedom for us both. Here, take your ring back. Give me mine.

Helmer: That too?

Nora: That too.

Helmer: There it is.

Nora: Good. Well, now it's all over. I'm putting the keys here. The maids know all about keeping up the house—better than I do. Tomorrow, after I've left town, Kristine will stop by to pack up everything that's mine from home. I'd like those things shipped up to me.

Helmer: Over! All over! Nora, won't you ever think about me?

Nora: I'm sure I'll think of you often, and about the children and the house here.

Helmer: May I write you?

Nora: No—never. You're not to do that.

Helmer: Oh, but let me send you—

Nora: Nothing. Nothing.

Helmer: Or help you if you need it.

Nora: No. I accept nothing from strangers.

Helmer: Nora — can I never be more than a stranger to you?

Nora (picking up her overnight bag): Ah, Torvald — it would take the greatest miracle of all —

Helmer: Tell me the greatest miracle!

Nora: You and I both would have to transform ourselves to the point that — Oh, Torvald, I've stopped believing in miracles.

Helmer: But I'll believe. Tell me! Transform ourselves to the point that — ?

Nora: That our living together could be a true marriage. *(She goes out down the hall.)*

Helmer (sinks down on a chair by the door, face buried in his hands): Nora! Nora! *(Looking about and rising.)* Empty. She's gone. *(A sudden hope leaps in him.)* The greatest miracle — ?

From below, the sound of a door slamming shut.

CONSIDERATIONS FOR CRITICAL THINKING AND WRITING

1. FIRST RESPONSE. What is the significance of the play's title?

2. Nora lies several times during the play. What kinds of lies are they? Do her lies indicate that she is not to be trusted, or are they a sign of something else about her personality?

3. What kind of wife does Helmer want Nora to be? He affectionately calls her names such as "lark" and "squirrel." What does this reveal about his attitude toward her?

4. Why is Nora "pale with terror" at the end of Act I? What is the significance of the description of the Christmas tree now "stripped of ornament, [with] burned-down candle stubs on its ragged branches" that opens Act II? What other symbols are used in the play?

5. What is Dr. Rank's purpose in the play?

6. How does the relationship between Krogstad and Mrs. Linde serve to emphasize certain qualities in the Helmers' marriage?

7. Is Krogstad's decision not to expose Nora's secret convincing? Does his shift from villainy to generosity seem adequately motivated?

8. Why does Nora reject Helmer's efforts to smooth things over between them and start again? Do you have any sympathy for Helmer?

9. Would you describe the ending as essentially happy or unhappy? Is the play more like a comedy or a tragedy?

10. Ibsen once wrote a different ending for the play to head off producers who might have been tempted to change the final scene to placate the public's sense of morality. In the second conclusion, Helmer forces Nora to look in on their sleeping children. This causes her to realize that she cannot leave her family even though it means sacrificing herself. Ibsen called this version of the ending a "barbaric outrage" and didn't use it. Which ending do you prefer? Why?

11. Ibsen believed that a "dramatist's business is not to answer questions, but only to ask them." What questions are raised in the play? Does Ibsen propose any specific answers?

12. What makes this play a work of realism? Are there any elements that seem not to be realistic?

CONNECTIONS TO OTHER SELECTIONS

1. What does Nora have in common with the protagonist in Gail Godwin's "A Sorrowful Woman" (p. 33)? What significant differences are there between them?

2. Explain how Torvald's attitude toward Nora is similar to the men's attitudes toward women in Susan Glaspell's *Trifles* (p. 1172). Write an essay exploring how the assumptions the men make about women in both plays contribute to the plays' conflicts.

3. Write an essay that compares and contrasts Nora's response to the social and legal expectations of her society with Antigone's in Sophocles' play (p. 1267). To what values does each character pledge her allegiance?

PERSPECTIVE

HENRIK IBSEN (1828–1906)

Notes for A Doll House   *1878*

There are two kinds of spiritual law, two kinds of conscience, one in man and another, altogether different, in woman. They do not understand each other; but in practical life the woman is judged by man's law, as though she were not a woman but a man.

The wife in the play ends by having no idea of what is right or wrong; natural feeling on the one hand and belief in authority on the other have altogether bewildered her.

A woman cannot be herself in the society of the present day, which is an exclusively masculine society, with laws framed by men and with a judicial system that judges feminine conduct from a masculine point of view.

She has committed forgery, and she is proud of it; for she did it out of love for her husband, to save his life. But this husband with his commonplace principles of honor is on the side of the law and looks at the question from the masculine point of view.

Spiritual conflicts. Oppressed and bewildered by the belief in authority, she loses faith in her moral right and ability to bring up her children. Bitterness. A mother in modern society, like certain insects who go away and die when she has done her duty in the propagation of the race. Love of life, of home, of husband and children and family. Now and then a womanly shaking off of her thoughts. Sudden return of anxiety and terror. She must bear it all alone. The catastrophe approaches, inexorably, inevitably. Despair, conflict, and destruction.

From From Ibsen's Workshop, translated by A. G. Chater

CONSIDERATIONS FOR CRITICAL THINKING AND WRITING

1. Given the ending of *A Doll House*, what do you think of Ibsen's early view in his notes that "the wife in the play ends by having no idea of what is right or wrong" (para. 2)? Would you describe Nora as "altogether bewildered" (para. 2)? Why or why not?

2. "A woman cannot be herself in the society of the present day, which is an exclusively masculine society" (para. 3). Why is this statement true of Nora? Explain why you agree or disagree that this observation is accurate today.

3. How does oppressive "authority" (para. 5) loom large for Nora? What kind of authority creates "spiritual conflicts" (para. 5) for her?

More perspectives appear in the next chapter, "Critical Case Study: Henrik Ibsen's *A Doll House,*" page 1627.

The Proposal: A Jest in One Act

Anton Chekhov, grandson of a serf and son of an unsuccessful grocer, was born in Taganrog, a small town in southern Russia. He studied medicine at Moscow University and began practicing in 1884. During his medical training, he wrote short stories to support himself and his family (one of the stories, "The Lady with the Pet Dog," appears on p. 185). Within a few years Chekhov had published two well-received collections of short stories. After this he practiced medicine only occasionally, continuing to treat his poor neighbors without charge. His compassion and generosity are also reflected in his ability to create sympathetic, convincing characters in his literary works.

Chekhov's first significant success in the theater was *The Seagull* (1896), which was produced by the Moscow Art Theater under the direction of Konstantin Stanislavsky, a champion of realistic methods of acting. *The Seagull* and Chekhov's three other major plays, *Uncle Vanya* (1899), *The Three Sisters* (1901), and *The Cherry Orchard* (1903), are studies of the changing texture of Russian life at the turn of the century. His characters come from a cross-section of society, ranging from valiant but ineffectual aristocrats to noble peasants. The future seems bleak for everyone because there is no energy or direction: civil government is merely officious, intellectuals are too self-absorbed, and the church has retreated to backward-looking tradition.

In contrast to Ibsen's plays, little appears to happen in Chekhov's major dramas. They lack the sense of inevitable direction intrinsic to the well-made play. Although Ibsen's characters are typically riddled with uncertainties, they take decisive actions or are forcefully acted upon. But in a Chekhov play changes, if any, are measured in small, seemingly inconsequential actions. He creates a slice of life onstage, in which characters frequently talk around issues or past each other so that direct confrontations — the makings of dramatic moments — are relatively rare. Therefore, we must listen carefully to the characters' small talk if we are to follow their deepest concerns. Chekhov uses this method intentionally to mirror the circumstances of most people's lives. He avoids heroics and extreme actions in favor of daily lives. Chekhov does incorporate some melodramatic elements in his plays, but they occur offstage and are subordinated to his interest in subtleties of character.

Before he wrote his major works of tragicomic realism, Chekhov also wrote brief farces, or "jests," as he called them. The following play, *The Proposal,* is a one-act comedy filled with the kind of humor associated with the incongruities of farce, in which character and actions are exaggerated. The play begins simply enough when a man comes to a father to ask for his daughter's hand in marriage, but complications quickly develop that lead to a series of comic misunderstandings.

ANTON CHEKHOV (1860–1904)

The Proposal: A Jest in One Act   *1888*

TRANSLATED BY ELISAVETA FEN

CHARACTERS IN THE PLAY

Choobukov, Stepan Stepanovich, a landowner
Natalyia Stepanovna (Natasha), his daughter, aged twenty-five
Lomov, Ivan Vassilievich, a landowner and neighbor of Choobukov, a healthy, well-
     nourished but hypochondriacal person

SCENE: *The action takes place on the estate of Choobukov*

> *The drawing-room in Choobukov's house. Choobukov and Lomov; the latter enters wearing evening dress and white gloves.*

Choobukov (going to meet him): My dearest friend, fancy seeing you! Ivan Vas-
     silievich! I'm so glad! *(Shakes hands.)* Well, this is a real surprise, dear old
     boy! . . . How are you?
Lomov: Thank you. And how are you, pray?
Choobukov: We're getting on reasonably well, my cherub — thanks to your
     prayers and all that. . . . Please do sit down. . . . You know it's too bad of
     you to forget your neighbors, old fellow. But, my dear friend, why all this
     formality? Tails, gloves, and all the rest of it! Are you going visiting, or
     what, dear boy?
Lomov: No, I've only come to see you, my dear Stepan Stepanovich.
Choobukov: Then why wear tails, dear boy? As though you were making a for-
     mal call on New Year's day!
Lomov: The fact is, you see. . . . *(Takes his arm.)* I've come to ask a favor of you,
     my dear Stepan Stepanovich — if I'm not causing too much trouble. I've
     taken the liberty of seeking your help more than once in the past, and
     you've always, so to speak. . . . But forgive me, I'm in such a state. . . . I'll
     take a drink of water, my dear Stepan Stepanovich. *(Drinks water.)*
Choobukov (aside): He's come to ask for money! I shan't give him any! *(To
     Lomov.)* What's the matter, my dear young fellow?
Lomov: You see, my dear Stepanych. . . . Forgive me, Stepan, my dear. . . . I
     mean I'm in such a state of nerves — as you can see. . . . In short, you're the

only man who can possibly help me, though, of course, I haven't done anything to deserve it, and . . . and I have no right to count on your assistance. . . .

Choobukov: Oh, don't spin it out, dear boy! Out with it! Well?

Lomov: Yes, yes. . . . I'll tell you straight away. . . . The fact is that I've come to ask for the hand of your daughter, Natalyia Stepanovna.

Choobukov (joyfully): Ivan Vassilievich! My dearest friend! Say it again — I didn't quite hear you!

Lomov: I have the honor to ask. . . .

Choobukov (interrupting him): My dearest chap! . . . I am so very glad, and so forth. . . . Yes, indeed — and all that sort of thing. *(Embraces and kisses him.)* I've wished it for a long time. It always has been my wish. *(Sheds a tear.)* I've always loved you as if you were my own son, my dearest fellow! May God grant you love and sweet concord, and all the rest of it. As for myself, I've always wished. . . . But why am I standing here like an idiot? I'm stunned with joy, simply stunned! Oh, with all my heart. . . . I'll go and call Natasha, and so on. . . .

Lomov (moved): My dear Stepan Stepanych, what do you think she'll say? May I count on her consenting?

Choobukov: She not consent to it? — and you such a good-looker, too! I bet she's up to her ears in love with you, and so forth. . . . I'll tell her straight away! *(Goes out.)*

Lomov (alone): I'm cold. . . . I'm trembling all over as if I were going in for an examination. The main thing is to make up your mind. If you think too long, keep talking and hesitating and waiting for the ideal woman or for real true love, you'll never get married. Brr! . . . I'm cold! Natalyia Stepanovna is an excellent housekeeper, educated, not bad-looking. . . . What more do I want? But I'm in such a state that I'm beginning to have noises in my head. . . . *(Drinks water.)* Yet I mustn't stay single. In the first place, I'm thirty-five already — a critical age, so to speak. Secondly, I must have an ordered, regular life. . . . I've got a heart disease, with continual palpitations. . . . I flare up so easily, and I'm always getting terribly agitated. . . . Even now my lips are trembling and my right eyelid's twitching. . . . But the worst thing is my sleep. No sooner do I get into bed and start dropping off to sleep than something stabs me in my left side. Stab! and it goes right through my shoulder to my head. . . . I jump up like a madman, walk about for a bit and lie down again. . . . But directly I start dozing off, there it goes again in my side — stab! And the same thing happens twenty times over. . . .

Enter Natalyia.

Natalyia: Oh, so it's you! And Papa said: go along, there's a customer come for the goods. How do you do, Ivan Vassilievich?

Lomov: How do you do, my dear Natalyia Stepanovna?

Natalyia: Excuse my wearing this apron and not being properly dressed. We're shelling peas for drying. Why haven't you been to see us for so long? Do sit down. . . .

They sit down.

Will you have some lunch?

Lomov: No, thank you, I've already had lunch.

Natalyia: Won't you smoke? Here are some matches. . . . It's a magnificent day, but yesterday it rained so hard that the men did nothing all day. How many ricks did you manage to get in? Would you believe it, I was so set on getting it done that I had the whole meadow cut, and now I almost feel sorry — I'm afraid the hay may rot. It might have been better to wait. But what's all this? I believe you're wearing tails! This is something new! Are you going to a ball or something? By the way, you've changed — you're better looking! . . . But really, why are you dressed up like this?

Lomov (in agitation): You see, dear Natalyia Stepanovna. . . . The fact is that I've decided to ask you to . . . listen to me. . . . Naturally, you'll be surprised, possibly even angry, but I. . . . *(Aside.)* How dreadfully cold it is!

Natalyia: What is it then? *(A pause.)* Well?

Lomov: I'll try to be brief. You are aware, of course, my dear Natalyia Stepanovna, that I've had the honor of knowing your family a long time — from my very childhood, in fact. My late aunt and her husband — from whom, as you know, I inherited the estate — always entertained a profound respect for your father and your late mother. The family of the Lomovs and the family of the Choobukovs have always been on the friendliest and, one might almost say, on intimate terms. Besides, as you are aware, my land is in close proximity to yours. Perhaps you will recollect that my Volovyi meadows lie alongside your birch wood.

Natalyia: Excuse me, but I must interrupt you there. You say "my" Volovyi meadows. . . . But are they really yours?

Lomov: Yes, mine. . . .

Natalyia: Well, what next! The Volovyi meadows are ours, not yours!

Lomov: No, they're mine, dear Natalyia Stepanovna.

Natalyia: That's news to me. How do they come to be yours?

Lomov: What do you mean, how? I'm speaking of the Volovyi meadows that lie like a wedge between your birth wood and the Burnt Swamp.

Natalyia: But yes, of course. . . . They're ours.

Lomov: No, you're mistaken, my dear Natalyia Stepanovna, they are mine.

Natalyia: Do come to your senses, Ivan Vassilievich! How long have they been yours?

Lomov: What do you mean by "how long"? As long as I can remember — they've always been ours.

Natalyia: Well, there you must excuse me for disagreeing.

Lomov: You can see it in the documents, my dear Natalyia Stepanovna. It's true that the Volovyi meadows were a matter of dispute at one time, but now everyone knows that they're mine. There's really no need to argue about it. If I may explain — my aunt's grandmother handed over those meadows to your great grandfather's peasants for their use, rent free, for an indefinite period, in return for their firing her bricks. Your great grandfather's peasants used the meadows rent free for forty years or so and got accustomed to looking upon them as their own . . . and then when the settlement was made after the emancipation. . . .

Natalyia: But it wasn't at all as you say! Both my grandfather and my great grandfather considered that their land reached to the Burnt Swamp — so the Volovyi meadows must have been ours. So why argue about it? I can't understand you. It's really rather annoying!

Lomov: I'll show you the documents, Natalyia Stepanovna!

Natalyia: No, you must be just joking, or trying to tease me. . . . What a surprise indeed! We've owned the land for something like three hundred years, and now suddenly someone declares that the land isn't ours! Forgive me, Ivan Vassilievich, but I just can't believe my own ears. . . . I set no value on those meadows. They're not more than fifteen acres, and they're only worth about three hundred rubles, but it's the injustice of it that disgusts me! You can say what you like, but I can't tolerate injustice.

Lomov: Do hear me out, I implore you! Your father's grandfather's peasants, as I've already had the honor of telling you, fired bricks for my aunt's grandmother. My aunt's grandmother, wishing to do something for them. . . .

Natalyia: Grandfather, grandmother, aunt. . . . I don't understand anything about it! The meadows are ours, that's all!

Lomov: They're mine!

Natalyia: They're ours! You can go on trying to prove it for two days, you can put on fifteen dress suits if you like, but they're still ours, ours, ours! . . . I don't want what's yours, but I have no desire to lose what's mine. . . . You can please yourself!

Lomov: I don't want the meadows, Natalyia Stepanovna, but it's a matter of principle. If you wish, I'll give them to you as a present.

Natalyia: But I'm the one who could make a present of them to you — because they're mine! . . . All this is very strange, Ivan Vassilievich, to say the least of it! Till now we've always regarded you as a good neighbor, a friend of ours. Last year we lent you our threshing machine, and because of that we had to finish threshing our own corn in November. And now you're treating us as if we were gypsies! You're making me a present of my own land! Forgive me, but this isn't neighborly conduct! To my mind it's almost impertinent, if you want to know. . . .

Lomov: You mean to say then that I'm a usurper? I've never stolen other people's land, Madam, and I won't allow anyone to accuse me of it. . . . *(Goes rapidly to the decanter and drinks water.)* The Volovyi meadows are mine!

Natalyia: That's not true, they're ours!

Lomov: They're mine!

Natalyia: It isn't true! I'll prove it to you! I'll send my men to mow those meadows today.

Lomov: What's that?

Natalyia: My men will be working there today!

Lomov: I'll kick them out!

Natalyia: You daren't do that!

Lomov (clutches at his heart): The Volovyi meadows are mine! Don't you understand that? Mine!

Natalyia: Don't shout, please! You can shout and choke with rage when you're at home, but please don't overstep the mark here!

Lomov: If it weren't for these dreadful agonizing palpitations, Madam — if it weren't for the throbbing in my temples, I should speak to you very differently! *(Shouts.)* The Volovyi meadows are mine!

Natalyia: Ours!

Lomov: Mine!

Natalyia: Ours!
Lomov: Mine!

Enter Choobukov.

Choobukov: What's all this? What are you shouting about?
Natalyia: Papa, please explain to this gentleman: to whom do the Volovyi meadows belong—to him or to us?
Choobukov (to Lomov): The meadows are ours, dear chap.
Lomov: But forgive me, Stepan Stepanych, how do they come to be yours? At least you might be reasonable! My aunt's grandmother gave over the meadows to your grandfather's peasants for temporary use without payment. The peasants had the use of the land for forty years and got accustomed to regarding it as their own. But when the settlement was made. . . .
Choobukov: Pardon me, my dear friend. . . . You forget that it was just because there was a dispute and so on about these meadows that the peasants didn't pay rent to your grandmother, and all the rest of it. . . . And now every dog knows that they're ours—yes, really! You can't have seen the plans!
Lomov: But I'll prove to you that they're mine!
Choobukov: You won't prove it, my dear man.
Lomov: Yes, I will!
Choobukov: But why shout, my dear boy? You won't prove anything by shouting! I don't want what is yours, but I've no intention of letting go of what's mine. Why should I? If it comes to that, my dear friend—if you're thinking of starting a dispute about the meadows and all the rest of it, I'd sooner make a present of them to the peasants than to you. So that's that!
Lomov: I don't understand this! What right have you to give away someone else's property?
Choobukov: Permit me to decide whether I have the right or not! And really, young man, I'm not used to being spoken to in that tone, and so forth. . . . I'm twice your age, young man, and I beg you to speak to me without getting excited, and all that. . . .
Lomov: No, you're simply taking me for a fool and laughing at me! You call my land yours, and then you expect me to stay cool and talk to you in the ordinary way. Good neighbors don't behave in this way, Stepan Stepanych! You're not a neighbor, you're a usurper!
Choobukov: What's that? What did you say?
Natalyia: Papa, send the men to mow the meadows at once!
Choobukov (to Lomov): What was it you said, sir?
Natalyia: The Volovyi meadows are ours, and I won't give them up! I won't, I won't!
Lomov: We shall see about that! I'll prove to you in court that they're mine.
Choobukov: In court? You take it to court, sir, and all the rest of it! You do it! I know you—you've really just been waiting for a chance to go to law, and all that. It comes natural to you—this petty niggling. Your family always had a weakness for litigation. All of them!
Lomov: Please don't insult my family! The Lomovs have all been honest men, and not one of them has ever been on trial for embezzling money like your uncle!

Choobukov: Every member of the Lomov family has been mad!

Natalyia: Every one of them — every one!

Choobukov: Your grandfather was a dipsomaniac, and your youngest aunt, Nastasyia Mihailovna — yes, it's a fact — ran away with an architect, and all the rest of it. . . .

Lomov: And your mother was deformed! *(Clutches at his heart.)* This shooting pain in my side! . . . The blood's gone to my head. . . . Holy Fathers! Water!

Choobukov: Your father was a gambler and a glutton!

Natalyia: Your aunt was a scandal-monger — and a rare one at that!

Lomov: My left leg's paralyzed. . . . And you're an intriguer. . . . Oh, my heart! . . . And it's an open secret that before the elections you. . . . There are flashes in front of my eyes. . . . Where's my hat? . . .

Natalyia: It's mean! It's dishonest! It's perfectly vile!

Choobukov: And you're just a malicious, double-faced, mean fellow! Yes, you are!

Lomov: Here it is, my hat. . . . My heart. . . . Which way do I go? Where's the door? Oh! I believe I'm dying. . . . I've lost the use of my leg. . . . *(Walks to the door.)*

Choobukov (calling after him): I forbid you to set foot in my house again!

Natalyia: Take it to court! We shall see!

> *Lomov goes out staggering.*

Choobukov: The devil take him! *(Walks about in agitation.)*

Natalyia: Have you ever seen such a cad? Trust good neighbors after that!

Choobukov: The ridiculous scarecrow! The scoundrel!

Natalyia: The monster! Grabs other people's land, then dares to abuse them into the bargain!

Choobukov: And this ridiculous freak, this eyesore — yes, he has the impertinence to come here and make a proposal and all the rest of it! Would you believe it? A proposal!

Natalyia: What proposal?

Choobukov: Yes, just fancy! He came to propose to you.

Natalyia: To propose? To me? But why didn't you tell me that before?

Choobukov: That's why he got himself up in his tail-coat. The sausage! The shrimp!

Natalyia: To me? A proposal? Oh! *(Drops into a chair and moans.)* Bring him back! Bring him back! Oh, bring him back!

Choobukov: Bring whom back?

Natalyia: Be quick, be quick! I feel faint! Bring him back! *(Shrieks hysterically.)*

Choobukov: What is it? What do you want? *(Clutches at his head.)* What misery! I'll shoot myself! I'll hang myself! They've worn me out!

Natalyia: I'm dying! Bring him back!

Choobukov: Phew! Directly. Don't howl. *(Runs out.)*

Natalyia (alone, moans): What have we done! Bring him back! Bring him back!

Choobukov (runs in): He's coming directly, and all the rest of it. Damnation take him! Ugh! You can talk to him yourself; I don't want to, and that's that!

Natalyia (moans): Bring him back!

Choobukov (shouts): He's coming, I tell you! What a job it is, O Lord, to be a grown-up daughter's father.° I'll cut my throat! Yes, indeed, I'll cut my throat! We've abused the man, we've insulted him, we've kicked him out, and it was all your doing—your doing!

Natalyia: No, it was yours!

Choobukov: So now it's my fault! What next!

Enter Lomov.

Lomov (exhausted): These dreadful palpitations.... My leg feels numb...a shooting pain in my side....

Natalyia: Forgive us, we were rather hasty, Ivan Vassilievich....I remember now: the Volovyi meadows really are yours.

Lomov: My heart's going at a terrific rate.... The meadows are mine.... Both my eyelids are twitching....

Natalyia: Yes, they're yours, yours.... Sit down....

They sit down.

We were wrong.

Lomov: To me it's a matter of principle.... I don't value the land, but I value the principle....

Natalyia: That's it, the principle.... Let's talk about something else.

Lomov: Especially as I have proof. My aunt's grandmother gave over to your father's grandfather's peasants....

Natalyia: Enough, enough about that.... *(Aside.)* I don't know how to begin.... *(To him.)* Will you soon be going shooting?

Lomov: I expect to go grouse shooting after the harvest, dear Natalyia Stepanovna.... Oh, did you hear? Just fancy—what bad luck I've had! My Tryer—you know him—he's gone lame.

Natalyia: What a pity! What was the cause of it?

Lomov: I don't know.... He may have dislocated his paw, or he may have been bitten by other dogs.... *(Sighs.)* My best dog, to say nothing of the money! You know, I paid Mironov a hundred and twenty-five rubles for him.

Natalyia: You paid too much, Ivan Vassilievich.

Lomov: Well, I think it was very cheap. He's a marvelous dog!

Natalyia: Papa paid eighty-five rubles for his Flyer, and Flyer is better than your Tryer by far.

Lomov: Flyer better than Tryer? Come, come! *(Laughs.)* Flyer better than Tryer!

Natalyia: Of course, he's better! It's true that Flyer's young—he's hardly a full-grown dog yet—but for points and cleverness even Volchanyetsky hasn't got a better one.

Lomov: Excuse me, Natalyia Stepanovna, but you forget that he's got a pug-jaw, and a dog with pug-jaw can never grip properly.

Natalyia: A pug-jaw? That's the first I've heard of it.

Lomov: I assure you, his lower jaw is shorter than the upper one.

Natalyia: Why, did you measure it?

A quotation from *The Misfortune of Being Clever,* by Griboyedov. It had become so much a part of ordinary speech that quotation marks were omitted by Chekhov.

Lomov: Yes. He's all right for coursing, of course, but when it comes to gripping, he's hardly good enough.

Natalyia: In the first place our Flyer is a pedigree dog — he's the son of Harness and Chisel — whereas your Tryer's coat has got such a mixture of colors that you'd never guess what kind he is. Then he's as old and ugly as an old hack. . . .

Lomov: He's old, but I wouldn't take five of your Flyers for him. . . . I wouldn't think of it! Tryer is a real dog, but Flyer . . . it's absurd to go on arguing. . . . Every sportsman has any number of dogs like your Flyer. Twenty-five rubles would be a lot to pay for him.

Natalyia: There's some demon of contradiction in you today, Ivan Vassilievich. First you pretend that the meadows are yours, and now you're saying that Tryer is better than Flyer. I don't like it when people say what they don't really believe. After all, you know perfectly well that Flyer is a hundred times better than your . . . well, your stupid Tryer. So why say the opposite?

Lomov: I can see, Natalyia Stepanovna, that you think I'm either blind or a fool. Won't you understand that your Flyer has a pug-jaw?

Natalyia: That isn't true.

Lomov: He has a pug-jaw.

Natalyia (shouts): It's not true! . . .

Lomov: What are you shouting for, Madam?

Natalyia: Why are you talking nonsense? This is quite revolting! It's time your Tryer was shot, and you're comparing him to Flyer!

Lomov: Excuse me, I can't continue this argument. I have palpitations.

Natalyia: I've noticed that the people who understand least about shooting are the ones who argue most about it.

Lomov: Madam, please be silent. . . . My heart's bursting. . . . *(Shouts.)* Be quiet!

Natalyia: I won't be quiet till you admit that Flyer is a hundred times better than your Tryer.

Lomov: He's a hundred times worse! It's time he was dead, your Flyer! Oh, my head . . . my eyes . . . my shoulder! . . .

Natalyia: As for your idiot Tryer — I don't need to wish him dead: he's half-dead already!

Lomov (weeping): Be quiet! My heart's going to burst.

Natalyia: I won't be quiet!

Enter Choobukov.

Choobukov: Now what is it?

Natalyia: Papa, tell us frankly, on your honor: which dog's the better — our Flyer or his Tryer?

Lomov: Stepan Stepanych, I implore you, tell us just one thing: has your Flyer got a pug-jaw, or hasn't he? Yes or no?

Choobukov: Well, what if he has? As if it mattered! Anyway, there's no better dog in the whole district, and all that.

Lomov: But my Tryer is better, isn't he? On your honor!

Choobukov: Don't get excited, my dear boy. . . . Let me explain. . . . Your Tryer, of course, has his good points. . . . He's a good breed, he's got strong legs, he's well built and all the rest of it. But if you really want to know, my dear friend, the dog has two serious faults: he's old and he's snub-nosed.

Lomov: Excuse me, I've got palpitations. . . . Let us look at the facts. . . . Perhaps you'll remember that when we hunted in the Maruskin fields my Tryer kept up with the Count's Spotter, while your Flyer was a good half-mile behind.

Choobukov: He dropped behind because the Count's huntsman hit him with his whip.

Lomov: He deserved it. All the other dogs were chasing the fox, but Flyer started worrying the sheep.

Choobukov: That's not true! . . . My dear friend, I lose my temper easily, so I do beg you, let's drop this argument. The man hit him because people are always jealous of other people's dogs. . . . Yes, everyone hates the other man's dog! And you, sir, are not innocent of that either! Yes! For instance, as soon as you notice that someone's dog is better than your Tryer, you immediately start something or other . . . and all the rest of it. . . . You see, I remember everything!

Lomov: So do I!

Choobukov (mimics him): So do I! And what is it you remember?

Lomov: Palpitations. . . . My leg's paralyzed. . . . I can't. . . .

Natalyia (mimics him): Palpitations. . . . What sort of a sportsman are you? You ought to be lying on the stove in the kitchen squashing blackbeetles instead of hunting foxes! Palpitations indeed!

Choobukov: Yes, honestly, hunting's not your line at all! With your palpitations and all that, you'd be better at home than sitting on horseback being jolted about. It wouldn't matter if you really hunted, but you only go out so that you can argue, or get in the way of other people's dogs, and all the rest of it. . . . I get angry easily, so let's stop this conversation. You're just not a sportsman, and that's all there is to it.

Lomov: What about you — are you a sportsman? You only go out hunting to make up to the Count, and intrigue against other people. . . . Oh, my heart! You're an intriguer!

Choobukov: What! I — an intriguer? *(Shouts.)* Be silent!

Lomov: Intriguer!

Choobukov: Milksop! Puppy!

Lomov: You old rat! Hypocrite!

Choobukov: Hold your tongue, or I'll shoot you with a dirty gun like a partridge! Windbag!

Lomov: Everyone knows — oh, my heart! — that your wife used to beat you! . . . My leg . . . my head . . . flashes in front of my eyes . . . I'm going to fall down. . . . I'm falling. . . .

Choobukov: And your housekeeper has got you under her thumb!

Lomov: Oh! oh! oh! . . . My heart's burst! My shoulder's gone. . . . Where's my shoulder? . . . I'm dying! *(Drops into an armchair.)* A doctor! *(Faints.)*

Choobukov: Milksop! Puppy! Windbag! I'm feeling faint. *(Drinks water.)* Faint!

Natalyia: A sportsman indeed! You don't even know how to sit on a horse! *(To her father.)* Papa! What's the matter with him? Papa! Look, Papa! *(Shrieks.)* Ivan Vassilievich! He's dead.

Choobukov: I feel faint! . . . I'm suffocating! Give me air!

Natalyia: He's dead! *(Shakes Lomov by the sleeve.)* Ivan Vassilych! Ivan Vassilych! What have we done! He's dead! *(Drops into an armchair.)* Doctor, doctor! *(Sobs and laughs hysterically.)*

Choobukov: What now? What's the matter? What do you want?

Natalyia (moans): He's dead! . . . Dead!

Choobukov: Who's dead? *(Glancing at Lomov.)* He really is dead! My God! Water! Doctor! *(Holds a glass of water to Lomov's lips.)* Take a drink! . . . No, he won't drink. . . . So he's dead and all that. . . . What an unlucky man I am! Why don't I put a bullet through my brain? Why didn't I cut my throat long ago? What am I waiting for? Give me a knife! Give me a gun!

Lomov makes a slight movement.

I believe he's coming round. . . . Do have a drink of water! That's right. . . .

Lomov: Flashes before my eyes . . . a sort of mist. . . . Where am I?

Choobukov: You'd better get married as soon as possible and — go to the devil. . . . She consents. *(Joins their hands.)* She consents, and all the rest of it. I give you my blessing, and so forth. Only leave me alone!

Lomov: Eh? What? *(Getting up.)* Who?

Choobukov: She consents! Well? Kiss each other and . . . and the devil take you!

Natalyia (moans): He's alive. . . . Yes, yes, I consent. . . .

Choobukov: Come now, kiss each other!

Lomov: Eh? Who? *(Kisses Natalyia.)* I am so pleased! . . . Excuse me, what's it all about? Ah! yes, I understand. . . . My heart . . . flashes . . . I'm so happy, Natalyia Stepanovna. . . . *(Kisses her hand.)* My leg's numb. . . .

Natalyia: I . . . I'm happy too. . . .

Choobukov: What a load off my back! . . . Ugh!

Natalyia: But . . . all the same, you must admit it now: Tryer is not as good a dog as Flyer.

Lomov: He's better!

Natalyia: He's worse!

Choobukov: There! Family happiness has begun! Bring the champagne!

Lomov: He's better!

Natalyia: He's worse, worse, worse!

Choobukov (trying to shout them down): Champagne! Bring the champagne!

Curtain

CONSIDERATIONS FOR CRITICAL THINKING AND WRITING

1. FIRST RESPONSE. Is it possible to determine who actually owns the Volovyi meadows? Why is this an important issue?

2. In the opening scene, what does Choobukov assume Lomov wants from him at the very start of their meeting? What does this reveal about Choobukov?

3. What does the state of Lomov's health suggest about his character?

4. When Natalyia's father tells her there is someone to see her, he says, "There's a customer come for the goods." Why is this offhand comment a particularly significant line in this play?

5. How does the manner in which Natalyia and Lomov argue over the Volovyi meadows reveal their sensibilities?

6. How does the argument about the dogs repeat the pattern established in the argument about the Volovyi meadows?

7. How do you interpret Choobukov's description of the union between Natalyia and Lomov as the beginning of "family happiness"?

8. Comment on the appropriateness of the play's title.

CONNECTIONS TO OTHER SELECTIONS

1. How does marriage in Ibsen's *A Doll House* (p. 1564) and *The Proposal* reflect larger social issues in each play?

2. Discuss the purpose of the humor in the scenes from *Seinfeld* (p. 1199) and *The Proposal*. Does the humor in each work suggest a hopeful or pessimistic assessment of the characters' relationships?

3. Read the section on Marxist criticism (p. 2033) in Chapter 37, "Critical Strategies for Reading." Write an essay discussing how you think a Marxist critic would approach *The Proposal*.

PERSPECTIVE

ANTON CHEKHOV (1860–1904)

On What Artists Do Best   *1888*

In conversation with my literary colleagues I always insist that it is not the artist's business to solve problems that require a specialist's knowledge. It is a bad thing if a writer tackles a subject he does not understand. We have specialists for dealing with special questions: it is their business to judge of the commune, of the future, of capitalism, of the evils of drunkenness, of boots, of the diseases of women. An artist must judge only of what he understands, his field is just as limited as that of any other specialist — I repeat this and insist on it always. That in his sphere there are no questions, but only answers, can be maintained only by those who have never written and have had no experience of thinking in images. An artist observes, selects, guesses, combines — and this in itself presupposes a problem: unless he had set himself a problem from the very first there would be nothing to conjecture and nothing to select. To put it briefly, I will end by using the language of psychiatry: if one denies that creative work involves problems and purposes, one must admit that an artist creates without premeditation or intention, in a state of abberation; therefore, if an author boasted to me of having written a novel without a preconceived design, under a sudden inspiration, I should call him mad.

You are right in demanding that an artist should take an intelligent attitude to his work, but you confuse two things: *solving a problem and stating a problem correctly*. It is only the second that is obligatory for the artist. . . . It is the business of the judge to put the right questions, but the answers must be given by the jury according to their own lights.

From a letter to A. S. Souvorin, October 27, 1888,
in *Letters of Anton Tchekhov to His Family and Friends*,
translated by Constance Garnett

CONSIDERATIONS FOR CRITICAL THINKING AND WRITING

1. Explain whether you agree with Chekhov that an artist's "field is just as limited as that of any other specialist" (para. 1). Write an essay on Chekhov's assertion that "it is not the artist's business to solve problems" (para. 1).

2. How does the humor in *The Proposal* reflect Chekhov's insistence that his job is to "put the right questions" (para. 2) rather than to answer them?

33

Critical Case Study: Henrik Ibsen's *A Doll House*

This chapter provides several critical approaches to Henrik Ibsen's *A Doll House,* which appears in Chapter 32, page 1564. There have been numerous critical approaches to this play because it raises so many issues relating to matters such as relationships between men and women, history, and biography, as well as imagery, symbolism, and irony. The following critical excerpts offer a small and partial sample of the possible biographical, historical, mythological, psychological, sociological, and other perspectives that have attempted to shed light on the play (see Chapter 37, "Critical Strategies for Reading," for a discussion of a variety of critical methods). They should help you to enjoy the play more by raising questions, providing insights, and inviting you to delve further into the text.

The following letter offers a revealing vignette of the historical contexts for *A Doll House.* Professor Richard Panofsky of the University of Massachusetts–Dartmouth has provided the letter and this background information: "The translated letter was written in 1844 by Marcus (1807–1865) to his wife Ulrike (1816–1888), after six children had been born. This upper-middle-class Jewish family lived in Hamburg, Germany, where Marcus was a doctor. As the letter implies, Ulrike had left home and children: the letter establishes conditions for her to return. A woman in upper-class society of the time had few choices in an unhappy marriage. Divorce or separation meant ostracism; as Marcus writes, 'your husband, children, and the entire city threaten indifference or even contempt.' And she could not take a job, as she would have no profession to step into. In any case, Ulrike did return home. Between 1846 and 1857 the marriage produced eight more children. Beyond what the letter shows, we do not know the reasons for the separation or what the later marriage relationship was like."

PERSPECTIVES

A Nineteenth-Century Husband's Letter to His Wife   1844

Dear Wife,   June 23, 1844

You have sinned greatly — and maybe I too; but this much is certain: Adam sinned after Eve had already sinned. So it is with us; you, alone, carry the guilt of all the misfortune which, however, I helped to enlarge later by my behavior. Listen now, since I still believe certain things to be necessary in order that we may have a peaceful life. If we want not only to be content for a day but forever, you will have to follow my wishes. So examine yourself and determine if you are strong enough to conquer your false ambitions and your stubbornness to submit to all the conditions, the fulfillment of which I cannot ignore. Every sensible person will tell you that all I ask of you is what is easily understood. If you insist on remaining stubborn, then do not return to my house, for you will never be happy with me; your husband, children, and the entire city threaten indifference or even contempt.

But if you decide to act *sensibly* and *correctly,* that is *justly* and *kindly,* then be certain that many in the world will envy you.

I am including here the paper which I read to you in front of the rabbi; ask anyone in your residence if the wishes expressed by me are not quite reasonable, and are of a kind to which every wife can agree for the welfare of domestic happiness. In any case, act in a way you think best.

When you decide to return, write to tell me on which day and hour you depart from Berlin and give me your itinerary whether by way of Kuestrin and Pinne or by way of Wollstein. I will then meet you at Wollstein or Pinne. I expect you will bring Solomon with you.

Don't travel unprepared. If you need money, ask your father.

May God enlighten your heart and mind

I remain your so far unhappy,   [Marcus]

Greetings to my parents, brothers, and sisters; also your brother. Show them what you wish, this letter, the enclosure, whatever you want. The children are fortunately healthy.

If you want to return with joy and peace, write me by return mail. In that case, I would rather send you a carriage. Maybe Madam Fraenkel will come along. . . .

[Enclosure]

My wife promises — for which every wife is obligated to her husband — to follow my wishes in everything and to strictly obey my orders. It is already self-evident that our marital relations have often been disturbed by the fact that my wife does not follow my wishes but believes herself to be entitled to act on her own, even if this is totally against my orders. In order not to have to remind my wife every second what my wishes are regarding homemaking and public conduct—wishes which I have often expressed—I want to make here a few rules which shall serve as a code of conduct. A home is best run if the work for each hour is planned ahead of time, if possible.

Servants get up no later than 5:00 A.M. in summer and 6:00 A.M. in winter, the children an hour later. The cook prepares breakfast. The nursemaid puts out clothes for every child, prepares water and sponge, cleans the combs, etc. The cook should stay in the kitchen unless there is time to clean the rooms. At least once a week the rooms should be cleaned whenever possible, but not all on the same day.

Every Wednesday, the people in the house should do a laundry. Every last Wednesday in the month, there shall be a large laundry with an outside washer-woman. At least every Monday, the seamstress shall come into the house to fix what is necessary.

Every Thursday or Friday, bread is baked for the week; I think it is best to buy grain and have it ground, but to knead it at home.

Every Friday special bread (Barches) should be bought for the evening meal.

The kitchen list will be prepared and discussed every Thursday evening, jointly, by me and my wife; but my wish is to be decisive.

After this, provisions are to be bought every Friday at the market. For this purpose, my wife, herself, will go to the market on Fridays, accompanied by a servant; she can substitute a special woman who does errands (*Faktorfrau*) if she wishes, but not a servant.

All expenditures have to be written down daily and punctually.

The children receive a bath every Thursday evening. The children's clothes must be kept in a specially appointed chest, with a separate compartment for each child with the child's name upon it. The boys' suits and girls' dresses are to be kept separately. To keep used laundry, there must be a hamper easily accessible. Equally important is the food storage box in which provisions are kept in order, locked and safe from vermin.

The kitchen should be kept in order. Once a week all woodwork and copper must be scoured. The lights and lamps have to be cleaned daily. Toward servants, one has to be strict and just. Therefore, one should not call them names which aren't suitable for a decent wife. One should give them enough nourishing food. Disobedience and obstinacy are to be referred to me.

My wife will never make visits in my absence. However, she should visit the synagogue every Saturday—at least once a month; also she should go for a walk with the children at least once a week.

CONSIDERATIONS FOR CRITICAL THINKING AND WRITING

1. Describe the tone of Marcus's letter to his wife. To what extent does he accept responsibility for their separation? What significant similarities and differences do you find between Marcus and Torvald Helmer?

2. Read the discussion on historical criticism in Chapter 37, "Critical Strategies for Reading" (p. 2031). How do you think a new historicist would use this letter to shed light on *A Doll House*?

3. Write a response to the letter from what you imagine the wife's point of view to be.

4. No information is available about this couple's marriage after Ulrike returned home. In an essay, speculate on what you think their relationship was like later in their marriage.

BARRY WITHAM (B. 1939) AND
JOHN LUTTERBIE (B. 1948)

Witham and Lutterbie describe how they use a Marxist approach to teach *A Doll House* in their drama class, in which they teach plays from a variety of critical perspectives.

A Marxist Approach to A Doll House   *1985*

A principal tenet of Marxist criticism is that human consciousness is a product of social conditions and that human relationships are often subverted by and through economic considerations. Mrs. Linde has sacrificed a genuine love to provide for her brothers, and Krogstad has committed a crime to support his children. Anne-Marie, the maid, has also been the victim of her economic background. Because she's "a girl who's poor and gotten in trouble," her relationship with her child has been interrupted and virtually destroyed. In each instance the need for money is linked with the ability to exist. But while the characters accept the social realities of their misfortunes, they do not appear to question how their human attitudes have been thoroughly shaped by socioeconomic considerations.

Once students begin to perceive how consciousness is affected by economics, a Marxist reading of Ibsen's play can illuminate a number of areas. Krogstad, for example, becomes less of a traditional villain when we realize that he is fighting for his job at the bank "as if it were life itself." And his realization of the senselessness of their lives is poignantly revealed when he reflects on Mrs. Linde's past, "all this simply for money." Even Dr. Rank speaks about his failing health and imminent death in entirely financial terms. "These past few days I've been auditing my internal accounts. Bankrupt! Within a month I'll probably be laid out and rotting in the churchyard."

All these characters, however, serve as foils for the central struggle between Nora and Torvald and highlight the pilgrimage that Nora makes in the play. At the outset two things are clear: (1) Nora is enslaved by Torvald in economic terms, and (2) she equates personal freedom with the acquisition of wealth. The play begins joyfully not only because it is the holiday season but also because Torvald's promotion to bank manager will ensure "a safe, secure job with a comfortable salary." Nora is happy because she sees the future in wholly economic terms. "Won't it be lovely to have stacks of money and not a care in the world?"

What she learns, however, is that financial enslavement is symptomatic of other forms of enslavement — master-slave, male-female, sexual objectification, all of which characterize her relationship with Torvald — and that money is no guarantee of happiness. At the end of the play she renounces not only her marital vows but also her financial dependence because she has discovered that personal and human freedom are not measured in economic terms.

This discovery also prompts her to reexamine the society of which she is a part and leads us into a consideration of the ideology in the play. In what sense has Nora committed a criminal offense in forging her father's name? Is it indeed just that she should be punished for an altruistic act, one that cost her dearly both in terms of self-denial and the destruction of her family? Ibsen's defense of Nora is clear, of course, and his implicit indictment of a society that encourages this kind of injustice stimulates a discussion of the assumptions that created the law.

One of the striking things about *A Doll House* is how Anne-Marie accepts her alienation from her child as if it were natural, given the circumstances of class and money. It does not occur to her that laws were framed by other people and thus are capable of imperfection and susceptible to change. Nora broke a law that not only tries to stop thievery (the appropriation of capital) by outlawing forgery but also discriminates against anyone deemed a bad risk. Question leads to question as the class investigates why women were bad risks and why they had difficulty finding employment. It becomes obvious that the function of women in this society was not "natural" but artificial, a role created by their relationship to the family and by their subservience to men. In the marketplace they were a labor force expecting subsistence wages and providing an income to supplement that earned by their husbands or fathers.

An even clearer picture of Nora's society emerges when the Marxist critic examines those features or elements that are not in the play. These "absences" become valuable clues in understanding the ideology in the text. In the words of Fredric Jameson, absences are

> terms or nodal points implicit in the ideological system which have, however, remained unrealized in surface of the text, which have failed to become manifest in the logic of the narrative, and which we can therefore read as what the text represses.[1]

The notion of absences is particularly intriguing for students, who learn quickly to apply it to such popular media as films and television (what can we learn about the experience of urban black Americans from sitcoms like *Julia* and *The Jeffersons*?). Absent from *A Doll House* is Nora's mother, an omission that ties her more firmly to a male-dominated world and the bank owners who promoted Torvald. These absences shape our view because they form a layer of reality that is repressed in the play. And an examination of this "repressed" material leads us to our final topic of discussion: What is the relation between this play and the society in which it was created and produced?

Most Marxist critics believe that there are only three possible answers: the play supports the status quo, argues for reforms in an essentially sound system, or advocates a radical restructuring. Though these options are seemingly reductive, discussion reveals the complexities of reaching any unanimous agreement, and students frequently disagree about Ibsen's intentions regarding reform or revolution. Nora's leaving is obviously a call for change, but many students are not sure whether this leave-taking is a way forward or a

---

[1] Fredric Jameson, *The Political Unconscious: Narrative as a Socially Symbolic Act* (Ithaca: Cornell UP, 1981), p. 48.

cul-de-sac for a system that is thoroughly controlled by the prevailing power structure. . . .

Viewing the play through the lens of Marxist atheists does make one thing clear. Nora's departure had ramifications for her society that went beyond the marriage bed. By studying the play within the context of its socioeconomic structure, we can see how the ideology in the text affects the characters and how they perpetuate the ideology. The conclusion of *A Doll House* was a challenge to the economic superstructures that had controlled and excluded the Noras of the world by manipulating their economic status and, by extension, their conscious estimation of themselves and their place in society.

From "A Marxist Approach to *A Doll House*"
in *Approaches to Teaching Ibsen's* A Doll House

CONSIDERATIONS FOR CRITICAL THINKING AND WRITING

1. To what extent do you agree or disagree with the Marxist "tenet" (para. 1) that "consciousness is affected by economics" (para. 2)?

2. Do you think that Nora's "leave-taking is a way forward or a cul-de-sac for a system that is thoroughly controlled by the prevailing power structure"? Explain your response.

3. Consider whether "A Nineteenth-Century Husband's Letter to His Wife" (p. 1628) supports or challenges Witham and Lutterbie's Marxist reading of *A Doll House.*

CAROL STRONGIN TUFTS (B. 1947)

A Psychoanalytic Reading of Nora   *1986*

I am not a member of the Women's Rights League. Whatever I have written has been without any conscious thought of making propaganda. I have been more the poet and less the social philosopher than people generally seem inclined to believe. . . . To me it has seemed a problem of mankind in general. And if you read my books carefully you will understand this. . . . My task has been the *description of humanity.* To be sure, whenever such a description is felt to be reasonably true, the reader will read his own feelings and sentiments into the work of the poet. These are then attributed to the poet; but incorrectly so. Every reader remolds the work beautifully and neatly, each according to his own personality. Not only those who write but also those who read are poets. They are collaborators.[1]

To look again at Ibsen's famous and often-quoted words — his assertion that *A Doll House* was not intended as propaganda to promote the cause of women's rights — is to realize the sarcasm aimed by the playwright at those nineteenth-century "collaborators" who insisted on viewing his play as a treatise and Nora, his heroine, as the romantic standard-bearer for the feminist cause. Yet there is also a certain irony implicit in such a realization, for direc-

---

[1] Speech delivered at the Banquet of the Norwegian League for Women's Rights, Christiana, 26 May 1898, in *Ibsen: Letters and Speeches,* ed. Evert Sprinchorn (New York: Hill and Wang, 1964), p. 337.

tors, actors, audiences, and critics turning to this play a little over one hundred years after its first performance bring with them the historical, cultural, and psychological experience which itself places them in the role of Ibsen's collaborators. Because it is a theatrical inevitability that each dramatic work which survives its time and place of first performance does so to be recast in productions mounted in succeeding times and different places, *A Doll House* can never so much be simply reproduced as it must always be re-envisioned. And if the spectacle of a woman walking out on her husband and children in order to fulfill her "duties to (her)self" is no longer the shock for us today that it was for audiences at the end of the nineteenth century, a production of *A Doll House* which resonates with as much immediacy and power for us as it did for its first audiences may do so through the discovery within Ibsen's text of something of our own time and place. For in *A Doll House*, as Rolf Fjelde has written, "(i)t is the entire house . . . which is on trial, the total complex of relationships, including husband, wife, children, servants, upstairs and downstairs, that is tested by the visitors that come and go, embodying aspects of the inescapable reality outside."[2] And a production which approaches that reality through the experience of Western culture in the last quarter of the twentieth century may not only discover how uneasy was Ibsen's relationship to certain aspects of the forces of Romanticism at work in his own society, but, in so doing, may also come to fashion *A Doll House* which shifts emphasis away from the celebration of the Romantic belief in the sovereignty of the individual to the revelation of an isolating narcissism—a narcissism that has become all too familiar to us today.[3]

The characters of *A Doll House* are, to be sure, not alone in dramatic literature in being self-preoccupied, for self-preoccupation is a quality shared by characters from Oedipus to Hamlet and on into modern drama. Yet if a contemporary production is to suggest the narcissistic self-absorption of Ibsen's characters, it must do so in such a way as to imply motivations for their actions and delineate their relationships with one another. Thus it is important to establish a conceptual framework which will provide a degree of precision for the use of the term "narcissism" in this discussion so as to distinguish it from the kind of self-absorption which is an inherent quality necessarily shared by all dramatic characters. For that purpose, it is useful to turn to the criteria established by the Task Force on Nomenclature and Statistics of the American Psychiatric Association for diagnosing the narcissistic personality:

A. Grandiose sense of self-importance and uniqueness, e.g., exaggerates achievements and talents, focuses on how special one's problems are.
B. Preoccupation with fantasies of unlimited success, power, brilliance, beauty, or ideal love.
C. Exhibitionistic: requires constant attention and admiration.

[2] Rolf Fjelde, Introduction to *A Doll House*, in Henrik Ibsen, *The Complete Major Prose Plays* (New York: Farrar, Straus, Giroux, 1978), p. 121.
[3] For studies of the prevalence of the narcissistic personality disorder in contemporary psychoanalytic literature, see Otto F. Kernberg, *Borderline Conditions and Pathological Narcissism* (New York: J. Aronson, 1975); Heinz Kohut, *The Analysis of the Self* (New York: International Universities Press, 1971); and Peter L. Giovachinni, *Psychoanalysis of Character Disorders* (New York: J. Aronson, 1975). See also Christopher Lasch, *The Culture of Narcissism* (New York: Norton, 1979), for a discussion of narcissism as the defining characteristic of contemporary American society.

   D. Responds to criticism, indifference of others, or defeat with either cool in-
       difference, or with marked feelings of rage, inferiority, shame, humiliation,
       or emptiness.
   E. At least two of the following are characteristics of disturbances in inter-
       personal relationships:
      1. Lack of empathy: inability to recognize how others feel, e.g., unable to
         appreciate the distress of someone who is seriously ill.
      2. Entitlement: expectation of special favors without assuming reciprocal
         responsibilities, e.g., surprise and anger that people won't do what he
         wants.
      3. Interpersonal exploitiveness: takes advantage of others to indulge own
         desires for self-aggrandizement, with disregard for the personal in-
         tegrity and rights of others.
      4. Relationships characteristically vacillate between the extremes of over-
         idealization and devaluation.[4]

These criteria, as they provide a background against which to consider Nora's
relationship with both Kristine Linde and Dr. Rank, will serve to illuminate
not only those relationships themselves, but also the relationship of Nora
and her husband which is at the center of the play. Moreover, if these criteria
are viewed as outlines for characterization — but not as reductive psychoanalytic constructs leading to "case studies" — it becomes possible to discover
a Nora of greater complexity than the totally sympathetic victim turned
romantic heroine who has inhabited most productions of the play. And,
most important of all, as Nora and her relationships within the walls of
her "doll house" come to imply a paradigm of the dilemma of all human relationships in the greater society outside, the famous sound of the slamming
door may come to resonate even more loudly for us than it did for the audiences of the nineteenth century with a profound and immediate sense of irony
and ambiguity, an irony and ambiguity which could not have escaped Ibsen
himself.

             From "Recasting *A Doll House:* Narcissism as Character Motivation
                 in Ibsen's Play," *Comparative Drama,* Summer 1986

[4] Task Force on Nomenclature and Statistics, American Psychiatric Association, *DSM-III:
Diagnostic Criteria Draft* (New York, 1978), pp. 103–04.

CONSIDERATIONS FOR CRITICAL THINKING AND WRITING

   1. What is Tufts's purpose in arguing that Nora be seen as narcissistic?
   2. Using the criteria of the American Psychiatric Association, consider Nora's
      personality. Write an essay either refuting the assertion that she has a nar-
      cissistic personality or supporting it.
   3. How does Tufts's reading compare with Joan Templeton's feminist reading
      of Nora in the perspective that follows? Which do you find more convinc-
      ing? Why?

JOAN TEMPLETON (B. 1940)

This feminist perspective summarizes the arguments against reading
the play as dramatization of a feminist heroine.

Is A Doll House *a Feminist Text?*

A Doll House *is no more about women's rights than Shakespeare's* Richard II *is about the divine right of kings, or* Ghosts *about syphilis. . . . Its theme is the need of every individual to find out the kind of person he or she is and to strive to become that person.*[1] Ibsen has been resoundingly saved from feminism, or, as it was called in his day, "the woman question." His rescuers customarily cite a statement the dramatist made on 26 May 1898 at a seventieth-birthday banquet given in his honor by the Norwegian Women's Rights League:

> I thank you for the toast, but must disclaim the honor of having consciously worked for the women's rights movement. . . . True enough, it is desirable to solve the woman problem, along with all the others; but that has not been the whole purpose. My task has been the description of humanity.[2]

Ibsen's champions like to take this disavowal as a precise reference to his purpose in writing *A Doll House* twenty years earlier, his "original intention," according to Maurice Valency.[3] Ibsen's biographer Michael Meyer urges all reviewers of *Doll House* revivals to learn Ibsen's speech by heart,[4] and James McFarlane, editor of *The Oxford Ibsen*, includes it in his explanatory material on *A Doll House*, under "Some Pronouncements of the Author," as though Ibsen had been speaking of the play.[5] Whatever propaganda feminists may have made of *A Doll House*, Ibsen, it is argued, never meant to write a play about the highly topical subject of women's rights; Nora's conflict represents something other than, or something more than, woman's. In an article commemorating the half century of Ibsen's death, R. M. Adams explains, "*A Doll House* represents a woman imbued with the idea of becoming a person, but it proposes nothing categorical about women becoming people; in fact, its real theme has nothing to do with the sexes."[6] Over twenty years later, after feminism had resurfaced as an international movement, Einar Haugen, the doyen of American Scandinavian studies, insisted that "Ibsen's Nora is not just a woman arguing for female liberation; she is much more. She embodies the comedy as well as the tragedy of modern life."[7] In the Modern Language Association's *Approaches to Teaching* A Doll House, the editor speaks disparagingly of "reductionist views of *(A Doll House)* as a feminist drama." Summarizing a "major theme" in the volume as "the need for a broad view of the play and a condemnation of a static approach," she warns that discussions of the play's "connection with feminism" have value only if they are monitored, "properly channeled and kept firmly linked to Ibsen's text."[8]

Removing the woman question from *A Doll House* is presented as part of a corrective effort to free Ibsen from his erroneous reputation as a writer of thesis

---

[1] Michael Meyer, *Ibsen* (Garden City: Doubleday, 1971), 457. [This is not the Michael Meyer who is editor of *The Bedford Introduction to Literature.*]
[2] Henrik Ibsen, *Letter and Speeches*, ed. and trans. Evert Sprinchorn (New York: Hill, 1964), 337.
[3] Maurice Valency, *The Flower and the Castle: An Introduction to Modern Drama* (New York: Schocken, 1982), 151.
[4] Meyer, 774.
[5] James McFarlane, "*A Doll's House*: Commentary" in *The Oxford Ibsen*, ed. McFarlane (Oxford UP, 1961), V, 456.
[6] R. M. Adams, "The Fifty-First Anniversary," *Hudson Review* 10 (1957), 416.
[7] Einar Haugen, *Ibsen's Drama: Author to Audience* (Minneapolis: U of Minnesota P, 1979), vii.
[8] Yvonne Shafer, ed., *Approaches to Teaching Ibsen's* A Doll House (New York: MLA, 1985), 32.

plays, a wrongheaded notion usually blamed on Shaw, who, it is claimed, mistakenly saw Ibsen as the nineteenth century's greatest iconoclast and offered that misreading to the public as *The Quintessence of Ibsenism.* Ibsen, it is now de rigueur to explain, did not stoop to "issues." He was a poet of the truth of the human soul. That Nora's exit from her dollhouse has long been the principal international symbol for women's issues, including many that far exceed the confines of her small world, is irrelevant to the essential meaning of *A Doll House,* a play, in Richard Gilman's phrase, "pitched beyond sexual difference."[9] Ibsen, explains Robert Brustein, "was completely indifferent to (the woman question) except as a metaphor for individual freedom."[10] Discussing the relation of *A Doll House* to feminism, Halvdan Koht, author of the definitive Norwegian Ibsen life, says in summary, "Little by little the topical controversy died away; what remained was the work of art, with its demand for truth in every human relation."[11]

Thus, it turns out, the *Uncle Tom's Cabin* of the women's rights movement is not really about women at all. "Fiddle-faddle," pronounced R. M. Adams, dismissing feminist claims for the play.[12] Like angels, Nora has no sex. Ibsen meant her to be Everyman.

From "The *Doll House* Backlash: Criticism, Feminism, and Ibsen,"
PMLA, January, 1989

[9] Richard Gilman, *The Making of Modern Drama* (New York: Farrar, 1972), 65.
[10] Robert Brustein, *The Theatre of Revolt* (New York: Little, 1962), 105.
[11] Halvdan Koht, *Life of Ibsen* (New York: Blom, 1971), 323.
[12] Adams, 416.

CONSIDERATIONS FOR CRITICAL THINKING AND WRITING

1. According to Templeton, what kinds of arguments are used to reject *A Doll House* as a feminist text?

2. From the tone of the summaries provided, what would you say is Templeton's attitude toward these arguments?

3. Read the section on feminist criticism in "Critical Strategies for Reading" (p. 2036), and write an essay addressing the summarized arguments as you think a feminist critic might respond.

QUESTIONS FOR WRITING
Applying a Critical Strategy

This section offers advice about developing an argument that draws on the different strategies, or schools of literary theory, covered in Chapter 37. The following list of questions and suggestions will help you to apply one or more of these critical strategies to a work in order to shed light on it. Following the questions is a sample paper based on *A Doll House* (p. 1564).

There are many possible lenses through which to read a literary work. The Perspectives, Complementary Critical Readings, and Critical Case Studies in this anthology suggest a variety of approaches — including formalist, biographical, psychological, Marxist, new historicist, feminist, mythological, reader-response, and deconstructionist strategies — that can be used to explore the effects, meanings, and significances of a poem, short story, or play (see Chapter 37 for a discussion of these strategies).

Once you have generated a central idea about a work, you will need to choose the critical approach(es) that will allow you to develop your argument. In the following sample paper, the writer chose a New Historicist approach because she was interested in speculating about what Nora faced after she left her husband on the other side of the slammed door in *A Doll House*. By using evidence external to the play, from a letter written by a nineteenth-century husband to his wife, the writer was able to recreate some of the historical context for *A Doll House* in order to argue that Nora's leaving home is a more risky, problematic action than her simple declaration of freedom from her husband. This historical approach allowed the writer to offer a substantive argument about what Nora might have faced beyond the slammed door.

Regardless of the approach — or combination of approaches — you find helpful, it is essential that you be thoroughly familiar with the text of the literary work before examining it through the lens of a particular critical strategy. Without a strong familiarity with the literary work you will not be able to judge the accuracy and validity of a critic's arguments, and you might find your own insights immediately superseded by those of the first critic you read. For additional advice on how to incorporate material from critical essays into your writing without losing track of your own argument about a work, see Questions for Writing: Incorporating the Critics (p. 501).

1. Which of the critical strategies discussed in Chapter 37 seems the most appropriate to the literary work under consideration? Why do you prefer one particular approach over another? Do any critical strategies seem especially inappropriate? Why?

2. Does the historical context of a literary work suggest that certain critical strategies, such as Marxism or feminism, might be particularly productive?

3. Does the literary work reflect or challenge the cultural assumptions contemporary to it in such a way as to suggest a critical approach for your paper?

4. Does the author comment on his or her own literary work in letters, interviews, or lectures? If so, how might these comments help you to develop an approach for your paper?

5. Are you able to formulate an interpretation of the work you want to discuss before reading the critics extensively? If so, how might the critics' discussions help you to develop, enhance, or qualify your argument about how to interpret the work?

6. If you haven't developed an argument before reading the critics, how might some exploratory reading lead you into significant questions and controversial issues that would offer topics that could be developed into a thesis?

7. If you are drawing on the work of a number of critics, how are their critical strategies — whether formalist, biographical, psychological, historical, or other — relevant to your own? How can you use their insights to support your own argument?

8. Is it possible and desirable to combine approaches — such as psychological and historical or biographical and feminist — so that multiple perspectives can be used to support your argument?

9. If the strategies or approaches the critics use to interpret the literary work tend to be similar, are there questions and issues that have been neglected or ignored that can become the focus of your argument about the literary work?

10. If the critics' approaches are very different from one another, is there a way to use those differences to argue your own critical approach that allows you to support one critic rather than another or to resolve a controversy among the critics?

11. Is your argument adequately supported with specific evidence from the literary text? Have you been careful not to avoid discussing parts of the text that do not seem to support your argument?

12. Is your own discussion of the literary text free of simple plot summary? Does each paragraph include a thesis statement that advances your argument rather than merely consisting of facts and plot summary?

13. Have you accurately and fairly represented the critics' arguments?

14. Have you made your own contributions, qualifications, or disagreements with the critics clear to your reader?

A SAMPLE PAPER

On the Other Side of the Slammed Door in **A Doll House**

The following sample paper focuses on the magnitude of Nora Helmer's decision to leave her husband in *A Doll House*. Kathy Atner uses a New Historicist perspective to show just how difficult Nora's decision would have been in the context of nineteenth-century attitudes toward marriage and women. The paper develops an argument primarily from evidence supplied by "A Nineteenth-Century Husband's Letter to His Wife" (p. 1628). By drawing on a source that ordinarily might have been ignored by literary critics, Atner is able to suggest how difficult Nora's life would have been after abandoning her husband and family. This historical strategy is combined with a feminist perspective that gives the modern reader a greater understanding of the issues Nora must inevitably confront once she slams the door shut on her conventional and accepted life as devoted wife and mother. By using both New Historicist and feminist perspectives, Atner suggests that twentieth-century readers should be sensitive to the tragic as well as the heroic dimension of Nora's life.

Kathy Atner
Professor Porter
English 216
April 8, 19--

On the Other Side of the Slammed Door
in A Doll House

Nora Helmer's decision to leave her family in Henrik
Ibsen's 1879 play A Doll House reflects the dilemma faced
by many nineteenth-century women who were forced either to
conform to highly restrictive gender roles or to abandon
these roles in order to realize their value as individuals. Although Ibsen brings his audience to the moment that
Nora chooses to disregard her social role and opt for her
"freedom," his play does not clearly reveal the true fate
of women who followed Nora's path in the nineteenth century. Historically, most women who chose not to acquiesce
to the socially prescribed roles of marriage were treated
as unnatural creatures and shunned by the respectable public. An actual letter, written in 1844 by Marcus to his
estranged wife, Ulrike, reveals the effects of this severe
social condemnation (1628). His letter implies the desperate fate that inevitably befalls women who reject their
prescribed duties as wives and mothers. Through Marcus's
letter to his wife, the painful ramifications of Nora's
decision to accommodate her own personal desires instead
of those of her family become even more poignant, courageous, and tragic.

In the nineteenth century, women had few alternatives
to marriage, and women who "failed" at marriage were
thought to have failed in their most important duty. In
his letter, Marcus articulates society's deep disgust for
women who reject what it believes is the sacred female
role of homemaker. His letter, while on one level an angry

condemnation of his wife's "stubbornness" (1628) and a
cruelly condescending list of conditions to be met on her
return, is on another level a plea for her to accept again
the role that society has assigned her. He is clearly
shaken by his wife's abandonment and interprets it as a
betrayal of a social "law" or tradition, which, to Marcus's mind, ought to be carved in stone. He responds to
this betrayal by demanding complete obedience from his
wife in the form of a promise "to follow in my wishes in
everything and to strictly obey my orders" (1628). Only
when she acquiesces to his conditions and returns to her
role as docile and obedient wife will Marcus in turn be
able to resume the comfortably familiar, socially sanctioned role of dominant, morally superior husband.

   Like Ulrike, Nora decides to leave the security and
comfort of her restrictive domestic life to try to become
a human being. Ibsen neglects, however, to show his audience the actual result of that decision. At the conclusion
of A Doll House, Nora slams the door on her past life,
hoping to begin a new life that will somehow be more satisfying. Yet the modern audience has no genuine sense of
what she may have found beyond that door, and perhaps neither did Nora. Through Ulrike's story, however, the reader
understands the historical truth that the world awaiting
Nora was hostile and unsympathetic. Marcus warns his wife
that "your husband, your children, and the entire city
threaten indifference or even contempt" (1628) if she refuses to return immediately to her socially acceptable
domestic role. This pressure to conform, combined with the
bleak prospects of a single woman, results in Ulrike's
ultimate choice to keep up "appearances" rather than further subject herself to a contemptuous world that neither
wants nor understands her. Although we cannot know Nora's

fate after she leaves Torvald, we may assume that her future would be as bleak as Ulrike's and that the pressure
to return to her domestic life would be equally strong.

When A Doll House was first produced in 1879, audiences had no more sympathy for Nora's predicament than
they did for the real-life stories of women such as
Ulrike. As Errol Durbach points out, in the nineteenth
century, Ibsen's play "did not precipitate heated debate about feminism, women's rights, or male domination.
The sound and the fury were addressed to the very question . . . What credible wife and mother would ever walk out
this way on her family?" (14). A great many readers and
audience members tended to side with Torvald, who seemed,
to them, the innocent victim of Nora's consuming selfishness. The audience's repulsion toward Nora's apparently
"unnatural" action of abandoning her family mirrors the
responses of Marcus and Torvald Helmer, the bereft, perplexed, and angry husbands. Nora and Ulrike radically disrupt their husbands' perceptions of family relationships
by walking out of their lives, preferring to recognize
their own needs before any others. These women suggest
that Torvald's claim that "before all else, you're a wife
and mother" (1609) may not necessarily be true for all
women, but their brave rejections of domestic life cannot
force society to condone their behavior.

Ibsen maintains that A Doll House is not about
women's rights specifically but encompasses a more universal "description of humanity" (Letters 337). In showing a
human being trying to create a new identity for herself,
however, Ibsen reveals the extent to which people are
trapped in societal norms and expectations. Nora's
acknowledgment that she "can't go on believing what the
majority says, or what's written in books" (1609) suggests

a profound social upheaval that has the potential to subvert long-established gender roles. If Nora and Ulrike
relinquish the role of the subservient and helpless wife,
then Torvald and Marcus can no longer play the role of
the dominating, protective husband. Without this role, the
men are as helpless as they want their wives to be, and
the traditional gender expectations are no longer beyond
question. Yet the historical reality is that in spite of
Nora's daring escape from her oppressive family, the world
was not ready to accommodate women who rejected their feminine duties. Ulrike was thwarted in her attempt to free
herself from her family; history suggests that Nora may
have met a similar fate.

    Modern audiences tend to see Nora as a strong, ad-
mirable woman who is courageous enough to sacrifice
everything in order to fulfill her own needs as an individual and as a woman. She shatters gender stereotypes
through her defiant disregard for all that society demands
of her. Yet, taken in the context of nineteenth-century
life, perhaps Nora's story is more tragic than we might
initially like to believe. Ulrike's story, told through
her husband's letter, suggests that in a time of turbulent
social upheaval, what was interpreted as a collapse of
what we now call "family values" was shocking, scandalous,
and deeply frightening to many. In the nineteenth century,
Nora was not the sympathetic character that she is today;
instead, she symbolized many negative attributes--what
Marcus calls "false ambition" and "stubbornness" (1628)--
that were often ascribed to women. Ulrike's forced return
to her role as dutiful wife and mother suggests that society was quick to punish disobedient women and that the
slamming door at the end of A Doll House was not necessarily the sound of freedom for Nora.

Atner 5

Works Cited

Durbach, Errol. <u>A Doll's House: Ibsen's Myth of Transfor-</u>
<u>mation</u>. Boston: Twayne, 1991.

Ibsen, Henrik. <u>A Doll House</u>. Trans. Rolf Fjelde. Meyer
1564-1612.

---. <u>Letters and Speeches</u>. Ed. and trans. Evert
Sprinchorn. New York: Hill, 1964. 337.

Meyer, Michael, ed. <u>The Bedford Introduction to Literature</u>.
5th ed. Boston: Bedford/St. Martin's, 1999.

"A Nineteenth-Century Husband's Letter to His Wife." Meyer
1628-1629.

34

Experimental Trends
in Drama

BEYOND REALISM

Realistic drama has remained popular throughout the twentieth century, but from its beginnings it has been continually challenged by nonrealistic modes of theater. By the end of the nineteenth century, playwrights reacting against realism began to develop a variety of new approaches to setting, action, and character. Instead of creating a slice of life onstage, modern experimental playwrights drew on purely theatrical devices, ranging from stark sets and ritualistic actions to symbolic characterizations and audience participation. In general, such devices were designed to jar audiences' expectations and to heighten their awareness that what appeared before them was indeed a theatrical production. A glimpse of some of the nonrealistic movements in drama suggests how the possibilities for affecting audiences have been broadened by experimental theater.

Symbolist drama rejected the realists' assumption that life can be understood objectively and scientifically. The symbolists emphasized a subjective, emotional response to life because they believed that ultimate realities can be recognized only intuitively. Since absolute truth cannot be directly perceived, symbolists such as the Belgian playwright Maurice Maeterlinck (1862–1949) sought to express spiritual truth through settings, characters, and actions that suggest a transcendent reality. Maeterlinck's most famous symbolist play, *Pelléas and Mélisande* (1892), is a story of love and vengeance that includes mysterious forebodings, symbolic objects, and unexplained powerful forces. The elements of the play make no attempt to create the texture of ordinary life.

Other playwrights — such as William Butler Yeats (1865–1939) in Ireland, Paul Claudel (1868–1955) in France, Leonid Andreyev (1871–1919) in Russia, and Federico García Lorca (1898–1936) in Spain — also used some of the techniques associated with symbolist plays, but the movement never enjoyed wide popularity because audiences often found the plays' action too vague and their language too cryptic. Nevertheless, symbolist drama had an important influence on the work of subsequent playwrights, such as Tennessee Williams's *The Glass Menagerie* (p. 1864) and Arthur Miller's *Death of a Salesman* (p. 1795); these dramatists effectively used symbols in plays that contain both realistic and nonrealistic qualities.

Another nonrealistic movement, known as ***expressionism,*** was popular from the end of World War I until the mid-1920s. Expressionist playwrights emphasized the internal lives of their characters and deliberately distorted reality by creating an outward manifestation of an inner state of being. The late plays of Swedish dramatist August Strindberg (1849-1912) anticipate expressionistic techniques. Strindberg's preface to *A Dream Play* (1902) reflects the impact that Freudian psychology would eventually have on the theater:

> The author has tried to imitate the disconnected but seemingly logical form of the dream. Anything may happen; everything is possible and probable. Time and space do not exist. On an insignificant background of reality, imagination designs and embroiders novel patterns: a medley of memories, experiences, free fancies, absurdities, and improvisations.

In such nonrealistic drama the action does not have to proceed chronologically because the playwright dramatizes the emotional life of the characters, which blends the past with the present rather than moving in a fixed, linear way. This fluidity of development can be seen in the *flashbacks* of Williams's *The Glass Menagerie* and Miller's *Death of a Salesman*.

The *epic theater* of Bertolt Brecht (1898-1956) is, like symbolism and expressionism, a long way from the realistic elements in Ibsen's *A Doll House*. Brecht kept a distance between his characters and the audience. This strategy of alienation was designed to alert audiences to important social problems that might be overlooked if an individual's struggles became too emotionally absorbing. Brecht's drama, by casting new light on chronic human problems such as poverty, injustice, and war, was a means to convey hope and evidence that society could be changed for the better. Brecht called his drama "epic" to distinguish it from Aristotle's notion of drama. The episodic structure was designed to prevent the audience from being swept up in the action or losing themselves in an inevitable tragedy. Instead, Brecht wanted the audience to analyze the action and realize that certain consequences weren't inevitable but could be avoided. This distancing, the dramatization of societal issues, and the use of loosely connected scenes sometimes narrated by a kind of stage manager are the hallmarks of "epic" drama.

Epic theater revels in stylized theatricality. The major action in *The Caucasian Chalk Circle*, for example, consists of a play within a play. Brecht's dramas use suggestive rather than detailed settings, and their scenery and props are frequently changed as the audience watches. His actors make clear that they are pretending to be characters. They may speak or sing in verse, address the audience, or comment on issues with other characters who are not participants in the immediate action. In brief, Brecht's theater is keenly conscious of itself as theater.

In contrast to this didactic theater, the ***theater of the absurd*** was a response to the twentieth century's loss of faith in reason, religion, and life itself. These doubts produced an approach to drama that emphasizes chaotic, irrational forces and portrays human beings as more the victims than the makers of their world.

Absurdists such as Samuel Beckett (1906–1989), French dramatist Eugène Ionesco (1912–1994), English playwright Harold Pinter (B. 1930), and American writer Edward Albee (B. 1928) employ a variety of approaches to drama, but they share some assumptions about what subjects are important. Absurdism challenges the belief that life is ordered and meaningful. Instead of positing traditional values that give human beings a sense of purpose in life, absurdists dramatize our inability to comprehend fully our identities and destinies. Unlike heroic characters such as Oedipus or Hamlet, who retain their dignity despite their defeats, the characters in absurdist dramas frequently seem pathetically comic as they drift from one destructive moment to the next. These ***antiheroes*** are often bewildered, ineffectual, deluded, and lost. If they learn anything, it is that the world isolates them in an existence devoid of God and absolute values.

The basic premise of absurdism—that life is meaningless—is often presented in a nonrealistic manner to disrupt our expectations. In a realistic play such as Ibsen's *A Doll House,* characters act pretty much the way we believe people behave. The motivation of these characters and the plausibility of their actions are comprehensible, but in an absurdist drama we are confronted with characters who appear in a series of disconnected incidents that lead to deeper confusion. What would we make of Nora if Ibsen had her appear in the final act costumed as a doll? This would be not only bizarre but unacceptable in a realistic play. However, it could make dramatic sense in an absurdist adaptation that sought to dramatize Nora's loss of identity and dehumanization as a result of her marriage.

Nora's appearance as a doll would, of course, be laughably inconsistent with what we judge to be real or reasonable. And yet we might find ourselves sympathizing with her situation. Suppose that instead of slamming the door and leaving her husband in the final scene, Nora moved stiffly about the room costumed as a doll while Helmer complacently sipped sherry and read the evening paper. Such an ending would suggest that she had been defeated by the circumstances in her life. Her condition— being nothing more than someone's toy—would be both absurd and pathetic. If we laughed at this scene, we would do so because Nora's situation is grotesquely humorous, a parody of her assumptions, hopes, and expectations. This is the world of ***tragicomedy,*** where laughter and pain coexist and where there is neither the happy resolution that typifies comic plots nor the transformational suffering that brings clarification to the tragic hero. It is the world dramatized, for example, in the opening scene of Harold Pinter's *The Dumb Waiter* when Ben tells Gus about an item he's read in the paper.

> *Ben:* A man of eighty-seven wanted to cross the road. But there was a lot of traffic, see? He couldn't see how he was going to squeeze through. So he crawled under a lorry [truck].
>
> *Gus:* He what?
>
> *Ben:* He crawled under a lorry. A stationary lorry.
>
> *Gus:* No?
>
> *Ben:* The lorry started and ran over him.
>
> *Gus:* Go on!
>
> *Ben:* That's what it says here.
>
> *Gus:* Get away.
>
> *Ben:* It's enough to make you want to puke, isn't it?
>
> *Gus:* Who advised him to do a thing like that?
>
> *Ben:* A man of eighty-seven crawling under a lorry!
>
> *Gus:* It's unbelievable.
>
> *Ben:* It's down here in black and white.
>
> *Gus:* Incredible.

As much as Gus finds the story difficult to believe and Ben is sickened by it, it is a fact that the old man was crushed under ridiculous circumstances. His death is unexpected, accidental, incomprehensible, and meaningless — except that what happened to the old man is, from an absurdist's perspective, really no different from what life has in store for all of us one way or the other.

An absurdist playwright may, as Pinter does, employ realistic settings and speech, but he or she goes beyond realistic conventions to challenge the rational assumptions we make about our lives. Pinter insists that "a play is not an essay." Background information, character motivation, action — nothing presented on an absurdist's stage is governed by the conventions of realism. The absurdists typically refuse to create the illusion of reality because there is, finally, no reality to imitate. If conversations in their plays are sometimes fragmented and seemingly inconsequential, the reason is that absurdists dramatize people's combined inability and unwillingness to communicate with one another. Indeed, Samuel Beckett's *Act without Words* contains no dialogue, and in his *Krapp's Last Tape* a single character addresses only his own tape-recorded voice. To some extent we must suspend common sense and logic if we are to appreciate the visions and voices in an absurdist play.

Although many other nonrealistic movements developed in the twentieth century, these four — symbolism, expressionism, epic theater, and the theater of the absurd — embrace the major differences between nonrealistic and realistic drama. The theater continually tests its own possibilities. In the 1960s and 1970s, for example, some acting companies in New York completely collapsed the usual distinctions between audience and actors. The Living Theater went even further by moving into the streets, where the actors and audiences engaged in dramatic political statements aimed at raising the social consciousness of people wherever they were. Some critics argued that this was not really theater but merely an exuberant kind of political rally. However, proponents of these productions—known as **guerrilla theater**—argued that protest drama is both politically and artistically valid. In any case, although today's playwrights seem considerably less inclined to take to the streets, there is a tolerance for a wide range of possible relationships between actors and audiences. Audiences (and readers) can expect symbolic characters, expressionistic settings, poetic language, monologues, and extreme actions in productions that also contain realistic elements. In *Route 1 & 9* (1981), a piece created by an experimental theater company called The Wooster Group, for example, audiences found themselves confronted with passages from Thornton Wilder's idealized version of America in *Our Town* that were coupled with a pornographic film and a black vaudeville act. This unlikely combination was used to comment on Wilder's conception of America in which issues of sex and race are largely ignored. Increasingly, experimental theater has cultivated an eclectic approach to drama, using a variety of media, cultures, playwrights, and even languages to enrich an audience's experience. Parts of Robert Wilson's *CIVIL warS* (1984)—a work never staged in its entirety in any one place—were performed in several countries, including France, Italy, and the United States, and drew on different languages as well as cultures to evoke a wide range of experiences from history, literature, myths, and even dreams. The Album of Contemporary Plays in Chapter 36 attests to the traditions and innovations that contemporary dramatists have incorporated into their dramatic art.

Krapp's Last Tape

Samuel Beckett was born near Dublin to a middle-class Irish-Protestant family. After graduating from Trinity College, Dublin, in 1927, he studied in Paris, where he met James Joyce and was influenced by Joyce's innovative use of language. There Beckett began his own experiments in poetry and fiction. He returned to Ireland to teach at Trinity College and earned an M.A. in 1931, but he left teaching the following year to travel in Europe. He permanently settled in Paris in the late 1930s. During this period his publications included two volumes of poetry, *Whoroscope* (1930) and *Echo's Bones* (1935); a collection of stories, *More Pricks Than Kicks* (1934); and a novel, *Murphy* (1938).

During World War II, Beckett's work for the French resistance made it necessary for him to flee German-occupied France, but he returned to Paris at the end of the war and began writing the works that would earn him the Nobel Prize for Literature in 1969. Writing mostly in French and translating his work into English later, Beckett produced both novels— *Molloy* (1951), *Malone Dies* (1951), *Watt* (1953), *The Unnamable* (1953), and *How*

It Is (1961) — and plays — *Waiting for Godot* (1952), *Endgame* (1957), *Krapp's Last Tape* (1958, first written in English), and *Happy Days* (1961).

These works are populated by characters who live meager, isolated existences that sometimes seem barely human. Yet their aspirations and desires are expressed in simple activities that are attempts to transcend the endless meaningless routines that make up their lives. In an illogical and absurdly comic world stripped of any lasting meaning, these characters appear in minimal settings, having little to say and even less to do.

Waiting for Godot, Beckett's most famous play, brought absurdist principles to popular audiences. Its seemingly pointless dialogue is spoken by two clownish vagabonds while they wait for a mysterious Mr. Godot, who never appears. The play has no clearly identifiable conflict; instead, the action tends to be random and repetitive. Nothing much happens, but there is tension nonetheless among strange characters who hope in an apparently hopeless world.

In *Krapp's Last Tape*, Beckett uses only one character onstage. The play is more than a monologue, however, because the protagonist engages in a kind of conversation with his own tape-recorded voice. Every year on his birthday Krapp has recorded his impressions of that year's events and methodically cataloged and indexed them. Krapp observes his sixty-ninth birthday by listening to portions of a tape he recorded thirty years earlier. Hence, there are two Krapps in the play: an elderly man and his younger self on tape. This device allows Beckett to present Krapp's relation to his past in an intriguing, complex manner; we witness a character thinking aloud with a part of himself he no longer knows. If the older Krapp appears strange to us, we should not overlook the fact that he is even stranger to himself.

SAMUEL BECKETT (1906–1989)
Krapp's Last Tape
1958

A PLAY IN ONE ACT

SCENE: *A late evening in the future.*

> *Krapp's den. Front center a small table, the two drawers of which open towards audience. Sitting at the table, facing front, i.e. across from the drawers, a wearish°*
> *old man: Krapp.*
>
> > *Rusty black narrow trousers too short for him. Rusty black sleeveless waistcoat, four capacious pockets. Heavy silver watch and chain. Grimy white shirt open at neck, no collar. Surprising pair of dirty white boots, size ten at least, very narrow and pointed.*
> >
> > *White face. Purple nose. Disordered gray hair. Unshaven.*
> >
> > *Very near-sighted (but unspectacled). Hard of hearing.*

wearish: Withered.

Cracked voice. Distinctive intonation.
Laborious walk.
On the table a tape-recorder with microphone and a number of cardboard boxes containing reels of recorded tapes.
Table and immediately adjacent area in strong white light. Rest of stage in darkness.
Krapp remains a moment motionless, heaves a great sigh, looks at his watch, fumbles in his pockets, takes out an envelope, puts it back, fumbles, takes out a small bunch of keys, raises it to his eyes, chooses a key, gets up and moves to front of table. He stoops, unlocks first drawer, peers into it, feels about inside it, takes out a reel of tape, peers at it, puts it back, locks drawer, unlocks second drawer, peers into it, feels about inside it, takes out a large banana, peers at it, locks drawer, puts keys back in his pocket. He turns, advances to edge of stage, halts, strokes banana, peels it, drops skin at his feet, puts end of banana in his mouth and remains motionless, staring vacuously before him. Finally he bites off the end, turns aside, and begins pacing to and fro at edge of stage, in the light, i.e. not more than four or five paces either way, meditatively eating banana. He treads on skin, slips, nearly falls, recovers himself, stoops and peers at skin and finally pushes it, still stooping, with his foot over the edge of stage into pit. He resumes his pacing, finishes banana, returns to table, sits down, remains a moment motionless, heaves a great sigh, takes keys from his pockets, raises them to his eyes, chooses key, gets up and moves to front of table, unlocks second drawer, takes out a second large banana, peers at it, locks drawer, puts back keys in his pocket, turns, advances to edge of stage, halts, strokes banana, peels it, tosses skin into pit, puts end of banana in his mouth, and remains motionless, staring vacuously before him. Finally he has an idea, puts banana in his waistcoat pocket, the end emerging, and goes with all the speed he can muster backstage into darkness. Ten seconds. Loud pop of cork. Fifteen seconds. He comes back into light carrying an old ledger and sits down at table. He lays ledger on table, wipes his mouth, wipes his hands on the front of his waistcoat, brings them smartly together and rubs them.

Krapp (briskly): Ah! (*He bends over ledger, turns the pages, finds the entry he wants, reads.*) Box . . . thrree . . . spool . . . five. (*He raises his head and stares front. With relish.*) Spool! (*Pause.*) Spooool! (*Happy smile. Pause. He bends over table, starts peering and poking at the boxes.*) Box . . . thrree . . . thrree . . . four . . . two . . . (*with surprise*) nine! good God! . . . seven . . . ah! the little rascal! (*He takes up box, peers at it.*) Box thrree. (*He lays it on table, opens it, and peers at spools inside.*) Spool . . . (*he peers at ledger*) . . . five (*he peers at spools*) . . . five . . . five! . . . ah! the little scoundrel! (*He takes out a spool, peers at it.*) Spool five. (*He lays it on table, closes box three, puts it back with the others, takes up the spool.*) Box thrree, spool five. (*He bends over the machine, looks up. With relish.*) Spooool! (*Happy smile. He bends, loads spool on machine, rubs his hands.*) Ah! (*He peers at ledger, reads entry at foot of page.*) Mother at rest at last . . . Hm . . . The black ball . . . (*He raises his head, stares blankly front. Puzzled.*) Black ball? . . . (*He peers again at ledger, reads.*) The dark nurse . . . (*He raises his head, broods, peers again at ledger, reads.*) Slight improvement in bowel condition . . . Hm . . . Memorable . . . what? (*He peers closer.*) Equinox, memorable equinox. (*He raises his head, stares blankly front. Puzzled.*) Memorable equinox? . . . (*Pause. He shrugs his shoulders, peers again at ledger, reads.*) Farewell to — (*he turns the page*) — love.

He raises his head, broods, bends over machine, switches on, and assumes listening posture; i.e. leaning forward, elbows on table, hand cupping ear towards machine, face front.

Tape *(strong voice, rather pompous, clearly Krapp's at a much earlier time):* Thirty-nine today, sound as a — *(Settling himself more comfortably he knocks one of the boxes off the table, curses, switches off, sweeps boxes and ledger violently to the ground, winds tape back to beginning, switches on, resumes posture.)* Thirty-nine today, sound as a bell, apart from my old weakness, and intellectually I have now every reason to suspect at the ... *(hesitates)* ... crest of the wave — or thereabouts. Celebrated the awful occasion, as in recent years, quietly at the Winehouse. Not a soul. Sat before the fire with closed eyes, separating the grain from the husks. Jotted down a few notes, on the back of an envelope. Good to be back in my den, in my old rags. Have just eaten I regret to say three bananas and only with difficulty refrained from a fourth. Fatal things for a man with my condition. *(Vehemently.)* Cut 'em out! *(Pause.)* The new light above my table is a great improvement. With all this darkness round me I feel less alone. *(Pause.)* In a way. *(Pause.)* I love to get up and move about in it, then back here to ... *(hesitates)* ... me. *(Pause.)* Krapp.

Pause.

The grain, now what I wonder do I mean by that, I mean ... *(hesitates)* ... I suppose I mean those things worth having when all the dust has — when all *my* dust has settled. I close my eyes and try and imagine them.

Pause. Krapp closes his eyes briefly.

Extraordinary silence this evening, I strain my ears and do not hear a sound. Old Miss McGlome always sings at this hour. But not tonight. Songs of her girlhood, she says. Hard to think of her as a girl. Wonderful woman though. Connaught, I fancy. *(Pause.)* Shall I sing when I am her age, if I ever am? No. *(Pause.)* Did I sing as a boy? No. *(Pause.)* Did I ever sing? No.

Pause.

Just been listening to an old year, passages at random. I did not check in the book, but it must be at least ten or twelve years ago. At that time I think I was still living on and off with Bianca in Kedar Street. Well out of that, Jesus yes! Hopeless business. *(Pause.)* Not much about her, apart from a tribute to her eyes. Very warm. I suddenly saw them again. *(Pause.)* Incomparable! *(Pause.)* Ah well ... *(Pause.)* These old P.M.s are gruesome, but I often find them — *(Krapp switches off, broods, switches on)* — a help before embarking on a new ... *(hesitates)* ... retrospect. Hard to believe I was ever that young whelp. The voice! Jesus! And the aspirations! *(Brief laugh in which Krapp joins.)* And the resolutions! *(Brief laugh in which Krapp joins.)* To drink less, in particular. *(Brief laugh of Krapp alone.)* Statistics. Seventeen hundred hours, out of the preceding eight thousand odd, consumed on licensed premises alone. More than 20%, say 40% of his waking life. *(Pause.)* Plans for a less ... *(hesitates)* ... engrossing sexual life. Last illness of his father. Flagging pursuit of happiness. Unattainable laxation. Sneers at what he calls his youth and thanks to God that it's over. *(Pause.)* False ring there. *(Pause.)* Shadows of the opus ... magnum. Closing with a — *(brief laugh)* — yelp to Providence. *(Prolonged laugh in which Krapp joins.)* What remains of all that misery? A girl in a shabby green coat, on a railway-station platform? No?

Pause.

When I look —

Krapp switches off, broods, looks at his watch, gets up, goes backstage into darkness. Ten seconds. Pop of cork. Ten seconds. Second cork. Ten seconds. Third cork. Ten seconds. Brief burst of quavering song.

Krapp (sings): Now the day is over,
        Night is drawing nigh-igh,
        Shadows — °

Fit of coughing. He comes back into light, sits down, wipes his mouth, switches on, resumes his listening posture.

Tape: — back on the year that is gone, with what I hope is perhaps a glint of the old eye to come, there is of course the house on the canal where mother lay a-dying, in the late autumn, after her long viduity° *(Krapp gives a start),* and the — *(Krapp switches off, winds back tape a little, bends his ear closer to machine, switches on)* — a-dying, after her long viduity, and the —

Krapp switches off, raises his head, stares blankly before him. His lips move in the syllables of "viduity." No sound. He gets up, goes backstage into darkness, comes back with an enormous dictionary, lays it on table, sits down and looks up the word.

Krapp (reading from dictionary): "State — or condition of being — or remaining — a widow — or widower." *(Looks up. Puzzled.)* Being — or remaining? . . . *(Pause. He peers again at dictionary. Reading.)* "Deep weeds of viduity . . . Also of an animal, especially a bird . . . the vidua or weaver-bird . . . Black plumage of male . . ." *(He looks up. With relish.)* The vidua-bird!

Pause. He closes dictionary, switches on, resumes listening posture.

Tape: — bench by the weir from where I could see her window. There I sat, in the biting wind, wishing she were gone. *(Pause.)* Hardly a soul, just a few regulars, nursemaids, infants, old men, dogs. I got to know them quite well — oh by appearance of course I mean! One dark young beauty I recollect particularly, all white and starch, incomparable bosom, with a big black hooded perambulator, most funereal thing. Whenever I looked in her direction she had her eyes on me. And yet when I was bold enough to speak to her — not having been introduced — she threatened to call a policeman. As if I had designs on her virtue! *(Laugh. Pause.)* The face she had! The eyes! Like . . . *(hesitates)* . . . chrysolite! *(Pause.)* Ah well . . . *(Pause.)* I was there when — *(Krapp switches off, broods, switches on again)* — the blind went down, one of those dirty brown roller affairs, throwing a ball for a little white dog, as chance would have it. I happened to look up and there it was. All over and done with, at last. I sat on for a few moments with the

---

Now . . . Shadows: From the hymn "Now the Day Is Over" by Sabine Baring-Gould (1834–1924), author of "Onward, Christian Soldiers."
viduity: Widowhood.

ball in my hand and the dog yelping and pawing at me. *(Pause.)* Moments. Her moments, my moments. *(Pause.)* The dog's moments. *(Pause.)* In the end I held it out to him and he took it in his mouth, gently, gently. A small, old, black, hard, solid rubber ball. *(Pause.)* I shall feel it, in my hand, until my dying day. *(Pause.)* I might have kept it. *(Pause.)* But I gave it to the dog.

Pause.

Ah well . . .

Pause.

Spiritually a year of profound gloom and indigence until that memorable night in March, at the end of the jetty, in the howling wind, never to be forgotten, when suddenly I saw the whole thing. The vision, at last. This I fancy is what I have chiefly to record this evening, against the day when my work will be done and perhaps no place left in my memory, warm or cold, for the miracle that . . . *(hesitates)* . . . for the fire that set it alight. What I suddenly saw then was this, that the belief I had been going on all my life, namely — *(Krapp switches off impatiently, winds tape forward, switches on again)* — great granite rocks the foam flying up in the light of the lighthouse and the wind-gauge spinning like a propellor, clear to me at last that the dark I have always struggled to keep under is in reality my most — *(Krapp curses, switches off, winds tape forward, switches on again)* — unshatterable association until my dissolution of storm and night with the light of the understanding and the fire — *(Krapp curses louder, switches off, winds tape forward, switches on again)* — my face in her breasts and my hand on her. We lay there without moving. But under us all moved, and moved us, gently, up and down, and from side to side.

Pause.

Past midnight. Never knew such silence. The earth might be uninhabited.

Pause.

Here I end —

Krapp switches off, winds tape back, switches on again.

— upper lake, with the punt, bathed off the bank, then pushed out into the stream and drifted. She lay stretched out on the floorboards with her hands under her head and her eyes closed. Sun blazing down, bit of a breeze, water nice and lively. I noticed a scratch on her thigh and asked her how she came by it. Picking gooseberries, she said. I said again I thought it was hopeless and no good going on, and she agreed, without opening her eyes. *(Pause.)* I asked her to look at me and after a few moments — *(pause)* — after a few moments she did, but the eyes just slits, because of the glare. I bent over her to get them in the shadow and they opened. *(Pause. Low.)* Let me in. *(Pause.)* We drifted in among the flags and stuck. The way they went down, sighing, before the stem! *(Pause.)* I lay down across her with my face in her breasts and my hand on her. We lay there without moving. But under us all moved, and moved us, gently, up and down, and from side to side.

Pause.

Past midnight. Never knew—

Krapp switches off, broods. Finally he fumbles in his pockets, encounters the banana, takes it out, peers at it, puts it back, fumbles, brings out the envelope, fumbles, puts back envelope, looks at his watch, gets up and goes backstage into darkness. Ten seconds. Sound of bottle against glass, then brief siphon. Ten seconds. Bottle against glass alone. Ten seconds. He comes back a little unsteadily into light, goes to front of table, takes out keys, raises them to his eyes, chooses key, unlocks first drawer, peers into it, feels about inside, takes out reel, peers at it, locks drawer, puts keys back in his pocket, goes and sits down, takes reel off machine, lays it on dictionary, loads virgin reel on machine, takes envelope from his pocket, consults back of it, lays it on table, switches on, clears his throat, and begins to record.

Krapp: Just been listening to that stupid bastard I took myself for thirty years ago, hard to believe I was ever as bad as that. Thank God that's all done with anyway. *(Pause.)* The eyes she had! *(Broods, realizes he is recording silence, switches off, broods. Finally.)* Everything there, everything, all the—*(Realizes this is not being recorded, switches on.)* Everything there, everything on this old muckball, all the light and dark and famine and feasting of . . . *(hesitates)* . . . the ages! *(In a shout.)* Yes! *(Pause.)* Let that go! Jesus! Take his mind off his homework! Jesus! *(Pause. Weary.)* Ah well, maybe he was right. *(Pause.)* Maybe he was right. *(Broods. Realizes. Switches off. Consults envelope.)* Pah! *(Crumples it and throws it away. Broods. Switches on.)* Nothing to say, not a squeak. What's a year now? The sour cud and the iron stool. *(Pause.)* Revelled in the word spool. *(With relish.)* Spoool! Happiest moment of the past half million. *(Pause.)* Seventeen copies sold, of which eleven at trade price to free circulating libraries beyond the seas. Getting known. *(Pause.)* One pound six and something, eight I have little doubt. *(Pause.)* Crawled out once or twice, before the summer was cold. Sat shivering in the park, drowned in dreams and burning to be gone. Not a soul. *(Pause.)* Last fancies. *(Vehemently.)* Keep 'em under! *(Pause.)* Scalded the eyes out of me reading *Effie* again, a page a day, with tears again. Effie . . . *(Pause.)* Could have been happy with her, up there on the Baltic, and the pines, and the dunes. *(Pause.)* Could I? *(Pause.)* And she? *(Pause.)* Pah! *(Pause.)* Fanny came in a couple of times. Bony old ghost of a whore. Couldn't do much, but I suppose better than a kick in the crutch. The last time wasn't so bad. How do you manage it, she said, at your age? I told her I'd been saving up for her all my life. *(Pause.)* Went to Vespers once, like when I was in short trousers. *(Pause. Sings.)*

Now the day is over,
Night is drawing nigh-igh,
Shadows—*(coughing, then almost inaudible)*—of the evening
Steal across the sky.

(Gasping.) Went to sleep and fell off the pew. *(Pause.)* Sometimes wondered in the night if a last effort mightn't—*(Pause.)* Ah finish your booze now and get to your bed. Go on with this drivel in the morning. Or leave it at that. *(Pause.)* Leave it at that. *(Pause.)* Lie propped up in the dark—and wander. Be again in the dingle on a Christmas Eve, gathering holly, the redberried. *(Pause.)* Be again on Croghan on a Sunday morning, in the haze, with the bitch, stop and listen to the bells. *(Pause.)* And so on. *(Pause.)* Be

again, be again. *(Pause.)* All that old misery. *(Pause.)* Once wasn't enough for you. *(Pause.)* Lie down across her.

Long pause. He suddenly bends over machine, switches off, wrenches off tape, throws it away, puts on the other, winds it forward to the passage he wants, switches on, listens staring front.

Tape: — gooseberries, she said. I said again I thought it was hopeless and no good going on, and she agreed, without opening her eyes. *(Pause.)* I asked her to look at me and after a few moments — *(pause)* — after a few moments she did, but the eyes just slits, because of the glare. I bent over her to get them in the shadow and they opened. *(Pause. Low.)* Let me in. *(Pause.)* We drifted in among the flags and stuck. The way they went down, sighing, before the stem! *(Pause.)* I lay down across her with my face in her breasts and my hand on her. We lay there without moving. But under us all moved, and moved us, gently, up and down, and from side to side.

Pause. Krapp's lips move. No sound.

Past midnight. Never knew such silence. The earth might be uninhabited.

Pause.

Here I end this reel. Box — *(pause)* — three, spool — *(pause)* — five. *(Pause.)* Perhaps my best years are gone. When there was a chance of happiness. But I wouldn't want them back. Not with the fire in me now. No, I wouldn't want them back.

Krapp motionless staring before him. The tape runs on in silence.

Curtain

CONSIDERATIONS FOR CRITICAL THINKING AND WRITING

1. FIRST RESPONSE. Why do you think the play is set in "a late evening in the future" rather than the present?

2. What does Krapp's physical description reveal about him?

3. Why does Krapp make tape recordings? How does he use them?

4. What is the effect of the many pauses in the play?

5. What are Krapp's attitudes toward his earlier perceptions about life? Compare and contrast the sixty-nine-year-old Krapp with the thirty-nine-year-old on the tape.

6. What career hopes did the younger Krapp have? How do you know whether he was successful?

7. How does Krapp, in retrospect, seem to feel about his life?

8. Although Krapp is obviously not a conventional dramatic hero, is there anything heroic about what he says or does? How do you respond to him?

9. What do you make of the play's title? A student once suggested that if the play were to have a subtitle, Beckett could have used the heading of one of Krapp's ledger entries: "Farewell to love." Explain whether this proposed subtitle reflects the play's major concerns.

10. Do you think the sixty-nine-year-old Krapp changes or develops during the play? In the final scene, how does he act differently from the way he behaved in the opening scene?

CONNECTIONS TO OTHER SELECTIONS

1. Write an essay in which you explore some important similarities or differences between Krapp and Willy Loman in Arthur Miller's *Death of a Salesman* (p. 1795) or the narrator in Robert Frost's "The Road Not Taken" (p. 976).

2. Compare and contrast the use of tape recorders in *Krapp's Last Tape* and David Henry Hwang's *M. Butterfly* (p. 1675). Do you think the tape recorders heighten or lessen the dramatic effects of each play?

PERSPECTIVE

MARTIN ESSLIN (B. 1918)

On the Theater of the Absurd   1961

Concerned as it is with the ultimate realities of the human condition, the relatively few fundamental problems of life and death, isolation and communication, the Theater of the Absurd, however grotesque, frivolous, and irreverent it may appear, represents a return to the original, religious function of the theater — the confrontation of man with the spheres of myth and religious reality. Like ancient Greek tragedy and the medieval mystery plays and baroque allegories, the Theater of the Absurd is intent on making its audience aware of man's precarious and mysterious position in the universe.

The difference is merely that in ancient Greek tragedy — and comedy — as well as in the medieval mystery play and the baroque *auto sacramental,* the ultimate realities concerned were generally known and universally accepted metaphysical systems, while the Theater of the Absurd expresses the absence of any such generally accepted cosmic system of values. Hence, much more modestly, the Theater of the Absurd makes no pretense at explaining the ways of God to man. It can merely present, in anxiety or with derision, an individual human being's intuition of the ultimate realities as he experiences them; the fruits of one man's descent into the depths of his personality, his dreams, fantasies, and nightmares.

While former attempts at confronting man with the ultimate realities of his condition projected a coherent and generally recognized version of the truth, the Theater of the Absurd merely communicates one poet's most intimate and personal intuition of the human situation, his own *sense of being,* his individual vision of the world. This is the *subject matter* of the Theater of the Absurd, and it determines its *form,* which must, of necessity, represent a convention of the stage basically different from the "realistic" theater of our time.

As the Theater of the Absurd is not concerned with conveying information or presenting the problems or destinies of characters that exist outside the author's inner world, as it does not expound a thesis or debate ideological propositions, it is not concerned with the representation of events, the narration of the fate or the adventures of characters, but instead with the presentation of one individual's basic situation. It is a theater of situation as against a theater of events in sequence, and therefore it uses a language based on patterns of concrete images rather than argument and discursive speech. And since it is trying to present a sense of being, it can neither investigate nor solve problems of conduct or morals.

From *The Theatre of the Absurd*

CONSIDERATIONS FOR CRITICAL THINKING AND WRITING

1. What does Esslin see as the essential difference between the theater of the absurd and Greek or medieval theaters in terms of their treatment of "ultimate realities" (para. 1)?

2. To what extent does Esslin's description of the theater of the absurd apply to *Krapp's Last Tape*?

3. Here's one to stretch your imagination: Take Krapp's "situation" and write a summary of how you think Sophocles, Shakespeare, or Ibsen might have developed it into a play. Consider, for example, what the focus of the conflict would be and how the story would end.

Rodeo

Jane Martin is a pseudonym. The author's identity is known only to a handful of administrators at the Actors Theatre of Louisville who handle permissions for productions and reprints of the play. *Rodeo* is one of eleven monologues in *Talking With.* . . . Martin has also published other plays including *Coup/Clucks* (1982), *What Mama Don't Know* (1988), and *Cementville* (1991).

Although only one character appears in *Rodeo,* the monologue is surprisingly moving as she describes what the rodeo once was, how it has changed, and what it means to her. At first glance the subject matter may not seem very promising for drama, but the character's energy, forthrightness, and colorful language transform seemingly trivial details into significant meanings.

JANE MARTIN
Rodeo   *1981*

A young woman in her late twenties sits working on a piece of tack. Beside her is a Lone Star beer in the can. As the lights come up we hear the last verse of a Tanya Tucker song or some other female country-western vocalist. She is wearing old worn jeans and boots plus a long-sleeved workshirt with the sleeves rolled up. She works until the song is over and then speaks.

Big Eight: Shoot — Rodeo's just goin' to hell in a handbasket. Rodeo used to be somethin'. I loved it. I did. Once Daddy an' a bunch of 'em was foolin' around with some old bronc over to our place and this ol' red nose named

Cinch got bucked off and my Daddy hooted and said he had him a nine-year-old girl, namely me, wouldn't have no damn trouble cowboyin' that horse. Well, he put me on up there, stuck that ridin' rein in my hand, gimme a kiss, and said, "Now there's only one thing t' remember Honey Love, if ya fall off you jest don't come home." Well I stayed up. You gotta stay on a bronc eight seconds. Otherwise the ride don't count. So from that day on my daddy called me Big Eight. Heck! That's all the name I got anymore . . . Big Eight.

Used to be fer cowboys, the rodeo did. Do it in some open field, folks would pull their cars and pick-ups round it, sit on the hoods, some ranch hand'd bulldog him some rank steer and everybody'd wave their hats and call him by name. Ride us some buckin' stock, rope a few calves, git throwed off a bull, and then we'd jest git us to a bar and tell each other lies about how good we were.

Used to be a family thing. Wooly Billy Tilson and Tammy Lee had them five kids on the circuit. Three boys, two girls and Wooly and Tammy. Wasn't no two-beer rodeo in Oklahoma didn't have a Tilson entered. Used to call the oldest girl Tits. Tits Tilson. Never seen a girl that top-heavy could ride so well. Said she only fell off when the gravity got her. Cowboys used to say if she landed face down you could plant two young trees in the holes she'd leave. Ha! Tits Tilson.

Used to be people came to a rodeo had a horse of their own back home. Farm people, ranch people—lord, they *knew* what they were lookin' at. Knew a good ride from a bad ride, knew hard from easy. You broke some bones er spent the day eatin' dirt, at least ya got appreciated.

Now they bought the rodeo. Them. Coca-Cola, Pepsi Cola, Marlboro damn cigarettes. You know the ones I mean. Them. Hire some New York faggot t' sit on some ol' stuffed horse in front of a sagebrush photo n' smoke that junk. Hell, tobacco wasn't made to smoke, honey, it was made to chew. Lord wanted ya filled up with smoke he would've set ya on fire. Damn it gets me!

There's some guy in a banker's suit runs the rodeo now. Got him a pinky ring and a digital watch, honey. Told us we oughta have a watchamacallit, choriographus or somethin', some ol' ballbuster used to be with the Ice damn Capades. Wants us to ride around dressed up like Mickey Mouse, Pluto, crap like that. Told me I had to haul my butt through the barrel race done up like Minnie damn Mouse in a tu-tu. Huh uh, honey! Them people is so screwed-up they probably eat what they run over in the road.

Listen, they got the clowns wearin' Astronaut suits! I ain't lyin'. You know what a rodeo clown does! You go down, fall off whatever—the clown runs in front of the bull so's ya don't git stomped. Pin-stripes, he got 'em in space suits tellin' jokes on a microphone. First horse see 'em, done up like the Star Wars went crazy. Best buckin' horse on the circuit, name of Piss 'N' Vinegar, took one look at them clowns, had him a heart attack and died. Cowboy was ridin' him got hisself squashed. Twelve hundred pounds of coronary arrest jes fell right through 'em. Blam! Vio con dios. Crowd thought that was funnier than the astronauts. I swear it won't be long before they're strappin' ice-skates on the ponies. Big crowds now.

Ain't hardly no ranch people, no farm people, nobody I know. Buncha disco babies and dee-vorce lawyers—designer jeans and day-glo Stetsons. Hell, the whole bunch of 'em wears French perfume. Oh it smells like money now! Got it on the cable T and V—hey, you know what, when ya rodeo yer just bound to kick yerself up some dust—well now, seems like that fogs up the ol' TV camera, so they told us a while back that from now on we was gonna ride on some new stuff called Astro-dirt. Dust free. Artificial damn dirt, honey. Lord have mercy.

Banker Suit called me in the other day said "Lurlene . . ." "Hold it," I said, "Who's this Lurlene? Round here they call me Big Eight." "Well, Big Eight," he said, "My name's Wallace." "Well that's a real surprise t' me," I said, "Cause aroun' here everybody jes calls you Dumb-ass." My, he laughed real big, slapped his big ol' desk, an' then he said I wasn't suitable for the rodeo no more. Said they was lookin' fer another type, somethin' a little more in the showgirl line, like the Dallas Cowgirls maybe. Said the ridin' and ropin' wasn't the thing no more. Talked on about floats, costumes, dancin' choreog-aphy. If I was a man I woulda pissed on his shoe. Said he'd give me a lifetime pass though. Said I could come to his rodeo any time I wanted.

Rodeo used to be people ridin' horses for the pleasure of people who rode horses—made you feel good about what you could do. Rodeo wasn't worth no money to nobody. Money didn't have nothing to do with it! Used to be seven Tilsons riding in the rodeo. Wouldn't none of 'em dress up like Donald damn Duck so they quit. That there's the law of gravity!

There's a bunch of assholes in this country sneak around until they see ya havin' fun and then they buy the fun and start in sellin' it. See, they figure if ya love it, they can sell it. Well you look out, honey! They want to make them a dollar out of what you love. Dress *you* up like Minnie Mouse. Sell your rodeo. Turn *yer* pleasure into Ice damn Capades. You hear what I'm sayin'? You're jus' merchandise to them, sweetie. You're jus' merchandise to them.

Blackout.

CONSIDERATIONS FOR CRITICAL THINKING AND WRITING

1. FIRST RESPONSE. Big Eight is presented as an old-fashioned rodeo type. What associations or stereotypes do you have about such people? What assumptions do you make about them? How does the author use those expectations to heighten your understanding of Big Eight's character?

2. How has the rodeo changed from how it "used to be"? How do you account for those changes?

3. Comment on Big Eight's use of language. Why is it appropriate for her character?

4. How would you describe Big Eight's brand of humor? How does it affect your understanding of her?

5. How do your feelings about Big Eight develop during the course of the monologue?

6. What does the rodeo mean to Big Eight?

CONNECTIONS TO OTHER SELECTIONS

1. Compare and contrast a Shakespeare monologue from either *Hamlet* (p. 1383) or *A Midsummer Night's Dream* (p. 1327) with the style and content of *Rodeo*.

2. In an essay discuss the nostalgic tone in *Rodeo* and Stephen Crane's short story "The Bride Comes to Yellow Sky" (p. 250). In your response consider each work's treatment of the West.

3. Compare the attitudes expressed about merchandising in *Rodeo* with those expressed in Arthur Miller's *Death of a Salesman* (p. 1795).

From Twilight: Los Angeles, 1992

Born in Baltimore in 1950, Anna Deavere Smith is a playwright, actor, and performance artist who teaches drama at Stanford University. Her one-woman play *Fires in the Mirror: Crown Heights, Brooklyn, and Other Identities* (1992) won an Obie Award and is part of an ongoing series titled *On the Road: A Search for American Character.* This series also includes *Twilight: Los Angeles, 1992,* which was published in 1994. Both works are based on interviews Smith conducted that she developed into scripts, using the interviewees' own words, and subsequently performed. Smith has described *Twilight* as "the product of [her] search for the character of Los Angeles in the wake of the Rodney King verdict." In this infamous case, four Los Angeles Police Department officers were found not guilty of beating King, though one count of excessive force was successfully prosecuted against one officer. Because the beating had been captured on videotape and broadcast repeatedly on nationally televised programs, the case became a lightning rod for racial issues in the United States.

On April 29, 1992, the same day the verdict was televised live, violence erupted in central Los Angeles, where fires raged over a twenty-five-block area. The next day looting and fires spread to South Los Angeles, Koreatown, Hollywood, Beverly Hills, and other locations. By May 3, there were reports of 58 deaths, nearly 2,400 injuries, more than 12,000 arrests, and around 3,000 damaged businesses. In the published version of *Twilight,* Smith includes some fifty voices of people with varying backgrounds and racial identities. These multiethnic voices speak from many points of view, including those of a policeman, a citizen's group activist, a member of a defense committee, a merchant, a reporter, a student, and an artist.

The many voices that appear in *Twilight* represent Smith's effort to have us hear the complexity and the many identities that inform discussions about race in the United States. In her introduction to *Twilight,* she points out that "few people speak of a language about race that is not their own. If more of us could actually speak from another point of view, like speaking another language, we could accelerate the flow of ideas." Here are four of the voices she includes in *Twilight.*

ANNA DEAVERE SMITH (B. 1950)

From Twilight: Los Angeles, 1992   *1994*

WHEN I FINALLY GOT MY VISION / NIGHTCLOTHES

Michael Zinzun, representative, Coalition Against Police Abuse

> *In his office at Coalition Against Police Abuse. There are very bloody and disturbing photographs of victims of police abuse. The most disturbing one was a man with part of his skull blown off and part of his body in the chest area blown off, so that you can see the organs. There is a large white banner with a black circle and a panther. The black panther is the image from the Black Panther Party. Above the circle is "All Power to the People." At the bottom is "Support Our Youth, Support the Truce."*

I witnessed police abuse.
It was
about one o'clock in the morning
and, um, I was asleep,
like
so many of the other neighbors,
and I hear this guy calling out for help.
So myself and other people came out in socks
and gowns
and, you know,
nightclothes
and we came out so quickly we saw the police had this brother
handcuffed
and they was beatin' the shit out of him!
You see,
Eugene Rivers was his name
and, uh,
we had our community center here
and they was doin' it right across the street from it.
So I went out there 'long with other people and we demanded they stop.
They tried to hide him by draggin' him away and we followed him
and told him they gonna stop.
They singled me out.
They began Macing the crowd, sayin' it was hostile.
They began
shootin' the Mace to get everybody back.
They singled me out.
I was handcuffed.
Um,
when I got Maced I moved back
but as I was goin' back I didn't go back to the center,
I ended up goin' around this . . .

it was a darkened
unlit area.
And when I finally got my vision
I said I ain't goin' this way with them police behind me,
so I turned back around, and when I did,
they Maced me again
and I went down on one knee
and all I could do was feel all these police stompin' on my back.

(He is smiling.)

And I was thinkin . . . I said
why, sure am glad they got them soft walkin' shoes on,
because when the patrolmen, you know, they have them
cushions,
so every stomp,
it wasn't a direct hard old . . .
yeah
type thing.
So
then they handcuffed me.
I said they . . .
well,
I can take this,
we'll deal with this tamarr° [sic],
and they handcuffed me.
And then one of them lifted my
head up —
I was on my stomach —
he lifted me from behind
and hit me with a billy club
and struck me in the
side of the head,
which give me about forty stitches —
the straight billy club,
it wasn't a
P-28, the one with the side handle.
Now, I thought in my mind, said hunh,
they couldn't even knock me out,
they in trouble now.
You see what I'm sayin'?
'Cause I knew what we were gonna do,
'cause I dealt with police abuse
and I knew how to organize.
I say they couldn't even knock me out,
and so as I was layin' there
they was all standin' around me.
They still was Macing, the crowd was gettin' larger and larger and
larger
and more police was comin'.
One these pigs stepped outta the crowd with his flashlight,

tamarr: Tomorrow.

caught me right in my eye,
and you can still see the stitches *(he lowers his lid and shows it)*
and
exploded the optic nerve to the brain,
ya see,
and boom *(he snaps his fingers)*
that was it.
I couldn't see no more since then.
I mean, they . . .
they took me to the hospital
and the doctor said, "Well, we can sew this eyelid up and these
stitches here
but
I don't think we can do nothin' for that eye."
So when I got out I got a CAT scan,
you know,
and
they said,
"It's gone."
So I still didn't understand but I said
well,
I'm just gonna keep strugglin'.
We mobilized
to the point where we were able
to get two officers fired,
two officers had to go to trial,
and
the city on an eye
had to cough up one point two million dollars
and so
that's why
I am able to be here every day,
because that money's bein' used to further the struggle.
I ain't got no big Cadillac,
I ain't got no gold . . .
I ain't got no
expensive shoes or clothes.
What we do have
is an opportunity to keep struggling and to do research and to
organize.

THEY

Jason Sanford, actor

> *A rainstorm in February 1993. Saturday afternoon. We are in an office at the Mark Taper Forum. Lamplight. A handsome white man in his late twenties wearing blue jeans and a plaid shirt and Timberland boots. He played tennis in competition for years and looks like a tennis player.*

Who's they?
That's interesting.
'cause the they is
a combination of a lot of things.
Being brought up in Santa Barbara,
it's a little bit different saying "they" than being brought up in,
um,
LA,
I think,
'cause
being brought up in Santa Barbara
you don't see a lot of blacks.
You see Mexicans,
you see some Chinese,
but you don't see blacks.
There was maybe two black people in my school.
I don't know, you don't say
black
or you don't say
Negro
or,
no,
yeah,
you really don't.
I work with one.
Um,
because
of what I look like
I don't know if I'd been beaten.
I sure the hell would have been arrested
and pushed down on the ground.
I don't think it would have gone as far.
It wouldn't have.
Even the times that I have been arrested
they always make comments
about God, you look like Mr.,
uh,
all-American white boy.
That has actually been said to me
by a . . . by a
cop.
Ya know,
"Why do you have so many warrants?"
Ya know . . .
"Shouldn't you be takin' care of this?"
Ya know . . .
"You look like an all-American white boy.
You look responsible."
And
I remember being arrested in Santa Barbara one time

and
driving back
in the cop car
and having a conversation about tennis
with the cops.
So,
ah,
I'm sure I'm seen by the police totally different
than a black man.

NATIONAL GUARD

Julio Menjivar, lumber salesman and driver

> *Near South Central, beautiful birds, traffic, hammering. In a kind of patio outside*
> *the backyard. A covered patio. Saturday morning. Very sunny. We sit on a bench.*
> *His BMW in the background. A man from El Salvador, in his late twenties. Later*
> *his mother and grandmother come to be photographed with him.*

And then,
a police passed by
and said,
that's fine,
that's fine
that you're doing that.
Anyway,
it's your neighborhood.
They were just like laughing or I don't know—
LAPD.
Black and white.
They just passed by and said it
in the radio:
Go for it.
Go for it,
it's your neighborhood.
I was only standing there
watching what was
happening.
And then
suddenly
jeeps came
from everywhere,
from all directions,
to the intersection.
Trucks
and
the National Guard.
And they threw all of
the people on the ground.
They threw

everybody down
and I was
in the middle of
a group.
They lifted me by my
arm like this.
First he told me to get up.
He said ugly things to me.
And as you see,
I'm a little fat,
so I couldn't get up.
They called me stupid.
He said, said,
many ugly things.
He said,
"Get up motherfucker, get up. Get up!"
Then he kicked me in the back.
He said,
"Come on, fat fucker,
get up."
Then I heard my wife
and my father
calling my name,
"Julio, Julio, Julio."
And then
my mother
and my sister and my wife,
they tried to go to the corner
and my mother
They almost shoot
them, almost shot them.
They were
pissed off,
too angry.
The National Guard.
They almost shot
my mom,
my wife,
and my sister
for try . . .
They will ask everybody questions
and the other guys don't know how to speak English.
Then the police don't like that.
So slap 'em in the face —
that guy got slapped three times.
An RTD bus came
and parked here
in the street,
and they put all of

us on it.
They took us to a station,
Southwest.
Young people
that got arrested.
Uh,
there was this guy crying and this other guy crying
because too tight,
too tight
the handcuffs.
And I felt very bad,
very bad.
Never never
in my life have I
been arrested.
Never
in my life.
Not in El Salvador.
This is the first time
I been in jail.
I was real scared,
yeah, yeah.
'Cause you got all these criminals
over there.
I'm not a criminal.
It's a lot of crazy people out there,
too many.
So I sit down.
So I barely close my eyes
and they went back —
pow pow pow pow pow
come on come on get up get up
come on get up,
and they had us
on our knees
for two hours.
I was praying,
yeah,
I was praying, yeah.
Yeah, that's true
I was praying.
I was thinking of all the
bad that could happen.
Yeah.
Now I have a record.
Aha, and a two-hundred-fifty-dollar
fine
and probation for
three years.

SWALLOWING THE BITTERNESS

Mrs. Young-Soon Han, former liquor store owner

A house on Sycamore Street in Los Angeles just south of Beverly. A tree-lined street. A quiet street. It's in an area where many Hasidic Jews live as well as yuppie types. Mrs. Young-Soon Han's living room is impeccable. Dark pink-and-apricot rug and sofa and chairs. The sofa and chairs are made of a velour. On the back of the sofa and chairs is a Korean design. A kind of circle with lines in it, a geometric design. There is a glass coffee table in front of the sofa. There is nothing on the coffee table. There is a mantel with a bookcase, and a lot of books. The mantel has about thirty trophies. These are her nephew's. They may be for soccer. On the wall behind the sofa area, a series of citations and awards. These are her ex-husband's. They are civic awards. There are a couple of pictures of her husband shaking hands with official-looking people and accepting awards. In this area is also a large painting of Jesus Christ. There is another religious painting over the archway to the dining room. There are some objects hanging on the side of the archway. Long strips and oval shapes. It is very quiet. When we first came in, the television was on, but she turned it off.

She is sitting on the floor and leaning on the coffee table. When she hits her hand on the table, it sounds very much like a drum. I am accompanied by two Korean American graduate students from UCLA.

Until last year
I believed America is the best.
I still believe it.
I don't deny that now
because I'm a victim,
but
as
the year ends in '92
and we were still in turmoil
and having all the financial problems
and mental problems.
Then a couple months ago
I really realized that
Korean immigrants were left out
from this
society and we were nothing.
What is our right?
Is it because we are Korean?
Is it because we have no politicians?
Is it because we don't
speak good English?
Why?
Why do we have to be left out?

    (She is hitting her hand on the coffee table.)

We are not qualified to have medical treatment.
We are not qualified to get, uh,
food stamp

(she hits the table once),
not GR
(hits the table once).
no welfare
(hits the table once).
Anything.
Many Afro-Americans
(two quick hits)
who never worked
(one hit),
they get
at least minimum amount
(one hit),
of money
(one hit)
to survive
(one hit).
We don't get any!
(Large hit with full hand spread.)
Because we have a car
(one hit)
and we have a house.
(Pause six seconds.)
And we are high taxpayers.
(One hit.)
(Pause fourteen seconds.)
Where do I finda [sic] justice?
Okay, Black people
probably
believe they won
by the trial?°
Even some complains only half right?
justice was there.
But I watched the television
that Sunday morning,
early morning as they started.
I started watch it all day.
They were having party and then they celebrated,

In April 1993, a federal court trial, launched after the 1992 state court acquittals, resulted in the conviction of two Los Angeles police officers for violating King's civil rights.

all of South-Central
all the churches.
They finally found that justice exists
in this society.
Then where is the victims' rights?
They got their rights.
By destroying innocent Korean merchants . . .
They have a lot of respect,
as I do,
for
Dr. Martin King?
He is the only model for Black community.
I don't care Jesse Jackson.
But
he was the model
of nonviolence.
Nonviolence?
They like to have hiseh [sic] spirits.
What about last year?
They destroyed innocent people.

    (Five-second pause.)

And I wonder if that is really justice

    (and a very soft "uh" after "justice," like "justicah," but very quick)

to get their rights
in this way.

    (Thirteen-second pause.)

I waseh swallowing the bitternesseh,
sitting here alone
and watching them.
They became all hilarious

    (three-second pause)

and, uh,
in a way I was happy for them
and I felt glad for them.
At leasteh they got something back, you know.
Just let's forget Korean victims or other victims
who are destroyed by them.
They have fought
for their rights

    (one hit simultaneous with the word "rights")

over two centuries

    (one hit simultaneous with "centuries")

and I have a lot of sympathy and understanding for them.
Because of their effort and sacrificing,
other minorities, like Hispanic
or Asians,
maybe we have to suffer more

by mainstream.
You know,
that's why I understand,
and then
I like to be part of their
'joyment.
But . . .
That's why I had mixed feeling
as soon as I heard the verdict.
I wish I could
live together
with eh Blacks,
but after the riots
there were too much differences.
The fire is still there —
how do you call it? —
igni . . .
igniting fire.

(She says a Korean phrase phonetically: "Dashi yun gi ga nuh.")

It's still dere.
It canuh
burst out anytime.

CONSIDERATIONS FOR CRITICAL THINKING AND WRITING

1. FIRST RESPONSE. How does Smith's arrangement of her interviewees' words on the page affect your reading of what they have to say? Choose one character to illustrate your response.

2. How might Michael Zinzun's story be regarded as a kind of play in miniature? Consider the setting, conflict, plot, climax, resolution, and conclusion, as well as the protagonist and antagonist.

3. What does Jason Sanford's account of his encounters with the police reveal about race relations?

4. Compare and contrast Julio Menjivar's experience with the police with Michael Zinzun's.

5. Why is Mrs. Young-Soon Han bitter about her life in the United States? Describe how her mood changes over the course of her interview. Why do you think Smith included the pauses in the interview?

6. Write a dialogue between any two of the characters on a topic you think would be important to them.

CONNECTIONS TO OTHER SELECTIONS

1. Compare and contrast one of Smith's monologues with the style and content of Jane Martin's *Rodeo* (p. 1657).

2. In an essay discuss the attitudes toward race expressed in Smith's monologues with those expressed in Lorraine Hansberry's *A Raisin in the Sun* (p. 1730).

3. Discuss the significance of violence and its relation to the themes in the *Twilight* monologues and Shakespeare's *Hamlet* (p. 1383).

35

Cultural Case Study: David Henry Hwang's *M. Butterfly*

Formalist readings of plays examine how various elements — such as setting, exposition, dialogue, characterization, conflict, subplot, climax, resolution, and other literary techniques — create patterns that contribute to the play's meanings or themes. This kind of close reading emphasizes the intrinsic elements of a work to describe and appreciate how it is artistically unified. Rather than taking the social, political, and economic contexts of a play into account, formalist critics focus on how literary elements within the play interact to produce a coherent and carefully made work of art. A formalist, for example, might approach Susan Glaspell's *Trifles* (p. 1172) by discussing how its opening setting establishes the play's tone. More than a whodunit, *Trifles* examines the nature of Mrs. Wright's married life rather than her guilt or innocence concerning the death of her husband. In the opening scene, the stage directions make clear the stark, gloomy kitchen that evokes the hard life Mr. Wright imposed on his wife. Through this cold environment, the Wrights' difficult relationship is subtly recapitulated by the dark, disordered setting. A formalist's analysis would be concerned with how the setting frames the theme rather than with the actual conditions of living on a midwestern farm in the early twentieth century. Recently, however, there has been an increased interest among literary critics in the historical and cultural contexts of texts.

Like literary historians, cultural critics examine the historical circumstances relevant to a work, but they do not emphasize only major events or famous historical figures. A literary historian would be intrigued by the fact that Glaspell's *Trifles* was written to complete a theater bill that featured several one-act plays by Eugene O'Neill produced by the Provincetown Players on Cape Cod, Massachusetts, in 1916. Glaspell's relationship to O'Neill, generally regarded as one of America's greatest dramatists, certainly would not escape the interest of a cultural critic, but such a critic might find even more revealing Glaspell's experiences as a newspaper reporter covering a murder trial in Iowa. She recalls that she "never forgot going to the kitchen of a woman who had been locked up [for murder] in town." The interests of cultural critics embrace popular culture as well as "high culture." A cultural critic is likely to find more relevant to *Trifles* the Federal Farm Loan Bank Act passed in 1916 than O'Neill's *Bound East for Cardiff*, one of the 1916 one-act plays written for the Provincetown Players.

The documents that follow Hwang's *M. Butterfly* in this chapter suggest how cultural criticism can be used to ask new questions of a literary work. They include a plot synopsis of Giacomo Puccini's opera *Madame Butterfly*, the newspaper source for *M. Butterfly*, a photograph of Shi Pei Pu (model for Hwang's Song Liling) dressed in the costume of a Chinese opera star, a review of a performance of *M. Butterfly*, and an interview with Hwang. These documents provide a glimpse of some approaches that a cultural critic might use to contextualize *M. Butterfly* historically in order to offer a wider and deeper understanding of the play.

DAVID HENRY HWANG
(B. 1957)

Born in Los Angeles, David Henry Hwang is the son of immigrant Chinese American parents; his father worked as a banker, and his mother was a professor of piano. Educated at Stanford University, from which he earned his B.A. in English in 1979, he became interested in theater after attending plays at the American Conservatory in San Francisco. His marginal interest in a law career quickly gave way to his involvement in the engaging world of live theater. By his senior year, he had written and produced his first play, *FOB* (an acronym for "fresh off the boat"), which marked the beginning of a meteoric rise as a playwright. After a brief stint as a writing teacher at a Menlo Park high school, Hwang attended the Yale University School of Drama from 1980 to 1981. Although he didn't stay to complete a degree, he studied theater history before leaving for New York City, where he thought the professional theater would provide a richer education than the student workshops at Yale.

In New York Hwang's work received a warm reception. In 1980 an off-Broadway production of *FOB* won an Obie Award for the best new play of the season. The play incorporates many of Hwang's characteristic concerns as a playwright. Growing up in California as a Chinese American made him politically conscious during his college years in the late 1970s;

this interest in his Chinese roots is evident in the central conflicts of *FOB*, which focuses on a Chinese immigrant's relationship with two Chinese American students he meets in Los Angeles. The immigrant quickly learns that he is expected to abandon much of his Chinese identity if he is to fit into mainstream American culture. The issues that arise between East and West are played out with comic effect in a Western theater but enriched and complicated by Hwang's innovative use of a Chinese theatrical tradition that portrays major characters as figures from Chinese mythology.

Chinese American life is also the focus of *The Dance and the Railroad* and *Family Devotions,* both produced off-Broadway in 1981. *The Dance and the Railroad,* set in the nineteenth century, focuses on two immigrant Chinese men working on the transcontinental railroad and attempting to sort out their pasts while confronting new identities and uncertain futures in America. Hwang mirrors the characters' conflicts in the play's form by creating a mixture of Eastern and Western theater and incorporating the nonrealistic modes of Chinese opera. *Family Devotions* examines an established affluent Chinese American family in the twentieth century through the lens of a television sitcom. The problems faced by immigrants living hyphenated lives are comically played out through the interaction of a visiting Communist uncle from China and his great-nephew, who struggles to find an authentic identity amid his family's materialism and Christianity. Hwang's early plays are populated with Chinese Americans attempting to find the center of their own lives as they seesaw between the conventions, traditions, and values of East and West.

Hwang's next two dramas, produced in 1983, consist of two one-act plays set in Japan. Together they are titled *Sound and Beauty,* but each has its own title — *The House of Sleeping Beauties* and *The Sound of a Voice.* In these plays Hwang moves away from tales of Chinese American immigrants and themes of race and assimilation to stories about tragic love based on Japanese materials. Although Hwang was successful in having additional plays produced in the mid-1980s and won prestigious fellowships from the Guggenheim Foundation and the National Endowment for the Arts, it was not until 1988, when *M. Butterfly* was produced on Broadway, that he achieved astonishing commercial success as well as widespread acclaim. His awards for this play include the Outer Critics Circle Award for best Broadway play, the Drama Desk Award for best new play, the John Gassner Award for best American play, and the Tony Award for best play of the year. By the end of 1988, Hwang was regarded by many critics as the most talented young playwright in the United States, and since then *M. Butterfly* has been staged in theaters around the world.

According to Hwang, *M. Butterfly* was inspired by newspaper accounts of an espionage trial. In his "Playwright's Notes" he cites an excerpt from the *New York Times* for May 11, 1986 (see p. 1723 for the entire news report). Hwang takes this fascinating true story of espionage and astonishing sexual misidentification and transforms it into a complex treatment of social, political, racial, cultural, and sexual issues that has dazzled both audiences and readers with its remarkable eroticism, insights, and beauty.

CHRONOLOGY

1957 Born on August 11 in Los Angeles, California.

1975–1979 Attends Stanford University, graduates with a B.A. in English.

1978 First play, *FOB*, produced at Stanford.

1979 Teaches at a high school in Menlo Park, California.

1980–81 Attends Yale University School of Drama.

1980 Wins Obie Award for *FOB*.

1981 *The Dance and the Railroad* and *Family Devotions* produced in New York City.

1983 *The House of Sleeping Beauties* and *The Sound of a Voice* produced off-Broadway; publishes *Broken Promises: Four Plays*; awarded Rockefeller Fellowship.

1984 Awarded a Guggenheim Fellowship.

1985 Awarded a National Endowment for the Arts Fellowship.

1986 *Rich Relations* produced off-Broadway; *As the Crow Flies* produced in Los Angeles.

1987 *My American Son*, a television drama, airs on Home Box Office.

1988 *M. Butterfly* produced on Broadway and wins the Outer Critics Circle Award, Drama Desk Award, John Gassner Award, and Tony Award; establishes the American Playwrights Project; *1000 Airplanes on the Roof* produced in Vienna, Austria.

1989 Publishes *1000 Airplanes on the Roof*.

1990 Publishes *FOB and Other Plays*.

1991 *Bondage* produced.

1992 *Face Value* and *The Voyage* (libretto for opera) produced.

1997 *Seven Years in Tibet* (screenplay for film).

DAVID HENRY HWANG (B. 1957)

M. Butterfly   1988

THE CHARACTERS

Rene Gallimard
Song Liling
Marc/Man No. 2/Consul Sharpless
Renee/Woman at Party/Pinup Girl
Comrade Chin/Suzuki/Shu-Fang
Helga
Toulon/Man No. 1/Judge
Dancers

TIME AND PLACE

*The action of the play takes place in a Paris prison in the present, and, in recall,
during the decade 1960–1970 in Beijing, and from 1966 to the present in Paris.*

PLAYWRIGHT'S NOTES

*A former French diplomat and a Chinese opera singer have been sentenced to six
years in jail for spying for China after a two-day trial that traced a story of clandestine love and mistaken sexual identity. . . .*

> *Mr. Boursicot was accused of passing information to China after he fell in love
with Mr. Shi, whom he believed for twenty years to be a woman.*

— The New York Times, *May 11, 1986*

*This play was suggested by international newspaper accounts of a recent espionage
trial. For purposes of dramatization, names have been changed, characters created,
and incidents devised or altered, and this play does not purport to be a factual
record of real events or real people.*

> *I could escape this feeling
> With my China girl . . .*
> *—David Bowie & Iggy Pop*

ACT I

SCENE I

M. Gallimard's prison cell. Paris. 1988.

> *Lights fade up to reveal Rene Gallimard, sixty-five, in a prison cell. He wears
a comfortable bathrobe and looks old and tired. The sparsely furnished cell contains a wooden crate, upon which sits a hot plate with a kettle and a portable tape
recorder. Gallimard sits on the crate staring at the recorder, a sad smile on his face.*

> *Upstage Song, who appears as a beautiful woman in traditional Chinese garb,
dances a traditional piece from the Peking Opera, surrounded by the percussive
clatter of Chinese music.*

> *Then, slowly, lights and sound cross-fade; the Chinese opera music dissolves
into a Western opera, the "Love Duet" from Puccini's* Madame Butterfly. *Song
continues dancing, now to the Western accompaniment. Though her movements
are the same, the difference in music now gives them a balletic quality.*

> *Gallimard rises, and turns upstage towards the figure of Song, who dances
without acknowledging him.*

Gallimard: Butterfly, Butterfly . . .

> *He forces himself to turn away, as the image of Song fades out, and talks to us.*

Gallimard: The limits of my cell are as such: four-and-a-half meters by five.
There's one window against the far wall; a door, very strong, to protect me
from autograph hounds. I'm responsible for the tape recorder, the hot
plate, and this charming coffee table.

When I want to eat, I'm marched off to the dining room — hot, steaming slop appears on my plate. When I want to sleep, the light bulb turns

itself off—the work of fairies. It's an enchanted space I occupy. The French—we know how to run a prison.

But, to be honest, I'm not treated like an ordinary prisoner. Why? Because I'm a celebrity. You see, I make people laugh.

I never dreamed this day would arrive. I've never been considered witty or clever. In fact, as a young boy, in an informal poll among my grammar school classmates, I was voted "least likely to be invited to a party." It's a title I managed to hold on to for many years. Despite some stiff competition.

But now, how the tables turn! Look at me: the life of every social function in Paris. Paris? Why be modest: My fame has spread to Amsterdam, London, New York. Listen to them! In the world's smartest parlors. I'm the one who lifts their spirits!

With a flourish, Gallimard directs our attention to another part of the stage.

SCENE II

A party. 1988.
Lights go up on a chic-looking parlor, where a well-dressed trio, two men and one woman, make conversation. Gallimard also remains lit; he observes them from his cell.

Woman: And what of Gallimard?
Man 1: Gallimard?
Man 2: Gallimard!
Gallimard (to us): You see? They're all determined to say my name, as if it were some new dance.
Woman: He still claims not to believe the truth.
Man 1: What? Still? Even since the trial?
Woman: Yes. Isn't it mad?
Man 2 (laughing): He says . . . it was dark . . . and she was very modest!

The trio break into laughter.

Man 1: So—what? He never touched her with his hands?
Man 2: Perhaps he did, and simply misidentified the equipment. A compelling case for sex education in the schools.
Woman: To protect the National Security—the Church can't argue with that.
Man 1: That's impossible! How could he not know?
Man 2: Simple ignorance.
Man 1: For twenty years?
Man 2: Time flies when you're being stupid.
Woman: Well, I thought the French were ladies' men.
Man 2: It seems Monsieur Gallimard was overly anxious to live up to his national reputation.
Woman: Well, he's not very good-looking.
Man 1: No, he's not.
Man 2: Certainly not.
Woman: Actually, I feel sorry for him.
Man 2: A toast! To Monsieur Gallimard!
Woman: Yes! To Gallimard!

Man 1: To Gallimard!

Man 2: Vive la différence!

They toast, laughing. Lights down on them.

Scene III

M. Gallimard's cell.

Gallimard (smiling): You see? They toast me. I've become a patron saint of the socially inept. Can they really be so foolish? Men like that — they should be scratching at my door, begging to learn my secrets! For I, Rene Gallimard, you see, I have known, and been loved by . . . the Perfect Woman.

Alone in this cell, I sit night after night, watching our story play through my head, always searching for a new ending, one which redeems my honor, where she returns at last to my arms. And I imagine you — my ideal audience — who come to understand and even, perhaps just a little, to envy me.

He turns on his tape recorder. Over the house speakers, we hear the opening phrases of Madame Butterfly.

Gallimard: In order for you to understand what I did and why, I must introduce you to my favorite opera: *Madame Butterfly.* By Giacomo Puccini. First produced at La Scala, Milan, in 1904, it is now beloved throughout the Western world.

As Gallimard describes the opera, the tape segues in and out to sections he may be describing.

Gallimard: And why not? Its heroine, Cio-Cio-San, also known as Butterfly, is a feminine ideal, beautiful and brave. And its hero, the man for whom she gives up everything, is — *(He pulls out a naval officer's cap from under his crate, pops it on his head, and struts about.)* — not very good-looking, not too bright, and pretty much a wimp: Benjamin Franklin Pinkerton of the U.S. Navy. As the curtain rises, he's just closed on two great bargains: one on a house, the other on a woman — call it a package deal.

Pinkerton purchased the rights to Butterfly for one hundred yen — in modern currency, equivalent to about . . . sixty-six cents. So, he's feeling pretty pleased with himself as Sharpless, the American consul, arrives to witness the marriage.

Marc, wearing an official cap to designate Sharpless, enters and plays the character.

Sharpless/Marc: Pinkerton!

Pinkerton/Gallimard: Sharpless! How's it hangin'? It's a great day, just great. Between my house, my wife, and the rickshaw ride in from town, I've saved nineteen cents just this morning.

Sharpless: Wonderful. I can see the inscription on your tombstone already: "I saved a dollar, here I lie." *(He looks around.)* Nice house.

Pinkerton: It's artistic. Artistic, don't you think? Like the way the shoji screens slide open to reveal the wet bar and disco mirror ball? Classy, huh? Great for impressing the chicks.

Sharpless: "Chicks"? Pinkerton, you're going to be a married man!

Pinkerton: Well, sort of.

Sharpless: What do you mean?

Pinkerton: This country—Sharpless, it is okay. You got all these geisha girls running around—

Sharpless: I know! I live here!

Pinkerton: Then, you know the marriage laws, right? I split for one month, it's annulled!

Sharpless: Leave it to you to read the fine print. Who's the lucky girl?

Pinkerton: Cio-Cio-San. Her friends call her Butterfly. Sharpless, she eats out of my hand!

Sharpless: She's probably very hungry.

Pinkerton: Not like American girls. It's true what they say about Oriental girls. They want to be treated bad!

Sharpless: Oh, please!

Pinkerton: It's true!

Sharpless: Are you serious about this girl?

Pinkerton: I'm marrying her, aren't I?

Sharpless: Yes—with generous trade-in terms.

Pinkerton: When I leave, she'll know what it's like to have loved a real man. And I'll even buy her a few nylons.

Sharpless: You aren't planning to take her with you?

Pinkerton: Huh? Where?

Sharpless: Home!

Pinkerton: You mean, America? Are you crazy? Can you see her trying to buy rice in St. Louis?

Sharpless: So, you're not serious.

Pause.

Pinkerton/Gallimard (as Pinkerton): Consul, I am a sailor in port. *(As Gallimard.)* They then proceed to sing the famous duet, "The Whole World Over."

The duet plays on the speakers. Gallimard, as Pinkerton, lip-syncs his lines from the opera.

Gallimard: To give a rough translation: "The whole world over, the Yankee travels, casting his anchor wherever he wants. Life's not worth living unless he can win the hearts of the fairest maidens, then hotfoot it off the premises ASAP." *(He turns towards Marc.)* In the preceding scene, I played Pinkerton, the womanizing cad, and my friend Marc from school . . . *(Marc bows grandly for our benefit.)* played Sharpless, the sensitive soul of reason. In life, however, our positions were usually—no, always—reversed.

SCENE IV

École Nationale.° Aix-en-Provence. 1947.

Gallimard: No, Marc, I think I'd rather stay home.

Marc: Are you crazy?! We are going to Dad's condo in Marseilles! You know what happened last time?

Gallimard: Of course I do.

École Nationale: National School.

Marc: Of course you don't! You never know. . . . They stripped, Rene!

Gallimard: Who stripped?

Marc: The girls!

Gallimard: Girls? Who said anything about girls?

Marc: Rene, we're a buncha university guys goin' up to the woods. What are we gonna do — talk philosophy?

Gallimard: What girls? Where do you get them?

Marc: Who cares? The point is, they come. On trucks. Packed in like sardines. The back flips open, babes hop out, we're ready to roll.

Gallimard: You mean, they just — ?

Marc: Before you know it, every last one of them — they're stripped and splashing around my pool. There's no moon out, they can't see what's going on, their boobs are flapping, right? You close your eyes, reach out — it's grab bag, get it? Doesn't matter whose ass is between whose legs, whose teeth are sinking into who. You're just in there, going at it, eyes closed, on and on for as long as you can stand. *(Pause.)* Some fun, huh?

Gallimard: What happens in the morning?

Marc: In the morning, you're ready to talk some philosophy. *(Beat.)* So how 'bout it?

Gallimard: Marc, I can't . . . I'm afraid they'll say no — the girls. So I never ask.

Marc: You don't have to ask! That's the beauty — don't you see? They don't have to say yes. It's perfect for a guy like you, really.

Gallimard: You go ahead . . . I may come later.

Marc: Hey, Rene — it doesn't matter that you're clumsy and got zits — they're not looking!

Gallimard: Thank you very much.

Marc: Wimp.

Marc walks over to the other side of the stage, and starts waving and smiling at women in the audience.

Gallimard (to us): We now return to my version of *Madame Butterfly* and the events leading to my recent conviction for treason.

Gallimard notices Marc making lewd gestures.

Gallimard: Marc, what are you doing?

Marc: Huh? *(Sotto voce.)* Rene, there're a lotta great babes out there. They're probably lookin' at me and thinking, "What a dangerous guy."

Gallimard: Yes — how could they help but be impressed by your cool sophistication?

Gallimard pops the Sharpless cap on Marc's head, and points him offstage. Marc exits, leering.

SCENE V

M. Gallimard's cell.

Gallimard: Next, Butterfly makes her entrance. We learn her age — fifteen . . . but very mature for her years.

Lights come up on the area where we saw Song dancing at the top of the play. She appears there again, now dressed as Madame Butterfly, moving to the "Love Duet." Gallimard turns upstage slightly to watch, transfixed.

Gallimard: But as she glides past him, beautiful, laughing softly behind her fan, don't we who are men sigh with hope? We, who are not handsome, nor brave, nor powerful, yet somehow believe, like Pinkerton, that we deserve a Butterfly. She arrives with all her possessions in the folds of her sleeves, lays them all out, for her man to do with as he pleases. Even her life itself—she bows her head as she whispers that she's not even worth the hundred yen he paid for her. He's already given too much, when we know he's really had to give nothing at all.

Music and lights on Song out. Gallimard sits at his crate.

Gallimard: In real life, women who put their total worth at less than sixty-six cents are quite hard to find. The closest we come is in the pages of these magazines. *(He reaches into his crate, pulls out a stack of girlie magazines, and begins flipping through them.)* Quite a necessity in prison. For three or four dollars, you get seven or eight women.

    I first discovered these magazines at my uncle's house. One day, as a boy of twelve. The first time I saw them in his closet . . . all lined up—my body shook. Not with lust—no, with power. Here were women—a shelfful—who would do exactly as I wanted.

The "Love Duet" creeps in over the speakers. Special comes up, revealing, not Song this time, but a pinup girl in a sexy negligee, her back to us. Gallimard turns upstage and looks at her.

Girl: I know you're watching me.
Gallimard: My throat . . . it's dry.
Girl: I leave my blinds open every night before I go to bed.
Gallimard: I can't move.
Girl: I leave my blinds open and the lights on.
Gallimard: I'm shaking. My skin is hot, but my penis is soft. Why?
Girl: I stand in front of the window.
Gallimard: What is she going to do?
Girl: I toss my hair, and I let my lips part . . . barely.
Gallimard: I shouldn't be seeing this. It's so dirty. I'm so bad.
Girl: Then, slowly, I lift off my nightdress.
Gallimard: Oh, god. I can't believe it. I can't—
Girl: I toss it to the ground.
Gallimard: Now, she's going to walk away. She's going to—
Girl: I stand there, in the light, displaying myself.
Gallimard: No. She's—why is she naked?
Girl: To you.
Gallimard: In front of a window? This is wrong. No—
Girl: Without shame.
Gallimard: No, she must . . . like it.
Girl: I like it.
Gallimard: She . . . she wants me to see.
Girl: I want you to see.
Gallimard: I can't believe it! She's getting excited!
Girl: I can't see you. You can do whatever you want.
Gallimard: I can't do a thing. Why?
Girl: What would you like me to do . . . next?

Lights go down on her. Music off. Silence, as Gallimard puts away his magazines. Then he resumes talking to us.

Gallimard: Act Two begins with Butterfly staring at the ocean. Pinkerton's been called back to the U.S., and he's given his wife a detailed schedule of his plans. In the column marked "return date," he's written "when the robins nest." This failed to ignite her suspicions. Now, three years have passed without a peep from him. Which brings a response from her faithful servant, Suzuki.

Comrade Chin enters, playing Suzuki.

Suzuki: Girl, he's a loser. What'd he ever give you? Nineteen cents and those ugly Day-Glo stockings? Look, it's finished! Kaput! Done! And you should be glad! I mean, the guy was a woofer! He tried before, you know—before he met you, he went down to geisha central and plunked down his spare change in front of the usual candidates—everyone else gagged! These are hungry prostitutes, and they were not interested, get the picture? Now, stop slathering when an American ship sails in, and let's make some bucks—I mean, yen! We are broke!

Now, what about Yamadori? Hey, hey—don't look away—the man is a prince—figuratively, and, what's even better, literally. He's rich, he's handsome, he says he'll die if you don't marry him—and he's even willing to overlook the little fact that you've been deflowered all over the place by a foreign devil. What do you mean, "But he's Japanese"? What do you think you are? You think you've been touched by the whitey god? He was a sailor with dirty hands!

Suzuki stalks offstage.

Gallimard: She's also visited by Consul Sharpless, sent by Pinkerton on a minor errand.

Marc enters, as Sharpless.

Sharpless: I hate this job.

Gallimard: This Pinkerton—he doesn't show up personally to tell his wife he's abandoning her. No, he sends a government diplomat . . . at taxpayers' expense.

Sharpless: Butterfly? Butterfly? I have some bad—I'm going to be ill. Butterfly, I came to tell you—

Gallimard: Butterfly says she knows he'll return and if he doesn't she'll kill herself rather than go back to her own people. *(Beat.)* This causes a lull in the conversation.

Sharpless: Let's put it this way . . .

Gallimard: Butterfly runs into the next room, and returns holding—

Sound cue: a baby crying. Sharpless, "seeing" this, backs away.

Sharpless: Well, good. Happy to see things going so well. I suppose I'll be going now. Ta ta. Ciao. *(He turns away. Sound cue out.)* I hate this job. *(He exits.)*

Gallimard: At that moment, Butterfly spots in the harbor an American ship—the *Abramo Lincoln!*

Music cue: "The Flower Duet." Song, still dressed as Butterfly, changes into a wedding kimono, moving to the music.

Gallimard: This is the moment that redeems her years of waiting. With Suzuki's help, they cover the room with flowers—

Chin, as Suzuki, trudges onstage and drops a lone flower without much enthusiasm.

Gallimard: — and she changes into her wedding dress to prepare for Pinkerton's arrival.

Suzuki helps Butterfly change. Helga enters, and helps Gallimard change into a tuxedo.

Gallimard: I married a woman older than myself — Helga.

Helga: My father was ambassador to Australia. I grew up among criminals and kangaroos.

Gallimard: Hearing that brought me to the altar —

Helga exits.

Gallimard: — where I took a vow renouncing love. No fantasy woman would ever want me, so, yes, I would settle for a quick leap up the career ladder. Passion, I banish, and in its place — practicality!

But my vows had long since lost their charm by the time we arrived in China. The sad truth is that all men want a beautiful woman, and the uglier the man, the greater the want.

Suzuki makes final adjustments of Butterfly's costume, as does Gallimard of his tuxedo.

Gallimard: I married late, at age thirty-one. I was faithful to my marriage for eight years. Until the day when, as a junior-level diplomat in puritanical Peking, in a parlor at the German ambassador's house, during the "Reign of a Hundred Flowers,"° I first saw her . . . singing the death scene from *Madame Butterfly.*

Suzuki runs offstage.

SCENE VI

German ambassador's house. Beijing. 1960.

The upstage special area now becomes a stage. Several chairs face upstage, representing seating for some twenty guests in the parlor. A few "diplomats" — Renee, Marc, Toulon — in formal dress enter and take seats.

Gallimard also sits down, but turns towards us and continues to talk. Orchestral accompaniment on the tape is now replaced by a simple piano. Song picks up the death scene from the point where Butterfly uncovers the hara-kiri knife.

Gallimard: The ending is pitiful. Pinkerton, in an act of great courage, stays home and sends his American wife to pick up Butterfly's child. The truth, long deferred, has come up to her door.

Song, playing Butterfly, sings the lines from the opera in her own voice — which, though not classical, should be decent.

Song: "Con onor muore / chi non puo serbar / vita con onore."

Gallimard (simultaneously): "Death with honor / Is better than life / Life with dishonor."

Reign of a Hundred Flowers: A brief period in 1957 when freedom of expression was allowed in China.

The stage is illuminated; we are now completely within an elegant diplomat's residence. Song proceeds to play out an abbreviated death scene. Everyone in the room applauds. Song, shyly, takes her bows. Others in the room rush to congratulate her. Gallimard remains with us.

Gallimard: They say in opera the voice is everything. That's probably why I'd never before enjoyed opera. Here . . . here was a Butterfly with little or no voice — but she had the grace, the delicacy . . . I believed this girl. I believed her suffering. I wanted to take her in my arms — so delicate, even I could protect her, take her home, pamper her until she smiled.

Over the course of the preceding speech, Song has broken from the upstage crowd and moved directly upstage of Gallimard.

Song: Excuse me. Monsieur . . . ?

Gallimard turns upstage, shocked.

Gallimard: Oh! Gallimard. Mademoiselle . . . ? A beautiful . . .
Song: Song Liling.
Gallimard: A beautiful performance.
Song: Oh, please.
Gallimard: I usually —
Song: You make me blush. I'm no opera singer at all.
Gallimard: I usually don't like *Butterfly*.
Song: I can't blame you in the least.
Gallimard: I mean, the story —
Song: Ridiculous.
Gallimard: I like the story, but . . . what?
Song: Oh, you like it?
Gallimard: I . . . what I mean is, I've always seen it played by huge women in so much bad makeup.
Song: Bad makeup is not unique to the West.
Gallimard: But, who can believe them?
Song: And you believe me?
Gallimard: Absolutely. You were utterly convincing. It's the first time —
Song: Convincing? As a Japanese woman? The Japanese used hundreds of our people for medical experiments during the war, you know. But I gather such an irony is lost on you.
Gallimard: No! I was about to say, it's the first time I've seen the beauty of the story.
Song: Really?
Gallimard: Of her death. It's a . . . a pure sacrifice. He's unworthy, but what can she do? She loves him . . . so much. It's a very beautiful story.
Song: Well, yes, to a Westerner.
Gallimard: Excuse me?
Song: It's one of your favorite fantasies, isn't it? The submissive Oriental woman and the cruel white man.
Gallimard: Well, I didn't quite mean . . .
Song: Consider it this way: what would you say if a blonde homecoming queen fell in love with a short Japanese businessman? He treats her cruelly, then goes home for three years, during which time she prays to his picture and turns down marriage from a young Kennedy. Then, when she learns he

PLAYS IN PERFORMANCE

TOP: *At center stage is Jocasta (Ching Valdes/Aran) in a scene from the 1993 production of* Oedipus the King *(p. 1224) at Philadelphia's Wilma Theater, directed by Blanka Zizka and Jiri Zizka. Copyright © T. Charles Erikson.*
BOTTOM: *Martha Henry as Antigone (p. 1267) in a scene from the 1971 production at the Repertory Theatre of Lincoln Center. Martha Swope © Time Inc.*

RIGHT: *Oberon, King of the Fairies (William Hurt), and Puck (Marcell Rosenblatt) in a scene from the 1982 New York Shakespeare Festival Central Park production of* A Midsummer Night's Dream *(p. 1327). Martha Swope © Time Inc.*
BELOW: *The "play within the play" scene from* Hamlet *(p. 1383). N. R. Farbman, Life Magazine © Time Inc.*

ABOVE AND LEFT:
*Two scenes from a
November 1995 A.R.T.
production in Cam-
bridge, Massachusetts,
of* The Tempest
*(p. 1483), directed
by Ron Daniels.*
ABOVE: *Prospero
(Paul Freeman)
recounts the story
of the shipwreck to
Miranda (Gilsig
Jessalyn) in Act I,
Scene II.* **LEFT:** *(left
to right) Stephano
(Charles Levin),
Caliban (Jack Willis),
and Trinculo(Thomas
Derrah) just after
they meet for the first
time in Act II, Scene
II. Copyright © T.
Charles Erickson.*

ABOVE: *Owen Teale and Janet McTeer in two scenes from the 1997 Bill Kenwright London production of* A Doll House *(p. 1564) performed at New York's Belasco Theater—winner of the 1997 Tony Award for Best Revival of a Play.*

ABOVE: *Hume Cronyn as Krapp in the 1972 Repertory Theatre of Lincoln Center production of* Krapp's Last Tape *(p. 1649). Martha Swope © Time Inc.*
LEFT: *Margo Martindale in* Rodeo *(p. 1657), during the Sixth Annual Humana Festival of New American Plays, at the Actor's Theatre of Louisville, Kentucky, in 1982. Katherine Wisniewski, photographer.*

TOP AND ABOVE: *Anna Deavere Smith portraying two characters from her play* Twilight: Los Angeles, 1992 *(p. 1661).* Martha Swope © Time Inc.

LEFT: *John Lithgow and B. D. Wong in M.* Butterfly *(p. 1675). This award-winning play opened on Broadway at the Eugene O'Neill Theatre in 1988. Joan Marcus, photographer.*

ABOVE RIGHT: *Sydney Poitier and Ruby Dee (and unknown actor, on the left) in a March 1959 performance of* A Raisin in the Sun *(p. 1730). Gordon Parks,* Life Magazine *© Time Inc.*

RIGHT: *Willy (Lee J. Cobb) with sons Hap (Cameron Mitchell) and Biff (Arthur Kennedy) in* Death of a Salesman *(p. 1795). W. Eugene Smith,* Life Magazine *© 1949 Time Inc.*

TOP LEFT: *Amanda (Ruby Dee) and Tom (Jonathan Earl Peck) in the 1989 Arena Stage production of* The Glass Menagerie *(p. 1864).*

TOP RIGHT: *Chris Chamberlin, Bob Lussier, Monica Merkel, and Peter Pecora play a number of characters during this February 1998 performance of William Seebring's* The Original Last Wish Baby *(p. 1944) at Baby Jupiter's in New York City. The production was directed by the author and produced by Annette Pecora.*

BOTTOM: *Charles Dutton in* The Piano Lesson *(p. 1962), at a 1989 performance at the Kennedy Center, Washington D.C.*

has remarried, she kills herself. Now, I believe you would consider this girl to be a deranged idiot, correct? But because it's an Oriental who kills herself for a Westerner—ah!—you find it beautiful.

Silence.

Gallimard: Yes . . . well . . . I see your point . . .

Song: I will never do Butterfly again, Monsieur Gallimard. If you wish to see some real theater, come to the Peking Opera sometime. Expand your mind.

Song walks offstage. Other guests exit with her.

Gallimard (to us): So much for protecting her in my big Western arms.

SCENE VII

M. Gallimard's apartment. Beijing. 1960.
Gallimard changes from his tux into a casual suit. Helga enters.

Gallimard: The Chinese are an incredibly arrogant people.

Helga: They warned us about that in Paris, remember?

Gallimard: Even Parisians consider them arrogant. That's a switch.

Helga: What is it that Madame Su says? "We are a very old civilization." I never know if she's talking about her country or herself.

Gallimard: I walk around here, all I hear every day, everywhere is how *old* this culture is. The fact that "old" may be synonymous with "senile" doesn't occur to them.

Helga: You're not going to change them. "East is east, west is west, and . . ." whatever that guy said.

Gallimard: It's just that—silly. I met . . . at Ambassador Koening's tonight—you should've been there.

Helga: Koening? Oh god, no. Did he enchant you all again with the history of Bavaria?

Gallimard: No. I met, I suppose, the Chinese equivalent of a diva. She's a singer in the Chinese opera.

Helga: They have an opera, too? Do they sing in Chinese? Or maybe—in Italian?

Gallimard: Tonight, she did sing in Italian.

Helga: How'd she manage that?

Gallimard: She must've been educated in the West before the Revolution. Her French is very good also. Anyway, she sang the death scene from *Madame Butterfly.*

Helga: Madame Butterfly! Then I should have come. *(She begins humming, floating around the room as if dragging long kimono sleeves.)* Did she have a nice costume? I think it's a classic piece of music.

Gallimard: That's what *I* thought, too. Don't let her hear you say that.

Helga: What's wrong?

Gallimard: Evidently the Chinese hate it.

Helga: She hated it, but she performed it anyway? Is she perverse?

Gallimard: They hate it because the white man gets the girl. Sour grapes if you ask me.

Helga: Politics again? Why can't they just hear it as a piece of beautiful music? So, what's in their opera?

Gallimard: I don't know. But, whatever it is, I'm sure it must be *old.*

Helga exits.

SCENE VIII

> *Chinese opera house and the streets of Beijing. 1960.*
> *The sound of gongs clanging fills the stage.*

Gallimard: My wife's innocent question kept ringing in my ears. I asked around, but no one knew anything about the Chinese opera. It took four weeks, but my curiosity overcame my cowardice. This Chinese diva—this unwilling Butterfly—what did she do to make her so proud?

    The room was hot, and full of smoke. Wrinkled faces, old women, teeth missing—a man with a growth on his neck, like a human toad. All smiling, pipes falling from their mouths, cracking nuts between their teeth, a live chicken pecking at my foot—all looking, screaming, gawking . . . at her.

The upstage area is suddenly hit with a harsh white light. It has become the stage for the Chinese opera performance. Two dancers enter, along with Song. Gallimard stands apart, watching. Song glides gracefully amidst the two dancers. Drums suddenly slam to a halt. Song strikes a pose, looking straight at Gallimard. Dancers exit. Light change. Pause, then Song walks right off the stage and straight up to Gallimard.

Song: Yes. You. White man. I'm looking straight at you.

Gallimard: Me?

Song: You see any other white men? It was too easy to spot you. How often does a man in my audience come in a tie?

Song starts to remove her costume. Underneath, she wears simple baggy clothes. They are now backstage. The show is over.

Song: So, you are an adventurous imperialist?

Gallimard: I . . . thought it would further my education.

Song: It took you four weeks. Why?

Gallimard: I've been busy.

Song: Well, education has always been undervalued in the West, hasn't it?

Gallimard (laughing): I don't think that's true.

Song: No, you wouldn't. You're a Westerner. How can you objectively judge your own values?

Gallimard: I think it's possible to achieve some distance.

Song: Do you? *(Pause.)* It stinks in here. Let's go.

Gallimard: These are the smells of your loyal fans.

Song: I love them for being my fans, I hate the smell they leave behind. I too can distance myself from my people. *(She looks around, then whispers in his ear.)* "Art for the masses" is a shitty excuse to keep artists poor. *(She pops a cigarette in her mouth.)* Be a gentleman, will you? And light my cigarette.

Gallimard fumbles for a match.

Gallimard: I don't . . . smoke.
Song (lighting her own): Your loss. Had you lit my cigarette, I might have blown a puff of smoke right between your eyes. Come.

> *They start to walk about the stage. It is a summer night on the Beijing streets. Sounds of the city play on the house speakers.*

Song: How I wish there were even a tiny café to sit in. With cappuccinos, and men in tuxedos and bad expatriate jazz.
Gallimard: If my history serves me correctly, you weren't even allowed into the clubs in Shanghai before the Revolution.
Song: Your history serves you poorly, Monsieur Gallimard. True, there were signs reading "No dogs and Chinamen." But a woman, especially a delicate Oriental woman — we always go where we please. Could you imagine it otherwise? Clubs in China filled with pasty, big-thighed white women, while thousands of slender lotus blossoms wait just outside the door? Never. The clubs would be empty. *(Beat.)* We have always held a certain fascination for you Caucasian men, have we not?
Gallimard: But . . . that fascination is imperialist, or so you tell me.
Song: Do you believe everything I tell you? Yes. It is always imperialist. But sometimes . . . sometimes, it is also mutual. Oh — this is my flat.
Gallimard: I didn't even —
Song: Thank you. Come another time and we will further expand your mind.

> *Song exits. Gallimard continues roaming the streets as he speaks to us.*

Gallimard: What was that? What did she mean, "Sometimes . . . it is mutual"? Women do not flirt with me. And I normally can't talk to them. But tonight, I held up my end of the conversation.

Scene IX

> *Gallimard's bedroom. Beijing. 1960.*
> *Helga enters.*

Helga: You didn't tell me you'd be home late.
Gallimard: I didn't intend to. Something came up.
Helga: Oh? Like what?
Gallimard: I went to the . . . to the Dutch ambassador's home.
Helga: Again?
Gallimard: There was a reception for a visiting scholar. He's writing a six-volume treatise on the Chinese revolution. We all gathered that meant he'd have to live here long enough to actually write six volumes, and we all expressed our deepest sympathies.
Helga: Well, I had a good night too. I went with the ladies to a martial arts demonstration. Some of those men — when they break those thick boards — *(she mimes fanning herself)* whoo-whoo!

> *Helga exits. Lights dim.*

Gallimard: I lied to my wife. Why? I've never had any reason to lie before. But what reason did I have tonight? I didn't do anything wrong. That night, I had a dream. Other people, I've been told, have dreams when angels appear. Or dragons, or Sophia Loren in a towel. In my dream, Marc from school appeared.

Marc enters, in a nightshirt and cap.

Marc: Rene! You met a girl!

Gallimard and Marc stumble down the Beijing streets. Night sounds over the speakers.

Gallimard: It's not that amazing, thank you.

Marc: No! It's so monumental, I heard about it halfway around the world in my sleep!

Gallimard: I've met girls before, you know.

Marc: Name one. I've come across time and space to congratulate you. *(He hands Gallimard a bottle of wine.)*

Gallimard: Marc, this is expensive.

Marc: On those rare occasions when you become a formless spirit, why not steal the best?

Marc pops open the bottle, begins to share it with Gallimard.

Gallimard: You embarrass me. She . . . there's no reason to think she likes me.

Marc: "Sometimes, it is mutual"?

Gallimard: Oh.

Marc: "Mutual"? "Mutual"? What does that mean?

Gallimard: You heard?

Marc: It means the money is in the bank, you only have to write the check!

Gallimard: I am a married man!

Marc: And an excellent one too. I cheated after . . . six months. Then again and again, until now — three hundred girls in twelve years.

Gallimard: I don't think we should hold that up as a model.

Marc: Of course not! My life — it is disgusting! Phooey! Phooey! But, you — you are the model husband.

Gallimard: Anyway, it's impossible. I'm a foreigner.

Marc: Ah, yes. She cannot love you, it is taboo, but something deep inside her heart . . . she cannot help herself . . . she must surrender to you. It is her destiny.

Gallimard: How do you imagine all this?

Marc: The same way you do. It's an old story. It's in our blood. They fear us, Rene. Their women fear us. And their men — their men hate us. And, you know something? They are all correct.

They spot a light in a window.

Marc: There! There, Rene!

Gallimard: It's her window.

Marc: Late at night — it burns. The light — it burns for you.

Gallimard: I won't look. It's not respectful.

Marc: We don't have to be respectful. We're foreign devils.

Enter Song, in a sheer robe, her face completely swathed in black cloth. The "One Fine Day" aria creeps in over the speakers. With her back to us, Song mimes attending to her toilette. Her robe comes loose, revealing her white shoulders.

Marc: All your life you've waited for a beautiful girl who would lay down for you. All your life you've smiled like a saint when it's happened to every other man you know. And you see them in magazines and you see them in movies. And you wonder, what's wrong with me? Will anyone beautiful ever want me? As the years pass, your hair thins and you struggle to hold on to even your hopes. Stop struggling, Rene. The wait is over. *(He exits.)*

Gallimard: Marc? Marc?

At that moment, Song, her back still towards us, drops her robe. A second of her naked back, then a sound cue: a phone ringing, very loud. Blackout, followed in the next beat by a special up on the bedroom area, where a phone now sits. Gallimard stumbles across the stage and picks up the phone. Sound cue out. Over the course of his conversation, area lights fill in the vicinity of his bed. It is the following morning.

Gallimard: Yes? Hello?

Song (offstage): Is it very early?

Gallimard: Why, yes.

Song (offstage): How early?

Gallimard: It's . . . it's 5:30. Why are you — ?

Song (offstage): But it's light outside. Already.

Gallimard: It is. The sun must be in confusion today.

Over the course of Song's next speech, her upstage special comes up again. She sits in a chair, legs crossed, in a robe, telephone to her ear.

Song: I waited until I saw the sun. That was as much discipline as I could manage for one night. Do you forgive me?

Gallimard: Of course . . . for what?

Song: Then I'll ask you quickly. Are you really interested in the opera?

Gallimard: Why, yes. Yes I am.

Song: Then come again next Thursday. I am playing *The Drunken Beauty*. May I count on you?

Gallimard: Yes. You may.

Song: Perfect. Well, I must be getting to bed. I'm exhausted. It's been a very long night for me.

Song hangs up; special on her goes off. Gallimard begins to dress for work.

SCENE X

Song Liling's apartment. Beijing. 1960.

Gallimard: I returned to the opera that next week, and the week after that . . . she keeps our meetings so short — perhaps fifteen, twenty minutes at most. So I am left each week with a thirst which is intensified. In this way, fifteen weeks have gone by. I am starting to doubt the words of my friend Marc. But no, not really. In my heart, I know she has . . . an interest in me. I suspect this is her way. She is outwardly bold and outspoken, yet her heart is shy and afraid. It is the Oriental in her at war with her Western education.

Song (offstage): I will be out in an instant. Ask the servant for anything you want.

Gallimard: Tonight, I have finally been invited to enter her apartment. Though the idea is almost beyond belief, I believe she is afraid of me.

Gallimard looks around the room. He picks up a picture in a frame, studies it. Without his noticing, Song enters, dressed elegantly in a black gown from the twenties. She stands in the doorway looking like Anna May Wong. °

Song: That is my father.
Gallimard (surprised): Mademoiselle Song . . .

She glides up to him, snatches away the picture.

Song: It is very good that he did not live to see the Revolution. They would, no doubt, have made him kneel on broken glass. Not that he didn't deserve such a punishment. But he is my father. I would've hated to see it happen.
Gallimard: I'm very honored that you've allowed me to visit your home.

Song curtseys.

Song: Thank you. Oh! Haven't you been poured any tea?
Gallimard: I'm really not—
Song (to her offstage servant): Shu-Fang! Cha! Kwai-lah! *(To Gallimard.)* I'm sorry. You want everything to be perfect—
Gallimard: Please.
Song: —and before the evening even begins—
Gallimard: I'm really not thirsty.
Song: —it's ruined.
Gallimard (sharply): Mademoiselle Song!

Song sits down.

Song: I'm sorry.
Gallimard: What are you apologizing for now?

Pause; Song starts to giggle.

Song: I don't know!

Gallimard laughs.

Gallimard: Exactly my point.
Song: Oh, I am silly. Light-headed. I promise not to apologize for anything else tonight, do you hear me?
Gallimard: That's a good girl.

Shu-Fang, a servant girl, comes out with a tea tray and starts to pour.

Song (to Shu-Fang): No! I'll pour myself for the gentleman!

Shu-Fang, staring at Gallimard, exits.

Gallimard: You have a beautiful home.
Song: No, I . . . I don't even know why I invited you up.
Gallimard: Well, I'm glad you did.

Song looks around the room.

Song: There is an element of danger to your presence.
Gallimard: Oh?

Anna May Wong (1905–1961): Chinese American actor known for her exotic beauty and most often cast as a villain.

Song: You must know.

Gallimard: It doesn't concern me. We both know why I'm here.

Song: It doesn't concern me either. No . . . well perhaps . . .

Gallimard: What?

Song: Perhaps I am slightly afraid of scandal.

Gallimard: What are we doing?

Song: I'm entertaining you. In my parlor.

Gallimard: In France, that would hardly—

Song: France. France is a country living in the modern era. Perhaps even ahead of it. China is a nation whose soul is firmly rooted two thousand years in the past. What I do, even pouring the tea for you now . . . it has . . . implications. The walls and windows say so. Even my own heart, strapped inside this Western dress . . . even it says things—things I don't care to hear.

Song hands Gallimard a cup of tea. Gallimard puts his hand over both the teacup and Song's hand.

Gallimard: This is a beautiful dress.

Song: Don't.

Gallimard: What?

Song: I don't even know if it looks right on me.

Gallimard: Believe me—

Song: You are from France. You see so many beautiful women.

Gallimard: France? Since when are the European women—?

Song: Oh! What am I trying to do, anyway?!

Song runs to the door, composes herself, then turns towards Gallimard.

Song: Monsieur Gallimard, perhaps you should go.

Gallimard: But . . . why?

Song: There's something wrong about this.

Gallimard: I don't see what.

Song: I feel . . . I am not myself.

Gallimard: No. You're nervous.

Song: Please. Hard as I try to be modern, to speak like a man, to hold a Western woman's strong face up to my own . . . in the end, I fail. A small, frightened heart beats too quickly and gives me away. Monsieur Gallimard, I'm a Chinese girl. I've never . . . never invited a man up to my flat before. The forwardness of my actions makes my skin burn.

Gallimard: What are you afraid of? Certainly not me, I hope.

Song: I'm a modest girl.

Gallimard: I know. And very beautiful. *(He touches her hair.)*

Song: Please—go now. The next time you see me, I shall again be myself.

Gallimard: I like you the way you are right now.

Song: You are a cad.

Gallimard: What do you expect? I'm a foreign devil.

Gallimard walks downstage. Song exits.

Gallimard (to us): Did you hear the way she talked about Western women? Much differently than the first night. She does—she feels inferior to them—and to me.

SCENE XI

The French embassy. Beijing. 1960.
   Gallimard moves towards a desk.

Gallimard: I determined to try an experiment. In *Madame Butterfly*, Cio-Cio-San fears that the Western man who catches a butterfly will pierce its heart with a needle, then leave it to perish. I began to wonder: had I, too, caught a butterfly who would writhe on a needle?

Marc enters, dressed as a bureaucrat, holding a stack of papers. As Gallimard speaks, Marc hands papers to him. He peruses, then signs, stamps, or rejects them.

Gallimard: Over the next five weeks, I worked like a dynamo. I stopped going to the opera, I didn't phone or write her. I knew this little flower was waiting for me to call, and, as I wickedly refused to do so, I felt for the first time that rush of power — the absolute power of a man.

Marc continues acting as the bureaucrat, but he now speaks as himself.

Marc: Rene! It's me.

Gallimard: Marc — I hear your voice everywhere now. Even in the midst of work.

Marc: That's because I'm watching you — all the time.

Gallimard: You were always the most popular guy in school.

Marc: Well, there's no guarantee of failure in life like happiness in high school. Somehow I knew I'd end up in the suburbs working for Renault and you'd be in the Orient picking exotic women off the trees. And they say there's no justice.

Gallimard: That's why you were my friend?

Marc: I gave you a little of my life, so that now you can give me some of yours. *(Pause.)* Remember Isabelle?

Gallimard: Of course I remember! She was my first experience.

Marc: We all wanted to ball her. But she only wanted me.

Gallimard: I had her.

Marc: Right. You balled her.

Gallimard: You were the only one who ever believed me.

Marc: Well, there's a good reason for that. *(Beat.)* C'mon. You must've guessed.

Gallimard: You told me to wait in the bushes by the cafeteria that night. The next thing I knew, she was on me. Dress up in the air.

Marc: She never wore underwear.

Gallimard: My arms were pinned to the dirt.

Marc: She loved the superior position. A girl ahead of her time.

Gallimard: I looked up, and there was this woman . . . bouncing up and down on my loins.

Marc: Screaming, right?

Gallimard: Screaming, and breaking off the branches all around me, and pounding my butt up and down into the dirt.

Marc: Huffing and puffing like a locomotive.

Gallimard: And in the middle of all this, the leaves were getting into my mouth, my legs were losing circulation, I thought, "God. So this is *it*?"

Marc: You thought that?

Gallimard: Well, I was worried about my legs falling off.

Marc: You didn't have a good time?

Gallimard: No, that's not what I—I had a great time!

Marc: You're sure?

Gallimard: Yeah. Really.

Marc: 'Cuz I wanted you to have a good time.

Gallimard: I did.

> *Pause.*

Marc: Shit. *(Pause.)* When all is said and done, she was kind of a lousy lay, wasn't she? I mean, there was a lot of energy there, but you never knew what she was doing with it. Like when she yelled "I'm coming!" — hell, it was so loud, you wanted to go, "Look, it's not that big a deal."

Gallimard: I got scared. I thought she meant someone was actually coming. *(Pause.)* But, Marc?

Marc: What?

Gallimard: Thanks.

Marc: Oh, don't mention it.

Gallimard: It was my first experience.

Marc: Yeah. You got her.

Gallimard: I got her.

Marc: Wait! Look at that letter again!

> *Gallimard picks up one of the papers he's been stamping, and rereads it.*

Gallimard (to us): After six weeks, they began to arrive. The letters.

> *Upstage special on Song, as Madame Butterfly. The scene is underscored by the "Love Duet."*

Song: Did we fight? I do not know. Is the opera no longer of interest to you? Please come — my audiences miss the white devil in their midst.

> *Gallimard looks up from the letter, towards us.*

Gallimard (to us): A concession, but much too dignified. *(Beat; he discards the letter.)* I skipped the opera again that week to complete a position paper on trade.

> *The bureaucrat hands him another letter.*

Song: Six weeks have passed since last we met. Is this your practice — to leave friends in the lurch? Sometimes I hate you, sometimes I hate myself, but always I miss you.

Gallimard (to us): Better, but I don't like the way she calls me "friend." When a woman calls a man her "friend," she's calling him a eunuch or a homosexual. *(Beat; he discards the letter.)* I was absent from the opera for the seventh week, feeling a sudden urge to clean out my files.

> *Bureaucrat hands him another letter.*

Song: Your rudeness is beyond belief. I don't deserve this cruelty. Don't bother to call. I'll have you turned away at the door.

Gallimard (to us): I didn't. *(He discards the letter; bureaucrat hands him another.)* And then finally, the letter that concluded my experiment.

Song: I am out of words. I can hide behind dignity no longer. What do you want? I have already given you my shame.

Gallimard gives the letter back to Marc, slowly. Special on Song fades out.

Gallimard (to us): Reading it, I became suddenly ashamed. Yes, my experiment had been a success. She was turning on my needle. But the victory seemed hollow.

Marc: Hollow?! Are you crazy?

Gallimard: Nothing, Marc. Please go away.

Marc (exiting, with papers): Haven't I taught you anything?

Gallimard: "I have already given you my shame." I had to attend a reception that evening. On the way, I felt sick. If there is a God, surely he would punish me now. I had finally gained power over a beautiful woman, only to abuse it cruelly. There must be justice in the world. I had the strange feeling that the ax would fall this very evening.

Scene XII

Ambassador Toulon's residence. Beijing. 1960.
        Sound cue: party noises. Light change. We are now in a spacious residence.
Toulon, the French ambassador, enters and taps Gallimard on the shoulder.

Toulon: Gallimard? Can I have a word? Over here.

Gallimard (to us): Manuel Toulon. French ambassador to China. He likes to think of us all as his children. Rather like God.

Toulon: Look, Gallimard, there's not much to say. I've liked you. From the day you walked in. You were no leader, but you were tidy and efficient.

Gallimard: Thank you, sir.

Toulon: Don't jump the gun. Okay, our needs in China are changing. It's embarrassing that we lost Indochina. Someone just wasn't on the ball there. I don't mean you personally, of course.

Gallimard: Thank you, sir.

Toulon: We're going to be doing a lot more information-gathering in the future. The nature of our work here is changing. Some people are just going to have to go. It's nothing personal.

Gallimard: Oh.

Toulon: Want to know a secret? Vice-Consul LeBon is being transferred.

Gallimard (to us): My immediate superior!

Toulon: And most of his department.

Gallimard (to us): Just as I feared! God has seen my evil heart—

Toulon: But not you.

Gallimard (to us): —and he's taking her away just as . . . *(To Toulon.)* Excuse me, sir?

Toulon: Scare you? I think I did. Cheer up, Gallimard. I want you to replace LeBon as vice-consul.

Gallimard: You—? Yes, well, thank you, sir.

Toulon: Anytime.

Gallimard: I . . . accept with great humility.

Toulon: Humility won't be part of the job. You're going to coordinate the revamped intelligence division. Want to know a secret? A year ago, you would've been out. But the past few months, I don't know how it happened, you've become this new aggressive confident . . . thing. And they also tell me you get along with the Chinese. So I think you're a lucky man, Gallimard. Congratulations.

They shake hands. Toulon exits. Party noises out. Gallimard stumbles across a darkened stage.

Gallimard: Vice-consul? Impossible! As I stumbled out of the party, I saw it written across the sky: There is no God. Or, no — say that there is a God. But that God . . . understands. Of course! God who creates Eve to serve Adam, who blesses Solomon with his harem but ties Jezebel to a burning bed° — that God is a man. And he understands! At age thirty-nine, I was suddenly initiated into the way of the world.

SCENE XIII

Song Liling's apartment. Beijing. 1960.
  Song enters, in a sheer dressing gown.

Song: Are you crazy?
Gallimard: Mademoiselle Song —
Song: To come here — at this hour? After . . . after eight weeks?
Gallimard: It's the most amazing —
Song: You bang on my door? Scare my servants, scandalize the neighbors?
Gallimard: I've been promoted. To vice-consul.

  Pause.

Song: And what is that supposed to mean to me?
Gallimard: Are you my Butterfly?
Song: What are you saying?
Gallimard: I've come tonight for an answer: are you my Butterfly?
Song: Don't you know already?
Gallimard: I want you to say it.
Song: I don't want to say it.
Gallimard: So, that is your answer?
Song: You know how I feel about —
Gallimard: I do remember one thing.
Song: What?
Gallimard: In the letter I received today.
Song: Don't.
Gallimard: "I have already given you my shame."
Song: It's enough that I even wrote it.
Gallimard: Well, then —
Song: I shouldn't have it splashed across my face.
Gallimard: — if that's all true —
Song: Stop!
Gallimard: Then what is one more short answer?
Song: I don't want to!

God who creates Eve . . . burning bed: Eve, Adam, Solomon, and Jezebel are biblical characters. See Gen. 2:18–25; I Kings 11:1–8; and II Kings 9:11–37.

Gallimard: Are you my Butterfly? *(Silence; he crosses the room and begins to touch her hair.)* I want from you honesty. There should be nothing false between us. No false pride.

Pause.

Song: Yes, I am. I am your Butterfly.

Gallimard: Then let me be honest with you. It is because of you that I was promoted tonight. You have changed my life forever. My little Butterfly, there should be no more secrets: I love you.

He starts to kiss her roughly. She resists slightly.

Song: No . . . no . . . gently . . . please, I've never . . .
Gallimard: No?
Song: I've tried to appear experienced, but . . . the truth is . . . no.
Gallimard: Are you cold?
Song: Yes. Cold.
Gallimard: Then we will go very, very slowly.

He starts to caress her; her gown begins to open.

Song: No . . . let me . . . keep my clothes . . .
Gallimard: But . . .
Song: Please . . . it all frightens me. I'm a modest Chinese girl.
Gallimard: My poor little treasure.
Song: I am your treasure. Though inexperienced, I am not . . . ignorant. They teach us things, our mothers, about pleasing a man.
Gallimard: Yes?
Song: I'll do my best to make you happy. Turn off the lights.

Gallimard gets up and heads for a lamp. Song, propped up on one elbow, tosses her hair back and smiles.

Song: Monsieur Gallimard?
Gallimard: Yes, Butterfly?
Song: "Vieni, vieni!"
Gallimard: "Come, darling."
Song: "Ah! Dolce notte!"
Gallimard: "Beautiful night."
Song: "Tutto estatico d'amor ride il ciel!"
Gallimard: "All ecstatic with love, the heavens are filled with laughter."

He turns off the lamp. Blackout.

ACT II

SCENE I

M. Gallimard's cell. Paris. 1988.
    Lights up on Gallimard. He sits in his cell, reading from a leaflet.

Gallimard: This, from a contemporary critic's commentary on *Madame Butterfly:* "Pinkerton suffers from . . . being an obnoxious bounder whom every man in the audience itches to kick." Bully for us men in the audience! Then, in the same note: "Butterfly is the most irresistibly appealing of Puccini's 'Little Women.' Watching the succession of her humiliations is like watching a child under torture." *(He tosses the pamphlet over his shoulder.)* I suggest that, while we men may all want to kick Pinkerton, very few of us would pass up the opportunity to *be* Pinkerton.

Gallimard moves out of his cell.

Scene II

Gallimard and Butterfly's flat. Beijing. 1960.
        We are in a simple but well-decorated parlor. Gallimard moves to sit on a sofa, while Song, dressed in a cheongsam,° enters and curls up at his feet.

Gallimard (to us): We secured a flat on the outskirts of Peking. Butterfly, as I was calling her now, decorated our "home" with Western furniture and Chinese antiques. And there, on a few stolen afternoons or evenings each week, Butterfly commenced her education.
Song: The Chinese men — they keep us down.
Gallimard: Even in the "New Society"?
Song: In the "New Society," we are all kept ignorant equally. That's one of the exciting things about loving a Western man. I know you are not threatened by a woman's education.
Gallimard: I'm no saint, Butterfly.
Song: But you come from a progressive society.
Gallimard: We're not always reminding each other how "old" we are, if that's what you mean.
Song: Exactly. We Chinese — once, I suppose, it is true, we ruled the world. But so what? How much more exciting to be part of the society ruling the world today. Tell me — what's happening in Vietnam?
Gallimard: Oh, Butterfly — you want me to bring my work home?
Song: I want to know what you know. To be impressed by my man. It's not the particulars so much as the fact that you're making decisions which change the shape of the world.
Gallimard: Not the world. At best, a small corner.

Toulon enters, and sits at a desk upstage.

Scene III

French embassy. Beijing. 1961.
        Gallimard moves downstage, to Toulon's desk. Song remains upstage, watching.

Toulon: And a more troublesome corner is hard to imagine.
Gallimard: So, the Americans plan to begin bombing?
Toulon: This is very secret, Gallimard: yes. The Americans don't have an embassy here. They're asking us to be their eyes and ears. Say Jack Kennedy

---

cheongsam: A fitted dress with side slits in the skirt.

signed an order to bomb North Vietnam, Laos. How would the Chinese react?

Gallimard: I think the Chinese will squawk —

Toulon: Uh-huh.

Gallimard: — but, in their hearts, they don't even like Ho Chi Minh.°

Pause.

Toulon: What a bunch of jerks. Vietnam was *our* colony. Not only didn't the Americans help us fight to keep them, but now, seven years later, they've come back to grab the territory for themselves. It's very irritating.

Gallimard: With all due respect, sir, why should the Americans have won our war for us back in fifty-four if we didn't have the will to win it ourselves?

Toulon: You're kidding, aren't you?

Pause.

Gallimard: The Orientals simply want to be associated with whoever shows the most strength and power. You live with the Chinese, sir. Do you think they like Communism?

Toulon: I live in China. Not with the Chinese.

Gallimard: Well, I —

Toulon: *You* live with the Chinese.

Gallimard: Excuse me?

Toulon: I can't keep a secret.

Gallimard: What are you saying?

Toulon: Only that I'm not immune to gossip. So, you're keeping a native mistress? Don't answer. It's none of my business. *(Pause.)* I'm sure she must be gorgeous.

Gallimard: Well . . .

Toulon: I'm impressed. You had the stamina to go out into the streets and hunt one down. Some of us have to be content with the wives of the expatriate community.

Gallimard: I do feel . . . fortunate.

Toulon: So, Gallimard, you've got the inside knowledge — what *do* the Chinese think?

Gallimard: Deep down, they miss the old days. You know, cappuccinos, men in tuxedos —

Toulon: So what do we tell the Americans about Vietnam?

Gallimard: Tell them there's a natural affinity between the West and the Orient.

Toulon: And that you speak from experience?

Gallimard: The Orientals are people too. They want the good things we can give them. If the Americans demonstrate the will to win, the Vietnamese will welcome them into a mutually beneficial union.

Toulon: I don't see how the Vietnamese can stand up to American firepower.

Gallimard: Orientals will always submit to a greater force.

Toulon: I'll note your opinions in my report. The Americans always love to hear how "welcome" they'll be. *(He starts to exit.)*

Gallimard: Sir?

Toulon: Mmmm?

Gallimard: This . . . rumor you've heard.

Ho Chi Minh (1890–1969): First president of North Vietnam (1945–1969).

Toulon: Uh-huh?

Gallimard: How . . . widespread do you think it is?

Toulon: It's only widespread within this embassy. Where nobody talks because everybody is guilty. We were worried about you, Gallimard. We thought you were the only one here without a secret. Now you go and find a lotus blossom . . . and top us all. *(He exits.)*

Gallimard (to us): Toulon knows! And he approves! I was learning the benefits of being a man. We form our own clubs, sit behind thick doors, smoke — and celebrate the fact that we're still boys. *(He starts to move downstage, towards Song.)* So, over the —

Suddenly Comrade Chin enters. Gallimard backs away.

Gallimard (to Song): No! Why does she have to come in?

Song: Rene, be sensible. How can they understand the story without her? Now, don't embarrass yourself.

Gallimard moves down center.

Gallimard (to us): Now, you will see why my story is so amusing to so many people. Why they snicker at parties in disbelief. Please — try to understand it from my point of view. We are all prisoners of our time and place. *(He exits.)*

SCENE IV

Gallimard and Butterfly's flat. Beijing. 1961.

Song (to us): 1961. The flat Monsieur Gallimard rented for us. An evening after he has gone.

Chin: Okay, see if you can find out when the Americans plan to start bombing Vietnam. If you can find out what cities, even better.

Song: I'll do my best, but I don't want to arouse his suspicions.

Chin: Yeah, sure, of course. So, what else?

Song: The Americans will increase troops in Vietnam to 170,000 soldiers with 120,000 militia and 11,000 American advisors.

Chin (writing): Wait, wait, 120,000 militia and —

Song: — 11,000 American —

Chin: — American advisors. *(Beat.)* How do you remember so much?

Song: I'm an actor.

Chin: Yeah. *(Beat.)* Is that how come you dress like that?

Song: Like what, Miss Chin?

Chin: Like that dress! You're wearing a dress. And every time I come here, you're wearing a dress. Is that because you're an actor? Or what?

Song: It's a . . . disguise, Miss Chin.

Chin: Actors, I think they're all weirdos. My mother tells me actors are like gamblers or prostitutes or —

Song: It helps me in my assignment.

Pause.

Chin: You're not gathering information in any way that violates Communist Party principles, are you?

Song: Why would I do that?

Chin: Just checking. Remember: when working for the Great Proletarian State, you represent our Chairman Mao in every position you take.

Song: I'll try to imagine the Chairman taking my positions.

Chin: We all think of him this way. Good-bye, comrade. *(She starts to exit.)* Comrade?

Song: Yes?

Chin: Don't forget: there is no homosexuality in China!

Song: Yes, I've heard.

Chin: Just checking. *(She exits.)*

Song (to us): What passes for a woman in modern China.

> *Gallimard sticks his head out from the wings.*

Gallimard: Is she gone?

Song: Yes, Rene. Please continue in your own fashion.

SCENE V

Beijing. 1961–1963.
   Gallimard moves to the couch where Song still sits. He lies down in her lap, and she strokes his forehead.

Gallimard (to us): And so, over the years 1961, '62, '63, we settled into our routine, Butterfly and I. She would always have prepared a light snack and then, ever so delicately, and only if I agreed, she would start to pleasure me. With her hands, her mouth . . . too many ways to explain, and too sad, given my present situation. But mostly we would talk. About my life. Perhaps there is nothing more rare than to find a woman who passionately listens.

> *Song remains upstage, listening, as Helga enters and plays a scene downstage with Gallimard.*

Helga: Rene, I visited Dr. Bolleart this morning.

Gallimard: Why? Are you ill?

Helga: No, no. You see, I wanted to ask him . . . that question we've been discussing.

Gallimard: And I told you, it's only a matter of time. Why did you bring a doctor into this? We just have to keep trying — like a crapshoot, actually.

Helga: I went, I'm sorry. But listen: he says there's nothing wrong with me.

Gallimard: You see? Now, will you stop — ?

Helga: Rene, he says he'd like you to go in and take some tests.

Gallimard: Why? So he can find there's nothing wrong with both of us?

Helga: Rene, I don't ask for much. One trip! One visit! And then, whatever you want to do about it — you decide.

Gallimard: You're assuming he'll find something defective!

Helga: No! Of course not! Whatever he finds — if he finds nothing, we decide what to do about nothing! But go!

Gallimard: If he finds nothing, we keep trying. Just like we do now.

Helga: But at least we'll know! *(Pause.)* I'm sorry. *(She starts to exit.)*

Gallimard: Do you really want me to see Dr. Bolleart?

Helga: Only if you want a child, Rene. We have to face the fact that time is running out. Only if you want a child. *(She exits.)*

Gallimard (to Song): I'm a modern man, Butterfly. And yet, I don't want to go.
    It's the same old voodoo. I feel like God himself is laughing at me if I can't
    produce a child.
Song: You men of the West—you're obsessed by your odd desire for equality.
    Your wife can't give you a child, and *you're* going to the doctor?
Gallimard: Well, you see, she's already gone.
Song: And because this incompetent can't find the defect, you now have to
    subject yourself to him? It's unnatural.
Gallimard: Well, what is the "natural" solution?
Song: In Imperial China, when a man found that one wife was inadequate, he
    turned to another—to give him his son.
Gallimard: What do you—? I can't . . . marry you, yet.
Song: Please. I'm not asking you to be my husband. But I am already your wife.
Gallimard: Do you want to . . . have my child?
Song: I thought you'd never ask.
Gallimard: But, your career . . . your—
Song: Phooey on my career! That's your Western mind, twisting itself into
    strange shapes again. Of course I love my career. But what would I love
    most of all? To feel something inside me—day and night—something I
    know is yours. *(Pause.)* Promise me . . . you won't go to this doctor. Who is
    this Western quack to set himself as judge over the man I love? I know who
    is a man, and who is not. *(She exits.)*
Gallimard (to us): Dr. Bolleart? Of course I didn't go. What man would?

Scene VI

Beijing. 1963.
    Party noises over the house speakers. Renee enters, wearing a revealing gown.

Gallimard: 1963. A party at the Austrian embassy. None of us could remember
    the Austrian ambassador's name, which seemed somehow appropriate.
    (To Renee.) So, I tell the Americans, Diem° must go. The U.S. wants to be
    respected by the Vietnamese, and yet they're propping up this nobody
    seminarian as her president. A man whose claim to fame is his sister-in-
    law imposing fanatic "moral order" campaigns? Oriental women—when
    they're good, they're very good, but when they're bad, they're Christians.
Renee: Yeah.
Gallimard: And what do you do?
Renee: I'm a student. My father exports a lot of useless stuff to the Third
    World.
Gallimard: How useless?
Renee: You know. Squirt guns, confectioner's sugar, Hula Hoops . . .
Gallimard: I'm sure they appreciate the sugar.
Renee: I'm here for two years to study Chinese.
Gallimard: Two years!
Renee: That's what everybody says.
Gallimard: When did you arrive?
Renee: Three weeks ago.

Diem: Ngo Dinh Diem (1901-1963), president of South Vietnam (1955-1963), assassinated in
a coup d'état supported by the United States.

Gallimard: And?

Renee: I like it. It's primitive, but . . . well, this is the place to learn Chinese, so here I am.

Gallimard: Why Chinese?

Renee: I think it'll be important someday.

Gallimard: You do?

Renee: Don't ask me when, but . . . that's what I think.

Gallimard: Well, I agree with you. One hundred percent. That's very farsighted.

Renee: Yeah. Well of course, my father thinks I'm a complete weirdo.

Gallimard: He'll thank you someday.

Renee: Like when the Chinese start buying Hula Hoops?

Gallimard: There're a billion bellies out there.

Renee: And if they end up taking over the world — well, then I'll be lucky to know Chinese too, right?

> *Pause.*

Gallimard: At this point, I don't see how the Chinese can possibly take —

Renee: You know what I *don't* like about China?

Gallimard: Excuse me? No — what?

Renee: Nothing to do at night.

Gallimard: You come to parties at embassies like everyone else.

Renee: Yeah, but they get out at ten. And then what?

Gallimard: I'm afraid the Chinese idea of a dance hall is a dirt floor and a man with a flute.

Renee: Are you married?

Gallimard: Yes. Why?

Renee: You wanna . . . fool around?

> *Pause.*

Gallimard: Sure.

Renee: I'll wait for you outside. What's your name?

Gallimard: Gallimard. Rene.

Renee: Weird. I'm Renee too. *(She exits.)*

Gallimard (to us): And so, I embarked on my first extra-extramarital affair. Renee was picture perfect. With a body like those girls in the magazines. If I put a tissue paper over my eyes, I wouldn't have been able to tell the difference. And it was exciting to be with someone who wasn't afraid to be seen completely naked. But is it possible for a woman to be *too* uninhibited, *too* willing, so as to seem almost too . . . masculine?

> *Chuck Berry°blares from the house speakers, then comes down in volume as Renee enters, toweling her hair.*

Renee: You have a nice weenie.

Gallimard: What?

Renee: Penis. You have a nice penis.

Gallimard: Oh. Well, thank you. That's very . . .

Renee: What — can't take a compliment?

Gallimard: No, it's very . . . reassuring.

Renee: But most girls don't come out and say it, huh?

Chuck Berry: Influential American rock 'n' roll musician whose first recording came out in 1955.

Gallimard: And also . . . what did you call it?

Renee: Oh. Most girls don't call it a "weenie," huh?

Gallimard: It sounds very —

Renee: Small, I know.

Gallimard: I was going to say, "young."

Renee: Yeah. Young, small, same thing. Most guys are pretty, uh, sensitive about that. Like, you know, I had a boyfriend back home in Denmark. I got mad at him once and called him a little weeniehead. He got so mad! He said at least I should call him a great big weeniehead.

Gallimard: I suppose I just say "penis."

Renee: Yeah. That's pretty clinical. There's "cock," but that sounds like a chicken. And "prick" is painful, and "dick" is like you're talking about someone who's not in the room.

Gallimard: Yes. It's a . . . bigger problem than I imagined.

Renee: I — I think maybe it's because I really don't know what to do with them — that's why I call them "weenies."

Gallimard: Well, you did quite well with . . . mine.

Renee: Thanks, but I mean, really *do* with them. Like, okay, have you ever looked at one? I mean, really?

Gallimard: No, I suppose when it's part of you, you sort of take it for granted.

Renee: I guess. But, like, it just hangs there. This little . . . flap of flesh. And there's so much fuss that we make about it. Like, I think the reason we fight wars is because we wear clothes. Because no one knows — between the men, I mean — who has the biggest . . . weenie. So, if I'm a guy with a small one, I'm going to build a really big building or take over a really big piece of land or write a really long book so the other men don't know, right? But, see, it never really works, that's the problem. I mean, you conquer the country, or whatever, but you're still wearing clothes, so there's no way to prove absolutely whose is bigger or smaller. And that's what we call a civilized society. The whole world run by a bunch of men with pricks the size of pins. *(She exits.)*

Gallimard (to us): This was simply not acceptable.

> *A high-pitched chime rings through the air. Song, dressed as Butterfly, appears in the upstage special. She is obviously distressed. Her body swoons as she attempts to clip the stems of flowers she's arranging in a vase.*

Gallimard: But I kept up our affair, wildly, for several months. Why? I believe because of Butterfly. She knew the secret I was trying to hide. But, unlike a Western woman, she didn't confront me, threaten, even pout. I remembered the words of Puccini's *Butterfly:*

Song: "Noi siamo gente avvezza / alle piccole cose / umili e silenziose."

Gallimard: "I come from a people / Who are accustomed to little / Humble and silent." I saw Pinkerton and Butterfly, and what she would say if he were unfaithful . . . nothing. She would cry, alone, into those wildly soft sleeves, once full of possessions, now empty to collect her tears. It was her tears and her silence that excited me, every time I visited Renee.

Toulon (offstage): Gallimard!

> *Toulon enters. Gallimard turns towards him. During the next section, Song, up center, begins to dance with the flowers. It is a drunken, reckless dance, where she breaks small pieces off the stems.*

Toulon: They're killing him.

Gallimard: Who? I'm sorry? What?

Toulon: Bother you to come over at this late hour?

Gallimard: No . . . of course not.

Toulon: Not after you hear my secret. Champagne?

Gallimard: Um . . . thank you.

Toulon: You're surprised. There's something that you've wanted, Gallimard. No, not a promotion. Next time. Something in the world. You're not aware of this, but there's an informal gossip circle among intelligence agents. And some of ours heard from some of the Americans —

Gallimard: Yes?

Toulon: That the U.S. will allow the Vietnamese generals to stage a coup . . . and assassinate President Diem.

> *The chime rings again. Toulon freezes. Gallimard turns upstage and looks at Butterfly, who slowly and deliberately clips a flower off its stem. Gallimard turns back towards Toulon.*

Gallimard: I think . . . that's a very wise move!

> *Toulon unfreezes.*

Toulon: It's what you've been advocating. A toast?

Gallimard: Sure. I consider this a vindication.

Toulon: Not exactly. "To the test. Let's hope you pass."

> *They drink. The chime rings again. Toulon freezes. Gallimard turns upstage, and Song clips another flower.*

Gallimard (to Toulon): The test?

Toulon (unfreezing): It's a test of everything you've been saying. I personally think the generals probably will stop the Communists. And you'll be a hero. But if anything goes wrong, then your opinions won't be worth a pig's ear. I'm sure that won't happen. But sometimes it's easier when they don't listen to you.

Gallimard: They're your opinions too, aren't they?

Toulon: Personally, yes.

Gallimard: So we agree.

Toulon: But my opinions aren't on that report. Yours are. Cheers.

> *Toulon turns away from Gallimard and raises his glass. At that instant Song picks up the vase and hurls it to the ground. It shatters. Song sinks down amidst the shards of the vase, in a calm, childlike trance. She sings softly, as if reciting a child's nursery rhyme.*

Song (repeat as necessary): "The whole world over, the white man travels, setting anchor, wherever he likes. Life's not worth living, unless he finds, the finest maidens, of every land . . . "

> *Gallimard turns downstage towards us. Song continues singing.*

Gallimard: I shook as I left his house. That coward! That worm! To put the burden for his decisions on my shoulders!

   I started for Renee's. But no, that was all I needed. A schoolgirl who would question the role of the penis in modern society. What I wanted was revenge. A vessel to contain my humiliation. Though I hadn't seen her in several weeks, I headed for Butterfly's.

Gallimard enters Song's apartment.

Song: Oh! Rene . . . I was dreaming!

Gallimard: You've been drinking?

Song: If I can't sleep, then yes, I drink. But then, it gives me these dreams which — Rene, it's been almost three weeks since you visited me last.

Gallimard: I know. There's been a lot going on in the world.

Song: Fortunately I am drunk. So I can speak freely. It's not the world, it's you and me. And an old problem. Even the softest skin becomes like leather to a man who's touched it too often. I confess I don't know how to stop it. I don't know how to become another woman.

Gallimard: I have a request.

Song: Is this a solution? Or are you ready to give up the flat?

Gallimard: It may be a solution. But I'm sure you won't like it.

Song: Oh well, that's very important. "Like it?" Do you think I "like" lying here alone, waiting, always waiting for your return? Please — don't worry about what I may not "like."

Gallimard: I want to see you . . . naked.

Silence.

Song: I thought you understood my modesty. So you want me to — what — strip? Like a big cowboy girl? Shiny pasties on my breasts? Shall I fling my kimono over my head and yell "ya-hoo" in the process? I thought you respected my shame!

Gallimard: I believe you gave me your shame many years ago.

Song: Yes — and it is just like a white devil to use it against me. I can't believe it. I thought myself so repulsed by the passive Oriental and the cruel white man. Now I see — we are always most revolted by the things hidden within us.

Gallimard: I just mean —

Song: Yes?

Gallimard: — that it will remove the only barrier left between us.

Song: No, Rene. Don't couch your request in sweet words. Be yourself — a cad — and know that my love is enough, that I submit — submit to the worst you can give me. *(Pause.)* Well, come. Strip me. Whatever happens, know that you have willed it. Our love, in your hands. I'm helpless before my man.

Gallimard starts to cross the room.

Gallimard: Did I not undress her because I knew, somewhere deep down, what I would find? Perhaps. Happiness is so rare that our mind can turn somersaults to protect it.

At the time, I only knew that I was seeing Pinkerton stalking towards his Butterfly, ready to reward her love with his lecherous hands. The image sickened me, pulled me to my knees, so I was crawling towards her like a worm. By the time I reached her, Pinkerton . . . had vanished from my heart. To be replaced by something new, something unnatural, that flew in the face of all I'd learned in the world — something very close to love.

He grabs her around the waist; she strokes his hair.

Gallimard: Butterfly, forgive me.

Song: Rene . . .

Gallimard: For everything. From the start.
Song: I'm . . .
Gallimard: I want to —
Song: I'm pregnant. *(Beat.)* I'm pregnant. *(Beat.)* I'm pregnant.

> Beat.

Gallimard: I want to marry you!

SCENE VII

> *Gallimard and Butterfly's flat. Beijing. 1963.*
> Downstage, Song paces as Comrade Chin reads from her notepad. Upstage,
> Gallimard is still kneeling. He remains on his knees throughout the scene, watching it.

Song: I need a baby.
Chin (from pad): He's been spotted going to a dorm.
Song: I need a baby.
Chin: At the Foreign Language Institute.
Song: I need a baby.
Chin: The room of a Danish girl. . . . What do you mean, you need a baby?!
Song: Tell Comrade Kang — last night, the entire mission, it could've ended.
Chin: What do you mean?
Song: Tell Kang — he told me to strip.
Chin: Strip?!
Song: Write!
Chin: I tell you, I don't understand nothing about this case anymore. Nothing.
Song: He told me to strip, and I took a chance. Oh, we Chinese, we know how to gamble.
Chin (writing): ". . . told him to strip."
Song: My palms were wet, I had to make a split-second decision.
Chin: Hey! Can you slow down?!

> Pause.

Song: You write faster, I'm the artist here. Suddenly, it hit me — "All he wants is for her to submit. Once a woman submits, a man is always ready to become 'generous.'"
Chin: You're just gonna end up with rough notes.
Song: And it worked! He gave in! Now, if I can just present him with a baby. A Chinese baby with blond hair — he'll be mine for life!
Chin: Kang will never agree! The trading of babies has to be a counterrevolutionary act!
Song: Sometimes, a counterrevolutionary act is necessary to counter a counterrevolutionary act.

> Pause.

Chin: Wait.
Song: I need one . . . in seven months. Make sure it's a boy.
Chin: This doesn't sound like something the Chairman would do. Maybe you'd better talk to Comrade Kang yourself.
Song: Good. I will.

> Chin gets up to leave.

Song: Miss Chin? Why, in the Peking Opera, are women's roles played by men?
Chin: I don't know. Maybe, a reactionary remnant of male —
Song: No. *(Beat.)* Because only a man knows how a woman is supposed to act.

> *Chin exits. Song turns upstage, towards Gallimard.*

Gallimard (calling after Chin): Good riddance! *(To Song.)* I could forget all that betrayal in an instant, you know. If you'd just come back and become Butterfly again.
Song: Fat chance. You're here in prison, rotting in a cell. And I'm on a plane, winging my way back to China. Your President pardoned me of our treason, you know.
Gallimard: Yes, I read about that.
Song: Must make you feel . . . lower than shit.
Gallimard: But don't you, even a little bit, wish you were here with me?
Song: I'm an artist, Rene. You were my greatest . . . acting challenge. *(She laughs.)* It doesn't matter how rotten I answer, does it? You still adore me. That's why I love you, Rene. *(She points to us.)* So — you were telling your audience about the night I announced I was pregnant.

> *Gallimard puts his arms around Song's waist. He and Song are in the positions they were in at the end of Scene VI.*

Scene VIII

> *Same.*

Gallimard: I'll divorce my wife. We'll live together here, and then later in France.
Song: I feel so . . . ashamed.
Gallimard: Why?
Song: I had begun to lose faith. And now, you shame me with your generosity.
Gallimard: Generosity? No, I'm proposing for very selfish reasons.
Song: Your apologies only make me feel more ashamed. My outburst a moment ago!
Gallimard: Your outburst? What about my request?!
Song: You've been very patient dealing with my . . . eccentricities. A Western man, used to women freer with their bodies —
Gallimard: It was sick! Don't make excuses for me.
Song: I have to. You don't seem willing to make them for yourself.

> *Pause.*

Gallimard: You're crazy.
Song: I'm happy. Which often looks like crazy.
Gallimard: Then make me crazy. Marry me.

> *Pause.*

Song: No.
Gallimard: What?
Song: Do I sound silly, a slave, if I say I'm not worthy?
Gallimard: Yes. In fact you do. No one has loved me like you.
Song: Thank you. And no one ever will. I'll see to that.
Gallimard: So what is the problem?

Song: Rene, we Chinese are realists. We understand rice, gold, and guns. You are a diplomat. Your career is skyrocketing. Now, what would happen if you divorced your wife to marry a Communist Chinese actress?

Gallimard: That's not being realistic. That's defeating yourself before you begin.

Song: We conserve our strength for the battles we can win.

Gallimard: That sounds like a fortune cookie!

Song: Where do you think fortune cookies come from!

Gallimard: I don't care.

Song: You do. So do I. And we should. That is why I say I'm not worthy. I'm worthy to love and even to be loved by you. But I am not worthy to end the career of one of the West's most promising diplomats.

Gallimard: It's not that great a career! I made it sound like more than it is!

Song: Modesty will get you nowhere. Flatter yourself, and you flatter me. I'm flattered to decline your offer. *(She exits.)*

Gallimard (to us): Butterfly and I argued all night. And, in the end, I left, knowing I would never be her husband. She went away for several months — to the countryside, like a small animal. Until the night I received her call.

A baby's cry from offstage. Song enters, carrying a child.

Song: He looks like you.

Gallimard: Oh! *(Beat; he approaches the baby.)* Well, babies are never very attractive at birth.

Song: Stop!

Gallimard: I'm sure he'll grow more beautiful with age. More like his mother.

Song: "Chi vide mai / a bimbo del Giappon . . . "

Gallimard: "What baby, I wonder, was ever born in Japan" — or China, for that matter —

Song: ". . . occhi azzurrini?"

Gallimard: "With azure eyes" — they're actually sort of brown, wouldn't you say?

Song: "E il labbro."

Gallimard: "And such lips!" *(He kisses Song.)* And such lips.

Song: "E i ricciolini d'oro schietto?"

Gallimard: "And such a head of golden" — if slightly patchy — "curls?"

Song: I'm going to call him "Peepee."

Gallimard: Darling, could you repeat that because I'm sure a rickshaw just flew by overhead.

Song: You heard me.

Gallimard: "Song Peepee"? May I suggest Michael, or Stephan, or Adolph?

Song: You may, but I won't listen.

Gallimard: You can't be serious. Can you imagine the time this child will have in school?

Song: In the West, yes.

Gallimard: It's worse than naming him Ping Pong or Long Dong or —

Song: But he's never going to live in the West, is he?

Pause.

Gallimard: That wasn't my choice.

Song: It is mine. And this is my promise to you: I will raise him, he will be our child, but he will never burden you outside of China.

Gallimard: Why do you make these promises? I want to be burdened! I want a scandal to cover the papers!

Song (to us): Prophetic.

Gallimard: I'm serious.

Song: So am I. His name is as I registered it. And he will never live in the West.

Song exits with the child.

Gallimard (to us): Is it possible that her stubbornness only made me want her more? That drawing back at the moment of my capitulation was the most brilliant strategy she could have chosen? It is possible. But it is also possible that by this point she could have said, could have done . . . anything, and I would have adored her still.

SCENE IX

Beijing. 1966.
A driving rhythm of Chinese percussion fills the stage.

Gallimard: And then, China began to change. Mao became very old, and his cult became very strong. And, like many old men, he entered his second childhood. So he handed over the reins of state to those with minds like his own. And children ruled the Middle Kingdom° with complete caprice. The doctrine of the Cultural Revolution° implied continuous anarchy. Contact between Chinese and foreigners became impossible. Our flat was confiscated. Her fame and my money now counted against us.

Two dancers in Mao suits and red-starred caps enter, and begin crudely mimicking revolutionary violence, in an agitprop fashion.

Gallimard: And somehow the American war went wrong too. Four hundred thousand dollars were being spent for every Viet Cong° killed; so General Westmoreland's° remark that the Oriental does not value life the way Americans do was oddly accurate. Why weren't the Vietnamese people giving in? Why were they content instead to die and die and die again?

Toulon enters. Percussion and dancers continue upstage.

Toulon: Congratulations, Gallimard.

Gallimard: Excuse me, sir?

Toulon: Not a promotion. That was last time. You're going home.

Gallimard: What?

Toulon: Don't say I didn't warn you.

Gallimard: I'm being transferred . . . because I was wrong about the American war?

Toulon: Of course not. We don't care about the Americans. We care about your mind. The quality of your analysis. In general, everything you've predicted here in the Orient . . . just hasn't happened.

Middle Kingdom: The royal domain of China during its feudal period.   *Cultural Revolution:* The reform campaign of 1965–1967 to purge counterrevolutionary thought in China that challenged Mao Zedong.   *Viet Cong:* Member of the National Liberation Front of South Vietnam, against which U.S. forces were fighting.   *General Westmoreland:* William Westmoreland (b. 1914), commander of American troops in Vietnam from 1964 to 1968.

Gallimard: I think that's premature.

Toulon: Don't force me to be blunt. Okay, you said China was ready to open to Western trade. The only thing they're trading out there are Western heads. And, yes, you said the Americans would succeed in Indochina. You were kidding, right?

Gallimard: I think the end is in sight.

Toulon: Don't be pathetic. And don't take this personally. You were wrong. It's not your fault.

Gallimard: But I'm going home.

Toulon: Right. Could I have the number of your mistress? *(Beat.)* Joke! Joke! Eat a croissant for me.

Toulon exits. Song, wearing a Mao suit, is dragged in from the wings as part of the upstage dance. They "beat" her, then lampoon the acrobatics of the Chinese opera, as she is made to kneel onstage.

Gallimard (simultaneously): I don't care to recall how Butterfly and I said our hurried farewell. Perhaps it was better to end our affair before it killed her.

Gallimard exits. Percussion rises in volume. The lampooning becomes faster, more frenetic. At its height, Comrade Chin walks across the stage with a banner reading: "The Actor Renounces His Decadent Profession!" She reaches the kneeling Song. At the moment Chin touches Song's chin, percussion stops with a thud. Dancers strike poses.

Chin: Actor-oppressor, for years you have lived above the common people and looked down on their labor. While the farmer ate millet—

Song: I ate pastries from France and sweetmeats from silver trays.

Chin: And how did you come to live in such an exalted position?

Song: I was a plaything for the imperialists!

Chin: What did you do?

Song: I shamed China by allowing myself to be corrupted by a foreigner . . .

Chin: What does this mean? The People demand a full confession!

Song: I engaged in the lowest perversions with China's enemies!

Chin: What perversions? Be more clear!

Song: I let him put it up my ass!

Dancers look over, disgusted.

Chin: Aaaa-ya! How can you use such sickening language?!

Song: My language . . . is only as foul as the crimes I committed . . .

Chin: Yeah. That's better. So—what do you want to do . . . now?

Song: I want to serve the people!

Percussion starts up, with Chinese strings.

Chin: What?

Song: I want to serve the people!

Dancers regain their revolutionary smiles, and begin a dance of victory.

Chin: What?!

Song: I want to serve the people!!

Dancers unveil a banner: "The Actor Is Re-Habilitated!" Song remains kneeling before Chin, as the dancers bounce around them, then exit. Music out.

SCENE X

> *A commune. Hunan Province. 1970.*

Chin: How you planning to do that?

Song: I've already worked four years in the fields of Hunan, Comrade Chin.

Chin: So? Farmers work all their lives. Let me see your hands.

> *Song holds them out for her inspection.*

Chin: Goddamn! Still so smooth! How long does it take to turn you actors into good anythings? Hunh. You've just spent too many years in luxury to be any good to the Revolution.

Song: I served the Revolution.

Chin: Serve the Revolution? Bullshit! You wore dresses! Don't tell me — I was there. I saw you! You and your white vice-consul! Stuck up there in your flat, living off the People's Treasury! Yeah, I knew what was going on! You two . . . homos! Homos! Homos! *(Pause; she composes herself.)* Ah! Well . . . you will serve the people, all right. But not with the Revolution's money. This time, you use your own money.

Song: I have no money.

Chin: Shut up! And you won't stink up China anymore with your pervert stuff. You'll pollute the place where pollution begins — the West.

Song: What do you mean?

Chin: Shut up! You're going to France. Without a cent in your pocket. You find your consul's house, you make him pay your expenses —

Song: No.

Chin: And you give us weekly reports! Useful information!

Song: That's crazy. It's been four years.

Chin: Either that, or back to rehabilitation center!

Song: Comrade Chin, he's not going to support me! Not in France! He's a white man! I was just his plaything —

Chin: Oh yuck! Again with the sickening language? Where's my stick?

Song: You don't understand the mind of a man.

> *Pause.*

Chin: Oh no? No I don't? Then how come I'm married, huh? How come I got a man? Five, six years ago, you always tell me those kind of things, I felt very bad. But not now! Because what does the Chairman say? He tells us *I'm* now the smart one, you're now the nincompoop! *You're* the blockhead, the harebrain, the nitwit! You think you're so smart? You understand "The Mind of a Man"? Good! Then *you* go to France and be a pervert for Chairman Mao!

> *Chin and Song exit in opposite directions.*

SCENE XI

> *Paris. 1968–1970.*
> *Gallimard enters.*

Gallimard: And what was waiting for me back in Paris? Well, better Chinese food than I'd eaten in China. Friends and relatives. A little accounting, regular schedule, keeping track of traffic violations in the suburbs. . . .

And the indignity of students shouting the slogans of Chairman Mao at me — in French.

Helga: Rene? Rene? *(She enters, soaking wet.)* I've had a . . . problem.

(She sneezes.)

Gallimard: You're wet.

Helga: Yes, I . . . coming back from the grocer's. A group of students, waving red flags, they —

Gallimard fetches a towel.

Helga: — they ran by, I was caught up along with them. Before I knew what was happening —

Gallimard gives her the towel.

Helga: Thank you. The police started firing water cannons at us. I tried to shout, to tell them I was the wife of a diplomat, but — you know how it is . . . *(Pause.)* Needless to say, I lost the groceries. Rene, what's happening to France?

Gallimard: What's — ? Well, nothing, really.

Helga: Nothing?! The storefronts are in flames, there's glass in the streets, buildings are toppling — and I'm wet!

Gallimard: Nothing! . . . that I care to think about.

Helga: And is that why you stay in this room?

Gallimard: Yes, in fact.

Helga: With the incense burning? You know something? I hate incense. It smells so sickly sweet.

Gallimard: Well, I hate the French. Who just smell — period!

Helga: And the Chinese were better?

Gallimard: Please — don't start.

Helga: When we left, this exact same thing, the riots —

Gallimard: No, no . . .

Helga: Students screaming slogans, smashing down doors —

Gallimard: Helga —

Helga: It was all going on in China, too. Don't you remember?!

Gallimard: Helga! Please! *(Pause.)* You have never understood China, have you? You walk in here with these ridiculous ideas, that the West is falling apart, that China was spitting in our faces. You come in, dripping of the streets, and you leave water all over my floor. *(He grabs Helga's towel, begins mopping up the floor.)*

Helga: But it's the truth!

Gallimard: Helga, I want a divorce.

Pause; Gallimard continues mopping the floor.

Helga: I take it back. China is . . . beautiful. Incense, I like incense.

Gallimard: I've had a mistress.

Helga: So?

Gallimard: For eight years.

Helga: I knew you would. I knew you would the day I married you. And now what? You want to marry her?

Gallimard: I can't. She's in China.

Helga: I see. You know that no one else is ever going to marry me, right?

Gallimard: I'm sorry.

Helga: And you want to leave. For someone who's not here, is that right?

Gallimard: That's right.

Helga: You can't live with her, but still you don't want to live with me.

Gallimard: That's right.

> *Pause.*

Helga: Shit. How terrible that I can figure that out. *(Pause.)* I never thought I'd say it. But, in China, I was happy. I knew, in my own way, I knew that you were not everything you pretended to be. But the pretense — going on your arm to the embassy ball, visiting your office and the guards saying, "Good morning, good morning, Madame Gallimard" — the pretense . . . was very good indeed. *(Pause.)* I hope everyone is mean to you for the rest of your life. *(She exits.)*

Gallimard (to us): Prophetic.

> *Marc enters with two drinks.*

Gallimard (to Marc): In China, I was different from all other men.

Marc: Sure. You were white. Here's your drink.

Gallimard: I felt . . . touched.

Marc: In the head? Rene, I don't want to hear about the Oriental love goddess. Okay? One night — can we just drink and throw up without a lot of conversation?

Gallimard: You still don't believe me, do you?

Marc: Sure I do. She was the most beautiful, et cetera, et cetera, blasé, blasé.

> *Pause.*

Gallimard: My life in the West has been such a disappointment.

Marc: Life in the West is like that. You'll get used to it. Look, you're driving me away. I'm leaving. Happy, now? *(He exits, then returns.)* Look, I have a date tomorrow night. You wanna come? I can fix you up with —

Gallimard: Of course. I would love to come.

> *Pause.*

Marc: Uh — on second thought, no. You'd better get ahold of yourself first.

> *He exits; Gallimard nurses his drink.*

Gallimard (to us): This is the ultimate cruelty, isn't it? That I can talk and talk and to anyone listening, it's only air — too rich a diet to be swallowed by a mundane world. Why can't anyone understand? That in China, I once loved, and was loved by, very simply, the Perfect Woman.

> *Song enters, dressed as Butterfly in wedding dress.*

Gallimard (to Song): Not again. My imagination is hell. Am I asleep this time? Or did I drink too much?

Song: Rene!

Gallimard: God, it's too painful! That you speak?

Song: What are you talking about? Rene — touch me.

Gallimard: Why?

Song: I'm real. Take my hand.

Gallimard: Why? So you can disappear again and leave me clutching at the air? For the entertainment of my neighbors who —?

Song touches Gallimard.

Song: Rene?

Gallimard takes Song's hand. Silence.

Gallimard: Butterfly? I never doubted you'd return.

Song: You hadn't . . . forgotten —?

Gallimard: Yes, actually, I've forgotten everything. My mind, you see — there wasn't enough room in this hard head — not for the world *and* for you. No, there was only room for one. *(Beat.)* Come, look. See? Your bed has been waiting, with the Klimt° poster you like, and — see? The *xiang lu*° you gave me?

Song: I . . . I don't know what to say.

Gallimard: There's nothing to say. Not at the end of a long trip. Can I make you some tea?

Song: But where's your wife?

Gallimard: She's by my side. She's by my side at last.

Gallimard reaches to embrace Song. Song sidesteps, dodging him.

Gallimard: Why?!

Song (to us): So I did return to Rene in Paris. Where I found —

Gallimard: Why do you run away? Can't we show them how we embraced that evening?

Song: Please. I'm talking.

Gallimard: You have to do what I say! I'm conjuring you up in *my* mind!

Song: Rene, I've never done what you've said. Why should it be any different in your mind? Now split — the story moves on, and I must change.

Gallimard: I welcomed you into my home! I didn't have to, you know! I could've left you penniless on the streets of Paris! But I took you in!

Song: Thank you.

Gallimard: So . . . please . . . don't change.

Song: You know I have to. You know I will. And anyway, what difference does it make? No matter what your eyes tell you, you can't ignore the truth. You already know too much.

Gallimard exits. Song turns to us.

Song: The change I'm going to make requires about five minutes. So I thought you might want to take this opportunity to stretch your legs, enjoy a drink, or listen to the musicians. I'll be here, when you return, right where you left me.

Song goes to a mirror in front of which is a wash basin of water. She starts to re- move her makeup as stagelights go to half and houselights come up.

Klimt: Gustav Klimt (1863–1918), Austrian painter in the art nouveau style, whose most fa- mous painting is *The Kiss.*   *xiang lu:* Incense burner.

ACT III

SCENE I

A courthouse in Paris. 1986.
   As he promised, Song has completed the bulk of his transformation onstage by the time the houselights go down and the stagelights come up full. As he speaks to us, he removes his wig and kimono, leaving them on the floor. Underneath, he wears a well-cut suit.

Song: So I'd done my job better than I had a right to expect. Well, give him some credit, too. He's right — I was in a fix when I arrived in Paris. I walked from the airport into town, then I located, by blind groping, the Chinatown district. Let me make one thing clear: whatever else may be said about the Chinese, they are stingy! I slept in doorways three days until I could find a tailor who would make me this kimono on credit. As it turns out, maybe I didn't even need it. Maybe he would've been happy to see me in a simple shift and mascara. But . . . better safe than sorry.
   That was 1970, when I arrived in Paris. For the next fifteen years, yes, I lived a very comfy life. Some relief, believe me, after four years on a fucking commune in Nowheresville, China. Rene supported the boy and me, and I did some demonstrations around the country as part of my "cultural exchange" cover. And then there was the spying.

Song moves upstage, to a chair. Toulon enters as a judge, wearing the appropriate wig and robes. He sits near Song. It's 1986, and Song is testifying in a courtroom.

Song: Not much at first. Rene had lost all his high-level contacts. Comrade Chin wasn't very interested in parking-ticket statistics. But finally, at my urging, Rene got a job as a courier, handling sensitive documents. He'd photograph them for me, and I'd pass them on to the Chinese embassy.
Judge: Did he understand the extent of his activity?
Song: He didn't ask. He knew that I needed those documents, and that was enough.
Judge: But he must've known he was passing classified information.
Song: I can't say.
Judge: He never asked what you were going to do with them?
Song: Nope.

   Pause.

Judge: There is one thing that the court — indeed, that all of France — would like to know.
Song: Fire away.
Judge: Did Monsieur Gallimard know you were a man?
Song: Well, he never saw me completely naked. Ever.
Judge: But surely, he must've . . . how can I put this?
Song: Put it however you like. I'm not shy. He must've felt around?
Judge: Mmmmm.
Song: Not really. I did all the work. He just laid back. Of course we did enjoy more . . . complete union, and I suppose he *might* have wondered why I was always on my stomach, but. . . . But what you're thinking is, "Of course a

wrist must've brushed . . . a hand hit . . . over twenty years!" Yeah. Well, Your Honor, it was my job to make him think I was a woman. And chew on this: it wasn't all that hard. See, my mother was a prostitute along the Bundt before the Revolution. And, uh, I think it's fair to say she learned a few things about Western men. So I borrowed her knowledge. In service to my country.

Judge: Would you care to enlighten the court with this secret knowledge? I'm sure we're all very curious.

Song: I'm sure you are. *(Pause.)* Okay, Rule One is: Men always believe what they want to hear. So a girl can tell the most obnoxious lies and the guys will believe them every time — "This is my first time" — "That's the biggest I've ever seen" — or *both,* which, if you really think about it, is not possible in a single lifetime. You've maybe heard those phrases a few times in your own life, yes, Your Honor?

Judge: It's not my life, Monsieur Song, which is on trial today.

Song: Okay, okay, just trying to lighten up the proceedings. Tough room.

Judge: Go on.

Song: Rule Two: As soon as a Western man comes into contact with the East — he's already confused. The West has sort of an international rape mentality towards the East. Do you know rape mentality?

Judge: Give us your definition, please.

Song: Basically, "Her mouth says no, but her eyes say yes."

The West thinks of itself as masculine — big guns, big industry, big money — so the East is feminine — weak, delicate, poor . . . but good at art, and full of inscrutable wisdom — the feminine mystique.

Her mouth says no, but her eyes say yes. The West believes the East, deep down, *wants* to be dominated — because a woman can't think for herself.

Judge: What does this have to do with my question?

Song: You expect Oriental countries to submit to your guns, and you expect Oriental women to be submissive to your men. That's why you say they make the best wives.

Judge: But why would that make it possible for you to fool Monsieur Gallimard? Please — get to the point.

Song: One, because when he finally met his fantasy woman, he wanted more than anything to believe that she was, in fact, a woman. And second, I am an Oriental. And being an Oriental, I could never be completely a man.

Pause.

Judge: Your armchair political theory is tenuous, Monsieur Song.

Song: You think so? That's why you'll lose in all your dealings with the East.

Judge: Just answer my question: did he know you were a man?

Pause.

Song: You know, Your Honor, I never asked.

Scene II

Same.

    Music from the "Death Scene" from Butterfly *blares over the house speakers. It is the loudest thing we've heard in this play.*

    Gallimard enters, crawling towards Song's wig and kimono.

Gallimard: Butterfly? Butterfly?

Song remains a man, in the witness box, delivering a testimony we do not hear.

Gallimard (to us): In my moment of greatest shame, here, in this courtroom — with that . . . person up there, telling the world. . . . What strikes me especially is how shallow he is, how glib and obsequious . . . completely . . . without substance! The type that prowls around discos with a gold medallion stinking of garlic. So little like my Butterfly.

Yet even in this moment my mind remains agile, flip-flopping like a man on a trampoline. Even now, my picture dissolves, and I see that . . . witness . . . talking to me.

Song suddenly stands straight up in his witness box, and looks at Gallimard.

Song: Yes. You. White man.

Song steps out of the witness box, and moves downstage towards Gallimard. Light change.

Gallimard (to Song): Who? Me?

Song: Do you see any other white men?

Gallimard: Yes. There're white men all around. This is a French courtroom.

Song: So you are an adventurous imperialist. Tell me, why did it take you so long? To come back to this place?

Gallimard: What place?

Song: This theater in China. Where we met many years ago.

Gallimard (to us): And once again, against my will, I am transported.

Chinese opera music comes up on the speakers. Song begins to do opera moves, as he did the night they met.

Song: Do you remember? The night you gave your heart?

Gallimard: It was a long time ago.

Song: Not long enough. A night that turned your world upside down.

Gallimard: Perhaps.

Song: Oh, be honest with me. What's another bit of flattery when you've already given me twenty years' worth? It's a wonder my head hasn't swollen to the size of China.

Gallimard: Who's to say it hasn't?

Song: Who's to say? And what's the shame? In pride? You think I could've pulled this off if I wasn't already full of pride when we met? No, not just pride. Arrogance. It takes arrogance, really — to believe you can will, with your eyes and your lips, the destiny of another. *(He dances.)* C'mon. Admit it. You still want me. Even in slacks and a button-down collar.

Gallimard: I don't see what the point of —

Song: You don't? Well maybe, Rene, just maybe — I want you.

Gallimard: You do?

Song: Then again, maybe I'm just playing with you. How can you tell? *(Reprising his feminine character, he sidles up to Gallimard.)* "How I wish there were even a small café to sit in. With men in tuxedos, and cappuccinos, and bad expatriate jazz." Now you want to kiss me, don't you?

Gallimard (pulling away): What makes you — ?

Song: — so sure? See? I take the words from your mouth. Then I wait for you to come and retrieve them. *(He reclines on the floor.)*

Gallimard: Why?! Why do you treat me so cruelly?

Song: Perhaps I *was* treating you cruelly. But now—I'm being nice. Come here, my little one.

Gallimard: I'm not your little one!

Song: My mistake. It's who am *your* little one, right?

Gallimard: Yes, I—

Song: So come get your little one. If you like, I may even let you strip me.

Gallimard: I mean, you were! Before . . . but not like this!

Song: I was? Then perhaps I still am. If you look hard enough. *(He starts to remove his clothes.)*

Gallimard: What—what are you doing?

Song: Helping you to see through my act.

Gallimard: Stop that! I don't want to! I don't—

Song: Oh, but you asked me to strip, remember?

Gallimard: What? That was years ago! And I took it back!

Song: No. You postponed it. Postponed the inevitable. Today, the inevitable has come calling.

> *From the speakers, cacophony: Butterfly mixed in with Chinese gongs.*

Gallimard: No! Stop! I don't want to see!

Song: Then look away.

Gallimard: You're only in my mind! All this is in my mind! I order you! To stop!

Song: To what? To strip? That's just what I'm—

Gallimard: No! Stop! I want you—!

Song: You want me?

Gallimard: To stop!

Song: You know something, Rene? Your mouth says no, but your eyes say yes. Turn them away. I dare you.

Gallimard: I don't have to! Every night, you say you're going to strip, but then I beg you and you stop!

Song: I guess tonight is different.

Gallimard: Why? Why should that be?

Song: Maybe I've become frustrated. Maybe I'm saying "Look at me, you fool!" Or maybe I'm just feeling . . . sexy. *(He is down to his briefs.)*

Gallimard: Please. This is unnecessary. I know what you are.

Song: You do? What am I?

Gallimard: A—a man.

Song: You don't really believe that.

Gallimard: Yes I do! I knew all the time somewhere that my happiness was temporary, my love a deception. But my mind kept the knowledge at bay. To make the wait bearable.

Song: Monsieur Gallimard—the wait is over.

> *Song drops his briefs. He is naked. Sound cue out. Slowly, we and Song come to the realization that what we had thought to be Gallimard's sobbing is actually his laughter.*

Gallimard: Oh god! What an idiot! Of course!

Song: Rene—what?

Gallimard: Look at you! You're a man! *(He bursts into laughter again.)*

Song: I fail to see what's so funny!

Gallimard: "You fail to see—!" I mean, you never did have much of a sense of humor, did you? I just think it's ridiculously funny that I've wasted so much time on just a man!

Song: Wait. I'm not "just a man."

Gallimard: No? Isn't that what you've been trying to convince me of?

Song: Yes, but what I mean—

Gallimard: And now, I finally believe you, and you tell me it's not true? I think you must have some kind of identity problem.

Song: Will you listen to me?

Gallimard: Why?! I've been listening to you for twenty years. Don't I deserve a vacation?

Song: I'm not just any man!

Gallimard: Then, what exactly are you?

Song: Rene, how can you ask—? Okay, what about this?

He picks up Butterfly's robes, starts to dance around. No music.

Gallimard: Yes, that's very nice. I have to admit.

Song holds out his arm to Gallimard.

Song: It's the same skin you've worshipped for years. Touch it.

Gallimard: Yes, it does feel the same.

Song: Now—close your eyes.

Song covers Gallimard's eyes with one hand. With the other, Song draws Gallimard's hand up to his face. Gallimard, like a blind man, lets his hands run over Song's face.

Gallimard: This skin, I remember. The curve of her face, the softness of her cheek, her hair against the back of my hand . . .

Song: I'm your Butterfly. Under the robes, beneath everything, it was always me. Now, open your eyes and admit it—you adore me. *(He removes his hand from Gallimard's eyes.)*

Gallimard: You, who knew every inch of my desires—how could you, of all people, have made such a mistake?

Song: What?

Gallimard: You showed me your true self. When all I loved was the lie. A perfect lie, which you let fall to the ground—and now, it's old and soiled.

Song: So—you never really loved me? Only when I was playing a part?

Gallimard: I'm a man who loved a woman created by a man. Everything else— simply falls short.

Pause.

Song: What am I supposed to do now?

Gallimard: You were a fine spy, Monsieur Song, with an even finer accomplice. But now I believe you should go. Get out of my life!

Song: Go where? Rene, you can't live without me. Not after twenty years.

Gallimard: I certainly can't live with you—not after twenty years of betrayal.

Song: Don't be stubborn! Where will you go?

Gallimard: I have a date . . . with my Butterfly.

Song: So, throw away your pride. And come . . .

Gallimard: Get away from me! Tonight, I've finally learned to tell fantasy from reality. And, knowing the difference, I choose fantasy.

Song: I'm your fantasy!

Gallimard: You? You're as real as hamburger. Now get out! I have a date with my Butterfly and I don't want your body polluting the room! *(He tosses Song's suit at him.)* Look at these — you dress like a pimp.

Song: Hey! These are Armani slacks and — ! *(He puts on his briefs and slacks.)* Let's just say . . . I'm disappointed in you, Rene. In the crush of your adoration, I thought you'd become something more. More like . . . a woman.

But no. Men. You're like the rest of them. It's all in the way we dress, and make up our faces, and bat our eyelashes. You really have so little imagination!

Gallimard: You, Monsieur Song? Accuse me of too little imagination? You, if anyone, should know — I am pure imagination. And in imagination I will remain. Now get out!

Gallimard bodily removes Song from the stage, taking his kimono.

Song: Rene! I'll never put on those robes again! You'll be sorry!

Gallimard (to Song): I'm already sorry! *(Looking at the kimono in his hands.)* Exactly as sorry . . . as a Butterfly.

Scene III

M. Gallimard's prison cell. Paris. 1988.

Gallimard: I've played out the events of my life night after night, always searching for a new ending to my story, one where I leave this cell and return forever to my Butterfly's arms.

Tonight I realize my search is over. That I've looked all along in the wrong place. And now, to you, I will prove that my love was not in vain — by returning to the world of fantasy where I first met her.

He picks up the kimono; dancers enter.

Gallimard: There is a vision of the Orient that I have. Of slender women in cheongsams and kimonos who die for the love of unworthy foreign devils. Who are born and raised to be the perfect women. Who take whatever punishment we give them, and bounce back, strengthened by love, unconditionally. It is a vision that has become my life.

Dancers bring the washbasin to him and help him make up his face.

Gallimard: In public, I have continued to deny that Song Liling is a man. This brings me headlines, and is a source of great embarrassment to my French colleagues, who can now be sent into a coughing fit by the mere mention of Chinese food. But alone, in my cell, I have long since faced the truth.

And the truth demands a sacrifice. For mistakes made over the course of a lifetime. My mistakes were simple and absolute — the man I loved was a cad, a bounder. He deserved nothing but a kick in the behind, and instead I gave him . . . all my love.

Yes — love. Why not admit it all? That was my undoing, wasn't it? Love warped my judgment, blinded my eyes, rearranged the very lines on my face . . . until I could look in the mirror and see nothing but . . . a woman.

Dancers help him put on the Butterfly wig.

Gallimard: I have a vision. Of the Orient. That, deep within its almond eyes, there are still women. Women willing to sacrifice themselves for the love of a man. Even a man whose love is completely without worth.

Dancers assist Gallimard in donning the kimono. They hand him a knife.

Gallimard: Death with honor is better than life . . . life with dishonor. *(He sets himself center stage, in a seppuku position.)* The love of a Butterfly can withstand many things — unfaithfulness, loss, even abandonment. But how can it face the one sin that implies all others? The devastating knowledge that, underneath it all, the object of her love was nothing more, nothing less than . . . a man. *(He sets the tip of the knife against his body.)* It is 1988. And I have found her at last. In a prison on the outskirts of Paris. My name is Rene Gallimard — also known as Madame Butterfly.

Gallimard turns upstage and plunges the knife into his body, as music from the "Love Duet" blares over the speakers. He collapses into the arms of the dancers, who lay him reverently on the floor. The image holds for several beats. Then a tight special up on Song, who stands as a man, staring at the dead Gallimard. He smokes a cigarette; the smoke filters up through the lights. Two words leave his lips.

Song: Butterfly? Butterfly?

Smoke rises as lights fade slowly to black.

CONSIDERATIONS FOR CRITICAL THINKING AND WRITING

1. FIRST RESPONSE. Do you think Gallimard is a sympathetic or despicable character? Does he have any redeeming qualities? Explain why or why not.

2. In addition to Gallimard, which other characters in the play reveal prejudices of one kind or another? What is the nature of these prejudices?

3. How does Gallimard's response to Song's letters reveal his attitudes toward her?

4. What purpose do Marc and Helga serve in the play?

5. What are some of the explanations for Gallimard's belief that Song is a woman? Which is the most plausible?

6. Why does Gallimard link magazine centerfold models with Asian women?

7. How does the structure of the play help to reinforce its themes?

8. Discuss the role reversal that takes place in the final scene.

9. Is *M. Butterfly* a comedy or a tragedy or something else?

10. Some critics have faulted *M. Butterfly* for the heavy-handed way in which Hwang links Western sexism to the events in Vietnam rather than letting the audience draw its own conclusions. In what ways do you think the play too polemical, and how do you feel the story carries its themes effectively?

CONNECTIONS TO OTHER SELECTIONS

1. At first glance Rene Gallimard and Sophocles' Oedipus in *Oedipus the King* (p. 1224) are very different kinds of characters, but how might their situations — particularly their discoveries about themselves — be compared? What significant similarities do you find in these two characters? Explain whether you think Gallimard can be seen as a tragic character.

2. Compare the function of Puccini's *Madame Butterfly* in *M. Butterfly* with that of the play within the play in Shakespeare's *Hamlet* (p. 1383). How are these internal dramatic actions used to comment on the events of each larger play? How is role playing relevant to the theme of each play?

3. Compare and contrast the way women are represented in *M. Butterfly* and Yukio Mishima's short story "Patriotism" (p. 593).

4. Write an essay comparing Gallimard's illusions with those of Amanda in Tennessee Williams's *The Glass Menagerie* (p. 1864).

DOCUMENTS

A Plot Synopsis of Madame Butterfly 1964

Madama Butterfly

Opera in 2 acts by Puccini; text by Giacosa and Illica, after David Belasco's drama (1900) on the story by John Luther Long, possibly based on a real event. Prod. Milan, Sc., 17 Feb. 1904, with Storchio, Zenatello, De Luca, when it was a fiasco. New version (three acts) prod. Brescia, Grande, 28 May 1904, with Krusceniski, cond. Toscanini; London, C.G., 10 July 1905 with Destinn, Caruso, Scotti; Washington, D.C., Belasco Theatre, 15 Oct. 1906, by Savage Company.

Act I. Goro (tenor), the Japanese marriage broker, is showing Pinkerton (tenor), lieutenant of the U.S. Navy, the little house he has leased for him and his Japanese child-bride, Cio-Cio-San (Madama Butterfly). The American Consul Sharpless (baritone) comes to see Pinkerton who tells him jokingly that he is going to marry in Japanese fashion for 999 years; and he drinks to the day he will marry an American girl. Sharpless warns Pinkerton that Butterfly really loves him and has renounced her religion to marry him. Butterfly (soprano) and her friends appear and the wedding ceremony takes place. In the midst of the celebrations the Bonze, a Japanese priest and her uncle, arrives and denounces her for giving up her religion. Pinkerton comforts the weeping Butterfly, and the act ends with an extended love duet.

Act 2. Scene I. Three years have passed, and the faithful Butterfly still awaits Pinkerton. She tries to convince her servant Suzuki (mezzo) in the famous aria "Un bel dì vedremo" that he will return. Sharpless now comes to see Butterfly with a letter from Pinkerton telling him that he is indeed returning. She is so thrilled with the prospect of seeing Pinkerton again that Sharpless is unable to tell her that Pinkerton will be bringing his new American wife. Goro appears with Prince Yamadori, a wealthy suitor. Sharpless tries to persuade her to accept Yamadori's proposal. He asks Butterfly what she would do if Pinkerton was never to return. She replies that she would kill herself, and then brings in the child she has borne Pinkerton. The harbor cannon announces the arrival of a ship — it is Pinkerton's. Butterfly, with Suzuki, decks the house with flowers; she then puts on her wedding dress, and they watch for Pinkerton's arrival. Night falls.

Act 2. *Scene 2.* After an intermezzo, the curtain rises to show Suzuki and the baby asleep, with Butterfly still waiting. Suzuki awakens and persuades her to rest. Pinkerton now arrives, and when Suzuki sees the American woman with him she guesses the truth. He sings a farewell to the little dwelling he had loved so well, and thrusting some money into Sharpless's hand leaves him to resolve the situation as best he can. Butterfly enters, and seeing Suzuki in tears, and then Kate Pinkerton, realizes what has happened. Kate begs her to let them have the child, and Butterfly agrees on condition that Pinkerton comes to collect him. Butterfly bids him a tearful farewell and then stabs herself. As she falls dying to the floor, Pinkerton's voice is heard calling her name. He enters the house to fetch his son just as Butterfly expires.

From Harold Rosenthal and John Warrack,
Concise Oxford Dictionary of Opera

CONSIDERATIONS FOR CRITICAL THINKING AND WRITING

1. In Act I, Scene iii, Gallimard sits alone in his prison cell and directly tells the audience that "In order for you to understand what I did and why, I must introduce you to my favorite opera: *Madame Butterfly.* By Giacomo Puccini." Why is the opera so central to telling Gallimard's story?

2. What does Gallimard's account of the opera emphasize? What details are foregrounded? Are any significant elements of the plot left out?

3. Is Gallimard to be more identified with Pinkerton or Butterfly? Explain your response.

4. Listen to a recording of *Madame Butterfly.* How does the music affect your understanding of the play?

RICHARD BERNSTEIN (B. 1944)
The News Source for M. Butterfly   1986

France Jails Two in Odd Case of Espionage

Paris, May 10. A former French diplomat and a Chinese opera singer have been sentenced to six years in jail for spying for China after a two-day trial that traced a story of clandestine love and mistaken sexual identity.

A member of the French counterespionage service said at the trial, which ended Tuesday, that the operation to collect information on France was carried out by a Chinese Communist Party intelligence unit that no longer exists.

The Chinese government has denied any involvement in the case.

The case has been the talk of Paris lately, not so much because of the charge of spying itself as because of the circumstances. The case centered on a love affair between a young French diplomat, Bernard Boursicot, now forty-one years old, who was stationed in Peking two decades ago, and a popular Chinese opera singer, Shi Peipu, forty-six.

Mr. Boursicot was accused of passing information to China after he fell in love with Mr. Shi, whom he believed for twenty years to be a woman.

Testimony in the trial indicated that the affair began in 1964 when Mr. Boursicot, then twenty years old, was posted at the French Embassy in Peking as an accountant. There he met Mr. Shi, a celebrated singer at the Peking Opera, where female roles have, according to tradition, often been played by men.

Mr. Shi was a well-known cultural figure in Peking and one of the few individuals allowed by the Chinese authorities to have contacts with foreigners.

According to testimony, Mr. Shi told Mr. Boursicot at a reception in the French Embassy in Peking that he was actually a woman.

A love affair between the two ensued to the point where, after several months, Mr. Shi told Mr. Boursicot that he was pregnant; later he announced to the apparently credulous Mr. Boursicot that he had had a son, Shi Dudu, that the diplomat had fathered.

Asked by the trial judge how he could have been so completely taken in, Mr. Boursicot said: "I was shattered to learn that he is a man, but my conviction remains unshakable that for me at that time he was really a woman and was the first love of my life. And then, there was the child that I saw, Shi Dudu. He looked like me."

Further explaining his sexual misidentification of Mr. Shi, Mr. Boursicot said their meetings had been hasty affairs that always took place in the dark.

"He was very shy," Mr. Boursicot said. "I thought it was a Chinese custom."

Mr. Boursicot's espionage activities began in 1969, when he returned to Peking after a three-year absence. By then, China was at the height of the Cultural Revolution, and it was virtually impossible for foreigners to have personal relations with Chinese citizens.

Mr. Boursicot testified that a member of the Chinese secret service, whom he said he knew only as "Kang," approached him and said he could continue to see Mr. Shi if he provided intelligence information from the French Embassy. Mr. Boursicot apparently believed that if he refused to comply, Mr. Shi would be persecuted.

Mr. Boursicot was accused of having turned over some 150 documents to Shi Peipu, who passed them on to "Kang." Mr. Boursicot said at the trial that the materials were generally not sensitive and were publicly available.

Later, from 1977 to 1979, Mr. Boursicot was posted at the French Embassy in Ulan Bator in Mongolia, where one of his duties was to make a weekly trip to Peking with the diplomatic pouch. He said he made photocopies of the documents in the diplomatic pouch and turned them over to Mr. Shi.

The case was uncovered in 1983 when Mr. Shi, accompanied by his putative son, Shi Dudu, was allowed to leave China. He lived in Paris with Mr. Boursicot, who said he continued to believe that Mr. Shi was a woman.

The arrival of a Chinese citizen in the home of a former French diplomat attracted the attention of the French counterespionage service. When the French police questioned Mr. Boursicot about his relations with Mr. Shi, he disclosed his spying activities.

From the *New York Times*, May 11, 1986

CONSIDERATIONS FOR CRITICAL THINKING AND WRITING

1. What details of the news story does Hwang use? Which does he ignore?
2. Explain whether your knowledge of its source has any effect on your understanding or enjoyment of *M. Butterfly*.

3. Write a response to this explanation of the relationship: Mr. Shi "was very shy," Mr. Boursicot said. "I thought it was a Chinese custom" (para. 12).

Shi Pei Pu in The Story of the Butterfly

CONSIDERATIONS FOR CRITICAL THINKING AND WRITING

1. Shi Pei Pu plays a central role as a source for Song Liling's character in *M. Butterfly* (see "The News Source for *M. Butterfly*," p. 1723). This photograph shows him as he appeared in the opera production of *The Story of the Butterfly*, in which he played the role of a girl who dresses up as a boy and falls in love with another boy. Does this photograph confirm or damage Boursicot's/Gallimard's credibility when he says he believed his object of love to be a woman?

2. How does this image of Shi Pei Pu evoke ideas, feelings, and attitudes about the East? Does Song Liling's character confirm or refute the image presented in the photograph? Explain your response.

FRANK RICH (B. 1949)

A Theater Review of M. Butterfly   *1988*

M. Butterfly, A Story of a Strange Love, Conflict, and Betrayal

It didn't require genius for David Henry Hwang to see that there were the makings of a compelling play in the 1986 newspaper story that prompted him to write *M. Butterfly*. Here was the incredible true-life tale of a career French foreign service officer brought to ruin — conviction for espionage — by a bizarre 20-year affair with a Beijing Opera diva. Not only had the French diplomat failed to recognize that his lover was a spy; he'd also failed to figure out that "she" was a he in drag. "It was dark, and she was very modest," says Gallimard (John Lithgow), Mr. Hwang's fictionalized protagonist, by half-joking way of explanation. When we meet him in the prison cell where he reviews his life, Gallimard has become, according to his own understatement, "the patron saint of the socially inept."

But if this story is a corker, what is it about, exactly? That's where Mr. Hwang's imagination, one of the most striking to emerge in the American theater in this decade, comes in, and his answer has nothing to do with journalism. This playwright, the author of *The Dance and the Railroad* and *Family Devotions,* does not tease us with obvious questions such as is she or isn't she?, or does he know or doesn't he? Mr. Hwang isn't overly concerned with how the opera singer, named Song Liling (B. D. Wong), pulled his hocus-pocus in the boudoir, and he refuses to explain away Gallimard by making him a closeted, self-denying homosexual. An inversion of Puccini's *Madama Butterfly,* M. Butterfly is also the inverse of most American plays. Instead of reducing the world to an easily digested cluster of sexual or familial relationships, Mr. Hwang cracks open a liaison to reveal a sweeping, universal meditation on two of the most heated conflicts — men versus women, East versus West — of this or any other time.

The play's form — whether the clashing and blending of Western and Eastern cultures or of male and female characters — is wedded to its content. It's Mr. Hwang's starting-off point that a cultural icon like *Madama Butterfly* bequeaths the sexist and racist roles that burden Western men: Gallimard believes he can become "a real man" only if he can exercise power over a beautiful and submissive woman, which is why he's so ripe to be duped by Song Liling's impersonation of a shrinking butterfly. Mr. Hwang broadens his message by making Gallimard an architect of the Western foreign policy in Vietnam. The diplomat disastrously reasons that a manly display of American might can bring the Viet Cong to submission as easily as he or Puccini's Pinkerton can overpower a Madama Butterfly.

Lest that ideological leap seem too didactic, the playwright shuffles the deck still more, suggesting that the roles played by Gallimard and Song Liling run so deep that they cross the boundaries of nations, cultures, revolutions, and sexual orientations. That Gallimard was fated to love "a woman created by a man" proves to be figuratively as well as literally true: we see that the male culture that inspired his "perfect woman" is so entrenched that the attitudes of *Madama Butterfly* survive in his cherished present-day porno magazines. Nor is the third world, in Mr. Hwang's view, immune from adopting the roles it condemns in foreign devils. We're sarcastically told that men continue to play women in Chinese opera because "only a man knows how a woman is supposed to act." When Song Liling reassumes his male "true self," he still must play a submissive Butterfly to Gallimard—whatever his or Gallimard's actual sexual persuasions—unless he chooses to play the role of aggressor to a Butterfly of his own.

Mr. Hwang's play is not without its repetitions and its overly explicit bouts of thesis mongering. When the playwright stops trusting his own instinct for the mysterious, the staging often helps out. Using Eiko Ishioka's towering, blood-red Oriental variant on the abstract sets Mr. Dexter has employed in *Equus* and the Metropolitan Opera *Dialogues of the Carmelites,* the director stirs together Mr. Hwang's dramatic modes and settings until one floats to a purely theatrical imaginative space suspended in time and place. That same disorienting quality can be found in Mr. Wong's Song Liling—a performance that, like John Lone's in the early Hwang plays, finds even more surprises in the straddling of cultures than in the blurring of genders.

From the *New York Times,* March 21, 1988

CONSIDERATIONS FOR CRITICAL THINKING AND WRITING

1. What do you think Rich means when he says that "The play's form . . . is wedded to its content" (para. 3)?

2. Why doesn't Rich judge the play to be "too didactic" (para. 4)? What saves the play from excessive didacticism?

3. Explain why you agree or disagree that the play "is overly explicit" and indulges in "bouts of thesis mongering" (para. 5).

4. See the film version of *M. Butterfly* (on video tape), and write a review of it.

DAVID SAVRAN (B. 1950)

An Interview with David Henry Hwang   *1988*

Savran: You strongly historicize the personal story [in *M. Butterfly*], comparing various imperialist ventures, like Vietnam, with Boursicot's sexual imperialism.

Hwang: What I was trying to do in *Butterfly*—I didn't really know this except in retrospect—was to link imperialism, racism, and sexism. It necessitates a certain historical perspective.

Savran: And a look at the mythologies created to justify them.

Hwang: Particularly Puccini's *Madame Butterfly.*

Savran: So the play is really focused on two systems of domination, the cultural and the sexual.

Hwang: Cultural superiority is essentially economic. Whatever country dominates the world economically determines what culture is, for a while. There's a lag, because the country gets to determine the culture even after somebody else takes over economically. It still has the mystique of being the old culture, whether it's Britain or the United States. Probably the next world power is going to be Japan. You can't deal with cultural mystique unless you deal with political mystique, political power.

Savran: I was interested in how you handled the fact that Boursicot's mistress, Shi Peipu, is really a man. That makes for the reversal at the end, the fact that Shi turns out to be Pinkerton.

Hwang: That's the axis on which the play turns. Insofar as this is possible, I would like to seduce the audience during the first act into believing that Shi is a woman. We're so conditioned to think in certain ways about Oriental women and the relationship of the West to the East, that I think it would be fun to get into the audience's head in the first act, in a very reactionary way, and then blow it out later. I don't know to what degree that's possible because anyone who goes to see this play, especially if it runs any length of time, will probably know what it's about. But I still think it can work on some level.

Savran: So you want Shi played by a man?

Hwang: Definitely. You have to create the illusion for the audience, you have to trick them. It's dirty pool if you give them a woman and say, this is a woman, and later, when he appears as a man, you give them a man. You have to play by the rules. If you're saying that Boursicot was seduced by a man, then you have to seduce the audience with a man. *Butterfly* runs the risk of indulging the sin it condemns, like violent movies that are supposedly antiviolence. If you cast a woman in that role, you'd condemn the oppression of women by oppressing a woman in a very attractive way on the stage. If you oppress a woman who actually is a man, it's much more interesting.

From *In Their Own Voices*

CONSIDERATIONS FOR CRITICAL THINKING AND WRITING

1. Why does Hwang think it is essential that Shi/Song be played by a man? Discuss whether you agree or disagree with his assessment of who should play the role.

2. Consider your response to Song as you read the play. How does knowing that Song is actually a man rather than a woman affect your response to him and to Gallimard?

3. Write an essay that discusses the ways in which Hwang weaves his concerns about imperialism, racism, and sexism into the play.

36

A Collection of Plays

A Raisin in the Sun

Lorraine Hansberry, the youngest of four children raised by African American parents who migrated from the South, was born in Chicago, Illinois. Her father was a successful businessman who provided the family with a comfortable middle-class home where distinguished blacks such as W. E. B. Du Bois, Langston Hughes, Duke Ellington, and Paul Robeson visited. Her mother was politically active and served as a ward commissioner for the Republican Party. When Hansberry was eight years old, the family bought a house in a white neighborhood, challenging segregationist real estate practices that excluded blacks. The Hansberrys endured violent hostility while fighting a lower court eviction and with the support from the National Association for the Advancement of Colored People won a victory in the U.S. Supreme Court.

After graduating from the segregated public schools of Chicago, Hansberry studied at the University of Wisconsin for two years but in 1950 moved to New York City. There she attended classes at the New School for Social Research and wrote for *Freedom*, a radical Harlem periodical published by Paul Robeson. During the course of her brief career, ended by cancer when she was only thirty-four years old, Hansberry remained a committed civil rights activist.

She began writing *A Raisin in the Sun* in 1956. It was produced on Broadway in 1959, bringing her international recognition. At the age of twenty-eight, Hansberry was the first black female playwright to be produced on Broadway, and the play was awarded the New York Drama Critics Circle Award for Best Play of the Year in competition with such successful dramatists as Eugene O'Neill and Tennessee Williams. *A Raisin in the Sun* has been translated into more than thirty languages and produced around the world. Among Hansberry's other writings are *The Movement: Documentary of a Struggle for Equality* (1964); *The Sign in Sidney Brustein's Window* (1965), a play in production at the time of her death; *To Be Young, Gifted and Black* (1969), a play published posthumously; and *Lorraine Hansberry: The Collected Last Plays* (1983).

In *A Raisin in the Sun*, Hansberry does not flinch from the tough realities that confronted African Americans contemporary to her. Racism, segregation, and a lack of economic opportunities seem brutally to mock the aspirations of her characters. Yet Hansberry sustained a sense of optimism owing to the growing activism of the civil rights movement during the 1950s. The play explores the difficulties of a black working-class family's struggle to overcome the racism and poverty in their lives and makes a connection between their efforts and the struggles of African countries to become free from colonialism. Her characters retain their humanity and dignity in the face of fierce social pressures and individual crises. Her realistic portrayal of racial issues, family conflicts, and relations between men and women presents a hostile world but also one that is capable of change. Her work, she once wrote, was about "not only what *is* but what is *possible.*"

The following poem by Langston Hughes (1902–1967) is the source for the play's title and serves as a fitting introduction to many of the issues dramatized in *A Raisin in the Sun*.

Harlem (A Dream Deferred)

What happens to a dream deferred?

> Does it dry up
> Like a raisin in the sun?
> Or fester like a sore —
> And then run?
> Does it stink like rotten meat?
> Or crust and sugar over —
> Like a syrupy sweet?

> Maybe it just sags
> Like a heavy load.

Or does it explode?

> — Langston Hughes

LORRAINE HANSBERRY (1930–1965)

A Raisin in the Sun   *1959*

CHARACTERS (in order of appearance)

Ruth Younger
Travis Younger
Walter Lee Younger, brother

Beneatha Younger
Lena Younger, Mama
Joseph Asagai
George Murchison
Mrs. Johnson
Karl Lindner
Bobo
Moving Men

The action of the play is set in Chicago's Southside, sometime between World War II
and the present.

ACT I

SCENE I. *[Friday morning.]*

The Younger living room would be a comfortable and well-ordered room if it were
not for a number of indestructible contradictions to this state of being. Its furnishings are typical and undistinguished and their primary feature now is that they
have clearly had to accommodate the living of too many people for too many
years—and they are tired. Still, we can see that at some time, a time probably no
longer remembered by the family (except perhaps for Mama), the furnishings of
this room were actually selected with care and love and even hope—and brought to
this apartment and arranged with taste and pride.

That was a long time ago. Now the once loved pattern of the couch upholstery
has to fight to show itself from under acres of crocheted doilies and couch covers
which have themselves finally come to be more important than the upholstery. And
here a table or a chair has been moved to disguise the worn places in the carpet; but
the carpet has fought back by showing its weariness, with depressing uniformity,
elsewhere on its surface.

Weariness has, in fact, won in this room. Everything has been polished,
washed, sat on, used, scrubbed too often. All pretenses but living itself have long
since vanished from the very atmosphere of this room.

Moreover, a section of this room, for it is not really a room unto itself, though
the landlord's lease would make it seem so, slopes backward to provide a small
kitchen area, where the family prepares the meals that are eaten in the living room
proper, which must also serve as dining room. The single window that has been
provided for these "two" rooms is located in this kitchen area. The sole natural light
the family may enjoy in the course of a day is only that which fights its way through
this little window.

At left, a door leads to a bedroom which is shared by Mama and her daughter,
Beneatha. At right, opposite, is a second room (which in the beginning of the life of
this apartment was probably a breakfast room) which serves as a bedroom for
Walter and his wife, Ruth.

Time: Sometime between World War II and the present.

Place: Chicago's Southside.

At Rise: It is morning dark in the living room. Travis is asleep on the make-
down bed at center. An alarm clock sounds from within the bedroom at right, and
presently Ruth enters from that room and closes the door behind her. She crosses
sleepily toward the window. As she passes her sleeping son she reaches down and

shakes him a little. At the window she raises the shade and a dusky Southside morn-
ing light comes in feebly. She fills a pot with water and puts it on to boil. She calls to
the boy, between yawns, in a slightly muffled voice.

Ruth is about thirty. We can see that she was a pretty girl, even exceptionally
so, but now it is apparent that life has been little that she expected, and disappoint-
ment has already begun to hang in her face. In a few years, before thirty-five even,
she will be known among her people as a "settled woman."

She crosses to her son and gives him a good, final, rousing shake.

Ruth: Come on now, boy, it's seven thirty! *(Her son sits up at last, in a stupor of*
sleepiness.) I say hurry up, Travis! You ain't the only person in the world got
to use a bathroom! *(The child, a sturdy, handsome little boy of ten or eleven,*
drags himself out of the bed and almost blindly takes his towels and "today's clothes"
from drawers and a closet and goes out to the bathroom, which is in an outside hall
and which is shared by another family or families on the same floor. Ruth crosses to
the bedroom door at right and opens it and calls in to her husband.) Walter
Lee! . . . It's after seven thirty! Lemme see you do some waking up in there
now! *(She waits.)* You better get up from there, man! It's after seven thirty I
tell you. *(She waits again.)* All right, you just go ahead and lay there and next
thing you know Travis be finished and Mr. Johnson'll be in there and
you'll be fussing and cussing round here like a madman! And be late too!
(She waits, at the end of patience.) Walter Lee — it's time for you to GET UP!

She waits another second and then starts to go into the bedroom, but is apparently
satisfied that her husband has begun to get up. She stops, pulls the door to, and
returns to the kitchen area. She wipes her face with a moist cloth and runs her
fingers through her sleep-disheveled hair in a vain effort and ties an apron around
her housecoat. The bedroom door at right opens and her husband stands in the
doorway in his pajamas, which are rumpled and mismated. He is a lean, intense
young man in his middle thirties, inclined to quick nervous movements and erratic
speech habits — and always in his voice there is a quality of indictment.

Walter: Is he out yet?

Ruth: What you mean *out?* He ain't hardly got in there good yet.

Walter (wandering in, still more oriented to sleep than to a new day): Well, what was
you doing all that yelling for if I can't even get in there yet? *(Stopping and*
thinking.) Check coming today?

Ruth: They *said* Saturday and this is just Friday and I hopes to God you ain't
going to get up here first thing this morning and start talking to me 'bout
no money — 'cause I 'bout don't want to hear it.

Walter: Something the matter with you this morning?

Ruth: No — I'm just sleepy as the devil. What kind of eggs you want?

Walter: Not scrambled. *(Ruth starts to scramble eggs.)* Paper come? *(Ruth points*
impatiently to the rolled up Tribune on the table, and he gets it and spreads it out
and vaguely reads the front page.) Set off another bomb yesterday.

Ruth (maximum indifference): Did they?

Walter (looking up): What's the matter with you?

Ruth: Ain't nothing the matter with me. And don't keep asking me that this
morning.

Walter: Ain't nobody bothering you. *(Reading the news of the day absently again.)*
Say Colonel McCormick is sick.

Ruth (affecting tea-party interest): Is he now? Poor thing.

Walter (sighing and looking at his watch): Oh, me. *(He waits.)* Now what is that boy doing in that bathroom all this time? He just going to have to start getting up earlier. I can't be being late to work on account of him fooling around in there.

Ruth (turning on him): Oh, no he ain't going to be getting up no earlier no such thing! It ain't his fault that he can't get to bed no earlier nights 'cause he got a bunch of crazy good-for-nothing clowns sitting up running their mouths in what is supposed to be his bedroom after ten o'clock at night . . .

Walter: That's what you mad about, ain't it? The things I want to talk about with my friends just couldn't be important in your mind, could they?

He rises and finds a cigarette in her handbag on the table and crosses to the little window and looks out, smoking and deeply enjoying this first one.

Ruth (almost matter of factly, a complaint too automatic to deserve emphasis): Why you always got to smoke before you eat in the morning?

Walter (at the window): Just look at 'em down there . . . Running and racing to work . . . *(He turns and faces his wife and watches her a moment at the stove, and then, suddenly.)* You look young this morning, baby.

Ruth (indifferently): Yeah?

Walter: Just for a second — stirring them eggs. Just for a second it was — you looked real young again. *(He reaches for her; she crosses away. Then, drily.)* It's gone now — you look like yourself again!

Ruth: Man, if you don't shut up and leave me alone.

Walter (looking out to the street again): First thing a man ought to learn in life is not to make love to no colored woman first thing in the morning. You all some eeeevil people at eight o'clock in the morning.

Travis appears in the hall doorway, almost fully dressed and quite wide awake now, his towels and pajamas across his shoulders. He opens the door and signals for his father to make the bathroom in a hurry.

Travis (watching the bathroom): Daddy, come on!

Walter gets his bathroom utensils and flies out to the bathroom.

Ruth: Sit down and have your breakfast, Travis.

Travis: Mama, this is Friday. *(Gleefully.)* Check coming tomorrow, huh?

Ruth: You get your mind off money and eat your breakfast.

Travis (eating): This is the morning we supposed to bring the fifty cents to school.

Ruth: Well, I ain't got no fifty cents this morning.

Travis: Teacher say we have to.

Ruth: I don't care what teacher say. I ain't got it. Eat your breakfast, Travis.

Travis: I *am* eating.

Ruth: Hush up now and just eat!

The boy gives her an exasperated look for her lack of understanding, and eats grudgingly.

Travis: You think Grandmama would have it?

Ruth: No! And I want you to stop asking your grandmother for money, you hear me?

Travis (outraged): Gaaaleee! I don't ask her, she just gimme it sometimes!

Ruth: Travis Willard Younger—I got too much on me this morning to be—
Travis: Maybe Daddy—
Ruth: Travis!

The boy hushes abruptly. They are both quiet and tense for several seconds.

Travis (presently): Could I maybe go carry some groceries in front of the supermarket for a little while after school then?
Ruth: Just hush, I said. *(Travis jabs his spoon into his cereal bowl viciously, and rests his head in anger upon his fists.)* If you through eating, you can get over there and make up your bed.

The boy obeys stiffly and crosses the room, almost mechanically, to the bed and more or less folds the bedding into a heap, then angrily gets his books and cap.

Travis (sulking and standing apart from her unnaturally): I'm gone.
Ruth (looking up from the stove to inspect him automatically): Come here. *(He crosses to her and she studies his head.)* If you don't take this comb and fix this here head, you better! *(Travis puts down his books with a great sigh of oppression, and crosses to the mirror. His mother mutters under her breath about his "slubbornness.")* 'Bout to march out of here with that head looking just like chickens slept in it! I just don't know where you get your slubborn ways . . . And get your jacket, too. Looks chilly out this morning.
Travis (with conspicuously brushed hair and jacket): I'm gone.
Ruth: Get carfare and milk money—*(Waving one finger.)*—and not a single penny for no caps, you hear me?
Travis (with sullen politeness): Yes'm.

He turns in outrage to leave. His mother watches after him as in his frustration he approaches the door almost comically. When she speaks to him, her voice has become a very gentle tease.

Ruth (mocking; as she thinks he would say it): Oh, Mama makes me so mad sometimes, I don't know what to do! *(She waits and continues to his back as he stands stock-still in front of the door.)* I wouldn't kiss that woman good-bye for nothing in this world this morning! *(The boy finally turns around and rolls his eyes at her, knowing the mood has changed and he is vindicated; he does not, however, move toward her yet.)* Not for nothing in this world! *(She finally laughs aloud at him and holds out her arms to him and we see that it is a way between them, very old and practiced. He crosses to her and allows her to embrace him warmly but keeps his face fixed with masculine rigidity. She holds him back from her presently and looks at him and runs her fingers over the features of his face. With utter gentleness—.)* Now—whose little old angry man are you?
Travis (the masculinity and gruffness start to fade at last): Aw gaalee—Mama . . .
Ruth (mimicking): Aw—gaaaaalleeeee, Mama! *(She pushes him, with rough playfulness and finality, toward the door.)* Get on out of here or you going to be late.
Travis (in the face of love, new aggressiveness): Mama, could I *please* go carry groceries?
Ruth: Honey, it's starting to get so cold evenings.
Walter (coming in from the bathroom and drawing a make-believe gun from a make-believe holster and shooting at his son): What is it he wants to do?
Ruth: Go carry groceries after school at the supermarket.
Walter: Well, let him go . . .
Travis (quickly, to the ally): I have to—she won't gimme the fifty cents . . .

Walter (to his wife only): Why not?

Ruth (simply, and with flavor): 'Cause we don't have it.

Walter (to Ruth only): What you tell the boy things like that for? *(Reaching down into his pants with a rather important gesture.)* Here, son —

> *He hands the boy the coin, but his eyes are directed to his wife's. Travis takes the money happily.*

Travis: Thanks, Daddy.

> *He starts out. Ruth watches both of them with murder in her eyes. Walter stands and stares back at her with defiance, and suddenly reaches into his pocket again on an afterthought.*

Walter (without even looking at his son, still staring hard at his wife): In fact, here's another fifty cents . . . Buy yourself some fruit today — or take a taxicab to school or something!

Travis: Whoopee —

> *He leaps up and clasps his father around the middle with his legs, and they face each other in mutual appreciation; slowly Walter Lee peeks around the boy to catch the violent rays from his wife's eyes and draws his head back as if shot.*

Walter: You better get down now — and get to school, man.

Travis (at the door): O.K. Good-bye.

> *He exits.*

Walter (after him, pointing with pride): That's *my* boy. *(She looks at him in disgust and turns back to her work.)* You know what I was thinking 'bout in the bathroom this morning?

Ruth: No.

Walter: How come you always try to be so pleasant!

Ruth: What is there to be pleasant 'bout!

Walter: You want to know what I was thinking 'bout in the bathroom or not!

Ruth: I know what you thinking 'bout.

Walter (ignoring her): 'Bout what me and Willy Harris was talking about last night.

Ruth (immediately — a refrain): Willy Harris is a good-for-nothing loudmouth.

Walter: Anybody who talks to me has got to be a good-for-nothing loud-mouth, ain't he? And what you know about who is just a good-for-nothing loudmouth? Charlie Atkins was just a "good-for-nothing loudmouth" too, wasn't he! When he wanted me to go in the dry-cleaning business with him. And now — he's grossing a hundred thousand a year. A hundred thousand dollars a year! You still call *him* a loudmouth!

Ruth (bitterly): Oh, Walter Lee . . .

> *She folds her head on her arms over the table.*

Walter (rising and coming to her and standing over her): You tired, ain't you? Tired of everything. Me, the boy, the way we live — this beat-up hole — every-thing. Ain't you? *(She doesn't look up, doesn't answer.)* So tired — moaning and groaning all the time, but you wouldn't do nothing to help, would you? You couldn't be on my side that long for nothing, could you?

Ruth: Walter, please leave me alone.

Walter: A man needs for a woman to back him up . . .

Ruth: Walter —

Walter: Mama would listen to you. You know she listen to you more than she do me and Bennie. She think more of you. All you have to do is just sit down with her when you drinking your coffee one morning and talking 'bout things like you do and — *(He sits down beside her and demonstrates graphically what he thinks her methods and tone should be.)* — you just sip your coffee, see, and say easy like that you been thinking 'bout that deal Walter Lee is so interested in, 'bout the store and all, and sip some more coffee, like what you saying ain't really that important to you — And the next thing you know, she be listening good and asking you questions and when I come home — I can tell her the details. This ain't no fly-by-night proposition, baby. I mean we figured it out, me and Willy and Bobo.

Ruth (with a frown): Bobo?

Walter: Yeah. You see, this little liquor store we got in mind cost seventy-five thousand and we figured the initial investment on the place be 'bout thirty thousand, see. That be ten thousand each. Course, there's a couple of hundred you got to pay so's you don't spend your life just waiting for them clowns to let your license get approved —

Ruth: You mean graft?

Walter (frowning impatiently): Don't call it that. See there, that just goes to show you what women understand about the world. Baby, don't *nothing* happen for you in the world 'less you pay *somebody* off!

Ruth: Walter, leave me alone! *(She raises her head and stares at him vigorously — then says, more quietly.)* Eat your eggs, they gonna be cold.

Walter (straightening up from her and looking off): That's it. There you are. Man say to his woman: I got me a dream. His woman say: Eat your eggs. *(Sadly, but gaining in power.)* Man say: I got to take hold of this here world, baby! And a woman will say: Eat your eggs and go to work. *(Passionately now.)* Man say: I got to change my life, I'm choking to death, baby! And his woman say — *(In utter anguish as he brings his fists down on his thighs.)* — Your eggs is getting cold!

Ruth (softly): Walter, that ain't none of our money.

Walter (not listening at all or even looking at her): This morning, I was lookin' in the mirror and thinking about it . . . I'm thirty-five years old; I been married eleven years and I got a boy who sleeps in the living room — *(Very, very quietly.)* — and all I got to give him is stories about how rich white people live . . .

Ruth: Eat your eggs, Walter.

Walter (slams the table and jumps up): —DAMN MY EGGS—DAMN ALL THE EGGS THAT EVER WAS!

Ruth: Then go to work.

Walter (looking up at her): See—I'm trying to talk to you 'bout myself— *(Shaking his head with the repetition.)* — and all you can say is eat them eggs and go to work.

Ruth (wearily): Honey, you never say nothing new. I listen to you every day, every night and every morning, and you never say nothing new. *(Shrugging.)* So you would rather *be* Mr. Arnold than be his chauffeur. So—I would *rather* be living in Buckingham Palace.

Walter: That is just what is wrong with the colored woman in this world . . . Don't understand about building their men up and making 'em feel like they somebody. Like they can do something.

Ruth (drily, but to hurt): There *are* colored men who do things.

Walter: No thanks to the colored woman.

Ruth: Well, being a colored woman, I guess I can't help myself none.

> *She rises and gets the ironing board and sets it up and attacks a huge pile of rough-dried clothes, sprinkling them in preparation for the ironing and then rolling them into tight fat balls.*

Walter (mumbling): We one group of men tied to a race of women with small minds!

> *His sister Beneatha enters. She is about twenty, as slim and intense as her brother. She is not as pretty as her sister-in-law, but her lean, almost intellectual face has a handsomeness of its own. She wears a bright-red flannel nightie, and her thick hair stands wildly about her head. Her speech is a mixture of many things; it is different from the rest of the family's insofar as education has permeated her sense of English—and perhaps the Midwest rather than the South has finally—at last—won out in her inflection; but not altogether, because over all of it is a soft slurring and transformed use of vowels which is the decided influence of the Southside. She passes through the room without looking at either Ruth or Walter and goes to the outside door and looks, a little blindly, out to the bathroom. She sees that it has been lost to the Johnsons. She closes the door with a sleepy vengeance and crosses to the table and sits down a little defeated.*

Beneatha: I am going to start timing those people.

Walter: You should get up earlier.

Beneatha (her face in her hands. She is still fighting the urge to go back to bed): Really—would you suggest dawn? Where's the paper?

Walter (pushing the paper across the table to her as he studies her almost clinically, as though he has never seen her before): You a horrible-looking chick at this hour.

Beneatha (drily): Good morning, everybody.

Walter (senselessly): How is school coming?

Beneatha (in the same spirit): Lovely. Lovely. And you know, biology is the greatest. *(Looking up at him.)* I dissected something that looked just like you yesterday.

Walter: I just wondered if you've made up your mind and everything.

Beneatha (gaining in sharpness and impatience): And what did I answer yesterday morning—and the day before that?

Ruth (from the ironing board, like someone disinterested and old): Don't be so nasty, Bennie.

Beneatha (still to her brother): And the day before that and the day before that!

Walter (defensively): I'm interested in you. Something wrong with that? Ain't many girls who decide—

Walter and Beneatha (in unison): —"to be a doctor."

> *Silence.*

Walter: Have we figured out yet just exactly how much medical school is going to cost?

Ruth: Walter Lee, why don't you leave that girl alone and get out of here to work?

Beneatha (exits to the bathroom and bangs on the door): Come on out of there, please!

She comes back into the room.

Walter (looking at his sister intently): You know the check is coming tomorrow.

Beneatha (turning on him with a sharpness all her own): That money belongs to Mama, Walter, and it's for her to decide how she wants to use it. I don't care if she wants to buy a house or a rocket ship or just nail it up somewhere and look at it. It's hers. Not ours — *hers.*

Walter (bitterly): Now ain't that fine! You just got your mother's interest at heart, ain't you, girl? You such a nice girl — but if Mama got that money she can always take a few thousand and help you through school too — can't she?

Beneatha: I have never asked anyone around here to do anything for me!

Walter: No! And the line between asking and just accepting when the time comes is big and wide — ain't it!

Beneatha (with fury): What do you want from me, Brother — that I quit school or just drop dead, which!

Walter: I don't want nothing but for you to stop acting holy 'round here. Me and Ruth done made some sacrifices for you — why can't you do something for the family?

Ruth: Walter, don't be dragging me in it.

Walter: You are in it — Don't you get up and go work in somebody's kitchen for the last three years to help put clothes on her back?

Ruth: Oh, Walter — that's not fair . . .

Walter: It ain't that nobody expects you to get on your knees and say thank you, Brother; thank you, Ruth; thank you, Mama — and thank you, Travis, for wearing the same pair of shoes for two semesters —

Beneatha (dropping to her knees): Well — I *do* — all right? — thank everybody! And forgive me for ever wanting to be anything at all! *(Pursuing him on her knees across the floor.)* FORGIVE ME, FORGIVE ME, FORGIVE ME!

Ruth: Please stop it! Your mama'll hear you.

Walter: Who the hell told you you had to be a doctor? If you so crazy 'bout messing 'round with sick people — then go be a nurse like other women — or just get married and be quiet . . .

Beneatha: Well — you finally got it said . . . It took you three years but you finally got it said. Walter, give up; leave me alone — it's Mama's money.

Walter: He was my father, too!

Beneatha: So what? He was mine, too — and Travis' grandfather — but the insurance money belongs to Mama. Picking on me is not going to make her give it to you to invest in any liquor stores — *(Under breath, dropping into a chair.)* — and I for one say, God bless Mama for that!

Walter (to Ruth): See — did you hear? Did you hear!

Ruth: Honey, please go to work.

Walter: Nobody in this house is ever going to understand me.

Beneatha: Because you're a nut.

Walter: Who's a nut?

Beneatha: You — you are a nut. Thee is mad, boy.

Walter (looking at his wife and his sister from the door, very sadly): The world's most backward race of people, and that's a fact.

Beneatha (turning slowly in her chair): And then there are all those prophets who would lead us out of the wilderness — *(Walter slams out of the house.)* — into the swamps!

Ruth: Bennie, why you always gotta be pickin' on your brother? Can't you be a little sweeter sometimes? *(Door opens. Walter walks in. He fumbles with his cap, starts to speak, clears throat, looks everywhere but at Ruth. Finally:)*

Walter (to Ruth): I need some money for carfare.

Ruth (looks at him, then warms; teasing, but tenderly): Fifty cents? *(She goes to her bag and gets money.)* Here — take a taxi!

Walter exits. Mama enters. She is a woman in her early sixties, full-bodied and strong. She is one of those women of a certain grace and beauty who wear it so unobtrusively that it takes a while to notice. Her dark-brown face is surrounded by the total whiteness of her hair, and, being a woman who has adjusted to many things in life and overcome many more, her face is full of strength. She has, we can see, wit and faith of a kind that keep her eyes lit and full of interest and expectancy. She is, in a word, a beautiful woman. Her bearing is perhaps most like the noble bearing of the women of the Hereros of Southwest Africa — rather as if she imagines that as she walks she still bears a basket or a vessel upon her head. Her speech, on the other hand, is as careless as her carriage is precise — she is inclined to slur everything — but her voice is perhaps not so much quiet as simply soft.

Mama: Who that 'round here slamming doors at this hour?

She crosses through the room, goes to the window, opens it, and brings in a feeble little plant growing doggedly in a small pot on the window sill. She feels the dirt and puts it back out.

Ruth: That was Walter Lee. He and Bennie was at it again.

Mama: My children and they tempers. Lord, if this little old plant don't get more sun than it's been getting it ain't never going to see spring again. *(She turns from the window.)* What's the matter with you this morning, Ruth? You looks right peaked. You aiming to iron all them things? Leave some for me. I'll get to 'em this afternoon. Bennie honey, it's too drafty for you to be sitting 'round half dressed. Where's your robe?

Beneatha: In the cleaners.

Mama: Well, go get mine and put it on.

Beneatha: I'm not cold, Mama, honest.

Mama: I know — but you so thin . . .

Beneatha (irritably): Mama, I'm not cold.

Mama (seeing the make-down bed as Travis has left it): Lord have mercy, look at that poor bed. Bless his heart — he tries, don't he?

She moves to the bed Travis has sloppily made up.

Ruth: No — he don't half try at all 'cause he knows you going to come along behind him and fix everything. That's just how come he don't know how to do nothing right now — you done spoiled that boy so.

Mama (folding bedding): Well — he's a little boy. Ain't supposed to know 'bout housekeeping. My baby, that's what he is. What you fix for his breakfast this morning?

Ruth (angrily): I feed my son, Lena!

Mama: I ain't meddling — *(Under breath; busy-bodyish.)* I just noticed all last week he had cold cereal, and when it starts getting this chilly in the fall a child ought to have some hot grits or something when he goes out in the cold —

Ruth (furious): I gave him hot oats — is that all right!

Mama: I ain't meddling. *(Pause.)* Put a lot of nice butter on it? *(Ruth shoots her an angry look and does not reply.)* He likes lots of butter.

Ruth (exasperated): Lena —

Mama (to Beneatha. Mama is inclined to wander conversationally sometimes): What was you and your brother fussing 'bout this morning?

Beneatha: It's not important, Mama.

> *She gets up and goes to look out at the bathroom, which is apparently free, and she picks up her towels and rushes out.*

Mama: What was they fighting about?

Ruth: Now you know as well as I do.

Mama (shaking her head): Brother still worrying hisself sick about that money?

Ruth: You know he is.

Mama: You had breakfast?

Ruth: Some coffee.

Mama: Girl, you better start eating and looking after yourself better. You almost thin as Travis.

Ruth: Lena —

Mama: Un-hunh?

Ruth: What are you going to do with it?

Mama: Now don't you start, child. It's too early in the morning to be talking about money. It ain't Christian.

Ruth: It's just that he got his heart set on that store —

Mama: You mean that liquor store that Willy Harris want him to invest in?

Ruth: Yes —

Mama: We ain't no business people, Ruth. We just plain working folks.

Ruth: Ain't nobody business people till they go into business. Walter Lee say colored people ain't never going to start getting ahead till they start gambling on some different kinds of things in the world — investments and things.

Mama: What done got into you, girl? Walter Lee done finally sold you on investing.

Ruth: No. Mama, something is happening between Walter and me. I don't know what it is — but he needs something — something I can't give him any more. He needs this chance, Lena.

Mama (frowning deeply): But liquor, honey —

Ruth: Well — like Walter say — I spec people going to always be drinking themselves some liquor.

Mama: Well — whether they drinks it or not ain't none of my business. But whether I go into business selling it to 'em *is,* and I don't want that on my ledger this late in life. *(Stopping suddenly and studying her daughter-in-law.)* Ruth Younger, what's the matter with you today? You look like you could fall over right there.

Ruth: I'm tired.

Mama: Then you better stay home from work today.

Ruth: I can't stay home. She'd be calling up the agency and screaming at them, "My girl didn't come in today—send me somebody! My girl didn't come in!" Oh, she just have a fit . . .

Mama: Well, let her have it. I'll just call her up and say you got the flu—

Ruth (laughing): Why the flu?

Mama: 'Cause it sounds respectable to 'em. Something white people get, too. They know 'bout the flu. Otherwise they think you been cut up or something when you tell 'em you sick.

Ruth: I got to go in. We need the money.

Mama: Somebody would of thought my children done all but starved to death the way they talk about money here late. Child, we got a great big old check coming tomorrow.

Ruth (sincerely, but also self-righteously): Now that's your money. It ain't got nothing to do with me. We all feel like that—Walter and Bennie and me— even Travis.

Mama (thoughtfully, and suddenly very far away): Ten thousand dollars—

Ruth: Sure is wonderful.

Mama: Ten thousand dollars.

Ruth: You know what you should do, Miss Lena? You should take yourself a trip somewhere. To Europe or South America or someplace—

Mama (throwing up her hands at the thought): Oh, child!

Ruth: I'm serious. Just pack up and leave! Go on away and enjoy yourself some. Forget about the family and have yourself a ball for once in your life—

Mama (drily): You sound like I'm just about ready to die. Who'd go with me? What I look like wandering 'round Europe by myself?

Ruth: Shoot—these here rich white women do it all the time. They don't think nothing of packing up they suitcases and piling on one of them big steamships and—swoosh!—they gone, child.

Mama: Something always told me I wasn't no rich white woman.

Ruth: Well—what are you going to do with it then?

Mama: I ain't rightly decided. *(Thinking. She speaks now with emphasis.)* Some of it got to be put away for Beneatha and her schoolin'—and ain't nothing going to touch that part of it. Nothing. *(She waits several seconds, trying to make up her mind about something, and looks at Ruth a little tentatively before going on.)* Been thinking that we maybe could meet the notes on a little old two-story somewhere, with a yard where Travis could play in the summertime, if we use part of the insurance for a down payment and everybody kind of pitch in. I could maybe take on a little day work again, few days a week—

Ruth (studying her mother-in-law furtively and concentrating on her ironing, anxious to encourage without seeming to): Well, Lord knows, we've put enough rent into this here rat trap to pay for four houses by now . . .

Mama (looking up at the words "rat trap" and then looking around and leaning back and sighing—in a suddenly reflective mood—): "Rat trap"—yes, that's all it is. *(Smiling.)* I remember just as well the day me and Big Walter moved in here. Hadn't been married but two weeks and wasn't planning on living here no more than a year. *(She shakes her head at the dissolved dream.)* We was going to set away, little by little, don't you know, and buy a little place out in Morgan Park. We had even picked out the house. *(Chuckling a little.)* Looks right dumpy today. But Lord, child, you should know all the dreams I had 'bout buying that house and fixing it up and making me a little garden in the back — *(She waits and stops smiling.)* And didn't none of it happen.

Dropping her hands in a futile gesture.

Ruth *(keeps her head down, ironing):* Yes, life can be a barrel of disappointments, sometimes.

Mama: Honey, Big Walter would come in here some nights back then and slump down on that couch there and just look at the rug, and look at me and look at the rug and then back at me — and I'd know he was down then . . . really down. *(After a second very long and thoughtful pause; she is seeing back to times that only she can see.)* And then, Lord, when I lost that baby — little Claude — I almost thought I was going to lose Big Walter too. Oh, that man grieved hisself! He was one man to love his children.

Ruth: Ain't nothin' can tear at you like losin' your baby.

Mama: I guess that's how come that man finally worked hisself to death like he done. Like he was fighting his own war with this here world that took his baby from him.

Ruth: He sure was a fine man, all right. I always liked Mr. Younger.

Mama: Crazy 'bout his children! God knows there was plenty wrong with Walter Younger — hard-headed, mean, kind of wild with women — plenty wrong with him. But he sure loved his children. Always wanted them to have something — be something. That's where Brother gets all these notions, I reckon. Big Walter used to say, he'd get right wet in the eyes sometimes, lean his head back with the water standing in his eyes and say, "Seem like God didn't see fit to give the black man nothing but dreams — but He did give us children to make them dreams seem worthwhile." *(She smiles.)* He could talk like that, don't you know.

Ruth: Yes, he sure could. He was a good man, Mr. Younger.

Mama: Yes, a fine man — just couldn't never catch up with his dreams, that's all.

Beneatha comes in, brushing her hair and looking up to the ceiling, where the sound of a vacuum cleaner has started up.

Beneatha: What could be so dirty on that woman's rugs that she has to vacuum them every single day?

Ruth: I wish certain young women 'round here who I could name would take inspiration about certain rugs in a certain apartment I could also mention.

Beneatha *(shrugging):* How much cleaning can a house need, for Christ's sakes.

Mama *(not liking the Lord's name used thus):* Bennie!

Ruth: Just listen to her — just listen!

Beneatha: Oh, God!

Mama: If you use the Lord's name just one more time —

Beneatha *(a bit of a whine):* Oh, Mama —

Ruth: Fresh — just fresh as salt, this girl!

Beneatha *(drily):* Well — if the salt loses its savor —

Mama: Now that will do. I just ain't going to have you 'round here reciting the scriptures in vain — you hear me?

Beneatha: How did I manage to get on everybody's wrong side by just walking into a room?

Ruth: If you weren't so fresh —

Beneatha: Ruth, I'm twenty years old.

Mama: What time you be home from school today?

Beneatha: Kind of late. *(With enthusiasm.)* Madeline is going to start my guitar lessons today.

Mama and Ruth look up with the same expression.

Mama: Your *what* kind of lessons?

Beneatha: Guitar.

Ruth: Oh, Father!

Mama: How come you done taken it in your mind to learn to play the guitar?

Beneatha: I just want to, that's all.

Mama (smiling): Lord, child, don't you know what to do with yourself? How long it going to be before you get tired of this now — like you got tired of that little play-acting group you joined last year? *(Looking at Ruth.)* And what was it the year before that?

Ruth: The horseback-riding club for which she bought that fifty-five-dollar riding habit that's been hanging in the closet ever since!

Mama (to Beneatha): Why you got to flit so from one thing to another, baby?

Beneatha (sharply): I just want to learn to play the guitar. Is there anything wrong with that?

Mama: Ain't nobody trying to stop you. I just wonders sometimes why you has to flit so from one thing to another all the time. You ain't never done nothing with all that camera equipment you brought home —

Beneatha: I don't flit! I — I experiment with different forms of expression —

Ruth: Like riding a horse?

Beneatha: — People have to express themselves one way or another.

Mama: What is it you want to express?

Beneatha (angrily): Me! *(Mama and Ruth look at each other and burst into raucous laughter.)* Don't worry — I don't expect you to understand.

Mama (to change the subject): Who you going out with tomorrow night?

Beneatha (with displeasure): George Murchison again.

Mama (pleased): Oh — you getting a little sweet on him?

Ruth: You ask me, this child ain't sweet on nobody but herself — *(Under breath.)* Express herself!

They laugh.

Beneatha: Oh — I like George all right, Mama. I mean I like him enough to go out with him and stuff, but —

Ruth (for devilment): What does *and stuff* mean?

Beneatha: Mind your own business.

Mama: Stop picking at her now, Ruth. *(She chuckles — then a suspicious sudden look at her daughter as she turns in her chair for emphasis.)* What DOES it mean?

Beneatha (wearily): Oh, I just mean I couldn't ever really be serious about George. He's — he's so shallow.

Ruth: Shallow — what do you mean he's shallow? He's *rich!*

Mama: Hush, Ruth.

Beneatha: I know he's rich. He knows he's rich, too.

Ruth: Well — what other qualities a man got to have to satisfy you, little girl?

Beneatha: You wouldn't even begin to understand. Anybody who married Walter could not possibly understand.

Mama (outraged): What kind of way is that to talk about your brother?

Beneatha: Brother is a flip — let's face it.

Mama (to Ruth, helplessly): What's a flip?

Ruth (glad to add kindling): She's saying he's crazy.

Beneatha: Not crazy. Brother isn't really crazy yet — he — he's an elaborate neurotic.

Mama: Hush your mouth!

Beneatha: As for George. Well. George looks good — he's got a beautiful car and he takes me to nice places and, as my sister-in-law says, he is probably the richest boy I will ever get to know and I even like him sometimes — but if the Youngers are sitting around waiting to see if their little Bennie is going to tie up the family with the Murchisons, they are wasting their time.

Ruth: You mean you wouldn't marry George Murchison if he asked you someday? That pretty, rich thing? Honey, I knew you was odd —

Beneatha: No I would not marry him if all I felt for him was what I feel now. Besides, George's family wouldn't really like it.

Mama: Why not?

Beneatha: Oh, Mama — The Murchisons are honest-to-God-real-*live*-rich colored people, and the only people in the world who are more snobbish than rich white people are rich colored people. I thought everybody knew that. I've met Mrs. Murchison. She's a scene!

Mama: You must not dislike people 'cause they well off, honey.

Beneatha: Why not? It makes just as much sense as disliking people 'cause they are poor, and lots of people do that.

Ruth (a wisdom-of-the-ages manner. To Mama): Well, she'll get over some of this —

Beneatha: Get over it? What are you talking about, Ruth? Listen, I'm going to be a doctor. I'm not worried about who I'm going to marry yet — if I ever get married.

Mama and Ruth: If!

Mama: Now, Bennie —

Beneatha: Oh, I probably will . . . but first I'm going to be a doctor, and George, for one, still thinks that's pretty funny. I couldn't be bothered with that. I am going to be a doctor and everybody around here better understand that!

Mama (kindly): 'Course you going to be a doctor, honey, God willing.

Beneatha (drily): God hasn't got a thing to do with it.

Mama: Beneatha — that just wasn't necessary.

Beneatha: Well — neither is God. I get sick of hearing about God.

Mama: Beneatha!

Beneatha: I mean it! I'm just tired of hearing about God all the time. What has He got to do with anything? Does He pay tuition?

Mama: You 'bout to get your fresh little jaw slapped!

Ruth: That's just what she needs, all right!

Beneatha: Why? Why can't I say what I want to around here, like everybody else?

Mama: It don't sound nice for a young girl to say things like that — you wasn't brought up that way. Me and your father went to trouble to get you and Brother to church every Sunday.

Beneatha: Mama, you don't understand. It's all a matter of ideas, and God is just one idea I don't accept. It's not important. I am not going out and be immoral or commit crimes because I don't believe in God. I don't even think about it. It's just that I get tired of Him getting credit for all the things the human race achieves through its own stubborn effort. There simply is no blasted God—there is only man and it is *He* who makes miracles!

Mama absorbs this speech, studies her daughter, and rises slowly and crosses to Beneatha and slaps her powerfully across the face. After, there is only silence and the daughter drops her eyes from her mother's face, and Mama is very tall before her.

Mama: Now—you say after me, in my mother's house there is still God. *(There is a long pause and Beneatha stares at the floor wordlessly. Mama repeats the phrase with precision and cool emotion.)* In my mother's house there is still God.
Beneatha: In my mother's house there is still God.

A long pause.

Mama *(walking away from Beneatha, too disturbed for triumphant posture. Stopping and turning back to her daughter)*: There are some ideas we ain't going to have in this house. Not long as I am at the head of this family.
Beneatha: Yes, ma'am.

Mama walks out of the room.

Ruth *(almost gently, with profound understanding)*: You think you a woman, Bennie—but you still a little girl. What you did was childish—so you got treated like a child.
Beneatha: I see. *(Quietly.)* I also see that everybody thinks it's all right for Mama to be a tyrant. But all the tyranny in the world will never put a God in the heavens!

She picks up her books and goes out. Pause.

Ruth *(goes to Mama's door)*: She said she was sorry.
Mama *(coming out, going to her plant)*: They frightens me, Ruth. My children.
Ruth: You got good children, Lena. They just a little off sometimes—but they're good.
Mama: No—there's something come down between me and them that don't let us understand each other and I don't know what it is. One done almost lost his mind thinking 'bout money all the time and the other done commence to talk about things I can't seem to understand in no form or fashion. What is it that's changing, Ruth.
Ruth *(soothingly, older than her years)*: Now . . . you taking it all too seriously. You just got strong-willed children and it takes a strong woman like you to keep 'em in hand.
Mama *(looking at her plant and sprinkling a little water on it)*: They spirited all right, my children. Got to admit they got spirit—Bennie and Walter. Like this little old plant that ain't never had enough sunshine or nothing—and look at it . . .

She has her back to Ruth, who has had to stop ironing and lean against something and put the back of her hand to her forehead.

Ruth *(trying to keep Mama from noticing)*: You . . . sure . . . loves that little old thing, don't you? . . .

Mama: Well, I always wanted me a garden like I used to see sometimes at the back of the houses down home. This plant is close as I ever got to having one. *(She looks out of the window as she replaces the plant.)* Lord, ain't nothing as dreary as the view from this window on a dreary day, is there? Why ain't you singing this morning, Ruth? Sing that "No Ways Tired." That song always lifts me up so — *(She turns at last to see that Ruth has slipped quietly to the floor, in a state of semiconsciousness.)* Ruth! Ruth honey — what's the matter with you . . . Ruth!

Curtain.

SCENE II. *[The following morning.]*

It is the following morning; a Saturday morning, and house cleaning is in progress at the Youngers'. Furniture has been shoved hither and yon and Mama is giving the kitchen-area walls a washing down. Beneatha, in dungarees, with a handkerchief tied around her face, is spraying insecticide into the cracks in the walls. As they work, the radio is on and a Southside disk-jockey program is inappropriately filling the house with a rather exotic saxophone blues. Travis, the sole idle one, is leaning on his arms, looking out of the window.

Travis: Grandmama, that stuff Bennie is using smells awful. Can I go downstairs, please?

Mama: Did you get all them chores done already? I ain't seen you doing much.

Travis: Yes'm — finished early. Where did Mama go this morning?

Mama (looking at Beneatha): She had to go on a little errand.

The phone rings. Beneatha runs to answer it and reaches it before Walter, who has entered from bedroom.

Travis: Where?

Mama: To tend to her business.

Beneatha: Haylo . . . *(Disappointed.)* Yes, he is. *(She tosses the phone to Walter, who barely catches it.)* It's Willie Harris again.

Walter (as privately as possible under Mama's gaze): Hello, Willie. Did you get the papers from the lawyer? . . . No, not yet. I told you the mailman doesn't get here till ten-thirty . . . No, I'll come there . . . Yeah! Right away. *(He hangs up and goes for his coat.)*

Beneatha: Brother, where did Ruth go?

Walter (as he exits): How should I know!

Travis: Aw come on, Grandma. Can I go outside?

Mama: Oh, I guess so. You stay right in front of the house, though, and keep a good lookout for the postman.

Travis: Yes'm. *(He darts into bedroom for stickball and bat, reenters, and sees Beneatha on her knees spraying under sofa with behind upraised. He edges closer to the target, takes aim, and lets her have it. She screams.)* Leave them poor little cockroaches alone, they ain't bothering you none! *(He runs as she swings the spraygun at him viciously and playfully.)* Grandma! Grandma!

Mama: Look out there, girl, before you be spilling some of that stuff on that child!

Travis (safely behind the bastion of Mama): That's right — look out, now! *(He exits.)*

Beneatha (drily): I can't imagine that it would hurt him — it has never hurt the roaches.

Mama: Well, little boys' hides ain't as tough as Southside roaches. You better get over there behind the bureau. I seen one marching out of there like Napoleon yesterday.

Beneatha: There's really only one way to get rid of them, Mama —

Mama: How?

Beneatha: Set fire to this building! Mama, where did Ruth go?

Mama (looking at her with meaning): To the doctor, I think.

Beneatha: The doctor? What's the matter? *(They exchange glances.)* You don't think —

Mama (with her sense of drama): Now I ain't saying what I think. But I ain't never been wrong 'bout a woman neither.

> *The phone rings.*

Beneatha (at the phone): Hay-lo . . . *(Pause, and a moment of recognition.)* Well — when did you get back! . . . And how was it? . . . Of course I've missed you — in my way . . . This morning? No . . . house cleaning and all that and Mama hates it if I let people come over when the house is like this . . . You *have?* Well, that's different . . . What is it — Oh, what the hell, come on over . . . Right, see you then. *Arrividerci.*

> *She hangs up.*

Mama (who has listened vigorously, as is her habit): Who is that you inviting over here with this house looking like this? You ain't got the pride you was born with!

Beneatha: Asagai doesn't care how houses look, Mama — he's an intellectual.

Mama: Who?

Beneatha: Asagai — Joseph Asagai. He's an African boy I met on campus. He's been studying in Canada all summer.

Mama: What's his name?

Beneatha: Asagai, Joseph. Ah-sah-guy . . . He's from Nigeria.

Mama: Oh, that's the little country that was founded by slaves way back . . .

Beneatha: No, Mama — that's Liberia.

Mama: I don't think I never met no African before.

Beneatha: Well, do me a favor and don't ask him a whole lot of ignorant questions about Africans. I mean, do they wear clothes and all that —

Mama: Well, now, I guess if you think we so ignorant 'round here maybe you shouldn't bring your friends here —

Beneatha: It's just that people ask such crazy things. All anyone seems to know about when it comes to Africa is Tarzan —

Mama (indignantly): Why should I know anything about Africa?

Beneatha: Why do you give money at church for the missionary work?

Mama: Well, that's to help save people.

Beneatha: You mean save them from *heathenism* —

Mama (innocently): Yes.

Beneatha: I'm afraid they need more salvation from the British and the French.

> *Ruth comes in forlornly and pulls off her coat with dejection. They both turn to look at her.*

Ruth (dispiritedly): Well, I guess from all the happy faces — everybody knows.

Beneatha: You pregnant?

Mama: Lord have mercy, I sure hope it's a little old girl. Travis ought to have a sister.

Beneatha and Ruth give her a hopeless look for this grandmotherly enthusiasm.

Beneatha: How far along are you?

Ruth: Two months.

Beneatha: Did you mean to? I mean did you plan it or was it an accident?

Mama: What do you know about planning or not planning?

Beneatha: Oh, Mama.

Ruth (wearily): She's twenty years old, Lena.

Beneatha: Did you plan it, Ruth?

Ruth: Mind your own business.

Beneatha: It is my business — where is he going to live, on the *roof? (There is silence following the remark as the three women react to the sense of it.)* Gee — I didn't mean that, Ruth, honest. Gee, I don't feel like that at all. I — I think it is wonderful.

Ruth (dully): Wonderful.

Beneatha: Yes — really.

Mama (looking at Ruth, worried): Doctor say everything going to be all right?

Ruth (far away): Yes — she says everything is going to be fine . . .

Mama (immediately suspicious): "She" — What doctor you went to?

Ruth folds over, near hysteria.

Mama (worriedly hovering over Ruth): Ruth honey — what's the matter with you — you sick?

Ruth has her fists clenched on her thighs and is fighting hard to suppress a scream that seems to be rising in her.

Beneatha: What's the matter with her, Mama?

Mama (working her fingers in Ruth's shoulders to relax her): She be all right. Women gets right depressed sometimes when they get her way. *(Speaking softly, expertly, rapidly.)* Now you just relax. That's right . . . just lean back, don't think 'bout nothing at all . . . nothing at all —

Ruth: I'm all right . . .

The glassy-eyed look melts and then she collapses into a fit of heavy sobbing. The bell rings.

Beneatha: Oh, my God — that must be Asagai.

Mama (to Ruth): Come on now, honey. You need to lie down and rest awhile . . . then have some nice hot food.

They exit, Ruth's weight on her mother-in-law. Beneatha, herself profoundly disturbed, opens the door to admit a rather dramatic-looking young man with a large package.

Asagai: Hello, Alaiyo —

Beneatha (holding the door open and regarding him with pleasure): Hello . . . *(Long pause.)* Well — come in. And please excuse everything. My mother was very upset about my letting anyone come here with the place like this.

Asagai (coming into the room): You look disturbed too . . . Is something wrong?

Beneatha (still at the door, absently): Yes . . . we've all got acute ghetto-itus. *(She smiles and comes toward him, finding a cigarette and sitting.)* So — sit down! No!

Wait! *(She whips the spraygun off sofa where she had left it and puts the cushions back. At last perches on arm of sofa. He sits.)* So, how was Canada?

Asagai (a sophisticate): Canadian.

Beneatha (looking at him): Asagai, I'm very glad you are back.

Asagai (looking back at her in turn): Are you really?

Beneatha: Yes—very.

Asagai: Why?—you were quite glad when I went away. What happened?

Beneatha: You went away.

Asagai: Ahhhhhhhh.

Beneatha: Before—you wanted to be so serious before there was time.

Asagai: How much time must there be before one knows what one feels?

Beneatha (stalling this particular conversation. Her hands pressed together, in a deliberately childish gesture): What did you bring me?

Asagai (handing her the package): Open it and see.

Beneatha (eagerly opening the package and drawing out some records and the colorful robes of a Nigerian woman): Oh Asagai! . . . You got them for me! . . . How beautiful . . . and the records too! *(She lifts out the robes and runs to the mirror with them and holds the drapery up in front of herself.)*

Asagai (coming to her at the mirror): I shall have to teach you how to drape it properly. *(He flings the material about her for the moment and stands back to look at her.)* Ah—Oh-pay-gay-day, oh-gbah-mu-shay. *(A Yoruba exclamation for admiration.)* You wear it well . . . very well . . . mutilated hair and all.

Beneatha (turning suddenly): My hair—what's wrong with my hair?

Asagai (shrugging): Were you born with it like that?

Beneatha (reaching up to touch it): No . . . of course not.

She looks back to the mirror, disturbed.

Asagai (smiling): How then?

Beneatha: You know perfectly well how . . . as crinkly as yours . . . that's how.

Asagai: And it is ugly to you that way?

Beneatha (quickly): Oh, no—not ugly . . . *(More slowly, apologetically.)* But it's so hard to manage when it's, well—raw.

Asagai: And so to accommodate that—you mutilate it every week?

Beneatha: It's not mutilation!

Asagai (laughing aloud at her seriousness): Oh . . . please! I am only teasing you because you are so very serious about these things. *(He stands back from her and folds his arms across his chest as he watches her pulling at her hair and frowning in the mirror.)* Do you remember the first time you met me at school? . . . *(He laughs.)* You came up to me and you said—and I thought you were the most serious little thing I had ever seen—you said: *(He imitates her.)* "Mr. Asagai—I want very much to talk with you. About Africa. You see, Mr. Asagai, I am looking for my *identity!*"

He laughs.

Beneatha (turning to him, not laughing): Yes—

Her face is quizzical, profoundly disturbed.

Asagai (still teasing and reaching out and taking her face in his hands and turning her profile to him): Well . . . it is true that this is not so much a profile of a Hollywood queen as perhaps a queen of the Nile—*(A mock dismissal of the im-*

portance of the question.) But what does it matter? Assimilationism is so popular in your country.

Beneatha (wheeling, passionately, sharply): I am not an assimilationist!

Asagai (the protest hangs in the room for a moment and Asagai studies her, his laughter fading): Such a serious one. *(There is a pause.)* So — you like the robes? You must take excellent care of them — they are from my sister's personal wardrobe.

Beneatha (with incredulity): You — you sent all the way home — for me?

Asagai (with charm): For you — I would do much more . . . Well, that is what I came for. I must go.

Beneatha: Will you call me Monday?

Asagai: Yes . . . We have a great deal to talk about. I mean about identity and time and all that.

Beneatha: Time?

Asagai: Yes. About how much time one needs to know what one feels.

Beneatha: You see! You never understood that there is more than one kind of feeling which can exist between a man and a woman — or, at least, there should be.

Asagai (shaking his head negatively but gently): No. Between a man and a woman there need be only one kind of feeling. I have that for you . . . Now even . . . right this moment . . .

Beneatha: I know — and by itself — it won't do. I can find that anywhere.

Asagai: For a woman it should be enough.

Beneatha: I know — because that's what it says in all the novels that men write. But it isn't. Go ahead and laugh — but I'm not interested in being someone's little episode in America or — *(With feminine vengeance.)* — one of them! *(Asagai has burst into laughter again.)* That's funny as hell, huh!

Asagai: It's just that every American girl I have known has said that to me. White — black — in this you are all the same. And the same speech, too!

Beneatha (angrily): Yuk, yuk, yuk!

Asagai: It's how you can be sure that the world's most liberated women are not liberated at all. You all talk about it too much!

Mama enters and is immediately all social charm because of the presence of a guest.

Beneatha: Oh — Mama — this is Mr. Asagai.

Mama: How do you do?

Asagai (total politeness to an elder): How do you do, Mrs. Younger. Please forgive me for coming at such an outrageous hour on a Saturday.

Mama: Well, you are quite welcome. I just hope you understand that our house don't always look like this. *(Chatterish.)* You must come again. I would love to hear all about — *(Not sure of the name.)* — your country. I think it's so sad the way our American Negroes don't know nothing about Africa 'cept Tarzan and all that. And all that money they pour into these churches when they ought to be helping you people over there drive out them French and Englishmen done taken away your land.

The mother flashes a slightly superior look at her daughter upon completion of the recitation.

Asagai (taken aback by this sudden and acutely unrelated expression of sympathy): Yes . . . yes . . .

Mama (smiling at him suddenly and relaxing and looking him over): How many miles is it from here to where you come from?

Asagai: Many thousands.

Mama (looking at him as she would Walter): I bet you don't half look after yourself, being away from your mama either. I spec you better come 'round here from time to time to get yourself some decent homecooked meals . . .

Asagai (moved): Thank you. Thank you very much. *(They are all quiet, then —)* Well . . . I must go. I will call you Monday, Alaiyo.

Mama: What's that he call you?

Asagai: Oh — "Alaiyo." I hope you don't mind. It is what you would call a nickname, I think. It is a Yoruba word. I am a Yoruba.

Mama (looking at Beneatha): I — I thought he was from — *(Uncertain.)*

Asagai (understanding): Nigeria is my country. Yoruba is my tribal origin —

Beneatha: You didn't tell us what Alaiyo means . . . for all I know, you might be calling me Little Idiot or something . . .

Asagai: Well . . . let me see . . . I do not know how just to explain it . . . The sense of a thing can be so different when it changes languages.

Beneatha: You're evading.

Asagai: No — really it is difficult . . . *(Thinking.)* It means . . . it means One for Whom Bread — Food — Is Not Enough. *(He looks at her.)* Is that all right?

Beneatha (understanding, softly): Thank you.

Mama (looking from one to the other and not understanding any of it): Well . . . that's nice . . . You must come see us again — Mr. —

Asagai: Ah-sah-guy . . .

Mama: Yes . . . Do come again.

Asagai: Good-bye.

He exits.

Mama (after him): Lord, that's a pretty thing just went out here! *(Insinuatingly, to her daughter.)* Yes, I guess I see why we done commence to get so interested in Africa 'round here. Missionaries my aunt Jenny!

She exits.

Beneatha: Oh, Mama! . . .

She picks up the Nigerian dress and holds it up to her in front of the mirror again. She sets the headdress on haphazardly and then notices her hair again and clutches at it and then replaces the headdress and frowns at herself. Then she starts to wriggle in front of the mirror as she thinks a Nigerian woman might. Travis enters and stands regarding her.

Travis: What's the matter, girl, you cracking up?

Beneatha: Shut up.

She pulls the headdress off and looks at herself in the mirror and clutches at her hair again and squinches her eyes as if trying to imagine something. Then, suddenly, she gets her raincoat and kerchief and hurriedly prepares for going out.

Mama (coming back into the room): She's resting now. Travis, baby, run next door and ask Miss Johnson to please let me have a little kitchen cleanser. This here can is empty as Jacob's kettle.

Travis: I just came in.

Mama: Do as you told. *(He exits and she looks at her daughter.)* Where you going?

Beneatha (halting at the door): To become a queen of the Nile!

> *She exits in a breathless blaze of glory. Ruth appears in the bedroom doorway.*

Mama: Who told you to get up?

Ruth: Ain't nothing wrong with me to be lying in no bed for. Where did Bennie go?

Mama (drumming her fingers): Far as I could make out—to Egypt. *(Ruth just looks at her.)* What time is it getting to?

Ruth: Ten twenty. And the mailman going to ring that bell this morning just like he done every morning for the last umpteen years.

> *Travis comes in with the cleanser can.*

Travis: She say to tell you that she don't have much.

Mama (angrily): Lord, some people I could name sure is tight-fisted! *(Directing her grandson.)* Mark two cans of cleanser on the list there. If she that hard up for kitchen cleanser, I sure don't want to forget to get her none!

Ruth: Lena—maybe the woman is just short on cleanser—

Mama (not listening): —Much baking powder as she done borrowed from me all these years, she could of done gone into the baking business!

> *The bell sounds suddenly and sharply and all three are stunned—serious and silent—midspeech. In spite of all the other conversations and distractions of the morning, this is what they have been waiting for, even Travis, who looks helplessly from his mother to his grandmother. Ruth is the first to come to life again.*

Ruth (to Travis): Get down them steps, boy!

> *Travis snaps to life and flies out to get the mail.*

Mama (her eyes wide, her hand to her breast): You mean it done really come?

Ruth (excited): Oh, Miss Lena!

Mama (collecting herself): Well . . . I don't know what we all so excited about 'round here for. We known it was coming for months.

Ruth: That's a whole lot different from having it come and being able to hold it in your hands . . . a piece of paper worth ten thousand dollars . . . *(Travis bursts back into the room. He holds the envelope high above his head, like a little dancer, his face is radiant and he is breathless. He moves to his grandmother with sudden slow ceremony and puts the envelope into her hands. She accepts it, and then merely holds it and looks at it.)* Come on! Open it . . . Lord have mercy, I wish Walter Lee was here!

Travis: Open it, Grandmama!

Mama (staring at it): Now you all be quiet. It's just a check.

Ruth: Open it . . .

Mama (still staring at it): Now don't act silly . . . We ain't never been no people to act silly 'bout no money—

Ruth (swiftly): We ain't never had none before—OPEN IT!

> *Mama finally makes a good strong tear and pulls out the thin blue slice of paper and inspects it closely. The boy and his mother study it raptly over Mama's shoulders.*

Mama: Travis! *(She is counting off with doubt.)* Is that the right number of zeros?

Travis: Yes'm . . . ten thousand dollars. Gaalee, grandmama, you rich.

Mama (She holds the check away from her, still looking at it. Slowly her face sobers into a mask of unhappiness): Ten thousand dollars. *(She hands it to Ruth.)* Put it away somewhere, Ruth. *(She does not look at Ruth; her eyes seem to be seeing something somewhere very far off.)* Ten thousand dollars they give you. Ten thousand dollars.

Travis (to his mother, sincerely): What's the matter with Grandmama — don't she want to be rich?

Ruth (distractedly): You go on out and play now, baby. *(Travis exits. Mama starts wiping dishes absently, humming intently to herself. Ruth turns to her, with kind exasperation.)* You've gone and got yourself upset.

Mama (not looking at her): I spec if it wasn't for you all . . . I would just put that money away or give it to the church or something.

Ruth: Now what kind of talk is that. Mr. Younger would just be plain mad if he could hear you talking foolish like that.

Mama (stopping and staring off): Yes . . . he sure would. *(Sighing.)* We got enough to do with that money, all right. *(She halts then, and turns and looks at her daughter-in-law hard; Ruth avoids her eyes and Mama wipes her hands with finality and starts to speak firmly to Ruth.)* Where did you go today, girl?

Ruth: To the doctor.

Mama (impatiently): Now, Ruth . . . you know better than that. Old Doctor Jones is strange enough in his way but there ain't nothing 'bout him make somebody slip and call him "she" — like you done this morning.

Ruth: Well, that's what happened — my tongue slipped.

Mama: You went to see that woman, didn't you?

Ruth (defensively, giving herself away): What woman you talking about?

Mama (angrily): That woman who —

Walter enters in great excitement.

Walter: Did it come?

Mama (quietly): Can't you give people a Christian greeting before you start asking about money?

Walter (to Ruth): Did it come? *(Ruth unfolds the check and lays it quietly before him, watching him intently with thoughts of her own. Walter sits down and grasps it close and counts off the zeros.)* Ten thousand dollars — *(He turns suddenly, frantically to his mother and draws some papers out of his breast pocket.)* Mama — look. Old Willy Harris put everything on paper —

Mama: Son — I think you ought to talk to your wife . . . I'll go on out and leave you alone if you want —

Walter: I can talk to her later — Mama, look —

Mama: Son —

Walter: WILL SOMEBODY PLEASE LISTEN TO ME TODAY!

Mama (quietly): I don't 'low no yellin' in this house, Walter Lee, and you know it — *(Walter stares at them in frustration and starts to speak several times.)* And there ain't going to be no investing in no liquor stores.

Walter: But, Mama, you ain't even looked at it.

Mama: I don't aim to have to speak on that again.

A long pause.

Walter: You ain't looked at it and you don't aim to have to speak on that again? You ain't even looked at it and *you* have decided — *(Crumpling his papers.)* Well, *you* tell that to my boy tonight when you put him to sleep on the living-room couch . . . *(Turning to Mama and speaking directly to her.)*

Yeah — and tell it to my wife, Mama, tomorrow when she has to go out of here to look after somebody else's kids. And tell it to *me,* Mama, every time we need a new pair of curtains and I have to watch *you* go out and work in somebody's kitchen. Yeah, you tell me then!

Walter starts out.

Ruth: Where you going?
Walter: I'm going out!
Ruth: Where?
Walter: Just out of this house somewhere —
Ruth (getting her coat): I'll come too.
Walter: I don't want you to come!
Ruth: I got something to talk to you about, Walter.
Walter: That's too bad.
Mama (still quietly): Walter Lee — *(She waits and he finally turns and looks at her.)* Sit down.
Walter: I'm a grown man, Mama.
Mama: Ain't nobody said you wasn't grown. But you still in my house and my presence. And as long as you are — you'll talk to your wife civil. Now sit down.
Ruth (suddenly): Oh, let him go on out and drink himself to death! He makes me sick to my stomach! *(She flings her coat against him and exits to bedroom.)*
Walter (violently flinging the coat after her): And you turn mine too, baby! *(The door slams behind her.)* That was my biggest mistake —
Mama (still quietly): Walter, what is the matter with you?
Walter: Matter with me? Ain't nothing the matter with *me!*
Mama: Yes there is. Something eating you up like a crazy man. Something more than me not giving you this money. The past few years I been watching it happen to you. You get all nervous acting and kind of wild in the eyes — *(Walter jumps up impatiently at her words.)* I said sit there now, I'm talking to you!
Walter: Mama — I don't need no nagging at me today.
Mama: Seem like you getting to a place where you always tied up in some kind of knot about something. But if anybody ask you 'bout it you just yell at 'em and bust out the house and go out and drink somewheres. Walter Lee, people can't live with that. Ruth's a good, patient girl in her way — but you getting to be too much. Boy, don't make the mistake of driving that girl away from you.
Walter: Why — what she do for me?
Mama: She loves you.
Walter: Mama — I'm going out. I want to go off somewhere and be by myself for a while.
Mama: I'm sorry 'bout your liquor store, son. It just wasn't the thing for us to do. That's what I want to tell you about —
Walter: I got to go out, Mama —

He rises.

Mama: It's dangerous, son.
Walter: What's dangerous?
Mama: When a man goes outside his home to look for peace.

Walter (beseechingly): Then why can't there never be no peace in this house then?

Mama: You done found it in some other house?

Walter: No — there ain't no woman! Why do women always think there's a woman somewhere when a man gets restless. *(Picks up the check.)* Do you know what this money means to me? Do you know what this money can do for us? *(Puts it back.)* Mama — Mama — I want so many things . . .

Mama: Yes, son —

Walter: I want so many things that they are driving me kind of crazy . . . Mama — look at me.

Mama: I'm looking at you. You a good-looking boy. You got a job, a nice wife, a fine boy, and —

Walter: A job. *(Looks at her.)* Mama, a job? I open and close car doors all day long. I drive a man around in his limousine and I say, "Yes, sir; no, sir; very good, sir; shall I take the Drive, sir?" Mama, that ain't no kind of job . . . that ain't nothing at all. *(Very quietly.)* Mama, I don't know if I can make you understand.

Mama: Understand what, baby?

Walter (quietly): Sometimes it's like I can see the future stretched out in front of me — just plain as day. The future, Mama. Hanging over there at the edge of my days. Just waiting for me — a big, looming blank space — full of *nothing*. Just waiting for *me*. But it don't have to be. *(Pause. Kneeling beside her chair.)* Mama — sometimes when I'm downtown and I pass them cool, quiet-looking restaurants where them white boys are sitting back and talking 'bout things . . . sitting there turning deals worth millions of dollars . . . sometimes I see guys don't look much older than me —

Mama: Son — how come you talk so much 'bout money?

Walter (with immense passion): Because it is life, Mama!

Mama (quietly): Oh — *(Very quietly.)* So now it's life. Money is life. Once upon a time freedom used to be life — now it's money. I guess the world really do change . . .

Walter: No — it was always money, Mama. We just didn't know about it.

Mama: No . . . something has changed. *(She looks at him.)* You something new, boy. In my time we was worried about not being lynched and getting to the North if we could and how to stay alive and still have a pinch of dignity too . . . Now here come you and Beneatha — talking 'bout things we ain't never even thought about hardly, me and your daddy. You ain't satisfied or proud of nothing we done. I mean that you had a home; that we kept you out of trouble till you was grown; that you don't have to ride to work on the back of nobody's streetcar — You my children — but how different we done become.

Walter (a long beat. He pats her hand and gets up): You just don't understand, Mama, you just don't understand.

Mama: Son — do you know your wife is expecting another baby? *(Walter stands, stunned, and absorbs what his mother has said.)* That's what she wanted to talk to you about. *(Walter sinks down into a chair.)* This ain't for me to be telling — but you ought to know. *(She waits.)* I think Ruth is thinking 'bout getting rid of that child.

Walter (slowly understanding): — No — no — Ruth wouldn't do that.

Mama: When the world gets ugly enough — a woman will do anything for her family. *The part that's already living.*

Walter: You don't know Ruth, Mama, if you think she would do that.

Ruth opens the bedroom door and stands there a little limp.

Ruth (beaten): Yes I would too, Walter. *(Pause.)* I gave her a five-dollar down payment.

There is total silence as the man stares at his wife and the mother stares at her son.

Mama (presently): Well — *(Tightly.)* Well — son, I'm waiting to hear you say something . . . *(She waits.)* I'm waiting to hear how you be your father's son. Be the man he was . . . *(Pause. The silence shouts.)* Your wife say she going to destroy your child. And I'm waiting to hear you talk like him and say we a people who give children life, not who destroys them — *(She rises.)* I'm waiting to see you stand up and look like your daddy and say we done give up one baby to poverty and that we ain't going to give up nary another one . . . I'm waiting.

Walter: Ruth — *(He can say nothing.)*

Mama: If you a son of mine, tell her! *(Walter picks up his keys and his coat and walks out. She continues, bitterly.)* You . . . you are a disgrace to your father's memory. Somebody get me my hat!

Curtain.

ACT II

SCENE I

TIME: *Later the same day.*

     At rise: Ruth is ironing again. She has the radio going. Presently Beneatha's bedroom door opens and Ruth's mouth falls and she puts down the iron in fascination.

Ruth: What have we got on tonight!

Beneatha (emerging grandly from the doorway so that we can see her thoroughly robed in the costume Asagai brought): You are looking at what a well-dressed Nigerian woman wears — *(She parades for Ruth, her hair completely hidden by the headdress; she is coquettishly fanning herself with an ornate oriental fan, mistakenly more like Butterfly than any Nigerian that ever was.)* Isn't it beautiful? *(She promenades to the radio and, with an arrogant flourish, turns off the good loud blues that is playing.)* Enough of this assimilationist junk! *(Ruth follows her with her eyes as she goes to the phonograph and puts on a record and turns and waits ceremoniously for the music to come up. Then, with a shout—)* OCOMOGOSIAY!

Ruth jumps. The music comes up, a lovely Nigerian melody. Beneatha listens, enraptured, her eyes far way— "back to the past." She begins to dance. Ruth is dumfounded.

Ruth: What kind of dance is that?

Beneatha: A folk dance.

Ruth (Pearl Bailey): What kind of folks do that, honey?

Beneatha: It's from Nigeria. It's a dance of welcome.

Ruth: Who you welcoming?

Beneatha: The men back to the village.
Ruth: Where they been?
Beneatha: How should I know—out hunting or something. Anyway, they are coming back now . . .
Ruth: Well, that's good.
Beneatha (with the record):

> Alundi, alundi
> Alundi alunya
> Jop pu a jeepua
> Ang gu soooooooooo
> Ai yai yae . . .
> Ayehaye—alundi . . .

Walter comes in during this performance; he has obviously been drinking. He leans against the door heavily and watches his sister, at first with distaste. Then his eyes look off—"back to the past"—as he lifts both his fists to the roof, screaming.

Walter: YEAH . . . AND ETHIOPIA STRETCH FORTH HER HANDS AGAIN! . . .
Ruth (drily, looking at him): Yes—and Africa sure is claiming her own tonight. *(She gives them both up and starts ironing again.)*
Walter (all in a drunken, dramatic shout): Shut up! . . . I'm diggin them drums . . . them drums move me! . . . *(He makes his weaving way to his wife's face and leans in close to her.)* In my heart of hearts—*(He thumps his chest.)*—I am much warrior!
Ruth (without even looking up): In your heart of hearts you are much drunkard.
Walter (coming away from her and starting to wander around the room, shouting): Me and Jomo . . . *(Intently, in his sister's face. She has stopped dancing to watch him in this unknown mood.)* That's my man, Kenyatta. *(Shouting and thumping his chest.)* FLAMING SPEAR! HOT DAMN! *(He is suddenly in possession of an imaginary spear and actively spearing enemies all over the room.)* OCOMO-GOSIAY . . .
Beneatha (to encourage Walter, thoroughly caught up with this side of him): OCOMO-GOSIAY, FLAMING SPEAR!
Walter: THE LION IS WAKING . . . OWIMOWEH!

He pulls his shirt open and leaps up on the table and gestures with his spear.

Beneatha: OWIMOWEH!
Walter (on the table, very far gone, his eyes pure glass sheets. He sees what we cannot, that he is a leader of his people, a great chief, a descendant of Chaka, and that the hour to march has come): Listen, my black brothers—
Beneatha: OCOMOGOSIAY!
Walter: —Do you hear the waters rushing against the shores of the coast-lands—
Beneatha: OCOMOGOSIAY!
Walter: —Do you hear the screeching of the cocks in yonder hills beyond where the chiefs meet in council for the coming of the mighty war—
Beneatha: OCOMOGOSIAY!

And now the lighting shifts subtly to suggest the world of Walter's imagination, and the mood shifts from pure comedy. It is the inner Walter speaking: the Southside chauffeur has assumed an unexpected majesty.

Walter: — Do you hear the beating of the wings of the birds flying low over the mountains and the low places of our land —

Beneatha: OCOMOGOSIAY!

Walter: — Do you hear the singing of the women, singing the war songs of our fathers to the babies in the great houses? Singing the sweet war songs! *(The doorbell rings.)* OH, DO YOU HEAR, MY *BLACK* BROTHERS!

Beneatha (completely gone): We hear you, Flaming Spear —

Ruth shuts off the phonograph and opens the door. George Murchison enters.

Walter: Telling us to prepare for the GREATNESS OF THE TIME! *(Lights back to normal. He turns and sees George.)* Black Brother!

He extends his hand for the fraternal clasp.

George: Black Brother, hell!

Ruth (having had enough, and embarrassed for the family): Beneatha, you got company — what's the matter with you? Walter Lee Younger, get down off that table and stop acting like a fool . . .

Walter comes down off the table suddenly and makes a quick exit to the bathroom.

Ruth: He's had a little to drink . . . I don't know what her excuse is.

George (to Beneatha): Look honey, we're going to the theater — we're not going to be *in* it . . . so go change, huh?

Beneatha looks at him and slowly, ceremoniously, lifts her hands and pulls off the headdress. Her hair is close-cropped and unstraightened. George freezes midsentence and Ruth's eyes all but fall out of her head.

George: What in the name of —

Ruth (touching Beneatha's hair): Girl, you done lost your natural mind? Look at your head!

George: What have you done to your head — I mean your hair!

Beneatha: Nothing — except cut it off.

Ruth: Now that's the truth — it's what ain't been done to it! You expect this boy to go out with you with your head all nappy like that?

Beneatha (looking at George): That's up to George. If he's ashamed of his heritage —

George: Oh, don't be so proud of yourself, Bennie — just because you look eccentric.

Beneatha: How can something that's natural be eccentric?

George: That's what being eccentric means — being natural. Get dressed.

Beneatha: I don't like that, George.

Ruth: Why must you and your brother make an argument out of everything people say?

Beneatha: Because I hate assimilationist Negroes!

Ruth: Will somebody please tell me what assimila-whoever means!

George: Oh, it's just a college girl's way of calling people Uncle Toms — but that isn't what it means at all.

Ruth: Well, what does it mean?

Beneatha (cutting George off and staring at him as she replies to Ruth): It means someone who is willing to give up his own culture and submerge himself completely in the dominant, and in this case *oppressive* culture!

George: Oh, dear, dear, dear! Here we go! A lecture on the African past! On
  our Great West African Heritage! In one second we will hear all about
  the great Ashanti empires; the great Songhay civilizations; and the great
  sculpture of Bénin — and then some poetry in the Bantu — and the whole
  monologue will end with the word *heritage!* *(Nastily.)* Let's face it, baby,
  your heritage is nothing but a bunch of raggedy-assed spirituals and some
  grass huts!
Beneatha: GRASS HUTS! *(Ruth crosses to her and forcibly pushes her toward the bedroom.)* See there . . . you are standing there in your splendid ignorance
  talking about people who were the first to smelt iron on the face of the
  earth! *(Ruth is pushing her through the door.)* The Ashanti were performing
  surgical operations when the English — *(Ruth pulls the door to, with Beneatha
  on the other side, and smiles graciously at George. Beneatha opens the door and
  shouts the end of the sentence defiantly at George.)* — were still tatooing themselves with blue dragons! *(She goes back inside.)*
Ruth: Have a seat, George. *(They both sit. Ruth folds her hands rather primly on her
  lap, determined to demonstrate the civilization of the family.)* Warm, ain't it? I
  mean for September. *(Pause.)* Just like they always say about Chicago
  weather: if it's too hot or cold for you, just wait a minute and it'll change.
  (She smiles happily at this cliché of clichés.) Everybody say it's got to do with
  them bombs and things they keep setting off. *(Pause.)* Would you like a
  nice cold beer?
George: No, thank you. I don't care for beer. *(He looks at his watch.)* I hope she
  hurries up.
Ruth: What time is the show?
George: It's an eight-thirty curtain. That's just Chicago, though. In New York
  standard curtain time is eight forty.

He is rather proud of this knowledge.

Ruth (properly appreciating it): You get to New York a lot?
George (offhand): Few times a year.
Ruth: Oh — that's nice. I've never been to New York.

*Walter enters. We feel he has relieved himself, but the edge of unreality is still with
him.*

Walter: New York ain't got nothing Chicago ain't. Just a bunch of hustling
  people all squeezed up together — being "Eastern."

He turns his face into a screw of displeasure.

George: Oh — you've been?
Walter: Plenty of times.
Ruth (shocked at the lie): Walter Lee Younger!
Walter (staring her down): Plenty! *(Pause.)* What we got to drink in this house?
  Why don't you offer this man some refreshment. *(To George.)* They don't
  know how to entertain people in this house, man.
George: Thank you — I don't really care for anything.
Walter (feeling his head; sobriety coming): Where's Mama?
Ruth: She ain't come back yet.
*Walter (looking Murchison over from head to toe, scrutinizing his carefully casual tweed
  sports jacket over cashmere V-neck sweater over soft eyelet shirt and tie, and soft*

slacks, finished off with white buckskin shoes): Why all you college boys wear them faggoty-looking white shoes?

Ruth: Walter Lee!

George Murchison ignores the remark.

Walter (to Ruth): Well, they look crazy as hell—white shoes, cold as it is.

Ruth (crushed): You have to excuse him—

Walter: No he don't! Excuse me for what? What you always excusing me for! I'll excuse myself when I needs to be excused! *(A pause.)* They look as funny as them black knee socks Beneatha wears out of here all the time.

Ruth: It's the college *style,* Walter.

Walter: Style, hell. She looks like she got burnt legs or something!

Ruth: Oh, Walter—

Walter (an irritable mimic): Oh, Walter! Oh, Walter! *(To Murchison.)* How's your old man making out? I understand you all going to buy that big hotel on the Drive? *(He finds a beer in the refrigerator, wanders over to Murchison, sipping and wiping his lips with the back of his hand, and straddling a chair backwards to talk to the other man.)* Shrewd move. Your old man is all right, man. *(Tapping his head and half winking for emphasis.)* I mean he knows how to operate. I mean he thinks *big,* you know what I mean, I mean for a *home,* you know? But I think he's kind of running out of ideas now. I'd like to talk to him. Listen, man, I got some plans that could turn this city upside down. I mean think like he does. *Big.* Invest big, gamble big, hell, lose *big* if you have to, you know what I mean. It's hard to find a man on this whole Southside who understands my kind of thinking—you dig? *(He scrutinizes Murchison again, drinks his beer, squints his eyes and leans in close, confidential, man to man.)* Me and you ought to sit down and talk sometimes, man. Man, I got me some ideas . . .

Murchison (with boredom): Yeah—sometimes we'll have to do that, Walter.

Walter (understanding the indifference, and offended): Yeah—well, when you get the time, man. I know you a busy little boy.

Ruth: Walter, please—

Walter (bitterly, hurt): I know ain't nothing in this world as busy as you colored college boys with your fraternity pins and white shoes . . .

Ruth (covering her face with humiliation): Oh, Walter Lee—

Walter: I see you all all the time—with the books tucked under your arms—going to your *(British A—a mimic.)* "clahsses." And for what! What the hell you learning over there? Filling up your heads—*(Counting off on his fingers.)*—with the sociology and the psychology—but they teaching you how to be a man? How to take over and run the world? They teaching you how to run a rubber plantation or a steel mill? Naw—just to talk proper and read books and wear them faggoty-looking white shoes . . .

George (looking at him with distaste, a little above it all): You're all wacked up with bitterness, man.

Walter (intently, almost quietly, between the teeth, glaring at the boy): And you—ain't you bitter, man? Ain't you just about had it yet? Don't you see no stars gleaming that you can't reach out and grab? You happy?—You contented son-of-a-bitch—you happy? You got it made? Bitter? Man, I'm a volcano. Bitter? Here I am a giant—surrounded by ants! Ants who can't even understand what it is the giant is talking about.

Ruth (passionately and suddenly): Oh, Walter — ain't you with nobody!
Walter (violently): No! 'Cause ain't nobody with me! Not even my own mother!
Ruth: Walter, that's a terrible thing to say!

> *Beneatha enters, dressed for the evening in a cocktail dress and earrings, hair natural.*

George: Well — hey — *(Crosses to Beneatha; thoughtful, with emphasis, since this is a reversal.)* You look great!
Walter (seeing his sister's hair for the first time): What's the matter with your head?
Beneatha (tired of the jokes now): I cut it off, Brother.
Walter (coming close to inspect it and walking around her): Well, I'll be damned. So that's what they mean by the African bush . . .
Beneatha: Ha ha. Let's go, George.
George (looking at her): You know something? I like it. It's sharp. I mean it really is. *(Helps her into her wrap.)*
Ruth: Yes — I think so, too. *(She goes to the mirror and starts to clutch at her hair.)*
Walter: Oh no! You leave yours alone, baby. You might turn out to have a pin-shaped head or something!
Beneatha: See you all later.
Ruth: Have a nice time.
George: Thanks. Good night. *(Half out the door, he reopens it. To Walter.)* Good night, Prometheus!

> *Beneatha and George exit.*

Walter (to Ruth): Who is Prometheus?
Ruth: I don't know. Don't worry about it.
Walter (in fury, pointing after George): See there — they get to a point where they can't insult you man to man — they got to go talk about something ain't nobody never heard of!
Ruth: How do you know it was an insult? *(To humor him.)* Maybe Prometheus is a nice fellow.
Walter: Prometheus! I bet there ain't even no such thing! I bet that simple-minded clown —
Ruth: Walter —

> *She stops what she is doing and looks at him.*

Walter (yelling): Don't start!
Ruth: Start what?
Walter: Your nagging! Where was I? Who was I with? How much money did I spend?
Ruth (plaintively): Walter Lee — why don't we just try to talk about it . . .
Walter (not listening): I been out talking with people who understand me. People who care about the things I got on my mind.
Ruth (wearily): I guess that means people like Willy Harris.
Walter: Yes, people like Willy Harris.
Ruth (with a sudden flash of impatience): Why don't you all just hurry up and go into the banking business and stop talking about it!
Walter: Why? You want to know why? 'Cause we all tied up in a race of people that don't know how to do nothing but moan, pray and have babies!

> *The line is too bitter even for him and he looks at her and sits down.*

Ruth: Oh, Walter . . . *(Softly.)* Honey, why can't you stop fighting me?

Walter (without thinking): Who's fighting you? Who even cares about you?

> *This line begins the retardation of his mood.*

Ruth: Well — *(She waits a long time, and then with resignation starts to put away her things.)* I guess I might as well go on to bed . . . *(More or less to herself.)* I don't know where we lost it . . . but we have . . . *(Then, to him.)* I — I'm sorry about this new baby, Walter. I guess maybe I better go on and do what I started . . . I guess I just didn't realize how bad things was with us . . . I guess I just didn't really realize — *(She starts out to the bedroom and stops.)* You want some hot milk?

Walter: Hot milk?

Ruth: Yes — hot milk.

Walter: Why hot milk?

Ruth: 'Cause after all that liquor you come home with you ought to have something hot in your stomach.

Walter: I don't want no milk.

Ruth: You want some coffee then?

Walter: No, I don't want no coffee. I don't want nothing hot to drink. *(Almost plaintively.)* Why you always trying to give me something to eat?

Ruth (standing and looking at him helplessly): What *else* can I give you, Walter Lee Younger?

> *She stands and looks at him and presently turns to go out again. He lifts his head and watches her going away from him in a new mood which began to emerge when he asked her "Who cares about you?"*

Walter: It's been rough, ain't it, baby? *(She hears and stops but does not turn around and he continues to her back.)* I guess between two people there ain't never as much understood as folks generally thinks there is. I mean like between me and you — *(She turns to face him.)* How we gets to the place where we scared to talk softness to each other. *(He waits, thinking hard himself.)* Why you think it got to be like that? *(He is thoughtful, almost as a child would be.)* Ruth, what is it gets into people ought to be close?

Ruth: I don't know, honey. I think about it a lot.

Walter: On account of you and me, you mean? The way things are with us. The way something done come down between us.

Ruth: There ain't so much between us, Walter . . . Not when you come to me and try to talk to me. Try to be with me . . . a little even.

Walter (total honesty): Sometimes . . . sometimes . . . I don't even know how to try.

Ruth: Walter —

Walter: Yes?

Ruth (coming to him, gently and with misgiving, but coming to him): Honey . . . life don't have to be like this. I mean sometimes people can do things so that things are better . . . You remember how we used to talk when Travis was born . . . about the way we were going to live . . . the kind of house . . . *(She is stroking his head.)* Well, it's all starting to slip away from us . . .

> *He turns her to him and they look at each other and kiss, tenderly and hungrily. The door opens and Mama enters — Walter breaks away and jumps up. A beat.*

Walter: Mama, where have you been?

Mama: My—them steps is longer than they used to be. Whew! *(She sits down and ignores him.)* How you feeling this evening, Ruth?

Ruth shrugs, disturbed at having been interrupted and watching her husband knowingly.

Walter: Mama, where have you been all day?

Mama (still ignoring him and leaning on the table and changing to more comfortable shoes): Where's Travis?

Ruth: I let him go out earlier and he ain't come back yet. Boy, is he going to get it!

Walter: Mama!

Mama (as if she has heard him for the first time): Yes, son?

Walter: Where did you go this afternoon?

Mama: I went downtown to tend to some business that I had to tend to.

Walter: What kind of business?

Mama: You know better than to question me like a child, Brother.

Walter (rising and bending over the table): Where were you, Mama? *(Bringing his fists down and shouting.)* Mama, you didn't go do something with that insurance money, something crazy?

The front door opens slowly, interrupting him, and Travis peeks his head in, less than hopefully.

Travis (to his mother): Mama, I—

Ruth: "Mama I" nothing! You're going to get it, boy! Get on in that bedroom and get yourself ready!

Travis: But I—

Mama: Why don't you all never let the child explain hisself.

Ruth: Keep out of it now, Lena.

Mama clamps her lips together, and Ruth advances toward her son menacingly.

Ruth: A thousand times I have told you not to go off like that—

Mama (holding out her arms to her grandson): Well—at least let me tell him something. I want him to be the first one to hear . . . Come here, Travis. *(The boy obeys, gladly.)* Travis—*(She takes him by the shoulder and looks into his face.)*—you know that money we got in the mail this morning?

Travis: Yes'm—

Mama: Well—what you think your grandmama gone and done with that money?

Travis: I don't know, Grandmama.

Mama (putting her finger on his nose for emphasis): She went out and she bought you a house! *(The explosion comes from Walter at the end of the revelation and he jumps up and turns away from all of them in a fury. Mama continues, to Travis.)* You glad about the house? It's going to be yours when you get to be a man.

Travis: Yeah—I always wanted to live in a house.

Mama: All right, gimme some sugar then—*(Travis puts his arms around her neck as she watches her son over the boy's shoulder. Then, to Travis, after the embrace.)* Now when you say your prayers tonight, you thank God and your grandfather—'cause it was him who give you the house—in his way.

Ruth (taking the boy from Mama and pushing him toward the bedroom): Now you get out of here and get ready for your beating.

Travis: Aw, Mama—

Ruth: Get on in there — *(Closing the door behind him and turning radiantly to her mother-in-law.)* So you went and did it!

Mama (quietly, looking at her son with pain): Yes, I did.

Ruth (raising both arms classically): PRAISE GOD! *(Looks at Walter a moment, who says nothing. She crosses rapidly to her husband.)* Please, honey — let me be glad . . . you be glad too. *(She has laid her hands on his shoulders, but he shakes himself free of her roughly, without turning to face her.)* Oh, Walter . . . a home . . . a home. *(She comes back to Mama.)* Well — where is it? How big is it? How much it going to cost?

Mama: Well —

Ruth: When we moving?

Mama (smiling at her): First of the month.

Ruth (throwing back her head with jubilance): Praise God!

Mama (tentatively, still looking at her son's back turned against her and Ruth): It's — it's a nice house too . . . *(She cannot help speaking directly to him. An imploring quality in her voice, her manner, makes her almost like a girl now.)* Three bedrooms — nice big one for you and Ruth . . . Me and Beneatha still have to share our room, but Travis have one of his own — and *(With difficulty.)* I figure if the — new baby — is a boy, we could get one of them double-decker outfits . . . And there's a yard with a little patch of dirt where I could maybe get to grow me a few flowers . . . And a nice big basement . . .

Ruth: Walter honey, be glad —

Mama (still to his back, fingering things on the table): 'Course I don't want to make it sound fancier than it is . . . It's just a plain little old house — but it's made good and solid — and it will be *ours*. Walter Lee — it makes a difference in a man when he can walk on floors that belong to *him* . . .

Ruth: Where is it?

Mama (frightened at this telling): Well — well — it's out there in Clybourne Park —

Ruth's radiance fades abruptly, and Walter finally turns slowly to face his mother with incredulity and hostility.

Ruth: Where?

Mama (matter-of-factly): Four o six Clybourne Street, Clybourne Park.

Ruth: Clybourne Park? Mama, there ain't no colored people living in Clybourne Park.

Mama (almost idiotically): Well, I guess there's going to be some now.

Walter (bitterly): So that's the peace and comfort you went out and bought for us today!

Mama (raising her eyes to meet his finally): Son — I just tried to find the nicest place for the least amount of money for my family.

Ruth (trying to recover from the shock): Well — well — 'course I ain't one never been 'fraid of no crackers, mind you — but — well, wasn't there no other houses nowhere?

Mama: Them houses they put up for colored in them areas way out all seem to cost twice as much as other houses. I did the best I could.

Ruth (struck senseless with the news, in its various degrees of goodness and trouble, she sits a moment, her fists propping her chin in thought, and then she starts to rise, bringing her fists down with vigor, the radiance spreading from cheek to cheek again): Well — well — All I can say is — if this is my time in life — MY TIME — to say good-bye — *(And she builds with momentum as she starts to circle the room with an exuberant, almost tearfully happy release.)* — to these Goddamned cracking walls! — *(She pounds the walls.)* — and these marching roaches! — *(She wipes at an imaginary army of marching roaches.)* — and this cramped little closet which ain't now or never was no kitchen! . . . then I say it loud and good, HALLELUJAH! AND GOOD-BYE MISERY . . . I DON'T NEVER WANT TO SEE YOUR UGLY FACE AGAIN! *(She laughs joyously, having practically destroyed the apartment, and flings her arms up and lets them come down happily, slowly, reflectively, over her abdomen, aware for the first time perhaps that the life therein pulses with happiness and not despair.)* Lena?

Mama *(moved, watching her happiness)*: Yes, honey?

Ruth *(looking off)*: Is there — is there a whole lot of sunlight?

Mama *(understanding)*: Yes, child, there's a whole lot of sunlight.

Long pause.

Ruth *(collecting herself and going to the door of the room Travis is in)*: Well — I guess I better see 'bout Travis. *(To Mama.)* Lord, I sure don't feel like whipping nobody today!

She exits.

Mama *(the mother and son are left alone now and the mother waits a long time, considering deeply, before she speaks)*: Son — you — you understand what I done, don't you? *(Walter is silent and sullen.)* I — I just seen my family falling apart today . . . just falling to pieces in front of my eyes . . . We couldn't of gone on like we was today. We was going backwards 'stead of forwards — talking 'bout killing babies and wishing each other was dead . . . When it gets like that in life — you just got to do something different, push on out and do something bigger . . . *(She waits.)* I wish you say something, son . . . I wish you'd say how deep inside you you think I done the right thing —

Walter *(crossing slowly to his bedroom door and finally turning there and speaking measuredly)*: What you need me to say you done right for? *You* the head of this family. You run our lives like you want to. It was your money and you did what you wanted with it. So what you need for me to say it was all right for? *(Bitterly, to hurt her as deeply as he knows is possible.)* So you butchered up a dream of mine — you — who always talking 'bout your children's dreams . . .

Mama: Walter Lee —

He just closes the door behind him. Mama sits alone, thinking heavily.

Curtain.

SCENE II

TIME: *Friday night, a few weeks later.*

   At rise: Packing crates mark the intention of the family to move. Beneatha and George come in, presumably from an evening out again.

George: O.K. . . . O.K., whatever you say . . . *(They both sit on the couch. He tries to kiss her. She moves away.)* Look, we've had a nice evening; let's not spoil it, huh? . . .

He again turns her head and tries to nuzzle in and she turns away from him, not with distaste but with momentary lack of interest; in a mood to pursue what they were talking about.

Beneatha: I'm *trying* to talk to you.

George: We always talk.

Beneatha: Yes—and I love to talk.

George (exasperated; rising): I know it and I don't mind it sometimes . . . I want you to cut it out, see—The moody stuff, I mean. I don't like it. You're a nice-looking girl . . . all over. That's all you need, honey, forget the atmosphere. Guys aren't going to go for the atmosphere—they're going to go for what they see. Be glad for that. Drop the Garbo routine. It doesn't go with you. As for myself, I want a nice—*(Groping.)*—simple *(Thoughtfully.)*—sophisticated girl . . . not a poet—O.K.?

He starts to kiss her, she rebuffs him again and he jumps up.

Beneatha: Why are you angry, George?

George: Because this is stupid! I don't go out with you to discuss the nature of "quiet desperation" or to hear all about your thoughts—because the world will go on thinking what it thinks regardless—

Beneatha: Then why read books? Why go to school?

George (with artificial patience, counting on his fingers): It's simple. You read books—to learn facts—to get grades—to pass the course—to get a degree. That's all—it has nothing to do with thoughts.

A long pause.

Beneatha: I see. *(He starts to sit.)* Good night, George.

George looks at her a little oddly, and starts to exit. He meets Mama coming in.

George: Oh—hello, Mrs. Younger.

Mama: Hello, George, how you feeling?

George: Fine—fine, how are you?

Mama: Oh, a little tired. You know them steps can get you after a day's work. You all have a nice time tonight?

George: Yes—a fine time. A fine time.

Mama: Well, good night.

George: Good night. *(He exits. Mama closes the door behind her.)* Hello, honey. What you sitting like that for?

Beneatha: I'm just sitting.

Mama: Didn't you have a nice time?

Beneatha: No.

Mama: No? What's the matter?

Beneatha: Mama, George is a fool—honest. *(She rises.)*

Mama (hustling around unloading the packages she has entered with. She stops): Is he, baby?

Beneatha: Yes.

Beneatha makes up Travis's bed as she talks.

Mama: You sure?

Beneatha: Yes.

Mama: Well—I guess you better not waste your time with no fools.

Beneatha looks up at her mother, watching her put groceries in the refrigerator. Finally she gathers up her things and starts into the bedroom. At the door she stops and looks back at her mother.

Beneatha: Mama—

Mama: Yes, baby —
Beneatha: Thank you.
Mama: For what?
Beneatha: For understanding me this time.

> *She exits quickly and the mother stands, smiling a little, looking at the place where Beneatha just stood. Ruth enters.*

Ruth: Now don't you fool with any of this stuff, Lena —
Mama: Oh, I just thought I'd sort a few things out. Is Brother here?
Ruth: Yes.
Mama (with concern): Is he —
Ruth (reading her eyes): Yes.

> *Mama is silent and someone knocks on the door. Mama and Ruth exchange weary and knowing glances and Ruth opens it to admit the neighbor, Mrs. Johnson,[1] who is a rather squeaky wide-eyed lady of no particular age, with a newspaper under her arm.*

Mama (changing her expression to acute delight and a ringing cheerful greeting): Oh — hello there, Johnson.
Johnson (this is a woman who decided long ago to be enthusiastic about EVERYTHING in life and she is inclined to wave her wrist vigorously at the height of her exclamatory comments): Hello there, yourself! H'you this evening, Ruth?
Ruth (not much of a deceptive type): Fine, Mis' Johnson, h'you?
Johnson: Fine. *(Reaching out quickly, playfully, and patting Ruth's stomach.)* Ain't you starting to poke out none yet! *(She mugs with delight at the over familiar remark and her eyes dart around looking at the crates and packing preparation; Mama's face is a cold sheet of endurance.)* Oh, ain't we getting ready round here, though! Yessir! Lookathere! I'm telling you the Youngers is really getting ready to "move on up a little higher!" — Bless God!
Mama (a little drily, doubting the total sincerity of the Blesser): Bless God.
Johnson: He's good, ain't He?
Mama: Oh yes, He's good.
Johnson: I mean sometimes He works in mysterious ways . . . but He works, don't He!
Mama (the same): Yes, he does.
Johnson: I'm just soooooo happy for y'all. And this here child — *(About Ruth.)* looks like she could just pop open with happiness, don't she. Where's all the rest of the family?
Mama: Bennie's gone to bed —
Johnson: Ain't no . . . *(The implication is pregnancy.)* sickness done hit you — I hope . . . ?
Mama: No — she just tired. She was out this evening.
Johnson (all is a coo, an emphatic coo): Aw — ain't that lovely. She still going out with the little Murchison boy?
Mama (drily): Ummmm huh.
Johnson: That's lovely. You sure got lovely children, Younger. Me and Isaiah talks all the time 'bout what fine children you was blessed with. We sure do.
Mama: Ruth, give Mis' Johnson a piece of sweet potato pie and some milk.

---

[1]This character and the scene of her visit were cut from the original production and early editions of the play.

Johnson: Oh honey, I can't stay hardly a minute—I just dropped in to see if there was anything I could do. *(Accepting the food easily.)* I guess y'all seen the news what's all over the colored paper this week . . .

Mama: No—didn't get mine yet this week.

Johnson (lifting her head and blinking with the spirit of catastrophe): You mean you ain't read 'bout them colored people that was bombed out their place out there?

Ruth straightens with concern and takes the paper and reads it. Johnson notices her and feeds commentary.

Johnson: Ain't it something how bad these here white folks is getting here in Chicago! Lord, getting so you think you right down in Mississippi! *(With a tremendous and rather insincere sense of melodrama.)* 'Course I thinks it's wonderful how our folk keeps on pushing out. You hear some of these Negroes round here talking 'bout how they don't go where they ain't wanted and all that—but not me, honey! *(This is a lie.)* Wilhemenia Othella Johnson goes anywhere, any time she feels like it! *(With head movement for emphasis.)* Yes I do! Why if we left it up to these here crackers, the poor niggers wouldn't have nothing—*(She clasps her hand over her mouth.)* Oh, I always forgets you don't 'low that word in your house.

Mama (quietly, looking at her): No—I don't 'low it.

Johnson (vigorously again): Me neither! I was just telling Isaiah yesterday when he come using it in front of me—I said, "Isaiah, it's just like Mis' Younger says all the time—"

Mama: Don't you want some more pie?

Johnson: No—no thank you; this was lovely. I got to get on over home and have my midnight coffee. I hear some people say it don't let them sleep but I finds I can't close my eyes right lessen I done had that laaaast cup of coffee . . . *(She waits. A beat. Undaunted.)* My Goodnight coffee, I calls it!

Mama (with much eye-rolling and communication between herself and Ruth): Ruth, why don't you give Mis' Johnson some coffee.

Ruth gives Mama an unpleasant look for her kindness.

Johnson (accepting the coffee): Where's Brother tonight?

Mama: He's lying down.

Johnson: MMmmmmm, he sure gets his beauty rest, don't he? Good-looking man. Sure is a good-looking man! *(Reaching out to pat Ruth's stomach again.)* I guess that's how come we keep on having babies around here. *(She winks at Mama.)* One thing 'bout Brother, he always know how to have a *good* time. And sooooooo ambitious! I bet it was his idea y'all moving out to Clybourne Park. Lord—I bet this time next month y'all's names will have been in the papers plenty—*(Holding up her hands to mark off each word of the headline she can see in front of her.)* "NEGROES INVADE CLYBOURNE PARK—BOMBED!"

Mama (she and Ruth look at the woman in amazement): We ain't exactly moving out there to get bombed.

Johnson: Oh honey—you know I'm praying to God every day that don't nothing like that happen! But you have to think of life like it is—and these here Chicago peckerwoods is some baaaad peckerwoods.

Mama (wearily): We done thought about all that Mis' Johnson.

Beneatha comes out of the bedroom in her robe and passes through to the bathroom. Mrs. Johnson turns.

Johnson: Hello there, Bennie!

Beneatha (crisply): Hello, Mrs. Johnson.

Johnson: How is school?

Beneatha (crisply): Fine, thank you. *(She goes out.)*

Johnson (insulted): Getting so she don't have much to say to nobody.

Mama: The child was on her way to the bathroom.

Johnson: I know—but sometimes she act like ain't got time to pass the time of day with nobody ain't been to college. Oh—I ain't criticizing her none. It's just—you know how some of our young people gets when they get a little education. *(Mama and Ruth say nothing, just look at her.)* Yes—well. Well, I guess I better get on home. *(Unmoving.)* 'Course I can understand how she must be proud and everything—being the only one in the family to make something of herself. I know just being a chauffeur ain't never satisfied Brother none. He shouldn't feel like that, though. Ain't nothing wrong with being a chauffeur.

Mama: There's plenty wrong with it.

Johnson: What?

Mama: Plenty. My husband always said being any kind of a servant wasn't a fit thing for a man to have to be. He always said a man's hands was made to make things, or to turn the earth with—not to drive nobody's car for 'em—or—*(She looks at her own hands.)* carry they slop jars. And my boy is just like him—he wasn't meant to wait on nobody.

Johnson (rising, somewhat offended): Mmmmmmmmmm. The Youngers is too much for me! *(She looks around.)* You sure one proud-acting bunch of colored folks. Well—I always thinks like Booker T. Washington said that time—"Education has spoiled many a good plow hand"—

Mama: Is that what old Booker T. said?

Johnson: He sure did.

Mama: Well, it sounds just like him. The fool.

Johnson (indignantly): Well—he was one of our great men.

Mama: Who said so?

Johnson (nonplussed): You know, me and you ain't never agreed about some things, Lena Younger. I guess I better be going—

Ruth (quickly): Good night.

Johnson: Good night. Oh—*(Thrusting it at her.)* You can keep the paper! *(With a trill.)* 'Night.

Mama: Good night, Mis' Johnson.

Mrs. Johnson exits.

Ruth: If ignorance was gold . . .

Mama: Shush. Don't talk about folks behind their backs.

Ruth: You do.

Mama: I'm old and corrupted. *(Beneatha enters.)* You was rude to Mis' Johnson, Beneatha, and I don't like it at all.

Beneatha (at her door): Mama, if there are two things we, as a people, have got to overcome, one is the Klu Klux Klan—and the other is Mrs. Johnson. *(She exits.)*

Mama: Smart aleck.

The phone rings.

Ruth: I'll get it.

Mama: Lord, ain't this a popular place tonight.

Ruth (at the phone): Hello — Just a minute. *(Goes to door.)* Walter, it's Mrs. Arnold. *(Waits. Goes back to the phone. Tense.)* Hello. Yes, this is his wife speaking . . . He's lying down now. Yes . . . well, he'll be in tomorrow. He's been very sick. Yes — I know we should have called, but we were so sure he'd be able to come in today. Yes — yes, I'm very sorry. Yes . . . Thank you very much. *(She hangs up. Walter is standing in the doorway of the bedroom behind her.)* That was Mrs. Arnold.

Walter (indifferently): Was it?

Ruth: She said if you don't come in tomorrow that they are getting a new man . . .

Walter: Ain't that sad — ain't that crying sad.

Ruth: She said Mr. Arnold has had to take a cab for three days . . . Walter, you ain't been to work for three days! *(This is a revelation to her.)* Where you been, Walter Lee Younger? *(Walter looks at her and starts to laugh.)* You're going to lose your job.

Walter: That's right . . . *(He turns on the radio.)*

Ruth: Oh, Walter, and with your mother working like a dog every day —

A steamy, deep blues pours into the room.

Walter: That's sad too — Everything is sad.

Mama: What you been doing for these three days, son?

Walter: Mama — you don't know all the things a man what got leisure can find to do in this city . . . What's this — Friday night? Well — Wednesday I borrowed Willy Harris' car and I went for a drive . . . just me and myself and I drove and drove . . . Way out . . . way past South Chicago, and I parked the car and I sat and looked at the steel mills all day long. I just sat in the car and looked at them big black chimneys for hours. Then I drove back and I went to the Green Hat. *(Pause.)* And Thursday — Thursday I borrowed the car again and I got in it and I pointed it the other way and I drove the other way — for hours — way, way up to Wisconsin, and I looked at the farms. I just drove and looked at the farms. Then I drove back and I went to the Green Hat. *(Pause.)* And today — today I didn't get the car. Today I just walked. All over the Southside. And I looked at the Negroes and they looked at me and finally I just sat down on the curb at Thirty-ninth and South Parkway and I just sat there and watched the Negroes go by. And then I went to the Green Hat. You all sad? You all depressed? And you know where I am going right now —

Ruth goes out quietly.

Mama: Oh, Big Walter, is this the harvest of our days?

Walter: You know what I like about the Green Hat? I like this little cat they got there who blows a sax . . . He blows. He talks to me. He ain't but 'bout five feet tall and he's got a conked head and his eyes is always closed and he's all music —

Mama (rising and getting some papers out of her handbag): Walter —

Walter: And there's this other guy who plays the piano . . . and they got a sound. I mean they can work on some music . . . They got the best little combo in the world in the Green Hat . . . You can just sit there and drink and listen to them three men play and you realize that don't nothing matter worth a damn, but just being there —

Mama: I've helped do it to you, haven't I, son? Walter I been wrong.

Walter: Naw — you ain't never been wrong about nothing, Mama.

Mama: Listen to me, now. I say I been wrong, son. That I been doing to you what the rest of the world been doing to you. *(She turns off the radio.)* Walter — *(She stops and he looks up slowly at her and she meets his eyes pleadingly.)* What you ain't never understood is that I ain't got nothing, don't own nothing, ain't never really wanted nothing that wasn't for you. There ain't nothing as precious to me . . . There ain't nothing worth holding on to, money, dreams, nothing else — if it means — if it means it's going to destroy my boy. *(She takes an envelope out of her handbag and puts it in front of him and he watches her without speaking or moving.)* I paid the man thirty-five hundred dollars down on the house. That leaves sixty-five hundred dollars. Monday morning I want you to take this money and take three thousand dollars and put it in a savings account for Beneatha's medical schooling. The rest you put in a checking account — with your name on it. And from now on any penny that come out of it or that go in it is for you to look after. For you to decide. *(She drops her hands a little helplessly.)* It ain't much, but it's all I got in the world and I'm putting it in your hands. I'm telling you to be the head of this family from now on like you supposed to be.

Walter (stares at the money): You trust me like that, Mama?

Mama: I ain't never stop trusting you. Like I ain't never stop loving you.

She goes out, and Walter sits looking at the money on the table. Finally, in a decisive gesture, he gets up, and, in mingled joy and desperation, picks up the money. At the same moment, Travis enters for bed.

Travis: What's the matter, Daddy? You drunk?

Walter (sweetly, more sweetly than we have ever known him): No, Daddy ain't drunk. Daddy ain't going to never be drunk again . . .

Travis: Well, good night, Daddy.

The father has come from behind the couch and leans over, embracing his son.

Walter: Son, I feel like talking to you tonight.

Travis: About what?

Walter: Oh, about a lot of things. About you and what kind of man you going to be when you grow up . . . Son — son, what do you want to be when you grow up?

Travis: A bus driver.

Walter (laughing a little): A what? Man, that ain't nothing to want to be!

Travis: Why not?

Walter: 'Cause, man — it ain't big enough — you know what I mean.

Travis: I don't know then. I can't make up my mind. Sometimes Mama asks me that too. And sometimes when I tell her I just want to be like you — she says she don't want me to be like that and sometimes she says she does. . . .

Walter (gathering him up in his arms): You know what, Travis? In seven years you going to be seventeen years old. And things is going to be very different with us in seven years, Travis. . . . One day when you are seventeen I'll come home — home from my office downtown somewhere —

Travis: You don't work in no office, Daddy.

Walter: No — but after tonight. After what your daddy gonna do tonight, there's going to be offices — a whole lot of offices. . . .

Travis: What you gonna do tonight, Daddy?

Walter: You wouldn't understand yet, son, but your daddy's gonna make a transaction . . . a business transaction that's going to change our lives. . . . That's how come one day when you 'bout seventeen years old I'll come home and I'll be pretty tired, you know what I mean, after a day of conferences and secretaries getting things wrong the way they do . . . 'cause an executive's life is hell, man — *(The more he talks the farther away he gets.)* And I'll pull the car up on the driveway . . . just a plain black Chrysler, I think, with white walls — no — black tires. More elegant. Rich people don't have to be flashy . . . though I'll have to get something a little sportier for Ruth — maybe a Cadillac convertible to do her shopping in. . . . And I'll come up the steps to the house and the gardener will be clipping away at the hedges and he'll say, "Good evening, Mr. Younger." And I'll say, "Hello, Jefferson, how are you this evening?" And I'll go inside and Ruth will come downstairs and meet me at the door and we'll kiss each other and she'll take my arm and we'll go up to your room to see you sitting on the floor with the catalogues of all the great schools in America around you. . . . All the great schools in the world! And — and I'll say, all right son — it's your seventeenth birthday, what is it you've decided? . . . Just tell me where you want to go to school and you'll *go*. Just tell me, what it is you want to be — and you'll *be* it. . . . Whatever you want to be — Yessir! *(He holds his arms open for Travis.)* You just name it, son . . . *(Travis leaps into them.)* and I hand you the world!

Walter's voice has risen in pitch and hysterical promise and on the last line he lifts Travis high.

Blackout.

SCENE III

TIME: *Saturday, moving day, one week later.*

    Before the curtain rises, Ruth's voice, a strident, dramatic church alto, cuts through the silence.

    It is, in the darkness, a triumphant surge, a penetrating statement of expectation: "Oh, Lord, I don't feel no ways tired! Children, oh, glory hallelujah!"

    As the curtain rises we see that Ruth is alone in the living room, finishing up the family's packing. It is moving day. She is nailing crates and tying cartons. Beneatha enters, carrying a guitar case, and watches her exuberant sister-in-law.

Ruth: Hey!

Beneatha (putting away the case): Hi.

Ruth (pointing at a package): Honey — look in that package there and see what I found on sale this morning at the South Center. *(Ruth gets up and moves to the package and draws out some curtains.)* Lookahere — hand-turned hems!

Beneatha: How do you know the window size out there?

Ruth (who hadn't thought of that): Oh — Well, they bound to fit something in the whole house. Anyhow, they was too good a bargain to pass up. *(Ruth slaps her head, suddenly remembering something.)* Oh, Bennie — I meant to put a special note on that carton over there. That's your mama's good china and she wants 'em to be very careful with it.

Beneatha: I'll do it.

Beneatha finds a piece of paper and starts to draw large letters on it.

Ruth: You know what I'm going to do soon as I get in that new house?

Beneatha: What?

Ruth: Honey—I'm going to run me a tub of water up to here . . . *(With her fingers practically up to her nostrils.)* And I'm going to get in it—and I am going to sit . . . and sit . . . and sit in that hot water and the first person who knocks to tell *me* to hurry up and come out—

Beneatha: Gets shot at sunrise.

Ruth (laughing happily): You said it, sister! *(Noticing how large Beneatha is absentmindedly making the note):* Honey, they ain't going to read that from no airplane.

Beneatha (laughing herself): I guess I always think things have more emphasis if they are big, somehow.

Ruth (looking up at her and smiling): You and your brother seem to have that as a philosophy of life. Lord, that man—done changed so 'round here. You know—you know what we did last night? Me and Walter Lee?

Beneatha: What?

Ruth (smiling to herself): We went to the movies. *(Looking at Beneatha to see if she understands.)* We went to the movies. You know the last time me and Walter went to the movies together?

Beneatha: No.

Ruth: Me neither. That's how long it been. *(Smiling again.)* But we went last night. The picture wasn't much good, but that didn't seem to matter. We went—and we held hands.

Beneatha: Oh, Lord!

Ruth: We held hands—and you know what?

Beneatha: What?

Ruth: When we come out of the show it was late and dark and all the stores and things was closed up . . . and it was kind of chilly and there wasn't many people on the streets . . . and we was still holding hands, me and Walter.

Beneatha: You're killing me.

Walter enters with a large package. His happiness is deep in him; he cannot keep still with his newfound exuberance. He is singing and wiggling and snapping his fingers. He puts his package in a corner and puts a phonograph record, which he has brought in with him, on the record player. As the music, soulful and sensuous, comes up he dances over to Ruth and tries to get her to dance with him. She gives in at last to his raunchiness and in a fit of giggling allows herself to be drawn into his mood. They dip and she melts into his arms in a classic, body-melting "slow drag."

Beneatha (regarding them a long time as they dance, then drawing in her breath for a deeply exaggerated comment which she does not particularly mean): Talk about— olddddddddddd-fashionedddddddd—Negroes!

Walter (stopping momentarily): What kind of Negroes?

He says this in fun. He is not angry with her today, nor with anyone. He starts to dance with his wife again.

Beneatha: Old-fashioned.

Walter (as he dances with Ruth): You know, when these *New Negroes* have their convention — *(Pointing at his sister.)* — that is going to be the chairman of the Committee on Unending Agitation. *(He goes on dancing, then stops.)* Race, race, race! . . . Girl, I do believe you are the first person in the history of the entire human race to successfully brainwash yourself. *(Beneatha breaks up and he goes on dancing. He stops again, enjoying his tease.)* Damn, even the N double A C P takes a holiday sometimes! *(Beneatha and Ruth laugh. He dances with Ruth some more and starts to laugh and stops and pantomimes someone over an operating table.)* I can just see that chick someday looking down at some poor cat on an operating table and before she starts to slice him, she says . . . *(Pulling his sleeves back maliciously.)* "By the way, what are your views on civil rights down there? . . ."

He laughs at her again and starts to dance happily. The bell sounds.

Beneatha: Sticks and stones may break my bones but . . . words will never hurt me!

Beneatha goes to the door and opens it as Walter and Ruth go on with the clowning. Beneatha is somewhat surprised to see a quiet-looking middle-aged white man in a business suit holding his hat and a briefcase in his hand and consulting a small piece of paper.

Man: Uh — how do you do, miss. I am looking for a Mrs. — *(He looks at the slip of paper.)* Mrs. Lena Younger? *(He stops short, struck dumb at the sight of the oblivious Walter and Ruth.)*

Beneatha (smoothing her hair with slight embarrassment): Oh — yes, that's my mother. Excuse me. *(She closes the door and turns to quiet the other two.)* Ruth! Brother! *(Enunciating precisely but soundlessly: "There's a white man at the door!" They stop dancing, Ruth cuts off the phonograph, Beneatha opens the door. The man casts a curious quick glance at all of them.)* Uh — come in please.

Man (coming in): Thank you.

Beneatha: My mother isn't here just now. Is it business?

Man: Yes . . . well, of a sort.

Walter (freely, the Man of the House): Have a seat. I'm Mrs. Younger's son. I look after most of her business matters.

Ruth and Beneatha exchange amused glances.

Man (regarding Walter, and sitting): Well — My name is Karl Lindner . . .

Walter (stretching out his hand): Walter Younger. This is my wife — *(Ruth nods politely.)* — and my sister.

Lindner: How do you do.

Walter (amiably, as he sits himself easily on a chair, leaning forward on his knees with interest and looking expectantly into the newcomer's face): What can we do for you, Mr. Lindner!

Lindner (some minor shuffling of the hat and briefcase on his knees): Well — I am a representative of the Clybourne Park Improvement Association —

Walter (pointing): Why don't you sit your things on the floor?

Lindner: Oh — yes. Thank you. *(He slides the briefcase and hat under the chair.)* And as I was saying — I am from the Clybourne Park Improvement Association and we have had it brought to our attention at the last meeting that

you people — or at least your mother — has bought a piece of residential
property at — *(He digs for the slip of paper again.)* — four o six Clybourne
Street . . .

Walter: That's right. Care for something to drink? Ruth, get Mr. Lindner a beer.

Lindner (upset for some reason): Oh — no, really. I mean thank you very much,
but no thank you.

Ruth (innocently): Some coffee?

Lindner: Thank you, nothing at all.

Beneatha is watching the man carefully.

Lindner: Well, I don't know how much you folks know about our organization. *(He is a gentle man; thoughtful and somewhat labored in his manner.)* It is
one of these community organizations set up to look after — oh, you
know, things like block upkeep and special projects and we also have what
we call our New Neighbors Orientation Committee . . .

Beneatha (drily): Yes — and what do they do?

Lindner (turning a little to her and then returning the main force to Walter): Well — it's
what you might call a sort of welcoming committee, I guess. I mean they,
we — I'm the chairman of the committee — go around and see the new
people who move into the neighborhood and sort of give them the low-
down on the way we do things out in Clybourne Park.

Beneatha (with appreciation of the two meanings, which escape Ruth and Walter): Un-
huh.

Lindner: And we also have the category of what the association calls — *(He
looks elsewhere.)* — uh — special community problems . . .

Beneatha: Yes — and what are some of those?

Walter: Girl, let the man talk.

Lindner (with understated relief): Thank you. I would sort of like to explain this
thing in my own way. I mean I want to explain to you in a certain way.

Walter: Go ahead.

Lindner: Yes. Well. I'm going to try to get right to the point. I'm sure we'll all
appreciate that in the long run.

Beneatha: Yes.

Walter: Be still now!

Lindner: Well —

Ruth (still innocently): Would you like another chair — you don't look comfortable.

Lindner (more frustrated than annoyed): No, thank you very much. Please.
Well — to get right to the point, I — *(A great breath, and he is off at last.)* I am
sure you people must be aware of some of the incidents which have happened in various parts of the city when colored people have moved into
certain areas — *(Beneatha exhales heavily and starts tossing a piece of fruit up and
down in the air.)* Well — because we have what I think is going to be a unique
type of organization in American community life — not only do we deplore that kind of thing — but we are trying to do something about it. *(Beneatha stops tossing and turns with a new and quizzical interest to the man.)* We
feel — *(gaining confidence in his mission because of the interest in the faces of the
people he is talking to.)* — we feel that most of the trouble in this world, when
you come right down to it — *(He hits his knee for emphasis.)* — most of the
trouble exists because people just don't sit down and talk to each other.

Ruth (nodding as she might in church, pleased with the remark): You can say that again, mister.

Lindner (more encouraged by such affirmation): That we don't try hard enough in this world to understand the other fellow's problem. The other guy's point of view.

Ruth: Now that's right.

Beneatha and Walter merely watch and listen with genuine interest.

Lindner: Yes — that's the way we feel out in Clybourne Park. And that's why I was elected to come here this afternoon and talk to you people. Friendly like, you know, the way people should talk to each other and see if we couldn't find some way to work this thing out. As I say, the whole business is a matter of *caring* about the other fellow. Anybody can see that you are a nice family of folks, hard working and honest I'm sure. *(Beneatha frowns slightly, quizzically, her head tilted regarding him.)* Today everybody knows what it means to be on the outside of *something.* And of course, there is always somebody who is out to take advantage of people who don't always understand.

Walter: What do you mean?

Lindner: Well — you see our community is made up of people who've worked hard as the dickens for years to build up that little community. They're not rich and fancy people; just hard-working, honest people who don't really have much but those little homes and a dream of the kind of community they want to raise their children in. Now, I don't say we are perfect and there is a lot wrong in some of the things they want. But you've got to admit that a man, right or wrong, has the right to want to have the neighborhood he lives in a certain kind of way. And at the moment the overwhelming majority of our people out there feel that people get along better, take more of a common interest in the life of the community, when they share a common background. I want you to believe me when I tell you that race prejudice simply doesn't enter into it. It is a matter of the people of Clybourne Park believing, rightly or wrongly, as I say, that for the happiness of all concerned that our Negro families are happier when they live in their *own* communities.

Beneatha (with a grand and bitter gesture): This, friends, is the Welcoming Committee!

Walter (dumfounded, looking at Lindner): Is this what you came marching all the way over here to tell us?

Lindner: Well, now we've been having a fine conversation. I hope you'll hear me all the way through.

Walter (tightly): Go ahead, man.

Lindner: You see — in the face of all the things I have said, we are prepared to make your family a very generous offer . . .

Beneatha: Thirty pieces and not a coin less!

Walter: Yeah?

Lindner (putting on his glasses drawing a form out of the briefcase): Our association is prepared, through the collective effort of our people, to buy the house from you at a financial gain to your family.

Ruth: Lord have mercy, ain't this the living gall!

Walter: All right, you through?

Lindner: Well, I want to give you the exact terms of the financial arrangement—

Walter: We don't want to hear no exact terms of no arrangements. I want to know if you got any more to tell us 'bout getting together?

Lindner (taking off his glasses): Well—I don't suppose that you feel . . .

Walter: Never mind how I feel—you got any more to say 'bout how people ought to sit down and talk to each other? . . . Get out of my house, man.

He turns his back and walks to the door.

Lindner (looking around at the hostile faces and reaching and assembling his hat and briefcase): Well—I don't understand why you people are reacting this way. What do you think you are going to gain by moving into a neighborhood where you just aren't wanted and where some elements—well—people can get awful worked up when they feel that their whole way of life and everything they've ever worked for is threatened.

Walter: Get out.

Lindner (at the door, holding a small card): Well—I'm sorry it went like this.

Walter: Get out.

Lindner (almost sadly regarding Walter): You just can't force people to change their hearts, son.

He turns and puts his card on a table and exits. Walter pushes the door to with stinging hatred, and stands looking at it. Ruth just sits and Beneatha just stands. They say nothing. Mama and Travis enter.

Mama: Well—this all the packing got done since I left out of here this morning. I testify before God that my children got all the energy of the *dead!* What time the moving men due?

Beneatha: Four o'clock. You had a caller, Mama.

She is smiling, teasingly.

Mama: Sure enough—who?

Beneatha (her arms folded saucily): The Welcoming Committee.

Walter and Ruth giggle.

Mama (innocently): Who?

Beneatha: The Welcoming Committee. They said they're sure going to be glad to see you when you get there.

Walter (devilishly): Yeah, they said they can't hardly wait to see your face.

Laughter.

Mama (sensing their facetiousness): What's the matter with you all?

Walter: Ain't nothing the matter with us. We just telling you 'bout the gentleman who came to see you this afternoon. From the Clybourne Park Improvement Association.

Mama: What he want?

Ruth (in the same mood as Beneatha and Walter): To welcome you, honey.

Walter: He said they can't hardly wait. He said the one thing they don't have, that they just *dying* to have out there is a fine family of fine colored people! *(To Ruth and Beneatha.)* Ain't that right!

Ruth (mockingly): Yeah! He left his card—

Beneatha (handing card to Mama): In case.

Mama reads and throws it on the floor—understanding and looking off as she draws her chair up to the table on which she has put her plant and some sticks and some cord.

Mama: Father, give us strength. *(Knowingly—and without fun.)* Did he threaten us?

Beneatha: Oh—Mama—they don't do it like that any more. He talked Brotherhood. He said everybody ought to learn how to sit down and hate each other with good Christian fellowship.

She and Walter shake hands to ridicule the remark.

Mama (sadly): Lord, protect us . . .

Ruth: You should hear the money those folks raised to buy the house from us. All we paid and then some.

Beneatha: What they think we going to do—eat 'em?

Ruth: No, honey, marry 'em.

Mama (shaking her head): Lord, Lord, Lord . . .

Ruth: Well—that's the way the crackers crumble. *(A beat.)* Joke.

Beneatha (laughingly noticing what her mother is doing): Mama, what are you doing?

Mama: Fixing my plant so it won't get hurt none on the way . . .

Beneatha: Mama, you going to take *that* to the new house?

Mama: Un-huh—

Beneatha: That raggedy-looking old thing?

Mama (stopping and looking at her): It expresses ME!

Ruth (with delight, to Beneatha): So there, Miss Thing!

Walter comes to Mama suddenly and bends down behind her and squeezes her in his arms with all his strength. She is overwhelmed by the suddenness of it and, though delighted, her manner is like that of Ruth and Travis.

Mama: Look out now, boy! You make me mess up my thing here!

Walter (his face lit, he slips down on his knees beside her, his arms still about her): Mama . . . you know what it means to climb up in the chariot?

Mama (gruffly, very happy): Get on away from me now . . .

Ruth (near the gift-wrapped package, trying to catch Walter's eye): Psst—

Walter: What the old song say, Mama . . .

Ruth: Walter—Now?

She is pointing at the package.

Walter (speaking the lines, sweetly, playfully, in his mother's face):
I got wings . . . you got wings . . .
All God's Children got wings . . .

Mama: Boy—get out of my face and do some work . . .

Walter:
When I get to heaven gonna put on my wings,
Gonna fly all over God's heaven . . .

Beneatha (teasingly, from across the room): Everybody talking 'bout heaven ain't going there!

Walter (to Ruth, who is carrying the box across to them): I don't know, you think we ought to give her that . . . Seems to me she ain't been very appreciative around here.

Mama (eying the box, which is obviously a gift): What is that?

Walter (taking it from Ruth and putting it on the table in front of Mama): Well — what you all think? Should we give it to her?

Ruth: Oh — she was pretty good today.

Mama: I'll good you —

She turns her eyes to the box again.

Beneatha: Open it, Mama.

She stands up, looks at it, turns and looks at all of them, and then presses her hands together and does not open the package.

Walter (sweetly): Open it, Mama. It's for you. *(Mama looks in his eyes. It is the first present in her life without its being Christmas. Slowly she opens her package and lifts out, one by one, a brand-new sparkling set of gardening tools. Walter continues, prodding.)* Ruth made up the note — read it . . .

Mama (picking up the card and adjusting her glasses): "To our own Mrs. Miniver — Love from Brother, Ruth, and Beneatha." Ain't that lovely . . .

Travis (tugging at his father's sleeve): Daddy, can I give her mine now?

Walter: All right, son. *(Travis flies to get his gift.)*

Mama: Now I don't have to use my knives and forks no more . . .

Walter: Travis didn't want to go in with the rest of us, Mama. He got his own. *(Somewhat amused.)* We don't know what it is . . .

Travis (racing back in the room with a large hatbox and putting it in front of his grandmother): Here!

Mama: Lord have mercy, baby. You done gone and bought your grandmother a hat?

Travis (very proud): Open it!

She does and lifts out an elaborate, but very elaborate, wide gardening hat, and all the adults break up at the sight of it.

Ruth: Travis, honey, what is that?

Travis (who thinks it is beautiful and appropriate): It's a gardening hat! Like the ladies always have on in the magazines when they work in their gardens.

Beneatha (giggling fiercely): Travis — we were trying to make Mama Mrs. Miniver — not Scarlett O'Hara!

Mama (indignantly): What's the matter with you all! This here is a beautiful hat! *(Absurdly.)* I always wanted me one just like it!

She pops it on her head to prove it to her grandson, and the hat is ludicrous and considerably oversized.

Ruth: Hot dog! Go, Mama!

Walter (doubled over with laughter): I'm sorry, Mama — but you look like you ready to go out and chop you some cotton sure enough!

They all laugh except Mama, out of deference to Travis's feelings.

Mama (gathering the boy up to her): Bless your heart — this is the prettiest hat I ever owned — *(Walter, Ruth, and Beneatha chime in — noisily, festively, and insincerely congratulating Travis on his gift.)* What are we all standing around here for? We ain't finished packin' yet. Bennie, you ain't packed one book.

The bell rings.

Beneatha: That couldn't be the movers . . . it's not hardly two good yet —

Beneatha goes into her room. Mama starts for door.

Walter (*turning, stiffening*): Wait — wait — I'll get it.

He stands and looks at the door.

Mama: You expecting company, son?

Walter (*just looking at the door*): Yeah — yeah . . .

Mama looks at Ruth, and they exchange innocent and unfrightened glances.

Mama (*not understanding*): Well, let them in, son.

Beneatha (*from her room*): We need some more string.

Mama: Travis — you run to the hardware and get me some string cord.

Mama goes out and Walter turns and looks at Ruth. Travis goes to a dish for money.

Ruth: Why don't you answer the door, man?

Walter (*suddenly bounding across the floor to embrace her*): 'Cause sometimes it hard to let the future begin! (*Stooping down in her face.*)

> *I got wings! You got wings!*
> *All God's children got wings!*

He crosses to the door and throws it open. Standing there is a very slight little man in a not-too-prosperous business suit and with haunted frightened eyes and a hat pulled down tightly, brim up, around his forehead. Travis passes between the men and exits. Walter leans deep in the man's face, still in his jubilance.

> *When I get to heaven gonna put on my wings,*
> *Gonna fly all over God's heaven . . .*

The little man just stares at him.

> *Heaven —*

Suddenly he stops and looks past the little man into the empty hallway.

Where's Willy, man?

Bobo: He ain't with me.

Walter (*not disturbed*): Oh — come on in. You know my wife.

Bobo (*dumbly, taking off his hat*): Yes — h'you, Miss Ruth.

Ruth (*quietly, a mood apart from her husband already, seeing Bobo*): Hello, Bobo.

Walter: You right on time today . . . Right on time. That's the way! (*He slaps Bobo on his back.*) Sit down . . . lemme hear.

Ruth stands stiffly and quietly in back of them, as though somehow she senses death, her eyes fixed on her husband.

Bobo (*his frightened eyes on the floor, his hat in his hands*): Could I please get a drink of water, before I tell you about it, Walter Lee?

Walter does not take his eyes off the man. Ruth goes blindly to the tap and gets a glass of water and brings it to Bobo.

Walter: There ain't nothing wrong, is there?

Bobo: Lemme tell you —

Walter: Man — didn't nothing go wrong?

Bobo: Lemme tell you — Walter Lee. (*Looking at Ruth and talking to her more than to Walter.*) You know how it was. I got to tell you how it was. I mean first I

got to tell you how it was all the way . . . I mean about the money I put in,
Walter Lee . . .

Walter (with taut agitation now): What about the money you put in?

Bobo: Well—it wasn't much as we told you—me and Willy—*(He stops.)* I'm
sorry, Walter. I got a bad feeling about it. I got a real bad feeling about
it . . .

Walter: Man, what you telling me about all this for? . . . Tell me what happened in Springfield . . .

Bobo: Springfield.

Ruth (like a dead woman): What was supposed to happen in Springfield?

Bobo (to her): This deal that me and Walter went into with Willy—Me and
Willy was going to go down to Springfield and spread some money 'round
so's we wouldn't have to wait so long for the liquor license . . . That's what
we were going to do. Everybody said that was the way you had to do, you
understand, Miss Ruth?

Walter: Man—what happened down there?

Bobo (a pitiful man, near tears): I'm trying to tell you, Walter.

Walter (screaming at him suddenly): THEN TELL ME, GODDAMMIT . . .
WHAT'S THE MATTER WITH YOU?

Bobo: Man . . . I didn't go to no Springfield, yesterday.

Walter (halted, life hanging in the moment): Why not?

Bobo (the long way, the hard way to tell): 'Cause I didn't have no reasons to . . .

Walter: Man, what are you talking about!

Bobo: I'm talking about the fact that when I got to the train station yesterday
morning—eight o'clock like we planned . . . Man—*Willy didn't never show
up.*

Walter: Why . . . where was he . . . where is he?

Bobo: That's what I'm trying to tell you . . . I don't know . . . I waited six
hours . . . I called his house . . . and I waited . . . six hours . . . I waited in
that train station six hours . . . *(Breaking into tears.)* That was all the extra
money I had in the world . . . *(Looking up at Walter with the tears running
down his face.)* Man, *Willy is gone.*

Walter: Gone, what you mean Willy is gone? Gone where? You mean he went
by himself. You mean he went off to Springfield by himself—to take care
of getting the license—*(Turns and looks anxiously at Ruth.)* You mean maybe
he didn't want too many people in on the business down there? *(Looks to
Ruth again, as before.)* You know Willy got his own ways. *(Looks back to Bobo.)*
Maybe you was late yesterday and he just went on down there without you.
Maybe—maybe—he's been callin' you at home tryin' to tell you what happened or something. Maybe—maybe—he just got sick. He's somewhere—
he's got to be somewhere. We just got to find him—me and you got
to find him. *(Grabs Bobo senselessly by the collar and starts to shake him.)* We
got to!

Bobo (in sudden angry, frightened agony): What's the matter with you, Walter!
When a cat take off with your money he don't leave you no road maps!

Walter (turning madly, as though he is looking for Willy in the very room): Willy! . . .
Willy . . . don't do it . . . Please don't do it . . . Man, not with that
money . . . Man, please, not with that money . . . Oh, God . . . Don't let it
be true . . . *(He is wandering around, crying out for Willy and looking for him or
perhaps for help from God.)* Man . . . I trusted you . . . Man, I put my life in

your hands . . . *(He starts to crumple down on the floor as Ruth just covers her face in horror. Mama opens the door and comes into the room, with Beneatha behind her.)* Man . . . *(He starts to pound the floor with his fists, sobbing wildly.)* THAT MONEY IS MADE OUT OF MY FATHER'S FLESH —

Bobo (standing over him helplessly): I'm sorry, Walter . . . *(only Walter's sobs reply. Bobo puts on his hat.)* I had my life staked on this deal, too . . .

He exits.

Mama (to Walter): Son — *(She goes to him, bends down to him, talks to his bent head.)* Son . . . Is it gone? Son, I gave you sixty-five hundred dollars. Is it gone? All of it? Beneatha's money too?

Walter (lifting his head slowly): Mama . . . I never . . . went to the bank at all . . .

Mama (not wanting to believe him): You mean . . . your sister's school money . . . you used that too . . . Walter? . . .

Walter: Yessss! All of it . . . It's all gone . . .

There is total silence. Ruth stands with her face covered with her hands; Beneatha leans forlornly against a wall, fingering a piece of red ribbon from the mother's gift. Mama stops and looks at her son without recognition and then, quite without thinking about it, starts to beat him senselessly in the face. Beneatha goes to them and stops it.

Beneatha: Mama!

Mama stops and looks at both of her children and rises slowly and wanders vaguely, aimlessly away from them.

Mama: I seen . . . him . . . night after night . . . come in . . . and look at that rug . . . and then look at me . . . the red showing in his eyes . . . the veins moving in his head . . . I seen him grow thin and old before he was forty . . . working and working and working like somebody's old horse . . . killing himself . . . and you — you give it all away in a day — *(She raises her arms to strike him again.)*

Beneatha: Mama —

Mama: Oh, God . . . *(She looks up to Him.)* Look down here — and show me the strength.

Beneatha: Mama —

Mama (folding over): Strength . . .

Beneatha (plaintively): Mama . . .

Mama: Strength!

Curtain.

ACT III

TIME: *An hour later.*

At curtain, there is a sullen light of gloom in the living room, gray light not unlike that which began the first scene of Act I. At left we can see Walter within his room, alone with himself. He is stretched out on the bed, his shirt out and open, his arms under his head. He does not smoke, he does not cry out, he merely lies there, looking up at the ceiling, much as if he were alone in the world.

In the living room Beneatha sits at the table, still surrounded by the now almost ominous packing crates. She sits looking off. We feel that this is a mood struck perhaps an hour before, and it lingers now, full of the empty sound of profound disappointment. We see on a line from her brother's bedroom the sameness of their attitudes. Presently the bell rings and Beneatha rises without ambition or interest in answering. It is Asagai, smiling broadly, striding into the room with energy and happy expectation and conversation.

Asagai: I came over . . . I had some free time. I thought I might help with the packing. Ah, I like the look of packing crates! A household in preparation for a journey! It depresses some people . . . but for me . . . it is another feeling. Something full of the flow of life, do you understand? Movement, progress . . . It makes me think of Africa.

Beneatha: Africa!

Asagai: What kind of a mood is this? Have I told you how deeply you move me?

Beneatha: He gave away the money, Asagai . . .

Asagai: Who gave away what money?

Beneatha: The insurance money. My brother gave it away.

Asagai: Gave it away?

Beneatha: He made an investment! With a man even Travis wouldn't have trusted with his most worn-out marbles.

Asagai: And it's gone?

Beneatha: Gone!

Asagai: I'm very sorry . . . And you, now?

Beneatha: Me? . . . Me? . . . Me, I'm nothing . . . Me. When I was very small . . . we used to take our sleds out in the wintertime and the only hills we had were the ice-covered stone steps of some houses down the street. And we used to fill them in with snow and make them smooth and slide down them all day . . . and it was very dangerous, you know . . . far too steep . . . and sure enough one day a kid named Rufus came down too fast and hit the sidewalk and we saw his face just split open right there in front of us . . . And I remember standing there looking at his bloody open face thinking that was the end of Rufus. But the ambulance came and they took him to the hospital and they fixed the broken bones and they sewed it all up . . . and the next time I saw Rufus he just had a little line down the middle of his face . . . I never got over that . . .

Asagai: What?

Beneatha: That that was what one person could do for another, fix him up— sew up the problem, make him all right again. That was the most marvelous thing in the world . . . I wanted to do that. I always thought it was the one concrete thing in the world that a human being could do. Fix up the sick, you know—and make them whole again. This was truly being God . . .

Asagai: You wanted to be God?

Beneatha: No—I wanted to cure. It used to be so important to me. I wanted to cure. It used to matter. I used to care. I mean about people and how their bodies hurt . . .

Asagai: And you've stopped caring?

Beneatha: Yes—I think so.

Asagai: Why?

Beneatha (bitterly): Because it doesn't seem deep enough, close enough to what
ails mankind! It was a child's way of seeing things — or an idealist's.

Asagai: Children see things very well sometimes — and idealists even better.

Beneatha: I know that's what you think. Because you are still where I left off.
You with all your talk and dreams about Africa! You still think you can
patch up the world. Cure the Great Sore of Colonialism — *(Loftily, mocking
it.)* with the Penicillin of Independence — !

Asagai: Yes!

Beneatha: Independence *and then what?* What about all the crooks and thieves
and just plain idiots who will come into power and steal and plunder the
same as before — only now they will be black and do it in the name of the
new Independence — WHAT ABOUT THEM?!

Asagai: That will be the problem for another time. First we must get there.

Beneatha: And where does it end?

Asagai: End? Who even spoke of an end? To life? To living?

Beneatha: An end to misery! To stupidity! Don't you see there isn't any real
progress, Asagai, there is only one large circle that we march in, around
and around, each of us with our own little picture in front of us — our
own little mirage that we think is the future.

Asagai: That is the mistake.

Beneatha: What?

Asagai: What you just said — about the circle. It isn't a circle — it is simply a
long line — as in geometry, you know, one that reaches into infinity. And
because we cannot see the end — we also cannot see how it changes. And it
is very odd but those who see the changes — who dream, who will not give
up — are called idealists . . . and those who see only the circle — we call *them*
the "realists"!

Beneatha: Asagai, while I was sleeping in that bed in there, people went out and
took the future right out of my hands! And nobody asked me, nobody
consulted me — they just went out and changed my life!

Asagai: Was it your money?

Beneatha: What?

Asagai: Was it your money he gave away?

Beneatha: It belonged to all of us.

Asagai: But did you earn it? Would you have had it at all if your father had not
died?

Beneatha: No.

Asagai: Then isn't there something wrong in a house — in a world — where all
dreams, good or bad, must depend on the death of a man? I never thought
to see *you* like this, Alaiyo. You! Your brother made a mistake and you are
grateful to him so that now you can give up the ailing human race on account of it! You talk about what good is struggle, what good is anything!
Where are we all going and why are we bothering!

Beneatha: AND YOU CANNOT ANSWER IT!

Asagai (shouting over her): I LIVE THE ANSWER! *(Pause.)* In my village at home
it is the exceptional man who can even read a newspaper . . . or who ever
sees a book at all. I will go home and much of what I will have to say will
seem strange to the people of my village. But I will teach and work and
things will happen, slowly and swiftly. At times it will seem that nothing
changes at all . . . and then again the sudden dramatic events which make

history leap into the future. And then quiet again. Retrogression even. Guns, murder, revolution. And I even will have moments when I wonder if the quiet was not better than all that death and hatred. But I will look about my village at the illiteracy and disease and ignorance and I will not wonder long. And perhaps . . . perhaps I will be a great man . . . I mean perhaps I will hold on to the substance of truth and find my way always with the right course . . . and perhaps for it I will be butchered in my bed some night by the servants of empire . . .

Beneatha: The martyr!

Asagai (he smiles): . . . or perhaps I shall live to be a very old man, respected and esteemed in my new nation . . . And perhaps I shall hold office and this is what I'm trying to tell you, Alaiyo: perhaps the things I believe now for my country will be wrong and outmoded, and I will not understand and do terrible things to have things my way or merely to keep my power. Don't you see that there will be young men and women — not British soldiers then, but my own black countrymen — to step out of the shadows some evening and slit my then useless throat? Don't you see they have always been there . . . that they always will be. And that such a thing as my own death will be an advance? They who might kill me even . . . actually replenish all that I was.

Beneatha: Oh, Asagai, I know all that.

Asagai: Good! Then stop moaning and groaning and tell me what you plan to do.

Beneatha: Do?

Asagai: I have a bit of a suggestion.

Beneatha: What?

Asagai (rather quietly for him): That when it is all over — that you come home with me —

Beneatha (staring at him and crossing away with exasperation): Oh — Asagai — at this moment you decide to be romantic!

Asagai (quickly understanding the misunderstanding): My dear, young creature of the New World — I do not mean across the city — I mean across the ocean: home — to Africa.

Beneatha (slowly understanding and turning to him with murmured amazement): To Africa?

Asagai: Yes! . . . *(smiling and lifting his arms playfully.)* Three hundred years later the African Prince rose up out of the seas and swept the maiden back across the middle passage over which her ancestors had come —

Beneatha (unable to play): To — to Nigeria?

Asagai: Nigeria. Home. *(Coming to her with genuine romantic flippancy.)* I will show you our mountains and our stars; and give you cool drinks from gourds and teach you the old songs and the ways of our people — and, in time, we will pretend that — *(Very softly.)* — you have only been away for a day. Say that you'll come — *(He swings her around and takes her full in his arms in a kiss which proceeds to passion.)*

Beneatha (pulling away suddenly): You're getting me all mixed up —

Asagai: Why?

Beneatha: Too many things — too many things have happened today. I must sit down and think. I don't know what I feel about anything right this minute.

She promptly sits down and props her chin on her fist.

Asagai (*charmed*): All right, I shall leave you. No — don't get up. (*Touching her, gently, sweetly.*) Just sit awhile and think . . . Never be afraid to sit awhile and think. (*He goes to door and looks at her.*) How often I have looked at you and said, "Ah — so this is what the New World hath finally wrought . . ."

He exits. Beneatha sits on alone. Presently Walter enters from his room and starts to rummage through things, feverishly looking for something. She looks up and turns in her seat.

Beneatha (*hissingly*): Yes — just look at what the New World hath wrought! . . . Just look! (*She gestures with bitter disgust.*) There he is! *Monsieur le petit bourgeois noir*° — himself! There he is — Symbol of a Rising Class! Entrepreneur! Titan of the system! (*Walter ignores her completely and continues frantically and destructively looking for something and hurling things to floor and tearing things out of their place in his search. Beneatha ignores the eccentricity of his actions and goes on with the monologue of insult.*) Did you dream of yachts on Lake Michigan, Brother? Did you see yourself on that Great Day sitting down at the Conference Table, surrounded by all the mighty bald-headed men in America? All halted, waiting, breathless, waiting for your pronouncements on industry? Waiting for you — Chairman of the Board! (*Walter finds what he is looking for — a small piece of white paper — and pushes it in his pocket and puts on his coat and rushes out without ever having looked at her. She shouts after him.*) I look at you and I see the final triumph of stupidity in the world!

The door slams and she returns to just sitting again. Ruth comes quickly out of Mama's room.

Ruth: Who was that?
Beneatha: Your husband.
Ruth: Where did he go?
Beneatha: Who knows — maybe he has an appointment at U.S. Steel.
Ruth (*anxiously, with frightened eyes*): You didn't say nothing bad to him, did you?
Beneatha: Bad? Say anything bad to him? No — I told him he was a sweet boy and full of dreams and everything is strictly peachy keen, as the ofay kids say!

Mama enters from her bedroom. She is lost, vague, trying to catch hold, to make some sense of her former command of the world, but it still eludes her. A sense of waste overwhelms her gait; a measure of apology rides on her shoulders. She goes to her plant, which has remained on the table, looks at it, picks it up and takes it to the window sill and sits it outside, and she stands and looks at it a long moment. Then she closes the window, straightens her body with effort and turns around to her children.

Mama: Well — ain't it a mess in here, though? (*A false cheerfulness, a beginning of something.*) I guess we all better stop moping around and get some work done. All this unpacking and everything we got to do. (*Ruth raises her head slowly in response to the sense of the line; and Beneatha in similar manner turns*

Monsieur le petit bourgeois noir: Mr. Black Bourgoisie (French).

very slowly to look at her mother.) One of you all better call the moving people and tell 'em not to come.

Ruth: Tell 'em not to come?

Mama: Of course, baby. Ain't no need in 'em coming all the way here and having to go back. They charges for that too. *(She sits down, fingers to her brow, thinking.)* Lord, ever since I was a little girl, I always remembers people saying, "Lena — Lena Eggleston, you aims too high all the time. You needs to slow down and see life a little more like it is. Just slow down some." That's what they always used to say down home — "Lord, that Lena Eggleston is a high-minded thing. She'll get her due one day!"

Ruth: No, Lena . . .

Mama: Me and Big Walter just didn't never learn right.

Ruth: Lena, no! We gotta go. Bennie — tell her . . .

She rises and crosses to Beneatha with her arms outstretched. Beneatha doesn't respond.

Tell her we can still move . . . the notes ain't but a hundred and twenty-five a month. We got four grown people in this house — we can work . . .

Mama (to herself): Just aimed too high all the time —

Ruth (turning and going to Mama fast — the words pouring out with urgency and desperation): Lena — I'll work . . . I'll work twenty hours a day in all the kitchens in Chicago . . . I'll strap my baby on my back if I have to and scrub all the floors in America and wash all the sheets in America if I have to — but we got to MOVE! We got to get OUT OF HERE!!

Mama reaches out absently and pats Ruth's hand.

Mama: No — I sees things differently now. Been thinking 'bout some of the things we could do to fix this place up some. I seen a second-hand bureau over on Maxwell Street just the other day that could fit right there. *(She points to where the new furniture might go. Ruth wanders away from her.)* Would need some new handles on it and then a little varnish and it look like something brand-new. And — we can put up them new curtains in the kitchen . . . Why this place be looking fine. Cheer us all up so that we forget trouble ever come . . . *(To Ruth.)* And you could get some nice screens to put up in your room round the baby's bassinet . . . *(She looks at both of them pleadingly.)* Sometimes you just got to know when to give up some things . . . and hold on to what you got . . .

Walter enters from the outside, looking spent and leaning against the door, his coat hanging from him.

Mama: Where you been, son?

Walter (breathing hard): Made a call.

Mama: To who, son?

Walter: To The Man. *(He heads for his room.)*

Mama: What man, baby?

Walter (stops in the door): The Man, Mama. Don't you know who The Man is?

Ruth: Walter Lee?

Walter: The Man. Like the guys in the streets say — The Man. Captain Boss — Mistuh Charley . . . Old Cap'n Please Mr. Bossman . . .

Beneatha (suddenly): Lindner!

Walter: That's right! That's good. I told him to come right over.

Beneatha (fiercely, understanding): For what? What do you want to see him for!

Walter (looking at his sister): We going to do business with him.

Mama: What you talking 'bout, son?

Walter: Talking 'bout life, Mama. You all always telling me to see life like it is. Well—I laid in there on my back today . . . and I figured it out. Life just like it is. Who gets and who don't get. *(He sits down with his coat on and laughs.)* Mama, you know it's all divided up. Life is. Sure enough. Between the takers and the "tooken." *(He laughs.)* I've figured it out finally. *(He looks around at them.)* Yeah. Some of us always getting "tooken." *(He laughs.)* People like Willy Harris, they don't never get "tooken." And you know why the rest of us do? 'Cause we all mixed up. Mixed up bad. We get to looking 'round for the right and the wrong; and we worry about it and cry about it and stay up nights trying to figure out 'bout the wrong and the right of things all the time . . . And all the time, man, them takers is out there operating, just taking and taking. Willy Harris? Shoot—Willy Harris don't even count. He don't even count in the big scheme of things. But I'll say one thing for old Willy Harris . . . he's taught me something. He's taught me to keep my eye on what counts in this world. Yeah—*(Shouting out a little.)* Thanks, Willy!

Ruth: What did you call that man for, Walter Lee?

Walter: Called him to tell him to come on over to the show. Gonna put on a show for the man. Just what he wants to see. You see, Mama, the man came here today and he told us that them people out there where you want us to move—well they so upset they willing to pay us *not* to move! *(He laughs again.)* And—and oh, Mama—you would of been proud of the way me and Ruth and Bennie acted. We told him to get out . . . Lord have mercy! We told the man to get out! Oh, we was some proud folks this afternoon, yeah. *(He lights a cigarette.)* We were still full of that old-time stuff . . .

Ruth (coming toward him slowly): You talking 'bout taking them people's money to keep us from moving in that house?

Walter: I ain't just talking 'bout it, baby—I'm telling you that's what's going to happen!

Beneatha: Oh, God! Where is the bottom! Where is the real honest-to-God bottom so he can't go any farther!

Walter: See—that's the old stuff. You and that boy that was here today. You all want everybody to carry a flag and a spear and sing some marching songs, huh? You wanna spend your life looking into things and trying to find the right and the wrong part, huh? Yeah. You know what's going to happen to that boy someday—he'll find himself sitting in a dungeon, locked in forever—and the takers will have the key! Forget it, baby! There ain't no causes—there ain't nothing but taking in this world, and he who takes most is smartest—and it don't make a damn bit of difference *how*.

Mama: You making something inside me cry, son. Some awful pain inside me.

Walter: Don't cry, Mama. Understand. That white man is going to walk in that door able to write checks for more money than we ever had. It's important to him and I'm going to help him . . . I'm going to put on the show, Mama.

Mama: Son—I come from five generations of people who was slaves and sharecroppers—but ain't nobody in my family never let nobody pay 'em no money that was a way of telling us we wasn't fit to walk the earth. We ain't never been that poor. *(Raising her eyes and looking at him.)* We ain't never been that — dead inside.

Beneatha: Well — we are dead now. All the talk about dreams and sunlight that goes on in this house. It's all dead now.

Walter: What's the matter with you all! I didn't make this world! It was give to me this way! Hell, yes, I want me some yachts someday! Yes, I want to hang some real pearls 'round my wife's neck. Ain't she supposed to wear no pearls? Somebody tell me — tell me, who decides which women is suppose to wear pearls in this world. I tell you I am a *man* — and I think my wife should wear some pearls in this world!

This last line hangs a good while and Walter begins to move about the room. The word "Man" has penetrated his consciousness; he mumbles it to himself repeatedly between strange agitated pauses as he moves about.

Mama: Baby, how you going to feel on the inside?

Walter: Fine! . . . Going to feel fine . . . a man . . .

Mama: You won't have nothing left then, Walter Lee.

Walter (coming to her): I'm going to feel fine, Mama. I'm going to look that son-of-a-bitch in the eyes and say — *(He falters.)* — and say, "All right, Mr. Lindner — *(He falters even more.)* — that's *your* neighborhood out there! You got the right to keep it like you want! You got the right to have it like you want! Just write the check and — the house is yours." And — and I am going to say — *(His voice almost breaks.)* "And you — you people just put the money in my hand and you won't have to live next to this bunch of stinking niggers! . . ." *(He straightens up and moves away from his mother, walking around the room.)* And maybe — maybe I'll just get down on my black knees . . . *(He does so; Ruth and Bennie and Mama watch him in frozen horror.)* "Captain, Mistuh, Bossman — *(Groveling and grinning and wringing his hands in profoundly anguished imitation of the slow-witted movie stereotype.)* A-hee-hee-hee! Oh, yassuh boss! Yassssssuh! Great white — *(Voice breaking, he forces himself to go on.)* — Father, just gi' ussen de money, fo' God's sake, and we's — we's ain't gwine come out deh and dirty up yo' white folks neighborhood . . ." *(He breaks down completely.)* And I'll feel fine! Fine! FINE! *(He gets up and goes into the bedroom.)*

Beneatha: That is not a man. That is nothing but a toothless rat.

Mama: Yes — death done come in this here house. *(She is nodding, slowly, reflectively.)* Done come walking in my house on the lips of my children. You what supposed to be my beginning again. You — what supposed to be my harvest. *(To Beneatha.)* You — you mourning your brother?

Beneatha: He's no brother of mine.

Mama: What you say?

Beneatha: I said that that individual in that room is no brother of mine.

Mama: That's what I thought you said. You feeling like you better than he is today? *(Beneatha does not answer.)* Yes? What you tell him a minute ago? That he wasn't a man? Yes? You give him up for me? You done wrote his epitaph too — like the rest of the world? Well, who give you the privilege?

Beneatha: Be on my side for once! You saw what he just did, Mama! You saw him — down on his knees. Wasn't it you who taught me to despise any man who would do that? Do what he's going to do?

Mama: Yes — I taught you that. Me and your daddy. But I thought I taught you something else too . . . I thought I taught you to love him.

Beneatha: Love him? There is nothing left to love.

Mama: There is *always* something left to love. And if you ain't learned that, you ain't learned nothing. *(Looking at her.)* Have you cried for that boy today? I don't mean for yourself and for the family 'cause we lost the money. I mean for him: what he been through and what it done to him. Child, when do you think is the time to love somebody the most? When they done good and made things easy for everybody? Well then, you ain't through learning — because that ain't the time at all. It's when he's at his lowest and can't believe in hisself 'cause the world done whipped him so! When you starts measuring somebody, measure him right, child, measure him right. Make sure you done taken into account what hills and valleys he come through before he got to wherever he is.

Travis bursts into the room at the end of the speech, leaving the door open.

Travis: Grandmama — the moving men are downstairs! The truck just pulled up.

Mama (turning and looking at him): Are they, baby? They downstairs?

She sighs and sits. Lindner appears in the doorway. He peers in and knocks lightly, to gain attention, and comes in. All turn to look at him.

Lindner (hat and briefcase in hand): Uh — hello . . .

Ruth crosses mechanically to the bedroom door and opens it and lets it swing open freely and slowly as the lights come up on Walter within, still in his coat, sitting at the far corner of the room. He looks up and out through the room to Lindner.

Ruth: He's here.

A long minute passes and Walter slowly gets up.

Lindner (coming to the table with efficiency, putting his briefcase on the table and starting to unfold papers and unscrew fountain pens): Well, I certainly was glad to hear from you people. *(Walter has begun the trek out of the room, slowly and awkwardly, rather like a small boy, passing the back of his sleeve across his mouth from time to time.)* Life can really be so much simpler than people let it be most of the time. Well — with whom do I negotiate? You, Mrs. Younger, or your son here? *(Mama sits with her hands folded on her lap and her eyes closed as Walter advances. Travis goes closer to Lindner and looks at the papers curiously.)* Just some official papers, sonny.

Ruth: Travis, you go downstairs —

Mama (opening her eyes and looking into Walter's): No. Travis, you stay right here. And you make him understand what you doing, Walter Lee. You teach him good. Like Willy Harris taught you. You show where our five generations done come to. *(Walter looks from her to the boy, who grins at him innocently.)* Go ahead, son — *(She folds her hands and closes her eyes.)* Go ahead.

Walter (at last crosses to Lindner, who is reviewing the contract): Well, Mr. Lindner. *(Beneatha turns away.)* We called you — *(There is a profound, simple groping quality in his speech.)* — because, well, me and my family *(He looks around and shifts from one foot to the other.)* Well — we are very plain people . . .

Lindner: Yes —

Walter: I mean — I have worked as a chauffeur most of my life — and my wife here, she does domestic work in people's kitchens. So does my mother. I mean — we are plain people . . .

Lindner: Yes, Mr. Younger —

Walter (really like a small boy, looking down at his shoes and then up at the man): And — uh — well, my father, well, he was a laborer most of his life. . . .

Lindner (absolutely confused): Uh, yes — yes, I understand. *(He turns back to the contract.)*

Walter (a beat; staring at him): And my father — *(With sudden intensity.)* My father almost *beat a man to death* once because this man called him a bad name or something, you know what I mean?

Lindner (looking up, frozen): No, no, I'm afraid I don't —

Walter (a beat. The tension hangs; then Walter steps back from it): Yeah. Well — what I mean is that we come from people who had a lot of *pride.* I mean — we are very proud people. And that's my sister over there and she's going to be a doctor — and we are very proud —

Lindner: Well — I am sure that is very nice, but —

Walter: What I am telling you is that we called you over here to tell you that we are very proud and that this — *(Signaling to Travis.)* Travis, come here. *(Travis crosses and Walter draws him before him facing the man.)* This is my son, and he makes the sixth generation our family in this country. And we have all thought about your offer —

Lindner: Well, good . . . good —

Walter: And we have decided to move into our house because my father — my father — he earned it for us brick by brick. *(Mama has her eyes closed and is rocking back and forth as though she were in church, with her head nodding the Amen yes.)* We don't want to make no trouble for nobody or fight no causes, and we will try to be good neighbors. And that's *all* we got to say about that. *(He looks the man absolutely in the eyes.)* We don't want your money. *(He turns and walks away.)*

Lindner (looking around at all of them): I take it then — that you have decided to occupy . . .

Beneatha: That's what the man said.

Lindner (to Mama in her reverie): Then I would like to appeal to you, Mrs. Younger. You are older and wiser and understand things better I am sure . . .

Mama: I am afraid you don't understand. My son said we was going to move and there ain't nothing left for me to say. *(Briskly.)* You know how these young folks is nowadays, mister. Can't do a thing with 'em! *(As he opens his mouth, she rises.)* Good-bye.

Lindner (folding up his materials): Well — if you are that final about it . . . there is nothing left for me to say. *(He finishes, almost ignored by the family, who are concentrating on Walter Lee. At the door Lindner halts and looks around.)* I sure hope you people know what you're getting into.

He shakes his head and exits.

Ruth (looking around and coming to life): Well, for God's sake — if the moving men are here — LET'S GET THE HELL OUT OF HERE!

Mama (into action): Ain't it the truth! Look at all this here mess. Ruth, put Travis' good jacket on him . . . Walter Lee, fix your tie and tuck your shirt in, you look like somebody's hoodlum! Lord have mercy, where is my plant? *(She flies to get it amid the general bustling of the family, who are deliberately trying to ignore the nobility of the past moment.)* You all start on down . . . Travis child, don't go empty-handed . . . Ruth, where did I put that box with my skillets in it? I want to be in charge of it myself . . . I'm going to make us the biggest dinner we ever ate tonight . . . Beneatha, what's the matter with them stockings? Pull them things up, girl . . .

The family starts to file out as two moving men appear and begin to carry out the heavier pieces of furniture, bumping into the family as they move about.

Beneatha: Mama, Asagai asked me to marry him today and go to Africa—

Mama (*in the middle of her getting-ready activity*): He did? You ain't old enough to marry nobody—(*Seeing the moving men lifting one of her chairs precariously.*) Darling, that ain't no bale of cotton, please handle it so we can sit in it again! I had that chair twenty-five years . . .

The movers sigh with exasperation and go on with their work.

Beneatha (*girlishly and unreasonably trying to pursue the conversation*): To go to Africa, Mama—be a doctor in Africa . . .

Mama (*distracted*): Yes, baby—

Walter: Africa! What he want you to go to Africa for?

Beneatha: To practice there . . .

Walter: Girl, if you don't get all them silly ideas out your head! You better marry yourself a man with some loot . . .

Beneatha (*angrily, precisely as in the first scene of the play*): What have you got to do with who I marry!

Walter: Plenty. Now I think George Murchison—

Beneatha: George Murchison! I wouldn't marry him if he was Adam and I was Eve!

Walter and Beneatha go out yelling at each other vigorously and the anger is loud and real till their voices diminish. Ruth stands at the door and turns to Mama and smiles knowingly.

Mama (*fixing her hat at last*): Yeah—they something all right, my children . . .

Ruth: Yeah—they're something. Let's go, Lena.

Mama (*stalling, starting to look around at the house*): Yes—I'm coming. Ruth—

Ruth: Yes?

Mama (*quietly, woman to woman*): He finally come into his manhood today, didn't he? Kind of like a rainbow after the rain . . .

Ruth (*biting her lip lest her own pride explode in front of Mama*): Yes, Lena.

Walter's voice calls for them raucously.

Walter (*off stage*): Y'all come on! These people charges by the hour, you know!

Mama (*waving Ruth out vaguely*): All right, honey—go on down. I be down directly.

Ruth hesitates, then exits. Mama stands, at last alone in the living room, her plant on the table before her as the lights start to come down. She looks around at all the walls and ceilings and suddenly, despite herself, while the children call below, a great heaving thing rises in her and she puts her fist to her mouth to stifle it, takes a final desperate look, pulls her coat about her, pats her hat, and goes out. The lights dim down. The door opens and she comes back in, grabs her plant, and goes out for the last time.

Curtain.

CONNECTIONS TO OTHER SELECTIONS

1. The play's title is a line from the Langston Hughes poem that introduces the play (p. 1730). Explain how the context of the entire poem helps to explain the play's title and its major concerns.

2. Consider Lena Younger's role as a mother in *A Raisin in the Sun*. Explain why you think she is nurturing or overbearing. Compare her character with Amanda Wingfield's in Tennessee Williams's *The Glass Menagerie* (p. 1864).

3. Write an essay that compares the dreams the Youngers struggle to realize with those of the Lomans in Arthur Miller's *Death of a Salesman* (p. 1795). What similarities and differences about the nature of each family's dreams do you find in the plays?

4. In an essay compare the economic, social, and moral pressures on the families in *A Raisin in the Sun* and August Wilson's *The Piano Lesson* (p. 1962). How does each family cope with these pressures? Discuss which family you think is more successful in confronting them.

PERSPECTIVE

THOMAS P. ADLER (B. 1943)

The Political Basis of Lorraine Hansberry's Art   1994

During Lorraine's high school years, the Hansberry home welcomed such luminaries in the black movement as W. E. B. Du Bois, the sociologist and author of the classic *Souls of Black Folk* (1903), under whom Lorraine would study African history; Paul Robeson, the prominent Shakespearean actor and activist with whom she would work on the journal *Freedom* in the early 1950s; Langston Hughes, the leading poet and playwright of the Harlem Renaissance and author of the poem, "A Dream Deferred," a line from which would provide the title for *A Raisin in the Sun;* and her uncle, William Leon Hansberry, an early professor of African studies who became Lorraine's mentor after her father's death. She always subscribed to the Pan-Africanist notion that the destinies of the African and African-American peoples are intertwined. Throughout her brief life she affirmed the responsibility of the writer to speak for those without public voice who share in one or another aspect of her "otherness" — biological, racial, sociocultural — and face oppression because of it.

"The Negro Writer and His Roots: Toward a New Romanticism," written in 1959, contains Lorraine Hansberry's aesthetic credo, outlining facets of her dramatic theory and analyzing the sources of her political radicalism. For her the writer's vocation is ordinarily inseparable from a political agenda. She asserts the duty of black authors to dispel a number of myths or "illusions rampant in contemporary American culture," challenging first "the notion put forth that art is not, and *should* not and, when it is at its best, CANNOT possibly be 'social.'" Ibsen's well-made problem plays exemplify Hansberry's dictum, following Arthur Miller, "that there are *no* plays which are not social and no plays that do not have a thesis." She singles out three additional destructive illusions subverting the American mindset: that somehow people can "exist independent of the world around them"; that the homogeneity in American society allows "one huge sprawling middle class" to be regarded as universally representative of what is a pluralistic and diverse culture and world; and, finally "that there exists an inexhaustible period of time" during which this "nation may leisurely resurrect the promise of our Constitution and begin to institute the equality of man."

Hansberry professes a balanced perspective on the topic of race, rejecting destructive stereotypes on both sides. Blacks as well as whites can be slaves to "ridiculous money values," to a perverted notion of "acquisition for the sake of acquisition" that elevates materialism over the possession of self and personal freedom. Blacks as well as whites can romanticize "the black bourgeoisie" and "Negro urban life," idealizing as eccentric and attractive what is actually evil and diseased. Blacks as well as whites can be politically naive, turning over their cause to those ambitious for power. Finally, well-meaning blacks might try to deny their "slave past or . . . sharecropper and ghetto present [as] an affront to every Negro who wears a shirt and tie" rather than analyze their history of oppression as a step toward overcoming it. Hansberry's analysis reveals a society in need of radical transformation, one still deficient in guaranteeing voting rights to all its citizens, one without equal job opportunities, one where lynchings still occur (she mentions Emmett Till, kidnapped and murdered in 1955), and one committed to racial genocide, since "the social and economic havoc wreaked on the American Negro takes some ten to fifteen years off the life-expectancy of our people." For these reasons, "the Negro writer has a role to play in shaming, if you will, the conscience of the people and the present national government."

From American Drama, 1940–1960: A Critical History

CONSIDERATIONS FOR CRITICAL THINKING AND WRITING

1. To what extent does *A Raisin in the Sun* reveal Hansberry's concern about the three "destructive illusions" that Adler quotes in the second paragraph?

2. How does *A Raisin in the Sun* reflect Hansberry's belief that "the Negro writer has a role to play in shaming . . . the conscience of the people and the present national government" (para. 3)?

3. In an essay discuss whether you agree or disagree that Ibsen's *A Doll House* (p. 1564) and Miller's *Death of a Salesman* (p. 1795) "exemplify" Hansberry's assertion that "there are *no* plays which are not social and no plays that do not have a thesis" (para. 2).

Death of a Salesman

Arthur Miller was born in New York City to middle-class Jewish parents. His mother was a teacher and his father a clothing manufacturer. In 1938 he graduated from the University of Michigan, where he had begun writing plays. Six years later his first Broadway play, *The Man Who Had All the Luck*, closed after only a few performances, but *All My Sons* (1947) earned the admiration of both critics and audiences. This drama of family life launched his career, and his next play was even more successful. *Death of a Salesman* (1949) won a Pulitzer Prize and established his international reputation so that Miller, along with Tennessee Williams, became one of the most successful American playwrights of the 1940s and 1950s. During this period, his plays included an adaptation of Henrik Ibsen's *Enemy of the People* (1951), *The Crucible* (1953), and *A View from the Bridge* (1955). Among his later works are *The Misfits* (1961, a screenplay), *After the Fall* (1964), *Incident at Vichy* (1964), *The Price* (1968), *The Creation of the World and Other Business* (1972), *The Archbishop's Ceiling* (1976), *The American Clock* (1980), *Time Bends* (1987, essays), *The Ride Down Mt. Morgan* (1991), and *Broken Glass* (1994).

In *Death of a Salesman* Miller's concerns and techniques are similar to those of social realism. His characters' dialogue sounds much like ordinary speech and deals with recognizable family problems ranging from feelings about one another to personal aspirations. Like Ibsen and Chekhov, Miller places his characters in a social context so that their behavior within the family suggests larger implications: the death of this salesman raises issues concerning the significance and value of the American dream of success.

Although such qualities resemble some of the techniques and concerns of realistic drama, Miller also uses other techniques to express Willy Loman's thoughts. In a sense, the play allows the audience to observe what goes on inside the protagonist's head. (At one point Miller was going to title the play *The Inside of His Head.*) When Willy thinks of the past, we see those events reenacted on stage in the midst of present events. This reenactment is achieved through the use of symbolic nonrealistic sets that appear or disappear as the stage lighting changes to reveal Willy's state of mind.

Willy Loman is in many ways an ordinary human being — indeed, painfully so. He is neither brilliant nor heroic, and his life is made up of unfulfilled dreams and self-deceptions. Yet Miller conceived of him as a tragic figure because, as he wrote in "Tragedy and the Common Man" (see p. 1860), "the common man is as apt a subject for tragedy . . . as kings." Willy's circumstances are radically different from those of Oedipus or Hamlet, but Miller manages to create a character whose human dignity evokes tragic feelings for many readers and viewers.

ARTHUR MILLER (B. 1915)

Death of a Salesman   1949
Certain private conversations in two acts and a requiem

CAST

Willy Loman	Uncle Ben
Linda	Howard Wagner
Biff	Jenny
Happy	Stanley
Bernard	Miss Forsythe
The Woman	Letta
Charley	

SCENE: *The action takes place in Willy Loman's house and yard and in various places he visits in the New York and Boston of today.*

Throughout the play, in the stage directions, left and right mean stage left and stage right.

ACT I

A melody is heard, played upon a flute. It is small and fine, telling of grass and trees and the horizon. The curtain rises.

Before us is the Salesman's house. We are aware of towering, angular shapes behind it, surrounding it on all sides. Only the blue light of the sky falls upon the house and forestage; the surrounding area shows an angry glow of orange. As more light appears, we see a solid vault of apartment houses around the small, fragile-seeming home. An air of the dream clings to the place, a dream rising out of reality. The kitchen at center seems actual enough, for there is a kitchen table with three chairs, and a refrigerator. But no other fixtures are seen. At the back of the kitchen there is a draped entrance, which leads to the living-room. To the right of the kitchen, on a level raised two feet, is a bedroom furnished only with a brass bedstead and a straight chair. On a shelf over the bed a silver athletic trophy stands. A window opens onto the apartment house at the side.

Behind the kitchen, on a level raised six and a half feet, is the boys' bedroom, at present barely visible. Two beds are dimly seen, and at the back of the room a dormer window. (This bedroom is above the unseen living-room.) At the left a stairway curves up to it from the kitchen.

The entire setting is wholly or, in some places, partially transparent. The roof-line of the house is one-dimensional; under and over it we see the apartment buildings. Before the house lies an apron, curving beyond the forestage into the orchestra. This forward area serves as the back yard as well as the locale of all Willy's imaginings and of his city scenes. Whenever the action is in the present the actors observe the imaginary wall-lines, entering the house only through its door at the left. But in the scenes of the past these boundaries are broken, and characters enter or leave a room by stepping "through" a wall onto the forestage.

From the right, Willy Loman, the Salesman, enters, carrying two large sample cases. The flute plays on. He hears but is not aware of it. He is past sixty years of age, dressed quietly. Even as he crosses the stage to the doorway of the house, his exhaustion is apparent. He unlocks the door, comes into the kitchen, and thankfully lets his burden down, feeling the soreness of his palms. A word-sigh escapes his lips— it might be "Oh, boy, oh, boy." He closes the door, then carries his cases out into the living-room, through the draped kitchen doorway.

Linda, his wife, has stirred in her bed at the right. She gets out and puts on a robe, listening. Most often jovial, she has developed an iron repression of her exceptions to Willy's behavior—she more than loves him, she admires him, as though his mercurial nature, his temper, his massive dreams and little cruelties, served her only as sharp reminders of the turbulent longings within him, longings which she shares but lacks the temperament to utter and follow to their end.

Linda (*hearing Willy outside the bedroom, calls with some trepidation*): Willy!
Willy: It's all right. I came back.
Linda: Why? What happened? (*Slight pause.*) Did something happen, Willy?

Willy: No, nothing happened.

Linda: You didn't smash the car, did you?

Willy (with casual irritation): I said nothing happened. Didn't you hear me?

Linda: Don't you feel well?

Willy: I'm tired to the death. *(The flute has faded away. He sits on the bed beside her, a little numb.)* I couldn't make it. I just couldn't make it, Linda.

Linda (very carefully, delicately): Where were you all day? You look terrible.

Willy: I got as far as a little above Yonkers. I stopped for a cup of coffee. Maybe it was the coffee.

Linda: What?

Willy (after a pause): I suddenly couldn't drive any more. The car kept going off onto the shoulder, y'know?

Linda (helpfully): Oh. Maybe it was the steering again. I don't think Angelo knows the Studebaker.

Willy: No, it's me, it's me. Suddenly I realize I'm goin' sixty miles an hour and I don't remember the last five minutes. I'm—I can't seem to—keep my mind to it.

Linda: Maybe it's your glasses. You never went for your new glasses.

Willy: No, I see everything. I came back ten miles an hour. It took me nearly four hours from Yonkers.

Linda (resigned): Well, you'll just have to take a rest, Willy, you can't continue this way.

Willy: I just got back from Florida.

Linda: But you didn't rest your mind. Your mind is overactive, and the mind is what counts, dear.

Willy: I'll start out in the morning. Maybe I'll feel better in the morning. *(She is taking off his shoes.)* These goddam arch supports are killing me.

Linda: Take an aspirin. Should I get you an aspirin? It'll soothe you.

Willy (with wonder): I was driving along, you understand? And I was fine. I was even observing the scenery. You can imagine, me looking at scenery, on the road every week of my life. But it's so beautiful up there, Linda, the trees are so thick, and the sun is warm. I opened the windshield and just let the warm air bathe over me. And then all of a sudden I'm goin' off the road! I'm tellin' ya, I absolutely forgot I was driving. If I'd've gone the other way over the white line I might've killed somebody. So I went on again—and five minutes later I'm dreamin' again, and I nearly—*(He presses two fingers against his eyes.)* I have such thoughts, I have such strange thoughts.

Linda: Willy, dear. Talk to them again. There's no reason why you can't work in New York.

Willy: They don't need me in New York. I'm the New England man. I'm vital in New England.

Linda: But you're sixty years old. They can't expect you to keep traveling every week.

Willy: I'll have to send a wire to Portland. I'm supposed to see Brown and Morrison tomorrow morning at ten o'clock to show the line. Goddammit, I could sell them! *(He starts putting on his jacket.)*

Linda (taking the jacket from him): Why don't you go down to the place tomorrow and tell Howard you've simply got to work in New York? You're too accommodating, dear.

Willy: If old man Wagner was alive I'd a been in charge of New York now! That man was a prince, he was a masterful man. But that boy of his, that Howard, he don't appreciate. When I went north the first time, the Wagner Company didn't know where New England was!

Linda: Why don't you tell those things to Howard, dear?

Willy (encouraged): I will, I definitely will. Is there any cheese?

Linda: I'll make you a sandwich.

Willy: No, go to sleep. I'll take some milk. I'll be up right away. The boys in?

Linda: They're sleeping. Happy took Biff on a date tonight.

Willy (interested): That so?

Linda: It was so nice to see them shaving together, one behind the other, in the bathroom. And going out together. You notice? The whole house smells of shaving lotion.

Willy: Figure it out. Work a lifetime to pay off a house. You finally own it, and there's nobody to live in it.

Linda: Well, dear, life is a casting off. It's always that way.

Willy: No, no, some people — some people accomplish something. Did Biff say anything after I went this morning?

Linda: You shouldn't have criticized him, Willy, especially after he just got off the train. You mustn't lose your temper with him.

Willy: When the hell did I lose my temper? I simply asked him if he was making any money. Is that a criticism?

Linda: But, dear, how could he make any money?

Willy (worried and angered): There's such an undercurrent in him. He became a moody man. Did he apologize when I left this morning?

Linda: He was crestfallen, Willy. You know how he admires you. I think if he finds himself, then you'll both be happier and not fight any more.

Willy: How can he find himself on a farm? Is that a life? A farmhand? In the beginning, when he was young, I thought, well, a young man, it's good for him to tramp around, take a lot of different jobs. But it's more than ten years now and he has yet to make thirty-five dollars a week!

Linda: He's finding himself, Willy.

Willy: Not finding yourself at the age of thirty-four is a disgrace!

Linda: Shh!

Willy: The trouble is he's lazy, goddammit!

Linda: Willy, please!

Willy: Biff is a lazy bum!

Linda: They're sleeping. Get something to eat. Go on down.

Willy: Why did he come home? I would like to know what brought him home.

Linda: I don't know. I think he's still lost, Willy. I think he's very lost.

Willy: Biff Loman is lost. In the greatest country in the world a young man with such — personal attractiveness, gets lost. And such a hard worker. There's one thing about Biff — he's not lazy.

Linda: Never.

Willy (with pity and resolve): I'll see him in the morning; I'll have a nice talk with him. I'll get him a job selling. He could be big in no time. My God! Remember how they used to follow him around in high school? When he smiled at one of them their faces lit up. When he walked down the street . . . *(He loses himself in reminiscences.)*

Linda (trying to bring him out of it): Willy, dear, I got a new kind of American-type cheese today. It's whipped.

Willy: Why do you get American when I like Swiss?

Linda: I just thought you'd like a change —

Willy: I don't want a change! I want Swiss cheese. Why am I always being contradicted?

Linda (with a covering laugh): I thought it would be a surprise.

Willy: Why don't you open a window in here, for God's sake?

Linda (with infinite patience): They're all open, dear.

Willy: The way they boxed us in here. Bricks and windows, windows and bricks.

Linda: We should've bought the land next door.

Willy: The street is lined with cars. There's not a breath of fresh air in the neighborhood. The grass don't grow any more, you can't raise a carrot in the back yard. They should've had a law against apartment houses. Remember those two beautiful elm trees out there? When I and Biff hung the swing between them?

Linda: Yeah, like being a million miles from the city.

Willy: They should've arrested the builder for cutting those down. They massacred the neighborhood. *(Lost.)* More and more I think of those days, Linda. This time of year it was lilac and wisteria. And then the peonies would come out, and the daffodils. What fragrance in this room!

Linda: Well, after all, people had to move somewhere.

Willy: No, there's more people now.

Linda: I don't think there's more people. I think —

Willy: There's more people! That's what's ruining this country! Population is getting out of control. The competition is maddening! Smell the stink from that apartment house! And another one on the other side . . . How can they whip cheese?

On Willy's last line, Biff and Happy raise themselves up in their beds, listening.

Linda: Go down, try it. And be quiet.

Willy (turning to Linda, guiltily): You're not worried about me, are you, sweetheart?

Biff: What's the matter?

Happy: Listen!

Linda: You've got too much on the ball to worry about.

Willy: You're my foundation and my support, Linda.

Linda: Just try to relax, dear. You make mountains out of molehills.

Willy: I won't fight with him any more. If he wants to go back to Texas, let him go.

Linda: He'll find his way.

Willy: Sure. Certain men just don't get started till later in life. Like Thomas Edison, I think. Or B. F. Goodrich. One of them was deaf. *(He starts for the bedroom doorway.)* I'll put my money on Biff.

Linda: And Willy — if it's warm Sunday we'll drive in the country. And we'll open the windshield, and take lunch.

Willy: No, the windshields don't open on the new cars.

Linda: But you opened it today.

Willy: Me? I didn't. *(He stops.)* Now isn't that peculiar! Isn't that a remarkable — *(He breaks off in amazement and fright as the flute is heard distantly.)*

Linda: What, darling?

Willy: That is the most remarkable thing.

Linda: What, dear?

Willy: I was thinking of the Chevy. *(Slight pause.)* Nineteen twenty-eight . . .
when I had that red Chevy — *(Breaks off.)* That funny? I coulda sworn I was
driving that Chevy today.

Linda: Well, that's nothing. Something must've reminded you.

Willy: Remarkable. Ts. Remember those days? The way Biff used to simonize
that car? The dealer refused to believe there was eighty thousand miles on
it. *(He shakes his head.)* Heh! *(To Linda.)* Close your eyes, I'll be right up. *(He
walks out of the bedroom.)*

Happy (to Biff): Jesus, maybe he smashed up the car again!

Linda (calling after Willy): Be careful on the stairs, dear! The cheese is on the
middle shelf! *(She turns, goes over to the bed, takes his jacket, and goes out of the
bedroom.)*

*Light has risen on the boys' room. Unseen, Willy is heard talking to himself, "Eighty
thousand miles," and a little laugh. Biff gets out of bed, comes downstage a bit, and
stands attentively. Biff is two years older than his brother Happy, well built, but in
these days bears a worn air and seems less self-assured. He has succeeded less, and
his dreams are stronger and less acceptable than Happy's. Happy is tall, powerfully
made. Sexuality is like a visible color on him, or a scent that many women have
discovered. He, like his brother, is lost, but in a different way, for he has never allowed himself to turn his face toward defeat and is thus more confused and hard-
skinned, although seemingly more content.*

Happy (getting out of bed): He's going to get his license taken away if he keeps
that up. I'm getting nervous about him, y'know, Biff?

Biff: His eyes are going.

Happy: No, I've driven with him. He sees all right. He just doesn't keep his
mind on it. I drove into the city with him last week. He stops at a green
light and then it turns red and he goes. *(He laughs.)*

Biff: Maybe he's color-blind.

Happy: Pop? Why he's got the finest eye for color in the business. You know
that.

Biff (sitting down on his bed): I'm going to sleep.

Happy: You're not still sour on Dad, are you, Biff?

Biff: He's all right, I guess.

Willy (underneath them, in the living-room): Yes, sir, eighty thousand miles —
eighty-two thousand!

Biff: You smoking?

Happy (holding out a pack of cigarettes): Want one?

Biff (taking a cigarette): I can never sleep when I smell it.

Willy: What a simonizing job, heh!

Happy (with deep sentiment): Funny, Biff, y'know? Us sleeping in here again?
The old beds. *(He pats his bed affectionately.)* All the talk that went across
those two beds, huh? Our whole lives.

Biff: Yeah. Lotta dreams and plans.

Happy (with a deep and masculine laugh): About five hundred women would like to know what was said in this room.

They share a soft laugh.

Biff: Remember that big Betsy something — what the hell was her name — over on Bushwick Avenue?

Happy (combing his hair): With the collie dog!

Biff: That's the one. I got you in there, remember?

Happy: Yeah, that was my first time — I think. Boy, there was a pig! *(They laugh, almost crudely.)* You taught me everything I know about women. Don't forget that.

Biff: I bet you forgot how bashful you used to be. Especially with girls.

Happy: Oh, I still am, Biff.

Biff: Oh, go on.

Happy: I just control it, that's all. I think I got less bashful and you got more so. What happened, Biff? Where's the old humor, the old confidence? *(He shakes Biff's knee. Biff gets up and moves restlessly about the room.)* What's the matter?

Biff: Why does Dad mock me all the time?

Happy: He's not mocking you, he —

Biff: Everything I say there's a twist of mockery on his face. I can't get near him.

Happy: He just wants you to make good, that's all. I wanted to talk to you about Dad for a long time, Biff. Something's — happening to him. He — talks to himself.

Biff: I noticed that this morning. But he always mumbled.

Happy: But not so noticeable. It got so embarrassing I sent him to Florida. And you know something? Most of the time he's talking to you.

Biff: What's he say about me?

Happy: I can't make it out.

Biff: What's he say about me?

Happy: I think the fact that you're not settled, that you're still kind of up in the air . . .

Biff: There's one or two other things depressing him, Happy.

Happy: What do you mean?

Biff: Never mind. Just don't lay it all to me.

Happy: But I think if you just got started — I mean — is there any future for you out there?

Biff: I tell ya, Hap, I don't know what the future is. I don't know — what I'm supposed to want.

Happy: What do you mean?

Biff: Well, I spent six or seven years after high school trying to work myself up. Shipping clerk, salesman, business of one kind or another. And it's a measly manner of existence. To get on that subway on the hot mornings in summer. To devote your whole life to keeping stock, or making phone calls, or selling or buying. To suffer fifty weeks of the year for the sake of a two-week vacation, when all you really desire is to be outdoors, with your shirt off. And always to have to get ahead of the next fella. And still — that's how you build a future.

Happy: Well, you really enjoy it on a farm? Are you content out there?

Biff (with rising agitation): Hap, I've had twenty or thirty different kinds of jobs since I left home before the war, and it always turns out the same. I just realized it lately. In Nebraska when I herded cattle, and the Dakotas, and Arizona, and now in Texas. It's why I came home now, I guess, because I realized it. This farm I work on, it's spring there now, see? And they've got about fifteen new colts. There's nothing more inspiring or—beautiful than the sight of a mare and a new colt. And it's cool there now, see? Texas is cool now, and it's spring. And whenever spring comes to where I am, I suddenly get the feeling, my God, I'm not gettin' anywhere! What the hell am I doing, playing around with horses, twenty-eight dollars a week! I'm thirty-four years old, I oughta be makin' my future. That's when I come running home. And now, I get here, and I don't know what to do with myself. *(After a pause.)* I've always made a point of not wasting my life, and everytime I come back here I know that all I've done is to waste my life.

Happy: You're a poet, you know that, Biff? You're a—you're an idealist!

Biff: No, I'm mixed up very bad. Maybe I oughta get married. Maybe I oughta get stuck into something. Maybe that's my trouble. I'm like a boy. I'm not married. I'm not in business, I just—I'm like a boy. Are you content, Hap? You're a success, aren't you? Are you content?

Happy: Hell, no!

Biff: Why? You're making money, aren't you?

Happy (moving about with energy, expressiveness): All I can do now is wait for the merchandise manager to die. And suppose I get to be merchandise manager? He's a good friend of mine, and he just built a terrific estate on Long Island. And he lived there about two months and sold it, and now he's building another one. He can't enjoy it once it's finished. And I know that's just what I would do. I don't know what the hell I'm workin' for. Sometimes I sit in my apartment—all alone. And I think of the rent I'm paying. And it's crazy. But then, it's what I always wanted. My own apartment, a car, and plenty of women. And still, goddammit, I'm lonely.

Biff (with enthusiasm): Listen, why don't you come out West with me?

Happy: You and I, heh?

Biff: Sure, maybe we could buy a ranch. Raise cattle, use our muscles. Men built like we are should be working out in the open.

Happy (avidly): The Loman Brothers, heh?

Biff (with vast affection): Sure, we'd be known all over the counties!

Happy (enthralled): That's what I dream about, Biff. Sometimes I want to just rip my clothes off in the middle of the store and outbox that goddam merchandise manager. I mean I can outbox, outrun, and outlift anybody in that store, and I have to take orders from those common, petty sons-of-bitches till I can't stand it any more.

Biff: I'm tellin' you, kid, if you were with me I'd be happy out there.

Happy (enthused): See, Biff, everybody around me is so false that I'm constantly lowering my ideals . . .

Biff: Baby, together we'd stand up for one another, we'd have someone to trust.

Happy: If I were around you—

Biff: Hap, the trouble is we weren't brought up to grub for money. I don't know how to do it.

Happy: Neither can I!

Biff: Then let's go!

Happy: The only thing is — what can you make out there?

Biff: But look at your friend. Builds an estate and then hasn't the peace of mind to live in it.

Happy: Yeah, but when he walks into the store the waves part in front of him. That's fifty-two thousand dollars a year coming through the revolving door, and I got more in my pinky finger than he's got in his head.

Biff: Yeah, but you just said —

Happy: I gotta show some of those pompous, self-important executives over there that Hap Loman can make the grade. I want to walk into the store the way he walks in. Then I'll go with you, Biff. We'll be together yet, I swear. But take those two we had tonight. Now weren't they gorgeous creatures?

Biff: Yeah, yeah, most gorgeous I've had in years.

Happy: I get that any time I want, Biff. Whenever I feel disgusted. The trouble is, it gets like bowling or something. I just keep knockin' them over and it doesn't mean anything. You still run around a lot?

Biff: Naa. I'd like to find a girl — steady, somebody with substance.

Happy: That's what I long for.

Biff: Go on! You'd never come home.

Happy: I would! Somebody with character, with resistance! Like Mom, y'know? You're gonna call me a bastard when I tell you this. That girl Charlotte I was with tonight is engaged to be married in five weeks. *(He tries on his new hat.)*

Biff: No kiddin'!

Happy: Sure, the guy's in line for the vice-presidency of the store. I don't know what gets into me, maybe I just have an overdeveloped sense of competition or something, but I went and ruined her, and furthermore I can't get rid of her. And he's the third executive I've done that to. Isn't that a crummy characteristic? And to top it all, I go to their weddings! *(Indignantly, but laughing.)* Like I'm not supposed to take bribes. Manufacturers offer me a hundred-dollar bill now and then to throw an order their way. You know how honest I am, but it's like this girl, see. I hate myself for it. Because I don't want the girl, and, still, I take it and — I love it!

Biff: Let's go to sleep.

Happy: I guess we didn't settle anything, heh?

Biff: I just got one idea that I think I'm going to try.

Happy: What's that?

Biff: Remember Bill Oliver?

Happy: Sure, Oliver is very big now. You want to work for him again?

Biff: No, but when I quit he said something to me. He put his arm on my shoulder, and he said, "Biff, if you ever need anything, come to me."

Happy: I remember that. That sounds good.

Biff: I think I'll go to see him. If I could get ten thousand or even seven or eight thousand dollars I could buy a beautiful ranch.

Happy: I bet he'd back you. 'Cause he thought highly of you, Biff. I mean, they all do. You're well liked, Biff. That's why I say to come back here, and we both have the apartment. And I'm tellin' you, Biff, any babe you want . . .

Biff: No, with a ranch I could do the work I like and still be something. I just wonder though. I wonder if Oliver still thinks I stole that carton of basketballs.

Happy: Oh, he probably forgot that long ago. It's almost ten years. You're too sensitive. Anyway, he didn't really fire you.

Biff: Well, I think he was going to. I think that's why I quit. I was never sure whether he knew or not. I know he thought the world of me, though. I was the only one he'd let lock up the place.

Willy (below): You gonna wash the engine, Biff?

Happy: Shh!

Biff looks at Happy, who is gazing down, listening. Willy is mumbling in the parlor.

Happy: You hear that?

They listen. Willy laughs warmly.

Biff (growing angry): Doesn't he know Mom can hear that?

Willy: Don't get your sweater dirty, Biff!

A look of pain crosses Biff's face.

Happy: Isn't that terrible? Don't leave again, will you? You'll find a job here. You gotta stick around. I don't know what to do about him, it's getting embarrassing.

Willy: What a simonizing job!

Biff: Mom's hearing that!

Willy: No kiddin', Biff, you got a date? Wonderful!

Happy: Go on to sleep. But talk to him in the morning, will you?

Biff (reluctantly getting into bed): With her in the house. Brother!

Happy (getting into bed): I wish you'd have a good talk with him.

The light on their room begins to fade.

Biff (to himself in bed): That selfish, stupid . . .

Happy: Sh . . . Sleep, Biff.

Their light is out. Well before they have finished speaking, Willy's form is dimly seen below in the darkened kitchen. He opens the refrigerator, searches in there, and takes out a bottle of milk. The apartment houses are fading out, and the entire house and surroundings become covered with leaves. Music insinuates itself as the leaves appear.

Willy: Just wanna be careful with those girls, Biff, that's all. Don't make any promises. No promises of any kind. Because a girl, y'know, they always believe what you tell 'em, and you're very young, Biff, you're too young to be talking seriously to girls.

Light rises on the kitchen. Willy, talking, shuts the refrigerator door and comes downstage to the kitchen table. He pours milk into a glass. He is totally immersed in himself, smiling faintly.

Willy: Too young entirely, Biff. You want to watch your schooling first. Then when you're all set, there'll be plenty of girls for a boy like you. (He smiles broadly at a kitchen chair.) That so? The girls pay for you? (He laughs.) Boy, you must really be makin' a hit.

Willy is gradually addressing—physically—a point offstage, speaking through the wall of the kitchen, and his voice has been rising in volume to that of a normal conversation.

Willy: I been wondering why you polish the car so careful. Ha! Don't leave the hubcaps, boys. Get the chamois to the hubcaps. Happy, use newspaper on the windows, it's the easiest thing. Show him how to do it, Biff! You see, Happy? Pad it up, use it like a pad. That's it, that's it, good work. You're doin' all right, Hap. *(He pauses, then nods in approbation for a few seconds, then looks upward.)* Biff, first thing we gotta do when we get time is clip that big branch over the house. Afraid it's gonna fall in a storm and hit the roof. Tell you what. We get a rope and sling her around, and then we climb up there with a couple of saws and take her down. Soon as you finish the car, boys, I wanna see ya. I got a surprise for you, boys.

Biff *(offstage)*: Whatta ya got, Dad?

Willy: No, you finish first. Never leave a job till you're finished—remember that. *(Looking toward the "big trees.")* Biff, up in Albany I saw a beautiful hammock. I think I'll buy it next trip, and we'll hang it right between those two elms. Wouldn't that be something? Just swingin' there under those branches. Boy, that would be . . .

Young Biff and Young Happy appear from the direction Willy was addressing. Happy carries rags and a pail of water. Biff, wearing a sweater with a block "S," carries a football.

Biff *(pointing in the direction of the car offstage)*: How's that, Pop, professional?

Willy: Terrific. Terrific job, boys. Good work, Biff.

Happy: Where's the surprise, Pop?

Willy: In the back seat of the car.

Happy: Boy! *(He runs off.)*

Biff: What is it, Dad? Tell me, what'd you buy?

Willy *(laughing, cuffs him)*: Never mind, something I want you to have.

Biff *(turns and starts off)*: What is it, Hap?

Happy *(offstage)*: It's a punching bag!

Biff: Oh, Pop!

Willy: It's got Gene Tunney's signature on it!

Happy runs onstage with a punching bag.

Biff: Gee, how'd you know we wanted a punching bag?

Willy: Well, it's the finest thing for the timing.

Happy *(lies down on his back and pedals with his feet)*: I'm losing weight, you notice, Pop?

Willy *(to Happy)*: Jumping rope is good too.

Biff: Did you see the new football I got?

Willy *(examining the ball)*: Where'd you get a new ball?

Biff: The coach told me to practice my passing.

Willy: That so? And he gave you the ball, heh?

Biff: Well, I borrowed it from the locker room. *(He laughs confidentially.)*

Willy *(laughing with him at the theft)*: I want you to return that.

Happy: I told you he wouldn't like it!

Biff *(angrily)*: Well, I'm bringing it back!

Willy *(stopping the incipient argument, to Happy)*: Sure, he's gotta practice with a regulation ball, doesn't he? *(To Biff.)* Coach'll probably congratulate you on your initiative!

Biff: Oh, he keeps congratulating my initiative all the time, Pop.

Willy: That's because he likes you. If somebody else took that ball there'd be an uproar. So what's the report, boys, what's the report?

Biff: Where'd you go this time, Dad? Gee we were lonesome for you.

Willy (pleased, puts an arm around each boy and they come down to the apron): Lonesome, heh?

Biff: Missed you every minute.

Willy: Don't say? Tell you a secret, boys. Don't breathe it to a soul. Someday I'll have my own business, and I'll never have to leave home any more.

Happy: Like Uncle Charley, heh?

Willy: Bigger than Uncle Charley! Because Charley is not — liked. He's liked, but he's not — well liked.

Biff: Where'd you go this time, Dad?

Willy: Well, I got on the road, and I went north to Providence. Met the Mayor.

Biff: The Mayor of Providence!

Willy: He was sitting in the hotel lobby.

Biff: What'd he say?

Willy: He said, "Morning!" And I said, "You got a fine city here, Mayor." And then he had coffee with me. And then I went to Waterbury. Waterbury is a fine city. Big clock city, the famous Waterbury clock. Sold a nice bill there. And then Boston — Boston is the cradle of the Revolution. A fine city. And a couple of other towns in Mass., and on to Portland and Bangor and straight home!

Biff: Gee, I'd love to go with you sometime, Dad.

Willy: Soon as summer comes.

Happy: Promise?

Willy: You and Hap and I, and I'll show you all the towns. America is full of beautiful towns and fine, upstanding people. And they know me, boys, they know me up and down New England. The finest people. And when I bring you fellas up, there'll be open sesame for all of us, 'cause one thing, boys: I have friends. I can park my car in any street in New England, and the cops protect it like their own. This summer, heh?

Biff and Happy (together): Yeah! You bet!

Willy: We'll take our bathing suits.

Happy: We'll carry your bags, Pop!

Willy: Oh, won't that be something! Me comin' into the Boston stores with you boys carryin' my bags. What a sensation!

Biff is prancing around, practicing passing the ball.

Willy: You nervous, Biff, about the game?

Biff: Not if you're gonna be there.

Willy: What do they say about you in school, now that they made you captain?

Happy: There's a crowd of girls behind him everytime the classes change.

Biff (taking Willy's hand): This Saturday, Pop, this Saturday — just for you, I'm going to break through for a touchdown.

Happy: You're supposed to pass.

Biff: I'm takin' one play for Pop. You watch me, Pop, and when I take off my helmet, that means I'm breakin' out. Then you watch me crash through that line!

Willy (kisses Biff): Oh, wait'll I tell this in Boston!

> *Bernard enters in knickers. He is younger than Biff, earnest and loyal, a worried boy.*

Bernard: Biff, where are you? You're supposed to study with me today.

Willy: Hey, looka Bernard. What're you lookin' so anemic about, Bernard?

Bernard: He's gotta study, Uncle Willy. He's got Regents next week.

Happy (tauntingly, spinning Bernard around): Let's box, Bernard!

Bernard: Biff! *(He gets away from Happy.)* Listen, Biff, I heard Mr. Birnbaum say that if you don't start studyin' math, he's gonna flunk you, and you won't graduate. I heard him!

Willy: You better study with him, Biff. Go ahead now.

Bernard: I heard him!

Biff: Oh, Pop, you didn't see my sneakers! *(He holds up a foot for Willy to look at.)*

Willy: Hey, that's a beautiful job of printing!

Bernard (wiping his glasses): Just because he printed University of Virginia on his sneakers doesn't mean they've got to graduate him, Uncle Willy!

Willy (angrily): What're you talking about? With scholarships to three universities they're gonna flunk him?

Bernard: But I heard Mr. Birnbaum say—

Willy: Don't be a pest, Bernard! *(To his boys.)* What an anemic!

Bernard: Okay, I'm waiting for you in my house, Biff.

> *Bernard goes off. The Lomans laugh.*

Willy: Bernard is not well liked, is he?

Biff: He's liked, but he's not well liked.

Happy: That's right, Pop.

Willy: That's just what I mean. Bernard can get the best marks in school, y'understand, but when he gets out in the business world, y'understand, you are going to be five times ahead of him. That's why I thank Almighty God you're both built like Adonises.° Because the man who makes an appearance in the business world, the man who creates personal interest, is the man who gets ahead. Be liked and you will never want. You take me, for instance. I never have to wait in line to see a buyer. "Willy Loman is here!" That's all they have to know, and I go right through.

Biff: Did you knock them dead, Pop?

Willy: Knocked 'em cold in Providence, slaughtered 'em in Boston.

Happy (on his back, pedaling again): I'm losing weight, you notice, Pop?

> *Linda enters, as of old, a ribbon in her hair, carrying a basket of washing.*

Linda (with youthful energy): Hello, dear!

Willy: Sweetheart!

Linda: How'd the Chevy run?

Willy: Chevrolet, Linda, is the greatest car ever built. *(To the boys.)* Since when do you let your mother carry wash up the stairs?

Biff: Grab hold there, boy!

Happy: Where to, Mom?

Linda: Hang them up on the line. And you better go down to your friends, Biff. The cellar is full of boys. They don't know what to do with themselves.

Adonis: In Greek mythology a young man known for his good looks and favored by Aphrodite, goddess of love and beauty.

Biff: Ah, when Pop comes home they can wait!

Willy (laughs appreciatively): You better go down and tell them what to do, Biff.

Biff: I think I'll have them sweep out the furnace room.

Willy: Good work, Biff.

Biff (goes through wall-line of kitchen to doorway at back and calls down): Fellas! Everybody sweep out the furnace room! I'll be right down!

Voices: All right! Okay, Biff.

Biff: George and Sam and Frank, come out back! We're hangin' up the wash! Come on, Hap, on the double! *(He and Happy carry out the basket.)*

Linda: The way they obey him!

Willy: Well, that's training, the training. I'm tellin' you, I was sellin' thousands and thousands, but I had to come home.

Linda: Oh, the whole block'll be at that game. Did you sell anything?

Willy: I did five hundred gross in Providence and seven hundred gross in Boston.

Linda: No! Wait a minute, I've got a pencil. *(She pulls pencil and paper out of her apron pocket.)* That makes your commission . . . Two hundred — my God! Two hundred and twelve dollars!

Willy: Well, I didn't figure it yet, but . . .

Linda: How much did you do?

Willy: Well, I — I did — about a hundred and eighty gross in Providence. Well, no — it came to — roughly two hundred gross on the whole trip.

Linda (without hesitation): Two hundred gross. That's . . . *(She figures.)*

Willy: The trouble was that three of the stores were half closed for inventory in Boston. Otherwise I woulda broke records.

Linda: Well, it makes seventy dollars and some pennies. That's very good.

Willy: What do we owe?

Linda: Well, on the first there's sixteen dollars on the refrigerator —

Willy: Why sixteen?

Linda: Well, the fan belt broke, so it was a dollar eighty.

Willy: But it's brand new.

Linda: Well, the man said that's the way it is. Till they work themselves in, y'know.

They move through the wall-line into the kitchen.

Willy: I hope we didn't get stuck on that machine.

Linda: They got the biggest ads of any of them!

Willy: I know, it's a fine machine. What else?

Linda: Well, there's nine-sixty for the washing machine. And for the vacuum cleaner there's three and a half due on the fifteenth. Then the roof, you got twenty-one dollars remaining.

Willy: It don't leak, does it?

Linda: No, they did a wonderful job. Then you owe Frank for the carburetor.

Willy: I'm not going to pay that man! That goddam Chevrolet, they ought to prohibit the manufacture of that car!

Linda: Well, you owe him three and a half. And odds and ends, comes to around a hundred and twenty dollars by the fifteenth.

Willy: A hundred and twenty dollars! My God, if business don't pick up I don't know what I'm gonna do!

Linda: Well, next week you'll do better.

Willy: Oh, I'll knock 'em dead next week. I'll go to Hartford. I'm very well liked in Hartford. You know, the trouble is, Linda, people don't seem to take to me.

They move onto the forestage.

Linda: Oh, don't be foolish.

Willy: I know it when I walk in. They seem to laugh at me.

Linda: Why? Why would they laugh at you? Don't talk that way, Willy.

Willy moves to the edge of the stage. Linda goes into the kitchen and starts to darn stockings.

Willy: I don't know the reason for it, but they just pass me by. I'm not noticed.

Linda: But you're doing wonderful, dear. You're making seventy to a hundred dollars a week.

Willy: But I gotta be at it ten, twelve hours a day. Other men—I don't know—they do it easier. I don't know why—I can't stop myself—I talk too much. A man oughta come in with a few words. One thing about Charley. He's a man of few words, and they respect him.

Linda: You don't talk too much, you're just lively.

Willy (smiling): Well, I figure, what the hell, life is short, a couple of jokes. *(To himself.)* I joke too much! *(The smile goes.)*

Linda: Why? You're—

Willy: I'm fat. I'm very—foolish to look at, Linda. I didn't tell you, but Christmas time I happened to be calling on F. H. Stewarts, and a salesman I know, as I was going in to see the buyer I heard him say something about—walrus. And I—I cracked him right across the face. I won't take that. I simply will not take that. But they do laugh at me. I know that.

Linda: Darling . . .

Willy: I gotta overcome it. I know I gotta overcome it. I'm not dressing to advantage, maybe.

Linda: Willy, darling, you're the handsomest man in the world—

Willy: Oh, no, Linda.

Linda: To me you are. *(Slight pause.)* The handsomest.

From the darkness is heard the laughter of a woman. Willy doesn't turn to it, but it continues through Linda's lines.

Linda: And the boys, Willy. Few men are idolized by their children the way you are.

Music is heard as behind a scrim, to the left of the house, The Woman, dimly seen, is dressing.

Willy (with great feeling): You're the best there is, Linda, you're a pal, you know that? On the road—on the road I want to grab you sometimes and just kiss the life outa you.

The laughter is loud now, and he moves into a brightening area at the left, where The Woman has come from behind the scrim and is standing, putting on her hat, looking into a "mirror" and laughing.

Willy: 'Cause I get so lonely—especially when business is bad and there's nobody to talk to. I get the feeling that I'll never sell anything again, that I won't make a living for you, or a business, a business for the boys. *(He talks*

through The Woman's subsiding laughter; The Woman primps at the "mirror.")
There's so much I want to make for —

The Woman: Me? You didn't make me, Willy. I picked you.

Willy (pleased): You picked me?

The Woman (who is quite proper-looking, Willy's age): I did. I've been sitting at that desk watching all the salesmen go by, day in, day out. But you've got such a sense of humor, and we do have such a good time together, don't we?

Willy: Sure, sure. *(He takes her in his arms.)* Why do you have to go now?

The Woman: It's two o'clock . . .

Willy: No, come on in! *(He pulls her.)*

The Woman: . . . my sisters'll be scandalized. When'll you be back?

Willy: Oh, two weeks about. Will you come up again?

The Woman: Sure thing. You do make me laugh. It's good for me. *(She squeezes his arm, kisses him.)* And I think you're a wonderful man.

Willy: You picked me, heh?

The Woman: Sure. Because you're so sweet. And such a kidder.

Willy: Well, I'll see you next time I'm in Boston.

The Woman: I'll put you right through to the buyers.

Willy (slapping her bottom): Right. Well, bottoms up!

The Woman (slaps him gently and laughs): You just kill me, Willy. *(He suddenly grabs her and kisses her roughly.)* You kill me. And thanks for the stockings. I love a lot of stockings. Well, good night.

Willy: Good night. And keep your pores open!

The Woman: Oh, Willy!

> *The Woman bursts out laughing, and Linda's laughter blends in. The Woman disappears into the dark. Now the area at the kitchen table brightens. Linda is sitting where she was at the kitchen table, but now is mending a pair of her silk stockings.*

Linda: You are, Willy. The handsomest man. You've got no reason to feel that —

Willy (coming out of The Woman's dimming area and going over to Linda): I'll make it all up to you, Linda, I'll —

Linda: There's nothing to make up, dear. You're doing fine, better than —

Willy (noticing her mending): What's that?

Linda: Just mending my stockings. They're so expensive —

Willy (angrily, taking them from her): I won't have you mending stockings in this house! Now throw them out!

> *Linda puts the stockings in her pocket.*

Bernard (entering on the run): Where is he? If he doesn't study!

Willy (moving to the forestage, with great agitation): You'll give him the answers!

Bernard: I do, but I can't on a Regents! That's a state exam! They're liable to arrest me!

Willy: Where is he? I'll whip him, I'll whip him!

Linda: And he'd better give back that football, Willy, it's not nice.

Willy: Biff! Where is he? Why is he taking everything?

Linda: He's too rough with the girls, Willy. All the mothers are afraid of him!

Willy: I'll whip him!

Bernard: He's driving the car without a license!

> *The Woman's laugh is heard.*

Willy: Shut up!

Linda: All the mothers —

Willy: Shut up!

Bernard (backing quietly away and out): Mr. Birnbaum says he's stuck up.

Willy: Get outa here!

Bernard: If he doesn't buckle down he'll flunk math! *(He goes off.)*

Linda: He's right, Willy, you've gotta —

Willy (exploding at her): There's nothing the matter with him! You want him to be a worm like Bernard? He's got spirit, personality . . .

> As he speaks, Linda, almost in tears, exits into the living-room. Willy is alone in the kitchen, wilting and staring. The leaves are gone. It is night again, and the apartment houses look down from behind.

Willy: Loaded with it. Loaded! What is he stealing? He's giving it back, isn't he? Why is he stealing? What did I tell him? I never in my life told him anything but decent things.

> Happy in pajamas has come down the stairs; Willy suddenly becomes aware of Happy's presence.

Happy: Let's go now, come on.

Willy (sitting down at the kitchen table): Huh! Why did she have to wax the floors herself? Everytime she waxes the floors she keels over. She knows that!

Happy: Shh! Take it easy. What brought you back tonight?

Willy: I got an awful scare. Nearly hit a kid in Yonkers. God! Why didn't I go to Alaska with my brother Ben that time! Ben! That man was a genius, that man was success incarnate! What a mistake! He begged me to go.

Happy: Well, there's no use in —

Willy: You guys! There was a man started with the clothes on his back and ended up with diamond mines!

Happy: Boy, someday I'd like to know how he did it.

Willy: What's the mystery? The man knew what he wanted and went out and got it! Walked into a jungle, and comes out, the age of twenty-one, and he's rich! The world is an oyster, but you don't crack it open on a mattress!

Happy: Pop, I told you I'm gonna retire you for life.

Willy: You'll retire me for life on seventy goddam dollars a week? And your women and your car and your apartment, and you'll retire me for life! Christ's sake, I couldn't get past Yonkers today! Where are you guys, where are you? The woods are burning! I can't drive a car!

> Charley has appeared in the doorway. He is a large man, slow of speech, laconic, immovable. In all he says, despite what he says, there is pity, and, now, trepidation. He has a robe over pajamas, slippers on his feet. He enters the kitchen.

Charley: Everything all right?

Happy: Yeah, Charley, everything's . . .

Willy: What's the matter?

Charley: I heard some noise. I thought something happened. Can't we do something about the walls? You sneeze in here, and in my house hats blow off.

Happy: Let's go to bed, Dad. Come on.

> Charley signals to Happy to go.

Willy: You go ahead, I'm not tired at the moment.

Happy (to Willy): Take it easy, huh? *(He exits.)*

Willy: What're you doin' up?

Charley (sitting down at the kitchen table opposite Willy): Couldn't sleep good. I had a heartburn.

Willy: Well, you don't know how to eat.

Charley: I eat with my mouth.

Willy: No, you're ignorant. You gotta know about vitamins and things like that.

Charley: Come on, let's shoot. Tire you out a little.

Willy (hesitantly): All right. You got cards?

Charley (taking a deck from his pocket): Yeah, I got them. Someplace. What is it with those vitamins?

Willy (dealing): They build up your bones. Chemistry.

Charley: Yeah, but there's no bones in a heartburn.

Willy: What are you talkin' about? Do you know the first thing about it?

Charley: Don't get insulted.

Willy: Don't talk about something you don't know anything about.

They are playing. Pause.

Charley: What're you doin' home?

Willy: A little trouble with the car.

Charley: Oh. *(Pause.)* I'd like to take a trip to California.

Willy: Don't say.

Charley: You want a job?

Willy: I got a job, I told you that. *(After a slight pause.)* What the hell are you offering me a job for?

Charley: Don't get insulted.

Willy: Don't insult me.

Charley: I don't see no sense in it. You don't have to go on this way.

Willy: I got a good job. *(Slight pause.)* What do you keep comin' in here for?

Charley: You want me to go?

Willy (after a pause, withering): I can't understand it. He's going back to Texas again. What the hell is that?

Charley: Let him go.

Willy: I got nothin' to give him, Charley, I'm clean, I'm clean.

Charley: He won't starve. None a them starve. Forget about him.

Willy: Then what have I got to remember?

Charley: You take it too hard. To hell with it. When a deposit bottle is broken you don't get your nickel back.

Willy: That's easy enough for you to say.

Charley: That ain't easy for me to say.

Willy: Did you see the ceiling I put up in the living-room?

Charley: Yeah, that's a piece of work. To put up a ceiling is a mystery to me. How do you do it?

Willy: What's the difference?

Charley: Well, talk about it.

Willy: You gonna put up a ceiling?

Charley: How could I put up a ceiling?

Willy: Then what the hell are you bothering me for?

Charley: You're insulted again.

Willy: A man who can't handle tools is not a man. You're disgusting.

Charley: Don't call me disgusting, Willy.

    Uncle Ben, carrying a valise and an umbrella, enters the forestage from around the right corner of the house. He is a stolid man, in his sixties, with a mustache and an authoritative air. He is utterly certain of his destiny, and there is an aura of far places about him. He enters exactly as Willy speaks.

Willy: I'm getting awfully tired, Ben.

    Ben's music is heard. Ben looks around at everything.

Charley: Good, keep playing; you'll sleep better. Did you call me Ben?

    Ben looks at his watch.

Willy: That's funny. For a second there you reminded me of my brother Ben.

Ben: I only have a few minutes. *(He strolls, inspecting the place. Willy and Charley continue playing.)*

Charley: You never heard from him again, heh? Since that time?

Willy: Didn't Linda tell you? Couple of weeks ago we got a letter from his wife in Africa. He died.

Charley: That so.

Ben (chuckling): So this is Brooklyn, eh?

Charley: Maybe you're in for some of his money.

Willy: Naa, he had seven sons. There's just one opportunity I had with that man . . .

Ben: I must make a train, William. There are several properties I'm looking at in Alaska.

Willy: Sure, sure! If I'd gone with him to Alaska that time, everything would've been totally different.

Charley: Go on, you'd froze to death up there.

Willy: What're you talking about?

Ben: Opportunity is tremendous in Alaska, William. Surprised you're not up there.

Willy: Sure, tremendous.

Charley: Heh?

Willy: There was the only man I ever met who knew the answers.

Charley: Who?

Ben: How are you all?

Willy (taking a pot, smiling): Fine, fine.

Charley: Pretty sharp tonight.

Ben: Is mother living with you?

Willy: No, she died a long time ago.

Charley: Who?

Ben: That's too bad. Fine specimen of a lady, Mother.

Willy (to Charley): Heh?

Ben: I'd hoped to see the old girl.

Charley: Who died?

Ben: Heard anything from Father, have you?

Willy (unnerved): What do you mean, who died?

Charley (taking a pot): What're you talkin' about?

Ben (looking at his watch): William, it's half-past eight!

Willy (as though to dispel his confusion he angrily stops Charley's hand): That's my build!

Charley: I put the ace —

Willy: If you don't know how to play the game I'm not gonna throw my money away on you!

Charley (rising): It was my ace, for God's sake!

Willy: I'm through, I'm through!

Ben: When did Mother die?

Willy: Long ago. Since the beginning you never knew how to play cards.

Charley (picks up the cards and goes to the door): All right! Next time I'll bring a deck with five aces.

Willy: I don't play that kind of game!

Charley (turning to him): You ought to be ashamed of yourself!

Willy: Yeah?

Charley: Yeah! *(He goes out.)*

Willy (slamming the door after him): Ignoramus!

Ben (as Willy comes toward him through the wall-line of the kitchen): So you're William.

Willy (shaking Ben's hand): Ben! I've been waiting for you so long! What's the answer? How did you do it?

Ben: Oh, there's a story in that.

Linda enters the forestage, as of old, carrying the wash basket.

Linda: Is this Ben?

Ben (gallantly): How do you do, my dear.

Linda: Where've you been all these years? Willy's always wondered why you —

Willy (pulling Ben away from her impatiently): Where is Dad? Didn't you follow him? How did you get started?

Ben: Well, I don't know how much you remember.

Willy: Well, I was just a baby, of course, only three or four years old —

Ben: Three years and eleven months.

Willy: What a memory, Ben!

Ben: I have many enterprises, William, and I have never kept books.

Willy: I remember I was sitting under the wagon in — was it Nebraska?

Ben: It was South Dakota, and I gave you a bunch of wild flowers.

Willy: I remember you walking away down some open road.

Ben (laughing): I was going to find Father in Alaska.

Willy: Where is he?

Ben: At that age I had a very faulty view of geography, William. I discovered after a few days that I was heading due south, so instead of Alaska, I ended up in Africa.

Linda: Africa!

Willy: The Gold Coast!

Ben: Principally diamond mines.

Linda: Diamond mines!

Ben: Yes, my dear. But I've only a few minutes —

Willy: No! Boys! Boys! *(Young Biff and Happy appear.)* Listen to this. This is your Uncle Ben, a great man! Tell my boys, Ben!

Ben: Why, boys, when I was seventeen I walked into the jungle, and when I was twenty-one I walked out. *(He laughs.)* And by God I was rich.

Willy (to the boys): You see what I been talking about? The greatest things can happen!

Ben (glancing at his watch): I have an appointment in Ketchikan Tuesday week.

Willy: No, Ben! Please tell about Dad. I want my boys to hear. I want them to know the kind of stock they spring from. All I remember is a man with a big beard, and I was in Mamma's lap, sitting around a fire, and some kind of high music.

Ben: His flute. He played the flute.

Willy: Sure, the flute, that's right!

New music is heard, a high, rollicking tune.

Ben: Father was a very great and a very wild-hearted man. We would start in Boston, and he'd toss the whole family into the wagon, and then he'd drive the team right across the country; through Ohio, and Indiana, Michigan, Illinois, and all the Western states. And we'd stop in the towns and sell the flutes that he'd made on the way. Great inventor, Father. With one gadget he made more in a week than a man like you could make in a lifetime.

Willy: That's just the way I'm bringing them up, Ben — rugged, well liked, all-around.

Ben: Yeah? *(To Biff.)* Hit that, boy — hard as you can. *(He pounds his stomach.)*

Biff: Oh, no, sir!

Ben (taking boxing stance): Come on, get to me. *(He laughs.)*

Willy: Go to it, Biff! Go ahead, show him!

Biff: Okay! *(He cocks his fists and starts in.)*

Linda (to Willy): Why must he fight, dear?

Ben (sparring with Biff): Good boy! Good boy!

Willy: How's that, Ben, heh?

Happy: Give him the left, Biff!

Linda: Why are you fighting?

Ben: Good boy! *(Suddenly comes in, trips Biff, and stands over him, the point of his umbrella poised over Biff's eye.)*

Linda: Look out, Biff!

Biff: Gee!

Ben (patting Biff's knee): Never fight fair with a stranger, boy. You'll never get out of the jungle that way. *(Taking Linda's hand and bowing):* It was an honor and a pleasure to meet you, Linda.

Linda (withdrawing her hand coldly, frightened): Have a nice — trip.

Ben (to Willy): And good luck with your — what do you do?

Willy: Selling.

Ben: Yes. Well . . . *(He raises his hand in farewell to all.)*

Willy: No, Ben, I don't want you to think . . . *(He takes Ben's arm to show him.)* It's Brooklyn, I know, but we hunt too.

Ben: Really, now.

Willy: Oh, sure, there's snakes and rabbits and — that's why I moved out here. Why, Biff can fell any one of these trees in no time! Boys! Go right over to where they're building the apartment house and get some sand. We're gonna rebuild the entire front stoop now! Watch this, Ben!

Biff: Yes, sir! On the double, Hap!

Happy (as he and Biff run off): I lost weight, Pop, you notice?

Charley enters in knickers, even before the boys are gone.

Charley: Listen, if they steal any more from that building the watchman'll put the cops on them!

Linda (to Willy): Don't let Biff . . .

> *Ben laughs lustily.*

Willy: You shoulda seen the lumber they brought home last week. At least a dozen six-by-tens worth all kinds a money.

Charley: Listen, if that watchman —

Willy: I gave them hell, understand. But I got a couple of fearless characters there.

Charley: Willy, the jails are full of fearless characters.

Ben (clapping Willy on the back, with a laugh at Charley): And the stock exchange, friend!

Willy (joining in Ben's laughter): Where are the rest of your pants?

Charley: My wife bought them.

Willy: Now all you need is a golf club and you can go upstairs and go to sleep. *(To Ben).* Great athlete! Between him and his son Bernard they can't hammer a nail!

Bernard (rushing in): The watchman's chasing Biff!

Willy (angrily): Shut up! He's not stealing anything!

Linda (alarmed, hurrying off left): Where is he? Biff, dear! *(She exits.)*

Willy (moving toward the left, away from Ben): There's nothing wrong. What's the matter with you?

Ben: Nervy boy. Good!

Willy (laughing): Oh, nerves of iron, that Biff!

Charley: Don't know what it is. My New England man comes back and he's bleedin', they murdered him up there.

Willy: It's contacts, Charley, I got important contacts!

Charley (sarcastically): Glad to hear it, Willy. Come in later, we'll shoot a little casino. I'll take some of your Portland money. *(He laughs at Willy and exits.)*

Willy (turning to Ben): Business is bad, it's murderous. But not for me, of course.

Ben: I'll stop by on my way back to Africa.

Willy (longingly): Can't you stay a few days? You're just what I need, Ben, because I — I have a fine position here, but I — well, Dad left when I was such a baby and I never had a chance to talk to him and I still feel — kind of temporary about myself.

Ben: I'll be late for my train.

> *They are at opposite ends of the stage.*

Willy: Ben, my boys — can't we talk? They'd go into the jaws of hell for me, see, but I —

Ben: William, you're being first-rate with your boys. Outstanding, manly chaps!

Willy (hanging on to his words): Oh, Ben, that's good to hear! Because sometimes I'm afraid that I'm not teaching them the right kind of — Ben, how should I teach them?

Ben (giving great weight to each word, and with a certain vicious audacity): William, when I walked into the jungle, I was seventeen. When I walked out I was twenty-one. And, by God, I was rich! *(He goes off into darkness around the right corner of the house.)*

Willy: . . . was rich! That's just the spirit I want to imbue them with! To walk into a jungle! I was right! I was right! I was right!

*Ben is gone, but Willy is still speaking to him as Linda, in nightgown and robe,
enters the kitchen, glances around for Willy, then goes to the door of the house, looks
out, and sees him. Comes down to his left. He looks at her.*

Linda: Willy, dear? Willy?

Willy: I was right!

Linda: Did you have some cheese? *(He can't answer.)* It's very late, darling.
Come to bed, heh?

Willy *(looking straight up):* Gotta break your neck to see a star in this yard.

Linda: You coming in?

Willy: Whatever happened to that diamond watch fob? Remember? When Ben
came from Africa that time? Didn't he give me a watch fob with a diamond in it?

Linda: You pawned it, dear. Twelve, thirteen years ago. For Biff's radio correspondence course.

Willy: Gee, that was a beautiful thing. I'll take a walk.

Linda: But you're in your slippers.

Willy *(starting to go around the house at the left):* I was right! I was! *(Half to Linda,
as he goes, shaking his head.)* What a man! There was a man worth talking to.
I was right!

Linda *(calling after Willy):* But in your slippers, Willy!

*Willy is almost gone when Biff, in his pajamas, comes down the stairs and enters
the kitchen.*

Biff: What is he doing out there?

Linda: Sh!

Biff: God Almighty, Mom, how long has he been doing this?

Linda: Don't, he'll hear you.

Biff: What the hell is the matter with him?

Linda: It'll pass by morning.

Biff: Shouldn't we do anything?

Linda: Oh, my dear, you should do a lot of things, but there's nothing to do,
so go to sleep.

Happy comes down the stairs and sits on the steps.

Happy: I never heard him so loud, Mom.

Linda: Well, come around more often; you'll hear him. *(She sits down at the table
and mends the lining of Willy's jacket.)*

Biff: Why didn't you ever write me about this, Mom?

Linda: How would I write to you? For over three months you had no address.

Biff: I was on the move. But you know I thought of you all the time. You know
that, don't you, pal?

Linda: I know, dear, I know. But he likes to have a letter. Just to know that
there's still a possibility for better things.

Biff: He's not like this all the time, is he?

Linda: It's when you come home he's always the worst.

Biff: When I come home?

Linda: When you write you're coming, he's all smiles, and talks about the future, and — he's just wonderful. And then the closer you seem to come, the
more shaky he gets, and then, by the time you get here, he's arguing, and

he seems angry at you. I think it's just that maybe he can't bring himself to — to open up to you. Why are you so hateful to each other? Why is that?

Biff (evasively): I'm not hateful, Mom.

Linda: But you no sooner come in the door than you're fighting!

Biff: I don't know why. I mean to change. I'm tryin', Mom, you understand?

Linda: Are you home to stay now?

Biff: I don't know. I want to look around, see what's doin'.

Linda: Biff, you can't look around all your life, can you?

Biff: I just can't take hold, Mom. I can't take hold of some kind of a life.

Linda: Biff, a man is not a bird, to come and go with the springtime.

Biff: Your hair . . . *(He touches her hair.)* Your hair got so gray.

Linda: Oh, it's been gray since you were in high school. I just stopped dyeing it, that's all.

Biff: Dye it again, will ya? I don't want my pal looking old. *(He smiles.)*

Linda: You're such a boy! You think you can go away for a year and . . . You've got to get it into your head now that one day you'll knock on this door and there'll be strange people here —

Biff: What are you talking about? You're not even sixty, Mom.

Linda: But what about your father?

Biff (lamely): Well, I meant him too.

Happy: He admires Pop.

Linda: Biff, dear, if you don't have any feeling for him, then you can't have any feeling for me.

Biff: Sure I can, Mom.

Linda: No. You can't just come to see me, because I love him. *(With a threat, but only a threat, of tears.)* He's the dearest man in the world to me, and I won't have anyone making him feel unwanted and low and blue. You've got to make up your mind now, darling, there's no leeway any more. Either he's your father and you pay him that respect, or else you're not to come here. I know he's not easy to get along with — nobody knows that better than me — but . . .

Willy (from the left, with a laugh): Hey, hey, Biffo!

Biff (starting to go out after Willy): What the hell is the matter with him? *(Happy stops him.)*

Linda: Don't — don't go near him!

Biff: Stop making excuses for him! He always, always wiped the floor with you. Never had an ounce of respect for you.

Happy: He's always had respect for —

Biff: What the hell do you know about it?

Happy (surlily): Just don't call him crazy!

Biff: He's got no character — Charley wouldn't do this. Not in his own house — spewing out that vomit from his mind.

Happy: Charley never had to cope with what he's got to.

Biff: People are worse off than Willy Loman. Believe me, I've seen them!

Linda: Then make Charley your father, Biff. You can't do that, can you? I don't say he's a great man. Willy Loman never made a lot of money. His name was never in the paper. He's not the finest character that ever lived. But he's a human being, and a terrible thing is happening to him. So attention must be paid. He's not to be allowed to fall into his grave like an old dog. Attention, attention must be finally paid to such a person. You called him crazy —

Biff: I didn't mean—

Linda: No, a lot of people think he's lost his—balance. But you don't have to be very smart to know what his trouble is. The man is exhausted.

Happy: Sure!

Linda: A small man can be just as exhausted as a great man. He works for a company thirty-six years this March, opens up unheard-of territories to their trademark, and now in his old age they take his salary away.

Happy (indignantly): I didn't know that, Mom.

Linda: You never asked, my dear! Now that you get your spending money someplace else you don't trouble your mind with him.

Happy: But I gave you money last—

Linda: Christmas time, fifty dollars! To fix the hot water it cost ninety-seven fifty! For five weeks he's been on straight commission, like a beginner, an unknown!

Biff: Those ungrateful bastards!

Linda: Are they any worse than his sons? When he brought them business, when he was young, they were glad to see him. But now his old friends, the old buyers that loved him so and always found some order to hand him in a pinch—they're all dead, retired. He used to be able to make six, seven calls a day in Boston. Now he takes his valises out of the car and puts them back and takes them out again and he's exhausted. Instead of walking he talks now. He drives seven hundred miles, and when he gets there no one knows him any more, no one welcomes him. And what goes through a man's mind, driving seven hundred miles home without having earned a cent? Why shouldn't he talk to himself? Why? When he has to go to Charley and borrow fifty dollars a week and pretend to me that it's his pay? How long can that go on? How long? You see what I'm sitting here and waiting for? And you tell me he has no character? The man who never worked a day but for your benefit? When does he get the medal for that? Is this his reward—to turn around at the age of sixty-three and find his sons, who he loved better than his life, one a philandering bum—

Happy: Mom!

Linda: That's all you are, my baby! *(To Biff.)* And you! What happened to the love you had for him? You were such pals! How you used to talk to him on the phone every night! How lonely he was till he could come home to you!

Biff: All right, Mom. I'll live here in my room, and I'll get a job. I'll keep away from him, that's all.

Linda: No, Biff. You can't stay here and fight all the time.

Biff: He threw me out of this house, remember that.

Linda: Why did he do that? I never knew why.

Biff: Because I know he's a fake and he doesn't like anybody around who knows!

Linda: Why a fake? In what way? What do you mean?

Biff: Just don't lay it all at my feet. It's between me and him—that's all I have to say. I'll chip in from now on. He'll settle for half my pay check. He'll be all right. I'm going to bed. *(He starts for the stairs.)*

Linda: He won't be all right.

Biff (turning on the stairs, furiously): I hate this city and I'll stay here. Now what do you want?

Linda: He's dying, Biff.

Happy turns quickly to her, shocked.

Biff (after a pause): Why is he dying?

Linda: He's been trying to kill himself.

Biff (with great horror): How?

Linda: I live from day to day.

Biff: What're you talking about?

Linda: Remember I wrote you that he smashed up the car again? In February?

Biff: Well?

Linda: The insurance inspector came. He said that they have evidence. That all these accidents in the last year — weren't — weren't — accidents.

Happy: How can they tell that? That's a lie.

Linda: It seems there's a woman . . . *(She takes a breath as):*

⎰ *Biff (sharply but contained):* What woman?

⎱ *Linda (simultaneously):* . . . and this woman . . .

Linda: What?

Biff: Nothing. Go ahead.

Linda: What did you say?

Biff: Nothing. I just said what woman?

Happy: What about her?

Linda: Well, it seems she was walking down the road and saw his car. She says that he wasn't driving fast at all, and that he didn't skid. She says he came to that little bridge, and then deliberately smashed into the railing, and it was only the shallowness of the water that saved him.

Biff: Oh, no, he probably just fell asleep again.

Linda: I don't think he fell asleep.

Biff: Why not?

Linda: Last month . . . *(With great difficulty.)* Oh, boys, it's so hard to say a thing like this! He's just a big stupid man to you, but I tell you there's more good in him than in many other people. *(She chokes, wipes her eyes.)* I was looking for a fuse. The lights blew out, and I went down the cellar. And behind the fuse box — it happened to fall out — was a length of rubber pipe — just short.

Happy: No kidding?

Linda: There's a little attachment on the end of it. I knew right away. And sure enough, on the bottom of the water heater there's a new little nipple on the gas pipe.

Happy (angrily): That — jerk.

Biff: Did you have it taken off?

Linda: I'm — I'm ashamed to. How can I mention it to him? Every day I go down and take away that little rubber pipe. But, when he comes home, I put it back where it was. How can I insult him that way? I don't know what to do. I live from day to day, boys. I tell you, I know every thought in his mind. It sounds so old-fashioned and silly, but I tell you he put his whole life into you and you've turned your backs on him. *(She is bent over in chair, weeping, her face in her hands.)* Biff, I swear to God! Biff, his life is in your hands!

Happy (to Biff): How do you like that damned fool!

Biff (kissing her): All right, pal, all right. It's all settled now. I've been remiss. I know that, Mom. But now I'll stay, and I swear to you, I'll apply myself. *(Kneeling in front of her, in a fever of self-reproach.)* It's just — you see, Mom, I don't fit in business. Not that I won't try. I'll try, and I'll make good.

Happy: Sure you will. The trouble with you in business was you never tried to please people.

Biff: I know, I —

Happy: Like when you worked for Harrison's. Bob Harrison said you were tops, and then you go and do some damn fool thing like whistling whole songs in the elevator like a comedian.

Biff (against Happy): So what? I like to whistle sometimes.

Happy: You don't raise a guy to a responsible job who whistles in the elevator!

Linda: Well, don't argue about it now.

Happy: Like when you'd go off and swim in the middle of the day instead of taking the line around.

Biff (his resentment rising): Well, don't you run off? You take off sometimes, don't you? On a nice summer day?

Happy: Yeah, but I cover myself!

Linda: Boys!

Happy: If I'm going to take a fade the boss can call any number where I'm supposed to be and they'll swear to him that I just left. I'll tell you something that I hate to say, Biff, but in the business world some of them think you're crazy.

Biff (angered): Screw the business world!

Happy: All right, screw it! Great, but cover yourself!

Linda: Hap, Hap!

Biff: I don't care what they think! They've laughed at Dad for years, and you know why? Because we don't belong in this nuthouse of a city! We should be mixing cement on some open plain, or — or carpenters. A carpenter is allowed to whistle!

Willy walks in from the entrance of the house, at left.

Willy: Even your grandfather was better than a carpenter. (*Pause. They watch him.*) You never grew up. Bernard does not whistle in the elevator, I assure you.

Biff (as though to laugh Willy out of it): Yeah, but you do, Pop.

Willy: I never in my life whistled in an elevator! And who in the business world thinks I'm crazy?

Biff: I didn't mean it like that, Pop. Now don't make a whole thing out of it, will ya?

Willy: Go back to the West! Be a carpenter, a cowboy, enjoy yourself!

Linda: Willy, he was just saying —

Willy: I heard what he said!

Happy (trying to quiet Willy): Hey, Pop, come on now . . .

Willy (continuing over Happy's line): They laugh at me, heh? Go to Filene's, go to the Hub, go to Slattery's, Boston. Call out the name Willy Loman and see what happens! Big shot!

Biff: All right, Pop.

Willy: Big!

Biff: All right!

Willy: Why do you always insult me?

Biff: I didn't say a word. (*To Linda.*) Did I say a word?

Linda: He didn't say anything, Willy.

Willy (going to the doorway of the living-room): All right, good night, good night.

Linda: Willy, dear, he just decided . . .

Willy (to Biff): If you get tired hanging around tomorrow, paint the ceiling I put up in the living-room.

Biff: I'm leaving early tomorrow.

Happy: He's going to see Bill Oliver, Pop.

Willy (interestedly): Oliver? For what?

Biff (with reserve, but trying, trying): He always said he'd stake me. I'd like to go into business, so maybe I can take him up on it.

Linda: Isn't that wonderful?

Willy: Don't interrupt. What's wonderful about it? There's fifty men in the City of New York who'd stake him. *(To Biff.)* Sporting goods?

Biff: I guess so. I know something about it and —

Willy: He knows something about it! You know sporting goods better than Spalding, for God's sake! How much is he giving you?

Biff: I don't know, I didn't even see him yet, but —

Willy: Then what're you talkin' about?

Biff (getting angry): Well, all I said was I'm gonna see him, that's all!

Willy (turning away): Ah, you're counting your chickens again.

Biff (starting left for the stairs): Oh, Jesus, I'm going to sleep!

Willy (calling after him): Don't curse in this house!

Biff (turning): Since when did you get so clean?

Happy (trying to stop them): Wait a . . .

Willy: Don't use that language to me! I won't have it!

Happy (grabbing Biff, shouts): Wait a minute! I got an idea. I got a feasible idea. Come here, Biff, let's talk this over now, let's talk some sense here. When I was down in Florida last time, I thought of a great idea to sell sporting goods. It just came back to me. You and I, Biff — we have a line, the Loman Line. We train a couple of weeks, and put on a couple of exhibitions, see?

Willy: That's an idea!

Happy: Wait! We form two basketball teams, see? Two water-polo teams. We play each other. It's a million dollars' worth of publicity. Two brothers, see? The Loman Brothers. Displays in the Royal Palms — all the hotels. And banners over the ring and the basketball court: "Loman Brothers." Baby, we could sell sporting goods!

Willy: That is a one-million-dollar idea!

Linda: Marvelous!

Biff: I'm in great shape as far as that's concerned.

Happy: And the beauty of it is, Biff, it wouldn't be like a business. We'd be out playin' ball again . . .

Biff (enthused): Yeah, that's . . .

Willy: Million-dollar . . .

Happy: And you wouldn't get fed up with it, Biff. It'd be the family again. There'd be the old honor, and comradeship, and if you wanted to go off for a swim or somethin' — well, you'd do it! Without some smart cooky gettin' up ahead of you!

Willy: Lick the world! You guys together could absolutely lick the civilized world.

Biff: I'll see Oliver tomorrow. Hap, if we could work that out . . .

Linda: Maybe things are beginning to —

Willy (wildly enthused, to Linda): Stop interrupting! *(To Biff.)* But don't wear sport jacket and slacks when you see Oliver.

Biff: No, I'll—

Willy: A business suit, and talk as little as possible, and don't crack any jokes.

Biff: He did like me. Always liked me.

Linda: He loved you!

Willy (to Linda): Will you stop! *(To Biff.)* Walk in very serious. You are not applying for a boy's job. Money is to pass. Be quiet, fine, and serious. Everybody likes a kidder, but nobody lends him money.

Happy: I'll try to get some myself, Biff. I'm sure I can.

Willy: I see great things for you kids, I think your troubles are over. But remember, start big and you'll end big. Ask for fifteen. How much you gonna ask for?

Biff: Gee, I don't know—

Willy: And don't say "Gee." "Gee" is a boy's word. A man walking in for fifteen thousand dollars does not say "Gee!"

Biff: Ten, I think, would be top though.

Willy: Don't be so modest. You always started too low. Walk in with a big laugh. Don't look worried. Start off with a couple of your good stories to lighten things up. It's not what you say, it's how you say it—because personality always wins the day.

Linda: Oliver always thought the highest of him—

Willy: Will you let me talk?

Biff: Don't yell at her, Pop, will ya?

Willy (angrily): I was talking, wasn't I?

Biff: I don't like you yelling at her all the time, and I'm tellin' you, that's all.

Willy: What're you, takin' over this house?

Linda: Willy—

Willy (turning on her): Don't take his side all the time, goddammit!

Biff (furiously): Stop yelling at her!

Willy (suddenly pulling on his cheek, beaten down, guilt ridden): Give my best to Bill Oliver—he may remember me. *(He exits through the living-room doorway.)*

Linda (her voice subdued): What'd you have to start that for? *(Biff turns away.)* You see how sweet he was as soon as you talked hopefully? *(She goes over to Biff.)* Come up and say good night to him. Don't let him go to bed that way.

Happy: Come on, Biff, let's buck him up.

Linda: Please, dear. Just say good night. It takes so little to make him happy. Come. *(She goes through the living-room doorway, calling upstairs from within the living-room.)* Your pajamas are hanging in the bathroom, Willy!

Happy (looking toward where Linda went out): What a woman! They broke the mold when they made her. You know that, Biff?

Biff: He's off salary. My God, working on commission!

Happy: Well, let's face it: he's no hot-shot selling man. Except that sometimes, you have to admit, he's a sweet personality.

Biff (deciding): Lend me ten bucks, will ya? I want to buy some new ties.

Happy: I'll take you to a place I know. Beautiful stuff. Wear one of my striped shirts tomorrow.

Biff: She got gray. Mom got awful old. Gee, I'm gonna go in to Oliver tomorrow and knock him for a—

Happy: Come on up. Tell that to Dad. Let's give him a whirl. Come on.

Biff (steamed up): You know, with ten thousand bucks, boy!

Happy (as they go into the living-room): That's the talk, Biff, that's the first time I've heard the old confidence out of you! *(From within the living-room, fading off.)* You're gonna live with me, kid, and any babe you want just say the word . . . *(The last lines are hardly heard. They are mounting the stairs to their parents' bedroom.)*

Linda *(entering her bedroom and addressing Willy, who is in the bathroom. She is straightening the bed for him):* Can you do anything about the shower? It drips.

Willy *(from the bathroom):* All of a sudden everything falls to pieces! Goddam plumbing, oughta be sued, those people. I hardly finished putting it in and the thing . . . *(His words rumble off.)*

Linda: I'm just wondering if Oliver will remember him. You think he might?

Willy *(coming out of the bathroom in his pajamas):* Remember him? What's the matter with you, you crazy? If he'd've stayed with Oliver he'd be on top by now! Wait'll Oliver gets a look at him. You don't know the average caliber any more. The average young man today — *(he is getting into bed)* — is got a caliber of zero. Greatest thing in the world for him was to bum around.

Biff and Happy enter the bedroom. Slight pause.

Willy *(stops short, looking at Biff):* Glad to hear it, boy.

Happy: He wanted to say good night to you, sport.

Willy *(to Biff):* Yeah. Knock him dead, boy. What'd you want to tell me?

Biff: Just take it easy, Pop. Good night. *(He turns to go.)*

Willy *(unable to resist):* And if anything falls off the desk while you're talking to him — like a package or something — don't you pick it up. They have office boys for that.

Linda: I'll make a big breakfast —

Willy: Will you let me finish? *(To Biff.)* Tell him you were in the business in the West. Not farm work.

Biff: All right, Dad.

Linda: I think everything —

Willy *(going right through her speech):* And don't undersell yourself. No less than fifteen thousand dollars.

Biff *(unable to bear him):* Okay. Good night, Mom. *(He starts moving.)*

Willy: Because you got a greatness in you, Biff, remember that. You got all kinds a greatness . . . *(He lies back, exhausted. Biff walks out.)*

Linda *(calling after Biff):* Sleep well, darling!

Happy: I'm gonna get married, Mom. I wanted to tell you.

Linda: Go to sleep, dear.

Happy *(going):* I just wanted to tell you.

Willy: Keep up the good work. *(Happy exits.)* God . . . remember that Ebbets Field game? The championship of the city?

Linda: Just rest. Should I sing to you?

Willy: Yeah. Sing to me. *(Linda hums a soft lullaby.)* When that team came out — he was the tallest, remember?

Linda: Oh, yes. And in gold.

Biff enters the darkened kitchen, takes a cigarette, and leaves the house. He comes downstage into a golden pool of light. He smokes, staring at the night.

Willy: Like a young god. Hercules — something like that. And the sun, the sun all around him. Remember how he waved to me? Right up from the field, with the representatives of three colleges standing by? And the buyers I brought, and the cheers when he came out—Loman, Loman, Loman! God Almighty, he'll be great yet. A star like that, magnificent, can never really fade away!

The light on Willy is fading. The gas heater begins to glow through the kitchen wall, near the stairs, a blue flame beneath red coils.

Linda *(timidly):* Willy dear, what has he got against you?

Willy: I'm so tired. Don't talk any more.

Biff slowly returns to the kitchen. He stops, stares toward the heater.

Linda: Will you ask Howard to let you work in New York?

Willy: First thing in the morning. Everything'll be all right.

Biff reaches behind the heater and draws out a length of rubber tubing. He is horrified and turns his head toward Willy's room, still dimly lit, from which the strains of Linda's desperate but monotonous humming rise.

Willy *(staring through the window into the moonlight):* Gee, look at the moon moving between the buildings!

Biff wraps the tubing around his hand and quickly goes up the stairs.

Curtain

ACT II

Music is heard, gay and bright. The curtain rises as the music fades away. Willy, in shirt sleeves, is sitting at the kitchen table, sipping coffee, his hat in his lap. Linda is filling his cup when she can.

Willy: Wonderful coffee. Meal in itself.

Linda: Can I make you some eggs?

Willy: No. Take a breath.

Linda: You look so rested, dear.

Willy: I slept like a dead one. First time in months. Imagine, sleeping till ten on a Tuesday morning. Boys left nice and early, heh?

Linda: They were out of here by eight o'clock.

Willy: Good work!

Linda: It was so thrilling to see them leaving together. I can't get over the shaving lotion in this house!

Willy *(smiling):* Mmm—

Linda: Biff was very changed this morning. His whole attitude seemed to be hopeful. He couldn't wait to get downtown to see Oliver.

Willy: He's heading for a change. There's no question, there simply are certain men that take longer to get—solidified. How did he dress?

Linda: His blue suit. He's so handsome in that suit. He could be a—anything in that suit!

Willy gets up from the table. Linda holds his jacket for him.

Willy: There's no question, no question at all. Gee, on the way home tonight I'd like to buy some seeds.

Linda (laughing): That'd be wonderful. But not enough sun gets back there. Nothing'll grow any more.

Willy: You wait, kid, before it's all over we're gonna get a little place out in the country, and I'll raise some vegetables, a couple of chickens . . .

Linda: You'll do it yet, dear.

Willy walks out of his jacket. Linda follows him.

Willy: And they'll get married, and come for a weekend. I'd build a little guest house. 'Cause I got so many fine tools, all I'd need would be a little lumber and some peace of mind.

Linda (joyfully): I sewed the lining . . .

Willy: I could build two guest houses, so they'd both come. Did he decide how much he's going to ask Oliver for?

Linda (getting him into the jacket): He didn't mention it, but I imagine ten or fifteen thousand. You going to talk to Howard today?

Willy: Yeah. I'll put it to him straight and simple. He'll just have to take me off the road.

Linda: And Willy, don't forget to ask for a little advance, because we've got the insurance premium. It's the grace period now.

Willy: That's a hundred . . . ?

Linda: A hundred and eight, sixty-eight. Because we're a little short again.

Willy: Why are we short?

Linda: Well, you had the motor job on the car . . .

Willy: That goddam Studebaker!

Linda: And you got one more payment on the refrigerator . . .

Willy: But it just broke again!

Linda: Well, it's old, dear.

Willy: I told you we should've bought a well-advertised machine. Charley bought a General Electric and it's twenty years old and it's still good, that son-of-a-bitch.

Linda: But, Willy —

Willy: Whoever heard of a Hastings refrigerator? Once in my life I would like to own something outright before it's broken! I'm always in a race with the junkyard! I just finished paying for the car and it's on its last legs. The refrigerator consumes belts like a goddam maniac. They time those things. They time them so when you finally paid for them, they're used up.

Linda (buttoning up his jacket as he unbuttons it): All told, about two hundred dollars would carry us, dear. But that includes the last payment on the mortgage. After this payment, Willy, the house belongs to us.

Willy: It's twenty-five years!

Linda: Biff was nine years old when we bought it.

Willy: Well, that's a great thing. To weather a twenty-five year mortgage is —

Linda: It's an accomplishment.

Willy: All the cement, the lumber, the reconstruction I put in this house! There ain't a crack to be found in it any more.

Linda: Well, it served its purpose.

Willy: What purpose? Some stranger'll come along, move in, and that's that. If only Biff would take this house, and raise a family . . . *(He starts to go.)* Good-by, I'm late.

Linda (suddenly remembering): Oh, I forgot! You're supposed to meet them for dinner.

Willy: Me?

Linda: At Frank's Chop House on Forty-eighth near Sixth Avenue.

Willy: Is that so! How about you?

Linda: No, just the three of you. They're gonna blow you to a big meal!

Willy: Don't say! Who thought of that?

Linda: Biff came to me this morning, Willy, and he said, "Tell Dad, we want to blow him to a big meal." Be there six o'clock. You and your two boys are going to have dinner.

Willy: Gee whiz! That's really somethin'. I'm gonna knock Howard for a loop, kid. I'll get an advance, and I'll come home with a New York job. God-dammit, now I'm gonna do it!

Linda: Oh, that's the spirit, Willy!

Willy: I will never get behind a wheel the rest of my life!

Linda: It's changing, Willy, I can feel it changing!

Willy: Beyond a question. G'by, I'm late. *(He starts to go again.)*

Linda (calling after him as she runs to the kitchen table for a handkerchief): You got your glasses?

Willy (feels for them, then comes back in): Yeah, yeah, got my glasses.

Linda (giving him the handkerchief): And a handkerchief.

Willy: Yeah, handkerchief.

Linda: And your saccharine?

Willy: Yeah, my saccharine.

Linda: Be careful on the subway stairs.

She kisses him, and a silk stocking is seen hanging from her hand. Willy notices it.

Willy: Will you stop mending stockings? At least while I'm in the house. It gets me nervous. I can't tell you. Please.

Linda hides the stocking in her hand as she follows Willy across the forestage in front of the house.

Linda: Remember, Frank's Chop House.

Willy (passing the apron): Maybe beets would grow out there.

Linda (laughing): But you tried so many times.

Willy: Yeah. Well, don't work hard today. *(He disappears around the right corner of the house.)*

Linda: Be careful!

As Willy vanishes, Linda waves to him. Suddenly the phone rings. She runs across the stage and into the kitchen and lifts it.

Linda: Hello? Oh, Biff! I'm so glad you called, I just . . . Yes, sure, I just told him. Yes, he'll be there for dinner at six o'clock, I didn't forget. Listen, I was just dying to tell you. You know that little rubber pipe I told you about? That he connected to the gas heater? I finally decided to go down the cellar this morning and take it away and destroy it. But it's gone! Imagine? He took it away himself, it isn't there! *(She listens.)* When? Oh, then you took it. Oh — nothing, it's just that I'd hoped he'd taken it away himself. Oh, I'm not worried, darling, because this morning he left in such high spirits, it was like the old days! I'm not afraid any more. Did Mr. Oliver see you? . . . Well, you wait there then. And make a nice impression on him, darling. Just don't perspire too much before you see him. And have a nice time with Dad. He may have big news too! . . . That's right, a New York job. And be sweet to him tonight, dear. Be loving to him. Because he's only a little boat looking for a harbor. *(She is trembling with sorrow and joy.)* Oh, that's wonderful, Biff, you'll save his life. Thanks, darling. Just put your arm around him when he comes into the restaurant. Give him a smile. That's the boy . . . Good-by, dear. . . . You got your comb? . . . That's fine. Good-by, Biff dear.

In the middle of her speech, Howard Wagner, thirty-six, wheels in a small typewriter table on which is a wire-recording machine and proceeds to plug it in. This is on the left forestage. Light slowly fades on Linda as it rises on Howard. Howard is intent on threading the machine and only glances over his shoulder as Willy appears.

Willy: Pst! Pst!

Howard: Hello, Willy, come in.

Willy: Like to have a little talk with you, Howard.

Howard: Sorry to keep you waiting. I'll be with you in a minute.

Willy: What's that, Howard?

Howard: Didn't you ever see one of these? Wire recorder.

Willy: Oh. Can we talk a minute?

Howard: Records things. Just got delivery yesterday. Been driving me crazy, the most terrific machine I ever saw in my life. I was up all night with it.

Willy: What do you do with it?

Howard: I bought it for dictation, but you can do anything with it. Listen to this. I had it home last night. Listen to what I picked up. The first one is my daughter. Get this. *(He flicks the switch and "Roll Out the Barrel" is heard being whistled.)* Listen to that kid whistle.

Willy: That is lifelike, isn't it?

Howard: Seven years old. Get that tone.

Willy: Willy: Ts, ts. Like to ask a little favor if you . . .

The whistling breaks off, and the voice of Howard's daughter is heard.

His Daughter: "Now you, Daddy."

Howard: She's crazy for me! *(Again the same song is whistled.)* That's me! Ha! *(He winks.)*

Willy: You're very good!

The whistling breaks off again. The machine runs silent for a moment.

Howard: Sh! Get this now, this is my son.

His Son: "The capital of Alabama is Montgomery; the capital of Arizona is Phoenix; the capital of Arkansas is Little Rock; the capital of California is Sacramento . . ." *(and on, and on).*

Howard (holding up five fingers): Five years old, Willy!

Willy: He'll make an announcer some day!

His Son (continuing): "The capital . . ."

Howard: Get that—alphabetical order! *(The machine breaks off suddenly.)* Wait a minute. The maid kicked the plug out.

Willy: It certainly is a—

Howard: Sh, for God's sake!

His Son: "It's nine o'clock, Bulova watch time. So I have to go to sleep."

Willy: That really is—

Howard: Wait a minute! The next is my wife.

They wait.

Howard's Voice: "Go on, say something." *(Pause.)* "Well, you gonna talk?"

His Wife: "I can't think of anything."

Howard's Voice: "Well, talk — it's turning."

His Wife (shyly, beaten): "Hello." *(Silence.)* "Oh, Howard, I can't talk into this . . ."

Howard (snapping the machine off): That was my wife.

Willy: That is a wonderful machine. Can we —

Howard: I tell you, Willy, I'm gonna take my camera, and my bandsaw, and all my hobbies, and out they go. This is the most fascinating relaxation I ever found.

Willy: I think I'll get one myself.

Howard: Sure, they're only a hundred and a half. You can't do without it. Supposing you wanna hear Jack Benny, see? But you can't be at home at that hour. So you tell the maid to turn the radio on when Jack Benny comes on, and this automatically goes on with the radio . . .

Willy: And when you come home you . . .

Howard: You can come home twelve o'clock, one o'clock, any time you like, and you get yourself a Coke and sit yourself down, throw the switch, and there's Jack Benny's program in the middle of the night!

Willy: I'm definitely going to get one. Because lots of time I'm on the road, and I think to myself, what I must be missing on the radio!

Howard: Don't you have a radio in the car?

Willy: Well, yeah, but who ever thinks of turning it on?

Howard: Say, aren't you supposed to be in Boston?

Willy: That's what I want to talk to you about, Howard. You got a minute? *(He draws a chair in from the wing.)*

Howard: What happened? What're you doing here?

Willy: Well . . .

Howard: You didn't crack up again, did you?

Willy: Oh, no. No . . .

Howard: Geez, you had me worried there for a minute. What's the trouble?

Willy: Well, tell you the truth, Howard. I've come to the decision that I'd rather not travel any more.

Howard: Not travel! Well, what'll you do?

Willy: Remember, Christmas time, when you had the party here? You said you'd try to think of some spot for me here in town.

Howard: With us?

Willy: Well, sure.

Howard: Oh, yeah, yeah. I remember. Well, I couldn't think of anything for you, Willy.

Willy: I tell ya, Howard. The kids are all grown up, y'know. I don't need much any more. If I could take home — well, sixty-five dollars a week, I could swing it.

Howard: Yeah, but Willy, see I —

Willy: I tell ya why, Howard. Speaking frankly and between the two of us, y'know — I'm just a little tired.

Howard: Oh, I could understand that, Willy. But you're a road man, Willy, and we do a road business. We've only got a half-dozen salesmen on the floor here.

Willy: God knows, Howard, I never asked a favor of any man. But I was with the firm when your father used to carry you in here in his arms.

Howard: I know that, Willy, but —

Willy: Your father came to me the day you were born and asked me what I thought of the name of Howard, may he rest in peace.

Howard: I appreciate that, Willy, but there just is no spot here for you. If I had a spot I'd slam you right in, but I just don't have a single solitary spot.

He looks for his lighter. Willy has picked it up and gives it to him. Pause.

Willy (with increasing anger): Howard, all I need to set my table is fifty dollars a week.

Howard: But where am I going to put you, kid?

Willy: Look, it isn't a question of whether I can sell merchandise, is it?

Howard: No, but it's a business, kid, and everybody's gotta pull his own weight.

Willy (desperately): Just let me tell you a story, Howard —

Howard: 'Cause you gotta admit, business is business.

Willy (angrily): Business is definitely business, but just listen for a minute. You don't understand this. When I was a boy — eighteen, nineteen — I was already on the road. And there was a question in my mind as to whether selling had a future for me. Because in those days I had a yearning to go to Alaska. See, there were three gold strikes in one month in Alaska, and I felt like going out. Just for the ride, you might say.

Howard (barely interested): Don't say.

Willy: Oh, yeah, my father lived many years in Alaska. He was an adventurous man. We've got quite a little streak of self-reliance in our family. I thought I'd go out with my older brother and try to locate him, and maybe settle in the North with the old man. And I was almost decided to go, when I met a salesman in the Parker House. His name was Dave Singleman. And he was eighty-four years old, and he'd drummed merchandise in thirty-one states. And old Dave, he'd go up to his room, y'understand, put on his green velvet slippers — I'll never forget — and pick up his phone and call the buyers, and without ever leaving his room, at the age of eighty-four, he made his living. And when I saw that, I realized that selling was the greatest career a man could want. 'Cause what could be more satisfying than to be able to go, at the age of eighty-four, into twenty or thirty different cities, and pick up a phone, and be remembered and loved and helped by so many different people? Do you know? when he died — and by the way he died the death of a salesman, in his green velvet slippers in the smoker of the New York, New Haven, and Hartford, going into Boston — when he died, hundreds of salesmen and buyers were at his funeral. Things were sad on a lotta trains for months after that. *(He stands up. Howard has not looked at him.)* In those days there was personality in it, Howard. There was respect, and comradeship, and gratitude in it. Today, it's all cut and dried, and there's no chance for bringing friendship to bear — or personality. You see what I mean? They don't know me any more.

Howard (moving away, to the right): That's just the thing, Willy.

Willy: If I had forty dollars a week — that's all I'd need. Forty dollars, Howard.

Howard: Kid, I can't take blood from a stone, I —

Willy (desperation is on him now): Howard, the year Al Smith° was nominated, your father came to me and —

Al Smith: Democratic candidate for president of the United States in 1928 who lost the election to Herbert Hoover.

Howard (starting to go off): I've got to see some people, kid.

Willy (stopping him): I'm talking about your father! There were promises made across this desk! You mustn't tell me you've got people to see — I put thirty-four years into this firm, Howard, and now I can't pay my insurance! You can't eat the orange and throw the peel away — a man is not a piece of fruit! *(After a pause.)* Now pay attention. Your father — in 1928 I had a big year. I averaged a hundred and seventy dollars a week in commissions.

Howard (impatiently): Now, Willy, you never averaged —

Willy (banging his hand on the desk): I averaged a hundred and seventy dollars a week in the year of 1928! And your father came to me — or rather, I was in the office here — it was right over this desk — and he put his hand on my shoulder —

Howard (getting up): You'll have to excuse me, Willy, I gotta see some people. Pull yourself together. *(Going out.)* I'll be back in a little while.

On Howard's exit, the light on his chair grows very bright and strange.

Willy: Pull myself together! What the hell did I say to him? My God, I was yelling at him! How could I! *(Willy breaks off, staring at the light, which occupies the chair, animating it. He approaches this chair, standing across the desk from it.)* Frank, Frank, don't you remember what you told me that time? How you put your hand on my shoulder, and Frank . . . *(He leans on the desk and as he speaks the dead man's name he accidentally switches on the recorder, and instantly:)*

Howard's Son: ". . . of New York is Albany. The capital of Ohio is Cincinnati, the capital of Rhode Island is . . . " *(The recitation continues.)*

Willy (leaping away with fright, shouting): Ha! Howard! Howard! Howard!

Howard (rushing in): What happened?

Willy (pointing at the machine, which continues nasally, childishly, with the capital cities): Shut it off! Shut it off!

Howard (pulling the plug out): Look, Willy . . .

Willy (pressing his hands to his eyes): I gotta get myself some coffee. I'll get some coffee . . .

Willy starts to walk out. Howard stops him.

Howard (rolling up the cord): Willy, look . . .

Willy: I'll go to Boston.

Howard: Willy, you can't go to Boston for us.

Willy: Why can't I go?

Howard: I don't want you to represent us. I've been meaning to tell you for a long time now.

Willy: Howard, are you firing me?

Howard: I think you need a good long rest, Willy.

Willy: Howard —

Howard: And when you feel better, come back, and we'll see if we can work something out.

Willy: But I gotta earn money, Howard. I'm in no position to —

Howard: Where are your sons? Why don't your sons give you a hand?

Willy: They're working on a very big deal.

Howard: This is no time for false pride, Willy. You go to your sons and you tell them that you're tired. You've got two great boys, haven't you?

Willy: Oh, no question, no question, but in the meantime . . .

Howard: Then that's that, heh?

Willy: All right, I'll go to Boston tomorrow.

Howard: No, no.

Willy: I can't throw myself on my sons. I'm not a cripple!

Howard: Look, kid, I'm busy this morning.

Willy (grasping Howard's arm): Howard, you've got to let me go to Boston!

Howard (hard, keeping himself under control): I've got a line of people to see this morning. Sit down, take five minutes, and pull yourself together, and then go home, will ya? I need the office, Willy. *(He starts to go, turns, remembering the recorder, starts to push off the table holding the recorder.)* Oh, yeah. Whenever you can this week, stop by and drop off the samples. You'll feel better, Willy, and then come back and we'll talk. Pull yourself together, kid, there's people outside.

Howard exits, pushing the table off left. Willy stares into space, exhausted. Now the music is heard — Ben's music — first distantly, then closer, closer. As Willy speaks, Ben enters from the right. He carries valise and umbrella.

Willy: Oh, Ben, how did you do it? What is the answer? Did you wind up the Alaska deal already?

Ben: Doesn't take much time if you know what you're doing. Just a short business trip. Boarding ship in an hour. Wanted to say good-by.

Willy: Ben, I've got to talk to you.

Ben (glancing at his watch): Haven't the time, William.

Willy (crossing the apron to Ben): Ben, nothing's working out. I don't know what to do.

Ben: Now, look here, William. I've bought timberland in Alaska and I need a man to look after things for me.

Willy: God, timberland! Me and my boys in those grand outdoors!

Ben: You've a new continent at your doorstep, William. Get out of these cities, they're full of talk and time payments and courts of law. Screw on your fists and you can fight for a fortune up there.

Willy: Yes, yes! Linda, Linda!

Linda enters as of old, with the wash.

Linda: Oh, you're back?

Ben: I haven't much time.

Willy: No, wait! Linda, he's got a proposition for me in Alaska.

Linda: But you've got — *(To Ben.)* He's got a beautiful job here.

Willy: But in Alaska, kid, I could —

Linda: You're doing well enough, Willy!

Ben (to Linda): Enough for what, my dear?

Linda (frightened of Ben and angry at him): Don't say those things to him! Enough to be happy right here, right now. *(To Willy, while Ben laughs.)* Why must everybody conquer the world? You're well liked, and the boys love you, and someday — *(to Ben)* — why, old man Wagner told him just the other day that if he keeps it up he'll be a member of the firm, didn't he, Willy?

Willy: Sure, sure. I am building something with this firm, Ben, and if a man is building something he must be on the right track, mustn't he?

Ben: What are you building? Lay your hand on it. Where is it?

Willy (hesitantly): That's true, Linda, there's nothing.
Linda: Why? *(To Ben.)* There's a man eighty-four years old —
Willy: That's right, Ben, that's right. When I look at that man I say, what is
    there to worry about?
Ben: Bah!
Willy: It's true, Ben. All he has to do is go into any city, pick up the phone, and
    he's making his living and you know why?
Ben (picking up his valise): I've got to go.
Willy (holding Ben back): Look at this boy!

> *Biff, in his high school sweater, enters carrying suitcase. Happy carries Biff's shoulder guards, gold helmet, and football pants.*

Willy: Without a penny to his name, three great universities are begging for
    him, and from there the sky's the limit, because it's not what you do, Ben.
    It's who you know and the smile on your face! It's contacts, Ben, contacts!
    The whole wealth of Alaska passes over the lunch table at the Commodore Hotel, and that's the wonder, the wonder of this country, that a
    man can end with diamonds here on the basis of being liked! *(He turns to
    Biff.)* And that's why when you get out on that field today it's important.
    Because thousands of people will be rooting for you and loving you. *(To
    Ben, who has again begun to leave.)* And Ben! when he walks into a business
    office his name will sound out like a bell and all the doors will open to
    him! I've seen it, Ben, I've seen it a thousand times! You can't feel it with
    your hand like timber, but it's there!
Ben: Good-by, William.
Willy: Ben, am I right? Don't you think I'm right? I value your advice.
Ben: There's a new continent at your doorstep, William. You could walk out
    rich. Rich! *(He is gone.)*
Willy: We'll do it here, Ben! You hear me? We're gonna do it here!

> *Young Bernard rushes in. The gay music of the Boys is heard.*

Bernard: Oh, gee, I was afraid you left already!
Willy: Why? What time is it?
Bernard: It's half-past one!
Willy: Well, come on, everybody! Ebbets Field next stop! Where's the pennants?
    (He rushes through the wall-line of the kitchen and out into the living-room.)
Linda (to Biff): Did you pack fresh underwear?
Biff (who has been limbering up): I want to go!
Bernard: Biff, I'm carrying your helmet, ain't I?
Happy: I'm carrying the helmet.
Bernard: How am I going to get in the locker room?
Linda: Let him carry the shoulder guards. *(She puts her coat and hat on in the
    kitchen.)*
Bernard: Can I, Biff? 'Cause I told everybody I'm going to be in the locker
    room.
Happy: In Ebbets Field it's the clubhouse.
Bernard: I meant the clubhouse. Biff!
Happy: Biff!
Biff (grandly, after a slight pause): Let him carry the shoulder guards.
Happy (as he gives Bernard the shoulder guards): Stay close to us now.

Willy rushes in with the pennants.

Willy *(handing them out):* Everybody wave when Biff comes out on the field. *(Happy and Bernard run off.)* You set now, boy?

The music has died away.

Biff: Ready to go, Pop. Every muscle is ready.

Willy *(at the edge of the apron):* You realize what this means?

Biff: That's right, Pop.

Willy *(feeling Biff's muscles):* You're comin' home this afternoon captain of the All-Scholastic Championship Team of the City of New York.

Biff: I got it, Pop. And remember, pal, when I take off my helmet, that touchdown is for you.

Willy: Let's go! *(He is starting out, with his arm around Biff, when Charley enters, as of old, in knickers.)* I got no room for you, Charley.

Charley: Room? For what?

Willy: In the car.

Charley: You goin' for a ride? I wanted to shoot some casino.

Willy *(furiously):* Casino! *(Incredulously.)* Don't you realize what today is?

Linda: Oh, he knows, Willy. He's just kidding you.

Willy: That's nothing to kid about!

Charley: No, Linda, what's goin' on?

Linda: He's playing in Ebbets Field.

Charley: Baseball in this weather?

Willy: Don't talk to him. Come on, come on! *(He is pushing them out.)*

Charley: Wait a minute, didn't you hear the news?

Willy: What?

Charley: Don't you listen to the radio? Ebbets Field just blew up.

Willy: You go to hell! *(Charley laughs. Pushing them out.)* Come on, come on! We're late.

Charley *(as they go):* Knock a homer, Biff, knock a homer!

Willy *(the last to leave, turning to Charley):* I don't think that was funny, Charley. This is the greatest day of his life.

Charley: Willy, when are you going to grow up?

Willy: Yeah, heh? When this game is over, Charley, you'll be laughing out of the other side of your face. They'll be calling him another Red Grange. Twenty-five thousand a year.

Charley *(kidding):* Is that so?

Willy: Yeah, that's so.

Charley: Well, then, I'm sorry, Willy. But tell me something.

Willy: What?

Charley: Who is Red Grange?

Willy: Put up your hands. Goddam you, put up your hands!

Charley, chuckling, shakes his head and walks away, around the left corner of the stage. Willy follows him. The music rises to a mocking frenzy.

Willy: Who the hell do you think you are, better than everybody else? You don't know everything, you big, ignorant, stupid . . . Put up your hands!

Light rises, on the right side of the forestage, on a small table in the reception room of Charley's office. Traffic sounds are heard. Bernard, now mature, sits whistling to himself. A pair of tennis rackets and an overnight bag are on the floor beside him.

Willy (offstage): What are you walking away for? Don't walk away! If you're going to say something say it to my face! I know you laugh at me behind my back. You'll laugh out of the other side of your goddam face after this game. Touchdown! Touchdown! Eighty thousand people! Touchdown! Right between the goal posts.

> *Bernard is a quiet, earnest, but self-assured young man. Willy's voice is coming from right upstage now. Bernard lowers his feet off the table and listens. Jenny, his father's secretary, enters.*

Jenny (distressed): Say, Bernard, will you go out in the hall?

Bernard: What is that noise? Who is it?

Jenny: Mr. Loman. He just got off the elevator.

Bernard (getting up): Who's he arguing with?

Jenny: Nobody. There's nobody with him. I can't deal with him any more, and your father gets all upset everytime he comes. I've got a lot of typing to do, and your father's waiting to sign it. Will you see him?

Willy (entering): Touchdown! Touch — *(He sees Jenny.)* Jenny, Jenny, good to see you. How're ya? Workin'? Or still honest?

Jenny: Fine. How've you been feeling?

Willy: Not much any more, Jenny. Ha, ha! *(He is surprised to see the rackets.)*

Bernard: Hello, Uncle Willy.

Willy (almost shocked): Bernard! Well, look who's here! *(He comes quickly, guiltily, to Bernard and warmly shakes his hand.)*

Bernard: How are you? Good to see you.

Willy: What are you doing here?

Bernard: Oh, just stopped by to see Pop. Get off my feet till my train leaves. I'm going to Washington in a few minutes.

Willy: Is he in?

Bernard: Yes, he's in his office with the accountant. Sit down.

Willy (sitting down): What're you going to do in Washington?

Bernard: Oh, just a case I've got there, Willy.

Willy: That so? *(Indicating the rackets.)* You going to play tennis there?

Bernard: I'm staying with a friend who's got a court.

Willy: Don't say. His own tennis court. Must be fine people, I bet.

Bernard: They are, very nice. Dad tells me Biff's in town.

Willy (with a big smile): Yeah, Biff's in. Working on a very big deal, Bernard.

Bernard: What's Biff doing?

Willy: Well, he's been doing very big things in the West. But he decided to establish himself here. Very big. We're having dinner. Did I hear your wife had a boy?

Bernard: That's right. Our second.

Willy: Two boys! What do you know!

Bernard: What kind of a deal has Biff got?

Willy: Well, Bill Oliver — very big sporting-goods man — he wants Biff very badly. Called him in from the West. Long distance, carte blanche, special deliveries. Your friends have their own private tennis court?

Bernard: You still with the old firm, Willy?

Willy (after a pause): I'm — I'm overjoyed to see how you made the grade, Bernard, overjoyed. It's an encouraging thing to see a young man really — really — Looks very good for Biff — very — *(He breaks off, then.)* Bernard — *(He is so full of emotion, he breaks off again.)*

Bernard: What is it, Willy?

Willy (small and alone): What — what's the secret?

Bernard: What secret?

Willy: How — how did you? Why didn't he ever catch on?

Bernard: I wouldn't know that, Willy.

Willy (confidentially, desperately): You were his friend, his boyhood friend. There's something I don't understand about it. His life ended after that Ebbets Field game. From the age of seventeen nothing good ever happened to him.

Bernard: He never trained himself for anything.

Willy: But he did, he did. After high school he took so many correspondence courses. Radio mechanics; television; God knows what, and never made the slightest mark.

Bernard (taking off his glasses): Willy, do you want to talk candidly?

Willy (rising, faces Bernard): I regard you as a very brilliant man, Bernard. I value your advice.

Bernard: Oh, the hell with the advice, Willy. I couldn't advise you. There's just one thing I've always wanted to ask you. When he was supposed to graduate, and the math teacher flunked him —

Willy: Oh, that son-of-a-bitch ruined his life.

Bernard: Yeah, but, Willy, all he had to do was go to summer school and make up that subject.

Willy: That's right, that's right.

Bernard: Did you tell him not to go to summer school?

Willy: Me? I begged him to go. I ordered him to go!

Bernard: Then why wouldn't he go?

Willy: Why? Why! Bernard, that question has been trailing me like a ghost for the last fifteen years. He flunked the subject, and laid down and died like a hammer hit him!

Bernard: Take it easy, kid.

Willy: Let me talk to you — I got nobody to talk to. Bernard, Bernard, was it my fault? Y'see? It keeps going around in my mind, maybe I did something to him. I got nothing to give him.

Bernard: Don't take it so hard.

Willy: Why did he lay down? What is the story there? You were his friend!

Bernard: Willy, I remember, it was June, and our grades came out. And he'd flunked math.

Willy: That son-of-a-bitch!

Bernard: No, it wasn't right then. Biff just got very angry, I remember, and he was ready to enroll in summer school.

Willy (surprised): He was?

Bernard: He wasn't beaten by it at all. But then, Willy, he disappeared from the block for almost a month. And I got the idea that he'd gone up to New England to see you. Did he have a talk with you then?

Willy stares in silence.

Bernard: Willy?

Willy (with a strong edge of resentment in his voice): Yeah, he came to Boston. What about it?

Bernard: Well, just that when he came back — I'll never forget this, it always mystifies me. Because I'd thought so well of Biff, even though he'd always taken advantage of me. I loved him, Willy, y'know? And he came back after that month and took his sneakers — remember those sneakers with "University of Virginia" printed on them? He was so proud of those, wore them every day. And he took them down in the cellar, and burned them up in the furnace. We had a fist fight. It lasted at least half an hour. Just the two of us, punching each other down the cellar, and crying right through it. I've often thought of how strange it was that I knew he'd given up his life. What happened in Boston, Willy?

Willy looks at him as at an intruder.

Bernard: I just bring it up because you asked me.

Willy (angrily): Nothing. What do you mean, "What happened?" What's that got to do with anything?

Bernard: Well, don't get sore.

Willy: What are you trying to do, blame it on me? If a boy lays down is that my fault?

Bernard: Now, Willy, don't get—

Willy: Well, don't—don't talk to me that way! What does that mean, "What happened?"

Charley enters. He is in his vest, and he carries a bottle of bourbon.

Charley: Hey, you're going to miss that train. *(He waves the bottle.)*

Bernard: Yeah, I'm going. *(He takes the bottle.)* Thanks, Pop. *(He picks up his rackets and bag.)* Good-by, Willy, and don't worry about it. You know. "If at first you don't succeed . . ."

Willy: Yes, I believe in that.

Bernard: But sometimes, Willy, it's better for a man just to walk away.

Willy: Walk away?

Bernard: That's right.

Willy: But if you can't walk away?

Bernard (after a slight pause): I guess that's when it's tough. *(Extending his hand.)* Good-by, Willy.

Willy (shaking Bernard's hand): Good-by, boy.

Charley (an arm on Bernard's shoulder): How do you like this kid? Gonna argue a case in front of the Supreme Court.

Bernard (protesting): Pop!

Willy (genuinely shocked, pained, and happy): No! The Supreme Court!

Bernard: I gotta run. 'By, Dad!

Charley: Knock 'em dead, Bernard!

    Bernard goes off.

Willy (as Charley takes out his wallet): The Supreme Court! And he didn't even mention it!

Charley (counting out money on the desk): He don't have to—he's gonna do it.

Willy: And you never told him what to do, did you? You never took any interest in him.

Charley: My salvation is that I never took any interest in any thing. There's some money—fifty dollars. I got an accountant inside.

Willy: Charley, look . . . *(With difficulty.)* I got my insurance to pay. If you can manage it—I need a hundred and ten dollars.

Charley doesn't reply for a moment; merely stops moving.

Willy: I'd draw it from my bank but Linda would know, and I . . .

Charley: Sit down, Willy.

Willy (moving toward the chair): I'm keeping an account of everything, remember. I'll pay every penny back. *(He sits.)*

Charley: Now listen to me, Willy.

Willy: I want you to know I appreciate . . .

Charley (sitting down on the table): Willy, what're you doin'? What the hell is goin' on in your head?

Willy: Why? I'm simply . . .

Charley: I offered you a job. You can make fifty dollars a week. And I won't send you on the road.

Willy: I've got a job.

Charley: Without pay? What kind of a job is a job without pay? *(He rises.)* Now, look, kid, enough is enough. I'm no genius but I know when I'm being insulted.

Willy: Insulted!

Charley: Why don't you want to work for me?

Willy: What's the matter with you? I've got a job.

Charley: Then what're you walkin' in here every week for?

Willy (getting up): Well, if you don't want me to walk in here —

Charley: I am offering you a job.

Willy: I don't want your goddam job!

Charley: When the hell are you going to grow up?

Willy (furiously): You big ignoramus, if you say that to me again I'll rap you one! I don't care how big you are! *(He's ready to fight.)*

   Pause.

Charley (kindly, going to him): How much do you need, Willy?

Willy: Charley, I'm strapped. I'm strapped. I don't know what to do. I was just fired.

Charley: Howard fired you?

Willy: That snotnose. Imagine that? I named him. I named him Howard.

Charley: Willy, when're you gonna realize that them things don't mean anything? You named him Howard, but you can't sell that. The only thing you got in this world is what you can sell. And the funny thing is that you're a salesman, and you don't know that.

Willy: I've always tried to think otherwise, I guess. I always felt that if a man was impressive, and well liked, that nothing —

Charley: Why must everybody like you? Who liked J. P. Morgan? Was he impressive? In a Turkish bath he'd look like a butcher. But with his pockets on he was very well liked. Now listen, Willy, I know you don't like me, and nobody can say I'm in love with you, but I'll give you a job because — just for the hell of it, put it that way. Now what do you say?

Willy: I — I just can't work for you, Charley.

Charley: What're you, jealous of me?

Willy: I can't work for you, that's all, don't ask me why.

Charley (angered, takes out more bills): You been jealous of me all your life, you damned fool! Here, pay your insurance. *(He puts the money in Willy's hand.)*

Willy: I'm keeping strict accounts.

Charley: I've got some work to do. Take care of yourself. And pay your insurance.

Willy (moving to the right): Funny, y'know? After all the highways, and the trains, and the appointments, and the years, you end up worth more dead than alive.

Charley: Willy, nobody's worth nothin' dead. *(After a slight pause.)* Did you hear what I said?

Willy stands still, dreaming.

Charley: Willy!

Willy: Apologize to Bernard for me when you see him. I didn't mean to argue with him. He's a fine boy. They're all fine boys, and they'll end up big—all of them. Someday they'll all play tennis together. Wish me luck, Charley. He saw Bill Oliver today.

Charley: Good luck.

Willy (on the verge of tears): Charley, you're the only friend I got. Isn't that a remarkable thing? *(He goes out.)*

Charley: Jesus!

Charley stares after him a moment and follows. All light blacks out. Suddenly raucous music is heard, and a red glow rises behind the screen at right. Stanley, a young waiter, appears, carrying a table, followed by Happy, who is carrying two chairs.

Stanley (putting the table down): That's all right, Mr. Loman, I can handle it myself. *(He turns and takes the chairs from Happy and places them at the table.)*

Happy (glancing around): Oh, this is better.

Stanley: Sure, in the front there you're in the middle of all kinds a noise. Whenever you got a party, Mr. Loman, you just tell me and I'll put you back here. Y'know, there's a lotta people they don't like it private, because when they go out they like to see a lotta action around them because they're sick and tired to stay in the house by theirself. But I know you, you ain't from Hackensack. You know what I mean?

Happy (sitting down): So how's it coming, Stanley?

Stanley: Ah, it's a dog's life. I only wish during the war they'd a took me in the Army. I coulda been dead by now.

Happy: My brother's back, Stanley.

Stanley: Oh, he come back, heh? From the Far West.

Happy: Yeah, big cattle man, my brother, so treat him right. And my father's coming too.

Stanley: Oh, your father too!

Happy: You got a couple of nice lobsters?

Stanley: Hundred per cent, big.

Happy: I want them with the claws.

Stanley: Don't worry, I don't give you no mice. *(Happy laughs.)* How about some wine? It'll put a head on the meal.

Happy: No. You remember, Stanley, that recipe I brought you from overseas? With the champagne in it?

Stanley: Oh, yeah, sure. I still got it tacked up yet in the kitchen. But that'll have to cost a buck apiece anyways.

Happy: That's all right.

Stanley: What'd you, hit a number or somethin'?

Happy: No, it's a little celebration. My brother is — I think he pulled off a big deal today. I think we're going into business together.

Stanley: Great! That's the best for you. Because a family business, you know what I mean? — that's the best.

Happy: That's what I think.

Stanley: 'Cause what's the difference? Somebody steals? It's in the family. Know what I mean? (*Sotto voce.*°) Like this bartender here. The boss is goin' crazy what kinda leak he's got in the cash register. You put it in but it don't come out.

Happy (raising his head): Sh!

Stanley: What?

Happy: You notice I wasn't lookin' right or left, was I?

Stanley: No.

Happy: And my eyes are closed.

Stanley: So what's the —?

Happy: Strudel's comin'.

Stanley (catching on, looks around): Ah, no, there's no —

> He breaks off as a furred, lavishly dressed girl enters and sits at the next table. Both follow her with their eyes.

Stanley: Geez, how'd ya know?

Happy: I got radar or something. (*Staring directly at her profile.*) Oooooooo . . . Stanley.

Stanley: I think that's for you, Mr. Loman.

Happy: Look at that mouth. Oh, God. And the binoculars.

Stanley: Geez, you got a life, Mr. Loman.

Happy: Wait on her.

Stanley (going to the girl's table): Would you like a menu, ma'am?

Girl: I'm expecting someone, but I'd like a —

Happy: Why don't you bring her — excuse me, miss, do you mind? I sell champagne, and I'd like you to try my brand. Bring her a champagne, Stanley.

Girl: That's awfully nice of you.

Happy: Don't mention it. It's all company money. (*He laughs.*)

Girl: That's a charming product to be selling, isn't it?

Happy: Oh, gets to be like everything else. Selling is selling, y'know.

Girl: I suppose.

Happy: You don't happen to sell, do you?

Girl: No, I don't sell.

Happy: Would you object to a compliment from a stranger? You ought to be on a magazine cover.

Girl (looking at him a little archly): I have been.

> Stanley comes in with a glass of champagne.

Happy: What'd I say before, Stanley? You see? She's a cover girl.

Stanley: Oh, I could see, I could see.

Happy (to the Girl): What magazine?

Girl: Oh, a lot of them. (*She takes the drink.*) Thank you.

Sotto voce: Softly, "under the breath" (Italian).

Happy: You know what they say in France, don't you? "Champagne is the drink of the complexion" — Hya, Biff!

> *Biff has entered and sits with Happy.*

Biff: Hello, kid. Sorry I'm late.
Happy: I just got here. Uh, Miss — ?
Girl: Forsythe.
Happy: Miss Forsythe, this is my brother.
Biff: Is Dad here?
Happy: His name is Biff. You might've heard of him. Great football player.
Girl: Really? What team?
Happy: Are you familiar with football?
Girl: No, I'm afraid I'm not.
Happy: Biff is quarterback with the New York Giants.
Girl: Well, that is nice, isn't it? *(She drinks.)*
Happy: Good health.
Girl: I'm happy to meet you.
Happy: That's my name. Hap. It's really Harold, but at West Point they called me Happy.
Girl (now really impressed): Oh, I see. How do you do? *(She turns her profile.)*
Biff: Isn't Dad coming?
Happy: You want her?
Biff: Oh, I could never make that.
Happy: I remember the time that idea would never come into your head. Where's the old confidence, Biff?
Biff: I just saw Oliver —
Happy: Wait a minute. I've got to see that old confidence again. Do you want her? She's on call.
Biff: Oh, no. *(He turns to look at the Girl.)*
Happy: I'm telling you. Watch this. *(Turning to the Girl.)* Honey? *(She turns to him.)* Are you busy?
Girl: Well, I am . . . but I could make a phone call.
Happy: Do that, will you, honey? And see if you can get a friend. We'll be here for a while. Biff is one of the greatest football players in the country.
Girl (standing up): Well, I'm certainly happy to meet you.
Happy: Come back soon.
Girl: I'll try.
Happy: Don't try, honey, try hard.

> *The Girl exits. Stanley follows, shaking his head in bewildered admiration.*

Happy: Isn't that a shame now? A beautiful girl like that? That's why I can't get married. There's not a good woman in a thousand. New York is loaded with them, kid!
Biff: Hap, look —
Happy: I told you she was on call!
Biff (strangely unnerved): Cut it out, will ya? I want to say something to you.
Happy: Did you see Oliver?
Biff: I saw him all right. Now look, I want to tell Dad a couple of things and I want you to help me.
Happy: What? Is he going to back you?

Biff: Are you crazy? You're out of your goddam head, you know that?

Happy: Why? What happened?

Biff (breathlessly): I did a terrible thing today, Hap. It's been the strangest day I ever went through. I'm all numb, I swear.

Happy: You mean he wouldn't see you?

Biff: Well, I waited six hours for him, see? All day. Kept sending my name in. Even tried to date his secretary so she'd get me to him, but no soap.

Happy: Because you're not showin' the old confidence, Biff. He remembered you, didn't he?

Biff (stopping Happy with a gesture): Finally, about five o'clock, he comes out. Didn't remember who I was or anything. I felt like such an idiot, Hap.

Happy: Did you tell him my Florida idea?

Biff: He walked away. I saw him for one minute. I got so mad I could've torn the walls down! How the hell did I ever get the idea I was a salesman there? I even believed myself that I'd been a salesman for him! And then he gave me one look and — I realized what a ridiculous lie my whole life has been! We've been talking in a dream for fifteen years. I was a shipping clerk.

Happy: What'd you do?

Biff (with great tension and wonder): Well, he left, see. And the secretary went out. I was all alone in the waiting-room. I don't know what came over me, Hap. The next thing I know I'm in his office — paneled walls, everything. I can't explain it. I — Hap, I took his fountain pen.

Happy: Geez, did he catch you?

Biff: I ran out. I ran down all eleven flights. I ran and ran and ran.

Happy: That was an awful dumb — what'd you do that for?

Biff (agonized): I don't know, I just — wanted to take something, I don't know. You gotta help me, Hap, I'm gonna tell Pop.

Happy: You crazy? What for?

Biff: Hap, he's got to understand that I'm not the man somebody lends that kind of money to. He thinks I've been spiting him all these years and it's eating him up.

Happy: That's just it. You tell him something nice.

Biff: I can't.

Happy: Say you got a lunch date with Oliver tomorrow.

Biff: So what do I do tomorrow?

Happy: You leave the house tomorrow and come back at night and say Oliver is thinking it over. And he thinks it over for a couple of weeks, and gradually it fades away and nobody's the worse.

Biff: But it'll go on forever!

Happy: Dad is never so happy as when he's looking forward to something!

Willy enters.

Happy: Hello, scout!

Willy: Gee, I haven't been here in years!

Stanley has followed Willy in and sets a chair for him. Stanley starts off but Happy stops him.

Happy: Stanley!

Stanley stands by, waiting for an order.

Biff (going to Willy with guilt, as to an invalid): Sit down, Pop. You want a drink?

Willy: Sure, I don't mind.

Biff: Let's get a load on.

Willy: You look worried.

Biff: N-no. *(To Stanley.)* Scotch all around. Make it doubles.

Stanley: Doubles, right. *(He goes.)*

Willy: You had a couple already, didn't you?

Biff: Just a couple, yeah.

Willy: Well, what happened, boy? *(Nodding affirmatively, with a smile.)* Everything go all right?

Biff (takes a breath, then reaches out and grasps Willy's hand): Pal . . . *(He is smiling bravely, and Willy is smiling too.)* I had an experience today.

Happy: Terrific, Pop.

Willy: That so? What happened?

Biff (high, slightly alcoholic, above the earth): I'm going to tell you everything from first to last. It's been a strange day. *(Silence. He looks around, composes himself as best he can, but his breath keeps breaking the rhythm of his voice.)* I had to wait quite a while for him, and—

Willy: Oliver.

Biff: Yeah, Oliver. All day, as a matter of cold fact. And a lot of—instances—facts, Pop, facts about my life came back to me. Who was it, Pop? Who ever said I was a salesman with Oliver?

Willy: Well, you were.

Biff: No, Dad, I was a shipping clerk.

Willy: But you were practically—

Biff (with determination): Dad, I don't know who said it first, but I was never a salesman for Bill Oliver.

Willy: What're you talking about?

Biff: Let's hold on to the facts tonight, Pop. We're not going to get anywhere bullin' around. I was a shipping clerk.

Willy (angrily): All right, now listen to me—

Biff: Why don't you let me finish?

Willy: I'm not interested in stories about the past or any crap of that kind because the woods are burning, boys, you understand? There's a big blaze going on all around. I was fired today.

Biff (shocked): How could you be?

Willy: I was fired, and I'm looking for a little good news to tell your mother, because the woman has waited and the woman has suffered. The gist of it is that I haven't got a story left in my head, Biff. So don't give me a lecture about facts and aspects. I am not interested. Now what've you got to say to me?

Stanley enters with three drinks. They wait until he leaves.

Willy: Did you see Oliver?

Biff: Jesus, Dad!

Willy: You mean you didn't go up there?

Happy: Sure he went up there.

Biff: I did. I—saw him. How could they fire you?

Willy (on the edge of his chair): What kind of a welcome did he give you?

Biff: He won't even let you work on commission?

Willy: I'm out! *(Driving.)* So tell me, he gave you a warm welcome?

Happy: Sure, Pop, sure!

Biff (driven): Well, it was kind of—

Willy: I was wondering if he'd remember you. *(To Happy.)* Imagine, man doesn't see him for ten, twelve years and gives him that kind of a welcome!

Happy: Damn right!

Biff (trying to return to the offensive): Pop, look—

Willy: You know why he remembered you, don't you? Because you impressed him in those days.

Biff: Let's talk quietly and get this down to the facts, huh?

Willy (as though Biff had been interrupting): Well, what happened? It's great news, Biff. Did he take you into his office or'd you talk in the waiting-room?

Biff: Well, he came in, see, and—

Willy (with a big smile): What'd he say? Betcha he threw his arm around you.

Biff: Well, he kinda—

Willy: He's a fine man. *(To Happy.)* Very hard man to see, y'know.

Happy (agreeing): Oh, I know.

Willy (to Biff): Is that where you had the drinks?

Biff: Yeah, he gave me a couple of—no, no!

Happy (cutting in): He told him my Florida idea.

Willy: Don't interrupt. *(To Biff.)* How'd he react to the Florida idea?

Biff: Dad, will you give me a minute to explain?

Willy: I've been waiting for you to explain since I sat down here! What happened? He took you into his office and what?

Biff: Well—I talked. And—and he listened, see.

Willy: Famous for the way he listens, y'know. What was his answer?

Biff: His answer was—*(He breaks off, suddenly angry.)* Dad, you're not letting me tell you what I want to tell you!

Willy (accusing, angered): You didn't see him, did you?

Biff: I did see him!

Willy: What'd you insult him or something? You insulted him, didn't you?

Biff: Listen, will you let me out of it, will you just let me out of it!

Happy: What the hell!

Willy: Tell me what happened!

Biff (to Happy): I can't talk to him!

> *A single trumpet note jars the ear. The light of green leaves stains the house, which holds the air of night and a dream. Young Bernard enters and knocks on the door of the house.*

Young Bernard (frantically): Mrs. Loman, Mrs. Loman!

Happy: Tell him what happened!

Biff (to Happy): Shut up and leave me alone!

Willy: No, no! You had to go and flunk math!

Biff: What math? What're you talking about?

Young Bernard: Mrs. Loman, Mrs. Loman!

> *Linda appears in the house, as of old.*

Willy (wildly): Math, math, math!

Biff: Take it easy, Pop!

Young Bernard: Mrs. Loman!

Willy (furiously): If you hadn't flunked you'd've been set by now!

Biff: Now, look, I'm gonna tell you what happened, and you're going to listen to me.

Young Bernard: Mrs. Loman!

Biff: I waited six hours —

Happy: What the hell are you saying?

Biff: I kept sending in my name but he wouldn't see me. So finally he . . . *(He continues unheard as light fades low on the restaurant.)*

Young Bernard: Biff flunked math!

Linda: No!

Young Bernard: Birnbaum flunked him! They won't graduate him!

Linda: But they have to. He's gotta go to the university. Where is he? Biff! Biff!

Young Bernard: No, he left. He went to Grand Central.

Linda: Grand — You mean he went to Boston!

Young Bernard: Is Uncle Willy in Boston?

Linda: Oh, maybe Willy can talk to the teacher. Oh, the poor, poor boy!

Light on house area snaps out.

Biff (at the table, now audible, holding up a gold fountain pen): . . . so I'm washed up with Oliver, you understand? Are you listening to me?

Willy (at a loss): Yeah, sure. If you hadn't flunked —

Biff: Flunked what? What're you talking about?

Willy: Don't blame everything on me! I didn't flunk math — you did! What pen?

Happy: That was awful dumb, Biff, a pen like that is worth —

Willy (seeing the pen for the first time): You took Oliver's pen?

Biff (weakening): Dad, I just explained it to you.

Willy: You stole Bill Oliver's fountain pen!

Biff: I didn't exactly steal it! That's just what I've been explaining to you!

Happy: He had it in his hand and just then Oliver walked in, so he got nervous and stuck it in his pocket!

Willy: My God, Biff!

Biff: I never intended to do it, Dad!

Operator's Voice: Standish Arms, good evening!

Willy (shouting): I'm not in my room!

Biff (frightened): Dad, what's the matter? *(He and Happy stand up.)*

Operator: Ringing Mr. Loman for you!

Willy: I'm not there, stop it!

Biff (horrified, gets down on one knee before Willy): Dad, I'll make good, I'll make good. *(Willy tries to get to his feet. Biff holds him down.)* Sit down now.

Willy: No, you're no good, you're no good for anything.

Biff: I am, Dad, I'll find something else, you understand? Now don't worry about anything. *(He holds up Willy's face.)* Talk to me, Dad.

Operator: Mr. Loman does not answer. Shall I page him?

Willy (attempting to stand, as though to rush and silence the Operator): No, no, no!

Happy: He'll strike something, Pop.

Willy: No, no . . .

Biff (desperately, standing over Willy): Pop, listen! Listen to me! I'm telling you something good. Oliver talked to his partner about the Florida idea. You listening? He — he talked to his partner, and he came to me . . . I'm going to be all right, you hear? Dad, listen to me, he said it was just a question of the amount!

Willy: Then you . . . got it?

Happy: He's gonna be terrific, Pop!

Willy (trying to stand): Then you got it, haven't you? You got it! You got it!

Biff (agonized, holds Willy down): No, no. Look, Pop. I'm supposed to have lunch with them tomorrow. I'm just telling you this so you'll know that I can still make an impression, Pop. And I'll make good somewhere, but I can't go tomorrow, see?

Willy: Why not? You simply —

Biff: But the pen, Pop!

Willy: You give it to him and tell him it was an oversight!

Happy: Sure, have lunch tomorrow!

Biff: I can't say that —

Willy: You were doing a crossword puzzle and accidentally used his pen!

Biff: Listen, kid, I took those balls years ago, now I walk in with his fountain pen? That clinches it, don't you see? I can't face him like that! I'll try elsewhere.

Page's Voice: Paging Mr. Loman!

Willy: Don't you want to be anything?

Biff: Pop, how can I go back?

Willy: You don't want to be anything, is that what's behind it?

Biff (now angry at Willy for not crediting his sympathy): Don't take it that way! You think it was easy walking into that office after what I'd done to him? A team of horses couldn't have dragged me back to Bill Oliver!

Willy: Then why'd you go?

Biff: Why did I go? Why did I go! Look at you! Look at what's become of you!

> *Off left, The Woman laughs.*

Willy: Biff, you're going to lunch tomorrow, or —

Biff: I can't go. I've got no appointment!

Happy: Biff, for . . . !

Willy: Are you spiting me?

Biff: Don't take it that way! Goddammit!

Willy (strikes Biff and falters away from the table): You rotten little louse! Are you spiting me?

The Woman: Someone's at the door, Willy!

Biff: I'm no good, can't you see what I am?

Happy (separating them): Hey, you're in a restaurant! Now cut it out, both of you! *(The girls enter.)* Hello, girls, sit down.

> *The Woman laughs, off left.*

Miss Forsythe: I guess we might as well. This is Letta.

The Woman: Willy, are you going to wake up?

Biff (ignoring Willy): How're ya, miss, sit down. What do you drink?

Miss Forsythe: Letta might not be able to stay long.

Letta: I gotta get up very early tomorrow. I got jury duty. I'm so excited! Were you fellows ever on a jury?

Biff: No, but I been in front of them! *(The girls laugh.)* This is my father.

Letta: Isn't he cute? Sit down with us, Pop.

Happy: Sit him down, Biff!

Biff (going to him): Come on, slugger, drink us under the table. To hell with it! Come on, sit down, pal.

On Biff's last insistence, Willy is about to sit.

The Woman (now urgently): Willy, are you going to answer the door!

The Woman's call pulls Willy back. He starts right, befuddled.

Biff: Hey, where are you going?

Willy: Open the door.

Biff: The door?

Willy: The washroom . . . the door . . . where's the door?

Biff (leading Willy to the left): Just go straight down.

Willy moves left.

The Woman: Willy, Willy, are you going to get up, get up, get up, get up?

Willy exits left.

Letta: I think it's sweet you bring your daddy along.

Miss Forsythe: Oh, he isn't really your father!

Biff (at left, turning to her resentfully): Miss Forsythe, you've just seen a prince walk by. A fine, troubled prince. A hard-working, unappreciated prince. A pal, you understand? A good companion. Always for his boys.

Letta: That's so sweet.

Happy: Well, girls, what's the program? We're wasting time. Come on, Biff. Gather round. Where would you like to go?

Biff: Why don't you do something for him?

Happy: Me!

Biff: Don't you give a damn for him, Hap?

Happy: What're you talking about? I'm the one who —

Biff: I sense it, you don't give a good goddamn about him. *(He takes the rolled-up hose from his pocket and puts it on the table in front of Happy.)* Look what I found in the cellar, for Christ's sake. How can you bear to let it go on?

Happy: Me? Who goes away? Who runs off and —

Biff: Yeah, but he doesn't mean anything to you. You could help him — I can't! Don't you understand what I'm talking about? He's going to kill himself, don't you know that?

Happy: Don't I know it! Me!

Biff: Hap, help him! Jesus . . . help him . . . Help me, help me, I can't bear to look at his face! *(Ready to weep, he hurries out, up right.)*

Happy (starting after him): Where are you going?

Miss Forsythe: What's he so mad about?

Happy: Come on, girls, we'll catch up with him.

Miss Forsythe (as Happy pushes her out): Say, I don't like that temper of his!

Happy: He's just a little overstrung, he'll be all right!

Willy (off left, as The Woman laughs): Don't answer! Don't answer!

Letta: Don't you want to tell your father —

Happy: No, that's not my father. He's just a guy. Come on, we'll catch Biff, and, honey, we're going to paint this town! Stanley, where's the check! Hey, Stanley!

They exit. Stanley looks toward left.

Stanley (calling to Happy indignantly): Mr. Loman! Mr. Loman!

Stanley picks up a chair and follows them off. Knocking is heard off left. The Woman enters, laughing. Willy follows her. She is in a black slip; he is buttoning his shirt. Raw, sensuous music accompanies their speech.

Willy: Will you stop laughing? Will you stop?

The Woman: Aren't you going to answer the door? He'll wake the whole hotel.

Willy: I'm not expecting anybody.

The Woman: Whyn't you have another drink, honey, and stop being so damn self-centered?

Willy: I'm so lonely.

The Woman: You know you ruined me, Willy? From now on, whenever you come to the office, I'll see that you go right through to the buyers. No waiting at my desk any more, Willy. You ruined me.

Willy: That's nice of you to say that.

The Woman: Gee, you are self-centered! Why so sad? You are the saddest, self-centeredest soul I ever did see-saw. *(She laughs. He kisses her.)* Come on inside, drummer boy. It's silly to be dressing in the middle of the night. *(As knocking is heard.)* Aren't you going to answer the door?

Willy: They're knocking on the wrong door.

The Woman: But I felt the knocking. And he heard us talking in here. Maybe the hotel's on fire!

Willy (his terror rising): It's a mistake.

The Woman: Then tell him to go away!

Willy: There's nobody there.

The Woman: It's getting on my nerves, Willy. There's somebody standing out there and it's getting on my nerves!

Willy (pushing her away from him): All right, stay in the bathroom here, and don't come out. I think there's a law in Massachusetts about it, so don't come out. It may be that new room clerk. He looked very mean. So don't come out. It's a mistake, there's no fire.

The knocking is heard again. He takes a few steps away from her, and she vanishes into the wing. The light follows him, and now he is facing Young Biff, who carries a suitcase. Biff steps toward him. The music is gone.

Biff: Why didn't you answer?

Willy: Biff! What are you doing in Boston?

Biff: Why didn't you answer? I've been knocking for five minutes, I called you on the phone—

Willy: I just heard you. I was in the bathroom and had the door shut. Did anything happen home?

Biff: Dad—I let you down.

Willy: What do you mean?

Biff: Dad . . .

Willy: Biffo, what's this about? *(Putting his arm around Biff.)* Come on, let's go downstairs and get you a malted.

Biff: Dad, I flunked math.

Willy: Not for the term?

Biff: The term. I haven't got enough credits to graduate.

Willy: You mean to say Bernard wouldn't give you the answers?

Biff: He did, he tried, but I only got a sixty-one.

Willy: And they wouldn't give you four points?

Biff: Birnbaum refused absolutely. I begged him, Pop, but he won't give me those points. You gotta talk to him before they close the school. Because if he saw the kind of man you are, and you just talked to him in your way,

I'm sure he'd come through for me. The class came right before practice, see, and I didn't go enough. Would you talk to him? He'd like you, Pop. You know the way you could talk.

Willy: You're on. We'll drive right back.

Biff: Oh, Dad, good work! I'm sure he'll change it for you!

Willy: Go downstairs and tell the clerk I'm checkin' out. Go right down.

Biff: Yes, sir! See, the reason he hates me, Pop — one day he was late for class so I got up at the blackboard and imitated him. I crossed my eyes and talked with a lithp.

Willy (laughing): You did? The kids like it?

Biff: They nearly died laughing!

Willy: Yeah? What'd you do?

Biff: The thquare root of thixthy twee is . . . (*Willy bursts out laughing; Biff joins him.*) And in the middle of it he walked in!

Willy laughs and The Woman joins in offstage.

Willy (without hesitation): Hurry downstairs and —

Biff: Somebody in there?

Willy: No, that was next door.

The Woman laughs offstage.

Biff: Somebody got in your bathroom!

Willy: No, it's the next room, there's a party —

The Woman (enters, laughing. She lisps this): Can I come in? There's something in the bathtub, Willy, and it's moving!

Willy looks at Biff, who is staring open-mouthed and horrified at The Woman.

Willy: Ah — you better go back to your room. They must be finished painting by now. They're painting her room so I let her take a shower here. Go back, go back . . . (*He pushes her.*)

The Woman (resisting): But I've got to get dressed, Willy, I can't —

Willy: Get out of here! Go back, go back . . . (*Suddenly striving for the ordinary*): This is Miss Francis, Biff, she's a buyer. They're painting her room. Go back, Miss Francis, go back . . .

The Woman: But my clothes, I can't go out naked in the hall!

Willy (pushing her offstage): Get outa here! Go back, go back!

Biff slowly sits down on his suitcase as the argument continues offstage.

The Woman: Where's my stockings? You promised me stockings, Willy!

Willy: I have no stockings here!

The Woman: You had two boxes of size nine sheers for me, and I want them!

Willy: Here, for God's sake, will you get outa here!

The Woman (enters holding a box of stockings): I just hope there's nobody in the hall. That's all I hope. (*To Biff.*) Are you football or baseball?

Biff: Football.

The Woman (angry, humiliated): That's me too. G'night. (*She snatches her clothes from Willy, and walks out.*)

Willy (after a pause): Well, better get going. I want to get to the school first thing in the morning. Get my suits out of the closet. I'll get my valise. (*Biff doesn't move.*) What's the matter? (*Biff remains motionless, tears falling.*) She's a buyer. Buys for J. H. Simmons. She lives down the hall — they're painting.

You don't imagine — *(He breaks off. After a pause.)* Now listen, pal, she's just a buyer. She sees merchandise in her room and they have to keep it looking just so . . . *(Pause. Assuming command.)* All right, get my suits. *(Biff doesn't move.)* Now stop crying and do as I say. I gave you an order. Biff, I gave you an order! Is that what you do when I give you an order? How dare you cry! *(Putting his arm around Biff.)* Now look, Biff, when you grow up you'll understand about these things. You mustn't — you mustn't overemphasize a thing like this. I'll see Birnbaum first thing in the morning.

Biff: Never mind.

Willy (getting down beside Biff): Never mind! He's going to give you those points. I'll see to it.

Biff: He wouldn't listen to you.

Willy: He certainly will listen to me. You need those points for the U. of Virginia.

Biff: I'm not going there.

Willy: Heh? If I can't get him to change that mark you'll make it up in summer school. You've got all summer to —

Biff (his weeping breaking from him): Dad . . .

Willy (infected by it): Oh, my boy . . .

Biff: Dad . . .

Willy: She's nothing to me, Biff. I was lonely, I was terribly lonely.

Biff: You — you gave her Mama's stockings! *(His tears break through and he rises to go.)*

Willy (grabbing for Biff): I gave you an order!

Biff: Don't touch me, you — liar!

Willy: Apologize for that!

Biff: You fake! You phony little fake! You fake! *(Overcome, he turns quickly and weeping fully goes out with his suitcase. Willy is left on the floor on his knees.)*

Willy: I gave you an order! Biff, come back here or I'll beat you! Come back here! I'll whip you!

Stanley comes quickly in from the right and stands in front of Willy.

Willy (shouts at Stanley): I gave you an order . . .

Stanley: Hey, let's pick it up, pick it up, Mr. Loman. *(He helps Willy to his feet.)* Your boys left with the chippies. They said they'll see you home.

A second waiter watches some distance away.

Willy: But we were supposed to have dinner together.

Music is heard, Willy's theme.

Stanley: Can you make it?

Willy: I'll — sure, I can make it. *(Suddenly concerned about his clothes.)* Do I — I look all right?

Stanley: Sure, you look all right. *(He flicks a speck off Willy's lapel.)*

Willy: Here — here's a dollar.

Stanley: Oh, your son paid me. It's all right.

Willy (putting it in Stanley's hand): No, take it. You're a good boy.

Stanley: Oh, no, you don't have to . . .

Willy: Here — here's some more, I don't need it any more. *(After a slight pause.)* Tell me — is there a seed store in the neighborhood?

Stanley: Seeds? You mean like to plant?

As Willy turns, Stanley slips the money back into his jacket pocket.

Willy: Yes. Carrots, peas . . .

Stanley: Well, there's hardware stores on Sixth Avenue, but it may be too late now.

Willy (anxiously): Oh, I'd better hurry. I've got to get some seeds. *(He starts off to the right.)* I've got to get some seeds, right away. Nothing's planted. I don't have a thing in the ground.

Willy hurries out as the light goes down. Stanley moves over to the right after him, watches him off. The other waiter has been staring at Willy.

Stanley (to the waiter): Well, whatta you looking at?

The waiter picks up the chairs and moves off right. Stanley takes the table and follows him. The light fades on this area. There is a long pause, the sound of the flute coming over. The light gradually rises on the kitchen, which is empty. Happy appears at the door of the house, followed by Biff. Happy is carrying a large bunch of long-stemmed roses. He enters the kitchen, looks around for Linda. Not seeing her, he turns to Biff, who is just outside the house door, and makes a gesture with his hands, indicating "Not here, I guess." He looks into the living-room and freezes. Inside, Linda, unseen, is seated, Willy's coat on her lap. She rises ominously and quietly and moves toward Happy, who backs up into the kitchen, afraid.

Happy: Hey, what're you doing up? *(Linda says nothing but moves toward him implacably.)* Where's Pop? *(He keeps backing to the right, and now Linda is in full view in the doorway to the living-room.)* Is he sleeping?

Linda: Where were you?

Happy (trying to laugh it off): We met two girls, Mom, very fine types. Here, we brought you some flowers. *(Offering them to her.)* Put them in your room, Ma.

She knocks them to the floor at Biff's feet. He has now come inside and closed the door behind him. She stares at Biff, silent.

Happy: Now what'd you do that for? Mom, I want you to have some flowers—

Linda (cutting Happy off, violently to Biff): Don't you care whether he lives or dies?

Happy (going to the stairs): Come upstairs, Biff.

Biff (with a flare of disgust, to Happy): Go away from me! *(To Linda.)* What do you mean, lives or dies? Nobody's dying around here, pal.

Linda: Get out of my sight! Get out of here!

Biff: I wanna see the boss.

Linda: You're not going near him!

Biff: Where is he? *(He moves into the living-room and Linda follows.)*

Linda (shouting after Biff): You invite him for dinner. He looks forward to it all day — *(Biff appears in his parents' bedroom, looks around, and exits.)* — and then you desert him there. There's no stranger you'd do that to!

Happy: Why? He had a swell time with us. Listen, when I — *(Linda comes back into the kitchen)* — desert him I hope I don't outlive the day!

Linda: Get out of here!

Happy: Now look, Mom . . .

Linda: Did you have to go to women tonight? You and your lousy rotten whores!

Biff re-enters the kitchen.

Happy: Mom, all we did was follow Biff around trying to cheer him up! *(To Biff.)* Boy, what a night you gave me!

Linda: Get out of here, both of you, and don't come back! I don't want you tormenting him any more. Go on now, get your things together! *(To Biff.)* You can sleep in his apartment. *(She starts to pick up the flowers and stops herself.)* Pick up this stuff, I'm not your maid any more. Pick it up, you bum, you!

Happy turns his back to her in refusal. Biff slowly moves over and gets down on his knees, picking up the flowers.

Linda: You're a pair of animals! Not one, not another living soul would have had the cruelty to walk out on that man in a restaurant!

Biff (not looking at her): Is that what he said?

Linda: He didn't have to say anything. He was so humiliated he nearly limped when he came in.

Happy: But, Mom, he had a great time with us —

Biff (cutting him off violently): Shut up!

Without another word, Happy goes upstairs.

Linda: You! You didn't even go in to see if he was all right!

Biff (still on the floor in front of Linda, the flowers in his hand; with self-loathing): No. Didn't. Didn't do a damned thing. How do you like that, heh? Left him babbling in a toilet.

Linda: You louse. You . . .

Biff: Now you hit it on the nose! *(He gets up, throws the flowers in the wastebasket.)* The scum of the earth, and you're looking at him!

Linda: Get out of here!

Biff: I gotta talk to the boss, Mom. Where is he?

Linda: You're not going near him. Get out of this house!

Biff (with absolute assurance, determination): No. We're gonna have an abrupt conversation, him and me.

Linda: You're not talking to him!

Hammering is heard from outside the house, off right. Biff turns toward the noise.

Linda (suddenly pleading): Will you please leave him alone?

Biff: What's he doing out there?

Linda: He's planting the garden!

Biff (quietly): Now? Oh, my God!

Biff moves outside, Linda following. The light dies down on them and comes up on the center of the apron as Willy walks into it. He is carrying a flashlight, a hoe, and handful of seed packets. He raps the top of the hoe sharply to fix it firmly, and then moves to the left, measuring off the distance with his foot. He holds the flashlight to look at the seed packets, reading off the instructions. He is in the blue of night.

Willy: Carrots . . . quarter-inch apart. Rows . . . one-foot rows. *(He measures it off.)* One foot. *(He puts down a package and measures off.)* Beets. *(He puts down another package and measures again.)* Lettuce. *(He reads the package, puts it down.)* One foot — *(He breaks off as Ben appears at the right and moves slowly down to him.)* What a proposition, ts, ts. Terrific, terrific. 'Cause she's suffered, Ben, the woman has suffered. You understand me? A man can't go out the way he came in, Ben, a man has got to add up to something. You can't, you can't — *(Ben moves toward him as though to interrupt.)* You gotta consider, now. Don't answer so quick. Remember, it's a guaranteed twenty-thousand-dollar proposition. Now look, Ben, I want you to go through the ins and outs of this thing with me. I've got nobody to talk to, Ben, and the woman has suffered, you hear me?

Ben (standing still, considering): What's the proposition?

Willy: It's twenty thousand dollars on the barrelhead. Guaranteed, gilt-edged, you understand?

Ben: You don't want to make a fool of yourself. They might not honor the policy.

Willy: How can they dare refuse? Didn't I work like a coolie to meet every premium on the nose? And now they don't pay off? Impossible!

Ben: It's called a cowardly thing, William.

Willy: Why? Does it take more guts to stand here the rest of my life ringing up a zero?

Ben (yielding): That's a point, William. *(He moves, thinking, turns.)* And twenty thousand — that *is* something one can feel with the hand, it is there.

Willy (now assured, with rising power): Oh, Ben, that's the whole beauty of it! I see it like a diamond, shining in the dark, hard and rough, that I can pick up and touch in my hand. Not like — like an appointment! This would not be another damned-fool appointment, Ben, and it changes all the aspects. Because he thinks I'm nothing, see, and so he spites me. But the funeral — *(Straightening up.)* Ben, that funeral will be massive! They'll come from Maine, Massachusetts, Vermont, New Hampshire! All the old-timers with the strange license plates — that boy will be thunder-struck, Ben, because he never realized — I am known! Rhode Island, New York, New Jersey — I am known, Ben, and he'll see it with his eyes once and for all. He'll see what I am, Ben! He's in for a shock, that boy!

Ben (coming to the edge of the garden): He'll call you a coward.

Willy (suddenly fearful): No, that would be terrible.

Ben: Yes. And a damned fool.

Willy: No, no, he mustn't, I won't have that! *(He is broken and desperate.)*

Ben: He'll hate you William.

The gay music of the Boys is heard.

Willy: Oh, Ben, how do we get back to all the great times? Used to be so full of light, and comradeship, the sleigh-riding in winter, and the ruddiness on his cheeks. And always some kind of good news coming up, always something nice coming up ahead. And never even let me carry the valises in the house, and simonizing, simonizing that little red car! Why, why can't I give him something and not have him hate me?

Ben: Let me think about it. *(He glances at his watch.)* I still have a little time. Remarkable proposition, but you've got to be sure you're not making a fool of yourself.

Ben drifts off upstage and goes out of sight. Biff comes down from the left.

Willy (suddenly conscious of Biff, turns and looks up at him, then begins picking up the packages of seeds in confusion): Where the hell is that seed? *(Indignantly.)* You can't see nothing out here! They boxed in the whole goddamn neighborhood!

Biff: There are people all around here. Don't you realize that?

Willy: I'm busy. Don't bother me.

Biff (taking the hoe from Willy): I'm saying good-by to you, Pop. *(Willy looks at him, silent, unable to move.)* I'm not coming back any more.

Willy: You're not going to see Oliver tomorrow?

Biff: I've got no appointment, Dad.

Willy: He put his arm around you, and you've got no appointment?

Biff: Pop, get this now, will you? Everytime I've left it's been a fight that sent me out of here. Today I realized something about myself and I tried to explain it to you and I — I think I'm just not smart enough to make any sense out of it for you. To hell with whose fault it is or anything like that. *(He takes Willy's arm.)* Let's just wrap it up, heh? Come on in, we'll tell Mom. *(He gently tries to pull Willy to left.)*

Willy (frozen, immobile, with guilt in his voice): No, I don't want to see her.

Biff: Come on! *(He pulls again, and Willy tries to pull away.)*

Willy (highly nervous): No, no, I don't want to see her.

Biff (tries to look into Willy's face, as if to find the answer there): Why don't you want to see her?

Willy (more harshly now): Don't bother me, will you?

Biff: What do you mean, you don't want to see her? You don't want them calling you yellow, do you? This isn't your fault; it's me, I'm a bum. Now come inside! *(Willy strains to get away.)* Did you hear what I said to you?

Willy pulls away and quickly goes by himself into the house. Biff follows.

Linda (to Willy): Did you plant, dear?

Biff (at the door, to Linda): All right, we had it out. I'm going and I'm not writing any more.

Linda (going to Willy in the kitchen): I think that's the best way, dear. 'Cause there's no use drawing it out, you'll just never get along.

Willy doesn't respond.

Biff: People ask where I am and what I'm doing, you don't know, and you don't care. That way it'll be off your mind and you can start brightening up again. All right? That clears it, doesn't it? *(Willy is silent, and Biff goes to him.)* You gonna wish me luck, scout? *(He extends his hand.)* What do you say?

Linda: Shake his hand, Willy.

Willy (turning to her, seething with hurt): There's no necessity to mention the pen at all, y'know.

Biff (gently): I've got no appointment, Dad.

Willy (erupting fiercely): He put his arm around . . . ?

Biff: Dad, you're never going to see what I am, so what's the use of arguing? If I strike oil I'll send you a check. Meantime forget I'm alive.

Willy (to Linda): Spite, see?

Biff: Shake hands, Dad.

Willy: Not my hand.

Biff: I was hoping not to go this way.

Willy: Well, this is the way you're going. Good-by.

Biff looks at him a moment, then turns sharply and goes to the stairs.

Willy (stops him with): May you rot in hell if you leave this house!

Biff (turning): Exactly what is it that you want from me?

Willy: I want you to know, on the train, in the mountains, in the valleys, wherever you go, that you cut down your life for spite!

Biff: No, no.

Willy: Spite, spite, is the word of your undoing! And when you're down and out, remember what did it. When you're rotting somewhere beside the railroad tracks, remember, and don't you dare blame it on me!

Biff: I'm not blaming it on you!

Willy: I won't take the rap for this, you hear?

Happy comes down the stairs and stands on the bottom step, watching.

Biff: That's just what I'm telling you!

Willy (sinking into a chair at the table, with full accusation): You're trying to put a knife in me — don't think I don't know what you're doing!

Biff: All right, phony! Then let's lay it on the line. *(He whips the rubber tube out of his pocket and puts it on the table.)*

Happy: You crazy —

Linda: Biff! *(She moves to grab the hose, but Biff holds it down with his hand.)*

Biff: Leave it there! Don't move it!

Willy (not looking at it): What is that?

Biff: You know goddam well what that is.

Willy (caged, wanting to escape): I never saw that.

Biff: You saw it. The mice didn't bring it into the cellar! What is this supposed to do, make a hero out of you? This supposed to make me sorry for you?

Willy: Never heard of it.

Biff: There'll be no pity for you, you hear it? No pity!

Willy (to Linda:) You hear the spite!

Biff: No, you're going to hear the truth — what you are and what I am!

Linda: Stop it!

Willy: Spite!

Happy (coming down toward Biff): You cut it now!

Biff (to Happy): The man don't know who we are! The man is gonna know! *(To Willy.)* We never told the truth for ten minutes in this house!

Happy: We always told the truth!

Biff (turning on him): You big blow, are you the assistant buyer? You're one of the two assistants to the assistant, aren't you?

Happy: Well, I'm practically —

Biff: You're practically full of it! We all are! And I'm through with it. *(To Willy.)* Now hear this, Willy, this is me.

Willy: I know you!

Biff: You know why I had no address for three months? I stole a suit in Kansas City and I was in jail. *(To Linda, who is sobbing.)* Stop crying. I'm through with it.

Linda turns away from them, her hands covering her face.

Willy: I suppose that's my fault!

Biff: I stole myself out of every good job since high school!

Willy: And whose fault is that?

Biff: And I never got anywhere because you blew me so full of hot air I could never stand taking orders from anybody! That's whose fault it is!

Willy: I hear that!

Linda: Don't, Biff!

Biff: It's goddam time you heard that! I had to be boss big shot in two weeks, and I'm through with it!

Willy: Then hang yourself! For spite, hang yourself!

Biff: No! Nobody's hanging himself, Willy! I ran down eleven flights with a pen in my hand today. And suddenly I stopped, you hear me? And in the middle of that office building, do you hear this? I stopped in the middle of that building and I saw — the sky. I saw the things that I love in this world. The work and the food and time to sit and smoke. And I looked at the pen and said to myself, what the hell am I grabbing this for? Why am I trying to become what I don't want to be? What am I doing in an office, making a contemptuous, begging fool of myself, when all I want is out there, waiting for me the minute I say I know who I am! Why can't I say that, Willy? *(He tries to make Willy face him, but Willy pulls away and moves to the left.)*

Willy (with hatred, threateningly): The door of your life is wide open!

Biff: Pop! I'm a dime a dozen, and so are you!

Willy (turning on him now in an uncontrolled outburst): I am not a dime a dozen! I am Willy Loman, and you are Biff Loman!

Biff starts for Willy, but is blocked by Happy. In his fury, Biff seems on the verge of attacking his father.

Biff: I am not a leader of men, Willy, and neither are you. You were never anything but a hard-working drummer who landed in the ash can like all the rest of them! I'm one dollar an hour, Willy! I tried seven states and couldn't raise it. A buck an hour! Do you gather my meaning? I'm not bringing home any prizes any more, and you're going to stop waiting for me to bring them home!

Willy (directly to Biff): You vengeful, spiteful mut!

Biff breaks from Happy. Willy, in fright, starts up the stairs. Biff grabs him.

Biff (at the peak of his fury): Pop, I'm nothing! I'm nothing, Pop. Can't you understand that? There's no spite in it any more. I'm just what I am, that's all.

Biff's fury has spent itself, and he breaks down, sobbing, holding on to Willy, who dumbly fumbles for Biff's face.

Willy (astonished): What're you doing? What're you doing? *(To Linda.)* Why is he crying?

Biff (crying, broken): Will you let me go, for Christ's sake? Will you take that phony dream and burn it before something happens? *(Struggling to contain himself, he pulls away and moves to the stairs.)* I'll go in the morning. Put him — put him to bed. *(Exhausted, Biff moves up the stairs to his room.)*

Willy (after a long pause, astonished, elevated): Isn't that — isn't that remarkable? Biff — he likes me!

Linda: He loves you, Willy!

Happy (deeply moved): Always did, Pop.

Willy: Oh, Biff! *(Staring wildly.)* He cried! Cried to me. *(He is choking with his love, and now cries out his promise.)* That boy — that boy is going to be magnificent!

Ben appears in the light just outside the kitchen.

Ben: Yes, outstanding, with twenty thousand behind him.

Linda (sensing the racing of his mind, fearfully, carefully): Now come to bed, Willy. It's all settled now.

Willy (finding it difficult not to rush out of the house): Yes, we'll sleep. Come on. Go to sleep, Hap.

Ben: And it does take a great kind of a man to crack the jungle.

In accents of dread, Ben's idyllic music starts up.

Happy (his arm around Linda): I'm getting married, Pop, don't forget it. I'm changing everything. I'm gonna run that department before the year is up. You'll see, Mom. *(He kisses her.)*

Ben: The jungle is dark but full of diamonds, Willy.

Willy turns, moves, listening to Ben.

Linda: Be good. You're both good boys, just act that way, that's all.

Happy: 'Night, Pop. *(He goes upstairs.)*

Linda (to Willy): Come, dear.

Ben (with greater force): One must go in to fetch a diamond out.

Willy (to Linda, as he moves slowly along the edge of the kitchen, toward the door): I just want to get settled down, Linda. Let me sit alone for a little.

Linda (almost uttering her fear): I want you upstairs.

Willy (taking her in his arms): In a few minutes, Linda. I couldn't sleep right now. Go on, you look awful tired. *(He kisses her.)*

Ben: Not like an appointment at all. A diamond is rough and hard to the touch.

Willy: Go on now. I'll be right up.

Linda: I think this is the only way, Willy.

Willy: Sure, it's the best thing.

Ben: Best thing!

Willy: The only way. Everything is gonna be — go on, kid, get to bed. You look so tired.

Linda: Come right up.

Willy: Two minutes.

Linda goes into the living-room, then reappears in her bedroom. Willy moves just outside the kitchen door.

Willy: Loves me. *(Wonderingly.)* Always loved me. Isn't that a remarkable thing? Ben, he'll worship me for it!

Ben (with promise): It's dark there, but full of diamonds.

Willy: Can you imagine that magnificence with twenty thousand dollars in his pocket?

Linda (calling from her room): Willy! Come up!

Willy (calling into the kitchen): Yes! Yes. Coming! It's very smart, you realize that, don't you, sweetheart? Even Ben sees it. I gotta go, baby. 'By! 'By! *(Going over to Ben, almost dancing.)* Imagine? When the mail comes he'll be ahead of Bernard again!

Ben: A perfect proposition all around.

Willy: Did you see how he cried to me? Oh, if I could kiss him, Ben!

Ben: Time, William, time!

Willy: Oh, Ben, I always knew one way or another we were gonna make it, Biff and I!

Ben *(looking at his watch):* The boat. We'll be late. *(He moves slowly off into the darkness.)*

Willy *(elegiacally, turning to the house):* Now when you kick off, boy, I want a seventy-yard boot, and get right down the field under the ball, and when you hit, hit low and hit hard, because it's important, boy. *(He swings around and faces the audience.)* There's all kinds of important people in the stands, and the first thing you know . . . *(Suddenly realizing he is alone.)* Ben! Ben, where do I . . . ? *(He makes a sudden movement of search.)* Ben, how do I . . . ?

Linda *(calling):* Willy, you coming up?

Willy *(uttering a gasp of fear, whirling about as if to quiet her):* Sh! *(He turns around as if to find his way; sounds, faces, voices, seem to be swarming in upon him and he flicks at them, crying.)* Sh! Sh! *(Suddenly music, faint and high, stops him. It rises in intensity, almost to an unbearable scream. He goes up and down on his toes, and rushes off around the house.)* Shhh!

Linda: Willy?

There is no answer. Linda waits. Biff gets up off his bed. He is still in his clothes. Happy sits up. Biff stands listening.

Linda *(with real fear):* Willy, answer me! Willy!

There is the sound of a car starting and moving away at full speed.

Linda: No!

Biff *(rushing down the stairs):* Pop!

As the car speeds off, the music crashes down in a frenzy of sound, which becomes the soft pulsation of a single cello string. Biff slowly returns to his bedroom. He and Happy gravely don their jackets. Linda slowly walks out of her room. The music has developed into a dead march. The leaves of day are appearing over everything. Charley and Bernard, somberly dressed, appear and knock on the kitchen door. Biff and Happy slowly descend the stairs to the kitchen as Charley and Bernard enter. All stop a moment when Linda, in clothes of mourning, bearing a little bunch of roses, comes through the draped doorway into the kitchen. She goes to Charley and takes his arm. Now all move toward the audience, through the wall-line of the kitchen. At the limit of the apron, Linda lays down the flowers, kneels, and sits back on her heels. All stare down at the grave.

REQUIEM

Charley: It's getting dark, Linda.

Linda doesn't react. She stares at the grave.

Biff: How about it, Mom? Better get some rest, heh? They'll be closing the gate soon.

Linda makes no move. Pause.

Happy *(deeply angered):* He had no right to do that. There was no necessity for it. We would've helped him.

Charley *(grunting):* Hmmm.

Biff: Come along, Mom.

Linda: Why didn't anybody come?

Charley: It was a very nice funeral.

Linda: But where are all the people he knew? Maybe they blame him.

Charley: Naa. It's a rough world, Linda. They wouldn't blame him.

Linda: I can't understand it. At this time especially. First time in thirty-five years we were just about free and clear. He only needed a little salary. He was even finished with the dentist.

Charley: No man only needs a little salary.

Linda: I can't understand it.

Biff: There were a lot of nice days. When he'd come home from a trip; or on Sundays, making the stoop; finishing the cellar; putting on the new porch; when he built the extra bathroom; and put up the garage. You know something, Charley, there's more of him in that front stoop than in all the sales he ever made.

Charley: Yeah. He was a happy man with a batch of cement.

Linda: He was so wonderful with his hands.

Biff: He had the wrong dreams. All, all, wrong.

Happy (almost ready to fight Biff): Don't say that!

Biff: He never knew who he was.

Charley (stopping Happy's movement and reply. To Biff): Nobody dast blame this man. You don't understand: Willy was a salesman. And for a salesman, there is no rock bottom to the life. He don't put a bolt to a nut, he don't tell you the law or give you medicine. He's a man way out there in the blue, riding on a smile and a shoeshine. And when they start not smiling back — that's an earthquake. And then you get yourself a couple of spots on your hat, and you're finished. Nobody dast blame this man. A salesman is got to dream, boy. It comes with the territory.

Biff: Charley, the man didn't know who he was.

Happy (infuriated): Don't say that!

Biff: Why don't you come with me, Happy?

Happy: I'm not licked that easily. I'm staying right in this city, and I'm gonna beat this racket! *(He looks at Biff, his chin set.)* The Loman Brothers!

Biff: I know who I am, kid.

Happy: All right, boy. I'm gonna show you and everybody else that Willy Loman did not die in vain. He had a good dream. It's the only dream you can have — to come out number-one man. He fought it out here, and this is where I'm gonna win it for him.

Biff (with a hopeless glance at Happy, bends toward his mother): Let's go, Mom.

Linda: I'll be with you in a minute. Go on, Charley. *(He hesitates.)* I want to, just for a minute. I never had a chance to say good-by.

Charley moves away, followed by Happy. Biff remains a slight distance up and left of Linda. She sits there, summoning herself. The flute begins, not far away, playing behind her speech.

Linda: Forgive me, dear. I can't cry. I don't know what it is, but I can't cry. I don't understand it. Why did you ever do that? Help me, Willy, I can't cry. It seems to me that you're just on another trip. I keep expecting you. Willy, dear, I can't cry. Why did you do it? I search and search and I search, and I can't understand it, Willy. I made the last payment on the house today. Today, dear. And there'll be nobody home. *(A sob rises in her throat.)* We're free and clear. *(Sobbing more fully, released.)* We're free. *(Biff comes slowly toward her.)* We're free . . . We're free . . .

Biff lifts her to her feet and moves out up right with her in his arms. Linda sobs quietly. Bernard and Charley come together and follow them, followed by Happy. Only the music of the flute is left on the darkening stage as over the house the hard towers of the apartment buildings rise into sharp focus, and

The Curtain Falls

CONNECTIONS TO OTHER SELECTIONS

1. Compare and contrast Willy Loman with Polonius in Shakespeare's *Hamlet* (p. 1383). To what extent is each character wise, foolish, deluded, and hypocritical? Explain why Loman can be seen as a tragic character while Polonius cannot be.

2. Read Tato Laviera's poem "AmeRícan" (p. 918), and compare its treatment of the American dream with the one in *Death of a Salesman*. How do the tones of the two works differ?

3. What similarities do you find between the endings of *Death of a Salesman* and August Wilson's *The Piano Lesson* (p. 1962)? Are the endings happy, unhappy, or something else?

PERSPECTIVES

ARTHUR MILLER (B. 1915)

Tragedy and the Common Man   1949

In this age few tragedies are written. It has often been held that the lack is due to a paucity of heroes among us, or else that modern man has had the blood drawn out of his organs of belief by the skepticism of science, and the heroic attack on life cannot feed on an attitude of reserve and circumspection. For one reason or another, we are often held to be below tragedy — or tragedy above us. The inevitable conclusion is, of course, that the tragic mode is archaic, fit only for the very highly placed, the kings or the kingly, and where this admission is not made in so many words it is most often implied.

I believe that the common man is as apt a subject for tragedy in its highest sense as kings were. On the face of it this ought to be obvious in the light of modern psychiatry, which bases its analysis upon classic formulations, such as the Oedipus and Orestes complexes, for instance, which were enacted by royal beings, but which apply to everyone in similar emotional situations.

More simply, when the question of tragedy in art is not at issue, we never hesitate to attribute to the well-placed and the exalted the very same mental processes as the lowly. And finally, if the exaltation of tragic action were truly a property of the high-bred character alone, it is inconceivable that the mass of mankind should cherish tragedy above all other forms, let alone be capable of understanding it.

As a general rule, to which there may be exceptions unknown to me, I think the tragic feeling is evoked in us when we are in the presence of a character who is ready to lay down his life, if need be, to secure one thing—his sense of personal dignity. From Orestes to Hamlet, Medea to Macbeth, the underlying struggle is that of the individual attempting to gain his "rightful" position in his society.

Sometimes he is one who has been displaced from it, sometimes one who seeks to attain it for the first time, but the fateful wound from which the inevitable events spiral is the wound of indignity, and its dominant force is indignation. Tragedy, then, is the consequence of a man's total compulsion to evaluate himself justly.

In the sense of having been initiated by the hero himself, the tale always reveals what has been called his "tragic flaw," a failing that is not peculiar to grand or elevated characters. Nor is it necessarily a weakness. The flaw, or crack in the character, is really nothing—and need be nothing—but his inherent unwillingness to remain passive in the face of what he conceives to be a challenge to his dignity, his image of his rightful status. Only the passive, only those who accept their lot without active retaliation, are "flawless." Most of us are in that category.

But there are among us today, as there always have been, those who act against the scheme of things that degrades them, and in the process of action, everything we have accepted out of fear or insensitivity or ignorance is shaken before us and examined, and from this total onslaught by an individual against the seemingly stable cosmos surrounding us—from this total examination of the "unchangeable" environment—comes the terror and the fear that is classically associated with tragedy.

More important, from this total questioning of what has been previously unquestioned, we learn. And such a process is not beyond the common man. In revolutions around the world, these past thirty years, he has demonstrated again and again this inner dynamic of all tragedy.

Insistence upon the rank of the tragic hero, or the so-called nobility of his character, is really but a clinging to the outward forms of tragedy. If rank or nobility of character was indispensable, then it would follow that the problems of those with rank were the particular problems of tragedy. But surely the right of one monarch to capture the domain from another no longer raises our passions, nor are our concepts of justice what they were to the mind of an Elizabethan king.

The quality in such plays that does shake us, however, derives from the underlying fear of being displaced, the disaster inherent in being torn away from our chosen image of what and who we are in this world. Among us today this fear is as strong, and perhaps stronger, than it ever was. In fact, it is the common man who knows this fear best.

Now, if it is true that tragedy is the consequence of a man's total compulsion to evaluate himself justly, his destruction in the attempt posits a wrong or an evil in his environment. And this is precisely the morality of tragedy and its lesson. The discovery of the moral law, which is what the enlightenment of tragedy consists of, is not the discovery of some abstract or metaphysical quantity.

The tragic right is a condition of life, a condition in which the human personality is able to flower and realize itself. The wrong is the condition which suppresses man, perverts the flowing out of his love and creative instinct. Tragedy enlightens—and it must, in that it points the heroic finger at the enemy of man's freedom. The thrust for freedom is the quality in tragedy which exalts. The revolutionary questioning of the stable environment is what terrifies. In no way is the common man debarred from such thoughts or such actions.

Seen in this light, our lack of tragedy may be partially accounted for by the turn which modern literature has taken toward the purely psychiatric view of life, or the purely sociological. If all our miseries, our indignities, are born and bred within our minds, then all action, let alone the heroic action, is obviously impossible.

And if society alone is responsible for the cramping of our lives, then the protagonist must needs be so pure and faultless as to force us to deny his validity as a character. From neither of these views can tragedy derive, simply because neither represents a balanced concept of life. Above all else, tragedy requires the finest appreciation by the writer of cause and effect.

No tragedy can therefore come about when its author fears to question absolutely everything, when he regards any institution, habit, or custom as being either everlasting, immutable, or inevitable. In the tragic view the need of man to wholly realize himself is the only fixed star, and whatever it is that hedges his nature and lowers it is ripe for attack and examination. Which is not to say that tragedy must preach revolution.

The Greeks could probe the very heavenly origin of their ways and return to confirm the rightness of laws. And Job could face God in anger, demanding his right, and end in submission. But for a moment everything is in suspension, nothing is accepted, and in this stretching and tearing apart of the cosmos, in the very action of so doing, the character gains "size," the tragic stature which is spuriously attached to the royal or the high born in our minds. The commonest of men may take on that stature to the extent of his willingness to throw all he has into the contest, the battle to secure his rightful place in his world.

There is a misconception of tragedy with which I have been struck in review after review, and in many conversations with writers and readers alike. It is the idea that tragedy is of necessity allied to pessimism. Even the dictionary says nothing more about the word than that it means a story with a sad or unhappy ending. This impression is so firmly fixed that I almost hesitate to claim that in truth tragedy implies more optimism in its author than does comedy, and that its final result ought to be the reinforcement of the onlooker's brightest opinions of the human animal.

For, if it is true to say that in essence the tragic hero is intent upon claiming his whole due as a personality, and if this struggle must be total and without reservation, then it automatically demonstrates the indestructible will of man to achieve his humanity.

The possibility of victory must be there in tragedy. Where pathos rules, where pathos is finally derived, a character has fought a battle he could not possibly have won. The pathetic is achieved when the protagonist is, by virtue of his witlessness, his insensitivity, or the very air he gives off, incapable of grappling with a much superior force.

Pathos truly is the mode for the pessimist. But tragedy requires a nicer balance between what is possible and what is impossible. And it is curious, although edifying, that the plays we revere, century after century, are the tragedies. In them, and in them alone, lies the belief — optimistic, if you will — in the perfectibility of man.

It is time, I think, that we who are without kings, took up this bright thread of our history and followed it to the only place it can possibly lead in our time — the heart and spirit of the average man.

From *Theater Essays of Arthur Miller*

CONSIDERATIONS FOR CRITICAL THINKING AND WRITING

1. According to Miller, why is there a "lack" (para. 1) of tragedy in modern literature? Why do psychological and sociological accounts of human behavior limit the possibilities for tragedy?

2. Why is the "common man" (para. 2) a suitable subject for tragedy? How does Miller's view of tragedy compare with Aristotle's (p. 1303)?

3. What distinction does Miller make between tragedy and pathos? Which term best characterizes Willy Loman in *Death of a Salesman*? Explain why.

ARTHUR MILLER (B. 1915)

On Biff and Willy Loman 1950

A serious theme is entertaining to the extent that it is not trifled with, not cleverly angled, but met in head-on collision. [The audience] will not consent to suffer while the creators stand by with tongue in cheek. They have a way of knowing. Nobody can blame them.

And there have been certain disappointments, one above all. I am sorry the self-realization of the older son, Biff, is not a weightier counterbalance to Willy's disaster in the audience's mind.

And certain things are more clearly known, or so it seems now. We want to give of ourselves, and yet all we train for is to take, as though nothing less will keep the world at a safe distance. Every day we contradict our will to create, which is to give. The end of man is not security, but without security we are without the elementary condition of humaneness.

To me the tragedy of Willy Loman is that he gave his life, or sold it, in order to justify the waste of it. It is the tragedy of a man who did believe that he alone was not meeting the qualifications laid down for mankind by those clean-shaven frontiersmen who inhabit the peaks of broadcasting and advertising offices. From those forests of canned goods high up near the sky, he heard the thundering command to succeed as it ricocheted down the newspaper-lined canyons of his city, heard not a human voice, but a wind of a voice to which no human can reply in kind, except to stare into the mirror at a failure.

From the *New York Times*, February 5, 1950

CONSIDERATIONS FOR CRITICAL THINKING AND WRITING

1. Discuss what you think Miller has in mind when he refers to Biff's "self-realization" (para. 2).

2. According to Miller, what influences Willy to make him feel like a failure?

3. How is Miller's description of "the tragedy of Willy Loman" (para. 4) dramatized in the play?

The Glass Menagerie

Thomas Lanier Williams, who kept his college nickname, Tennessee, was born in Columbus, Mississippi, the son of a traveling salesman. In 1918 the family moved to St. Louis, Missouri, where his father became the sales manager of a shoe company. Williams's mother, the daughter of an Episcopal clergyman, was withdrawn and genteel in contrast to his aggressive father, who contemptuously called him "Miss Nancy" as a way of mocking his weak physical condition and his literary pursuits. This family atmosphere of repression and anger makes its way into many of Williams's works through characterizations of domineering men and psychologically vulnerable women.

Williams began writing in high school and at the age of seventeen published his first short story in *Weird Tales*. His education at the University of Missouri was interrupted when he had to go to work in a shoe factory. This "living death," as he put it, led to a nervous breakdown, but he eventually resumed his studies at Washington University and finally graduated from the University of Iowa in 1938. During his college years, Williams wrote one-act plays; in 1940 his first full-length play, *Battle of Angels,* opened in Boston, but none of these early plays achieved commercial success. In 1945, however, *The Glass Menagerie* won large, enthusiastic audiences as well as the Drama Critics' Circle Award, which marked the beginning of a series of theatrical triumphs for Williams including *Streetcar Named Desire* (1947), *The Rose Tattoo* (1950), *Cat on a Hot Tin Roof* (1955), *Suddenly Last Summer* (1958), and *The Night of the Iguana* (1961).

The Glass Menagerie reflects Williams's fascination with characters who face lonely struggles in emotionally and financially starved environments. Although Williams's use of colloquial southern speech is realistic, the play also employs nonrealistic techniques, such as shifts in time, projections on screens, music, and lighting effects, to express his characters' thoughts and inner lives. (Williams describes these devices in his production notes to the play; see p. 1908.) As much as these techniques are unconventional, Williams believed that they represented "a more penetrating and vivid expression of things as they are." The lasting popularity of *The Glass Menagerie* indicates that his assessment was correct.

TENNESSEE WILLIAMS (1911–1983)

The Glass Menagerie

1945

nobody, not even the rain, has such small hands
—E. E. Cummings

LIST OF CHARACTERS

Amanda Wingfield, the mother. A little woman of great but confused vitality clinging frantically to another time and place. Her characterization must be carefully created, not copied from type. She is not paranoiac, but her life is paranoia. There is much to admire in Amanda, and as much to love and pity as there is to laugh at. Certainly she has endurance and a kind of heroism, and though her foolishness makes her unwittingly cruel at times, there is tenderness in her slight person.

Laura Wingfield, her daughter. Amanda, having failed to establish contact with reality, continues to live vitally in her illusions, but Laura's situation is even graver. A childhood illness has left her crippled, one leg slightly shorter than the other, and held in a brace. This defect need not be more than suggested on the stage. Stemming from this, Laura's separation increases till she is like a piece of her own glass collection, too exquisitely fragile to move from the shelf.

Tom Wingfield, her son. And the narrator of the play. A poet with a job in a warehouse. His nature is not remorseless, but to escape from a trap he has to act without pity.

Jim O'Connor, the gentleman caller. A nice, ordinary, young man.

SCENE: *An alley in St. Louis.*
PART I: *Preparation for a Gentleman Caller.*
PART II: *The Gentleman Calls.*
TIME: *Now and the Past.*

SCENE I

The Wingfield apartment is in the rear of the building, one of those vast hivelike conglomerations of cellular living-units that flower as warty growths in overcrowded urban centers of lower middle-class population and are symptomatic of the impulse of this largest and fundamentally enslaved section of American society to avoid fluidity and differentiation and to exist and function as one interfused mass of automatism.

The apartment faces an alley and is entered by a fire-escape, a structure whose name is a touch of accidental poetic truth, for all of these huge buildings are always burning with the slow and implacable fires of human desperation. The fire-escape is included in the set—that is, the landing of it and steps descending from it.

The scene is memory and is therefore nonrealistic. Memory takes a lot of poetic license. It omits some details; others are exaggerated, according to the emotional value of the articles it touches, for memory is seated predominantly in the heart. The interior is therefore rather dim and poetic.

At the rise of the curtain, the audience is faced with the dark, grim rear wall of the Wingfield tenement. This building, which runs parallel to the footlights, is flanked on both sides by dark, narrow alleys which run into murky canyons of tangled clotheslines, garbage cans, and the sinister latticework of neighboring fire-escapes. It is up and down these side alleys that exterior entrances and exits are made, during the play. At the end of Tom's opening commentary, the dark tenement wall slowly reveals (by means of a transparency) the interior of the ground floor Wingfield apartment.

Downstage is the living room, which also serves as a sleeping room for Laura, the sofa unfolding to make her bed. Upstage, center, and divided by a wide arch or second proscenium with transparent faded portieres (or second curtain), is the dining room. In an old-fashioned what-not in the living room are seen scores of transparent glass animals. A blown-up photograph of the father hangs on the wall of the living room, facing the audience, to the left of the archway. It is the face of a very handsome young man in a doughboy's First World War cap. He is gallantly smiling, ineluctably smiling, as if to say, "I will be smiling forever."

The audience hears and sees the opening scene in the dining room through both the transparent fourth wall of the building and the transparent gauze portieres of the dining-room arch. It is during this revealing scene that the fourth wall slowly ascends, out of sight. This transparent exterior wall is not brought down again until the very end of the play, during Tom's final speech.

The narrator is an undisguised convention of the play. He takes whatever license with dramatic convention as is convenient to his purposes.

Tom enters dressed as a merchant sailor from alley, stage left, and strolls across the front of the stage to the fire-escape. There he stops and lights a cigarette. He addresses the audience.

Tom: Yes, I have tricks in my pocket, I have things up my sleeve. But I am the opposite of a stage magician. He gives you illusion that has the appearance of truth. I give you truth in the pleasant disguise of illusion. To begin with, I turn back time. I reverse it to that quaint period, the thirties, when the huge middle class of America was matriculating in a school for the blind. Their eyes had failed them, or they had failed their eyes, and so they were having their fingers pressed forcibly down on the fiery Braille alphabet of a dissolving economy. In Spain there was revolution. Here there was only shouting and confusion. In Spain there was Guernica.° Here there were disturbances of labor, sometimes pretty violent, in otherwise peaceful cities such as Chicago, Cleveland, Saint Louis. . . . This is the social background of the play.

(Music.)

The play is memory. Being a memory play, it is dimly lighted, it is sentimental, it is not realistic. In memory everything seems to happen to music. That explains the fiddle in the wings. I am the narrator of the play, and also a character in it. The other characters are my mother, Amanda, my sister, Laura, and a gentleman caller who appears in the final scenes. He is the most realistic character in the play, being an emissary from a world of reality that we were somehow set apart from. But since I have a poet's weakness for symbols, I am using this character also as a symbol; he is the long delayed but always expected something that we live for. There is a fifth character in the play who doesn't appear except in this larger-than-life photograph over the mantel. This is our father who left us a long time ago. He was a telephone man who fell in love with long distances; he gave up his job with the telephone company and skipped the light fantastic out of town. . . . The last we heard of him was a picture post-card from Mazatlán, on the Pacific coast of Mexico, containing a message of two words — "Hello — Good-bye!" and no address. I think the rest of the play will explain itself. . . .

Amanda's voice becomes audible through the portieres.

(Legend on screen: "Où sont les neiges."°)
He divides the portieres and enters the upstage area.

Guernica: A town in northern Spain destroyed by German bombers in 1937 during the Spanish Civil War.
Où sont les neiges: Part of a line from a poem by the French medieval writer François Villon; the full line translates, "Where are the snows of yesteryear?"

Amanda and Laura are seated at a drop-leaf table. Eating is indicated by gestures without food or utensils. Amanda faces the audience.

Tom and Laura are seated in profile.

The interior has lit up softly and through the scrim we see Amanda and Laura seated at the table in the upstage area.

Amanda (calling): Tom?

Tom: Yes, Mother.

Amanda: We can't say grace until you come to the table!

Tom: Coming, Mother. *(He bows slightly and withdraws, reappearing a few moments later in his place at the table.)*

Amanda (to her son): Honey, don't *push* with your *fingers.* If you have to push with something, the thing to push with is a crust of bread. And chew — chew! Animals have sections in their stomachs which enable them to digest food without mastication, but human beings are supposed to chew their food before they swallow it down. Eat food leisurely, son, and really enjoy it. A well-cooked meal has lots of delicate flavors that have to be held in the mouth for appreciation. So chew your food and give your salivary glands a chance to function!

Tom deliberately lays his imaginary fork down and pushes his chair back from the table.

Tom: I haven't enjoyed one bite of this dinner because of your constant directions on how to eat it. It's you that makes me rush through meals with your hawklike attention to every bite I take. Sickening — spoils my appetite — all this discussion of animals' secretion — salivary glands — mastication!

Amanda (lightly): Temperament like a Metropolitan star! *(He rises and crosses downstage.)* You're not excused from the table.

Tom: I am getting a cigarette.

Amanda: You smoke too much.

Laura rises.

Laura: I'll bring in the blanc mange.

He remains standing with his cigarette by the portieres during the following.

Amanda (rising): No, sister, no, sister — you be the lady this time and I'll be the darky.

Laura: I'm already up.

Amanda: Resume your seat, little sister — I want you to stay fresh and pretty — for gentlemen callers!

Laura: I'm not expecting any gentlemen callers.

Amanda (crossing out to kitchenette. Airily): Sometimes they come when they are least expected! Why, I remember one Sunday afternoon in Blue Mountain — *(Enters kitchenette.)*

Tom: I know what's coming!

Laura: Yes. But let her tell it.

Tom: Again?

Laura: She loves to tell it.

Amanda returns with bowl of dessert.

Amanda: One Sunday afternoon in Blue Mountain — your mother received — *seventeen!* — gentlemen callers! Why, sometimes there weren't chairs enough to accommodate them all. We had to send the nigger over to bring in folding chairs from the parish house.

Tom (remaining at portieres): How did you entertain those gentlemen callers?

Amanda: I understood the art of conversation!

Tom: I bet you could talk.

Amanda: Girls in those days *knew* how to talk, I can tell you.

Tom: Yes?

(Image: Amanda as a girl on a porch greeting callers.)

Amanda: They knew how to entertain their gentlemen callers. It wasn't enough for a girl to be possessed of a pretty face and a graceful figure — although I wasn't slighted in either respect. She also needed to have a nimble wit and a tongue to meet all occasions.

Tom: What did you talk about?

Amanda: Things of importance going on in the world! Never anything coarse or common or vulgar. *(She addresses Tom as though he were seated in the vacant chair at the table though he remains by portieres. He plays this scene as though he held the book.)* My callers were gentlemen — all! Among my callers were some of the most prominent young planters of the Mississippi Delta — planters and sons of planters!

Tom motions for music and a spot of light on Amanda.
Her eyes lift, her face glows, her voice becomes rich and elegiac.
(Screen legend: "Où sont les neiges.")

There was young Champ Laughlin who later became vice-president of the Delta Planters Bank. Hadley Stevenson who was drowned in Moon Lake and left his widow one hundred and fifty thousand in Government bonds. There were the Cutrere brothers, Wesley and Bates. Bates was one of my bright particular beaux! He got in a quarrel with that wild Wainright boy. They shot it out on the floor of Moon Lake Casino. Bates was shot through the stomach. Died in the ambulance on his way to Memphis. His widow was also well-provided for, came into eight or ten thousand acres, that's all. She married him on the rebound — never loved her — carried my picture on him the night he died! And there was that boy that every girl in the Delta had set her cap for! That beautiful, brilliant young Fitzhugh boy from Green County!

Tom: What did he leave his widow?

Amanda: He never married! Gracious, you talk as though all of my old admirers had turned up their toes to the daisies!

Tom: Isn't this the first you mentioned that still survives?

Amanda: That Fitzhugh boy went North and made a fortune — came to be known as the Wolf of Wall Street! He had the Midas touch, whatever he touched turned to gold! And I could have been Mrs. Duncan J. Fitzhugh, mind you! But — I picked your *father!*

Laura (rising): Mother, let me clear the table.

Amanda: No dear, you go in front and study your typewriter chart. Or practice your shorthand a little. Stay fresh and pretty! — It's almost time for our gentlemen callers to start arriving. *(She flounces girlishly toward the kitchenette.)* How many do you suppose we're going to entertain this afternoon?

Tom throws down the paper and jumps up with a groan.

Laura (alone in the dining room): I don't believe we're going to receive any, Mother.

Amanda (reappearing, airily): What? No one — not one? You must be joking! *(Laura nervously echoes her laugh. She slips in a fugitive manner through the half-open portieres and draws them gently behind her. A shaft of very clear light is thrown on her face against the faded tapestry of the curtains.) (Music: "The Glass Menagerie" under faintly.) (Lightly.)* Not one gentleman caller? It can't be true! There must be a flood, there must have been a tornado!

Laura: It isn't a flood, it's not a tornado, Mother. I'm just not popular like you were in Blue Mountain. . . . *(Tom utters another groan. Laura glances at him with a faint, apologetic smile. Her voice catching a little.)* Mother's afraid I'm going to be an old maid.

(The scene dims out with "Glass Menagerie" music.)

SCENE II

"Laura, Haven't You Ever Liked Some Boy?"

On the dark stage the screen is lighted with the image of blue roses.
   Gradually Laura's figure becomes apparent and the screen goes out.
   The music subsides.
   Laura is seated in the delicate ivory chair at the small clawfoot table.
   She wears a dress of soft violet material for a kimono — her hair tied back from her forehead with a ribbon.
   She is washing and polishing her collection of glass.
   Amanda appears on the fire-escape steps. At the sound of her ascent, Laura catches her breath, thrusts the bowl of ornaments away, and seats herself stiffly before the diagram of the typewriter keyboard as though it held her spellbound. Something has happened to Amanda. It is written in her face as she climbs to the landing: a look that is grim and hopeless and a little absurd.
   She has on one of those cheap or imitation velvety-looking cloth coats with imitation fur collar. Her hat is five or six years old, one of those dreadful cloche hats that were worn in the late twenties, and she is clasping an enormous black patent-leather pocketbook with nickel clasp and initials. This is her full-dress outfit, the one she usually wears to the D.A.R.°
   Before entering she looks through the door.
   She purses her lips, opens her eyes wide, rolls them upward, and shakes her head.
   Then she slowly lets herself in the door. Seeing her mother's expression Laura touches her lips with a nervous gesture.

Laura: Hello, Mother, I was — *(She makes a nervous gesture toward the chart on the wall. Amanda leans against the shut door and stares at Laura with a martyred look.)*

Amanda: Deception? Deception? *(She slowly removes her hat and gloves, continuing the swift suffering stare. She lets the hat and gloves fall on the floor — a bit of acting.)*

D.A.R.: Daughters of the American Revolution; members must document that they have ancestors who served the patriots' cause in the Revolutionary War.

Laura (shakily): How was the D.A.R. meeting? *(Amanda slowly opens her purse and removes a dainty white handkerchief, which she shakes out delicately and delicately touches to her lips and nostrils.)* Didn't you go to the D.A.R. meeting, Mother?

Amanda (faintly, almost inaudibly): — No. — No. *(Then more forcibly.)* I did not have the strength — to go to the D.A.R. In fact, I did not have the courage! I wanted to find a hole in the ground and hide myself in it forever! *(She crosses slowly to the wall and removes the diagram of the typewriter keyboard. She holds it in front of her for a second, staring at it sweetly and sorrowfully — then bites her lips and tears it in two pieces.)*

Laura (faintly): Why did you do that, Mother? *(Amanda repeats the same procedure with the chart of the Gregg Alphabet.°)* Why are you —

Amanda: Why? Why? How old are you, Laura?

Laura: Mother, you know my age.

Amanda: I thought that you were an adult; it seems that I was mistaken. *(She crosses slowly to the sofa and sinks down and stares at Laura.)*

Laura: Please don't stare at me, Mother.

Amanda closes her eyes and lowers her head. Count ten.

Amanda: What are we going to do, what is going to become of us, what is the future?

Count ten.

Laura: Has something happened, Mother? *(Amanda draws a long breath and takes out the handkerchief again. Dabbing process.)* Mother, has — something happened?

Amanda: I'll be all right in a minute. I'm just bewildered — *(count five)* — by life. . . .

Laura: Mother, I wish that you would tell me what's happened.

Amanda: As you know, I was supposed to be inducted into my office at the D.A.R. this afternoon. *(Image: A swarm of typewriters.)* But I stopped off at Rubicam's Business College to speak to your teachers about your having a cold and ask them what progress they thought you were making down there.

Laura: Oh. . . .

Amanda: I went to the typing instructor and introduced myself as your mother. She didn't know who you were. Wingfield, she said. We don't have any such student enrolled at the school! I assured her she did, that you had been going to classes since early in January. "I wonder," she said, "if you could be talking about that terribly shy little girl who dropped out of school after only a few days' attendance?" "No," I said, "Laura, my daughter, has been going to school every day for the past six weeks!" "Excuse me," she said. She took the attendance book out and there was your name, unmistakably printed, and all the dates you were absent until they decided that you had dropped out of school. I still said, "No, there must have been some mistake! There must have been some mix-up in the records!" And she said, "No — I remember her perfectly now. Her hand shook so that she couldn't hit the right keys! The first time we gave a speed-test, she broke down completely — was sick at the stomach and almost had to be carried into the wash-room! After that morning she never showed up any more.

Gregg Alphabet: System of shorthand symbols invented by John Robert Gregg.

We phoned the house but never got any answer" — while I was working at Famous and Barr, I suppose, demonstrating those — Oh! I felt so weak I could barely keep on my feet. I had to sit down while they got me a glass of water! Fifty dollars' tuition, all of our plans — my hopes and ambitions for you — just gone up the spout, just gone up the spout like that. *(Laura draws a long breath and gets awkwardly to her feet. She crosses to the Victrola, and winds it up.)* What are you doing?

Laura: Oh! *(She releases the handle and returns to her seat.)*

Amanda: Laura, where have you been going when you've gone out pretending that you were going to business college?

Laura: I've just been going out walking.

Amanda: That's not true.

Laura: It is. I just went walking.

Amanda: Walking? Walking? In winter? Deliberately courting pneumonia in that light coat? Where did you walk to, Laura?

Laura: It was the lesser of two evils, Mother. *(Image: Winter scene in park.)* I couldn't go back up. I — threw up — on the floor!

Amanda: From half past seven till after five every day you mean to tell me you walked around in the park, because you wanted to make me think that you were still going to Rubicam's Business College?

Laura: It wasn't as bad as it sounds. I went inside places to get warmed up.

Amanda: Inside where?

Laura: I went in the art museum and the bird-houses at the Zoo. I visited the penguins every day! Sometimes I did without lunch and went to the movies. Lately I've been spending most of my afternoons in the Jewel-box, that big glass house where they raise the tropical flowers.

Amanda: You did all this to deceive me, just for the deception? *(Laura looks down.)* Why?

Laura: Mother, when you're disappointed, you get that awful suffering look on your face, like the picture of Jesus' mother in the museum!

Amanda: Hush!

Laura: I couldn't face it.

> Pause. A whisper of strings.
>   *(Legend: "The Crust of Humility.")*

Amanda (hopelessly fingering the huge pocketbook): So what are we going to do the rest of our lives? Stay home and watch the parades go by? Amuse ourselves with the glass menagerie, darling? Eternally play those worn-out phonograph records your father left as a painful reminder of him? We won't have a business career — we've given that up because it gave us nervous indigestion! *(Laughs wearily.)* What is there left but dependency all our lives? I know so well what becomes of unmarried women who aren't prepared to occupy a position. I've seen such pitiful cases in the South — barely tolerated spinsters living upon the grudging patronage of sister's husband or brother's wife! — stuck away in some little mousetrap of a room — encouraged by one in-law to visit another — little birdlike women without any nest — eating the crust of humility all their life! Is that the future that we've mapped out for ourselves? I swear it's the only alternative I can think of! It isn't a very pleasant alternative, is it? Of course — some girls *do* marry. *(Laura twists her hands nervously.)* Haven't you ever liked some boy?

Laura: Yes. I liked one once. *(Rises.)* I came across his picture a while ago.

Amanda (with some interest): He gave you his picture?
Laura: No, it's in the year-book.
Amanda (disappointed): Oh — a high-school boy.

(Screen image: Jim as a high-school hero bearing a silver cup.)

Laura: Yes. His name was Jim. *(Laura lifts the heavy annual from the clawfoot table.)* Here he is in *The Pirates of Penzance.*
Amanda (absently): The what?
Laura: The operetta the senior class put on. He had a wonderful voice and we sat across the aisle from each other Mondays, Wednesdays, and Fridays in the Aud. Here he is with the silver cup for debating! See his grin?
Amanda (absently): He must have had a jolly disposition.
Laura: He used to call me — Blue Roses.

(Image: Blue roses.)

Amanda: Why did he call you such a name as that?
Laura: When I had that attack of pleurosis — he asked me what was the matter when I came back. I said pleurosis — he thought that I said Blue Roses! So that's what he always called me after that. Whenever he saw me, he'd holler, "Hello, Blue Roses!" I didn't care for the girl that he went out with. Emily Meisenbach. Emily was the best-dressed girl at Soldan. She never struck me, though, as being sincere. . . . It says in the Personal Section — they're engaged. That's — six years ago! They must be married by now.
Amanda: Girls that aren't cut out for business careers usually wind up married to some nice man. *(Gets up with a spark of revival.)* Sister, that's what you'll do!

Laura utters a startled, doubtful laugh. She reaches quickly for a piece of glass.

Laura: But, Mother —
Amanda: Yes? *(Crossing to photograph.)*
Laura (in a tone of frightened apology): I'm — crippled!

(Image: Screen.)

Amanda: Nonsense! Laura, I've told you never, never to use that word. Why, you're not crippled, you just have a little defect — hardly noticeable, even! When people have some slight disadvantage like that, they cultivate other things to make up for it — develop charm — and vivacity — and — *charm!* That's all you have to do! *(She turns again to the photograph.)* One thing your father had *plenty of* — was *charm!*

Tom motions to the fiddle in the wings.
(The scene fades out with music.)

SCENE III

(Legend on the screen: "After the Fiasco —")
Tom speaks from the fire-escape landing.

Tom: After the fiasco at Rubicam's Business College, the idea of getting a gentleman caller for Laura began to play a more important part in Mother's calculations. It became an obsession. Like some archetype of the universal unconscious, the image of the gentleman caller haunted our small apartment. . . . *(Image: Young man at door with flowers.)* An evening at home rarely passed without some allusion to this image, this specter, this hope. . . . Even when he wasn't mentioned, his presence hung in Mother's preoccupied look and in my sister's frightened, apologetic manner—hung like a sentence passed upon the Wingfields! Mother was a woman of action as well as words. She began to take logical steps in the planned direction. Late that winter and in the early spring—realizing that extra money would be needed to properly feather the nest and plume the bird—she conducted a vigorous campaign on the telephone, roping in subscribers to one of those magazines for matrons called *The Home-maker's Companion*, the type of journal that features the serialized sublimations of ladies of letters who think in terms of delicate cuplike breasts, slim, tapering waists, rich, creamy thighs, eyes like wood-smoke in autumn, fingers that soothe and caress like strains of music, bodies as powerful as Etruscan sculpture.

(Screen image: Glamour *magazine cover.)*
    Amanda enters with phone on long extension cord. She is spotted in the dim stage.

Amanda: Ida Scott? This is Amanda Wingfield! We *missed* you at the D.A.R. last Monday! I said to myself: She's probably suffering with that sinus condition! How is that sinus condition? Horrors! Heaven have mercy!—You're a Christian martyr, yes, that's what you are, a Christian martyr! Well, I just now happened to notice that your subscription to the *Companion's* about to expire! Yes, it expires with the next issue, honey!—just when that wonderful new serial by Bessie Mae Hopper is getting off to such an exciting start. Oh, honey, it's something that you can't miss! You remember how *Gone with the Wind* took everybody by storm? You simply couldn't go out if you hadn't read it. All everybody *talked* was Scarlett O'Hara. Well, this is a book that critics already compare to *Gone with the Wind*. It's the *Gone with the Wind* of the post-World War generation!—What?—Burning?—Oh, honey, don't let them burn, go take a look in the oven and I'll hold the wire! Heavens—I think she's hung up!

(Dim out.)
    (Legend on screen: "You think I'm in love with Continental Shoemakers?")
    Before the stage is lighted, the violent voices of Tom and Amanda are heard. They are quarreling behind the portieres. In front of them stands Laura with clenched hands and panicky expression.
    A clear pool of light on her figure throughout this scene.

Tom: What in Christ's name am I—
Amanda *(shrilly)*: Don't you use that—
Tom: Supposed to do!
Amanda: Expression! Not in my—
Tom: Ohhh!
Amanda: Presence! Have you gone out of your senses?
Tom: I have, that's true, *driven* out!
Amanda: What is the matter with you, you—big—big—IDIOT!
Tom: Look—I've got *no thing*, no single thing—
Amanda: Lower your voice!
Tom: In my life here that I can call my own! Everything is—

Amanda: Stop that shouting!

Tom: Yesterday you confiscated my books! You had the nerve to —

Amanda: I took that horrible novel back to the library—yes! That hideous book by that insane Mr. Lawrence.° *(Tom laughs wildly.)* I cannot control the output of diseased minds or people who cater to them — *(Tom laughs still more wildly.)* BUT I WON'T ALLOW SUCH FILTH BROUGHT INTO MY HOUSE! No, no, no, no, no!

Tom: House, house! Who pays rent on it, who makes a slave of himself to —

Amanda (fairly screeching): Don't you DARE to —

Tom: No, no, *I* mustn't say things! *I've* got to just —

Amanda: Let me tell you —

Tom: I don't want to hear any more! *(He tears the portieres open. The upstage area is lit with a turgid smoky red glow.)*

> *Amanda's hair is in metal curlers and she wears a very old bathrobe, much too large for her slight figure, a relic of the faithless Mr. Wingfield.*
>
> *An upright typewriter and a wild disarray of manuscripts are on the drop-leaf table. The quarrel was probably precipitated by Amanda's interruption of his creative labor. A chair lying overthrown on the floor.*
>
> *Their gesticulating shadows are cast on the ceiling by the fiery glow.*

Amanda: You *will* hear more, you —

Tom: No, I won't hear more, I'm going out!

Amanda: You come right back in —

Tom: Out, out, out! Because I'm —

Amanda: Come back here, Tom Wingfield! I'm not through talking to you!

Tom: Oh, go —

Laura (desperately): Tom!

Amanda: You're going to listen, and no more insolence from you! I'm at the end of my patience! *(He comes back toward her.)*

Tom: What do you think I'm at? Aren't I supposed to have any patience to reach the end of, Mother? I know, I know. It seems unimportant to you, what I'm *doing*—what I *want* to do—having a little *difference* between them! You don't think that—

Amanda: I think you've been doing things that you're ashamed of. That's why you act like this. I don't believe that you go every night to the movies. Nobody goes to the movies night after night. Nobody in their right minds goes to the movies as often as you pretend to. People don't go to the movies at nearly midnight, and movies don't let out at two A.M. Come in stumbling. Muttering to yourself like a maniac! You get three hours' sleep and then go to work. Oh, I can picture the way you're doing down there. Moping, doping, because you're in no condition.

Tom (wildly): No, I'm in no condition!

Amanda: What right have you got to jeopardize your job? Jeopardize the security of us all? How do you think we'd manage if you were —

Tom: Listen! You think I'm crazy *about* the *warehouse*! *(He bends fiercely toward her slight figure.)* You think I'm in love with the Continental Shoemakers? You think I want to spend fifty-five *years* down there in that—*celotex interior!* with—*fluorescent—tubes!* Look! I'd rather somebody picked up a crowbar and battered out my brains—than go back mornings! I *go!* Every time you

---

Mr. Lawrence: D. H. Lawrence (1885–1930), English poet and novelist who advocated sexual freedom.

come in yelling that God damn *"Rise and Shine!" "Rise and Shine!"* I say to myself "How *lucky dead* people are!" But I get up. I *go!* For sixty-five dollars a
month I give up all that I dream of doing and being *ever!* And you say self—
self's all I ever think of. Why, listen, if self is what I thought of, Mother, I'd be
where he is—! *(Pointing to father's picture.)* As far as the system of transportation reaches! *(He starts past her. She grabs his arm.)* Don't grab at me, Mother!
Amanda: Where are you going?
Tom: I'm going to the *movies!*
Amanda: I don't believe that lie!
Tom (crouching toward her, overtowering her tiny figure. She backs away, gasping): I'm
going to opium dens! Yes, opium dens, dens of vice and criminals' hang-
outs, Mother. I've joined the Hogan gang, I'm a hired assassin, I carry a
tommy-gun in a violin case! I run a string of cat-houses in the Valley! They
call me Killer, Killer Wingfield, I'm leading a double-life, a simple, honest
warehouse worker by day, by night a dynamic *czar* of the *underworld, Mother.*
I go to gambling casinos, I spin away fortunes on the roulette table! I wear a
patch over one eye and a false mustache, sometimes I put on green whiskers.
On those occasions they call me—*El Diablo!*° Oh, I could tell you things to
make you sleepless! My enemies plan to dynamite this place. They're going
to blow us all sky-high some night! I'll be glad, very happy, and so will you!
You'll go up, up on a broomstick, over Blue Mountain with seventeen gentlemen callers! You ugly—babbling old—*witch....* *(He goes through a series of
violent, clumsy movements, seizing his overcoat, lunging to the door, pulling it fiercely
open. The women watch him, aghast. His arm catches in the sleeve of the coat as he
struggles to pull it on. For a moment he is pinioned by the bulky garment. With an
outraged groan he tears the coat off again, splitting the shoulders of it, and hurls it
across the room. It strikes against the shelf of Laura's glass collection, there is a tinkle of
shattering glass. Laura cries out as if wounded.)*

(Music legend: "The Glass Menagerie.")

Laura (shrilly): My glass!—menagerie.... *(She covers her face and turns away.)*

*But Amanda is still stunned and stupefied by the "ugly witch" so that she barely
notices this occurrence. Now she recovers her speech.*

Amanda (in an awful voice): I won't speak to you—until you apologize! *(She
crosses through portieres and draws them together behind her. Tom is left with
Laura. Laura clings weakly to the mantel with her face averted. Tom stares at her
stupidly for a moment. Then he crosses to shelf. Drops awkwardly to his knees to collect the fallen glass, glancing at Laura as if he would speak but couldn't.)*

"The Glass Menagerie" steals in as
    (The scene dims out.)

SCENE IV

The interior is dark. Faint light in the alley.
    *A deep-voiced bell in a church is tolling the hour of five as the scene
commences.*

El Diablo: The devil (Spanish).

Tom appears at the top of the alley. After each solemn boom of the bell in the tower, he shakes a little noise-maker or rattle as if to express the tiny spasm of man in contrast to the sustained power and dignity of the Almighty. This and the unsteadiness of his advance make it evident that he has been drinking.

As he climbs the few steps to the fire-escape landing light steals up inside. Laura appears in night-dress, observing Tom's empty bed in the front room.

Tom fishes in his pockets for the door-key, removing a motley assortment of articles in the search, including a perfect shower of movie-ticket stubs and an empty bottle. At last he finds the key, but just as he is about to insert it, it slips from his fingers. He strikes a match and crouches below the door.

Tom (*bitterly*): One crack — and it falls through!

Laura opens the door.

Laura: Tom! Tom, what are you doing?

Tom: Looking for a door-key.

Laura: Where have you been all this time?

Tom: I have been to the movies.

Laura: All this time at the movies?

Tom: There was a very long program. There was a Garbo picture and a Mickey Mouse and a travelogue and a newsreel and a preview of coming attractions. And there was an organ solo and a collection for the milk-fund — simultaneously — which ended up in a terrible fight between a fat lady and an usher!

Laura (*innocently*): Did you have to stay through everything?

Tom: Of course! And, oh, I forgot! There was a big stage show! The headliner on this stage show was Malvolio the Magician. He performed wonderful tricks, many of them, such as pouring water back and forth between pitchers. First it turned to wine and then it turned to beer and then it turned to whiskey. I know it was whiskey it finally turned into because he needed somebody to come up out of the audience to help him, and I came up — both shows! It was Kentucky Straight Bourbon. A very generous fellow, he gave souvenirs. (*He pulls from his back pocket a shimmering rainbow-colored scarf.*) He gave me this. This is his magic scarf. You can have it, Laura. You wave it over a canary cage and you get a bowl of gold-fish. You wave it over the gold-fish bowl and they fly away canaries. . . . But the wonderfullest trick of all was the coffin trick. We nailed him into a coffin and he got out of the coffin without removing one nail. (*He has come inside.*) There is a trick that would come in handy for me — get me out of this 2 by 4 situation! (*Flops onto bed and starts removing shoes.*)

Laura: Tom — Shhh!

Tom: What you shushing me for?

Laura: You'll wake up Mother.

Tom: Goody, goody! Pay 'er back for all those "Rise an' Shines." (*Lies down, groaning.*) You know it don't take much intelligence to get yourself into a nailed-up coffin, Laura. But who in hell ever got himself out of one without removing one nail?

As if in answer, the father's grinning photograph lights up.
    (Scene dims out.)
    Immediately following: The church bell is heard striking six. At the sixth stroke the alarm clock goes off in Amanda's room, and after a few moments we hear her

calling: *"Rise and Shine! Rise and Shine! Laura, go tell your brother to rise and shine!"*

Tom (sitting up slowly): I'll rise — but I won't shine.

The light increases.

Amanda: Laura, tell your brother his coffee is ready.

Laura slips into front room.

Laura: Tom! it's nearly seven. Don't make Mother nervous. *(He stares at her stupidly. Beseechingly.)* Tom, speak to Mother this morning. Make up with her, apologize, speak to her!

Tom: She won't to me. It's her that started not speaking.

Laura: If you just say you're sorry she'll start speaking.

Tom: Her not speaking — is that such a tragedy?

Laura: Please — please!

Amanda (calling from kitchenette): Laura, are you going to do what I asked you to do, or do I have to get dressed and go out myself?

Laura: Going, going — soon as I get on my coat! *(She pulls on a shapeless felt hat with nervous, jerky movement, pleadingly glancing at Tom. Rushes awkwardly for coat. The coat is one of Amanda's, inaccurately made-over, the sleeves too short for Laura.)* Butter and what else?

Amanda (entering upstage): Just butter. Tell them to charge it.

Laura: Mother, they make such faces when I do that.

Amanda: Sticks and stones may break my bones, but the expression on Mr. Garfinkel's face won't harm us! Tell your brother his coffee is getting cold.

Laura (at door): Do what I asked you, will you, will you, Tom?

He looks sullenly away.

Amanda: Laura, go now or just don't go at all!

Laura (rushing out): Going — going! *(A second later she cries out. Tom springs up and crosses to the door. Amanda rushes anxiously in. Tom opens the door.)*

Tom: Laura?

Laura: I'm all right. I slipped, but I'm all right.

Amanda (peering anxiously after her): If anyone breaks a leg on those fire-escape steps, the landlord ought to be sued for every cent he possesses! *(She shuts door. Remembers she isn't speaking and returns to other room.)*

As Tom enters listlessly for his coffee, she turns her back to him and stands rigidly facing the window on the gloomy gray vault of the areaway. Its light on her face with its aged but childish features is cruelly sharp, satirical as a Daumier° print. (Music under: "Ave Maria.")

Tom glances sheepishly but sullenly at her averted figure and slumps at the table. The coffee is scalding hot; he sips it and gasps and spits it back in the cup. At his gasp, Amanda catches her breath and half turns. Then catches herself and turns back to window.

Tom blows on his coffee, glancing sidewise at his mother. She clears her throat. Tom clears his. He starts to rise. Sinks back down again, scratches his head, clears his throat again. Amanda coughs. Tom raises his cup in both hands to blow on it, his

---

Daumier: Honoré Daumier (1808–1879), French caricaturist, lithographer, and painter who mercilessly satirized bourgeois society.

eyes staring over the rim of it at his mother for several moments. Then he slowly sets the cup down and awkwardly and hesitantly rises from the chair.

Tom (hoarsely): Mother. I—I apologize. Mother. *(Amanda draws a quick, shuddering breath. Her face works grotesquely. She breaks into childlike tears.)* I'm sorry for what I said, for everything that I said, I didn't mean it.

Amanda (sobbingly): My devotion has made me a witch and so I make myself hateful to my children!

Tom: No, you *don't.*

Amanda: I worry so much, don't sleep, it makes me nervous!

Tom (gently): I understand that.

Amanda: I've had to put up a solitary battle all these years. But you're my right-hand bower! Don't fall down, don't fail!

Tom (gently): I try, Mother.

Amanda (with great enthusiasm): Try and you will SUCCEED! *(The notion makes her breathless.)* Why, you—you're just *full* of natural endowments! Both of my children—they're *unusual* children! Don't you think I know it? I'm so— proud! Happy and—feel I've—so much to be thankful for but—Promise me one thing, son!

Tom: What, Mother?

Amanda: Promise, son, you'll—never be a drunkard!

Tom (turns to her grinning): I will never be a drunkard, Mother.

Amanda: That's what frightened me so, that you'd be drinking! Eat a bowl of Purina!

Tom: Just coffee, Mother.

Amanda: Shredded wheat biscuit?

Tom: No. No, Mother, just coffee.

Amanda: You can't put in a day's work on an empty stomach. You've got ten minutes—don't gulp! Drinking too-hot liquids makes cancer of the stomach. . . . Put cream in.

Tom: No, thank you.

Amanda: To cool it.

Tom: No! No, thank you, I want it black.

Amanda: I know, but it's not good for you. We have to do all that we can to build ourselves up. In these trying times we live in, all that we have to cling to is—each other. . . . That's why it's so important to—Tom, I—I sent out your sister so I could discuss something with you. If you hadn't spoken I would have spoken to you. *(Sits down.)*

Tom (gently): What is it, Mother, that you want to discuss?

Amanda: Laura!

Tom puts his cup down slowly.
    (Legend on screen: "Laura.")
    (Music: "The Glass Menagerie.")

Tom: —Oh.—Laura . . .

Amanda (touching his sleeve): You know how Laura is. So quiet but—still water runs deep! She notices things and I think she—broods about them. *(Tom looks up.)* A few days ago I came in and she was crying.

Tom: What about? ·

Amanda: You.

Tom: Me?

Amanda: She has an idea that you're not happy here.

Tom: What gave her that idea?

Amanda: What gives her any idea? However, you do act strangely. I—I'm not criticizing, understand *that!* I know your ambitions do not lie in the warehouse, that like everybody in the whole wide world—you've had to—make sacrifices, but—Tom—Tom—life's not easy, it calls for—Spartan endurance! There's so many things in my heart that I cannot describe to you! I've never told you but I—*loved* your father. . . .

Tom (gently): I know that, Mother.

Amanda: And you—when I see you taking after his ways! Staying out late—and—well, you *had* been drinking the night you were in that—terrifying condition! Laura says that you hate the apartment and that you go out nights to get away from it! Is that true, Tom?

Tom: No. You say there's so much in your heart that you can't describe to me. That's true of me, too. There's so much in my heart that I can't describe to *you!* So let's respect each other's—

Amanda: But, why—*why,* Tom—are you always so *restless?* Where do you go to, nights?

Tom: I—go to the movies.

Amanda: Why do you go to the movies so much, Tom?

Tom: I go to the movies because—I like adventure. Adventure is something I don't have much of at work, so I go to the movies.

Amanda: But, Tom, you go to the movies *entirely too much!*

Tom: I like a lot of adventure.

> *Amanda looks baffled, then hurt. As the familiar inquisition resumes he becomes hard and impatient again. Amanda slips back into her querulous attitude toward him.*
> *(Image on screen: Sailing vessel with Jolly Roger.)*

Amanda: Most young men find adventure in their careers.

Tom: Then most young men are not employed in a warehouse.

Amanda: The world is full of young men employed in warehouses and offices and factories.

Tom: Do all of them find adventure in their careers?

Amanda: They do or they do without it! Not everybody has a craze for adventure.

Tom: Man is by instinct a lover, a hunter, a fighter, and none of those instincts are given much play at the warehouse!

Amanda: Man is by instinct! Don't quote instinct to me! Instinct is something that people have got away from! It belongs to animals! Christian adults don't want it!

Tom: What do Christian adults want, then, Mother?

Amanda: Superior things! Things of the mind and the spirit! Only animals have to satisfy instincts! Surely your aims are somewhat higher than theirs! Than monkeys—pigs—

Tom: I reckon they're not.

Amanda: You're joking. However, that isn't what I wanted to discuss.

Tom (rising): I haven't much time.

Amanda (pushing his shoulders): Sit down.

Tom: You want me to punch in red° at the warehouse, Mother?

Amanda: You have five minutes. I want to talk about Laura.

---

punch in red: Be late for work.

(Legend: "Plans and Provisions.")

Tom: All right! What about Laura?

Amanda: We have to be making plans and provisions for her. She's older than you, two years, and nothing has happened. She just drifts along doing nothing. It frightens me terribly how she just drifts along.

Tom: I guess she's the type that people call home girls.

Amanda: There's no such type, and if there is, it's a pity! That is unless the home is hers, with a husband!

Tom: What?

Amanda: Oh, I can see the handwriting on the wall as plain as I see the nose in front of my face! It's terrifying! More and more you remind me of your father! He was out all hours without explanation—Then *left! Good-bye!* And me with the bag to hold. I saw that letter you got from the Merchant Marine. I know what you're dreaming of. I'm not standing here blindfolded. Very well, then. Then *do it!* But not till there's somebody to take your place.

Tom: What do you mean?

Amanda: I mean that as soon as Laura has got somebody to take care of her, married, a home of her own, independent—why, then you'll be free to go wherever you please, on land, on sea, whichever way the wind blows! But until that time you've got to look out for your sister. I don't say me because I'm old and don't matter! I say for your sister because she's young and dependent. I put her in business college—a dismal failure! Frightened her so it made her sick to her stomach. I took her over to the Young People's League at the church. Another fiasco. She spoke to nobody, nobody spoke to her. Now all she does is fool with those pieces of glass and play those worn-out records. What kind of a life is that for a girl to lead!

Tom: What can I do about it?

Amanda: Overcome selfishness! Self, self, self is all that you ever think of! *(Tom springs up and crosses to get his coat. It is ugly and bulky. He pulls on a cap with earmuffs.)* Where is your muffler? Put your wool muffler on! *(He snatches it angrily from the closet and tosses it around his neck and pulls both ends tight.)* Tom! I haven't said what I had in mind to ask you.

Tom: I'm too late to—

Amanda (catching his arms—very importunately. Then shyly.): Down at the warehouse, aren't there some—nice young men?

Tom: No!

Amanda: There *must* be—*some.*

Tom: Mother—

Gesture.

Amanda: Find out one that's clean-living—doesn't drink and—ask him out for sister!

Tom: What?

Amanda: For *sister!* To *meet!* Get *acquainted!*

Tom (stamping to door): Oh, my *go-osh!*

Amanda: Will you? *(He opens door. Imploringly.)* Will you? *(He starts down.)* Will you? *Will* you, dear?

Tom (calling back): YES!

Amanda closes the door hesitantly and with a troubled but faintly hopeful expression.

(Screen image: Glamour *magazine cover.)*
Spot Amanda at phone.

Amanda: Ella Cartwright? This is Amanda Wingfield! How are you, honey? How is that kidney condition? *(Count five.)* Horrors! *(Count five.)* You're a Christian martyr, yes, honey, that's what you are, a Christian martyr! Well, I just happened to notice in my little red book that your subscription to the *Companion* has just run out! I knew that you wouldn't want to miss out on the wonderful serial starting in this new issue. It's by Bessie Mae Hopper, the first thing she's written since *Honeymoon for Three.* Wasn't that a strange and interesting story? Well, this one is even lovelier, I believe. It has a sophisticated society background. It's all about the horsey set on Long Island!

(Fade out.)

SCENE V

(Legend on screen: "Annunciation.") Fade with music.
    It is early dusk of a spring evening. Supper has just been finished in the Wingfield apartment. Amanda and Laura in light-colored dresses are removing dishes from the table, in the upstage area, which is shadowy, their movements formalized almost as a dance or ritual, their moving forms as pale and silent as moths.
    Tom, in white shirt and trousers, rises from the table and crosses toward the fire-escape.

Amanda (as he passes her): Son, will you do me a favor?
Tom: What?
Amanda: Comb your hair! You look so pretty when your hair is combed! *(Tom slouches on sofa with evening paper. Enormous caption "Franco Triumphs."°)* There is only one respect in which I would like you to emulate your father.
Tom: What respect is that?
Amanda: The care he always took of his appearance. He never allowed himself to look untidy. *(He throws down the paper and crosses to fire-escape.)* Where are you going?
Tom: I'm going out to smoke.
Amanda: You smoke too much. A pack a day at fifteen cents a pack. How much would that amount to in a month? Thirty times fifteen is how much, Tom? Figure it out and you will be astounded at what you could save. Enough to give you a night-school course in accounting at Washington U! Just think what a wonderful thing that would be for you, son!

Tom is unmoved by the thought.

Tom: I'd rather smoke. *(He steps out on landing, letting the screen door slam.)*
Amanda (sharply): I know! That's the tragedy of it. . . . *(Alone, she turns to look at her husband's picture.)*

"Franco Triumphs": In January 1939 the Republican forces of Francisco Franco (1892–1975) defeated the Loyalists, ending the Spanish Civil War.

(Dance music: "All the World Is Waiting for the Sunrise!")

Tom (to the audience): Across the alley from us was the Paradise Dance Hall. On evenings in spring the windows and doors were open and the music came outdoors. Sometimes the lights were turned out except for a large glass sphere that hung from the ceiling. It would turn slowly about and filter the dusk with delicate rainbow colors. Then the orchestra played a waltz or a tango, something that had a slow and sensuous rhythm. Couples would come outside, to the relative privacy of the alley. You could see them kissing behind ash-pits and telephone poles. This was the compensation for lives that passed like mine, without any change or adventure. Adventure and change were imminent in this year. They were waiting around the corner for all these kids. Suspended in the mist over the Berchtesgaden,° caught in the folds of Chamberlain's° umbrella—In Spain there was Guernica! But here there was only hot swing music and liquor, dance halls, bars, and movies, and sex that hung in the gloom like a chandelier and flooded the world with brief, deceptive rainbows. . . . All the world was waiting for bombardments!

Amanda turns from the picture and comes outside.

Amanda (sighing): A fire-escape landing's a poor excuse for a porch. *(She spreads a newspaper on a step and sits down, gracefully and demurely as if she were settling into a swing on a Mississippi veranda.)* What are you looking at?

Tom: The moon.

Amanda: Is there a moon this evening?

Tom: It's rising over Garfinkel's Delicatessen.

Amanda: So it is! A little silver slipper of a moon. Have you made a wish on it yet?

Tom: Um-hum.

Amanda: What did you wish for?

Tom: That's a secret.

Amanda: A secret, huh? Well, I won't tell mine either. I will be just as mysterious as you.

Tom: I bet I can guess what yours is.

Amanda: Is my head so transparent?

Tom: You're not a sphinx.

Amanda: No, I don't have secrets. I'll tell you what I wished for on the moon. Success and happiness for my precious children! I wish for that whenever there's a moon, and when there isn't a moon, I wish for it, too.

Tom: I thought perhaps you wished for a gentleman caller.

Amanda: Why do you say that?

Tom: Don't you remember asking me to fetch one?

Amanda: I remember suggesting that it would be nice for your sister if you brought home some nice young man from the warehouse. I think I've made that suggestion more than once.

Tom: Yes, you have made it repeatedly.

Amanda: Well?

Berchtesgaden: A resort in the German Alps where Adolf Hitler had a heavily protected villa.
Chamberlain: Neville Chamberlain (1869–1940), British prime minister who sought to avoid war with Hitler through a policy of appeasement.

Tom: We are going to have one.
Amanda: What?
Tom: A gentleman caller!

> *(The Annunciation is celebrated with music.)*
> Amanda rises.
> *(Image on screen: Caller with bouquet.)*

Amanda: You mean you have asked some nice young man to come over?
Tom: Yep. I've asked him to dinner.
Amanda: You really did?
Tom: I did!
Amanda: You did, and did he — *accept?*
Tom: He did!
Amanda: Well, well — well, well! That's — lovely!
Tom: I thought that you would be pleased.
Amanda: It's definite, then?
Tom: Very definite.
Amanda: Soon?
Tom: Very soon.
Amanda: For heaven's sake, stop putting on and tell me some things, will you?
Tom: What things do you want me to tell you?
Amanda: Naturally I would like to know when he's *coming!*
Tom: He's coming tomorrow.
Amanda: Tomorrow?
Tom: Yep. Tomorrow.
Amanda: But, Tom!
Tom: Yes, Mother?
Amanda: Tomorrow gives me no time!
Tom: Time for what?
Amanda: Preparations! Why didn't you phone me at once, as soon as you asked him, the minute that he accepted? Then, don't you see, I could have been getting ready!
Tom: You don't have to make any fuss.
Amanda: Oh, Tom, Tom, Tom, of course I have to make a fuss! I want things nice, not sloppy! Not thrown together. I'll certainly have to do some fast thinking, won't I?
Tom: I don't see why you have to think at all.
Amanda: You just don't know. We can't have a gentleman caller in a pig-sty! All my wedding silver has to be polished, the monogrammed table linen ought to be laundered! The windows have to be washed and fresh curtains put up. And how about clothes? We have to *wear* something, don't we?
Tom: Mother, this boy is no one to make a fuss over!
Amanda: Do you realize he's the first young man we've introduced to your sister? It's terrible, dreadful, disgraceful that poor little sister has never received a single gentleman caller! Tom, come inside! *(She opens the screen door.)*
Tom: What for?
Amanda: I want to ask you some things.
Tom: If you're going to make such a fuss, I'll call it off, I'll tell him not to come.

Amanda: You certainly won't do anything of the kind. Nothing offends people worse than broken engagements. It simply means I'll have to work like a Turk! We won't be brilliant, but we'll pass inspection. Come on inside. *(Tom follows, groaning.)* Sit down.

Tom: Any particular place you would like me to sit?

Amanda: Thank heavens I've got that new sofa! I'm also making payments on a floor lamp I'll have sent out! And put the chintz covers on, they'll brighten things up! Of course I'd hoped to have these walls re-papered. . . . What is the young man's name?

Tom: His name is O'Connor.

Amanda: That, of course, means fish — tomorrow is Friday! I'll have that salmon loaf — with Durkee's dressing! What does he do? He works at the warehouse?

Tom: Of course! How else would I —

Amanda: Tom, he — doesn't drink?

Tom: Why do you ask me that?

Amanda: Your father *did*!

Tom: Don't get started on that!

Amanda: He *does* drink, then?

Tom: Not that I know of!

Amanda: Make sure, be certain! The last thing I want for my daughter's a boy who drinks!

Tom: Aren't you being a little premature? Mr. O'Connor has not yet appeared on the scene!

Amanda: But will tomorrow. To meet your sister, and what do I know about his character? Nothing! Old maids are better off than wives of drunkards!

Tom: Oh, my God!

Amanda: Be still!

Tom (leaning forward to whisper): Lots of fellows meet girls whom they don't marry!

Amanda: Oh, talk sensibly, Tom — and don't be sarcastic! *(She has gotten a hairbrush.)*

Tom: What are you doing?

Amanda: I'm brushing that cow-lick down! What is this young man's position at the warehouse?

Tom (submitting grimly to the brush and the interrogation): This young man's position is that of a shipping clerk, Mother.

Amanda: Sounds to me like a fairly responsible job, the sort of a job *you* would be in if you just had more *get-up*. What is his salary? Have you got any idea?

Tom: I would judge it to be approximately eighty-five dollars a month.

Amanda: Well — not princely, but —

Tom: Twenty more than I make.

Amanda: Yes, how well I know! But for a family man, eighty-five dollars a month is not much more than you can just get by on. . . .

Tom: Yes, but Mr. O'Connor is not a family man.

Amanda: He might be, mightn't he? Some time in the future?

Tom: I see. Plans and provisions.

Amanda: You are the only young man that I know of who ignores the fact that the future becomes the present, the present the past, and the past turns into everlasting regret if you don't plan for it!

Tom: I will think that over and see what I can make of it.

Amanda: Don't be supercilious with your mother! Tell me some more about this — what do you call him?

Tom: James D. O'Connor. The D. is for Delaney.

Amanda: Irish on *both* sides! *Gracious!* And doesn't drink?

Tom: Shall I call him up and ask him right this minute?

Amanda: The only way to find out about those things is to make discreet inquiries at the proper moment. When I was a girl in Blue Mountain and it was suspected that a young man drank, the girl whose attentions he had been receiving, if any girl *was,* would sometimes speak to the minister of his church, or rather her father would if her father was living, and sort of feel him out on the young man's character. That is the way such things are discreetly handled to keep a young woman from making a tragic mistake!

Tom: Then how did you happen to make a tragic mistake?

Amanda: That innocent look of your father's had everyone fooled! He *smiled —* the world was *enchanted!* No girl can do worse than put herself at the mercy of a handsome appearance! I hope that Mr. O'Connor is not too good-looking.

Tom: No, he's not too good-looking. He's covered with freckles and hasn't too much of a nose.

Amanda: He's not right-down homely, though?

Tom: Not right-down homely. Just medium homely, I'd say.

Amanda: Character's what to look for in a man.

Tom: That's what I've always said, Mother.

Amanda: You've never said anything of the kind and I suspect you would never give it a thought.

Tom: Don't be suspicious of me.

Amanda: At least I hope he's the type that's up and coming.

Tom: I think he really goes in for self-improvement.

Amanda: What reason have you to think so?

Tom: He goes to night school.

Amanda (beaming): Splendid! What does he do, I mean study?

Tom: Radio engineering and public speaking!

Amanda: Then he has visions of being advanced in the world! Any young man who studies public speaking is aiming to have an executive job some day! And radio engineering? A thing for the future! Both of these facts are very illuminating. Those are the sort of things that a mother should know concerning any young man who comes to call on her daughter. Seriously or — not.

Tom: One little warning. He doesn't know about Laura. I didn't let on that we had dark ulterior motives. I just said, why don't you come have dinner with us? He said okay and that was the whole conversation.

Amanda: I bet it was! You're eloquent as an oyster. However, he'll know about Laura when he gets here. When he sees how lovely and sweet and pretty she is, he'll thank his lucky stars he was asked to dinner.

Tom: Mother, you mustn't expect too much of Laura.

Amanda: What do you mean?

Tom: Laura seems all those things to you and me because she's ours and we love her. We don't even notice she's crippled any more.

Amanda: Don't say crippled! You know that I never allow that word to be used!

Tom: But face facts, Mother. She is and — that's not all —

Amanda: What do you mean "not all"?

Tom: Laura is very different from other girls.

Amanda: I think the difference is all to her advantage.

Tom: Not quite all — in the eyes of others — strangers — she's terribly shy and lives in a world of her own and those things make her seem a little peculiar to people outside the house.

Amanda: Don't say peculiar.

Tom: Face the facts. She is.

(The dance-hall music changes to a tango that has a minor and somewhat ominous tone.)

Amanda: In what way is she peculiar — may I ask?

Tom (gently): She lives in a world of her own — a world of — little glass ornaments, Mother. . . . *(Gets up. Amanda remains holding brush, looking at him, troubled.)* She plays old phonograph records and — that's about all — *(He glances at himself in the mirror and crosses to door.)*

Amanda (sharply): Where are you going?

Tom: I'm going to the movies. *(Out screen door.)*

Amanda: Not to the movies, every night to the movies! *(Follows quickly to screen door.)* I don't believe you always go to the movies! *(He is gone. Amanda looks worriedly after him for a moment. Then vitality and optimism return and she turns from the door. Crossing to portieres.)* Laura! Laura! *(Laura answers from kitchenette.)*

Laura: Yes, Mother.

Amanda: Let those dishes go and come in front! *(Laura appears with dish towel. Gaily.)* Laura, come here and make a wish on the moon!

Laura (entering): Moon — moon?

Amanda: A little silver slipper of a moon. Look over your left shoulder, Laura, and make a wish! *(Laura looks faintly puzzled as if called out of sleep. Amanda seizes her shoulders and turns her at angle by the door.)* Now! Now, darling, *wish!*

Laura: What shall I wish for, Mother?

Amanda (her voice trembling and her eyes suddenly filling with tears): Happiness! Good Fortune!

The violin rises and the stage dims out.

SCENE VI

(Image: High-school hero.)

Tom: And so the following evening I brought Jim home to dinner. I had known Jim slightly in high school. In high school Jim was a hero. He had tremendous Irish good nature and vitality with the scrubbed and polished look of white chinaware. He seemed to move in a continual spotlight. He was a star in basketball, captain of the debating club, president of the senior class and the glee club and he sang the male lead in the annual light operas. He was always running or bounding, never just walking. He seemed always at the point of defeating the law of gravity. He was shooting with such velocity through his adolescence that you would logically expect him to arrive at nothing short of the White House by the time he was thirty. But Jim apparently ran into more interference after his graduation from Soldan. His speed had definitely slowed. Six years after he left high school he was holding a job that wasn't much better than mine.

(Image: Clerk.)

He was the only one at the warehouse with whom I was on friendly terms. I was valuable to him as someone who could remember his former glory, who had seen him win basketball games and the silver cup in debating. He knew of my secret practice of retiring to a cabinet of the washroom to work on poems when business was slack in the warehouse. He called me Shakespeare. And while the other boys in the warehouse regarded me with suspicious hostility, Jim took a humorous attitude toward me. Gradually his attitude affected the others, their hostility wore off, and they also began to smile at me as people smile at an oddly fashioned dog who trots across their paths at some distance.

I knew that Jim and Laura had known each other at Soldan, and I had heard Laura speak admiringly of his voice. I didn't know if Jim remembered her or not. In high school Laura had been as unobtrusive as Jim had been astonishing. If he did remember Laura, it was not as my sister, for when I asked him to dinner, he grinned and said, "You know, Shakespeare, I never thought of you as having folks!"

He was about to discover that I did. . . .

(Light upstage.)
(Legend on screen: "The Accent of a Coming Foot.")
Friday evening. It is about five o'clock of a late spring evening which comes "scattering poems in the sky."
A delicate lemony light is in the Wingfield apartment.
Amanda has worked like a Turk in preparation for the gentleman caller. The results are astonishing. The new floor lamp with its rose-silk shade is in place, a colored paper lantern conceals the broken light fixture in the ceiling, new billowing white curtains are at the windows, chintz covers are on chairs and sofa, a pair of new sofa pillows make their initial appearance.
Open boxes and tissue paper are scattered on the floor.
Laura stands in the middle with lifted arms while Amanda crouches before her, adjusting the hem of the new dress, devout and ritualistic. The dress is colored and designed by memory. The arrangement of Laura's hair is changed; it is softer and more becoming. A fragile, unearthly prettiness has come out in Laura: she is like a piece of translucent glass touched by light, given a momentary radiance, not actual, not lasting.

Amanda (impatiently): Why are you trembling?
Laura: Mother, you've made me so nervous!
Amanda: How have I made you nervous?
Laura: By all this fuss! You make it seem so important!
Amanda: I don't understand you, Laura. You couldn't be satisfied with just sitting home, and yet whenever I try to arrange something for you, you seem to resist it. *(She gets up.)* Now take a look at yourself. No, wait! Wait just a moment — I have an idea!

Laura: What is it now?

Amanda produces two powder puffs which she wraps in handkerchiefs and stuffs in Laura's bosom.

Laura: Mother, what are you doing?
Amanda: They call them "Gay Deceivers"!
Laura: I won't wear them!
Amanda: You will!
Laura: Why should I?
Amanda: Because, to be painfully honest, your chest is flat.
Laura: You make it seem like we were setting a trap.
Amanda: All pretty girls are a trap, a pretty trap, and men expect them to be. *(Legend: "A Pretty Trap.")* Now look at yourself, young lady. This is the prettiest you will ever be! I've got to fix myself now! You're going to be surprised by your mother's appearance! *(She crosses through portieres, humming gaily.)*

Laura moves slowly to the long mirror and stares solemnly at herself.
    A wind blows the white curtains inward in a slow, graceful motion and with a faint, sorrowful sighing.

Amanda (off stage): It isn't dark enough yet. *(She turns slowly before the mirror with a troubled look).*

(Legend on screen: "This Is My Sister: Celebrate Her with Strings!" Music.)

Amanda (laughing, off): I'm going to show you something. I'm going to make a spectacular appearance!
Laura: What is it, Mother?
Amanda: Possess your soul in patience — you will see! Something I've resurrected from that old trunk! Styles haven't changed so terribly much after all. . . . *(She parts the portieres.)* Now just look at your mother! *(She wears a girlish frock of yellowed voile with a blue silk sash. She carries a bunch of jonquils — the legend of her youth is nearly revived. Feverishly.)* This is the dress in which I led the cotillion. Won the cakewalk twice at Sunset Hill, wore one spring to the Governor's ball in Jackson! See how I sashayed around the ballroom, Laura? *(She raises her skirt and does a mincing step around the room.)* I wore it on Sundays for my gentlemen callers! I had it on the day I met your father — I had malaria fever all that spring. The change of climate from East Tennessee to the Delta — weakened resistance — I had a little temperature all the time — not enough to be serious — just enough to make me restless and giddy! Invitations poured in — parties all over the Delta! — "Stay in bed," said Mother, "you have fever!" — but I just wouldn't. — I took quinine but kept on going, going! — Evenings, dances! — Afternoons, long, long rides! Picnics — lovely! — So lovely, that country in May. — All lacy with dogwood, literally flooded with jonquils! — That was the spring I had the craze for jonquils. Jonquils became an absolute obsession. Mother said, "Honey, there's no more room for jonquils." And still I kept bringing in more jonquils. Whenever, wherever I saw them, I'd say, "Stop! Stop! I see jonquils!" I made the young men help me gather the jonquils! It was a joke, Amanda and her jonquils! Finally there were no more vases to hold them, every available space was filled with jonquils. No vases to hold them? All right, I'll hold them myself! And then I — *(She stops in front of the*

picture.) (Music.) met your father! Malaria fever and jonquils and then—
this—boy. . . . *(She switches on the rose-colored lamp.)* I hope they get here before it starts to rain. *(She crosses upstage and places the jonquils in bowl on
table.)* I gave your brother a little extra change so he and Mr. O'Connor
could take the service car home.

Laura (with altered look): What did you say his name was?

Amanda: O'Connor.

Laura: What is his first name?

Amanda: I don't remember. Oh, yes, I do. It was—Jim!

Laura sways slightly and catches hold of a chair.
        (Legend on screen: "Not Jim!")

Laura (faintly): Not—Jim!

Amanda: Yes, that was it, it was Jim! I've never known a Jim that wasn't nice!

(Music: Ominous.)

Laura: Are you sure his name is Jim O'Connor?

Amanda: Yes. Why?

Laura: Is he the one that Tom used to know in high school?

Amanda: He didn't say so. I think he just got to know him at the warehouse.

Laura: There was a Jim O'Connor we both knew in high school—*(Then, with effort.)* If that is the one that Tom is bringing to dinner—you'll have to excuse me, I won't come to the table.

Amanda: What sort of nonsense is this?

Laura: You asked me once if I'd ever liked a boy. Don't you remember I showed
you this boy's picture?

Amanda: You mean the boy you showed me in the year-book?

Laura: Yes, that boy.

Amanda: Laura, Laura, were you in love with that boy?

Laura: I don't know, Mother. All I know is I couldn't sit at the table if it was
him!

Amanda: It won't be him! It isn't the least bit likely. But whether it is or not,
you will come to the table. You will not be excused.

Laura: I'll have to be, Mother.

Amanda: I don't intend to humor your silliness, Laura. I've had too much
from you and your brother, both! So just sit down and compose yourself
till they come. Tom has forgotten his key so you'll have to let them in,
when they arrive.

Laura (panicky): Oh, Mother—*you* answer the door!

Amanda (lightly): I'll be in the kitchen—busy!

Laura: Oh, Mother, please answer the door, don't make me do it!

Amanda (crossing into kitchenette): I've got to fix the dressing for the salmon.
Fuss, fuss—silliness!—over a gentleman caller!

Door swings shut. Laura is left alone.
        (Legend: "Terror!")
        She utters a low moan and turns off the lamp—sits stiffly on the edge of the
sofa, knotting her fingers together.
        (Legend on screen: "The Opening of a Door!")
        Tom and Jim appear on the fire-escape steps and climb to landing. Hearing
their approach, Laura rises with a panicky gesture. She retreats to the portieres.

The doorbell. Laura catches her breath and touches her throat. Low drums.

Amanda *(calling):* Laura, sweetheart! The door!

Laura stares at it without moving.

Jim: I think we just beat the rain.

Tom: Uh-huh. *(He rings again, nervously. Jim whistles and fishes for a cigarette.)*

Amanda *(very, very gaily):* Laura, that is your brother and Mr. O'Connor! Will you let them in, darling?

Laura crosses toward kitchenette door.

Laura *(breathlessly):* Mother — you go to the door!

Amanda steps out of kitchenette and stares furiously at Laura. She points imperiously at the door.

Laura: Please, please!

Amanda *(in a fierce whisper):* What is the matter with you, you silly thing?

Laura *(desperately):* Please, you answer it, *please!*

Amanda: I told you I wasn't going to humor you, Laura. Why have you chosen this moment to lose your mind?

Laura: Please, please, please, you go!

Amanda: You'll have to go to the door because I can't!

Laura *(despairingly):* I can't either!

Amanda: Why?

Laura: I'm *sick!*

Amanda: I'm sick, too — of your nonsense! Why can't you and your brother be normal people? Fantastic whims and behavior! *(Tom gives a long ring.)* Preposterous goings on! Can you give me one reason — *(Calls out lyrically.)* COMING! JUST ONE SECOND! — why should you be afraid to open a door? Now you answer it, Laura!

Laura: Oh, oh, oh . . . *(She returns through the portieres. Darts to the Victrola and winds it frantically and turns it on.)*

Amanda: Laura Wingfield, you march right to that door!

Laura: Yes — yes, Mother!

A faraway, scratchy rendition of "Dardanella" softens the air and gives her strength to move through it. She slips to the door and draws it cautiously open.
Tom enters with the caller, Jim O'Connor.

Tom: Laura, this is Jim. Jim, this is my sister, Laura.

Jim *(stepping inside):* I didn't know that Shakespeare had a sister!

Laura *(retreating stiff and trembling from the door):* How — how do you do?

Jim *(heartily extending his hand):* Okay!

Laura touches it hesitantly with hers.

Jim: Your hand's cold, Laura!

Laura: Yes, well — I've been playing the Victrola . . .

Jim: Must have been playing classical music on it! You ought to play a little hot swing music to warm you up!

Laura: Excuse me — I haven't finished playing the Victrola . . .

She turns awkwardly and hurries into the front room. She pauses a second by the Victrola. Then catches her breath and darts through the portieres like a frightened deer.

Jim (grinning): What was the matter?

Tom: Oh — with Laura? Laura is — terribly shy.

Jim: Shy, huh? It's unusual to meet a shy girl nowadays. I don't believe you ever mentioned you had a sister.

Tom: Well, now you know. I have one. Here is the *Post Dispatch.* You want a piece of it?

Jim: Uh-huh.

Tom: What piece? The comics?

Jim: Sports! *(Glances at it.)* Ole Dizzy Dean is on his bad behavior.

Tom (disinterest): Yeah? *(Lights cigarette and crosses back to fire-escape door.)*

Jim: Where are *you* going?

Tom: I'm going out on the terrace.

Jim (goes after him): You know, Shakespeare — I'm going to sell you a bill of goods!

Tom: What goods?

Jim: A course I'm taking.

Tom: Huh?

Jim: In public speaking! You and me, we're not the warehouse type.

Tom: Thanks — that's good news. But what has public speaking got to do with it?

Jim: It fits you for — executive positions!

Tom: Awww.

Jim: I tell you it's done a helluva lot for me.

(Image: Executive at desk.)

Tom: In what respect?

Jim: In every! Ask yourself what is the difference between you an' me and men in the office down front? Brains? — No! — Ability? — No! Then what? Just one little thing —

Tom: What is that one little thing?

Jim: Primarily it amounts to — social poise! Being able to square up to people and hold your own on any social level!

Amanda (off stage): Tom?

Tom: Yes, Mother?

Amanda: Is that you and Mr. O'Connor?

Tom: Yes, Mother.

Amanda: Well, you just make yourselves comfortable in there.

Tom: Yes, Mother.

Amanda: Ask Mr. O'Connor if he would like to wash his hands.

Jim: Aw — no — no — thank you — I took care of that at the warehouse. Tom —

Tom: Yes?

Jim: Mr. Mendoza was speaking to me about you.

Tom: Favorably?

Jim: What do you think?

Tom: Well —

Jim: You're going to be out of a job if you don't wake up.

Tom: I am waking up —

Jim: You show no signs.

Tom: The signs are interior.

(Image on screen: The sailing vessel with Jolly Roger again.)

Tom: I'm planning to change. (*He leans over the rail speaking with quiet exhilaration. The incandescent marquees and signs of the first-run movie houses light his face from across the alley. He looks like a voyager.)* I'm right at the point of committing myself to a future that doesn't include the warehouse and Mr. Mendoza or even a night-school course in public speaking.

Jim: What are you gassing about?

Tom: I'm tired of the movies.

Jim: Movies!

Tom: Yes, movies! Look at them — *(A wave toward the marvels of Grand Avenue.)* All of those glamorous people — having adventures — hogging it all, gobbling the whole thing up! You know what happens? People go to the *movies* instead of *moving*! Hollywood characters are supposed to have all the adventures for everybody in America, while everybody in America sits in a dark room and watches them have them! Yes, until there's a war. That's when adventure becomes available to the masses! *Everyone's* dish, not only Gable's! Then the people in the dark room come out of the dark room to have some adventures themselves — Goody, goody — It's our turn now, to go to the South Sea Island — to make a safari — to be exotic, far-off — But I'm not patient. I don't want to wait till then. I'm tired of the *movies* and I am *about* to *move*!

Jim (incredulously): Move?

Tom: Yes.

Jim: When?

Tom: Soon!

Jim: Where? Where?

(Theme three: Music seems to answer the question, while Tom thinks it over. He searches among his pockets.)

Tom: I'm starting to boil inside. I know I seem dreamy, but inside — well, I'm boiling! Whenever I pick up a shoe, I shudder a little thinking how short life is and what I am doing! — Whatever that means. I know it doesn't mean shoes — except as something to wear on a traveler's feet! *(Finds paper.)* Look —

Jim: What?

Tom: I'm a member.

Jim (reading): The Union of Merchant Seamen.

Tom: I paid my dues this month, instead of the light bill.

Jim: You will regret it when they turn the lights off.

Tom: I won't be here.

Jim: How about your mother?

Tom: I'm like my father. The bastard son of a bastard! See how he grins? And he's been absent going on sixteen years!

Jim: You're just talking, you drip. How does your mother feel about it?

Tom: Shhh — Here comes Mother! Mother is not acquainted with my plans!

Amanda (enters portieres): Where are you all?

Tom: On the terrace, Mother.

They start inside. She advances to them. Tom is distinctly shocked at her appearance. Even Jim blinks a little. He is making his first contact with girlish Southern vivacity and in spite of the night-school course in public speaking is somewhat thrown off the beam by the unexpected outlay of social charm.

Certain responses are attempted by Jim but are swept aside by Amanda's gay laughter and chatter. Tom is embarrassed but after the first shock Jim reacts very warmly. Grins and chuckles, is altogether won over.

(Image: Amanda as a girl.)

Amanda (coyly smiling, shaking her girlish ringlets): Well, well, well, so this is Mr.
  O'Connor. Introductions entirely unnecessary. I've heard so much about
  you from my boy. I finally said to him, Tom — good gracious! — why don't
  you bring this paragon to supper? I'd like to meet this nice young man at the
  warehouse! — Instead of just hearing him sing your praises so much! I don't
  know why my son is so stand-offish — that's not Southern behavior! Let's sit
  down and — I think we could stand a little more air in here! Tom, leave the
  door open. I felt a nice fresh breeze a moment ago. Where has it gone?
  Mmm, so warm already! And not quite summer, even. We're going to burn
  up when summer really gets started. However, we're having — we're having a
  very light supper. I think light things are better fo' this time of year. The
  same as light clothes are. Light clothes an' light food are what warm weather
  calls fo'. You know our blood gets so thick during th' winter — it takes a
  while fo' us to *adjust* ou'selves! — when the season changes. . . . It's come so
  quick this year. I wasn't prepared. All of a sudden — heavens! Already summer! — I ran to the trunk an' pulled out this light dress — Terribly old! Historical almost! But feels so good — so good an' co-ol, y'know. . . .
Tom: Mother —
Amanda: Yes, honey?
Tom: How about — supper?
Amanda: Honey, you go ask Sister if supper is ready! You know that Sister is in
  full charge of supper! Tell her you hungry boys are waiting for it. *(To Jim.)*
  Have you met Laura?
Jim: She —
Amanda: Let you in? Oh, good, you've met already! It's rare for a girl as sweet
  an' pretty as Laura to be domestic! But Laura is, thank heavens, not only
  pretty but also very domestic. I'm not at all. I never was a bit. I never could
  make a thing but angel-food cake. Well, in the South we had so many servants. Gone, gone, gone. All vestiges of gracious living! Gone completely! I
  wasn't prepared for what the future brought me. All of my gentlemen
  callers were sons of planters and so of course I assumed that I would be
  married to one and raise my family on a large piece of land with plenty of
  servants. But man proposes — and woman accepts the proposal! — To vary
  that old, old saying a little bit — I married no planter! I married a man
  who worked for the telephone company! — that gallantly smiling gentleman over there! *(Points to the picture.)* A telephone man who — fell in love
  with long distance! — Now he travels and I don't even know where! — But
  what am I going on for about my — tribulations! Tell me yours — I hope
  you don't have any! Tom?
Tom (returning): Yes, Mother?
Amanda: Is supper nearly ready?
Tom: It looks to me like supper is on the table.
Amanda: Let me look — *(She rises prettily and looks through portieres.)* Oh, lovely —
  But where is Sister?
Tom: Laura is not feeling well and she says that she thinks she'd better not
  come to the table.
Amanda: What? — Nonsense! — Laura? Oh, Laura!
Laura (off stage, faintly): Yes, Mother.
Amanda: You really must come to the table. We won't be seated until you come
  to the table! Come in, Mr. O'Connor. You sit over there and I'll — Laura?

Laura Wingfield! You're keeping us waiting, honey! We can't say grace until you come to the table!

The back door is pushed weakly open and Laura comes in. She is obviously quite faint, her lips trembling, her eyes wide and staring. She moves unsteadily toward the table.
(Legend: "Terror!")
Outside a summer storm is coming abruptly. The white curtains billow inward at the windows and there is a sorrowful murmur and deep blue dusk.
Laura suddenly stumbles — She catches at a chair with a faint moan.

Tom: Laura!

Amanda: Laura! *(There is a clap of thunder.) (Legend: "Ah!") (Despairingly.)* Why, Laura, you *are* sick, darling! Tom, help your sister into the living room, dear! Sit in the living room, Laura — rest on the sofa. Well! *(To the gentleman caller.)* Standing over the hot stove made her ill! — I told her that it was just too warm this evening, but — *(Tom comes back in. Laura is on the sofa.)* Is Laura all right now?

Tom: Yes.

Amanda: What *is* that? Rain? A nice cool rain has come up! *(She gives the gentleman caller a frightened look.)* I think we may — have grace — now . . . *(Tom looks at her stupidly.)* Tom, honey — you say grace!

Tom: Oh . . . "For these and all thy mercies —" *(They bow their heads, Amanda stealing a nervous glance at Jim. In the living room Laura, stretched on the sofa, clenches her hand to her lips, to hold back a shuddering sob.)* God's Holy Name be praised —

(The scene dims out.)

SCENE VII

A Souvenir

Half an hour later. Dinner is just being finished in the upstage area, which is concealed by the drawn portieres.
As the curtain rises Laura is still huddled upon the sofa, her feet drawn under her, her head resting on a pale blue pillow, her eyes wide and mysteriously watchful. The new floor lamp with its shade of rose-colored silk gives a soft, becoming light to her face, bringing out the fragile, unearthly prettiness which usually escapes attention. There is a steady murmur of rain, but it is slackening and stops soon after the scene begins; the air outside becomes pale and luminous as the moon breaks out.
A moment after the curtain rises, the lights in both rooms flicker and go out.

Jim: Hey, there, Mr. Light Bulb!

Amanda laughs nervously.
(Legend: "Suspension of a Public Service.")

Amanda: Where was Moses when the lights went out? Ha-ha. Do you know the answer to that one, Mr. O'Connor?

Jim: No, Ma'am, what's the answer?

Amanda: In the dark! *(Jim laughs appreciatively.)* Everybody sit still. I'll light the
    candles. Isn't it lucky we have them on the table? Where's a match? Which
    of you gentlemen can provide a match?
Jim: Here.
Amanda: Thank you, sir.
Jim: Not at all, Ma'am!
Amanda: I guess the fuse has burnt out. Mr. O'Connor, can you tell a burnt-
    out fuse? I know I can't and Tom is a total loss when it comes to mechan-
    ics. *(Sound: Getting up: Voices recede a little to kitchenette.)* Oh, be careful you
    don't bump into something. We don't want our gentleman caller to break
    his neck. Now wouldn't that be a fine howdy-do?
Jim: Ha-ha! Where is the fuse-box?
Amanda: Right here next to the stove. Can you see anything?
Jim: Just a minute.
Amanda: Isn't electricity a mysterious thing? Wasn't it Benjamin Franklin who
    tied a key to a kite? We live in such a mysterious universe, don't we? Some
    people say that science clears up all the mysteries for us. In my opinion it
    only creates more! Have you found it yet?
Jim: No, Ma'am. All these fuses look okay to me.
Amanda: Tom!
Tom: Yes, Mother?
Amanda: That light bill I gave you several days ago. The one I told you we got
    the notices about?
Tom: Oh. — Yeah.

    (Legend: "Ha!")

Amanda: You didn't neglect to pay it by any chance?
Tom: Why, I —
Amanda: Didn't! I might have known it!
Jim: Shakespeare probably wrote a poem on that light bill, Mrs. Wingfield.
Amanda: I might have known better than to trust him with it! There's such a
    high price for negligence in this world!
Jim: Maybe the poem will win a ten-dollar prize.
Amanda: We'll just have to spend the remainder of the evening in the nine-
    teenth century, before Mr. Edison made the Mazda lamp!
Jim: Candlelight is my favorite kind of light.
Amanda: That shows you're romantic! But that's no excuse for Tom. Well, we
    got through dinner. Very considerate of them to let us get through dinner
    before they plunged us into everlasting darkness, wasn't it, Mr. O'Connor?
Jim: Ha-ha!
Amanda: Tom, as a penalty for your carelessness you can help me with the dishes.
Jim: Let me give you a hand.
Amanda: Indeed you will not!
Jim: I ought to be good for something.
Amanda: Good for something? *(Her tone is rhapsodic.)* You? Why, Mr. O'Connor,
    nobody, *nobody's* given me this much entertainment in years — as you
    have!
Jim: Aw, now, Mrs. Wingfield!
Amanda: I'm not exaggerating, not one bit! But Sister is all by her lone-
    some. You go keep her company in the parlor! I'll give you this lovely old

candelabrum that used to be on the altar at the church of the Heavenly Rest. It was melted a little out of shape when the church burnt down. Lightning struck it one spring. Gypsy Jones was holding a revival at the time and he intimated that the church was destroyed because the Episcopalians gave card parties.

Jim: Ha-ha.

Amanda: And how about coaxing Sister to drink a little wine? I think it would be good for her! Can you carry both at once?

Jim: Sure. I'm Superman!

Amanda: Now, Thomas, get into this apron!

> *The door of kitchenette swings closed on Amanda's gay laughter; the flickering light approaches the portieres.*
>
> *Laura sits up nervously as he enters. Her speech at first is low and breathless from the almost intolerable strain of being alone with a stranger.*
>
> *(Legend: "I Don't Suppose You Remember Me at All!")*
>
> *In her first speeches in this scene, before Jim's warmth overcomes her paralyzing shyness, Laura's voice is thin and breathless as though she has run up a steep flight of stairs.*
>
> *Jim's attitude is gently humorous. In playing this scene it should be stressed that while the incident is apparently unimportant, it is to Laura the climax of her secret life.*

Jim: Hello, there, Laura.

Laura (faintly): Hello. *(She clears her throat.)*

Jim: How are you feeling now? Better?

Laura: Yes. Yes, thank you.

Jim: This is for you. A little dandelion wine. *(He extends it toward her with extravagant gallantry.)*

Laura: Thank you.

Jim: Drink it — but don't get drunk! *(He laughs heartily. Laura takes the glass uncertainly; laughs shyly.)* Where shall I set the candles?

Laura: Oh — oh, anywhere . . .

Jim: How about here on the floor? Any objections?

Laura: No.

Jim: I'll spread a newspaper under to catch the drippings. I like to sit on the floor. Mind if I do?

Laura: Oh, no.

Jim: Give me a pillow?

Laura: What?

Jim: A pillow!

Laura: Oh . . . *(Hands him one quickly.)*

Jim: How about you? Don't you like to sit on the floor?

Laura: Oh — yes.

Jim: Why don't you, then?

Laura: I — will.

Jim: Take a pillow! *(Laura does. Sits on the other side of the candelabrum. Jim crosses his legs and smiles engagingly at her.)* I can't hardly see you sitting way over there.

Laura: I can — see you.

Jim: I know, but that's not fair, I'm in the limelight. *(Laura moves her pillow closer.)* Good! Now I can see you! Comfortable?

Laura: Yes.

Jim: So am I. Comfortable as a cow. Will you have some gum?

Laura: No, thank you.

Jim: I think that I will indulge, with your permission. *(Musingly unwraps it and holds it up.)* Think of the fortune made by the guy that invented the first piece of chewing gum. Amazing, huh? The Wrigley Building is one of the sights of Chicago. — I saw it summer before last when I went up to the Century of Progress. Did you take in the Century of Progress?

Laura: No, I didn't.

Jim: Well, it was quite a wonderful exposition. What impressed me most was the Hall of Science. Gives you an idea of what the future will be in America, even more wonderful than the present time is! *(Pause. Smiling at her.)* Your brother tells me you're shy. Is that right, Laura?

Laura: I — don't know.

Jim: I judge you to be an old-fashioned type of girl. Well, I think that's a pretty good type to be. Hope you don't think I'm being too personal — do you?

Laura (hastily, out of embarrassment): I believe I *will* take a piece of gum, if you — don't mind. *(Clearing her throat.)* Mr. O'Connor, have you — kept up with your singing?

Jim: Singing? Me?

Laura: Yes. I remember what a beautiful voice you had.

Jim: When did you hear me sing?

(Voice offstage in the pause.)

Voice (offstage): O blow, ye winds, heigh-ho,
                A-roving I will go!
                I'm off to my love
                With a boxing glove —
                Ten thousand miles away!

Jim: You say you've heard me sing?

Laura: Oh, yes! Yes, very often . . . I — don't suppose you remember me — at all?

Jim (smiling doubtfully): You know I have an idea I've seen you before. I had that idea soon as you opened the door. It seemed almost like I was about to remember your name. But the name that I started to call you — wasn't a name! And so I stopped myself before I said it.

Laura: Wasn't it — Blue Roses?

Jim (springs up, grinning): Blue Roses! My gosh, yes — Blue Roses! That's what I had on my tongue when you opened the door! Isn't it funny what tricks your memory plays? I didn't connect you with the high school somehow or other. But that's where it was; it was high school. I didn't even know you were Shakespeare's sister! Gosh, I'm sorry.

Laura: I didn't expect you to. You — barely knew me!

Jim: But we did have a speaking acquaintance, huh?

Laura: Yes, we — spoke to each other.

Jim: When did you recognize me?

Laura: Oh, right away!

Jim: Soon as I came in the door?

Laura: When I heard your name I thought it was probably you. I knew that Tom used to know you a little in high school. So when you came in the door — Well, then I was — sure.

Jim: Why didn't you *say* something, then?

Laura (breathlessly): I didn't know what to say, I was — too surprised!

Jim: For goodness' sakes! You know, this sure is funny!

Laura: Yes! Yes, isn't it, though . . .

Jim: Didn't we have a class in something together?

Laura: Yes, we did.

Jim: What class was that?

Laura: It was — singing — Chorus!

Jim: Aw!

Laura: I sat across the aisle from you in the Aud.

Jim: Aw.

Laura: Mondays, Wednesdays, and Fridays.

Jim: Now I remember — you always came in late.

Laura: Yes, it was so hard for me, getting upstairs. I had that brace on my leg — it clumped so loud!

Jim: I never heard any clumping.

Laura (wincing in the recollection): To me it sounded like — thunder!

Jim: Well, well, well. I never even noticed.

Laura: And everybody was seated before I came in. I had to walk in front of all those people. My seat was in the back row. I had to go clumping all the way up the aisle with everyone watching!

Jim: You shouldn't have been self-conscious.

Laura: I know, but I was. It was always such a relief when the singing started.

Jim: Aw, yes, I've placed you now! I used to call you Blue Roses. How was it that I got started calling you that?

Laura: I was out of school a little while with pleurosis. When I came back you asked me what was the matter. I said I had pleurosis — you thought I said Blue Roses. That's what you always called me after that!

Jim: I hope you didn't mind.

Laura: Oh, no — I liked it. You see, I wasn't acquainted with many — people. . . .

Jim: As I remember you sort of stuck by yourself.

Laura: I — I — never had much luck at — making friends.

Jim: I don't see why you wouldn't.

Laura: Well, I — started out badly.

Jim: You mean being —

Laura: Yes, it sort of — stood between me —

Jim: You shouldn't have let it!

Laura: I know, but it did, and —

Jim: You were shy with people!

Laura: I tried not to be but never could —

Jim: Overcome it?

Laura: No, I — I never could!

Jim: I guess being shy is something you have to work out of kind of gradually.

Laura (sorrowfully): Yes — I guess it —

Jim: Takes time!

Laura: Yes —

Jim: People are not so dreadful when you know them. That's what you have to remember! And everybody has problems, not just you, but practically everybody has got some problems. You think of yourself as having the only problems, as being the only one who is disappointed. But just look around you and you will see lots of people as disappointed as you are. For instance, I hoped when I was going to high school that I would be further along at this time, six years later, than I am now — You remember that wonderful write-up I had in *The Torch*?

Laura: Yes! *(She rises and crosses to table.)*

Jim: It said I was bound to succeed in anything I went into! *(Laura returns with the annual.)* Holy Jeez! *The Torch!* *(He accepts it reverently. They smile across it with mutual wonder. Laura crouches beside him and they begin to turn through it. Laura's shyness is dissolving in his warmth.)*

Laura: Here you are in *Pirates of Penzance!*

Jim (wistfully): I sang the baritone lead in that operetta.

Laura (rapidly): So — *beautifully!*

Jim (protesting): Aw —

Laura: Yes, yes — beautifully — beautifully!

Jim: You heard me?

Laura: All three times!

Jim: No!

Laura: Yes!

Jim: All three performances?

Laura (looking down): Yes.

Jim: Why?

Laura: I — wanted to ask you to — autograph my program.

Jim: Why didn't you ask me to?

Laura: You were always surrounded by your own friends so much that I never had a chance to.

Jim: You should have just —

Laura: Well, I — thought you might think I was —

Jim: Thought I might think you was — what?

Laura: Oh —

Jim (with reflective relish): I was beleaguered by females in those days.

Laura: You were terribly popular!

Jim: Yeah —

Laura: You had such a — friendly way —

Jim: I was spoiled in high school.

Laura: Everybody — liked you!

Jim: Including you?

Laura: I — yes, I — I did, too — *(She gently closes the book in her lap.)*

Jim: Well, well, well! — Give me that program, Laura. *(She hands it to him. He signs it with a flourish.)* There you are — better late than never!

Laura: Oh, I — what a — surprise!

Jim: My signature isn't worth very much right now. But some day — maybe — it will increase in value! Being disappointed is one thing and being discouraged is something else. I am disappointed but I'm not discouraged. I'm twenty-three years old. How old are you?

Laura: I'll be twenty-four in June.

Jim: That's not old age.

Laura: No, but —

Jim: You finished high school?

Laura (with difficulty): I didn't go back.

Jim: You mean you dropped out?

Laura: I made bad grades in my final examinations. *(She rises and replaces the book and the program. Her voice strained.)* How is — Emily Meisenbach getting along?

Jim: Oh, that kraut-head!

Laura: Why do you call her that?

Jim: That's what she was.

Laura: You're not still — going with her?

Jim: I never see her.

Laura: It said in the Personal Section that you were — engaged!

Jim: I know, but I wasn't impressed by that — propaganda!

Laura: It wasn't — the truth?

Jim: Only in Emily's optimistic opinion!

Laura: Oh —

> *(Legend: "What Have You Done since High School?")*
> *Jim lights a cigarette and leans indolently back on his elbows smiling at Laura with a warmth and charm which light her inwardly with altar candles. She remains by the table and turns in her hands a piece of glass to cover her tumult.*

Jim (after several reflective puffs on a cigarette): What have you done since high school? *(She seems not to hear him.)* Huh? *(Laura looks up.)* I said what have you done since high school, Laura?

Laura: Nothing much.

Jim: You must have been doing something these six long years.

Laura: Yes.

Jim: Well, then, such as what?

Laura: I took a business course at business college —

Jim: How did that work out?

Laura: Well, not very — well — I had to drop out, it gave me — indigestion —

Jim laughs gently.

Jim: What are you doing now?

Laura: I don't do anything — much. Oh, please don't think I sit around doing nothing! My glass collection takes up a good deal of my time. Glass is something you have to take good care of.

Jim: What did you say — about glass?

Laura: Collection I said — I have one — *(She clears her throat and turns away again, acutely shy.)*

Jim (abruptly): You know what I judge to be the trouble with you? Inferiority complex! Know what that is? That's what they call it when someone low-rates himself! I understand it because I had it, too. Although my case was not so aggravated as yours seems to be. I had it until I took up public speaking, developed my voice, and learned that I had an aptitude for science. Before that time I never thought of myself as being outstanding in any way whatsoever! Now I've never made a regular study of it, but I have a friend who says I can analyze people better than doctors that make a profession of it. I don't claim that to be necessarily true, but I can sure guess a person's psychology, Laura! *(Takes out his gum.)* Excuse me, Laura. I always take it out when the flavor is gone. I'll use this scrap of paper to wrap it in. I know how it is to get it stuck on a shoe. Yep — that's what I judge to be your principal trouble. A lack of confidence in yourself as a person. You don't have the proper amount of faith in yourself. I'm basing that fact on a number of your remarks and also on certain observations I've made. For instance that clumping you thought was so awful in high school. You say that you even dreaded to walk into class. You see what you did? You dropped out of school, you gave up an education because of a clump, which as far as I know was practically nonexistent! A little physical defect is what you have. Hardly noticeable even! Magnified thousands of times by imagination! You know what my strong advice to you is? Think of yourself as *superior* in some way!

Laura: In what way would I think?

Jim: Why, man alive, Laura! Just look about you a little. What do you see? A world full of common people! All of 'em born and all of 'em going to die! Which of them has one-tenth of your good points! Or mine! Or anyone else's, as far as that goes — Gosh! Everybody excels in some one thing. Some in many! *(Unconsciously glances at himself in the mirror.)* All you've got to do is discover in *what!* Take me, for instance. *(He adjusts his tie at the mirror.)* My interest happened to lie in electrodynamics. I'm taking a course in radio engineering at night school, Laura, on top of a fairly responsible job at the warehouse. I'm taking that course and studying public speaking.

Laura: Ohhhh.

Jim: Because I believe in the future of television! *(Turning back to her.)* I wish to be ready to go up right along with it. Therefore I'm planning to get in on the ground floor. In fact, I've already made the right connections and all that remains is for the industry itself to get under way! Full steam — *(His eyes are starry.)* Knowledge — Zzzzzp! Money — Zzzzzzp! — Power! That's the cycle democracy is built on! *(His attitude is convincingly dynamic. Laura stares at him, even her shyness eclipsed in her absolute wonder. He suddenly grins.)* I guess you think I think a lot of myself!

Laura: No — o-o-o, I —

Jim: Now how about you? Isn't there something you take more interest in than anything else?

Laura: Well, I do — as I said — have my — glass collection —

A peal of girlish laughter from the kitchen.

Jim: I'm not right sure I know what you're talking about. What kind of glass is it?

Laura: Little articles of it, they're ornaments mostly! Most of them are little animals made out of glass, the tiniest little animals in the world. Mother calls them a glass menagerie! Here's an example of one, if you'd like to see it! This one is one of the oldest. It's nearly thirteen. *(He stretches out his hand.)* *(Music: "The Glass Menagerie.")* Oh, be careful — if you breathe, it breaks!

Jim: I'd better not take it. I'm pretty clumsy with things.

Laura: Go on, I trust you with him! *(Places it in his palm.)* There now — you're holding him gently! Hold him over the light, he loves the light! You see how the light shines through him?

Jim: It sure does shine!

Laura: I shouldn't be partial, but he is my favorite one.

Jim: What kind of thing is this one supposed to be?

Laura: Haven't you noticed the single horn on his forehead?

Jim: A unicorn, huh?

Laura: Mmm-hmmm!

Jim: Unicorns, aren't they extinct in the modern world?

Laura: I know!

Jim: Poor little fellow, he must feel sort of lonesome.

Laura (smiling): Well, if he does he doesn't complain about it. He stays on a shelf with some horses that don't have horns and all of them seem to get along nicely together.

Jim: How do you know?

Laura (lightly): I haven't heard any arguments among them!

Jim (grinning): No arguments, huh? Well, that's a pretty good sign! Where shall I set him?

Laura: Put him on the table. They all like a change of scenery once in a while!

Jim (stretching): Well, well, well, well — Look how big my shadow is when I stretch!

Laura: Oh, oh, yes — it stretches across the ceiling!

Jim (crossing to door): I think it's stopped raining. *(Opens fire-escape door.)* Where does the music come from?

Laura: From the Paradise Dance Hall across the alley.

Jim: How about cutting the rug a little, Miss Wingfield?

Laura: Oh, I —

Jim: Or is your program filled up? Let me have a look at it. *(Grasps imaginary card.)* Why, every dance is taken! I'll have to scratch some out. *(Waltz music: "La Golondrina.")* Ahhh, a waltz! *(He executes some sweeping turns by himself then holds his arms toward Laura.)*

Laura (breathlessly): I — can't dance!

Jim: There you go, that inferiority stuff!

Laura: I've never danced in my life!

Jim: Come on, try!

Laura: Oh, but I'd step on you!

Jim: I'm not made out of glass.

Laura: How — how — how do we start?

Jim: Just leave it to me. You hold your arms out a little.

Laura: Like this?

Jim: A little bit higher. Right. Now don't tighten up, that's the main thing about it — relax.

Laura (laughing breathlessly): It's hard not to.

Jim: Okay.

Laura: I'm afraid you can't budge me.

Jim: What do you bet I can't? *(He swings her into motion.)*

Laura: Goodness, yes, you can!

Jim: Let yourself go, now, Laura, just let yourself go.

Laura: I'm —

Jim: Come on!

Laura: Trying.

Jim: Not so stiff — Easy does it!

Laura: I know but I'm —
Jim: Loosen th' backbone! There now, that's a lot better.
Laura: Am I?
Jim: Lots, lots better! *(He moves her about the room in a clumsy waltz.)*
Laura: Oh, my!
Jim: Ha-ha!
Laura: Goodness, yes you can!
Jim: Ha-ha-ha! *(They suddenly bump into the table. Jim stops.)* What did we hit on?
Laura: Table.
Jim: Did something fall off it? I think —
Laura: Yes.
Jim: I hope it wasn't the little glass horse with the horn!
Laura: Yes.
Jim: Aw, aw, aw. Is it broken?
Laura: Now it is just like all the other horses.
Jim: It's lost its —
Laura: Horn! It doesn't matter. Maybe it's a blessing in disguise.
Jim: You'll never forgive me. I bet that that was your favorite piece of glass.
Laura: I don't have favorites much. It's no tragedy, Freckles. Glass breaks so
    easily. No matter how careful you are. The traffic jars the shelves and
    things fall off them.
Jim: Still I'm awfully sorry that I was the cause.
Laura (smiling): I'll just imagine he had an operation. The horn was removed
    to make him feel less — freakish! *(They both laugh.)* Now he will feel more at
    home with the other horses, the ones that don't have horns . . .
Jim: Ha-ha, that's very funny! *(Suddenly serious.)* I'm glad to see that you have a
    sense of humor. You know — you're — well — very different! Surprisingly
    different from anyone else I know! *(His voice becomes soft and hesitant with a
    genuine feeling.)* Do you mind me telling you that? *(Laura is abashed beyond
    speech.)* You make me feel sort of — I don't know how to put it! I'm usually
    pretty good at expressing things, but — This is something that I don't
    know how to say! *(Laura touches her throat and clears it — turns the broken uni-
    corn in her hands.)* *(Even softer.)* Has anyone ever told you that you were
    pretty?

Pause: Music.

(Laura looks up slowly, with wonder, and shakes her head.) Well, you are! In a
very different way from anyone else. And all the nicer because of the difference, too. *(His voice becomes low and husky. Laura turns away, nearly faint with
the novelty of her emotions.)* I wish that you were my sister. I'd teach you to
have some confidence in yourself. The different people are not like other
people, but being different is nothing to be ashamed of. Because other
people are not such wonderful people. They're one hundred times one
thousand. You're one times one! They walk all over the earth. You just stay
here. They're common as — weeds, but — you — well, you're — *Blue Roses!*

(Image on screen: Blue Roses.)
    (Music changes.)

Laura: But blue is wrong for — roses . . .
Jim: It's right for you — You're — pretty!

Laura: In what respect am I pretty?

Jim: In all respects — believe me! Your eyes — your hair — are pretty! Your hands are pretty! *(He catches hold of her hand.)* You think I'm making this up because I'm invited to dinner and have to be nice. Oh, I could do that! I could put on an act for you, Laura, and say lots of things without being very sincere. But this time I am. I'm talking to you sincerely. I happened to notice you had this inferiority complex that keeps you from feeling comfortable with people. Somebody needs to build your confidence up and make you proud instead of shy and turning away and — blushing — Somebody ought to — ought to — *kiss* you, Laura! *(His hand slips slowly up her arm to her shoulder.) (Music swells tumultuously.) (He suddenly turns her about and kisses her on the lips. When he releases her Laura sinks on the sofa with a bright, dazed look. Jim backs away and fishes in his pocket for a cigarette.) (Legend on screen: "Souvenir.")* Stumble-john! *(He lights the cigarette, avoiding her look. There is a peal of girlish laughter from Amanda in the kitchen. Laura slowly raises and opens her hand. It still contains the little broken glass animal. She looks at it with a tender, bewildered expression.)* Stumble-john! I shouldn't have done that — That was way off the beam. You don't smoke, do you? *(She looks up, smiling, not hearing the question. He sits beside her a little gingerly. She looks at him speechlessly — waiting. He coughs decorously and moves a little farther aside as he considers the situation and senses her feelings, dimly, with perturbation. Gently.)* Would you — care for a — mint? *(She doesn't seem to hear him but her look grows brighter even.)* Peppermint — Life Saver? My pocket's a regular drug store — wherever I go . . . *(He pops a mint in his mouth. Then gulps and decides to make a clean breast of it. He speaks slowly and gingerly.)* Laura, you know, if I had a sister like you, I'd do the same thing as Tom. I'd bring out fellows — introduce her to them. The right type of boys of a type to — appreciate her. Only — well — he made a mistake about me. Maybe I've got no call to be saying this. That may not have been the idea in having me over. But what if it was? There's nothing wrong about that. The only trouble is that in my case — I'm not in a situation to — do the right thing. I can't take down your number and say I'll phone. I can't call up next week and — ask for a date. I thought I had better explain the situation in case you misunderstood it and — hurt your feelings. . . . *(Pause. Slowly, very slowly, Laura's look changes, her eyes returning slowly from his to the ornament in her palm.)*

Amanda utters another gay laugh in the kitchen.

Laura (faintly): You — won't — call again?

Jim: No, Laura, I can't. *(He rises from the sofa.)* As I was just explaining, I've — got strings on me, Laura, I've — been going steady! I go out all the time with a girl named Betty. She's a home-girl like you, and Catholic, and Irish, and in a great many ways we — get along fine. I met her last summer on a moonlight boat trip up the river to Alton, on the *Majestic.* Well — right away from the start it was — love! *(Legend: Love!) (Laura sways slightly forward and grips the arm of the sofa. He fails to notice, now enrapt in his own comfortable being.)* Being in love has made a new man of me! *(Leaning stiffly forward, clutching the arm of the sofa, Laura struggles visibly with her storm. But Jim is oblivious, she is a long way off.)* The power of love is really pretty tremendous! Love is something that — changes the whole world, Laura! *(The storm abates a little and Laura leans back. He notices her again.)* It happened that Betty's aunt took sick, she got a wire and had to go to Centralia. So Tom—when he asked me to dinner—I naturally just accepted the invitation, not knowing that you— that he—that I—*(He stops awkwardly.)* Huh—I'm a stumble-john! *(He flops back on the sofa. The holy candles in the altar of Laura's face have been snuffed out! There is a look of almost infinite desolation. Jim glances at her uneasily.)* I wish that you would—say something. *(She bites her lip which was trembling and then bravely smiles. She opens her hand again on the broken glass ornament. Then she gently takes his hand and raises it level with her own. She carefully places the unicorn in the palm of his hand, then pushes his fingers closed upon it.)* What are you— doing that for? You want me to have him?—Laura? *(She nods.)* What for?

Laura: A—souvenir . . .

> She rises unsteadily and crouches beside the Victrola to wind it up.
> *(Legend on screen: "Things Have a Way of Turning Out So Badly.")*
> *(Or image: "Gentleman caller waving good-bye!—Gaily.")*
> At this moment Amanda rushes brightly back in the front room. She bears a pitcher of fruit punch in an old-fashioned cut-glass pitcher and a plate of maca-roons. The plate has a gold border and poppies painted on it.

Amanda: Well, well, well! Isn't the air delightful after the shower? I've made you children a little liquid refreshment. *(Turns gaily to the gentleman caller.)* Jim, do you know that song about lemonade?
"Lemonade, lemonade
Made in the shade and stirred with a spade—
Good enough for any old maid!"

Jim (uneasily): Ha-ha! No—I never heard it.

Amanda: Why, Laura! You look so serious!

Jim: We were having a serious conversation.

Amanda: Good! Now you're better acquainted!

Jim (uncertainly): Ha-ha! Yes.

Amanda: You modern young people are much more serious-minded than my generation. I was so gay as a girl!

Jim: You haven't changed, Mrs. Wingfield.

Amanda: Tonight I'm rejuvenated! The gaiety of the occasion, Mr. O'Connor! *(She tosses her head with a peal of laughter. Spills lemonade.)* Oooo! I'm baptiz-ing myself!

Jim: Here—let me—

Amanda (setting the pitcher down): There now. I discovered we had some mara-schino cherries. I dumped them in, juice and all!

Jim: You shouldn't have gone to that trouble, Mrs. Wingfield.

Amanda: Trouble, trouble? Why it was loads of fun! Didn't you hear me cut-ting up in the kitchen? I bet your ears were burning! I told Tom how out-done with him I was for keeping you to himself so long a time! He should have brought you over much, much sooner! Well, now that you've found your way, I want you to be a very frequent caller! Not just occasional but all the time. Oh, we're going to have a lot of gay times together! I see them coming! Mmm, just breathe that air! So fresh, and the moon's so pretty! I'll skip back out—I know where my place is when young folks are having a—serious conversation!

Jim: Oh, don't go out, Mrs. Wingfield. The fact of the matter is I've got to be going.

Amanda: Going, now? You're joking! Why, it's only the shank of the evening, Mr. O'Connor!

Jim: Well, you know how it is.

Amanda: You mean you're a young workingman and have to keep working-men's hours. We'll let you off early tonight. But only on the condition that next time you stay later. What's the best night for you? Isn't Saturday night the best night for you workingmen?

Jim: I have a couple of time-clocks to punch, Mrs. Wingfield. One at morning, another one at night!

Amanda: My, but you *are* ambitious! You work at night, too?

Jim: No, Ma'am, not work but — Betty! *(He crosses deliberately to pick up his hat. The band at the Paradise Dance Hall goes into a tender waltz.)*

Amanda: Betty? Betty? Who's — Betty! *(There is an ominous cracking sound in the sky.)*

Jim: Oh, just a girl. The girl I go steady with! *(He smiles charmingly. The sky falls.)*

(Legend: "The Sky Falls.")

Amanda (a long-drawn exhalation): Ohhhh . . . Is it a serious romance, Mr. O'Connor?

Jim: We're going to be married the second Sunday in June.

Amanda: Ohhhh — how nice! Tom didn't mention that you were engaged to be married.

Jim: The cat's not out of the bag at the warehouse yet. You know how they are. They call you Romeo and stuff like that. *(He stops at the oval mirror to put on his hat. He carefully shapes the brim and the crown to give a discreetly dashing effect.)* It's been a wonderful evening, Mrs. Wingfield. I guess this is what they mean by Southern hospitality.

Amanda: It really wasn't anything at all.

Jim: I hope it don't seem like I'm rushing off. But I promised Betty I'd pick her up at the Wabash depot, an' by the time I get my jalopy down there her train'll be in. Some women are pretty upset if you keep 'em waiting.

Amanda: Yes, I know — The tyranny of women! *(Extends her hand.)* Good-bye, Mr. O'Connor. I wish you luck — and happiness — and success! All three of them, and so does Laura — Don't you, Laura?

Laura: Yes!

Jim (taking her hand): Good-bye, Laura. I'm certainly going to treasure that souvenir. And don't you forget the good advice I gave you. *(Raises his voice to a cheery shout.)* So long, Shakespeare! Thanks again, ladies — Good night!

He grins and ducks jauntily out.

Still bravely grimacing, Amanda closes the door on the gentleman caller. Then she turns back to the room with a puzzled expression. She and Laura don't dare to face each other. Laura crouches beside the Victrola to wind it.

Amanda (faintly): Things have a way of turning out so badly. I don't believe that I would play the Victrola. Well, well — well — Our gentleman caller was engaged to be married! Tom!

Tom (from back): Yes, Mother?

Amanda: Come in here a minute. I want to tell you something awfully funny.

Tom (enters with macaroon and a glass of the lemonade): Has the gentleman caller gotten away already?

Amanda: The gentleman caller has made an early departure. What a wonderful joke you played on us!

Tom: How do you mean?

Amanda: You didn't mention that he was engaged to be married.

Tom: Jim? Engaged?

Amanda: That's what he just informed us.

Tom: I'll be jiggered! I didn't know about that.

Amanda: That seems very peculiar.

Tom: What's peculiar about it?

Amanda: Didn't you call him your best friend down at the warehouse?

Tom: He is, but how did I know?

Amanda: It seems extremely peculiar that you wouldn't know your best friend was going to be married!

Tom: The warehouse is where I work, not where I know things about people!

Amanda: You don't know things anywhere! You live in a dream; you manufacture illusions! *(He crosses to door.)* Where are you going?

Tom: I'm going to the movies.

Amanda: That's right, now that you've had us make such fools of ourselves. The effort, the preparations, all the expense! The new floor lamp, the rug, the clothes for Laura! All for what? To entertain some other girl's fiancé! Go to the movies, go! Don't think about us, a mother deserted, an unmarried sister who's crippled and has no job! Don't let anything interfere with your selfish pleasure! Just go, go, go — to the movies!

Tom: All right, I will! The more you shout about my selfishness to me the quicker I'll go, and I won't go to the movies!

Amanda: Go, then! Then go to the moon — you selfish dreamer!

> *Tom smashes his glass on the floor. He plunges out on the fire-escape, slamming the door. Laura screams — cut by door.*
> *Dance-hall music up. Tom goes to the rail and grips it desperately, lifting his face in the chill white moonlight penetrating the narrow abyss of the alley.*
> *(Legend on screen: "And So Good-Bye . . .")*
> *Tom's closing speech is timed with the interior pantomime. The interior scene is played as though viewed through sound-proof glass. Amanda appears to be making a comforting speech to Laura who is huddled upon the sofa. Now that we cannot hear the mother's speech, her silliness is gone and she has dignity and tragic beauty. Laura's dark hair hides her face until at the end of the speech she lifts it to smile at her mother. Amanda's gestures are slow and graceful, almost dancelike, as she comforts the daughter. At the end of her speech she glances a moment at the father's picture — then withdraws through the portieres. At close of Tom's speech, Laura blows out the candles, ending the play.*

Tom: I didn't go to the moon, I went much further — for time is the longest distance between two places — Not long after that I was fired for writing a poem on the lid of a shoe-box. I left Saint Louis. I descended the steps of this fire-escape for a last time and followed, from then on, in my father's footsteps, attempting to find in motion what was lost in space — I traveled around a great deal. The cities swept about me like dead leaves, leaves that were brightly colored but torn away from the branches. I would have stopped, but I was pursued by something. It always came upon me unawares, taking me altogether by surprise. Perhaps it was a familiar bit of music. Perhaps it was only a piece of transparent glass—Perhaps I am walking along a street at night, in some strange city, before I have found companions. I pass the lighted window of a shop where perfume is sold. The window is filled with pieces of colored glass, tiny transparent bottles in delicate colors, like bits of a shattered rainbow. Then all at once my sister touches my shoulder. I turn around and look into her eyes. . . . Oh, Laura, Laura, I tried to leave you behind me, but I am more faithful than I intended to be! I reach for a cigarette, I cross the street, I run into the movies or a bar, I buy a drink, I speak to the nearest stranger—anything that can blow your candles out! *(Laura bends over the candles)*—for nowadays the world is lit by lightning! Blow out your candles, Laura—and so good-bye . . .

She blows the candles out.
(The Scene Dissolves.)

CONNECTIONS TO OTHER SELECTIONS

1. Discuss the symbolic significance of the glass menagerie in Williams's play and the piano in August Wilson's *The Piano Lesson* (p. 1962). How do the objects' symbolic values contribute to the theme of each play?

2. Compare and contrast the nonrealistic techniques that Williams uses with those used by Arthur Miller in *Death of a Salesman* (p. 1795).

3. Write an essay that compares Tom's narrative function in *The Glass Menagerie* with that of the Chorus in Sophocles' *Oedipus the King* (p. 1224) and *Antigone* (p. 1267).

PERSPECTIVES

TENNESSEE WILLIAMS (1911–1983)

Production Notes to The Glass Menagerie   1945

Being a "memory play," *The Glass Menagerie* can be presented with unusual freedom of convention. Because of its considerably delicate or tenuous material, atmospheric touches and subtleties of direction play a particularly important part. Expressionism and all other unconventional techniques in drama have only one valid aim, and that is a closer approach to truth. When a play employs unconventional techniques, it is not, or certainly shouldn't be, trying to escape its responsibility of dealing with reality, or interpreting experience, but is actually or should be attempting to find a closer approach, a more penetrating and vivid expression of things as they are. The straight realistic play with its genuine Frigidaire and authentic ice cubes, its characters that speak exactly as its audience speaks, corresponds to the academic landscape and has the same virtue of a photographic likeness. Everyone should know nowadays the unimportance of the photographic in art: that truth, life, or reality is an organic thing which the poetic imagination can represent or suggest, in essence, only through transformation, through changing into other forms than those which were merely present in appearance.

These remarks are not meant as a preface only to this particular play. They have to do with a conception of a new, plastic theater which must take the place of the exhausted theater of realistic conventions if the theater is to resume vitality as a part of our culture.

The Screen Device. There is *only one important difference between the original and acting version of the play* and that is the *omission* in the latter of the device which I tentatively included in my *original* script. This device was the use of a screen on which were projected magic-lantern slides bearing images or titles. I do not regret the omission of this device from the present Broadway production. The extraordinary power of Miss Taylor's° performance made it suitable to have the utmost simplicity in the physical production. But I think it may be interesting to some readers to see how this device was conceived. So I am putting it into the published manuscript. These images and legends, projected from behind, were cast on a section of wall between the front-room and dining-room areas, which should be indistinguishable from the rest when not in use.

The purpose of this will probably be apparent. It is to give accent to certain values in each scene. Each scene contains a particular point (or several) which is structurally the most important. In an episodic play, such as this, the basic structure or narrative line may be obscured from the audience; the effect may seem fragmentary rather than architectural. This may not be the fault of the play so much as a lack of attention in the audience. The legend or image upon the screen will strengthen the effect of what is merely allusion in the writing and allow the primary point to be made more simply and lightly than if the entire responsibility were on the spoken lines. Aside from this structural value, I think the screen will have a definite emotional appeal, less definable but just as important. An imaginative producer or director may invent many other uses for this device than those indicated in the present script. In fact the possibilities of the device seem much larger to me than the instance of this play can possibly utilize.

The Music. Another extra-literary accent in this play is provided by the use of music. A single recurring tune, "The Glass Menagerie," is used to give emotional emphasis to suitable passages. This tune is like circus music, not when you are on the grounds or in the immediate vicinity of the parade, but when you are at some distance and very likely thinking of something else. It seems under those circumstances to continue almost interminably and it weaves in and out of your preoccupied consciousness; then it is the lightest, most delicate music in the world and perhaps the saddest. It expresses the surface vivacity of life with the underlying strain of immutable and inexpressible sorrow. When you look at a piece of delicately spun glass you think of two things: how beautiful it is and how easily it can be broken. Both of those ideas should be woven into the recurring tune, which dips in and out of the play as if it were carried on a wind that changes. It serves as a thread of connection and allusion between the narrator with his separate point in time and space and the subject of his story. Between each episode it returns as reference to the emotion, nostalgia, which is the first condition of the play. It is primarily Laura's music and therefore comes out most clearly when the play focuses upon her and the lovely fragility of glass which is her image.

Miss Taylor's: Laurette Taylor (1884–1946) played the role of Amanda in the original Broadway production.

The Lighting. The lighting in the play is not realistic. In keeping with the atmosphere of memory, the stage is dim. Shafts of light are focused on selected areas or actors, sometimes in contradistinction to what is the apparent center. For instance, in the quarrel scene between Tom and Amanda, in which Laura has no active part, the clearest pool of light is on her figure. This is also true of the supper scene, when her silent figure on the sofa should remain the visual center. The light upon Laura should be distinct from the others, having a peculiar pristine clarity such as light used in early religious portraits of female saints or madonnas. A certain correspondence to light in religious paintings, such as El Greco's,° where the figures are radiant in atmosphere that is relatively dusky, could be effectively used throughout the play. (It will also permit a more effective use of the screen.) A free, imaginative use of light can be of enormous value in giving a mobile, plastic quality to plays of a more or less static nature.

El Greco (1541–1614): Greek painter who worked primarily in Spain and is known for the unearthly lighting in his large canvases.

CONSIDERATIONS FOR CRITICAL THINKING AND WRITING

1. What was your response to the screen device as you read the play? Do you think the device would enhance a production of the play or prove to be a distraction?

2. How does Williams's description of music and lighting serve as a summary of the play's tone? Does this tone come through in your reading of the play or is it dependent upon the music and lighting? Explain your answer.

3. Explain whether you agree with Williams's assertion that "theater of realistic conventions" is "exhausted" (para. 2).

TENNESSEE WILLIAMS (1911–1983)
On Theme
1948

For a writer who is not intentionally obscure, and never, in his opinion, obscure at all, I do get asked a hell of a lot of questions which I can't answer. I have never been able to say what was the theme of my play and I don't think I've ever been conscious of writing with a theme in mind. I am always surprised when, after a play has opened, I read in the papers what the play is about. . . . I am thankful for these highly condensed and stimulating analyses, but it would never have occurred to me that that was the story I was trying to tell. Usually when asked about a theme, I look vague and say, "It is a play about life. . . ."

From *Where I Live: Selected Essays,* edited by Christine R. Day

CONSIDERATIONS FOR CRITICAL THINKING AND WRITING

1. Williams's disclaimer invites the inevitable question: What is the theme of *The Glass Menagerie?* Write an essay that answers this question.

2. Discuss whether you think it is likely (or possible) to write a play without "a theme in mind."

AN ALBUM OF WORLD LITERATURE
From Molly Sweeney

Born in County Tyrone, Northern Ireland, Brian Friel is regarded as one of Ireland's major playwrights. Before becoming a full-time playwright in the early 1960s, Friel taught school, but his early successes launched him into an impressive writing career. His plays focus on Irish characters making their way in circumscribed family situations, through unpromising circumstances and politically oppressed times. Among his plays are *Philadelphia, Here I Come!* (1964), *The Loves of Cass McGuire* (1966), *The Mundy Scheme* (1969), *The Freedom of the City* (1973), *Translations* (1980), and *Dancing at Lughnasa* (1990), which won a Tony Award.

In *Molly Sweeney*, Friel tells the story of a blind woman living in the small, dreary town of Ballybeg, County Donegal. Molly is faced with the prospect of regaining her sight, but she's not certain what she might lose in the process. Unlike her husband Frank and her doctor Mr. Rice, who are eager for her to see again, Molly is filled with uncertainties, and her doubts prove to be justified by the end of the play. Molly's final words are delivered from an institution; she no longer knows whether she can see or not, but she also no longer cares:

> . . . what I think I see may be fantasy or indeed what I take to be imagined may very well be real — what's Frank's term? — external reality. Real — imagined — fact — fiction — fantasy — reality — there it seems to be. And it seems to be all right. And why should I question any of it any more?

All three characters remain on stage for the entire play and tell the story of Molly's vision in a series of shifting monologues. The following excerpt is taken from the beginning of Act Two, which recounts Molly's response to a successful operation.

BRIAN FRIEL (IRELAND / B. 1929)
From Molly Sweeney   *1994*

CHARACTERS

Molly Sweeney
Frank Sweeney
Mr. Rice

ACT TWO

Molly: The morning the bandages were to be removed a staff nurse spent half an hour preparing me for Mr. Rice. It wasn't really her job, she told me; but this was my big day and I had to look my best and she was happy to do it.

So she sponged my face and hands. She made me clean my teeth again. She wondered did I use lipstick — maybe just for today? She did the best she could with my hair, God help her. She looked at my fingernails and suggested that a touch of clear varnish would be nice. She straightened the bow at the front of my nightdress and adjusted the collar of my dressing-gown. She put a dab of her own very special perfume on each of my wrists — she got it from a cousin in Paris. Then she stood back and surveyed me and said, "Now. That's better. You'll find that from now on — if everything goes well of course — you'll find that you'll become very aware of your appearance. They all do for some reason. Don't be nervous. You look just lovely. He'll be here any minute now."

I asked her where the bathroom was.

"At the end of the corridor. Last door on the right. I'll bring you."

"No," I said. "I'll find it."

I didn't need to go to the bathroom. I just wanted to take perhaps a last walk; in my own world; by myself.

I don't know what I expected when the bandages would be removed. I think maybe I didn't allow myself any expectations. I knew that in his heart Frank believed that somehow, miraculously, I would be given the perfect vision that sighted people have, even though Mr. Rice had told us again and again that my eyes weren't capable of that vision. And I knew what Mr. Rice hoped for: that I would have partial sight. "That would be a total success for me" is what he said. But I'm sure he meant it would be great for all of us.

As for myself, if I had any hope, I suppose it was that neither Frank nor Mr. Rice would be too disappointed because it had all become so important for them.

No, that's not accurate either. Yes, I did want to see. For God's sake of course I wanted to see. But that wasn't an expectation, not even a mad hope. If there was a phantom desire, a fantasy in my head, it was this. That perhaps by some means I might be afforded a brief excursion to this land of vision; not to live there — just to visit. And during my stay to devour it again and again and again with greedy, ravenous eyes. To gorge on all those luminous sights and wonderful spectacles until I knew every detail intimately and utterly — every ocean, every leaf, every field, every star, every tiny flower. And then, oh yes, then to return home to my own world with all that rare understanding within me forever.

No, that wasn't even a phantom desire. Just a stupid fantasy. And it came into my head again when that poor nurse was trying to prettify me for Mr. Rice. And I thought to myself: It's like being back at school — I'm getting dressed up for the annual excursion.

When Mr. Rice did arrive, even before he touched me, I knew by his quick, shallow breathing that he was far more nervous than I was. And then as he took off the bandages his hands trembled and fumbled.

"There we are," he said. "All off. How does that feel?"

"Fine," I said. Even though I felt nothing. Were all the bandages off?

"Now, Molly. In your own time. Tell me what you see."

Nothing. Nothing at all. Then out of the void a blur; a haze; a body of mist; a confusion of light, color, movement. It had no meaning.

"Well?" he said. "Anything? Anything at all?"

I thought: Don't panic; a voice comes from a face; that blur is his face; look at him.

"Well? Anything?"

Something moving; large; white; the nurse? And lines, black lines, vertical lines. The bed? The door?

"Anything, Molly?" A bright light that hurt. The window maybe?

"I'm holding my hand before your eyes, Molly. Can you see it?"

A reddish blob in front of my face; rotating; liquefying; pulsating. Keep calm. Concentrate.

"Can you see my hand, Molly?"

"I think so . . . I'm not sure. . . ."

"Now I'm moving my hand slowly."

"Yes . . . yes. . . ."

"Do you see my hand moving?"

"Yes . . ."

"What way is it moving?"

"Yes . . . I do see it . . . up and down . . . up and down . . . Yes! I see it! I do! Yes! Moving up and down! Yes yes yes!"

"Splendid!" he said. "Absolutely splendid! You are a clever lady!"

And there was such delight in his voice. And my head was suddenly giddy. And I thought for a moment—for a moment I thought I was going to faint.

Frank: There was some mix-up about what time the bandages were to be removed. At least I was confused. For some reason I got it into my head that they were to be taken off at eight in the morning, October 8, the day after the operation. A Wednesday, I remember, because I was doing a crash course in speed reading and I had to switch from the morning to the afternoon class for that day.

So; eight o'clock sharp; there I was sitting in the hospital, all dickied up—the good suit, the shoes polished, the clean shirt, the new tie, and with my bunch of flowers, waiting to be summoned to Molly's ward.

The call finally did come—at a quarter to twelve. Ward 10. Room 17. And of course by then I knew the operation was a disaster.

Knocked. Went in. Rice was there. And a staff nurse, a tiny little woman. And an Indian man—the anaesthetist, I think. The moment I entered he rushed out without saying a word.

And Molly. Sitting very straight in a white chair beside her bed. Her hair pulled away back from her face and piled up just here. Wearing a lime green dressing gown that Rita Cairns had lent her and the blue slippers I got her for her last birthday.

There was a small bruise mark below her right eye.

I thought: How young she looks, and so beautiful, so very beautiful.

"There she is," said Rice. "How does she look?"

"She looks well."

"Well? She looks wonderful! And why not? Everything went brilliantly! A complete success! A dream!"

He was so excited, there was no trace of the posh accent. And he bounced up and down on the balls of his feet. And he took my hand and shook it as if he were congratulating me. And the tiny staff nurse laughed and said "Brilliant! Brilliant!" and in her excitement knocked the chart off the end of the bed and then laughed even more.

"Speak to her!" said Rice. "Say something!"

"How are you?" I said to Molly.

"How do I look?"

"You look great."

"Do you like my black eye?"

"I didn't notice it," I said.

"I'm feeling great," she said. "Really. But what about you?"

"What do you mean?"

"Did you manage all right on your own last night?"

I suppose at that moment and in those circumstances it did sound a bit funny.

Anyhow Rice laughed out loud and of course the staff nurse; and then Molly and I had to laugh, too. In relief, I suppose, really . . .

Then Rice said to me,

"Aren't you going to give the lady her flowers?"

"Sorry," I said. "I got Rita to choose them. She said they're your favorite."

Could she see them? I didn't know what to do. Should I take her hand and put the flowers into it?

I held them in front of her. She reached out confidently and took them from me.

"They're lovely," she said. "Thank you. Lovely."

And she held them at arm's length, directly in front of her face, and turned them round. Suddenly Rice said,

"What color are they, Molly?"

She didn't hesitate at all.

"They're blue," she said. "Aren't they blue?"

"They certainly are! And the paper?" Rice asked. "What color is the wrapping paper?"

"Is it . . . yellow?"

"Yes! So you know some colors! Excellent! Really excellent!"

And the staff nurse clapped with delight.

"Now—a really hard question, and I'm not sure I know the answer to it myself. What sort of flowers are they?"

She brought them right up to her face. She turned them upside down. She held them at arm's length again. She stared at them—peered at them really—for what seemed an age. I knew how anxious she was by the way her mouth was working.

"Well, Molly? Do you know what they are?"

We waited. Another long silence. Then suddenly she closed her eyes shut tight. She brought the flowers right up against her face and inhaled in quick gulps and at the same time, with her free hand, swiftly, deftly felt the stems and the leaves and the blossoms. Then with her eyes still shut tight she called out desperately, defiantly,

"They're cornflowers! That's what they are! Cornflowers! Blue corn-flowers! Centaurea!"

Then for maybe half a minute she cried. Sobbed really.

The staff nurse looked uneasily at Rice. He held up his hand.

"Cornflowers, indeed. Splendid," he said very softly. "Excellent. It has been a heady day. But we're really on our way now, aren't we?"

I went back to the hospital again that night after my class. She was in buoyant form. I never saw her so animated.

"I can see, Frank!" she kept saying. "Do you hear me?—I can see!" Mr.

Rice was a genius! Wasn't it all wonderful? The nurses were angels! Wasn't I thrilled? She loved my red tie—it was red, wasn't it? And everybody was so kind. Dorothy and Joyce brought those chocolates during their lunch break. And old Mr. O'Neill sent that Get Well card—there—look—on the window sill. And didn't the flowers look beautiful in that pink vase? She would have the operation on the left eye just as soon as Mr. Rice would agree. And then, Frank, and then and then and then and then—oh, God, what then!

I was so happy, so happy for her. Couldn't have been happier for God's sake.

But just as on that first morning in Rice's bungalow when the only thing my mind could focus on was the smell of fresh whiskey off his breath, now all I could think of was some—some—some absurd scrap of information a Norwegian fisherman told me about the eyes of whales.

Whales for God's sake!

Stupid information. Useless, off-beat information. Stupid, useless, quirky mind . . .

Molly was still in full flight when a nurse came in and said that visiting time was long over and that Mrs. Sweeney needed all her strength to face tomorrow.

"How do I look?"

"Great," I said.

"Really, Frank?"

"Honestly. Wonderful."

"Black eye and all?"

"You wouldn't notice it," I said.

She caught my hand.

"Do you think . . . ?"

"Do I think what?"

"Do you think I look pretty, Frank?"

"You look beautiful," I said. "Just beautiful."

"Thank you."

I kissed her on the forehead and, as I said good night to her, she gazed intently at my face as if she were trying to read it. Her eyes were bright; unnaturally bright; burnished. And her expression was open and joyous. But as I said good night I had a feeling she wasn't as joyous as she looked.

Mr. Rice: When I look back over my working life I suppose I must have done thousands of operations. Sorry—performed. Bloomstein always corrected me on that: "Come on, you bloody bogman! We're not mechanics. We're artists. We perform." (*He shrugs his shoulders in dismissal.*)

And of those thousands I wonder how many I'll remember.

I'll remember Dubai. An Arab gentleman whose left eye had been almost pecked out by one of his peregrines and who sent his private jet to New York for Hans Girder and myself. The eye was saved, really because Girder was a magician. And we spent a week in a palace of marble and gold and played poker with the crew of the jet and lost every penny of the ransom we had just earned.

And I'll remember a city called Frankfort in Kentucky; and an elderly lady called Busty Butterfly who had been blinded in a gas explosion.

Hiroshi Matoba and I "performed" that operation. A tricky one, but he and I always worked well together. And Busty Butterfly was so grateful that she wanted me to have her best racehorse and little Hiroshi to marry her.

And I'll remember Ballybeg. Of course I'll remember Ballybeg. And the courageous Molly Sweeney. And I'll remember it not because of the operation — the operation wasn't all that complex; nor because the circumstances were special; nor indeed because a woman who had been blind for over forty years got her sight back. Yes, yes, yes, I'll remember it for all those reasons. Of course I will. But the core, the very heart, of the memory will be something different, something altogether different.

Perhaps I should explain that after that high summer of my thirty-second year — that episode in Cairo — the dinner party for Maria — Bloomstein's phone call — all that tawdry drama — my life no longer . . . cohered. I withdrew from medicine, from friendships, from all the consolations of work and the familiar; and for seven years and seven months — sounds like a fairy tale I used to read to Aisling — I subsided into a terrible darkness. . . .

But I was talking of Molly's operation and my memory of that. And the core of that memory is this. That for seventy-five minutes in the theater on that blustery October morning, the darkness miraculously lifted, and I performed — I watched myself do it — I performed so assuredly and with such skill, so elegantly, so efficiently, so economically — yes, yes, yes, of course it sounds vain — vanity has nothing to do with it — but suddenly, miraculously all the gifts, all the gifts were mine again, abundantly mine, joyously mine; and on that blustery October morning I had such a feeling of mastery and — how can I put it? — such a sense of playfulness for God's sake that I knew I was restored. No, no, no, not fully restored. Never fully restored. But a sense that a practical restoration, perhaps a restoration to something truer — that was possible. Yes, maybe that was possible. . . .

Yes, I'll remember Ballybeg. And when I left that dreary little place, that's the memory I took away with me. The place where I restored her sight to Molly Sweeney. Where the terrible darkness lifted. Where the shaft of light glanced off me again.

Molly: Mr. Rice said he couldn't have been more pleased with my progress. He called me his Miracle Molly. I liked him a lot more as the weeks passed.

And as usual Rita was wonderful. She let me off work early every Monday, Wednesday and Friday. And I'd dress up in this new coat I'd bought — a mad splurge to keep the spirits up — brilliant scarlet with a matching beret — Rita said I could be seen from miles away, like a distress signal — anyhow in all my new style I'd walk to the hospital on those three afternoons — without my cane! — and sometimes that was scary, I can tell you. And Mr. Rice would examine me and say, "Splendid, Molly! Splendid!" And then he'd pass me on to a psychotherapist, Mrs. O'Connor, a beautiful looking young woman according to Frank, and I'd do all sorts of tests with her. And then she'd pass me on to George, her husband, for more tests — he was a behavioral psychologist, if you don't mind, a real genius apparently — the pair of them were writing a book on me. And then I'd go back to Mr. Rice again and he'd say "Splendid!" again. And then I'd walk home — still no cane! — and have Frank's tea waiting for him when he'd get back from the library.

I can't tell you how kind Frank was to me, how patient he was. As soon as tea was over, he'd sit at the top of the table and he'd put me at the bottom and he'd begin my lesson.

He'd put something in front of me — maybe a bowl of fruit — and he'd say,

"What have I got in my hand?"

"A piece of fruit."

"What sort of fruit?"

"An orange, Frank. I know the color, don't I?"

"Very clever. Now, what's this?"

"It's a pear."

"You're guessing."

"Let me touch it."

"Not allowed. You already have your tactical engrams. We've got to build up a repertory of visual engrams to connect with them."

And I'd say, "For God's sake stop showing off your posh new words, Frank. It's a banana."

"Sorry. Try again."

"It's a peach. Right?"

"Splendid!" he'd say in Mr. Rice's accent. "It certainly is a peach. Now, what's this?"

And he'd move on to knives and forks, or shoes and slippers, or all the bits and pieces on the mantelpiece for maybe another hour or more. Every night. Seven nights a week.

Oh, yes, Frank couldn't have been kinder to me.

Rita, too. Even kinder. Even more patient.

And all my customers at the health club, the ones who had massages regularly, they sent me a huge bouquet of pink-and-white tulips. And the club I used to swim with, they sent me a beautiful gardening book. God knows what they thought — that I'd now be able to pick it up and read it? But everyone was great, just great.

Oh, yes, I lived in a very exciting world for those first weeks after the operation. Not at all like that silly world I wanted to visit and devour — none of that nonsense.

No, the world that I now saw — half-saw, peered at really — it was a world of wonder and surprise and delight. Oh, yes; wonderful, surprising, delightful. And joy — such joy, small unexpected joys that came in such profusion and passed so quickly that there was never enough time to savor them.

But it was a very foreign world, too. And disquieting; even alarming. Every color dazzled. Every light blazed. Every shape an apparition, a specter that appeared suddenly from nowhere and challenged you. And all that movement — nothing ever still — everything in motion all the time; and every movement unexpected, somehow threatening. Even the sudden sparrows in the garden, they seemed aggressive, dangerous.

So that after a time the mind could absorb no more sensation. Just one more color — light — movement — ghostly shape — and suddenly the head imploded and the hands shook and the heart melted with panic. And the only escape — the only way to live — was to sit absolutely still; and shut the eyes tight; and immerse yourself in darkness; and wait. Then when the hands were still and the heart quiet, slowly open the eyes again. And emerge. And try to find the courage to face it all once more.

I tried to explain to Frank once how — I suppose how *terrifying* it all was. But naturally, naturally he was far more concerned with teaching me practical things. And one day when I mentioned to Mr. Rice that I didn't think I'd find things as unnerving as I did, he said in a very icy voice, "And what sort of world did you expect, Mrs. Sweeney?"

Yes, it was a strange time. An exciting time, too — oh, yes, exciting. But so strange. And during those weeks after the operation I found myself thinking more and more about my mother and father, but especially about my mother and what it must have been like for her living in that huge, echoing house.

Mr. Rice: I operated on the second eye, the left eye, six weeks after the first operation. I had hoped it might have been a healthier eye. But when the cataract was removed, we found a retina much the same as in the right: traces of pigmentosa, scarred macula, areas atrophied. However, with both eyes functioning to some degree, her visual field was larger and she fixated better. She could now see from a medical point of view. From a psychological point of view she was still blind. In other words she now had to learn to see.

CONNECTIONS TO OTHER SELECTIONS

1. Discuss the themes of *Molly Sweeney* and Samuel Beckett's *Krapp's Last Tape* (p. 1649). What kind of recognition or understanding do the protagonists have at the end of each play?

2. Discuss the significance of blindness in *Molly Sweeney* and in Sophocles' *Oedipus the King* (p. 1224). How is blindness used for symbolic purposes in each play?

3. In an essay compare Brian Friel's techniques for revealing characters in *Molly Sweeney* with Jane Martin's *Rodeo* (p. 1657). What important similarities and differences do you find in the playwrights' use of monologues?

The Strong Breed

Born Oluwole Akinwande Soyinka in the western Nigerian town of Akinwande, Wole Soyinka has embodied in his life and art the contradictions and tensions that can often seem inevitable for the European-educated, English-speaking, African writer. "Selective eclecticism," he once said, is "the right of every productive being." Although he has written and published novels and poetry, Soyinka is most renowned as a playwright whose work often focuses on the tragic consequences of a clash between colonial and tribal values. Educated at Leeds University in England, he subsequently began an active career as a playwright as well as a political reformer and social critic. His autobiography *The Man Died* (1973) records his experiences as a political prisoner in Nigeria.

Soyinka's many plays include *The Swamp Dwellers* (1958), *The Invention* (1959), *The Lion and the Jewel* (1959), *A Dance of Forests* (1960), *The Strong Breed* (1963), *Madmen and Specialists* (1970), and *Death and the King's Horseman*

(1976). He has also written two novels and three volumes of poetry. In 1986 he was awarded the Nobel Prize for Literature.

Like nearly all of Soyinka's writing, *The Strong Breed* is steeped in African tribal culture and tradition, but the play's abiding concern for human suffering and social justice invites all readers to step into the small village in which one "night's work" changes the lives of its inhabitants.

WOLE SOYINKA (NIGERIA / B. 1934)
The Strong Breed   1963

CHARACTERS

Eman, a stranger
Sunma, Jaguna's daughter
Ifada, an idiot
A Girl
Jaguna
Oroge
Attendant Stalwarts, the villagers

From Eman's past—

Old Man, his father
Omae, his betrothed
Tutor
Priest
Attendants, the villagers

The scenes are described briefly, but very often a darkened stage with lit area will not only suffice but is necessary. Except for the one indicated place, there can be no break in the action. A distracting scene-change would be ruinous. A mud house, with space in front of it. Eman, in light buba° and trousers, stands at the window, looking out. Inside, Sunma is clearing the table of what looks like a modest clinic, putting the things away in a cupboard. Another rough table in the room is piled with exercise books, two or three worn textbooks, etc. Sunma appears agitated. Outside, just below the window, crouches Ifada. He looks up with a shy smile from time to time, waiting for Eman to notice him.

Sunma (hesitant): You will have to make up your mind soon, Eman. The lorry leaves very shortly.

As Eman does not answer, Sunma continues her work, more nervously. Two villagers, obvious travelers, pass hurriedly in front of the house, the man has a small raffia° sack, the woman a cloth-covered basket, the man enters first, turns, and urges the woman who is just emerging to hurry.

Sunma (seeing them, her tone is more intense): Eman, are we going or aren't we? You will leave it till too late.
Eman (quietly): There is still time—if you want to go.

buba: Traditional long shirt.
raffia: Woven palm.

Sunma: If I want to go . . . and you?

Eman makes no reply.

Sunma (bitterly): You don't really want to leave here. You never want to go away — even for a minute.

Ifada continues his antics. Eman eventually pats him on the head and the boy grins happily. Leaps up suddenly and returns with a basket of oranges, which he offers Eman.

Eman: My gift for today's festival enh?

Ifada nods, grinning.

Eman: They look ripe — that's a change.

Sunma (she has gone inside the room. Looks round the door): Did you call me?

Eman: No. *(She goes back.)* And what will you do tonight, Ifada? Will you take part in the dancing? Or perhaps you will mount your own masquerade?

Ifada shakes his head, regretfully.

Eman: You won't? So you haven't any? But you would like to own one.

Ifada nods eagerly.

Eman: Then why don't you make your own?

Ifada stares, puzzled by this idea.

Eman: Sunma will let you have some cloth you know. And bits of wool . . .

Sunma (coming out): Who are you talking to, Eman?

Eman: Ifada. I am trying to persuade him to join the young maskers.

Sunma (losing control): What does he want here? Why is he hanging round us?

Eman (amazed): What . . . ? I said Ifada, Ifada.

Sunma: Just tell him to go away. Let him go and play somewhere else!

Eman: What is this? Hasn't he always played here?

Sunma: I don't want him here. *(Rushes to the window.)* Get away, idiot. Don't bring your foolish face here any more, do you hear? Go on, go away from here . . .

Eman (restraining her): Control yourself, Sunma. What on earth has got into you?

Ifada, hurt and bewildered, backs slowly away.

Sunma: He comes crawling round here like some horrible insect. I never want to lay my eyes on him again.

Eman: I don't understand. It *is* Ifada you know, Ifada! The unfortunate one who runs errands for you and doesn't hurt a soul.

Sunma: I cannot bear the sight of him.

Eman: You can't do what? It can't be two days since he last fetched water for you.

Sunma: What else can he do except that? He is useless. Just because we have been kind to him. . . . Others would have put him in an asylum.

Eman: You are not making sense. He is not a madman, he is just a little more unlucky than other children. *(Looks keenly at her.)* But what is the matter?

Sunma: It's nothing. I only wish we had sent him off to one of those places for creatures like him.

Eman: He is quite happy here. He doesn't bother anyone and he makes himself useful.

Sunma: Useful! Is that one of any use to anybody? Boys of his age are already earning a living but all he can do is hang around and drool at the mouth.

Eman: But he does work. You know he does a lot for you.

Sunma: Does he? And what about the farm you started for him! Does he ever work on it? Or have you forgotten that it was really for Ifada you cleared that brush. Now you have to go and work it yourself. You spend all your time on it and you have no room for anything else.

Eman: That wasn't his fault. I should first have asked him if he was fond of farming.

Sunma: Oh, so he can choose? As if he shouldn't be thankful for being allowed to live.

Eman: Sunma!

Sunma: He does not like farming but he knows how to feast his dumb mouth on the fruits.

Eman: But I want him to. I encourage him.

Sunma: Well keep him. I don't want to see him any more.

Eman (after some moments): But why? You cannot be telling all the truth. What has he done?

Sunma: The sight of him fills me with revulsion.

Eman (goes to her and holds her): What really is it? *(Sunma avoids his eyes.)* It is almost as if you are forcing yourself to hate him. Why?

Sunma: That is not true. Why should I?

Eman: Then what is the secret? You've even played with him before.

Sunma: I have always merely tolerated him. But I cannot any more. Suddenly my disgust won't take him any more. Perhaps . . . perhaps it is the new year. Yes, yes, it must be the new year.

Eman: I don't believe that.

Sunma: It must be. I am a woman, and these things matter. I don't want a mis-shape near me. Surely for one day in the year, I may demand some whole-someness.

Eman: I do not understand you.

> *Sunma is silent.*

It was cruel of you. And to Ifada who is so helpless and alone. We are the only friends he has.

Sunma: No, just you. I have told you, with me it has always been only an act of kindness. And now I haven't any pity left for him.

Eman: No. He is not a wholesome being.

> *He turns back to looking through the window.*

Sunma (half-pleading): Ifada can rouse your pity. And yet if anything, I need more kindness from you. Every time my weakness betrays me, you close your mind against me . . . Eman . . . Eman . . .

> *A Girl comes in view, dragging an effigy by a rope attached to one of its legs. She stands for a while gazing at Eman. Ifada, who has crept back shyly to his accustomed position, becomes somewhat excited when he sees the effigy. The Girl is unsmiling. She possesses, in fact, a kind of inscrutability which does not make her hard but is unsettling.*

Girl: Is the teacher in?

Eman (smiling): No.

Girl: Where is he gone?

Eman: I don't really know. Shall I ask?

Girl: Yes, do.

Eman (turning slightly): Sunma, a girl outside wants to know . . .

> *Sunma turns away, goes into the inside room.*

Eman: Oh. (*Returns to the girl, but his slight gaiety is lost.*) There is no one at home who can tell me.

Girl: Why are you not in?

Eman: I don't really know. Maybe I went somewhere.

Girl: All right. I will wait until you get back.

> *She pulls the effigy to her, sits down.*

Eman (slowly regaining his amusement): So you are ready for the new year.

Girl (without turning round): I am not going to the festival.

Eman: Then why have you got that?

Girl: Do you mean my carrier? I am unwell you know. My mother says it will take away my sickness with the old year.

Eman: Won't you share the carrier with your playmates?

Girl: Oh, no. Don't you know I play alone? The other children won't come near me. Their mothers would beat them.

Eman: But I have never seen you here. Why don't you come to the clinic?

Girl: My mother said No.

> *Gets up, begins to move off.*

Eman: You are not going away?

Girl: I must not stay talking to you. If my mother caught me . . .

Eman: All right, tell me what you want before you go.

Girl (stops. For some moments she remains silent): I must have some clothes for my carrier.

Eman: Is that all? You wait a moment.

> *Sunma comes out as he takes down a buba from the wall. She goes to the window and glares almost with hatred at the Girl. The Girl retreats hastily, still impassive.*

By the way, Sunma, do you know who that girl is?

Sunma: I hope you don't really mean to give her that.

Eman: Why not? I hardly ever use it.

Sunma: Just the same don't give it to her. She is not a child. She is as evil as the rest of them.

Eman: What has got into you today?

Sunma: All right, all right. Do what you wish.

> *She withdraws. Baffled, Eman returns to the window.*

Eman: Here . . . will this do? Come and look at it.

Girl: Throw it.

Eman: What is the matter? I am not going to eat you.

Girl: No one lets me come near them.

Eman: But I am not afraid of catching your disease.

Girl: Throw it.

> *Eman shrugs and tosses the buba. She takes it without a word and slips it on the effigy, completely absorbed in the task. Eman watches for a while, then joins Sunma in the inner room.*

Girl (after a long, cool survey of Ifada): You have a head like a spider's egg, and your mouth dribbles like a roof. But there is no one else. Would you like to play?

Ifada nods eagerly, quite excited.

Girl: You will have to get a stick.

Ifada rushes around, finds a big stick, and whirls it aloft, bearing down on the carrier.

Girl: Wait. I don't want you to spoil it. If it gets torn I shall drive you away. Now, let me see how you are going to beat it.

Ifada hits it gently.

Girl: You may hit harder than that. As long as there is something left to hang at the end.

She appraises him up and down.

You are not very tall . . . will you be able to hang it from a tree?

Ifada nods, grinning happily.

Girl: You will hang it up and I will set fire to it. *(Then, with surprising venom.)* But just because you are helping me, don't think it is going to cure you. I am the one who will get well at midnight, do you understand? It is my carrier and it is for me alone. *(She pulls at the rope to make sure that it is well attached to the leg.)* Well don't stand there drooling. Let's go.

She begins to walk off, dragging the effigy in the dust. Ifada remains where he is for some moments, seemingly puzzled. Then his face breaks into a large grin and he leaps after the procession, belaboring the effigy with all his strength. The stage remains empty for some moments. Then the horn of a lorry is sounded and Sunma rushes out. The hooting continues for some time with a rhythmic pattern. Eman comes out.

Eman: I am going to the village . . . I shan't be back before nightfall.

Sunma (blankly): Yes.

Eman (hesitates): Well what do you want me to do?

Sunma: The lorry was hooting just now.

Eman: I didn't hear it.

Sunma: It will leave in a few minutes. And you did promise we could go away.

Eman: I promised nothing. Will you go home by yourself or shall I come back for you?

Sunma: You don't even want me here?

Eman: But you have to go home, haven't you?

Sunma: I had hoped we would watch the new year together—in some other place.

Eman: Why do you continue to distress yourself?

Sunma: Because you will not listen to me. Why do you continue to stay where nobody wants you?

Eman: That is not true.

Sunma: It is. You are wasting your life on people who really want you out of their way.

Eman: You don't know what you are saying.

Sunma: You think they love you? Do you think they care at all for what you— or I—do for them?

Eman: *Them?* These are your own people. Sometimes you talk as if you were a stranger too.

Sunma: I wonder if I really sprang from here. I know they are evil and I am not. From the oldest to the smallest child, they are nourished in evil and unwholesomeness in which I have no part.

Eman: You knew this when you returned?

Sunma: You reproach me then for trying at all?

Eman: I reproach you with nothing. But you must leave me out of your plans. I can have no part in them.

Sunma (nearly pleading): Once I could have run away. I would have gone and never looked back.

Eman: I cannot listen when you talk like that.

Sunma: I swear to you, I do not mind what happens afterwards. But you must help me tear myself away from here. I can no longer do it by myself. . . . It is only a little thing. And we have worked so hard this past year . . . surely we can go away for a week . . . even a few days would be enough.

Eman: I have told you, Sunma . . .

Sunma (desperately): Two days, Eman. Only two days.

Eman (distressed): But I tell you I have no wish to go.

Sunma (suddenly angry): Are you so afraid then?

Eman: Me? Afraid of what?

Sunma: You think you will not want to come back.

Eman (pitying): You cannot dare me that way.

Sunma: Then why don't you leave here, even for an hour? If you are so sure that your life is settled here, why are you afraid to do this thing for me? What is so wrong that you will not go into the next town for a day or two?

Eman: I don't want to. I do not have to persuade you, or myself, about anything. I simply have no desire to go away.

Sunma (his quiet confidence appears to incense her): You are afraid. You accuse me of losing my sense of mission, but you are afraid to put yours to the test.

Eman: You are wrong, Sunma. I have no sense of mission. But I have found peace here and I am content with that.

Sunma: I haven't. For a while I thought that too, but I found there could be no peace in the midst of so much cruelty. Eman, tonight at least, the last night of the old year . . .

Eman: No, Sunma. I find this too distressing; you should go home now.

Sunma: It is the time for making changes in one's life, Eman. Let's breathe in the new year away from here.

Eman: You are hurting yourself.

Sunma: Tonight. Only tonight. We will come back tomorrow, as early as you like. But let us go away for this one night. Don't let another year break on me in this place . . . you don't know how important it is to me, but I will tell you, I will tell you on the way . . . but we must not be here today, Eman, do this one thing for me.

Eman (sadly): I cannot.

Sunma (suddenly calm): I was a fool to think it would be otherwise. The whole village may use you as they will but for me there is nothing. Sometimes I think you believe that doing anything for me makes you unfaithful to some part of your life. If it was a woman then I pity her for what she must have suffered.

Eman winces and hardens slowly. Sunma notices nothing.

Keeping faith with so much is slowly making you inhuman. *(Seeing the change in Eman.)* Eman. Eman. What is it?

As she goes towards him, Eman goes into the house.

Sunma *(apprehensive, follows him):* What did I say? Eman, forgive me, forgive me please.

Eman remains facing into the slow darkness of the room. Sunma, distressed, cannot decide what to do.

I swear I didn't know. . . . I would not have said it for all the world.

A lorry is heard taking off somewhere nearby. The sound comes up and slowly fades away into the distance. Sunma starts visibly, goes slowly to the window.

Sunma *(as the sound dies off, to herself):* What happens now?
Eman *(joining her at the window):* What did you say?
Sunma: Nothing.
Eman: Was that not the lorry going off?
Sunma: It was.
Eman: I am sorry I couldn't help you.

Sunma, about to speak, changes her mind.

Eman: I think you ought to go home now.
Sunma: No, don't send me away. It's the least you can do for me. Let me stay here until all the noise is over.
Eman: But are you not needed at home? You have a part in the festival.
Sunma: I have renounced it; I am Jaguna's eldest daughter only in name.
Eman: Renouncing one's self is not so easy—surely you know that.
Sunma: I don't want to talk about it. Will you at least let us be together tonight?
Eman: But . . .
Sunma: Unless you are afraid my father will accuse you of harboring me.
Eman: All right, we will go out together.
Sunma: Go out? I want us to stay here.
Eman: When there is so much going on outside?
Sunma: Some day you will wish that you went away when I tried to make you.
Eman: Are we going back to that?
Sunma: No. I promise you I will not recall it again. But you must know that it was also for your sake that I tried to get us away.
Eman: For me? How?
Sunma: By yourself you can do nothing here. Have you not noticed how tightly we shut out strangers? Even if you lived here for a lifetime, you would remain a stranger.
Eman: Perhaps that is what I like. There is peace in being a stranger.
Sunma: For a while perhaps. But they would reject you in the end. I tell you it is only I who stand between you and contempt. And because of this you have earned their hatred. I don't know why I say this now, except that somehow, I feel that it no longer matters. It is only I who have stood between you and much humiliation.
Eman: Think carefully before you say any more. I am incapable of feeling indebted to you. This will make no difference at all.
Sunma: I ask for nothing. But you must know it all the same. It is true I hadn't the strength to go by myself. And I must confess this now, if you had come with me, I would have done everything to keep you from returning.

Eman: I know that.

Sunma: You see, I bare myself to you. For days I had thought it over, this was to be a new beginning for us. And I placed my fate wholly in your hands. Now the thought will not leave me, I have a feeling which will not be shaken off, that in some way, you have tonight totally destroyed my life.

Eman: You are depressed, you don't know what you are saying.

Sunma: Don't think I am accusing you. I say all this only because I cannot help it.

Eman: We must not remain shut up here. Let us go and be part of the living.

Sunma: No. Leave them alone.

Eman: Surely you don't want to stay indoors when the whole town is alive with rejoicing.

Sunma: Rejoicing! Is that what it seems to you? No, let us remain here. Whatever happens I must not go out until all this is over.

There is silence. It has grown much darker.

Eman: I shall light the lamp.

Sunma (eager to do something): No, let me do it.

> *She goes into the inner room. Eman paces the room, stops by a shelf, and toys with the seeds in an "ayo" board,° takes down the whole board and places it on a table, playing by himself.*
>
> *The Girl is now seen coming back, still dragging her "carrier." Ifada brings up the rear as before. As he comes round the corner of the house two men emerge from the shadows. A sack is thrown over Ifada's head, the rope is pulled tight rendering him instantly helpless. The Girl has reached the front of the house before she turns round at the sound of scuffle. She is in time to see Ifada thrown over the shoulders and borne away. Her face betraying no emotion at all, the Girl backs slowly away, turns, and flees, leaving the "carrier" behind. Sunma enters, carrying two kerosene lamps. She hangs one up from the wall.*

Eman: One is enough.

Sunma: I want to leave one outside.

> *She goes out, hangs the lamp from a nail just above the door. As she turns she sees the effigy and gasps. Eman rushes out.*

Eman: What is it? Oh, is that what frightened you?

Sunma: I thought . . . I didn't really see it properly.

> *Eman goes towards the object, stoops to pick it up.*

Eman: It must belong to that sick girl.

Sunma: Don't touch it.

Eman: Let's keep it for her.

Sunma: Leave it alone. Don't touch it, Eman.

Eman (shrugs and goes back): You are very nervous.

Sunma: Let's go in.

Eman: Wait. (*He detains her by the door, under the lamp.*) I know there is something more than you've told me. What are you afraid of tonight?

Sunma: I was only scared by that thing. There is nothing else.

Eman: I am not blind, Sunma. It is true I would not run away when you wanted me to, but that doesn't mean I do not feel things. What does tonight really mean that it makes you so helpless?

---

ayo board: A game.

Sunma: It is only a mood. And your indifference to me . . . let's go in.

Eman moves aside and she enters; he remains there for a moment and then follows. She fiddles with the lamp, looks vaguely round the room, then goes and shuts the door, bolting it. When she turns, it is to meet Eman's eyes, questioning.

Sunma: There is a cold wind coming in.

Eman keeps his gaze on her.

Sunma: It *was* getting cold.

She moves guiltily to the table and stands by the ayo board, rearranging the seeds. Eman remains where he is a few moments, then brings a stool and sits opposite her. She sits down also and they begin to play in silence.

Sunma: What brought you here at all, Eman? And what makes you stay?

There is another silence.

Sunma: I am not trying to share your life. I know you too well by now. But at least we have worked together since you came. Is there nothing at all I deserve to know?

Eman: Let me continue a stranger—especially to you. Those who have much to give fulfill themselves only in total loneliness.

Sunma: Then there is no love in what you do.

Eman: There is. Love comes to me more easily with strangers.

Sunma: That is unnatural.

Eman: Not for me. I know I find consummation only when I have spent myself for a total stranger.

Sunma: It seems unnatural to me. But then I am a woman. I have a woman's longings and weaknesses. And the ties of blood are very strong in me.

Eman (smiling): You think I have cut loose from all these—ties of blood.

Sunma: Sometimes you are so inhuman.

Eman: I don't know what that means. But I am very much my father's son.

They play in silence. Suddenly Eman pauses, listening.

Eman: Did you hear that?

Sunma (quickly): I heard nothing . . . it's your turn.

Eman: Perhaps some of the mummers are coming this way.

Eman, about to play, leaps up suddenly.

Sunma: What is it? Don't you want to play any more?

Eman moves to the door.

Sunma: No. Don't go out, Eman.

Eman: If it's the dancers I want to ask them to stay. At least we won't have to miss everything.

Sunma: No, no. Don't open the door. Let us keep out everyone tonight.

A terrified and disordered figure bursts suddenly round the corner, past the window and begins hammering at the door. It is Ifada. Desperate with terror, he pounds madly at the door, dumb-moaning all the while.

Eman: Isn't that Ifada?

Sunma: They are only fooling about. Don't pay any attention.

Eman (looks round the window): That is Ifada. *(Begins to unbolt the door.)*

Sunma (pulling at his hands): It is only a trick they are playing on you. Don't take any notice, Eman.

Eman: What are you saying? The boy is out of his senses with fear.

Sunma: No, no. Don't interfere, Eman. For God's sake don't interfere.

Eman: Do you know something of this then?

Sunma: You are a stranger here, Eman. Just leave us alone and go your own way. There is nothing you can do.

Eman (he tries to push her out of the way but she clings fiercely to him): Have you gone mad? I tell you the boy must come in.

Sunma: Why won't you listen to me, Eman? I tell you it's none of your business. For your own sake do as I say.

> *Eman pushes her off, unbolts the door. Ifada rushes in, clasps Eman round the knees, dumb-moaning against his legs.*

Eman (manages to rebolt the door): What is it, Ifada? What is the matter?

> *Shouts and voices are heard coming nearer the house.*

Sunma: Before it's too late, let him go. For once, Eman, believe what I tell you. Don't harbor him or you will regret it all your life.

> *Eman tries to calm Ifada, who becomes more and more abject as the outside voices get nearer.*

Eman: What have they done to him? At least tell me that. What is going on, Sunma?

Sunma (with sudden venom): Monster! Could you not take yourself somewhere else?

Eman: Stop talking like that.

Sunma: He could have run into the bush couldn't he? Toad! Why must he follow us with his own disasters!

Voices outside: It's here. . . . Round the back. . . . Spread, spread . . . this way . . . no, head him off . . . use the bush path and head him off . . . get some more lights . . .

> *Eman listens. Lifts Ifada bodily and carries him into the inner room. Returns at once, shutting the door behind him.*

Sunma (slumps into a chair, resigned): You always follow your own way.

Jaguna (comes round the corner followed by Oroge and three men, one bearing a torch): I knew he would come here.

Oroge: I hope our friend won't make trouble.

Jaguna: He had better not. You, recall all the men and tell them to surround the house.

Oroge: But he may not be in the house after all.

Jaguna: I know he is here . . . *(To the men.)* . . . go on, do as I say.

> *He bangs on the door.*

Teacher, open your door . . . you two stay by the door. If I need you I will call you.

> *Eman opens the door.*

Jaguna (speaks as he enters): We know he is here.

Eman: Who?

Jaguna: Don't let us waste time. We are grown men, teacher. You understand me and I understand you. But we must take back the boy.

Eman: This is my house.

Jaguna: Daughter, you'd better tell your friend. I don't think he quite knows our ways. Tell him why he must give up the boy.

Sunma: Father, I . . .

Jaguna: Are you going to tell him or aren't you?

Sunma: Father, I beg you, leave us alone tonight . . .

Jaguna: I thought you might be a hindrance. Go home then if you will not use your sense.

Sunma: But there are other ways . . .

Jaguna (turning to the men): See that she gets home. I no longer trust her. If she gives trouble carry her. And see that the women stay with her until all this is over.

Sunma departs, accompanied by one of the men.

Jaguna: Now, teacher . . .

Oroge (restrains him): You see, Mister Eman, it is like this. Right now, nobody knows that Ifada has taken refuge here. No one except us and our men — and they know how to keep their mouths shut. We don't want to have to burn down the house, you see, but if the word gets around, we would have no choice.

Jaguna: In fact, it may be too late already. A carrier should end up in the bush, not in a house. Anyone who doesn't guard his door when the carrier goes by has himself to blame. A contaminated house should be burnt down.

Oroge: But we are willing to let it pass. Only, you must bring him out quickly.

Eman: All right. But at least you will let me ask you something.

Jaguna: What is there to ask? Don't you understand what we have told you?

Eman: Yes. But why did you pick on a helpless boy? Obviously he is not willing.

Jaguna: What is the man talking about? Ifada is a godsend. Does he have to be willing?

Eman: In my home, we believe that a man should be willing.

Oroge: Mister Eman, I don't think you quite understand. This is not a simple matter at all. I don't know what you do, but here, it is not a cheap task for anybody. No one in his senses would do such a job. Why do you think we give refuge to idiots like him? We don't know where he came from. One morning, he is simply there, just like that. From nowhere at all. You see, there is a purpose in that.

Jaguna: We only waste time.

Oroge: Jaguna, be patient. After all, the man has been with us for some time now and deserves to know. The evil of the old year is no light thing to load on any man's head.

Eman: I know something about that.

Oroge: You do? *(Turns to Jaguna, who snorts impatiently.)* You see I told you so, didn't I? From the moment you came I saw you were one of the knowing ones.

Jaguna: Then let him behave like a man and give back the boy.

Eman: It is you who are not behaving like men.

Jaguna (advances aggressively): That is a quick mouth you have . . .

Oroge: Patience, Jaguna . . . if you want the new year to cushion the land there must be no deeds of anger. What did you mean, my friend?

Eman: It is a simple thing. A village which cannot produce its own carrier contains no men.

Jaguna: Enough. Let there be no more talk or this business will be ruined by some rashness. You . . . come inside. Bring the boy out, he must be in the room there.

Eman: Wait.

The men hesitate.

Jaguna (hitting the nearer one and propelling him forward): Go on. Have you changed masters now that you listen to what he says?

Oroge (sadly): I am sorry you would not understand, Mister Eman. But you ought to know that no carrier may return to the village. If he does, the people will stone him to death. It has happened before. Surely it is too much to ask a man to give up his own soil.

Eman: I know others who have done more.

Ifada is brought out, abjectly dumb-moaning.

Eman: You can see him with your own eyes. Does it really have meaning to use one as unwilling as that?

Oroge (smiling): He shall be willing. Not only willing but actually joyous. I am the one who prepares them all, and I have seen worse. This one escaped before I began to prepare him for the event. But you will see him later tonight, the most joyous creature in the festival. Then perhaps you will understand.

Eman: Then it is only a deceit. Do you believe the spirit of a new year is so easily fooled?

Jaguna: Take him out. *(The men carry out Ifada.)* You see, it is so easy to talk. You say there are no men in this village because they cannot provide a willing carrier. And yet I heard Oroge tell you we only use strangers. There is only one other stranger in the village, but I have not heard him offer himself. *(Spits.)* It is so easy to talk is it not?

He turns his back on him. They go off, taking Ifada with them, limp and silent. The only sign of life is that he strains his neck to keep his eyes on Eman till the very moment that he disappears from sight. Eman remains where they left him, staring after the group.

A blackout lasting no more than a minute. The lights come up slowly, and Ifada is seen returning to the house. He stops at the window and looks in. Seeing no one, he bangs on the sill. Appears surprised that there is no response. He slithers down on his favorite spot, then sees the effigy still lying where the Girl had dropped it in her flight. After some hesitation, he goes towards it, begins to strip it of the clothing. Just then the Girl comes in.

Girl: Hey, leave that alone. You know it's mine.

Ifada pauses, then speeds up his action.

Girl: I said it is mine. Leave it where you found it. *(She rushes at him and begins to struggle for possession of the carrier.)* Thief! Thief! Let it go, it is mine. Let it go. You animal, just because I let you play with it. Idiot! Idiot!

The struggle becomes quite violent. The Girl is hanging to the effigy and Ifada lifts her with it, flinging her all about. The Girl hangs on grimly.

Girl: You are spoiling it . . . why don't you get your own? Thief! Let it go, you thief!

Sunma comes in walking very fast, throwing apprehensive glances over her shoulder. Seeing the two children, she becomes immediately angry. Advances on them.

Sunma: So you've made this place your playground. Get away, you untrained pigs. Get out of here.

Ifada flees at once, the Girl retreats also, retaining possession of the carrier.
Sunma goes to the door. She has her hand on the door when the significance of Ifada's presence strikes her for the first time. She stands rooted to the spot, then turns slowly round.

Sunma: Ifada! What are you doing here?

Ifada is bewildered. Sunma turns suddenly and rushes into the house, flying into the inner room and out again.

Eman! Eman! Eman!

She rushes outside.

Where did he go? Where did they take him?

Ifada distressed, points. Sunma seizes him by the arm, drags him off.

Take me there at once. God help you if we are too late. You loathsome thing, if you have let him suffer . . .

Her voice fades into other shouts, running footsteps, banged tins, bells, dogs, etc., rising in volume.
It is a narrow passageway between two mudhouses. At the far end one man after another is seen running across the entry, the noise dying off gradually.
About halfway down the passage, Eman is crouching against the wall, tense with apprehension. As the noise dies off, he seems to relax, but the alert, hunted look is still in his eyes, which are ringed in a reddish color. The rest of his body has been whitened with a floury substance. He is naked down to the waist, wears a baggy pair of trousers, calf-length, and around both feet are bangles.

Eman: I will simply stay here till dawn. I have done enough.

A window is thrown open and a woman empties some slop from a pail. With a startled cry Eman leaps aside to avoid it and the woman puts out her head.

Woman: Oh, my head. What have I done! Forgive me, neighbor . . . Eh, it's the carrier! *(Very rapidly she clears her throat and spits on him, flings the pail at him and runs off, shouting.)* He's here. The carrier is hiding in the passage. Quickly, I have found the carrier!

The cry is taken up and Eman flees down the passage. Shortly afterwards his pursuers come pouring down the passage in full cry. After the last of them come Jaguna and Oroge.

Oroge: Wait, wait. I cannot go so fast.

Jaguna: We will rest a little then. We can do nothing anyway.

Oroge: If only he had let me prepare him.

Jaguna: They are the ones who break first, these fools who think they were born to carry suffering like a hat. What are we to do now?

Oroge: When they catch him I must prepare him.

Jaguna: He? It will be impossible now. There can be no joy left in that one.

Oroge: Still, it took him by surprise. He was not expecting what he met.

Jaguna: Why then did he refuse to listen? Did he think he was coming to sit down to a feast? He had not even gone through one compound before he bolted. Did he think he was taken round the people to be blessed? A woman, that is all he is.

Oroge: No, no. He took the beating well enough. I think he is the kind who would let himself be beaten from night till dawn and not utter a sound. He would let himself be stoned until he dropped dead.

Jaguna: Then what made him run like a coward?

Oroge: I don't know. I don't really know. It is a night of curses, Jaguna. It is not many unprepared minds will remain unhinged under the load.

Jaguna: We must find him. It is a poor beginning for a year when our own curses remain hovering over our homes because the carrier refused to take them.

They go. The scene changes. Eman is crouching beside some shrubs, torn and bleeding.

Eman: They are even guarding my house . . . as if I would go there, but I need water . . . they could at least grant me that . . . I can be thirsty too . . . *(He pricks his ears.)* . . . there must be a stream nearby . . . *(As he looks round him, his eyes widen at a scene he encounters.)*

An Old Man, short and vigorous looking, is seated on a stool. He also is wearing calf-length baggy trousers, white. On his head, a white cap. An attendant is engaged in rubbing his body with oil. Round his eyes, two white rings have already been marked.

Old Man: Have they prepared the boat?

Attendant: They are making the last sacrifice.

Old Man: Good. Did you send for my son?

Attendant: He's on his way.

Old Man: I have never met the carrying of the boat with such a heavy heart. I hope nothing comes of it.

Attendant: The gods will not desert us on that account.

Old Man: A man should be at his strongest when he takes the boat, my friend. To be weighed down inside and out is not a wise thing. I hope when the moment comes I shall have found my strength.

Enter Eman, a wrapper round his waist and a danski° over it.

Old Man: I meant to wait until after my journey to the river, but my mind is so burdened with my own grief and yours I could not delay it. You know I must have all my strength. But I sit here, feeling it all eaten slowly away by my unspoken grief. It helps to say it out. It even helps to cry sometimes.

He signals to the attendant to leave them.

Come nearer . . . we will never meet again, son. Not on this side of the flesh. What I do not know is whether you will return to take my place.

Eman: I will never come back.

Old Man: Do you know what you are saying? Ours is a strong breed, my son. It is only a strong breed that can take this boat to the river year after year and

---

danski: A garment.

wax stronger on it. I have taken down each year's evils for over twenty years. I hoped you would follow me.

Eman: My life here died with Omae.

Old Man: Omae died giving birth to your child and you think the world is ended. Eman, my pain did not begin when Omae died. Since you sent her to stay with me, son, I lived with the burden of knowing that this child would die bearing your son.

Eman: Father.

Old Man: Don't you know it was the same with you? And me? No woman survives the bearing of the strong ones. Son, it is not the mouth of the boaster that says he belongs to the strong breed. It is the tongue that is red with pain and black with sorrow. Twelve years you were away, my son, and for those twelve years I knew the love of an old man for his daughter and the pain of a man helplessly awaiting his loss.

Eman: I wish I had stayed away. I wish I never came back to meet her.

Old Man: It had to be. But you know now what slowly ate away my strength. I awaited your return with love and fear. Forgive me then if I say that your grief is light. It will pass. This grief may drive you now from home. But you must return.

Eman: You do not understand. It is not grief alone.

Old Man: What is it then? Tell me, I can still learn.

Eman: I was away twelve years. I changed much in that time.

Old Man: I am listening.

Eman: I am unfitted for your work, father. I wish to say no more. But I am totally unfitted for your call.

Old Man: It is only time you need, son. Stay longer and you will answer the urge of your blood.

Eman: That I stayed at all was because of Omae. I did not expect to find her waiting. I would have taken her away, but hard as you claim to be, it would have killed you. And I was a tired man. I needed peace. Because Omae was peace, I stayed. Now nothing holds me here.

Old Man: Other men would rot and die doing this task year after year. It is strong medicine which only we can take. Our blood is strong like no other. Anything you do in life must be less than this, son.

Eman: That is not true, father.

Old Man: I tell you it is true. Your own blood will betray you, son, because you cannot hold it back. If you make it do less than this, it will rush to your head and burst it open. I say what I know, my son.

Eman: There are other tasks in life, father. This one is not for me. There are even greater things you know nothing of.

Old Man: I am very sad. You only go to give to others what rightly belongs to us. You will use your strength among thieves. They are thieves because they take what is ours, they have no claim of blood to it. They will even lack the knowledge to use it wisely. Truth is my companion at this moment, my son. I know everything I say will surely bring the sadness of truth.

Eman: I am going, father.

Old Man: Call my attendant. And be with me in your strength for this last journey. A-ah, did you hear that? It came out without my knowing it; this is indeed my last journey. But I am not afraid.

Eman goes out. A few moments later, the attendant enters.

Attendant: The boat is ready.

Old Man: So am I.

He sits perfectly still for several moments. Drumming begins somewhere in the distance, and the Old Man sways his head almost imperceptibly. Two men come in bearing a miniature boat, containing an indefinable mound. They rush it in and set it briskly down near the Old Man, and stand well back. The Old Man gets up slowly, the attendant watching him keenly. He signs to the men, who lift the boat quickly onto the Old Man's head. As soon as it touches his head, he holds it down with both hands and runs off, the men give him a start, then follow at a trot. As the last man disappears Oroge limps in and comes face to face with Eman—as carrier—who is now seen still standing beside the shrubs, staring into the scene he has just witnessed. Oroge, struck by the look on Eman's face, looks anxiously behind him to see what has engaged Eman's attention. Eman notices him then, and the pair stare at each other. Jaguna enters, sees him and shouts, "Here he is," rushes at Eman, who is whipped back to the immediate and flees, Jaguna in pursuit. Three or four others enter and follow them. Oroge remains where he is, thoughtful.

Jaguna (reenters): They have closed in on him now, we'll get him this time.

Oroge: It is nearly midnight.

Jaguna: You were standing there looking at him as if he was some strange spirit. Why didn't you shout?

Oroge: You shouted didn't you? Did that catch him?

Jaguna: Don't worry. We have him now. But things have taken a bad turn. It is no longer enough to drive him past every house. There is too much contamination about already.

Oroge (not listening): He saw something. Why may I not know what it was?

Jaguna: What are you talking about?

Oroge: Hm. What is it?

Jaguna: I said there is too much harm done already. The year will demand more from this carrier than we thought.

Oroge: What do you mean?

Jaguna: Do we have to talk with the full mouth?

Oroge: S-sh . . . look!

Jaguna turns just in time to see Sunma fly at him, clawing at his face like a crazed tigress.

Sunma: Murderer! What are you doing to him? Murderer! Murderer!

Jaguna finds himself struggling really hard to keep off his daughter. He succeeds in pushing her off and striking her so hard on the face that she falls to her knees. He moves on her to hit her again.

Oroge (comes between): Think what you are doing, Jaguna, she is your daughter.

Jaguna: My daughter! Does this one look like my daughter? Let me cripple the harlot for life.

Oroge: That is a wicked thought, Jaguna.

Jaguna: Don't come between me and her.

Oroge: Nothing in anger—do you forget what tonight is?

Jaguna: Can you blame me for forgetting?

Draws his hand across his cheek—it is covered with blood.

Oroge: This is an unhappy night for us all. I fear what is to come of it.

Jaguna: Let's go. I cannot restrain myself in this creature's presence. My own daughter . . . and for a stranger . . .

They go off. Ifada, who came in with Sunma and had stood apart, horror-stricken, comes shyly forward. He helps Sunma up. They go off, he holding Sunma bent and sobbing.

> *Enter Eman—as carrier. He is physically present in the bounds of this next scene, a side of a round thatched hut. A young girl, about fourteen, runs in, stops beside the hut. She looks carefully to see that she is not observed, puts her mouth to a little hole in the wall.*

Omae: Eman . . . Eman . . .

Eman—as carrier—responds, as he does throughout the scene, but they are unaware of him.

Eman (from inside): Who is it?

Omae: It is me, Omae.

Eman: How dare you come here!

Two hands appear at the hole and, pushing outwards, create a much larger hole through which Eman puts out his head. It is Eman as a boy, the same age as the girl.

Go away at once. Are you trying to get me into trouble!

Omae: What is the matter?

Eman: You. Go away.

Omae: But I came to see you.

Eman: Are you deaf? I say I don't want to see you. Now go before my tutor catches you.

Omae: All right. Come out.

Eman: Do what!

Omae: Come out.

Eman: You must be mad.

Omae (sits on the ground): All right, if you don't come out I shall simply stay here until your tutor arrives.

Eman (about to explode, thinks better of it and the head disappears. A moment later he emerges from behind the hut): What sort of a devil has got into you?

Omae: None. I just wanted to see you.

Eman (his mimicry is nearly hysterical): "None. I just wanted to see you." Do you think this place is the stream where you can go and molest innocent people?

Omae (coyly): Aren't you glad to see me?

Eman: I am not.

Omae: Why?

Eman: Why? Do you really ask me why? Because you are a woman and a most troublesome woman. Don't you know anything about this at all? We are not meant to see any woman. So go away before more harm is done.

Omae (flirtatious): What is so secret about it anyway? What do they teach you?

Eman: Nothing any woman can understand.

Omae: Ha ha. You think we don't know eh? You've all come to be circumcised.

Eman: Shut up. You don't know anything.

Omae: Just think, all this time you haven't been circumcised, and you dared make eyes at us women.

Eman: Thank you—woman. Now go.

Omae: Do they give you enough to eat?

Eman (testily): No. We are so hungry that when silly girls like you turn up, we eat them.

Omae (feigning tears): Oh, oh, oh, he's abusing me. He's abusing me.

Eman (alarmed): Don't try that here. Go quickly if you are going to cry.

Omae: All right, I won't cry.

Eman: Cry or no cry, go away and leave me alone. What do you think will happen if my tutor turns up now?

Omae: He won't.

Eman (mimicking): "He won't." I suppose you are his wife and he tells you where he goes. In fact this is just the time he comes round to our huts. He could be at the next hut this very moment.

Omae: Ha-ha. You're lying. I left him by the stream, pinching the girls' bottoms. Is that the sort of thing he teaches you?

Eman: Don't say anything against him or I shall beat you. Isn't it you loose girls who tease him, wiggling your bottoms under his nose?

Omae (going tearful again): A-ah, so I am one of the loose girls, eh?

Eman: Now don't start accusing me of things I didn't say.

Omae: But you said it. You said it.

Eman: I didn't. Look, Omae, someone will hear you and I'll be in disgrace. Why don't you go before anything happens.

Omae: It's all right. My friends have promised to hold your old rascal tutor till I get back.

Eman: Then go back right now. I have work to do. *(Going in.)*

Omae (runs after and tries to hold him. Eman leaps back, genuinely scared): What is the matter? I was not going to bite you.

Eman: Do you know what you nearly did? You almost touched me!

Omae: Well?

Eman: Well! Isn't it enough that you let me set my eyes on you? Must you now totally pollute me with your touch? Don't you understand anything?

Omae: Oh, that.

Eman (nearly screaming): It is not "oh that." Do you think this is only a joke or a little visit like spending the night with your grandmother? This is an important period of my life. Look, these huts, we built them with our own hands. Every boy builds his own. We learn things, do you understand? And we spend much time just thinking. At least, I do. It is the first time I have had nothing to do except think. Don't you see, I am becoming a man. For the first time, I understand that I have a life to fulfill. Has that thought ever worried you?

Omae: You are frightening me.

Eman: There. That is all you can say. And what use will that be when a man finds himself alone—like that? *(Points to the hut.)* A man must go on his own, go where no one can help him, and test his strength. Because he may find himself one day sitting alone in a wall as round as that. In there, my mind could hold no other thought. I may never have such moments again to myself. Don't dare to come and steal any more of it.

Omae (this time, genuinely tearful): Oh, I know you hate me. You only want to drive me away.

Eman (impatiently): Yes, yes, I know I hate you—but go.

Omae (going, all tears. Wipes her eyes, suddenly all mischief): Eman.

Eman: What now?

Omae: I only want to ask one thing . . . do you promise to tell me?

Eman: Well, what is it?

Omae (gleefully): Does it hurt?

She turns instantly and flees, landing straight into the arms of the returning tutor.

Tutor: Te-he-he . . . what have we here? What little mouse leaps straight into the beak of the wise old owl eh?

Omae struggles to free herself, flies to the opposite side, grimacing with distaste.

Tutor: I suppose you merely came to pick some fruits eh? You did not sneak here to see any of my children.

Omae: Yes, I came to steal your fruits.

Tutor: Te-he-he . . . I thought so. And that dutiful son of mine over there. He saw you and came to chase you off my fruit trees didn't he? Te-he-he . . . I'm sure he did, isn't that so, my young Eman?

Eman: I was talking to her.

Tutor: Indeed you were. Now be good enough to go into your hut until I decide your punishment. *(Eman withdraws.)* Te-he-he . . . now now, my little daughter, you need not be afraid of me.

Omae (spiritedly): I am not.

Tutor: Good. Very good. We ought to be friendly. *(His voice becomes leering.)* Now this is nothing to worry you, my daughter . . . a very small thing indeed. Although of course if I were to let it slip that your young Eman had broken a strong taboo, it might go hard on him, you know. I am sure you would not like that to happen, would you?

Omae: No.

Tutor: Good. You are sensible, my girl. Can you wash clothes?

Omae: Yes.

Tutor: Good. If you will come with me now to my hut, I shall give you some clothes to wash, and then we will forget all about this matter eh? Well, come on.

Omae: I shall wait here. You go and bring the clothes.

Tutor: Eh? What is that? Now now, don't make me angry. You should know better than to talk back at your elders. Come now.

He takes her by the arm, and tries to drag her off.

Omae: No no, I won't come to your hut. Leave me. Leave me alone, you shameless old man.

Tutor: If you don't come I shall disgrace the whole family of Eman, and yours too.

Eman reenters with a small bundle.

Eman: Leave her alone. Let us go, Omae.

Tutor: And where do you think you are going?

Eman: Home.

Tutor: Te-he-he . . . As easy as that eh? You think you can leave here any time you please? Get right back inside that hut!

Eman takes Omae by the arm and begins to walk off.

Tutor: Come back at once.

He goes after him and raises his stick. Eman catches it, wrenches it from him, and throws it away.

Omae (hopping delightedly): Kill him. Beat him to death.

Tutor: Help! Help! He is killing me! Help!

Alarmed, Eman clamps his hand over his mouth.

Eman: Old tutor, I don't mean you any harm, but you mustn't try to harm me either. *(He removes his hand.)*

Tutor: You think you can get away with your crime. My report shall reach the elders before you ever get into town.

Eman: You are afraid of what I will say about you? Don't worry. Only if you try to shame me, then I will speak. I am not going back to the village anyway. Just tell them I have gone, no more. If you say one word more than that I shall hear of it the same day and I shall come back.

Tutor: You are telling me what to do? But don't think to come back next year because I will drive you away. Don't think to come back here even ten years from now. And don't send your children. *(Goes off with threatening gestures.)*

Eman: I won't come back.

Omae: Smoked vulture! But Eman, he says you cannot return next year. What will you do?

Eman: It is a small thing one can do in the big towns.

Omae: I thought you were going to beat him that time. Why didn't you crack his dirty hide?

Eman: Listen carefully, Omae . . . I am going on a journey.

Omae: Come on. Tell me about it on the way.

Eman: No, I go that way. I cannot return to the village.

Omae: Because of that wretched man? Anyway you will first talk to your father.

Eman: Go and see him for me. Tell him I have gone away for some time. I think he will know.

Omae: But, Eman . . .

Eman: I haven't finished. You will go and live with him till I get back. I have spoken to him about you. Look after him!

Omae: But what is this journey? When will you come back?

Eman: I don't know. But this is a good moment to go. Nothing ties me down.

Omae: But, Eman, you want to leave me.

Eman: Don't forget all I said. I don't know how long I will be. Stay in my father's house as long as you remember me. When you become tired of waiting, you must do as you please. You understand? You must do as you please.

Omae: I cannot understand anything, Eman. I don't know where you are going or why. Suppose you never came back! Don't go, Eman. Don't leave me by myself.

Eman: I must go. Now let me see you on your way.

Omae: I shall come with you.

Eman: Come with me! And who will look after you? Me? You will only be in my way, you know that! You will hold me back and I shall desert you in a strange place. Go home and do as I say. Take care of my father and let him take care of you. *(He starts going but Omae clings to him.)*

Omae: But, Eman, stay the night at least. You will only lose your way. Your father, Eman, what will he say? I won't remember what you said . . . come
back to the village . . . I cannot return alone, Eman . . . come with me as
far as the crossroads.

*His face set, Eman strides off and Omae loses balance as he increases his pace.
Falling, she quickly wraps her arms around his ankle, but Eman continues
unchecked, dragging her along.*

Omae: Don't go, Eman . . . Eman, don't leave me, don't leave me . . . don't
leave your Omae . . . don't go, Eman . . . don't leave your Omae . . .

*Eman—as carrier—makes a nervous move as if he intends to go after the vanished
pair. He stops but continues to stare at the point where he last saw them. There is
stillness for a while. Then the Girl enters from the same place and remains looking
at Eman. Startled, Eman looks apprehensively round him. The Girl goes nearer
but keeps beyond arm's length.*

Girl: Are you the carrier?
Eman: Yes, I am Eman.
Girl: Why are you hiding?
Eman: I really came for a drink of water . . . er . . . is there anyone in front of
the house?
Girl: No.
Eman: But there might be people in the house. Did you hear voices?
Girl: There is no one here.
Eman: Good. Thank you. *(He is about to go, stops suddenly.)* Er . . . would you . . .
you will find a cup on the table. Could you bring me the water out here?
The water pot is in a corner.

*The Girl goes. She enters the house, then, watching Eman carefully, slips out and
runs off.*

Eman (sitting): Perhaps they have all gone home. It will be good to rest. *(He
hears voices and listens hard.)* Too late. *(Moves cautiously nearer the house.)*
Quickly, girl, I can hear people coming. Hurry up. *(Looks through the window.)* Where are you? Where is she? *(The truth dawns on him suddenly and he
moves off, sadly.)*

Enter Jaguna and Oroge, led by the Girl.

Girl (pointing): He was there.
Jaguna: Ay, he's gone now. He is a sly one is your friend. But it won't save him
forever.
Oroge: What was he doing when you saw him?
Girl: He asked me for a drink of water.
Jaguna: ⎫
Oroge: ⎭ Ah! *(They look at each other.)*
Oroge: We should have thought of that.
Jaguna: He is surely finished now. If only we had thought of it earlier.
Oroge: It is not too late. There is still an hour before midnight.
Jaguna: We must call back all the men. Now we need only wait for him — in the
right place.
Oroge: Everyone must be told. We don't want anyone heading him off again.

Jaguna: And it works so well. This is surely the help of the gods themselves, Oroge. Don't you know at once what is on the path to the stream?

Oroge: The sacred trees.

Jaguna: I tell you it is the very hand of the gods. Let us go.

An overgrown part of the village. Eman wanders in, aimlessly, seemingly uncaring of discovery. Beyond him, an area lights up, revealing a group of people clustered round a spot, all the heads are bowed. One figure stands away and separate from them. Even as Eman looks, the group breaks up and the people disperse, coming down and past him. Only three people are left, a man (Eman) whose back is turned, the village Priest, and the isolated one. They stand on opposite sides of the grave, the man on the mound of earth. The Priest walks round to the man's side and lays a hand on his shoulder.

Priest: Come.

Eman: I will. Give me a few moments here alone.

Priest: Be comforted.

They fall silent.

Eman: I was gone twelve years but she waited. She whom I thought had too much of the laughing child in her. Twelve years I was a pilgrim, seeking the vain shrine of secret strength. And all the time, strange knowledge, this silent strength of my child-woman.

Priest: We all saw it. It was a lesson to us; we did not know that such goodness could be found among us.

Eman: Then why? Why the wasted years if she had to perish giving birth to my child? *(They are both silent.)* I do not really know for what great meaning I searched. When I returned, I could not be certain I had found it. Until I reached my home and I found her a full-grown woman, still a child at heart. When I grew to believe it, I thought, this, after all, is what I sought. It was here all the time. And I threw away my new-gained knowledge. I buried the part of me that was formed in strange places. I made a home in my birthplace.

Priest: That was as it should be.

Eman: Any truth of that was killed in the cruelty of her brief happiness.

Priest (looks up and sees the figure standing away from them, the child in his arms. He is totally still): Your father — he is over there.

Eman: I knew he would come. Has he my son with him?

Priest: Yes.

Eman: He will let no one take the child. Go and comfort him, priest. He loved Omae like a daughter, and you all know how well she looked after him. You see how strong we really are. In his heart of hearts the old man's love really awaited a daughter. Go and comfort him. His grief is more than mine.

The Priest goes. The Old Man has stood well away from the burial group. His face is hard and his gaze unswerving from the grave. The Priest goes to him, pauses, but sees that he can make no dent in the man's grief. Bowed, he goes on his way.

Eman, as carrier, walks towards the graveside, the other Eman having gone. His feet sink into the mound and he breaks slowly on to his knees, scooping up the sand in his hands and pouring it on his head. The scene blacks out slowly.

Enter Jaguna and Oroge.

Oroge: We have only a little time.

Jaguna: He will come. All the wells are guarded. There is only the stream left him. The animal must come to drink.

Oroge: You are sure it will not fail — the trap, I mean.

Jaguna: When Jaguna sets the trap, even elephants pay homage — their trunks downwards and one leg up in the sky. When the carrier steps on the fallen twigs, it is up in the sacred trees with him.

Oroge: I shall breathe again when this long night is over.

They go out.

Enter Eman — as carrier — from the same direction as the last two entered. In front of him is a still figure, the Old Man as he was, carrying the dwarf boat.

Eman (joyfully): Father.

The figure does not turn round.

Eman: It is your son. Eman. *(He moves nearer.)* Don't you want to look at me? It is I, Eman. *(He moves nearer still.)*

Old Man: You are coming too close. Don't you know what I carry on my head?

Eman: But, father, I am your son.

Old Man: Then go back. We cannot give the two of us.

Eman: Tell me first where you are going.

Old Man: Do *you* ask that? Where else but to the river?

Eman (visibly relieved): I only wanted to be sure. My throat is burning. I have been looking for the stream all night.

Old Man: It is the other way.

Eman: But you said . . .

Old Man: I take the longer way, you know now I must do this. It is quicker if you take the other way. Go now.

Eman: No, I will only get lost again. I shall go with you.

Old Man: Go back, my son. Go back.

Eman: Why? Won't you even look at me?

Old Man: Listen to your father. Go back.

Eman: But father!

He makes to hold him. Instantly the Old Man breaks into a rapid trot. Eman hesitates, then follows, his strength nearly gone.

Eman: Wait, father. I am coming with you . . . wait . . . wait for me, father . . .

There is a sound of twigs breaking, of a sudden trembling in the branches. Then silence.

The front of Eman's house. The effigy is hanging from the sheaves. Enter Sunma. Still supported by Ifada, she stands transfixed as she sees the hanging figure. Ifada appears to go mad, rushes at the object, and tears it down. Sunma, her last bit of will gone, crumbles against the wall. Some distance away from them, partly hidden, stands the Girl, impassively watching. Ifada hugs the effigy to him, stands above Sunma. The Girl remains where she is, observing. Almost at once, the villagers begin to return, subdued and guilty. They walk across the front, skirting the house as widely as they can. No word is exchanged. Jaguna and Oroge eventually appear. Jaguna, who is leading, sees Sunma as soon as he comes in view. He stops at once, retreating slightly.

Oroge (almost whispering): What is it?
Jaguna: The viper.

> *Oroge looks cautiously at the woman.*

Oroge: I don't think she will even see you.
Jaguna: Are you sure? I am in no frame of mind for another meeting with her.
Oroge: Let's go home.
Jaguna: I am sick to the heart of the cowardice I have seen tonight.
Oroge: That is the nature of men.
Jaguna: Then it is a sorry world to live in. We did it for them. It was all for their own common good. What did it benefit me whether the man lived or died? But did you see them? One and all they looked up at the man and words died in their throats.
Oroge: It was no common sight.
Jaguna: Women could not have behaved so shamefully. One by one they crept off like sick dogs. Not one could raise a curse.
Oroge: It was not only him they fled. Do you see how unattended we are?
Jaguna: There are those who will pay for this night's work!
Oroge: Ay, let us go home.

> *They go off. Sunma, Ifada, and the Girl remain as they are, the light fading slowly on them.*

CONNECTIONS TO OTHER SELECTIONS

1. Compare and contrast Eman's role as a scapegoat with that of Oedipus in Sophocles' *Oedipus the King* (p. 1224).

2. How does the use of flashbacks provide essential information about the two protagonists in *The Strong Breed* and in Miller's *Death of a Salesman* (p. 1795)?

3. Read the discussion of mythological criticism (p. 2037) in Chapter 37, "Critical Strategies for Reading." Explain what you think a mythological critic would have to say about *The Strong Breed*.

PERSPECTIVE

JAMES GIBB

Ritual Sacrifice in The Strong Breed   *1986*

The Strong Breed is a serious play of considerable substance, it shows a moment of spiritual growth in a community and provides excellent theater. Eman brings the growth, for when faced by moral choices he rises to the occasion and sacrifices himself for his convictions. He insults the men of the village and ridicules the practice of using a vulnerable and unwilling carrier. He argues that "the spirit of a new year [will not be] fooled" by an unwilling carrier. Challenged to be "a man" himself and discovering that Jaguna has captured Ifada, he offers himself: he becomes a willing sacrifice. In this there are deliberate parallels to the self-sacrifice of Christ and of the Yoruba deity Obatala, and the drama takes on the qualities of a passion play. From the reaction of the villagers it is clear that Eman's sacrificial death has an impact on the community. The final mood indicates that a climax has been reached and passed, those who have been part of it will never be the same again. This new year provides opportunities for a new beginning in Jaguna's village.

From *Wole Soyinka*

Considerations for Critical Thinking and Writing

1. What parallels can you find between the self-sacrifice of Eman and that of Christ?

2. Use the library to learn about the Yoruba deity Obatala. How does the story of Obatala figure in the action of *The Strong Breed?*

3. Write an essay on the impact of Eman's death on the community.

4. Do you agree with Gibb's interpretation of the ending? Are there "opportunities for a new beginning in Jaguna's village"? Explain why or why not.

AN ALBUM OF CONTEMPORARY PLAYS
The Original Last Wish Baby

William Seebring grew up in an area of Ohio commonly referred to as the Rustbelt and now widely regarded as the fast-food capital of the world. After leaving a factory job where he assembled prototype emission control systems for the automobile industry, Seebring drove a 1965 Pontiac Le-Mans to Brooklyn, New York, where he took up structural drawing. Adopting the pseudonym Douglas Michael, Seebring published a series of underground comic books titled *Tales from the Outerboroughs* as well as an illustrated full-color travel guide to fictitious lands that was published by a magazine catering to lonely hearts. After selling his Pontiac for a slightly used Honda Accord, Seebring moved his family to upstate New York to raise chickens and adapt his comics into stage plays. Other plays include *Das Wolfkin,* a darkly comic fairy tale written in an invented language, and *The Geldings,* a Western spoof about cowboys without genitals. Under his assumed name, Seebring has dabbled in numerous pursuits, including literary agent and country and western songwriter.

WILLIAM SEEBRING (B. 1956)

The Original Last Wish Baby

1995

THE SETS

> Aside from a podium, the action of the play is best staged with pools of lighting and minor propping.

THE CAST

> There are more than 40 characters, and almost all are speaking parts. However, the play can be performed with as few as four actors. A suggested breakdown of parts follows:

Narrator

Actor #2: Executive, Specialist #1, Network Exec #1, Terry Collins, Customer #1, Glam Entertainment Marketeer, Newsboy, Phoney Last Wish Baby, Judge, Pundit #1, Surgeon #3, Right-to-Extended-Lifer #2, Congregant #2, Diner, Politician #1

Actor #3: Nurse, Mrs. Kornfeld, Product Demonstrator, Welda Mae Forms, Network Exec #3, Waitress, Glam Entertainment Exec, Pundit #3, Surgeon #2, Congregant #1, Corpse, Right-to-Extended-Lifer #1, Pollster

Actor #4: Doctor, Assistant, Man, Specialist #2, Network Exec #2, Customer #2, Glam Entertainment Pitchman, Guatemalan Cleaning Woman, Lawyer, Daryl Wayne Trebleau, Pundit #2, Surgeon #1, Maitre d', Preacher, Woman in Black, Politician #2

> We hear "tha-dump, bump — tha-dump, bump." The steady, rhythmic beat of a human heart. A special light comes up on a podium and the Narrator at stage right. The Narrator opens a large storybook.

Narrator: The Original Last Wish Baby, as researched, recorded, and revised by William Seebring. Cleveland, Ohio. Or, more specifically, the third-floor maternity room of the Holy Name Hospital on Cleveland's impoverished West Side where, at precisely seven-oh-one P.M. —

> Turns page. We hear a baby crying.

A baby was born. Not just any baby, but the infamous, original, Last Wish Baby. The baby born without a heart.

> Lights up on a Doctor and Nurse. The Nurse is cradling a bundled infant.

Doctor: What's this about a baby with no heart? Good heavens, that's impossible.
Nurse: Check for yourself, Doctor.
Doctor: Nothing, no pulse. Not a sound.

> The bundled baby squirms in the Nurse's arms.

And yet, this baby clearly mimics life. A freak.
Nurse (softly): No. A miracle.
Doctor: What's that?
Nurse: A miracle . . . the baby is a miracle.
Doctor: A miracle? This is Cleveland. It'll be a miracle if the mother's insured.

> Lights down on the maternity ward.

Narrator: Not only were the baby's parents uninsured, the identity of the baby's father was unknown. However, the birth mother's name was given as Welda Mae Forms, a thirty-one-year-old unemployed cosmetologist. At the time, little else was known about Ms. Forms, but word of her remarkable progeny spread quickly from the maternity ward to the scrub rooms to the hospital's administrative offices, where a larger picture began to emerge.

Lights up on the hospital's administrative Executive and his Assistant.

Executive: A baby born without a heart? Sounds awful. Sounds *really* awful.

Assistant: Maybe not as bad as you think.

Executive: C'mon, Chet. How the hell do ya' window dress a missing heart? God knows we've had our share of high-risk deliveries here at Holy Name — little baby heads get smushed, tiny baby limbs get . . . it's messy, terrible, makes me shudder. But delivering a baby and not the heart — good God! *(Beat.)* What's our liability on something like that?

Assistant: Well, here's the thing, sir . . . the baby is alive.

Executive: Alive? Without a heart? But that's . . . that . . .

Assistant: Impossible? Yes. Nevertheless, it's —

Executive: What, some kind of weird, autoneuron tremors? Good God, is that what passes for life these days?

Assistant: The baby is fully functioning, quite spirited, and has a healthy appetite, I might add.

Executive: For how long? An hour, maybe two?

Assistant: Who can say? But even if the baby were to, God forbid. . . . Its short life could, with the right spin, be played out as the most incredible P.R. story of our time. What's more, the timing couldn't have been more . . . fortuitous . . . sir.

Executive: What, the Sprach/Klockenheimer takeover?

Assistant: Precisely the kind of thing that could triple our name factor overnight. A miracle . . . and it happened here, in *our* hospital, under the care and guidance of *our* health care professionals. Think of it, sir. "Holy Name, the get-well place where miracles happen."

Executive: "The get-well place where miracles happen.". . . Now there's a ball with some bounce to it! Call Delores Childs at Channel Five. If we can dazzle her, there's a good chance we could make the six o'clock news!

Assistant: She's on her way, sir.

Executive: Good boy. Oh, one other thing . . . the heart? Did anyone ever *find* the heart?

Assistant: No. Actually, as far as we know, there never was a heart.

Lights down on the administrative offices.

Narrator: In point of fact, there was a heart. However, through one of those unfathomable anomalies which defy all logic yet govern most things, the heart was delivered separately by a surprised New Jersey woman on her way home from the store.

Lights up on a Man and Mrs. Kornfeld. Mrs. Kornfeld steps forward carrying a Nordstrom's bag and then stops to hail a taxi when something like a beefsteak tomato falls from her skirt. The man regards it.

Man: Yo, Miss . . . Lady! You dropped something.

Mrs. Kornfeld looks back.

Mrs. Kornfeld: Oh-my-god, what is it!

The thumping heart is heard. Lights fade on Mrs. Kornfeld as she bends to retrieve the heart.

Narrator: That something would soon be determined to be the baby's heart. However, at that particular moment, the New Jersey woman, later identified as Mrs. Sydney Kornfeld and soon to become known as "The Baby Heart Mom," was not yet aware of the miracle baby story unfolding in Cleveland.

Lights up on a Product Demonstrator with a Tupperware container, a beefsteak tomato, and a can of peaches.

As for Mrs. Kornfeld, she fortuitously retrieved the baby heart and returned immediately to her home in Paramus, where, as the demonstrator shall faithfully recreate, she placed the pulsating vital organ into a clear, air-tight, number-seven Tupperware container, which she then filled with a high-fructose, low-sodium, heavy syrup drained from a can of Libby's yellow-cling sliced peaches. After burping for a tight seal, Mrs. Kornfeld placed the container in the crisper drawer of her refrigerator where, according to product designers, the heart could have been stored indefinitely and would remain every bit as fresh and vigorous as the moment she delivered it.

Lights down on the Product Demonstrator.

Meanwhile, back in Cleveland, ever more adept medical specialists were brought in to examine the so-called miracle baby.

Lights up on the maternity ward as Two Medical Specialists look into a crib and we hear a giggling baby.

Specialist #1: Coo-chee-coo-chee-cooo.

Specialist #2: No pulse. No pressure. This baby doesn't have a heart.

Specialist #1: I'll be damned.

Specialist #2: And yet . . . this baby is alive.

The Hospital's Executive Assistant enters. He appears agitated.

Assistant: Doctors, please, the press conference. They're waiting.

Lights down on the maternity ward.

Lights up as the specialists and assistant take their places at a table facing the audience. The table skirt advertises the Holy Name Hospital and its new slogan. The Narrator assumes the role of reporter.

Questions for the doctors?

Narrator: Yes. A living baby without a heart? How is this possible?

Specialist #2: Technically, it's not.

Specialist #1: The baby should be dead.

Specialist #2: In fact, the baby could die any minute.

Assistant: It's a miracle is what it is! And it happened right here in our —

Narrator: What about the baby's mom?

Assistant: What about her?

Narrator: I'd like to hear her side of the story. I'd like to ask her a few questions.

Assistant (horrified): What, you mean *talk* with her?

Narrator: Why not?

Assistant: No reason, uh, well, actually — that's impossible. I'm sorry, we're just, she's just — she's in recovery right now.

Lights down on the press conference.

Narrator: In fact, Welda Mae Forms was not in recovery. The so-called Baby Mom was not only alert and well rested, she was, much to the dismay of hospital staffers, quite lucid and most outspoken.

Lights up on Welda Mae Forms, the Executive, and the Assistant. Welda paces like a trapped animal. The Executive and Assistant hover.

Welda Mae Forms: What the hell's going on here! And where's my damn kid! I come into this dump to pop off another slug, which is the last thing I need, and you-all got me strapped down so I can't even see Oprah — big as she is!

Executive: Ms. Forms, please, please calm down. There's something we have to tell you.

Welda Mae Forms: What, is my baby dead or deformed or some damn thing?

Assistant: Uh, well, Miss Forms, actually, it's *more* than that.

Welda Mae Forms: Huh? Was that a hard question, or are you really as stupid as you look? Listen-here, lapdog. Tell your fat-ass boss that as far as I'm concerned I could care less if the little maggot's dead or mutated — hell, I never wanted one tuh begin with. Tried to have it flushed out in one of them clinics, but them damn bible-thumpers chased me away —

Executive (aghast): You were going to . . . ! Cleveland's miracle baby . . . ?

Welda Mae Forms: So I figured I'd drown the slug in booze. Well, did it work or what?

Executive: Ms. Forms, you've got to understand. . . . You've made medical history here today.

Welda Mae Forms: Hee-doggie! Do tell, the little maggot's got three heads? Two weenies? Five titties? What?!

Assistant: This is insane. We can't put *that* before the public. She'll ruin everything!

Lights down on Welda Mae's hospital room.

Narrator: Meanwhile, at that very moment, the afternoon press conference was being fed via satellite to network studios in New York.

We hear the squelch of computer modems linking. Then lights up on a roomful of Network Execs.

Network Exec #1 (tears a fax from a machine): Can this be for real — a baby without a heart?!

Network Exec #2: The affiliate swears it's true.

Network Exec #3: Regardless, it's too late to break tonight.

Network Exec #1: Are you nuts! This stuff goes on immediately.

Network Exec #3: But, but we're airing a live feed from the White House!

Network Exec #2: Who cares? A baby without a heart! Now that's news!

Lights down on the Network Execs.

Narrator: And news it was. Within the hour, satellite-beaming reporters from around the world had descended on Cleveland like the plague, and every last one of them wanted one thing — a baby mom exclusive. Hospital officials acted with both haste and prudence.

Lights up on Welda Mae's hospital room. Welda is still under restraint.

Welda Mae Forms: Let me outta' here! You hear me? Let me out!

Terry Collins, a foppish man with a long scarf around his neck, enters and assesses Welda with dread.

Terry Collins (carefully): Hello, Ms. Forms.

Welda Mae Forms: Who are you? What do ya' want?

Terry Collins: My name is Terry Collins, and I've been hired to be your image consultant.

Welda Mae Forms: Oh yeah? Well, does that mean you can reach up there and change the channel on that pile a' crap TV? Because that's all I've been trying to get from the lazy turds in white that run around here all day. And do they listen? Hell no. Channel five—wrestling. You get me Bone-Crusher on the tube and lay a six-pack of Huedey Gold 'side my pillow here and I'll be so happy I could pee green.

Terry Collins: Oh my, I see I have my work cut out for me.

Lights down on Welda's room.

Narrator: Terry Collins proved he was worth every penny of his hefty makeover fee. In short order, Ms. Welda Mae Forms was polished, enlightened, and coiffured. At long last, cameras were admitted into her room, and a nation known for its thirst of spectacle tuned in.

Lights up on Welda. She's no longer restrained, and her appearance has been transformed. Terry Collins stands in the shadows like a nervous stage mother.

Welda Mae Forms (her hands folded as if in prayer): With the Lord's help, my precious, precious baby will live. Of course, I can't begin to thank all you wonderful little people out there who have kept me and my baby in your thoughts and prayers. Bless you. Bless you all.

Lights down on Welda.

Narrator: With that one newsbit, the groundswell of public emotion became unquenchable. Overnight, Cleveland's miracle tot became America's most adored critical-list baby. There were news conferences every morning and afternoon, and updates on the baby's condition flashed every hour on the hour, but it wasn't enough. Americans not only wanted to know more: they wanted to know what more they could do. . . .

Lights up on a lunch counter somewhere deep in rural America.

Waitress: And they say that baby could die any moment.

Customer #1: Hate to see that baby die and me not knowing if they was *something* I coulda' done.

Customer #2: By Gawd, I'd give my left nut for that sweet, little innocent lamb.

Waitress: Hell, Ross, baby don't need a go-nad. That baby needs a heart!

Customer #2: Can't give baby my heart. But I'd give that baby anything else. Anything a'tall.

Customer #1: You know, I hear baby likes to watch big-time wrestling! What say we call the hospital and see if we could buy that baby a brand-new color TV! Now wouldn't that make us all feel a sight better?

Lights down on the lunch counter.

Narrator: Calls from like-minded Americans jammed the hospital's switchboard. It was reported that in a single twenty-four-hour period more than twenty thousand color TVs were bought and delivered. Corporate America stood up and took note. Syndicate giant Glam Entertainment culled their best minds and put forward a most alluring concept.

Lights up on an executive board meeting. The Pitchman stands before an easel scrawled with dollar signs.

Glam Entertainment Pitchman: Every night we'll feature the baby's mom, what's her name —

Glam Entertainment Marketeer: Welda Mae Forms.

Glam Entertainment Exec: Welda Mae? Where do you gotta' go to get a name like that?

Glam Entertainment Marketeer: Welda, last stop before Zelda.

Glam Entertainment Pitchman: Whatever. We get her, and we call it "The Last Wish Baby Show." See, every night mom stands in front of the camera holding little baby no-heart in her arms like this, and she's pouting 'cause the docs are telling her how the baby's supposed to die any minute, but — and here's the kicker — before baby goes, baby's made this one last wish . . . get it? Baby's last wish — Last Wish Baby!

Eyes widen with delight. Lights down on the meeting.

Narrator: A deal was proffered and quickly struck with Ms. Forms and her people. That very night, "The Last Wish Baby Show" blew out the ratings board with a whopping seventy-five share. Even more notable, the show's seamless tie-in with corporate sponsors set an industry standard.

Lights up on Welda. She is clutching a cloth-wrapped bundle of baby in her arms.

Welda Mae Forms: Poor, poor baby. Baby doesn't have a heart. Doctors say baby might have to leave us all for heaven any minute now.

The baby cries.

What's that, Baby . . . ?

Welda leans in to the baby and then returns her gaze to the cameras.

Awww. Baby wishes some nice person out there would buy us a, uh . . . a Sony XRK-35 Digital Game System.

Narrator (as the studio announcer): That's right folks, the Sony game system could be Baby's Last Wish. Poor, poor baby. So open up that heart God so kindly gave you, and call the 1-800 number you see now on your screen.

Lights down on "The Last Wish Baby Show."

Lights up on Mrs. Kornfeld's kitchen as a Guatemalan Cleaning Woman removes a Tupperware container.

Meanwhile, in a certain kitchen in Paramus, New Jersey, a certain Guatemalan cleaning woman was wiping down a certain refrigerator when she made an unusual discovery.

Guatemalan Cleaning Woman: Eeeeee! Mios Dios! Eeeee!

Mrs. Kornfeld enters.

Mrs. Kornfeld: What? Que? Que esta? What the hell is it?

Guatemalan Cleaning Woman: Esta la corazón de la niño con *last wish!*

Mrs. Kornfeld: What? What are you talking about?

Guatemalan Cleaning Woman: Niño! Niño con last wish! Niño con last wish!

Mrs. Kornfeld: Baby? You mean *that* baby? That Last Wish Baby? The one on TV? Give me that! *(Studies the heart for a moment.)* Oh-my-God, it's alive! I have the baby heart! What should I do? What should I do?

Guatemalan Cleaning Woman: Llama de medico! Pronto! Pronto!

Mrs. Kornfeld: Call a doctor?! Are you crazy? This is big, really big! I'm calling Howard Stern!

Mrs. Kornfeld reaches for the phone. Lights down.

Narrator: Mrs. Kornfeld's call to the popular radio shock jock was quickly put through, and she not only revealed that she possessed what she believed was the Last Wish Baby's heart, but listeners also learned her cup size and that she enjoyed lesbian sex while a sophomore at Harley Dickerson University. Meanwhile, word of the whereabouts of the newly discovered baby heart spread fast and a race, of sorts, was on. EMS crews were the first on the scene, but no sooner had they readied the baby heart for shipment to Cleveland, when . . . the lawyers arrived.

Lights up on a Lawyer waving a writ.

Lawyer: Halt! Court order!

Lights down on the lawyer.

Narrator: Motions were made. Injunctions issued. Larger questions loomed. The battle for custody of the Last Wish Baby had begun.

We hear the thumping heart.

The hearing to determine the rightful custodial parents of the Last Wish Baby had barely opened when legal fees threatened to exceed even Ms. Welda Mae Forms's recently fatted purse strings. However, with the "Baby Show" still posting record ratings, Ms. Forms saw fit to make full use of her forum.

Lights up on Welda.

Welda Mae Forms (angelic): Poor, poor precious baby. Baby doesn't have a heart . . . know why? Hmmm? *(Bitter.)* 'Cause some East Coast floozy has got it and won't hand it over unless I give her half a' baby's royalties on the —

The baby cries. Welda looks at it.

Yeah, what do you want? *(A beat to compose herself.)* Awww, but of course, my sweet little precious baby.

Welda looks up and smiles for the camera.

Baby wishes there was some nice, pro-bono law firm out there who would take Baby's rightful mother's custody case and, when that was all settled and a certain individual from a certain so-called *Garden State* was financially ruined, that same nice law firm might just be retained to negotiate with those shysters at Glum Entertainment for a more favorable contract . . . idn't that what baby wants? Yes, baby's so sweet. I just hope and pray this won't be baby's last wish.

Lights down on Welda.

Narrator: But no sooner had Welda Mae and her people retained new legal counsel than a shocking courtroom revelation hit the newsstands.

Lights up on a Newsboy hawking his papers.

Newsboy: Read all about it! "Last Wish Baby Show" Hoax! Read all about it!

Lights down on the newsboy.

Narrator: Unsealed court documents alleged that "The Last Wish Baby Show" Baby was not the real Last Wish Baby, the baby born without a heart, but, rather, a sixteen-year-old unemployed actor with a glandular condition. Americans shuddered. Did this mean the Original Last Wish Baby was dead? Or, Heaven forbid, was there even an original Last Wish Baby in the first place? Congressional spouses convened a hearing and demanded answers.

Lights up on a hearing room. Welda Mae, the Hospital's Executive Assistant, and the Phoney Last Wish Baby are seated together under a glaring light. The Narrator serves as inquisitor.

Come forward. State your full name and occupation for the record, please.

Phoney Last Wish Baby: Look, pal, you can't nail this one on me! I'm not even equity! The only reason I signed on to this sham was 'cause the lady there got me tanked up, then threatened to put my nuts in the grinder if I didn't —

Welda Mae Forms: Shut your trap you little —

Phoney Last Wish Baby: Who are you calling little!? The only thing little around here is your heart! You wanna' know why her kid's got no heart? I'll tell ya' why —

Welda Mae Forms: How dare you! And you said you loved me!

Assistant: Stop it! Okay, look, it was all my fault. I agreed to pull the baby from the show, and I was the one who okayed it when the Forms woman wanted to hire the little guy. But I only went along with it 'cause the doctors insisted on keeping the baby in intensive care. That's the God's-honest truth. There really is a Last Wish Baby, there really is a baby without a heart! I can prove it! I swear to God, I can prove it!

Lights down on the hearing room.

Narrator: Needless to say, Americans were skeptical and demanded that proof. Thus, the following night, "The Last Wish Baby Show" aired live from the Holy Name Hospital's pediatric intensive care unit. Viewers held their breath as the Baby Mom ushered the cameras toward the swinging doors which led to Baby's chamber.

Lights up on a hospital corridor. Welda Mae and the Assistant are wearing scrubs. Welda Mae motions for the camera to follow her.

Welda Mae Forms: Shhh. Be quiet. This way, please.

Daryl Wayne Trebleau pushes his way toward Welda.

Assistant: Watch it, he's got a gun!

> *Blackout. Four shots are fired, and Welda screams. We then hear the high-pitched hum of the Emergency Broadcast System. Lights come up on the Narrator.*

Narrator: Four shots, each one following its own fatal trajectory, were fired into the torso and cranial cavity of the woman most Americans knew only as the Last Wish Baby Mom.

> *Lights up on Daryl Wayne Trebleau as he faces forward and then turns for a profile.*

The assailant was identified as Daryl Wayne Trebleau, a slope-shouldered itinerant floral designer from nearby Loraine, Ohio, and, purportedly, the man many believed to be the Last Wish Baby Dad.

> *Daryl steps forward as if on the witness stand.*

Daryl Wayne Trebleau never uttered a single word in his own defense. Rather, he expressed himself through artfully designed floral arrangements.

> *Daryl holds up a floral bouquet.*

Mr. Trebleau's "Not competent to stand trial bouquet" was a lovely and eloquent display of mums, gladioli, and forty-four magnum shell casings set in a handsome earthenware bowl. Meanwhile, in another court in another state, the judge in the custody hearing for the Last Wish Baby had reached a verdict.

> *Lights down on Daryl Wayne Trebleau. Lights up on a Judge.*

Judge: As per the dictates of the honorable State of New Jersey, Court of Domestic Relations, I, Judge Maliss T. Ward Nunn, have found as follows: Said infant, herein-and-ever-after known as "The Original Last Wish Baby," shall be granted ward status of this court and thereby ordered to be joined immediately with heart. So be it, so help us God.

> *The Judge pounds his gavel. Lights down.*

Narrator: With "The Last Wish Baby Show" having been abruptly pulled from the airwaves, no effort was made to appeal the Judge's decision. Thus, a medical team of the nation's leading cardiovascular surgeons were assembled to carry out the court's wishes and, with God's blessing, prolong the baby's life. Meanwhile, high-minded pontificators from the academic, medical, and legal communities pondered the implications of it all for the benefit of viewers at home.

> *Lights up on a television round-table show.*

Pundit #1: The baby phenomenon speaks directly to who we are as a nation.

Pundit #2: And who we, as a nation, are not.

Pundit #3: Yes, who we are and who we are not.

Pundit #1: But *more* to who we are than who we are not.

Pundit #3: Then again, I think one could say this whole baby phenomenon says even more *still* to where we, as a nation, are going than where we, as a nation, have been.

Pundit #2: Or not been.

Pundit #1: Or not, not been.

Pundit #2: Or not been, not-been-not.

Pundit #3: Yes, not-been-not. But not, been-been, not-not, been-not-been.

Pundit #1: Been-not-been been-not. But not-been, been-not-been-been.

Pundit #2: Nor been.

Pundit #1: Nor been-been.

Narrator: We interrupt this program to bring you a special Last Wish Baby medical update. We take you now, *live,* directly to the Hoppenscotch Medical Center in Tarmac, New Jersey.

Lights down on the Pundits. Lights up on a team of Surgeons.

Surgeon #1: The operation to implant the baby heart into the Last Wish Baby was both a success and . . .

Surgeon #2: A failure.

Surgeon #1: The heart was successfully sutured and continues to pump vigorously. Unfortunately, the baby . . .

Surgeon #3: The baby, for reasons we do not fully understand, has ceased all other life-sustaining functions and appears to be in a rapid state of . . .

Surgeon #2: Decay.

Surgeon #1: Decay.

Surgeon #3: Decay.

Lights down on the Surgeons. We hear the thumping of the baby heart.

Narrator: There was no denying it. The Original Last Wish Baby, the baby born without a heart, was now and irretrievably a dead baby but — one with a very healthy heart. And that presented doctors and lawyers with an entirely new set of problems. For one, the baby could not be considered legally dead unless the heart were either stopped or removed. However, if the baby was not legally dead, then removing or stopping the heart would be, in a word, murder. Therefore, despite all appearances to the contrary, the Last Wish Baby was, in the eyes of the law, very much alive. Further, this being a democratic society, it did not take long for Americans to gaze upon their own dearly departed loved ones and find similar cause to stretch the definition of what constitutes life . . . and death.

The thumping fades. Lights up in a restaurant.

Maitre d': Chatterwok, party of four, your table is ready. Chatterwok, party of four —

A Diner wheels in a well-dressed Corpse on a two-wheeler. The Maitre d' is appalled.

Excusez-moi, monsieur! Excusez — Yo! What in God's name do you think you're doing?

Diner: Look here, buddy. . . . My wife may look a little ripe to you, but she's still getting mail, and *that,* in my opinion, qualifies her for your early bird special. Oh, and, uh, nonsmoking section, please.

Lights down on the restaurant.

Narrator: Suddenly, Americans became embroiled in an entirely new moral debate — when did life end? The question was not at all as simple as it sounded. After all, who in this country can say with any real certainty when life begins?

Lights up on a Preacher as he takes the pulpit with two swaying Congregants on either side.

Preacher: The Bible, my friends, is very specific with regard to one thing.
Congregant #1: Tell it now!
Preacher: No bones about it! It says so right here!
Congregant #2: Hallelujah!
Preacher: It says, "dust to dust"!
Congregant #1: Dust to dust!
Congregant #2: Hallelujah!
Preacher: Say it with me, everybody!
Preacher and Congregants: Dust to dust!

Lights down on the Preacher.

Narrator: With these words, the "Right to Extended Life" movement was born. Also known as "Antifuneralists," the movement cannily usurped the image of the Last Wish Baby and made it their own. Soon, that image was being bandied about as a symbol of protest in nearly every cemetery and crematorium in the country.

Lights up on a funeral as a Woman in Black stands over an open grave. The Narrator joins her and offers a shoulder in comfort.

Narrator: Bill was . . . he was a decent guy. A sensible guy. The kind of guy who let you know where he stood even when everything else around just got weirder and weirder—

Two Right to Extended Lifers enter and march around. They are wearing Last Wish Baby/Antifuneralist tee-shirts.

Right to Extended Lifer #1: Burial is murder! Burial is murder! Burial is murder!
Right to Extended Lifer #2: Save the undead! Save the undead! Save the undead!

The Woman in Black shrieks. Lights down on the funeral. The Woman and the Right to Extended Lifers exit. The Narrator remains downstage.

Narrator: Despite their innocent-looking symbol, the movement stressed confrontation. Funeral homes were fire-bombed. Morticians and embalmers were forced to conceal their identities. Even limo drivers were suspect. Many believed reason would prevail and took comfort in the fact that the movement failed to win mainstream support. However, the ranks of the Antifuneralists continued to swell as old members never died off and new recruits were always just a few shovelfuls away. Inevitably, highly paid political pollsters were the first to see the writing on the wall.

The Narrator backs off and returns to the podium. Lights up on a political party meeting of Politicians and their Pollster.

Politician #1: Speaking for my constituents, I say, cut the heart out of that damned baby and you kill the movement. It's that simple!
Pollster: You're dead wrong. Give them what they want. Embrace these people *now,* and they might remember you in the fall.
Politician #2: But that's insane. We'd be giving the right to vote to the dead!
Pollster: Dead, alive—c'mon, this is America—what's the difference?

Lights down on the political meeting.

Narrator: And so, in an historic Rose Garden ceremony, President Lance Ito signed the so-called Last Wish Baby Bill into law. The bill not only granted the living-impaired the right to vote but also guaranteed entitlements and protections historically denied to members of this community, a community long regarded by many narrow-minded Americans as sloven, listless, and, euphemistically speaking, somewhat aromatic. *(Beat.)*

As the years passed and the American political spectrum calcified, living-impaired voters inevitably sought a candidate from among their own ranks. Republican strategists boldly exhumed a former California vote-getter whose appeal cut across party lines and living tissue.

The cast steps forward and fervently wave small American flags.

During his first news conference as President, the newly reelected Ronald Reagan announced his plan to fund and build a massive protective shield, which he claimed would act as a deterrent to foreign aggression and help staunch the flow of illegal immigration.

They gradually lose their enthusiasm as we get some indication of a massive shield descending upon them. Lighting and/or perhaps a black scrim being lowered can achieve this effect.

When completed, the shield did more than defend American shores. It stood as a symbol to all that here was a nation entombed, whose people sought no light to guide them and silenced any sound which might stir them. *(Beat.)* Except one . . .

We hear the growing sound of the thump-thump-thumping of the baby heart.

The never-ceasing, ever-pumping, always-thumping heart of the Original Last Wish Baby.

The thumping continues as lights slowly fade to black.

End of Play.

CONNECTIONS TO OTHER SELECTIONS

1. Compare the tone of the humor in *The Original Last Wish Baby* with that of either Larry David's *Seinfeld* episode "The Pitch" (p. 1199) or Wendy Wasserstein's *Tender Offer* (p. 1956).

2. Discuss the implicit social commentary in *The Original Last Wish Baby* and in Anna Deavere Smith's *Twilight: Los Angeles, 1992* (p. 1661).

3. Write an essay comparing the satire in *The Original Last Wish Baby* with the satire in T. Coraghessan Boyle's "Carnal Knowledge" (p. 276). Which satire do you find more effective? Explain why.

Tender Offer

Born in Brooklyn, New York, in 1950, Wendy Wasserstein studied at Mount Holyoke College, City College of New York, and the Yale School of Drama. A resident of Greenwich Village, she is also a resident playwright off-Broadway, at New York's Playwrights Horizon Theatre where many of her plays have been performed before audiences receptive to Wasserstein's humorous treatment of feminist issues. Among her plays are *Uncommon Women* (1977), *Isn't It Romantic* (1980), *The Sisters Rosenzweig* (1993), and the enormously successful *The Heidi Chronicles* (1988), which won numerous honors including a Tony Award, a Pulitzer Prize, and the New York Drama Critics' Circle Award. In 1990 her book of essays, *Bachelor Girl*, was published. She has received National Endowment for the Arts and Guggenheim grants in support of her work.

    Tender Offer, which appeared in a special issue of one-act plays in the spring 1991 *Antaeus*, is a brief but absorbing treatment of the tentative relationship between a father and daughter. Characteristic of Wasserstein's work, this play uses humor deftly to present a serious moment that requires a "good deal" to resolve it.

WENDY WASSERSTEIN (B. 1950)

Tender Offer   *1991*

A girl of around nine is alone in a dance studio. She is dressed in traditional leotards and tights. She begins singing to herself, "Nothing Could Be Finer Than to Be in Carolina." She maps out a dance routine, including parts for the chorus. She builds to a finale. A man, Paul, around thirty-five, walks in. He has a sweet, though distant, demeanor. As he walks in, Lisa notices him and stops.

Paul: You don't have to stop, sweetheart.
Lisa: That's okay.
Paul: Looked very good.
Lisa: Thanks.
Paul: Don't I get a kiss hello?
Lisa: Sure.
Paul (embraces her): Hi, Tiger.
Lisa: Hi, Dad.
Paul: I'm sorry I'm late.
Lisa: That's okay.
Paul: How'd it go?
Lisa: Good.
Paul: Just good?
Lisa: Pretty good.
Paul: "Pretty good." You mean you got a lot of applause or "pretty good" you could have done better?
Lisa: Well, Courtney Palumbo's mother thought I was pretty good. But you know the part in the middle when everybody's supposed to freeze and the big girl comes out. Well, I think I moved a little bit.
Paul: I thought what you were doing looked very good.
Lisa: Daddy, that's not what I was doing. That was tap-dancing. I made that up.
Paul: Oh. Well it looked good. Kind of sexy.
Lisa: Yuch!
Paul: What do you mean "yuch"?

Lisa: Just yuch!

Paul: You don't want to be sexy?

Lisa: I don't care.

Paul: Let's go, Tiger. I promised your mother I'd get you home in time for dinner.

Lisa: I can't find my leg warmers.

Paul: You can't find your what?

Lisa: Leg warmers. I can't go home till I find my leg warmers.

Paul: I don't see you looking for them.

Lisa: I was waiting for you.

Paul: Oh.

Lisa: Daddy.

Paul: What?

Lisa: Nothing.

Paul: Where do you think you left them?

Lisa: Somewhere around here. I can't remember.

Paul: Well, try to remember, Lisa. We don't have all night.

Lisa: I told you. I think somewhere around here.

Paul: I don't see them. Let's go home now. You'll call the dancing school tomorrow.

Lisa: Daddy, I can't go home till I find them. Miss Judy says it's not professional to leave things.

Paul: Who's Miss Judy?

Lisa: She's my ballet teacher. She once danced the lead in *Swan Lake,* and she was a June Taylor dancer.

Paul: Well, then, I'm sure she'll understand about the leg warmers.

Lisa: Daddy, Miss Judy wanted to know why you were late today.

Paul: Hmmmmmmmm?

Lisa: Why were you late?

Paul: I was in a meeting. Business. I'm sorry.

Lisa: Why did you tell Mommy you'd come instead of her if you knew you had business?

Paul: Honey, something just came up. I thought I'd be able to be here. I was looking forward to it.

Lisa: I wish you wouldn't make appointments to see me.

Paul: Hmmmmmmm.

Lisa: You shouldn't make appointments to see me unless you know you're going to come.

Paul: Of course I'm going to come.

Lisa: No, you're not. Talia Robbins told me she's much happier living without her father in the house. Her father used to come home late and go to sleep early.

Paul: Lisa, stop it. Let's go.

Lisa: I can't find my leg warmers.

Paul: Forget your leg warmers.

Lisa: Daddy.

Paul: What is it?

Lisa: I saw this show on television, I think it was WPIX Channel 11. Well, the father was crying about his daughter.

Paul: Why was he crying? Was she sick?

Lisa: No. She was at school. And he was at business. And he just missed her, so he started to cry.

Paul: What was the name of this show?

Lisa: I don't know. I came in in the middle.

Paul: Well, Lisa, I certainly would cry if you were sick or far away, but I know that you're well and you're home. So no reason to get maudlin.

Lisa: What's maudlin?

Paul: Sentimental, soppy. Frequently used by children who make things up to get attention.

Lisa: I am sick! I am sick! I have Hodgkin's disease and a bad itch on my leg.

Paul: What do you mean you have Hodgkin's disease? Don't say things like that.

Lisa: Swoosie Kurtz, she had Hodgkin's disease on a TV movie last year, but she got better and now she's on *Love Sidney.*

Paul: Who is Swoosie Kurtz?

Lisa: She's an actress named after an airplane. I saw her on *Live at Five.*

Paul: You watch too much television; you should do your homework. Now, put your coat on.

Lisa: Daddy, I really do have a bad itch on my leg. Would you scratch it?

Paul: Lisa, you're procrastinating.

Lisa: Why do you use words I don't understand? I hate it. You're like Daria Feldman's mother. She always talks in Yiddish to her husband so Daria won't understand.

Paul: *Procrastinating* is not Yiddish.

Lisa: Well, I don't know what it is.

Paul: Procrastinating means you don't want to go about your business.

Lisa: I don't go to business. I go to school.

Paul: What I mean is you want to hang around here until you and I are late for dinner and your mother's angry and it's too late for you to do your homework.

Lisa: I do not.

Paul: Well, it sure looks that way. Now put your coat on and let's go.

Lisa: Daddy.

Paul: Honey, I'm tired. Really, later.

Lisa: Why don't you want to talk to me?

Paul: I do want to talk to you. I promise when we get home we'll have a nice talk.

Lisa: No, we won't. You'll read the paper and fall asleep in front of the news.

Paul: Honey, we'll talk on the weekend, I promise. Aren't I taking you to the theater this weekend? Let me look. *(He takes out appointment book.)* Yes. Sunday. *Joseph and the Amazing Technicolor Raincoat* with Lisa. Okay, Tiger?

Lisa: Sure. It's *Dreamcoat.*

Paul: What?

Lisa: Nothing. I think I see my leg warmers. *(She goes to pick them up, and an odd-looking trophy.)*

Paul: What's that?

Lisa: It's stupid. I was second best at the dance recital, so they gave me this thing. It's stupid.

Paul: Lisa.

Lisa: What?

Paul: What did you want to talk about?

Lisa: Nothing.

Paul: Was it about my missing your recital? I'm really sorry, Tiger. I would have liked to have been here.

Lisa: That's okay.

Paul: Honest?

Lisa: Daddy, you're prostrastinating.

Paul: I'm procrastinating. Sit down. Let's talk. So. How's school?

Lisa: Fine.

Paul: You like it?

Lisa: Yup.

Paul: You looking forward to camp this summer?

Lisa: Yup.

Paul: Is Daria Feldman going back?

Lisa: Nope.

Paul: Why not?

Lisa: I don't know. We can go home now. Honest, my foot doesn't itch anymore.

Paul: Lisa, you know what you do in business when it seems like there's nothing left to say? That's when you really start talking. Put a bid on the table.

Lisa: What's a bid?

Paul: You tell me what you want and I'll tell you what I've got to offer. Like Monopoly. You want Boardwalk, but I'm only willing to give you the Railroads. Now, because you are my daughter I'd throw in Water Works and Electricity. Understand, Tiger?

Lisa: No. I don't like board games. You know, Daddy, we could get Space Invaders for our home for thirty-five dollars. In fact, we could get an Osborne System for two thousand. Daria Feldman's parents . . .

Paul: Daria Feldman's parents refuse to talk to Daria, so they bought a computer to keep Daria busy so they won't have to speak in Yiddish. Daria will probably grow up to be a homicidal maniac lesbian prostitute.

Lisa: I know what that word *prostitute* means.

Paul: Good. *(Pause.)* You still haven't told me about school. Do you still like your teacher?

Lisa: She's okay.

Paul: Lisa, if we're talking try to answer me.

Lisa: I am answering you. Can we go home now, please?

Paul: Damn it, Lisa, if you want to talk to me . . . Talk to me!

Lisa: I can't wait till I'm old enough so I can make my own money and never have to see you again. Maybe I'll become a prostitute.

Paul: Young lady, that's enough.

Lisa: I hate you, Daddy! I hate you! *(She throws her trophy into the trash bin.)*

Paul: What'd you do that for?

Lisa: It's stupid.

Paul: Maybe I wanted it.

Lisa: What for?

Paul: Maybe I wanted to put it where I keep your dinosaur and the picture you made of Mrs. Kimbel with the chicken pox.

Lisa: You got mad at me when I made that picture. You told me I had to respect Mrs. Kimbel because she was my teacher.

Paul: That's true. But she wasn't my teacher. I liked her better with the chicken pox. *(Pause.)* Lisa, I'm sorry. I was very wrong to miss your recital, and you don't have to become a prostitute. That's not the type of profession Miss Judy has in mind for you.

Lisa (mumbles): No.

Paul: No. *(Pause.)* So Talia Robbins is really happy her father moved out?

Lisa: Talia Robbins picks open the eighth-grade lockers during gym period. But she did that before her father moved out.

Paul: You can't always judge someone by what they do or what they don't do. Sometimes you come home from dancing school and run upstairs and shut the door, and when I finally get to talk to you, everything is "okay" or "fine." Yup or nope?

Lisa: Yup.

Paul: Sometimes, a lot of times, I come home and fall asleep in front of the television. So you and I spend a lot of time being a little scared of each other. Maybe?

Lisa: Maybe.

Paul: Tell you what. I'll make you a tender offer.

Lisa: What?

Paul: I'll make you a tender offer. That's when one company publishes in the newspaper that they want to buy another company. And the company that publishes is called the Black Knight because they want to gobble up the poor little company. So the poor little company needs to be rescued. And then a White Knight comes along and makes a bigger and better offer so the shareholders won't have to tender shares to the Big Black Knight. You with me?

Lisa: Sort of.

Paul: I'll make you a tender offer like the White Knight. But I don't want to own you. I just want to make a much better offer. Okay?

Lisa (sort of understanding): Okay. *(Pause. They sit for a moment.)* Sort of, Daddy, what do you think about? I mean, like when you're quiet what do you think about?

Paul: Oh, business usually. If I think I made a mistake or if I think I'm doing okay. Sometimes I think about what I'll be doing five years from now and if it's what I hoped it would be five years ago. Sometimes I think about what your life will be like, if Mount Saint Helens will erupt again. What you'll become if you'll study penmanship or word processing. If you speak kindly of me to your psychiatrist when you are in graduate school. And how the hell I'll pay for your graduate school. And sometimes I try and think what it was I thought about when I was your age.

Lisa: Do you ever look out your window at the clouds and try to see which kinds of shapes they are? Like one time, honest, I saw the head of Walter Cronkite in a flower vase. Really! Like look don't those kinda look like if you turn it upside down, two big elbows or two elephant trunks dancing?

Paul: Actually still looks like Walter Cronkite in a flower vase to me. But look up a little. See the one that's still moving? That sorta looks like a whale on a thimble.

Lisa: Where?

Paul: Look up. To your right.

Lisa: I don't see it. Where?

Paul: The other way.

Lisa: Oh, yeah! There's the head and there's the stomach. Yeah! *(Lisa picks up her trophy.)* Hey, Daddy.

Paul: Hey, Lisa.

Lisa: You can have this thing if you want it. But you have to put it like this, because if you put it like that it is gross.

Paul: You know what I'd like? So I can tell people who come into my office why I have this gross stupid thing on my shelf, I'd like it if you could show me your dance recital.

Lisa: Now?

Paul: We've got time. Mother said she won't be home till late.

Lisa: Well, Daddy, during a lot of it I freeze and the big girl in front dances.

Paul: Well, how 'bout the number you were doing when I walked in?

Lisa: Well, see, I have parts for a lot of people in that one, too.

Paul: I'll dance the other parts.

Lisa: You can't dance.

Paul: Young lady, I played Yvette Mimimeux in a *Hasty Pudding Show.*

Lisa: Who's Yvette Mimimeux?

Paul: Watch more television. You'll find out. *(Paul stands up.)* So I'm ready. *(He begins singing.)* "Nothing could be finer than to be in Carolina."

Lisa: Now I go. In the morning. And now you go. Dum-da.

Paul (obviously not a tap dancer): Da-da-dum.

Lisa (whines): Daddy!

Paul (mimics her): Lisa! Nothing could be finer . . .

Lisa: That looks dumb.

Paul: Oh, yeah? You think they do this better in *The Amazing Minkcoat?* No way! Now you go — da da da dum.

Lisa: Da da da dum.

Paul: If I had Aladdin's lamp for only a day, I'd make a wish . . .

Lisa: Daddy, that's maudlin!

Paul: I know it's maudlin. And here's what I'd say:

Lisa and Paul: I'd say that "nothing could be finer than to be in Carolina in the mooooooooooornin'."

CONNECTIONS TO OTHER SELECTIONS

1. Compare the fathers in *Tender Offer* and Sylvia Plath's poem "Daddy" (p. 1113). What conflicts are associated with the father in each work? To what extent are the conflicts resolved or not resolved?

2. *Tender Offer* and Jane Martin's *Rodeo* (p. 1657) are extremely brief dramatic works that present conflicts in which business serves as an antagonist. Write an essay on the nature of the conflicts in each play and how business is the source of those conflicts.

The Piano Lesson

August Wilson, who, as a young poet, "wanted to be Dylan Thomas," has become in recent years a major force in the American theater. He has projected a sequence of ten plays that will chronicle the African American experience in the United States in each decade of the twentieth century. *Ma Rainey's Black Bottom,* the first of these to be completed, premiered at the Yale Repertory Theatre in 1984, went to Broadway shortly thereafter, and eventually won the New York Drama Critics' Circle Award. The plays that have so far followed are *Fences* (1985), *Joe Turner's Come and Gone* (1986), *The Piano Lesson* (1987), *Two Trains Running* (1989), and *Seven Guitars* (1996).

Born in Pittsburgh, Pennsylvania, Wilson grew up in the Hill, a black neighborhood to which his mother had come from North Carolina. His white father never lived with the family. Wilson quit school at sixteen and worked in a variety of menial jobs, meanwhile submitting poetry to a number of local publications. He didn't begin to find his writing voice, however, until he moved to Minneapolis–St. Paul, where he founded the Black Horizons Theatre Company in 1968 and later started the Playwrights Center. He supported himself during part of this time by writing skits for the Science Museum of Minnesota.

The Piano Lesson — awarded a Pulitzer Prize in 1990 — offers comedy as well as serious examination of an African American family's spiritual heritage.

AUGUST WILSON (B. 1945)

The Piano Lesson   *1990*

CHARACTERS

Doaker Charles	Lymon
Berniece, Doaker's niece	Avery
Maretha, Berniece's eleven-year-old daughter	Wining Boy
Boy Willie	Grace

SETTING: *The action of the play takes place in the kitchen and parlor of the house where Doaker Charles lives with his niece, Berniece, and her eleven-year-old daughter, Maretha. The house is sparsely furnished, and although there is evidence of a woman's touch, there is a lack of warmth and vigor. Berniece and Maretha occupy the upstairs rooms. Doaker's room is prominent and opens onto the kitchen. Dominating the parlor is an old upright piano. On the legs of the piano, carved in the manner of African sculpture, are masklike figures resembling totems. The carvings are rendered with a grace and power of invention that lifts them out of the realm of craftsmanship and into the realm of art. At left is a staircase leading to the upstairs.*

ACT I

SCENE I

The lights come up on the Charles household. It is five o'clock in the morning. The dawn is beginning to announce itself, but there is something in the air that belongs to the night. A stillness that is a portent, a gathering, a coming together of something akin to a storm. There is a loud knock at the door.

Boy Willie *(offstage, calling):* Hey, Doaker . . . Doaker! *(He knocks again and calls.)* Hey Doaker! Hey, Berniece! Berniece!

Doaker enters from his room. He is a tall, thin man of forty-seven, with severe features, who has for all intents and purposes retired from the world though he works full-time as a railroad cook.

Doaker: Who is it?
Boy Willie: Open the door, nigger! It's me . . . Boy Willie!
Doaker: Who?
Boy Willie: Boy Willie! Open the door!

Doaker opens the door and Boy Willie and Lymon enter. Boy Willie is thirty years old. He has an infectious grin and a boyishness that is apt for his name. He is brash and impulsive, talkative, and somewhat crude in speech and manner. Lymon is twenty-nine. Boy Willie's partner, he talks little, and then with a straightforwardness that is often disarming.

Doaker: What you doing up here?
Boy Willie: I told you, Lymon. Lymon talking about you might be sleep. This is Lymon. You remember Lymon Jackson from down home? This my Uncle Doaker.
Doaker: What you doing up here? I couldn't figure out who that was. I thought you was still down in Mississippi.
Boy Willie: Me and Lymon selling watermelons. We got a truck out there. Got a whole truckload of watermelons. We brought them up here to sell. Where's Berniece? (*Calls.*) Hey, Berniece!
Doaker: Berniece up there sleep.
Boy Willie: Well, let her get up. (*Calls.*) Hey, Berniece!
Doaker: She got to go to work in the morning.
Boy Willie: Well she can get up and say hi. It's been three years since I seen her. (*Calls.*) Hey, Berniece! It's me . . . Boy Willie.
Doaker: Berniece don't like all that hollering now. She got to work in the morning.
Boy Willie: She can go on back to bed. Me and Lymon been riding two days in that truck . . . the least she can do is get up and say hi.
Doaker (*looking out the window*): Where you all get that truck from?
Boy Willie: It's Lymon's. I told him let's get a load of watermelons and bring them up here.
Lymon: Boy Willie say he going back, but I'm gonna stay. See what it's like up here.
Boy Willie: You gonna carry me down there first.
Lymon: I told you I ain't going back down there and take a chance on that truck breaking down again. You can take the train. Hey, tell him Doaker, he can take the train back. After we sell them watermelons he have enough money he can buy him a whole railroad car.
Doaker: You got all them watermelons stacked up there no wonder the truck broke down. I'm surprised you made it this far with a load like that. Where you break down at?
Boy Willie: We broke down three times! It took us two and a half days to get here. It's a good thing we picked them watermelons fresh.
Lymon: We broke down twice in West Virginia. The first time was just as soon as we got out of Sunflower. About forty miles out she broke down. We got it going and got all the way to West Virginia before she broke down again.
Boy Willie: We had to walk about five miles for some water.

Lymon: It got a hole in the radiator but it runs pretty good. You have to pump the brakes sometime before they catch. Boy Willie have his door open and be ready to jump when that happens.

Boy Willie: Lymon think that's funny. I told the nigger I give him ten dollars to get the brakes fixed. But he thinks that funny.

Lymon: They don't need fixing. All you got to do is pump them till they catch.

> *Berniece enters on the stairs. Thirty-five years old, with an eleven-year-old daughter, she is still in mourning for her husband after three years.*

Berniece: What you doing all that hollering for?

Boy Willie: Hey, Berniece, Doaker said you was asleep. I said at least you could get up and say hi.

Berniece: It's five o'clock in the morning and you come in here with all this noise. You can't come like normal folks. You got to bring all that noise with you.

Boy Willie: Hell, I ain't done nothing but come in and say hi. I ain't got in the house good.

Berniece: That's what I'm talking about. You start all that hollering and carry on as soon as you hit the door.

Boy Willie: Aw, hell, woman, I was glad to see Doaker. You ain't had to come down if you didn't want to. I come eighteen hundred miles to see my sister I figure she might want to get up and say hi. Other than that you can go back upstairs. What you got, Doaker? Where your bottle? Me and Lymon want a drink. *(To Berniece.)* This is Lymon. You remember, Lymon Jackson from down home.

Lymon: How you doing, Berniece? You look just like I thought you looked.

Berniece: Why you all got to come in hollering and carrying on? Waking the neighbors with all that noise.

Boy Willie: They can come over and join the party. We fixing to have a party. Doaker, where your bottle? Me and Lymon celebrating. The Ghosts of the Yellow Dog got Sutter.

Berniece: Say what?

Boy Willie: Ask Lymon, they found him the next morning. Say he drowned in his well.

Doaker: When this happen, Boy Willie?

Boy Willie: About three weeks ago. Me and Lymon was over in Stoner County when we heard about it. We laughed. We thought it was funny. A great big old three-hundred-and-forty-pound man gonna fall down his well.

Lymon: It remind me of Humpty Dumpty.

Boy Willie: Everybody say the Ghosts of the Yellow Dog pushed him.

Berniece: I don't want to hear that nonsense. Somebody down there pushing them people in their wells.

Doaker: What was you and Lymon doing over in Stoner County?

Boy Willie: We was down there working. Lymon got some people down there.

Lymon: My cousin got some land down there. We was helping him.

Boy Willie: Got near about a hundred acres. He got it set up real nice. Me and Lymon was down there chopping down trees. We was using Lymon's truck to haul the wood. Me and Lymon used to haul wood all around them parts. *(To Berniece.)* Me and Lymon got a truckload of watermelons out there. *(Berniece crosses to the window to the parlor.)* Doaker, where your bottle?

I know you got a bottle stuck up in your room. Come on, me and Lymon want a drink.

Doaker exits into his room.

Berniece: Where you all get that truck from?

Boy Willie: I told you it's Lymon's.

Berniece: Where you get the truck from, Lymon?

Lymon: I bought it.

Berniece: Where he get that truck from, Boy Willie?

Boy Willie: He told you he bought it. Bought it for a hundred and twenty dollars. I can't say where he got that hundred and twenty dollars from . . . but he bought that old piece of truck from Henry Porter. *(To Lymon.)* Where you get that hundred and twenty dollars from, nigger?

Lymon: I got it like you get yours. I know how to take care of money.

Doaker brings a bottle and sets it on the table.

Boy Willie: Aw hell, Doaker got some of that good whiskey. Don't give Lymon none of that. He ain't used to good whiskey. He liable to get sick.

Lymon: I done had good whiskey before.

Boy Willie: Lymon bought that truck so he have him a place to sleep. He down there wasn't doing no work or nothing. Sheriff looking for him. He bought that truck to keep away from the sheriff. Got Stovall looking for him too. He down there sleeping in that truck ducking and dodging both of them. I told him come on let's go up and see my sister.

Berniece: What the sheriff looking for you for, Lymon?

Boy Willie: The man don't want you to know all his business. He's my company. He ain't asking you no questions.

Lymon: It wasn't nothing. It was just a misunderstanding.

Berniece: He in my house. You say the sheriff looking for him, I wanna know what he looking for him for. Otherwise you all can go back out there and be where nobody don't have to ask you nothing.

Lymon: It was just a misunderstanding. Sometimes me and the sheriff we don't think alike. So we just got crossed on each other.

Berniece: Might be looking for him about that truck. He might have stole that truck.

Boy Willie: We ain't stole no truck, woman. I told you Lymon bought it.

Doaker: Boy Willie and Lymon got more sense than to ride all the way up here in a stolen truck with a load of watermelons. Now they might have stole them watermelons, but I don't believe they stole that truck.

Boy Willie: You don't even know the man good and you calling him a thief. And we ain't stole them watermelons either. Them old man Pitterford's watermelons. He give me and Lymon all we could load for ten dollars.

Doaker: No wonder you got them stacked up out there. You must have five hundred watermelons stacked up out there.

Berniece: Boy Willie, when you and Lymon planning on going back?

Boy Willie: Lymon say he staying. As soon as we sell them watermelons I'm going on back.

Berniece (starts to exit up the stairs): That's what you need to do. And you need to do it quick. Come in here disrupting the house. I don't want all that loud carrying on around here. I'm surprised you ain't woke Maretha up.

Boy Willie: I was fixing to get her now. *(Calls.)* Hey, Maretha!

Doaker: Berniece don't like all that hollering now.

Berniece: Don't you wake that child up!

Boy Willie: You going up there . . . wake her up and tell her her uncle's here. I ain't seen her in three years. Wake her up and send her down here. She can go back to bed.

Berniece: I ain't waking that child up . . . and don't you be making all that noise. You and Lymon need to sell them watermelons and go on back.

Berniece exits up the stairs.

Boy Willie: I see Berniece still try to be stuck up.

Doaker: Berniece alright. She don't want you making all that noise. Maretha up there sleep. Let her sleep until she get up. She can see you then.

Boy Willie: I ain't thinking about Berniece. You hear from Wining Boy? You know Cleotha died?

Doaker: Yeah, I heard that. He come by here about a year ago. Had a whole sack of money. He stayed here about two weeks. Ain't offered nothing. Berniece asked him for three dollars to buy some food and he got mad and left.

Lymon: Who's Wining Boy?

Boy Willie: That's my uncle. That's Doaker's brother. You heard me talk about Wining Boy. He play piano. He done made some records and everything. He still doing that, Doaker?

Doaker: He made one or two records a long time ago. That's the only ones I ever known him to make. If you let him tell it he a big recording star.

Boy Willie: He stopped down home about two years ago. That's what I hear. I don't know. Me and Lymon was up on Parchman Farm doing them three years.

Doaker: He don't never stay in one place. Now, he been here about eight months ago. Back in the winter. Now, you subject not to see him for another two years. It's liable to be that long before he stop by.

Boy Willie: If he had a whole sack of money you liable never to see him. You ain't gonna see him until he get broke. Just as soon as that sack of money is gone you look up and he be on your doorstep.

Lymon (noticing the piano): Is that the piano?

Boy Willie: Yeah . . . look here, Lymon. See how it got all cash money. He don't know I found out the most Stovall how it's carved up real nice and polished and everything? You never find you another piano like that.

Lymon: Yeah, that look real nice.

Boy Willie: I told you. See how it's polished? My mama used to polish it every day. See all them pictures carved on it? That's what I was talking about. You can get a nice price for that piano.

Lymon: That's all Boy Willie talked about the whole trip up here. I got tired of hearing him talking about the piano.

Boy Willie: All you want to talk about is women. You ought to hear this nigger, Doaker. Talking about all the women he gonna get when he get up here. He ain't had none down there but he gonna get a hundred when he get up here.

Doaker: How your people doing down there, Lymon?

Lymon: They alright. They still there. I come up here to see what it's like up here. Boy Willie trying to get me to go back and farm with him.

Boy Willie: Sutter's brother selling the land. He say he gonna sell it to me. That's why I come up here. I got one part of it. Sell them watermelons and get me another part. Get Berniece to sell that piano and I'll have the third part.

Doaker: Berniece ain't gonna sell that piano.

Boy Willie: I'm gonna talk to her. When she see I got a chance to get Sutter's land she'll come around.

Doaker: You can put that thought out of your mind. Berniece ain't gonna sell that piano.

Boy Willie: I'm gonna talk to her. She been playing on it?

Doaker: You know she won't touch that piano. I ain't never known her to touch it since Mama Ola died. That's over seven years now. She say it got blood on it. She got Maretha playing on it though. Say Maretha can go on and do everything she can't do. Got her in an extra school down at the Irene Kaufman Settlement House. She want Maretha to grow up and be a schoolteacher. She say she good enough she can teach on the piano.

Boy Willie: Maretha don't need to be playing on no piano. She can play on the guitar.

Doaker: How much land Sutter got left?

Boy Willie: Got a hundred acres. Good land. He done sold it piece by piece, he kept the good part for himself. Now he got to give that up. His brother come down from Chicago for the funeral . . . he up there in Chicago got some kind of business with soda fountain equipment. He anxious to sell the land, Doaker. He don't want to be bothered with it. He called me to him and said cause of how long our families done known each other and how we been good friends and all, say he wanted to sell the land to me. Say he'd rather see me with it than Jim Stovall. Told me he'd let me have it for two thousand dollars cash money. He don't know I found out the most Stovall would give him for it was fifteen hundred dollars. He trying to get that extra five hundred out of me telling me he doing me a favor. I thanked him just as nice. Told him what a good man Sutter was and how he had my sympathy and all. Told him to give me two weeks. He said he'd wait on me. That's why I come up here. Sell them watermelons. Get Berniece to sell that piano. Put them two parts with the part I done saved. Walk in there. Tip my hat. Lay my money down on the table. Get my deed and walk on out. This time I get to keep all the cotton. Hire me some men to work it for me. Gin my cotton. Get my seed. And I'll see you again next year. Might even plant some tobacco or some oats.

Doaker: You gonna have a hard time trying to get Berniece to sell that piano. You know Avery Brown from down there, don't you? He up here now. He followed Berniece up here trying to get her to marry him after Crawley got killed. He been up here about two years. He call himself a preacher now.

Boy Willie: I know Avery. I know him from when he used to work on the Willshaw place. Lymon know him too.

Doaker: He after Berniece to marry him. She keep telling him no but he won't give up. He keep pressing her on it.

Boy Willie: Avery think all white men is bigshots. He don't know there some white men ain't got as much as he got.

Doaker: He supposed to come past here this morning. Berniece going down to the bank with him to see if he can get a loan to start his church. That's why I know Berniece ain't gonna sell that piano. He tried to get her to sell it to help him start his church. Sent the man around and everything.

Boy Willie: What man?

Doaker: Some white fellow was going around to all the colored people's houses looking to buy up musical instruments. He'd buy anything. Drums. Guitars. Harmonicas. Pianos. Avery sent him past here. He looked at the piano and got excited. Offered her a nice price. She turned him down and got on Avery for sending him past. The man kept on her about two weeks. He seen where she wasn't gonna sell it, he gave her his number and told her if she ever wanted to sell it to call him first. Say he'd go one better than what anybody else would give her for it.

Boy Willie: How much he offer her for it?

Doaker: Now you know me. She didn't say and I didn't ask. I just know it was a nice price.

Lymon: All you got to do is find out who he is and tell him somebody else wanna buy it from you. Tell him you can't make up your mind who to sell it to, and if he like Doaker say, he'll give you anything you want for it.

Boy Willie: That's what I'm gonna do. I'm gonna find out who he is from Avery.

Doaker: It ain't gonna do you no good. Berniece ain't gonna sell that piano.

Boy Willie: She ain't got to sell it. I'm gonna sell it. I own just as much of it as she does.

Berniece (offstage, hollers): Doaker! Go on get away. Doaker!

Doaker (calling): Berniece?

> *Doaker and Boy Willie rush to the stairs, Boy Willie runs up the stairs, passing Berniece as she enters, running.*

Doaker: Berniece, what the matter? You alright? What's the matter?

> *Berniece tries to catch her breath. She is unable to speak.*

Doaker: That's alright. Take your time. You alright. What's the matter? *(He calls.)* Hey, Boy Willie?

Boy Willie (offstage): Ain't nobody up here.

Berniece: Sutter . . . Sutter's standing at the top of the steps.

Doaker (calls): Boy Willie!

> *Lymon crosses to the stairs and looks up. Boy Willie enters from the stairs.*

Boy Willie: Hey Doaker, what's wrong with her? Berniece, what's wrong? Who was you talking to?

Doaker: She say she seen Sutter's ghost standing at the top of the stairs.

Boy Willie: Seen what? Sutter? She ain't seen no Sutter.

Berniece: He was standing right up there.

Boy Willie (entering on the stairs): That's all in Berniece's head. Ain't nobody up there. Go on up there, Doaker.

Doaker: I'll take your word for it. Berniece talking about what she seen. She say Sutter's ghost standing at the top of the steps. She ain't just make all that up.

Boy Willie: She up there dreaming. She ain't seen no ghost.

Lymon: You want a glass of water, Berniece? Get her a glass of water, Boy Willie.

Boy Willie: She don't need no water. She ain't seen nothing. Go on up there and look. Ain't nobody up there but Maretha.

Doaker: Let Berniece tell it.

Boy Willie: I ain't stopping her from telling it.

Doaker: What happened, Berniece?

Berniece: I come out of my room to come back down here and Sutter was standing there in the hall.

Boy Willie: What he look like?

Berniece: He look like Sutter. He look like he always look.

Boy Willie: Sutter couldn't find his way from Big Sandy to Little Sandy. How he gonna find his way all the way up here to Pittsburgh? Sutter ain't never even heard of Pittsburgh.

Doaker: Go on, Berniece.

Berniece: Just standing there with the blue suit on.

Boy Willie: The man ain't never left Marlin County when he was living . . . and he's gonna come all the way up here now that he's dead?

Doaker: Let her finish. I want to hear what she got to say.

Boy Willie: I'll tell you this. If Berniece had seen him like she think she seen him she'd still be running.

Doaker: Go on, Berniece. Don't pay Boy Willie no mind.

Berniece: He was standing there . . . had his hand on top of his head. Look like he might have thought if he took his hand down his head might have fallen off.

Lymon: Did he have on a hat?

Berniece: Just had on that blue suit . . . I told him to go away and he just stood there looking at me . . . calling Boy Willie's name.

Boy Willie: What he calling my name for?

Berniece: I believe you pushed him in the well.

Boy Willie: Now what kind of sense that make? You telling me I'm gonna go out there and hide in the weeds with all them dogs and things he got around there . . . I'm gonna hide and wait till I catch him looking down his well just right . . . then I'm gonna run over and push him in. A great big old three-hundred-and-forty-pound man.

Berniece: Well, what he calling your name for?

Boy Willie: He bending over looking down his well, woman . . . how he know who pushed him? It could have been anybody. Where was you when Sutter fell in his well? Where was Doaker? Me and Lymon was over in Stoner County. Tell her, Lymon. The Ghosts of the Yellow Dog got Sutter. That's what happened to him.

Berniece: You can talk all that Ghosts of the Yellow Dog stuff if you want. I know better.

Lymon: The Ghosts of the Yellow Dog pushed him. That's what the people say. They found him in his well and all the people say it must be the Ghosts of the Yellow Dog. Just like all them other men.

Boy Willie: Come talking about he looking for me. What he come all the way up here for? If he looking for me all he got to do is wait. He could have saved himself a trip if he looking for me. That ain't nothing but in Berniece's head. Ain't no telling what she liable to come up with next.

Berniece: Boy Willie, I want you and Lymon to go ahead and leave my house. Just go on somewhere. You don't do nothing but bring trouble with you everywhere you go. If it wasn't for you Crawley would still be alive.

Boy Willie: Crawley what? I ain't had nothing to do with Crawley getting killed. Crawley three time seven. He had his own mind.

Berniece: Just go on and leave. Let Sutter go somewhere else looking for you.

Boy Willie: I'm leaving. Soon as we sell them watermelons. Other than that I ain't going nowhere. Hell, I just got here. Talking about Sutter looking for me. Sutter was looking for that piano. That's what he was looking for. He had to die to find out where that piano was at . . . If I was you I'd get rid of it. That's the way to get rid of Sutter's ghost. Get rid of that piano.

Berniece: I want you and Lymon to go on and take all this confusion out of my house!

Boy Willie: Hey, tell her, Doaker. What kind of sense that make? I told you, Lymon, as soon as Berniece see me she was gonna start something. Didn't I tell you that? Now she done made up that story about Sutter just so she could tell me to leave her house. Well, hell, I ain't going nowhere till I sell them watermelons.

Berniece: Well why don't you go out there and sell them! Sell them and go on back!

Boy Willie: We waiting till the people get up.

Lymon: Boy Willie say if you get out there too early and wake the people up they get mad at you and won't buy nothing from you.

Doaker: You won't be waiting long. You done let the sun catch up with you. This the time everybody be getting up around here.

Berniece: Come on, Doaker, walk up here with me. Let me get Maretha up and get her started. I got to get ready myself. Boy Willie, just go on out there and sell them watermelons and you and Lymon leave my house.

Berniece and Doaker exit up the stairs.

Boy Willie (calling after them): If you see Sutter up there . . . tell him I'm down here waiting on him.

Lymon: What if she see him again?

Boy Willie: That's all in her head. There ain't no ghost up there. *(Calls.)* Hey, Doaker . . . I told you ain't nothing up there.

Lymon: I'm glad he didn't say he was looking for me.

Boy Willie: I wish I would see Sutter's ghost. Give me a chance to put a whupping on him.

Lymon: You ought to stay up here with me. You be down there working his land . . . he might come looking for you all the time.

Boy Willie: I ain't thinking about Sutter. And I ain't thinking about staying up here. You stay up here. I'm going back and get Sutter's land. You think you ain't got to work up here. You think this the land of milk and honey. But I ain't scared of work. I'm going back and farm every acre of that land.

Doaker enters from the stairs.

I told you there ain't nothing up there, Doaker. Berniece dreaming all that.

Doaker: I believe Berniece seen something. Berniece level-headed. She ain't just made all that up. She say Sutter had on a suit. I don't believe she ever seen Sutter in a suit. I believe that's what he was buried in, and that's what Berniece saw.

Boy Willie: Well, let her keep on seeing him then. As long as he don't mess with me. *(Doaker starts to cook his breakfast.)* I heard about you, Doaker. They say you got all the women looking out for you down home. They be looking to see you coming. Say you got a different one every two weeks. Say they be fighting one another for you to stay with them. *(To Lymon.)* Look at him, Lymon. He know it's true.

Doaker: I ain't thinking about no women. They never get me tied up with them. After Coreen I ain't got no use for them. I stay up on Jack Slattery's place when I be down there. All them women want is somebody with a steady payday.

Boy Willie: That ain't what I hear. I hear every two weeks the women all put on their dresses and line up at the railroad station.

Doaker: I don't get down there but once a month. I used to go down there every two weeks but they keep switching me around. They keep switching all the fellows around.

Boy Willie: Shakespeare can't turn that railroad loose. He was working the railroad when I was walking around crying for sugartit. My mama used to brag on him.

Doaker: I'm cooking now, but I used to line track. I pieced together the Yellow Dog stitch by stitch. Rail by rail. Line track all up around there. I lined track all up around Sunflower and Clarksdale. Wining Boy worked with me. He helped me put in some of that track. He'd work it for six months and quit. Go back to playing piano and gambling.

Boy Willie: How long you been with the railroad now?

Doaker: Twenty-seven years. Now, I'll tell you something about the railroad. What I done learned after twenty-seven years. See, you got North. You got West. You look over here you got South. Over there you got East. Now, you can start from anywhere. Don't care where you at. You got to go one of them four ways. And whichever way you decide to go they got a railroad that will take you there. Now, that's something simple. You think anybody would be able to understand that. But you'd be surprised how many people trying to go North get on a train going West. They think the train's supposed to go where they going rather than where it's going.

   Now, why people going? Their sister's sick. They leaving before they kill somebody . . . and they sitting across from somebody who's leaving to keep from getting killed. They leaving cause they can't get satisfied. They going to meet someone. I wish I had a dollar for every time that someone wasn't at the station to meet them. I done seen that a lot. In between the time they sent the telegram and the time the person get there . . . they done forgot all about them.

   They got so many trains out there they have a hard time keeping them from running into each other. Got trains going every whichaway. Got people on all of them. Somebody going where somebody just left. If everybody stay in one place I believe this would be a better world. Now what I done learned after twenty-seven years of railroading is this . . . if the train stays on the track . . . it's going to get where it's going. It might not be where you going. If it ain't, then all you got to do is sit and wait cause the train's coming back to get you. The train don't never stop. It'll come back every time. Now I'll tell you another thing . . .

Boy Willie: What you cooking over there, Doaker? Me and Lymon's hungry.

Doaker: Go on down there to Wylie and Kirkpatrick to Eddie's restaurant.

Coffee cost a nickel and you can get two eggs, sausage, and grits for fifteen cents. He even give you a biscuit with it.

Boy Willie: That look good what you got. Give me a little piece of that grilled bread.

Doaker: Here . . . go on take the whole piece.

Boy Willie: Here you go, Lymon . . . you want a piece?

He gives Lymon a piece of toast. Maretha enters from the stairs.

Boy Willie: Hey, sugar. Come here and give me a hug. Come on give Uncle Boy Willie a hug. Don't be shy. Look at her, Doaker. She done got bigger. Ain't she got big?

Doaker: Yeah, she getting up there.

Boy Willie: How you doing, sugar?

Maretha: Fine.

Boy Willie: You was just a little old thing last time I seen you. You remember me, don't you? This your Uncle Boy Willie from down South. That there's Lymon. He my friend. We come up here to sell watermelons. You like watermelons? *(Maretha nods.)* We got a whole truckload out front. You can have as many as you want. What you been doing?

Maretha: Nothing.

Boy Willie: Don't be shy now. Look at you getting all big. How old is you?

Maretha: Eleven. I'm gonna be twelve soon.

Boy Willie: You like it up here? You like the North?

Maretha: It's alright.

Boy Willie: That there's Lymon. Did you say hi to Lymon?

Maretha: Hi.

Lymon: How you doing? You look just like your mama. I remember you when you was wearing diapers.

Boy Willie: You gonna come down South and see me? Uncle Boy Willie gonna get him a farm. Gonna get a great big old farm. Come down there and I'll teach you how to ride a mule. Teach you how to kill a chicken, too.

Maretha: I seen my mama do that.

Boy Willie: Ain't nothing to it. You just grab him by his neck and twist it. Get you a real good grip and then you just wring his neck and throw him in the pot. Cook him up. Then you got some good eating. What you like to eat? What kind of food you like?

Maretha: I like everything . . . except I don't like no black-eyed peas.

Boy Willie: Uncle Doaker tell me your mama got you playing that piano. Come on play something for me. *(Boy Willie crosses over to the piano followed by Maretha.)* Show me what you can do. Come on now. Here . . . Uncle Boy Willie give you a dime . . . show me what you can do. Don't be bashful now. That dime say you can't be bashful. *(Maretha plays. It is something any beginner first learns.)* Here, let me show you something. *(Boy Willie sits and plays a simple boogie-woogie.)* See that? See what I'm doing? That's what you call the boogie-woogie. See now . . . you can get up and dance to that. That's how good it sound. It sound like you wanna dance. You can dance to that. It'll hold you up. Whatever kind of dance you wanna do you can dance to that right there. See that? See how it go? Ain't nothing to it. Go on you do it.

Maretha: I got to read it on the paper.

Boy Willie: You don't need no paper. Go on. Do just like that there.

Berniece: Maretha! You get up here and get ready to go so you be on time. Ain't no need you trying to take advantage of company.

Maretha: I got to go.

Boy Willie: Uncle Boy Willie gonna get you a guitar. Let Uncle Doaker teach you how to play that. You don't need to read no paper to play the guitar. Your mama told you about the piano? You know how them pictures got on there?

Maretha: She say it just always been like that since she got it.

Boy Willie: You hear that, Doaker? And you sitting up here in the house with Berniece.

Doaker: I ain't got nothing to do with that. I don't get in the way of Berniece's raising her.

Boy Willie: You tell your mama to tell you about that piano. You ask her how them pictures got on there. If she don't tell you I'll tell you.

Berniece: Maretha!

Maretha: I got to get ready to go.

Boy Willie: She getting big, Doaker. You remember her, Lymon?

Lymon: She used to be real little.

> *There is a knock on the door. Doaker goes to answer it. Avery enters. Thirty-eight years old, honest and ambitious, he has taken to the city like a fish to water, finding in it opportunities for growth and advancement that did not exist for him in the rural South. He is dressed in a suit and tie with a gold cross around his neck. He carries a small Bible.*

Doaker: Hey, Avery, come on in. Berniece upstairs.

Boy Willie: Look at him . . . look at him . . . he don't know what to say. He wasn't expecting to see me.

Avery: Hey, Boy Willie. What you doing up here?

Boy Willie: Look at him, Lymon.

Avery: Is that Lymon? Lymon Jackson?

Boy Willie: Yeah, you know Lymon.

Doaker: Berniece be ready in a minute, Avery.

Boy Willie: Doaker say you a preacher now. What . . . we supposed to call you Reverend? You used to be plain old Avery. When you get to be a preacher, nigger?

Lymon: Avery say he gonna be a preacher so he don't have to work.

Boy Willie: I remember when you was down there on the Willshaw place planting cotton. You wasn't thinking about no Reverend then.

Avery: That must be your truck out there. I saw that truck with them watermelons, I was trying to figure out what it was doing in front of the house.

Boy Willie: Yeah, me and Lymon selling watermelons. That's Lymon's truck.

Doaker: Berniece say you all going down to the bank.

Avery: Yeah, they give me a half day off work. I got an appointment to talk to the bank about getting a loan to start my church.

Boy Willie: Lymon say preachers don't have to work. Where you working at, nigger?

Doaker: Avery got him one of them good jobs. He working at one of them skyscrapers downtown.

Avery: I'm working down there at the Gulf Building running an elevator. Got a pension and everything. They even give you a turkey on Thanksgiving.

Lymon: How you know the rope ain't gonna break? Ain't you scared the rope's gonna break?

Avery: That's steel. They got steel cables hold it up. It take a whole lot of breaking to break that steel. Naw, I ain't worried about nothing like that. It ain't nothing but a little old elevator. Now, I wouldn't get in none of them airplanes. You couldn't pay me to do nothing like that.

Lymon: That be fun. I'd rather do that than ride in one of them elevators.

Boy Willie: How many of them watermelons you wanna buy?

Avery: I thought you was gonna give me one seeing as how you got a whole truck full.

Boy Willie: You can get one, get two. I'll give you two for a dollar.

Avery: I can't eat but one. How much are they?

Boy Willie: Aw, nigger, you know I'll give you a watermelon. Go on, take as many as you want. Just leave some for me and Lymon to sell.

Avery: I don't want but one.

Boy Willie: How you get to be a preacher, Avery? I might want to be a preacher one day. Have everybody call me Reverend Boy Willie.

Avery: It come to me in a dream. God called me and told me he wanted me to be a shepherd for his flock. That's what I'm gonna call my church . . . The Good Shepherd Church of God in Christ.

Doaker: Tell him what you told me. Tell him about the three hobos.

Avery: Boy Willie don't want to hear all that.

Lymon: I do. Lots a people say your dreams can come true.

Avery: Naw. You don't want to hear all that.

Doaker: Go on. I told him you was a preacher. He didn't want to believe me. Tell him about the three hobos.

Avery: Well, it come to me in a dream. See . . . I was sitting out in this railroad yard watching the trains go by. The train stopped and these three hobos got off. They told me they had come from Nazareth and was on their way to Jerusalem. They had three candles. They gave me one and told me to light it . . . but to be careful that it didn't go out. Next thing I knew I was standing in front of this house. Something told me to go knock on the door. This old woman opened the door and said they had been waiting on me. Then she led me into this room. It was a big room and it was full of all kinds of different people. They looked like anybody else except they all had sheep heads and was making noise like sheep make. I heard somebody call my name. I looked around and there was these same three hobos. They told me to take off my clothes and they give me a blue robe with gold thread. They washed my feet and combed my hair. Then they showed me these three doors and told me to pick one.

I went through one of them doors and that flame leapt off that candle and it seemed like my whole head caught fire. I looked around and there was four or five other men standing there with these same blue robes on. Then we heard a voice tell us to look out across this valley. We looked out and saw the valley was full of wolves. The voice told us that these sheep people that I had seen in the other room had to go over to the other side of this valley and somebody had to take them. Then I heard another voice say, "Who shall I send?" Next thing I knew I said, "Here I am. Send me." That's when I met Jesus. He say, "If you go, I'll go with you." Something told me to say, "Come on. Let's go." That's when I woke up. My head still felt like it was on fire . . . but I had a peace about myself that was hard to explain. I knew right then that I had been filled with the Holy Ghost and called to be a servant of the Lord. It took me a while before I could accept that. But then a lot of little ways God showed me that it was true. So I became a preacher.

Lymon: I see why you gonna call it the Good Shepherd Church. You dreaming about them sheep people. I can see that easy.

Boy Willie: Doaker say you sent some white man past the house to look at that piano. Say he was going around to all the colored people's houses looking to buy up musical instruments.

Avery: Yeah, but Berniece didn't want to sell that piano. After she told me about it . . . I could see why she didn't want to sell it.

Boy Willie: What's this man's name?

Avery: Oh, that's a while back now. I done forgot his name. He give Berniece a card with his name and telephone number on it, but I believe she throwed it away.

Berniece and Maretha enter from the stairs.

Berniece: Maretha, run back upstairs and get my pocketbook. And wipe that hair grease off your forehead. Go ahead, hurry up.

Maretha exits up the stairs.

How you doing, Avery? You done got all dressed up. You look nice. Boy Willie, I thought you and Lymon was going to sell them watermelons.

Boy Willie: Lymon done got sleepy. We liable to get some sleep first.

Lymon: I ain't sleepy.

Doaker: As many watermelons as you got stacked up on that truck out there, you ought to have been gone.

Boy Willie: We gonna go in a minute. We going.

Berniece: Doaker. I'm gonna stop down there on Logan Street. You want anything?

Doaker: You can pick up some ham hocks if you going down there. See if you can get the smoked ones. If they ain't got that get the fresh ones. Don't get the ones that got all that fat under the skin. Look for the long ones. They nice and lean. *(He gives her a dollar.)* Don't get the short ones lessen they smoked. If you got to get the fresh ones make sure that they the long ones. If they ain't got them smoked then go ahead and get the short ones. *(Pause.)* You may as well get some turnip greens while you down there. I got some buttermilk . . . if you pick up some cornmeal I'll make me some cornbread and cook up them turnip greens.

Maretha enters from the stairs.

Maretha: We gonna take the streetcar?

Berniece: Me and Avery gonna drop you off at the settlement house. You mind them people down there. Don't be going down there showing your color. Boy Willie, I done told you what to do. I'll see you later, Doaker.

Avery: I'll be seeing you again, Boy Willie.

Boy Willie: Hey, Berniece . . . what's the name of that man Avery sent past say he want to buy the piano?

Berniece: I knew it. I knew it when I first seen you. I knew you was up to something.

Boy Willie: Sutter's brother say he selling the land to me. He waiting on me now. Told me he'd give me two weeks. I got one part. Sell them watermelons get me another part. Then we can sell the piano and I'll have the third part.

Berniece: I ain't selling that piano, Boy Willie. If that's why you come up here you can just forget about it. *(To Doaker.)* Doaker, I'll see you later. Boy Willie ain't nothing but a whole lot of mouth. I ain't paying him no mind. If he come up here thinking he gonna sell that piano then he done come up here for nothing.

Berniece, Avery, and Maretha exit the front door.

Boy Willie: Hey, Lymon! You ready to go sell these watermelons. *(Boy Willie and Lymon start to exit. At the door Boy Willie turns to Doaker.)* Hey, Doaker . . . if Berniece don't want to sell that piano . . . I'm gonna cut it in half and go on and sell my half.

Boy Willie and Lymon exit.

The lights go down on the scene.

Scene II

The lights come up on the kitchen. It is three days later. Wining Boy sits at the kitchen table. There is a half-empty pint bottle on the table. Doaker busies himself washing pots. Wining Boy is fifty-six years old. Doaker's older brother, he tries to present the image of a successful musician and gambler, but his music, his clothes, and even his manner of presentation are old. He is a man who looking back over his life continues to live it with an odd mixture of zest and sorrow.

Wining Boy: So the Ghosts of the Yellow Dog got Sutter. That just go to show you I believe I always lived right. They say every dog gonna have his day and time it go around it sure come back to you. I done seen that a thousand times. I know the truth of that. But I'll tell you outright . . . if I see Sutter's ghost I'll be on the first thing I find that got wheels on it.

Doaker enters from his room.

Doaker: Wining Boy!

Wining Boy: And I'll tell you another thing . . . Berniece ain't gonna sell that piano.

Doaker: That's what she told him. He say he gonna cut it in half and go on and sell his half. They been around here three days trying to sell them watermelons. They trying to get out to where the white folks live but the truck keep breaking down. They go a block or two and it break down again. They trying to get out to Squirrel Hill and can't get around the corner. He say soon as he can get that truck empty to where he can set the piano up in there he gonna take it out of here and go sell it.

Wining Boy: What about them boys Sutter got? How come they ain't farming that land?

Doaker: One of them going to school. He left down there and come North to school. The other one ain't got as much sense as that frying pan over yonder. That is the dumbest white man I ever seen. He'd stand in the river and watch it rise till it drown him.

Wining Boy: Other than seeing Sutter's ghost how's Berniece doing?

Doaker: She doing alright. She still got Crawley on her mind. He been dead three years but she still holding on to him. She need to go out here and let one of these fellows grab a whole handful of whatever she got. She act like it done got precious.

Wining Boy: They always told me any fish will bite if you got good bait.

Doaker: She stuck up on it. She think it's better than she is. I believe she messing around with Avery. They got something going. He a preacher now. If you let him tell it the Holy Ghost sat on his head and heaven opened up with thunder and lightning and God was calling his name. Told him to go out and preach and tend to his flock. That's what he gonna call his church. The Good Shepherd Church.

Wining Boy: They had that joker down in Spear walking around talking about he Jesus Christ. He gonna live the life of Christ. Went through the Last Supper and everything. Rented him a mule on Palm Sunday and rode through the town. Did everything . . . talking about he Christ. He did everything until they got up to that crucifixion part. Got up to that part and told everybody to go home and quit pretending. He got up to the crucifixion part and changed his mind. Had a whole bunch of folks come down here to see him get nailed to the cross. I don't know who's the worse fool. Him or them. Had all them folks come down there . . . even carried the cross up this little hill. People standing around waiting to see him get nailed to the cross and he stop everything and preach a little sermon and told everybody to go home. Had enough nerve to tell them to come to church on Easter Sunday to celebrate his resurrection.

Doaker: I'm surprised Avery ain't thought about that. He trying every little thing to get him a congregation together. They meeting over at his house till he get him a church.

Wining Boy: Ain't nothing wrong with being a preacher. You got the preacher on one hand and the gambler on the other. Sometimes there ain't too much difference in them.

Doaker: How long you been in Kansas City?

Wining Boy: Since I left here. I got tied up with some old gal down there. *(Pause.)* You know Cleotha died.

Doaker: Yeah, I heard that last time I was down there. I was sorry to hear that.

Wining Boy: One of her friends wrote and told me. I got the letter right here. *(He takes the letter out of his pocket.)* I was down in Kansas City and she wrote and told me Cleotha had died. Name of Willa Bryant. She say she know cousin Rupert. *(He opens the letter and reads:)*

> Dear Wining Boy: I am writing this letter to let you know Miss Cleotha Holman passed on Saturday the first of May she departed this world in the loving arms of her sister Miss Alberta Samuels. I know you would want to know this and am writing as a friend of Cleotha. There have been many hardships since last you seen her but she survived them all and to the end was a good woman whom I hope have God's grace and is in His Paradise. Your cousin Rupert Bates is my friend also and he give me your address and I pray this reaches you about Cleotha. Miss Willa Bryant. A friend.

(He folds the letter and returns it to his pocket.) They was nailing her coffin shut by the time I heard about it. I never knew she was sick. I believe it was that yellow jaundice. That's what killed her mama.

Doaker: Cleotha wasn't but forty-some.

Wining Boy: She was forty-six. I got ten years on her. I met her when she was sixteen. You remember I used to run around there. Couldn't nothing keep me still. Much as I loved Cleotha I loved to ramble. Couldn't nothing keep me still. We got married and we used to fight about it all the time. Then one day she asked me to leave. Told me she loved me before I left. Told me, Wining Boy, you got a home as long as I got mine. And I believe in my heart I always felt that and that kept me safe.

Doaker: Cleotha always did have a nice way about her.

Wining Boy: Man that woman was something. I used to thank the Lord. Many a night I sat up and looked out over my life. Said, well, I had Cleotha. When it didn't look like there was nothing else for me, I said, thank God, at least I had that. If ever I go anywhere in this life I done known a good woman. And that used to hold me till the next morning. *(Pause.)* What you got? Give me a little nip. I know you got something stuck up in your room.

Doaker: I ain't seen you walk in here and put nothing on the table. You done sat there and drank up your whiskey. Now you talking about what you got.

Wining Boy: I got plenty money. Give me a little nip.

Doaker carries a glass into his room and returns with it half-filled. He sets it on the table in front of Wining Boy.

Wining Boy: You hear from Coreen?

Doaker: She up in New York. I let her go from my mind.

Wining Boy: She was something back then. She wasn't too pretty but she had a way of looking at you made you know there was a whole lot of woman there. You got married and snatched her out from under us and we all got mad at you.

Doaker: She up in New York City. That's what I hear.

The door opens and Boy Willie and Lymon enter.

Boy Willie: Aw hell . . . look here! We was just talking about you. Doaker say you left out of here with a whole sack of money. I told him he wasn't going see you till you got broke.

Wining Boy: What you mean broke? I got a whole pocketful of money.

Doaker: Did you all get that truck fixed?

Boy Willie: We got it running and got halfway out there on Centre and it broke down again. Lymon went out there and messed it up some more. Fellow told us we got to wait till tomorrow to get it fixed. Say he have it running like new. Lymon going back down there and sleep in the truck so the people don't take the watermelons.

Lymon: Lymon nothing. You go down there and sleep in it.

Boy Willie: You was sleeping in it down home, nigger! I don't know nothing about sleeping in no truck.

Lymon: I ain't sleeping in no truck.

Boy Willie: They can take all the watermelons. I don't care. Wining Boy, where you coming from? Where you been?

Wining Boy: I been down in Kansas City.

Boy Willie: You remember Lymon? Lymon Jackson.

Wining Boy: Yeah, I used to know his daddy.

Boy Willie: Doaker say you don't never leave no address with nobody. Say he got to depend on your whim. See when it strike you to pay a visit.

Wining Boy: I got four or five addresses.

Boy Willie: Doaker say Berniece asked you for three dollars and you got mad and left.

Wining Boy: Berniece try and rule over you too much for me. That's why I left. It wasn't about no three dollars.

Boy Willie: Where you getting all these sacks of money from? I need to be with you. Doaker say you had a whole sack of money . . . turn some of it loose.

Wining Boy: I was just fixing to ask you for five dollars.

Boy Willie: I ain't got no money. I'm trying to get some. Doaker tell you about Sutter? The Ghosts of the Yellow Dog got him about three weeks ago. Berniece done seen his ghost and everything. He right upstairs. (*Calls.*) Hey Sutter! Wining Boy's here. Come on, get a drink!

Wining Boy: How many that make the Ghosts of the Yellow Dog done got?

Boy Willie: Must be about nine or ten, eleven or twelve. I don't know.

Doaker: You got Ed Saunders. Howard Peterson. Charlie Webb.

Wining Boy: Robert Smith. That fellow that shot Becky's boy . . . say he was stealing peaches . . .

Doaker: You talking about Bob Mallory.

Boy Willie: Berniece say she don't believe all that about the Ghosts of the Yellow Dog.

Wining Boy: She ain't got to believe. You go ask them white folks in Sunflower County if they believe. You go ask Sutter if he believe. I don't care if Berniece believe or not. I done been to where the Southern cross the Yellow Dog and called out their names. They talk back to you, too.

Lymon: What they sound like? The wind or something?

Boy Willie: You done been there for real, Wining Boy?

Wining Boy: Nineteen thirty. July of nineteen thirty I stood right there on that spot. It didn't look like nothing was going right in my life. I said everything can't go wrong all the time . . . let me go down there and call on the Ghosts of the Yellow Dog, see if they can help me. I went down there and right there where them two railroads cross each other . . . I stood right there on that spot and called out their names. They talk back to you, too.

Lymon: People say you can ask them questions. They talk to you like that?

Wining Boy: A lot of things you got to find out on your own. I can't say how they talked to nobody else. But to me it just filled me up in a strange sort of way to be standing there on that spot. I didn't want to leave. It felt like the longer I stood there the bigger I got. I seen the train coming and it seem like I was bigger than the train. I started not to move. But something told me to go ahead and get on out the way. The train passed and I started to go back up there and stand some more. But something told me not to do it. I walked away from there feeling like a king. Went on and had a stroke of luck that run on for three years. So I don't care if Berniece believe or not. Berniece ain't got to believe. I know cause I been there. Now Doaker'll tell you about the Ghosts of the Yellow Dog.

Doaker: I don't try and talk that stuff with Berniece. Avery got her all tied up in that church. She just think it's a whole lot of nonsense.

Boy Willie: Berniece don't believe in nothing. She just think she believe. She believe in anything if it's convenient for her to believe. But when that convenience run out then she ain't got nothing to stand on.

Wining Boy: Let's not get on Berniece now. Doaker tell me you talking about selling that piano.

Boy Willie: Yeah . . . hey, Doaker, I got the name of that man Avery was talking about. The man's what's fixing the truck gave me his name. Everybody know him. Say he buy up anything you can make music with. I got his name and his telephone number. Hey, Wining Boy, Sutter's brother say he selling the land to me. I got one part. Sell them watermelons get me the second part. Then . . . soon as I get them watermelons out that truck I'm gonna take and sell that piano and get the third part.

Doaker: That land ain't worth nothing no more. The smart white man's up here in these cities. He cut the land loose and step back and watch you and the dumb white man argue over it.

Wining Boy: How you know Sutter's brother ain't sold it already? You talking about selling the piano and the man's liable to sold the land two or three times.

Boy Willie: He say he waiting on me. He say he give me two weeks. That's two weeks from Friday. Say if I ain't back by then he might gonna sell it to somebody else. He say he wanna see me with it.

Wining Boy: You know as well as I know the man gonna sell the land to the first one walk up and hand him the money.

Boy Willie: That's just who I'm gonna be. Look, you ain't gotta know he waiting on me. I know. Okay. I know what the man told me. Stoval already down tried to buy the land from him and he told him no. The man say he waiting on me . . . he waiting on me. Hey, Doaker . . . give me a drink. I see Wining Boy got his glass. *(Doaker exits into his room.)* Wining Boy, what you doing in Kansas City? What they got down there?

Lymon: I hear they got some nice-looking women in Kansas City. I sure like to go down there and find out.

Wining Boy: Man, the women down there is something else.

> *Doaker enters with a bottle of whiskey. He sets it on the table with some glasses.*

Doaker: You wanna sit up here and drink up my whiskey, leave a dollar on the table when you get up.

Boy Willie: You ain't doing nothing but showing your hospitality. I know we ain't got to pay for your hospitality.

Wining Boy: Doaker say they had you and Lymon down on the Parchman Farm. Had you on my old stomping grounds.

Boy Willie: Me and Lymon was down there hauling wood for Jim Miller and keeping us a little bit to sell. Some white fellows tried to run us off of it. That's when Crawley got killed. They put me and Lymon in the penitentiary.

Lymon: They ambushed us right there where that road dip down and around that bend in the creek. Crawley tried to fight them. Me and Boy Willie got away but the sheriff got us. Say we was stealing wood. They shot me in my stomach.

Boy Willie: They looking for Lymon down there now. They rounded him up and put him in jail for not working.

Lymon: Fined me a hundred dollars. Mr. Stovall come and paid my hundred dollars and the judge say I got to work for him to pay him back his hundred dollars. I told them I'd rather take my thirty days but they wouldn't let me do that.

Boy Willie: As soon as Stovall turned his back, Lymon was gone. He down there living in that truck dodging the sheriff and Stovall. He got both of them looking for him. So I brought him up here.

Lymon: I told Boy Willie I'm gonna stay up here. I ain't going back with him.

Boy Willie: Ain't nobody twisting your arm to make you go back. You can do what you want to do.

Wining Boy: I'll go back with you. I'm on my way down there. You gonna take the train? I'm gonna take the train.

Lymon: They treat you better up here.

Boy Willie: I ain't worried about nobody mistreating me. They treat you like you let them treat you. They mistreat me I mistreat them right back. Ain't no difference in me and the white man.

Wining Boy: Ain't no difference as far as how somebody supposed to treat you. I agree with that. But I'll tell you the difference between the colored man and the white man. Alright. Now you take and eat some berries. They taste real good to you. So you say I'm gonna go out and get me a whole pot of these berries and cook them up to make a pie or whatever. But you ain't looked to see them berries is sitting in the white fellow's yard. Ain't got no fence around them. You figure anybody want something they'd fence it in. Alright. Now the white man come along and say that's my land. Therefore everything that grow on it belong to me. He tell the sheriff, "I want you to put this nigger in jail as a warning to all the other niggers. Otherwise first thing you know these niggers have everything that belong to us."

Boy Willie: I'd come back at night and haul off his whole patch while he was asleep.

Wining Boy: Alright. Now Mr. So and So, he sell the land to you. And he come to you and say, "John, you own the land. It's all yours now. But them is my berries. And come time to pick them I'm gonna send my boys over. You got the land . . . but them berries, I'm gonna keep them. They mine." And he go and fix it with the law that them is his berries. Now that's the difference between the colored man and the white man. The colored man can't fix nothing with the law.

Boy Willie: I don't go by what the law say. The law's liable to say anything. I go by if it's right or not. It don't matter to me what the law say. I take and look at it for myself.

Lymon: That's why you gonna end up back down there on the Parchman Farm.

Boy Willie: I ain't thinking about no Parchman Farm. You liable to go back before me.

Lymon: They work you too hard down there. All that weeding and hoeing and chopping down trees. I didn't like all that.

Wining Boy: You ain't got to like your job on Parchman. Hey, tell him, Doaker, the only one got to like his job is the waterboy.

Doaker: If he don't like his job he need to set that bucket down.

Boy Willie: That's what they told Lymon. They had Lymon on water and everybody got mad at him cause he was lazy.

Lymon: That water was heavy.

Boy Willie: They had Lymon down there singing *(sings):*

> O Lord Berta Berta O Lord gal oh-ah
> O Lord Berta Berta O Lord gal well

Lymon and Wining Boy join in.

> Go 'head marry don't you wait on me oh-ah
> Go 'head marry don't you wait on me well
> Might not want you when I go free oh-ah
> Might not want you when I go free well

Boy Willie: Come on, Doaker. Doaker know this one.

As Doaker joins in the men stamp and clap to keep time. They sing in harmony with great fervor and style.

> O Lord Berta Berta O Lord gal oh-ah
> O Lord Berta Berta O Lord gal well
>
> Raise them up higher, let them drop on down oh-ah
> Raise them up higher, let them drop on down well
> Don't know the difference when the sun go down oh-ah
> Don't know the difference when the sun go down well
>
> Berta in Meridan and she living at ease oh-ah
> Berta in Meridan and she living at ease well
> I'm on old Parchman, got to work or leave oh-ah
> I'm on old Parchman, got to work or leave well
>
> O Alberta, Berta, O Lord gal oh-ah
> O Alberta, Berta, O Lord gal well
>
> When you marry, don't marry no farming man oh-ah
> When you marry, don't marry no farming man well
> Everyday Monday, hoe handle in your hand oh-ah
> Everyday Monday, hoe handle in your hand well
>
> When you marry, marry a railroad man, oh-ah
> When you marry, marry a railroad man, well
> Everyday Sunday, dollar in your hand oh-ah
> Everyday Sunday, dollar in your hand well
>
> O Alberta, Berta, O Lord gal oh-ah
> O Alberta, Berta, O Lord gal well

Boy Willie: Doaker like that part. He like that railroad part.

Lymon: Doaker sound like Tangleye. He can't sing a lick.

Boy Willie: Hey, Doaker, they still talk about you down on Parchman. They ask me, "You Doaker Boy's nephew?" I say, "Yeah, me and him is family." They treated me alright soon as I told them that. Say, "Yeah, he my uncle."

Doaker: I don't never want to see none of them niggers no more.

Boy Willie: I don't want to see them either. Hey, Wining Boy, come on play some piano. You a piano player, play some piano. Lymon wanna hear you.

Wining Boy: I give that piano up. That was the best thing that ever happened to me, getting rid of that piano. That piano got so big and I'm carrying it around on my back. I don't wish that on nobody. See, you think it's all fun being a recording star. Got to carrying that piano around and man did I get slow. Got just like molasses. The world just slipping by me and I'm walking around with that piano. Alright. Now, there ain't but so many places you can go. Only so many road wide enough for you and that piano. And that piano get heavier and heavier. Go to a place and they find out you play piano, the first thing they want to do is give you a drink, find you a piano, and sit you right down. And that's where you gonna be for the next eight hours. They ain't gonna let you get up! Now, the first three or four years of that is fun. You can't get enough whiskey and you can't get enough women and you don't never get tired of playing that piano. But that only last so long. You look up one day and you hate the whiskey, and you hate the women, and you hate the piano. But that's all you got. You can't do nothing else. All you know how to do is play that piano. Now who am I? Am I me? Or am I the piano player? Sometime it seem like the only thing to do is shoot the piano player cause he the cause of all the trouble I'm having.

Doaker: What you gonna do when your troubles get like mine?

Lymon: If I knew how to play it, I'd play it. That's a nice piano.

Boy Willie: Whoever playing better play quick. Sutter's brother say he waiting on me. I sell them watermelons. Get Berniece to sell that piano. Put them two parts with the part I done saved . . .

Wining Boy: Berniece ain't gonna sell that piano. I don't see why you don't know that.

Boy Willie: What she gonna do with it? She ain't doing nothing but letting it sit up there and rot. That piano ain't doing nobody no good.

Lymon: That's a nice piano. If I had it I'd sell it. Unless I knew how to play like Wining Boy. You can get a nice price for that piano.

Doaker: Now I'm gonna tell you something, Lymon don't know this . . . but I'm gonna tell you why me and Wining Boy say Berniece ain't gonna sell that piano.

Boy Willie: She ain't got to sell it! I'm gonna sell it! Berniece ain't got no more rights to that piano than I do.

Doaker: I'm talking to the man . . . let me talk to the man. See, now . . . to understand why we say that . . . to understand about the piano . . . you got to go back to slavery time. See, our family was owned by a fellow named Robert Sutter. That was Sutter's grandfather. Alright. The piano was owned by a fellow named Joel Nolander. He was one of the Nolander brothers from down in Georgia. It was coming up on Sutter's wedding anniversary and he was looking to buy his wife . . . Miss Ophelia was her name . . . he was looking to buy her an anniversary present. Only thing with him . . . he ain't had no money. But he had some niggers. So he asked Mr. Nolander to see if maybe he could trade off some of his niggers for that piano. Told him he would give him one and a half niggers for it. That's the way he told him. Say he could have one full grown and one half grown. Mr. Nolander agreed only he say he had to pick them. He didn't want Sutter to give him just any old nigger. He say he wanted to have the pick of the litter. So Sutter lined up his niggers and Mr. Nolander looked them over and out of the whole bunch he picked my grandmother . . . her name was Berniece . . . same like Berniece . . . and he picked my daddy when he wasn't nothing but a little boy nine years old. They made the trade off and Miss Ophelia was so happy with that piano that it got to be just about all she would do was play on that piano.

Wining Boy: Just get up in the morning, get all dressed up and sit down and play on that piano.

Doaker: Alright. Time go along. Time go along. Miss Ophelia got to missing my grandmother . . . the way she would cook and clean the house and talk to her and what not. And she missed having my daddy around the house to fetch things for her. So she asked to see if maybe she could trade back that piano and get her niggers back. Mr. Nolander said no. Said a deal was a deal. Him and Sutter had a big falling out about it and Miss Ophelia took sick to the bed. Wouldn't get out of bed in the morning. She just lay there. The doctor said she was wasting away.

Wining Boy: That's when Sutter called our granddaddy up to the house.

Doaker: Now, our granddaddy's name was Boy Willie. That's who Boy Willie's named after . . . only they called him Willie Boy. Now, he was a worker of wood. He could make you anything you wanted out of wood. He'd make you a desk. A table. A lamp. Anything you wanted. Them white fellows around there used to come up to Mr. Sutter and get him to make all kinds of things for them. Then they'd pay Mr. Sutter a nice price. See, everything my granddaddy made Mr. Sutter owned cause he owned him. That's why when Mr. Nolander offered to buy him to keep the family together Mr. Sutter wouldn't sell him. Told Mr. Nolander he didn't have enough money to buy him. Now . . . am I telling it right, Wining Boy?

Wining Boy: You telling it.

Doaker: Sutter called him up to the house and told him to carve my grandmother and my daddy's picture on the piano for Miss Ophelia. And he took and carved this . . . *(Doaker crosses over to the piano.)* See that right there? That's my grandmother, Berniece. She looked just like that. And he put a picture of my daddy when he wasn't nothing but a little boy the way he remembered him. He made them up out of his memory. Only thing . . . he didn't stop there. He carved all this. He got a picture of his mama . . . Mama Esther . . . and his daddy, Boy Charles.

Wining Boy: That was the first Boy Charles.

Doaker: Then he put on the side here all kinds of things. See that? That's when him and Mama Berniece got married. They called it jumping the broom. That's how you got married in them days. Then he got here when my daddy was born . . . and here he got Mama Esther's funeral . . . and down here he got Mr. Nolander taking Mama Berniece and my daddy away down to his place in Georgia. He got all kinds of things what happened with our family. When Mr. Sutter seen the piano with all them carvings on it he got mad. He didn't ask for all that. But see . . . there wasn't nothing he could do about it. When Miss Ophelia seen it . . . she got excited. Now she had her piano and her niggers too. She took back to playing it and played on it right up till the day she died. Alright . . . now see, our brother Boy Charles . . . that's Berniece and Boy Willie's daddy . . . he was the oldest of us three boys. He's dead now. But he would have been fifty-seven if he had lived. He died in 1911 when he was thirty-one years old. Boy Charles used to talk about that piano all the time. He never could get it off his mind. Two or three months go by and he be talking about it again. He be talking about taking it out of Sutter's house. Say it was the story of our whole family and as long as Sutter had it . . . he had us. Say we was still in slavery. Me and Wining Boy tried to talk him out of it but it wouldn't do any good. Soon as he quiet down about it he'd start up again. We seen where he wasn't gonna get it off his mind . . . so, on the Fourth of July, 1911 . . . when Sutter was at the picnic what the county give every year . . . me and Wining Boy went on down there with him and took the piano out of Sutter's house. We put it on a wagon and me and Wining Boy carried it over into the next county with Mama Ola's people. Boy Charles decided to stay around there and wait until Sutter got home to make it look like business as usual.

Now, I don't know what happened when Sutter came home and found the piano gone. But somebody went up to Boy Charles's house and set it on fire. But he wasn't in there. He must have seen them coming cause he went down and caught the 3:57 Yellow Dog. He didn't know they was gonna come down and stop the train. Stopped the train and found Boy Charles in the boxcar with four of them hobos. Must have got mad when they couldn't find the piano cause they set the boxcar afire and killed everybody. Now, nobody know who done that. Some people say it was Sutter cause it was his piano. Some people say it was Sheriff Carter. Some people say it was Robert Smith and Ed Saunders. But don't nobody know for sure. It was about two months after that that Ed Saunders fell down his well. Just upped and fell down his well for no reason. People say it was the ghost of them who burned up in the boxcar that pushed him in his well. They started calling them the Ghosts of the Yellow Dog. Now, that's how all that got started and that why we say Berniece ain't gonna sell that piano. Cause her daddy died over it.

Boy Willie: All that's in the past. If my daddy had seen where he could have traded that piano in for some land of his own, it wouldn't be sitting up here now. He spent his whole life farming on somebody else's land. I ain't gonna do that. See, he couldn't do no better. When he come along he ain't had nothing he could build on. His daddy ain't had nothing to give him. The only thing my daddy had to give me was that piano. And he died over giving me that. I ain't gonna let it sit up there and rot without trying to do something with it. If Berniece can't see that, then I'm gonna go ahead and sell my half. And you and Wining Boy know I'm right.

Doaker: Ain't nobody said nothing about who's right and who's wrong. I was just telling the man about the piano. I was telling him why we say Berniece ain't gonna sell it.

Lymon: Yeah, I can see why you say that now. I told Boy Willie he ought to stay up here with me.

Boy Willie: You stay! I'm going back! That's what I'm gonna do with my life! Why I got to come up here and learn to do something I don't know how to do when I already know how to farm? You stay up here and make your own way if that's what you want to do. I'm going back and live my life the way I want to live it.

Wining Boy gets up and crosses to the piano.

Wining Boy: Let's see what we got here. I ain't played on this thing for a while.

Doaker: You can stop telling that. You was playing on it the last time you was through here. We couldn't get you off of it. Go on and play something.

Wining Boy sits down at the piano and plays and sings. The song is one which has put many dimes and quarters in his pocket, long ago, in dimly remembered towns and way stations. He plays badly, without hesitation, and sings in a forceful voice.

Wining Boy (singing):

    I am a rambling gambling man
    I gambled in many towns
    I rambled this wide world over
    I rambled this world around
    I had my ups and downs in life
    And bitter times I saw
    But I never knew what misery was
    Till I lit on old Arkansas.

    I started out one morning
    to meet that early train
    He said, "You better work for me
    I have some land to drain.
    I'll give you fifty cents a day,
    Your washing, board and all
    And you shall be a different man
    In the state of Arkansas."

    I worked six months for the rascal
    Joe Herrin was his name
    He fed me old corn dodgers
    They was hard as any rock
    My tooth is all got loosened
    And my knees begin to knock
    That was the kind of hash I got
    In the state of Arkansas.

    Traveling man
    I've traveled all around this world
    Traveling man
    I've traveled from land to land
    Traveling man
    I've traveled all around this world
    Well it ain't no use
    writing no news
    I'm a traveling man.

The door opens and Berniece enters with Maretha.

Berniece: Is that . . . Lord, I know that ain't Wining Boy sitting there.

Wining Boy: Hey, Berniece.

Berniece: You all had this planned. You and Boy Willie had this planned.

Wining Boy: I didn't know he was gonna be here. I'm on my way down home. I stopped by to see you and Doaker first.

Doaker: I told the nigger he left out of here with that sack of money, we thought we might never see him again. Boy Willie say he wasn't gonna see him till he got broke. I looked up and seen him sitting on the doorstep asking for two dollars. Look at him laughing. He know it's the truth.

Berniece: Boy Willie, I didn't see that truck out there. I thought you was out selling watermelons.

Boy Willie: We done sold them all. Sold the truck too.

Berniece: I don't want to go through none of your stuff. I done told you to go back where you belong.

Boy Willie: I was just teasing you, woman. You can't take no teasing?

Berniece: Wining Boy, when you get here?

Wining Boy: A little while ago. I took the train from Kansas City.

Berniece: Let me go upstairs and then I'll cook you something to eat.

Boy Willie: You ain't cooked me nothing when I come.

Berniece: Boy Willie, go on and leave me alone. Come on, Maretha, get up here and change your clothes before you get them dirty.

Berniece exits up the stairs, followed by Maretha.

Wining Boy: Maretha sure getting big, ain't she, Doaker. And just as pretty as she want to be. I didn't know Crawley had it in him.

Boy Willie crosses to the piano.

Boy Willie: Hey, Lymon . . . get up on the other side of this piano and let me see something.

Wining Boy: Boy Willie, what is you doing?

Boy Willie: I'm seeing how heavy this piano is. Get up over there, Lymon.

Wining Boy: Go on and leave that piano alone. You ain't taking that piano out of here and selling it.

Boy Willie: Just as soon as I get them watermelons out that truck.

Wining Boy: Well, I got something to say about that.

Boy Willie: This my daddy's piano.

Wining Boy: He ain't took it by himself. Me and Doaker helped him.

Boy Willie: He died by himself. Where was you and Doaker at then? Don't come telling me nothing about this piano. This is me and Berniece's piano. Am I right, Doaker?

Doaker: Yeah, you right.

Boy Willie: Let's see if we can lift it up, Lymon. Get a good grip on it and pick it up on your end. Ready? Lift!

As they start to move the piano, the sound of Sutter's Ghost is heard. Doaker is the only one to hear it. With difficulty they move the piano a little bit so it is out of place.

Boy Willie: What do you think?

Lymon: It's heavy . . . but you can move it. Only it ain't gonna be easy.

Boy Willie: It wasn't that heavy to me. Okay, let's put it back.

The sound of Sutter's Ghost is heard again. They all hear it as Berniece enters on the stairs.

Berniece: Boy Willie . . . you gonna play around with me one too many times. And then God's gonna bless you and West is gonna dress you. Now set that piano back over there. I done told you a hundred times I ain't selling that piano.

Boy Willie: I'm trying to get me some land, woman. I need that piano to get me some money so I can buy Sutter's land.

Berniece: Money can't buy what that piano cost. You can't sell your soul for money. It won't go with the buyer. It'll shrivel and shrink to know that you ain't taken on to it. But it won't go with the buyer.

Boy Willie: I ain't talking about all that, woman. I ain't talking about selling my soul. I'm talking about trading that piece of wood for some land. Get something under your feet. Land the only thing God ain't making no more of. You can always get you another piano. I'm talking about some land. What you get something out the ground from. That's what I'm talking about. You can't do nothing with that piano but sit up there and look at it.

Berniece: That's just what I'm gonna do. Wining Boy, you want me to fry you some pork chops?

Boy Willie: Now, I'm gonna tell you the way I see it. The only thing that makes that piano worth something is them carvings Papa Willie Boy put on there. That's what make it worth something. That was my great-granddaddy. Papa Boy Charles brought that piano into the house. Now, I'm supposed to build on what they left me. You can't do nothing with that piano sitting up here in the house. That's just like if I let them watermelons sit out there and rot. I'd be a fool. Alright now, if you say to me, Boy Willie, I'm using that piano. I give out lessons on it and that help me make my rent or whatever. Then that be something else. I'd have to go on and say, well, Berniece using that piano. She building on it. Let her go on and use it. I got to find another way to get Sutter's land. But Doaker say you ain't touched that piano the whole time it's been up here. So why you wanna stand in my way? See, you just looking at the sentimental value. See, that's good. That's alright. I take my hat off whenever somebody say my daddy's name. But I ain't gonna be no fool about no sentimental value. You can sit up here and look at the piano for the next hundred years and it's just gonna be a piano. You can't make more than that. Now I want to get Sutter's land with that piano. I get Sutter's land and I can go down and cash in the crop and get my seed. As long as I got the land and the seed then I'm alright. I can always get me a little something else. Cause that land give back to you. I can make me another crop and cash that in. I still got the land and the seed. But that piano don't put out nothing else. You ain't got nothing working for you. Now, the kind of man my daddy was he would have understood that. I'm sorry you can't see it that way. But that's why I'm gonna take that piano out of here and sell it.

Berniece: You ain't taking that piano out of my house. *(She crosses to the piano.)* Look at this piano. Look at it. Mama Ola polished this piano with her tears for seventeen years. For seventeen years she rubbed on it till her hands bled. Then she rubbed the blood in . . . mixed it up with the rest of the blood on it. Every day that God breathed life into her body she rubbed and cleaned and polished and prayed over it. "Play something for me, Berniece. Play something for me, Berniece." Every day. "I cleaned it up for you, play something for me, Berniece." You always talking about your daddy but you ain't never stopped to look at what his foolishness cost your mama. Seventeen years' worth of cold nights and an empty bed. For what? For a piano? For a piece of wood? To get even with somebody? I look at you and you're all the same. You, Papa Boy Charles, Wining Boy, Doaker, Crawley . . . you're all alike. All this thieving and killing and thieving and killing. And what it ever lead to? More killing and more thieving. I ain't never seen it come to nothing. People getting burned up. People getting shot. People falling down their wells. It don't never stop.

Doaker: Come on now, Berniece, ain't no need in getting upset.

Boy Willie: I done a little bit of stealing here and there, but I ain't never killed nobody. I can't be speaking for nobody else. You all got to speak for yourself, but I ain't never killed nobody.

Berniece: You killed Crawley just as sure as if you pulled the trigger.

Boy Willie: See, that's ignorant. That's downright foolish for you to say something like that. You ain't doing nothing but showing your ignorance. If the nigger was here I'd whup his ass for getting me and Lymon shot at.

Berniece: Crawley ain't knew about the wood.

Boy Willie: We told the man about the wood. Ask Lymon. He knew all about the wood. He seen we was sneaking it. Why else we gonna be out there at night? Don't come telling me Crawley ain't knew about the wood. Them fellows come up on us and Crawley tried to bully them. Me and Lymon seen the sheriff with them and give in. Wasn't no sense in getting killed over fifty dollars' worth of wood.

Berniece: Crawley ain't knew you stole that wood.

Boy Willie: We ain't stole no wood. Me and Lymon was hauling wood for Jim Miller and keeping us a little bit on the side. We dumped our little bit down there by the creek till we had enough to make a load. Some fellows seen us and we figured we better get it before they did. We come up there and got Crawley to help us load it. Figured we'd cut him in. Crawley trying to keep the wolf from his door . . . we was trying to help him.

Lymon: Me and Boy Willie told him about the wood. We told him some fellows might be trying to beat us to it. He say let me go back and get my thirty-eight. That's what caused all the trouble.

Boy Willie: If Crawley ain't had the gun he'd be alive today.

Lymon: We had it about half loaded when they come up on us. We seen the sheriff with them and we tried to get away. We ducked around near the bend in the creek . . . but they was down there too. Boy Willie say let's give in. But Crawley pulled out his gun and started shooting. That's when they started shooting back.

Berniece: All I know is Crawley would be alive if you hadn't come up there and got him.

Boy Willie: I ain't had nothing to do with Crawley getting killed. That was his own fault.

Berniece: Crawley's dead and in the ground and you still walking around here eating. That's all I know. He went off to load some wood with you and ain't never come back.

Boy Willie: I told you, woman . . . I ain't had nothing to do with . . .

Berniece: He ain't here, is he? He ain't here! *(Berniece hits Boy Willie.)* I said he ain't here. Is he? *(Berniece continues to hit Boy Willie, who doesn't move to defend himself, other than back up and turning his head so that most of the blows fall on his chest and arms.)*

Doaker (grabbing Berniece): Come on, Berniece . . . let it go, it ain't his fault.

Berniece: He ain't here, is he? Is he?

Boy Willie: I told you I ain't responsible for Crawley.

Berniece: He ain't here.

Boy Willie: Come on now, Berniece . . . don't do this now. Doaker get her. I ain't had nothing to do with Crawley . . .

Berniece: You come up there and got him!

Boy Willie: I done told you now. Doaker, get her. I ain't playing.
Doaker: Come on, Berniece.

> *Maretha is heard screaming upstairs. It is a scream of stark terror.*

Maretha: Mama! . . . Mama!

> *The lights go down to black. End of Act I.*

ACT II

SCENE I

> *The lights come up on the kitchen. It is the following morning. Doaker is ironing the pants to his uniform. He has a pot cooking on the stove at the same time. He is singing a song. The song provides him with the rhythm for his work and he moves about the kitchen with the ease born of many years as a railroad cook.*

Doaker:
Gonna leave Jackson Mississippi
and go to Memphis
and double back to Jackson
Come on down to Hattiesburg
Change cars on the Y.D.
coming through the territory to
Meridian
and Meridian to Greenville
and Greenville to Memphis
I'm on my way and I know where

Change cars on the Katy
Leaving Jackson
and going through Clarksdale
Hello Winona!
Courtland!
Bateville!
Como!
Senitobia!
Lewisberg!
Sunflower!
Glendora!
Sharkey!
And double back to Jackson
Hello Greenwood
I'm on my way to Memphis
Clarksdale
Moorhead
Indianola
Can a highball pass through?
Highball on through sir
Grand Carson!

Thirty First Street Depot
Fourth Street Depot
Memphis!

Wining Boy enters carrying a suit of clothes.

Doaker: I thought you took that suit to the pawnshop.

Wining Boy: I went down there and the man tell me the suit is too old. Look at this suit. This is one hundred percent silk! How a silk suit gonna get too old? I know what it was he just didn't want to give me five dollars for it. Best he wanna give me is three dollars. I figure a silk suit is worth five dollars all over the world. I wasn't gonna part with it for no three dollars so I brought it back.

Doaker: They got another pawnshop up on Wylie.

Wining Boy: I carried it up there. He say he don't take no clothes. Only thing he take is guns and radios. Maybe a guitar or two. Where's Berniece?

Doaker: Berniece still at work. Boy Willie went down there to meet Lymon this morning. I guess they got that truck fixed, they been out there all day and ain't come back yet. Maretha scared to sleep up there now. Berniece don't know, but I seen Sutter before she did.

Wining Boy: Say what?

Doaker: About three weeks ago. I had just come back from down there. Sutter couldn't have been dead more than three days. He was sitting over there at the piano. I come out to go to work . . . and he was sitting right there. Had his hand on top of his head just like Berniece said. I believe he broke his neck when he fell in the well. I kept quiet about it. I didn't see no reason to upset Berniece.

Wining Boy: Did he say anything? Did he say he was looking for Boy Willie?

Doaker: He was just sitting there. He ain't said nothing. I went on out the door and left him sitting there. I figure as long as he was on the other side of the room everything be alright. I don't know what I would have done if he had started walking toward me.

Wining Boy: Berniece say he was calling Boy Willie's name.

Doaker: I ain't heard him say nothing. He was just sitting there when I seen him. But I don't believe Boy Willie pushed him in the well. Sutter here cause of that piano. I heard him playing on it one time. I thought it was Berniece but then she don't play that kind of music. I come out here and ain't seen nobody, but them piano keys moving a mile a minute. Berniece need to go on and get rid of it. It ain't done nothing but cause trouble.

Wining Boy: I agree with Berniece. Boy Charles ain't took it to give it back. He took it cause he figure he had more right to it than Sutter did. If Sutter can't understand that . . . then that's just the way that go. Sutter dead and in the ground . . . don't care where his ghost is. He can hover around and play on the piano all he want. I want to see him carry it out the house. That's what I want to see. What time Berniece get home? I don't see how I let her get away from me this morning.

Doaker: You up there sleep. Berniece leave out of here early in the morning. She out there in Squirrel Hill cleaning house for some bigshot down there at the steel mill. They don't like you to come late. You come late they won't give you your carfare. What kind of business you got with Berniece?

Wining Boy: My business. I ain't asked you what kind of business you got.

Doaker: Berniece ain't got no money. If that's why you was trying to catch her. She having a hard enough time trying to get by as it is. If she go ahead and marry Avery . . . he working every day . . . she go ahead and marry him they could do alright for themselves. But as it stands she ain't got no money.

Wining Boy: Well, let me have five dollars.

Doaker: I just give you a dollar before you left out of here. You ain't gonna take my five dollars out there and gamble and drink it up.

Wining Boy: Aw, nigger, give me five dollars. I'll give it back to you.

Doaker: You wasn't looking to give me five dollars when you had that sack of money. You wasn't looking to throw nothing my way. Now you wanna come in here and borrow five dollars. If you going back with Boy Willie you need to be trying to figure out how you gonna get train fare.

Wining Boy: That's why I need the five dollars. If I had five dollars I could get me some money. *(Doaker goes into his pocket.)* Make it seven.

Doaker: You take this five dollars . . . and you bring my money back here too.

Boy Willie and Lymon enter. They are happy and excited. They have money in all of their pockets and are anxious to count it.

Doaker: How'd you do out there?

Boy Willie: They was lining up for them.

Lymon: Me and Boy Willie couldn't sell them fast enough. Time we got one sold we'd sell another.

Boy Willie: I seen what was happening and told Lymon to up the price on them.

Lymon: Boy Willie say charge them a quarter more. They didn't care. A couple of people give me a dollar and told me to keep the change.

Boy Willie: One fellow bought five. I say now what he gonna do with five watermelons? He can't eat them all. I sold him the five and asked him did he want to buy five more.

Lymon: I ain't never seen anybody snatch a dollar fast as Boy Willie.

Boy Willie: One lady asked me say, "Is they sweet?" I told her say, "Lady, where we grow these watermelons we put sugar in the ground." You know, she believed me. Talking about she had never heard of that before. Lymon was laughing his head off. I told her, "Oh, yeah, we put the sugar right in the ground with the seed." She say, "Well, give me another one." Them white folks is something else . . . ain't they, Lymon?

Lymon: Soon as you holler watermelons they come right out their door. Then they go and get their neighbors. Look like they having a contest to see who can buy the most.

Wining Boy: I got something for Lymon.

Wining Boy goes to get his suit. Boy Willie and Lymon continue to count their money.

Boy Willie: I know you got more than that. You ain't sold all them watermelons for that little bit of money.

Lymon: I'm still looking. That ain't all you got either. Where's all them quarters?

Boy Willie: You let me worry about the quarters. Just put the money on the table.

Wining Boy (entering with his suit): Look here, Lymon . . . see this? Look at his eyes getting big. He ain't never seen a suit like this. This is one hundred percent silk. Go ahead . . . put it on. See if it fit you. *(Lymon tries the suit coat on.)* Look at that. Feel it. That's one hundred percent genuine silk. I got that in Chicago. You can't get clothes like that nowhere but New York and Chicago. You can't get clothes like that in Pittsburgh. These folks in Pittsburgh ain't never seen clothes like that.

Lymon: This is nice, feel real nice and smooth.

Wining Boy: That's a fifty-five-dollar suit. That's the kind of suit the bigshots wear. You need a pistol and a pocketful of money to wear that suit. I'll let you have it for three dollars. The women will fall out of their windows they see you in a suit like that. Give me three dollars and go on and wear it down the street and get you a woman.

Boy Willie: That looks nice, Lymon. Put the pants on. Let me see it with the pants.

> *Lymon begins to try on the pants.*

Wining Boy: Look at that . . . see how it fits you? Give me three dollars and go on and take it. Look at that, Doaker . . . don't he look nice?

Doaker: Yeah . . . that's a nice suit.

Wining Boy: Got a shirt to go with it. Cost you an extra dollar. Four dollars you got the whole deal.

Lymon: How this look, Boy Willie?

Boy Willie: That look nice . . . if you like that kind of thing. I don't like them dress-up kind of clothes. If you like it, look real nice.

Wining Boy: That's the kind of suit you need for up here in the North.

Lymon: Four dollars for everything? The suit and the shirt?

Wining Boy: That's cheap. I should be charging you twenty dollars. I give you a break cause you a homeboy. That's the only way I let you have it for four dollars.

Lymon (going into his pocket): Okay . . . here go the four dollars.

Wining Boy: You got some shoes? What size you wear?

Lymon: Size nine.

Wining Boy: That's what size I got! Size nine. I let you have them for three dollars.

Lymon: Where they at? Let me see them.

Wining Boy: They real nice shoes, too. Got a nice tip to them. Got pointy toe just like you want.

> *Wining Boy goes to get his shoes.*

Lymon: Come on, Boy Willie, let's go out tonight. I wanna see what it looks like up here. Maybe we go to a picture show. Hey, Doaker, they got picture shows up here?

Doaker: The Rhumba Theater. Right down there on Fullerton Street. Can't miss it. Got the speakers outside on the sidewalk. You can hear it a block away. Boy Willie know where it's at.

> *Doaker exits into his room.*

Lymon: Let's go to the picture show, Boy Willie. Let's go find some women.

Boy Willie: Hey, Lymon, how many of them watermelons would you say we got left? We got just under a half a load . . . right?

Lymon: About that much. Maybe a little more.

Boy Willie: You think that piano will fit up in there?

Lymon: If we stack them watermelons you can sit it up in the front there.

Boy Willie: I'm gonna call that man tomorrow.

Wining Boy (returns with his shoes): Here you go . . . size nine. Put them on. Cost
    you three dollars. That's a Florsheim shoe. That's the kind Staggerlee
    wore.

Lymon (trying on the shoes): You sure these size nine?

Wining Boy: You can look at my feet and see we wear the same size. Man, you
    put on that suit and them shoes and you got something there. You ready
    for whatever's out there. But is they ready for you? With them shoes on
    you be the King of the Walk. Have everybody stop to look at your shoes.
    Wishing they had a pair. I'll give you a break. Go on and take them for two
    dollars.

Lymon pays Wining Boy two dollars.

Lymon: Come on, Boy Willie . . . let's go find some women. I'm gonna go up-
    stairs and get ready. I'll be ready to go in a minute. Ain't you gonna get
    dressed?

Boy Willie: I'm gonna wear what I got on. I ain't dressing up for these city nig-
    gers.

Lymon exits up the stairs.

That's all Lymon think about is women.

Wining Boy: His daddy was the same way. I used to run around with him. I
    know his mama too. Two strokes back and I would have been his daddy!
    His daddy's dead now . . . but I got the nigger out of jail one time. They was
    fixing to name him Daniel and walk him through the Lion's Den. He got in
    a tussle with one of them white fellows and the sheriff lit on him like white
    on rice. That's how the whole thing come about between me and Lymon's
    mama. She knew me and his daddy used to run together and he got in jail
    and she went down there and took the sheriff a hundred dollars. Don't get
    me to lying about where she got it from. I don't know. The sheriff *looked at
    that hundred dollars and turned his nose up.* Told her, say, "That ain't gonna do
    him no good. You got to put up another hundred on top of that." She
    come up *there and got me where I was playing at this saloon* . . . said she had all
    but fifty dollars and asked me if I could help. Now the way I figured it . . .
    without that fifty dollars the sheriff was gonna turn him over to Parch-
    man. The sheriff turn him over to Parchman it be three years before any-
    body see him again. Now I'm gonna say it right . . . I will give anybody fifty
    dollars to keep them out of jail for three years. I give her the fifty dollars
    and she told me to come over to the house. I ain't asked her. I figure if she
    was nice enough to invite me I ought to go. I ain't had to say a word. She in-
    vited me over just as nice. Say, "Why don't you come over to the house?"
    She ain't had to say nothing else. Them words rolled off her tongue just as
    nice. I went on down there and sat about three hours. Started to leave and
    changed my mind. She grabbed hold to me and say, "Baby, it's all night
    long." That was one of the shortest nights I have ever spent on this earth! I
    could have used another eight hours. Lymon's daddy didn't even say noth-
    ing to me when he got out. He just looked at me funny. He had a good

notion something had happened between me an' her. L. D. Jackson. That was one bad-luck nigger. Got killed at some dance. Fellow walked in and shot him thinking he was somebody else.

Doaker enters from his room.

Hey, Doaker, you remember L. D. Jackson?

Doaker: That's Lymon's daddy. That was one bad-luck nigger.

Boy Willie: Look like you ready to railroad some.

Doaker: Yeah, I got to make that run.

Lymon enters from the stairs. He is dressed in his new suit and shoes, to which he has added a cheap straw hat.

Lymon: How I look?

Wining Boy: You look like a million dollars. Don't he look good, Doaker? Come on, let's play some cards. You wanna play some cards?

Boy Willie: We ain't gonna play no cards with you. Me and Lymon gonna find some women. Hey, Lymon don't play no cards with Wining Boy. He'll take all your money.

Wining Boy (to Lymon): You got a magic suit there. You can get you a woman easy with that suit . . . but you got to know the magic words. You know the magic words to get you a woman?

Lymon: I just talk to them to see if I like them and they like me.

Wining Boy: You just walk right up to them and say, "If you got the harbor I got the ship." If that don't work ask them if you can put them in your pocket. The first thing they gonna say is, "It's too small." That's when you look them dead in the eye and say, "Baby, ain't nothing small about me." If that don't work then you move on to another one. Am I telling him right, Doaker?

Doaker: That man don't need you to tell him nothing about no women. These women these days ain't gonna fall for that kind of stuff. You got to buy them a present. That's what they looking for these days.

Boy Willie: Come on, I'm ready. You ready, Lymon? Come on, let's go find some women.

Wining Boy: Here, let me walk out with you. I wanna see the women fall out their window when they see Lymon.

They all exit and the lights go down on the scene.

Scene II

The lights come up on the kitchen. It is late evening of the same day. Berniece has set a tub for her bath in the kitchen. She is heating up water on the stove. There is a knock at the door.

Berniece: Who is it?

Avery: It's me, Avery.

Berniece opens the door and lets him in.

Berniece: Avery, come on in. I was just fixing to take my bath.

Avery: Where Boy Willie? I see that truck out there almost empty. They done sold almost all them watermelons.

Berniece: They was gone when I come home. I don't know where they went off to. Boy Willie around here about to drive me crazy.

Avery: They sell them watermelons . . . he'll be gone soon.

Berniece: What Mr. Cohen say about letting you have the place?

Avery: He say he'll let me have it for thirty dollars a month. I talked him out of thirty-five and he say he'll let me have it for thirty.

Berniece: That's a nice spot next to Benny Diamond's store.

Avery: Berniece . . . I be at home and I get to thinking you up here an' I'm down there. I get to thinking how that look to have a preacher that ain't married. It makes for a better congregation if the preacher was settled down and married.

Berniece: Avery . . . not now. I was fixing to take my bath.

Avery: You know how I feel about you, Berniece. Now . . . I done got the place from Mr. Cohen. I get the money from the bank and I can fix it up real nice. They give me a ten cents a hour raise down there on the job . . . now Berniece, I ain't got much in the way of comforts. I got a hole in my pockets near about as far as money is concerned. I ain't never found no way through life to a woman I care about like I care about you. I need that. I need somebody on my bond side. I need a woman that fits in my hand.

Berniece: Avery, I ain't ready to get married now.

Avery: You too young a woman to close up, Berniece.

Berniece: I ain't said nothing about closing up. I got a lot of woman left in me.

Avery: Where's it at? When's the last time you looked at it?

Berniece (stunned by his remark): That's a nasty thing to say. And you call yourself a preacher.

Avery: Anytime I get anywhere near you . . . you push me away.

Berniece: I got enough on my hands with Maretha. I got enough people to love and take care of.

Avery: Who you got to love you? Can't nobody get close enough to you. Doaker can't half say nothing to you. You jump all over Boy Willie. Who you got to love you, Berniece?

Berniece: You trying to tell me a woman can't be nothing without a man. But you alright, huh? You can just walk out of here without me — without a woman — and still be a man. That's alright. Ain't nobody gonna ask you, "Avery, who you got to love you?" That's alright for you. But everybody gonna be worried about Berniece. "How Berniece gonna take care of herself? How she gonna raise that child without a man? Wonder what she do with herself. How she gonna live like that?" Everybody got all kinds of questions for Berniece. Everybody telling me I can't be a woman unless I got a man. Well, you tell me, Avery — you know — how much woman am I?

Avery: It wasn't me, Berniece. You can't blame me for nobody else. I'll own up to my own shortcomings. But you can't blame me for Crawley or nobody else.

Berniece: I ain't blaming nobody for nothing. I'm just stating the facts.

Avery: How long you gonna carry Crawley with you, Berniece? It's been over three years. At some point you got to let go and go on. Life's got all kinds of twists and turns. That don't mean you stop living. That don't mean you cut yourself off from life. You can't go through life carrying Crawley's ghost with you. Crawley's been dead three years. Three years, Berniece.

Berniece: I know how long Crawley's been dead. You ain't got to tell me that. I just ain't ready to get married right now.

Avery: What is you ready for, Berniece? You just gonna drift along from day to day. Life is more than making it from one day to another. You gonna look up one day and it's all gonna be past you. Life's gonna be gone out of your hands — there won't be enough to make nothing with. I'm standing here now, Berniece — but I don't know how much longer I'm gonna be standing here waiting on you.

Berniece: Avery, I told you . . . when you get your church we'll sit down and talk about this. I got too many other things to deal with right now. Boy Willie and the piano . . . and Sutter's ghost. I thought I might have been seeing things, but Maretha done seen Sutter's ghost, too.

Avery: When this happen, Berniece?

Berniece: Right after I came home yesterday. Me and Boy Willie was arguing about the piano and Sutter's ghost was standing at the top of the stairs. Maretha scared to sleep up there now. Maybe if you bless the house he'll go away.

Avery: I don't know, Berniece. I don't know if I should fool around with something like that.

Berniece: I can't have Maretha scared to go to sleep up there. Seem like if you bless the house he would go away.

Avery: You might have to be a special kind of preacher to do something like that.

Berniece: I keep telling myself when Boy Willie leave he'll go on and leave with him. I believe Boy Willie pushed him in the well.

Avery: That's been going on down there a long time. The Ghosts of the Yellow Dog been pushing people in their wells long before Boy Willie got grown.

Berniece: Somebody down there pushing them people in their wells. They ain't just upped and fell. Ain't no wind pushed nobody in their well.

Avery: Oh, I don't know. God works in mysterious ways.

Berniece: He ain't pushed nobody in their wells.

Avery: He caused it to happen. God is the Great Causer. He can do anything. He parted the Red Sea. He say I will smite my enemies. Reverend Thompson used to preach on the Ghosts of the Yellow Dog as the hand of God.

Berniece: I don't care who preached that. Somebody down there pushing them people in their wells. Somebody like Boy Willie. I can see him doing something like that. You ain't gonna tell me that Sutter just upped and fell in his well. I believe Boy Willie pushed him so he could get his land.

Avery: What Doaker say about Boy Willie selling the piano?

Berniece: Doaker don't want no part of that piano. He ain't never wanted no part of it. He blames himself for not staying behind with Papa Boy Charles. He washed his hands of that piano a long time ago. He didn't want me to bring it up here — but I wasn't gonna leave it down there.

Avery: Well, it seems to me somebody ought to be able to talk to Boy Willie.

Berniece: You can't talk to Boy Willie. He been that way all his life. Mama Ola had her hands full trying to talk to him. He don't listen to nobody. He just like my daddy. He get his mind fixed on something and can't nobody turn him from it.

Avery: You ought to start a choir at the church. Maybe if he seen you was doing something with it — if you told him you was gonna put it in my church — maybe he'd see it different. You ought to put it down in the church and start a choir. The Bible say "Make a joyful noise unto the Lord." Maybe if Boy Willie see you was doing something with it he'd see it different.

Berniece: I done told you I don't play on that piano. Ain't no need in you to keep talking this choir stuff. When my mama died I shut the top on that piano and I ain't never opened it since. I was only playing it for her. When my daddy died seem like all her life went into that piano. She used to have me playing on it . . . had Miss Eula come in and teach me . . . say when I played it she could hear my daddy talking to her. I used to think them pictures came alive and walked through the house. Sometime late at night I could hear my mama talking to them. I said that wasn't gonna happen to me. I don't play that piano cause I don't want to wake them spirits. They never be walking around in this house.

Avery: You got to put all that behind you, Berniece.

Berniece: I got Maretha playing on it. She don't know nothing about it. Let her go on and be a schoolteacher or something. She don't have to carry all of that with her. She got a chance I didn't have. I ain't gonna burden her with that piano.

Avery: You got to put all of that behind you, Berniece. That's the same thing like Crawley. Everybody got stones in their passway. You got to step over them or walk around them. You picking them up and carrying them with you. All you got to do is set them down by the side of the road. You ain't got to carry them with you. You can walk over there right now and play that piano. You can walk over there right now and God will walk over there with you. Right now you can set that sack of stones down by the side of the road and walk away from it. You don't have to carry it with you. You can do it right now. (*Avery crosses over to the piano and raises the lid.*) Come on, Berniece . . . set it down and walk away from it. Come on, play "Old Ship of Zion." Walk over here and claim it as an instrument of the Lord. You can walk over here right now and make it into a celebration.

Berniece moves toward the piano.

Berniece: Avery . . . I done told you I don't want to play that piano. Now or no other time.

Avery: The Bible say, "The Lord is my refuge . . . and my strength!" With the strength of God you can put the past behind you, Berniece. With the strength of God you can do anything! God got a bright tomorrow. God don't ask what you done . . . God ask what you gonna do. The strength of God can move mountains! God's got a bright tomorrow for you . . . all you got to do is walk over here and claim it.

Berniece: Avery, just go on and let me finish my bath. I'll see you tomorrow.

Avery: Okay, Berniece. I'm gonna go home. I'm gonna go home and read up on my Bible. And tomorrow . . . if the good Lord give me strength tomorrow . . . I'm gonna come by and bless the house . . . and show you the power of the Lord. (*Avery crosses to the door.*) It's gonna be alright, Berniece. God say he will soothe the troubled waters. I'll come by tomorrow and bless the house.

The lights go down to black.

Scene III

Several hours later. The house is dark. Berniece has retired for the night. Boy Willie enters the darkened house with Grace.

Boy Willie: Come on in. This my sister's house. My sister live here. Come on, I ain't gonna bite you.

Grace: Put some light on. I can't see.

Boy Willie: You don't need to see nothing, baby. This here is all you need to see. All you need to do is see me. If you can't see me you can feel me in the dark. How's that, sugar?

He attempts to kiss her.

Grace: Go on now . . . wait!

Boy Willie: Just give me one little old kiss.

Grace (pushing him away): Come on now. Where I'm gonna sleep at?

Boy Willie: We got to sleep out here on the couch. Come on, my sister don't mind. Lymon come back he just got to sleep on the floor. He run off with Dolly somewhere he better stay there. Come on, sugar.

Grace: Wait now . . . you ain't told me nothing about no couch. I thought you had a bed. Both of us can't sleep on that little old couch.

Boy Willie: It don't make no difference. We can sleep on the floor. Let Lymon sleep on the couch.

Grace: You ain't told me nothing about no couch.

Boy Willie: What difference it make? You just wanna be with me.

Grace: I don't wanna be with you on no couch. Ain't you got no bed?

Boy Willie: You don't need no bed, woman. My granddaddy used to take women on the backs of horses. What you need a bed for? You just want to be with me.

Grace: You sure is country. I didn't know you was this country.

Boy Willie: There's a lot of things you don't know about me. Come on, let me show you what this country boy can do.

Grace: Let's go to my place. I got a room with a bed if Leroy don't come back there.

Boy Willie: Who's Leroy? You ain't said nothing about no Leroy.

Grace: He used to be my man. He ain't coming back. He gone off with some other gal.

Boy Willie: You let him have your key?

Grace: He ain't coming back.

Boy Willie: Did you let him have your key?

Grace: He got a key but he ain't coming back. He took off with some other gal.

Boy Willie: I don't wanna go nowhere he might come. Let's stay here. Come on, sugar. *(He pulls her over to the couch.)* Let me heist your hood and check your oil. See if your battery needs charging.

He pulls her to him. They kiss and tug at each other's clothing. In their anxiety they knock over a lamp.

Berniece: Who's that . . . Wining Boy?

Boy Willie: It's me . . . Boy Willie. Go on back to sleep. Everything's alright. *(To Grace.)* That's my sister. Everything's alright, Berniece. Go on back to sleep.

Berniece: What you doing down there? What you done knocked over?

Boy Willie: It wasn't nothing. Everything's alright. Go on back to sleep. *(To Grace.)* That's my sister. We alright. She gone back to sleep.

They begin to kiss. Berniece enters from the stairs dressed in a nightgown. She cuts on the light.

Berniece: Boy Willie, what you doing down here?

Boy Willie: It was just that there lamp. It ain't broke. It's okay. Everything's alright. Go on back to bed.

Berniece: Boy Willie, I don't allow that in my house. You gonna have to take your company someplace else.

Boy Willie: It's alright. We ain't doing nothing. We just sitting here talking. This here is Grace. That's my sister Berniece.

Berniece: You know I don't allow that kind of stuff in my house.

Boy Willie: Allow what? We just sitting here talking.

Berniece: Well, your company gonna have to leave. Come back and talk in the morning.

Boy Willie: Go on back upstairs now.

Berniece: I got an eleven-year-old girl upstairs. I can't allow that around here.

Boy Willie: Ain't nobody said nothing about that. I told you we just talking.

Grace: Come on . . . let's go to my place. Ain't nobody got to tell me to leave but once.

Boy Willie: You ain't got to be like that, Berniece.

Berniece: I'm sorry, Miss. But he know I don't allow that in here.

Grace: You ain't got to tell me but once. I don't stay nowhere I ain't wanted.

Boy Willie: I don't know why you want to embarrass me in front of my company.

Grace: Come on, take me home.

Berniece: Go on, Boy Willie. Just go on with your company.

Boy Willie and Grace exit. Berniece puts the light on in the kitchen and puts on the teakettle. Presently there is a knock at the door. Berniece goes to answer it. Berniece opens the door. Lymon enters.

Lymon: How you doing, Berniece? I thought you'd be asleep. Boy Willie been back here?

Berniece: He just left out of here a minute ago.

Lymon: I went out to see a picture show and never got there. We always end up doing something else. I was with this woman she just wanted to drink up all my money. So I left her there and came back looking for Boy Willie.

Berniece: You just missed him. He just left out of here.

Lymon:. They got some nice-looking women in this city. I'm gonna like it up here real good. I like seeing them with their dresses on. Got them high heels. I like that. Make them look like they real precious. Boy Willie met a real nice one today. I wish I had met her before he did.

Berniece: He come by here with some woman a little while ago. I told him to go on and take all that out of my house.

Lymon: What she look like, the woman he was with? Was she a brown-skinned woman about this high? Nice and healthy? Got nice hips on her?

Berniece: She had on a red dress.

Lymon: That's her! That's Grace. She real nice. Laugh a lot. Lot of fun to be with. She don't be trying to put on. Some of these women act like they the Queen of Sheba. I don't like them. Grace ain't like that. She real nice with herself.

Berniece: I don't know what she was like. He come in here all drunk knocking over the lamp, and making all kind of noise. I told them to take that somewhere else. I can't really say what she was like.

Lymon: She real nice. I seen her before he did. I was trying not to act like I seen her. I wanted to look at her a while before I said something. She seen me when I come into the saloon. I tried to act like I didn't see her. Time I looked around Boy Willie was talking to her. She was talking to him kept looking at me. That's when her friend Dolly came. I asked her if she wanted to go to the picture show. She told me to buy her a drink while she thought about it. Next thing I knew she done had three drinks talking about she too tired to go. I bought her another drink, then I left. Boy Willie was gone and I thought he might have come back here. Doaker gone, huh? He say he had to make a trip.

Berniece: Yeah, he gone on his trip. This is when I can usually get some peace and quiet, Maretha asleep.

Lymon: She look just like you. Got them big eyes. I remember her when she was in diapers.

Berniece: Time just keep on. It go on with or without you. She going on twelve.

Lymon: She sure is pretty. I like kids.

Berniece: Boy Willie say you staying . . . what you gonna do up here in this big city? You thought about that?

Lymon: They never get me back down there. The sheriff looking for me. All because they gonna try and make me work for somebody when I don't want to. They gonna try and make me work for Stovall when he don't pay nothing. It ain't like that up here. Up here you more or less do what you want to. I figure I find me a job and try to get set up and then see what the year brings. I tried to do that two or three times down there . . . but it never would work out. I was always in the wrong place.

Berniece: This ain't a bad city once you get to know your way around.

Lymon: Up here is different. I'm gonna get me a job unloading boxcars or something. One fellow told me say he know a place. I'm gonna go over there with him next week. Me and Boy Willie finish selling them watermelons I'll have enough money to hold me for a while. But I'm gonna go over there and see what kind of jobs they have.

Berniece: You shouldn't have too much trouble finding a job. It's all in how you present yourself. See now, Boy Willie couldn't get no job up here. Somebody hire him they got a pack of trouble on their hands. Soon as they find that out they fire him. He don't want to do nothing unless he do it his way.

Lymon: I know. I told him let's go to the picture show first and see if there was any women down there. They might get tired of sitting at home and walk down to the picture show. He say he wanna look around first. We never did get down there. We tried a couple of places and then we went to this saloon where he met Grace. I tried to meet her before he did but he beat me to her. We left Wining Boy sitting down there running his mouth. He told me if I wear this suit I'd find me a woman. He was almost right.

Berniece: You don't need to be out there in them saloons. Ain't no telling what you liable to run into out there. This one liable to cut you as quick as that one shoot you. You don't need to be out there. You start out that fast life you can't keep it up. It makes you old quick. I don't know what them women out there be thinking about.

Lymon: Mostly they be lonely and looking for somebody to spend the night with them. Sometimes it matters who it is and sometimes it don't. I used to be the same way. Now it got to matter. That's why I'm here now. Dolly liable not to even recognize me if she sees me again. I don't like women like that. I like my women to be with me in a nice and easy way. That way we can both enjoy ourselves. The way I see it we the only two people like us in the world. We got to see how we fit together. A woman that don't want to take the time to do that I don't bother with. Used to. Used to bother with all of them. Then I woke up one time with this woman and I didn't know who she was. She was the prettiest woman I had ever seen in my life. I spent the whole night with her and didn't even know it. I had never taken the time to look at her. I guess she kinda knew I ain't never really looked at her. She must have known that cause she ain't wanted to see me no more. If she had wanted to see me I believe we might have got married. How come you ain't married? It seem like to me you would be married. I remember Avery from down home. I used to call him plain old Avery. Now he Reverend Avery. That's kinda funny about him becoming a preacher. I like when he told about how that come to him in a dream about them sheep people and them hobos. Nothing ever come to me in a dream like that. I just dream about women. Can't never seem to find the right one.

Berniece: She out there somewhere. You just got to get yourself ready to meet her. That's what I'm trying to do. Avery's alright. I ain't really got nobody in mind.

Lymon: I get me a job and a little place and get set up to where I can make a woman comfortable I might get married. Avery's nice. You ought to go ahead and get married. You be a preacher's wife you won't have to work. I hate living by myself. I didn't want to be no strain on my mama so I left home when I was about sixteen. Everything I tried seem like it just didn't work out. Now I'm trying this.

Berniece: You keep trying it'll work out for you.

Lymon: You ever go down there to the picture show?

Berniece: I don't go in for all that.

Lymon: Ain't nothing wrong with it. It ain't like gambling and sinning. I went to one down in Jackson once. It was fun.

Berniece: I just stay home most of the time. Take care of Maretha.

Lymon: It's getting kind of late. I don't know where Boy Willie went off to. He's liable not to come back. I'm gonna take off these shoes. My feet hurt. Was you in bed? I don't mean to be keeping you up.

Berniece: You ain't keeping me up. I couldn't sleep after that Boy Willie woke me up.

Lymon: You got on that nightgown. I likes women when they wear them fancy nightclothes and all. It makes their skin look real pretty.

Berniece: I got this at the five-and-ten-cents store. It ain't so fancy.

Lymon: I don't too often get to see a woman dressed like that. *(There is a long pause. Lymon takes off his suit coat.)* Well, I'm gonna sleep here on the couch. I'm supposed to sleep on the floor but I don't reckon Boy Willie's coming back tonight. Wining Boy sold me this suit. Told me it was a magic suit. I'm gonna put it on again tomorrow. Maybe it bring me a woman like he say. *(He goes into his coat pocket and takes out a small bottle of perfume.)* I almost forgot I had this. Some man sold me this for a dollar. Say it come from Paris. This is the same kind of perfume the Queen of France wear. That's what he told me. I don't know if it's true or not. I smelled it. It smelled good to me. Here . . . smell it see if you like it. I was gonna give it to Dolly. But I didn't like her too much.

Berniece (takes the bottle): It smells nice.

Lymon: I was gonna give it to Dolly if she had went to the picture with me. Go on, you take it.

Berniece: I can't take it. Here . . . go on you keep it. You'll find somebody to give it to.

Lymon: I wanna give it to you. Make you smell nice. *(He takes the bottle and puts perfume behind Berniece's ear.)* They tell me you supposed to put it right here behind your ear. Say if you put it there you smell nice all day. *(Berniece stiffens at his touch. Lymon bends down to smell her.)* There . . . you smell real good now. *(He kisses her neck.)* You smell real good for Lymon.

He kisses her again. Berniece returns the kiss, then breaks the embrace and crosses to the stairs. She turns and they look silently at each other. Lymon hands her the bottle of perfume. Berniece exits up the stairs. Lymon picks up his suit coat and strokes it lovingly with the full knowledge that it is indeed a magic suit. The lights go down on the scene.

SCENE IV

It is late the next morning. The lights come up on the parlor. Lymon is asleep on the sofa. Boy Willie enters the front door.

Boy Willie: Hey, Lymon! Lymon, come on get up.

Lymon: Leave me alone.

Boy Willie: Come on, get up, nigger! Wake up, Lymon.

Lymon: What you want?

Boy Willie: Come on, let's go. I done called the man about the piano.

Lymon: What piano?

Boy Willie (dumps Lymon on the floor): Come on, get up!

Lymon: Why you leave, I looked around and you was gone.

Boy Willie: I come back here with Grace, then I went looking for you. I figured you'd be with Dolly.

Lymon: She just want to drink and spend up your money. I come on back here looking for you to see if you wanted to go to the picture show.

Boy Willie: I been up at Grace's house. Some nigger named Leroy come by but I had a chair up against the door. He got mad when he couldn't get in. He went off somewhere and I got out of there before he could come back. Berniece got mad when we came here.

Lymon: She say you was knocking over the lamp busting up the place.

Boy Willie: That was Grace doing all that.

Lymon: Wining Boy seen Sutter's ghost last night.

Boy Willie: Wining Boy's liable to see anything. I'm surprised he found the right house. Come on, I done called the man about the piano.

Lymon: What he say?

Boy Willie: He say to bring it on out. I told him I was calling for my sister, Miss Berniece Charles. I told him some man wanted to buy it for eleven hundred dollars and asked him if he would go any better. He said yeah, he would give me eleven hundred and fifty dollars for it if it was the same piano. I described it to him again and he told me to bring it out.

Lymon: Why didn't you tell him to come and pick it up?

Boy Willie: I didn't want to have no problem with Berniece. This way we just take it on out there and it be out the way. He wanted to charge twenty-five dollars to pick it up.

Lymon: You should have told him the man was gonna give you twelve hundred for it.

Boy Willie: I figure I was taking a chance with that eleven hundred. If I had told him twelve hundred he might have run off. Now I wish I had told him twelve-fifty. It's hard to figure out white folks sometimes.

Lymon: You might have been able to tell him anything. White folks got a lot of money.

Boy Willie: Come on, let's get it loaded before Berniece come back. Get that end over there. All you got to do is pick it up on that side. Don't worry about this side. You wanna stretch you' back for a minute?

Lymon: I'm ready.

Boy Willie: Get a real good grip on it now.

The sound of Sutter's Ghost is heard. They do not hear it.

Lymon: I got this end. You get that end.

Boy Willie: Wait till I say ready now. Alright. You got it good? You got a grip on it?

Lymon: Yeah, I got it. You lift up on that end.

Boy Willie: Ready? Lift!

The piano will not budge.

Lymon: Man, this piano is heavy! It's gonna take more than me and you to move this piano.

Boy Willie: We can do it. Come on — we did it before.

Lymon: Nigger — you crazy! That piano weighs five hundred pounds!

Boy Willie: I got three hundred pounds of it! I know you can carry two hundred pounds! You be lifting them cotton sacks! Come on lift this piano!

They try to move the piano again without success.

Lymon: It's stuck. Something holding it.

Boy Willie: How the piano gonna be stuck? We just moved it. Slide you' end out.

Lymon: Naw — we gonna need two or three more people. How this big old piano get in the house?

Boy Willie: I don't know how it got in the house. I know how it's going out though! You get on this end. I'll carry three hundred and fifty pounds of it. All you got to do is slide your end out. Ready?

They switch sides and try again without success. Doaker enters from his room as they try to push and shove it.

Lymon: Hey, Doaker . . . how this piano get in the house?

Doaker: Boy Willie, what you doing?

Boy Willie: I'm carrying this piano out of the house. What it look like I'm doing? Come on, Lymon, let's try again.

Doaker: Go on let the piano sit there till Berniece come home.

Boy Willie: You ain't got nothing to do with this, Doaker. This my business.

Doaker: This is my house, nigger! I ain't gonna let you or nobody else carry nothing out of it. You ain't gonna carry nothing out of here without my permission!

Boy Willie: This is my piano. I don't need your permission to carry my belongings out of your house. This is mine. This ain't got nothing to do with you.

Doaker: I say leave it over there till Berniece comes home. She got part of it too. Leave it set there till you see what she say.

Boy Willie: I don't care what Berniece say. Come on, Lymon. I got this side.

Doaker: Go on and cut it half in two if you want to. Just leave Berniece's half sitting over there. I can't tell you what to do with your piano. But I can't let you take her half out of here.

Boy Willie: Go on, Doaker. You ain't got nothing to do with this. I don't want you starting nothing now. Just go on and leave me alone. Come on, Lymon. I got this end.

Doaker goes into his room. Boy Willie and Lymon prepare to move the piano.

Lymon: How we gonna get it in the truck?

Boy Willie: Don't worry about how we gonna get it on the truck. You got to get it out the house first.

Lymon: It's gonna take more than me and you to move this piano.

Boy Willie: Just lift up that end, nigger!

Doaker comes to the doorway of his room and stands.

Doaker (quietly, with authority): Leave that piano set over there till Berniece come back. I don't care what you do with it then. But you gonna leave it sit over there right now.

Boy Willie: Alright . . . I'm gonna tell you this, Doaker, I'm going out of here . . . I'm gonna get me some rope . . . find me a plank and some wheels . . . and I'm coming back. Then I'm gonna carry that piano out of here . . . sell it and give Berniece half the money. See . . . now that's what I'm gonna do. And you . . . or nobody else is gonna stop me. Come on, Lymon . . . let's go get some rope and stuff. I'll be back, Doaker.

Boy Willie and Lymon exit. The lights go down on the scene.

SCENE V

The lights come up. Boy Willie sits on the sofa, screwing casters on a wooden plank. Maretha is sitting on the piano stool. Doaker sits at the table playing solitaire.

Boy Willie (to Maretha): Then after that them white folks down around there started falling down their wells. You ever seen a well? A well got a wall around it. It's hard to fall down a well. You got to be leaning way over.

Couldn't nobody figure out too much what was making these fellows fall down their well . . . so everybody says the Ghosts of the Yellow Dog must have pushed them. That's what everybody called them four men what got burned up in the boxcar.

Maretha: Why they call them that?

Boy Willie: Cause the Yazoo Delta railroad got yellow boxcars. Sometime the way the whistle blow sound like an old dog howling so the people call it the Yellow Dog.

Maretha: Anybody ever see the Ghosts?

Boy Willie: I told you they like the wind. Can you see the wind?

Maretha: No.

Boy Willie: They like the wind you can't see them. But sometimes you be in trouble they might be around to help you. They say if you go where the Southern cross the Yellow Dog . . . you go to where them two railroads cross each other . . . and call out their names . . . they say they talk back to you. I don't know, I ain't never done that. But Uncle Wining Boy he say he been down there and talked to them. You have to ask him about that part.

Berniece has entered from the front door.

Berniece: Maretha, you go on and get ready for me to do your hair. *(Maretha crosses to the steps.)* Boy Willie, I done told you to leave my house. *(To Maretha.)* Go on, Maretha.

Maretha is hesitant about going up the stairs.

Boy Willie: Don't be scared. Here, I'll go up there with you. If we see Sutter's ghost I'll put a whupping on him. Come on, Uncle Boy Willie going with you.

Boy Willie and Maretha exit up the stairs.

Berniece: Doaker — what is going on here?

Doaker: I come home and him and Lymon was moving the piano. I told them to leave it over there till you got home. He went out and got that board and them wheels. He say he gonna take that piano out of here and ain't nobody gonna stop him.

Berniece: I ain't playing with Boy Willie. I got Crawley's gun upstairs. He don't know but I'm through with it. Where Lymon go?

Doaker: Boy Willie sent him for some rope just before you come in.

Berniece: I ain't studying Boy Willie or Lymon — or the rope. Boy Willie ain't taking that piano out this house. That's all there is to it.

Boy Willie and Maretha enter on the stairs. Maretha carries a hot comb and a can of hair grease. Boy Willie crosses over and continues to screw the wheels on the board.

Maretha: Mama, all the hair grease is gone. There ain't but this little bit left.

Berniece (gives her a dollar): Here . . . run across the street and get another can. You come straight back, too. Don't you be playing around out there. And watch the cars. Be careful when you cross the street. *(Maretha exits out the front door.)* Boy Willie, I done told you to leave my house.

Boy Willie: I ain't in you' house. I'm in Doaker's house. If he ask me to leave then I'll go on and leave. But consider me done left your part.

Berniece: Doaker, tell him to leave. Tell him to go on.

Doaker: Boy Willie ain't done nothing for me to put him out of the house. I told you if you can't get along just go on and don't have nothing to do with each other.

Boy Willie: I ain't thinking about Berniece. *(He gets up and draws a line across the floor with his foot.)* There! Now I'm out of your part of the house. Consider me done left your part. Soon as Lymon come back with that rope, I'm gonna take that piano out of here and sell it.

Berniece: You ain't gonna touch that piano.

Boy Willie: Carry it out of here just as big and bold. Do like my daddy would have done come time to get Sutter's land.

Berniece: I got something to make you leave it over there.

Boy Willie: It's got to come better than this thirty-two-twenty.

Doaker: Why don't you stop all that! Boy Willie, go on and leave her alone. You know how Berniece get. Why you wanna sit there and pick with her?

Boy Willie: I ain't picking with her. I told her the truth. She the one talking about what she got. I just told her what she better have.

Berniece: That's alright, Doaker. Leave him alone.

Boy Willie: She trying to scare me. Hell, I ain't scared of dying. I look around and see people dying every day. You got to die to make room for somebody else. I had a dog that died. Wasn't nothing but a puppy. I picked it up and put it in a bag and carried it up there to Reverend C. L. Thompson's church. I carried it up there and prayed and asked Jesus to make it live like he did the man in the Bible. I prayed real hard. Knelt down and everything. Say ask in Jesus' name. Well, I must have called Jesus' name two hundred times. I called his name till my mouth got sore. I got up and looked in the bag and the dog still dead. It ain't moved a muscle! I say, "Well, ain't nothing precious." And then I went out and killed me a cat. That's when I discovered the power of death. See, a nigger that ain't afraid to die is the worse kind of nigger for the white man. He can't hold that power over you. That's what I learned when I killed that cat. I got the power of death too. I can command him. I can call him up. The white man don't like to see that. He don't like for you to stand up and look him square in the eye and say, "I got it too." Then he got to deal with you square up.

Berniece: That's why I don't talk to him, Doaker. You try and talk to him and that's the only kind of stuff that comes out his mouth.

Doaker: You say Avery went home to get his Bible?

Boy Willie: What Avery gonna do? Avery can't do nothing with me. I wish Avery would say something to me about this piano.

Doaker: Berniece ain't said about that. Avery went home to get his Bible. He coming by to bless the house see if he can get rid of Sutter's ghost.

Boy Willie: Ain't nothing but a house full of ghosts down there at the church. What Avery look like chasing away somebody's ghost?

Maretha enters the front door.

Berniece: Light that stove and set that comb over there to get hot. Get something to put around your shoulders.

Boy Willie: The Bible say an eye for an eye, a tooth for a tooth, and a life for a life. Tit for tat. But you and Avery don't want to believe that. You gonna pass up that part and pretend it ain't in there. Everything else you gonna agree with. But if you gonna agree with part of it you got to agree with all of it. You can't do nothing halfway. You gonna go at the Bible halfway. You gonna act like that part ain't in there. But you pull out the Bible and open it and see what it say. Ask Avery. He a preacher. He'll tell you it's in there. He the Good Shepherd. Unless he gonna shepherd you to heaven with half the Bible.

Berniece: Maretha, bring me that comb. Make sure it's hot.

Maretha brings the comb. Berniece begins to do her hair.

Boy Willie: I will say this for Avery. He done figured out a path to go through life. I don't agree with it. But he done fixed it so he can go right through it real smooth. Hell, he liable to end up with a million dollars that he done got from selling bread and wine.

Maretha: OWWWWWW!

Berniece: Be still, Maretha. If you was a boy I wouldn't be going through this.

Boy Willie: Don't you tell that girl that. Why you wanna tell her that?

Berniece: You ain't got nothing to do with this child.

Boy Willie: Telling her you wished she was a boy. How's that gonna make her feel?

Berniece: Boy Willie, go on and leave me alone.

Doaker: Why don't you leave her alone? What you got to pick with her for? Why don't you go on out and see what's out there in the streets? Have something to tell the fellows down home.

Boy Willie: I'm waiting on Lymon to get back with that truck. Why don't you go on out and see what's out there in the streets? You ain't got to work tomorrow. Talking about me . . . why don't you go out there? It's Friday night.

Doaker: I got to stay around here and keep you all from killing one another.

Boy Willie: You ain't got to worry about me. I'm gonna be here just as long as it takes Lymon to get back here with that truck. You ought to be talking to Berniece. Sitting up there telling Maretha she wished she was a boy. What kind of thing is that to tell a child? If you want to tell her something tell her about that piano. You ain't even told her about that piano. Like that's something to be ashamed of. Like she supposed to go off and hide somewhere about that piano. You ought to mark down on the calendar the day that Papa Boy Charles brought that piano into the house. You ought to mark that day down and draw a circle around it . . . and every year when it come up throw a party. Have a celebration. If you did that she wouldn't have no problem in life. She could walk around here with her head held high. I'm talking about a big party!

Invite everybody! Mark that day down with a special meaning. That way she know where she at in the world. You got her going out here thinking she wrong in the world. Like there ain't no part of it belong to her.

Berniece: Let me take care of my child. When you get one of your own then you can teach it what you want to teach it.

Doaker exits into his room.

Boy Willie: What I want to bring a child into this world for? Why I wanna bring somebody else into all this for? I'll tell you this . . . If I was Rockefeller I'd have forty or fifty. I'd make one every day. Cause they gonna start out in life with all the advantages. I ain't got no advantages to offer nobody. Many is the time I looked at my daddy and seen him staring off at his hands. I got a little older I know what he was thinking. He sitting there saying, "I got these big old hands but what I'm gonna do with them? Best I can do is make a fifty-acre crop for Mr. Stovall. Got these big old hands capable of doing anything. I can take and build something with these hands. But where's the tools? All I got is these hands. Unless I go out here and kill me somebody and take what they got . . . it's a long row to hoe for me to get something of my own. So what I'm gonna do with these big old hands? What would you do?"

    See now . . . if he had his own land he wouldn't have felt that way. If he had something under his feet that belonged to him he could stand up taller. That's what I'm talking about. Hell, the land is there for everybody. All you got to do is figure out how to get you a piece. Ain't no mystery to life. You just got to go out and meet it square on. If you got a piece of land you'll find everything else fall right into place. You can stand right up next to the white man and talk about the price of cotton . . . the weather, and anything else you want to talk about. If you teach that girl that she living at the bottom of life, she's gonna grow up and hate you.

Berniece: I'm gonna teach her the truth. That's just where she living. Only she ain't got to stay there. *(To Maretha.)* Turn you' head over to the other side.

Boy Willie: This might be your bottom but it ain't mine. I'm living at the top of life. I ain't gonna just take my life and throw it away at the bottom. I'm in the world like everybody else. The way I see it everybody else got to come up a little taste to be where I am.

Berniece: You right at the bottom with the rest of us.

Boy Willie: I'll tell you this . . . and ain't a living soul can put a come back on it. If you believe that's where you at then you gonna act that way. If you act that way then that's where you gonna be. It's as simple as that. Ain't no mystery to life. I don't know how you come to believe that stuff. Crawley didn't think like that. He wasn't living at the bottom of life. Papa Boy Charles and Mama Ola wasn't living at the bottom of life. You ain't never heard them say nothing like that. They would have taken a strap to you if they heard you say something like that. *(Doaker enters from his room.)* Hey, Doaker . . . Berniece say the colored folks is living at the bottom of life. I tried to tell her if she think that . . . that's where she gonna be. You think you living at the bottom of life? Is that how you see yourself?

Doaker: I'm just living the best way I know how. I ain't thinking about no top or no bottom.

Boy Willie: That's what I tried to tell Berniece. I don't know where she got that from. That sound like something Avery would say. Avery think cause the white man give him a turkey for Thanksgiving that makes him better than everybody else. That's gonna raise him out of the bottom of life. I don't need nobody to give me a turkey. I can get my own turkey. All you have to do is get out my way. I'll get me two or three turkeys.

Berniece: You can't even get a chicken let alone two or three turkeys. Talking about get out your way. Ain't nobody in your way. *(To Maretha.)* Straighten your head, Maretha! Don't be bending down like that. Hold your head up! *(To Boy Willie.)* All you got going for you is talk. You' whole life that's all you ever had going for you.

Boy Willie: See now . . . I'll tell you something about me. I done strung along and strung along. Going this way and that. Whatever way would lead me to a moment of peace. That's all I want. To be as easy with everything. But I wasn't born to that. I was born to a time of fire.

   The world ain't wanted no part of me. I could see that since I was about seven. The world say it's better off without me. See, Berniece accept that. She trying to come up to where she can prove something to the world. Hell, the world a better place cause of me. I don't see it like Berniece. I got a heart that beats here and it beats just as loud as the next fellow's. Don't care if he black or white. Sometime it beats louder. When it beats louder, then everybody can hear it. Some people get scared of that. Like Berniece. Some people get scared to hear a nigger's heart beating. They think you ought to lay low with that heart. Make it beat quiet and go along with everything the way it is. But my mama ain't birthed me for nothing. So what I got to do? I got to mark my passing on the road. Just like you write on a tree, "Boy Willie was here."

   That's all I'm trying to do with that piano. Trying to put my mark on the road. Like my daddy done. My heart say for me to sell that piano and get me some land so I can make a life for myself to live in my own way. Other than that I ain't thinking about nothing Berniece got to say.

There is a knock at the door. Boy Willie crosses to it and yanks it open thinking it is Lymon. Avery enters. He carries a Bible.

Boy Willie: Where you been, nigger? Aw . . . I thought you was Lymon. Hey, Berniece, look who's here.

Berniece: Come on in, Avery. Don't you pay Boy Willie no mind.

Boy Willie: Hey . . . Hey, Avery . . . tell me this . . . can you get to heaven with half the Bible?

Berniece: Boy Willie . . . I done told you to leave me alone.

Boy Willie: I just ask the man a question. He can answer. He don't need you to speak for him. Avery . . . if you only believe on half the Bible and don't want to accept the other half . . . you think God let you in heaven? Or do you got to have the whole Bible? Tell Berniece . . . if you only believe in part of it . . . when you see God he gonna ask you why you ain't believed in the other part . . . then he gonna send you straight to Hell.

Avery: You got to be born again. Jesus say unless a man be born again he cannot come unto the Father and who so ever heareth my words and believeth them not shall be cast into a fiery pit.

Boy Willie: That's what I was trying to tell Berniece. You got to believe in it all. You can't go at nothing halfway. She think she going to heaven with half the Bible. *(To Berniece.)* You hear that . . . Jesus say you got to believe in it all.

Berniece: You keep messing with me.

Boy Willie: I ain't thinking about you.

Doaker: Come on in, Avery, and have a seat. Don't pay neither one of them no mind. They been arguing all day.

Berniece: Come on in, Avery.

Avery: How's everybody in here?

Berniece: Here, set this comb back over there on that stove. *(To Avery.)* Don't pay Boy Willie no mind. He been around here bothering me since I come home from work.

Boy Willie: Boy Willie ain't bothering you. Boy Willie ain't bothering nobody. I'm just waiting on Lymon to get back. I ain't thinking about you. You heard the man say I was right and you still don't want to believe it. You just wanna go and make up anythin'. Well there's Avery . . . there's the preacher . . . go on and ask him.

Avery: Berniece believe in the Bible. She been baptized.

Boy Willie: What about that part that say an eye for an eye a tooth for a tooth and a life for a life? Ain't that in there?

Doaker: What they say down there at the bank, Avery?

Avery: Oh, they talked to me real nice. I told Berniece . . . they say maybe they let me borrow the money. They done talked to my boss down at work and everything.

Doaker: That's what I told Berniece. You working every day you ought to be able to borrow some money.

Avery: I'm getting more people in my congregation every day. Berniece says she gonna be the Deaconess. I get me my church I can get married and settled down. That's what I told Berniece.

Doaker: That be nice. You all ought to go ahead and get married. Berniece don't need to be by herself. I tell her that all the time.

Berniece: I ain't said nothing about getting married. I said I was thinking about it.

Doaker: Avery get him his church you all can make it nice. *(To Avery.)* Berniece said you was coming by to bless the house.

Avery: Yeah, I done read up on my Bible. She asked me to come by and see if I can get rid of Sutter's ghost.

Boy Willie: Ain't no ghost in this house. That's all in Berniece's head. Go on up there and see if you see him. I'll give you a hundred dollars if you see him. That's all in her imagination.

Doaker: Well, let her find that out then. If Avery blessing the house is gonna make her feel better . . . what you got to do with it?

Avery: Berniece say Maretha seen him too. I don't know, but I found a part in the Bible to bless the house. If he is here then that ought to make him go.

Boy Willie: You worse than Berniece believing all that stuff. Talking about . . . if he here. Go on up there and find out. I been up there I ain't seen him. If you reading from that Bible gonna make him leave out of Berniece imagination, well, you might be right. But if you talking about . . .

Doaker: Boy Willie, why don't you just be quiet? Getting all up in the man's business. This ain't got nothing to do with you. Let him go ahead and do what he gonna do.

Boy Willie: I ain't stopping him. Avery ain't got no power to do nothing.

Avery: Oh, I ain't got no power. God got the power! God got the power over everything in His creation. God can do anything. God say, "As I commandeth so it shall be." God said, "Let there be light," and there was light. He made the world in six days and rested on the seventh. God's got a wonderful power. He got power over life and death. Jesus raised Lazareth from the dead. They was getting ready to bury him and Jesus told him say, "Rise up and walk." He got up and walked and the people made great rejoicing at the power of God. I ain't worried about him chasing away a little old ghost!

There is a knock at the door. Boy Willie goes to answer it. Lymon enters carrying a coil of rope.

Boy Willie: Where you been? I been waiting on you and you run off somewhere.

Lymon: I ran into Grace. I stopped and bought her drink. She say she gonna go to the picture show with me.

Boy Willie: I ain't thinking about no Grace nothing.

Lymon: Hi, Berniece.

Boy Willie: Give me that rope and get up on this side of the piano.

Doaker: Boy Willie, don't start nothing now. Leave the piano alone.

Boy Willie: Get that board there, Lymon. Stay out of this, Doaker.

> *Berniece exits up the stairs.*

Doaker: You just can't take the piano. How you gonna take the piano? Berniece ain't said nothing about selling that piano.

Boy Willie: She ain't got to say nothing. Come on, Lymon. We got to lift one end at a time up on the board. You got to watch so that the board don't slide up under there.

Lymon: What we gonna do with the rope?

Boy Willie: Let me worry about the rope. You just get up on this side over here with me.

> *Berniece enters from the stairs. She has her hand in her pocket where she has Crawley's gun.*

Avery: Boy Willie . . . Berniece . . . why don't you all sit down and talk this out now?

Berniece: Ain't nothing to talk out.

Boy Willie: I'm through talking to Berniece. You can talk to Berniece till you get blue in the face, and it don't make no difference. Get up on that side, Lymon. Throw that rope around there and tie it to the leg.

Lymon: Wait a minute . . . wait a minute, Boy Willie, Berniece got to say. Hey, Berniece . . . did you tell Boy Willie he could take this piano?

Berniece: Boy Willie ain't taking nothing out of my house but himself. Now you let him go ahead and try.

Boy Willie: Come on, Lymon, get up on this side with me. *(Lymon stands undecided.)* Come on, nigger! What you standing there for?

Lymon: Maybe Berniece is right, Boy Willie. Maybe you shouldn't sell it.

Avery: You all ought to sit down and talk it out. See if you can come to an agreement.

Doaker: That's what I been trying to tell them. Seem like one of them ought to respect the other one's wishes.

Berniece: I wish Boy Willie would go on and leave my house. That's what I wish. Now, he can respect that. Cause he's leaving here one way or another.

Boy Willie: What you mean one way or another? What's that supposed to mean? I ain't scared of no gun.

Doaker: Come on, Berniece, leave him alone with that.

Boy Willie: I don't care what Berniece say. I'm selling my half. I can't help it if her half got to go along with it. It ain't like I'm trying to cheat her out of her half. Come on, Lymon.

Lymon: Berniece . . . I got to do this . . . Boy Willie say he gonna give you half of the money . . . say he want to get Sutter's land.

Berniece: Go on, Lymon. Just go on . . . I done told Boy Willie what to do.

Boy Willie: Here, Lymon . . . put that rope over there.

Lymon: Boy Willie, you sure you want to do this? The way I figure it . . . I might be wrong . . . but I figure she gonna shoot you first.

Boy Willie: She just gonna have to shoot me.

Berniece: Maretha, get on out the way. Get her out the way, Doaker.

Doaker: Go on, do what your mama told you.

Berniece: Put her in your room.

> *Maretha exits to Doaker's room. Boy Willie and Lymon try to lift the piano. The door opens and Wining Boy enters. He has been drinking.*

Wining Boy: Man, these niggers around here! I stopped down there at Seefus. . . . These folks standing around talking about Patchneck Red's coming. They jumping back and getting off the sidewalk talking about Patchneck Red this and Patchneck Red that. Come to find out . . . you know who they was talking about? Old John D. from up around Tyler! Used to run around with Otis Smith. He got everybody scared of him. Calling him Patchneck Red. They don't know I whupped the nigger's head in one time.

Boy Willie: Just make sure that board don't slide, Lymon.

Lymon: I got this side. You watch that side.

Wining Boy: Hey, Boy Willie, what you got? I know you got a pint stuck up in your coat.

Boy Willie: Wining Boy, get out the way!

Wining Boy: Hey, Doaker. What you got? Gimme a drink. I want a drink.

Doaker: It look like you had enough of whatever it was. Come talking about "What you got?" You ought to be trying to find somewhere to lay down.

Wining Boy: I ain't worried about no place to lay down. I can always find me a place to lay down in Berniece's house. Ain't that right, Berniece?

Berniece: Wining Boy, sit down somewhere. You been out there drinking all day. Come in here smelling like an old polecat. Sit on down there, you don't need nothing to drink.

Doaker: You know Berniece don't like all that drinking.

Wining Boy: I ain't disrespecting Berniece. Berniece, am I disrespecting you? I'm just trying to be nice. I been with strangers all day and they treated me like family. I come in here to family and you treat me like a stranger. I don't need your whiskey. I can buy my own. I wanted your company, not your whiskey.

Doaker: Nigger, why don't you go upstairs and lay down? You don't need nothing to drink.

Wining Boy: I ain't thinking about no laying down. Me and Boy Willie fixing to party. Ain't that right, Boy Willie? Tell him, I'm fixing to play me some piano. Watch this.

> *Wining Boy sits down at the piano.*

Boy Willie: Come on, Wining Boy! Me and Lymon fixing to move the piano.

Wining Boy: Wait a minute . . . wait a minute. This a song I wrote for Cleotha. I wrote this song in memory of Cleotha.

> *He begins to play and sing.*

Hey little woman what's the matter with you now
Had a storm last night and blowed the line all down

> Tell me how long
> Is I got to wait
> Can I get it now
> Or must I hesitate
>
> It takes a hesitating stocking in her hesitating shoe
> It takes a hesitating woman wanna sing the blues
>
> Tell me how long
> Is I got to wait
> Can I kiss you now
> Or must I hesitate.

Boy Willie: Come on, Wining Boy, get up! Get up, Wining Boy! Me and Lymon's fixing to move the piano.

Wining Boy: Naw . . . Naw . . . you ain't gonna move this piano.

Boy Willie: Get out the way, Wining Boy.

> *Wining Boy, his back to the piano, spreads his arms out over the piano.*

Wining Boy: You ain't taking this piano out the house. You got to take me with it!

Boy Willie: Get on out the way, Wining Boy! Doaker get him!

> *There is a knock on the door.*

Berniece: I got him, Doaker. Come on, Wining Boy. I done told Boy Willie he ain't taking the piano.

> *Berniece tries to take Wining Boy away from the piano.*

Wining Boy: He got to take me with it!

> *Doaker goes to answer the door. Grace enters.*

Grace: Is Lymon here?

Doaker: Lymon.

Wining Boy: He ain't taking that piano.

Berniece: I ain't gonna let him take it.

Grace: I thought you was coming back. I ain't gonna sit in that truck all day.

Lymon: I told you I was coming back.

Grace (sees Boy Willie): Oh, hi, Boy Willie. Lymon told me you was gone back down South.

Lymon: I said he was going back. I didn't say he had left already.

Grace: That's what you told me.

Berniece: Lymon, you got to take your company someplace else.

Lymon: Berniece, this is Grace. That there is Berniece. That's Boy Willie's sister.

Grace: Nice to meet you. *(To Lymon.)* I ain't gonna sit out in that truck all day. You told me you was gonna take me to the movie.

Lymon: I told you I had something to do first. You supposed to wait on me.

Berniece: Lymon, just go on and leave. Take Grace or whoever with you. Just go on get out my house.

Boy Willie: You gonna help me move this piano first, nigger!

Lymon (to Grace): I got to help Boy Willie move the piano first.

> *Everybody but Grace suddenly senses Sutter's presence.*

Grace: I ain't waiting on you. Told me you was coming right back. Now you got to move a piano. You just like all the other men. *(Grace now senses some-*

thing.) Something ain't right here. I knew I shouldn't have come back up in this house.

Grace exits.

Lymon: Hey, Grace! I'll be right back, Boy Willie.
Boy Willie: Where you going, nigger?
Lymon: I'll be back. I got to take Grace home.
Boy Willie: Come on, let's move the piano first!
Lymon: I got to take Grace home. I told you I'll be back.

Lymon exits. Boy Willie exits and calls after him.

Boy Willie: Come on, Lymon! Hey . . . Lymon! Lymon . . . come on!

Again, the presence of Sutter is felt.

Wining Boy: Hey, Doaker, did you feel that? Hey, Berniece . . . did you get cold? Hey, Doaker . . .
Doaker: What you calling me for?
Wining Boy: I believe that's Sutter.
Doaker: Well, let him stay up there. As long as he don't mess with me.
Berniece: Avery, go on and bless the house.
Doaker: You need to bless that piano. That's what you need to bless. It ain't done nothing but cause trouble. If you gonna bless anything go on and bless that.
Wining Boy: Hey, Doaker if he gonna bless something let him bless everything. The kitchen . . . the upstairs. Go on and bless it all.
Boy Willie: Ain't no ghost in this house. He need to bless Berniece's head. That's what he need to bless.
Avery: Seem like that piano's causing all the trouble. I can bless that. Berniece, put me some water in that bottle.

Avery takes a small bottle from his pocket and hands it to Berniece, who goes into the kitchen to get water. Avery takes a candle from his pocket and lights it. He gives it to Berniece, as she gives him the water.

Hold this candle. Whatever you do make sure it don't go out.

O Holy Father we gather here this evening in the Holy Name to cast out the spirit of one James Sutter. May this vial of water be empowered with thy spirit. May each drop of it be a weapon and a shield against the presence of all evil and may it be a cleansing and blessing of this humble abode.

Just as Our Father taught us how to pray so He say, "I will prepare a table for you in the midst of mine enemies," and in His hands we place ourselves to come unto his presence. Where there is Good so shall it cause Evil to scatter to the Four Winds.

He throws water at the piano at each commandment.

Get thee behind me, Satan! Get thee behind the face of Righteousness as we Glorify His Holy Name! Get thee behind the Hammer of Truth that breaketh down the Wall of Falsehood! Father. Father. Praise. Praise. We ask in Jesus' name and call forth the power of the Holy Spirit as it is written. . . . *(He opens the Bible and reads from it.)* I will sprinkle clean water upon thee and ye shall be clean.

Boy Willie: All this old preaching stuff. Hell, just tell him to leave.

Avery continues reading throughout Boy Willie's outburst.

Avery: I will sprinkle clean water upon you and you shall be clean: from all your uncleanliness, and from all your idols, will I cleanse you. A new heart also will I give you, and a new spirit will I put within you: and I will take out of your flesh the heart of stone, and I will give you a heart of flesh. And I will put my spirit within you, and cause you to walk in my statutes, and ye shall keep my judgments, and do them.

Boy Willie grabs a pot of water from the stove and begins to fling it around the room.

Boy Willie: Hey Sutter! Sutter! Get your ass out this house! Sutter! Come on and get some of this water! You done drowned in the well, come on and get some more of this water!

Boy Willie is working himself into a frenzy as he runs around the room throwing water and calling Sutter's name. Avery continues reading.

Boy Willie: Come on, Sutter! (*He starts up the stairs.*) Come on, get some water! Come on, Sutter!

The sound of Sutter's Ghost is heard. As Boy Willie approaches the steps he is suddenly thrown back by the unseen force, which is choking him. As he struggles he frees himself, then dashes up the stairs:

Boy Willie: Come on, Sutter!

Avery (continuing): A new heart also will I give you and a new spirit will I put within you: and I will take out of your flesh the heart of stone, and I will give you a heart of flesh. And I will put my spirit within you, and cause you to walk in my statutes, and ye shall keep my judgments, and do them.

There are loud sounds heard from upstairs as Boy Willie begins to wrestle with Sutter's Ghost. It is a life-and-death struggle fraught with perils and faultless terror. Boy Willie is thrown down the stairs. Avery is stunned into silence. Boy Willie picks himself up and dashes back upstairs.

Avery: Berniece, I can't do it.

There are more sounds heard from upstairs. Doaker and Wining Boy stare at one another in stunned disbelief. It is in this moment, from somewhere old, that Berniece realizes what she must do. She crosses to the piano. She begins to play. The song is found piece by piece. It is an old urge to song that is both a commandment and a plea. With each repetition it gains in strength. It is intended as an exorcism and a dressing for battle. A rustle of wind blowing across two continents.

Berniece (singing):
> I want you to help me
> I want you to help me
> I want you to help me
> I want you to help me
> I want you to help me
> I want you to help me
> Mama Berniece
> I want you to help me
> Mama Esther

I want you to help me
Papa Boy Charles
I want you to help me
Mama Ola
I want you to help me

I want you to help me
I want you to help me
I want you to help me
I want you to help me
I want you to help me
I want you to help me
I want you to help me
I want you to help me

The sound of a train approaching is heard. The noise upstairs subsides.

Boy Willie: Come on, Sutter! Come back, Sutter!

Berniece begins to chant:

Berniece:
Thank you.
Thank you.
Thank you.

A calm comes over the house. Maretha enters from Doaker's room. Boy Willie enters on the stairs. He pauses a moment to watch Berniece at the piano.

Berniece:
Thank you.
Thank you.

Boy Willie: Wining Boy, you ready to go back down home? Hey Doaker, what time the train leave?

Doaker: You still got time to make it.

Maretha crosses and embraces Boy Willie.

Boy Willie: Hey Berniece . . . if you and Maretha don't keep playing on that piano . . . ain't no telling . . . me and Sutter both liable to be back.

He exits.

Berniece: Thank you.

The lights go down to black.

CONNECTIONS TO OTHER SELECTIONS

1. Discuss the significance of custom and the past in *The Piano Lesson* and Wole Soyinka's *The Strong Breed* (p. 1919).

2. In an essay discuss the importance of African heritage in *The Piano Lesson* and Lorraine Hansberry's *A Raisin in the Sun* (p. 1730).

3. How might the narrator's experience in Ralph Ellison's "Battle Royal" (p. 223) be used to shed light on the conflicts in *The Piano Lesson?*

CRITICAL THINKING AND WRITING

37

Critical Strategies
for Reading

CRITICAL THINKING

Maybe this has happened to you: the assignment is to write an analysis of some aspect of a work — let's say, Nathaniel Hawthorne's *The Scarlet Letter* — that interests you and takes into account critical sources that comment on and interpret the work. You cheerfully begin research in the library but quickly find yourself bewildered by several seemingly unrelated articles. The first traces the thematic significance of images of light and darkness in the novel; the second makes a case for Hester Prynne as a liberated woman; the third argues that Arthur Dimmesdale's guilt is a projection of Hawthorne's own emotions; and the fourth analyzes the introduction, "The Custom-House," as an attack on bourgeois values. These disparate treatments may seem random and capricious — a confirmation of your worst suspicions that interpretations of literature are hit-or-miss excursions into areas that you know little about or didn't know even existed. But if you understand that the four articles are written from four different perspectives — formalist, feminist, psychological, and Marxist — and that the purpose of each is to enhance your understanding of the novel by discussing a particular element of it, then you can see that the articles' varying strategies represent potentially interesting ways of opening up the text that might otherwise never have occurred to you. There are many ways to approach a text, and a useful first step is to develop a sense of direction, an understanding of how a perspective — your own or a critic's — shapes a discussion of a text.

This chapter offers an introduction to critical approaches to literature by outlining a variety of strategies for reading fiction, poetry, or drama. These strategies include approaches that have long been practiced by readers who have used, for example, the insights gleaned from biography and history to illuminate literary works as well as more recent approaches, such as those used by gender, reader-response, and deconstructionist critics. Each of these perspectives is sensitive to point of view, symbol, tone, irony, and other literary elements that you have been studying, but each also casts those elements in a special light. The formalist approach emphasizes how the elements within a work achieve their effects, whereas biographical and psychological approaches lead outward from the work to consider the author's life and other writings. Even broader approaches, such as historical and cultural perspectives, connect the work to historic, social, and economic forces. Mythological readings represent the broadest approach because they discuss the cultural and universal responses readers have to a work.

Any given strategy raises its own types of questions and issues while seeking particular kinds of evidence to support itself. An awareness of the assumptions and methods that inform an approach can help you to understand better the validity and value of a given critic's strategy for making sense of a work. More important, such an understanding can widen and deepen the responses of your own reading.

The critical thinking that goes into understanding a professional critic's approach to a work is not foreign to you because you have already used essentially the same kind of thinking to understand the work itself. You have developed skills to produce a literary *analysis* that, for example, describes how a character, symbol, or rhyme scheme supports a theme. These same skills are also useful for reading literary criticism because they allow you to keep track of how the parts of a critical approach create a particular reading of a literary work. When you analyze a story, poem, or play by closely examining how its various elements relate to the whole, your *interpretation* — your articulation of what the work means to you as supported by an analysis of its elements — necessarily involves choosing what you focus on in the work. The same is true of professional critics.

Critical readings presuppose choices in the kinds of materials that are discussed. An analysis of the setting of John Updike's "A & P" (p. 576) would probably focus on the oppressive environment the protagonist associates with the store rather than, say, the economic history of that supermarket chain. (For a student's analysis of the setting in "A & P," see p. 2089.) The economic history of a supermarket chain might be useful to a Marxist critic concerned with how class relations are revealed in "A & P," but for a formalist critic interested in identifying the unifying structures of the story, such information would be irrelevant.

The Perspectives, Complementary Critical Readings, and Critical Case Studies in this anthology offer opportunities to read critics using a wide variety of approaches to analyze and interpret texts. In the Critical Case Study on Ibsen's *A Doll House* (Chapter 33), for instance, Carol Strongin Tufts (p. 1632) offers a psychoanalytic reading of Nora that characterizes her as a narcissistic personality rather than as a feminist heroine. The criteria she uses to evaluate Nora's behavior are drawn from the language used by the American Psychiatric Association. In contrast, Joan Templeton (p. 1635) places Nora in the context of women's rights issues to argue that Nora must be read from a feminist perspective if the essential meaning of the play is to be understood. Each of these critics raises different questions,

examines different evidence, and employs different assumptions to interpret Nora's character. Being aware of those differences—teasing them out
so that you can see how they lead to competing conclusions—is a useful
way to analyze the analysis itself. What is left out of an interpretation is
sometimes as significant as what is included. As you read the critics, it's
worth reminding yourself that your own critical thinking skills can help
you to determine the usefulness of a particular approach.

The following overview of critical strategies for reading is neither exhaustive in the types of critical approaches covered nor complete in its presentation of the complexities inherent in them, but it should help you to
develop an appreciation of the intriguing possibilities that attend literary
interpretation. The emphasis in this chapter is on ways of thinking about
literature rather than on daunting lists of terms, names, and movements.
Although a working knowledge of critical schools may be valuable and
necessary for a fully informed use of a given critical approach, the aim here
is more modest and practical. This chapter is no substitute for the shelves
of literary criticism that can be found in your library, but it does suggest
how readers using different perspectives organize their responses to texts.

The summaries of critical approaches that follow are descriptive, not
evaluative. Each approach has its advantages and limitations. In practice,
many critical approaches overlap and complement each other, but those
matters are best left to further study. Like literary artists, critics have their
personal values, tastes, and styles. The appropriateness of a specific critical
approach will depend, at least in part, on the nature of the literary work
under discussion as well as on your own sensibilities and experience. However, any approach, if it is to enhance understanding, requires sensitivity,
tact, and an awareness of the various literary elements of the text, including, of course, its use of language.

Successful critical approaches avoid eccentric decodings that reveal so-
called hidden meanings that are not only hidden but totally absent from
the text. For a parody of this sort of critical excess, see "A Parodic Interpretation of 'Stopping by Woods on a Snowy Evening'" (p. 1003), in which
Herbert R. Coursen Jr. has some fun with a Robert Frost poem and Santa
Claus while making a serious point about the dangers of overly ingenious
readings. Literary criticism attempts, like any valid hypothesis, to account
for phenomena—the text—without distorting or misrepresenting what it
describes.

THE LITERARY CANON:
DIVERSITY AND CONTROVERSY

Before looking at the various critical approaches discussed in this
chapter, it makes sense to consider first which literature has been traditionally considered worthy of such analysis. The discussion in the Introduction called The Changing Literary Canon (p. 5) may have already

alerted you to the fact that in recent years many more works by women, minorities, and writers from around the world have been considered by scholars, critics, and teachers to merit serious study and inclusion in what is known as the literary canon. This increasing diversity has been celebrated by those who believe that multiculturalism taps new sources for the discovery of great literature while raising significant questions about language, culture, and society. At the same time, others have perceived this diversity as a threat to the established, traditional canon of Western culture.

The debates concerning who should be read, taught, and written about have sometimes been acrimonious as well as lively and challenging. Bitter arguments have been waged recently on campuses and in the press over what has come to be called *political correctness.* Two main camps have formed around these debates — liberals and conservatives (the appropriateness of these terms is debatable, but the oppositional positioning is unmistakable). The liberals are said to insist on encouraging tolerant attitudes about race, class, gender, and sexual orientation, and opening up the curriculum to multicultural texts from Asia, Africa, Latin America, and elsewhere. These revisionists, seeking a change in traditional attitudes, are sometimes accused of trying to substitute ideological dogma for reason and truth and to intimidate opposing colleagues and students into silence and acceptance of their politically correct views. The conservatives are also portrayed as ideologues; in their efforts to preserve what they regard as the best from the past, they fail to acknowledge that Western classics, mostly written by white male Europeans, represent only a portion of human experience. These traditionalists are seen as advocating values that are neither universal nor eternal but merely privileged and entrenched. Conservatives are charged with ignoring the political agenda that their values represent and that is implicit in their preference for the works of canonical authors such as Homer, Virgil, Shakespeare, Milton, Tolstoy, and Faulkner. The reductive and contradictory nature of this national debate between liberals and conservatives has been neatly summed up by Katha Pollitt: "Read the conservatives' list and produce a nation of sexists and racists — or a nation of philosopher kings. Read the liberals' list and produce a nation of spiritual relativists — or a nation of open-minded world citizens" ("Canon to the Right of Me . . . ," *The Nation,* Sept. 23, 1991, p. 330).

These troubling and extreme alternatives can be avoided, of course, if the issues are not approached from such absolutist positions. Solutions to these issues cannot be suggested in this limited space, and, no doubt, solutions will evolve over time, but we can at least provide a perspective. Books — regardless of what list they are on — are not likely to unite a fragmented nation or to disunite a unified one. It is perhaps more useful and accurate to see issues of canonicity as reflecting political changes rather than being the primary causes of them. This is not to say that books don't have an impact on readers — that *Uncle Tom's Cabin,* for instance, did not galvanize antislavery sentiments in nineteenth-century America — but that book lists do not by themselves preserve or destroy the status quo.

It's worth noting that the curricula of American universities have always undergone significant and, some would say, wrenching changes. Only a little more than one hundred years ago there was strong opposition to teaching English, as well as other modern languages, alongside programs dominated by Greek and Latin. Only since the 1920s has American literature been made a part of the curriculum, and just five decades ago including twentieth-century writers such as James Joyce, Virginia Woolf, Franz Kafka, and Ernest Hemingway in the curriculum was regarded with raised eyebrows. New voices do not drown out the past; they build on it and eventually become part of the past as newer writers take their place beside them. Neither resistance to change nor a denial of the past will have its way with the canon. Though both impulses are widespread, neither is likely to dominate the other because there are too many reasonable, practical readers and teachers who instead of replacing Shakespeare, Melville, and other canonical writers have supplemented them with neglected writers from Western and other cultures. These readers experience the current debates about the canon not as a binary opposition but as an opportunity to explore important questions about continuity and change in our literature, culture, and society.

FORMALIST STRATEGIES

Formalist critics focus on the formal elements of a work — its language, structure, and tone. A formalist reads literature as an independent work of art rather than as a reflection of the author's state of mind or as a representation of a moment in history. Historic influences on a work, an author's intentions, or anything else outside the work are generally not treated by formalists (this is particularly true of the most famous modern formalists, known as the *New Critics,* who dominated American criticism from the 1940s through the 1960s). Instead, formalists offer intense examinations of the relationship between form and meaning within a work, emphasizing the subtle complexity of how a work is arranged. This kind of close reading pays special attention to what are often described as *intrinsic* matters in a literary work, such as diction, irony, paradox, metaphor, and symbol, as well as larger elements, such as plot, characterization, and narrative technique. Formalists examine how these elements work together to give a coherent shape to a work while contributing to its meaning. The answers to the questions formalists raise about how the shape and effect of a work are related come from the work itself. Other kinds of information that go beyond the text — biography, history, politics, economics, and so on — are typically regarded by formalists as *extrinsic* matters, which are considerably less important than what goes on within the autonomous text.

Poetry especially lends itself to close readings because a poem's relative brevity allows for detailed analyses of nearly all its words and how they achieve their effects. For a student's formalist reading of how a pervasive sense of death is worked into a poem, see "A Reading of Dickinson's 'There's a certain Slant of light'" (p. 2084).

Formalist strategies are also useful for analyzing drama and fiction. In his well-known essay "The World of *Hamlet*," Maynard Mack explores Hamlet's character and predicament by paying close attention to the words and images that Shakespeare uses to build a world in which appearances mask reality and mystery is embedded in scene after scene. Mack points to recurring terms, such as *apparition, seems, assume,* and *put on,* as well as repeated images of acting, clothing, disease, and painting, to indicate the treacherous surface world Hamlet must penetrate to get to the truth. This pattern of deception provides an organizing principle around which Mack offers a reading of the entire play:

> Hamlet's problem, in its crudest form, is simply the problem of the avenger: he must carry out the injunction of the ghost and kill the king. But this problem . . . is presented in terms of a certain kind of world. The ghost's injunction to act becomes so inextricably bound up for Hamlet with the character of the world in which the action must be taken — its mysteriousness, its baffling appearances, its deep consciousness of infection, frailty, and loss — that he cannot come to terms with either without coming to terms with both.

Although Mack places *Hamlet* in the tradition of revenge tragedy, his reading of the play emphasizes Shakespeare's arrangement of language rather than literary history as a means of providing an interpretation that accounts for various elements of the play. Mack's formalist strategy explores how diction reveals meaning and how repeated words and images evoke and reinforce important thematic significances.

For an example of a work in which the shape of the plot serves as the major organizing principle, let's examine Kate Chopin's "The Story of an Hour" (p. 10), a two-page short story that takes only a few minutes to read. With the story fresh in your mind, consider how you might approach it from a formalist perspective. A first reading probably results in surprise at the story's ending: a grieving wife "afflicted with a heart trouble" suddenly dies of a heart attack, not because she's learned that her kind and loving husband has been killed in a terrible train accident but because she discovers that he is very much alive. Clearly, we are faced with an ironic situation since there is such a powerful incongruity between what is expected to happen and what actually happens. A likely formalist strategy for analyzing this story would be to raise questions about the ironic ending. Is this merely a trick ending, or is it a carefully wrought culmination of other elements in the story so that in addition to creating surprise the ending snaps the story shut on an interesting and challenging theme? Formalists value such complexities over simple surprise effects.

A second, closer reading indicates that Chopin's third-person narrator presents the story in a manner similar to Josephine's gentle attempts to break the news about Brently Mallard's death. The story is told in "veiled hints that [reveal] in half concealing." But unlike Josephine, who tries to protect her sister's fragile heart from stress, the narrator seeks to reveal Mrs. Mallard's complex heart. A formalist would look back over the story for signs of the ending in the imagery. Although Mrs. Mallard grieves immediately and unreservedly when she hears about the train disaster, she soon begins to feel a different emotion as she looks out the window at "the tops of trees . . . all aquiver with the new spring life." This symbolic evocation of renewal and rebirth — along with "the delicious breath of rain," the sounds of life in the street, and the birds singing — causes her to feel, in spite of her own efforts to repress her thoughts and emotions, "free, free, free!" She feels alive with a sense of possibility, with a "clear and exalted perception" that she "would live for herself" instead of for and through her husband.

It is ironic that this ecstatic "self-assertion" is interpreted by Josephine as grief, but the crowning irony for this "goddess of Victory" is the doctors' assumption that she dies of joy rather than of the shock of having to abandon her newly discovered self once she realizes her husband is still alive. In the course of an hour, Mrs. Mallard's life is irretrievably changed: her husband's assumed accidental death frees her, but the fact that he lives and all the expectations imposed on her by his continued life kill her. She does, indeed, die of a broken heart, but only Chopin's readers know the real ironic meaning of that explanation.

Although this brief discussion of some of the formal elements of Chopin's story does not describe all there is to say about how they produce an effect and create meaning, it does suggest the kinds of questions, issues, and evidence that a formalist strategy might raise in providing a close reading of the text itself.

BIOGRAPHICAL STRATEGIES

A knowledge of an author's life can help readers understand his or her work more fully. Events in a work might follow actual events in a writer's life just as characters might be based on people known by the author. Ernest Hemingway's "Soldier's Home" (p. 145) is a story about the difficulties of a World War I veteran named Krebs returning to his small hometown in Oklahoma, where he cannot adjust to the pious assumptions of his family and neighbors. He refuses to accept their innocent blindness to the horrors he has witnessed during the war. They have no sense of the brutality of modern life; instead they insist he resume his life as if nothing has happened. There is plenty of biographical evidence to indicate that Krebs's unwillingness to lie about his war experiences reflects Hemingway's own responses on his return to Oak Park, Illinois, in 1919. Krebs, like Hemingway, finds he has to leave the sentimentality, repressiveness, and smug complacency that threaten to render his experiences unreal: "the world they were in was not the world he was in."

An awareness of Hemingway's own war experiences and subsequent disillusionment with his hometown can be readily developed through available biographies, letters, and other works he wrote. Consider, for example, this passage from *By Force of Will: The Life and Art of Ernest Hemingway*, in which Scott Donaldson describes Hemingway's response to World War I:

> In poems, as in [*A Farewell to Arms*], Hemingway expressed his distaste for the first war. The men who had to fight the war did not die well:
>
>> Soldiers pitch and cough and twitch —
>>> All the world roars red and black;
>> Soldiers smother in a ditch,
>>> Choking through the whole attack.
>
> And what did they die for? They were "sucked in" by empty words and phrases —
>
>> King and country,
>> Christ Almighty,
>> And the rest,
>> Patriotism,
>> Democracy,
>> Honor —
>
> which spelled death. The bitterness of these outbursts derived from the distinction Hemingway drew between the men on the line and those who started the wars that others had to fight.

This kind of information can help to deepen our understanding of just how empathetically Krebs is presented in the story. Relevant facts about Hemingway's life will not make "Soldier's Home" a better written story than it is, but such information can make clearer the source of Hemingway's convictions and how his own experiences inform his major concerns as a storyteller.

Some formalist critics — some New Critics, for example — argue that interpretation should be based exclusively on internal evidence rather than on any biographical information outside the work. They argue that it is not possible to determine an author's intention and that the work must stand by itself. Although this is a useful caveat for keeping the work in focus, a reader who finds biography relevant would argue that biography can at the very least serve as a control on interpretation. A reader who, for example, finds Krebs at fault for not subscribing to the values of his hometown would be misreading the story, given both its tone and the biographical information available about the author. Although the narrator never *tells* the reader that Krebs is right or wrong for leaving town, the story's tone sides with his view of things. If, however, someone were to argue otherwise, insisting that the tone is not decisive and that Krebs's position is problematic, a reader familiar with Hemingway's own reactions could refute that argument with a powerful confirmation of Krebs's instincts to withdraw. Hence, many readers find biography useful for interpretation.

However, it is also worth noting that biographical information can complicate a work. Chopin's "The Story of an Hour" presents a repressed wife's momentary discovery of what freedom from her husband might mean to her. She awakens to a new sense of herself when she learns of her husband's death, only to collapse of a heart attack when she sees that he is alive. Readers might be tempted to interpret this story as Chopin's fictionalized commentary about her own marriage because her husband died twelve years before she wrote the story and seven years before she began writing fiction seriously. Biographers seem to agree, however, that Chopin's marriage was evidently satisfying to her and that she was not oppressed by her husband and did not feel oppressed.

Moreover, consider this diary entry from only one month after Chopin wrote the story (quoted by Per Seyersted in *Kate Chopin: A Critical Biography*):

> If it were possible for my husband and my mother to come back to earth, I feel that I would unhesitatingly give up everything that has come into my life since they left it and join my existence again with theirs. To do that, I would have to forget the past ten years of my growth — my real growth. But I would take back a little wisdom with me; it would be the spirit of perfect acquiescence.

This passage raises provocative questions instead of resolving them. How does that "spirit of perfect acquiescence" relate to Mrs. Mallard's insistence that she "would live for herself"? Why would Chopin be willing to "forget the past ten years of . . . growth" given her protagonist's desire for "self-assertion"? Although these and other questions raised by the diary entry cannot be answered here, this kind of biographical perspective certainly adds to the possibilities of interpretation.

Sometimes biographical information does not change our understanding so much as it enriches our appreciation of a work. It matters, for instance, that much of John Milton's poetry, so rich in visual imagery, was written after he became blind; and it is just as significant — to shift to a musical example — that a number of Ludwig van Beethoven's greatest works, including the Ninth Symphony, were composed after he succumbed to total deafness.

PSYCHOLOGICAL STRATEGIES

Given the enormous influence that Sigmund Freud's psychoanalytic theories have had on twentieth-century interpretations of human behavior, it is nearly inevitable that most people have some familiarity with his ideas concerning dreams, unconscious desires, and sexual repression, as well as his terms for different aspects of the psyche — the id, ego, and superego. Psychological approaches to literature draw on Freud's theories and other psychoanalytic theories to understand more fully the text, the writer, and the reader. Critics use such approaches to explore the motivations of characters and the symbolic meanings of events, while biographers speculate about a writer's own motivations — conscious or unconscious — in a literary work. Psychological approaches are also used to describe and analyze the reader's personal responses to a text.

Although it is not feasible to explain psychoanalytic terms and concepts in so brief a space as this, it is possible to suggest the nature of a psychological approach. It is a strategy based heavily on the idea of the existence of a human unconscious — those impulses, desires, and feelings that a person is unaware of but that influence emotions and behavior.

Central to a number of psychoanalytic critical readings is Freud's concept of what he called the *Oedipus complex,* a term derived from Sophocles' tragedy *Oedipus the King* (p. 1224). This complex is predicated on a boy's unconscious rivalry with his father for his mother's love and his desire to eliminate his father in order to take his father's place with his mother. The female version of the psychological conflict is known as the *Electra complex,* a term used to describe a daughter's unconscious rivalry for her father. The name comes from a Greek legend about Electra who avenged the death of her father, Agamemnon, by plotting the death of her mother. In *The Interpretation of Dreams,* Freud explains why *Oedipus the King* "moves a modern audience no less than it did the contemporary Greek one." What unites their powerful attraction to the play is an unconscious response:

> There must be something which makes a voice within us ready to recognize the compelling force of destiny in the *Oedipus.* . . . His destiny moves us only because it might have been ours — because the oracle laid the same curse upon us before our birth as upon him. It is the fate of all of us, perhaps, to direct our first sexual impulse towards our mother and our first hatred and our first murderous wish against our father. Our dreams convince us that this is so. King Oedipus, who slew his father Laius and married his mother Jocasta, merely shows us the fulfillment of our own childhood wishes . . . and we shrink back from him with the whole force of the repression by which those wishes have since that time been held down within us.

In this passage Freud interprets the unconscious motives of Sophocles in writing the play, Oedipus in acting within it, and the audience in responding to it.

A further application of the Oedipus complex can be observed in a classic interpretation of *Hamlet* by Ernest Jones, who used this concept to explain why Hamlet delays in avenging his father's death. This reading has been tightly summarized by Norman Holland, a recent psychoanalytic critic, in *The Shakespearean Imagination.* Holland shapes the issues into four major components:

> One, people over the centuries have been unable to say why Hamlet delays in killing the man who murdered his father and married his mother. Two, psychoanalytic experience shows that every child wants to do just exactly that. Three, Hamlet delays because he cannot punish Claudius for doing what he

himself wished to do as a child and, unconsciously, still wishes to do: he would be punishing himself. Four, the fact that this wish is unconscious explains why people could not explain Hamlet's delay.

Although the Oedipus complex is, of course, not relevant to all psychological interpretations of literature, interpretations involving this complex do offer a useful example of how psychoanalytic critics tend to approach a text. (For Freud's discussion of *Hamlet*, see p. 1546.)

The situation in which Mrs. Mallard finds herself in Chopin's "The Story of an Hour" is not related to an Oedipus complex, but it is clear that news of her husband's death has released powerful unconscious desires for freedom that she had previously suppressed. As she grieved, "something" was "coming to her and she was waiting for it, fearfully." What comes to her is what she senses about the life outside her window; that's the stimulus, but the true source of what was to "possess her," which she strove to "beat . . . back with her [conscious] will" is her desperate desire for the autonomy and fulfillment she had been unable to admit did not exist in her marriage. A psychological approach to her story amounts to a case study in the destructive nature of self-repression. Moreover, the story might reflect Chopin's own views of her marriage — despite her conscious statements about her loving husband. And what about the reader's response? How might a psychological approach account for different responses in female and male readers to Mrs. Mallard's death? One needn't be versed in psychoanalytic terms to entertain this question.

HISTORICAL STRATEGIES

Historians sometimes use literature as a window onto the past because literature frequently provides the nuances of a historic period that cannot be readily perceived through other sources. The characters in Harriet Beecher Stowe's *Uncle Tom's Cabin* (1852) display, for example, a complex set of white attitudes toward blacks in mid-nineteenth-century America that is absent from more traditional historic documents, such as census statistics or state laws. Another way of approaching the relationship between literature and history, however, is to use history as a means of understanding a literary work more clearly. The plot pattern of pursuit, escape, and capture in nineteenth-century slave narratives had a significant influence on Stowe's plotting of action in *Uncle Tom's Cabin*. This relationship demonstrates that the writing contemporary to an author is an important element of the history that helps to shape a work. There are many ways to talk about the historical and cultural dimensions of a work. Such readings treat a literary text as a document reflecting, producing, or being produced by the social conditions of its time, giving equal focus to the social milieu and the work itself. Four historical strategies that have been especially influential are literary history criticism, Marxist criticism, new historicist criticism, and cultural criticism.

Literary History Criticism

Literary historians shift the emphasis from the period to the work. Hence a literary historian might also examine mid-nineteenth-century abolitionist attitudes toward blacks to determine whether Stowe's novel is representative of those views or significantly to the right or left of them. Such a study might even indicate how closely the book reflects racial attitudes of twentieth-century readers. A work of literature may transcend time to the extent that it addresses the concerns of readers over a span of decades or centuries, but it remains for the literary historian a part of the past in which it was composed, a past that can reveal more fully a work's language, ideas, and purposes.

Literary historians move beyond both the facts of an author's personal life and the text itself to the social and intellectual currents in which the author composed the work. They place the work in the context of its time (as do many critical biographers, who write "life and times" studies), and sometimes they make connections with other literary works that may have influenced the author. The basic strategy of literary historians is to illuminate the historic background in order to shed light on some aspect of the work itself.

In Hemingway's "Soldier's Home" we learn that Krebs had been at Belleau Wood, Soissons, the Champagne, St. Mihiel, and the Argonne. Although nothing is said of these battles in the story, they were among the bloodiest battles of the war; the wholesale butchery and staggering casualties incurred by both sides make credible the way Krebs's unstated but lingering memories have turned him into a psychological prisoner of war. Knowing something about the ferocity of those battles helps us account for Krebs's response in the story. Moreover, we can more fully appreciate Hemingway's refusal to have Krebs lie about the realities of war for the folks back home if we are aware of the numerous poems, stories, and plays published during World War I that presented war as a glorious, manly, transcendent sacrifice for God and country. Juxtaposing those works with "Soldier's Home" brings the differences into sharp focus.

Similarly, a reading of William Blake's poem "London" (p. 762) is less complete if we do not know of the horrific social conditions — the poverty, disease, exploitation, and hypocrisy — that characterized the city Blake laments in the late eighteenth century.

One last example: the repression expressed in the lines on Mrs. Mallard's face is more distinctly seen if Chopin's "The Story of an Hour" is placed in the context of "the women's question" as it continued to develop in the 1890s. Mrs. Mallard's impulse toward "self-assertion" runs parallel with a growing women's movement away from the role of long-suffering housewife. This desire was widely regarded by traditionalists as a form of dangerous selfishness that was considered as unnatural as it was immoral.

It is no wonder that Chopin raises the question of whether Mrs. Mallard's sense of freedom owing to her husband's death isn't a selfish, "monstrous joy." Mrs. Mallard, however, dismisses this question as "trivial" in the face of her new perception of life, a dismissal that Chopin endorses by way of the story's ironic ending. The larger social context of this story would have been more apparent to Chopin's readers in 1894 than it is to readers in the 1990s. That is why an historical reconstruction of the limitations placed on married women helps to explain the pressures, tensions, and momentary — only momentary — release that Mrs. Mallard experiences.

Marxist Criticism

Marxist readings developed from the heightened interest in radical reform during the 1930s, when many critics looked to literature as a means of furthering proletarian social and economic goals, based largely on the writings of Karl Marx. *Marxist critics* focus on the ideological content of a work — its explicit and implicit assumptions and values about matters such as culture, race, class, and power. Marxist studies typically aim at revealing and clarifying ideological issues and also correcting social injustices. Some Marxist critics have used literature to describe the competing socioeconomic interests that too often advance capitalist money and power rather than socialist morality and justice. They argue that criticism, like literature, is essentially political because it either challenges or supports economic oppression. Even if criticism attempts to ignore class conflicts, it is politicized, according to Marxists, because it supports the status quo.

It is not surprising that Marxist critics pay more attention to the content and themes of literature than to its form. A Marxist critic would more likely be concerned with the exploitive economic forces that cause Willy Loman to feel trapped in Miller's *Death of a Salesman* (p. 1795) than with the playwright's use of nonrealistic dramatic techniques to reveal Loman's inner thoughts. Similarly, a Marxist reading of Chopin's "The Story of an Hour" might draw on the evidence made available in a book published only a few years after the story by Charlotte Perkins Gilman titled *Women and Economics: A Study of the Economic Relation between Men and Women as a Factor in Social Evolution* (1898). An examination of this study could help explain how some of the "repression" Mrs. Mallard experiences was generated by the socioeconomic structure contemporary to her and how Chopin challenges the validity of that structure by having Mrs. Mallard resist it with her very life. A Marxist reading would see the protagonist's conflict as not only an individual issue but part of a larger class struggle.

New Historicist Criticism

Since the 1960s a development in historical approaches to literature known as *new historicism* has emphasized the interaction between the historic context of a work and a modern reader's understanding and interpretation of the work. In contrast to many traditional literary historians, however, new historicists attempt to describe the culture of a period by reading many different kinds of texts that traditional historians might have previously left for economists, sociologists, and anthropologists. New historicists attempt to read a period in all its dimensions, including political, economic, social, and aesthetic concerns. These considerations could be used to explain the pressures that destroy Mrs. Mallard. A new historicist might examine the story and the public attitudes toward women contemporary to "The Story of an Hour" as well as documents such as suffragist tracts and medical diagnoses to explore how the same forces — expectations about how women are supposed to feel, think, and behave — shape different kinds of texts and how these texts influence each other. A new historicist might, for example, examine medical records for evidence of "nervousness" and "hysteria" as common diagnoses for women who led lives regarded as too independent by their contemporaries.

Without an awareness of just how selfish and self-destructive Mrs. Mallard's impulses would have been in the eyes of her contemporaries, twentieth-century readers might miss the pervasive pressures embedded not only in her marriage but in the social fabric surrounding her. Her death is made more understandable by such an awareness. The doctors who diagnose her as suffering from "the joy that kills" are not merely insensitive or stupid; they represent a contrasting set of assumptions and values that are as historic and real as Mrs. Mallard's yearnings.

New historicist criticism acknowledges more fully than traditional historical approaches the competing nature of readings of the past and thereby tends to offer new emphases and perspectives. New historicism reminds us that there is not only one historic context for "The Story of an Hour." Those doctors reveal additional dimensions of late-nineteenth-century social attitudes that warrant our attention, whether we agree with them or not. By emphasizing that historical perceptions are governed, at least in part, by our own concerns and preoccupations, new historicists sensitize us to the fact that the history on which we choose to focus is colored by being reconstructed from our own present moment. This reconstructed history affects our reading of texts.

Cultural Criticism

Cultural critics, like new historicists, focus on the historical contexts of a literary work, but they pay particular attention to popular manifestations of social, political, and economic contexts. Popular culture — mass-produced and consumed cultural artifacts, today ranging from advertising to popular fiction to television to rock music — and "high" culture are given equal emphasis. A cultural critic might be interested in looking at how Baz Luhrmann's movie version of *Romeo and Juliet* (1996) was influenced by the fragmentary nature of MTV videos. Adding the "low" art of everyday life to "high" art opens up previously unexpected and unexplored areas of criticism. Cultural critics use widely eclectic strategies drawn from new historicism, psychology, gender studies, and deconstructionism (to name only a handful of approaches) to analyze not only literary texts but radio talk shows, comic strips, calendar art, commercials, travel guides, and baseball cards. Because all human activity falls within the ken of cultural criticism, nothing is too minor or major, obscure or pervasive, to escape the range of its analytic vision.

Cultural criticism also includes *postcolonial criticism,* the study of cultural behavior and expression in relationship to the formerly colonized world. Postcolonial criticism refers to the analysis of literary works written by writers from countries and cultures that at one time were controlled by colonizing powers — such as Indian writers during or after British colonial rule. The term also refers to the analysis of literary works written about colonial cultures by writers from the colonizing country. Many of these kinds of analyses point out how writers from colonial powers sometimes misrepresent colonized cultures by reflecting more their own values: Joseph Conrad's *Heart of Darkness* (published in 1899) represents African culture differently than Chinua Achebe's *Things Falling Apart* does, for example. Cultural criticism and postcolonial criticism represent a broad range of approaches to examining race, gender, and class in historical contexts in a variety of cultures.

A cultural critic's approach to Chopin's "The Story of an Hour" might emphasize how the story reflects the potential dangers and horrors of train travel in the 1890s or it might examine how heart disease was often misdiagnosed by physicians or used as a metaphor in Mrs. Mallard's culture for a variety of emotional conditions. Each of these perspectives can serve to create a wider and more informed understanding of the story. For a sense of the range of documents used by cultural critics to shed light on literary works and the historical contexts in which they are written and read, see the Cultural Case Studies on James Joyce's "Eveline" for fiction (p. 507), Julia Alvarez's "Queens, 1963" for poetry (p. 1060), and David Henry Hwang's *M. Butterfly* for drama (p. 1672).

GENDER STRATEGIES

Gender critics explore how ideas about men and women — what is masculine and feminine — can be regarded as socially constructed by particular cultures. According to some critics, sex is determined by simple biological and anatomical categories of male or female, and gender is determined by a culture's values. Thus, ideas about gender and what constitutes masculine and feminine behavior are created by cultural institutions and conditioning. A gender critic might, for example, focus on Chopin's characterization of an emotionally sensitive Mrs. Mallard and a rational, composed husband in "The Story of an Hour" as a manifestation of socially constructed gender identity in the 1890s. Gender criticism expands categories and definitions of what is masculine or feminine and tends to regard sexuality as more complex than merely masculine or feminine, heterosexual or homosexual. Gender criticism, therefore, has come to include gay and lesbian criticism as well as feminist criticism. Although there are complex and sometimes problematic relationships among these approaches because some critics argue that heterosexuals and homosexuals are profoundly biologically different, gay and lesbian criticism, like feminist criticism, can be usefully regarded as a subset of gender criticism.

Feminist Criticism

Like Marxist critics, *feminist critics* reading "The Story of an Hour" would also be interested in Charlotte Perkins Gilman's *Women and Economics: A Study of the Economic Relation between Men and Women as a Factor in Social Evolution* (1898) because they seek to correct or supplement what they regard as a predominantly male-dominated critical perspective with a feminist consciousness. Like other forms of sociological criticism, feminist criticism places literature in a social context, and, like those of Marxist criticism, its analyses often have sociopolitical purposes — explaining, for example, how images of women in literature reflect the patriarchal social forces that have impeded women's efforts to achieve full equality with men.

Feminists have analyzed literature by both men and women in an effort to understand literary representations of women as well as the writers and cultures that create them. Related to concerns about how gender affects the way men and women write about each other is an interest in whether women use language differently from the way men do. Consequently, feminist critics' approach to literature is characterized by the use of a broad range of disciplines, including history, sociology, psychology, and linguistics, to provide a perspective sensitive to feminist issues.

A feminist approach to Chopin's "The Story of an Hour" might explore the psychological stress created by the expectations that marriage imposes on Mrs. Mallard, expectations that literally and figuratively break her heart. Given that her husband is kind and loving, the issue is not her being married to Brently but her being married at all. Chopin presents marriage as an institution that creates in both men and women the assumed "right to impose a private will upon a fellow-creature." That "right," however, is seen, especially from a feminist perspective, as primarily imposed on women by men. A feminist critic might note, for instance, that the protagonist is introduced as "Mrs. Mallard" (we learn that her first name is Louise only later); she is defined by her marital status and her husband's name, a name whose origin from the Old French is related to the word *masle*, which means "male." The appropriateness of her name points up the fact that her emotions and the cause of her death are interpreted in male terms by the doctors. The value of a feminist perspective on this work can be readily discerned if a reader imagines Mrs. Mallard's story being told from the point of view of one of the doctors who diagnoses the cause of her death as a weak heart rather than as a fierce struggle.

Gay and Lesbian Criticism

Gay and lesbian critics focus on a variety of issues, including how homosexuals are represented in literature, how they read literature, and whether sexuality and gender are culturally constructed or innate. Gay critics have produced new readings and discovered homosexual concerns in writers such as Herman Melville and Henry James, while lesbian critics have done the same for the works of writers such as Emily Dickinson and Toni Morrison. A lesbian reading of "The Story of an Hour," for example, might consider whether Mrs. Mallard's ecstatic feeling of relief — produced by the belief that her marriage is over owing to the presumed death of her husband — isn't also a rejection of her heterosexual identity. Perhaps her glimpse of future freedom, evoked by feminine images of a newly discovered nature "all aquiver with the new spring of life," embraces a repressed new sexual identity that "was too subtle and elusive to name" but that was "approaching to possess her" no matter how much she "was striving to beat it back with her will." Although gay and lesbian readings often raise significant interpretive controversies among critics, they have opened up provocative discussions of seemingly familiar texts.

MYTHOLOGICAL STRATEGIES

Mythological approaches to literature attempt to identify what in a work creates deep universal responses in readers. Whereas psychological critics interpret the symbolic meanings of characters and actions in order to understand more fully the unconscious dimensions of an author's mind, a character's motivation, or a reader's response, mythological critics (also frequently referred to as *archetypal critics*) interpret the hopes, fears, and expectations of entire cultures.

In this context myth is not to be understood simply as referring to stories about imaginary gods who perform astonishing feats in the causes of love, jealousy, or hatred. Nor are myths to be judged as merely erroneous, primitive accounts of how nature runs its course and humanity its affairs. Instead, literary critics use myths as a strategy for understanding how human beings try to account for their lives symbolically. Myths can be a window onto a culture's deepest perceptions about itself because myths attempt to explain what otherwise seems unexplainable: a people's origin, purpose, and destiny.

All human beings have a need to make sense of their lives, whether they are concerned about their natural surroundings, the seasons, sexuality, birth, death, or the very meaning of existence. Myths help people organize their experiences; these systems of belief (less formally held than religious or political tenets but no less important) embody a culture's assumptions and values. What is important to the mythological critic is not the validity or truth of those assumptions and values; what matters is that they reveal common human concerns.

It is not surprising that although the details of mythic stories vary enormously, the essential patterns are often similar because these myths attempt to explain universal experiences. There are, for example, numerous myths that redeem humanity from permanent death through a hero's resurrection and rebirth. The resurrection of Jesus symbolizes for Christians the ultimate defeat of death and coincides with the rebirth of nature's fertility in spring. Features of this rebirth parallel the Greek myths of Adonis and Hyacinth, who die but are subsequently transformed into living flowers; there are also similarities that connect these stories to the reincarnation of the Indian Buddha or the rebirth of the Egyptian Osiris. Important differences exist among these stories, but each reflects a basic human need to limit the power of death and to hope for eternal life.

Mythological critics look for underlying, recurrent patterns in literature that reveal universal meanings and basic human experiences for readers regardless of when or where they live. The characters, images, and themes that symbolically embody these meanings and experiences are called **archetypes.** This term designates universal symbols, which evoke deep and perhaps unconscious responses in a reader because archetypes bring with them our hopes and fears since the beginning of human time. Surely one of the most powerfully compelling archetypes is the death and rebirth theme that relates the human life cycle to the cycle of the seasons. Many others could be cited and would be exhausted only after all human concerns were catalogued, but a few examples can suggest some of the range of plots, images, and characters addressed.

Among the most common literary archetypes are stories of quests, initiations, scapegoats, meditative withdrawals, descents to the underworld, and heavenly ascents. These stories are often filled with archetypal images — bodies of water that may symbolize the unconscious or eternity or baptismal rebirth; rising suns, suggesting reawakening and enlightenment; setting suns, pointing toward death; colors such as green, evocative of growth and fertility, or black, indicating chaos, evil, and death. Along the way are earth mothers, fatal women, wise old men, desert places, and paradisal gardens. No doubt your own reading has introduced you to any number of archetypal plots, images, and characters.

Mythological critics attempt to explain how archetypes are embodied in literary works. Employing various disciplines, these critics articulate the power a literary work has over us. Some critics are deeply grounded in classical literature, whereas others are more conversant with philology, anthropology, psychology, or cultural history. Whatever their emphases, however, mythological critics examine the elements of a work in order to make larger connections that explain the work's lasting appeal.

A mythological reading of Sophocles' *Oedipus the King,* for example, might focus on the relationship between Oedipus's role as a scapegoat and the plague and drought that threaten to destroy Thebes. The city is saved and the fertility of its fields restored only after the corruption is located in Oedipus. His subsequent atonement symbolically provides a kind of re-birth for the city. Thus, the plot recapitulates ancient rites in which the well-being of a king was directly linked to the welfare of his people. If a leader was sick or corrupt, he had to be replaced in order to guarantee the health of the community.

A similar pattern can be seen in the rottenness that Shakespeare ex-poses in Hamlet's Denmark. *Hamlet* reveals an archetypal pattern similar to that of *Oedipus the King:* not until the hero sorts out the corruption in his world and in himself can vitality and health be restored in his world. Hamlet avenges his father's death and becomes a scapegoat in the process. When he fully accepts his responsibility to set things right, he is swept away along with the tide of intrigue and corruption that has polluted life in Denmark. The new order—established by Fortinbras at the play's end—is achieved precisely because Hamlet is willing and finally able to sacrifice himself in a necessary purgation of the diseased state.

These kinds of archetypal patterns exist potentially in any literary pe-riod. Consider how in Chopin's "The Story of an Hour" Mrs. Mallard's life parallels the end of winter and the earth's renewal in spring. When she feels a surge of new life after grieving over her husband's death, her own sensibilities are closely aligned with the "new spring life" that is "all aquiver" outside her window. Although she initially tries to resist that re-newal by "beat[ing] it back with her will," she cannot control the life force that surges within her and all around her. When she finally gives herself to the energy and life she experiences, she feels triumphant—like a "goddess of Victory." But this victory is short lived when she learns that her hus-band is still alive and with him all the obligations that made her marriage feel like a wasteland. Her death is an ironic version of a rebirth ritual. The coming of spring is an ironic contrast to her own discovery that she can no longer live a repressed, circumscribed life with her husband. Death turns out to be preferable to the living death that her marriage means to her. Al-though spring will go on, this "goddess of Victory" is defeated by a devas-tating social contract. The old, corrupt order continues, and that for Chopin is a cruel irony that mythological critics would see as an unnatural disruption of the nature of things.

READER-RESPONSE STRATEGIES

Reader-response criticism, as its name implies, focuses its attention on the reader rather than the work itself. This approach to literature describes what goes on in the reader's mind during the process of reading a text. In a sense, all critical approaches (especially psychological and mythological criticism) concern themselves with a reader's response to literature, but there is a stronger emphasis in reader-response criticism on the reader's active construction of the text. Although many critical theories inform reader-response criticism, all ***reader-response critics*** aim to describe the reader's experience of a work: in effect we get a reading of the reader, who comes to the work with certain expectations and assumptions, which are either met or not met. Hence the consciousness of the reader — produced by reading the work — is the subject matter of reader-response critics. Just as writing is a creative act, reading is, since it also produces a text.

Reader-response critics do not assume that a literary work is a finished product with fixed formal properties, as, for example, formalist critics do. Instead, the literary work is seen as an evolving creation of the reader's as he or she processes characters, plots, images, and other elements while reading. Some reader-response critics argue that this act of creative reading is, to a degree, controlled by the text, but it can produce many interpretations of the same text by different readers. There is no single definitive reading of a work, because the crucial assumption is that readers create rather than discover meanings in texts. Readers who have gone back to works they had read earlier in their lives often find that a later reading draws very different responses from them. What earlier seemed unimportant is now crucial; what at first seemed central is now barely worth noting. The reason, put simply, is that two different people have read the same text. Reader-response critics are not after the "correct" reading of the text or what the author presumably intended; instead they are interested in the reader's experience with the text.

These experiences change with readers; although the text remains the same, the readers do not. Social and cultural values influence readings, so that, for example, an avowed Marxist would be likely to come away from Miller's *Death of a Salesman* with a very different view of American capitalism than that of, say, a successful sales representative, who might attribute Willy Loman's fall more to his character than to the American economic system. Moreover, readers from different time periods respond differently to texts. An Elizabethan — concerned perhaps with the stability of monarchical rule — might respond differently to Hamlet's problems than would a twentieth-century reader well versed in psychology and concepts of what Freud called the Oedipus complex. This is not to say that anything goes, that Miller's play can be read as an amoral defense of cheating and rapacious business practices or that *Hamlet* is about the dangers of living away from home. The text does, after all, establish some limits that allow us to reject certain readings as erroneous. But reader-response critics do reject formalist approaches that describe a literary work as a self-contained object, the meaning of which can be determined without reference to any extrinsic matters, such as the social and cultural values assumed by either the author or the reader.

Reader-response criticism calls attention to how we read and what influences our readings. It does not attempt to define what a literary work means on the page but rather what it does to an informed reader, a reader who understands the language and conventions used in a given work. Reader-response criticism is not a rationale for mistaken or bizarre readings of works but an exploration of the possibilities for a plurality of readings shaped by the readers' experience with the text. This kind of strategy can help us understand how our responses are shaped by both the text and ourselves.

Chopin's "The Story of an Hour" illustrates how reader-response critical strategies read the reader. Chopin doesn't say that Mrs. Mallard's marriage is repressive; instead, that troubling fact dawns on the reader at the same time that the recognition forces its way into Mrs. Mallard's consciousness. Her surprise is also the reader's because although she remains in the midst of intense grief, she is on the threshold of a startling discovery about the new possibilities life offers. How the reader responds to that discovery, however, is not entirely controlled by Chopin. One reader, perhaps someone who has recently lost a spouse, might find Mrs. Mallard's "joy" indeed "monstrous" and selfish. Certainly that's how Mrs. Mallard's doctors — the seemingly authoritative diagnosticians in the story — would very likely read her. But for other readers — especially late-twentieth-century readers steeped in feminist values — Mrs. Mallard's feelings require no justification. Such readers might find Chopin's ending to the story more ironic than she seems to have intended because Mrs. Mallard's death could be read as Chopin's inability to envision a protagonist who has the strength of her convictions. In contrast, a reader in 1894 might have seen the ending as Mrs. Mallard's only escape from the repressive marriage her husband's assumed death suddenly allowed her to see. A late-twentieth-century reader probably would argue that it was the marriage that should have died rather than Mrs. Mallard, that she had other alternatives, not just obligations (as the doctors would have insisted), to consider.

By imagining different readers we can imagine a variety of responses to the story that are influenced by the readers' own impressions, memories, or experiences with marriage. Such imagining suggests the ways in which reader-response criticism opens up texts to a number of interpretations. As one final example, consider how readers' responses to "The Story of an Hour" would be affected if it were printed in two different magazines, read in the context of either *Ms.* or *Good Housekeeping.* What assumptions and beliefs would each magazine's readership be likely to bring to the story? How do you think the respective experiences and values of each magazine's readers would influence their readings? For a sample reader-response student paper on "The Story of an Hour," see page 14.

DECONSTRUCTIONIST STRATEGIES

Deconstructionist critics insist that literary works do not yield fixed, single meanings. They argue that there can be no absolute knowledge about anything because language can never say what we intend it to mean. Anything we write conveys meanings we did not intend, so the deconstructionist argument goes. Language is not a precise instrument but a power whose meanings are caught in an endless web of possibilities that cannot be untangled. Accordingly, any idea or statement that insists on being understood separately can ultimately be "deconstructed" to reveal its relations and connections to contradictory and opposite meanings.

Unlike other forms of criticism, deconstructionism seeks to destabilize meanings instead of establishing them. In contrast to formalists such as the New Critics, who closely examine a work in order to call attention to how its various components interact to establish a unified whole, deconstructionists try to show how a close examination of the language in a text inevitably reveals conflicting, contradictory impulses that "deconstruct" or break down its apparent unity.

Although deconstructionists and New Critics both examine the language of a text closely, deconstructionists focus on the gaps and ambiguities that reveal a text's instability and indeterminacy, whereas New Critics look for patterns that explain how the text's fixed meaning is structured. Deconstructionists painstakingly examine the competing meanings within the text rather than attempting to resolve them into a unified whole.

The questions deconstructionists ask are aimed at discovering and describing how a variety of possible readings are generated by the elements of a text. In contrast to a New Critic's concerns about the ultimate meaning of a work, a deconstructionist is primarily interested in how the use of language — diction, tone, metaphor, symbol, and so on — yields only provisional, not definitive, meanings. Consider, for example, the following excerpt from an American Puritan poet, Anne Bradstreet. The excerpt is from "The Flesh and the Spirit" (1678), which consists of an allegorical debate between two sisters, the body and the soul. During the course of the debate, Flesh, a consummate materialist, insists that Spirit values ideas that do not exist and that her faith in idealism is both unwarranted and insubstantial in the face of the material values that earth has to offer — riches, fame, and physical pleasure. Spirit, however, rejects the materialistic worldly argument that the only ultimate reality is physical reality and pledges her faith in God:

> Mine eye doth pierce the heavens and see
> What is invisible to thee.
> My garments are not silk nor gold,
> Nor such like trash which earth doth hold,
> But royal robes I shall have on,
> More glorious than the glist'ring sun;
> My crown not diamonds, pearls, and gold,
> But such as angels' heads enfold
> The city where I hope to dwell,
> There's none on earth can parallel;
> The stately walls both high and strong,
> Are made of precious jasper stone;
> The gates of pearl, both rich and clear,
> And angels are for porters there;

> The streets thereof transparent gold,
> Such as no eye did e'er behold;
> A crystal river there doth run,
> Which doth proceed from the Lamb's throne.

A deconstructionist would point out that Spirit's language — her use of material images such as jasper stone, pearl, gold, and crystal — cancels the explicit meaning of the passage by offering a supermaterialistic reward to the spiritually faithful. Her language, in short, deconstructs her intended meaning by employing the same images that Flesh would use to describe the rewards of the physical world. A deconstructionist reading, then, reveals the impossibility of talking about the invisible and spiritual worlds without using materialistic (that is, metaphoric) language. Thus Spirit's very language demonstrates a contradiction and conflict in her conviction that the world of here and now must be rejected for the hereafter. Her language deconstructs her meaning.

Deconstructionists look for ways to question and extend the meanings of a text. A deconstructionist might find, for example, the ironic ending of Chopin's "The Story of an Hour" less tidy and conclusive than would a New Critic, who might attribute Mrs. Mallard's death to her sense of lost personal freedom. A deconstructionist might use the story's ending to suggest that the narrative shares the doctors' inability to imagine a life for Mrs. Mallard apart from her husband.

As difficult as it is controversial, deconstructionism is not easily summarized or paraphrased. For an example of deconstructionism in practice and how it differs from New Criticism, see Andrew P. Debicki's "New Criticism and Deconstructionism: Two Attitudes in Teaching Poetry" (p. 2050).

SELECTED BIBLIOGRAPHY

Given the enormous number of articles and books written about literary theory and criticism in recent years, the following bibliography is necessarily highly selective. Even so, it should prove useful as an introduction to many of the issues associated with the critical strategies discussed in this chapter. For a general encyclopedic reference book that describes important figures, schools, and movements, see *The Johns Hopkins Guide to Literary Theory and Criticism,* edited by Michael Grodin and Martin Kreiswirth (Baltimore: Johns Hopkins UP, 1994); and for its concise discussions, see Ross Murfin and Supryia M. Ray, *The Bedford Glossary of Critical and Literary Terms* (Boston: Bedford/St. Martin's, 1998).

Canonical Issues

"The Changing Culture of the University." Special Issue. *Partisan Review* 58 (Spring 1991): 185–410.

Gates, Henry Louis, Jr. *The Signifying Monkey*. New York: Oxford UP, 1988.

Greenblatt, Stephen, and Giles Gunn. *Redrawing the Boundaries: The Transformation of English and American Literary Studies*. New York: MLA, 1992.

Lauter, Paul. *Canons and Contexts*. New York: Oxford UP, 1991.

"The Politics of Liberal Education." Special Issue. *South Atlantic Quarterly* 89 (Winter 1990): 1–234.

Sykes, Charles J. *The Hollow Men: Politics and Corruption in Higher Education*. Washington, DC: Regnery Gateway, 1990.

Formalist Strategies

Brooks, Cleanth. *The Well Wrought Urn: Studies in the Structure of Poetry*. New York: Reynal and Hitchcock, 1947.

Crane, Ronald Salmon. *The Languages of Criticism and the Structure of Poetry*. Toronto: U of Toronto P, 1953.

Eliot, Thomas Stearns. *The Sacred Wood: Essays in Poetry and Criticism*. London: Methuen, 1920.

Fekete, John. *The Critical Twilight: Explorations in the Ideology of Anglo-American Literary Theory from Eliot to McLuhan*. London: Routledge, 1977.

Lemon, Lee T., and Marion J. Reis, eds. *Russian Formalist Criticism: Four Essays*. Lincoln: U of Nebraska P, 1965.

Ransom, John Crowe. *The New Criticism*. Norfolk, CT: New Directions, 1941.

Wellek, René, and Austin Warren. *Theory of Literature*. New York: Harcourt, Brace and World, 1949.

Biographical and Psychological Strategies

Bleich, David. *Subjective Criticism*. Baltimore: Johns Hopkins UP, 1978.

Bloom, Harold. *The Anxiety of Influence*. New York: Oxford UP, 1975.

Brennan, Teresa. *The Interpretation of the Flesh: Freud and Femininity*. New York: Routledge, 1994.

Crews, Frederick. *Out of My System: Psychoanalysis, Ideology, and Critical Method*. New York: Oxford UP, 1975.

——. *The Sins of the Fathers: Hawthorne's Psychological Themes*. New York: Oxford UP, 1966.

Felman, Shoshana. *Writing and Madness (Literature/Philosophy/Psychoanalysis)*. Ithaca: Cornell UP, 1985.

——, ed. *Literature and Psychoanalysis: The Question of Reading: Otherwise*. Baltimore: Johns Hopkins UP, 1981.

Freud, Sigmund. *The Standard Edition of the Complete Psychological Works*. 24 vols. 1940–1968. London: Hogarth Press and the Institute of Psychoanalysis, 1953.

Holland, Norman. *The Dynamics of Literary Response*. New York: Oxford UP, 1968.

Jones, Ernest. *Hamlet and Oedipus.* New York: Doubleday, 1949.

Lacan, Jacques. *Écrits: A Selection.* Trans. Alan Sheridan. New York: Norton, 1977.

——. *The Four Fundamental Concepts of Psychoanalysis.* Trans. Alan Sheridan. London: Penguin, 1980.

Lesser, Simon O. *Fiction and the Unconscious.* Chicago: U of Chicago P, 1957.

Skura, Meredith Anne. *The Literary Use of the Psychoanalytic Process.* New Haven: Yale UP, 1981.

Zizek, Slavoj. *Looking Awry: An Introduction to Jacques Lacan through Popular Culture.* Cambridge: MIT P, 1991.

Historical Strategies, Including Marxist, New Historicist, and Cultural Strategies

Ang, Ien. *Watching Television.* New York: Routledge, 1991.

Armstrong, Nancy. *Desire and Domestic Fiction.* New York: Oxford UP, 1987.

Ashcroft, Bill, Ga Breth Griffiths, and Helen Tiffin, eds. *The Post-Colonial Studies Reader.* New York: Routledge, 1995.

Bhabha, Homi K. *The Location of Culture.* New York: Routledge, 1994.

Dollimore, Jonathan. *Radical Tragedy: Religion, Ideology and Power in the Drama of Shakespeare and His Contemporaries.* Brighton, Eng.: Harvester, 1984.

Frow, John. *Marxist and Literary History.* Cambridge: Harvard UP, 1986.

Geertz, Clifford. *The Interpretation of Cultures: Selected Essays.* New York: Basic, 1973.

Greenblatt, Stephen. *Renaissance Self-Fashioning: From More to Shakespeare.* Chicago: U of Chicago P, 1980.

——. *Shakespearean Negotiations: The Circulation of Social Energy in Renaissance England.* Berkeley: U of California P, 1985.

Lindenberger, Herbert. *Historical Drama: The Relation of Literature and Reality.* Chicago: U of Chicago P, 1975.

McGann, Jerome. *The Beauty of Inflections: Literary Investigations in Historical Method and Theory.* Oxford: Clarendon, 1985.

Storey, John, ed. *What Is Cultural Studies?* New York: St. Martin's, 1996.

White, Hayden. *Tropics of Discourse: Essays in Cultural Criticism.* Baltimore: Johns Hopkins UP, 1978.

Williams, Raymond. *Marxism and Literature.* Oxford: Oxford UP, 1977.

Gender Strategies, Including Feminist and Gay and Lesbian Strategies

Ablelove, Henry, Michèle Aina Barale, and David M. Halperin, eds. *The Lesbian and Gay Studies Reader.* New York: Routledge, 1993.

Baym, Nina. *Feminism and American Literary History.* New Brunswick: Rutgers UP, 1992.

Beauvoir, Simone de. *The Second Sex.* Trans. H. M. Parshley. New York: Knopf, 1972. Trans. of *Le deuxième sexe.* Paris: Gallimard, 1949.

Benstock, Shari, ed. *Feminist Issues and Literary Scholarship.* Bloomington: Indiana UP, 1987.

Cixous, Hélène, and Catherine Clément. *The Newly Born Woman.* Trans. Betsy Wing. Minneapolis: U of Minnesota P, 1986.

Edelman, Lee. *Homographesis: Essays in Gay Literary and Cultural Theory.* New York: Routledge, 1994.

Fetterley, Judith. *The Resisting Reader: A Feminist Approach to American Fiction.* Bloomington: Indiana UP, 1978.

Flynn, Elizabeth A., and Patrocino P. Schweickert. *Gender and Reading: Essays on Readers, Texts, and Contexts.* Baltimore: Johns Hopkins UP, 1986.

Gilbert, Sandra M., and Susan Gubar. *The Madwoman in the Attic: The Woman Writer and the Nineteenth-Century Literary Imagination.* New Haven: Yale UP, 1979.

Irigaray, Luce. *This Sex Which Is Not One.* Ithaca: Cornell UP, 1985. Trans. of *Ce sexe qui n'en est pas un.* Paris: Éditions de Minuit, 1977.

Jagose, Annamarie. *Queer Theory.* Victoria: Melbourne UP, 1996.

Kolodny, Annette. "Some Notes on Defining a 'Feminist Literary Criticism.'" *Critical Inquiry* 2 (1975): 75–92.

Millett, Kate. *Sexual Politics.* New York: Avon, 1970.

Sedgwick, Eve Kosofsky. *Epistemology of the Closet.* Berkeley: U of California P, 1990.

Showalter, Elaine. *A Literature of Their Own: British Women Novelists from Brontë to Lessing.* Princeton: Princeton UP, 1977.

Smith, Barbara. *Toward a Black Feminist Criticism.* New York: Out and Out, 1977.

Mythological Strategies

Bodkin, Maud. *Archetypal Patterns in Poetry.* London: Oxford UP, 1934.

Frye, Northrop. *Anatomy of Criticism: Four Essays.* Princeton: Princeton UP, 1957.

Jung, Carl Gustav. *Complete Works.* Ed. Herbert Read, Michael Fordham, and Gerhard Adler. 17 vols. New York: Pantheon, 1953–.

Reader-Response Strategies

Booth, Wayne C. *The Rhetoric of Fiction.* 2nd ed. Chicago: U of Chicago P, 1983.

Eco, Umberto. *The Role of the Reader: Explorations in the Semiotics of Texts.* Bloomington: Indiana UP, 1979.

Escarpit, Robert. *Sociology of Literature.* Painesville, OH: Lake Erie College P, 1965.

Fish, Stanley. *Is There a Text in This Class? The Authority of Interpretive Communities.* Cambridge: Harvard UP, 1980.

Freund, Elizabeth. *The Return of the Reader: Reader-Response Criticism.* London: Methuen, 1987.

Holland, Norman N. *The Critical I.* New York: Columbia UP, 1992.

———. *Five Readers Reading.* New Haven: Yale UP, 1975.

Iser, Wolfgang. *The Implied Reader: Patterns of Communication in Prose Fiction from Bunyan to Beckett.* Baltimore: Johns Hopkins UP, 1974.

Jauss, Hans Robert. "Literary History as a Challenge to Literary Theory." *Toward an Aesthetics of Reception.* Trans. Timothy Bahti. Minneapolis: U of Minnesota P, 1982. 3–46.

Rosenblatt, Louise. *Literature as Exploration.* 1938. New York: MLA, 1983.

Suleiman, Susan, and Inge Crosman, eds. *The Reader in the Text: Essays on Audience and Interpretation.* Princeton: Princeton UP, 1980.

Tompkins, Jane P., ed. *Reader-Response Criticism: From Formalism to Post-Structuralism.* Baltimore: Johns Hopkins UP, 1980.

Deconstructionist and Other Poststructuralist Strategies

Barthes, Roland. *The Rustle of Language.* New York: Hill and Wang, 1986.

Culler, Jonathan. *On Deconstruction: Theory and Criticism after Structuralism.* Ithaca: Cornell UP, 1982.

de Man, Paul. *Blindness and Insight.* New York: Oxford UP, 1971.

Derrida, Jacques. *Of Grammatology.* 1967. Baltimore: Johns Hopkins UP, 1976.

———. *Writing and Difference.* 1967. Chicago: U of Chicago P, 1978.

Foucault, Michel. *Language, Counter-Memory, Practice.* Ithaca: Cornell UP, 1977.

———. *The Order of Things: An Archaeology of the Human Sciences.* 1966. London: Tavistock, 1970.

Gasche, Rodolphe. "Deconstruction as Criticism." *Glyph* 6 (1979): 177–216.

Hartman, Geoffrey H. *Criticism in the Wilderness.* New Haven: Yale UP, 1980.

Johnson, Barbara. *The Critical Difference: Essays in the Contemporary Rhetoric of Reading.* Baltimore: Johns Hopkins UP, 1980.

Martin, Bill. *Humanism and Its Aftermath: The Shared Fate of Deconstructionism and Politics.* Atlantic Highlands, NJ: Humanities, 1995.

Melville, Stephen W. *Philosophy Beside Itself: On Deconstruction and Modernism.* Theory and History of Literature 27. Minneapolis: U of Minnesota P, 1986.

Royle, Nicholas. *After Derrida.* Manchester: Manchester UP, 1995.

Said, Edward W. *The World, the Text, and the Critic.* Cambridge: Harvard UP, 1983.

Smith, Barbara Herrnstein. *On the Margins of Discourse: The Relation of Literature to Language.* Chicago: U of Chicago P, 1979.

PERSPECTIVES ON CRITICAL READING

SUSAN SONTAG (B. 1933)

Against Interpretation   *1964*

Like the fumes of the automobile and of heavy industry which befoul the urban atmosphere, the effusion of interpretations of art today poisons our sensibilities. In a culture whose already classical dilemma is the hypertrophy of the intellect at the expense of energy and sensual capability, interpretation is the revenge of the intellect upon art.

Even more. It is the revenge of the intellect upon the world. To interpret is to impoverish, to deplete the world—in order to set up a shadow world of "meanings." It is to turn *the* world into *this* world. ("This world"! As if there were any other.)

The world, our world, is depleted, impoverished enough. Away with all duplicates of it, until we again experience more immediately what we have. . . .

In most modern instances, interpretation amounts to the philistine refusal to leave the work of art alone. Real art has the capacity to make us nervous. By reducing the work of art to its content and then interpreting *that,* one tames the work of art. Interpretation makes art manageable, conformable.

This philistinism of interpretation is more rife in literature than in any other art. For decades now, literary critics have understood it to be their task to translate the elements of the poem or play or novel or story into something else.

From *Against Interpretation*

CONSIDERATIONS FOR CRITICAL THINKING AND WRITING

1. What are Sontag's objections to "interpretation"? Explain whether you agree or disagree with them.

2. In what sense does interpretation make art "manageable" and "conformable" (para. 4)?

3. In an essay explore what you take to be both the dangers of interpretation and its contributions to your understanding of literature.

JUDITH FETTERLEY (B. 1938)

A Feminist Reading of "A Rose for Emily"   *1978*

"A Rose for Emily" [p. 72] is a story not of a conflict between the South and the North or between the old order and the new; it is a story of the patriarchy North and South, new and old, and of the sexual conflict within it. As Faulkner himself has implied, it is a story of a woman victimized and betrayed by the system of sexual politics, who nevertheless has discovered, within the structures that victimize her, sources of power for herself. . . . "A Rose for Emily" is the story of how to murder your gentleman caller and get away with it. Faulkner's story is an analysis of how men's attitudes toward women turn back upon themselves; it is a demonstration of the thesis that it is impossible to oppress without in turn being oppressed, it is impossible to kill without creating the conditions for your own murder. "A Rose for Emily" is the story of a *lady* and of her revenge for that grotesque identity. . . .

Not only is "A Rose for Emily" a supreme analysis of what men do to women by making them ladies; it is also an exposure of how this act in turn defines and recoils upon men. This is the significance of the dynamic that Faulkner establishes between Emily and Jefferson. And it is equally the point of the dynamic implied between the tableau of Emily and her father and the tableau which greets the men who break down the door of that room in the region above the stairs. When the would-be "suitors" finally get into her father's house, they discover the consequences of his oppression of her, for the violence contained in the rotted corpse of Homer Barron is the mirror image of the violence represented in the tableau, the back-flung front door flung back with a vengeance. Having been consumed by her father, Emily in turn feeds off Homer Barron, becoming, after his death, suspiciously fat. Or, to put it another way, it is as if, after her father's death, she has reversed his act of incorporating her by incorporating and becoming him, metamorphosed from the slender figure in white to the obese figure in black whose hair is "a vigorous iron-gray, like the hair of an active man." She has taken into herself the violence in him which thwarted her and has reenacted it upon Homer Barron.

That final encounter, however, is not simply an image of the reciprocity of violence. Its power of definition also derives from its grotesqueness, which makes finally explicit the grotesqueness that has been latent in the description of Emily throughout the story: "Her skeleton was small and spare: perhaps that was why what would have been merely plumpness in another was obesity in her. She looked bloated, like a body long submerged in motionless water, and of that pallid hue. Her eyes, lost in the fatty ridges of her face, looked like two small pieces of coal pressed into a lump of dough." The impact of this description depends on the contrast it establishes between Emily's reality as a fat, bloated figure in black and the conventional image of a lady—expectations that are fostered in the town by its emblematic memory of Emily as a slender figure in white and in us by the narrator's tone of romantic invocation and by the passage itself. Were she not expected to look so different, were her skeleton not small and spare, Emily would not be so grotesque. Thus, the focus is on the grotesqueness that results when stereotypes are imposed upon reality. And the implication of this focus is that the real grotesque is the stereotype itself. If Emily is both lady and grotesque, then the syllogism must be completed thus: the idea of a lady is grotesque. So Emily is metaphor and mirror for the town of Jefferson; and when, at the end, the town folk finally discover who and what she is, they have in fact encountered who and what they are.

From *The Resisting Reader: A Feminist Approach to American Fiction*

CONSIDERATIONS FOR CRITICAL THINKING AND WRITING

1. Discuss Fetterley's claim that Emily Grierson is a victim of a "system of sexual politics" (para. 1). What details of the story support this view?

2. What are the consequences of Emily's oppression by her father? How are the men in the story affected by it?

3. Write an essay that supports or refutes Fetterley's argument that "A Rose for Emily" is an implicitly feminist story about "the patriarchy North and South" (para. 1).

ANNETTE KOLODNY (B. 1941)

On the Commitments of Feminist Criticism 1980

If feminist criticism calls anything into question, it must be that dog-eared myth of intellectual neutrality. For what I take to be the underlying spirit or message of any consciously ideologically premised criticism — that is, that ideas are important *because* they determine the ways we live, or want to live, in the world — is vitiated by confining those ideas to the study, the classroom, or the pages of our books. To write chapters decrying the sexual stereotyping of women in our literature, while closing our eyes to the sexual harassment of our women students and colleagues; to display Katharine Hepburn and Rosalind Russell in our courses on "The Image of the Independent Career Women in Film," while managing not to notice the paucity of female administrators on our own campus; to study the women who helped make universal enfranchisement a political reality, while keeping silent about our activist colleagues who are denied promotion or tenure; to include segments on "Women in the Labor Movement" in our American studies or women's studies courses, while remaining willfully ignorant of the department secretary fired for efforts to organize a clerical workers' union; to glory in the delusions of "merit," "privilege," and "status" which accompany campus life in order to insulate ourselves from the millions of women who labor in poverty — all this is not merely hypocritical; it destroys both the spirit and the meaning of what we are about.

From "Dancing through the Minefield: Some Observations on the Theory, Practice, and Politics of a Feminist Literary Criticism," *Feminist Studies* 6, 1980

CONSIDERATIONS FOR CRITICAL THINKING AND WRITING

1. Why does Kolodny reject "intellectual neutrality" as a "myth"? Explain whether you agree or disagree with her point of view.

2. Kolodny argues that feminist criticism can be used as an instrument for social reform. Discuss the possibility and desirability of her position. Do you think other kinds of criticism can and should be used to create social change?

ANDREW P. DEBICKI (B. 1934)

New Criticism and Deconstructionism: Two Attitudes in Teaching Poetry 1985

[Let's] look at the ways in which a New Critic and a deconstructivist might handle a poem. My first example, untitled, is a work by Pedro Salinas, which I first analyzed many years ago and which I have recently taught to a group of students influenced by deconstruction:

> Sand: sleeping on the beach today
> and tomorrow caressed
> in the bosom of the sea:
> the sun's today, water's prize tomorrow.
> Softly you yield

to the hand that presses you
and go away with the first
courting wind that appears.
Pure and fickle sand,
changing and clear beloved,
I wanted you for my own,
and held you against my chest and soul.
But you escaped with the waves, the wind, the sun,
and I remained without a beloved,
my face turned to the wind which robbed her,
and my eyes to the far-off sea in which she had
green loves in a green shelter.

My original study of this poem, written very much in the New Critical tradition, focused on the unusual personification of sand and beloved and on the
metaphorical pattern that it engendered. In the first part of the work, the
physical elusiveness of sand (which slips through one's hand, flies with the wind,
moves from shore to sea) evokes a coquettish woman, yielding to her lover and
then escaping, running off with a personified wind, moving from one being to
another. Watching these images, the reader gradually forgets that the poem is
metaphorically describing sand and becomes taken up by the unusual correspondences with the figure of a flirting woman. When in the last part of the
poem the speaker laments his loss, the reader is drawn into his lament for a
fickle lover who has abandoned him.

Continuing a traditional analysis of this poem, we would conclude that
its unusual personification/metaphor takes us beyond a literal level and leads
us to a wider vision. The true subject of this poem is not sand, nor is it a flirt
who tricks a man. The comparison between sand and woman, however, has
made us feel the elusiveness of both, as well as the effect that this elusiveness
has had on the speaker, who is left sadly contemplating it at the end of the
poem. The poem has used its main image to embody a general vision of fleetingness and its effects.

My analysis, as developed thus far, is representative of a New Critical study.
It focuses on the text and its central image, it describes a tension produced
within the text, and it suggests a way in which this tension is resolved so as to
move the poem beyond its literal level. In keeping with the tenets of traditional
analytic criticism, it shows how the poem conveys a meaning that is far richer
than its plot or any possible conceptual message. But while it is careful not to reduce the poem to a simple idea or to an equivalent of its prose summary, it does
attempt to work all of its elements into a single interpretation which would satisfy every reader . . . : it makes all of the poem's meanings reside in its verbal
structures, and it suggests that those meanings can be discovered and combined
into a single cohesive vision as we systematically analyze those structures.

By attempting to find a pattern that will incorporate and resolve the
poem's tensions, however, this reading leaves some loose ends, which I noticed
even in my New Critical perspective — and which I found difficult to explain. To
see the poem as the discovery of the theme of fleetingness by an insightful
speaker, we have to ignore the fanciful nature of the comparison, the whimsical
attitude to reality that it suggests, and the excessively serious lament of the
speaker, which is difficult to take at face value — he laments the loss of *sand* with
the excessive emotion of a romantic lover! The last lines, with their evocation of

the beloved/sand in an archetypal kingdom of the sea, ring a bit hollow. Once we notice all of this, we see the speaker as being somehow unreliable in his strong response to the situation. He tries too hard to equate the loss of sand with the loss of love, he paints himself as too much of a romantic, and he loses our assent when we realize that his rather cliché declarations are not very fitting. Once we become aware of the speaker's limitations, our perspective about the poem changes: we come to see its "meaning" as centered, not on the theme of fleetingness as such, but on a portrayal of the speaker's exaggerated efforts to embody this theme in the image of sand.

For the traditional New Critic, this would pose a dilemma. The reading of the poem as a serious embodiment of the theme of evanescence is undercut by an awareness of the speaker's unreliability. One can account for the conflict between readings, to some extent, by speaking of the poem's use of irony and by seeing a tension between the theme of evanescence and the speaker's excessive concern with an imaginary beloved (which blinds him to the larger issues presented by the poem). That still leaves unresolved, however, the poem's final meaning and effect. In class discussions, in fact, a debate between those students who asserted that the importance of the poem lay in its engendering the theme of fleetingness and those who noted the absurdity of the speaker often ended in an agreement that this was a "problem poem" which never resolved or integrated its "stresses" and its double vision. . . .

The deconstructive critic, however, would not be disturbed by a lack of resolution in the meanings of the poem and would use the conflict between interpretations as the starting point for further study. Noting that the view of evanescence produced by the poem's central metaphor is undercut by the speaker's unreliability, the deconstructive critic would explore the play of signification that the undercutting engenders. Calling into question the attempt to neatly define evanescence, on the one hand, and the speaker's excessive romanticism on the other, the poem would represent, for this critic, a creative confrontation of irresoluble visions. The image of the sand as woman, as well as the portrayal of the speaker, would represent a sort of "seam" in the text, an area of indeterminacy that would open the way to further readings. This image lets us see the speaker as a sentimental poet, attempting unsuccessfully to define evanescence by means of a novel metaphor but getting trapped in the theme of lost love, which he himself has engendered; it makes us think of the inadequacy of language, of the ways in which metaphorical expression and the clichés of a love lament can undercut each other.

Once we adopt such a deconstructivist perspective, we will find in the text details that will carry forward our reading. The speaker's statement that he held "her" against his "chest and his soul" underlines the conflict in his perspective: it juggles a literal perspective (he rubs sand against himself) and a metaphorical one (he reaches for his beloved), but it cannot fully combine them — "soul" is ludicrously inappropriate in reference to the former. The reader, noting the inappropriateness, has to pay attention to the inadequacy of language as used here. All in all, by engendering a conflict between various levels and perspectives, the poem makes us feel the incompleteness of any one reading, the way in which each one is a "misreading" (not because it is wrong, but because it is incomplete), and the creative lack of closure in the poem. By not being subject to closure, in fact, this text becomes all the more exciting: its view of the possibilities and limitations of metaphor, language, and perspective seems more valuable than any static portrayal of "evanescence."

The analyses I have offered of this poem exemplify the different classroom approaches that would be taken by a stereotypical New Critic, on the one hand, and a deconstructive critic on the other. Imbued with the desire to come to an overview of the literary work, the former will attempt to resolve its tensions (and probably remain unsatisfied with the poem). Skeptical of such a possibility and of the very existence of a definable "work," the latter will focus on the tensions that can be found in the text as vehicles for multiple readings. Given his or her attitude to the text, the deconstructive critic will not worry about going beyond its "limits" (which really do not exist). This will allow, of course, for more speculative readings; it will also lead to a discussion of ways in which the text can be extended and "cured" in successive readings, to the fact that it reflects on the process of its own creation, and to ways in which it will relate to other texts.

From *Writing and Reading DIFFERENTLY: Deconstruction*
and the Teaching of Composition and Literature,
edited by G. Douglas Atkins and Michael L. Johnson

CONSIDERATIONS FOR CRITICAL THINKING AND WRITING

1. Explain how the New Critical and deconstructionist approaches to the Salinas poem differ. What kinds of questions are raised by each? What elements of the poem are focused on in each approach?

2. Write an essay explaining which reading of the poem you find more interesting. In your opening paragraph define what you mean by "interesting."

3. Choose one of the critical strategies for reading discussed in this chapter and discuss Salinas's poem from that perspective.

BROOK THOMAS (B. 1947)

A New Historical Approach to Keats's "Ode on a Grecian Urn" 1987

The traditional reception of the poem invites a discussion of its implied aesthetic. The poem's aesthetic is, however, intricately linked to its attitude to the past. The urn is, after all, Keats's "sylvan historian." To ask what sort of history a piece of art presents to us is, of course, to raise one of the central questions of historical criticism. It also opens up a variety of directions to take in historicizing the teaching of literature. . . .

To ask what history the urn relates to the reader easily leads to a discussion of how much our sense of the past depends upon art and the consequences of that dependency. These are important questions, because even if our students have little knowledge of the past or even interest in it, they do have an attitude toward it. A poem like Keats's "Ode" can help them reflect upon what that attitude is and on how it has been produced.

Such a discussion also offers a way to raise what critics have traditionally seen as the poem's central conflict: that between the temporal world of man and the atemporal world of art. The urn records two different visions of the past, both at odds with what we normally associate with historical accounts. On the one hand, it preserves a beauty that resists the destructive force of time. On the other, it records a quotidian scene populated by nameless people rather than the account of "famous" personages and "important" events our students often associate with traditional histories. Art, Keats seems to suggest, both keeps alive a sense of beauty in a world of change *and* gives us a sense of the felt life of the past. But in its search for a realm in which truth and beauty coexist, art risks freezing the "real" world and becoming a "cold pastoral," cut off from the very felt life it records. In dramatizing this conflict Keats's "Ode" allows students to see both art's power to keep the past alive and its tendency to distort it.

Chances are, however, that not all students share Keats's sense of the relationship between art and history. Rather than demonstrate their lack of "aesthetic appreciation," this difference can open up another direction to pursue in discussing the poem. To acknowledge a difference between our present attitude and the one embodied by Keats's poem is to call into question the conditions that have contributed to the changed attitude. Thus, if the first approach to the poem aims at having students reflect generally upon the influence art has on our attitude toward the past, this approach demands that we look at the specific historical conditions that help shape our general attitude toward both art and the past. In the case of the "Ode," this can lead to a discussion of the economic and political conditions of early nineteenth-century England that helped shape Keats's image of ancient Greece. On the one hand, there was England's self-image as the inheritor of ancient Greece's republican institutions and, on the other, a nostalgia for a harmonious pastoral world in contrast to the present state of industrialized, fragmented British society. Thus, the two versions of the past offered by Keats's sylvan historian — the aesthetic one in which harmony and beauty are preserved and the democratic one in which the life of everyday people is recorded — are related to specific historical conditions at the time Keats wrote. The challenge for our students — and for us — would be to speculate on how our attitudes towards art and history are shaped by our historical moment — how that moment is different from and similar to Keats's.

A third way to teach the poem historically is to concentrate on the urn itself as a historical as well as aesthetic object. "Where," we might ask our students, "would Keats have seen such an urn?" Most likely someone will respond, "A museum." If so, we are ready to discuss the phenomenon of the rise of the art museum in eighteenth- and nineteenth-century Europe, how cultural artifacts from the past were removed from their social setting and placed in museums to be contemplated as art. Seemingly taking us away from Keats's poem, such a discussion might be the best way to help our students understand Keats's aesthetic, for they will clearly see that in Keats's poem an urn that once had a practical social function now sparks aesthetic contemplation about the nature of truth, beauty, and the past. If we ask why the urn takes on this purely aesthetic function in a society that was increasingly practical, our students might start to glimpse how our modern notion of art has been defined in response to the social order.

To consider the urn a historical as well as an aesthetic object is also to raise political questions. For how, we might ask, did a Grecian urn (or the Elgin marbles, if we were to teach another Keats poem) end up in England in the first place? Such a question moves us from Keats's image of ancient Greece to a consideration of Greece in the early nineteenth century, and to how a number of Englishmen who sympathized with its struggle for liberation at the same time pillaged its cultural treasures and set them on display in London to advertise Britain's "advanced" cultural state. Thus, a very simple historical question about Keats's urn can force us to consider the political consequences of our cultural heritage. As Walter Benjamin warned, the cultural treasures that we so love have an origin we should not contemplate without horror: "They owe their existence not only to the efforts of the great minds and talents who have created them, but also to the anonymous toil of their contemporaries. There is no document of civilization which is not at the same time a document of barbarism" ("Theses on the Philosophy of History" in *Illuminations*, 256).

If we consider the task of historical scholarship to recreate the conditions of the past so that we can recover the author's original intention, the questions I have asked about Keats's "Ode" are not valid ones to ask. Clearly my questions are not primarily directed at recovering that intention. Instead, I am treating Keats's poem as social text, one that in telling us about the society that produced it also tells us about the society we inhabit today. This approach is not to say that we should completely abandon the effort to recover Keats's intention, but that, as in the case of formalist criticism, we need to go beyond the traditional historical scholar's efforts. We need to try both to reconstruct the author's intention — for instance, what Keats thought about art and history — and to read against the grain of his intention.

From "The Historical Necessities for — and Difficulties with — New Historical Analysis in Introductory Literature Courses," *College English*, September 1987

CONSIDERATIONS FOR CRITICAL THINKING AND WRITING

1. Summarize the three historical approaches to "Ode on a Grecian Urn" (p. 741) Thomas describes. Which do you consider the most interesting? Explain why.

2. Write an essay that explores Thomas's claim that "a very simple historical question about Keats's urn can force us to consider the political consequences of our cultural heritage" (para. 6).

3. Choose another poem from this anthology and treat it as a "social text" (para. 7). What kinds of questions can you ask about it that suggest the poem's historical significance?

PETER RABINOWITZ (B. 1944)
On Close Readings   1988

Belief in close reading may be the nearest thing literary scholars have to a shared critical principle. Academics who teach literature tend to accept as a matter of course that good reading is slow, attentive to linguistic nuance (especially figurative language), and suspicious of surface meanings.

Close reading is a fundamental link between the New Critics and the Yale deconstructionists. Indeed, deconstructionist J. Hillis Miller has gone so far as to characterize what he saw as an attack on close reading by Gerald Graff as "a major treason against our profession." Similarly, what Naomi Schor calls "clitoral" feminist criticism, and its "hermeneutics focused on the detail," is a variant of close reading. So is much reader-response criticism.

Despite its broad acceptance by scholars, however, close reading is not the natural, the only, or always the best way to approach a text. I'm not suggesting that it should never be taught or used. But I do want to argue that close reading rests on faulty assumptions about how literature is read, which can lead, especially in the classroom, to faulty prescriptions about how it *ought* to be read.

The fact is that there are a variety of ways to read, all of which engage the reader in substantially different kinds of activity. Which kind depends in part on the reader and his or her immediate purpose. Teasing out the implicit homoerotic tendencies in Turgenev's *Asya*, for instance, is a different activity from trying to determine its contribution to the development of first-person narrative techniques. In part, the way one reads also varies from text to text. Different authors, different genres, different periods, different cultures expect readers to approach texts in different ways.

The bias in academe toward close reading reduces that multiplicity. While all close readers obviously don't read in exactly the same way, the variations have a strong family resemblance. Their dominance in the aristocracy of critical activity — virtually undiminished by the critical revolutions of the last twenty years — can skew evaluation, distort interpretation, discourage breadth of vision, and separate scholars from students and other ordinary readers.

David Daiches was not being eccentric when he argued that literary value depends on the "degree to which the work lends itself" to the kind of reading demanded by New Critical theory. The schools in vogue may change, but we still assign value to what fits our prior conceptions of reading, and the academically sanctioned canon consequently consists largely of texts that respond well to close reading.

Once you give priority to close reading, you implicitly favor figurative writing over realistic writing, indirect expression over direct expression, deep meaning over surface meaning, form over content, and the elite over the popular. In the realm of poetry, that means giving preference to lyric over narrative poems, and in the realm of fiction, to symbolism and psychology over plot. Such preferences, in turn, devalue certain voices. A writer directly confronting brute oppression, for instance, is apt to be ranked below another who has the luxury minutely to explore the details of subtle middle-class crises. Thus, for a close reader, the unresonant prose of Harriet Wilson's *Our Nig* will automatically make the novel seem less "good" than Henry James's more intricate *What Maisie Knew*, although the racist brutality endured by Ms. Wilson's heroine is arguably more important for our culture — and thus more deserving of our consideration — than the affluent sexual merry-go-round that dizzies Maisie.

It would be bad enough if the preference for close reading simply meant that texts that didn't measure up were chucked onto a noncanonical pile — then, at least, the rebellious could rummage through the rejects. But close reading also has an insidious effect on interpretation. Not only do we reject many works that don't fit; more damaging, we also twist many others until they *do* fit.

Yet we fail to recognize the magnitude of this distortion. One of the major problems with much current critical practice is the tendency to underestimate the extent to which texts can serve as mirrors — not of the external world but of the reader, who is apt to find in a text not what is really there but what he expects or wants to find. . . .

When reading for class, many students read closely, but few continue the practice once they've left college. In fact, most people — including teachers — who really enjoy literature recognize that close reading is a special kind of interpretive practice. Literary scholars are apt to make a distinction between "real reading" and "reading for fun"; most nonacademic readers are likely to divide "real reading" from "reading for class." In either case, an artificial split is created between academe and "real life," which leads to theories that devalue the kinds of reading (and therefore the kinds of books) that engage most readers most of the time.

If I'm against close reading, then what am I for? The obvious alternative is pluralism.

We can legitimately show our students that different writers in different social, historical, and economic contexts write for different purposes and with different expectations. Likewise, we can teach our students that different readers (or the same reader under different circumstances) read for different reasons.

We must also give our students actual practice in various kinds of reading. For example, an introductory literature course should include many different sorts of texts: long novels as well as lyric poems; realistic (even didactic) works as well as symbolic ones; writing aimed at a broad audience as well as at a literate elite. The course should also include different kinds of tasks. Students should learn to approach a given text in several different ways, at least some of which arise out of their personal and cultural situations. Most important, we must help our students to be self-conscious about what they are doing, and to realize that every decision about how to read opens certain doors only by closing others.

It is not simply that learning new, less rigid ways of reading increases the number of works we can enjoy and learn from. More important, learning to read in different ways allows us to enjoy a wider range of texts and gain new perspectives on our cultural assumptions. Only such flexible reading leads to intellectual growth, for it is only that kind of reading that can enable us to be conscious of — and therefore able to deal effectively with — the narrowness of "standard" interpretive techniques.

> From "Our Evaluation of Literature Has Been Distorted
> by Academe's Bias toward Close Readings of Texts,"
> *Chronicle of Higher Education,* April 6, 1988

CONSIDERATIONS FOR CRITICAL THINKING AND WRITING

1. Why does Rabinowitz object to the bias toward close reading as the primary way to approach a literary work? Explain why you agree or disagree.

2. According to Rabinowitz, how does a critical emphasis on close reading affect the formation of the canon?

3. In an essay discuss Rabinowitz's observation that an emphasis on close reading "devalue[s] the kinds of reading (and therefore the kinds of books) that engage most readers most of the time" (para. 10).

HARRIET HAWKINS (B. 1939)

Should We Study King Kong *or* King Lear? 1988

There is nothing either good or bad, but thinking makes it so.
—*Hamlet*

Troilus: *What's aught but as 'tis valued?*
Hector: *But value dwells not in particular will:*
　It holds its estimate and dignity
　As well wherein 'tis precious of itself
　As in the prizer.
—*Troilus and Cressida*

To what degree is great literature—or bad literature—an artificial category? Are there any good—or bad—reasons why most societies have given high status to certain works of art and not to others? Could Hamlet be right in concluding that there is *nothing* either good or bad but thinking—or critical or ideological discourse—makes it so? Or are certain works of art so precious, so magnificent—or so trashy—that they obviously ought to be included in the canon or expelled from the classroom? So far as I know, there is not now any sign of a critical consensus on the correct answer to these questions either in England or in the United States.

In England there are, on the one hand, eloquent cases for the defense of the value of traditional literary studies, like Dame Helen Gardner's last book, *In Defence of the Imagination*. On the other hand, there are critical arguments insisting that what really counts is not what you read, but the way that you read it. You might as well study *King Kong* as *King Lear*, because what matters is not the script involved, but the critical or ideological virtues manifested in your own "reading" of whatever it is that you are reading. Reviewing a controversial book entitled *Re-Reading English*, the poet Tom Paulin gives the following account of the issues involved in the debate:

> The contributors are collectively of the opinion that English literature is a dying subject and they argue that it can be revived by adopting a "socialist pedagogy" and introducing into the syllabus "other forms of writing and cultural production than the canon of literature" . . . it is now time to challenge "hierarchical" and "elitist" conceptions of literature and to demolish the bourgeois ideology which has been "naturalised" as literary value. . . . They wish to develop "a politics of reading" and to redefine the term "text" in order to admit newspaper reports, songs, and even mass demonstrations as subjects for tutorial discussion. Texts no longer have to be books: indeed, "it may be more democratic to study *Coronation Street* [England's most popular soap opera] than *Middlemarch*."

However one looks at these arguments, it seems indisputably true that the issues involved are of paramount critical, pedagogical, and social importance. There are, however, any number of different ways to look at the various arguments. So far as I am, professionally, concerned, they raise the central question, "Why should any of us still study, or teach, Shakespeare's plays (or *Paradise Lost* or *The Canterbury Tales*)?" After all, there are quite enough films, plays, novels, and poems being produced today (to say nothing of all those "other forms of writing," including literary criticism, that are clamoring for our attention) to satisfy anyone interested in high literature, or popular genres, or any form of "cultural production" whatsoever. They also raise the obviously reflexive question: "Assuming that all traditionally 'canonized' works were eliminated, overnight, from the syllabus of every English department in the world, would not comparable problems of priority, value, elitism, ideological pressure, authoritarianism, and arbitrariness almost(?) immediately arise with reference to *whatever* works — of whatsoever kind and nature — were substituted for them?"

If, say, the place on the syllabus currently assigned to *King Lear* were reassigned to *King Kong*, those of us currently debating the relative merits of the Quarto, the Folio, or a conflated version of *King Lear* would, *mutatis mutandis*,° have to decide whether to concentrate classroom attention on the "classic" version of *King Kong*, originally produced in 1933, or to focus on the 1974 remake (which by now has many ardent admirers of its own). Although classroom time might not allow the inclusion of both, a decision to exclude either version might well seem arbitrary or authoritarian and so give rise to grumbles about the "canon." Moreover, comparable questions of "canonization" might well arise with reference to other films excluded from a syllabus that included either version (or both versions) of *King Kong*. For example: why assign class time to *King Kong* and not to (say) *Slave Girls of the White Rhinoceros?* Who, if any, of us has the right to decide whether *King Lear* or *King Kong* or the *Slave Girls* should, or should not, be included on, or excluded from, the syllabus? And can the decision to include, or exclude, any one of them be made, by any one of us, on any grounds whatsoever that do *not* have to do with comparative merit, or comparative value judgments, or with special interests — that is, with the aesthetic or ideological priorities, preferences, and prejudices of the assigners of positions on whatever syllabus there is? And insofar as most, if not all, of our judgments and preferences are comparative, are they not, inevitably, hierarchical?

Is there, in fact, any form of endeavor or accomplishment known to the human race — from sport to ballet to jazz to cooking — wherein comparative standards of excellence comparable to certain "hierarchical" and "elitist" conceptions of literature are nonexistent? Even bad-film buffs find certain bad films more gloriously bad than others. And, perhaps significantly given its comparatively short lifetime, the avant-garde cinema has, by now, produced snobs to rival the most elitist literary critic who ever lived, such as the one who thus puts down a friend who likes ordinary Hollywood films:

> Ah that's all right for you, I know the sort you are, but give me a private job that's shot on faded sepia sixteen millimetre stock with non-professional actors . . . no story and dialogue in French *any day of the week.*

What is striking about this snob's assumption is how characteristic it is of a long tradition of critical elitism that has consistently sneered at popular genres (e.g., romance fiction, soap operas, horror films, westerns, etc.) that are tainted by the profit motive and so tend to "give the public what it wants" in the way of sentimentality, sensationalism, sex, violence, romanticism, and the like.

From "*King Lear* to *King Kong* and Back: Shakespeare and Popular Modern Genres" in *"Bad" Shakespeare: Revaluations of the Shakespeare Canon,* edited by Maurice Charney

mutatis mutandis: Substituting different terms (Latin).

CONSIDERATIONS FOR CRITICAL THINKING AND WRITING

1. Do you agree or disagree that "great literature — or bad literature — [is] an artificial category" (para. 1)? Explain why.

2. Why would problems of "priority, value, elitism, ideological pressure, authoritarianism, and arbitrariness" (para. 3) probably become issues for evaluating any new works that replaced canonized works?

3. Write an essay in which you argue for (or against) studying popular arts (for example, the *Seinfeld* script on p. 1199) beside the works of classic writers such as Shakespeare.

MORRIS DICKSTEIN (B. 1940)

On the Social Responsibility of the Critic   *1993*

Many critics today, as if in violent reaction to the reading habits of the ordinary citizen, are haunted by the fear of becoming the passive consumer of ideological subtexts or messages. As the country grew more conservative in the eighties, many academic critics turned more radical, and this led to an onslaught by national magazines and media pundits on political correctness, the supposed left-wing and multicultural orthodoxy in American universities.

Here we encounter a number of puzzling paradoxes about "reading" in America today. As reading diminishes — not in absolute terms but in relation to other ways of receiving information — as reading loses its hold on people, the metaphor of reading constantly expands. Molecular biologists like Robert Pollack talk about "reading DNA," the structure of genetic transmission in each living cell. Students of urban life discuss "the city as text" and how to read it, as they did at a conference I attended in 1989. Film scholars publish books about "how to read a film" reflecting on our constantly expanding (and increasingly undifferentiated) notion of what constitutes a text. And literary critics over the past sixty years have developed ever more subtle and complex ways of reading those texts, often using obscure, specialized language that itself resists being read.

As educators worry about the role of video and electronic media in displacing the written word, as the skills of ordinary readers seem to languish, the sophistication and territorial ambition of academic readers continue to grow, widening a split that has been one of the hallmarks of the modern period. The common reader still exists, but many professional readers dissociate themselves on principle from the habits of the tribe: they deliberately read against the grain of the text, against common sense, against most people's way of reading — indeed, against their own way of reading in their ordinary lives. If the reader of *Scarlett* or *Gone with the Wind* reads passively, wanting to be possessed and carried away by a book, as by an old-fashioned movie or piece of music, the critical reader, influenced by theory and by the new historicism, has developed an active, aggressive, even adversarial approach to writing. What Paul Ricoeur in his book on Freud calls the "hermeneutics of suspicion" has become a primary feature of academic criticism, which aims above all to disclose the institutional pressures and ideological formations that speak through texts and influence us as we read.° . . .

What . . . read: Paul Ricoeur (B. 1913), a French philosopher and critic, author of *Freud and Philosophy: An Essay on Interpretation* (1970). Hermeneutics refers to the theory and method of perceiving and interpreting texts.

Our advanced criticism is especially marked by the suspicion and the hostility with which it performs such operations: its failure to distinguish art from propaganda, literature from advertising; its fierce resistance to the mental framework of the works it examines. "All right, what's wrong with this book?" asks one programmatically suspicious instructor of the students in her humanities class, to make sure they don't get taken in by those "great" books. Some of our recent ideological criticism turns the social understanding of literature, which can be intrinsically valuable, into an all too predictable exercise in debunking and demystification. . . .

The role of the critic is not to read notionally and cleverly, and certainly not to castigate writers for their politics, but to raise ordinary reading to its highest power — to make it more insightful, more acute, without losing touch with our deepest personal responses. It is ironic to speak for the social responsibility of the writer while betraying the public sphere of reading. Criticism, even academic criticism, is neither a sect nor a priesthood but ultimately a public trust, mediating between artists or writers and their often puzzled audience. . . .

A naive reading, anchored in wonder, must remain an indispensable moment of a more self-conscious reading, not just a piece of scaffolding to be kicked away as our suspicion and professionalism take over. We need a better balance between the naive and suspicious readers in ourselves: between the willing suspension of disbelief and our ability to withhold ourselves and read skeptically; between our appreciation of art and our wary knowledge of its persuasive power; between a sympathy for the author as an individual like ourselves — working out creative problems, making contingent choices — and our critical sense of a literary work as the discursive formation of a cultural moment.

From "Damaged Literacy: The Decay of Reading," *Profession 93*

CONSIDERATIONS FOR CRITICAL THINKING AND WRITING

1. Do you think video and electronic media are "displacing the written word" (para. 3)? What evidence can you point to in your own experience that refutes or supports this claim?

2. What do you think Dickstein means when he refers to academic criticism as "a public trust" (para. 5)? What should the function of criticism be, according to Dickstein? In what sense is the role of the critic "to raise ordinary reading to its highest power" (para. 5)?

3. What criticism does Dickstein level against contemporary literary criticism? Explain why you agree or disagree with his perspective.

WENDY STEINER (B. 1949)

On the Critics' Readership
1998

The question of audience today is extremely perplexing. During the first few decades of the century, there were genuine "people of letters," who wrote for very broad audiences. Their writing reflected the commonality of intellectual life among writers and artists, academics, cultural journalists, and arts professionals. In Europe, this model is still very much intact.

However, in North America by the 1960s when I was in school and college, the academy had become hopelessly self-regarding. The assumption was that academic concerns were too sophisticated and specialized for "the masses," a term that by this time included those outside of academia who would before have been included in the category of the intelligentsia. Academia was becoming "professionalized," by which people meant that no one would teach in a university who did not have a PhD and did not produce scholarly articles and books. By the 1970s one heard rumors that assistant professors who published in the *New York Times Book Review* would never be taken seriously for tenure, and of course there were examples like Eric Segal, whose screenplay for *Yellow Submarine* and whose novel *Love Story* were supposed to have disqualified him for tenure in Classics at Yale.

The story has been told over and over, especially by right-wing detractors of academia: that the rise of theory in the 1980s finished the process of professional isolation. Theory allowed some academics to speak across disciplines, and so achieve a more prominent position in the university and, by smart media management, outside it, than any intellectuals had achieved since the 1920s and 1930s. But unlike the people of letters, the theorists' writings were unintelligible to the general public, and often to each other. The scandals in the arts and the university of the late 1980s and 1990s (Mapplethorpe,° political correctness, the antipornography movement) are a direct reflection of the hostility that now exists between art experts and the public.

At this point, academics (or at least *this* academic) are bewildered as to whom they should address. Those with political agendas, such as the various ethnic and gender specialists, are torn between the stance of the "public intellectual," with the suspicions it raises about the self-interest rather than public interest being served, and the stance of the communitarian teacher, a stance that seems sentimental and unrigorous in light of the professional standards of the academy. And with a disastrous job market for PhDs, even those academics with no particular political agenda have trouble understanding who cares about their work. Does intellectual life go on anywhere but in universities? Will the general culture continue to support the humanities and the arts? If theory was a dead end and scholars are in oversupply, is there an audience for research even within the academy itself? These questions have not as yet produced satisfying answers.

From "Thinking in Public: A Forum," in
American Literary History, Spring 1998

Mapplethorpe: Robert Mapplethorpe (1946–1989), a controversial art photographer.

CONSIDERATIONS FOR CRITICAL THINKING AND WRITING

1. According to Steiner, how has the audience for academic criticism changed during the twentieth century? What caused these changes?

2. Why do you think Steiner believes "academics . . . are bewildered as to whom they should address"?

3. Write an essay in which you respond to Steiner's question: "Does intellectual life go on anywhere but in the universities?"

38

Reading and Writing

THE PURPOSE AND VALUE
OF WRITING ABOUT LITERATURE

Introductory literature courses typically include three components — reading, discussion, and writing. Students usually find the readings a pleasure, the class discussions a revelation, and the writing assignments — at least initially — a little intimidating. Writing an analysis of Melville's use of walls in "Bartleby, the Scrivener" (p. 113), for example, may seem considerably more daunting than making a case for animal rights or analyzing a campus newspaper editorial that calls for grade reforms. Like Bartleby, you might want to respond with "I would prefer not to." Literary topics are not, however, all that different from the kinds of papers assigned in English composition courses; many of the same skills are required for both. Regardless of the type of paper, you must develop a thesis and support it with evidence in language that is clear and persuasive.

Whether the subject matter is a marketing survey, a political issue, or a literary work, writing is a method of communicating information and perceptions. Writing teaches. But before writing becomes an instrument for informing the reader, it serves as a means of learning for the writer. An essay is a process of discovery as well as a record of what has been discovered. One of the chief benefits of writing is that we frequently realize what we want to say only after trying out ideas on a page and seeing our thoughts take shape in language.

More specifically, writing about a literary work encourages us to be better readers because it requires a close examination of the elements of a short story, poem, or play. To determine how plot, character, setting, point of view, style, tone, irony, or any number of other literary elements function in a work, we must study them in relation to one another as well as separately. Speed-reading won't do. To read a text accurately and validly — neither ignoring nor distorting significant details—we must return to the work repeatedly to test our responses and interpretations. By paying attention to details and being sensitive to the author's use of language, we develop a clearer understanding of how the work conveys its effects and meanings.

Nevertheless, students sometimes ask why it is necessary or desirable to write about a literary work. Why not allow stories, poems, and plays to speak for themselves? Isn't it presumptuous to interpret Hemingway, Dickinson, or Shakespeare? These writers do, of course, speak for themselves, but they do so indirectly. Literary criticism seeks not to replace the text by explaining it but to enhance our readings of works by calling attention to elements that we might have overlooked or only vaguely sensed.

Another misunderstanding about the purpose of literary criticism is that it crankily restricts itself to finding faults in a work. Critical essays are sometimes mistakenly equated with newspaper and magazine reviews of recently published works. Reviews typically include summaries and evaluations to inform readers about a work's nature and quality, but critical essays assume that readers are already familiar with a work. Although a critical essay may point out limitations and flaws, most criticism—and certainly the kind of essay usually written in an introductory literature course—is designed to explain, analyze, and reveal the complexities of a work. Such sensitive consideration increases our appreciation of the writer's achievement and significantly adds to our enjoyment of a short story, poem, or play. In short, the purpose and value of writing about literature are that doing so leads to greater understanding and pleasure.

READING THE WORK CLOSELY

Know the piece of literature you are writing about before you begin your essay. Think about how the work makes you feel and how it is put together. The more familiar you are with how the various elements of the text convey effects and meanings, the more confident you will be explaining whatever perspective on it you ultimately choose. Do not insist that everything make sense on a first reading. Relax and enjoy yourself; you can be attentive and still allow the author's words to work their magic on you. With subsequent readings, however, go more slowly and analytically as you try to establish relations between characters, actions, images, or whatever else seems important. Ask yourself why you respond as you do. Think as you read, and notice how the parts of a work contribute to its overall nature. Whether the work is a short story, poem, or play, you will read relevant portions of it over and over, and you will very likely find more to discuss in each review if the work is rich.

It's best to avoid reading other critical discussions of a work before you are thoroughly familiar with it. There are several good reasons for following this advice. By reading interpretations before you know a work, you deny yourself the pleasure of discovery. That is a bit like starting with the last chapter in a mystery novel. But perhaps even more important than protecting the surprise and delight that a work might offer is that a premature reading of a critical discussion will probably short-circuit your own responses. You will see the work through the critic's eyes and have to struggle with someone else's perceptions and ideas before you can develop your own.

Reading criticism can be useful, but not until you have thought through your own impressions of the text. A guide should not be permitted to become a tyrant. This does not mean, however, that you should avoid background information about a work—for example, that Joyce Carol Oates's story "The Lady with the Pet Dog" was based on a similar story by Anton Chekhov. Knowing something about the author as well as historic and literary contexts can help to create expectations that enhance your reading.

ANNOTATING THE TEXT AND JOURNAL NOTE TAKING

As you read, get in the habit of making marginal notations in your textbook. If you are working with a library book, use note cards and write down page or line numbers so that you can easily return to annotated passages. Use these cards to record reactions, raise questions, and make comments. They will freshen your memory and allow you to keep track of what goes on in the text.

Whatever method you use to annotate your texts—whether writing marginal notes, highlighting, underlining, or drawing boxes and circles around important words and phrases—you'll eventually develop a system that allows you to retrieve significant ideas and elements from the text. Another way to record your impressions of a work—as with any other experience—is to keep a journal. By writing down your reactions to characters, images, language, actions, and other matters in a reading journal, you can often determine why you like or dislike a work or feel sympathetic or antagonistic to an author or discover paths into a work that might have eluded you if you hadn't preserved your impressions. Your journal notes and annotations may take whatever form you find useful; full sentences and grammatical correctness are not essential (unless they are to be handed in and your instructor requires that), though they might allow you to make better sense of your own reflections days later. The point is simply to put in writing thoughts that you can retrieve when you need them for class discussion or a writing assignment. Consider the following student annotation of the first twenty-four lines of Andrew Marvell's "To His Coy Mistress" (p. 729) and the journal entry that follows it:

Annotated Text

If we had time . . .

(Had we but world enough, and time,   *Waste life and you*
This coyness, lady, were no (crime.)°   *steal from yourself.*
We would sit down, and think which way
To walk, and pass our long love's day.
Thou by the Indian (Ganges') side   5
Shouldst rubies find; I by the tide
Of (Humber) would complain.° I would   *Measurements*   *write love songs*
Love you ten years before the Flood,   *of time*
And you should, if you please, refuse
Till the conversion of the Jews.   10
My vegetable love should grow,°   *slow, unconscious growth*
Vaster than empires, and more slow;
An hundred years should go to praise
Thine eyes and on thy forehead gaze,
Two hundred to adore each breast,   15
But thirty thousand to the rest:
An age at least to every part,
And the last age should show your heart.
For, lady, you deserve this state,
Nor would I love at lower rate.   20

contrast river and desert images

(But) at my back I always hear   *Lines move faster here—*
Time's wingèd chariot hurrying near;   *tone changes*
And yonder all before us lie
(Deserts) of vast (eternity.)——*This eternity rushes in.*

Journal Note

He'd be patient and wait for his "mistress" if they had
the time--sing songs, praise her, adore her, etc. But they
don't have that much time according to him. He <u>seems</u> to be
patient but he actually begins by calling patience--her coy-
ness--a "crime." Looks to me like he's got his mind made up
from the beginning of the poem. Where's her response? I'm not
sure about him.

This journal note responds to some of the effects noted in the annotations of the poem; it's an excellent beginning for making sense of the
speaker's argument in the poem.

Taking notes will preserve your initial reactions to the work. Many
times first impressions are the best. Your response to a peculiar character
in a story, a striking phrase in a poem, or a subtle bit of stage business in a
play might lead to larger perceptions. The student paper on John Updike's
"A & P" (p. 2089), for example, began with the student writing "how come?"
next to the story's title in her textbook. She thought it strange that the title
didn't refer to a character or the story's conflict. That annotated response

eventually led her to examine the significance of the setting, which became the central idea of her paper.

You should take detailed notes only after you've read through the work. If you write too many notes during the first reading, you're likely to disrupt your response. Moreover, until you have a sense of the entire work, it will be difficult to determine how connections can be made among its various elements. In addition to recording your first impressions and noting significant passages, characters, actions, and so on, you should consult the Questions for Responsive Reading and Writing about fiction (p. 41), poetry (p. 711), and drama (p. 1211). These questions can assist you in getting inside a work as well as organizing your notes.

Inevitably, you will take more notes than you finally use in the paper. Note taking is a form of thinking aloud, but because your ideas are on paper you don't have to worry about forgetting them. As you develop a better sense of a potential topic, your notes will become more focused and detailed.

CHOOSING A TOPIC

If your instructor assigns a topic or offers a choice from among an approved list of topics, some of your work is already completed. Instead of being asked to come up with a topic about *Antigone*, you may be asked to write a three-page essay that specifically discusses "Antigone's decision to defy Creon." You also have the assurance that a specified topic will be manageable within the suggested number of pages. Unless you ask your instructor for permission to write on a different or related topic, be certain to address yourself to the assignment. An essay that does not discuss Antigone's decision but instead describes her relationship with her sister would be missing the point. Notice too that there is room even in an assigned topic to develop your own approach. One question that immediately comes to mind is whether Antigone is justified in defying Creon's authority. Assigned topics do not relieve you of thinking about an aspect of a work, but they do focus your thinking.

At some point during the course, you may have to begin an essay from scratch. You might, for example, be asked to write about a short story that somehow impressed you or that seemed particularly well written or filled with insights. Before you start considering a topic, you should have a sense of how long the paper will be because the assigned length can help to determine the extent to which you should develop your topic. Ideally, the paper's length should be based on how much space you deem necessary to present your discussion clearly and convincingly, but if you have any doubts and no specific guidelines have been indicated, ask. The question is important; a topic that might be appropriate for a three-page paper could be too narrow for ten pages. Three pages would probably be adequate for a discussion of why Emily murders Homer in Faulkner's "A Rose for Emily." Conversely, it would be futile to try to summarize Faulkner's use of the South in his fiction in even ten pages; this would have to be narrowed to something like "Images of the South in 'A Rose for Emily.'" Be sure that the topic you choose can be adequately covered in the assigned number of pages.

Once you have a firm sense of how much you are expected to write, you can begin to decide on your topic. If you are to choose what work to write about, select one that genuinely interests you. Too often students pick a story, poem, or play because it is mercifully short or seems simple. Such works can certainly be the subjects of fine essays, but simplicity should not be the major reason for selecting them. Choose a work that has moved you so that you have something to say about it. The student who wrote about "A & P" was initially attracted to the story's title because she had once worked in a similar store. After reading the story, she became fascinated with its setting because Updike's descriptions seemed so accurate. Her paper then grew out of her curiosity about the setting's purpose. When a writer is engaged in a topic, the paper has a better chance of being interesting to a reader.

After you have settled on a particular work, your notes and annotations of the text should prove useful for generating a topic. The paper on "The A & P as a State of Mind" developed naturally from the notes (p. 2087) that the student jotted down about the setting and antagonist. If you think with a pen in your hand, you are likely to find when you review your notes that your thoughts have clustered into one or more topics. Perhaps there are patterns of imagery that seem to make a point about life. There may be scenes that are ironically paired or secondary characters who reveal certain qualities about the protagonist. Your notes and annotations on such aspects can lead you to a particular effect or impression. Having chuckled your way through "A & P," you may discover that your notations about the story's humor point to a serious satire of society's values.

DEVELOPING A THESIS

When you are satisfied that you have something interesting to say about a work and that your notes have led you to a focused topic, you can formulate a *thesis,* the central idea of the paper. Whereas the topic indicates what the paper focuses on (the setting in "A & P"), the thesis explains what you have to say about the topic (because the intolerant setting of "A & P" is the antagonist in the story, it is crucial to our understanding of Sammy's decision to quit his job). The thesis should be a complete sentence (though sometimes it may require more than one sentence) that establishes your topic in clear, unambiguous language. The thesis may be revised as you get further into the topic and discover what you want to say about it, but once the thesis is firmly established, it will serve as a guide for you and your reader because all the information and observations in your essay should be related to the thesis.

One student on an initial reading of Andrew Marvell's "To His Coy Mistress" (p. 729) saw that the male speaker of the poem urges a woman to love now before time runs out for them. This reading gave him the impression that the poem is a simple celebration of the pleasures of the flesh, but on subsequent readings he underlined or noted these images: "Time's wingèd chariot hurrying near"; "Deserts of vast eternity"; "marble vault"; "worms"; "dust"; "ashes"; and these two lines: "The grave's a fine and private place, / But none, I think, do there embrace."

By listing these images associated with time and death, he established an inventory that could be separated from the rest of his notes on point of view, character, sounds, and other subjects. Inventorying notes allows patterns to emerge that you might have only vaguely perceived otherwise. Once these images are grouped, they call attention to something darker and more complex in Marvell's poem than a first impression might suggest.

These images may create a different feeling about the poem, but they still don't explain very much. One simple way to generate a thesis about a literary work is to ask the question "why?" Why do these images appear in the poem? Why does Hamlet hesitate to avenge his father's death? Why does Hemingway choose the Midwest as the setting of "Soldier's Home"? Your responses to these kinds of questions can lead to a thesis.

Writers sometimes use freewriting to help themselves explore possible answers to such questions. It can be an effective way of generating ideas. Freewriting is exactly that: the technique calls for nonstop writing without concern for mechanics or editing of any kind. Freewriting for ten minutes or so on a question will result in fragments and repetitions, but it can also produce some ideas. Here's an example of a student's response to the question about the images in "To His Coy Mistress":

```
He wants her to make love. Love poem. There's little time.
Her crime. He exaggerates. Sincere? Sly? What's he want?
She says nothing--he says it all. What about deserts,
ashes, graves, and worms? Some love poem. Sounds like an
old Vincent Price movie. Full of sweetness but death
creeps in. Death--hurry hurry! Tear pleasures. What
passion! Where's death in this? How can a love poem be so
ghoulish? She does nothing. Maybe frightened? Convinced?
Why death? Love and death--time--death.
```

This freewriting contains several ideas; it begins by alluding to the poem's plot and speaker, but the central idea seems to be death. This emphasis led the student to five potential thesis statements for his essay about the poem:

1. "To His Coy Mistress" is a difficult poem.
2. Death in "To His Coy Mistress."
3. There are many images of death in "To His Coy Mistress."
4. "To His Coy Mistress" celebrates the pleasures of the flesh, but it also recognizes the power of death to end that pleasure.
5. On the surface, "To His Coy Mistress" is a celebration of the pleasures of the flesh, but this witty seduction is tempered by a chilling recognition of the reality of death.

The first statement is too vague to be useful. In what sense is the poem difficult? A more precise phrasing, indicating the nature of the difficulty, is needed. The second statement is a topic rather than a thesis. Because it is not a sentence, it does not express a complete idea about how the poem treats death. Although this could be an appropriate title, it is inadequate as a thesis statement. The third statement, like the first one, identifies the topic, but even though it is a sentence, it is not a complete idea that tells us anything significant beyond the fact it states. After these preliminary attempts to develop a thesis, the student remembered his first impression of the poem and incorporated it into his thesis statement. The fourth thesis is a useful approach to the poem because it limits the topic and indicates how it will be treated in the paper: the writer will begin with an initial impression of the poem and then go on to qualify it. However, the fifth thesis is better than the fourth because it indicates a shift in tone produced by the ironic relationship between death and flesh. An effective thesis, like this one, makes a clear statement about a manageable topic and provides a firm sense of direction for the paper.

Most writing assignments in a literature course require you to persuade readers that your thesis is reasonable and supported with evidence. Papers that report information without comment or evaluation are simply summaries. A plot summary of Shakespeare's *The Tempest*, for example, would have no thesis, but a paper that discussed how Prospero's oppression of Caliban represents European imperialism and colonialism would argue a thesis. Similarly, a paper that merely pointed out the death images in "To His Coy Mistress" would not contain a thesis, but a paper that attempted to make a case for the death imagery as a grim reminder of how vulnerable flesh is would involve persuasion. In developing a thesis, remember that you are expected not merely to present information but to argue a point.

ARGUING ABOUT LITERATURE

An argumentative essay is designed to make persuasive your interpretation of a work. Arguing about literature doesn't mean that you're engaged in an angry, antagonistic dispute (though controversial topics do sometimes engender heated debates; see, for example, Joan Templeton's comments in the Critical Case Study on Ibsen's *A Doll House* [p. 1635]). Instead, argumentation requires that you present your interpretation of a work (or a portion of it) by supporting your discussion with clearly defined terms, ample evidence, and a detailed analysis of relevant portions of the text.

If you have a choice, it's generally best to write about a topic that you feel strongly about. If you're not fascinated by Bartleby the Scrivener's haunting presence in Melville's short story, then perhaps you'll find chilling Emily Grierson's behavior in Faulkner's "A Rose for Emily," or maybe you can explain why Bartleby's character is so excruciatingly boring to you. If your essay is to be interesting and convincing, what is important is that it be written from a strong point of view that persuasively argues your evaluation, analysis, and interpretation of a work. It is not enough to say that you like or dislike a work; instead you must give your reader some ideas and evidence that can be accepted or rejected based on the quality of the answers to the questions you raise.

One way to come up with persuasive answers is to generate good questions that will lead you further into the text and to critical issues related to it. Notice how the Perspectives, Complementary Critical Readings, Critical Case Studies, and Cultural Case Studies in this anthology raise significant questions and issues about texts from a variety of points of view. Moreover, the Critical Strategies for Reading summarized in Chapter 37 can be a resource for raising questions that can be shaped into an argument, and the Questions for Writing: Incorporating the Critics (p. 501) can help you to incorporate a critic's perspective into your own argument. The following lists of questions for the critical approaches covered in Chapter 37 should be useful for discovering arguments you might make about a short story, poem, or play. The page number that follows each heading refers to the discussion in the anthology for that particular approach.

Formalist Questions (p. 2025)

1. How do various elements of the work — plot, character, point of view, setting, tone, diction, images, symbol, and so on — reinforce its meanings?
2. How are the elements related to the whole?
3. What is the work's major organizing principle? How is its structure unified?
4. What issues does the work raise? How does the work's structure resolve those issues?

Biographical Questions (p. 2027)

1. Are facts about the writer's life relevant to your understanding of the work?
2. Are characters and incidents in the work versions of the writer's own experiences? Are they treated factually or imaginatively?
3. How do you think the writer's values are reflected in the work?

Psychological Questions (p. 2029)

1. How does the work reflect the author's personal psychology?
2. What do the characters' emotions and behavior reveal about their psychological states? What types of personalities are they?
3. Are psychological matters such as repression, dreams, and desire presented consciously or unconsciously by the author?

Historical Questions (p. 2031)

1. How does the work reflect the period in which it is written?
2. What literary or historical influences helped to shape the form and content of the work?
3. How important is the historical context to interpreting the work?

Marxist Questions (p. 2033)

1. How are class differences presented in the work? Are characters aware or unaware of the economic and social forces that affect their lives?
2. How do economic conditions determine the characters' lives?
3. What ideological values are explicit or implicit?
4. Does the work challenge or affirm the social order it describes?

New Historicist Questions (p. 2033)

1. What kinds of documents outside the work seem especially relevant for shedding light on the work?
2. How are social values contemporary to the work reflected or refuted in the work?
3. How does your own historical moment affect your reading of the work and its historical reconstruction?

Cultural Studies Questions (p. 2034)

1. What does the work reveal about the cultural behavior contemporary to it?
2. How does popular culture contemporary to the work reflect or challenge the values implicit or explicit in the work?

3. What kinds of cultural documents contemporary to the work add to your reading of it?
4. How do your own cultural assumptions affect your reading of the work and the culture contemporary to it?

Gender Studies Questions (p. 2035)

1. How are the lives of men and women portrayed in the work? Do the men and women in the work accept or reject these roles?
2. Is the form and content of the work influenced by the author's gender?
3. What attitudes are explicit or implicit concerning heterosexual, homosexual, or lesbian relationships? Are these relationships sources of conflict? Do they provide resolutions to conflicts?
4. Does the work challenge or affirm traditional ideas about men and women and same-sex relationships?

Mythological Questions (p. 2037)

1. How does the story resemble other stories in plot, character, setting, or use of symbols?
2. Are archetypes presented, such as quests, initiations, scapegoats, or withdrawals and returns?
3. Does the protagonist undergo any kind of transformation such as a movement from innocence to experience that seems archetypal?
4. Do any specific allusions to myths shed light on the text?

Reader-Response Questions (p. 2039)

1. How do you respond to the work?
2. How do your own experiences and expectations affect your reading and interpretation?
3. What is the work's original or intended audience? To what extent are you similar to or different from that audience?
4. Do you respond in the same way to the work after more than one reading?

Deconstructionist Questions (p. 2041)

1. How are contradictory and opposing meanings expressed in the work?
2. How does meaning break down or deconstruct itself in the language of the text?
3. Would you say that ultimate definitive meanings are impossible to determine and establish in the text? Why? How does that affect your interpretation?
4. How are implicit ideological values revealed in the work?

These questions will not apply to all texts; and they are not mutually exclusive. They can be combined to explore a text from several critical perspectives simultaneously. A feminist approach to Kate Chopin's "The Story of an Hour" could also use Marxist concerns about class to make observations about the oppression of women's lives in the historical context of the nineteenth century. Your use of these questions should allow you to discover significant issues from which you can develop an argumentative essay that is organized around clearly defined terms, relevant evidence, and a persuasive analysis.

ORGANIZING A PAPER

After you have chosen a manageable topic and developed a thesis, a central idea about it, you can begin to organize your paper. Your thesis, even if it is still somewhat tentative, should help you decide what information will need to be included and provide you with a sense of direction.

Consider again the sample thesis in the section on developing a thesis:

On the surface, "To His Coy Mistress" is a celebration of the pleasures of the flesh, but this witty seduction is tempered by a chilling recognition of the reality of death.

This thesis indicates that the paper can be divided into two parts — the pleasures of the flesh and the reality of death. It also indicates an order: because the central point is to show that the poem is more than a simple celebration, the pleasures of the flesh should be discussed first so that another, more complex, reading of the poem can follow. If the paper began with the reality of death, its point would be anticlimactic.

Having established such a broad and informal outline, you can draw on your underlinings, margin notations, and note cards for the subheadings and evidence required to explain the major sections of your paper. This next level of detail would look like the following:

1. Pleasures of the flesh
   Part of the traditional tone of love poetry
2. Recognition of death
   Ironic treatment of love
   > Diction
   > Images
   > Figures of speech
   > Symbols
   > Tone

This list was initially a jumble of terms, but the student arranged the items so that each of the two major sections leads to a discussion of tone. (The student also found it necessary to drop some biographical information from his notes because it was irrelevant to the thesis.) The list indicates that the first part of the paper will establish the traditional tone of love poetry that celebrates the pleasures of the flesh, while the second part will present a more detailed discussion about the ironic recognition of death. The emphasis is on the latter because that is the point to be argued in the paper. Hence, the thesis has helped to organize the parts of the paper, establish an order, and indicate the paper's proper proportions.

The next step is to fill in the subheadings with information from your notes. Many experienced writers find that making lists of information to be included under each subheading is an efficient way to develop paragraphs. For a longer paper (perhaps a research paper), you should be able to develop a paragraph or more on each subheading. On the other hand, a shorter paper may require that you combine several subheadings in a paragraph. You may also discover that while an informal list is adequate for a brief paper, a ten-page assignment could require a more detailed outline. Use the method that is most productive for you. Whatever the length of the essay, your presentation must be in a coherent and logical order that allows your reader to follow the argument and evaluate the evidence. The quality of your reading can be demonstrated only by the quality of your writing.

WRITING A DRAFT

The time for sharpening pencils, arranging your desk, and doing almost anything else instead of writing has ended. The first draft will appear on the page only if you stop avoiding the inevitable and sit, stand up, or lie down to write. It makes no difference how you write, just so you do. Now that you have developed a topic into a tentative thesis, you can assemble your notes and begin to flesh out whatever outline you have made.

Be flexible. Your outline should smoothly conduct you from one point to the next, but do not permit it to railroad you. If a relevant and important idea occurs to you now, work it into the draft. By using the first draft as a means of thinking about what you want to say, you will very likely discover more than your notes originally suggested. Plenty of good writers don't use outlines at all but discover ordering principles as they write. Do not attempt to compose a perfectly correct draft the first time around. Grammar, punctuation, and spelling can wait until you revise. Concentrate on what you are saying. Good writing most often occurs when you are in hot pursuit of an idea rather than in a nervous search for errors.

To make revising easier, leave wide margins and extra space between lines so that you can easily add words, sentences, and corrections. Write on only one side of the paper. Your pages will be easier to keep track of that way, and, if you have to clip a paragraph to place it elsewhere, you will not lose any writing on the other side.

If you are working on a word processor, you can take advantage of its capacity to make additions and deletions as well as move entire paragraphs by making just a few simple keyboard commands. Some software programs can also check spelling and certain grammatical elements in your writing. It's worth remembering, however, that though a clean copy fresh off a printer may look terrific, it will read only as well as the thinking and writing that have gone into it. Many writers prudently store their data on disks and print their pages each time they finish a draft to avoid losing any material because of power failures or other problems. These printouts are also easier to read than the screen when you work on revisions.

Once you have a first draft on paper, you can delete material that is unrelated to your thesis and add material necessary to illustrate your points and make your paper convincing. The student who wrote "The A & P as a State of Mind" wisely dropped a paragraph that questioned whether Sammy displays chauvinistic attitudes toward women. Although this is an interesting issue, it has nothing to do with the thesis, which explains how the setting influences Sammy's decision to quit his job. Instead of including that paragraph, she added one that described Lengel's crabbed response to the girls so that she could lead up to the A & P "policy" he enforces.

Remember that your initial draft is only that. You should go through the paper many times — and then again — working to substantiate and clarify your ideas. You may even end up with several entire versions of the paper. Rewrite. The sentences within each paragraph should be related to a single topic. Transitions should connect one paragraph to the next so that there are no abrupt or confusing shifts. Awkward or wordy phrasing or unclear sentences and paragraphs should be mercilessly poked and prodded into shape.

Writing the Introduction and Conclusion

After you have clearly and adequately developed the body of your paper, pay particular attention to the introductory and concluding paragraphs. It's probably best to write the introduction — at least the final version of it — last, after you know precisely what you are introducing. Because this paragraph is crucial for generating interest in the topic, it should engage the reader and provide a sense of what the paper is about. There is no formula for writing effective introductory paragraphs because each writing situation is different — depending on the audience, topic, and approach — but if you pay attention to the introductions of the essays you read, you will notice a variety of possibilities. The introductory paragraph to "The A & P as a State of Mind," for example, is a straightforward explanation of why the story's setting is important for understanding Updike's treatment of the antagonist. The rest of the paper then offers evidence to support this point.

Concluding paragraphs demand equal attention because they leave the reader with a final impression. The conclusion should provide a sense of closure instead of starting a new topic or ending abruptly. In the final paragraph about the significance of the setting in "A & P," the student brings together the reasons Sammy quit his job by referring to his refusal to accept Lengel's store policies. At the same time she makes this point, she also explains the significance of Sammy ringing up the "No Sale" mentioned in her introductory paragraph. Thus, we are brought back to where we began, but we now have a greater understanding of why Sammy quits his job. Of course, the body of your paper is the most important part of your presentation, but do remember that first and last impressions have a powerful impact on readers.

Using Quotations

Quotations can be a valuable means of marshaling evidence to illustrate and support your ideas. A judicious use of quoted material will make your points clearer and more convincing. Here are some guidelines that should help you use quotations effectively.

1. Brief quotations (four lines or fewer of prose or three lines or fewer of poetry) should be carefully introduced and integrated into the text of your paper with quotation marks around them:

> According to the narrator, Bertha "had a reputation for strictness." He tells us that she always "wore dark clothes, dressed her hair simply, and expected contrition and obedience from her pupils."

For brief poetry quotations, use a slash to indicate a division between lines:

> The concluding lines of Blake's "The Tyger" pose a disturbing question: "What immortal hand or eye / Dare frame thy fearful symmetry?"

Lengthy quotations should be separated from the text of your paper. More than three lines of poetry should be double spaced and centered on the page. More than four lines of prose should be double spaced and indented ten spaces from the left margin, with the right margin the same as for the text. Do *not* use quotation marks for the passage; the indentation indicates that the passage is a quotation. Lengthy quotations should not be used in place of your own writing. Use them only if they are absolutely necessary.

2. If any words are added to a quotation, use brackets to distinguish your addition from the original source:

> "He [Young Goodman Brown] is portrayed as self-righteous and disillusioned."

Any words inside quotation marks and not in brackets must be precisely those of the author. Brackets can also be used to change the grammatical structure of a quotation so that it fits into your sentence:

> Smith argues that Chekhov "present[s] the narrator in an ambivalent light."

If you drop any words from the source, use ellipses to indicate the omission:

"Early to bed . . . makes a man healthy, wealthy, and wise."

Use ellipses following a period to indicate an omission at the end of a sentence:

"Early to bed and early to rise makes a man healthy. . . ."

Use a single line of spaced periods to indicate the omission of a line or more of poetry or more than one paragraph of prose:

> Nothing would sleep in that cellar, dank as a ditch,
> Bulbs broke out of boxes hunting for chinks in the dark,
> . . . .
> Nothing would give up life:
> Even the dirt kept breathing a small breath.

3. You will be able to punctuate quoted material accurately and confidently if you observe these conventions.

Place commas and periods inside quotation marks:

"Even the dirt," Roethke insists, "kept breathing a small breath."

Even though a comma does not appear after "dirt" in the original quotation, it is placed inside the quotation mark. The exception to this rule occurs when a parenthetical reference to a source follows the quotation:

"Even the dirt," Roethke insists, "kept breathing a small breath" (11).

Punctuation marks other than commas or periods go outside the quotation marks unless they are part of the material quoted:

What does Roethke mean when he writes that "the dirt kept breathing a small breath"?

Yeats asked, "How can we know the dancer from the dance?"

REVISING AND EDITING

Put some distance—a day or so if you can—between yourself and each draft of your paper. The phrase that seemed just right on Wednesday may be revealed as all wrong on Friday. You'll have a better chance of detecting lumbering sentences and thin paragraphs if you plan ahead and give yourself the time to read your paper from a fresh perspective. Through the process of revision, you can transform a competent paper into an excellent one.

Begin by asking yourself if your approach to the topic requires any rethinking. Is the argument carefully thought out and logically presented? Are there any gaps in the presentation? How well is the paper organized? Do the paragraphs lead into one another? Does the body of the paper deliver what the thesis promises? Is the interpretation sound? Are any relevant and important elements of the work ignored or distorted to advance the thesis? Are the points supported with evidence? These large questions should be addressed before you focus on more detailed matters. If you uncover serious problems as a result of considering these questions, you'll probably have quite a lot of rewriting to do, but at least you will have the opportunity to correct the problems — even if doing so takes several drafts.

A useful technique for spotting awkward or unclear moments in the paper is to read it aloud. You might also try having a friend read it aloud to you. If your handwriting is legible, your friend's reading — perhaps accompanied by hesitations and puzzled expressions — could alert you to passages that need reworking. Having identified problems, you can readily correct them on a word processor or on the draft, provided you've skipped lines and used wide margins. The final draft you hand in should be neat and carefully proofread for any inadvertent errors.

The following checklist offers questions to ask about your paper as you revise and edit it. Most of these questions will be familiar to you; however, if you need help with any of them, ask your instructor or review the appropriate section in a composition handbook.

Revision Checklist

1. Is the topic manageable? Is it too narrow or too broad?
2. Is the thesis clear? Is it based on a careful reading of the work?
3. Is the paper logically organized? Does it have a firm sense of direction?
4. Is your argument persuasive?
5. Should any material be deleted? Do any important points require further illustration or evidence?
6. Does the opening paragraph introduce the topic in an interesting manner?
7. Are the paragraphs developed, unified, and coherent? Are any too short or long?
8. Are there transitions linking the paragraphs?
9. Does the concluding paragraph provide a sense of closure?
10. Is the tone appropriate? Is it unduly flippant or pretentious?
11. Is the title engaging and suggestive?
12. Are the sentences clear, concise, and complete?
13. Are simple, complex, and compound sentences used for variety?
14. Have technical terms been used correctly? Are you certain of the meanings of all the words in the paper? Are they spelled correctly?
15. Have you documented any information borrowed from books, articles, or other sources? Have you quoted too much instead of summarizing or paraphrasing secondary material?
16. Have you used a standard format for citing sources (see p. 2106)?
17. Have you followed your instructor's guidelines for the manuscript format of the final draft?
18. Have you carefully proofread the final draft?

When you proofread your final draft, you may find a few typographical errors that must be corrected but do not warrant retyping an entire page. Provided there are not more than a handful of such errors throughout the page, they can be corrected as shown in the following passage. This example condenses a short paper's worth of errors; no single passage should be this shabby in your essay:

```
To add a letter or word, use a caret on the line where the
                 is
addition^needed. To delete a word draw a single line through
t̶h̶r̶o̶u̶g̶h̶ it. Run-on words are separated by a vertical|line,
and inadvertent spaces are closed like t͡his. Transposed
letters are indicated this w̃ãỹ. New paragraphs are noted
with the sign ¶ in front of where the next paragraph is to
begin.¶Unless you . . .
```

These sorts of errors can be minimized by using correction fluids or tapes while you type. If you use a word processor, you can eliminate such errors completely by simply entering corrections as you proofread on the screen.

MANUSCRIPT FORM

The novelist and poet Peter De Vries once observed that he very much enjoyed writing but that he couldn't bear the "paper work." Behind this playful pun is a half-serious impatience with the mechanics of it all. You may feel some of that too, but don't let your thoughtful, carefully revised paper trip over minor details. The final draft you hand in to your instructor should not only read well but look neat. If your instructor does not provide specific instructions concerning the format for the paper, follow these guidelines:

1. Papers (particularly long ones) should be typed on 8½ by 11-inch paper in double space. Avoid transparent paper such as onionskin; it is difficult to read and write comments on. The ribbon should be dark and the letters on the machine clear. If you compose on a word processor with a dot-matrix printer, be certain that the dots are close enough together to be legible. And don't forget to separate your pages and remove the strips of holes on each side of the pages if your printer uses a continuous paper feed. If your instructor accepts handwritten papers, write legibly in ink on only one side of a wide-lined page.

2. Use a one-inch margin at the top, bottom, and sides of each page. Unless you are instructed to include a separate title page, type your name,

instructor's name, course number and section, and date on separate lines one inch below the upper-left corner of the first page. Double space between these lines and then center the title two spaces below the date. Do not underline or put quotation marks around your paper's title, but do use quotation marks around the titles of poems, short stories, or other brief works, and underline the titles of books and plays (for instance, Racial Stereotypes in "Battle Royal" and *The Piano Lesson*). Begin the text of your paper two spaces below the title. If you have used secondary sources, list them on a separate page at the end of the paper. Center the heading "Notes" or "Works Cited" one inch from the top of the page and then double space between it and the entries.

3. Number each page consecutively, beginning with page 2, a half inch from the top of the page in the upper-right corner.

4. Gather the pages with a paper clip rather than staples, folders, or some other device. That will make it easier for your instructor to handle the paper.

TYPES OF WRITING ASSIGNMENTS

The types of papers most frequently assigned in literature classes are explication, analysis, and comparison and contrast. Most writing about literature involves some combination of these skills. This section includes a sample explication, an analysis, and a comparison and contrast paper. For a sample research paper that demonstrates a variety of strategies for documenting outside sources, see page 2113. For genre-based assignments, see the sample papers for writing about fiction (p. 43), poetry (p. 714), and drama (p. 1213).

Explication

The purpose of this approach to a literary work is to make the implicit explicit. *Explication* is a detailed explanation of a passage of poetry or prose. Because explication is an intensive examination of a text line by line, it is mostly used to interpret a short poem in its entirety or a brief passage from a long poem, short story, or play. Explication can be used in any kind of paper when you want to be specific about how a writer achieves a certain effect. An explication pays careful attention to language — the connotations of words, allusions, figurative language, irony, symbol, rhythm, sound, and so on. These elements are examined in relation to one another and to the overall effect and meaning of the work.

The simplest way to organize an explication is to move through the passage line by line, explaining whatever seems significant. It is wise to avoid, however, an assembly-line approach that begins each sentence with

"In line one (two, three) . . . ." Instead, organize your paper in whatever way best serves your thesis. You might find that the right place to start is with the final lines, working your way back to the beginning of the poem or passage. The following sample explication on Dickinson's "There's a certain Slant of light" does just that. The student's opening paragraph refers to the final line of the poem in order to present her thesis. She explains that though the poem begins with an image of light, it is not a bright or cheery poem but one concerned with "the look of Death." Since the last line prompted her thesis, that is where she begins the explication.

You might also find it useful to structure a paper by discussing various elements of literature, so that you have a paragraph on connotative words followed by one on figurative language and so on. However your paper is organized, keep in mind that the aim of an explication is not simply to summarize the passage but to comment on the effects and meanings produced by the author's use of language in it. An effective explication (the Latin word *explicare* means "to unfold") displays a text to reveal how it works and what it signifies. Although writing an explication requires some patience and sensitivity, it is an excellent method for coming to understand and appreciate the elements and qualities that constitute literary art.

A SAMPLE EXPLICATION

A Reading of Dickinson's "There's a certain Slant of light"

The sample paper by Bonnie Katz is the result of an assignment calling for an explication of about 750 words on any poem by Emily Dickinson. Katz selected "There's a certain Slant of light."

EMILY DICKINSON (1830–1886)

There's a certain Slant of light — c. *1861*

There's a certain Slant of light,
Winter Afternoons —
That oppresses, like the Heft
Of Cathedral Tunes —

Heavenly Hurt, it gives us — 5
We can find no scar,
But internal difference,
Where the Meanings, are —

None may teach it — Any —
'Tis the Seal Despair —   10
An imperial affliction
Sent us of the Air —

When it comes, the Landscape listens —
Shadows — hold their breath —
When it goes, 'tis like the Distance   15
On the look of Death —

This essay comments on every line of the poem and provides a coherent reading that relates each line to the speaker's intense awareness of death. Although the essay discusses each stanza in the order that it appears, the introductory paragraph provides a brief overview explaining how the poem's images contribute to its total meaning. In addition, the student does not hesitate to discuss a line out of sequence when it can be usefully connected to another phrase. This is especially apparent in the third paragraph, in her discussion of stanzas 2 and 3. The final paragraph describes some of the formal elements of the poem. It might be argued that this discussion could have been integrated into the previous paragraphs rather than placed at the end, but the student does make a connection in her concluding sentence between the pattern of language and its meaning.

Several other matters are worth noticing. The student works quotations into her own sentences to support her points. She quotes exactly as the words appear in the poem, even Dickinson's irregular use of capital letters. When something is added to a quotation to clarify it, it is enclosed in brackets so that the essayist's words will not be mistaken for the poet's: "Seal [of] Despair." A slash is used to indicate line divisions as in "imperial affliction / Sent us of the Air." And, finally, because the essay focuses on a short poem, it is not necessary to include line numbers, though they would be required in a study of a longer work.

Bonnie Katz
Professor Quiello
English 109-2
October 26, 19--

                A Reading of Dickinson's
             "There's a certain Slant of light"

     Because Emily Dickinson did not provide titles for
her poetry, editors follow the customary practice of using
the first line of a poem as its title. However, a more appropriate title for "There's a certain Slant of light,"
one that suggests what the speaker in the poem is most
concerned about, can be drawn from the poem's last line,
which ends with "the look of Death." Although the first
line begins with an image of light, nothing bright, carefree, or cheerful appears in the poem. Instead, the predominant mood and images are darkened by a sense of
despair resulting from the speaker's awareness of death.

     In the first stanza, the "certain Slant of light" is
associated with "Winter Afternoons," a phrase that connotes the end of a day, a season, and even life itself.
Such light is hardly warm or comforting. Not a ray or
beam, this slanting light suggests something unusual or
distorted and creates in the speaker a certain slant on
life that is consistent with the cold, dark mood that winter afternoons can produce. Like the speaker, most of us
have seen and felt this sort of light: it "oppresses" and
pervades our sense of things when we encounter it. Dickinson uses the senses of hearing and touch as well as sight
to describe the overwhelming oppressiveness that the
speaker experiences. The light is transformed into sound
by a simile that tells us it is "like the Heft / Of Cathedral Tunes." Moreover, the "Heft" of that sound--the slow,
solemn measures of tolling church bells and organ music--

weighs heavily on our spirits. Through the use of shifting
imagery, Dickinson evokes a kind of spiritual numbness
that we keenly feel and perceive through our senses.

By associating the winter light with "Cathedral
Tunes," Dickinson lets us know that the speaker is concerned about more than the weather. Whatever it is that
"oppresses" is related by connotation to faith, mortality,
and God. The second and third stanzas offer several suggestions about this connection. The pain caused by the
light is a "Heavenly Hurt." This "imperial affliction /
Sent us of the Air" apparently comes from God above, and
yet it seems to be part of the very nature of life. The
oppressiveness we feel is in the air, and it can neither
be specifically identified at this point in the poem nor
be eliminated, for "None may teach it--Any." All we know
is that existence itself seems depressing under the weight
of this "Seal [of] Despair." The impression left by this
"Seal" is stamped within the mind or soul rather than
externally. "We can find no scar," but once experienced
this oppressiveness challenges our faith in life and its
"Meanings."

The final stanza does not explain what those "Meanings" are, but it does make clear that the speaker is
acutely aware of death. As the winter daylight fades,
Dickinson projects the speaker's anxiety onto the surrounding landscape and shadows, which will soon be engulfed by the darkness that follows this light: "the
Landscape listens-- / Shadows--hold their breath." This
image firmly aligns the winter light in the first stanza
with darkness. Paradoxically, the light in this poem illuminates the nature of darkness. Tension is released when
the light is completely gone, but what remains is the despair that the "imperial affliction" has imprinted on the

speaker's sensibilities, for it is "like the Distance / On
the look of Death." There can be no relief from what that
"certain Slant of light" has revealed because what has
been experienced is permanent--like the fixed stare in the
eyes of someone who is dead.

The speaker's awareness of death is conveyed in
a thoughtful, hushed tone. The lines are filled with fluid
l and smooth s sounds that are appropriate for the quiet,
meditative voice in the poem. The voice sounds tentative
and uncertain--perhaps a little frightened. This seems to
be reflected in the slightly irregular meter of the lines.
The stanzas are trochaic with the second and fourth lines
of each stanza having five syllables, but no stanza is
identical because each works a slight variation on the
first stanza's seven syllables in the first and third
lines. The rhymes also combine exact patterns with variations. The first and third lines of each stanza are not
exact rhymes, but the second and fourth lines are exact so
that the paired words are more closely related: Afternoons, Tunes; scar, are; Despair, Air; and breath, Death.
There is a pattern to the poem, but it is unobtrusively
woven into the speaker's voice in much the same way that
"the look of Death" is subtly present in the images and
language of the poem.

Analysis

The preceding sample essay shows how an explication examines in detail the important elements in a work and relates them to the whole. An analysis, however, usually examines only a single element—such as plot, character, point of view, symbol, tone, or irony—and relates it to the entire work. An analytic topic separates the work into parts and focuses on a specific one; you might consider "Point of View in 'A Rose for Emily,'" "Patterns of Rhythm in Browning's 'My Last Duchess,'" or "The Significance of Fortinbras in *Hamlet*." The specific element must be related to the work as a whole or it will appear irrelevant. It is not enough to point out that there are many death images in Marvell's "To His Coy Mistress"; the images must somehow be connected to the poem's overall effect.

Whether an analytic paper is just a few pages or many, it cannot attempt to discuss everything about the work it is considering. Only those elements that are relevant to the topic can be treated. This kind of focusing makes the topic manageable; this is why most papers that you write will probably be some form of analysis. Explications are useful for a short passage, but a line-by-line commentary on a story, play, or long poem simply isn't practical. Because analysis allows you to consider the central effect or meaning of an entire work by studying a single important element, it is a useful and common approach to longer works.

A SAMPLE ANALYSIS

The A & P as a State of Mind

Nancy Lager's paper analyzes the setting in John Updike's "A & P" (the entire story appears on p. 576). The assignment simply asked for an essay of approximately 750 words on a short story written in the twentieth century. The approach was left to the student.

The idea for this essay began with Lager asking herself why Updike used "A & P" as the title. The initial answer to the question was that "the setting is important in this story." This answer was the rough beginning of a tentative thesis. What still had to be explained, though, was how the setting is important. To determine the significance of the setting, Lager jotted down some notes based on her underlinings and marginal notations:

A & P
"usual traffic"
lights and tile
"electric eye"
shoppers like "sheep," "houseslaves," "pigs"
"Alexandrov and Petrooshki" — Russia

New England Town
typical: bank, church, etc.
traditional
conservative
proper
near Salem — witch trials
puritanical
intolerant

Lengel
"manager"
"doesn't miss that much" (like lady shopper)

Sunday school
"It's our policy"
spokesman for A & P values

From these notes Lager saw that Lengel serves as the voice of the A & P. He is, in a sense, a personification of the intolerant atmosphere of the setting. This insight led to another version of her thesis statement: "The setting of 'A & P' is the antagonist of the story." That explained at least some of the setting's importance. By seeing Lengel as a spokesman for "A & P" policies, she could view him as a voice that articulates the morally smug atmosphere created by the setting. Finally, she considered why it is significant that the setting is the antagonist, and this generated her last thesis: "Because the intolerant setting of 'A & P' is the antagonist in the story, it is crucial to our understanding of Sammy's decision to quit his job." This thesis sentence does not appear precisely in these words in the essay, but it is the backbone of the introductory paragraph.

The remaining paragraphs consist of details that describe the A & P in the second paragraph, the New England town in the third, Lengel in the fourth, and Sammy's reasons for quitting in the concluding paragraph. Paragraphs 2, 3, and 4 are largely based on Lager's notes, which she used as an outline once her thesis was established. The essay is sharply focused, well organized, and generally well written. In addition, it suggests a number of useful guidelines for analytic papers:

1. Only those points related to the thesis are included. In another type of paper the role of the girls in the bathing suits, for example, might have been considerably more prominent.

2. The analysis keeps the setting in focus while at the same time indicating how it is significant in the major incident in the story — Sammy's quitting.

3. The title is a useful lead into the paper; it provides a sense of what the topic is. In addition, the title is drawn from a sentence (the final one of the first paragraph) that clearly explains its meaning.

4. The introductory paragraph is direct and clearly indicates the paper will argue that the setting serves as the antagonist of the story.

5. Brief quotations are deftly incorporated into the text of the paper to illustrate points. We are told what we need to know about the story as evidence is provided to support ideas. There is no unnecessary plot summary. Because "A & P" is only a few pages in length and is an assigned topic, page numbers are not included after quoted phrases. If the story were longer, page numbers would be helpful for the reader.

6. The paragraphs are well developed, unified, and coherent. They flow naturally from one to another. Notice, for example, the smooth transition worked into the final sentence of the third paragraph and the first sentence of the fourth paragraph.

(Text continues on page 2091.)

Nancy Lager
Professor Taylor
English 102-12
April 1, 19--

The A & P as a State of Mind

The setting of John Updike's "A & P" is crucial to
our understanding of Sammy's decision to quit his job.
Although Sammy is the central character in the story and
we learn that he is a principled, good-natured nineteen-
year-old with a sense of humor, Updike seems to invest as
much effort in describing the setting as he does in Sammy.
The setting is the antagonist and plays a role that is as
important as Sammy's. The title, after all, is not "Youthful Rebellion" or "Sammy Quits" but "A & P." Even though
Sammy knows that his quitting will make life more difficult for him, he instinctively insists on rejecting what
the A & P comes to represent in the story. When he rings
up a "No Sale" and "saunter[s]" out of the store, he
leaves behind not only a job but the rigid state of mind
associated with the A & P.

Sammy's descriptions of the A & P present a setting
that is ugly, monotonous, and rigidly regulated. The fluorescent light is as blandly cool as the "checkerboard
green-and-cream rubber-tile floor." We can see the uniformity Sammy describes because we have all been in chain
stores. The "usual traffic" moves in one direction (except
for the swimsuited girls, who move against it), and
everything is neatly ordered and categorized in tidy
aisles. The dehumanizing routine of this environment is
suggested by Sammy's offhand references to the typical
shoppers as "sheep," "houseslaves," and "pigs." They seem
to pace through the store in a stupor; as Sammy tells us,
not even dynamite could move them.

Lager 2

The A & P is appropriately located "right in the middle" of a proper, conservative, traditional New England town north of Boston. This location, coupled with the fact that the town is only five miles from Salem, the site of the famous seventeenth-century witch trials, suggests a narrow, intolerant social atmosphere in which there is no room for stepping beyond the boundaries of what is regarded as normal and proper. The importance of this setting can be appreciated even more if we imagine the action taking place in, say, a mellow suburb of southern California. In this prim New England setting, the girls in their bathing suits are bound to offend somebody's sense of propriety.

As soon as Lengel sees the girls, the inevitable conflict begins. He embodies the dull conformity represented by the A & P. As "manager," he is both the guardian and enforcer of "policy." When he gives the girls "that sad Sunday-school-superintendent stare," we know we are in the presence of the A & P version of a dreary bureaucrat who "doesn't miss that much." He is as unsympathetic and unpleasant as the woman "with rouge on her cheeks and no eyebrows" who pounces on Sammy for ringing up her "HiHo crackers" twice. Like the "electric eye" in the doorway, her vigilant eyes allow nothing to escape their notice. For Sammy the logical extension of Lengel's "policy" is the half-serious notion that one day the A & P might be known as the "Great Alexandrov and Petrooshki Tea Company." Sammy's connection between what he regards as mindless "policy" and Soviet oppression is obviously an exaggeration, but the reader is invited to entertain the similarities anyway.

The reason Sammy quits his job has less to do with defending the girls than with his own sense of what it

Lager 3

means to be a decent human being. His decision is not an
easy one. He doesn't want to make trouble or disappoint
his parents, and he knows his independence and self-
reliance (the other side of New England tradition) will
make life more complex for him. In spite of his own hesitations, he finds himself blurting out "Fiddle-de-doo"
to Lengel's policies and in doing so knows that his
grandmother "would have been pleased." Sammy's "No Sale"
rejects the crabbed perspective on life that Lengel represents as manager of the A & P. This gesture is more than
just a negative, however, for as he punches in that last
entry on the cash register, "the machine whirs 'pee-pul.'"
His decision to quit his job at the A & P is an expression
of his refusal to regard policies as more important than
people.

7. Lager makes excellent use of her careful reading and notes by finding revealing connections among the details she has observed. The store's "electric eye," for instance, is related to the woman's and Lengel's watchfulness.
8. As events are described, the present tense is used. This avoids awkward tense shifts and lends an immediacy to the discussion.
9. The concluding paragraph establishes the significance of why the setting should be seen as the antagonist and provides a sense of closure by referring again to Sammy's "No Sale," which has been mentioned at the end of the first paragraph.
10. In short, Lager has demonstrated that she has read the work closely, has understood the relation of the setting to the major action, and has argued her thesis convincingly by using evidence from the story.

Comparison and Contrast

Another essay assignment in literature courses often combined with analytic topics is the type that requires you to write about similarities and differences between or within works. You might be asked to discuss "How Sounds Express Meanings in May Swenson's 'A Nosty Fright' and Lewis

Carroll's 'Jabberwocky,'" or "Sammy's and Stokesie's Attitudes about Conformity in Updike's 'A & P.'" A *comparison* of either topic would emphasize their similarities, while a *contrast* would stress their differences. It is possible, of course, to include both perspectives in a paper if you find significant likenesses and differences. A comparison of Andrew Marvell's "To His Coy Mistress" and Richard Wilbur's "A Late Aubade" would, for example, yield similarities because each poem describes a man urging his lover to make the most of their precious time together; however, important differences also exist in the tone and theme of each poem that would constitute a contrast. (You should, incidentally, be aware that the term *comparison* is sometimes used inclusively to refer to both similarities and differences. If you are assigned a comparison of two works, be sure that you understand what your instructor's expectations are; you may be required to include both approaches in the essay.)

When you choose your own topic, the paper will be more successful — more manageable — if you write on works that can be meaningfully related to each other. Although Robert Herrick's "To the Virgins, to Make Much of Time" and Shakespeare's *Hamlet* both have something to do with hesitation, the likelihood of anyone making a connection between the two that reveals something interesting and important is remote — though perhaps not impossible if the topic were conceived imaginatively and tactfully. That is not to say that comparisons of works from different genres should be avoided, but the relation between them should be strong, as would a treatment of African American identity in M. Carl Holman's "Mr. Z" and August Wilson's *The Piano Lesson*. Choose a topic that encourages you to ask significant questions about each work; the purpose of a comparison or contrast is to understand the works more clearly for having examined them together. Despite the obvious differences between Henrik Ibsen's *A Doll House* and Gail Godwin's "A Sorrowful Woman," the two are closely related if we ask why the wife in each work withdraws from her family.

Choose works to compare or contrast that intersect with each other in some significant way. They may, for example, be written by the same author, in the same genre, or about the same subject. Perhaps you can compare their use of some technique, such as irony or point of view. Regardless of the specific topic, be sure to have a thesis that allows you to organize your paper around a central idea that argues a point about the two works. If you merely draw up a list of similarities or differences without a thesis in mind, your paper will be little more than a series of observations with no apparent purpose. Keep in the foreground of your thinking what the comparison or contrast reveals about the works.

There is no single way to organize comparative papers since each topic is likely to have its own particular issues to resolve, but it is useful to be aware of two basic patterns that can be helpful with a comparison, a contrast, or a combination of both. One method that can be effective for relatively short papers consists of dividing the paper in half, first discussing one work and then the other. Here, for example, is a partial informal outline for a discussion of Sophocles' *Oedipus the King* and Shakespeare's *Hamlet;* the topic is a comparison and contrast: "Oedipus and Hamlet as Tragic Figures."

1. Oedipus
   a. The nature of the conflict
   b. Strengths and stature
   c. Weaknesses and mistakes
   d. What is learned
2. Hamlet
   a. The nature of the conflict
   b. Strengths and stature
   c. Weaknesses and mistakes
   d. What is learned

This organizational strategy can be effective provided that the second part of the paper combines the discussion of Hamlet with references to Oedipus so that the thesis is made clear and the paper unified without being repetitive. If the two characters were treated entirely separately, then the discussion would be merely parallel rather than integrated. In a lengthy paper, this organization probably would not work well because a reader would have difficulty remembering the points made in the first half as he or she reads on.

Thus, for a longer paper it is usually better to create a more integrated structure that discusses both works as you take up each item in your outline. Here is the second basic pattern using the elements in the partial outline just cited:

1. The nature of the conflict
   a. Oedipus
   b. Hamlet
2. Strengths and stature
   a. Oedipus
   b. Hamlet
3. Weaknesses and mistakes
   a. Oedipus
   b. Hamlet
4. What is learned
   a. Oedipus
   b. Hamlet

This pattern allows you to discuss any number of topics without requiring that your reader recall what you first said about the conflict Oedipus confronts before you discuss Hamlet's conflicts fifteen pages later. However you structure your comparison or contrast paper, make certain that a reader can follow its elements and keep track of its thesis.

A SAMPLE COMPARISON

The Struggle for Women's Self-Definition in A Doll House *and* M. Butterfly

The following paper was written in response to an assignment that required a comparison and contrast — about 750 words — of two assigned plays. The student chose to write an analysis of how the women in each play resist being defined by men.

Although these two plays are fairly lengthy, Monica Casis's brief analysis of them is satisfying because she specifically focuses on the women's struggle for self-definition. After introducing the topic in the first paragraph, she takes up *A Doll House* and *M. Butterfly* in a pattern similar to the first outline suggested for "Oedipus and Hamlet as Tragic Figures." Notice how Casis works in subsequent references to *A Doll House* as she discusses *M. Butterfly* so that her treatment is integrated and we are reminded why she is comparing and contrasting the two works. Though this brief paper cannot address all the complexities and subtleties of gender definition in the plays, her final paragraph sums up her points without being repetitive and reiterates the thesis with which she began.

Monica Casis

Professor Matthews

English 105-4

November 4, 19--

The Struggle for Women's Self-Definition in

A Doll House and M. Butterfly

Though Henrik Ibsen's A Doll House (1879) and David Henry Hwang's M. Butterfly (1988) were written more than one hundred years apart and portray radically different characters in settings and circumstances that are foreign to one another, both plays raise similar questions about the role of women and how they are defined in their respective worlds. Each play presents a woman who initially seems to be without a strong identity as she attempts to conform to her partner's ideals of the perfect

woman in an effort to be accepted and loved. However, at
the same time Ibsen's Nora Helmer and Hwang's Song Liling
are resourceful, cunning, and manipulative. Though the
plays seem to be about the emergence of each woman's
identity--Nora's refusal to be only a dutiful housewife
and devoted mother and Song's refusal to be a woman at
all(!)--these women are from the beginning stronger and
more autonomous than their partners ever imagine them
to be. Even so, that does not lead to their ability to
define themselves as either completely autonomous or as
women.

In A Doll House Nora is treated as her father's, then
her husband's, doll. She is called "squirrel," "spendthrift," and "lark" and is admonished for such things as
eating sweets or asking her husband to take her ideas into
consideration. Torvald's concept of the ideal woman is a
showpiece who can dress up, recite, and dance. As a mother
she only plays with her children, since she has Anne-Marie
to take care of them. As a housewife, she has no control
over the household finances and is given an allowance by
her husband.

Although Nora externally conforms to her husband's
expectations, she has the strength and resourceful courage
to borrow money for a trip to Italy to save her husband's
life and does odd jobs in order to pay the debt that she
has committed forgery to secure. She is proud of her secret of sacrificing for the family. She refers to herself
as a frivolous, helpless, dependent woman in order to coax
her husband into giving her money or to steer him away
from the mailbox carrying Krogstad's incriminating letter.
Nora is constantly lying in order to please her husband.
So although in one instance we see Nora as a woman trapped
within her husband's definition of her, the reader is also

aware that Nora uses his expectations to achieve her own goals. Once Nora sees and understands her superficiality and selfishness--that Torvald is concerned with only what might threaten him--she realizes she must abandon the confines of his definitions of her.

In a similar manner Song plays on the needs of Gallimard. To Gallimard, the perfect woman is one who is "beautiful" and "brave" but most important one whom he can dominate and control. Song is Asian, which underlies the cultural prejudice that she is expected to be subservient, quiet, faithful, and obedient. When Gallimard refers to her as Butterfly, she loses her individual identity as Nora loses hers within her pet names.

By the end of the play the reader is aware that Song is, in fact, a man working as a spy to obtain important military information from Gallimard. In order to keep hidden this secret identity, Song acts as he believes men desire women to be. As a woman Song refers to her "shame" or modesty so that Gallimard will not undress her. She pretends that she has a need to know everything he knows when in reality she is appeasing his ego and passing on military information to his enemies. Song tells Gallimard that she is trying to act "modern" and "manly" but cannot. In actuality Song is an actor who is acting the way a Chinese woman is assumed to act. When Song observes that "Once a woman submits, a man is always ready to become 'generous'" (1706; all page references are to the class text, The Bedford Introduction to Literature, 5th ed.), she is actually describing her method of control. Like Nora, the "woman" Song appeals to her mate's egotistical needs in order to fulfill her own personal goals and, in this case, the needs of her political allegiances. Just as Nora is Torvald's doll in need of care and protection,

Song is Gallimard's doll, beautiful and seemingly willing
to accede to his every desire.

The turning point in these plays occurs when Nora and
Song are faced with their dramatically changed relationships with their mates. Nora becomes convinced that she
will corrupt her children and home with the guilt she
bears--not for borrowing the vacation money but for being
with a man she no longer knows. When Torvald learns of the
truth from Krogstad, he regards her as a liar, hypocrite,
and criminal and therefore repudiates her. Once Nora realizes the selfishness of her husband, she also realizes she
cannot go on living the lie of being his ideal. Nora must
leave her husband and children in order to search for an
identity commensurate with her strengths. In M. Butterfly
the controlling roles are switched when Gallimard admits
that he loves Song and intends to marry her. It is when
Song refuses marriage and determines the future of the
child that Gallimard openly gives up control (which he
never truly had). He supports Song and the child, divorces
Helga, and passes classified information to Song. Once
Song has total control, she emerges as a man, free from
any of Gallimard's efforts to define her.

When Nora and Song come to terms with themselves,
their situations are, however, no less problematic than
when they falsely fulfilled the definition imposed on
them. Nora leaves to pursue what may seem to some readers
selfish desires, however necessary they are. In Ibsen's
world, if a woman is not an obedient wife, mother, and
nurturer, she defies definition. Similarly, Song's cruelty
toward Gallimard and her revelation that she is not what
he seems totally destroys Gallimard's image of Song as a
woman, but we must understand that under the weight of
that destruction Song's identity as a woman disappears,

just as Nora does when she slams the door of the doll
house she rejects. It seems that unless a man defines what
a woman is in these two plays, the strong and resourceful
woman must disappear rather than be allowed to redefine
herself.

39

The Literary
Research Paper

A close reading of a primary source such as a short story, poem, or play can give insights into a work's themes and effects, but sometimes you will want to know more. A published commentary by a critic who knows the work well and is familiar with the author's life and times can provide insights that otherwise may not be available. Such comments and interpretations — known as *secondary sources* — are, of course, not a substitute for the work itself, but they often can take you into a work further than if you made the journey by yourself.

After imagination, good sense, and energy, perhaps the next most important quality for writing a research paper is the ability to organize material. A research paper on a literary topic requires a writer to take account of quite a lot at once: the text, ideas, sources, and documentation techniques all make demands on one's efforts to present a topic clearly and convincingly.

The following list should give you a sense of what goes into creating a research paper. Although some steps on the list can be folded into one another, they offer an overview of the work that will involve you:

1. Choosing a topic
2. Finding sources
3. Evaluating sources
4. Taking notes
5. Developing a thesis
6. Organizing an outline
7. Writing drafts
8. Revising
9. Documenting sources
10. Preparing the final draft and proofreading

Even if you have never written a research paper, you most likely have already had experience choosing a topic, developing a thesis, organizing an outline, and writing a draft that you then revised, proofread, and handed in. Those skills represent six of the ten items on the list. This chapter briefly reviews some of these steps and focuses on the remaining tasks, unique to research paper assignments.

CHOOSING A TOPIC

Chapter 38 discussed the importance of reading a work closely and taking careful notes as a means of generating topics for writing about literature. If you know a work well and record your understanding of it in notes, you'll have impressions and ideas to choose from for potential topics. You may find it useful to review the information on pages 2064–2066 before reading the advice about putting together a research paper in this chapter.

The student author of the sample research paper "How the Narrator Cultivates a Rose for Emily" (p. 2113) was asked to write a five-page paper that demonstrated some familiarity with published critical perspectives on a Faulkner story of his choice. Before looking into critical discussions of the story, he read "A Rose for Emily" several times, taking notes and making comments in the margin of his textbook on each reading.

What prompted his choice of "A Rose for Emily" was a class discussion in which many of his classmates found the story's title inappropriate or misleading because they could not understand how and why the story constituted a tribute to Emily given that she murdered a man and slept with his dead body over many years. The gruesome surprise ending revealing Emily as a murderer and necrophiliac hardly seemed to warrant a rose and a tribute for the central character. Why did Faulkner use such a title? Only after having thoroughly examined the story did the student go to the library to see what professional critics had to say about this question.

FINDING SOURCES

Whether your college library is large or small, its reference librarians can usually help you locate secondary sources about a particular work or author. Unless you choose a very recently published story, poem, or play about which little or nothing has been written, you should be able to find commentaries about a literary work efficiently and quickly. Here are some useful reference sources that can help you to establish both an overview of a potential topic and a list of relevant books and articles.

Annotated List of References

Baker, Nancy L. *A Research Guide for Undergraduate Students: English and American Literature.* 2nd ed. New York: MLA, 1985. Especially designed for students; a useful guide to reference sources.

Bryer, Jackson, ed. *Sixteen Modern American Authors: A Survey of Research and Criticism.* New York: Norton, 1973. Extensive bibliographic essays on Sherwood Anderson, Willa Cather, Hart Crane, Theodore Dreiser, T. S. Eliot, William Faulkner, F. Scott Fitzgerald, Robert Frost, Ernest Hemingway, Eugene O'Neill, Ezra Pound, Edwin Arlington Robinson, John Steinbeck, Wallace Stevens, William Carlos Williams, and Thomas Wolfe.

Corse, Larry B., and Sandra B. Corse. *Articles on American and British Literature: An Index to Selected Periodicals, 1950–1977.* Athens, OH: Swallow, 1981. Specifically designed for students using small college libraries.

Eddleman, Floyd E., ed. *American Drama Criticism: Interpretations, 1890–1977.* 2nd ed. Hamden, CT: Shoe String, 1979. Supplement 1984.

Elliot, Emory, et al. *Columbia Literary History of the United States.* New York: Columbia UP, 1988. This updates the discussions in Spiller (below) and reflects recent changes in the canon.

Harner, James L. *Literary Research Guide: A Guide to Reference Sources for the Study of Literature in English and Related Topics.* 2nd ed. New York: MLA, 1993. A selective but extensive annotated guide to important bibliographies, abstracts, databases, histories, surveys, dictionaries, encyclopedias, and handbooks; an invaluable research tool with extensive, useful indexes.

Holman, C. Hugh, and William Harmon. *A Handbook to Literature.* 6th ed. New York: Macmillan, 1992. A thorough dictionary of literary terms that also provides brief, clear overviews of literary movements such as Romanticism.

Kuntz, Joseph M., and Nancy C. Martinez. *Poetry Explication: A Checklist of Interpretation since 1925 of British and American Poems Past and Present.* Boston: Hall, 1980.

MLA International Bibliography of Books and Articles on Modern Language and Literature. New York: MLA, 1921–. Compiled annually; a major source for articles and books.

The New Cambridge Bibliography of English Literature. 5 vols. Cambridge, Eng.: Cambridge UP, 1967–77. An important source on the literature from A.D. 600 to 1950.

The Oxford History of English Literature. 13 vols. Oxford, Eng.: Oxford UP, 1945–, in progress. The most comprehensive literary history.

The Penguin Companion to World Literature. 4 vols. New York: McGraw-Hill, 1969–71. Covers classical, Asian, African, European, English, and American literature.

Preminger, Alex, and T. V. F. Brogan, eds. *The New Princeton Encyclopedia of Poetry and Poetics.* Princeton: Princeton UP, 1993. Includes entries on technical terms and poetic movements.

Rees, Robert, and Earl N. Harbert. *Fifteen American Authors before 1900: Bibliographic Essays on Research and Criticism.* Madison: U of Wisconsin P, 1971. Among the writers covered are Stephen Crane and Emily Dickinson.

Spiller, Robert E., et al. *Literary History of the United States.* 4th ed. 2 vols. New York: Macmillan, 1974. Coverage of literary movements and individual writers from colonial times to the 1960s.

Walker, Warren S. *Twentieth-Century Short Story Explication.* 3rd ed. Hamden, CT: Shoe String, 1977. A bibliography of criticism on short stories written since 1800; supplements appear every few years.

These sources are available in the reference sections of most college libraries; ask a reference librarian to help you locate them.

Electronic Sources

Researchers can locate materials in a variety of sources, including card catalogs, specialized encyclopedias, bibliographies, and indexes to periodicals. Many libraries now also provide computer searches that are linked to a database of the libraries' holdings. This can be an efficient way to establish a bibliography on a specific topic. If your library has such a service, consult a reference librarian about how to use it and to determine whether it is feasible for your topic. If a computer service is impractical, you can still collect the same information from printed sources.

In addition to the many electronic databases ranging from your library's computerized holdings to the many specialized CD-ROMs available, such as *MLA International Bibliography* (a major source for articles and books on literary topics), there are also numerous sources now available on the Internet. Although the Internet does not yet provide much in-depth scholarly literary criticism, it can be useful for finding overviews of topics in encyclopedias or dictionaries, and it is especially useful for finding up-to-date information on contemporary writers. Browsing on the Net can be absorbing as well as informative, but unless you have plenty of time to spare, don't wait until the last minute to locate your electronic sources. Unless you're familiar with using search engines and narrowing menu selections, you might find yourself choosing from thousands of potential documents if you enter an unqualified entry such as "Charles Dickens." Once you are familiar with the Net, however, you'll find its research potential both fascinating and rewarding.

The details you'll need to conduct research on the Internet go beyond the scope of this chapter, but you can find the necessary information in a free online version of *Research and Documentation in the Electronic Age* at the Bedford Books Web site at <http://www.bedfordstmartins.com/rd/index.html>. This booklet offers detailed information for researching literary topics on the Internet and provides examples of how to document these sources (basic examples are also provided in this book on pp. 2108–2111). This site also includes "Bedford Links to Resources in Literature," which provides annotated research links to professionally maintained sites about selected authors, specific works, and literary periods.

EVALUATING SOURCES AND TAKING NOTES

Evaluate your sources for their reliability and the quality of their evidence. Check to see whether an article or book has been superseded by later studies; try to use up-to-date sources. A popular magazine article will probably not be as authoritative as an article in a scholarly journal. Sources that are well documented with primary and secondary materials usually indicate that the author has done his or her homework. Books printed by university presses and established trade presses are preferable to books privately printed. But there are always exceptions. If you are uncertain about how to assess a book, try to find out something about the author. Are there any other books listed in the card catalog that indicate the author's expertise? What do book reviews say about the work? Three valuable indexes to book reviews of literary studies are *Book Review Digest, Book Review Index,* and *Index to Book Reviews in the Humanities.* Your reference librarian can show you how to use these important tools for evaluating books. Reviews can be a quick means to gain a broad perspective on writers and their works because reviewers often survey previous approaches to the topic under discussion.

A cautionary note: assessing online sources can be more problematic than evaluating print sources because anyone with a computer and online access can publish on the Internet. Be sure to determine the nature of your sources and their authority. Is the site the work of a professional or an amateur? Is the information likely to be reliable? Is it documented? Before placing your trust in an Internet source, make sure that it warrants your confidence.

As you prepare a list of reliable sources relevant to your topic, record the necessary bibliographic information so that it will be available when you make up the list of works cited for your paper. (See the sample bibliography card on page 2104.) For a book include the author, complete title, place of publication, publisher, and date. For an article include author, complete title, name of periodical, volume number, date of issue, and page numbers.

Once you have assembled a tentative bibliography, you will need to take notes on your readings. If you are not using a word processor, use 3 by 5-, 4 by 6-, or 5 by 8-inch cards for note taking. They are easy to manipulate and can be readily sorted after you establish subheadings for your paper. Be sure to keep track of where the information comes from by writing the author's name and page number on each note card. If you use more than one work by the same author, include a brief title as well as the author's name. (See the sample note card on page 2104.)

The sample note card records the source of information (the complete publishing information is on the bibliography card) and provides a heading that will allow easy sorting later on. Notice that the information is summarized rather than quoted in large chunks. The student also includes a short note asking himself whether this will be relevant to the topic — the meaning of the title of "A Rose for Emily." (As it turned out, this was not directly related to the topic, so it was dropped.)

> Minter, David. <u>William</u>
> <u>Faulkner: His Life and Work.</u>
> Baltimore, MD: Johns Hopkins
> UP, 1980.

Sample bibliography card for a book.

Note cards can combine quotations, paraphrases, and summaries; you can also use them to cite your own ideas and give them headings so that you don't lose track of them. As you take notes, try to record only points relevant to your topic. Although the sample card on Scribner's rejection of "A Rose for Emily" wasn't used in the paper, it might have been. At least that fact was an interesting possibility, even if it wasn't, finally, worth developing.

> **On the publication of "A Rose for Emily" Minter 116**
>
> Minter describes "A Rose" as "one of Faulkner's
> finest short stories" yet it was rejected at
> Scribner's when Faulkner submitted it.
>
> [Can I work this in?]

Sample note card.

DEVELOPING A THESIS AND ORGANIZING THE PAPER

As the notes on "A Rose for Emily" accumulated, the student sorted them into topics, including:

1. Publication history of the story
2. Faulkner on the title of "A Rose for Emily"
3. Is Emily simply insane?
4. The purpose of Emily's servant
5. The narrator
6. The townspeople's view of Emily
7. The surprise ending
8. Emily's admirable qualities
9. Homer's character

The student quickly saw that items 1, 4, and 9 were not directly related to his topic concerning the significance of the story's title. The remaining numbers (2, 3, 5, 6, 7, 8) are the topics taken up in the paper. The student had begun his reading of secondary sources with a tentative thesis that stemmed from his question about the appropriateness of the title. That "why" shaped itself into the expectation that he would have a thesis something like this: "The title justifies Emily's murder of Homer because . . ."

The assumption was that he would find information that indicated some specific reason. But the more he read, the more he discovered that it was possible to speak only about how the narrator prevents the reader from making a premature judgment about Emily rather than justifying her actions. Hence, he wisely changed his tentative thesis to this final thesis: "The narrator describes incidents and withholds information in such a way as to cause the reader to sympathize with Emily before her crime is revealed." This thesis helped the student explain why the title is accurate and useful rather than misleading.

Because the assignment was relatively brief, the student did not write up a formal outline but instead organized his stacks of usable note cards and proceeded to write the first draft from them.

REVISING

After writing your first draft, you should review the advice and revision checklist on pages 2078–2080 so that you can read your paper with an objective eye. Two days after writing his next-to-last draft, the writer of "How the Narrator Cultivates a Rose for Emily" realized that he had allotted too much space for critical discussions of the narrator that were not directly related to his approach. He wanted to demonstrate a familiarity with these studies, but it was not essential that he summarize or discuss them. He corrected this by consolidating parenthetical references: "Though a number of studies discuss the story's narrator (see, for example, Kempton; Sullivan; and Watkins). . .". His earlier draft had included summaries of these studies that were tangential to his argument. The point is that he saw this himself after he took some time to approach the paper from a fresh perspective.

DOCUMENTING SOURCES

You must acknowledge the use of a source when you (1) quote someone's exact words, (2) summarize or borrow someone's opinions or ideas, or (3) use information and facts that are not considered to be common knowledge. The purpose of this documentation is to acknowledge your sources, to demonstrate that you are familiar with what others have thought about the topic, and to provide your reader access to the same sources. If your paper is not adequately documented, it will be vulnerable to a charge of *plagiarism* — the presentation of someone else's work as your own. Conscious plagiarism is easy to avoid; honesty takes care of that for most people. However, there is a more problematic form of plagiarism that is often inadvertent. Whether inadequate documentation is conscious or not, plagiarism is a serious matter and must be avoided. Papers can be evaluated only by what is on the page, not by their writers' intentions.

Let's look more closely at what constitutes plagiarism. Consider the following passage quoted from John Gassner's introduction to *Four Great Plays by Henrik Ibsen* (New York: Bantam, 1959), p. viii:

> Today it seems incredible that *A Doll's House°* should have created the furor it did. In exploding Victorian ideals of feminine dependency the play seemed revolutionary in 1879. When its heroine Nora left her home in search of self-development it seemed as if the sanctity of marriage had been flouted by a playwright treading the stage with cloven-feet.

Now read this plagiarized version:

> *A Doll's House* created a furor in 1879 by blowing up Victorian ideals about a woman's place in the world. Nora's search for self-fulfillment outside her home appeared to be an attack on the sanctity of marriage by a cloven-footed playwright.

Though the writer has shortened the passage and made some changes in the wording, this paragraph is basically the same as Gassner's. Indeed, several of his phrases are lifted almost intact. Even if a parenthetical reference had been included at the end of the passage and the source included in

---

Rolf Fjelde, whose translation is included in Chapter 32, renders the title as *A Doll House* in order to emphasize that the whole household, including Torvald as well as Nora, lives an unreal, doll-like existence.

"Works Cited," the language of this passage would still be plagiarism because it is presented as the writer's own. Both language and ideas must be acknowledged.

Here is an adequately documented version of the passage:

> John Gassner has observed how difficult it is for today's readers to comprehend the intense reaction against *A Doll's House* in 1879. When Victorian audiences watched Nora walk out of her stifling marriage, they assumed that Ibsen was expressing a devilish contempt for the "sanctity of marriage" (viii).

This passage makes absolutely clear that the observation is Gassner's, and it is written in the student's own language with the exception of one quoted phrase. Had Gassner not been named in the passage, the parenthetical reference would have included his name: (Gassner viii).

Some mention should be made of the notion of common knowledge before we turn to the standard format for documenting sources. Observations and facts that are widely known and routinely included in many of your sources do not require documentation. It is not necessary to cite a source for the fact that Alfred, Lord Tennyson, was born in 1809 or that Ernest Hemingway loved to fish and hunt. Sometimes it will be difficult for you to determine what common knowledge is for a topic that you know little about. If you are in doubt, the best strategy is to supply a reference.

There are two basic ways to document sources. Traditionally, sources have been cited in footnotes at the bottom of each page or in endnotes grouped together at the end of the paper. Here is how a portion of the sample paper would look if footnotes were used instead of parenthetical documentation:

```
As Heller points out, before we learn of Emily's bizarre be-
havior, we see her as a sympathetic--if antiquated--figure
in a town whose life and concerns have passed her by; hence,
"we are disposed to see Emily as victimized."[1]

    [1]Terry Heller, "The Telltale Hair: A Critical Study of
William Faulkner's 'A Rose for Emily,'" Arizona Quarterly 28
(1972): 306.
```

Unlike endnotes, which are double spaced throughout under the title of "Notes" on separate pages at the end of the paper, footnotes appear four spaces below the text. They are single spaced with double spaces between notes.

No doubt you will have encountered these documentation methods in your reading. A different style is recommended, however, in the Modern Language Association's *MLA Handbook for Writers of Research Papers,* Fourth Edition (1995). This style employs parenthetical references within the text of the paper; these are keyed to an alphabetical list of works cited at the end of the paper. This method is designed to be less distracting for the reader. Unless you are instructed to follow the footnote or endnote style for documentation, use the parenthetical method explained in the next section.

The List of Works Cited

Items in the list of works cited are arranged alphabetically according to the author's last name and indented five spaces after the first line. This allows the reader to locate quickly the complete bibliographic information for the author's name cited within the parenthetical reference in the text. The following are common entries for literature papers and should be used as models. If some of your sources are of a different nature, consult the *MLA Handbook for Writers of Research Papers,* Fourth Edition (New York: MLA, 1995); or, for the latest updates, check MLA's Web site at <http://www.mla.org>.

A BOOK BY ONE AUTHOR

Hendrickson, Robert. The Literary Life and Other Curiosities. New York: Viking, 1981.

Notice that the author's name is in reverse order. This information, along with the full title, place of publication, publisher, and date, should be taken from the title and copyright pages of the book. The title is underlined to indicate italics and is also followed by a period. If the city of publication is well known, it is unnecessary to include the state. Use the publication date on the title page; if none appears there, use the copyright date (after ©) on the back of the title page.

A BOOK BY TWO AUTHORS

Horton, Rod W., and Herbert W. Edwards. Backgrounds of American Literary Thought. 3rd ed. Englewood Cliffs: Prentice, 1974.

Only the first author's name is given in reverse order. The edition number appears after the title.

A BOOK WITH MORE THAN THREE AUTHORS

Abrams, M. H., et al., eds. The Norton Anthology of English Literature. 5th ed. 2 vols. New York: Norton, 1986. Vol. 1.

The abbreviation *et al.* means "and others." It is used to avoid having to list all fourteen editors of this first volume of a two-volume work.

A WORK IN A COLLECTION BY THE SAME AUTHOR

```
O'Connor, Flannery. "Greenleaf." The Complete Stories. By
    O'Connor. New York: Farrar, 1971. 311-34.
```

Page numbers are given because the reference is to only a single story in the collection.

A WORK IN A COLLECTION BY DIFFERENT WRITERS

```
Frost, Robert. "Design." The Bedford Introduction to Litera-
    ture. Ed. Michael Meyer. 5th ed. Boston: Bedford/St.
    Martin's, 1999. 993.
```

A TRANSLATED BOOK

```
Grass, Günter. The Tin Drum. Trans. Ralph Manheim. New York:
    Vintage-Random, 1962.
```

AN INTRODUCTION, PREFACE, FOREWORD, OR AFTERWORD

```
Johnson, Thomas H. Introduction. Final Harvest: Emily Dick-
    inson's Poems. By Emily Dickinson. Boston: Little,
    Brown, 1961. vii-xiv.
```

This cites the introduction by Johnson. Notice that a colon is used between the book's main title and subtitle. To cite a poem in this book use this method:

```
Dickinson, Emily. "A Tooth upon Our Peace." Final Harvest:
    Emily Dickinson's Poems. Ed. Thomas H. Johnson. Boston:
    Little, Brown, 1961. 110.
```

AN ENCYCLOPEDIA

```
"Wordsworth, William." The New Encyclopedia Britannica.
    1984 ed.
```

Because this encyclopedia is organized alphabetically, no page number or other information is given, only the edition number (if available) and date.

AN ARTICLE IN A MAGAZINE

```
Morrow, Lance. "Scribble, Scribble, Eh, Mr. Toad." Time 24
    Feb. 1986: 84.
```

The citation for an unsigned article would begin with the title and be alphabetized by the first word of the title other than "a," "an," or "the."

An Article in a Scholarly Journal with Continuous Pagination beyond a Single Issue

Mahar, William J. "Black English in Early Blackface
    Minstrelsy: A New Interpretation of the Sources of Min-
    strel Show Dialect." American Quarterly 37 (1985):
    260-85.

Because this journal uses continuous pagination instead of separate pagination for each issue, it is not necessary to include the month, season, or
number of the issue. Only one of the quarterly issues will have pages num-
bered 260-85. If you are not certain whether a journal's pages are num-
bered continuously throughout a volume, supply the month, season, or
issue number, as in the next entry.

An Article in a Scholarly Journal with Separate Pagination for Each Issue

Updike, John. "The Cultural Situation of the American
    Writer." American Studies International 15 (Spring
    1977): 19-28.

By noting the spring issue, the entry saves a reader looking through each
issue of the 1977 volume for the correct article on pages 19 to 28.

An Article in a Newspaper

Ziegler, Philip. "The Lure of Gossip, the Rules of History."
    New York Times 23 Feb. 1986: sec. 7: 1+.

This citation indicates that the article appears on page 1 of section 7 and
continues onto another page.

A Lecture

Stern, Milton. "Melville's View of Law." English 270 class
    lecture. University of Connecticut, Storrs, 12 Mar.
    1992.

Letter, E-Mail, or Interview

Vellenga, Carolyn. Letter to the author. 9 Oct. 1997.
Harter, Stephen P. E-mail to the author. 28 Dec. 1997.
McConagha, Bill. Personal interview [or Telephone
    interview]. 4 March 1998.

If a source appears in print as well as in an electronic format, provide
the same publication information you would for printed sources — the

title of the electronic source, the medium (such as "CD-ROM"), the name of the distributor, and the date of publication. If it does not appear in print form, or if you don't have all or some of the information, provide as much as you have along with the date of access and the electronic address. You need to provide all the information necessary for your readers to find the source themselves.

CD-ROM Issued Periodically

```
Aaron, Belèn V. "The Death of Theory." Scholarly Book
    Reviews 4.3 (1997): 146-47. ERIC. CD-ROM. SilverPlatter.
    Dec. 1997.
```

CD-ROM Issued in a Single Edition

```
Sideman, Bob, and Donald Sheehy. "The Risk of Spirit."
    Robert Frost: Poems, Life, Legacy. CD-ROM. Vers. 1.0.
    New York: Holt, 1997.
```

Electronic Web Site

```
Cody, David. "Dickens: A Brief Biography." World Wide Web.
    13 Feb. 1998. <http://www.stg.brown.edu/projects/
    hypertext/landow/victorian/dickens/dickensbio1.html>.
```

Electronic Newsgroup

```
Kathman, David. "Shakespeare's Literacy--or Lack of." 3 Mar.
    1998. Newsgroup. <humanities.lit.authors.shakespeare>.
```

Parenthetical References

A list of works cited is not an adequate indication of how you have used sources in your paper. You must also provide the precise location of quotations and other information by using parenthetical references within the text of the paper. You do this by citing the author's name (or the source's title if the work is anonymous) and the page number:

```
Collins points out that "Nabokov was misunderstood by early
reviewers of his work" (28).
```

or

```
Nabokov's first critics misinterpreted his stories
(Collins 28).
```

Either way a reader will find the complete bibliographic entry in the list of works cited under Collins's name and know that the information cited in the paper appears on page 28. Notice that the end punctuation comes after the parentheses.

If you have listed more than one work by the same author, you would add a brief title to the parenthetical reference to distinguish between them. You could also include the full title in your text:

```
Nabokov's first critics misinterpreted his stories (Collins,
"Early Reviews" 28).
```

or

```
Collins points out in "Early Reviews of Nabokov's
Fiction" that his early work was misinterpreted by
reviewers (28).
```

There can be many variations on what is included in a parenthetical reference, depending on the nature of the entry in the list of works cited. But the general principle is simple enough: provide enough parenthetical information for a reader to find the work in "Works Cited." Examine the sample research paper for more examples of works cited and strategies for including parenthetical references. If you are puzzled by a given situation, ask your reference librarian to show you the *MLA Handbook*.

A SAMPLE RESEARCH PAPER

How the Narrator Cultivates a Rose for Emily

The following research paper by Tony Groulx follows the format described in the *MLA Handbook for Writers of Research Papers*, Fourth Edition (1995). This format is discussed in the preceding section on documentation and in Chapter 38 in the section on manuscript form (p. 2080). Though the sample paper is short, it illustrates many of the techniques and strategies useful for writing an essay that includes secondary sources. (Faulkner's "A Rose for Emily" is reprinted on p. 72.)

Tony Groulx

Professor Hugo

English 109-3

December 3, 19--

How the Narrator Cultivates a Rose for Emily

William Faulkner's "A Rose for Emily" is an absorbing
mystery story whose chilling ending contains a gruesome
surprise. When we discover, along with the narrator and
townspeople, what was left of Homer Barron's body, we may
be surprised or not, depending on how carefully we have
been reading the story and keeping track of details such
as Emily Grierson's purchase of rat poison and Homer's
disappearance. Probably most readers anticipate finding
Homer's body at the end of the story because Faulkner
carefully prepares the groundwork for the discovery as the
townspeople force their way into that mysterious upstairs
room where a "thin, acrid pall as of the tomb seemed to
lie everywhere" (78). But very few readers, if any, are
prepared for the story's final paragraph, when we realize
that the strand of "iron-gray hair" (the last three words
of the story) on the second pillow indicates that Emily
has slept with Homer since she murdered him. This last
paragraph produces the real horror in the story and an
extraordinary revelation about Emily's character.

The final paragraph seems like the right place to
begin a discussion of this story because the surprise ending not only creates a powerful emotional effect in us but
also raises an important question about what we are to
think of Emily. Is this isolated, eccentric woman simply
mad? All the circumstantial evidence indicates that she is
a murderer and necrophiliac, and yet Faulkner titles the
story "A Rose for Emily," as if she is due some kind of
tribute. The title somehow qualifies the gasp of horror

that the story leads up to in the final paragraph. Why would anyone offer this woman a "rose"? What's behind the title?

Faulkner was once directly asked the meaning of the title and replied:

> Oh it's simply the poor woman had had no life at all. Her father had kept her more or less locked up and then she had a lover who was about to quit her, she had to murder him. It was just "A Rose for Emily"--that's all. (qtd. in Gwynn and Blotner 87-88)

This reply explains some of Emily's motivation for murdering Homer, but it doesn't actually address the purpose and meaning of the title. If Emily killed Homer out of a kind of emotional necessity--out of a fear of abandonment--how does that explain the fact that the title seems to suggest that the story is a way of paying respect to Emily? The question remains.

Whatever respect the story creates for Emily cannot be the result of her actions. Surely there can be no convincing excuse made for murder and necrophilia; there is nothing to praise about what she does. Instead, the tribute comes in the form of how her story is told rather than what we are told about her. To do this Faulkner uses a narrator who tells Emily's story in such a way as to maximize our sympathy for her. The grim information about Emily's "iron-gray hair" on the pillow is withheld until the very end and not only to produce a surprise but to permit the reader to develop a sympathetic understanding of her before we are shocked and disgusted by her necrophilia.

Significantly, the narrator begins the story with Emily's death rather than Homer's. Though a number of studies discuss the story's narrator (see, for example, Kempton; Sullivan; and Watkins), Terry Heller's is one of the most comprehensive in its focus on the narrator's effects on the readers' response to Emily. As Heller points out, before we learn of Emily's bizarre behavior we see her as a sympathetic--if antiquated--figure in a town whose life and concerns have passed her by; hence, "we are disposed to see Emily as victimized" (306). Her refusal to pay her taxes is an index to her isolation and eccentricity, but this incident also suggests a degree of dignity and power lacking in the town officials who fail to collect her taxes. Her encounters with the officials of Jefferson--whether in the form of the sneaking aldermen who try to cover up the smell around her house or the druggist who unsuccessfully tries to get her to conform to the law when she buys arsenic--place her in an admirable light because her willfulness is based on her personal strength. Moreover, it is relatively easy to side with Emily when the townspeople are described as taking pleasure in her being reduced to poverty as a result of her father's death because "now she too would know the old thrill and the old despair of a penny more or less" (75). The narrator's account of their pettiness, jealousy, and inability to make sense of Emily causes the reader to sympathize with Emily's eccentricities before we must judge her murderous behavior. We admire her for taking life on her own terms, and the narrator makes sure this response is in place prior to our realization that she also takes life.

We don't really know much about Emily because the narrator arranges the details of her life so that it's difficult to know what she's been up to. We learn, for example, about the smell around the house before she buys the poison and Homer disappears, so that the cause-and-

effect relationship among these events is a bit slippery
(for a detailed reconstruction of the chronology, see Mc-
Glynn and Nebecker's revision of McGlynn's work), but the
effect is to suspend judgment of Emily. By the time we
realize what she has done, we are already inclined to see
her as outside community values almost out of necessity.
That's not to say that the murdering of Homer is justified
by the narrator, but it is to say that her life maintains
its private--though no longer secret--dignity. Despite the
final revelation, Emily remains "dear, inescapable, impervious, tranquil, and perverse" (77).

　　The narrator's "rose" to Emily is his recognition that
Emily is all these things--including "perverse." She evokes
"a sort of respectful affection for a fallen monument" (72).
She is, to be sure, "fallen" but she is also somehow cen-
tral--a "monument"--to the life of the community. Faulkner
does not offer a definitive reading of Emily, but he does
have the narrator pay tribute to her by attempting to provide a complex set of contexts for her actions--contexts
that include a repressive father, resistance to a changing
South and impinging North, the passage of time and its influence on the present, and relations between men and women
as well as relations between generations. Robert Crosman
discusses the narrator's efforts to understand Emily:

> The narrator is himself a "reader" of Emily's
> story, trying to put together from fragments a
> complete picture, trying to find the meaning of
> her life in its impact upon an audience, the
> citizens of Jefferson, of which he is a member.
> (212)

The narrator refuses to dismiss Emily as simply mad or to
treat her life as merely a grotesque, sensational horror
story. Instead, his narrative method brings us into her

life before we too hastily reject her, and in doing so it offers us a complex imaginative treatment of fierce determination and strength coupled with illusions and shocking eccentricities. The narrator's rose for Emily is paying her the tribute of placing that "long strand of iron-gray hair" in the context of her entire life.

Works Cited

Crosman, Robert. "How Readers Make Meaning." College Literature 9 (1982): 207-15.

Faulkner, William. "A Rose for Emily." The Bedford Introduction to Literature. Ed. Michael Meyer. 5th ed. Boston: Bedford/St. Martin's, 1999. 72-78.

Gwynn, Frederick, and Joseph Blotner, eds. Faulkner in the University: Class Conferences at the University of Virginia, 1957-58. Charlottesville: U of Virginia P, 1959.

Heller, Terry. "The Telltale Hair: A Critical Study of William Faulkner's 'A Rose for Emily.'" Arizona Quarterly 28 (1972): 301-18.

Kempton, K. P. The Short Story. Cambridge: Harvard UP, 1954. 104-06.

McGlynn, Paul D. "The Chronology of 'A Rose for Emily.'" Studies in Short Fiction 6 (1969): 461-62.

Nebecker, Helen E. "Chronology Revised." Studies in Short Fiction 8 (1971): 471-73.

Sullivan, Ruth. "The Narrator in 'A Rose for Emily.'" The Journal of Narrative Technique 1 (1971): 159-78.

Watkins, F. C. "The Structure of 'A Rose for Emily.'" Modern Language Notes 69 (1954): 508-10.

40

Taking Essay
Examinations

PREPARING FOR AN ESSAY EXAM

Keep Up with the Reading

The best way to prepare for an examination is to keep up with the reading. If you begin the course with a commitment to completing the reading assignments on time, you will not have to read in a frenzy and cram just days before the test. The readings will be a pleasure, not a frantic ordeal. Moreover, you will find that your instructor's comments and class discussion will make more sense to you and that you'll be able to participate in class discussion. As you prepare for the exam, you should be rereading texts rather than reading for the first time. It may not be possible to reread everything, but you'll at least be able to scan a familiar text and reread passages that are particularly important.

Take Notes and Annotate the Text

Don't rely exclusively on your memory. The typical literature class includes a hefty amount of reading, so unless you take notes, annotate the text with your own comments, and underline important passages, you're likely to forget material that could be useful for responding to an examination question (see pp. 2065–2067 for a discussion of these matters). The more you can retrieve from your reading, the more prepared you'll be for reviewing significant material for the exam. These notes can be used to illustrate points that were made in class. By briefly quoting an important phrase or line from the text you can provide supporting evidence that will make your argument convincing. Consider, for example, the difference between writing that "Marvell's speaker in 'To His Coy Mistress' says that they won't be able to love after they die" and writing that "the speaker intones that 'The grave's a fine and private place / But none, I think, do there embrace.'" No one expects you to memorize the entire poem, but recalling a few lines here and there can transform a sleepy generality into an illustrative, persuasive argument.

Anticipate Questions

As you review the readings, keep in mind the class discussions and the focus provided by your instructor. Class discussions and the instructor's emphasis often become the basis for essay questions. You may not see the exact same topics on the exam, but you might find that the matters you've discussed in class will serve as a means of responding to an essay question. If, for example, class discussion of John Updike's "A & P" (see p. 576) centered on the story's small-town New England setting, you could use that conservative, traditional, puritanical setting to answer a question such as "Discuss how the conflicts that Sammy encounters in 'A & P' are related to the story's theme." A discussion of the intolerant rigidity of this New England town could be connected to A & P "policy" and the crabbed values associated with Lengel that lead to Sammy's quitting his job in protest of such policies. The point is that you'll be well prepared for an essay exam when you can shape the material you've studied so that it is responsive to whatever kinds of reasonable questions you encounter on the exam. Reasonable questions? Yes, your instructor is more likely to offer you an opportunity to demonstrate your familiarity with and understanding of the text than to set a trap that, for instance, demands you discuss how Updike's work experience as an adolescent informs the story when no mention was ever made of that in class or in your reading.

You can also anticipate questions by considering the generic Questions for Responsive Reading and Writing about fiction (p. 41), poetry (p. 711), and drama (p. 1211) and the questions in Arguing about Literature (p. 2071), along with the Questions for Writing about an Author in Depth (p. 965). Not all of these questions will necessarily be relevant to every work that you read, but they cover a wide range of concerns that should allow you to organize your reading, note taking, and reviewing so that you're not taken by surprise during the exam.

Studying with a classmate or a small group from class can be a stimulating and fruitful means of discovering and organizing the major topics and themes of the course. This method of brainstorming can be useful not only for studying for exams but throughout the semester for understanding and reviewing course readings. And, finally, you needn't be shy about asking your instructor what types of questions might appear on the exam and how best to study for them. You may not get a very specific reply, but almost any information is more useful than none.

TYPES OF EXAMS

Closed-Book versus Open-Book Exams

Closed-book exams require more memorization and recall than open-book exams, which permit you to use your text and perhaps even your notes to answer questions. Dates, names, definitions, and other details play less of a role in an open-book exam. An open-book exam requires no less preparation, however, because you'll need to be intimately familiar with the texts and the major ideas, themes, and issues that you've studied in order to quickly and efficiently support your points with relevant, specific evidence. Since every student has the same advantage of having access to the text, preparation remains the key to answering the questions. Some students find open-book exams more difficult than closed-book tests because they risk spending too much time reading, scanning, and searching for material and not enough time writing a response that draws on the knowledge and understanding that their reading and studying has provided them. It's best to limit the time you allow yourself to review the text and notes so that you devote an adequate amount of time to getting your ideas on paper.

Essay Questions

Essay questions generally fall within one of the following categories. If you can recognize quickly what is being asked of you, you will be able to respond to them more efficiently.

1. **Explication** Explication calls for a line-by-line explanation of a passage of poetry or prose that considers, for example, diction, figures of speech, symbolism, sound, form, and theme in an effort to describe how language creates meaning. (For a more detailed discussion of explication, see p. 2081.)

2. **Definition** Defining a term and then applying it to a writer or work is a frequent exam exercise. Consider: "Define *romanticism*. To what extent can Hawthorne's *The Scarlet Letter* be regarded as a romantic story?" This sort of question requires that you first describe what constitutes a romantic literary work and then explain how *The Scarlet Letter* does (and doesn't) fit the bill.

3. **Analysis** An analytical question focuses on a particular part of a literary work. You might be asked, for example, to analyze the significance of images in Diane Ackerman's poem "A Fine, a Private Place" (p. 734). This sort of question requires you to discuss a specific element of the poem and also to explain how that element contributes to the poem's overall effect. (For a more detailed discussion of analysis, see pp. 2086–2091.)

4. **Comparison and Contrast** Comparison and contrast calls for a discussion of the similarities and/or differences between writers, works, or elements of works — for example, "Compare and contrast Lengel's sensibilities

in John Updike's 'A & P' (p. 576) with John Wright's in Susan Glaspell's *Trifles* (p. 1172)." Despite the obvious differences in age and circumstances between these characters, a discussion of their responses to people — particularly to women — reveals some intriguing similarities. (For a more detailed discussion of comparison and contrast, see pp. 2091–2093.)

5. **Discussion of a Critical Perspective**   A brief quotation by a critic about a work is usually designed to stimulate a response that requires you to agree with, disagree with, or qualify a critic's perspective. Usually it is not important whether you agree or disagree with the critic; what matters is the quality of your argument. Think about how you might wrestle with this assessment of Robert Frost written by Lionel Trilling: "The manifest America of Mr. Frost's poems may be pastoral; the actual America is tragic." With some qualifications (surely not all of Frost's poems are "tragic") this could provide a useful way of talking about a poem such as "Mending Wall" (p. 979).

6. **Imaginative Questions**   To a degree every question requires imagination regardless of whether it's being asked or answered. However, some questions require more imaginative leaps to arrive at the center of an issue than others do. Consider, for example, the intellectual agility needed to respond to this question: "How do you think Dickens's Mr. Gradgrind from *Hard Times* and the narrator of Frost's 'Mending Wall' would respond to Sammy's character in Updike's 'A & P'?" As tricky as this triangulation of topics may seem, there is plenty to discuss concerning Gradgrind's literal-mindedness, the narrator's imagination, and Sammy's rejection of "policy." Or try a simpler but no less interesting version: "How do you think Frost would review Marvell's 'To His Coy Mistress' and Ackerman's 'A Fine, a Private Place'?" Such questions certainly require detailed, reasoned responses, but they also leave room for creativity and even wit.

STRATEGIES FOR WRITING ESSAY EXAMS

Your hands may be sweaty and your heart pounding as you begin the exam, but as long as you're prepared and you keep in mind some basic strategies for writing essay exams, you should be able to respond to questions with confidence and a genuine sense of accomplishment.

1. Before you begin writing, read through the entire exam. If there are choices to be made, make certain you know how many questions must be answered (only one out of four, not two). Note how many points each question is worth; spend more time on the two worth forty points each, and perhaps leave the twenty-point question for last.

2. Budget your time. If there are short-answer questions, do not allow them to absorb you so that you cannot do justice to the longer essay questions. Follow the suggested time limits for each question; if none is

offered, then create your own schedule in proportion to the points allotted for each question.

3. Depending on your own sensibilities, you may want to begin with the easiest or hardest questions. It doesn't really matter which you begin with as long as you pace yourself to avoid running out of time.

4. Be sure that you understand the question. Does it ask you to compare and/or contrast, define, analyze, explicate, or use some other approach? Determine how many elements there are to the question so that you don't inadvertently miss part of the question. Do not spend time copying the question.

5. Make some brief notes about how you plan to answer the question; even a simple list of what you'll need to cover can serve as a useful outline.

6. Address the question; avoid unnecessary summaries or irrelevant asides. Focus on the particular elements enumerated or implied by the question.

7. After beginning the essay, write a clear thesis that describes the major topics you will discuss: "*The Scarlet Letter* is typical of Hawthorne's concerns as a writer owing to its treatment of sin, guilt, isolation, and secrecy."

8. Support and illustrate your answer with specific, relevant references to the text. The more specificity — the more you demonstrate a familiarity with the text (rather than simply provide a plot summary) — the better the answer.

9. Don't overlap and repeat responses to questions; your instructor will recognize such padding. If two different questions are about the same work or writer, demonstrate the breadth and depth of your knowledge of the subject.

10. Allow time to proofread and to qualify and to add more supporting material if necessary. At this final stage, too, it's worth remembering that Mark Twain liked to remind his readers that the difference between the right word and the almost right word is the difference between lightning and a lightning bug.

Glossary of Literary Terms

Accent The emphasis, or STRESS, given a syllable in pronunciation. We say *"syl-lable"* not *"syllable,"* *"emphasis"* not *"emphasis."* Accents can also be used to emphasize a particular word in a sentence: *Is* she con*tent* with the *con*tents of the *yel*low *pack*age? See also METER.

Act A major division in the action of a play. The ends of acts are typically indicated by lowering the curtain or turning up the houselights. Playwrights frequently employ acts to accommodate changes in time, setting, characters onstage, or mood. In many full-length plays, acts are further divided into scenes, which often mark a point in the action when the location changes or when a new character enters. See also SCENE.

Allegory A narration or description usually restricted to a single meaning because its events, actions, characters, settings, and objects represent specific abstractions or ideas. Although the elements in an allegory may be interesting in themselves, the emphasis tends to be on what they ultimately mean. Characters may be given names such as Hope, Pride, Youth, and Charity; they have few if any personal qualities beyond their abstract meanings. These personifications are not symbols because, for instance, the meaning of a character named Charity is precisely that virtue. See also SYMBOL.

Alliteration The repetition of the same consonant sounds in a sequence of words, usually at the beginning of a word or stressed syllable: *"descending dew drops"; "luscious lemons."* Alliteration is based on the sounds of letters, rather than the spelling of words; for example, *"keen"* and *"car"* alliterate, but *"car"* and *"cite"* do not. Used sparingly, alliteration can intensify ideas by emphasizing key words, but when used too self-consciously, it can be distracting, even ridiculous, rather than effective. See also ASSONANCE, CONSONANCE.

Allusion A brief reference to a person, place, thing, event, or idea in history or literature. Allusions conjure up biblical authority, scenes from Shakespeare's plays, historic figures, wars, great love stories, and anything else that might enrich an author's work. Allusions imply reading and cultural experiences shared by the writer and reader, functioning as a kind of shorthand whereby the recalling of something outside the work supplies an emotional or intellectual context, such as a poem about current racial struggles calling up the memory of Abraham Lincoln.

Ambiguity Allows for two or more simultaneous interpretations of a word, phrase, action, or situation, all of which can be supported by the context of a work. Deliberate ambiguity can contribute to the effectiveness and richness of a work, for example, in the open-ended conclusion to Hawthorne's "Young Goodman Brown." However, unintentional ambiguity obscures meaning and can confuse readers.

Anagram A word or phrase made from the letters of another word or phrase, as "heart" is an anagram of "earth." Anagrams have often been considered merely an exercise of one's ingenuity, but sometimes writers use anagrams to conceal proper names or veiled messages, or to suggest important connections between words, as in "hated" and "death."

Anapestic meter See FOOT.

Antagonist The character, force, or collection of forces in fiction or drama that opposes the PROTAGONIST and gives rise to the conflict of the story; an opponent of the protagonist, such as Claudius in Shakespeare's play *Hamlet*. See also CHARACTER, CONFLICT.

Antihero A protagonist who has the opposite of most of the traditional attributes of a hero. He or she may be bewildered, ineffectual, deluded, or merely pathetic. Often what antiheroes learn, if they learn anything at all, is that the world isolates them in an existence devoid of God and absolute values. Yossarian from Joseph Heller's *Catch-22* is an example of an antihero. See also CHARACTER.

Apostrophe An address, either to someone who is absent and therefore cannot hear the speaker or to something nonhuman that cannot comprehend. Apostrophe often provides a speaker the opportunity to think aloud.

Approximate rhyme See RHYME.

Archetype A term used to describe universal symbols that evoke deep and sometimes unconscious responses in a reader. In literature, characters, images, and themes that symbolically embody universal meanings and basic human experiences, regardless of when or where they live, are considered archetypes. Common literary archetypes include stories of quests, initiations, scapegoats, descents to the underworld, and ascents to heaven. See also MYTHOLOGICAL CRITICISM.

Aside In drama, a speech directed to the audience that supposedly is not audible to the other characters onstage at the time. When Hamlet first appears onstage, for example, his aside "A little more than kin, and less than kind!" gives the audience a strong sense of his alienation from King Claudius. See also SOLILOQUY.

Assonance The repetition of internal vowel sounds in nearby words that do not end the same, for example, "asleep under a tree," or "each evening." Similar endings result in rhyme, as in "asleep in the deep." Assonance is a strong means of emphasizing important words in a line. See also ALLITERATION, CONSONANCE.

Ballad Traditionally, a ballad is a song, transmitted orally from generation to generation, that tells a story and that eventually is written down. As such, ballads usually cannot be traced to a particular author or group of authors. Typically, ballads are dramatic, condensed, and impersonal narratives, such as "Bonny Barbara Allan." A **literary ballad** is a narrative poem that is written in deliberate imitation of the language, form, and spirit of the traditional ballad, such as Keats's "La Belle Dame sans Merci." See also BALLAD STANZA, QUATRAIN.

Ballad stanza A four-line stanza, known as a QUATRAIN, consisting of alternating eight- and six-syllable lines. Usually only the second and fourth lines rhyme (an *abcb* pattern). Coleridge adopted the ballad stanza in "The Rime of the Ancient Mariner."

All in a hot and copper sky
The bloody Sun, at noon,
Right up above the mast did stand,
No bigger than the Moon.

See also BALLAD, QUATRAIN.

Biographical criticism An approach to literature which suggests that knowledge of the author's life experiences can aid in the understanding of his or her work. While biographical information can sometimes complicate one's interpretation of a work, and some formalist critics (such as the New Critics) disparage the use of the author's biography as a tool for textual interpretation, learning about the life of the author can often enrich a reader's appreciation for that author's work. See also CULTURAL CRITICISM, FORMALIST CRITICISM, NEW CRITICISM.

Blank verse Unrhymed iambic pentameter. Blank verse is the English verse form closest to the natural rhythms of English speech and therefore is the most common pattern found in traditional English narrative and dramatic poetry from Shakespeare to the early twentieth century. Shakespeare's plays use blank verse extensively. See also IAMBIC PENTAMETER.

Cacophony Language that is discordant and difficult to pronounce, such as this line from John Updike's "Player Piano": "never my numb plunker fumbles." Cacophony ("bad sound") may be unintentional in the writer's sense of music, or it may be used consciously for deliberate dramatic effect. See also EUPHONY.

Caesura A pause within a line of poetry that contributes to the rhythm of the line. A caesura can occur anywhere within a line and need not be indicated by punctuation. In scanning a line, caesuras are indicated by a double vertical line (‖). See also METER, RHYTHM, SCANSION.

Canon Those works generally considered by scholars, critics, and teachers to be the most important to read and study, which collectively constitute the "masterpieces" of literature. Since the 1960s, the traditional English and American literary canon, consisting mostly of works by white male writers, has been rapidly expanding to include many female writers and writers of varying ethnic backgrounds.

Carpe diem The Latin phrase meaning "seize the day." This is a very common literary theme, especially in lyric poetry, which emphasizes that life is short, time is fleeting, and that one should make the most of present pleasures. Robert Herrick's poem "To the Virgins, to Make Much of Time" employs the *carpe diem* theme.

Catharsis Meaning "purgation," *catharsis* describes the release of the emotions of pity and fear by the audience at the end of a tragedy. In his *Poetics,*

Aristotle discusses the importance of catharsis. The audience faces the misfortunes of the protagonist, which elicit pity and compassion. Simultaneously, the audience also confronts the failure of the protagonist, thus receiving a frightening reminder of human limitations and frailties. Ultimately, however, both these negative emotions are purged, because the tragic protagonist's suffering is an affirmation of human values rather than a despairing denial of them. See also TRAGEDY.

Character, characterization A character is a person presented in a dramatic or narrative work, and characterization is the process by which a writer makes that character seem real to the reader. A **hero** or **heroine,** often called the PROTAGONIST, is the central character who engages the reader's interest and empathy. The ANTAGONIST is the character, force, or collection of forces that stands directly opposed to the protagonist and gives rise to the conflict of the story. A **static character** does not change throughout the work, and the reader's knowledge of that character does not grow, whereas a **dynamic character** undergoes some kind of change because of the action in the plot. A **flat character** embodies one or two qualities, ideas, or traits that can be readily described in a brief summary. They are not psychologically complex characters and therefore are readily accessible to readers. Some flat characters are recognized as **stock characters;** they embody stereotypes such as the "dumb blonde" or the "mean stepfather." They become types rather than individuals. **Round characters** are more complex than flat or stock characters, and often display the inconsistencies and internal conflicts found in most real people. They are more fully developed, and therefore are harder to summarize. Authors have two major methods of presenting characters: **showing** and **telling. Showing** allows the author to present a character talking and acting, and lets the reader infer what kind of person the character is. In **telling,** the author intervenes to describe and sometimes evaluate the character for the reader. Characters can be convincing whether they are presented by showing or by telling, as long as their actions are motivated. **Motivated action** by the characters occurs when the reader or audience is offered reasons for how the characters behave, what they say, and the decisions they make. **Plausible action** is action by a character in a story that seems reasonable, given the motivations presented. See also PLOT.

Chorus In Greek tragedies (especially those of Aeschylus and Sophocles), a group of people who serve mainly as commentators on the characters and events. They add to the audience's understanding of the play by expressing traditional moral, religious, and social attitudes. The role of the chorus in dramatic works evolved through the sixteenth century, and the chorus occasionally is still used by modern playwrights such as T. S. Eliot in *Murder in the Cathedral.* See also DRAMA.

Cliché An idea or expression that has become tired and trite from overuse, its freshness and clarity having worn off. Clichés often anesthetize readers, and are usually a sign of weak writing. See also SENTIMENTALITY, STOCK RESPONSES.

Climax See PLOT.

Closet drama A play that is written to be read rather than performed onstage. In this kind of drama, literary art outweighs all other considerations. See also DRAMA.

Colloquial Refers to a type of informal diction that reflects casual, conversational language and often includes slang expressions. See also DICTION.

Comedy A work intended to interest, involve, and amuse the reader or audience, in which no terrible disaster occurs and that ends happily for the main characters. **High comedy** refers to verbal wit, such as puns, whereas **low comedy** is generally associated with physical action and is less intellectual. **Romantic comedy** involves a love affair that meets with various obstacles (like disapproving parents, mistaken identities, deceptions, or other sorts of misunderstandings) but overcomes them to end in a blissful union. Shakespeare's comedies, such as *A Midsummer Night's Dream,* are considered romantic comedies.

Comic relief A humorous scene or incident that alleviates tension in an otherwise serious work. In many instances these moments enhance the thematic significance of the story in addition to providing laughter. When Hamlet jokes with the gravediggers we laugh, but something hauntingly serious about the humor also intensifies our more serious emotions.

Conflict The struggle within the plot between opposing forces. The PROTAGONIST engages in the conflict with the ANTAGONIST, which may take the form of a character, society, nature, or an aspect of the protagonist's personality. See also CHARACTER, PLOT.

Connotation Associations and implications that go beyond the literal meaning of a word, which derive from how the word has been commonly used and the associations people make with it. For example, the word *eagle* connotes ideas of liberty and freedom that have little to do with the word's literal meaning. See also DENOTATION.

Consonance A common type of near rhyme that consists of identical consonant sounds preceded by different vowel sounds: *home, same; worth, breath.* See also RHYME.

Contextual symbol See SYMBOL.

Controlling metaphor See METAPHOR.

Convention A characteristic of a literary genre (often unrealistic) that is understood and accepted by audiences because it has come, through usage and time, to be recognized as a familiar technique. For example, the division of a play into acts and scenes is a dramatic convention, as are soliloquies and asides. FLASHBACKS and FORESHADOWING are examples of literary conventions.

Conventional symbol See SYMBOL.

Cosmic irony See IRONY.

Couplet Two consecutive lines of poetry that usually rhyme and have the same meter. A **heroic couplet** is a couplet written in rhymed iambic pentameter.

Crisis A turning point in the action of a story that has a powerful effect on the protagonist. Opposing forces come together decisively to lead to the climax of the plot. See also PLOT.

Cultural criticism An approach to literature that focuses on the historical as well as social, political, and economic contexts of a work. Popular culture — mass produced and consumed cultural artifacts ranging from advertising to popular fiction to television to rock music — is given equal emphasis as "high culture." Cultural critics use widely eclectic strategies such as new historicism, psychology, gender studies, and deconstructionism to analyze not only literary texts but everything from radio talk shows, comic strips, calendar art, commercials, to travel guides and baseball cards. See also HISTORICAL CRITICISM, MARXIST CRITICISM, POSTCOLONIAL CRITICISM.

Dactylic meter See FOOT.

Deconstructionism An approach to literature which suggests that literary works do not yield fixed, single meanings, because language can never say exactly what we intend it to mean. Deconstructionism seeks to destabilize meaning by examining the gaps and ambiguities of the language of a text. Deconstructionists pay close attention to language in order to discover and describe how a variety of possible readings are generated by the elements of a text. See also NEW CRITICISM.

Denotation The dictionary meaning of a word. See also CONNOTATION.

Dénouement A French term meaning "unraveling" or "unknotting," used to describe the resolution of the plot following the climax. See also PLOT, RESOLUTION.

Dialect A type of informational diction. Dialects are spoken by definable groups of people from a particular geographic region, economic group, or social class. Writers use dialect to contrast and express differences in educational, class, social, and regional backgrounds of their characters. See also DICTION.

Dialogue The verbal exchanges between characters. Dialogue makes the characters seem real to the reader or audience by revealing firsthand their thoughts, responses, and emotional states. See also DICTION.

Diction A writer's choice of words, phrases, sentence structures, and figurative language, which combine to help create meaning. **Formal diction** consists of a dignified, impersonal, and elevated use of language; it follows the rules of syntax exactly and is often characterized by complex words and lofty tone. **Middle diction** maintains correct language usage, but is less elevated than formal diction; it reflects the way most educated people speak. **Informal diction** represents the plain language of everyday use, and often includes idiomatic expressions, slang, contractions, and many simple, common words. **Poetic diction** refers to the way poets sometimes employ an elevated diction that deviates significantly from the common speech and writing of their time, choosing words for their supposedly inherent poetic qualities. Since the eighteenth century, however, poets have been incorporating all kinds of diction in their work and so there is no longer an automatic distinction between the language of a poet and the language of everyday speech. See also DIALECT.

Didactic poetry Poetry designed to teach an ethical, moral, or religious lesson. Michael Wigglesworth's Puritan poem *Day of Doom* is an example of didactic poetry.

Doggerel A derogatory term used to describe poetry whose subject is trite and whose rhythm and sounds are monotonously heavy-handed.

Drama Derived from the Greek word *dram*, meaning "to do" or "to perform," the term *drama* may refer to a single play, a group of plays ("Jacobean drama"), or to all plays ("world drama"). Drama is designed for performance in a theater; actors take on the roles of characters, perform indicated actions, and speak the dialogue written in the script. **Play** is a general term for a work of dramatic literature, and a **playwright** is a writer who makes plays.

Dramatic irony See IRONY.

Dramatic monologue A type of lyric poem in which a character (the speaker) addresses a distinct but silent audience imagined to be present in the poem in such a way as to reveal a dramatic situation and, often unintentionally, some aspect of his or her temperament or personality. See also LYRIC.

Dynamic character See CHARACTER.

Editorial omniscience See NARRATOR.

Electra complex The female version of the Oedipus complex. *Electra complex* is a term used to describe the psychological conflict of a daughter's unconscious rivalry with her mother for her father's attention. The name comes from the Greek legend of Electra, who avenged the death of her father, Agamemnon, by plotting the death of her mother. See also OEDIPUS COMPLEX, PSYCHOLOGICAL CRITICISM.

Elegy A mournful, contemplative lyric poem written to commemorate someone who is dead, often ending in a consolation. Tennyson's *In Memoriam*, written on the death of Arthur Hallam, is an elegy. *Elegy* may also refer to a serious meditative poem produced to express the speaker's melancholy thoughts. See also LYRIC.

End rhyme See RHYME.

End-stopped line A poetic line that has a pause at the end. End-stopped lines reflect normal speech patterns and are often marked by punctuation. The first line of Keats's "Endymion" is an example of an end-stopped line; the natural pause coincides with the end of the line, and is marked by a period:

A thing of beauty is a joy forever.

English sonnet See SONNET.

Enjambment In poetry, when one line ends without a pause and continues into the next line for its meaning. This is also called a **run-on line**. The transition between the first two lines of Wordsworth's poem "My Heart Leaps Up" demonstrates enjambment:

My heart leaps up when I behold
   A rainbow in the sky:

Envoy See SESTINA.

Epic A long narrative poem, told in a formal, elevated style, that focuses on a serious subject and chronicles heroic deeds and events important to a culture or nation. Milton's *Paradise Lost*, which attempts to "justify the ways of God to man," is an epic. See also NARRATIVE POEM.

Epigram A brief, pointed, and witty poem that usually makes a satiric or humorous point. Epigrams are most often written in couplets, but take no prescribed form.

Epiphany In fiction, when a character suddenly experiences a deep realization about himself or herself; a truth which is grasped in an ordinary rather than a melodramatic moment.

Escape literature See FORMULA LITERATURE.

Euphony *Euphony* ("good sound") refers to language that is smooth and musically pleasant to the ear. See also CACOPHONY.

Exact rhyme See RHYME.

Exposition A narrative device, often used at the beginning of a work, that provides necessary background information about the characters and their circumstances. Exposition explains what has gone on before, the relationships between characters, the development of a theme, and the introduction of a conflict. See also FLASHBACK.

Extended metaphor See METAPHOR.

Eye rhyme See RHYME.

Falling action See PLOT.

Falling meter See METER.

Farce A form of humor based on exaggerated, improbable incongruities. Farce involves rapid shifts in action and emotion, as well as slapstick comedy and extravagant dialogue. Malvolio, in Shakespeare's *Twelfth Night,* is a farcical character.

Feminine rhyme See RHYME.

Feminist criticism An approach to literature that seeks to correct or supplement what may be regarded as a predominantly male-dominated critical perspective with a feminist consciousness. Feminist criticism places literature in a social context and uses a broad range of disciplines, including history, sociology, psychology, and linguistics, to provide a perspective sensitive to feminist issues. Feminist theories also attempt to understand representation from a woman's point of view and to explain women's writing strategies as specific to their social conditions. See also GAY AND LESBIAN CRITICISM, GENDER CRITICISM, SOCIOLOGICAL CRITICISM.

Figures of speech Ways of using language that deviate from the literal, denotative meanings of words in order to suggest additional meanings or effects. Figures of speech say one thing in terms of something else, such as when an eager funeral director is described as a vulture. See also METAPHOR, SIMILE.

First-person narrator See NARRATOR.

Fixed form A poem that may be categorized by the pattern of its lines, meter, rhythm, or stanzas. A sonnet is a fixed form of poetry because by definition it must have fourteen lines. Other fixed forms include LIMERICK, SESTINA, and VILLANELLE. However, poems written in a fixed form may not always fit into categories precisely, because writers sometimes vary traditional forms to create innovative effects. See also OPEN FORM.

Flashback A narrated scene that marks a break in the narrative in order to inform the reader or audience member about events that took place before the opening scene of a work. See also EXPOSITION.

Flat character See CHARACTER.

Foil A character in a work whose behavior and values contrast with those of another character in order to highlight the distinctive temperament of that character (usually the protagonist). In Shakespeare's *Hamlet*, Laertes acts as a foil to Hamlet, because his willingness to act underscores Hamlet's inability to do so.

Foot The metrical unit by which a line of poetry is measured. A foot usually consists of one stressed and one or two unstressed syllables. An *iambic foot*, which consists of one unstressed syllable followed by one stressed syllable ("away"), is the most common metrical foot in English poetry. A *trochaic foot* consists of one stressed syllable followed by an unstressed syllable ("lovely"). An *anapestic foot* is two unstressed syllables followed by one stressed one ("understand"). A *dactylic foot* is one stressed syllable followed by two unstressed ones ("desperate"). A *spondee* is a foot consisting of two stressed syllables ("dead set"), but is not a sustained metrical foot and is used mainly for variety or emphasis. See also IAMBIC PENTAMETER, LINE, METER.

Foreshadowing The introduction early in a story of verbal and dramatic hints that suggest what is to come later.

Form The overall structure or shape of a work, which frequently follows an established design. Forms may refer to a literary type (narrative form, short story form) or to patterns of meter, lines, and rhymes (stanza form, verse form). See also FIXED FORM, OPEN FORM.

Formal diction See DICTION.

Formalist criticism An approach to literature that focuses on the formal elements of a work, such as its language, structure, and tone. Formalist critics offer intense examinations of the relationship between form and meaning in a work, emphasizing the subtle complexity in how a work is arranged. Formalists pay special attention to diction, irony, paradox, metaphor, and symbol, as well as larger elements such as plot, characterization, and narrative technique. Formalist critics read literature as an independent work of art rather than as a reflection of the author's state of mind or as a representation of a moment in history. Therefore, anything outside of the work, including historical influences and authorial intent, is generally not examined by formalist critics. See also NEW CRITICISM.

Formula literature Often characterized as "escape literature," formula literature follows a pattern of conventional reader expectations. Romance novels, westerns, science fiction, and detective stories are all examples of formula literature; while the details of individual stories vary, the basic ingredients of each kind of story are the same. Formula literature offers happy endings (the hero "gets the girl," the detective cracks the case), entertains wide audiences, and sells tremendously well.

Found poem An unintentional poem discovered in a nonpoetic context, such as a conversation, news story, or advertisement. Found poems serve as re-

minders that everyday language often contains what can be considered poetry, or that poetry is definable as any text read as a poem.

Free verse Also called *open form poetry,* free verse refers to poems characterized
by their nonconformity to established patterns of meter, rhyme, and
stanza. Free verse uses elements such as speech patterns, grammar, emphasis, and breath pauses to decide line breaks, and usually does not rhyme. See
OPEN FORM.

Gay and lesbian criticism An approach to literature that focuses on how homosexuals are represented in literature, how they read literature, and
whether sexuality, as well as gender, is culturally constructed or innate. See
also FEMINIST CRITICISM, GENDER CRITICISM.

Gender criticism An approach to literature that explores how ideas about
men and women — what is masculine and feminine — can be regarded as socially constructed by particular cultures. Gender criticism expands categories and definitions of what is masculine or feminine and tends to regard
sexuality as more complex than merely masculine or feminine, heterosexual
or homosexual. See also FEMINIST CRITICISM, GAY AND LESBIAN CRITICISM.

Genre A French word meaning kind or type. The major genres in literature
are poetry, fiction, drama, and essays. Genre can also refer to more specific
types of literature such as comedy, tragedy, epic poetry, or science fiction.

Haiku A style of lyric poetry borrowed from the Japanese that typically presents an intense emotion or vivid image of nature, which, traditionally, is
designed to lead to a spiritual insight. Haiku is a fixed poetic form, consisting of seventeen syllables organized into three unrhymed lines of five,
seven, and five syllables. Today, however, many poets vary the syllabic count
in their haiku. See also FIXED FORM.

Hamartia A term coined by Aristotle to describe "some error or frailty" that
brings about misfortune for a tragic hero. The concept of hamartia is
closely related to that of the tragic flaw: both lead to the downfall of the
protagonist in a tragedy. Hamartia may be interpreted as an internal weakness in a character (like greed or passion or HUBRIS); however, it may also
refer to a mistake that a character makes that is based not on a personal
failure, but on circumstances outside the protagonist's personality and
control. See also TRAGEDY.

Hero, heroine See CHARACTER.

Heroic couplet See COUPLET.

High comedy See COMEDY.

Historical criticism An approach to literature that uses history as a means of
understanding a literary work more clearly. Such criticism moves beyond
both the facts of an author's personal life and the text itself in order to examine the social and intellectual currents in which the author composed
the work. See also CULTURAL CRITICISM, MARXIST CRITICISM, NEW HISTORI-
CISM, POSTCOLONIAL CRITICISM.

Hubris or Hybris Excessive pride or self-confidence that leads a protagonist
to disregard a divine warning or to violate an important moral law. In

tragedies, hubris is a very common form of hamartia. See also HAMARTIA, TRAGEDY.

Hyperbole A boldly exaggerated statement that adds emphasis without intending to be literally true, as in the statement "He ate everything in the house." Hyperbole (also called **overstatement**) may be used for serious, comic, or ironic effect. See also FIGURES OF SPEECH.

Iambic meter See FOOT.

Iambic pentameter A metrical pattern in poetry which consists of five iambic feet per line. (An iamb, or iambic foot, consists of one unstressed syllable followed by a stressed syllable.) See also FOOT, METER.

Image A word, phrase, or figure of speech (especially a SIMILE or a METAPHOR) that addresses the senses, suggesting mental pictures of sights, sounds, smells, tastes, feelings, or actions. Images offer sensory impressions to the reader and also convey emotions and moods through their verbal pictures. See also FIGURES OF SPEECH.

Implied metaphor See METAPHOR.

In medias res See PLOT.

Informal diction See DICTION.

Internal rhyme See RHYME.

Irony A literary device that uses contradictory statements or situations to reveal a reality different from what appears to be true. It is ironic for a firehouse to burn down, or for a police station to be burglarized. **Verbal irony** is a figure of speech that occurs when a person says one thing but means the opposite. **Sarcasm** is a strong form of verbal irony that is calculated to hurt someone through, for example, false praise. **Dramatic irony** creates a discrepancy between what a character believes or says and what the reader or audience member knows to be true. **Tragic irony** is a form of dramatic irony found in tragedies such as *Oedipus the King*, in which Oedipus searches for the person responsible for the plague that ravishes his city and ironically ends up hunting himself. **Situational irony** exists when there is an incongruity between what is expected to happen and what actually happens due to forces beyond human comprehension or control. The suicide of the seemingly successful main character in Edwin Arlington Robinson's poem "Richard Cory" is an example of situational irony. **Cosmic irony** occurs when a writer uses God, destiny, or fate to dash the hopes and expectations of a character or of humankind in general. In cosmic irony, a discrepancy exists between what a character aspires to and what universal forces provide. Stephen Crane's poem "A Man Said to the Universe" is a good example of cosmic irony, because the universe acknowledges no obligation to the man's assertion of his own existence.

Italian sonnet See SONNET.

Limerick A light, humorous style of fixed form poetry. Its usual form consists of five lines with the rhyme scheme *aabba*; lines 1, 2, and 5 contain three feet, while lines 3 and 4 usually contain two feet. Limericks range in subject matter from the silly to the obscene, and since Edward Lear popularized them in the nineteenth century, children and adults have enjoyed these comic poems. See also FIXED FORM.

Limited omniscience See POINT OF VIEW.

Line A sequence of words printed as a separate entity on the page. In poetry, lines are usually measured by the number of feet they contain. The names for various line lengths are as follows:

monometer: one foot	pentameter: five feet
dimeter: two feet	hexameter: six feet
trimeter: three feet	heptameter: seven feet
tetrameter: four feet	octameter: eight feet

The number of feet in a line, coupled with the name of the foot, describes the metrical qualities of that line. See also END-STOPPED LINE, ENJAMBMENT, FOOT, METER.

Literary ballad See BALLAD.

Literary symbol See SYMBOL.

Low comedy See COMEDY.

Lyric A type of brief poem that expresses the personal emotions and thoughts of a single speaker. It is important to realize, however, that although the lyric is uttered in the first person, the speaker is not necessarily the poet. There are many varieties of lyric poetry, including the DRAMATIC MONOLOGUE, ELEGY, HAIKU, ODE, and SONNET forms.

Marxist criticism An approach to literature that focuses on the ideological content of a work — its explicit and implicit assumptions and values about matters such as culture, race, class, and power. Marxist criticism, based largely on the writings of Karl Marx, typically aims at not only revealing and clarifying ideological issues but also correcting social injustices. Some Marxist critics use literature to describe the competing socioeconomic interests that too often advance capitalist interests such as money and power rather than socialist interests such as morality and justice. They argue that literature and literary criticism are essentially political because they either challenge or support economic oppression. Because of this strong emphasis on the political aspects of texts, Marxist criticism focuses more on the content and themes of literature than on its form. See also CULTURAL CRITICISM, HISTORICAL CRITICISM, SOCIOLOGICAL CRITICISM.

Masculine rhyme See RHYME.

Melodrama A term applied to any literary work that relies on implausible events and sensational action for its effect. The conflicts in melodramas typically arise out of plot rather than characterization; often a virtuous individual must somehow confront and overcome a wicked oppressor. Usually, a melodramatic story ends happily, with the protagonist defeating the antagonist at the last possible moment. Thus, melodramas entertain the reader or audience with exciting action while still conforming to a traditional sense of justice. See SENTIMENTALITY.

Metaphor A metaphor is a figure of speech that makes a comparison between two unlike things, without using the word *like* or *as*. Metaphors assert the identity of dissimilar things, as when Macbeth asserts that life *is* a "brief candle." Metaphors can be subtle and powerful, and can transform people, places, objects, and ideas into whatever the writer imagines them to be. An **implied metaphor** is a more subtle comparison; the terms being compared are not so specifically explained. For example, to describe a stubborn man unwilling to leave, one could say that he was "a mule standing his ground." This is a fairly explicit metaphor; the man is being compared to a mule. But to say that the man "brayed his refusal to leave" is to create an implied metaphor, because the subject (the man) is never overtly identified as a mule. Braying is associated with the mule, a notoriously stubborn creature, and so the comparison between the stubborn man and the mule is sustained. Implied metaphors can slip by inattentive readers who are not sensitive to such carefully chosen, highly concentrated language. An **extended metaphor** is a sustained comparison in which part or all of a poem consists of a series of related metaphors. Robert Francis's poem "Catch" relies on an extended metaphor that compares poetry to playing catch. A **controlling metaphor** runs through an entire work and determines the form or nature of that work. The controlling metaphor in Anne Bradstreet's poem "The Author to Her Book" likens her book to a child. **Synecdoche** is a kind of metaphor in which a part of something is used to signify the whole, as when a gossip is called a "wagging tongue," or when ten ships are called "ten sails." Sometimes, synecdoche refers to the whole being used to signify the part, as in the phrase "Boston won the baseball game." Clearly, the entire city of Boston did not participate in the game; the whole of Boston is being used to signify the individuals who played and won the game. **Metonymy** is a type of metaphor in which something closely associated with a subject is substituted for it. In this way, we speak of the "silver screen" to mean motion pictures, "the crown" to stand for the king, "the White House" to stand for the activities of the president. See also FIGURES OF SPEECH, PERSONIFICATION, SIMILE.

Meter When a rhythmic pattern of stresses recurs in a poem, it is called *meter.* Metrical patterns are determined by the type and number of feet in a line of verse; combining the name of a line length with the name of a foot concisely describes the meter of the line. **Rising meter** refers to metrical feet which move from unstressed to stressed sounds, such as the iambic foot and the anapestic foot. **Falling meter** refers to metrical feet which move from stressed to unstressed sounds, such as the trochaic foot and the dactylic foot. See also ACCENT, FOOT, IAMBIC PENTAMETER, LINE.

Metonymy See METAPHOR.

Middle diction See DICTION.

Motivated action See CHARACTER.

Mythological criticism An approach to literature that seeks to identify what in a work creates deep universal responses in readers, by paying close attention to the hopes, fears, and expectations of entire cultures. Mythological critics (sometimes called *archetypal critics*) look for underlying, recurrent patterns in literature that reveal universal meanings and basic human experiences for readers regardless of when and where they live. These critics attempt to explain how archetypes (the characters, images, and themes that symbolically embody universal meanings and experiences) are embodied in literary works in order to make larger connections that explain a particular work's lasting appeal. Mythological critics may specialize in areas such as classical literature, philology, anthropology, psychology, and cultural history, but they all emphasize the assumptions and values of various cultures. See also ARCHETYPE.

Naive narrator   See NARRATOR.

Narrative poem   A poem that tells a story. A narrative poem may be short or long, and the story it relates may be simple or complex. See also BALLAD, EPIC.

Narrator   The voice of the person telling the story, not to be confused with the author's voice. With a **first-person narrator,** the *I* in the story presents the point of view of only one character. The reader is restricted to the perceptions, thoughts, and feelings of that single character. For example, in Melville's "Bartleby, the Scrivener," the lawyer is the first-person narrator of the story. First-person narrators can play either a major or a minor role in the story they are telling. An **unreliable narrator** reveals an interpretation of events that is somehow different from the author's own interpretation of those events. Often, the unreliable narrator's perception of plot, characters, and setting becomes the actual subject of the story, as in Melville's "Bartleby, the Scrivener." Narrators can be unreliable for a number of reasons: they might lack self-knowledge (like Melville's lawyer), they might be inexperienced, they might even be insane. **Naive narrators** are usually characterized by youthful innocence, such as Mark Twain's Huck Finn or J. D. Salinger's Holden Caulfield. An **omniscient narrator** is an all-knowing narrator who is not a character in the story and who can move from place to place and pass back and forth through time, slipping into and out of characters as no human being possibly could in real life. Omniscient narrators can report the thoughts and feelings of the characters, as well as their words and actions. The narrator of *The Scarlet Letter* is an omniscient narrator. **Editorial omniscience** refers to an intrusion by the narrator in order to evaluate a character for a reader, as when the narrator of *The Scarlet Letter* describes Hester's relationship to the Puritan community. Narration that allows the characters' actions and thoughts to speak for themselves is called **neutral omniscience.** Most modern writers use neutral omniscience so that readers can reach their own conclusions. **Limited omniscience** occurs when an author restricts a narrator to the single perspective of either a major or minor character. The way people, places, and events appear to that character is the way they appear to the reader. Sometimes a limited omniscient narrator can see into more than one character, particularly in a work that focuses on two characters alternately from one chapter to the next. Short stories, however, are frequently limited to a single character's point of view. See also PERSONA, POINT OF VIEW, STREAM-OF-CONSCIOUSNESS TECHNIQUE.

Near rhyme   See RHYME.

Neutral omniscience   See NARRATOR.

New Criticism   An approach to literature made popular between the 1940s and the 1960s that evolved out of formalist criticism. New Critics suggest that detailed analysis of the language of a literary text can uncover important layers of meaning in that work. New Criticism consciously downplays the historical influences, authorial intentions, and social contexts that surround texts in order to focus on explication—extremely close textual analysis. Critics such as John Crowe Ransom, I. A. Richards, and Robert Penn Warren are commonly associated with New Criticism. See also FOR-MALIST CRITICISM.

New historicism An approach to literature that emphasizes the interaction between the historic context of the work and a modern reader's understanding and interpretation of the work. New historicists attempt to describe the culture of a period by reading many different kinds of texts and paying close attention to many different dimensions of a culture, including political, economic, social, and aesthetic concerns. They regard texts not simply as a reflection of the culture that produced them but also as productive of that culture playing an active role in the social and political conflicts of an age. New historicism acknowledges and then explores various versions of "history," sensitizing us to the fact that the history on which we choose to focus is colored by being reconstructed from our present circumstances. See also HISTORICAL CRITICISM.

Objective point of view See POINT OF VIEW.

Octave A poetic stanza of eight lines, usually forming one part of a sonnet. See also SONNET, STANZA.

Ode A relatively lengthy lyric poem that often expresses lofty emotions in a dignified style. Odes are characterized by a serious topic, such as truth, art, freedom, justice, or the meaning of life; their tone tends to be formal. There is no prescribed pattern that defines an ode; some odes repeat the same pattern in each stanza, while others introduce a new pattern in each stanza. See also LYRIC.

Oedipus complex A Freudian term derived from Sophocles' tragedy *Oedipus the King*. It describes a psychological complex that is predicated on a boy's unconscious rivalry with his father for his mother's love and his desire to eliminate his father in order to take his father's place with his mother. The female equivalent of this complex is called the **Electra complex.** See also ELECTRA COMPLEX, PSYCHOLOGICAL CRITICISM.

Off rhyme See RHYME.

Omniscient narrator See NARRATOR.

One-act play A play that takes place in a single location and unfolds as one continuous action. The characters in a one-act play are presented economically and the action is sharply focused. See also DRAMA.

Onomatopoeia A term referring to the use of a word that resembles the sound it denotes. *Buzz, rattle, bang,* and *sizzle* all reflect onomatopoeia. Onomatopoeia can also consist of more than one word; writers sometimes create lines or whole passages in which the sound of the words helps to convey their meanings.

Open form Sometimes called "free verse," open form poetry does not conform to established patterns of METER, RHYME, and STANZA. Such poetry derives its rhythmic qualities from the repetition of words, phrases, or grammatical structures, the arrangement of words on the printed page, or by some other means. The poet E. E. Cummings wrote open form poetry; his poems do not have measurable meters, but they do have rhythm. See also FIXED FORM.

Organic form Refers to works whose formal characteristics are not rigidly predetermined but follow the movement of thought or emotion being expressed. Such works are said to grow like living organisms, following their own individual patterns rather than external fixed rules that govern, for example, the form of a SONNET.

Overstatement See HYPERBOLE.

Oxymoron A condensed form of paradox in which two contradictory words are used together, as in "sweet sorrow" or "original copy." See also PARADOX.

Paradox A statement that initially appears to be contradictory but then, on closer inspection, turns out to make sense. For example, John Donne ends his sonnet "Death, Be Not Proud" with the paradoxical statement "Death, thou shalt die." To solve the paradox, it is necessary to discover the sense that underlies the statement. Paradox is useful in poetry because it arrests a reader's attention by its seemingly stubborn refusal to make sense.

Paraphrase A prose restatement of the central ideas of a poem, in your own language.

Parody A humorous imitation of another, usually serious, work. It can take any fixed or open form, because parodists imitate the tone, language, and shape of the original in order to deflate the subject matter, making the original work seem absurd. Anthony Hecht's poem "Dover Bitch" is a famous parody of Matthew Arnold's well-known "Dover Beach." Parody may also be used as a form of literary criticism to expose the defects in a work. But sometimes parody becomes an affectionate acknowledgment that a well-known work has become both institutionalized in our culture and fair game for some fun. For example, Peter De Vries's "To His Importunate Mistress" gently mocks Andrew Marvell's "To His Coy Mistress."

Persona Literally, a *persona* is a mask. In literature, a *persona* is a speaker created by a writer to tell a story or to speak in a poem. A persona is not a character in a story or narrative, nor does a persona necessarily directly reflect the author's personal voice. A persona is a separate self, created by and distinct from the author, through which he or she speaks. See also NARRATOR.

Personification A form of metaphor in which human characteristics are attributed to nonhuman things. Personification offers the writer a way to give the world life and motion by assigning familiar human behaviors and emotions to animals, inanimate objects, and abstract ideas. For example, in Keats's "Ode on a Grecian Urn," the speaker refers to the urn as an "unravished bride of quietness." See also METAPHOR.

Petrarchan sonnet See also SONNET.

Picture poem A type of open form poetry in which the poet arranges the lines of the poem so as to create a particular shape on the page. The shape of the poem embodies its subject; the poem becomes a picture of what the poem is describing. Michael McFee's "In Medias Res" is an example of a picture poem. See also OPEN FORM.

Plausible action See CHARACTER.

Play See DRAMA.

Playwright See DRAMA.

Plot An author's selection and arrangement of incidents in a story to shape the action and give the story a particular focus. Discussions of plot include not just what happens, but also how and why things happen the way they do. Stories that are written in a **pyramidal pattern** divide the plot into three essential parts. The first part is the **rising action,** in which complication creates some sort of conflict for the protagonist. The second part is the **climax,** the moment of greatest emotional tension in a narrative, usually marking a turning point in the plot at which the rising action reverses to become the falling action. The third part, the **falling action** (or RESOLUTION) is characterized by diminishing tensions and the resolution of the plot's conflicts and complications. *In medias res* is a term used to describe the common strategy of beginning a story in the middle of the action. In this type of plot, we enter the story on the verge of some important moment. See also CHARACTER, CRISIS, RESOLUTION, SUBPLOT.

Poetic diction See DICTION.

Point of view Refers to who tells us a story and how it is told. What we know and how we feel about the events in a work are shaped by the author's choice of point of view. The teller of the story, the narrator, inevitably affects our understanding of the characters' actions by filtering what is told through his or her own perspective. The various points of view that writers draw upon can be grouped into two broad categories: (1) the third-person narrator uses *he, she,* or *they* to tell the story and does not participate in the action; and (2) the first-person narrator uses *I* and is a major or minor participant in the action. In addition, a second-person narrator, *you,* is also possible, but is rarely used because of the awkwardness of thrusting the reader into the story, as in "You are minding your own business on a park bench when a drunk steps out and demands your lunch bag." An **objective point of view** employs a third-person narrator who does not see into the mind of any character. From this detached and impersonal perspective, the narrator reports action and dialogue without telling us directly what the characters think and feel. Since no analysis or interpretation is provided by the narrator, this point of view places a premium on dialogue, actions, and details to reveal character to the reader. See also NARRATOR, STREAM-OF-CONSCIOUSNESS TECHNIQUE.

Postcolonial criticism An approach to literature that focuses on the study of cultural behavior and expression in relationship to the colonized world. Postcolonial criticism refers to the analysis of literary works written by writers from countries and cultures that at one time have been controlled by colonizing powers — such as Indian writers during or after British colonial rule. Postcolonial criticism also refers to the analysis of literary works written about colonial cultures by writers from the colonizing country. Many of these kinds of analyses point out how writers from colonial powers sometimes misrepresent colonized cultures by reflecting more their own values. See also CULTURAL CRITICISM, HISTORICAL CRITICISM, MARXIST CRITICISM.

Problem play Popularized by Henrik Ibsen, a problem play is a type of drama that presents a social issue in order to awaken the audience to it. These plays usually reject romantic plots in favor of holding up a mirror that reflects not simply what the audience wants to see but what the playwright sees in them. Often, a problem play will propose a solution to the problem that does not coincide with prevailing opinion. The term is also used to refer to certain Shakespeare plays that do not fit the categories of tragedy, comedy, or romance. See also DRAMA.

Prologue The opening speech or dialogue of a play, especially a classic Greek play, that usually gives the exposition necessary to follow the subsequent action. Today the term also refers to the introduction to any literary work. See also DRAMA, EXPOSITION.

Prose poem A kind of open form poetry that is printed as prose and represents the most clear opposite of fixed form poetry. Prose poems are densely compact and often make use of striking imagery and figures of speech. See also FIXED FORM, OPEN FORM.

Prosody The overall metrical structure of a poem. See also METER.

Protagonist The main character of a narrative; its central character who engages the reader's interest and empathy. See also CHARACTER.

Psychological criticism An approach to literature that draws upon psychoanalytic theories, especially those of Sigmund Freud or Jacques Lacan to understand more fully the text, the writer, and the reader. The basis of this approach is the idea of the existence of a human unconscious — those impulses, desires, and feelings about which a person is unaware but which influence emotions and behavior. Critics use psychological approaches to explore the motivations of characters and the symbolic meanings of events, while biographers speculate about a writer's own motivations — conscious or unconscious — in a literary work. Psychological approaches are also used to describe and analyze the reader's personal responses to a text.

Pun A play on words that relies on a word's having more than one meaning or sounding like another word. Shakespeare and other writers use puns extensively, for serious and comic purposes; in *Romeo and Juliet* (III.i.101), the dying Mercutio puns, "Ask for me tomorrow and you shall find me a grave man." Puns have serious literary uses, but since the eighteenth century, puns have been used almost purely for humorous effect. See also COMEDY.

Pyramidal pattern See PLOT.

Quatrain A four-line stanza. Quatrains are the most common stanzaic form in the English language; they can have various meters and rhyme schemes. See also METER, RHYME, STANZA.

Reader-response criticism An approach to literature that focuses on the reader rather than the work itself, by attempting to describe what goes on in the reader's mind during the reading of a text. Hence, the consciousness of the reader — produced by reading the work — is the actual subject of reader-response criticism. These critics are not after a "correct" reading of the text or what the author presumably intended; instead, they are interested in the reader's individual experience with the text. Thus, there is no single definitive reading of a work, because readers create rather than discover absolute meanings in texts. However, this approach is not a rationale for mistaken or bizarre readings, but an exploration of the possibilities for a plurality of readings. This kind of strategy calls attention to how we read and what influences our readings, and what that reveals about ourselves.

Recognition The moment in a story when previously unknown or withheld information is revealed to the protagonist, resulting in the discovery of the truth of his or her situation and, usually, a decisive change in course for that character. In *Oedipus the King*, the moment of recognition comes when Oedipus finally realizes that he has killed his father and married his mother.

Resolution The conclusion of a plot's conflicts and complications. The resolution, also known as the **falling action,** follows the climax in the plot. See also DÉNOUEMENT, PLOT.

Revenge tragedy See TRAGEDY.

Reversal The point in a story when the protagonist's fortunes turn in an unexpected direction. See also PLOT.

Rhyme The repetition of identical or similar concluding syllables in different words, most often at the ends of lines. Rhyme is predominantly a function of sound rather than spelling; thus, words that end with the same vowel sounds rhyme, for instance, *day, prey, bouquet, weigh,* and words with the same consonant ending rhyme, for instance *vain, feign, rein, lane.* Words do not have to be spelled the same way or look alike to rhyme. In fact, words may look alike but not rhyme at all. This is called **eye rhyme,** as with *bough* and *cough,* or *brow* and *blow.*

End rhyme is the most common form of rhyme in poetry; the rhyme comes at the end of the lines.

> It runs through the reeds
>   And away it proceeds,
> Through meadow and glade,
>   In sun and in shade.

The **rhyme scheme** of a poem describes the pattern of end rhymes. Rhyme schemes are mapped out by noting patterns of rhyme with small letters: the first rhyme sound is designated *a,* the second becomes *b,* the third *c,* and so on. Thus, the rhyme scheme of the stanza above is *aabb.* **Internal rhyme** places at least one of the rhymed words within the line, as in "Dividing and gliding and sliding" or "In mist or cloud, on mast or shroud." **Masculine rhyme** describes the rhyming of single-syllable words, such as *grade* or *shade.* Masculine rhyme also occurs where rhyming words of more than one syllable, when the same sound occurs in a final stressed syllable, as in *defend* and *contend, betray* and *away.* **Feminine rhyme** consists of a rhymed stressed syllable followed by one or more identical unstressed syllables, as in *butter, clutter; gratitude, attitude; quivering, shivering.* All the examples so far have illustrated **exact rhymes,** because they share the same stressed vowel sounds as well as sharing sounds that follow the vowel. In **near rhyme** (also called **off rhyme, slant rhyme,** and **approximate rhyme**), the sounds are almost but not exactly alike. A common form of near rhyme is CONSONANCE, which consists of identical consonant sounds preceded by different vowel sounds: *home, same; worth, breath.*

Rhyme scheme See RHYME.

Rhythm A term used to refer to the recurrence of stressed and unstressed sounds in poetry. Depending on how sounds are arranged, the rhythm of a poem may be fast or slow, choppy or smooth. Poets use rhythm to create pleasurable sound patterns and to reinforce meanings. Rhythm in prose arises from pattern repetitions of sounds and pauses that create looser rhythmic effects. See also METER.

Rising action See PLOT.

Rising meter See METER.

Romantic comedy See COMEDY.

Round character See CHARACTER.

Run-on line See ENJAMBMENT.

Sarcasm See IRONY.

Satire The literary art of ridiculing a folly or vice in order to expose or correct it. The object of satire is usually some human frailty; people, institutions, ideas, and things are all fair game for satirists. Satire evokes attitudes of amusement, contempt, scorn, or indignation toward its faulty subject in the hope of somehow improving it. See also IRONY, PARODY.

Scansion The process of measuring the stresses in a line of verse in order to determine the metrical pattern of the line. See also LINE, METER.

Scene In drama, a scene is a subdivision of an ACT. In modern plays, scenes usually consist of units of action in which there are no changes in the setting or breaks in the continuity of time. According to traditional conventions, a scene changes when the location of the action shifts or when a new character enters. See also ACT, CONVENTION, DRAMA.

Script The written text of a play, which includes the dialogue between characters, stage directions, and often other expository information. See also DRAMA, EXPOSITION, PROLOGUE, STAGE DIRECTIONS.

Sentimentality A pejorative term used to describe the effort by an author to induce emotional responses in the reader that exceed what the situation warrants. Sentimentality especially pertains to such emotions as pathos and sympathy; it cons readers into falling for the mass murderer who is devoted to stray cats, and it requires that readers do not examine such illogical responses. Clichés and stock responses are the key ingredients of sentimentality in literature. See also CLICHÉ, STOCK RESPONSES.

Sestet A stanza consisting of exactly six lines. See also STANZA.

Sestina A type of fixed form poetry consisting of thirty-six lines of any length divided into six sestets and a three-line concluding stanza called an ENVOY. The six words at the end of the first sestet's lines must also appear at the ends of the other five sestets, in varying order. These six words must also appear in the envoy, where they often resonate important themes. An example of this highly demanding form of poetry is Elizabeth Bishop's "Sestina." See also SESTET.

Setting The physical and social context in which the action of a story occurs. The major elements of setting are the time, the place, and the social environment that frames the characters. Setting can be used to evoke a mood or atmosphere that will prepare the reader for what is to come, as in Nathaniel Hawthorne's short story "Young Goodman Brown." Sometimes, writers choose a particular setting because of traditional associations with that setting that are closely related to the action of a story. For example, stories filled with adventure or romance often take place in exotic locales.

Shakespearean sonnet See SONNET.

Showing See CHARACTER.

Simile A common figure of speech that makes an explicit comparison between two things by using words such as *like, as, than, appears,* and *seems:* "A sip of Mrs. Cook's coffee is like a punch in the stomach." The effectiveness of this simile is created by the differences between the two things compared. There would be no simile if the comparison were stated this way: "Mrs. Cook's coffee is as strong as the cafeteria's coffee." This is a literal translation because Mrs. Cook's coffee is compared with something like it — another kind of coffee. See also FIGURES OF SPEECH, METAPHOR.

Situational irony See IRONY.

Slant rhyme See RHYME.

Sociological criticism An approach to literature that examines social groups, relationships, and values as they are manifested in literature. Sociological approaches emphasize the nature and effect of the social forces that shape power relationships between groups or classes of people. Such readings treat literature as either a document reflecting social conditions or a product of those conditions. The former view brings into focus the social milieu; the latter emphasizes the work. Two important forms of sociological criticism are Marxist and feminist approaches. See also FEMINIST CRITICISM, MARXIST CRITICISM.

Soliloquy A dramatic convention by means of which a character, alone onstage, utters his or her thoughts aloud. Playwrights use soliloquies as a convenient way to inform the audience about a character's motivations and state of mind. Shakespeare's Hamlet delivers perhaps the best known of all soliloquies, which begins: "To be or not to be." See also ASIDE, CONVENTION.

Sonnet A fixed form of lyric poetry that consists of fourteen lines, usually written in iambic pentameter. There are two basic types of sonnets, the Italian and the English. The **Italian sonnet,** also known as the **Petrarchan sonnet,** is divided into an octave, which typically rhymes *abbaabba,* and a sestet, which may have varying rhyme schemes. Common rhyme patterns in the sestet are *cdecde, cdcdcd,* and *cdccdc.* Very often the octave presents a situation, attitude, or problem that the sestet comments upon or resolves, as in John Keats's "On First Looking into Chapman's Homer." The **English sonnet,** also known as the **Shakespearean sonnet,** is organized into three quatrains and a couplet, which typically rhyme *abab cdcd efef gg.* This rhyme scheme is more suited to English poetry because English has fewer rhyming words than Italian. English sonnets, because of their four-part organization, also have more flexibility with respect to where thematic breaks can occur. Frequently, however, the most pronounced break or turn comes with the concluding couplet, as in Shakespeare's "Shall I compare thee to a

summer's day?" See also COUPLET, IAMBIC PENTAMETER, LINE, OCTAVE, QUA-
TRAIN, SESTET.

Speaker   The voice used by an author to tell a story or speak a poem. The speaker is often a created identity, and should not automatically be equated with the author's self. See also NARRATOR, PERSONA, POINT OF VIEW.

Spondee   See FOOT.

Stage directions   A playwright's written instructions about how the actors are to move and behave in a play. They explain in which direction characters should move, what facial expressions they should assume, and so on. See also DRAMA, SCRIPT.

Stanza   In poetry, *stanza* refers to a grouping of lines, set off by a space, that usually has a set pattern of meter and rhyme. See also LINE, METER, RHYME.

Static character   See CHARACTER.

Stock character   See CHARACTER.

Stock responses   Predictable, conventional reactions to language, characters, symbols, or situations. The flag, motherhood, puppies, God, and peace are common objects used to elicit stock responses from unsophisticated audiences. See also CLICHÉ, SENTIMENTALITY.

Stream-of-consciousness technique   The most intense use of a central consciousness in narration. The stream-of-consciousness technique takes a reader inside a character's mind to reveal perceptions, thoughts, and feelings on a conscious or unconscious level. This technique suggests the flow of thought as well as its content; hence, complete sentences may give way to fragments as the character's mind makes rapid associations free of conventional logic or transitions. James Joyce's novel *Ulysses* makes extensive use of this narrative technique. See also NARRATOR, POINT OF VIEW.

Stress   The emphasis, or accent, given a syllable in pronunciation. See also ACCENT.

Style   The distinctive and unique manner in which a writer arranges words to achieve particular effects. Style essentially combines the idea to be expressed with the individuality of the author. These arrangements include individual word choices as well as matters such as the length of sentences, their structure, tone, and use of irony. See also DICTION, IRONY, TONE.

Subplot   The secondary action of a story, complete and interesting in its own right, that reinforces or contrasts with the main plot. There may be more than one subplot, and sometimes as many as three, four, or even more, running through a piece of fiction. Subplots are generally either analogous to the main plot, thereby enhancing our understanding of it, or extraneous to the main plot, to provide relief from it. See also PLOT.

Suspense   The anxious anticipation of a reader or an audience as to the outcome of a story, especially concerning the character or characters with whom sympathetic attachments are formed. Suspense helps to secure and sustain the interest of the reader or audience throughout a work.

Symbol   A person, object, image, word, or event that evokes a range of additional meaning beyond and usually more abstract than its literal significance. Symbols are educational devices for evoking complex ideas without having to resort to painstaking explanations that would make a story more like an essay than an experience. **Conventional symbols** have meanings that are widely recognized by a society or culture. Some conventional symbols are the Christian cross, the Star of David, a swastika, or a nation's flag. Writers use conventional symbols to reinforce meanings. Kate Chopin, for example, emphasizes the spring setting in "The Story of an Hour" as a way of suggesting the renewed sense of life that Mrs. Mallard feels when she thinks herself free from her husband. A **literary** or **contextual symbol** can be a setting, character, action, object, name, or anything else in a work that maintains its literal significance while suggesting other meanings. Such symbols go beyond conventional symbols; they gain their symbolic meaning within the context of a specific story. For example, the white whale in Melville's *Moby-Dick* takes on multiple symbolic meanings in the work, but these meanings do not automatically carry over into other stories about whales. The meanings suggested by Melville's whale are specific to that text; therefore, it becomes a contextual symbol. See also ALLEGORY.

Synecdoche See METAPHOR.

Syntax The ordering of words into meaningful verbal patterns such as phrases, clauses, and sentences. Poets often manipulate syntax, changing conventional word order, to place certain emphasis on particular words. Emily Dickinson, for instance, writes about being surprised by a snake in her poem "A narrow Fellow in the Grass," and includes this line: "His notice sudden is." In addition to the alliterative hissing s-sounds here, Dickinson also effectively manipulates the line's syntax so that the verb *is* appears unexpectedly at the end, making the snake's hissing presence all the more "sudden."

Telling See CHARACTER.

Tercet A three-line stanza. See also STANZA, TRIPLET.

Terza rima An interlocking three-line rhyme scheme: *aba, bcb, cdc, ded,* and so on. Dante's *The Divine Comedy* and Frost's "Acquainted with the Night" are written in terza rima. See also RHYME, TERCET.

Theme The central meaning or dominant idea in a literary work. A theme provides a unifying point around which the plot, characters, setting, point of view, symbols, and other elements of a work are organized. It is important not to mistake the theme for the actual subject of the work; the theme refers to the abstract concept that is made concrete through the images, characterization, and action of the text. In nonfiction, however, the theme generally refers to the main topic of the discourse.

Thesis The central idea of an essay. The thesis is a complete sentence (although sometimes it may require more than one sentence) that establishes the topic of the essay in clear, unambiguous language.

Tone The author's implicit attitude toward the reader or the people, places, and events in a work as revealed by the elements of the author's style. Tone may be characterized as serious or ironic, sad or happy, private or public, angry or affectionate, bitter or nostalgic, or any other attitudes and feelings that human beings experience. See also STYLE.

Tragedy A story that presents courageous individuals who confront powerful forces within or outside themselves with a dignity that reveals the breadth and depth of the human spirit in the face of failure, defeat, and even death. Tragedies recount an individual's downfall; they usually begin high and end low. Shakespeare is known for his tragedies, including *Macbeth, King Lear, Othello,* and *Hamlet.* The **revenge tragedy** is a well-established type of drama that can be traced back to Greek and Roman plays, particularly through the Roman playwright Seneca (c. 3 B.C.–A.D. 63). Revenge tragedies basically consist of a murder that has to be avenged by a relative of the victim. Typically, the victim's ghost appears to demand revenge, and invariably madness of some sort is worked into subsequent events, which ultimately end in the deaths of the murderer, the avenger, and a number of other characters. Shakespeare's *Hamlet* subscribes to the basic ingredients of revenge tragedy, but it also transcends these conventions because Hamlet contemplates not merely revenge but suicide and the meaning of life itself. A **tragic flaw** is an error or defect in the tragic hero that leads to his downfall, such as greed, pride, or ambition. This flaw may be a result of bad character, bad judgment, an inherited weakness, or any other defect of character. **Tragic irony** is a form of dramatic irony found in tragedies such as *Oedipus the King,* in which Oedipus ironically ends up hunting himself. See also COMEDY, DRAMA.

Tragic flaw See TRAGEDY.

Tragic irony See IRONY, TRAGEDY.

Tragicomedy A type of drama that combines certain elements of both tragedy and comedy. The play's plot tends to be serious, leading to a terrible catastrophe, until an unexpected turn in events leads to a reversal of circumstance, and the story ends happily. Tragicomedy often employs a romantic, fast-moving plot dealing with love, jealousy, disguises, treachery, intrigue, and surprises, all moving toward a melodramatic resolution. Shakespeare's *Merchant of Venice* is a tragicomedy. See also COMEDY, DRAMA, MELODRAMA, TRAGEDY.

Triplet A tercet in which all three lines rhyme. See also TERCET.

Trochaic meter See FOOT.

Understatement The opposite of hyperbole, *understatement* (or litotes) refers to a figure of speech that says less than is intended. Understatement usually has an ironic effect, and sometimes may be used for comic purposes, as in Mark Twain's statement, "The reports of my death are greatly exaggerated." See also HYPERBOLE, IRONY.

Unreliable narrator See NARRATOR.

Verbal irony See IRONY.

Verse A generic term used to describe poetic lines composed in a measured rhythmical pattern, that are often, but not necessarily, rhymed. See also LINE, METER, RHYME, RHYTHM.

Villanelle A type of fixed form poetry consisting of nineteen lines of any length divided into six stanzas: five tercets and a concluding quatrain. The first and third lines of the initial tercet rhyme; these rhymes are repeated in each subsequent tercet (*aba*) and in the final two lines of the quatrain (*abaa*). Line 1 appears in its entirety as lines 6, 12, and 18, while line 3 reappears as lines 9, 15, and 19. Dylan Thomas's "Do not go gentle into that good night" is a villanelle. See also FIXED FORM, QUATRAIN, RHYME, TERCET.

Well-made play A realistic style of play that employs conventions including plenty of suspense created by meticulous plotting. Well-made plays are tightly and logically constructed, and lead to a logical resolution that is favorable to the protagonist. This dramatic structure was popularized in France by Eugène Scribe (1791–1861) and Victorien Sardou (1831–1908) and was adopted by Henrik Ibsen. See also CHARACTER, PLOT.

Dagoberto Gilb. "Love in L.A." from *The Magic of Blood* by Dagoberto Gilb. Copyright © 1993 by the University of New Mexico Press. Story originally published in *Buffalo*. Reprinted by permission.

Gail Godwin. "A Sorrowful Woman." Originally appeared in *Esquire* Magazine in 1971. Copyright © 1971 by Gail Godwin. Reprinted by permission of John Hawkins & Associates, Inc.

Mark Halliday. "Young Man on Sixth Avenue" from *The Pushcart Prize XXI: 1997 Best of the Small Presses* (Pushcart Press, 1996), pp. 358–60. Originally appeared in *Chicago Review* 1995. Copyright © 1995 by Mark Halliday. Reprinted by permission of the author.

Robert Hampson. "On the Reader's Expectations in 'How I Met My Husband' " from "Johnny Panic and the Pleasures of Disruption" in *Re-Reading the Short Story*. Claire Hanson, editor. Copyright © Claire Hanson. Reprinted with permission of St. Martin's Press, Inc., and MacMillan Press, Ltd.

Bessie Head. "The Prisoner Who Wore Glasses" from *Tales of Tenderness and Power* (Heinemann International, 1990). Copyright © the Estate of Bessie Head.

Ernest Hemingway. "Soldier's Home." Reprinted with permission of Scribner, a Division of Simon & Schuster, from *In Our Time* by Ernest Hemingway. Copyright © 1925 by Charles Scribner's Sons. Copyright renewed 1953 by Ernest Hemingway.

Jane Hiles. "Blood Ties in 'Barn Burning' " from "Kinship and Heredity in Faulkner's 'Barn Burning.' " *Mississippi Quarterly*, v. 38, No. 3 (Summer 1985), pp. 329–37. Copyright © 1985 Mississippi State University, Mississippi State, Mississippi. Reprinted by permission of *Mississippi Quarterly: The Journal of Southern Culture*.

Gish Jen. "In the American Society." Copyright © 1986 by Gish Jen. First published in *Southern Review*. Reprinted by permission of the author.

Ruth Prawer Jhabvala. "The Englishwoman." Copyright © 1972 R. Prawer Jhabvala. Used by permission of Harriet Wasserman Literary Agency, Inc., as agent for the author.

Charles Johnson. "Exchange Value" from *The Sorcerer's Apprentice* by Charles Johnson. Copyright © 1986 Charles Johnson. Reprinted with the permission of Scribner, a Division of Simon & Schuster.

Franz Kafka. "A Hunger Artist" from *Franz Kafka: The Complete Stories* by Franz Kafka, edited by Nahum N. Glatzer. Copyright © 1946, 1947, 1948, 1949, 1954, 1958, 1971 by Schocken Books, Inc. Reprinted by permission of Schocken Books, distributed by Pantheon Books, a division of Random House, Inc.

Claire Kahane. "The Function of Violence in O'Connor's Fiction" from "Flannery O'Connor's Rage of Vision," *American Literature*, 46:1 (March 1974). Copyright 1974, Duke University Press. Reprinted with permission.

Thomas E. Kennedy. "On Morality and Revenge in 'Killings.' " Reprinted with permission of Twayne Publishers, an imprint of Simon & Schuster Macmillan, from *Andre Dubus: A Study of the Short Fiction* by Thomas E. Kennedy. Copyright © 1988 by G. K. Hall & Company.

Edward Kessler. "On O'Connor's Use of History" from *Flannery O'Connor and the Language of Apocalypse*. Copyright © 1986 by Princeton University Press. Reprinted by permission of Princeton University Press.

Jamaica Kincaid. "Girl" from *At the Bottom of the River* by Jamaica Kincaid. Copyright © 1983 by Jamaica Kincaid. Reprinted by permission of Farrar, Straus & Giroux, Inc.

Stephen King. "Suffer the Little Children" from *Nightmares and Dreamscapes* by Stephen King (NY: Viking, 1993); pp. 95–108. Copyright © 1993 by Stephen King. Reprinted by permission of Penguin Putnam, Inc.

D. H. Lawrence. "The Horse Dealer's Daughter" from *Complete Short Stories of D. H. Lawrence* by D. H. Lawrence. Copyright 1922 by Thomas B. Seltzer, Inc., renewed 1950 by Frieda Lawrence. Used by permission of Viking Penguin, a division of Penguin Putnam Inc.

Naguib Mahfouz. "The Answer Is No" from *The Time and the Place and Other Stories* by Naguib Mahfouz. Copyright © 1991 by the American University in Cairo Press. Used by permission of Doubleday, a division of Bantam Doubleday Dell Publishing Group, Inc.

Mordecai Marcus. "What Is an Initiation Story?" from *The Journal of Aesthetics and Art Criticism* 19.2, pp. 222–23. Reprinted by permission of the publisher.

W. R. Martin. "On Prue's Suppressed Passions" from *Alice Munro: Paradox and Parallel* (University of Alberta Press, 1987). Reprinted by permission of University of Alberta Press.

Dan McCall. "On the Lawyer's Character in 'Bartleby the Scrivener' " from *The Silence of Bartleby* by Dan McCall (Cornell UP, 1989). Reprinted by permission of Cornell University Press.

Lorraine McMullen. "On Munro's Ironic Humor in 'An Ounce of Cure' " from " 'Shameless, Marvellous, Shattering Absurdity': The Humour of Paradox in Alice Munro" in *Probable Fictions: Alice Munro's Narrative Acts*, edited by Louis K. MacKendrick. Reprinted by permission of ECW Press.

Susan Minot. "Lust" from *Lust and Other Stories* by Susan Minot. Copyright © 1989 by Susan Minot. Reprinted by permission of Houghton Mifflin Co./Seymour Lawrence. All rights reserved.

Yukio Mishima. "Patriotism," translated by Geoffrey W. Sargent from *Death in Midsummer*. Copyright © 1966 New Directions Publishing Corporation. Reprinted by permission of New Directions Publishing Corporation.

Tania Modleski. "The Popularity of Romance Novels" from *Loving with a Vengeance: Mass-Produced Fantasies for Women*. Copyright © 1982. Reprinted by permission of The Shoe String Press, Inc.

Bharati Mukherjee. "The Tenant" from *The Middleman and Other Stories* by Bharati Mukherjee. Copyright © 1988 by Bharati Mukherjee. Used by permission of Grove/Atlantic, Inc.

Alice Munro. "An Ounce of Cure" from *Dance of the Happy Shades* by Alice Munro. Copyright © 1968 by Alice Munro. Originally published by McGraw-Hill Ryerson Limited. Reprinted by arrangement with the Virginia Barber Literary Agency, Inc. and McGraw-Hill Ryerson. All rights reserved. "How I Met My Husband" from *Something I've Been Meaning to Tell You* by Alice Munro. Copyright © 1974 by Alice Munro. Originally published by McGraw-Hill Ryerson Limited. Reprinted by arrangement with the Virginia Barber Literary Agency, Inc. All rights reserved. "Miles City, Montana" from *The Progress of Love* by Alice Munro. Copyright © 1986 by Alice

Munro. Reprinted by permission of Alfred A. Knopf, Inc., and by permission of McClelland & Stewart, Inc. *The Canadian Publishers*. "Munro on Narration in 'An Ounce of Cure'" from "Author's Commentary" in *Sixteen by Twelve: Short Stories by Canadian Writers*, ed. John Metcalf. Originally published by McGraw-Hill Ryerson Limited. Reprinted by arrangement with the Virginia Barber Literary Agency, Inc.. All rights reserved. "Prue" from *The Moons of Jupiter* by Alice Munro. Copyright © 1978, 1982 by Alice Munro. Reprinted by permission of Alfred A. Knopf, Inc., and Macmillan Canada.

Fae Myenne Ng. "A Red Sweater." Originally appeared in *The American Voice*, 1987. Reprinted by permission of Donadio and Ashworth, Inc. Copyright © 1987 by Fae Myenne Ng.

Joyce Carol Oates. "The Lady with the Pet Dog" from *Marriages and Infidelities* by Joyce Carol Oates (Vanguard Press, 1972). Copyright © 1972 by Joyce Carol Oates. Reprinted by permission of John Hawkins & Associates, Inc. "The Night Nurse," published in *Ploughshares* Vol. 19, #4 (Winter 1993-94). Copyright © 1994 by The Ontario Review, Inc. Reprinted by permission of John Hawkins & Associates, Inc.

Tim O'Brien. "How to Tell a True War Story." Copyright © 1987 by Tim O'Brien. Originally published in *Esquire* Magazine. Reprinted by permission of the author.

Flannery O'Connor. "A Good Man Is Hard to Find" from *A Good Man Is Hard to Find and Other Stories*. Copyright © 1953 by Flannery O'Connor and renewed 1981 by Regina O'Connor. "Good Country People" from *A Good Man Is Hard to Find and Other Stories*. Copyright © 1955 by Flannery O'Connor and renewed 1983 by Regina O'Connor. Reprinted by permission of Harcourt Brace & Company. "Revelation" and "The Turkey" from *The Complete Stories* by Flannery O'Connor. Copyright © 1971 by the Estate of Mary Flannery O'Connor. Reprinted by permission of Farrar, Straus & Giroux, Inc. "O'Connor on Faith" excerpted from "Letter to 'A'," 20 July 1955, from *The Habit of Being: Letters of Flannery O'Connor* edited by Sally Fitzgerald. Copyright © 1979 by Regina O'Connor. Reprinted by permission of Farrar, Straus & Giroux, Inc. "O'Connor on the Materials of Fiction" from "The Nature and Aim of Fiction," "O'Connor on the Use of Exaggeration and Distortion" from "Novelist and Believer," and "O'Connor on Theme and Symbol" from "Writing Short Stories," all from *Mystery and Manners* by Flannery O'Connor. Copyright © 1969 by the Estate of Mary Flannery O'Connor. Reprinted by permission of Farrar, Straus & Giroux, Inc.

James Quinn and Ross Baldessarini. "A Psychological Reading of 'The Birthmark'" from "'The Birthmark': a Deathmark," *University of Hartford Studies in Literature* 13 (1981). Reprinted by permission.

Leon Rooke. "Sweethearts." First published in the *Mississippi Review*. Copyright © 1996 by Leon Rooke. Reprinted by permission of the Bukowski Agency.

Catherine Sheldrick Ross. "On the Reader's Experience in Reading Munro's Stories" from "Alice Munro" in *Canadian Writers Since 1960: First Series*, edited by W. H. New. Gale Research, 1986. Reprinted by permission of Gale Research.

Bi Shumin. "Broken Transformers." Translation by Shi Junbao, copyright © 1993. Reprinted by permission of Panda Books/China Books & Periodicals.

David Updike. "Summer" from *Out on the Marsh* by David Updike. Copyright © 1988 by David Updike. Reprinted by permission of David R. Godine, Publisher, Inc.

John Updike. "A & P" from *Pigeon Feathers and Other Stories* by John Updike. Copyright © 1962 by John Updike. Reprinted by permission of Alfred A. Knopf, Inc. Originally appeared in *The New Yorker*.

Karen Van Der Zee. "A Secret Sorrow." Copyright © 1981 by Karen Van Der Zee. All rights reserved. Reproduction with the permission of the publisher, Harlequin Books S.A.

Gore Vidal. "The Popularity of the Tarzan Books" from "Tarzan Revisited," *Esquire* Magazine (December 1963). Reprinted by permission of the William Morris Agency, Inc., on behalf of the author. Copyright © 1963 by Literary Creation Enterprises, Inc..

Fay Weldon. "IND AFF, or Out of Love in Sarajevo." Copyright © 1988 by Fay Weldon. First published in *The Observer* magazine (7 August 1988). Reprinted by permission of the author.

Eudora Welty. "On the Plots of 'The Bride Comes to Yellow Sky' and 'Miss Brill'" from "The Reading and Writing of Short Stories" by Eudora Welty. Copyright © 1949 by Eudora Welty, renewed 1977 by Eudora Welty. Reprinted by permission of Russell & Volkening as agents for Eudora Welty.

Gayle Edward Wilson. "Conflict in 'Barn Burning'" from "'Being Pulled Two Ways': The Nature of Sarty's Choice in 'Barn Burning.'" *Mississippi Quarterly*, v. 24, No. 3 (Summer 1971), pp. 279-88. Copyright © 1971 Mississippi State University, Mississippi State, Mississippi. Reprinted by permission of *Mississippi Quarterly: The Journal of Southern Culture*.

Tobias Wolff. "Powder" from *The Night in Question* by Tobias Wolff. Copyright © 1996 by Tobias Wolff. Reprinted by permission of Alfred A. Knopf, Inc.

George Woodcock. "On Symbolism in Munro's Fiction" excerpted from pp. 133-34 of *Northern Spring: The Flowering of Canadian Literature* by George Woodcock, © 1987, published by Douglas & McIntyre. Reprinted by permission.

POETRY

Diane Ackerman. "A Fine, a Private Place" from *Jaguar of Sweet Laughter* by Diane Ackerman. Copyright © 1991 by Diane Ackerman. Reprinted by permission of Random House, Inc.

Anna Akhmatova. "Dedication" from *Anna Akhmatova: Selected Poems*, trans. Richard McKane. Copyright © 1967 by Richard McKane, Blookdaxe Books, Ltd.

Claribel Alegría. "I Am Mirror" from *Sobrevito* by Claribel Alegría. Reprinted by permission of the author.

Elizabeth Alexander. "Harlem Birthday Party" from *Ploughshares*, Spring 1996, vol. 22, no. 1, p. 6. Reprinted by permission of the author.

Julia Alvarez. "Queens, 1963" from *The Other Side/El Otro Lado* by Julia Alvarez. Copyright © 1995 by Julia Alvarez. Published by Plume Penguin, an imprint of Dutton, a Division of Penguin USA and originally in hardcover by Dutton Signet. Reprinted by permission of Susan Bergholz Literary Services, New York. All rights reserved. "Woman's Work" from *Homecoming: New and Collected Poems*, NAL/Dutton, 1996.

A. R. Ammons. "Coward" from *Diversifications* by A. R. Ammons. Copyright © 1975 by A. R. Ammons. Reprinted by permission of W. W. Norton & Co., Inc.

Charles R. Anderson. "Eroticism in 'Wild Nights—Wild Nights!'" from *Emily Dickinson's Poetry: Stairway of Surprise*, Holt, Rhinehart, and Winston, 1960. Reprinted with permission of the author.

Maya Angelou. "Africa" from *Oh Pray My Wings Are Gonna Fit Me Well* by Maya Angelou. Copyright © 1975 by Maya Angelou. Reprinted by permission of Random House, Inc.

Katerina Anghelaki-Rooke. "Jealousy" from *Daughters of Sappho: Contemporary Greek Women Poets*. Ed. and trans. Rae Dalven. Associated University Presses, Fairleigh Dickinson UP, 1994. Reprinted with permission of Associated University Presses.

Richard Armour. "Going to Extremes" from *Light Amour* by Richard Armour. Reprinted by permission of Kathleen Armour.

Margaret Atwood. "Bored" and "February" from *Morning in the Burned House*. Copyright © 1995 by Margaret Atwood. Reprinted by permission of Houghton Mifflin Company and McClelland & Stewart, Inc., The Canadian Publishers. All rights reserved. "you fit into me" from *Power Politics* by Margaret Atwood (Toronto: House of Anansi Press, 1971). Reprinted with permission of Stoddard Publishing Co., Limited, Canada.

W.H. Auden. "The Unknown Citizen" from *W.H. Auden: Collected Poems* by W.H. Auden, ed. by Edward Mendelson. Copyright © 1940 and renewed 1968 by W.H. Auden. Reprinted by permission of Faber & Faber Ltd.

Margaret Avison. "Tennis" from *The Dumbfounding* by Margaret Avison. Copyright © 1966 by Margaret Avison. Reprinted by permission of W. W. Norton & Company, Inc.

Jimmy Santiago Baca. "Green Chile" by Jimmy Santiago Baca, from *Black Mesa Poems*. Copyright © 1989 by Jimmy Santiago Baca. Reprinted by permission of New Directions Publishing Corp.

Amiri Baraka. "SOS" from *Selected Poetry of Amiri Baraka/Leroi Jones*. Copyright © 1979 by Amiri Baraka.

Richard K. Barksdale. "On Censoring 'Ballad of the Landlord'" from *Langston Hughes: The Poet and His Critics* by Richard K. Barksdale. American Library Association, 1977.

Regina Barreca. "Nighttime Fires" from *The Minnesota Review* (Fall, 1986). Reprinted by permission of the author.

Matsuo Bashō. "Under cherry trees" from *Japanese Haiku*, trans. by Peter Beilenson, Series I. Copyright © 1955-56, Peter Beilenson, Editor. Reprinted by permission of Peter Pauper Press.

Michael L. Baumann. "The 'Overwhelming Question' for Prufrock" excerpted from "Let Us Ask What Is It?" *Arizona Quarterly* 37 (Spring 1981): 47-58.

Robin Becker. "Shopping" from *All American Girl* by Robin Becker. Copyright © 1996. Reprinted by permission of the University of Pittsburgh Press.

Paula Bennett. "On 'I heard a Fly buzz—when I died—'" excerpt from *Emily Dickinson: Woman Poet* by Paula Bennett. Reprinted with permission of the University of Iowa Press.

Elizabeth Bishop. "Manners," "Sestina," and "The Fish" from *The Complete Poems 1927-1979* by Elizabeth Bishop. Copyright © 1979, 1983 by Alice Helen Methfessel. Reprinted by permission of Farrar, Straus & Giroux, Inc.

Sophie Cabot Black. "August" copyright © 1994 by Sophie Cabot Black. Reprinted from *The Misunderstanding of Nature* with the permission of Graywolf Press, Saint Paul, Minnesota.

Robert Bly. "Sitting Down to Dinner" and "Snowbanks North of the House" from *The Man in the Black Coat Turns* by Robert Bly. Copyright © 1981, 1988 by Robert Bly. Used by permission of Georges Borchardt, Inc., for the author, and Doubleday, a division of Bantam Doubleday Dell Publishing Group, Inc. "Snowfall in the Afternoon" and "Waking from Sleep" reprinted from *Silence in the Snowy Fields*, by Robert Bly, Wesleyan University Press, Middletown, CT, 1962. Copyright © 1962 by Robert Bly. Reprinted with his permission. "On 'Snowbanks North of the House'" reprinted by permission of the author. "Youth" (translation of Neruda's "Juventud") from *Neruda & Vallejo: Selected Poems*. Ed. Robert Bly. Beacon Press, 1993. Copyright © 1993 by Robert Bly.

Roo Borson. "Talk" from *Night Walk: Selected Poems* by Roo Borson (Oxford University Press, 1994). Reprinted by permission of the author.

Marilyn Bowering. "Wishing Africa" from *Sleeping with Lambs* by Marilyn Bowering.

Anne Bradstreet. "Before the Birth of One of Her Children" from *The Works of Anne Bradstreet*, ed. by Jeannine Hensley. Cambridge, Mass.: Harvard University Press. Copyright © 1967 by the President and Fellows of Harvard College.

Joseph Brodsky. "Love Song" from *So Forth* by Joseph Brodsky. Copyright © 1996 by the Estate of Joseph Brodsky. Reprinted by permission of Farrar, Straus & Giroux, Inc.

Gwendolyn Brooks. "The Mother" and "We Real Cool" from *Blacks* (Chicago, IL: Third World Press, 1987). Copyright © 1987 and 1991 by Gwendolyn Brooks.

Joseph Bruchac. "Ellis Island." Reprinted by permission of the Barbara S. Kouts Literary Agency.

Rosario Castellanos. "Chess" translated by Maureen Ahern from *A Rosario Castellanos Reader*, ed. and trans. by Maureen Ahern. Fondo de Cultura Econimica. Copyright © 1988. Reprinted by permission of the University of Texas Press.

Helen Chasin. "The Word Plum" from *Coming Close and Other Poems* by Helen Chasin. Copyright © 1968 by Yale University Press.

David Chinitz. "The Romanticization of Africa in the 1920s" excerpted from "Rejuvenation through Joy: Langston Hughes, Primitivism, and Jazz" by David Chinitz from *American Literary History* Spring 1997, vol. 9, no. 1, pp. 60-78. Reprinted by permission of Oxford University Press.

John Ciardi. "Suburban" from *For Instance* by John Ciardi. Copyright © 1979 by Jon Ciardi. Reprinted by permission of W. W. Norton & Company, Inc.

Lucille Clifton. "come home from the movies" and "for deLawd" copyright © 1986 by Lucille Clifton. Reprinted from *Good Woman: Poems and a Memoir 1969-1990,* by Lucille Clifton, with the permission of BOA Editions, Ltd., Rochester, NY.

Edmund Conti. "Pragmatist" from *Light Year '86.* Reprinted by permission of the author.

Herbert R. Coursen Jr. "A Parodic Interpretation of 'Stopping by Woods on a Snowy Evening'" excerpted from "The Ghost of Christmas Past: 'Stopping by Woods on a Snowy Evening'" by Herbert R. Coursen Jr. from *College English,* December 1962. Originally published by the National Council of Teachers of English.

Sally Croft. "Home-Baked Bread" from *Light Year '86.* Reprinted by permission of the author.

Victor Hernández Cruz. "Anonymous" from *Rhythm, Content and Flavor* by Victor Hernández Cruz, © 1969. Reprinted by permission of the author.

Countee Cullen. "On Racial Poetry" from *Opportunity: A Journal of Negro Life,* February 1926 issue. Copyright © 1926 by *Opportunity Magazine;* copyright renewed 1954 by Ida M. Cullen. "Yet Do I Marvel" from *Color* by Countee Cullen. Copyright © 1925 by Harper & Brothers; copyright renewed 1953 by Ida M. Cullen. Reprinted by permission of GRM Associates, Inc., Agents for the Estate of Ida M. Cullen.

E. E. Cummings. "Buffalo Bill 's," "in Just-," "l(a," "next to of course god america i," "she being Brand," and "since feeling is first" from *Complete Poems: 1904–1962* by E. E. Cummings, edited by George J. Firmage. Copyright 1923, 1925, 1926, 1931, 1935, 1938, 1939, 1940, 1944, 1945, 1946, 1947, 1948, 1949, 1950, 1951, 1952, 1953, 1954. Copyright © 1955, 1956, 1957, 1958, 1959, 1960, 1961, 1962, 1963, 1966, 1967, 1968, 1972, 1973, 1974, 1975, 1976, 1977, 1978, 1979, 1980, 1981, 1982, 1983, 1984, 1985, 1986, 1987, 1988, 1989, 1990, 1991 by the Trustees for the E. E. Cummings Trust. Copyright © 1973, 1976, 1978, 1979, 1981, 1983, 1985, 1991 by George James Firmage. Reprinted by permission of Liveright Publishing Corporation.

Jim Daniels. "Short-order Cook" from *Places/Everyone.* Copyright © 1985. Winner of the 1985 Brittingham Prize in Poetry. Reprinted by permission of The University of Wisconsin Press.

Peter De Vries. "To His Importunate Mistress." Reprinted by permission of the Estate of Peter De Vries and the Watkins/Loomis Agency. Originally published in *The New Yorker.*

Mary di Michele. "As in the Beginning" from *Necessary Sugar,* Oberon Press, 1984. Copyright © 1984 by Mary di Michele. Reprinted by permission of the author.

James Dickey. "Deer Among Cattle" from *Poems, 1957–1967* by James Dickey. Wesleyan UP, 1978.

Emily Dickinson. "A Bird came down the Walk—," "A Light exists in Spring," "After great pain, a formal feeling comes—," "Because I could not stop for Death—," "From all the Jails the Boys and Girls," "I cannot dance upon my Toes—" "I dwell in Possibility—," "I felt a Cleaving in my Mind—," "I heard a Fly buzz—when I died—," "I never saw a Moor—," "I read my sentence—steadily—," "I taste a liquor never brewed—," "If I shouldn't be alive," "I'm Nobody! Who are you?," "Much Madness is divinest Sense—," "Of Bronze— and Blaze—," "One need not be a Chamber— to be Haunted—," "Safe in their Alabaster Chambers— (1859 version)," "Safe in their Alabaster Chambers— (1861 version)," "Success is counted sweetest," "Tell all the Truth but tell it slant—," "The Grass so little has to do—," "The Soul selects her own Society—," "The Thought beneath so slight a film—," "This is my letter to the World," "This was a Poet—It is That," "What Soft— Cherubic Creatures—," and "'Heaven'—is what I cannot reach!" Reprinted by permission of the publishers and the Trustees of Amherst College from *The Poems of Emily Dickinson,* Thomas H. Johnson, ed., Cambridge, Mass.: The Belknap Press of Harvard University Press, Copyright © 1951, 1955, 1979, 1983 by the President and Fellows of Harvard College.

Emily Dickinson. "After great pain, a formal feeling comes—" and "I dwell in Possibility—" from *The Complete Poems of Emily Dickinson* by Thomas H. Johnson. Copyright © 1929, 1935 by Martha Dickinson Bianchi. Copyright © renewed 1957, 1963 by Mary L. Hampson. By permission of Little, Brown and Company.

Emily Dickinson. "Description of Herself" and excerpt from a letter to Thomas Wentworth Higginson from August 20, 1862 reprinted by permission of the publishers from *The Letters of Emily Dickinson,* edited by Thomas J. Johnson. Cambridge, Mass.: The Belknap Press of Harvard University Press, Copyright © 1958, 1986 by the President and Fellows of Harvard College.

Chitra Banerjee Divakaruni. "Indian Movie, New Jersey" from the *Indiana Review,* 1990. Copyright © by Chitra Banerjee Divakaruni. Reprinted by permission of the author.

Gregory Djanikian. "When I First Saw Snow." Reprinted from *Gregory Djanikian: Falling Deeply Into America* by permission of Carnegie Mellon University Press. Copyright © 1989 by Gregory Djanikian.

David Donnell. "The Canadian Prairies View of Literature" from *Settlements* by David Donnell. Used by permission, McClelland & Stewart, Inc. *The Canadian Publishers.*

Bernard Duyfhuizen. " 'To His Coy Mistress': On How a Female Might Respond" excerpted from "Textual Harassment of Marvell's Coy Mistress: The Institutionalization of Masculine Criticism," *College English* (April 1988). Copyright © 1988 by the National Council of Teachers of English.

Cornelius Eady. "The Supremes." Reprinted from *Cornelius Eady: The Gathering of my Name* by permission of Carnegie Mellon University Press. Copyright © 1991 by Cornelius Eady.

George Eliot. "In a London Drawingroom" from *George Eliot, Collected Poems,* Ed. Lucien Jenkins. Skoob Books Publishing LTD, London, 1989. Reprinted by permission.

James A. Emanuel. "Hughes's Attitudes toward Religion" from "Christ in Alabama: Religion in the Poetry of Langston Hughes" in *Modern Black Poets,* Ed. Donald B. Gibson.

Louise Erdrich. "Windigo" from *Jacklight* by Louise Erdrich. Copyright © 1984 by Louise Erdrich. Reprinted by permission of Henry Holt & Co., Inc.

Martín Espada. "Coca-Cola and Coco Frío" from *City of Coughing and Dead Radiators* by Martín Espada. Copyright © 1993 by Martín Espada. Reprinted by permission of W. W. Norton & Company, Inc. "Latin Night at the Pawn Shop" from *Rebellion is the Circle of a Lover's Hands* by Martín Espada. Curbstone Press, 1990. Reprinted by permission of Curbstone Press, Inc.

Barbara Everett. "The Problem of Tone in Prufrock" excerpted from "In Search of Prufrock," *Critical Quarterly* 16 (Summer, 1974).

Ruth Fainlight. "Flower Feet." Copyright © Ruth Fainlight. Originally in The New Yorker, July 10, 1989.

Faiz Ahmed Faiz. "If You Look at the City from Here" from *Faiz Ahmed Faiz, The True Subject*, trans. Naomi Lazard. Copyright © 1988 Princeton UP.

Blanche Farley. "The Lover Not Taken" from *Light Year '86*. Reprinted by permission of the author.

Kenneth Fearing. "AD" from *New and Collected Poems* by Kenneth Fearing (Indiana University Press, 1956).

Carolyn Forché. "The Colonel" from *The Country Between Us* by Carolyn Forché. Copyright © 1981 by Carolyn Forché. Reprinted by permission of The Virginia Barber Literary Agency.

Robert Francis. "Catch" and "The Pitcher" copyright © 1950, 1953 by Robert Francis. From *The Orb Weaver*, copyright © 1950, 1953 by Robert Francis. Wesleyan University Press. Reprinted by permission of the University Press of New England. "On 'Hard' Poetry" reprinted from *The Satirical Rogue of Poetry* by Robert Francis (Amherst: University of Massachusetts Press, 1968), copyright © 1968 by Robert Francis.

Robert Frost. "Acquainted with the Night," "Come In," "Design," "Fire and Ice," "Neither Out Far nor In Deep," "Nothing Gold Can Stay," "Once by the Pacific," "Stopping by Woods on a Snowy Evening," "The Most of It," "The Silken Tent," and "Two Tramps in Mud Time" from *The Poetry of Robert Frost* by Robert Frost. Copyright © 1936, 1942, 1951, © 1956 by Robert Frost. Copyright © 1964, 1970 by Lesley Frost Ballantine. Copyright © 1923, 1928, © 1969 by Henry Holt & Co., Inc. Reprinted by permission of Henry Holt & Co., Inc. "In White" from *The Dimensions of Robert Frost* by Reginald L. Cook. Copyright © 1958 by Reginald L. Cook. "On the Living Part of a Poem" from *A Swinger of Birches: A Portrait of Robert Frost* by Sidney Cox. Copyright © 1957 by New York University Press. Reprinted with permission of New York University Press. "On the Way to Read a Poem" from "Poetry and School" by Robert Frost in *The Atlantic Monthly*, June 1951. Reprinted by permission of the Estate of Robert Frost. "On the Figure a Poem Makes" from *The Selected Prose of Robert Frost*, edited by Hyde Cox and Edward Connery Lathem. Copyright © 1946, 1956, 1959 by Robert Frost. Copyright © 1949, 1954, © 1966 by Henry Holt & Co., Inc. Reprinted by permission of Henry Holt & Co., Inc.

Deborah Garrison. "She Was Waiting to Be Told." Copyright © 1990 by Deborah Garrison. Originally appeared in *The New Yorker*. Reprinted by permission of the author.

Donald B. Gibson. "The Essential Optimism of Hughes and Whitman," excerpt from "The Good Black Poet and the Good Gray Poet: The Poetry of Hughes and Whitman" in *Langston Hughes — Black Genius: A Critical Evaluation* by Donald B. Gibson. William Morrow, 1971. Reprinted with permission of the author.

Sandra M. Gilbert and Susan Gubar. "On Dickinson's White Dress" excerpted from *The Madwoman in the Attic*, Yale University Press, 1979. Reprinted by permission of Yale University Press.

Allen Ginsberg. "First Party at Ken Kesey's with Hell's Angels" from *Collected Poems 1947-1980* by Allen Ginsberg. Copyright © 1965 by Allen Ginsberg. Reprinted by permission of HarperCollins Publishers, Inc.

Louise Glück. "The School Children" from *The House on Marshland*. Copyright © 1971, 1972, 1973, 1974, 1975 by Louise Glück. First published by The Ecco Press in 1989. Reprinted by permission of The Ecco Press.

Donald J. Greiner. "On What Comes 'After Apple-Picking'" from "The Indispensable Robert Frost" by Donald J. Greiner. Excerpted with permission of G. K. Hall & Co., an imprint of Simon & Schuster Macmillan, from *Critical Essays on Robert Frost*, edited by Philip L. Gerber. Copyright © 1982 by Philip L. Gerber.

H. D. [Hilda Doolittle]. "Heat" by H. D., from *Collected Poems, 1912-1944*. Copyright © 1982 by The Estate of Hilda Doolittle. Reprinted by permission of New Directions Publishing Corp.

Marilyn Hacker. "Groves of Academe" from *Winter Numbers* by Marilyn Hacker. Copyright © 1994 by Marilyn Hacker. Originally published in *Open Places*. Reprinted with permission of Marilyn Hacker and W. W. Norton & Co., Inc.

Rachel Hadas. "The Red Hat" from *Halfway Down the Hall: New and Selected Poems*. Copyright © 1997 by Rachel Hadas. Reprinted by permission of The University Press of New England.

Donald Hall. "My Son, My Executioner" from *Old and New Poems* by Donald Hall. Copyright © 1990 by Donald Hall. Reprinted by permission of Ticknor & Fields/Houghton Mifflin Company. All rights reserved. An earlier version of "Letter with No Address" appeared in *Ploughshares*, Winter 1996-97, vol. 22, no. 4, pp. 109-113. Reprinted with permission of the author.

Mark Halliday. "Graded Paper" from *The Michigan Quarterly Review*. Reprinted by permission of the author.

Joy Harjo. "Fishing" from June 21, 1991 Op-Ed page of the *New York Times*. Copyright © 1991 by The New York Times Company. Reprinted by permission.

Michael S. Harper. "Grandfather." Reprinted by permission of the author.

Robert Hass. "A Story About the Body" from *Human Wishes* by Robert Hass. Copyright © 1989 by Robert Hass. First published by The Ecco Press in 1989. Reprinted by permission of The Ecco Press. "Happiness" from *Sun Under Wood* by Robert Hass. Copyright © 1996 by Robert Hass. First Published by The Ecco Press in 1989. Reprinted by permission of The Ecco Press.

William Hathaway. "Oh, Oh" from *Light Year '86*. This poem was originally published in *The Cincinnati Poetry Review*.

Robert Hayden. "Those Winter Sundays" copyright © 1966 by Robert Hayden, from *Angle of Ascent: New and Selected Poems* by Robert Hayden. Reprinted by permission of Liveright Publishing Corporation.

Seamus Heaney. "Mid-term Break" from *Poems 1965-1975* by Seamus Heaney. Copyright © 1980 by Seamus Heaney. Reprinted by permission of Farrar, Straus & Giroux, Inc. "The Pitchfork" from *Seeing Things* by Seamus Heaney. Copyright © 1991 by Seamus Heaney. Reprinted by permission of Farrar, Straus & Giroux, Inc.

Anthony Hecht. "The Dover Bitch" from *Collected Earlier Poems* by Anthony Hecht. Copyright © 1990 by Anthony D. Hecht. Reprinted by permission of Alfred A. Knopf., Inc.

Judy Page Heitzman. "The Schoolroom on the Second Floor of the Knitting Mill." Copyright © 1991 by Judy Page Heitzman. Originally in *The New Yorker,* December 2, 1992, p. 102.

William Heyen. "The Trains" from *The Host: Selected Poems 1965-1990,* by William Heyen. Reprinted by permission of Time Being Books. Copyright © 1994 by Time Being Press. All Rights Reserved.

Thomas Wentworth Higginson. "On Meeting Dickinson for the First Time" from *The Letters of Emily Dickinson,* ed. Thomas H. Johnson. Cambridge, Mass.: The Belknap Press of Harvard University Press. Copyright © 1958, 1986 by the President and Fellows of Harvard University.

Conrad Hilberry. "The Frying Pan" first appeared in *Field 19* (Fall, 1978). Reprinted by permission of Oberlin College Press.

Edward Hirsch. "Fast Break" from *Wild Gratitude* by Edward Hirsch. Reprinted by permission of Alfred A. Knopf, Inc.

Jane Hirshfield. "The Lives of the Heart" from *The Lives of the Heart* published by HarperCollins. Copyright © 1997 by Jane Hirshfield. First appeared in *The Yale Review,* January, 1997, vol. 85, no. 1. Used by permission.

Linda Hogan. "Hunger" from *The Book of Medicines* by Linda Hogan, Coffee House Press, 1993. Copyright © 1993 by Linda Hogan. Used by permission of the publisher. "Song for My Name" from *Calling Myself Home* by Linda Hogan (Greenfield Review Press).

Margaret Holley. "Peepers" from *Morning Star* by Margaret Holley. Copyright © 1992 by Margaret Holley. Reprinted by permission of Copper Beach Press.

M. Carl Holman. "Mr. Z." Reprinted by permission of the Estate of M. Carl Holman.

A. E. Housman. "Is my team ploughing," "Loveliest of trees, the cherry now," "To an Athlete Dying Young," and "When I was one-and-twenty" from *The Collected Poems of A. E. Housman.* Copyright © 1939, 1949 © 1965 by Holt, Rinehart and Winston. Copyright © 1967, 1968 by Robert E. Symons. Reprinted by permission of The Society of Authors as the literary representative of the Estate of A. E. Housman.

Carolynn Hoy. "In the Summer Kitchen" from *Ariel,* vol. 24:2, April 1993. Reprinted with permission of The Board of Governors, University of Calgary.

Andrew Hudgins. "Seventeen" from *The Glass Hammer.* Copyright © 1994 by Andrew Hudgins. Reprinted by permission of Houghton Mifflin Company. All rights reserved. "Elegy for My Father, Who Is Not Dead" from *The Never-Ending.* Copyright © 1991 by Andrew Hudgins. Reprinted by permission of Houghton Mifflin Company. All rights reserved.

Langston Hughes. "Ballad of the Landlord," "Cross," "Danse Africaine," "Dinner Guest: Me," "doorknobs," "Dream Boogie," "Dream Variations," "Formula," "Frederick Douglass: 1817-1895," "Harlem (Dream Deferred)," "I, Too," "Jazzonia," "Johannesburg Mines," "Juke Box Love Song," "Lenox Avenue: Midnight," "Midnight Raffle," "Negro," "Note on Commercial Theatre," "Old Walt," "Red Silk Stockings," "Rent-Party Shout: For a Lady Dancer," "The English," "The Negro Speaks of Rivers," "The Weary Blues," "Theme for English B," and "Un-American Investigators," from *Collected Poems* by Langston Hughes. Copyright © 1994 by the Estate of Langston Hughes. Reprinted by permission of Alfred A. Knopf., Inc. "On Harlem Rent Parties" text excerpt from "When the Negro Was in Vogue" from *The Big Sea* by Langston Hughes. Copyright © 1940 by Langston Hughes. Copyright renewed © 1968 by Arna Bontemps and George Houston Bass. Reprinted by permission of Hill and Wang, a division of Farrar, Straus & Giroux, Inc. "On Racial Shame and Pride" excerpt from "The Negro Artist and the Racial Mountain" by Langston Hughes. Reprinted with permission from the June 23, 1926 issue of *The Nation.*

Paul Humphrey. "Blow" from *Light Year '86.* Reprinted with permission of the author.

Bonnie Jacobsen. "On Being Served Apples" from *Stopping for Time.* Reprinted by permission of Green Tower Press.

Mark Jarman. "Unholy Sonnet" from *The New Criterion,* April 1993. Reprinted by permission of the author.

Randall Jarrell. "The Death of the Ball Turret Gunner" from *The Complete Poems.* Copyright © 1969 by Mrs. Randall Jarrell. Reprinted by permisison of Farrar, Straus & Giroux, Inc.

Onwuchekwa Jemie. "On Universal Poetry" from *Langston Hughes* by Onwuchekwa Jemie. Copyright © 1985 by Columbia University Press. Reprinted with permission of the publisher.

Alice Jones. "The Foot." Reprinted by permission of the author.

Donald Justice. "Order in the Streets " from *Losers Weepers* by Donald Justice. Reprinted by permission of the author.

Katherine Kearns. "On the Symbolic Setting of 'Home Burial'" excerpt from "The Place Is the Asylum: Women and Nature in Robert Frost's Poetry" in *American Literature 59* (May 1987). Copyright © 1991 by Duke University Press. Reprinted by permission of Duke University Press.

Aron Keesbury. "Song to a Waitress." Copyright 1997 by Aron Keesbury, Boston, MA. Reprinted by permission of the author.

Karl Keller. "Robert Frost on Dickinson" from *The Only Kangaroo among the Beauty: Emily Dickinson in America.* Copyright © 1979. The Johns Hopkins University Press.

X. J. Kennedy. "A Visit from St. Sigmund." Copyright © 1993 by X. J. Kennedy. Originally published in *Light, The Quarterly of Light Verse.* Reprinted by permission of the author and *Light.*

Jane Kenyon. "The Blue Bowl" and "Surprise" copyright © 1996 by Jane Kenyon. Reprinted from *Otherwise: New & Selected Poems* with the permission of Graywolf Press, Saint Paul, Minnesota.

Maxine Hong Kingston. "Restaurant" from *The Iowa Review 12* (Spring/Summer, 1981). Reprinted by permission of the author.

Galway Kinnell. "After Making Love We Hear Footsteps" and "Blackberry Eating" from *Three Books.* Copyright © 1993 by Galway Kinnell. Originally published in *Mortal Acts, Mortal Words* (1980). Reprinted by permission

Elaine Mitchell. "Form" from *Light 9* (Spring 1994). Reprinted by permission of the author.

N. Scott Momaday. "The Bear." Copyright © 1992 by N. Scott Momaday. From *In the Presence of The Sun* by N. Scott Momaday. Reprinted by permission of St. Martin's Press Incorporated.

Janice Townley Moore. "To a Wasp." Reprinted by permission of the author.

Marianne Moore. "Poetry." Reprinted with the permission of Simon & Schuster from *Collected Poems of Marianne Moore*. Copyright © 1935 by Marianne Moore. Copyright renewed © 1963 by Marianne Moore and T. S. Eliot.

Robert Morgan. "Mountain Graveyard" from *Sigodlin*, copyright © 1990 by Robert Morgan. Wesleyan University Press. Reprinted by permission of the University Press of New England. "On the Shape of a Poem" from *Epoch* (Fall/Winter 1983). Reprinted by permission of the author.

Joan Murray. "Play-By-Play." Reprinted by permission from *The Hudson Review*, Vol. XLIX, No. 4 (Winter 1997). Copyright © 1997 by Joan Murray.

Pablo Neruda. "Juventud (to be printed in Spanish)" from *Neruda & Vallejo: Selected Poems*. Ed. Robert Bly. Beacon Press, 1993. "Youth" from *Canto General* by Pablo Neruda, tr. Jack Schmitt, University of California Press, 1991. "Sweetness Always" from *Extravagaria* by Pablo Neruda, translated by Alastair Reid. English translation copyright © 1974, by Alastair Reid. Reprinted by permission of Farrar, Straus & Giroux, Inc.

John Frederick Nims. "Love Poem" from *Selected Poems*. Copyright © 1982 by the University of Chicago. Reprinted by permission of the Publisher.

Alden Nowlan. "The Bull Moose" from *An Exchange of Gifts* by Alden Nowlan. Reprinted with the permission of Stoddart Publishing Co. Limited, Canada.

Sharon Olds. "Rite of Passage" and "Sex without Love" from *The Dead And The Living* by Sharon Olds. Copyright © 1983 by Sharon Olds. Reprinted by permission of Alfred A. Knopf., Inc.

Michael Ondaatje. "To a Sad Daughter" from *The Cinnamon Peeler* by Michael Ondaatje. Copyright © 1989 by Mongrel Corporation. Reprinted by permission of Alfred A. Knopf, Inc.

Wilfred Owen. "Arms and the Boy" and "Dulce et Decorum Est" by Wilfred Owen from *The Collected Poems of Wilfred Owen*. Copyright © 1963 by Chatto & Windus, Ltd. Reprinted by permission of New Directions Publishing Corp.

Dorothy Parker. "One Perfect Rose" copyright 1929, renewed © 1957 by Dorothy Parker, from *The Portable Dorothy Parker* by Dorothy Parker, Introduction by Brenda Gill. Used by permission of Viking Penguin, a division of Penguin Books USA Inc.

Linda Pastan. "Marks." Copyright © 1978 and 1981 by Linda Pastan from *PM/AM: New and Selected Poems* by Linda Pastan. Reprinted by permission of W. W. Norton & Co., Inc.

Octavio Paz. "The Street" from *Early Poems 1935-1955*. Reprinted with permission of Indiana University Press.

Molly Peacock. "Desire" from Molly Peacock, *Raw Heaven*. Random House, 1984.

Laurence Perrine. "The limerick's never averse" from *A Limerick's Always A Verse: 200 Original Limericks* by Laurence Perrine. Copyright © 1990 by Harcourt Brace & Company.

Stephen Perry. "Blue Spruce." Copyright © 1991 by Stephen Perry. Originally in *The New Yorker*, January 28, 1991, pp. 34-35.

Marge Piercy. "Barbie Doll" and "The Secretary Chant" from *Circles on the Water* by Marge Piercy. Copyright © 1982 by Marge Piercy. Reprinted by permission of Alfred A. Knopf, Inc.

Sylvia Plath. "Daddy" from *The Collected Poems* by Sylvia Plath, ed. Ted Hughes. "Metaphors" from *Crossing the Water* by Sylvia Plath. Copyright © 1960 by Ted Hughes. Copyright renewed. "Mirror" from *The Collected Poems* by Sylvia Plath, ed. Ted Hughes. Originally appeared in *The New Yorker*. All reprinted by permission of Faber & Faber, Ltd. and HarperCollins Publishers, Inc. "Mushrooms" from *The Colossus and Other Poems* by Sylvia Plath. Copyright © 1960 by Sylvia Plath. Reprinted by permission of Alfred A. Knopf, Inc.

Ezra Pound. "In a Station of the Metro" from *Personae*. Copyright © 1926 by Ezra Pound. Reprinted by permission of New Directions Publishing Corp.

Jim Powell. "Artfully adorned Aphrodite, deathless" from *Sappho A Garland: The Poems and Fragments of Sappho*. Copyright © by Jim Powell. Reprinted by permission of Farrar, Straus & Giroux, Inc.

Wyatt Prunty. "Elderly Lady Crossing on Green" from *The Run of the House*, page 18. Copyright © 1993. The Johns Hopkins University Press.

"Queens: The 'Fair' Borough" (originally titled "Cariello Glorifies Queens as Example of Gracious Living"), *New York Times*, July 18, 1963. Copyright © 1963 by The New York Times Company. Reprinted by permission.

Henry Reed. "Naming of Parts" and "Lessons of War" (1. Naming of the Parts) from *Henry Reed: Collected Poems*, ed. Jon Stallworthy. Copyright © 1991 by the Executor of Henry Reed's Estate. Reprinted by permission of Oxford University Press.

Marny Requa. "An Interview with Julia Alvarez" from "The Politics of Fiction," *Frontera* 5 (1997): n. pdg. On-line. Internet. 29 Jan. 1997.

David S. Reynolds. "Popular Literature and 'Wild Nights—Wild Nights!'" from *Beneath the American Renaissance* by David S. Reynolds. Copyright © 1988 by David S. Reynolds. Reprinted by permission of Alfred A. Knopf, Inc.

Adrienne Rich. "Living in Sin." Copyright © 1993, 1955 by Adrienne Rich from *Collected Early Poems: 1950-1970* by Adrienne Rich. Reprinted by permission of W. W. Norton & Company, Inc.

Rainer Maria Rilke. "The Panther" from *The Selected Poetry of Rainer Maria Rilke* by Rainer Maria Rilke, edited & translated by Stephen Mitchell. Copyright © 1982 by Stephen Mitchell. Reprinted by permission of Random House, Inc.

Alberto Ríos. "Seniors" from *Five Indiscretions*. Copyright © 1985 by Alberto Ríos. Reprinted by permission of the author.

Theodore Roethke. "My Papa's Waltz" and "Root Cellar" copyright © 1954 by Theodore Roethke. From *The Collected Poems of Theodore Roethke* by Theodore Roethke. Used by permission of Doubleday, a division of Bantam Doubleday Dell Publishing Group, Inc.

Frederik L. Rusch. "Society and Character in 'The Love Song of J. Alfred Prufrock'" from "Approaching Literature through the Social Psychology of Erich Fromm" in *Psychological Perspectives on Literature: Freudian Dissidents and Non-Freudians,* edited by Joseph Natoli. Copyright © 1984.

Mary Jo Salter. "Welcome to Hiroshima" from *Henry Purcell in Japan* by Mary Jo Salter. Copyright © 1984 by Mary Jo Salter. Reprinted by permission of Alfred A. Knopf, Inc.

Indira Sant. "Household Fires" from *Sixteen Modern Indian Poems,* eds. A. K. Ramanujan and Vinay Dharwadker, copyright © 1989. Reprinted by permission of *Daedalus, Journal of the American Academy of Arts and Sciences* from the issue entitled "Another India," Fall 1989, vol. 118, No. 4.

Jack Schmitt. "Youth (translation of Neruda's 'Juventud')" from *Pablo Neruda, Canto General* tr. Jack Schmitt, University of California Press, 1991.

Elisabeth Schneider. "Hints of Eliot in Prufrock" from "Prufrock and After: The Theme of Change," *PMLA 87* (1982): 11033–1117.

Louis Simpson. "In the Suburbs" from *At the End of the Open Road* by Louis Simpson. Wesleyan UP, 1963. Reprinted by permission of the University Press of New England.

David R. Slavitt. "Titanic" from *Big Nose* by David R. Slavitt. Copyright © 1983 by David R. Slavitt. Reprinted by permission of Louisiana State University Press.

Ernest Slyman. "Lightning Bugs" from *Sometime the Cow Kick Your Head, Light Year 88/89.* Reprinted by permission of the author.

David Solway. "Windsurfing." Reprinted by permission of the author.

Cathy Song. "The White Porch (moved from collection)" from *Picture Bride.* Copyright © 1983 by Yale University Press.

Gary Soto. "Behind Grandma's House," "Black Hair," and "Mexicans Begin Jogging" from *New and Selected Works* by Gary Soto. Copyright © 1995, published by Chronicle Books. Reprinted by permission of the publisher.

Wole Soyinka. "Future Plans" from *A Shuttle in the Crypt* by Wole Soyinka. Copyright © 1972 by Wole Soyinka. Reprinted by permission of Hill and Wang, a division of Farrar, Straus & Giroux, Inc. "Telephone Conversation" from *Ibadan,* volume 10, November 1960, p. 34.

Bruce Springsteen. "Streets of Philadelphia." Reprinted with permission.

William Stafford. "Traveling through the Dark." Copyright © 1977 William Stafford from *Stories That Could Be True* (Harper & Row). Reprinted by permission of The Estate of William Stafford.

Timothy Steele. "An Aubade" and " Waiting for the Storm" from *Sapphics and Uncertainties: Poems, 1970-1986* by Timothy Steele. University of Arkansas Press, 1995. Reprinted by permission of the University of Arkansas Press

Jim Stevens. "Schizophrenia" originally appeared in *Light: The Quarterly of Light Verse* (Spring 1992). Copyright © 1992 by Jim Stevens. Reprinted by permission of the author.

Wallace Stevens. "The Emperor of Ice-Cream" from *Collected Poems* by Wallace Stevens. Copyright © 1923 and renewed 1951 by Wallace Stevens. Reprinted by permission of Alfred A. Knopf, Inc.

Robert Sward. "A Personal Analysis of 'The Love Song of J. Alfred Prufrock'" from *Touchstones: American Poets on a Favorite Poem,* eds. Robert Pack and Jay Parini, Middlebury College Press. Published by UP New England.

May Swenson. "A Nosty Fright." Copyright © 1984 by May Swenson. Reprinted by permission of the Estate of May Swenson.

Wislawa Szymborska. "End and Beginning" translated by Joseph Brodsky. Originally appeared in *The Times Literary Supplement* (December 31, 1993). Copyright © 1993, Times Supplements, Limited.

Dylan Thomas. "Do not go gentle into that good night" and "The Hand That Signed the Paper" by Dylan Thomas from *Poems of Dylan Thomas.* Copyright © 1952 by the Trustees for the Copyrights of Dylan Thomas. Reprinted by permission of New Directions Publishing Corp. "On the Words in Poetry" by Dylan Thomas from *Quite Early One Morning.* Copyright © 1964 by New Directions Publishing Corp. Reprinted by permission of New Directions Publishing Corp.

Mabel Loomis Todd. "The Character of Amherst" from *The Years and Hours of Emily Dickinson,* volume 2, by Jay Leda. Copyright © 1960 by Yale University Press.

Jean Toomer. "Reapers" from *Cane* by Jean Toomer. Copyright © 1923 by Boni & Liveright, renewed 1951 by Jean Toomer. Reprinted by permission of Liveright Publishing Corporation.

Steven C. Tracy. "A Reading of 'The Weary Blues'" from *Langston Hughes and the Blues* by Steven C. Tracy. Copyright © 1988 by the Board of Trustees of the University of Illinois. Reprinted with permission of The University of Illinois Press.

Tomas Transtromer. "April and Silence" translated by Robin Fulton. First published in *The Kenyon Review New Series,* Summer 1991, vol. 12, no. 3. Copyright © Robin Fulton. Reprinted by permission.

Lionel Trilling. "On Frost as a Terrifying Poet." Copyright © 1959 by Lionel Trilling, reprinted by permission of the Wylie Agency, Inc.

John Updike. "Dog's Death" from *Midpoint and Other Poems* by John Updike. Copyright © 1969 by John Updike. Reprinted by permission of Alfred A. Knopf, Inc. "Player Piano" from *Collected Poems 1953-1993* by John Updike. Copyright © 1993 by John Updike. Reprinted by permission of Alfred A. Knopf., Inc.

Derek Walcott. "The Virgins" from *Sea Grapes* by Derek Walcott. Copyright © 1976 by Derek Walcott. "The Road Taken" excerpt from "The Road Taken" by Derek Walcott from *Homage to Robert Frost* by Joseph Brodsky, Seamus Heaney, and Derek Walcott. Copyright © 1996 by the Estate of Joseph Brodsky. Reprinted by permission of Farrar, Straus & Giroux, Inc.

DRAMA

Cynthia P. Gardiner. "The Function of the Chorus in *Antigone*" from *The Sophoclean Chorus: A Study of Character and Function* by Cynthia P. Gardiner. Copyright © 1978 by Cynthia P. Gardiner. Reprinted by permission of the author.

Lorraine Hansberry. *A Raisin in the Sun*. Copyright © 1958 by Robert Nemiroff, as an unpublished work. Copyright © 1959, 1966, 1984 by Robert Nemiroff. Reprinted by permission of Random House, Inc.

David Henry Hwang. *M. Butterfly*. Copyright © 1986, 1987, 1988 by David Henry Hwang. Used by permission of Dutton Signet, a division of Penguin Putnam Inc.

Henrik Ibsen. *A Doll House* from *The Complete Major Prose Plays of Henrik Ibsen* by Henrik Ibsen, translated by Rolf Fjelde. Translation copyright © 1965, 1970, 1978 by Rolf Fjelde. Used by permission of Dutton Signet, a division of Penguin Putnam Inc.

David Ives. "Sure Thing" from *All in the Timing* by David Ives. Copyright © 1994 by David Ives. Reprinted by permission of Vintage Books, a Division of Random House, Inc.

Russell Jackson. "A Film Diary of the Shooting of Kenneth Branagh's *Hamlet*" from *Hamlet* by Kenneth Branagh, William Shakespeare, and Russell Jackson. Copyright © 1996 by W. W. Norton & Co. Reprinted by permission of W. W. Norton & Co.

Lisa Jardine. "On Boy Actors in Female Roles" from *Still Harping on Daughters: Women and Drama in the Age of Shakespeare* by Lisa Jardine. Copyright © 1983, 1989 by Lisa Jardine. Reprinted by permission of the publisher, Columbia University Press.

James R. Kincaid. "On the Value of Comedy in the Face of Tragedy" from "Who Is Relieved by Comic Relief?" in *Annoying the Victorians* (New York: Routledge, 1995). Reprinted by permission of the author.

Bernard Knox. "On Oedipus and Human Freedom" from "Introduction" by Bernard Knox, copyright © 1982 by Bernard Knox. From *Three Theban Plays* by Sophocles, translated by Robert Fagles. Translation copyright © 1982 by Robert Fagles. Used by permission of Viking Penguin, a division of Penguin Putnam Inc.

Jan Kott. "On Producing *Hamlet*" from *Shakespeare: Our Contemporary* by Jan Kott. Copyright © 1964 by Panstwowe Wydawnictwo Naukowe and Doubleday, a division of Bantam, Doubleday, Dell Publishing Group, Inc. Used by permission of Doubleday, a division of Bantam Doubleday Dell Publishing Group, Inc.

Jane Martin. *Rodeo*. Copyright © 1982 by Alexander Speer, as Trustee. Reprinted by permission. CAUTION: Professionals and amateurs are hereby warned that *Rodeo* is subject to a royalty. It is fully protected under the copyright laws of the United States of America, the British Commonwealth, including Canada, and all other countries of the Copyright Union. All rights, including professional, amateur, motion pictures, recitation, lecturing, public reading, radio broadcasting, television, and the rights of translation into foreign languages are strictly reserved. In its present form the play is dedicated to the reading public only. Particular emphasis is laid on the question of amateur or professional readings, permission and terms for which must be secured in writing from Samuel French, Inc., 45 West 25th Street, New York, NY 10010.

Arthur Miller. *Death of a Salesman*. Copyright © 1949, renewed © 1977 by Arthur Miller. Used by permission of Viking Penguin, a division of Penguin Putnam Inc. "On Biff and Willy Loman," *New York Times* (February 5, 1959). Copyright © 1959 by Arthur Miller. Reprinted by permission of the *New York Times* and International Creative Management, Inc. "Tragedy and the Common Man." Copyright © 1959 by Arthur Miller. Reprinted by permission of International Creative Management, Inc. Copyright © 1949, renewed © 1977 by Arthur Miller, from *The Theater Essays of Arthur Miller*, edited by Robert Martin. Used by permission of Viking Penguin, a division of Penguin Putnam Inc.

Louis Montrose. "On Amazonian Mythology in *A Midsummer Night's Dream*" from " 'Shaping Fantasies': Figurations of Gender and Power in Elizabethan Culture." Copyright © 1983 by The Regents of the University of California. Reprinted from *Representations* Vol. 2 (Spring 1983), pp. 133-35, by permission of the publisher and the author.

Geoffrey O'Brien. "On *Seinfeld* as Sitcom Money-Maker" from "Sein of the Times," *New York Review of Books*, August 14, 1997. Reprinted with permission from *The New York Review of Books*. Copyright © 1997 Nyrev, Inc.

Frank Rich. "A Theater Review of *M. Butterfly*" from "*M. Butterfly*, a Story of a Strange Love and Betrayal," *New York Times*, March 21, 1988. Copyright © 1988 by The New York Times Company. Reprinted by permission.

Harold Rosenthal. "A Plot Synopsis of *Madame Butterfly*" from *The Concise Oxford Dictionary of Opera* by Harold Rosenthal and John Warrack (1964). Reprinted by permission of Oxford University Press.

Muriel Rukeyser. "On *Oedipus the King*." Originally titled "Myth," from *Out of Silence* (Evanston, IL: TriQuarterly Books, 1992). Copyright © Muriel Rukeyser. Reprinted by permission of William Rukeyser.

Maurice Sagoff. "A Humorous Distillation of *Antigone*" from *Shrinklits*. Copyright © 1970, 1980 by Maurice Sagoff. Used by permission of Workman Publishing Company Co., Inc., New York. All Rights Reserved.

David Savran. "An Interview with David Henry Hwang" from *In Their Own Words: Contemporary American Playwrights* by David Savran. Copyright © 1988 by David Savran. Used by permission of Theatre Communications Group.

William Seebring. *The Original Last Wish Baby*. Copyright © 1995 by Douglas Michael. Reprinted by permission. CAUTION: Professionals and amateurs are hereby warned that *The Original Last Wish Baby* is subject to a royalty. The play is fully protected under the copyright laws of the United States of America, the British Empire, including Canada, and all other countries covered by the International Copyright Union and the Universal Copyright Convention. All rights, including professional, amateur, motion picture, radio and/or television broadcast, and any other form of electronic transmission are strictly reserved by the author. No portion of the play may be published, reprinted in any publication, or copied for any reason without the permission of the author, c/o of the author's agent. No performances, professional, stock or amateur, of this play may be given without the written permission of the author. All inquiries should be addressed to Frieda Fishbein Associates, P.O. Box 723, Bedford, NY 10506, (914) 234-7232.

William Shakespeare. *A Midsummer Night's Dream, Hamlet, Prince of Denmark,* and *The Tempest* from *The Complete Works of Shakespeare,* 4th ed. by David Bevington. Copyright © 1992 by HarperCollins Publishers, Inc. Reprinted by permission of Addison Wesley Educational Publishers, Inc.

Anna Deavere Smith. From *Twilight: Los Angeles, 1992* by Anna Deavere Smith. Copyright © 1994 by Anna Deavere Smith. Used by permission of Doubleday, a division of Bantam Doubleday Dell Publishing Group, Inc.

Sophocles. *Antigone* and *Oedipus the King* from *Three Theban Plays* by Sophocles, translated by Robert Fagles. Translation copyright © 1982 by Robert Fagles. Used by permission of Viking Penguin, a division of Penguin Putnam Inc. "Another Translation of a Scene from *Oedipus the King*" from *Oedipus the King,* translated by J. T. Sheppard. Copyright 1920 by Cambridge University Press. Reprinted with the permission of Cambridge University Press.

Wole Soyinka. *The Strong Breed.* Copyright © Oxford University Press 1964. Reprinted from *Collected Plays 1* (1973) by permission of Oxford University Press.

Joan Templeton. "Is *A Doll House* a Feminist Text?" from "The *Doll House* Backlash: Criticism, Feminism, and Ibsen." Reprinted by permission of the Modern Language Association of America from *PMLA* 104. Copyright © 1989 by the Modern Language Association.

Carol Strongin Tufts. "A Psychoanalytic Reading of Nora" from "Recasting *A Doll House:* Narcissism as Character Motivation in Ibsen's Play." Originally published in *Comparative Drama* (Summer 1986). Reprinted by permission of the publisher.

Alden T. Vaughan. "Caliban as a Sociopolitical Symbol," *Massachusetts Review* (Summer 1988). Reprinted by permission of the author.

Wendy Wasserstein. *Tender Offer.* Copyright © 1991 by Wendy Wasserstein. First appeared in *Antaeus* 66 (Spring 1991). Reprinted by permission of the author.

Tennessee Williams. *The Glass Menagerie* (play and production notes). Copyright © 1945 by Tennessee Williams and Edwina D. Williams. Copyright renewed 1973 by Tennessee Williams. Reprinted by permission of Random House, Inc. "On Theme" from *Where I Live.* Copyright © 1978 by Tennessee Williams. Reprinted by permission of New Directions Publishing Corporation.

August Wilson. *The Piano Lesson.* Copyright © 1988, 1990 by August Wilson. Used by permission of Dutton Signet, a division of Penguin Putnam Inc.

Barry Witham and John Lutterbie. "A Marxist Approach to *A Doll House.*" Reprinted by permission of the Modern Language Association of America from *Approaches to Teaching Ibsen's* A Doll House, edited by Yvonne Shafer. Copyright © 1985 by the Modern Language Association.

LITERARY THEORY

Andrew P. DeBicki. "New Criticism and Deconstructionism: Two Attitudes in Teaching Poetry" from *Writing and Reading Differently: Deconstruction and the Teaching of Composition and Literature,* edited by G. Douglas Atkins and Michael L. Johnson. Copyright © 1985 by the University Press of Kansas. Reprinted by permission.

Emily Dickinson. "There's a certain Slant of light." Reprinted by permission of the publishers and the Trustees of Amherst College from *The Poems of Emily Dickinson,* Thomas H. Johnson, ed., Cambridge, Mass.: The Belknap Press of Harvard University Press. Copyright © 1951, 1955, 1979, 1983 by the President and Fellows of Harvard College.

Morris Dickstein. "On the Social Responsibility of the Critic" from "Damaged Literacy: The Decay of Reading." Reprinted by permission of the Modern Language Association of America from *Profession 93.* Copyright © 1993 by the Modern Language Association.

Judith Fetterley. "A Feminist Reading of 'A Rose for Emily'" from *The Resisting Reader: A Feminist Approach to American Fiction* by Judith Fetterley. Copyright © 1978. Reprinted by permission of the Indiana University Press.

Harriet Hawkins. "Should We Study *King Kong* or *King Lear?*" from "From *King Lear* to *King Kong* and Back: Shakespeare in Popular Modern Genres" in *Bad Shakespeare: Revelations of the Shakespeare Canon,* edited by Maurice Cherney (Fairleigh Dickinson University Press, 1988). Reprinted by permission of Associated University Presses.

Annette Kolodny. "On the Commitments of Feminist Criticism" from "Dancing through the Minefield: Some Observations on the Theory, Practice, and Politics of a Feminist Literary Criticism." Feminist Studies 6 (1980). Copyright © 1979 by Annette Kolodny. All rights reserved. Reprinted by permission of the author.

Peter Rabinowitz. "On Close Readings" from *Pedagogy Is Politics: Literary Theory and Critical Thinking.* Copyright © 1992 by the Board of Trustees of the University of Illinois. Used with the permission of the University of Illinois Press.

Susan Sontag. "Against Interpretation" from *Against Interpretation* by Susan Sontag. Copyright © 1964, 1966; and copyright renewed 1994 by Susan Sontag. Reprinted by permission of Farrar, Straus & Giroux, Inc.

Wendy Steiner. "On the Critics' Readership" from "Thinking in Public: A Forum," *American Literary History,* Spring 1998. Copyright © 1998 by Wendy Steiner. Reprinted by permission of Oxford University Press and Wendy Steiner.

Brook Thomas. "A New Historical Approach to Keats's 'Ode on a Grecian Urn'" from "The Historical Necessities for — and Difficulties with — New Historical Analysis in Introductory Literature Courses," *College English* (September 1987). Copyright © 1987 by the National Council of Teachers of English. Reprinted with permission.

Index of First Lines

Index of Authors and Titles

Index of Terms

Boldface numbers refer to the Glossary of Literary Terms